THE INTERNATIONAL
WHO'S WHO IN POETRY

1974–1975

THE INTERNATIONAL WHO'S WHO IN POETRY

HON. GENERAL EDITOR:
ERNEST KAY, D.Litt., F.R.S.A.

EDITORIAL AND ADVISORY BOARD:
MADELINE MASON
Poet and Lecturer (USA)

CHARLES A. WAGNER
Executive Secretary, The Poetry Society of America

JOHN ATHEY ROEBUCK
Author and Administrator (England)

FRANCES CLARK HANDLER
National Poetry Day Committee (USA)

LORENA SIMON
Poet and Benefactor (USA)

JOHN WOODWARD
Poet and Editor (England)

KRISHNA SRINIVAS
World Poetry Society Intercontinental (India)

AMADO M. YUZON
United Poets Laureate International (Philippines)

LOU LuTOUR
Poet and Broadcaster (USA)

LARRY FARSACE
Editor and Publisher (USA)

ORVILLE CROWDER MILLER
Poet and Educator (USA)

ARMANDO TRONI
Centro Studi e Scambi Internatzionali (Italy)

EDITORIAL MANAGER:
Judy Boothroyd

ASSOCIATE EDITORS:
Georgina Reynolds; Geoffrey Handley-Taylor, Ph.D., F.R.S.L.

APPENDICES EDITOR:
Bernadette Lalonde, M.A. (Canada)

EDITOR, U.S. STATE POETRY SOCIETIES SECTION:
Marvin Davis Winsett, L.H.D., F.I.A.L.,
F.R.S.A. (Dallas, Texas, USA)

HEAD OF RESEARCH:
Pamela A. Derby

All communications to: I.W.W.P., International Biographical Centre,
Cambridge CB2 3QP, England

Sir John Betjeman
Poet-Laureate of the United Kingdom

INTERNATIONAL WHO'S WHO IN POETRY

FOURTH EDITION
1974-1975

Edited by
ERNEST KAY

Dedicated, by permission, to

SIR JOHN BETJEMAN
Poet Laureate of the United Kingdom

with a Memoir on his life and work
by
GEOFFREY HANDLEY-TAYLOR, Ph.D., F.R.S.L.

INTERNATIONAL WHO'S WHO IN POETRY
Cambridge and London, England

I SBN 0 900332 29 8

Library of Congress Catalog Card Number: 59-16302

TYPESET BY COMPUTATYPE (UK) LTD. FORT WILLIAM
PRINTED OFFSET LITHO AND BOUND IN GREAT BRITAIN BY
THE CAMBRIDGE UNIVERSITY PRESS

CONTENTS

	Page
FOREWORD BY THE HON. GENERAL EDITOR	7
A MEMOIR ON SIR JOHN BETJEMAN	10
BIOGRAPHICAL SECTION	13
I.W.W.P. POETRY AWARDS	518
PHOTOGRAPHIC APPENDIX	577

APPENDIX A: 609
Recipients of the Queen's (King's) Gold Medal for Poetry
Poets Laureate of the United Kingdom
Oxford University Professors of Poetry
Official State Poets Laureate of the U.S.A.

APPENDIX B: 618
International Societies

APPENDIX C: 646
American Poetry Societies
The National Federation of State Poetry Societies
State Poetry Societies of the U.S.A.
Poetry Societies (other than State) in the U.S.A.

APPENDIX D: 692
Poetry Societies in the United Kingdom

APPENDIX E: 716
Poetry Societies other than in the U.K. or U.S.A.

APPENDIX F: 726
Magazines and Publishers interested in Poetry

APPENDIX G: 779
Poetry Awards, Prizes and Contests.

APPENDIX H: 802
Poetry on Record and Tape

APPENDIX I: 835
Poetry Recordings at the Library of Congress.

APPENDIX J: 861
The Second World Congress of Poets

PSEUDONYMS OF INCLUDED POETS   870

FOREWORD BY THE HON. GENERAL EDITOR

It hardly seems possible that two years and three months have gone by since I wrote my Foreword to the Third Edition of the *International Who's Who in Poetry* in January 1972. Yet, much has happened during this time. In 1972 I recorded, with deep regret, the deaths of two members of our Editorial and Advisory Board – Gustav Davidson of New York City, and Alice Miller of Lancashire, England, both of whom had been associated with the *International Who's Who in Poetry* since before the First Edition was published in 1958. I must now sadly report the death of another founder-member of the Editorial and Advisory Board – Martin-Saint-René, of Paris, France.

Martin-Saint-René, who was born in 1888, was the founder of the Académie Française de la Poésie, a director of the Victor Hugo Foundation and a member of dozens of important literary associations in his native France and elsewhere. He will be sadly missed, not least of all by us at the *International Who's Who in Poetry*.

In May 1972 the death occurred of Cecil Day-Lewis, C.B.E., Poet-Laureate of the United Kingdom, who succeeded John Masefield, O.M., to that office in 1968. He was 68 and had been in poor health for a long time. His second marriage to Jill Balcon, the actress, increased his interest in spoken poetry and he became one of the most outstanding poetry readers of his time. Cecil Day-Lewis was equally famous as his "other self" under the pseudonym of Nicholas Blake, writer of many fine detective novels.

Three other distinguished English poets also died – William Plomer, C.B.E., aged 69; Teresa Hooley, 85; and Edmund Blunden, C.B.E., 77.

William Plomer, who narrowly missed appointment as Poet-Laureate of the United Kingdom in succession to the late Cecil Day-Lewis, won the Queen's Gold Medal for Poetry in 1963. It was he who "discovered" Ian Fleming and, without his constant encouragement, James Bond would never have been created.

Teresa Hooley wrote poetry for more than seventy years. Her obituary notice in the London *Times* described her simply as "Teresa Hooley, poet" and printed, in her memory, these lines from one of her poems:

Fame is a rocket, going out with a bang and a spark;
Love a spent comet, streaming from dark to dark;
Only the cresset of Faith remains at the end
To guide the pilgrim's feet to the house of a Friend.

Edmund Blunden was a prolific and distinguished poet who found real fame during World War II with "Shells by a Stream", published in 1944 and containing some of his most mature poems. He was elected Oxford University Professor of Poetry in 1966 in succession to Robert Graves.

Other deaths included two eminent New Zealand poets, Charles Brasch, 64, founder and for twenty years editor of the quarterly "Landfall"; and James K. Baxter, 46, whose first collection of poetry was published when he was 18 years old; and Lionello Fiumi, 79, the Italian poet who was the author of more than sixty books of poetry, prose and criticism.

One of the greatest of all losses to poetry was the death of the American poet and teacher, Mark Van Doren. A notable Annual Dinner of the Poetry

Society of America at The Plaza, New York City, in April 1973, was a fine memorial to him. Six of his former students paid tribute from the dais: Allen Ginsberg was on crutches, following an accident, but this did not deter him from speaking at length about what he owed to Mark Van Doren. My wife, my daughter and myself, who were present, were most moved on this occasion.

From the sad to the glad, and on to a few milestones in poetry (selected at random) which I feel should be recorded here.

On October 10 1972 it was announced that Queen Elizabeth II had appointed Sir John Betjeman as her Poet-Laureate to succeed the late Cecil Day-Lewis. This Edition of the *International Who's Who in Poetry* is dedicated, by permission, to Sir John and includes an essay on him by Geoffrey Handley-Taylor, under the appropriate title, "Poet of the People".

At the famed National Eisteddfod of Wales in August 1973 Alan Lloyd Roberts, a bookseller aged 25, was awarded both the crown and the bardic chair for poetry – the first time since 1915 that both honours have gone to one poet. His 300-line poem, in the traditional strict metre, expressed his deep concern for minority groups. The only other double winner was Sir T.H. Parry-Williams in both 1912 and 1915.

In October 1973 President Senghor, of the Republic of Senegal, West Africa, received, as a poet, the degree of D. Litt. from Oxford University. The President is a distinguished poet in his own right and has also translated T.S. Eliot and Gerard Manley Hopkins into French. The literary stature of President Senghor is well known but how many, I wonder, realize that Marcelino dos Santos, leader of the Frelimo liberation movement in Mozambique, is also a fine poet? And who would believe that a General Election in the United Kingdom would result in a poet as First Lady? Yet this is what happened in March 1974 when Harold Wilson again became Prime Minister. His wife, Mary, is a noted and popular poet who has been able to pay off the mortgage on their holiday home in the Isles of Scilly (the most southerly and westerly point of the British Isles) from the proceeds of her published poetry.

The International Who's Who in Poetry $1,000 Awards, which were introduced with the publication of the Second Edition (1970-1971) and repeated with the Third Edition (1973-1973), were increased to $2,500 for this Fourth Edition (1974-1975) and the full results (with winning poems) are given elsewhere in this book. The First Prize winners, so far, are:

1970-1971 : Dorothy Lee Richardson (U.S.A.)
1972-1973 : Shared between Julia Mary Webley and Leonard Clark (both U.K.)
1974-1975 : Madeline Mason (U.S.A.)

My very good friends, Boshra and Nadia Makar, of Jersey City, New Jersey, U.S.A., have added to the Awards by donating $500 for a young poet, under 21 years of age, who really needs the money for the pursuance of poetry. This, the Charles Baudelaire Award (after the French poet, 1821-1867), has been won by Julia Mary Webley whose poems are printed in the *IWWP* Awards Appendix which follows the biographical section. Julia is only 17 years old: she has collected $900 from the *International Who's Who in Poetry* already. I believe she will go far and that is why I sponsored her (successfully) for Student Membership of the Poetry Society of America.

Since the publication of the Third Edition of the *International Who's Who in Poetry* the most dramatic domestic event, from my point of view, was the moving of our headquarters from London to Cambridge in the summer of 1972. For some years we had been at Artillery Mansions, Victoria Street, London, an old Victorian building midway between the Palace of Westminster and Buckingham Palace but, alas, it was announced that the property was to be demolished in the interests of "progress" and that an hotel would be built in its place. We could have no security of tenure: we could be thrown out at six months' notice.

My colleagues and I therefore decided that, rather than risk this uncertainty, we should find alternative accommodation. Rents in Central London had become prohibitive ($25 a square foot would be "cheap" and now it is far higher), so we opted to leave London and move to a University City. Cambridge proved by far the most suitable and we were fortunate to acquire, on a 21-year lease, the International Biographical Centre right in the centre of the City of Cambridge. The move took from August to October 1972 to complete.

But we are now very happy to be in Cambridge and we have been successful in recruiting an excellent staff of more than forty men and women. Unfortunately, we lost most of our London staff, including Jean Bubbers, the Executive Editor of the Third Edition of the *International Who's Who in Poetry*. I therefore decided to take on the task of Executive Editor as well as Hon. General Editor for this Fourth Edition: the results of my efforts are now in your hands.

Let me say right away that I could never have produced this Fourth Edition without the unswerving help and allegiance of my associates. I offer my warmest personal thanks to them: Bernadette Lalonde, Research Assistant, who is responsible for most of the Appendices; Geoffrey Handley-Taylor and Georgina Reynolds, who have compiled the biographies; Judy Boothroyd, Editorial Manager, who has meticulously kept press deadlines; Veronica Mann, my Personal Secretary, who has written hundreds of letters to biographees; Marvin Davis Winsett (Dallas, Texas) for all his research into American Poetry Societies and Poets-Laureate; Tim Phillips, Printer to the Cambridge University Press, for the excellent end-product.

This Fourth Edition of the *International Who's Who in Poetry* is, by far, the largest and most comprehensive yet: it contains some 4,500 biographies and bibliographies of *living* poets from more than fifty countries and many new as well as updated Appendices. In my view this is the most important Who's Who of poets in existence.

Every questionnaire returned to me has been carefully examined and typescripts of entries have been sent to included poets, for correction, so as to establish a very high degree of accuracy. Even so, it is possible that some errors may appear: if so, my apologies in advance.

International Biographical Centre,
Cambridge,
England.
April, 1974

SIR JOHN BETJEMAN

Poet of the people

By Geoffrey Handley-Taylor

On Wednesday morning, 25th of October, 1972, in the royal church of St. Martin-in-the-Fields, Trafalgar Square, London, the newly-appointed Poet Laureate, Sir John Betjeman, undertook his first major public appearance. Supporting the arm of the late Poet Laureate's widow he attended the spectacular broadcast Memorial Service for his predecessor, C. Day-Lewis, C.B.E., who died in May of that year.

Betjeman's elevation to the Laureateship, in keeping with recent tradition, achieved considerable press, radio and television coverage in the United Kingdom and elsewhere within a few hours of his appointment on Tuesday, 10th of October, 1972. The announcements were headed variously from "Betjeman plans to be an "angry" Poet Laureate", "Sir John Summoned", "Betjeman to wait for the right muse", "Summoned by Bells", "Chronicler of London Life", "Betjeman is made Poet Laureate", "Of anthems and executives", "Betjeman is poet to enjoy Laureateship", "Sweetness and Light", "Summoned by Success" to "Sir John Betjeman: Poet Laureate in Ordinary who felt humbled". Perhaps the most appropriate banner heading appeared in the *Yorkshire Evening Post* one month after the Poet Laureate's appointment. It read simply: "Betjeman – poet of the people".

In every aspect Sir John Betjeman is a poet of the people. Few men and women in the United Kingdom today, at one time or another, have not read words from his compassionate and lively pen. Similarly, few men and women in the United Kingdom have not seen this eloquent writer of verse beaming or questing on the television screen. His championship of countless good causes, no less, at once endears him to the broad face of the world at large. Assuredly deserving of record are the words appearing in *The Times* (London) some weeks before his appointment. In a leader headed "Worthy of a tun of sack" the writer commends Sir John thus:

He is one of the few poets since Kipling and Newbolt to become not only known by name but even to be sometimes quoted. He has done for girl athletes what Kipling did for private soldiers. And the extraordinary thing about the Betjeman story is that, though the scope of his popularity owes a great deal to television, he has never modified his style to win a wider audience. It is public taste that has changed. Verses which were first admired by a small group of his intellectual contemporaries are now spread around every Christmas from uncle to niece and nephew to aunt with the same abandon that earlier was accorded to the works of Rupert Brooke or Elroy Flecker. It is a remarkable development, and the laureateship would be a fitting seal to it. There is also the not unimportant consideration that Sir John is more likely to produce verse worthy of a public occasion than is anyone else. Back comes the argument – does it matter? Of course it does. We lack the excitement they enjoy in France of measuring up candidates for the Academy or for the literary prizes; we have not the privilege that belongs to the Swedish Academy of Literature of making every year an absolute and bountiful literary judgment. But those who speak the tongue that Shakespeare spake can at least have their attention turned from time to time to the current state of poetry in their midst.

In an interview at Trebetherick in Cornwall, the day he was appointed to office, Sir John jokingly announced he was choosing the traditional butt of sack rather than the £27 ($65) in lieu. That, plus his £70 ($168) annual salary, would seem to be a meagre pittance for a post of such historic renown, but as was noted in "Some Reflections upon Poets Laureate of the United Kingdom, Their Appointments, and Their Problems" *(IWWP*, third edition, 1972-1973), the Poet Laureateship carries with it a useful number of fringe opportunities for additional income-raising, or, that was the experience of the long-reigning John Masefield, O.M. We need not fear, therefore, the prospect of seeing a begging cap being handed around to support the royal keeper of the British muse.

Given good health, so sadly denied his well-loved predecessor, C. Day-Lewis, John Betjeman has a unique and privileged opportunity further to popularise poetry. As a greatly-loved public figure as well as being a best-selling poet, by virtue of his easy style and uninvolved approach to the subjects of his choice, he is at once understood. Thus his term of Poet Laureateship is unlikely to escape the notice of the common man and it is, after all, in the hands of the common man that poetry power is best assured a durable vibrance and a universal custodianship.

INTERNATIONAL
WHO'S WHO IN POETRY

AALI, Jamiluddin, pen name **AALI,** b. 1 Jan. 1926. Banker. Education: Grad., Delhi Univ., 1944; Fellowship holder of UNESCO, 1961. Currently Development Adviser, Nat. Bank of Pakistan. Memberships: Ctrl. Sec., Pakistan Writers Guild, 1959-63; Acting Sec.-Gen., ibid, 1963-67; Sec.-Gen., 1967-70; Ctrl. Comm., 1970–; Soc. for Advancement of Urdu lang. Published works: Gazlen, Dohay, Geet (coll. of poetry), 1957; Dunya Meray Aagay (The World in Front of Me), prose travelogue of world tours, 1963. Has edited 30 publs. of Urdu Soc. & republished Standard English Urdu Dictionary, of same soc., 1967. Contbr. to var. Urdu publs. & anthols. Has initiated many Pakistani awards in Poetry inclng: Nat. Bank Prize, United Bank Prize, & was Sec. of all Prize Panels, 1960-70. Address: Nat. Bank of Pakistan, Head Office, Karachi, Pakistan.

AANDERAA, Jorunn, b. 12 Sept. 1934. Copy Editor; Literary Critic. Educ.: Univ. of Oslo, Norway; Tchrs. Trng. Course; Courses in lang. & lit. Positions held: Primary Schl. Tchr., 4 yrs.; worked in Information Serv., Univ. Bookshop, 5 yrs.; Copy Ed., Norwegian Univ. Press; Lit. Critic for newspaper 'Nationen, 1970–. Memberships: Norwegian Authors Assn.; Norwegian Authors Ctr.; Artists' Assn.; Norwegian Assn. for Lit. Critics. Published works: Hansen pa jorden, 1966; Tidssignalet, 1967; TIL, 1969. Contbr. to: Dagbladet; Aftenposten; Universitas, & var. anthols. Honours, awards: Oslo Commune's Grant for young authors; Artists' Assn. 'Blom' Grant for Literature; Welhavens Legacy. Address: Grimstadgt 24 B, Oslo 4, Norway.

ABBASI, Tanveer, b. 7 Dec. 1934. Medical Practitioner. Education: M.B., B.S., Sind Univ., 1960. Memberships: Sec., Sindhi Sub Region, Pakistan Writers Guild, 1959; Sec., All Sind Sindhi Adabi Sangat, 1967; Ctrl. Exec. Pakistan Writers Guild, 1969–; Advisory Bd., Inst. of Sindology, Sind Univ. Published works: Ragoon Thiyoon Rabab (poems), 1958; Shair (poems), 1970. Contbr. to: Mehran; Naeen Zindagi; Barsaat; Sojhro; Sohni; Agte Kadam; Hilale Pakistan; Rooh Rehan; Malir Digest. Honours, awards: Best Book of Sindhi Poetry by Pakistan Writers Guild, 1970. Address: Sarmad House, Khairpur, Sind, Pakistan.

ABBOTT, Keith George, b. 2 Feb. 1944. Poet. Education: B.A., San Francisco State, 1968; M.A., Western Washington State, 1974. Married, 1 daughter. Positions held: Ed., Blue Suede Shoes, 1969-74; Chmn. of Engl. Dept., Palma H.S., 1971-72; Poet-in-Res., Sisykou Coll., 1972; Poet for Poetry-in-the-Schools, Calif., 1972-73. Published works: (poetry) Dumptruck, 1967; Moving Postures, 1969; Putty, 1971; Joi de Vivre, 1972; Red Lettuce, 1974; (prose fiction) Hero Pills, 1971; (novel) Gush, 1974. Contbr. to: The World; NEW; Choice; Tri-Qtly.; Poetry Northwest; Telephone; Measure; The Fault; Titmouse Review; Strange Faeces, etc. Honours, awards: Poets Fndn. Grant, 1972; CCLM Grants, 1971, '72, '73; Squaw Valley Writers Fellowship, 1973. Address: 1146 Sutter, Berkeley, CA 94707, U.S.A.

ABBOTT, Mason, b. 3 Oct. 1920. Cashier. Married with one son. Var. positions with Brewery inclng.: Order Mgr.; Gen. Office Mgr.; Br. Cashier. Contbr. to: Omens, 1972; The Shore, 1972 & 73; Viewpoints, 1972; New Headland, 1972; Centre 17, 1973; Pink Peace, 1972 & 73; Expression One, 1972; Poetry Forum, 1970; New Bond Anthol., 1970; New Poets, 1970 & 71; Treasury of Modern Poets, 1972 & 71; Seasons of Song, 1971; The Tavistock Collection, 1970; New Times Poetry, 1970. Address: 13 Helme Dr., Kendal, Westmorland, U.K.

ABDULJABBAR, Ahmad, b. 1921. Diplomat. Education: B.A., Political Science, Am. Univ. of Beirut, Lebanon. Has contributed to all Saudi Arabian newspapers as well as 'Al-Adeeb' lit. jrl. of Beirut. Address: c/o Saudi Arabian Embassy, Rome, Italy.

ABEL, Irene Marie, b. ∠3 Apr. 1931. Housewife. Education: De Paul Univ., Chicago Ill., 1950-51. Married John F. Abel, 5 children. Memberships: 2nd V.P., The Pa. Poetry Soc., 1971, '72, '73, '74; Chmn., Educ. Comm., ibid, 1972, '73, '74; Pegasus Contest Chmn., 1973-74; Penn Laurel, 1972–; Phila. Writers' Conf., 1970–. Published works: Parquet Circle, 1973; Poems for my Friends (children's poems), 1974. Contbr. to: Rendezvous; The Bulletin (Brussels); Prize Poems of the Pa. Poetry Soc.; Cat Mag.; Limnos; The Harrison Mid-Monthly Review; Humpty-Dumpty. Honours, awards: Hon. Mention, Pa. Poetry Soc., 1971 & '73; 2nd Prize, The Phila. Writers' Conf., 1971. Address: 10 Cherry Ln., Wynnewood, PA 19096, U.S.A.

ABRAM, Theresa, pen name **TWA.** Teacher. Education: B.S., Langston Univ., Okla.; M.A., Univ. of Okla., Norman. Memberships: Organized Philomatheons Club, Langston Univ. & 1st Pres. of same; Coun. for Matrons New Zion Bapt. Ch.; Chmn., Intermediate Dept. of State Tchrs. Assn.; Regl. Chmn., Zeno Club of Phi Delta Kappa; Poetry Socs. of Okla. & Ill.; Centro Studi e Scambi Int, etc. Published works: Abrams Treasures (book of poetry), 1967; Rhythm & Animals (book of poetry for children), 1970. Contbr. to: Black Dispatch, Okla. City; Tulsa Eagle; Church Bulletin, St. John's Bapt. Ch.; Black Voices; Modern Images, etc. Honours, awards: 1st prize for humorous writing, State Poetry Soc., 1969; Hon. Mention, ibid, 1971. Address: 2333 N.E. 22, Oklahoma City, OK 73111, U.S.A.

ABRAMOFF, Asya, pen name **ASYA,** b. 11 Apr. 1926. Pianist; Poetess; Painter. Education: Dip. of Musical School, Harbin, China. Memberships: Soc. of Russian Writers in Israel. Published works: 18 poems written in Russian, transl. into Hebrew by I. Zmora. Contbr. to: Hapoel Hazair; Davar Liladim; Davar Hapoelet; Mibifnim; Shdemoth; Russkaya Misl (Paris); Russkoye Slovo (N.Y.); Moznaim; Siman Kriah. Address: Smiliansky St. 31, Nathanya, Israel.

ABSE, Dannie, b. 22 Sept. 1923. Poet. Education: St. Illtyd's Coll., Cardiff; Univ. of S. Wales & Mon.: King's Coll., London; Westminster Hosp., London; MRCS; LRCP. Published works: After Every Green Thing, 1949; Walking Under Water, 1952; Ash On A Young Man's Sleeve, 1954; Some Corner Of An English Field, 1956; Tenants of the House, 1957; Poems, Golders Green, 1962; A Small Desperation, 1968; Selected Poems, 1970. Contbr. to: New Yorker; Encounter; BBC; etc. Awards: Charles Henry Foyle Award, 1960. Address: 85 Hodford Road, London N.W.11, U.K.

ABU-MUATI, Sa'ad I., b. 1934. Educational Administrator. Education: M.A., Public Administration. Positions held: Sev. positions in Education; Currently Dir. Gen. of Primary & Intermediate Educ., Min. of

Educ., Riyadh, Saudi Arabia. Has contributed to most Saudi Arabian periodicals. Address: c/o Min. of Educ., Riyadh, Saudi Arabia.

ACCONCI, Vito, b. 24 Jan. 1940. Lecturer; Editor. Educ: A.B., Coll. of the Holy Cross, Worcester, Mass., 1962; M.F.A., Univ. of Iowa, 1964. Positions held: Lectr., Schl. of Visual Arts, N.Y.C.; Co-Ed., 0 to 9 Magazine, N.Y.C. Published works: Four Book, 1968; Transference: Roget's Thesaurus, 1969. Contbr. to: Paris Review; Young American Poets (anthology), 1968. Honours, awards: Woodrow Wilson Fellowship, 1962; Grants from Nat. Co-ordinating Council of Literary Magazines, 1968. Address: 102 Christopher St., New York, NY 10014, U.S.A.

ACKERSON, Duane Wright, Jr., b. 17 Oct. 1942. Teacher of Creative Writing & English. Education: Geo. Wash. Univ., Wash. D.C., U.S.A., 1960-63; B.A. in Engl., Univ. of Ore., 1964; M.F.A., ibid, 1967. Married Catherine McFarland, 1 daughter. Positions held: Tchng. Asst. in Engl., Univ. of Ore., 1964-67; Rdr., Northwest Review, 1965-66; Asst. Ed., ibid, 1966-67; Instr. of Engl., Salem Coll., Winston-Salem, N.C., 1967-68; Instr. & Asst. Prof. of Engl., Idaho State Univ., 1968–; Ed., The Dragonfly, 1969–; Dir. of Creative Writing, Idaho State Univ., 1970–; Coordinator, Poetry in the Schls. for Idaho, 1970-71. Memberships incl.: Bd. Dirs., Pacific N.W. Coll. Engl. Assn., 1970-71; Coordinating Coun. of Lit. Mags., 1972–. Published works: UA Flight to Chicago, 1971; Inventory, 1971; Poems About Hard Times, 1971; Works: Edson Benedikt Ackerson, 1972; Old Movie House, 1972; Weathering, 1973. Contbr. to many poetry reviews, mags., etc. Address: Box 147, Idaho State Univ., Pocatello, ID 83201, U.S.A.

ACKLEY, Randall William, b. 9 Aug. 1931. Teacher; Poet; Humanist. Education: B.A., magna cum laude, 1962, Univ. of Minn.; Ph.D. Cand. 1965, Rice Univ.; Ph.D., 1974, Union Grad. School. Married; 4 children. Positions held: Instr.-Assoc. Prof., Univ. of Minn.; Univ. of Texas, Austin; Univ. of Utah; Univ. of the Americas; Univ. of Texas, El Paso; St. Mary's Coll. 1961-72; Faculty, Navajo Community Coll., Tsaile, Ariz., 1973. Also Acad. Dean, Candle Coll. (external degree prog.), Shreveport, La. Publisher/Ed., Quetzal: a journal of native American arts, and, Director, Southwest Poets Conference; Poetry Ed., Conradiana; Cons. Ed., Pembroke Mag. Memberships: Fellow, Int. Poetry Soc.; Polish Inst. Letters & Sci.; Southwest Poets Conference (founder, 1969, and director); Chmn., Assn. for Studies in Am. Indian Lits. Published works: Troll Songs, 1971; Sea Troll Songs, 1974. Contbr. to: St. Andrews Review; Pembroke Mag.; Poetry Review; Southern Poetry Review; Out of Sight; Cafe Solo; Measure; Last Journal of the Tibetan Kite Soc.; The Pilot; Quetzal; West Coast Poetry Review; Akwasasne Notes; Indian Histn.; Carolina Indian Voice; Rocky Mtn. Poetry Review; Inscape. Recip., Hon. Litt.D., Rochdale Coll., 1971. Address: Tsaile, AZ 86503, USA.

ACORN, Milton, b. 1923. Editor. Positions held: Editor, Moment Magazine, Montreal, P.Q., Canada. Published works: In Love and Anger, 1957; The Brain's the Target, 1960; Against A League of Liars, 1960; Jawbreakers, 1963; Selected Poems, 1969. Contbr. to: Tamarack Review; Fiddlehead; Delta; Canadian Forum; Poetry '62 (anthology), 1961. Address: c/o The Place, Stanley St., Montreal, P.Q., Canada.

ADAM, Helen, b. 2 Dec. 1909. Journalist. Educ: Univ. of Edinburgh, Scotland; Navin Academy. Published works: The Queen o'Crow Castle, 1958; Ballads, 1961; San Francisco's Burning, 1963. Contbr. to: Exantis; Poetry; (anthologies) Anthology of Irish Verse, 1948; New American Poetry, 1960; A Poetry Folio, 1963. Recip., Ingram Merrill Award.

ADAM, Ian William, b. 14 Nov. 1932. University Lecturer. Education: B.A., Alta. Univ., 1955; M.A., London Univ., 1960. Married, 3 children. Positions held: Asst. Prof., Univ. of Calgary, 1960-67; Assoc. Prof., ibid, 1967–. Published works: Encounter, 1973. Contbr. to: Prism Int.; Seven Persons Repository; Fiddlehead; Edge; New; Wascana Review; West Coast Review; Delta; Canadian Forum. Address: Dept. of Engl., Univ. of Calgary, Calgary, Alta., Canada T2N 1N4.

ADAMS, Anna Theresa, pen name, **ADAMS, Anna,** b. 9 Mar. 1926. Ceramicist; Artist. Education: Harrow Schl. of Art, U.K., 1939-46; Hornsey Schl. of Art, 1948-50. Married Norman Adams, 2 sons (Jacob & Benjamin). Positions held: P/t Tchr. of Art, var. schls. in London, Manchester & Settle; Designer, Chelsea Pottery, 1952-56. Mbr., Yorkshire Poets Assn. Published works: Journey through Winter, 1969; A Rainbow Plantation, 1971; Memorial Tree, 1972. Contbr. to: Phoenix (Manchester); Platform; Volt; Pennine Platform; New Headland; Outposts. Address: 'Butts', Horton-in-Ribblesdale, Settle, Yorks., U.K.

ADAMS, Barbara, pen names **ADAMS, Barbara Block & ADAMS, B.B.,** b. 23 Mar. 1932. College English Instructor. Education: B.S., State Univ. of N.Y. at New Paltz; M.A., ibid; currently working on Ph.D., N.Y. Univ. Married, 2 sons, 2 daughters. Positions held: Third Grade Tchr., Marlboro, N.Y., 1962-67 & Newburgh, N.Y., 1967-69; Instr. of Engl., Orange Co. Community Coll., Middletown, N.Y., 1970-74. Member, N.Y. Poetry Forum. Contbr. to: Bitterroot; Lilith; Conradiana; Poet Lore. Honours, awards: Finalist, Bitterroot Poetry Contest, 1973. Address: 57 Coach Lane, Newburgh, NY 12550, U.S.A.

ADAMS, Georgia B., b. 28 Mar. 1926. Administrative Assistant (Graphic Arts). Pub. The Silver Flute (poetry). Contributor to: Berks Italo-American; Gazeta Readingska; Gold Star Family Album; Gold Star Family Anthologies; Our Daily Bread; Cathedral Press publications; Grace & Hope Evangel; Gospel Herald; Mennonite Press publications; Ideals; Favorites Sacred Songs; Sing My Heart; Voices in Worship; Bible Heroes; John Sergey Sings; The Saviour Has Come; New Songs for Special Occasions. Poems regularly read on miscellaneous radio stations. Address: 867 Delta Avenue, Northmont, Reading, Penna. 19605, USA.

ADAMS, Hazard, b. 15 Feb. 1926. Professor of English. Education: B.A., Princeton Univ., U.S.A., 1948; M.A., Univ. of Wash., 1949; Ph.D., ibid, 1953. Positions held: U.S. Marine Corps, 1943-45, 1951; Instr., Engl., Cornell Univ., 1952-56; Asst. Prof. of Engl., Univ. of Tex., 1956-59; Asst. Prof. of Engl., Univ. of Tex., 1956-59; Vis. Assoc. Prof. Engl., Wash. Univ., 1959; Assoc. Prof. to Prof., Mich. State Univ., 1959-64; Prof. Engl., Univ. of Calif., Irvine, 1964-73. Memberships: MLA; Philological Assn. of the Pacific Coast; Am. Soc. for Aesthetics. Has written books of criticism & novels. Contbr. to: Quicksilver; Michigan's Voice; Poetry Northwest; Poetry; American Scholar. Address: 1121 Oxford Lane, Newport Beach, CA 92660, U.S.A.

ADAMS, Kaywynne, b. 31 Jul. 1936. Writer. Education: McKendree Coll., Lebanon, Ill.; Univ. of Leiden, Netherlands; Indiana State Univ. Married; 2 s. Membership: Poetry Soc. of America. Contbr. to: Best Poems of 1972; Poetry (Chicago); North American Review; Prairie Schooner; Northeast. Awarded Christensen Award from Prairie Schooner for best group of poems in Vol. XLV., 1971-72. Address: 800 S. 4th St., Terre Haute, IN 47807, USA.

ADAMS, Leonie, b. 9 Dec. 1899. Teacher; Writer; Poet. Education: A.B., Barnard Coll., 1922. Widow of William E. Troy. Positions held: Tchr., Writing &/or Lit., Wash. Sq. Coll., 1930-32, Sarah Lawrence Coll., 1933-34, Bennington Coll., 1935-37 & 1941-44, N.J. Coll. for Women (Douglass), 1946-48, Columbia Univ. Gen. Studies, 1947-68; Cons. in Poetry, Lib. of Congress, 1948-49 & at Wash. Sq. Coll. of N.Y.U., 1953-54; New Schl. for Soc. Rsch., 1950; Vis. Prof. of Poetry, Univ. of Wash., 1960 & '69, Trinity Coll.,

Hartford, 1960, Purdue Univ., 1971-72; Staff, Breadloaf Writers' Conf., 1956-59; Fulbright Lectr., Toulouse & in Spain (USIS), 1954-55. Memberships: PEN; Nat. Inst. of Arts & Letters, 1951–; Sec., ibid, 1959-61. Published works: Those Not Elect, 1925; High Falcon & Other Poems, 1929; This Measure, 1933; Lyrics of François Villon (Ed. w. intro. & transl.), 1932; Poems, a Selection, 1954, '59. Contbr. to var. reviews & newspapers. Honours, awards: Award, lyric poetry, Nat. Inst. of Arts & Letters, 1949; D.Litt., N.J. Coll. for Women, 1950; Harriet Monroe Award for Lit., Univ. of Chicago, 1954; Bollinger Prize in Poetry, 1954; Shelley Mem. Award, 1954; Acad. of Am. Poets Fellowship, 1959; Brandeis Medal & Award for Poetry, 1969; Mark Rothke Fndn. Grant, 1972, etc. Address: Candlewood Mt., New Milford, CT 06776, U.S.A.

ADAMS, Peter Robert Charles, pen name **ADAMS, Perseus,** b. 11 Mar. 1933, Cape Town, S. Africa. English Teacher. Education: B.A., Psychol. & Engl., Univ. of Cape Town; Secondary Tchrs. Cert., ibid. Positions held: Jr. Clerk; Psychologist; Journalist; Tchr. Published works: The Land at my Door, 1964; Grass for the Unicorn, 1972. Contbr. to: Standpunte; Contrast; The New African; The Lion & the Impala; Cape Argus; EP Herald; New Coin; New Nation; Poetry, USA; Encounter, UK; Rhodesian Poetry; The South African Book of Verse; Penguin Anthol. of S.A. Verse; P.E.N. Anthol., 1968. African Writing Today; Commonwealth Poetry. Awards: The South African Poetry Prize, 1964; The Eastern Province Poetry Prize, 1964; The Festival of Rhodesia Poetry Prize, 1970; 2nd Prize, John Keats Mem. Poetry Competition (London), 1972. Address: 2 Wellesley Court, Durban Rd., Wynberg, Cape Town, S.ªAfrica.

ADAMSON, Margot Robert, b. 1898. Published works: A Year of War and Other Poems, 1917; The Desert and the Sown and Other Poems, 1921; Up on the Hill of Fairlight, 1925; A Northern Holiday, 1928; The Forester's Wife, 1931; (translations) A Treasury of Middle English Verse, 1930; The Degrees of Knowledge, 1937; True Humanism, 1938; (novels) Render Unto Ceasar, 1934; A Rope of Sand, 1965. Contbr. to Modern Scottish Poetry (anthology), 1966.

ADCOCK, Fleur, b. 10 Feb. 1934. Librarian. Education: various schools in UK and New Zealand; M.A. (in classics) from Victoria Univ. of Wellington, N.Z. Divorced; 2 s. Positions held: Library positions in Univ. of Otago, Alexander Turnbull Library, Wellington, and (currently) Foreign and Commonwealth Office, London. Published works: The Eye of the Hurrican, 1964; Tigers, 1967; High Tide in the Garden, 1971. Contbr. to: Listener; New Statesman; Encounter; London Mag.; Times Lit. Supp.; Ambit; Landfall; Islands; Malahat Review. Also BBC. Awards: Wellington Festival Poetry Prize, 1961; NZ State Lit. Fund Award, 1964; Buckland Award (NZ), 1968; Jessie MacKay Prize (NZ), 1968 and 1971; Arts Council Publication Grant, 1971. Address: 14 Lincoln Rd., London N2 9DL, UK.

ADELMAN, Gary S., b. 1 Jul. 1935. Associate Professor of Engl. Lit. Education: B.A., Univ. of Mich.; M.A., Ph.D., Columbia Univ., NYC. Married Bette Orovan Adelman, 5 children (Katherine, John, Carrie, James, Madeline). Positions held: Instr. of Engl., Brooklyn Coll., 1958-63; Asst. Prof. of Engl., Univ. of Ill., 1963-1970, and Assoc. Prof., 1970–. Member, World Poetry Soc. Pubs.: Honey Out of Stone, 1970; Political Poems, 1968. Contrib. to: Prairie Schooner; New Orleans Review; D.H. Lawrence Review; Poet. Recip. 2nd prize, Hart Crane Poetry Award, 1967. Address: 910 W. White St., Champaign, Ill. 61820, USA.

ADKINS, Joseph Carroll, b. 29 Nov. 1933. Engineer of Long Range Planning. Education: B.S., Mech. Engrng., La. State Univ. Positions held: Mech. Engr. then Engr. of Long Range Planning, Ark. La. Gas Co. Memberships: Past Nat. Corres. Sec., Past Chapt. Pres. & currently Recording Sec., Nat. Soc. of Arts & Letters, Shreveport Chapt; D'Oyly Carte Opera Trust Ltd., London, U.K.; Gilbert & Sullivan Soc., London;

Bd. Govs. & Sec., The Gilbert & Sullivan Soc. of Shreveport; La. State Poetry Soc.; Acad. of Am. Poets. Editor: Shreveport Chapt. NSAL Newsletter (w. poems each issue), 1971-74; Gilbert & Sullivan Soc. of Shreveport 'D'Oyly Card' (w. poems each issue) 1973-74. Contbr. to: IWWP Anthol.; R.C. Modeler; Modeler's Jrnl.; Sharks Sparks; Ark-La. News. Address: Box 1734, Shreveport, LA 71102, U.S.A.

ADLER, Carol Ellen, b. 5 Dec. 1938. Writer. Education: Brandeis Univ.; A.B., Univ. of Mich. Married Samuel Adler, 2 daughters. Memberships: Editl. Bd., Jewish Roots, 1974–; Nat. Poetry Soc.; Rochester Poetry Soc. Has written sev. short stories, children's books & two novels. Contbr. to: European Judaism (London); Jewish Qtly. (London); Reconstructionist; Jewish Roots; Cimarron Review; Miss. Review; Law & Arts Review; People; Mundus Artium; Fellowship in Prayer; Amanuensis; Reform Judaism; Jean's Jrnl.; Janus SCTH; Eclipse. Translations of Israel Emiot appeared in Jewish Ledger, etc. Address: 54 Railroad Mills Rd., Pittsford, NY 14534, U.S.A.

ADLER, (Kinbor) Marnie Faustine, pen name **ADLER, Marnie,** b. 4 Feb. 1924. Poet; Tutor English and Speech Therapy. Education: Student of Psychol., Hunter College. Married to Dan Adler; 2 children. Member, Poetry Soc. of America; West Va. Poetry Soc.; Nat. Fed. of State Poetry Socs. Inc.; Affil. of Acad. of American Poets; Fellow, Internat. Poetry Soc., UK., Former correspondent, Poesie Vivante International, and member. Contrib. to: Int. Who's Who in Poetry Anthology 1972; P.V. Anthol.; Internat. Poetry Soc. Anthology; Poesie Vivante Int. Tribune: No. 24/67, No. 27/68; Chirimo/Rhodesia, 1969; Second Poesie Vivante Anthology, etc. Recipient Int. Who's Who in Poetry Cert. of Merit; Karta of Award, 1969. Address: 24 Farrell Street, Long Beach, N.Y. 11561, USA.

ADZOVIC, Kathryn Battles, b. 8 Oct. 1943. Teacher; Housewife. Education: B.A., Elmhurst Coll., 1967; McCormick Theol. Sem. Positions held: Engl. & Lit. Tchr., 1967-68; Sales, Lane Bryant, Marshal Field & Bonwit Teller, 1968-71. Contbr. to: Intermission Mag., 1968; Collage, Lit. mag., 1968; Patterns, anthol., 1971. Address: 211 Liberty, Apt. 9, Wauconda, IL 60084, U.S.A.

AGARONIAN, Leon Roman, pen names **NIRAPO, NIRAGO,** b. 29 June 1941. Author; Poet; Professor; Journalist. Education: CUNY, N.Y.; State Univ. of N.Y.; Sorbonne, Paris, France; N.Y. Univ.; Univ. of Barcelona, Spain. Positions held: Author; Poet; Professor. Memberships: Poetry Soc. of Am.; Univ. Alumni Club Lit. Soc. Published works: Alive Dust Shell, 1968; Spengalam, 1973. Contbr. to: N.Y. Times; Bachaet; Poet Lore; News Review. Honours, awards: Alumni Award; Stipend Bourse; U.N. Award for Peace. Address: Pageant-Poseidon Ltd., C44 Pacifica St., Brooklyn, N.Y., U.S.A.

AGREN, Sven Gösta, b. 3 Aug. 1936. Author; Film Director. Education: Ph.D., Stockholm Univ., Sweden, 1971. Member of Bd., Finlands Svenska Författaretörening. Published works: Kraft och tanke, 1955; Jordlös bonde, 1956; Folkvargarna, 1958; Bergsväg, 1959; Emigrantresan, 1960; Ett brev fran Helsingfors, 1961; Din makt är alltför stor, 1962; Stig upp pa bergen, 1963; Kungörelser, 1965; ''Agren'', 1968; Cellens dagrar, 1970; Dan Anderssons väg, 1970; Kärlek som i allting bor, 1971; Massmöte pa jorden, 1972; Han kommer, han kommer, 1973. Address: Handelsespl. 42, Vasa, Finland.

AHARONI, Arie, b. 27 Oct. 1923. Author. Education: Humanities in the Hebrew Univ. of Jerusalem. Married, 3 children. Member of Kibbutz Beit-Alfa, Israel. Memberships: Acum (Soc. of Authors, Composers of Israel); The KibbzAuthors Org. Published works: (Translations into Hebrew) A Cloud in Trousers, by V. Mayakovsky, 1960, '66; Anthology of Young Russian Poetry, 1962; Three Poems, by A.S. Pushkin, 1962;

Oresteia, by Aeschylus, 1967; Under Milk Wood, by Dylan Thomas, 1965; Anna Sniyegina, by S. Yesenin, 1966; Twenty Poems, by A. Vozhesensky, 1967; Sky in the Grass, by R. Fishman, 1968; Troilus & Cressida, by W. Shakespeare, 1971; A Legend on the Rain, by B. Akhmadulina, 1973. Contbr. to: (mags.) Hedim; Mibifnim; Ofek; Behinot; (newspapers) Al-Hamishmar; Ma'ariv; Davar; Ha'arez; Lamerhav. Address: Kibbutz Biet-Alfa, 19140, Israel.

AHERN, Tom, b. 3 Aug. 1947. Writer. Education: M.A. & B.A. in Engl. Lit., Brown Univ., Providence, R.I., U.S.A. Positions held: Co-Ed., Eye Witness (Cambridge); Columnist, Point-in-Time; Ed., Diana's Bi Monthly. Published works: The Transcript, 1973; The Strangulation of Dreams, 1973; Sphincter, 1973. Contbr. to: Ghost Dance; Center; Telephone; Eye Witness; Tottel's; Curtains; Diana's Bi Monthly; Brown Sweater; The Point; Margins; The Transubstantiations of the John Barton Wolgamot Soc.; Occident; Point-in-Time; The Lit. Supplement; The Providence Review, etc. Recip., The Pinky Tincture Grant, 1972. Address: 71 Elmgrove Ave., Providence, RI 02906, U.S.A.

AHLFORS, Bengt Gunnar Richard, b. 28 Dec. 1937. Theatre Director; Playwright. Education: M.A., Lit. & Pol. Sci., Helsinki Univ., Finland. Memberships: Finland's Svenska Författareförening; Finland's Dramatikerförbund; Sveriges Dramatikerförbund. Published works: Sanger & Dikter (songs & poems), 1971; Songs in Plays, TV Programs, etc. Address: St. Robertsgatan 16 A9, 00120 Helsingfors 12, Finland.

AHLO, Börje Walter, b. 19 Nov. 1932. Writer. Memberships: Finland's Swedish Author Assn.; Osterbottens Lit. Assn. Published works: i debutdiktantologin Tre – (w. Carl-Erik Ström & Dan Sundell), 1968; I skuggan av ditt leende, 1972. Contbr. to: Horizon; Hembygden; Capital News; Jakobstad's News, etc. Honours, awards: 200 Mark, Jakobstad Culture Comm. Grant, 1969; 300 Mark, ibid, 1971; 600 Mark, 1973; 1000 Mark, Swedish Culture Fund's Author Grant, 1970; 2000 Mark, ibid, 1973; 1000 Mark, Min. of Educ's. Lib. Grant, 1973. Address: Lindskogsgatan 26, 68620 Jakobstad 2, Finland.

AHLO, Walter Johannes, b. 15 Apr. 1907. Writer. Married Heidi Birgine Lillqvist, 1932, 3 children. Positions held incl: Sailor; Salesman, etc. Memberships: Finland's Swedish Author Assn.; Osterbottens Lit. Assn. Published works: (prose) En sjömans liv, (A Sailor's Life), 1964; Pa mafa runt jorden (Wandering around the World), 1967; Tidlös förtröstan (Timeless Comfort), 1971; Tillfällets Skickelse, 1973; 30 short stories in var. newspapers; lyric poetry; 4 plays, local & Osterbottniska Radio. Contbr. to: Jakobstad News; Vasabladet; Alands News; Capital News; Osterbottningen; Hembygden; Skrivarna; Pedersöre. Honours, awards: 1000 Mark, Lib. Grant, 1968, '71, '73; 3000 Mark, Wainsteinska Fndn., 1971; 1000 Mark, Culture Fund, Helsingfors, 1970; 400 Mark, Jakobstad Town Distribution, 1973; 1000 Mark, Art Commn., Vasa Co., 1973. Address: Lindskogsgatan 26, 68620 Jakobstad 2, Finland.

AHMAD, Zia Nisar, pen name **ZIA JALLUNDHRI,** b. 2 Feb. 1923. Civil Servant. Education: B.A., (Hons.), Govt. Coll., Lahore (Univ. of the Punjab), 1942; M. A. (Engl.Lit.), ibid, 1945. Positions held: Lectr. in Engl., Islamia Coll., Lahore, 1945; Programme Producer, All India Radio, 1945-47; Programme Producer, Radio Pakistan, 1947-49; Exec. Appts. in the Post Office Dept., 1950-65; Dir., Pakistan Coun. for Nat. Integration, 1965-57; Dpty. Dir. Gen., Post Office Dept., 1967–. Memberships: held var. offices, Halqa-i-Arbab-i-Zauq; Govng. Body, Arts Coun. of Pakistan, Karachi, 1967-70; Writers' Guild of Pakistan. Published works: Sar-i-Sham (First coll. of Poems), 1955; Na-Rasa (Second coll. of Poems), 1966. Contbr. to the leading lit. jrnls. of the country, particularly Fanoon, Auraq, Naya Daur, Savera, Naqoosh, Humayun & Adabi Dunya; also rep. in var. anthols. of poems published in Pakistan & India, especially in the selections of the best poems of the year from 1942

onwards. Recip., Halqa-i-Arbab-i-Zauq's Prize for the best Urdu poem, 1945. Address: Deputy Dir. Gen., Pakistan Post Office, Karachi, Pakistan.

AHMAD SHAH, Nadeem, pen name **AHMAD NADEEM QASIMI,** b. 20 Nov. 1916. Editor; Poet. Education: B.A., Univ. of the Punjab, Pakistan. Positions held: Ed., children's weekly 'Phool' & women's weekly 'Tehzib-I-Niswan', Lahore, 1942-45; Ed., monthly lit. mag. 'Adab-I-Latif', Lahore, 1943-46; Ed., lit. qtly. 'Sawera', Lahore, 1947-48; Ed., monthly lit. mag. 'Nuqoosh', Lahore, 1948-50; Ed., The Daily 'Imroze', Lahore, 1953-59; Ed., monthly 'Funoon', Lahore, 1963–. Memberships: Sec. Gen., The Pakistan Progressive Writers' Assn., 1949-54; Chmn., Afro-Asian Writers' Liaison Comm.; Pakistan Writers' Guild. Published works: Rim Jhim, 1940; Jalal-o-Jamal, 1947; Shola-e-Gul, 1953; Dasht-e-Wafa, 1963; Moheet, 1974. Contbr. to: Daily Imroze; Daily Jang; Daily Hurriyat; Daily Pakistan Times; Daily Dawn; Naya Daur; Seep, etc. Honours, awards: Adamji Lit. Prize of Poetry, 1964; Pride of Performance in Lit., 1968. Address: Ed. of The Funoon, 47 Anarkali, Lahore, Pakistan.

AHSAN, Syed Ali, b. 26 Mar. 1922. University Vice-Chancellor. Education: M.A. Engl., Univ. of Dacca, 1944. Married, 4 children. Positions held: Rdr. & Hd. of the Dept. of Bengali, Univ. of Karachi, 1953-60; Dir., Bengali Acad., Dacca, 1960-66; Dean of the Fac. of Arts, Univ. of Chittagong, 1967-68, '68-69, '69-70; Prof. & Hd. of the Dept. of Bengali, Univ. of Chittagong; V. Chancellor, Jahangirnagar Univ., 1972–. Memberships: Bengali Acad.; MLA (USA); Int. PEN. Published works incl: (poetry) Chahar Darwesh (The Four Mendicants), a narrative poem in Bengali, 1945; Anek Akash (Many Skies), a book of lyrics; Ekak Sandhyai Basanta (Spring on a Lonely Evening), poems; Shahasha Sacakita (Suddenly in a Tremour), poems; Uchcharan (Utterances), poems; var. rsch. publs., adaptations & transl. & edited jrnls., books & anthols. Contbr. to o'seas jrnls. Honours, awards: Bengali Acad. Award for Poetry, 1968; Dawood Prize for Original Research, 1969. Has attended var. int. congresses & acted as Adviser to UNESCO. Address: Vice-Chancellor's Residence, 119–B Dhanmondi Residential Area, Rd. No.2, Dacca 5, Bangladesh.

AHTI, Risto Tapani, b. 27 Aug. 1943. Poet. Studied literature & English at Oulu Univ. Married Pia Kristina, 1 daughter (Kukka Matleena). Member, Suomen Kirjailijaliitto. Published works: Talvi on harha, 1967; Runoja, 1969; Unilaulu, 1972. Contbr. to: Parnasso. Recip. prize Kordelin, 1972. Address: Valkkyla VI B 11, Oulu 10, Finland.

AIG-IMOUKHUEDE, Frank Abiodun, b. 8 Jan. 1935. Film-maker; Free-lance Journalist. Education: Igbobi Coll., Lagos, Nigeria; Univ. Coll., Ibadan; Film Inst. of India, Poona; B.A. Hons. (Lond.), English; Dip. in Cinematography. Positions held: Sr. Feature Writer, Daily Express; Info. Officer, Western Nigeria, then Mid-Western Nigeria; Scriptwriter, Fed. Film Unit. Author of Day of Sasswood, 1965; sev. radio plays, humorous essays, & Ikeke (play). Contbr. to: Flamingo; W. African Pilot; The Horn & the Beacon (Univ. Coll. of Ibadan). Address: Fed. Film Unit, Min. of Information, Ikoyi, Lagos, Nigeria, WA.

AIKEN, Conrad Potter, b. 1889. Poet. Education: A.B., Harvard Coll., Mass. Positions held: Contbng. Ed., The Dial (jrnl.) 1917-19; Instr., Harvard Coll., 1927-28; Cons. in Poetry, Lib. of Congress, 1950-51, '51-52. Published works: Earth Triumphant, 1914; Turns and Movies, 1916; The Jig of Forslin, 1916; Nocturne of Remembered Spring, 1917; The Charnel Rose, 1918; The House of Dust, 1920; Punch–the Immortal Liar, 1921; Priapus and the Pool, 1922; The Pilgrimage of Festus, 1923; Senlin–A Biography, 1925; Scepticisms, 1919; Bring! Bring! and other stories, 1925; Blue Voyage, 1927; Costumes By Eros, 1928; Selected Poems, 1929; John Deth and other poems, 1930; The Coming Forth By Day Of Osiris Jones, 1931; Preludes for Memnon, 1931; Great Circle, 1933; Among the Lost

People, 1934; Landscape West of Eden, 1934; King Coffin, 1935; Time In The Rock, 1936; A Heart For The Gods Of Mexico, 1939; The Conversation–or Pilgrim's Progress, 1939; And In The Human Heart, 1940; Brownstone Eclogues, 1942; The Soldier, 1944; The Kid, 1947; The Divine Pilgrim, 1949; Skylight One, 1949; The Short Stories of Conrad Aiken, 1950; Ushant–An Essay (autobiography), 1952; Collected Poems, 1953; A Letter From Li Po, 1955; Mr. Arcularis, 1957; Sheepfold Hill, 1958; A Reviewer's ABC, 1958; Collected Criticism, 1958; Collected Short Stories, 1960; Selected Poems, 1961; The Morning Song of Lord Zero, 1963; A seisure of Limericks, 1964; Cats and Bats and Things with Wings, 1965; Tom, Sue and the Clock, 1966; Thee, 1967; Collected Poems, 1916-1970, 1970; Collected Criticism, 1968; Ushant: an Essay, 1971; the Clerk's Jrnl: An Undergrad. Poem, 1971; Ed., the following: Modern American Poets, 1922; Selected Poems of Emily Dickinson, 1924; American Poetry 1671-1928 (anthol.), 1929. Contbr. to the following jrnls. & anthols: Poets on Poetry, 1965; Athenaeum; Nation; London Mercury; Dial; New Republic; Freeman; New Freeman; Criterion; New Criterion; Atlantic; etc. Honours & Awards: Pulitzer Prize, 1930; Shelley Mem. Award, 1930; Nat. Book Award, 1954; Bollinger Prize, 1956; Fellowship, Acad. of Am. Poets, 1957; Gold Medal for Poetry, Nat. Inst. of Arts & Letters, 1958; Nat. medal for Lit., 1969. Address: c/o Oxford Univ. Press, 37 Dover St., London, W1, UK.

AILOR, Hazel Lea Nowell, pen names **NOWELL, Hazel Lea & AILOR, Hazel Nowell,** b. 18 May 1911. Homemaker. Education: B.A., Engl.–Soc.Scis., La. Tech., Ruston, La., 1936; postgrad. work, Engl.–Educ., ibid, 1936-37; Sociol. of Relig., SMU, Dallas, Tex. Married James W. Ailor, 3 children (1 dec.) Positions held: Dir. of Methodist Student work, La. Tech.; Sec. to Dean of Schl. of Arts & Scis.; Sec. to Dean of Women, SMU; Field Wkr., La Dept. of Public Welfare, 1 yr.; Supvsr., Home-Hosp. for unwed mothers, 5 yrs.; Reporter & Features, weekly newspaper, etc. Memberships: Laramore Rader Poetry Grp.; Acad. of Am. Poets; Pres., Sigma Tau Delta; Chi Delta Phi. Contbr. to: The White Heron, anthol., 1937; The Mansfield Enterprise; Pine Cones; Guideposts; The Christian Herald; Orbit, etc. Honours, awards incl: Sigma Tau Delta Poetry Award, 1937; Carrie Baines Yeiser Poetry Award, Barry Coll., 1968; Vivian Laramore Rader special monthly awards, June 1967, June 1970, Summer 1972. Address: 2311 Second Ave., Lake Charles, LA 70601, U.S.A.

AKALIN, Lûtfullah Sami, b. 2 Nov. 1924. Educator. Education: grad., Fac. of Lit., Univ. of Ankara, Turkey; doctorate, Fac. of Lit., Univ. of Istanbul. Positions held: Tchr. of literature & language arts in var. senior high schls., 1949-72; Instr. of Folklore & Folk-Literature, Univ. of Istanbul, Fac. of Economical Scis., Dept. of Jrnlsm., 1973-74. Rep. of Turkish Poets Assn. at the Second World Congress of Poets, Taipei, Taiwan, Rep. of China, 1973. Published works: Halit Ziya, 1953, '62; Mehmet Rauf, 1953; Erzurum Bilmeceleri (Turkish Folk-Riddles from Oral Traditions), 1954; Japon Şiiri (an anthol. of Japanese Poetry in Turkish version), 1962; Çin Şiiri (an anthol. of Chinese poetry in Turkish version), 1964; Edebiyat Terimleri Sözlüğü (A Dictionary of Turkish & World Lit. Terms), 1966, '70, '72; Dede Korkut, 1968; Türk Manileri, vols. I & II (an anthol. of Turkish Folk Poetry), 1972. Contbr. to var. mags. Honours, awards: Chancellor of the 2nd World Congress of Poets, Taipei, Taiwan & recip. of the Dectrum Award, 1973. Address: Vefa Lisesi Edebiyat Oğretmeni, Vefa-Istanbul, Turkey.

AKAVYAHU, Itzhak, b. 24 May 1918. Germany. Teacher; Writer; Poet; Translator. Positions held: Tchr., HS; Co-ed., Carmelit, since 1967. Memberships: Hebrew Writers Assoc. in Israel; PEN Ctr., Israel. Published works: Mar'eh Wa Siah (Sight and Utterance), 1952; Manginat Hatzot (Midnight Melody), 1961; Hattarat Nedarim (Abrogation of Vows), 1963; Etzli Babayit (With Me At My Home), 1969; The Image

of the Father in Contemporary Hebrew Poetry (Essay), 1969. Translations: Sonnets from the Portuguese, by Elizabeth Barrett Browning, 1964; Poésies Choisies, Henri Michaux, 1965; Le Retour de L'Enfant Prodigue, by André Gide, 1970; Aphorismen, by Georg Ch. Lichtenberg, 1970; also trans. for broadcast & theater; poetry criticism in periodicals. Contbr. to: Gilyonot; Moznayim; Meassef; Carmelit. Awards: 1st Prize, Competition for a Hebrew poem about Israel or a biblical topic, Hebrew Section, BBC, London. Address: 5 Koresh St., Haifa 33726, Israel.

AKESSON, Sonja, b. 19 Apr. 1926. Writer. Member, Sveriges Forfattarforbund. Published works: Situatoner, 1957; Glasveranda, 1959; Leva Livef, 1961; Husfrid, 1963; Ute skiner solen, 1965; Jag bor i Sverige, 1966; Man far vara glad och Sacka Gud, 1967; Pris, 1968; Hagdängor, 1969; Ljuvor sexfiofal, 1970; Dödens ungar, 1973; three book with Jarl Hammorberg-Akesson – Hrolande dikter/nej sa fan heller, 1967; Kandis, 1969; Ha, vi är ja väg, 1972. Honours, awards: Ferlinpriset, De Nros Pris. Address: Hertig Knutsgatan 43C, 302 50 Halmstad, Sweden.

AKINS, Terese. Poet; Reader; Speaker. Education: Compton Coll.; Poetry & Creative Writing, Inst. of Lifetime Learning, Long Beach. Married Herbert Vancefield Akins, 1 son. Positions held: Demonstrator of Chemical Cleaner, Walkers, Long Beach; Sales & Service, Studio Girl Cosmetics & Avon Cosmetics; Front Desk Receptionist, St. Francis Hosp., Lynwood, Calif., etc. Memberships: 4th V.P., State Bd., Calif. Fed. of Chaparral Poets; Jr.–Sr. H.S. Contest Chmn. for Calif., ibid, 1974; Fndr. & 1st Pres., Apollo Chapt.; Fndr., Publicity & Mbrship Chmn., Orpheus Chapt., Lakewood; Poetry Dir., Long Beach Writers Club, etc. Rep. in following anthols: From Sea to Sea in Song, 1965 & '66; Velvet Paws in Print, 1967; Yearbook of Modern Poetry, 1971; Lyrics of Love, 1972; Outstanding Contemporary Poetry, 1972 & '73, etc. Contbr. to many mags. & jrnls. inclng: Clifton's Food for Thought; Fireflower; Am. Bard; Pegasus Prances; Haiku Highlights; Jean's Jrnl.; Modern Images; Major Poets; Poetry of the Year. Honours, awards incl: Dlp. of Merit, Centro Studi e Scambi, 1969; Medal of Hon.; Diploma di Benemerenza, 1972; Cert. of Merit for Disting. Serv. in Field of Poetry, Am. Poet's Fellowship Soc., 1973. Address: 4748 Oliva Ave., Lakewood, CA 90712, U.S.A.

AL-ABIDEEN, Ali Zain, b. 1923. Businessman. Education: Military Cert., Cavalry. Positions held: Col., King Abdulaziz Military Acad., Riyadh, ret'd. Contbr. to all Saudi Arabian periodicals. Address: c/o Higher Comm. for Scis., Arts & Literature, Ministry of Education, Riyadh, Saudi Arabia.

AL-BAWARDI, Saad, b. 1929. Civil Servant. Self educated. Published works: Sev. volumes of poetry in Arabic. Contbr. to all Saudi Arabian newspapers. Recip. of Short Story Prize sponsored by 'Al-Bilad', newspaper. Address: Saudi Arabian Cultural Bureau, P.O.B. 2583, Beirut, Lebanon.

ALBERT, Mimi, b. 18 June 1940. Writer; College Instructor. Education: Philos. & Anthropol., Hunter Coll., N.Y., 1963; M.F.A. in Writing, Columbia Univ., N.Y.C., 1969. Positions held: Instr., Fordham Univ., 1969-70; Instr., Creative Writing, Lit., College Composition, Brooklyn Coll., 1970-75. Contbr. to: The Above Ground Review; Remember Our Fire; The Transatlantic Review; The Phoenix; Pequod; Moving Out; Off Our Backs; Our Town; Palehorse Review. Address: P.O. Box 389, Cooper Stn., N.Y., NY 10003, U.S.A.

ALBERTS, Lily S. Krug, b. 19 Nov. 1890. Artist & Writer. Positions held: Lab. Techn.; Writer. Published works: (books of poetry) Married to Life, 1968; Don't Count The Wrinkles, 1970; Leisure is Treasure, 1973. Contbr. to: Oakland Tribune; Berkeley Gazette; var. periodicals in U.S.A., Australia, N. Zealand & Germany. Recip., prize from Radio Stn. in Va. (poems also read over the air). Address: 531 Kenyon Ave.,

Berkeley, Kensington, CA, U.S.A.

ALDAN, Daisy, b. 17 Sept. 1923. Poet; Educator. Education: B.A., Hunter Coll., U.S.A.; M.A., Brooklyn Coll.; N.Y. Univ.; Litt.D., Univ. of Karachi. Positions held: Tchr., H.S. of Art & Design, 1948–; Regular Dramatic Show, Columbia Broadcasting System, 1934-56; Publisher, small press, 1953–; Ed., Folder Mag. of the Arts, 1953-59; Ed., Two Cities, 1961-62; Ed., var. poetry anthols., Tchr., Creative Writing, Emerson Coll., Sussex, U.K., summer 1971. Mbr. var. orgs. inclng. PEN & on Exec. Bd. of Poetry Soc. of Am. Published works incl: (poems) The Destruction of Cathedrals, 1964, 2nd ed.; 1970; Seven:Seven, 1967; The Masks are Becoming Faces, 1967; Breakthrough, 1971; Love Poems of Daisy Aldan, 1972; Stones, 1973; special edns. of poetry in calligraphy, Or Learn to Walk on Water, 1970; Journey, 1970; A New Folder: Americans: Poems & Drawings, 1962; Poems from India, 1969; The Death Experience of Manes, 5 act play in verse by A. Steffen, transl. from German, 1971. Num. individual poems included in major periodicals in USA, Switz., England, France, Spain, Italy, India. Rep. in num. anthols. inclng: Am. Lit. Anthol.; Poems in a Time Revolution; 53 Am. Poets Today; New Orlando Anthol.; Golden Blade Anthol. Many translations inclng: French poetry From Denerval to Valery, transl. of Rimbaud, Baudelaire, DeNerval, Mallarme, Apollinaire; An Anthol. of Medieval Lyrics. Has given lectures at univs. & instns. & poetry readings at univs., colls., libs. etc. & on radio stns. Recordings made for Lib. of Congress & Harvard Univ. Lamont Poetry Colls. Honours, awards incl: Nat. Fndn. of the Arts Poetry Prize; 1st Prize Poetry, Rochester Fest. of Arts. Address: 325 E. 57 St., N.Y., NY 10022, U.S.A.

ALDERDICE, Eve, b. 18 Dec. 1922. Housewife. Married James C. Alderdice, 1 son, 3 daughters. Positions held: Sec. Asst. to husband, A & B Heating & Cooling Co. Memberships: Ky. State Poetry Soc.; Purchase Poets Club. Contbr. to: Ladies Home Jrnl.; Saturday Evening Post; Pegasus; Bardic Echoes; Playgirl Mag.; The News, Paducah Ky. Weekly Newspaper, & other small mags. & regional newspapers. Honours, awards: Winner, Ky. State Poetry Contest, 1970-72, & var. other poetry mentions. Address: 525 South 6th, Mayfield, KY 42066, U.S.A.

ALDREDGE, Georgie Redden, b. 25 Dec. 1919, Kansas City, Kan., USA. Financial Planner; Shop Owner. Married, Charles S. Aldredge, 1 d. Positions held: Sec., Beaumont Indep. Schls., 1953-59; Ed., Ch. News, N. End Meth. Ch. & Educ. Asst., 1960-65; Financial Planner, Waddell & Reed, Inc., 1966-69; Co-Operator, Aldredge Cupboard, Vidor, Tex. Memberships: Beaumont Chap., Poetry Soc. of Tex. Contbr. to: Poetry, Classical & Contemporary, 1969; The Church School. Recip., 1st place, Beaumont City Contest, Beaumont Writers Club for Festival of Arts, 1969. Address: 2005 Primrose, Beaumont, Tex. 77703, USA.

ALDRICH, Mark Joseph, b. 18 Jan. 1953. English Student. Education: currently studying for Bachelor's degree in Engl., Univ. of Calif., Los Angeles. Has held var. positions inclng. Lib. Asst. in Periodicals Dept. at Pierce Coll. Lib. Memberships: Pierce Coll. Poetry Workshop, 1971–. Contbr. to: Direction, 1972 & '73; Poetry of the Year; Best in Poetry; Poetry of Our Time; Aesop's Feast Mag.; Univ. of Tampa Review; Cape Rock Jrnl.; Reach Out, etc. Address: 1114 12th St., No. 308 (c/o Hayes), Santa Monica, CA 90403, U.S.A.

ALDRICH, Sonia Gretchen, b. 10 April 1894. Education: Music, Franklin Coll., 1910-13; Safety Engineering & Personal Industrial Relations Illinois U. Ext., 1941-42; Special Instructions: Voice, 1917; Interpretive Dancing, 1923-25; Dramatic Art, 1925-27; Psychology & Personal Relations, 1938-39; Radio Speech, 1947; Supervisor Development 1950-53; Methods Development, Procedural Analysis, & Fundamentals of Supervision, 1961. Married Clifford F. Aldrich (deceased). Positions held: 1947-64, Supervisory Budget Analyst, US Naval Air Station,

Corpus Christi, Texas, 1946-47, Statistical Draftsman, City of Corpus Christi; 1930-37, Accountant, Chase Nat. Bank, NYC; 1928-29, Columnist, Scripps-Howard Newspapers, Toledo, Ohio. Memberships: Poetry Soc. of Texas; Byliners of Corpus Christi; Nat. Assoc. of Supervisors, Dept. of Defense; Internat. Platform Assoc.; Smithsonian Associates. Contbr. to: Anthol. of American Poetry, 1959; This Friendly Shore, 1955; Visions in Verse, 1967; Franklin Star (Indiana); Indianapolis News; Cats Mag. Awards: Southwest Writers Conference, 1947, 1960, 1961. Address: 1114 Seventh St., Apt. 2, Corpus Christi, TX 78404, USA.

ALDRIDGE, Adele, b. 12 Aug. 1934. Artist; Painter; Printmaker; Poet (Concrete). Education: Parsons Schl. of Design, N.Y.C., 1954-56; Chicago Art Inst., Chicago, 1960; Cert., Silvermine Coll. of Art, 1965-68. Published works: Not Poems, 1972; Changes (graphic interpretation of the I Ching), 1972; I Ching Meditations, Hexagram 1, 1973, & Hexagram 2, 1974. Contbr. to: Aphra; Black Maria; Viva; Assembling; Konglomerati; Omen. Address: 31 Chapel Lane, Riverside, CT 06878, U.S.A.

ALECKOVIC, Mira, b. 2 Feb. 1924. Editor. Educ: Fac. of Philos., Belgrade; Ecole Superieure de Fouchet, Sorbonne, France. 3 children. Positions held: Ed., children's mag., 1939; Participated in the Resistance, WW II; Ed. & Chief Ed., num. children's reviews & Jeunesse literary review; Dir., l'Epoque, literary page of Borba newspaper; Dir., Liaison, Mlado Pokolenje & Zmai Review. Memberships: Sec., Assn. of Serbian Writers, 1947-53; Comm. of Serbian Writers; COMES Comm.; Comm., PEN Club; V.P., Serbian Writers; V.P., Pres., Union of Yugoslav Writers, 1969-73; V.P., Cultural Assn. of Yugoslavia-France. Published works incl: (poetry) Trois printemps, 1949; Traces sans pas, 1953; Clairière, 1956; Peu il y a d'amour, 4 eds.; Nuit cette la dernière, 1960; Que la ne soit l'amour, 3 eds., 1970; Poèmes, 3 eds., 1957; (romans) Pourquoi tu maudit le fleuve, 1955; L'aube, 1963. Contbr. to num. newspapers & reviews. Honours, awards incl: 1st Prize, Youth Newspaper, Belgrade, 1945; Poetry Prize, Serbian Repub., 1950; Chevalier, Legion of Hon., 1971; num. Yugoslavian awards. Address: Bulevar Revolucije 17, 11000 Belgrade, Yugoslavia.

AL-EISA, Mohammad Fahd, b. 1923. Diplomat. Positions held: Dir., Income Tax & Zakat Dept.; Deputy Min., Ministry of Labour; Saudi Arabian Ambassador in Mauretania. Published works: one volume of Arabic poetry. Rep. in 'Contemporary Poets of Nejd' anthol. Address: Saudi Arabian Embassy, Nouachott, Mauretania.

AL-EISA, Mokbel, b. 1932. Diplomat; Civil Servant. Education: Licence in Law. Positions held: w. the Diplomatic Corps; Counselor, Ministry of Foreign Affairs. Has published one volume of poetry in Arabic. Contbr. to: Saudi Arabian newspapers; 'Al-Abddeb' lit. jrnl.; var. other lit. jrnls. published in the Arab world. Address: Ministry of Foreign Affairs, Jidda, Saudi Arabia.

ALEIXANDRE, Vicente, b. 26 Apr. 1898. Writer. Education: Lic. Derecho, Univ. of Madrid, Spain. Memberships: Real Academia Espanola; Academie du Monde Latin (Paris); The Hispanic Soc. of America (N.Y.); Academia de Ciencias y Artes de Puerto Rico; Real Academia de Bellas Artes de S. Telmo (Malaga); Academia Hispanoamericana (Bogota). Published works: (books) Ambito, 1928; Esdadas Como Labios, 1932; Pasion de la Tierra, 1935; La Destruccion o El Amor, 1935; Sombra del Paraiso, 1944; Mundo A Solas, 1950; Poemas Paradisiacos, 1952; Nacimiento Ultimo, 1953; Historia del Corazon, 1954; Mis Poemas Mejores, 1957; Poemas Amorosos, 1960; En Un Vasto Dominio, 1962; Retratos con Nombre, 1965; Obras Completas, 1968; Poemas de la Consumacion, 1968; Poesia Superrealista, 1971. Recip., Premio Nacional de Literatura, 1933. Address: Velintonia 3, Madrid 3, Spain.

ALEXANDER, Elizabeth, b. 22 Feb. 1902. Secretary

(retired). Education: Southern Methodist Univ.; Univ. of Colorado; Voice – Washington, DC. Positions held: Sec. Gen., American Tank Car Corp., Dallas (subsid. of Chicago); during WWII worked for US Gov., French and South African Gov. Supply Mission; Sec., American Assoc. of Univ. Women. Memberships: Texas Poetry Soc.; Coleman Shakespeare Club (Sec.); DAR's (Capt. Wm. Buckner chapter, local chairman Nat. Defense, and Historian). Address: 721 West College Ave., Coleman, TX 76834, USA.

ALEXANDER, Floyce Milton, b. 31 Dec. 1938. Teaching Assistant; Editor. Education: B.A., Univ. of Wash., Seattle, 1962; M.A., Wash. State Univ., Pullman, 1971; M.F.A., Univ. of Mass., Amherst, 1974. Married Karenlee Clarke. Positions held: Ed., Wash. State Univ. Press, Pullman, 1963-70; Tchng. Asst., Wash. State Univ. Dept. of Engl., 1970-71; Tchng. Asst., Univ. of Mass., Rhetoric Dept., 1972-74. Published works: (poems) Ravines, 1971; Machete, 1972; (in manuscript) Episodes on the Floor of the Sky (book of poems); Bottom Falling Out of the Dream (book of poems); Wine Blood: The Lamentations (a book-length poem); A Book of Survivors (in progress). Contbr. to many mags., reviews, jrnls. Address: 131 Summer St., P.O. Box 600, North Amherst, MA 01059, U.S.A.

ALEXANDER, Frances L., b. 12 Feb. 1888, Blanco, Texas. Teacher; Author. Education: B.A., Baylor Univ., 1911; M.A., Columbia Univ. Positions held: Tchr., Maths., HS, San Marcos, Tex., 1911-14; Maths. Tchr., Port Arthur, Tex., 1914-18; Prof. of Engl., Kingsville, Tex., 1925-46; Instr., Univ. of Tex., 1946-48. Memberships: Poetry Soc. of Tex.; Poetry Soc. of Am.; Tex. Inst. of Letters. Published works: Seven White Birds, 1937; Mother Goose on Rio Grande, 1943; Time at the Window, 1946; Conversations with a Lamb; Mary Charlotte Alexander; Choc the Chachalaca; Pebbles from a Broken Jar; The Diamond Tree. Contbr. to: Survey Graphic; Literary Digest; New York Sun; Oregonian; etc. Awards: Tex. Inst. of Letters Award, 1946; Prize, Tex. Poetry Soc., 1948; Southwestern Schlship. to Univ. of Texas for Mother Goose on Rio Grande. Address: 2708 Enfield Rd., Austin, Texas.

ALFTAN, Robert Magnus, b. 8 June 1940. Writer of poetry & Plays. Education: commercial schools in London, U.K. & Helsinki, Finland, 1961-64. Memberships: Finland's Svenska Författareförening; Suomen näytelmäkirjailijaliitto; Finland's Dramatikerförbund, etc. Published works: Splitter, 1964; Nollpunkter/Tyngdpunkter, 1966; Vida Gavlar, 1968; Gränsfall, 1970. Contbr. to: Ung Generation, 1963; FBT, 1965-68; Horisont, 1965–; Tuli Mies Tupestaan, 1964; Läntinen, 1973; First, 1966. Honours, awards: Studentbladets Lyriktävling, 1963. Address: Tempelgatan 12 A 19, 00100 Helsinki 10, Finland.

AL-GHAZZAWI, Ahmad Ibrahim, b. 1902. Vice Chairman, Consultative Council, Mecca. Has published sev. vols. of poetry, mostly in praise of Arab Kings and leaders. Has contributed to all Saudi Arabian periodicals over a period of sixty years. Address: The Consultative Council, Mecca, Saudi Arabia.

ALGOSAIBI, Ghazi Abdulrahman, b. 1940. Professor at Riyadh University. Education: Ph.D. Married, 2 children. Published works: Three volumes of poetry published in 1960, '65 & '71. Contbr. to 'Riyadh' daily newspaper and 'Al-Adwa' newspaper printed in Bahrain. Address: c/o Coll. of Commerce, Riyadh Univ., Riyadh, Saudi Arabia.

AL-HIJJI, Hamad, b. 1937. Poet. Published works: Modern Nejdi Poets, a collection of verse. Address: c/o Higher Council for Science, Literature & Arts, Min. of Education, Riyadh, Saudi Arabia.

ALIGER, Margarita, b. 7 Oct. 1915. Odessa, USSR. Writer; Poet; Translator; Journalist. Education: Grad.,

Moscow Lit. Institute. Married to Composer, killed WWII. Memberships: Bd., Writers' Union of USSR; Cumunita Europea degli Scrittori. Published works: The Year of Birth, 1938; Railway, 1939; Stones & Grasses, 1940; Memories of the Brave, 1942; Zoja, 1943; A Few Steps, 1964; Rhymes & Poems, 2 vols., 1970; The Blue Hour, 1970. Contbr. to: Novy Mir; Literaturnaja Gazeta; Chudogestvennaja Literatura, etc. Recip. of State Prize for Art & Lit., USSR, 1943; The Badge of Honour, 1939; Order of the Red Banner of Labour, 1965; The Rumanian Medal; The Bulgarian Order of Cyril and Metody. Address: Lavrushinskipereulok 17 kw 41, Moscow JH-17, USSR.

ALI KHAN (Mir) Naqi, pen name **SAQIB,** b. 29 Nov. 1938. Education: In accordance with royal tradition, was educated in the palace under the guidance of experts in Urdu, Arabic, Persian and English. Personal details: Grandson of H.E.H. the Nizam VII, the late, Sir Mir Osman Ali Khan, of Hyderabad; Son of Prince Taqi Jah Bahadur, 6th son of H.E.H. the Nizam of Hyderabad. Made an independent beneficiary in H.E.H. the Nizam's Family Trust, 1950; Made an ultimate beneficiary in H.E.H. the Nizam's Family Jewellery Trust, 1958. Membership: Urdu Writers' Guild, India. Published works: The Eternal Imprint (poems in Urdu), 1964; Book of the Dawn, 1971; The Inaccessible Desert, 1973. English translation of selections from the third Urdu collection entitled, Spring of Solitude, in progress. Contbr. to: Siasat; Rahnumae Deccan; Milap; Deccan Chronicle; Tahreek; Ajkal; Hayat; Naya Daur; Shabkoon; Pasban; Shair; Blitz; Andhra Pradesh; Hamari Zaban; Funoon; Alshuja. Lyrics have been recorded by H.M.V. Address: "Zar Afshan", 10-2-289/7 Shanti Nagar, Hyderabad 28, Andhra Pradesh, India.

AL-JALHAM, Abdulla Ibrahim, b. 1930. Civil Servant. Education: B.A., Coll. of Arabic Lang., Riyadh. Positions held: Sev. positions in the field of Education; currently Dir. of the Technical Dept. in the Social Affairs Dept., Min. of Labour. Member, Literary Club, Onaiza, Saudi Arabia. Contbr. to sev. Saudi Arabian periodicals. Address: c/o Ministry of Labour, Dept. of Social Affairs, Riyadh, Saudi Arabia.

ALKAZI, Roshen, b. 12 Aug. 1923. Art Centre Director. Married. Positions held: Costume Designer, Theatre Grp. and Theatre Unit, India, 1945-64; Dir., Kunika-Chemould Art Ctr., 1968–. Published works: Seventeen Poems: Poems 1961-65, 1965. Contbr. to: Thought; Sunday Times; Eastern Horizon; Writers Workshop Miscellany (anthology), 1966. Address: C 442, Defence Colony, New Delhi, India.

ALLAF, Ibrahim Khalil, b. 1931. Poet; Company Director. Education: Licence, Dar al-Ulum, Cairo Univ., Egypt, 1953. Positions held: Director of the factory which manufactures the covering for the Holy Ka'ba in Mecca. Published works: 4 vols. of Arabic poetry. Contbr. to all the newspapers in Saudi Arabia. Address: c/o Kiswat al-Ka'ba Factory, Mecca, Saudi Arabia.

ALLANA, Ghulam Ali, b. 22 Aug. 1906. Government Representative; Poet; Author. Education: D.J. Sind College, Karachi; Ferguson Coll., Poona. Positions held: Pres., Karachi Muslim League, 1940; Gen. Sec., Sind Provincial Muslim League, 1938; Finance Sec., All Pakistan Muslim League, 1958; Mbr., Karachi Municipal Corp., 20 yrs.; Mayor, City of Karachi, 1948; Mbr., W. Pakistan Legislative Assembly, 1957; Mbr., Gov. Body, Int. Labour Org., Geneva, 1948-57; Pres., Int. Org. of Employers, Brussels, 1956; V. Chmn., Econ. Comm., Gen. Assembly of U.N., 1962; Has rep. Pakistan at about 30 int. confs. & comms.; Acting Ldr., Pakistan Del. to Gen. Assembly of U.N., 1962; Acad. Coun., Univ. of Karachi, 1972, etc. Published works incl: Incense & Echoes (Selected Poems); Thus Spake Man (Selected Poems); Reflections on Respect, Reverence & Revolt; Some of My Yesterdays (transl. into Urdu & Sindhi); A Rosary of Islamic Readings (compiled & edited); Bazgasht (transl. of Poems into

Urdu); The Silent Hour (Selected Poems). Poems publd. in 4 anthols. in U.K. & U.S.A. Recip. num. hons. & awards inclng: Fellow, Royal Soc. of Arts, U.K.; Gold Medal, Pres. Macapagal of the Philippines, for Poetry; Ph.D., Barcelona, Spain; Conferred The Freedom of the City, or The Golden Key, or civic hons by cities of San Francisco, Buffalo, Phila., Patterson, Paris, Prague, Rome, Geneva. Address: P.O. Box 4825, Karachi, Pakistan.

ALLEN, Alma, pen name ALLEN, Billie, b. 13 Feb. 1912. Post Office Clerk; Writer. Education: H.S., Ark,; course in Creative Writing, Imperial Coll. Married, 2 sons (1 dec.), 2 daughters. Positions held: Bookkeeper; P.O. Clerk. Memberships: Nat. Writer's Assn., Denver, Colo.; Poet's Tape Exchange, Lynchburg, Va.; IPA; Am. Poetry League; Poetry Soc. of Tex., San Antonio Chapt.; Desert Writers Workshop of Imperial Valley, Calif. Published works: Won't You Walk Into My Parlor, 1966. Contbr. to: Poems of Patriotism & Peace, 1967 (poems: The Test of Greatness & Freedom That Can Destroy); Orphic Lute; Penman Mag.; The Nutmegger; Jean's Jrnl.; Enterprise, Canada; Writer's Notes & Quotes; Calif. Writer; Haiku Mag.; Modern Haiku; The Piggot Banner; The Calipatria Herald. Honours, awards: 1st Pl., Poets Tape Exchange, workshop tape, 1967; 2nd Pl. Award, PTE Workshop, 1966; 5th Hon. Mention, Haiku, Calif. Fed. of Chaparral Poets, 1967; Modern Haiku Spec. Mention, 1970. Address: P.O. Box 6134, Calipatria, CA 92233, U.S.A.

ALLEN, Dick, b. 18 Aug. 1939. Poet; Writer; Director of Creative Writing and Assoc. Professor of English. Education: A.B., Syracuse Univ., 1961; M.A., 1963. and post-M.A. work, 1962-64, Brown Univ. Married Loretta Negridge; 2 children. Positions held: Teaching Asst., 1962-63, Teaching Associate, 1963-64, Brown Univ.; Instr. of Engl., & Creative Writing, Wright State Univ., 1964-68; Editor-in-Chief, The Mad River Review, 1966-68; Asst. Prof., Dept. of Engl., 1968-71, Assoc. Prof. & Director of Creative Writing, since 1972, Univ. of Bridgeport. Memberships: Contributing Editor, American Poetry Review; Member, Editorial Bd., Diactics (S.F.W.A.). Published works: Anon and Various Time Machine Poems, 1971; Science Fiction: The Future (ed. HBJ), 1971; Detective Fiction: Crime and Compromise (co-ed., HBJ) 1974. Contbr. to sev. journals and magazines, etc. Awards: Hart Crane Mem. Poetry Fellowship, 1965; Acad. of American Poets Prize, 1963; Union League Arts and Civic Prize (poetry), 1970; Robert Frost Fellowship in Poetry, 1972. Address: Dept. of Engl., Univ. of Bridgeport, Bridgeport, CT 06602, USA.

ALLEN, Roberta (Ethridge), b. 0 Nov. 1908. Freelance Writer; Poet. Education: B.A., Miss. Woman's Coll. (now Wm. Carey Coll.); short story writing, Columbia Univ., N.Y.C. Married Arthur Abele Allen, 2 sons. Positions held: Substitute Tchr., Little Rock Public Schls., 1951-54; Freelance Writer, Poet, Little Rock, 1954–; etc. Block Warden Civil Defense, Miami, 1941-43, Cammack Village, 1954-60. Memberships incl: Pres., Ark. Pioneer Br., Nat. League of Am. Pen Women, 1962-64 (office each yr.); Exec. Bd., Treas., Ark. Writers' Conf.; Pres., Poets' Roundtable of Ark., 1971-72; Newsletter Ed., ibid, 1972-74, etc. Contbr. to: Poetry by Poets' Roundtable of Ark., 1970-74; The Latchstrings Poetry Column, N. Little Rock Times; Poets' Forum; Home Life Mag.; The Ark. Baptist News mag.; The Ark. Methodist, etc. Recip. many awards for poetry inclng: Award of Merit, Poets' Roundtable of Ark., 1972; 2nd pl., anthol. contest., ibid, 1973. Address: 6604 Kenwood Rd., Little Rock, AR 72207, U.S.A.

ALLEN, Samuel Washington, pen name VESEY, Paul, b. 9 Dec. 1917. Professor of English. Education: A.B., Fisk Univ., 1938; J.D., Harvard Law Schl., 1941; grad. study, New Schl. for Soc. Rsch., N.Y. & the Sorbonne, Paris. Positions held: Govt. Atty., N.Y.C. & Wash. D.C.; Avalon Prof. of Humanities, Tuskegee Inst., 1968-70; Vis. Prof. of Engl., Wesleyan Univ., 1970-71; Prof. of Engl., Boston Univ., 1971–. Published works:

Elfenbein Zahne (Ivory Tusks), a bilingual vol. of poetry w. epilogue & transl. by Jahnheinz Jahn. Heidelberg, 1956; (translations) Orphee Noir, by Jean-Paul Sartre, 1951, '60; Africa, by Aime Cesaire, 1972; Elegy for Martin Luther King by Leopold Senghor; var. essays. Contbr. to: Presence Africaine; Black Orpheus; Black World. Address: Dept. of Engl., Boston Univ., Boston, MA 02215, U.S.A.

ALLEN, Steve, pen name STEVENS, William Christopher, b. 26 Dec. 1921. Comedian, author, composer, lyricist, actor, pianist, vocalist. Married Jayne Meadows, 1.s. Bill (William Christopher); 3 s. by 1st marriage, Steve Jr., Brian, David. Star of Steve Allen Show. Publications include: Windfall, 1947; Wry on the Rocks, 1956; A Flash of Swallows'' (as William Christopher Stevens), 1971. Contrib. to: Atlantic Monthly; Saturday Review, etc. Address: 15201 Burbank Blvd., Van Nuys, Calif. 91401, USA.

ALLEN, Velta Myrle, b. 9 Feb. 1898. Writer & Artist. Education: La Verne Coll., Calif., Univ. of Calif. Bus. Coll. Positions as civilian, US Army. Memberships: Nat. Cancer Rsch.; Calif. Hist. Soc.; Calif. Chaparral Poets; Alliance of Fine Arts; Child Security, Inc.; Am. Composer, Authors & Artists; Poets of the Pacific; Am. British Poets; Nat. Emerson Soc., Am. Poetry League; LuVailean Poetry Club; Long Beach Music Club; Nat. Hymn Soc.; Nat. Travel Club; La. State Poetry Soc.; Long Beach Writers Club; Internat. Acad. of Poets; Ina Coolbrith Soc.; Hist. Soc. of Pomona Valley, Inc.; Poets of the Pacific; The Poets Haven; Midwest Fed. of Chaparral Poets; Centro Studi e Scambi Internazionali; Long Beach Hobby Council; YWCA; YMCA of Long Beach. Published works: Within Adobe Walls, 1948; Random Treasure, 1949; No Narrow Grooves, 1954; Meditation on a Hilltop, 1967; Me and My Shadows, 1947; Toward the Horizon, 1951; Paleography & Scroll Painting, 1964; Etcetera, 1973. Contbr. of numerous articles, stories & poems to various mags. Designer of greeting cards, mag. covers, personalized hand-lettered, scroll-drawn art-work, etc. Perm. displays of art in many museums & colls., plus pvte. collections. Address: 846 Termino Ave., Long Beach, Calif. 90804, USA.

ALLEY, Rewi, b. 2 Dec. 1897. Writer. Education: Christchurch Boy's HS, Canterbury, NZ. Positions held: Soldier, NZEF, WWI; Farmer, until 1926; Factory Inspector, Shanghai, until 1938; Organizer, Chinese Industrial Cooperatives; Headmaster, Sandan Bailie School, West Kansu, until 1953; Writer, Peking. Published works: Gung Ho, 1948; Leaves from a Sandan Notebook, 1948; This is China Today, 1951; Fragments of Living Peking, 1955; Beyond the Withered Oak Ten Thousand Saplings Grow, 1962; The Mistake, 1965; What is Sin, 1967; Poems of Protest, 1968; Upsurge, 1969, '70; Man To Be, 1970. Translations from Chinese: Peace Through the Ages, 1953; The People Speak Out, 1954; Lament of a Soldier's Life, 1956; The People Sing, 1958; Tu Fu Selected Poems, 1962; Poems of Revolt, 1962; The Eighteen Laments, 1963. Contbr. to: Eastern Horizon, Hong Kong Ta Kung Pao, Hong Kong; New Zealand Monthly Review. Address: 1 Yung Ke Road, Peking, China.

ALLISON, Winifred Kathleen, pen name ALLISON, Kathleen, b. 23 Apr. 1923. Housewife; Freelance Writer. Married, 2 sons. Positions held: Shop Asst.; Hairdresser; L/Corporal, A.T.S.; Bought Ledger Clerk; p/t Clerk/Asst.; Clerk Typist; Invoice Clerk, Credit Accounts, S. Electricity Bd. Memberships: Fndr. Fellow, Int. Poetry Soc.; Fndr. Mbr., Ealing Writers' Circle (also Sec.); Past Mbr., Poetry Soc., Earls Court; Poetry Grp., Ealing. Contbr. to: Writers' Review Anthol. (Poetry Anthol. No.1), 1972; Int. Poetry Soc. 1st Anthol.; Harrow Observer; Hayes Post; Scrip; Writers' Review; Hillingdon Writer; Good Reading; New Writing; Competitors Jrnl.; Pony; Loving; The Seasons; Rainbow; Stanza; Breakthru Anthol. Address: 17 Barn Close, Northolt, Middx. UB5 6NA, U.K.

ALLOTT, Kenneth, b. 1912. Journalist; Editor; Teacher. Education: King's Coll., Durham Univ.; St. Edmund Hall, Oxford. Positions held: Asst. Ed., New Verse, London, 1938-39; Tchr., Liverpool Univ. 1947–; currently, A.C. Bradley Sr. Lectr., Engl. Lit.; Gen. Ed., Penguin Series, Pelican Book of English Prose. Published works include: Poems, 1938; The Ventriloquist's Doll, 1943; The Rhubarb Tree, 1937; (plays) A Room with a View, 1951; The Publican's Story, 1953; (Lit. Crit.) Jules Verne, 1940; The Art of Graham Greene, 1951; Matthew Arnold, 1955. Ed. & Contbr., numerous other publs. Address: The University, Liverpool, UK.

AL-MANSOUR, Abdulrahman Mohammad, b. 1925. Merchant. Education: Licence, Coll. of Arabic Lang., Al-Azhar Univ., Cairo; Dip. in Educ. & Psychol., Ain Shams Univ., Cairo. Positions held: Dir., Labour Office, Dammam, Saudi Arabia; currently in Business. Rep. in the 'Contemporary Poets of Nejd' anthol. Address: c/o Higher Committee for Arts & Sciences, Ministry of Education, Riyadh, Saudi Arabia.

AL-OBAID, Abdulrahman Abdulkarim, b. 1933. Businessman. Positions held: Personnel, Ministry of Educ., Eastern Province. Memberships: Hon. Mbr., Riyadh Univ. Soc. for Hist. & Archaeol.; Editl. Comm., Saudi Arabian Geographical Dictionary. Published works: Historical & Geographical studies in Arabic; Critical studies of Saudi Arabian poetry. Contbr. to most Saudi Arabian publs. Address: P.O. B. 949, Dammam, Saudi Arabia.

AL-OQAILY, Mohammad Ahmad, b. 1916. Merchant. Positions held: Sev. government positions; Currently, Businessman. Published works: Eight printed volumes in the fields of history, religion, geography, popular literature and biography. Contbr. to all Saudi Arabian newspapers & periodicals. Address: Al-Oqaily Company, Jizan, Saudi Arabia.

AL-OTHAIMEEN, Abdulla Salih, b. 1936. University Professor. Education: Doctorate, Shaikh Mohammad Abdulwahhab Higher Inst., Riyadh, Saudi Arabia. Position held: Prof., Riyadh Univ. Rep. in the 'Contemporary Poets of Nejd' anthol. Address: c/o Higher Council for the Arts & Sciences, Ministry of Education, Riyadh, Saudi Arabia.

AL-OTHAMEEN, Salih Ahmad, b. 1938. Educator. Education: Intermediate Cert. plus private study. Has held var. positions in Education. Published works: Rays of Hope (vol. of poetry). Contbr. to all Saudi Arabian newspapers. Address: Education District Office, Onaiza, Saudi Arabia.

AL-QURASHI, Hassan Abdulla, b. 1927. Civil Servant/Diplomatic Corps. Education: B.A., Hist., Riyadh Univ. Positions held: Sev. high posts in the Min. of Finance & Economy. Memberships: Al-Yamamah Jrnlsts. Soc., Riyadh. Published works: Eleven vols. of Arabic poetry; sev. vols. of literary & critical studies. Contbr. to all the Saudi Arabian periodicals. Recip., 'Al-Bilad' newspaper award. Address: c/o Ministry of Foreign Affairs, Jidda, Saudi Arabia.

AL-SANOUSI, Mohammad Ali, b. 1923. Journalist & Correspondent. Education: Intermediate Cert. Positions held: Head, Customs Dept., Jizan; Mayor, Jizan; Head, Electricity Company, Jizan. Contbr. to most Saudi Arabian newspapers & periodicals. Honours, awards: Prize for Military Songs Competition; Riyadh Newspaper Comp. Prize; 3 Prizes from the Ministry of Information. Address: Jizan, Saudi Arabia.

AL-Saud (His Royal Highness), Abdulla Faisal, b. 1921. Businessman. Self Educated. Personal details: Eldest son-of H.M. King Faisal Abdulaziz Al-Saud, King of Saudi Arabia. Positions held: Deputy to the King's Representative in the Hejaz; Minister of the Interior; Minister of Health. Memberships: Writers' Soc., Lebanon; Delegate to World Conference of Writers.

Published works: One volume of Arabic poetry; sev. volumes currently in press. Contbr. to: 'Al-Arabi', a Kuwaiti monthly publication; many other Arabic periodicals inclng. all the publs. of Saudi Arabia. Address: Jidda, Saudi Arabia.

AL-SHIBL, Mohammad Sulaiman, b. 1929. Teacher. Education: B.A., Sharia College, Mecca, 1953. Contbr. to all Saudi Arabian newspapers. Address: c/o Aziziya Secondary Schl., Mecca, Saudi Arabia.

ALTA, b. 22 May 1942. Writer. Education: Univ. of Calif., Berkeley, 2 yrs. Married, 2 daughters. Positions held: Co-Ed., Aldebaran Review; Co-Ed., It Ain't Me, Babe; Publisher, Shameless Hussy Press. Published works: Freedom's in Sight, 1969, '70; Letters to Women, 1970; Song of the Wife, Song of the Mistress, 1971; Burn This & Memorize Yourself, 1971, '73; Poems & Prose By Alta, 1972, '74; No Visible Means of Support, 1971; I Am Not a Practising Angel, 1974. Contbr. to num. anthols., mags., reviews inclng: Anthol. of Underground Poetry; Chicago Seed; From Feminism to Liberation; Every Woman; Country Press; California Living; Children of the Moon; Hayward Daily Review; Kaleidoscope; Manroot; San Francisco Bay Guardian; Second Coming. Address: Box 424 San Lorenzo, CA 94580, U.S.A.

ALTMAN, Mary, b. 15 Jan. 1931. Housewife. Education: B.S., Wayne State Univ., Detroit, Mich.; Postgrad. courses in Humanities & Educ.; Elem. Tchng. Cert., State of Mich. Married Larry Altman, 1 son. Positions held: Auditorium Tchr., Detroit Public Schls.; Creative Drama Tchr., Adult Educ., Troy, Mich.; Freelance Educl. Writing, Sci. Rsch. Assn.; Ed., Troy Times Children's Page, Mich.; Writer, Educational Media, Inc., Detroit. Memberships: World Poetry Soc.; Ky. State Poetry Soc.; Poetry Soc. of Mich. Contbr. to: Poet Mag.; Ky. State Poetry Soc. Anthol.; Troy Times Children's Page. Address: 489 Evaline, Troy, MI 48084, U.S.A.

ALVAREZ, Alfred, b. 5 Aug. 1929. Writer, Critic & Poetry Editor. Education: Oundle Schl.: B.A., Corpus Christi Coll., Oxford, 1952; M.A., ibid, 1956. Married 1, Ursula Barr, 1956, 1s., Div., 1962; 2, Anne Adams, 1966, 1s., 1d. Positions held: Sr. Rsch. Scholar, Corpus Christi Coll., Oxford, & Rsch. Scholar, Goldsmiths' Co., 1952-53, 1954-55; Procter Vis. Fellow, Princeton Univ., USA, 1953-54; Vis. Fellow, Rockefeller Fndn., 1955-56, 1958; Vis. Lectr. & Christian Gauss Seminars, Princeton, 1957-58; D.H. Lawrence Fellow, Univ. Of NM, 1958; Drama Critic, New Statesman, 1959–; Vis. Prof., Brandeis Univ., 1960 & NY State Univ., Buffalo, 1966; Poetry Ed., The Observer; Advsry. Ed., Penguin Mod. European Poets. Published works include: The Shaping Spirit (Am. Edition called, Stewards of Excellence), 1958; The School of Donne, 1961; The New Poetry, 1962 (Ed. & introd.); Fantasy Poets, 1952 (Pamphlet); The End of It, 1958 (Pamphlet); 12 Poems, 1968 (Pamphlet); Lost, 1968; Penguin Modern Poets, 18, 1970; Apparition, 1971; Beyond All This Fiddle, 1968; The Review, 1968 (Pamphlet); The Anarchist, 1969 (Filmscript); The Savage God, A Study of Suicide, 1971. Contbr. to the following anthols., jrnls., mags., etc: New Statesman; Observer; Kenyon Review; Partisan Review; Listener; Passim; Twentieth Century, etc. Honours, awards: Vachel Lindsay Prize for Poetry, Poetry, Chicago, 1961. Address: c/o The Observer, London, EC4, UK.

ALYEA, Dorothy C., b. 8 Oct. 1898. Writer. Education: B.A., Wellesley, 1919. Married, 2 children. Mbr., Pen & Brush. Published works: (books) All My Argument, 1935; Beach Fire, 1951; Asst. Poetry Editor, Forum Mag., 1924-26; Editor, Poetry Column, "All That Glitters" Oranges Mag., 1936; Contbr. to num. publs. Honours, awards incl: 1st Prize, Rochester Festival of Religious Arts, 1967. Address: 77 Highland Ave., Montclair, NJ, U.S.A.

ALYN, Marc, b. 18 Mar. 1937. Writer; Literary Critic. Education: College of Reims, France. Married Claude Argelier. Positions held: Lit. Critic, l'hebdomadaire

Arts, 1960-64; Poetry Critic, Figaro littéraire & Figaro, 1964–; Ed. in Chief, Formes et Langages. Memberships: Pres., Actuelles-Formes et Langages, 1969–; Société des Gens de Lettres; PEN CLUB; Comm. Dir., France-Yugoslavia, Writers of Champagne; Editl. Comm., int. review, Books Abroad, U.S.A. Published works: (poetry) Le Temps des Autres, 1957; Cruels divertissements, 1957; Délébiles, 1962; Nuit majeure, 1968; Infini au-delà, 1972; var. critical books on Mauriac, Dylan Thomas, Nerval, De Richaud, Kosovel etc. & La Nouvelle poésie française, 1968; Le Grand suppositoire (w. Lawrence Durrell), 1972; (theatre) Le Grand labyrinthe, 1972, etc. Contbr. to var. lit. reviews & articles in "Le Figaro". Honours, awards: Prix Max Jacob, 1957; Prix International Camille Engelmann, 1971; Prix Guillaume Apollinaire, 1973. Address: Mas des Poiriers, 30700 Uzes, France.

AMABILE, George, b. 29 May 1936. University Teacher. Education: A.B., Amherst Coll., Mass., 1957; M.A., Univ. of Minn., 1961; Ph.D., Univ. of Conn., Storrs., 1969. Positions held: Tchng Asst., Univ. of Conn.; Lectr., Univ. of Manitoba; Asst. Prof., ibid; Vis. Writer in Res., Univ. of British Columbia; Assoc. Prof., Univ. of Manitoba. Member, League of Canadian Poets. Published works: Blood Ties, 1972. Editor: The Far Point; The Penny Paper; Northern Light. Rep. in following anthols: Best Poems of 1964, 1965; The Young Am. Poets, 1968; The New Yorker Book of Poems, 1970; Open Skull Anthol.; Canadian Poems for Children, 1972, etc. Contbr. to many mags. inclng: Canadian Dimension; The Fiddlehead; Harper's; Modern Poetry Studies; New Orleans Review; N.C. Qtly.; The Prairie Schooner; CBC Anthol. Honours, awards: Anna Von Helmholz Phelan Prize, 1960; Canada Coun. Grant, 1968 & 69. Address: 272 Ash St., Winnipeg, Manitoba, Canada.

AMEERUDDIN, Syed, b. 5 Dec. 1942. Poet & Professor. Education: M.A., Engl., Aligarh Univ., India; student of Film Direction, Fily & TV Inst. of India, Poona. Positions held: Asst. Prof., Post Grad. Dept. of Engl., The New Coll., Madras; Asian Ed., Poet, an international monthly; Poetry Cons., Kalaingyer Int. Memberships: World Poetry Soc. Intercontinental, U.S.A.; Sec.-Gen., All India Poets Meet, Madras, 1973; Sec., Poets Workshop, Madras. Published works: What the Himalaya said .. And Other Poems, 1972; The Dreadful Doom to Come .. And Other Poems, 1973. Contbr. to: Poet; Thought; Kalaingyer Int.; Gujarat Samachar; Rambler, etc. Guest Ed., Indo-Anglian Number of Poet, 1973. Contbr. to Mini-Max & A Jrnl. of Indian Writing in Engl. Recip., Disting. Serv. Citadal, World Poet Award, World Poetry Soc. Intercontinental, 1973. Address: 14 Mirza Ghulam Hussain Ali Khan St., Royapettah, Madras 600014, India.

AMES, Barbara Dorothy, pen name **TAWNY,** b. 30 Apr. 1922. Housewife; Previously Stage Actress. Education: Grad., Am. Acad. Dramatic Art. Married w. children. Member, Vivienne Laramore Rader Poetry Grp. Contbr. to: Shell Qtly., 1973; Miami Times, Poets Corner; McCall's; Mademoiselle; M.S. mag.; Good Housekeeping; Family Circle; Livenight Publ.; Christian Sci. Monitor. Address: 445 N.E. 163 St., N. Miami Beach, FL 33162, U.S.A.

AMES, Bernice, b. 22 Feb. 1915. Housewife & Poet. Married. Memberships: Poetry Soc. of Am.; PEN, Los Angeles; Calif. Guild of Writers; Nat. League of Am. Pen Women, Santa Monica; Pres., Santa Monica Writers Club, 1962-64. Published works: Where the Light Bends, 1955; In Syllables of Stars, 1958; Antelope Bread, 1966. Contbr. to: Prairie Schooner; Southwest Review; Poetry Northwest; Western Humanities Review; Georgia Review; Accent; Approach; Midwest Quarterly; Yankee; Lyric; Spirit; Arizona Quarterly; Commonweal; NY Times; NY Herald Tribune; Chicago Tribune; Christian Science Monitor; Cimarron Review; Nimrod; Epos; Literary Review; N. American Review; Kansas Quarterly; W. Coast Review; Saturday Evening Post; University Review; Outposts (UK); Fiddlehead (Canada); Voices.

Honours: James Joyce Award, 1967; Wroxton Fellowship, 1967; Ariz. Quarterly Short Story Award, 1967; Cecil Hemley Award, 1971. Address: 12223 Dunoon Lane, Los Angeles, Calif. 90049, USA.

AMIDON, Bill, pen names, **TAYLOR, Jessie; MORGAN, Patrick,** b. 30 June 1935. Writer. Education: HS. Positions held: various, including, Editor; Copy-Editor; Actor; Proof-Reader; Optician; Typist; Promotion & Publicity, etc. Author of seven novels; short stories; essays; articles; two plays (produced). Address: 532 East 5th St., New York, NY 10009, USA.

AMIR-PINKERFELD, Anda, pen name **BAT-HEDVA,** b. 26 June 1902. Writer; Poet; Education: Univs. of Lwow & Leipzig. Widow, 1 son, 1 daughter. Memberships: Israel Writers Assn.; PEN; AKUM, Writers & Composers Assn. Published works: Piesni Zycia, 1921; Yamin Doverim, 1930; Youval, 1933; Githit, 1936; Doodayim, 1936; Meolam, 1937; Gadish, 1942; Gadish Vaomer, 1948; Ahat, 1950; Tehiyot, 1960; has also written 8 books of poetry & 4 books of prose for children. Contbr. to: Davar; Moznayim; Children's Davar. Honours, awards: Bialik prize for Children's Poems, 1933; Rupin's prize for 'Ahat' (epics), 1951. Address: 87 Ahad Haam, Tel Aviv, Israel.

AMIS, Kingsley William, b. 16 Apr. 1922. Author. Educ: St. John's, Oxford. Married (1) Hilary Ann Bardwell, 1948, 2 sons, 1 daughter; (2) Elizabeth Jane Howard, 1965. Positions held: Served in Army, 1942-45; Lectr., Engl., Univ. Coll. of Swansea, 1949-61; Fellow, Peterhouse, Cambridge, 1961-63. Published works: A Frame of Mind (verse), 1953; Lucky Jim (novel), 1954; That Uncertain Feeling (novel), 1955; A Case of Samples (verse), 1956; I Like it Here (novel), 1958; Take a Girl Like You (novel), 1960; New Maps of Hell (belle-lettres), 1960; My Enemy's Enemy (short stories), 1962; One Fat Englishman (novel), 1963; The James Bond Dossier (belles-lettres), 1965; The Egyptologists (novel), w. Robert Conquest, 1965; The Anti-Death League (novel), 1966; A Look Round the Estate (poems), 1967; (as Robert Markham) Colonel Sun (novel), 1968; I Want it Now (novel), 1968; The Green Man (novel), 1969; What Became of Jane Austen? (belles-lettres), 1970; Girl, 20 (novel), 1971; On Drink (belles-lettres), 1972; The Riverside Villas Murder (novel), 1973; Ending Up (novel), 1974. Contbr. to: Spectator; New Statesman; Encounter; London Mag.; Listener; Observer, etc. Address: c/o A.D. Peters & Co., 10 Buckingham St., London W.C.2, U.K.

AMMONS, A(rchie) R(andolph), b. 18 Feb. 1926. Associate Professor of English. Education: B.S. in Gen. Sci., Wake Forest Coll., NC. Published works: Ommateum, 1955; Expressions of Sea Level, 1964; Corsons Inlet, 1965; Tape For The Turn of the Year, 1965; Northfield Poems, 1966; Selected Poems, 1968. Contbr. to: The Hudson Review; Accent; Poetry (Chicago); Chelsea; NY Times; Nation; Choice; Apple; Epoch; Lillabulero; Poetry NW; Emerson Review; Compass Review, et. Honours: Guggenheim Fellowship, 1966-67; Traveling Fellowship of the Am. Acad. of Arts & Letters, 1967-68. Address: Engl. Dept., Cornell Univ., Ithaca, NY 14850, USA.

AMOAKO, Alex Agyarko, pen name **AMOAKO, Kwabena,** b. 15 July 1941. Teacher. Education: B.A., English Univ. of Ghana, 1965; Post grad. Dip. in English Studies, Univ. of Leeds, 1966; M.Phil. in English Course, London Univ., 1966-68. Positions held: Engl. Master, Saint Augustine's Coll., Cape Coast, Ghana, 1968-69; Sr. Engl. Master, Opoku Ware Secondary Schl., Kumasi, Ghana, 1970. Member, Caribbean Artists Movement, London, 1967-68. Contbr. to: Newsletter of Caribbean Artists Movement, 1967. Address: Opoku Ware Secondary Schl., P.O. Box 849, Kumasi, Ghana.

AMPRIMOZ, Alexandre, b. 14 Aug. 1948. University Instructor. Education: Bac.Math., Univ. Aix Marseille, 1966; D.U.E.S.P.C., ibid, 1967; Math.Sup., Math.Spe.,

Prytanee Militaire, 1968; grad. studies, Univ. of Toronto, Canada, 1969; L.F.I. Tchng. Cert., Univ. of Ottawa, 1969; M.A., Univ. of Windsor, 1970; grad. studies, Univ. of Western Ont., 1973. Married Jeannette. Positions held: Tchr., Assumption Coll., Schl., Windsor, 1968-72; Instr., Univ. of Western Ont., London, 1972-. Mbr., Int. Poetry Soc. Published works: Jiva & Other Poems, 1971, 2nd printing, 1972; Initiation A Menke Katz, 1972; Re & Other Poems, 1972; Visions, 1973; Odes to the Skeleton, 1974; An Island in the Heart & Other Dialogues, 1973; Selected Poems, 1973. Other publs. in French: Veritas – Feuillets poetiques et litteraires – Niort, 1963; La Vierge de l'Ocean – Cahiers du cercle des poetes Rochelais, 1963; Solutions – L'education mathematiques, 1964; sev. short stories, articles & book reviews. Contbr. to: Bitterroot; Prism; The Lance; Orion; Poetry Australia, etc. Address: Box 186 Sandwich P.O., Windsor, Ont., Canada N9C, 3Z1.

AMYX, Katherine McClure, b. 29 Oct. 1901. Poet. Education: Old State Normal Inst., Morehead, Ky.; State Cert. Tchng. Married Ova B. Amyx, 1 son. Positions held: Schl. Tchr., 4 yrs.; Postmistress, 17 yrs.; Previewer, Viking Press, 2 yrs. & Random House, 2 yrs. Memberships: Bd. Dirs., Ky. State Poetry Soc.; Nat. Fed. of State Poetry Socs.; Past State Pres., Nat. League of Am. Pen Women; Chmn., South Ctrl. States; Poetry Ed., Pen Woman, 2 yrs.; Past Mbr., The Poetry Soc. of London. Published works: (books of poetry) The Changing Hills, 1959; Eastward in Eden, 1972; Wedding of the Waters, 1973. Contbr. to num. anthols., newspapers, mags. in U.S.A., Canada & U.K. Recip. of over 50 poetry prizes. Address: P.O. Box 89, Grassy Creek, KY 41435, U.S.A.

ANAMIKA, b. 15 Aug. 1940. Freelance Writer; Poet. Education: M.A. in Hindi Lang. & Lit. Published works: Many poems in Hindi & English; Translator of sev. poems, short stories & articles from English & Panjabi into Hindi. Contbr. to: Eastern Horizon (Hong Kong); Radar (Europe); Dharanyug; Bharli; Basanti; Afkal & many others. Recip., 1st Prize, Tagore Centenary Medal, 1962. Address: 26/53 W.E.A., New Delhi 5, India.

ANDERS, Lois-Long, b. 27 Nov. 1907. Writer. Education: A.B., Wellesley Coll.; special courses at Univ. of N.C., Chapel Hill., N.Y. Advt. Club., Publicity Club of N.Y. Married Col. Sterling H. Anders. Positions held: Advt. Asst. & Mgr., Loeser's Dept. Store, Brooklyn, N.Y.; Hd. of Fashion Advt., The Hecht Co., Wash., D.C.; Ed., Princeton Alumni Weekly, N.J.; Advt. & Promotion Mgr., Previews Inc., N.Y.C.; Copy Chief, Friend-Reiss Advt. Agency, N.Y.C.; P.R. Mgr., Creative Playthings, Princeton, N.J.; Hd. of Anders P.R. Services, Princeton, N.J. Memberships: Delaware Valley Poets (Br. of N.J. State Poetry Soc.); Co-Chmn., Creative Writing Dept. (N.J. Federated) Women's Club of Princeton; Mbr., Lit. Dept, ibid; Lit. Study Grp., Princeton Women's Coll. Club. Contbr. to: Poetry Soc. Column., Statesville (N.C.) Record; Echoes of Parnassus Column (N.J. Poetry Soc.), Times-Bulletin, Boonton, N.J.; Princeton Herald; The Clubwoman, etc. Recip., award, N.J. State Fed. of Women's Clubs Creative Writing Contest, 1965, '66, '68. Address: 601 Lake Dr., Princeton, NJ 08540, U.S.A.

ANDERS, Mattie, b. 20 Oct. 1909 at Moreland, Alabama. Housewife. Education: Danville HS; Albright Business Coll. Married to Hilliard L. Anders (decd), 2 s. Contbr. to: Decatur Daily. Address: 1310 Pinehurst St., Hartsville, AL 35640, USA.

ANDERSEN, Inez Elliott, b. 19 Mar. 1899. Teacher (retired); Poet; Writer. Educ.: B.S., M.A., Geo. Peabody Coll., Nashville, Tenn. Married to Holger W. Andersen. Positions held: Pub. Schl. Tchr., Birmingham, Ala., 1918-20, '24-33; Asst. Dir. of Curric., ibid, 1935-37; Sub. Tchr., Ark. State Univ., Jonesboro, 1937-41; Educ. Workshop, Pan Am. Coll., Edinburgh, Tex., 1943. Memberships: World Poetry Soc.-Intercontinental, 1969-; Nat. League Am. Pen

Women, Memphis, 1948-; Dir., Southcentral Regional Poetry Workshop, 1961 & SE. Br., 1965; Dir., Tenn. State Conven. Poetry Workshop, 1969, 1971; Memphis Br. Recording Sec., 1958-60, 1972-74; Hist., 1964-66; Parliamentarian, 1966-68, '68-70; Histn., Memphis Br., AAUW, 1963-65; Chmn., Memphis Br. Creative Writing Grp., 1956; Nat. Poetry Soc. Am., 1947; Poetry Soc. Tenn., 1953-; Recording Sec., ibid, 1953-54; Dir., 1957-58; Official Reader, 1955-; on Panel of Critics, 1956-; Histn., 1969-71, Tenn. Touring Poets, 1970-72, Tenn. Vox Poetica, 1972; Chap., Tenn. Woman's Press & Authors Club, 1968; Mbr., Poetry Panels (Speaker) Ala. Writers' Conclave, 1966, '69; Ala. State Poetry Soc., 1970-. Published works incl: Books, Sections of Language Journeys Series, 1938 & '39; Never Send to Know, 1962; The Poetry Society of Tennessee, 1953-69, A History, 1969; Anthols., Silver Spur, 1942; Cenizo Spray, 1947; Silver Spur V-Yucca Trail, 1951; One Hundred Poems, 1956; Memphis Poems by Memphis Poets, 1969; Memorabilia, 1965; A Book of the Year, Poetry Soc. Tenn., 1955-; Pancontinental Premier Poets, 1970; Poems by Poets, 1973. Contbr. to: Commercial Appeal; Unitarian Calendar; Arkansas Times; Memphis Mirror; Campus & Church; Pen Wheel; Broadcaster; Commercial News, Danville, Ill.; Messenger; Pen Woman; Christian Advocate; Motive; Cats; Am. Courier; Chipmunk; Living Quill; Beat of Wings; Reflections; Peabody Reflector; Verse Craft; Modern Images; Poet; Grade Tchr.; Highroad; S. & W.; Sampler; Old Hickory Review; Ala. Sunday Mag. Honours include: 1st prize, Memorabilia (int. comp.), 1965; 4th prize, B. Babcock Mem. Contest, Ark. Pioneer Br., Nat. League Am. Pen Women, 1969; num. prizes, Mid-South Poetry Festival, 1960-; num. prizes, Poetry Soc. Tenn. contests; frequent Kenneth L. Beaudoin Gemstone Awards, One of 5 readers on WKNO-TV Memphis & the Muse prog., 1969; Chosen 'Most Outstanding Writer', Memphis Br., Nat. League Am. Pen Women, 1963, '69; World Poetry Award, World Poetry Soc., 1970; Hon. Mbr., Poetry Soc. of Tenn., 1973; 2nd Prize, Kaleidograph Award, Nat. Fedn. of State Poetry Socs., 1973. Address: 3587 Cowden Ave., Memphis, Tenn. 38111, USA.

ANDERSON, Elsie (Mrs.), b. 15 Jan. 1918. Housewife, formerly expediter and proof reader. Pubs. Rambling Thoughts, 1970; Vagabond Thoughts, 1971; Transient Thoughts, 1972. Contrib. to: Orphic Lute; Nutmegger; The Saint; Echoes; Bay Shore Breeze; Haiku Highlights; Angels; Poetry Prevue; Encore; Quoin; Russell Times; Normal News; Southwest Times Record; Conroe County Courier; Accademie International Leonardo da Vinci; American Mosaic (anthol.); Crawford County Courier; Daily Independent; Sunrise Sunset Silhouette; Apercu; Fairy's Poetry Corner; Words with Wings; Southwest Breeze; Creative Urge; Bardic Echoes; Star Journal. Hon. Mention: Golden Circle, Haiku Contest, Lamoni, Iowa, 1966; Dip. of Merit: Studio Leonardo da Vinci, 1969, 1972, 1973; Cert. of Appreciation from Arizona State Univ., 1970. Address: 1803 Maryland Street, Los Angeles, California 90057, USA.

ANDERSON, Jon, b. 4 July 1940. Teacher; Poet. Education: B.S., Northeastern Univ., Boston, Mass., U.S.A.; M.F.A., Univ. of Iowa, Iowa City. Positions held: at Univ. of Iowa; Portland Univ.; Ohio Univ.; Univ. of Pittsburgh. Published works: Looking for Jonathan, 1968; Death & Friends, 1971; Stories (poems), 1973; In Sepia, 1974. Contbr. to: Iowa Review; Ohio Review; New Yorker; Poetry; Field, etc. Nominated for Nat. Book Award, 1972. Address: Engl. Dept., Univ. of Pittsburgh, Pittsburgh, PA, U.S.A.

ANDERSON, Lila Pauline Gage, pen name **GAGE, Paul,** b. 18 Nov. 1921. Artist; Poet; Housewife. Married to Chester Anderson. Positions held: Sales Clerk; Rep. for Avon Cosmetics. Memberships: Charter Mbr., Smithsonian Inst., Wash. D.C.; Past Dir., Okmulgee Art Guild; currently Sec., ibid. Contbr. to: Tehachapi News, Calif., 1948-49. One man Exhib. of paintings, Okmulgee Pub. Lib., 1971 & 73. Address: 600 N. Morton, Okmulgee, OK 74447, U.S.A.

ANDERSON, Patrick John McAlister, b. 4 Aug. 1915. Head of English Department. Educ: B.A., Worcester Coll., Oxford, U.K.; M.A., ibid; M.A., Columbia Univ., U.S.A. Positions held: Former Pres., Oxford Union; Asst. Prof., McGill Univ., Montreal, P.Q., Canada, 1948-50; Lectr., Univ. of Malaya, 1950-52; Lectr., Dudley Trng. Coll., Worcestershire, U.K., 1954-57; Prin. Lectr., Engl. Dept., Trent Park Coll. of Educ., Barnet, U.K., 1967; Hd. of Dept., ibid, 1968–. Published works: On This Side of Nothing, 1932; A Tent for April, 1945; The White Centre, 1946; The Colour As Naked, 1953. Contbr. to: Poetry; New York Times; Preview; Canadian Forum; The Listener; Times Literary Supplement; (Anthologies) Book of Canadian Poetry, 1948; Canadian Poetry in English, 1954; Poetry of the Forties, 1968. Recip., Commonwealth Fellowship, 1938-40. Address: Field House, Gosfield Lake, Halstead, Essex, U.K.

ANDERSON, Violet Louise, pen name **ANDERSON, Violet,** b. 16 Nov. 1906. Housewife. Education: B.A., Univ. of Toronto, Canada; Tchng. degree, Conservatory of Music. Positions held: Past Ed., 4 or 5 books on pub. affairs. Published works: The Ledge, 1957; In the Balance, 1967. Contbr. to: Canadian Forum; Fiddlehead; Northern Review; Canadian Poetry Mag.; Saturday Night; Poetry. Address: 137 Buckingham Ave., Toronto 12, Ontario, Canada.

ANDERSON, Virginia Rose (Cronin), pen name **HILL, Hyacinthe (Dame),** b. 24 May 1920. Poet; Educator; Painter; Astrologer. Education: A.B., cum laude, Brooklyn Coll., NYC; M.A., Hunter Coll.; Ph.D. studies, Fordham Univ. Married to John Anderson. Positions held; Tchr., NYC Bd. of Educ.; NY State Assn. in Performing Arts and Humanities Educ. Memberships: Exec. Bd., Poetry Soc. of Am., 1968-72; Fndr. Mbr., Acad of Am. Poets; World Poetry Soc. Intercontinental; United Poet Laureates Int.; MLA; Poetry Soc. London; AAUW; Nat. League Am. Pen Women; Alpha Delta Kappa. Published works incl: Shoots of a Vagrant Vine, 1950; Promethea, 1957; Through a Flaming Hoop, 1971. Over 1500 poems published worldwide plus short stories & articles. Contbr. to: Astrological Review; Colo. Review; Outposts; Ariz. Highways; Chicago Tribune; Denver Post; Fantasy & Sci. Fiction; Laurel Leaves; Negro Hist. Bulletin; NY Herald Tribune; Peacemaker; Pegasus; The Poet, Madras; The Poet, Glasgow; Proteus Quarterly; Quaderne di Poesia, Rome; The Sharian, London; Shi'r, Beirut; Epos; Searchlight, San Francisco; The Villager; Townlights. Honours include: Ph.D. honoris causa, Northern Pontifical Acad., 1969; Doct., Great China Arts Coll., Hong Kong; HD, Int. Acad. of Sovereign Order of Alfred the Great, UK; awards, Poetry Soc. of Am., 1958–; Hon. Int. Poet Laureateship, UPLI with Poets' Golden Laurel Wreath Crown, by ex-Pres. of Philippines C.P. Garcia, plus Karta & Gold Medal, Dip. & Medal of Honour, Centro Studi E. Scambi, Rome, 1968; Dip. Medal of Honour, Int. Acad. Leonardo da Vinci, 1968; Gold Commemorative Medal from Shah of Iran, 1972; Guest Editor, Great American World Poets (N. Atlantic Ed.), 1973; Guest of Honor, World Congress of Poets, Taipei, 1973; Poet Laureate, ibid; Magus w. Hon. Life Mbrship., Cosmosynthesis League, Australia. work chosen by US Info. Off. to be translated into other langs. Work being collected by L.S. Thompson, Dir. of Libs., Margaret I. King Lib., Lexington, Ky. Address: 166 Hawthorne Ave., Yonkers, NY 10705, USA.

ANDRE, Michael, b. 31 Aug. 1946. Writer. Education: B.A., McGill Univ., 1968; M.A., Univ. of Chicago, 1969; Ph.D., Columbia Univ., 1974. Positions held: Film Critic, Montreal Gazette, 1968; Lectr., City Coll., 1973; Editl. Assoc., Art News, 1973–. Memberships: C.C.L.M.; COSMEP. Published works: Get Serious, 1973. Contbr. to: Unmuzzled Ox; Assembling; Little Magazine; Greenfield Review; Bleb; Far Point; Telephone; Chicago Seed; West End; The Stone; Some; Dragonfly; Invisible City; Page; Amphora. Address: c/o Unmuzzled Ox, Box 374 Planetarium Stn., N.Y., NY 10024, U.S.A.

ANDREW, Warren, b. 19 July 1910. Educator; Physician. Education: B.A., Carleton Coll., 1932; M.S., Brown Univ., 1933; Ph.D., Yale Univ., 1936; M.D., Baylor Coll. Med., 1943. Positions held: Instr. of Anatomy, Univ. of Ga., 1936-39; Asst. Prof., Baylor Coll. of Med., 1939-43; Assoc. Prof., Southwestern Med. Coll., 1943-47; Chmn. of Anatomy Dept., Geo. Wash. Univ., 1947-52, Bowman Gray Schl. of Med., 1952-58 & Ind. Univ., 1958-71. Member, Poets' Corner, Indianapolis. Contbr. to: Stylus Lit. Mag., Cornucopia; Ball State Lit. Mag.; Forum; Sat. Evening Post. Recip., Award in Sesquicentennial of Indiana, 1966. Address: 5275 N. Capitol Ave., Indianapolis, IN 46208, U.S.A.

ANDREWS, John Williams, b. 10 Nov. 1898. Writer; Lawyer. Education: A.B., Yale Univ., 1920; J.D., 1926. Married 1) Elizabeth Robert, div., 1 son, 2) Miriam Benton Wise. Positions held: Freelance Writer, 1932–; Assoc. w. Hist. Dept., Yale Univ., 1938-40; Chief Fedl. State Rels. Sect., U.S. Dept. of Justice, Wash., 1942-48; Trial Atty., Anti-Trust Div., Dept. of Justice, 1948-50; w. Hill & Knowlton, Inc., P.R. Coun., 1952-53; Pres., Andrews Assocs. Inc., 1954-62; Pres., Lit. Publsrs. Fndn., Boston; Dir., Cooper Hill Writers' Conf., E. Dover. Memberships: Fellow, Timothy Dwight Coll., Yale Univ., 1938-40; V.-Chmn., Trustee, Lingnan Univ., Canton, China; V.P., Bd. Dirs., Wash. Housing Assn., 1947-52; Pres., ibid, 1952; Dir., Wash. Inst. of Mental Hygiene, 1951-52; Poetry Soc. of Am. Published works: History of the Founding of Wolf's Head, 1934; Prelude to Icaros, 1936; Georgia Transport (verse play for radio), 1938; A Ballad of Channel Crossings, 1940; First Flight, the Story of the Wright Brothers at Kitty Hawk, N.C.; Hill Country North, a Vermont Cycle, 1965; A.D. Twenty-One Hundred, A Narrative of Space, Legends of Flight, Triptych for the Atomic Age. Contbr. of articles & poems to var. publs. Ed.-in-Chief, Poet Lore; Ed., St. Lawrence Sea Way Fact Sheet, 1958-61. Honours, awards: co-recipient, Robert Frost Narration Poetry Award, 1963. Address: 52 Cranbury Rd., Westport, CT 06830, USA.

ANDREWS, Lyman, b. 2 Apr. 1938. Lecturer in American Studies, The University, Leicester. Education: Brandeis Univ., 1956-1960; King's Coll., London, 1960-1961; Univ. of Calif., Berkeley, 1961-1963. Positions held: Fulbright Scholar, 1960-1961; Woodrow Wilson Fellow, 1961-1962; Teaching Fellow, Univ. of Calif., 1962-1963; Phelan Fellow, Univ. of Calif., 1963-1964; Temporary Lecturer, Univ. of Wales, 1964-1965. Memberships: P.E.N.; Nat. Poetry Centre, London. Published works: Ash Flowers, 1958; Fugitive Visions, 1962; The Death of Mayakovsky & Other Poems, 1968; Kaleidoscope: New & Selected Poems, 1973. Anthologised in UK, USA, France, and Jugoslavia. Contbr. to: The Sunday Times (regular poetry critic). Poems appear in: Encounter; Partisan Review; Poetry Review; Transatlantic Review; Minnesota Review, etc. Awards: Warren Poetry Prize, 1959; 1960; Brandeis Lyric Poetry Prize, 1960. Address: Dept. of Engl., The Univ., Leicester LEI 7RH, UK.

ANDREWS, Miriam Wise. Poet; Editor; Critic. Education: Oberlin Conserv. of Music; Univ. of Akron; Kent State Univ. Married John Williams Andrews. Positions held: Poetry Ed., Scripps-Howard; Book & Arts Ed., ibid; Information Specialist, U.S. Census Bureau; Mng. Ed., Am. Red Cross Jr. Mags.; currently Assoc. Ed., Poet Lore & Cooper Hill Writers Conf. Memberships: Poetry Soc. of Am.; Am. Poetry Therapy Assn.; Boston Authors' Club. Published works: Fifty Poems, 1970; Oases, 1974. Contbr. to: Am. Forests; McCall's; Good Housekeeping; Paris Tribune; Chicago Tribune; Educational Forum; Sat. Review; Poet Lore; Yankee; var. Radio & TV scripts, etc. Recip., 'Best Beyond Ohio' Award, Ohio Poetry Day, 1968. Address: (winter) Box 688, Westport, CT 06880, (summer) Wind Rapids, East Doves, VT 05351, U.S.A.

ANDREWS, Rose Ellen, b. 20 Nov. 1882. Retired

Teacher. Education: Bellingham State Normal, Wash., U.S.A. Positions held: in Wenatchee, Wash. & rural schls. in the State of Wash.; Tchr., Metina, Tex. & Tyler, Tex. Memberships: Poetry Soc. of Tex.; Int. Mark Twain Soc. Published works: The Glory in Common Things, 1938; Always the Rainbow, 1970; The Glory in Common Things, 2nd ed., 1972. Contbr. to: The Poetry Digest Annual Anthol. of Verse, 1939; Am. Voices, 1939; The Poetry House Anthol., 1938; Contemporary Am. Poets, 1936; North Am. Book of Verse; Biog. Dict. of Contemporary Poets; The Paebar Anthol.; The Southern Churchman; Holland's Mag.; Winnsboro News. Address: Box 24, Winnsboro, TX 75494, U.S.A.

ANGELES, Carlos A, b. 25 May 1921. Public Relations Manager. Educ: Univ. of the Philippines, Diliman, Quezon City. Married with seven children. Positions held: Chief of Bur., Int. News Serv., Manila, 1948-58; Press Asst., 1958-59; P.R. Mgr., Pan Am. World Airways, Manila, 1959-. Published works: A Stun of Jewels, 1963. Contbr. to: Literary Apprentice; Sunday Times Magazine; Chronicle Magazine; Mirror Magazine; (anthologies) Six Filipino Poets, 1954; Doveglion Book of Philippine Poetry, 1963; Asian P.E.N. Anthology, 1965; New Writing from the Philippines, 1966. Honours, awards: Philippine Cultural Heritage Award in Literature, 1964; Palanca Mem. Award in Literature, 1964. Address: 141 Pinatubo Street, Mandaluyong, Rizal, Philippines.

ANGLE, Lily D., b. 23 July 1922. Library Clerk. Married, 1 daughter. Memberships: Pres., Saturday Scribes; Sec.-Treas., Kans. Chapt., Chaparral Poets; Publicity Chmn., Kansas Authors Club, 5th District. Published works: Soul & I, 1962. Contbr. to: Bardic Echoes; Denver Post; Kansas Kernels; Jean's Jrnl.; Midwest Chaparral; Christian Home; Purpose; Poet. Recip. prizes from Chaparral Poetry Contest, Kans. Authors' Club Poetry Contest & Kans. Poetry Contests. Address: 3610 Country Club Pl., Wichita, KS 67208, U.S.A.

ANGOFF, Charles, b. 22 Apr. 1902. Professor of English, Author, Poet. Education: Harvard, A.B., 1923; Fairleigh Dickinson Univ., Litt.D., 1966. Since, 1952, Prof. of Engl. at Fairleigh Dickinson Univ.; Editor, The Literary Review, since 1957; Chief Editor, Fairleigh Dickinson Univ. Press, since 1967. Member: Authors League of America; International P.E.N.; Poetry Soc. of America (President, 1968-72); Jewish Book Council of America; Fellow, Jewish Acad. of Arts and Sciences, USA.; Fellow, Boston Univ. Libraries, USA. Publications: About 40 books of poetry, fiction, history, criticism, essays; books of poetry: The Bell of Time, 1967; Memoranda for Tomorrow, 1970; Prayer at Midnight, 1971; Season of Mists, 1971; novel: 9th in the Polonsky saga; The Tone of the Twenties, 1969, essays. Contrib. to virtually all important mags. and newspapers in USA and other English-speaking countries – including: The Atlantic Monthly; The New Yorker; NY Times; The Southwest Review; The Prairie Schooner, etc. Recip. Author Award, NJ Assoc. of Teachers of English, for Memoranda for Tomorrow, 1970, also for Prayer at Midnight and Season of Mists, 1971. Awarded medal for distinguished service to poetry, Poetry Soc. of America, April, 1973. Address: 140 West 86th St., Apt. 14B., New York, NY 10024, USA.

ANHAVA, Tuomas, b. 5 June 1927. Writer & Translator. Education: M.A., Univ. of Helsinki, 1947. Positions held: Poetry & Fiction Ed., Finland's three leading publishing houses, 1948-61; Ed.-in-Chief, Parnasso Lit. Mag., 1966-; Prof. of Arts, 1970-; Mbr., Admin. Coun., Werner Söderström Oy Publishers, 1972-. Memberships: Bd. Mbr., Finnish Soc. of Authors, 1956-62; Chmn., Coun. of Lit. Socs. in Finland, 1970-. Published works: Runoja, 1953; Runoja 1955, 1955; 36 runoa, 1958; Runoja 1961, 1961; Kuudes kirja, 1966; Runot, 1951-66, 1967; (in foreign transl.) In the Dark, Move Slowly (transl. Anselm Hollo), 1969; Wiersze (transl. Natalia Baschmakoff), 1972. Translations incl: William Blake,

Taivaan ja helvetin avioliitto (The Marriage of Heaven & Hell), 1959; Saint-John Perse, Anabasis, 1960; St. Jerzy Lec, Vastakarvaan (selected aphorisms), 1968; Gunnar Björling, Kosmos valmiiksi kirjoitettu (selected poetry), 1972; Bo Carpelan, Runoja (selected poetry), 1974. Honours, awards: State Award for Literature, 1956; The Otava Award for Poetry, 1961; The Tammi Award for Translations, 1963; State Award for Translators, 1968 & 73; The Pro Finlandia Medal, 1968. Address: Tehtaankatu 7 B 14, 00140, Helsinki 14, Finland.

ANJANEYULU, Hemlata, b. 29 June 1925. Journalist; Writer; Broadcaster. Education: M.A. (Hindi); Sangeet Ratna (Hindustani Vocal Music). Positions held: V. Prin., Sri Ram Sangeet Vidyalaya, Raipur, M.P., 1945-47; Staff Artist, AIR, Allahabad, 1949-57; Announcer/Translator, Radio Moscow, 1957-60; Madras Corres., Aaj (Hindi daily from Varanasi), Madhuri (Times of India grp., fortnightly, Bombay), Thought (Engl. weekly, New Delhi); Writer & Jrnlst. Published works: (books) Poetry of Mahadevi Verma, 1949 (in press); Veeresalingam (Hindi transl. of the monograph by V.R. Narla), 1971; The Story of Mahasharata (Hindi transl. for N.B.T.); Looking Again at Indian Art (Hindi transl. for Publications Div., Govt. of India); Bhartiya Kavita (1958-59) 11 poems from Telugu to Hindi, coll. of own poetry; var. essays. Contbr. to: Amrita Patrika; Bharat; Haj; Aai Dhara; Nav Bharat Times; Andhra Pradesh, etc. Honours, awards: Chandra Mohdni Kaul Meml. Gold Medal; sev. prizes for music. Address: 'Saketa', 42 Mandavalli St., Madras 600028, India.

ANNAND, James King, b. 2 Feb. 1908. Teacher. Education: St. Bernard's Elem. School; Broughton Secondary School; Univ. of Edinburgh (M.A., Hons. History, 1930); Moray House Training Coll. Married, Beatrice Violet Lindsay; 4 d. Positions held: Asst. (Engl. and History), James Clark Secondary School, 1932-49 (in Royal Navy, 1941-46); Tutor in Social Science, Regent Road Coll. of Further Education, 1949-53; Principal Teacher of History, James Clark School, 1953-58; Headmaster, Whithorn Secondary School, 1959-62; Principal Teacher of History, Firrhill Secondary School, 1962-71. Memberships: Scottish Centre Internat. P.E.N.; Lallans Soc.; English Assoc. Published works: Sing it Aince for Pleisure, 1965; Two Voices, 1968; Twice for Joy, 1973; Early Lyrics by Hugh MacDiarmid (edited), 1968. Contbr. to: Akros; Broughton Mag.; Bulletin; Burns Chronicle; Chapman; Eve. Dispatch; English; Gambit; Glasgow Herald; Labour Standard; Lines Review; New Shetlander; Press and Journal; Saltire Review; Scotia Review; Scots Mag.; Scotsman; Scottish Mountaineering Club Journal; Southern Reporter; The Student; Voice of Scotland; Weekly Scotsman. Recip. Burns Chronicle Award, 1955. Address: 174 Craigleith Rd., Edinburgh EH4 2EE, Scotland, UK.

ANNAND, Peter Geoffrey Grant, pen name **ANNAND, Peter,** b. 28 May, 1949. Lawyer. Education: B.A. (1st class hons. Engl.), LL.B., Univ. of Queensland, Australia. Born in Brisbane, where lived until 1972. Temp. in UK reading for a postgraduate degree in law at Magdalen Coll., Oxford. Co-editor of Makar, literary mag., with Martin Duwell, since 1969. Published work: The long-distance poets' entry into heaven, 1973. Contbr. to: (Australia) The Australian; Linq; Makar; Meanjin; Poetry Australia; Southerly; Saturday Club Book of Poetry; Westerly; Galmahra; (UK) Cut; Oxford Poetry Mag. Address: Magdalen Coll., Oxford OX1 4AU, UK.

ANNOH, Kwesi Godfried, b. 4 June 1944. Journalist. Education: Ghana Inst. of Langs.; Ghana Inst. of Jrnlsm.; Alliance Française du Ghana; Advance Trng. Course in Jrnlsm. w. A.F.P., Paris. Positions held: Reporter & Acting Foreign Ed., Daily Graphic. Memberships: Nat. Assn. of Writers (Ghana); Ghana Assn. of Writers; Ghana Jrnlsts. Assn. Has written approx. 45 poems & is currently compiling them for publ. Contbr. to Gems of Modern British Poetry, vol. 3, 1972. Poems read on Ghana TV. Recip., Book Prize,

Gems of Modern British Poetry, vol. 3, 1972. Address: Daily Graphic (Editl.), P.O. Box 742, Accra, Ghana.

ANSEN, Alan, b. 23 Jan. 1922. Poet. Education: A.B., M.A., Harvard, 1942. Positions held: Sec., W.H. Auden, 1949-53. Published works: The Old Religion, 1959; Disorderly Houses, 1961; Field Report, 1961; Field Report, 1963; Believe & Tremble, 1963; Day by Day, 1966. Contbr. to: Partisan Review; Hudson Review; The Hasty Papers; Two Worlds; Solus Locus; Of Poetry & Power; Poems on Poetry. Address: 19 Alopekees St., Kolonaki, Athens 139, Greece.

ANTIN, David, 1 Feb. 1932. Curator; Director. Positions held: Formerly Ed., Some/Thing Magazine, NY; Curator & Director, Gallery, Univ. of Calif., San Diego. Published works: Definitions, 1967; Autobiography, 1967; Code of Flag Behavior, 1968. Contbr. to: Stony Brook Journal; Some/Thing; Caterpillar; Trobar; Kayak; El Corno Emplumado; (anthology) Antipiugiu, 1966. Honours, awards: Longview Award, 1960; Herbert Lehmann Fellowship, 1966-68. Address: 201 Pacific Ave., Solana Beach, CA 92075, U.S.A.

ANYIDOHO, Kofi, b. 25 July 1947. Teacher. Education: Ghana Tchrs. Cert. 'A', Accra Trng. Coll., 1968; Specialist Cert. in Engl., First Class, Advanced Tchr. Trng. Coll. Positions held: Elem. Schl. Tchr. at Nkoranza Local Authority Middle Schl. in the Brong Ahafo region of Ghana, 1968-70; Tchr. of Engl., Achimota Schl., Achimota, Ghana, 1972-. Memberships: Fndn. Mbr., Creative Writers' Assn. of Ghana & currently Sec. to 'The Foundation' (made up of old members); Former Asst. Gen. Sec., Ghana Assn. of Writers; Fndr. Mbr., Nat. Assn. of Writers; Sec., Writers' Club, Advanced Tchr. Trng. Coll., Winneba; Pres., Writers' Club, Accra Trng. Coll.; currently Patron, Writers' Club, Achimota Schl. Published works: The Things I Have to Say (coll. of poetry under consideration). Contbr. to: Talent for Tomorrow, annual anthol. of Creative Writers' Assn., 3rd, 5th, 6th & 7th edns. Frequently featured in Radio Ghana's 'Literary Corner' and 'Writers' Own'. Many public recitals. Address: Achimota School, P.O. Box 11, Achimota, Ghana.

APPLEBY, Wilfrid Morrison, b. 3rd July 1892. Philatelist. Positions held: Stamp Dealer, 1928-70, now semi-retired; Founder & Editor, Guitar News; Trustee, British Esperanto Association; Associate Editor, Envoi, 1968-69. Memberships: Founder & Chairman, Poetry Soc. of Cheltenham, 1967; Founder & Secretary, The Rhymsters' Poetry Soc., Essex, 1912; West Country Writers' Association; The Poetry Soc., Inc., London; Philatelic Traders' Soc. Ltd.; Founder, International Classic Guitar Association; Hon. Fellow, Socs. of Classic Guitar of NY & Boston; Rotary Club. Publications: Treatise on the evolution of the classic guitar; Life-Colour, 1971. Contbr. to: The Bookman; Titbits; Guitar News, Outposts; Breakthru; Mitre Press Spring Anthologies, 1968-69; Imprint; The Guitar Bulletin (Sydney, Australia); British Esperantist; British Jeweller; Frets (Japan) (w. profile article); Nature Poetry II, etc. Honours: 1st and 2nd prizes, Poetry Section, Birmingham Music Festival, 1968. Address: 47 Clarence St., Cheltenham, Glos., UK.

APPLEMAN, Philip, b. 8 Feb. 1926. Poet; Novelist; Professor of English. Education: B.S., Northwestern Univ., 1950; A.M., Univ. of Mich., 1951; Fulbright Student, Univ. of Lyon, France, 1951-52; Ph.D., Northwestern Univ., 1955. Married Marjorie Appleman. Positions held: Instr., Ind. Univ., Bloomington, 1955-58; Asst. Prof., ibid, 1958-62; Assoc. Prof., 1962-67; Prof., 1967-; Instr. in World Lit. & Philos., Int. Schl. of Am., 1960-61, 1962-63; Field Dir., 1962-63; Vis. Prof. of Engl., State Univ. of N.Y., 1973; Vis. Prof. of Engl., Columbia Univ., 1974. Memberships: PEN; Acad. of Am. Poets; Poetry Soc. of Am. Published works: Kites on a Windy Day, 1967; Summer Love & Surf, 1968. Contbr. to: Antioch Review; Beloit Poetry Jrnl.; Harper's Magazine; Lit. Review; Mass. Review; The Nation; New Republic;

N.Y. Qtly.; Partisan Review, etc. Honours, awards: Ind. Authors' Day Award, 1968; Ferguson Meml. Award, 1969; Midland Poetry Award, 1969; Christopher Morley Award, Poetry Soc. of Am., 1970. Address: Dept. of Engl., Ind. Univ., Bloomington, IN 47401, U.S.A.

APRONTI, Eric Ofoe, pen name **JAWA,** b. 9 Jan. 1940. University Lecturer. Education: B.A., London, Univ. of Ghana, 1962; P.G. Dip. in Engl. Studies, Leeds Univ., 1964; Ph.D. in General Linguistics & Phonetics, Univ. of London, 1967. Married, 3 sons, 1 daughter. Positions held: Rsch. Fellow in Lang. & Lit., Inst. of African Studies, Univ. of Ghana, 1967-. Memberships: Pres., Ghana Assn. of Writers, 1970; Co-Ed., OKYEAME, Ghana's Lit. Mag., 1968-. Published works: The Writing of Dangme (monograph), 1969. Contbr. to: Transitions Mag.; Okyeame Mag.; Modern Poetry from Africa, 1966; Legon Observer; New Voices of the Commonwealth, 1968. Address: Inst. of African Studies, Univ. of Ghana, Legon, Ghana.

ARAB, Hussain bin Ali. Retired Government Official. Education: Certificate from the Religious Institute, Mecca. Positions held: Newspaper Editor; Deputy Minister, Ministry of the Interior; Employee, Ministry of Pilgrimage & Religious Endowments. Has written two volumes of poetry. Address: Jidda, Saudi Arabia.

ARCHER, Eva L., pen name **VAN CREME, Rachel,** b. 1 Apr. 1887. Teacher. Writer. Positions held: Teacher, Public Schools of West Va.; Writer; Poet; Poetry Judge. Memberships include: Hon. Member, Eugene Field Soc., 1945; Charter Member, West Va. Poetry Soc., 1948; Chairman, West Va. Nat. Poetry Day, 1950. Pubs. Echoes from the Valley; Songs from the Hills; Mood Melodies. Contrib. to: Ideals; Christian Advocate; Seattle Times; Bremerton Sun; Whittier Coll. Year Book; West Va. Club Woman; Marietta Times; Seydall Quarterly; Don McNeil's Radio Prog.; Centennial Verse of W. Va., 1963; also sev. anthologies. Recip. various prizes. Address: 102 4½ St., Williamstown, West Va. 26187, USA.

ARCHER, Lee Ola, pen name **LEOLA,** b. 30 Jan. 1901. Columnist; Feature Writer. Education: Univ. of Tennessee, Knoxville; Conservatory of Music, Lexington, Kentucky. Positions held: Teacher, Creative Writing, Knoxville YWCA, 1965-; Pres., East Tennessee Baptist Hospital Auxiliary of Volunteer Services for 3 yrs., 1966-69; Pres., Up-town Opti-Mrs. Club, 1960-61; Teacher, Adult Bible Class, West Hills Baptist Church, 1962-. Memberships: Tenn. Womans Press and Authors Club (vice-pres., now serving as chaplain); Knoxville Branch, Nat. League of American Pen Women (former Branch and State Pres., at present serving as Chairman of Short Story Workshop). Published works: White Ship Sailing (poems), 1940; Write This Way – Folks, 1971. Contbr. to: NY Times; Knoxville News-Sentinel; Knoxville Journal; The Oregonian; Lexington Herald; Lexington Leader; West Side Story; Home Life; War Cry; Progressive Woman; Progressive Farmer; Christian Home; Open Windows; Adult Leader; Sunday School Times, and numerous church bulletins. Recip. 1st Prize in poetry, Tenn. Womans Press and Authors Club for best poem for State of Tennessee, Oct., 1972; 1st Prize for best poem, Nat. League of American Pen Women, 1970; 1st Prize for best poem submitted at Writers Conference, Ridgecrest, N.C. in 1952. Address: 825 Whitehall Rd., Knoxville, TN 37919, USA.

ARCHER, Louise (Nellie Louise Barnes), pen name **STREET, Louise,** b. 9 Nov. 1939. Saleswoman. Education: HS, and studied creative writing under Robert Shaver, Fresno City Coll. Now divorced; 2 children. Contbr. to: Angel Hour Mag.; Nutmegger Poetry Club Mag.; Internat. Who's Who in Poetry Anthol. Address: 3872 E. Ashcroft Ave., Fresno, CA 93726, USA.

ARDEN, Susan, b. 19 Dec. 1912. Typist; Researcher. Education: Bus. Coll. Memberships: Corres. Sec., The Fictioneers (a lit. club); Pacific Northwest Writers'

Conf. Rep. in following anthols: Cavalcade of Poetry, 1963; Rhyme Time For the Very Young, 1965; Versatility in Verse, 1965; Melody of the Muse, 1964. Contbr. to: Angel Hour; Angel Michael; Jr. World; The Christian Bd. of Publ.; Jean's Jrnl.; Friday Harbor Jrnl.; Tacoma News Tribune; Washington Verse. Honours, awards: First prize, Fictioneers Poetry Contest, 1971; Hon. mention, ibid, 1974. Address: 2814 N.E. 55th, Apt. 3, Seattle, WA, U.S.A.

ARDENT, Claude. Poet; Director, "Journees de Poésie", Orleans. Memberships: Sociétaire, Société des Gens de Lettres; Société des Auteurs et Compositeurs. Published works: (poems) Du Val en Beauce, caractères, 1958; Fait de soleil, silvaire, 1964; Baignes de Vert, profils littéraires, 1964; Au Val du Ciel, traces, 1969; Cet antérieur présent, St. Germain des prés, 1969; Entre, formes et langages, 1972; Capristics, formes et langages, 1974. Contbr. to République du Centre. Address: 21 rue Jeanne d'Arc, Orleans 45000, France.

AREF, Mahmoud, b. 1909. Positions held: Member, Consultative Council. Contbr. to all Saudi Arabian periodicals. Address: c/o Higher Council for Arts & Sciences, Ministry of Education, Riyadh, Saudi Arabia.

ARGOW, Sylvia, pen name **MELETUSA.** Secretary. Education: N.Y. Univ. and City of N.Y. Univ., studied economics, law, accounting. Positions held: Gaynes, Inc.; Star Machine Mfrs.; Dayton Metal Prod. Inc.; Freelance since 1961. Memberships include: Bronx Brush & Palette Art Soc.; Eastern Centre of the Poetry Soc. (London); World Poets' Resource Centre; Internat. Clover Poetry Assoc. (Danae); Bronx Council on the Arts; N.Y. Woman's Press Club (corresponding sec.); American Poets Fellowship Soc.; Nat. Bus. and Prof. Council; World Poetry Soc. Internat.; Centro Studi e Scambi Internazionali; Poetry Soc. Inc. (London); Mark Twain Soc. (N.Y.); Shore Nat. Network of Poets Soc.; Internat. Centre of N.Y.; Nat. Poetry Day Com. Inc. of the Fla. State Poetry Soc. Inc.; Nat. Shut-In Soc.; Internat. Poetry Soc. (Foundation Fellow-Designate); N.Y. Poetry Forum (historian). Contrib. to: Taft Review; Prairie Poets; American Poets; Poetry Prevue; Shore Record; Coney Island Times; Driftwood East; United Poets; Poet, 1973; Prairie Poet Year 1973; United Poets Laureate; Quaderni di Poesia; Dawn Anthology; Pan Continental Premier Poets; Lyrics of Love; Outstanding Contemporary Poetry; Shore Poetry Anthology; Written Word 13; Gato of Calif.; Ankh Jrnl.; Open Window – 1973; Williamsburg Times. Donor of the Sylvia Argow Sonnet Award in the N.Y. Poetry Forum Contest & Argonelle Award. Address: 2075 Grand Concourse, Bronx, N.Y. 10453, USA.

ARGRAVES, Hugh Oliver, b. 7 July 1922. Artist; Poet. Education: Beloit Coll., Wis. Memberships: Co-Fndr., Am. Acad. of Poets; Hon., Mark Twain Soc. Contbr. to: New Directions in Prose & Poetry, 1942; Collected Poetry, 1940-60, 1960; Four Poems, 1966; Poems, 1966; Year Book of Modern Poetry, 1971; Flame. Address: 519 N. Main St., Rockford, Ill. 61103, USA.

ARMSTRONG, Keith Francis Whitfield, pen names **CARM MAC & KEITH X,** b. 7 Apr. 1950. Musician; Artist; Poet; Part time Journalist. Positions held: Ed., In (Int. Poetry mag.), 1966; Chmn., Oxford YCND, 1968-69; Sec., Oxford Arts Lab. proj., 1969; Ldr., The Trip Company of G.B. Unlimited. Published works incl: Dreams, 1968; (Anthols.) Poetry for Peace, vol. 2, Breakthru, 1967; New Poems & Poems in Honour, Dock Leaves, 1967; Its World that Make the Love Go Round, Corgi, 1968; Miniposterpoem, 1969; Three poemfolder, 1970; Womb Wow, 1971. Contbr. to: Breakthru; Riding West; The Journal; It; Firebird; Flame; Imprint; Informer; Oxford Mail; Poetry Workshop; Second Aeon; Tamarisk; Somethings; Oz; Moonshine; Alla. Honours, awards: 3rd pl., Manifold Fire Comp., 1967. Address: 16 Davenant Rd., Oxford, U.K.

ARMSTRONG, Marion, b. 16 July 1916. Teacher of English. Education: B.A., Vassar Coll.; M.A., Columbia Univ.; Ph.D. cand., N.Y. Univ. Married, 2 children. Positions held: Tchr. of Engl. in two N.Y. private schls.; Exec. Chmn. of Engl. Dept., 19 yrs.; Film Reviewer for Christian Century Mag., 1966-72. Member, Poetry Soc. of Am. Published works: Tabret & Harp, 1967. Contbr. to: Sat. Review; Punch; Christian Century; The Living Ch.; NAIS Mag.; Vassar Review; Vassar Little Mag., etc. Address: 315 West 106th St., N.Y., NY 10025, U.S.A.

ARMSTRONG, Naomi Young, b. 17 Oct. 1918. Teacher; Actress; Poetess. Education: B.S. in Speech-Theatre, Northwestern Univ., 1961; Assoc. in Arts, Woodrow Wilson Jr. Coll., 1957. Divorced, 1 daughter. Positions held: Fiscal & Acctng. Clerk, Bureau of Public Debt, 1955-56; Information/Receptionist/Expediter, Internal Revenue Serv., 1956-59; Caseworker, Cook Co. Dept. of Public Aid, 1961; Certified Tchr., Chicago Public Schls., 1962–. Memberships: Elected Judge, 2nd World Congress of Poets; Life Mbr., IBA; Life Mbr., World Poets Resource Ctr. & Poetry Soc. of England; Life Mbr., Int. Platform Assn. & a member of its Poetry & Hospitality Comm.; Centro Studi e Scambi Int.; Bd. Trustees, World Univ.; Past Basileus, Sigma Gamma Rho. Published works: Expression I, 1973; A Child's Easter, 1971. Contbr. to: New Voices in Am. Poetry, 1972; World Poets No. 4 & Am. Voice Poetry, 1971. Recip. 3 awards from Second World Congress of Poets, 1973. Address: 9257 South Burnside Ave., Chicago, IL 60619, U.S.A.

ARMSTRONG, Phyllis Eleanor, pen names, **ARMSTRONG, Phil; LINGARD, Christopher,** b. 25 March 1910. Librarian – Special Assistant for Poetry to Chair of Poetry, Library of Congress, Washington DC, USA. Education: privately tutored in England and Canada; received formal education in England and USA. Personal details: born of English parents; became US citizen, 1949. Positions held: Physical Ed. Teacher; Private English Day School Teacher; Statistician, Dept. of Justice & Census Bureau; Research, Library of Congress; WWII Code & Cypher Officer, W.R.N.S., 1942-45, with Combined Chiefs of Staff, Washington & Canada. Hon. discharged on disability, Nov. 1945; (Awarded the King's Badge); Special Asst. for Poetry, Lib. of Congress, 1946-70. Retired. Memberships: Internat. Poetry Soc., UK (Founder Fellow); Acad. of American Poets; Amos R. Koontz Memorial Foundation (Fellowship); Washington Writers League. Published works: A Witness in Washington, 1972; LP Recording of Poetry Reading in Lib. of Congress Recording Studio. Contbr. to: The Silver Treasury of Light Verse, etc. Recip. Amos R. Koontz Memorial Foundation Distinguished Service Plaque for outstanding service to literature in the Library of Congress Poetry Office, 1946-70 (1970). Address: 5614 29th Ave., Queen's Chapel Manor, Hyattsville, MD 20782, USA.

ARMSTRONG, Robert, b. 22 Apr. 1901. Poet; Author; Lecturer. Education: London Schl. of Econs., U.K., 1924-26; Civil Serv. Entrance, 1926. Married, 2 sons. Positions held: H.M. Inspector of Taxes, 1926-61; Sec. & Treas., The Poetry Soc. & Nat. Poetry Ctr., 1962-67. Memberships: Chmn., Poetry Soc. of G.B., 1948-50 & 1961; Dir., ibid, 1962-67; V.P., 1967–; Pres., The York Poetry Soc., 1968–; Pres., The Order of Druids & Bards, 1968–; Coun. Mbr., Anglo Finnish Soc., 1957–; Am. Poetry Soc., 1967–. Published works: Seventeen Poems, 1950; Entr'acte, Poems, 1955; Collected Lyrical Poems for the Blind, 1957; Exchange of Hearts, 1954; The Ghosts of Highgate Hill, 1966; Finnish Christmas Songs, 1972; The Poetic Vision (essays & lectures), 1973. Contbr. to: The Poetry Review; Weekly Scotsman; British Weekly; The Times; Times Lit. Supplement; Evening Standard; New Statesman; The New Beacon; Qtly. Record; The Critic, Chicago; The Kaleva, Finland, etc. Honours, awards: Civil Serv. Essay Prize, 1924; Gold Medal, Dining Club of N.Y. Editors & TV Producers, 1968; Transatlantic Award, Manifold Soc., 1968; Poem of the Year Cit.,

The Flame Assn., U.S.A., 1957. Address: 16 Harford Walk, Hampstead Gdn. Suburb, London N2, U.K.

ARNER, Samuel De Walt, b. 17 June 1900, Vandergrift Heights, Pa. Education: Dips., Law, Theol., Premedics; Painting under Philbrick, San Antonio, Robert Graham, Denver & George Frederick Gleich, Palm Springs. Positions held: Military Duty; Fndr., San Jacinto Studio, Calif.; Archeologist, Mexico, Ctrl. Am., Ecuador; Fndr. & Curator, Mus. of Antiquities & Art, Cathedral City, Calif. Memberships: Am. Inst. Fine Arts; Calif. Acad. Scis.; Archaeol. Inst. of Am.; Archaeol. Soc. of NM; Am. Mus. Nat. Hist. Contbr. of poems to local newspapers & mags., also to Internat. Who's Who in Poetry Anthol., 1972. Address: PO Box 687, Cathedral City, Calif. 92234, USA.

ARNETT, Thomas Lewis, b. 10 May 1935. Writer. Education: Univ. of Sask., Canada. Published works: TV: She Shows Me Everything; Defrosting the Arts; Sounds Like Music; The Sound Collectors; Sounds Together (a series for tchng. music to children); Radio: The Last Book of the Last Prophet; Ballad of a Thin Man; The Game; The Island of Quadra & Vancouver; Tekhionwake; The Tin Housekeeper (two episodes); To Laugh or to Cry; Bernard Mergandieler (musical); Thesula; Trying Too Hard (sound-poetry drama); Whatever Happened to Alice (stereo); Seance (stereo); var. educl. film scripting & promotional writing for film companies; num. articles in newspapers & mags.; worked for Margaret MacLeod on the writing of Cuthbert Grant & Folk Songs of Old Manitoba; hundreds of published photographs. Has written num. poems which have been published in mags. in Canada, U.S.A. & G.B. & read at over 100 profl. readings. Has made num. personal appearances on radio & TV, reading own poetry. Mbr. & past Exec. Mbr., League of Canadian Poets. Address: RR1, Cooks Town, Ont., Canada LOL 1LO.

ARNSTEIN, Flora J., b. 10 Aug. 1885. Teacher. Education: Univ. of Calif. at Berkeley; San Francisco State Coll. Teacher Elementary School. Member, Poetry Soc. of America. Pubs.: Adventure Into Poetry, 1951, subsequently reprinted as: Children Write Poetry; Poetry in the Elementary Classroom, subsequently reprinted as: Children & Poetry. Contrib. to: NY Times; London Mercury; Poetry World; Antioch Review; Accent; Prairie Schooner; Nation; Northwestern Review, etc. Recip. Poetry Soc. of America awards, 1954, 1960, 1961. Address: 30 Cragmont Av., San Francisco, Calif., 94116, USA.

ARROWSMITH, William Ayres, b. 13 Apr. 1924. Professor of Classics. Education: B.A., Princeton; B.A. (Oxon.), 1951; M.A. (Oxon.), 1958; Ph.D., Princeton, 1958. Married w. 2 children. Positions held: Instr. in Classics, Princeton Univ., 1951-53 & Wesleyan Univ., 1953-54; Asst. Prof. of Classics, Univ. of Calif., 1954-56; Assoc. Prof. of Classics, Univ. of Tex., 1958-59; Prof. of Classics, 1960-70; Univ. Prof., Univ. of Tex., 1966-70; Univ. Prof. & Prof. of Classics, Boston Univ., 1972–. Memberships: Bd. Mbr., National Translation Ctr., 1964-69; Fndng. Ed., The Hudson Review, 1948-60; Fndng. Ed., Arion, 1962–; Ed., Delos; Contbng. Ed., Am. Poetry Review; Contbng. Ed., Mosaic. Published works: Translations (verse) of Euripides, Heracles, Cyclops, Bacahae, Hecuba, Orestes, 1960; Translation of Aristophanes Birds, 1961; Clouds, 1963; Ed., The Complete Greek Comedy, 1960-70; Ed., The New Greek Tragedy, 1973–. Contbr. to: Botteghe Oscure; Am. Poetry Review; The Hudson Review; The Sewanee Review; Arion, etc. Recip., 9 hon. degrees. Address: RD 1, Box 311, Lincoln, VT 05443, U.S.A.

ARSEGUEL Gérard, b. 26 Feb. 1940. Professor of Literature. Mbr., Editl. Comm., review 'Manteia'. Published works: Persian Wood, 1966; Une Méthode de Discours un la Lumiere, 1968; Pluriels, 1969 (illustrations, Jacques Gastinel). Contbr. to: L'Arc – Action poetique; Les Cahiers du Sud; Manteia; Da Nouvelle revue Française; Art Vivant. Address: c/o Manteia, 39 Allies Leon Gambetta, 13 Marseille 1, France.

ARVIDSON, Leonore Charnofsky, b. 17 Dec. 1925. Poet. Education: B.A., Univ. of Calif. at Los Angeles, 1948; grad. studies, ibid. Married Alvin B. Arvidson, Jr., 1 son, 1 daughter. Positions held: Editl. Dept., Los Angeles Daily News, 3 yrs.; Rdr. & Rsch. Asst., UCLA Spanish Dept., 3 yrs.; Elem. Schl. Tchr., Los Angeles City Schls., 1 yr.; Aide, Los Angeles Co. Public Lib., 5 yrs.; Docent (Volunteer), Calif. Mus. of Sci. & Industry, 3 yrs. Memberships: Fndng. Mbr., PAN Ltd., Beverly Hills, Calif.; UCLA Poetry Workshop; Mbr., Editl. Bd., Pandemonium, 1973. Participant, Andrew W. Thornhill Poetry Symposium, 1974 & to var. poetry readings. Contbr. to Pandemonium, poetry jrnl. Address: 808 Broom Way, Los Angeles, CA 90049, U.S.A.

ASALACHE, Khadambi. Published works: A Calabash of Life (novel), 1967. Contbr. to: Transition; (anthologies) Commonwealth Poems of Today, 1967; New Voices of the Commonwealth, 1968.

ASCOOP, Hubert, pen name **MEYLAND, Frank,** b. 26 Aug. 1920. Medical Prospector. Education: Hist. & Hist. of Arts, Univ. of Ghent. Married Mary Jane Hallaert, 3 sons. Memberships: Soc. of Flemish Authors; PEN Club; Lit. Commn., Provincie Oostvlaanderen; Jury Mbr. for Lit. Prizes in East Flanders; V.P., Comm. for Flemish Days of Poetry. Published works: (poetry) Andante, 1942; Memoria, 1943: Gestamelde Elegieën, 1946, 2nd edn., 1957; Mors et Vita, 1947; Aendachtigh, 1953; Op Fluistertoon, 1962. Contbr. to: Dietsche Warande en Belfort; Nieuwe Stemmen; Roeping; many anthols. Recip., Prize of Flemish Days of Poetry, 1947. Address: Warnefordstr. 2, 9110 St. Amandsberg, Belgium.

ASH, Sarah Leeds, b. 20 Nov. 1904. Author; Teacher. Education: Illman-Carter Unit, Univ. of Pa., Philadelphia. Married, H. Dickson Ash. Positions held: Tchr., Pub. Schls., Atlantic City, NJ; Sponsor, Creative Writing Group, 1941-50. Memberships: Poetry Soc. of Am.; Nat. League Am. Pen Women; Colonial Dames of Am.; Pa. Poetry Soc.; Society of Friends. Published works: Changeless Shore, 1962; Little Things, 1942; Moment of Time, 1972. Contbr. to: Good Housekeeping; Parade; Saturday Evening Post; NY Times; Voices; Peacock Alley; Poetry Chap Book; Hollands; Am. Weave; Detroit Times; Yachting; Times Chronicle; The Friend; The Golden Year; The Pen Woman; Forward; Sonnet Sequences; Suburban Life; Work Sheet Dir.; Golden Harvest; Voices Int.; Milady; Between the Book Ends; Poems of Pa. Anthol. Recip. of numerous poetry awards from Poetry Soc. of Am.; Pa. Poetry Soc., NLAPW, etc. Address: West Nook, Wyncote, Pa. 19095, USA.

ASHBERY, John Lawrence, b. 28 July 1927. Author & Critic. Education: B.A., Harvard Coll., Cambridge, Mass., 1949; M.A., Columbia Univ., 1951. Positions held: Copywriter, Oxford Univ. Press N.Y.C., 1951-54; McGraw-Hill Book Co., N.Y.C., 1954-55; Art Critic, European edn., N.Y. Herald Tribune, Paris, France, 1960-65; Paris Corres., Art News, N.Y.C., 1964-65; Art Critic, Art International, Lugano, Switz., 1961-64; Ed., Locus Solus, Lans-en-Vercors, France, 1960-62; Ed., Art & Literature, Paris, France, 1963-67; Exec. Ed., Art News, N.Y.C., 1965-72. Published works incl: Turandot & Other Poems, 1953; Some Trees, 1956, '70; The Poems, 1960; The Tennis Court Oath, 1962; Rivers & Mountains, 1966 (nominated for Nat. Book Award); Selected Poems, 1967; Three Madrigals, 1968; Sunrise in Suburbia, 1968; Fragment, 1969; The Double Dream of Spring, 1970; The New Spirit, 1970; Penguin Modern Poets 19, 1971; Three Poems, 1972; (novel w. James Schuyler) Nest of Ninnies, 1969; (plays) The Heroes (one act), 1952; The Compromise (3 acts), 1955; The Philosopher (one act), 1964; var. translations & other works. Rep. in many anthols. & contbr. to num. mags. & jrnls. Recip. var. awards inclng: Nat. Inst. Arts & Letters Award, 1969; Shelley Award, PSA, 1973. Address: c/o Georges Borchardt, Inc., 145 East 52nd St., N.Y., NY 10022, U.S.A.

ASHBROOK, John. Child Psychologist. Education: B.Sc., Psychol., Manchester Univ.; M.A., Child Psychol., Nottingham Univ. Married, 2 children. Positions held: currently Child Psychol., Lancashire Co. Coun. Published works: Death Duties, 1968. Contbr. to: Poetry Wales; Critical Survey: Phoenix. Recip., Poetry comp. prizes, Critical Qtly., 1967 & '68. Address: 4 Park Gate Ave., Withington, Manchester 20, U.K.

ASHCROFT, Nell, b. 23 June 1927. Assistant Company Secretary. Education: Ormskirk Grammar School; Private Commercial College, Southport. Married; 1 s. Positions held (since 1945): various secretarial appointments; With textile organisation, 1957, Director's Secretary, 1960, Sec. to Company Chairman, 1968, Staff Benefits Officer; since 1973, Asst. Company Sec., brickmaking organisation. Membership: Lancs. Authors' Assoc. Published work: private collection printed and sold for charity (650 copies), 1970. Contbr. to: Prize Poets of Spring, 1969; Poetry Gems, 1972. Address: 15 New St., Eccleston, Chorley, Lancs., UK.

ASHE, John Harold, b. 4 Sep. 1907. Accountant. Pubs. Songs of Sentiment, 1968. Well-known as Australia's most versatile songwriter. Country songs include: Game as Ned Kelly; Harry the Breaker; The Old Pioneers. L.P. Recordings: Island Songs of the Great Barrier Reef; Fair Dinkum Aussie Fun; Fair Dinkum Mate. Address: 409 Walker Street, Townsville, Q. 4810, Australia.

ASHER, Frances Ellsworth, b. 3 May 1902. Housewife; Free-lance Writer. Married to Robert G. Asher. Positions held: w. Am. Red Cross Home Serv., 1959-66; Chmn., Fndr., local Poetry Workshop, 1952-54. Memberships: Poetry Soc. of Colo., 1935–; Nat. Honor Soc., 1918; Past Pres., Fed. Woman's Club, 1958-60; Chap., Eastern Star Chapt., 3 yrs.; Contbng. Poetry Ed., Nat. Peace Officers Assn. Published works: 4 copyrighted songs, words & music; some safety versus pub. monthly in Nat. Peace Officers Mag., 1954–; 2 poems in Silver Souvenir Anthol., 1953; Along the Overland Trail (play). Contbr. to: Colo. Club Woman; Sterling Parm Jrnl. Advocate; Spotlight; The Key; Mo. State Patrol Mag.; Delta Paper; Montrose Paper; Eljebel Shrine mag.; Denver Post; Sterling Advocate; Blue Moon mag.; Colo. News; Nat. Peace Officer's mag.; Nat. Sheriff's mag.; Conn. Vox-Cop; Pueblo Chieftain; Denver Police Jrnl.; Motor Vehicle Spotlight; local & Denver radio stns.; Kansas City Poetry mag.; Rocky Mtn. News.; Grand Junction Sentinel; Buzza-Cardoza Greeting Cards; Golden Harvest Anthol. Honours: awarded over 50 prizes, Poetry Soc. of Colo. contests, 1939–; Annual Sweepstakes Award, 1957; 2nd & 1st prizes, Colo. Fed. Women's Club, 1958, '59; 1st prize for short stories and plays, 1959. Address: Country Club Mobile Manor, 113-A Shady Lane, Eustis, Fla. 32726, USA.

ASHFORD, Shirley Ann, pen name **ASHFORD, Shirley Agin,** b. 23 Sept. 1935. Housewife. Married, 4 children. Contbr. to: World Call; Christian; Poet. Address: 520 South Washington, Iola, KS 66749, U.S.A.

ASHI, Abdulwahhab, b. 1923. Retired Civil Servant. Has held var. governmental positions. Contbr. to all Saudi Arabian periodicals. Address: c/o Higher Committee for Arts & Sciences, Ministry of Education, Riyadh, Saudi Arabia.

ASHLEY, Nova Trimble, b. 10 Jul. 1911. Poet, Freelance Writer of Fiction and Non-Fiction. Education: Selden Rural High School; College courses and Creative Writing courses at Wichita State Univ. Married to James E. Ashley. Children: Keith E.; Kenneth L.; Joyce (Mrs. Donald C. Olson); James K. (deceased). Insurance Supervisor, Wesley Medical Center, Wichita, 1952-70. Pres., Wichita Branch, Nat. League of American Pen Women, Inc., 1973-74; Member: Nat. Fed. of Press Women, Inc. (State and Wichita Branches); Internat. Platform Assoc.; Kansas Authors Club; Friends of the Library, Wichita; Wichita Line Women; Poetry Soc. of America. Pubs. Through an Ocean of Gold, 1963; Coffee with Nova, 1966; Loquacious Mood, 1970; Haps and Mishaps, 1973. Contrib. to more than 100 newspapers, magazines, etc. including: Good Housekeeping; McCall's; Guideposts; Reader's Digest; Saturday Evening Post; Kansas Quarterly; Together, etc. Recipient of more than 100 poetry prizes, including Kansas Authors Club (1960 to 1973); Nat. Fed. of Press Women; Nat. League of American Pen Women; New York Poetry Forum; Pennsylvania Poetry Society (1968 to 1973); Midwest Chaparral contests, 1972, and many others; Kansas Poet of the Year, Midwest Chaparral Poetry Soc., 1969, 1970, 1973; "Prayer for Peace" sonnet (Nat. Press Women), 1968. Address: 2101 S. Glendale Avenue, Wichita, Kansas 67218, USA.

ASHONG-KATAI, Selby, b. 29 June 1946. Insurance Manager. Education: B.A. (Hons.) Hist.; studying at Chartered Insurance Inst. Married, 1 son. Positions held: Air Traffic Control Asst., 1964-67; Marine Mgr., Commercial Union Assurance Co. of Ghana Ltd. Memberships: Org. Sec., Ghana Assn. of Writers; Exec. Mbr., Gtr. Accra Region, Nat. Assn. of Writers; V.P., Univ. of Ghana Writers Forum, etc. Published works: Confessions of a Bastard, coll. of prize-winning stories, 1974; A Sonata of Broken Bones, coll. of prize-winning poems, 1974; Zogbane, a pamphlet of 5 poems; 'Sons & Lovers' (D.H. Lawrence), simplified, 1974. Contbr. to: The Voice; The Sunday Mirror; Growth; The Spectator. Honours, awards: The Nehru Prize, 1968/69, '69/70; The Gurrey Prize, 1970; African Arts Mag. Award (Calif. Univ.) Address: P.O. Box 5080, Accra, Ghana.

ASHONG-KATAI, Setheli Tettey, b. 31 Jan. 1947. Tax Official. Education: UNESCO Cert. on Book Production (Publishing & Writing). Positions held: Cmdr. of Administration, Finance & Organisation, Pan African Youth Movement of Ghana, 1972; Sec.-Gen., Juju Theatre, 1973–; Tax Official, Ctrl. Revenue Dept., Accra. Memberships: V.P., Ghana Assn. of Writers, 1971-73; Special Presidential Asst., ibid, 1973; currently First Organising Sec.; Nat. Assn. of Writers, Ghana. Contbr. to Growth Lit. Mag.; Panymo Mag.; Annual Congress, Ghana Assn. of Writers' Brochure, 1973; Evening News; Radio Ghana (External Service); Ghana TV; Poetry evenings at the theatre & Ghana's Higher institutions. Address: P.O. Box 5080, Accra-North P.O., Accra, Ghana.

ASHOUR, Gladys Brierly, pen name **ASHOUR, Brierly,** b. 10 Sept. 1906. Freelance Writer; Lecturer; Educator (Instructor). Education: A.B., 1946, M.A., 1948, Univ. of Missouri at Kansas City; Grad. Study, George Washington Univ. and Catholic Univ. of America, Washington, DC. Widow of Gerald Raymond Ashour; 2 d. Positions held: Teacher, K.C. Pub. Schools, 1945-52; Tech. Librarian, Human Resources Research Office, Washington, DC, 1954-58; Head Librarian, Emerson Research Lab., Silver Spring, 1958-59; Childrens Librarian, Montgomery County, Md, 1962; Instr. in Creative Writing, Inst. Lifetime Learning, American Assoc. of Retired Persons, 1967–. Memberships: N.L.A.P.W. (Nat. Pres., Nat. Registrar, Nat. Membership Chairman, Pres. Baltimore Branch, MD State Pres.); Nat. Writers Club; Internat. Platform Assoc. (Poet Laureate, 1971-72); Poetry Soc. (London) Eastern Center; Nat. Story League (Sec., Vice-Pres., and Yearbook Editor, Wash. Chapt.); Soc. of Childrens Book Writers; Missouri Writers Guild (Pres., Kansas City Chapter); Maryland Poetry Soc. Contbr. to: Home Life; Quaker Life; Christian Herald; Orphans Messenger; War Cry; The Friend; St. Anthony Messenger; Phi Delta Gamma Journal; The Instructor; The Grade Teacher; Highlights for Children; Humpty Dumpty's Mag.; Primary Treasure; Child Life; Denver Post Round Up; Hyacinths & Biscuits; Int. Who's Who in Poetry Anthol., etc. Has sold over 400 poems to nat. publications. Address: 10610 Mantz Rd., Silver Spring, MD 20903, USA.

ASI, Harry, b. 29 Aug. 1922. Electrical Draftsman. Education: Langs. & Lit., Univ. of Toronto, Canada,

1955-56; Art & Archaeol., ibid, 1960-62. Memberships: Sec., Estonian Lit. Soc. in Geislingen, W. Germany, 1948-51; Pres., Estonian Lit. Soc., Toronto, Canada, 1969-70; PEN Club, Stockholm, 1965–. Published works: (colls. of poetry) Sódalane Värsivibuga (Warrior with Verbal Arrow & Bow), 1950; Tuisosóitsa (Blizzard Rider), 1952; Kuivalgus Kaob (If Light Vanishes), 1954; Heiastused (Reflections), 1959; Epigramme Ehk Kaksgrammieepikat (Epigrams), 1960; Oölille laul (Song of the Nocturnal Flower), 1971; (novel) Pärast plahvatust (After the Explosion), 1967 (book design, cover & illustrations by the author). Contbr. to criticism on art, drama, lit. & poetry in Estonian newspapers, periodicals & mags. since 1954. Active artist since 1962 & participant in a number of exhibs. as well as two one-man shows. Honours, awards: Visnapuu Prize for Pärast plahvatust, 1967 & for Oölille laul, 1972; Estonian Poet Laureate for 1968 & 1972. Address: 57 Rawlinson Ave., Apt. 105, Toronto, Ont. M4P 2N1, Canada.

ASTEL, Arnfrid, b. 9 July 1933. Editor. Education: studied biology & philology in Freiburg & Heidelberg. Positions held: Private Tutor, Heidelberg & Cologne; Publsr. of lit. works, Saarbrucken, 1967–; Publisher, Lyrische Hefte, periodical; Broadcasting Ed. Memberships: Verband deutscher Schriftsteller (VS); RFFU (Rundfunkgewerkschaft); PEN. Published works: Lyrische Hefte, Zeitschrift für Gedichte, 1959; Notstand, 100 Epigramme, 1968; Kläranlage, 100 neue Epigramme, 1970; Ho Chi Minh, Gefängnistagebuch, 1970; Zwischen den Stühlen sitzt der Liberale auf seinem Sessel, Epigramme und Arbeitsgerichtsurteile, 1974. Contbr. to: Akzente; Neue deutsche Literatur (DDR); Neue deutsche Hefte; Kursbuch. Address: 66 Saarbrücken, St. Ingberter Str. 52, German Fed. Repub.

ATCHLEY, Dana Winslow, pen names, **ACE SPACE CO; SPACECO,** b. 15 April 1941. Artist; Poet; Teacher. Education: Dartmouth Coll., B.A. (with distinction), 1963; Yale Univ., B.F.A., 1964, M.F.A., 1965. Positions held: Instr. Marlboro Coll., 1963-65; Instr., Maryland Inst. of Art, 1966-69; Asst. Prof., Univ. of Victoria, 1969-71; Freelance consultant and teacher/lecturer, 1971-74. Published works: ABC Design, 1965; This Book is a Movie (anthol.), 1971; Six Rusticated, Walleyed Poems (in conjunction with Jonathan Williams), 1969; Blues & Roots, Rue and Bluets (in conjunction with Jonathan Williams & Nick Dean), 1971; Cows/Clouds, 1971; Word Pack, 1971. Since all work is in the area of visual poetry, most of it appears in exhibition format including the following exhibitions: Expo/Internacional de Novisima Poesia, Buenos Aires, 1969; Internat. Exposition of Visual & Phonetic Poetry, Stedelijk Museum, Amsterdam, 1970; 1st Bienale de Artes Graficas, Cali Colombia, 1971; Concrete/Post Concrete Show, Plattsburgh, NY, 1971; Artist's Books, Univ. of Calif., Berkeley, 1973. Honours: Purchase Prize: 6th Burnaby Printshow, 1971. Address: Box 183, Crested Butte, CO 81224, USA.

ATHAS, Daphne, b. 19 Nov. 1923. Author & Lecturer. Education: A.B., Univ. of NC; Harvard Schl. of Educ. Positions held: Tchr. of the Blind; Service Club Dir., USAF, Ruislip, UK, 1954-58; Coord. of Programmed Learning, Tech. Inst., Hillsboro, NC., USA; Lectr., Dept. of Engl., Prog. of Creative Writing, Univ. of NC, 1968-71. Memberships: Authors League; Poetry International: N.C. Lit. and Hist. Assoc. Published works: Weather of the Heart, 1947; Fourth World, 1956; Ding Dong Bell (Sit on the Earth), 1957; Greece by Prejudice, 1963; Entering Ephesus, 1971. Contbr. to: Botteghe Oscure; Transatlantic Review; Envoi; Int. Poet; SC Review; New World Writing; Beloit Poetry Jrnl.; Carolina Quarterly; Grit; The Brompton Poets. Honours, Awards: 2nd Prize, Observer Play Contest, 1957; MacDowell Fellowship, 1962; Scholarship, Nat. Council Arts & Humanities, 1968; Time Magazine Ten Best List for Fiction, 1971; Sir Walter Raleigh Award for Fiction, 1972; Fulbright Award, 1973. Address: Box 224, Chapel Hill, NC. 27514, USA.

ATKINS, Jack, b. 30 Aug. 1923. Educator. Education: Business Coll. Training (private, church school); Univ. of Utah, Salt Lake City, B.A., Engl.; Univ. of Wyoming, Laramie, M.A., School Admin. Both parents born in UK, naturalized Americans. Positions held: Librarian (School). St. Michael's HS, Santa Fe, 1965–; Engl. Teacher, Tuba City HS., Ariz., 1965 (for half-year); Engl. Teacher, Sunnyside HS., Tucson, Ariz., 1963-64; District School Supt., Moorcroft, Wyoming, 1962-63. Published work: Some Early Life and Poems of Jack Atkins, 1973. Contbr. to: Flagstaff Daily Sun; The New Mexican; The Encore. Also poem selected for Nat. Poetry Anthol. for the years 1966-73 (8 poems in course of 8 yrs.). Address: 1973 Ildefonso Rd., Santa Fe, NM 87501, USA.

ATKINS, Russell, b. 25 Feb. 1926. Poet & Composer. Education: Cleveland Schl. of Art; study w. Milton Fox Paul Travis; Cleveland Mus. Schl. Settlement; Cleveland Inst. of Mus., 1945; study w. J. Harold Bron. Positions held: Fndr. & Ed., Free Lance Mag., 1950; Publicity Mgr. & Asst. to the Dir., The Sutphen Schl. of Mus., 1957-60; Invited to Breadloaf Writers Conf., 1956; Cons. for federally funded Industrialization Ctrs. Writing Workshop Prog., 1967-69; Cons. for Educl. TV, WVIZ, 1969-71 & for Karamu Theatre's Poetry Confs.; Cons. for Cleveland Bd. of Ed. Writers-in-schools Prog.; Writer in Res., Cuyahoga C. Coll., 1973; Writing Instr., Karamu Ctr., 1972-73. Memberships incl: Cleveland State Univ. Poetry Forum; Affil., Iowa Univ. Writing Workshop, 1953-54; COSMEP. Published works: Phenomena, 1961; Objects, 1963; Objects 2, 1963; Heretofore, 1968; The Nail, 1971; Presentations, 1969; 'I Stand Far to the East' (sheet mus.), 1969. Contbr. to var. jrnls. & anthols. Work read by Marianne Moore on WEVD 'The World in Books', 1950. Address: 6005 Grand Ave., Cleveland, OH 44104, U.S.A.

ATWOOD, Margaret, b. 18 Nov. 1939. Writer. Education: B.A., Univ. of Toronto, 1961; A.M., Radcliffe, 1962. Positions held: Teacher, Univ. of British Columbia; Sir George Williams(Montreal); Univ. of Alberta; York Univ., Toronto; Univ. of Toronto, Writer-in-Residence, 1972-73. Member, League of Canadian Poets. Pubs.: Double Persephone, 1961; The Circle Game, 1966; The Animals in That Country, 1968; The Journals of Susanna Moodie, 1970; Procedures for Underground, 1970; Power Politics, 1971; (novels): The Edible Woman, 1969; Surfacing, 1972; (criticism): Survival: A Thematic Guide to Canadian Literature, 1972. Contrib. to: The New Yorker; The Atlantic Monthly; Poetry (Chicago); Mademoiselle; The Nation; NY Times; Aphra; Kayak; Field; New; Tamarack Review; Prism International; Canadian Forum; Quarry; Blackfish; Northern Journal; Exile; Blew Ointment, etc., etc. Recip. Governor General's Award, 1966; 1st Prize, Centennial Poetry Competition, 1968; Union Poetry Prize, Poetry, 1969. Address: Box 1401, Alliston, Ont., Canada.

AUCHTERLONIE, Dorothy, b. 28 May 1915. University Lecturer in Engl. and Australian Literature. Education: Sunderland, UK.; Univ. of Sydney, M.A., hons. Married to Henry Mackenzie Green, author of definitive History of Australian Literature, former Librarian, Univ. of Sydney (dec'd 1962); 1 s., 1 d. Positions held: Teacher in private schools; News Editor, Australian Broadcasting Commission, Brisbane, 1942-44; Headmistress, Presbyterian Girls Coll., Warwick, Queensland; Lecturer, Monash Univ., 1960-63; Senior Lecturer, Australian Nat. Univ., 1964-72. Member, Australian Soc. of Authors. Pubs.: Kaleidoscope, 194: The Dolphin, 1967; Ulysses Bound, 1973. Contrib. to: Meanjin Qtly.; Quadrant; Melbourne Age; Sydney Morning Herald; The Bulletin; Spirit; Canberra Times; The Australian Transition; Australian Poetry (annual), etc. Address: Box 41, P.O. Hackett, A.C.T., Australia.

AUGUSTINE, Jane, b. 6 Apr. 1931. University Teacher. Education: A.B., Bryn Mawr Coll.; M.A., Wash. Univ.; doctoral study, Univ. of Colo. Married Anthony J. Morley, 3 sons, 1 daughter. Positions held: Grad. Asst., Wash. Univ., St. Louis, Mo.; Instr. in Engl.,

Webster Coll., Webster Groves, Mo.; Adjunct Lectr. in Speech, John Jay Coll., N.Y.C. Member, Poetry Soc. of Am. Contbr. to: A Gallery of Pictorial Poetry (anthol.), 1974; S.C. Review; Hanging Loose; 8 x 10 Art Portfolio; Greenfield Review; For Now; Third & Fourth Assembling. Visual poems exhibited in An International Cyclopedia of Plans & Occurrences at Va. Commonwealth Univ. Articles on three women poets in 1974 revision of Contemporary Poets. Short story in Aphra, 1973. Recip., 1st Prize, Browning Soc. of Calif., 1948. Address: Rt. 1, Box 57A, Westcliffe, CO 81252, U.S.A.

AUSALA, Margarita, b. 13 Jul. 1914. Writer and Journalist. Education: Philology & Art, Univ. of Riga, Latvia. Married, 2 d., 1 s. Positions held: Sec. for monthly mag. issued by the Ministry of Education and Culture, Latvia; Deputy Head, Information Dept., Latvian Council in Gt. Britain; Press Officer, Latvian Welfare Fund in Gt. Britain. Memberships: Exec. Member, Latvian Song Festivals in G.B. and Europe; Latvian Press Soc.; Ramave-Latvian Academicians; Internat. P.E.N. Club, Engl. Centre; Internat. P.E.N. Club, Latvian Centre (Perm. Internat. delegate); Internat. Fed. of Free Journalists; UPLI (Vice-Pres.); Internat. Poetry Soc. (Fellowship); Council for American-European Cooperation, Latvian Rep.; Hon. Life Mbr., Cosmosynthesis League; C.S.S.I. (Internat. Committee). Published works: Perlu zvejnieks (essays), 1943; Patiesibas vins (poems), 1965; several pamphlets. Contbr. to: Latvija (US and Canada, Asst. Editor); Laiks; Londonas Avize; Latvija; Cela Zimes; Jauna Gaita; Zintis; Laurel Leaves; etc. Awards: Gold Medal, UPLI, donated by Pres. of Philippines, Ferd. Marcos, for Jose Rizal's transl.; Gold Badge of Distinction, Fu Hsiang Kang Coll., Taiwan; Gold Laurel Wreath, UPLI; Internat. Acad. of Philippines, D.L.Litt., 1968; Univ. of Karachi, H.L.D., 1971; Advisor of the Second World Congress of Poets, in Taiwan, 1973. Address: 243 Rockingham Rd., Corby, Northamptonshire NN17 2AB, UK.

AUSTIN, Aurelia, b. 21 Jan. 1912. Business Woman. Education: Southern Bus. Univ., Atlanta, Ga.; Emory Univ., Atlanta; Art, Music, Poetry, pvte. classes. Positions held: Tchr., Music; Sec. to Exec. V.P., Ashcraft-Wilkinson Co., 1957-60; Sec. to Pres., Duval Sales Corp, 1960-65; Sec. to Chmn., ibid, 1965–. Memberships: Sec., Houston Br., Nat. League of Am. Pen Women; 1972-73; Ed., anthol. of poetry, ibid, 1974; V.P. & Past Trustee, Ga. Writers Assn. (Charter Mbr.), Atlanta; Past Pres., Atlanta Writers Club; Past V.P., Atlanta Br., Nat. League Am. Pen Women; Past Pres., The Manuscript Club, Atlanta. Published works: Bright Feathers (vol. of poetry), 1958; Leaves of Life (anthol. of poetry), 1964; Georgia Boys with Stonewall Jackson (histl. vol.), 1967; anthol. of poetry for Houston Br., Nat. League Am. Pen Women, in process of being edited & printed. Contbr. to: Poet; Georgia Mag.; Georgia Review; Seydell Quarterly; The Westminster Mag., etc. Recip. var. hons. & awards. Address: 526 Hardendorf Ave., N.E., Atlanta, GA 30307, U.S.A.

AUSTIN, Juanita Chandler, b. 12 Mar. 1915. Homemaker; Former Teacher. Education: B.S. Educ., West Tenn. State Tchrs. Coll., Memphis, Tenn. Married Robert L. Austin, 1 son. Positions held: Tchr., Memphis, 1938-42; Asst. Airway Traffic Controller, Memphis, 1942-44. Memberships: Sec., Penrock Writers' Grp., Waupun, Wis., 1970-72. Contbr. to: Waupun Leader News; Appleton Post Crescent; Appleton Post Crescent View; Together Mag.; Edge; Cyclo-flame; Friends Jrnl.; Boston Globe; Wis. Hist. in Poetry; Ripon C'wealth Press; The Republican; Farm Wife News; Quidnunc. Address: 122 South West St., Brandon, WI 53919, U.S.A.

AUSTIN, Maxine Sanford, b. 24 Oct. 1910. Education: Randolph-Macon Woman's Coll., Lynchburg, Va.; transferred to Univ. of Oklahoma, A.B., 1931; Social Education courses Phillips Univ., Enid, Oklahoma, Summer 1931; Grad. courses in creative writing, Oklahoma Univ., 1963-1973. Married, David Marsden

Austin; 2 children. Positions held: Organiser and Director children's choir, First Presbyterian Church, Chickasha, 1937-38; Director and actor, Enid Little Theatre, 1952-56; Teacher, Children's Drama Class, First Presbyterian Church; guest lecturer on poetry Enid HS Creative Writing Classes, 1972, 1973. Memberships: Poetry Soc. of Oklahoma; Oklahoma Writers Fed.; Enid Writers Club (Pres., 1972-73); Staff of The Cherokee Strip Journal, 1971-73. Published works: This Land is Our Land (co-author, pageant play, produced 1968); The Spring of the Spirit (poems), 1972. Contbr. to: Enid Daily Eagle; The Daily Oklahoman; Manila Bulletin, Philippines. Awards: 1st Prize, Enid Writers Club Poetry contest, 1973; Pegasus Award (best book of poetry published in 1972) by Oklahoma Writers Fed. Address: 1505 Osage Dr., Enid, OK 73701, USA.

AVALLE-ARCE (Marques de la Lealtad), Juan Bautista, b. 13 May 1927. University Professor. Education: A.B., Harvard Univ., U.S.A., 1951; M.A., ibid, 1952; Ph.D., 1955. Positions held: Tchng. Fellow, Harvard Univ.; Asst. & Assoc. Prof., Romance Langs., Ohio State Univ.; Prof. & Sophia Smith Prof., Hispanic Studies, Smith Coll.; William Rand Kenan Jr. Prof., Romance Langs., Univ. of N.C., Chapel Hill. Memberships incl: MLA; Renaissance Soc. of Am.; Mediaeval Acad. of Am.; Modern Humanities Rsch. Assn.; Centro de Estudios Jacobeos. Published works: El Inca Garcilaso en sus Comentarios, 1963, 2nd ed., 1970; Cervantes: Three Exemplary Novels, 1964; Bernal Francés y su romance, 1966; El Persiles de Cervantes, 1969; Los Entremeses de Cervantes, 1970; Don Juan Valera: Morsamor, 1970; El cronista Pedro de Escavias. Una vida del siglo XV, 1972; Suma cervantina, 1973; Temas medievales hispánicos, 1973; El Peregrino de Lope de Vega, 1973; Narradores hispanoamericanos de hoy, 1973; Nuevos deslindes cervantinos, 1973. Contbr. to var. jrnls., reviews etc. Recip. num. honours & awards inclng: Kt. of Mark Twain, 1973. Address: Euskaletxea, 3904 Garrett Rd., Durham, NC 27707, U.S.A.

AVIDAN, David, b. 21 Feb. 1934. Poet; Playwright; Script-writer; Journalist; Filmmaker; Painter; Electronic Composer. Positions held: Hd. of var. expmtl. orgs. such as The Israeli Brainpower Ctr., Tel Aviv; Sr. Ed., var. weeklies & dailies, Israel. Bd. Mbr., Film & TV Dirs. Guild in Israel. Memberships: Poetry Soc. of Am.; Hebrew Assn. of Writers in Israel; Acum Ltd.; Assn. of Painters & Sculptors in Israel, etc. Published works incl: Megaovertone, selected poems transl. from Hebrew by author, 1952-66; No, poems, miniessays & comments accompanying author's plastic works; also nine vols. of poetry in Hebrew: B'razim Arufei S'fatayim, 1954; Be'ayot Ishiyot, 1957; Sikkum Beinayim, 1960; Shirei Lahats, 1962; Mashehu Bishvil Mishehu, selected poems, 1952-64, 1964; Shirim Bilti Efshariyim & Doah Ishi Al Massa LSD, 1968; Shirim Hitsoniyim, 1970; Shirim Shimushiyim, 1973; one vol. of plays, David Avidan Maggish Teatron Mufshat, 1965. Films: You Name It, 1968; Split, 1969; Sex, 1971. Two one-man art exhibs. & a number of collective exhibs., 1968-70. Rep. in var. anthols. Honours, awards incl: A. Abraham Woursell Prize, 1971; Israel's Prime Minister's Annual Prize, 1973. Address: 11 Shimshon St., Tel Aviv 64354, Israel.

AVI-SHAUL, Mordechay, b. 17 May 1898. Poet; Novelist; Translator of Classical Literature. Education: Tchrs. Trng. Coll.; Hebrew Univ., Inst. for Jewish Studies. Married, 3 children. Positions held: Associate w. Ketubim, lit. weekly, 1928-33; Fndng. Mbr. of LEPAC (Levant Publishing Co.) & Assoc. Ed. of KEDEM lit. bulletin, 1943-44; Ed., Thmurot (The Turning Tide) for problems of art & society, 1951; Jt-Ed., Shalom, periodical of Israeli Peace Movement. Memberships: P.E.N. Centre in Israel; Fndr. Mbr., Israel League for Human & Civil Rights, 1935; currently V. Chmn., ibid; World Peace Council. Published works: Ba'azikim, 1932; Juggernaut, 1945; Ballad on Peace, 1966; Israel Landscape, prose poems, 1956; The Necklace, 1928; Songs of Impatience, 1960, etc. Translations incl: J.W. Goethe:

Die Leiden des Jungen Werther; Heine: Poetry; Bertolt Brecht: Selected Poems; Mihály Babits: The Book of Yonah. Contbr. to var. mags. & lit. supplements of newspapers. Honours, awards incl: Tchernichovsky Prize for Classical Translation, 1957; ACUM Prize for Belles-lettres, 1966; Max Nordau Prize for Classical Translation, 1967; Memorial Medal of PEN Ctr. in Hungary, 1970. Address: 8 Kiryat Sefer St., Tel-Aviv 65277, Israel.

AVISON, Margaret Kirkland, b. 1918. Educ: Univ. of Toronto, Ont., Canada. Published works: Winter Sun, 1960; The Dumbfounding, 1966. Contbr. to: Canadian Poetry; Canadian Forum; (anthologies) Other Canadians: An Anthology of the New Poetry in Canada 1940-46, 1947; Canadian Poetry in English, 1954; Oxford Book of Canadian Verse, 1960; Poetry '62, 1961; Penguin Book of Canadian Verse, 1967. Honours, awards: Guggenheim Fellowship in Poetry, 1956-57; Governor-General's Award, 1960.

AWAD, Mohammad Hassan, b. 1906. Government Official. Education: Secondary Certificate. Positions held: Has held thirteen different posts in the Saudi Arabian Government, in the Municipalities, Law Cts., Advisory Councils, Development Bds., Printing and Publishing Councils; Has founded and is Director General of a business. Contbr. to all Saudi Arabian newspapers. Recip., BBC Poetry Prize. Address: Jidda, East (in front of Imad Exhibition), Saudi Arabia.

AWOONOR, Kofi, b. 13 Mar. 1935. Teacher. Education: Univ. of Ghana; Univ. of London, U.K. Positions held: Lectr., Univ. of Ghana; Dir., Ghana Film Corp.; Asst. Prof., State Univ. of New York, Stony Brook, USA. Published works: Rediscovery, 1964; Night of my Blood, 1970; Messages, 1970; This Earth, My Brother, 1971. Contbr. to the following anthols. & jrnls: Transition; Eastern Horizon; Modern Poetry from Africa; Commonwealth Poets of Today; Younger Poets of the Commonwealth; African Writing Today; A Book of African Verse. Translations of Poetry in Chinese, French, Russian & Swedish. Recip. of Gurrey Prize, 1959. Address: Dept. of English, State Univ. of New York, Stony Brook, NY 11790, USA.

AYRES, Donald S., b. 17 Sep. 1946. Member: Contemporary Poets of South Jersey. Pubs. Contemporary Poets of South Jersey, 1968; Down, 1969. Address: 421 E. Oak Street, Millville, New Jersey 08332, USA.

AZCONA-CRANWELL, Elena-Inés Gurpegui–, pen name **AZCONA-CRANWELL, Elizabeth,** b. 1937. Writer; Translator; Journalist; Style Corrector. Education: M.A., Schl. of Philos. & Letters, Univ. of Buenos Aires. Positions held: Prof. of Modern Lit., Univ. of Santa Maria del Buen Ayre; Writer of radio programmes about Contemporary Lit., LRA Radio Nacional & LS, 1 Radio Municipal; Corrector of Style for Am. Embassy. Member, Sociedad Argentina de Escritores. Published works: (books of poetry) Capitulo sin Presencia, 1955; La vida disgregada, 1966; Poemas, 1960; Los riesgos y el vacío, 1960; De los opuestos, 1966; Imposbilidad del lenguaje, 1972; (fiction) La vuelta de los equinoccios (has won two awards). Contbr. to var. jrnls., mags., etc. Honours, awards: Consejo del Escritor prize; 1st Prize, Fondo Nacional de las artes & Prize Municipal, 1966; Fellowship, Univ. of Iowa, sponsored by State Dept. Address: Marcelo T. de Alvear 1277, Piso 11 Dto 105, Buenos Aires, Argentina.

B

BABALOLA, Adeboye Solomon Oladele, pen name **LOWLY, Sable,** b. 17 Dec. 1926. University Teacher and Researcher. Education: Igbobi Coll., Lagos, 1938-43; Achimota Coll., Ghana, 1944-46; Queen's Coll., Cambridge, UK, 1948-51; School of Oriental and African Studies, Univ. of London, UK, 1961-63; M.A. (Cantab.), Ph.D. (London). Positions held: Asst.

Master, Igbobi Coll., Lagos, 1946-48, 1952-57; Principal, Igbobi Coll., Lagos, 1958-61; Lecturer in Yoruba, Univ. of Ife, 1962-64; Snr. Lecturer in African Studies, Univ. of Lagos, 1964-68, and Prof. of African Languages and Literatures, since 1969. Memberships: Yoruba Poetry Soc., Lagos (Pres.). Published works: Olokun: 1-10, 1957-73; Ewi Iwoyi, 1969; An Anthol. of West African Verse, 1958. Contbr. to: Poet; West African Mag.; African Affairs. Recip. 1st Prize in Yoruba Poetry, Lagos Festival of Arts, 1954. Address: Dept. of African Languages & Literatures, Univ. of Lagos, Lagos, Nigeria.

BABCOCK, Alberta, pen name **RAAMAH, Ingra,** b. 2 May 1910. Artist & Writer. Education: Univ. of Mich.; Ph.D., Int. Univ., Quebec, Canada. Positions held: Art Dir., Art Agency in Detroit; Freelance Artist in Chicago; Disney Artist; M.G.M. Artist; Warner Bros. Tchr. & Artist; Prof. of Art, Citrus Coll.; Owner of Glendora Art Gall. & Schl. Designed & painted 100 murals. Num. one-man shows. Memberships: Los Angeles Pen Womens Club; Fndr. & Life Mbr. of Desert Art Ctr.; Mid Valley Art League; Pre., Allied Arts Coun., 6 yrs.; currently Chmn. of the Bd., ibid. Published works: The Enchanted Carousel, 1969. Contbr. to: Detroit Free Press; Cyclo-Flame; Avalon Anthols.; Glendora Press; New Church Messenger; Cyclotron; Poet, India; Radio broadcasts. Honours, awards: Placed 3rd, Int. Book Ms. Award, 'Echoes from Eden', 1963; 1st prize, Hon. Mention, Cyclo-Flame; num. Gold Cups, Ribbons, etc. Address: 1500 Compromise Line Rd., Glendora, CA, U.S.A.

BABER, Mae Tjepkema, b. 28 Sept. 1910. Housewife; Poet; Columnist; Freelance Writer. Married Alfred E. Baber. Memberships: Penrock Writer's Club; Wisc. Fellowship of Poets; Nat. Fellowship of State Poetry Socs.; Hon. Rep. in U.S.A., Centro Studi e Scambi Int.; Am. Fellowship of Poets; World Poetry Soc.; active in prayer & church grps. Published works: Country Echoes from Edgewood Acres, 1961. Rep. in the following anthols: The Mind Create, 1961; Hearts Secrets, 1962; Treasures of Parnassus, 1962; Sing Loud for Loveliness, 1962; Fragments of Faith, 1963; Melody of the Muse, 1964; Flame Annual, 1965; American Poets, 1966, '68; Golden Harvest, 1967, '68; Poets, 1968; Badge of Promise, 1968; Poems Out of Wisconsin III, 1967; Okla. Poetry, 1968; Bouquet of Poems, 1968; Grandma's Treasures, 1968; Wis. History in Poetry, 1969, '70; Yearbook of Modern Poetry, 1971; Outstanding Contemporary Poetry, 1972. Contb. to many jrnls., newspapers, etc. inclng. Poet, India. Recip. var. awards inclng.: 1st pl., Wis. Fellowship of Poets Trav. Trophy Award, 1969 & 3rd pl., 1972. Address: R.R. 2, Brandon, WI 53919, U.S.A.

BACHRACH, Yvonne Iny, pen name **INY, Yvonne,** b. 11 Jan. 1927. Writer; Interpreter; Translator. Education: B.S., Pol. Sci., Georgetown Univ., Wash. D.C.; Cambridge Schl. of T.V., N.Y. Married, 2 sons. Positions held: part time work reporting and translating for a newspaper; Document Translator for Dept. of Agriculture, Wash. D.C. Memberships: N.Y. Poetry Forum; U.N. Assn.; Alliance Française de New York. Published works: Nature & Sentiments; Poems of a Quivering Heart; The Child is the Father of the Man; (TV Plays) Signorella; The San Francisco Conference. Address: 1036 Park Ave., N.Y., NY 10028, U.S.A.

BACKSTROM, Lars David, b. 18 Peb. 1925. Writer. Education: studied Scand. langs., English, Comp. Lit., Univ. of Uppsala; Fil.lic., comp. lit., Uppsala. Positions held: Ed., Ord & Bild, 1962-70; Vis. Lectr., Univ. of Wis., Madison, 1968; Ed., Författarförlagets Tidskrift, 1970-73. Memberships: Mbr., Writers' Cooperative House, 1970–; active in Författarcentrum (Writers' Ctr.) & Swedish Union of Writers. Published works: Sammanfattning (Summary), 1952; K.D. Logrens dikter (K.D. Logren's Poems), 1955; Världen omkring oss (The World Around Us), 1962; Oppen stad (Open City), 1967. Selections: Sammanfattning. Dikter, 1946-54, 1963; Den som flyr det privata kan inte forsta det allmänna. Dikter, 1957-67, 1971. Translations: Det trekantiga päronet (The Triangular Pear, poems by Chairil Anwar, Indonesia, Ted Hughes, G.B., Andrei Voznesensky, USSR). Criticism (mainly of poetry): Under välfärdens yta (Under the Surface of Welfare), 1959; Erik Lindegren (monograph of the Swedish poet), 1962; Klippbok (Cuttings), 1965; Litteraturpolitik (Literary Politics), 1970; Minnen fran den nya klassen (Memoirs from the New Class), autobiog., 1972. Contbr. to num. newspapers, reviews, etc. Address: Osterplan 15B, S–753 31 Uppsala, Sweden.

BADMAN, May, pen name IVIMY, May. Poet & Poetry Organiser. Married R.F. Badman, 2 children. Memberships: Mbr. of Exec., St. Albans Arts Assn. 1966– & of The Poetry Soc., The Nat. Poetry Ctr., 1965-72; Hon. Treas., Poetry Soc., 1968-72; The English Assn.; Critical Quarterly Soc.; Fndr., Org., Treas. & Sec., Ver Poets. Published works: Night is Another World, 1964; Midway This Path, 1966. Contbr. to: Without Adam, anthol., 1967; 'Poemcards', 1973; 'Poemsounds', 1973; 'Thoughtshapes'; Poetry Review; Time & Tide; Tribune; Workshop Poetry. Honours, awards: Prize Chapbook of Poems, Manifold, 1966. Address: 61 & 63 Chiswell Green Ln., St. Albans, Herts., U.K.

BADTKE, Frances, pen names GRAY, Rosemary & BRADFORD, Jan, b. 11 July 1919. Writer. Education: Grad., Prospect Hall. Secretarial Schl.; Univ. of Wis.; var. Univ. Jrnlsm. postal courses. Published works: Former Ed., im-PRESS-ions & ex-PRESS-ions, publ. of Wis. Press women; Former Women's Ed., Door County Advocate, semi-weekly paper; Ed., The Peninsula, publ. of Door County Histl. Soc., issued each yr. Memberships: Wis. Fellowship of Poets; State Sec., 2 rs. & Ed. of monthly news bulletin, Wis. Press Women; Nat. Fed. of Press Women; Wis. Regional Writers; Door Co. Writers. Publications: Packer Wives Cookbook; Eagle Lighthouse. Contbr. to: Door Co. Advocate; Shore Anthol., 1971; Wis. Hist. in Poetry, Book 3. Address: Rte. 1, Forestville, WI 54213, U.S.A.

BAGLIORE, Virginia, b. 14 Mar. 1931. Housewife; Poet. Education: N.Y. Univ., 1952-53; studied poetry w. Kimon Friar; poetry workshops w. Ann Di Bella. Married James Bagliore, 2 daughters. Positions held: Comptometer Operator, N.Y. Life Insurance Co., 1949-52; N.Y. Model for Bonwit Teller, Saks Fifth Avenue, B. Altman Bergdon & Goodman, 1952-56. Memberships: Corres. Sec., Nat. League of Am. Pen Women; Avalon Mbrship, World Poet's Resource Ctr. Inc.; N.Y. Poetry Forum. Contbr. to: Southwest-Times Record; Images; Poet; Bitterroot; Poetry Prevue; Cyclo-flame; Shore Review; Legend; Merlin's Magic; The Symbolist. Honours, awards: The Louise Bogan Meml. Award, for 'The Dream that Marries Every Day', 1972 & Hon. Mention for 'Eulogy on a Statue of an Indian Brave, 1973. Address: 2048 E. 56 St., Brooklyn, NY 11234, USA.

BAHLING, Naida Esther, b. 12 Sept. 1912. Home Maker; Artist. Education: Calif. Coll. of Arts & Crafts. Positions held: Dental Asst. & X-ray Techn.; Dental Surgeon's Nurse; Private Art Tchr.; Artist & Homemaker. Memberships: IPA; UPA; Rep. of C.S.S.I. & Accademia Int. 'Leonardo da Vinci'; Int. Poetry Soc.; Calif. Fed. of Chaparral Poets; Pres., Sec. & Treas., Camellia Chapt., ibid; Int. Quill & Scroll; Am. Poets Fellowship Soc. Published works: (books of poetry) Just for You; Rambling Thoughts, both 1935; Voice from the Heart, 1971; Thought Parades, 1972; Fragmented Seasons, Haiku-1973 & Poetry Potpourri, 1973 (both illustrated by author). Contbr. to: Japan Forum; Calif. Fed. of Chaparral Newsletter; Oakland Tribune; Calif. Sunshine; Swordsman Review; Am. Bard; Prairie Poet; United Poets; Am. Poet; The Yearbook of Modern Poetry, 1939; CSSI Anthols., 1971 & 72, & var. other mags. & anthols. in U.S.A. & Italy. Honours, awards: Haiku Award (First), Camellia Poets, 1971; First & Second pl., Dec. Contest, ibid, 1971; Third pl., Dec. Contest, 1972; Gold Medal (La Scala Gall.) for 'Voice From The Heart'. Address: 871 48th St., Sacramento, CA 95819, U.S.A.

BAIGENT, Beryl, pen name, "SNOWDON", b. 16 Dec. 1937. Housewife. Education: Grove Park Girls GS, Wrexham, N. Wales, UK; Secretarial Course , Leicester, UK; Dept. of Education Leadership Course, held at Geneva Park, Orillia, Ontario, Canada. Personal details: born in village of Llay, Denbighshire, N. Wales. Married Alan Baigent, 1963, in Leicester, UK; 3 d. (Amanda, Nicola, Krista). Positions held: Comptometer Operator, Llay, N. Wales, also Leicester; Sec., Leicester; Reporter, Ingersoll Times, Ontario, Canada; Instr. of a Rhythmic Exercise & Yoga Course for women in night school. Memberships: World Poetry Soc. Intercontinental; United Amateur Press Assoc.; Kentucky State Poetry Soc. (former member). Published work: The Quiet Village, 1972. Contbr. to: Townswoman; This England; Friendly Way; Bluenose Rambler; Alberta Year Book (1970, '72, '73); Poetry Preview; Driftwood East; Echoes of Love (1971 Anthol.); These are my Jewels (1972 Anthol.); Poetry of Our Times (1971 Anthol.); Poet W.P.S.I.; Ingersoll Times; Dutton Advance; Lambeth News Star; Premier Poets (1973 Anthol.). Awards: Best poem of the month, United Amateur Press Assoc., May, 1973; Cert. from Personal Poetry Broadcasts, Winchester, Va.; Red Rose Award from (group) Add Enchantment, for a sonnet; Poet of the month, May, 1972, Friendly Way Mag., Minnesota. Address: 137 Byron Avenue, Thamesford, Ontario NOM 2MO, Canada.

BAIL, Grace Shattuck, b. 17 Jan. 1898, Cherry Creek, NY. Music Teacher; Poetry Editor. Education: Darlington Sem.; Dana Schl. of Music, Univ. of Youngstown, 1919. Positions held: Pvte. Tchr., Piano, Violin, Conneaut, Ohio, 1920-24, San Bernardino, 1930-44, Costa Mesa, Newport Beach area, 1944-49, Anaheim, Calif., 1950-60, Beaumont, 1954–; Tchr., Violin, Brethren Schl., 1967–; Poetry Ed., own column, Canzoni, in Banning Record & Beaumont Gazette. Memberships: Calif. Fed. Chaparral Poets; Nat. Music Chmn. & Dir., Composers, Authors, Artists of Am.; Nat. League Am. Pen Women; Mich. Poetry Soc.; Am. Poetry League; World Poetry Day. Published works: Arethusa, 1945; Singing Heart, 1948; Daily Bread, 1952; Phantasy, 1954: Whispering Leaves, 1957; For the Dreamer, 1965; Heartstrings, 1968; Golden Days, 1970. Contbr. to: The Oregonian; The American Bard; Denver Post; The Archer; The Swordsman Review; Listen Mag.; Arizona Highways; Hartford Courant; Los Angeles Examiner; San Francisco Examiner; Peninsula Poets. Honours & Awards: Silver Medal Edwin Markam Award, 1961; Bronze Medal & 4 hon. certs., Centro Studi E Scambi; Gold Medal, Int. Poets' Shrine, 1969. Address: 873½ Beaumont Ave., Beaumont, Calif. 92223, USA.

BAILEY, Alfred Goldsworthy, b. 18 Mar. 1905. University Professor & Vice President. Education: B.A., Univ. of New Brunswick; M.A. & Ph.D., Univ. of Toronto; Post doctoral overseas scholarship to London Schl. of Econs. & Pol. Sci., from Royal Soc. of Canada. Positions held: City Ed., Fredericton Daily Mail, 1927; Staff Writer, Toronto Mail & Empire, 1930; Asst. Dir., N.B. Mus., 1935-38; Prof. & Hd., Dept. of Hist., Univ. of N.B., 1938-69; Dean of Arts, ibid, 1946-64; Hon. Libn., 1946-61; V.P. (Academic), 1965-70; Innis Vis. Prof., Univ. of Toronto, 1955-56. Memberships: League of Canadian Poets; Fndr. & Mbr. of Bliss Carman Soc.; Publsr. & Co. Fndr., The Fiddlehead. Published works: (poetry) Songs of the Saguency, 1927; Tao: A Ryerson Poetry Chap book, 1930; Border River, 1952; Thanks for a Drowned Island, etc. Contbr. to: Fiddlehead; Dalhousie Review; Poetry Commonwealth; Canadian Forum; Canadian Poetry Mag.; Queens Qtly.; Northern Review, etc. Address: Dept. of Hist., Univ. of New Brunswick, Fredericton, N.B., Canada.

BAIN, Edna Margaret, b. 16 Dec. 1913. Cook; Housekeeper. Divorced, 2 daughters. Memberships: Int. Clover Poetry Assn.; Laurel Publishers Int. Poetry Symposium. Contbr. to: The Children's Friend; Encore Mag., Albuquerque; Hyacinths & Biscuits; Major Poets; Cyclofame; Adult Bible Teacher; Kenneth Kwint Anthol.; Jean's Jrnl.; El Viento Valley Publs.;

The Creative Urge; The Little Flower Mag.; Golden Anthol. of Poetry; All Time Favorite Poetry; Kansas Jrnl., etc. Honours, awards: Hon. Award, World of Writers Club, 1968; 4th Prize, 1969 & 3rd Prize, 1971, Clover Int. Poetry Award; Cert. of Merit, Personal Poetry, 1969 & J. Mark Press, 1970 & '69; Hon. Award, Laurel Publsrs., 1970. Address: 954 South Ardmore, Apt. 211, Los Angeles, CA 90005, U.S.A.

BAINES, Keith, b. 20 Jan. 1923. Poet. Published works: Longmous Green, 1964; 'Goldensheep'. Contbr. to var. periodicals. Poems recorded for British Inst. (w. Harvard Univ.) in Contemporary British Poets Series. Address: 7 Willow Rd., London NW3, U.K.

BAIRD, Alexander, b. 1925. Lecturer. Educ: Liverpool Inst. H.S., U.K.; Emmanuel Coll., Cambridge, 1943. Positions held: Served in WWII, Italy, Egypt, Iraq; Lectr., Engl. Lit., Univ. of Hiroshima, Japan, 1959-62; Worked with British Coun. until 1965. Published works: Poems, 1963; (novels) The Micky Hunters, 1957; The Unique Sensation, 1959. Contbr. to: London Magazine; Listener; Texas Quarterly; New Poems (anthology), 1960 & '62. Recip., Felicia Hemans Prize for Lyric Verse, 1954.

BAKER, Howard, b. 5 Apr. 1905. Writer; Orange and Olive Farmer, and Farm Cooperative Officer. Education: Whittier Coll., Calif., B.A., 1927; Stanford Univ., Calif., M.A., 1929; The Sorbonne, Paris, 1929-31; Univ. of Calif., Berkeley, Ph.D., 1937. Married, Dorothy (Dodds) Baker, novelist, 1930; children: Ellen Branson Baker, Joan Baker Fry. Dorothy Baker, deceased, 1968. Remarried to Virginia De Camp Beattie, 1969. Positions held: Briggs-Copeland Instr., Harvard Univ., Cambridge, Mass., 1937-43; Visiting Prof., Univ. of Calif., Berkeley, 1958-59; Visiting Prof., Univ. of Calif., Davis, 1963-67; Pres., Grand View Heights Citrus Assoc., 1960–; Pres., Tulare Kern Citrus Exchange, 1968–. Memberships: Ford Madox Ford's Sonnet Soirees, Paris, 1929-30; English Club, Berkeley, Calif., 1931-37; Phi Beta Kappa, 1937–: The Barn Theater, Porterville, Calif., 1948– (Founding Member and occasional Pres.); Archaeological Inst. of America; Soc. for the Promotion of Hellenic Studies; American Farm Bureau. Published works: A Letter from the Country & Other Poems, 1941; Ode to the Sea and Other Poems, 1966; Orange Valley (novel), 1931; Trio (play, with Dorothy Baker, Belasco Theater, NY, 1944; Los Angeles and San Francisco, 1945); The Ninth Day (play, with Dorothy Baker, Columbia TV, 1957; The Gate Theatre, Dublin, 1962, etc.); Induction to Tragedy (Lit. Criticism), 1939. Contbr. to: The Gyroscope; Southern Review; Poetry; NM Qtly.; Understanding Poetry, 1960; Twelve Poets of the Pacific, 1937; The Oxford Book of American Verse, 1950; A Western Sampler, 1963; Sewanee Review, etc. Awards: Prize poem, The Southern Review, 1935; Award, NM Qtly. Review, 1966; Phelan Fellowship, Univ. of Calif., 1933-35; Guggenheim Fellowship, 1944. Address: Rte. 1, Box 11, Terra Bella, CA 93270, USA.

BAKER, Sheridan, b. 10 July 1918. Professor of English; Editor. Education: A.B., Univ. of Calif., Berkeley, 1939; M.A., ibid, 1946; Ph.D., 1950. Personal details: m. 1, Helen Barker, 1946, 1 d., divorced 1954; m. 2, Sally Baubie Sandwick, 1955, 1 stepdaughter, 1 s. Positions held: Seaman-Lt. Cmdr., USN (destroyers), 1940-46; Tchng. Asst., Engl., Univ. of Calif., 1946-49; Lectr., ibid, 1949-50; Instr., Univ. of Mich., 1950-57; Asst. Prof., ibid, 1957-61; Assoc. Prof., 1961-64; Prof., 1964–; Ed., Michigan Quarterly Review, 1964-71. Memberships: Pres., Mich. Acad. Sci., Arts & Letters, 1963-64; Ed., Papers, 1954-61; MLA; Coll. Engl. Assn. Contbr. to: Beloit Poetry Journal; New Yorker; Michigan Quarterly Review; Epoch; Univ. of Kansas City Review; Edge; Northwest Review; Inscape; Arbor; Voices; New York Herald Tribune (European Edit.); Ernest Hemingway, An Introduction and Interpretation, 1967. Awards: named among the Top Fifty Living American Poets, Epoch, 1966. Address: 2688 Provincial Dr., Ann Arbor, Michigan 48104, USA.

BALASUBRAHMANYAM, Vaidyanathan, b. 6 Apr. 1926. Indian Civil Servant. Education: M.A., Engl., Madras Presidency Coll., India, 1946. Married, 3 s., 1 d. Positions held: Tchr., Engl. Lit., Madras Univ., 1947-49; w. Indian Admin. Serv., Bihar State, 1950-58; New Delhi, 1959-64; Sec. to Bihar Govt.; currently Commnr. for Dep. Enquiries, Patna. Author of Verses, 1971. Address: 44 Cutcherry Rd., Mylapore, Madras 4, India.

BALDWIN, Bertha Marjorie, pen name, **BALDWIN, Marjorie.** Educational & Clinical Psychologist. Education: B.A. Hons., Philos., Univ. Coll., London, 1938; Exchange Fellowship in Philos., Univ. of Louvain, Belgium, 1939-40; Child Guidance Training, Guy's Hosp., London, UK; Fellow of Trinity Coll. of Music (Speech & Drama), 1961. Positions held: Educ. Psychol., Hampshire Child Guidance Service, 1945; Child Psychotherapist, City of Nottingham CGC, 1950-60; Educ. Psychol., Royal Philanthropic Soc.'s Schl. for Boys, Redhill, Surrey, 1960-65; Sr. Psychol., ibid, 1965–. Memberships: Poetry Bd., Manifold, 1965–; Poetry Soc., UK; Poetry Soc. of Am., 1967; Internat. Poetry Soc. (Founder Fellow, 1973–); Keats-Shelley Mem. Assn. Published works: To Early White Narcissi, 1953; Poems & Translations, 1961; The Slain Unicorn & Other Poems, 1965. Contbr. to the following anthols., jrnls., etc: Poetry of Today, 1945; Stroud Festival Anthol., 1967; Laudamus Te, 1967; Without Adam, 1968; Look Through a Diamond, 1970; Doves For The Seventies, 1969; The Londoner, 1971; Outposts; Poetry Review; Manifold; Ukrainian Review; Sussex Life; Nature; Orbis Anthol.; Speech; N. Am. Mentor; Bitterroot; Daily Independent, Ashland, KY., USA; Advance Monticellonian, Ark.; Internat. Who's Who in Poetry Anthol., 1973; Prayers for Today, 1973; The House That Jack Built (anthol.) 1973; LAMDA Anthol. of Verse & Prose, Vol. VIII, 1973. Honours: 1st Prize, Ivan Franko Int. Competition, Assoc. of Ukrainians in GB, 1966. Address: Old School Cottage, Colgate, Horsham, Sussex RH12 4SY, UK.

BALDWIN, Mary, b. 10 June 1908. Housewife. Married, 2 daughters. Memberships: Fndr. Fellow, Int. Poetry Soc.; World Poetry Soc. Intercontinental; Leicester Writers' Club; Melton Mowbray Writers' Club. Published works: The Second Spark, 1966; Lark Rise, 1971; Sparks Flying Upward, 1974; Ed., Elizabeth Goudge anthol. 'The Ten Gifts', 1969. Contbr. to: The Field; The Orcadian; This England; Church News; Orbis (IPS); Methodist Mag.; Poet (WPSI); United Writers' Poetry Anthol.; New Poems & Poems in Honour; World Poetry Soc. Anthol.; Int. Poetry Soc. Anthol. A number of poems have been read on Radio Leicester. Recip., Prize in Lit. Comp. of the United Writers, 1972. Address: Lark Rise, Debdale Hill, Old Dalby, Melton Mowbray, Leics., U.K.

BALDWIN, Mary Newton, b. 26 June 1903. Housewife. Education: Ph.B., Univ. of Vt., 1924; courses at St. Michael's Coll., Winooski, Vt., Universidad Internacional, Santander, Spain, etc. Married, James Gordon Baldwin. Memberships: Poetry Soc. of Am.; Nat. League of Am. Penwomen; Poetry Soc. of Vt.; Fndr. & Past Pres., ibid, & a former Ed. of their poetry mag., The Mountain Troubadour. Published works: Here in These Hills, 1946, 2nd printing, 1947. Contbr. to: Sat. Evening Post; Christian Sci. Monitor; N.Y. Times; N.Y. Herald Tribune; The Vermonter, etc. & sev. anthols. Recip., Durham Chapbook Award, 1946 & var. poetry prizes, 1940-69. Address: 59 Fairway Dr., Ormond Beach, FL 32074, U.S.A.

BALESTRIERI, Peter Dominic, b. 9 June 1953. Poet; Clown. Education: Pius XI H.S., 1971; student of oriental philos. & religion, principally Taoism & Zen. Positions held: Ed., Menagerie Mag.; Poet, Wis. Arts Council's 'Poetry in the Schools' prog. Memberships: Wis. Poetry Alliance. Published works: jub jub, 1970; jub jub II, 1970; Sol-leks, 1971; All of a sudden .. everything! 1971. Contbr. to: The Open Door; Cheap & Fast; Menagerie. Recip. var. grants. Address: Oscar Bueno, 3520 N. 84th St., Milwaukee, WI 53222, U.S.A.

BALKENBUSH   Michael   Leo,   pen   name,

BALKENBUSH, Michael, b. 28 Feb. 1908, Linn, Mo. Poetry Therapist. Education: High School. Positions held: Secretarial work: entered Franciscan Order, 1942, withdrew 1971. Member of Catholic Poetry Soc. of Am. while in existence. Publs: Lines of a Senior Citizen & an Epic of the Soul; Empire of Dragons. Address: Old Mission, Santa Barbara, Calif. 93105, USA.

BALL, David, b. 27 Feb. 1937. Poet and Teacher. Education: Docteur en Littérature Générale et Comparée, Université de Paris (Sorbonne); Licence ès Lettres, Sorbonne; B.A., Brandeis Univ.; Fulbright Scholar in Strasbourg and Paris, 1959-60; French Government Fellowship, Paris, 1967-69; French Government Fellowship, Paris, 1967-60. Married, 1 s. Positions held: Lecturer in French Language and Literature, Smith Coll., 1969-71, and Asst. Prof., 1971-. Published works: We Just Wanted To Tell You, 1963; Two Poems, 1964; New Topoi, 1972. Contbr. to: The Atlantic Monthly; Locus Solus; The World; Jazz Poems; Telephone; Toothpaste; Ploughshares; Juillard; Gum; Blue Pig; Canards du Siècle Présent; Shelter; Doones; Poet & Critic; Rhinozeros; Poor. Old. Tired. Horse; Collection 7 Supplement; The; Imago; The Lit. Supplement; The Wivenhoe Park Review; Outburst; Damascus Road. Award: Eugene M. Warren Prize at Brandeis Univ., 1957 and 1958. Address: 108 South St., A–10, Northampton, MA 01060, USA.

BALL, Nelson, b. 14 Jan. 1942. Library Assistant. Educ: Univ. of Waterloo, Ont., Canada. Married Barbara Caruso, 1965. Positions held: Forest Ranger, Dept. of Lands and Forests, White River, Ont., 1963; Lib. Asst., Univ. of Toronto Lib., 1967–. Published work: Room of Clocks, 1965; Beaufort's Scale, 1967; Sparrows, 1968; Force Movements, 1969. Contbr. to: Is; Hyphid; Canadian Forum; Ant's Forefoot; El Corno Emplumado; (anthologies) Thumbprints, 1969; A Canadian Folio, 1969. Address: Toronto, Ont., Canada.

BALLARD, Juliet Lyle Brooke (Mrs. Lyttleton W.), b. 6 Feb. 1913. Poet. Education: A.B., Randolph-Macon Woman's Coll., 1934; Cert. of Social Case Work, Richmond Prof. Inst., 1938. Assoc. Ed. A.R.E. Journal (Assoc. for Research and Enlightenment, Inc.) 1966-70; Assoc. Ed. A.R.E. Children's Mag., 1970. Editor, Treasure Trove (A.R.E. children's qtly.) 1971-73. Memberships: C.A.A.A.; Am. Poetry League. Published works: Under a Tropic Sun, 1945; Winter Has Come, 1945; The Ballad of the Widow's Flag (official poem of The Star-Spangled Flag House Assoc., Baltimore, Md.), 1956. Contbr. to Composers, Authors & Artists of America; Wings; Nature Mag.; Canadian Poetry; Poems for Our Time; Moccasin; Driftwind; The Raven; The Lantern; Blue Moon; Kaleidograph; l'Alouette; Silver Star; The Searchlight; With Rhyme and Reason; American Poet; Greetings; A.R.E. Journal; Coronet, etc. Honours: Participant in various radio progs., Lib exhibits of poems, 1955, 1956, 1958. Awards from poetry journals, and winner of lit. org. contests; 1st Prize, Saucier Lyric Award, Nat. Fed. of State Poetry Socs., 1965; included in Syracuse Univ. Lib MS Coll., 1964–. Address: 2217 Wake Forest St., Virginia Beach, VA 23451, USA.

BAN, Eva Maria, pen name **BAN, Eva,** b. 16 Mar. 1932, Ijui, Rio Grande do Sul, Brazil. Writer; Journalist; Poet. Education: Master's Degree, Tchng., Cruz Alta, Rio Grande do Sul, Brazil; Med., Grad. Univ. of Curitiba, 2 years; Law, Univ. of Porto Alegre, 3 years; Ph.D., Jrnlsm. (Philos., Grad. Schl., Univ. of Rio de Janeiro); Langs., Lausanne, Switzerland. Personal details: Father, Adalberto Bán, M.D. (Hungarian); m. to Danilo Martinovich, painter. Positions held: Writing as HS, student in 'O Comercio', Carazinho, Brazil; Reporter, 'Folha da Tarde', 'Correio do Porvo', Porto Alegre; Star Reporter, 'A Noite Ilustrada'; 'Diário da Noite'; 'O Cruzeiro'; 'Jornal do Comercio', etc. Rio de Janeiro. Memberships: Poetry Soc. of Am.; Acad. of Letters of Rio Grande do Sul; Brazilian Press Assn.; Brazilian Poetry Soc.; Overseas Press Club; Foreign Press Assn., NY, USA; Int. Soc. of Poets, Rio de Janeiro,

Brazil; Union of Free-lance Writers, ibid; Internat. Assoc. of Journalists. Published Works include: Oriental Poems, Pamphlet–'Poemas Orientais', 1948; Death and I, Pamphlet–'A Morte e Eu', 1952; Center of World, Pamphlet–'Centro do Mundo', 1957; Green Boy, Book–'Menino Verde', 1967; Tempo do Amanhã–'Tomorrow Time', 1971. Contbr. to the following newspapers & jrnls.: O Comercio; Imprensa Universitária de Curitiba; Jornal Universitário Rio Grandense; Carioca; Figurino; Revista Lady; Estado de São Paulo; A Cigarra; Letras e Arte; Diário da Noite; Folha da Tarde; Jornal do Comercio; Jornal do Brasil; O Cruzeiro, (Brazil); Chicago Tribune's Sunday Mag., (USA) & Népszabadság, (Hungary); Poet Lore. Honours, awards: Best Radio Prog., Poetry, Porto Alegre, 1949; Best Oriental Poems Judged by Readers, 1950; Best Reporting, 1953; Poetry Dir., Brazilian Press Assn., 1955-67; 5 awards for Short Stories: O Globo, 1958; Diário de Noticias, 1963; Revista Lady, 1961; Diário Serrano, 1947; Editor Savio Antunes, 1964; Guest of Honour, Poetry Readings, Dept. of Arts & Letters Conf., Univ. of Porto Alegre, 1965; Poetry Readings, Budapest, Hungary, 1964; Brazilian Embassy, Rome, Italy, 1964; 2 awards in painting: Silver Medal & Trip to Bahia, 1967; Best Poem, Green Boy, Brazil, 1966; 3 awards in Jrnlsm: Best Chronicle, Carioca, 1950; Best Police Reporting, Manchete, 1952; Best Foreign Report, O Jornal, 1964; York Internat. Poetry Contest, UK., 1972; Brazilian Delegate to 3rd Internat. Conf. of Journalists, Greece, 1973; Recip. (1973) of one of Poet Lore's Stephen Vincent Benet Narrative Poetry Awards. Address: The Mayflower, Suite 908, 15 Central Park W. at 61st St., New York, NY 10023, USA.

BANGS, Helen Hutton, b. 7 Feb. 1905, Phoenix, Ariz. Housewife. Education: Univ. of Calif. at LA, 3 yrs. Personal details: m. to Scholer Bangs, poet & ed., 1928, 3 s. Memberships: Pres., Calif. Fed. of Chaparral Poets, 1958-61; Pres., Aeolian Chapt., ibid, 1955-56; Tumbleweed Chapt., 1962; Sec., Treas., Robert W. Service Chapt.; Poets Haven; Ina Coolbrith Circle; World Poetry Day; Acad. of Am. Poets; Am. Poetry League; Organized and directed Children's Poetry Fair (CFCP), 1960-73. Contbr. to: The American Bard; The Archer; Cats Magazine; Los Angeles Daily News; Quaderini di Poesia; From Sea to Sea in Song; Ina Coolbrith Anthology; Aeolian Song; Ghosts of the Stagecoach Station; American Poets Best Vol..I;.Haiku.& Vol. 1; Haiku & Tanka, Vol. 1 & 2; The Wagging Tail, 1969. Honours & Awards: 1st Place, Haiku, Calif. Fed. Chaparral Poets Annual Contest, 1957; 2nd Place, Dramatic Monologue, ibid, 1964; Gold Medal, Int. Poets Shrine, 1971. Address: 362 E. Michelle St., W. Covina, Calif. 91790, USA.

BANKS, David Francis, b. 10 Oct. 1943. Student. Education: Philos. & Theol., Ushaw Coll. (a Roman Catholic Sem.), 1957-67; Philos., Churchill Coll., Cambridge Univ., 1972–. Married Christiane, 1973. Positions held: worked in Approved Schl. for 6 months, 1967; Civil Servant, 5 yrs.; Painter. Currently J.C.R. Pres., Churchill Coll., Cambridge. Contbr. to: Ludd's Mill; Platform; Ostrich; Wayfarers; Next Wave Poets; Fresca; Eureka (Sweden); A Xmas Anthol.; Continuum; Glass Onion; Out of Sight; Really; Words. Address: 28 Sunnyside Rd., London W.5, U.K.

BANTLEMAN, Lawrence, pen name **LINGAM,** b. 8 Aug. 1942. Positions held: Writer, The Century, New Delhi, India, 1963-67. Published works: Graffiti, 1962; Kanchenjunga, 1967. Contbr. to: (anthology) Young Commonwealth Poets '65, 1965. Address: Montreal, P.Q., Canada.

BANTOCK, Gavin Marcus August, b. 4 July 1939. English Lecturer. Education: M.A. Engl. & Dip. Ed., New Coll., Oxford Univ., UK, 1960-64. Positions held: Hd. of Engl. Depts., various schls., UK; Lectr., Reitaku Univ., Japan. Member of Soc. of Authors. Published works: Christ (poem in 26 parts), 1966; A New Thing Breathing, 1969. Contbr. to: Poetry Review, London; Tri-Quarterly, USA; Spectator. Awards: Richard Hillary Award, 1964; Alice Hunt-Bartlett Award, 1966; Eric

Gregory Award, 1969. Address: The Grey Cottage, 36 Bittell Road, Barnt Green, Nr. Birmingham, U.K.

BARADI, Mauro, pen name **UHURU,** b. 22 Aug. 1899. Lawyer. Education: Univ. of the Philippines HS, 1919; School of Economics & Government, Nat. Univ., Washington, DC, (A.B., 1931; M.A., 1933); Philippine Law School (LL.B., 1923); Nat. Univ. Law School, Washington, DC. (M.P.L., 1930; LL.M., 1930; S.J.D., 1932); special courses, Columbia Univ., New York, NY, and American Univ., Washington, DC. Married, Eden Guevara; 4 children (Perla; Mauro, Jr.; Jose; Patria). Positions held: Legal Counsel, Senate of the Philippines, 1952; Phil. Rep. and Chairman, UN Advisory Council for Italian Somaliland; Phil. Ambassador to Nigeria; Cameroon; Ghana; Liberia; Sierra Leone; Delegate, 1971 Constitutional Convention (Manila and Quezon City); Editor, The Cabletow (official organ of the Grand Lodge of Philippines, Manila (1945-55)); Columnist, Ilocos Times, and The Star Reporter, Manila. Published work: Life's Message to Youth, 1932; Poems, 1935-1972. Contbr. to: The Tribune; Philippines Herald; Manila Times; The Examiner (Quezon City), also articles, poems and other writings published in American and Hawaiian newspapers. Recip. 1st Prize, Declamation Contest, 1919 (Manila); 1st Prize, Poetry Contest (Arroyo Silver Cup), 1927 (Manila); Gold Medal, Public Speaking Contest, 1930 (Washington, DC); Plaque for distinguished service as Editor, The Cabletow, 1955 (Manila); Gold Medal Award, UPLI, 1967 (Manila). Address: Villa Eden, 338 Rodriguez Ave., Mangahan, Pasig, Rizal D-721, Philippines.

BARANYI, Ferenc, b. 24 Jan. 1937. Teacher, French & Italian Literature; Post. Education: Budapest Univ., Hungary, 1962; Poitiers Univ., France, 1967. Positions held: Egyetemi Lapok (mag.), 1962-68; Ifjusági Magazin (youth mag.), 1968-69; Magyar Ifjuság (youth mag.), 1969. Memberships: Hungarian Writers Assn.; Hungarian Pen Club. Publications: (essay) The 'Endecasillabo' of Dante, 1966; (poetry) Villamok balladajá (Ballad of Thunderbolts), 1962; Hazateres (Going Home), 1964; Az a mere⎰ + /˘¼§˘˘g (That is Courage), 1966; Tul az ejszakań (Over the Night), 1969; Változó szelek (Changing Winds), 1972; Fiancee supposed to be a Horse, 1972. The House is Bleeding (pending publ.) Contbr. to: Oj Irás, Hungary; Kortárs, Hungary; Europa Letteraria, Italy; La Fiera Lettereria, Italy; Action Poétique, France; De Tafel Rond, Netherlands; Republik, Yugoslavia; Inosztrannaja Literatura, USSR; Ogonjok, USSR. Address: Budapest, XIV. Báróczy u. 15/a l. 1, Hungary.

BARBOUR, Douglas Fleming, b. 21 Mar. 1940. Professor of English. Education: B.A., Acadia Univ., N.S., 1962; M.A., Dalhousie Univ., N.S., 1964; Ph.D. pending from Queen's Univ., Ont. Married. Positions held: Asst. Prof. of Engl., Univ. of Alta., 1969-. Chmn., League of Canadian Poets, 1972-74. Published works: Land Fall, 1971; A Poem as long as the Highway, 1971; White, 1972; Songbook, 1973; He. & She. &., 1974. Contbr. to: Canadian Forum; Quarry; Queen's Qtly.; Fiddlehead; Prism Int.; West Coast Review; Another Poetry Mag.; The Far Point; Copperfield; Antigonish Review; Grain; Oasis; Mainline; Impulse; Cloven Hoof; Ariel; Open Spaces; Waves; Truck; Tuatara; Ganglia; Black Moss; Galley Sail Review; Talon; CBC. Address: 10808 – 75th Ave., Edmonton, Alta., Canada T6E 1K2.

BARCOCK, George, b. 30 May 1918. Education: Scholarship in Engl., Ruskin Coll., Oxon.; Morley Coll.; Pianoforte, Metropolitan Acad. of Music; Hugh Myddelton Schl. of Langs.; French, City of London Coll.; Oxford Arts & Technol.; London Coll. of Printing (for Camera operating in Litho & Typographical Design); Southampton Arts & Crafts (Electronics in Printing); Southampton Univ. (Computer Ctr.); A.C.P. Positions held: Advtng. w. London Press Exchange; Asst. Prodn. Mgr., Laytons; Hd. Rdr. of Baytree Press & Cox & Sharlands, Soton; 2nd Violin, Cowley Community Orch.; currently Rdr. for The Guardian, London; has taught English to Italians. Memberships: The Calder Valley Poetry Soc., Yorks.; Fndr. Fellow &

on Editl. Bd., Int. Poetry Soc.; Past Mbr., Gaybirds Concert Party, Andover, Hants. Contbr. to: The Parnassian; Sussex Life; Orbis; Print in Britain; The Int. Printing Corp. House Jrnl.; The Andover Congl. Ch. Mag.; anthol. published by Robin Gregory of the Int. Poetry Soc. Poems broadcast on BBC Radio Brighton 'Wordsound'. Recip., The George Camp Meml. Prize in Class 1, 1973. Address: 33 Lansdowne Pl., Hove, Sussex BN3 1HF, U.K.

BARD, William E., b. 8 June 1892. Retired Minister; Poet. Education: B.A., Southern Meth. Univ., Dallas, Tex.; Postgrad. work, ibid. Positions held: Meth. Pastor, various parts of Tex.; Rating Specialist & Contact Supvsr., US Vet. Admin.; Poet Laureate of Tex., 1967-. Memberships: Councillor, VP, Poetry Soc. of Tex.; Pres., ibid., 1966-; Charter Mbr., Tex. Inst. of Letters, 1936-; Mbr., Advisory Board, Poet Lore; VP, US East, United Poets Laureate Int.; Vachel Lindsay Assn.; Nat. Fed. of State Poetry Socs.; Acad. of Am. Poets. Published works: Fountain Unsealed, 1933; A Little Flame Blown, 1934; Feather in the Sun, 1959; This Land This People, 1966; Burning Embers, 1971; As a Wild Bird Returning, 1973. Contbr. to num. anthols. since 1933, inclng. recently: Surf, Stars & Stone, 1961; Avalon Golden Book, 1961; Avalon Anthol. of Tex. Poets, 1963; Anthol. of Am. Poetry, No. VII, 1965; Poet's Parade, 1963; Nat. Fed. of State Poetry Socs. Anthol., 1967. Contbr. to num. lit. jrnls., inclng: Laurel Leaves; Poetry Review (London); Yearbook, Poetry Soc. of Tex. (various yrs.); The Midland; The Circle; The Forge; Kaleidograph; Troubadour; The Harp; Westward; West; The Torchbearer; Dallas News; Southwester; Denver Post; 9uicksilver; South & West; Voices; Southwest Review; The Lyric; Poet Lore; The Lantern; Encore; Creativity, etc. Honours: Tex. Centennial Award, Kaleidograph, 1936; Various awards, Poetry Soc. of Tex.; Greatness & World Leadership Award, UPLI, 1967; Bronze Medal of Achievement, ibid, 1968; Avalon Presidential Citation for Excellence in Poetry, 1969; Dr. of Humane Letters (h.c.), 1969. Address: 11132 Pinocchio Dr., Dallas, Tex. 75229, USA.

BARFIELD, Stephen Leonard, pen name **BARFIELD, Steve,** b. 23 Nov. 1946. Poet. Education: B.A., Univ. of Tampa; post grad. study, Univ. of Ga., 2 yrs. Positions held: Asst. Ed., Poetry Review, 1966-69; Rsch. Asst. to Coleman Barks working on 'Little Magazines' in America. Mbr., Immanentist Poetry Movement. Published works: Skullgrin, 1969; New Generation of Poets Anthol., 1971; Banjo's Carnival, 1973; The Immanentist Anthology, 1973; Mantras: An Anthology of Immanentist Poetry, 1973. Contbr. to: Intermision; Cardinal; Encore; Poetry Review; U.T. Review; Ghost Dance; Gnosis; Univ. of S. Fla. Review; Ann Arbor Review; Abraxas; Poet Lore. Address: 4408 Carlyle Rd., Tampa, FL 33615, U.S.A.

BARKAN, Stanley Howard, b. 20 Nov. 1936. Educator; Editor; Publisher. Education: B.Ed., Univ. of Miami, 1962; M.A., NY Univ., 1967; Ph.D. Cand., ibid., 1967-. Positions held: Tchr., creative writing, Engl., Engl. as a second language, mass media, & Swahili; Ed., El Verano, San Miguel Mex.; Dir., Engl. as a second lang., Greek Ctr., NYC, USA; Ed., Language News, 1969-73; Lectr., Engl. as a second lang., Swahili, LI Univ., 1970; Chairman, Cross-Cultural Communications Inst., LI Univ., 1971-72; Publisher, Cross-Cultural Communications, 1972-73; Assoc. Ed., Bitterroot, 1972-. Memberships: ASCAP; Publs. Comm., Am. Soc. Geolinguistics; Bd. of Dirs., ibid, 1970; Am. Dialect Soc.; Am. Name Soc.; Int. Linguistics Assoc.; Int. Soc. of Gen. Semantics; MLA; Nat. Council of Tchrs. of Engl.; NYC Assoc. for For. Lang. Tchrs.; NYS TESOLBEA; Kappa Delta Pi; Phi Delta Kappa; Shakespeare Assoc. of Am.; Esperanto League of N. America; Int. Platform Assoc.; NY Poetry Forum. Published works: The American Hototogisu: Original Haiku in English, 1969; incl. in Internat. Festival of Poetry, LIU, 1972 & Internat. Festival of Poetry & Art, Internat. Center, 1973; creator of 'apostrophe' verse form anthologized in Handbook on Haiku and Other Form Poems, 1970. Contbr. to:

Bardic Echoes; Bitterroot; Cultural Horizons; Educational Forum; Fireflower; Haiku Highlights; Haiku Spotlight; Haiku West; Highpoints; Human Voice Qtly.; Janus SCTH; Modern Haiku; Nat. Poetry Anthol.; Poet Lore; Washington Square Review; Washington Square Journal; The Writer; El Verano; El Vocero del Norte; Shantih. Honours: Internat. Who's Who in Poetry, 1970-71; 1972-73. Address: 239 Wynsum Ave., Merrick, NY 11566, USA.

BARKER, Eric, b. 9 July 1905. Self-employed. Published works: The Planetary Heart, 1942; Directions in the Sun, 1955; In Easy Dark, 1958; A Ring of Willows, 1961; Looking for Water, 1964. Contbr. to: Harper's Magazine; Harper's Bazaar; Saturday Review; Nation; New York Times; Atlantic; American Scholar; Yale Review; Poetry; Beloit Poetry Journal; (anthologies) Music Makers, 1945; Unseen Wings, 1949; A Garland for Dylan Thomas, 1963. Honours, awards: Borestone Mountain Poetry Awards, 1955 & '57; Shelley Memorial Award, 1962. Address: Big Sur, CA, U.S.A.

BARKER, George Granville, b. 26 Feb. 1913. Writer; Educator. Education: Marlborough Rd. Schl., Chelsea, London. Positions held: Prof. of Engl. Lit., Imperial Tohoku Univ., Japan, 1939-41; Arts Fellow, York Univ., 1966. Fellow, Soc. for Preservation of Ancient Monuments. Published works: Poems, 1933; Alanna Autumnal, 1933; Calamiterror, 1935; Janus, 1935; Lament & Triumph, 1940; News of the World, 1950; The True Confession of George Barker, 1950; Collected Poems, 1957; Two Plays, 1962; The View From a Blind I, 1962; The New Confession, 1963; Dreams of a Summer Night, 1965. Awards: Borestone Poetry Prize, 1967; Guinness Poetry Prize, 1962. Address: Bintry House, Itteringham, Aylsham, Norfolk, U.K.

BARKER, Max Samuel, b. 5 March 1912. College Educator, Division of Fine Arts Chairman. Education: Grad., West Union HS, Iowa; B.A., Upper Iowa Coll., Fayette; M.A., Univ. of Iowa, Iowa City; work toward Doctorate: Community Coll Education, Univ. of Iowa; Creative Writing, Drake Univ; Eastern Cultures, Univ. of Northern Iowa. Married, Wilma Louise Sauerbry; 1 d. (Laura Louise). Positions held: HS & Jr. Coll. Music Supervisor, Aurora, Fairbank and Independence, Iowa; During WW 11, Instr. at 3 British Flight Training School, Miami, Oklahoma; moved to Tulsa, Oklahoma as Registrar and Dean of Men for Spartan School of Aeronautics owned by J. Paul Getty; Instr. for Marshalltown Community Schools; Music Chairman and Div. of Fine Arts Chairman, Marshalltown Community Coll.; poetry editor; chairman of T.R. Poetry Contests; pres. of BIFCO Corporation. Memberships: Acad. of American Poets; Nat. Commissioner, Boy Scouts of America; A.A.P.A.; U.A.P.A.; Poetry Soc. of Michigan; Poetry Soc. of South Carolina; Appalacian Studies Center; Assoc. for Poetry Therapy; Clover Internat. Poetry Assoc.; Music Educators Nat. Conference; Iowa Poetry Assoc. (1st Vice-Pres.); Iowa Music Educators; Iowa Bandmasters Assoc.; Rotary Internat.; Central Iowa Art, Theater & Drama Assocs.; Civic & Community Music Assocs.; Oratorio Soc. Published works: Prairie Man, 1971; Prairie Carnival, 1972; Propositions for Peace (Pulitzer Prize nomination), 1973; Poem Patterns, 1973; Poetry for People Under Pressure, 1973. Contbr. to: Times Republican; Campus News Today; Rotary Shaft; Iowa Music Educators; Lyrical Iowa; North American Mentor; Modern Haiku; Scimitar & Song; Green Gate; Charas; Midwest Poetry (anthol.); All-Time Favorite Poetry; Hyacinths & Biscuits; Mennonite Publishing House; Youth Alive; Appalcian Studies Center; Merlin's Magic; Cycloflame; Modern Images; Orphic Lute; Cardinal; Bardic Echoes; Jean's Journal; Prairie Poet; Haiku Highlights; American Poet; NY Poetry Forum; College Concerts; Poets Corner; Poem Patterns; United Poets; Glowing Lanternes; Dragonfly; The Archer; Tweed; Japan Forum; Bouquet of Poems; WHMC Radio Station; KFJB-AM & FM; Poetry of the Year; Peninsula Poets, and many others. Awards: 1970, Hon., Iowa

Poetry Assoc. Lyrical Iowa; 1971, 1st, Words of Eisenhower, College Concerts; 1972, Special, North American Mentor; 1973, 2nd, Robert Martin Award, NY Poetry Forum. Address: 509 N. 16th St., Marshalltown, IA 50158, USA.

BARKER, Squire Omar, pen names, SQUIRES, Phil & CANUSI, Jose, b. 16 June 1894, Virginia. Writer. Education: B.A., New Mexico Highlands Univ., 1924; Hon. Dr. of Lit., ibid, 1961. Positions held: Cowhand; Tchr. of Engl., Tularos & Santa Rosa, NM. High Schools & NM Highlands Univ. Memberships: Pres., Western Writers' of Am., 1958-59; Am. Poetry League; Poetry Soc. of Tex.; Poetry Soc. of NM; Published works: Winds of the Mountains, 1922; Buckaroo Ballads, 1929; Born to Battle, 1950; Cattleman's Steak Book; Sunlight Through the Trees, 1954; Songs of the Saddlemen, 1954; Little World Apart, 1966; Rawhide Rhymes, 1968. Contbr. to: Saturday Evening Post; New York Times; Western Horseman; Wall Street Journal-Denver Post; Cosmopolitan; Red Book; Country Gentlemen; Progressive Farmer; Chicago Tribune; American Bard; From Sea to Sea in Song; Horse Lover's Mag.; Chronicle of the Horse; Short Stories; Western Story Mag.; Today's Education; The Cattleman; Signature of the Sun, 1950; Yucca Land, 1958; Legends & Tales of the Old West, 1964; A Festival of Poetry, 1965. Awards: Justin Golden Boot Awards, 1960; Western Writers of Am. Spur Award, 1967; Levi Straus Golden Saddleman Awards, 1967. Address: 1118-9th St., Las Vegas, NM 87702, USA.

BARKS, Herbert B., b. 1 Jul. 1933. President, Baylor School. Education: B.A., Univ. of Chattanooga; B.D., M.V.D., Columbia Seminary; D.D., King Coll.; Grad. work at Univ. of Hamburg, Germany. Father was Headmaster of Baylor School, Chattanooga, and nationally known educator. Positions held: Asst. Pastor, First Presbyterian Church, Sheveport, La.; Interim Pastor, Anglican Church, Hamburg, Germany; Snr. Pastor, Grandview Presbyterian Church, Glendale, Calif.; Snr. Pastor, First Presbyterian Church, Lynchburg, Va. Published work: Words Are No Good If The Game Is Solitare, 1971. Contbr. to: Presbyterian Outlook (series of poems); Faith At Work mag., series of poems and articles, etc. Awarded Red Ribbon, script for film, 1971, American Film Festival, NYC. Address: Baylor School, P.O. Box 1337, Chattanooga, TN 37401, USA.

BARNARD, Mary, b. 6 Dec. 1909. Educ: B.A., Reed Coll., Portland, Ore. Positions held: Curator, Poetry Collection, Lockwood Mem. Lib., Buffalo, NY, 1939-43; Rsch. Asst. to Carl Van Doren, 1943-50. Published works: Five Young American Poets (w. others), 1940; A Few Poems, 1952; Sappho: A New Translation, 1958. Contbr. to: Origin; New Yorker. Recip., Levinson Award, 1935. Address: 7100 Evergreen Hwy., Vancouver, WA, U.S.A.

BARNARD, Wilhelmus (Willem), pen name GUILLAUME VAN DER GRAFT, b. 15 Aug. 1920. Clergyman. Education: Rijksuniversiteit, Leiden; Rijksuniversiteit, Utrecht. Married Christina van Malde, 1 son, 2 daughters. Positions held: Ministry at Hardenberg, 1946-50 & Nijmegen, 1950-54; Scholarship (Prof. de G. van der Leeuw-Fndn.), 1954–; Curacy at Rozendaal, 1962–. Memberships: Maatschappij der Nederlandse Letterkunde; PEN; Vereniging van Letterkundigen. Published works: (as G. van der Graft) many colls. of poetry inclng. In Exilio, 1946; Mythologisch, 1950; Vogels en Vissen, 1953; Woorden van Brood, 1957; Collected Poems (Gedichten), 1961; (as W. Barnard) many hymns, De Tale Kanaans, 1963; contbns. to Liedboek voor de Kerken, 1973; Na Veertig, (poems), 1973. Contbr. to Maatstaf; De Gids; Wending; Inde Waagschaal; Woord en Dienst. Honours, awards: Arnhem, 1950; Maatschappij van Letterkunde (Van der Hoogtprijs), 1954; Amsterdam, 1957; Hon.degree, R.U., Utrecht, 1966. Address: c/o de Pastorie de Rozendaal, (Gld) Netherlands.

BARNES, Eunice, b. 5 July 1914. English Teacher.

Education: B.S., Univ. of So. Miss., Hattiesburg. Positions held: Taught Engl., Williamsburg H.S., Covington Co. & Puckett H.S., Rankin Co., Miss.; Engl. Tchr., Runnelstown H.S., Miss.; Taught Jr. H.S. Engl. Hattiesburg, Miss. Memberships: Miss. Poetry Soc.; Jackson Co. Writers Unlimited (has served as Sec., V.P. & Treas.); Centro Studi e Scambi Int., Rome, Italy. Contbr. to: Toward the Stars, Miss. Poetry Soc., 1944 & 49; Lyric Mississippi, 1955; Dance of the Muse, 1970; Yearbook of Modern Poetry, 1971; Lyrics of Love, 1972; Poet, India, 1973; Quaderni Di Poesia, Rome, 1973; Outstanding Contemporary Poetry, 1972; Word Craft, 1971; Jackson Daily; Clarion Ledger; Advance Monticellonian; Miss. Poetry Soc. Jrnl., etc. Honours, awards: 2nd pl., Miss. Poetry Soc. Contest, 1944; 2nd pl., South Miss. Poet Laureate Award, 1967; 1st pl., Writers Unlimited Semiannual Comp. for Poetry, 1971; 1st pl. in Poetry, Hope Div., Poem of the Yr. Award, Inky Trails Publs., 1973. Address: 712 Irving St., Pascagoula, MS 39567, U.S.A.

BARNES, Mary Jane, b. 23 Apr. 1913. Teacher. Education: A.B., Morehead State Univ., 1942; M.A., Ariz. State Univ., 1948. Married twice, 3 sons (1 dec.) Positions held: Tchr., elem. & sec. schls. of Greenup Co., Ky., 1933-42; Tchr., Raceland H.S., Ky., 1942-45; Tchr., elem. & sec. schls. in Phoenix & Mesa, Ariz., 1945-48; Tchr., Pierce Joint Union H.S., Arbuckle, Calif., 1949-50; Tchr. of Engl., Liberty Union H.S., Brentwood, Calif., 1950-73. Memberships: World Poetry Soc.; Calif. State Poetry Soc.; Ky. State Poetry Soc.; Flatwoods Poetry Soc., Ky.; Centro Studi e Scambi Int. Published works: (books of poetry) The Opposite Shore, 1961; Delta Portraits, 1962; 2nd printing, 1973; A Puff of Smoke, 1969; (booklet of sonnets) Song of a Quester, 1964. Contbr. to num. mags., newspapers & anthols. inclng: Quill & Quair; Haiku & Tanka; Nat. Poetry Anthol.; CTA Jrnl.; Am. Bard; Midwest Chaparral; The Writer's Voice; Hoosier Challenger. Honours, awards: Poet Laureate of Brentwood; nom. to Accademia Internazionale, Rome; one of six poets to be honored by Centro Studi e Scambi in dedication of int. book of poems. Address: 425 Pippo Ave., Brentwood, CA 94513, U.S.A.

BARNETT, Mary, pen name **WILLS, C. M.** (for competitions etc.), b. 28 Nov. 1910. Teacher (now Housewife). Education: Whitchurch HS for Girls; Edge Hill Training Coll., Liverpool; further courses for teaching at Balliol Coll. (Oxford), Loughborough, Scarborough, and Moreton Hall, near Oswestry. Positions held: Teaching at Highley, Whitchurch, and Shrewsbury. Memberships: English Assoc.; Poetry Soc.; Ass. member, Poets' Workshop (London); Attingham Writer's (Sec.), Attingham Park, Shropshire (Coll. of Adult Education). Contbr. to: The Shropshire Mag.; Orbis; Swing Back (Anthol. Orbis); Anglo-Welsh Review; I.P.S. (Orbis) Anthol. 1974; six poems broadcast (Midland Poets). Awards: Final considerations in the Premium & Greenwood Competitions (Poetry Review); Commended, Summa Cum Laude, in John Masefield Memorial Competition (Manifold); Poem selected and read (London) Poetry Soc. Members' Work, Dec., 1961. Address: 9 Meadow View Rd., Whitchurch, Shropshire, UK.

BARNHILL, Myrtle Annie, pen name **BARNHILL, Myrtle Fait,** b. 10 July 1896. Librarian; School Teacher. Education: A.B., Miss. Coll., Clinton; Bapt. Theol. Sem., Louisville, Ky.; post grad. work, State Univ., Austin, Tex. Married David Hinds Barnhill, 2 daughters. Positions held: Ch. Missionary, San Antonio, Tex.; Libn., Baylor Univ., Waco, Tex.; Math Tchr., Hitchcock & La Marque, Tex. Memberships incl: Tex. Womens Press; Tex. State Tchrs. Assn.; Tex. Poetry Assn.; Am. Poetry League; Centro Studi e Scambi Int.; Alpha Delta Kappa. Published works: (books of poems) Life's Overtones, 1963; Afterglow, 1964; Alchemy of Love, 1970; Interlude, 1973. Has written & published 4 booklets of Devotionals, Through a Glass Darkly, Thy Kingdom Come, These Our Children, A Teacher's Soliloquy. Contbr. to: Am. Poetry League anthols. & qtly. bulletins; Midwestern Chaparral Poetry Assn. qtly. bulletins; Bapt. Standard;

Waco News Tribune; Tex. State Tchrs. Assn. mag., etc. Honours, awards: 2nd pl., Tex. Press Women, 1965; Cert. of Merit, IWWP, 1971; Diploma di Benemerenza, Acad. Leonardo da Vinci, 1972. Address: 2630 Camp Circle, P.O. Box 183, La Marque, TX 77568, U.S.A.

BARNHORST, Colin Gregory, b. 24 Apr. 1942. Educational Administrator. Education: B.A., Univ. of Tex., Arlington, 1968; Ed.M., Temple Univ., Phila., Pa., 1971. Positions held: USAF, 1959-61; Student, 1962-68; Math Instr., Tilden Middle Schl., Phila., 1968-71; Dir., Reading Rsch. Fndn., Phila., 1971; Dir., Ctr. for Developmental Learning, Phila., 1972; Math Instr., Booth Schl., Rosemont, Pa., 1971-72; Doctoral Student, 1972–. Memberships: 1st Pres., Dallas Poetry Soc., Tex., 1967-68; Fndr., ibid, 1967; Fndr., Mid-Cities Poetry Soc. of Tex.; Pa. Poetry Soc.; Fndr. & Coord., Creativity Workshop, Univ. of Tex., Arlington. Ed., Creativity, Dallas, 1967-68. Contbr. to: Arlington News (regular Sunday Column); Grand Prairie News; Arlington Review; Book of the Year, 1968. Honours: 1st Pl., Monthly Contest, Poetry Soc. of Tex., Feb. 1968. Address: 6832 Grebe Pl., Philadelphia, PA 19142, U.S.A.

BARO, Gene, b. 1924. Teacher. Positions held: Tchr., Bennington Coll., U.S.A. Published works: Northwind and Other Poems, 1959; A View of Water, 1965; Claes Oldenberg and Gene Baro, 1968. Editor: Beat Poems, 1961; Famous American Poems, 1962; After Appomattox: The Image of the South in Its Fiction, 1963; Modern American Stories, 1963. Contbr. to: New Yorker; Discovery; New Poets of England and America (anthology), 1962. Address: Bennington, VT, U.S.A.

BAROTT, Lois, b. 28 Apr. 1928. Homemaker. Positions held: w. Sperry-Univac Computer Mfg., Roseville, Minn. Member, Midwest Fed. of Chaparral Poets. Address: Rte. 1, Box 13, Shafer, MN 55074, U.S.A.

BARRANDA, Natividad 'Natty' Gatbonton, pen names **AGAPE, Fedelis & SHANTIH, Philia.** Professor; Educator; Lawyer; Poet; Writer. Education: A.A., Legazni Colls., Philippines, 1950; LL.B., Far Eastern Univ., Manila, 1954; M.A., De Pauw Univ., Ind., U.S.A., 1961; Ph.D., Claremont Grad. Schl. & Univ. Ctr., Calif. 1968. Positions held: Law prac., Manila, 1950-56; Youth Dir., Ed.-in-Chief, Filipino Christian Youth Mag., 1956-57; Student Dir., Meth. Soc. Ctr., Manila, Coun. of Univ. Students, etc., 1958-59; Asst. Prof., Dept. of Philos. & Religion, Wilberforce Univ., Ohio, 1967-69; Vis. Lectr., Int. Studies Prog., Ctrl. State Univ., Wilberforce, Ohio, 1968-69; Assoc. Prof., Dept. of Philos. & Religion, Wilberforce Univ., 1969; Vis. Lectr., Edinboro State Coll., Pa., 1969-70, etc. Published works: (books & booklets) Together We Worship; Hands Across the Sea, 1958; On Counselling & Counsellors, 1957; Dare We Worship; Love Unfolding; Spoonful of Love, poems, 1967; var. other books co-edited & published in the Philippines & var. books pending publication in the U.S.A. Has written legal & devotional articles. Recip. of num. hons. & awards inclng: Teacher of the Year, Univ. Fac., Wilberforce Univ. Students, 1967-68; Ford Fndn. Award, 1969. Address: Unit 7, Xenia Meadows, 1012 Frederick Dr., Xenia, OH 45385, U.S.A.

BARRETT, William M., b. 1 June 1900. Lawyer; Educator; Lecturer; Critic on Modern Poetry. Education: City Coll., Univ. of N.Y.; Fordham Law Schl. Positions held: Law Practice, N.Y.C. & Ohio; Lectured on Modern Poetry in num. colls. & sec. schls. Memberships: Pres., Ohio Poetry Soc., 2 yrs.; Pres., Akron Poetry Grp.; helped to edit The Ohio Poetry Anthol. w. G. Abbey. Published works: A Lawyers Phantasy; Song of the Warsaw Ghetto; The Farmers Daughter (verse play); Aint you got no Shame; Lopsided Halo; And all the World Wondered; Crossway to Heaven (play); This Unbegotten Paradise; Ed., An Anthol. of Contemporary Ohio Poetry – A Tenderfoot in Paradise, 1973. Contbr. to:

Poet Lore; The Am. Bookman; Laurel Leaves; Orbis; Writer's Voice; Guardino's Gazette; Pegasus, etc. Honours, awards: Dr. of Liberal Arts, World Univ., Gtr. China Arts Coll., 1970; Hon Poet, United Poets Laureate Int., 1968; Ph.D., Free Univ. of Asia, 1968. Address: 3490 N.W. 23rd St., Ft. Lauderdale, FL 33311, U.S.A.

BARROW, Raymond, b. 1920. Civil Servant. Educ: Belize City, British Honduras; St. Catharine's Coll., Cambridge, U.K. Contbr. to: Caribbean Verse (anthology), 1967.

BARROWS, Anita, b. 13 Jan. 1947. Poet & Translator. Education: B.A., San Francisco State Coll., U.S.A., 1969; M.A., Boston Univ., 1970. Married Richard Friedman. Positions held: Tchr., Shasta Schl., Sausalito, Calif., 1969; Tchr., Poetry in the Schools, Calif., 1972; Tchr., Univ. of Calif., Berkeley, 1972, '74. Published works: Poems Until Now (pamphlet), 1968; Emigration (book), 1972. Contbr. to: Aphra; Dryad; Invisible City; Grecourt Review; Univ. of Kansas City Review; New Mag.; Transfer; Open Coll.; European Judaism; Am. Poetry Review; No More Masks (anthol.); Rising Tides (anthol.) Honours, awards: Prize, Atlantic Mag., 1964 & from New Mag., 1972. Address: c/o Joseph Barrows, 1390 Stevenson Rd., Hewlett, NY 11557, U.S.A.

BARROWS, Margaret Hamilton, pen names, **STEVENS, Leslie; GRAY, Douglas,** b. 6 Sept. 1920. Composer-Lyricist. Education: St. 7imothy's School, Maryland, 1935-1939; Sarah Lawrence Coll., 1939-41, (2 yr. diploma). Positions held: Pres., Detroit, Mich., Branch, Sarah Lawrence Alumnae Assoc., 1943-44; Staff Asst., Red Cross Foreign Inquiry Service, 1943-44 on Lay Jury of Detroit Artists Market, 1951-52; Pres., Women's Farm Home Advisory Comm. of Southern States Co-oper., 1954–; Chairman, Life Membership Council of World Poets Resource Center, 1970, also member of Bd. of Directors, 1970-1973; also Chairman, Internat. Poets Workshop, World Poets Resource Center; Regional Plan Assoc. of NYC (member); Christian Crusade (member Nat. Advisory Bd.); American Security Council (member Nat. Advisory Bd.); Intercontinental Biographical Assoc. (Life Fellow). Contbr. to: World Poets Qtly.; Great World Poets Anthol.; Words and Music of songs extensively copyrighted. Awards: 1st Art Prize, St. Timothy's School, 1938; 1st Prize, Stage Design from Jr. League of Detroit, 1941; Hon. Ph.D., 1971, for work in the Arts (Colorado State Christian Coll.); Essay Award, World Poets Resource Center; Song "Living With the Arts" (written by Dr. Margaret Hamilton Barrows) given by Mrs. Onassis to Kennedy Memorial Library at Harvard Univ. Address: 500 East 77 St., New York, NY 10021, USA.

BARTANA, Ortsion, b. 12 May 1949. Education: B.A. in Philosophy and Hebrew Lit., and M.A. in Hebrew Lit., Tel-Aviv Univ. Teacher of Hebrew Lit. in Tel-Aviv Univ. Pubs: Every Tree Has Its Heaven, 1967. Contrib. to many Israeli literature magazines, etc. Address: Dept. of Hebrew Literature, Tel-Aviv Univ., Tel-Aviv, Israel.

BARTHOLOMEW, Edna, pen name (occasionally) **STANLEY, Alison,** b. 3 Dec. 1904. Retired Teacher. Education: B.A. (Hons.), Univ. of Leeds, U.K., 1925. Positions held: Tchr., Saltburn Primary Schl. Memberships: Editl. Panel, ENVOI, 1972–; Middlesbrough Writers' Group; Fndr. Mbr., Middlesbrough 20+ Poetry Grp. Published works: The Bells of Middlesmoor, 1972. Contbr. to: Homes & Gardens; Envoi; The Dalesman; Headland; Manifold; Intak; Breakthru; Sunday Companion; Hearing; New Melody; E. Riding Bystander; Rainbow; Country Life; (anthols.) London Anthol.; Laudamus Te; 3 Writers' Review Annuals. Honours, awards: 1st Prize, Ivan Franko Meml. Comp., 1966; Manifold Century Scholarship, 1969; Rainbow Poet of the Yr., 1970. Address: 66 Windy Hill Ln., Marske-by-the-Sea, Redcar, Teesside TS11 7HA, U.K.

BARTON, Geraldine Dolores, pen name **BARTON, Geri,** b. 3 Feb. 1927. Housewife. Married, 2 children (Barbara & Gary). Positions held: Dictaphone Operator, Borden Milk Co., 1943-45; Asst. Supvsr., Book-of-the-Month Club, Booksellers Div., 1945-47. Memberships: Haiku Soc. of Am., N.Y.; Am. Soc. of Composers, Authors & Publishers, N.Y.; Long Island Writers; United Amateur Press. Published works: Paumanok – a Mag. of Long Island Living, 1973 (monthly feature 'Paumanoems'). Contbr. to: Modern Haiku; Haiku West; Dragonfly, a Qtly. of Haiku Highlights; Janus-SCTH; Tejas; Verdure; Friendship Ferry. Honours, awards: Haiku Award, Haiku Highlights, 1972; Haiku of the Yr. Award, Dragonfly, 1973 & others. Address: 14 Elwood Ave., Hicksville, NY 11801, U.S.A.

BARTURA, Avrahàm Elièser, pen names **BERGMANN, A., BEREG, Eli, DAHARI, A.,** & Others, b. 12 Sept. 1907. Linguist; Administrator; Writer & Publisher; Pedagogue. Education: Econ. Coll., Nuremberg; Tchrs. Coll., Wurzburg. Married, 1 son. Positions held: Prin., Jewish Schl., Stettin; Jrnlst., Haaretz Daily, Tel-Aviv (& other papers); Prin. schls: Ekron, Magdiel, Jerusalem, Israel; Dir., Pedag. Neve Hadassa Youth Village, Israel; Dir., Jewish Agency, Dept. for Culture & Educ., W. Germany; Rep., Youth Alia for S. Am.; Dir. of Info. Dept. & Linguist; Advisor of Israel Broadcasting Serv.; Chief Red. of Hatzofe-Liyeladim (Children's Weekly); & Alumot (Sci. Monthly); Ed., Min. of Educ. & Culture. Published works: Children of the Town, The Three of Makhlul, a.o. books for Youth & Children, 1927-56; Germany Diary & Journey in Sweden & Lapland, 1962, '63; A School Near the Border, 1963, '64; Peace from the Mountains, 1968; Jerusalem in the Eyes of its Beholders, 1970; High Skies, Diary Jerusalem & Germany, 1910-31, 1971; var. articles & translations; chapts. in The History of the Jewish Community in Jerusalem. Recip., Award, Min. of Educ. & Culture, 1971. Address: 7 Qiryat Moshe St., Jerusalem, Israel.

BART-WILLIAMS, Gaston, b. 1938. Positions held: Fndr., African Youth Cultural Soc., W. Africa, 1958; Sierre Leone Rep., World Assembly of Youth, Mali Republic, 1959, Commonwealth Theatre Conf., Commonwealth Poets' Conf., London, U.K., 1965. Contbr. to: Black Orpheus; Meanjin; New Statesman; Outposts; London Magazine; (anthologies) Young Commonwealth Poets '65, 1965; New Poems, 1966; Commonwealth Poems of Today, 1967; New Voices of the Commonwealth, 1968; Poetry from Africa, 1968. Honours, awards: All Africa Short Story Award, 1962-63; Michael Karolyi International Award, 1963; German London Embassy Cultural Grant, 1964.

BARZE, Marguerite Enlow, occasional pen name **BLANK, Margaret,** b. 31 August 1895. Writer; Lecturer; Book Reviewer. Education: Rollins Schl. of Speech, Rollins Coll., Winter Pk., Fla.; Creative Writing, Univ. of Ala. Married to Roland Detling Barze, 2 s. Positions held: Book Review Broadcaster, WSB, Atlanta, Ga.; Columnist, Thing or Three, N. Ga. newspaper; Lectr. on Handwriting & Personality. Memberships: Pres., Atlanta Writers' Club; Prose Chmn., ibid.; Instr., Ga. Writers' Assn.; Pres., Daytona Beach Br., Nat. League Am. Penwomen; currently Treas., ibid.; Poetry Soc. of Am.; Fla. State Poetry Soc.; State Poetry Chmn., NLAPW; Co-Sponsor, Ronald-Barze Poetry Group, 1966–. Published works: This I Give to You, 1966, '69, '73. Contbr. to: NY Herald Tribune; Poet Lore; Chicago Tribune; Miami Herald; The Lyric; The Muse; Flamingo; Sonnet Sequences; Writer's Digest; Penwoman; Penpoint; American Bard; Selected Poems (Fla. State Poetry Soc.), 1966-71; Memorial Books, Fla. State Poetry Soc.; New Hampshire News; Orlando; Fla. Poets Book, 1940; Poem; The Christian; Housewife; She; Poetry Prevue; Mod. Am. Sonnets; Westminster Mag.; Scimitar & Song, etc. Honours: 1st Prize, Nat. Bernie Babcock Mem. Contest, 1967; 1st Prizes, NLAWP State Conf. & Daytona Br. Annual Contest; 1st Prize, NY Poetry Forum, 1970; 1st Prize, Poetry Soc. of Ga., 1972; PSA Diamond Jubilee Anthology, 1972.

Address: 917 N. Oleander Ave., Daytona Beach, Fla. 32018, USA.

BARZELAY, Walter Moshe, b. 1 Dec. 1924. Poet & Writer. Positions held: Ed., Literary Page, Israeli daily, Kol-Ha'am, 1963-64; Co-Ed., Ocarina, Madras, Int. Edn., 1972–; Ed., Sandra Fowler: In the Shape of Sun, 1973. Memberships: World Poetry Soc.; Nat. Dir., Israeli Chap., ibid; Poetry Soc., London. Published works: N. Guillen's Selected Verse, 1962: A Tinge of Purple, (verse), 1967; Variations on a Theme, (verse), 1970; Semantics of the Heart, (verse), 1971; Guest Ed., Israeli Number of Poet, Madras; From Past Nights' Shores, (verse), 1973. Rep. in the following anthols: Spring Anthol., 1972; Premier Poets (U.S.A.), 1970; Eight Israeli Poets, 1973; Friendship Trail (U.S.A.), 1970. Contbr. to: Poet (India); Al-Hamishmar; Al-Ittihad; Al-Jedid; Poetry Soc., Accent, etc. Poems have been transl. into Arabic, Portuguese, Italian, Swedish, Japanese, Russian & Iddish. Honours, awards: Disting. Serv. Cit., World Poetry Soc., 1970 & 72; Degree of World Poetry Translator Laureate & Bronze Medal, World Acad. of Langs. & Lit.; Sponsors' Award, Kans. Poetry Contest. Address: P.O. Box 26 464, Tel-Aviv, Israel.

BASHAM, Jessie Lena, b. 28 Jan. 1910. Housewife. Education: Grad., Jena H.S., La., 1926. Married William Basham, 1931, 3 children, 6 grandchildren. Positions held: Tchr., Adult Sunday Schl. Classes, Eddy Justiss Meml. Meth. Ch., Trout, La., 15 yrs. Mbr., La. State Poetry Soc. Contbr. to: The Jena Times; The La. State Poetry Soc. Yr. Book, 1973; poem, Life's Tragic Dream, published in I.W.W.P. Anthol., 1973. Honours, awards: 3rd pl., for humorous poem, La. State Poetry Soc. Fest., 1971; 3rd pl., historical poem, ibid; 3rd pl., La. State Poetry Soc. Spring Fest., 1972. Address: Rt.1, Trout, LA 71371, U.S.A.

BASHFORD, Rosemary, pen name **FROBISHER, Mark.** Private Secretary. Positions held: Sec., Registry (Senate Div.), Univ. of Birmingham, U.K.; Sec. to Prof. of Physiological Chem., Fac. of Med., ibid; Sec. to Regl. Dir., Birmingham Region of John Laing Construction Ltd. Memberships: Org. Comm., Poetry Day, 1967 & 70. Contbr. to: Priapus; Envoi; Scrip; Manifold; Expression. Address: Flat 2, 35 Melton Rd., Kings Heath, Birmingham B14 7DA, U.K.

BASS, Clara May, pen name, **OVERY, Claire May,** b. 11 May 1910. Poet. Education: Wintringham Grammar School, Grimsby, Lincs.; studied ballet, singing, piano. Personal details: Married to D.L. Bass; 1 s. (Anthony Donald William). Positions held: Proprietor, Ladies Hairdroooing ootablichmont, 1927 37; Teacher of Singing, 1945-50. Memberships: Int. Comm. Mbr., C.S.S.I. (Rome); Internat. Poetry Soc. (Fndr. Fellow); Soc. of Authors; Grimsby Amateur Operatic Soc. Published works: Dreams of a Singer, 1963; Living Poetry, 1968; Major and Minor, 1971; Trio, 1973; Quintet, 1974. Contbr. to: Internat. Poetry Mag.; Orbis; Expression One, 1971-72; Nature Poetry 1 & 2; Poetry Mag. Headland, 1970; Grimsby News, 1974; Collected Poems; Poetry City & Machine Age; Love Poetry; Grimsby Eve. Telegraph; Grimsby News; Parnassus; Internat. Poetry Mag. Breakthru; 1st Int. Poetry Soc. Anthol., 1974; Quaderni de Poesia (anthol.), etc. Recip. Long Service Medal, Operatic Soc.; various prizes, certificates for singing, pianoforte, 1922, 1923-24, 1951. Address: 68 L'Estrange St., Cleethorpes, Lincs., UK.

BATES, Ronald Gordon Nudell, b. 3 Apr. 1944. Professor of English. Education: Public and HS, Regina, Saskatchewan; B.A., M.A., Ph.D., Univ. of Toronto, Ont. Married; 3 children. Served, Canadian Army, 1943-45. Positions held: Lektor, Uppsala Univ., Sweden; Instr., Univ. of Toronto; Instr., Lecturer, Ast. Prof., Assoc. Prof., Prof., Univ. of Western Ont. London, Ont. Membership: League of Canadian Poets (member, Exec. Committee for 1 yr.). Published works: The Wandering World, 1959; The Unimaginable Circus, Theatre and Zoo, 1961; Changes, 1968; Translator, Man Without A Road, by Erik Lindegren.

Contbr. to: Northern Review; Canadian Poetry; Canadian Forum; Contemporary Verse; Tamarack Review; Prism International; Times Lit. Supp (London, UK). Address: Dept. of Engl., Univ. of Western Ont., London, Ont., Canada.

BATH, Raymond, b. 19 Feb. 1931. Translator. Education: Master of Econ. Sci. Positions held: Ed., Falaises, 1965; Belgian Ed. of Les Cahiers d'Action d'Art, 1970; Fndr., Concours Internationaux de Poésie et de Prose Raymond Bath, 1968. Memberships: Chmn., Le Groupe Belge de l'Action d'Art; Artistic Councillor, Le Groupe Belge de l'Academie Européenne des Arts; Int. Mgmt., Centro Studi e Scambi, Rome; V. Chmn. of Hon., Les Jeunesses Culturelles; Hon. Mbr., Centre Culturel d'Orient, Alexandria & La Haute Academie Litteraire et Artistique de France. Published works: Dessins d'Enfant, 1963; Poemes sur Orbite, 1964; Shera, 1965; Poèmes de Mauvais Poil, 1966; Les Pendus de Sainte-Eulalie, 1969; Le Psaltérion d'Airain, 1970; Job, 1971; Tête-à-queue, 1972; Requiem pour une Sorcière, 1972; Frok, 1973. Contbr. to var. mags., jrnls. in Belgium, France, Italy, Germany, Canada, U.S.A., etc. Honours, awards incl: Silver Medal of La Haute Académie Artistique et Littéraire de France, 1970; Gold Medal of the Educative Ability of La Fédération Nationale de l'Encouragement Français au Dévouement, 1972; Gold Medal, Artistic Worth, Académie Européenne des Arts, 1973. Address: rue Goor, 57, B-6080, Montignies-sur-Sambre, Belgium.

BATTAGLIA, Elizabeth Louise, pen name **BATTAGLIA, Bette,** b. 27 Feb. 1925, Pigua, Ohio. Housewife. Personal details: m. to Vito Battaglia, 1945, 2 s., 1 d. Positions held: Draftsman. Member of Poetry Soc. of Mich; Member, American Poets Fellowship Society. Published works: The Blood of Roses, 1968. Contbr. to the following anthols. & newspapers: American Poets Best Nos. 3 & 4; Almanac; Coney Island Times; Williamsburg Press; Crawford Co. Courier; News Tribune; The Nutmegger; Haiku Highlights; American Bard; Peninsula Poets; Bardic Echoes; The Angels; The Green World; The Muse; Caravan; Scimitar & Song; Notes & Quotes; Glory; Ladies Home Jrnl.; Family Weekly; Sault Ste. Marie Newspapers. Awards: 2nd Prize, Dyer-Ives Fndn. Contest, 1971. Address: 3106 Cascade Rd. SE, Grand Rapids, Mich. 49506, USA.

BATUSIC, Slavko, pen name **BELAN,** b. 2 June 1902. Institute Manager. Education: B.A. & Ph.D., Univ. of Zagreb, Yugoslavia; studied at Univ. of the Sorbonne & Ecole du Louvre, Paris. Positions held: var. positions in the Croatian Nat. Theatre, Zagreb, 1921-45; Mgr., Theatre Archives & Museum, Zagreb, 1945-50; Prof. of Acad. of Theatrical Arts, Zagreb, 1950-72; Mgr., Inst. for Theatrical Arts. Memberships: Yugoslav Acad. of Scis. & Arts; Soc. of Writers of Croatia; PEN Club, Croatian Ctr. Published works: (coll. of poems) 23 Poems, 1938; (short stories) Cuda i čarolije (Wonder & Magic), 1931; (novels) Na dragom tragu (On a Deer Track), 1933; Argonauti (Argonauts), 1936; Laterna (Magic Lantern), 1958; (play) Komorni trio (Chamber Trio), 1938; (travel) Kroz zapadne zemlje i gradove (Through Western Countries & Towns), 1932; Od Kandije do Hammerfesta (From Candia to Hammerfest), 1937; Od Siene do Haarlema (From Siena to Haarlem), 1941; Rembrandtu u pohode (A Visit to Rembrandt), 1952; Pejzaži i vedute (Landscapes & Sights), 1959; (critical studies) Stanislavski u Zagrebu (Stanislavski in Zagreb), 1948; (An outline of History of Art) Umjetnost u slici (Art in Pictures), 1957, etc. Contbr. to var. jrnls., mags. in Europe. Honours, awards: Lit. Prize of Town of Zagreb, 1959; Vladimir Nazor Prize, Republic of Croatia, 1971. Address: Boskovićeva 32, Zagreb, Yugoslavia.

BAUCOM, Margaret Dean, pen name, **BAUCOM, Margaret,** b. 25 Sept. 1909. Freelance Writer; Poet. Education: HS; Journalism; private; Ph.D. (h.c.), Colorado State Christian Coll., 1972. Married, Hiram Bascom Baucom (dec.); 1 d. (Mrs. James Preston

Brown, Jr.). Positions held: Owner & Operator, B. & M. Motor Co., 1950-53; Columnist, Feature Writer, The Union Mail; Women's Editor, Columnist, Feature Writer, The Monroe Enquirer; Advertising Column, Around Town Shopping with Margaret Baucom (Monroe Enquirer Journal); Assoc. Editor, The Carolinas Genealogical Soc. Bulletin; current, Freelance Writer-Poet. Memberships: World Poetry Soc. Intercontinental; American Poets Fellowship Soc.; United Poets Laureate Int.; Mattoon Branch, NLAPW; Santa Cruz Chapt., Calif. Chaparral Poets; Ill. State Poetry Soc.; Internat. Poetry Soc. (UK); CSSI; NC Press Women Inc., Nat. Fed. of Press Women, Inc.; Huguenot Soc.; Col. Dames of 17th Century; DAR; United Daughters of the Confederacy; Carolinas Genealogical Soc.; Union County Hist. Soc.; Monroe Women's Club (Org. Pres.); Monroe Ladies Golf Club; Monroe Garden Club (Past Pres.), and others. Contbr. to numerous anthols., mags., journals, inclng. Mood Magic, 1974. Awards and Honours: several, including Etta Caldwell Harris Poetry Award, 1st Prize, 1962; 1st Prize, Ill. State Poetry Soc. Contest, 1972, etc. Address: 710 South Hayne St., Monroe, NC 28110, USA.

BAUER, Walter, b. 4 Nov. 1904. Professor of German. Education: Tchrs. Coll., Germany; B.A. & M.A., Univ. in Canada, 1954-58. Positions held: Public Schl. Tchr., Instr., Lectr., Asst. Prof., Assoc. Prof., Special Lectr. Memberships: P.E.N.; Deutsche Akademie fur Sprache und Dichtung; League of Canadian Poets. Published works: Kameraden, zu euch spreche ich, 1929; Stimme aus dem Leunawerk, 1930; Dammerung wird Tag, 1947; Mein blaues Oktavheft, 1954; Nachtwachen des Tellerwaschers, 1957; Klopfzeichen, 1962; Fragment vom Hahnenschrei, 1966; The Price of Morning, 1968. Contbr. to: Neue Rundschau; Deutsche Rundschau; Neue deutsche Literatur; Frankfurter Hefte; Neue deutsche Hefte; Tamarack Review, etc. Address: 95 Redpath Ave., Apt.15A, Toronto, Ont. M4S 2K1, Canada.

BAVIN, Frances (E. Laurie Horsley), b. 21 Dec. 1907. Freelance Journalist. Education: Governess, and Private Schools, West Indies, Cusacks Coll., U.K. Married, 2 s. Positions held: Asst. Beauty Editor, Amalgamated Press. Memberships: Poetry Soc. (UK.); Yorkshire Poetry Soc. Contbr. to: BBC (London and Overseas); Chambers Journal; John O'London's; Daily Mail; Poetry Review; The Perfume Booklet; Women's Pictorial; British Bandsman (also poem sung at the Royal Albert Hall); Troubadour; Radio Sheffield; Yorkshire Poets, etc. Award: 2nd Prize, Yorkshire Poets' Competition. Address: 117 Bannerdale Rd., Sheffield, Yorkshire S7 2DQ, UK.

BAXTER, Audrey Earl, b. 4 April 1935. Director of Evangelism, First Presbyterian Church, Huntington, West Va. Education: Graduated Magna Cum Laude, Marshall Univ., Huntington, West Va.; Grad. work at Marshall Univ.; Attended Wordsworth Seminar at Rydal Mt., U.K., 1972. Married to Prof. Curtis Baxter. Children: 1 son. Asst. Personnel Director, Anderson Newcomb Dept. Store, Huntington, West Va., 1956-59; Teacher, Public School, Huntington, 1962-63; Director of Evangelism, First Presbyterian Church, Huntington, 1965-. Member, The Huntington Poetry Guild; West Virginia Poetry Soc.; Nat. Fed. of State Poetry Societies. Poems published locally, 1964-73. Contib. to: Herald Advertiser (Huntington); Infinity Review. Awarded 1st place in West Va. State Women's Club Contest, 1973. Address: 1555 Fifth Avenue, Huntington, West Va., 25701, USA.

BAYBARS, Taner, pen name BAYLISS, Timothy, b. 18 June 1936. British Council Official. Married. Positions held: (all w. Brit. Coun.) in Books Dept., 1956-66; Book Exhibs. Dept., 1966-67; Periodicals Dept., 1967-72; Book Promotion Dept., 1972- (runs the Brit. Coun's O'seas Reviews Scheme). Memberships: Poetry Soc.; Advsry Panel, ibid. Published works: Mendilin Ucundakiler, 1954; To Catch a Falling Man, 1963; A Trap for the Burglar, 1965; Selected Poems of Nazim Hikmet, 1967; Plucked in a Far-off Land, 1970; The

Moscow Symphony (N Hikmet), 1970; Modern Poetry in Translation: Turkish (Ed.), 1971; The Day Before Tomorrow (N Hikmet), 1972. Contbr. to: Times Lit. Supplement; Critical Qtly.; Ambit; Listener; London Mag.; Delos; Modern Poetry in Translation; Samphire; num. Canadian & Am. mags. & anthols. Address: 69 Onslow Gdns., Muswell Hill, London N10 3JY, U.K.

BAYLEY, Urla Marjorie, pen names SUBURBANITE, ROSHER, Rosamund, b. 29 Nov. 1924. Housewife. Member, United Amateur Press; Scotian Pen Guild; Editor of Friendship Ferry (monthly). Pubs. Around the Year in Rhyme, 1967; Rural Riches, 1971; City Sadness, 1971; Lanternes and Lesser Lights, 1970; Pondering the Parables, 1972; Searching the Seasons, 1972. Contrib. to: Alberta Poetry Yr. Book; Fur and Feathers; Pegasus; Amber; Bluenose Rambler; Christian Living; Hyacinths and Biscuits; Inky Trails; Kansas Kernals; Encore; Verdure; Dragonfly; Modern Haiku; Poetry Prevue; Driftwood East; Tejas (Texas); Olive Hill News (Kentucky); Durango-Cortez Herald (Colorado), etc. Awards include: UAP Transatlantic Conventional Poetry, 1973, 1st prize; SEOX Pattern Poetry (Tejas), 1972, 1st prize; Spring Poem Inky Trails Grand Prize, 1973, etc. Address: 91 Barford Road, Rexdale, Ontario M9W 4H8, Canada.

BAYLISS, John Clifford, pen name CLIFFORD, John, b. 4 Oct. 1919. Editor. Education: M.A., St. Catharine's Coll., Cambridge. Positions held: Asst. Prin., Colonial Office, 1946-49; Ed., Macmillan & Co., 1949-52; Sr. Edit. Officer, Northern Rhodesia & Nyasaland Publs. Bur., Lusaka, 1952-59; Admnstr., Brit. Govt.'s Low-Priced Book Scheme, 1959-. Published works include: Indications (w. others), 1943; The White Knight, 1944; Call Wind To Witness, 1945; A Romantic Miscellany (w. D. Stafford), 1946; Ed. & Contbr., various other publs. Address: London, UK.

BAZLEY, Rosemary, b. 15 July 1900. Housewife; Teacher. Married. Positions held: A.T.S., 2 yrs.; p/t Lectr. (German), Kidderminster Coll. of Further Ed., 6 yrs.; Pvte. Tchr. of German. Memberships: Writers Guild; Worcester Writers' Circle; Int. Poetry Soc.; Girl Guide Movement, 1921- as District & Div. Commnr., Co. Ranger Advisor, Co. Trefoil Guild Recorder. Published works: (poetry booklets) Shadow Pantomime, 1960; Pride of the Evening, 1963; Turn of the Year, 1968; Run of the Mill, 1972; (poems) Peacock Parade, 1966; Resurgent, 1968; Cats on my Coffin, 1970. Broadcasts (BBC Midland Poets Series) Flying Swan, 1960; To a Deaf Friend, 1964; Unrest, 1965; (Brit. Forces Broadcasting Serv.) Interviewed Cologne, 1968 & 70. Contbr. to var. mags., jrnls. inclng: Homes & Gardens; Envoi; The Lady. Honours, awards: Prize, Envoi Mag.; 1965; Prize, Anglo-Welsh Comp., 1969. Has taken part in var. public readings of own work. Address: High Beeches, 32 Chaddesley Rd., Kidderminster, Worcs., U.K.

BEAN, Doralee Jemmett, pen name JEMMETT, Doralee, b. 17 Apr. 1947. Clerk-Typist. Education: Coll. of Idaho, Caldwell, 1965-67; B.A., Idaho State Univ., Pocatello, 1969. Married Larry R. Bean. Positions held: Tchng. Asst. in Remedial Summer Prog., Homedale Elem. Schl., Homedale, Idaho, summers 1968 & '69; Receptionist, Doremus & Co., San Francisco, Calif., 1969; Deputy Clerk, Fourth District Court, Ada Co., Idaho, 1970-73; Sr. Clerk-Typist, Institutional Services Div., Univ. of Idaho, 1973-. Member, World Poetry Soc. Intercontinental. Contbr. to: The Idaho Daily Statesman; Poet. Address: Rt. No. 1, Viola, ID 83872, U.S.A.

BEARD, Amy Carolina, pen name, BEARD, Amy Carol, b. 1 Aug. 1909. Former Business Woman. Education: Livingston High School, Calif.; Southern Calif. Coll. of Bus., Los Angeles. Personal details: Married; maternal side trace ancestry back to Reigning House of Stuart, Scotland, UK. Positions held: Steno-Sec., 1927-43; with WAC, US Army, 1943-45; Exec. Sec., -1963. Memberships: AAPA; UAPA; The Bards; World Poetry Soc.; UAP; Clover Poetry

Assn. Author of Thoughts from a Lonely Hill, 1970. Contbr. to: (Anthols.), Echoes of Laughter; Magical World of Holidays; The New Poetry; Quorum of Cats; A Rainbow of Wishes; Echoes of Love; 1970 Anthol. of Contemporary Poets; Quaderni di Poesia; Tower by the Sea; Great American World; (Jrnls.), Altoona Mirror; Bay Shore Breeze; Echoes; Fellowship in Prayer; Images; Mendocino-Robin; Nutmegger; Poetry Prevue; PFFST. Publ. Enterprises; Saint; Tejas; Words With Wings; Pancontinental Premier Poets. Honours: Sr. Poet Award, The Saint, 1968; Merit Award, NY State Poetry Contest, 1968; Cert. of Merit, Laurel Publrs. Int. Poetry Symposium, Centro Studi e Scambi Int. Address: 5734 Rimbank Ave., Pico Rivera, Calif. 90660, USA.

BEARMAN, Louisa Maud, b. 27 Mar. 1899. Housewife. Married, 2 sons, 1 daughter. Member, Lancashire Authors Assn. Published works: Bits & Pieces, 1972; Larger Addition, 1973. Contbr. to: Lancashire Life; The Record; Has read poetry six times on the radio & twice on television. Address: 22 Park Row, Eagley Bank, Andrew Lane, Bolton, Lancs., U.K.

BEARN, Pierre, b. 15 June 1902. Poet; Novelist; Lecturer. Married Gabrielle Messant. Memberships: Pres., Syndicat des Ecrivains; Dir., Comm., Société des Gens de Lettres; Commission dela professionnalité à la Confederation des travailleurs intellectuels; Commn. of Authors' Rights, Min. of Cultural Affairs; Commn. Sociale du Centre National des Lettres; Fndr., Mandat des Poètes, 1950; Dir. & Ed., La Passerelle review. Published works: Mains sur la mer, 1941; Mes cent Amériques, 1944; Couleurs d'usine, 1951; Couleurs de cendre, 1952; Couleurs intimes, 1953; Couleurs d'ébène, 1953; Couleurs nocturnes; Dialogues de mon amour; Couleurs de mer, 1962; Passantes 1; Passantes 2 illustré par Zadkine, 1966; Couleurs Piégées, 1973; Etude sur Paul Fort, 1950 etc. Contbr. to: Revue Art et Poesie & other poetry publs. Honours, awards incl: Grand prix internationale de poésie, 1970; Grand prix Broquette-Gonin, 1973. Address: 60 rue Monsieur le Prince, 75006 Paris, France.

BEATTIE, Pamela Elizabeth, b. 7 Oct. 1932. Poet. Married. Memberships: Coun. Mbr., Int. Poetry Soc.; Editl. Bd., Orbis; Pellow, Int. Poetry Soc. Published works: Beyond the Minotaur, 1969. Contbr. to: BBC Radio Birmingham; BBC Midland Poets; Cornish Review; Orbis Anthol.; Poetry & Audience; Anglo-Welsh Review; The Lady; She; Country Life; Birmingham Post; Shelter Anthol. 'The House That Jack Built'; Ore; Scrip; Kidderminster Times; Envoi; Country Quest; Orbis; Ambit; Dodo; Outposts; Samphire; Nursing Mirror. Address: Chapel Farm, Menith Wood, Worcester WR6 6UG, U.K.

BEAUDOIN, Kenneth Lawrence, pen names **BOYCE, McKinley, CHATTELERAULT, Victor de & TODANY, Alex de,** b. 12 Dec. 1913. Chief Clerk, Criminal Intelligence Bureau, Memphis Police Dept. Memberships: Workshop Dir., Tenn. Poetry Soc., 1953–; V. Chancellor, Nat. Fed. of Poetry Socs., 1966; V.P., South & West, Inc., 1965–; Sec., Memphis & Shelby Co. Histl. Commn., 1965–; Lit. Panel, Tenn. Arts Commn., 1971–. Published works: Selected Poems & Eye Poems, 1970; Discourses on Poetry, 1971; New Look Trio (w. Sue Abbott Boyd), 1968; Rhythmic Landscape, 1967; Book of the Hours, 1965; Poets, S.E.U.S. (for World Poetry Soc.), 1971-72; 16 Eye Poems, 1963, etc. Contbr. to: South & West; The Muse; The Paper, Dallas; Star Webb Papers, Chadwick, N.J.; Tenn. Poetry Jrnl.; The Old Hickory Review, Jackson; Florida, And ..., Gainesville; Kast; Attack; Subteranneans, Tokyo, Japan, & others. Honours, awards: South & West Award, 1967; Cit., World Poetry Soc., 1971 & 72. Address: 1298 Jefferson Ave., Memphis, TN 38104, U.S.A.

BEAUDRY, Glenn Wesley, b. 14 Oct. 1931. Teacher. Education: LA High School, 1949; U.C.L.A., 1949-50; L.A. City Coll., 1956; B.A. Anthrop., Mexico City Coll.,

1958; San Francisco State Coll., (M.A., English), 1966. Positions held: Engl., Instr., E.T.S.U., 1966-68; Chairman, Cr. Wr., V.A., 1968-70; Engl. Instr., S.M.U., 1970-72; Director, Montessori School, Commerce, Texas (currently). Memberships: Poetry Soc. of Texas; Alaska Poetry Soc.; Affiliation of State Poetry Socs.; Poetry Soc. of America; Internat. Poet's Laureate. Contbr. to: Haiku '64; Poetry: Classical & Contemporary, 1969; Commerce Journal; Fairbanks News-Miner; Prism International; Wascana Review; Western Review, etc. Recip. Hon. Mention: Phelan Award, San Francisco, California, 1967. Address: 2501 Mayo, Commerce, TX 75428, USA.

BEAVER, Bruce, b. 14 Feb. 1928. Writer. Positions held: p/t Journalist; Full time Author. Memberships: Contbng. Ed., Poetry Australia; Australian Soc. of Authors. Published works: Under the Bridge, 1961; Seawall & Shoreline, 1964; Open at Random, 1967; Letters to Live Poets, 1969; Lauds & Plaints, 1974. Contbr. to: (Australia) The Age; The Australian; Australian Poetry 1964-73; Australian Poetry Now; Australian Writing Today; A Book of Australian Verse; The Bulletin; Free Poetry; The Ear in a Wheatfield; Hemisphere; Highway; Leatherjacket 2; Meanjin; Modern Australian Poetry; New Impulses in Australian Poetry; Overland; The Pluralist; The Penguin Book of Australian Verse; Poetry Australia; Poetry Mag.; Poet's Choice; Quadrant; Southerly; Sydney Morning Herald; Verse in Australia; The Vital Decade; We Took Their Orders & Are Dead; (N.Z.) Arena; Image; Landfall; Mate; (U.S.A.) Borestone Awards 1966. Honours, awards: 1st prize, Poetry Mag. Award, 1964; 3rd prize, Capt. Cook Bi-Centenary Poetry Award, 1970; Grace Leven Prize for Poetry, 1970; Poetry Soc. of Australia Annual Book Award, 1970. Address: 15/14-16 Malvern Ave., Manly, N.S.W. 2095, Australia.

BECK, Peter Lockhart, b. 17 Apr. 1955. Student. Education: Liverpool Univ., 1973–. Contbr. to: Hampshire Poets; Phoenix; The Trumpeter; The Hart (Cowplain); The Purbrookian; The Portsmouth News. Ed., school mag. 'Purbrookian', 1972-73; Dir. of 'Under Milk Wood' by Dylan Thomas, at Purbrook, 1973. Poems broadcast on BBC Radio Schools' Prog. 'Books, Plays & Poems'. Honours, awards: 1st Prize, Nat. Schools' Brass Band Assn. Poetry Comp., 1971; Runner-up, Daily Mirror Lit. Comp., 1971; 2nd Prize, Portsmouth Festival Poetry Comp., 1972; 2nd Prize, Dorothy Manger Poetry Comp., 1973. Address: 200 Park Ave., Purbrook, Portsmouth, Hants. PO7 5EZ, U.K.

BECK, Richard, b. 9 June 1897, Reydarfjordur, Eastern Iceland. University Professor. Education: Grad. State Coll. of Iceland, Reykjavik; M.A., Ph.D., Cornell Univ., USA. Personal details: Son of a farm owner, emigrated to Canada in 1921 & USA in 1922; Res. of Canada since 1967. Positions held: Asst. Prof. of Engl. ffSt. Olaf Coll., Northfield, Minn., 1926-27; Assoc. Prof., ibid, 1927-28; Prof. of Engl. & Hd. of Dept., Thiel Coll., Greenville, Pa., 1928-29; Prof., Scandinavian Langs. & Lit., Univ. of ND, 1929-67. Memberships: Poetry Soc. of Am.; Past VP, Am. Poetry League; World Poetry Soc. Intercontinental; Hon., Midwest Assn. of Chaparral Poets; Soc. of Icelandic Authors; Hon., Icelandic Lit. Soc.; Corres., Icelandic Acad. of Sci.; Pres., Icelandic Nat. League of Am., 1940-46, '57-63; Pres., Soc. for Advancement of Scandinavian Study, 1940-42, '50-52 & '57-58. Published Works incl: Ljodmal (poems in Icelandic), 1929; Icelandic Lyrics (compiler), 1930 & '56; Icelandic Poems & Stories (compiler), 1943 & '68; History of Icelandic Poets 1800-1940, 1950; Vid ljodal indir, 1959; A Sheaf of Verses, 3rd edit., 1966. Contbr. to Minneapolis Tribune; The Winnipeg Free Press; The Free Press Prairie Farmer; The Grand Forks; Herald; Poet Lore; Norge-Canada; The American-Scandinavian Review; Poet; The Lutheran; ND Quarterly; The Icelandic Canadian; Midwest Chaparral; Annual of the Icelandic National League; etc. Honours: D.Phil., Univ. of Iceland, 1961; D.Litt., Univ. of ND, 1969; Kt., 1st Class, Royal Order of St. Olaf, 1939; Kt. Order of Falcon, 1939; Cmdr. Order of

Falcon, 1944; Gold Medal, Iceland, 1944; Danish Liberty Medal, 1946; Medal of Merit, Norsemen's Fed., 1957. Address: 28 Marlborough St., Victoria, BC, Canada.

BECKETT, Samuel (Barclay), b. 13 Apr. 1906. Writer. Education: M.A., Trinity Coll., Dublin, Eire; D.Lit. Positions held: Reader in English, Ecole Normale Superieure, 1928-30; Reader in French, Trinity Coll., Dublin, -1938. Published works: Essays on Joyce, 1929; Essays on Proust, 1931; (poems) More Pricks than Kicks, 1934; Echo's Bones and Other Precipitates, 1935; Murphy, 1938; Molloy, 1951; Malone Meurt, 1952; l'Innommable, 1953; Watt, 1953; Textes pour rien, 1955; Comment c'est, 1960; Imagination morte, imaginez, 1965; Tetes Mortes, 1967; Un Recueil de Poemes, 1968. (Plays) Waiting for Godot, 1952; Fin de Partie suivie de Acte sans parole, 1957; All That Fall, 1957; Krapp's Last Tape, 1960; Happy Days, 1963; Embers, 1959; Words & Music, 1961; Cascando, 1964; Essay: Proust, 1965; No's Knife: Collected Shorter Prose, 1945-66, 1967. Honours, awards: Nobel Prize for Literature, 1969. Address: c/o Grove Press Inc., 80 University Place, New York, NY 10003, U.S.A.

BEDEAU, Rosemary, pen name **SAINT-LO, Michèle.** Writer. Mbrships: Société des gens de lettres; Société des auteurs et compositeurs dramatiques; Société des Auteurs, Compositeurs et Editeurs. Published works: Les mains du temps, poèmes; 11 radio plays; Le coeur fou (novel); Le poids du bonheur (novel); Une liaison (novel); La vie qui bat (novel); Un cri silencieux (novel); La folle du logis (novel); La Majesté nue (novel); Les Inséparables (novel); Le refuge (novel). Contbr. to: Revue de la Table ronde; Les nouvelles littéraires; Réforme. Honours, awards: Award for 'Les mains du temps', Acad. Rhodanienne of Letters; num. other awards for novels inclng. Grand Prix du roman, 1969. Address: 17 Rue de Clignancourt, 75018 Paris, France.

BEECHER, John, b. 22 Jan. 1904. University Professor & Lecturer. Education: B.A., Univ. of Ala., U.S.A.; Harvard Univ.; Univ. of Paris (Sorbonne); M.A., Univ. of Wis.; Univ. of N.C. Positions held: Steel Wkr. & Mettallurgist, U.S. Steel Corp., B'ham, Ala.; Instr., Dartmouth Coll.; Instr., Univ. of Wis., 1927-33; Field Admnstr., var. U.S. Govt. Agencies, 1934-43; Ship's Off., WWII; Ed., Staff Writer, B'ham News & Age-Herald, N.Y. Post, Nat. Inst. of Soc. Rels., San Francisco Chronicle, Ramparts Mag.; on Facs. of Calif. State Univ., San Francisco, Ariz. State Univ., Univ. of Santa Clara, Miles Coll., Ala., St. John's Univ., Minn., North Shore Community Coll. & Assumption Coll., Mass.; Currently, Vis. Scholar, Duke Univ. Published works: And I Will Be Heard, 1940; Here I Stand, 1941; Land of the Free, 1956; Observe the Time, 1956; In Egypt Land, 1960; Phantom City, 1961; Report to the Stockholders, 1962; To Live & Die in Dixie, 1966; Hear the Wind Blow! 1968; Complete Works & Papers issued by Microfilming Corp., 1973; Collected Poems to be publ. 1974. Contbr. to num. mags., jrnls. etc. Honours, awards: L.H.D., Ill. Coll., 1948; Western Books Exhibitions, 1960, 61, 63; Outstanding Academic Book Choice, 1967. Address: P.O. Box 2521, Durham, NC 27705, U.S.A.

BEELER, Janet Nadina, b. 30 Sept. 1937. Teacher. Education: A.A., Stephens Coll., Columbia, Mo., 1957; B.A., Goucher Coll., Balt., Md., 1959; M.A., Cleveland State Univ., Ohio, 1974. Married, 3 children. Member, Cleveland State Univ. Poetry Forum. Published works: How to Walk Water, 1973. Contbr. to: Antaeus; Cardinal; Poet Lore; Perspective; New Orleans Review; Mademoiselle (short story); The O. Henry Awards Best Short Stories, 1960. Honours, awards: Winner, Seventeen Mag. Poetry Contest, 1957; Winner, Atlantic Mag. student supplement, 1958; Winner, Mademoiselle Mag. short story contest, 1959; Winner of CSU Poetry Scholarship Comp., 1973. Address: 1954 Woodward Ave., Cleveland Heights, OH 44118, U.S.A.

BEER, Patricia, b. 4 Nov. 1924. University Lecturer. Education: Exeter Univ.; St. Hugh's Coll., Oxford; B.A. (London), B.Litt. (Oxon). Married to Damien Parsons, Architect. Positions held: Lectr., Engl., Univ. of Padua, Italy, 1946-48; Brit. Inst. in Rome, 1948; Ministero Aeronautica, Rome, 1950; Sr. Lectr., Goldsmiths' Coll., London Univ., 1962-68; Full-time Writer. Published works include: Loss of the Magyar, 1959; The Survivors, 1963; Just Like the Resurrection, 1967; Mrs. Beer's House (autobiog.), 1968. Contbr. to many anthols. Address: 1 Lutton Terr., Flask Walk, London, NW3, UK.

BEGLEY, Carl Edward, b. 4 Nov. 1928. Psychologist. Education: Ph.D., Univ. of Ky., U.S.A., 1961. Memberships: Fndr. & Pres., Dylan Thomas Poetry Club; Poetry Soc. of Jacksonville, Fla. Contbr. to: Psychology (A Jrnl.); Psychological Analysis of Poem, vol. V, 1968; Prose & poetry to Int. Jrnl. of Symbology, vol. II, 1971; Poetry to Voices (A Jrnl. of Am. Acad. of Psychotherapy), vol. IX, 1973. Address: 6240 Brooks Circle S, Jacksonville, FL 32211, U.S.A.

BEHBAHANI, Simin, b. 1927. Teacher; Poetess. Education: Grad., Law, Tehran. m Married Hassan Behbahani. Positions held: Teacher, Tehran High Schls. Associated w. the Iran Daneshvaran Literary Soc. which was founded by her mother, Mrs. Fakhr Adel Khalat-Bari. Published works: (colls. of poems) The Broken Seh-Tar; Foot Step; Chandelier, etc. Address: c/o Press Attache, Imperial Iranian Embassy, 16 Princes Gate, London S.W.7., U.K.

BEHRMAN, Carol H. Freelance Writer; Educator. Education: B.S. in Ed., City Coll. of NY.; Grad. studies at Teachers Coll., Columbia Univ., NY. Positions held: HS Teacher, NYC; Freelance Writer; Teacher, Middle School, Glen Ridge, NJ. Membership: Soc. of Children's Book Writers. Contbr. to: NY Times; Cyclatron; Writer's Notes & Quotes; Pet Life; Orphic Lute; The Muse; Jean's Journal. Awards: Writer's Digest Poetry Contest, 1970; Fair Lawn Arts Festival – Poetry, 1969. Address: 325 Howard Ave., Fair Lawn, NJ 07410, USA.

BEIER, (Horst Ulrich) Ulli, pen name **IJIMERE, Obotunde,** b. 30 Jul. 1922. University Lecturer. Education: London Univ., B.A. (Hons.), 1948. Married to Georgiana Beier (artist); 2 s. Positions held: Tutor, Extra Mural Dept., Univ. of Ibadan, Nigeria, 1951-66; Sen. Lecturer in Lit., Univ. of Papua, New Guinea, 1967-71; Director, Inst. of African Studies, Univ. of Ife, Nigeria, since 1971. Published works: Yoruba Poetry, 1960; African Poetry, 1963; Yoruba Poetry, 1970; Editor, Black Orpheus, 1957-66; Editor, Kovave, 1968-71; Editor, Papua Pocket Poets, 1967-71. Address: Inst. of African Studies, Univ. of Ife, Nigeria.

BEISSEL, Henry Eric, b. 12 Apr. 1929. Professor of English. Education: Univ. of Cologne, Germany; Univ. of London, UK.; Univ. of Toronto, Canada; B.A. (1958), M.A. (1960), both Univ. of Toronto. Twice married; 3 children. Positions held: Teaching Fellow, Univ. of Toronto, 1958-60; Lektor, Univ. of Munich, Germany, 1960-62; Lecturer, Univ. of Alberta, Canada, 1962-64; Visiting Prof., Univ. of the West Indies, Trinidad, 1964-1966; Assoc. Prof., Sir George Williams Univ., Montreal, 1966-. Member: Canadian Authors & Composers Assoc.; League of Canadian Poets; Playwrights Co-op. Pubs.: Witness the Heart, 1963; New Wings for Icarus, 1966; The Price of Morning, 1968; Face on the Dark, 1970; The World is a Rainbow (children's poetry set to music by W. Bottenberg); Inook and the Sun (verse play), 1973; Editor, 1963-69, Edge, a Journal of the Arts, Poetry & Politics. Contrib. to: Edge; West Coast Review; Prism International; Tamarack Review; Quarry; Volume 67; Fiddlehead; Contemporary Literature in Translation; Modern Poetry in Translation; Bim; Stand; Mundus Artium, etc. Also represented in anthols.: Modern Canadian Verse; The Blasted Pine, etc. Recip. Norma Epstein Award for Poetry, 1958; Davidson Creative Writing Award, 1959; Canada Council Awards in 1967, 1969, and 1973. Address: 4158 Oxford Ave., Montreal 260,

Quebec, Montreal.

BELART, Gerard Simon, b. 10 Apr. 1946. Poet; Translator. Education: Acad. of Fine Arts, Rotterdam, The Hague, Antwerp; 3 yrs. private study, Comparative Lit. with the American poet, Harold Norse. Positions held: Ed., Cold Turkey Press, 1967-74. Published works: D/D, 1967; Ouroboros (collected poems 1965-70), 1970; Dronken mirakels en andere offere, selected poems of Charles Bukowski in Dutch transl.; Mensengedichten, by Cesare Vallejo in Dutch transl.; De Verandering, 3 poems by Allen Ginsberg in Dutch transl.; De Duende: theorie en divertissement, by F.G. Lorca in Dutch transl.; Cold Turkey/Klacto Present (a record of 10 Am. poets reading own work). Contbr. to: The San Francisco Earthquake; Aous (Switz.); Klactoveedsedsteen (Germany); Labris (Belgium); Wurm (S. Africa). Recip., Grants from the Rotterdam Arts Fndn., 1971, '72 & '73. Address: 17b Schietbaanlaan, Rotterdam 3003, Holland.

BELITT, Ben, b. 2 May 1911. Professor. Educ: B.A., Univ. of Va., Charlottesville, 1932; M.A., ibid, 1934. Positions held: Served, U.S. Army, 1942-44; Ed.-Scenarist, Combat Film Sec., U.S. Army Signal Corps Photographic Ctr., 1945-46; Asst. Literary Ed., The Nation, N.Y.C., 1937-38; Tchr., 1938-42 and 1947-; Currently Prof. of Lit. and Langs., ibid. Published works: The Five-Fold Mesh, 1938; Wilderness Stair, 1955; Nowhere But Light, 1970; (translations) Four Poems by Rimbaud: The Problem of Translation, 1948; Poet in New York: Federico Garcia Lorca, 1955; Selected Poems of Pablo Neruda, 1961; Selected Poems of Rafael Alberti, 1965; Pablo Neruda: A New Decade, 1969. Contbr. to: Poetry; Virginia Quarterly Review; New Yorker; New Republic; (anthologies) Trial Balances, 1935; This Generation, 1949; Best Poems of 1967: The Borestone Mountain Poetry Awards, 1968. Honours, awards: Shelley Memorial Award in Poetry, 1936; Guggenheim Fellowship, 1946; Oscar Blumenthal Award, 1956; Brandeis Creative Arts Award in Poetry, 1962. Address: Bennington Coll., Bennington, VT 05201, U.S.A.

BELL, Barbara, b. 7 May 1920. Journalist. Positions held: Freelance Writer, 1954-62; Commentator, Radio Stn. WFLR, Dundee, N.Y., 1961 & 62, 65-; Feature Writer, Reporter, Photographer, Ithaca Jrnl., Ithaca, N.Y., 1962-. Published works: Little Tales from Little Schuyler, 1962; Ballad of Bertie, 1966 (poetry); More Tales from Little Schuyler, 1967; To My Grandson & Other Poems, 1969; Glance Backward, 1970. Contbr. to: Midwest Chaparral Poets publs.; Blue River Poetry Mag.; Am. Poetry League Bulletins; The Am. Bard; Housier Challenger; many newspapers, etc. Recip., B.M. Heth Award, 1958. Address: R.D.1, Irelandville Rd., Watkins Glen, NY 14891, U.S.A.

BELL, Birdie Leona White. Housewife & Poet. Married John Wesley Bell. Positions held: Nurse; Kindergarten Teacher; Home Demonstration Agent; Teacher of Elocution, Public Speaking & Program Direction in community. Memberships: Odessa Chap., Poetry Soc. of Tex.; Odessa Chap., Creative Writers of Tex.; Spiritual Chmn., Women's Soc. of Christian Service. Contbr. to: Manna in the Morning, 1943; Praise & Worship Hymnal (lyrics), 1940; Sayer Dailey Headlight; Sayer Sun; Erick Democrat; Capper's Weekly. Honours, awards: Cit. for Poetry, Poetry Soc. of Tex., 1969; Cert. for Musical Compositions, 1969; Recognition, Odessa Fine Arts Assn., 1969. Address: 2703 N. Hancock, Odessa, TX 79760, U.S.A.

BELL, Charles G(reenleaf), b. 31 Oct. 1916. Professor; Writer. Education: B.S., Univ. of Va., U.S.A., 1936; B.A., Oxford Univ., 1938; B.Litt., ibid 1939; M.A., 1966. Married, 5 daughters. Positions held: Instr. & Asst. Prof. of Engl., Iowa State Coll. Ames, Iowa, 1940-45; Asst. Prof. of Engl., Princeton Univ., 1945-49; Asst. Prof. of Humanities, Univ. of Chicago, 1949-56; Tutor, St. John's Coll., Annapolis, Md., 1956-67; Poet in Res., Univ. of Rochester, N.Y., Spring, 1967; Tutor, St. John's Coll., Santa Fe, N.M., 1967-; Guest Prof. to var. o'seas Univs. Published

works incl: Verse: Songs for a New America, 1953, rev. 1966; Delta Return, 1956, rev. 1969; Novels: The Married Land, 1962; The Half Gods, 1968; Short Stories: The Fall of Candida, 1959; The Open Door, 1962. Ency. Brit. Film 'The Spirit of Rome.' Rep. in the following anthols.: New Poems by American Poets, 1953, '57; Modern Love Poems, 1961; Erotic Poetry, 1963. Contbr. to num. periodicals, profl. jrnls. & reviews. Recip. var. scholarships & grants. Address: 1260 Canyon Rd., Santa Fe, NM 87501, U.S.A.

BELL, Ian (Wright), b. 21 Aug. 1913. H.M. Diplomatic Service (retired). Education: Canford School, 1927-30; St. Peter's Hall (now College), Oxford, 1932-35 (Hons. degree in Mod. Langs. (French & German)). Married, Ruth Waterfield (d. of E. H. Waterfield, I.C.S. (decd.)), 3 s. Positions held: H.M. Vice-Consul, Valparaiso, 1938-40, and Montevideo, 1940-45; Foreign Office, 1946-49; First Sec., Addis Ababa, 1949-53; H.M. Consul, Innsbruck, 1953-54; First Sec., Prague, 1954-56; Counsellor, Jedda, 1956; Official Sec., Canberra, 1957-59; H.M. Consul-General, Lyon, 1960-65; H.M. Ambassador, Santo Domingo, 1965-69; H.M. Consul-General, Stuttgart, 1969-73. Founding member and first Hon. Sec. of the English Club, Oxford. Published work: The Scarlet Flower, 1947. Contbr. to: Times Lit. Supp. (sev. reviews of mod. French poetry). Awarded C.B.E. (1964). Address: Liveras House, Broadford, Isle of Skye IV49 9AA, Scotland.

BELL, Martin, pen name, **OATES, Titus,** b. 2 Feb. 1918. University Lecturer. Education: Southampton Univ. Positions held: 1st Lt., Corp.-Acting Sgt., Royal Engrs., 1939-46; Mgr., Army saw mill, Lebanon, 2 years; Tchr., London Shls., 1946-67; Fndr., The Group, London, 1966; Gregory Fellow in Poetry, Leeds Univ., 1967-; Part-time Lectr., Leeds Coll. of Art, 1968-. Published works: Collected Poems, 1938-67, 1967; Letters From Cyprus, 1970. Contbr. to the following anthols.: Penguin Modern Poets 3, 1962; New Poems, PEN Anthol., 1958; Guinness Book of Verse, 1959; A Group Anthol., 1963. Awards. Address: 3 Moorland Ave., Leeds 6, Yorkshire, U.K.

BELL, Marvin, b. 3 Aug. 1937. Teacher at the University of Iowa. Education: B.A., Alfred Univ.; Syracuse Univ.; M.A., Univ. of Chgo.; M.F.A., Univ. of Iowa. Positions held: Ed. & Publisher, Statements, 1959-64; Poetry Ed., The North American Review, 1964-69; Poetry Ed., The Iowa Review, 1969-. Published works: Poems for Nathan & Saul (pamphlet), 1966; Things We Dreamt We Died for, 1966; A Probable Volume of Dreams, 1969; Woo Havoc (Pamphlet), 1971; The Escape Into You (probable title), pending publication, 1971. Contbr. to: Poetry; The New Yorker; The Nation; New American Review; Stand; The Virginian Quarterly Review; Tri-Quarterly; Northwest Review; Field; Harper's Bazaar; The North American Review; Choice; Chicago Review; The Carleton Miscellany, etc. Awards: Lamont Poetry Award, The Acad. of Am. Poets, 1969; Bess Hokin Award, Poetry Mag., 1969; 2nd Prize, Emily Clark Balch Awards, The Virginian Quarterly Review, 1969. Address: Writers Workshop: EPB, Univ. of Iowa, Iowa City, Iowa 52240, USA.

BELL, Vera, b. 16 June 1906. Retired Civil Servant; Writer. Education: Columbia Univ. Schl. of Lib. Serv., N.Y.C., U.S.A.; Dip. in Archaeol., London Univ., U.K. Married, 2 sons, 1 daughter. Positions held: Clerical Asst., Govt. of Jamaica; Exec. Officer, The Water Commn., Jamaica; Ed., The Welfare Reporter, Jamaica Social Welfare Commn. Member, Prehistoric Soc., London. Author, Ogog - Epic Poem, 1971. Contbr. to: Focus, Jamaica (anthol.), 1948; Independence Anthology of Jamaica Literature, 1962; New Ships - an Anthology of West Indian Poems, 1971; Life Lines - One hundred poems for Jr. Sec. Schls. (Anthol.), 1972; World Union Mag., India; The Beacon. Address: The Old Rectory, Halkyn, Flintshire, U.K.

BELLAMY, Virginia (Woods) (Mrs. Francis R.

Bellamy), pen names, HALL, Ibby; MACKALL, Virginia Woods, b. 5 April 1890. Writer. Education: Friends Acad.; Girls Latin School, Baltimore, Maryland; Peabody Conservatory, Baltimore, Maryland. Positions held: numerous freelance editorial, songwriting, also musical publicity, musical critic of records for "The Musician", etc. Published works: Book of Songs; The Never-Lonely Child Composer: Carl Engle; (operettas): The Fairy Rose; The Runaway Song. Contbr. to: (anthols.) Braithwaite, 1923, Christopher Morley's "The Bowling Green", 1924; Oliver Hereford's "Poems from Life", 1923; New Yorker, 1935; (newspapers, journals): Sunday School Times; Measure; Conning Tower – NY Tribune; NY Eve. Post; Womans Home Companion; Ladies Home Journal; Life; The Nation; Sat. Review; New Republic; New Yorker; Commonweal; CS Monitor; Scribner's Commentator, etc. Awards: Pen & Brush (sev. 1sts, between 1938-51); sev. prizes from Fellowship of Maine Poets, 1956-1973. Address: Box 281, (Water Street), Castine, ME 04421, USA.

BELLERBY, Frances. Poet. Published works: Plash Mill, poems, 1946; The Blightening Cloud & Other Poems, 1949; The Stone Angel & The Stone Man, poems, 1958; The Stuttering Water & Other Poems, 1970; Selected Poems, Ed. by Charles Causley, 1970; The First-Known & Other Poems, 1974. Contbr. to: John o'London's; Country Life; Orion; Observer; The Spectator; West Country Mag.; The Wind & The Rain; The Listener; Cornish Review; Outposts; Public Opinion; Poetry & Poverty; The New Statesman; New Soundings (Third prog., BBC); London Mag.; Truth; The Poetry Review; Edward Blishen's Miscellany 3, etc.

BELLMAN, Samuel I(rving), b. 28 Sept. 1926. University Professor. Education: B.A., Univ. of Texas, Austin, 1947; M.A., Wayne Univ., Detroit, Mich., 1951; Ph.D., Ohio State Univ., Columbus, 1955. Positions held: Instr., Fresno (Calif.) State Coll., 1955-57; Asst. Prof. Calif. State Polytechnic Coll., San Luis Obispo, 1957-59; Asst. Prof. to Full Prof., Calif. State Polytechnic Univ., Pomona, 1959 to present; Visiting Prof., Univ. of So. Calif., Summer, 1968. Contrib. to: Descant; Ill. Qtly.; Lake Superior Review; Improving College & Univ. Instruction; CEA Critic; Calif. English Journal; Datamation; Golden Quill Anthol.; Internat. Who's Who in Poetry Anthol.; Satire News-letter; Yearbook of Mod. Poetry; The Muse; Haiku Highlights; etc., etc. Address: Dept. of Engl. and Modern Langs., Calif. State Polytechnic Univ., Pomona, Calif. 91768, USA.

BELOOF, Robert Lawrence, b. 30 Dec. 1923. Professor. Educ: M.A., Northwestern Univ., Evanston; Ph.D., ibid; M.A., Middlebury Coll. Married to Ruth LaBarre; four children. Positions held: Former Chmn., Dept. of Rhetoric, Univ. of Calif.; Prof. of Rhetoric, ibid, current position. Published works: The One-Eyed Gunner and Other Portraits, 1956; Ed., The Performing Voice in Literature, 1966. Honours, awards: Fund for the Advancement of Education Fellowship, 1951; Institute of Fine Arts Fellowships, Univ. of Calif., 1963-64 & 1968-69. Address: Dept. of Rhetoric, Univ. of Calif., Berkeley, CA 94720, USA.

BENEDICT, Rex, b. 27 June 1920. Writer. Education: B.A., NW State Univ., Alva, Okla. Positions held incl: Lt., USN, Published works: In The Green-Grass Time, 1969; Moonwash, 1969; Nights in the Gardens of Glebe, 1969; Epitaph for a Lady, 1970; Haloes for Heroes, 1971. Contbr. to Italia Domani; Glebe. Address: 23 West 88th St., New York, NY 10024, USA.

BENEDIKT, Michael, b. 26 May 1937, NY. Editor; Writer. Education: B.A., NY Univ., 1957; M.A., Colombia Univ., 1961. Positions held: Assoc. Ed., Horizon Press, 1959-61; Assoc. Ed., Art News, 1963–; NY Corres., Art International, 1965-67; Guggenheim Fellowship in Poetry, 1968; Fac., Bennington Coll. 1968-69; Fac., Sarah Lawrence Coll., 1969–. Published works: The Body, 1968; Sky, 1970; Mole Notes, 1971. Ed. & Translator of: Modern French

Theatre: The Avant-Garde, Dada & Surrealism, 1964 & •'66; Ring Around the World: Selected Poems of Jean L'Anselme, 1967, UK edit., 1967; Post-War German Theatre, 1966, UK edit, 1968; Modern Spanish Theatre, 1968; Theatre Experiment, 1967; Twenty-Two Poems of Robert Desnos, 1971; Surrealism, Prose & Poetry, 1972. Contbr. to: The Modern Poets: An American British Selection; The Major Young Poets; Contemporary American Poetry; The Contemporary American Poets: 1940 & After; Another Poetry Anthology; American Literary Anthology III & IV; Expanded Poetry; The Young American Poets; Medieval Age; The Grand Eccentrics; The New Music; Minimal Art; Poetry; Partisan Review; New American Review; Paris Review; Quarterly Review of Literature; Chelsea; Choice; Transatlantic Review; The Sixties; Lillabulero; Iowa Review; Stand; The Kenyon Review; Tri-Quarterly Sumac; Ambit; The London Magazine. Honours & Awards: Hokin Award for Poetry, 1968; Judge, Lamont Contest, Acad. of Am. Poets, 1970-72. Address: 315 W. 98th St., New York, NY 10025, USA.

BENET, Laura, b. June 1884. Author. Positions held: Settlement Wkr., Spring St. Settlement, N.Y.C.; Asst., Book Sect., N.Y. Sun; Substitute Book Reviewer, N.Y. Times. Memberships: Poetry Soc. of Am.; Hon. Mbr., Pen & Brush Club; Craftsman; Cleaman Poets. Published works: Fairy Bread, 1920; Goods & Chattels, 1930; Noah's Dave, 1922; The Boy, Shelley; The Hidden Valley; Enchanting Tennyson; Young Edgar Allan Poe; Washington Irving; Emily Dickinson; Coleridge; Thackeray. Contbr. to: N.Y. Herald Tribune; N.Y. Times; Voices; Famous Poets Young People; Famous Essayists; Story Tellers; New England Poets; Famous Am. Humorists. Recip. Hon.Litt.D., 1969. Address: Hotel van Rensselaer, 17th E. 11th St., N.Y., NY 10003, U.S.A.

BENISH, (Sister) Janet Claughton, pen name **JANET, Sister, CC,** b. 20 May 1921. Member, Contemplatives of the Cross, part of the Good Sheperd Congregation, 1956–. Education: Extension Courses, Univ. of Wash. & Seattle Univ. Positions held: Sec.; Acct.; Tchr. of office machines, dictaphone, typing, comptometer, etc. Co-author with Maggi Nolan of Angels' Advocates, 1968. Contbr. to: Oregon Jrnl.; Lancaster Sunday News; Spirit; Contemplative Review; Portland Oregonian; Spokane, Inland Register; The Bible Today; Inland Catholic Register. Address: West 3804 Indian Trail Rd., Spokane, Wash. 99208, USA.

BENJAMIN, Grace Lyon (Mrs.), born 18th January 1894. Housewife, Poet and Artist. Education: Oberlin Coll.; New Haven Normal School, 1916. Memberships: Nat. League Am. Pen Women; Copley Soc. of Artists; South Shore Art Assoc.; N.H. Poetry Soc.; Mass Poetry Soc.; Am. Poetry League. Publications: Invitation to New England, 1963. Contbr. to: Boston Herald Trader; Christian Science Monitor; Am. Home Mag.; Gourmet; Youth Instr.; Am. Bard; From Sea to Sea in Song (anthol.); Seydell Quarterly; Hartford Times; Pacific Anthol., '66; Denver Post; Ohio Motorist, etc. Exhibitions: Copley Galls; Boston Art Festival, 1953; 2nd Prize, Oils, Pen Women Nat. Contest; 3 one-man shows; exhib. in many group shows. Honours: 1st Prize, Mass. State Poetry Soc. Address: 16 Hilldale Rd., S. Weymouth, Mass. 02190, U.S.A.

BENNETT, Gertrude Ryder, b. Brooklyn, NY. Writer; Author. Education: B.S., NY Univ.; M.A., Columbia Univ. Married, Rev. Frank Curtis Williams. Memberships: Poetry Soc. of America (Executive Bd.); Vice Pres., Nat. League of American Pen Women; Long Island Hist. Soc.; Women Poets; Brooklyn Poetry Circle; Pa. Poetry Soc.; W. Va. Poetry Soc. Published works: Etched in Words; The Harvesters, 1967; Ballads of Colonial Days, 1972. Contbr. to leading mags. Honours, Awards: Arthur Davison Ficke Award, Poetry Soc. Am., 1960, '63; Carl Sandburg Award, NC Poetry Soc.; Blanch Whiting Keysner Mem. Award, Pa. Poetry Soc., 1967; Evans Spencer Wall Mem. Contest, Fed. of State, Poetry Socs., 1966; Poetry Fellowships of Me., 1966; Norfolk

Prize, Poetry Soc. Va.; 1st Prize, Poet's Study Club of Terre Haute Contest, 1970; 2nd Prize, 1970 & 1st Prize, 1971, Annual Anne Lloyd Mem. Award, Women Poets; 2nd Prize, Ruth Mason Rice Mem. Contest, 1970; 1st Prize, Lady Graham Contest, Nat. League of Am. Pen Women, 1970; 2nd Prize, Henry W. Shoemaker Mem. Award, Pa. Poetry Soc., 1970; 3rd Prize, Edna Shoemaker Award, 1971; 1st Prize, Blanche Whiting Keysner Mem. Award & 1st Prize, Edna Groff Diehl Award, Pa. Poetry Soc., 1971. Address: 1669 E. 22 St., Brooklyn, NY 11229, USA.

BENNETT, John Frederic, b. 20 Mar. 1920. Professor of English. Education: B.A., Oberlin Coll., 1947; M.A., Univ. of Wis., 1950; Ph.D., ibid, 1956. Married (2nd) Elizabeth Jones, 2 daughters. Positions held: Tchng. Asst., Univ. of Wis., 1948-53; Instr., Engl., Ind. Univ., 1953-58; Asst. Prof., Beloit Coll., 1958-59; Assoc. Prof., Rockford Coll., 1959-62; Prof., ibid, 1962-68; Chmn., Engl. Dept., 1960-68; Prof. of Engl., St. Norbert Coll., 1968-70; Bernard H. Pennings Disting. Prof. of Engl., 1970-. Member, Melville Soc. Published works: Once We Thought: An Anthol. of Oberlin Verse (Ed.), 1941; The Zoo Manuscript, 1968; Griefs & Exultations, 1970; The Struck Leviathan/Poems on Moby Dick, 1970; Knights & Squires/More Poems on Moby Dick, 1972; Dinner in the Union Lunch (in Ms.) Contbr. to var. reviews, jrnls., anthols. Recip. var. hons. & awards inclng: Midland Poetry Award, 1971. Address: 526 Karen Lane, Green Bay, WI 54301, U.S.A.

BENNETT, Pamela Ann, b. 19 Jan. 1943. Consultant Research Astrologer. Education: Gidea Park School, Romford, Essex; Musgrave School, Lowfell, Co. Durham; Withington Girls' School, Manchester; High Wycombe HS, Bucks.; Central School of Speech and Drama, London; External Course of the Faculty of Astrological Studies (cert. and dip., D.F. Astrol. S., 1973). Married, Robert Frederick Bennett; 2 s. Other occupation: antique print colourist. Positions held: 1973, Sec. to the Council of the Astrological Assoc. of G.B.; Asst. Tutor, Mayo School of Astrology; Tutor to Classes, Kent Group, Astrological Assoc.; 1974, Editor of "Transit", Ast. Assoc. Newsletter. Memberships: Poets of Deal (Chairman), etc. Published work: Triad (with Clinton Voist and Anthony R. Martin), 1972. Contbr. to: Pink Peace; Viewpoints; Centre 17; also to various astrological publications. Address: 47 Sydney Rd., Walmer, Deal, Kent CT14 9JW, UK.

BENNETT, Paul Lewis, b. 10 Jan. 1921. Professor of English. Education: B.A., Ohio Univ., Athens, 1942; M.A., Harvard Univ., 1947. Married to Martha Jeanne Leonhart, 1941, 2 s. Positions held: Ensign-Lt., USNR, 1942-45; Instr., Samuel Adams Schl. of Soc. Studies, Boston, 1945-46; Instr. in Engl., Univ. of Me., 1946-47; Instr.-Prof., Denison Univ., 1947-. Memberships: Franco-Calliopean Lit. Soc.; Exec. Comm., Ohioana Poetry Soc. Contbr. to the following jrnls. & mags: Saturday Evening Post; Ladies' Home Journal; English Journal; Beloit Poetry Journal; The Nation; College English; Arlington Quarterly; Georgia Review; Colorado Quarterly; Quixote; American Weave; Nimrod. Apptd. Creative Writing Fellow, 1973-74, Nat. Endowment for the Arts. Address: 1281 Burg St., Granville, Ohio 43023, USA.

BENNETT, Raine Edward, b. 23 Oct. 1891. Executive Director, Islands Research Foundation. Education: Military Acads.; Univ. of Santa Clara; Hastings Coll. of Law; Stanford Univ. Positions held: Founded, Islands Research Fndn., 1944; currently Exec. Dir., ibid, & has offices in N.Y.C. & Wash. D.C. He has lectured extensively on islandography; Ed., Wasp, San Francisco's oldest weekly. Memberships: Poetry Soc. of Am.; Overseas Press Club of America; The Lambs; Fndr., Am. Arts Fndn.; Commentator, Nat. Broadcasting Co. Published works: Vagrant Vanities, 1970; The Talisman, drama, Forest Theatre Soc., Carmel, Calif., 1917 & Univ. of Calif., 1919; South Sea Idol, Columbia Theatre, San Francisco, 1916. Contbr. to: Islandography: A New Study, Oceans Mag., 1971;

The Madonna of Passion Isle, Am. weekly, 1962; The Green Gown, Catholic mag., 1960; The Wasp; Don Passé (George Sterling), The Lit. Review, 1971-72; Radio Ed., L.A. Evening Express, 1940-42. Address: Prospect Tower, Tudor City, N.Y., NY 10017, U.S.A.

BENNETT, Sandra, pen name **BENNETT, Stefanie,** b. 6 May 1945. Writer. Positions held: Australian Rep., Caveman Press, New Zealand; Editl. Rdr., The Saturday Club Book of Poetry Qtly. Memberships: Jt. Fndr., North Qld. Adult Educ. Ctr. Qtly. 'In Print'; The Poetry Soc. of Australia. Published works: Blackbirds of Superstition (32 page selection of poetry & graphics), 1972; Madam Blackboots, 1974. Contbr. to: Living Daylights; The Australian; Nation Review; Refractory Girl; Westerly; Australian Univ. Qtly.; Overland; Sat. Club Book of Poetry; Makar; Expression; Vox; Outback Press Anthol., etc. Has also had topical articles published. Honours, awards: Runner-up, The Vera A. Bladen Poetry Award, 1971-72; Poem of the Year Award, Adult Educ. Ctr. Qtly., N. Qld., 1973. Address: 26 Breillat St., Annandale, Sydney 2038, N.S.W., Australia.

BENNETT-COVERLEY, Simone Louise, pen name **BENNETT, Louise,** b. 7 Sept. 1919. Kingston, Jamaica. Writer; Broadcaster. Education: St. Simons Coll., Jamaica; Excelsior Coll.; Sociol., Friends Coll.; Royal Acad. of Dramatic Art, London, UK. Married to Eric Coverley, Draughtsman & Impresario. Positions held: Weekly Columnist, The Daily Gleaner, Jamaica, 1940-; Res. Artiste, Caribbean Carnival, BBC, London, UK, 1945-46; Drama Tchr., Excelsior Coll., 1947-49; Res. Artiste & Compere, West Indies Sect., BBC, Lonodn, 1950-55; Script Writer & Artiste, TV, Radio & Theatre, Jamaica, & Little Theatre Movement, ibid. Member of Jamaica PEN. Published works: Verses in Jamaican Dialect, 1942; Dialect Verses, 1943; Lulu Say, Dialect Verses with Glossary, 1952; Folk Stories & Verses, with Glossary, 1952; Folk Stories & Verses, 1957; Laugh with Louise, 1961; Jamaica Labrish, 1966. Contbr. to: Sunday Gleaner; Independence Anthology of Jamaica; Breaklight; Bite In. Awards: MBE, for work in Jamaica Lit. & Theatre, 1960; Musgrave Silver Medal, Inst. of Jamaica, 1965. Address: Enfield House, Gordon Town, Jamaica, West Indies.

BENTLEY, Beth Rita, b. 7 Oct. 1928. Writer; Teacher. Education: B.A., Univ. of Minn.; M.A., Univ. of Mich. Married Nelson Bentley, 2 children. Positions held: Instr., Bellevue Coll., Engl. Dept. Memberships: Acad. of Am. Poets; Dir., Pacific N.W. Poets Reading series. Published works: Phone Calls From the Dead, 1971; Field of Snow, 1973. Contbr. to: Sewanee Review; New Yorker; Atlantic; Nation; Sat. Review; Paris Review; Lit. Review; Mass. Review; N.Y. Qtly.; Poetry North West; Jeopardy; Prairie Schooner; Choice; World Over; Audience; Ten Seattle Poets (anthol.); Poets Dozen (anthol.); Borestone Mt. Best Poems, 1966 & 67 (anthol.); Love Poems (anthol.) & others. Honours, awards: N.W. Booksellers Award, 1971; Gov's Award, 1971. Address: 8762 25th Pl. N.E., Seattle, WA 98115, U.S.A.

BENTON, Patricia, b. 20 Mar. 1907. Writer & Musician. Education: Columbia Univ.; Westchester Conservatory of Music. Positions held: Cons. in Poetry, Dept. of Pub. Instrn., Ariz.; Organizer & Dir., Ariz. Poetry Workshop. Memberships: Fndr. Pres., Ariz. Chap., Nat. Soc. of Arts & Letters; Fndr. Pres., Empire State Chap., ibid.; Past Pres., Phoenix Chap., Nat. League Am. Pen Women; Past. Pres., NYC Br., ibid.; Vice-Pres., Composers, Authors, Artists of Am.; Ariz. State Pres., ibid., 1968-; Vice-Pres., Mark Twain Soc. of NY; State Dir., Nat. Poetry Day of Ariz., 1955-59; State Dir., Nat. Poetry Day, NY State, 1960-; NY Woman's Press Club; Nat. Assoc. Composers & Conductors; Poetry Soc. of Am.; Dramatists Guild; Authors Guild; Internat. Platform Assoc.; Nat. Arts Council; Creative Club of NY; Cath. Poetry Soc.; Hon. Vice-Pres., Centro Studi e Scambi Internazionali (Italy); Hon. Internat. Mbr., Beta Sigma Phi; Fellow, Royal Soc. of Arts, London. Published works: Of the

Heart's Own Telling, 1966; Manhattan Mosaic, 1964; Love Has Many Faces, 1965; A Friend is For Always, 1963; Gift of Christmas, 1964; Love is– 1963; Barkie the Dog, 1964; Magic of Christmas, 1965; Merry Go Sounds at the Zoo, 1961; Arizona the Turquoise Land, 1958; Cradle of the Sun, 1956; Medallion Southwest, 1954; The Young Corn Rises, 1953; Signatures in the Sand, 1952; The Miracle of Roses (play); Star Child Series, 12 books, 1970. Contbr. to: NY Times; Christian Science Monitor; Spirit; Chatelaine; Good Housekeeping; Ariz. Highways; The Arizonian. Honours, Awards: Complete perm. collection established at Boston Univ., 1965; The Whispering Earth 1 of 50 Books of the Year, 1950; Ariz., The Turquoise Land nominated for Pulitzer Prize in Letters, 1960; Poet of the Year, NY Woman's Press Club, 1960-62. Address: 7849 E. Glen Rosa, Scottsdale, Ariz. 85251, USA, or c/o Frederick Fell, Publisher, 386 Park Ave. South, New York, NY 10016, USA.

BERANOVA, Jana, b. 2 May 1932. Poet; Actress. Education: Inst., Prague, Czechoslovakia; Cambridge Univ. Schl. Cert., U.K.; Doct., Econs., Univ. of Rotterdam, Holland. Positions held: w. Min. of Interior, The Hague, –1973; Reader of poetry to school children; Presenter of poems on Stage; Dramatiser of books on stage. Memberships: Lit. Workshop, Rotterdam Arts Fndn.; Comm., Artists Club, Rotterdam. Published works: gramophone record with poetry, 1971; mag. w. translated poems of Miroslav Holub, 1971; Jantje zag eens mensen hangen (book w. poems), 1972; book of poems in preparation; dramatization of 'The Book I' by Bert Schierbeek, for the stage, 1973; var. radio & TV progs. Contbr. to: De Havenloods; Rotterdams Parool; Vrije Volk; Algemeen Dagblad; Avenue Literair; Vrij Nederland; book of poetry publ. by Rotterdam Art Fndn., 1971; (poetry) Je zult van vuur zijn, 1973; photobook of Rotterdam, introduced by one of her poems, 1973; translations of poems by Miroslav Holub & Vasko Popa in book to be publ. 1974. Participant, Poetry Int. Festival, Rotterdam, 1973. Address: Joost Banckertsplaats 31, Rotterdam, The Netherlands.

BERG, Helen Christina, pen name **BERG, Nina Stevenson,** b. 26 Jan. 1911. Housewife. Married, 4 children. Memberships: Sask. Poetry Soc.; Vancouver Poetry Soc. Published works: (booklet) Rhymes & Reasons, 1972. Contbr. to: Family Herald Mag.; Free Press (Winnipeg); Western Producer (Saskatoon, Sask.); Vancouver Sun; Vancouver Province. Honours, awards: 2nd prize, Vancouver Sun Contest, 1956; 1st prize, Sask. Poetry Soc., 1958; 2nd prize, Van. Poetry Soc., 1971. Address: R.R.1, Gould Ave., Summerland, B.C., Canada VOH 1ZO.

BERG, Maryleona (Ecklin), b. 19 May 1922. Corsetiere. Education: HS, night school, home study, Grad., Monica Boyce course in Versification, Nat. School of Poetry, also private lessons. Married, Lloyd H. Berg; 3 s. Positions held: Clerk; Waitress; Bookkeeper; during WWII rolled rocket powder; Writer of feature article (currently) for Amateur Writer's Journal, publish Rambling and Haiku Happenings for United Amateur Press; also edited Ruddy Haiku Hunt, an anthol. for U.A.P. Memberships: United Amateur Press-Mailer, Convention Welcoming Committee; Iowa Poetry Day Assoc., membership committee; Iowa Poetry Assoc., "reader", Midwest Chaparral, Membership Committee, Southwest Iowa Writers, one of the founders, Assoc. for Poetry Therapy, Poet's Study Club of Terre Haute, Friendship Ferry Canada, Writer's Correspondence Club, Speak Out Literary Assoc., Japan Soc. (Haiku) NYC., Iowa Rep. of Western World Haiku Soc. Contbr. to: Scimitar & Song; Cyclo-Flame; Lyrical Iowa; Kansas Kernels; Inky Trails; Insight; New Dimensions; Jean's Journal; Poet's Nook; N. Am. Mentor; Hyacinths & Biscuits; Janus-SCTH; Quintessence; Fellowship in Prayer; Special Song; Robbins Song; Tweed, Australia; Creativity Newsletter; Bardic Echoes; The Archer; Major Poets; Land 'O Lakes Mirror; Japan Forum; Tweed; Haiku Highlights; Haiku Mag.; Haiku West;

Modern Haiku; Weekly Jrnl., Whittier, Calif.; Marshalltown Times-Republican; Atlantic Farm Monthly; Omaha World-Herald; Des Moines Register; Harlan Iowa News-Advertizer; Journal-Enquirer (Grayson, Ky.); Olive Hill Times (Ky.); Cumberland Enterprise. Awards: Jean's Journal, 1st, Light Verse, May, 1972; Hon. Mention, Iowa Poetry Day Assoc., 1972, 1973; 4th Sonnet, Creativity Newsletter, 1973; 1st, Light Verse, Marshalltown Times-Republican; 1st, Cinquain, Bardic Echoes, 1973; Book, Dragonfly, 1973; Poem on Lyndon Baines Johnson in The Johnson Library, Texas; Poet's file, Iowa State Traveling Library; 1st, Hebrew Poetry, Speak Out Literary Assn., 1973. Address: Rt. 2, Wiota, IA 50274, USA.

BERG, Stephen, b. 2 Aug. 1934. Teacher. Educ: Univs. of Pa., Boston, Ind.; B.A., Univ. of Iowa, 1959. Married; Two daughters. Positions held: Former Instr., Engl., Temple Univ., Phila.; Currently Tchr., Phila. Coll. of Art. Published works: Berg-Goodman-Mezey, 1957; Bearing Weapons, 1963; Ed. (w. R. Mezey), Naked Poetry: Recent American Poetry in Open Forms, 1969. Contbr. to: Poetry; New Yorker; North American Review; Tri-Quarterly; Naked Poetry (anthology), 1969.

BERG, Viola Jacobson, b. 29 Sept. 1918. Secretary. Education: Grad., Union Grove HS, Wis.; Continuation School, Racine, Wis.; Courses, Nassau County Extension, State Univ. of NY; 2 courses by private tutor in the writing of poetry. Married to Howard Berg; 4 children. Positions held: Sec., Marshall Field & Co., Zion, Ill.; Bookkeeper, Hamilton-Beach, Inc., Racine, Wis.; Sec. to the Pres. & Treas., Rainfair, Racine, Wis.; Sec. and Asst. Librarian, L.I. Lutheran HS, Brookville, NY, also teacher of poetry writing at L.I. HS for 3 semesters; currently, Sec. to the Principal of the L.I. Christian Schools. Memberships: L.I. Writers (Vice-Pres., 1970-71), also member of many nat., state, and internat. socs. Published works: The Heart of Things, 1968; Wings of Good Tidings, 1969; Move That Mountain, 1969; Harvest of the Heart, 1969; Pathways for the Poet (in course of publication), etc. Contbr. to many anthols., newspapers, journals. Recip. of numerous awards, citations, certificates, etc. Address: 5 Roosevelt Av., Malverne, NY 11565, USA.

BERGE, Carol. Writer (Novelist). Positions held: Ed., Center Mag. for expmtl. prose; Novelist & short story writer. Memberships: Authors League & Guild; PEN; Bd. of Dirs., Cosmep, 1971-73. Published works: Lumina, 1963; The Vulnerable Island, 1964; Poems Made of Skin, 1968; Circles, As In the Eye, 1969; The Chambers, 1969; An American Romance, 1969; The Unfolding, 1969; Poems About Women: From a Soft Angle, 1971; A Couple Called Moebius (stories); Acts of Love: An American Novel, 1973. Contbr. to: The Nation; Origin; Beloit Poetry Jrnl.; East Village Other; Village Voice; Poetry (Chicago); Yale Lit. Mag.; Beatitude East; For Now; Poetmeat, etc. Honours, awards: CCLM Comms., 1971, '73; MacDowell Colony Fellowship, residence, 1971, '73; CENTER Mag. grants for publication, CCLM – NY State Coun. on the Arts, 1971, 72, 73; Fulbright Alternate, 1974. Address: Box 698, Woodstock, NY 12498, U.S.A.

BERGE, Hans C. ten, b. 24 Dec. 1938. Writer/Poet. Memberships: Soc. of Dutch Lit., Leyden; Writers' Union. Published works: Poolsneeuw (poetry), 1964; Swartkrans (poetry), 1966; Personages (poetry), 1967; Canaletto & Other Stories, 1969; Gedichten (poems), 1969; Yugao, A Tale & 5 Noh-plays (intro., transl. & commentaries on the plays), 1969; Translation of the Izu Dancer by Yasunari Kawabata, 1969; 15 Cantos of Ezra Pound (transl. & commentaries), 1970; Een geval van verbeelding (novel), 1970; Hommage aan de Nahua (sacred songs of the Nahua-Indians from Ancient Mexico), 1971; Poëzie van de Azteken (intro., transl. & commentaries), 1972; De witte sjamaan (poetry), 1973. De dood is de jager, 1974. Contbr. to lit. reviews & weeklies. Fndr. & Ed., lit. qtly., Raster, 1967-73. Honours, awards: Van der Hoogt Prize, Soc. of Dutch Lit., 1968; Prose-Prize of the City of

Amsterdam, 1971; Special prize by the Jan Campert Fndn. of the City of The Hague, 1972. Address: c/o Uitgeverij De Bezige Bij, Van Miereveldstraat 1, Amsterdam Z, The Netherlands.

BERGFELD, Annabelle Wagner, b. 30 Aug. 1903. Retired Teacher. Education: Edinboro State Tchrs. Coll., Pa.; M.A., B.A., Rutgers Univ., New Brunswick, NJ. Positions held: Tchr., Elementary Schls., Pa., NY, NJ. Memberships: NJ, Pa., Ariz. Poetry Socs.; Int. Platform Assn. Contbr. to: Humanist; Cyclo-Flame; Avalon Anthol.; Scimitar & Song; Dalhousie Review; New York Times; Herald Tribune; Spirit; Catalyst; Vision; Georgia Magazine; Long Island Magazine; American Weave; Garret; Chipmunk; Sign; Baltimore Scene; Messenger; Cardinal; New Athenaeum, etc. Awards: Va. Poetry Soc., 1971; Nat. Fed. State Poetry Socs., 1971, etc. Address: 563 Francis Rd., Bricktown, NJ 08723, USA.

BERKLEY, Constance Elaine Gresham, b. 12 Nov. 1931. Lecturer. Education: Howard Univ.; B.A., Columbia Univ., 1971; M.A., ibid, 1972; currently working on Doctorate, N.Y. Univ. Positions held: Lectr. in Black Studies, Fordham Univ., p/t 1972; Lectr. in Black Studies, Vassar Coll., p/t 1972-73; Lectr., ibid, two thirds time, 1973–. Memberships: N.Y. Coun. of the Arts (Lectr. under its aegis); Harlem Writers' Guild, 1962–; Negro Ensemble Dramatists Workshop, 1970–. Published works: Night Comes Softly, Ed., Nikki Giovanni, 1970; GlowChild, Ed., Ruby Dee, 1972. Contbr. to: People in Poetry, 1969; Poems by Blacks, Vol. I, 1971 & Vol. II, 1972; Penumbra; Black Sun; Freedomways Mag.; New World Review; The Fiddlehead; Roots; Black Collegian; Sane Newsletters; Lefferts Manor Civic Assn. Newsletter; Am. Dialog; var. Xmas cards. Honours, awards: Woodstock, poetry fest. under aegis of N.Y. State Coun. of the Arts, summer 1972. Address: 54 Glasco Turnpike, Woodstock. NY 12498, U.S.A.

BERKSON, Bill, b. 30 Aug. 1939. Poet. Education: Brown Univ.; Columbia Univ.; New Schl. of Soc. Rsch. Positions held: Edit. work, Artnews; Mus. of Mod. Art, NY; WNDT-TV; Tchr., New Schl. Soc. Rsch. & Yale Univ.; Ed., Best & Company, 1970; Editor, Big Sky Mag. and Big Sky Books, 1972–. Published works: Saturday Night: Poems 1960-61, 1961; Shining Leaves, 1968; Terrace Fence, 1972; 2 Serious Poems & 1 Other (w. Larry Fagin), 1972; Untitled (Ants), 1973; The Hymns of St. Bridget (w. Frank O'Hara), 1973; Recent Visitors, 1973; Blue Is The Hero, 1974. Contbr. to: The World; Paris Review; Poetry; Locus Solus; Sugar Mountain; Art in America; On the Mesa; Adventures in Poetry; The Ant's Forefoot; Angel Hair; Mercure de France, etc. Awards & Honours: Dylan Thomas Mem. Award, 1959; Poets Fndn. Grant, 1968. Address: Box 272, Bolinas, Calif. 94924, USA.

BERLIND, Bruce (Peter), b. 17 July 1926. University Professor. Education: Grad., The Mercersburg Acad., Pa., 1943; A.B., Princeton Univ., 1947; M.A., The Johns Hopkins Univ., 1950; Ph.D., ibid, 1958. Married 1) Doris Lidz, div., 2) Mary Dirlam, 5 children. Positions held: Jr. Instr. of Engl., The Johns Hopkins Univ., 1948-50, '52-54; Instr. of Engl., Colgate Univ., 1954-58; Asst. Prof., 1958-63; Assoc. Prof., 1963-66; Prof., 1966–; Chmn. of the Dept., 1969-72; Vis. Assoc. Prof. & Poet-in-Res., Univ. of Rochester, 1966. Member, Poetry Soc. of Am. Published works: Three Larks for a Loony, 1957; Ways of Happening, 1959; Companion Pieces, 1971. Contbr. to: The Beloit Poetry Jrnl.; Chicago Review; Epoch; The Grecourt Review; The Hopkins Review; Poetry (Chicago); The N.Y. Herald Tribune; Sage; Mass. Review; Blue Grass; Qtly. Review of Lit.; Transatlantic Review; Vortex, etc. Recip. Grants from Lucius N. Littauer Fndn., 1958, '59 & Colgate Univ. Rsch. Coun., 1970. Address: Box 237, Hamilton, NY 13346, U.S.A.

BERNARD, Oliver Owen, b. 6 Dec. 1925. Teacher. Education: Univ. of London Goldsmiths' Coll., 1950-53; Ctrl. Schl. of Speech & Drama, 1970-71. Positions held: Advt. Copy Writer, 1958-64; Tchr. in var. Grammar & Comprehensive Schls. in Suffolk, 1964–; Drama tchng. & play prodn., 1967–. Member, London Poetry Secretariat, 1972–. Published works: Country Matters & Other Poems, 1960; Rimbaud Collected Poems (transl., ed., intro.), 1962; Appollinaire Selection (transl., ed., intro.), 1965. Contbr. to: Poetry (Chicago); Encounter; Botteghe Oscure; Gemini; Times Lit. Supplement; The Listener; Child Educ.; Ambit; Mabon (North Wales); anthols. in U.S.A., S. Africa, Aust. & U.K. Address: The Walnut Tree, Banham, Norwich NOR.O5X, Norfolk, U.K.

BERNE, Stanley, b. 8 June 1923. Professor; Author. Education: B.S., Rutgers Univ., 1951; M.A., N.Y. Univ. 1952; grad. study, La. State Univ., 1958-62. Married Arlene Zekowski, 1953. Positions held: Asst. Prof., Eastern N.M. Univ., Portales, 1963-67; Assoc. Prof. in Engl., ibid, 1968–. Memberships: PEN; COSMEP; CCLM (Coordinating Coun. of Little Mags., a br. of Nat. Endowment for the Arts); Pres., Am.-Canadian Publishers Ltd.; New England Small Press Assn.; Comm. of Small Mags., Eds., and Publrs. Published works: A First Book of the Neo-Narrative, 1954; Cardinals & Saints, 1958; The Dialogues, 1962; The Multiple Modern Gods & Other Stories, 1964; The Unconscious Victorious & Other Stories, 1968; The New Rubaiyat of Stanley Berne, 1973. Contbr. to: Ed., Richard Kostelanetz, Breakthrough Fictioneers, 1973; Tigers Eye; New World Writing No. 11; S.D. Review; Kayak; Denver Qtly., etc. Address: Dept. of Engl., Eastern N.M. Univ., Portales, NM 88130, U.S.A.

BERRIGAN, (Fr.) Daniel, S.J., b. 1921. Member Society of Jesus. Published works: Time Without Number, 1957; Encounters, 1960; The World For Wedding Ring, 1962; False Gods, Real Men, 1966; No One Walks Waters, 1966; Love, Love at the End, 1968; Night Flight to Hanoi, 1968. Contbr. to (anthologies) From One Word, 1950; Joyce Kilmer's Anthology of Catholic Poets, 1955; Sealed unto the Day, 1955; Twentieth Century American Poetry, 1963. Address: Cornell Univ., Taylor Hall, Ithaca, NY, U.S.A.

BERRIGAN, Edmund J., Jr., pen name **BERRIGAN, Ted,** b. 15 Nov. 1934. Editor; Lecturer. Educ: B.A., Univ. of Tulsa, Okla., 1959; M.A., ibid, 1962. Married to Sandra Alper, two children. Positions held: Tchr., Poetry Workshop, St. Marks Art Proj., N.Y.C., 1966-67; Vis. Lectr., Writer's Workshop, Univ. of Iowa, 1968–; Ed., C Mag. & C Press, N.Y.C. Published works: The Sonnets, 1967; Bean Spasms, 1967; Many Happy Returns, 1968; Seventeen: Collected Plays (w. Ron Padgett), 1965. Contbr. to: Angel Hair; Mother; World; (anthologies) Young American Poets, 1968; Fuck You, 1968; Sparklers, 1969. Recip., Poetry Foundation Award, 1964. Address: 407 South Capitol, Iowa City, IA, U.S.A.

BERRY, Francis, b. 23 Mar. 1915. University Professor. Education: Hereford Cathedral School, Dean Close School, and the Universities of London (B.A. 1 cl. hons.), and Exeter (M.A.). Married, Nancy Melloney Graham in 1947 (dec'd, 1967); 1 s., 1 d. Positions held: successively Asst. Lecturer, Lecturer, Senior Lecturer, Reader, and Prof. in Dept. of Engl. Lit., Univ. of Sheffield, 1947-70; Prof. of Engl., Univ. of London, Royal Holloway Coll., since 1970. Fellow, Royal Soc. of Literature. Published works: Gospel of Fire, 1933; Snake in the Moon, 1936; The Iron Christ, 1938; Fall of a Tower, 1943; Murdock and Other Poems, 1947; The Galloping Centaur, 1952, reprinted 1970; Morant Bay and Other Poems, 1961; Ghosts of Greenland, 1966. Contbr. to: The Observer; The Listener; New Statesman; Life and Letters Today; Critical Qtly.; Wind and The Rain; The Tablet; The Northern Review; Times Lit. Supp.; BBC programmes. Address: Dept. of Engl., Royal Holloway Coll., Englefield Green, Surrey, UK.

BERRY, James, b. 28 Sept. 1924. Telegraphist. Positions held: Butler/Gardener & Insurance Agent in Jamaica; Farm Wkr. in U.S.A. during the war; Dental Mechanic & O'seas Telegraphist in London. Memberships: Hendon Arts Together; Poets'

Workshop, Nat. Poetry Ctr. Contbr. to: All Sorts and Conditions of Men, a use of English anthol., 1967; Other Voices Other Places, an anthol. of Third World poetry, 1972; Sunday Gleaner, Jamaica; Tribune; The Listener; Bim; Poetry Review; Savacou; Caribbean Artists Movement Newsletter; Afras, etc. Address: 28 Eastholm, Golders Green, London NW11 6LR, U.K.

BERRY, Wendell, b. 5 Aug. 1934. Educator. Educ: A.B., Univ. of Ky.; M.A., ibid. Married Tanya Amyx, 1957; Two children. Positions held: Mbr., Dept. of Engl., Univ. of Ky., 1964–. Published works: The Broken Ground, 1964; Openings, 1968; Findings, 1969; (novels) Nathan Coulter, 1960; A Place on Earth, 1967; The Long-Legged House (essay), 1969. Contbr. to: (anthologies) American Poetry, 1965; Poetry Southeast, 1968. Honours, awards: Guggenheim Fellowship, 1961-62; Rockefeller Foundation Grant, 1965-66. Address: Port Royal, KY 40058, U.S.A.

BERTINI, Aharon, pen name **BERTINI, K.A.,** b. 14 June 1903. Teacher of Literature; Writer. Education: Licence ès Lettres, Sorbonne, Paris. Member of the Board of the Hebrew Writers Assn. in Israel. Published works: Faded Yesterday, 1940; From Night till Morning, 1951; Mirrs on the Ash, 1954; Blue Path, 1961; A Bottle Upon the Waters, 1969. Contbr. to: Literary supplements of all newspapers. Editor of the monthly review 'Moznaim', 1964-70. Honours, awards: Akum Prize, 1959; Fichman Prize, 1966; Valenrod Prize, 1973. Address: 19 Veidat Kattowitz, Tel-Aviv, Israel.

BERTOLINO, James Dean, b. 4 Oct. 1942. Poet; Teacher. Education: Wash. State Univ.; Univ. of Wis. at Madison; B.A. Wis. State Univ.; M.F.A., Cornell Univ. Positions held: Pizza Cook; Mural Painter; Bartender; Bookstore Clerk & Receiving Mgr.; House Painter; Horseback Riding Trail-Guide; Ed., Publr., Abraxas (poetry Mag.); Tchr., Creative Writing, Wash. State Univ., 1970-71 & Cornell Univ., 1971-72. Teaching Asst. 1971-73, and Lecturer in Creative Writing, 1973-74, Cornell Univ. Mbr. Bd. of Directors, The Print Center, Inc., NY; Mbr. Coordinating Coul of Lit. Mags., NY.; Mbr: Perceptivists Grp., Madison, Wis. Published works: Maize, 1968; Day Of Change, 1968; Drool, 1968; Mr. Nobody, 1969; Stone-Marrow, 1969; Ceremony, 1969; The Executrix of Weirds, 1969; Becoming Human, 1970; The Blood Vision, 1971; Employed, 1972; Edging Through, 1972; Soft Rock, 1973; Making Space for Our Living, 1973. Ed. of Northwest Poets (anthol.), 1968. Contbr. to: Poetry, Chicago; Apple; Lillabulero; Foxfire; Cafe Solo; Poetry Bag; Red Cedar Review; Quartet; Cormoran Y Delfin, Argentina; West Coast Review; Kaleidoscope; Captain May I; Doones; Suction; Driftwood; Druid; Human Voice; Drunken Boat; Northwest Review; Witwoud, Copenhagen; Folio; Chicago Seed; San Francisco Oracle; Dragonfly; Quixote; Counterpoint; Cottonwood Review; Mandala; Hartford Courant; Prism; Makar; Hey Lady; Amalgamated Holding Co.; Mano Mano; Carrots & Peas; New Poetry Out Of Wise., 1969; The Living Underground; Goliards; Univ. of Portland Review; Wis. Review; Toucan; Galley Sail; Cronopios; Road Apple; Trace; Pebble; etc. Recip. of award for poetry, Book of the Month Club, 1970; Summer Research Fellowship (Creative Writing), Cornell Univ., 1972; Winner, Discovery '72 Poetry Comp., Poetry Center, YM-YWHA, NYC., 1972. Address: Dept. of English, Cornell Univ., Ithaca, New York 14850, USA.

BERTRAM, James Munro, b. 11 Aug. 1910. University Teacher. Education: Auckland Univ., New Zealand; New Coll., Oxford Univ., U.K.; Yenching Univ., Peking. Married. Positions held: Acting Press Attaché, British Embassy, Chung King; Sr. Lectr., Engl., later Prof., Victoria Univ. of Wellington, New Zealand. Memberships: Pres., New Coll. Essay Soc.; Comm. & Delegate, PEN (N.Z. Ctr.) Published works: Occasional Verses, 1971. Contbr. to: Phoenix; Landfall; N.Z. Listener. Address: 30 Park Rd., Belmont, Lower Hutt, New Zealand.

BESSEMER, Auriel, b. 27 Feb. 1909. Poet; Mural, Landscape, Portrait Painter and Illustrator; Art Teacher; Writer-Lecturer. Education: Western Reserve Acad., 1924-27; Columbia Univ., 1927-30; Master Inst. of United Arts (Roerich Museum), 1931-33; Nat. Acad. of Design Schools & Art Students League, 1927-30. Positions held: Founder & Dir., Gallery of Modern Masters, Washington, DC, 1936-42; WVS Govt. Serv., II Art Teacher, Nat. Art School, 1945-46; Jean Morgan Art School, NYC, 1947-49; Roerich Acad. of Arts, NYC, 1948-52; Pan Am. Art School, NYC, 1949-51; Catan-Rose Art Inst., Forest Hills, NY & Montclair School of Art, NJ, 1950; Painter of murals for public buildings, railway and other private cos., 1931-61; Staff Artist & Illustrator for The Summit Lighthouse, publications dept., Colorado Springs, 1972-73, engaged in illus. of books, pamphlets, etc. Contbr. to many anthols., journals; (also illus. to several books), etc., including: Voice Universal; The Beacon; The Writer's Voice; Washington Post; New Age Interpreter; Cyclo-Flame: Avalon Anthols.; Contemp. Am. Men Poets; Poetry House Anthol.; Arte, Internat. Art Mag.; D.I.B. Mag.; Enciclopedia Internazionale, 1970-71; Climb The Highest Mountain (28 illus.); Light From Heavenly Lanterns (10 illus.), etc. Recip. sev. awards, including: Toch Prize, Nat. Acad. of Design School, 1930; Tiffany Fndn. Scholarship, 1932; 1st Hon. Mention, Chaloner Prize Comp., 1932; Silver Medal (1970), and Gold Medal (1972), with 2 Hon. Diplomas, Tommaso Campenella Internat. Acad., Rome; Certs. of Merit, D.I.B. (1970); I.W.W.P. (1970). Address: c/o The Summit Lighthouse, First & Broadmoor, Colorado Springs, CO 80906, USA.

BEST, John, b. 11 Feb. 1929. Manufacturer. Education: Christ's Coll., Cambridge Univ. Published works: Poems & Drawings in Mud Time, in collab. w. G. Rigby Graham, 1960; Nine Gnats, in collab. w. G. Rigby Graham, 1964. Contbr. to: Delta; Ophir (S. Africa); Muse; Outsider; Extra Verse; Midland Read (an omnibus compiled by West Midlands Arts Assn.); BBC Midland Poets Prog., etc. Address: 16 Oak Hill Dr., Birmingham B15 3UG, U.K.

BETANZOS-SANTOS, Manuel, b. 12 Jan. 1933. Writer and Teacher. Education: Licentiate in Philos. and Letters, Univ. of Madrid; Cert. in Brazilian Studies; Dip. in Portuguese Studies, Univ. of Coimbra; studies in French, Engl., and Italian; doctoral courses and research in comparative poetry. Born in Galicia (Spain), and brought up in Canary Islands. Positions held: Teaching appts. in various univs. and schools, mainly in the Province of Quebec. Memberships: League of Canadian Poets (Quebec Area Rep. on Exec., 1970-72); Circulo Internacional de Poetas de Latinoamérica (Perú) (member of Hon. Committee); Soc. Argentina de Letras, Artes y Ciencias (Hon. member); Galaxia 71 (Organo de Escritores de Venezuela). Published works: Por la arcilla de tu silencio, 1960; Como piedras en la otra orilla, 1964; Arbol amante, 1964; Tala, poemas de la guerra indiferente, 1967; Canción del nino en la ventana, 1970; Se hizo dura la faz de la tierra (section of Doce jóvenes poetas espanoles, El Bardo), 1967; Torre Tavira, 1973; Saludo a la humanidad (poster), 1968; Editor, Boreal – poesía española en el Canada, 1965–. Contbr. to: Poesie eclair du monde entier, 1967; Volvox, 1972; West Coast Review; Contemp. Literature in Translation; Maguey; American Literary Accents; Ghost Dance; Vanguardia; Mensaje; Poesia Española; Bahía; La mano en el cajón; Azor; Alberdi; Cormorán y Delfín; Espiral; Yes; Booster and Blaster; El Caballo de Fuego, etc. Recip. Canada Council Awards, 1972 and 1973 (Canadian poetry in Spanish trans.). Address: P.O. Box 262, Victoria Station, Montreal H32 2V5, Quebec, Canada.

BETJEMAN, (Sir) John, b. 1906. Poet and Author. Education: Marlborough College; Oxford Univ., U.K. Married, 1 s., 1 d. Positions held: U.K. Press Attache, Dublin, Ireland, 1941-42; Admiralty, 1943. Appointed Poet Laureate of U.K., October 1972. Published works: Mount Zion; Ghastly Good Taste; Continual

Dew; An Oxford University Chest; Shell Guides to Cornwall and Devon; Antiquarian Prejudice; Old Lights for New Chancels; Selected Poems (Heinemann Award, 1948); First and Last Loves; A Few Late Chrysanthemums; Summoned by Bells; High and Low; English Love Poems; London's Historic Railway Stations; etc. Honours, awards: Queen's Gold Medal for Poetry, 1960; C.B.E., 1969; K.B.E.; 1969; Albert Medal, Royal Society of Arts, 1973. Address: 43 Cloth Fair, London EC1A 7JJ, U.K.

BETTIN, Doris J., pen name, **D.J.,** b. 14 May 1914. Housewife & Poet. Married, Earl E. Bettin; 2 s., 2 d. Memberships: Wisconsin Fellowship of Poets; Nat. Fed. of State Poetry Socs.; Acad. of American Poets; Wisconsin Regional Writers; The Shawand Area Writers. Contbr. to numerous journals, publications, etc. Recip. of sev. awards. Address: 76 N. Main St., Clintonville, WI 54929, USA.

BEZWODA, Eva Susanne, b. 23 Aug. 1942. Teacher. Educ: Hons. degree, Engl. Married Robert Royston, 1969. Positions held: Worked in Lib.; Tchr., Engl. & German; Teaches Privately at present. Contbr. to: Purple Renoster; New Coin; Wurm; New Nation. Recip., Nottcutt Memorial Prize, Univ. of Natal, 1962. Address: 34 Second Ave., Parktown N., Johannesburg, South Africa.

BHARATI, Yogi Shuddhananda, b. 11 May 1897. Poet. Positions held: Tchr. of Engl. & Sci.; joined Tilak & Gandhiji; for 25 yrs. was steeped in Yogic Silence at the feet of Sri Aurobindo & wrote var. poetic works. Lyrical poems broadcast on radio & are largely sung in concerts; they have been recorded & sold by HMV & other record cos. Translator of poets & novelists, e.g. Kalidasa, Kamban, Victor Hugo, Racine, Corneille, Shakespeare, Moliere, Goethe, Homer, Virgille, Dante. Published works incl: 20 poetic works, 42 dramas, 15 novels, 40 biographies, 20 works on Yoga & philos., 8 science works, 5 travel literatures, 10 histl. works & many essays, letters, talks etc. English works incl: The Gospel of Perfect Life: Experiences of a pilgrim soul; Secrets of Sama Yoga; Yoga For All; Soul Sings; Lights on Better Life; The Grand Epic of Saivism; Tirukural Couplets; Yogi & His Words; Voice of Tayumanar; Sri Aurobindo & His Yoga; Sri Krishna & His Gospel; Cross Roads. Awarded title Kavi Yogi Seer Poet, by His Holiness Narasimhe Bharati the Sankaracharya, 1912; recip. var. other hons. Address: Pres., Yoga Samaj, Adyar, Madras 600020, India.

BHASKARAN, M.P., pen name **Rhada & Manjula,** b. 22 Dec. 1921. Professor of English. Education: B.A., Madras Christian Coll., Tambaran, Tamil Nadu, S. India; Presidency Coll., Madras; Univ. of Leeds. Positions held: Tutor in Engl.; Jr. Officer, Madras Snowball; Prof., Reg. Inst. of Engl., Bangalore. Published works include: The Dancer and the Ring, 1962. Contbr. to the following anthols., jrnls., mags., etc: The Illustrated Weekly of India, Bombay; Beloit Poetry Jrnl., USA; Thought, Delhi; Asian Laughter; Asia Soc., NY; Writers' Workshop Miscellany, Calcutta; Swarajya, Madras; The Hindu, Madras; Deccan Herald, Bangalore. Address: Reg. Inst. of Engl., 6A Cunningham Rd., Bangalore 1-B, S. India.

BHATTACHARYA, Jagadish, pen name **COLLEGE-BOY,** b. 23 Jan. 1912. Teacher. Education: M.A. (Modern Indian Langs.), Calcutta Univ. Positions held: Prin., Bengabasi Coll. of Commerce, Calcutta; Pt.-time Lectr. on Tagori Lit., Rubindra Bharati Univ., Calcutta; Mbr. of the Senate & Acad. Coun., Calcutta Univ., 1954-61. Memberships: Fndr.-Sec., 'Kabisatra' (Soc. of Poets), 1966–; V.P., Bangiya Sahitya Parisad (Acad. of Bengali Lit.), 1971-72. Published works: Astadashi, 1933; Kshanasaswati (The Moment Eternal), 1942; Blackboard (ps. 'College-Boy), 1943; Premke Mrityuke (To Love, to Death), 1969; Ekti Alom Pakhi (A Bird of Light), 1972. Contbr. to all leading mags. & periodicals of West Bengal. Address: 10 Raja Rajkrishna St., Calcutta 6, India.

BIALY, Harvey, b. 23 May 1945. Student. Educ: Grad.,

Bard Coll., Annandale-on-Hudson, 1966; Working on Ph.D., Univ. of Calif. Married. Positions held: Poet-in-Residence, Mills Coll., Oakland, 1967. Published works: Love's Will, 1968; The Geronimo Poem, 1969; Susanna Martin, 1970. Contbr. to: Caterpillar; El Corno Emplumado; Io; Tufts Literary Magazine; Matter; Where Is Vietnam (anthology), 1967. Address: 1654 Fifth Street, Berkeley, CA 94710, U.S.A.

BIAMONTE, Edgar Louis, b. 9 Jan. 1930. English Teacher; Jazz Piano Player. Education: B.A., Queens Coll., 1961; M.S., Elmira Coll., 1968; David Mannes Coll. of Music, 1949. Positions held: English Tchr. Memberships: Ky. State Poetry Soc.; World Poetry Soc.; Int. Poetry Assn. Published works: Beyond These Flaming Leaves, 1974. Contbr. to: The Am. Bard; Bachet Mag.; Ball State College Forum; Bardic Echoes; Beyond Baroque; Cardinal Poetry Qtly.; Cycloflame; Dekalb Lit. Jrnl.; Encore; Fine Arts Discovery; Four Quarters; Inky Trails; New Voices in the Wind Anthol.; Outstanding Contemporary Poets Anthol.; Poet; Major Poets; Clover Coll. of Verse, etc. Recip. var. poetry prizes inclng: 1st prize, S.C. Poetry Soc., 1970; Hon. Mention & 1st prize, Ky. State Poetry Contest, 1972; Cert. of Merit, Int. Clover Poetry Assn., 1973. Address: 461 S. Hill Rd., Spencer, NY 14883, U.S.A.

BIDGOOD, Ruth, b. 20 July 1922. Writer; Housewife. Education: St. Hugh's Coll., Oxford Univ., U.K. Married, 3 children. Positions held: WRNS; Sub-Ed., Chambers Ency. Published works: The Given Time (poetry), 1972; one of six poets in 'Sestet', 1973. Contbr. to: Poetry Wales; The Anglo-Welsh Review; The London Welshman; Planet; Manifold; Candelabrum; Ore; Country Life; Country Quest; The Countryman; Poems 71 (anthol.); Poems 72 (anthol.); Poems 73 (anthol.). Address: Tyhaiarn, Abergwesyn, Llanwrtyd Wells, Breconshire, U.K.

BIEBUYCK, Francine (Lauryssen), pen name **WACKEN, Françoise,** b. 8 Dec. 1928. Writer. Education: Belgian Baccalaureat; Humanities, Greco-Latines. Married Marc Biebuyck, 3 children. Positions held: i/c of the Lib. of the Association des Amis de Georges Linze. Memberships: Association des Ecrivains Belges; Scriptores Catholici; Association des Amis de Georges Linze. Published works: (poems) Solfige Intérieur, 1970; Point d'Orgue, 1973; Chiendent, 1974; (novel) Comme un poisson hors de l'eau; Ceux des bruyeres (in prep.) Contbr. to: Faloises; Aqua; Eurêka; Le Travailleur; Marginales, etc. Honours, awards: Medaille de bronze, Momenturn, Switz., 1972; Award of Hon., City of Charleroi, 1972. Address: 4 Ieperstraat, 8140 Staden, Belgium.

BIELSKI, Alison Joy, b. 24 Nov. 1925. Writer; Housewife. Educ: Newport H.S.; Secretarial Trng. Married, two children. Positions held: Pvte. Sec., Press Off., Bristol Aeroplane Co., 1945; Welfare Sec., British Red Cross, 1964. Published works: Twentieth Century Flood, 1964; Shapes and Colours, 1969; The Story of the Welsh Dragon (children's book), 1968. Contbr. to: Anglo-Welsh Review; Country Quest; Poetry Wales; Poetry Review; London Welshman; Outposts; (anthologies) Best Poems of 1964 and 1967: The Borestone Mountain Poetry Awards, 1965, 1968; Young Commonwealth Poets '65, 1965; Commonwealth Poems of Today, 1967; New Voices of the Commonwealth, 1968. Recip., Premium Prize, Poetry Review, 1961. Address: Flat 2, Seaman's Rooms, Harbour, Tenby, Pembrokeshire, Wales.

BIERLAIRE, Christian, b. 26 Mar. 1937. Head Schoolmaster. Member, Belgian Writers Assn. Published works: Effigies d'un monde, 1963; Cinq légendes légendaires, 1968; De l'âtre qui s'éteint, 1970; L'Arche et le Déluge (poems), 1969; L'Hostie Noire, 1969; (Theatre Plays in Walloon dialect) Il n'y a rien de pis (1 act), 1968; Les voisins (3 acts), 1969; Ceux de maintenant (3 acts), 1973; Le Canari (3 acts), 1972; La machine (3 acts), 1973. Honours, awards: Grand Prix Littéraire de Wallonie, 1970; Prix

Engelman, 1972; Médaille de la ville de Cannet, 1972. Address: Rue Durieux, No. 16, B-5001, Belgrade, Yugoslavia.

BIGELOW, Faye Scoggins, pen name, **SCOGGINS, Faye,** b. 23 March 1898. Teacher. Education: M.A., B.A., West Texas Univ., Canyon, Texas; A.S.U., Tempe, Arizona. Positions held: Teaching appts. in Texas; HS Engl. & Music, Florence, Arizona; HS Engl., Counseling, Glendale, Arizona; Engl., Glendale Community Coll., Arizona. Memberships: Delta Kappa Gamma (vice-pres.); Arizona State Poetry Assoc. Published works: Topping the Heights (poems), 1969. Contbr. to: Nat. Anthol. of Poetry, 1959, 1960, 1961, 1962, 1965, 1967; Delta Kappa Gamma Handbook, 1967, 1968, 1969, 1970; Poet; Glendale News; Salt River Teachers Assoc. News; Phoenix .Gazette. Awards: Freedoms Foundation Class-room Teachers Award, 1960; Principal Award for Glendale High, 1960-62 (Freedoms Foundation); Certificate awarded by Veterans of Foreign Wars, 1963, 1964, 1965. Address: 2823 West Rancho Dr., Phoenix, AZ 85017, USA.

BILLINGS, Peggy, b. 10 Sept. 1928. Education: B.S., Millsaps Coll., Jackson, Miss.; M.A., Columbia Univ., N.Y.C.; additional study at Yale Univ., Inst. of Far Eastern Langs., New Haven, Conn. & Scarritt Coll., Nashville, Tenn. Positions held: Social Worker, Pusan Social Ctr., Pusan, Rep. of Korea, 1953; Dir., Tai Wha Soc. Ctr., Seoul, 1954; Sec. for Racial Justice, United Methodist Women, N.Y.C., U.S.A., 1963; Asst. Gen. Sec., Sect. of Christian Soc. Rels., United Meth. Women, 1968–; Vis. Prof. of Religion & Society, Chandler Schl. of Theol., Emory Univ., 1972-73. Contbr. to: Certain Days Are Islands; Motive Mag. Address: 257 Central Park West, N.Y., NY 10024, U.S.A.

BINSFELD, Edmund Louis, b. 25 Aug. 1909. Clergyman. Education: A.B., St. Joseph Coll., Rensselaer, Ind.; St. Charles Sem., Carthagena, Ohio; M.S. in L.S., Rosary Coll., River Forest, Ill.; Cert., Am. Univ., Wash., D.C. Positions held: Curate after Ordination, 1937; Instr., St. Rose Convent, Lac Crosse, Wis., 1938-43; Instr., St. Angela Acad., Iowa, 1943-48; Libn., Brunnerdale Sem., Canton, Ohio, 1948-50, '57-63; Libn., Carthagena, Ohio, 1951-57. Published works: Dream Dust, 1931. Contbr. to: America; Spirit; Land & Home; Spokesman; Cath. World; Lyric; Today; Delta Epsilon Sigma Bull.; Fiddlehead; Carolina Qtly.; Sponsa Regis; Nanzan Herald; Sign; Limbo; Husk; St. Anthony Messenger; Christian Century; Ajax; Ariz. Qtly.; P.B. Messenger. Recip. of poetry awards. Address: P.O. Box 87, Crookston, MN 56716, USA.

BIRCH, Leo Bedrich, b. 7 Feb. 1902. Educator. Education: Gymnasium, Prague, Czechoslovakia, 1912-20; Univs. in Vienna, Heidelberg, Paris, 1920-29. Positions held: Prof. of Gymnasium in Vienna, Austria, 1930-38; Industl. positions, N.Y., 1940-64. Memberships: World Poetry Soc. Intercontinental; Centro Studi e Scambi Int.; The Int. Poetry Soc.; Avalon World Arts Acad. Published works: The Old & the New Adam, 1969; Poems & Translations: Mallarmé, Valéry, Péguy, 1971. Contbr. to: The Poet; Orbis; Cyclo-flame; The Poets Guild; The Writers Guild; Imprints; Cardinal; Moon Age Poets; Hoosier-Challenger; Grassroots; IWWP Anthol., 1971. Address: 1487 Teller Ave., Bronx, NY 10457, U.S.A.

BIRD, Harold F., pen name LITTLEBIRD, Harold, b. 28 May 1951. Poet; Pottery Maker. Education: Inst. of Am. Indian Arts in Santa Fe, N.M., 1969; apprenticeship in pottery, Santa Fe, 1970-71. Married Gloria Castillo Bird, 2 daughters. Contbr. to: A Directory of Am. Poets, Poets & Writers, Inc., 1973; Writer's Reader; N.M. Review; Alcheringa; Coyote's Jrnl.; My Music Reaches to the Sky, 1973; var. anthols. Produced a documentary film on living Am. Indian Craftsmen (incl. Harold Littlebird working on pottery, sound track of him singing traditional Indian songs & reciting his own poetry), Sveriges Radio-TV 2, Stockholm, Sweden, 1972. Participates in many poetry readings. Honours, awards: Special Award, Scottsdale Nat. Poetry Contest, 1968; 1st pl., N.M. Poetry Soc., 1970, etc. Address: General Delivery, Paguate, NM 87040, U.S.A.

BIRKELBACH, Marie (Mary) Ruth, b. 17 May 1935. Real Estate Salesperson; Writer. Education: Southwestern Univ., Georgetown, Tex.; Southern Meth. Univ., Dallas; Tex. Univ., Austin; Art Students League, N.Y.C. Licensed, Assoc. Mbr., Austin Bd. of Realtors; Affil., Tex. Assn. of Realtors & Nat. Assn. of Realtors. Positions held: Food Supvsr., Driskill Hotel, 2 yrs. Sec., Southwestern Univ. Poetry Soc., 1971. Recip., award, Southern Meth. Univ. Arts fest. for poem 'Grace' & short story 'Man & a Rose', 1957. Address: Rte. 1, Box 14, Georgetown, TX 78626, U.S.A.

BIRNEY, Earle, b. 13 May 1904. Writer. Education: B.A., Univ. of B.C., Canada, 1926; M.A., Toronto Univ., 1927; Ph.D., ibid, 1936. Positions held: Instr., Univ. of Utah, 1930-34; Lectr. & Asst. Prof. of Engl., Univ. of Toronto, 1936-42; Personnel Selection Off., Canadian Active Army, 1942-45 (Ret'd as Major); Supvsr., For. Lang. European Broadcasts, Radio Canada, 1945-46; Prof., Mediaeval Lit., Univ. of B.C., 1946-62; Hd. of Creative Writing Dept., ibid, 1962-65; Writer in Res., Univ. of Toronto, 1965-67, Univ. of Waterloo, 1967-68; Regents Prof. of Creative Writing, Univ. of Calif., 1968; Freelance Writer, broadcaster, poetry reader, 1968–. Memberships: League of Canadian Poets; Writers' Union of Canada. Published works: David, 1942; Now is Time, 1945; Strait of Anian, 1948; Trial of a City, 1952; Ice Cod Bell or Stone, 1962; Near False Creek Mouth, 1964; Selected Poems, 1965; Pnomes, Jukollages & Other Stunzas, 1968; Memory No Servant, 1968; Poetry of Earle Birney, 1969; Four Parts Sand, 1971 (co-author); The Bear on the Delhi Road, 1973; What's So Big About Green? 1973. Contbr. to over 200 jrnls. in U.K., U.S.A., Australia & elsewhere. Honours, awards: Gov. Gen's Medal for best book of Poetry in Canada, 1942 & 45; Borestone Mt. first prize for best poem in Engl. lang. periodical, 1951; recip. var. fellowships & grants. Address: c/o McClelland & Stewart Ltd., 25 Hollinger Rd., Toronto, Ont. M4B 3G2, Canada.

BIRRELL, Verla Leone, b. 24 Nov. 1903. Artist; Poet; Lecturer; Teacher. Education: B.S., Univ. of Utah, 1929; M.F.A., Claremont Grad. Schl., Calif., 1941; Ed.D. (Fine Arts), Columbia Univ., N.Y., 1967. Positions held: Tchr., Payson H.S., Utah, 1928-30, & Irving Jr. H.S., Utah, 1930-37; Asst. Prof., Brigham Young Univ., 1937-48; Assoc. Prof., Univ. of Utah, S.L.C., 1948-72; Emeritus Prof., Univ. of Utah, 1972–. Memberships: Treas., Nat. League of Am. Penwomen, 1964; League of Utah Writers; Utah Poetry Soc.; Reader's Guild; Alice Louis Reynolds Club. Contbr. to: Utah Sings, Vol.II, Salt Lake City, 1943; Poetry Digest Anthol., 1945; Deseret News, 1948; Utah Sings Collection, Vol.III, 1953; Salt Lake Tribune, 1969; Driftwood, Ore., 1969. Recip., prizes in fine arts. Address: 2004 Wasatch Dr., Salt Lake City, UT 84108, U.S.A.

BISHOP, Elizabeth, b. 8 Feb. 1911. Poet. Education: A.B., Vassar Coll. Positions held: Cons. in Poetry, Lib. of Congress, 1949-50. Mbr., Am. Inst. of Arts & Letters. Published works: North and South; Poems; The Diary of Helena Morley (transl. from the Portuguese); A Cold Spring; Selected Poems; Questions of Travel, 1965. Contbr. to: Life & Letters Today; Partisan Review; New Yorker; etc. Honours, awards: Guggenheim Fellowship; Shelley Mem. Award; Amy Lowell Fellowship; Partisan Review Fellowship, etc.; Pulitzer Prize for Poetry, 1956. Address: c/o Chatto & Windus Ltd., 40-42 William IV St., London, WC2, UK.

BISHOP, Mary Cameron, pen name, **BISHOP, Mary C.,** b. 20 Apr. 1906. Secretary (retired). Education: 4 yrs. HS; 6 mths. Business Coll.; 6 mths. course in Journalism (by corres.), NY. Newspaper Inst. of America. Married; 3 s. Positions held: Telephone

Operator; Stenographer; Secretary (Dept.); Private Sec. Memberships: Pacific Northwest Writers Association, USA; United Amateur Press Org., USA. Contbr. to: Alberta Poetry Yearbook (Canadian Authors Assoc., Alberta Branch), 1941, 1949, 1950, 1951, 1962, 1963, 1966, 1967, 1969, 1970, 1971, 1972, 1973; Vancouver Sun; Edmonton Journal; Winnipeg Free Press; United Church "Observer"; Blue Nose Rambler; Yukon "Fire Flower"; also items published in various amateur papers of the United Amateur Press; Friendly Way Mag.; Guardino's Gazette (Brooklyn, NY). Awards: Hon. Mention in Misc. Prose Division of Trans-Atlantic 6th Annual Competition, Apr., 1973. Address: 1427 Dublin St., New Westminster, British Columbia, Canada.

BISHOP, Mary Elizabeth, pen name **PIPER, Ivonne,** b. 8 Apr. 1930. Housewife; Painter. Education: Swansea Schl. of Art & Crafts, Wales. Contbr. to: Envoi 41, & 46; Cheltenham Poets; Expression One, No. 27; Anglo-Welsh Review, Nos. 46 & 49; Poetry Wales; Planet 16; People Within, an anthol.; var. short stories broadcast by BBC. Honours, awards: Prize of 'Spring Anthology 1969' awarded by mbr. of Cheltenham Poetry Soc.; Prose Prize Winner, comp. sponsored by the Welsh Arts Coun., 1971. Address: 64 Park Ave., Longlevens, Gloucester, U.K.

BISINGER, Gerald, b. 8 June 1936. Publisher; Critic. Education: Univ. of Vienna, Austria. Positions held: responsible for the poetry publs. in the Vienna cultural mag. 'Neue Wege', 1962-70; w. Literarisches Colloquium Berlin, 1964–. Memberships: Bd. Dirs. (Berlin delegate), Grazer Autorenversammlung; Verband deutscher Schriftsteller, Berlin. Published works: 5 kurze Gedichte für Kenner, 1968; 7 Gedichte zum Vorlesen, 1968; 7 Neue Gedichte/7 Nuove Poesie, 1971. Contbr. to: Aachener Nachrichten (Aachen); Akzente (Munich); Antologia Geiger (Torino); Dimension (Austin, Tex.); Literatur und Kritik (Salsburg); Manuskripte (Graz); Neue deutsche Hefte (Berlin); Neue Rundschau (Frankfurt/Main); Neue Wege (Vienna); Podium; Protokolle (Vienna & Munich); Stillere Heimat; Tam Tam; Tintenfisch; Typos; Wespennest, etc. Address: Blissestrasse 50, D–1000 Berlin 31, German Fed. Repub.

BISSELL, Olin Cecil, pen names **BISSELL, O. & BISSELL, Ole,** b. 1 Aug. 1909. Retired Teacher. Education: B.Schl. Music, Morningside Coll., U.S.A., 1930-32; Grad. work, Drake Univ. Positions held: Tchr., pub. schls. in Iowa & Wyoming, 15 yrs.; The Vernon Co., 20 yrs. Memberships: Sec.-Treas. & at times has held all offs., Jasper Co. Writers, Inc.; Iowa Poetry Assn. Contbr. to: Lyrical Iowa (15 edns.), 1909–; The Clover Collection of Verse, 1971–. Has 3 copyrighted songs. Address: 1720 N. 4th Ave. W., Newton, IA 50208, U.S.A.

BISSETT, Bill, 23 Nov. 1939. Writer; Painter. Published works: we sleep inside each other all, 1966; Fires in the Tempul, 1967; where is miss florence riddle, 1967; what poetiks, 1967; Gossamer Bed Pan, 1967; Of th Land/Divine Service, 1968; Awake in the Red Desert, 1968; Killer Whale, 1969. Films: In Search of Innocence, 1963; Strange Grey Day This, 1964; Poets of the 60's, 1967. Contbr. to: Canadian Forum; Tamarack Review; Fiddlehead; Alphabet; Once Again (anthology), 1968. Recip., Canada Council Grants, 1967 & '68. Address: 1611 Yew Street, Vancouver 9, B.C., Canada.

BISTRITZKY, Nathan, b. 1896. Author-Novelist; Dramatist; Philosopher; Poet & Essayist. Published works: A Vision of Man (philosophical work); Days & Nights (novel about Kibbutz life); (nine historic dramas grouped in three vols.) Vol. 1, The Mystery of the Vision; Vol. 2, The Mystery of the Birth; Vol. 3, The Mystery of Man; (translations from Spanish) Don Quixote; Pablo Neruda (much of the poet's works); (original book on South America) Enchanted Continent. Var. essays on philosophical & literary subjects. Elected to the Academia Real de Bellas Letres de Espana. Address: 9 Mevo Yoram St.,

Jerusalem, Israel.

BIVONA, Francesco, b. 23 Nov. 1908. Writer of plays, novels, poetry, essays. Education: Grad., Manhattan Community Coll., N.Y.C., U.S.A. Published works: Agony of Faust, a poetic drama in 4 acts. Poems incl: Abandoned Poems, 1959; Moon Wash, 1960; Paper World & Other Poems, 1963; Sonnets From A Sicilian, 1967; Seeds in the Desert, 1967; Samara, Poems in the Greek Manner, 1969. Published short stories incl: Four Stories, 1950; Stolen Laughter, 1954; Running Mouse, 1964. Contbr. to: The Messenger; Singing San Juan; Guardino's Gazette, etc. Address: 12 Belvidere St., Brooklyn, NY 11206, U.S.A.

BLACK, David Macleod, b. 8 Nov. 1941. Writer. Education: M.A. Philos., Edinburgh Univ., U.K.; M.A. Religious Studies, Lancaster Univ. Published works: Theory of Diet, 1966; With Decorum, 1967; A Dozen Short Poems, 1968; The Educators, 1969; The Old Hag, 1972. Contbr. to: Penguin Modern Poets II, 1968; Akros; Lines Review; Scottish Int. Honours, awards: Scottish Arts Coun. Poetry Award, 1967; Arts Coun. of G.B. Award, 1969; Scottish Arts Coun. Publication Award, 1969. Address: c/o Barrie & Jenkins Ltd., 24 Highbury Cres., London N.5., U.K.

BLACK, Wilma Elizabeth Fritz, pen name **BLACK, Wilma Fritz,** b. 19 Feb. 1903. Teacher. Education: HS grad.; Milwaukee, Downer Coll.; Univ. of Wisconsin (degree in Elem. Education (and Art Minor)), 1965. Married; 3 children. Positions held: Teacher, elem., 2 yrs. Cambridge, Wisconsin; Teacher, 3 yrs. in remedial reading, Columbus, Wisconsin Public Schools; also taught 4 yrs. (part-time) County Teachers Coll., course in Art. Memberships: Wisconsin Regional Writers; Wisconsin Fellowship of Poets. Contbr. to: (anthols.) Northern Spring, 1956; Undergraduate Verse, 1950; A Wisconsin Harvest, 1966; Poems Out of Wisconsin, 1961; Poems Out of Wisconsin, III, 1967; New Poetry Out of Wisconsin, 1969; Wisconsin History in Poetry, Books I, II, III. Contbr. to: Creative Wisconsin; Hawthorn Leaves; Portage Register; Ideals; Standard Publishing program books; Review Publishing Mag.; Nuggets, etc. Awards: All-College Contests (short story, song), Milwaukee, Downer, 1921; 1st Prize, Wis. Regional Writers, 1958, also 2nd prize in poetry, 1950. Address: R.F.D. 3, Columbus, WI 53925, USA.

BLACKBURN, Beatrice Bray, pen name, **LLOYD, J.B.,** b. 6 Sept. 1906. Teacher. Education: B.A., Univ. of Okla., Norman; M.A., Eastern N.M. Univ., Partales. Married, Horace L. Blackburn, 1 d. Positions held: Tchr., HS, Daris, Madill & Walters, Okla.; Tchr., Lereland & Muleshoe, Tex.; E. Ctrl. State Coll., Ada, Okla. Memberships: VP, Muleshoe Area Poetry Soc.; Tex. State Poetry Soc. Contbr. to the following anthols. & jrnls: Nat. H.S. Poetry Assoc. Anthol. for Teachers, 1952, 53, 54, 59, 60, 62, 63, 64. Nat. Photolith Mag.; Muleshoe Jrnl.; study clubs; ch. & tchrs. grps.; org. grps. Honours, Awards: Poet Laureate, Fed. Study Club Caprock Dist., 1967-68, '68-69, '69-70; Winner, Fed. Study Clubs Dist. Poetry Contest, 1971. Address: 302 E. Elm, Muleshoe, Texas 79347, USA.

BLACKBURN, Paul, 24 Nov. 1926. Editor; Lecturer. Educ: B.A., Univ. of Wis., 1950; New York Univ.; Univ. of Toulouse, France, 1954-55. Married to Joan D. Miller, one child. Positions held: Served U.S. Army, 1945-47; Lecteur Americain, Univ. of Toulouse, France, 1955-56; Assoc. Ed., New International Yearbook, 1959-62; Poetry Ed., The Nation, N.Y.C. 1962; Assoc. Ed., World Scope Encyclopedia Yearbook, 1963-65; Staff Mbr. in Poetry, Aspen Writers' Workshop, 1966-67; Poet-In-Residence, CCNY, 1966-67; Lectr., Engl., ibid, 1968–; Free Lance Ed., Writer, Translator, 1968–. Published works: The Dissolving Fabric, 1955; The Nets, 1961; Sing-Song, 1966; The Cities, 1967. Contbr. to: Caterpillar; New Yorker; Poetry; (anthologies) New American Poetry, 1960; Where Is Vietnam?, 1967; New Modern Poetry, 1967. Translations: Proensa, 1953; Poem of Cid, 1966; Hunk of Skin, 1968. Honours, awards: Fulbright

Fellowship, 1954-56; Guggenheim Fellowship in Poetry, 1967-68. Address: 19 E 7th St., New York, NY 10003, U.S.A.

BLACKBURN, Thomas, b. 1916. Poet. Education: M.A., Durham Univ. Positions held: Gregory Fellow of Poetry, Univ. of Leeds, 1956-58; Sr. Lectr., Coll. of St. Mark & St. John. Published works: The Outer Darkness, 1951; The Holy Stone, 1954; In The Fire, 1956; The Next Word, 1958; A Breathing Space, 1964; A Smell of Burning, 1961; The Price of an Eye (crit.); Judas Tree, 1967; Robert Browning, 1968; A Clip of Steel, 1969. Contbr. to: New Statesman; London Mag.; Listener; BBC; Times Lit. Supplement. Address: 4 Luttrell Ave., London S.W.15, U.K.

BLACKHALL, David (Scott), b. 9 May 1910. Writer and Broadcaster. Membership: Soc. of Authors. Published works: Alms for Oblivion (poetry), 1957; This House Had Windows (autobiography), 1961, 1962; The Way I See It (autobiography), 1971. Contbr. to: various poetry mags.; The Times, etc. Address: 9 Melrose Ave., Borehamwood, Herts., UK.

BLADEN, Peter Louis, b. 28 Aug. 1922. Poet. Education: M.A., School of Modern Literature, Univ. of Melbourne. Since 1968, dealer in antiques, books, etc., and owner of Bruse's Hall, a Centre offering hospitality to creative artists and writers. Memberships: International PEN. From 1967-72, editor and publisher, Expression Australian Qtly. Published works: Selected Poems, 1946; The Old Ladies at Newington, 1953; Masque for a Modern Minstrel, 1962; Island Trilogy, 1970; Lazy Walkabout, 1954; The Christmas Card Murders, 1974. Awards: 1st Prize, in the long poem section, Commonwealth Jubilee Literary Competitions, for "The Old Ladies at Newington", 1951. Address: P.O. Box 19, Quorn, South Australia 5433.

BLANCHARD, André Louis François, b. 3 Oct. 1906. General Telecommunications Engineer. Education: Licencié ès sciences; Licencié en Droit. Married, 4 children. Memberships: V.P. Société des Gens de Lettres; Pres., Maison de Poésie. Published works: Les Figures et les Songes, 1938; Entre Jour et Nuit, 1939; Ligne de Vie, 1943; Capitale, 1945; Baroques et Classiques, 1947; Ton silence, O Joie, 1949; Petit bestiaire moral et fabuleux, 1951; De la St. Pierre à la St. Jean, 1952; Glossaire incongru, 1954; Si loin qu'on aille, 1962; Vivre est un jeu, 1965; Trésor de la poésie baroque et précieuse, 1969; De nuit et d'oubli, 1973; Itinéraire de Jean Second, 1940; Jean Second et ses poèmes sur l'exécution de Thomas More, 1973. Contbr. to: La Muse Française; Points et Contrepoints; Caractères; Ecclesia; Laudes; Les Cahiers du Sud; La Revue des Deux Mondes, etc. Honours, awards: var. Prizes of the Acad. Française & the Soc. des Gens de Lettres; Prix Moreas, 1940; Grand Prix de la Maison de Poésie, 1968. Address: 17 Rue Philibert Delorme, 75017, Paris, France.

BLAND, Peter, b. 12 May 1934. Free-lance Actor; Writer. Education: Victoria Univ., Wellington, New Zealand. Positions held: Talks Producer, NZ Broadcasting Corp.; Sr. Journalist, NZ Listener; Assoc. Artistic Dir., Downstage Theatre Co., Wellington, NZ. Published works: Habitual Fevers, 1958; Domestic Interiors, 1964; My Side of the Story, 1964. Contbr. to: London Mag.; Landfall; NZ Listener; English; Mate; NZ Poetry Yearbooks, 1958-64; (anthols.) Recent NZ Poetry; London Mag. Poems, 1966. Honours: Macmillan-Browne Prize, Creative Writing, Univ. of NZ, 1958; Melbourne Arts Festival Lit. Award, 1960; Fellowship in Drama, Queen Elizabeth II Arts Coun., NZ, 1968. Address: c/o Vincent Shaw Organization, 39A Welbeck St., London W1, UK.

BLANKENSHIP, Frank (Anthony), pen name **BLANKENSHIP, F. Anthony,** b. 23 June 1918. Salesman. Education: Shurtleff Coll., Alton, Ill. Married, 3 daughters, 1 son. Positions held: Ed., Labor World Newspaper, 1946-1948; Salesman, Montgomery Ward & Sears Roebuck, 1948-1951;

Famous Writers Schl., Westport, Conn., –1972. Member, Sigma Tau Delta. Published works: (poems) The Three Little Birds, 1972; Liquid Love, 1973; Blind, 1973; Amongst the Stars, 1973; The Sail, 1973. Contbr. to: Labor World; Harper's mag.; The Am. Scholar; New Orleans Review; The Smith; Our Family; Tri Qtly. Univ. Hall, Northwestern Univ., etc. Address: 746 Harvard Ave. No. 4, Santa Clara, CA 95051, U.S.A.

BLANKENSHIP, Gladys Elizabeth, b. 28 July 1905. Teacher. Education: Grad., Eastern Montana Coll. of Educ.; Northeastern Coll., Chicago, Ill., 1 yr.; B.S. Married, 1 son, 1 daughter. Membership: Ariz. State Poetry Soc.; World Poetry Soc. Intercontinental. Published works: (books of poetry) From the Crow Country, 1966; Pot Luck, 1965. Contbr. to Poet, 1973. Honours, awards: 1st pl., Mont. Press Women State Wide Contest & 2nd pl., Nat. Fed. of Press Women for 'Pot Luck', 1967; 1st. pl., Mont. Press Women Contest & 3rd pl., Nat. Fed. of Press Women for 'From the Crow Country', 1966. Address: Dayton, WY 82836, U.S.A.

BLASEN, Robin, pen name **AVALON,** b. 18 May 1925. Poet. Education: B.A., Berkeley Univ.; M.A. & M.L.S., ibid. Positions held: Prof., Simon Fraser Univ., British Columbia. Memberships: League of Canadian Poets. Published works include: The Moth Poem, 1964; Les Chimères, 1965; Cups, 1969; Holy Forest, 1970. Contbr. to num. publications, inclng: Georgia Straight, BC underground newspaper. Honours, awards: Poetry Soc., 1964; Canada Coun. Award, 1970. Address: 2247 Bellevue Ave., W. Vancouver, British Columbia, Canada.

BLAZER, John Allison, b. 18 Apr. 1930. Clinical Psychologist. Education: B.A., Andrew Jackson Univ., 1954; A.A., Cumberland Univ., 1958; B.S., Coll. of William & Mary, 1959; M.S., Richmond Prof. Inst., ibid, 1960; M.A., Burton Coll., 1960; Ph.D., Free Prot. Episc. Univ., 1962; Sc.D. (Hon.) Burton Coll., 1965; Ph.D., (Hon.) Ohio Christian Coll., 1970. Positions held: Pvte. Prac. of Psychol., 1962; Pres., The Psychological Press, 1962–; Staff Psychol., Mental Hlth. Clin., Mem. Hosp., Bristol, Va.-Tenn., 1963-64; Schl. Psychol., Bristol, Tenn., 1963-64; Ed., Psychology–A Jrnl. of Human Behaviour, 1963–; Dir., Bristol Family Guidance Ctr., Va., 1964; Sr. Clin. Psychol., Mental Hlth. Clin., Chatham Co. Hlth. Dept., Savannah, Ga., 1964–; Cons., Bayview Psychol. Servs., Portsmouth, Va., 1964–; Instr., Am. Univ. 1966; Lectr., Med. Coll. of Ga., 1966-67; Personnel Dir., Wachtel's Physicians Supply Co., Savannah, 1968–; Dir., Children's Learning Ctr., Savannah, 1969–; Personnel Cons., Candler Gen. Hosp., ibid, 1969-70; Assoc. Psych., Smith & Assocs., 1969–. Published works: Lyrics of Love, 1963; Fragments of Faith, 1963; Melody of the Muse, 1964; Rhyme Time, 1964; Versatility in Verse, 1965; A Burst of Trumpets, 1966; The Soul & The Singer, 1968; New Voices in the Wind, 1969. Contbr. to: The Cumberland Collegian; Proscript; The Miami Hurricane; Tempo; Anthol. (Am. Coll. Poetry Soc.); Poetry Parade; The Muse. Address: PO Box 6495, Station C, Savannah, Ga. 31405, USA.

BLIGHT, Frederick John, pen name **BLIGHT, John,** b. 30 July 1913. Poet; Qualified Accountant. Married Beverley D'Arcy-Irvine, 2 daughters. Positions held: Orchardist & Swagman before WWII; Public Acct., –1941; Sr. Price Control Officer, WWII; Cost Acct. & Mbr. of Timber Inquiry Commn., 1949-50; Company Dir., –1968; Crown employee, –1973. Memberships: Australian Soc. of Accts.; Australian Soc. of Authors. Published works: (poetry books) The Old Pianist, 1945; The Two Suns Met, 1954; A Beachcomber's Diary, 1963; My Beachcombing Days, 1968. Contbr. to: The Bulletin, Sydney; The Age, Melbourne; The Australian, Sydney; The Sydney Morning Herald; Nation Review, Melbourne; Meanjin, Melbourne; Poetry Mag., S.A.; Makar, Univ. of Qld.; Linq, James Cook Univ., Townsville, etc. Rep. in num. anthols. Honours, awards: Myer Award for Poetry, 1965; Mary Gilmore Award, 1956; Lit. Bd., Australian Coun. for the Arts, Long-term Grant, 1973. Address: 34 Greenway

St., The Grange 4051, Brisbane, Qld., Australia.

BLOCK, Allan, b. 6 Oct. 1923. Poet; Musician; Leathercrafter. Education: Univ. of Wis., U.S.A., 3 yrs.; Columbia Univ., 1 yr. Owner of leathercraft business in N.Y.C. for 20 yrs.; currently engaged in similar work, New Hampshire. Mbr., New England Poetry Club. Published works: The Swelling Under the Waves (13 poems – pamphlet), 1948; In Noah's Wake (60 poems – book), 1972. Contbr. to: The Nation; The New Republic; Poetry (Chicago); Northwest Review; The N.Y. Times; The New Am. Review; Commonweal; Prairie Schooner; The Harvard Advocate; Tiger's Eye; Christian Sci. Monitor; Boston Globe; Mass. Review, etc. Honours, awards: 2nd prize, Yankee Mag., 1970; inclusion, Best Poems of 1970, Borestone Mountain, 1970. Address: Quarry Rd., Francestown, NH 03043, U.S.A.

BLOEDORN, Hartmut, b. 3 July 1936. Construction Worker. Education: studied Germanistic sociology, geography & studies in philos. at Univ. Positions held: Nursing Orderly; part time Tchr.; Photographer, etc. Published works: short stories and poems in German newspapers (in German lang.), 1971-73; sev. short stories in the Edmonton Jrnl., 1972. Contbr. to: Alberta Courier (in German). Address: 9104 – 129 B. Ave., Edmonton, Alta., Canada T5E OP5.

BLOOM, Clare Celia, b. 21 Oct. 1915. Housewife; Poet; University Staff Member. Education: p/t student, Univ. of N.M. Married Clifton Blom, 2 sons, 1 daughter. Positions held: Mgr.-Staff Mbr., Univ. of N.M.; Administration, Coffee Shop, Univ. of N.M. Memberships: Portsmouth Lit. Club, Va.; Corres. Sec., N.M. Poetry Soc.; Nat. Fed. of State Poetry Socs. Contbr. to: Encore Mag.; Sunstone Review; Bitterroot; Southwest Heritage; Mustang Review; Thunderbird; N.M. Mag.; Poetry Forum; Poet, India; Santa Fe Writes; Albuquerque Herald. Poetry recorded for Tape Lib., Engl. Dept., M.V. Mahila Coll., Rajkat, India. Recip. Hon. Mention, Poetry Contest, 1972. Address: 8008 Hannett Ave. N.E., Albuquerque, NM 87110, U.S.A.

BLUM, Ray Owen, b. 23 Nov. 1944. Teacher. Education: B.A., Loyola Univ., 1972; M.A. cand., Univ. of Wis., 1973; also studied at San Francisco State Univ.; Univ. of Md.; Tatchikawa Univ. Married, 1 daughter. Positions held: U.S. Navy, 4 yrs.; Theatrical Dir., New Orleans Civic Theatre, 1972 season; Lutheran H.S. (Engl. & Drama), New Orleans, La., 1973–; Jesuit H.S. (Engl.), New Orleans, 1972-73. Memberships: New Orleans Poetry Forum; New Orleans Poetry Soc. Published works: New Orleans Poets – an Anthology, 1972, original play, presented 1962. Contbr. to: Red Beans & Rice; Vieux Carrie Courier; Wonewoc Review; Pogo; New Orleans Review; Men of the South. Address: 307 South Dupre St., New Orleans, La., U.S.A.

BLUMENKRON, Carmen Virginia (Mrs. Carmen Blumenkron Bernard), pen name, **BLUMENKRON, Carmen,** b. 3 June 1920. Writer; Translator; Volunteer Social Worker; Poet. Education: Private Engl. and Amer. Schools in Mexico; Mt. Mary Coll., Milwaukee, Wis.; Barat Coll. of the Sacred Heart, Lake Forest, Ill. (B.A., Magna Cum Laude & other Honours). Studied singing with Mme. Rosa Raisa in Chicago. Grad. work: Northwestern Univ's School of Speech, Evanston, Ill.; Universidad Nacional de Mexico & El Colegio de Mexico; also studies at the Alliance Francaise & Goethe Inst. Personal details: Born in NYC of Mexican & American parents. Positions held: Volunteer teacher, School for the Blind, Mexico; Co-director, Anahuac Machinery Co. & Talleres America (industrial plant). Appeared in sev. motion pictures. Voice-dubbing for films. Free-lance Writing. Radio & TV writing, including TV series in Spanish, " Musica, USA", sponsored by US Info. Service. Volunteer work of various kinds, specially with orphans. Translation (inclng. poetry) & interpreting in diverse fields. Work for Internat. Audio-visual Cooperative Movement, etc. Memberships: Acad. of American Poets; Catholic Poetry Soc. of America; (formerly) Radio Writers' Guild, of Authors League of America; Delta Epsilon Sigma; (formerly) associated with Centro Mexicano de Escritores; Nat. & Internat. Bd. of Directors of "Our Little Brothers & Sisters" (Father Wasson's complex of homes & schools for orphans, Mexico); Chaplain, Mexico Chapter, DAR; Mexican North-American Cultural Inst. Published works: Spearhead Toward the Dawn, 1973; award-winning radio play "Villa de Reyes", 1945. Contbr. to: New Voices in American Poetry, 1973; Horizons; Forest Leaves; Sat Sandesh; Mexican Life; American Soc. Review (Mexico); Vistas: Sunday Suppl. of "The News" of Mexico, etc. Honours: All-American Honor Award, Nat. Scholastic Press Assoc., 1945; Northwestern Annual Award for Writing, 1945. New Voices in American Poetry, 1973. Address: Ave. San Francisco 609, Colonia Del Valle, Mexico 12, D.F., Mexico.

BLUMENTHAL, Ilse Rosa, pen name **BLUMENTHAL-WEISS,** b. 14 Oct. 1899. Librarian. Education: State Registered Gym. Instr. Widow of Dr. Herbert Blumenthal, 1 son (dec.), 1 daughter. Positions held: Freelance Writer & contbr. to German broadcasts, 1933–, & later to Dutch & Swizz. broadcasts. Lectrs. on Lit. at Am. univs. Memberships: PEN; SDS, Sitz Zuerich (Schutzverband deutscher Schriftsteller). Published works: Gesicht und Maske, poems, 1929; Mahnmal, poems, 1960; Das Schluesselwunder, poems, 1954; Jahrbuch fuer Juedische Geschichte und Literatur 1936: 13 Gedichte aus einem Ms., Wir Leben. Contbr. to: Berliner Tageblatt und Vossische Zeitung; Deutschen Rundschau; Emuna-Horizonte, etc. & radio programmes. Address: 35–15, 75th St., Jackson Heights, NY 11372, U.S.A.

BLUNDELL, Gordon James, b. 6 Sept. 1912. Fruit Farm Worker. Memberships: The Poetry Soc.; The English Assn. Published works: The Swan & Other Poems, 1965. Contbr. to: Southern Television; Competitors Jrnl.; The Countryman; Time & Tide; Hellas; Envoi; Manifold; Jongleur; Tait's Quarterly; Phoenix; Rainbow; English; John o'London's Weekly; New Statesman; Church Times; Spectator; Candelabrum; (anthols.) The Sleep Book; Springtime, Yet More Comic & Curious Verse; New Statesman Competition Anthol.; Sestet; Candelabrum Anthol. No.1. Honours, awards: Poetry Soc. Holmes Poem of Place Prize, 1951; Poetry Soc. Howard Parsons Epigram Prize, 1952; Poetry Soc. Quarterly Premium Prize, 1951 & 61. Address: Lane's End, East Malling, Nr. Maidstone, Kent ME19 6JG, U.K.

BLUNDELL, Rachel Mary, b. 9 July 1930. Teacher. Education: Tchr. Trng., Coventry Coll. of Educ.; A.L.A.M.; T.C. Positions held: Sec. in local Govt.; Drama Libn. with Glos. County Lib.; Tchr./Libn. at Secondary Schl. in Stroud. Memberships: Cheltenham Poetry Soc.; Bristol Arts Ctr. Published works: Out of the Shell, 1971; Sunshine & Shadow, 1973/74. Rep. in following anthols: People Within, 1973; Mosaic, 1974. Address: Church Cottage, Walkley Hill, Rodborough, Stroud, Gloucestershire, U.K.

BLY, Robert Elwood, b. 23 Dec. 1926. Poet and Publisher. Education: A.B., Harvard, magna cum laude, 1950; M.A., Univ. of Iowa, 1956. Married to Carol McLean, 4 children. Positions held: Instr., Univ. of Iowa, 1955; Instr., Queens Coll., 1959; Publisher and editor, The Sixties Press, and subsequently, The Seventies Press. Publications: Silence in the Snowy Fields, 1962; A Light Around the Body, 1967; The Morning Glory, 1970; The Teeth Mother Naked at Last, 1970; Sleepers Joining Hands, 1973; Jumping Out of Bed, 1973, also many books of translations of Spanish, Norwegian, Swedish, German and French poetry. Contrib. to numerous journals, etc. Recip. Nat. Book Award (for: Light Around the Body), 1967; Guggenheim Fellowship (twice); Amy Lowell Fellowship, grant from Nat. Inst. of Arts and Letters. Address: The Seventies Press, Madison, Minn. 56256, USA.

BOADELLA, David, b. 6 July 1931. Headmaster;

Lecturer; Writer. Education: B.A., Univ. Coll., London, U.K., 1950-53; M.Ed., Univ. of Nottingham, 1955-58. Married Elsa Corbluth, 2 children. Positions held: Hd. Tchr., Abbotsbury Schl., Dorset, 1963–; Ed., Energy & Character, Jrnl. of Bio-energetic Rsch., 1970–; Assoc. Mbr., Inst. of Bio-energetic Analysis, N.Y., 1971–. Memberships: Sec. of Literary & Debating Soc., Beckenham, 1948-49; Fndr. Mbr., Chesil Poets, Dorset; Weymouth & Bridport Arts Socs. Published works: The Spiral Flame, 1958; Coming of Age, 1972; Wilhelm Reich, 1973. Contbr. to: Outposts; Phoenix; Poetry Workshop; Poetry Nottingham; Voice; Splatt. Address: Abbotsbury, Weymouth, Dorset, U.K.

BOAL, Charles Denis, b. 23 Mar. 1946. Pilot. Education: B.S., Biology, Grove City Coll., Pa. Member: Fellowship of Professional Poets; Centro Studi e Scambi Internazionali. Publication: Invitation to Dream, 1973. Contrib. to: Gato; Poetry Parade; Cardinal Poetry Qtly.; Poetry of our Times; Best in Poetry; American Scenes; Reach Out; Best Poets of the 20th Cent.; Notable American Poets; Denver Post's Poetry Forum. Address: 216 Haymaker Rd., Monroeville, Pa. 15146, USA.

BOATRIGHT, Philip, b. 26 June 1934. Editor & Publisher of Steppenwolf Jrnl. Education: B.A., Univ. of Omaha. Published works: 14 Poems, 1960; The Chambered Distances (poems), 1962; The Visionary Eye (poems), 1962. Contbr. of poems & book reviews to var. jrnls. Address: P.O. Box 55045, Omaha, NB 68155, U.S.A.

BOCKIUS, William Lawrence, b. 16 Nov. 1924. Teacher. Education: B.A., Columbia Univ.; studied at Rutgers Univ.; Bennington Coll.; currently M.A. cand. at Manhattanville Coll., Purchase, N.Y. Married Julianne McMillan, 2 daughters. Positions held: Freelance Actor, director, stage-manager in the theatre & television, appearing off B'way & in Hollywood; Tchr., Engl. & Dramatics, The Rye Country Day Schl., Rye, N.Y., 1968–, etc. Member, The Lambs Actors' Club, N.Y.C. Writer of play, 'Thanks for the Use of the Hall', produced in Rye, N.Y., 1969. Work-in-Progress: 'We Take the Ridge' (vol. of poetry). Contbr. to: Omega Lit. Mag.; Metaphor Poetry Mag.; Nat. Poetry Anthol. Recip., 2nd prize, Westchester Co. 1973 Greenburgh Arts Coun. Poetry Awards. Address: RD2 Pound Ridge, N.Y. 10576, U.S.A.

BODE, Carl, b. 14 Mar. 1911. University Professor. Education: Ph.B., Univ. of Chicago, 1933; Ph.D., Northwestern Univ., 1941. Positions held: Asst. Prof. of Engl., UCLA, 1946-47; Prof. of Engl., Univ. of Md., 1947–; Cultural Attache, Am. Embassy to G.B., 1957-59 (on leave from Univ. of Md.) Memberships: Fellow, Royal Soc. of Lit., U.K.; PEN, U.K. & U.S.A. Published works: The Sacred Seasons, 1953, reprinted 1972; The Calendar of Love, 1959; The Man Behind You, 1959 (U.K.) & 1960 (USA). Contbr. to: New Statesman; Times Lit. Supplement; London Mag.; Contemporary Review; English; John o'Londons; Am. Scholar; Carleton Miscellany; Encounter; Critical Qtly.; Dryad; Dare; Nation; New Republic; Southern Review; Tri-Qtly.; Time & Tide; Transatlantic Review; Saturday Review, etc. Honours, awards: Northwestern Poetry Prize, 1940 & 41; Newson Prize, 1959; Fieldstone Award for Religious Poetry, 1965. Address: c/o Dept. of Engl., Univ. of Md., College Pk., MD 20742, U.S.A.

BODINE, Franklynn, b. 24 Feb. 1910. Kindergarten Teacher. Education: grad., Tex. Womens Univ., Denton, 1931; post grad. work, A & M Univ., College Stn., Tex. & Lamar Univ., Beaumont. Married, 4 children. Positions held: Tchr., 4th grade, 1932; Taught a Children's Bible Class, Nessler Civic Ctr., 13 yrs.; Taught Conversational Engl., Coll. of the Mainland, Texas City, 2 yrs. & Bodine's Christian Kindergarten, 6 yrs. Memberships: Dee Walker Poetry Club, Texas City; Int. Union of Associations, Rome, Italy. Contbr. to: IWWP Anthol.; The Spring Anthol., 1972; My Favorite Poems Anthol., 1944; Dance of the Muse Anthol., 1970; From Sea to Sea In Song, 1970; Am. Poetry League Bulletin; Ralls Banner newspaper.

Address: 2207 1st Ave. North, Texas City, TX 77590, U.S.A.

BOER, Charles, b. 25 June 1939. Assistant Professor. Educ: A.B., Western Reserve Univ., Cleveland; M.A., Harvard Univ.; Ph.D., S.U.N.Y., Buffalo. Positions held: The Fulbright Fellow, Medieval Studies, Univ. of Florence, Italy, 1961-62; Asst. Prof., Engl. & Comparative Lit., The Univ. of Conn., Storrs, U.S.A., 1966–. Published works: The Odes, 1969. Address: Knowlton Hill, Storrs, CT, U.S.A.

BOGGS, Beverly Creech, b. 30 Nov. 1917. Primary Public School Teacher. Education: Marshall Univ., Huntington, W.Va., 1936-38; Morehead State Univ., 1938-39; A.B., ibid, 1963; postgrad. work, Youngstown State Univ., Ohio, 1965-73. Married James H. Boggs, 1 son. Positions held: Inspector; Receptionist; Records Disposition Clerk; School Teacher. Memberships: Nat. Fed. of State Poetry Socs.; Ky. State Poetry Soc.; Flatwoods Poetry Soc.; World Poetry Soc. Intercontinental. Published works: Incidents & Impressions, 1969; The Yoke of Reality, 1973. Contbr. to: Ashland Daily Independent; The Russell Times; The Written Word Anthol. No. 8; Odyssey No. 2; The Forever Bear; Poet. Honours, awards: The Jesse Stuart Award of Excellence, 1971; 1st pl. in Haiku Contest, 1970; A Guest of Hon. at Authors' Tea & Open House given by the Trumbull Co. Histl. Soc. (Ohio) & The Martha Kinny Cooper Ohioana Lib. Assn., 1971. Address: 3266 Curtis, S.E., Warren, OH 44484, U.S.A.

BOGUE, Lucile Maxfield, b. 20 Apr. 1911. Educator; Author. Education: A.A., Colo. Coll., 1932; B.A., Univ. of Northern Colo., 1934; Grad., Coll. Int., Cannes, France; Sophia Univ., Tokyo, Japan; Univ. of Colo., Boulder, USA; Univ. of Berkeley; M.A., San Francisco State Coll., 1972. Married to Arthur Bogue, 1935, 2 d. Positions held: Pub. Schl. Tchr., 1934-62; Pres. & Fndr., Yampa Valley Coll. (now Alpine Campus of US Int. Univ.), 1962-66; Dir. of Guidance, Am. Schl. in Japan, Tokyo, 1966-68; Dean, Anna Head Schl., Oakland, Calif., 1968-71. Member, Calif. Writers Club; Secretary, World Citizens League, USA; Member, Dramatists Guild. Author of Typhoon, Typhoon!, 1970. Contbr. to: Denver Post; St. Anthony's Messenger; Good Housekeeping; Country Poet; Children's Activities; Jack & Jill; Highlights for Children; Ideals; Scimitar; Extension. Address: 2611 Brooks, El Cerrito, Calif. 94530, USA.

BOHRS, Mary Ann (Mrs. Harry Bohrs, Jr.), born 7th November 1934. Housewife & Poet. Education: B.A. cum laude, Baylor Univ., 1956. Memberships: St. Davids Christian Writers' Assoc.; Poetry Soc. of Tex.; Hightstown, East Windsor Writers' Forum. Staff mbr. & Ed., Water Wheel, 1969 Writers' Conf. Publications: Ironing Board Altars, 1969. Contbr. to: Badge of Promise Anthol., 1958; Philadelphia Bull.; Sun Mag.; Hearthstone; Baptist Leader; Adventure Time. Honours: 2nd Prize, Poetry Div., St. David's Christian Writers' Conf., 1967. Address: 360 S. Main St., Hightstown, N.J. 08520, U.S.A.

BOISSEAU, Marie-Antoinette-Albertine, pen name **BOISSEAU, Albertine,** b. 18 Mar. 1900. Secretary; Poet; Teacher. Educ: Cert., Enseignement Superieur, 1917; Spanish Lang. Study, Univ. Laval. m. William Georges Boisseau, 1928 (dec. 1949), 1 s., 1 d. Positions held: Pvte. Instr., Gov's. children, Ile d'Anticosti, 1919-20; French Tchr., 1917-27; Sec., Nat. Defense, Valcartier, 5 yrs.; Sec., Quebec Govt., 15 yrs.; Sec. Gen., ibid, 1966-68; Judge, Literary Contest, Collège de Merici, Quebec. Memberships: Past Mbr., Quebec Histl. Soc. & Soc. of Canadian Writers. Published work: Chants d'Automne, 1957. Contbr. to: Poètes du Québec; Quelques Poètes étrangers de langue française; Odes à Paris; Le Soleil; L'Action catholique; Belle province; l'Evangéline; Le Foyer rural. Honours, awards incl: Laureate, Soc. of French-Canadian Poets, 1954; Dip. of Hon., French Literary Studies Club, Malines, Belgium, 1960. Address: 1135

Ave. Moncton, Quebec, P.Q., Canada.

BOITEL ADAMS, Carmen, pen name **ADAMS, Carmen Boitel,** b. 3 Apr. 1920. Housewife. Education: Utica HS., NY.; Katherine Gibbs Sec. School., NYC. Positions held: Anglo Bank, Modesto, Calif. Memberships: American Poetry League; Ariz. State Poetry Soc.; Pierson Metler Associates, Major Poets Chapter. Published works: Twenty Little Lyrics, 1969; Quiet Reflections, 1971; With Love, 1971. Conbr. to: Ideals; Medford News; Poet's Guild Anthol.; American Bard; American Poetry League. Address: 345 W. Cambridge Ave., Phoenix, AZ 85003, USA.

BOLAND, Eavan Aisling, b. 24 Sept. 1944. Lecturer. Educ: Hons. Degree, Trinity Coll., Dublin, Ireland; New York; London. Positions held: Jr. Lectr., Engl. Lit., Trinity Coll., Dublin, 1967-68. Published works: New Territory, 1967. Contbr. to: Dublin Magazine; Irish Times. Recip., Macaulay Fellowship in Poetry, Irish Arts Council, 1968. Address: 60 Ailesbury Road, Donny-brook, Dublin 4, Ireland.

BOLD, Alan Norman, b. 20 Apr. 1943. Writer. Education: Edinburgh Univ. Positions held: Garage Hand; Apprentice Baker; Swimming Instr.; Jrnlst., The Times Educational Supplement. Published works: Society Inebrious, 1965; The Voyage, 1966; To Find the New, 1967; A Perpetual Motion Machine, 1969; Penguin Modern Poets 15, 1969; The State of the Nation, 1969; The Penguin Book of Socialist Verse, 1970; He Will Be Greatly Missed, 1971; A Century of People, 1971; A Pint of Bitter, 1971; The Auld Symie, 1971; A Lunar Event, 1973; Hammer & Thistle, 1973. Contbr. to: Transatlantic Review; The Scotsman; Stand; Times Lit. Supplement; Tribune; Agenda; Poetry Review; Akros; Scotia Review; Contrasts; N.Y. Times. Recip., Scottish Arts Coun. Award, 1967. Address: 19 Gayfield Sq., Edinburgh EH1 3NX, U.K.

BOLLS, Imogene, b. 25 Sept. 1938. University Instructor. Education: B.A., Engl., Kan. State Univ., Manhattan, 1960; M.A., Engl. & Comp. Lit., Univ. of Utah, 1962. Married to Univ. Biol. Prof., 1 d. Positions held: Instr., French, Kan. State Univ., 1960; Tching. Asst., Engl., Univ. of Utah, 1960-62; Instr., conversational French to Army Personnel, 1962-63; Instr., Engl., Wittenberg Univ., Ohio, 1963-64; Part-time Instr., ibid, 1965–. Contbr. to: Ball State University Forum; Cape Rock Journal; Cimarron Review; The Georgia Review; Florida Quarterly; Kansas Quarterly; Laurel Review; Midwest Quarterly; Perspective; Poet Lore; The Poetry Bag; Prairie Schooner; Roanoke Review; The South Carolina Review; Southern Humanities Review; Western Review. Address: Dept. of English, Wittenberg Univ., Springfield, Ohio 45501, USA.

BOLTON, Frederic James, pen name **BOLTON, Deric,** b. 12 June 1908. Research Chemist. Education: B.Sc., Birkbeck Coll., London Univ., 1934; FRIC. Positions held: Rsch. Chemist, Works Mgr., Tech. Dir., J.F. MacFarlan & Co. Ltd., Edinburgh, 1937-62; Co. Trng. Off., Macfarlan Smith Ltd., 1962-71. Memberships: Chmn., Soc. of Chem. Ind., Edinburgh Sect., 1951-53, '72-73; V.Chmn., 1970-73 & Hon Treas., 1955-65, Scottish Assn. for the Speaking of Verse, Edinburgh Br.; Poetry Soc., etc. Published works: A View from Ben More, 1972; Glasgow Central Station, 1972; The Wild Uncharted Country (A scientific pilgrimage), 1973. Contbr. to: Akros; Elders; Glasgow Herald; Nature; New Athenian Broadsheet; Outposts; Poetry of To-day; Rotary; Scotsman; Scottish Poetry IV; BBC Scottish Life & Letters (radio). Recip., 2nd prize, Scottish Assn. for the Speaking of Verse, Poetry Comp., Edinburgh, 1965. Address: 17 Wester Coates Ave., Edinburgh EH12 5LS, U.K.

BOLTON, Rosemary de Brissac, pen name **DOBSON, Rosemary de Brissac,** b. 18 June 1920. Writer. Education: Art Studies, Sydney Univ., NSW. Married. Positions held: Tchr.; Ed. Work, Book Publing. firms. Mbr. of Australian lit. socs. Published works: In a Convex Mirror, 1944; Cock Crow, 1965; The Ship of Ice, 1948; L'Enfant au Cacatoes–Child with a Cockatoo, 1955; Autour du Monde, 1967; Selected Poems. Contbr. to nearly all editions of Australian Poetry (annual anthol.), to the Penguin Book of Australian Verse, & numerous other anthols., Australia, UK, USA, & USSR. Honours, awards: Sydney Morning Herald Poetry Prize, for the Ship of Ice, 1946; Sidney Meyer Award for Poetry, 1966. Address: c/o Angus & Robertson Ltd., 22 George St., Sydney, NSW 2000, Australia.

BOND, Deborah Mary, b. 5 Aug. 1949. Education: Lady Margaret Hall, Oxford Univ. Contbr. to Daily Telegraph Young Writer of the Year Book, 1969. Address: Summer Ct., Football Green, Hornsea, Yorks. HU18 1RA, U.K.

BOND, Harold, b. 2 Dec. 1939, Boston, Mass., USA. Editor; Teacher. Education: A.B., Engl.-Jrnlism, Northeastern Univ., Boston, 1962; M.F.A., Creative Writing, Univ. of Iowa, Iowa City, 1967. Positions held: Dir., Poetry Workshop, Ctr. for Adult Educ., Cambridge, 1968–; Ed., Ararat Mag., 1969-70; Currently on Ed. Bd.; Instr., Prog. of Poetry Workshops in Pub. Schls., Mass. Coun. on the Arts & Humanities, 1971–; Various ed. positions, newspaper & book publng. Published works: Co-author, 3x3, 1969; The Northern Wall, 1969; Dancing on Water, 1970; Fragments of an Earlier Life, 1974. Contbr. to the following mags. & anthols: The Young Am. Poets, 1968; Speaking for Ourselves: Am. Ethnic Writing, 1969; The New Yorker Book of Poems, 1969; Ararat: A Decade of Armenian-Am. Writing, 1969; Eleven Boston Poets, 1970; East Coast Poets, 1971; Getting Into Poetry, 1972; New Voices in Am. Poetry, 1973; Outside/Inside, 1973; Shake the Kaleidoscope, 1973; Boston Anthol. of Poets, 1973; New Yorker; Harper's Mag.; Sat. Review; New Republic; N. Am. Review; Iowa Review; Carleton Miscellany; Choice; Boston Review of the Arts; Yankee, etc. Awards: 1st Prize, Armenian Allied Arts Assn. Poetry Competition, 1963, '64, '65; 1st Prize, Kan. City Star Awards, 1967, '68. Address: 11 Chestnut St., Melrose, Mass. 02176, USA.

BONINE, Vivian, pen names **SMALL, Mary Vivian, BONINE, Vivian Small & BONINE, Vivian Way,** b. 28 Sept. 1912. Film Technician; Poetry Editor; Critic. Education: Tex. Woman's Univ., Denton Co., 1929-30; West Tex. State Univ., Randall Co., 1931-43, etc. Married 1) Morris W. Small, 2 daughters, 2) Arvel Earl Bonine. Positions held: Film Technician, Technicolor Corp., Inc., Hollywood, 1945-71; Land Owner-rentals, 1919–; Farm Mgr. (cotton cattle), 1960–; Poetry Editor; Critic, Judge, 1966–. Memberships incl: Charter & Life Mbr., Ralls Histl. Mus., Inc., 1969–; Life Mbr., Pasadena Writers' Club, 1967–; Life Mbr., Poetry Soc. of Tex., 1973–; Pres., Pasadena Writers' Club, 1963-66. Published works: Sparks (brochure of poetry), 1958; Scriptorium Arboretum (author, ed., publsr., a writers' workshop mag.), 1963-68; Silver Ashes (book of poetry), 1971. Contbr. to num. jrnls., mags., anthols. inclng: IWWP Anthol., 1972; Calif. State Poetry Qtly., 1972; The Poet's Nook, Weekly Jrnl. Publs., 1971-73; Poet (Madras, India). Var. radio broadcasts. Recip. var. honours & awards inclng: Award of Hon, United Poets Laureate Int.; 1st prize for Song Parady, Dec. 1972 & 2nd prize, Serious Verse contest, Spring 1973, Writers' Club of Pasadena. Address: 2556 North La Presa Ave., Rosemead, CA 91770, U.S.A.

BONNETTE, Jeanne, b. 29 Dec. 1907. Housewife; Poet. Education: Univ. of Chgo.; Cosmopolitan Schl. of Music; Hazel Sharp Schl. of Dance. Personal details: m. to Arthur E. Bonnette; Father, Assoc. Conductor of Chgo. Symph. Orch.; Mother, singer, organist. Positions held: Educ. TV Producer of 8 weeks of poetry readings & 15 weeks of art series, KNME, Albuquerque; Dir., N.M. Art League; Publicity Dir., Albuquerque Little Theatre. Memberships: Poetry Soc. of America; Nat. League Am. Pen Women; Recording Sec., Nat. Fed. State Poetry Socs.; Am. Acad. Poets; 2nd VP, NM Poetry Soc.; 2nd VP, NM Hist. Outdoor Drama Soc.; South & West, Inc.

Published works: Colored Sails, 1930; Seven Stars, 1939; Chess Game & Other Poems, 1952; Oh, The Wide Sky! 1968; In This Place, 1971. Contbr. to: Chicago Tribune; Christian Science monitor; Denver Post; Poet Lore; Poet; Lyric, South & West; Voices International; Some Haystacks Don't Ever Have Any Needle, 1968; American Haiku; NM Quarterly; Western Review; Tulsa Poetry Quarterly; Ann Arbor Review; Poetry Parade; Mustang Review; Child Life; NM Magazine; IWWP Anthol., 1973. Awards: Voices Int., 1967; various, Nat. League of Am. Pen Women, 1970, '71; Mason Sonnet Award, Va. Poetry Soc., 1971; NM Poetry Soc., Sonnet, 1971; N.M. Press Women Zia Award, June, 1972; 1st Award, Nat. Fed. of State Poetry Socs. Contest, June, 1972. Address: Coronado Village No. 235, 8901 W. Frontage Rd. NE, Albuquerque, NM 87113, USA.

BOO, Maureen Hyun, b. 17 July 1937. Medical Researcher; Histo-Chemist. Memberships: Acad. of Am. Poets; Nat. Fed. of State Poetry Socs.; Centro Studi e Scambi Int. Contbr. to: Oregonian; Poetry in View; The Smith; St. Andrews Review; Weid; Capper's Weekly; Ensign; Journal; Crossroad Newsletter; Bardic; Year Book of Modern Poetry; Archer, & others. Address: 6022 S. Drexel, Chicago, IL 60637, U.S.A.

BOOKER, Clifford Harvey, pen names **HARVEY-BOOKER, C. & EMPIRE-STATEMENT,** b. 10 June 1950. Artist. Education: Bolton Coll. of Art & Design, U.K.; Newcastle Coll. of Art. Published works: Calfmellow Revisited, 1974. Contbr. to: Pink Peace; Bogg; Myrixia. Address: c/o Rustington, 12 Catterick Dr., Little Lever, Bolton, Lancs., U.K.

BOOTH, Martin, b. 1944. Poet; Editor; Educator. Education: studied Natural Scis., Coll. of Educ., London; Schoolmaster Fellowship, St. Peter's Coll., Oxford, 1973. Positions held: Specialist Tchr. of Engl. Lit. & Lang., var. schools; currently tchng. in a sr. grammar schl. in the East Midlands & lecturing on a programme for Am. undergrads. in the Univ. of Oxford; Fndr., The Sceptre Press, 1968; Ed. w. Anthony Rudolf, Poetry Review, 1971; Fndr., Omphalos Press w. Hugh Lander, 1973. Memberships: Gen. Coun., Poetry Soc. of G.B., 1968 (has held other offices); Sec., The Poets' Workshop, London, 1967-70; Regl. Arts Coun. Lit. Advisory Panel, 1972; Assn. of Little Presses. Published works: Paper Pennies & Other Poems, 1967; A Winnowing of Silence, 1970; The Crying Embers, 1971; Pilgrims & Petitions, 1971; On the death of Archdeacon Broix, 1972; Coronis, 1973; Teller, 1973; Brevities, 1974; Unpublished poems & drafts of James Elroy Flecker: discovered & edited by Martin Booth, from original manuscripts, 1971. Contbr. to num. mags., reviews in G.B. & abroad, & radio broadcasts. Regular contbr. to Tribune, reviewing poetry & novels; The Teacher, verse & educl. books, w. some children's novels, & he has reviewed for Poetry Review, etc. Recip. many lit. awards inclng: Guinness Award for Poetry, Stroud Fest., 1970; President's Prize, York Int. Poetry Fest., 1973. Address: c/o Sceptre Press, 15 Keats Way, Rushden, Northants NN10 9BJ, U.K.

BOOTH, Philip, b. 8 Oct. 1925. Poet; Teacher. Education: A.B., Dartmouth, 1948; M.A., Columbia, 1949. Married Margaret Tillman, 3 daughters. Positions held: Instr. in Engl., Bowdoin Coll. & Dartmouth Coll.; Asst. Prof., Wellesley Coll.; Assoc. Prof., Syracuse Univ.; Prof. of Engl., ibid. Member, Am. PEN. Published works: (colls. of poetry) Letter from a Distant Land, 1957; The Islanders, 1961; Weathers & Edges, 1966; Margins (New & Selected Poems), 1970. Ed: The Dark Island, 1960; Syracuse Poems, 1965 & '70. Contbr. to: The Sat. Review; The Christian Sci. Monitor; N.Y. Times Book Review; The Contemporary Poet as Artist & Critic; Master Poems of the English Language; The London Mag.; Hudson Review, etc. Rep. in many anthols. inclng: New Poems by Am. Poets; The Modern Poets; The Chicago Review Anthol. Var. TV & Radio readings & public readings at schls. & univs. Recip. var. honours & awards inclng: Bess Hokin Prize, 1955; D.Litt., Colby

Coll., 1968; Theodore Roethke Prize, 1970. Address: Dept. of Engl., Syracuse Univ., Syracuse, NY 13210, U.S.A.

BORDNER, Marie S., b. 27 Aug. 1906. Writer; Advertising Copywriter. Widow, 1 son. Positions held: Asst. Adv. Mgr., Pomeroys Reading; Fashion Copywriter, Snellenburgs, Phila., Pa.; Lit Bros., Phila.; Adv. Agencies; Freelance Reporter, Readings Times & others. Memberships: Nat League of Am. Pen Women; Pa. Poetry Soc.; Fellow, Int. Poetry Soc. Published works: Star Dust Book, 1928; The Silver Shadow Book, 1970. Contbr. to: A Goodly Heritage, 1968; Kaleidoscope; The Galleon; The Spotlight; Phila. Bulletin; Bucks County Life. Honours, awards: Geo. Washington Hon. Medal, Freedom Fndn., Valley Forge, 1968; Liberty Bell poem accepted by U.S. Park Serv. to hang permanently in Independence Hall Complex; 2nd Prize for sonnet, Nat. League of Am. Pen Women, 1972. Address: 78 Mercer Ave., Doylestown, PA, U.S.A.

BORGMANN, Helena Rose, b. 6 June 1898. Retired Clerk. Positions held: w. Grant Co. Health Dept., Williamstown, Ky., 1938-40; WP-AFB, Statistical, 1942-68; Church of Resurrection, 1969 & 70; Self employed, 1972–. Memberships: Comm., Poetry Reading Circle, Dayton; Poets Round Table, Terre Haute, Ind.; Ind. Soc. of Poetry Clubs; Council on Aging, Lexington, Ky.; Writers' Workshop Over 57. Contbr. to: Orphic Lute; Tweed Mag., Australia, 1972; Kans. Kernels; Columbus Dispatch; Major Poets, Tremont, Ill.; Friendly Way Mag.; South West Breeze; Hyacinths And Biscuits, etc. Recip. var. poetry awards inclng: Sylvia Martin Award, UAPA. Address: 225 N. Ludlow St., Dayton, OH 45402, U.S.A.

BORREGAARD, Ebbe, b. 1933. Served in U.S. Army. Published works: The Wapitis, 1960. Contbr. to: New American Poetry, 1960.

BORRELL, Dorothy Elizabeth, pen names (poetry) **BORRELL, D.E.** & (other work) **FINN, D.E.,** b. 10 July 1928. English Teacher. Education: B.A., Durham Univ.; Dip. in Educ. Married Hugh Finn, 2 sons. Positions held: Lectr. in Educ., Univ. of Rhodesia, 1958; Editl. Bd., Rhodesian Poetry, 1958–. Cons., Nat. Archives on the work of Arthur Shearly Cripps, the missionary poet. Memberships: Chmn., Poetry Soc. of Rhodesia, 1967-71; Salisbury Arts Coun., 1964-70; English Acad. of Southern Africa, 1970-74; Sec., PEN Int., Rhodesia Ctr., 1969-72; Nat. Anthem Comm., Rhodesia, 1970-73. Ed.: Poetry in Rhodesia: 75 Years, 1968; Beneath a Rhodesian Sky, 1972. Rep. in the following: New South African Writing, 1968, '69; New Poems, 1970 (Ed. Stallworthy, Heany & Brownjohn, London, 1971). Regular contbr. to New Coin, Rhodesian Poetry, 1956-72, Chirimo, Two-Tone, etc. Runner-up, PEN Rhodesia Book Ctr. Award for Lit., 1972. Address: 22 Bradfield Rd., Hillside, Salisbury, E.61, Rhodesia.

BORTONE, (Fr.) Fernando, S.J., b. 13 Dec. 1902. Jesuit Father. Education: degree in philos., the Pontifical Gregorian Univ., 1929. Positions held: sent as Missionary to China, by Soc. of Jesus, 1931; Tchr., Sinology, Peking, 1939-41; Philos. & Religion at Pengpu, 1942-48; Latin, Shanghai, 1948-49; Prof., Sonology, Libera Universita di Paestum, 1973. Memberships incl: United Poets Laureate Int. (Italian-Chinese poet in Res.), 1967; Free World Int. Acad., 1970; Sovereign Order of St. John. of Jerusalem (Kts. of Malta); Athenaeum Academiae Gentium 'Pro Pace' (Radiestesia Medica). Author of num. works in Italian & Chinese inclng: Per l'avvenire dei Giovani, 3rd ed., 1962; L'Invito di Gesu, 2nd ed., 1962; I canti dell'esilio, 1963; P. Matteo Ricci, S.J., Un grande italiano nella Cina impenetrabile (1552-1610), 2nd ed., 1965; Salmi in metrica italiana, 3rd ed., 1969; Alla Corte do Pechino: Due secoli di eroismi per la fede cattolica in Cina (1601-1813), 1969; Salmi e Cantici meditati, 5th ed., 1972. Has written film scripts on life of Fr. Matteo Ricci, S.J., the Apostle of China whose cause for beautification he has forwarded. Recip. of many decorations & lit awards of merit inclng: 6 Gold Medals for biog. of P. Matteo Ricci, S.J., Rome, 1965-67; 2 Gold Medals for I Salmi e Cantici Meditati, Rome, 1966-68; Award of U.N. Day, Philippines, 1967; Commendatore al merito della Repubblica Italiana, 1971. Address: via del Quizinale 29, 00187 Rome, Italy.

BOSE, Buddhadeva, b. 30 Nov. 1908. University Professor. Education: B.A., Dacca Univ., 1930; M.A., ibid, 1931. Married Protiva Shome. Positions held: Lectr. in Engl., Ripon (now Surendranath) Coll., Calcutta, 1934-45; Fulbright Vis. Prof., U.S.A., 1953-54; Prof. & Chmn. of Comparative Lit., Jadarpur Univ., Calcutta, 1956-63; Vis. Prof., U.S. Univs., 1961, '63-65. Member, Int. PEN. Has written numerous works & contributed to many jrnls., newspapers, jrnls. etc. Edited, poetry quarterly, Kavita, 1935-60. Honours, awards: Sahitya Akademi Award, Govt. of India; Awarded Padmabhushan, Govt. of India. Address: 364/19 Netaji S.C. Bose Rd., Calcutta 47, India.

BOSE, Suddha Sattwa, b. 1 Mar. 1921. College Principal. Education: B.A., 1941; M.A., 1948. Positions held: Lectr., Netaji Subhas Coll., 1949-52; Lectr., Charn Chandra Coll., 1952-60; Lectr., Deshbandhu Coll., 1955-62; Prin., ibid, 1962-. Memberships: Life Mbr., Banga Sahitya Sammelan, All India Juvenile Lit. Assn. & Sisu Sahitya Parishad; Bangla Sahitya Akad.; Past Mbr., Nikhil Bharat Banga Sahitya Sammelan. Fndr., 1941 & Ed., poetry jrnl. 'EKAK', 1941. Contbr. to most Bengali papers & jrnls. Address: 10/3C Nepal Bhattacharya St., Calcutta 26, India.

BOSLEY Keith, b. 16 Sept. 1937. Poet; Translator. Education: B.A. Hons. French, Reading. Published works: The Possibility of Angels, 1969; sev. books of verse translation inclng. French (An Idiom of Night, selection from Pierre Jean Jouve, 1968), Vietnamese (The War Wife, anthol. covering 200 yrs., 1972), Finnish (The Song of Aino, epic ballad, 1973), Hebrew (The Song of Songs, 1974). Contbr. to num. mags. inclng: Encounter; Agenda; The Listener; The Young British Poets; radio programmes; anthols. Address: 108 Upton Rd., Slough SL1 2AW, U.K.

BOSQUET, Alain (Anatole Bisk), b. 28 Mar. 1919. Poet & Critic. Education: Univ. Libre de Bruxelles, 1938-40; M.A., Univ. of Paris, 1951. Married Norma Caplan. Positions held: served w. Belgian, French & U.S. Armies, 1940-45; Editl. Sec., La Voix de France, N.Y.C., 1942-43; served w. Allied Control Coun., Berlin, then Dept. of State, 1945-51; Lit. Dir., Editions Calmann-Lévy, 1956-72; Prof. French Lit., Brandeis Univ., 1958-59; Prof. Am. Lit., Univ. of Lyons, 1959-60; Prof. Poetry, Univ. of Wis., 1970; Columnist, Combat, 1953-; Critic, ORTF, 1956-; Columnist, Le Monde, 1961-. Memberships: Acad. of Alsace; Acad. of Brazil. Published works: La vie est clandestine, 1945; A la mémoire de ma planète, 1948; Langue morte, 1951; Quel royaume oublié, 1955; Premier Testament, 1957; Deuxième Testament, 1959; Maitre Objet, 1952; Quatre Testaments et Autres Poèmes, 1967; 100 Notes pour une Solitude, 1970; Notes pour un amour, 1972. Contbr. to var. reviews. Honours, awards incl: Prix Interallié for La Confession Mexicaine, 1965; Grand Prix de Poésie de l'Académie Française for Quatre Testaments et Autres Poèmes. Address: 32 rue de Laborde, 75008 Paris, France.

BOSTOK, Janice Mae, b. 9 Apr. 1942. Editor; Plantation Owner. Married, 1 son, 1 daughter. Positions held: Ed., TWEED, a small mag. interested in Haiku, Tanka, Haibun & general poetry; Jt. Owner, Banana Plantation. Memberships: Poetry Soc. of Australia; Australian Soc. of Authors; World Poetry Soc. Contbr. to: Haiku Mag.; Modern Haiku; Haiku Highlights; Dragonfly; Haiku West; Janus-SCTH; Byways (U.K.); Voices Int.; Encore; Special Song; Orphic Lute; Bardic Echoes; Sunburst; Bitterroot; Haiku Happening; UAP Yrly. Contest Coll., 1972; View; Valley Views; The Muse; Hyacinths & Biscuits; Imprints Quarterly; Speak Out; Poetry Nippon (Japan); Poet (India); Spectrum; Poets of Australia, 1972 & 73

(anthol.); Ruddy Haiku Hunt (UAP Haiku anthol.), 1973. Address: P.O. Box 304, Murwillumbah, N.S.W. 2484, Australia.

BOTHWELL, Shirley Marie, pen name **BOTHWELL, Shirley Oakes,** b. 8 Apr. 1936. Housewife; Writer. Education: Mars Hill Junior College, and 13 yrs. private studies at College level. 3 yrs. U.S. Navy. Member, Non-Eu Lit. Soc., Mars Hill College. Pubs. Nineteen Songs, 1964; Living Lyrics (poems), 1967. Contrib. to: Progressive Farmer; National Beta Club Journal. Nat. Beta Club Award, 1950-55; 2nd place, Jesse Stuart Awards, Prog. Farmer Mag. Address: 8056 Milton Avenue, Baltimore, Maryland 21207, USA.

BOTSFORD, Talitha, b. 21 Sep. 1901. Musician, Artist, Writer. Education: Ithaca Conservatory of Music, Ithaca, N.Y. Member, ASCAP. Pubs. Short Stems, 1964; Mini Verse, 1970. Contrib. to: Elmira Sunday Telegram; Reader's Digest; Milady; Chemung Valley Reporter; Grit; Am. Artist. Appointed Hon. Member in Kiwanis Club for "Hymn to the Flag", 1971. Address: 1718 W. Church Street, Elmira, N.Y., 14905, USA.

BOTTOMS, Mollie Ruth, b. 26 Sept. 1901. Retired Teacher. Education: B.S., Geo. Peabody Coll. for Tchrs., Nashville, Tenn., 1927; M.A., ibid, 1929. Positions held: Taught grades 1-3, Oakdale Schl., nr. Athens, Ala., 1920-21; Tchr., Walker Co. H.S., Jasper, Ala., 1924-25; Engl. Tchr., Ala. Coll. Trng. Schl., 1926-28, Geo. Peabody Coll. for Tchrs., 1929-30; Assoc. Prof., Ctrl. State Coll., Edmond, Okla., 1930-39 & '40-47; Taught, Geo. Peabody Coll. for Tchrs., 1947-49. Memberships incl: Fac. Sponsor, Chi Gamma Chapt. of Sigma Tau Delta, 1932-39; Okla. Poetry Soc., 1935-39 & '58-73; Pres., Edmond Poetry Soc., 1946-47; Nat. Poetry Soc. Contbr. to: Fac. Ed., Moving Fingers, a coll. anthol., 1934; Fac. Sponsor & Ed., Anthol. of Poetry, 1935, 36, 37, 38, 39, Chi Gamma Chapt. of Sigma Tau Delta; The Peabody Reflector & Alumni News; Spinners; Sat. Review of Lit.; Okla. Tchr.; Poetry Awards, 1949. Address: P.O. Box 53, Edmond, OK 73034, U.S.A.

BOTTRALL, (Francis James) Ronald, b. 2 Sept. 1906. Retired Diplomat. Education: Cambridge Univ., U.K., 1925-29; Commonwealth Fellow, Princeton Univ., U.S.A., 1931-33. Married 1) Margaret S. Smith, div., 1 son, 2) Margot P. Samuel. Positions held: Lectr. in Engl., Helsingfors Univ., Finland, 1929-31; Johore Prof. of Engl. Lang. & Lit., Singapore, 1933-37; Dir. of Priorites, Air Ministry, 1940-41; British Coun. Rep. in Sweden, 1941-44, Italy, 1945-50, Brazil, 1954-56, Greece, 1957-59, Japan, 1959-61 (& Cultural Counsellor, Brit. Embassy, Tokyo); Controller of Educ., Brit. Coun., London, 1950-54; Chief, Fellowships & Trng. Br. of FAO of the U.N., Rome, 1963-65. Fellow, Royal Soc. of Lit. Member, PEN. Published works: The Loosening, 1931; Festivals of Fire, 1934; The Turning Path, 1939; Farewell & Welcome, 1945; Selected Poems, 1946; The Palisades of Fear, 1949; Adam Unparadised, 1954; Collected Poems, 1961; Day & Night, 1974; Poems 1955-73, 1974. Contbr. to num. mags., anthols., etc. Honours, awards: CBE, 1949; Coronation Medal, 1953; Theocritus Int. Poetry Prize & Medal, City of Siracusa, Sicily, 1954; Grand Off., Order of Merit, Rep. of Italy, 1973; Kt., Order of St. John of Jerusalem, 1972. Address: Via delle Quattro Fontane 16, 00184 Rome, Italy.

BOUGHTWOOD, Alice Marian, pen name **SID,** b. 14 Oct. 1897. Teacher, Science. Education: B.S., Simmons Coll., Boston, 1928; M.A. Educ., Columbia Univ., N.Y., 1933. Positions Held: Bishop Coll., Texas; Homemaking Schol., Quincy, Mass.; E. Boston High Schl., Boston. Memberships: Assoc., New England Poetry Club, Boston, Mass.; The Acad. of Am. Poets. Author of Mathematical Music, 1967; Gleanings, 1973. Contrib. to: Patriot Ledger, Quincy; Morning Herald, Boston; Am. Mentor Mag.; Poet, India; Manifold; American Bard; Mature Years; Cardinal; Muse; Boston Mag.; Swordsman Review; Bitterroot; Echoes; Wisconsin Poetry Mag.; Hoosier Challenger; Orphic

Lute; Writers Notes & Quotes; Nat. Retired Teachers Journal; Cyclo-Flame; 4 Avaolon Anthols. Personal Poetry, WBUX. Honours: Midget Pegasus Award, 1965; Read at The Poetry Soc., Inc., UK., 1966; Annual Mentor Poetry Award, 1967; 2nd Prize, Manifold No. 23, 1967; 1st Prize, Manifold, No. 26, 1968; Avalon Presidential Award, 1969; 2 Hon. Mentions, Flame Anthol.; 2 Citations, Alice M. Boughtwood Citation, ibid; sev. book awards; North American Mentor, 1972; 2 certificates of awards, 1972; 1 book prize, 1972. Address: 1000 Southern Artery, North Wing, Apt. 612, Quincy, Mass. 02169, USA.

BOUILLON, Georges, b. 14 June 1915. Professor. Education: Licence en Philosophie et Lettres, Univ. of Liege, Belgium, 1937. Positions held: Fndr.-Dir., Revue & Publishing House, La Dryade. Mbr., Société européenne de Culture. Published works: (art) Visages; Camille Barthélemy; Albert Raty; Marie Howet; (poems) Poemes choisis; Hymnes et Ballades; (other books) Humanisme d'un homme quelconque, I, II & III; Souviens-toi; Paroles d'un incroyant. Recip., Prix de Litterature des Arts en Europe, Brussels, 1971, & Prix de l'essai des Ecrivains de Wallonie, Charleroi. Address: La Dryade, B-6762, Vieux-Virton, Belgium.

BOULTON, Marjorie, b. 7 May 1924. Writer. Education: B.A., Somerville Coll., Oxford, 1944; M.A., ibid, 1947; B.Litt., 1948; currently reading for D.Phil. Positions held: Asst. Engl. Mistress, High Schl. for Girls, Westcliff-on-Sea, 1944-46; Lectr., Drake Hall Emergency Trng. Coll., 1948-50; Lectr., Northern Counties Coll., Hexham, 1950-55; V. Prin., ibid, 1955-62; Prin., Charlotte Mason Coll., Ambleside, 1962-70. Memberships: Soc. of Authors; Engl. Assn.; Oxford Univ. Poetry Soc. Published works: (poems in Esperanto) Preliminaries, 1949; Kontralte, 1955; Cent Gojkantoj, 1957; Eroj, 1959. Contbr. to num. Esperanto mags. Honours, awards: Esperanto Author of the Year, 1958; var. prizes for original & translated poetry in Esperanto. Address : 36 Stockmore St., Oxford, OX4 1JT, U.K.

BOURAOUI, Hédi André, b. 16 July 1932. University Professor; Writer. Education: Licence ès lettres, Univ. of Toulouse; M.A., Indiana Univ. (Engl. & Am. Lit.); Ph.D., Cornell Univ. (Romance Studies). Positions held: Has taught at Cornell Univ., Wells Coll., Rosary Coll., Ithaca Coll. & York Univ. Memberships: Pres., Toronto Chapt., Am. Assn. of Tchrs. of French; MLA; Comparative Lit. Assn.; Canadian Assn. of Semiotic Rsch.; World Poetry Soc. Published works: Musocktail, 1966; Tremblé, 1969; Immensément Croisés: poème dramatique, 1969; Eclate Module, 1972; Vésuviade & L'Icônaison, to be publd. Contbr. to: Rythmes et Couleurs; Edge; Waves; Voodoo; Substance; Sud. Address: French Lit. Dept., Founders 130, York Univ., 4700 Keele St., Downsview, Ont., Canada M3J 1P3.

BOURGUIBA, (President) Habib Ben Ali, b. 3 Aug. 1903. President of the Republic of Tunisia. Educ: Dip., Lit., Pol. Sci. & Law; Lic. Law, Free Schl. of Pol. Sci., Univ. of Paris, France. Positions held: Mbr., Destour Party, 1921; Fndr., Neo-Destour Party, 1934; Arrested for pol. reasons, 1934-36, 1938-43 & 1952-54; Returned to Tunisia, 1955; Pres., Tunisian Nat. Assembly, Prime Minister & Pres. of the Coun., 1956-59; Minister of For. Affairs & Defence, 1959; Pres., Destour Socialist Party & Rep. of Tunisia, 1957-. Published works: Le Destour et la France, 1937; La Tunisie et La France, 1954. Honours, awards: Ordre du Sang; Ordre de la Confiance en diamants. Address: The Presidency, Palace, Tunis, Tunisia.

BOUSONO, Carlos, b. 9 May 1923. Professor at the University of Madrid. Education: Dr. Philos. & Letters. Published works: (books of poetry) Subida al Amor, 1945; Primavera de la Muerte, 1946; Hacia otre Luz, 1952; Noche del Sentido, 1956; Invasion de la Realidad, 1962; Oda en la Ceniza, 1967; Las Monedas contra la Losa, 1973. Honours, awards: Critics prize for 'Oda en la Ceniza', best poetry book, 1967; Critics

prize for 'Las Monedas contra la Losa', best poetry book, 1973. Address: Reyes Magos, 10-10-B, Madrid 9, Spain.

BOWEN, Iris O'Neal, b. 18 May 1915. Home Maker. Married, 5 children. Positions held: Tchr., 4 & 5 Grades, Salem, Ark., 1937-38; Tchr., Jr.-High, Floral, Ark., 1939-40; in business w. husband (Bowen Food Markets), 1940-. Memberships: Nat. Bd., Nat. Fed. of State Poetry Socs.; Histn., Nat. League of Am. Pen Women; Treas., Poets' Round Table of Ark., 4 yrs.; Pres., ibid, 2 yrs.; Histn., Libn., Chmn., Nat. Poetry Day, 4 yrs.; Ozark Writers & Artists Guild; Authors, Composers, Artists of Ark. Contbr. to: Life & Health; Homelife; Jack & Jill; Open Windows; Poetry Soc. of Okla. Anthol.; Poets Roundtable of Ark. Anthols., 1962-73; Improvement Era; Today's People, Saline Co. News; Ark. Gazette; Southwest Times Record, etc. Recip. num. poetry awards inclng: Sybil Nash Abrams Award, 1971; 1st & 3rd pl., Ozark Writers & Artists Guild, 1971; 1st, sonnet, Ark. Poetry Day, 1972; 1st, light verse, Ark. Arts Fest., 1973. Address: 406 W. L, N. Little Rock, AR 72116, U.S.A.

BOWEN, John Charles Edward, b. 8 Oct. 1909. Poet; Orientalist. Education: Charterhouse; B.A., Oriel Coll., Oxford Univ. Positions held: served in Indian Army (6th D.C.O. Lancers) & Indian Political Service, 1932-47, & as a District Commnr. in the Bechuanaland Protectorate & in Northern Nigeria, 1950-63. Comm. Mbr., Guildford & West Surrey Br., Poetry Soc. Published works: Grim & Gay (under ps. 'Lancer'), 1941; Poems from the Persian, 1948, currently in its 3rd edn.; The Golden Pomegranate: A Selection from the Poetry of the Mogul Empire in India 1526-1858, 1957, republished 1966; A New Selection From the Rubaiyat of Omar Khayyam, 1961; Poems, 1968; A Journey to the Heart of Asia, 1972; Translation or Travesty? An enquiry into Robert Graves' version of some Rubaiyat of Omar Khayyam, 1973. Contbr. to: Blackwoods Mag.; The Spectator; Argosy; The Contemporary Review; Asian Affairs; The Civil & Military Gazette, etc. Address: 22 High St., Petersfield, Hants. GU32 3JL, U.K.

BOWERING, George, b. 1 Dec. 1939. Professor of English. Education: B.A., Univ. of B.C., Canada, 1960; M.A., 1963. Positions held: Instr., Univ. of Calgary, 1963-66; Writer in Res., Sir George Williams Univ., Montreal, 1967-68; Asst. Prof., ibid, 1967-71. VP, Nihilist Party of Canada, 1966. Published works: Touch: Selected Poems, 1960-70, 1971; Geneve, 1971; George, Vancouver, 1970; Rocky Mountain Foot, 1969; The Gangs of Kosmos, 1969. Contbr. to: London Mag.; Atlantic Monthly; Scrip; Tlaloc; Fiddlehead; Tamarack Review; Sum; San Francisco Review; Tish; Imago; The Spero; Open Letter; Ophir; Prism Int.; Sun; Dalhousie Review; 0 to 9; Malahat Review; Is; Island; Ant's Forefoot; Io; Sumac; Iron; Quarry; Queen's Quarterly; West Coast Review. Honours, Awards: Brissendon Award, 1961; Gov. Gen.'s Award, 1969; Canada Coun. Sr. Arts Award, 1971. Address: 2249 York Ave., Vancouver 9, B.C., Canada.

BOWERS, Edgar, b. 2 Mar. 1924. Teacher. Education: B.A., Univ. of North Carolina, 1947; M.A., Ph.D., Stanford Univ., 1949, 1953. Positions held: Duke Univ., 1952; Harpur College (SUNY), 1955; U.C., Santa Barbara, 1958. Pubs. The Form of Loss, 1956; The Astronomers, 1965; Living Together: New and Selected Poems, 1973. Contrib. to: Factotum; Hudson Review; Western Review; Sewanee Review; Southern Review; New Statesman; Virginia Quarterly; Poetry. Awards include: Jones Fellowship (Stanford), 1948; Sewanee Review Award, 1954; Guggenheim Fellowship, 1958, 1969; Creative Arts Award, U.C., 1963. Address: 1502 Miramar Beach, Santa Barbara, Calif. 93108, USA.

BOXER, Avi, b. 8 Sept. 1932. Ghost Writer & Private Tutor. Education: B.A., Sir Geo. Williams Univ. Married Sheila Mary Ross, 2 sons. Positions held: Proofreader; Copywriter; Advertising Mgr.; Creative Dir. of an

Advertising Agency. Member, League of Canadian Poets, etc. Published works: No Address (book of poems), 1972. Rep. in following anthols: Poets 56, 1956; Love Where The Nights Are Long, 1962. Contbr. to: Artisan, London, U.K.; The Canadian Forum; Catapult, Montreal, Canada; Cataract, Montreal; CIV/n, Montreal; Contact, Toronto; Delta, Montreal; Exchange, Montreal; The Fiddlehead, Fredericton; The Lit. Review, Fairleigh Dickinson Univ., U.S.A.; Tribune, London, U.K., etc. Honours, awards: Bd. of Govs. Gold Medal for Creative Expression, Sir. Geo. Williams Univ., 1965; Canada Coun. Award, 1972 & '73. Address: 2084 Decarie Blvd., Apr. 6, Montreal Quebec, 260, Canada.

BOYARS, Arthur, b. 1925. Editor. Education: Wadham Coll., Oxford. Positions held: Ed., Mandrake, 1946-57; Ed., Int. Lit. Annual; Free-lance Reviewer. Published works: Poems, 1944; Poems, 1953. Contbr. to the following anthols: Poetry Now, 1956; New Poets of England & America, 1962; New Poetry, 1962.

BOYD, Melba Joyce, pen name **BOYD, Melba J.,** b. 2 Apr. 1950. Asst. Editor at Broadside Press, Detroit. Education: B.A., Western Michigan Univ., 1971 (Major in Engl. Lit., Minor in Communications Arts and Sciences)., M.A. (Engl. Lit.), 1972. Positions held: Grad. Asst. for the Martin Luther King Program at Western Mich. Univ., 1971-72; Editorial Asst. at Broadside Press, 1972; Teacher, Cass Tech. HS, Detroit, 1972-73; Instr., Wayne County Community Coll., 1973-; Asst. Editor at Broadside Press, 1973-. Membership: African Image Makers' Workshop (founding member). Published works: Broadside Series No. 66 "1965", 1972; Broadside Series No. 68 "To Darnell And Johnny", 1973; Boyd, Brown and Bethune (prose and poetry), 1974. Contbr. to: Maisha Mag. Address: 18846 Charest, Detroit, MI 48234, USA.

BOYER, Gwen, pen name, **BOYER, Gwen Roberts,** b. 7 Nov. 1910. Public Librarian (retired). Education: HS Grad., Hammond, Indiana; Moody Bible Inst., Chicago, Illinois; Library Training, Indiana Univ. Married to Frank A. Boyer; 1 s. (David); also 2 Korean foster sons, and 1 Indonesian foster daughter. Positions held: Adult and Children's work, Hammond Public Library, Indiana, 13 yrs.; Hospital Library work, 4 yrs.; Head, Dyer Public Library, Indiana, 17 yrs.; Church Libry librarian and oganizer, 20 yrs; Poetry Editor, WCAE-TV Journal, St. John, Indiana (currently). Memberships: Lake County Poetry Club (served as Pres., Vice-Pres., Treas., Historian, Chairman annual School Contests); Dyer Chamber of Commerce (3 yrs. director); Nat. Council For the Encouragement of Patriotism, Inc. (served as Treas. and Chaplain, Asst. Parade Chairman); Indiana State Fed. of Poetry Clubs; UPLI; American Bus. Women's Assoc.; American Poetry League; Midwest Fed. of Chaparral Poets; (Co-Chairman) Salvation Army Service Unit; Brewer Library, Richland Center, Wisconsin (Trustee). Contbr. to: (anthols) The Soul Sings, 1973; Midwest Poetry, 1973; Yearbook of Mod. Poetry, 1973; Lyrics of Love, 1973 (and many others 1945-1972), also contbr. to many newspapers, journals. Composers of three hymns (one translated into various languages). Recip. numerous awards, honours: Poet Laureate Indiana State Poets, 1957-58; Doct., Karachi, Pakistan, and others. Address: 418 Keilman St., Dyer, IN 46311, USA.

BOYLE, Kay, b. 19 Feb. 1903. Professor. Educ: Cincinnati Conservatory of Music; Ohio Mechanics Inst. Widow, six children. Positions held: Prof., San Fran. State Coll., 1963-. Memberships: National Inst. of Arts and Letters. Published works: A Glad Day, 1938; American Citizen, 1944; Collected Poems, 1962; (novels) Year Before Last, 1932; Death of a Man, 1936; A Frenchman Must Die, 1946; Generation Without Farewell, 1960; (short stories) Wedding Day, 1930; The First Lover, 1933; Thirty Stories, 1946; Nothing Ever Breaks Except the Heart, 1966. Contbr. to: Harvard Advocate; Southern Review; (anthologies) Anthology for the Enjoyment of Poetry, 1939; Anthology of American Poetry, 1941; Poetry of the Negro, 1949. Recip., Two Guggenheim Fellowships. Address: c/o A. Watkins, Inc., 77 Park Ave., New York, NY 10016, U.S.A.

BOYSON, Emil, b. 4 Sept. 1897. Author & Translator. Memberships: The Norwegian Acad. of Lang. & Lit.; Norwegian Authors Assn. Published works: Poems, privately printed, 1920; Varsler & Möter, 1934; Tegn & Tydning, 1935; Gjemt i Mörket, 1939; Sjelen & Udyret, 1946; Gjenkjennelse, 1957; Selected Poems, 1959; European Poetry, 1965; Seventy Poems, 1974. Address: c/o Gyldendal Norsk Forlag, Oslo, Norway.

BRADBURY, Malcolm (Stanley), b. 7 Sept. 1932. University Lecturer. Education: B.A., Univ. of Leicester; M.A., Queen Mary Coll., London; Ph.D., Manchester Univ. Positions held: Staff Tutor, Engl., Hull Univ., 1959-61; Lectr., Engl., Birmingham Univ., 1961-64; Am. Coun. of Learned Societies Fellow, Harvard Univ., Cambridge, Mass., USA, 1965; Sr. Lectr. – Rdr., Engl. & Am. Lit., Univ. of East Anglia, Norwich, UK; Vis. Fellow, All Souls Coll., Oxford, 1969. Published works: Two Poets: Allan Rodway, Malcolm Bradbury, 1966; (novels) Eating People is Wrong, 1959; Stepping Westward, 1965; (Lit. Crit.) Evelyn Waugh, 1962; Contbr., Universities Poetry Two, 1959. Address: Lockington House Cottage, Lockington, Nr. Driffield, East Yorkshire, UK.

BRADDY, Haldeen, b. 22 Jan. 1908. Professor of English. Education: Ph.D., NY Univ., 1934. Professor of Engl., Univ. of Texas at El Paso. Member: Modern Language Assoc. of America; Shakespeare Assoc. of America; The Westerners; Kappa Sigma. Pubs.: Chaucer and the French Poet Graunson, 1947, 2nd ed. 1968; Glorious Incense, Fulfillment of Edgar Allan Poe, 1953, 1968; Cock of the Walk, Legend of Pancho Villa, 1955, 1970; Hamlet's Wounded Name, 1964; Pancho Villa in Mexico, 1965; Pershing's Mission in Mexico, 1966; Pancho Villa Rides Again, 1967; Chaucer's Parlement of Foules, 1969; Geoffrey Chaucer: Literary & Historical Studies, 1971; Mexico and the Old Southwest, 1971; Three Dimensional Poe, 1973. Contrib. to: American Poetry Anthol., 1926; Houston Gargoyle; Poets Mag.; Texas Writers of Today; New Mexico Qtly.; Kaleidograph; NY Herald Tribune; Sewanee Review; The Lyric; Living Poetry; Albatross; Crescendo; Interim; Poems Southwest; Amigos. Address: 2109 Arizona Ave., El Paso, Texas 79930, USA.

BRADLEY, Gladys, pen name **KEIGHLEY, Gladys,** b. 7 July 1910. Housewife & Freelance Journalist. Married Harold Frank Bradley, 2 daughters. Positions held: Civil Servant. Memberships: Fndr. Mbr., Sec., V.P. & Chmn., Worcester Writers Circle; Jt. Ed., Prospect; Jt. Ed., Worcester Anthology '71. Published works: (book) The Pegasus Book of Trees, 1971. Contbr. to: BBC Midland Poets, 1917; BBC Radio Birmingham (Poems of the Worcester Area 1971), 1972; Spirit of the Trees Anthol.; Worcester Anthol., 1971; Heart of England Anthol.; My Garden; Homes & Gardens; Worcester Evening News; Yorkshire Herald; West Riding Mag.; Children's Britannica, etc. Address: 41 Bromwich Rd., Worcester, U.K.

BRADLEY, Harold Frank, b. 29 June 1904. Retired School Headmaster. Education: Worcester Royal Grammar Schl.; St. Peter's Coll., Saltley, Birmingham, U.K. Married Gladys Keighley, 2 daughters. Positions held: Asst. Master at schls. in Coventry & Worcester; Press Sec., Worcester City Tchrs. Assn., N.U.T.; Pres., ibid; Headmaster, St. Paul's Primary Schl., Worcester. Memberships: Fndr. Mbr., Folio Ed. & V.P., Worcester Writers' Circle; Jt. Ed., Prospect; Jt. Ed., Worcester Anthol. '71. Contbr. to: BBC Midland Poets (num. broadcasts); BBC Radio B'ham; Chamber's Jrnl.; Arena Qtly. (N.Z.); Heart of England Anthol.; Int. Youth Review; Prospect; Poems of the Worcester Area; The Jongleur; Worcester Evening News; Platform One; Verse; Worcester Anthol. '71, etc. Honours, awards: James Howard Gilmore Award, 1951; 2nd prize, Reflections, N.Y., 1953. Address: 41 Bromwich Rd., Worcester, U.K.

BRADLEY, Maurice, pen name **El Troubadour,** b. 28 Aug. 1897. Retired Civil Servant. Contbr. to: the Sunday Express; Fairyland Tales; Child Education; People's Jrnl., Devon Life; New Melody; Manifold; Envoi; Headland; Yorkshire Dialect Soc.; BBC; Stroud Fest. Poems, 1967. Address: 1 Sunnyside, Chawleigh, Chulmleigh, North Devon EX18 7EZ, U.K.

BRADLEY, Samuel McKee, b. 6 Feb. 1917. College Teacher; Professor of American & African Literature. Education: A.B., Morehead State Univ., Ky.; M.A., Univ. of Wash., Seattle; Univ. of Pa. Positions held: Engl. Instr., Duke Univ., 1945-46; Asst. Prof., Engl., Florence State Coll., Ala., 1947-49, Lincoln Univ., Pa., 1950-54, Lebanon Valley Coll., Pa., 1956-60; Assoc. Prof., Engl., St. Augustine's Coll., N.C., 1966-70; Dir. of Engl. Studies, African Inst., Lincoln Univ., 1960-65; Asst. Prof., Am. & African Lit., Kutztown State Coll., Pa., 1970-. Published works: Men – In Good Measure, 1966; Alexander & One World, 1967; Three New Soviet Poets, transl. w. M. Bogojavlensky, 1968; Manspell/Godspell, 1973. Contbr. to num. mags., jrnls., reviews inclng: Antigonish Review; Antioch Review; Commonweal; Kenyon Review; Ill. Qtly.; Meanjin Qtly.; Nation; Ohio Review; S.C. Qtly. Honours, awards: Fellow in Humanities, Duke Univ., 1969-70. Address: RD1, Box 584, HoneyBrook, PA 19344, U.S.A.

BRADSHAW, Irene Amelia (Mrs. Francis), pen name **BRADSHAW, Irene A.,** b. 15 Aug. 1915. Housewife. Education: State Teachers Coll., Eau Claire, Wisconsin. Positions held: Teacher, Eau Claire County, 1934-36; Co-owner and office manager, Downey Body Works, Downey, Calif., 1947-1970. Memberships: C.S.S.I.; American Poetry League; American Poets Fellowship Soc.; Calif. Fed. Chaparral Poets; Live Oak Chapter, C.F.C.P. (Pres., 1970-71); Orpheus Chapter, C.F.C.P.; Major Poets Chapter, Pierson Mettler Associates. Published work: Monument to Memory, 1973. Contbr. to: (anthols.) Dance of the Muse; Yearbook of Mod. Poetry; Outstanding Contemporary Poetry; From Sea to Sea in Song; Leaves from the Live Oak; (newspapers) The Daily Telegram; Call-Enterprise; (magazines, journals) American Bard; Jean's Journal; Haiku Highlights; The Archer, APL Bulletin; Bits & Pieces; Food for Thot; Tweed; American Poet; Creativity Newsletter; The Delvings; Wisconsin Centennial Album; Major Poets; Prairie Poet; Rainbow; United Poets. Address: 8232 Noren St., Downey, CA 90240, USA.

BRADY, Derek Kingsley, pen name **BRADY, D. Kingsley,** b. 17 Sept. 1935. Civil and Environmental Engineer. Education: B.E. (Civil), Univ. of Auckland, N.Z., 1957; M.S. (Engr.), Johns Hopkins Univ., Baltimore, USA, 1961; Ph.D., ibid., 1971. Positions held: Engineer, Ministry of Works, Wellington, N.Z., 1957-66; Research Scientist, Johns Hopkins Univ., Baltimore, 1966-74. Membership: Maryland State Poetry Soc. Contbr. to: Takapuna Grammar School Mag.; Auckland Univ. Engineering Soc. Proceedings. Awards: 1st Prize for Humorous Verse, TGS., 1951; 2nd Hon. Mention, MSPS Contest, 1968. Address: 136 Overbrook Rd., Baltimore, MD 21212, USA.

BRAINARD, Franklin Emory, b. 20 June 1920. Teacher. Poet. Education: B.A., Jamestown Coll., N.D.; M.A., Univ. of N.D., Grand Forks; Tchr. educ. courses at Dickinson State Tchrs. Coll., N.D. Married, 3 children. Positions held: Cook & steward, merchant ships, 1943-45; Tchr., Deadwood H.S., S.D., 1946-56; Tchr. & later Poet-in-Res., Mounds View Public Schls., 1956-72. Published works: Poems (pamphlet), 1952; Raingatherer (booklet), 1973. Contbr. to: The Hornbook Mag.; Educational Forum; Jewish Frontier; Chicago Jewish Forum; Plainsong; Epos; The Midwest Qtly.; Black Flag; Café Solo; The Hiram Poetry Review; Today's Health; Preview, etc. Address: 1901 17th St. N.W., New Brighton, MN 55112, U.S.A.

BRAND, Millen, b. 19 Jan. 1906. Writer. Education: B.A., Columbia Coll., U.S.A., 1929; B.Litt., Columbia Schl. of Jrnlsm., 1929. Married, 4 children. Positions

held: Copywriter, N.Y. Telephone Co.; Instr., N.Y. Univ.; Ed., Crown Publishers, 1953-. Memberships: Authors League; PEN; Soc. of Am. Historians. Published works: Dry Summer in Provence, 1966; Local Lives, 1974. Contbr. to: Accent; Agape; Am. Dialog; the Am. Pen; Am. Poetry Review; Am. Swedish Histl. Fndn. Yrbook; Am. Weave; Beloit Poetry Jrnl.; Book Week; Calif. Qtly.; Chelsea; Chicago Choice; El Corno Emplumado; N.Y. Times; the New Yorker; Nexus; The Outsider; Pembroke Mag.; Poetry; Poetry Pilot; Queens Qtly.; Southern Poetry Review, etc. Address: 242 E. 77th St., N.Y., NY 10021, U.S.A.

BRANDI, John, b. 5 Nov. 1943. Poet & Forester. Education: B.F.A., Univ. of Calif., San Fernando Valley, 1965. Positions held: Ed., Designer, Eclipse Mag., Univ. of Calif., San Fernando Valley, 1964-65. Published works include: Poem Afternoon in A Square of Guadalajara, 1970; Desde Alla, 1970; Poems of Venice and LA, 1971; Field Notes from Alaska, 1971; One Week of Mornings at Dry Creek, 1971; Y Aun Hay Mas, 1972; Narrowgauge to Riobamba, 1973; San Fran. Lastday Homebound Hangover Highway Blues, 1973; A Partial Exploration of Palo Flechado Canyon, 1973. Contbr. to the following jrnls., mags., etc.: Los Angeles Free Press; Tree Jrnls. I, II, III; Portland State Review; Cranium; Christopher's, San Francisco & Santa Barbara, Calif.; Measure; Lips; Tractor; Vagabond; Atlantic Monthly; Quetzal; Chelsea. Maguey Mag.; Kayak; Desert Review, San Francisco, Santa Cruz, NM. Recip. 1971 Poetry Award, Portland State Review. Address: Box 356, Guadalupita, NM 87722, USA.

BRANDSTAETTER, Roman, b. 3 Jan. 1906. Writer. Education: Ph.D., Fac. of Philos., Jagiellonian Univ. at Krakow. Married. Positions held: Tchr. of Polish lang.; Mbr. of an editl. staff; Cultural Attaché, Polish Embassy, Rome, Italy, 1947-48; Lit. Mgr., Polish State Theatre at Poznan & the State Opera, 1948-50. Memberships: Polish Writers' Assn.; currently Mngmt. Mbr., Polish PEN Ctr.; Corres. Mbr., Académie Rhodanienne des Lettres; Hon. Mbr., Académie des Poetes de Rhoranie, 1968. Published works: (poetry) Yokes, 1928; The Way Upwards, 1931; Knots & Swords, 1933; The Kingdom of the Third Temple, 1934; Lights & Darks of Jerusalem, 1934; The Song about my Christ, 1960, '63, '65, '69 & '74; Two Muses, 1965; The Hymns on Our Lady, 1963, '65, '69, '74; (prose) The Chronicles of Assissi, 1947, '57, '59; Jesus of Nazareth, 4 vols., 1967-73; (dramas) Silence, 1957; Downfall of the Stone House, St. Francis Theatre, Moonlight Drama & The Weeping Odysseus in one vol., St. Francis Theatre & Other Dramas, 1958; Death on the Shore of Artemis, 1961; Medea, 1961; Calm, 1961; The Day of Wrath, 1962; The Twilight of the Demons, 1964, etc. Var. translations. Contbr. to var. jrnls. in Poland. Honours, awards incl: Bronze Medal, Académie Rhodanienne des Lettres, 1963; Polish-Am. Prize of the Alfred Jurzykowski Fndn., 1970; PEN Club Prize, 1973; Kt. of the Order of Poland's Revival; Hon. Citizen of the town of Zakopane. Address: Winogrady 37/6, 61-663 Poznan, Poland.

BRANTLEY, Dora, b. 3 Jan. 1890. Beautician (retired). Education: Grammar School; School of Beauty Culture; North Dade College, Miami. Contrib. to: Poet Lore, vol. 19; Haiku Highlights. Address: 12781 Westview Drive, Miami, Florida 33167, USA.

BRASE, Paul Yngve, b. 22 Nov. 1943. Poet; Teacher. Education: B.A., Bethany Coll., Lindsborg, Kan., 1966. Positions held: Substitute Tchr., Denver Public Schls.; Poetry Cons., Colo. Coun. on the Arts, Nevada Coun. of the Arts; Poet in Res., Tacoma Public Schls., Tacoma, Wash. Contbr. to: West Coast Poetry Review. Address: c/o 984 S. Race St., Denver, CO 80209, U.S.A.

BRATHWAITE, L. Edward, b. 11 May 1930. Writer; University Lecturer. Education: Harrison Coll., Barbados; Barbados Scholarship, 1949; Pembroke Coll., Cambridge Univ., U.K., 1950-54; B.A., 1953;

Cert. of Educ., 1954; Ph.D., 1968. Positions held: Educ. Office, Min. of Educ., Ghana, 1955-62; Res. Tutor, Dept. of Extra-Mural Studies, Univ. of W.I., St. Lucia, 1962-63; Lectr., Dept. of Hist., ibid, Mona, Jamaica, 1963–. Memberships: Fndr., Sec., Caribbean Artists Movement; Anglo-Am. Historian Conf., Univ. of London, 1966; Anglo-Am. Poets' Conf.; PEN Int. Published works: The People Who Came, Bk.1, 1968 & Bk. II (Ed. & co-author), 1969; The Folk Culture of Jamaican Slaves, 1969; The Development of Creole Society in Jamaica, 1770-1820, 1969; Four Plays for Primary Schools, 1964; Odale's Choice (play), 1967; Rights of Passage (a long poem), 1967; Masks (a long poem), 1968; Island (a long poem), 1969; The Making of a Drum, from 'Masks' (gramaphone record), 1968; Rights of Passage (gramaphone record), 1969; Masks, 1973; Islands, 1973; The Arrivants, 1973. Contbr. to num. jrnls., reviews, anthols. inclng: Poetry From Cambridge, 1947-50, 1950; Young Commonwealth Poets, '65; New Poems, 1965; New Poems, 1966; Twelve Poets, 1967; Commonwealth Poems of Today, 1967; New Voices of the Commonwealth, 1968; The Sun's Eye, 1968; Penguin Modern Poets 15, 1969; N.Y. Times Anthol. of Poetry, 1969; Times Educ. Supplement; Contemporary Poets of the Engl. Lang.; Caribbean Voice; Sunday Gleaner, Jamaica; N.Y. Times; London Mag.; Sunday Times; London. Ed., Iouanaloa, 1963; Co-Ed., Bim., 1965–; Ed., Newsletter, Caribbean Artists Movement, 1966-68; Co-Ed., Comment, 1968; Co-Ed., Savacou. Has read poetry at num. festivals., univs. etc. in U.K., W.I., U.S.A. Num. Radio & TV broadcasts. Honours, awards: Poetry Book Soc. Recommend. (Rights of Passage), 1967; Hampstead Arts Fest. Poetry Prize, U.K., 1967; Arts Coun. of G.B. Poetry Bursary, 1967; Cholmondeley Award, 1970; Guggenheim Fndn. Fellowship, 1971; Bussa Award, 1973. Address: Dept. of Hist., Univ. of West Indies, Mona, Kingston 7, Jamaica, W.I.

BRATT, B.A. Eyvind, b. 30 July 1907. Diplomatist. Education: Ph.D., Univ. of Uppsala, Sweden; Law degree, Univ. of Stockholm. Positions held: Entered Swedish Foreign Serv. in 1931; Swedish Ambassador to Persia; Min. in S. Africa, & Ethopia; Consul General, Berlin; currently First Swedish Ambassador to Ireland. Member, Irish PEN Club. Published works: Arcadia Ethiopica, 1962; Persiska dikter, 1970 (transl. from Russian of S. Esienin's 'Persian Motives'). A number of transl. of French, Engl., Russian poetry as well as own poems in the Swedish papers 'Svenska Dagbladet', 'Sydsvenska Dagbladet', & the lit. review 'Lyrikvännen'. Also a few Engl. transl. in Irish & Engl. papers such as 'Broadsheet' & in connection w. interviews in 'Irish Press' & 'Sunday Mirror'. Honours, awards: Hon. mention of 'Arcadia Ethiopia' among best turned out prints publd. by Swedish Lit. Soc. 'Bokvännen'. Address: Ballymadun, Ashbourne, Co. Meath, Ireland.

BRATT, Nina Elois, pen name **ABBOTT, Anne,** b. 19 Nov. 1942. Businesswoman. Education: Miss. State Coll. for Women, Columbus, 2 yrs.; psychol., Univ. of S. Ala., Mobile; currently studying Drafting at Jackson Co. Jr. Coll., Gautier, Miss. Married Charles B. Bratt, 1 daughter (Heather). Positions held: Admin. Asst., Jackson Co. ASCS; Libn., Jackson Co. Law Lib.; Mgr., Western Union Substation; Litton Ship Systems. Memberships: Pres., Writers Unlimited, Pascagoula, 1968; Contest Chmn., ibid, 1973; South & West Grp. Contbr. to: South & West Mag., 1972 & '73; Legend, 1972; Poems by Poets Anthol., 1974; Poet, 1973; The Log, 1972; The Paper, 1972. Recip. Award, Mid-South Poetry Fest., 1971. Address: P.O. Box 461, Moss Point, MS 39563, U.S.A.

BRATTMAN, Steven Ronald, pen names, **BRATT, Ronald, BART, Gunther & GREEN, Thomas,** b. 17 Mar. 1948, LA, Calif., USA. Education: B.A., UCLA. Positions held: Logkeeper, KHJ-TV, Channel 9, LA: Coord., KHJ-TV, ibid; Audience Rels., Hollywood Video Ctr., Lit. Aide, MGM. Mbrships: Alpha Mu Gamma; Defenders of Wildlife. Published works: Media, 1973; The Beastly Book, 1971; Negaflap, 1971;

On the Moon, 1971; The Great War, 1971. Contbr. to the following jrnls. & anthols: Envoi; Two Tone; Zahir; Major Poets Quarterly; Scrip; Cardinal; Message; Fireflower; Cycloflame; Personal Poetry WEFG-FM; Yearbook of Mod. Poetry; Contemporary Am. Poetry. Address: 1664 S. Crescent Heights Blvd., Los Angeles, Calif. 90035, USA.

BRAULT, Jacques, b. 29 Mar. 1933. University Professor. Education: B.A.; B. Philos.; M.A. Positions held: Prof., Univ. of Montreal, Canada. Member, Editl. Comm., Revues Liberté & Etudes Francaises. Published works: Trinôme, 1957; Mémoire, 1965; Suite Fratenelle, 1970; La Poésie ce Matin, 1971, '73. Contbr. to: Liberté; Les Herbes Rouges; Ellipse; Le Devoir; Le Monde, Paris; Les Lettres Nouvelles; Esprit; West Coast Review; Souschasnit; Le Journal des Poètes; Commune Mesure, etc. Honours, awards: Province de Québec, 1965; Prix, France-Canada, 1968; Lauréat du Collège Poétique de Menton. Address: 3799 rue Kent, Montreal, Quebec, Canada H3S 1N4.

BRAUN, Felix, b. 4 Nov. 1885. Writer; University Professor. Education: Dr.phil., Univ. of Vienna, Austria. Positions held: Prof., Univ. of Palermo & Padua, Italy; Prof. of Extra Mural Studies, U.K. Memberships: PEN Austria; Deutsche Akademie fur Spuads und Dichtung, Darmstadt; Oesterreichischer Kunstsenat, Vienna. Has written many books (poetry, novels, stories, dramas, translations, essays). Honours, awards: State Prize of Austria; Prize of the Town of Vienna, etc. Address: A 1190 Vienna, Geistingergasse 1, Austria.

BRAUN, Henry, b. 25 July 1930. Assistant Professor of English. Education: B.A., French Lit., M.A., Engl. & Am. Lit., Brandeis Univ., Waltham, Mass.; Buffalo Univ., N.Y.; Boston Univ., Mass.; Fulbright Scholar, France, 1955-56. Married w. 2 daughters. Positions held: Guide & Lectr., Isabella Stewart Gardner Museum, Boston, 1960-65; Instructor in Engl., Univ. of Maine, 1963-65; Currently, Asst. Prof., Engl., Temple Univ., Phila. Published works: The Vergil Woods, 1968. Contbr. to (Jrnls.): Prairie Schooner; Massachusetts Review; War Registers League Peace Calendar; Chelsea; Nation; Midstream; Poetry. Address: 325 Wellesley Rd., Philadelphia, PA 19119, USA.

BRAUTIGAN, Richard, b. 30 Jan. 1935. Published works: The Return of the Rivers, 1957; The Galilee Hitch-Hiker, 1958; The Octopus Frontier, 1960; The Pill Versus the Springhill Mine Disaster, 1968; (novels) In Watermelon Sugar, 1970; The Confederate General from Big Sur, 1965; Trout Fishing In America, 1970. Address: San Francisco, CA, U.S.A.

BRAYBROOKE, Neville Patrick Bellairs, b. 1928. Writer. Education: Ampleforth Coll. Positions held: Ed., Chamber's Encyclopaedia, 1947. Memberships: Soc. of Authors; Writers Action Group. Published works: Ed The Wind & the Rain, quarterly, 1940-51; T.S. Eliot: A symposium for his 70th birthday, 1958; Partridge in a Pear Tree: A Christmas Anthol., 1960; Letters of J.R. Ackerley, 1974; This is London, 1953; London Green: a history of the Royal Parks, 1959; The Isler: a novel, 1960; The Delicate Investigation: a play, 1969. Contbr. to: Encounter; The Listener; New Statesman; The Observer; Spectator; The Times; Times Lit. Supplement; Sunday Times; Sunday Telegraph. Address: Grove House, Castle Rd., Cowes, I.O.W., U.K.

BRAZER, Joan Miller, b. 26 Sept. 1937. Journalist. Education: Univ. of Md., 1955-56; A.A., Dade Jr. Coll., Miami, Fla., 1967; poetry course, Barry Coll., Miami, Fla. Divorced, 3 children. Positions held: Book Reviewer, Miami News; Columnist, Jewish Floridian Newspaper; Book Reviewer, Miami Herald; Stringer for Tropic (mag. sect. of Miami Herald); Entertainment & Feature Ed., Coral Gables Times & Guide; Entertainment Writer, Ft. Lauderdale News. Memberships: Laramore-Rader Poetry Soc.; Sigma

Delta Chi; Fla. Press Club. Contbr. to: Penman Mag.; Am. Bard; Human Voice Qtly.; Encore Mag.; Haiku Highlights; Poetry Parade; El Viente; Words on the Wind; Coral Gables Times; The Guide; Miami Beach Sun Reporter. Honors, awards: Laramore-Rader Poetry Prize, 1967; Prize Winner for Poetry, State of Fla., 1969; Award, Miami Herald & Coun. for Continuing Educ. of Women, 1969; Selected to read own poetry at Vizcaya Gdns. & Miami Libs. celebrating World Poetry Day, 1970, '71, '72. Address: 5250 N.E. 6th Ave., Ft. Lauderdale, FL, U.S.A.

BRECHBUHL, Beat, b. 28 July 1939. Writer; Artist. Married, 1 daughter. Positions held: Editor; Production Mgr., large Zurich Publishing House; Freelance Writer & Artist, 1971–. Memberships: Internationaler Schutzverband deutschsprachiger Schriftsteller. Published works: Spiele um Pan, poems, 1962; Die Stiere, narrative, 1963; Lakonische Reden, poems, 1964; Gesunde Predigt eines Dorfbewohners, poems, 1966; Die Bilder und ich, poems, 1968; Die Litanei von den Bremsklötzen, poems, 1969; Auf der Suche nach den Enden des Regenbogens, poems, 1970; Kneuss, novel, 1970; Der geschlagene Hund pisst an die Säulen des Tempels, poems, 1972; Meine Füsse lauf ich ab bis an die Knie, poems, 1973; Beat Brechbühls Branchenbuch, poems, 1974; Nora und der Kümmerer, novel, 1974. Contbr. to: Weltwoche, Zurich; Akzente, Munich; Dimension, Austin, Tex.; Uj iras, Budapest; Manuskripte, Graz. Recip. some hons. & awards. Address: Belsitostrasse 20, CH-8645 Jona-Rapperswil, Switzerland.

BREEDLOVE, Mildred Matthews, b. 27 May 1904. Writer, Poet. Married. Positions held: Ranching, Nev., 1959-63; Appointed Poet Laureate of Nev., 1957; Re-appointed, 1959; Resigned, 1966. Memberships: Nat. League of Am. Pen Women; Organizer, Pres., Nev. Poetry Soc., 1961–; Nev. State Chmn., Nat. Fed. of State Poetry Socs., 1961–; State Chmn., Nat. Poetry Day Comm., Inc. Published works: Those Desert Hills and Other Poems, 1959; A Study of Rhyme and Rhythmn in Creative Expression, 1959; Nevada (narrative poem), 1963. Contbr. to: Nature; Ariz. Highways; Desert Mag.; Am. Opinion; Empire Mag.; Las Vegas Sun; Oregonian; Kan. City Star; etc. 'The Portrait of Nevada', words by Mildred Breedlove & music by Antonio Morelli, performed by Las Vegas Pops Concert Orch. w. Univ. of Nev. Las Vegas Singing Chorus & guest soloists, 1969. Honours, awards: Achievement Award, Nat. League of Am. Pen Women, 1953; ibid, 1957; Outstanding Citizen's Award, Nev. Savings & Loan, for the poem 'Nevada', 1963; Best Poem (any lang.) Award, United Poets Laureate Int., for the poem 'Nevada', 1964; Gold Laurel Wreath, Medal, United Poets Laureate Int., 1965. Address: 2271 Davidson, San Bernadino, Calif. 92405, USA.

BREEN, Barry Andrew, pen name **BREEN, B.A.,** b. 15 July 1938. English Teacher. Education: B.A., Dip. Ed., Melbourne Univ., Australia. Married, 3 sons, 1 daughter. Positions held: Sr. Engl. Tchr., Shepparton H.S., 1964-65; Sr. Engl. Tchr., Camperdown H.S., 1966-73; Lit. Ed., The Secondary Tchr., 1966-73; Sr. Master, Camperdown H.S., 1969-73. Memberships: Sec. Engl. Standing Comm., 1967-73; Soc. of Authors; Vic. Fellowship of Australian Writers. Published works: Behind My Eyes, 1968; Interim, 1973. Has edited var. anthols. for schls. Contbr. to: The Age; The Australian; Nation Review; The Bulletin; Hemisphere; Meanjin Quarterly; Overland; Poetry Australia; New Poetry; Quadrant; The Secondary Tchr.; Westerly; The Penguin Book of Australian Poetry, etc. Recip., Poetry Mag. Award, 1968. Address: 9 Campbell St., Camperdown, Vic 3260, Australia.

BREHM, Edythe Lucille, b. 3 Sept. 1904. Educator. Education: A.B., Univ. of Tex.; grad. courses in Educational Psychol. & course in Poetics. Married Harold E. Brehm, 1 son. Positions held: H.S. Tchr., Harlingen, Tex., 1926-27; Bible Instr., McAllen H.S. 1937-41; H.S. Tchr., ibid, 1942-72 (ret'd); Substitute

Tchng. Memberships: McAllen Study Club, 1927-41, '72–; Delta Kappa Gamma Soc.; Past Mbr., Valley Byliners; Past Mbr., Coun. for Promotion of Poetry in Tex.; Sponsor of H.S. Lit.-feature mag., 25 yrs.; Past Mbr., McAllen Chapt., AAUW; Past Mbr., Zonta Int. Published works: Heartwrought Filigree, 1943; Heritage of Song, 1945; The Christmas Story, 1956. Contbr. to: Singing Quill; Span; Driftwind; Sun Dial; Fla. Mag. of Verse; Candor; Flatbush Mag.; Carmel Pine Cone; Hartford Times; N.Y. Herald Tribune; Oregonian; Tampa Tribune, etc. Honours, awards: Wildlife Mag. Book Prize, 1946; Prairie Wings Third Prize (Editor's Prize), Sept.-Oct. issue, 1947. Address: 400 Quince Circle, McAllen, TX 78501, U.S.A.

BREIGHNER, Harry Daniel, Sr. pen names **DEE, H., BREIGHNER, H. Daniel,** b. 27 Feb. 1909. Business Owner and Manager, Promotions. Education: High School, US Navy H.C.T.S., Motel Training School. Positions held: Standard Oil Co., dealer, 22 yrs.; Theater Mgr.; Motel Manager, 6 yrs., Major Dept. Store Security, and App. Mgr. Member: U.A.P. Pubs. Lincoln Country, 1968; Memories, 1967; Mini History, 1969; Poetry in Action for Christ, 1971; Along Lincoln's Trail, 1973; Great Moments in Vacationland USA, 1973. Contrib. to: Dewitt County Observer; Santa Ana Register; Anthol. of California Poets, 1969; Anthology of Railroad Poems, 1970; Sunshine Magazine, 1971; Poetry Parade, 1967, 1968; The Batterseam, 1973; Gato Magazine; Golden Anthol. of Poetry, 1973, etc. Recipient, Outstanding Achievement Award, 1973. Address: 2627 East LaPalma No. 138, Anaheim, Calif. 92806, USA.

BREMSER, Ray, b. 22 Feb. 1934. Poet. Educ: Correspondence Course, Journalism, Univ. of Okla., 1956-57. Married, one child. Positions held: Served with U.S.A.F. Published works: Poems of Madness, 1965; Angel, 1967; Drive Suite, 1968. Contbr. to: Partisan Review; Chicago Review; Exodus; (anthologies) New American Poetry, 1960; Beat Scene, 1960.

BRENNAN, Henry, pen names **LE FER BRUN & ETAIN WHITETHOUGHT,** b. 27 Sept. 1906. Retired. Contbr. to: A Girdle of Song (Commonwealth Anthol.); Jindyworobak Anthol.; New Zealand Poetry Yearbook; Poet (New Zealand Number); Poet (Pacific Number); Sydney Bulletin; New Zealand Listener; Thirteen Poets; Arena; 2 NZEF Times; Auckland Star; New Zealand Best Poems; Art in New Zealand; Here & Now; The Wooden Horse. Address: 90 Hutton St., Otahuhu 6, Auckland, New Zealand.

BRENNAN, Joseph Payne, b. 20 Dec. 1918. Writer. Positions held: Assistant Editor, Theatre News; 26th "Yankee" Division, World War II; Library Asst., Yale Univ., 1946-1973; Editor-Publisher, Essence, 1950-1973; Editor-Publisher, Macabre, 1957-1973. Member: Poetry Soc. of America; New England Poetry Club. Pubs.: Heart of Earth, 1950; The Humming Stair, 1953; The Wind of Time, 1962; Nightmare Need, 1964; Edges of Night (forthcoming). Contrib. to: The American Scholar; American Vanguard; Anthol. of Magazine Verse; Beloit Poetry Journal; Best Poems Annual; Chicago Review; N.Y. Times; Univ. Review; Yale Literary Magazine. Anthol. appearances include: Albermarle Book of Mod. Verse for Schools; The Owl Book; Every Child's Book of Verse; Fire & Sleet & Candlelight; The Various Light, etc. Recipient: Hartshorne Award, 1957; Leonora Speyer Mem. Award (Poetry Soc. of America), 1961. Address: 26 Fowler St., New Haven, Conn. 06515, USA.

BRENNER, Reeve Robert, pen name, **BAR NER, R.,** b. 20 May 1936. Rabbi. Education: A.B., CCNY; B.H.L., M.A., Rabbi, Hebrew Union Coll., Jewish Inst. of Religion, NY. Married to Joyce Rosman, 3 children. Positions held: Instr., St. Vincent Coll. & Seminary, Pa.; Rabbi, Princeton Jewish Center, NJ; Rabbi, Temple Israel, Staten Island, NY; Rabbi, Genesis Hebrew Center, Tuckahoe, NY (current). Published work: A Goodly Heritage, 1967. Contbr. to: Variant Mag.; Jewish Spectator; Pennsylvania Poetry Anthol.;

Internat. Who's Who in Poetry Anthol. Awards: Brooklyn Coll. Poetry Prize, 1956; Binder Mem. Award, 1964. Address: Genesis Hebrew Center, 25 Oakland Ave., Tuckahoe, NY 10707, USA.

BRENT, Josephine Stresen-Reuter, b. 30 Aug. 1911. Lecturer. Education: Art Inst. of Chicago; Lewis Inst., 1935-36; Univ. of Chicago, Down Town Coll., 1935; B.A., 1936. Divorced, 1 son, 1 daughter. Positions held: Art Supvsr., Saint Sabina's Schl., Chicago, 1946-49, St. Basel's Schl., 1948-49; Art & Engl. Tchr. (Sub.), High Schools in Chicago, 1949-52; Private Art Tutor, Holland, Mich., 1953-55; Lecturer on Antiques, 1958-73. Memberships: Poetry Soc. of Mich., 1959-73; Bd. Mbr., South Shore Hosp. Guild, 1962-65; Pres., Christine Van Raalte Questers, 1962; Sec., ibid, 1964. Contbr. to: Peninsula Poets Mag., 1959-71; Ludington Daily News, 1962; Argentine Prize Poets Mag., 1962. Honours, awards: 3rd prize, Argentine Poetry Contest, 1962; 1st prize, humor, Peninsula Poets, 1971. Address: 600 Midway Ave., Holland, MI 49423, U.S.A.

BRETCHES, Ethel Elizabeth, b. 25 Feb. 1909. Retired Secretary. Education: Independence H.S., Kansas; Lacaze Acad. of Langs., Wash. D.C. Positions held: Sec., law office, 1928-34; worked for U.S. Dept. of Agric. until 1947; Sec. Asst., Missionary Educ. Dept. & Foreign Div. of the United Christian Missionary Soc., Indpls., Ind., 1948; Agric. Dept., then Atomic Energy Commn. until retirement in 1959. Memberships: Kansas Authors Club; Sec., Third Dist. of Kansas Authors; Sec.-Treas., Verdigris Valley Writers, ibid; Poets Study Club of Terre Haute, Ind. Contbr. to: Vital Christianity; Poets' Page of The News, Paducah, Ky. Recip. 3rd prize, Third Dist. Kans. Authors Contest, 1973, & var. hon. mentions. Address: 213 West Locust St., Independence, KS 67301, U.S.A.

BRETTELL, Noel Harry, b. 3 July 1908. Retired Schoolmaster. Education: B.A., Univ. of Birmingham, U.K., 1930. Positions held: Headmaster of Rural Schls. in Rhodesia. Memberships: PEN Int., Rhodesia & S. Africa Ctrs.; Poetry Soc. of Rhodesia; English Assn. Published works: Bronze Frieze, Poems mostly Rhodesia, 1950. Contbr. to: Two Tone (Rhodesia); New Coin & Standpunte (S. Africa); Chirimo (Rhodesia); Oxford Book of S. African Poetry; Rhodesian Poetry; Commonwealth Anthol. Recip. First Award of PEN 'Book Ctr.' Award, 1972. Address: P.O. Bonda, via Umtali, Rhodesia.

BREW, Kwesi, b. 27 May 1928. Diplomat; Poet. Education: B.A. (Gen), Univ. Coll. of Ghana, 1953. Positions held: Asst. Govt. Agt. (Asst. Dist. Commnr.), 1953-54; Govt. Agt., Kete Krachi, 1954; Asst. Sec., Pub. Service Commn., 1955; For. Ser. Officer, 1957; 3rd Sec., Ghana High Commn., London, & Ghana Embassy, Paris, 1958; 2nd Sec., Ghana High Commn., New Delhi, 1959; Counsellor, Ghana Embassy, Moscow, 1962; Dir., Div. of Middle E. & Asia, Min. of For. Affairs; Dir., UN & Int. Orgs., ibid; Dir., Div. of Western & European Affairs; Dir., Div. of Protocol; Mbr., Ghana Deleg., Int. Atomic Energy Agcy., Vienna, 1960-61; Ghana Ambassador to Mexico, 1964; Ambassador-Designate, Karachi, 1966; Ambassador to Senegal, 1966; Alternate Hd., Deleg. to Econ. Conf., Dakar, 1968. Author of Shadows of Laughter, 1968. Contbr. to: Voices of Ghana; Voices of the Commonwealth; New World Writings; Schwarzer Orpheus; Ghana Review; Malahat Review No. 6 (Univ. of Victoria, BC., Canada); Outpost; Presence Africaine; Times Lit. Supplement; Okyeame; Poems From Black Africa; Mod. Poetry for Africa; African Writing Today; West African Verse; Zuka–a Jrnl. of E. African Creative Writing; New Writing From Zambia No. 2. Active in the theatre, taking the leading role in the Ghana Nat. Theatre's prod. of Our Town, by T. Wilder, & in other prods. Honours: Winner, poetry competition, The Engl. Soc., Univ. Coll. of Ghana, 1949. Address: Embassy of Ghana, 23 Ave. Maginot, Dakar, Senegal.

BREWER, Kenneth Wayne, b. 28 Nov. 1941. Educator. Education: B.A., Western N.M. Univ., Silver City, 1965;

M.A., N.M. State Univ., Las Cruces, 1967; Ph.D., Univ. of Utah, Salt Lake City, 1973. Married Carol Ann Hayton, 1 son, 1 daughter. Positions held: Engl. Tchr., Las Cruces H.S., N.M., 1968; Instr. in Engl. Utah State Univ., Logan, 1969-72; Asst. Prof. in Engl., ibid, 1973–. Member, Rocky Mountain Modern Lang. Assn. Published works: (books) Places, Shadows, Dancing People, 1969; Catching Light, 193. Contbr. to: Poetry Northwest; Dragonfly; Western Humanities Review; Westigan Review; Fragments; Egg; Puerto Del Sol; Hanging Loose; Arx; Desperado; Grande Ronde Review, etc. Recip., Hon. Mention, Poetry Contest, Utah State Fine Arts Inst., 1973. Address: Engl. Dept., 32, Utah State Univ., Logan, UT 84322, U.S.A.

BREWER, Wilmon, b. 1 Apr. 1895. Author. Education: Hingham Center School; Country Day School, Newton; Harvard Univ. (A.B. magna cum laude, 1917; A.M., 1920; Ph.D., 1925). Married, Katharine Hay More (d. of poet, Brookes More). Positions held: 2nd Lt., Infantry, 1918-19; Instr. Harvard, 1923-24; Chairman, Parish Committee, 1st Parish, Hingham, 1934-1936; Pres., American Poetry Assoc., 1939-41; Pres., Boston Authors Club, 1944-46; Lecturer, Cooper Hill Writers' Conference, Dover, Vt. 1968-70; Memberships: New England Poetry Club; Manuscript Club of Boston; Modern Lang. Assoc.; Dante Soc. of America; Shakespeare Assoc. of America; Internat. Platform Assoc.; Internat. Inst. of Arts and Letters. Published works: Dante's Ecologues, 1927 (2nd ed., 1961); Ovid's Metamorphoses in European Culture (Volume One 1933, Volume Two 1941, Volume Three 1957) Companion Volumes to Ovid's Metamorphoses in blank verse by Brookes More; Adventures in Verse, 1945 (2nd ed., 1963); Sonnets and Sestinas, 1937; New Adventures, 1950; Adventures Further, 1958; Still More Adventures, 1966. Contbr. to: American Poetry Assoc. anthols., 1930, 1933, 1938, 1942; Principal Poets of the World (London), 1932; Chapbook of the Maine Writers' Conference, No. 4, 5, 6, 7, 8, 9, 10, 11, and many other anthols. Edited, The Twentieth Anniversary volume of the American Poetry Assoc. Awarded Rhyme 'n' Rhythm, 1947, 100-dollar prize; Made double record of poems for the Woodbury Poetry Room, Harvard Univ., 1964. Address: Great Hill, Hingham, MA 02043, USA.

BREWSTER, Elizabeth Winifred, b. 26 Aug. 1922. Librarian; Teacher. Member of League of Canadian Poets. Published works: East Coast, 1951; Lillooet, 1954; Roads, 1957; Passage of Summer, 1969; Sunrise North, 1972. Contbr. to: Alphabet; Canadian Forum; Fiddlehead; Far Point; Poetry, Chgo.; Prism; Queen's Quarterly; Quarry, etc. Recip. of E.J. Pratt gold medal, 1954; Canada Coun. Sr. Arts Award, 1971-72. Address: Dept. of English, Univ. of Saskatchewan, Saskatoon, Sask., Canada.

BRIDGES, Mary Winifred, b. 30 July 1929. Textile Worker. Married, 4 sons, 7 daughters. Member, Calder Valley Poetry Soc. Published works: A Random Collection of Poems, 1968; Poems, 1972. Contbr. to: Lancashire Evening Telegraph; Harwood Advertiser; Three Towns Gazette; Raleigh Jrnl.; Blackburn Times; Parnassian; Accrington Observer. Address: 28 Springfield Rd., Gt. Harwood, Nr. Blackburn, Lancs., U.K.

BRIERLEY, Patricia Anne, pen name **MARTLAND, Patricia,** b. 6 Jan. 1929. Education: Public School. Married, 1 s., 1 d. Member, Editorial Panel of Envoi; Reviewer for Scrip. Published works: The Fox of Stone, 1963; A Song at the Centre, 1970. Contbr. to: Breakthru; Breakthru Publications; It's World That Makes The Love Go Round; Envoi; New Headland; Outposts; Poetry of the Circle in the Square; Scrip. Address: 40 Barrington Rd., Letchworth, Herts. SG6 3TQ, UK.

BRIGGS, John, pen name **CASSEGRAIN, William,** b. 8 Jan. 1945. Teacher; Screenwriter. Education: B.A., Wesleyan Univ., 1968; M.A., NY Univ., 1972. Positions held; Instructor, The New School; Tchr., Irvington HS; Police Reporter, Hartford Courant; currently writing film scripts; Ed., Reflection, 1967; Ed., NY Poetry, 1970; Mng. Ed., NY Quarterly, 1971–. Publ: The Logic of Poetry (co-author with Richard Monaco), 1974. Contbr. to: New American Poetry; Yearbook of Modern Poetry, 1971; NY Poetry; The Iowa Review; The Guild; The Cardinal; WBAI, NY. Honours & Awards: Poetry Scholarship, Ind. Univ. Writers Conf., 1962; Hon. mention, NY Poetry Soc. of Am., 1962. Address: 346 W. 56th St., New York, NY 10019, USA.

BRIGHAM, Besmilr, b. 28 Sept. 1923. Writer. Education: B.Jrnlsm., Mary Hardin-Baylor Coll., Belton, Tex., 1945; New Schl. for Soc. Rsch., NY, 1954-57. Personal details: m. to Roy C. Brigham; Great-great-grandfather was a Miss. Choctaw. Memberships: Acad. of Am. Poets; Poetry Soc. of Am. Published works: Agony Dance: Death of the Dancing Dolls, 1969; Heaved from the Earth, 1971. Contbr. to the following anthols. & jrnls: 31 New American Poets; New Directions in Prose & Poetry 21 & 23; I Love You All Day, It is that Simple (anthol.); New Generation: Poetry, 1971; Their Place in the Heat, 1971; Borestone Mountain Poetry Awards Annual: Best Poems of 1970; The Belly of the Shark, 1973; Rising Tides: Twentieth Century Am. Women Poets, 1973; Am. Women Poets – Colonial to Contemporary; Contemporary Am. Women Poets, 1973; Only Let There Be Peace, 1973; The Atlantic; Harper's Bazaar; The New York Times; Southern Review; Southwest Review; The Carolina Quarterly; Wisconsin Review; West Coast Review; North American Review; Red Clay Reader; Hiram Poetry Review; Ann Arbor Review; Crazy Horse; Beloit Poetry Journal; The Little Review; Confrontation; Univ. of Tampa Poetry Review; Arx; Descant; Prairie Schooner; New American & Canadian Poetry; Sumac; South Florida Poetry Journal; Foxfire; Extensions; Apple; Abraxas; Road Apple Review; Hanging Loose; Fragments; Hearse;Epos; South & West; Cafe Solo; The Outsider; El Corno Emplumada; Open Letter; Monk's Pond; Is; Symptom; Consumption; Loveletter; Ninth Circle; Camels Coming; The Camel's Hump; Magdalene Syndrome Gazette; Seizure; Granite; PEN: an International Quarterly. Recip. of Fellowship-Grant, Nat. Endowment for the Arts, 1970; PEN Emergency Grant, 1972; Carnegie Foundation Emergency Grant, 1972. Recording for Library of Congress Collection of Poets, 1972. Address: Rte 1, Horatio, Ark. 71842, USA.

BRILLIANT, Alan, b. 22 May 1936. Founder/Director, Unicorn Press. Educ: B.A., Columbia Univ., 1959. Married Teo Savory, 1958. Positions held: Publisher, Pan Magazine, 1956-58; Publisher, Bread, Mexico, 1959; Founder-Director, Unicorn Press, 1966. Published works: At Trial, 1968; Searching for Signs, 1969; Selected Poems of Garcia Lorca (translation), 1969. Contbr. to: Fiddlehead; Unicorn Folio; Unicorn Journal; Trace; Columbia Review; Poetry Review. Address: c/o Unicorn Press, 317 East de la Guerra, Santa Barbara, CA 93101, U.S.A.

BRINNIN, John Malcolm, b. 1916. Poet, Critic. Education: Univ. of Mich.; Harvard Univ. Positions held: Dir., The Poetry Ctr., NY, 1949-56; State Dept. Lectr., Europe, 1954, '56, '61. Published works: The Garden is Political, 1942; The Lincoln Lyrics, 1942; No Arch, No Triumph, 1945; The Sorrows of Cold Stone, 1951; Dylan Thomas in America (biog.), 1955; Gertrude Stein and her World, 1960; William Carlos Williams (crit.), 1963; Selected Poems, 1963; Emily Dickinson, 1961; Casebook on Dylan Thomas, 1961; The Modern Poets, 1963. Contbr. to: New Yorker; Atlantic; Harper's; Saturday Review; Mademoiselle; Poetry, Chicago; etc. Address: c/o Little, Brown & Co., 34 Beacon St., Boston, Mass. 02106, USA.

BRITT, Alan William, b. 3 Mar. 1950. Poet. Education: B.A., Univ. of Tampa. Married Joyce Lavery Britt. Positions held: Asst. Ed., Poetry Review, 1968-70; Poetry Cons. for UT Review, 1972–; Tchr. in Poetry in The Public Schools Program, 1973. Mbr., Immanentist Poetry Movement. Published works: (poetry books) I Ask For Silence, Also, 1969; We Follow Night, 1973. Rep. in following anthols: The Living Underground: An Anthology of Contemporary Poetry, 1969; New Generation; Poetry, 1971; Recycle This Poem: Poems on Ecology, 1971; Poetry Ventured, 1972; The Immanentist Anthology: Art of the Superconscious, 1973; Poetry Americana, 1973; Mantras: An Anthology of Immanentist Poetry, 1973. Contbr. of poetry to num. jrnls., reviews, mags. inclng: UT Review; The Windless Orchard; Ann Arbor Review; S. Fla. Review; Poet Lore; Now Save The Dead; Tampa Times; Poetry Review; De Nova; Encore. Honours, awards: Top 5 winner, Annual Univ. of S. Fla. Poetry Fest., 1969; 2nd pl., Annual Beaux Arts Poetry & Folk Fest., 1971. Address: 4408 Carlyle Rd., Tampa, FL 33615, U.S.A.

BROBST, Sarah Elizabeth Heiney, pen name **BROBST, Sarah H. & 'JUSTA NABOR',** b. 19 Feb. 1903. Housewife; Secretary; Newspaper Columnist; Retired Editor. Married Nathan B. Brobst, 1 daughter. Positions held: Sec., 1921-27; Ed., Safety Sentinel monthly, 1942-46; Columnist, Dear Neighbor, Nazareth Item, 1946-69. Memberships: World Poetry Day, 1963-70; Am. Poetry League, 1965–. Contbr. to: From Sea to Sea in Song; A Goodly Heritage; Poems of Pennsylvania; Yearbook of Modern Poetry, 1971. Wrote three church dedication hymns in 1962, & one for church dedication, St. Petersburg, U.M. Ch., 1972. Honours, awards: Hon. Mention, World Poetry Day, 1964; 3rd Prize, ibid, 1966; Hon. Mention, Am. Poetry League, 1967 & '73. Address: 5620 Cedar St. N.E., St. Petersburg, FL 33703, U.S.A.

BROCK, Edwin, b. 19 Oct. 1927. Advertising Writer. Married (1), 1 s., 1 d.; (2) Elizabeth Brock, 1 d. Positions held: Publrs. Officer Jr., Royal Navy, 1945-47; Edit. Asst., Trade Paper, 1947-51; Metropolitan Police Constable, 1951-59; Advt. Agcys., 1959–; Poetry Ed., Ambit, monthly lit. & arts mag., 1961–. Published works: An Attempt at Exorcism, 1959; A Family Affair, 1960; With Love From Judas, 1963; Penguin Mod. Poets 8, 1966; Fred's Primer, 1969; A Cold Day at the Zoo, 1970. Contbr. to: Observer; New Statesman; Critical Quarterly; Ambit; many univ. mags., anthols. & schl. textbooks in UK & elsewhere. Address: 13 Finch Way, The Street, Brundall, Norfolk, UK.

BROCK, Mary Frances Spalding, b. 26 Nov. 1905. Poet. Education: studied poetry at Cambridge Univ., U.K., Univ. of Colo., Boulder, U.S.A., Univ. of New Mex., Albuquerque. Pres., Poetry Soc. of Colo., 1971-73. Contbr. to: The Denver Post; True Confessions; New Mexico Qtly. Honours, awards: First Prize, Workshop Contest of Colo. Poetry Soc., 1971; First Prize, poem on Colorado, Wolcott Schl., 1921. Address: 955 Eudora St., Apt. 908, Denver, CO 80220, U.S.A.

BRODEY, James Miles, pen names **TAYLOR, Ann & FEMORA,** b. 30 Nov. 1942. Editor. Educ: N.Y. Univ.; New Schl. for Soc. Rsch. Married to Tandy Brodey. Positions held: Music Ed., The East Village Other, N.Y., 1966-67; Music Ed., Los Angeles Free Press, 1967. Published works: Four Summer Poets (w. others), 1962; Fleeing Madly South, 1967; Identikit, 1967; Long Distance Quote, 1968. Contbr. to: Paris Review; World; Angel Hair; Ravioli; San Francisco Earthquake; (anthologies) Young American Writers, 1968; World Anthology, 1969; Sparklers, 1969. Honours, awards: Dylan Thomas Poetry Award, 1966; Poets' Foundation Grant, 1967. Address: 2308 West 4th St., Los Angeles, CA, U.S.A.

BRODSKY, Nina-Anna, b. 13 June 1892. Painter; Stage Designer. Education: pupil of Herman Struck, Berlin; painting, studio of Youon & Doodin & the Stroganov Schl., Moscow, 1911; Dip. in Painting, Acad. of Weimar, 1912-14; New Art Studio, Petrograd, 1916; student of Prof. Grabar, College de France & the Sorbonne, Paris, 1952-63. Positions held: Nurse, War Hosp., Kiev, 1915; Asst. Keeper, State Mus. of Ukraine, 1918-19; first scenographic work, Berlin, 1926; Chief Scenographer, Municipal Theatre, Basle, 1930-33; introduced projection to Theatre du Chatelet, Paris, 1936; var. work, Comedie Francaise; Portraits &

Restoration, Toulouse, 1940-42. Var. commns. inclng. life-size reprodn. of a Doura-Europos fresco, Jewish Mus. in Paris. Memberships: Societe des Auteurs, Compositeurs et Editeurs de Musique, Paris; Société d'Archeologie Francaise, 1970; Institut d'Etudes Slaves, 1970. Published works: three small colls. of poetry edited in Berlin – Hobocembe, Pouza & Hebog, 1931, '32, '33; Hanporem, personal coll., Paris, 1968. Contbr. to: Cahiers du Sud; Esprit, Paris; Poesie Vivante, Geneva; Poet, etc. Var. transl. Address: 17 rue Poliveau, 75005 Paris, France.

BROMIGE, David Mansfield, b. 22 Oct. 1933. Writer. Education: B.A., Univ. of B.C., Canada, 1962; M.A., Univ. of Calif., Berkeley, U.S.A., 1964. Married 1) Ann Livingston, div& 2) Joan Peacock, div., 1 son, 3) Sherril Jaffe. Positions held: Taught at Univ. of B.C., summer 1964, Univ. of Calif., Berkeley, 1965-70, Calif. Coll. of Arts & Crafts, 1970; currently tchng. at Calif. State Coll., Sonoma, 1970–. Memberships: Exec., U.C. Berkeley, Rhymers Club, 1966-68; Fac. Advisor to Calif. State Coll., Sonoma, Rhymers Club, 1970–. Published works: The Gathering, 1965; Please, Like Me, 1968; The Ends of the Earth, 1969; The Quivering Roadway, 1969; In His Image, 1970; Threads, 1970; The Fact So Of Itself, 1971; They Are Eyes, 1972; Three Stories, 1973; Birds of the West, 1973; Tight Corners & What's Around Them, 1974. Rep. in following anthols: Best Poems of 1962: Borestone Mt. Poetry Awards, 1963; Out of the War Shadow, 1967; Earth Air Fire & Water, 1970; Mark in Time, 1970; A Caterpillar Anthol., 1971; 3rd Am. Lit. Anthol., 1971; Open Poetry, 1973. Contbr. to many mags., reviews. Honours, awards incl: Canada Coun. Awards, 1965-66, '66-67, '72-73; James Phelan Award in Lit., Univ. of Calif., 1966-67; Discovery Award, Nat. Endowment for the Arts, 1969. Address: 880 First St., Sebastopol, CA 95472, U.S.A.

BROOKER, Irene, pen name **GLEM,** b. 28 Apr. 1921. Housewife. Positions held: Shorthand Typist/Telephonist, Solicitors offices, –1942. Memberships: Brentwood Writers Circle, Essex. Contbr. to: Stock Press (local mag.) Address: 32 Dakyn Dr., Stock, Ingatestone, Essex CM4 1TA, U.K.

BROOKS, Frederick. Poet. Education: B.A. in Hist. & Psychol.; M.A. in Engl. Lit.; Dip. in Jrnlsm. Published works: A Happy Christmas Carol (poems), 1973; Charles Dickens – Brandy for BOZ, 5 act play on the life & loves of the celebrated novelist; Rocket to the Moon, poems on the Apollo moon flights; Frank Sinatra Sing to Me, poems, forthcoming; GBS, play on GBS, forthcoming. Contbr. to: Illustrated Weekly of India; Thought, New Delhi; Shankar's Weekly, New Delhi; The Nagpur Times; Poet. Address: 11B, Flat No. 3, Appadurai Naicker St., Ayanavaram, Madras City 600023, India.

BROOKS, Gwendolyn, b. 1917. Poet Laureate of Illinois. Education: Wilson Jr. Coll. Married to Henry Blakely, 1 s., 1 d. Positions held: Poet-in-Res., Univ. of Wis., Madison; Tchr., Northeastern Ill., State Coll.; Tchr., Elmhurst Coll., Ill. & Columbia Coll., Chgo. Published works: A Street In Bronzeville, 1945; Annie Allen, 1949; Bronzeville, Boys & Girls; The Bean Eaters; Selected Poems; Maud Martha; In the Mecca. Honours & Awards: Citation, Am. Acad. Arts & Letters, 1946; Guggenheim Fellowships, 1946 & '47; Invited to read for Nat. Poetry Festival, Lib. of Congress, 1962; Poet Laureate of Ill., 1968–. Address: Northeastern Ill. State Coll., Chgo., Ill. 60625, USA.

BROOKS, John. Novelist. Education: M.A., Emmanuel Coll., Cambridge Univ. Memberships: Soc. of Authors; Treas., West Country Writers Assn., 1972–. Published works: Hat; The Expert. Contbr. to: Poetry Unicorn; Courier; The Lady; Country Fair. Recip., Poetry Award, Cheltenham Fest. of Lit., 1968. Address: 7 Clifton Close, Bristol BS8 3LR, U.K.

BROOKS, Nigel Anthony Langhorn, b. 10 Apr. 1952. Computer Consultant. Education: B.Sc., Maths., Univ. of Exeter, U.K. Memberships: Poetry Soc., Inc. of

G.B.; Judge, Tornado Enterprises Poetry Comp., 1968. Ed., Versewise, 1968. Contbr. to: Bardic Echoes; The Spring Anthol.; Manifold; The Ukranian Thought; The Angels; Laudamuste (Manifold Anthol.); Voices Int. Recip., Benjamin Award (Manifold), 1966. Address: 28 Orchard Dr., Tonbridge, TN10 4LG, Kent, U.K.

BROPHY, James Joseph, pen name **BROPHY, Jim,** b. 21 Jul. 1912. Certified Public Accountant; Real Estate Investor. Education: DePaul Univ., Chicago, Illinois. Married, 1933; Divorced, 1967; 8 children; Married Barbara Black, 1972. Positions held: Jr. Accountant, Price Waterhouse and Co.; Audit Supervisor, U.S. Steel Corp.; Manager, Peat, Marwick, Mitchell and Co.; President, Dallas Land Investors, Inc. Memberships: Poetry Soc. of Texas; Illinois Poetry Soc.; American Poets Fellowship Soc.; World Poetry Soc. Published work: Taking A Stand, 1969. Contbr. to: Prairie Poet; Poet; The American Poet; Major Poets; United Poets. Awards: Clover Collection of Verse; Pierson Mettler Associates. Address: 3611 Oak Lawn, Dallas, TX 75219, USA.

BROSSARD, Nicole, b. 27 Nov. 1943. Teacher. Education: M.A. in Lit., Univ. of Montreal. Positions held: Sec. in an insurance co., 1962-63; Tchr., 1968-72. Co-Dir. & Co.Fndr. of lit. review, La Barre du Jour, 1965-73. Published works: Poetry: Aube à la saison, 1965; Mordre en sa chair, 1966; L'écho bouge beau, 1968; Suite logique, 1970; Le centre blanc, 1970; Novels: Un livre, 1970; Sold out, 1973; Prose: Mécanique jongleuse, 1973. Contbr. to: La Barre du Jour; Passe-Partout; Liberté; Ether; Stratégie; L'illettré; Hobe-Québec; Lettres et Ecritures; Ellipse; Sexus; Génération; Métamorphoses; Europe; Opus international; Dimensions. Address: 665, rue Crevier, Montreal 379, Quebec, Canada.

BROUGHTON, James, b. 10 Nov. 1913. Poet; Playwright; Filmmaker; Teacher. Education: B.A., Stanford Univ., Calif., 1936. Married, 2 children. Positions held: Prof. in Creative Arts, Calif. State Univ., San Francisco; Instr. in Filmmaking, San Francisco Art Inst. Published works: (books) The Playground, 1949; The Ballad f Mad Jenny, 1949; Musical Chairs, 1950; An Almanac for Amorists, 1955; True & False Unicorn, 1957; The Right Playmate, 1964; The Water Circle, 1965; Tidings, 1965; Look in Look Out, 1968; High Kukus, 1969; A Long Undressing, 1971. Films: Mother's Day, 1948; Adventures of Jimmy, 1950; Four in the Afternoon, 1951; Loony Tom the Happy Lover, 1951; The Pleasure Garden, 1953; The Bed, 1968; Nuptiae, 1969; The Golden Positions, 1970; This is It, 1971; Dreamwood, 1972. Plays: Summer Fury, 1957; Burning Questions, 1958; The Last Word, 1959; The Rites of Women, 1959; Bedlam, 1969. Rep. in sev. anthols. Recordings: San Francisco Poets, 1958; The Bard & The Harper, 1965. Honours, awards: James D. Phelan Award in Lit., 1948; Prix du fantasie poetique, Cannes Film Fest., 1954; Hautpreis der Kursfilmtage, Oberhausen, Germany, 1968 & many others. Address: P.O. Box 183, Mill Valley, CA 94941, U.S.A.

BROUGHTON, T. Alan, b. 9 June 1936. Professor of English. Education: Harvard Univ.; Juilliard Schl. of Mus.; B.A., Swarthmore Coll., 1962; M.A., Univ. of Wash., 1964. Positions held: Tchng. Asst., Univ. of Wash., 1962-64; Instr., Sweet Briar Coll., 1964-66; Asst., Assoc., Full Prof., Univ. of Vt., 1966–. Member, Phi Beta Kappa. Published works: The Skin And All (poems w. prints by Bill Davison, Geo. Little & Stinehour Presses), 1972. Contbr. to: AAUP Bulletin; Abraxas/5 Anthol.; Am. Weave; Barat Review; Beloit Poetry Jrnl.; Bitterroot; The Blackbird Circle; Caryatid; Christian Sci. Monitor; Cimarron; Commonweal; Confrontation; Dekalb Lit. Arts Jrnl.; Descant; Discourse; Essence; Fla. Qtly.; Poet Lore; Poetry Northwest; Prairie Schooner, etc. Honours, awards: 2nd prize, Yankee 1971 Annual Poetry Awards; Best Poems of 1972, Borestone Mountain Poetry Awards. Address: Engl. Dept., Univ. of Vt., 315 Old Mill, Burlington, VT 05401, U.S.A.

BROWN, Alice Needham Very, pen name **VERY, Alice,** b. 25 Feb. 1894. Writer & Editor. Education: A.B., Wellesley, 1916. Married Edmund R. Brown. Positions held: Literary Agent; Editor; Writer. Published works: The Human Abstract, 1936; Round-the-Year Plays for Children, 1955; Write on the Water, 1973. Contbr. to: Carmel Pine Cone; Cats Mag.; New Church Messenger; New England Home; Plays; Poet Lore; Springfield Register; The World in Books; var. other mags. Address: 10 Edge Hill Rd., Sharon, MA 02067, U.S.A.

BROWN, Annice Harris, b. 6 Aug. 1897. Homemaker. Married, 3 children. Memberships: Poetry Soc. of Colo., 1956–; Sterling Poetry Workshop, 1956-62; Fort Collins Poetry Workshop, 1963–; Chmn., ibid, 4 yrs. & currently Asst. Chmn.; Colo. Comm. for Jr. Contests, 6 yrs.; Colo. Annuals Comm., 4 yrs. Published works: Thank You Lord, for Little Things (coll. of verses), 1973. Contbr. to: The Denver Post; Capper's; Fed. of Womens Clubs Biennial; The Bapt. Woman; Union Sunday Schl. Assn. Recip. num. poetry awards inclng: 18 first place awards, 8 2nd place awards, 20 third place awards. Address: 1002 West Mountain Ave., Fort Collins, CO 80521, U.S.A.

BROWN, Clemson, pen name **HANNIBAL RA,** b. 25 Aug. 1939. Artist. Education: B.A., City Univ. of N.Y.C., U.S.A. Married, 2 children. Positions held: Co-ordinator of cultural activities for children in Harlem (sponsored by the Police Athletic League), 1968; Dir., 'Our Place', a community centre; currently, Exec. Dir., Intercultural Workshop. Art Exhibis. incl: Studio Musem, Harlem, N.Y.; The Bowery Savings Bank; Tucker Gall.; Rockland Palace; NU-Arts Gall.; Acts of Art Gall.; Black Arts Celebration, Boston, Mass. Memberships: World Poets; Sec., The Young Lions Lodge No. 15 A.F.A.M. Published works: Poems of Soul (book); Hook Your Roots in Earth (book); Poems of Love (pamphlets); Speak Love to Her (pamphlet); Contbr. to: Black Pride; Amsterdam News; 40 Acres & a Mule; Village Voice, etc. Address: 789 Croes Ave., Bronx, NY 10472, U.S.A.

BROWN, George Mackay, b. 17 Oct. 1921. Poet. Education: Edinburgh Univ. (read Engl. Lit. & did Post-graduate work on Gerard Manley Hopkins). Published works: The Storm, 1954; Loaves & Fishes, 1959; The Year of the Whale, 1965; The Five Voyages of Arnor, 1966; Twelve Poems, 1968; Other: A Calendar of Love, 1967; A Time to Keep, 1969; An Orkney Tapestry, 1969. Contbr. to (Anthols.): An Anthology of Orkney Verse, 1949; Guiness Book of Poetry, 1960; New Poets of England and America, 1962; Modern Scottish Poetry, 1966; Oxford Book of Scottish Verse, 1966; A Book of Scottish Verse, 1967; (Jrnls.): New Statesman; Poor. Old. Tired. Horse; Scotsman; Lines Review; Paris Review; Atlantic. Hons: Arts Council Award for Poetry, 1966; Soc. of Authors Travel Award, 1968. Address: 3 Mayburn Court, Stromness, Orkney, Scotland, UK.

BROWN, Gladys Mungen, pen names, **MUNGINNI, Gladys; BROWN, Gladys Lefferts,** b. 21 Feb. 1926 at Alexandria, Virginia, USA. Poet; Writer; Sculptor; Artist; Playwright; Actress; Composer; Lecturer; Translator; Drama Critic. Education: Columbia Univ.; Sorbonne (Paris); Alexandria Inst. of Music; American Acad. Dramatic Arts; Theatre Guild Drama School. Married to Capt. Charles Lefferts Brown. Positions held: Drama Critic, Amer. Review Mag.; Bd. of Directors, NY Poetry Forum; Asst. to Poetry Soc. of Amer. Workshop (under Gustav Davidson); Laurel Films, staff writer; Advertising Mgr., Southern Molasses Co.; Pres., Little Gardens Club; Director, Childrens Flower Show; Publicity Director, Greenwich Village Outdoor Show; Archaeological Asst. to Baron Walram Von Schoeler, Peru. Memberships: Poetry Soc. of America; CAAA; NY Poetry Forum (Bd. of Directors); ASCAP; Actors Equity. Published works: Pegasus In The Seventies, 1973; Review in Rhyme (anthol.), 1973; Drama Critic, Amer. Review Mag.; Le Flambeau, 1973; Shadow Against The Night, 1972; Maine (State), 1970 (anthol.); Richmond Times; King

Features; United Press; Brooklyn Daily Eagle; Adventure Mag. Awards: for Free Form, Anthol.: Pegasus In The Seventies, 1973; Best Religious Poem, NY Poetry Forum, 1972. Address: 60 Gramercy Park North (Apt. 6K), New York, NY 10010, USA.

BROWN, Ina Ladd, b. 14 May 1906 at Sebec, Maine, USA. Legal Secretary. Education: Sebec GS; Foxcroft Acad., Dover-Foxcroft, Maine; Shaw Business Coll., Portland, Maine. Married Harold Prescott Brown (deceased 1968). Positions held: Sec., office of Clerk of Courts, Piscataquis County, Dover-Foxcroft, Maine, 1921-29; Sec. officed US Commissioner, Bangor, Maine, 1929-31; Sec. Justices & Chief Justice, Supreme Judicial Court of Maine, 1931-42; Sec. office Bangor City Manager, 1942-44; Sec. to Treas., Univ. of Maine, 1944-46; Sec. Chr. of Bd., and Treas. Bangor Savings Bank, 1945-55; Sec. legal office, Mitchell & Ballou, Bangor, Maine, 1955–. Memberships: Pine Tree Branch (Maine) of NLAPW (past member, V.P. and Sec.); Poetry Fellowship of Maine (member, past Pres. and Exec. Sec.); Poetry Soc. of New Hampshire; Maine Writers Research Club (now inactive – former member); Maine Writers Conference (member, active participant); Bangor Civic Theatre, Maine (member, past Pres., etc.). Published works: Merry-go-Round, 1943; Just for Luck, 1946; More of the Same, 1949; As Time Goes By, 1951; Homespun, 1960; Leaves on the Wind, 1963; Cross-Roads, 1970; (all poetry) Johnny Cake & Gingerbread, 1953 (prose essays and short stories) Dear David, Dark Music, Bitter Bread (plays), 1952, 1954, 1955. Contbr. to: Down East Mag.; New Hampshire Profiles; American Weave; Golden Quill Anthols.; Pen Women Mag.; Maine Writers Conf. Chapbooks; Westminster Mag.; Kansas City Star; Columbus Sunday Citizen; Pacific Spectator; Arizona Highways; Husson Coll. Review; CS Monitor; Blue Moon Mag.; Portland Sunday Telegram; Eve. Post; Maine Islands; Rockland Courier-Gazette; Moosehead Gazette; Piscataquis Observer; Quatrain Digest; Kaleidoscope; Pathfinder, etc. Awards: 15 First Prizes, Maine Writers Conference, and Richard Recchia Award; many 1st prizes, Poetry Fellowship of Maine; 1 first award, Poetry Soc. of New Hampshire; awards from Nat. Assoc. of American Pen Women. Address: 14 Garland St., Bangor, ME 04401, USA.

BROWN, James Goldie, b. 21 May 1901. School Teacher. Education: M.A., Engl., French, Hist., Canterbury Univ., New Zealand. Positions held: Asst., Wairarapa HS; Hdmaster., Western Province Schl., Fiji; Housemaster, Mt. Albert Grammar Schl., Auckland. Member of Auckland English Soc. Published works: Verse for You Book I, 1956, Book II, 1958, Book III, 1958; School Certificate Revision in English, 1957; Revision in English for University Entrance, 1961; The Poetry Lesson, 1964; From Frankenstein to Andromeda, 1966; Modern Verse for You (w. Prof. P.W. Day), 1968; English Grammar, a Linguistic Study (jt. author), 1968; You and the Public–Letters & Reports on Public Relations, 1970. Address: 243 Blockhouse Bay Rd., Auckland 7, New Zealand.

BROWN, Kathleen Pearl, b. 3 Dec. 1902. Teacher. Education: A.B., Southwestern Coll., Winfield, Kans.; M.A., Colo. State, Greeley. Positions held: Deputy Tax Collector, Mo., 12 yrs.; Chief Clerk, Agriculture Assn., Mo., 9 yrs.; Tchr., Engl. & Maths., Kans., 14 yrs.; Tchr. of Engl. & Maths., W. Indies, 11 yrs.; currently tchng. in Grenada. Contbr. to Poet, India. Address: 329 Carner Ave., Marion, OH 43302, U.S.A.

BROWN, Lyn (Ingoldsby). Education: Univ. of Sydney, M.A. (1946). Married to F.C. Brown. Memberships: Australian Soc. of Authors; Fellowship of Australian Writers; N.S.W. Assoc. of Univ. Women Graduates (affiliated with Internat. Fed. of Univ. Women). Published works: Late Summer, 1970; Listen! It's Poetry. Give It a Go (in collab. with Joan Baldwin), 1973; Jacaranda and Illawarra Flame, 1973. Address: 24 Seaforth Ave., Oatley, NSW 2223, Australia.

BROWN, Margaret Elizabeth Snow, pen name

BROWN, Marel, b. 17 Dec. 1899. Writer, Poet. Married to Alex B. Brown, native of Aberdeen, Scotland. Memberships: Atlanta Branch, Nat. League of American Pen Women, since 1940; served as Branch Pres., 1950-52, State Pres., 1948-50; National League Fifth V. Pres., 1952-54; and Nat. Historian, 1954-56, also appointed sev. nat. craft chairmanships; Ladies Burns Club, pres., 1946-47; Georgia Fed. of Women's Clubs, state poetry chairman, 1942-44; State Fine Arts Chairman, 1944-46; Rader Poetry Group of Miami, Fla.; Atlanta Writers Club, since 1937; Ga. Writers Assoc.; Dixie Council of Authors and Journalists; Poetry Soc of Ga., Poetry Soc. of America. Pubs. Red Hills, 1941; Hearth-Fire, 1943; Fence Corners, 1952; The Shape of a Song, 1968; Three Wise Women of the East, 1970; Lilly May and Dan, 1946; The Greshams of Greenway, 1952; The Cherry Children, 1956. Contrib. to: Home Life; Christian Herald; Christian Science Monitor; Christian Advocate; Christmas (Annual); Nature Mag.; Sunday Digest; Ga. Mag.; Poet; Manifold; Atlanta Journal, etc. Recip. of several prizes, awards, including Nat. League of Pen Women Biennial contests (prize for best Mason Sonnet, 1968), etc. Address: 1938 N. Decatur Rd., N.E., Atlanta, Ga. 30307, USA.

BROWN, Murray, b. 23 Mar. 1934. One-Man Theater Artist; Translator of Danish Literature; Poet; Writer. Education: A.B., Univ. of Southern Calif., 1955; grad. work at UCLA & NYU, 1955 & '61. Positions held: Recreation Ldr.; Sports Ed. (Coll. daily); Bank Teller; Post Office Clerk; Asst. Mgr., Movie Theater; Public Schl. Tchr.; Translator; One-Man Theater Performer. Performed one-man theater on Great Literature at N.Y.C. Town Hall, & of Edgar Allan Poe off-Broadway, Brooklyn Acad. of Mus. Performed over 400 one-man theater shows at colls. & univs. in U.S.A., Canada & Europe. Has given extensive poetry recitals & read poetry on radio, ABC & Danish TV. Member, Poetry Soc. of Am. Published works: The Whirling Sun, 1958; I Journey Onward, 1963; Six American Poets, 1964; Hans Christian Andersen: Poems (transl. into English), 1972; Inner Fire, 1973; Mother & Son (novelette); Hamlet & Ophelia (new play drawn from Shakespeare's complete works). Contbr. to var. mags. & anthols. Recip., Lithgow Osborne Fellowship, 1968, '69. Address: 1113 Euclid Ave., Berkeley, CA 94709, U.S.A.

BROWN, Rita Mae, b. 28 Nov. 1944. Writer; Feminist Revolutionary. Education: B.A., N.Y. Univ., U.S.A., 1968; Cinematography Cert., Schl. of Visual Arts, N.Y., 1969; Ph.D. in progress. Positions held: Tchng. Asst., Greek & Latin, N.Y. Univ., 1966-68; Photo Ed., Sterling Publications, N.Y.C., 1968-70; Vis. Fac., Federal City Coll., Wash. D.C., 1970-71; Vis. Fellow, Inst. for Policy Studies, Wash. D.C., 1971-73; Vis. Fac., Feminist Studies, Goddard Coll., Vermont, Sept.-Dec., 1973. Published works: Rubyfruit Jungle, 1973; Songs to a Handsome Woman, 1973; The Hand That Cradles the Rock, 1971; Out of the Closets (anthol.), 1973; No More Masks (anthol.), 1973; Sisterhood is Powerful, 1970; The New Woman, 1970. Contbr. to: MS Mag.; Liberation Mag.; December Mag.; Aphra Mag.; Women: A Journal of Liberation; Amazon Quarterly; Off Our Backs; The Furies; Goodbye to All That; Cassandra. Recip., Award for best Engl. transl. of a Latin poem, N.Y. Univ., 1967. Address: Inst. for Policy Studies, 1520 New Hampshire Ave. N.W., Wash. D.C. 20036, U.S.A.

BROWN, Rosalie Moore, pen name **MOORE, Rosalie,** b. 8 Oct. 1910. Teacher. Education: B.A., Univ. of Calif., Berkeley, 1932; M.A., ibid, 1934. Widow of Wm. L. Brown, 3 daughters. Positions held: Radio Script Writer & Announcer, Oakland Tribune KLX Radio Stn.; Newspaper Writer & Columnist, The Leader & Monitor, San Francisco; Book Reviewer; Music Tchr. & Mbr., Calif. Music Tchrs. Assn.; Instr., Coll. of Marin, 1965-. Memberships: Poetry Soc. of Am.; Phi Beta Kappa; Activist Poetry Group of the Bay Area, San Francisco. Published works: Grasshopper's Man & Other Poems, 1949, New edit., 1971; 10 children's books written w. husband incl: The Forest Fireman; Whistle Punk; Big

Rig; The Boy Who Got Mailed; Department Store Ghost. Contbr. to: Yale Review; Poetry (Chicago); New World Writing; Commonweal; Southern Poetry Review; Works; Chicago Tribune; New Yorker; Mark In Time, anthol.; Rising Tides, anthol., 1973. Recip. var. honours & awards inclng: 1st award, Poetry Soc. of Am., 1948; Guggenheim Fellowships in Creative Writing, 1950, 1951; Vachel Lindsay Award, Poetry (Chicago), 1958. Address: 11 Crescent Ln., Fairfax, CA 94930, U.S.A.

BROWNE, Michael Dennis, b. 28 May 1940. University Teacher. Education: B.A., 1st Class Hons., Modern Langs., Hull Univ.; Tchrs. Cert., Oxford Univ.; M.A. Hons., Univ. of Iowa. Positions held: Vis. Lectr., Creative Writing, Univ. of Iowa, Iowa City, 1967-68; Adjunct Asst. Prof., Columbia Univ. Schl. of the Arts, N.Y., Fall Semester, 1968; Tchr., Bennington Coll., Bennington, Vt., 1969-. Published works: The Wife of Winter, 1970; Librettos for Music by David Lord: How the Stars Were Made, 1967; The Wife of Winter, 1968; The Sea Journey, 1969. Contbr. to (Anthols.): New Poems, 1968; Best Poems of 1967: The Borestone Mountain Poetry Awards, 1968; (Jrnls.): New Yorker; Kayak; Tri-Quarterly; North American Review; Silo. Hons: Fulbright Scholarship, 1965; Hallmark Honor Prize for Poetry, 1967. Address: Bennington Coll., Bennington, VT, USA.

BROWNE, William, pen name **TELOIS, Maurice,** b. 1935. College Professor. Education: B.A., M.A. (twice); currently completing Ph.D. dissertation. Married, 4 children. Positions held: Assoc. Prof. of Sociol., J.C. Smith Univ., Charlotte, N.C.; Lectr., Psychol., N.C. Univ., Charlotte; Lectr., CUNY, Brooklyn; currently Fac. Mbr., Am. Studies Dept., Ramapo Coll., N.J. & Horace Mann Prep. Schl., Bronx. Memberships: Am. Acad. of Negro Writers; Red Clay Poets; Black Poets of N.Y.; N.Y. Poetry Workshop. Contbr. to: Eleven Charlotte Poets, 1971; Am. Negro Poetry, 1967; The Treewell, 1972; Veritas, 1972; Haiku (record), 1970; Phylon, 1960; Pittsburgh Courier, 1956-60; Amsterdam News, 1959-61; Echo Mag., 1963; Beacon, 1962; Tan, C.B.S. Stage 2, 1967. Recip., Nat. Coun. of the Arts Award, 1970. Address: 231 W. 246th St., Bronx, NY 10471, U.S.A.

BROWNFIELD, J.R., b. 31 May 1926. Professor of English. Education: Am. Univ. of Berlin, Germany; B.A., Hamilton Coll., Clinton, N.Y., U.S.A.; M.A., Lit., LeHigh Univ., Bethlehem, Pa. Positions held: Grad. Asst., LeHigh Univ.; Instr., Univ. of Vt., Burlington; Asst. Prof., Norwich Univ., Northfield, Vt.; Asst. Prof., Chicago City Coll., Ill.; Co-ed., Patterns, int. poetry mag., 1955-60. Author of The Far Cry of Silence, 1970. Contbr. to: Poetry Australia; Message (France); Expression (UK); Outpost (UK); Breakthru (UK); Beloit Poetry Jrnl.; Carolina Qtly.; Patterns; Gnosos; College English; Centaur; Inditer; Borestone Mountain Best Poems of 1955. Address: 632 East 159th Ct., South Holland, IL 60473, U.S.A.

BROWNJOHN, Alan Charles, pen name **BERRINGTON, John,** b. 28 July 1931. Lecturer. Education: Merton Coll., Oxford, UK. Positions held: Schl. Tchr., now Lectr., Coll. of Educ.; Mbr., Wandsworth Borough Council, 1962-65. Memberships: Chmn., Poets Workshop, London, 1970-71; Mbr. of Council & Exec. Comm. Poetry Soc., London, 1967-69; Literature Panel, Arts Council of GB, 1968-. Published works: The Railings, 1961; The Lions' Mouths, 1967; Sandgrains on a Tray, 1969; Penguin Mod. Poets 14, 1969; Warriors Career, 1972. Contbr. to: New Statesman; Observer; Spectator; Ambit; Listener; London Mag.; Encounter; Outposts; Times Lit. Supplement, etc. The Railings was Recommended by the Poetry Book Soc. Address: 2 Belsize Park, London, NW3, UK.

BROWNLOW, David Timothy, pen name **BROWNLOW, Timothy,** b. 11 June 1941. Academic. Education: B.A. Hons., Trinity Coll., Dublin, 1963; Higher Dip. in Educ., 1965; M.A., 1969. Positions held: School Master, St. Columba's Coll., Rathfarnham, Co.

Dublin, 1963-69; Co-Ed., The Dublin Mag., 1963-69. Published works: The Hurdle Ford, 1964; Figures Out of Mist, 1966. Contbr. to: The Irish Times; Hibernia; The Dublin Mag.; The Kilkenny Mag.; Irish Univ. Review; Hermathena (Trinity Coll., Dublin); Ariel, etc. Address: The Cottage, Caulcott Lodge, Caulcott, Nr. Lower Heyford, Oxon., U.K.

BROWNSTEIN, Michael, b. 25 Aug. 1943. Poet. Education: B.A., 1966; Fulbright Scholar, Paris, France, 1967-68. Published works include: Highway to the Sky, 1969; Brainstorms, 1971 (stories & prose poems); Behind the Wheel, 1967 (pamphlets); 30 Pictures, Poems, 1971. Contbr. to the following jrnls. & mags.; Paris Review; Rolling Stone; Poetry; Chelsea Review; Angel Hair; The World; The Harris Review; etc. Honours, awards: Frank O'Hara Award, 1969; Grant, Poets' Fndn., 1967. Address: c/o The Poetry Project, St. Mark's Church, 10th St. & 2nd Ave., New York, NY 10003, USA.

BRUBECK, David Warren, b. 6 Dec. 1920. Musician. Educ: B.A., Univ. of Pacific, 1942; Ph.D., Univ. of Pacific & Fairfield Univ.; Postgrad., Mills Coll., 1946-49. Married Iola Whitlock, 1942; six children. Positions held: Pianist, dance bands & small jazz trio, 1946-49; Formed Trio, 1950; Formed Dave Brubeck Quartet, 1951; Concert tours in U.S.A., 1953–; Toured Europe, Middle East, Australia. Memberships: Poetry Soc. of Am.; Fellow, Int. Inst. of Arts and Scis; Mbr., Broadcast Music, Inc.; Phi Mu Alpha. Compositions: The Light In The Wilderness; The Gates of Justice, Truth (Cantatas); Elementals (Symphony); over 100 jazz compositions. Honours, awards: First place in popularity poll, 1953-55; 1st place in critics poll, Downbeat Mag., 1953; Named one of California's five outstanding young men, 1957; Winner jazz polls conducted by Downbeat, Melody Maker, Cashbox, Playboy mags., 1962. Address: c/o Sutton Artists Inc., 505 Park Ave., New York, NY 10022, U.S.A.

BRUCE, Charles, b. 11 May 1906. Port Shoreham, NS, Canada. Writer. Education: B.A., 1927. Positions held: War Corres.; Reporter, Halifax Chronicle, 1927; Ed., Gen. Supt., Canadian Press, 1928-63. Published works: Wild Apples, 1927; Tomorrows Tide, 1932; Grey Ship Moving, 1945; The Flowing Summer, 1947; The Mulgrave Road, 1957; 2 novels. Contbr. to: Sat. Eve. Post; Chamber's Jrnl.; Harper's Mag.; Sat. Review; MacLean's Mag.; Sat. Night; Poetry Chicago; Ladies Home Jrnl.; Canadian Poetry Mag. Honours, Awards: Gov. Gen's Award, 1951; D.Litt., Mt. Allison Univ., NB, 1952. Address: 40 Farnham Ave., Toronto 190, Ont., Canada.

BRUCE, George Robert, b. 10 Mar. 1909. Writer. Education: M.A., Aberdeen Univ., 1932. Married Elizabeth Duncan, 2 children (David & Marjorie). Positions held: Asst. Master & then Deputy Head Master, Engl. Dept., High Schl., Dundee, 1935-46; Prog. Producer, BBC Aberdeen, 1947-56; Talks Producer (Documentary) BBC Edinburgh, 1956-70; First Fellow in Creative Writing, Glasgow Univ., 1971-73. Theatre Critic in Scotland for the Sunday Times; Dir. of a number of documentary art films. Published works: Sea Talk, 1944; Selected Poems, 1947; Landscapes & Figures, 1967; Collected Poems, 1970; Scottish Sculpture Today w. T.S. Halliday, 1947; var. lit. criticism inclng. Neil M. Gunn. Works rep. in num. anthols. inclng: The New British Poets; Modern Scottish Poetry, 1946 & 66; The Oxford Book of Scottish Verse, 1966; The Book of Scottish Verse, 1967; Poetry of the Forties, 1968; Scottish Poetry; vols. 1-6, 1966-72. Ed., The Scottish Lit. Revival & The Scottish Poetry Anthologies. Awaiting publication: The Book of the Edinburgh Festival & in press, Anne Redpath – a monograph of the Scottish Artist. Recip. Scottish Arts Coun. Award, 1967 & 70. Address: 25 Warriston Cres., Edinburgh EH3 5LB, U.K.

BRUCE, Lennart, b. 21 Feb. 1919. Poet. Married Sonja. Published works: Making The Rounds, 1967; Observations, 1968; Moments of Doubt, 1969; Mullioned Window, 1970; Robot Failure, 1971;

Exposure, 1972; Letter of Credit, 1973. Address: 1815 Jones Street, Apt. 4, San Francisco, CA 94109, U.S.A.

BRUCE, Robert, Sr., b. 19 May 1888. Engineer. Education: Invernrie Acad., Aberdeenshire, U.K.; Robert Gordon's Coll., Aberdeen. Married, 1 son, 1 daughter. Positions held: Draughtsman, Invernrie; Chief Draughtsman, Darlington; Chief Draughtsman Docks & Inland Waterways, Hull. Published works: Wm. Thom, the Invernrie Poet – A New Look, 1970. Address: 15 Deneside Rd., Darlington, Co. Durham, U.K.

BRUCHAC, Joseph Edward, III, b. 16 Oct. 1942. Teacher & Writer. Education: B.A., Cornell Univ., 1965; M.A., Syracuse Univ., 1966; SUNY, Albany, 1971-72; currently completing doctorate through Union Grad. Schl. (Antioch Coll.) Positions held: Tchr. in Ghana in Tchrs. for W. Africa Prog., 1966-69; Instr. in Engl., Skidmore Coll., 1969-73; p/t Creative Writing Tchr., Gt. Meadows Correctional Facility, 1972-73. Memberships: Poetry Soc. of Am.; Bd. Mbr., COSMEP. Published works: The Duval Lectures, poetry pamphlet, 1965; Indian Mountain & Other Poems, 1971; The Buffalo in the Syracuse Zoo, 1972. Contbr. to: The Nation; Am. Poetry Review; Shenandoah; Chelsea; Sumac; Ohio Review; New; New Letters; Epoch; Carleton Miscellany; Miss. Review; Journal 31; Invisible City; Bitterroot, etc. Honours, awards: Morrison Poetry Prize, Cornell Univ., 1965; Syracuse Univ. Writing Fellowship, 1966; N.Y. State Creative Artists Prog. Serv. Grant, 1972-73; Poetry Soc. of Am. Monthly Prize, 1972. Address: Greenfield Ctr., NY 12833, U.S.A.

BRUCHER, Roger-André, b. 2 Sept. 1930. Poet; Head of Works, Royal Library of Belgium. Educ: Licence en philologie romane, Univ. of Liège; E.M.D.S. Dip., Libn. & Bibliographer. Positions held: Currently, Dir. of Works, Royal Lib. of Belgium; Dir., Bur. of Documentation on French Writers of Belgium. Memberships: Luxembourg Acad.; PEN Club; Assn. of Belgian Writers; Comms., Scriptores catholici. Published works: Rites pour une clarté, 1958; Vigiles de la rigueur, 1961; Chair de l'hiver; Assomption pour le sable, 1974. Honours, awards: Franz De Wever Prize, 1965; Malpertuis Prize, Royal Acad. of French Lang. & Lit., 1966. Address: 16 Ave. des Abeilles, 1050 Brussels, Belgium.

BRUNET, Yves-Gabriel, b. 29 Mar. 1938. Writer; Professor; Critic. Educ: B.A., Coll. St. Marie, Montreal, 1959; M.A., Univ. of Montreal, 1961. Positions held: Prof., French, Univ. & Pre-Univ. Levels, 1965-70; Prof., Author of Courses in Oral Expression & Communication in the Theatre, Nat. Theatre Schl. of Canada, Montreal, 1972–; Literary Critic, La Revue des Arts et des Lettres radio prog., Montreal, 1964-65; Researcher, daily variety prog., Radio-Canada, 1966-67; Free-lance writer, var. mags.; Film Narrator. Memberships: Parti Québécois (movement for Quebec independence) & Fndr.-Dir. of monthly jrnl. Published works: Les Hanches Mauves, 1961; Les Métamorphoses d'Aphrodite et Epitre aux Poetes, 1968; Les Hanches Mauves, 1961; Les Nuits Humiliées, 1962; Poésies I, 1973; L'eau Filosofale, 1963-64; La Grande Queste, 1965-68; Poésies II, 1974; L'Athanor, 1974. Contbr. to var. anthols. & mags. Address: 678 Ave. Outremont, Cite d'Outremont, Montreal, P.Q. H2V 3M9, Canada.

BRUTUS, Dennis (Vincent), b. 28 Nov. 1924. Professor of English. Education: B.A., C.E.D., Fort Hare Univ., South Africa; Part LL.B., Witwatersrand Univ., South Africa. Personal details: Exiled from South Africa, 1966, after imprisonment on Robben Island for opposition to apartheid, 1964; Writings banned in South Africa; married, 8 children. Positions held: HS Tchr.; Jrnlst.; Vis. Prof., Univ. of Denver, Colo., USA; Dir., Campaign for the Release of South African Political Prisoners; Pres., South African Non-racial Olympic Comm. (SAN-ROC). Mbr. of various socs. Published works include: Modern Poetry From Africa; African Writing Today; Protest: Conflict in

African Literature; Seven South African Poets; Presence Africaine Encounter; Black Orpheus; New Edinburgh Review, etc. Honours, awards: Mbari Prize for African Poetry. Address: Engl. Dept., Northwestern Univ., Evanston, Ill. 60201, USA.

BRYANT, Frederick James, Jr. Casework Supervisor. Education: B.A., Lincoln Univ.; currently studying for M.A. at Temple Univ. Married Marianne Brady. Positions held: Casework Supvsr., State of Pa. Published works: Songs From Ragged Streets, 1974. Rep. in following anthols: Black Fire, 1968; The New Black Poetry, 1969; Extension, 1969; To Gwen, With Love, 1971; New Black Voices, 1972; You Better Believe It, 1973; America: 20th Century Poetry: Landscapes of the Mind, 1973; The Poetry of Black America: Anthology of the 20th Century, 1973. Contbr. to: The Jrnl. of Black Poetry, 1968; Negro Digest, 1969; Nickel Review, 1969; Black Poets Write On, 1970; The Greenfield Review, 1971; Shore Poetry Anthol., 1971. Honours, awards: Eichelberger Prize, 1965; Silvera Award, 1966. Address: 1625 Griffith St., 2nd fl., Philadelphia, PA 19111, U.S.A.

BRYANT, Helen, b. 24 Jan. 1906. Writer. Educated: Haberdasher Aske's Girls School, London (U.K.); Lycee de Jeunes Filles de Versailles, France. Positions held: account exec. in various advertising agencies in N.Y.C. Member, Poetry Soc. of America; N.Y. Women Poets; Wisconsin Fellowship of Poets. Contib. to: Poetry; Poet Lore; The Lyric; N.Y. Times; Christian Sci. Monitor; North American Mentor; Social Education; Kent Messenger; Manifold; The Diamond Anthol. of the Poetry Soc. of America. Awards: Poetry Soc. of America, 1973, John W. Gassner Mem. Award; Lyric 1971 Mem. Prize; Ca. Poetry Soc. 1972 Monday Prize; Lyric 1967 Leitch Mem. Prize; Nat. Fed. of State Poetry Soc. prizes; 1st prize, Modern division, 1967, 2nd prize, Modern division, 1968. Address: 240 South Blvd., Nyack, NY 10960, USA.

BRZOSTOWSKA, Janina, b. 9 July 1907. Poetess. Education: Fac. of Polish Philol. & Lit., Jagiellonian Univ. of Kraków. Married, 1 son. Positions held: Translator of Ancient Greek lang. (Sapho), German Poetry (Rilke & others) & Slavonic Poetry. Memberships: Union of Polish Writers; PEN Club; 'Comes'. Published works: Szczęście w cudzym mieście (Happiness in Strange Town), 1926; O ziemi i miłości (About Land & Love), 1937; Erotyki (Erotics), 1928; Zbór poetów (Assembly of Poets); Najpiękniejsza z przygód (The Most Beautiful Adventure), 1928; Naszyjnik (Necklace), 1938; Żywioł i śpiew (Element & Song), 1939; Płomień w cierniach (Flamo in Thorne), 1947; Collection of Poems, 1957; Zanim noc (Before the Night), 1961; Sofona (transl.), 1960; Giordano Bruno, 1953; Nienazwany czas (The Unnamed Time), 1953; Ochrona światla (Defense of the Night), 1968; Pozdrowienia (Greetings), 1969. Contbr. to: Kultura; Nowa Kultura; Miesięcznik Literacki; Twórczość; Kamena; Poezja. Address: J. Dabrowskiego 75 m. 113, 02-586 Warsaw, Poland.

BUCHAN, Tom, b. 19 June 1931. Writer. Education: Univ. of Glasgow, U.K. Married Emma Chapman, 3 children. Positions held: Assoc. Prof. of Engl. Lit., Madras Christian Coll., Madras, S. India, 1957-58; Warden, Community House, Glasgow, 1958-59; Sr. Lectr. in Engl. & Drama, Clydebank Tech. Coll., 1967-70; Ed., Scottish International, 1973; Playwright & Theatre Director. Plays & Musicals incl: Tell Charlie Thanks for the Truss, 1972; Knox & Mary, 1972; The Great Northern Welly Boot Show, 1972. Published works: Ikons, 1958; Dolphins at Cochin, 1969; Exorcism, 1972; Poems 1969-72, 1973. Contbr. to: The Scotsman; The Glasgow Herald; The London Mag.; Scottish Int.; The Listener; Lines Review; Int. Times; Cracker. Recip., Scottish Arts Coun. Award, 1969 & Bursary, 1970. Address: 10 Pittville St., Edinburgh EH15 2BY, U.K.

BUCHANAN, George, b. 9 Jan. 1904. Poet. Education: Campbell Coll., & Queen's Univ., Belfast. Married 1952 (wife dec.), 2 daughters. Positions held: Editl. Staff,

The Times, 1930-35; Drama Critic, Columnist, News Chronicle, 1935-38; Operations Off., RAF Coastal Cmd., 1940-45. Memberships: Société Européene de Culture; PEN; Poetry Soc.; Irish Lit. Soc. (London). Published works: Bodily Responses, 1958; Conversation with Strangers, 1961; Annotations, 1970; Minute-book of a City, 1972. Contbr. to: Critical Quarterly; Honest Ulsterman; Second Aeon; Poetry Nation; Transatlantic Review; Dublin Mag.; Irish Statesman. Address: 27 Ashley Gdns., Westminster SW1P 1QD, U.K.

BUCHMAN, Marion (Mrs. Harold Buchman). Poet; Lecturer; Teacher. Positons held: Lectr., St. John's Coll., Johns Hopkins Univ., Rider Coll., Essex Community Coll., Morgan State Coll., Alice Loyd Coll., & Peabody Inst. of Music. Memberships: Poetry Soc. of Am.; Discussion Ldr., ibid.; Acad. of Am. Poets; Poetry Soc. of Gt. Britain; London Writer Circle; Md. Council of Engl. Tchrs.; Md. State Poetry Soc. Publications: A Voice in Ramah, 1960. Contbr. to: (Anthols.) Poets of Today; 7 Poets & the War; Timeless Treasures; Tribute to Triumph Esoteric Anthol.; Poetry Americana; Mentor Poetry of the 60's; Festival Poems, 1967 (Stroud Festival Poetry Competition, Glos., U.K.); Workshop Directory; Md. Engl. Jrnl.; Manifold; Laudamus Te; Emily Dickinson Anthol.; Vagabond; (Jrnls.) N.Y. Times; N.Y. Herald Tribune; Redbook; McCall's; Crisis; Chicago Tribune Sunday Mag.; Poet Lore; Twigs; Writer; Cat; Voices Int.; Prairie Poet; Am. Judaism; N.H. News Sunday Poetry Review; Sunpapers; Poetry Soc. of Am. Sheets; Hoosier Challenger. Poetry Dial; Bip; Student Outlook; Reflections; Stanza; Midland Poetry Review; Albatross; Talaria; Folio; N. Am. Mentor Mag.; Scimitar & Song; Ariz. Quarterly; Westminster Mag.; Hearth Songs; Different; Flame; Rainbow; Accent; Piggot Banner; Voices; Manifold; Oregonian. Awards: Stroud Festival Poetry Competition, U.K., 1967; Ivan Franko Mem. Award, U.K., 1967; 1st Prize, Soc. of Am. Poets, 1949; Pegasus Award, Poets Workshop of Calif., San Jose; Md. State Poetry Soc. Awards; Awards, Deep South Writers Conf. Poetry Competition, 1969; Cheltenham Prize, Guinness Award, U.K., 1969. Address: 3912 Fords Lane, 203, Baltimore, Md. 21215, USA.

BUCKINGHAM, Peter Allan, b. 24 Oct. 1938. Letterpress Compositor. Education: Bishop Vesey's Grammar Schl., Sutton Coldfield; Birmingham Univ. Positions held: Librarian; Printer. Member, Birmingham Poetry Ctr. Contbr. to: Poetry Review; var. mags. Address: 126 Slade Road, Erdington, Birmingham 23, U.K.

BUCKINGHAM, Ray Eugene, b. 2 Mar. 1908. Cemetarian. Education: DePauw Univ. Married, 1 son, 4 daughters. Positions held: Mgr., City Cemetery, Union City, Ind. & Oak Grove Cemetery, Delaware, Ohio, ret'd 1973. Memberships: Pres., Verse Writers Guild of Ohio, 1971-74; Ed. of their poetry qtly., The Dream Shop, 4 yrs; Ohioana Lib. Assn. Published works: It Could Be Verse, 1961; Under One Roof, 1971; The Birds Come to Oak Grove, 1972. Contbr. to: The Rotarian; Palm; Elbeetee; Dream Shop; Modern Haiku; Am. Haiku; Haiku Highlights; Blue Print; Legend; My Best to You; Just Rays; Reach Out, etc. Address: 285 North Sandusky St. (15), Delaware, OH 43015, U.S.A.

BUCKLEY, Vincent Thomas, b. 8 July 1925. Teacher. Educ: St. Patrick's Coll., E. Melbourne, Australia; B.A. & M.A., Univ. of Melbourne; Univ. of Cambridge, U.K. Married, two children. Positions held: First Lockie Fellow in Australian Lit. and Creative Writing, Univ. of Melbourne, Australia, 1958-60; Dept. of Engl., ibid 1967–. Published works: The World's Flesh, 1954; Masters in Israel, 1959; Arcady and Other Places, 1966; Ed., Eight by Eight, 1963; (literary criticism) Essays in Poetry, Mainly Australian, 1957; Poetry and Morality, 1960; Poetry and the Sacred, 1968. Contbr. to: (anthologies) Young Commonwealth Poets, '65, 1965; Modern Australian Writing, 1966. Honours, awards: Australian Literature Society Gold Medal,

1959; Myer Award for Poetry, 1967. Address: Melbourne, Victoria, Australia.

BUCKNER, Sally Beaver, b. 3 Nov. 1931. College Instructor. Education: A.B., Engl., UNC–G, 1953; M.A., Engl., NCSU, 1970. Married Robert L. Buckner, 3 children. Positions held: Tchr., Arlington Jr. High, Gastonia, N.C., 1953-54; Tchr., Goldsboro Sr. High, N.C., 1959-60; Kindergarten Tchr., The Protestant Schl., Goldsboro, 1962-65; Columnist, Goldsboro News-Argus, 1964-65; Staff Writer, The Raleigh Times, N.C., 1968-70; Grad. Tchng. Asst., N.C.S.U., 1968-70; Instr., Peace Coll., Raleigh, 1970–. Poet-in-Res., Juvenile Evaluation Ctr., Swannanoa, N.C. 3 yrs. Mbr., Poets-in-the-Schools prog., N.C. public schls. Contbr. to: The Raleigh News & Observer; The Goldsboro News-Argus; Together; Christian Century; The Adult Tchr.; Roundtable; Wesley Qtly.; Cardinal; The Rebel; The Windhover; Christian Home; Hi-Times; Workers with Youth; The Educational Forum; Great, Great, Great!; Camellian; Southern Pines Pilot; Southern Poetry Review. Honours, awards: Best poem, Windhover, 1969. Address: 3231 Birnamwood Rd., Raleigh, NC 27607, U.S.A.

BUELL, Frederick Henderson, b. 17 Nov. 1942. Associate Professor. Education: B.A., Yale Univ., 1964; Ph.D., Cornell Univ., 1970; Yale Law Schl., 1964-65; Die Freie Universität, W. Berlin, 1969. Positions held: Instr., Dept. of Engl., Queens Coll., Flushing, NY, 1970-71; Asst. Prof., Dept. of Engl., Queens Coll., 1971-73; Assoc. Prof., ibid, 1974. Published works: Theseus And Other Poems, 1971. Contbr. to: Poetry; Epoch Mag.; Modern Occasions; Centennial Review; Wind Mag.; Women's Studies. Honours, awards: Acad. of Am. Poets Prize, Cornell Univ., 1970; 2nd Prize, Epoch Mag. Yearly Poetry Contest, 1971; Nat. Endowment for the Arts Fellowship, 1972-73. Address: Dept. of English, Queens Coll., Flushing, NY 11367, U.S.A.

BUFFINGTON, Tiny Louise, pen names **BUFF, Lou & MYHHB, Cesi,** b. 6 May 1925. Teacher; Lecturer; Poet. Education: B.A., Engl., Married, 1 daughter. Positions held: Textile Wkr.; Saleslady; Guitarist; String Band; Tchr., Fla., Ala. & Ark. Schl. Systems; Tchr., Harding Coll. Acad., Ark. Memberships: United Amateur Press Assn.; Ala. State Poetry Soc.; Nat. Fed. of State Poetry Socs.; Ala. Writers' Conclave; Int. Poetry Soc.; The Pensters; Centro Studi e Scambi; Nat. Comm. for Haiku Evaluation, Am. Haiku Mag. Published works: Armchair Treasures, 1971; Southern Echoes (pending publ.) Contbr. to: Nat. Poetry Anthol., 1969; Poems by Poets' Roundtable of Ark. (3 anthols.), 1966, 67, 68; The Sampler, 1970, 71, 72, 73; Silhouettes of Life; Garland of Verse, 1971; Medley of Poetry; Anthol. of Ala. Poets 1971; Summertime Anthol., 1972; Friendships Garden of Verse, 1972; Author Poet; U.A.P. Packet; Ark. State Mag., etc. Recip. sev. poetry awards. Poet-in-Res. at J.H.S. for five weeks (sponsored by grant from Ala. State Coun. on the Arts & Humanities & the Nat. Endowment for the Arts, Wash. D.C. Address: 400 W. 1st Ave., Jay, FL 32565, U.S.A.

BUKHARI, Farigh (Ahmed Shah), b. 11 Nov. 1917. Journalist. Memberships: Sec.-Gen., Progressive Writers Org., 1947-54; Sec.-Gen., Peace Comm. of Pakistan, 1953-54; Sec.-Gen., Anjuman Taro-e-Urdu, N.W.F.P., Pakistan, 1954-70; Gov. of Pak China Friendship, N.W.F.P., Peshawar, Pakistan, 1955-72; Sec.-Gen., Idara-e-Ilm-o-Fun, N.W.F.P., Pakistan, 1970-74; Ctrl. Exec. Mbr., Pakistan Writers' Guild, 1960-61, '64-65, '68-69; Provincial Exec. Mbr., ibid, 1962-63, '66-67, '70-71; Sec.-Gen., Working Jrnlst., N.W.F.P., Pakistan, 1973-74; Judge, Habir Bank Lit. Prize of Pakistan, 1969-74 & of Adam Ji Lit. Prize, 1973. Published works: (poetry books) Zero Bum, Sheshe-ke-Parhan, Ayat-e-Zindgi, & Khushbu ka Safer, all in Urdu; Nawian Rawan, in Hindko; (prose) Aurat Ka Gunah (short stories); Pushtu Loak Geet (folk lore); Sarhad Ke Loak Geet (folk lore); Pushtu Shairi (transl. Pushtu); Adabiat-e-Sarhad (Hist. of Urdu Lit.); Attak Ke Us Par (Book on Pushtu culture);

Pathanoke-Roman (folk stories); Bacha Khan (biog.) Ed. of monthlies, weeklies & dailies in Pakistan & contbr. to all lit. mags., jrnls. & newspapers in Pakistan & India, 1935–. Honours, awards: Habib Bank Annual Prize for Pushtu Poetic transl., 1968; Abasin Art Council's Annual Prize, 1970; Pakistan Arts Fac. Annual Prize for Best Film Drama, 1974. Address: Ed., 'Sang-e-Meel', 8 Cinema Rd., Peshawar, Pakistan.

BUKOWSKI, Charles, b. 16 Aug. 1920. Newspaper Columnist. Education: Studied Journalism, Los Angeles City Coll., 1939-41. Divorced w. 1 child. Has held num. positions; Currently writes Column for Open City, Los Angeles. Published works: Flower, Fist and Bestial Wall, 1959; Longshot Poems for Broke Players, 1961; Run with the Hunted, 1962; It Catches My Heart in Its Hands, 1963; Cold Dogs in the Courtyard, Crucifix in a Deathhand, 1965; At Terror Street and Agony Way, 1968; Poems ritten Before Jumping out of an 8-story Window, 1968; Penguin Modern Poets 13 (w. others), 1969; Other: Confessions of a Man Insane Enough to Live with Beasts, 1965. Contbr. to (Anthols.): Poets of Today, 1964; (Jrnls.): Outsider; San Francisco Review; Open City; Hearse. Recip., Loujon Press Award.

BULIN, Beatrice Stephenson, b. 25 June 1922. Poet; Houswife; Communication Worker (retired). Education: Teague HS; Navarro Jnr. Coll.; extension work and seminars at various colls. Positions held: Dow Chemical Co., Freeport, Texas, 1942-46; Communications Worker, Bell Telephone System, 1952-59; Chief Operator, Telco., 1959-62, Toll and Traffic Chief, 1962. Memberships: World Poetry Soc. Intercontinental; American Poetry League; Poetry Soc. of Texas; Waco Poetry Soc., Palestine Poetry Chapter. Contbr. to: Penwheels, 1967-68; Teague Chronicle; Nat. Letter Carrier; Bouquet of Poems; Tisdale Anthol.; American Poetry League Bulletin; Collection of Prayer Poems, 1972; Poet (India); Anthols. in Browning Library, Baylor Univ. Awards: Poetry Soc. of Texas, Christmas, 1970; Cloverleaf Hon. Mention, 1969. Address: Box 466, Teague, TX 75860, USA.

BULLINS, Ed, b. 2 July 1935. Writer. Education: Wm. Penn Bus. Inst., Phila., Pa.; L.A. City Coll., Calif.; S.F. State Coll., Calif. Positions held: Res. Playwright, Lafayette Theatre, Harlem, N.Y.C.; Ed., Black Theatre Mag., Harlem. Memberships: Dramatist Guild; PEN. Published works: Five Plays by Ed Bullins, 1968; The Duplex, 1970; The Hungered One, 1971; Four Dynamic Plays, 1972; The Theme is Blackness, 1973; The Reluctant Rapist, 1973. Contbr. to: Black World Mag.; The Jrnl. of Black Poetry. Honours, Awards: American Place Theater grant, 1968; Vernon Rice Award, 1968; Rockefeller Foundation grants, 1969, 1971, 1973; Guggenheim Fellowship, 1970. Address: 932 E. 212th St., Bronx, NY 10469, U.S.A.

BULLIS, Jerald, b. 5 May 1944. Assistant Professor. Education: A.B., Wash. Univ., U.S.A.; M.A. & Ph.D., Cornell Univ. Positions held: Asst. Prof. of Engl., Lawrence Univ., 1970–. Published works: An Eclogue: Pastoral Meditation, 1971 (pamphlet edn. w. a 'Prefatory Note' by A.R. Ammons); Taking Up The Serpent (book of poems), 1973. Contbr. to: Apple; Beloit Poetry Jrnl.; Epoch; Hudson Review; Monmouth Review; North American Review; Pebble; Poetry Now; Quarterly Review of Lit.; Riverrun; Southern Poetry Review; Yale Review; Hearse; Wind; Borestone Mountain Poetry Awards Annual volumes, Best Poems of 1970 & '71. Honours, awards: Acad. of Am. Poets 1st Prize, Cornell Univ., 1969; Grant, Nat. Endowment for the Arts, 1972-73. Address: Dept. of Engl., Main Hall, Lawrence Univ., Appleton, WI 54911, U.S.A.

BULLOCK, Marie Leontine Graves b. 30 June 1911. Executive; Housewife. Education: Sorbonne, Paris; Columbia Univ., USA, 1933-37; Juilliard Schl. of Music, 1937; Hayden Planetarium, 1952-53. Married to Hugh Bullock. Positions held: Fndr., Acad. of Am. Poets, 1934; Pres., ibid, 1939; Mbr., Bd. of Dirs., Edward MacDowell Assoc.; Mbr., Bd. of Dirs., Exec.

Comm., Theodore Roosevelt Assoc.; Ex-officio Mbr., Pres., Advisory Comm. on Arts, John F. Kennedy Ctr. for the Performing Arts; Chmn., Belles Lettres Comm., Office of Cultural Affairs, City of NY, 1964; Dir., Calvin Bullock Ltd.; Bd. of Gvnrs., Colony Club, 1968–; Mbr., Visiting Comm., Dept. of Astronomy, Harvard Coll., 1968. Honours: King's Medal for Service in the Cause of Freedom, 1948; Gold Medal, Nat. Inst. of Soc. Scis., 1961; Award for Distinguished Service to the Arts, Nat. Inst. of Arts & Letters; Assoc. Officer, St. John of Jerusalem. Address: 1030 5th Ave., New York, NY 10028, USA.

BULLOCK, Michael Hale. b. 19 Apr. 1918. University Professor. Education: Hornsey Coll. of Art, UK; Regent St. Polytechnic Schl. of Langs. Married, 2 children. Writing Dept., Univ. of B.C., Canada. Memberships. Chmn., Translators Assn., London, UK, 1963-67; Mgmt. Comm., Soc. of Authors, 1968; Exec. Comm., Engl. Ctr., PEN, 1968; Ed., Prism International. Published works: Transmutations, 1938; Sunday is a Day of Incest, 1960; World Without Beginning Amen!, 1963 and 1973; Zwei Stimmen in meinem Mund, 1967; A Savage Darkness, 1969; Green Beginning Black Ending, 1971; Black Wings White Dead, 1974. Contbr. to: Encounter; London Mag.; Adam Int. Review; Prism Int.; Mundus Artium; The Far Point; New Orleans Review; Prairie Schooner; Expression; Canadian Fiction Magazine; Arts in Society; Madrona; Perspectives; Tamarack Review; Gradiva; Brumes Blondes; Oasis; Contemporary Literature in Translation; Modern Poetry in Translation; Neue deutsche Hefte; Akzente; Mademoiselle. Translations: Poems of Solitude (w. Jerome Chen), 1961 & '70; Invisible Hands (by Karl Krolow), 1969; Foreign Bodies (by Karl Krolow), 1969; Astrologer in the Underground (by Andrzej Busza), 1971. Address: 3836 West 18 Ave., Vancouver 8, British Columbia, Canada.

BUNAO, G Burce, pen name **DEL MUNDO, Oscar,** b. 3 Aug. 1926. Managing Editor. Educ: B.A., Univ. of The Philippines. Married Fe S. Buenavides, seven children. Positions held: Public Relations Exec., Operation Brotherhood, Laos; Bd. of Dirs., Filipino Acad. of Movie Arts and Sciences, Philippines; Managing Ed., Weekly Women's Magazine, Manila. Published works: The Quiver and the Fear, 1968. Contbr. to: Sunday Times Magazine; Mirror Magazine; Weekly Graphic; Chronicle Magazine; Philippines Free Press; Nation. Recip., Palanca Memorial Award for Poetry in English, 1967-68. Address: Pres. Quinino, Industrial Valley, Marikina, Rizal, Philippines.

BUNCH, David Roosevelt, pen name, **GROUPE, Darryl R.** Freelance Writer and former USAF Cartographer. Education: Lowry City HS; Central Missouri Univ. (formerly Cent. Missouri State Coll.), 1939-43, B.S., 1946; Washington Univ., 1946-49, M.A., 1949; further grad. study at Washington Univ., including admission to candidacy for Ph.D., 1949-50; State Univ. of Iowa Dept. of Engl. and Writer's Workshop, 1951-52. Married Phyllis Geraldine Flette; 2 children. Positions held: Navig. Cadet, 1943, Radio Op., 1944-46, Photogrammetrist, 1954-57, Professional Cartographer, Aeronautical Chart & Info. Center, and Defense Mapping Agency Aerospace Center, 1957-73 (all in service of USAF). Memberships: Alpha Phi Sigma Hon. Fraternity; Science Fiction Writers of America (Charter Member). Contbr. to: many journals, anthols. etc., including: Mag. of Fantasy & Science Fiction; Epos; Jean's Journal; Scimitar & Song; Ground Zero, a Mag. of Poetry; Writer's Notes & Quotes; The Galley Sail Review; Kauri; The Archer; Cyclotron; Caravan; L.A. Mag.; Orphic Lute; Poetry Digest; Hoosier Challenger; Today The Stars; Fiddlehead; Flame; The Kansas City Poetry Mag.; Different; The Oregonian; The Evening Star; Zane Grey Western Mag., and sev. others. Recip. of sev. awards in Scimitar & Song's contests; 4th place in the Promethean Lamp's 11,000-dollar Poetry Contest; Cert. of Merit, Internat. Who's Who in Poetry, etc. Address: 2021 South Compton, St. Louis, MO 63104, USA.

BUNTING, Basil, b. 1 Mar. 1900. Poet. Education: Ackworth Schl.; Leighton Park Schl.; Wormwood Scrubs; London Schl. Econs. Positions held: Asst. Ed., Transatlantic Review, Paris, France, 1920's; Music critic, The Outlook, London, U.K.; currently Tchr., Univ. of Durham, England. Published works: Redimiculum Matellarum; Poems 1950; The Spoils, 1964; First Book of Odes, 1965; Loquitur, 1965; Briggflatts, 1966; What the Chairman told Tom, 1967; Two Poems, 1967; Collected Poems, 1968. Gramophone Record: Briggflatts (L.P.). Address: Shadingfield, Wylam, Northumberland, UK.

BUNTING, Karen, b. 16 Sept. 1938. Poet. Education: B.A., Radcliffe Coll., Cambridge, Mass., 1960; Brown Univ. Grad. Schl., Providence, R.I., 1962. Positions held: Owner-Mgr. of Latin Am. import shop in Boston, Mass.; Tchr. & Officer of Mid-Peninsula Free Univ. in Palo Alto, Calif.; Mbr., Bd. of Dirs., Wildlife Conservation Coalition, San Francisco, Calif. Memberships: Poetry Soc. of Am.; past mbr., New England Poetry Club, Mass. Contbr. to: The Diamond Anthol., 1971 (as Karen Marmon); Open Places; Dryad; Sequoia; The Sunstone Review; Stonecloud. Address: 53 Homer Ln., Menlo Pk., CA 94025, U.S.A.

BUONOCORE, Michaelina, occasional pen name **CORTNEY, Michelle,** b. 2 Jan. 1919. Public Relations; Private Secretary. Education: New Schl. of Soc. Rsch., N.Y.; City Coll. of City of N.Y. Married Charles Maria Fonck. Positions held: Collaborator, Gabriel Pascal, Prod. & Dir.; Assoc. w. S.N. Behrman, Gustav Davidson & Conde Nast Publs., Inc., N.Y.; currently Pvte. Sec., firm of Int. Attys., N.Y. Asst., The Golden Year Anthol. (1910-1960) by Gustav Davidson; Asst., Deep Haven, by Cornel Lengyel. Memberships: Poetry Soc. of Am.; Eastern Ctr., Poetry Soc. of London; World Poets' Rsch. Ctr.; Casa Italian, Columbia Univ. A short vol. of Poetry & Neapolitan Folklore is now in progress. Contbr. of column 'Centre Aisle' to Uptown News Sentinel, & serialized column 'Man & the Theatre'. Address: Bldg. 2, Apt. 13G, 2141 Crotona Ave., Bronx, NY 10457, U.S.A.

BUONTEMPO, Amante, b. 15 Oct. 1920. Roman Catholic Priest, Advocate of the Sacred Roman Rota. Education: Seminary of Malta, 1934-43; Royal Univ. of Malta, 1943-46; Nottingham Univ., 1946-47; Pontifical Lateran Univ., Rome, 1949-53; Studium Sacrae Romanae Rotae, 1951-54. Became Doctor of Canon and Civil Laws (J.U.D.) in 1953, and Advocate of the Sacred Roman Rota in 1954. Personal details: Ordained Priest in 1946. Positions held: Curate; out-door speaker and spiritual director, Catholic Evidence Guild (St. Barnabas Cathedral, Nottingham, 1946-47); Teacher at the Minor Seminary, Malta, 1947-49; Interpreter and sub-secretary of one of the main Commissions of the First Internat. Catholic Congress on Problems of Rural Life (Castelgandolfo, June–July, 1951); Canon, Colleg. Chapter of St. Paul Shipwrecked, Valletta, 1952–. Chancellor, same Chapter, 1956-61; Parish Priest, 1963-66; Dean of same Chapter, 1964–; Curia examiner in Canon Law, 1959–; Member of Deputation in the Dept. of Marriage Legacies, 1961–; Chaplain to House of Representatives, Malta, 1962-71; Officer-in-charge "Unione Cattolica San Giuseppe", 1972–. Published works: I was called (in Maltese, Engl., and Italian), 1967; I have won, 1968; "Si vis pacem cane semper" (If you want peace sing all the time) (in Engl., and Italian), 1973. Contbr. to: Il-Malti; The Malta Cultural Inst. Bulletin; Lehen is-Sewwa; In-Nazzjon Taghna. Honours & Awards: 2nd Prize and special mention, public competition for Maltese Poetry, 1941; also 2nd and 3rd Prizes, 1945; Cert. of Merit, Internat. Who's Who in Poetry, 1971; Dip. of Merit, "Reportage" (Rome), also 2nd Prize in Italian Poetry, 1972; Special mention for a poetical anthol. in Italian, in competition, "Picenum", Montalto Marche, Italy, 1972; Special mention, in competition, "Gli Amici dei Sacri Lari", Bergamo, Italy, 1972. Address: 55 St. Paul St., Valletta, Malta G.C.

BURDEN, Jean, b. 1 Sept. 1914. Freelance Writer & Editor. Education: B.A., Univ. of Chicago, U.S.A. Positions held: P.R. & Admin., Meals for Millions Fndn., 1956-65; Jean Burden & Assocs., 1967-; Taught Poetry Workshop, Pasadena City Coll., & privately; Has lectured on poetry & read her poems at many colls. & univs. Has read her poems over the air in L.A., Berkeley, N.Y. & Boston & on TV in L.A. Fellow, MacDowell Colony, 1973. Published works: Naked As The Glass, 1963; Journey Toward Poetry (essays about poetry), 1966. Poetry Ed., Yankee, a New England mag., 1955-. Has recorded poems for Lib. of Congress. Contbr. to: Poetry (Chicago); Saturday Review; The Am. Scholar; Shenandoah; Southern Review; Va. Qtly.; Prairie Schooner; Beloit Poetry Jrnl.; Choice; The Critic; Southwest Review; Epoch; Outposts; Salmagundi; Coastlines; Experiment; N.Y. Times; Poetry Chapbook, etc. Num. articles in jrnls. & mags. Honours, awards: 1st Prize, Borestone Mountain Poetry Awards Anthol. Address: 1129 Beverly Way, Altadena, CA 91001, U.S.A.

BURFORD, William Skelly, b. 20 Feb. 1927. Professor of English. Educ: B.A., Amherst Coll., 1949; M.A., Johns Hopkins Univ., Baltimore, 1956; Ph.D., ibid, 1966. Married to Lolah Egan, three children. Asst. & Assoc. Prof., Engl., Univ. of Tex., Austin, 1958-65; Assoc. Prof., Humanities, Univ. of Montana, Missoula, 1966-68; Prof., Engl., Tex. Christian Univ., Fort Worth, 1968-. Published works: Man Now, 1954; Faccia Della Terra, 1960; A World, 1962; A Beginning, 1966; Ed. & Translator (w. Christopher Middleton), The Poet's Vocation: Selections from Letters of Holderlin, Rimbaud, and Hart Crane, 1967. Contbr. to: Poetry; Nation; Partisan Review; Texas Quarterly; (anthologies) Perspectives USA 12, 1955; Poesia Americana del Dopoguerra, 1958; Out of the War Shadow, 1967; An Anthology of Current Poetry, 1967. Honours, awards: Irene Glasscock Memorial Award for Poetry, 1949; Fulbright Fellowship, 1952; Philadelphia Art Inst. Award for Poetry, 1953. Address: 3000 Gambrell, Fort Worth, TX, U.S.A.

BURGESS, Charles S., b. 19 Aug. 1924. Poet; University Teacher. Education: B.A., Vanderbilt Univ.; M.A., Middlebury (Breadloaf); Ph.D. cand., Columbia Univ. Positions held: Depts. of Engl., Kans. State Coll., Pittsburg, Centenary Coll. for Women, William Paterson Coll.; currently Lectr., N.Y. Univ. Mbr., Poetry Soc. of Am.; Critic, ibid, 1972. Contbr. to: New Poems by Am. Poets, 1958; Kansas Renaissance, 1960; The New Yorker; The Midwest Qtly.; Gadfly; Quest; articles in Kansas Folklore, Jrnl. of Irish Lit.; Folklore in the Schools. Address: 718 North Broadway, Yonkers, NY 10701, U.S.A.

BURGEVIN, Mabel Beatrice Honor, b. 17 June 1877. Housewife. Education: Hunter Coll., NYC, etc. Married George Burgevin, noted florist and maker of gardens, ex-President of Bank; 6 s. 3 d. Published work: Once Upon a Time (collection of poems and essays). Contbr. to: Spirit (mag.); Columbia Univ. paper. Address: The Benedictine Senior Residence, 105 Mary's Ave., Kingston, NY 12401, USA.

BURGHARD, Shirley Mae, pen name **SALENA,** b. 7 June 1931. Registered Nurse. Education: Grad., Orange County Community Coll., School of Nursing in 1956, Middletown, NY. (L.P.N.; R.N.; A.A.S.; B.A.). Currently attending Syracuse Univ. and majoring in Engl. Lit. Positions held: various (within field of nursing): medical, surgical, obstetrical, private duty, summer camp nurse, Red Cross nurse, etc. Editor/Publisher of Constructive Action for Good Health Mag. for past 14 yrs. (75th issue recently published). Memberships: American Poetry Therapy Assoc.; American Amateur Press Assoc.; Coordinating Council of Lit. Mags.; Committee of Small Mag. Editors and Publishers. Contbr. to: United Amateur Press; Constructive Action for Good Health Mag. (has poetry section); Wind Midwest Mag.; Syracuse New Times; Associated Rational Thinkers Newsletter. Work for poetry therapy widely publicised in many newspapers, journals. Address: Windridge Farm, West Genesee Turnpike, Elbridge, NY 13060, USA.

BURKE, Kenneth Duva, b. 5 May 1897. Lecturer. Educ: Ohio State Univ., Columbus, 1916-17; Columbia Univ., 1917-18. Married Elizabeth Batterham, five children. Positions held: Music Critic, The Dial, N.Y.C., 1927-29; Music Critic, The Nation, 1934-35; Lectr., New Schl. for Soc. Rsch., 1937, Univ. of Chgo., Princeton Univ., Kenyon Coll., Ind. Univ., Drew Univ., Pa. State Univ., Central Wash. State Coll., & Harvard Univ. Memberships: Am. Acad. of Arts & Letters; Am. Acad. of Arts & Scis. Published works: Book of Moments: Poems 1915-1954, 1954; Collected Poems 1915-1967, 1968; Toward a Better Life (novel), 1932; (short stories) The White Oxen: 1924; The Complete White Oxen; Collected Short Fiction, 1968; (literary criticism) The Philosophy of Literary Forms, 1957; Language as Symbolic Action: Essays on Life, Literature and Method, 1966. Honours, awards: The Dial Award, 1928; Guggenheim Fellowship, 1935; Nat. Inst. of Arts & Letters Grant, 1946; Rockefeller Fndn. Grant, 1966. Address: Andover, NJ, U.S.A.

BURKHOLDER, Esther York, pen name **YORK, Esther Baldwin,** b. 27 Dec. 1911. Freelance Writer; Editor; Poet. Education: B.A., Univ. of Calif. at Los Angeles. Married Ray E. Burkholder, 1 daughter. Positions held: Part owner, gift shop, 1943-51; Ed., Food for Thot (house organ Clifton Restaurant chain), 1943-. Memberships: V.P., Corres. Sec. State Bd., Pres. & Sec. of Hollywood Chapt., Calif. Fed. of Chaparral Poets; Poets of the Pacific; V.P., Prog. Chmn., Glendale Poetry Forum. Published works: (vol. of poems) Scarf of Stars, 1953; (booklet of poems) Beyond this Hour, 1974. Rep. in following anthols. & textbooks: Reading-Literature, book 3, 1950; Heroic Heights, 1967; These Are Our Horizons, VIII; Harp Strings Swept by Many Hands; Evening Incense; Stars in Our Pool; The Unsung; A Laugh a Day; Keys for Happiness; Masterpieces of Religious Verse, etc. Contbr. to num. jrnls., newspapers inclng: Sat. Evening Post; Ladies Home Jrnl.; Good Housekeeping; The Am. Bard; Catholic Home Jrnl.; Harbor Lights. Recip. many poetry hons. & awards inclng: Gold Medal, Int. Poets Shrine, 1970; Gordon W. Norris Award, 1973. Address: 1478 Westerly Terr., Los Angeles, CA 90026, U.S.A.

BURMESTER, Ruth (Seymour), b. 15 Apr. 1907. Retired Educator. Education: Sauk Co. Tchrs. Coll.; Stevens Point Tchrs. Coll. Married, 3 sons. Positions held: Tchr. in rural schls., 1925-30; Tchr. in city schl., 1954-69. Memberships: Sauk Co. Regl. Writers; Wis. Regl. Writers; Wis. Fellowship of Poets. Contbr. to: Creative Wis.; New Poetry Out of Wis.; Wis. Hist. in Poetry, Bk.2. Honours, awards: 1st Hon. Mention, Wis. Regl. Writers Contest, 1962; 1st prize, Madison Area Writers Workshop Contest, 1971; 1st prize & Jade Ring, Wis. Regl. Writers Contest, 1973. Address: 547 Myrtle St., Reedsburg, WI, U.S.A.

BURNETT, Alfred David, b. 15 Aug. 1937. University Librarian. Education: George Watson's Boys' Coll., Edinburgh, 1945-55; Edinburgh Univ., 1955-59; Univ. of Strathclyde, 1963-64. Positions held: Library Asst., Glasgow Univ. Library, 1959-64; Asst. Librarian, Durham Univ. Library, 1964-. Memberships: Bibliographical Soc.; Lib. Assn.; Poetry Book Soc. Published works: Mandala, 1967; Diversities, 1968; A ballad upon a wedding, 1969; Columbaria, 1971; Shimabara, 1972; Thirty snow poems, 1973; Fescennines, 1973. Address: Senior Common Room, Grey Coll., Univ. of Durham, Durham, UK.

BURNIAUX, Constant, b. 1 Aug. 1892. Writer; Journalist; Teacher. Education: Tchrs. Trng. Coll., Brussels; self-taught in Latin, Italian & Spanish. Married, 1 son. Positions held: Tchr., 1912-14 & 1919-39; Attached to Health Sect. of Belgian Army during WWI; Jrnlst., 1932-. Memberships: Hon. Dir., Belgian Royal Acad. of French Lang. & Lit., 1945-; V.P., Belgian Sect., PEN Int.; Bd. Mbr., Assn. of Belgian Writers. Published works incl: Poèmes en prose, 1918-

26, 1927; Poèmes en prose, 1927-29, 1932; Ondes Courtes, 1951; La Poesie du roman, 1958; Poèmes choisis, 1961; Voyages, 1962; Recherche sur la poesie de la nouvelle, 1962; Poesie, 1922-63, 1965; D'Humour et d'Amour – Proses poetiques, 1968. Contbr. to: Le Journal des Poets, Brussels; Realismo lirico, Milan; Il giormale dei Poeti, Rome; Marginales, Brussels & num. mags. Has received important prizes for his romance work inclng: Prix Beernaert (Royal Belgian Acad.), 1931; Prix Malpertuis, ibid, 1944; Grand prix triennal du Roman du Gouvernement belge, 1945. Has had sev. works dedicated to him. Address: 61 Ave. Commandant Lothaire, 1040 Brussels, Belgium.

BURNS, James (Jim), b. 19 Feb. 1936. Poet. Married, div., 2 sons. Published works: Some Poems, 1965; Some More Poems, 1966; My Sad Story & Other Poems, 1967; The Store Of Things, 1969; Types, 1970; A Single Flower, 1972; Leben in Preston, 1973. Contbr. to: Ambit; Tribune; Samphire; Evergreen Review; Transatlantic Review; Akros; Poetry Review; Priapus; Pink Peace; Second Aeon; Cambridge Opinion; Grosseteste Review; The Honest Ulsterman; Phoenix; Imprint; Continuum; Poetry & Audience; The Curiously Strong; The Open Letter (Canada); Capella (Eire); Sum (USA); Poetry Review (USA); Twentieth Century; Tlaloc; Solstice; Chelsea (USA); Work (USA); Driftwood Quarterly; New Voice; Smoky Hill Review (USA); Grass Eye; Scop Sheet; Prism; Guerilla (USA); Human Voice Quarterly (USA); Clare Market Review; Matrix; Paperway, etc. Address: 7 Ryelands Cres., Larches Estate, Preston, Lancs. PR2 1PX, U.K.

BURNS, Robert Grant, b. 3 Oct. 1938. Poet & Musician. Education: Juilliard Schl. of Music, 1956-57 (piano w. Rosina Lhevinne & Josef Raieff); Baylor Univ., 1957-60 (drama w. Paul Baker); Univ. of Tex. at Austin, 1963-66 (piano w. Dalies Frantz & Charles Rosen); ethnomusicol. w. Norma McLeod & Marcia Herndon, 1973. Positions held: Poetry Cons., Tex. Commn. on the Arts & Humanities, 1973. Published works: Quiet World/Mundo Tranquilo, 1967. Contbr. to: The New Yorker; The Nation; Chelsea; Carolina Qtly.; Carleton Miscellany; The Ladies Home Jrnl.; Poetry; Beloit Poetry Jrnl.; Pegasus; etc. Honours, awards: 1st prize in Poetry, Seventeen Mag., 1958, Baylor Univ., 1960 & Univ. of Tex., 1966; Poetry Award, Nat. Endowment for the Arts, 1969; Dobie-Paisano Fellowship of Tex., 1970. Address: Q Ranch, 11311 Q Ranch Rd., Austin, TX 78759, U.S.A.

BURNS, Vincent Godfrey, pen name, BURNS, Bobby, b. 17 Oct. 1893. Poet; Author; Lecturer. Education: B.S., Penn State Univ.; A.M., Harvard Univ.; B.D. Union Theol. Seminary. Twice married to (1) Edna Rodenberger (2) Katharine Howard; children: Barbara, Vincent, David. Positions held: Minister of 5 churches; Teacher in 3 High Schools; Publisher. Memberships: Founder, Maryland State Poetry Soc.; President, C.A.A.A.; Founder, Maryland State Soc. of the Cultural Arts. Published works: The Story of Old Glory; The Men Who Broke a Thousand Chains; An American Poet Speaks; Out Of These Chains; Poetry For Young Americans; America, I Love You; Redwood and Other Poems; Female Convict; I am a Fugitive from a Chain Gang (book and film); Thirteen Songs; Ballads of the Free State Bard; Songs of the Free State Bards; The Sunny Side of Life; Heart on Fire; World on Fire; Poetry Is Fun; Memories & Melodies of Maryland; Maryland's Revolutionary Hero; Red Fuse on a World Bomb; The Master's Message for the New Day; Four Tests of a Loyal American; Flame Against the Night; New Light on the Lindbergh Kidnapping Mystery; Red Harvest; Still Life. Contbr. to: Ideals Mag.; Christ & Fine Arts (anthol.); Sunshine Mag.; War Cry. Honours: Apptd. Poet Laureate of Maryland, June 1962; Apptd. Poet Laureate of America, Feb., 1955 (Freedoms Foundation); Apptd. Poet Laureate of America, Apr., 1973 (World Poetry Therapy Convention, NYC). Address: 304 Epping Way, Epping Forest, Annapolis, MD 21401, USA.

BURNSHAW, Stanley (Alfred), b. 20 June, 1906.

Writer and Editor. Education: B.A., Univ. of Pittsburgh, 1925; M.A., Cornell Univ., 1933; Attended (also) Columbia Univ., N.Y., N.Y. Univ., Univ. de Poitiers, Sorbonne (Paris). Married; 1 d., and two step-children (through remarriage to Lydia Chaitkin, 1943). Positions held: Blaw-Knox Co., Penna., 1925-27: advertising; 1928-32: advertising, in N.Y.C.; 1934-37: assoc. editor, New Masses (wkly. mag.); 1937-38: vice-pres., ed.-in-chief, The Cordon Co., Inc.; 1939-58: pres., ed.-in-chief, The Dryden Press, Inc.; 1958-68: vice-pres., Holt, Rinehart & Winston, Inc. Faculty, N.Y. Univ., part-time, 1958-62. Member: P.E.N. (N.Y.) and Authors' League (N.Y.). Pubs: Poems, 1927; The Great Dark Love, 1932; The Iron Land, 1936; Early and Late Testament, 1952; Caged in an Animal's Mind, 1963; In the Terrified Radiance, 1972; Also: The Revolt of the Cats in Paradise, 1945; The Hero of Silence, 1965; The Bridge, 1945; André Spire and His Poetry, 1933; The Seamless Web, 1970; Editor, The Poem Itself (anthol. translations), 1960; Editor, The Modern Hebrew Poem Itself, 1966. Contrib. to: Atlantic Monthly; Saturday Review; Poetry; Sewanee Review; The American Scholar; Mass. Review, etc. Recip. Nat. Inst. of Arts & Letters, award for creative work, $3,000.00, 1971. Address: RFD Vineyard Haven, Martha's Vineyard, Mass. 02568, USA.

BURROW, Royal Douglass, b. 3 Dec. 1935. Editor and Publisher. Education: B.A., Ouachita Baptist Univ., 1957; M.A., in English, Univ. of Arkansas, 1959; M.A., in French, Univ. of Arkansas, 1966. Sec.-Treas., University-City Poetry Club, 1967-70; Southwestern Rep. for Prairie Press Books, 1968–; Head of Burro Books, 1969–. Member, Ark. Poets' Roundtable; Council of Ozark Artists and Craftsmen; Ozark Writers and Artists Guild; Ill. State Poetry Soc.; Poetry Soc. of London (UK). Pubs. The Ageless Ozarks, 1966; The Bums, The Athletes, 1967; Alabaster, 1968; Oedipus And Medea, 1969; Trail of Tears, 1969; The Battle of Pea Ridge; Far-Out Fables, 1972. Contrib. to: South and West; Contemp. Poets of Arkansas, Vols. I-III; Bitterroot; The Denver Post; Personal Poetry, Vols. I and II; Moon-Age Poets; Manifold; American Bard. Awards include: Poet of the Future, (Ark. Poetry Day), 1965; 2nd place, Lit. Award, Soc. of Ark. Authors, Composers and Artists, 1969; APFS Certificate for Contribution to Poetry Publications, 1973. Address: 1400 North Jefferson, El Dorado, Ark. 71730, USA.

BURROWS, Miles James Edwin, b. 18 Feb. 1936. Teacher. Education: Wadham Coll., Oxford Univ.; Univ. Coll. Hosp. Med. Schl. Married with 2 children. Published works: A Vulture's Egg, 1966. Contbr. to: The Listener; New Statesman; The Times Lit. Supplement. Address: 24 Hertford St., Cambridge, U.K.

BURTON, Cleo May, pen name BURTON, Cleo M., b. 16 June 1904. Homemaker. Education: High School. Widow; 2 s., 1 d. Positions held: Sunday School Teacher; T.U. Director; Choir Member; Principal of Vacation Bible School; Prayer Chairman of W.M.S.; Past Matron, Order of Eastern Star of Texas; Director of Music. Memberships: Poetry Soc. of Texas, and Garland Chapter; Writer's Workshop of Garland (current Pres., and formerly Reporter). Published works (songs): Our Jesus, 1964; Jesus Is Always With Me, 1964; Jesus Is My Saviour, 1965; Look Up To The Windows Of Heaven, 1965; I Want The Whole Wide World To Know, 1966; Lift Up Your Eyes and Pray, 1966. Contbr. to: Baptist Standard; Temple Baptist Church paper; Skyview Baptist Church paper in Austin; AsspciationAssociational Paper of Northern Area, Bay City, Mich.; Progressive Life Mag. Winner of awards from local chapter, Poetry Soc. of Texas, inclng. Human Relationship award. Address: 2121 South Glenbrook Dr., Apt. 9, Garland, TX 75041, USA.

BURTON, Mary. Poet; Composer; Artist. Education: Texas Tech. Univ.; Stephen F. Austin Univ.; Angelina Coll. Married to C.R. Burton; 1 s., 2 d. Positions held: East Texas Writers' Assn., Prog. Chairman, and Chairman of Poetry Day activities for Lufkin. Memberships: Avalon; Poetry Soc. of Texas; Houston

Chapter, Poetry Soc. of Texas; Acad. of American Poets; Lufkin Art League (Bulletin Editor); Tex. Fine Arts Assn.; CSSI (Hon. Rep.). Contbr. to: Cyclo-Flame; A Book of The Year; Bouquets of Poems; Listen/Hear; Lufkin Art League Bulletin; Lufkin News; KLUF Radio. Recip. of sev. awards. Address: 803 Johnson St., Lufkin, TX 75901, USA.

BURTON, Wilma, pen name, **BURTON, Wilma Wicklund,** b. 1 Dec. 1912. Editor-in-chief; Executive Secretary. Education: Roosevelt, Des Moines, Iowa; numerous poetry workshops attended and taught: Bedford Writing Center; Green Lake Writers' Conference; Salt Lake City Writers' Conference; 1st Writers' Conf. for Blind, for Dialogue, Inc., 1973; Judson Coll. Communications Conference; Mid-Admin. Cong., Denver, 1973; Biennial Cong., Miami, 1974, etc. Personal details: Married to Wilfred LaRue Burton, Director of Sacred Music Dept., Moody Bible Inst., Chicago; 3 children. Positions held: Div. Supervisor, Bankers Life Insurance, 1932-39; Medical Sec., 1939-40; Exec. Sec., Gen. Manager, John Deere, 1947-48; Edit. Asst., Hitchcock Publishing, 1954-55; Exec. Sec., Pres., YFC, Int'l., 1955-60; Exec. Sec., Gen. Director, Greater Europe Mission, 1961-73. Memberships: Poetry Ed., Pen Woman Mag. (NLAPW), 1972-73; Ed.-in-chief, ibid, 1974–; Memorial Chairman, NLAPW, 1972-73; Workshop Chairman, Poets & Patrons of Chicago, 1973-74; Sec., Chicago Poets, 1973-74; Pres., DuPage Poets; 1970-72; Poetry Ed., Church News of Chicago, 1973; State Chaplain, NLAPW for Illinois, 1973-74. Published works: Christmas is a Miracle!, 1966; Awarding Winning Poetry, 1973; Poem-Prayers for Monday Morning, 1974. Contbr. to: Gospel Messenger; Ideals; Moody Monthly; Christianity Today; Gospel Light; Scripture Press Publications; The Christian Family; The Rotarian; Chicago Church News; Progressive Women; Poet Lore; Good Housekeeping; Seven; The Pen Woman. Awards: Special Award, Stephen Vincent Benet Narrative Contest, Poet Lore, 1973; 1st Place, Shakespearean Sonnet, Deep South Writers' Contest, also NLAPW, 1973; 2nd Place, Boston Branch Contest, NLAPW, 1973; 1st Place, Pike's Peak Lyric Contest, 1972; 1st Place, Ark. State Sonnet Contest, 1972; 1st Place, Experimental Sonnet, Chicago Poets & Patrons, 1972; 1st Place, Lyric, Chicago Poets & Patrons, 1971; Grand Prize, Clement Stone Award, Poets & Patrons Contest, 1970; First Place, Love Lyric, Georgia State Poetry Contest, 1970. Address: 519 North President, Wheaton, IL 60187, USA.

BURUCOA, Christiane, b. 28 Sept. 1909. Writer; Poet. Married, 3 children. Memberships: Societe des Poets Francais; Société des Gens de Lettres; Syndicat des Ecrivains; Syndicat des Critiques; Academie des Jeux Floraux de Toulouse; Academie des Ecrivains Mediterraneens Montpellier. Published works: (poetry) Infrarimes, 1948; Antares, 1951; L'Heritier, 1953, '55; L'Oeil, 1957; L'Ombre et la Proie, 1958; Artizarra, 1962; Astrolabe, 1965; Altitudes, 1970; var. prose works. Contbr. to: Les Cahiers du Sud; Le Journal des Poetes; La Tour du Feu; Temps des Hommes; Points et Contrepoints, etc. Honours, awards incl: Prix J.J. Weis de l'Academie Française, 1966; Prix de Wolmar, ibid, 1971; Prix Hennequin de la Société des Gens de Lettres, 1973. Address: 68 Avenue Jean Jaurés, 12100 Millau, France.

BUSCALFERRI, Fabiano, b. 6 July 1920. Professor of Latin and Italian. Educ: Univ. of Florence, Italy. Positions held: Prof., Italian, Latin, & History, Istituto Magistrale R. Lambruschini, Montalcino, Siena. Memberships: Centro Studi e Scambi Internazionali; Acad. Leonardo da Vinci, Roma; Int. Acad. of Cultural Propaganda. Published works incl: Sabbie Lunari, 1951; Sabbie Terrestri, 1956; E Passano I Giorni, 1969. Contbr. to: Alla Bottega, Milan; Relations Latines, Naples; Battaglia Letteraria, Messina. Honours, awards incl: Gold Medal, 3rd Int. Poetry & Prose Contest, G. Ungaretti, 1972; Tied for 1st Prize, Città di Sulmona Poetry Prize, 1969; Citation, Alla Bottega Contest, Milan, 1973; 5th Prize, 2nd Int. Poetry & Prose Contest, Sorrento, 1973, etc. Address:

Via del Pino 5/A, 53024 Montalcino (Siena), Italy.

BUSCHING, (Mrs.) Mary Louise, pen name, **BUSCHING, Mary Wood,** b. 9 July 1925. Assistant to County Librarian, Gorman Public Schools, Texas. Education: HS. grad; Grad., Telephone Telegraph School, Springfield, Missouri; various courses poetry, English, psychology, etc. Positions held: various, and currently Asst. to County Librarian, Gorman Public Schools, Gorman, Texas. Memberships: 3rd Vice-Pres., Sec. & Treas., Iowa Poetry Day Assoc.; 2nd Vice-Pres.; Sec. & Treas. ibid; Vice-Regent, Midwest Fed. Chaparral Poets; Poetry Soc. of Texas, CSSI; Life Mbr., Iowa Poetry Day Assoc.; Acad. of Am. Poets; UPLI. Published works: Castle of Dreams, 1952; River's Bend, 1964. Contbr. to: De Leon Free Press; Gorman Progress; Tipton Conservative; Mechanicsville & Stanwood Herald. Honours: 1st Place Friendship Div., Southwestern Writer's Conference, Corpus Christi, Texas, 1950; 3rd Place, Iowa Poetry Day Assoc.; CAAA, 1954-55; Critics Award, Midwest Chaparral Poets, 1963, etc. Address: Route 1, Gorman, TX 76454, USA.

BUSTA, Christine, b. 23 Apr. 1915. Librarian. Education: studied Engl. & German philol., Univ. of Vienna. Married Maximilian Dimt. Positions held: Supplementary Tchr., commercial Acad., WWII; Interpreter & ENSA hostel Matron for Brit. Occupation troops in Austria, 1945-46; Private Tchr., 1946-50; Libn., pub. libs. of Vienna, 1950–. Memberships: Austrian Fed. of Writers; Austrian PEN Ctr.; Droste Soc., Münster, etc. Published works incl: Der Regenbawnr, 1951; Lampe und Delphin, 1955; Die Schoune der Vogel, 1958; Die Steruerminhle, 1958; Das andere Schof, 1959; Unterwegs tu alteron Feuern, 1965. Contbr. of many anthols., mags., reviews, in many countries. Recip. many honours & awards inclng: Austrian State Prize for Children's Lit., 1959; Prize of the City of Vienna for Young People's books, 1959; Dip. of Merit of the Christian Andersen Prize, 1960; Great Prize of the City of Vienna for Poetry, 1964; Great Austrian State Prize for Poetry, 1969. Address: Leop. Ristergasse 5/4/23, A1050, Vienna V, Austria.

BUTCHER, Grace, b. 18 Jan. 1934. Poet; Teacher; Athlete. Educ: B.A., Hiram Coll., Hiram, Ohio, U.S.A., 1966; M.A., Kent State Univ., 1967. Positions held: Instr., Cleveland State Univ., Cleveland, Ohio, 1967-68; Instr., Kent State Univ., 1968–; Athlete; track career, 1949–; pioneered the dev. of distance running for women in the U.S., 1957–; U.S. Half-Mile Women's Champion, Indoors, 1958, '60; Outdoors, Champ., 1959; U.S. Record Holder, Half-Mile Run, Indoors, 1958-61; U.S. Half-Mile Record Holder, Outdoors, 1959; A.A.U. All American, 1958-60; Middle Atlantic A.A.U. Cross Country Champion, 1963; Ohio & Lake Erie Cross Country Champ., 1968. Memberships: Ohio Poets Assn.; Nat. Coun. of Tchrs. of Engl.; Amateur Athletic Union of the U.S. Published works: The Bright Coloured Dark, 1966; More Stars than Room For, 1966; Rumors of Ecstasy..Rumors of Death, 1971. Contbr. to: Antioch Review; Coll. English; A Review of Gen. Semantics; Ohioana; Penny Papers; Free Lance; Ole; Midwest; Am. Weave; Dust; Lyric; Trace; Polemic; Poucan; Hika; Small Pond; Sparrow; The Smith; Jeopardy; Northeast; Experiment; Epos; Random House Anthol.; In the Time of Revolution; Viking Press Am. Lit. Anthol. III; Rising Tides Anthol., 1973, etc. Honours, awards: Vachel Lindsay Poetry Prize, Hiram Coll., 1962-66; Abbie M. Cops Nat. Sonnet Comp/. Olivet Fine Arts Fest., 1967; Nat. Endowment for the Arts Award, 1969. Address: P.O. Box 274, Chardon, OH 44024, U.S.A.

BUTLER, Bill, b. 3 Nov. 1934. Writer; Publisher. Published works: Byrne's Atlas, 1968, etc. Contbr. to: Scotsman; Guardian; Spectator; It; Friends; Frendz; Time Out. Recip., Nat. Fndn. for the Arts Award, 1970. Address: 50 Gloucester Rd., Brighton BN1 4AQ, Sussex, U.K.

BUTLER, Honor Florence Hellen, b. 4 Jan. 1918.

Doctor's Receptionist. Widow. Positions held: Tchr.; Schl. Sec.; Medical Sec.Sec.-Receptionist. Memberships: The Poetry Soc.; The West Country Writers' Assn. Contbr. to: Berkshire Mercury; Pulse (Med. Jrnl.); Popular Gardening; Weyfarers (Guildford Poets Press); Southern TV (for Epilogue). Address: Ferndale, Soke Rd., Silchester, Reading RG7 2PA, U.K.

BUTLER, Michael Gregory, b. 1 Nov. 1935. University Lecturer. Education: M.A. (Cantab.); Dip. Ed. (Oxon.); Ph.D. (CNAA); F.I.L. Married, 1 son, 1 daughter. Positions held: Asst. Master, King's Schl., Worcester, U.K. & Reuchlin Gymnasium, Pforzheim, Germany; Hd. of German, Ipswich Schl., U.K.; Lectr. in German, Univ. of Birmingham. Memberships: Lit. Advisory Panel, West Midlands Arts Assn. Published works: Nails & Other Poems, 1964; Ed., Samphire, 1968–. Contbr. to: Migrant; Ukrainian Review; Samphire; Vagabond (Munich); Universities Poetry; Mica (Calif.); Poetry Review; BBC; Sceptre Press. Recip., Taras Schevchenko Meml. Prize, 1961. Address: 45 Westfields, Catshill, Bromsgrove, U.K.

BUTTRESS, Noëline E. Barry, pen name, **BARRY, Noëline,** b. 25 Dec. 1915. Writer. Education: St. Cyprian's Schl., Cape Town, S. Africa; Tchng. Dip., Tchrs. Training Coll., Bulawayo. Married w. 2 s. Positions held: Head Mistress, Plumtree Primary Schl., Rhodesia; Farming, Concession, Rhodesia, 20 yrs.; Sr. Mistress, Highfield Secondary African Schl., Salisbury. Memberships: Past, London Poetry Soc.; Salisbury Poetry Soc., 1952–; PEN Club, Salisbury. Published works: Bundu, 1957; The Poetry Society's Verse-Speaking Anthology, 1957; People & Poetry, 1966; New Voices of the Commonwealth, (ed. Howard Sergeant), 1968. Ed., Teerera, Young Writers' Club Mag., Highfield Schl. Contbr. to: Rhodesian Poetry; Two-Tone; John O'London; Poetry Review, UK; Fiddlehead, Canada; Poet, India; Contemporary Poets of the English Language, 1969. Awards: Book of the Year, London Poetry Soc., 1957; Special Prize, Poetry Soc. of Natal, 1956. Address: Highfield Secondary School, P.O. Highfield, Salisbury, Rhodesia.

BUXBAUM, Martin, b. 27 June 1912. Director of Communications & Editor of Table Talk Magazette. Education: Columbia Tech., 1934-38; Scholarship, Newman Sudduth Art Schl., 1938. Married Alice Lee Lyons, 2 sons, 6 daughters. Positions held: Ed., Hechinger Co., Wash. D.C., 1933-38; Timekeeper, Diamond Construction Co., Wash. D.C., 1938-39; Freelance Writer, Photographer, 1939-41; Ed., mags., Engrng. & Rsch. Corp., Riverdale, Md., 1941-45; So. Dairies Corp., Wash. D.C., 1945-53; Ed., Table Talk, Marriott Corp., 1953 & Dir. of Communications, 1953–. Memberships: Md. Poetry Soc.; Int. Platform Assn.; Counselor, Sunshine Mag., 1968–; Assoc. Ed., Playtime Mag.,· 1970–. Published works: Rivers of Thought, 1958; The Underside of Heaven, 1963; The Unsung, 1964, vol. II, 1965; Whispers in the Wind, 1966; Once Upon a Dream, 1970; The Warm World, 1974; (prose) Around Our House, 1968; Fifteen Years of Table Talk, 1973. Contbr. to var. mags. Honours, awards: Syracuse Univ. estab. Martin Buxbaum Manuscript Coll., 1960–; Named Poet of Yr., State of Md., 1967; Lizette Woodward Reese Poetry Award, 1968; Recip., Geo. Wash. Medal of Hon., Freedoms Fndn., 1967, 70, 71, 72; Ky. Col., 1971. Address: 7819 Custer Rd., Bethesda, MD 20014, U.S.A.

BYRD, Larry (Dale), b. 30 Aug. 1947. Photographer. Education: Univ. of Maryland in Europe; Jefferson State Jr. Coll. in Birmingham, Alabama. Positions held: Editor, Jefferson News Mag., Birmingham, Ala., 1971, and Literary Editor, 1972. Owner of Creative Photography, Birmingham, Ala. Published works: Chocolate Machine Guns and Turquoise Fantasia, 1972; Children of the Morning (co-author), 1971. Address: 2600 Stouts Rd., Fultondale, AL 35068, USA.

BYRON, Brenda Valerie, b. 13 Mar. 1923. Housewife. Married, 6 children. Positions held: Reporter on provincial newspaper; p/t Freelance Writer (short stories, mostly for radio, newspaper & mag. articles, & children's material). Member, Nottingham Writers' Club; Comm. Mbr. & Ed. of club mag., 'Scribe'. Published works: Landscape With Pylons, 1961. Contbr. to: Poetry Review; Envoi; Headland; Scrip; Country Life; The Lady; This England; Wascana Review (Canada); John Bull; Manifold; Scottish Sec. Schls. Mag.; Orbis; Woman & Home; Notts. Weekly Guardian; Nottigham Guardian Jrnl.; var. children's publs. & many BBC local & nat. radio progs. Address: Halcyon, Nicker Hill, Keyworth, Nottingham NG12 5ED, U.K.

BYRON, Stuart, b. 9 May 1941. Film Critic. Education: B.A. (Hist.), Wesleyan Univ., Middletown, Conn., 1963. Positions held: Assoc. Ed., Independent Film Jrnl., N.Y., 1963-65; Dir. of Advt. & Publicity, Pathé Contemporary Films, N.Y., 1955-56; Staff Writer, Publicity Dept., Embassy Pictures, N.Y., 1966-67; Reporter-reviewer, Variety, N.Y., 1967-69; Asst. to the President, Natoma Productions, Inc., N.Y., 1969-70; Film Ed., The Real Paper, Cambridge, Mass., 1973–; Instr., Orson Welles Film Schl., Cambridge, Mass., summer 1973. Contbr. to: N.Y. Times; Transatlantic Review; Approach; Epos; Poets at Wesleyan, 1962; Wagner Lit. Mag. Address: 1167 Boylston St., Apt. 17, Boston, MA 02215, U.S.A.

C

CABANISS, Alice, b. 20 June 1934. Teacher & Advisor of Student Newspaper. Education: B.A., Winthrop Coll.; The Citadel, S.C. Positions held: Prog. Dir., WQSN Radio, Charleston; Advt. Copywriter, Tobias Advt. Agency, Charleston; Instr., Dept. of Engl., Wando H.S., Mt. Pleasant, S.C. Memberships: Treas., Bd. Dirs., Ed., Yearbook, Poetry Soc., of S.C. Contbr. to: var. schl. periodicals; Yearbook, Poetry Soc. of S.C., Charleston; S.C. Mag., Columbia; The New South, Atlanta; The Brown Bag, Greensboro; S.C. Review, Greenville. Recip. num. prizes from Poetry Soc. of S.C., 1965-71. Address: 334 Molasses Ln., Mt. Pleasant, SC 29464, U.S.A.

CABRAL, Olga, b. 14 Sept. 1910, West Indies. Writer. Education: High School Graduate; sev. art courses; largely self-educated. Personal details: of Portuguese descent, m. to Aaron Kurtz, (d.), Yiddish Poet. Positions held: Formerly Art Gallery Owner; currently Editorial secretary. Member of Poetry Soc. of America. Published works: Cities & Deserts, 1959; The Evaporated Man, 1968; Tape Found in a Bottle, 1971. Contbr. to the following anthols: Poets of Today, 1964; Where Is Vietnam? 1907, Poems of Protest Old & New, 1968; The Writing on the Wall, 1969; Live Poetry, 1971; The Diamond Anthology, 1971; Points of Departure, 1972; Imaginative Literature, 1973; Open Poetry, 1973; From the Belly of the Shark, 1973. Co-winner, Emily Dickinson Award of Poetry Soc. of America, 1971. Address: Box 6110, San Francisco, Calif. 94101, USA.

CACCIATORE, Edoardo, b. 18 Nov. 1912. Writer. Education: Univ. of Rome, Italy. Published works: Graduali, 1953; La Restituzione, 1955; Lo Specchio e La Trottola, 1960; Tutti i Poteri, 1969. Contbr. to: Botteghe Oscure; Tempo Presente. Address: 26 Piazza di Spagna, Rome, Italy.

CACCIATORE, Vera. Writer. Education: Dr. in Lit. & Philos., Rome Univ., Italy. Married Edoardo Cacciatore. Positions held: Curator of the Keats-Shelley Meml. House in Rome. Hon. Mbr., Poetry Soc. of Am. Published works: La Vendita All'Asta (short stories), 1953; La Palestra (short stories), 1961; La Forza Motrice (novel), 1968; Shelley & Byron at Pisa (essay), 1961; A Room in Rome (essay), 1970. Honours, awards: M.B.E. Address: Piazza di Spagna 26, Rome, Italy.

CADDEL, Richard Ivo, b. 13 July 1949. Librarian. Education: B.A. in Mus. Engl. & Hist., Newcastle Univ.;

L.A. exams in Librarianship, Newcastle Polytechnic. Positions held: Barman, Queen's Head, Wigmore, Kent, & Blyford; Sr. Lib. Asst., Durham Univ. Lib. Published works: Icarus etc. (poems), 1969; Heron (poems), 1973. Contbr. to: Make; Penny Make; Samphire; P/S (Midnag); Makaris; Blue Front Door; Ostrich; Day Anywhere Ticket; Grosseteste Review; Pig Sample Pack; Coel; Ashes. Address: 16 Rothbury Terr., Heaton, Newcastle upon Tyne 6, U.K.

CADWALLADER, Mary Rue (Molly), b. 23 Jan. 1944. Student. Education: Univ. of Hartford, 1 yr.; courses at Tulane Univ., New Orleans & La. State Univ.; currently studying poetry, short story writing & playwriting at La. State Univ. Positions held: Math Tchr., Runnels Pre-School (Montasori method). Member, New Orleans Poetry Soc. Contbr. to: La. State Poetry Soc. Yearbook, 1973; New Orleans Poetry Soc. Yearbook, 1974. Address: 1520 Steele Blvd., Baton Rouge, LA 70808, U.S.A.

CAHILL, Mary-Paula, pen name PAULA. Retired Freelance Writer. Education: Tchr. Trng., Binghamton, N.Y., U.S.A., 5 yrs.; Adult Educ. in Creative Writing, 5 yrs. Married. Positions held: Tchr., N.Y. State & Pa., 5 yrs.; Pvte. Tutoring. Memberships: Sec. of Manuscript, Nat. League of Am. Pen Women; Org., Writers Workshop of Tucson & a Past Pres. of Ariz. State Poetry Soc., Tucson; The Rimers; World Poetry Soc. Published works: Heart-Beats, 1959 (poems); The Desert Speaks, 1968 (book of poems); Vagabond Gold, 1971 (book of poems); The Voice of Paula, 1973 (book of poems). Contbr. to Binghamton Sun, N.Y.; Endicott Bulletin, N.Y.; Jrnl. of Lifetime Living; Family Times, etc. Honours, awards: 1st prize, expmtl. verse, Nat. Fed. of State Poetry Socs. & many other prizes. Address: 2381 West Nebraska St., Tucson, AZ, U.S.A.

CAINE, Marcella Barbara, b. 28 June 1915. Businesswoman. Education: Business Coll., sev. yrs. Widow, 2 children. Positions held: Sec.; Owns & rents real estate – houses. Memberships: Sec., Ore. State Poetry Assn. Contbr. to: Circle Forum, a mag. of reversible poetry; Shore Publs. anthol.; Dorothy Dalton's newspaper columns, Menasha, Wis.; Jean's Jrnl.; Clackamas River Rhymes; Medford Mail Tribune; Hyacinths & Biscuits; Tweed; Dragonfly; Modern Maturity mag.; Driftwood Mag.; Oregonian poetry columns; The Wick mag., Utah; Fate mag.; Modern Haiku; Mexican World; Valley View; Fireflower, Yukon, Canada; Sunburst; Haiku Bylines, U.K.; The Bard; Zodiac mag. of Pyramid Pub.; Cyclo-flame, etc. Recip. var. poetry awards. Address: 935 N.E. 126th Ave., Portland, OR, U.S.A.

CAIRNCROSS, George Thomas Richard, b. 13 Jan. 1938. Businessman. Education: James Graham Coll. of Educ. Positions held: Bank Cashier; Soldier; Freelance Artist; Art Tchr.; Tailor & Outfitter; Ed.; Bogg Mag.; Hd. of Fiasco Publs. Published works & anthol. contbns: Nature Poetry, 1966; Poetry for Peace, 1967; Vibrations, 1967; Its World that Makes the Love Go Round, 1968; Next Wave 2, 1970; Next Wave 3, 1971; Anthol. of Students Poetry, 1968; It Was Only the Other Day, 1971; The Nightcrawlers, 1969; In Concert, 1973; Being a Lunatic is No Easy Thing, 1973; Poems by George Cairncross & John Elsberg, 1973; The Pineapple in the Fruit Machine, 1973; Mighty Joe Young by George Cairncross & Joe Hirst, 1973. Contbr. to: Somethings; Gaga; Centre 17; Bogg; Your Friendly Fascist; 1D; Platform (Hants); Gargantua; Viewpoints; Scrip; Moonshine, etc. Address: 31 Belle Vue St., Filey, East Yorks., U.K.

CALCUTT, John David, b. 9 Sept. 1950. Teacher. Education: West Midlands Coll. of Educ., 1968. Married. Memberships: Sub-Comm., Birmingham Poetry Ctr. (Has run, under the direction of the Ctr., evenings of Music, Poetry, Drama, Dance, etc. at The Fitters Arms in Walsall). Contbr. to: Envoi; Lines; Scrip; The Little Word Machine; Oasis; Nucleus '73; Dodo; Grosseteste Review; Pink Peace; Cornhill Mag.; Expression One; Midland Read; Transgravity Press;

Radix; Mag. of West Midlands Arts Assn.; Chapman; Muse; Platform; New Headland; Strath; Radio Birmingham (Jim Green's prog. 'The Poets'). Address: 202A Birmingham Rd., Walsall, Staffs, U.K.

CALDWELL, Gala Ray, b. 16 Mar. 1914. Education: undergrad. work, Univ. of Ark., Fayetteville. Contbr. to: Jean's Jrnl.; Poet; Tempo; Over the Ozarks; Creative Review; Encore; Hyacinths & Biscuits; Am. Bard; Poetry Preview; Bardic Echoes; United Poet; Dragonfly; Young's Anthol., etc. Recip. var. poetry awards & prizes. Address: 603 N. 6th St., Thayer, MO 65791, U.S.A.

CALKINS, A. Jean, pen name **GOLDEN, Rima,** b. 12 Mar. 1933. Editor; Poet; Publisher. Married to Tracy Jay Calkins, 5 children. Positions held: Stenographer; Dental Asst.; Pvte. Sec.; Ed.; Publisher. Memberships: Am. Poets Fellowship Soc.; World Poetry Soc. Intercontinental; Am. Poetry League; Int. Poetry League. Author of Dawn of Promise, 1967. Ed., Jean's Jrnl. of Poems, 1963–; Haiku Highlights, 1965-72. Contbr. to: Altoona Mirror; Poets' Bulletin; Echoes; American Poet; Memorabilia Anthology; The Saint; Haiku Highlights; Echoes of Laughter; Quintessence; Jean's Jrnl.; Writer's Notes & Quotes; Prairie Poet; The Angels: Steuben Courier; Harbor Lights; Ophic Lute; These Are My Jewels; J & C Transcripts Christmas Anthols.; Mitre Press Anthology. Honours: 3rd Place, Poets' Tape Exchange, Poetry Contest, 1966; 1st Place, Quintessence Mag. Contest, 1967; 1st Place, Rondelet Contest, Down Ink Lane, 1966; 1st Haiku Contest, Poets' Tape Exchange, 1970. Address: PO Box 15, Kanona, NY 14856, USA.

CALLOW, Philip Kenneth, b. 26 Oct. 1924. Writer. Education: St. Luke's Coll., Exeter, U.K. Has taught occasionally at art schls. & has lectured and given readings from own work at colls., festivals & univs. in U.K. & U.S.A. Memberships: Poetry Secretariat, London & Nat. Poetry Secretariat. Published works: (novels) Yours; Flesh of Morning: The Bliss Body; Going to the Moon; Clipped Wings; A Pledge for the Earth; Common People; Native Ground; The Hosanna Man; (poetry) Bare Wires, 1972; The Real Life, 1965; Turning Point, 1962; (works in progress) Book on the life of D.H. Lawrence & a new novel. Contbr. to: The Listener; New Statesman; Tribune; Stand; BBC Radio. Address: Little Thatch, Haselbury, nr. Crewkerne, Somerset, U.K.

CALVELLO, Michael Anthony, b. 27 Feb. 1940. English Teacher. Education: B.A., Calif. State Univ., San Francisco; M.A., Creative Writing, in progress. Married Gail Calvello, 2 children. Positions held: Engl. Tchr. Member, The N.Y. Poetry Forum. Contbr. to: Mother's Hen Publication, Gypsy Table, No.4, summer 1973. Recip., Award, Franklin's Tales Poetry Contest, San Francisco, 1973. Address: 5 Lafayette St., Caribou, ME 04736, U.S.A.

CAMERON, (Mrs.) Bella, b. 8 Aug. 1918. Retired Businesswoman. Memberships: Hon. Sec., Blackpool Friendship Club (resigned after 15 yrs.); Hon. Sec., Blackpool Good Samaritans, 13 yrs.; Past Asst. Sec., Blackpool & Fylde Welfare Soc.; Publicity & Press Off. for Congl. mag. & org.; Leonardo da Vinci Acad.; Corrispondente, Hon. Rep., Centro Studi e Scambi; Avalon World Arts Acad.; Am. Poetry League; Int. Poetry Soc., etc. Rep. in following anthols: London Anthol., 1967; Spring Anthol., 1968; Corgi Books, 1968; Laudamus Te, 1967; Peace Poems, 1967; City & Machine Age Poetry, 1968; Love Poems Anthol., 1968; Nature Poetry, 1968; Spring Anthols., 1969, 70, 71, 72, 73; Mosaic Enterprises Chapbook, U.S.A., 1972; Phoenix Fires Anthol., 1973; IWWP Anthol., 1973; Quaderni di Poesia Anthol., Italy, 1972 & 73, etc. Contbr. to num. mags. inclng: Orbis; Scrip; Expression One; Poet India; Manifold; Viewpoints; Cyclo-Flame; Platform; Am. Poetry League Bulletin. Poems broadcast on Radio Blackburn & I.O.M.; interviewed on both; work broadcast in Germany & Ark., U.S.A. Recip. num. poetry awards. Address: 398 Talbot Rd., Blackpool, Lancs. FY3 7AY, U.K.

CAMPBELL, Alistair Te Ariki, b. 25 June 1925, Rarotonga, Cook Islands. Editor. Education: Victoria Univ. of Wellington, New Zealand. Positions held: Tchr.; Ed., Schl. Publs. Br., Dept. of Educ. Formerly Treas., PEN, New Zealand. Published books: Mine Eyes Dazzle, 1950, '51, '56; Sanctuary of Spirits, 1963; Wild Honey, 1964; Blue Rain, 1967. Contbr. to: Hilltop; Arachne; The New Zealand Listener; Numbers; Landfall; New Zealand Poetry Year Book; Poetry Australia; Poetry New Zealand. Address: 4 Rawhiti Rd., Pukerua Bay, Wellington, New Zealand.

CAMPBELL, David, b. 1915. Farmer. Education: Arts Graduate, Cambridge Univ., UK. Positions held: Played football for England; Pilot, RAAF, WWII; Farmer, Bungendore, NSW. Published works: Speak With the Sun, 1949; The Miracle of Mullion Hill, 1956; Poems, 1962; Evening Under Lamplight (short stories), 1959. Honours, awards: DFC & Bar. Address: Palerang, Bungendore, N.S.W., Australia.

CAMPBELL, George. Published works: First Poems, 1940; A Play Without Scenery. Contbr. to: (anthologies) Caribbean Literature, 1966; Carribean Verse, 1967; (Jrnls.): Focus.

CANE, Julia Elizabeth Dickinson, b. 2 Feb. 1905. Teacher of Biology, Physiology & Physical Education; First Aid & Water Safety Instructor. Education: B.Sc., Battle Creek Coll., Mich., 1929; Tex. Tech., Lubbock, Tex., 1939 & '40; Incarnate Word Coll., San Antonio, Tex., 1956-70. Widow of Joel Cane. Positions held: Water Safety Instr., San Antonio Country Club, 1924; Governess, W.K. Kellog family, 1927; Phys. Educ. Tchr., Detroit Pub. Schls., 1929-30; Phys. Dir., YWCA, Kalamazoo, Mich., 1929; Tchr., Lubbock, Tex., Pub. Schls., 1940-47; Tchr. of Sci., San Antonio Pub. Schls., 1947-72. Memberships: San Antonio Poetry Soc., 1970–; Am. Poetry League; Soc. Chmn., local Poetry Soc. Contbr. to: San Antonio Poetry Soc. Mag., 1971-73; San Antonio Poetry League; poems published by the Edison H.S. Student Coun., San Antonio, 1973. Recip. var. poetry awards. Address: 335 Freiling Dr., San Antonio, TX 78213, U.S.A.

CANELLOS, George, pen name **DELPHIS, Phoebus,** b. 27 July 1909. Pensioner of Chamber of Commerce, Athens. Education: Lit., Univ. of Athens, Greece. Positions held: Pres., Delphic Org. Mbr., Greek Poets Soc. Published works: Tilling of Wrath, poems, 1948; The Man With Hoe, poems, 1943; Solitude of Stone, 1948; Greek Poems Contemporaneous; Vigilance Poems, 1956; Eniochos, 1973; Rose of Apollo, 1973; Heliconia Symphonia, 1973. Contbr. to var. newspapers, reviews, mags., in Greece, Europe & Am. Honours, awards: 4 Gold Medals; Accademico dell'Accademia Internazionale 'Neocastrum' Calabria, 1961; Premio Nazionale di Poesia "Magna Grecia", 1971; Premio per poesia 'Concorso Nazionale Aurelio Cassiodoro', 1970. Address: Mousson & Lascou, Psychico, Athens, Greece.

CANFIELD, Joan Giltner, pen names **SHERRARD, Dave, HAWTRE, Sharon Howard & HAINES, Stacy Shannon,** b. 22 Nov. 1921. Freelance Writer. Education: Univ. of Iowa, Iowa City; Buena Vista Coll., Storm Lake, Iowa; Penn Coll., Oskaloosa; Drake Univ., Des Moines. Memberships: Histn., Alpha Chapt., Des Moines, Iowa; Am. Poetry League, Phoenix; Patron, Lyrical Iowa, New London; Nat. League of Am. Pen Women; Int. Org. of Writers. Published works: The Ming Tree, 1951; All About Pan, 1957; Panorama, 1960; In Indigo Ink, 1970; Bronzed Masque, 1970; Green Moth of Summer, 1973; On Wellington Commons, 1973; Immortal Carousel, 1973; Tinfoil Clown, 1973; Red Cardinal Sing, 1974; Of Clowns & Carnivals, 1974; Ovals in a Picture Frame, 1974; Sequestered New Orleans, 1974; Green Shutters, 1974; They Call Me Punchinello, 1974; The Dual Image, 1974; To Goya with Love, 1974; Bal Masque, 1974, etc. Contbr. to: Quintessence; Am. Poet; United Poet; World Poet; Driftwood East; Olive Hill Times; The Amateur Writers Jrnl.; Harlo Anthol., 1973-74, etc. Honours, awards: Carthage Press Award for 'The

Tudor Image', 1961, etc. Address: 4815 Harwood Dr., Des Moines, IA 50312, U.S.A.

CANNADY, Criss Ellen, pen name **CANNADY, Criss E.,** b. 22 Oct. 1951. Library Assistant. Education: Calif. State Univ. at Northridge, and Univ. of Calif. at Irvine. Contrib. to: Irvine Humanities Review, 1973; Artifax, 1972; Gate Magazine, 1970; Nat. Poetry Press, 1970; Nat. Poetry Press (special edition), 1970. Co-winner, Acad. of American Poets Prize (1st place), 1971. Address: 6840 Firmament Ave., Van Nuys, Calif. 91406, USA.

CANNON, M., pen names **MINERVA & WOLFE,** Paris. Freelance Writer; Poet; Essayist; Novelist. Education: Columbia Univ., N.Y.; Univ. of Miami, Fla. Married. Positions held: Sec. to husband; Freelance Writer. Memberships: Poetry Soc. of Am.; Acad. of Am. Poets; Centro Studi e Scambi Int.; Leonardo da Vinci; Fellow, Int. Poetry Soc., 1973; Western World Haiku Soc., 1974. Published works: Running From the Wind; Of Gossamer Wings; Jewels of the Judean Hills; Nostradamus; Prophet of France (novel in progress). Contbr. to following jrnls. & anthols: Am. Bard; Am. Poet; Bitterroot; Hartford Courant; Jean's Jrnl.; Haiku Highlights; Dragonfly; Imprints Qtly.; The Saint; Modern Images; The Symbolist; Voices Int.; New Poetry; Poet Lore; Prairie; United Poets; Valley Views; Cycloflame; Best in Poetry 1969; Am. Poet 1968, '69; These Are My Jewels, 1969; All Time Favorite Poetry, 1970; New Voices in the Wind, 1970; A Quorum of Cats; Golden Quill Anthol., 1971; Yearbook of Modern Poetry, 1971; Outstanding Contemporary Poetry, 197; New Anthol. of Int. Poetry Soc., 1973. Honours, awards: 1st prize, Fla. state-wide poetry, 1967; 2nd prize, Haiku Highlights, 1969; 1st prize, ibid, 1970; Love Poem Award, Poet Lore, 1971; Descriptive Poem Award, ibid, 1972. Address: 9120 S.W. 32nd St., Miami, FL 33165, U.S.A.

CANNON, Maureen, b. 4 Nov. 1922. Housewife. Education: B.A., Barnard Coll., 1943. Married, 2 daughters. Positions held: Corres., Book-of-the-Month Club, 1943-52; Office Worker for James P. Cannon Co., 1969–; Asst. in Schl. Lib., many volunteer positions inclng. working with schl. children in verse & Editing the Bergen Poets Anthology. Memberships: Poetry Soc. of Am.; Pa. Poetry Soc.; Ga. Poetry Soc.; Poets' Study Club of Terre Haute, Ind.; Bergen Poets, N.J. Rep. in the following anthols: Poems for the Early Grades, 1972; Poetry Soc. of Am. Diamond Anthol., 1971; Ga. Poetry Soc. 50th Anniversary Anthol., 1973; Bergen Poets Anthol., 1973; IWWP, 1972. Contbr. to: McCalls; Good Housekeeping; Ladies Home Jrnl.; Saturday Evening Post; Lyric; Pen; Am. Jrnl. of Nursing; Am. Baby; Girl Talk; Verse in View; Christian Sci. Monitor; Hartford Courant; Reader's Digest; Modern Bride; Improvement Era; Catholic World, etc. Honours, awards: Grand Prix, Nat. Fed. State Poetry Socs., 1967; 1st Prize, Trad., Nat. Fed. State Poetry Soc., 1968; 1st Prize, light verse, ibid, 1969; 1st Prize, light verse, Deep South Writer's Conf., 1970 & Pa. Poetry Soc., 1970; Va. Prize, Lyric, 1971; 1st Prize, Terre Haute Poets Study Club, 1971, W. Va. Poetry Soc. Contest, 1972 & NFSPS, 1973, Arizona Poetry Soc., 1973. Address: 258 Steilen Ave., Ridgewood, NJ 07450, U.S.A.

CANON, Julia H., b. 7 Aug. 1889. Teacher. Education: Maryville Coll., Maryville, Tennessee; Eastern New Mexico Univ., A.B. Positions held: Teacher, Public Schools, New Mexico, 20 yrs., etc. Membership: Poetry Soc. of Colorado. Contbr. to: W.C.T.U. Messenger; Protestant Herald; Colorado Club Woman; Golden Harvest (anthol.), 1971. Address: 1300 South Gaylord St., Denver, CO 80210, USA.

CANTONI, Louis Joseph, b. 22 May 1919. Educator; Poet. Education: A.B., Univ. of Calif., Berkeley, 1946; M.S.W., Univ. of Michigan, Ann Arbor, 1949., Ph.D., ibid, 1953. Married; 2 children. Positions held: Conf. Ldr., Psychol. Tchr., Counselor, Gen. Motors Inst., Flint, Michigan, 1951-56; Assoc. Prof. to Prof., Dir. of Rehab. Counseling, Wayne State Univ., Detroit,

Michigan, 1956–. Memberships: Chmn., Coun. of Rehab. Counselor Educators; Pres., Mich. Rehab. Assoc.; Pres., Detroit Rehab. Assoc.; Fellow, American Assoc. for the Advancement of Science; Mbr., Am. Philos. Assoc.; Am. Psychol. Assoc.; Am. Personnel & Guidance Assoc.; Nat. Rehabilitation Assoc.; World Poetry Soc. Intercontinental; South & West; Poetry Soc. of Michigan; Fndr., Acad. of Am. Poets. Published works: With Joy I Called You, 1969; sev. profl. books in counseling and rehab., including: Counseling Your Friends (co-authored with Lucile Cantoni), 1961. Contbr. to many journals, including: Am. Assoc. of Univ. Professors Bulletin; Bardic Echoes; Cape Rock Qtly.; Cathedral Digest; The Clearing House; Church and Home; Daily Collegian; Education; A Review of General Semantics; Graduate Comment; The Green World; Hartford Courant; The Human Voice; Insight – Interdisciplinary Studies of Man; Legend; Michigan Qtly. Review; Modern Images; The Muse; Michigan Rehab. Assoc. Digest; Newman Review; Pegasus; Peninsula Poets; The Personalist; Poet (India); Tulsa Poetry Qtly.; Univ. of Windsor Review; Verdure; The Vocational Guidance Qtly.; Voices Internat. Address: 2591 Woodstock Dr., Detroit, MI 48203, USA.

CAPASSO, Aldo, b. 13 Aug. 1909. Writer. Education: Dr. of Letters. Married Florette Morand. Published works: Il passo del cigno, 1931; Il paese senja tempo, 1934; A la nuit, 1935; Poemes choisis, 1942; Per non moline, 1947; Folmi che d'autenno, 1951; Fredici recitative, 1956; Recitativi quasi me ditajiorni, 1958; L'eclair et la duree, 1964; Pour enchanter la mort, 1965. Contbr. to: Il Conveyno; L'Italia Cetteraria; La Repubblica; Il sentiro dell'Arte; La Nacion; Jrnl. des Poetes, etc. Honours, awards incl: Premio della Ginestra, 1948; Premio Murano, 1950; Premio Delfo, 1960; Frouda d'Oro, Sileno d'Oro plusieurs medailles en or. Address: Piazza del Consolato 6, Altare (Savona), Liguria, Italy.

CAPENERHURST, Ralph George, b. 22 Sept. 1925. Supplies Officer. Education: Kenley Bible Coll. Married, 2 children. Served in British Army in France, Egypt, Palestine, 1943-47. Memberships: Panel Writer, Redemption Tidings. Published works: You in Your Small Corner, 1967; God at Ground Level, 1972. Contbr. to: Redemption Tidings; Life of Faith; Latimer House; Crusade. Address: Maranatha, 39 Empress Rd., Derby DE3 6TD, U.K.

CARBERRY, H.D., b. 1921. Lecturer. Educ: Jamaica; England. Positions held: Ex-Pres., West Indian Students Union, London, U.K.; Lectr., University of the West Indies, Mona, Jamaica. Published works: A West Indian in England (w. Dudley Thomas), 1950. Contbr. to: Sun's Eye (anthology), 1968.

CARD, Jane Ridgley, b. 17 July 1912. Health Educator. Education: Grad. study in Psychol., Claremont Grad. Schl. & Univ. of Southern Calif.; Masters in Public Hlth., UCLA. Married, 3 children. Positions held: Tchr., 1955-65; Psychological Counceling, 1965-70; Dir. of Hlth. Educ., 1970-73. Mbr., Small Press Review. Publisher of poetry mag., Hyacinths & Biscuits, 4 times a yr., 1969–. Contbr. to: Hyacinths & Biscuits; Quickenings in Trillium Land; Crown Jewels Schaeffer Ambulance Trade Paper; Small Press Review. Recip., Award, lit. contest, L.A. State Coll., 1952. Address: Box 392, Brea, CA 92621, U.S.A.

CAREME, Maurice Jean-Baptiste, b. 12 May 1899. Writer. Education: Royal Conservatory, Brussels, Belgium. Tchr. until 1942. Memberships: Assn. of Belgian Writers; Pen Club Int.; Société Internationale des auteurs et compositeurs. Published works: 63 illustrations pour un jeu de l'oie, 1925; Hôtel bourgeois, 1926; Reflects d'hélices, 1932; Mère, 1935; Petite flore, 1937; Femme, 1946; La Lanterne magique, 1947; Petites Légendes, 1949; La Maison blanche, 1949; La Voix du Silence, 1951; L'Eau passe, 1953; Volière, 1953; Le Semeur de rêves, 1953; Images perdues, 1954; Le Voleur d'etincelles, 1956;

Heure de grâce, 1957; Pigeon vole, 1958; L'oiseleur, 1959; La cage aux grillons, 1959; La flûte au verger, 1960; La grange bleue, 1961; Pomme de reinette, 1962; Le mât de cocagne, 1963; La Bien-aimée, 1965; Brabant, 1967; Entre deux mondes, 1970; Mer du Nord, 1971; L'Envers du Miroir, 1973; Le Moulin de Papier, 1973, etc. Honours, awards incl: Chevalier ordre Leopold; Officier de l'ordre de la Couronne; Prix de poésie religieuse, 1957; Grand prix international de poésie à Paris, 1968; Prince en poésie, 1972, etc. Address: 14 Avenue Nellie Melba, 1070 Brussels, Belgium.

CAREW, Rivers Verain, b. 17 Oct. 1935. Farmer Journalist. Education: St. Columba's Coll., Rathfarnham, Co. Dublin; B.A., B.Agric., Dublin Univ., 1956; M.A., 1960. Married, 3 daughters. Member, Int. Assn. for the Study of Anglo-Irish Lit. Published works: Figures Out of Mist (w. Timothy Brownlow). Contbr. to: Irish Times; Dublin Mag.; Kilkenny Mag.; A Review of English Lit. Address: Killyon Manor, Hill of Down, Co. Meath, Ireland.

CARMEL, Hilda Anne. Professional Artist. Education: City Coll. of New York; N.Y. Univ. Art Students League. Married, 2 children. Positions held: Corres. Sec., Artists Equity Assn. of N.Y.; Pres., League of Present Day Artists; Visual Arts Co-Chmn., Bronx Coun. on the Arts, N.Y.; Sec. of Metropolitan Painters & Sculptors, –1974. Memberships: N.Y. Poetry Forum; Spafaswap (poetry mag.) Contbr. to: Composers, Authors & Artists, 1971; Centro Studi e Scambi Int., 1971; Spafaswap Mag., 1970-72; Art World Mag., 1972. Recip., Hon. Mention, N.Y. Poetry Forum, 1973. Address: 3210 Fairfield Ave., Riverdale, NY 10463, U.S.A.

CARNEY, James Patrick, b. 17 May 1914. Professor of Celtic. Education: Grad. in Celtic Studies, Univ. Coll., Dublin; post grad. studies in Germany. Positions held: worked in research, Dublin Inst. for Advanced Studies, 1941–; currently Prof. of Celtic, ibid; Vis. Prof., Uppsala, Sweden, 1950-52; Vis. Prof., U.C.L.A., 1965-67. Published works: Medieval Irish Lyrics, selected & transl. by James Carney, 1967. Address: 45 Garville Ave., Rathgar, Dublin 6, Ireland.

CAROTHERS, Robert Lee, b. 3 Sept. 1942. Professor of English. Education: B.S., Edinboro State Coll., 1965; M.A., Kent State Univ., 1966; Ph.D., ibid, 1969. Positions held: Fellow, Kent State Univ.; Instr., Asst. Prof., Assoc. Prof. & Prof., Edinboro State Coll. Published works: Poems for the End of Something, 1969; Freedom & Other Times, 1972. Contbr. to: Am. Weave; Podium; Polemic; Congress; Icon; The Penguin Review; The Hiram Poetry Review; Toucan; Wrenches; New; Canadian & Am. Poetry; Small Ponds; A Cleveland Sampler; Poetry Cleveland; The Buddhist Newsletter; The Kent Qtly.; Debut, etc. Honours, awards: Kent Qtly. Award for Poetry, 1966; Hart Crane-Alice Crane Williams Award for Poetry, 1967. Address: P.O. Box 184, Edinboro, PA 16412, U.S.A.

CARPELAN, Bo G.B., b. 25 Oct. 1926. Writer; Assistant Chief Librarian. Education: Ph.D., Helsinki Univ., Finland, 1960. Married Barbro Eriksson, 1 son, 1 daughter. Memberships: PEN; Finnish-Swedish Writers Assn. Published works: Som en dunkel värme, 1946; Du mörka överlevande, 1947; Variationer, 1950; Minus sju, 1952; Objekt för ord, 1954; Landshapets förvandlingar, 1957; Den svala dagen, 1961; 73 dikter, 1966; Garden, 1969; Källan, 1973. Contbr. to sev. reviews in Scandinavia. Recip. sev. awards inclng: Finnish States Award, 1970; Swedish Acad. Finland Prize, 1972. Address: Nyckelpigvägen 2B, Hagalund, Finland.

CARPENTER, Anthony John, b. 11 Oct. 1944. Claims Negotiator & Semi-Professional Photographer. Positions held: Radio & TV Salesman, 1961; Backstage Stage Asst., 'Blitz', West End, 1962; Sales Asst./Stock Control Keeper, Motor Accessory Shop, Gloucester, 1962-64; joined London Plays Group

'Dialogue Enterprise' & helped present plays & poetry readings, 1966; w. North Thames Gas, 1966; Insurance Rep., then i/c Claims Dept. as Claims Mgr., private insurance broking co., Gloucester, 1968; Claims Negotiator, Nat. Insurance Grp. of Cos., Gloucester & opened a Studio for wedding & portrait photography, 1973. Member, Cheltenham Poetry Soc. Published works: The Poetical Works of Anthony John Carpenter, 1972. Address: The Studio, 264 Barton St., Gloucester, U.K.

CARPENTER, Joyce Frances, b. 4 Oct. 1926. Actress. Positions held: Actress, TV, Films, West End Theatre; Held part of Betty Brook, Bob Dale's Sec., Mrs. Dale's Diary, BBC radio, 6 yrs.; Writer, poetry, short stories, 1969–. Memberships: Hon. Sec., Cath. Poetry Soc.; London Writers' Circle; The Keys Cath. Writers' Soc.; The Poetry Soc. Contbr. to: New Bard Anthol., 1971; All People are Poets, 1971; The Orbis Verse Anthol., 1971; Int. Who's Who in Poetry Anthol., 1972; Int. Poetry Soc. Anthol., 1974; The Tablet; Irish Times; Headland Poetry Mag.; Aquarius Poetry Mag.; Envoi; Viewpoints; Orbis; Sussex Life; New Writing; Chichester Observer; Writers Digest; The Dalesman; Writers Review; Monday World; Country Quest; Kansas Kernels Poetry Mag.; Hyacinths & Biscuits (USA); Meaning in Life Anthol.; Anthol. of Love Poems (USA); The Lady; Unity Mag. (USA); Cork Weekly Newspaper; Village Review Poetry Mag.; Platform (poetry mag.). Poems read on BBC Radio Soap Box Prog., 1972 & '73 & on BBC Radio Medway 'Listen' Prog. Honours, awards: Cert. of Merit, The Writers' Poetry Contest, 1970; 4th Prize, United Writers' Poetry Comp., 1970 & 2nd prize 1972; 1st prize, London Writers' Circle Annual Poetry Comp., 1973; 4th prize, Platform Poetry Competition, 1973. Address: Flat 1, 44 Lansdowne Rd., Holland Pk., London W.11 2LU, U.K.

CARPENTER, Margaret Haley. Author; Editor. Education: B.A., Univ. of Richmond. Vice Pres., Virginia Humanities Foundation. Memberships: Poetry Soc. of America; Poetry Soc. (UK); Poetry Soc. of Virginia; Vachel Lindsay Assoc. (Adv. Board). Published works: Poems, by Marion Cummings (Edited), 1957; Journey into Time, by David Morton (Edited), 1958; Anthol. of Magazine Verse for 1958 (Edited, with W.S. Braithwaite); Sara Teasdale, A Biography (Author), 1960. (Song of Sara, with music by Daniel Jahn, based on Sara Teasdale, A Biography, presented on Cape Cod, 1972, and in NYC, 1973). Contbr. to: (anthols.) The Diamond Anthol.; The Golden Year; Invitation to the City; Lyric Va. Today; Anthol. of Mag. Verse; Golden Quill Anthol.; (newspapers and journals) Country Life; Outposts; Poetry Review; Spirit; The Lyric; Good Housekeeping; NY Times; NY Herald Tribune; The Canadian Poet; Voices; Recurrence; English; The Cresset; Irene Leacne Memorial, etc. Awards: Greenwood Prize (Poetry Soc., UK), 1957; Co-winner, Arthur D. Ficke Award (PSA), 1956; many 1st prize awards from various sources, the latest being the Keats Memorial Sonnet Prize, 1972; the James & Helen Duff Memorial Prize, 1973; the Nancy Byrd Turner Prize, 1973. Appointed Hon. Daughter of Mark Twain, 1970. Address: 1032 Cambridge Cres., Norfolk, VA 23508, USA.

CARPENTER, Maurice, pen name **CARPENTER, Miles,** b. 25 Sept. 1911. Poet; Retired Teacher. Education: London Univ.; Bristol Aeroplane Factory. Married three times, 4 children. Positions held: Teaching posts in Barnstaple, Wotton, Norfolk, London, etc. Memberships: West Country Writers Assn.; Fellow, Int. Poetry Soc.; Poetry Soc. Published works: IX Poems, 1935; The Tall Interpreter, 1946; Gentle Exercise, 1950; Black Ballads & Love Words, 1971; Verses of my Sixtieth Year, 1972; Orpheus Expresso (a Play for a Youth Theatre), 1972; Reverie on Cadbury Rings (A Play for six voices), 1973; A Chaos to Tame, 1973. Poems & Drama produced on BBC Third Prog. & BBC West Region. Contbr. to: Poetry Review; Outposts; London Mag.; West Country Mag.; Unicorn; Arena; Our Time; Anvil; Poetry London; Poetry Qtly.; Aquarius; Faber Book of 20th

Century Verse; Methuen New Anthol. of Modern Verse; Penguin Mid-Century Verse; Frontiers of Going; Unicorn Anthol.; Peninsula; 600 Years of Bristol Poetry; Int. Poetry Soc. Anthol. Honours, awards: Atlantic Award for Lit., 1948; Shakespeare Quatercentenary Prize (Poetry Soc.), 1964; Greenwood 2nd Prize, 1949. Address: 'A Chaos to Tame', 74 High St., Wootton Bassett, Wilts., U.K.

CARR, Ray de la Montanye, b. 26 Apr. 1902, Spartanburg, SC. Independent Publisher's Representative (Advertising); Writer; Lecturer; Poet; Presbyterian Minister. Education: A.B., Davidson Coll., NC; B.D. & Th.M., UTS, Richmond, Va.; Univ. of Va. Positions held: Indep. publr.'s rep., NYC; Ldr. of Great Book Seminars, Great Books Fndn. & NY Pub. Lib.; Preacher at NY Chs.; Tchr., Bronx Bible Class; Lectr. on & reader of Poetry. Memberships: Poetry Soc. of Am.; Cath. Poetry Soc.; World Poetry Soc., Int.; NY Poetry Forum; Brooklyn Poetry Soc.; Greenwich Village Poetry Soc.; Hon. Chap., Lectr., N.Y. Chapt., United Daughters of the Confederacy; Lectr., Lollard R. Wolfe Club & Donnell Lib.; Contbr. to: Am. Bard; Am. Courier; Am. Poetry Mag.; Anthol. 1; Anthol. 2; Blue Moon; Boston Post; Caravan; Charleston News & Courier; Christian Herald; Chaparral Writer; Driftwind; Fawnlight; Hippocrene; Lantern; Parade Bulletin; Pegasus; Poetry Digest; Poet's Log Book; New Review; Reflections; Scimitar & Song; Spirit-Bull.; Step-Ladder; Weaver; Westminster Mag.; Flatbush Mag.; Leader Observer; St. Clare's Hosp. Bull.; NY Times; New Poetry Digest; NE Courier, etc. Poetry & writings on file in Lib. for perm. record, Univ. of Syracuse, NY. Address: 663 Fifth Ave., New York, NY 10022, USA.

CARRIER, Constance, b. 29 July 1908. Teacher. Education: B.A., Smith Coll., 1929; M.A., Trinity Coll., 1940. Positions held: Instr. of Engl., French, Latin, Sr. H.S., New Britain & Hall H.S., West Hartford; Instr., Classics, Summer Workshop, Tufts Univ. Published works: The Middle Voice, 1955; The Poems of Propertius, 1963; The Poems of Tibullus, 1968; The Angled Road, 1973. Contbr. to: New Yorker Mag.; New York Qtly.; Am. Scholar; The Nation; Poetry; Chicago Tribune Poetry; Yankee; Concerning Poetry; Counter/Measures; Christian Sci. Monitor; The Atlantic Monthly; Beloit Poetry Jrnl.; N.M. Qtly.; Approach. Honours, awards: Lamont Award, 1955; var. awards in '40's, Poetry Soc. of Am.; 3rd pl., 1970, 2nd pl., 1971, Chicago Tribune; Approach Award, 1969. Address: 225 West Main St., New Britain, CT 06052, U.S.A.

CARRIER, Warren, b. 3 July 1918. College Dean. Education: A.B., Miami Univ.; M.A., Harvard Univ.; Ph.D., Occidental Coll. Positions held: Prof. of Engl., Chmn., Engl. Dept., Univ. of Montana; Assoc. Dean, Rutgers Univ.; Dean, Coll. of Arts & Letters, San Diego State Univ. Published works include: The Cost of Love, 1953; Toward Montebello, 1966. Contbr. to the following anthols., jrnls., mags., etc: Poetry; Kenyon Review; Va. Qtly.; Poetry N.W.; N.W. Review; Qtly. Review of Lit.; Epoch; Prism Int.; Western Review; Colo. Qtly., etc. Honours, awards: Cash Award, Nat. Fndn. for the Arts, 1968. Address: Office of the Dean, San Diego State Coll., San Diego, Calif. 92115, USA.

CARROLL, Paul, b. 15 July 1927. Poet; Critic; Teacher; Editor. Education: M.A., Engl. Language & Literature, Univ. of Chicago, 1952. Positions held: Lecturer in Humanities, Notre Dame Univ. & Univ. of Chicago, 1952-59; Instr., Engl., Loyola Univ., 1957-59; Editor, Big Table Magazine, 1959-61; Editor, WFMT, Chicago, 1961-64; Editor, Inst. of Philosophical Research, Chicago, 1964-67; Editor, Big Table Books, Chicago, 1968-71; Visiting Poet, Writers Workshop, Univ. of Iowa, 1966-67; Visiting Poet & Critic, State Univ. of NY at Buffalo, Summer, 1968; Visiting Poet, Branford Coll., Yale Univ., Spring, 1969; Prof. of Engl., and Chairman, The Prog. for Writers, Univ. of Ill. at Chicago Circle, since 1968. Published works: Odes, 1968; The Luke Poems, 1971; The Poem In Its Skin (criticism), 1968; (Editor) The Young American Poets,

1968. Contbr. to: The New Yorker; Beloit Poetry Journal; Accent; Choice; Big Table; Chicago Review; The Nation; Paris Review; Evergreen Review; Poetry; Locus/Solus; Origin; Black Mountain Review. Address: Dept. of Engl., Univ. of Illinois at Chicago Circle, Chicago, IL 60680, USA.

CARRUTH, Hayden, b. 3 Aug. 1921. Freelance writer & editor. Educ: B.A., Univ. of N. C., Chapel Hill, 1943; M.A., Univ of Chicago, 1947. Married to Rose Marie Dorn, two children. Positions held: Ed., Poetry, Chicago, 1949-50; Book Ed., var. publishers; Currently Freelance Writer & Ed. Published works: The Crow and The Heart, 1959; Journey to a Known Place, 1962; The Norfolk Poems of Hayden Carruth, 1962; North Winter, 1964; Contra Mortem, 1967. Contbr. to: Poetry; Virginia Quarterly Review; Hudson Review; Kenyon Review; Kayak; (anthologies) Best Poems of 1960, '62, '66, '68: The Borestone Mountain Poetry Awards, 1961, '63, '67, '69; On Writing, By Writers, 1966; From the Hungarian Revolution, 1966; New Modern Poetry, 1967; American Literary Anthology 2, 1969. Editor: Contemporary American Poetry, 1969; A New Directions Reader (w. James Laughlin), 1964. Honours, awards: Bess Hokin Prize, 1954; Vachel Lindsay Prize, 1956; Levinson Prize, 1958; Morton Zabel Prize, 1968; Eunice Tietjens Memorial Prize, 1964; Harriet Monroe Poetry Prize, 1960; Bolligen Fndn. Fellowship, 1963; Guggenheim Fellowship, 1965. Address: Johnson, VT, U.S.A.

CARSON, Herbert L., b. 3 Oct. 1929. Professor. Education: B.A., Univ. of Pittsburgh, 1953; M.A., Columbia, 1955; Ph.D., Univ. of Minn., 1959. Married, 3 children. Positions held: Tchr., Orange HS, NJ, 1953-55; Instr., Minn., 1956-59; Instr., Neb., 1959-60; Asst. Prof. to Prof., Ferris State Coll., Mich., 1960-. Memberships: Poetry Soc. of Mich.; Acad. Am. Poets; Poetry Soc. of America. Published works: Steps in Successful Speaking; The Impact of Fiction (co-author). Contbr. to: Carolina Quarterly; Kans. Quarterly; Brainstormer; Quarterly Jrnl. of Speech; The Cresset; Today's Speech; The Personalist; Coll. Compositions & Communication; Western Speech; Central States Speech Jrnl.; Jrnl. of Aesthetics & Art Criticism; Goodly Co; Angel Hour; Experiment; Quixote; Soliloquy; Classical Outlook; Western Review; Pa. Hist.; Folio; Laurel Review; Bardic Echoes; Flame; Peninsula Poets; Forum; The Archer; Encore; The Muse; Angel; Am. Bard; Driftwood; Swordsman Review, etc. Address: 823 Cherry Ave., Big Rapids, Mich. 49307, USA.

CARSON, Robert, pen name **MARR, Lem,** b. 24 Oct. 1904. Retired Accountant. Education: Oklahoma State Univ., 1924-27. Memberships: Fellow, Internat. Poetry Soc.; Nat. Fed. of State Poetry Socs.; Poetry Soc. of Oklahoma; Centro Studi e Scambi Internazionali; Southwesterners Workshop. Pub. Crossing the Field (book of poetry), 1972. Contib. to: The Oklahoma Messenger; Harlow's Weekly; The Daily Oklahoman. Awards include: Poetry Soc. of Okla.: 1st place, The Adelia Clifton Award, 1969; 2nd place, Annual Award, 1969; Hon. Mention, Jennie Harris Oliver Award, 1969; 1st place, Nat. Fed. of State Poetry Socs. Frontier Award, 1970. Address: 1824 West Cleveland, Guthrie, Okla. 73044, USA.

CARTER, Esther Lee, b. 18 Aug. 1897. Writer. Education: Univ. of Wash. Married Lee J. Carter, dec., 1 son & 1 daughter, dec. Memberships: Nat. League of Am. Pen Women; Washington Poetry Assn.; Seattle Poetcrafters. Published works incl: Olympian. Contbr. to many mags. & jrnls. Address: 140 Circle Dr., Panorama City, Olympia, WA 98503, U.S.A.

CARTER, Frances Tunnell, b. 21 May 1922. Professor. Education: B.S., Univ. of So. Miss.; M.S., Univ. of Tenn.; Ed.D., Univ. of Ill.; additional studies, Univ. of Dayton & Fla. State Univ. Married John T. Carter, 2 children. Positions held: Elem. Schl. Tchr.; H.S. Tchr.; Tchr.; Wood Jr. Coll., East Ctrl. Jr. Coll., Clarke Memorial Jr. Coll.; Prof., Samford Univ. (Educ. & Psychol.); Guest Prof., Hong Kong Baptist Coll.

Memberships: Past Pres., B'ham Br., Nat. Assn. of Am. Penwomen; B'ham Quill Club; Ala. State Poetry Soc.; Centro Studi e Scambi Int. (Hon. Rep.) Published works: Sammy in the Country, 1960; 'Tween-Age Ambassador, 1970; co-author, Sharing Times Seven, 1971; Ten articles on child dev. & educ. in var. mags.; sev. articles & stories for children. Contbr. to: Author/Poet; Poetry Anthologies (about 4); The Sampler (about 4 vols.); The Current; Distaff. Recip., 1st prize, for poem published in Author Poet, 1971. Address: Schl. of Educ., Samford Univ., Birmingham, AL 35209, U.S.A.

CARTER, Graeme, pen names, **BOLLARD and CLOACA,** b. 1947. Student. Co-Ed., Sandwiches Mag.; Co-Ed., Peninsula Mag., Univ. of Kent. Published works: Now Look Here, 1973. Contbr. to: Sunday Times; Sandwiches; Peninsula. Address: 66B Whitstable Rd., Canterbury, Kent, CT2 8EB, U.K.

CARTER, James G(rafton), b. 26 Jan. 1917. Professor of Accounting. Education: M.S., Michigan State Univ., 1951; B.S., Miami Univ., Oxford, Ohio, 1940; C.P.A., Ohio, 1951. Married to Jean H. Whipple; three children: Katharine Jean, James Whipple, Charles Grafton. Professor, chigan State Univ., 1949-53; Practice as C.P.A., 1954-57; Professor, Univ. of Georgia, 1958-59; Professor, Western Michigan Univ., 1959-61; Director, Applied Education in Accounting, 1962-65; Professor, Franklin University, 1966-; Practice as Certified Public Accountant, 1966-. Member, Ohioana Library Association. Author, The Sign of the Empty Cross, 1974. Address: 2500 Wickliffe Road, Columbus, Ohio 43221, USA.

CARTER, Marion, b. 31 Jan. 1924. Poet; Artist; Writer; Housewife. Education: Darwen Tech. Coll. (further educ. courses). Married, 4 children. Positions held: Pianist; Artist. Contbr. to: Rev. Tait's Quarterly; Darwen News; Darwen Advertiser; Poets of Symbol (anthol.); Competitors Jrnl.; Wilson Bros. Greeting Card Verse; Symbol Writers Mag. Address: 88A Birch Hall Ave., Darwen BB3 0JB, Lancs. U.K.

CARTER, Martin Wylde, b. 1927. United Nations Representative. Educ: Queen's Coll., Georgetown, Guyana. Positions held: Clerk, Civil Service, four years; Representative, Guyana, United Nations. Published works: The Hill of Fire Glows Red, 1951; To a Dead Slave, 1951; The Kind Eagle, 1952; The Hidden Man, 1952; Poems of Resistance from British Guiana, 1954. Contbr. to (anthology) Young Commonwealth Poets '65, 1965. Address: United Nations, New York, NY, U.S.A.

CARVER, Raymond C., b. 25 May 1938. Writer. Education: A.B., Humboldt State Coll., 1963; grad. work, Univ. of Iowa, Sacramento State Univ., San Jose State Univ. & Tel Aviv Univ. Married, 1 son, 1 daughter. Positions held: Coll. Textbook Ed., Sci. Rsch. Assocs., Inc., Palo Alto, Calif., 1967-70; Lectr. in Creative Writing, Univ. of Calif., Santa Cruz, 1970-72; Vis. Lectr., Dept. of Engl., Univ. of Calif., Berkeley, 1972-73; Vis. Lectr., Writers Workshop, Univ. of Iowa, 1973-. Published works: Near Klamath, 1968; Winter Insomnia, 1970; Foreign & Domestic, 1974. Rep. in following anthols: New Voices in Am. Poetry, 1973; Literature, 1973; Ways of Looking at Poetry, 1974. Short stories published in many mags. & anthols. Honours, awards: Nat. Endowment for the Arts Award, 1970; Joseph Henry Jackson Award, 1971; Wallace Stegner Creative Writing Award Fellowship, Stanford Univ., 1972-73. Address: 22272 Cupertino Rd., Cupertino, CA 95014, U.S.A.

CASEY, Michael, b. 1947. Poet. Published works: Obscenities, 1972. Contbr. to: The New York Times; The Nation; America. Recip., Yale Younger Poet Award, 1972. Address: c/o Yale Univ. Press, 92A Yale Stn., New Haven, CT 06520, U.S.A.

CASEY, Vivian M., b. 16 Mar. 1926. Social Worker (Child Care). Memberships: Life Danae Mbr., Int. Clover Poetry Assn.; N.Y. Poetry Forum. Published works: Stop! Think It Over (Clover Book of Anthol.), 1973; The Wrath of God (Algiers Sentinel), 1967. Address: P.O. Box 6279, New Orleans, LA 70174, U.S.A.

CASH, Peter Maurice, b. 31 Dec. 1949. Postgraduate Student of English. Education: Univ. of Nottingham, 1968–. Positions held: Ed., 'Gong', 1970-72; Ed., 'Poetry Nottingham', 1972–; Editl. Bd., 'Orbis', 1972–. Memberships: The Poetry Soc.; The Nottingham Poetry Soc.; The International Poetry Soc. Published works: Something to Write Home About, 1971. Contbr. to: Workshop; Outposts; Lincolnshire Writers; Orbis; Tribune; Contrasts; Gong; Scrip; New Headland; Poetry Nottingham. Honours, awards: Skegness Arts Fest. Poetry Prize, 1967; Kirke White Poetry Prize, 1970; Lake Aske Meml. Award, 1971; Platform Poetry Prize, 1972; Workshop Poetry Prize II, 1973. Address: Wayncroft, Croft Ln., Wainfleet, Nr. Skegness, Lincolnshire PE24 4PA, U.K.

CASSIDY, Vincent Harold, pen name, **CASSIDY, Vin,** b. 10 Sept. 1923. Professor of History. Education: B.A., M.A., Ph.D., Univ. of North Carolina. Married to Amy Page. Positions held: Assoc. Prof. of History, USL., Lafayette, Louisiana, 1960-65; Bd. and Staff member, Deep South, Writer's Conference, 1961-68; Sec.-Treas., Lafayette Civic Theatre, Inc., Louisiana, 1965-69; Coll. Coordinator, Deep South Writer's Conference, 1966-67, and elected Permanent Bd. Member, 1968; Assoc. Editor, Attakapas Gazette, 1968-69; Prof. of History, Univ. of Akron, 1969. Memberships: Southwest Louisiana Poetry Soc. (Pres., 1967-69); Louisiana State Poetry Soc. (3rd Vice-Pres., 1968-69). Contbr. to: Saturday Eve. Post; One Nation Under God (anthol.); Archer; Arizona Qtly.; Ball State U. Forum; Bitterroot; Border; Caravan; Cardinal Poetry Qtly.; Carolina Qtly.; Dust; Fiddlehead; New Lantern Club Review; Nexus; Quoin; Trace. Recip. 1st place Poetry Book Award, Deep South Writers' Conference, 1964. Address: 569 Weber Ave., Akron, OH 44303, USA.

CASSITY, Turner, b. 12 Jan. 1929. Librarian. Education: A.B., Millsaps Coll.; M.A., Stanford Univ.; M.S., Columbia Univ. Positions held: Assoc. Libn., Transvaal Provincial Lib., 1958-60; Assoc. Libn., Emory Univ. Lib., 1962–. Published works: Watchboy, What of the Night? 1966; Steeplejacks in Babel, 1973. Contbr. to: Poetry; Southern Review; Kenyon Review; Univ. of Denver Qtly.; Poem; New Am. Review; North Am. Review. Recip., Levinson Prize (Poetry), 1971. Address: Emory Univ., Robert W. Woodruff Lib., Atlanta, GA 30322, U.S.A.

CATHCART, Mildred Dooley, b. 28 June 1915. Teacher; Writer. Education: Grad., Centerville HS and Centerville Jr. Coll.; Iowa Wesleyan Coll., Mount Pleasant; Grad. B.S., Drake Univ., Des Moines, Iowa. Married John C. Cathcart; children (Kerry Lee and Jean Marie). Positions held: Teacher, Jerome School, Iowa; Receptionist, Chicago, Ill.; Teacher, Seymour Community Jr. HS, Iowa. Memberships: Des Moines Branch, NLAPW (State Pres.); Iowa Poetry Day Assoc.; Alpha Chapter, Des Moines Poetry Soc. of Iowa; CSSI (Exec. Bd.); Internat. Platform Assoc.; Iowa Fed. Club Woman. Published works: Life of Jesus, 1956; God's Gifts, 1956; Easter Book of Poems, 1957. Contbr. to: Farm Journal; Des Moines Sunday Register; Capper's Weekly; Kitchen Klatter; Iowa Poetry Assoc.; Alpha Poetry Chapter; Iowa Poetry Day Assoc.; Iowa Fed. Club Woman. Recip. of sev. awards and honours. Address: RR 3, Centerville, IA 52544, USA.

CATO, Nancy Fotheringham, b. 11 Mar. 1917. Writer. Education: Presbyterian Girls' College; Adelaide Univ. & S.A. Schl. of Arts. Married Eldred Norman, 3 children. Positions held: Jrnlst.; Grape-picker; Art Critic; Ed., 2 Anthols.; Asst. Ed., Hudson's Poetry, 1947-48. Memberships: Fndr. Mbr., Lyrebird Writers (Sydney) Poets' Cooperative Publishing Venture; V.P., S.A. Fellowship of Writers; Coun. Mbr., Authors' Soc. of Australia; former mbr., Poetry Soc. of Australia;

F.A.W. of Queensland. Published works: The Darkened Window, 1950; The Dancing Bough, 1957; Ed., Jindyworobak Anthol., 1950. Contbr. to: Sydney Bulletin; Poetry Australia; Poetry (S.A.); Meanjin Quarterly; Quadrant; Southerly; Australian Poetry; A. & R. Anthol.; Australian Poet (Moscow); The Australian; Canberra Times; Melbourne Age; Sydney Morning Herald; Overland; Vision; The Women Poets in Engl., etc. Honours, awards: Tennyson Medal for Engl. Lt., 1934; Northern Territory Poetry Prize, 1961; Farmers' Poetry Prize, 1964. Address: Nairana, Noosa Heads, Queensland 4567, Australia.

CAULFIELD, Francis, b. 3 Jul. 1907. Retired. Education: Lees Council School, Cross Roads; St. Anne's Roman Catholic School, Keighley. Memberships: Internat. Poetry Soc. (Fellow); Pennine Poets. Published work: Long Errand, 1973. Contbr. to: Pennine Platform; Headlands. Address: 232 West Lane, Keighley, Yorks., UK.

CAUSLEY, Charles (Stanley), b. 24 Aug. 1917. Poet; Teacher. Education: Launceston Nat. School; Horwell Grammar School, Launceston; Launceston Coll.; Peterborough Training Coll. Born Launceston, Cornwall; Served in Royal Navy, 1940-46. Positions held: Teaching in Cornwall, 1947-73; Currently, Visiting Fellow in Poetry (1973-74), University of Exeter, Devon. Memberships: Vice-Pres., Poetry Soc. (UK); Vice-Pres., West Country Writers' Assoc.; Fellow, Royal Soc. of Literature (since 1958). Published works: Hands to Dance, 1951; Farewell, Aggie Weston, 1951; Survivor's Leave, 1953; Union Street, 1957; Johnny Alleluia, 1961; Underneath the Water, 1968; Figure of 8, 1969; Figgie Hobbin, 1971; The Tail of the Trinosaur, 1973. As editor, verse anthols: Peninsula, 1957; Dawn & Dusk, 1962; Rising Early, 1964; Modern Folk Ballads, 1966; The Puffin Book of Magic Verse, 1974. Penguin Modern Poets 3 (with George Barker and Martin Bell), 1962; Pergamon Poets X (with Laurie Lee), 1970. Contbr. to: New Statesman; The Spectator; The Listener; The Times; The Times Lit. Supp.; Encounter; The Sunday Times; The Observer; The Tablet; The London Mag.; Harpers Bazaar; Outposts; Tribune; Ladies' Home Journal; The Transatlantic Review; The Poetry Review; BBC, etc. Awards: The Queen's Gold Medal for Poetry, 1967; Soc. of Authors' Travelling Scholarships, 1954 and 1966; Cholmondeley Award for Poetry, 1971. Address: 2 Cyprus Well, Launceston, Cornwall, UK.

CAVALCANTE, E. Salome, pen name **CAVALCANTE, Salome Diehl,** b. 19 Apr. 1904. Poet; Composer; Amateur Artist (ret'd). Education: Grad., Burrows Schl. of Music. Widow of Anthony Cavalcante, 2 sons, 1 daughter. Memberships: Pittsburg Poetry Soc.; Carlisle Poets' Workshop; Pa. State Poetry Soc.; Nat. Fed. of State Poetry Soc.; Harrisburg Manuscript Club; V.P., Carlisle Poets' Workshop. Published works: (book of poetry) Golden Moments, 1972. Contbr. to: Ideal Mag.; Jewels for Advent. Honours, awards: 1st Jury Award for 'The Secret Known', Pitts. Poetry Soc., 1957; 2nd Jury Award for 'Faith', ibid, 1959; Third popular pl., 'The Golden Door', 1969; 2nd Hon. Mention, 'The Sound of Fall', 1972; 1st Hon. Mention, 'The Old Apple Tree', 1972. Address: 8108 Lake Terr. No. 7, Louisville, KY 40222, U.S.A.

CAVENAUGH, Irene Amy (Ransom), b. 23 June 1892. Poet. Education: Eastbourne Ladies Coll., U.K.; 'Avalon', Dresden, Germany; Royal Coll. of Music, London. Widow of P.H.C. Cavenaugh, 1 son, 3 daughters. Member, Salisbury Poetry Circle. Contbr. to: Prism; The Lady; The Window; Salisbury Circle Poets. Poem, 'Prayer', was set to music as an anthem. Address: 30A The Close, Salisbury, Wilts., U.K.

CAWEIN, Madison, pen names **PORDELLORAR, Adrian & DE HERANCOUR, Julian,** b. 18 Mar. 1904. Consultant in Physics & TV Design. Education: B.S., Physics, Univ. of Ky., 1924; grad. study, Cornell Univ., 1934-25. Married 1) Jane Walker 2) Ursula Maurer, 1 son (M.J. Cawein, III). Positions held: w. Westinghouse Lamp, N.J., 1925; Hazeltine Corp., N.Y.,

1930-38; Andrea Radio Corp, 1939; Mgr. of Rsch., Farnsworth TV & Radio, 1940-48; Cons., G.E., Admiral, Diamond Power, Dumont, 1948-59; V.P., Grimson Color (TV), 1959-60; Sr. Engr., Fairchild Cam. & Inst. Corp., 1960-69. Memberships: Univ. of Ky Tusitalia, 1923; Poetry Soc. of Am., 1958-62. Published works: The Conqueror, Weird Tales, 1925; Studies in Symbolism, 1937; The Red King Lies a-Dreaming, 1940; Halloween, a poem, 1972. Contbr. to num. jrnls. & mags. Address: 27 Hussa Pl., Denville, NJ 07834, U.S.A.

CAWS, Ian Victor, b. 19 Mar. 1945. Social Worker. Education: Churcher's Coll.; Petersfield & North-Western Polytechnic. Positions held: Trainee Social Welfare Officer, 1967; Social worker, 1970; Social worker with the Deaf, 1973, all with West Sussex Co. Council. Contbr. to: Phoenix; Tablet; Southern Arts Review; English; New Headland; Hampshire Poets; New Fire; Scrip; Village Review. Recip., Eric Gregory Award, 1973. Address: 35 Woodgate Pk., Westergate, Chichester, Sussex PO20 6QP, U.K.

CERAVOLO, Joseph, b. 22 Apr. 1937. Poet and Civil Engineer. Education: B. Civil Engrng., City Coll. of N.Y. Married Mona da Vinci, 3 children. Positions held: Civil Engr., Porter & Ripa Assocs. Published works: Fits of Dawn, 'C' edns., 1965; Wild Flowers Out of Gas, 1966; Spring In This World of Poor Mutts, 1968. Contbr. to: Anthol. of N.Y. Poets, 1970; Poets of the N.Y. Schl., Univ. of Pa., 1969; World Anthol., 1970; Lines; Locus Solus; Adventures in Poetry; The World; Angel Hair; Paris Review, etc. Honours, awards: Nat. Endowment Award, 1972; Poets Fndn. Award, 1962, '63, '64, '66, '67; Frank O'Hara Fndn. Award, 1968. Address: 65 Spruce St., Bloomfield, NJ 07003, U.S.A.

CEROVA, Carlo (Carlo Alberto Viva), b. 15 July 1941. Painter. Education: Liceo Classico. Memberships: Accademia Tiberiana; Accademia de 'I 500'; Accademicus ex Classe; Accademia Gentium Populorum Progressio; Accademia Int. Leonardo da Vinci; Accademia Legion d'Oro; Accademia B. Franklin; Comitato Studio Europeo per l'Arte e la Cultura; Burckhardt Basel, Switz. Published works: Andare Senza Fine, 1970; Specialmente la Sera, 1974. Honours, awards: Trofeo Numana Ars; Winner of Int. Lit. Comp. 'Text-Book'. Address: Via C. Battisti 10, I 73010 Sogliano Cavour, Italy.

CHAFFIN, Lillie D., pen names **CHAFFIN, Randall & DAY, Lila.** Author; Librarian; Writer-in-Residence. Education: B.S., Akron Univ., Pikeville Coll.; M.A., Eastern Ky. Univ. Married Thomas Chaffin. Positions held: Elem. & H.S. Tchr.; Elem. & H.S. Libn.; Creative Writing Instr., Univ. of Ky.; Freelance Lectr.; Writer-in-Res., Pikeville Coll.; Author, Libn., Johns Creek H.S.; Assoc. Ed., The Pen Woman; Poetry Ed., Twigs Mag. Published works: Lines & Points, 1965; A Stone for Sisyphus, 1967; First Notes, 1969; Bear Weather, 1969; In My Backyard, 1969. Contbr. to: Christian Sci. Monitor; Cregonian; Kan. City Star; Approach; Bitterroot; Fiddlehead; Ideals; Jack & Jill; Humpty Dumpty; Child Life; Manifold; Poem; Trace; Shenandoah; Encounter; Cardinal; Tangent; Wormwood; Poetry Dial; Moonstone; Lyric; Poet Lore; New Orleans Jrnl.; Poetry Venture, etc. Honours, awards incl: Poet of Yr., Alice Lloyd Coll., 1968; Ky. Col., 1969; Child Study Assn. of Am. Award, 1971. Address: Box 42 Meta Stn., Pikeville, KY 41501, U.S.A.

CHAI, Chun-Shih, pen name **CHUNG-LEI,** b. 24 Oct. 1920. Editor & Publisher. Education: B.A., China Univ.; grad., Army Acad. Married, 1 son. Positions held: served in the Military for 12 yrs., ret'd as Col., 1937-49; Exec. Dir. of Chinese Writers & Artists Assn., Chinese Cinema & Drama Assn., Chinese Poets Assn., 1955-; V.P., Second World Congress of Poets, 1973; Deputy Publisher & Ed.-in-Chief of Central Monthly. Published works: The Spark of Life, 1951; Under the Blue-Sky & Bright Sun Flag, 1955; Great Rudder, 1956; The Green Memory, 1960; The Maiden & the Soldier, 1964; This Generation, 1968; Poems from a Wandering Man, 1972; The Territory of Spring, 1973. Contbr. to: Ctrl.

Daily News; China Daily News; Shin-sheng Daily News; Ctrl. Monthly; China Lit. Monthly; Chinese Lit.; New Lit. Monthly; New Poem Today; The Vineyard Mag.; The Laurel Mag., etc. Honours, awards: Awards, Comm. of the Chinese Arts & Lit., 1952 & '54; Award given by Dr. Sun Yat-sen, Acad. & Cultural Fndn., 1967. Address: P.O. Box 55, Taipei, Taiwan, Rep. of China.

CHAILLIE, M. Jean Humphrey, pen name **CHAILLIE, Jean Humphrey,** b. 23 Jan. 1925. Poet; Drama Director; Playwright. Positions held: Pvte. Sec., Photographer's Model, Aircraft Riveter, Newspaper Ed., TV Dir., Optometrist Asst., Drama Dir. & Creative Writing Instr. Memberships incl: St. Joseph Creative Writers Club; Mary Alicia Owen Story Tellers' League; Poetry Chmn., Nat. League of Am. Pen Women; Dir., Theatre Arts Club; Producer, Writer, Scottsdale Community Players; Poetry Soc. of Australia; Charter Mbr., Ariz. Poetry Soc.; Am. Poetry League. Published works: Melodies from a Jade Harp, 1968; Ballet on the Wind, 1969; Spring Anthol. (London), 1970; 1st & 2nd Biennial Anthols., World Poetry Soc. Int., 1971-72; From Sea to Sea in Song, 1972; Sing, Naked Spirit, 1970. Contbr. to: The Sunshine Press; Kans. City Poetry Mag.; St. Joseph, Mo. News-Press; The Jrnl.-St. Joseph, Mo.; Phoenix Fires; Owl Express; Poet's Reed; And Their Voices Shall Be Heard; The Searchlight; The Evening Light; Scimitar & Song; Ideals, etc. Recip. num. poetry prizes inclng: 1st Prize, Am. Mosaic Poets, 1972; 1st Hon. Mention, Ariz. State Poetry Soc. Award, 1973. Address: 4549 E. Montecito Ave., Phoenix, AZ 85018, U.S.A.

CHAKRAVARTI, Prithvindra, b. 18 Nov. 1933. Teacher. Education: B.A., Visvabharati Univ., 1953; M.A., ibid, 1935; Ph.D., Calcutta Univ., India, 1962. Married, 3 children. Positions held: Prof. of Modern Langs. & Lit., City Coll., Calcutta, 1956-62; Lectr. & Vis. Asst. Prof. in South Asian Studies, Univ. of Chicago, 1962-66; Sr. Lectr. in Lit., Univ. of Papua New Guinea, 1967-. Published works: Sand Sun Water (21 poems in Engl.), 1970; Chharaachhatris (36 nonsense rimes in Bengali), 1970; Haanser Chha Baker Chha (16 poems in Bengali), 1970; Inni Binni (19 poems), 1970. Contbr. to: Indian Lit., New Delhi; Kovave, Brisbane; Delos, Ariz.; Chaturanga, Calcutta; Uttarsuri, Calcutta; Maharaj, Calcutta; Transition, Accra; Poet, Madras. Ed., Papua Pocket Poets, vols. 26-40, 1971-73. Address: Box 4820, University P.O., Papua New Guinea.

CHAKRAVORTY, Jagannath, pen name **JE-CHEE,** b. 12 Aug. 1924. University Educator. Education: B.A., Calcutta Univ., India, 1943; M.A., ibid, 1945; Ph.D., Jadarpur Univ., Calcutta, 1966. Positions held: Asst. Prof. & Hd., Dept. of Engl., Darjeeling Govt. Coll., W. Bengal; currently Rdr. of Engl., Jadarpur Univ., Calcutta. Memberships: Indian PEN; Asiatic Soc., Calcutta; Int. Shakespeare Assn., U.K. Published works:Nagar Sandhya, 1945-46; Karar Prarthana, 1949-50; Madadiganta, 1961; Parkstreeter Statue, 1969; Nihsarter nam Sundari, 1970; Kolkata Koltata, Kolkata, 1973. Ed., Bengali Literature, 1968. Contbr. to num. newspapers & mags. inclng: Hindusthan Standard; Indian Literature; Desh; Amrita; La Poesie; O Kabita; Lekha O Rikha. Address: Dept. of Engl., Jadavpur Univ., Calcutta 700032, India.

CHALLIS, C. Gordon, 3 July 1932. Clinical Psychiatrist. Educ: M.A., Univ. of New Zealand, Wellington. Married, 1959; two children. Positions held: Psychiatric Social Worker, Pororua Hosp., Wellington, 1960-62 & Memorial Hosp., Hastings, 1962-66. Clin. Psychiatrist, ibid, 1966-. Published works: Building, 1963. Contbr. to: Landfall; (anthologies) New Zealand Poetry Yearbook, 1957-62, 1964; Best Poems of 1960 and 1962; Borestone Mountain Poetry Awards, 1961, '63; Young Commonwealth Poets '65, 1965. Address: 510 Huia St., Hastings, New Zealand.

CHAMBERLAIN, Geraldine Laura Sandford, b. 25 Aug. 1912. Former Secretary. Education: Diocesan Coll., Auckland, New Zealand. Married Edward E. Chamberlain, 1 son. Positions held: Former Sec., King's Coll., Auckland. Memberships: World Poetry

Soc. Intercontinental; New Zealand Women Writers Soc.; New Zealand Penwomens Club; Convener, Poetry Workshop, ibid, 1970 & '71; Poetry Soc., New Zealand; Convener, Poetry Workshop, Hawkes Bay New Writers. Contbr. to: Poet; New Zealand Listener; Eve Mag.; New Zealand Farmer; Penpoint; Northland; New Zealand Home Jrnl.; New Zealand Women's Weekly; Forest & Bird; New Zealand Mercury; Manuka Blossoms, anthol. Honours, awards: Edna Macky Cup for Poetry, N.Z. Penwomen's Club, 1968 & '70; var. prizes in mag. comps. Address: Arden, Kopanga Rd., Havelock North, New Zealand.

CHAMBERLAIN, Kent (Clair), b. 22 Jan. 1943. Student, Bookkeeper, Merritt Davis Coll. of Commerce. Education: Ashland Senior H.S.; Writer's Digest Short Fiction Course; Merritt Davis Coll. of Commerce. Memberships include: World Poetry Soc. Intercontinental; Centro Studi e Scambi Internazionali; The Acad. Inter. Leonardo da Vinci; Nat. Writers Club; Internat. Songwriters Union; American Poets Fellowship Soc.; Internat. Poetry Soc.; Illinois State Poetry Soc.; Laurel Publishers Internat. Poetry Symposium; Internat. Clover Poetry Assoc. Pubs. Ship Bound for Where (1971); Collage (1969); Sweet Seventies (1972); American Poets Fellowship Soc. Anthol. (1972); Grains of Sand (1971); Dawn: the Birth of Day (1972); 70 Poets (1970). Contrib. to: Intro (ed.-in-chief); Akahi Hoi; The Cooperator; Ghost Dance 16; Circular Causation; Poet; Poets; Inner Well; Modern Images; Medford Mail Tribune; Willow Leaves; Beau-Cocoa; American Poet; Lincoln Log; Elementary English; Poetry Parade; Encore; Silk Screen; Hartford Courant; All-Time Favorites; Bachaet; Personal Poetry; Orion; Little Flower, etc. Honours: Trophy, 1972-73; Cover Poet, Jan.-Feb.-Mar. 1973, American Poet; 3rd prize, 1972 Environment Contest, Major Poets Nat. Awards & Pubs. Mrs. Pierson Mettler Associates (1869-1937); 5th prize, Spencer Book Company's 1969 Poetry Parade Contest. Address: 625 Holly St., Ashland, Oregon 97520, USA.

CHAMIEL, Haim Itzchak, pen names, BEN EPHRAIM & AVNIRA, b. 18 Jan. 1917. Writer; Educator; Poet; Lecturer. Education: M.A. & Ph.D., Hebrew Univ., Jerusalem. Positions held: Tchr. & Headmaster, Hebrew Schl., 1936-38; Tchr. & Youth Ldr., Palestine, 1939-44; Educ. Publs., Youth Dept., Jewish Agency, Jerusalem, 1944-51; Dir., Dept of Torah Educ. & Culture, 1951–; Univ. Lectr., Hebrew Lit., 1956-58; Univ. Lectr., Educ., 1968–. Member, ACUM, Israel. Published works: Meofek al Ofek, 1952; Avivim, 1958; Nof Adam, 1954; The Discovery of the Well (play); Moked Venir, 1960; Nerot Moledet, 1966; Benofei Hayorn, 1966. Contbr. to: Hatzofe; Mabua; State & Nation; Maariv; Mitzpe; Beshivateinu; Peoiot; Hadashot; Shalom, etc. Honours, awards: Klausner Prize, Tel Aviv, 1950; Rudolf Kaplan Prize & Ashlag Prize, Hebrew Univ., 1954. Address: 7a Narkis, Jerusalem, Israel.

CHAMPAGNE, Paul, b. 6 Mar. 1894. Professor of Humanities & Literature. Education: Dr. of Philos. & Letters. Positions held: Prof., l'Athénée Royal, Tournai, then Mons; Prof., l'Académie des Beaux-Arts, Mons. Mbr., Assn. of Belgian Writers. Published works: Noces Spirituelles, Paris, 1913; Les Yeux Clos, Brussels-Paris, 1936; Hainaut, Mon beau Pays, Brussels, 1942; La Marche à laLumière, Mons, 1949; Des Croix, des Fleurs, Mons, 1953; Quand l'Ame chante, Brussels, 1964; L'Eau Pure, Brussels, 1972. Honours, awards: Médaille de Vermeil, Académie française, 1929; Lauréat, Académie royale, 1930; Lauréat des Scriptores catholici, 1952; Médaille de bronze, Académie française, 1942; Laureat, Académie Nationale de Bordeaux, Prix Lelande & Prix Moreau, 1966; Prix du Hainaut, 1957; Prix Bouvier-Parvillez, 1949. Address: 12 rue Notre-Dame Débonnaire, Mons 7000, Belguim.

CHANCELLOR, Mabel M., b. 26 Jan. 1893. Teacher; Executive; Social Worker; Poet. Widow. Positions held: Fndr. & Owner, Alton Voc. Coll., Ill.; Dir., Hillcrest Br., YWCA, Alton; w. US Civil Serv. & Army Intelligence Corps, 20 yrs.; engaged in Soc. Service ac-

tivities w. Sr. Citizens; Chmn., Planning & Zoning Commn., Cockrell Hill; VA Hosp. & Children, Inc. Memberships: Poet Laureate, Dallas Pen Women; Pres., Dallas Pen Women, 1971-72-73; Recording Sec., Poetry Soc. of Tex., 1965-67; Am. Assn. Retired Persons; Retired Tchrs. Club; Nat. Assn. Retired Persons; Dir., Golden Chefs of Dallas, Sr. Citizens; Perm. Rep., Tex. Fine Arts Commn., Cockrell Hill; Fndng., Acad. Am. Poets. Published works: Lights & Shadows, 1966. Contbr. to: Good Old Days Mag.; Macoupin Co. Enquirer; Ill. State Jrnl.; NY Times; Cyclo-Flame Mag., & various anthols., etc. Composer of num. songs, both publd. & unpubld. Honours: Citation for Outstanding Contbns. to Poetry, United Poets Laureate Int.; Philippines, 1969; Outstanding Sr. Citizen, Oak Cliff, 1970; Nominee, Poet Laureate of Tex., 1973; also num. poetry prizes. Address: 3930 Dempster Ave., Dallas, Tex. 75211, USA.

CHANDLER, Rose Wiley, b. 3 Oct. 1921. Poet; Teacher. Education: Eastern Ky. Univ., Richmond, Ky.; Univ. of Ky., Lexington, Ky. Married, 2 d. Memberships: Am. Acad. of Poets; Nat. Fed. State Poetry Socs.; Int. Platform Soc.; Sec., Ky. State Poetry Soc., 1968; Sec. & Pres., ibid, 1970; Pres., 1971; Advsr., Johnson & Co. Poetry Soc. Contbr. to: Clover Anthol., 1969; Second Flight, 1969; Ky. Harvest, 1967; Legend of Ky. State Poetry Soc.; Ashland Daily Independent; Huntington Herald Despatch; Greenup News; Paintsville Herald. Honours & Awards: Special mention, Clover Int. Contest, 1969; Cert. of Recognition, Ky. State Poetry Soc., 1970; Hon. Cert., Murray State Univ. Creative Writing Workshop; Jesse Stuart Award of Excellence; Cert., Personal Poetry Radio Stn. Address: Jefferson Ave., Paintsville, Ky. 41240, USA.

CHANDRAKANT, Deotalé, b. 7 Nov. 1936. Teacher. Education: M.A. (Hindi). Positions held: Jrnlst.; Tchr., Hindi Lit., sev. colls.; currently, Prof. of Hindi, Govt. Post Grad. Coll., Ratlam, India. Published works: The Fever Under the Bones; translations of poems published in Marathi, Gujrati & English. Contbr. to: Nishedha (anthol. of 11 modern Hindi poets), 1972; Aalochna; Kalpna; Kavita; Athwa; Aavesh; Aaveg; Lahar; Dharmyuga, etc. Address: Prof. in Hindi, Govt. Post Grad. Coll., Ratlam, (M.P.), India.

CHANG, Wei-Han, pen name SHUN-OU, b. 29 Nov. 1886. Member, Control Yuan, Rep. of China. Education: Yunnan Provincial Political Sci. Coll.; Tokyo Imperial Univ. Widower, 2 sons, 2 daughters. Positions held: Sec., Gen. Szechwan Mil. Govt. H.Q., 1917-18; Prof., Yunnan Univ.; Mayor, Kunming, 1922-28; Commnr., Yunnan Prov. Govt.; Hd., Dept. of Civil Affairs, ibid, 1929-31; Mbr. & Sec. Gen., Legislation Yuan, 1931-38; V. Min. of Interior Affairs, 1939-46; Inspector Gen., Yunnan-Kweichow Area, 1946-48; Prof., New Asia Coll., H.K., 1951-52; V.P., Control Yuan, 1965-72; Acting Pres., ibid, 1972-73. Memberships: Assn. of Chinese Letters; Head, Poetry Rsch. Inst., China Acad. Published works: City Planning & Constitutionalism, 1929; The Essentials of Administration Law, 1930; The Essentials of the Local Self-Government, 1931; Collected Poems, 1957; Annual Poem Collection, since 1940. Contbr. to: Chung Hua Poetry Monthly; Tzu Yu Evening News; Ta Huw Evening News; Min Tzu Evening News; Tzu Yu Tan Monthly. Recip., Chung Shan Lit. & Arts Award for Superior Achievement in Poetry, 1973. Address: c/o Control Yuan. Taipei, Taiwan, Rep. of China.

CHANG TEH-CHUNG, pen name, CHANG MO, b. 20 Dec. 1931. Editor. Education: Cheng-Mei HS, Nanking City. Married to Lu Pin-Chun; 2 d. Positions held: Public Information Officer (with rank of Lt.Com.), Chinese Navy Hs.; Editor, The Epoch Poetry Qtly. Membership: China's Artists' & Writers' Assoc. Published works: Edge of Purple (poems), 1964; A Reflection on Modern Poetry (critical essays), 1967; Scenery in Rise (poems), 1971. Contbr. to: Epoch Poetry Qtly.; Modern Literature; Young Lion Literature Monthly; Modern Chinese Poetry (an English anthol.). Address: 54-2 Lane 239, Wu Hsien St., Taipei, Taiwan,

Repub. of China.

CHANG WAN-HSI, pen name, **MO JEN,** b. 6 June 1920. Secretariat Specialist, and Associate Professor. Education: Grad., Chinese Military Acad. Married; 2 s., 3 d. Positions held: Newspaper Editor; General Editor; Assoc. Prof. of Colleges; Specialist of the Secretariat of the Nat. Assembly; Assoc. Prof. of Soochow Univ. Membership: Poetry Soc. of the Rep. of China. Published works: The Flames of Freedom, 1950; Lament for My Mother Country, 1952; Selected Poems of Mo Jen, 1972. Address: The Secretariat of the Nat. Assembly, City Hall, Taipei, Taiwan, Repub. of China.

CHANNON, James Edward Grey, b. 19 Mar. 1915. Medical Practitioner. Education: Sydney Univ. & Royal Prince Alfred Hosp., Sydney. Positions held: Medical Officer, Australian Army, 1942-46 (served in New Guinea); Private Medical Prac., 1946-; Medical Officer, Australian Antarctic Expedition, Mawson, 1958. Memberships: Fellowship of Australian Writers. Contbr. to: Sydney Bulletin; (anthols.) This Land; This World. Recip., Special Prize, Fellowship of Australian Writers Poetry Comp., 1959. Address: 15 Bailey St., Woody Point, Australia 4019.

CHANOVER, E. Pierre, b. 10 Dec. 1932. Professor. Education: Acad. Dip., Brooklyn Coll., N.Y., 1953; B.A., ibid, 1957; M.A., Univ. of Kans., 1959. Positions held: Asst. Instr., Univ. of Kans. Dept. of French, 1957-59; Tchr. of French, Garden City H.S., N.Y., 1959-; Prof. of French, (Evening) Inst. Français, N.Y.C., 1960-63; Rdr. of French, Educl. Testing Serv., CEEB, Princeton, N.J., Adv. Placement Prog., 1962-64; Prof. of Comp. & Conv., N.D.E.A. French Inst., Pace Coll., N.Y.C., Summer, 1963 & Guest Lectr., Wells Coll., Aurora, N.Y.; Dir. of Int. Level & Inst. of French, Peace Corps Trng. Prog., Princeton Univ., Summer, 1964, '66; Vis. Instr., Hofstra Univ., Summer, 1965, '67, '68; Campus Prin., Univ. of Dijon, France, Summer, 1970-71. Memberships incl: Pres., L.I. Chapt., Am. Assn. of Tchrs. of French, 1964-67; N.Y. State Fed. of For. Lang. Tchrs.; MLA. Guest Speaker at var. confs. Published works: Ches les Français, 1969; Ce Monde des Français, 1970; Clapotis d'Outre-Mer (book of poems), 1971; The Marquis de Sade: A Bibliography, 1973. Contbr. to: The Psychoanalytic Review; Amenophis (Belgium); French Review; Prairie Poet; Bachaet; United Poets, etc. Recip., 1st prize, Walt Whitman Poetry Contest, Huntington, N.Y., 1970. Address: 6 Seton St., Huntington Stn., NY 11746, U.S.A.

CHAPPELL, Fred D., b. 28 May 1936. University Professor & Writer-in-Residence. Education: B.A., Duke Univ., 1961; M.A., ibid, 1964. Married Susan Nicholls, 1 son. Positions held: Instr.-Prof., Univ. of N.C. at Greensboro, 1964-; Writer-in-Res., ibid. Memberships: Southeastern Renaissance Assn.; MLA; S. Atlantic MLA. Published works: The World Between the Eyes, 1971; River, 1975. Contbr. to: Paris Review; Southern Poetry Review; Am. Scholar; Transatlantic Review; Carolina Qtly. Honours, awards: Roanoke-Chowan Poetry Award, 1972; The North Carolina Literary & Historical Assn. Award, 1973. Address: Dept. of Engl., Univ. of N.C. at Greensboro, Greensboro, NC 27412, U.S.A.

CHAPPELL, Inez Celeste, b. 25 July 1911. Freelance Writer. Education: Secretarial Schl., Tyler, Tex.; Telegraph course, San Angelo, Tex., 1936. Positions held: Bank Sec., Republic Natl., Dallas, Tex.; Branch Officer Mgr., Western Union (5 States). Memberships: Poetry Soc. of Tex.; Councillor for Lasnor Co., ibid, 1964-73; Art Study Club, Paris, Tex., 1959-. Contbr. to: Dallas Morning News; La Grange Jrnl.; Lasnor Co. Echo. Recip., Nortex Prix, Poetry Soc. of Tex. Address: 3246 Cleveland St., Paris, TX 75460, U.S.A.

CHAPPUIS, Pierre, b. 6 Jan. 1930. Professor. Education: Univ. of Geneva. Married, 3 children. Positions held at Gymnase Cantonal, Neuchâtel. Member, Groupe d'Olten. Published works: Ma femme

ô mon tombeau, 1969; Pommier impudique, 1970; L'Autre Versant, 1971; Michel Leiris, essay & texts, 1974. Contbr. to: Les Lettres Nouvelles (Paris); Liberté (Montreal); Sud (Marseille); La Revue de Belles-Lettres (Geneva); Le Journal de Genève; critical essays of poetry to var. lit. jrnls. Address: 3 rue de l'Orangerie, 2000 Neuchâtel, Switzerland.

CHARLTON, Geoffrey Norman, b. 16 Aug. 1943. Teacher. Education: B.Educ., Birmingham Univ., U.K., 1972. Positions held: Asst. Tchr. of Engl., Engl. Dept., Nether Stowe Comprehensive Schl., Lichfield, Staffs. Memberships: Fndr. Mbr., Birmingham Poetry Ctr.; Ed., Muse Poetry Mag., B.P.C. mag. of Midlands poetry, 1971-; Former Ed., Somethings mag.; Former Sec., Birmingham Arts Lab. Writers' Grp.; Rdr. for Second City Poets (B.P.C.), 1971-; Fndr. Mbr., Fitters Arms Club, Walsall, 1973-. Contbr. to: Breakthru mag., Sussex; Somethings mag., Birmingham; Centaur mag., City of Birmingham Coll. of Educ.; Muse mag., B.P. Ctr. Address: 150 Lichfield Rd., Rushall, Walsall WS4 1ED, U.K.

CHASE, Otta Louise, b. 8 July 1909. Housewife; Poet. Married to Hunter E. Chase. Positions held: Treas., Tax Collector, Town of Sweden, Me., 1957; Town Clerk & Registrar of Voters, ibid, 1959-. Memberships: Pres., Pine Tree Br., Nat. League of Am. Pen Women; Poetry Fellowship of Me.; Poetry Soc. of NH; Ala. State Poetry Soc.; Fla. State Poetry Soc.; New Writing Club of Nova Scotia. Pub. November Violets, 1973. Contbr. to the following anthologies: From One Bright Spark, 1959; State of Maine Writers' Conf. Chap-Book, 1963, '64, '66, '67, '68, '69; Melody of the Muse, 1964; Golden Harvest, 1968; Personal Poetry Anthology, 1969; Ala. Samplet, 1969; Golden Quill Anthology, 1970. Contbr. to: Am. Legion Mag.; Am. Weave; Poetry Digest; Snowy Egret; Flamingo; Grange Herald; Frostbite; Linda; Tempo. Harbor Lights; Town Crier; Weekly Bible Reader; Children's Friend; Innovator; Boston Globe; Bridgton News; Carroll County Enterprise; Pegasus; Granite State News; NH Sunday News; Nantucket Inquirer & Mirror. Honours: 1st Prize, Poetry Soc. of NH, 1967, '69; 1st Prize, Poetry Fellowship of Me., 1965; 1st Prize, Sesquicentennial Contest, Ala. State Poetry Soc., 1969; 3rd Prize, Ky. State Poetry Soc.; George Washington Hon. Medal Award, Freedoms Fndn., 1963, '65, '67; 1st Prize, NFSPS, Histl. Narrative Blank Verse Nat. Contests, 1973; 1st Prize, Triolet, Ky. State Poetry Soc. Nat. Contests, 1973. Address: R.F.D. No. 2, Harrison, Maine 04040, USA.

CHASIN, Helen. Teacher. Educ: B.A., Radcliffe Coll., Cambridge, Mass.; Studied writing w. Robert Lowell, Robert Fitzgerald & John Frederick Nims. Divorced, two children. Positions held: Teacher, Emerson Coll., Boston, 1966-; Scholar in Creative Writing, Radcliffe Inst. for Independent Study, 1968-70. Published works: Coming Close and Other Poems, 1968. Honours, awards: Bread Loaf Writers' Conference Poetry Scholar, 1965; Atlantic Monthly Young Poet, 1966; Bread Loaf Poetry Writers' Conf. Fellow, 1968. Address: Radcliffe Inst. for Independent Study, 3 James St., Cambridge, MA 02138, U.S.A.

CHATFIELD, Eugene Hale, born 26th March 1936. Educator; Editor; Poet. Education: B.A., Wesleyan Univ., 1957; A.M., Rutgers Univ., 1963. Positions held: Lt. USNR, 1957-60; Grad. Fellow, Rutgers Univ., 1960-62; Sales Supvsr., Olivetti-Underwood, 1962-64; Asst. Prof. of Engl., Hiram Coll., Ohio; Dean of Students, 1971-; Assoc. Prof. of Engl., 1973-; Ed., Hiram Poetry Review. Memberships: Chmn., Poetry Advisory Panel to the Ohio Arts Council, 1968-72; Ohio Poets' Assoc. Publications: The Young Country & Other Poems, 1959; Teeth, 1967; At Home, 1971. Contbr. to: Beloit Poetry Jrnl.; N.M. Quarterly; San Francisco Review; Signet; Audit; The Sparrow; Views; Impetus; Wormwood Review; Antioch Review; Epos; Outcry; N.W. Review; Sciamachy; Univ. Review; Synapse; Nexus; Poet & Critic; Verb; Northeast; Trace; Am. Weave; Folio; New Am. & Canadian Poetry. Made 10-show educ. TV series, NBC-TV, 1968. Address: P.O.

Box 162, Hiram, Ohio 44234, U.S.A.

CHATTERJEE, Margaret, b. 13 Sept. 1925. University Educator. Education: Exhibitioner, Somerville Coll., Oxford Univ., 1943-46; Ph.D., Delhi Univ., India. Married, 3 children. Positions held: has been teaching philos. at Delhi Univ. since 1956; currently Rdr. & Hd. of the Dept. of Philos. Published works: The Spring & the Spectacle, 1967; Towards the Sun, 1970; The Sandalwood Tree, 1972. Contbr. to: Hindustan Standard (Calcutta daily); Illustrated Weekly of India; Hemisphere (Australia); Span (Anthol. publ. in Canberra); Thought (Delhi periodical); Mainstream (Delhi periodical); Poet (Madras); Struggle (Calcutta); Mahfil (USA); Searchlight (Patna daily). Address: Dept. of Philos., Delhi Univ., Delhi, India.

CHATTOPADHYAYA, Harindranath, b. 2 Apr. 1898. Writer. Education: Cambridge Univ. Positions held: Member of Indian Parliament, 1952-57. Rep. India at the Conf. of 30 World Poets at 1967 EXPO, Montreal. Producer (Emeritus) A.I.R. & Television 'Kismet'. Published works: The Feast of Youth, 1918; Magic Tree, 1922; Wizard's Masks; Strange Journey, 1936; The Dark Well, 1939; Edgeways & the Saint, 1946; Spring in Winter, 1956; Masks & Farewells, 1961; Virgins & Vineyards, 1967. Contbr. to almost all newspapers & mags. in India. Works translated into most of the languages of India & some foreign languages inclng. Chinese & Russian. The Govt. of India has made a documentary on his life and work. Recip., Padma Bhushan Award for Lit. Address: Flat No. 10, Carter Rd., Bandra, Bombay 50, India.

CHATURVEDI, Jagdish, b. 13 Jan. 1933. Research Officer. Education: M.A. (Hindi), 1955. Married, 1 son, 2 daughters. Positions held: Lectr. in Hindi, Madhar Coll., Ujjain, 1955; Lectr. in Hindi, Coll. of Sci., Nagpur, 1956; Script Writer, All India Radio, Bhopal, 1957; Rsch. Asst., Min. of Educ. & Social Welfare, New Delhi, 1959-71; Rsch. Officer, Ctrl. Hindi Directorate, Min. of Educ. & Soc. Welfare, New Delhi, 1971–. Memberships: Sec., Hindi Sahitya Parishad, Ujjain, 1955; Participated in All India Poets Conf., Calcutta, 1968. Published works: Ed., Prarambh (An anthol. of Modern Hindi Poets), 1963; Ed., Modern Kavita (An anthol. of Modern Indian poets), 1964; Akavita (An anthol. of Young Hindi poets, 6 vols.), 1965-66; Ed., Sankalan (An anthol. of Indian poets), 1967; Vijap (poetry coll.), 1967; Itihas Hants (poetry coll.), 1970; Nishedh (An anthol. of poets of protest), 1972. Contbr. to var. jrnls. & mags. in India. Recip., All India Sur Award for poetry coll. 'Itihas Hanta', 1971. Address: 27/23 East Patel Nagar, New Delhi 8, India.

CHAUDHURI, Sukanta, b. 23 June 1950. Teacher. Education: Presidency Coll., Calcutta, 1967-70; Univ. Coll., Oxford, 1970-72. Positions held: Prof. of Engl., Presidency Coll., Calcutta, 1973–. Associated with Writers Workshop, Calcutta. Published works: Poems, 1967; The Glass King & Other Poems, 1970. Contbr. to: Writers Workshop Miscellany, Calcutta; Books Abroad, Oklahoma; "2000", Oxford. Address: DA 211, Bidhan Nagar, Calcutta 64, India.

CHAZAI, Franco, b. 28 Apr. 1910. Professor. Education: Univs. of Lyons & Paris, France. Personal details: Son of Louis Chazai, poet & writer. Positions held: Dir. & Fndr., Momentum Review (the voice of poets for a united Europe & world peace). Memberships: World Coun. for Culture; 15 acads. Published works: Poemes italiens, 8 vols.; Récits de guerre; Roman pour la jeunesse. Hons. & Awards: Chevalier for lit. merits, Belgian-Hispanic Order; Silver medal for European merit; 2 gold medals for poetry, Pres. of Italian Republic, 1963 & '67; many others. Address: 6828 Balerna, Switzerland.

CHEDID, Andrée, b. 1920. Writer. Education: B.A. Published works: (poetry) Textes pour une figure, 1949; Textes pour un poème, 1950; Textes pour le vivant, 1953; Textes pour la Terre aimée, 1955; Terre et Poésie, 1956; Terre regardée, 1957; Seul, le visage, 1960; Lubies, 1962; Double-Pays, 1965; Contre-Chant, 1969; Visage Premier, 1972; Fêtes et Lubies, 1973; Prendre Corps, 1973; (novels) Le sommeil délivré, 1952; Jonathan, 1955; Le Sixième jour, 1960, 2nd ed. '72; Le survivant, 1963; L'autre, 1969; La Cité fertile, 1972; (Short Stories) L'étroite peau, 1965; Liban (essay); (theatre) Bérénice d'Egypte; Les Nombres; Le Montreur, etc. Contbr. to var. jrnls. & to radio & TV. Honours, awards: Prix Louise Labbé, 1965; Aigle d'or de la Poésie, International Book Festival, Nice, 1972. Address: 121 Boulevard St. Germain, Paris 6e, France.

CHEESMAN, Willard L., b. 28 Mar. 1912. Patent Agent. Education: Chemical Engr., Purdue Univ., U.S.A., 1934; grad. study, Univ. of Louisville & Geo. Wash. Univ. Positions held: Surveyor, 1935; Chemical Engr., 1935-37; Meteorologist, 1937-40; Patent Examiner, 1940-46; Patent Agent, 1946–. Contbr. to: Purdue Scrivener; Palms; Poet Lore; Orphic Lute; Am. Bard; The Muse; Verdure; Prairie Poet; Driftwood; Driftwood East; Am. Poet; Poetry Preview. Recip., Poet Lore Special Award, 1971 & 72. Address: 135 East Candlewyck, Apt. 222, Kalamazoo, MI 49001, U.S.A.

CHEFFEY, Jessie Annis, b. 24 July 1895. Retired Teacher. Education: Wash. Co. Normal Schl.; Ohio Univ.; Dip., Chautauqua Schl. of Nursing. Positions held: Schl. Tchr., Righteous Ridge, all grades, 1921-22; Fairview Schl. in Morgan Co., all grades, 1923-24; Children's Home, Primary grades, 1924-25; Center Bend Schl., all grades, 1927-28. Member, Avalon World Arts Acad. & Hon. Mbr., The Eugene Field Soc., 1943. Published works: Jewels by the Wayside, 1942 (book of verse). Poems have been read on the Ohio Broadcasting Prog. Contbr. to: The Martha Kinney Cooper Lib.; Scimitar & Song; The Cinn. Enquirer; The Ohio Farmer; The Ohio Alumnus; The Parish Visitor; Ohio Poetry Day Anthol.; World's Fair Anthol.; Cycloflame; Avalon Anthol., etc. Recip. var. hons. & awards inclng. Dip., Centro Studi e Scambi, Rome, Italy, 1970. Address: Cedar Nook, Box 223, Waterford, OH 45786, U.S.A.

CHEN, Hsiu-Hsi, b. 15 Dec. 1921. Housewife. Education: Grad., Taiwan Acad. for Girls. Married to a bank manager; 2 s., 2 d. Positions held: Director, Li Poetry Mag., 1963; Rep. of New Poems of Republic of China, 1970; Exec. Director of China Art & Literature Assoc., 1971; Speaker on Taiwan TV Forum, 1973; Exec. Director of 2nd World Congress of Poetry, 1973. Published works: Japanese Classical Poetry, 1970; Chinese Modern Poetry, 1971 (2nd edition, 1971); Big Leaves (trans. from Chinese to English), 1972; Children's Poems, 1973. Contbr. to: Taiwan Daily News; Folkways of Taiwan; Youth of Freedom Mag.; Mag. of Japan; Mag. of Vietnam. Address: 2nd Floor, 11 Alley 78, Lane 362, Sung Chiang Rd., Taipei, Taiwan, Repub. of China.

CHEN, Mai-tze, b. 16 Nov. 1914. Sr. Assistant, Office of the President of the Republic of China; University Professor. Education: B.A., Northwestern Univ., Sian; Grad. of Central Training Corps, Nanking; Grad. of Ke Min Shih Chien Research Inst., Taipei. Personal details: a native of Mienhsien, Shensi Province, China. Married; 4 s., 7 d. Positions held: Prof., Ming Tzu Univ., Shansi; Sec., Peiping Hs. of Chairman of Military Commission of Nat. Government; Sec., Peiping Office of Chairman of Nat. Government; Prof., Univ. of Communications, Peiping; Sec., Office of the Pres. of the Republic of China; Sr. Asst. ibid; Prof. College of Law Commerce; Soochow Univ.; Chung Hsing Univ.; Military Law College, Officers Foreign Language School, Tamkang Coll. of Arts & Sciences, and Chinese Cultural Coll.; Commissioner for Higher & Special Civil Service Examination; Research Fellow, School of Poetry of Chinese Academic Inst. Memberships: Lit. Assoc. of China; Chun Jen Poetry Assoc.; Ying Ming Poetry Assoc.; Instr., Assoc. of Free Chinese Poets; Standing Member, Preparation Committee for 2nd World Congress of Poets (Judge for same Congress; Deputy Chief, Chinese Delegation). Contbr. to: 1st Anthol. of Ying Ming

Poetry Assoc., 1961; 2nd Anthol. of Ying Ming Poetry Assoc., 1969; Anthol. of Chinese & Engl. Poems by Members of Assoc. of Free Chinese Poets, 1973; Chang Liu; Taiwan Shih Tan; Friend of Poetry & Essays; Bulletin of Chou Huei; College Poems; Poetry Soc. Monthly; Central Daily News; Ta Hua Eve. News; Hsin Sheng Pao; Chung Hua Daily News; Min Tzu Eve. News; Tzu Li Eve. News. Honours & Awards: Patriotic Poet (elected by Assoc. of Free Chinese Poets, 1965); Nat. Poet (elected by Nat. Congress of Poets, 1965); Dip. & Medal of Hon. Int. Poet Laureate, awarded by Dr. Yuzon on behalf of Pres. Marcos, Philippines, 1973. Address: 14-1 Jen Ai St., Yunghochen, Taipeihsien, Taiwan, Republic of China.

CHEN, Min-Hwa, b. 7 Sept. 1932. TV Programmer. Education: Providence Coll.; Grad. from Modern Poetry Research Class. Married to architect; 3 children. Positions held: Editor-in-Chief, The Vineyard (poetry quarterly). Memberships: Chinese Poetry Soc. (Member of Bd. of Directors); Chinese Women Writers Club; UPLI (Hon. member). Published works: The Daisy, 1967; Through the Crystal Glass, 1971; Strings at the Window, 1972; As Dawn Whistles Over the Sea, 1973. Contbr. to: Chinese Daily Newspaper; The Vineyard; Central Monthly Mag.; Chinese Poetry; Poet; The Sandcutters; Kansas Kernels. Awards: Service Award, Chinese Poetry Soc., 1968; Mod. Poetry Prize Citation, World Poetry Soc. Intercontinental, 1972; Lit. Medal, Chinese Writers' & Artists' Assoc., 1971; Lyric Poet Laureate, UPLI, 1973; Modern Poetry Prize, Education Ministry Culture Division, 1971; Distinguished Asian Lyric Poet, Comm. on Arts & Culture, Repub. of Philippines, 1972. Address: 71-16, Section, Chung Hsiau East Rd., Taipei, Taiwan, Repub. of China.

CHENEY, L. Stanley, b. 12 Apr. 1928. Writer; Photographer; Illustrator. Education: Eastern New Mexico University, Portales, N.M., 1950; Long Beach City Coll., Long Beach, Calif.; active student Oriental Art. Positions held: Labourer; Soldier; Clerk; Author; Photographer. Membership: Pres., Avalon Acad. of World Arts; Mbr. & Rep., World Poetry Soc.; Ariz. State Poetry Soc.; Am. Poetry League; Free Verse Ed., The Swordsman Review, 1966-70. North Jersey Poetry Soc. Published works: Footsteps Across The Page, 1963; Nijo Castle, 1965; Walk With Me, 1966; How Soon The Night, 1968. Contbr. to the following anthols., jrnls., mags., etc: Canadian Poetry Mag.; Fireflower; Haiku; Voice of Poetry; West Coast Review; Manifold; Spring Anthology (UK); Accademia Internazionale Bouquet of Poems (Italy); Let's Have A Chat (Japan); Am. Bard; Am. Courier; Am. Haiku; Am. Poetry League Bulletin; Am. Poets' Best; Am. Songbird; Am. Weave; And Their Voices Shall Be Heard; Angel Favourites; Angel Hour; Angels; Anthology of Desert Poetry; Anthology of Verse; Ardentia B Verba; Author/Poet; Avalon Book of the Year; Badge of Promise; Bardic Echoes; Bay Shore Breeze; Bell's Letters; Ben Trovato; Bitterroot; Bluebook of Am. Poetry; Boonton Times Bulletin; Border; Calamus; Calif. Writer; Calif. Writer's Mag.; Caravan; Caravel; Cardinal Poetry Quarterly; Choice of the Angels; Commemorative Anthology; Conception; Creative Hodgepodge; Creative Review; Cyclo-Flame; Cyclotron; Delight Mag.; Diversion; Down Ink Lane; Driftwood; Dust; Echoes; Ellisonian Echoes; Encore; Explorer; Exploring; Flame; Flame Annual; Fragments of Faith; Friendship Trail; From Sea to Sea; Golden Circle; Green World; Guild; Haiku Anthology; Haiku Highlights; Hiku West; Heart's Secrets; Hoosier Challenger; Human Voice; Imprints Quarterly; Inky Trails; Int. Writers Newsletter; Jacinth; Jet & Jade; Jean's Jrnl. of Poems; Kansas City Poetry Mag.; Karyn; Kauri; Ladies' Delight Mag.; Liberty Bell; Macabre; Major Poetry; Melodies From A Jade Harp; Melody of the Muse; Mendocino Robin; Merlin's Magic; Mid-Century Anthology of Prose & Poetry; Mod. Am. Lyrics; Mod. Images; Muse; Nat. Weekly Poetry Letter; New Anthenaeum; Anthology of N. Am. Mentor Poetry; The Notebook; Nutmegger Poetry Club; On Wings of Song; Prange County Writer; Penman Mag.; Penny-A-Thought; Phylis Mag.; Piggott

Banner; Pixie Angel; Poems of Patriotism & Peace; Poetidings; Poetry Club Mag.; Poetry Desert Inspired; Poetry Dial Anthology; Poetry Digest; Poetry Prevue; Poet's Bulletin; Poets of Am. Anthology; El Portal; Prairie Poet; Quintessence; Quoin; Rays; Renaissance; Robin; Sandcutters; Scimitar & Song; Scrivener; Seydell Quarterly; Sing Loud for Loveliness; 68 Poets; Small World Monthly; Stem; Stepping Stones to Faith; Sunrise-Sunset-Silhouette; Swordsman Review; Tangent; These Are My Jewels; Trace; Treasures of Parnassus; United Poets; Versatility in Verse; Verse of Staten Island; Voices Int.; Warriors of Eternity; Windfall; Wisc. Poetry Mag.; Wormwood Review; Worksheet Directory; Written Word; Writer; Writer's Notes & Quotes; Writer's Voice; You; Poet, India; Japan Forum, Japan; Ariz. Highways; Animals; Modern Haiku; The Poet's Guild. Over 1000 poems & sev. hundred photos, illustrations, articles, essays & stories publd. in comm. & lit. mags., newspapers, anthol., etc., 1958-71. Honours, awards: Cinquanin Poet of the Year, Swordsman Review, 1968; Lilith Lorraine Award, Poem of the Year, Cyclo-Flame, 1966; 5th Place, N. Am. Mentor Nat. Contest, 1966; Featured Poet, Scimitar & Song, 1970; Disting. Serv. Citation for poem: The River United, World Poetry Soc., 1970; Citation for lit. contbns. to the Am. Mosaic Collect., Hayden Lib., Ariz. State Univ., 1970; Golden Atom Poem of the Year Award for The Eagle has landed, 1970. Address: PO Box 9053; San Diego, Calif. 92109, USA.

CHERPILLOD, Gaston, b. 24 Oct. 1925. Writer. Education: studied at Fac. of Arts, Univ. of Lausanne; Licence en lettres. Positions held: Tchr. of French Lit. Member, Group d'Olten. Published works: L'Insurgent, poems; Agrest Agression, poems; Retour ni Consigne, poems; Le Chêne Brûlé, autobiog.; Promotion Staline, pamphlet; Alma Mater, récit; Le Gour Noir, contes; Les Avatars de Juste Palinod, comédie. Contbr. to: Gazette de Lausanne; Alliance Culturelle Romande; Domaine Suisse; Rencontre; La Tour de Feu. Address: 8 rue de Plan, 1023 Crissier, Switzerland.

CHESTER, Laura (Chapman), b. 13 Apr. 1949. Writer. Education: Univ. of New Mex., 2 yrs. Married Geoff Young, 1969. Co-Ed., Stooge, small poetry mag. Member, Best Friends. Published works: Tiny Talk (poetry pamphlet), 1972; The All Night Salt Lick (small book co-authored w. Geoff Young), 1972; Rising Tides (Co-Ed.), 1973. Contbr. to: Discourse; Stooge; Folio; Thunderbird; Road Apple Review; Quetzal; Changes; Velvet Glove; Measure; Clear Creek; Best Friends; Fervent Valley; The Lamp In The Spine; Manroot; Center; 2 Charlies; Cafe Solo; Nevermind; I Love You All Day It Is That Simple; 20th Century Women Poets, etc. Honours, awards: Steloff Poetry Prize, Skidmore Coll.; Kappa Alpha Theta Award for Poetry, UNM. Address: 4063 Petit Road, Oconomowoc Lake, WI 53066, U.S.A.

CHESTERMAN, Jean, pen name **KENWARD, Jean,** b. 10 May 1920. Lecturer in Creative Writing. Education: Central Schl. of Speech & Drama, London. Married, 2 sons, 1 daughter. Positions held: Lectr. in Creative Writing, Harrow Schl. of Art. Mbr., Gtr. London Arts Assn. Published works: Book of Rhymes; Rain; Flight of Words; The Forest, 1972; Rag Bag Book, 1973. Contbr. to: Poetry Review; The Countryman; Countrylife; Books; Outposts; The Lady. Contbr. of rhymes, guitar songs, & stories, BBC schls. progs. for 5-7 yr. olds. Honours, awards: 3 times winner of Poetry Review Premium Prize. Address: 15 Shire Lane, Chorleywood, Herts., U.K.

CHEYFITZ, Eric, b. 17 June 1941. Teacher; Musician. Education: M.A., in Creative Writing, The Johns Hopkins Univ., 1974. Positions held: Cons. in Poetry, Ctr. for Urban Educ., Winter, 1968-69; Poet-in-Res., Baltimore Co. Public Schls., 1973-74. Contbr. to: Times Lit. Supplement; Esquire; The Review; Stand; Per Se; Image, a textbook on language, 1973. Address: 4502 Frederick Ave., Baltimore, MD 21229, U.S.A.

CHIARO, Lee, pen name **CHIARO, Lee Bain,** b. 6 July 1927. Homemaker. Education: Baylor Univ., Waco, Tex., 1944-45; A.A., Southern Colo. State Coll., 1961-67. Married twice, 3 children. Positions held: Volunteer Tchr. of Retarded Children; Private Tutor of Reading & Lang. skills. Member, N.Y. Poetry Forum. Contbr. to: Poets of America Anthol., 1966; Prospectus, So. Colo. State Coll., 1964, '65; Beacon, publ. of Pueblo Assn. for Retarded Children. Poetry selections read by Dean Budge Threlkheld at Colo. State Penitentiary & read on Radio Stn. K.C.S.J., Pueblo, Colo. Address: 2327 Cortez Rd., Pueblo, CO 81003, U.S.A.

CHIDAMBARAM, Meera, b. 20 Sept. 1951. Poetry Editor. Education: B.A. Econs., Stella Maris Coll., Madras, India; M.A., Engl. Lit., ibid. Positions held: Poetry Ed. of College Students Mag., 1972-73. Memberships: Pres. of Literary Soc., Schl., 1967; Editl. Bd., Coll., 1968-70; Poetry Workshop Conducted by Mr. R. Parthasarathy of Oxford Univ. Press, Madras. Contbr. to: Stella Maris Coll. Mag.; Udaya – Students Mag.; Poet; Minimax. Address: H-28, Green Pk. Ext., New Delhi – 16, India.

CHILD, Philip Albert Gillett, b. 19 Jan. 1898. Emeritus Professor. Educ: B.A., Univ. of Toronto, Ont., Canada; Cambridge Univ., U.K.; A.M., Harvard Univ., U.S.A.; Ph.D., ibid. Married Gertrude Potts, two children. Positions held: Served WWI; Instr., Univ. of B.C., Canada & Harvard Univ., U.S.A.; Chancellor's Professor of Engl., Trinity Coll., Univ. of Toronto, Canada; Currently Emeritus Prof., ibid. Published works: The Victorian House and Other Poems, 1951; The Wood of the Nightingale, 1965; (novels) The Village of Souls, 1948; God's Sparrows, 1937; Blow Wind, Come Wrack, 1945; Day of Wrath, 1945; Mr. Ames Against Time, 1949. Contbr. to: Univ. of Toronto Quarterly; Queen's Quarterly; Dalhousie Review; Canadian Poetry In English (anthology), 1954. Honours, awards: Sr. Arts Fellowship for Poetry; Ryerson Fiction Awards, 1945 & '49; Governor-General's Award for Fiction, 1949. Address: Trinity Coll., Hoskin Ave., Toronto 5, Ont., Canada.

CHILDRESS, William, b. 5 Feb. 1933. Journalist; Travel-Outdoors Columnist; Editor. Education: B.A., Fresno State Coll., Calif., 1965; M.F.A., Univ. of Iowa, Iowa City, 1968. Married; 3 s. Positions held: Coll. Instr., 1968-69; Editor/Writer, Nat. Geographic Mag., 1969-70; fulltime professional writer since 1970. Membership: Poetry Soc. of America. Published works: Burning The Years (poems), 1971; Lobo (poems), 1972; Cowboys & Indians, 1974. Contbr. to: Age of Chivalry, 1969; Vacationland USA, 1970; Poetry; Harper's; The Kenyon Review; The Southern Review; North American Review; Mademoiselle; NM Qtly.; Ariz. Qtly.; Georgia Review; Prairie Schooner; The Reporter; Chicagoland; Chicago Tribune Mag.; The Smith; Human Voice; Goddard Journal; Hearse; The Writer; The Far Point; Mad River Review; America; Win; Westways; Nugget; Some; Haystacks Don't Have Any Needle; American Forever New; New Poets; British & American; Down at the Santa Fe Depot; 20 Fresno Poets; Lib. of Congress Ms. of American War Poetry; Midland 2; Sounds & Silences; Little Mag. Poetry; HV Anthol.; Man; Adam; Gent; Pebble; Poetry Now; Fragments; Good Housekeeping; December Mag.; St. Anthony Messenger; The Reporter; Valley; Dude; Snowgoer; American Hunter; Points; Milwaukee Journal; Sat. Eve. Post; Holiday; Better Homes & Gardens; True; Field & Stream; Saga (Field Editor, 1972-); Inland; Hunting; Nat. Geographic; Nevada Highways; Wheels Afield, and many others. Hons. and Awards: Hon. mention, Joseph Henry Jackson Award, 1965; Hon. mention & Cash Award, ibid, 1967; Fellowship to Univ. of Iowa Writer's Workshop, 1966; Stephen Vincent Benet Award, 1969; Devins Award in Poetry, 1971; 500–dollars Carnegie Grant, 1972, and 2nd Prize, best single poem, P.S.A., 1972. Address: Rte. 1, Box 194, Anderson, MO 64831, USA.

CHILDS, (Sister) Maryanna (Mary Claire), pen name

CHILDS, C. Sand, b. 16 Jan. 1910. Dominican Sister; College Professor. Education: B.A., St. Mary of the Springs Coll., Columbus, Ohio; M.A., Engl., Cath. Univ. of Am., Wash. DC, 1948. Positions held: Grade Schl. Tchr.; High Schl. Tchr.; Coll. & Univ. Prof.; Chmn., Engl. Dept., Ohio Dominican Coll., Columbus, Ohio, 1947-67. Guest Prof. of Writing, Loretto Heights Coll., Colo.; Dominican Coll., Dublin, Ireland; Georgetown Univ., Wash. DC; Coll. of the Holy Names, Calif.; Aquinas Coll., Mich.; Capital Univ., Ohio; Wright State Univ., Ohio, summers, 1960-70. Memberships: Cath. Poetry Soc.; Ohio Poetry Day; MLA. Published works: The Littlest Angel & Other Legends, 1942; My Little Book of Thanks, 1957; My Mary Book, 1959; My Little Book of Manners, 1963; With Love & Laughter, 1960, & '64; With Joy & Gladness, 1964; The Sounds of Ireland, 1969. Contbr. to over 35 mags., jrnls., etc. inclng: America; American Childhood; Catholic Digest; Catholic World; Columbia; Extension; Holy Name Journal; Josephinum Review; Irish Spotlight; Scholastic; Sign; Spirit; Our Sunday Visitor; Liguorian; The Priest; The Catholic Traveler. Poems included in 12 anthols. inclng: Contemporary Ohio Poets; Columbia Poetry; With Harp & Lute. Awards: Advsr.'s Medal, Cath. Schl. Press Assn., 1960; Kts. of Columbus Travel Grant, 1961; American Irish Foundation Author's Grant, 1965; Internat. Who's Who in Poetry Award, 1972. Address: Ohio Dominican Coll., Columbus, Ohio, 43219, USA.

CHILTON, Teresa Ann, pen name **CHILTON, Tracey,** b. 26 July 1935. Housewife. Education: Tech. Trng., Ochsner Clinic, New Orleans, La. Married, 1 son, 1 daughter. Positions held: EEG Tech. at: Ochsner Clinic, New Orleans, La., St. Anthonys Hosp., Denver, Colo., Sacred Heart Hosp., Pensacola, Fla. Member, La. State Poetry Soc. Contbr. to: Louisiana Poets (selected to appear in La. Poets Showcase); We Sing. Honours, awards: Hon. Mention, Deep South Writers & Artist Conf., La. State Univ. in New Orleans, 1973; Hon. Mention & 3rd prize, Spring Poetry Fest., New Orleans, 1973. Address: 3717 Simone Gardens, Apt. F., Metairie, LA 70002, U.S.A.

CHISM, James Richard III, b. 10 July 1945. Antique Dealer. Education: Keystone Secretarial & Bus. Admin. Schl., Springfield, Pa., 2 yrs. Positions held: Stock Clerk; Tutor; Antique Dealer. Memberships: Bd. Dirs., Prog. Chmn., Lions Int., Newport Lions Club; Pa. Poetry Soc., Keysner Chapt.; Pa. State Antique Assn. Contbr. to: 'Coin of the least Denomination', mag., London, U.K.; Holy Comforter Church Bulletin (Epis.); Keystone Sec. & Bus. Schl. Mag. 'The Keys'. Address: P.O. Box 36, Newport, PA 17074, U.S.A.

CHRISTESEN, C(lement) B(yrne), b. 28 Oct. 1911. Editor. Educ: King's Coll., Univ. of Queensland, Australia. Married to Nina Maximoff. Positions held: Publicist, Queensland Govt., 1935-41; Journalist, Australian, Engl. and Am. newspapers; T.V. & Radio commentator; Lectr., Australian Lit., Univs. of Queensland, Melbourne, & Tasmania; Fndr. & Ed., Meanjin Quarterly, 1940-. Memberships: V.P., Australian Soc. of Authors, Fellowship of Australian Writers & Australian Coun. for Civil Liberties; UNESCO Letters Comm. Published works: North Coast, 1943; South Coast, 1944; Dirge and Lyrics, 1945. Editor: Australian Heritage, 1949, '67; Coast to Coast: Australian Stories, 1953-54, 1955; On Native Grounds: Australian Writing from Meanjin Quarterly, 1968. Contbr. to: Poetry Australia; Poetry Chapbook; Voices; (anthologies) A Book of Australian Verse, 1945; Modern Australian Poetry, 1946; Poetry of Australia, 1956. Honours, awards: O.B.E., Gold Medal, 1966. Address: c/O Univ. of Melbourne, Parkville, Victoria, Australia 3052.

CHRISTIAENS, André, b. 24 Mar. 1905. Teacher. Mbr., P.E.N. Club. Published works: Te Brussel bij dag en nacht, 1933; De Algemene Regel, 1934; Irrequietum, 1937; Uit de toren, 1937; Angsten in het Westen, 1968; Onvindbaar land, 1968. Contbr. to: Forum; Groot – Nederland; Spectator; De Nieuwe Gids; De Standaard, etc. Recip., Poëzieprijs

Merendree, 1947. Address: Blauwe-Vogellaan 27, 1150 Brussels, Belgium.

CHRISTIAN, Nonie Winifred Sophie, b. 4 Mar. 1908. Teacher. Married Major C.G.H. Christian R.A. (Ret'd). Positions held: Tchr. of Speech & Drama, St. Probus Schl., Salisbury, 1950-66. Member, Poetry Soc., London, Brighton & Salisbury. Published works: Hampshire Muse (in conjunction with Walter Hewitt), 1952. Contbr. to: Poetry Review; Poetry of To-day; The Field; Fishing Gazette; Salisbury Circle Poets. Address: Clare Cottage, 29 Folkestone Rd., Salisbury, U.K.

CHRISTIE, Phillippa Mary, pen name BERLYN, Phillippa, b. 8 Oct. 1923. Freelance Journalist & Poet. Married Prof. Dick Christie, 5 children. Positions held: Political commentator, Feature Writer, var. S. African & Rhodesian jrnls. & for syndicate Agency, Camara Press. Memberships: PEN Ctr., Rhodesia; Shona & Sindebele Writers Assn.; Comm., Rhodesian Poetry Soc.; Editl. Bd. & Assoc. Editl., Two Tone, Rhodesia, Envoi, London, South & West, U.S.A. & Ocarina, India. Published works: Rhodesia Beleaguered Country, 1966; Rhodesian Panorama (co-author), 1968; Conversational Shona, 1969; This is Rhodesia, 1969. Rep. in following anthols: New South African Writing, 1964, '65, '66, '67; Commonwealth Poems of Today, 1967; New Voices of the Commonwealth, 1968; Rhodesian Poetry Review, 1966, '68, '70, '72, etc. Contbr. to: London Mag.; Outposts; Tribune; Manifold; Bitterroot; Poet, & many others. Honours, awards: Religious Poetry Award, Manifold, 1967. Dagobert Award for Best Prose Work by a known poet, 1967; Ford Fndn. Grant (Nat. Translation Ctr.) for transl. work Shona Poetry. Address: Tandara, Farthing Hill, Highlands, Salisbury NE71, Rhodesia.

CHUNG, Tin-wen, pen name FAN-TS'AO, b. 29 Apr. 1914. Congressman; Editorial Writer; Columnist; Poet. Education: LL.B., Chinese Univ., Shanghai, China, 1932; LL.B., Kyoto Imperial Univ., Japan, 1936. Married Miss Shang, 2 sons, 2 daughters. Positions held: Prof., Fu Tan Univ., Shanghai, China, 1936; Editor-in-Chief, Tien-Hsia Daily News, Shanghai, 1937; Editor-in-Chief, Kwangsi Daily News, Kweilin, 1938; Major-Gen., Sino-Japanese War, 1940-45; currently Mbr., Nat. Assembly of the Rep. of China, Chief Editorialist, Independence Evening Post, Editorialist, United Daily News & China Times, & Sec.-Gen., Taipei Civil Press Assn. Memberships incl: Pres., Chinese Poets Assn.; Dir., Int. PEN, Chinese Ctr.; Hon. Mbr., Lit. Union & Presidial Comm., W. Germany; Hon. Life Mbr., The Cosmosynthesis League, Aust.; Hon. Mbr., United Poets Laureate Int., Philippines; Rep. of World Poets' Resource Ctr., U.S.A. Official del. to var. confs. & Pres. of 2nd World Congress of Poets, Taipei, Taiwan, 1973. Published works incl: Three Years, 1940; The Minstreal, 1951; Mountains & Rivers-Reminiscences of the Mainland, 1956; A Nosegay of White Flowers, 1956; The Flag, 1962; The Monsoon, 1967; Plateau & other poems, 1973. Contbr. to var. mags., jrnls., newspapers etc. Recip. num. hons. & awards inclng: Sun Yat-sen Meml. Award, 1967; Hon. Chinese Poet Laureate, United Poets Laureate Int., 1976; LL.D., Int. Acad., U.K., 1969; Litt.D., Univ. Libre, Pakistan, 1973; Disting. Serv. Cit., World Poetry Soc. Intercontinental, U.S.A., 1972. Address: P.O. Box 58508, Taipei, Taiwan, Rep. of China.

CIARDI, John Anthony, b. 24 June 1916. Lecturer; Editor. Educ: Bates Coll., Lewiston; A.B., Tufts Coll., Medford, 1938; M.A., Univ. of Mich., 1939. Married Myra Judith Hostetter, three children. Positions held: Tchr., Univ. of Kan. City, 1940-42, Harvard Univ., 1946-53, Rutgers Univ., 1953-61; Lectr., Bread Loaf Writers' Conf., 1947–; Dir., ibid, 1956–; Poetry Ed., Saturday Review, 1956–. Memberships: Fellow, Nat. Inst. of Arts & Letters; Fellow, Am. Acad. of Arts & Scis & Am. Acad. of Arts & Letters; Former Pres., Nat. Coll. Engl. Assn. Published works: Homeward to America, 1940; Other Skies, 1947; Live Another Day, 1949; I Marry You: A Sheaf of Love Poems, 1958; Thirty-Nine Poems, 1959; In Fact, 1962; Person to Person, 1964; This Strangest Everything, 1966; An Alphabestiary, 1967; Num. books of Children's Verse and Literary Criticism. Contbr. to: Atlantic Monthly; New Yorker; Harper's; (anthologies) Poems of Doubt and Belief, 1964; Today's Poets, 1964; Modern Ballads and Story Poems, 1965. Honours, awards: D. Litt., Tufts Coll., 1960; L.L.D., Ursinus Coll., 1964; New England Poetry Cup Golden Rose Trophy, 1948; Harriet Monroe Mem. Prize, 1955. Address: Metuchen, NJ, U.S.A.

CILLIERS, Charl J(ean) F(rancois), b. 25 Jan. 1941. Translator. Education: Engineer's Diploma; B.A. (Afrikaans, Psychology, Criminology). Married, 1. s. (Eugene). Lecturer in Electronics, GPO Training Centre, Pretoria, 1959-67; Parliamentary Translator, Cape Town, 1968-73. Pub. West-Falling Light, 1971. Contrib. to: Two Roads (anthol.); Seismograph. Also contrib. to: De Arte; Ophir; Wurm; New Nation; Contrast; New Coin; Chirimo; Poet; Standpunte; Unisa English Studies; etc. Address: P.O. Box 15, Cape Town, South Africa.

CLANCY, Barbara Anne, pen name KIM, b. 1 June 1923. Homemaker; Writer; Poet. Education: Calif. State Coll., Fullerton, Calif., U.S.A. Married William H. Clancy. Positions held: Sec.; Receptionist, W. Valley Coll., Saratoga, Calif. Memberships: N.J. Poetry Soc.; Am. Poetry League. Contbr. to: Am. Bard; Writer's Notes & Quotes; Am. Poetry League Bulletin; Sea to Sea in Song, 1970, 71; N.J. Poetry Soc. Anthol., 1970; Explorer; Orange County Writer; Fullerton News Tribune; Postidings. Address: 1394 Piland Dr., San Jose, CA 95130, U.S.A.

CLARK, China, b. 11 Sept. 1952. Playwrite. Education: Central State Univ.; Am. Acad. for Dramatic Arts; Martha Graham Schl. of Contemporary Dance; Am. Mime Theatre; Columbia Univ. Positions held: Consultant to Columbia University's Urban Ctr. Memberships: Poets & Writers of Am.; Am. Acad. of Poets. Published works: Poems from China, 1971. Contbr. to: Essence Mag., 1973; Black American, 1973; Black Collegian, 1972; The Sunday Sun, 1972; San Francisco Intersection; Yardbird Reader Anthol., 1973; Hny Anthol., 1972. Recip., Woolrich Fndn. Fellowship, 1973-74. Address: 22 Hudson Terr., Edgewater, NJ, U.S.A.

CLARK, Gladys P., b. 27 Feb. 1909. Poet; Artist; Business Woman (retired). Education: Special courses, Western Ill. Univ.; Poetry technique and oil painting in Adult Education. Married to Frank B. Clark; 3 children. Memberships: Charter member, Camellia Poets (Sec. & Treas. 1965-68; Pres., 1971-73); Calif. Fed. Chaparral Poets; UPLI; CSSI; Sacramento Poetry Club (Sec. & Treas., 1965, Pres., 1967-68). Published works: Singing Silhouettes, 1970, 1972. Contbr. to: Sacramento Poets Qtly.; Spring Bouquet (Lds. Art Festival, 1972); American Bard; Angels; Swordsman Review; Messenger; Laurel Leaves, and numerous anthols. Awards: Dr. of Arts & Letters (hon.); 1st & 2nd Prize, Camellia Poets, 1965-67, 1968-72; 1st Prizes in Sacramento Poets Contest, 1964-66; 1967, 1968, 1970, 1972; 3 artistic diplomas from Dr. Armando Troni, CSSI, Rome. Address: 6435 Orange Ave., 26A, Sacramento, CA 95823, USA.

CLARK, John Pepper, b. 1935. Editorial Writer; Lecturer. Educ: Ibadan Univ., Nigeria; Grad. student, Princeton Univ., U.S.A., 1962. Positions held: Fndr. & Ed., The Horn, 1962; Editorial Writer, Daily Express, Lagos, Nigeria; Lectr., African Lit., Univ. of Lagos. Published works: Poems, 1962; A Reed in the Tide, 1965; (plays) Song of a Goat, 1962; Three Plays: Song of a Goat, The Masquerade, The Raft, 1964. Contbr. to: Transition; (anthologies) Seven African Writers, 1962; A Book of African Verse, 1964; West African Verse, 1967; New Voices of the Commonwealth, 1968.

CLARK, Leonard, b. 1 Aug. 1905. Writer; Poet. Education: Normal Coll., Bangor. Married Jane Callow, 2 children. Positions held: Tchr., Glos. & London, U.K. 1922-28, 1930-36; H.M. Insp. of Schls.,

1936-70; Mbr., Lit. Panel, Arts Coun. of G.B. Fellow, Royal Soc. Lit. Freeman, City of London. Published works: (poetry) Poems, 1942; Passage to the Pole, 1944; Rhandanim, 1945; The Mirror & Other Poems, 1948; XII Poems, 1948; English Morning & Other Poems, 1953; Selected Poems, 1940-57, 1958; Drums & Trumpets, 1962; Daybreak: A First Book of Poems for Children, 1964; The Year Round: A Second Book of Poems for Children, 1965; Fields & Territories, 1967; Good Company: Poems for Children, 1968; Flutes & Cymbals: Poetry for the Young, 1968; Near & Far: Poems for Children, 1969; Here & There: Poems for Children, 1969; Secret as Toads; (prose) The Life & Work of Alfred Williams, 1945, '69; Walter de la Mare, 1960; A Fool in the Forest, 1965; Grateful Caliban, Autobiog., 1968; Co-Translator, The Zemganno Brothers, 1957; (ed.), Quiet as Moss: 36 Poems by Andrew Young, 1959; The Collected Poems of Andrew Young, 1959; Common Ground, 1964; The Poetry of Nature, 1965; Complete Poems of Walter de la Mare, 1969; Poems by Children, 1970. Latest books: Secret As Toads, Poems for Children, 1972; Sark Discovered, rev. edn., 1971; Poems of Ivor Gurney (ed.), 1973; Four Seasons, Poems for Children, 1974; The Broad Atlantic, Poems, 1974; The Hearing Heart, Poems, 1973; Great & Familiar, 1974; Mr. Pettigrew's Harvest Festival, 1974. Contbr. to: New Poems, PEN Anthol., 1960, '65; From Darkness to Light, 1964; Oxford Miscellany, 1967, '68; Poetry of the Forties, 1968; Outposts; Poetry Review. Honours, awards: Jt-winner, IWWP Poetry Award, 1972; Kt. of St. Sylvester. Address: 50 Cholmeley Cres., London N.6., U.K.

CLARK, Mary Carter, b. 3 June 1912. Printer. Education: Blackburn Technical Coll.; Harrison Inst., Blackburn; Guest's Bus. Trng. Coll., Blackburn; Special Tchrs. Dip., Commercial Tchrs. Trng. Coll., Bournemouth; Pitman's Shorthand Tchrs. Dip.; Typewriting Tchrs. Dip., Inc. Phonographic Soc.; Dip. for Women Supvsrs. in Engrng. Married James Clark. Positions held: Sec. to Sales Mgmt., Van den Berghs & Jurgens, Manchester, 1937-40; Sec. to Hd. Buyer, Supvsr. of Main Off. Typists' Pool, The Bristol Aeroplane Co. Ltd., Clayton-le-Moors, 1940-45; formed Clarke's Typewriting Bureau, 1945; formed partnership w. husband in printing bus., The Bridge press, 1951. Mbr., The Lancashire Authors Assn., 20 yrs. published works: Mary's Miscellany; Meander with Mary, prose & verse, 1971. Contbr. to: The Accrington Observer & Times; The Lancashire Evening Telegraph; also var. broadcasts on Radio Blackburn. Recip., 3rd prize, Lancs. Authors' Cup Comp., 1963. Address: 15 Jubilee St., Oswaldtwistle, Nr. Accrington, Lancs., U.K.

CLARK, Robert John, pen name CLARK, Robert, b. 12 Oct. 1911. Solicitor. Education: LL.B., King's Coll. and University of Adelaide, Australia, 1933. Married Dorothy Mavis Johnson, 1 daughter, 1 son. Co-Ed. of Verse in Australia, 1958-62. Mbr., Australian Soc. of Authors & the Poetry Soc. of Australia. Published works: The Dogman & other poems, 1962; Segments of the Bowl, 1968; selected & edited A Window At Night, the poems of Max Harris w. a critical intro., 1967. Contbr. to: The Australian; Australian Broadcasting Commn.; Australian Letters; Illustrated Weekly of India; Meanjin Quarterly; New York Times Book Review; Overland; Overseas; Poetry; Quadrant; Southerly; The Sydney Morning Herald; Verve; Westerly; poems included in num. anthols. Recip., 1st Prize, Poetry Sect., Sydney Morning Herald Lit. Comp., 1956. Address: Hill Rd., Montacute, S. Australia 5134.

CLARK, Thomas A., b. 16 April 1944. Editor. Positions held: Ed., Bo Heem E Um, Dorset, U.K.; Full time poet. Published works: Alexander's Gaze, 1968; The Secrecy of the Totally, 1969. Contbr. to: Akros; Lines Review; Tlaloc; (anthologies) Scottish Poetry One, Two, Three, 1966, '67, '68. Address: 3 South St., Sherborne, Dorset, U.K.

CLARK, Tom, b. 1 Mar. 1941. Poetry Editor. Educ: B.A., Univ. of Mich., 1963; Univ. of Cambridge, U.K.;

Univ. of Essex. Married Angelica Heinegg, 1968; one child. Positions held: Instr., Am. Poetry, Univ. of Essex, 1966-67; Poetry Ed., The Paris Review, 1963–. Published works: Airplanes, 1966; The Sand Burg, 1966; Bun, 1967; Stones, 1969; The Emperor of the Animals (play), 1967. Contbr. to: Poetry; Paris Review; Angel Hair; (anthologies) Young American Writers, 1968; Contemporary American Poets, 1969; Sparklers, 1969. Honours, awards: Univ. of Mich. Hopwood Prize for Poetry, 1963; Fulbright Grant, 1963-65; Bess Hokin Prize, 1966; George Dillon Prize, 1968; Poets' Fndn. Award, 1967; Rockefeller Grant, 1968. Address: Box 6, Cherry Rd., Bolinas, CA 94924, U.S.A.

CLARKE, Austin, b. 9 May 1896. Freelance Reviewer & Broadcaster. Educ: Belvedere Coll., Dublin, Ireland; Univ. Coll., Dublin. Positions held: Lectr., Engl., Univ. Coll., Dublin, 1917-21; Asst. Ed., Argosy, London, 1929; Freelance Reviewer & Broadcaster. Memberships: Pres., Irish P.E.N., 1939-42 & '46-49; Fndn. Mbr., Irish Acad. of Letters, 1932 & Pres., 1952-54; Chmn., Dublin Verse Speaking Soc. and Lyric Theatre Co. Published works: Pilgrimage and Other Poems, 1929; Collected Poems, 1936; Night and Morning, 1938; Later Poems, 1961; Flight to Africa and Other Poems, 1963; Old-Fashioned Pilgrimage, 1967; A Sermon on Swift, 1969; (novels) The Bright Temptation, 1932; The Singing Men at Cashel, 1936; The Sun Dances at Easter, 1952. Contbr. to: (anthologies) Oxford Book of Irish Verse, 1958; New Poets of Ireland, 1963; New Modern Poetry, 1967. Honours, awards: Nat. Award for Poetry; Gregory Medal, 1968. Address: Bridge House, Templeogue, Dublin 14, Ireland.

CLARKE, Peter Edward, (earlier poems appeared under the name KUMALO), b. 2 June 1929. Graphic Artist & Painter; Book Illustrator. Studied Art in Holland, 1962-63. Has exhibited paintings widely in S. Africa, Europe, America & Australia. Contbr. of poems to: (anthols.) An African Treasury, 1960; Poems From Black Africa, 1963; Junior Voices, 1971; Teachers Read-Aloud Anthology, 1971; (mags.) South African Outlook, 1973; New Nation, 1973; Contrast, 1973; also included in 'Living Language', a series of broadcasts by the B.B.C., 1968. Has read own poetry at seminar, Univ. of Cape Town, 1972. Address: 14 Alpha Way, Ocean View, Fish Hoek, C.P., South Africa.

CLARKE, Sylvia Storla, b. 4 June 1903. Public Health Nurse (R.N.). Education: Pub. Health Cert. & Licensed Audiometrist; B.S., Nursing Chico State, Grad. Frances E. Willard Hospital, Chicago, Ill., Post Grad. Anaesthetist, Chicago Lying-In Hospital, Chicago; Fiction Writing, Northwestern Univ.; studied Poetry with Clement Wood. Positions held: Public Health Dept., Chico, 7 yrs.-Chico City Schools, 6½ yrs., plus Admin. positions in hospitals in Chicago; also 7 yrs. with Western Electric as Industrial Nurse. Memberships: Butte Co. Branch Nat. League of American Penwomen (Pres.); Poet's Forum, Chicago; Iota Sigma Epsilon, Writers' Sorority, Northwestern Univ.; Poetry Soc. of America. Contbr. to: Detroit News; Chicago Tribune; Parent-Teacher's Mag.; Children's Friend; Christian Living; The Humanist; The Lyric, etc. Awards: Dorrance Poetry Award; Mary O'Connor Award; Francis W. Reid Award; Lyric Foundation Award; Sonnet Award – Author's and Artist's Club of Chattanooga, Tenn.; currently co-editor of book, Butte Remembers (a publication of Butte Co. Branch, Nat. League of American Penwomen), also contbr. to same. Address: 1505 Citrus Ave., Chico, CA 95926, USA.

CLARKE, Verna Mary, b. 18 Oct. 1919. Medical Welfare Officer. Education: Washington Med. Ctr., Wash. D.C., U.S.A.; Hon. Dip., Nat. Schl. Dress Design, Chicago, U.S.A.; Literary Tutor, Gordon Pittaway (Author & Dramatist), Melbourne, Vic., Australia. Widow of John Flavien Clarke, 1 daughter. Positions held: Med. Record Libn., Havre de Grace Hosp., Md., U.S.A., 1947-50; Med. Welfare Officer, Royal Children's Hosp., Brisbane, Aust., 1954–.

Memberships: Am. Assn. of Med. Record Libns.; Comm. Mbr., Fellowship of Australian Writers', Brisbane Br.; Ed. & Publsr., Poets of Australia 1972, Poets of Australia 1973 & Poets of Australia 1974-75 (in compilation); Fndr. & Dir., Queensland Writers' Workshop. Published works: Love is the Soul of the Man, 3 act Musical, script, lyrics & melodies, performed in Brisbane for one week, May 1972 & second season in Redcliffe 1973; Power of the Purse, 3 act drama, to be produced in Brisbane in 1975; Body, Mind & Soul, novel, in press. Contbr. to 'Spectrum', Writers' Workshop lit. mag. Address: 31 Salkeld St., Tarragindi, Qld. 4121, Australia.

CLAUDEL, Calvin André, b. 7 July 1909. Professor of Languages. Education: B.A. & M.A., Tulane Univ., 1931-32; Ph.D., Univ. of N.C., 1947; Dip., Sorbonne, 1962. Married Alice Moser Claudel. Positions held: Language Tchr. in New Orleans High Schools, 1932-66; Chmn. of Romance Langs., West Va. Wesleyan, 1966-69; Prof. of French & Spanish, Salisbury Coll., 1969-72; Asst. Prof. of French & Spanish, Eastern Shore Community Coll., 1972-. Memberships: Pres., La. State Poetry Soc., 1965-66; Chancellor, Nat. Fed. of State Poetry Socs., 1968-69. Contbr. to: Lyric Louisiana, vol. III, 1965; Piggott Banner; Oaks & Acorns; Iconograph; Univ. of N.M. Qtly.; Int. Lit. Qtly.; Qtly. Review of Lit.; La. Histl. Qtly.; New Laurel Review; The Wash. Coll. Review. Guest Ed., The New Laurel Review, 1972. Address: 56 West Kearsarge Circle, Wallops Island, VA 23337, U.S.A.

CLAYRE, Alasdair, b. 9 Oct. 1935. Writer; Television Producer; Singer. Education: Winchester Coll., 1948-54; Christ Ch., Oxford Univ., 1956-59. Positions held: Prize Fellow, All Souls Coll., Oxford, 1959-; Production Dir., Arts Fac., BBC Open Univ. TV, 1970-. Published works: (poetry) A Fire By The Sea; (poetry & Music) Adam & The Beasts; (anthol.) A Hundred Folk Songs & New Songs. Contbr. to: London Mag.; Broadside; Sing, etc. Address: 38 West Hill Court, Millfield Lane, London N.6, U.K.

CLEMENT, Mary Brown (Edna), b. 13 Apr. 1904. Married. Member: Nat. League of American Pen Women (various offices held, including: Nev. State Pres., Las Vegas Branch Pres., Vice-Pres., Treas., Sec., Membership Chairman). Publication: Black and Silver, 1944. Contrib. to: Okla. City Times; American Author; Ariz. Highways; World Fair Anthology, 1938, etc. Address: 2402 Marlin Av., Las Vegas, Nevada 89101, USA.

CLEMENT, Robert Allen, b. 18 Dec. 1947 at Dover, Delaware, USA. Retail Salesman. Education: Grad. Collins HS, Oak Hill, W.Va.; student, W.Va. Inst. of Tech., Montgomery, W.Va., 1966-69. Positions held: with Street Dept., City of Montgomery, 2 summers; Student, 1966-69; House Painter; presently with Hills Dept. Store, Div. of SCOA Industries, Beckley, W.Va. Memberships: W.Va. Poetry Soc.; Beckley Chapter of W.Va. Poetry Soc. (vice-pres.); Internat. Platform Assoc., 1971-72. Contbr. to: Fayette Tribune; Montgomery Herald; Echoes of the W.Va. Poetry Soc.; Internat. Who's Who in Poetry Anthol., 1972; Young America Sings, 1965; Songs of Youth, 1966; Voice of America, 1967; Poetry Parade; W.Va. Poetry Soc. News-Letter; Souvenir Brochure (1972), Convention of W.Va. Poetry Soc. at Beckley. Awards: Prize for most literary contributions to Sr. Engl. Class, Collins HS, 1966; Prize-winning poems at 1971 & 1973 Conventions of W.Va. Poetry Soc. Address: Box 836, Beckley, WV 25801, USA.

CLEMO, Reginald John (Jack), b. 11 Mar. 1916. Poet. Education: Trethosa Council School, St. Austell, 1922-29. Son of Reginald Clemo, clay-kiln worker, and Eveline Clemo, farmer's daughter. Married to Ruth Grace Peaty. Memberships: Hon. member, West Country Writers' Assoc.; Bard of Cornish Gorsedd. Published works: The Clay Verge, 1951; The Map of Clay, 1961; Cactus on Carmel, 1967; The Echoing Tip, 1971. Contbr. to: Poetry Review; Transatlantic Review; The Twentieth Century; Aquarius; Workshop

New Poetry; Malahat Review; Cornish Review. Recip. of Arts Council Festival Poetry Prize, 1951; Civil List Pension, 1961. Address: Goonamarris, St. Stephen's, St. Austell, Cornwall, UK.

CLENDENNING, Anna Martha Utterback, pen names **AUSTIN, A. Nash, CLENDENNING, Anne,** b. 4 Oct. 1908. Senior Mechanical Engineer. Educated: Marshall Univ., Huntington, West Va., L.A. City College, Los Angeles. Editor, Poetry Soc. of West Virginia; Treasurer, California Fed. of Chaparral Poets; Sec., Southern California Poetry Soc. Pubs. Crumbs (1956), Darling Beast (1960). Contrib. to: Huntington Herald Advertiser; Good Housekeeping Magazine; The American Bard; The Archer; Echoes of West Virginia; Kaliedograph; Swoardsman Press. Recipient of Awards from Southern Calif. Poetry Soc., 1960; Calif. Fed. of Chaparral Poets, 1954, 1960, 1962; West Virginia Poetry Soc., 1966, 1968, 1969, 1970. Address: 2837 Sunset Place, Los Angeles, Calif. 90005, USA.

CLEVE, Anders Zachris, b. 25 July 1937. Teacher of History. Education: Univ. degree in History. Married, 2 children. Has held var. tchng. posts. Memberships: Finland's Svenska författareförening; Eino Leino Seura; Finland's PEN Club. Published works incl: Dagen, 1955; Det bara ansiktet, 1956 (1 collection of short stories, 3 novels). Recip. sev. prizes for short stories & novels. Address: Lappviksgatan 31 A4, 00180 Helsingfors 18, Finland.

CLIMENHAGA, Joel, b. 9 April 1922. Teacher; Poet; Playwright; Actor; Director; Lecturer; Editor. Education: Messiah Coll., Pennsylvania; Chaffey Coll., Calif.; Pomona Coll., Calif.; Univ. of Calif. at Los Angeles; Stanford Univ., B.A., 1953, M.A., 1958. Personal details: born at Bulawayo, Rhodesia; married to Zoe Motter, 4 children. Positions held: Director of Drama, Central Dauphin HS, Pennsylvania; Director, Creative Writing, Wilmington Coll., Ohio; Director, Southern Ohio Writers Workshop; Assoc. Prof. of Playwriting, Univ. of NC; Lecturer in Playwriting, Southern Writers Workshop, Univ. of Georgia; Chairman, Dept. of Speech & Drama, Culver-Stockton Coll., Missouri; Director, Mississippi Valley Writers Conference; Director of Theatre, Kansas State Univ; Director of New Play Prog., Kansas State Univ.; Editor, Transient Press; Editor, Greenage Press. Memberships: American Community Theatre Assoc.; American Poetry League; American Theatre Assoc. (Advisory Council; Bd. Directors; Internat. Liaison Project; Latin-American Theatre Project; Chairman, Playwrights' Prog., 1960-65); Children's Theatre Conf., Internat. Platform Assoc.; Prairie Playwrights Project; Secondary School Theatre Conf.; Theta Alpha Phi Nat. Hon. Frat. of Theatre Arts (Vice-Pres., 1966-68, Pres., 1968-72); World Poetry Soc. Intercontinental. Published works: Heathen Pioneer, 1956; Marriage Wheel, 1963; Hawk and Chameleon, 1972; Belief in Chaos, 1973; One Candle is Light Enough Forever, 1973; Angel Who Has Taken Us by the Hand, 1974; The Age of Pollution, 1974. Contbr. to many anthols., mags., etc. Awards: Sam. Goldwyn Award for Creative Writing, 1st Prize, 1955; Sam. French Nat. Collegiate Playwriting Competition, 1st Prize, 1956; Rockefeller Playwriting Grant, 1955-56; Field-Hotaling Fellowship, 1962, 1967. Address: 210 South 10th St., Manhattan, KS 66502, USA.

CLOUSER, Carolyn Ruth (Eppley), pen name **CLOUSER, Carolyn E.,** b. 20 Oct. 1927. Legal Secretary; Housewife. Education: Ctrl. Pa. Bus. Coll., Harrisburg. Married William H. Clouser, 3 daughters. Memberships: Pa. Poetry Socs., affil. w. Nat. Fed. of State Poetry Socs.; Midwest Fed. of Chaparral Poets; Am. Poetry League. Contbr. to: Sunday Patriot-News, Hbg., Pa.; The Evening News, Hbg., Pa.; The News-Sun, Newport, Pa.; The Altoona Mirror, Altoona, Pa.; Am. Poetry League Bulletin; A Goodly Heritage; Midwest Chaparral Mag.; The Hoosier Challenger; Swordsman Review; Past The Flame of Words; Echoes of Faith (vol. of religious poetry); also var. vols. of From Sea to Sea in Song. Recip. var. poetry awards inclng: 1st Hon. Mention, Margaret Deland

Meml. Contest, Pa. Poetry Soc., 1966 & Col. Shoemaker Meml. Contest, 1967. Address: P.O. Box 27, Newport, PA 17074, U.S.A.

CLOUTS, Sydney David, b. 10 Jan. 1926. Research Fellow. Educ: South African Coll. Schl.; B.A., Univ. of Cape Town. Married, three children. Positions held: Rsch. Fellow, Inst. of the Study of Engl., Africa, 1969–. Published works: One Life, 1966. Contbr. to: Contrast; New Coin; Transatlantic Review; Listener; (anthologies) Poets in South Africa, 1958; A Book of South African Verse, 1959; Penguin Book of South African Verse, 1968; Inscapes, 1969. Honours, awards: Ingrid Jonker Prize, 1968; Olive Schreiner Award, 1968. Address: Rhodes Univ., Grahamstown, South Africa.

CLUYSENAAR, Anne Alice Andrée, b. 15 Mar. 1936, Belgium. University Lecturer. Education: M.A., Engl. & French, Trinity Coll., Dublin, Eire, 1957; Dip. in Gen. Linguistics, Edinburgh Univ., Scotland, UK, 1964. Personal details: Took Irish Citizenship, 1962; d. of John Cluysenaar, abstract painter. Positions held: Lectrship. in Engl., Manchester Univ., 1958; Trinity Coll., Dublin, 1962; King's Coll., Aberdeen, 1964-65; Lectr., Lit., Stylistics & Gen. Linguistics, Lancaster Univ., 1966–; Poetry Reviewer, Stand. Published works: A Fan of Shadows, 1967; Nodes, 1971; Bill Morey, 1972; Introduction to Structural Stylistics, 1972. Contbr. to: Icarus; Delta; University Poetry; Satis; Irish Times; Hibernia; Evening News, Edinburgh; Aberdeen Univ. Review; Continuum. The Dubliner; The Dublin Magazine; Poetry Ireland; Tri-Quarterly; Irish TV & Radio. Address: c/o Dept. of English, Univ. of Lancaster, Bailrigg, Lancaster, Lancs., UK.

COBB, James R., b. 6 Dec. 1945. Educator & Writer. Education: B.A.; M.A., Western Ky. Univ., Bowling Green, 1968. Positions held: College Instructor. Contbr. to publs. in U.S.A. & India. Address: Continuing Educ. Dept., Univ. of Northern Colo., Greeley, CO, U.S.A.

COBB, Winifred Mary Bradley, pen name (for song lyrics), **KENT, Allison,** b. 27 Aug. 1906. Teacher; Writer. Education: B.A., Texas Tech. Univ.; M.A., Eastern N.M. Univ. Has held various teaching positions in Texas and New Mexico. Memberships: Poetry Soc. of Texas; Centro Studi e Scambi Internazionali; Nat. Education Assoc.; N.M. Education Assoc. Pubs. The Greening Branch, 1964; Spin the Golden Thread, 1966; Let the Mountains Stand, 1971. Contrib. to: Terry County Herald (Texas); State Line Tribune (Texas). Address: 1717 E. 21st St., Clovis, N.M. 88101, USA.

COBBING, Bob, b. 30 July 1920. Poet. Positions held: Co-ed., Writers Forum Series. Memberships: Council & Exec. Comm., The Poetry Soc. Published works: Massacre of the Innocents, 1963; ABC in Sound, 1965; Eyearun, 1966; Chamber Music, 1966; Kurrirrurriri, 1967; So, 1968; Octo, 1969; Whisper Piece (Whississippi), 1969; Why Shiva has Ten Arms, 1969. Contbr. to: And; Approaches; Arc; Exit; Extraverse; Futura; Isis; Its; Labris; Link; Marrahwannah; Neue Texte; Ou; Poetdoos; Second Amaranth; Second Aeon; Tlaloc; Solstice; Vertigo; Workshop; Young Commonwealth Poets, 1965; Concrete Poetry; Britain Canada USA, 1965; Anthol. of Concrete Poetry, 1967; Once Again, 1968; Experimentalni Poezie (Czechoslovakia), 1968; Pamphlet 2–Wjississippi, 1969; 12 Days (of Xmas), 1970. Also on several gramophone records. Address: 262 Randolph Ave., London W9, UK.

COBEAN, Charles Scott, b. 13 Dec. 1952. Student. Education: Randolph-Macon Coll.; Vanderbilt Univ., Nashville, Tn. Positions held: Music & Drama Critic, The Yellow Jacket, 1970-71; Ed., On Mag., 1973–. Member, Washington Literary Soc. Contbr. to: Poem Mag.; On Mag.; Versus; Private Poetry Review; The Yellow Jacket. Honours, awards: 1st prize, Norfolk Art Show; 1st prize, Westchester Poetry Contest, 1973;

Hon. Mention, Acad. of Am. Poets, 1972. Address: Box 5327, Stn. B., Vanderbilt Univ., Nashville, TN 37235, U.S.A.

COBERLY, Lenore McComas, b. 23 Feb. 1925. Writer; Housewife; Consultant. Education: B.S. in Bus. Admin., West Va. Univ.; M.A. in Bus. Admin., Univ. of Pittsburgh. Married. Positions held: Instr., Univ. of Wis., Commerce Dept.; Adult Educ. Specialist, Project Head Start; Instr., Madison Area Tech. Coll.; Cons., Midwest Region, Head Start. Memberships: Wis. Fellowship of Poets; Nat. Fed. of State Poetry Socs.; Wis. Acad. of Scis., Arts & Letters. Published works: Drink from a Sulphur Well, 1973. Contbr. to: The Capital Times, Madison, Wis.; Hawk & Whipporwill Recalled; World Poets; From the Hills; other newspapers and jrnls. Honours, awards: Third Prize, Perfect Poems Contest, World Poets, 1973; 'Drink from a Sulphur Well' was purchased by Felix Pollak for the Rare Books Collection of the Univ. of Wis., 1974. Address: 4114 N. Sunset Court, Madison, WI 53705, U.S.A.

COBLENTZ, Stanton A(rthur), b. 24 Aug. 1896. Writer; Editor. Education: A.B., Univ. of Calif. at Berkeley, 1917; M.A., ibid, 1919. Positions held: Writer, daily feature poems, San Francisco Examiner, 1919-20; Book Reviewer, NY Times, Sun, etc., & Free-lance Writer, 1920-38; Ed., Wings, a Quarterly of Verse, 1933-60. Mbr., Poetry Soc. of Am. Published works: The Thinker & Other Poems, 1923; The Lone Adventurer, 1926; Shadows on a Wall, 1930; Songs by the Wayside, 1938; The Pageant of Man, 1936; Senator Goose, 1940; Songs of the Redwoods, 1933; Winds of Chaos, 1942; Green Vistas, 1943; The Mountains of the Sleeping Maiden, 1946; Garnered Sheaves, 1949; Time's Travellers, 1952; From a Western Hilltop, 1954; Out of Many Songs, 1958; Atlantis & Other Poems, 1960; Redwood Poems, 1961; Aesop's Fables (rhymed versions), 1968; The Pageant of the New World, 1968. Compiler of five anthols. of verse. Author of 8 books about poetry, including: My Life in Poetry, 1959; The Poetry Circus, 1967. Contbr. to: NY Times; NY Sun; NY Herald-Trib.; Christian Century; Am. Mercury; Los Angeles Times; etc. Honours: Lyric Fndn. Award for Trad. Poetry, 1953; Silver Medal for Poetry, Commonwealth Club of Calif., 1953. Address: 5380 Cribari Crest, San Jose, Calif. 95135, USA.

COCHRAN, (George) Leonard (Hunter), b. 19 Aug. 1928. Roman Catholic Priest (member of the Order of Friars Preachers, popularly known as the Dominicans). Education: B.A.(Phil.); M.A.(Theol.); M.A.(Engl.) Chairman, Engl. Dept., Fenwick High School, Oak Park, Ill., 1965-1969; 1973–; Prof. of Logic, Fenwick High School, 1967–; Sub-Prior, St. Dominic's Priory, 1968-71. Member: Baker Street Irregulars; Hugo's Companions; Poetry Soc. of America. Contrib. to: Spirit; American Haiku; College English; Poetry (Chicago); Catholic World; Chicago Tribune Magazine. Address: Priory of St. Dominic & St. Thomas, 7200 West Division, River Forest, Ill. 60305, USA.

CODE, Grant Hyde, b. 2 Mar. 1896. Actor. Education: Public Schools in Wisconsin, Illinois, Ohio; HS in Ohio, Pennsylvania; Coll. Harvard, A.B., 1918; Post grad. study, Univ. of Toulouse, France, and Harvard; Military training, Plattsburgh Barracks, NY. Positions held: Lieut. Infantry, 1st Div., AEF, WWI; Teacher of Engl., Boston Univ., Harvard Coll., Radcliffe Coll., and Univ. of Delaware; ran general research bureau; director, Soc. of Arts & Crafts, Boston; Asst. to Committee for Region Four Public Works Art Project; Officer, American Fed. of Arts; Editor of Publications, Brooklyn Museums; Founder and Curator of Dance Center, Brooklyn Museum; Editor of Dance Observer; Editorial work for NY publishers; Actor stage, films and TV since 1953. (Made stage debut 1910 and frequently acted as an amateur before becoming a professional actor). Published short stories, plays, poems, and critical articles. Memberships: Actors Equity Assoc.; Screen Actors Guild; American Fed. of

TV and Radio Artists; Authors' League, etc. Published works: Volume One, 1924; Volume Two, 1925; This Undying Quest, 1971; Chalk Marks, 1973. Contbr. to: Poetry, a mag. of verse; NY Times; Providence Journal; New Republic; American Poetry Journal; American Poetry Mag.; Commonweal; Gyroscope; Hound & Horn; Internat. Theatre; Lyrica; Pagany; Temp; Unicorn; Voices; Gandhi Marg.; Milwaukee Arts Monthly; Hawk and Whippoorwill; (anthols.): Poetry out of Wisconsin; Poetry from Wisconsin; Fire and Sleet and Candlelight. Address: Hotel St. Francis, 124 West 47th St., New York, NY 10036, USA.

COE, Minna, b. 12 Feb. 1896. Poet. Education: Cert. of Completion, Univ. of Oregon, Normal School, 1915; Voice Study with Yeatman-Griffith, NYC, and Ely Cohen, Paris. Married Willard Coe. Extenisve musical career as opera singer, conductor, voice teacher, musical director, author and narrator, etc. Positions held, also: Voice Teacher of prof. artists for opera, TV., radio and concert, 1918-72; Head, Voice Dept., Ellison-White Conservatory of Music, Reed Coll., Portland, Oregon, 1920-37; Voice Coach French Repertoire with conductor, Ely Cohen, Opera-Comique, Paris, 1929; Founder; Sponsor, etc. of many musical organizations, and holder of many Offices therein; TV Panelist: CBS, NBC, KCET, 1962-66, and Star of Wolper Prods. documentary films: Story of a Patroness, 1963; The Imposters, 1966. Memberships, many, including: Faculty Club, UCLA (Life Member). Published works: Humanity Ensnared (Thesis for Symposium at UCLA, Los Angeles), 1965; Born Enthusiastic (poetry), 1967. Author of poems set to music. Honours: Ph.D. (h.c.), Colorado State Christian Coll, 1973., etc. Address: 1650 North Amalfi Dr., Pacific Palisades, CA 90272, USA.

COE, Miriam, b. 1 July 1902. Writer; Librarian. Education: English and American Schools, Colls., and Univs., including Fine and Performing Arts. Personal details: Sister of Harold Maurice Cohen, C.B.E., M.D., UK. Positions held: Sec. to John Ogden & Co., Shipbrokers, Liverpool, UK; Teacher of Violin Playing; Writer for Liverpool Express; Originated system for teaching music relating color in visual art to color in sound; Originated System for Teaching Music; Lecturer at WHAM, Rochester, NY (Psychology of Music); Inventions for the Implementation of Adjuncts in the Construction of Typewriters; Estab. w. Adolphe A. Berle Sr. pvte. schl. in Manhattan; Lectr., LSU Free Univ. Careers Series; Commercial Artist; Librarian; Song-writer; Poet; Author; Lexicographer (self-employed). Memberships: Little Theatre Group, Liverpool Psychological Soc., Liverpool, UK.; Smithsonian Inst.; S. & W., Inc. Poetry Soc.; American Historical Soc.; American Sociological Assoc.; American Assoc. of Political & Social Sciences; Nat. Assoc. of Museums; American Public Health Assoc.; Louisiana Art & Artists Guild; Louisiana Water Color Soc.; American Dickens League (Hon. Life Member); Unified Art of Chicago; Mystery Club of NY; Sociology Club of Louisiana State Univ.; American Judicature Soc.; American Soc. of Photogrammetry; Am. Lib. Assn.; American Assoc. of School Librarians; Louisiana Library Assoc.; Southwestern & Southeastern Library Assocs.; Alumna Winthrop Palmer Library School; Alpha Beta Alpha ISU. Published works: Anthol. of World Literature; Psychology of Music; Poems for the Young; Miscellaneous Poems; (Children's Stories) Children of Other Lands; Animal Stories, etc.; Highschool Librarian's Manual; A Sociological Cyclopedia; Dictionary of Photogrammetry & Related Terms; Careers in Art; Haiku: East/West; Pitirim Sorokin: His Life and Work; National Anthem "Our Land". Awards: 1st, 2nd, and 3rd Prizes, also cash, pearls, trophies, and Hon. Mentions, at Deep South Penwomen's Annual Conferences, La. Art Commn., La. Art & Artists Guild, LSU, etc. Address: P.O. Box 18184 Univ. Station, Baton Rouge, LA 70803, USA.

COFFIN, Ellen, pen name **MAGELLAN, Ellen; ANN, Avocado,** b. 20 Apr. 1949. Music Teacher. Education: Grad., Columbus School for Girls; attended

Bennington Coll.; Univ. of E. Anglia; Grad., Hollins Coll. Married, David P. Coffin. Positions held: Salesgirl, antique store; Hostess, at art exhibtions; Receptionist, Central Ohio Medical Clinic; Music Teacher, Boxwood School. Membership: Hollins Coll. Lit. Soc. Contbr. to: Poet Lore; Cargoes; Early Hours; Concepts. Awards: Nancy Thorp Prize (Hollins Coll.), 1967, 1970; Ohio Poetry Soc. Prize, 1967; Rye Beach Writers Conference Award, 1967; Poet Lore, Descriptive Poem Award, 2nd Prize, 1969, and Hon. Mention, for Love Poetry, 1971. Address: 834 S. Cassingham Rd., Columbus, OH 43209, USA.

COGHILL, Rhoda, b. 1903. Teacher. Educ: B.A., Univ. of Dublin, Ireland. Positions held: Music Tchr., Dublin Royal Acad. of Irish Music. Published works: Bright Hillside, 1948; Time Is a Squirrel, 1956. Contbr. to: (anthologies) 1000 Years of Irish Poetry, 1953; The Oxford Book of Irish Verse, 1958. Address: c/o Acad. of Music, Dublin, Ireland.

COGSWELL, Frederick William, pen name **COGSWELL, Fred,** b. 8 Nov. 1917. Professor of English. Fducation: B.A., 1949, M.A., 1950, Univ. of New Brunswick; Ph.D., 1952, Edinburgh Univ. Married, 2 d. Positions held: Asst. Prof., Dept. of English, U.N.B., 1952, Assoc. Prof., 1957, Prof., 1962. Memberships: Independent Publishers Assoc. (Regional Representative, 1972-73); League of Canadian Poets (Regional Representative, since 1970); International P.E.N.; Canadian Authors Assoc.; Editor, The Fiddlehead, 1952-66; Publisher and Editor, Fiddlehead Poetry Books, 1954-1973. Pubs. The Stunted Strong, 1954; The Haloed Tree, 1957; The Testament of Cresseid (trans.), 1958; Descent from Eden, 1959; Lost Dimension, 1960; Star People, 1968; One Hundred Poems of Modern Quebec (Ed. and trans.), 1970; A Second Hundred Poems of Modern Quebec (Ed. and trans.), 1971; Immortal Plowman, 1970; In Praise of Chastity, 1971; The Chains of Liliput, 1971; The House Without a Door, 1973; Confrontation (trans.), 1973; Five New Brunswick Poets (Ed. and Cont.), 1966. Contrib. to: Saturday Review; New World Writing; New Statesman and Nation; Colorado Qtly.; Origin; Canadian Forum; The Fiddlehead; Pan; Northern Review; Queens Qtly.; Poetry (Australia); Outposts; Poetry Review; The Poet (India); Adam; Venture; Delta; Whetstone; Contemporary Verse; Venture; Saltire Review; The Literary Review; South and West; Pegasus; Inferno; Salt; Osiris, etc. Awarded Gold Medal, Poet's International in 1960's. Address: 769 Reid St., Fredericton, N.B., Canada.

COHEN, Aaron, E., b. 2 July 1937. Proxy Clerk. Member, New Hampshire Poetry Soc. Publications: Masquerade (narrative poem), 1969; Night City, 1973. Contrib. to: Earlham College newspaper; Provincetown Qtly.; N.H. Poetry Soc. Newsletter; Color and Rhyme. Awarded Hon. Membership to Poetry Soc. of N.H., 1969-70. Address: 1 Bank St., New York, NY 10014, USA.

COHEN, Diana Paula, b. 3 Sept. 1942. Art Teacher. Education: A.A.S., Fashion Inst. of Technol., 1962; B.S., N.Y. Univ., 1972; currently working for M.A., ibid. Positions held: Tchr., Fashion Art & Design, Fashion Inst. of Technol., N.Y.C., 1969-74 (p/t); Tchr., Fashion Illustration, Posters, Lettering, High Schl. of Art & Design, N.Y.C., 1972; Tchr., Drawing, Painting, Flat Design, Basic Art, High Schl. of Fashion Industries, N.Y.C., 1972-73; Org. var. workshops in Art for Nursery-into-Elem. Schl. Child, Brooklyn Museum, N.Y.C., 1973; Speaker at var. conferences; Fashion illustrator on staff & freelance; Art Del. to Educ. Coun., N.Y. Univ. Memberships: Nat. Soc. of Arts & Letters; N.Y. Poetry Forum; N.Y. City Art Tchrs. Assn. Published works: Education Violet Review, 1972; Articles, 1972; Light, vol.1, no.1, 1973. Honours, awards: St. Gaudens Medal, 1960; Cert. of Merit, Student Coun., N.Y. Univ., 1972. Address: 98-45, 57th Ave., Queens, NY 11368, U.S.A.

COHEN, Jean, b. 23 July 1924. Professor. Education: Sorbonne, Paris. 6 sons. Positions held: Tchr., Lycee d'Oran; i/c Rsch., Nat. Ctr. of Sci. Rsch.; Asst. Master, Sorbonne; Docteur en Philosophie. Published works: Structure du Langage poetique, 1966; L'obscurite de Mallarmé, 1962; La Theorie du Roman de René Girard, 1963; La Comparaison poetique, 1968; Theorie de la Figure, 1970; Poesie et Motivation, 1972. Honours, awards: Laureat de l'Academie des Sciences morales et politiques. Address: 162 Boulevard de Grenelle, 75015, Paris, France.

COHEN, Leonard. Poet; Novelist; Musician, Songwriter. Ecucation: McGill Univ., Montreal, P.Q., Canada; Columbia Univ., N.Y., U.S.A. Published works: Let Us Compare Mythologies, 1956; Flowers for Hitler, 1964; Parasites of Heaven, 1966; The Favourite Game, 1963; The Spice-Box of Earth, 1965; Beautiful Losers (novel); Selected Poems 1956-68, 1969. Gramophone Records: The Songs of Leonard Cohen (LP); Songs From A Room (LP). Songs widely performed by Nina Simone, Judy Collins, Buffie St. Marie, etc. Address: c/o Jonathan Cape Ltd., 30 Bedford Sq., London, WC1, UK.

COHEN, William Howard, b. 13 Aug. 1927. Professor; Poet. Education: B.A., M.A., Univ of Fla.; Univ. of Chgo.; Emory Univ.; Ph.D., Southern Ill. Univ., 1970. Positions held: Tchr., Andrew Jackson HS; Ga. State Coll.; Southern Ill. Univ.; Oglethorpe Coll.; currently Prof. of Engl. & Humanities & Poet-in-Residence, Alice Lloyd Coll., Pippa Passes, Ky.; Resident poet, Lotts Creek Community School, Cordia, Ky., 1971-72; Visiting Prof. World Literature, Winston-Salem St. U., 1973. Memberships: Gvrng. Bd., Int. Rep., Ky. State Poetry Soc.; Poetry Soc. of Am. Published works: A House In The Country, 1962; The Hill Way Home, 1965; To Walk In Seasons, 1971; An Introduction to Japanese Haiku, 1969; Mexico 68: The New World of Man, 1971; To Walk in Seasons, 1972. Contbr. to: Poet Lore; Lit. East & West; Southern Humanities Review; Am. Haiku; Haiku (Canada): Haiku West (also co-ed.); Green World; Green River; Approaches; Parallax; Contemporary Ky. Poetry; Ky. Harvest; Ky. Authors; Minority of One; Am. Mosaic; First Flight; Second Flight; Poetry Dial; Poetry Dial Anthol.; New Souls; Poetry Trans-World; Pegasus; Am. Bard; Haiku Highlights; El Universal (Mexico City); El Nacional (Mexico City); La Prensa (Mexico City); Egyptian; Hollow Harvest; Blue Print; Mountain Life & Work; XIXth Olympic Games Anthol. (Mexico City); Grass Roots. Awards: Int. Prize for A Poem On Peace, Disciples of Christ Fellowship; US Olympic Poet, Games of the XIXth Olympiad, Mexico City, 1968. Address: Poet's Park, Rt. 2, Box 52, Carterville, Ill. 62918, USA.

COLE, Audrey, pen name **LAWRENCE, Audrey,** b. 12 Mar. 1938. Fashion Writer. Trained in rep. as Actress, Dancer & Elocutionist. Positions held: Fashion Writer. Membership: Sec., Brentwood Writers' Circle. Has had plays for children & poems performed at festivals, & has won many competitions & awards for poetry reading & Shakespeare at the City Lit. Inst. Address: 9 Park Rd., Brentwood, Essex, U.K.

COLE, Barry, b. 13 Nov. 1936. Civil Servant. Married Rita Linihan, three children. Positions held: Employed w. Govt. Serv., 1964-. Published works: Blood Ties, 1967; Ulysses in the Town of Coloured Glass, 1968; Moonsearch; The Visitors, 1970; (novels) A Run Across the Island, 1970, Joseph Winter's Patronage, 1969; The Search for Rita, 1970; The Evacuees (essay), 1968. Contbr. to: Listener; New Worlds; Spectator; Times Literary Supplement; London Magazine; New Statesman; Transatlantic Review; (anthologies) Scottish Poetry One, Two, Three, 1966, '67, '68; New Poems, 1968; Holding Your Eight Hands, 1969; Children of Albion, 1969; Penguin Book of Postwar British Verse, 1970. Address: 18 Great Percy St., Finsbury, London W.C.1, U.K.

COLE, Eddie-Lou, b. 2 Feb. 1909. Poet and Illustrator. Education: HS, Livingston, Montana; Creative Writing and Poetry; Sacramento City Coll.; Poetry: Univ. of Calif. at Berkeley (extension). Married (1) Laurence A.

Cole, decd; married (2) Ray W. Howard; 1 s., 1 d. Positions held: Retired State Employee, Editor & feature writer, State Employee Chap. 58 magazine; Poetry column, Harlequin Press; Illustrator, Promethian Lamp. Memberships: WPSI.; Major Poets; PMA.; NFSPS.; Calif. Writers Club; El Camino Poets Chapter; CFCP: Ina Coolbrith Circle. Published works: Of Winter, 1962; Pinions to the Sun, 1963, 2nd edition, 1965; Shadows on Sundials, 1966; The Great Wall (self illustrated with Sumi E), 1968; Strange, 1972. Contbr. to: Internat. Who's Who in Poetry Anthol., 1973; Year Book of Modern Poetry; Voices International, and many others. Awards: First and Grand prize, Olympic Gold Medals and Laurel Wreath, 1972; Ad Schuster Citation, Berkeley Poets, 1965 and 1966; 93 poems have won State, National, or International awards, including 9 Grand Prizes. Address: 1841 Garden Highway, Sacramento, CA 95833, USA.

COLE, E(ugene) R(oger), b. 14 Nov. 1930. Freelance Writer & Critic. Education: B.A., St. Edward's Coll., 1954; M.Div., Sulpician Sem. of the Northwest, 1958; A.B., Ctrl. Wash. State Coll., 1959; M.A., Seattle Univ., 1970. Positions held: Chmn., Engl. Dept., Yakima Ctrl. H.S., 1959-66; Chmn., Engl. Dept., Marquette H.S., 1966-69; Instr., Engl., Philos., Humanities, 1959-69; Poetry Critic for the Nat. Writers Club, 1969-. Memberships: Authors Guild, Inc.; Poetry Soc. of Am.; Poetry Soc., London; Acad. of Am. Poets; Nat. Writers Club; Nat. Fed. of State Poetry Socs.; Western World Haiku Soc. Published works: Selected Poems, 1975. Acting Ed., Experiment: An International Review of New Poetry. Rep. in the following anthols: The Golden Yr., 1960; La Poesie Contemporaine aux Etats-Unis, 1962; Best Broadcast Poetry, 1969; Adam Among the Television Trees, 1971; Nor All Your Wit, 1973; Nat. Fed. Anthol., 1974. Contbr. to: Sat. Review; The Personalist; The Beloit Poetry Jrnl.; Western Humanities Review; N.M. Qtly.; Ga. Review; La Voix des Poetes (Paris); Poetry Review; Discourse; Compass Review; The Dalhousie Review; Modern Am. Sonnet; Southern Humanities Review; The Free Lance; Miss. Review; Am. Bard; Northwest Review; Poet Lore, etc. Recip., Dragonfly Haiku Commentary Award, 1974. Address: 26301 Shirley Ave., Euclid, OH 44132, U.S.A.

COLE, Katherine Cecelia Keller, pen name **COLE, Casey,** b. 5 Aug. 1937. Housewife. Married, 2 sons, 2 daughters. Memberships: Treas., Portage Writers' Workshop, 3 yrs.; Wis. Regl. Writers' Assn.; Wis. Fellowship of Poets; Nat. Fed. of Poets. Published works: Family Album of Poetry, 1969. Contbr. to: Portage Daily Register; Appleton Post Cresent; Haiku Highlights; Shake Shingle; Upstream-Downstream, anthol. Address: Box 584, Cross Village, MI 53901, U.S.A.

COLE, Thomas Casilear, b. 23 July 1888. Artist – Portrait Painter. Education: Grad., Riverview Mil. Acad., Poughkeepsie, N.Y.; Harvard Univ., 1 yr.; studied Art, Schl. of the Mus. of Pine Arts, Boston, Mass. & at Julien Acad., Paris, France. Positions held: Instr. in Portrait Painting, Phoenix Art Inst., N.Y.; Instr. in Portrait & Figure Painting, N.Y. Schl. of Fine & Indl. Art, N.Y.C. Mbr., The Poetry Soc. of Am. Contbr. to: The Boston Herald; Boston Evening Transcript; Christian Sci. Monitor; Boston Post; Wellesley Townsman; New England Mag.; The Craftsman Mag.; N.Y. Times; N.Y. Herald Tribune. Address: 939 Eighth Ave., N.Y., NY 10019, U.S.A.

COLE, William, b. 20 Nov. 1919. Anthologist of Poetry. Married, 4 children. Positions held: Publicity Dir., Alfred A. Knopf, publisher; Publicity Dir. & Ed., Simon & Schuster; Conducts column, Trade Winds, for Saturday Review/World Mag. Memberships: PEN, 1953-; V.P., U.S. Ctr., ibid, 2 terms; Poetry Soc. of Am.; Authors Guild. Anthols. incl: The Poet's Tales, 1971; Poetry Brief, 1971; Pick Me Up, 1972; Oh, That's Ridiculous! 1972; Oh, How Silly! 1970; Poems from Ireland, 1972; ...And Be Merry! 1972; Poems One Line & Longer, 1973. Books: A Cat-Hater's Handbook,

1963; Frances Face-Maker, 1963; What's Good for a Six-year-old? 1965; What's Good for a Five-year-old? 1968; What's Good for a Four-year-old? 1967; What's Good for a Three-year-old? 1972; Uncoupled Couplets: A Game of Rhymes, 1966; That Pest, Jonathan, 1970; Aunt Bella's Umbrella, 1970. Var. anthols. in collaboration with others. Contbr. to: The New Yorker; The Atlantic Monthly; The Saturday Review; Book Week; The Irish Times, etc. Address: 201 West 54 St., N.Y., NY 10019, U.S.A.

COLEMAN, (Rev.) Alvis Moreland, b. 20 Sept. 1927. Methodist Minister. Education: Assoc. in Science, North Texas Agric. Coll., 1946; B.A. in Journalism, North Texas State Coll., 1949; B.D., Perkins School of Theol., S.M.U., 1952; other studies at SMU, Kilgore JC, Iliff School of Theol.; East Texas Bapt. Married, Wanda Linville Coleman; 4 children. Positions held: (Pastoral appts.) Winnsboro Circuit; Canton Circuit; Call and Watson's Chapel, Sabine Pass; St. Andrew's Ch., Groves; Hardwick Ch., Longview; Crockett Place Ch., Galveston; Velasco and Oyster Creek Chs., Freeport; Summitt Ch., Marshall; Newton and Burkeville Chs.; Cameron Ch. with Tracy and Maysfield Chs. also. Currently Pastor of First United Methodist Ch., Rosenberg, Texas. Memberships: Chaplain, 111 Eng. Bn. Pt. Arthur, Texas., 1955-57; Pres., Groves Ministerial Assoc., 1955-57; Pres., Cameron Ministerial Assoc.; Cameron Day Care Center Pres. Reporter and Contbr. to Nurnberg Post-Spade, 1946-48. Address: 1418 Ward St., Rosenberg, TX 77471, USA.

COLEMAN, Eleanor Dorothy, b. 6 Feb. 1901. Writer of Poetry & Prose. Education: Erie Conservatory of Music. Widow of Arthur F. Coleman, 2 sons. Memberships: Am. Poetry League, 20 yrs.; Centro Studi e Scambi Int. published works: Pursuit of Happiness (book of poetry), 1952. Contbr. to many anthols.; Erie Times News. Poetry has been broadcast on Radio & used in TV broadcasts. Address: 3109 Liberty St., Erie, PA 16508, U.S.A.

COLEMAN, (Rev.) Elliott, b. 26 Sept. 1906. Minister of Religion; Professor. Educ: B.A., Wheaton Coll.; Princeton Theological Sem.; Gen. Theological Sem., N.Y.C.; St. Stephen's House, Oxford, U.K. Positions held: Ordained, Diaconate of the Episcopal Ch., 1942; Master, Asheville Schl., 1928-40; W. Henry Holt & Co., Inc., Publishers, 1943; W. Doubleday & Co., Inc., Publishers, 1944; Prof. of Engl. Writing & Dir. of Writing Seminars, The Johns Hopkins Univ., Baltimore, U.S.A., 1945–. Published works: The Poems of Elliott Coleman, 1936; An American in Augustland, 1940; Pearl Harbor, 1942; A Glass Darkly, 1952; 33 Night Sonnets, 1955; Mockingbirds at Fort McHenry, 1963; Broken Death, 1964; Rose Demonics: 1936-66, 1967; Ed., Lectures in Criticism, 1959; Ed., Poems of Byron, Keats & Shelley, 1968; Num. translations. Contbr. to: Poetry. Address: The Johns Hopkins Univ., Baltimore, MD 21218, U.S.A.

COLEMAN, Mary Ann, pen names COLEMAN, Mary Ann Braunlin, b. 3 Jan. 1928. Poet & Teacher. Education: Ind. Univ., 1945-48; B.S., Auburn Univ., 1950; studied poetry w. Paul Engle, Univ. of Iowa, 1954; Van Brock, Emory Univ., 1961; Marion Montgomery, Univ. of Ga., 1963; John Ciardi, Breadloaf Writers Conf., 1965 & James Dickey, Univ. of Fla., 1972. Married Oliver M. Coleman, Jr. Positions held: Elem. Schl. Tchr., Pompano, Fla., 1951-52 & in East Point, Ga., 1953-55; Welfare Wkr., Atlanta, Ga., 1952-53; Tchr. of Poetry Workshops for the Dixie Coun. of Authors & Jrnlsts., 1970 & '71, Dekalb Coll., Univ. of Ga. Ctr. for Continuing Educ., winter 1972 & '73, & for the Ga. Writers' Assn. at Emory-at-Oxford, 1973. Memberships: Poetry Soc. of Am.; Ga. Writers' Assn. Contbr. to var. reviews & mags. Recip. var. awards from Ga. Writers' Assn. for poetry. Address: 205 Sherwood Dr., Athens, GA, U.S.A.

COLLIE, Michael John, b. 8 Aug. 1929. Professor of English Literature. Education: St. Catharine's Coll., Cambridge. Married Joanne L'Heureux, 5 children.

Positions held: Tchng. at Univ. of Manitoba, Exter Univ., Mount Allison Univ.; currently at York Univ., Toronto, Canada, 1965–. Published works: Poems, 1959; Skirmish with Fact, 1960; The House, 1967; Kerdruc Notebook, 1972. Address: 2 Fowlmere Rd., Shepreth, Royston, Hertfordshire 5G8 6QG or Dept. of Engl., York Univ., Downsview, Ont., Canada.

COLLINS, Christopher, b. 8 July 1936. University Instructor. Education: B.A., St. Anselm's Coll., 1958; M.A., Univ. of Calif. at Berkeley, 1959; Ph.D., Columbia Univ., 1964. Positions held: at State Univ. of N.Y., 1963-65; City Univ. of N.Y., 1965-68; Chmn., Dept. of Engl., ibid, 1967-68; Assoc. Prof., N.Y. Univ., 1968–. Published works: Daphnis & Chloe (trans. w. critical intro.), 1972; The Uses of Observation (a study in Am. poetics & perception), 1971; The Act of Poetry (a practical intro. to the reading of poetry), 1970; Henry James: The Ambassadors (a short critical study of the novel), 1964. Contbr. to: The Logic of Poetry; The N.Y. Quarterly; The Nation; Epoch; N.Y. Poetry; The Univ. Review; Wis. Poetry Mag.; The Fiddlehead; The Gauntlet; The Nassau Review; New Am. Poetry (anthol.) Has been interviewed on the subject of contemporary poetry & has read own work on Radio Stns. WBAI & WNYC. Honours, awards: Mbr. of the Room, Cambridge Univ., U.K., 1970; N.Y. Univ. Arts & Sci. Grant, 1969, etc. Address: 244 E. Fifth St., N.Y., NY 10003, U.S.A.

COLLINS, John W., b. 2 Jan. 1939. Minister. Education: A.A., Fla. Coll., Tampa; courses in Engl., Psychol. & Liberal Arts at Univ. of Ala. & Univ. of Calif. at Los Angeles. Married, 3 children. Positions held: Minister in Fla., N.C., Ala. & Calif.; Sales positions in all those areas. Memberships: Recording Sec. & Treas., Pan; South & West; Major Poets Chapter, Pierson Mettler Assn.; Clover. Contbr. to: Mission Mag.; Bitterroot; Lunatic Fringe; Bridge (Troll); Encore; Clover; Poetry Venture; Community of Friends; Garden Island; Inland Writers Mag.; Pandemonium. Address: P.O. Box 24C45, Los Angeles, CA 90024, U.S.A.

COLLINSON, Laurence, b. 7 Sept. 1925. Poet; Playwright. Education: Tchng. Degree, Melbourne, Australia, 1953. Positions held: currently with Publs. Br., Victoria Educ. Dept. Published works: The Mood of Love, 1957; Who is Wheeling Grandma?, 1964. Sev. plays produced on stage, radio & TV. Honours: Elizabeth Theatre Trust Award, 1961; Soc. of Australian Authors Award, 1966. Address: c/o Angus & Robertson Ltd., 89 Castlereagh St., Sydney, Australia.

COLLYMORE, Frank Appleton, b. 7 Jan. 1893. Teacher. Education: Combermere School, Barbados. Married, 4 ds. Positions held: Asst. Master, Combermere School, 1910-49, Deputy Headmaster, 1950-58, Asst. Master (acting), 1958-63. Pubs. Thirty Poems, 1944; Beneath the Casmarinas, 1945; Flotsam, 1948; Collected Poems, 1959; Rhymed Ruminations on the Fauna of Barbados (light verse), 1968; Selected Poems, 1971. Contrib. to: Bim; Caribbean Voices (2 vols.); Commonwealth Poems of Today; The Sun's Eye; Talk of the Tamarinds, 1971; Honours awarded: O.B.E., 1958; Hon. M.A., (U.W.I., Mona, Jamaica), 1968. Address: Woodville, Chelsea Rd., St. Michael Barbados, W.1.

COLOMBO, John Robert, b. 24 Mar. 1936. Editor; Poet; Broadcaster; Writer. Education: Schl. of Grad. Studies, Univ. of Toronto, Canada. Married, 3 children. Positions held: Lectr., Atkinson Coll., York Univ.; Edit. Asst., Univ. of Toronto Press; Asst. Ed., The Ryerson Press; Sr. Cons. Ed., McClelland & Stewart. Memberships: 1st provisional co-ord, League of Canadian Poets; PEN. Published works: The Mackenzie Poems, 1965; The Great Wall of China, 1966; Abracadabra, 1967; Miraculous Montages, 1968; John Toronto, 1969; Neo Poems, 1970; The Great San Francisco Earthquake & Fire, 1971; Praise Poems, 1970; Leonardo's Lists, 1971; Colombo's Quotations: The Dictionary of Quotations of Interest to

Canadians, 1974. Ed. of the following: The Varsity Chapbook, 1959; Poetry 64/Poesie 64, 1963; New Direction in Canadian Poetry, 1970; How Do I Love Thee, 1971; Rhymes & Reasons, 1971. Contbr. to: The Atlantic Monthly; The Tamarack Review, etc. Awarded: Centennial Medal, Secretary of State, 1967. Address: 42 Dell Park Ave., Toronto M6B 2T6, Ontario, Canada.

COLONY, Horatio, b. 22 Sept. 1900. Writer; Poet. Education: Keene Public Schools; Phillips Exeter Acad.; Harvard Coll. Memberships: St. Botolph Club, Boston, Mass.; Authors Club, Boston, Mass.; Poetry Soc. of America; Poetry Soc. of N.H.; Catholic Poetry Soc.; Bostonian Soc. Pubs. Free Forester, a novel, 1935; A Brook of Leaves, 1935; Birth and Burial, 1939; Bacchus and Krishna, 1952; Young Malatesta, 1957; Three Loves the Same, 1961; The Early Land, 1962; The Flying Ones, 1964; Demon In Love, 1967; The Magic Child, 1968; Some Phoenix Blood, 1969; Flower Myth, 1970; The Amazon's Hero, 1973; Modern Library; Twentieth Cent. American Poetry; PSA Anthology; NH Poetry Soc. Anthology. Contrib. to: Quicksilver; The Lit. Review; Harvard Bulletin; World of Books; Spirit; Poet Lore; Harvard Advocate. Address: 199 Main St., Keene, N.H. 03431, USA.

COLQUHOUN, Ithell, b. 9 Oct. 1906. Painter & Writer. Education: Cheltenham Ladies' Coll., 1919-25; Slade Schl. of Fine Art, 1927-31; Univ. of London Dip. in Fine Art, 1930; private study in Paris & Athens. Mbr., West Country Writers' Assn. & Newlyn Soc. of Artists. Poetry Readings: sev. of surrealist poetry at the Int. Arts Ctr., London, 1942-44; Taliessin Poetry & Music Grp., London, 1952; Progressive League, London, 1953, '54; & Inst. of Contemporary Art, London, 1953; Hovel Theatre, Soho, London, 1955; Playgoers' Theatre, Penzance, 1963, '69, '70; Penzance Soc. of Arts, 1967, '69; St. Ives Arts Club (twice), 1968, etc. Illustrated & wrote the following: The Crying of the Wind, 1955; The Living Stones, 1957; Grimoire of the Entangled Thicket, 1973. Author of Goose of Hermogenes, 1961. Contbr. to: Soleils, Paris; Fantasmagie, Brussels; View, U.S.A.; Time & Tide; Adam; Poetry Quarterly; Poetry Review; The Glass; Grubb St.; Cornish Review; Ore; The Scillonian; The Bell; Other Voices; Transformation, etc. Honours: Bardess to the Clan Colquhoun. Address: Stone Cross Cottage, Paul, Penzance TR19 6TU, Cornwall, U.K.

COLTMAN, Paul Curtis, b. 14 Oct. 1917. Schoolmaster. Education: St. John's Coll., Oxford Univ., 1936-39. Married, 4 daughters. Positions held: Tchr. at Bradford Grammar Schl. & Steyming Grammar Schl. Member, Nat. Poetry Secretariat. Published works: The Pattern of Violence, 1968; Weald & Downland, 1974. Contbr. to: Priapus; Outposts; Poetry Review. Address: Standings, Mouse Lane, Steyning, Sussex, U.K.

COLVIN, Norma Lucille Thomas, pen name COLVIN, Norma Thomas, b. 4 Sept. 1915. Artist. Education: Art Ctr., L.A., Calif.; Art Mus. Art Schl., Portland, Ore.; Univ. of Alaska, Fairbanks. Married, 1 daughter. Positions held: Display Artist, Coldwaters, Phoenix, Ariz.; Photography Artist; L.A., Calif.; Display Artist, Meier & Frank, Portland; Fine Arts & Tchng., Alaska & Wash. States. Memberships: Wash. Poets Assn., 1 yr.; Tacoma Writers Club, 2 yrs. Contbr. to: Durango Herald, Colo.; also anthol. Recip., 1st pl., poetry, Tacoma Writers Club Award, 1973. Address: 6491 S. Eye St., Tacoma, WA, U.S.A.

COMBS, Elisha Trammell, Jr., pen name COMBS, Tram, b. 25 Sept. 1924. Poet; Book seller. Education: A.B., Univ. of Calif.; Cert. in Meteorology, Univ. of Chicago. Positions held: Oil Chem., Tidewater Assoc. Oil Co.; Owner-Mgr., Tram Combs, Books, VI. Memberships: PEN; Poetry Ctr., San Francisco State Coll. Published works: Pilgrim's Terrace, 1957; Artists Boys Cats, 1959; But Never Mind, 1961; Saint Thomas, 1965; Briefs, 1966. Contbr. to: Bim; VI review; Liberation; San Francisco Review; Kayak; The Home Jrnl.; St. Thomas. Address: Crystal Gade Eleven.

Charlotte Amalie, St. Thomas, U.S. Virgin Islands.

COMFORT, Alex(ander), b. 10 Feb. 1920. Poet & Novelist; Medical Biologist. Education: MRCS, LRCP Lond., 1944; M.B. B.Ch., Trinity Coll., Cambridge, 1944; M.A., 1945; D.C.H., Lond., 1945; Ph.D. (Biochem.) Lond., 1949; D.Sc. (Gerontology), Lond., 1963. Positions held: Med. & Hosp. Prac., 1944-48; Lectr. in Physiol., The London Hosp., 1948-51; Nuffield Rsch. Asst., Univ. Coll., London, 1951-54; Nuffield Rsch. Fellow in Bio. of Senescence, 1954-63; Dir., Med. Rsch. Council Rsch. Group in Ageing, Univ. Coll., 1963-. Published works: The Silver River, 1937; No Such Liberty, 1941; Into Egypt (play), 1942; France & Other Poems, 1942; A Wreath for the Living, 1943; The Almond Tree (novel), 1943; Cities of the Plain, 1943; The Powerhouse (novel), 1944; Elegies, 1944; The Song of Lazarus, 1945; Letters From an Outpost (stories), 1947; Art & Social Responsibility (essays), 1947; The Signal to Engage, 1947; Gengulphus, 1948; On this Side Nothing, 1948; First Year Physiological Technique (textbook), 1948; The Novel and Our Time (criticism), 1948; Barbarism & Sexual Freedom (essays), 1948; Sexual Behaviour in Society, 1950; The Pattern of the Future, 1950; Authority & Delinquency in the Modern State, 1950; And All But He Departed (poems), 1951; A Giant's Strength (novel), 1952; The Biology of Snescence, 1956; Darwin & the Naked Lady (essays), 1961; Come Out to Play, 1961; Haste to the Wedding (poems), 1961; Are You Sitting Comfortably? (songs), 1962; Sex & Society, 1963; The Biology of Ageing, 1964; The Koka Shastra (translation), 1964; The Process of Ageing, 1965; The Anxiety Makers, 1967. Address: c/o Routledge & Kegan Paul, Ltd., Broadway House, 68-74 Carter Lane, London EC4, UK.

CONGDON, Kirby, b. 13 Nov. 1924. Typesetter. Education: B.A., Columbia Coll.; grad. work, Columbia Univ. Positions held: Asst. to Lit. Agent; Editl. Asst., Collier's Ency.; Typesetter. Memberships: Comm., Small Mag. Editors & Presses. Published works: Iron Ark, A Bestiary, 1962; Juggernaut, 1966; A Key West Rebus, 1969; Dream-Work, 1970; Black Sun, 1973; Animals, 1974. Contbr. to: One; A New England Review; Poet; Athanor; Trace; The Fiddlehead; Am. Poetry Mag.; Theo; The Lookout; Wormwood; Comoran y Delfin; The Colo. Qtly.; Voices; Yankee; El Corno Emplumado; Dare; Americas; Poetmeat; Soho; Nickel Review; Amaranthus; The Smith; Nada; N.Y. Times; N.Y. Herald Tribune; The Christian Sci. Monitor; Key West Citizen, etc. Rep. in following anthols: Bluebeat; For Bill Butler; N.Y. Times Book of Verse; The East Side Scene; Open Poetry; In a Time of Revolution; The Writing on the Wall; The Male Muse; Inside Outer Space, etc. Address: Interim Books, P.O. Box 35, N.Y., NY 10014, U.S.A.

CONKEY, Virginia, b. 19 June 1939. Typist & Freelance Writer. Education: Business Coll., 6 months; Liberal Arts Coll., 1 yr. Member, Sons & Daughters of the Ore. Pioneers Assn. Contbr. to: Oregonian; Poet (India); Driftwood; Am. Bard; Swordsman Review; Muse; Cyclo-Flame; Am. Poet's Best, vol. IV; South & West; Cardinal; News Guard; Badge of Promise anthol.; Redmond Spokesman; Encore; Am. Poets, 1968; Major Poetry – Classical 500 in Poetry; Velvet Paws in Print, II; Bouquets of Poems (Italy). Honours, awards: 3rd pl., local Ore. contest, 1966; Hon. Mention, Nat. Contest, Writers Digest, 1967; Cert. of Merit, South & West, 1967; Award of Merit, Swordsman Review, 1967; var. book awards. Address: Star Rte. Box 392, Bonneville, OR 97008, U.S.A.

CONLEY, Robert Jackson, b. 29 Dec. 1940. College Educator. Education: B.A., Midwestern Univ., Wichita Falls, 1966; M.A., ibid, 1968. Positions held: Tchng. Asst., Engl. & Speech Dept., Midwestern Univ., 1966-68; Instr., Engl. Dept., Northern Ill. Univ., 1968-72; Instr., Engl., Dept., Southwest Mo. State Univ., 1972-. Published works: (textbooks) A Return to Vision; The Shadow Within; A Return to Vision, rev. edn.; The Essay; (all ed. w. Richard Cherry & Bernard Hirsch);

Poems for Comparison & Contrast, ed. w. R. Cherry. Co-ed./publisher, The Blackbird Circle. Has given profl. readings of his poetry at colls. around the U.S.A. Contbr. to: Pembroke Mag.; Quetzal; The Blue Cloud Quarterly; The Blackbird Circle; Indian Voice Mag.; Academy; The Cardinal Poetry Quarterly; From the Belly of the Shark (anthol.) Address: Rt. 1, Box 145–A, Brookline Stn., MO 65619, U.S.A.

CONN, Stewart, b. 5 Nov. 1936. Playwright. Education: Glasgow Univ., U.K. Married, 1 son. Positions held: BBC Drama Producer. Published works incl: Thunder in the Air, 1967; The Chinese Tower, 1967; Stoats in the Sunlight, 1968; An Ear to the Ground, 1972. Contbr. to: Poetry (Chicago); The Listener; The Observer; New Statesman; Critical Quarterly; The Scotsman; Poetry Book Soc. Supplement; var. anthols., etc. Honours, awards: E.C. Gregory (Leeds) Award, 1963; Scottish Arts Coun. Publication Award & Poetry Prize, 1968; Choice of the Poetry Book Soc. (An Ear to the Ground), 1972, etc. Address: c/o Radio Drama Dept., BBC, Broadcasting House, Queen Margaret Dr., Glasgow G12 8DN, U.K.

CONNAH, Margaret Heywood, b. 3 Jan. 1912. Clerk/Typist. Positions held: Dir., Women Personnel Sect., Qld. Div. of Australian Red Cross Soc., 10 yrs. (now ret'd.) Memberships: Comm. Mbr., Fellowship of Australian Writers, 1949-60, '68-72; V.P.; ibid, 1973–; Ed., Scope, monthly newsletter; Fndn. Mbr., Brisbane Writers' Grp. & 1st Hon. Sec.; Brisbane Music Club; Assoc. Mbr., Sunshine Coast Lit. Soc., 1972–; Soc. of Women Writers (Aust.), 1973–; Lyceum Club, Brisbane, 1973–. Co-Ed. & contbr. to: Softly Falls My Shadow, 1972. Rep. in following anthols: The Upward Flight, 1943; Qld. Writing, 1954 & '56; Never Kill a Dolphin, 1959; The Qld. Centenary Anthol., 1959; Square Poets, 1971; Brisbane Writers' Group Anthols., 1953-63. Contbr. to: The Brisbane Telegraph; The Courier-Mail; North Aust. Monthly; Prism; Endeavour; Scope, etc. Poems read on Aust. Broadcasting Commn. & commnd. for Anzac Day Broadcast. Personal appearance reading own poetry, Poets' Corner, TV Channel 9. Poems set to music by mbrs. of the Composers' Guild. Honours, awards incl: 1st prize, Poem Sect., Warana Writers' Conven. Comp., 1968 & Sunshine Coast Lit. Soc. Comp., 1972. Address: 15 Howie St., Eagle Junction, Qld. 4011, Australia.

CONNOR, Tony, pen name SPEAR, Bino, b. 16 Mar. 1930. Lecturer. Educ: M.A., Manchester Univ., U.K., 1968. Positions held: Served in the 5th Royal Inniskilling Dragoon Guards; Textile Designer, Manchester, 1944-60; Asst., Liberal Studies, Bolton Tech. Coll., 1961-64; Vis. Poet, Amherst Coll., U.S.A., 1967-68; Vis. Poet & Lectr., Wesleyan Univ., Middletown, 1968-69. Published works: With Love Somehow, 1962; Lodgers, 1965; Poems (w. Austin Clarke & Charles Tomlinson), 1966; Twelve Secret Poems, 1966; Kon in Springtime, 1968; Seven Last Poems from the Memoirs of Uncle Harry, 1969. Address: 16 Curzon Ave., Victoria Park, Manchester, 14, U.K.

CONQUEST, Robert, b. 15 Jul. 1917. Writer. Education: Winchester Coll.; Magdalen Coll., Oxford, M.A. Married; 2 s. Positions held: Private to Captain, Oxford & Bucks. Light Infantry, 1939-46; Diplomatic Service, HM Legation, Sofia, UK Delegation to the UN, Foreign Office, 1946-56; Fellow, L.S.E., 1956-58; Fellow Univ. of Buffalo, 1959-60; Lit. Editor, The Spectator, 1962-63; Fellow, Columbia Univ., 1964-65. Fellow, Royal Soc. of Literature. Published works: Poems, 1955; Between Mars and Venus, 1962; Arias from a Love Opera, 1969; New Lines, 1956 (edited), New Lines II, 1962 (edited). Contbr. to: Encounter; London Mag.; Twentieth Century Verse; Times Lit. Supp.; Spectator; New Statesmen; Outposts; Listener; Tribune; World Review; Observer; Time & Tide; Listen; Wave; Botteghe Oscure; Poetry Northwest; Beloit Poetry Journal; Polemic, etc. Recip. P.E.N. Brazil Prize, 1945; Festival of Britain Prize, Arts Council, 1951; O.B.E., 1955. Address: 4 York Mansions, Prince

of Wales Dr., London SW11, UK.

CONRAD, Berta Kaye, b. 4 Nov. 1909. Homemaker; Music Teacher. Education: Univ. of Utah, Salt Lake City; studied w. Concert Pianist, 10 yrs.; studied Voice, Harmony, Theory, Counterpoint, Keyboard Harmony. Married, 2 sons. Mbrship Chmn., Nev. Poetry Soc. Contbr. to: Poet (Great Am. World Poets,); South West Spring Edn., 1973. Address: P.O. Box 1147, McGill, NV 89318, U.S.A.

CONRAN, Anthony, b. 7 Apr. 1931, India. Research Fellow & Tutor. Education: Engl., Univ. of N Wales, UK. Positions held: Rsch. Asst.; Rsch. Fellow & Tutor, Univ. Coll. of N Wales, Bangor; Deleg., Taliesin Conf., Cardiff, 1969. Published works: Formal Poems, 1960; Metamorphoses, 1961; Sequence of the Blue Flower, 1961; Guernica, 1962; Icons, 1963; Asymptotes, 1963; A String o Blethers, 1963; Stelae, 1965; Collected Poems, 4 vols., 1965-67; Penguin Book of Welsh Verse, 1967; Claim Claim Claim, 1969; Dial a Poem, 1970; O. 125, Where is Thy Sting, 1971; Last Year We Built Together, 1971. Contbr. to: Poetry Mag.; Outposts; Critical Quarterly; Anglo-Welsh Review; Poetry Wales; Mabon; Time & Tide; Poetry Review; Welsh Serv., BBC. Honours, Awards: Welsh Comm. of the Arts Coun. Poetry Prize, 1958; Welsh Arts Coun. Bursary for Creative Writers, 1967; Dock Leaves Dylan Thomas Mem. Award, 1954. Address: 1 Frondirion, Allt Glanrafon, Bangor, Sir Gaernarfon, Wales, UK.

CONSTABLE, Patricia Ann, pen names, CONSTABLE, Patricia Anna; PATRICK, Connie, b. 6 Feb. 1934. Radio Sales Representative & Broadcaster. Education: GS; HS & classes at Indiana Univ. Southeast. Personal details: born in Indianapolis; married to Ray L. Constable; 2 s., 4 d. Positions held: Associated with Bobbs Merrill Publishing, 1958-59 as proof-reader, copy editor in law editorial; The Republic Newspaper in Columbus (assisted Soc. Editor and wrote news, 1967-68); Advertising Manager, Clark Co. Almanac (weekly newspaper, and wrote 3 cols. per week, 1971-72); Connie Creations Agency & WXUW Radio, since 1971. Memberships: Columbus Poetry Club, 1966-70 (Pres.); Indiana State Fed. of Poetry Clubs; Kentucky State Poetry Soc.; Southern Indiana Poets & Writers Soc. (founder of this group in 1970) (Pres.). Contbr. to: Indiana Sesquicentennial Poets, 1967; Poet; The Republic; Decatur County Monthly; Clark Co. Almanac; produced "Kaleidoscope" a daily poetry radio show on WREY-Radio in New Albany, Ind.; participated as hostess of show, etc; recently undertook special 1–hr broadcast on WXUW in a Rod McKuen Spolight. Awards: 2nd Place, Columbus Poetry Club, 1966; nominated for IWWP, 1973, etc. Address: Box 324, Jeffersonville, IN 47130, USA.

CONSTANT, (Baron), Jean Théophile Joseph, pen name CONSTANT DE HORION, b. 25 Jan. 1901. Professor; Attorney General. Education: Humanities (Greek, Latin), Collège Saint Servais, Liège; .D., Univ. of Liège. Positions held: Police Ct. Magistrate, Beaumont; Deputy Atty., First Magistrate's Ct. of Liège; First Deputy Solicitor Gen., Ct. of Appeal, Liège; Atty. Gen., Ct. of Appeal, Liège; Hon. Chief of the Chambers of the Min. of Justice; Pres., Benelux Commn. for the study & unification of Law; Doyen of the Fac. of Law of the Univ. of Liège; Prof. Emeritus, ibid; Pres., Schl. of Criminology. Published works: Du soleil et de l'ombre, 1919; Aventure (Ed. Ca ira), 1936; Aventure (Ed. Debresse, Paris), 1936, Preface by Georges Virres; La Guirlande dénouée, 1936. Contbr. to: Revue du Groupe d'Art Moderne de liège 1920-40; Da pensée Latine, Paris, 1920-30; Le Flambeau, Brussels; Le Thyrse, Brussels; Dante, Revue de Culture Latine, Paris; La Renaissance d'Occident, Brussels; L'espansion belge, Brussels; Books Abroad, Okla.; Revue de la Presse périodique, Brussels; L'expression française, Liege; Le Pays Natal (anthol.), 1972, etc. Honours, awards: Commandeur de l'Ordre des Palmes Académiques de France. Address: 227 rue Ferdinand Nicolay, 4310 Saint Nicolas lez, Liege, Belgium.

CONTOSKI, Victor J., b. 4 May 1936. Teacher. Education: B.A., Univ. of Minn., 1959; M.A., ibid, 1961; Ph.D., Univ. of Wis., 1969. Positions held: Fulbright Prof., Univ. of Lodz, Poland, 1963-64; Asst. Prof., Univ. of Kansas, 1969-73; Assoc. Prof., ibid, 1973–. Memberships: Modern Lang. Assn.; Soc. for the Study of Midwestern Lit. Published works: Four Contemporary Polish Poets, (translations), 1967; Astronomers, Madonnas, & Prophecies, (poetry), 1972; Broken Treaties, (poetry), 1973. Has published num. transl. of contemporary Polish poets. Contbr. to: Quixote; Kayak; North Stone Review; Minn. Review; Chicago Review; Midwest Qtly.; Hearse; Sumac; Prairie Schooner; Manhattan Review; Chelsea; Epoch; Hierophant; Hanging Loose. Honours, awards: Vanderwater Poetry Prize, Ohio State Univ., 1965; Edward H. Gardner Poetry Award, Univ. of Wis., 1966. Address: Engl. Dept., Kans. Univ., Lawrence, KS 66045, U.S.A.

COOK, Arlene E., pen name **COLE, Cannon,** b. 1 July 1936. Authoress. Education: A.A., Palomar Coll., San Marcos, Calif., 1955; B.A., San Diego State Coll., 1958; Life Tchng. Credential, Elem. Educ., State of Calif. Married Richard H. Cook, 3 children. Memberships: Past Pres., Escondido Br., Nat. League Am. Pen Women; Calif. Fed. Chaparral Poets. Co-author of The World of Long Ago, 1971. Contbr. to: Am. Haiku; Golden Circle; Haiku Highlights; Piggott Banner; Jean's Jrnl.; Bitterroot; Bardic Echoes; Am. Bard; Am. Jrnl. of Nursing; Animal Cavalcade. Honours, awards: Best of Issue, Haiku Highlights, 1966 & Bardic Echoes, twice in 1967. Address: P.O. Box 184, Escondido, CA 92025, U.S.A.

COOK, Gerald Lawrence, pen name **COOK, G.L.,** b. 29 Dec. 1940. Teacher of Composition & Creative Writing. Education: A.A., B.A. & M.A.T. Engl., Monmouth Coll., W. Long Branch, N.J. Positions held: Lectr. on Composition & Creative Writing, Monmouth Coll., 1966–73. Memberships: Poetry Soc. of Am.; MLA. Contbr. to: Genesis, anthol., 1962; Separate Voices, an anthol. of N.J. shore poets, 1966; Arena, a poetry broadsheet; Outside the Establishment, a poetry broadsheet; Monmouth Letters. Recip., 2nd prize, Jerry Thoms Meml. Poetry Contest, 1964. Address: Box 261 Navesink, NJ 07752, USA.

COOK, Gladys May, pen name **COOK, Gladys Moon,** b. 8 Apr. 1907. Writer of poetry & fiction. Education: Des Moines Univ., 1925-27; sev. courses in Jrnlsm., Northwestern Univ., Chicago campus; B.A., Communication Arts, Columbia Coll., 1967. Widow of Robert Neil Cook, 1 son (Bruce). Positions held: Actress, United Chautauquas, 1927; travelled w. repertoire Co., summer 1933; Salesman, A.C. McClurg & Co., Wholesalers, 1947; Bookkeeper, Russel Seeds Co., Advt., 1954-56; Bookkeeper, Perrin & Assocs., Advt., 1956-70. Memberships: Nat. League Am. Pen Women, Inc.; Soc. of Midland Authors; Pres., Poets of Chicago; Past Workshop Chmn., current Treas., Poets & Patrons, Inc.; var. offs., Iota Sigma Epsilon. Published works: Escape, a religious adventure book for boys. Contbr. to: Human Voice (anthol.); Yearbook of Modern Poetry, 1971; Outstanding Contemporary Poetry, 1972; Lyrics of Love (anthol.), 1972; Chicagoland's Award Winning Poetry, 1972; Poet Lore; Lyric; Human Voice Quarterly; Poet Mag.; Madras, India; Bardic Echoes; Am. Bard; The Muse; Poets Corner, Hartford Times, etc. Recip. num poetry awards, Intra Sorority Contest, Iota Sigma Epsilon; 4 first prizes, Poets & Patrons Annual Contest; Best of the Best, ibid, 1972. Address: 1628 W. Touhy Ave., Chicago, IL 60626, U.S.A.

COOK, Harold Lewis, b. 21 Mar. 1897. Episcopal Priest (Diocese of Mexico). Education: Union Coll., A.B., Schenectady, NY., USA., 1918; Emmanuel Coll., Cambridge Univ., 1920-22. Positions held: Instr. in English, Ga. Inst. of Tech., 1919-20; Northwestern Univ., 1922-25; Acting Headmaster, Chateau Neuvic and Park Lodge Schools, France, 1925-30; Head Engl. Dept., Avon Old Farms School, 1930-36; Training Director, Bendix Aviation Corp., 1941-53;

Management Consultant, 1953-58; Chairman, Business Division, Univ. of the State of N.Y. at Delhi, N.Y., 1958-62; Founder and Conductor, Poetry Workshop, Institute Allende, Mexico, 1960-70; Ordained to Holy Orders, 1970; Assisting Priest, St. Paul's Church, San Miguel de Allende, Mexico, since 1970. Pubs. Spell Against Death, 1933. Contrib. Introduction to Bibliography of Edna St. Vincent Millay, 1937. Contrib. to: (U.K.) Westminster Gazette; Spectator; New Witness; Voices; Chapbook; Colour; Today; (U.S.A.) Smart Set; Forum; Bookman; Touchstone; Harpers; Poetry, a mag. of verse; Dial; New Republic; Nation; Masses; Midland; Lyric; Contemporary Verse; Yale Review; New Yorker; Living Church. Anthologies: Best Poems of the Year (Thomas Moult); The Modern Muse; Silver Pennies, Poems for Young People; New Poetry (Harriet Monroe); Adventures in Poetry, etc. Appointed Guggenheim Fellow in Creative Writing, 1937. Address: Calle de Murillo 4, San Miguel de Allende, Gto. Mexico.

COOK, Michael, b. 12 Jan. 1950. Student. Education: studied Film, Northwestern Univ., Evanston, Ill., 1967-69; Mathematics, Hunter Coll., N.Y.C., 1972-74. Member, Poetry Soc. of Am. and Maths. Soc. of Am. Contbr. to: Spirit Mag.; Bridge Mag.; N.Y. Qtly.; Imprints Qtly. Address: Box 677, Stockbridge, MA 01262, U.S.A.

COOK, Ramona Graham, pen names **COOK, R. Graham & GRAHAM, Ramona,** Author. Education: Grad. in Music & Art (Normal Coll. Dip.) Positions held: Public Schl. Supvsr.; Head of Music Dept. in a State Normal of Ala. Member, Nat. League of Am. Pen Women; Nat. Pres., ibid, 1968-70. Published works: (poetry) Greetings from Boston, 1936; Hills of New England, 1946; What The Heart Creates, 1956; Aeolus Drives, 1969; Ballads from a Cart, 1970; (prose) With Uncle Thomas, 1967. Contbr. to num. mags., jrnls., etc. Recip. many poetry prizes. Address: 109 Main St., Rockport, MA 01966, U.S.A.

COOK, Stanley, b. 12 Apr. 1922. Educator. Education: Christ Ch., Oxford Univ., U.K. Married, 1 son, 2 daughters. Positions held: Tchng. posts at: Barrow-in-Furness Grammar Schl., Bury Grammar Schl. & Firth Park Schl., Sheffield; Lectr. in Dept. of Engl. Studies, Huddersfield Polytechnic. Chmn., Sheffield Authors Club. Published works: Form Photograph, 1971; Signs of Life, 1972. Contbr. to: Anglo-Welsh Review; Country Life; Countryman; English; The Listener; New Statesman; Phoenix; Poetry Review; Times Lit. Supplement; Transatlantic Review; Twentieth Century. Honours, awards: 1st in Hull Arts Ctr./BBC Comp., 1969; 1st In Cheltenham Fest. Poetry Comp., 1972. Address: 600 Barnsley Rd., Sheffield S5 6VA, U.K.

COOKE, Audrey, pen name **FRAZIER, April,** b. 18 Apr. 1926. Educator. Education: B.A., Engl., Marymount Coll., Tarrytown, NY., 1947; M.A., French, Laval Univ., Quebec, Canada, 1950; M.A., Engl., Bread Loaf School of Engl., Middlebury, Vt., 1971; Ph.D., French, Catholic Univ., Washington, D.C., 1960. Positions held: Academic Dean, Marymount Coll., Boca Raton, Fla., to 1966; Directress, Internat. School, Rome, Italy, to 1967; Senior Fellow in Engl. & French, Mackinac Coll., Mackinac Island, Mich., to 1969; Acting Headmistress, Chairman Language Dept., St. Margaret's School, to 1972; Asst. to Headmaster, Chairman Language Dept. St. Margaret's-McTernan School. Membership: World Poetry Soc. Published works: Patterns: A Modern Poetry Anthol., 1970; (in progress: Roman Ruins and Other People (poetry)). Contbr. to: Mexican Quarterly Review; Peninsula Poets; Poet; Poetry Parade; Bardic Echoes; Poetry Pageant. Awards: Summa Cum Laude award by World Poetry Soc., for: Roman Ruins (1970); Prize-winning poem in Writers Digest annual contest, 1969; Hon. mention in Writers Digest annual contest, 1968; Golden Scroll Award, Poetry Pageant, 1969; Special Recording Award from Five Star Music Masters, 1973. Address: 565 Chase Parkway, Waterbury, CT 06720,

USA.

COOKE, Diana (Lady Cooke), pen name **WITHERBY, Diana,** b. 19 Jan. 1915. Poet. Positions held: Staff, Horizon Mag., during WWII. Publications: Poems, 1954; The Heat & the Cold, 1965; Collected Poems, 1973. Contbr. to: Horizon; Encounter; London Mag.; Art & Lit.; Polemic; Penguin New Writing; New Statesman; Listener; Poetry Chicago; Peacock. Various broadcasts, 3rd Prog., BBC. Address: Rectory Farm, Plumpton, Towcester, Northamptonshire, U.K.

COOLEY, Peter John, b. 19 Nov. 1940. College Professor. Education: A.B., Shimer Coll., A.M., Univ. of Chicago; Ph.D., Univ. of Iowa. Positions held: Currently Assoc. Prof., Coll. of Creative Communication, Univ. of Wis.-Green Bay; Poetry Ed., North Am. Review. Published works: How To Go, pamphlet, 1968. Contbr. to: Esquire; Harper's; The New Yorker; The Am. Review; Partisan Review, etc. Address: 331 Skyline Blvd., Green Bay, WI 54302, U.S.A.

COOLIDGE, Clark, b. 26 Feb. 1939. Writer. Education: Brown Univ., 2 yrs. Personal details: Father, Prof. of Music, Brown Univ.; married Susan Hopkins, 1967, 1 d. Positions held: Musician (drums); Lab. Techn.; Disk Jockey; Libn.; Prod., Words, KPFA-FM, Berkeley, Calif. Published works: Flag Flutter & US Electric, 1966; Clark Coolidge, 1967; Ing, 1969; To Obtain the Value of the Cake Measure From Zero (w. Tom Veitch), 1970; Space, 1970; The So, 1970; Moroccan Variations, 1971. Contbr. to: Lines; Angelhair; The World; Paris Review; Juillard; The Herald; The Rolling Stone; Nice; Thrice; Adventures in Poetry; Yale Literary Magazine; The; Big Sky; Strange Faeces; Daily Planet; Art & Literature; Toothpaste; Cum; Elephant; Clothesline; Spectrum; Blue Pig; Ant's Forefoot; Telephone; University Review; Best & Co.; Insect Trust Gazette; Or; Wild Dog; Coyote's Journal; This; Tuatera; Floatingbear; 0 to 9; Bricoleur; Input; Aspen, etc. Awards: Am. Lit. Anthol. Award, 1968; Poets Fndn. Award, 1968. Address: Box 224, New Lebanon, New York 12125, USA.

COONEY, Ellen, b. 23 June 1948. Poet. Education: B.A., Lone Mountain Coll., San Francisco, U.S.A.; grad. work, San Francisco State Univ., Calif., 1973. Published works: Wednesday's Children, 1970. Contbr. to: St. Ignatius Bulletin, 1967; Poetry Pageant, 1969; Gay Sunshine, 1970; Evergreen Review, 1971 & 1973; Prism Int., 1971; Libera Mag., 1973; Aisling Mag., 1973. Address: 707 – 10th Ave., San Francisco, CA 94118, U.S.A.

COOPER, George William Noel, pen name **NOEL-COOPER, George,** b. 21 July 1896. Physician. Education: B.S., M.A., M.D., Fellow, Int. Coll. of Surg. Married, 1 s., 1 d. Positions held: Surgeon, USN, 1944-47; Fac. Mbr., USN Med. Schl., Tulane Univ., La. State Univ., Univ. of Ark., Loyola Univ., New Orleans, La. Memberships: Pres. (2 terms), La. State Poetry Soc., 1967-69; pres. Emeritus, ibid, 1969; Pres. (1 term), Nat. Writers Club of New Orleans, La., 1949-50; Manuscript Club of Atlanta, Ga.; Atlanta Writers Club; Wis. Fellowship of Poets; Mbr. of Bd., Nat. Fed. of State Poetry Socs.; Pres., New Orleans Chapt. No. 2, Int. Boswell Inst., 1968-69; Hon. Int. Rep., Centro Studi e Scambi Int. Published Works: Poems For Peace, 1949; Lace of Sonnets, 1961; Russianism or Christ, 1964. Contbr. to: NY Times; Atlanta Constitution; La. State Poetry Soc. Anthol., 1961; Wis. Fellowship of Poets Anthol., 1961; plus several poetry jrnls. & other anthols. Honours: Commissioned Poet Laureate of Louisiana by Governor Edwin W. Edwards, 15 Mar. 1973. 2nd Prize, Books of Verse, 1949; NY Times Award, 1950; Knight of Palmes Academiques for lit. & cultural works, France, 1961; Poet Laureate of 250th Anniv. Celebrations of New Orleans, La.; Medal & Dip., Centro Studi e Scambi Int., 1970. Address: 7307 St. Charles Ave., New Orleans, La. 70118, USA.

COOPER, Jane Marvel, b. 9 Oct. 1924. Teacher.

Educ: Vassar Coll., Poughkeepsie; B.A., Univ. of Wis.; M.A., Univ. of Iowa. Positions held: Tchr., Poetry & Creative Writing, Sarah Lawrence Coll., Bronxville, 1950-. Published works: The Weather of Six Mornings, 1969. Contbr. to: New Yorker; Transatlantic Review; (anthologies) Best Poems of 1957 & 1967: The Borestone Mountain Poetry Awards, 1958, '68; Midland, 1961; New Poets of England and America, 1962; American Poems, 1964; Modern Occasions, 1966. Honours, awards: Guggenheim Fellowship, 1960-61; Fellowships at Yaddo, 1958, '67 & '68; Lamont Poetry Prize, 1968. Address: c/o Sarah Lawrence Coll., Bronxville, NY 10708, U.S.A.

COOPER, Tennessee, b. 9 Nov. 1937. Education: HS graduate. Occupation: Vending Machine business. Membership: International Platform Assoc. Published work: Drifting, 1973. Contbr. to: Friendly Way; Author/Poet; Army Digest; Phoenix Fires; Major Poets; Best in Poetry; Clam; United Poet; Horizon; Address: 3810 8th St., N.W., Washington, DC 20011, USA.

COPE, Jack, b. 3 June 1913. Writer. Divorced, 2 sons. Positions held: Newspaperman in South Africa; Political Corres., Fleet St., London; Farmer, Natal, S. Africa; Fndr., 1960, of S. African lit. quarterly 'Contrast' & is still Editor; Gen. Ed., Mantis Editions of Southern African Poets, a series started in 1973. Member of South African PEN. Published works: Lyrics & Diatribes (poems), 1948; Marie (satire), 1949; Ed. (w. U. Krige) Penguin Book of South African Verse, 1968; Seismograph, New South African Verse & Other Writing; also published 7 novels, 3 vols. of stories; Translated (w. William Plomer) Selected Poems by Ingrid Jonker (from Afrikaans), 1968. Contbr. to: Poetry Commonwealth; Vandag; Izwi; Unisa English Studies. Address: El Dorado, P.O. Onrust River 7201, Cape, South Africa.

COPPEDGE, George Herman, Jr., pen name **JUBILATE,** b. 5 Sept. 1922. Poet; Taxi Dispatcher. Education: A.B., Washington Coll., 1943; Howard Univ. School of Religion; S.T.B., Temple Univ. 1952. Positions held: Methodist Minister, 1948-54; School Teacher, 1955-63; Social Worker, 1964-70; Taxi-Driver-Dispatcher, 1971-. Memberships: Internat. Platform Assoc.; Internat. Poetry Soc. Published works: World Cathedralic, 1968; George's Song, 1971. Contbr. to: Delaware Poets, 1960-61; Delaware State News; Coppedge Family Bulletin, Vol. XIII, July, 1962; Internat. Who's Who in Poetry Anthol., 1972-73; Nutrition Today; The Spring Anthol., 1973; Own radio show WKIK Leonardtown: Jubilate Speaks. Awards: Silver Pitcher, Annapolis Fine Arts Festival, Md. State Poetry Soc. 1971, etc. Address: Box 154, Valhalla, Lexington Park, MD 20653, USA.

CORBLUTH, Elsa, b. 2 Aug. 1928. Housewife & Clerk. Married David Boadella, 1 son, 1 daughter. Positions held: Asst. Libn., etc. Memberships: Chesil Poets, Dorset; The Poetry Soc.; Bridport Arts Soc.; Abbotsbury Players, drama soc. (Org. & Initiator). Published works: Stone Country, 1970. Contbr. to: Outposts; Workshop New Poetry; Phoenix; Envoi; Voice; Chesil. Recip., Arnold Vincent Bowen Prize for Lyric Poem, Poetry Soc., 1973. Address: 1 Back St., Abbotsbury, Weymouth, Dorset, U.K.

CORDELL, Ida Lee, b. 12 Nov. 1920. Poet. Education: 2 yrs. of study in Poetry. Married Dewey Cordell, 4 children. Member, Lit. Soc., Int. Platform Assn. of Cleveland Heights, Ohio. Published works: Echoes Along Rhythm Lane, 1969. Contbr. to: Jean's Jrnl.; Inky Trail; Ideals Mag.; Poetry Prevue; Poets Bulletin; Spafaswap; These are my Jewels Anthol.; Insight Mag.; Tejas Mag.; IWWP Anthol., etc. Recip. var. awards. Address: 30 Badger St., Greenville, SC 29605, U.S.A.

CORKE, Hilary, b. 1921. Freelance Writer. Educ: Charterhouse; Christ Church, Oxford, U.K. Married to Sylvia Bridges, four children. Positions held: Served in the Royal Artillery, 1941-45; Lectr., Cairo Univ., Egypt;

Lectr., Univ. of Edinburgh, Scotland; Freelance Writer, 1956–. Published works: The Early Drowned, 1961; Ed. (w. William Plomer & Anthony Thwaite), New Poems, 1961: The P.E.N. Anthology, 1961. Contbr. to: Encounter; London Magazine; Times Literary Supplement; Listener; New Yorker; Harper's Magazine; (anthologies) New Voices, 1959; An Anthology of Modern Verse 1940-60, 1961; Penguin Book of Contemporary Verse, 1962; New Lines II, 1963; Poetry Now, 1968. Address: Abinger Hammer, Surrey, U.K.

CORLEY, Viola C., pen name, CORLEY, Vi., b. 8 Oct. 1888. Art Teacher (retired). Education: Cocoran School of Art, Wahington, DC. Positions held: Art Teacher (23 yrs.). Memberships: Poetry Soc. of Texas (Member of Council). Published works: The G.I's. Travelled Texas; Man, 1949. Contbr. to many newspapers, magazines, etc. Recip. of sev. prizes, certificates, etc. Address: 1102 Orion Dr., Portland, TX 78374, USA.

CORMAN, Cid, b. 29 June 1924. Editor. Educ: Boston Latin Schl.; B.A., Tufts Coll., Medford, 1945; Univ. of Mich., 1946-47; Univ. of N.C., 1947; The Sorbonne, Paris, France, 1954-55. Married. Positions held: Taught in Europe & Japan; Ed., Origin periodical, Kyoto, Japan, 1951–. Published works: subluna, 1945; Thankgiving Ecologue, 1954; The Precisions, 1955; The Responses, 1956; Stances and Distances, 1957; The Marches, 1957; A Table in Provenance, 1958; The Descent from Daimonji, 1959; For Sure, 1959; In Good Time, 1964; In No Time, 1964; For You, 1966; For Granted, 1966; Words for Each Other, 1968; & Without End, 1968; No More, 1969; Plight, 1969; Livingdying, 1970. Honours, awards: Hopwood Award in poetry, 1946-47; Chapelbrook Fndn. Grant, 1967-69. Address: c/o Yamada Art Gallery, 253 Umemotocho, Shinmonzen, Higashiyama-ku, Kyoto, Japan.

CORNETT, Frances Boggs, pen name CORNETT, Fran, b. 27 Apr. 1937. Housewife. Education; two coll. level Engl. courses; attended sev. writing workshops. Married, 3 children. Memberships: Nat. Fed. of State Poetry Socs.; Bd. Dirs., Mbrship Chmn., Ky. State Poetry Soc.; Louisville Writers Club; Western World Haiku Soc. Contbr. to: Modern Haiku; Haiku Mag.; Haiku West; Dragonfly; Twigs & Wind Mag., etc. Honours, awards: Hon. Mention, Haiku Mag., 1970 & '71, Ky. State Poetry Soc., 1971 & Modern Haiku, 1971 & '72; 3rd pl., Ky. State Poetry Soc., 1973; 1st pl., Tejas, 1969. Address: 1754 Algonquin Parkway, Louisville, KY 40210, U.S.A.

CORNING, Howard McKinley, b. 23 Oct. 1896. Poet; Journalist; Historian; Librarian; Editor; Sales Promotion Executive. Memberships: Poetry Soc. of Am.; Pres., 4 terms, Ore. State Poetry Assoc. Published works: These People, 1926; The Mountain In The Sky, 1930; This Earth & Another Country, 1969. Contbr. to: Saturday Review; Nation; New Republic; Am. Mercury; Poetry (Chicago); Voices; NY Herald Trib.; NY Times; CS Monitor; Oregonian; Contemporary Verse; Lyric West; Frontier & Midland; Midwest Quarterly; Chicago Trib.; SD Review; Mod. Am. Poetry, 1930, 1936; The New Poetry, 1932; L.A.G. Strong's Best, 1927, etc. Honours: William Marion Reedy Award, Poetry Soc. of Am., 1965. Address: 1110 SE 16th Ave., Portland, Ore. 97214, USA.

CORNISH, Samuel James, 22 Dec. 1935. Consultant; Editor. Married Jean Cornish, 1967. Positions held: Served in Armed Forces, 1958-60; Former Ed., Chicory, Enoch Pratt Lib., Baltimore; Cons., Humanities Prog., Central Atlantic Regional Educational Laboratories, currently; Ed., Mimeo magazine, currently. Published works: In This Corner, 1961; People Under the Window, 1962; Generations, 1964; Angels, 1965; Winters, 1968; Missing Afternoon (essay), 1968; Co-Ed., Chicory. Contbr. to: Ann Arbor Review; Poetry Review; Journal of Black Poetry; (anthologies) Black Fire, 1968; New Black Poetry, 1969; American Literary Anthology 3, 1970. Recip., grant from Nat. Endowment for the Arts, 1967.

Address: 12 E. Read St., Baltimore, MD, U.S.A.

CORRINGTON, John William, b. 28 Oct. 1932. Professor of Literature. Education: A.B., 1956; M.A., Rice Univ., 1969; D.Phil., Univ. of Sussex, 1964. Married to Joyce Elaine Hooper, 4 children. Positions held: Asst. Prof., La. State Univ., 1960-65; Assoc. Prof., Loyola Univ., 1966–; Vis. Prof., Univ. of Calif., Berkeley, 1968. Published works: Where we are, 1962; Mr. Clean & other poems, 1963; The Anatomy of Love, 1964; Lines to the South, 1965. Contbr. to num. jrnls., mags., newspapers, etc. Honours: Charioteer Poetry Prize, 1962; Nat. Endowment for the Arts Award, 1967. Address: Rt. 1, Box 186, Covington, La. 70433, USA.

CORSO, Gregory, b. 26 Mar. 1930. Writer. Education: Grammar Schl. Positions held: Manual Laborer, 1950-51; w. Los Angeles Examiner, 1951-52; Merchant Seaman, 1952-53; Appeared in 2 Andy Warhol films; associated w. Allen Ginsberg, Jack Kerouac & Lawrence Ferlinghetti & the early Beat poets in Am. Published works: The Vestal Lady on Brattle & Other Poems, 1955; Bomb, 1958; Gasoline, 1958; Happy Birthday of Death, 1960; Long Live Man, 1962; Selected Poems, 1962; There Is Yet Time To Run Back Through Life & Expiate All That's Been Sadly Done, 1965. Contbr. to: A Controversy of Poets & Other anthols. & mags. Honours: Longview Award for poem Marriage; $1,000 award from Poetry Fndn. Address: c/o New Directions Publishing Corp., 333 6th Ave., New York, NY 10014, USA.

CORTEZ, Jayne, b. 5 Oct. 1936. Writer. Positions held: Guest Poet/Lecturer on Univ. & Coll. Campuses throughout the United States. Published works: Pisstained Stairs & the Monkey Man's Wares, 1969; Festivals & Funerals, 1971; Scarifications, 1973. Rep. in following anthols: We Speak as Liberators; Black Aesthetic; New Black Voices; Rock Against the Wind; The Poetry of Black America. Contbr. to: Confrontation; Discourses on Poetry; Pan African Jrnl.; Mundus Artium; Works; Black World; Black Dialogue; Umbra; Am. Dialogue; Essence Mag. Recip., The N.Y. State Coun. of the Arts C.A.P.s Award for Poetry, 1973. Address: P.O. Box 249, Village Stn., N.Y., NY 10014, U.S.A.

CORYLLIS, Peter, b. 19 July 1909. Writer. Married, 2 children. Positons held: Creator & Fndr., Kreis der Freunde; Publsr., Vier Groschenbogen; Memberships: Kogge; podinm Salzburg; Writers' Union; Saarbrücken Lit. Union; Regensburger Writers' Grp.; Turmbund Innsbruck, Tukan Munich, Wiesbaden. Published works incl: Rost auf Gottes Geboten, 1961; Der Himmel hat keine Gewehre, 1962; Und der Abgrund ist nicht das Ende, 1962, Die Schöpfung, 1961, '72, '74; Licht unterm Bröckenbogen, 1965; Menschen Gesichter Stationen, 1965; In den Segeln der Wind, 1966; So schön ist die Welt, 1967, '74; Neuestzeit Weihnachtslegende, 1968; Unterwegs, 1969; Unkenrufe und ein Quentchen Wahrheit, 1969; Salzburg, Das Wunder einer Stadt, 1970; Fresken, 1971; Hinter die Grünen Stachelwehr, 1974; Im Zeitenlauf, 1973; Zwischen Gestern und Morgen Leuchtet die Mitternacht, 1973; Meine Haut Atmet Herbst, 1974; Du im Du, 1973; Peter Coryllis in Vertonungen von Stephan Cosacchi, 1973; Im Kosmos daheim, 1974; Vagabunden-Brevier, 1973. Num. publs. in var. organs of Lit. press & major newspapers; num. translations. Honours, awards: Lit Prize, 125th Jubilee Year, Malkasten Dusseldorf; Trees for Israel – in Hon. of Mr. & Mrs. Peter Coryllis – planted by Dr. H.E. Nathorff, N.Y., 1973. Address: Postfach 1126/Peppermuhl 26, D 4408 Dulmen, German Fed. Repub.

COSGRAVE, Pearl-Joan, b. 2 May 1906. Writer-Lecturer. Education: B.Sc., A.M., Univ. of Nebraska, at Lincoln; grad. study further at Univ. of Denver, Colorado; Univ. of Chicago, Illinois; Univ. of Wisconsin at Madison; Colorado State Univ. at Fort Collins. Personal details: Daughter of the late Judge (Colonel) and Mrs. P. James Cosgrave. Positions held: various Coll. and Univ. teaching positions, and also business positions. Memberships: Internat. Poetry Soc., UK (Fellow); NLAPW, Omaha Branch; Nebraska Writers Guild (Pres. twice); Omaha Writers Conference (member of Panel, 1948); Chi Delta Phi., etc. Contbr. to: Prairie Schooner (Assoc. Ed., 1933-1937); Nature Mag. (now known as Nat. History Mag.); Internat. Who's Who in Poetry Anthol.; Selected Poems, 1967; Poetic Voice of America, 1940; Book of Modern Poetry, 1941, etc. Awards: UPLI, 1970, and others. Address: Century House, Lincoln, NB 68508, USA.

COTTON, John, b. 7 Mar. 1925. Headmaster. Education: B.A. (Hons.), London Univ., U.K. Married, 2 sons. Positions held: Ed., Priapus, a mag. of poetry & art, 1962-72; Headmaster, Highfield Comprehensive Schl., Hertfordshire, 1963–; Ed., The Private Library, 1969–. Memberships: Coun., The Poetry Soc., 1971–; Chmn., The Poetry Soc., 1972–. Published works: Outside the Gates of Eden, 1969; Poetry: Introduction 1, 1969; Old Movies & Other Poems, 1971; Photographs – a Sycamore Press Broadsheet, 1973. Contbr. to: Encounter; Observer; New Statesman; Tribune; Poetry Chicago; Outposts; The Poetry Review; Second Aeon; Phoenix; Priapus; Solstice; New Measure; Form; The Transatlantic Review; Fishpaste; Best S.F. No. 3 & 6 (Sphere Books); P.E.N. Anthologies, 1965 & 67. Honours, awards: 2nd Prize, Critical Quarterly Poetry Comp., 1963; 'Old Movies' recommended by the Poetry Book Soc., 1971; Publication Award, The Arts Coun. of G.B. Address: 37 Lombardy Dr., Berkhamsted, Herts., U.K.

COULET DU GARD, Rene, b. 29 Dec. 1919. Professor of Literature (French). Education: M.S., Univ. of Pa., U.S.A., 1963; Doctor's degree, Univ. of Besançon, France, 1966. Positions held: Prin., Ecole d'Apprentissage, Casablanca, Morocco, 1946-52; French Tchr., Kimberton Schl., U.S.A., 1957-62 & Ursinus Coll., 1962-63; French & Spanish, West Chester State Coll., Pa., 1963-66; Prof. of Lit., Univ. of Delaware, 1966–. Memberships: President des Amitiés iques Pétiques et Littéraires de Casablanca, Morocco; Sociétaire de la Société Culturelle et Philanthropique de France. Published works: Poémes pour Dire, 1960; L'Epopée Algérienne, vols. I, II, 1964, '67; Les Poèmes du Boueux, 1968; Feux Follets, 1969; L'Arithmosophie de Gérard de Nerval, essays, 1972; Reine, novel, 1973. Contbr. to: Les Echos du Monde; Creation et Critique; Sequences, etc. Honours, awards: 1st Prize, Academie des Jeux Floraux de Tunisie, 1953; Mention tres Honorable, Internationale des Arts et des Lettres, 1960; Silver Medal & Dip. of Hon., Lutece Int. Acad., Paris, 1973. Address: Lang. & Lit. Dept., Univ. of Delaware, Newark, DE 19711, U.S.A.

COULETTE, Henri, b. 11 Nov. 1927. Professor of English; Associate Editor. Educ: B.A., Los Angeles State Coll., 1952; M.F.A. & Ph.D., Univ. of Iowa, 1954. Married to Jacqueline Meredith. Positions held: Served in the U.S. Army, 1945-46; Lectr., Univ. of Iowa, 1957-59; Prof., Engl., Calif. State Coll., L.A., 1959–; Assoc. Ed., Midland. Published works: The War of the Secret Agents, 1966; Ed. (w. Philip Levine), Character and Crisis (essays), 1966. Contbr. to: New Yorker; Hudson Review; Paris Review; (anthologies) New Poets of England and America, 1957, '62; Poetry for Pleasure, 1960; Midland, 1961; Poet's Choice, 1962; Contemporary American Poets, 1969. Recip., Lamont Poetry Award, 1965. Address: 1901 Oxley St., S. Pasadena, CA, U.S.A.

COUPER, John Mill, b. 7 Sept. 1914. University Lecturer. Education: M.A., Aberdeen Univ., Scotland, UK, 1935; Ph.D., ibid, 1948. Positions held: Tchr., Scottish Schls., until 1951; Lectr. in Educ., Univ. of Qld., Australia, 1951-54; Hdmaster., Knox Grammar Schl., 1954-55; Lectr. in Engl., 3 colls. & univs., 1955–. Published works: East of Living, 1967; The Book of Bligh, 1969; The Thundering Good Today, 1970. Contbr. to: Meanjin; Southerly; Sydney Morning Herald; The Australian; The Bulletin; The Age; Westerly; Lines Review; Recip. of Moomba Prize for The Book of Bligh, 1970. Address: 9 Dudley St.,

Asquith, NSW, Australia 2078.

COUPEY, Pierre Louis Marcel, b. 17 Aug. 1942. Writer. Education: B.A., McGill Univ., 1964; M.A., Univ. of B.C., 1971; studied drawing at Academie Julian, Paris, 1965 & print-making, Atelier 17, 1965. Married, 2 children. Positions held: Fndng. Ed. w. Bill Bissett, Patrick Lane & Seymour Mayne, Verystone House Press, 1967; Fndng.Ed. w. Milton Acorn, Rick Kitaeff, Peter Hlookoff, The Georgia Straight, 1967; Fndng.Ed., The Western Gate, 1968; Ed., The Capilano Review, Capilano Coll., 1972–. Mbr., Canadian Artists Representation. Published works: Bring Forth the Cowards, 1964; Circle Without Center, 1968; Terminal Series, 1973. Rep. in the following anthols: The Penguin Book of Canadian Verse, 1967; To Every Thing There is a Season, 1968; West Coast Seen, 1969; Three Hours Later, 1973. Contbr. to sev. reviews & jrnls. Poetry readings at: McGill Univ.; UBC Fest. of Contemporary Arts; The Vancouver Art Gall., etc. Recip., sev. prizes, awards & grants inclng: Louis B. Shapiro Award for Poetry, McGill Univ., 1964; H.R. MacMillan Award for Poetry, UBC, 1966. Address: The Capilano Review, 2055 Purcell Way, N. Vancouver, B.C., Canada.

COUROUCLI, Jennifer Rosemary, b. 21 Aug. 1922. Housewife. Married, 2 daughters, 1 step-daughter, 1 step-son. Positions held: served in A.T.S., WWII; Voluntary Wkr. for the Greek Animal Welfare Fund. Published works: On This Athenian Hill, 1969. Contbr. to: The New York Times; The Hibernian; School Anthol. Address: Fokilidou 2, Athens 136, Greece.

COUSENS, Mildred, b. 29 May 1904. Housewife. Education: Grad., Radcliffe Coll., U.S.A.; further study, Harvard Univ. & at the Tufts poetry Workshop. Married Theodore W. Cousens. Positions held: Engl. Tchr., 1 yr. Memberships: Poetry Soc. of Am.; New England Poetry Club; Pres. for one term, Rochester, N.Y., Poetry Soc. Contbr. to: The Transatlantic Review; Hudson Review; Va. Qtly. Review; Literary Review; Prairie Schooner; Colo. Qtly.; Western Humanities Review; Beloit Poetry Jrnl.; Epos; Voices; The Lyric; South & West; Harper's Bazaar; Ladies Home Jrnl.; Hawk & Whippoorwill; Univ. Review; N.Y. Times; Christian Sci Monitor; Poet Lore; Chicago Tribune Mag.; Kans. City Star; The Humanist; The Am. Scholar; Sat. Review; Fiddlehead; Impetus; Audience; Educational Forum: Imprints Qtly.; New Hampshire Profiles; Bitterroot; Spirit; Christian Herald. Honours, awards: Gwendolyn Brooks Award, Approach, 1964; Phyllida Award, The Lyric, 1971; Love Poem Category Award, Poet Lore, 1971; Second Prize, National Federation State Poetry Societies' Grand Award, 1972; Special Mention, Stroud Festival Poetry Contest, 1973, etc. Address: 7 Craigie Circle, Apt. 42, Cambridge, MA 02138, U.S.A.

COUTERMASH, John H., pen names BYRON, Christopher, AUGUSTINE, Luther, BARRETT, Lucian, SANTAYANA, Adrian & McLAREN, Davis, b. 23 Mar. 1942. Little Magazine Publisher & Editor. Education: Danbury State Tchrs. Coll., Conn., 1 yr. Married, 1 son. Has held var. positions, & is currently the Publisher, Editor of The Lunatic Fringe. Contbr. to: Island Lantern, 1972; Speak Out, 1972; Action, 1971-74; Wind, 1973; Spafaswap, 1972; Bachaet, 1969-71; Encore, 1973; Tejas, 1972; South & West, 1970-73; The Clock, 1971-72; The Lunatic Fringe; The Raiford Record, 1972-73; Invictus, 1972-73, etc. Recip. var. poetry awards. Address: Highview Rd., Pound Ridge, NY 10576, U.S.A.

COUTSOHERAS, John, b. 1904. Poet; Politician. Education: Univ. of Athens; Univ. of Paris, Sorbonne. Positions held: Lawyer, Athens, 1927; Athens City Councillor, 1945: V.P., YMCA, Greece, 1948: Pres., Soc. of Greek Problems, 1956; V.P., Hippocratic Int. Fndn., 1960–; Pioneer for the rural social insurances in Greece, & the vote for women; V.P., Int. Fndn. for the Delphic Amphicyonies, 1965–: Past Mbr., Greek Comm. for the Rights of Man; Past Mbr. of Parliament, Greece. Memberships: Pres., PEN, Greece; Fndr. of the Int. Ctr. of the World Citizen – Cosmopolitis; V.P., Friends of Contemporary Theatre; Comm. Mbr., Greek Lit. Assn.; Comm. Mbr., Lit. League of 'Parnassus'; Hon. Comm. in France of the Syndicat des Journalistes et Ecrivains, Cercle Int. de la Pensée et des Arts Français, & Arts et Poésie; Published works: Thoughts & Echoes, 1942; Blue Breaths, 1949; Greek Nights, 1954; Poesie et Langage, 1954; The Supper of Bethany, 1959; The March of the Lilies, 1959; Jordan the Ever Running, 1960: Smoke Spiring up, 1960: Faccia a Faccia, 1960: The Golgotha, 1961; Markos Evgenikos, 1964: Autour de la Poesie, 1965; The Man and the Sea, 1965: The Charioteer, 1966: Hommes Pour Les Droits de l'homme, levez-vous, 1969; Avec l'aile de la mouette et le trident de Poseidon, 1972. Contbr. to: Le Journal des Poetes; Il Giornale dei Poeti: Poesie et Langage; Voix des Poetes; Sequences; Poesie Vivante; Scarabee; Revue Independante; Signior Si; Masques et Visages: Relations Latines; Peau de Serpent; Das Lied des Parnass; Parabels Freie Akadamies der Kunste in Hamburg; Ubersetzen; Caracola. Honours, awards: Medaglia d'oro di Poesia, Rome, 1969; Prix 'Auguste Marin', Belgium, 1970: Grand Prix de la Poesie libre. des Journalistes et Ecrivains, Paris, 1970 (for his poetical manifesto 'Men for Human Rights, Arise!', rep. at the official award by René Cassin, Nobel Peace Prize & Pres. of European Ct. of Human Rights); Grand Prix Intern. de Poésie du Cercle Int., de la Pensée et des Arts Français, 1970; Prix de la Palme d'Or de Paris-Critique, 1971; Chevalier de l'Ordre Celtique 1971. Medaille d'Or du CIPAF 1972 etc. Address: 60 a Skoufa St., Athens 144, Greece.

COWLEY, Malcolm, b. 24 Aug. 1898. Writer; Editor. Education: A.B., Harvard Univ., 1920. Married, Muriel Maurer, 1932, 1 s. Positions held: Lit. Ed., New Republic, 1929-44; Lit. Advsr., Viking Press, 1948–; Vis. Prof., various univs. Memberships: Pres., Nat. Inst. of Arts & Letters, 1956-59, '62-65; Chancellor, Am. Acad. Arts & Letters, 1968–. Published works: Blue Juniata, 1929; The Dry Season, 1941; Blue Juniata: Collected Poems, 1968. Contbr. to: Poetry Mag.; New Yorker; Harper's; Sat. Review; Southern Review, etc. Honours, Awards: Poetry Mag., 1927, '39; Nat. Endowment for the Arts, 1967. Address: Sherman, Conn. 06784, USA.

COX, Hardin Charles, pen name **NONNIE NU NU,** b. 4 Mar. 1928. Democratic State Representative. Education: A.B., Univ. of Mo., Columbia. Married Virginia Ann Heifner, 2 children (Charles & Mark). Positions held: Operator, General Insurance Agency, Cox & Son & the Hardin Cox Real Estate Brokerage, Farm Loan Agency, Rock Port, 15 yrs.; Treas., Farmers Mutual Ins. Co., Rock Port; Treas., Farmers Mutual Hail Insurance Co. & Farmers Mutual Windstorm Ins. Co., Columbia; Elected to House of Reps., 1964, re-elected in 1966 & '68; Chmn., Comm. on Flood Control & Soil Conservation, Mbr. of Elections & on State Parks & Recreation Comms., 75th Gen. Assembly. Memberships: Sigma Chi: Omicron Delta Kappa; QEBH; Ancient Free & Accepted Masons; Am. Legion; Mo. Univ. Alumni Assn.; Mo. Alumni Athletic Coun. Dist. No. 1. Address: 605 Bluff St., Rock Port, MO 64482, U.S.A.

COX, Joseph Mason Andrew, b. 12 July 1923. Poet; Writer; Inventor; Lawyer; College Lecturer. Education: B.A., Columbia Univ., U.S.A., 1945; LL.B., LaSalle Law Schl., 1949; Doctorate Art Psychol., China Art Coll., World Univ., 1972. Positions held: Reporter & Feature Writer, St. Thomas Daily News, N.Y. Age, N.Y. Post; Pres., Afro-Asian Purchasing Commn.; Lectr., The City Univ. of N.Y.; Asst. Prof., Medgar Evers Coll., ibid. Memberships: The Authors League of Am.; Former Exec. Bd., The Poetry Soc. of Am.; Poetry Soc. of London; Acad. of Am. Poets; United Poets Laureate Int.; Centro Studi e Scambi Int. Published works: The Shore Dimly Seen; The Search; The Cracked Wall; Ode to Dr. Martin Luther King, Jr.; The Collected Poetry of Joseph Mason Andrew Cox. Contbr. to: Spring Anthol. (England); Golden Quill Anthol.; Poems by Blacks; Etudes Litteraires; World Poets Quarterly;

The N.Y. Post; The Amsterdam News; The Afro-American; The Community News; The Moon Age Poets; Master Poets Quarterly; Bouquet of Poems, Centro Studi e Scambi Int. Honours, awards: Daniel S. Mead Int. Award, 1964; Pres. Johnson's Great Soc. Award (Writers), 1965; Moon Age Poetry Award, 1970; Fellow, Int. Poetry Soc.; World Poets Award, 1971; Int. Poet Laureate, 1972; U.S. Rep., World Poetry Conf., Expo 67, Montreal. Address: 353 W. 57th St., N.Y., NY 10019, U.S.A.

COXE, Louis Osborne, b. 15 Apr. 1918. Professor of English. Educ: B.A., Princeton Univ., 1940. Married, four children. Positions held: Served in the U.S.N., 1942-46; Pierce Prof. of Engl., Bowdoin Coll., Brunswick, 1955–. Published works: The Sea Faring, 1947; The Second Man, 1955; The Wilderness, 1958; The Middle Passage, 1960; The Last Hero, 1964; Nikal Seyn and Decoration Day, 1966; Billy Bud (play), 1962; Edwin Arlington Robinson (literary criticism), 1969. Honours, awards: Sewanee Review Fellowship, 1956; Fulbright Lectureship, 1959-60; Brandeis Univ. Creative Arts Award, 1962. Address: Bowdoin Coll., Brunswick, ME 04011, U.S.A.

COX, Naomi D., b. 14 Sept. 1906. Teacher. Education: M.A., Marshall Univ., Huntington, W. Va. Memberships: Parkersburg Poetry Soc. (Sec., 1972); West Va. State Poetry Soc. Published works: Poverty Poems, 1968; Mindy, 1973. Contbr. to: Poetry (Chicago); Poet (India); NEA Journal; WVEA Journal; American Poet; United Poet; American Poetry League; Major Poets; The Ravenswood New; Echoes of West Va. Awards: West Va. State Poetry Contest, 1971; Virginia Randall Lyric Award, 1960. Address: Rte. 1, Box 172, Ravenswood, WV 26164, USA.

COX, Patrick Brian, pen name **STUART, Kenneth,** b. 19 Apr. 1914. Author; Journalist; Poet; Public Relations. Education: B.A., Univ. of Melbourne, Australia, 1949; Dip. in Journalism, ibid, 1968; Dip. Supérieur d'Etudes Françaises Modernes (Paris), 1972. Positions held: Reporter, Reviewer, 'The Argus' & 'The Australasian', 1947-48; Contbg. Ed., 'New International Illustrated Encyclopaedia', 1953; currently Exec. Dir., Cosmos PR Enterprises; Critic, Nation-Wide Lit. Services, Melbourne, 1972–; Editor, Kaleidoscope, 1959– (suspended 1972). Memberships: Australian Corres., 'Le Bayou', Univ. of Houston, Tex., USA, 1953–; Del.-Gen. for Australasia, Academie Populaire de Litterature et Poesie (nr. Paris, France), 1958–; Del.-Gen. for Victoria, Poetry Soc. of Australia, 1957–; Regent in Australia, Avalon World Arts Acad., 1956–; Australian Poetry Lovers' Soc.; Melbourne Shakespeare Soc.; Fndr., Dir., Cosmosynthesis League & Int. Guild of Contemporary Bards; Fellow, Royal Soc. of Arts; Fellow, Int. Inst. of Arts & Letters; Pres., Melbourne Shakespeare Soc. 1972–; Acting Pres., Internat. P.E.N. (Melbourne), 1970; Hon. Life Fellow, Intercontinental Biographical Assoc., (1972). Published works: Hooded Falcon/Faucon Chaperonné (bilingual), 1957; Singing Forest, 1958; Roses Aflame, 1964; Lineaments, 1968; The Roseate Flame, 1971; Testament to Love, 1969; Collected Poems (forthcoming). Contbr. to: Week-End Review; Poetry & The Play; Melody; Poetry Review; Hong Kong Sunday Herald; Eastern Pictorial; Comment; Farrago; Focus; Arena; Pertinent; Argus; Australasian Post; Cath. Weekly; Language; Mia Mia Monthly; Indian Review; Marches de France; Quicksilver; Kaleidograph; Step Ladder; Different; Flame; Miscellaneous Man; I Efimerida ton Poiiton; Harmony; Prism; Revue Internationale de Culture Française; North Queensland Register; D.I.B. Monthly; The Swordsman Review; The Angels; Flame; Séquences; L'Encyclopédie Poétique; Présence; Art et Poésie; American Poet; Prairie Poet; United Poets; Laurel Leaves; Bedsitter; Quintessence; Bohemia; The Western Mail; The Countryman; Language; Melbourne Graduate; Melbourne Univ. Mag.; Present Opinion; Southerly; Australian Woman's Mirror; New Melody; London Anthol.; Outposts; The Poet; Poet (India); Experiment; Modernalia; The Muse; Kaleidoscope; Scintilla, and many others, including anthols. Honours: Grand Cross of the Emperor Justinian, Patriarchate of Alexandria; Apostolic Del. of the Ancient & Mystical Order of Antioch; Medals from Accademia Leonardo da Vinci, & Centro Studi e Scambi Internazionali; F.I.B.A., 1972; Hon. Poet Laureate (UPLI), 1965, with added gold medals and diplomas to 1970; Litt.D. (Univ. Libre, Asie), 1968; D.D. (Univ. Philotechnique, Mysore), 1960; Litt.D., LL.D. (Minerva), 1958, 1960; Contemporary Poets' Internat. Hall of Fame (UPLI), 1967; Dip. of Merit as Internat. Poet (Committee on Arts & Culture of the 1971 Consitutional Convention, Philippines), 1973; World Poetry Soc. Awards, etc., etc. Address: Box 2108-S, GPO, Melbourne, Victoria, Australia 3001.

CRAIG, Alexander, b. 22 Feb. 1923. Educator. Education: Univ. of Melbourne; Univ. of Iowa, USA with AIF, New Guinea, WWII. Tchr.; Univ. of Iowa; Dir., Creative Writing Prog., Colby Coll., Me., 1964-66; Lectr., Schl. of Engl. Studies, Macquarie Univ., NSW, Australia, 1967–. Published works: Far-back Country, 1954; The Living Sky, 1964. Address: c/o Angus & Robertson Ltd., 89 Castlereagh St., Sydney, Australia.

CRAMER, Hallie Agnes, pen name CRAMER, Hallie, b. 23 Jul. 1897. Sales Associate (retired). Education: Grades and HS, Toledo, Ohio; evening courses in creative writing, Toledo Univ.; 5 week-long writing workshops at Univ. of Kentucky. Married. Memberships: Toledo Chapter, Ohio Poetry Soc. (Charter member, and has held all offices); Ohioana Library Assoc.; Lasco Club (Lasalles) (Life Member); Friends of the Library (Toledo); Oral Arts Workshop; Acad. of American Poets. Published works: The Tapestry We Weave, 1971; Of Frost and Fire, 1972. Contbr. to: Second Spring (pub. of Writer's Workshop, 4 issues, 1969-70-71-72); Toledo Blade; Columbus Dispatch; Tampa Tribune; Poet; Poet Lore; Old Hickory Review; Bethany Press; The Christian; Telescope Messenger; Ohio Poetry Day brochure; Second Spring; Kentucky. Awards: Ohio Poetry Day winning poems: 1960; 1962; 1963; 1965; 1966; 1968; 1969; 1970; 1971; 1973. Interviewed & read her poetry on WSPD-TV Channel 13. Address: 2915 Midwood Ave., Toledo, OH 43606, USA.

CRANDALL, Norma, b. 20 Nov. 1907. Writer; Editor; Book Reviewer; Biographer; Literary Advisor. Education: Barnard Coll., Columbia Univ., N.Y.C., U.S.A.; Lycee, Paris, France. Positions held: Freelance Editl. Advsr. for N.Y. Publishers specializing in Engl. & French fiction & non fiction, beginning w. Harcourt Brace Co., N.Y.C., 1939-40. Memberships: Poetry Soc. of Am.; Bronte Soc. of England; Author's Guild N.Y.; Patron Acad. of Am. Poets; Barnard Coll. Club of N.Y.C. Published works: Emily Bronte: A Psychological Portrait, Kraus Reprint Co., N.Y., 1970. Contbr. of reviews, essays & articles to: The New Republic; The Nation; The New Leader; Trace; The North Am. Review; The New Review; N.Y. Times Book Review; The Humanist; The Chicago Review; The Readers' Digest (in collab. w. late husband); Town & Country Review (poetry), etc. A Dramatic Reading, An Evening with the Brontes, has been presented in many lib. & art gall. auditoriums. Address: Apt. 1B – 44 E. 63rd St., N.Y., NY 10021, U.S.A.

CRANWELL, Andrew, Jr., pen name CRANWELL, Andi, b. 29 Apr. 1954. Student. Education: Huddersfield Technical Coll.; Huddersfield Polytechnic. Memberships: Comm. Mbr., Inner Circle Poetry & Music Soc.; Fndr. Mbr., Ludd's Mill mag. Contbr. to Ludd's Mill mag. Address: 29 Blackmoorfoot Rd., Crosland Moor, Huddersfield, U.K.

CRAWFORD, John William, b. 2 Sept. 1936. Teacher. Education: B.A., Ouachita Univ., U.S.A., 1959; M.A., Drake Univ., 1962; Ph.D., Okla. State Univ., 1968. Positions held: H.S. Engl. Instr., Greene Co., Iowa, 1959-62; Instr. of Engl., Clinton Coll., Iowa, 1962-66; Assoc. Prof. of Engl., Henderson State Coll., Ark., 1967-73; Prof. of Engl., ibid, 1973–. Memberships: Ark. Roundtable; Ozark Writers' Guild; Int. Poetry Soc.

Contbr. to: Counterpoint; Iowa Poetry Jrnl.; Miss. Poetry Jrnl.; Ark. Roundtable Anthol.; Encore; Ark. Gazette; Little Rock Times; Contemporary Poets of Ark.; Cyclo-Flame, etc. Recip. var. poetry awards inclng. Iowa Poetry Assn. Hon. Awards. Address: Box H-2652, Henderson State Coll., Arkadelphia, AR 71923, U.S.A.

CRAWLEY, Margaret, b. 14 June 1942. Editorial Assistant. Married. Positions held: Quality control checking diodes & rectifiers for use in Radios, Computers, etc.; Sewing Machinist, Clothing factory; Editl. Asst., Greeting Card Co. Contbr. to: anthols. published by London Lit. Editions; Atlantic Press; Janay Publishing Co. Recip., 2nd Prize, Atlantic Press Poet of the Year, 1971. Address: 1 Treviot Close, Corby, Northants, U.K.

CREELEY, Robert White, b. 21 May, 1926. Teacher; Editor. Educ: Harvard Coll.; B.A., Black Mountain Coll., 1955; M.A., Univ. of N.M., Albuquerque, 1960. Married, three children. Positions held: Tchr., Black Mountain Coll., 1955-56, Univ. of N.M., 1961-62, 1963-66, 1968-69, Univ. of B.C., Canada, 1962-63; Tchr., Dept. of Engl., S.U.N.Y., Buffalo, U.S.A., 1966–; Former Assoc. Ed., Fragmente, Freiburg im Breisgau, Germany; Former Ed., Black Mountain Review, seven years. Published works: Le Fou, 1952; The Immoral Proposition, 1953; All That Is Lovely in Men, 1955; If You, 1956; The Whip, 1957; A Form of Women, 1959; For Love: Poems, 1950-1960, 1962; Words: Poems, 1967; The Finger, 1968; The Charm: Early and Uncollected Poems, 1968; 5 Numbers, 1969; Divisions and Other Early Poems, 1969; Pieces, 1969. Contbr. to: Nation; Evergreen Review; New Directions Annual; Poetry; (anthologies) New American Poets, 1960; Contemporary American Poetry, 1962; American Poems, 1964; Today's Poets, 1964; American Poetry, 1965. Address: c/o Dept. of English, S.U.N.Y., Buffalo, NY, U.S.A.

CRENNER, James, b. 10 Feb. 1938. Assistant Professor. Educ: B.A., St. Vincent Coll., Latrobe, 1959; M.A., Univ. of Iowa, 1961, M.F.A., 1962, Ph.D., 1967. Married to Catherine Lybarger, three children. Positions held: Asst. Prof., Engl., Hobart & William Smith Colls., Geneva, 1967–; Am. Lit. Cons., N.Y. State Dept. of Educ., Coll. Proficiency Examinations Comm., 1967–. Published works: The Ageing Ghost, 1964. Contbr. to: Poetry; (anthologies) Poets of the Midwest, 1966; Best Poems of 1966: The Borestone Mountain Poetry Awards, 1967; Midland II, 1970. Honours, awards: Woodrow Wilson Fellowship, 1959-60 & 1965-66; Acad. of Am. Poets Student Prize for Univ. of Iowa Writers' Workshop, 1966; Community Colls. of the Finger Lakes Grant, 1968. Address: Town Line Rd., R.D. No. 1, Lyons, NY 14456, U.S.A.

CREWS, Judson (Campbell), b. 30 June 1917. Teacher; Psychologist; Sociologist; Poet. Education: A.B., M.A., Baylor Univ., Waco, Tex.; Kinzinger Field Schl. of Art, Taos. Married to Mildred Crews. Positions held: Grad. Asst., Dept. of Sociol., Baylor Univ., 1941-42; Med. Corps, Admin. & Supply, Trainer of enlisted personnel, US Army, 1942-44; Consumer Market Rschr., Stewart, Dougal & Assocs., NY, 1948; Printer-Publr., The Taos Star, El Crepusculo, & The Taos News, 1948-66; formerly Ed., various jrnls., inclng: Vers Libre, Taos, Motive, The Flying Fish, Suck-Egg Mule, The Deer and Dachshund, Poetry Taos, & The Naked Ear; Edit. Asst., Crescendo, & Gale; Publr., Motive Press; Bibliophilist, Motive Book Shop, Waco, Tex., 1938–; Casewkr., El Paso Co. Child Welfare; Psychotherapist in Community Mental Hlth.; Tchr., Wharton Co. Jr. Coll. Memberships: Am. Civil Liberties Union; Southern Sociol. Soc.; Southwestern Soc. Sci. Assn.; Southwestern Sociol. Assn.; Tex. Jr. Coll. Tchrs. Assn. Published works: Psalms For A Late Season, 1942; The Southern Temper, 1946; No Is The Night, 1949; The Anatomy of Prosperine, 1955; The Wrath Wrenched Splendor of Love Poems, 1956; The Heart in Naked Hunger, 1958; The Ogres Who Were His Henchmen, 1958; Inwade to Briney Garth (w. nudes by Eric Gill), 1960; The Feel of Sun & Air Upon

Her Body, 1960; Patrocinio Barela– Taos Wood Carver (w. Mildred Tolbert Crews & Wendell B. Anderson), 1962; A Unicorn When Needs Be, 1963; Hermes Past The Hour, 1963; Selected Poems, 1964; You, Mark Antony, Navigator Upon The Nile, 1964; Angels Falls, They Are Towers, 1965; The Stones of Kanorak, 1966; Come Curse The Moon; To Wed Beneath The Sun. Contbr. to: Poetry, Chicago; Accent; Black Mountain Review; Circle; Departure; Death; Experiment; Evergreen Review; Golden Goose; Hearse; Merlin, Paris; Outsider; New Mexico Quarterly; Southwest Review; Mass. Review; Prairie Schooner; Phoenix; Points, Paris; Tiger's Eye; Voices; Wormwood; Yugen; Carolina Quarterly; Per Se; Interim; Simbolica; Miscellaneous Man; Inferno; Blue Guitar; Whetstone; Epos; Inscape; Beloit Poetry Jrnl.; Fresco; Poetry Dial; Inland; Genesis West; S. Dak. Review; Desert Review; The Window, London; Shenandoah; Trace; The Rag; Space City; Nola Express; Hey Lady; Brass Ring; Hyperion; Wind; The Stone; Aldebaran Review; Back Door; Desperado; The Drunken Boat; Wordjock, etc. Address: Community Mental Health Serv., PO Box 936, Gallup, New Mexico, 87301, USA.

CRISWELL, Ronald, pen name **THERFU,** b. 18 Feb. 1942. Poet; Songwriter. Education: Jefferson Community Coll., Louisville, Ky. Positions held: Ed., student newspaper 'The Quadrangle'; Assoc. Ed., The Louisville Gazette, 1971-72. Memberships: World Poetry Soc.; The Ky. State Poetry Soc. Contbr. to: Poet Mag., 1972; Pegasus, 1972; Handsel, 1972; Playgirl, 1973; The Louisville Gazette, 1972; The Lietchfield Gazette, 1972; The Quadrangle. Address: 441 North 29th St., Louisville, KY 40212, U.S.A.

CROBAUGH, Emma Adelia, pen name **CROBAUGH, Emma,** b. 24. Jan. 1903. Housewife; Poet. Education: Martha Washington Coll.; Ground Instr. Cert, Civil Aeronautics Assn. Married Dr. Clyde Crobaugh, 1 son. Positions held: Rsch. Supvsr., Signal Corps, USAF, WWII. Memberships: Int. Platform Assn.; Past V.P., Cleveland Br., Composers, Authors & Artists of Am.; Poetry Soc. of Am.; Poetry Soc. of Mich.; Acad. of Am. Poets; World Poetry Soc. Int.; Nat. League of Am. Pen Women; UPLI; Centro Studi e Scambi Int.; Am. Poets Fellowship Soc.; Avalon World Arts Acad.; Poetry Soc. of S.C.; Ky. State Poetry Soc.; Poetry Soc. of Miss.; Tampa Symph. Guild; Ohio Poetry Soc.; Ohioana Lib. Assn.; Poetry Socs. of Fla., Tex., N.H., Okla., Ariz., Pa., Md., N.M., Ill., La., W. Va.; Poetry Fellowship of Me.; Me. Writers' Rsch. Club; Portland Women's Lit. Union; Parkville Arts & Lit. Club; Int. Acad. of Poets (London), etc. Published works: Crystal & Wine, 1959. Contbr. to num. nat. & int. mags. inclng: Africana; Am. Haiku; Am. Bard; Am. Woavo; Bardic Echoes; Bitterroot; Cardinal; Cleveland Plain Dealer; Columbus Citizen; Coop. Consumer; Congregationalist; Cyclo-flame; Extension; Flatbush; Golden Quill; Goliards; Hartford Courant; Hartford Times; Mod. Images; Muse; Poet; Peninsula Poets; Laurel Leaves; Scimitar & Song; Seydell Qtly.; Encore; Poetry Venture; Pegasus; Literary Review; North Am. Mentor. Recip. num. hons. & awards inclng: many first prizes from Composers, Authors & Artists of Am., Poetry Soc. of Tex., Poetry Soc. of S.C., Nat. Fed. State Poetry Socs., Okla. Poetry Soc.; U.N. Day Philippines Nat. Celebration Award of Hon., 1967; Holds title, Hon. Am-African Poet Laureate. Listed in num. ref. books. Address: Seagate of Highland 821–C, 3300 S. Ocean Blvd., Delray Beach, FL 33444, U.S.A.

CROCKER, Eloise Metcalf, b. 3 Feb. 1913. Housewife. Married H.E. Crocker. Positions held: Past Matron, Order of Eastern Star; Mbr. of Official Bd. of Meth. Church; Church Schl. Tchr. Memberships: Charter Mbr., Ala. State Poetry Soc.; Affiliate, Nat. Fed. of Poetry Socs.; De Kalb Co. Poetry Grp. Has written hymns, anthems & popular songs. Contbr. to: The World's Fair Anthology of Verse; The Chattanooga Times; The Lookout; The Samplers. Recip., Hon. Mention, A.S.P.S. Sonnet Contest, 1971. Address: Valley Head, AL 35989, U.S.A.

CRONIN, Anthony, b. 1926. Editor. Positions held:

Assoc. Ed., The Bell, Dublin, Ireland; Lit. Ed., Time and Tide, London, U.K. Published works: Poems, 1957; The Life of Riley (novel), 1966; A Question of Modernity (literary criticism), 1964. Contbr. to: (anthologies) Faber Book of Twentieth Century Verse, 1953; Mavericks, 1957; New Poets of Ireland, 1963; Mid-Century, 1965.

CROOKE, Joan Theresa, pen name **COLLEDGE, Margaret,** b. 26 Mar. 1920. Retired Army Officer. Education: St. Winefride's Convent; Shrewsbury Tech. Coll. Positions held: var. appts. on Staff & at Regimental Duty, British Army; ret'd as Major, Women's Royal Army Corps. Past Mbr., Poetry Soc. Recip., Gold Medal of the Poetry Soc. for Verse Speaking, 1958. Address: Cranham, 20 Longden Rd., Shrewsbury, Salop, U.K.

CROPPER, Margaret, b. 29 Aug. 1886. Poetess. Member, Soc. of Authors. Published works: Poems, 1914; The Broken Hearthstone; The Springing Well; The End of the Road; Anthony Broom; Collected Poems. Contbr. to: Country Life; The Old Westminster Gazette. Address: Laurel Cottage, Burneside, Kendal, Westmorland, U.K.

CROSBY, Tempe Fenn, Genealogist/Historian. Education: Louisiana State Univ. Positions held: Miss. Insurance Agency; Ext. Serv., Louisiana State Univ. Co-ordinator, Creative Writing Grp. Published works: of one & many, 1966; Who's Afraid of Being Adam? 1969; Certain Days Are Islands, 1971; Journeyman, 1971; Poems by Poets, 1973. Contbr. to: Verbatim, Fellowship Bulletins; Poet. Address: 3246 Conway Dr., Baton Rouge, LA 70809, U.S.A.

CROSNO, Maude Davis, b. 7 Aug. 1904. English & U.S. History Instructor. Education: B.A., Engl., Univ. of N.M., 1928; M.A., Engl., 1942; Positions held: Jr. H.S. Tchr., Albuquerque Public Schl., 1928-69; Soc. Ed., Albuquerque Jrnl., pt.-time, 1940's; Sponsor, Schl. Paper, Circa, 1935-60; Chmn., Comm. to write a New Mex. Guide for Tchrs., 1952; Del., NMEA Coun., Circa, 1958; Freelance Writer. Memberships: Phi Kappa Phi; Phi Alpha Theta; Recording Sec., N.M. Poetry Soc., 1969-74; Mavericks, a workshop writers' grp. of limited mbrship, 1957-74; Histn. & Newsletter Ed., N.M. Press Women, 1970-72; Albuquerque Press Club, 1971-74. Co-author of Discovering New Mexico, 1950. Writer & Revisor of articles on 'New Mexico' for Collier's Ency., 1960-70. Contbr. to: N.M. Qtly.; Western Review; N.M. Mag.; South & West; Poet; Encore & Sunstone Review. Honours, awards: Katherine Mather Simms Award, 1928; 1st Prize in patterned verse, N.M. Poetry Soc., 1973, etc. Address: 1114 Pampas Pl. S.E., Albuquerque, NM 87108, U.S.A.

CROSS, Rae B. Freelance Writer. Education: Grad., Colo. Springs HS., Blair's Business Coll., Colo. Springs; A.B., Univ. of Colo., Greeley, Colorado. Married to George W. Cross (now deceased). Positions held: HS Teacher, Engl., Latin, Spanish, commercial subjects, for 15 yrs.; Sec. and Tutor, Colo. Christian Home, Denver; Sec., Boys' Div., Denver YMCA.; Sec. and Creative Writing, Colo. Springs, YWCA. Memberships: Nat. League of American Pen Women (Pikes Peak Branch); Colo. Authors' League; Poetry Soc. of Colorado; Poetry Fellowship, Colo. Springs; Women in Communications (formerly Theta Sigma Phi). Contbr. to: Improvement Era; Hearthstone; Wee Wisdom; Aspire; New; Weekly Unity; Primary Treasure; Little Friend; Grit; Capper's Weekly; Children's Friend; Sunshine; Christian Home; War Cry; Young Crusader; National Enquirer. Awards: 5 awards, Poetry Soc. of Colo., 1973; Awards in both serious and light verse, Poetry Fellowship, 1973; 5 awards (out of possible 6) in essay contest; 1973 awards from poetry societies of Nebraska, Indiana, Boston. Address: 1701 W. Colo. Avenue, Colo. Springs, CO 80904, USA.

CROSSLEY-HOLLAND, Kevin John William, b. 7 Feb. 1941. Publisher; Writer. Education: BA, St. Edmund

Hall, Oxford Univ., U.K. Married Ruth Marris, 2 sons by first marriage. Positions held: Ed., Macmillan & Co. Ltd., Publishers; Gregory Fellow in Poetry, Univ. of Leeds; Talks Producer, BBC; Editl. Dir., Victor Gollancz Ltd., Publishers. Mbr., Poetry Soc. (one time Mbr. of Gen. Comm.) Published works: On Approval (booklet), 1959; My Son (booklet), 1966; Aldernty: The Nunnery (booklet), 1969; The Rain-Giver, 1972; The Battle of Maldon & Other Old English Poems (transl.), 1965; Beowulf (transl.), 1968; Storm & Other Old English Riddles (transl.), 1970. Contbr. to many mags., jrnls. in G.B. & U.S.A. Recip., Arts Coun. Award, 1972. Address: c/o Deborah Rogers, Lit. Agency, 29 Goodge St., London W.1., U.K.

CRUICKSHANK, Helen Burness, pen names **A.M.V. & A.N.A.,** b. 15 May 1886. Retired Civil Servant. Education: Montrose Acad., Scotland, UK. Positions held: Civil Servant, Post Office Savings Bank, London, 10 yrs.; Exec. Officer, Hlth. Dept., St. Andrews House, Edinburgh. Memberships: Hon. Sec., Scottish Ctr., PEN, 7 yrs.; Life, Saltire Soc., Edinburgh; Hon., Scottish Assn. for Speaking of Verse; Hon., Assn. for Scottish Lit. Studies, 1970. Published works: Up the Noran Water; Sea Buckthorn; Ponnage Pool; Collected Poems, 1971. Contbr. to approx. 12 anthols. & to: Glasgow Herald; Country Life; Time & Tide; Poetry Review; Punch; Edinburgh Evening News. Honours & Awards: Scottish Arts Coun. Award, 1969; Hon. M.A., Edinburgh Univ., 1970. Address: 4 Hillview Terrace, Corstorphine, Edinburgh 12, Scotland, UK.

CRUTTWELL, Elizabeth Josephine Vernon, b. 5 Mar. 1905. Poet. Married. Published collections: The Just Proportion; Lyrics from Hampton Court; Bird-in-Hand; Pisces to Virgo; Lyme Bay; Breakfast in Eden. Contbr. to: New York Herald Tribune; Manifold. Address: Hogshill House, Beaminster, Dorset, U.K.

CRUZ, Victor Hernandez, b. 1949. Positions held: Former Ed., Umbra mag.; Associated with Gut-Theatre, E. Harlem, currently. Published works: Papo Got His Gun, 1966; Snaps, 1969. Contbr. to: Umbra; Evergreen Review; Ramparts; Review of Books; (anthologies) Black Fire, 1968; New Black Poetry, 1969. Address: c/o Random House Publishers, 457 Madison Ave., New York, NY 10022, U.S.A.

CUBA, Ivan, b. 15 Sept. 1920. Art Professor. Education: Fac. of Fine Arts & Architecture, Univ. of Auckland, New Zealand, 6 years. Positions held: Past Chmn., late L. Pitcher's Organisation, N.Z.; Past Dir., Amalgamated Plastics, N.Z.; Past Dir., Orange Int. Acad.; currently Pres., New Zealand Temple of Arts Mus.; Hon. Dir., Profl. Arts Universal Assn. for Australia & Pacific Islands. Memberships: Life Fellow, Institut Des Arts et des Lettres, Switzerland (Geneva & Paris), 1963; Friends of the Lib. Univ. of Mo., U.S.A. Published works: (poetic works) Skits & Frenic; Democius; Realms of the Spiral Stairway. Books in most univ. & other main libs. in the English speaking countries. Recip. var. hons. Address: P.O. Box 5199, Auckland, New Zealand.

CUDE, Jean Ring, b. 17 Mar. 1906. Positions held: Poetry Ed., Winston-Salem Jrnl. & Twin City Sentinel, 1957-67; Owner, Mgr., Beauty Salon for 20 yrs., ret'd. Memberships: Acad. of Am. Poets; N.C. Poetry Coun.; N.C. Lit. & Hist. Soc.; N.C. Poetry Soc. Contbr. to: A Time for Poetry, 1966; Silver Echoes, 1959; Bay Leaves, 1970, '71; Winston-Salem Poets, 1944-52; Quaker Life; Terse Verse (syndicated column); prepared poetry scripts for Radio Educ. Coun., 1958, '59. Honours, awards: Narrative Poetry Contest, N.C. Fed. of Women's Clubs, 1952, '56, '58, & Sonnet Contest, 1973; N.C. Poetry Coun. Contest, 1968, '70; N.C. Poetry Soc. Contest, 1970, '72. Address: 622 Summit St., Winston-Salem, NC 27101, U.S.A.

CULLA, Daniel, pen names **KUYA, QLA, ULLA K,** b. 28 Jan. 1945. Teacher; Writer. Positions held: Tchr.; Officer Wkr.; Chief Asst.; Writer; Printer; a clandestine cabal Ed., Hoja Muerta. Memberships: Poetry Edinburgh; Jornal do Felgueiras. Published works: Ojo

de Dios Ojo Ojo; Hoja Muerta. Contbr. to: Poetry Edinburgh; Gargantua; Mole; Private Eye; Norte; Chick; Spoir; INFO iac; Formica Nera; Les lettres grec; Tridente; La Pata de Palo; Patterns; Cardinal; Astral Projection; The Phoenix; Moving On; Quintessence; Bardic Echoes; Special Song, etc. Address: Gral Ricardos, 70–Madrid–19, Spain.

CUMBERLEGE, Marcus Crossley, b. 23 Dec. 1938. Teacher. Educ: B.A., St. John's Coll., Oxford, U.K. Married, one child. Positions held: Worked with British Coun., Lima, Peru, 1957-58 & 1962-63; Worked in Advertising, London, U.K., 1964-68; Tchr., Engl. Lang., Lycée Int., St. Germain-en-Laye, France, 1968–. Published works: Oases, 1968. Contbr. to: New Measure; Poetry; Review; Expression; Aylesford Review; Dublin Magazine; Contemporary Literature In Translation; Twelve Poets (anthology), 1967. Recip., Eric Gregory Award, 1966. Address: Lycée International, 78 St. Germain-en-Laye, France.

CUMBO, Kattie M., b. 3 Nov. 1938. Public Relations Executive. Education: A.A., Long Is. Univ., 1969; B.A., ibid, 1970; Cert., African-Caribbean Studies, Univ. of the West Indies, 1970. Positions held: Dev. & carried out community & pub. rels. to advance the progs. of the Fund for the Republic, L.I. Univ., Ertec Int., Success Chemical Co., Afro-Am. Civic Serv. Employees, Liberator Mag., etc., 1963–; Staff Communications Asst./Admin., African Am. Inst., 1966-67; Asst. to Dir. of Prog., Moorish Sci. Temple. Oceanhill Brownsville, summer 1967; Sec. to the Assoc. Dean of the Grad. Schl. of Bus. Admin., L.I. Univ., 1967-69; Exec. Dir., N.Y. Sect., Am. Camping Assn., 1972-74. Memberships: Women in Communications (var. offices); Harlem Writers' Guild; Bd. Dirs., Alonzo Players. Contbr. to: Galaxy of Black Writings, (an anthol. of poetry, prose & essays), 1970; Nine Black Poets, 1968; Black Outloud, 1970; Black Works, 1970-72; Crow; Afro-Am.; African Opinion; Ghanaian Times; Morning Post, Lagos, Nigeria, etc. Honours, awards: Poet-in-Res., Wilmington, Del., Dec. 1973. Address: 191 Willoughby St., Brooklyn, NY 11201, U.S.A.

CUMMINGS, Norva Thurston Thomas, b. 1 July 1916. Writer; Poet. Education: B.A., The Pa. State Univ., 1939; Univ. of Pa. Schl. of Law, 1939-40. Married, 1 son, 1 daughter. Positions held: Instr., Pol. Sci., The Pa. State Univ., 1940-44. Memberships: Life Mbr., Poetry Soc. of Am.; Nat. Arts Club; Centro Studi e Scambi Int.; Pa. Poetry Soc.; Nat. Fed. State Poetry Socs. Published works: Dear Anne, With Love, 1967. Contbr. to IWWP Anthol. Address: Bethlehem Pike & Stump Rd., North Wales, PA 19454, U.S.A.

CUNNINGHAM, James Vincent, b. 23 Aug. 1911. Professor of English. Educ: A.B., Stanford Univ., 1934; Ph.D., ibid, 1945. Married to Jessie MacGregor Campbell, one child. Positions held: Tchr., Stanford Univ., 1937-45, Univ. of Hawaii, 1945-46, the Univ. of Chgo., 1946-52, Univ. of Va., Charlottesville, 1952-53; Prof. of Engl., Brandeis Univ., Waltham, 1953–. Published works: The Helmsman, 1942; The Judge Is Fury, 1947; Doctor Drink, 1950; The Exlusions of a Rhyme: Poems and Epigrams, 1960; To What Strangers, What Welcome, 1964; Some Salt, 1967; (literary criticism) Woe or Wonder, 1951; Tradition and Poetic Structure, 1960. Contbr. to: (anthologies) New Poems by American Poets, 1953; A Silver Treasury of Light Verse, 1957; Modern Verse in English, 1958; A Poetry Sampler, 1962; Erotic Poetry, 1963; Poetry in English, 1963; Poems on Poetry, 1965; Studying Poetry, 1965. Recip., Guggenheim Fellowship, 1959-60 & 1967-68. Address: c/o Dept. of English, Brandeis Univ., Waltham, MA 02154, U.S.A.

CURNOW, Thomas Allen Monro, b. 17 June 1911. University Teacher. Education: B.A., Univ. of Canterbury, New Zealand; Litt. D., Univ. of Auckland. Positions held: Lit. Staff, The Press, Christchurch, NZ, 1936-48; News Chronicle, London, UK, 1949; Lectr. in Engl., Univ. of Auckland, 1951; Assoc. Prof., ibid, 1967. Published works: Enemies, Poems 1934-36,

1937; Not in Narrow Seas, 1939; Island & Time, 1941; Sailing or Drowning, 1943; Jack Without Magic, 1946; At Dead Low Water, 1949; The Axe, 1949; A Book of New Zealand Verse, (ed.) 2 edits., 1945 & '51; Penguin Book of New Zealand Verse (ed.), 1960; A Small Room with Large Windows, 1962. Contbr. to: New Zealand Listener; Landfall; Poetry (Chgo.); New World New Writing (NY); Penguin New Writing; The Times Literary Supplement. Awards: Jessie Mackay Mem. Prize for yr's. best verse publ. in NZ, 1957 & '62. Address: 62 Tohunga Crescent. Parnell, Auckland, New Zealand.

CURREY, Ralph Nixon, pen name **CURREY, R.N.,** b. 14 Dec. 1907. Retired Schoolmaster. Education: Wadham Coll., Oxford Univ., 1927-30; Trng. Dept., Oxford, 1930-31; M.A. (Hons.), Modern Hist. at Oxford; Dip. in Educ., Oxford. Married Stella Martin, 2 sons. Positions held: Subaltern, Royal Artillery, transferred to Educ. Corps. (for war publs.), finished w. rank of Major, WWII; Hd. of Engl. Dept., Colchester Royal Grammar Schl., 1946-72. Memberships: Fellow, Royal Soc. of Lit., 1970-; Pres., Suffolk Poetry Soc., 1967-; Mbr., Lit. Panel of the Eastern Arts Assn., 1972-; Mbr., PEN. Published works: Tiresias & Other Poems, 1940; This Other Planet, 1945; Poems from India (ed. w. R.V. Gibson) – Forces Anthol., 1945, '46; Indian Landscape, 1947; Formal Spring (verse transl. of French Renaissance poets), 1950, '69; Poets of the 1939-45 War, 1960, rev. '67; Between Two Worlds (verse play), 1948, '51; Early Morning in Vaaldorp (verse play), 1961; The Africa We Knew, 1973. Contbr. to: Listener; London Mag.; New Statesman; Observer; Poetry (Chicago); Sunday Times; Times Lit. Supplement; Spectator; Punch, & many more. Honours, awards: Prize, Viceroy's Poetry Prize, 1945; S. African Poetry Prize, 1959. Address: 3 Beverley Road, Colchester, Essex, U.K.

CURRY, Frances Mae, b. 19 Feb. 1918. Librarian. Positions held: Pastry Chef; File Clerk; Expediter in Office Supplies co.; Dept. Hd., Addressograph Dept., Am. Acad. of Pediatrics; currently Libn., ibid. Member, Poets & Patrons, Chicago. Honours, awards: 2nd pl., First time contbr. to Poets & Patrons, 1967; First Hon. Mention in the Div. for Award Winners Comp., ibid, 1973. Address: 1725 Brown Ave., Evanston, IL 60201, U.S.A.

CURTIS, Edith Roelker, b. 29 July 1893. Biographer. Education: Miss Porter's School, Farmington, Connecticut, 1909-12; Radcliffe Coll., Cambridge, Mass., 1919-22. Married Charles Pelham Curtis, Jr.; 5 children. Memberships: Boston Branch, NLAPW (Pres. 1956); Mass. State, NLAPW (Pres., 1957); NH Poetry Soc. Writers Conference, 1966, 1967 (on Staff); Nat. Authors League & Guild, NYC; Boston Authors' Club (V.P., 1967, Pres., 1968, 1969); Marquis Biog. Library Soc.; Poet Lore's Writers Conference, 1968 (on Staff). Published works: 3 historical biogs.; 2 short novels. Contbr. to: Poet Lore; Poetry Review; Boston Herald; Hartford Courant; The Golden Quill Anthol.; Forest Notes; Peterborough Transcript; Keene Sentinel; Keene Shopper; Hartford Times; Charleston News & Courier, etc. Papers held in Archives, Smith Coll. Library, Northampton, Mass. Awards: 1st Prize, Boston Branch, NLAPW. Address: Box 71, Dublin, NH 03444, USA.

CURTIS, Walter Alan, b. 4 July 1941. Data Clerk. Education: B.A., Engl., Portland State Univ. Positions held: Ed., The Hoodoo Times. Published works: The Erotic Flying Machine, 1971; Angel Pussy, 1970. Contbr. to: The Atlantic Monthly; Evergreen Review. Address: 15270 S. Holcomb Blvd., Oregon City, OR, U.S.A.

CUTLER, Bruce, b. 8 Oct. 1930. University Professor. Education: Northwestern Univ., 1947-49; B.A., Univ. of Iowa, 1951; M.S., Kans. State Univ., 1957; Universita degli Studi, Naples, 1957-58. Married Tina, 3 children. Positions held: Instr. in Engl., Kans. State Univ., 1958-60; Instr. in Engl., Wichita State Univ., 1960-62; Asst. Prof. of Engl., ibid, 1962-64; Assoc. Prof., 1964-67; Prof. of Engl., 1967-; Disting. Prof. of Humanities,

1973-. Member, Guild, Am. Poets Series, 1972-. Published works: The Year of the Green Wave, 1960; A West Wind Rises, 1962; Sun City, 1964; A Voyage to America, 1967. Ed. of: The Arts at the Grass Roots, 1968; In That Day, 1969. Advisory Ed., Kansas Qtly. Mbr., Advisory Bd., Nimrod. Contbr. to: Poetry; N.Y. Times; Canadian Forum; Prairie Schooner, etc. Recip., 1st book poetry prize, Univ. of Neb. Press, 1960 & 1st prize, Heart of Am. poetry awards, 1964. Address: Dept. of Engl., Wichita State Univ., Wichita, KS 67208, U.S.A.

CUTLER, Ivor, b. 15 Jan. 1923. Teacher. Positions held: Tchr., A.S. Neill's Summerhill Schl., Two years; Teacher for twenty years. Published works: A Seal Is a Sheep Without Feet, 1970; (recordings) Get Away From the Wall; Who Tore Your Trousers?, 1962; Ludo, 1967. Contbr. to: Ambit; Workshop Two; Twentieth Century; Tribune; Sunday Times; New Statesman. Address: 21 Laurier Road, London, N.W.5, U.K.

CVITAN, Dalibor, b. 20 Dec. 1934. Writer. Education: Classic langs., Univ. of Philos. Positions held: Ed. 'Umjetnost i dijete', mag. for theory of children's art; Ed. 'Telegram', weekly cultural mag. Memberships: Sec., Assn. of Croatian Authors, 1968-70; Croatian PEN. Published works: Posljednji kupač, poems, 1957; Apo thallátes, poems, 1969; Ironični Narcis, criticism & essays, 1971. Contbr. to: Forum; Republika; Telegram; Krugovi; Kolo, etc. Recip., Prize of Zagreb for criticism & essays (for book 'Ironični Narcis'), 1972. Address: Djurkov put 16, Gracani, 41000 Zagreb, Yugoslavia.

D

DAHL, Ronald Albin, b. 31 May 1938. Assistant Professor. Educ: B.F.A., Calif. Coll. of Arts and Crafts, Oakland; M.F.A., San Francisco Art Inst. Positions held: Instr., San Francisco Art Inst., 1964; Co-ordinator of Insights, San Francisco Mus. of Art teenage workshop, 1965-67; Dir., Art & Ecol. Mexico, 1968; Co-ordinator, Symbol Projection Orientation Nourished and Guided Ecologically, 1968; Asst. Prof., Fine Art, Calif. Coll. of Arts & Crafts, 1968-. Published works: From Horsehead Nebula to Here, 1965. Contbr. to: Loveletter; Sponge; Best Poems of 1965: The Borestone Mountain Poetry Awards (anthology), 1966. Address: 5283 Broadway Terrace, Oakland, CA, U.S.A.

DALE, Peter John, b. 21 Aug. 1938. Teacher; Writer. Education: B.A., St. Peter's Coll., Oxford Univ. Positions held: Asst. Tchr., Howden C.S. Schl., E. Yorks, 1964-65; Asst. Tchr., Glastonbury C.S. Schl., Morden, Surrey, 1965-72; Hd. of Engl., Hinchley Wood C.S. Schl., 1972-; Assoc. Ed., Agenda. Published works: Walk From The House, 1962; The Storms, 1968; Mortal Fire, 1970; The Legacy of François Villon, (transl.), 1971; Villon (transl.), 1973; Poems of Villon, (bilingual ed.) 1975. Contbr. to: Meridian; The Review; Stand; Shenandoah; Southern Review; Modern Occasions (essay); The New Statesman; The Times Lit. Supplement. Recip., Arts Coun. Bursary, 1969-70. Address: 10 Selwood Rd., Sutton, Surrey, U.K.

DALLAS, Charlotte Holmes, pen name **HOLMES Charlotte,** b. 25 Nov. 1935. Cold-Type Compositor, Freelance Journalist. Education: B.M., B.A., from Sul Ross State Univ., Alpine, Texas. Married, William L. Dallas. Positions held: HS Engl. Teacher; Newspaper Reporter; Editor, The Canyon Lake Times. Memberships: Avalon World Arts Acad.; Poetry Soc. of Texas (Councillor); Nat. Fed. of State Poetry Socs.; Poets, Unlimited (Co-Founder). Published works: Of Men and Milestones, 1969. Contbr. to: Flame; Lit. Calender; Dawn; Modernalia; Am. Bard; Cyclo-Flame; Imprints Qtly.; Cardinal Poetry Qtly.; Quintessence; Lilac City Lyrics, etc. Awards: Ralph Cheyney Mem. Prize, 1952; Avalon Conf. Award for Rhymed Verse, 1957; Vietnam Prize, Poetry Soc. of Texas, 1968; Critics Choice for February, 1969; Poetry & Opera

Comp., Dallas Grand Opera Assoc., 1969; Sonja Fojtik Award, Poetry Soc. of Texas, 1970. Address: 1201 W. Woodlawn, San Antonio, TX 78201, USA.

DALLAS, Ruth, b. 29 Sept. 1919. Writer. Published works: Country Road & Other Poems, 1953; The Turning Wheel, 1961; Experiment in Form, 1964; Day Book: Poems of a Year, 1966; Shadow Show, 1968; also writes books for children (The Children in the Bush, etc.) Contbr. to: Landfall (NZ Qtly.); Islands (NZ Qtly.); N.Z. Listener; Review, Univ. of Otago; Experiment, Victoria Univ.; Poetry Commonwealth; Meanjin Qtly., Australia; Poetry Australia; N.Z.B.C. & B.B.C. Honours, awards: N.Z. Lit. Fund Achievement Award, 1962; Robert Burns Fellowship at Univ. of Otago, N.Z., 1968. Address: 448 Leith St., Dunedin, New Zealand.

DALTON, Dorothy, b. 25 Sept. 1915. Poet. Married Roy Kuehn, 2 daughters. Positions held: Physicians' Asst.; N.Y. Public Lib. Clerk; X-Ray Techn., Women's Army Corps-Medics; Freelance Writer; Ed., Poetry View. Mbr., Ore. State Poetry Soc. & the Poetry Society of America. Published works: Poems, 1967; Midnight, and Counting, 1973. Contbr. to: Saturday Evening Post; McCall's; Good Housekeeping; Abraxas; Beloit Poetry Jrnl.; Blackbird Circle; Charas; Dust; Descant; Epos; Encounter; Fla. Quarterly; Folio; Foxfire; Galley Sail Review; Human Voice; Impetus; Legend; Midwest; New College; N.M. Quarterly; The N.Y. Quarterly; Odyssey; Poet Lore; Red Cedar Review; Southern Poetry Review; Oregonian Verse; South & West; Trace; Tweed; Tulsa Poetry Quarterly; Voices; Wisc. Review; Wormwood; Dragonfly; Rune; Sign; Poet (India); Outposts (G.B.), etc. Recip. var. poetry awards inclng: First Hon. Mention, Ga. Poetry Soc., 1973. Address: 1125 Valley Rd., Menasha, WI 54952, U.S.A.

DALVEN, Rae, b. 25 Apr. 1904. Professor Emeritus; Translator; Writer. Education: B.A., Hunter Coll., N.Y., 1925; M.A., N.Y. Univ., 1928; M.F.A. (Playwriting), Yale Drama Schl., 1941; Ph.D. (Engl.), N.Y. Univ., 1961. Positions held: Engl. Tchr., N.Y. City System at the Jr. H.S. & H.S. levels, & for the past twenty years has taught at the College level; Asst. Prof. of Drama, Fisk Univ., Nashville, Tenn., 1952-53; Engl. Instr., Fairleigh Dickinson, 1957-60; Adjunct Prof. of Engl., Pace Coll., 1962-68; Chmn. of Engl. Dept. & Prof. of Engl., Ladycliff Coll., 1962-73. Memberships: Poetry Soc. of Am.; Authors League of Am.; MLA, –1973; Am. Theatre Assn., –1973. Published works: Poems (transl. of 90 poems from the Greek by Joseph Eliyia), 1944; Modern Greek Poetry (anthol.), 1949, '71; The Complete Poems of Cavafy, 1961; Anna Comnena (biog.), 1972. Contbr. to: Poetry (Chicago); Odyssey; Sat. Review of Lit.; The Noiseless Spider, etc. Honours, awards: Recip., three grants to write a book on the Jews of Ioannina, Greece, two from the Meml. Fndn. for Jewish Culture and one from the Nat. Fndn. for Jewish Culture, 1967, '68, '69; Poetry Prize, in memory of the Yiddish poet Jacob Glatstein for transl. which appeared in the August issue of Poetry mag., 1972; Elected to the Hall of Fame by the Hunter Coll. Alumni Assn., 1973. Address: 11 Fifth Ave., N.Y., NY 10003, U.S.A.

DALY, Betty Miller, b. 25 Sept. 1926. Medical Assistant. Education: Business Coll.; Medical Pathol. Technol. Positions held: employed, Merrill, Lynch, Pierce, Fenner & Beane, Stock Brockerage; employed, Bowman Gray Schl. of Med., Yale Univ. Med. Schl., Am. Oncologic Hosp., Phila. Gen. Hosp. & Rex Hosp. Memberships: Poetry Soc. of Am.; Am. Pen Women; Nat. Fed. of State Poetry Socs.; The Acad. of Am. Poets; has held offices of Pres., Corres. Sec., Mbrship Chmn., Treas., N.C. Poetry Soc. Published works: As A Woman Thinketh, 1958; A Time for Poetry (Anthol.), 1966. Contbr. to: Instructor; Home Life; Fellowship in Prayer; Bay Leaves; Award Winning Poems; Sanford Herald; Charlotte Observor; Winston-Salem Jrnl. & Sentinal, etc. Honours, awards: Sidney Lanier Award (sonnets), 1967, '68, '69; Caldwell W. Nixon Award (for children), 1967, '68, '69, '70; Thomas McDill Award (gen. category), 1970; Writers Roundtable Award (gen. category), 1971, etc. Address: Box 108, Broadway, NC 27505, U.S.A.

D'AMBROSIO, Vinnie-Marie, b. 5 Apr. 1928. Teacher. Education: B.A., Smith Coll.; M.A., Brooklyn Coll.; Doctoral candidate, NY Univ. Positions held: Instr., Engl. Dept., Brooklyn Coll.; Director of Poetry Readings, Brooklyn Museum. Memberships: Poetry Soc. of America; NY Poets Coop. Published work: Life of Touching Mouths, 1971. Contbr. to various newspapers, magazines, etc. Awards: Acad. of American Poets at N.Y.U., 1st prize, 1967; Poetry Soc. of America, Christopher Morley Memorial Award, 1972. Address: 405 Parkside Ave., Brooklyn, NY 11226, USA.

DAME, Hazel Stevens, b. 22 Dec. 1904. Homemaker. Education: B.L., Northwestern Univ., Evanston, Ill. (Schl. of Speech), 1926. Widow of James Stokes Dame, 2 sons. Positions held: Hd. of the Dept. of Dramatics, Elmhurst Coll., Ill., 1929. Memberships: Scribblers; Nat. League of Am. Pen Women; Poetry Soc. of Am.; Hon. Mbr., Mark Twain Soc. Published works: (book of poems) This Too-Brief Moment, 1950. Contbr. to: Bookfellow Anthols.; Anthol. of Contemporary Poetry; Chicago Poets; Am. Haiku; Chicago Tribune Line o' Type; The Pen Woman; The Wind Listens, etc. Honours, awards: 1st prize, 11th Dist., Ill. Fed. Womens Club (Serious Poetry); Cash Award & Hon. Mention, Poets & Patrons, 1973, etc. Address: 159 Cottage Hill Ave., Elmhurst, IL 60126, U.S.A.

DANA, Robert, b. 2 June 1929. Professor of English. Educ: A.B., Drake Univ., Des Moines, 1951; M.A., State Univ. of Iowa, 1953; Studied w. Karl Shapiro, John Berryman, Robert Lowell. Married to Mary K., three children. Positions held: Instr., Engl. Dept., Cornell Coll., Mount Vernon, 1953; Currently Prof., Engl., ibid, Ed., Hillside Press, 1957-67 & North American Review, Mount Vernon, 1963-68. Published works: My Glass Brother, 1957; The Dark Flags of Waking, 1964; Journeys from the Skin, 1966; Some Versions of Silence, 1967. Contbr. to: Poetry; Nation; New York Times; New Yorker; Paris Review; (anthologies) Homage to Baudelaire, 1959; Poetry for Pleasure, 1960; Midland, 1961. Honours, awards: Danforth Teacher Study Grant, 1959-60; Rinehart Fndn. Fellowship for Poetry, 1960-61; Ford ACM Non-Western Studies Grant, 1966-67. Address: 219 Seventh Ave. North, Mount Vernon, IA 52314, U.S.A.

DANIELLS, Roy, b. 6 Apr. 1902. Professor of English. Education: B.A., Univ. of B.C., Canada; M.A. & Ph.D., Univ. of Toronto. Married Laurenda Francis, 2 children (Susan, Sara). Positions held: Hd. of Dept. of Engl., Univ. of Manitoba, 1937-46; Hd. of Dept. of Engl., Univ. of B.C., 1948-65; Prof. of Engl., ibid, 1965-. Memberships: Pres., Royal Soc. of Canada, 1970-71. Published works: Deeper into the Forest, 1948; The Chequered Shade, 1963. Recip., Lorne Pierce Medal, 1970. Address: Dept. of Engl., Univ. of B.C., Vancouver, Canada.

DANNER, Margaret Essie, b. 12 Jan. 1915. Poet-in-Residence. Educ: Loyola Univ., Chicago; Roosevelt Univ., Chicago. Married. Positions held: Former Asst. Ed., Poetry; Former Poet-in-residence, Wayne State Univ., Detroit; Poet-in-residence, Virginia Union Univ., Richmond, currently. Published works: Impressions of African Art Forms, 1960; To Flower, 1963; Poem, Counterpoem (w. Dudley Randall), 1966; Iron Lace, 1968; Ed., Brass Horses, 1968 & Regroup, 1969. Contbr. to: Negro Digest; Bahai' World Order; Poetry; Accent; Chicago Review (anthologies) La Poesie Negro-Americaine, 1966; Kaleidoscope, 1967. Honours, awardes: Poetry Workshop Award, 1945; John Hay Whitney Fellowship, 1951; Harriet Tubman Award, 1956; Am. Soc. of African Culture Grant, 1960. Address: 626 E. 102 Place, Chicago, IL, U.S.A.

DARBY, Edith M., pen name **GREENFIELD, Bernadotte,** b. 19 Sept. 1906. Government Clerk-

Typist. Education: Grad. Atlantic City HS, 1926. Positions held: Legal Sec.; business woman; real estate broker for number of yrs.; now government employee. Memberships: Past. Chmn. State of NJ Nat. Poetry Day, Inc.; Am. Acad. of Poets; Past Chmn. for Lit. Dept. for Woman's Research Club of A.C., now Vice-Pres.; Hon. Rep. for CSSI (Rome); Member, ASCAP, etc. Contbr. to: Nat. Poetry Day Anthol., 1965; Bouquet of Poems, 1969, 1972-73; Poets of Am., 1964, 1966; Internat. Who's Who in Poetry Anthol., 1972; Yogi World Cong., New Delhi, India, paper accepted; Song (in collab. with Randy Oness) appearing in Christmas Album, 1973. Awards: Bronze Medal (CSSI), 1971 for work in the arts and sciences, also CSSI Award, 1972 for poem "New Jersey" (which also received 3rd prize from Womens Club of Asbury). Address: 210 Cedarcrest Av., Pleasantville, NJ 08232, USA.

DARCY, Louise S., b. 14 Oct. 1907. Poet. Education: Boston Univ., Mass. Married, 2 children. Memberships: Poetry Soc. of Am.; Poetry Fellowship of Me. Contbr. to: The N.Y. Times; The Christian Sci. Monitor; The Educational Forum; Quartet; The Ladies Home Jrnl.; Woman's Weekly (U.K.); Driftwood; many other newspapers, mags., anthols, etc. Recip. prizes from the State Poetry Soc. & from poetry mags. Address: 149 South St., Biddeford, ME 04005, U.S.A.

DARLINGTON, Andrew John, b. 18 Sept. 1947. Printer. Education: Hull Coll. of Technol., U.K., Leeds Polytechnic. Positions held: Art Ed., Ludds Mill. Mbr., Inner Circle Arts Co-operative, Huddersfield. Published works: Deaf Eyes, 1973; Positive Negative, 1973. Contbr. to: Abbey, U.S.A.; Anthol.-2; Aspect-9, U.S.A.; B.B. Eccles Rides Out; Bogg; Both Sides Now; Breakthru; Centre Seventeen; Circle in the Square; Contac; Continuum; Dark Areas, Australia; Dharma, Australia; Durango Cortez Herald, U.S.A.; Dodo; Eureka, Sweden; Field, Australia; Gargantua; Gegenschein, Australia; Genesis; Global Tapestry; Headland; In Concert; Ludds Mill; Moonshine; New Headland; Next Wave Poets; Poetry & Audience, No. 2 vol. 19; Poetry Nippon, Japan; Roots; Sad Traffic; Saturday Club Book of Poetry, Australia; Second Coming, vol. 2, U.S.A.; York Poetry; Your Friendly Fascist, Australia; also num. reviews, articles, art-work & works of fiction & broadcast for 'Radio Humberside', 1972. Address: 44 Spa Croft Rd., Teall St., Ossett, West Yorks. WF5 OHE, U.K.

DART, Robert Paul, b. 7 Nov. 1895. Retired. Education: grad., Univ. of Calif.; studied music, Univ. of Ore. Positions held: Mbr. of Asiatic Dept., Mus. of Fine Arts, Boston, Mass. Mbr. & Past Treas., The Far Eastern Ceramic Grp. Published works: Book of Poems, 1971. Contbr. to The Christian Sci. Monitor, Boston. Address: 104 W. Calle Crespis, Apt. 5, Santa Barbara, CA 93105, U.S.A.

DARUWALLA, Bejan, b. 11 Jul. 1931. Professor of English, also professional astro-numero-palmist. Education: M.A., Engl. Guest Editor of the first Indian Number of "Poet". Published works: Wheel of Fire, 1966; Poet (Indian Number), 1967; "21" (poems), 1973; Poet (Gujarat Regional Number), 1973. Om Shanti (song) recorded by Cathedral Recording Co., U.S.A. Columnist, Eve's Weekly, Star & Style, and Gujarat Samachar. Contbr. to: Indian Writing in English; Sunday Standard; Mirror; South & West; American Poetry League; Words with Wings; Muse; Cyclo-Flame; Sea to Sea in Song; Hoosier Challenger; Mississippi Journal; Flame Anthol.; Border; Explorer; Sunday Manila Times. Awards: Poet-in-residence, Manila, Philippines, 1969; Merit Cert., CSSI., 1969; World Poetry Award, 1970-71, and 1973-74; Poet of the Month, Cyclo-Flame, 1973. Address: Firdos, Shāhibag, Ahmedabad 4, India.

DARUWALLA, Keki Nasserwanji, b. 24 Jan. 1937. Indian Police Service. Education: M.A. (Engl. Lit.) Positions held: Supt. of Police, Bara Banki; Supt. of Police, Anti-Dacoity Operations, Agra; Supt. of Police, Fatehgarh; currently Asst. Inspector Gen. of Police,

U.P. Published works: Under Orion, 1970; Apparition in April, 1971. Rep. in the following anthols: Poetry East West, 1966; Indian Poetry in English, 1947-72; Contemporary Indian Poetry in English; Modern Indian Poetry in English; Writers Workshop; recent anthol. on Indian Poetry brought out by Prof. Howard McCord. Contbr. of poems & short stories to: Antioch Review; Poet Lore; Voices Int.; Poetry Australia; Poetry India; Atlantic Review; Trace; Illustrated Weekly of India; Times of India. Recip., State Award for Poetry, 1972. Address: c/o Inspector Gen. of Police, Uttar Pradesh, 1 Tilak Marg, Lucknow, India.

DAS, Deb Kumar, b. 22 Dec. 1935. Instructor in Adult Education. Educ: B.A., St. Xavier's Coll., Calcutta, India; B.A. & M.A., Queens' Coll., Cambridge, U.K. Positions held: Instr., Basic Adult Educ., in a Black ghetto in the U.S.A. Published works: The Night Before Us, 1958; Through a Glass Darkly, 1964; The Eyes of Autumn, 1968; The Four Labyrinths, 1969. Contbr. to: Writers Workshop Miscellany; Illustrated Weekly of India; (anthologies) Commonwealth Poems of Today, 1967; New Voices of the Commonwealth, 1968; Poetry from India, 1969. Address: Seattle, WA, U.S.A.

DAS, Lakshahira, b. 2 Feb. 1933. Educator. Education: B.A., 1950; M.A. Educ., 1953; Ph.D., Educ., 1973. Married Prof. Ramcharan Das, 3 sons. Positions held: Hd. of Dept. of Educ., Cotton Coll., Gauhati, Assam, India, 1959; Prof., ibid, 1971. Memberships: Past Mbr., Exec. Comm., Assam Sahitya Sabha; Past Mbr., Gauhati Sahitya Sabha; Ex-Pres., Assam Radio Artists Assn.; Pres., Kavi Chakra. Published works: Prathama (lyrics), 1950; Surseturu (lyrics), 1956; Pranganga (poem), 1957; Mayurpankhi (lyrics), 1968; Pis Duaredi Sit (poem), 1974. Contbr. to: Ramdhenu; Manideep; Prahari; New Voice; Asom Bani; Dainik Asom; Asom Batori; Mahekiya Kavita; Nilachal; Amar Pratinidhi; Arunachal. Address: Dept. of Educ., Cotton Coll., P.O. Gauhati 1, Assam, India.

DAS, Salilendra Nath, pen name DAS, S.N., b. 18 Nov. 1931. University Educator. Education: M.A. in English. Positions held: Sr. Lectr. in Engl. Lit., N.A.S. College. Contbr. to: Poet, an int. monthly (poems: Soul to Itself, Yet Ascetic Heart, They Brand You, Bastard, When I think of the Long Days). Recip., Distinguished Service Cit., World Poetry Soc. Intercontinental, 1973. Address: N.A.S. College, Meerut, Uttar Pradesh, India.

DASH, Jack Brien, b. 23 Apr. 1907. Retired Docker. Lecturer. Positions held: currently serving on T.U.C. leadership as exec. mbr. of British Pensioners Action Coun. in support of T U C campaign to raise living standards of Britain's O.A.P.'s; Exec. Mbr., British Pensioners Act Council; Lectures on the Labour Movement. Hon. Mbr., English Poetry Soc. Published works: Elder; Artist & Author, Good Morning Brothers (biography). Contbr. to: Times; Express; Radio recital, BBC, London Broadcasting; Capital Radio. Holder of T.U.C.'s highest award. Address: 96 Latham House, Westport St., Tower Hamlet, London E.1 ORD, U.K.

DASH, Rama Chandra, b. 4 Aug. 1948. English Lecturer. Education: B.A., S.C.S. Coll., Puri, Orissa, 1969; M.A. in Engl. Lit., Ravenshaw Coll., Cuttack, Orissa, 1971. Positions held: Lectr. in Engl., Govt. Evening Coll., Sambalpur, Orissa. Contbr. to: Annual Mag. of the Govt. Evening Coll., Sambalpur (To-Night); The Mirror, Bombay; The Jhankar (Oriya Mag.), Cuttack, Orissa; The Saptarsi (Oriya Mag.), Sambalpur, Orissa; many poems published in Oriya lang., 1966-74. Honours, awards: First prizes in Oriya & Engl. in the Annual Poems Comp. sponsored by S.C.S. Coll., Puri, Orissa, 1968 & '69; First prize for Oriya Poem in the Poem Comp. sponsored by a local Club at Puri, Orrisa. Address: Lectr. in Engl., Govt. Evening Coll., Sambalpur, Orissa, India.

DATHORNE, Oscar Ronald, b. 19 Nov. 1934. Professor of English. Educ: Queen's Coll., Georgetown, Guyana; Univ. of London, U.K.; Ph.D., Univ. of Sheffield. Married to Hildegard Ostermaier, two children. Positions held: Former UNESCO Advsr. in Engl. to Govt. of Sierra Leone; Prof., Engl., Njala Univ. Coll., Univ. of Sierra Leone, West Africa, 1968–. Published works: (novels) Dumplings in the Soup, 1963; The Scholar Man, 1964. Editor: Caribbean Narrative, 1965; Caribbean Verse, 1967; African Poetry, 1969; Africa in Prose, 1969. Contbr. to: Phylon; London Magazine; Times Literary Supplement; New African; (anthologies) Young Commonwealth Poets '65, 1965; Commonwealth Poems of Today, 1967; New Voices of the Commonwealth, 1968. Address: 8904/Friedberg bei Augsburg, Luberstrasse 2, Germany.

DATTA, Amaresh, b. Feb. 1920. University Professor. Education: M.A. & Ph.D. Married, 5 sons. Positions held: Lectr. in Engl.; Asst. Prof. of Engl.; Rdr. in Engl.; Prof. of Engl. & Dean of the Fac. of Arts, Gauhati Univ. Memberships: Am. Studies Assn., Phila., Pa., U.S.A. Published works: Shakespeare's Tragic Vision & Art, 1963; Captive Moments – a book of verse, 1971. Contbr. to: Quest; East & West; Illustrated Weekly of India; Thought; Prabuddha Bharata; Writers' Workshop; Indo-Anglian Poetry – an anthol.; Il Giornale Dei Poeti, Rome; Ocarina; Poet. Recip., highest prize, Int. Poetry Comp., Int. Assn. of Poetry, Rome, 1951. Address: Gauhati Univ., Gauhati-14, Assam, India.

d'AURIA, Gemma Abkazoff, pen name **d'AURIA, Gemma,** Poet; Dramatist; Sculptor; Archaeologist. Education: Univ. of Pa.; R.I. Schl. of Design; Sartain Schl. of Art; Pa. Acad. of Fine Arts; Albert Newman Schl. of the Dance; Elizabetta Menzelli Schl. of Ballet. Positions held: Asst. in Paleontology & Archaeology, Santa Barbara Mus. of Natural Hist.; an Ed. of the Borestone Poetry Awards Anthol. of Best Poems. Memberships: Bd. of Trustees, Poets of the Pacific; Writers Guild of Am., West, Inc. Published works: Resurrection at Sundown; High Noon (vol. of poems), 1949; Soliloquies of Stephen Foster, 1947 (also Radio broadcast on KHJ); Litany of Loreto – a recording, verse sequence w. Roger Wagner Choir. Contbr. to: Sat. Review of Lit.; Voices; Motive; Spirit; Prairie Schooner; Yankee; N.M. Qtly.; N.Y. Herald Tribune; Los Angeles Times: Joyce Kilmer's Anthol., 1955; Music in Miniature, 1942; Borestone Mountain Poetry Awards Anthol., 1952, '53, '54, & '56; Epos Anthol., 1956; New Orlando Poetry Anthol., 1958, etc. Address: 2361 Allview Terr. West, Hollywood, CA 90068, U.S.A.

DAVE, Mukund R., pen name **URRAGI,** b. 15 Aug. 1939. Lecturer in English. Education: M.A., Engl. Lit., Gujarat Univ., 1965. Positions held: Secondary Schl. Tchr., 1957-59; H.S. Tchr., 1959-65; Coll. Lectr., 1965– (recognised post-grad. Tchr. in Engl. & Am. Lit., 1970–) Memberships: World Poetry Soc. Intercontinental, U.S.A.; Am. Studies Rsch. Ctr., Hyderabad, India; Jt. Sec., Saurashtra Univ. Area Engl. Tchrs.' Assn., Rajkot, India. Contbr. to: Poetry India; Poet; Thought; Ocarina; Vishwa-Vigyan; Chetna; Tantrum; Jansatta; The Western Times; Ful-Chhab. Guest Ed., Tantrum, 1974. Recip., Distinguished Serv. Cit. Award, World Poetry Soc. Intercontinental, 1973. Address: Vasant, Setubandh Soc., Behind M.V. Mahila Coll., Rajkot 360001, India.

DAVEY, Frank, b. 19 Apr. 1940. Associate Professor of English. Education: B.A., Univ. of B.C., Canada; M.A., ibid; Ph.D., Univ. of So. Calif. Married Helen Simmons, div. 1969, 2) Linda Tallentire, 2 children (Michael & Sara). Positions held: Tchng. Asst., Univ. of B.C., Canada, 1961-63; Lectr., Royal Rds. Mil. Coll., 1963-66; Asst. Prof., ibid. 1967-70; Writer-in-Res., Sir Geo. Williams Univ., 1969-70; Asst. Prof., York Univ., 1970-72; Assoc. Prof., ibid, 1972–. Published works: D-Day & After, 1962; City of the Gulls & Sea, 1964; Bridge Force, 1965; The Scarred Hull, 1966; Weeds, 1970; Four Myths for Sam Perry, 1970; Griffon, 1972; King of Swords, 1972; l'An Trentiesme, 1972; Arcana, 1973. Contbr. to: Tish; Delta; The Canadian Forum; Prism; Evidence; South & West; Blue Grass; Mountain; Lahar Hindi Monthly; The Fiddlehead;

Island; Sum; Imago; Genesis West; The Literary Review; Magdalene Syndrome Gazette, etc. Recip., Macmillan Prize, 1962. Address: 395 Elm Rd., Toronto, Ont., Canada M5M 3W3.

DAVIDS, Jennifer, b. 15 Oct. 1945. Teacher. Educ: Tchr. Trng. Coll., South Africa, 1963-65. Positions held: Factory Worker, 1967; Tchr., Primary Schl., Cape Town, 1968–. Contbr. to: New Coin; Contrast; New Nation. Address: Cape Town, S. Africa.

DAVIE, Donald (Alfred), b. 17 July 1922. University Professor. Education: St. Catherine's Coll., Cambridge. Positions held: Lectr., Engl., Trinity Coll., Dublin, 1950-54; Fellow, ibid, 1954-57; Vis. Prof., Univ. of Calif., Berkeley, 1957-58; Lectr., Engl., Cambridge Univ., 1958-59; Fellow, Gonville & Caius Coll., Cambridge, 1959-64; Pro-Vice-Chancellor, Univ. of Essex, 1965-68; Prof., Engl., Stanford Univ., Calif., USA, 1968–. Published works: Brides of Reason, 1955; A Winter Talent, 1957; The Forest of Lithuania, 1959; A Sequence of Francis Parkman, 1961; New & Selected Poems, 1961; Events & Wisdoms: Poems 1957-63, 1965. Ed. & Contbr., numerous publs. Address: Dept. of Engl., Stanford Univ., Stanford, Calif. 94305, USA.

DAVIES, P(iers) A(nthony) D(avid), b. 15 June 1941. Barrister, Solicitor, Poet. Education: LL.B., Auckland Univ., NZ.; Dip. of Engl. & Comparative Law, City of London Coll., UK. Memberships: NZ rep., Workshop Two, London, UK.; Int. Correspondent, Poesie Vivante, Geneva; Centro Studi e Scambi Internazionali, Rome; Poetry Soc., UK. Published works: East And Other Gong Songs, 1967; Day Trip From Mount Meru, 1969; Diaspora Performed, 1971. Contbr. to: Hark; Hornsey Journal; Poetry One; Ophir; NZ Overseas; Workshop; Continuum; Earwig; Scrip; Poesie Vivante; UNISA English Studies; Internat. Who's Who in Poetry Anthol.; Poet Lore. Address: P.O. Box 1479, Auckland, NZ.

DAVIS, Carol Beery, b. 15 Sept. 1890. Music Teacher (Piano, Pipe Organ). Education: Chattanooga School of Music, Tenn.; Kofler School of Music, Dayton, Ohio; Univ. of Washington (4 yrs.). Positions held: Church organist, since 1904, and for Northern Light Presbyterian Church for 35 yrs.; sometime Pres., Pioneers of Alaska; Pres., Juneau-Douglas Concert Assoc. Memberships: Creative Writers Group, Juneau (Charter Member, and Pres. (for 8 yrs.)); Poetry Soc. of Alaska, Inc. (orig. organizer; Pres. (for 8 yrs.), and now Pres. Emeritus. Published works: Alaska's Flag (now in 3rd edition); Songs of the Totem; Alaska Driftwood, 1953; One Hundred Years of Alaskan Poetry, 1967 (associated with compilation, for Alaska Centennial); Home is North (forthcoming). Contbr. to: Alaska Mag.; Poet; Country Poet; Alaska Empire; Life & Health Mag.; Anthol. of American Poetry; One Hundred Years of Alaskan Poetry; Spring Anthol.; American Mosaic; Oregonian Sunday Supp.; Modern American Sonnet. Awards: Silver Cup, for Legends of Alaska Contest in Poetry; Gold and Silver Medallion plaques from Alaska Purchase Centennial Commission, 1967; Appointed Poet Laureate of Alaska, by Alaska State Legislature, 1967; Cert. from UPLI, 1968; Pres. Emeritus, Poetry Soc. of Alaska, Inc.; other hons.: Mother of Alaska, by American Mothers Committee, 1952, and Woman of the Year, by Juneau Rotary Club, 1965. Address: 114 E. 6th St., Juneau, AK 99801.

DAVIS, Jeff Ray, b. 17 Nov. 1906. Retired Financial Management Analyst; Educator. Education: B.A. & M.A., N. Tex. State Univ., Denton, Tex.; further study at Univ. of Tex., Austin, Tex. A & M, Tex. Tech. & Baylor Univ. Positions held: Coll. Tchr. of Engl., Tarleton Coll., Baylor, Grand Canyon Coll., Phoenix, Ariz., Ark. A & M., 1949-57; Financial Mgmt. Analyst, Dept. of Housing & Urban Dev., 1957-73. Member, Poetry Soc. of Tex. Published works: Autumn Bud, 1959; Winter Thaw, 1966; Spring Glory, 1970. Contbr. to: Avesta; Bapt. Standard; Anthol. of Poetry for Teachers; Fort Worth Press. Recip., Offer Lan & Willie

Davis Award, Poetry Soc. of Tex. Address: 422 N. Denton St., Gainesville, TX 76240, U.S.A.

DAVIS, Maralee, (Mary Elizabeth G. Gibson), b. 9 Jan. 1924. Writer; Poet; Real Estate Saleswoman. Married 1) Francis Charles Davis, div. 2) David Joel Thibault, div. 3) William Carter Gibson. Positions held: Owner, Real Estate Bus.; Dairy Farmer w. 1st husband; Sec., The Collegian, Univ. of Mass. student newspaper; Amherst Jrnl. Record; Greenfield Recorder; w. WHYN-Radio-TV, Springfield; w. WTTT-Radio, Amherst; Radio Sales, WHMP-AM-FM, Northampton; Speaker & Rdr., Vt. Writers' Sem., 1970; WMUL-TV series, 1970, Morris Harvey Coll., 1970 & '71. Memberships: Fndr., Western Mass. Writers' Guild; Asst. Ed., Newsletter, Poetry Soc. of NH; Ariz. State Poetry Soc.; World Poetry Soc.; W. Va. Poetry Soc.; Va. Poetry Soc.; League of Vt. Writers; Ga. State Poetry Soc.; Fla. State Poetry Soc. Published works: Soliloquy's Virgin, 1964; The Valley of Self, 1969; Christmas – A Season of Heart, 1969; Compiled anthol. Collage of Emily. Contbr. to: Ballet on the Wind (anthol.), 1969; Golden Quill Press Anthol., 1969, '70, '71; Manchester Sunday News, NH; Greenfield Recorder Gazette; Herald Advertiser; Ariz. State Poetry Soc. Anthol.; Premier Poets; Poet, 1970; Hartford Courant; The Traveller; Springfield Sunday Republican; Morris Harvey Coll. Anthols., 1970-72. Honours, awards: Writers' Scholarship, Springfield Writers' Conf., Suffield, Conn., 1961; Awards from Nat. Fed. of Poetry Socs.; Cit., World Poetry Soc., 1970; Nom. of the Valley of Self to World Poet Archives. Address: P.O. Box 697, Amherst, MA 01002, U.S.A.

DAVIS, Marjorie Aline, b. 21 May 1928. Housewife. Education: Business College, and Baylor University, Waco. Married to Robert F. Davis. Pres., Women Missionary Union, 1968-69; Superintendent, Kindergarten Church Training, 1969-70; Program Chairman, Adult Church Training, 1970; Asst. Church Librarian, 1971; Pres., Adult Church Training, 1973. Member, Poetry Soc. of Texas; Nat. Fed. of State Poetry Societies; Waco Chapter, Poetry Soc.; Major Poets Chapter; San Antonio International Poetry Society; Poetry Soc. of Centro Studi e Scambi Internazionali; The American Poets Fellowship Soc.; The Acad. of American Poets. Pubs. include: Thoughts in Poetry, 1970. Contrib. to publications of Centro Studi e Scambi Internazionali; Poetry Soc. of Texas; Waco Youth Cultural Centre; Texas Collection, Baylor Univ., etc. Awarded Certificate of Merit, 1972. Address: 2400 Austin Avenue, Waco, Texas 76701, USA.

DAVIS, Mary Octavia Roberta. Illustrates under name of **DUTZ.** b. 11 May 1901. Teacher; Writer; Painter; Musician. Education: B.A. English, Our Lady of Lake Coll., San Antonio; Grad. Federal Art School; Grad. Famous Writers School; Attended Univ. of Texas, Austin; C.I.A., School Industrial Arts, Denton, Texas. Member: Poetry Soc. of Texas; Poetry Soc. of San Antonio (Music Chairman); Art League, Hondo, Texas; Conservation Soc. King William Area, San Antonio; Delta Kappa Gamma – Beta Chapter San Antonio. Pubs. Red Sky, 1936; 2 anthologies, 1936-37; text book on literature, 1938; Waves of Thought, 1970. Contrib. to: Houston Chronicle; Hollands Magazine; Fletcher's Farming; Palms Magazine; Grade Teacher; Normal Instructor; Torch Bearer; Awards include: Major Donald J. Crocker Award, 1st in 1968, 69, 71., Monthly prize Texas Poetry Soc., Austin; 8 1st prizes Texas Poetry Soc., 1960-73; 2 1st prizes 1972-73, San Antonio Poetry Soc.; Presented songs and poem to Teachers Council; Presented Indian Cantata arranged for San Antonio Poetry Soc., 1972. Addresses: (Summer) P.O. Box 236, Hondo, Texas 78861, USA; (Sept. to June) 125 Adams, San Antonio, Texas 78210, USA.

DAVIS, Raecile Gwaltney, b. 5 Feb. 1910. Teacher of Business Education. Education: Howard Coll., Samford Univ.; Tchrs. Cert., Speedwriting Inst., N.Y.C. Married Fred Alvis Davis, 2 daughters Elizabeth Anne

Cosper (dec.), Sandra Patricia Barksdale. Positions held: Tchr. of Bus. Educ. for many years. Memberships: Recording Sec., Corres. Sec., Ala. Writers Conclave; First Dir. of Jr. Clubs, Third Dist., Ala. Fed. Women's Clubs, Org. 1962; Prog. Chmn., The Quill Club of Birmingham; Prog. Chmn., The Woman's Club of Birmingham; Gen. Sec., The Ala. Poetry Soc.; Nat. Inst. Arts and Letters. Contbr. to: Anthol. So. Poetry, 1971; Anthol. Ala. Poets, 1971; The Sampler, vol. 5, Spring 1973 & '74; Progressive Farmer; Ideals; B'ham. News; Poetry Taped, Ala. Poetry Soc., 1974. Honours, awards incl: Histl. Awards, Ala. Writers' Conclave, 1968, '69; Morrison Silver Bowl Award, AFWC, 1974; Wrote and directed pageant celebrating 50th anniversary, Ala. Writers' Conclave, 1974. Address: 5621 Sixth Ave. South, Birmingham, AL 35212, U.S.A.

DAVIS, William Virgil, b. 26 May 1940. Professor of English. Education: A.B., Ohio Univ., 1962; B.D., The Pittsburgh Theological Sem., 1965; M.A., Ohio Univ., 1965; M. Div., The Pittsburgh Theological Sem., 1971; Ph.D., Ohio Univ., 1967. Married. Positions held: Asst. Prof. of Engl., Ohio Univ., 1967-68, Ctrl. Conn. State Coll., 1968-71; Tunxis Community Coll., 1971-72 & The Univ. of Ill., 1972–. Rep. in following anthols: The Best In Poetry, 1969; New Generation; Poetry, 1971, etc. Contbr. to: Poetry; The Nation; Mich. Quarterly Review; The Mass. Review; Shenandoah; North Am. Review; Chelsea; Minn. Review; The Carleton Miscellany; The Centennial Review; Epoch; The Univ. Review; Arion's Dolphin; Prairie Schooner; Prism; The Fiddlehead, etc. Honours: Scholar in Poetry, Bread Loaf Writers' Conf., 1970. Address: Apt. 204, 415 South Lombard Ave., Oak Park, IL 60302, U.S.A.

DAVISON, Peter Hubert, b. 27 June 1928. Poet; Editor. Education: A.B., Harvard Univ., 1949; St. John's Coll., Cambridge Univ., 1949-50. Married, Jane Auchincloss Truslow, 1959. Positions held: Asst. Ed., Harcourt, Brace & Co., 1950-51, '53-55; US Army, 1951-53; Asst. to Dir., Harvard Univ. Press, 1955-56; Assoc. Ed., Atlantic Monthly Press, 1956-59; Exec. Ed., ibid, 1959-64; Dir., 1964–. Published works: The Breaking of the Day, 1964; The City & the Island, 1966; Pretending to be Asleep, 1970. Dark Houses, 1971. Contbr. to: Harper's; Encounter; Atlantic; New Yorker; Poetry; Hudson Review; Partisan Review; Southern Review; Kenyon Review; Epoch; Antioch Review; Antalus; Mill Mountain Review; Choice; The Reporter; Breve; American Scholar; num. anthols. Winner in Comp., Yale Series & Younger Poets, 1963. Address: 11 Mellow St., Cambridge, Mass. 02138, USA.

DAWE, Bruce, b. 15 Feb. 1930. Teacher. Education: Melbourne & Queensland Univs.; B.A.; Litt.B., Univ. of New England. Positions held: currently Lectr. in Literature, Darling Downs Inst. of Advanced Educ., Darling Heights, Toowoomba, Queensland. Published works: No Fixed Address, 1962; A Need of Similar Name, 1965; An Eye for a Tooth, 1967; Beyond the Subdivisions, 1969; Heat-Wave, 1970; Condolences of the Season, 1971; Poets on Record No. 5. Contbr. to: Twentieth Century Review; Southerly; Southern Review; Makar; Australian Poetry; Westerly; Meanjin; Poetry Mag.; Overland; Poetry Australia; The Australian; The Age; The Sydney Morning Herald; Hemisphere; Lot's Wife; Australian Letters; Bulletin; Sunday Observer; Oz; Spirit, U.S.A., etc. Honours, awards: Myer Poetry Prize, 1966 & 69; Ampol Arts Award for Creative Lit., 1969. Address: 30 Cumming St., Toowoomba, Qld. 4350, Australia.

DAWE, Thomas, b. 24 Oct. 1940. Assistant Professor of English. Education: B.A. (Ed.), Memorial Univ. of Nfld.; B.A., ibid; completing M.A. in Romantics. Married, 1 son, 1 daughter. Positions held: Tchr., Lewisporte, Nfld.; V.P., ibid; Lectr., Memorial Univ.; Asst. Prof., Junior Div., ibid. Memberships: World Poetry Soc.; Nfld. Writers' Guild; Nfld. Art Assn. Published works: Connections, 1972. Contbr. to: Baffles of Wind & Tide (anthol.); Poet; Atlantic Advocate; Fiddlehead; The Far Point; Other Voices; Canadian Poetry; Quarry; Pluck; The Small Pond;

Nfld. Stories & Ballads; Nfld. Quarterly, etc. Honours, awards: Awards for narrative poetry, short story & art, Nfld. Arts & Letters Comps., 1968, 69, 70, 71, 72, 73; Elizabeth Burton Poetry Prize, 1972. Address: English Dept., Jr. Div., Memorial Univ., St. John's, Nfld., Canada.

DAWES, Neville, b. 16 June 1926. Senior Lecturer. Educ: Jamaica Coll., Kingston; M.A., Oriel Coll., Oxford. Married, six children. Positions held: Ed., Okyeame, Accra, Ghana; Vis. Prof., Engl., Univ. of Guyana, 1963-64; Sr. Lectr., Engl., ibid, 1965–. Published works: In Sepia, 1957; (novel) The Last Enchantment, 1960. Contbr. to: Bim; Focus; (anthologies) Schwarzer Orpheus, 1964; Young Commonwealth Poets '65, 1965; Caribbean Voices, 1966; Sun's Eye, 1968. Address: Univ. of Ghana, Accra, Ghana.

DAWSON, Marjorie, b. 16 Apr. 1896. Teacher. Education: M.A., Liverpool Univ. Positions held: Tchr., Thetford Girls' Grammar Schl., Norfolk (Engl. & French); Engl. Tchr., Heanor Grammar Schl., Derbyshire. Memberships: Hon. Sec. Gen., Poetry Lovers' Fellowship; Poetry Soc. Contbr. to: Poetry Review; Poetry of To-day. Honours, awards: Poetry Review Cash Prize for 'In Memory of John Keats', 1921; Poetry of To-day Book Prize for 'The Robin's Song, 1925. Address: 56 Raikes Parade, Blackpool F71 4EX, Lancs., U.K.

DAWSON, Martha Morgan, pen names **MORGAN, Mary Martha,** & **FEHR, Martha Morgan,** b. 30 Aug. 1908. Writer; Advertiser. Education: Colo. Univ., Boulder; Denver Univ., Colo. Positions held: Free-lance Writer; Religious Advertiser. Memberships: Colo. Poetry Soc., Committee Chairman; Denver Women's Press Club, Pres., 1973-74. Contrib. to: The Denver Post; Aspire Magazine. Address: 1515 E. 9th Ave., Apt. 109, Denver, Colo. 80218, USA.

DAY, Audrey Grace, b. 9 July 1940. Training Supervisor. Memberships: Orbis Poetry Soc.; Strand Poetry Club. Contbr. to: The Autumn Anthol., 1969; A Treasury of Modern Poets, 1970; New Poetry, 1971; Editors Choice, 1972; The Florwain Book of Poetry, 1973; Poetry, 1973. Address: 'Redvers', 127 Queen Mary Ave., Cleethorpes, Lincolnshire, U.K.

DAYTON, Irene, b. 6 Aug. 1922. Poet. Education: Roberts Wesleyan Coll. Married Benjamin B. Dayton, 2 sons (David & Glenn). Memberships: Poetry Soc. of Am.; Pres., Rochester Poetry Soc., 1960-62 & 70-72; Int. Platform Assn.; Advsry. Mbr., Marquis Biographical Lib. Soc. Published works: (books of poetry) The Sixth Sense Quivers, 1970 & The Panther's Eye, 1974. Contbr. to poetry jrnls. & lit. mags. in U.S.A., Europe & Japan inclng: The Lit. Review; The Midwest Quarterly; The Chicago Tribune Sunday Mag.; Malahat Review; Dimensions in Am. Judaism; Black Mountain Review; Mod. Age; Adam, an Inter. Quarterly; Jrnls. of Vacuum Sci., Japan; Poetry Australia. Honours, awards: Poetry Award, Religious Fest. of Religious Art, 1959 & 60; Guinness Poetry Award, Cheltenham Fest. of Lit., U.K., 1963. Address: 209 S. Hillandale Dr., East Flat Rock, NC 28726, U.S.A.

DEAGON, Ann Fleming, b. 19 Jan. 1930. Teacher of Classics. Education: B.A., Birmingham-Southern Coll., 1950; M.A., Univ. of N.C., 1951; Ph.D., ibid, 1954. Married Dr. Donald D. Deagon, 2 daughters. Positions held: Grad. Asst. & Kenan Fellow, Univ. of N.C., 1950-54; Asst. Prof. of Classics, Furman Univ., 1954-56; Assoc. Prof. of Classics, Guilford Coll., 1956–. Memberships: N.C. Poetry Soc.; Greensboro Writers Club. Contbr. to many jrnls., reviews inclng: Beloit Poetry Jrnl.; Carleton Miscellany; Carolina Qtly.; Crucible; Encore; Matrix; Miss. Review; New Laurel Review; Southern Poetry Review; Western Humanities Review; Wormwood Review. Recip. many poetry hons. & awards inclng. sev. from Nat. Fed. of State Poetry Socs., Ala. State Poetry Soc., Poetry Coun. of N.C. Address: 802 Woodbrook Dr., Greensboro, NC

27410, U.S.A.

DEAL, Susan Lynn, pen name **DEAL, Susan Strayer,** b. 21 Feb. 1948. Student; Poet. Education: Inter Am. Univ., San Juan, Puerto Rico; B.A., Kearney State Coll., Neb., 1973. Married Steven L. Deal. Positions held: Lit. Ed., Kearney State Coll. Mag., 1973. Co-ed. & publisher, poetry mag. Chevnozem. Contbr. to: North Platte Coll. Knight's Page, 1966-67; The Antler, Kearney State Coll., 1970 & '73; Encore, N.M.; Aspect, Mass.; Poetry of Our Times, N.Y.; Cyclo-Flame, Tex.; Chernozem, Neb. Address: 611, 11th St., Gothenburg, NB 69138, U.S.A.

DE BARBOZA CARNEYRO E FONSECA, Arthur Lambert, pen name **DE FONSECA, Arthur Lambert,** b. 7 Nov. 1922. Writer; Poet; Gentleman-Farmer. Educ: Classical Univ., Porto; Art Study, Ecole de Beaux-Arts, Porto & Lisbon. Mbrships: Geographical Soc. of Lisbon; Teilhard de Chardin Soc. of Brussels; Assn. of Men of Letters, Porto. Published works incl: (poetry) Elegras e outros Poemas, 3rd ed., 1964; Continuidades Poéticas, 2nd ed.,1972; Requiem e VI Cauçoés de Morte, 1965; Salmos e Oraçoés, 3rd ed., 1970; La Torche, 1973; (prose) O II Cerco de Dio, 3rd ed., 1971; Lear Cadeao, 2nd ed., 1971; Dialogo en o Silencos, 1973. Contbr. to: Le Journal des Poètes; Il Giornale dei Poeti; The Bridge; Veuto Nuovo; Nouvelle Europe; United Daily News, Taiwan, etc. Invited to speak at num. int. poetry congresses. Address: Casa do Barral, Paço de Sousa, Portugal.

DE BELDER, J.L., b. 18 June 1912. Editor, Redactor, Encyclopaedia Winkler Prins & Founder & Ldr. of the Colibrant Publications for Poetry, 1950–. Education: Hist. of Art, Univ. Marburg/Lahn; Jrnlsm. Married, 4 sons. Positions held: Jrnlst.; Tchr.; Publisher. Memberships: PEN Club; Die Kogge; Assn. of Flemish Authors. Published works: (poetry) De gesloten kamer, 1939; Epimenides ontwaken, 1943; Ballade der onzekerheden, 1949; Recitatief, 1951; Ki Fong, een Chinese suite, 1956; Van zuilen, sneeuw en rozen, 1964; (translations) R.M. Rilke (poems), 1936; Friedrich Hölderlin (poems), 1943; De ballade van Reading, Oscar Wilde, 1950; A. Sully Prudhomme (poems), 1962; 'Serres chaudes' of Maurice Maeterlinck (poems), 1962; (anthols.) Van 20 dichters, 1959; Flämische Lyrik, 1960; Zoete, lieve, soevereine (Vlaamse minnelyriek), 1970; (essays) Inleiding tot 'Friedrich Hölderlin, Gedichten en fragmenten, 1943; A. Sully Prudhomme of de abdicatie van het hart, 1962; also prose & var. contbns. to jrnls., etc. Honours, awards: Guido Gezelle Prize, 1957; Prize, Lit. Critique, Oost Vlaanderen, 1959. Address: Rode Beukendreef 17, B. 9831, Deurle-Leie, Belgium.

DE BOLT, William Walter, b. 11 Mar. 1909. Minister, United Church of Christ. Education: A.B., Jefferson Coll.; Southern Meth. Univ.; B.D., Th.D., Burton Coll. & Seminary. Minister of following chs: Baker, Ore.; Douglas, Wyo.; Ontario, Ore.; Butte, Mont.; Chester, Neb.; Trenton, Neb. Memberships: Mich. Poetry Soc.; World Poetry Soc. Interncontinental; Cath. Poetry Soc.; Am. Poetry League; Idaho Poet's Guild. Published works: Reflections, 1930; Aery Shapes, 1936; Vials of Verse, 1937; Drifted Dreams, 1937; Through The Lattice, 1944, '61; Lighted Lanterns, 1952; Green Before The Sun, 1960; Mist From The Earth, 1969; Bricks Without Straw, 1971; Daughters of Music, 1973. Contbr. to: Forum (Univ. of Houston); Forum (Ball State Univ.); Prairie Schooner (Univ. of Neb.); Laurel Review; Pulpit; Nat. Cath. Reporter; Int. Poetry Review; Alaska Review; Time of Singing; The Christian Century; Am. Bard; Archer; United Poets; Peninsula Poets; Midwest Quarterly; Kansas Quarterly; Poet (India), etc. Honours & Awards: The Geneva Booher Award (nat.), 1965; The Russel Petit Askue Prize, 1968; 2nd Place, Nat. Contest, Ariz. Poetry Soc., 1969, & many other prizes & awards. Address: Trenton, Neb. 69044, USA.

DECAUNES, Lucien Daniel, pen name **DECAUNES, Luc,** b. 4 Jan. 1913. Poet; Author. Educ: Cert., Singing Tchr.; Cert., Adv. Studies, Psychol. m. (1) Cécile

Eluard, 1938 (div. 1946); (2) Andrée-Claude Lacôte, 1955, 1 s. Positions held: Fndg. Dir., Soutes Revue, 1935-38, 1952-53; Mbr., Superior Coun. of Inquiry into Nat. Educ., 1946-48; Fndg. Dir., Theatre sans visage Troupe, 1953-55; Dir., Radio Dakar, 1957-59; Chief Ed., Dossiers Documentaires, 1962-66; Chief Ed., Tep-Actualité, 1963–; Dir., Clefs Collect., 1962–. Published works incl: L'Indicatif présent, 1938; A l'oeil nu, 1941; Le Coeur en Ordre, 1943; L'Air Natal, 1944; Le Sens du Mystère, 1946; Droit de Regard, 1951; Baudelaire, 1952; L'Amour sans preuves, 1959; Raisons Ardentes, 1964; Paul Eluard, 1965; La Poésie Romantique, 1973. Contbr. to: La Hune; Esprit; Europe; Cahiers du Sud; Mercure de France; Marginales, etc. Address: 3 Sq. Beethoven, 93100 Montreuil, France.

DE CHAZAL, Malcolm, b. 12 Sept. 1902. Engineer. Education: Royal Coll., Curepipe, Mauritius; Agric. Engrng., Baton Rouge, La., U.S.A. Positions held: Agric. Engr., Cuba; Agric. Engr., Mauritius; Telephone Engr. in the Telecommunications Dept. Member, Acad. of Mauritians Writers. Is also a painter, specializing in humouristic designs in poster-paint & has held exhibs. in London, U.S.A., Johannesburg, Paris & Dakar. Published works: Books of 'Pensées', I 1940, II 1942, III 1942, IV 1943, V 1944, VI 1944; Sens Plastique, 1948; Plastic Sense (transl., Irwing J. Weiss, Herder & Herder, U.S.A.), 1971; La Vie Filtrée, 1949; Sens Magique, 1957; Poëmes, 1968. Contbr. to: Le Mauricien; L'Express; Advance; Poèmes d'aujourd'hui pour les enfants de maintenant, Jacques Charpentreau; Le livre d'Or de la Poèsie française, Pierre Seghers. Address: Curepipe, Mauritius.

DECKER, Esther Bailey, b. 12 Sept. 1913. Retired Office Manager. Education: Bus. Coll., Salina, Kans. Widow. Positions held: Sec.; Asst. Mgr.; Mgr. of Insurance Office; Hurricane Disaster Chmn. for Am. Red Cross. Active in civic affairs. Memberships: NAPA; NJPA; Modern Haiku. Contbr. to: Orphic Lute; J.C. Transcripts; Nutmegger; Modern Haiku; Haiku West; The Ferry; Quoin; Jean's Jrnl.; Denver Post; Grit; Salina Jrnl.; Little Angel; Pixie Angel; Image; Haiku Highlights; Imprints; Christian Religion; Highlights for Children, etc. Recip. var. certs. from mags. Address: P.O. Box 331, Rockport, TX 78382, U.S.A.

de CLIPPELE, Antoine, b. 7 Dec. 1885. Emeritus Premier President of Belgian Supreme Court. Educ: Doct., Law; Licence, Pol. & Soc. Scis. Married, 8 children. Positions held incl: Served in World War I, 1914-18; Lawyer, Ct. of Appeals, Brussels, 1909; Dpty. Atty. to King, 1919; Advsr., Court of Appeals, Ghent, 1938; Advsr., Supreme Ct., 1946; Pres., then Premier Pres., ibid, 1946. Mbr., Soc. of Belgian Writers. Published works: Poèmes au fil des heures, 1971; Nostalgies et aspirations, 1971. Contbr. to: Journal des Tribunaux; Anthologie de 1947; Journal de l'Académie des Poètes; La Coupe d'Ambroisie. Honours, awards: Prix Voltaire, 1942; 1st Prize for Songs, Soc. of Friends of Petrach. Address: Mussenstraat 16, 9000 Ghent, Belgium.

DEDERICK, Robert, b. 27 Sept. 1919. Solicitor. Married, 1 son, 3 daughters. Positions held: Solicitor, 1947-51; Legal staff of Shell Mex & BP Grp. in S. Africa, 1952–. Memberships: V.P., Cape Town Writers' Club; Comm. Mbr., Owl Club, Cape Town. Published works: The Quest & other Poems, 1968; A Lucid Interval, 1974. Represented in following anthols: Penguin Book of South African Verse, 1968; Inscapes, 1970; Seismograph, 1971; Outridings, 1972; Ah Big Yaws, 1973; IWWP, 1973. Contbr. to: Standpunte; New Coin; Contrast; New Nation; Cape Times; 'English'; Lion & Impala; Torque. Honours, awards: State Poetry Prize, S. Africa, 1967; Thomas Pringle Award for Creative Writing, 1971. Address: 82 Camp Ground Rd., Rondebosch 7700, Cape Town, S. Africa.

DEEBLE, Russell John. Director of Publishing Firm. Educated in Melbourne & Adelaide, Australia.

Positions held: Literary Ed., Young Modern Mag., Adelaide; Free Lance Reviewer of theatre and books for Melbourne newspapers; Dir., Still Earth Publications, currently. Published works: War Babies, 1965; Trip to Light Blue, 1968; High on a Horse with Wax Wings, 1969; Dictionary of Poetics, 1969. Contbr. to: Meanjin; Overland; Mok; Westerly; Young Writers in Australia (anthology), 1968. Address: Still Earth Publications, 84 Bridge St., Richmond, Victoria, Australia, 3121.

DEEMER, Bill, b. 4 Mar. 1945. Published works: Poems, 1964; Diana, 1966; The King's Bounty, 1968. Recip., National Endowment for the Arts award, 1968.

DEFENBAUGH, Helena Cheney, b. 24 Apr. 1907. Housewife; Ex-Legal Secretary. Education: Bus. Coll.; Univ. of N.M. Married Leo Defenbaugh. Positions held: Sec., Albuquerque Civic Coun.; var. State & Govt. offices over the years; Legal Sec., Eva C. Thomas, Atty., 10 yrs. Memberships: Nat. Fed. of State Poetry Socs. Inc.; N.M. Poetry Soc.; Former Mbr., 'Mavericks'. Published works: Trio, 1973; A Rose to Bloom, 1972. Contbr. to: New Hampshire Troubadour; Health City Sun; N.M. Mag.; Christian Sci. Monitor; Encore; Quintessence; Inky Trails; Sunburst; Kansas Kernels; Tejas; Poet (India); South & West (N.M. edn.) Honours, awards: 2nd prize, State Contest, sponsored by C.T. French, late 1930's; Book Award, Quintessence, 1972; Cert. of Appreciation, 1972; Poet of the Month, Inky Trails, 1972; 1st prize, Faith Contest, sponsored by Caroline Kotowicz, 1972. Address: 1620 Arcadian Trail, N.W. Albuquerque, NM 87107, U.S.A.

DEFFRY, Frank, b. 4 July 1938. Educ: Univ. of Chicago. Married & Separated, one child. Published works: Two States of Mine, 1969; As Near as I Can Tell, 1969; "Does God Have Blue Eyes" (short story), in Seared Eye, 1968. Contbr. to: Spiro; Love-Letter; Nexus; New. Address: 975 N. Point, San Francisco, CA 94109, U.S.A.

DEFLANDRE, Maurice, b. 31 May 1900. Pensioned Official of the Belgian State. Memberships: Assn. of Belgian Writers (A.E.B.), 1956–; Association Royale des Ecrivains wallons dialectaux & francophones (A.R.E.W.), 1972–. Contbr. of poetry to newspapers, reviews, jrnls., periodicals inclng: La Revue Nationale (Brussels); Belext (Brussels); anthologies of the 'Editions de la Revue Moderne', Paris; many others. Address: Avenue du Sacré-Coeur, 53, 1090 Brussels, Belgium.

deFORD, Sara Whitcraft, b. 9 Nov. 1916. College Professor of English. Education: B.A., 1936, M.A., 1938, Mount Holyoke; Ph.D., 1942, Yale. Positions held: Instr. in Engl., Barnard Coll., 1942-46; Prof. (various ranks), Goucher College, 1946–, and Full Prof. since 1957. Pubs. The Return to Eden, 1941; The City of Love, 1956; On Oran's Eyes (verse play), 1964. Contrib. to: Catholic World; Poetry; Saturday Review; Arizona Qtly.; AAUW Mag.; Christian Sci. Monitor; New York Times; Friends Journal, CEA Critic, etc. Awards: Sigma Theta Chi Alumnae Poetry Prize (Mt. Holyoke), 1935; Albert Stanburrough Cook Prize (Yale), 1941; Eugene F. Saxton Fellowship, 1946; Fulbright Fellowships to Japan, 1954, 1961; Two prizes from Arizona Qtly., 1964, 1971; AAUW prize, 1953; Wings Prize, 1948. Address: Goucher College, Towson, Md. 21204, USA.

DE FREES, Mary Madeline, formerly **SISTER MARY GILBERT,** b. 18 Nov. 1919. Teacher; Writer. Education: B.A., Marylhurst Coll., 1948; M.A., Univ. of Ore., 1951. Member of the Sisters of the Holy Names of Jesus & Mary 1936-73. Positions held: Tchr., Ore. elem. schls., 1938-42, high schls., 1942-48; Instr., Holy Names Coll., Spokane, Wash. (later re-named Fort Wright Coll.), 1950-55; Asst. Prof., ibid, 1955-63; Assoc. Prof., 1963-67; Vis. Assoc. Prof., Univ. of Mont., 1967-69; Assoc. Prof., 1969-72; Prof., 1972–; Vis. Instr. & Writer-in-Res., Seattle Univ., 1965-66. Published works: From the Darkroom, 1964;

Domesticating Two Landscapes, 1975. Rep. in following anthols: No More Masks! 1973; Rising Tides: Twentieth Century Am. Women Poets, 1973; Borestone Mountain Poetry Awards: Best Poems of 1960, Best Poems of 1965. Contbr. to: Am. Review; New Republic; Commonweal; The Nation; Poetry Northwest; N.Y. Times; Sat. Review; Sewanee Review; Minn. Review; Lit. Review; The Human Voice, etc. Co-winner of Abbie M. Copps Prize, Garfield Lake Review, 1973. Recip., Hon. LL.D., Gonzaga Univ., 1959. Address: 135 E. Central Ave., Missoula, MT 59801, U.S.A.

DEGANI, Asarel, pen name **DEGANI, Assi,** b. 9 May 1935. Printer. Education: B.A., Hebrew & Engl. Lit., Hebrew Univ. of Jerusalem. Married, 3 children. Contbr. to: Keshet; Me'assef Yerushalayim; Davar; Egoz; Pi-Ha'Aton, etc. Address: P.O. Box 7198, Jerusalem 91070, Israel.

DE GROOT, Jan Hendrik, pen names **SIKKEMA, Haje & J. ten MUTSAERT,** b. 13 Mar. 1901. Writer. Positions held: Operator, Govt. Telegraph Head Office, Amsterdam, 1919-35; Freelance Author, 1935-37; Asst., Lib. of the Royal Dutch Acad. of Scis., Amsterdam, 1938-44; Ed., daily newspaper, Amsterdam-Arnhem, 1945-48; Public Relations Officer, 1949-66; Drama Critic; Reviewer of Literature; Rdr.-Advisor for publishing firms on transl. of novels from Engl., German & French. Memberships incl: Soc. of Dutch Lit., Leiden; Union of Dutch Authors, Amsterdam; PEN, Dutch Ctr.; Die Kogge, European Authors Club. Published works: (poetry) Lentezon, 1927; Sprongen, 1928; Vaart, 1931; Rond de Wereld, 1931; Verloren Liedjes, 1933; Polonaise, 1934; Botsing, 1937; Een bos boterblommen, 1941; Jeremia, 1941; Herfstvacantie, 1941; De Visvangst, 1944; (ps. Haje Sikkema) Strophen op zingende soldaten, 1944; Moederkoren, 1945; Vice-Versa, 1955; Op de man af, 1961; Signalen tegen de hemel, 1968; var. prose works, as well as drama & essays. Contbr. to many jrnls., newspapers, anthols. Sev. translations. Honours, awards incl: Amsterdam Poetry Prize, 1946; Govtl. award for continuation of literature during WWII, 1946. Address: Gabrielstr. 6311, Arnhem 6002, Netherlands.

DEGUY, Michel, b. 23 May 1930. University Professor. Education: Agrégation de Philosophie. Positions held: Prof., University of Paris. Memberships: Comité de lecture des éditions Gallimard; Comité de la revue Critique. Published works: Fragment du Cadastre, 1960; Poèmes de la Presqu' ile, 1962; Biefs, 1964; Actes, 1966; Oui Dire, 1966; Figurations, 1969; Poèmes 1960-70, 1973; Tombeau de DuBellay, 1973, also Les Meurtrières, 1959; Le Monde de Thomas Mann, 1962; Histoire des Rechutes, 1968. Contbr. to: Nouvelle revue française; Critique; La Revue de Poésie; Esprit; Les Cahiers de l'Herne, etc. Honours, awards: Prix Fénéon, 1960; Prix Max Jacob, 1962. Address: 48 rue de Vaugirard, Paris 75006, France.

DEHN, Paul Edward, b. 5 Nov. 1912. Screenwriter; Opera-Librettist; Lyricist; Poet. Educ: B.A., Brasenose Coll., Oxford, U.K. Positions held: War Service, 1939-45; Film Critic, London Nat. Newspapers, 1936-63; Writer, Film-Scripts, lyrics & sketches for many West End revues; After 1963 concentrated on screenplays (Goldfinger, The Spy Who Came in From the Cold, etc.) Currently screenwriter, opera-librettist, lyricist and poet. Memberships: Councillor, Royal Soc. for the Protection of Birds; Pres., London Critics' Circle, 1956. Published works: The Day's Alarm, 1949; Romantic Landscape, 1952; Quake, Quake, Quake, 1960; The Fern on the Rock: Collected Poems, 1965. Contbr. to: Listener, New Statesman, Time and Tide; Horizon; Spectator; Outposts; Punch; (anthologies) Modern Verse, 1940; For Those Who Are Alive, 1946; Voice of Poetry (1930-50), 1950; Guinness Book of Poetry, 1958; Poetry of War, 1965; Modern Love Poems, 1966. Honours, awards: Hollywood Academy Award for Best Original Story, 1952; Cheltenham Festival Poetry Prize, 1957. Address: 19 Bramerton Street, London, S.W.3, U.K.

DEI-ANANG, Michael Francis, b. 16 Oct. 1909. Poet; Historian; Educationist. Education: B.A., London Univ., 1936; Postgrad. Dip. in Educ., ibid, 1938. Positions held: Sec. to the Gov.-Gen. of Ghana, Chief of State Protocol., 1957-58; Perm. Sec., Ministry of Foreign Affairs, Ghana, 1958-60; Hd. of African Affairs Secretariat, Ghana, 1961; Ambassador Extraordinary & Plenipotentiary, 1961-66; Nuffield Fndn. Rsch. Fellow, London Univ., 1970; African Cons. 'Sesame Street', N.Y., 1971; Disting. Vis. Prof., State Univ. of N.Y., 1970; Prof., Depts. of Hist. & African & Afro-Am. Studies, 1971; Chmn., African & Afro-Am. Studies Dept., 1973. Memberships incl: Fellow, Royal Econ. Soc., U.K.; Poetry Soc.; World Poetry Soc. Intercontinental; Fndr. Mbr., OKYEAME (Ghana Lit. Mag.) Published works inc: Okonkronni Augustino; Wayward Lines from Africa, poems; Africa Speaks, poems transl. into French, German, Hebrew, Russian; Ghana Semi-Tones, poems; Okomfo Anokye's Golden Stool, play; Ghana Glory, poems; Ghana Resurgent (Histl. sketch of Ghana); Man's Inhumanity to Man, (History); Two Faces of Africa (in collab., poems); Administration of Ghana's Foreign Policy 1957-66; var. works in prep. Honours, awards incl: Gold Coast Drama Award, 1954; Play, The Golden Stool, produced before Queen Elizabeth II in Ghana, 1961; Disting. Serv. Cit., World Poetry Soc., 1972; F.I.B.A., 1973. Permanent Address: 'Awonkae Fie', Mampong – Akwapim, Ghana, W. Africa. Present Address: Dept. of African and Afro-Am. Studies, SUNY, Brockport, NY 14420, USA.

DELAET, Jean, b. 4 Jan. 1904. Retired Professor. Education: Ecole normale pour instituteurs; Specialized in Education. Memberships: Editl. Sec., Courrier Des Poètes (mag.), 1936-39; Dir., Tribune du Journal Des Poètes, 1953-56; Réalisateur de l'hommage à Pierre-Louis Flouquet, 1936. Published works: Les Aventures extraordinaires de Billy Dum, I – Le Roi des Robbers, 1936, II – Monoo l'Insaisissable, 1938, III – Johnny Goudron, 1954; La Légende des Ailes, 1949. Contbr. to: Journal des Poètes; L'Avant-Garde; Le Thyrse, special issue on René Verboom. Address: Zeelaan No. 144, 8470 De Panne, Belgium.

DELGADO, Abelardo, pen name **ABELARDO,** b. 27 Nov. 1931. Health Director. Education: B.S. in Secondary Educ., Univ. of Tex. at El Paso, 1962. Married Dolores Estrada, 8 children. Positions held: Youth Worker, 1954-64; Prof., 1962-64; Organizer, 1965-69; Migrant Prog. Dir., 1969-71; Philos. Prof., 1971-72; Pres., Barrio Publs. On Editl. Bd. of: Mitcla Publs.; Nosotros Mag.; La Luz Mag.; Totinem Publs. Published works: Chicano (poetry), 1970; Los Cuatro (poetry), 1971; The Chicano Movement (prose-text), 1972; Mortal Sin Kit (poetry), 1972; Reflexiones (poetry), 1972; Bajo El Sol de Aztlán (poetry), 1973. Contbr. to: La Luz Mag.; Nosotros Mag.; El Gallo Newspapers; El Burro Coll. Mag.; Aztlán (book); La Raza (book). Plays written & directed: Revolucion, 1956; Young Mr. X, 1957; The Day Before Wednesday, 1958. Address: 1915 3rd St., Kirkland, WA 98033, U.S.A.

DEL GRANADO, Javier, b. 27 Feb. 1913. Writer. Education: La Salle Coll., Cochabamba, Bolivia. Memberships: Elected to Bolivian Acad. of Language; Corresponding Mbr., Royal Spanish Acad.; Foreign Mbr. French Acad. of Poetry; Int. Acad. of Leadership; Hispanic Cultural Inst.; Interam. Assoc. of Writers; Vice-Pres., Int. Union of Poet Laureates; Pres., Soc. of Writers & Artists of Bolivia; occasional Tournament Pres., Bolivian Floral Games. Published works: Rosas Pálidas, 1939; Canciones de la Tierra, 1945; Antologia Boliviana, 1948; Cochabamba, 1959; Evocación del Valle, 1964; La Parábola del Aguila, 1967; Antologica Poética de le Flor Natural, 1969; Estampas Liricas; Poemas Epicos. Contbr. to: El Imparcial; El Pais; Presna Libre; Los Tiempos; El Diario; La Razón; Presencia; La Prensa. Honours: Primer Accesit, Juegos Florales, Santa Cruz, 1939; Jazmín de Plata, Juegos Florales, Cochabamba, 1941; Primer Premio Nacional de Poesía, Diploma de Honor, Congreso Eucarístico, Cochabamba, 1941; Primer Premio

Nacional de Poesía, Diploma de Honor, Flor Natural, Laurel de Oro y Banda del Gay Saber, Juegos Florales, La Paz, 1943; Primer Premio Sudamaricano de Poesia 'Cesar Vallejo', Diploma de Honor y Medalla de Oro del Sol de Los Incas, Lima, 1947; Diploma y Medalla, Rea Academia Espanola, Madrid, 1952; Primer Premio Continental de Poesía 'Ruben Darïo', Diploma de Honor de la Asociasión Interamericana de Escritores, Plaqueta de la Embajada de Nicaragua, Buenos Aires, 1954; Primer Premio Intercontinental de Poesía, Juegos Florales Hispano-Luso-Americanos, Buenos Aires, 1959; Corona de Laureles de Oro, impuesta por el Excmo. Sr. General Don René Barrientos Ortuno, Presidente da la República de Bolivia, 1965; Pergamino de Honor y Titulo de 'Poeta Laureado Continental', otorgado por la Unión Internacional de Poetas Laureados, Quezon City, Philipines, 1965; Condecoracion de la 'Gran Orden de la Educación Boliviana', otorgada por el Supremo Gobierne, Sucre, 1967. Address: Casilla 10, Cochabamba, Bolivia.

DELIA, Joseph, b. 1 Apr. 1900. Jesuit Priest. Education: St. Aloysius Coll., Malta; philos., Granada, Spain; theol., Dublin, Ireland. Joined Soc. of Jesus, 1917. Positions held: Rector, St. Aloysius Coll., 1934-47; Mbr., Bd. of Educ., Malta, 1943-60; Spiritual Advsr. of the Malta Union of Tchrs., 1945-62. Memberships: Pioneer Mbr., Acad. of the Maltese Lang. (Akkademja tal-Malti). Published works: Leggendi (Legends), 1st ed., 1958, 2nd ed., 1964, 3rd ed., 1972; Meta tohlom il-Qalb (When the Heart Dreams), 1962. Has written verses in Maltese, Italian, Latin, Spanish, English, classical Greek. Contbr. to: Lil Hbiebna. Address: St. Philip's Rectory, Senglia, Malta, G.C.

DELISA, Emilia (Valente), Executive, Poet & Assistant Professor to husband, Prof. Dr. Victor V. DeLisa, B.S.M., Director-Owner of the Lakeland Music Ctr. and the Conservatory of Music & Arts. Positions held: Dir., Fndr. of following; Hartford Poetry League; American Jr. Poetry Soc.; Cultural Club of town of Courtlandt. Memberships: United Poets Laureate Int.; Nat. Day Poetry Comm.; World Poetry Day; Community Hosp.; Putnam Valley League of Women Voters; Am. Soc. of Composers, Authors & Publishers; The Preserver; Int. Platform Assoc.; Eastern Ctr. of Poetry Soc. of London, UK.; Scenic Hudson River. Contbr. of poetry to: Hartford Courant; Hartford Times; Peekskill Evening Star; Patent Trader; Craton News; Laurel Leaves; Int. Hall of Fame Poets; Flamingo; The Preserver; Anthol. of Verse, 1964; Poets Leaves (UPLI int. poetry mag.). Honours: Good Citizenship, DAR, 1942; 1st Prize Poetry, Dr. G.D. Saul, Univ. of Conn., 1957; "Lloyd McLean Roberts", World Poetry Day, 1962; Karta of Award, Philippines, 1966; Presidential Medal, F.E. Marcos, Philippines, 1966; Mayor A.J. Villegas (Medallion), Gatpuno's Int. Poetry, Philippines, 1966; Dr. D.S. La Madrid, Pres., Philippine Assoc. of Drs. of Civil Law & Int. Acad. of Leadership, the following: Outstanding Am. Cultural Poetry Ctr. of Youth; Prof. Dr. & Mme. DeLisa, Outstanding Couple of Poetry & Music of NY (from UN Day); Outstanding Lyric Poetess (from World Poetry Day); Cert. of Merit, DIB, 1967; Citation, DAV Chapt. 137, 1967; Dr. Rizal's Postrer Adios, Sondrio dialect transl., Gold Medal & Karta, 1968; Golden Laurel Wreath & Gold Medal, Dr. Lorena Simon, 1968; UPLI Karta, Poet in Residence for Budding Parnassians, 1968. Attended World Congress of Poets, UPLI, Manila, Philippines, 1969. Address: Renee Gate Rt. 6, Peekskill, NY 10566, USA.

DELIUS, Anthony Ronald St. Martin, b. 11 June 1916. Journalist & Broadcaster. Education: Rhodes Univ., Grahamstown, S. Africa. Married, 1 son, 1 daughter. Positions held: Captain, S.A. Army, 1939-45; Reporter, Evening Post, Port Elizabeth, 1946-49; Ldr.-Writer, Cape Times, Cape Town, 1950-54; Freelance Corres. & Broadcaster, Africa, Britain & U.S.A., 1954-57; Africa & Parliamentary Columnist, Cape Times, 1958-66; S.A. Morning Press Corres. in U.S.A. & Britain, 1967; B.B.C. Africa Service, 1968-. Mbr., PEN. Published works: Unknown Border; 1954; The Last

Division, 1959; A Corner of the World, 1962; Black South-Easter, 1966. Contbr. to: Poetry Commonwealth; Vandag; Standpunte; Contrast; New Yorker; New Coin; B.B.C. Recip. (w. R.N. Currey) S.A. Poetry Prize (Educ. Dept.), 1960. Address: B.B.C. External Service, Bush House, London E.C.4., U.K.

DE LONGCHAMPS, Joanne Laurie, b. 7 Jan. 1923. Poet. Education: Univ. of Nev., Reno. Married Galen Edward de Longchamps, 1 son. Positions held: Lectr. in Poetry, Univ. of Nev., Reno, 1962, 1971-. Member, Poetry Soc. of Am. Published works: (poetry books) And Ever Venus, 1944; Eden Under Glass, 1957; The Hungry Lions, 1963; The Wishing Animal, 1970. Contbr. of over 300 poems to mags., newspapers, anthols., 1944-. Honours, awards: Reynolds Lyric Award, Poetry Soc. of Am., 1954; Carolina Qtly. Award, Univ. of N.C., 1959; Borestone Mountain Poetry Awards (individual poems), 1953, '55, '59, '65. Address: P.O. Box 2526, Reno, NV 89505, U.S.A.

DELORKO, Olinko, b. 30 Jan. 1910. Teacher & Writer. Education: Grad., Fac. of Philos., Zagreb, 1935; study tours in Paris, 1938, Florence, 1939, Rome, 1956. Positions held: Tchr., Yugoslav Lit., Medium Tech. Schl., Zagreb, 1937-41 & at Medium Med. Schl., Zagreb, 1948-49; engaged in study of Croatian oral poetry, Inst. of Nat. Art. Memberships: PEN, 1940-; Union of Croatian Writers, 1955-. Published works: (colls. of poems) Pjesme, 1944; Rastužena Euterpa, 1937; Razigrani vodoskoci, 1940; Uznosite slutnje, 1944; Izgaranja, 1958; Svijetli i tamni sati, 1961; Lirski Eden, 1965; (transl.) Colls. of Poems by Dante, Petrarca & Michaelangelo (from Italian to Croatian) etc. Contbr. to var. lit. jrnls. Recip., Prize 'S.S. Kranjčević' for the coll. of poems 'Razigrani vodoskoci (Dancing Fountains), 1941. Address: Vramčeva St. 15/IId, Zagreb 41000, Yugoslavia.

DeMARIA, Robert, b. 28 Sept. 1928. Novelist. Education: B.A., Columbia Coll., 1948; M.A., Columbia Univ., 1949; Ph.D., ibid, 1959. Married 1) Maddalena Buzzeo, 1 son (Robert Jr.), 2) Ellen Hope Meyer, 3 children (Nikolas, Amanda & Michael). Positions held: Instr., Univ. of Ore., 1949-52; Asst. Prof. of Engl., Hofstra Univ., 1952-61; Assoc. Dean, The New Schl. for Social Rsch., 1961-64; Ed., Macmillan Co., 1959-61; Prof. of Engl., Dowling Coll., 1965-; Dir., Mediterranean Inst., Spain, 1969-70; Ed., Mediterranean Review. Memberships: PEN Am. Ctr.; The Authors Guild; MLA. Published works: Sea Sketches, 1955; God is a Woman, 1974; (novels) Carnival of Angels; Clodia; Don Juan in Lourdes; The Satyr; The Decline & Fall of America; The Atheist. Contbr. to: The Word; Talaria; Northern Review; Open Secrets; The Mediterranean Review; Antaeus; Suffolk Times; Southwest Review; New Leader, Renaissance Faire; The Am. Bard. Address: Orient, N.Y. 11957, U.S.A.

DEMETILLO, Ricaredo D., b. 2 June 1920. Associate Professor. Education: A.B., Engl., Silliman Univ., 1947; M.F.A. in Creative Writing, Iowa, 1952. Positions held: Instr. & Asst. Prof., Silliman Univ., 1947-49; '52-55; Instr., Univ. of the Philippines, 1955; Asst. Prof., U.P., 1958; Assoc. Prof. of Humanities, ibid, 1968; Chmn., Humanities Dept., 1960-62. Memberships: Co-Fndr., Sands & Coral, Silliman Univ., 1948; Philippine Writers' Assn.; Univ. of the Philippines Writers' Club, 1956-; Int. PEN. Published works: No Certain Weather, book, 1956; La Via: A Spiritual Journey, 1958; Barber in Panay: An Epic, 1961; The Authentic Voice of Poetry, criticism, 1961; Daedalus & Other Poems, 1961; Masks & Signature, 1968; The Scare-Crow Christ, 1973. Contbr. to var. jrnls., mags., reviews. Honours, awards: The Art Assn. of the Philippines Award for Art Criticism; Univ. of Philippines Golden Jubilee Award for Poetry, 1958; The Republic Cultural Heritage Award for Poetry & Lit. Criticism, 1968; The Outstanding Sillimanian Award, 1973; The Palanca First Prize Award for Drama, 1973, etc. Address: T 1416 Area 14, Univ. of the Philippines, Diliman, Quezon City, Philippines.

DEMUS, Klaus, b. 30 May 1927. Keeper, Picture Gallery, Kunsthistorisches Museum, Vienna. Education: Humanistisches Gymnasium; Dr. phil. (Hist. of Art), Univ. of Vienna. Published works: Das schwere Land, 1958; Morgennacht, 1969. Contbr. to: Merkur; Akzente; Die Neue Rundschau; Botteghe Oscure; Jahresring. Address: Rennweg 4, Vienna III, Austria.

de MUYNCK, Rémy, pen name **SAINT-REMY,** b. 22 Dec. 1913. Painter; Poet; Essayist. Positions held: Naval Officer; Translator; Editor; Publisher; Painter; Poet; Essayist. Memberships: Accademia Internazionale Leonardo da Vinci, Rome; Centro Studi e Scambi Int., Rome; l'Association des Ecrivains Belges; Lid van de Vereniging van Vlaamse Letterkundigen, etc. Published works: Les Poèmes de Georges, 1958; Echanges Poétiques, 1962; Lao-Tseu: Tao te King ou la Jonction Suprême, 1962; Tcheng-Tsan: Le Poème de la Foi Eprouveé et de l'Esprit Illuminé, 1964; Velazquez, quatre prolégomènes et un fragment d'essai, 1965; Les Quatrains de Thalie, 1966; Six poètes néerlandais (Herman Gorter, Jan-Hendrik Leopold, Jan Slauerhoff, Hendrik Marsman, Gerrit Achterberg, Adriaan Roland Holst), 1971; poietikos ou la relation entre la poésie et la peinture, 1972; Polumetis, poèmes néerlandais, 1972. Contbr. to var. jrnls. Honours, awards: Prix de la traduction par A.R., 1965; Prix A. Michot de l'Académie royale de Langue et de Littérature Françaises de Belgique, 1962 & 67; Chevalier, l'Ordre de la Couronne. Address: Leopoldstraat 61, 2000 Antwerpen, Belgium.

DEN BOER, James D., b. 21 Aug. 1937. Writer; Editor. Education: A.B., Calvin Coll., 1960; M.A., Univ. of Calif., 1969. Married, 1 son, 1 daughter. Positions held: Information Officer, U.S. Public Hlth. Serv., 1963-67; Grad. student, 1967-69; Asst. Dir., Unicorn Press, 1968-69; Sr. Staff, White House Conf. on Children & Youth, 1970-71; Travel & writing, U.S. & Canada, 1971-72; Freelance Writer, 1972-73; Rsch. Information Officer, Univ. of Calif., 1973–. Published works: Learning The Way, 1968; Trying To Come Apart, 1971; Nine Poems, 1972. Contbr. to: Northwest Review; North Am. Review; Poetry Northwest; Concerning Poetry; Spectacle; Mad River Review; Holy Door; Art & Literature; Fiddlehead; Green River Review; Colo. Qtly., etc. Honours, awards incl: U.S. Award of the Int. Poetry Forum, 1967; Grant, Nat. Inst. of Arts & Letters, 1971; Grant, Carnegie Fund for Authors, 1973, Authors League of Am., 1973. Address: 1804 Loma St., Santa Barbara, CA 93103, U.S.A.

DENBY, Edwin Orr, b. 4 Feb. 1903. Free-lance Critic; Essayist. Educ: Harvard Univ., 1919-22; Schule Helleran-Laxenburg, Austria, 1925-27. Positions held: Dancer & Choreographer, 1920s–; Dance Critic, Modern Music, 1938-42; Dance Critic, New York Herald Tribune, 1942-45; Free-lance Critic & Essayist, 1946–. Published works: In Public, In Private, 1948; Mediterranean Cities, 1956; Looking at the Dance (criticism), 1949; Dancers, Buildings, and People in the Street (essays), 1965. Contbr. to: (anthologies) Penguin Book of Sonnets, 1943; A Little Treasury of Modern Poetry: English and American, 1950; Palgrave's Golden Treasury, 1953; Faber Book of Modern American Verse, 1956; Modern Verse, 1958; Erotic Poetry, 1963; A Book of Love Poems, 1965. Address: 145 W. 21st St., New York, NY 10011, U.S.A.

DENEKA, Paul, b. 25 July 1954. Student. Education: currently attending Univ. of Minn. majoring in Chemical Engrng. Contbr. to: Minneapolis Argus; Sphere. Recip., Polly Hart MFCP Award from Mid-west Fed. of Chaparral Poets (Minn. Chapt.) Address: 908 – 27th Ave. N.E., Minneapolis, MN 55418, U.S.A.

DENES, Kiss, b. 1 Jan. 1936. Poet. Education: Jrnlst. Schl., 1962. Positions held: Libn., Jrnlst., Translator of poems from Finnish. Memberships: Hungarian Writer Union; Hungarian Jrnlst. Union. Published works: (poetry books) Roomwall Drew in the Dust, 1962; My Face is the Earth, 1965; From Face to Face, 1970; Blue Blue Blue, 1973; (youth novels) Indians of Kite-hill, 1970; The Last Indian Summer, 1972; Falcontime, 1973. Contbr. to: Kortárs; Jelenkor; Alföld; Tiszatáj; Uj Irás; Elet és Irodalom; Népszava; Magyar Hirlap; Népszabadság; Ifjusági Magazin; Nök Lapja; Képes Ujság; Napjaink, etc. Address: 1065 Budapest VI, Bajcsy-Zsilinszky ut 35. III.e. 31, Hungary.

DENIN, Susan (Mrs.), born 24th April 1931. Housewife & Poet. Education: B.S., Brooklyn Coll., N.Y. Positions held: La. Rsch. Asst. Mbr., Ore. State Poetry Assoc. Contbr. to: Am. Bard; Cardinal; Driftwood; Haiku Highlights; Leprechaun Review; Medford Mail Trib.; Oregonian; Personal Poetry Anthol. N.Y. Rep., Pixie Angel. Address: Rt. 1, Box 169, Molalla, Ore. 97038, U.S.A.

DENISSEN, Frans, pen name (formerly), **DE VREESE, Dani,** b. 7 Sept. 1947. Professor of Italian. Positions held: Translator of TV programmes; Prof. of Italian, Antwerp Inst. of Translators & Interpreters; Editor, Labris (literary mag.). Published works: Concerto voor Tamtam, 1963; Zingend tot giftig toe, 1965; Uit Adem Gesneden, 1966; Aubaden bij het Laatste Licht, 1969. Contbr. to: Labris; Yang; Dietsche Warande & Belfort, Nieuw Vlaams Tijdschrift. Address: Oude Steenweg 70, 2000 Antwerpen, Belgium.

DENNEY, Reuel Nicholas, b. 13 Apr. 1913. Professor of American Studies. Educ: B.A., Darmouth Coll., Hanover, 1932. Married Ruth Lois Norton, 1938; one child. Positions held: Factory clerk and Tchr., 1932-42; Contbng. Ed., Time Mag., N.Y.C., 1943-45; Assoc. Ed., Fortune Mag., 1945-46; Prof., Social Scis., Univ. of Chgo., 1947-61; Prof., American Studies, Univ. of Hawaii, Honolulu, 1961–. Published works: The Connecticut River, 1939; In Praise of Adam, 1963; The Lonely Crowd: A Study of the Changing American Character (w. David Riesman & Nathan Glazen), 1950. Contbr. to: Poetry; New Republic; Hudson Review; (anthologies) A New Anthology of Modern Verse, 1938; Pocket Anthology of American Verse, 1955; Twentieth Century American Poetry, 1963. Honours, awards: Eunice·Tietjens Prize, 1953; Nat. Inst. of Arts and Letters Prize, 1968. Address: Apt. 315, Diamond Head Ambassador Apts., 2957 Kalakaua Ave., Honolulu, HI 96815, U.S.A.

DENNIS BROWNE, Michael, b. 28 May 1940. Teacher. Education: B.A., Hull Univ., U.K., 1962; Min. of Educ. Tchrs. Cert., 1963; Worcester Coll., Oxford Univ., 1962-63; M.A., Univ. of Iowa, U.S.A., 1967. Positions held: Vis. Lectr. in Creative Writing, Univ. of Iowa, 1967-68; Adjunct Asst. Prof., Schl. of the Arts, Columbia Univ., Pall 1968; Mbr. of Lit. Dept. Bennington Coll., Vt., 1969-71; Asst. Prof., Univ. of Minn., Minneapolis, 1971–. Published works: The Wife of Winter, London & N.Y., 1970; Libretti (music by David Lord) How the Stars Were Made, 1967; The Wife of Winter, 1970; The Sea Journey, 1970; Non Songs, 1973/74. Contbr. to: The New Yorker; Tri-Qtly.; North Am. Review; The Am. Review; Antaeus; Crazy Horse; The Iowa Review; Pen New Poems 1965, '67; Best Poems of 1967, '69; The New Yorker Book of Poems; Under Thirty; Loves, etc; Oh, That's Ridiculous!, & others. Address: Dept. of Engl., Univ. of Minn., Minneapolis, MN 55455, U.S.A.

DE NOLA, Jean-Paul, b. 13 May 1931. University Professor; Literary Critic. Education: Free Univ. of Brussels (Dr. of Romanic Philology); Univs. of Siena, Perugia, Lille. Positions held: Teacher sev. High Schools; Prof. High Commercial Inst. (Brussels); Lecturer Univ. of Messina. Memberships: Accademia Peloritana dei Pericolanti, Messina; Biennales Internationales de Poésie (Knocke); Assoc. Internationale des Etudes Françaises, Paris. Published works: Les Poètes de la Rue des Sols, 1963; Les 3 Visages de la Belgique Littéraire, 1965; Cromatismo di Marcel Thiry, 1967; Deux Etudes sur Domenico Tempio, 1971; Echos Shakespeariens dans la Poésie Française, 1972; Robert Goffin Poète, 1973. Contbr. to various newspapers, reviews. Address: 79 Viale Regina Margherita, I 98100, Messina, Italy.

DENOMME, Robert Thomas, b. 17 May 1930. Professor of French Literature (Poetry). Education: A.B., Assumption Coll., 1952; M.A., Boston Univ., 1953; Dip., Univ. of Paris, 1959; Ph.D., French & Romance Philol., Columbia Univ., 1962. Positions held: Asst. Prof., French, Univ. of Va., U.S.A., 1962-64; Asst. Prof., French, Univ. of Chicago, 1964-66; Assoc. Prof., French, Univ. of Va., 1966-69; Prof. of French Lit., ibid, 1970-. Memberships: Advisory Bd., Nineteenth-Century French Studies; Standing Comm. on Bibliography, MLA of Am.; Studies Awards Comm., S. Atlantic MLA of Am. Published works: Nineteenth-Century French Romantic Poets (book), 1969; The French Parnassian Poets (book), 1972; Leconte de Lisle (book), 1973; The Motif of the 'Poète maudit' in Musset's Lorenzaccio (art); L'Esprit Createur, 1965; The Essential Rimbaud (art), Sewanee Review, 1971. Honours, awards: Fulbright Scholar for France, 1959; Sesquicentennial Fellowship & Assoc. in Ctr. for Adv. Studies, Univ. of Va., 1971-72. Address: Dept. of French Lit., Univ. of Va., Charlottesville, VA 22903, U.S.A.

de NORONHA, Leslie, b. 9 June 1926. Copy Chief. Educ: St. Xavier's Coll., Bombay, India; Grant Med. Coll., ibid; M.B. & B.S., Univ. of Bombay; D.T.M. & Hy., London Schl. of Tropical Med. and Hygiene, U.K. Positions held: Held num. hosp. positions in U.K., 1954-58 and in U.S.A., 1959-60; Copy Chief, Ethical Advertising, Bombay, India, 1960-; Hd., Creative Unit, Glaxo Labs. Ltd., ibid, 1960-. Published works: Poems, 1965; Short Stories, 1966. Contbr. to: Quest; Writers Workshop Miscellany; Modern Indian Poetry in English (anthology), 1969. Address: Springfield, 10th Road TPS IV, Almeida Park, Bandra, Bombay 50, India.

DENSON, Alan. Writer; Poet. Positions held: Ed. of the U.K. statutory Register of Veterinary Surgeons (which he reconstructed both as to contests & arrangement), 1960-65. Published works: (colls. of poetry) Impetuous Poems, 1968; Solitary Intimate Voices, 1970; Broken Imagery, 1970; (other books) Letters from AE (Edited & Annotated), 1961; Printed Writings by George W. Russell (AE): A Bibliography & Iconography, 1961; Thomas Bodkin & His Family: A Bio-Bibliographical Survey, 1966; James H. Cousins & Margaret E. Cousins: Bio-Bibliographical Survery, 1967; John Hughes, R.H.A. (1865-1941) Sculpto: A Documentary Biography, 1969; W.J. Leech, R.H.A. (1881-1968) His Life & Work, vol.1, 1968, vol.2, 1969; Ronald Falck, A Yorkshire Artist, 1970; Poems by Charles A. Weekes (Edited & Annotated), 1970; George W. Russell (AE): Collected Poems (Edited & Annotated) in prep; etc. Contbr. of articles, reviews & poems to var. jrnls., newspapers, reviews. Has prepared var. works for publication. Address: 'Denbrae', Dudwick, Ellon, Aberdeenshire AB4 9YS, U.K.

DEPEW, Wally (Wallace M.), b. 5 Jan. 1938. Poet; Artist; Photographer; Writer. Education: A.A., Keystone J.C., La Plume, Pa., 1957; B.A., Drew Univ., Madison, N.J., 1959; A.A., Sacramento C.C., Calif., 1974. Married Linda Bandt Depew. Positions held: Asst. to Ed., Poetry London, N.Y., 1964; Ed., Publsr., Poetry Newsletter, 1964-68; Mag. Review Ed. of Small Press Review, 1966-68; Ed., Publsr., PN2, PN3, & Books From PN, 1968-; Ed., Dust Mag., 1970-72; Asst. Dir., Omega Gall., Sacramento, Calif., 1973-. Published works: Black Marks, 1967; Scream Poem, 1969; Bounce Poem, 1969; Once, 1970; Morning Drop, 1973; Lobelia, 1973; Mumble a Sparrow, 1973; Ladderbook Piece, 1972; Grey G, 1974; Empo, 1974; 100 Poems, 1974; 9 Essays on Concrete Poems, 1974, etc. Contbr. to: Tri Qtly.; The Realist; Wormwood Review; Ole; Avalanche; Dust; Runcible Spoon; Grand Ronde Review; Akwesasne Notes; Small Press Review; Nexus; Kontexts; Down Here; Assembling. Address: 819 Seventeenth St., Sacramento, CA 95814, U.S.A.

DEPIERRIS, Jean-Louis, b. 28 Dec. 1931. Institute Director. Educ: Sorbonne, Paris, France; Univs. of Clermont-Ferrand & Tours. Positions held: Press Attaché, Min. of Finances, 1953; Art Critic, French Radio & TV, 1956-65; Collaborated w. Grand Larousse of the French Lang., 1964-66; Rdr., Univ. of Sarajevo, Yugoslavia, 1966-68, Univ. of Split, 1968; Dir., French Inst., Split, 1971-. Mbr., Soc. of Men of Letters. Published works incl: Analogies, 1952; L'Esprit de la Terre, 1955; Naufragé du Bestiaire, 1957; Ce Crissement de Faulx, 1960; Ragusi, 1960; Fer de Lance, 1965; Quand le Mauve se plisse, 1969; Nouvelle Poésie Française, 1971; Poèmes de l'Année, 1971. Contbr. to num. revues inclng: Jrnl. des Poètes; Pont de l'Epée; Tour de Feu; Sens plastique; Simoun; Marginales; Cahiers de Jeunesse. Honours, awards: Poets' Mandate, 1961; René-Guy Cadou, 1961; Antonin Artaud, 1971. Address: Institut Français, Marmontova 3, Split 58000, Yugoslavia.

DE PIFTRO, Albert, pen name **LOREL, Phil,** b. 11 Sept. 1913. Professor; Lawyer; Poet. Education: B.B.A., LL.B., J.S.D. Positions held: Lawyer, Prof., Nassau Community Coll. Member of the Poetry Society of America. Fellow, International Poetry Society. Published works: Moments in Passing, 1967; Sounds of Shadow, 1970; Island City, 1970: of hush and whispers, 1972. Contbr. to following anthols. & reviews: Spirit; Southwest Times Record; The Catholic World; South & West; Voices International; Cardinal Poetry Quarterly, etc. Honours: Hon. Mention, 2nd Prize, Rochester Festival of Religious Arts, 1965. Address: 230 Kilburn Rd., Garden City, Long Island, NY 11530, USA.

DE POORTERE, Estelle Julienne Marie Hortense, Professor of French. Memberships: Deleg., Arts, Scis., & Letters, Paris; French Poets, Paris; Comm., 'Prométhée', Paris; Comm., C.I.P.A.F.; Deleg., F.N.E.F.D., Liège; Soc. of Belgian Writers; Deleg., Courrier des Marches; Acad. Berrichonne; Academia de Torino, Rome. Published works incl: Les Echos, 1933; L'Eternelle Absence, 1934; Rêve de Papillon, 1936; Kitski (novel), 1947; Christ, seul porteur de toute la Vérité, 1950; La Harpe Eolienne, 1972. Contbr. to: Le Courrier Vauclusien; L'Atrium; Présence des Art et des Lettres; Le Courrier des Marches; Prométhée; Falaises; Les Poètes et leurs Amis. Honours, awards incl: Gold Medal, Arts, Scis., & Letters, Paris, 1965; Gold Palm of Educl. Merit, Liège, 1967; Given the title, Princess of Poets, w. 8 1st prizes in 12 competitions, Friends of Petrarch; Gold Medal for 'Sous la Lampe de Jade', 1971; num. awards for poetry. Address: 502 Kortrijksesteenweg, Ghent 9000, Belgium.

de RADZITZKY d'OSTROWICK, (Baron), Carlos, pen name **de RADZITZKY, Carlos,** b. 7 June 1915. Poet; Jazz Critic; Collagist. Education: Philos. & Letters, St Louis Univ., Brussels. Memberships: Gen. Sec., PEN Club of Belgium, French Br.; Assn. of Belgian Writers; Soc. des Gens de Lettres de France; Bd. of Jrnl. of Poetry; Advisor, Biennales de Poésie de Knokke. Published works: Harmonika saloon, 1934; A vol d'oiseau, 1936; Dormeuse, 1937; Le fond de l'eau, 1942; Ophélie, 1955; Poèmes choisis, 1963; Désert secret, 1965; Les semeurs de feu, 1968; Le commun des mortels, 1973. Contbr. to: Le journal des poètes; Marginales; Contravento (Portugal), etc. Recip., Prix Denayer, Académie Royale de Belgique, 1966. Address: Avenue Fond'Roy 110, 1180 Brussels, Belgium.

DER HOVANESSIAN, Diana. Poet. Education: A.B., Boston Univ.; courses at Radcliffe & Harvard Grad. Schl. of Educ. & Univ. of Utah. Positions held: Poet in Res., Newton Public Schls. & Quincy Schls. under a grant from the Nat. Coun. of Arts & Humanities; Ed., Young America. Memberships: Sec., New England Poetry Club; Mbrship Chmn., New England Poetry Club; Poetry Soc. of Am. Published works: booklet of translations of the works of Hovanes Shiraz, 1973. Contbr. to: Harpers; N.Y. Times; Nation; Mademoiselle; Louisiana Review; Western Humanities Review; Granite; Ararat; Armenian Review; N.Y. Herald Tribune; Paris Tribune; Look; Wall Street Jrnl.; Ladies Home Jrnl.; Good Housekeeping; McCall's;

Yankee; Sail; Christian Sci. Monitor. Recip., St. Vartan's Medal. Address: 2 Farrar St., Cambridge, MA 02138, U.S.A.

DESANKA, Maksimović, b. 16 May 1898. Writer. Education: Fac. of Arts & Scis., Belgrade Univ.; Sorbonne, Paris, 1 yr. Widow of Sergej Slastikov. Positions held: Prof., Grammar Schl., Obrenovac, Dubrovniku & Belgrade; Writer. Memberships: Union of Serbian Writers; Serbian Acad. of Scis. & Arts, 1965–; Soc. of French Friends; Soc. of Norwegian Friends; Soc. for Protection of Children; Directorate, Matica, Serbian. Published works: Pjesme, 1924; Zeleni Vitez, 1930; Gozba na Livadi, 1932; Nove Pesme, 1936; Pesnik i Zavičaj, 1945; Reka Pomoćnica, 1949; Otadžbino Tu Sam, 1950; Miris Zemlje, 1954; Zarobljenik Snova, 1960; Tražim Pomilovanje, 1964; Sabrana Dela, 1969; Neman Više Vremena, 1973. Contbr. to var. jrnls. Recip. many honours & awards inclng: Award of ZMAJ from Matica Serbian for the coll. 'Miris zemlje', 1959; Order of Russia; Order of the Republic w. Golden Wreath (1st class); Award AVNOJ-a, 1970; Award of ZMAJ, Novi Sad for book 'Nemam više vremena', 1973. Address: Generala Zdanova 6, Belgrade, Yugoslavia.

DESHMUKHYA, Ramendra, b. 20 Sept. 1917. Medical Representative. Education: M.A., Bengali Lit., Univ. of Calcutta, 1942; Dip., Advt. Prac. & Admin., Schl. of Careers, Kensington, London. Married, 1 son, 1 daughter. Positions held: served A.R.P., WWII; Staff Reporter, Jugantar, a Daily Paper of Calcutta, 1945-47; Med. Propagandist under B.I. Co., Bombay, 1949-50; currently Med. Rep., Burroughs Wellcome & Co. (I) Ltd., 1951–; Assoc. Ed., Ocarina, Madras. Published works: Dhan Khet, 1945; Bahni Bangla, 1949; Shata Puspa, 1961; Mahakash; also novels, story-books for children & a book on travel. Contbr. to anthols., jrnls., newspapers, reviews, mags., periodicals. Address: Flat Y/7, 76/2 Bidhan Sarani, Calcutta 700006, India.

DESHPANDE, Gauri, b. 11 Feb. 1942. Writer; Editor; Journalist. Education: M.A., Engl. Lit., Poona Univ., 1966. Divorced, 2 children. Positions held: Engl. Lectr. (Undergrad.); Rsch. Scholar; Engl. Lectr. (Postgrad.); Sub-Ed., The Illustrated Weekly of India; Editl. Asst., Opinion. Published works: Between Births, 1967; Lost Love, 1970; Beyond the Slaughterhouse, 1972; Modern Indian Poetry in English (Ed.), 1973. Contbr. to: Quest; Opinion; The Illustrated Weekly of India; Dialogue India; Poet; Mahfil (Chicago). Address: 2/7 Skyscraper 'B', Warden Rd., Bombay 26, India 400026.

DESICH, Helen Cynthia, b. 5 June 1925. Personnel Staffing Clerk. Education: Sociol., Univ. of Minn., 1954-58. Positions held: Bank Remitter; Clerk Typist; Biller; Nurse; Personnel Staffing Clerk. Memberships: Mnpls. Poetry Soc. Histn.; Young Women's Christian Assn.; Midwest Fed. of Chaparral Poets; Mnpls. Soc. of Fine Arts; Minn. League of Poets. Contbr. to: Mocassin; Mnpls. Tribune; Mnpls. Argus. Honours, awards: Hon. Mention, WWTC Radio-Haiku Contest, 1967; 1st prize, Sawyers Award, 1971; Cash Award-Agency 'Basic Staffing Handbook', co-authored w. Lil Bluml, 1973. Address: 1000 West Franklin, Minneapolis, MN 55405, U.S.A.

DE SOUZA, Eunice, b. 1 Aug. 1940. Lecturer in English. Education: B.A., Univ. of Bombay; M.A., Marquette Univ., Wis., U.S.A. Contbr. to: Opinion; Opinion Lit. Qtly.; Times Weekly; Gray Book. Address: Dept. of Engl., St. Xavier's Coll., Mahapallika Marg, Bombay 1, India.

DESPAIN, Wilma Morley, writing symbol, **The Pearl,** b. 18 Aug. 1914. Housewife. Married, 3 sons, 1 daughter. Has held var. Church positions. Memberships: State Bd. Mbr., League of Utah Writers, 4 yrs.; Pres., Sevier Valley Chapt., ibid; Utah State Poetry Soc.; Counselor, Stake Relief Soc. of Gunnison Stake, 9 yrs.; Chmn. of Histl. Comm., ibid; Bd. Mbr., Sanpete Co. Histl. Soc. Co-Publisher of the yearly book 'Saga of the Sanpitch'; Weekly column in Gunnison Valley News, also a 'Wilma's Whimsical

Whims' in same paper. Contbr. to: Poetry Parade; Gato's; Relief Soc. Mag.; Gunnison Valley News; Friend, children's mag.; Ensign; Golden Boy, etc. Honours, awards incl: 3rd pl., League of State Contests, light verse & serious narrative verse, 1973; 1st pl., essay 'Torches on Time', 1973, etc. Address: P.O. Box 172, Centerfield, UT 84622, U.S.A.

DETTMERS, Howard, A., b. 21 Apr. 1893. Educator. Education: Univ. of Okla.; Educ. degree, Eastern Wash. State Coll.; Theol. Educ., Theol. Schls. in Bangor & Chicago; Degree in Philos. and Theol. Positions held: Missionary; Writer; Instructor of Retarded. Memberships: a State Chmn., Nat. Thanksgiving Assn.; Am. Poetry League; Am. Bard; Midwest Chaparral; Hon. Mbr., Eugene Field Soc., 1946. Contbr. to: New Poets 1948; Nat. Thanksgiving Soc. Vol. 1950; From Sea to Sea in Song, 1972; The Congregationalist; The Christian Advocate; The Friend; The Am. Bard; Am. Poetry Bulletin & Annual; Midwest Chaparral; The Muse; Ideals; Spokane Chronicle; Detroit News, etc. Recip. var. poetry awards & hons. inclng: 1st pl. Award, Midwest Chaparral, 1973; 1st pl., Famous Am. Poetry Contest, 1973. Address: Mt. Angel Towers, Mt. Angel, OR 97362, U.S.A.

DEUTSCH, Babette, b. 22 Sept. 1895. Writer. Education: A.B., Barnard Coll., 1917. Married to Avrahm Yarmolinsky. Positions held: Lectr. in Engl., Columbia Univ., NY, 1944–; Hon. Cons., Lib. of Congress, 1961-67. Memberships: Nat. Inst. Art & Letters; PEN. Published works: Banners (verse), 1919; Honey Out of the Rock (verse), 1925; A Brittle Heaven (novel), 1926; In Such a Night (novel), 1927; Potable Gold (criticism), 1929; Fire For The Night (verse), 1930; Epistle to Prometheus (verse), 1931; Mask of Silenus (novel), 1933; This Modern Poetry (criticism), 1935; One Part Love (verse), 1939; Heroes of the Kalevala (juvenile), 1940; It's a Secret! (juvenile), 1941; Walt Whitman, Builder for America (juvenile), 1941; The Welcome (juvenile), 1942; Rogue's Legacy (novel), 1942; Take Them, Stranger (verse), 1944; The Reader's Shakespeare (criticism), 1946; Poetry in Our Time (criticism), 1952, '56, '63, '64; Animal, Vegetable, Mineral (verse), 1954; Poetry Handbook, 1957, '64; Coming of Age: New & Selected Poems, 1959; Collected Poems, 1919-62, 1963; I Often Wish, 1966; The Collected Poems of Babette Deutsch, 1969. Co-author, Tales of Faraway Folk (juvenile), 1952; More Tales of Faraway Folk, 1964; The Steel Flea, 1964. Translator of sev. vols. of verse, inclng: The Twelve, by Alexander Blok; Eugene Onegin, by Pushkin; The Book of Hours, by Rilke; Two Centuries of Russian Verse, 1966. Contbr. to num. publs. Address: 300 W. 108th St., New York, NY 10025, USA.

DeVALL, Sally, b. 3 June 1920. Secretary to Physician. Memberships: C.S.S.I.; Hub Internat. Poetry Soc. Fellowship. Published work: Robert, 1972. Contbr. to: (anthols.) Echos of Faith; Yearbook of Mod. Poetry, 1971; Quorum of Cats, 1969; Contemp. American Love Scene, 1971; Velvet Paws in Print, 1967; New Poetry, 1967; Written Word Nos. 3, 4, 5 and 6; Poetry Pageant, 1969; Anthol. of NY Poets, 1969; Golden Anthol. of Poetry, 1970. Contbr. to: Angels; Angel Hour; Cats Mag.; Author-Poet; Bitterroot; Fireflower; Haiku Highlights; Harbor Lights; Jean's Journal; Merlin's Magic; Modern Images; Nutmegger; Nightshade; Ladies' Delight; Poetry Prevue; Encore; Pixie Angel; Quintessence; Sand Castles; Scimitar and Song Tempo; Sunrise Sunset Silhouette; Brass Ring; Major Poets; Southwest Breeze; Creative Review; Animal Lovers. Address: 45 Dove St., Albany, NY 12210, USA.

DEVANAYAGOM, D. Jacob, pen name **JACOB,** b. 27 Dec. 1944. Doctor. Education: Medical Grad., M.B., B.S., Medical Coll., Trivandrum, Kerala Univ. (Grad. 1968). Positions held: Resident Medical Officer, L.M.S. Boys Brigade Hospital, Kundara, 1970-71; Regimental Medical Officer, Indian Army, 1971–. Memberships: World Poetry Soc. Intercontinental, Ariz., USA.; P.E.N. Centre, Bombay, India. Published works: Deceptions (poetry); Selected Poems (1973). Contbr. to: Poet Intercontinental Monthly. Address: 21 Chellammal St., Shenoy Nagar P.O., Madras 30, India.

de VINCK, Catherine, b. 20 Feb. 1922. Poet. Education: Belgian Greco-Latin Humanities. Married to Baron Jose de Vinck, 6 children. Published works: A Time to Gather, selected poems, 1966/67; Ikon, 1972. In preparation: Selected poems, second series; 'A Liturgy'; A Book of Uncommon Prayers; 'Passion Play'. Contbr. of opening poem in 'A House of Good Proportion', Women in Literature, an anthol. by Michele Murray, 1973 & 'Restoration', Madonna Hse, Combermere, Ont., Canada. Address: 672 Franklin Turnpike, Allendale, NJ 07401, U.S.A.

DE VREE, Paul, b. 13 Nov. 1909. Professor in History. Education: Tchr., 1928, Aggregate, 1930, Lic. in History, Central Jury, Brussels, 1938. Married Mariette Versterren, 1 son (Frits). Positions held: Ed., De Tafelronde, 1953–; Pres., The Centre of Modern Art, 1959-69; Pres., Fugitive Cinema, 1967–; Co-Ed., Lotta Poetica, 1971–. Memberships: Poesia Visiva-Group, 1971–; Pen Club; Vereniging Van Schrÿverswerk Groepen, 1973–; Maatschappÿ Van Nederlandse Letterkunde; Paul van Ostaÿen – Genootschap; Rob. Roemans-Stichting. Published – works: Verzen en Kwatrÿnen, 1935; Het Blanke Waaien, 1937; Elegische Hymnen, 1937; Atmosfeer, 1938; Loutering, 1940; Zang in de Landouw, 1940; Het aards bedriff, 1942; Terra Firma, 1944; Tussen Twÿfel en Traan, 1946; Appassionato, 1953; Egelrond, 1956; Grondbeeldig, 1959; Explositieven, 1966; Zimprovisaties, 1968; Poëzie in Fusie, 1968; Verbaal Gelaat, 1970; Poëzien, 1971; Maskers, 1973. Contbr. to: Dietse Warande en Belfort; Vormen; Forum; De Tafelronde; Nul; L'Humidite, etc. Recip., Prize of the Province Antwerpen, 1935. Address: 46 Camille Huysmanslaan, 2020 Antwerp, Belgium.

DE VREEDE, Henny, pen name **DE VREEDE, Mischa,** b. 17 Sept. 1936. Author. Memberships: Vereniging van Letterkundigen; Maatschappij der Nederlandse Letterkunde; PEN. Published works: Morgen mooi weer maken, poetry, 1957; Met huid en hand, poetry, 1959, 5th edn., 1974; Al zeg ik het zelf, zei de Zwifzwaf, children's book, 1960; Eindeloos, novel, 1961, 2nd edn., 1974; Ham mag appels eten, children's book; Oorlog en liefde, short stories, 1963, re-edited, 1974; Binnen en buiten, poetry, 1968; Een stukje van de wereld, children's book, 1969; Onze eeuwige honger, novel, 1973; Een Hachelijk bestaan, autobiographical, 1974. Contbr. to: Podium; Maatstaf; Ruimte; Avenue; Jrnl. de Poetes; var. radio & TV progs. Honours, awards: Poezieprijs, Amsterdam, 1959. Address: Ceintuurbaan 229 111, Amsterdam 8, Netherlands.

DE VRIES, Carrow, b. 6 July 1906. Policeman. Education: Univ. of Michigan, 2 yrs. Member of Poetry Soc. of Mich. Published works: Hawthorn, 1967; Passing Butterflies, 1967; Moment of Flower & Leaf, 1967; Hawthorn, 1967; An Alphabet Book of Haiku and Tanka, 1973. Contbr. to: New Michigan Verse, 1940; Frontier & Midland; Prairie Schooner; Haiku; Haiku West; Haiku Highlights; American Haiku; The Archer; Sou'wester; SCTH Peninsula Poets; Snowy Egret. Awards: Hon. mention for Moment of Flower & Leaf; Midget Pegasus Award, 1968; Cert. of Appreciation, Hayden Lib., Ariz. State Univ., 1970. Address: RR 3, Holland, Mich. 49423, USA.

DE VRIES, Hendrik, b. 17 Aug. 1896. Poet; Essayist; Painter; Designer; Translator. Memberships: PEN; Maatschappij van Letterkunde; Vereniging van Letterkundigen (Hon. Mbr.) Published works: (poems) De Nacht, 1920; Vlamrood, 1922; Lofzangen, 1923; Silenen, 1928; Spaanse Volksliederen, 1931; Stormfakkels, 1933; Coplas, 1935; Geimproviseerd Bouquet, 1937; Nergal, 1937; Atlantische Balladen, 1937; Romantische Rhapsodie, 1939; Robijnen, 1944; Caprichos en Rijmcritieken, 1946; Tovertuin, 1946; Distels en Aloës, 1951; Gitaarfantasieën, 1955; Groninger Symphonie, 1957; Keur uit vroegere verzen, 1916-46, 1962; Iberia, 1964; Goyescos, 1971; (Spanish) Cantos extraviados del español groninguense, 1971; (Criticism) Vers tegen Vers, 1949; De Tweede Ronde, 1952. Contbr. to var. lit. jrnls. Honours, awards: Essayprijs van de Jan Campertstichting, 1950; Culturele prijs van de Provincie Groningen, 1961; Constantijn Huijgensprijs, 1962; Officer in the Order of Orange Nassau. Address: 't Woeste Hoekje, Onnerweg 87, Haren (GR.), Netherlands.

DEWHIRST, Ian, b. 17 Oct. 1936. Librarian. Education: Keighley Boys' Grammar School, 1948-1955; Univ. of Manchester, 1955-1958 (Hons. Engl.). Positions held: Hon. Gen. Sec., Yorkshire Dialect Soc., 1963–. Memberships: Internat. Poetry Soc.; Pennine Poets; Bronte Soc.; Yorkshire Dialect Soc. Published works: The Handloom Weaver, and Other Poems, 1965; Scar Top, and Other Poems, 1968. Contbr. to: Yorkshire Ridings Mag.; The Dalesman; Pennine Platform; Here Now; Headlands; Transactions of the Yorks. Dialect Soc. Address: 14 Raglan Ave., Fell Lane, Keighley, Yorkshire BD22 6BJ, UK.

DEY, Bishnu, b. 18 July 1909. Retired Professor of English. Education: M.A., Calcutta Univ., India. Positions held: Prof. of Engl., Ripon Coll., Calcutta, 1935-44; Prof. of Engl., Presidency Coll., ibid, 1944-47; Prof. of Engl., Ctrl. Calcutta Coll. (later Maulana Azad Coll.), 1947-69. Published works: Urbasi-O-Artemis, 1932; Chorabali, 1936; Purbolékh, 1941; 22nd June, 1942; Satbhai Champa, 1945; Roochi-o-Pragatee, 1946; Sandipér Char, 1947; Samudrérmauno (trans.), 1945; Anwista, 1950; Sahityér Bhabisyat, 1952; Nam Rékéchhi Komal Gandhar, 1953; Hébidéshi Phul (trans.), 1957; Paintings of Rabindranath Tagore, India & Modern Art, 1953; Aleékhya, 1958; Tumi Shudhu Panchisé Baisakh, 1958; Prodosh Das Gupta, his sculpture, 1961; Smriti-Satta-Bhabisyat, 1963; Satyendranath Bose – A Legend in his Lifetime, 1963; Sei Andhakar Chai, 1966; Rushati Panchasati, 1967; Itihasé Tragic Ullasé, 1967; Sambad Mulata Kabya, 1970; Rabi Karojjal Nijadéshé, 1973; & critical essays, trans., etc. Contbr. to all mags. published in India & to Indian Literature, Sahitya Akademi, Delhi. Awards: Sahitya Akademi Award, 1965; Soviet Land Award, 1970; Bharatiya Jnanpith, 1973. Address: 9/17 Fern Rd., Calcutta 19, India.

DHANRAJGIR, Indira Devi (Rajkumari Saheba Indira Devi Dhanrajgir), b. 17 Aug. 1930. Poet. Married G. Seshendra Sarma. Positions held: Mbr., Ctrl. Bd. of Film Censors, Govt. of India; Mbr., Script Comm., Film Finance Corp., Govt. of India; Dir., Ashoka Hotel Limited, Chanakyapuri, New Delhi (Govt. nominee); Pres., All India Women's Conf., North Andhra Br.; Mbr., Sahitya Akademy Urdu Comm.; Pres., Indian Langs. Forum, Goshamahal, Hyderabad, AP. Published works: The Apostle, 1964; Return Eternity, 1965; Yearning & Other Poems, 1966; Partings in Mimosa, 1966; Ritu Ghosh (transl.) long poem in Telugu by G. Seshendra Sarma; Meghdoot (transl.) Sanskrit Classic by Kalidasa, 1969; Sheshajyotsana (transl.) 20 poems in Telugu by G. Seshendra Sarma, 1972; The Commitment; The Tide, 1974. Contbr. to: Deccan Chronicle; Le Advance of Mauritius; Dialogue India; Mahfil, U.S.A., etc. Address: Gyan Bagh Palace, Goshamahal, Hyderabad 12, Andhra Pradesh, India.

DHONDT, Steven Thomas, b. 4 Aug. 1944. University Educator. Education: B.A., Engl., Adrian Coll., Mich., 1966; M.A., Engl., Utah State Univ., Logan, Utah, 1967; grad. work at var. univs. Positions held: Grad. Tchng. Asst., Dept. of Engl., Utah State Univ., 1966-67; Admin. Asst., The Grad. Schl., Bowling Green State Univ., 1967-68; Assoc. Dean, Fac. of Humanities & Soc. Scis. & Instr. in Engl., State Univ. of N.Y. Coll. at Buffalo, 1968–. Memberships: Mng. Ed., The College Engl. Assn.; The Modern Lang. Assn.; Lambda Iota Tau. Published works: First Reading, 1972. Contbr. to: Oblique; Raven; Elm Leaves; West Coast Poetry Review; Poem; Buffalo Evening News.

Honours, awards: 2nd pl., Adrian Coll. Poetry Prize, 1965; Contbr. in Poetry, Bread Loaf Nat. Writers' Conf., 1972; Logos Press Book of the Year, 1972. Address: 641 Forest Ave., Buffalo, NY 14222, U.S.A.

DIAMOND, Florence Jean, professional name, **PIELD, Jean,** b. 18 Oct. 1924. Teacher-Actress; Singer; Songwriter. Educ: B.A., Northwestern Univ., 1946; post grad. work at var. univs. Divorced, 1 son, 1 daughter. Positions held: Elem. Tchr., L.A. City Schls., 1950-74; Actress (Equity Prodns.), Hollywood, Calif., Las Palmas, Circle Theatre, Inglewood Playhouse, Ludlum Theatre; Var. Radio, TV, & Stage work. Memberships: Corres. Sec., Poetry Soc. of So. Calif., 1971-72; 2nd V.P., ibid, 1972-73; Pres., 1973-74; Mary Carr Moore Manuscript Club; Delta Kappa Gamma. Published works: '17 by Florence Jean', personal vol. of Haiku, 1974. Contbr. to: The Historian; Beverly Hills Mag.; Delta Kappa Gamma; Israel Today; Opportunity Knocks. & var. selections of the Poetry Soc. of So. Calif. Address: 226 So. Willaman Dr., Beverly Hills, CA 90021, U.S.A.

DICKEY, James, b. 2 Feb. 1923. Writer, Lecturer, Teacher, Poet. Education: Vanderbilt Univ.; B.A., 1949; M.A., 1950. Positions held: Engl. Tchr., Rice Univ., Houston, Tex.; ibid, Univ. of Fla.; Writer-in-Residence, Reed Coll., Portland, Ore.; Univ. of Wisc.; currently, Univ. of SC. Published works: Into The Stone, 1960; Drowning With Others, 1962; Helmets, 1964; Buckdancer's Choice, 1965; Poems 1957-67, 1967. Contbr. to: New Yorker; Encounter; Partisan Review; Poetry; Atlantic Monthly; Harper's Life; Sewanee Review; Yale Review; Va. Quarterly; Hudson Review; Kenyon Review; Shenandoah; Nation; Southern Review; Tex. Quarterly. Awards & Honours: Sewane Review Fellowship; Guggenheim Fellowship; Grant, Nat. Inst. of Arts & Letters; Longview Award, Melville Cene Award; Nat. Book Award; Chair of Poetry, Lib. of Congress. Address: 4620 Lelia's Ct., Lake Katherine, Columbia, SC 29206, USA.

DICKEY, R(obert) P(reston), pen name, **DICKEY, R.P.,** b. 24 Sept. 1936. Professor; Editor; Publisher; Poet. Fducation: M.A., Univ. of Mo. Positions held: Instr., Univ. of Mo., 1967-69; Asst. Prof., Southern Colo. State Coll., 1969–; Fndr., Ed., Poetry Bag (jrnl.), 1966–; Poetry Ed., Southern Colo. Standard. Publr. Published Works: Four Poets (w. Donald Drummond, Thomas McAfee & Donald Justice), 1967; Running Lucky, 1969; Acting Immortal, 1970; Homage to Ezra pound, 1971; Bufferoo the Prophet, 1971; Concise Dictionary of Lead River, 1972; The Basic Stuff of Poetry, 1972; Life-Cycle of Seven Songs, 1972; McCabe Wants Chimes, 1973; Minnequa, 1973. Contbr. to: Tambourine; Poets of the Midwest; Contemporary Poets of Am.; New Generation of Poets; Intro No. 2; Sat. Review; Commonweal; Prairie Schooner; Choice; Perspective; Poetry Northwest; Contact; Sou'wester; New England Review; Colo. State Review; Western Am. Literature; Mediterranean Review; Poetry Australia; The Nation; Southern Colo. Standard; Richmond (Va.) Mercury Book Review, etc. Awards: Mahan Award for Poetry, 1965, '66; Kan. City poetry Contests, 1966. Address: c/o Dept. of Engl., Southern Colo. State Coll., Pueblo, Colo., USA.

DICKEY, William, b. 15 Dec. 1928. University Professor. Education: B.A., Reed Coll., 1951; M.A., Harvard Univ., 1955; M.F.A., Univ. of Iowa, 1956; advanced study, Jesus Coll., Oxford. Phi Beta Kappa; Woodrow Wilson Fellow; Fulbright Fellow. Married, 1959, div. 1972. No children. Positions held: Managing Ed., Western Review; Man. Ed., Civil War History; Instr., Cornell Univ., and member edit. bd. of Epoch; Asst. Prof., Denison Univ.; Asst. Prof., San Francisco State Coll., now Calif. State Univ., San Francisco, where at present Prof. of Engl. and Creative Writing; Visiting Prof., Univ. of Hawaii, Spring, 1973. Memberships: Mod. Lang. Assoc.; Philological Assoc. of the Pacific Coast. Published works: Of the Festivity, 1959; Interpreter's House, 1964; Rivers of the Pacific Northwest, 1969; More Under Saturn, 1971. Contbr. to: Atlantic Monthly; Harper's; New Yorker; Hudson

Review; Kenyon Review; Poetry; Southern Review; Iowa Review; Minnesota Review; Carleton Miscellany; Epoch; Dubliner, etc. Awards: Union League Prize, Poetry; Commonwealth Club of Calif., silver medal, 1972. Address: Dept. of Engl., CA State Univ., San Francisco, CA 94132, USA.

DICKINSON, Ernest, b. 30 Oct. 1897. Retired. Positions held: Mgr., Boots Internal Audit; Sec., Boots Hlth. Ins. Soc.; Sec., Boots Savings Bank; Mgr., Nat. Ins. Off., Nottingham, Loughborough, Carlton. Memberships: Nottingham Poetry Soc. Published works: Donkey Brays on Parnassus; Montmartre, Mount of Temptation; Dickolympians; A Joseph Coat. Contbr. to: Berwick-on-Tweed Advertiser; Window; Nottingham Evening Post; Notts. Countryside. Also broadcasts on BBC & Radio Nottingham & poems read at festivals. Recip. of var. small poetry awards. Address: 6 Devonshire Cres., Sherwood, Nottingham NG5 2EU, U.K.

DICKINSON, Patric (Thomas), b. 26 Dec. 1914. Poet; Playwright; Free-lance Broadcaster. Education: St. Catherine's Coll., Cambridge. Positions held: Asst. Schoolmaster, 1936-39; Astists' Rifles, 1939-40; BBC, 1942-48; Acting Poetry Ed., ibid, 1945-48. Published works: The Seven Days of Jericho, 1944; Theseus & the Minotaur & Poems, 1946; Stone in the Midst & Poems, 1948; The Sailing Race, 1952; The Scale of Things, 1955; The World I See, 1960; This Cold Universe, 1964; A Round of Golf Courses, 1951; Aristophanes Against War, 1957; The Aenid of Vergil, 1960; A Durable Fire (play), 1962; The Good Minute (autobiog.), 1965. Anthologies: Soldiers' Verse, 1945; Byron (selected), 1949; Poems to Remember, 1958. Honours, awards: Atlantic Award in Lit., 1948. Address: 38 Church Sq., Rye, Sussex, U.K.

DICKSON, Robert Cook, b. 12 March 1910. College Professor. Education: B.A., & M.A., Ohio State Univ.; further study at Oxford and Edinburgh Univs.; studied art at Art Students League in NY and The Nat. Acad. School of Fine Arts in NY; studied sculpturing with Chaim Gross. Positions held: Prof. of Engl., and Chairman of the Dept. at the Baruch School of the City Univ. of NY.; owner and director, Elsinore Galleries in Portland and Denmark, Maine. Retired as Prof. Emeritus. Instr. of fighter pilots in WWII in England. Has exhibited paintings throughout the Eastern U.S. including NYC. Published works: Ten Poems, 1955; Primer For Dust & Other Poems, 1957; Poems, 1971. Contbr. to: The Candle: Voices; Home & Abroad; Talisman; NY Times; NY Times Book Review, etc. Address: Royal Crest Apts., 1814 Kuser Rd., Apt. 16, Hamilton Township, NJ 08690, USA.

DIENER, Mary Eleanor, b. 20 July 1929. Washington, DC, USA. Advertising, Public Relations; Poet-Journalist. Education: Internat. Coll. of Japan; For. Lang. Courses, Catholic Univ. of Am.; B.A., Manhattanville Coll., Purchase, NY; Teaching Certification in Engl., Public Relations & Advertising. Positions held: 1971 to present: Pres., Diener & Associates, Inc.; 1969-71. Account Rep., The Center for Market & Research, Sarasota; 1966-67; Editor, Display Ad. Manager & Sales Manager, The Citizen (weekly newspaper); 1956-62, Pres. of Assistencia Social de Vila Alpina; 1961-65, Feature Writer & Social Crit. Columnist, Brazil Herald; 1956-62, Director-Manager, a Shopping Service; 1953-54, Acted as Asst. to American Director, Cultural Union of Brazil-US; 1951-52; Member Econ. Staff, General Motors of Brazil; 1946-47, Civil Service Commission. Memberships: American Advertising Fed. (Director, SBV Branch); Florida Public Relations Assoc.; NLAPW, Sarasota Branch (Pres.); Women's Symphony Assoc. (Director, Parliamentarian); Internat. Platform Assoc.; Allied Arts Council of Sarasota (Director); Sarasota Florida Chamber of Commerce. Published works: Brazilian Guide, 1957; Laments (in Portuguese), 1963; When the Sun Goes Down, 1969. Contbr. to: Sarasota Herald Tribune; Sarasota Journal; The Citizen; The Pen Woman; Brazil Herald; Estado de Sao Paulo, etc. Address: P.O. Box

12052, Research Triangle Park, NC 27709, U.S.A.

DIGBY, Ronald Yarham, b. 7 Jan. 1900. Science Master. Education: B.Sc., Victoria Univ., Manchester, 1921; Royal Coll. of Sci., London. Positions held: Chemistry Master, Accrington Grammar Schl.; Lectr., Bamber Bridge Trng. Coll.; Lectr., Burnley Municipal Coll.; Biol. Master, Bacup & Rawtenstall Grammar Schl. Memberships: Life Mbr., Edwin Waugh Soc., Rochdale; Ed. 'The Record', qtly. mag. of The Lancs. Authors Assn., 1964–. Published works: Jt. author w. the late Alice Miller, Accrington Miscellany, 1970; Rossendale Anthology, 1969; Jt. author w. the late Harry Craven, Bacup Miscellany, 1972. Contbr. to The Record. Recip., The Scholes Cup for Dialect Poem, Lancs. Authors Assn., 1962. Address: 222 Stanley St., Accrington, Lancs., U.K.

DILAWAR, Husain, pen name **FIGAR, Dilawar,** b. 9 July 1928. Teacher; Journalist. Education: M.A., Econs., Agra Univ., India, 1963; M.A., Urdu, ibid, 1966. Positions held: Asst. Tchr., Islamia Coll., Budaun, U.P., India; Lectr., Haroon Coll., Karachi; Asst. Dir., Master Plan Dept., K.D.A., Karachi; Writer, 'Masawat', Karachi. Pres., Pakistan Peoples Poets. Published works: Hadsay, Collection of Ghazals, 1949; Shamate Aamal, poems, 1962, Aadab Arz, 1964 & Unglian Figar Apnee, 1972, all colls. of humorous & satirical poems. Contbr. to: Shama Monthly, Delhi; Nai Dunya Daily, Delhi; Siyasat Daily, Kanpur; Jasarat Daily, Karachi; Masawat Daily, Karachi, etc. Recip., Akbar Allahabadi Award from U.P. Govt. (India) on Shamat Aamal, 1962. Address: 5-B-3/17, Shahrah-e-Farhana, Nazimabad, Karachi, Pakistan.

DILKS, Linda Helen, pen name **ALICE G.A.,** b. 14 Mar. 1953. Lab. Assistant. Education: Camp Hill HS.; Lock Haven State Coll.; Dickenson Law Coll. Membership: Keysner Poetry Soc. of Harrisburg. Book in progress, Raintree Road. Contbr. to: Patriot News (Harrisburg, Pa.). Address: R. D. 3, Mechanicsburg, PA 17055, USA.

DINO, (Rev. Fr.) Isidoro D., pen name, **DUCE, Sacro.** b. 4 Apr. 1910. Catholic Priest; Seminary Dean & Professor; College President. Education: Holy Rosary Major Sem., Naga City; Jrnlsm. & Educ., Univ. of Santo Tomas, Manila; M.A., Engl., ibid, 1950; Ph.D., 1952; Ph.D., Educ., McKinley-Roosevelt, Chgo., USA. Positions held: Ordained Priest, 1937; Curate of Masbate; Provincial Corres., Debate-Mabuhay-Herald-Monday Mail chain of newspapers, 1938; Chap., I.X.L. Mining Co., Balete, Masbate; Acting Pastor, Baleno, Masbate; Chap., Masbate Guerilla Regiment; Chap., Replacement Battalion, Philippine Army, Tacloban., Leyte; Chap., 42nd Inf. Regt., Philippine Army, Calbayog, Samar; Zone Chap., Mindanao & Sulu, MPC, Camp Overton, Lanao; Asst. Chief Chap., GHQ, Philippine Constabulary, Camp Crame, Quezon City; Chap., Malacanang Guard Battalion, Manila; Chap., Victoriano Luna Gen. Hosp., Kamias, Quezon City; Area Chap., 1st Military Area, Philippine Army, Camp Olivas, Pampanga; Prin., Camp Olivas H.S., ibid; Prof. of Engl. & Philos., Colegio de la Milagrosa, Sorsogon; Pastor & Schl. Dir., Palanas, Masbate; Pres., Masbate Assn. Pvte. Schls. & Colls.; Pastor & Schl. Dir., Baleno, Masbate; Sem. Dean & Prof., Our Lady of Penafrancia Sem., Sorsogon; Pres., Bacon Annunciation Coll. Coop. Credit Union, Bacon, Sorsogon. Coll. Pres., Annunciation Coll. of Bacon, ibid; Director, Encinas Inst., Rizal, Gubat, Sorsogon, since 1972. Memberships: Sec., Philos. Lit. Soc., Holy Rosary Sem.; Bicol. Vernacular Guild; United Poets Laureate Int.; Pres., Hist. Assn., Sorsogon Province; Chmn., Cath. Educ. Assn. of Sorsogon, 1971; Comm. Chmn., World's Congress of Poets; Internat. Poetry Soc., UK (Fellow); CSSI (Rome); Internat. Acad. of Leadership; Hist. Assoc. of the Philippines; Philosophical Assn. of the Philippines; Philippine Assn. for Grad. Educ. Published poetry; My Lyre, 1940. Contbr. to: Laurel Leaves; Bicol Star; Bicolandia; Heraldo Bicol; La Defenza; The Philippine Commonweal; Seminarium; The Catechist; The Letran News; Thomasian; The

Quill; Mayon; Philippine Jrnl. of Education: The Crossroad. Awards & Honours: 1st Prize, XXXIII Int. Eucharistic Congress Essay Contest, Manila, 1937; Disting. Philippine Cath. Poet, Philippine Assn. Drs. Law, Int. Acad. Ldrship., United Poets Laureate Int., UN Day, Philippines, 1967; D. Litt., Free Univ. of Asia, Karachi, Pakistan, 1968; Gold Plaque of Decretum, World Congress of Poets, 1969; Dip. & Gold Medal, Int. Acad. Ldrship., ibid; Dip., Postrer Adios World Trans. Contest, United Poets Laureate Int.; Dr. of Historical Sciences (h.c.), 1970, Inst. Heraldico, Barcelona, Spain. Address: Annunciation Coll. of Bacon, Bacon, Sorsogon H-401, Philippines.

DINWIDDIE, Faye Love, b. 17 Sept. Poet; Lecturer; (former Social Worker). Education: Toledo Pub. Schools; Univ. of Toledo; Univ. of Michigan (School of Public Health). Personal details: Widow of Benjamin Dinwiddie; 1st marriage to John Foster; 1 child (John Love Foster, deceased). Positions held: Director, Dunbar Community Center, E. Toledo; Newspaper Columnist (syndicated – Negro Newspapers); Field Worker and Director of prog., "Better Pattern of Living", Toledo Public Health Assoc.; Case Worker, Lucas Co. Welfare Dept.; Family Counselor, Asst. Director, Acting Director, OEO Neighborhood Center; Editor, Community Orbit. Memberships: Poetry Soc. (UK); Ohio Poetry Soc., Toledo Chapter; CSSI; Nat. Writers Club; Black Writers Conference. Published work: Song of the Mute, 1970. Contbr. to: Advance Mag.; Before the Shadow; Negro News Weeklies, 1936-38; Ohio State Press; Ohio State News; Colorado Statesman; Toledo Press; Field of Daisies, 1967; Tilt The World, 1967-68. Address: 1908 Washington St., Toledo, OH 43624, USA.

DIOMEDE, Matthew, b. 8 June 1940. Teacher; Poet. Education: B.A., Fordham Coll.; M.S., Fordham Univ. Positions held: Teacher, NY and Conn., since 1962. Memberships: Poetry Soc. of New Hampshire; C.S.S.I. Contbr. to: (anthols.) Poetry of Our Time, 1970; New Voices in the Wind, 1969; Yearbook of Modern Poetry, 1971; Nat. Poetry Anthol. (1972 and 1973 editions); Black Cat Bone (shortly); Outstanding Contemporary Poetry, 1971; Internat. Who's Who in Poetry Anthol., 1972; (mags. and journals, etc.) Kansas Qtly.; Phylon; The Above Ground Review; Performing Arts Review; The Outcast; Spirit; NY English Record; Cardinal Poetry Qtly.; The Villager; Poetry Soc. of NH Newsletter; NY State Education; Hoosier Challenger; Creative Review; Fireflower; American Poet; United Poets; Cyclo-Flame; Bardic Echoes; Poetry Prevue; Encore; Nimrod; Tejas; Verdure; Painted Poetry Appreciation; Leatherneck; Blue Print; Prairie Poet; Poetry Parade; Haiku Highlights, etc. Awards: 2nd Prize, for a poem with no adjectives, at State of Maine Writers' Conference, 1970; Dip. and bronze medal of hon. from CSSI, 1972. Address: 21 Botany Lane, Stony Brook, Long Island, NY 11790, USA.

DIORIO, Margaret, b. 17 Sept. 1929. Poet. Education: Columbia Univ. Married, 2 children. Editor and founder of ICARUS, a poetry quarterly. Member, Poetry Soc. of Md. Published works: Morning Fugues (under maiden name, Margaret Toarello), 1953; Listening, 1971. Contbr. to: Cath. Worker; Beloit Poetry Journal; Books Abroad; Canadian Forum; Motive; Poet Lore; Poetry Qtly.; Lyric; New Frontiers; Folio; Pegasus; Westminster Mag.; Hartford Courant; Friends Journal; Poetry Chapbook; De Kalt Lit. Arts Journal; Understanding; Talaria. Address: 1015 Kenilworth Dr., Towson, MD 21204, USA.

di PRIMA, Diane, b. 6 Aug. 1934. Editor; Publisher. Educ: Swarthmore Coll., Pa., 1950-51. Married, three children. Positions held: Contbng. Ed., Kulchur, 1960-61; Ed., Floating Bear, N.Y.C., 1961–; Assoc. Ed., Signal Mag., 1963–; Ed. & Publr. (w. husband), Poets Press, N.Y.C., 1964–. Published works: This Kind of Bird Flies Backward, 1958; The New Handbook of Heaven, 1963; Poems for Freddie, 1966; Hiaku, 1967; Earthsong: Poems 1957-1959, 1968; (plays) Murder Cake, 1960; Paideuma, 1960; Like, 1964; (fiction) Dinners and Nightmares, 1961; The Calculus of

Variation, 1966; Spring and Autumn Annuals, 1966; (editor) Various Fables from Various Places, 1960; War Poems, 1968. Contbr. to: (anthologies) Beat Scene, 1960; Poems Now, 1966. Recip., Nat. Inst. of Arts and Letters Grant, 1965.

DISCH, Thomas Michael, pen name **DISCH, Tom,** b. 2 Feb. 1940. Freelance Writer and Editor. Education: 3 yrs., Washington Square Coll., NY Univ. Positions held: Lecturer (Winter and Spring quarter), 1973. Univ. of Minnesota. Published work: The Right Way to Figure Plumbing: 50 Poems 1962-1967, 1972. Contbr. to: Poetry (Chicago); American Review; Little Mag.; Epoch; Minnesota Review; Open Places; New Measure; Tribune; New Worlds; Seshita. Recip. The Union League Civic and Arts Foundation Award (for poems published in Poetry (Chicago)) in 1972. Address: c/o Brandt & Brandt, 101 Park Ave., New York, NY 10017, USA.

DITTO, Roy Waymon, pen name, **SOPHER, Phil O.,** b. 24 May 1895. Public Accountant and Income Tax Consultant. Education: HS, Gustine, Texas; School of Business Admin., Comanche, Texas; Buford School of Accounting, Banking & Finance, Dallas, Texas; Southern Methodist Univ., School of Banking, Business Admin. & Finance with Business Law & Income Tax; Univ. of Omaha, Special Work in Coll. Admin. Married; 2 d., 1 s. Positions held: Junior and Senior Accountant, 3 yrs., Alex Turner & Co., Chartered Accountants (UK); Entered Public Accounting field under own name until 1937; Corporate position as the Comptroller, Sec. & Treas., City Transportation Company to 1945; re-entered Public Accounting field for 10 yrs., then drafted to assist in founding Evangel (Liberal Arts) Coll., Springfield, Mo. (4 yrs.); returned to Texas, 1958, and continued in Public Accounting until retirement. Membership: Poetry Soc. of Texas (since 1934, and served 1 yr. on Exec. Bd.). Published works (in progress); Apples of Gold in Pictures of Silver; Mightier Than The Sword. Contbr. to: The Old Camp Meeting News (monthly column, 1935-40); Dallas Morning News; Daily Times Herald (Dallas); The Pentecostal Evangel (Springfield, Mo.); The Disabled American Veterans Mag.; Poetry of the Southwest (an anthol.); The Southwester. Recip. of bronze plaque "for contribution in establishment of Evangel College, 1954-58". Address: 2002 Swansee St., Dallas, TX 75232, USA.

DIVERS, Olive Alma, b. 28 Feb. 1906. School Teacher. Education: Schls. in Jackson Co., W.Va.; Jrnlsm. course, Newspaper Inst. of Am., 1950-51; poetry course w. Margarette Ball Dickson; Poet & Critic w. Purdue Univ. & Iowa State. Positions held: Poetry Instr., Examiner/Grader for Newspaper Inst. of Am., 1969/74; Freelance Writer for West Va. State Mag.; Jackson Herald, Ripley, W.Va.; Ravenswood News, W.Va. Memberships: Fndr. Fellow, Int. Poetry Soc., U.K.; United Poets Laureate Int., Philippines; Am. Poets Fellowship Soc.; Am. Poetry League; Nat. Fed. of State Poetry Socs.; Histn., W.Va. Poetry Soc., 1963-73; Histn., Parkersburg Chapt., ibid, 1962-73. Published works: Sparks from the Fiery Furnace, 1950; Laurel Twigs, 1966. Songs published or recorded: Gold Dust, 1957; Evening Solitaire, 1958; Eye Shadow, 1959; Tuck Away a Memory or Two, 1962; This Singing Heart of Mine, 1972. Contbr. to var. mags., jrnls., anthols. Honours, awards: First Poet Laureate, Am. Poets Fellowship Soc., 1964; Poet Laureate Trophy, 1965; W.Va. Appreciation Plaque, 1971; Gold Leaf Laurel Crown, Philippines, 1968, etc. Address: Rural Route 2, Box 34, Ravenswood, WV 26164, U.S.A.

DOANE, Myrtle, Caroline, b. 19 May 1914. Teacher; Freelance Writer. Education: Univ. of Me., Gorham, U.S.A., 2 yrs.; Univ. of N.H., Durham. Positions held: Kindergarten Tchr.; Bank Clerk, Lynn Instn. for Savings, Lynn, Mass.; Substitute Schl. Tchr., Me. Schl. Dist.; Freelance Writer. Memberships: Proj. Chmn., Poetry Fellowship of Me.; Me. Press, Radio, TV Women; Mbr. at Large, Nat. League of Am. Pen

Women. Published works: Lyrical Echoes of Freedom, 1966; Sounds of Maine, 1970; Sounds of Maine Revised & illustrated, 1973. Rep. in the following anthols: Poetry Parade, No.12, 1969; Moon Age Poets Anthol., 1970; Anthol. of Am. Poetry-X, Milestone edn., 1970; Moon Age Poets Anthol., 1970; Anthol. of Am. Poetry, 11, 1971; Outstanding Contemporary Poetry Anthol., 1972; Rock Ledge & Apple Blossoms, 1971; Garland of Verse, Thom Hendricks Poetry Anthol., 1971. Contbr. to var. newspapers. Recip. many awards for poetry inclng: 1st pl., State of Me. Writers' Conf.-Poetry Tournament, 1972. Address: R.F.D., Brownfield, ME 04010, U.S.A.

DOBYNS, Stephen J., b. 19 Feb. 1941. Writer. Education: B.A., Engl., Wayne State Univ., 1964; M.F.A., Creative Writing, Univ. of Iowa, 1967. Positions held: Engl. Instr., State Univ. of N.Y. at Brockport, 1968-69; General Assignment Reporter, The Detroit News, 1969-71; Vis. Lectr., Engl., Univ. of New Hampshire, 1973–. Published works: Concurring Beasts, 1972; A Man of Little Evils, (novel), 1973. Contbr. to: Cafe Solo; The Chicago Review; The English Record; The Iowa Review; Kayak; The Little Mag.; Minn. Review; North Am. Review; Northeast; Poetry; Poetry Northwest; Trace; The Wormwood Review, etc. Honours, awards: 'Concurring Beasts', The Lamont Poetry Selection for 1971, of the Acad. of Am. Poets. Address: 8 East St., Dover, NH 03820, U.S.A.

DOCKERAY, John Malcolm, pen name **DOCKERAY, Malcolm,** b. 2 Jan. 1927. Assistant Editor. Education: Royal Manchester Coll. of Music, 1943-45; A.R.M.C.M. Positions held: Asst. Sec., British Poetry-Drama Guild, 1950-52; Mbr., Editl. Bd., 1st Edn., Int. Who's Who in Poetry, 1957-58; Asst. to Hon. Gen. Ed., County Authors Today Series, 1971-73, etc. Memberships: Arts Theatre Club, London; Lancashire Authors' Assn. Contbr. to: The Spring Anthol., 1973; 'Twixt Thee & Me' (anthol.), 1973; Poems of Time & Place (anthol.), 1974; The Record (L.A.A.) Address: c/o Arts Theatre Club, 6-7 Great Newport St., London, W.C.2., U.K.

DODD, Arthur Edward, b. 29 May 1913. Author. Education: M.Sc., Ph.D., London Univ., U.K. Positions held: Information Officer, British Ceramic Rsch. Assn., Stoke-on-Trent, ret'd 1973. Published works: Poems from Belmont, 1955; Three Journeys, 1958; Words & Music, 1963; Weaver Hills, 1967; The Fifth Season, 1971. Verse Plays: The Flower-spun Web, 1960; To Build a Bridge, 1965. Contbr. to: Poetry Review; Country Life; Cheshire Life; Candelabrum. Address: Hall Lodge, Upper Ellastone, Ashbourne, Derbyshire, U.K.

DOLAN, Beth Evelyn (Rogler), b. 26 Mar. 1898. College Instructor; Technical Writer; Research Editor. Education: A.B., Washburn Univ., Topeka, Kan., 1920; M.A., Univ. of Mich., 1922. Married William P. Dolan, 1943. Positions held: Rsch. Supvsr., Chase Co. Hist. Soc., 1935-37; Asst. to Dean of Women, K.S.T.C., 1939-41; Sr. Interviewer, USES (Civil Serv. appt.), 1941-46; Univ. of Mo., McKendree Coll., 1951-56; Engl. Lang. Instr., For. Liaison Sect., Scott AFB, 1951-57; Engl. Instr., San Antonio Coll. Evening Div., 1958-68; Engl. & Personnel Instr., Lackland AFB, San Antonio, Tex., 1957-68; Tech. Writer, Tech. Writing Div., 1962-68; Engl. & Math. Instr., San Antonio Literacy Coun. (Adult Continuing Educ.), 1968–, etc. Memberships incl: Dir., Maywood Writers' Forum, Ill.; Poetry Soc. of Tex.; Chmn., Ways & Means Comm., Poetry Soc. of San Antonio. Published works: (textbook) English Composition: A Capsule Course in Effective Expression, 1968; Chase County Historical Sketches, vols. 1 & 2, 1940-43. Contbr. to: Nat. Poetry Anthol., 1950; Best Am. Poetry of 1938; Chase Co. Ldr-News; The Wichita Eagle, etc. Recip. var. awards. Address: 1122 Jewett St., San Antonio, TX 78237, U.S.A.

DOMIN, Hilde, b. 27 July 1912. Writer; Translator. Education: Studies of law, sociol., philos., econ. theory, Univs. of Heidelberg, Cologne, Berlin, Rome,

Florence; Ph.D., Florence, 1935. Married Erwin Walter Palm. Positions held: Univ. Prof., Univ. of Santo Domingo, 1948-53. Readings & lectures throughout Germany, 1961– and at the following: Harvard, Yale, Princeton, Ann Arbor, Johns Hopkins, Oberlin, Denver, Stanford, Houston, & other in the U.S.A., 1964-71; also in Canada, U.K., Holland, Italy, Luxembourg; Israel, France, Switz., Hungary. Memberships: PEN German Ctr.; Verband Deutscher Schriftsteller; Hon. Mbr., Heine Soc., Dusseldorf. Published works: (poetry) Nur eine Rose als Stütze, 1959; Rückkehr der Schiffe, 1962; Hier, 1964; Ich will dich, 1970; Höhlenbilder (Hundertdruck, with Heinz Mack), 1968; (theory) Wozu Lyrik heute. Dichtung und Leser in der gesteuerten Gesellschaft, 1968; (prose) Das zweite Paradies. Roman in Segmenten, 1968; Die andalusische Katze. Bericht, 1971; Von der Natur nicht vorgesehen. Auskünfte, 1974. Ed. var. publs. Contbr. to num. mags., jrnls., anthols. in Germany & abroad. Honours, awards: Ida Dehmel Prize; Droste Prize of the Town of Meersburg; Medal of the Heine Gesellschaft Dusseldorf. Address: Graimbergweg 5, 69 Heidelberg, German Fed. Repub.

DOMINY, Mary Louise, b. 31 Oct. 1925. Housewife. Education: Tex. Beauty Acad., Tyler, Tex., 1960; selected courses, Panola Jr. Coll., Carthage, Tex., 1970-73. Married Leon Ray Dominy. Memberships: Panola Co. Poetry Soc.; V.P., Rusk Co. Poetry Soc.; Mbrship. Chmn., Finance, Educ. Comm. Chmn., Tex. Poetry Soc. Contbr. to: Major Poets; Young Am. Sings; The Tex. Methodist; The Panola Watchman; The Panola Post; The Shreveport Times. Recip. First Prize for Patriotic verse, Rusk Co. Annual Awards, Dec. 1973. Address: Box 71, Carthage, TX 75633, U.S.A.

DOMS, André, b. 9 Mar. 1932. Professor. Published works: Poème des Anges, 1953; Chant de Lena, 1961; L'Ombre la Sentinelle, pre'ce'de' de Demeure successive, 1963; Matiere habitée, 1965; Cantata pour le vif des Temps, 1971; Selon plis et reflects, 1974; De samaille obscure, 1974. Contbr. to a number of Belgian & French jrnls. Regular Critic to reviews: Marginales; Fantasmagie; du Journal des Poètes. Address: 45 rue de Chastre, B 5872, Corroy-Le-Grand, Belgium.

DONDIEGO, Alice, b. 26 Mar. 1916. Education: B.A., Univ. of Ariz. Positions held: Med. Lab. Techn.; Sec., Med. Supply House; Mgr., Chem.-Phys. Store Rooms at Univ. of Ariz.; Owner & Mgr., Record Shop; Sec., 4-Dr. Clinic. Memberships: Mbrship Comm., Ariz. Poetry Soc.; Sec. Treas., Creative Writing Workshop; Am. Poetry League; Scotlon Pen Guild; United Amateur Press; Am. Amateur Press Assn. Published works: These Memories, 1973. Contbr. to newspapers, books, anthols., mags. inclng: From Sea to Sea in Song; Thoughts of Splendor; Wild Violets in the Snow; Golden Ours; The Barker Brigade; Bouquets of Poems; Tower by the Sea; Easter Prayer Poems; Haiku Anthol.; Birth of a Nation; Trilogy; Poet Directory; Valley Advertiser; Valley Center Index; Am. Poetry League Bulletin; Dragonfly; Tweed; Amber; Action; The Friendship Ferry; Inky Trails; Tots to Teens; Author/Poet. Recip. var. poetry hons. inclng: Hon. Mention, 1972 & First pl., 1973, Caroline Kotowicz Poetry Contest; one of three winning poems in The Barker Blaze, 1973. Address: 18 E. Garfield, Apt. 16, Phoenix, AZ 85004, U.S.A.

DONGALA, Boundzeki Emmanuel, b. 16 July 1941. Science Teacher. Education: B.A., Oberlin Coll., Ohio, U.S.A.; M.Sc., Rutgers Univ., N.J.; Doctorate in Chemistry, Université Louis Pasteur, Strasbourg, France. Contbng. Ed., The Activist, 1963-65 & Regular Contbr. to presence Africaine, 1968–. Published works: (novel) Un fusil dans la main, un poème dans la poche; vol. of poetry in preparation. Rep. in the following: Nouvelle Somme de Poésie du Monde Noir, 1967; Modern Poetry from Africa, 1966; French African Verse, 1972; Negritude, Black Poetry from the French, 1970. Address: Boite Postale 2181, Brazzaville, Rep. of the Congo.

DOR, Moshe, pen names, **M. BAR – YA'AKOV & M. DROMI,** b. 9 Dec. 1932. Journalist. Education: B.A. (Pol. Sci.), Tel Aviv Univ.; studied mod. hist. & pol. sci., Hebrew Univ. of Jerusalem & Tel Aviv Univ. Married, 2 children. Positions held: worked on sev. mags. & newspapers; w. Maariv, 1958–; currently Columnist & Feature Writer. Memberships: Past Mbr. (Dpty.Chmn., 1972), Hebrew Writers' Assn.; Israeli Journalists' Assn.; Dpty. Chmn., Acum (Israeli Assn. of Writers & Musicians), 1968-70; PEN Club of Israel. Published works: (in Hebrew) White Cypresses, 1954; If We Do & If We Don't, 1957; Order of Attachment, 1960; Crossing the Street, 1962; Cold & Ashes, poems of Paris, 1963; Nettles & Metal, 1965; Icarus the World, 1966; Baron Porcelli in Jerusalem, 1968; Selected Poems, 1970; Two books of poems for Children; Reading and Re-reading, a volume of Literary essays, 1970. Contbr. to num. mags., jrnls. Hon. Fellow in Writing, Univ. of Iowa, U.S.A. Address: 11 Brodetsky St., Ramat Aviv, Tel Aviv, Israel.

DORBIN, Sanford, pen name **DORBIN, Sandy,** b. 8 Dec. 1932. Head Reference Librarian, Univ. of Connecticut. Education: A.B. in Engl., M.L.S., from U.C.L.A. Positions held: in libraries of U.C.L.A., Univ. of Calif., Santa Barbara; Northern Arizona Univ.; currently: Head Ref. Librarian, Univ. of Connecticut. Editor and publisher of SCHIST, a journal of poetry and graphics. Published works: Family Life, and Others, 1968; Persona: Image Mirror Image, 1969; (Editor) The Days Run Away Like Wild Horses Over the Hills, poetry by Charles Bukowski, 1969; Remember: Ocelot, or Ochre, 1971; The Ruby Woods, 1971. Contbr. to: UCLA Daily Bruin; Per/Se; Thrust; Outcast; Cronopios; Ante; Haravec; Spectrum; Ghost Dance; Stooge; Pine Knots; Trace; After Noon; Soundings; The Wormwood Review; Out of Sight; Inscape; Bachy; Corduroy; Small Press Review; The Blackbird Circle; Huerfano; Schist. Address: P.O. Box 257, Willimantic, CT 06226, USA.

DORN, Edward, b. 2 Apr. 1929. Professor of Literature; Visiting Poet. Educ: Univ. of Ill.; Black Mountain Coll., N.C. Positions held: Vis. Prof., Am. Lit., Univ. of Essex, U.K., 1965-68; Vis. Poet, Univ. of Kansas, Lawrence, U.S.A., 1968–. Published works: The Newly Fallen, 1961; Hand Up, 1963; Geography, 1966; The North Atlantic Turbine, 1967; Gunslinger, Part I, 1968; Gunslinger, Part II, 1969; Gunslinger, Parts I and II, 1969; 24 Love Songs, 1969. Contbr. to: (anthologies) New American Poetry, 1960; A Controversy of Poets, 1965. Address: Lawrence, KS, U.S.A.

DOUGHERTY, Alma. Education: Draughons' Bus. Coll.; sev. courses in writing. Married, 5 children. Positions held: Sec.; Civil Serv. Positions held: Pres., Poets Roundtable of Ark.; Pres., Authors, Composers & Artists; Pres., Pioneer Br., Nat. League of Am. Penwomen; Pres., Prose Writers Workshop; currently State Pres., Nat. League of Am. Penwomen. Contbr. to: The Ark. Democrat; The Ark. Gazette; The Monticellonian; The Forum; North Little Rock Times; The Christian; The Ark. Churchman. Honours, awards incl. sev. from Poets Roundtable of Ark. in particular, 1st pl. & Best of Show in illustrated poetry, 1970; 5th pl., Nat. Contest for Penwomen, 1973; Alma K. Dougherty Award for Excellence in Creative Writing established, 1973. Address: 2111 Cumberland St., Little Rock, AR 72206, U.S.A.

DOWDEN, George Duncan, Jr., b. 15 Sept. 1932. Education: B.A., Bucknell Univ., 1957; M.A., N.Y. Univ., 1960. Positions held: Lectr. in Engl., N.Y. Univ., 1959 & Brooklyn Coll., 1960-63 & 1966. Published works: Flight From America, 1965; Because I Am Tired of the Night, 1966; Letters to English Poets, 1967; He, or Genesis, 1968; Birth Vision & Green Song, 1968; Poems from the Paintings of David Jenkins, 1969; Renew Jerusalem, 1969; This Is the Land of the Dead, the Island of the Blessed, 1970; A Bibliography of Works by Allen Ginsberg, 1971; New York; First Poems, 1971; Mukteshwari: The Way of Muktananda (transl.), 1972 & part II (transl.), 1973. Contbr. to num.

mags., jrnls., anthols. inclng: Anthol. of Little Mag. Poets; Asylum; Bo Heem E Um; The Wormwood Review; Second Aeon; Broadsheet; Rupambara Int. Poetry Number; Antigonish Review; The Children of Atlantis; Viet Nam Poeti Americani; Sat. Review, etc. Address: 11B Adelaide Cres., Hove, Sussex BN3 2JE, U.K.

DOWLING, Basil Cairns, b. 29 Apr. 1910. Schoolmaster. Education: M.A., Canterbury Univ., Christchurch; Diploma, NZ Lib. Schl. Positions held: Ref. Libn., then Dpty. Libn., Otago Univ.; Asst. Master, Downside Schl., Purley, UK; Hd., Engl. Dept., Raine's Fndn. Grammar Schl., London. Mbr., NZ Br., PEN. Published works: A Day's Journey, 1941; Signs & Wonders, 1944; Canterbury & Other Poems, 1949; Hatherley, 1968. Contbr. to: Landfall; NZ Listener; NZ Yearbook of the Arts; Times Lit. Supplement; Time & Tide; (anthols.) Penguin Book of NZ Verse; Anthol. of NZ Verse; The Albemarle Book of Modern Verse; Poems of Spirit & Action, etc. Honours: Jessie MacKay Mem. Award for Poetry, NZ, 1954. Address: 30C Shepherds Hill, Highgate, London N6, UK.

DOWLING, Dorothea Helena. Stenographer, State Government, Sydney. Education: Sydney Schl. of Ballet; Estelle Andersen Schl. of Ballet, Sydney; Margaret Saul Schl. of Ballet, London, U.K. Memberships: Poetry, Poets & People Soc., Sydney. Published works: When I Am Free; Twenty-One Poems; Proud Heritage; The Open Road; Candles Are For Christmas (2nd ed.); Bunny Slippers; Poems for Recitation; (U.K.) Candles Are For Christmas, 1st ed.; Selected Poems; More Poems. Contbr. to: Australian Broadcasting Commn. Poetry Progs.; Seydell Quarterly, USA/Belgium; Chambers' Jrnl., Edinburgh; Sydney Morning Herald (Mag. Sections); Stateworks, Sydney; var. other mags. Recip. var. hons. & awards inclng: Twice Winner of ANZAC DAY poems; Awarded Cultural Grant for 'Candles are.fo are For Christmas', in Carol form, set to music by Miriam Hyde; Many poems selected as Test Pieces in var. Eisteddfods inclng. The City of Sydney Eisteddfod. Address: 11/290 Old South Head Rd., Vaucluse, Sydney, NSW, Australia 2030.

DOWLING, Mavis Annette. Federal Government Stenographer. Education: State Conserv. of Music, Piano & Violin; Estelle Anderson Acad. of Ballet, Sydney; Sydney Schl. of Ballet (Gwen Sievers); Margaret Saul Schl. of Ballet, London, U.K. Member, Poets, Poetry & People Soc., Sydney. Published works: (Australia) The Open Road, (jointly w. Dorothea Dowling); Candles Are For Christmas, 2nd ed., (w. D. Dowling) – these were also set to music by Miriam Hyde & won a N.S.W. Govt. Cultural Grant; Bunny Slippers & Poems for Recitation (written by D. Dowling & illustrated by M. Dowling); (U.K.) Selected Poems; More Poems; Candles Are For Christmas, 1st ed. (all w. D. Dowling). Contbr. to: The B.P. Mag., Sydney; Sydney Morning Herald; The New Idea Mag., Melbourne; Seydell Quarterly; Chambers Jrnl.; Avon; The Sunday Sun, Sydney. Recip., var. prizes for poetry. Address: 11/290 Old South Head Rd., Vaucluse, N.S.W., Australia 2030.

DOWNES, Gwladys Violet, b. 22 Apr. 1915. University Professor. Education: Univs. of B.C. & Toronto, Canada & Sorbonne, Paris, France. Currently Prof. of French, Univ. of Victoria. Mbr., League of Canadian Poets. Published works: Lost Diver, 1955; When We Lie Together, 1973 (translations from French-Canadian poets). Contbr. to: Canadian Forum; Ellipse; Tamarack Review; Tuatara; Edge; Threshold (Belfast); Prism; Alphabet; Malahat; Fiddlehead. Address: 2621 Lincoln Rd., Victoria, B.C., Canada.

DOWNING, Eva C., b. 4 Feb. 1895. Housewife. Married J.H. Downing. Positions held: Schl. Tchr.; Saleslady. Memberships: Pen Women; Int. Poetry Soc.; Amateur Press Assn.; Christian Church Order of the Eastern Star; Treas., Federated Club; Troy Study Club, etc. Published works: three poetry books, 1950, '58, '66. Contbr. to: Cyclo-flame; Inky Trails; Creative

Review; Author & Poet, etc. Recip. var. poetry prizes. Address: 22 Kuhne Blvd., Troy, Missouri, U.S.A.

DOYLE, Charles (Desmond), pen names **DOYLE, Mike & DOYLE, Charles,** b. 18 Oct. 1928. University Teacher. Education: B.A., M.A., Ph.D. & Dip. Tchng., New Zealand; Yale Univ., 1967-68. Married Doran Ross Smithells, 3 sons, 1 daughter. Positions held: currently Assoc. Prof. of Engl., Univ. of Victoria, B.C., Canada. Mbr. League of Canadian Poets. Published works: (colls. of poetry) A Splinter of Glass, 1956; The Night Shift (w. others), 1957; Distances, 1963; A Sense of Place, 1965; Messages for Herod, 1965; Earth Meditations: 2, 1968; Quorum/Noah (w. R. Sward), 1970; Abandoned Sofa, 1971; Earth Meditations, 1971; Earthshot, 1972; Preparing for the Ark, 1973; Going On, 1973; (other publs.) Recent Poetry in New Zealand, 1965; Small Prophets & Quick Returns, 1966; R.A.K. Mason: A Critical Study, 1970. Rep. in over a dozen anthols. & contbr. to many mags., jrnls., reviews. Honours, awards: Jessie Mackay Meml. Award, 1955; MacMillan Brown Prize, 1956; UNESCO Int. Fellowship, 1958-59. Address: 759 Helvetia Cres., Victoria, B.C., Canada.

DOYLE, Winefride, pen names **BROOME, Winefride & BROOME, Joanna.** Clerical Officer. Widow, 2 sons. Positions held: Retired Clerical Officer, British Leyland Motors Ltd. Memberships: Lancashire Authors' Assn.; Preston Poets' Soc.; Leyland Writers'. Contbr. to: Preston Poets' Soc. anthol. 'Reflections', 1972; Fleetwood Music & Arts Fest. publ., 1972 & '73; Lancashire Life, 1973; Catholic Bulletin; Oldham Chronicle; British Leyland Motors Ltd. mag. Poems broadcast on Radio Blackburn. Honours, awards incl: 3rd prize, 1968, 1st prize, 1971, 3rd prize, 1971, Preston Writers'; Mackenzie Trophy 2nd pl., Preston Poets', 1968; 3rd pl., ibid, 1969; Pomfret Cup, 1st pl., 1970; Mackenzie Trophy, 1st pl., 1970; Pomfret Cup, 2nd pl., 1971; Mackenzie Trophy, 1st pl., 1972; 3rd pl., Batty Cup, Lancs. Authors' Assn., 1971; Writer of the Year, Rose Bowl, ibid, 1971. Address: 148 Eaves Ln., Chorley, Lancs. PR6 OTA, U.K.

DOYRAN, Turhan, b. 20 June 1926. Poet; Writer; Photographer. Educ: Univ. of Ankara, Turkey; Univ. of Grenoble, France; Studied film, Sorbonne, Univ. of Paris; Inst. of Adv. Int. Studies, Paris; Theatre, Ansaldi Acad.; Photography, Nat. Conservatory of Arts & Trades. Married, 1 daughter. Memberships: Acad. Leonardo da Vinci, Rome; Centro Studi e Scambi Int., Rome. Published works: (poetry) Şiirler, 1955; Şehir, 1959; Partir, 1962; Geçilmez, 1962; Le Jour, 1962; Il Faut Bien, 1962; Comme Autrefois, 1964; Je ne suis pas de Bologne, 1967; (theatre) Söz-La Parole, 1946; Onur, 1947; La Préméditation, Paris, 1961, Liège, 1965; Marée Haute, 1965; Le Mobile, 1967; Agaç-L'Arbre, 1967. Contbr. to: Yenisabah; Yeditepe; Les Débats; Varlik; Arkitekt; Yeniufuklar; Yucel; Gençlik; Varan; Turk Tityatrosu; Şairler Yapragi; Beraber; Seçilmiş Hikayeler; Kaynak.; La Revue du Caire; Le Pays du Lac; Le Bayou; La Voix des Poètes; Elan; Le Divan; La Licorne; Gyroscope; Séquences 62; Les Cahiers de Jean Tousseul; Jouvence; Signor Si; Paf; Thyrse, etc. Honours, awards: Prize for Photography, Cannes, 1958; Prize, Acad. Leonardo da Vinci, 1964. Address: 8 Rue du Cambodge, Paris 75020, France.

DRAKE, Albert Dee, b. 26 Mar. 1935. Associate Professor. Education: B.A., Engl., Univ. of Ore., Eugene, 1962; M.F.A., Engl., ibid, 1966. Married, 3 children. Positions held: Rsch. Asst., Ore. Rsch. Inst., 1962-63 & Dept. of Engl., Univ. of Ore., 1965; Tchng. Asst., Dept. of Engl., Univ. of Ore., 1965-66; Asst. Prof., Engl., Mich. State Univ., 1966-69; Assoc. Prof., ibid, 1969–; Writers' Digest Schl., 1973–. Memberships: COSMEP; CCLM. Published works: Crap Game, 1968; Michigan Signatures, Ed., 1968; 3 Northwest Poets, 1970; Poems, 1972; Riding Bike, 1973. Contbr. to: Poetry Northwest; Sumac; Shenandoah; December; Northwest Review; N.Y. Qtly.; S.D. Review; Wis. Review; Trace; The Fiddlehead; Cimarron Review, etc. Honours, awards: Julia Burgess Poetry Prize, 1961; E. Haycox Fiction

Award, 1st 1962, 2nd 1961; CCLM Grant, 1972; MSU Rsch. Grant, 1968. Address: Dept. of Engl., Mich. State Univ., East Lansing, MI 48824, U.S.A.

DRAKE, Barbara Ann, b. 13 Apr. 1939. Writer; Teacher. Education: B.A. in Engl., Univ. of Ore., Eugene, 1961; M.F.A. in Creative Writing, Engl., ibid, 1966. Positions held: Tchng. Asst., Univ. of Ore., 1961-62 & '64-66; Writer/Researcher, Ore. Curric. Study Ctr., 1965-66; Writer/Researcher, Holt, Rinehart & Winston, Publsrs. (Schl. Dept.), 1966-71; Tchr., Mich. State Univ. Evening Coll., Fall 1971 & Spring 1974; Freelance Writer, small press Ed./Publsr.; currently organising poetry workshops in public schls. for the Mich. Arts Coun., 1973-74. Published works: Narcissa Notebook, a chapbook, 1973. Contbr. to: Sumac; 10 Mich. Poets, 1972; Transpacific, 1969; Red Cedar Review, 1972; Maelstrom, 1968; Centennial Review, 1971; Human Voice Qtly.; Three Rivers Poetry Jrnl.; Wis. Review; Western Humanities Review; Best Poems of 1970/Borestone Mountain Poetry Awards, 1971, etc. Recip., Nat. Endowment for the Arts Creative Writing Grant, 1966. Address: 1790 Grand River Rd., Okemos, MI 48864, U.S.A.

DRAKE, Marjorie Davis Look, pen name, **DAVIS, Georgianna,** b. 5 June 1919. Writer; Typist; Printer; Editor. Education: Grad. HS, Washington Acad., East Machias, Maine; Attended law classes East Providence, Rhode Island & Sr. Classes (1½ yrs.) 1937-1938; during 7 yrs. of blindness studied Engl., Patterns in Writing, via mail, Hadley School for the Blind, Winnetka, Illinois, USA. Married; 1 d., 1 s. (adopted). Positions held: Chairman, Comm. on Education, Providence Branch, The Nat. Assoc. for the Advancement of Colored People. Memberships: Poetry Soc. of Maine; (past mbr.) Eastern Centre, World Poets Resource, NYC; United Amateur Press Assoc. (various positions from Ms. Manager, page typist, to the Presidency in 1972); NY Poetry Forum. Published works: printed own amateur pages monthly from 1967-72 (Driftwood Newsette), plus one issue, Pensations; Taproots (poems), 1968; Driftwood East (poetry mag., editor). Contbr. to many newspapers, journals, etc. Awards include Cups, Prizes, Certificates, and poetry read over radio, etc. Address: 95 Carter Av., Pawtucket, RI 02861, USA.

DRESSE DE LEBIOLES, Paul Charles Marie, pen name **DRESSE, Paul,** b. 24 Sept. 1901. Forest Owner. Educ: Ph.D., Univ. of Liège, Belgium. Positions held: Dir., Les Cahiers Monsans, literary review, Liège, & Audace, Brussels. Memberships: PEN Club, Brussels; Assn. of Belgian Writers. Published works incl: Préludes, 1924; Vingt-et-un Poèmes, 1931; Ternaires, 1938; Socles dans Bruxelles, 1947; Chants de la Quarantaine, 1948; Léopold II devant la mer, 1949; Chant Royal, 1950; L'Ange blessé, 1954; Seravalle, 1961; Caÿstre, 1969; (prose works on poets) Une poétesse moderne: Claude Chardon, 1937; Marcel Thiry: Evolution d'un Poète, 1935; Charles Maurras, poète, 1948; Goethe et Hugo, 1959; Plaisir au vers, 1965. Contbr. to num. publs. inclng: Spa-Saison; Le Vaillant; La Revue Latine: La Couronne; La Terre Wallonne; Les Cahiers Mosans; La Vie Wallonne; Septimanie; La Grive; Audace; La Revue Nationale, etc. Recip., Malpertuis Prize, Brussels, 1948, and Van Lerberghe Prize, Paris. Address: 134 Ave. Franklin Roosevelt, 1050 Brussels, Belgium.

DREW, Fraser Bragg Robert Brendan, b. 23 June 1913. Education: A.B., magna cum laude, Univ. of Vermont, 1933; A.M., Duke Univ., 1935; Ph.D., Univ. of Buffalo, 1952. Instr. in Latin and Engl., Green Mountain Coll., Vermont, 1936-39; Professor of Engl. and Irish Lit. State Univ. Coll., Buffalo, NY., 1945-; Disting. Teaching Prof., ibid. Memberships: Acad. of American Poets; Poetry Soc. of America; Irish American Cultural Inst.; American Committee for Irish Studies; Coll. English Assoc.; The Housman Soc. Published works: John Masefield, Interpreter of England and Englishmen, 1952; Some Contributions to the Bibliography of John Masefield, 1957; John Masefield's England: A Study of the National Themes

in His Work, 1973. Contbr. to: CS Monitor; Mod. Language Notes; Philological Qtly.; Colby Library Qtly.; Eire-Ireland; Ireland of the Welcomes; Western Humanities Review; Trace; Canadian Forum; Vermont History; In Britian; Library Journal; Spirit; Costerus; CEA Critic; NY State Education; Yale Library Gazette; Buffalo Eve. News Mag., etc. Address: 119 Thurston Ave., Kenmore, NY 14217, USA.

DRIVER, Charles Jonathan, pen name **DRIVER, C.J.,** b. 19 Aug. 1939. Teacher & Novelist. Education: B.A., Univ. of Cape Town, S. Africa, 1960; B.Ed., ibid, 1962; B.Phil., Trinity Coll., Oxford Univ., U.K., 1967. Married, 3 children. Positions held: Pres., Nat. Union of S. African Students, 1963-64; Housemaster, Int. 6th Form Ctr., Sevenoaks Schl., Kent, U.K., 1968-73; Dir. of 6th Form Studies, Matthew Humberstone Schl., Lincs., 1973-. Published works: (novels) Elegy for a Revolutionary, 1969; Send War in Our Time, O Lord, 1970; Death of Fathers, 1972; A Messiah of the Last Days, 1974; (poems) Seven South African Poets, 1971. Contbr. to: London Mag.; Contrast; The New African; New Coin; Groote Sihuur, etc. Address: c/o John Johnson, Aulkass Agent, 3 Albemarle St., London W.1., U.K.

DROZDOWSKI, Bohdan Otto, pen name **KRZEMIEN, Paweł,** b. 20 Nov. 1931. Writer; Journalist. Education: M.A., Yegellonian Univ., 1957. Married Bozena Dybowska, 2 sons. Positions held: Ed., Zycie literackie, 1956-59; Deputy Ed. in Chief, Współczesność, Warsaw, 1959-66; Deputy Dir. of The Polish Cultural Inst., London, 1966-70; Ed.-in-Chief of POEZJA, Warsaw, 1972-. Memberships: Polish Writers Union, 1958-; PEN Club, Warsaw. Published works: (poetry) Jest takie drzewo, 1956; Moja Polska, 1957; Południe i cien, 1960; Skarga do syna, 1962; Piołun, 1970; Wybór, 1974; Poezja wybrane, 1974; (books of essays) Epoka i reszta, 1967; Gry ludzkie, 1971; Zycie samo w sobie, 1973; (theatrical plays in verse) Serpentyna, 1960; Mazur kajdaniarski, 1971; 'Hamlet 70', Dialog 6, 1972; var. transl. of Shakespeare; Edited & partly translated 'Shakespeare – on Love', 1974; 6 novels, 14 plays & a book about Great Britain, 'Albion od środka', 1973. Contbr. to var. papers, mags., jrnls., anthols. in Poland, U.S.A., U.K., France, Sweden, Finland, Hungary, Bulgaria, etc. Honours, awards: Red Rose Award, Union of the Polish Students, 1959; The Ring – of the Red Rose Award, 1973. Address: Plac Konstytucji 6, m 89, Warsaw 00 550, Poland.

DRUCK, Kitty, b. 13 May 1919. Technical Writer; Scientific Abstractor. Education: B.A. in Biol., Austin Coll.; M.A. in Chemistry, Smith Coll. Married John U. Druck, 2 daughters. Positions held: Literature Chemist, duPont Co., 1948-52; Biol. Tchr. in private sec. schl., 1965-70; currently Freelance Abstractor for Qtly. Jrnl. of Alcohol Studies, Rutgers Univ., New Brunswick, N.J. & Tech. Writer on p/t basis for Logical Technical Services Corp., N.Y.C. Memberships: N.Y. Poetry Forum; V. Chmn., N.J. Poetry Soc., Delaware Valley Poets Sect.; currently Chmn., ibid. Contbr. to: New Laurel Review; N.J. Poetry Soc. Anthol., 1972, '73, & '74; Poet; Writers' Showcase; Times Bulletin, Boonton, N.J.; Edgar, schl. publ. of Bishop Flaget H.S., Ohio; etc. Recip., 2nd prize, French Form Contest, N.J. Poetry Soc., 1971. Address: 13 Penlaw Rd., Lawrenceville, NJ 08648, U.S.A.

DUBASH, Peshoton Sorabji-Goolbai, b. 20 May 1891. Retired Government Contractor: Writer; Scholar. Education: London & Bombay Matriculation; Dip., Electrometallurgy & Allied Scis. Positions held: Stevedoring & Gen. Contractor, 24 yrs.; V.P., La Fed. Int. des Corps Savants de Recherches, L'Academia Asiatica & Free Univ. of Asia, 1944-45; World Pres., ibid, 1955-66. Fndr., Int. Day Movement, 1923-. Memberships: Del., Karachi, Universal Esperanto Assn.; Past Chmn., Young Men's Zoroastrian Assn.; Inst. Soc. of Philol.; Sci & Fine Arts; Past Fellow, Royal Soc. of Arts; Past Fellow, Royal Meteorological Soc.; Past V.P., Empire Poetry League, London; Poet Laureate, United Poets Laureate Int., Philippines; Past

Mbr., Calder Valley Poets Soc. Published works: Dreaming; Rationalistic & Other Poems, 1917; Romance of Souls, 1918; Continuity – From Electrons to Infinity; Colour & The Child; Spiritual & Other Poems, 1936; Colour Psychology; Researches in Geometry; Lunalogy; Therapeutic IUses of New Radiation; The Coronation Padiations; Sewage Disposal by Fish Culture; A Theory of Colour Vision; Sum Digital Recurrence; Researches & Discoveries, etc. Contbr. to: Hindi Graphic; Shind Observer; Laurel Leaves, etc. Honours, awards: Bronze Medal, World Lit. Comp., Paris, France, 1924; Freeman, City of London; Chief Guest of Honour of "The Second World Congress of Poets" at Taipei, Taiwan; Laurel-Crowned and "Simon Memorial Prize for World Leadership" in 1973. Originated and founded "United Religions" 1972 – confirmed 1973 at Taipei, Taiwan. HSE Macapagal Gold Medal for Poetry & Laurel Crown, UpLI. Address: Villa Esperanta, 7 Katrak Parsee Colony, Karachi, Pakistan.

DUBE, Rodolphe, pen name, HERTEL, François, b. 31 May 1905. Professor of Literature & Philosophy; Writer. Education: Classical Coll., Canada; degrees in philos. & theol., Gregorian Univ., Rome, Italy. Positions held: Prof. of Lit., Jesuit Colls. in Canada, then Prof. of Philos.; Publisher of books & mags., Paris, France, 1957-69; Prof. of Lit., Queen's Univ., Kingston, Ont., Canada, 1966-67; Writer & occasionally Jrnlst.; Has given many lectures in Canadian & European univs. Mbr., L'Académie Canadienne-française. Published works from 1934-73: Les voix de mon rève; Axe et parallaxes; Strophes et catastrophes; Cosmos Quatorze; Mes naufrages; Jeux de mer et de soleil; Poèmes d'hier et d'aujourd 'hui, & many essays, short stories, comedies & novels. Ctbr. to: Rythmes et Couleurs (Paris); Amérique française (Canada); L'Information médicale (Canada), etc. Recip., Bronze Medal in Poetry, London Olympiades, 1945 & also a prize from the French Acad., etc. Address: 23 rue Blanche, Paris 9e, France.

DUBOYCE, Iva, b. 2 Feb. 1908. Housewife. Positions held: Schl. Tchr.; Clerk; Bookkeeper. Contbr. to: Family Herald; Sherbrooke Record; Author/Poet Mag.; The Golden Hours Anthol.; Between the Tides Anthol.; an Anthol. by Northwoods Press; also short stories & articles to farm mags. Recip., 2 prizes from Author/Poet Mag., 1972. Address: R.R.1, Knowlton, Quebec JOE 1VO, Canada.

DUBRAU, Louis, (Mrs. Louise Scheidt), b. 19 Nov. 1904. Writer. Education: Sorbonne, Paris, France. Memberships: Royal Acad. of French Lang. & Lit. of Belgium; V.P., Alliance Francaise of Belgium; Past Sec., PEN Club (French Speaking) of Belgium; Bd. Mbr., Association des Ecrivains Belges; Bd. Mbr., Biennales Internationales de Poesie. Published works: Présences, 1937; Abécédaire, 1939; Message, 1940; Pour une autre saison, 1948; Elégies, 1951; Ailleurs, 1956; Le temps réversible, 1958. Contbr. to: Jrnl. des poètes; Marginales; Thyrse; Revue Nationale; Revue Générale. Honours, awards: Prix Verhaeren (poetry), 1939; Prix Malpertuis (short novel), 1952; Prix Victor Rossel (novel), 1964. Address: 4 Avenue de la Forêt, 1050 Brussels, Belgium.

DUDEK, Louis, b. 6 Feb. 1918. Professor of English. Educ: B.A., McGill Univ., Montreal, P.Q., Canada, 1939; M.A., Columbia Univ., N.Y.C., 1946; Ph.D., ibid, 1955. Positions held: Tchr:, C.C.N.Y., 1946-51; Mbr., Engl. Dept., McGill Univ., 1951–, Prof. of Engl., currently; Former Ed., Delta Mag. & Publr., Contact Press, Toronto; Publr., Delta Press, Montreal, currently. Published works: Unit of Five (w. others), 1944; East of the City, 1944; The Searching Image, 1952; Twenty-Four Poems, 1952; The Transparent Sea, 1952; Europe, 1955; Laughing Stalks, 1958; Atlantis, 1967; (editor) Canadian Poems: 1850-1952 (w. Irving Layton), 1952; Poetry of Our Time: An Introduction to 20th Century Poetry Including Modern Canadian Poetry, 1965; The Making of Modern Poetry in Canada: Essential Articles on Contemporary Canadian Poetry in English (w. Michael Gnarowski),

1967. Contbr. to: (anthologies) Canadian Anthology, 1955; Book of Canadian Poetry, 1957; Penguin Book of Canadian Verse, 1958; Poetry of Our Time, 1965. Recip., Quebec Lit. Award, 1968. Address: 5 Ingleside Ave., Montreal 6, P.Q., Canada.

DUDLEY, Austin Edison, pen name LECERF, M. (criticism), b. 26 Oct. 1931. School Master. Education: Tchr. Trng., Saltley Coll. of St. Peter; Diocesan Trng. Coll., Derby; B.A., Open Univ., 1974. Married, 1 son, 1 daughter. Positions held: var. tchng. posts; Deputy Headmaster, St. Mary's R.C. Primary Schl., Walsall. Memberships: Poetry Soc.; Past Sec., Cannock Lit. Soc. of Staffs; Past Chmn., Rugeley Lit. Soc. Published works: Family Tree (11 poems), 1968. Contbr. to: Happy Landings anthol., 1970; Prism Int. (Canada); Poet (India); Southern Cross; Poetry Review; Outposts; Ambit; Anglo-Welsh Review; Breakthru; Quintessence (USA); Scrip; Chase; The Tablet; BBC Publs. & Listen with Mother prog.; Manifold, etc. Honours, awards: Poetry Day prize, 1967; Poetry Soc. Qtly. prize, 1967, etc. Address: Almadene, 20 Priory Rd., Hednesford, Staffs. WS12 5NX, U.K.

DUFFY, Maureen Patricia, pen name, CAYER, Patrick, b. 21 Oct. 1933. Writer. Education: B.A., Hons., Kings Coll., Univ. of London, UK, 1953-56. Published works: Lyrics for the Dog Hour, 1968; The Venus Touch, 1971. Contbr. to: The Listener; The Arts; Adam; Univ. of Stamford; Wave; Nova; Contact; The Sixties; Kan. City Review; Outposts; Poetry Soc. Review, etc. Address: 8 Roland Gardens, London, SW7, UK.

DUGAN, Alan, b. 12 Feb. 1923. Teacher. Educ: B.A., Mexico City Coll., 1951. Married Judith Shahn. Positions held: Faculty Mbr., Sarah Lawrence Coll., Bronxville, 1967–. Published works: Poems, 1961; Poems 2, 1963; Poems 3, 1967. Contbr. to: New Modern Poetry (anthology), 1967. Honours, awards: Pulitzer Prize, 1962; Nat. Book Award, 1962; Am. Acad. of Rome Fellowship, 1962; Guggenheim Fndn. Fellowship, 1963; Rockefeller Fndn. Fellowship, 1966-67. Address: 59 West 10th St., New York, NY 10011, U.S.A.

DUGGAN, Eileen. Former Teacher; Poet. Educ: M.A., Victoria Univ. of Wellington, N.Z., 1918. Positions held: Former Tchr., Jacob Joseph Schl. and Danariske H.S.; Lectr., Hist., Victoria Univ. of Wellington, one year. Published works: Poems, 1921; New Zealand Bird Songs, 1929; Poems, 1939; New Zealand Poems, 1940; More Poems, 1951. Contbr. to: (anthologies) Kowhai Gold, 1930; Old Clay Patch, 1949; New Zealand Farm and Station Verse, 1950; Poems, 1953; An Anthology of New Zealand Verse, 1956. Honours, awards: Honorary Fellowship, Royal Soc. of Letters, London, 1943; O.B.E.

DULAC, Margarita Walker, b. 12 Sept. 1922. Artist, Writer, Teacher. Education: B.S. cum laude, Northwestern Univ., 1942; M.A., Univ. of Chicago, 1944. Positions held: Head, Art Dept., De Kalb Township H.S., Ill., 1944-45; Prof., Painting; Heidelberg Univ., 1946-1949, US Army Extension Course; Art Instr., Andre Lhote Academie, Paris, 1949-51; Instr., Art, Academie Leger, Paris, 1951-1955; Art Critic, Jersey Journal, 1967-1970; Art Critic, the Herald, NYC., 1970–. Memberships: Poetry Soc. of America; Authors Guild; Kentucky Poetry Soc. Published works: Cyclorama, 1942. Contbr. to numerous newspapers and journals. Recip. numerous prizes for poetry (New Trier H.S., Winnetka, Ill.; Northwestern Univ.; Univ. of Chicago; Rochester Festival of Music and Arts; N.H. Poetry Soc.; Beaux Arts Gallery Festival, St. Petersburg, Fla.; Indiana Fed. of Poetry Socs.). Address: Box 334, Murray Hill Sta. P.O., New York, NY 10016, USA.

DUNCAN, Robert, b. 7 Jan. 1919. Lecturer, Education: Civilization of Middle Ages, Univ. of Calif., 1936-38 & '48-50. Positions held: Tchr., Black Mt. Coll., NC, 1956; Asst. Dir., Poetry Ctr., San Francisco State Coll.,

1956-57; Assoc. w. Creative Writing Workshop, Univ. of BC, Canada, 1963; Lectr., Advanced Poetry Workshop, San Francisco State Coll., 1965. Published works: Heavenly City, Earthly City, 1947; Medieval Scenes, 1950; Poems 1948-49, 1950; Caesar's Gate, 1956; Letters, 1958; Selected Poems, 1959; The Opening of the Field, 1960; Roots & Branches, 1964; Writing, Writing, 1964; The Years as Catches: First Poems, 1966; Bending the Bow, 1968. Honours & Awards: Union League Civic & Arts Fndn. Prize, 1957; Harriet Monroe Prize, 1961; Guggenheim Fellowship, 1963-64; Levinson Prize, 1964. Address: c/o New Directions Publishing Grp., 333 Sixth Ave., New York, NY 10014, USA.

DUNCAN, Ronald, b. 6 Aug. 1914. Poet. Education: Switzerland & Cambridge Univ., UK. Married, 1 s., 1 d. Positions held: Ed., Townsman, 1938-46; Fndr., Devon Festival of the Arts, 1953; Fndr., English Stage Co., 1955. Published works: The Dull Ass's Hoof, 1941; Postcards to Pulcenella, 1942; Journal of a Husbandman, 1944; This Way to the Tomb, 1946; The Rape of Lucretia, 1946; Home Made Home, 1947; Ben Jonson, 1947; Songs and Satires of the Earl of Rochester, 1948; Stratton (play), 1948; Beauty & the Beast, 1948; Pope's Letters, 1948; The Cardinal, 1949; The Mongrel & other poems, 1950; Tobacco Growing in England, 1950; Our Lady's Tumbler, 1951; Selected Writings of Mahatma Gandhi, 1951; The Blue Fox, 1951; Don Juan, 1952; Jan at the Blue Fox, 1952; Where I Live, 1953; The Death of Satan, 1954; Judas, 1959; The Solitudes & Other Poems, 1960; Judas, 1960; St. Spiv., 1960; Abelard & Heloise, 1961; Anthology of Classical Songs, 1962; All Men Are Islands (autobiog.), 1964; How To Make Enemies (Part II of autobiog.), 1968; The Catalyst, 1965; O-B-A-F-G, 1965; The Trojan Women, 1966; Unpopular Poems, 1969; The Perfect Mistress, 1969; Man (Part I), 1969; The Gift, 1970; Collected Plays, 1970; Man (Part II), 1971; Man (Part III), 1973. Sev. of above works produced on stage, latest prod. being Abelard and Heloise, 1973. Address: Welcombe, Nr. Bideford, Devon, UK.

DUNETZ, Lora. Registered Occupational Therapist. Education: M.A., Educ. of Handicapped; Cert. in Occupational Therapy; Diplôme, Ecole Pour Etrangers, Pau, France; Laval Univ., Canada. Positions held: Occupational Therapist; French Tchr., H.S., 4 yrs.; Tchr., Educable Retarded, 3 yrs.; Designing & direction writing of needlework for women's publs., sev. yrs. Memberships: Poetry Soc. of Am.; Chmn., Poetry Sect., Baltimore Writers' Forum, Md., 3 yrs.; Fellow, Int. Poetry Soc. Contbr. to the following newspapers & anthols: N.Y. Sun.; N.Y. Times; New Poems by Am. Poets; Epos; Imagi; Discovery 5; Poet Lore; Educational Forum; Inferno; New Mex. Quarterly; Experiment; Instructor; Children's Friend; Furioso; Christian Century; Commonweal; Lyric; Kaleidograph; Chicago Review; Audience; Mandala; Ga. Review. Address: Box 113, Riderwood, MD 21139, U.S.A.

DUNHAM, Kimberly, b. 18 Dec. 1942. Freelance Writer. Education: B.A., Engl. & French, W. Va. Univ. Married John Morton Krall, 2 sons. Memberships: Pres., Morgantown Poetry Soc., 1970-71; Treas., ibid, 1972-73; W. Va. Poetry Soc. Contbr. to: Mustang Review; Lake Superior Review: Best In Poetry, 1972; Infinity Review; From The Hills, 1972, El Viento; IWWP; Panorama; Poet Lore; Gallery Series IV; Quality Am. Poetry, 1973; The Christian; Scimitar & Song. Recip., High Commendation for 'Sea Salt', IWWP, 1972. Address: 673 Bellaire Dr., Morgantown, WV 26505, U.S.A.

DUNHAM, Sandra Martin, b. 24 Feb. 1938. Photo-Journalist. Education: Jrnlsm. corres. course, Newspaper Inst. of Am., N.Y., 3 yrs. Positions held: Pvte. Sec.; Staff Mbr. of Norway, Me., Advertiser-Democrat, Guy Gannett Newspapers, Portland, Me., Lewiston, Me., Daily Sun & The Western Mainer newspapers. Memberships: Poetry Fellowship of Me.; Poetry Soc. of New Hampshire; 2nd V.P., United

Amateur Press Assn., 1971-72; 1st V.P., ibid, 1972; Pres., ibid, 1973. Published works: Maine Street, 1971, '72, '73; Between You and Me, 1969; When the Warm Comes In (in process of publication). Contbr. to: Portland, Me., Sunday Telegram; Grit; Lady's Circle Mag.; Friendship Ferry; Nat. H.S. Anthol.; Poetry Fellowship of Me. Anthol.; Driftwood East, etc. Recip. var. poetry hons. & awards inclng: 1st prize, Canadian Kindness Poem Contest, 1971; 1st hon. mention, Poetry Fellowship of Me., 1972. Personal Poetry Broadcast, WEFG-FM, Virginia, 1973. Address: Bryant Pond, Rte. 1, ME 04219, U.S.A.

DUNN, Douglas Eaglesham, b. 23 Oct. 1942. Freelance Writer. Education: Scottish Schl. of Librarianship; B.A., Univ. of Hull. Positions held: worked in the following libs: Renfrew County Lib.; Andersonian Lib., Univ. of Strathclyde; Akron Pub. Lib., Ohio, U.S.A.; Joseph Black Chem. Lib., Univ. of Glasgow; Sir Brynmor Jones Lib., Univ. of Hull. Mbr., Writers' Action Grp. Published works: Terry Street, 1969; Backwaters, the Review, 1971; The Happier Life, 1972; Ed., New Poems 1972-73; in preparation; Contemporary Irish Writing (co-ed.); New British Poems, 1973; A Choice of Lord Byron's Verse, 1974. Contbr. to: the PEN Anthol.; New Statesman; The Listener; Spectator; Encounter; London Mag.; The Review; The New Yorker; Antaeus; Wave; Stand; Lines Review; Scottish Poetry, etc. Honours, awards: Gregory Award, 1968; Scottish Arts Coun. Publication Award, 1970; Somerset Maugham Award, 1972. Address: c/o Faber & Faber Ltd., 3 Queen Sq., London WC1N 3AU, U.K.

DUNN, Stephen Elliott, b. 24 June 1939. Poet; Professor. Education: B.A., Hofstra Univ., 1962; New Schl. Writing Workshops, 1964-66; M.A., Creative Writing, Syracuse Univ., 1970. Positions held: Semi-pro Basketball Player; Copywriter; Asst. Ed.; Tchr., Southwest Minn. State Coll. & Syracuse Univ. Published works: Five Impersonations (pamphlet), 1971; Looking for Holes in the Ceiling (book), 1974; Transitions. Contbr. to: New Voices In Am. Poetry (anthol.); The Atlantic; The New Republic; Poetry; Poetry Northwest; Kayak; Beloit Poetry Jrnl.; Hearse; The N.Y. Qtly.; The N.Y. Times; The North Am. Review; The Antioch Review; Shenandoah; Am. Poetry Review, etc. Honours, awards: Leonard O. Brown Prize, Syracuse Univ., 1969; Acad. of Am. Poets Award, 1970; Winner, Discovery '71, N.Y. Poetry Ctr.; Winner, Fla. Poetry Contest, 1972; Grant, Nat. Endowment for the Arts, 1973. Address: 307 Clarendon St., Syracuse, NY 13210, U.S.A.

DUQUE, Aquilino, b. 6 Jan. 1931. Translator for U.N. Agencies. Education: Legal studies at the Univs. of Seville, Spain, Cambridge (Trinity Hall), U.K. & SMU, Dallas, Tex., U.S.A. Married, 4 children. Published works: La calle de la luna, 1958; El campo de la verdad, 1958; De palabra en palabra, 1968; El invisible anillo, 1970. Transl: Roy Campbell, Poesías, Madrid, 1958; Ana Ajmátova, Requiem, Barcelona, 1966. Contbr. to: Insula; Papeles de Son Armadans; Cuadernos Hispanoamericanos; Poesia Española; Aljibe; Platero; Aljaba; Caracola; Litoral (segunda época); Revista de Occidente, etc. Honours, awards: Premio Leopoldo Panero, Instituto de Cultura Hispánica, 1967; Premio Fastenrath, Real Academia Española de la Lengua, 1972. Address: Lungotevere Ripa 6, 00153 Rome, Italy.

DURBEN, Maria-Magdalena, b. 8 July 1935. Writer; Editor; Secretary. Education: Pädagogische Hochschule Erfurt; Pädagogische Hochschule Berlin; mentor for tchrs. of German lang., Berlin. Married Wolfgang Durben. Positions held: Sec. of the Literary Union, 1967; Co-Ed., pancontinental mag. UNIO, 1968. Memberships: Ctrl. Comm., Lit. Union; United Poets Laureate International (UPLI); Hon. Member, The Cosmosynthesis League – Guild of Contemporary Bards, Melbourne; The Melbourne Shakespeare Society. Published works: 'Wenn der Schnee fällt', first 'Partnerbuch' (w. Wolfgang Durben), 1974. Contbr. to: Unio; Stahl, Stein und Wort (bibliophile documentation series, containing reproductions of sculptures in steel and marble together with short poems and short prose); Lyrik und Prosa, New-York; Luxembourg; w Europe, Prométhée, Paris; Wegwarten; Der Literat; Pages; Die Tat, Zürich, etc. Honours, awards: Chmn., Second World Congress of Poets, Taipei, Taiwan; Decretum of Award, ibid, 1973. Address: Schulstrasse 8, D–6639 Beckingen-Saar, German Fed. Repub.

DURBEN, Wolfgang, pen names **PASDELOUP, Jean-Marie (for poetry in French lang.), WILLIBALD, Graf (for comical poetry), & WENDOLIN (for painting & caricatures),** b. 12 Aug. 1933. Professor; Poet; Writer; Editor. Education: Saarbrücken Univ.; Paris Univ. (Sorbonne); Cambridge Univ. Married Maria-Magdalena Durben. Positions held: Tchr., Collège Colbert, Paris, 1954-55; Lectr., Svenska Folksuniversitetet vid Högskolan, Norrköping, 1956-58; Pres., Literary Union, 1956–; Pres., 'Youth Circle of the Lit. Union', 1962-70; Fndr. & Co-Ed. of the pancontinental mag. 'Unio' (fnd. 1963); Fndr. & Ed. of the 2 series 'Schüler schreiben (freiwillig)' & 'D Elèves Ecrivains', (fnd. 1971). Memberships: Lit. Union; Hon. Mbr., World Poetry Soc. Intercontinental; UPLI; Cosmosynthesis League; World Cultural Coun. Published works: Harte Lichter (poetry), 1956; Wenn die Flöhe niesen (comical poetry), 1960; Der einsame Narr (libretto for ballet), 1960; Ballade vom verliebten Narren (contbn. to the German Choral Fest. at Stuttgart), 1964; Was ist ein Gedicht? (critical essay), 1971; Manifesto for the Second World Congress of Poets in Taipei, 1973; Récolte de Patates et d'Etoiles (French poems), 1974; Wenn der Schnee fällt, first 'Partnerbuch' (w. Maria-Magdalena Durben), 1974; translator from French, Engl., Swedish & Italian (mainly poems); adaptor of poems & prose from var. langs. Contbr. to anthols., newspapers, periodicals, etc. Honours, awards: Saarländischer Erzählerpreis, 1964; Radio-Play Prizes, Ostdeutscher Kulturrat, Bonn, 1969 & '70; Decretum of Award, 2nd World Congress of Poets, Taipei, 1973; World Poetry Prize, ibid; Hon. Doct., World Univ., 1974. Address: Schulstrasse 8, D–6639 Beckingen-Saar, German Fed. Repub.

DURCAN, Paul, b. 16 Oct. 1944. Magazine Editor. Married. positions held: Co-Ed. (w. Martin Green), Two Rivers Mag. Published works: Endsville, 1967. Contbr. to: Poetry Ireland; Irish Press. Address: 28 Tottenham St., London, W.1, U.K.

DURHAM, Laura Mae, b. 18 Apr. 1915. Secretary. Education: Grad. of HS and Business Coll. Memberships: Poets' Roundtable of Ark. (Historian and Newsletter Editor); Poet's Roundtable of Southeast Ark. (Publicity Chairman and Newsletter Editor); Authors, Composers & Artists Soc. of Ark. (Vice-Pres.). Contbr. to: Ark. Gazette; Ark. Methodist Mag.; Bell's Letters (Gulfport, Mississippi); Latchstrings Poetry Column, The Times (North Little Rock, Ark.); Ashley County Leader, (Hamburg, Ark.); Poet's Forum (Benton, Ark.); News Observer (Crossett, Ark.). Awards: Perpetual Help Award (Aug., 1967); George Kock Appreciation Award, N.Y., Nov. 1967; Poets' Forum Award, Oct., 1968; Citation of Merit, Poets' Roundtable of Ark., Oct., 1968; State Annual Poetry Contest, Authors, Composers & Artists Soc. of Ark., 2nd Place, March, 1971; Annual Light Verse Award, Poets' Roundtable of Southeast Ark., Oct., 1972; Rosa Zagnoni Marinoni Memorial Award, 2nd place, Oct. 1972 (given in memory of the late Poet Laureate of Ark.). Address: 1009 West 3rd St., Apt. C., Little Rock, AR 72201, USA.

DURKEE, Joycelyn Joan, pen name, **LOWREY, Joy,** b. 15 March 1930. Glasscutter (Monograming Glass). Education: HS. Personal details: Married, 1951; 1 d.; Divorced, 1968. Positions held: Nurses Aid; Photography (studio work); Manager of Dept. in a Dept. Store. Memberships: Laurel Publishers Internat. Symposium. Contbr. to: Yearbook of Modern Poetry, 1972; Outstanding Contemp. Poetry, 1972; Lyrics of Love, 1972; Tower by the Sea. Recip. Hon. Award,

Cert. of Merit (Laurel Publishers), 1973. Address: P.O. Box 21, Oceanside, CA 92054, USA.

DURNFORD, Delova Stansell, b. 12 Mar. 1905. Abstracter & Title Insurance Researcher (ret'd). Education: summer course, Univ. of Fla.; sev. credit & non-credit courses in poetry at Fort Steilacoom Community Coll., Wash. Married Jack Durnford, 1 son. Positions held: w. Abstract Co. of Sarasota, Fla.; temporarily associated w. title companies in Calif., WWII Lawyers Title Ins. Co., Seattle, Wash. Memberships: Poetry Soc. of Am.; Wash. Poetry Assn.; Pacific Northwest Writers Conf.; Chmn. of Poetry Workshop, Tacoma Writers Club, Wash. Contbr. to: The Christian Sci. Monitor; The Muse; Washington Verse (longstanding column in the Tacoma News-Tribune); Washington State Poetry (anthol. publd. by Wash. State Poetry Fndn.) Has read own poetry at Pacific Northwest Writers Conf., Poetry Showcase, Allied Arts of Tacoma & the Tacoma Public Lib. Has also made tape & radio broadcast for Lib. Honours, awards incl: 1st Prize, Tacoma Writers' Club Poetry Contest, 1970. Address: 6012 Richard Pl., Sarasota, FL 33581, U.S.A.

DURRANT, Roy Turner, b. 4 Oct. 1925. Artist. Education: Schl. of Art, London, U.K. Published works: A Rag Book of Love, 1960. Address: 38 Hurst Park Ave., Cambridge, U.K.

DURRELL, Lawrence (George), pen name **NORDEN, Charles,** b. 27 Feb. 1912. Author. Educated in India & the U.K. Married three times, 2 daughters, 1 step-son, 1 step-daughter. Positions held: Tchr., Brit. Inst., Kalamata, Greece, 1940; Foreign Press Serv. Officer, Brit. Info. Office, Cairo, 1941-44; Press Attache, Alexandria, 1944-45; Dir. of P.R. for the Dodecanese Islands, 1947; Dir., Brit. Coun. Inst., Cordoba, Argentina, 1947-48; Press Attache, Brit. Legation, Belgrade, Yugoslavia, 1949-52; worked on script of Cleopatra, 20th Century-Fox, London, 1961. Published works incl: The Black Book, An Agon, Paris, 1938, U.S.A., 1960; Prospero's Cell: A Guide to the Landscape & Manners of the Island of Corcyra, 1945; Cefalu, 1947 (republished as The Dark Labyrinth, 1958); Cities, Plains, & People, 1946; A Key to Modern Poetry, 1952; On Seeming to Presume, 1948; White Eagles Over Serbia, 1957; My Family & Other Animals, 1956; Esprit de Corps, 1957; Stiff Upper Lip, 1958; Sappho (play), 1950 (produced in Hamburg, 1959 & Edinburgh, 1961); Acte, (play produced in Hamburg, 1962); An Irish Faust (play produced in Hamburg 1963); Bitter Lemons, 1957; The Alexandria Quartet, 1962; Selected Poems, 1957; Collected Poems, 1960; The Henry Miller Reader, 1959; Art & Outrage: A Correspondence about Henry Miller between Lawrence Durrell & Alfred Perles, (w. Alfred Perles), 1959. Recip., Duff Cooper Meml. Prize, U.K., 1957. Address: c/o National & Grindlay's Bank Ltd., 13 St. James's Sq., London S.W.1, U.K.

DURTAL, Jean, b. 16 Feb. 1905. Journalist; Lecturer. m. Serge Sandberg. Positions held: Jrnlst., for. politics; V.P., Independent Radical Party, before WW II; Lectr., Italy, Belgium, Switzerland, Africa, Near E. Memberships: PEN Club; Past V.P., Soc. of Men of Letters, France; Comm. Mbr., ibid, 1964-71; Soc. of French Poets; Bd. of Dirs., ibid; Fndg. Pres., French-Italian Union for Int. Coop.; Syndicate of Writers; Acad. of Angers. Published works incl: La Solitude Peuplée, 1937; Le Voile de Béatrice, 1948; Le Chef d'Orchestre, 1950; Chants Pour Athanael, 1968; Les Raisins de Septembre, 1971; Livre Blanc, 1973. Contbr. to: Climet; La femme et la Vie; Le Cerf volant; Revue du Liban. Honours, awards: François Coppée Prize, Acad. Française, 1970; Prize, Soc. of Men of Letters, 1954; Prize, Soc. of French Poets, 1971; Chevalier, Nat. Order of Merit; Off., Arts & Letters; Cmdr. of Merit, Italian Repub. Address: Les Grès, 1 Rue Ernest Renan, Sevres 92310, France.

DUSENBERY, Gail, b. 9 Mar. 1939. Magazine Editor. Educ: Cornell Univ., 1956-59; B.A., Univ. of Calif., 1963; San Francisco State Coll. Married to Walter

Dusenbery, 1961; Divorced, 1968. Positions held: Sec., 1966-68; Co-Fndr. & Co-Ed., The San Francisco Earthquake Mag., 1967. Published works: The Mark, 1967; The Sea-Gull, 1968. Contbr. to: Cow Mag.; Wild Dog; Oar Mag.; Poetry; R. C. Lion; Aldebaran Review; Akzente; (anthologies) Poems Read in the Spirit of Peace and Gladness, 1966; Out of the War Shadow, 1967; 31 New American Poets, 1969; Possibilities of Poetry, 1969. Honours, awards: Elizabeth Mills Crothers Short Story Award, 1963; Grove Press Scholarship, 1965. Address: 29-B Guy Place, San Francisco, CA 94105, U.S.A.

DUSSAUSSOIS, Monique, b. 13 Jan. 1947. Writer. Memberships: Titular Mbr., Association Royale des Ecrivains Wallons, Brussels; Fondation Charles Plisnier (Belgian Br. of l'Association Europeene de l'Ethnie française), Brussels; Association litteraire dialectale 'Les Scriveus du Cente'. Published works: Le Suicidaire (novel; coll. of poèms in prep. Contbr. to: Rif tout Dju; Falaises; El Mouchon d'Aunia; revue de Litterature dialectale, etc. Honours, awards: 4th Prize, Concours Prix Louis-Henri LeComte, 1972; Hon. Mention, Concours Internationaux Raymond Bath, 1972; 1st Hon. Mention, Prose, ibid; Prix de l'Escaut (Nouvelle), 1972; Prix du Beffroi (Theatre), 1972; Mention Prix des Jeunesses Culturelles, 1972; 2nd Prize, Concours International de Poésie Roger Desaise, 1973; 1st Prize, Poseie Libre de l'A.R.E.W., 1973; Prix des Critiques Wallons, 1973. Address: Rue Camille Lemonnier 2, B.7100 La Louviere, Belgium.

DUTTON, Geoffrey Piers Henry, b. 2 Aug. 1922. Writer and Farmer. Education: Geelong C. of E. Grammar School, 1932-39; Univ. of Adelaide, Magdalen Coll., Oxford (B.A., 1949). Positions held: Snr. Lecturer in Engl., Univ. of Adelaide, 1955-62; Visiting Fellow in Commonwealth Lit., Leeds, 1960; Visiting Prof., Kansas, 1963. Membership: Australian Soc. of Authors. Published works: Nightflight and Sunrise, 1944; Antipodes in Shoes, 1957; Flowers and Fury, 1962; Poems Soft and Loud, 1967; Findings and Keepings (Collected Poems), 1970; New Poems to 1972, 1972; Sev. books of translations from the Russian of Yevtushenko, Bella Akhmadulina. Contbr. to: Angry Penguins; Voices; Mandrake; Oxford Poetry; Meanjin; Southerly; Overland; Australian Letters; Quadrant; The Bulletin; The Age; The Sydney Morning Herald; The Australian; Ogonyok (Moscow, trans. by Y. Yevtushenko), etc. Recip. Grace Lieven Award, 1957. Address: Old Anlaby, Kapunda, South Australia 5373.

DUTTON, Paul (Cuthbert), b. 29 Dec. 1943. Advertising Copywriter. Education: Univ. of Western Ont., Canada. Positions held: Car washer/Factory Hand; Paper Mill Hand & Fork-lift Operator; Order Expeditor for Hotelware firm; Office Boy; Accounting Clerk; Book Clerk; Substitute Tchr.; Window Washer; Publisher's Ed.; Publisher's Advertising Copywriter. Mbr., League of Canadian Poets. Published works: Canadada (or Nada Canadada): an album of collaborative verbal & non-verbal poetry w. The Four Horsemen, a sonic poetry quartet consisting of himself, Rafael Barreto-Rivera, Steve McCaffery & Bp Nichol, 1972; 3 poems in an anthol. (Made in Canada: New Poems of the Seventies), 1970. Contbr. to: Catalyst; Ganglia; grOnk; runcible spoon; First Encounter; Earth & You; Gryphon; Kensington Market. Address: 82 Admiral Rd., Toronto, Ont., Canada M5R 2L6.

DYCUS, Frances W., pen name **DYCUS, Webb,** b. 18 Mar. 1919. Housewife & Poet. Married James Dycus, 1 son (James). Memberships: Poetry Soc. of Tenn., U.S.A.; Tenn. Press & Authors Club; United Amateur Press Assn.; Ky. State Poetry Soc. Published works: Come Sit With Me, 1969; Ed., The Blue Buck Banner, 1969-; a poem in One Hundred Poems, Poetry Soc. of Tenn. Anthol., 1956; a poem in Who Tells the Crocuses It's Spring? 1971. Contbr. to: Christian Living; Christian Science Monitor; Baptist Leader; North Little Rock Times; The South West Record; The Ensign; The Progressive Farmer; Country Living;

Outdoor World, etc. Recip., many prizes from Poetry Soc. of Tenn. Address: Duck River, TN 38454, U.S.A.

DYER, Roberta Coldren, b. 25 Aug. 1914. Counsellor-Educator. Education: American Conservatory of Music; North Park Coll., etc. Personal details: born near Dover, Delaware, USA. Positions held: Teacher of music (voice and theory); Investigator of religious cults; Counsellor, Educator in religion; Tutor in learning methods, music and art, also poetry, (piano); Lecturer; Writer. Memberships: Internat. Poetry Soc. (Fellow); Poets & Patrons (Workshop director); Poets Club of Chicago; Brownson Circle (Lit. & Drama Chairman); Brownson Poets; Women's Lit. Club of Chicago; Poetry Soc. (UK); Delta Omicron; American Poetry League; World Poetry Day; Pa. Poetry Soc.; Int. Acad. of Poets; Am. Poets Fellowship Soc.; Nat. Writers Club; Theosophical Soc. in Am.; Poetry Soc. of America; Hospitalized Veterans' Writing Project; Paragraph Club; The Quill Pushers. Published work: Message from Gabriel, 1961. Contbr. to various anthols., journals, newspapers. Recip. of sev. awards (Brownson Circle; Ill. Fed. Women's Clubs; Poets & Patrons; Am. Poetry League; Pa. Poet Soc; Internat. Who's Who in Poetry; Nat. Writers Club). Address: 1325 Manchester Rd., Wheaton, IL 60187, USA.

DYKES, James Elmore, b. 20 May 1919. Clergyman; Teacher; Editor. Education: B.A., Oakwood Coll.; Wayne State Univ.; Univ. of Pa.; Fisk Univ.; currently enrolled in a doctoral prog. (Educational Supervision with supporting studies in Mass Media Communications at Univ. of Miami, Coral Gables, Fla.). Positions held: Pastor, 7th Day Adventists, Detroit, 1946-48; Flint & Saginaw, Mich., 1948-52; Inkster, Mich., 1952-56; Fac., Pine Forge Inst., 1956-59; Ed.-in-Chief, Message Mag., 1960-67; Chmn., Engl. Dept., Pine Forge Acad., 1967-. Memberships: Associated Church Press; Nat. Council of Tchrs. of Engl. Internat. Poetry Soc. (Founding Fellow). Contbr. to: Voices of Freedom (anthology), 1941; Poetry of Freedom (anthology), 1940; Opportunity; NY Herald Tribune; Insight Mag.; Liberty Mag.; MV Kit for Youth; The Columbia Union Visitor; Signs of the Times; Signs (South Africa); Signs (Australia); Out Our Times (Poona, India). Honours: Nat. Poetry Ctr. Award, 1937; Jr. Poet Laureate of NYC. Address: Box 148, Oakwood Coll. Station, Huntsville, AL 35906, USA.

DYLAN, Bob, b. 24 May 1941. Singer; Composer. Married w. children. Memberships: Am. Soc. Composers, Authors & Publishers. Published works: Tarantula, 1966, '71; Writings & Drawings by Bob Dylan, 1973; num. music folios. Recip. num. awards for songs & albums in fields of popular music, folk & country music; recip. D. Mus., Princeton Univ., 1970. Address: Box 264, Cooper Station, N.Y., NY 10003, U.S.A.

E

EADIE, Thomas Michael, b. 21 Apr. 1941. Graduate Student. Educ: Trinity Coll. Schl.. Port Hope, Ont., Canada; B.A.. Queen's Univ., Kingston; Grad. Student, ibid, current. Positions held: Ed., Quarry Mag., Kingston, 1962-69. Published Works: The Beast with Three Backs (w. Colin Norman & Tom Marshall), 1965. Contbr. to: Fiddlehead; Canadian Forum; Canadian Poetry. Address: 208 Univ. Ave., Kingston, Ontario, Canada.

EARLEY, Jacqueline, pen name **JACKIE,** b. 17 Dec. 1939. Poet; Dramatist. Education: Art Study at Studio Museum, Harlem, 1 yr. & Art Students League; Hatha Yoga, 6 yrs. Positions held: Profl. Dancer; Actress; Dance Instr.; Creative Writing Tchr.; Yoga & Judo Instr., etc. Memberships: Harlem Cultural Coun.; Poets & Writers. Contbr. to: Soulscript, 1970; We Speak as Liberators, 1970; Jrnl. of Black Poetry, Nos. 10, 11, 12; Scholastic Mag., vol. 39, No. 7, 1971; Currents in Poetry, 1974. Honours, awards: Harlem Writers Grant, 1970; Inst. of Int. Education's Black

Artists to Africa Tour, 1972. Address: Poets & Writers, 201 West 54 St., N.Y., NY 10019, U.S.A.

EARLEY, Tom, b. 13 Sept. 1911. Former Schoolmaster; Writer; Lecturer. Education: Trinity Coll., Carmarthen. Memberships: Welsh Acad. of Writers, 1971; Poetry Soc., London. Published works: Welshman in Bloomsbury, 1966; 2nd impression 1968; The Sad Mountain, 1970, 2nd impression 1971. Contbr. to: Poetry Wales; Anglo-Welsh Review; Planet; Welsh Nation; London Welshman; Second Aeon; Country Quest; Breakthru; Poet; Outposts; Tribune; (anthols.) Doves for the Seventies; The Lilting House; Poems '69; Poetry for Peace; Storm of Bloods; Poems '72; If I Had A Hammer; Starting Point; Readings; Poems '73. A number of his poems have been read & discussed on the following: BBC Welsh Home Service; Harlech TV; BBC Radio 4; I.L.E.A. TV; Radio London; Gtr. London Arts Assn. (Dial-a-Poem); Welsh Arts Coun. (Dial-a-Poem). Address: 21 Bloomsbury Sq., London, W.C.1, U.K.

EATON, Burnham, b. 31 Mar. 1901. Writer of prose & poetry. Education: special courses at Curry Schl., Boston & Univ. of Mass. Married Rodney C. Eaton, 2 children. Positions held: Tchr. & Tutor in Poetry Writing; Rdr. of poetry & prose; gives talks & readings to clubs, schls. & on radio. Memberships: Pres., Sec., New England Poetry Club; Treas., Boston Br., Nat. League of Am. Pen Women; V.P., The Manuscript Club of Boston; Poetry Soc. of Am.; Acad. of Am. Poets. Published works: True Places, selected verse, 1955. Rep. in the following: Sing Out (lyrics for children's songs), 1956; Poetry Ventured Anthol., 1972; The Golden Year Anthol., 1945; Away We Go! (Anthol. of Children's verse); The Diamond Yr. Anthol., 1970. Contbr. to many mags., jrnls., newspapers inclng: N.Y. Times; N.Y. Herald-Tribune; Christian Sci. Monitor; Sat. Review; Prairie Schooner; Ladies' Home Jrnl.; Poet Lore; Am. Haiku; Voices; Am. Weave; Catholic World; Educational Forum; Good Housekeeping. Recip., Golden Rose of the New England Poetry Club, 1956 & Lyric Quarterly Prize, Leitch Meml. Prize, Poet Lore, 1967. Address: Prospect Hill Rd., Harvard, MA 01451, U.S.A.

EATON, Charles Edward, b. 25 June 1916. Poet & Short Story Writer. Educ: Duke Univ., 1932-33; A.B., Univ. of N.C., 1936; grad. work, Princeton, 1936-37; M.A., Harvard Univ., 1940. Married Isabel Patterson. Positions held: Instr. of Engl., Ruiz Gandia Schl., Ponce, Puerto Rico, 1937-38, & Univ. of Mo., 1940-42; Am. Vice Consul at the Am. Embassy in Rio de Janeiro, Brazil, 1942-46; Prof. of Creative Writing, Univ. of N.C., 1946-51. Memberships: Poetry Soc. of Am.; New England Poetry Club. Published works: (poetry) The Bright Plain, 1942; The Shadow of the Swimmer, 1951; The Greenhouse in the Garden, 1956; Countermoves, 1963; On the Edge of the Knife, 1970; (short stories) Write Me From Rio, 1959; The Girl from Ipanema, 1972; (art criticism) Karl Knaths, Five Decades of Painting, 1973. Contbr. to var. mags., jrls., reviews. Honours, awards: Ridgely Torrence Meml. Award, 1951; Gertrude Boatwright Harris Award, 1954; Ariz. Qtly. Award, 1956; Roanoke-Chowan Poetry Cup, 1970; Oscar Arnold Young Meml. Award, 1971; The Golden Rose, New England Poetry Club, 1972. Address: Merlin Stone, Woodbury, CT 06798, U.S.A.

EATON, Evelyn, b. 22 Dec. 1902. Novelist. Education: Heathfield, Ascot, U.K., 1916-20; Sorbonne Univ., France, 1920-21. Married Ernst Paul Richard Viedt, Dec. 1942, 1 daughter. Positions held: Lectr. in Engl., Schl. of Gen. Studies, Columbia Univ., U.S.A., 1949-51; Lectr. for Arts Prog., Assn. of Am. Colls., 1950-60; Vis. Lectr., Sweet Briar Coll., 1951-60; Vis. Prof. of Engl., Mary Wash. Coll., Univ. of Va., 1957-59; Adult Educ. Progs., 1955-60; TV Prog. sponsored by Univ. of Va., 1960; Writer in Res., Montalvo Assn., 1960 & 63, Deep Springs Coll., 1961 & Huntington Hartford Fndn., 1960 & 62; Vis. Lectr., Ohio Univ., 1962; Vis. Prof. in Engl., Pershing Coll., 1967; ret'd '68. Memberships incl: V.P., Canadian Authors' Assn., 1940-41; Pres.,

Pen & Brush, 1946-50; PEN; Poetry Soc. of Am. Published works: (novels) Summer Dust, 1938; Pray to the Earth, 1939: Quietly My Captain Waits, 1940; Restless Are the Sails, 1942; The Sea Is So Wide, 1943; In What Torn Ship, 1945; Give Me Your Golden Hand, 1950; Flight, 1954; I Saw My Mortal Sight, 1959; The King Is A Witch, 1965; Go Ask the River, 1969; (biog.) Heart in Pilgrimage, 1946; (short stories) Every Month Was May, 1946; The North Star is Nearer, 1949; (poetry) The Interpreter, 1923; The Small Hour, 1955; The Progression, 1967; Love Is Recognition, 1972. Contbr. to var. jrnls. Honours: 5 poems from The Small Hour performed at Fest. of Mod. Mus., Oberlin Conserv., 1960, Carnegie Hall, 1965; 10 Res. Fellowships, Macdowell Colony, 1946-69; Recip., John Masefield Award, 1923, etc. Address: 112 Rosedale Dr., Independence, CA 93526, U.S.A.

EATON, Lucy Ellen, b. 9 July 1905. Housewife; Poet. Education: Bible Coll., 1 yr.; Creative Writing, Selkirk Coll., 1 yr. Married, 3 sons. Positions held: Dressmaker; Newspaper Corres. for Leader-Post, 8 yrs.; Clerk-Typist & Key Punch Operator, Sask. Govt.; Advertising Dir. Memberships: Sask. Poetry Soc.; Alta. Canadian Author Assn. (Edmonton Br.); World Poetry Soc.; Int. Poetry (Clover) Assn.; Laurel Publishers Int. Poetry Symposium; Major Poets Chapt.; United Amateur Press. Published works: Mount up on Wings, 1971. Contbr. to: Regina Leader-Post; Moose Jaw Times-Herald; The Observer; Trail Times; Castlegar News; Poet; Friendship Ferry; Poet/Author; Over the Ozarks; Creative Review, etc. Recip. var. poetry prizes. Address: 101 4th Ave. N., Castlegar, B.C., Canada V1N 1M7

EBERHART, Richard, b. 5 Apr. 1904. Poet; Playwrite; Educator; Consultant; Lecturer; Executive. Education: B.A., Dartmouth Coll., U.S.A., 1926; B.A., St. John's Coll., Cambridge, U.K., 1929; M.A., ibid, 1933; Harvard Grad. Schl. of Arts & Scis., U.S.A., 1932-33. Positions held: Lt. – Lt. Cmdr., USNR, WWII; Asst. Mgr. to V.P., The Butcher Polish Co., Boston, Mass., 1946-52; currently Hon. V.P. & Mbr., Bd. Dirs., ibid; served as Poet-in-Res., Prof. or Lectr., Univ. of Wash., Univ. of Conn., Wheaton Coll., Norton, Mass., & Princeton, 1952-56; Prof. of Engl. & Poet-in-Res., Dartmouth Coll., 1956-68; Class of '25 Prof., ibid, 1968–; Cons. in Poetry, Lib. of Congress, 1959-61; Hon. Cons. in Am. Letters, ibid, 1963-69; Appointed by Pres. Eisenhower to Advsry. Comm. on the Arts for the Nat. Cultural Ctr., Wash. D.C. (now J.F. Kennedy Ctr. for Performing Arts), 1959–; Dir., Yaddo Corp., Saratoga Springs; Lectr. at sev. US Colls. & Univs. inclng. 1st annual mem. lecture on Robert Frost, San Fran. Pub. Lib., 1964; A Fndr. & 1st Pres., Poets' Theatre, Inc., Cambridge, Mass., 1950. Memberships: Hon. Pres., Poetry Soc. of Am., 1972; Poetry Int. 73, London; Fellow, Acad. of Am. Poets, 1969; Nat. Inst. of Arts & Letters; Nat. Acad. Arts & Scis.; The Century Club, N.Y.; Buck Harbor Yacht Club, S. Brookville, Me. Published works: A Bravery of Earth, 1930; Reading the Spirit, 1936; Song and Idea, 1940; Burr Oaks, 1947; Selected Poems, 1951; Undercliff, Poems 1946-53, 1953; Great Praises, 1957; Collected Poems, 1930-60, 1960; The Quarry, 1964; Shifts of Being, 1968; Collected Verse Plays, 1962; Richard Eberhart: Selected Poems 1930-65, 1965; Thirty-One Sonnets, 1967; Fields of Grace, 1972, etc. Verse adaptation of Justice Without Revenge, by Lope de Vega (re-entitled The Bride From Mantua) produced at Hopkins Ctr., Dartmouth Coll., 1964; Contbr. of book reviews & critical articles to US & for. jrnls. Richard Eberhart Reading His Poetry, recorded by Caedmon Records, 1968. Honours, awards: Pulitzer Prize, for Richard Eberhart: Selected Poems 1930-65, 1966; Harriet Monroe Meml. Prize; Harriet Monro Meml. Award (Univ. of Chicago); Shelley Meml. Prize; Grant, Nat. Inst. Arts & Letters; Co-winner, Bollingen Prize, Yale Univ. Lib., 1962; Hon. D.Litt., Dartmouth Coll., 1954; Hon. D.Litt., Skidmore Coll., 1966; Hon. D.Litt., Coll. of Wooster, 1969; Hon. D.Litt., Colgate Univ., 1974. Subject of a no. of critical works & appreciations. Address: 5 Webster Terr., Hanover, NH 03755, U.S.A.

EBNER, Jeannie (Mrs.), b. 17 Nov. 1918. Writer; Translator; Magazine Editor. Education: studied sculpture, Institute of Fine Arts, Vienna, 5 yrs. Positions held: Stenotypist, 3 yrs.; Freelance writer since 1949; Hon. Secretary, European Sculptors Symposium, Austria, 1967; Publisher & Sole Editor of the monthly magazine, Literatur und Kritik, since 1968. Memberships: Board, Austrian PEN Club; Committee, Gerhard Fritsch-Stiftung, Vienna; Board of Trustees, Willibald Prikheimer; Ges., Nürnberg; 'Die Kogge', lit. union, Minden, Westphalia; Board, IGOA (Interessengemeinschaft österr. Autoren), Vienna; Verband deutscher Ubersetzer; Deutscher Schriftstellerverband. Publications incl: Gesang an das Heute, 1952; Gedichte, 1965; (in anthologies): Stimmen der Gegenwart, 1952; Tür an Tür, 1951; Unter dem sapphischen Mond, 1957; Die Barke, 1957 & 63; Deutsche Lyrik, 1966; Wien im Gedicht, 1967; Irdene Schale, Poeten beten, 1968, etc. Contbr. to num. magazines and newspapers inclng: Wiener Zeitung; Die Presse, Vienna; Neue Deutsche Hefte; Deutsche Rundschau; Neue Rundschau; Hortulus, Switzerland. Honours & awards incl: Theodor-Körner-Stiftung Prize, Vienna, 1955; Förderungspreis d. Kulturamts, City of Vienna, 1961; Willibald Pirkheimer Medal, Nürnberg, 1962; Ludwig von Ficker Prize, 1967; Adalbert Stifter Medal, 1970; Prize for Literature, City of Vienna, 1971; Kulturpreis des Landes Nieder-Osterreich, 1972; Ubersetzerpreis zum Staatspreis, Austria, 1973. Address: Schlossgasse 3/8, Vienna V, Austria.

EBTEHAJ, Hushang, pen name SAYEH, H.A., b. 1927. Poet. Education: Grad., Tehran Univ. Published works: (collections) 'Naela' (Songs), 1956; 'Sarab' (Mirage), 1951; 'Shabgir, Siyah Mashq', 1956; 'Lezzat Nayafteh', & 'Zamin' (The Earth), 1954. Address: c/o Press Attache, Imperial Iranian Embassy, 16 Princes Gate, London S.W.7, U.K.

ECHENIQUE POSSE, María Elisa del Rosario, pen name ECHENIQUE POSSE, Mareli, b. 29 Aug. 1929. Professor. Educ: Maestra, 1946; Prof. Normal de Lit., Alejandro Carbó Normal Schl., 1949; Prof. of Theol.; Superior Inst. Religious Culture, 1953; License, Modern Letters, Nat. Univ. of Córdoba, 1973; studied w. Jorge Luis Borges, 1962; Hispanoamericana Lit., Univ. Santa María de los Bs. As., 1964; Philos., Cath. Univ. of Córdoba, 1967. Positions held: Prof., Lit., ENET No. 1; Prof., Castilian, Nat. Schl. for Girls, Gen. Manuel Belgrano; Prof., Argentinian Lit., Night Schl. for Women; Prof., Spanish Lit., Alejandro Carbó Normal Schl.; Instr., Prof., Relig., 1953–; Prof., Mod. Hispanoamerican Novel, Ext. Univ. Dept., Nat. Univ. of Río Cuarto, Córdoba, 1973; Dir., Cath. Action, 1946-64. Memberships incl: Assn. of Cath. Writers. Published works incl: Un Alto En El Camino, 1964; Elcistal sobre la roca; Pastora Moine. sev. essays. Contbr. to anthols: World Anthol. of Contemporary Poets, 1973; Antología de poetas cordobeses, Cuadernos de Biblioteca, 1973; Los Principios, Córdoba; Prairie Poets; Pennons of Pegasus, etc. Honours, awards: Poetry Prize, María Auxiliadora Parish literary contest; Prize, Nat. Fndn. of Arts, 1963; Vitori Hó World Poetry Prize and Plaque, 2nd World Congress of Poets, 1973; sev. awards for prose. Address: Lavalleja 1321, Dpto. 19, Barrio Cofico, Ciudad de Cordoba, Argentina.

ECHERUO, Michael Joseph Chukwudalu, b. 14 Mar. 1937. University Professor of English. Education: B.A., Univ. of Ibadan, Nigeria, 1960; M.A., Cornell Univ., U.S.A., 1963; Ph.D., ibid, 1965. Married Dr. Rose N. Echeruo, 4 children. Positions held: Lectr., 1961-70; Sr. Lectr., 1970-73; Prof., 1973–. Published works: Mortality, 1968. Contbr. to: Black Orpheus; Jrnl. of New African Lit. & Arts; Southern Review (Australia); N.Y. Times; Modern Poetry from Africa; New Voices of the Commonwealth. Recip., 1st prize, All-Africa Poetry Comp., 1962. Address: Dept. of Engl., Univ. of Nigeria, Nsukka, Nigeria.

ECKELS, Jon, pen name ASKIA AKHNATON. Poet; English Professor; Essayist. Education: B.A., Ind. Ctrl. Coll., Indianapolis, Ind.; B.D., Pacific Schl. of Religion, Berkeley, Calif.; Ph.D., Stanford Univ., Calif. Married, 1 son. Positions held: Minister, United Meth. Ch., 1964-68; Fndr. & Dir. of Summer Freedom Schls., 1967-68; Engl. Tchr., Mills Coll., 1968–; Afro-Am. Lit. Tchr., Merritt Coll., 1969-70. Published works: This Time Tomorrow, 1966; Black Dawn, 1966; Home Is Where The Soul Is, 1968; Black Right On, 1968; Our Business In The Street, 1970; Firesign – For the Free & Will Be, 1973; Stone Spirit Space, 1974. Contbr. to: Stanford Daily; Millstream; Merritt Coll. Newspaper; Reed Coll. Newspaper; Black Dialogue; Broadside Treasury; To Gwen With Love; Black Panther; Jrnl. of Black Poetry, etc. Address: Stanford Univ., Engl. Dept., Stanford, CA 94305, U.S.A.

ECKHART, Katherine Lawrence, pen name ECKHART, Katherine Nielsen, b. 7 June 1909. Teacher. Education: Bachelor's degree in Elem. Educ. Married Carl Eckhart. Positions held: Tchr., Rural Schl., grades 1-8, Elem. Schl., Grade 3, Elem. Schl., Grades 3, 4 & 5 in succeeding yrs.; Elem. & Jr. H.S., 15 yrs. in reading, Engl., spelling, geog. & hist. & Lang. arts & Soc. studies in grades 6, 7 & 8. Memberships: Poetry Int.; Nat. & Wash. State Educ. Socs. Contbr. to Centralia Daily Chronicle. & Poetry Int. Address: 1831 Cascade No. 2, Chehalis, WA 98532, U.S.A.

ECONOMOU, George, b. 24 Sept. 1934. IIniversity Professor. Education: A.B., Colgate Univ., 1956; M.A.(1957), Ph.D.(1967), Columbia Univ. Born in Great Falls, Montana, of Greek immigrant parents. Positions held: Prof. of Engl. and Comparative Lit., The Brooklyn Center, Long Island Univ. Has also taught at Wagner Coll.; Hunter Coll.; Columbia Univ. Published works: The Georgics, 1968; Landed Natures, 1969; Poems for Self Therapy, 1972. Contbr. to: The Nation; Maps; El Corno Emplumado; Caterpillar; Arion's Dolphin; Mulberry; Some/Thing; Poems from the Floating World; Trobar; Chelsea; Kulchur, and many anthols. Address: 606 West 116th St., New York, NY 10027, USA.

EDD, Karl, b. 24 Jan. 1926. Printer. Education: LL.B.; Ph.D. (hon.) Owner of Print Shop. Memberships: Colo. Authors' League; Mark Twain Lit. Fellowship. Published works: Ballad of Helen Smith Jones; Love is a Moment of Grace; Booker T; Billy the Kid (in process). Contbr. to approx. 60 jrnls., mags., reviews, etc. incIng: Am. Bard; Epoch; Poet Lore; Twigs; In Wyoming; Denver Post; Poet (India). Recip. var. poetry awards inclng: Top Hand Award, Colo. Poet Laureate Award; Mark Twain Soc. Lit. Award. Address: P.O. Box 9007, Denver, CO 80209, U.S.A.

EDFELT, Bo Johannes, b. 21 Dec. 1904. Poet; Literary Critic; Translator. Education: M.A., 1930; Ph.D., 1952; Dr.h.c., 1960. Positions held: Lit. Critic, Dageus Nyheter, 1943-68. Memberships: Swedish Academy; Corres. Mbr., German Acad. for Speech & Poetry; Corres. Mbr., Acad. for Sci. & Lit., Mainz. Published works: Högmässa, 1934; I denna natt, 1936; Vintern är lang, 1939; Sang för reskamrater, 1941; Elden och klyftan, 1943; Braddjupt eko, 1947; Hemliga slagfäit, 1952; Heinrich Heine (essay), 1955; Under Saturnus, 1956; Insyn, 1962; Adernät, 1968; Birger Sjöberg (essay), 1971; Profiler orh episoder (memoirs), 1973. Translations of Poetry: Der Schattenfischer (trans. by Nelly Sachs), 1958; Gedichte (by E. Furreg), 1963; I venti della vita (by C.F. Piazza), 1957. Contbr. to: Göteborgs Handels orh Sjöfartstidring; Dagens Nyheter; Ord och bild; Bonniers litterära Magasin; Nya Argus; Finsk tidskrift. Honours, awards: De nios pris, 1949; Ovralidspriset, 1951; Bellmanspriset, 1954; Boklotteriets stora pris, 1962; Henrik Steffens Prize, Germany, 1967. Address: Bergviksvägen 38, Rönninge, Sweden.

EDGAR, June Elizabeth, pen name EDGAR, Judy, b. 19 June 1936. Teacher. Education: B.A., Univ. of Natal; Scholarship, French Govt., for postgrad. studies at the Sorbonne, Paris; B.A. Hons., Univ. of S. Africa. Married, 1 son, 1 daughter. Positions held: Jrnlst., Salisbury, Rhodesia, 1959-60; Engl. & French

Tchr., Gwelo, Rhodesia, 1961 & '67-68; Lectr., Engl., African Tchr. Trng. Coll., 1970–; Engl. Tchr., Girls' Dominican Convent, Bulawayo. Memberships: The Poetry Soc., London; The Poetry Soc., Salisbury, Rhodesia. Contbr. to: Rhodesian Poetry; Poetry in Rhodesia; Two Tone; Illustrated Life Rhodesia; New Coin; PEN's New S. African Writing; Unisa English Studies; Bitterroot, U.S.A. Has had many poems broadcast by the S. African Broadcasting Corp. & the Rhodesian Broadcasting Corp. Grp. of Poems set to music (Song Cycle of Birds). Honours, awards: Natal Settlers' Poetry Prize; Two Tone's Annual Prize for the best poem in the sr. sect., 1973. Address: 174 Devonshire Cres., Llewellin Barracks, Rhodesia.

EDGERTON, Angie Rose, b. 14 Oct. 1891. Housewife; Poet. Education: Music & Drama, summer schl., Mich. State Univ. Married Leo Edmund Edgerton, 1 son. Memberships: Pres., Lansing, Mich. Poetry Club, 1958-59; Pres., Home Garden Club, 1962-63; West Side Lit. Club; Chmn., fund raising, Girl's Town; Poetry Soc. of Mich.; Nat. Fed. of State Poetry Socs.; Acad. of Am. Poets. Published works: Mosaics of the Mind (poetry book), 1962; two songs, words & music. Contbr. to: Jean's Jrnl.; Am. Bard; Swordsman Review; Seydel Quarterly, Belgium; Poet (India); Bouquet of Poems (Italy); IWWP Anthol.; Am. Poetry League; Bardic Echoes; Author Poet, etc. Honours, awards incl: Poet Laureate, Mich. Fed. Womens Clubs, 1950, 61, 63, 64; 1st Prize, Terza Rima, Calif. Fed. of Chaparral Poets, 1967; 1st Prize, Poetry Soc. of Mich., 1970 & Mosaic poem in Phoenix Fires, 1973. Address: 911 Middle St., Lansing, MI 48915, U.S.A.

EDINGER, Norma L., b. 8 Oct. 1904. Freelance Writer; Poet. Education: Northwestern Univ., Evanston, Ill.; Five yrs. study & performing for Red Path & also Chautaqua Jrnlsm. 1A, Freelance Writing, Ext. Urliv. of Wis. Married, 2 daughters. Positions held: Personnel Mgr., pvte. firm, Shawano, Wis., 1951-61; Monthly Radio Prog. slanted towards community hosp. & hlth., ibid, 1956-59; Pres., Hosp. Aux., 1956-58 & '72-74; Pres., County Histl. Soc. & Womens Presbyn. Assn., 1967-68 & '69-70. Memberships: Wis. Regl. Writers Assn.; Int. Fellowship of Poets; Wis. Fellowship of Poets; Shawano Regl. Writers; Am. Poets Fellowship Soc. Contbr. to: Saturday Evening Post; The Am. Poet; Pioneer Poet; Chicago Tribune; Wall St. Jrnl.; Ideals; The Scribblers; New Poetry Out of Wis., anthol. Address: 204 Humphrey Circle N., Shawano, WI 54166, U.S.A.

EDSON, Russell, b. 9 Apr. 1945. Writer; Print Maker (woodcuts). Education: Art Students League (Scholarship); New School for Social Research; Columbia Univ.; Black Mountain Coll. Positions held: Teacher in creative writing. Memberships: P.E.N.; Silermine Guild of Artists. Published works: Appearances, 1961; A Stone Is Nobody's, 1961; The Very Thing That Happens, 1964; The Brain Kitchen, 1965; What A Man Can See, 1969; The Childhood Of An Equestrian, 1973; The Clam Theater, 1973. Contbr. to: Akzente; Beloit Poetry Journal; il Caffe; Between Worlds; Caterpillar; Chelsea; Chicago Review; Doones; The Dragonfly; Eventorium Muse; Genesis West; The Goodly Co.; Iowa Review; Joglars; Kayak; Lillabulero; Lugano Review; Maps; Monks Pond; Mss.; The Nation; Nomad; North American Review; The Outsider; Pebble; Prairie Schooner; The Sixties; The Seventies; The Small Pond; Some/thing; Statements; Wormwood Review; TriQuarterly; Esquire Mag.; Crazy Horse; Hearse; NEW: American & Canadian Poetry; Ironwood; The Falcon; Field; Toothpick; Seneca Review; Unmuzzled Ox; Noise; Seizure; Bachy; Lemming; Madrona; Rivers Poetry Journal; Hawaii Lit. Review; Some; Clown War; Mosaic; Stooge; New Directions Annual, etc. Honored by the American P.E.N. for book "The Childhood of an Equestrian", Jan. 22, 1973. Address: 149 Weed Ave., Stamford, CT 06902, USA.

EDWARDS, Gene Mary, b. 26 Dec. 1915. Library Technician. Education: Grad., Hanford Union HS; attended Fresno State Coll.; Visalia Jr. Coll.; Has taken

various courses from Fresno State Coll.; Coll. of Sequoias; Reedley Coll. Positions held: "Car Hop" (waitress); laundry worker; bookkeeper; housewife; clerical asst.; clerk-typist, and currently library technician at Kings County Library. Membership: Nat. Writers Club. Contbr. to: (anthols.) This Way of Life; Haiku and Tanka; These Are My Jewels (6th annual); The Best in Poetry, 1968; Ardentia Verba; Velvet Paws in Print; The Wagging Tail; (mags.) American Haiku; Tangent; Haiku Highlights; Modern Haiku; American Bard; Swordsman Review; Dragon Fly; Janus-SCTH; Tweed. Address: P.O. Box 298, Hanford, CA 93230, USA.

EDWARDS, Michael, b. 29 Apr. 1938. University Senior Lecturer. Education: M.A., Ph.D., Christ's Coll., Cambridge Univ., U.K., 1957-63. Married, 1 son, 1 daughter. Positions held: Lectr. in French, Univ. of Warwick, 1965-73; Sr. Lectr. in Lit., Univ. of Essex, 1973–. Memberships: Exec. Mbr., Eastern Arts Assn.; London Poetry Secretariat. Published works: Common Place (BBC Radio 3), 1971; To Kindle the Starling, 1973. Contbr. to: Adam; Critical Qtly.; Delta; Listener; Poet (India); Prospice (Co-Ed.) Address: 30 Alma St., Wivenhoe, Essex CO7 9DN, U.K.

EDWORTHY, Joan, b. 16 Feb. 1921. School Teacher. Married, 1 son, 1 daughter. Memberships: V.P., Derby Poetry Soc.; Poetry Workshop Ldr., ibid. Contbr. to: John o'Londons; Manifold; Midland Poets, B.B.C.; Radio Derby, B.B.C. Honours, awards: Iris Harvey Scholarship, 1964 & 67; Second Prize, Netherseal Arts Fest. Open Comp. Address: 5 Park Grove, Derby, U.K.

EE, Tiang Hong, b. 13 Feb. 1933. Lecturer. Education: Univ. of Singapore; Univ. of Reading, UK. Married, 4 children. Positions held: Educ. Officer, Min. of Educ., 1956-63; Sr. Educ. Officer, ibid, 1963-69; Lectr., Educ. Admin., Fac. of Educ., Univ. of Malaya, Kuala Lumpur, Malaysia. Member of Raffles Soc., Univ. of Singapore. Published works: I of the Many Faces, 1960; The Flowering Tree, 1970; Seven Poets, Malaysia, Singapore, 1971-72. Contbr. to the following anthols. & mags: Commonwealth Poets of Today, 1967; New Voices of the Commonwealth, 1968; The Times Literary Supplement; Westerly; Tenggara; Focus; Tamesis; New Nation. Address: Faculty of Education, Univ. of Malaya, Kuala Lumpur, Malaysia.

EFROS, Israel Isaac, b. 28 May 1891. Professor; Poet; Essayist. Education: B.A., N.Y. Univ., 1913; M.A., Columbia Univ., 1914; Ph.D., ibid, 1915. Married Mildred Blaustein, 1 daughter. Positions held: Dean, Baltimore Hebrew Coll., 1918-29; Prof. of Semitics, Buffalo Univ., 1929-41; Prof. of Hebrew, Hunter Coll., 1941-55; Prof. of Philos., Dropsie Univ., 1941–; First Rector, Tel-Aviv Univ., 1955-62. Memberships: Pres., Israel PEN Club; Chmn., Israel Assn. of Hebrew Writers. Published works: Ancient Jewish Philosophy, 1964; The Problem of Space in Jewish Med. Philosophy, 1917; Philosophical Terms in the Moreh Nebukim, 1924; Maimonides Treatise on Logic, 1938; Studies in Med. Jewish Philos. (in press); Five books of Hebrew Verse, 1965, '72; Four books of Essays, 1968; translator of works into Hebrew. Recip. var. hons., prizes & awards inclng: Milo Prize, 1964; Tchernichovsky Prize, 1966; Bialik Prize, 1966; Hon. PH.D., Tel-Aviv Univ., 1971. Address: 11 Mapu St., P.O.B. 3436, Tel-Aviv, Israel.

EGAN, Alvie Mary, pen name **ANONA,** b. 26 Oct. 1918. Home Maker. Married James Egan, 5 sons, 2 daughters. Positions held: Freelance Reporter. Memberships: Hon. Sec., Cobram & District Arts Coun., 7 yrs.; Present Hon. Sec. & Trustee, The Australian Literature Soc. (est. 1899), 5 yrs.; Fellowship of Australian Writers; Adult Educ. Assn., 12 yrs.; Maroo Writers Grp. – A Constructive Criticism Forum. Contbr. to: 20th Century Literary Review, 1969-70; Let's Listen Again Anthol., 1966; Poetry Mag. (Poetry Soc. of Aust.), 1966; Vision Mag., 1971; Adult (Coun. of Adult Educ. Qtly.), 1964; Words (A.E.A. Annual), 1964; Nova Anthol., 1972; Cobram Courier; Master Mariners Jrnl. Var. Radio Broadcasts & a TV appearance. Poem read at Waratah Fest., Sydney, 1966. Address: Vermont St., Barooga, NSW 2739, Australia.

EGEA, Norma Edith, pen name **BOANERGES,** b. 19 Dec. 1946. Professor. Educ. Italian studies, Istituto di Cultura Italiana Dante Alighieri, 1964-65; Translator, French, Superior Inst. of Mod. Langs., 1964; Maestra, French, ibid, 1965; var. courses, Univ. of Córdoba; Licenciada en Literaturas Modernas, Fac. of Philos. & Humanities, Nat. Univ. of Córdoba, 1970; Specialist in French Lit., ibid; courses & seminars in musicotherapy & psychodrama. Positions held: Spanish & Hist. Prof., Secondary Commercial Coll. Aristóbulo del Valle; Prof., Secondary Schl., Patricias Argentinas; Prof., Justo José de Urquiza Mixed Secondary Schl.; Asst., Chair of French Lit., Fac. of Philos. & Humanities, Nat. Univ. of Córdoba. Contbr. to: Prairie Poet; Echoes of Parnassus; N.J. Poetry Soc. Anthol.; Am. Poetry Fellowship Soc. Anthol.; La Cachimba Ilusionada; United Poets. Address: Calle 5 No. 946, Barrio Talleres Este, Córdoba, Argentina.

EGELAND, Olga, b. 19 May 1923. Author. Education: Oslo Univ., Norway; Scuola Superiore Normale, Pisa, Italy (scholarship from Assn. for Norwegian Int. Youth Work). Positions held: Tchr., Grammar Schl. Memberships: Den Norske Forfatterforening; Norsk Forfattersentrum. Published works: (books of poetry) Lystavle, 1966; Orkestra, 1967; Lysnam, 1968; Speilspiral, 1969; Fase, 1970; Lyshugg, 1971; Miniatyrer, 1973; a pamphlet on poetry, 1973. Contbr. to: Aftenposten, Oslo; Dagbladet, Oslo; Stavanger Aftenblad, Stavanger; Samtiden, Oslo; Nemzetör, Munich, etc. Prose writings in Magasinet for Alle, Oslo. Honours, awards: The Sarpsborg Prize, 1968; The Ingeborg & Lars Osteras Bequest, 1969; Schou Scholarship, 1970; Govt. Scholarship, 1972-. Address: Hasselbakken 4, Oslo 7, Norway.

EGGEBRECHT, Jürgen, b. 17 Nov. 1898. Writer. Education: studied law & pol. sc. in Halle a/S, Berlin, Rostock, Würzburg. Married Elfi Stiehr, 3 children. Member, PEN, German Fed. Repub. Published works incl: Vogelkoie, 1949; Schwalbensturz, 1956; Zeichen in der Nacht, 1962; Ostern Eines Knaben 1971; Vaters Haus, Huldigung der Nördlichen Stämme, Erinnerungen, 1971; (radio) Colloquien und Städtebilder, etc. Contbr. to var. anthols. & newspapers inclng: Ma Anthologie Jüngster Lyrik, 1927; Junge Deutsche Lyrik, 1928; Das Fünfminutenlexikon, 1950; Widerspiel, Deutsche Lyrik, 1945, '61; Panorama Moderner Lyrik, 1965; M.A. Federjese, PEN Almanach, 1967; Süddeutsche Zeitung; Frankfurter Allgemeine Zeitung; Hannoversche Presse, Hannoversche Allgemeine; Die Tat (Schweiz). Address: Freystrasse 2/1, 8000 Munich 40, German Fed. Repub.

EGLINTON, Charles, b. 12 Sept. 1918. Journal Editor. Educ: Diocesan Coll., Rondebosch, Cape Town, South Africa; Univ. of Witwatersrand, Johannesburg. Married, one child. Positions held: Formerly worked as a ldr. writer, feature writer & lit. ed.; Ed., Optima, Johannesburg, current. Published works: Under the Horizon: Selected Poems 1944-1969, 1969. Contbr. to: Contrast; New Coin; (anthologies) Oxford Book of South African Verse, 1959; Penguin Book of Animal Verse, 1965; Penguin Book of South African Verse, 1968. Address: 22 Orange Road, Orchards, Johannesburg, South Africa.

EGLITE-BERZINS, Karina, pen name **EGLITE, Karina,** b. 6 Oct. 1911. Draughtswoman. Education: Gymnasium in Riga-Latvia; 2 yrs. Univ. in Riga-Latvia, reading philosophy (studies interrupted by WW 2). Married. Born Riga, Latvia; British subject since 1960. Positions held: Office work, Riga, Latvia, 1930-1944; Domestic work, UK., 1948-53; Draughtswoman 1954 until retirement. Memberships: Internat. Press Soc. (Fellow); Latvian Press Soc.; Nottingham Poetry Soc. Published works: Sirds (Latvian poems), 1971; Heart (English poems), 1972; Mana aizjuras paradize (Latvian poems), 1971. Contbr. to Latvian

newspapers: Latvija Vacija (Germany); Latvija Amerika (USA); Londonas Avize (UK), (mags.) Jauna Gaite (Canada); Nottingham Poetry Soc. Address: 170 Holme Rd., West Bridgford, Nottingham NG2 5AF, UK.

EGUDU, Romanus Nnagbo, b. 1 Feb. 1940. University Teacher. Education: Primary School at St. John's School, Ebe in Udi Div., Nigeria; St. Peter's School, Abor in Udi Div.; Teacher Training Coll., St. Charles Teacher Training Coll., Onitsha; B.A. (Hons.) Engl., Univ. of Nigeria, Nsukka; Ph.D. (Engl.), Michigan State Univ., East Lansing, Mich., USA. Married, 3 children. Positions held: 1957, Tutor in P.T.C., Aku, East Central State, Nigeria; 1958, Principal of P.T.C., Awhum, East Central State, Nigeria; 1959, Headmaster of St. Mary's School, Owo-Nike, East Central State, Nigeria; 1960, Tutor in C.I.C., Enugu; 1963, Principal, St. Paul's Secondary School, Eke. Now Senior Lecturer in Engl., Univ. of Nigeria, Nsukka. Memberships: Nigeria Engl. Studies Assoc.; Soc. for the Promotion of Igbo Language and Culture; African Rep., Journal of the New African Literature & Arts; Editorial Consultant, Conch: A Sociological Journal of African Cultures and Literatures. Published works: Poetic Heritage: Igbo Traditional Verse (with Dr. D. I. Nwoga), 1971; Igbo Traditional Verse, 1973; Four Modern West African Poets, 1974; Calabash of Wisdom and Other Igbo Stories, 1974. Contbr. to: Black Orpheus; Transition; Zeitgeist; Red Cedar Review; Prism International; Journal of the New African Literature & Arts; Conch; Presence Africaine; Comparative Lit. Studies; Ikorok; Ikenga; African Studies; The Python (anthol.); Modern Poetry from Africa (anthol.); New Voices from the Commonwealth (anthol.); African Voices (anthol.). Awards: 1966, 2nd Prize, Poetry Competition, Michigan State Univ., USA. Address: Dept. of Engl., Univ. of Nigeria, Nsukka, East Central State, Nigeria.

EHRENPREIS, Bernard, b. 10 May 1897. Retired Physician, Radiologist. Education: M.D., Med. Fac., Univ. of Vienna, Austria, 1922; post grad. internship at the General Hosp. X Ray Div., Holzknecht; Intern at BelleVue Hosp. & City Hosp., N.Y.C. Positions held: Asst. Roentgenologist, Kings Co. Hosp., 1925; Dir. of Radiol., ibid & Bushwick Hosp.; Attending Radiol. of the Brooklyn State Hosp., 1927- & Consulting since 1931; Radiol. Instr., L.I. Med. Schl., -1945; Clin. Prof. of Radiol., ibid, 1945-53; Dir. of all X-Ray Depts. of the City of N.Y., 1947-57; Memberships: AMA; Radiol. of North Am. Soc.; FACR. Published works: (poetry) Thorny Memories, 1961 (with four poems to music); num. med. papers & collab. on Book of ACRTA, 1951. Participant in Vivian Laramore Poetry Soc. reading at Surf Lib. & twice at the Lib., Miami Beach. Address: 910 West Ave., Apt. 1938, Miami Beach, FL 33139, U.S.A.

EHRMAN, Eva N., b. 10 Jan. 1902. Farm Wife; Music Teacher. Education: Ind. Univ. Ext., Kokomo; studied music under Agnes Lee Smith (piano) & Lalla Laymon (violin). Married, 1 son, 1 daughter. Positions held: Ch. Organist for many yrs. & Sunday Schl. Tchr.; Pvte. Mus. Tchr.; Pres., local Womens Christian Temperance Union; Pres., W.S.C.S. Worthy Matron, Order of the Eastern Star. Memberships: Junta Lit. Soc.; Kokomo Poetry Circle; Pres., ibid, 2 yrs., Sec., 2 yrs. & Contest Chmn., 1 yr. Contbr. to: Ariz. Highways; Christian Publng. Co.; Evangelical United Brethern; Hearthstone; Ideals; Meth. Publng. Co.; Rodeheaver Publng. Co.; Science of Mind; Southern Bapt. Convention; Union Signal; The Farm News; The Young Crusader; over 300 poems to more than 25 publs. Recip., 2nd pl., Kokomo Poetry Circle Contest, 1961 & 62; 4 hon. mentions, ibid, 1957, 59, 60, 65. Address: Box 315, R.R.1., Kokomo, IN 46901, U.S.A.

EHRMAN, George Loren, pen name **MANER, Loren,** b. 10 May 1901. Farmer. Education: Ind. Univ. Ext. in Kokomo. Married, 1 son, 1 daughter. Positions held: Farmer; Master, Masonic Lodge, 2 yrs; Tchr. of Sunday Schl. classes, 30 yrs. Memberships: Kokomo Poetry Circle, 1948-; Pres., ibid, 2 yrs., V.P., 2 yrs. & Contest Chmn., sev. times. Published works: Simple

Things, (illus. by Robert Ludwig) 1946; Mary of Bethany, (illus. by Betty Ehrman Maletich) 1961. Contbr. to: Ariz. Highways; Dakota Farmer; Hallmark; Ideals; Science of Mind; Hearthstone; Meth.; Southern Bapt.; Child Evangelism; Poet; The Farm News; The Young Crusader; over 1200 poems, articles & stories to more than 50 publs. Honours, awards: 1st pl., Kokomo Poetry Circle Contest, 1957 & 63; 2nd pl., ibid, 1957, 62, 65, 69; 3rd pl., 1960; nine hon. mentions. Address: Box 315, R.R.1, Kokomo, IN 46901, U.S.A.

EIBEL, Deborah, b. 25 June 1940. Teacher. Education: McGill Univ.; Radcliffe Coll.; The Johns Hopkins Univ. Positions held: The Walnut Hill School, Mass.; Univ. of N.C. at Greensboro; Haifa Coll., Israel; The Johns Hopkins Univ.; Loyola Coll., Montreal. Membership: Poetry Soc. of America. Published work: Kayak Sickness (selected poems: 1958-71), 1972. Contbr. to: (anthols.) Commonwealth Poems of Today, 1967; 40 Women Poets of Canada, 1971; The McGill Poetry Chapbook, 1959; New Poems of the Seventies, 1970; New Voices of the Commonwealth, 1968; PSA Diamond Anniversary Anthol., 1971; Soundings, 1971; Storm Warning, 1971; (journals) Approach; The Dalhousie Review; The Greensboro Review; The Green World; The Literary Review; The Lyric; The Malahat Review; The Red Clay Reader II; The Southwest Review; The Tamarack Review. Awards: The Arthur Davison Ficke Sonnet Award (Poetry Soc. of America), 1965. Address: 6657 Wilderton Ave., Montreal 251, Canada.

EIGELDINGER, Marc, b. 19 Dec. 1917. University Professor. Education: Baccalauréat littéraire, Gymnase de La Chaux-de-Fonds, 1936; Lic. ès lettres, Université de Neuchâtel, 1940; Doctorat ès lettres, ibid, 1943. Married, 2 children. Positions held: Prof., Gymnase de Neuchâtel, 1946; Chargé de cours, Université de Berne, –1962; Prof. of Modern French Lit., Université de Neuchâtel, –1963; Hon. Prof., Université de Berne, –1968; Doyen, Fac. of Letters, Université de Neuchâtel, 1969-73. Memberships: Société d'Histoire littéraire de la France; Société des écrivains suisses; Société J.-J. Rousseau; Amis de Vigny; Amis de Rimbaud; Fondation Ramuz. Published works: Le Pèlerinage du silence, 1941; Le Tombeau d'Icare, 1943 & '48; Prémices de la Parole, 1953; Terres vêtues de soleil, 1957; Mémoire de l'Atlantide, 1961; Les Chemins du Soleil, préface, Pierre Emmanuel of the Acad. Française, 1971. Contbr. to: Lettres; Revue de poésie contemporaine; Le Thyrse; Flammes vives; Phra; L'Univers de la poésie; Masa Tácerii. Directeur de la collection de poésie 'La mandragore qui chante' aux Editions de la Baconnière. Co-Directeur de la collection 'Langages' et des 'Etudes baudelairiennes' aux Editions de la Baconnière. Honours, awards: Prix de la Fondation Schiller suisse, 1958; Prix International de poésie 'Languedoc', 1958/1959. Address: 10 rue Dardel, 2072 Saint-Blaise, Switzerland.

EIGNER, Laurence Joel, pen name **EIGNER, Larry,** b. 7 Aug. 1927. Writer. Education: Mass. Hosp. Schl.; Corres. courses, Univ. of Chgo. Published works: From the Sustaining Air, 1953 & '67; Look at the Park, 1958; On My Eyes, 1960; The Music, The Rooms, 1965; The Memory of Yeats, Blake, 1965; Six Poems, 1967; Another Time in Fragments, 1967; Towards Autumn, 1967; Air the Trees, 1967; The Breath of Once Live Things In the Field with Poe, 1968; A Line that May Be Cut, 1968; Valleys Branches, 1969; What you Hear, 1971. Recip. of Poetry Award from The Poets' Fndn., 1965. Address: Massachusetts, USA.

EISENBERG, William David, b. 24 May 1930. College Teacher. Education: B.A., Univ. of Del., 1953; M.A., Lehigh Univ., 1955; Grad. Study, Duke Univ., 1955-58. Married Bonnie Louise Michaels, 2 sons. Positions held: Grad. Asst., Lehigh Univ., 1953-55; Grad. Rdr., Duke Univ., 1955-56; Temp. Asst. Prof., West Chester State Coll., Pa., 1959-60; Fac. Mbr. (now Assoc. Prof.), Bloomsburg State Coll., Pa., 1960–. Memberships: Wilmington, Del., Poetry Soc., 1959-63; Centro Studi e

Scambi Int., 1971–; International Poetry Society, 1972–. Published works: Moonshine: or the Ballad of Sneaky Pete, pamphlet, 1959; Forever is Not Long, pamphlet, 1972. Contbr. to: Wilmington Poetry Soc.; BSC Footnote; Haiku Highlights; Jean's Jrnl.: Univ. of Del. Alumni Bulletin. Address: 5380 Old Berwick Rd., Bloomsburg, PA 17815, U.S.A.

EITZEN, Margaret-Mary, pen names, **BRAHAN, Leigh; Dickie, M-M; EITZEN, Maggie,** b. 14 Oct. 1925. College Director of Public Information. Education: Grad., Adelphi Univ., Long Is., N.Y. Married Robert W. Eitzen, 2 daughters (Moira, Una). Positions held: Contbng. Ed., Assoc. Ed., Asst. Ed., Ed.-in-Chief, Bucks Co. Life mag.; Mng. Ed., N.J. Jrnl. of Optometry; Pres., County Publs., Inc.; Freelance Jrnlst.; Jrnlsm. Fac., Phoenix Coll. – Fac. Advsr., Student newspaper, Fac. Advsr., Lit. mag., Dir. of Public Information. Memberships incl: Ariz. Press Women (Nat. Fed. of Press Women); Phoenix Press Club; Am. Acad. of Poets; Ariz. State Poetry Soc.; Nat. League of Am. Pen Women; Past Pres., Phoenix Writers Club; Theta Sigma Pi; Am. Poetry League. Published works: (Co-Ed.), Ballet on the Wind, 1969; Sing Naked Spirit, 1970; Pancontinental Premier Poets, 1972. Contbr. to: Phila. Bulletin Mag.; Ariz. Mag.; Adelphi Quarterly; Home Life Mag.; Poet; Yearbook of Modern Poetry; Phoenix Fires; Haiku Highlights; Haiku; Premier Poets, & many more. Recip. var hons. & poetry prizes. Address: Box E–64, Phoenix Coll., 1202 West Thomas Rd., Phoenix, AZ 85013, U.S.A.

EKBAUM, Salme, b. 21 Oct. 1912. Writer. Education: Univ. of Tartu, Estonia. Memberships: Union of Estonian Writers Abroad; Estonian PEN; Int. PEN, Canadian Ctr. Published works: (books of poetry) Indian Summer, 1951; A Stone Crashing Into The Window, 1967; 13 books of prose fiction. Contbr. to many Estonian papers & mags. Address: 98 Galbraith Ave., Toronto 16, Ont., Canada M4B 2B7.

ELDAN, Anadad, b. 7 July 1924. Literature Teacher. Education: Jerusalem Univ., Israel. Married, 3 children. Positions held: Cultural Officer in the Kibbutz Movement. Memberships: Israeli Writer's Soc.; PEN. Published works: (poetry) Choshech Zorem Ufre (Darkness Flows & Fruit), 1959; Lo Besmachot Icalot (Not with Easy Joys), 1964; Lo Al Haeven Levada (Not by the Stone Alone), 1967; Levado Bezerm Hakaved (Lonely in the Heavy Stream), 1970; Folk-loric verse play for Fest. of Pesach, 1955 & Fest. of Svaoth, 1961. Contbr. to: lit. supplements of Israeli daily papers; Mibifnim; Achsav; Moznaim; Keshet. Poems translated into English, Italian, Spanish, Arabic, etc. Hon. Mbr., Int. Writing Prog., Univ. of Iowa, U.S.A. Address: Kibbutz Beeri, Doar Na, Hanegev, Israel.

ELDER, Gary M(ichael), b. 16 Apr. 1939. Writer. Published works: Arnulfsaga, 1970; Making Touch, 1971; Grosser Fagott Fugit, 1973. Contbr. to: The Angels; The Blackbird Circle; Cardinal Poetry Qtly.; Cloven Hoof; Dust; Entrails; Folio; Gato; The Goodly Co.; The Green World; Grist; Hyperion; Larvae du Golden Gate; Maelstrom; Masque; Mojo Navigator(e); Neo Poetry Anthol.; Open Places; Pyramid; Quetzal; S-B Gazette; Scimitar & Song; Scrivener Newsletter; The Smith; Snowy Egret; Tulsa Poetry Qtly.; The Vagabond; Worksheet Directory; Wormwood Review, etc. Address: 22 Ardith Lane, Alamo, CA 94507, USA.

ELDRIDGE, Jessie Cannon, pen name **KANE, Teddy,** b. 8 Mar. 1914. Poet. Married, 4 sons. Positions held: Poet; Homemaker; Typist; Owner of Kingston Telephone Answering Service; Ordained Min. of the Gospel. Memberships: Am. Poetry League; Mass. State Poetry Soc.; Nat. Fed. of State Poetry Socs.; World Poetry Day Soc.; Poesy Club. Published works: 25 books of poetry; To a Dream Aspiring, 1948; var. Short stories; (song) Whatsoever Things Are Lovely; Columnist of 'Thought Stretchers'. Contbr. to: From Sea to Sea in Song; Kennedy Anthol.; Anthol. of Am. Poetry, books I, II, III; Ladies Home Jrnl.; Seydell Qtly.; Haiku Highlights; Country Poet; Am. Bard, etc.

Honours, awards: 1st Prize, Mass. State Poetry Soc., 1968; 'Down East Poet' Danae Award; Poet Laureate of Kingston & Plymouth, Mass.; Dr. of Letters; Dr. of Divinity; many other prizes & citations. Address: 35 Maple St., Kingston, MA 02364, U.S.A.

ELLIOT, Alistair, b. 13 Oct. 1932. Librarian. Education: M.A.(Oxon.). Married, 2 s. Positions held: Asst. Librarian, Univ. of Keele; Acquisitions Librarian, Pahlavi Univ., Shiraz, Iran; Special Collections Librarian, Univ. of Newcastle upon Tyne. Published works: Translation of Alcestis, by Euripides, 1965; Translation of Peace, by Aristophanes, 1965; Air in the Wrong Place, 1968. Contbr. to: The Greek Anthol. (edited by Peter Jay), 1973; The Listener; Times Lit. Supp.; Encounter; New Poems (P.E.N. Club), 1962, etc. Address: 27 Hawthorn Rd., Newcastle upon Tyne NE3 4DE, UK.

ELLIOT, Jean Pirnie Robertson, pen name **ELLIOT, Jean,** b. 12 July 1901. Freelance Writer; Lecturer; Historian. Education: Nat. Acad. of Design, N.Y.C., U.S.A. Married R.Sherrard Elliot, Jr. Positions held: Designer of rugs, chintzes, etc.; Assoc. Ed., Bronxville Press; Conducted seminars on Origins of Alexandria for local Y.W.C.A.; Lectured on Anne Dudley Bradstreet to PSA. Memberships: former Sec. & Treas., Women Poets of N.Y.; non-res. Mbr., Nondescript Club of Bronxville (also former sec. & V.P.); Poetry Soc. of Va. Published works: Pictoral Guide to American Gardens (w. Col. Louis H. Frohman); A Starrier Coldness, 1973. Rep. in World Love Poetry, 1959. Contbr. to: The Lyric; Westchester Histn.; The Pen Woman; N.Y. Herald Tribune; Washington Star; Voices; The Villager. Has conducted workshops & made broadcasts & an hour's taping of poetry & criticism for the Lib. of Congress. Address: 323 South Fairfax St., Alexandria, VA 22314, U.S.A.

ELLIOTT, Elizabeth Ann, b. 5 Aug. 1932. Registered Professional Nurse. Education: St. Vincent's Hosp., Bridgeport, Conn., USA. Divorced, 2 daughters. Positions held: Obstetrical Supvsr., 9 yrs.; Charge Nurse, Outpatient Clinic, 5 yrs.; currently Nursing Co-ordinator for residential treatment ctr. for emotionally disturbed youth. Memberships: Poetry Soc. of Tex.; Fndr. & Mng. Dir. of Community Actors Theatre, New Braunfels, Tex. Contbr. to Cyclo Flame. Honours, awards: L.M. Wirtz Meml. Award, 1968; Editors Award, Cyclo Flame, 1968; Cyclotron Prize, 1969. Address: 322 Oakcrest Dr., New Braunfels, TX 78130, USA.

ELLIOTT, George P., b. 16 June 1918. University Professor. Education: B.A., Univ. of Calif., Berkeley, 1939; M.A., ibid, 1941. Married, 1 daughter. Positions held: Instr. then Asst. Prof., St. Mary's Coll., Calif.; Asst. Prof., Cornel Univ., Barnard Coll.; Lectr., Univ. of Iowa, Univ. of Calif., Berkeley; Prof., Syracuse Univ. Member, PEN. Published works: Eight American Poets, 1952; Fever & Chills, 1961; 14 Poems, 1964; From The Berkeley Hills, 1969. Ed: Fifteen Modern Am. Poets, 1956; Selected Poems of Winfield Townley Scott, 1967. Contbr. to: Qtly. Review; of Lit.; Epoch; The Poet; Furioso; Paris Review; The Quest; Departure; Whetstone; Vintage; Genesis West; Accent; Poetry; Hudson Review; Beloit Poetry Jrnl.; Mass. Review; Kayak; Dalhousie Review; Experiment; etc. Address: Engl. Dept., Syracuse Univ., Syracuse, NY 13210, U.S.A.

ELLIOTT, Harley, b. 29 July 1940. Art Instructor. Education: B.A., Kans. Wesleyan Univ., Salina, Kans., U.S.A.; M.A., N.M. Highlands Univ., Las Vegas. Married, 1 daughter. Positions held: Landscape Nursery Worker; Truck Driver; Warehouseman; Sign Designer & Signpainter; Book Designer; Teacher. Published works: Dark Country, 1971; Six Eyes Open (w. others), 1972; All Beautyfull & Foolish Souls, 1973; New Am. & Canadian Poetry (anthol.), 1972. Contbr. to: Abraxas; Aim; The Alternative Press; The Ark River Review; Back Door; Beloit Poetry Jrnl.; Bones; Brass Ring; Carolina Quarterly; Cottonwood Review; Epos; The Expatriate Review; The Falcon; Hearse; Intrepid; The Kans. Quarterly; Maelstrom; The Midwest

Quarterly; The N.Y. Quarterly; Northeast; Paradox; Second Coming; The S.C. Review; The Sunstone Review; Trace; Wis. Review; Wormwood Review & many others. Recip., The Lucille Medwick Award, N.Y. Quarterly, 1973. Address: 425 South Phillips, Salina, KS 67401, U.S.A.

ELLIS, Carolyn Hargus, pen name, **ELLIS, Carolyn,** b. in small rural community in Arkansas. Writer. Education: Arkansas State Normal Inst., now Ark. State Tchrs. Coll.; NY Univ. corres. course in Versification. Widow w. 2 d. Positions held: Tchr., Elementary Schl.; Receptionist, The Humble Oil & Refining Co., Houston, Tex., for 24 yrs; Columnist, The Humble Philosopher in The Humble Club Bulletin, ibid. Memberships: Poetry Soc. of Tex., Dallas; The Houston Chapter; The Scribblers' Club, Houston. Contbr. to the following anthols. & jrnls: Between the Book Ends, 1942; Prairie Schooner Caravan, 1943; Adventures in Poetry, 1946; That Eager Zest, 1961; The New York Times; The Washington Post; The Wall Street Journal; The Saturday Review of Literature; The Texas Literary Quarterly; The Christian Home; The Saturday Evening Post; Prairie Schooner; McCall's; Good Housekeeping; Cosmopolitan; The Ladies Home Journal; Reader's Digest; Peacock Alley; The St. Regis; Holland's; Radio Mirror; Between the Book Ends, 1942; Prairie Schooner Caravan, 1943; Adventures in Poetry, 1946; That Eager Zest, 1961; The American Magazine. Awards: Critic's Awards, A Book of the Year, Poetry Soc. of Tex., 1954, '58, '60, '62, '65, '66, '68; Annual Critic's Award, 1958, '68; Prizes in annual contests, 1955, '61, '63, '68, '69, '70, '71; The Kansas City Poetry Mag., 1946, '47; Poetry Prize, Profl. Chapt., Theta Sigma Phi, 1961; 1st Prize, ibid, 1962, '64. Address: 2015 Avenue P, Huntsville, Tex. 77340, USA.

ELLIS, Kenneth John, b. 19 Dec. 1945. Journalist. Education: Pulteney Grammar Schl., S. Australia. Positions held: Reporter, sub-editor, broadcaster, cabaret and children's entertainer. Mbr., P.E.N. Club English Ctre. Published works: London Doodles, 1973. Contbr. to: Westerly (Australia); Under 25 (anthology); Overland (Australia); Makar (Australia). Address: 39 Tanza Rd., London NW3, U.K.

ELLIS, Royston, b. 10 Feb. 1941. Author & Administrator. Positions held: Author, Poet, Lecturer, TV & Radio Commentator, 1957-61; Asst. Ed., Jersey News & Features Agency, 1961-63; Assoc. Ed., The Canary Islands Sun, 1963-66; Admnstr., Emerald Hillside Estates, Dominica, 1966–. Memberships: West India Comm.; Royal C'wealth Soc.; MCC; Windward Islands Cricket Bd. of Control; Dominica Nat. Sports Coun.; Dominica Arts Coun. Writers Workshop. Published works: Jiving to Gyp, 1959; Rave, 1960; A Seaman's Suitcase, 1963; The Rainbow Walking Stick, 1961; The Cherry Boy, 1967; (novels) The Flesh Merchants; The Rush at the End; Myself for Fame; Flesh Game; (biographies) Rebel; The Big Beat Scene; Drifting with Cliff Richard; The Shadows by Themselves. Contbr. to: Beat; Phoenix; Sphinx; Peace News; Daily Express; New Writing in the Caribbean; Generation X; Daily Mirror; Dominica Star; University mags.; BBC Radio & TV; U.K. Arts Coun. Poetry Shows; Ind. TV progs., etc. Honours, awards: Dominica Nat. Day Poetry Prizes, 1970, 1971 & 1973; Hon. Dukedom of Caribbean Island of Redonda. Address: BM Box 235, London WC1V 6XX, U.K. or P.O. Box 110, Dominica, W.I.

ELLISON, Kay, b. 22 Jul. 1922. Clerk for City-County Health Department, Victoria, Texas. Education: Grad., Patti Welder HS, Studied the writing of poetry with Clement Wood of Bozenkill, Delanson, NY. Married (now divorced), 5 children (Gloria, Clark, Clement, Lloyd, Boyd). Positions held: Bank, 16 yrs., Fire and Casualty Insurance, 10 yrs., and Dept. of Health since July, 1973. Memberships: Poetry Soc. of Texas; St. Francis Episcopal Church (and member of choir). Published work: Mood Segments, (poetry), 1973. Contbr. to: Victoria Advocate; Houston Post; Laredo Times; various anthols. – Important American Poets;

Int. Who's Who in Poetry; Thoughts in Poetry, 1972; Visions in Verse; Your Mother and Mine; – Different Mag.; Southwester Mag.; Kansas City Poetry Mag.; Poems also read over Radio Station KVIC (Victoria), and also over KTRH, in Houston, by Alec Bearov. Recip. of 3 monthly poetry prizes, 1971 and 1972, Poetry Soc. of Texas; Hon. Mention for poem pub. in Different (mag.); featured in Victoria Advocate (3 Sept. 1972); Interviewed and poems read over TV Station KX1X (Victoria). Address: P.O. Box 3248, Victoria, TX 77901, USA.

ELLYSON, Mary Holbert, b. 13 June 1904. School Teacher & Housewife. Education: Tchng. Cert., Glenville Normal Schl., 1925; Degree in Elem. Educ., Fairmont State Coll., 1954. Married Russell G. Ellyson. Positions held: Tchr., Clover Fork Schl., Lewis Co., 1922-23; Tchr., The Arnold Schl., Lewis Co., 1923-24; Taught 4th grade, Chriton Schl., Greenbrier Co., 1925-26; Tchr., Cooper Schl., Gilmer Co., 1926-28; Taught in Monongalia Co. for 5 yrs. & worked for Dept. of Public Assistance for sev. months. Member, Morgantown Br., West Va. Poetry Soc. Published works: (novels) It Might Have Been; Mud & Money. Contbr. of poems to Panorama, local newspaper mag. Address: Rt. 5, Box 294, The Briar Patch, Morgantown, WV 26505, U.S.A.

ELMSLIE, Kenward Gray, b. 27 Apr. 1929. Poet. Education: B.A., Harvard Coll., 1950. Memberships: ASCAP; Dramatists' Guild; Authors' Leage; AGAC. Published works: The Champ (poetry), 1968; Album (poetry & prose), 1969; Circus Nerves (poetry), 1971; Motor Disturbance (poetry), 1972; The Orchid Stories (novel), 1973; The Sweet Bye & Bye, (libretto), 1973; The Seagull (libretto), 1974; The Grass Harp (libretto), 1973. Contbr. to: Poetry (Chicago); Art & Literature; The World; Univ. Review; Nadada; The Paris Review; Locus Solus; Folder; Big Sky; Sesheta; Juillard; Angel Hair; Adventures in Poetry; Mother; Telephone; The Zodiac; ZZ. Honours, awards: Frank O'Hara Prize for Poetry, 1971; Nat. Coun. on the Arts Award, 1969; Ford Fndn. Grant; Houston Grand Opera Grant. Address: 104 Greenwich Ave., N.Y., NY 10011, U.S.A.

EMANUEL, James Andrew, Sr., b. 15 June 1921. University Professor. Education: B.A., Howard Univ., 1950; M.A., Northwestern Univ., 1953; Ph.D., Columbia Univ., 1962. Married, 1 son. Positions held: Confidential Asst. to Gen. B.O. Davis, Sr., Asst. Insp. Gen. of U.S. Army, Wash. D.C., 1942-44; Chief, Pre-Induction Sect., Chicago Army & Air Force Induction Stn., 1951-53; Instr., Harlem YWCA Bus. Schl., 1954-56; Fulbright Prof. of Am. Lit., Univ. of Grenoble, France, 1968-69; Vis. Prof., Univ. of Toulouse, France, 1971-73; Prof., Dept. of Engl., City Coll., City Univ. of N.Y. (on staff since 1957); Gen. Ed., Broadside Critics Series, 1969–. Published works: The Treehouse & Other Poems, 1968; Panther Man, 1970; (non-poetry) Langston Hughes, 1967; How I Write (co-author), 1972; Dark Symphony: Negro Literature in America (co-ed.), 1968, etc. Two vols. of poetry on tape. Contbr. to jrnls., newspapers, anthols. & textbooks & some have been transl. into French, Italian & Russian. Recip. var. hons. Address: c/o Dept. of Engl., City Coll. of N.Y., Convent Ave. at 138th St., N.Y., NY 10031, U.S.A.

EMERY, Raymond C., b. 11 Jan. 1918. English Professor. Education: B.A., Univ. of Wyoming, Laramie, 1935; M.A., ibid, 1940; Ph.D., Stanford Univ., Calif., 1951. Married, 4 sons. Positions held: Rural Schl. Tchr. in Neb.; Tchr. & Prin., Neb. H.S.'s; H.S. Engl. Tchr. & Asst. Prin., Laramie, Wyo.; A.F. Capt. & Engrng. Instr.; Engl. Dept. Chmn., Phoenix Coll., Ariz.; Curric. Dir., Phoenix Union H.S.'s & Phoenix Coll. Dist.; Engl. Prof., Ariz. State Univ. Memberships: World Poetry Soc. Int.; Am. Mosaic; Modern Haiku; Ariz. Poetry Soc.; Phoenix Poetry Soc.; Tri-City Poetry Grp. Published works incl: High Interest – Easy Reading for Jr. & Sr. H.S. Reluctant Readers, 1965; Six Young Arizona Writers, Ed., 1968; Behavioral Objectives in English for Slow Learners (a folio of articles), Ed., 1969; Nurenberg & Vietnam: An Am.

Tragedy (book review), 1971; Existentialism in the Classroom, 1971; English Themes Center on Vocational Guidance, 1973. Contbr. to: Poet; Pancontinental Premier Poets; Am. Haiku, etc. Address: 1019 E. Lemon, Tempe, AZ 85281, U.S.A.

EMERY, Sarah, b. 8 Aug. 1911. Teacher. Education: A.B., Emory Univ., 1933; M.A., Ohio State Univ., 1938; Ph.D., ibid, 1942. Married Stephen A. Emery, 2 sons. Positions held: Instr., Packer Collegiate Inst., 1943-46; Instr. of Philos., Syracuse Univ., 1946-47; Asst. Prof. of Philos., Duke Univ., 1951-52; Asst. Prof. of Engl., Univ. of Plano, 1967-69. Member, Poetry Soc. of Tex. Contbr. to: Georgia Review; Emory Univ. Qtly., etc. Address: P.O. Box 683, Denton, TX 76201, U.S.A.

EMILY, Geneva Hargis, pen name **EMILY, G.H.,** b. 2 May 1920. Education: B.A., Univ. of Ga., U.S.A., 1970. 4 sons. Mbr., Nashville, Tenn. Press & Authors Club. Contbr. to: Ky. Writers; Nat. Poetry Weekly; Hot Lead; Ga. Review; Aurora; DeKalb Lit. Arts Jrnl.; Stillpoint; Impression; New England Review; Calliope; Ga. Mag. Recip., Mrs. Clyde Lovejoy Stevens Award, Univ. of Ga. Dept. of Engl., 1970. Address: 175 Sunset Dr., Athens, GA 30601, U.S.A.

EMIOT, Israel (Israel Goldwasser), b. 15 Jan. 1909. Author. Education: Warsaw Yeshiva, & others; 8 yrs. of secular educ., inclng. the study of Polish, German, Russian & economics. Positions held: Author in Res., Jewish Community Ctr. of Rochester, N.Y.; Regular contbr. to The Daily Forward, 1958–; Ed., Jewish Roots. Hon. Mbr., Rochester Poetry Soc. Published works incl: Der Birobidjaner Inyen (The Biroibdjar Case), 1960; In Nigun Eingehert (Hearing the Melody), 1962; In Mitele Yorn (In Middle Ages), 1963; Fardekta Shpieglen (Covered Mirrors), 1964; Eider De Lesht Mich Ois (Before I Am Extinguished), 1966; Tzulib Di Tzen Umshuldige (For the Sake of Ten), 1969; in all, 13 books of poetry & prose. Contbr. to var. newspapers & jrnls. Honours, awards: Cassel's Prize in Mexico for Der Birobidjaner Inyen; The Jewish Book Council of America's Harry & Florence Kovner Meml. Award for In Nigun Eingehert; World Congress of Jewish Culture's Prize for Eider Du Lesht Mich Ois. Address: c/o Jewish Community Ctr. of Rochester, 1200 Edgwood Ave., Rochester, NY 14618, U.S.A.

EMME, Patricia Ann Sweeney, b. 12 Dec. 1935. Housewife. Education: Queens Coll. Married, 1 son, 1 daughter. Positions held: Freelance work for leading card cos. & mags. Mbr., Poetry Soc. of Tex. Works published by: Ideal Publs., 1967, 68, 69, 70, 71, 72, 73; Warner Press Publrs., 1965, 66, 67, 68, 69, 70, 71, 72, 73; Rust Craft Cards, 1965-73; Buzza Cards, 1962-70; American Greetings, 1970; Charmcraft Publs., 1965-71; Norcross Card Co., 1972 & 73; Paramount Card Co., 1970, 71, 72, 73. Contbr. to: This Day Mag.; Ideals; Warner Press Poetry Books; Treasury of Thoughts; Three-Four Mag., etc. Recip., Personal Poetry Radio Award, 1965, & 1st Prize, Harry Konner Award for Poetry, 1973. Address: 122-05-135th Ave., South Ozone Park, NY 11420, U.S.A.

EMMERT-WADSWORTH-WHITMORE, Alice **Elizabeth,** b. 8 Dec. 1918. Poet; Writer of Lyrics; Musician (singer, pianist, electric organist), etc. Education: Private studies in music; Reader of Literature; studied, Northwestern Univ., Rockford College, etc. Widow of Lt. R. Wadsworth; 1 s. (Michael R. Wadsworth). Positions held: Literature & Drama Office held in Woman's Club; Assoc. Member of Smithsonian Inst., Washington; Hon. Rep. of CSSI. Memberships: Acad. of American Poets; World Poetry Soc., Internat.; UPLI; CSSI; Poetry Soc. (UK); Nat. League of American Penwomen; American Fellowship Poetry Soc.; Florida State Poetry Soc., Inc.; Chaparral Poets of Calif.; Illinois State Poetry Soc. Published works: A Garland of Leis, 1971; Our Singing States, 1973. Contbr. to: Penny-A-Thought; Poet; Anthol. of Midwest Poets, 1972; Anthol. of All Favorite Poetry; Poets Corner, Brown County Newspaper; American Revolution Book; The American Poet; Ill. State Poetry Soc. Booklet; Prairie Poet; World Poet; Sterling Illinois

Newspaper; Nat. School of Poetry Anthol.; Purring-in-a-Pocket; Major Poets of Illinois; Cardinal; Soc. of Children's Book Writers; Lincoln Log. Awards: Lit. Contest, Lt. Verse 3rd place (State) also 2nd place winner for children 1966; First Award, Adult, 1968, (State of Illinois) Hon. Mention in Environment Contest, 1972; Internat. Contest 1971, Hon. Mention, (American Fellowship Soc.) Hon. Mention 1968 (State, Illinois). Address: 215 W. Morgan, Dixon, IL 61021, USA.

EMMS, Josepha Murray, b. 21 April 1894. Poet. Education: Girls' Latin School; Edith M. Herrick School of Expression; Univ. Extension courses, etc. Married to Edward Emms (b. Redditch, Worcs., UK.), now deceased; 1 d. Positions held: Dramatic Reader; Teacher of Expression; Dramatic Coach; Playwright; Poet; Judge of Poetry Contests. Memberships: American Poetry League; Poets' Haven; Midwest Chaparral; Agnes Carr Writers' Club of Boston; Reading Circle of The Whitman Woman's Club. Published work: April Music, 1962. Contbr. to: Spring Anthol. (UK); American Bard; Bouquet of Poems (CSSI); Midwest Chaparral; Poetry Prevue; The Muse; Swordsman Review; Ideals; The Archer; Wings; Herald of Life; New Athenaeum; CS Monitor; Prairie Poet; Youth's Instructor; Washington Eve. Star; Sonnet Sequences; American Weave; Kansas City Poetry Mag.; American Poet; American Poetry League Bulletin; Daily News Tribune; Southwest Times; Chromatones; Gospel Trumpet; Driftwood East; Sea To Sea In Song, and many others, including Internat. Who's Who in Poetry Anthol.; Yearbook of Mod. Poetry Anthol.; American Poetry Anthol. (books 1, 2, 3), etc. Recip. of numerous honours and awards. Address: 52 Alden St., Whitman, MA 02382, USA.

EMPSON, William, b. 27 Sept. 1906. University Professor. Education: Winchester & Magdalene Coll., Cambridge Univ., U.K. Positions held: Prof. of Engl. Lit. in Tokyo, Peking & Sheffield. Published works: Poems, 1935; The Gathering Storm, 1940; Collected Poems, 1955; Milton's God, 1961. Address: 1 Hampstead Hill Gdns., London NW3, U.K.

ENG, Stephen Richard, pen name, **BREDON, John,** b. 31 Oct. 1940. Neighborhood Planner and Organizer. Education: Grad. Central HS, USAF, Bushy Park, UK., 1958; Univ. of Maryland, Munich, Germany, 1958-59; Grad. A.B. in Engl. Lit., The George Washington Univ., Washington, DC, 1963; Grad. M.S. in Education, Portland State Univ., Oregon, 1973. Positions held: Claims adjustor, 1962-64; door-to-door salesman 1960-64; insurance salesman, 1964-65; ball bearings salesman, 1965-68; social caseworker, 1968-70; community organization and planning director, since 1970. (USAF, Hon. Discharge, 1969). Memberships: Broadcast Music, Inc., songwriter and publisher (since 1972); Am. Poetry League. Published works: edited and published, Elusive Butterfly and Other Lyrics, by Bob Lind, 1971; The Battle of Ft. Vancouver/Tomorrow's Rain, (record), 1972; Golden Eagle/Linda, Did You Ever Change Your Name? (record), 1973; The Verse Tarot (a verse translation of the 78 Greater and Lesser Arcana), 1974. Contbr. to: Ambrosia; American Bard; American Poet; Arkham Collector; Bachaet; Etchings & Odysseys; Express Mag.; Florida Notes; Gems; Green Book; Harbor Lights; Invictus; Jean's Journal; LA 22; Legend; Lincoln Log; Lunatic Fringe; Major Poets; Modern Images; Modern Utopian; Nyctalops; Orphic Lute; Poetry Parade; Poetry Prevue; Prairie Poet; The Poet's Guild; Poet's Nook; The Rufus; Special Song; Sunburst Anthol.; Texas Traveller; United Poets; Vancouver Columbian; Weekly Jrnl.; World Poets; Whispers from Armham; Yearbook of Modern Poetry, 1971; Those That Cared, 1972; The Spring Anthol., 1972, 1973; The Poets' Guild Anthol., 1972. Awards: Focus Poet in Bachaet, June, 1971; radio and television interviews concerning recorded song "The Battle of Ft. Vancouver", 1972; 1st Prize, The Rufus, Spring, 1973; American Poets Fellowship Soc. Cert. of Merit, 1973. Address: c/o Red Phoenix Music, P.O. Box 66315, Portland, OR 97266, USA.

ENGELS, John David, b. 19 Jan. 1931. Associate Professor of English. Educ: A.B., Univ. of Notre Dame, 1952; Univ. Coll., Dublin, Ireland; M.F.A., Univ. of Iowa, U.S.A., 1957. Married Gail Jochimsen, five children. Positions held: Served w. U.S.N., Caribbean, Mediterranean, Marshall Islands, 1952-55; Former Instr., Engl., St. Norbert Coll., W. DePere, U.S.A.; Assoc. Prof., Engl., St. Michael's Coll., Winooski, current. Published works: The Homer Mitchell Place, 1968; (literary criticism) A Guide to William Carlos Williams, 1969; A Checklist of William Carlos Williams, 1969; Writing Techniques, 1965; Co-Ed., Experience and Imagination (anthology), 1960. Contbr. to: Poetry; Reporter; Commonweal; Nation; Quarterly Review of Literature; Literary Review; (anthologies) Riverside Poetry 3, 1958; Poetry Out of Wisconsin, 1960; Midland, 1961. Recip., Poetry Schlrship., Bread Loaf Writers Conference, 1960. Address: R.F.D. 1, Box 247, North Williston, VT 95495, U.S.A.

ENGLAND, Gerald, b. 21 Dec. 1946. Editor. Positions held: Ed., Headland Mag., 1969-72; Dir., Headland Publs., 1970–; Sec., Yorkshire Poets Assn., 1971-73; Ed., Osgoldcross Review, 1973. Memberships: Fndr., Yorks. Poets Assn.; Coun. Mbr., Yorks. Dialect Soc.; Engl. Ctr., Int. PEN; Poets Conf.; Lewis Carroll Soc.; Sheffield Authors Club. Published works: Poetic Sequence for Five Voices, 1966; Mousings, 1970; The Wine The Women and The Song, 1972; For Her Volume One, 1972. Contbr. to: Pontefract & Castleford Express; St. John's Bulletin; New Melody; Tait's Quarterly; Platform (Yorks.); Breakthru; Bo Heem E Um; Manifold; It's World that makes the Love go Round; Whitwood Arts Assn. Anthol.; Bogg; Headland; Ludd's Mill; Yorks. Poets 72; Village Review; Wormwood Review; Spring Tide; Help; Crab Grass; IWWP Anthol.; Moonshine; Roots; Purston Parish Mag.; Hyacinths & Biscuits; Cork Examiner, & many others. Address: 50 Chiltern Dr., Ackworth, Pontefract WF7 7DW, U.K.

ENGLE, Paul (Hamilton), b. 12 Oct. 1908. University Professor. Education: B.A., Coe Coll., Cedar Rapids, Iowa, 1931; M.A., Univ. of Iowa, 1932; Rhodes Scholar, Merton Coll., Oxford Univ., UK, 1933-36. Married, (1) 2 d., (2) Hua Ling Nieh, novelist. Positions held: Fac., Univ. of Iowa, 1937–; Currently Clark Ansley Prof. of Creative Writing, ibid; Dir., Iowa Writers Workshop; Dir., Int. Writing Prog. Memberships: Nat. Coun. on the Arts, White House, Wash.DC; Vis., Rockefeller Fndn. to investigate the conditions of writers in Pakistan, India, Hong Kong, Taiwan, The Philippines & Japan; Am. Lit. Specialist, Dept. of State. Published works: Worn Earth, 1932; American Song, 1934; Corn; West of Midnight; American Child, 1945, '56, The Word of Love, Poems in Praise, 1959; A Woman Unashamed, 1965; Embrace, 1968. Contbr. to: Poetry; The Kenyon Review; The Sewanee Review; The Listener; Boteghe Oscure; Harper's; Atlantic Monthly; The New Yorker. Honours, Awards: Yale Series of Younger Poets Prize, 1932; Guggenheim Fellowships; Rockefeller Grant; Ford Fndn. Grant. Address: Int. Writing Prog., Univ. of Iowa, Iowa City, Iowa 52240, USA.

ENGLISH, Elizabeth Lois. Writer; Bank President. Positions held: Pres., Macksville State Bank, Kan. Memberships: Kan. Authors' Club; Int. Platform Assn.; Centro Studi e Scambi Int. Published works: Travel Memories of Europe; Of Dreams & Memories; Echoes in the Wind; Sunshine & Shadows; Leave Me My Dreams; O On Wings Of Faith; The Golden Stairway; The Poet & the Psalms; The Moving Story (free-verse version of the Bible); Heritage of Faith; The Miracle of Miracles; Of Course I've Paith; The Progress of the Pilgrim (free-verse version of Pilgrim's Progress); Wait, Wait for Yet A Little Longer; Philosophies of Nature; Bringing Home the Greek Gods & Goddess. Contbr. to IWWP Anthol. Recip., Hon. Ph.D., Colo. State Christian Coll., Evergreen, Colo., 1973. Address: Macksville, KS 67557, U.S.A.

ENGLISH, Maurice, b. 21 Oct. 1909. Director of Temple University Press. Educ: Harvard Coll. Married

Fanita Blumberg, 1946; two children. Positions held: Free-lance Journalist, U.S.A. & Europe, 1933-54; Ed.-in-Chief, Int. Div., Nat. Broadcasting Corp., 1941-43; Ed. & Publr., Chicago Mag., 1954-58; Mng. Ed., Univ. of Chgo. Press, 1961-63; Sr. Ed., ibid, 1963-69. Dir., Temple Univ. Press, Phila., 1969–. Published works: Midnight in the Century, 1964; The Saints of Illinois (play), 1968; Translator (w. others), Selected Poems of Eugenio Montale, 1967; Ed., The Testament of Stone, 1963. Contbr. to: (anthologies) New Yorker Book of Verse, 1935; One Hundred Modern Poems, 1949; Where Steel Winds Blow, 1969. Honours, awards: Ferguson Mem. Award, 1964; Fulbright Fellowship, 1966-67; U.S.A. Delegate to Les Biennales Int. de Poesie, Knokke-Le-Zoute, Belgium, 1965. Address: 1530 Locust St., Philadelphia, PA 19102, U.S.A.

ENRIGHT, D(ennis) J(oseph), b. 11 Mar. 1920. Publisher's editor; writer. Education: Leamington Coll.; Downing Coll., Cambridge. Married, 1 d. Positions held: Univ. posts in Egypt, England, Japan, Berlin, Bangkok; Prof. of Engl., Univ. of Singapore, 1960-70; Co-editor, Encounter (mag.), 1970-72; Editor, Chatto & Windus Ltd., 1973–. Fellow, Royal Soc. of Literature; Member, Soc. of Authors. Published works: The Laughing Hyena & Other Poems, 1953; Bread rather than Blossoms, 1956; Some Men Are Brothers, 1960; Additions, 1962; The Old Adam, 1965; Unlawful Assembly, 1968; Selected Poems, 1969; Daughters of Earth, 1972; Foreign Devils, 1972; The Terrible Shears, 1973. Contbr. to: Encounter; The Listener; London Mag.; New Statesman; Times Lit. Supp., etc. Address: c/o Chatto & Windus Ltd., 40-42 William IV St., London WC2, UK.

ENSLIN, Theodore Vernon, b. 25 Mar. 1925. Poet. Education: Episcopal Acad., Phila.; studied composition w. Nadia Boulanger, Cambridge Mass. Married Mildred Stout, div. 1961, 1 son, 1 daughter. 2) Alison Jose, 1 son. Has published poetry, criticism, etc. in nearly every 'little' & lit. mag. in U.S. & Canada as well as o'seas, and sev. non-technical articles concerning homoeopathic therapeutics. His work has been translated into German, French, Spanish, Portugese & Israeli. Wrote weekly column in a local newspaper, 1951-56. Four plays produced, one in 1966 & three in the summer of 1970 at the Hardware Poets Theater in N.Y. & Skitikuk Playhouse, Orono, Me. Published works incl: The Work Proposed, 1958; New Sharon's Prospect, 1962; The Place Where I Am Standing, 1964; This Do & The Talents, 1964; New Sharon's Prospect & Jrnls., 1965; To Come To Have Become, 1966; Characters In Certain Places, 1967; The Diabelli Variations, 1968; 2/30...6/31, 1968; Agreement & Back, 1969; Forms, Part One, 1970, Part Two, 1971, Part Three, 1972, Part Four, 1973; The Poems, 1971; Views, 1970; The Country of Our Consciousness, 1971; Etudes, 1972; Views, 1973; In The Keeper's House, 1973; The Swamp Fox, 1973; Sitlo, 1973. Rep. in six anthols. Num. reviews & articles in mags. Many readings at univs. & colls. Recip., Niemann Award, 1955. Address: R.F.D. 1, Temple, ME 04984, U.S.A.

ENTREKIN, Sue Wright, b. 15 Feb. 1916. Housewife. Education: Schls. & Colls. in S. Miss., U.S.A. Married, 3 children. Memberships: Universal Literary Club, Hattiesburg, Miss. (has held positions of Pres., V.P., Sec. & Reporter at var. times); Writers Unlimited, Pascagoula, Miss.; Chap., Gautier Garden Club. Published works: Butterflies in the Rain. Contbr. to: The Gautier Independent; Advance Monticellonian; Texas Newspaper of the Arts; Tejas Publications, Tex.; Poet India; Legend; Wordcraft; Miss. Poetry Jrnl.; Book of Prayer Poems. Honours, awards: 1st pl. in Narrative poetry & 2nd & 3rd places in other categories, Nationwide contest sponsored by Miss. Fest. of Arts, 1970; 1st, 2nd & 3rd places, var. club contests, 1971 & '72; 1st pl. poem for the Golden Age Convalescent Home, Grand Bay, Ala., 1972; Hon. Mention, Miss. Poetry Soc., 1971 & '72. Address: P.O. Box 264, Gautier, MS 39553, U.S.A.

ERB, Christopher, b. 26 May 1942. English Teacher.

Education: Jersey City State Coll., N.J. Member, Poetry Soc. of Am. Published works: (book) Osmosis, 1972. Contbr. to Keats Prize Poems, 1973. Recip., First prize for Elizabethan verse, Poetry Soc. of Am., 1973. Address: 30 West 27 St., Bayonne, NJ 07002, U.S.A.

ERCOLANI, Luigi Arcangelo, b. 25 May 1902. Franciscan Monk. Memberships incl: Richelieu Int. Acad., Paris; Acad. Tiberina, Rome; Acad. of Superior Study, Minera, Milan; Acad. Int. Leonardo da Vinci-Centro Studi e Scambi Int., etc. Published works incl: Canti Segreti, 1958; In Attesa Dell'Aurora, 1959; In Attesa Dell'Alba, 1960; Verso L'Alto, 1961; Voci di Un'Anima, 1961; Canti di Maggio, 1962; Petali Sparsi, 1962; Ultime Voci, 1962; Canti Del Vespero, 1963; Acqua Sorgiva, 1963; Canti Mariani, 1964; Voci Sacre, 1964; Ore Serene, 1965; Sotto Le Stelle, 1965; Nel Silenzio e Nella Pace, 1967; Momenti Lieti Della Vita Mia, 1969; Amor Che Spira, 1970; Quardando Lontano, 1971; Nel Segno Della Speranza, 1971; Palpiti Arcani, 1972; Luce e Calore, 1972; Come Fiamma, 1972; Pace e Liberta', 1973; Verso L'Azzurro, 1974; Oltre L'Orizzonte, 1974. Honours, awards incl: Europa Prize, 1970, '71; Golden Rose, Acad. of Pontzen, Naples, 1970-72; Trophy, Acad. of 500, Rome; Eternal City Prize, Rome, 1972, etc. Address: Via dei Cappuccini 32, 52046 Lucignano (Arezzo), Italy.

ERNE, Giovanni Bruno (Nino), pen name **ERNE, Nino,** b. 31 Oct. 1921. Writer; Television Reporter. Education: Dr. phil., Univs. of Berlin & Munich. Positions held: Interpreter 'Dramaturg' at theatre 'Kammerspiele' in Munich; Tchr. at Dramatic Art Schl.; Ed. of reviews; Tchr., Univ. of Aix-en-Provence, Marseille, France; Artistic Dir. of publng. houses in Frankfurt & Hamburg; Freelance Author, Reporter & Dir., TV, Hamburg, London & Rome; currently at Ctr. of 'Zweites Deutsches Fernsehen', Mainz. Memberships: PEN; VS Soc. of German Writers; Verwertungsgesellschaft Wort; E.T.A. Hoffmann-Gesellschaft. Published works: Der sinnende Bettler, 1947; Murmelpoeme, 1967; Brassens Texte 3, transl. & essay, 1969; Flötenkonzert und andere Kompositionen, 1971. Contbr. to num. mags., jrnls., newspapers, anthols., etc. Recip., First Prize for short story. Address: Ebersheimer Weg 37, 65 Mainz, German Fed. Repub.

ERSKINE, Edith Lanier, pen name **ERSKINE, Edith Deaderick,** b. 28 Sept. 1887. Poet; Substitute Teacher. Education: Southwestern Univ.; Berlitz Schl. of Langs., Chicago; Weaver Coll., N.C. Married John Vincent Erskine. Positions held: Tchr. of Folk & Aesthetic Dancing, YMCA, Mobile, Ala.; Subs. Tchr., Latin & French, Weaver Coll. & of Latin, Weaverville H.S.; Assoc. Latin Tchr., Weaverville H.S.; Subs. Tchr., Latin & French, Montreath Coll. & of Folk Dancing at Marshill Coll., N.C. Memberships incl: Am. Poetry League; Nat. League of Am. Pen Women; Pres., Asheville Chapt. & N.C. State Pres., ibid; Avalon Soc.; Am. Poetry Fellowship; Co-Fndr. & Hon. Mbr., Weaverville Book Club; Coun., Nat. Poetry Day, Asheville, N.C.; Daughters of the Am. Revolution. Published works: Clouds, Chords & Calico, 1943; The Regal Now, 1949; The Power Flows, 1950; Here They Live & Die, 1953; From Sea to Sky, 1954; The Millions Climb, 1958; Time Roads, 1962. Contbr. to: Avalon Publs.; Major Poets Spring Anthol.; World Poetry Day Anthol.; Cyclo-flame; Am. Poets; United Poets; Prairie Poets; Am. Poetry League Bulletin, etc. Address: 325 Patrick Ave., Merritt Island, FL 32952, U.S.A.

ESCALLIER, Emile, b. 28 Sept. 1906. Lawyer. Education: LL.D. Positions held: Pres., Acad. Delfinale, Grenoble; Pres., Ecrivain dauphinois, Grenoble; Pres. de la Société d'Etudes des Hautes-Alpes. Published works: Poémes de Jeunesse, 1942; Le destin tragique du troubadour Guillaume de Cabestan, 1935; Ce cher pays gavot, 1951; Dauphiné, 1963; Images du Dauphiné, 1965; Le tombeau de Marie, récit, 1966; Guide littéraire du Dauphiné, etc.

Co-Dir., des Çahiers de l'Alpe, Grenoble. Collaborator, régional & national revues. Honours, awards: Chevalier de la Legion d'honneur; Chevalier, l'Ordre des Arts et Lettres; Officier de l'Ordre au Mérite, de Malte. Address: 5 rue de Palanka, Grenoble 38000, France.

ESCALONA-ESCALONA, José Antonio, b. 1 Jan. 1917. Professor of Literature. Education: grad. in Caracas, Venezuela; postgrad. courses in Psychol. & Letters in Brazil. Positions held: Prof., sev. schls. in Caracas.; Prof., Inst. Pedagogico Nacional, Universidad Central & Escuela Militar de Venezuela, simultaneously with Dept. of Culture & Fine Arts, Min. of Educ.; currently Secretario General, Sociedad Bolivariana de Venezuela. Memberships: Grupo Literario 'Yunke' en San Cristobal, Venezuela, 1943; Editl. Hd., Revista Nacional de Cultura; former V.P., Asociacion de Escritores Venezolanos; Dir. of Publs., ibid, etc. Published works: Isla de Soledad, 1943; Soledad invadida, 1947; Angulo, 1954; La Generacion de la Esperanza, 1956; La Inefable Compania, 1956; Sombra del cuerpo del Amor, 1956; Columna de Papel, 1957; Biografia de Jose Antonio Maitin, 1958; Sanare Puramente Paraiso, 1962; Biografia de Andres Bello, 1969; rep. in Antologia General de la Poesia Venzolana, 1966 & Antologia de Mis I Poemas, 1969. Contbr. to var. jrnls., newspapers, mags. Honours, awards incl: Orden del Libertador en el grado de Comendador, 1969; Orden de Isabel la Catolica, 1970. Address: Apartado 874, Caracas, Venezuela.

ESHLEMAN, Clayton, b. 1 June 1935. Magazine Editor. Educ: B.A., Ind. Univ.; M.A., ibid. Divorced, one child. Positions held: Former Instr., Am. Lang. Inst., N.Y. Univ.; Ed., Caterpillar Mag., current. Published works: Mexico and North, 1961; The Chavin Illumination, 1965; Lachrymae Mateo, 1967; Walks, 1967; Brother Stones, 1968; The House of Okumura, 1968; A Pitchblende, 1969; Yellow River Record, 1969; (verse translations) Residence on Earth by Pablo Neruda, 1963; State of the Union by Aime Cesaire, 1966; Poemas Humanos/Human Poems by Cesar Vallejo, 1969. Contbr. to: Poetry; Nation; Origin; Haravec; Lit; (anthologies) Erotic Poetry, 1963; Poetas Norteamericanos, 1966; Poets for Peace, 1967. Honours, awards: Union League Civic & Arts Fndn. Prize, 1968; Nat. Translation Ctr. Awards for translating Cesar Vallejo; Coordinating Coun. of Literary Mags. Award. Address: 36 Greene St., New York, NY 10013, U.S.A.

ESKRIDGE, Audeen, pen name **ESKRIDGE, Audeen Bunyard,** b. 9 July 1914. Housewife. Education: Creative Poetry, Eastfield Coll., Dallas, Tex., U.S.A. Married James R. Eskridge, 3 children. Mbr., Poetry Soc. of Tex., 1964–. Contbr. to: Collier's Mag.; Reader's Digest; Red Book; Ladies Home Jrnl. Address: 2129 Prichard Lane, Dallas, TX 75227, U.S.A.

ESPINO, Federico Licsi, Jr., pen name **QUIXOTE DE EXTRAMUROS,** b. 10 Apr. 1939. Journalist. Education: B. Litt., Fac. of Philos. & Letters, Univ. of Santo Tomas, Manila, Philippines, 1959. Positions held: Proofreader, Manila Times, 1966; Editl. Asst., Mirror Mag., 1968; Asst. Ed., ibid, 1969-72. Pres., Catholic Writers Guild, 1959. Published works: Counterclockwise, Poems: 1965-69, 1969; Percussive Blood: Selected Stories, 1972; Puente del Diablo: A Poem in Three Movements, 1973. Contbr. to: Lit. East & West; Sands & Corral; Panitikan; The Diliman Review. Honours, awards: First prize, Tagalog Poetry, Palanca Meml. Awards, 1967; First prize, Engl. Poetry, ibid, 1969; First prize, Tagalog Poetry, Inst. of Nat. Lang. Contest, 1966. Address: 178 M.H. del Pilar, Palatiw, Pasig, Rizal, Philippines.

ESPINOZA, Rudolph L., pen name **ESPINOSA, Rudy,** b. 28 Sept. 1939. Writer. Education: A.B., Univ. of Calif. at Berkeley, 1971. Positions held: Job Developer-Counselor, Calif. Migrant Worker Proj., D-Q Univ., Davis, Calif.; currently Guest Lectr., Chicano Studies, Course-survey of Chicano Lit.,

Contra Costa J.C., San Pablo, Calif. Contbr. to: Warpath (Native-Am. newspaper), Berkeley, Calif., 1969; El Grito, 1969, '70, '71, '72; El Pocho Che, Oakland, Calif., 1970, '71; El Espejo (Mexican-Am. Lit. Anthol.), 4th ed., 1971; S.F. Examiner, San Francisco, 1972. Recip., Scholarship, Breadloaf Writers' Conf., Middlebury Coll., Vt., 1962. Address: 250 Drake St., San Francisco, CA 94112, U.S.A.

ESTEB, Adlai Albert, b. 17 Nov. 1901. Missionary; Editor; Teacher; Poet. Education: B.Th., Walla Walla Coll., 1931; M.A., Univ. of Calif.; Ph.D., Univ. of Southern Calif., 1944. Positions held: Missionary, China, 1923-37; Director, Lay Activities, Pacific Union, 1946-50; Assoc. Sec., Lay Activities Dept., Gen. Conf., Seventh Day Adventist Ch., 1950–; Ed., Go., Monthly Journal for Adventist Laymen, 1950–. Memberships: Pres., China Soc. of Southern Calif., 1946-50; Phi Beta Kappa; Phi Kai Phi; Phi Kappa Phi. Published works: Driftwood, 1947; Firewood, 1952; Sandalwood, 1955; Morning Manna, 1962; Rosewood, 1964; Scrapwood, 1967; Redwood, 1970; Kindle Kindness, 1971; What Christmas Means, 1971; When Sorrow Comes, 1973; Straight Ahead, (A daily devotional book), 1974. Contbr. to: Signs of the Times; These Times; Go; Review & Herald; The Ministry; Ideals. Honours: Poet Laureate, Seventh Day Adventist Ch., 1966–. Address: 8013 Sligo Creek Parkway, Washington, DC 20012, USA.

ETTER, David Pearson, pen name **ETTER, Dave,** b. 18 Mar. 1928. Book Editor. Education: B.A., Hist., Univ. of Iowa, 1953. Positions held: Ed., Northwestern Univ. Press, Evanston, Ill., 1961-63; Ed., Ency. Britannica, Chicago, Ill., 1964-68; Ed., Compton's Ency., Chicago, 1969-73; Freelance Ed., 1973–. Published works: (books) Go Read the River, 1966; The Last Train to Prophetstown, 1968; Strawberries, 1970; Voyages to the Inland Sea, 1971; Crabtree's Woman, 1972. Contbr. to: Chicago Review; Saturday Review; The Nation; Poetry Northwest; Minn. Review; San Francisco Review; Mass. Review; Prairie Schooner; Kans. Quarterly; Chelsea; Shenandoah; New Orleans Review; Tenn. Poetry Jrnl.; Focus/Midwest; S.D. Review, etc. Honours, awards: Midland Poetry Award, Soc. of Midland Authors, Chicago, 1967; Poetry Award, Friends of Lit., Chicago, 1967; Ill. Sesquicentennial Award for Poetry, 1968; Chicagoland Mag. Award for Poetry, 1968; Theodore Roethke Poetry Prize, Poetry Northwest Mag., 1971. Address: 416 South First St., Geneva, IL 60134, U.S.A.

EVANS, Abbie Huston, b. 20 Dec. 1881. Poet. Educ: B.A., Radcliffe Coll., 1913; M.A., ibid, 1918. Positions held: Staff Mbr., Settlement Music Schl., Phila., 1923-53. Memberships: Jury Mbr., Shelley Mem. Award, 1940; Jury Mbr., U.S. Award for Poetry, Int. Poetry Forum, 1967. Published works: Outcrop, 1928; The Bright North, 1938; Fact of Crystal, 1961. Contbr. to: Nation; New Yorker; (anthologies) A Little Treasury of Modern Poetry, 1946; Poems and Poetry, 1964; Various Light, 1964. Honours, awards: Guarantor's Prize, 1931; Loines Mem. Award, 1960; Golden Rose Award, 1965; Litt.D., 1961. Address: 414 Queen St., Philadelphia, PA 19147, U.S.A.

EVANS, David Allan, b. 11 Apr. 1940. College Teacher. Education: B.A., Morningside Coll., 1962; M.A., Univ. of Iowa, 1964. Positions held: Engl. Instr., Marshalltown Community Coll., 1963; Asst. Prof., Engl., Adams State Coll., Alamosa, Colo., 1966-68; Asst. Prof., Engl., S.D. State Univ., 1968–. Mbr., Poetry Soc. of Am. Contbr. of poems to: Poetry Northwest; Shenandoah; Esquire; Prairie Schooner; N.Y. Times; Kansas Quarterly; The Far Point; Hearse; North Am. Review; Ed., New Voices in American Poetry (has also poetry included), 1973; poem in Borestone Best Poems of 1969. Address: Engl. Dept., S.D. State Univ., Brookings, SD 57006, U.S.A.

EVANS, Gregory Morgan, b. 24 Apr. 1954. Student. Education: Sheffield Univ. (Engl. & Philos.) Positions held: Operating Theatre Attendant, Gen. Hosp. Memberships: Sec., Sheffield Univ. Arts Soc.; Co-Ed.,

Chrysalis, poetry mag. Contbr. to: Images; Muse; Chrysalis; Arrows; Gargantua, etc. Address: 35 Little Moor Hill, Smethwick, Warley, Worcs., U.K.

EVANS, John C., b. 2 Oct. 1901. Professor (Ret'd). Education: Mus.B., Huron Coll., S.D., U.S.A.; B.A., Eastern State Tchrs. Coll., Madison, S.D.; M.A., Univ. of Iowa. Married Agnes Braa, 1 daughter & 1 son. Positions held: H.S. Engl. Tchr., Akron, Colo. & Dassel, Minn.; H.S. Prin., Washburn, Wis. & Madison, Minn.; Assoc. Prof. of Engl., Neb. Wesleyan Univ., Lincoln, Neb.; Chmn., Engl. Dept., Two Harbors, Minn. Memberships: Neb. Poetry Soc.; Pres., Neb. Fed. of Coll. Engl. Tchrs.; Minn. Poetry League; Phi Sigma Pi; Delta Psi Omega. Rep. in following anthols: North Am. Book of Verse, 1932; Poems of Trees, 1932; Selected Anthology of Mag. Verse, 1933; Anthol. of S.D. Poets, 1935; Muse Anthol., 1938; Eros Anthol., 1939; Music Unheard Anthol., 1939; N.Am. Book of Verse, 1939; Sonnets (Anthol.), 1939. Contbr. to: Am. Agriculturist; Am. Poet; Augusta Chronicle, Ga.; Boaz Westminster; Caravel; Christian Sci. Monitor; Denver Post, Colo.; Golden Atom; The Rotarian; Scimitar & Song; United Poets; The Villager; Writer's Notes & Quotes & many others. Recip., Quarterly Prize, Lyric, & Ga. Prize, Lyric, 1968. Address: Rte.3, Box 72A, Ashland, WI 54806, U.S.A.

EVANS, Paul, b. 3 Jan. 1945. Published works: Current Affairs, 1970; True Grit, 1971; February, 1972. Recip., Alice Hunt Bartlett Prize, 1972 (Poetry Soc., London). Address: 13A Brunswick Pl., Hove, Sussex, U.K.

EVANS, Robert Daniel, b. 26 Jan. 1944. Art Historian. Education: B.A., Adelphi Univ.; M.A., Columbia Univ. Positions held: currently Co-Ed. of Painted Bride Qtly. Published works: 'Snort', pamphlet w. 3 other poets, 1973. Contbr. to: Kauri; Wis. Review; Aspect; Maguey; Hellcoal Annual; Temple Univ. Poetry Newsletter; Erratica; Painted Bride Qtly.; Thin Dime Poems; Gay Sunshine; Philadelphia Mag.; Merlin's Magic; Ampersand. Recip., Peter Stone Meml. Prize, 1963. Address: c/o Painted Bride Arts Ctr., 527 South St., Philadelphia, PA 19147, U.S.A.

EVANS DAVIES, Gloria, b. 17 Apr. 1932. Poet. Published works: Words – For Blodwen, 1962; Her Name Like The Hours, 1974. Contbr. to: var. anthols.; N.Y. Times; Times Lit. Supplement; Spectator; The Listener; BBC TV & Radio; HTV (progs. about her life & poems). Recip. of grant from the Gulbenkian Fndn. to write first book of poems & grants from the Royal Lit. Fund to write second and third books. Address: 25C High Street Superior, Brecon, S. Wales, U.K.

EVATT, Julia Katherine Eubanks, b. 23 July 1930. Writer & Editor. Education: Univ. of Ga., Atlanta Div., 1948-51. Married Donald L. Evatt, 4 children. Positions held: currently Asst. V.P., Georgia Int. Life Ins. Co., i/c of Public Relations; Treas.-Sec. of Southern Assn. of Business Communicators. Member, Georgia Writers' Assn. Contbr. to: DeKalb Lit. Arts Jrnl.; Prairie Schooner; This Issue; Poem; Quoin; Mnemosyne; Yes; Calliope; Lyric; Cobb County Times; Home Life; N.C. Anvil, etc. Honours, awards: Ga. Writers' Assn. Poetry Mss. Award, 1971 & '69; num. cash prizes from Ga. Writers' Assn. & Atlanta Writers' Club. Address: 1068 Azalea Circle, Marietta, GA 30062, U.S.A.

EVERETT, Graham L., b. 23 Dec. 1947. Writer/Poet. Education: B.A., Engl., Canisius Coll., Buffalo, N.Y., U.S.A. Positions held: Carpenter, summers of 1967-70; Child Care Wkr., 1970-71; Emotional Therapist, 1971-72; Tchr., winter, 1972-73; Drug Counselor, summer 1973; Tchr., Poetry, N.Y. State Prog. Poets-in-the-Schools. Memberships: Past Grp. Ldr., Dog Dish Writers Workshop; Past Asst. Dir., Centerville Conservatory, an educational org. & artists' community, Riverhead, N.Y. Published works: American States, prose & poetry, 1970; Rainbow Ride, poems, 1973. Ed., Street Mag. Contbr. to: Paradox Mag.; Quadrill Mag.; Street Mag.; 1973. Address: c/o James H. Everett, 28 Nadel Dr., Riverhead, NY 11901,

U.S.A.

EVERETT. Olivia, b. 14 Sept. 1914. Clerk in Harris County, Texas, Tax Office. Education: HS and Business Coll. Widow of Rufus Marshall Everett; 5 children. Memberships: Internat. Poetry Inst.; Poetry Soc. of Texas; Houston Chapter of Poetry Soc. of Texas; Major Poets Chapter of Pierson Mettler Associates. Published work: Come Walk With Me, 1970. Contbr. to: Houston Post; The Friendly Church Letter (Amarillo); numerous anthols.; Lyrics for Songs (Vamalco Music Publishing Co.); Lyrics for song (Cathedral Recording Co.). Recip. many awards from Internat. Poetry Inst., and Houston Chapter of Poetry Soc. of Texas. Address: 3318 Castledale, Houston, TX 77016, USA.

EVERSON, Ronald Gilmour, b. 18 N-v. 1903. Barrister; Poet. Education: B.A., Univ. of Toronto; Upper Canada Law Schl. Positions held: Mng. Dir.-Pres., Johnston, Everson & Charlesworth Ltd., Toronto & Montreal, 1936-63; Chmn., Communications–6 Inc., Toronto & Montreal, 1963-66; Mbr., League of Canadian Poets. Published works: Three Dozen Poems, 1957; A Lattice for Momos, 1958; Blind Man's Holiday, 1963; Four Poems, 1964; Wrestle With An Angel, 1965; Incident on Cote des Neiges, 1966; Raby Head, 1967; The Dark is Not So Dark, 1969; Selected Poems, 1970. Contbr. to: Poetry (Chicago); Sat. Review; Sewanee Review; NY Times Book Review; Tamarack Review; Atlantic Monthly; Poetry; Elizabeth; Adam (London); Prism Int.; Canadian Forum; Fiddlehead; Queen's Quarterly, etc. Recip., Arts Award, Canada Cou., 1971. Address: Suite 404, 4920 Maisonneuve, Montreal 215, Canada.

EVERSON, William Oliver, pen name **BROTHER ANTONINUS,** b. 10 Sept. 1912. Sacramento, Calif. Lecturer. Education: Fresno State Coll., 1931, 1934-35. Married twice, m. (3) Susanna Rickson. Positions held: Co-Fndr., Untide Press, Waldport, Ore., 1943; Dir., Fine Arts, ibid, 1944-45; Lay Brother, Dominican Order, 1951-69; Poet in Residence, Kresge Coll., Univ. of Calif., Santa Cruz, 1971–. Published Works Include: San Joaquin, 1939; The Masculine Dead, 1942; The Residual Years, 1948, '68; A Privacy of Speech, 1949; Triptych for the Living, 1951; The Crooked Lines of God, 1959; The Year's Declension, 1961; The Hazards of Holiness, 1962; The Blowing of the Seed, 1966; Single Source, 1966; The Rose of Solitude, 1967; In the Fictive Wish, 1967; The Springing of the Blade, 1968; Robinson Jeffers: Fragments of an Older Fury, 1968; A Canticle to the Waterbirds, 1968; The Last Crusade, 1969. Contbr. to the following anthols. & periodicals: Beat: Fine Anthologie, 1962; Today's Poets, 1964; San Francisco Renaissance, 1964; Studying Poetry, 1965; The New American Poetry, 1967; An Introduction to Literature, 1968; The Possibilities of Poetry, 1970; Literature in America, 1971; Two Ways of Seeing, 1971; Muse of Fire, 1971; The San Francisco Poets, 1971; Mark in Time, 1971; Atlantic Monthly; The Chicago Review; Saturday Review; Voices; Commonweal; Texas Quarterly, etc. Honours & Awards: Guggenheim Fellowships in Poetry, 1949; Silver Medal, C'wealth Club of Calif., 1967. Address: Saint Albert's Coll., 5890 Birch Court, Oakland, CA 94618, U.S.A.

EWART, Gavin (Buchanan), b. 4 Feb. 1916. Freelance Writer. Education: Wellington Coll., Berks., 1929-1933; Christ's Coll., Cambridge, 1934-1937, (B.A., 1937, M.A., 1942). Positions held: The British Council, 1946-1952; (War Service, 1940-1946); Advertising, 1952-1971; Freelance, 1971–. Memberships: The Poetry Soc.; The Soc. of Authors. Published works: Poems and Songs, 1939; Londoners, 1964; Throwaway Lines, 1964; Pleasures of the Flesh, 1966; The Deceptive Grin of the Gravel Porters, 1968; Twelve Apostles, 1970; The Gavin Ewart Show, 1971. Contbr. to: New Verse; The Listener; New Statesman; London Mag.; Ambit; The Times Lit. Supp.; Encounter; The Honest Ulsterman; Club Internat.; The Observer; The Sunday Times, etc. Awards: 1971 Cholmondeley Award for Poetry. Address: 57 Kenilworth Court,

Lower Richmond Rd., London SW15 1EN, UK.

EWING, Annemarie, b. 2 Apr. 1905. Teacher. Education: B.A., Univ. of PIttsburg, Pa.; Dip., Ecole Normale de Musique, Paris, France; M.A., Univ. of So. Calif., L.A., U.S.A. Positions held: Poetry Columnist, Christian Herald; Feature & Program Writer, Columbia Broadcasting System, N.Y.C.; Tchr., L.A. Harbor Coll. Memberships: Acad. of Am. Poets; Fed. of Chaparral Poets. Contbr. to: Poetry Folio, 1928; Poetry on the Air, 1947; New Poems by Am. Poets, 1954 & 57; Essentials of Modern English, 1961; 23 Calif. Poets, 1968; Discovery & Recollection, 1970; Yearbook of Modern Poetry, 1971; Shore Poetry Anthol., 1971; Outstanding Contemporary Poetry, 1972; Anglo-Welsh Review; Colo. Qtly.; Western Humanities Review; Ante; Encore; Folio; Good Housekeeping; Ladies Home Jrnl.; Lyric; Hyacinths & Biscuits; Major Poets; Poetry (India); Speak Out; Small Pond; Yes; Portland (Me.) Sunday Telegram, etc. Address: 2477 Cedar Ave., Long Beach, CA 90806, U.S.A.

EYNON, Marilyn Martha Theresa Scott, pen name **SCOTT, Marilyn Eynon,** b. 18 Feb. 1922. Secretary; Homemaker. Married, w. children. Positions held: Secl. work in Hosp., Wright Patterson A.F.B.; currently working in an elem. schl. Memberships: Poetry Soc. of Am.; Ohio Poetry Soc.; W. Va. Poetry Soc.; Poetry Soc. of Tex.; Treas. & Pres., Dayton Poets Round Table. Contbr. to: Anthol. of Mag. Verse, 1958; Commemorative Anthol., 1964; Spirit Mag.; The Lyric; Wings; Am. Weave; Poet Lore; Wis. Poetry Mag.; Am. Bard; Poetry Soc. of Tex. Book of the Year, 1973 & '74; N.Y. Times; N.Y. Herald Tribune; Wash. Evening Star; Chgo. Tribune Sunday Mag.; Columbus Dispatch; Cinn. Enquirer; Good Housekeeping; Family Circle, etc. Honours, awards: Silver Webb Award, 'Ohio Poet of the Yr.', 1965; Ohio Poetry Soc. Lyric Cup Award, 1961. Address: 771 Clareridge Ln., Centerville, OH 45459, U.S.A.

EZEKIEL, Nissim, b. 16 Dec. 1924. University Teacher. Education: M.A., Bombay Univ., India. Married Daisy Jacob, 2 daughters, 1 son. Positions held: Hd. of Engl. Dept., Mithibai Coll. of Arts, 1961-72; V.Prin., ibid, 1963-72; currently Rdr. in Am. Lit., Dept. of Engl., Univ. of Bombay. Memberships: P.E.N. All India Ctr. since 1955, & Exec. Comm. Mbr. since 1962; Hon. Sec., 1963-65 & 69-72; Gen. Coun., Sahitya Akademi & on the Panel for Engl. Published works: A Time to Change, 1952; Sixty Poems, 1953; The Third, 1958; The Unfinished Man, 1960; The Exact Name, 1965; Three Plays, 1969. Contbr. to: London Mag.; Adam Int.; Ariel; Poetry Australia; Literature East & West (U.S.A.); Quest; Literary Studies; Dialogue India, etc. Address: The Retreat, Bellasis Rd., Bombay 400008, India.

F

FABILLI, Mary, pen name **BLIGH, Aurora,** b. 16 Feb. 1914. Museum Associate Curator. Educ: A.B., Univ. of Calif. Positions held: Former Steel-Checker, Richmond; Former Art Tchr., Bentley Schl. & Y.M.C.A., Oakland, 1946-47; Educl. Asst., Oakland Public Mus., 1949–; Assoc. Curator, ibid, 1966–. Published works: The Old Ones, 1966; Aurora Bligh and Early Poems, 1935-1949, 1968. Contbr. to: Occident; Circle; Berkeley Miscellany; Ritual; Experimental Review; New Directions 8 (anthology), 1944. Address: Berkeley, CA, U.S.A.

FAINLIGHT, Harry. Published works: Sussicram, 1965. Contbr. to: Listener, Encounter; New Departures.

FAINLIGHT, Ruth Esther, b. 2 May 1931. Writer. Memberships: Soc. of Authors; London Poetry Secretariat; National Poetry Secretariat. Published works: A Forecast, A Fable, 1958; Cages, 1966, 67; To See The Matter Clearly, 1968, 69; 18 Poems from 1966, 1967; 3 Poets (w. Alan Sillitoe & Ted Hughes),

1971; The Regions Violence, 1973; 21 Poems, 1973. Contbr. to: The Observer; Sunday Times; New Yorker; N.Y. Times; Encounter; Poetry Chicago; Poetry Review; New Statesman; Times Literary Supplement; Outposts; Transatlantic Review; Southern Review; Sewanee Review; Aylsford Review; European Judaism; Mediterranean Review; Antaeus; The Scotsman; Work In Progress. Address: 14 Ladbroke Terr., London W.11, U.K.

FAIR, C.A., b. 19 NoV. 1923. Teacher & Lecturer in English Literature. Education: in Kenya & England; London Univ. Positions held: Tchng., Somerset, Nairobi; Lecturing, S. Africa; Co-Ed., 'New Coin Poetry', Grahamstown, S. Africa. Contbr. to: Contrast; New Coin; New Nation; Chirimo (Rhodesia); The Penguin Book of S. African Verse. Address: Engl. Dept., Rhodes Univ., Grahamstown, S. Africa 6140.

FAIRFAX, John, b. 9 Nov. 1930. Poet. Education: English Public School. Married; 2 s. Director, Phoenix Press; Poetry Publications; Co-Founder and Director, Arvon Foundation (creative writing centres). Published works: This I Say, 1966; The 5th Horseman of the Apocalypse, 1969; Stop and Listen, 1969; Double Image, 1972. Contbr. to: Times Lit. Supp.; Paris Review; Partisan Review; X Magazine; Panache; Time & Tide; BBC Poetry Programme; Wheelers Mag.; Two Cities; Poetry Review; Poetry Qtly.; Outposts; Southern Art Review; Look Mag.; Spectator. Recip. Gregory Poetry Award (twice). Address: The Thatched Cottage, Eling, Hermitage, Newbury, Berks. RG16 9XR, UK.

FAIZ, Ahmed Faiz, pen name **FAIZ,** b. 13 Feb. 1911. Writer; Administrator. Education: M.A. (Engl. Lit.), Punjab Univ., Lahore, 1933; M.A. (Arabic Lit.), ibid, 1934. Married, 2 daughters. Positions held: Lectr. in Engl. Lit., Amoritsar, Lahore, 1935-42; Officer, Indian Army, 1942-46; Chief Ed., Pakistan Times, Lahore, 1947-59; Dir., Pakistan Arts Coun., Lahore, 1959-62; Prin., Haroon Coll., Karachi, 1964-72; Chmn., Pakistan Nat. Coun. of Arts & Advisor to Govt. on Cultural Affairs, 1972–. Memberships: Sec., Indian Progressive Writers Assn., Punjab Provincial Br., 1936-42; Fndr. Mbr., Afro-Asian Writers Conf., 1958–; Editl. Br., Lotus Qtly. Published works: Poems by Faiz, 1971; (in Urdu) Naqsh-E-Faryadi, 1941; Wast-e-Saba, 1953; Zindan Nama, 1956; Daste-Tahe-Sang, 1966; Sare-Wadi-e-Sina, 1971. Contbr. of poems to most important lit. mags. in Pakistan & India. Translations have appeared in Russian, Czech., Hungarian, Chinese, Arabic, French, Italian, English, etc. Recip., Int. Lenin Prize, 1962. Address: Cons. on Cultural Affairs, Min. of Educ., Nat. Coun. of the Arts, 73-F/6-2 Islamabad, Pakistan.

FAKIH, Mohammad Hassan, b. 1913. Chairman, Administrative Board, Agricultural Bank, Riyadh. Published works: 'Man and Fate' (a volume of poetry in Arabic). Contbr. to all Saudi Arabian periodicals. Address: c/o Higher Committee for Arts & Sciences, Ministry of Education, Riyadh, Saudi Arabia.

FALK, Ruth C., b. 11 May 1913. Housewife. Education: N.Y. Univ. Ext.; Seminars at Columbia Univ., N.Y.C.; Master Poet-Tchr. Trng., Bergen Community Coll. Married, w. children. Positions held: Ed., Criterion, E.H.S. Lit. Mag.; Sec., Paterson, N.J. League of Women Voters; Resource Chmn. for Higher Educ. in N.J.; Regional Planning, Water Conservation in N.J. for Glen Rock, N.J. Memberships: Pres. & a Fndr. of Bergen Poets; World Poetry Soc. Intercontinental; N.J. Poetry Soc.; N.Y. Poetry Forum; Pa. Poetry Soc.; Project Poetry of North Jersey Cultural Coun., Bergen Community Coll. Works in prep: Habiru, a coll. & Miniatures in Mosaic, selection of Haiku. Contbr. to: N.J. Poetry Soc. Anthols., 1971, '72, '73, '74; Wm. Carlos Williams Anthol. of Paterson Lib., 1972; World Poet; Bergen Poet Anthol. I, 1973; Project Poetry Anthol., 1973; Y Poetry Roundtable of Bergen Co., 1971, '72, '73; Stone Country Fall, '74; Swordsman's Review; Haiku; Haiku Highlights; Patterns; Bitterroot; Poet Int., etc. Radio readings on WFDU, WPAT, CATV,

1973. Honours, awards incl: 1st prize, Ricepaper Haiku Contest, N.J. Poetry Soc. & 1st prize, French Form Contest, 1971; 1st prize, Haiku Contest, ibid, 1972. Address: 197 Delmar Ave., Glen Rock, NJ 07452, U.S.A.

FALKOWSKI, Edwin Andrzej, pen names **WA-NA-KA, KASTAN, A. & ANDRZEJ, E,** b. 3 Sept. 1911. Research Specialist. Education: Doctorate in Indian Studies, Indian Assn. of Am.; Doctorate in Divinity, Mayan Temple Church; Univ. of Wis.; Layton Schl. of Art.; Milwaukee Art Inst. Ordained Min. (Missionary), 1946. Positions held: Recreation Dir.; Scenic Designer; Puppeteer; N.C. Officer in Wis. Nat. Guard; Installation Engr.; Missionary & Rsch. Specialist, etc. Memberships incl: Calif. Fed. of Chaparral Poets; V.P., Robert Frost Chapt. & Ed. of their Frostorian, ibid; Ky. State Poetry Soc.; World Poetry Soc. Intercontinental; Fellow, Int. Poetry Soc., U.K. Contbr. to: Premier Poets Anthol., 1971-72; Orbis Anthol., U.K., 1973; Wash. Poets Assn., Finalists Anthol., 1973; Indian Voice; Sandcutters; Pegasus; Cyclo-Flame; Modern Haiku; Swordsman Review; Am. Bard; Poet; Dragonfly. Honours, awards incl: First, Ariz. State Poetry Soc., 1970 (annual Haiku); First, Edw. Markham Soc., San Jose, 1970 & '73 (annual Free Verse). Has read poems for CFCP & over radio stns. Address: 208 W. Latimer Ave., Campbell, CA 95008, U.S.A.

FALLER, Kevin, b. 4 July 1920. Writer; Journalist. Education: Grad., Nat. Univ. of Ireland, Galway. Memberships: Dublin Br. Rep., PEN; Treas., ibid, 1953. Published works: Lyric & Script, 1948; Ireland Lyrics, 1963. Contbr. to following anthols: A Concord of Harps, 1952; New Poets of Ireland, 1963; Love Poems of the Irish, 1969; Penguin Book of Irish Verse, 1970. Honours: Centenary Poem Prize; Book Assn. of Gt. Britain & Ireland, 1949. Address: 274 Cloutarf Rd., Dublin 3, Republic of Ireland.

FALLIS, Laurence Sidney, b. 28 May 1936. Historian. Education: A.B., Univ. of Mich., Ann Arbor, Mich., U.S.A., 1959; M.A., ibid, 1960; Ph.D., 1966. Married. Positions held: Instr., Univ. of Manitoba, Canada; Asst. Prof., Centre Coll.; Asst. Prof., Wis. State Univ.; Assoc. Prof., Univ. of W.Fla. Mbr., Poetry Soc. of N.M. Published works: Lion's Roar, 1973; Geronimo, 1973. Contbr. to: Abbey; Amaranthus; Apalachee Quarterly; Aspect; Bardic Echoes; Bleb; Blue Cloud Quarterly; Books Abroad; Cardinal Poetry Quarterly; Corduroy; Concerning Poetry; Encore; Invisible City; J. Mark Press Publs.; Jean's Jrnl.; Middle Way; Modern Images; Orion; Stoney Lonesome. Recip., Prize, Fla. State Univ. Poetry Contest, 1972. Address: Box 3 BD Univ. Park, Las Cruces, NM 88003, U.S.A.

FALLON, Padraic, b. 3 Jan. 1905. Retired Customs Official. Married Dorothea Maher, 1930; six children. Positions held: Former Customs Official, Wexford, U.K., forty years; Retired. Memberships: Irish Acad. of Letters. Published works: Collected Poems, 1969; The Seventh Step (play), 1954; The Shield of Steel (play), 1966. Contbr. to: Bell; Dublin Mag.; Irish Times; New Writing; New Statesman; Botteghe Oscure; (anthologies) New Irish Poets, 1948; An Anthology of Irish Verse, 1948; Oxford Book of Irish Verse, 1958.

FALLON, Peter, b. 26 Feb. 1951. Writer. Education: Glenstal Abbey, Murroe, Co. Limerick; Trinity Coll., Dublin. Published works: Among the Walls, 1970; Co-incidence of Flesh, 1972. Ed: Twenty-one, 1967; Capella, 1968; Poems, 1968; Gallery Books, 1970. Recording: Voices, 1974. Poems widely published in U.S.A., U.K., India, Ireland. Broadcast on radio & TV in Ireland, U.K. & the Continent. Address: 19 Oakdown Rd., Dublin 14, Ireland.

FANTUZZO, Carmen, religious pen name **SISTER MARY JEANNETTE,** & others, b. 12 Dec. 1920. Educator. Education: B.Ed., Duquesne Univ., 1959; State Tchng. Cert., 1973; M.Ed., Fairfield Univ., 1975. Member, Order of Apostles of the Sacred Heart of Jesus. Positions held: Taught in 7 schls.; Art

Coordinator, Kansas City, Mo.; Art & English Coordinator, New Castle, Pa. Member, Catholic Poetry Soc. of Am., N.Y.C., 1956–. Contbr. to: Lady of Sorrows, Chicago, 1955-57; Lady of Pompeii, N.Y., 1962-63; Catholic Schl. Jrnl., 1954-57; Catholic Educator, 1957; News Acts of the Apostles, 1974; Nat. Catholic Reporter, 1966-67, etc. Recip., 1st prize, Bronx County Contest, 1958. Address: St. Vitus Convent, 915 South Jefferson St., New Castle, PA, U.S.A.

FARDING, Leif Juhani, b. 21 May 1951. Poet. Education: Literature & Folklore studies, Univ. of Helsinki. Memberships: Suomen kirjailijaliitto (The Union of Finnish Authors); Suomen arvostelijain liitto (The Union of Finnish Critics). Published works: (books of poetry) Maailmaa mina rakastan, 1971; Luominen, 1972; Olen onnen poika, 1973. Contbr. to: Parnasso; Aika. Honours, awards: Prize, City of Vaasa, 1972; The Lib. Prize, 1972 & 73; The Union of Finnish Authors, 1973. Address: Tennistie 3 C 39, Tapiola 02100, Finland.

FARMILOE, Dorothy, b. 8 Sept. 1920. Teacher. Education: B.A. & M.A., Univ. of Windsor, Ont., Canada. Widow w. 3 children. Positions held: Tchr., St. Clair Coll., Windsor; Co-Fndr. & Co-Ed., Mainline Mag., an independent poetry mag. Published works: The Lost Island, 1966; Z1X3, 1967; Poems for Apartment Dwellers, 1970; Winter Orange Mood, 1972; Blue is the Colour of Death, 1973; Ed., Controverse, 9 Windsor Poems, 1972. Contbr. to: Adam Int. Review; America; Beloit Poetry Jrnl.; Black Moss; Canadian Forum; Fiddlehead; Intercourse; Mainline; Connexion; Other Voices; Salt; Tide; Visions 2020; Univ. of Windsor Review; West Coast Review; Windsor Salt; Temper of the Times; Women Poets, Canada. Honours: Featured on CBC Radio Prog., Anthology, 1971. Address: P.O. Box 61, Sandwich Post Office, Windsor, Ont., Canada.

FARRELL, James Thomas, Novelist. Education: Univ. of Chicago; N.Y. Univ.; Depaul Univ. Positions held: Boatsworth Prof., Richmond Univ.; Writer-in-Res., Glassboro State Coll. Member, Nat. Inst. of Arts & Letters. Published works: The Collected Poems of James T. Farrell; When Time Was Born. Recip., hon. degree from Miami Univ., Oxford, Ohio. Address: c/o Doubleday & Co., 277 Park Ave., N.Y., NY, U.S.A.

FARREN, Robert, b. 1909. Abbey Theatre Director. Educ: Christian Brothers' Schls.; St. Patrick's Coll., Drumcondra, Ireland; M.A., Nat. Univ. of Ireland. Positions held: Dir., Abbey Theatre, Dublin, 1940–; Controller, Gaelic Progs., Radio Eireann, ibid, currently. Published works: Thronging Feet, 1936; Time's Wall Asunder, 1939; The First Exile, 1944; Rime Gentleman Please, 1951; Selected Poems, 1951; (literart criticism) Towards an Appreciation of Poetry, 1947; The Course of Irish Verse in English, 1948. Contbr. to: (anthologies) 1000 Years of Irish Poetry, 1953; Oxford Book of Irish Verse, 1958. Address: c/o Abbey Theatre, Dublin, Rep. of Ireland.

FARRIS, William Wellington, b. 26 May 1931. Interior Designer. Education: A.B., Alma Coll., Mich. Positions held: Army Chaplain; Chapter Pres., Nat. Drama Praternity; Bus. Office Mgr.; var. minor positions. Memberships: The Nat. Writers Club; The Int. Platform Assn. Published works: Sunrise Pagan – Sunset Rebel (book of poetry), 1974. Contbr. to: The Stars & Stripes; Pine River Anthol.; The Orb; The Muse; Flame; Bardic Echoes; Treasures of Parnassus; Caravan; Sunburst. Address: 1920 Biarritz Dr., Miami Beach, FL 33141, U.S.A.

FARSACE, Duverne Konrick, pen name, **SUMMERS, Diana,** b. 20 Aug. 1923 at Jasper, Texas, USA. Poet; Teacher; Editor, Publishing Company Reader; Poetry Judge. Education: B.A., liberal arts, St. Mary's Dominican Coll., New Orleans, Louisiana, 1945. Married to Larry Farsace. Positions held: Librarian, New Orleans Public Library, City Bookmobile, 1945-56; Librarian, Rochester Public Library, City

Bookmobile, 1956-62; Advance Reader, Lawyer's Co-operative Publishing Co., 1962-66, and Sr. Advance Reader, 1966 to-date; Co-editor, Golden Atom Publications, since 1956. Memberships: Avalon World Arts Acad., director/teacher of poetry workshop, Sidney Lanier (New Orleans) Chapter, 1951-56, member, since 1947, contrib. editor, 1951-53, Asst. Nat. Councillor, 1953-55, Hon. Life Member, since 1952; Nat. Poetry Day, member since 1951, Chairman for Louisiana, 1956, World Poetry Day Committee member, since 1958, Nat. Asst. Director, since 1970; Co-Chairman, Rochester World Poetry Day, since 1958, and Co-Chairman, Rochester World & Nat. Poetry Day, since 1965; Asst. Chairman, Western NY State, Nat. Poetry Day, Inc., since 1966; Co-Judge, Rochester World Poetry Day contests, since 1958, also Fed. of State Poetry Socs., Contest, Baton Rouge, Louisiana, 1966; Cyclo-Flame (Avalon) Contest, 1969; The Nolacon, New Orleans World Science Fiction Convention, 1951; CAAA; League of Am. Pen Women, 1952-56; Nat. Poetry Soc. (Contrib. Editor of official organ); American Poetry League; Rochester Poetry Soc.; Acad. of American Poets (founder member); Marquis Biog. Soc. Published works: Flame of Freedom, 1952. Contbr. to many anthols., mags., etc. Poems read over radio in Mexico and Louisiana. Recip. numerous honours & awards, including Medal (with husband) from Pres. Marcos of the Philippines, 1968, etc. Address: c/o World Poetry Day Committee, P.O. Box 1101, Rochester, NY 14603, USA.

FARSACI, Litterio B. (Larry Farsace), pen name **'THE VERY YOUNG MAN',** b. 11 Feb. 1921. Poet; Editor; Stenographer-Radiologist. Education: grad., 1st Stenographic Schl., U.S. Army, Norfolk, Va., 1943; Dip., Radiology Course, U.S. Post Office, 1970. Married Duverne Konrick. Positions held: Estab., Golden Atom, 1939; U.S. Army, 1942-46; Publr./Ed., Stars (poetry mag.), A Golden Atom Publication, 1940–; Co-Fndr. w. wife, & Co-Chmn., Rochester World Poetry Day, 1958– (now Rochester World & Nat. Poetry Day, 1965–); Co-Judge, Rochester World Poetry Day Contests, 1958-1971. Memberships incl: Hon. Life Mbr., Avalon World Arts Acad., 1956–; World Poetry Day Comm., Phila., 1958–; Asst. Chmn., Western N.Y. State Nat. Poetry Day, Miami Beach, 1966–; Asst. Nat. Dir., World Poetry Day, 1970–; Fndr.-Mbr., Acad. of Am. Poets, 1969–; Editl. & Advsry. Bd., IWWP, 1973–; Delegate, World Poetry Congress, EXPO, Montreal, 1967, etc. Published works: Fleeting Moments, 1944; Star-Bound, 1944; Enchanting Reveries, 1949; author/composer, Be With Me & other song lyrics, 1952; (Ed./Publr.) Rochester in Poetry, Past & Present, 1958; Golden Atom Special Poetry Edn., 1959; Am. Beauty, 1965; Lilac City Lyrics; The Timeless Glory, 1972. Contbr. to many anthols. & jrnls. Poetry also read over radio stns. WBUX, WEFG-FM, WHPL-AM, etc. Recip., num. hons. inclng. Medal, with wife from Pres. Marcos of the Philippines, 1968. Address: c/o World Poetry Day Comm., P.O. Box 1101, Rochester, NY 14603, U.S.A.

FASSNIDGE, Christopher James, b. 6 Sept. 1939. Actor; Writer. Education: B.A., Christ Church, Oxford Univ., U.K.; postgrad. qualifications in Social Work, London Schl. of Econs. & Birmingham Univ. Married Virginia, 2 children. Positions held: Probation Officer, London Probation Serv., 1963-65; Tchr. of Engl., Drama, Social Studies, Film-making, Monkton Wyld Schl., Charmouth, Dorset; Actor/Writer w. Word & Action (Dorset) – service in drama, theatre & writing, 1973–. Published works: The Axe-head: a Collection of 41 poems, 1971; Vibrations: a one-act play, part one of 'Two Plays from Pandora's Box', 1973. Contbr. to: Spectator; Chesil, mag. of Chesil Poets. Address: 186, Newstead Road, Westham, Weymouth, Dorset, U.K.

FAULKNER, Peter William, pen name **FAULKNER, Pete,** b. 19 Jan. 1953. Art Student. Education: Dundee Coll. of Commerce, 1970-71; Bristol Coll. of Art, 1971-73; Dip. AD Illustration. Positions held: Reviewer, 'BOGG'. Contbr. to: Akros; Amazing Grace (poems & drawings); BOGG; Global Tapestry; Good Elf; Ludd's

Mill; Open Circle; Pommegranite; Scrip; Viewpoints; Somethings; Leaves; Sandwiches; Moonshine, etc. Sev. unpublished colls. of poems inclng: Between the Silences, 1970; The Smell of Rain, 1971. Chosen to appear at POEM 73 (a one day poetry festival held at Edinburgh Univ., 1973). Address: 'Amstel', Turfbeg Ave., Forfar, Angus, DD8 3LJ, U.K.

FAUST, Naomi. College Professor. Education: A.B., Bennett Coll., Greensboro, N.C.; M.A., Univ. of Mich., Ann Arbor; Ph.D., N.Y. Univ. Positions held at: Granard H.S., Gaffney, S.C.; Atkins H.S., Winston-Salem, N.C.; Bennett Coll., Greensboro, N.C.; Southern Univ., Scotlandville, La.; Morgan State Coll., Baltimore, Md.; Dudley H.S., Greensboro, N.C.; N.Y. City Public Schls.; Queens Coll., Flushing, N.Y. Memberships: World Poetry Soc. Intercontinental; The N.Y. Poetry Forum; South & West, Inc.; NEA; AAUP; Nat. Coun. of Tchrs. of Engl. Contbr. to: Poet; South & West Int. Lit. Qtly.; Poetry Prevue Mag.; Cyclo-flame Mag.; Poems by Blacks; Written Word; Nat. Poetry Anthol. Honours, awards: Prize & Cert. of Merit, Cooper Hill Writers Conf., 1970; Cert. of Merit, Poems by Blacks, 1970. Address: Queens Coll. of the City Univ. of N.Y., Flushing, NY 11367, U.S.A.

FAYE, Jean Pierre, b. 19 July 1925. Writer. Education: studied philos. & econs. Founder of the Collectif Change with Jacques Roubaud. Published works: Fleuve renversé, 1969; Couleurs pliées, 1965; Le change, 1968; Verres, 1970; Traits, 1971. Contbr. to: Review 'Change'; NRF; Mercure de France; Tel Quel; Lettres Françaises; Opus; Temps Moderne. Recip., Prix Renaudot.

FEASEY, Paul, b. 15 Mar. 1951. Driver. Member, Portsmouth Poetry Soc. Contbr. to Hampshire Poets, 1973. Address: 57 Copperfield House, Wingfield St., Landport, Portsmouth, Hants., U.K.

FEDDEN, Robin, b. 26 Nov. 1908. Deputy-Director General, The National Trust. Positions held: Ed., Personal Landscape, Cairo, 1942-45; Dpty.-Dir. Gen., The Nat. Trust, currently. Published works: Suicide: A Social and Historical Study, 1938; Land of Egypt, 1939; Syria, 1946; Crusader Castles, 1950; The Enchanted Mountains, 1962; Chantemesle, 1964; The Continuing Purpose: A History of the National Trust, Its Aims and Work, 1968; The White Country (Poetry), 1968; As the Unicorn (novel), 1933. Contbr. to: Personal Landscape, 1945; Poetry of the Forties, 1968. Address: 20 Eldon Rd., London, W.8, U.K.

FEDERMAN, Raymond, b. 15 May 1928. Writer; Professor of Literature. Education: B.A., Columbia Univ., 1957; M.A., Univ. of Calif. at Los Angeles, 1958; Ph.D., ibid, 1963. Married Erica Hubscher, 1 daughter. Positions held: Asst. Prof., Univ. of Calif. at Santa Barbara, 1961-64; Assoc. Prof., State Univ. of N.Y. at Buffalo, 1964-68; Prof., ibid, 1968–. Member, Bd. of Consultants, Coordinating Coun. of Lit. Mags., 1972–. Published works: Temporary Landscapes (bilingual poems), 1965; Among the Beasts/Parmi les Monstres (bilingual poems), 1967; Double or Nothing (novel), 1971; Amer Eldorado (novel), 1974. Contbr. to: Big Table; Evergreen Review; Genesis West; Westcoast Review; Adam; Tempest; Partisan Review; Uclan; Mica; Buffalo Evening News; Le Monde; (anthols.) Imaged Words & Worded Images; Breakthrough Fictioneers; Future's Fiction; One Summer, etc. Honours, awards: The France Steloff Fiction Prize, 1971; The Panache Expmt. Writing Prize, 1972. Address: 227 Depew Ave., Buffalo, NY 14214, U.S.A.

FEINMAN, Alvin, b. 21 Nov. 1929. College Teacher. Education: B.A., Brooklyn Coll., N.Y.C., 1951; M.A., Yale Univ., 1953; Fulbright Scholar, Heidelberg Univ., 1954-55. Positions held: Taught philos. & lit. at var. colls. & univs.; Member, Literature Fac., Bennington Coll., Vt., 1969–. Published works: Preambles & Other Poems, 1964. Contbr. to: Yale Review; Harper's; Silo. Rep. in following anthols. & colls.: Poems of Our moment; Pocket Book of Modern Verse; Pocket Anthology of American Verse; The Contemporary

American Poets, Shake the Kaleidescope. Address: c/o Bennington Coll., Bennington, VT 05201, U.S.A.

FEIRSTEIN, Frederick, b. 2 Jan. 1940. Writer. Education: B.A., Univ. of Buffalo, U.S.A., 1960; M.A. in Engl., N.Y.U., 1961; currently training to become a psychoanalyst at NPAP. Memberships: Dramatists Guild; Actors Studio Playwrights Unit. Published works: Survivors (poems), 1974; The Family Circle (a play), 1973. Contbr. to: Arts in Society; Beloit Poetry Jrnl.; Choice; Counter/Measures; Qtly. Review of Literature; The Nation; Shenandoah; Southwest Review; University Review. Address: 355 East 86th St., N.Y., NY 10028, U.S.A.

FELDMAN, Alan, b. 16 Mar. 1945. Assistant Professor. Education: A.B., Columbia Coll., U.S.A.; M.A., ibid; Ph.D., State Univ. of N.Y. at Buffalo. Married Nanette Hass, 1 child. Positions held: Tchr., N.Y. City Public Schls., 1966-70; Grad. Asst., State Univ. of N.Y., 1970-72; Asst. Prof., Framingham State Coll., 1972-. Chief Ed., Columbia Review. Published works: The Household, 1966; summer 1972 issue of Audit/Poetry. Contbr. to: New American Review; Columbia Review; Columbia Forum; Panache; Sun; First Issue; Mulberry; Charlie; College English. Address: Dept. of Engl., Framingham State Coll., Framingham, MA 01701, U.S.A.

FELDMAN, Irving Mordecai, b. 22 Sept. 1928. Teacher. Education: B.S.S.S., CCNY, U.S.A., 1950; M.A., Columbia Univ., 1953. Positions held: Instr. of Engl., Univ. of Puerto Rico, 1954-56; Lecteur américain, Univ. de Lyon, 1957-58; Asst. Prof. of Engl., Kenyon Coll., 1958-63; Prof. of Engl., State Univ. of N.Y., Buffalo, N.Y., 1964-. Published works: Works & Days, & Other Poems, 1961; The Pripet Marshes, & Other Poems, 1965; Magic Papers, & Other Poems, 1970; Lost Originals (poems), 1972. Contbr. to: New Yorker; Atlantic; Harper's Bazaar; Harper's Poetry; Commentary; Midstream; N.Y. Times; Saturday Review; New Am. Review; Am. Review; Partisan Review; Kenyon Review; Book Week; New Republic; Va. Quarterly Review; New World Writing, etc. Honours, awards: Kovner Prize, Jewish Book Soc. of Am., 1962; Nat. Inst. of Arts & Letters Grant, 1973; Guggenheim Fellowship, 1973. Address: Dept. of Engl., State Univ. of N.Y., Buffalo, NY 14214, U.S.A.

FELDMAN, Miroslav, b. 28 Dec. 1899. Doctor of Medicine; Writer. Education: Med. Fac., Vienna. Positions held: var. important positions as a doctor such as Chief of a Dept. & Dir. of a Hosp. Memberships: Pres., Assn. of Writers of Croatia; Pres., PEN, Zagreb Ctr. & Assn. of Yugoslavia. Published works: (colls. of poems) Iza sunca, 1920; Arhipelag snova, 1927; Ratna lirika, 1936; Poems, 1955; Pitat će kako je bilo, 1959; Izabrane pjesme, 1964; (Plays) Vožnja, 1927; Zec, 1932; Gospoda Dor, 1931; Profesor Zič, 1934; Na uglu, 1935; Srna, 1936; U pozadini, 1939; Iz mraka, 1946; Doci ce dan, 1947; Three plays, 1955; Drame, 1964. Contbr. to many periodicals, reviews & anthols. Honours, awards: Award, Assn. of Writers of Croatia for 'Poems', 1955; Demeter's Award for the play 'The Hare', 1933; Demeter's Award for the play 'In the Background', 1939; Vladimir Nazor Prize for his life's work, 1972. Address: Gajdekova 3, 41000 Zagreb, Yugoslavia.

FELDMAN, Ruth (Wasby), b. 21 May 1911. Poet; Translator. Education: B.A., Wellesley Coll., 1931; Poetry Workshops, Boston Univ. & Radcliffe. Memberships: Poetry Soc. of Am.; New England Poetry Club; Am. Translators' Assn. Published works: transl. from the Italian w. Brian Swann, The Collected Poems of Lucio Piccolo, 1973, Poetry, Quarterly Review of Literature, Texas Quarterly, Chelsea, Nation, Partisan Review, Books Abroad, Mundus Artium, Forum Italioum, Antaeus, Granite, New Directions Annual, Poetry Review; articles & short stories in Mediterranean Review. Contbr. to: N.Y. Times; N.Y. Times Book of Verse; Mich. Quarterly Review; The Lit. Review; Prairie Schooner; Yankee; Commonweal; Malahat Review; Colloquy; Arion's

Dolphin; Western Review; Southern Poetry Review; The New Renaissance; Poet Lore; United Church Herald; Voices; N.M. Mag.; New Orlando Anthol.; Denver Post Poetry Forum; South & West, etc. Honours, awards: Poet Lore Hon. Mention, 1970; Poetry Soc. of Am. Devil's Advocate Award, 1972, etc. Address: 221 Mt. Auburn St., Cambridge, MA 02138, U.S.A.

FELDMANN, Annette B., b. 7 Jan. 1919. Former Translator of French for U.S. Customs. Education: Phoenix Jr. Coll., Ariz.; Scholarship in Dramatic Workshop, New Schl. for Soc. Rsch.; Breadloaf Writers Conf.; Cooper Hill Writers' Conf. Memberships: Pres. & Fndr., Shelley Soc. of N.Y.; Keats-Shelley Meml. Assn. of N.Y.; Byron Soc.; N.Y. Histl. Soc.; Poetry Soc. of Am.; N.Y. Poetry Forum; Mark Twain Assn. Author of articles & travels in Greece, Italy, Turkey & Mexico concerning visits to archaeological & lit. sites. Formerly Poetry Ed. of Writers Voice. Contbr. to: Poet Lore; Bitterroot; South & West; New Orlando Poetry Anthol.; Hartford Courant; South & West; Wis. Poetry Mag.; Denver Post; 'La Rvue Moderne', Paris. Honours, awards: Winner, one act play contest; Winner, Third Prize, Phila. Writers Conf. Poetry recorded from Wis. Poetry Mag. Address: Apt. 322, 144-20-41st Ave., Flushing, NY 11355, U.S.A.

FELL, James Black, b. 14 Aug. 1892. Farmer. Education: Isle of Wight Coll., UK; Bedford Grammar Schl.; Scarborough Coll.; Pvte Tutors. Personal details: descendant of John Fell, Dean of Christ Ch., Fndr. of Oxford Univ. Positions held: Rep., Min. of Agric. on river bds., etc. Memberships: Poetry Soc.; VP, Geneva Arts Club. Published works: Song of Noel, 1961. Unpublished works: Christ Enthroned, epic poem; Sussex Poems; Essex Poems; Isle of Wight Prometheus, imaginative reconstruction of the Aeschylean Trilogy. Contbr. to: NY Times; Brighton Herald. Address: 1 Stanford Rd., Brighton, Sussex, UK.

FELSENFELD, Rosella Lee, b. 6 June 1941. Teacher; Poet. Education: B.A., Roosevelt Univ., Chicago, 1962; M.A., Engl., Northwestern Univ., Evanston, 1967; currently working on Ph.D., Univ. of Wis., Milwaukee. Married Herb Felsenfeld, 1 daughter. Positions held: Tchr., H.S., Chicago, Denver, Park Ridge, Ill. & Milwaukee for 8 yrs.; currently Tchng. Asst., Univ. of Wis., Milwaukee. Memberships: Wis. Poet in the Schls.; Past Mbr., Milwaukee Women's Poetry Collective; Women's Caucus of Modern Lang. Assn. Published works: People's Live's Honey, People's Lives, 1971; Sometimes Semeramis (book in progress). Contbr. to: Kaleidoscope; Bugle American; Amazon; Offstage Voice; Street Sheet. Featured in Bugle Am's Wis. Poets, 1972. Address: 2728 N. Prospect, Milwaukee, WI 53211, U.S.A.

FERICANO, Paul Francis, pen name **ANTHONY, P.F.,** b. 16 Jan. 1951. Freelance Writer. Education: Career Acad. Schl. of Broadcasting, San Francisco, Calif.; Univ. of Calif., Berkeley; Calif. State Coll., Hayward; San Francisco State Coll.; Skyline Coll., San Bruno. Married. Positions held: Radio Disc Jockey; Computer Operator; Poet/Lectr. var. High Schls., etc. Memberships: World Poetry Soc. Intercontinental; Int. Platform Assn.; Am. Poets Fellowship Soc. Contbr. to: Jean's Jrnl.; United Poets; The Am. Poet; Prairie Poet; Tweed; Penelope; Mary's Scrapbook; Poet; The Fringe Press; Kansas Kernels; Quintessence; Texas Traveler; The Creative Urge; Orphic Lute. Recip., 1st prize, Poetry & Fiction, AAUW, 1969. Address: 105 La Cruz, Apt. 17, Millbrae, CA 94030, U.S.A.

FERLINGHETTI, Lawrence, b. 24 Mar. 1919 or 1920. Writer; Poet. Education: A.B., Univ. of NC; M.A., Columbia Univ.; Doct., Sorbonne Univ., Paris, France, 1951. Positions held: w. Time Mag., after WWII; Tchr. of French, Adult Educ. Prog., San Francisco, USA; Fndr., City Lights Books; Co-Ed., Journal for the Protection of All Beings & Interim Pad; Ed., City Lights Annual Journal; Participant, w. Allen Ginsberg, Pan-

Am. Cultural Conf., Univ of Concepcion, Chile, S. Am. Published works: Pictures of the Gone World, 1955; Tentative Description of a Dinner Given to Promote the Impeachment of President Eisenhower, 1958; Starting from San Francisco, 1961 & '67; An Eye on the World, 1967; The Secret Meaning of Things, 1969; A Coney Island of the Mind; After the Cries of the Birds; Moscow in the Wilderness, Segovia in the Snow; Her; Routines; Unfair Arguments with Existence. Contbr. to: San Francisco Chronicle; Counterpoint; Inferno; Goad; Art Digest; California Quarterly; Miscellaneous Man; Nation; Hearse; Evergreen Review; Chicago Review; Big Table; L'Express; Les Lettres Nouvelles; Chelsea; Swank; Liberation; Outsider; Root & Branch; City Lights Journal; Carolina Quarterly; Les Temps Modernes; Fux Magascene; Isis; Cahiers des Midis, etc. Address: c/o New Direction Publishing Corp., 333 Sixth Ave., New York, NY 10014, USA.

FERNANDEZ, Daniel, b. 4 Apr. 1938. Proof Reader. Education: B.A., Columbia Coll., 1958. Married. Member, Bd., N.Y. Poetry Forum. Published works: Apples From Hesperides, 1971. Contbr. to: The Lyric; Apollo XI; Saratoga News. Honours, awards: 2nd Prize for poetic drama 'Phaedra' (produced at Villa Montalvo, 1968 & '69), Calif. Olympiad of the Arts, 1968; First prize for heroic drama 'Tupac Amaro, the Last of the Incas', ibid, 1972; Special Award for 'The Loves of Schopenhauer', 1972. Address: 601 West 176th St., N.Y., NY 10033, U.S.A.

FERNANDO, Joseph Patrick, b. 17 Mar. 1931. Government Tax Official. Education: B.A., Univ. of Ceylon, 1948; Harvard Univ., U.S.A., 1 yr. (studying Taxation, on scholarship given by Ceylon Govt.), 1972. Married, 4 children. Positions held: Tchr., Engl. & Latin, 1 yr.; Entered Public Service in 1953 & is currently Asst. Commnr. of Inland Revenue. Ed., Ceylon Sect., New Voices of the Commonwealth, 1965. Published works: The Return of Ulysses, 1955. Contbr. to: Poetry Peradeniya Univ. of Ceylon); Community (Jrnl. of Soc. & the Arts); Young C'wealth Poets '65; C'wealth Poems of Today, 1967; New Voices of the C'wealth, 1968; The Key of The Kingdom, vol. 4, anthol., 1963. Address: Dept. of Inland Revenue, New Secretariat, Republic Sq., Colombo, Sri Lanka.

FERRETT, Mabel, b. 30 Apr. 1917. Poet. Education: Tchrs. Cert. Married, 1 son. Currently working at the Red House Museum, Somersal, Cleckheaton, Yorks. Memberships: Libn., Yorks. Poets' Assn.; Comm. Mbr., Int. Poetry Soc.; Soc. of Women Writers & Journalists; Halifax Authors Circle; Fndr.-Pres., Spar Valley Histl. Soc. Published works: The Lynx-eyed Strangers, 1956; The Tall Tower, 1971. Ed. of qtly. mag., Pennine Platform, 1973–. Contbr. to: Yorkshire Observer; Chamber's Jrnl.; Yorkshire Life; The Dalesman; Yorkshire Observer Budget; John o'London's; Outposts; John Bull; Ore; Homes & Gardens; East Anglian Mag.; The Yorkshire Post; The Home Owner; Yorkshire Ridings Mag.; Pennine Anthol.; Pennine Platform; BBC; BBC Radio Leeds. Address: 2 Vernon Rd., Heckmondwike WF16 9LU, Yorks., U.K.

FERRIL, Thomas Hornsby, b. 25 Feb. 1896. Publisher; Editor. Educ: A.B., Colo. Coll., 1918. Married Helen R. Ferril. Positions held: Off., Air Serv.; Former Drama Critic, Denver Times; Employed w. Gt. Western Sugar Co., 1926–; Publr. & Ed., The Rocky Mountain Herald, 1939–. Memberships: Writers Conf., Colo. Univ. Published works: High Passage, 1926; Westering, 1934; Trial by Time, 1944; New and Selected Poems, 1952; Words for Denver, 1966; Ed., Rocky Mountain Herald Reader, 1966; And Perhaps Happiness (verse play), 1958; I Hate Thursday (essays), 1946. Contbr. to: (anthologies) Anthology of American Poetry, 1941; Eternal Sea, 1946; New Poems by American Poets, 1957; Golden Year, 1960. Honours, awards: Yale Series of Younger Poets Prize, 1926; Oscar Blumenthal Prize, 1937; Robert Frost Poetry Prize, 1960; Ridgely Torrence Prize, 1963; Hon. degrees

from Colo. Coll., Colo. Univ., Denver Univ. Address: 2123 Downing St., Denver, CO 80205, U.S.A.

FERRY, David Russell, pen name FERRY, David, b. 5 Mar. 1924. Professor of English. Education: B.A., Amherst Coll., 1948; M.A., Ph.D., Harvard Univ., 1949, 1955. Married, Anne Davidson, 2 children. Positions held: Instr. to Prof. of Engl., Wellesley Coll., and currently Sophie Chantal Hart Prof. of Engl. Member, Selection Committee, New England Poetry Circuit. Published work: On the Way to the Island, 1960. Contbr. to: The Kenyon Review; The New Yorker; The Nation; The Paris Review; The Partisan Review; Poetry, and many others. Address: Dept. of Engl., Wellesley Coll., Wellesley, MA 02181, USA.

FERTIG, Nelle, b. 1 Oct. 1919. Teacher. Education: A.B., Whittier Coll.; M.A., Cal. State Univ., Los Angeles. Personal details: Married to Dr. Norman R. Fertig (USC Associate Dean); 4 s. Positions held: Teacher (elem. School), 21 yrs.; Part-time Instr., Dept. Spec. Ed. Cal. State Univ., L.A., 5 yrs.; Instr. of Poetry and Creative Writing Class, Arroyo Adult School, 1 yr.; Instr. of Poetry Class, Coronado Adult Center, 2 yrs. Memberships: Acad. of American Poets; Calif. Fed of Chaparral Poets; Calif. State Poetry Soc.; Poetry Soc. of Texas; South & West, Inc; Ina Coolbrith Circle; Edwin Markham Poetry Soc.; Internat. Poetry Soc. Published work: The Brittle Distance, 1974. Contbr. to: Poet Lore; South & West; Descant; Calif. State Poetry Qtly.; Cardinal Poetry Qtly.; Imprints Qtly.; Legend; Poet (India); Poetry Parade; Quoin; Voices Internat.; The Swordsman Review; Siteman/Brodhead (radio-TV); American Bard; The Archer; Calif. English Journal; Cyclo-Flame; Modern Haiku; Haiku West; Janus-SCTH; Dragonfly; Encore; Alhambra Post-Advocate; Montebello Journal; Saline County Pacesetter; Rall's Banner, and various anthols. and yearbooks of Poetry Soc. of Texas, Florida State Poetry Soc., J. Mark Press, Ina Coolbrith Circle, South & West, Inc., etc. Awards: 1973: Nat. Fed. State Poetry Socs., book publication award (sponsored by South & West, Inc.), 3rd prize, 8 HM's; Deep South Writers & Artists Conference, 1st & 2nd prize, and HM; Arkansas Writers Conference, 2nd & 3rd prizes; C.F.C.P. annuals, 2nd prize, 2 HM's, commendable excellence; Edwin Markham, 3rd prize; CFCP monthlies: 1st prize & 2 HM's; 1972: CFCP annuals, Golden Pegasus Sweepstakes Award, 1st, 2nd & 3rd prizes; Poetry Soc. of Texas annuals, 6 1sts, 1 2nd, 4 3rd prizes; Edwin Markham, 1st and 3rd prizes; South & West Convention, 2nd prize; CFCP monthlies, 1st and 2nd prizes; 1st & 4th Prize, Calif. Fed. Chaparral Poets (Annual), 1969; two 1sts, a 6th, 8th & 11th, 1970; 1st, 5th, 9th, 10th, 1971; various placings in Open Monthlies, four 1sts, 2nd & 3rd, Poetry Soc. of Tex. (Annual), 1969; 1st, 2nd & three 3rds, 1970; 2nd, 5th & 7th in Grand Prix, NFSPS, 1970; 1st, free verse, Southwest Lit. Festival, 1970; two 3rd place Publishers' awards, 1968 & '69; 1st & 2nd, Edwin Markham Poetry Soc., 1970; 2nd, 1971; 2nd, Alhambra Post-Advocate & Aeolian Soc. Open Contest, 1968; Recip. of var. awards of Recognition, Achievement, Merit or Commendable Excellence; Anonymous Donor Award, Modern Haiku, 1971. Address: 11143 McGirk Ave., El Monte, CA 91731, USA.

FICOWSKI, Jerzy, b. 4 Sept. 1924. Writer. Education: Philos. & Sociol., Univ. of Warsaw, Poland. Memberships: Polish Lit. Union, 1948–; Gypsy Lore Soc., Edinburgh-Liverpool, 1949–; Mbr. of Presidium of Polish Writers Union, 1956-59; PEN Club, Polish Ctr., Warsaw, 1969–. Published works: (books of poetry) Olowiani Zolnierze, 1948; Zwierzenia, 1952; Po Polsku, 1955; Moje Strony Swiata, 1957; Makowskie Bajki, 1959; Amulety i Definicje, 1960; Pismo Obrazkowe, 1962; Ptak Poza Ptakiem, 1968; Wiersze Niektore, 1971; (poetry for children) Tecza na Niedziele, 1970; Daje Slowo Kolorowe, 1973, etc. Has translated var. works & his own poetry has been translated into French, Italian, German, Russian, Hebrew, etc. Contbr. to var. Polish mags., jrnls. Address: ul Zywnego 16/43, 02-701 Warsaw, Poland.

FIEDLER, Leslie A., b. 8 Mar. 1917. Professor of English. Education: B.A., N.Y. Univ., 1938; M.A., Univ. of Wis., 1939; Ph.D., ibid, 1941; post doctoral study, Harvard Univ., 1944, '47. Married Sally Andersen Fiedler, 8 children. Positions held: Montana State Univ., 1941-63; Chmn. of Dept., ibid, 1954-56; Prof. of Engl., SUNY, Buffalo, 1964– & Assoc. Fellow of the Calhoun Coll., Yale Univ.; Vis. Prof. at var. o'seas & Am. univs. Memberships: AAUP; MLA; English Inst.; PEN Club; Dante Soc. of Am. Published works: (books) Waiting for the End, 1964; Back to China, 1965; The Continuing Debate (w. Jacob Vinocur), 1964; Love & Death in the American Novel (rev. new edn.), 1966; The Last Jew in America, 1966; The Return of the Vanishing American, 1968; Nude Croquet & Other Stories, 1969; Being Busted, 1970; The Collected Essays of Leslie Fiedler, 1971; The Stranger in Shakespeare, 1972, & many others. Contbr. of num. critical & review articles as well as poetry & short fiction to periodicals in many countries. Honours, awards: Furioso Poetry Prize; Prize story reprinted in the Martha Foley Coll.; Prize awarded by the Nat. Inst. of Arts & Letters, 1957. Address: 154 Morris Ave., Buffalo, NY 14214, U.S.A.

FIELD, Edward. Writer. Published works: Stand Up, Friend, With Me, 1963; Variety Photoplays, 1967. Contbr. to: Evergreen Review; New York Review of Books; New American Review; New Directions; Annuals; New York Review of Sex & Politics; Gay Sunshine; Amigo; Jeopardy, etc. Awards: Lamont Award, 1962; Guggenheim Fellowship, 1963. Address: PO Box 72, Village PO, New York, NY 10014, USA.

FIELDS, Julia, b. 21 Jan. 1938. Housewife. Education: Knoxville Coll.; Middlebury Coll. Positions held: Tchr. of English in H.S., Birmingham, Ala., 1961-64; Tchr. of Poetic Arts, Hampton Inst., 1969-70. Published works: Poems, 1968; East of Moonlight, 1973. Contbr. to: The pilot; The Mass. Review; Black World; A History of the South; Essence, etc. Honours, awards: Woodrow Wilson Fellowship, 1968; Nat. Endowment for the Arts & Humanities Awards, 1969-70-71; Conrad Kent Rivers Award, 1973. Address: P.O. Box 209, Scotland Neck, NC 27874, U.S.A.

FIELEKE, Catharine Nicholson, b. 27 Sept. 1909. Freelance Writer. Education: Drury Coll.; Olivet Coll.; Univ. of Chicago, Ill. Widow, 7 children. Memberships: Social Chmn., Pres., Am. Pen Women, Chicago Br.; World Soc. of Poets Intercontinental; Nat. Writers Club; Am. Acad. of Poets; Chicago Poets & Patrons; Ill. State Poetry Soc. Contbr. to: Chicago Daily News; Am. Pen Woman Mag.; Ill. State Poetry Bulletin; Friends of Am. Lit., ibid; Int. Biographical Assn. Mag.; Poet; The Lyric; The Va. Qtly. Review, etc. Has written 22 scripts for educational tapes, comprising the Am. Poetry Series, produced & marketed by Imperial Int. Learning, of Kankakee, Ill. Recip. var. poetry prizes. Address: 312 Ohio St., Momence, IL 60954, U.S.A.

FIGUEROA, John Joseph Maria, b. 4 Aug. 1920. University Professor; Writer. Education: Holy Cross Coll., Worcester, Mass.; London Univ. & Ind. Univ.; A.B.; T.D.; M.A., (Lond.); Lit. Hum. D. Married Dorothy Alexander. Positions held: Lectr. in Engl. & Philos., London Univ., 1949-53; Sr. Lectr., Univ. of W. Indies, 1953-58; Vis. Prof., Ind. Univ., 1965-66; Prof. of Educ., Univ. of W. Indies, & Hd. of Dept. of Educ., 1958-72; Vis. Prof. & Cons., Univ. of Puerto Rico., Rio Piedras & Cayey, 1971-73; Prof. of Humanities, Cons. on Educ. Dev. & Community Learning, Caribbean Ctr. for Postgrad. Studies, 1973–. Memberships: PEN Int. (one time Pres. of the Jamaica PEN); Athaeneum Club, London. Published works: Blue Mountain Peak, 1944; Love Leaps Here, 1962; Designed, edited, collected, The Caribbean Voices Anthol.; Society Schools and Progress in the West Indies, 1971. Contbr. to: The London Mag.; Bim; Focus; America; C'wealth Poetry; Caribbean Qtly.; Jamaica Jrnl.; The Crusader; The Londinian; Revista Interamericana. Commnd. to write & read poem for C'wealth Fest. of Arts, London, 1965. Address: Caribbean Ctr. for Postgrad. Studies, P.O. Box 757, Caroline, Puerto

Rico 00630.

FIGUEROA, José-Angel, b. 28 Nov. 1946. Poet; Writer; Lecturer; Columnist; Teacher; Actor. Education: B.S., N.Y. Univ., 1965-70, '71-72; M.A., SUNY, Buffalo, 1971. Married Taina Lozano, 3 children. Positions held: Asst. Dir., Casita Maria Inc.; Dir., So. East BX St. Acad., 1970; Tchr.-Instr., Parkeast H.S.; Instr., CUNY & SUNY at Buffalo, & Columbia University's 'P.D.D.' Prog.; Unit Co-ordinator (Supvsr.-Admnstr.), Youth Enrichment Services (Urban League), 1972-73; Asst. Dir., Aspira Inc., 1973–. Memberships incl: Co-Fndr., Puerto Rican in the Arts; Past Mbr., Borinquen Artist Guild. Published works incl: (books) East 110th Street; Broadside Series 66 'X Pressing Feelings'; Boricua (poems from noo jork); (plays) The Lead Box That Couldn't Be Opened (adapted, edited, transl. & revised). Contbr. to var. jrnls., anthols., newspapers, mags. & also to Radio & TV. Recip. var. hons. Address: 751 Walton Ave., No. 26B, Bronx, NY 10451, U.S.A.

FILIPOFF, Boris, b. 6 Aug. 1905. Writer. Education: Leningrad Oriental Inst., U.S.S.R., 1924-28; Leningrad Inst. of Indl. Construction (Glavstroyprom), 1930-34. Positions held: Engrng. & Econ. Planning in Leningrad Construction Enterprises, 1928-36; Freelance Jrnlst. for the 'Voice of America', N.Y., 1951-54; Researcher, Publisher, Ed., Wash. D.C., 1954-68; Assoc. Prof., Am. Univ. Grad. Schl., Wash. D.C., 1968–; Ed. Published works: all books in Russian, publd. in the U.S.A. (poetry) Scythian Wind, 1959; Foul Weather, 1960; Burden of Time, 1961; Frontiers, 1962; Chills of Eternity, 1964; In 30 Years, 1973; (poetry & prose) The Dimmed Window, 1967; The Wind Turns Crisper, 1969; In Passing, 1970; Legends from the Times of Old, 1971. Contbr. to: Diasporas Muse, Germany (anthol.); Sodruzhestvo, U.S.A. (anthol.); Grani; Mosty, etc. Address: Am. Univ., Dept. of Lit. & Linguistics, Wash. D.C., U.S.A.

FINCH, Donald G., b. 30 June 1937. Poet. Education: Bradley Univ. Positions held: Radio operator in USAF.; Clerk, Peoria Post Office; Salesman. Membership: Peoria Poetry Club (past vice-pres.). Published works: On Strawberry Eve, 1972; She Waits For Me, 1972; A Dandelion Is Not A Rose, 1973. Contbr. to: Columns Northwest; Twigs; Univ. Review; Mississippi Review; The Villager; Human Voice Qtly.; Dust; The Christian; Nuggets; Cyclo-Flame; The Saint; Explorer; North American Mentor; Veterans Voices; Penman Mag.; The Archer; American Bard; Encore; etc. Awards: Writer of The Year Bell's Letters, 1967; 3rd place, Village Post Talent Search, 1966; Hon. Mention, Rochester Poetry Day, 1966; Feature write-up in The Muse, 1967; 2nd place, Kentucky State Poetry Soc. Contest, 1971. Address: The Jefferson House, 235 S.W. Jefferson At Liberty, Room 133, Peoria, IL 61602, USA.

FINCH, Peter, b. 6 Mar. 1947. Ex Local Government Employee. Married. Positions held: Ed., Second Aeon; Mgr., Oriel Bookshop, Welsh Arts Coun.; Writes small press column, Margins mag. Memberships: Coun. Mbr., Poetry Soc.; Treas., Assn. of Little Presses; Welsh Rep. of Poets Conference. Published works: Wanted, 1968; Pieces of the Universe, 1969; Cycle of the Suns, 1970; Beyond the Silence, 1970; An Alteration in the Way I Breathe, 1970; The Edge of Tomorrow, 1971; The End of the Vision, 1971; Whitesung, 1972; Blats, 1972; Antarktika, 1973. Contbr. to: Second Aeon; Transatlantic Review; Poetry Wales; Poetry Review; Anglo-Welsh Review; Planet; Strange Faeces; Oasis; Decal Review; Second Coming; Gargantua; Amazing Grace; Toyon Review; Ore; Pause; Bogg; Ophir, etc. Recip., Welsh Arts Coun. Bursary for Concrete Poetry, 1969. Address: 3 Maplewood Court, Maplewood Ave., Llandaf North, Cardiff CF4 2NB, U.K.

FINCH, Robert Duer Claydon, b. 14 May 1900. University Professor. Education: Univ. of Toronto, Canada & Sorbonne, Paris, France. Positions held:

successively Lectr., Asst. Prof., Assoc. Prof., Full Prof., Univ. of Toronto, Sect. of French Lang. & Lit., 1928-70; Prof. Emeritus, ibid, 1970–. Fndr. Mbr., League of Canadian Poets. Published works: (books) New Provinces (w. others), 1936; Poems, 1946; The Strength of the Hills, 1948; Acis in Oxford, 1959; Acis in Oxford (new edn.), 1961; Dover Beach Revisited, 1961; Silverthorn Bush, 1966. Contbr. to: Canadian Forum; Saturday Night; Living Age; Literary Digest; Poetry (Chicago); Canadian Poetry Mag.; The Fiddlehead; Here & Now, Toronto; SUR (S.Am.); Punch (U.K.); The Lit. Review (USA); Anthol. of Modern Canadian Poetry, 1942; The Book of Canadian Poetry, 1943; New Directions (N.Y.); Oxford Book of Canadian Verse, 1960, etc. Honours, awards: Gov. Gen's Prize (best book of verse for the year), 1946 & 61; Lorne Pierce Prize & Gold Medal, Royal Soc. of Canada, 1968, etc. Address: Massey Coll., Univ. of Toronto, Toronto M5S 2E1, Ont., Canada.

FINCH, Vivienne, b. 4 June 1946. Writer; Journalist. Positions held: Company Secretary; Translator. Memberships: Soc. of Women Writers & Jrnlsts.; The Poetry Soc. Published works: The Itinerant Dreamer, 1972. Contbr. to: Prospice; Little Word Machine; Roots; Pink Peace; Next Wave; Orbis; Scrip; Agog; Bogg; Contac; Envoi; Ataraxia; Overspill; Outposts; Osgoldcross Review; New Headland; Here Now; Gargantua; Oasis; Writers Review; Good Elf; Village Review. Address: 56 Blakes Ln., New Malden, Surrey KT3 6NX, U.K.

FINDLAY, Norman Edward, pen names & PAUL TARQUIN, b. 15 Aug. 1920. Accountancy Assistant. Positions held: served in a variety of clerical capacities w: British Railways; East Midlands Gas Brd.; Nottingham City Transport; Trent River Authority; RAF, 1941-45. Memberships: Sec., Nottingham Poetry Soc., U.K.; Nottingham Writers Club. Published works: Medals for the Terrace, 1974; Elephants in a Wild Garden, 1974. Contbr. to: Outposts; Punch; Envoi; Listener; Poetry Review; Scrip; Cornhill Mag.; Country Mag.; Breakthro'; BBC Radio progs. Work featured at many Festival poetry readings. Address: 82 Kentwood Rd., Sneinton Dale, Nottingham, U.K.

FINEFROCK, Thelma, b. 10 Oct. 1906. Educator. Education: Am. Coll. Phys. Ed., 1924-25; Dip., Wis. State Coll., 1927; B.A., Southwestern Coll., Winfield, Kan., 1935; post. grad. study at var. univs. inclng. Univs. of Ohio, So. Calif. & Colo. Married Lt. Col. Meryl K. Finefrock, 1 son (Michael). Positions held: Tchr. in pub. schls. in following States: Mich., 1927-29, Md., 1943-44, Ohio, 1955-57, Tex., 1958-59, Colo., 1957-58, Mass., 1959-63; Dir. of Phys. for Girls, Chilocco Indian Sohl. in Okla., 1929-42; Poetry Workshop, Univ. of Colo., Fall 1973. Memberships: Poetry Soc. of Am.; Colo. Authors League; Nat. League of Am. Pen Women; Children's Reading Round Table; Friends of the Lib; Charter Mbr., Hon. Mbr., Palmer Lake Little Art Grp., 1973. Published works: Poems of the Palmer Lake Poet, 1968. Contbr. to: The Sun, Colo. Springs; Hartford Courant; Christian Sci. Monitor; Denver Post; Human Voice Quarterly; Poetry Mag., Australia; Outposts, U.K.; Haiku Spotlight (Japan); Poet Lore; Ga. Poetry Soc. Annual; The Pen Women; Haiku (Canada); Modern Haiku; Peninsula Poets & many others. Honours, awards: Posey Award, State Poetry Soc. of Colo., 1966; Charles E. Tuttle Fellow, Rocky Mountain Writers Conf., Univ. of Colo., 1967; Jane Judge Meml. Award, Ga. Poetry Soc., 1968 & others. Address: Hope Cottage, Palmer Lake, CO 80133, U.S.A.

FINKEL, Donald, b. 21 Oct. 1929. Poet, Teacher. Education: B.S., Philos., M.A., Engl., Columbia Univ., NY. Married, Constance Urdang, 3 children. Positions held: Tchr., Univ. of Iowa; Tchr., Bard Coll.; Wash. Univ., St. Louis; Bennington Coll.; currently, Poet in Residence, Wash. Univ. Memberships: Authors' Guild; PEN Club. Published works: The Clothing's New Emperor (in Poets of Today VI); Scribner's 1959; Simeon, 1964; A Joyful Noise, 1966; Answer Back, 1968; The Garbage Wars, 1970. Contbr. to the

following jrnls. & anthols: Accent; Carleton Misc.; Glamour; Hudson Rev.; London Mag.; New Yorker; Paris Rev.; Perspective; Antaeus; Atlantic; Lillabulero; NM Quarterly; Poetry; Poetry NW; Qtly. Rev. of Lit.; Western Rev.; New Poets of England & America, 1st & 2nd selections; A Controversy of Poets; Rising Early; Modern Ballad & Story Poems; Poetry for Pleasure, etc. Honours, awards: Helen Bullis Prize, 1964; Guggenheim Fellowship, 1967-68; Nat. Endowment for the Arts Award. Address: 6943 Columbia Pl., St. Louis, Mo. 63130, USA.

FINLAY, Ian Hamilton, b. 28 Oct. 1925. Married, 2 children. Published works: num. books & booklets inclng: The Sea-Bed & Other Stories, 1958; The Dancers Inherit The Party, 1960; Concertina, 1962; Autumn Poem, 1966; Stonechats, 1967; Canal Game, 1967; Air Letters, 1968; A Boatyard, 1969; Rhymes for Lemons, 1970; A Sailor's Calendar, 1971; A Memory of Summer, 1971; From 'An Inland Garden', 1971; Sail/Sundial, 1972; Jibs, 1973; Butterflies, 1973; A Family, 1973; Straiks (by Ian Hamilton Finlay & Simon Cutts, drawings by Sydney Mck. Glen), 1973. Num. cards & folding cards inclng: Der Tag, (w. Ron Costley), 1973; Estuary Cupboards, (w. M. Harvey), 1973; The Sea's Waves, (lettering drawn by Stuart Barrie), 1973; Mid-Pacific Elements, 1973, etc. Poems have been published in: the Times Lit. Supplement; Nat. Review, U.S.A.; Lugano Review; Art Int.; Origin. One-Man Exhibs. of Concrete Poetry at: The Scottish Nat. Gall. of Mod. Art; Axiom Gall., London; The Richard Demarco Gall.; Nat. Maritime Mus., 1973. Address: Stonypath, Dunsyre, Lanark, U.K.

FINLEY, Dewey Gibson, pen names **FINLEY, Lora Dewey & ROSEN, Ayn,** b. 17 Feb. 1925. College Instructor. Education: B.A., Univ. of Okla., Norman, 1947; M.A., ibid, 1973. Divorced, 3 children. Positions held: Reporter, El Dorado Daily News & Evening Times, El Dorado, Ark., 1947-55 (Night Ed. part of that time); Staff Writer, Shreveport Times, La., 1955; Reporter, El Dorado Daily News & Times, 1955-61; Publs. Ed., Murphy Oil Corp., El Dorado, 1961-71. Memberships: South & West Inc.; Workshop Dir., Poetry Workshop, ibid, El Dorado, 1970-71. Published works: Tamaracks & Roses, 1973. Contbr. to: South & West; Voices Int.; Poet India; Love/Woman; Poetic License; Scimitar & Song; Encore; Lyrics of Love; Outstanding Contemporary Poetry Anthol.; Contemporary Am. Love Scene; Southwest Poetry 1971; Windmill. Honours, awards: Best Work in Progress, Ind. Univ. Writer's Conf., 1972; Rosa Zagnoni Meml. Award, Ozark Writers & Artists Guild, 1970; 3rd prize, Ozark Writers & Artists Guild, 1970; Vers Libre Award, South & West, 1972; 3rd pl., 6th Annual Okla. (Student) Poetry Contest, 1973. Address: 140 Spanish Gardens Apts., El Toro Dr., Huntsville, TX 77340, U.S.A.

FINN, Hugh Lauder, b. 26 Oct. 1925. Schoolmaster. Education: B.Sc. & Tchng. Dip., Rhodes Univ., S. Africa. Ifarried D.E. Borrell, 2 sons. Memberships: Past Chmn., Poetry Soc. of Rhodesia; P.E.N. Int.; Past Chmn., Salisbury Arts Coun.; V. Chmn., Nat. Arts Coun. of Rhodesia; Sec. of Steering Comm. for Nat. Arts Fndn. of Rhodesia. Contbr. to: New Poems 1954; New South African Writing; Poetry in Rhodesia; The Birds & Beasts Were There; Life is Poetry; New Coin; Standpunte; New Nation; Looking Back; De Arte; Poetry South; Rhodesian Poetry; Two Tone; Chirimo; Rhodesia Calls; Illustrated Life Rhodesia; Atlantic Monthly; Dalhousie Review; Fiddlehead; Canadian Poetry Mag.; Sydney Bulletin, etc. Address: 22 Bradfield Rd., Hillside, Salisbury E.61, Rhodesia.

FINNEGAN, (Sister) Mary Jeremy. Professor of English. Education: Ph.B., Univ. of Chicago, M.A., ibid.; Ph.D., Yale Univ. Member, Dominican Order, Congregation of the Most Holy Rosary, Sinsinawa, Wisconsin. Positions held: Instr., St. Clara Acad., Sinsinawa, Wisconsin; Member, Engl. Dept., Rosary Coll., River Forest, Ill.; Visiting Prof., Catholic Univ. of America, extension at San Rafael, Calif.; Trinity Coll., Washington; Prof. of Engl., Rosary Coll., River Forest,

III. Memberships: Poetry Club, Univ. of Chicago; Catholic Poetry Soc.; Mod. Lang. Assoc. Published work: Dialogue with an Angel, 1949. Contbr. to: Poetry Mag.; Atlantic; Saturday Review; Commonweal; Botteghe Oscure; America; Ladies' Home Journal; Zero; Lit. Review; Queen's Work; Skyline, Sponsa Regis, etc. Awards: John Billings Fiske Award, Univ. of Chicago, 1930; Katherine Tyndall Memorial Prize, Poetry Soc. of Va., 1967; Margaret Hayes Stickney Prize, ibid., 1967. Address: Rosary Coll., River Forest, IL., USA.

FINNIGAN, Joan. Freelance Writer. Educ: Carleton Univ., Ottawa, Ont., Canada; B.A., Queen's Univ., Kingston. Widowed, three children. Positions held: Former Tchr.; Former Reporter, Ottawa Jrnl.; Freelance Writer, Rsch. for Nat. Film Bd. of Canada, 1965-. Published works: Through the Glass Darkly, 1957; A Dream of Lillies, 1965; Entrance to the Green-House, 1968; It Was Warm and Sunny When I Set Out, 1970. Contbr. to: Queen's Quarterly; Quarry; Fiddlehead; Tamarack Review; (anthologies) Best Poems of 1957, 1959, 1961, 1963, 1965, 1967: The Borestone Mountain Poetry Awards, 1958, '60, '62, '64, '66, '68. Honours, awards: Canada Coun. Grants, 1965, '68, '69; Canada Coun. Sr. Arts Grant, 1967; Centennial Commn. Prize for Poetry, 1967. Address: 17 Parkwood Place, Kingston, Ontario, Canada.

FINNIN, Mary. Poet; Writer; Artist. Education: Melbourne Univ. Married to J.J. Connellan. Positions held: Tchr.; Industrial Rschr.; Hist. Rschr. Published works: A Beggar's Opera, 1938; Look Down, Olympians, 1939; Royal, 1941; Aims for Oblivion, 1947; The Shield of Place, 1957. Contbr. to: (anthol.) Modern Australian Verse, 1964. Address: 105 Mathoura Rd., Toorak, Victoria, Australia.

FINSTEIN, Max. Published works: Savanarola's Tune, 1959; There's Always a Moon in America, 1968. Contbr. to: Paris Review; Wild Dog; Writing 3 (anthology), 1964.

FIORENTINO, Luigi, b. 13 Feb. 1913. Writer; Professor of the History of Italian Literature. Education: Naples Univ., Italy; Dip. in Hispanic Studies; Laureate Man of Letters. Married Francisca Cruz Rosón. Positions held: Prof., Univs. of Siena & Trieste. Memberships: Corres., Acad. of Sci., Letters & Art, Palermo; Accademia degli Intronati di Siena, etc. Published works: Un fiume un amore (poetry), 1961; Occhio rosso occhio verde (poetry), 1969; Il balcone e le rondini: Bécquer nella vita e nella poesia (criticism), 1972; Storia della letteratura italiana, 1964-73. Contbr. to over 200 anthols., major newspapers &jrnls., Italian & foreign. Lectured in univs. & cultural instns., Europe & Middle East. Honours, awards: Isola d'Elba, 1949; San Pellegrino, 1950; Chianciano, 1951; Presidenza del Consiglio dei Ministri, 1956, '57, '60, '65, '69; Sileno d'Oro, 1964; Pisa, 1964; Le Muse, 1966; Renato Serra, 1973, etc. Address: Via di Malizia 38, Villa Gaia, 53100 Siena, Italy.

FIRTH, Florence, b. 25 Sept. 1893. Retired Teacher. Education: Grad., Trenton State Normal Schl., Trenton, N.J.; B.S., N.Y. Univ., 1934; M.A., ibid, 1937; study at var. other univs. Positions held: Tchr., Elem. schls., Harrison, N.J.; Ardmore, Pa., Garfield, N.J., Lahaina, Maui, Hawaii; Chmn., Poetry Comm. to plan Poetry Course of study for Plainfield Schls., Plainfield, N.J.; Tchr. of High or Secondary Schl., Engl. & Social Studies, Plainfield, N.J. (last 18 yrs.) Memberships: World Poetry Soc. Intercontinental, 1971-; Nat. Fed. State Poetry Socs., 1970; Sec., Musconetcong Chapt., N.J. Poetry Soc. Inc., 1970-; Charter Mbr., Creative Writing Club, Easton, Pa., 1970-. Published works: My Hawaiian Lei. Contbr. to var. newspapers, mags., anthols. inclng: The Swordsman Review; Poet; Am. Voices, 1939; Yearbook of Modern Poetry, 1971; Annual Anthol. of N.J. Poetry Soc., 1971, '72. Address: 685 Belvidere Rd., Phillipsburg, NJ 08865, U.S.A.

FISCHER, Barbara, pen names **IRVING, Joan,**

MORRIS, B.J., ALDER, B. & KELLY, Maureen, b. 25 Nov. 1943. Publisher/Editor. Education: Ph.D., Marlowe Univ. Married Martin Fischer, 1 son (Mark Jay). Positions held: Ed./Publr., PENMAN Mag., 1963-68; Ed./Publr., Poetry of the Year Quarterly anthols., simultaneously; Formed J. Mark Press, 1969; Fndr. & Dir., Nat. Schl. of Poetry, 1970; Taught Poetry, Continuing Ed. Prog., Deer Park H.S., 1972; N.Y. State's only approved corres. poetry schl., NSP, 1970; Host own TV Show, Creative World, Jan. 1974. Memberships: Fndr. & Pres., Suffolk Writers' Club, & Fellowship of Profl. Poets. Published works: Writers Rulebook, 1963; Successful Fiction & Poetry, 1965; Your Copyright Protection, 1966; Perfecting Your Poetry, 1967; Rhyme's Reason, 1968; Correspondence Poetry Course, 1969; Poetry Self-Taught, 1970; Amoung the Reeds, 1971; Selling Poetry, 1972; Poetry That Sold, 1972; Poetips, 1973. Rep. in following anthols: Ben Travato, 1963; Ardentia Verba, 1966; Best in Poetry, 1967, 68, 69, 70, 71, 72, 73; Poetry of Our Time; All-Time Favorite Poetry; American Scenes, 1968-74. Contbr. to var. jrnls. Honours, awards: Personal Poetry Broadcasts, 1969; Spencer Award, 1968; Emerson Award, 1968. Address: 133 West Sixth St., Deer Pk., NY 11729, U.S.A.

FISCHL, Ruth, pen name **KLEINER, Pesca,** b. 11 Apr. 1934. Teacher. Education: B.A., Engl., Queens Coll. of the City of N.Y., 1955; M.A., Ohio Univ., Athens, 1957. Married Robert Fischl, 1 son, 1 daughter. Positions held: Asst. in Engl., Ohio Univ.; Copy Rdr., Univ. of Mich.; Tchr., Ypsilanti, Mich.; Lectr., Phila. Coll. of Art. Memberships: V.P., Leaves of Grass Chapt., N.J. Poetry Soc., 1972-74. Contbr. to Unripe Fruits, N.J. Poetry Soc. Anthol., 1973. Recip. var. hons. Address: 305 Pembrook Ave., Moorestown, NJ 08057, U.S.A.

FISHER, Gillian Christine, pen name **BEECH, Norah,** b. 1 May 1949. Clerk Typist. Memberships: Basildon Poetry Grp.; Ver Poets. Contbr. to: Billericay Recorder; Basildon Arts Review; Poetry One; Ver Poets (pamphlets & mags.); Weyfarers; Poets World; Self Expression; Ver Poets Single Poets Series No. 2, 1972; Outposts; Ver Poets Broadsheet; Good Elf; Scrip. Address: 54 Beaufort Rd., Billericay, Essex, U.K.

FISHER, Mary Hannah Fahringer, b. 29 Jan. 1910. Artist; Craft Teacher; Writer. Education: Art Schl.; studied art, arts & crafts, Sculpture under private instructors. Memberships: Ariz. State Poetry Soc.; World Poetry Soc. Contbr. to: Friends Intelligencer; Rosicrucian Fellowship Mag.; World Poetry Soc.; Philadelphia Inquirer. Address: 831 N. Venice Ave., Tucson, AZ 85711, U.S.A.

FISHER, Roy, b. 11 June 1930. Lecturer. Memberships: Gen. Coun., The Poetry Soc.; Exec. Comm., Nat. Poetry Secretariat. Published works: City, 1961; Then Hallucinations, 1962; Ten Interiors, 1966; The Ship's Orchestra, 1967; The Memorial Fountain, 1969; Collected Poems, 1969; Titles, 1969; Metamorphoses, 1970; Correspondence, 1971; Matrix, 1971; The Cut Pages, 1971; Bluebeard's Castle, 1972. Contbr. to: Tarasque; The Birmingham Post; Mermaid; Poetry & Audience; Origin; The Poet; Stand; Sum; Poetry Now; Signature; Extra Verse; The Window; Delta; Combustion; The National Review; Mich. Qtly. Review; Tlaloc; Migrant; Mica; Samphire; Living Arts; The Outsider; Sixty One; Grosseteste Review; Clare Market Review; Black Country Meat; Blackga; The Yorks. Post; New Measure; Sad Traffic; Resuscitator; Kulchur; Cambridge Opinion; The Nation, & many others. Recip., Andrew Kelus Prize for Engl. Poetry, 1970. Address: Dept. of Am. Studies, Univ. of Keele, Keele, Staffs. ST5 5BG, U.K.

FISHER, Thomas Allen, pen names **NET, Thomas & FISHER, Allen,** b. 1 Nov. 1944. Poet; Editor. Positions held: Ed. & Part Dir., Aloes Books; Part Ed., Strange Faeces; Participant, Fluxshoe England West. Published works: Bavuska, 1969; Tree-Birst, 1970; Before Ideas, Ideas, 1971; Facece, 1972; Spaces for

Winter Solstice, 1972; Lines, Circles, Wheelbarrows, 1973; Creek in the Ceiling Beam, 1973; Sicily, 1973. Contbr. to: Fluxshoe; Catalogue 1972; Addenda, 1973; To Fluxshoe; 10 (U.S.A.); Poetry Review (London); Strange Faeces (London); Curtains (Yorkshire); Big Venus (London); IAC (Germany); Earthship (Southampton); Six Pack (USA & London). Address: 18 Hayes Court, New Park Rd., London SW2 4EX, U.K.

FISHMAN, Charles (Munro), b. 10 Jul. 1942. Education; B.A., M.A., in Literature, Hofstra Univ. Positions held: Instr. in Engl., SUNY at Farmingdale. Published works: Apparitions (forthcoming). Contbr. to: New Orleans Review; Journal 31; Epoch; Ghost Dance; NY Times; Kansas Qtly.; Wascana Review; NY Qtly.; Tractor; Cottonwood Review; Tree; Descant; Quarry; Cloven Hoof; Mediterranean Review; Malahat Review; Jewish Frontier; Catholic World; Jewish Exponent; Poet Lore; Quoin; Salmagundi; Roanoke Review; Bitterroot; Nimrod; Epos; Colorado Qtly.; Motive; Film Qtly.; Kauri; Dimensions in American Judaism; Maguey. Recip. Stephen Vincent Benet Narrative Poetry Awards Competition, 1969: 3rd Prize; Writers' Digest Creative Writing Contest, 1972: 1st Prize. Address: Horton Hall, SUNY at Farmingdale, Farmingdale, NY 11735, USA.

FITZ-GERALD, Carolyn, b. 1 Mar. 1932. Editor. Education: So. Meth. Univ.; B.S., Univ. of Tex. at Austin; Grad. Schl., ibid. Married, 4 children. Positions held: Ed., The Leslie Press; Ptnr., Writers Ink, advertising & public rels. Memberships: Theta Sigma Phi; Tex. Poetry Soc.; Okla Profl. Writers Assn. Published works: Everyday, Five Minutes With God, 1969. Contbr. to: Power; Presbyterian Survey; World Call; Texas Presbyterian; Youth Highlights. Recip., Religious Poetry Prize, Odessa Coll. Writers Roundup, 1967. Address: Box 4311, Midland, TX 79701, U.S.A.

FITZGERALD, Dorothy Hobson, b. 9 Nov. 1905. Instructor. Education: A.B., Hunter Coll., N.Y.C., 1934; M.A., N.Y. Univ., 1952. Married Alfred Fitzgerald, 1 son. Positions held: Fndr., Dir., Ed., Publsr., The League to Support Poetry, issuer of 12 brochures & 10 annual prize vols. of poetry, the Poetry Bulletin (1938-46) & the New Qtly. of Poetry (1946-48), 1936-49; Instr., Engl. Lit., Creative Writing, Human Rels., Packer Collegiate Inst., 1957-69; Instr., Lang. & Lit., New Schl. for Social Rsch., N.Y., 1960-66. Memberships: Exec. Bd., 1943-44 & '44-45, Poetry Soc. of Am.; Co-Chmn., Poetry Workshop, Pen & Brush Club, 1973-74; MLA. Published works: Celestial Interim, 1933; Let There Be Light, 1943; The Lion & the Unicorn, ready for publ. Rep. in following anthols: The Golden Book of Catholic Poetry; The Music Makers, 1945; Poetry Soo. of Am. Anthol., 1046; From the Four Winds, 1939; Seventeen & One, 1943; A Treasury of Favorite Poems, 1963. Contbr. to many mags., reviews, newspapers inclng: Pegasus; Va. Qtly. Review; Christian Sci. Monitor; N.Y. Herald Tribune; Portland Oregonian; Recent; The Ensign, 1972-73; Imprints Qtly.; Pen & Brush Bulletin. Recip., First prize, Pen & Brush Annual Poetry Contest, 1970 & '72 & 2nd prize, 1973. Address: 327 West 18th St., N.Y., NY 10011, U.S.A.

FITZGERALD, (George) Geoffrey, b. 23 Jul. 1923. Artist, Actor, Poet. Education: Dramatic Workshop, New School for Social Research, NYC. Served with USN in WW 11 (in the Mediterranean). Positions: Sundry acting engagements in the theatre; also professional poetry reader at universities, churches, hospitals, nursing homes, and Greenwich Village coffee shops. Membership: Poetry Soc. of America. Published work: Rockets in the Afternoon, 1946. Work in progress: full Ms. of lyric verse. Address: 333 E. 92nd St., New York, NY 10028, USA.

FITZGERALD, Robert David, b. 22 Feb. 1902. University Teacher. Education: Sydney Univ., Australia. Positions held: Supervising Surveyor, Dept. of Interior, Sydney (Retired); Lectr., Univ. of Tex., Austin, Tex., USA. Memberships: Fellow, Instn. of Surveyors, Australia; Australian Soc. of Authors.

Published works: The Greater Apollo, 1927: To Meet the Sun, 1929; Moonlight Acre, 1938; Heemskerck Shoals, 1949; Between Two Tides, 1952; This Night's Orbit, 1953; The Wind At Your Door, 1959; Southmost Twelve, 1962; Of Some Country, 1963; Selected Poems, 1963; Forty Years' Poems, 1965. Contbr. & Ed., various publs. Honours, awards: Australian Lit. Soc. Gold Medal, 1938; Fulbright Travel Grant, 1963; Ency. Britannica Award, 1965; OBE, 1951. Address: 4 Prince Edward Parade, Hunters Hill, NSW, Australia 2110.

FITZGERALD, Robert Stuart, b. 12 Oct. 1910. Professor. Educ: A.B., Harvard Univ., 1933; Trinity Coll., Cambridge, U.K., 1931-32. Married Sarah Morgan 1947; six children. Positions held: Reporter, N.Y. Herald Tribune, 1933-35; Staff Writer, Time Mag., 1936-40, '41-43, '46-49; Poetry Reviewer, New Republic, Washington, 1948-52; Served, U.S.N.R., 1943-46; Instr., Sarah Lawrence Coll., Bronxville, 1946-53; Instr., Princeton Univ., 1950-52; Fellow, Ind. Univ. Schl. of Letters, 1951–; Vis. Prof., Poetry & Poetics, Notre Dame Univ., 1957, Univ. of Wash., 1961, Mt. Holyoke Coll., 1964; Boylston Prof. of Rhetoric, Harvard Univ., 1965. Published works: Poems, 1935; A Wreath for the Sea, 1943; In the Rose of Time, 1956; numerous translations. Ed., The Aeneid of Virgil, 1965; The Collected Poems of James Agee, 1968; The Collected Short Prose of James Agee, 1969. Contbr. to: (anthologies) 100 Modern Poems, 1949; Modern Verse in English, 1958; Modern Poets, 1963. Honours, awards: Midland Author's Prize, 1931; Guggenheim Fellowship, 1953; Shelley Memorial Award, 1955; Ford Fndn. Grant, 1959; Fellow, Nat. Inst. of Arts & Letters, 1961 & Am. Acad. of Arts & Sci., 1962. Address: San Fortunato Della Collina, Perugia, Italy.

FITZGERALD-BUSH, Frank Shepard, b. 11 Oct. 1925. Historian. Education: San Francisco State Coll., Calif.; Univ. of Miami, Coral Gables; A.B. & M.A. Positions held: RCAF, 1943-44; Vol. Ambulancier, Am. Field Serv. attached to Brit. XIVth Army, India & Burma, 1944-45; US Marine Corps (res), 1948-51; USAF, 1951-55; Instr. of Hist., Fla. State Univ., 1961-64; Libn., Univ. of Miami, 1964-65; Libn. & Curator of Floridiana, John F. Kennedy Meml. Lib., Hialeah, 1966-71. Member, Laramore-Rader Poetry Grp., Miami, Fla., 1943–. Published works: Native Treasure, 1943; Sonnets in Search of Sequence, 1968; Remembered Spring, 1974; (pamphlet) Hechos son Amor, 1968. Contbr. to num. periodicals in U.S.A., U.K. & Ireland over past thirty yrs. Address: 3030 N.W. 171 St., Opa-Locka, FL 33055, U.S.A.

FITZHUGH, Jewell Durnice Kirby, b. 13 Sept. 1904. Retired Teacher; Newspaper Columnist; Feature Writer; Poet. Education: B.A., Ark. State Tchrs. Coll., Conway, 1931; grad. study, Geo. Peabody Coll., Nashville, Tenn., Scarritt Coll., Nashville & Univ. of Ark. Married Oscar Fitzhugh. Positions held: Classroom Tchr., –1963; Hd. of Engl. Dept., Mabelvale H.S., Ark. Memberships: Mbrship Chmn., Poets Roundtable of Ark.; Authors, Composers & Artists Soc.; Nat. League of Am. Pen Women; Ozark Writers Guild. Contbr. to: Democrat Enterprise; Ozark Spectator; Ark. Gazette; Ark. Methodist; Ark. Baptist; Saline County News-Pacesetter; N. Little Rock Times; Message Mag.; Piggott Banner; Ft. Smith Times Record; Voices Int.; Hot Springs News; The Paper. Honours, awards: 1st Prize, Democrat Enterprise Poetry Contest, 1941; Loving Cup Achievement Award, Ark. Authors, Composers & Artists Soc. Address: Rte. 1, Box 532, Mabelvale, AR 72103, U.S.A.

FITZSIMMONS, Thomas, b. 21 Oct. 1926. Professor of English. Education: Fresno State Coll., Calif., U.S.A., 1947-49; Sorbonne & Inst. de Sci. Pol., France, 1949-50; B.A., Engl. Lit., Stanford Univ., Calif., U.S.A., 1951; M.A., Engl. & Comp. Lit., Columbia Univ., N.Y., 1952. Married w. 2 sons. Positions held: Cons., Hist. Sect., Off. of Sec. of Defense, 1952; For. Affairs Writer & Ed., New Republic Mag.; Asst. Prof., Am. Univ.,

1955-59; Rsch. Chmn., HRAF, Yale Univ., 1955-56; Dir. of Rsch., ibid, 1956-58; Dir. & Ed., HRAF Press, 1958-59; Asst. Prof., Oakland Univ., 1959-60; Assoc. Prof., ibid, 1961-66; Prof. of Lit., 1966-; currently Vis. Prof., Tokyo Univ. of Educ., Keio Univ., Japan Women's Univ., Tokyo, Japan. Published works: USSR, 1960; Downinside, 1969; This Time, This Place, 1969; Zenjoints, 1970; Morningdew, 1970; Meditation Seeds, 1971; Japanese Poetry Now, 1971, new edn., 1973; Mooning, 1971. Contbr. to: Actual Size; Antioch Review; Astra; Beloit Poetry Jrnl.; Commonweal; East-West Review; The Floating Bear; Free Poems; Midstream; London Mag.; The Wisc. Review & many others. Recip. var. honours & awards inclng: Nat. Endowment for the Arts Award in Poetry, 1967. Address: 720 Westwood Dr., Birmingham, MI 48009, U.S.A.

FLAHERTY, Douglas, b. 25 Apr. 1939. University Instructor, Poet. Education: B.S., Merrimack Coll., Andover, Mass.; M.A., Univ. of Mass.; M.F.A., Univ. of Iowa. Positions held: Grower of carnation flowers; Truck Driver; Bus. Clerk; Ed.; Publr.; Tchr.; Univ. Instr.; Co-Ed., Road Apple Review (poetry mag.). Published works: The Elderly Battlefield Nurse, 1967; Just A Little Old Wood's Tale, 1969. Contbr. to: Colo. Quarterly; Descant; Expression; Folio; Fiddlehead; Open Places; Perspective; Quarterly Review of Lit.; Quartet: Poetry Northwest; New Mexico Quarterly; Southern Poetry Review; Outsider; Beloit Poetry Quarterly; Wisc. Review; Poetry Bag; S Fla. Review; Foxfire; etc. Awards: Hallmark Honor Award, judged by Robert Penn Warren. Address: 1525 Burdick, Oshkosh, Wis. 54901, USA.

FLAIG, Phyllis M., b. 7 Mar. 1898. Poet. Education: Northfield Sem., Mass.; special courses, Ind. Univ. Ext.; Technique of poetry from Vivian Laramore-Rader, Poet Laureate of Fla., and Gilbert Maxwell. Married Walter H. Flaig, 1 son, 1 daughter. Memberships: Poetry Soc. of Ga.; Laramore-Rader Poetry Grp.; former mbr., Nat. League of Am. Pen Women & Poetry Soc. of N.H. Contbr. to: Ladies Home Jrnl.; Good Housekeeping; Voices; N.Y. Times; Christian Sci. Monitor; Lyric, etc. Honours, awards incl: 1st Prize, Pa. Soc., 1965, Ga. Writers Assn. (for sonnet), 1969, N.H. Poetry Soc. (for Ballad), 1970; Hon. Mention, Ga. McIntire Meml. Prize, 1974. Address: 330 Romano Ave., Coral Gables, FL 33134, U.S.A.

FLAVELL, Adrian Donald, b. 22 Sept. 1951. Student. Education: Flinders Univ., Australia. Married. Fndr. & Editor, 'Fields' Poetry Mag., 1971-73. Contbr. to: On Dit; Fields; Your Friendly Fascist; Dharma; Contempa; Dark Areas; Tweed; Saturday Club Book of Poetry; Expression; Nova Anthology, 1972. Address: c/o P.O., Mylor, S.A. 5153, Australia.

FLEMING, Harold Lee, b. 16 June 1927. College Professor. Education: B.S., Ind. State Coll., Pa., U.S.A., 1950; M.A., Bread Loaf Schl. of Engl., Middlebury Coll., Vt. Positions held: Tchr., Penns Manor Schl., Clymer, Pa., 1950-60; Tchr., Abington South Campus, Pa., 1960-68; Assoc. Prof. of Engl., Montgomery County Community Coll., Blue Bell, Pa., 1968-. Published works: (textbooks) Composition: Models & Exercises, 1965; Models for Composition, 1968; English Grammar: Forms & Structures, 1971; (novel) Elizabeth Newt, 1967. Contbr. of poetry to num. mags., reviews inclng: Accent; The Denver Post; Fiddlehead; Folio; The Kenyon Review; The Mass. Review; New Orleans Poetry Jrnl.; N.Y. Herald Tribune; N.Y. Times; Paris Review; Penny Poems; Perspective; Poetry (Chicago); Poetry Northwest; Yankee; Prairie Schooner; Quarterly Review of Lit. Recip., Bread Loaf Fellowship, 1959. Address: Sunset Ave. RD 3, Norristown, PA 19401, U.S.A.

FLETCHER, Ian, b. 22 Aug. 1920. University Lecturer. Education: Goldsmith's Coll.; Univ. of London, UK. Positions held: Children's Libn., Borough of Lewisham, 1939-55; Univ. Lectr., Univ. of Reading, 1956-65; Reader in Engl. Lit., ibid, 1965-. Published

works: An Homily for Kenneth Topley, 1945; Orisons, 1947; Motets, 1962; Translation of the Hippolytus (w. D.S. Carne-Ross), 1966; The Milesian Intrusion, 1967. Contbr. to: Encounter; Times Literary Supplement; Plan; Nine; Poetry Quarterly; Poetry Review; Argna; Southern Review; Colonnade; Ariel; Tamesis; Poetry, London. Address: Flat 12, 12 Coley Ave., Reading, UK.

FLETCHER, Mary Frances, b. 11 Apr. 1907. Teacher. Education: B.A., La. Polytechnic Inst.; M.A., Univ. of Va.; Ph.D., La. State Univ. Positions held: Latin & Engl. Tchr., De Ridder H.S., 1926-27; Engl. Tchr., L. Charles H.S., 1927-40; worked at L.S.U., summers of 1940, 41, 42, 47; La. Tech. Univ., 1940-. Memberships: Pres., Coll. Writers Soc. of La., 1957-58 & 1967-68; Dir. of Deep South Writers Conf., 1967-68; Pres. of Coll. Engl. Assn. of S.C.M.L.A.; Sec. of Am. Lit., ibid; Danforth Panel, Columbia Univ., 1959; Am. Pen Women. Contbr. to: South-Central Mod. Lang. Bulletin; Rectangle; LEA; Nat. Poetry Anthol.; Ruston Writers Book. Winner, Delta Kappa Gamma Summer Award, 1947. Address: 1102 North Vienna, Ruston, LA 71270, U.S.A.

FLETCHER, Patricia Ann, pen name, **BUNIN, Patricia Ann.** Freelance Writer. Education: Radford Women's Coll., Radford, Va., USA. Married, Dennis A. Fletcher; 1 child. Positions held: Editor of HS newspaper, Granby HS Spectator; Feature Editor of coll. newspaper, Radford Grapurchat; Copywriter for WNOR AM/FM radio, Norfolk, Va.; Asst. to Promotion Manager, Topics Publ. Co., NYC.; Asst. Promotion Manager, Progressive Architecture Mag., Reinhold Publ. Co., NYC; Founder, Editor, Publisher of "the RUFUS", poetry qtly., P.O. Box 75982, Los Angeles, CA 90075. Published work: Rites Performed on This Body (poems), 1974. Contbr. to: All-Time Favorite Poetry Anthol.; Poetry Parade; Poetaster; Cardinal Poetry Qtly.; Bachaet; Orphic Lute; American Poet; United Poets; Prairie Poets; Quintessence; Hyacinths & Biscuits; American Voice Poetry; Shore Poetry Anthol.; Vista; World Poets; The Poets' Guild; Legend; Tejas; Poetry Prevue; The Written Word Anthol. No. 12. Awarded Cert. of Achievement for outstanding poetry by Anthols. of the Year (J. Mark Press), Nov. 1969. Address: P.O. Box 75982, Los Angeles, CA 90075, USA.

FLORIAN, Tibor, b. 12 Apr. 1908. Writer; Editor. Education: Fac. of Law, Univ. of Kolozsvar. Married, 5 children. Positions held: Writer; Poet; Lit. Ed. of the weekly 'Hungaria', Germany, 1947-49; Announcer, Radio Free Europe, Hungarian Desk, N.Y.C., 1950-60; Ed., ibid, 1961-74. Memberships incl: Kemény Zsigmond Literary Assn., Marosvásárhely, 1944; Pázmány Literary Assn., Kolozsvár, 1938; Hon. Treas., Int. PEN Ctr. for Writers in Exile, Am. Br., N.Y.; Asst. Sec., ibid, last 2 yrs.; Former Pres., Kossuth Publishing Co., Cleveland, Ohio; Int. Fed. of Jrnlsts.; Hungarian Helikon, Canada; Pres., Lit. Br. of the Arpád Acad., Cleveland, 1974. Published works: Above Clouds, Below Clouds, 1935; Sketches, 1936; In Christ's Shadow, trans. from Rumanian, 1938; The Stone Slabs are Broken, 1946; Above the Depth, 1948; New Poems, 1948. Rep. in following anthols: New Frontier, 1931; New Transsylvanian Anthol., 1937; Songs of God, 1939; Glittering Poems of Transsylvania, 1941; Poems of Migrant Hungarians, 1947; The Butterfly, 1947; Before Sunrise, 1948; Orökmécs, 1947; Poems of ten years, 1956; Do you know us?, 1971; Poets of Transsylvanian Helikon, 1973. Contbr. to num. newspapers, reviews, mags., jrnls., periodicals. Honours, awards incl: Silver Medal, Arpád Acad., Cleveland, Ohio, 1964; Gold Medal, ibid, 1973. Address: 3 Mountain View Dr., New Milford, CT 06776, U.S.A.

FONTAIN, (Rt. Rev. Archimandrite) Gregory, pen names **TARSICIO, Fray, CIFUENTES, Jaime & RENE, Danilo.** Missionary Priest; Language Instructor. Education: A.B., Ph.B., S.T.M., Colegio Seráfico; Colegio de los RR.HH. Maristas, Columbia; S.A. Eastern Theol. Sem., Phila., Pa. Positions held: Instr. in French, Seráfico Coll., Columbia, 1949-50; Latin,

French, Spanish, Episcopal Acad., 1958-61; Haddonfield Meml. H.S., 1961-62; Spanish, Latin, French, Spanish, German & Interlingua, Valley Forge Mil. Acad., 1962–; Advisor, Soc. of Ruben Dario, 1962-67; Rector, St. Peter & St. Paul Orthodox Cath. Ch., Phila., 1967-70; Spiritual Advisor, Orth. Cath. Fellowship, Bryn Mawr & Haverford Colls. Rep. to the Chaplancies Commn. of the Canonical Orth. Cath. Bishops in the Americas. Memberships incl: Fndr.- Mbr., Acad. of Am. Poets; Classic Soc. of Phila.; Centro Studi e Scambi. Published works: Seeds of Love (book), 1971. Contbr. to: Drita e Vertete; The Word; Solia; The Heritage; La Aurora; Sound Off; The Legionnaire; New Voices in Am. Poetry; Modern Day Poets & Authors; Man: When Born of Fire; Shore Poetry Anthol., etc. Recip. var. hons. & awards inclng: Gold Plaque from Broadway Spanish Ch., 1959. Address: P.O. Box 139, Wayne, PA 19087, U.S.A.

FORD, Betty Richards (Mrs.), b. 28 Dec. 1940. Vice-Pres., New Car Dealership. Education: Lenoir Coll., Hickory, NC; Sullins Col., Bristol, Va. Memberships: NC Poetry Soc. Contbr to: Red Clay Reader II, 1965; A Time For Poetry, 1966; Bay Leaves, 1966; NC Poetry Soc. Award Winning Poems, 1967; Internat. Who's Who in Poetry Anthol., 1972, also: The Am. Poet, 1968; The News & Observer, Raleigh, NC; Hickory Daily Record; Above Ground Review; Voices Internat.; Longview Journal; Carolina Country. Awards: SC Fiction & Poetry Conf., 1969; 2nd Place, Charlotte Writers Club, 1964; 1st Place, Hickory Writers Workshop, 1964; Congressional Dist. Award, NC Poetry Council, 1964, etc. Address: PO Box 1086, Hickory, NC 28601, USA.

FORD, Connie May, b. 22 Sept. 1912. Veterinary Surgeon. Education: Dip., Royal Veterinary Coll., London, U.K., 1933. Positions held: Private prac. (small animals), S.E. London, 1933-41; Women's Land Army in Scotland, 1942; Lab. posts, 1943-44; w. Min. of Agriculture Veterinary Investigation Serv., 1945-72. Memberships: Treas., Nottingham Poetry Soc., 1973; Leicester Poetry Soc.; Soc. of Civil Serv. Authors. Author, Wings and Water, 1973. Contbr. to: Poetry Nottingham; Breakthru; Manifold; Civil Service Hobbies Exhibitions, broadsheets, etc. Honours, awards: 1st prize, Annual Open Comp., Nottingham Poetry Soc., 1961; Prize, Herbert Spencer Poetry Comp. (Civil Serv. Authors), 1962; 1st prize, Spring Comp., Nottingham Poetry Soc., 1967; Masefield Meml. Prize, 1968. Address: 49 Rivermead, West Bridgford, Nottingham NG2 7RD, U.K.

FORD, Edsel, b. 30 Dec. 1928. Poet. Education: B.A., jrnlsm., Univ. of Ark., 1952. Positions held: Frequent readings of work; Advor., writing workshops. Memberships: Poetry Soc. of Am. Published works: The Manchild from Sunday Creek, 1956; A Thicket of Sky, 1961. Love Is the House It Lives In, 1965; Looking for Shiloh, 1968. Contbr. to: over 150 jrnls., incl. Saturday Rev.; NY Times; Macleans, Canada; Mademoiselle; Ladies' Home Jrnl.; Good Housekeeping; Western Humanities Rev.; McCall's; Christian Sci. Monitor; New Orleans Rev.; Tex. Qtly.; Country Beautiful, etc. Honours: 4 annual awards, Poetry Soc. of Am., incl. 3,500 dollar di Castagnola, 1966, & Dylan Thomas award, 1967; Looking for Shiloh won Devins Mem. Award, 1968. Address: 2021 S R St., Ft. Smith, Ark. 72901, USA.

FORD, Robert Arthur Douglass, b. 8 Jan. 1915. Diplomat. Educ: M.A., Cornell Univ., Ithaca. Married Maria Thereza Gomes. Positions held: Tchr., Hist., Cornell Univ., 1938-40; Joined Canadian Dept. of External Affairs, 1940; Canadian Ambassador to Yugoslavia, 1959-61; Canadian Ambassador to Soviet Union, 1964–. Published works: A Window on the North, 1956; The Solitary City, 1969; Recent Russian Poetry (literary criticism), 1965. Contbr. to: (anthologies) Canadian Poetry in English, 1954; Penguin Book of Canadian Verse, 1958. Honours, awards: Canadian Governor-General's Medal for Poetry, 1965; D. Litt., Univ. of Western Ontario. Address: The Canadian Embassy, Moscow, U.S.S.R.

FORDE, Alfred Nathaniel, b. 25 Dec. 1923. Permanent Government Secretary. Education: B.A. (London), 1947; Cert. of Educ. w. Merit (Southampton), 1955; Special Public Admin. Cert. (Carleton), 1960; Thomson Television Proficiency Cert. (Glasgow), 1965. Married Elna Christabel, 3 children. Positions held: Asst. Master at Sec. Schls. in Tobago & Grenada, W.I., 1944-57; Asst. Sec., Govt. of Barbados, 1957-63; Permanent Sec., ibid, 1963–, w. a secondment from 1965-68 as Gen. Mgr., Caribbean Broadcasting Corp., Barbados. Published works: Canes by the Roadside; Ed., Talk of the Tamarinds (anthol.), 1971. Contbr. to: Caribbean Voices; Young Commonwealth Poets, 1965; Caribbean Verse; BIM mag.; Kyk-Over-Al, etc. Address: Chedleigh, Black Rock, St. Michael, Barbados, W.I.

FORNES, Maria Irene, b. 14 May 1930. Playwright. Memberships: Pres., N.Y. Theater Strategy; Pres., Women's Theatre Council; Poets & Writers; The Dramatists Guild; The Authors Guild of Am.; ASCAP. Published works: Cuatro Obras de Teatro Cubano, 1961; Playwrights for Tomorrow (Tango Palace & The Successful Life of 3), 1966; The Bold New Women (Promenade), 1966; Eight Plays from Off-Off Broadway (The Successful Life of 3), 1966; The New Underground Theatre (Promenade), 1968; Yale Theatre Review (Dr. Kheal), 1968; The Best of Off-Off Broadway (Dr. Kheal), 1969; Concepts of Literature (Tango Palace), 1971; The Off-Off Broadway Book (Molly's Dream), 1972. Honours, awards: John Hay Whitney Fndn. Grant, 1961; Centro Mexicano de Escritores Grant, 1962; OADR Grant, 1965; Cintas Fndn. Grant, 1967; Yale Univ. Grant, 1967-68; Rockefeller Fndn. Grant, 1971; CAPS Grant, 1972; Guggenheim Fndn. Grant, 1973; OBIE Award (for Promenade & The Successful Life of 3), 1965. Address: 1 Sheridan Sq., N.Y., NY 10014, U.S.A.

FORSHAW, David Arnold, b. 25 Oct. 1939. Warehouseman. Married, 1 child. Memberships: Past Mbr., Lancashire Authors Assn.; Calder Vale Poetry Soc.; Fndr., The Tudor Soc. Published works: Stephen & Other Poems, 1968. Contbr. to: The Evening Telegraph; The Gt. Harwood & Rushton Times; The Daily Mail; The Parnassian; The Record. Recip., 1st prize Cert. of Merit, George Camp Meml. Comp., Calder Valley Poetry Soc., 1968. Address: 2 Russell Pl., Gt. Harwood, Lancs., U.K.

FORSS, Oscar Harald, b. 3 Oct. 1911. Author; Poet. Memberships: Bd. Mbr., Sveriges Författareförening, 1948-65; The Swedish Pen Club; Sveriges Författarforbund; Romantishe Forbundet. Published works: Trött Pupill, 1939; Mossa, 1939; Handen drömmer, 1940, Violetta skuggor, 1940; Portalen, 1941; Nyansernas älskare, 1943; Valda dikter, 1943; Bortöver havets langa smärta, 1945; Rannsakan, 1946: Den vittnesgille vaganten, 1947; Adanoi, 1950; Arpeggio, 1956; Kärlekens ögon, 1962; Skomakarstan, 1965; Paranssen i Sankta Klara, 1968; Romantisk aterkomst, 1971. Anthols: P.D.A. Atterbom Dikter, 1955; Svenska landskapsdikter, 1960. Contbr. to many Swedish publications. Honours, awards: De Nios Prize, 1949; The Pen Club Prize, 1968; Hjalmar Bergman-stipendiet, 1961; Lindingö stads stipendium, 1969; Stockholms stads stipendier, sev. times; ABF-stipendiet, 1964. Address: Lejonets Gata 371, 136 OO Handen, Sweden.

FORSYTH-SCOTT, Nancy, b. 21 June 1940. Poet; Actress; Model; Singer. Education: B.S., Northwestern Univ., 1960. Married, 3 children. Positions held: Editl. staff, N.Y. Qtly. Poetry Jrnl. Member, ASCAP; Poetry Soc. of Am.; N.Y. Poetry Forum. Published works: Going into the 16th Round (w. Peggy Garrison), 1974. Contbr. to: N.Y. Qtly., 1973; Assembling Anthol., 1972 & '73; Clown War, poetry mag., 1972, '73; For Now, 1973; Grande Ronde Review, 1973; Hyn Anthol., 1973; Friends Sem. Review, 1973; The Dragonfly, 1973; Noise Qtly., 1972; The Writer Mag., 1971; Feminist Newsletter, 1972; etc. Readings, incl: New Schl. for Soc. Rsch.; Friends Sem.; The Ctr. for Human Potential; The N.Y. Poets'

Cooperative. Has appeared in a CABLE TV prog. of poetry filmed at the Cafe Feenjon. Address: 1 Hillside Terr., Irvington-on-Hudson, NY 10533, U.S.A.

FORTNER, Ethel Nestell, b. 11 Feb. 1907. Author and Editor; (Educator, retired). Education: Univ. of Oregon, B.S. in Psychology; Advanced studies at Univ. of Calif. at Los Angeles, Columbia Univ., Univ. of Chicago. Married, Laurence W. Fortner. Positions held: Teacher, public schools, 1926-31; Principal, School for Blind, 1932-44; Supervisor, State Dept. of Education, 1945-48; Psychologist, 1950-64; Poetry Editor, 1968-71; Review Editor, 1972-. Memberships: Acad. of American Poets; Oregon State Poetry Assoc. (Bd. member); South & West, Inc. (Northwest Rep.); Mt. Hood Poetry Circle; Poetry Soc. of Tennessee. Published works: A Sudden Clarity (1st Ed., 2nd Ed., 1967; 3rd Ed., 1969) also published on Cassette, 1972; Clouds and Keepings, 1973. Contbr. to anthols.: Spring Anthol., 1967; Flame, 1944, 1945, 1946; Poems of Memory, 1964; Poems of Peace, 1966; Singing Mariners, 1966; Unique, 1969; Poetry-by-the-Sea, 1970; Northwest Poets, 1968. Contbr. to mags., newspapers, etc.: St. Andrew Review; Pembroke Mag.; Mississippi Review; New Laurel Review; Human Voice; Weid; Charas; Dragonfly; Encore; Etchings; Folio; Foxfire; Imprints Qtly.; Voices Internat.; South & West; Green World; Tulsa Poetry Qtly.; Swordsman Review; Spectroscope; Poet (India); Mustang Review; Jean's Journal; Driftwood; Dimension; Creative Review; Caravan; Christian Herald; Cardinal Poetry Qtly.; Bitterroot; American Bard; Poet Lore; Oregonian Verse; Medford Mail Tribune; Shorelines; Poet Trails; Redmond Spokesman; Words With Wings; Poetry Review; The Muse; Denver Post; Golden Echo; Poetry View; Words on the Wind; Focus on Poetry; Poetry of the Pacific Northwest. Awards: Voice of the Year publication Award, Olivant Press, 1967; 1st Place, Oregon State Poetry Assoc. Poetry Award, 1964; John Gould Fletcher Award, South West Lit. Festival, 1970; Service Awards, Oregon State Poetry Assoc., 1967, and South & West, 1969; Featured speaker for Nat. Fed. of State Poetry Socs., etc. Address: Route 1, Box 259, Estacada, OR 97023, USA.

FOSTER, Don, b. 17 July 1948. Poet. Education: B.A., N. Tex. State Univ. Published works: Laugh, 1971. Contbr. to: Tampa Poetry Review; Invisible City; Meatball; Showcase; Sandcastles; Sattvas Review; Desperado, etc. Address: Box 8867, NT Station, Denton, TX 76203, U.S.A.

FOUDAH, Ibrahim Ameen, b. 1913. Businessman. Positions held: One time Director of the Saudi Arabian Broadcasting System. Has written one volume 'of Arabic poetry (in manuscript). Contbr. to all Saudi Arabian publications. Address: c/o The Higher Council for Arts & Sciences, Ministry of Education, Riyadh, Saudi Arabia.

FOUNTAIN, Helen Van Alstyne, pen name **TYLER, Lillian,** b. 15 Oct. 1906. Teacher. Education: B.S. & Ed.M., Rutgers Univ., 1950, 1952; Cert of Adv. Study, Wesleyan Grad. Schl. for Tchrs., Middletown, Conn. 1962. Married Kenneth Pierce Fountain, 1 daughter. Positions held: Tchr., bedside patients, Bonnie Burn Sanitorium, 8 yrs.; w. Deerfield Schl., Mountainside, N.J., ret'd.; Lectr., TV & radio progs., Women's Clubs, civic grps.; Poetry Cons., Cooper Hill Writers' Conf. sponsored by Poet Lore, 1972-73. Memberships: Life Assoc. Mbr., Poetry Soc. of Am.; World Poetry Soc. Intercontinental; Fndr. Mbr., The Acad. of Am. Poets; London Poetry Soc., Eastern Ctr., USA; The N.Y. Poetry Forum; Haiku Soc. of Am.; Poetry Fellowship of Me.; N.J. Poetry Soc., Inc.; Pa. Poetry Soc., Inc. Published works: Star Quest, 1967; A Cage of Birds, 1970. Contbr. to: Granite Chips Anthol., 1964; Golden Quill Anthol., 1966-68, '69-70; Selected Poems (Fla. State Poetry Soc.), 1967-68; Am. Mosaic; New Light on Poetic Horizon (Ariz. State Poetry Soc.), 1968; Poet; Star-Borne; The Spring Anthol., 1970; Poetry Prevue; Swordsman Review; Quidnunc; Am. Weave; Poet Lore; Driftwood East; Me. Writers' Chapbook, 1973; Voices Int., 1973, etc. Honours: awards: Cit.,

N.J. Assn. Tchrs. of Engl., 1968; World Poet Award, World Poetry Soc. Intercontinental, 1970; 1st Awards, Poetry Fellowship of Me., 1972-73; Humorous Verse, Nat. Fed. of Women's Clubs, 1972; 1973 Bouts Rimes, Cooper Hill Writers' Conf. Address: 23 B Maryland Ave., Cedar Glen Lakes, Whiting, NJ 08759, U.S.A.

FOWLER, Gene, b. 5 Oct. 1931. Poet. Positions held: Poet in Res., Univ. of Wisconsin, Milwaukee, U.S.A., summer 1970. Published works: Field Studies, 1965; Quarter Tones, 1966; Shaman Songs, 1967; Fires, 1971. Rep. in following anthols: Peace & Gladness Anthol., 1965; Am. Lit. Anthol., 1970; 31 New Am. Poets, 1970; The Outsider 4/5. 1970; Toward a New America, 1971; The Shadow Within, 1973; New Am. Poetry, 1973; A Mark in Time, 1972. Contbr. to: Evergreen Review; Chicago Review; Minn. Review; S.D. Review; East Village; Dust; Wild Dog; Southern Review; S.F. Examiner-Chronicle; Hyperion; Amphora, etc. Recip. var. awards inclng: Awards, Nat. Endowment of Arts, 1967 & '70; Dymaxion Award, 1967. Address: 1321 19th Ave., San Francisco, CA 94122, U.S.A.

FOWLER, Sandra, b. 4 Feb. 1937. Writer and Poet. Education: Pranklin Inst., 1956; Palmer Inst. of Authorship, 1966. Positions held: Contributing Editor, Ocarina, since 1972. Memberships: CSSI (Hon. Rep.); United Poets (Hon. Member); World Poetry Soc. Intercontinental (Rep.-at-large); Avalon World Arts Acad.; American Poets Fellowship Soc.; Internat. Platform Assoc.; Kentucky Poetry Soc. Published work: In The Shape Of Sun (published in Israel, copyrighted 1972-73). Contbr. to numerous anthols. and journals. Recip. several awards and citations (Avalon; North American Mentor; Accademia Leonardo da Vinci; CSSI). Also Personal Poetry Radio Prog., 1967. Address: West Columbia, WV 25287, USA.

FOX, (Right Rev.) Bartholomew Ruxton, b. 27 July 1925. Monk in Holy Orders. Education: B.Sc., Fordham Univ.; M.A., Burton Seminary; Licencie en Theologic, Inst. Orthodox Francais; Philathea Seminary, Ind. Positions held: World Council of Chs. Liaison, 1969; UN Rep., 1968–; Nat. Council of Chs.; Sev. Pastorates. Memberships: Fellow, Royal Soc. of Arts (UK); Royal Soc. of Lit.; World Poetry Soc. Intercontinental; Overseas Press Club. Author of sev. unpublished mss. Contbr. to: Catholic Worker; Orthodixy; Kaleidescope, etc. Honours, awards: 1st Prize, Leinster Fleadh Ceoil Music Festival, Ireland, 1969. Address: Ch. Ctr. for UN, 777 UN Plaza, New York, NY 10017, USA.

FOX, Siv Cedering, b. 5 Feb. 1939. Poet. Married to Dr. David Fox, mathematician/Pres. of C.T.I.; 3 children. Positions held: Lecturer, Univ. of Mass., fall 1973. Memberships: Consultant to C.C.L.M., 1972–; Member, Poetry Soc. of America, 1969–. Published works: Cup of Cold Water, 1973; Letters from the Island, 1973; Det Blommande Trädet (The Flowering Tree), anthol., in Swedish, of Am. Indian poetry, 1973. Contbr. to: Partisan Review; Qtly. Review of Literature; Minnesota Review; Hawaii Review; Sumas; Dryad; The Literary Review; Mundus Artium; The Chicago Tribune; The NY Times; The Colorado Qtly.; The Prairie Schooner; First Issue; Mill Mountain Review; Anteaus; The NY Qtly., etc. Recip. William Marion Reedy Award, 1970; John Masefield Narrative Poetry Award, 1969; Annapolis Fine Arts Festival Poetry Prize, 1968. Address: Polly Park Rd., Rye, NY 10580, USA.

FOX, Theodore T., b. 9 Mar. 1899. Physician. Education: Grad. in Medicine, McGill Univ., Canada. Positions held: Attending Physn. at sev. Hospitals. Member, Poetry Soc. of Am.; Fellow of sev. academic socs. Published works: Book of Poems, 1972. Contbr. to: Christian Monitor; Hadoar; Eden. Address: 38 East 85 St., N.Y., NY 10021, U.S.A.

FOX HUTCHINSON, Juliet Mary, pen name **PHOENICE, Jay,** b. 13 Jan. 1911. Writer. Educated privately. Married, 1934, widowed, 1964. Positions held: Edit. Bd., Envoi Mag. Memberships: PEN Club; English Assn. Published works: Sea Climate, 1955; Lightfall, 1957; The Flower is Crowned, 1960; The Harbour, 1961; The Third Day (prose), 1963; A Rainbow of Paths, 1964; Peke Posy, 1967; From the Kyloe Hills, 1971. Contbr. to: Yorkshire Post; Glasgow Herald; Scotsman; Lady; Homes & Gardens; Field; Country Life; Tablet; Aylesford Rev.; NY Times; Herald Tribune; Ladies Home Jrnl.; Chatelaine; Saltire Rev.; Christian Science Monitor; English, Canadian Forum; Auckland Mirror; NY Times Anthol.; Yorkshire Post Anthol. Poems broadcast on BBC. Address: Kyloe Old Vicarage, Beal, Berwick on Tweed, UK.

FRANCIS, Marilyn A., b. 26 Jan. 1920. Poet. Education: B.S. in Commerce, Ohio Univ., Athens, Ohio, U.S.A., 1941. Positions held: Personnel & P.R., Western Elec. Co., N.J., 1941-45; Special Ins. invest., Retail Credit Co., N.J. & N.Y., 1945-51; Freelance Writer, 1951–; Dir., Winged Arts Gall., Sedona, Ariz., 1969-72; Sedona Ed., The Verde Ind., Cottonwood, Ariz., 1973. Memberships: Poetry Soc. of Am.; Nat. League of Am. Pen Women; past Pres., Phoenix Br., ibid; Nat. Writers Club; Centro Studi e Scambi, Rome, Italy. Published works: Thunder in the Superstitions, 1959; Tangents at Noon, 1960; Space for Sound, 1961; Mirror Without Glass, 1964; Symbols for Instants, 1965; Radius: Red Rocks, 1972. Contbr. to: The Saturday Evening Post; Christian Sci. Monitor; Denver Post; The Oregonian; Best Poems & Stories; The Fiddlehead; P.S.; Flame; Ariz. Highways; Desert Mag.; Conn. Lit. Review; The Looming Arts; The Arizonian; The Arizona Rep.; The Phoenix Gazette; Poems Southwest, etc. Honours, awards: Emerson Poem Prize, Ohio Univ., 1956; Achievement Award, Nat. Writers Club, 1958; Best Mss. Award, Southwest Writers Conf., 1960; Cited by Ohio Univ., 1961 & by Phoenix Arts Coun., 1968. Address: P.O. Box 196, Sedona, AZ 86336, U.S.A.

FRANCIS, Robert (Churchill). Writer. Education: A.B., Harvard Coll., 1923; Ed.M., Harvard Grad. School of Education, 1926. Published works: (poetry) Stand With Me Here, 1936; Valhalla and Other Poems, 1938; The Sound I Listened For, 1943-44; The Face Against the Glass, 1950; The Orb Weaver, 1960; Come Out Into the Sun: Poems New and Selected, 1965; (prose relating to poetry): The Satirical Rogue on Poetry (essays), 1968; The Trouble with Francis (autobiography), 1971; Frost: A Time to Talk (memoirs), 1972. Contbr. to: Virginia Qtly. Review; Massachusetts Review; Poetry (Chicago); Field; The New Yorker; The Atlantic Monthly; Harpers, etc. Awards: The Golden Rose of the New England Poetry Club, 1942; Phi Beta Kappa poet at Tufts Univ., 1955; Rome Prize Fellowship (Am. Acad. Arts & Letters), 1957-58; Phi Beta Kappa poet at Harvard Univ., 1960; Amy Lowell Poetry Traveling Scholarship, 1967-68; Hon. L.H.D., Univ. of Massachusetts, 1970. Address: Fort Juniper, 170 Market Hill Rd., Amherst, MA 01002, USA.

FRANICEVIC, Marin, b. 18 May 1911. Poet; Man of Letters; Lecturer on Literature. Education: Higher Schl. of Pedagogy, Zagreb.; Dr. of Lit., Fac. of Philos., Zagreb Univ. Married Ina Brajčić. Positions held: Schl. Tchr. in Dalmatia; Educl. & Cultural worker with the partisans, WWII; also Jrnlst.; Hd. of Dept., Min. of Educ., Rep. of Croatia; Ed. in Chief of the lit. jrnl. 'Republika'; Prof., Higher Schl. of Pedagogy; Referendary for Lit., Yugoslav Lexicographical Inst. in Zagreb (publishers of the Yugoslav Encys.) Memberships incl: Yugoslav Acad. of Scis. & Arts, Sec. for Contemporary Lit.; Lit. Soc. of Croatia; Assn. of Writers of Yugoslavia; PEN. Published works incl: (poetry in the lit. lang.) Na putu za novi grad, 1937; Zvijezda nad planinom, 1945 & '46; Prozor odškrinut podnevu, 1956; Nastanjene uvale, 1963; Sunčani sat, 1967; Pod istim suncem, 1969; (poetry in the čakavic dialect) Govorenje Mikule Trudnega, 1945; Bliščavci, 1954; I tako sunca, 1959; Vitar u korenu, 1963; Sve masline, 1971; (books of essays & studies) Pisci i problemi, 1948; O nekim problemima ritma, 1958;

Književnost juoe¨ucer i danas, 1959; Književne interpretacije, 1964; Cakavski pjesnici renesanse, 1969; Pjesnici i stoljeća, 1974. Contbr. to many lit. jrnls., newspapers, reviews. Honours, awards incl: Twice recip. Prize of the Republic of Croatia (1946 & '48); Twice recip., Prize of the City of Zagreb (1960 & '72); Order of Merit for the Nation; First Class Order of Work. Address: Rendićeva 28/II – VIII, 41000 Zagreb, Yugoslavia.

FRANK, Adassa, b. 11 Nov. 1924. Assistant Editor, Boston University Bulletins Office. Education: Boston University. Married to a mathematician (Mr. Irving); four children (2 boys, 2 girls). Member, New England Poetry Club, since 1961. Presently completing first book of poems. Contrib. to: Scimitar and Song (Cover poet, Nov. 1961); Wormwood Review; Yankee; University Review; Saturday Review; Virginia Quarterly Review; also in anthology of peace poems, Not from the Victor; Poets of the Boston Area, 1973. Won yearly lyric award, New England Poetry Club, 1964, 1972; Won scholarship to Breadloaf Writer's Conference, 1965; Placed 8th in U.S. in peace poem contest, 1964. Address: 8 Eldredge Street, Newton, Mass. 02158, USA.

FRANKHOUSER, Floyd Richard, pen name, **FRANKHOUSER, Floyd R.,** b. 16 Oct. 1944. Chief Scheduler in Production Control Dept., and Assistant to Supervisor. Education: various grade schools in Brecknock Twp. Lanc. Co. Pa., Garden Spot HS, 3 yrs. night school at Penn State Extension Coll. in Wyomissing, Pa. Personal details: Lay Reader at the Muddy Creek Evangelical Lutheran Church. Positions held: Shipping Dept. Clerk; General Office Clerk; Asst. Scheduler, Production Control Dept. and now Chief Scheduler, Production Control Dept. & Asst. to Supervisor at Geo. W. Bollman and Co., Inc. Memberships: CSSI; World Poetry Soc. Intercontinental (past member). Published works: Folk Singer, 1973; Beyond Shadows, 1974. Contbr. to: Ideals Mag.; Poet; Poetry Parade; Jean's Journal; Yearbook of Modern Poetry, 1971; Dance of the Muse; American Voice; Ardentia Verba; American Bard; Best in Poetry, 1969; Poetry Of Our Times, 1970; Time to Pause; Major Poets; World Poets; Bachaet; Premier Poets '71-72; Shore Poetry Anthol., 1971; All-Time Favorite Poetry, 1970; Outstanding Contemporary Poetry, 1972; Hoosier Challenger. Awards: Highly Commended (Internat. Who's Who in Poetry, 1972-73); 4th place prize, Poetry Parade, 12, 1969. Address: RFD 1, Denver, PA 17517, USA.

FRANZWA, Carol Ellis, b. 9 Nov. 1946. Poet. Education: B.A. in Drama, Univ. of Santa Clara, Calif., 1968; M.A. in Engl. & Creative Writing, San Francisco State Univ., Calif., 1972. Married Gregg Edward Franzwa. Memberships: Poetry Workshop of Rochester, N.Y.; Acad. of Am. Poets. Works ready for publication: No Peaches; Given. Contbr. to: West Coast Poetry Review; Worksheet; South. Honours, awards: Runner-up in the San Francisco State Univ. participation connected with the Acad. of Am. Poets, 1972. Address: 159 Commodore Parkway, Rochester, NY 14625, U.S.A.

FRASER, Douglas J(amieson), b. 12 Jan. 1910. Retired Insurance Clerk. Education: George Heriot's School, Edinburgh. Married, 2 sons, 1 daughter. Memberships: Scottish P.E.N.; Hon. Treas., Scottish Assoc. for the Speaking of Verse (Edinburgh Branch); Hon. Sec., Edinburgh Poetry Club. Published works: Landscape of Delight, 1967; Rhymes o'Auld Reekie, 1973. Contbr. to: Scots Mag.; Burns Chronicle; The Fireside Book; The Friendship Book (as David Hope). Awards incl: Consolation Prize, The Scotsman Burns Bi-Centenary Competition, 1959. Address: 2 Keith Terrace, Edinburgh EH4 3NJ, Scotland.

FRASER, George Sutherland, b. 1915. Critic, Poet. Education: St. Andrew's Univ.; M.A. Positions held: Army, 1939-45; Free-lance Writer, 1945-58; Cultural Adviser, UK Liaison Mission, Japan, 1950-51; Lectr., Univ. of Leicester. Published works: Home Town

Elegy, 1944; The Traveller Has Regrets, 1947; News From South America, 1948; The Modern Writer and His World, 1952; Vision and Rhetoric, 1960; Ezra Pound (crit.), 1960; Robert Burns (Ed.), 1960. Contbr. to: Times Lit. Supplement; Observer; New Statesman; Listener; Partisan Review; Poetry, Chicago; Commentary. Address: 19 Guildford Rd., Stoneygate, Leicester, U.K.

FRASER, Kathleen, b. 1937. Writer. Educ: Occidental Coll., L.A. Married Jack Marshall, one child. Published works: Change of Address, 1966; Stilts, Somersaults and Headstands (for children), 1968. Contbr. to: New Yorker; Young American Poets (anthology), 1968.

FRASER, Raymond Joseph, b. 8 May 1941. Writer. Positions held: Lab. Technician, 1962; Tchr., 1964-65; Newspaper Ed. & Features Writer, 1966-67; Freelance Writer, 1967-69; Stage Performer, 1971-72; Sea Captain, 1972-. Published works: Waiting for God's Angel, 1967; I've Laughed & Sung through the Whole Night Long seen the Summer Sunrise in the Morning, 1969; The More I Live, 1971. Contbr. to: Tom-Tom; Moncton Times; The Fiddlehead; Queen's Quarterly; Tamarack Review; Canadian Forum; West Coast Review; Intercourse; Alphabet; New American & Canadian Poetry; The Far Point; Mountain; Ingluvin; Delta; Duel; Salt; Other Voices; Floorboards; Mainline. Recip., Canada Coun. Arts Awards, 1969-70 & 1971-72. Address: 74 Howard St., Chatham, New Brunswick, Canada.

FREDIN, Lars Olof, b. 27 Mar. 1919. Published works: Utan villkor, 1944; Sangen om stranden i havet, 1946; Vindbrygga, 1954; Jordorgel, 1955; Det bla rummet, 1955; Den blinda jorden, 1957; Jordledning, 1961; Molnfonster, 1963; Rummet, 1965; Bilden, 196 Slagruten, 1967; Svit, 1968; Ur tradet, 1968; i Kvall i nett, 1 Ur grasboken, 1971; Fagelspranget, 1972; Rosen, 1973; Till fodel 1973. Contbr. to: Bonniers Litterara Nagasin (BLM); Ord och Bil Horisont; Lyrikvannen; Bockernas varld; Var Losen; VI; Dagens N Svenska Dagbladet; Arbetet; Handelstidningen; Sydsvenska Dagbla Byggnadsarbetaren; Metallarbetaren m.fl. Honours, awards: FIB's Lyrikklubbs Stipendium, 1970; Sveriges Radios Stipendium, 1972. Hägerstensvägen 123, 12648 Hagersten, Sweden.

FREED, Sara, b. 18 Oct. 1901. Retired Concert Pianist; Teacher of Music. Education: Grad., Leefson-Hille Conserv. of Music; student at Curtis Inst. Positions held: Pianist for Symphony Club Opera Co.; on Fac. of Settlement Music Schl.; Dir. & Choreographer, Riva Hoffman Schl. of Dancing; Official Pianist for Dancers' Guild; on Fac. of Schl. of Musical Art. Memberships: Penn Laurel Poets; Pa. Poetry Soc.; Poetry Soc. of Ga. Contbr. to: Evening Bulletin; Bulletin Almanac Annual (poems in calendar sect.), 1964-; Prize Poems of 1970; World Poetry Day Mag.; Music Jrnl. Honours, awards: Hon. Mention, Pa. Poetry Soc., 1970; Poems for Presser Home Fndrs. Day Celebration, 1969-. Address: 101 W. Johnson St., Philadelphia, PA 19144, U.S.A.

FREEMAN, Arthur, b. 31 July 1938. Professor of English. Education: A.B. & Ph.D., Harvard Univ. Positions held: Instr., Brown Univ.; Jr. Fellow, Harvard Univ.; Asst. Prof., Assoc. Prof., Prof., Boston Univ.; Ptnr., Ximenes Rare Books; Sr. Ptnr., Hofmann & Freeman (USA); Dir., Hofmann & Freeman Ltd. (UK); Am. Rep., Bernard Quaritch, Ltd. Memberships: Bibliographical Soc.; Renaissance Soc.; MLA; Malone Soc.; Bibliographical Soc. of the Univ. of Va.; Antiquarian Booksellers Assn. of Am.; Int. League of Antiquarian Booksellers. Published works: Izmir, 1959; Apollonian Poems, 1961; Estrangements, 1965; Assays of Bias, 1970. Contbr. to: Am. Scholar; Antioch Review; Atlantic; Audience; Audit; Harvard Advocate; Identity; Mosaic; New Campus Writing; N.Y. Times; N.Y. Times Book Review; New Yorker; Nuova Precenza; Paris Review; Ploughshares; Poetry (Chicago); Prospect; Saturday Review; Voices; William & Mary Review. Address: Dept. of Engl.,

Boston Univ., Boston, MA 02215, U.S.A.

FREEMAN, Helen Ruth, pen names **MORK, Helen Ruth & WEGMAN, Helen Ruth,** b. 26 Mar. 1917. Educator. Education: B.A., Wellesley Coll.; M.A., Columbia Univ. Married 1) Fice Mork, dec., 1 daughter, Elizabeth, 2) Bernard Freeman. Positions held: Tchr. of Engl., N.Y.C. High Schls., 1945-69; Asst. Prin., Supvsn. Engl., N.Y.C. H.S. (Washington Irving) 1969-; Chmn., N.Y.C. High Schl. Poetry Contest, 1970-. Memberships: Poetry Soc. of Am.; Acad. of Am. Poets; Composers, Authors & Artists of Am. Published works: A Pride of Poets (anthol. of student poetry), 1972. Contbr. to: Wellesley Mag.; Nat. Scholastic Press Anthol.; Columbia Press Bulletin; Composers, Authors & Artists of Am. Bulletin. Address: 7 Peter Cooper Rd., N.Y., NY 10010, U.S.A.

FREEMAN, John, pen name **FREEMAN, J.,** b. 27 June 1952. Wages & Accounts Clerk. Positions held: Ed., Contac Arts Mag. Memberships: Yorkshire Arts Assn.; Vision (Arts & Drama Grp.). Published work: Face to Face (mag.). Contbr. to: Contac; All People Are Poets; Bogg; Both Sides Now; Gargantua; Genesis; Headlands; Id; In Concert; Lines; Mallorn; Moonshine; Pink Peace; Viewpoints. Address: 6 Main View, Thorne Rd., Stainforth, Nr. Doncaster, Yorks. DN7 5BU, U.K.

FREER, Maureen, b. 2 Aug. 1933. Housewife; Company Director; Stud Cattle Breeder. Education: B.A., Univ. of Qld. Married Gerard Freer, 1 son, 5 daughters. Positions held: Company Sec., Superfoods Pty. Ltd., 1958-; Dir., Superfoods Pty. Ltd., Red Seal Pty. Ltd. & Freers Pty. Ltd., 1963-; Prin., Coottha Coottha Charolais Cattle Stud, 1969-. Memberships: Fed. Pres., Fellowship of Australian Writers, 1972-74; Qld. Pres., Fellowship of Aust. Writers, 1970-74; Toowoomba Ladies Lit. Soc. Published works: Ed. & Author, Square Poets, Brisbane 71 & Writers' Guide, Warana 73; The Speyed Bitch, in prep. Contbr. to: The Australian; The Sunday Australian; The Sydney Morning Herald; Meanjin Qtly.; Vision; New Poetry; Poetry Mag.; Vista; Quadrant. Honours, awards: Poetry Soc. of Aust. Award, 1968; Warana Fest. Poetry Award, 1970. Address: 'Coottha Coottha', 445 Simpsons Rd., Bardon, Brisbane, Qld., Australia 4065.

FREESTON, Nicholas, b. 28 Aug. 1907. Poet. Published works: Christmas Bells & Other Poems, 1950; House in the Croft & Other Poems, 1952; The First Christmas & Other Poems, 1953; Collected Poems, 1955; Poems, 1966. Poems set to music & published as songs. incl: A Bird Song Away; The Stream; The Thrush; They Sweeten Time. Appearances on Radio & TV reading own work. Contbr. to: Daily Mail; Daily Express; The Sun; Daily Mirror. Honours, awards: Philippines Presidential Gold Medal for lyric poetry, United Poets Laureat Int., 1965; Dr. Lit. Ldrship, Int. Acad. of Ldrship, Quezon Capital City, Philippines, 1967; 13 poetry awards. Address: 79 Barnes St., Clayton-le-Moors, Lancs., U.K.

FREIBERG, Kay Markus, b. 17 Jul. 1935. Commercial Artist; Illustrator; Graphic Designer. Education: A.A.S. (1956). School of Art & Design, Rochester Inst. of Technology. Married, Samuel Freiberg. Positions held: Freelance commercial artist and graphic designer for various newspapers, publishers, advertisers, etc. in printing industry. Number of paintings in private collections; several one-man shows; has undertaken work in restoration of paintings. Memberships: Pennsylvania Poetry Soc. (Editor of Newsletter, since 1970); Carlisle Poets Workshop (Contest Chairman, Animal Kingdom Competition, since 1971; Treas., 1973-74); Harrisburg Manuscript Club (Treas., since 1969); N.F.S.P.S. (1974 Convention Co-Chairman); Carlisle Art Assoc., and numerous civic organisations. Contbr. to: (anthols.): A Goodly Heritage, 1968; Prize Poems, 1973; Flood of '72, 1973. (newspapers, journals): Eve. Sentinel; Dillsburg Bulletin; West Shore Guide; Carlisle Guide; Mechanicsburg News; R.I.T. Reporter; The Courant; The Candle; The Eve. News; Yiddish

Lingo, etc. Recip. Gemstone Award, 1972, on campus contest at N.F.S.P.S. Convention, Louisville, Kentucky; First Prize, 1973, Sans Souci Contest Category of P.P.S. annual contests. Address: R.D. 4, Carlisle, PA 17013, USA.

FRENCH, Dolores Marie (Cristina), b. 2 Mar. 1932. Secretary; School Teacher. Education: Am. Fndn. of Dramatic Arts; Rider Coll.; Univ. of Pa. Positions held: Tchr., 1953-58; Sec., 1959-66; Court Sec., 1967–. Memberships: Avalon Poetry Soc.; Cotton Astrological Soc. & Psychical Rsch. Fndn.; Legal Secretaries Grp.; Spiritual Frontiers, Inc. Contbr. to: Young Publs., 1967, '68, '69, '70; Flame, 1959, '62, '65, '67; Avalon, 1959, '60, '68; Int. Poetry Soc., 1970-71, '72, '73. Recip., 4th Prize, Avalon Int. Contest, etc. Address: Main St., Juliustown, NJ 08042, U.S.A.

FRENCH, Florence Pitzer, b. 23 Feb. 1895. Teacher of English. Education: B.S., Oklahoma State Univ. Married to Logan French (deceased). Positions held: Teacher (16 yrs.); HS Principal; Past. Pres., Toastmistress, Stillwater; Corres. Sec., Stillwater Writers; Snr. Vice-Pres., V.F.W. Post 2027. Memberships: Oklahoma Writers Fed.; Stillwater Writers. Contbr. of poems to: Denver Post (Empire Mag.); Grit; Christianity Today; Message Mag.; Conquest; Christian Parents; Junior Guide; The Christian; Sunshine Mag.; Home Life; Sunday School Times; Daily Meditation; Unity; Boys & Girls; Golden Trumpet; Fellowship in Prayer; Hearthstone Mag.; Farmland Mag.; Christian Home Messenger; Warner Press; Adult Teacher; Church School Mag.; Gospel Messenger; Sunday School Banner; The Youth's Comrade; Vision; Church Management; Union Gospel Press; Pilgrim Pub. House; Grace and Glory; Builders; Bay Shore Breeze; Joy Bearer; Life and Health; Young Publications (anthologies); Royal Pub. Co. (Anthol. of American Poetry 1964); The Muse; The Green World; Cardinal Poetry Qtly.; Scimitar and Song; Reflections; Poetry Digest; Vital Christianity; also various greeting card poems for Hall Mark Co., and others. Awards: Deep South Poetry Award; Gift from Young Publications; Gift from Scimitar & Song Donor; Poem of the Month (Sunshine Mag.). Address: 513 S. Knoblock, Stillwater, OK 74074, USA.

FRENCH, Joan, b. 20 Nov. 1935. Actress; Writer. Education: Vincentian Inst., Albany, NY.; State Univ. of NY. at Albany; studied acting at Erwin Piscator's Dramatic Workshop, NY. Contbr. to: The Archer; Voices Internat.; Hyacinths & Biscuits; Modern Images; Shore Poetry Anthol.; Poetry of Our Time. Address: 427 East 73rd St., New York, NY 10021, USA.

FRIAR, Kimon, b. 18 Nov. 1911. Translator of Modern Greek Poetry; University Professor. Education: B.A., Univ. of Wis., U.S.A., 1934; M.A., Univ. of Mich., 1939; Fulbright Rsch. Schlr. in Modern Greek Lit., Univ. of Athens, 1954-55. Positions held: Tchr. at: State Univ. of Iowa, 1939-40; Adelphi Coll., Garden City, N.Y., 1940-45; Amherst Coll., 1945-46; The Poetry Ctr., N.Y.C., 1943-47 & '51-52; N.Y. Univ., 1952-53; Univ. of Minn., 1953-54; Univ. of Calif. at Berkeley, 1965; Ind. Univ., 1971; Univ. of Ill., 1971; Dir., The Poetry Ctr., N.Y.C., 1943-47; The Theater Circle of the Circle-in-the-Sq., N.Y.C., 1950-52. Ed., New Writing (Detroit), 1936; Ed., The Charioteer, An Am. Quarterly of Modern Greek Culture, 1960-61; Greek Heritage, Quarterly of Modern Greek Culture, 1961-64; Contbng. Critic, New Republic, 1952-54. Published works: The Poetry Center Presents, 1947; Modern Poetry: American & British (anthol. co-edited w. John Brinnin), 1951; The Odyssey: A Modern Sequel, by Nikos Kazantzakis, transl., 1958; The Saviors of God: Spiritual Exercises, by Nikos Kazantzakis, transl., 1961; With Face to the Wall: The Selected Poems of Miltos Sahtouris, transl., 1961; Modern Greek Poetry, (anthol.) transl., 1973; Ed. & translator of Greek Section: Bantam Book of Modern European Poetry, 1965, & many other translations. Contbr. of poetry to Poetry, Out of Wisconsin, 1937 & Midland, 1961 & var. other mags., jrnls. & reviews. Recip. var. hons. &

awards inclng: Gold Plaque & Hon. Dip., Greek Br. of the Int. Soc. of P.R., Athens. Address: Kallidromiou 10, Athens 706, Greece.

FRICK, Elizabeth, b. 18 Jan. 1913. Retired. Positions held: var. temp. positions, –1946; Sec., State Veterinarian, Kansas, 1946-53; Clerk I, Catalog Div., Houston Public Lib., 1954-71. Memberships: State Chapt., Poetry Soc. of Tex. & the Houston Chapt. of Poetry Soc. of Tex., 1966–. Published works: Edelweiss, a book of poetry, 1966. Contbr. to num. anthols., mags., newspapers & jrnls. inclng: Ardentia Verba, 1967; Best In Poetry, 1968; Personal Poetry, vol. 2, 1970; Variety in Verse, 1966; Dawn Series, vol. 1, 1972; Poetry, Classical & Contemporary, 1969; From the Heart of America, 1968; Poems of Presidents & Your Townsman, 1968; Anthology of American Poetry Book 8, 1966; Coalgate Record Register; the Houston Post. Recip. var. poetry awards inclng: Cert. of Merit, Centro Studi e Scambi, Int., Rome, 1972. Address: 212 Redan, Houston, TX 77009, U.S.A.

FRICKX, Robert, pen name **MONTAL, Robert,** b. 21 Jan. 1927. University Professor. Married, 1 son, 1 daughter. currently Prof., Univ. of Brussels (V.U.B.) Memberships: Assn. of Belgian Writers; S.A.B.A.M. Published works: La traque (roman), 1970; Introduction à la poésie française (essay), 1970; Lautréamont (essay), 1973; La littérature belge d'expression française (essay), 1973 (in collab. w. Robert Bruniaux). Contbr. to: Les cahiers du groupe; L'arche; Tijdschrift van de Vrije Universiteit Brussel; Moderne Encyclopedie der Wereldliteratuur. Address: Rue Auguste Van Zande 56, 1080 Brussels, Belgium.

FRIDAY, Marjorie H., pen name **MARGE,** b. 19 Nov. 1910. Retired Teacher. Education: Florence Univ., Ala.; Samford Univ., B'ham, Ala.; M.A. in Elem. Educ., Univ. of Ala. Married 1) W.A. Martin, dec., 1 son, 2) W.C. Friday. Positions held: Tchr., Carbon Hill & Walker Co. Schls., Selma City. Member, Ala. Poetry Soc. Address: Rt. 5, Box 352, Selma, AL 36701, U.S.A.

FRIEDENKRAFT, b. 27 Mar. 1945. Poet. Educ: Licencié ès Sci.; Licencié, Philos.; Docteur de Spécialité; Attended Ecole Normale Superieure. m. Wan Hua Goh-Chapouthier, 1 d. Published works incl: Un cadre à notre amour?, 1967; Complainte en forme de mélodie, 1969; Mélusine, ou Ta Saveur et Ma Lutte, 1971; La Saison avec Miralna, 1972; Un, deux trois, Nous n'irons au bois, in prep. Contbr. to: ACILECE Revue; Poésie Vivante Anthol., etc. Address: c/o Chapouthier, 11 bis Rue du Val de Grâce, 75005 Paris, France.

FRIEDLAND, David Lionel, b. 31 Oct. 1936. Poet. Educ: B.A., Witwatersrand Univ., S. Africa, 1969. Contbr. to: New Coin; Purple Renoster; Wurm; Penguin Book of South Africa Verse (anthology), 1968. Recip., Critique Mag. Poetry Prizes, 1956 & '61. Address: 2 Farfields, Elray St., Fairmount Ext., Johannesburg, South Africa.

FRIEDMAN, Florence Zirinsky, b. 17 Feb. 1905. Retired Executive. Education: Heffley Inst., Brooklyn, N.Y.; Columbia Univ.; New Schl. for Soc. Rsch. Widow, 2 children. Positions held: V.P., Friedman Silver Co., 1930-53; Pres., ibid, 1953-60; V.P. & Chmn. of Bd., Bogart Mfg. Co., 1953-63 (ret'd); Pres., Revere Silversmiths, ret'd 1959. Established a yearly Walt Whitman Award through the Poetry Soc. of Am., in memory of husband, Joseph Friedman, for the best definitive study of the poet and his work. Memberships: Poetry Soc. of Am.; O'seas Press Club; Poetry Workshop at Fairleigh Dickinson Univ.; Brooklyn Mus.; Sponsor, Brooklyn Soc. of Artists, Am. Horse Shows Assn. Voluntary speaker for charitable & civic orgs. & volunteer Libn. at Patients & Staff Lib., Roosevelt Hosp., N.Y.C. Address: 155 West 68 St., Apt. 1134, N.Y., NY 10023, U.S.A.

FRIEDMAN, John, pen names **PATER, Elias** and **FRIEDMAN, Elias,** b. 11 Mar. 1916. Member of the Carmelite Order; Writer. Educ: M.B., Ch.B., Med. Fac.,

Univ. of Capetown, S. Africa, 1938; Entered Carmelite Order (O.D.C.), London, 1947; Study of Philos. & Theol., Tarascon & Lyons, France, 1948-54; Ordained, 1953; Special study of Hebrew, Carmelite monastery Stella Maris, Haifa, Israel, 1954–. Positions held: Intern, var. hosps., S. Africa, 1938-40; S. African Med. Corps, 1940-45; Med. CO, Camp Hosp., Robben Is., Capetown, 1944-46. Published works: The Redemption of Israel, 1947, translated into Hebrew, 1949; Translator, French-Engl., The Diocese of the Latin Patriarchate of Jerusalem, 1963; In Praise of Night (poetry), 1969; Variations on Bialik Themes, 1970. Contbr. to: New Coin; Ephermerides Carmeliticae; Cape Times; Southern Cross; Jewish Affairs; Mary; Carmel; Voices; Cape Argus. Honours, awards: Acad. schlrships., Univ. of Capetown, 1934-38; Olive Schriener Debut Prize, S. African Acad. of Sci. & Art, 1971. Address: Stella Maris Monastery, P.O. Box 9047, Haifa 31090, Israel.

FRIEDMAN, Kenneth Scott, pen name **FRIEDMAN, Ken.** Artist; Writer; Educator. Education: B.A. & M.A., San Francisco State Univ.; var. other courses. Positions held: Mbr., FLUXUS Grp., 1966–; Dir. of FLUXUS West (rep. Fluxus in portions of U.S.A., Canada, U.K. & Germany), 1966–; Ed.-in-Chief, FLUXUS WEST publs. & of FLUXUS Editions, 1966–; Fac., San Francisco State Coll. Expmtl. Coll., 1966-69; Contbng. Writer, Underground, Wash., D.C., 1967; Taught Lit. of Surrealism & the Avant-Garde, Engl. Dept. & Expanded Arts, Radio-TV-Film Dept., San Fran. State Coll., 1967; served as Ed., contbng. or Assoc. Ed., many publs.; Special Sessional Lectr., Vis. Artist, Dept. of Visual Arts, Univ. of Sask., Canada, 1972; Prog. Dir. & Dir. of Gall. for de Benneville Pines, Calif., 1972-73, etc. Mbr., var. profl. socs. Has had num. one-man art exhibs. & participates in grp. shows. Works are rep. in var. public colls. Published works incl: Fugue, 1965; The Bowery of the Mind, 1966; The Dreams, 1967; Cleanliness Kit, 1968; Veranstaltung 1969; This Breathing Miracle; Corsage, 1970-71; An International Contact List of the Arts, 1972; The Aesthetics, 1973; Aestetica (tranl. into German), 1974. Contbr. to var. anthols., periodicals. Has given lectures, seminars, workshops at var. instns. Honours, awards incl: The Friedman Collection, created by Univ. of Calif. to hold & catalogue his writings; Grants from Neb. State Coun. on the Arts, 1973. Address: 6361 Elmhurst Dr., San Diego, CA 92120, U.S.A.

FRIEND, Robert, b. 25 Nov. 1913. University Lecturer. Education: B.A., Brooklyn Coll.; M.A., Harvard Univ., U.S.A.; Ph.D., The Hebrew Univ., Jerusalem, Israel. Positions held: Western Union Messenger Boy; Typist; Inspector of Fire Extinguishers; University Lecturer. Published works: Shadow on the Sun, 1941; Salt Gifts, 1964; The Practice of Absence, 1971. Contbr. to: Poetry; The New Yorker; Saturday Review; Encounter; The London Mag.; The Prairie Schooner; The Jerusalem Post; Epoch; The N.Y. Times; Partisan Review; The New Yorker Book of Poems; The New York Times Book of Verse. Recip., The Jeannette Sewell Poetry Award, 1940. Address: 13 Jabotinsky St., Jerusalem, Israel.

FRIES, Marjorie Fifield, pen name **FRIES, Mardi,** b. 31 Oct. 1933. Poet. Education: B.S., Beloit College, Wis., 1955. Married Richard O. Fries. Memberships: Sec., Wis. Fellowship of Poets. Contbr. to: New Poetry Out of Wisconsin, 1969; Poet: An International Monthly; The Hartford Courant; Encounters. Honours, awards: Nat. Fed. of State Poetry Socs: 2nd pl.; Beaudoin Gemstone Awards, 1971, Hon. Mention (3rd), Ariz. State Poetry Award, 1973, Hon. Mention (4th), 1972; Gemstone Award, Wausau Fest. of Arts Poetry Awards, 1972. Address: 3143 Cliffside Dr., La Crosse, WI 54601, U.S.A.

FRIGGIERI, Oliver, b. 27 Mar. 1947. Master of Maltese. Education: B.A., Univ. of Malta, 1968. Positions held: Master of Maltese, The Malta Lyceum; Lit. Ed., In-Nazzjon Taghna. Has lectured to students & the general public, presented a weekly lit. prog. on local radio, & is frequently invited to take part in cultural & lit. discussion on radio. Memberships: Pres., Movement for the Promotion of Lit., Malta; Ghaqda Letterarja Maltija; Akkademja tal-Malti; Fellow, Int. Poetry Soc., U.K. Ed., Il-Polz, literary mag. Co-Fndr., Mbr. Edit. Bd., Saghtar, nat. secondary schls. mag., 1971–. Published works: (poetry) Dhahen fl-imhuh, 1967; Analizi '70, 1970; Mas-sejha tat-tnabar, 1971; Malta – the new poetry, 1971; Dwal fil-persjani, 1972; (criticism) Kittieba ta' zmienna, 1970; Ir-ruh fil-kelma, 1973; Ruzar Briffa – l-ahhar poeziji u bijografija, 1973; (biog. of poets) Dun Karm – hajja u karattru, 1971; Ruzar Briffa – hajja u Karattru, 1972; (novel) Meta xejn ma jitbiddel. Contbr. to var. mags., jrnls. Recip., Italian Embassy Book prize for Italian, 1968. Address: 6 Gemini Court, New Street off Qormi Rd., Birkirkara, Malta.

FRITH, Nigel Andrew Silver, b. 30 Nov. 1941. Tutor of English Literature. Education: B.A., St. Catherine's Coll., Oxford, 1963; B.Litt., ibid, 1972. Positions held: Libn., History Fac. Lib., Oxford, 1963; Profl. Actor, Peter Dews Shakespeare Co., Ravinia Park, Chicago, 1964; Tutor of Engl. Lit., Coleg Harlech, N. Wales, 1965-68. Memberships: Fndr., The New Renaissance. Published works: The Lover's Annual, 1965: In This Wild Attic, 1972. Articles on the ideas of The New Renaissance in the Observer, Telegraph & Spectator. Broadcast on Radio 3. Address: 21 St. Andrew's Ln., Old Headington, Oxford, U.K.

FRITZ, Walter Helmut, b. 26 Aug. 1929. Writer. Education: Lit. & Philos., Univ. of Heidelberg, German Fed. Repub. Memberships: German Acad. for Speech & Poetry; Acad. for Sci. & Lit., Mainz; Bavarian Acad. of Fine Arts, Munich; PEN Club; Union of German Writers. Published works: Achtsam- sein, 1956; Veränderte Jahre, 1963; Umwege, 1964; Zwischenbemerkungen, 1965; Abweichung, 1965; Die Zuverlässigkeit der Unruhe, 1966; Bemerkungen zu einer Gegend, 1969; Die Verwechslung, 1970; Aus der Nähe, 1972; Die Beschaffenheit solcher Tage, 1972 Contbr. to: Neue Rundschau; Neue Deutsche Hefte; Frankfurter Hefte; Jahresring; Ensemble; Universitas; Neue Zürcher Zeitung: Stuttgarter Zeitung; Tagesspiegel and others. Honours, awards: Literature Prize of the City of Karlsruhe, 1960; Prize, Bavarian Acad. of Fine Arts, 1962; Heine-Taler, Lyrik Prize, 1966; Prize, Culture Circle, Fed. of German Industry, 1972. Address: Kolbergerstr. 2a, 75 Karlsruhe 1, German Fed. Repub.

FROST, Richard George, b. 8 Apr. 1929. Poet; Professor of English. Education: A.B., Calif. State Univ., San Jose, 1951; M.A., ibid, 1957. Married 1) Frances Atkins, 3 children, 2) Carol Kristin Kydd, 2 children. Positions held: Tchr. of Engl., Abraham Lincoln H.S., San Jose, Calif., 1952-56; Asst. in Engl., Calif. State Univ. at San Jose, 1956-57; Instr. of Engl., State Coll., Towson, Md., 1957-59; Mbr. of Engl. Dept., State Univ. Coll., Oneonta, N.Y., 1959–; Full Prof., 1972–; Poetry Ed., Satire Newsletter, 1964-74. Published works: Getting Drunk With The Birds, 1971; The Circus Villains, 1965. Contbr. to: Harper's Mag.; Poetry (Chicago); Sewanee Review; Carleton Miscellany; Prairie Schooner; The N.Y. Times; The N.Y. Herald Tribune; Mich. Qtly. Review; The Lit. Review, etc. Recip. var. grants & fellowships. Address: R.D. No. 2, Box 73, Otego, NY 13825, U.S.A.

FRUITS, Wanda Fae Hardin, pen name **NATHAN, Jo,** b. 2 Aug. 1930. Homemaker. Education: Oregon State Univ., Ore. Coll. of Educ., E. Ore. Coll., LBCC, Degree and grad. work in Elem. Education; grad. work in Writing, 1973. Positions held: Forest Lookout; Farmer; Library Aide; Teacher; Forest Dispatcher. Membership: Impact (Wisconsin group); Wordsmiths (local grp.). Contbr. to: Tweed (Australia); Lake Superior Review; Legend; Grande Rhonde Review; Herald & News, Klamath Falls; Democrat-Herald, Baker, Oregon; Lake County Examiner, Lakeview, Oregon. Awards: Hon. Mention, IMPACT contest, Summer, 1973, September, 1973. Address: 834 So. 4th St., Lakeview, OR 97630, USA.

FRUMKIN, Gene, b. 29 Jan. 1928. Author/Educator. Education: B.A. Engl., Univ. of Calif. at Los Angeles. Divorced, 2 children. Positions held: Lectr., Engl., Univ. of N.M., 1966-67; Asst. Prof. of Engl., ibid, 1967-71; Assoc. Prof. of Engl., 1971-. Member, Modern Lang. Assn.; AAUP. Published works: The Hawk & The Lizard, 1963; The Orange-Tree, 1965; The Rainbow-Walker, 1969; Dostoyevsky & Other Nature Poems, 1972; Locust Cry: Poems 1958-65, 1973. Contbr. to: The Nation; Saturday Review; Poetry (Chicago); Evergreen Review; Kayak; New Mexico Qtly.; Minn. Review; Chicago Review; N.Y. Herald Tribune; Choice; Chelsea; San Francisco Review; Calif. Qtly.; Beloit Poetry Jrnl.; Prairie Schooner; Cafe Solo; New Orleans Review; Dacotah Territory, etc. Address: 1332 Princeton Dr. N.E., Albuquerque, NM 87106, U.S.A.

FRY, Christopher, b. 18 Dec. 1907. Playwright. Fellow, Royal Soc. of Lit. Published works: The Boy with a Cart, 1939; The Firstborn, 1946; A Phoenix Too Frequent, 1945; The Lady's Not for Burning, 1949; Thor, with Angels, 1949; Venus Observed, 1950; A Sleep of Prisoners, 1951; The Dark is Light Enough, 1954; Cuztmantle, 1961; A Yard of Sun, 1970. Translations: Ring Round the Moon, 1950; The Lark, 1955; Tiger at the Gates, 1955; A Duel of Angels, 1968; Judith, 1959; Peer Gynt, 1970. Honours, awards: Foyle's Poetry Prize, 1950; The Queen's Gold Medal for Poetry, 1962; The Royal Society of Lit. Heinemann's Prize, 1962; Hon. Dip. of Arts (Manchester); etc. Address: c/o Emanuel Wax, 16 Cadogan Lane, London SW1, U.K.

FRY, L. Evelyn, pen name O'FRY, Evelyn Mills, b. 11 Feb. 1920. Secretary. Education: Assoc. in Sec. Sci., Landsale Schl. of Bus., Pa.; Nursing Schl., Univ. Hosp. Schl. of Nursing. Married twice, 3 children. Positions held: Secretarial jobs, Yale & Towne Lock, Refractory & Insulation Co., & Allan Wood Steel Co., Penco Div.; Private duty nursing, also floor duty in hospitals in Phila., & in Ga. as Staff Nurse; currently Sec., State Govt. Memberships: Nat. Fed. of State Poetry Socs.; Pa. Poetry Soc.; Harrisburg Manuscript Club. Contbr. to: Harrisburg Patriot; Bulloch County Times; Augusta Herald; Atlanta Jrnl.; Hyacinths & Biscuits, etc. Address: 134 N. 25 St., Camp Hill, PA 17011, U.S.A.

FUKUDA, Tsutomu, b. 24 Sept. 1905. Professor of English Literature & Language. Education: Osaka For. Lang. Coll. Tchrs. Inst.; D.Litt., Engl., Kansei Gakuin Univ., Japan; Fulbright Scholar to U.S.A., 1963. Married Toshie Tanaka, 5 children. Positions held: Lectr., Asst. Prof., Prof., Kirosaki Univ., 1951-59; Prof., Kobe Univ., 1959-69; Prof., Tezukayama Women's Jr. Coll., 1960-70; Prof., Kyoto Univ. of For. Studies, 1970-. Memberships: Decal, U.K.; V.P., Poetry Nippon, Nagoya, Japan; Editl. Cons., Orvis, U.K.; Far-East Ed., Poet, India. Published works: The Realm of Fancy, 65 vols., 1964-; Green & Gray, 1969; Heart & Art, 1970; English Translations of Japanese Poems, 1970-71; The Hanging Bridge, 1971. Contbr. to: An Anthology of Poetry for Children, 1970; IWWP Anthol., 1972; Listening to Japan, 1973; Poetry Nippon; Decal; Orbis; Poet; Ocarina; Tantrum; Tweed; Expression One; Shikai, Tokyo; Shikai, Nagoya (Haiku mag.); The Rising Generation; The Jrnl. of Current Engl.; Poetry Australia. Address: 3-17, 2-chome, Yakushidori, Nada, Kobe, Japan.

FUKUYAMA, Betty Marie (Adkins), b. 25 Feb. 1922. Teacher. Education: B.A., Boston Univ., 1947; M.A., Creative Writing, Univ. of Wash., Seattle, 1972. Married Tsutomu Tom Fukuyama, 5 children. Positions held: Tchr., Poetry Workshop, Fort Steilacoom Community Coll., Tacoma, 1969-; Tchr., Poetry Workshop, Western State Hosp., Ft. Steilacoom, Wash., 1973. Memberships: Sec., Wash. Poets Assn., 1971-; Pres., Tacoma Writers Club, 1964-66; Ore. State Poetry Assn., 1971-; Nat. League of Am. Pen Women, 1967-. Contbr. to: Am. Bard; Alaska Review; Bitterroot; Caravan; Des Moines Register; Christian Century; Greater Works; Green World; Lyrical Iowa; The Oregonian; Midwest Chaparral; Motive; Seydell Qtly.; Tacoma News Tribune, etc. Honours, awards: 1st, Ark. Br., Nat. League of Am. Pen Women 'Bernie Babcock Meml. Award', 1969; 3rd, Ore. State Poetry Assn., 1972. Address: 9920 Woodlawn Pl. Southwest, Tacoma, WA 98498, U.S.A.

FULKER, Tina, b. 3 July 1954. Window Displayer. Memberships: Ver Poets; Poets Vigilantes; Poetry Book Soc. Published works: Moonshine (booklet), 1971; Artist By The Shore (booklet), 1973. Contbr. to: Moonshine Poetry Mag. (in its 5th edn.); Bogg; Contac; Ludds Mill; Ver Poets Voices; Gargantua; Centre 17; Breath of Fresh Air; Shore (Cleveland Poetry Soc.); Sandwiches; Global Tapestry; Jo De Maggio; Radix; Circa; Next Wave (anthol.) Address: 6 Oxford Close, Edmonton, London N.9, U.K.

FULLER, John (Leopold), b. 1 Jan. 1937. Fellow of Magdalen Coll., Oxford. Education: St. Paul's School; New Coll., Oxford. Positions held: Visiting Lecturer, State Univ. of NY at Buffalo, 1962-63; Asst. Lecturer in Engl., Univ. of Manchester, 1963-66; Fellow and Tutor in Engl., Magdalen Coll., Oxford, 1966-. Published works: Fairground Music, 1961; The Tree that Walked, 1967; The Art of Love, 1968; The Labours of Hercules, 1969; The Wreck, 1970; Cannibals and Missionaries, 1972; Penguin Modern Poets 22, 1973; Epistles to Several Persons, 1973. Contbr. to: Agenda; Antaeus; The Review; Encounter; London Mag.; Spectator; New Statesman; Poetry (Chicago); Listener; New Yorker; NY Times; Times Lit. Supp.; Poesie Vivante, etc. Awards: Newdigate Prize, 1960; E.C. Gregory Award, 1965; Poetry Book Soc. Choice for The Tree that Walked, 1967. Address: Magdalen Coll., Oxford, UK.

FULLER, Roy Broadbent, b. 11 Feb. 1912. Solicitor, Poet. Positions held: Asst. Solicitor, Woolwich Equitable Bldg. Soc., UK, 1938-58; Solr., ibid, 1958-69; Dir., 1969; Prof. of Poetry, Univ. of Oxford, 1968. Memberships: Mbr. of Bd., Poetry Book Soc. Ltd.; Fellow, Royal Soc. of Lit. Published works: The Middle of a War, 1942; A Lost Season, 1944; Epitaphs & Occasions, 1949; Counterparts, 1954; Brutus' Orchard, 1957; The Second Curtain, 1953; Fantasy & Fugue, 1954; Image of a Society, 1956; The Ruined Boys, 1959; The Father's Comedy, 1961; The Perfect Fool, 1963; My Child, My Sister, 1965. Collected Poems, 1962; Buff, 1965; New Poems, 1968; Off Course, 1969. Contbr. to numerous publs. Honours, awards: Arts Coun. Prize, 1960; Duff Cooper Mem. Prize, 1969; CBE. Address: 37 Langton Way, London, SE3, UK.

FULTON, Robin, b. 6 May 1937. Poet, Editor. Education: M.A., Engl. Lang. & Lit., Edinburgh IUniv., Scotland, UK, 1955-59. Positions held: School Master, 1959-69: Writer's Fellowship, Edinburgh Univ., 1969-71; Ed., Lines Review, Scottish Lit. mag. Published works: (poetry) Instances, 1967; Inventories, 1969; The Spaces Between The Stones, 1971; The Man With The Surbahar, 1971; Tree-Lines, 1974; (translations) An Italian Quartet, 1966; Blok's 'Twelve', 1968; Five Swedish poets, 1972; Selected Poems of Lars Gustafsson, 1972; Selected poems of Gunnar Harding, 1973; Selected Poems of Tomas Transtromer, 1974; Selected Poems of Osten Sjöstrand, 1974; (edited) Lines Review (since 1967); Ten Scottish Poets, 1971; Trio: New Poets From Edinburgh, 1971; (criticism) Contemporary Scottish Poetry: Individuals and Contexts, 1974. Contbr. to: Studies in Scottish Literature; Scandinavica; Scottish Internat. Review; Shouts and Murmurs, 1963; Young Commonwealth Poets '65 (1965); Modern Scottish Poetry, 1966; The Scottish Literary Revival, 1968; Scottish Poetry, 1,2,1, 2, 3, Verse, 1969; Agenda; Akros; Critical Qtly.; English; Extra Verse: Glasgow Herald; Glasgow Rev.; Scotsman; Scottish Field; SSTA Mag.; Lines Rev.; New Saltire; Observer; Outposts; Poesie Vivante; Poetry Review; Tablet; Times Lit. Supp.: Transatlantic Rev.; Tribune; Yorks. Post; Poems read on BBC. Awards: 1966 shared Eric Gregory Award; 1969-71, Writer's Fellowship, Edinburgh Univ.; 1972, Scottish Arts Council Writer's

Bursary; 1973, Sveriges Författarfonden arbetsstipendium. Currently residing in Scandinavia.

G

GABRE-Medhin, Tsegaye, b. 17 Aug. 1936. Playwright; Poet; Director. Education: Ethiopian Church School; Elem. School; Gen. Wingate and Commercial High Schools; LL.B., Blackstone School of Law, Chicago; British Experimental Theatre at The Royal Court, 1959-60. Positions held: Asst. Librarian, Haile Selassie Addis Ababa Coll., 1957-59; Director, Haile Selassie 1 Theatre, 1961-71; now Research Fellow, Univ. of Dakar, Senegal, on African Art of Antiquities and writing on "Africa As Origin of Early Greek Theatre". Memberships: Soc. of African Cultures, and East African Rep.; Pres. of the Ethiopian Dramatists Union. Published works: Collection of English Poems, 1965; Translation in (verse) Amharic, Othello, 1963, Macbeth and Hamlet, 1969-70, and King Lear, 1970; Collection of Amharic Poems (Fire or Flower), 1973. Contbr. to: Ethiopia Observer; Presence Africaine; Ethiopian Dialogue; Transition; African Research; African Humanism; Scandinavian Culture; Henry: An Anthol. by World Poets, etc. Awards: Haile Selassie 1 Prize for Ethiopian Literature, 1967; Commander of the Senegal Nat. Order for Literary Merit, 1970. Address: P.O. Box 1024, Addis Ababa, Ethiopia.

GABRIEL, Louise Marsh, b. 13 Jan. 1897. Housewife; Writer; Public Speaker. Education: W.Va. Wesleyan Coll., 1941-42; Ohio Univ. Extension Courses. Married Cecil McClelland Gabriel, 2 sons. Positions held: Tchr., public & pvte. schls., 1917-20; Promotion Sec., W.Va. W.C.T.U.; Field Wkr., W.Va. W.C.T.U. & Ed., Yearbook, 1952-60; Contbng. Ed., Camping Int., 1960; Nat. Chaplain, Daughters of Am. Pioneers, 1963-64. Memberships: Pres., Parkersburg Chap., W.Va. Poetry Soc., 1967-70; Nat. Fed. Poetry Socs.; Affiliate, Acad. Am. Poets; Am. Poetry League; World Poetry Soc. Intercontinental, etc. Rep. in following anthols: Sea to Sea in Song, 1966-71; Spring Anthol., Mitre Press, 1969-72; Fchoes of W.Va., 1970; Yearbook Contemporary Poetry, 1971 & '72; Outstanding Contemporary Poetry, 1972; H.P.F.S.; 1972; Poems From the Hills, 1970-71. Contbr. to var. poetry mags. & other jrnls. Honours, awards incl: 1st prize, Cinquoin, W.Va. State, 1956; 1st pl., Little Kanawha Nature Contest, 1970 & 2nd, 1969; 1st pl., light verse, W.Va. State, 1970 & 2nd pl., historical, 1970. Address: 3107 Custer St., Parkersburg, WV 26101, U.S.A.

GABRIEL, Marie-Cruz, pen name **BRIAN,** b. 8 Aug. 1926. 1926, Hyderabad (Deccan), India, of Tamil stock. Teacher. Education: M.A., History. Positions held: Prin. of Coll.; Editor-in-Charge, Asia Publishing House, Calcutta, India; Lectr., Coll. of Tchr. Educ., Addis Ababa, Ethiopia. Member of Writers' Workshop, Calcutta. Author of Poems, 1968. Contbr. to Illustrated Weekly of India; Thought. Address: PO Box 2744, Addis Ababa, Ethiopia.

GAERTNER, Irene Kilbourne, pen name **KILBOURNE, Irene,** b. 30 Nov. Musician; Leatherworker. Education: HS Grad.; Night School, afterwards, and then Univ. Extension courses. Memberships: Poetry Soc. of Southern Calif. (and was Treas. for 16 yrs.); Calif. Fed. of Chaparral Poets; Nat. Sheet Music Soc. Published works include music (choral number, Windy Day), 1964; (orig. musical revue produced, 1964 (lyrics, music and sketches)). Contbr. to: The Lyric; The Writer; Sunset; CS Monitor; Weekly Unity Mag.; The Bard; Manuscript; Script; The Reviewer; The Spinners; Partisan; Westward; Dion; The Silver Bough; Pollen; Freelance Writer for greetings card companies; Poetry concerts with Classics Vocal Reading Group, and with The Olympian Players on recording tapes for the blind; also concerts, clubs, etc. Anthol. contbr. Internat. Who's Who in Poetry. Awards: Billings Award, 1st Prize 1957, 1961, 1963, Hon. Mention 1955 and 1960; Ben Field Award 1st

Prize 1965, 1968; Evans Award 4th Prize, 1962; Valley Writers' Council 2nd Prize, 1969; Calif. Fed. of Chaparral Poets contests, various prizes and hon. mentions 1947 to 1951. Address: 338 No. Kenmore Ave., Los Angeles, CA 90004, USA.

GALAI, Benjamin, b. 10 Apr. 1921. Journalist. Member, PEN, Israel. Published works: (poetry) With The Wind; Chesnuts; Third Return; Shores of Mercy; Voyage North: (novel) The Black Death; (for children) Bats of Acre; Armilos, King of Phillipi; Journey to the Land of the Camels; (jrnlsm.) Over A Cup of Coffee. Honours, awards: Ana Frank Prize; Fichman Prize; Lamdan Prize; Brener Prize; Shwimer Prize. Address: 111 Hatishbi St., Haifa, Israel.

GALE, Vi, b. Sweden. Free-lance Writer, Teacher of Creative Writing. Education: Univ. of Ore., Portland Ext.; Portland State Univ.; Lewis & Clark Coll.; Univ. of Colo. Positions held: Free-lance Writer, past 10 yrs.; Dir., Creative Writing Workshops, Portland YWCA, 1962-72; Writer-in-Residence, Eastern Ore. Coll., summer 1969; Writer-in-Res., Clatsop Community Coll., summer 1969; Selection Comm., NW Poetry Circuit, past 8 yrs. Memberships: Ore. State Poetry Assn.; Am. Acad. Poets. Published works: Several Houses, 1959; Love Always, 1965; 19 Ing Poems, 1970; Clouded Sea, 1971; Clear Water (forthcoming). Contbr. to: Poetry; Poetry NW; NW Rev.; Western Humanities; SW Rev.; Univ. of Portland Rev.; St. Andrews Review; New Orleans Poetry Jrnl.; Colo. Qtly.; Quarto; December; Elizabeth; Midwest, etc. Honours: Ore. Poetry Prize, 1964. Address: 407 Postal Bldg., Portland, Ore. 97204. USA.

GALIULO, Leonard Frank, b. 17 July 1940. College Professor. Education: B.A., Villanova Univ., U.S.A.; M.F.A., Univ. of Iowa. Positions held: Asst. Prof. of Engl., Mercy Coll., Dobbs Ferry, N.Y.; Instr. of Engl., Fredonia State Univ. & Columbus Coll. of Art & Design; Instr. of Music, Febbraio Schl. of Music. published works: Dust, 1971; Ego, 1972; The Smith, 1972; Alter-Ego, 1973. Contbr. to: New Voices in the Wind Anthol., 1970. Recip., Writing Grant to Univ. of Iowa Writers' Workshop, 1964. Address: 724 First St., Mamaroneck, NY 10543, U.S.A.

GALLER, David, b. 11 Mar. 1929. Writer. Education: B.A., New Schl. for Soc. Rsch., 1950; M.A., N.Y. Univ., 1959. Positions held: P.R. Writer, The Hertz Corp., N.Y.C.; Trade Mag. Ed., Spot Mag.; Instr. in Engl., N.Y. Univ.; Trade Book Production Mgr., W.W. Norton & Co. Published works: Leopards in the Temple, 1968 & Walls & Distances, 1959 (both books of poems). Three poems appear in New American Poetry, 1973. Contbr. to: The New Yorker; Esquire; The Nation; The N.Y. Times; Commentary; The Yale Review; Va. Quarterly Review; Kenyon Review; Sewanee Review; Accent; Origin; Neon; Hika; Epoch; Shawman; Beloit Poetry Jrnl.; The Reporter; Harper's Mag.; The Atlantic Monthly; Midstream; The Commonweal; Confrontation; Quarterly Review of Lit.; Shenandoah; The Ark; Poetry; Poetry Northwest; Chicago Review; Perspective; The Beat Anthol.; N.Y. Herald Tribune; Folio; Red Clay Rdr.; Folder, etc. Address: The MacMillan Co., 866 Third Ave., N.Y., NY 10022, U.S.A.

GALLIENNE, Margaret E(llen), b. 15 May 1913. Medical Secretary. Education: Commercial Coll., Barnstaple; Tech. Coll., Barnstaple; Cert. in Braille, Royal Nat. Inst. of Blind. Positions held: Civil Servant, 1935-42; Medical Secretary, firm of doctors, Barnstaple, 1942-; Sec., Barnstaple Soroptimist Club; Hon. Treas., Barnstaple Branch British Rheumatism & Arthritis Assoc. Memberships: Poetry Soc. of Michigan (USA); Wisconsin Regional Writers (USA); Assoc. of Medical Secretaries; N. Devon Samaritans; N. Devon Choral Soc. Contbr. to: Peninsula Poets. Address: Verdenne, Rock Park, Barnstaple, N. Devon, UK.

GALLOY, Alice, pen name **BELL, Viviane,** b. 9 Apr. 1923. Secretary; Journalist; Astrologer. Educ: Secretarial. musical & astrological studies. Positions held: Poet, 1943–; Jrnlst., Astrologer, 1970–; Poems and Role in "Sur deux notes", 1973-74, Mon cadavre sur un plateau, 1974. Memberships: PEN Club Int.; Assn. of Belgian Writers; Assn. of Walloon Writers; Poésie Vivante, Charleroi; Int. Union of Feminine Press. Published works: Rizières, 1950; Le Soleil Enrhumé, 1971; Le Trident de Neptune, 1972; La Lune Vagabonde, 1972; Vénus la Fugitive, 1972; Mars, mon fier amant, 1973. Contbr. to: Agence Economique et Financière; Peau de Serpent. Honours, awards incl: 2nd Prize, Poetry, Editions Regains, 1971; Grand Prix des Muses, Paris, 1972; 1st Int. Prose Prize, Sylarus, Italy, 1973; Odyssée Poetry Prize, Permanences Poétiques, Brussels, 1973; Gold Medal, Int. Club for Epistolary Rels., Paris, 1974. Address: 157 Rue Jourdan, 1060 Brussels, Belgium.

GALLUP, Richard John, pen name **DANGERFIELD, Harlan,** b. 3 July 1941. Playwright; Novelist; Musician; Poet. Educ: Tulane Univ., New Orleans; Columbia Univ. Married Carol Clifford, two children. Published works: Hinges, 1965; The Bingo: A Play in Five Acts, 1966. Contbr. to: Poetry; Angel Hair; World; Reindeer; Adventures in Poetry; Paris Review; Sparklers (anthology), 1969. Recip., Poets' Fndn. Award, 1966. Address: 54 East 3rd St., No. 2, New York, NY 10003, U.S.A.

GALVEZ, Luis R., b. 17 Apr. 1934. Translator. Education: Universidad Nacional de Ingeniería, Peru; Bachelor's degree in Hispanic Lits., Calif. State Univ., Northridge. Positions held: Tchng.; Coordinating of foreign lang. progs. for children; Translating (presently, the Diary of Anaïs Nin). Memberships: PAN; Co-Fndr. & First Pres., Sociedad de Cultura Hispánica. Recip. Award & Medal from the Nat. Assn. of Tchrs. of Spanish & Portuguese, for an original poem. Address: P.O. Box 24C45, Los Angeles, CA 90024, U.S.A.

GALVIN, Brendan James, b. 20 Oct. 1938. Poet; Professor of English. Education: B.S. in Natural Sci., Boston Coll., 1960; M.A. in Engl., Northeastern Univ., 1964; M.F.A., Engl., Univ. of Mass., 1968; Ph.D., ibid, 1970. Positions held: Instr. of Engl., Northeastern Univ.; Asst. Prof., Slippery Rock State Coll. & Ctrl. Conn. State Coll. Published works: (book) No Time for Good Reasons, 1974; (pamphlets) The Salt Farm, 1972; The Narrow Land, 1971. Contbr. to: Am. Review; Atlantic; College English; Concerning Poetry; Critical Qtly.; Epoch; Harper's; Hudson Review; Malahat Review; Mass. Review; The New Yorker; N.Y. Times; Northwest Review; Poetry Northwest; Monmouth Review; West Coast Review; The Fiddlehead; New England Review; Plainsong; Sage; Four Quarters; Falmouth Review; The Dragonfly. Radio Tape: The Poet Speaks, WGBH-FM, Boston, 1971. Address: 7 Webster Hill, New Britain, CT 06051, U.S.A.

GALVIN, Patrick, b. 15 Aug. 1927. Magazine Editor; Playwright. Married, two children. Positions held: Served, R.A.F.; Ed., Chanticleer Lit. Mag. Published works: Heart of Grace, 1958; Christ in London, 1960; (plays) And Him Stretched, 1961; Cry the Believers, 1962; Boy in the Smoke, 1965. Contbr. to: Irish Times; Irish Writing; Poetry Ireland; Irish Press; Stand; Observer; New Statesman; World Review; (anthologies) Prismatic Voices, 1958; Yet More Comic and Curious Verse, 1959; New Poets of Ireland, 1963; Various Light, 1964; Love Poems of the Irish, 1967.

GANGEMI, Kenneth, b. 23 Nov. 1937. Writer. Education: Engrng. degree, Rensselaer Polytechnic Inst., Troy, N.Y., 1959. Published works: (poetry) Lydia, 1970. Address: 211 East 5th St., N.Y., NY 10003, U.S.A.

GANNELLO, Alfreda Mavis, b. 17 Nov. 1926. Freelance Writer; Housewife. Education: Grade School; HS; College; Journalism. Married, Carmelo Charles Gannello, artist. Positions held: Clerk; Receptionist; Secretary. Memberships: Ill. State Poetry Soc.; American Poets Fellowship Soc.; Major Poets Chapter; Internat. Clover Poetry Assoc. Contbr.

to: (anthols.) Personal Poetry, 1970; Yearbook of Mod. Poetry, 1971; Midwest Poetry, 1972; (journals, Newspapers) Piggot Banner; Austinite; Words with Wings; Altooner Mirror; Jean's Journal; Cardinal; Robin; Tempo; Quintessence; Sparkling Gems; Avant Garde Poetry Journal; Southwest Times Record; Voices International; The Doings; Major Poets; American Poets; Prairie Poets; United Poets; Bitterroot; Creative Review; Time to Pause; The Villager; American Voice; Lincoln Log, etc. Awards: Title of Danae (1973) Internat. Clover Poetry Assoc.; Hon. Mention, Carlisle Poets Workshop (1973); 2 Prizes, Ill. State Poetry Soc. (1972). Address: 316 Washington Blvd., Oak Park, IL 60302, USA.

GARDEN, David Kenday, pen names, **BUDGIE; BURNS, Picasso,** b. 11 June 1949. Hospital Porter. Memberships: Poet's Vigilantes; Int. Poetry Soc. Poetry Soc. (UK.). Published works: several broadsheets, and: The Foolscap File; Satens Notebook, etc. Contbr. to various magazines. Address: 3 Mather Rd., Barton Estate, Headington, Oxford.

GARDNER, Donald Robert Hugh, b. 13 Sept. 1938. Former Lecturer; Writer. Educ: M.A. & B.Litt., Oxford Univ., U.K. Positions held: Lectr., Engl. Lit., Pace Coll., N.Y., U.S.A., 1964-66; Orgr., Poetry Workshop, Arts Lab., London, U.K., 1968. Published works: Peace Feelers and Other Poems, 1969; The Time of Dreams, 1969; El castillo de la pureza by Octavio Paz (translation), 1969. Contbr. to: Caterpillar; Vincent; For Now; El Corno Emplumado; Paris Review; Transatlantic Review; Ambit; London Magazine; Peace News; Con Cuba (anthology), 1969. Honours, awards: Rome Schlrship. in Mediaeval & Renaissance Studies, 1960; Creative Writing Fellowship, Helene Wurlitzer Fndn., 1966. Address: 14 Belitha Villas, Islington, London, N.1, U.K.

GARDNER, Isabella, b. 7 Sept. 1915. Education: Embassy Theatre School of Acting (Central School of Speech & Drama), Swiss Cottage, London, UK. Positions held: Associate Editor of Poetry Mag. in Chicago, 1953-56. Published works: Birthdays From The Ocean; The Looking Glass; West of Childhood. Contbr. to numerous anthols. and to: The New Yorker; Hudson Review; Sewanee Review; Kenyon Review; Furioso; Atlantic Monthly; Saturday Review; Mercury; Chicago Review; Minnesota Review; Encounter; Horizon, etc. Awards: Hazel Ferguson Award, Chicago, 1956. Address: 1305 Foothill Rd., Ojai, CA, USA.

GARDNER, Viola, b. 10 Feb. 1903. Retired Real Estate Broker. Education: B.S., K.C.T.C., Mo.; Grad., Tyler Commercial Coll., Tex. Married. Positions held: Self-employed real estate & Ins. broker; State Mgr., Children's Activities, Mo.; Poetry Ed., K.C. Jrnl. Post.; Asst. Ed., Am. Courier; Ed., Orphic Lute. Memberships: Regent, Mo. Chaparral Poets, 1957; Mo. Chmn., World Poetry Day; Hon. Mbr., Avalon Poets; Poetry Soc. of Tex. Published works: (books & anthols.) Immortal Cast; Poetry Need Not Beg; French Patterns; Bittersweet; Penny a Piece Poems; Where Petals Touch; Last Rose of Summer; When Violets Blue the Meadow; Down Paradise Lane; Love Poems by a Shy Violet; Ariel. Contbr. to: K.C. Star-Times; Am. Poetry; Avalon; Cycloflame; Quoin, etc. Address: 3815 Mercier, Kansas City, MO 64111, U.S.A.

GARFITT, Roger, b. 12 Apr. 1944. Lecturer; Freelance Writer. Education: Merton Coll., Oxford Univ. Married Priscilla Eckhard. Past Pres., Oxford Univ. Poetry Soc. Published works: Caught on Blue, 1970; Selected Poems, forthcoming 1974; critical essay in 'British Poetry Since 1960', 1972. Contbr. to: Ambit; Encounter; Isis; The Poetry Review; Poetry Nation; Solstice; Stand; T.L.S.; Poetry Now (BBC 3). Fiction Reviewer for the Listener. Poetry Critic of the London Mag. Recip., Dorothy Mauger Lit. Award, Portsmouth Fest., 1973, and Guinness Int. Poetry Prize, Stroud Festival, 1973. Address: South Weylands Farm, Esher Rd., Walton-on-Thames, Surrey, U.K.

GARLAND, Margaret J.C. Wolff, pen name **GARLAND, Margaret Wolff,** b. 5 Sept., 1907. Educator. Education: B.A., Iowa State Tchrs. Coll.; Cedar Falls; M.A., Univ. of Iowa, 1940; Adv. work at Univ. of Wis., Univ. of Minn., State Univ. of Kans., State Coll. of Iowa, Iowa State Univ., Ames. Widow of Earl S. Garland. Positions held: Tchr. of Engl., Jrnlsm. & Dramatics, Pub. H.S's, Cooper & New Hampton, Iowa; Tchr. of Engl. & Jrnlsm., Oelwein, Ft. Madison, Iowa, & Manitowoc, Wis.; Instr., Engl. & Jrnlsm., Wartburg Coll., Waverly, Iowa, 1946-50; Asst. Prof., ibid, 1950-65; Assoc. Prof., 1965-73; Emeritus, 1973–. Memberships incl: Pres., Waterloo-Cedar Rapids Br., Nat. League Am. Pen Women, 1960-62; Midwest Fed. of Chaparral Poets; Iowa Poetry Assn.; 2nd V.P., Iowa Poetry Day Assn., 1972–; Assn. for Educ. in Jrnlsm.; State Chmn., Nat. Coun. of Coll. Publs. Advisers, 1969-72; Western V.P., Alpha Phi Gamma. Clinic Judge of Poetry submitted to MFCP & IPDA for a number of years. Published works: (book of poems) The Good Wine, 1972. Contbr. to: Nat. Poetry Anthol., 1952-57; Lyrical Iowa, 1954–; IPDA Brochure of Poems, 1950–; The Pen Woman; Poet; Midwest Chaparral; Midland Schls. Mag.; Des Moines Register; The Castle. Recip. several poetry awards. Address: 1309 Second Ave. S.W., Waverly, IA 50677, U.S.A.

GARLICK, Raymond, b. 21 Sept. 1926. University Lecturer. Education: B.A., Univ. of Wales, 1944-48. Married Elin Jane Hughes w. 1 son, 1 daughter. Positions held: Fndr. & Ed., The Anglo-Welsh Review, Pembroke Dock, 1949-60; Sr. Lectr., Trinity Coll., Carmarthen, 1967–. Mbr., Literature Committee of the Welsh Arts Council. Published works: Poems from the Mountain-House, 1950; The Welsh-Speaking Sea, 1954; Blaenau Observed, 1957; Landscapes and Figures, 1964; A Sense of Europe: Collected Poems 1954-68, 1968; Literary Criticism: Anglo-Welsh Poetry from 1587 to 1800 (Dublin Magazine), 1954; The Interpreted Evening: A Note on Dylan Thomas's Pattern-Poem (Adam), 1956; Seventy Anglo-Welsh Poets (Welsh Anvil), 1964; Anglo-Welsh Literature (New Catholic Encyclopedia), 1964; An Anglo-Welsh Accidence (University of Wales Review), Welsh Poetry 1917-1967, 1969. Contbr. to (Anthols.): New Poems, 1954; Guiness Book of Poetry, 1958; John O'London's Anthology, 1961; Here Today, 1963; Welsh Voices, 1967; Lilting House, 1969; Poetry 69, 1969. Address: Bryn Isaf, Pentremeurig Rd., Camarthen, Wales.

GARNIER, Pierre, b. 9 Jan. 1928. Professor. Education: studied at the Univs. of Paris & Mainz; Lang. & Lit., Allemandes. Positions held: Chief Ed., reviews "Les Lettres", Revue du Spatialisme, 1963. Published works: Les Armes de la Terre, 1954; La Nuit est prisonnière des étoiles, 1958; Seconde Géographie, 1959; Sept poèmes extraits d'Ithaque, 1959; Les Synthèses, 1961; Poèmes mécaniques (w. Ilse Garnier) 1965; Prototypes – Textes pour une architecture (w. Ilse Garnier) 1965; Poèmes Franco-japonais (w. Seiichi Niikuni), 1966; Picardie – coupes poétiques, 1967; Minipoèmes, textes concrets pour enfants, 1967; Six odes concrètes à la Picardie, 1967; Othon III – Jeanne d'Arc (w. Ilse Garnier), 1967; Perpetuum mobile, 1968; Esquisses palatines (w. Ilse Garnier), 1971. Address: 14 rue Gresset, 80000 Amiens, France.

GARRETT, Florence Rome, b. 10 Sept. 1912. Author. Married. Granddaughter of Tom Rome who, with his brother Andrew, printed the first edition of Walt Whitman's Leaves of Grass. Positions held: professional accompanist; piano teacher; lecturer on poetry. Memberships: Nat. League of American Pen Women (Pres., Long Island Branch; Poetry Chairman, Conn. Pioneer Branch); Long Island Poetry Day (Chairman); Walt Whitman Birthplace Assoc. (Sec.); Fellow, Internat. Poetry Soc. Published works: Edge of Day, 1954; More Than The Quiet Pond, 1969. Contbr. to: Saturday Review; New Review; The Country Poet; Golden Circle; Wings; The Sparrow; Cats Mag.; NY Herald Tribune; Brooklyn Daily Eagle; New Milford Times; SCAF Poets of 1966; SCAF's Best Poems 1965; SCAF Poets of 1968; Golden Quill Anthol. 70.

71. Awards: Wings First, 1954; Sharon Creative Arts Foundation, 1965; Nat. League of Am. Pen Women Regs., 1952, 56, 66; Inclusi; n of poem to Walt Whitman in Trent Collection, Duke Univ. Address: Botsford Hill Rd., Roxbury, CT 06783, USA.

GARRETT, George Palmer, b. 11 June 1929. Professor of English; Director of Writing Program; Poetry Editor. Educ: B.A. & M.A., Princeton Univ. Married, three children. Positions held: Served, U.S. Army; Tchr., Wesleyan Univ., Middletown, 1957-60, Rice Univ., Houston, 1961-62, Univ. of Va., Charlottesville, 1962-67. Prof. of Engl. & Dir. of Writing Prog., Hollins Coll., 1967–; Poetry Ed. (w. B.S. Johnson), Transatlantic Review, 1958–; Co-Ed., The Hollins Critic, 1968–. Published works: The Reverend Ghost: Poems, 1957; The Sleeping Gypsy and Other Poems, 1958; For a Bitter Season: New and Selected Poems, 1967; (novels) The Finished Man, 1959; Which Ones are the Enemy?, 1961; Do, Lord, Remember Me, 1964; (short stories) King of the Mountain, 1958, In the Briar Patch, 1961. Contbr. to: Sewanee Review; Virginia Quarterly Review; Mademoiselle; (anthologies) New Poems by American Poets, 1957; Poets at Wesleyan, 1959; Southern Poetry Today; Seven Princeton Poets, 1963; A Decade of Poetry, 1969. Recip., num. grants and prizes. Address: Box 9661, Hollins Coll., VA 24020, U.S.A.

GARRIGUE, Jean, b. 8 Dec. 1914. Poetry Editor; Lecturer. Educ: B.A., Univ. of Chgo., 1937; M.F.A., Univ. of Iowa, 1943. Positions held: Instr., Bard Coll., Annandale-on-Hudson, 1951-52; Queen's Coll., Flushing, 1952-53; The New Schl. for Soc. Rsch., 1955-56, Univ. of Conn., 1960-61; Lectr., Poetry, Smith Coll., Northampton, 1965-66; Schol., Radcliffe Inst., Cambridge, 1968-70; Poetry Ed., The New Leader, N.Y.C., 1965–. Published works: Five Young American Poets (w. others), 1944; The Ego and the Centaur, 1947; The Monument Rose, 1953; A Water Walk by Villa d'Este, 1959; New and Selected Poems, 1967; (critical study) Marianne Moore, 1956; Festschrift for Marianne Moore's Seventy-Seventh Birthday (essay), 1965; works of fiction in sev. books. Contbr. to: Hudson Review; Nation; Harper's Bazaar; New Yorker; (anthologies) A Little Treasury of American Poetry, 1948; A Little Treasury of Modern Poetry, 1950; Modern Verse in English, 1958; Modern Poets, 1963; Twentieth Century American Poetry, 1963. Recip., numerous awards, fellowships & prizes. Address: 4 Jones St., New York, NY, U.S.A.

GARRISON, Margaret Ellen (Peggy), pen name **GARRISON, Peggy,** b. 9 Aug. 1938. Poet/Writer/Teacher. Education: B.S., Univ. of Wis., Milwaukee, U.S.A.; Univ. of Caen, France; the New Schl. for Social Rsch.; Univ. of Calif. Ext., San Francisco. Positions held: Taught a creative writing workshop at The Ctr. for Human Potential, N.Y.C. Spring Semester, 1973; Cons. for the Village Poetry Proj., N.Y.C., 1973-74. Featured Readings incl: N.Y. Univ.; New Schl. for Social Rsch.; Supernova Poetry Series; N.Y. Poets' Cooperative; The Women's Interart Ctr.; The Basement Coffee House; Friends Sem.; CABLE TV. Currently collaborating w. Nancy Scott on a series of readings & book of their selected poetry entitled, Going into the 16th Round. Contbr. to: The Wormwood Review; Choice Mag.; For Now; The Grande Ronde Review; Second Coming; The Dragonfly; The Angels; Clown War; Wellesley News; Quixote Mag.; The Friends Sem. Review; The Milwaukee Jrnl. Address: 74 E. 7th St., N.Y., NY 10003, U.S.A.

GARSON, Joel Schafer, b. 30 Jul. 1946. Student, Poet. Education: H.S., 1965; Cuyahaga Community Coll., 1965-1968; Kent State Beachwood Univ., 1968-1970. Positions held: Mbr. Ed. Staff, Everyman Lit. Mag., 1966; Feature & Poetry Ed., Commuter (jrnl.); Poetry Ed., Kent Quarterly, Kent State Univ. Mbr.: Cleveland Poetry Workshop. Contrib. to: Commuter; Everyman; Kent Quarterly; Haiku Highlights. Address: Coventry Books, 1832 Coventry Rd., Cleveland Hts., Ohio 44118, USA.

GARY, Lorena Marsh. University Professor; Poet; Lecturer. Education: A.B., Western Michigan Univ.; M.A., Univ. of Michigan; Univ. of Chicago; Duke Univ. Positions held: Principal, HS, Athens, Michigan, 3 yrs.; Principal, Hopkins HS, Michigan, 1 yr.; Assoc. Prof., Engl. Dept., Western Michigan Univ., Kalamazoo, Michigan; Lecturer, Univ. of Tennessee Writing Conference. Memberships: Acad. of American Poets; American Acad. of Arts & Science; League of American Pen Women; CAAA.; Michigan Poetry Soc.; New Hampshire Poetry Soc., etc. Contbr. to: Nat. Observer; Indianapolis Daily News; Chicago Tribune; Detroit News; Battle Creek Enquirer; Hartford Times; Atlanta Journal; South Atlantic Qtly.; Sewanee Review; The Christian Leader; New Hampshire Profiles; Michigan Educational Journal; Scimitar & Song; Peninsula Poet; CAAA., etc. Address: 471 W. South St., 2F, Kalamazoo, MI 49006, USA.

GASCOYNE, David Emory, b. 10 Oct. 1916. Writer. Education: Salisbury Cathedral Choir Schl., UK; Regent's St. Polytech. Fellow of Royal Soc. of Lit. Published works: Poems, 1937-42; A Vagrant, 1950; Night Thoughts, 1957; Collected Poems, 1965; Collected Verse Translations, 1970. Contbr. to: New Verse; New Writing; Poetry London; The New Statesman & Nation; The Times Litterary Supplement; Botteghe Oscure, Rome; Malahat Review; Adam. Address: 48 Oxford St., Northwood, Cowes, Isle of Wight, UK.

GASPARINI, Len, b. 13 July 1941. Poet; Playwright; Substitute Teacher. Married, 2 children. Positions held: Truck Driver; Sailor; Jrnlst.; Substitute Tchr. Mbr., League of Canadian Poets. Published works: Cutty Sark, 1970; Acknowledgement to Life: The Collected Poems of Bertram Warr, edited, 1970; Tunnel Bus to Detroit, 1971; The Somniloquist, 1972. Contbr. to: Antigonish Review; Quarry; Canadian Forum; Impulse; The Fiddlehead; Prism International; West Coast Review; Queen's Quarterly; New American & Canadian Poetry; Saturday Night; Mainline; Alive. Recip., Canada Coun. Grants, 1969 & 71 & Ont. Arts Coun. Grant, 1973. Address: 179 Hanna East, Windsor, Ont., Canada.

GAUSE, Emilyn, pen names, **LEEDS, Lynne; GAUSE, Lynne,** b. 22 July 1927. Freelance Writer & Newspaper Columnist. Education: Mars Hill Coll., NC; Northern Ill. Univ., DeKalb, Ill.; Cape Fear Tech. Inst.; Grad. of Journalism Class, Craven Community Coll., New Bern, NC. Personal details: d. of Boney L. Malpass and Myrtle Everett Malpass (d.); m. to Thomas Sneed Gause, 1 s., 1 d. Positions held: Sec. Editor, DeKalb Chronicle; Staff Writer, Asst. Women's Ed. & Women's Ed., Columnist; Freelance Feature Articles on retainer; Sec. to Chambr. of Comm., New Bern, NC; Writer, currently with Sun Journal, New Bern, NC.; 1st Vice-Pres., New Bern Civic Theater. Memberships: Internat. Poetry Soc. (UK); New Bern Civic Theater. Published works: Petals & Pages: Rhyme or Reason, 1965; Matu And Matsue, 1973. Contbr. to: Chicago Tribune; The Hanover Sun Newspaper; Inklings in Star News Newspapers Mag.; Three Ring Circus in DeKalb County Press; The Pipeline; The Mars Hill Proclaimer; Angel Hour; Orbis, etc., Wildlife in North Carolina. Awards: Angel & Pixie Awards, Spearman Publs.; 1st Prize, Calif. Poetry Day Contest, 1970; Saluted as Today's Outstanding North Carolina Citizen, WNCT TV. Address: P.O. Box 2724, New Bern, NC 28560, USA.

GAVRONSKY, Serge, b. 16 Aug. 1932. Professor of French. Education: A.B., Columbia Coll., 1954; M.A., ibid, 1955; Ph.D., 1965. Married, 1 daughter. Positions held: Assoc. Prof. of French, Barnard Coll., Columbia Univ. Memberships: Exec. Bd., Poetry Soc. of Am., 1970-72; Co-Fndr. & Am. Ed., Two Cities; N.Y. Rep., Plumed Horn; Lectr., Acad. of Am. Poets. Published works: Lectures et compte-rendu, poèmes, 1973; Where's Vietnam (anthol.), 1967; In a Time of Revolution (anthol.), 1971; Man in the Poetic Mode (anthol.), 1970. Contbr. to: Les Temps modernes; Siècle à mains; Liberté; Voix des poètes; Two Cities; Plumed Horn; Columbia Forum; Dada/Surrealism; Bread; Weed; Things; Eventorium Muse; Theo; Wormwood; Sparrow; Poet & Critic; Sundial; Radex; Fragments; First Issue; Nation. Recip., Gold Medal, York Coll., CUNY, 1970. Address: French Dept., Barnard Coll., Columbia Univ., N.Y., NY 10027, U.S.A.

GAY, Clara Flournoy, b. 19 Dec. 1907. Owner of Art Gallery. Education: Centenary Coll., Shreveport, La. Positions held: Owner & Operator, Art Galleries, New Orleans, La., 1943-70. Memberships: La. State Poetry Soc., New Orleans, La.; The Out Door Int. Poets & Writers; The Round Table Club. Contbr. to: newspapers in New Orleans, Shreveport, Natchitoches, Ark.; La. Heritage; Reader's Digest. Recip., Int. Boswell Inst. Award, Rome, Italy. Address: 507 Rosebud Dr., Natchitoches, LA 71457, U.S.A.

GAY, K.C., b. 12 Feb. 1912. Librarian; Curator. Positions held: Curator, Poetry Collection, Lockwood Meml. Lib., State Univ. of N.Y. at Buffalo. Address: Poetry Collection, Lockwood Meml. Lib., SUNYAB, Buffalo, NY 14214, U.S.A.

GAY, Thomas, b. 8 Oct. 1905. Editor; Writer; Teacher. Education: Scholar, Clifton Coll., Scholar, Magdalen Coll., Oxford, U.K. Positions held: Revenue Officer & Magistrate, India; Dist & Sessions Judge; Registrar of Bombay High Ct.; Chmn., Ind. Enquiry Comm.; Schl. Tchr. & Acting Prin.; Film Exec.; Advt. Exec.; Ed., mag.; Univ. Lectr. Translations of poems of R.V. Pandit into English; Voices of Peace, 1967; The Tamarind Leaf, 1967; The Moon The Moon, 1969; My Goa, 1971. Contbr. to: Times of India; Illustrated Weekly of India; The Hindu; The Clarion, etc. Address: Dev Kunj, Prabhat Road, Poona 411004, India.

GELDER, John Thomas, pen name **GELDER, Jack,** b. 5 Jan. 1947. Poet; Writer. Education: Sandbank Public School, Dunoon Grammar School; Alnwick Coll. of Education; Newcastle Univ. Memberships: Pennine Poets; West Highland Poets (Sec.); Joachim Sperber German-Scottish Soc.; Gaelic Soc. of Scotland. Published works: Beyond the Green Mountains, 1962; Alle Strassen Munden in Schwarze Verwesung, 1966; Dark Shadow, 1968; The Unreturning, 1970; The Erotic Image, 1973. Contbr. to: Pennine Anthol.; Voice of the West; Platform; West Highland Poetry Mag.; Headland; Dunoon Herald; Argyllshire Standard. Awards: The Black Onyx (Leicestershire); 1968; Carlisle Medal (Cumberland), 1970. Address: 8 Riverbank Rd., Alnmouth, Northumberland NE66 2RH, UK.

GELFOND, Rhoda, b. 15 May 1946. Education: B.A., Univ. of Pennsylvania, 1968; M.A. in Creative Writing, The Johns Hopkins Univ., 1970; Masters Degree in Creative Writing, Brown Univ., 1972. Positions held: Employed by Rhode Island Council on the Arts in Education to read own poetry in the high schools; employed by the Pennsylvania Council on the Arts as a poet in their "Poets-in-the-Schools" project. Membership: Pennsylvania Poetry Soc.; Acad. of Am. Poets. Published work: The First Trail, 1972. Contbr. to: Baltimore Sun; Pendulum; New Poets 1970; The Poetry Newsletter; Roanoke Review; Hellcoal Annual One; Hellcoal Annual Three; Instant Anthol. Awards: 1st prize in the Soc. for the Alumni of the Univ. of Penna. Poetry Contest, June, 1968; Co-winner, 1st prize, The Acad. of American Poets Award at Brown Univ., June, 1971; 1st prize, The Winfield Townley Scott Mem. Award. Address: 716 Ashbourne Rd., Philadelphia, PA 19117, USA.

GENSLER, Kinereth, b. 17 Sept. 1922. Poet. Education: B.A., Univ. of Chicago, 1943; M.A., Columbia Univ., 1946. Married Walter J. Gensler, 3 children. Positions held: Poetry Workshop Tchr. in Elem. Schl. in Framingham, Mass., 1971, '72, Medway, Mass., 1973 & Watertown, Mass., 1973 under aegis of the Mass. Coun. on the Arts & Humanities. Memberships: Mbrship Chmn., New England Poetry Club; Poetry Soc. of Am. Published works: Songs of Cyprus (principal translator), Govt. Printing Office of

Cyprus, 1970 under auspices of the Coun. of Europe. Contbr. to: Fire-Exit; New Orlando Poetry Anthol.; New Renaissance; N.Y. Times; Poems/Women; Poetry Northwest; Premiere; Sequoia; Stonecloud; Va. Qtly. Review; Yankee. Honours, awards: Annual Award, Poetry Soc. of Am., 1969; 2nd prize, Power Dalton Award, New England Poetry Club, 1973. Address: 45 Gale Rd., Belmont, MA 02178, U.S.A.

GENTZLER, Keith Richard, b. 12 Apr. 1937. Urban Planner. Education: B.S., Millersville State Coll., Pa., U.S.A.; M.R.P., Pa. State Univ. Married Rie, 3 children (Kim, David & Scott). Positions held: Surveyor & Carpenter, 1955-59; Tchr., 1962-63; Urban Planner, 1963-73. Memberships: Fndr., The Acad. of Am. Poets; Pa. Poetry Soc. Contbr. to: The Lancaster Independent Press; The Unsung, vol. 2. Address: 2920 Spring Valley Rd., Lancaster, PA 17601, U.S.A.

GEORGAKAS, Dan, b. 1 Mar. 1938. Writer. Education: B.A., Wayne State Univ., 1959; M.A., Univ. of Mich., 1960. Published works: And All Living Things Their Children, 1972; Prison Poetry, 1973; The Broken Hoop, 1973; Red Shadows, 1973; Zodiac, 1974; Motor City Blues, 1974. Assoc. Ed., Cineaste. Address: Box 841, N.Y., NY 10009, U.S.A.

GEORGE, Emery Edward, b. 8 May 1933. Educator. Education: B.A., Univ. of Mich., 1955; M.A., ibid, 1959; Ph.D., 1964. Positions held: Instr., Univ. of Ill., 1964-65; Asst. Prof., ibid, 1965-66; Asst. Prof., Univ. of Mich., 1966-69; Assoc. Prof., ibid, 1969-. Memberships: Int. PEN, 1966-; Poetry Soc. of Am., 1971-. Published works: (poetry) Mountainwild, 1974; A Gift of Nerve, in Prep.; (books) Ed., Friedrich Hölderlin: An Early Modern, 1972; Hölderlin's 'Ars Poetica': A Part-Rigorous Analysis of Information Structure in the Late Hymns, 1973; Co-Ed., Husbanding the Golden Grain: Studies in Honor of Henry W. Nordmeyer, 1973; 'Movable Metric, Translated Music: The Rubaiyát of Henry W. Nordmeyer', 1973; Ed., Digest of the Proceedings, Hölderlin Bicentennial Symposium, 1971. Translations incl: Sándor Weöres, 'Hölderlin' (trans. from Hungarian into German), Insel-Almanach auf das Jahr 1970: An Friedrich Hölderlin, Gedichte aus 180 Jahren deutsch-und fremdsprachiger Autoren, 1969; Three Poems by Aleksis Rannit in Baltic Literature: A Survey of Finnish, Estonian, Latvian & Lithuanian Literatures, 1970; Viacheslav Ivanov, 'Winter Sonnets' and 'Italian Sonnets', Russian Lit. Tri-Qtly., 1972. Contbr. of poems, articles, reviews to jrnls., mags., schol. works. Recip., Avery & Jule Hopwood Major Award in Poetry, Univ. of Mich., 1960. Address: 1485 Maywood, Ann Arbor, MI 48103, U.S.A.

GEORGE, Peggy, pen name **GEORGE, Margaret,** b. 5 Aug. 1919. Housewife. Education: Marlborough Grammar School. Married; 1 s. Positions held: Civil Service Assistant until 1946. Memberships: Internat. Poetry Soc. (Founder Fellow); Guildford & West Surrey Branch, Poetry Soc. (Committee Member); Poets Vigilantes (Co-Founder and London Area Rep.); London Writer Circle Poets (Co-Organiser); Wey Poets (Founder Member); Richmond Poetry Soc. Contbr. to: Nucleus; Radix; Weyfarers; Overspill; Centre 17; Envoi; Success; Oasis; Expression One; Platform; Humorous Hotchpotch; Internat. Poetry Soc. Anthol., 1973. Awards: 1st Prize, Success Competition, No. 28, Sept., 1973; 2nd Prize, Platform/Success Competition, November, 1973; 1st Prize, Success Yrly. Competition, 1973. Address: 1 Rayleigh Court, Kingston upon Thames, Surrey KT1 3NF, UK.

GEORGE, Phillip Williams, pen name **GEORGE, Phil,** b. 22 Mar. 1946. Student. Education: Inst. of Am. Indian Arts, Santa Fe., N.M.; Gonzaga Univ.; Univ. of Calif., Santa Cruz, 2 yrs.; Calif. State Univ., Long Beach, Winter quarter, 1974. Published works: Design For Good Reading, 1969. Contbr. to: Whispering Winds, Ed. Terry D. Allen, 1969; Time Mag., 1970; I Am An Indian, Canada Schl. Text, 1968; Amon Carter Mus. of Western Art, Travelling show, 1973. Honours,

awards: Achievement Award, Inst. of Am. Indian Arts, 1965; Vincent Price Award, 1965 & '66; Golden Eagle Award, La Grande Fest. of Indian Arts, 1965; Patricia Benton Award, 1966; N.M. State Univ. Cit., 2 - 1965, 1 - 1966; Gold Medal Award, Nat. Poetry Day, 1966; 1st pl., Scottsdale Nat. Indian Arts Exhib., 1970. Poetry read before Congress, May 1965 & on Dick Cavett TV Talk Shows. Address: 2022 East Gordon, Spokane, WA 99207, U.S.A.

GERBER, Daniel Frank, Jr., pen name **GERBER, Dan,** b. 12 Aug. 1940. Writer-Poet; Novelist; Journalist. Education: B.A., Michigan State Univ., 1962. Positions held: Poet in Residence, Thomas Jefferson Coll.; Poet in Residence, Michigan State Univ. Published works: Five Blind Men, 1969; The Revenant, 1971; Departure, 1973; American Atlas (novel), 1973; Out of Control (novel), 1974. Contbr. to: Arbraxas; December; Epos; Greenfield Review; Hearse; Mikro-Kismos; The Nation; The New Yorker; The Partisan Review; Pebble; Stony Brook Poetry Journal; Sumac; Voyages; Inscape; New Letters; Pembrook; Equal Time; Seizure; The Ohio Review; The Red Cedar Review; The Shore Review; The Dragonfly; Noise Qtly.; Granite; (anthols.) Inside Outer Space; Michigan Signatures; Poem of the Month Club. Departure, selected for reading over the BBC, 1974. Address: P.O. Box 39, Fremont, MI 49412, USA.

GERBER, Lewis, b. 29 Nov. 1935. Teacher of History. Education: B.A., Hist., N.Y. Univ.; doctoral prog., Intellectual Hist., N.Y. Univ., 3 yrs. Married Carole L. Inge. Memberships: Poetry Soc. of Am., N.Y.C.; Acad. of Am. Poets. First vol.' of poetry entitled 'Country of His Gentle Keeping'. Contbr. to: Poet Lore: Mich. Qtly. Review: S.D. Review; Centennial Review; Iowa Review; Bitterroot. Address: 300 East 71 St., N.Y., NY 10021 U.S.A.

GERHARDT, Ida Gerdina Margaretha, b. 11 May 1905. Author. Education: studied Greek & Latin; Dr. of Literature. Positions held: Tchr. of Greek & Latin. Member, Maatschappij der Nederlandse Letterkunde. Published works: Kosmos, 1940; Het Veerhuis, 1945; Buiten Schot, 1947; Kwatrijnen in bpdracht, 1947; Sonnetten van een Leraar, 1952; Het levend Monogram, 1955; De Argelozen, 1955; De Hovenier, 1961; De Slechtvalk, 1966; De Ravenvecr, 1970; Twee uur: de klokken anrwoordden elhaal, 1971; De Psalmen, transl. from Hebrew in collab. w. Dr. Marie van der Zeydr; Vijt Vuuistenen, 1974; Transl. of Vergil & Lucretius. Contbr. to var. jrnls. Honours, awards: Van der Hoogtprijs, 1945; Poezieprijs van de Stad Amsterdam, 1955, '61. '70; Marianne Philipsprijs, 1967; Martinus Nijhoffprijs, 1968; Culturele prijs van de Gemeente Arnhem, 1970. Address: Zutfense weg 120, Eefde, Netherlands.

GERSHON, Karen Tripp, b. 29 Aug. 1923. Poet. Published works: The Relentless Year, 1959; Selected Poems, 1966; We Came as Children (collective autobiography), 1966; Postscript: A Collective Account of the Lives of Jews in West Germany since 1945, 1969. Contbr. to: Critical Quarterly; Midstream; (anthologies) New Poems, P.E.N. Anthology, 1963 & '65; Best Poems of 1963: The Borestone Mountain Poetry Awards, 1964. Honours, awards: Arts Coun. Poetry Award, 1967; Jewish Chronicle Book Prize, 1967; Grant from Pres. of Israel, 1967; Pioneer Women Poetry Award, 1968. Address: Jerusalem, Israel.

GERSTNER, Edna Rachel, b. 17 Apr. 1914. Housewife. Education: A.B., Wheaton Coll., Ill.; M.A., Univ. of Pennsylvania; Grad. Work, Columbia Univ., NY. Married; 3 children. Positions held: Teacher, Engl. Lit., Monroe HS., Indiana. Membership: Fort Ligonier Poetry Soc. Published works: Song By The River (novel), 1960; Idalette (novel), 1963. Contbr. to: Fort Ligonier Poetry Review; Ideals. Recip. 1st Annual Award, Fort Ligonier Poetry Review, 1954, 1959. Address: R.D.I, Ligonier, PA 15658, USA.

GERVAIS, Charles Henry Marty, pen name **GERVAIS,**

C.H., b. 20 Oct. 1946. Education: B.A., Univ. of Guelph; M.A., Univ. of Windsor. Raised by Anglo-French parents in farm country of Essex county, Canada. Membership: League of Canadian Poets. Published works: Other Marriage Vows, 1969; A Sympathy Orchestra, 1970; Bittersweet, 1972. Contbr. to: Poetry Australia; Fiddlehead; Alive; West Coast Review; Tamarack Review; Canadian Forum; Globe and Mail; Windsor Star; Storm Warning; Touchings. Address: R.R.I, Coatsworth, Ont., Canada.

GESSWEIN, Alfred, b. 6 Jan. 1911. Writer. Married. Positions held: Publisher, Yearbook 'Konfigurationen', 1965–; Publisher & Ed., lit. periodical, 'Podium', 1971–. Memberships: Austrian PEN Club; Osterr. Schriftstellerverband; Literaturkreis 'Podium'. Published works: Leg in den Wind sein Herz, 1960; An den Schläfen der Hügel, 1965; Vermessenes Gebiet, 1967; Der gläserne November, 1968; Zwischen Topfbäumen, 1972. Contbr. to: Literatur und Kritik; Zeitschrift Neutralität (Bern); Dimension (Tex.) Recip., Theodor Körner Prize for Lit., 1963 & '66. Address: Radetzkystrasse 4/15, 1030 Vienna, Austria.

GHIGNA, Charles Vincent, pen name, **TEAGUE, Christopher,** b. 25 Aug. 1946. English Instructor, Freelance. Education: Florida State Univ.; Univ. of South Florida; Florida Atlantic Univ., B.A., M.Ed. 1 d. Positions held: Poetry Editor, English Journal NCTE Publ.; Engl. Instr., Cypress Lake School, Fort Myers; Creative Writing Instr., Edison Community Coll., Ft. Myers; Actor: Asolo State Theatre, Sarasota, Florida; Actors Repertory Theatre, Fort Myers; Edison Players, Fort Myers. Memberships: Gulf Coast Writers Guild (Charter Member). Published works: Plastic Tears (poems); Act One: A Dream Play (poems). Contbr. to: Coll. Engl.; The Writer; English Journal; Changing Education; Uptown Beat; Nat. Poetry Press; Gato; Internat. Who's Who in Poetry; Avant Garde Poetry Journal; Yearbook of Mod. Poetry; Adventure and More; Oyez; Sand Castles; Prize Poems (Pennsylvania Poetry Soc.); New Voices in the Wind; Plaintiff; Bachaet; Dance of the Muse; Bitterroot; Modern Images; Outstanding Contemporary Poetry; Marian Helpers Bulletin; Eclectic; Hyacinths & Biscuits; Poetic License; New Renaissance; Janus, etc. Hon. mention, The Writer, 1969. Address: 2366 E. Mall Dr., Apt. 110, Fort Myers, FL 33901, USA.

GHISELIN, Brewster, b. 13 June 1903. Retired University Professor. Education: A.B., UCLA, U.S.A., 1927; M.A., Univ. of Calif., Berkeley, 1928; grad. study, Oxford Univ., U.K., 1928-29 & at Univ. of Calif., Berkeley, 1931-33. Positions held: Instr. in Engl., Univ. of Utah, Salt Lake City, 1929-31, 1934-38; Lectr., ibid, 1938-39; Asst. Prof., 1939-46; Assoc. Prof., 1946-50; Prof., 1950-71; Prof. Emeritus, 1971–; Dir., annual Writers' Conf., 1947-66; Disting. Rsch. Prof., 1967-68; Supvsr., Index of Am. Design, Federal Art Proj., Utah, 1936. Published works: Against the Circle, 1946; The Nets, 1955; Images & Impressions (w. others), 1969; Country of the Minotaur, 1970. Contbr. to num. mags., jrnls., inclng: Poetry; Am. Prefaces; Story; The Phoenix; Measure; Hudson Review; Sewanee Review; Accent; The Am. Scholar; Encounter. Honours. awards: Award, Nat. Inst. Arts & Letters, 1970; Charles Redd Prize, Utah Acad. of Scis., Arts & Letters, 1970; Blumenthal-Leviton-Blonder Prize for poems publd. in 'Poetry', 1973. Address: Dept. of Engl., Univ. of Utah, Salt Lake City, UT 84112, U.S.A.

GHITELMAN, Hélène, b. 29 Nov. 1916. Translator; Correspondent. Education: Univ. of Liege, Belgium; painting, Académie des Beaux-Arts. Positions held: worked as corres. in six langs. for sev. European & Brazilian companies. Memberships: Centre Europeen de Diffusion de la Culture, 1960-62; Cercle d'Etudes Litteraires Francaises; Int. Corres. for Poésie Vivante (seat in Geneva, Switz.), in Rio de Janeiro, Brazil, 1964-67; Casa do Poeta, Sao Paulo, Brazil, 1963-65; PEN Int.; Assn. of Belgian Writers. Published works: Avec des Mots, poems, 1962; Bresil a Nu, poems, (foreword by Robert Goffin) 1970; Voix des Sortileges,

poems (foreword by Raymond Quinot), 1972. Collaborator of following reviews: Apollo; Signor Si; Scarabee; Presences; Fanal; Aonde Vamos (Brazil). Honours, awards: Dip. of Hon., Prix 'Le Souvenir de Nicole Houssa', 1961; Palme D'Or, (Acad. du Disque de Poésie) Neuilly-Sur-Seine, 1962; 1st Prize, Médaille d'Argent, Union Culturelle de France, Paris, 1973. Address: Rue Jourdan 75, B – 1060, Brussels, Belgium.

GHOSE, Amal pen name **ESOHG, Lama,** b. 14 Apr. 1928. Journalist. Positions held: Freelance Jrnlst., 1950; Officer i/c & Corres., Amrita Bazar Patrika (the English Nationalist Daily), Madras. Published works: Devabhumi Dakshin, a travelogue, 1962; Ruby & Rouge, first coll. of English Poems, 1969; Pebbles & Pearls, first novel in English, 1971; So Many Roses, 2nd coll. of English poems, 1972; Flames of Agonies, 3rd coll. of Poems in English, 1973; Art – I Adore, an art book in English, 1973. Address: The Nook, Jaisaras, Madras 600028, India.

GHOSE, Zulfikar, b. 13 Mar. 1935. Poet; Novelist; Critic. Education: B.A., Keele Univ. Published works: (poetry) The Loss of India, 1964; Jets From Orange, 1967; The Violent West, 1972; (fiction) The Contradictions, 1966; The Murder of Aziz Khan, 1967; The Incredible Brazilian: The Native, 1972; (short stories) Statement Against Corpses (w. B.S. Johnson), 1964; (autobiog.) Confessions of a Native-Alien, 1965. Contbr. to: Encounter; Illustrated Weekly of India; Atlantic Monthly; Critical Quarterly; Listener; London Mag.; Outposts; Spectator; New Statesman; N.Y. Times; Times Lit. Supplement; Transatlantic Review; Western Daily Press; Yale Review; Malahat Review; Pakistan Quarterly; Poetry Northwest; Prairie Schooner; Western Mail; Western Humanities Review; The Bulletin; Chirimo. Honours, awards: Special Award, B.C. Gregory Trust, 1963; Poetry Bursary, Arts Coun. of G.B., 1967; Publication Award, ibid, 1972. Address: c/o Harold Matson Co. Inc., 22 East 40th St., N.Y., NY 10016, U.S.A.

GIAMMARINO, Jaye, Secretary; Receptionist; Poet. Education: N.Y. City Coll.; Ext. Courses, Univ. of Minn.; Penn State Univ. – Ext. Courses; Phila. Writers Conf. & St. Davids Writers Conf. Married Dr. Michael A. Giammarino. Positions held: Sec-Receptionist; Jury Commnr., Chester Co., Pa., 1969–; Mbr., Bd. of St. Davids Writers Conf. & Phila. Writers Conf.; Dir. of Regl. Progs. for Am. Poets Fellowship Soc.; Taught, Techniques of Poetry Writing, at confs.; Judge, Poetry Contests. Memberships incl: Poetry Soc. of Am. Treas., Nat. League Am. Pen Women, 1968-71; Dir. of Regl. Progs., Am. Poets Fellowship Soc.; World Poetry Soc. Intercontinental, etc. Published works: The First Thaw, 1966; Wine in a Gold Cup, 1967; Sun of Reflection, 1970. Ed: Badge of Promise (anthol.), 1968 & Moon Age Poets 1970. Contbr. to: Fordham Univ. Review; South Fla. Review; Spirit; South & West; Voices Int: Laurel Review; Cyclo-flame; Pen Women; Spring Anthol; Poems by Poets; Hartford Courant; Poet Lore; Denver Post; Tweed; Archer; Major Poets; Legend; Bardic Echoes, & many other. Honours, awards: 2nd Poet Laureate of Am. Poets Fellowship Soc., 1967; Gold Cup, Am. Poets Fellowship Soc. 1967; Dr. Humane Letters, Int. Acad., Hull, U.K., 1970; Dir. of Regl. Progs. (APFS) 1969, & others. Address: 519 E. Lincoln Highway, Coatesville, PA 19320, U.S.A.

GIBBON, Monk, b. 15 Dec. 1896. Author. Education: St. Columba's Coll.; Hist., Keble Coll., Oxford Univ., UK; Ph.D., Dublin Univ., Eire. Married to Winifred Dingwall, 1928; 6 children. Positions held: Served in France, WWI; Tchr., N. Wales, Switzerland, Dorset & Ireland. Memberships: VP, Irish Acad. of Letters; Fellow, Royal Soc. of Lit. Published works: The Tremulous String, 1926; The Branch of Hawthorn Tree, 1927; For Daws to Peck At, 1929; Seventeen Sonnets, 1932; This Insubstantial Pageant, 1951; Selected Poems, 1972. Contbr. to: Spectator; Observer; Forum: Dublin Magazine; Irish Times. Recip. of Tailteann Silver Medal for Poetry, 1928. Address: 24 Sandycove Rd., Sandycove, Co. Dublin,

Republic of Ireland.

GIBBS, Barbara, b. 23 Sept. 1912. Poet; Writer. Educ: B.A., Stanford Univ., 1934; M.A., Univ. Calif., 1935. Second marriage to Francis Golffing. Positions held: Tchr., Bennington Coll., 1952-53. Published works: The Well, 1941; The Green Chapel, 1958; Poems Written in Berlin, 1959; Sev. articles of Literary Criticism in mags. Contbr. to: Poetry; New Republic; Southern Review; Rocky Mountain Review; Partisan Review; New Yorker; (anthologies) Twelve Poets of the Pacific, 1937; A Little Treasury of World Poetry, 1947; Flowers of Evil, 1955; An Anthology of French Poetry from Nerval to Valery, 1958. Honours, awards: Oscar Blumenthal Prize, 1949; Guggenheim Fellowship, 1955-57. Address: R.F.D. 1, Peterborough, NH 03458, U.S.A.

GIBBS, Jeanne Osborne, b. 1 June 1920. Poet and Writer. Education: B.A., Agnes Scott Coll., Decatur, Ga. Positions held: Editorial Staff, The Atlanta Constitution, 1942; Feature Writer and Proof Reader, The New London Day, 1943; Book Reviewer, The Atlanta Journal, 1945-48; Book Editor, Georgia (magazine), since 1957. Memberships: Phi Beta Kappa; World Poetry Soc. Intercontinental; C.S.S.I.; Poetry Soc. of Georgia; Georgia Writers Assoc. (Awards Committee); Atlanta Writers Club (Pres., 1949-50). Published work: The Other Side of the Water, 1970. Contbr. to: (anthols.) Pancontinental Poets, 1972; Songs from American Hearts, 1948; Gold from Many Minds, 1967, etc. Christmas Poems from Georgia Mag., 1970 (11 poems); First 500 Poems from Georgia Mag., 1964 (14 poems); (mags., journals) NY Times; NY Herald Tribune; The Writer; Hartford Courant; Denver Post; Atlanta Constitution; Georgia Mag.; Georgia Review; PTA Mag.; Poet; Emory Univ. Qtly.; Stained Glass (mag. of the Stained Glass Assoc. of America); DeKalb Lit. Arts Journal; Poetry Soc. of Ga. Yearbook; Seydell Qtly.; Prize Poems of the Nat. Fed. of State Poetry Socs., 1968; Georgia Farmers' and Consumers' Market Bulletin, etc. Awards: (for bk. of poetry, The Other Side of the Water) Author of the Year in Poetry, Dixie Council of Authors and Journalists, 1971; Literary Achievement Award, Georgia Writers Assoc., 1971; Aurelia Austin Writer of the Year in Poetry, Atlanta Writers Club, 1971. Robt. Martin Award in internat. contest, NY Poetry Forum, 1973; John Clare prize, nat. contest, Poetry Soc. of Georgia, 1955; Cert. of Excellence for poetry brochure, South & West, 1969, etc. Address: 809 Pinetree Dr., Decatur, GA 30030, USA.

GIBBS, Robert John, b. 3 Feb. 1930. English Teacher. Education: B.A., Univ. of New Brunswick, Canada, 1951; B.A., M.A., Selwyn Coll., Cambridge Univ., U.K., 1952-54; M.A., Univ. of N.B., 1963; Ph.D., ibid, 1970. Positions held: Tchr., N.B. Schls., 1954-63; Lectr., Asst. & Assoc. Prof., Univ. of N.B., 1963-; Ed., The Fiddlehead, 1971-; Dir. of Grad. Studies in Engl., Univ. of N.B., 1973-. Mbrships: Editl. Bd., The Fiddlehead, 1967-; Chmn. & Ed., ibid, 1970-; League of Canadian Poets. Published works: in Five New Brunswick Poets, 1962; The Road from Here, 1968; Earth Charms Heard So Early, 1970; A Dog in a Dream, 1971; A Kind of Wakefulness, 1973. Contbr. to: The Fiddlehead; West Coast Review; Quarry; The Canadian Forum; Intercourse; Salt; The Wascana Review; Prism International; The Literary Review; Poetry Australia; Copperfield; The Small Pond; Scruncheons; Urchin. Recip., Bliss Carman Prize, 1950. Address: Dept. of Engl., Univ. of New Brunswick, Fredericton, N.B., Canada.

GIBSON, Dorothy Violet, b. 20 Dec. 1915. Executive Civil Service Officer. Education: Dip. in Sociol., London Univ. Married Douglas Gibson, 2 children. Positions held: Sec. work.; Tchng.; Nursing; Social Work; Civil Servant, Customs & Excise. Memberships: Soc. of Civil Service Authors; Southend Poetry Grp.; V. Chmn., Southend W.E.A. Contbr. to: Greenwood Anthol., 1948; Civil Service Poetry, 1972 & 73; Country Life; My Garden; Observer; Poetry Review; New Venture, 1973, etc. Honours, awards: 1st Prize, Herbert Spencer Meml. Comp., 1970 & 71; 1st Prize, Southend Standard Poetry Comp., 1970; 2nd Prize, Civil Service Further Educ. Nat. Poetry Comp., 1972, etc. Address: 100 Olive Ave., Leigh-on-Sea, Essex, U.K.

GIBSON, Douglas, b. 1 Dec. 1910. Poet & Playwright. Married Dorothy Gibson, 2 children. Ed., lit. mag., Quest, 1937-40. Memberships: Player$Playwrights; Temp. Mbr., Writers Guild of G.B.; Speaker to schls. on poetry for Eastern Arts Assn. Published works: Winter Journey (poems), 1945; The Singing Earth, 1951; Markets for Verse, 1956/74. Rep. in num. anthols. inclng: One Voice; This Living Stone; Poems of this War; Retrospect; Best Poems of 1943; Poems for France; Greenwood Anthol.; John o'London's Anthol.; Albemarle Books of Modern Verse; N.Y. Times Anthol.; O'Seas Schl. Anthol.; Happy Landings; Points of Light; My kind of Rhymes, 1972; Fireside Book, 1973; Tapestry, 1974, & many others. Broadcasts for: BBC & Copenhagen Radio; S. African Broadcasting Corp., 1973; Dial a Poem (Gtr. London Arts Coun), 1972. Contbr. to var. mags. & jrnls. in U.K., U.S.A. & Italy. Address: 100 Olive Ave., Leigh-on-Sea, Essex, U.K.

GIFFORD, Barry Colby, b. 18 Oct. 1946. Poet and Novelist. Education: DeWitt Clinton Grammar School and Mather HS (Chicago); Univ. of Missouri (1 yr.); King's Coll., Cambridge Univ. (1 term). All other education at sea and on the road. Positions held: Seaman; Asst. to Senior Editor of London publishing house; Dance Hall Bouncer; Music Critic; Post Office Clerk; Logger; HS Baseball Coach; Truck Driver. Published works: The Blood of the Parade, 1967; No Enemy of Horses, 1970; A Boy's Novel, 1973; Kerouac's Town, 1973; Coyote Tantras, 1973; Persimmons: Poems for Paintings, 1973. Contbr. to: NY Times (Paris Edition); South Florida Poetry Journal; Cimarron Review; Lampeter Muse; Tribal Village; Arx; Madrugada; Florida Qtly.; Chicago Review; Beloit Poetry Journal; Wisconsin Review; Measure; Rain; Artisans' Almanak; Journal 31; Road Apple Review; Twigs (Appalachian Studies Center); Truck; Sumus; Rolling Stone; Jazz and Pop; Titmouse Review; Bastard Angel; For Now; Open Reading; Calif. Qtly.; Noise Qtly.; Cottonwood Review. Recip. Silverthorne Award for Poetry, 1968. Address: c/o Serendipity Bookshop, 1790 Shattuck Ave., Berkeley, CA 94709, USA.

GIFFORD, Kenneth Harril, b. 8 Mar. 1923. Queen's Counsel. Education: Scotch Coll. & Prince Alfred's Coll., Adelaide, Australia; Melbourne Univ. Married Elizabeth E.L. Caldwell, 1 son, 1 daughter. Positions held: Ed. for Victoria 'Jindyworabork' Publications, 1944-45; Queen's Counsel for the States of Victoria, Queensland & Tasmania, 1964. Published works: The Reluctant Lover (poetry), 1943; The Glad Season, 1944; Jindyworabork – Towards an Australian Culture, 1944. Contbr. to: Meanjin Papers; Jindyworabork Anthol.; Australian Poetry. Address: Owen Dixon Chambers, 205 William St., Melbourne, Australia.

GILBERT, Elizabeth, pen name **EL GILBERT,** b. 13 Jan. 1931. Businesswoman. Education: Grad., Am. Acad. of Dramatic Arts, N.Y.C. Positions held: w. Capitol Records, N.Y.C.; MGM Records, N.Y.C.; CBS Records, N.Y.C.; currently Asst. to John Hammond, V.P., Columbia Records, N.Y.C. Memberships: SOLA; UAP; AAPA; Ariz. State Poetry Soc. Contbr. to: Modern Images, 1973; Tweed, 1973; Nausea One, 1973; Nevermind, 1973; The Sandcutters, 1973; Raunchy Rock, 1973; Amsterdam News, 1972; Cave, 1973; Grande Ronde Review, 1973; Aspect, 1973; Black World, 1972; Broadside Series of Poetry, 1973; Apostrophe, 1973; Lunatic Fringe, 1972; Orphic Lute, 1973; Japan Forum, 1973; Touchstone, 1973; Calico Patches; Speak Out; The Poet's Guild; Spinner; Wines & Roses; San Francisco Phoenix, etc. Recip. many poetry awards inclng: Hon. Mention & 1st pl., Sola Contest, 1973; 1st place, personal div., Inky Trails, 1973; 3rd pl., N.M. State Poetry Contest, 1973. Address: 305 West 55 St., Apt. 28, N.Y., NY 10019,

U.S.A.

GILBERT, Jack Glenn, b. 17 Feb. 1925. Writer; Teacher. Educ: A.B., Univ. of Pittsburgh; M.A., San Fran. State Coll. Positions held: Associated w. Poetry Ctr. of San Fran. State Coll.; Tchr., var. colls. Published works: Views of Jeopardy, 1962. Contbr. to: (anthologies) Poets of Today, 1964; Poems on Poetry, 1965; New Modern Poetry, 1967. Honours, awards: Yale Series of Younger Poets Award, 1962; Guggenheim Fellowship in Poetry, 1964. Address: 5904 Stanton Ave., Pittsburgh, PA, U.S.A.

GILBERT, Robert L., pen name **DAHLHOUSE, The.,** b. 10 June 1947. Writer; Poet ffEducation: Illinois State Univ., Normal, B.S. (Major: Speech; Minor: English). Memberships: ASCAP; AGAC; AF of M. Contbr. to: Creative Review; El Viento; Cardinal Poet. Qtly.; Hyacinths and Biscuits; Lake Superior Review; Spafaswap; Inland Writers Mag.; The Vidette; The Conn. Critic; Jean's Journal; Reach Out; Bachaet; Merlin's Magic; Midwest Poetry 1972; Modern Images; All-Time Favorite Poet; Best Poets of 20th Cent.; Bitterroot; Some Friends; Poetry Eastwest, etc. Address: P.O. Box 3262, Hollywood, CA 90028, USA.

GILBURT, Samuel G., b. 13 Sept. 1910. Teacher; Poet. Education: B.S., CCNY, 1933; M.A., Columbia Univ., 1935. Positions held: Prin., Elem. Schl. 212, Brooklyn; Prin., Morrison Jr. H.S., Brooklyn; Opened new Coleman Jr. H.S. 271, Hawthorne Jr. H.S. 74, 1965; Asst. Prof., Grad. Schl. of Educ., L.I. Univ., 1957-67; Guest Lectr., CCNY & Pratt Inst., N.Y. Univ.; currently Prin., Nathaniel Hawthorne Jr. H.S. Memberships: Poetry Soc. of Am., 1960–; Nat. Poetry Soc., Los Angeles; Centro Studi e Scambi Int., Rome; Association for Poetry Therapy, 1973-74. Contbr. to: Clearing House; Intercom; High Points; Creative Writing; Queens Tchr.; Student Writer; Bridges to Understanding, etc. Recip., Merit Cert., Leonardo Soc. of Rome, 1973. Address: 6751 – 181 St., Fresh Meadows, NY 11365, U.S.A.

GILDNER, Gary, b. 22 Aug. 1938. Writer. Education: Michigan State Univ., B.A., 1960, M.A., 1961. Published works: First Practice, 1969; Digging for Indians, 1971; Nails (forthcoming). Contbr. to: American Review; Antioch Review; The Nation; Foxfire; Crazy Horse; Lillabulero; New American Review; Sumac; Epoch; December; Occident; Poetry Northwest; The North American Review; Red Clay Reader; Sage; Motive; Voyages; Field; Fiction International; Quartet; Perspective; Focus/Midwest; Hearse; Granite; Univ. of Windsor Review; Northwest Review; Discourse; Poetry Bag; TransPacific; Sunday Clothes; Contempora; New Letters; Southern Poetry Review; Wormwood Review; Kansas Qtly.; Red Cedar Review; The Miscellany; Premiere; The Above Ground Review; Black Door; Spectrum; CutBank, etc. Awards: Robert Frost Fellowship, 1970; Nat. Endowment Fellowship, 1971. Address: 2915 School St., Des Moines, IA 50311, USA.

GILFILLAN, Merrill, pen name **RICK DU CALME,** b. 14 May 1945. Education: B.A., Univ. of Mich., 1967; M.F.A., Univ. of Iowa, 1969. Published works: Truck, 1970; 9:15, 1970; Ten Cents, 1971; Skyliner, 1973. Contbr. to: The World; Search for Tomorrow; Blue Pig; Buffalo Stamps; Doones; Suction; Telephone; River Run; Clothesline; Just Before Sailing; Nadine; Calypso Revue; Poetry (Baton Rouge); Strange Faeces. Recip., Hopwood Award in Poetry, 1967. Address: c/o Larry Fagin, 437 E. 12th St., N.Y., NY, U.S.A.

GILL, David Lawrence William, b. 3 July 1934. Lecturer at College of Education. Education: B.A., Univ. Coll., London, 1955; Birmingham Univ., 1959-60; Postgrad. Cert. in Educ., ibid; B.A., London (Ext.), 1970. Married, 3 children. Positions held: Tchr., Bedales, Hampshire; Nyakasura Schl., Uganda; Magdalen Coll. Schl., Oxford; currently Lectr., Engl. Dept., Newland Park Coll. of Educ., Chalfont St. Giles, Bucks. Mbr., The Poetry Soc. Published works: Men Without Evenings, 1966; The Pagoda & Other Poems,

1969; Fifty Years of Ondra Lysohorsky (in prep.) Contbr. to: The Listener; The Observer; Tribune; Country Life; Encounter; John o'London's; English; The Use of English; Delta; Invicta; Informer; Index; Dimension; A.M.A. Jrnl.; Twentieth Century; The Critical Quarterly; Platform; Streetword. Recip., Birmingham Post Poetry Prize, 1959. Address: 33 Melbourne Rd., High Wycombe, Bucks., U.K.

GILL, M. Lakshmi, b. 24 May 1943. English Instructor; Writer. Educ: B.A., Western Wash. State Coll., Bellingham; M.A., Univ. of B.C., Canada. Married W.G. Godfrey. Positions held: Engl. Instr., Notre Dame Univ., Nelson, B.C., 1965-67. Published works: Rape of the Spirit, 1962; During Rain, I Plant Chrysanthemums, 1966; Confrontations, 1969. Contbr. to: Prism International; West Coast Review; Quarry; New Wave Canada (anthology), 1966. Address: Kingston, Ontario, Canada.

GILLET, Philippe Claude Marie Jean, pen name **SAINT GIL, Philippe,** b. 13 July 1923. General Manager. Education: Licence en droit, Paris Univ.; Ancien Eleve Ecole Polytechnique. Positions held: Engr., Entreprise SOFRA (Public Works), 1948-55; Mbr. of Mng. Staff, Société Poliet et Chausson, 1955-56; Commercial Mgr., Voyer S.A. (Steel Structures), 1957; Gen. Sub. Mgr., ibid, 1965; Gen. Mgr., 1967–. Mbr., Société des Gens de Lettres. Published works: (novels) La Meilleure Part; La Machine à Faire des Dieux; Le Barrage; (poetry) Dialogues à une voix. Honours, awards: Chevalier de la Légion d'Honneur; Chevalier de l'Ordre National du Mérite; Jean Cocteau Poetry Prize for 'Dialogues à une voix', 1965; Académie Française Prizes for 'La Meilleure Part', 1955, and 'Dialogues à une voix', 1967. Address: Résidence Saint James, 64 Rue de Longchamp, 92000 Neuilly sur Seine, France.

GILLIAM, Elizabeth M., b. 1 Mar. 1930. Poet; Artist. Education: Kansas City Art Inst., 1952; Mo. Univ.; Univ. of Bonn, W. Germany, 1957-58; Painting Atelier of Theodora Kane, Wash. D.C., 1962-65; Painting classes in Bangkok, Thailand, 1966-67 & '68-69; Poetry Workshops at Montalvo Ctr., Saratoga, Calif. & Writing classes at The Poets Corner, San Jose, 1969-74. Married Ronald R. Gilliam, 3 children. Positions held: at Hallmark Greeting Card Co.; Corps of Army Engrs.; VFW Womens' Aux. Mag.; Rand Corp., Santa Monica, 1955. Memberships: Robert Frost Chapt. of Chaparral Poets; World Poetry Soc.; Poetry Soc. of Southern Calif. Contbr. to: Pacifica Mag.; Int. Poet; Swordsmans Review. Occasional contest awards and poems read over Calif. radio stns. Address: 1194 West Vanderbilt, Sunnyvale, CA 94087, U.S.A.

GILLIAMS, Eugene, pen name **DE WILDE, Frans,** b. 18 Oct. 1889. Retired Teacher of English. Education: State Trng. Schl. for Tchrs., Lier, Belgium; Cert. in Engl., Municipal special lang. courses, Antwerp. Married twice, 1 son (dec.) Positions held: Schl. Tchr., Municipal Elem. Schl., Antwerp; Belgian Army, WWI; Postal Clerk, Bath, Somerset, U.K.; English Tchr., Higher Tech. Inst. for Commerce & Administration, City of Antwerp. Memberships: Union of Flemish Writers; Bd. of Administrators, Belgian Union of Tourist Writers. Published works: Intrede, 1919; De Weg door het Woud, 1921; Het Huis op de Vlakte, 1926; De Veuchtende Schone, 1930; Dichter en Burgerman, 1935; Droef Dagboek, 1937; Het Eenzaam Hart, 1939; In Memoriam, 1941; De Slotson, 1944; De Verloren Zoon, 1945; Het Antwoord, 1951; Voor de Stilte, 1959; Aards Avontuur, 1964. Contbr. to: Dietse Warande en Belfozt; Le Journal des Poètes; Vormen; Helicon, etc. Recip., Poetry Prize for Voor de Stilte, 1969 & Special Prize for Collected Poems, 1966, Province of Antwerp. Address: 118 Lange Lozanastraat, Antwerp, Belgium.

GILLIS, Everett Alden, b. 4 Mar. 1914. College Professor. Education: B.A., Tex. Christian Univ., 1936; M.A., ibid, 1939; Ph.D., Univ. of Tex., 1948. Married Lizzie Mae Allen Gillis. Positions held: Asst. Prof. of Engl., Tex. Coll. of Arts & Industries, 1947-49; Prof. of

Engl., Tex. Tech. Univ., 1949–; Chmn., Dept. of Engl., Tex. Tech. Univ., 1964-69. Memberships: The Poetry Soc., London; MLA of Am.; Am. Folklore Soc.; Nat. Coun. of Tchrs. of English; Nat. Writers Club; Tex. Inst. of Letters; V.P., Poetry Soc. of Tex., 1951; Pres., Tex. Folklore Soc., 1961; Pres., Southwestern Am. Lit. Assn., 1970. Published works: Ed., Sun & Wind, 1936; Hello the House, 1944; Who Can Retreat? 1944; Sunrise in Texas, 1949; Angles of the Wind, 1954; Ballads for Texas Heroes, 1963. Contbr. to: Kaleidoscope Mag.; Poet Lore; Dallas Morning News; Am. Poet; Descant; N.Y. Times, etc. Recip. var. poetry hons. & awards inclng: Critics Award Prize, 1946, '47; All State Poetry Prize, 1954; Lone Star Prize, 1948; Old South Prize, 1952, '58, '73. Address: Engl. Dept., Tex. Tech. Univ., Lubbock, TX 79409, U.S.A.

GILLMEISTER, Agnes Miner, b. 1 June 1906. Housewife. Education: Ext. course, Univ. of Calif., Berkeley. Memberships: Galley Slaves, Ink; Pres., sev. yrs., sec. & currently Hd., Poetry Sect., ibid; Avalon, Tex. Poetry Soc.; Int. Poetry Soc. Published works: A Calendar of Verse (for children), 1968. Contbr. to: Galley Slaves, Ink Yearbook, 1961; Caravan to Christmas, Galley Slaves, Ink Anthol., 1965; Words, Galley Slaves, Ink Anthol., 1971; IWWP; Cyclotron; Cyclo-Flame; Imprints Quarterly; Haiku Highlights; Jean's Jrnl.; Snowy Egret; War Cry; Cats Mag.; The Baptist Ldr.; Vision; Rochester Democrat & Chronicle; Syracuse Post, etc. Honours, awards: Midget Pegasus Award; John Vilkas Meml. Award, 1966. Address: 106 Lewis St., Geneva, NY 14456, U.S.A.

GINGELL, Benjamin Broughton Gingell, b. 15 Dec. 1924. Publisher. Education: Corpus Christi Coll., Oxford Univ.; Fulbright Lectr., Univ. of Ark., U.S.A. Positions held: appointed to Macmillan, N.Y., 1953-57; appointed to Longmans (Far East Ed.), 1957-59; Mgr. & Dir., Longman Rhodesia, 1959–. Memberships: Poetry Soc. of Rhodesia; Chmn., Rhodesia Ctr. of PEN Int., 1970-73; V.Chmn., Rhodesia PEN, 1973–. Published works incl: Human & All Human, 1946. Contbr. to: Outposts; Two Tone, Salisbury Rhodesia; Poetry Rhodesia; Beneath a Rhodesian Sky. Honours, awards: Keats Poetry Award, 1973; Prize winner in 1972 & 73, poems published (U.K.) Address: P.O. Box ST 125, Southerton, Salisbury, Rhodesia.

GINSBERG, Allen, b. 3 June 1926. Poet. Education: Columbia Coll., 1948. Published works: Howl, 1956; Kaddish & Other Poems, 1960; Empty Mirror, 1960; The Yage Letters, 1963; Reality Sandwiches, 1963; Airplane Dreams, 1968; Planet News, 1968; Ankor Wat, 1968; TV Baby Poems, 1968; Indian Journals, 1970; Fall of America, 1973. Contbr. to: Times Lit. Supplement; Partisan Review; Evergreen Review; Black Mountain Review. Honours, awards: Guggenheim Fellowship, 1963; Am. Acad. of Arts & Letters, 1969. Address: c/o City Lights, 261 Columbus Ave., San Francisco, CA 94133, USA.

GINSBERG, Louis, b. 1 Oct. 1895. College Teacher. Education: B.A., Rutgers, 1918; M.A., Columbia Univ., 1924. Married, 2 sons. Positions held at: Central H.S., Paterson, N.J., 1921-61; Rutgers Univ. Coll., 1949-73. Memberships: Poetry Soc. of Am. (formerly on Bd. of Dirs.) Published works: The Attic of the Past, 1920; The Everlasting Minute, 1937; Morning in Spring (w. intro. by son, Allen Ginsberg) 1970. Rep. in num. anthols. inclng: Modern Am. & British Poetry (3rd & 4th edns.); Poetry: Is Appreciation & Enjoyment; Yesterday & Today; Doorways to Poetry; Discovery I; Rittenhouse's Third Little Book of Modern Verse; Herzberg's This Is America; Kaplan's The World of Poetry; Lask's N.Y. Times Book of Verse. Contbr. to num. mags. inclng: The Atlantic Monthly; The Am. Scholar; Poetry (Chicago); The Sat. Review; Ladies Home Jrnl.; N.M. Qtly.; The Nation; The New Republic; Prairie Schooner; The Mass. Review; The Commonweal; Beloit Poetry Jrnl.; Mich. Qtly. Review; N.Y. Qtly.; Christian Sci. Monitor; The Fiddlehead; The New Statesman; Trace. Address: 490 Park Ave, 4a, Paterson, NJ 07504, U.S.A.

GIORNO, John, b. 4 Dec. 1936. Poet. Education: B.A., Columbia Univ., 1958. Published works: The American Book of the Dead, 1964; Poems by John Giorno, 1967; Balling Buddha, 1970; Cancer In My Left Ball, 1973. Originator of Dail-a-Poem at: The Architectural League of N.Y., 1969; The Mus. of Contemporary Art, Chicago, 1969; The Mus. of Modern Art, N.Y., 1970; The Phila. Mus. of Art, 1973. LP record produced: The Dial-a-Poem Poets (2 record Album), 1972; The Dial-a-Poem Poets Disconnected (2 record Album), 1974. Address: 222 Bowery, N.Y., NY 10012, U.S.A.

GIOSEFFI, Dorothy Daniela, pen name, **GIOSEFFI, Daniela,** b. 12 Feb. 1941. Poet; Playwright; Actress; Multi-Media Artist; Dancer. Education: M.F.A. in Drama & Playwriting, Catholic Univ. of America, 1965; B.A. (Engl.), Montclair State Coll., 1963; Pub. Schools in New Jersey. Personal details: formerly married to Richard Kearney; 1 d. Positions held: 1971-73, playwright (plays produced at The Cubiculo Theatre, NY, and theatre at St. Clement's, NY); 1964-69, prof. actress: stock, resident and classical repertory throughout USA; 1972–, Multi-Media Artist: State Council on the Arts, NY; 1973–, Birth Dancer: New Feminist Talent Associates, NYC. Memberships: Poetry Soc. of America; Actors' Equity Assoc.; The Long Island Historical Soc. (and founder/administrator of the Walt Whitman/Hart Crane Memorial Poetry Series at the L.I. Hist. Soc.). Published works: (featured in) Rising Tides, 20th Century American Women Poets, 1973; Contemporaries, 1972; Woman: The New Voice, 1973. Contbr. to: The Nation; The Paris Review; Chelsea; Choice; Ambit (UK); Dialog (Canada); Antaeus; MS.; NY Qtly.; New Letters; The Minnesota Review; Penumbra; Sun; Modern Poetry Studies; Assembling, etc. Awards: Grant from The Creative Artists Public Service Program of NY State Council on the Arts, 1972, for multi-media poetry. Address: 276 Henry St., Brooklyn, NY 11201, USA.

GISGES, Jan Maria, b. 15 Jan. 1914. Writer. Education: Polish lang. philol. Married Anna Strychalski, 2 daughters. Positions held: Tchr. of Polish Lang.; Hd. of a Dept. at the Min. of Culture & Art; Hd. of the Dept. of Lit., Min. of Culture & Art; Min., Sec., Main Bd. of The Polish Writers Union, 1951–. Published works: The Prisoner & Peasant, 1946; The Partisan Poem, 1948; The First Love, 1951; To Those Who Go Ahead, 1957; The Closest to the Heart, 1955; The Time of Ripening, 1956; The Larches, 1959; The Most Important Matters, 1965; The Day of the Peaceful Sun, 1967; The Foreboding, 1970; The Song of the Royal Castle, 1972. Contbr. to: Kamena; Kronika; Kuźnica; Wici; Mazury i Warmia; Morze; Nowa Kultura; Orka; Pomorze; Praca Swietlicowa, etc. Honours, awards: Golden Cross of Merit, 1956; Officer's Cross of The Order Polonia Restituta, 1963; Medal of Labour, 2nd class, 1966; Commander's Cross, Order Polonia Restituta, 1974. Address: ul.Krakowskie Przedmieście 87/89, 00–079 Warsaw, Poland.

GITTINGS, Robert William Victor, b. 1 Feb. 1911. Author. Education: Jesus Coll., Cambridge Univ., U.K. Married Jo Manton. Positions held: Fellow & Supvsr., Jesus Coll., Cambridge Univ., 1933-40; Producer/Scriptwriter, BBC, 1940-63; Independent Author & Lectr., 1963–. Fellow, Royal Soc. of Lit. of the U.K., 1955–. Published works incl: (poems) The Roman Road, 1932; Story of Psyche, 1937; Wentworth Place, 1950; Famous Meeting, 1953; This Tower My Prison, 1960; Matters of Love & Death, 1968; American Journey: 25 Sonnets, 1972; num. critical & biographical works. Rep. in following anthols: The Oxford Book of Twentieth Century Verse, 1973. Contbr. to: Times Lit. Supplement; The Listener; New Statesman; N.Y. Times; Outposts, etc. Recip. Greenwood Prize of the Poetry Soc., 1947. Address: Dodds, East Dean, Chichester, Sussex, U.K.

GIUSEPPI, Charles Stephen Neville, b. 26 Dec. 1909. Freelance Writer. Positions held: Sr. Clerk, Trinidad Civil Service (now retired). Memberships: Fndr. Mbr.,

Int. Poetry Soc., U.K. Published works: The Light of Thought, 1943; Selected Poems, 1972. Contbr. to: The Trinidad Guardian; The Sunday Express; The Beacon (Trinidad); The Forum (Barbados); Caribbean Quarterly. Rep. in following anthols: One Voice, 1969; Bite In, 1971; Best Poems of Trinidad, 1939. Address: 41A Green St., Arima, Trinidad, W.I.

GIVENS, Violet (Banks-Robinson), pen name, **GIVENS, V.,** b. 1 Jan. 1924. Teacher; Writer. Education: Univ. of Kentucky at Lexington, Ky., 1949-51; Univ. of Maryland, 1960-61; A.B., Heidelberg Univ., Germany, 1961; Post Grad. Study in Education, Univ. of Kentucky, 1966. Personal details: Married, 1943; widowed, 1952; Remarried, 1954; 2 d. Positions held: Asst. Editor, 1959, Page Editor, 1962, Sumter Daily Item, S.C.; Elem. Teacher, Sumter, 1963; Secondary Teacher, Hillcrest HS, Sumter, 1964; Secondary Teacher, Dunbar HS, Lexington, Ky., 1966; Head Start, Orlando, Fla., 1968; Secondary Teacher, New Albany, Ohio, 1971; Community Activities Editor, Tri-Community News, Gahanna, Ohio, 1972-. Memberships: World Poetry Soc.; Kentucky State Poetry Soc.; Verse Writers Guild of Ohio. (also active in League of Women Voters; PTA; Girl Scouts; American Red Cross (USA, UK, Germany), UN Assoc., USA; Nat. Org. for Women; Ohio Commission on Status of Women). Published work: Singings of the Damned, 1971. Contbr. to: Jean's Journal; North American Mentor; Haiku; Haiku West; Dream Shop; Kauri; Rainbow Qtly.; Stylus; Educational Forum; From The Other Side Of Silence; Podium; Ashland Ky. Daily Independent; Columbus Ohio Citizen-Journal; Pegasus; Twigs; Ave Maria; Right Now; Charlotte Observer; Aphra; MS.; Approaches, and others. Awards: 2nd Prize, The Saint Competition, 1968; 3rd Prize, Colorado Branch, Am. Soc. Penwomen, 1968; 1st Prize, Ky. Writers' Guild Poetry Competition, 1969; 3rd Prize, KSPS, and 1st Prize, KSPS, 1968; 1st Prize, Haiku and 3rd Prize Ohio Poetry Day, 1970. Address: 319 N. Hamilton Rd., Gahanna, OH 43230, USA.

GJELSNESS, Barent Rudolph, b. 1 Feb. 1936. Teacher; Editor. Education: B.A., Engl., The Univ. of Mich., 1958; M.A., Engl., ibid, 1961. Positions held: Lectr., N.D. State Univ., Fargo, N.D., 1961-62; Lectr., Univ. of Southern Calif., L.A., 1962-63; Fellow, The Huntington Hartford Fndn., Pacific Palisades, 1963-64; Instr., Eastern Mich. Univ., Ypsilanti, Mich., 1965-67; Instr., Washtenaw Community Coll., Ann Arbor, 1966-67; Lectr., Cochise Coll., Douglas, Ariz., 1967-71; Ed., Changes Mag., 1971-73. Published works: On The Raft (chapbook of poetry), 1970. Contbr. to: Kayak; New Directions Anthol. 25; Intransit; The Minn. Review; Inscape; The Desert Review; The Sage; The Seventies; Tuatara (Canada); Hearse; Abraxas; Lillabulero; Suenos (Mexico); The Road Apple Review; The Baleen Press Anthol.; Poetry of the Desert Southwest; Edge (N.Z.); Guabi, Jrnl. of the Tibetan Kite Soc., etc. Honours, awards: Kenyon Prize Scholar in Engl., 1953; Huntington Hartford Fndn. Fellowship, 1964. Address: Box 92, Bisbee, AZ 85603, U.S.A.

GJESSING, Ketil, b. 18 Feb. 1934. Evaluator of Manuscripts. Education: Mag. art. & Cand. philol, Oslo Univ. Positions held: Tchr., Atlantic Coll., St. Donat's Castle, Llantwit Major, Glam., S. Wales; Program Selector, Norwegian Broadcasting Corp. Memberships: Den Norske Forfatterforening; Norsk Forfattersentrum. Published works: (colls. of peotry) Kransen om et mote, 1962; Frostjern, 1968; Private steiner bl.a., 1970. Rep. in following anthols: Ti unge. Studentlyrikk, 1958; Nye navn i norsk kunst, 1962; I grenselandet, 1969. Contbr. to: (newspapers) Dagbladet; Aftenposten; (lit. periodicals) Vinduet; Filologen; Profil; (other periodicals) Pacifisten (Danish); Pax; Atlantic Coll. Mag. (British). Address: Betzy Kjelsbergs V. 15, Oslo 4, Norway.

GLADISH, David, b. 18 Mar. 1928. Professor. Education: B.A., Lake Forest Coll., 1950; M.A., Univ. of Ill., 1954; Ph.D., Univ. of Ill., 1961. Married, 3 children. Positions held: Prof., Engl., Franklin Coll., Ind., 1961-

72. Memberships: MLA; Renaissance Soc. Ed., Gondibert, Oxford Univ. Press, 1971. Contbr. to: Accent; Epos; I Love You All Day (anthol.); Since Feeling Is First (anthol.); Indiana Sesquicentennial Poets (anthol.), 1966. Honours, awards: 2nd pl., Indiana Sesquicentennial Poetry Contest, 1966. Address: St. James, MI 49782, U.S.A.

GLASER, Isabel Joshlin, b. 7 June 1929. Freelance Writer & Teacher. Education: Peabody Coll.; Randolph-Macon Woman's Coll.; Baldwin-Wallace; Kent State Univ. & Ohio Univ. Widow of M.W. Glaser, 2 children. Positions held: H.S. Tchr., 1951-53; Elem. Schl. Tchr., 8 yrs.; Freelance Writer, 1968-; Engl. & Hist. Tchr. & Freelance Writer, 1973-. Memberships: Recording Sec., Poetry Soc. of Tenn.; Nat. League of Am. Pen Women, Memphis, Tn., Br.; Ozark Writers-Artists Guild; Parliamentarian, Tenn. Woman's Press & Author's Club. Contbr. to: Better Thoughts, 1970; Tenn. Voices, 1971; Human Voice; SPAFASWAP; Cyclo-Flame; Old Hickory Review; Salem Headlight; The Ozarks Mountaineer; Valley Views; Hawk & Whippoorwill Recalled; Haiku Highlights; Modern Images; Muse; Miss. Review; Wind; The Small Pond; Together; Weekly Reader; The Christian Sci. Monitor; Bastian Review; Poets Forum; The Christian; The Pen Woman; Prairie Schooner; A Place for Poets; Light Lines & Rhymes; South & West; Voices Int.; Poems by Poets, 1973; NFSPS Prize Anthol., etc. Recip. var. poetry prizes & awards inclng: 1st pl., April & Annual Contest of Poetry Soc. of Tenn., 1973; 1st pl., Tennant Award, Nat. Fed. of State Poetry Socs., Inc. Address: 5383 Mason Rd., Memphis, TN 38117, U.S.A.

GLASGOW, Eric, b. 10 June 1924. Historical Researcher. Education: St. John's Coll., Cambridge Univ.; Manchester Univ. Positions held: School Tchr. for 20 yrs.; ret'd 1967; currently engaged in Historical Rsch., chiefly Nineteenth-Century England. Contbr. to: Spring Anthol., 1971, '72, '73; Treasury of Modern Poets of 1973. Address: 45 York Rd., Birkdale, Southport, Lancs. PR8 2AY, U.K.

GLASS, Helen Bernice (Lemansky), pen name **GLASS, Helen B.,** b. 17 Feb. 1912. Medical Technologist. Education: B.A., Chemistry; Minor in Education and Engl., additional credits in technology, education, and Spanish. Married to Mathew J.; 1 s. (Mathew George). Positions held: Medical Technologist, Carle Clinic, Ill.; Kaiser Foundation Hospital, Calif.; Substitute Teacher, Vacaville School System, Calif.; Medical Technologist, A.R. Kincaid, M.D., Calif., and Mills Prof. Lab., Calif. Memberships: Calif. Chaparral (El Camino Chapter; Laurel Chapter); Sacramento Poets; Ina Coolbrith Circle. Published work: Voice Prints, 1970. Contbr. to: Grapevine; The Bard; Yearbook of Modern Poetry, 1972; Ina Coolbrith Anthol., 1972; Sacramento Poets (4 qtly. issues). Awards: 1st, St. John's Festival of Arts, 1969; Ina Coolbrith, 1970, 1st Ballad, 1971, 1st Ballad, 2nd Lyric; Poets' Dinner, 1972, 1st Ballad; Calif. Chaparral: monthly, Honor. Ment., 1972, and Annual Convention, Hon. Ment., 1973. Address: 10760 Carlos Way, Rancho Cordova, CA 95670, USA.

GLASSBERG, Gwendolyn Revilda Kroman Darling, pen names, **KROMAN, G. G.; KROMAN, Gwen G.,** b. 19 March 1927 in Philadelphia, Pennsylvania, USA. Portrait Artist; Poet. Married to Rubin Glassberg. Memberships: Fellow, Int. Poetry Soc., U.K. Intercontinental Biographical Assoc.; World Poetry Soc. Intercontinental; Accademia Internazionale Leonardo da Vinci; Nat. Fed. of State Poetry Socs.; Pennsylvania Poetry Soc., Inc.; Pennsylvania Folklore Soc.; Acad. of American Poets (affiliate); American Poets Fellowship Soc.; American Poetry League; CSSI; Internat. Platform Assoc.; Chester Co. Art Assoc. Contbr. to: Badge of Promise, 1968; From Sea to Sea in Song, 1970, 1971; Moon Age Poets, 1970; Pa. Poetry Soc. Prize Poems; Prize Poems 1969, 1972, 1973; Premier Poets 1971-72; From Sea to Sea in Song 50th Anniv. Edition, 1972; Internat. Who's Who in Poetry Anthol., 1972; Poet; American Poet; Prairie Poet; United Poets; American Poetry League

Bulletin. Recip. of numerous prizes, certs. of merit, scholarship, medals etc. for poetry. Address: Sevenoaks East, Apt. 438, 302 E. Marshall St., West Chester, PA 19380, USA.

GLASSBURY, Betty Blanc. Poet; Artist (Ceramics); Singer; Linguist; Art Collector. Widow of Dr. John A. Glassbury, 1 daughter. Memberships: Pres., Composers League of Creative Arts; Century Theatre Club; Ziegfield Club; Pres., Composers, Authors & Artists of Am.; Poetry Forum. Contbr. to: Bardic Echoes; Conn. Review; Poetry Digest; Poetry Review; Pegasus. Address: 150 W. 55th St., N.Y., NY 10019, U.S.A.

GLASSCO, John, b. 15 Dec. 1909. Author. Education: Bishop's Coll. Schl., Lennoxville, Que.; McGill Univ., Montreal. Memberships: League of Canadian Poets; Authors League of Am.; Canadian Writers Union; PEN Int. Published works: (verse) The Deficit Made Flesh, 1958; A Point of Sky, 1964; Selected Poems, 1971; Montreal, 1973. Contbr. to: Canadian Forum; First Statement; Queens Qtly.; Poetry (Chicago); Tamarack Review; The New Yorker; Canadian Literature; This Quarter, etc. Honours, awards: Prix David (Quebec Provincial Prize), 1958; Governor General's Prize for Poetry, 1972. Address: Foster, Que, Canada.

GLAZE, Andrew (Louis), b. 21 Apr. 1920. Press Officer. Education: B.A., Harvard Coll., U.S.A., 1942. Married, 2 children. Positions held: 1st Lt., US Army; Reporter, Birmingham, Ala. Post Herald; Writer, Press Officer, British Tourist Authority. Published works: Lines, 1964; Damned Ugly Children, 1966. Contbr. to: Poetry (Chicago); Paris Review; Va. Qtly. Review; Qtly. Rev. Lit.; New Directions Annuals 12 & 26; New Am. Review; New Yorker; Sat. Review; Atlantic; Audience; Epos; Lilliburlero; Kayak; Boston Univ. Jrnl.; New Orleans Review; Denver Qtly.; Dialog; The Nation; Tri-Qtly.; Poetry Southeast; Tenn. Poetry Jrnl.; Occasional Windhover (England). Honours, awards: Eunice Tietjens Award Poetry Mag., 1952; Notable Books List Am. Lib. Assn., 1966, (Damned Ugly Children) best 60 books of yr. Address: 803 Ninth Ave., N.Y., NY 10019, U.S.A.

GLEASON, Madeline, b. 26 Jan. 1913. Poet; Painter; Playwright. Positions held: Employed by brokerage firm, 1944-68; Fndr., San Fran. Poetry Guild; Orgr., first poetry festival in America, 1947; Tchr., Master Workshop in Poetry, Poetry Center of San Fran. State Coll., 1959-60. Published works: Poems 1944, 1944; The Metaphysical Needle, 1949; Concerto for Bell and Telephone, 1957. Contbr. to: (anthologies) A New Folder, Americans, 1959; New American Poetry, 1960; 53 American Poets Today, 1968. Several exhibitions of paintings. Address: 2932 Larkin St., San Francisco, CA 94109, U.S.A.

GLEESON, Ingrid L., b. 20 Jan. 1930. Legal Secretary. Education: some college, business school, creative writing courses; HS Grad. Married; 3 children. Positions held: varied secretarial positions in US and abroad. Memberships: Bd. of Trustees, Pa. Poetry Soc., Inc., 1973–; Treas., Harrisburg chapt., Nat. Org. Women; American Business Womens Assoc., Keystone State Chapter, Harrisburg, Pa.; Penna. Poetry Soc. Inc. (Corresponding Sec., since 1969); Phila. Writers Conference; St. Davids Writers Conference. Contbr. to: Eve. News (Harrisburg); The American Bard; Girl Talk Mag.; German-American Studies (Univ. of Ohio); various little mags., etc. Ed., Keystone Flier, Am. Bus. Womens Assn., 1973-74. Awards: Inky Trails, 1969, Cert. of Merit; 1st prize (portrait), 1970, Prize Poems, Penna. Poetry Soc.; Hon. Mention (historical), 1972, Prize Poems, Penna. Poetry Soc.; 1st prize, 1972, Limerick Contest, Unit. Universalist Church; 1st prizes, Writers Conf. Address: 5 Birchwood Dr., Harrisburg, PA 17109, USA.

GLEN, Emilie Carolyn, pen name, **GLEN, Emilie.** Writer; Actress. Education: Juilliard School of Music (piano pupil of Ernest Hutcheson); Columbia Univ.; American Creative Theatre. Positions held: Macmillan

Pub. Co.; on staff of The New Yorker. Memberships: Poetry Soc. of America; UPLI; American Creative Theatre. Published works: Up to us Chickens, 1973; Laughing Lute; Mad Hatter, etc. Contbr. to: New Directions; New Folder; New Voices; The Golden Years; Best Articles & Short Stories; Best American Short Stories; Foley, Anthol. of American Verse; America's Poets Speak; Lyrics of Love, 1963; Poetry in the Round; Anthol. of American Poetry; New Orlando Anthol.; translations in sev. French mags.; also contbr. to: The Nation, NY Qtly.; The Lit. Review; Poetry Dial; Western Humanities Review; The Kansas Mag.; Georgia Review; NM Qtly. Review; Prairie Schooner; CS Monitor; The American Mercury; NY Herald Tribune; Beloit Poetry Journal; The Fiddlehead; The Goliards; Poetry Review; Poet Lore; Fine Arts, and many others. Recip. Stephen Vincent Benet Award for best narrative poem, 1969; Hon. doctorate in Arts & Letters, Free Univ. of Pakistan, and Internat. Acad. of Leadership, etc. Address: 77 Columbia St., New York, NY 10002, USA.

GLOVER, Denis James Matthews, b. 1912. Lecturer. Education: Christ's Coll.; A.B., Canterbury Univ. Coll., New Zealand. Positions held: Jrnlst., The Press, Christchurch. Lectr., Engl.; Fndr., Caxton Press, Christchurch; currently, Tutor, Typography, Tech. Corresp. Inst., Christchurch. Published works: Thistledown, 1935; Six Easy Ways of Dodging Debt Collectors, 1936; The Arraignment of Paris, 1937; Thirteen Poems, 1939; Cold Tongue, 1940; Recent Poems, 1941; The Wind & the Sand: Poems 1934-44, 1945; Summer Flowers, 1945; Arawata Bill: A Sequence of Poems, 1953; Since Then, 1957; Poetry Harbinger (w. R.A.D. Fairburn), 1958; Selected Poems, 1964; Enter Without Knocking, 1964. Contbr. to various anthols. Address: c/o The Tech. Corresp. Inst., Christchurch, New Zealand.

GLUCK, Louise Elisabeth, b. 22 Apr. 1943. Writer. Education: Columbia Univ., U.S.A. Positions held: Vis. Artist, Goddard Coll.; Vis. Lectr., Univ. of North Carolina, Greensboro. Published works: Firstborn, 1968. Contbr. to: New Yorker; The Atlantic; Poetry; The Iowa Review; The Goddard Jrnl.; Salmagundi; Gulf Stream. Honours, awards: Rockefeller Fndn. Grant, 1969; Nat. Endowment for the Arts Grant, 1970; Eunice Tietjens Meml. Prize (Poetry mag.), 1972. Address: c/o Daniel Glück, 966 Northfield Rd., Woodmere, NY 11598, U.S.A.

GNAROWSKI, Michael, b. 27 Sept, 1934. Academician. Education: B.A., McGill Univ., Canada; M.A., Univ. of Montreal; Ph.D., Univ. of Ottawa. Positions held: Lectr. in Engl., Univ. of Sherbrooke; Asst. Prof., Lakehead Univ.; Assoc. Prof., Sir Geo. Williams Univ.; Prof., Carleton Univ. Mbr., P.E.N. Int. (Montreal Br.) Published works: Postscript for St. James Street, 1965; The Gentlemen Are Also Lexicographers, 1969. Contbr. to: Yes; The Fiddlehead; The Canadian Forum; Delta; The Montreal Poet Booster & Blaster; Inner Space. Address: c/o English Dept., Carleton Univ., Ottawa, Ont., Canada.

GOACHER, Denis John, b. 9 June 1925. Published works: Clear Lake Comes From Enjoyment, 1959; Logbook, 1972; Transversions, 1973; One Paradise, 1974. Contbr. to: Times Lit. Supplement; Time & Tide; BBC 3rd Prog.; Grossesteste Review; Last Fly; Origin; Decal; The Antigonish Review; Second Aeon; British Coun. Recordings. Address: Dione House, Wembworthy, Chulmleigh, N. Devon, U.K.

GODBERT, Geoffrey Harold, b. 11 June 1937. Public Relations Executive. Education: Grammar School; Royal Manchester Coll. of Music. Formerly, journalist. Contbr. to: Poetry Review; Priapus; Wheeler's Review. Address: 15 Thayer St., London W1, UK.

GODDARD, Hazel Idella, pen name **GODDARD, Hazel Firth,** b. 12 Dec. 1911. Civil Servant. Widow, 1 son. Positions held: Rural schl. tchr.; Telephone Order Clerk; Stenographer in corres. section at Simpson-Sears; Sec. in Law office; Sec., Civil Serv.; p/t

Interviewer for Rsch. Co. Memberships: Sec.-Treas., N.S. Poetry Soc.; Editl. Bd., Atlantic Mirror; Ed., Innovator, a small mag.; Ed., Pegasus; Pres., Scotian Pen Guild; Ed., publs. AMBER & IDELIA. Published works: Prisms in Print, 1963; Hazelbough, 1970; Paper Plates & Poetry (in prep.) Contbr. to num. jrnls. & mags. inclng: Dartmouth Free Press; Halifax Chronicle-Herald; Canadiana; The Rufus; Friendship Ferry; Encore. Recip. var. poetry awards & prizes inclng: Donald G. French Prize; Friendship Ferry 'Places' Prize; Hon. Mention, United Amateur Poets' Assn., 1973. Address: Scotian Pen Guild, P.O. Box 173, Dartmouth, Nova Scotia, Canada.

GODSIFF, Patricia Mary, pen name to 1948 **SAUNDERS, Patricia M.,** b. 21 Aug. 1915. Writer; Broadcaster; Teacher. Education: M.A., Hons., Univs. of Canterbury & Victoria, N.Z., 1954. Married. Positions held: Greek Tutor, St. Faith's House of Sacred Learning; Engl. Lang. & Lit. Tchr., St. Margaret's Coll., Christchurch; Commnd. Writer, N.Z. Broadcasting Corp., 1948–; Admin. Clerk, Min. of Defence, RNZAF Base, Woodbourne, 1964-66; Tchr. of Engl., Soc. & Liberal Studies & Tchr.-Libn., Marlborough Girls' Coll., 1966–; Mbr., N.Z. Lit. Fund Advsry. Comm., 1970-74. Memberships: Exec. Mbr., NZ Ctr., PEN Int., 1969; Hon Mbr., World Poetry Soc. Intercontinental; Fellow & Rep. for Oceania; Societa Dante Alighieri, Rome, Italy; Circolo Italiano di Wellington, N.Z.; N.Z. Del., World Congress of Poets, Manila, Philippines, 1969. Published works: Arena, 1948; Inside Looking Out, 1964. Contbr. to anthols., jrnls. inclng: N.Z. Best Poems, 1942-45; Discovering N.Z. Writing, 1965; Pacific & Other Verse, 1969; Nelson Evening Mail; Landfall; N.Z. Listener; Poet Int. Performances: Choreographic Poems, danced by Barbara de Castro Ballet; Eclipse, 1960; Safari, 1962; Delinquent, 1964. Poetry Recital, Adelaide Fest. of Arts, 1966. Honours, awards: Co-winner, UNESCO Contest, 1945; Winner, N.Z. Listener Poem Contest to Celebrate Laureateship, 1968; H.L.D., Univ. Libre Asie, 1969; Pres. Marcos Medal, World Cong. of Poets, Manila, 1969. Address: 87 Agincourt St., Renwick, Marlborough, New Zealand.

GOEDICKE, Patricia McKenna, b. 21 June 1931. Writer. Education: B.A., Middlebury Coll., Vt., 1953; M.A., Ohio Univ., 1963. Married to Mr. Goedicke. Positions held: Publg. Asst., 1955-56; Instr., Creative writing & comp., 1963-68; Instr., Poetry, Hunter Coll., 1969–. Memberships: Poetry Soc. of Am. Publications: Between Oceans, 1968. Contbr. to: (jrnls.) Kenyon Rev.; Nation; NY Times; Western Rev.; Va. Qtly. Rev.; Accent: Colo. Qtly.; Prairie Schooner; Best Articles & Stories; Perspective; San Francisco Rev.; Beloit Poetry Jrnl.; Antioch Rev.; Saturday Rev.; Poetry NW; Am. Weave; December; Epos; Wormwood Rev.; Today; Northwestern Rev.; N. Am. Rev.; Ohio Rev.; Poet, India; Lotus; (anthols.) Borestone Mountain Poetry Anthol., best poems of 1968; New Orlando Poetry Anthols., 4 poems. NET TV appearances. Honours: 2nd Prize, Virginia Clark Balch Poetry Contest, 1968; Poem incl. in Am. Women Poets issue of Poet, India. Address: Apt. 1J, 552 Riverside Dr., New York, NY 10027, USA.

GOKAK, Vinayak Krishna, pen name VINAYAK, b. 10 Aug. 1909. Teacher & Educational Administrator. Education: B.A. & M.A., Bombay Univ., 1929 & '31; M.A., (Oxon), 1938. Married Sharada B. Betadur, 1930, 1 son, 2 daughters. Positions held: Asst. Prof. of Engl., F.C. Poona, 1931-34; Prof. of Engl., F.C. & Willn. Coll., Sangli, 1934-36 & 1938-40; Prof. & Prin., Willn. Coll., 1940-44; Univ. Prof. of Engl., Osmania Univ., 1944-46; Prin. & Prof., Visnagar Coll., Guz, 1946-49; R.C., Kolhapur, 1949-52; K.C., Dharwar, 1952-58; Dir., Ctrl. Inst. of Engl., Hyderabad, 1959-66; V. Chancellor, Bangalore Univ., 1966-69; Dir., Indian Inst. of Adv. Study, Simla, 1970-71; Chmn., All India Sathya Sai Educl. Org., 1971–. Memberships incl: Pres., All Karnatak Lit. Conf., 1957; PEN; Bharatiya Jnana Pith Selection Comm. Published works: The Song of Life, 1948; In Life's Temple, 1965; Ed., The Golden Treasury of Indo-Anglian Poetry, 1970; 18 publs. of poetry in Kannada, 1930–. Contbr. to: Poetry, Chicago; Thought, India, etc. Honours, awards incl: Sahitya Akademi Prize, 1960; D.Litt., Karnatak Univ., 1967 & Univ. of the Pacific, Calif., U.S.A., 1969. Address: Sai Educational Organizations, Brindavan, Whitefield, Bangalore, India.

GOLDEN, Ellen, b. 24 Oct. 1915. Songwriter. Has had several of her songs released. Contbr. to: Frontier Records; Cactus Records; Hyperbolic Records. Address: Rte. 3, Clinton, IN 47842, U.S.A.

GOLDEN, Virginia Preston, b. 1 Nov. 1913. Housewife. Education: B.A., Mills Coll., Calif., 1935; grad. study in French, summer schl., Middlebury Coll., Vt.; Univ. of Lausanne, summer 1966. Married Richard Golden, 3 sons. Positions held: Tchr. of French, Am. Assn. of Univ. Women, Calif., 1954-57; Tchr. of French, St. Matthews Church Schl., 1955-58. Memberships: Writers Workshop, David McDavid, San Jose, Calif., 1969–'73–'74; Calif. Fed. of Chaparrel Poets, 1970-74; World Poetry Soc., 1973-74. Contbr. to: Janus, SCTH; Bardic Echoes; These Are My Jewels, anthol., 1971; Swordsman Review; Bachaet; Poet. Translator of French poetry in Poet, Aug. 1973. Address: 171 Mapache Dr., Portola Valley, CA 94025, U.S.A.

GOLDENBERG, Marion Heather, pen name SPEARS, Heather, b. 29 Sept. 1934. Painter. Education: B.A., Univ. of B.C., Canada, 1956; 2nd yr. Dip., Vancouver Schl. of Art, 1956. Published works: Asylum Poems, 1956; The Danish Portraits, 1964; From the Inside, 1972. Contbr. to Prism International (Vancouver). Address: Ved Parken 5, 3740 Svaneke, Denmark.

GOLDMAN, Isaie, pseudonym for recordings paulyphonique, b. 29 Sept. 1914. Pharmacist. Positions held incl: Ed., Prod., Poésie Sonore (recorded poetry), Geneva. Contbr. to var. newspapers & broadcasts on radio. Address: 4 Rue Bonivard, Geneva, Switzerland.

GOLDMAN, Lloyd Nathaniel, b. 22 July 1937. College Teacher. Education: Wash. Univ., St. Louis, 1958; M.A., Rice Univ., Houston, 1960; Ph.D., Univ. of Ill., 1964. Married, 1 son. Positions held: Tennis Ct. Mgr. & Instr.; Record Libn.; Grad. Rsch. Asst., Tchng. Asst., Instr. (Engl.), City Coll. of N.Y.; Asst. Prof., L.I. Univ., Brooklyn; Assoc. Prof., Jersey City State Coll., 1968–; Adjunct Assoc. Prof., Brooklyn Coll. Contbr. to: Galley Sail Review; The Sparrow Mag.; The Minn. Review; Western Review; The Carleton Miscellany; Prairie Schooner; Poetry Bag; Confrontation; Sou'wester; The New Orleans Review; Crisis; N.Y. Times; Engl.; Polio; Epoch; Miss. Review; Voci Del Nostro Tempo. Recip., Hon. Mention, First Internationale of Poetry, Gradara, Italy, 1971. Address: Engl. Dept., Jersey City State Coll., Jersey City, NJ 07305, U.S.A.

GOLDMAN, Michael Paul, b. 11 May 1936. Assistant Professor of English. Educ: B.A., Columbia Coll., 1956; B.A., Clare Coll., Cambridge, U.K., 1958; M.A., Princeton Univ., 1960; Ph.D., ibid, 1962. Married Eleanor Bergstein, 1965. Positions held: Poetry Ed., The Nation, N.Y.C., 1965-68; Asst. Prof., Engl. & Comparative fiit., Columbia Univ., 1966–. Published works: First Poems, 1965; At the Edge, 1969; Sev. literary criticism articles in var. mags. Contbr. to: New Yorker; Kenyon Review; Massachusetts Review; Poetry; Of Poetry and Power (anthology), 1964. Address: 425 Riverside Dr., New York, NY 10025, U.S.A.

GOLDTHORPE, Judith Mary, pen name GOLDTHORPE, Judy, b. 15 June 1944. Lecturer in Educational Psychology. Education: M.A., Edinburgh Univ., 1965; Tchng. Cert. & Dip. Rel. Ed., Moray House, Edinburgh; currently completing M.Sc. at Bradford Univ. Positions held: Tchr. of Engl. (V.S.O.), Simanggang Sec. Schl., Sarawak, Malaysia, 1966-67; Tchr. of Engl., Boroughmuir Sec. Schl., Edinburgh (& ran drama grp.); Postgrad. Student at Schl. of Rsch. in Educ., Bradford Univ. & Lectr., Dunfermline Coll. of P.E., Edinburgh. Contbr. to: Intak (Jrnl. of Yorkshire

Poets Assn.); Yorkshire Poets '69; Osgoldcross Review; Envoi. Address: 10D Silverknowes Neuk, Edinburgh EH4 5QA, U.K.

GOLOB, Zvonimir, b. 19 Feb. 1927. Writer. Education: studied literature (Engl., Russian & Yugoslav) at Zagreb Univ. Positions held: Was Co-Ed. of lit. mag. 'Krugovi' and the cultural weekly 'Telegram', Zagreb. Founded a grp. of composers & poets known as 'Studio 64' where the Zagreb schl. of Chanson developed. Has contributed to int. exhibs. of art photography & has had four individual exhibitions. Memberships: Authors' Assn. of Croatia; COMES (Assn. of European Writers); PEN. Published works: Okovane oči, 1946; Nema sna, 1951; Afrika, 1957; Glas koji odjekuje hodnicima, 1957; Elegije, 1963; Kao stotinu ruža, 1970; Covjek i pas i druge šansone, 1971; Naga, 1971. Translator of poetry, esp. Spanish & Russian & has published sev. books of Croatian versions of foreign poets (Esenin, Lorca, Neruda, etc.) Contbr. to: Krugovi; Telegram; Republika; Forum; Kolo; Literatura; Hrvatski tjednik; Oko (Zagreb); Delo; Nova misao; Polja (Novi Sad), etc. Recip., Goran's Wreath for Poetry', 1973. Address: Cakovečka 3a, 41000 Zagreb, Yugoslavia.

GOM, Leona Marie, b. 29 Aug. 1946. Teacher. Education: B.Ed., Univ. of Alta., Edmonton, Canada, 1968; M.A., ibid, 1971. Positions held: Sessional Lectr., Dept. of Engl., Univ. of Alta., Edmonton, 1970-72. Mbr., League of Canadian Poets. Published works: Kindling, 1971. Contbr. to: The Canadian Forum; Dalhousie Review; West Coast Review; White Pelican; Other Voices; Quarry; Ingluvin; Queen's Quarterly; Fiddlehead; Artscanada; Forty Women Poets of Canada; 39 Below; The Western Producer; Vanguard; The Gateway; var. Radio progs. Address: c/o Mrs. M. Gom, Box 323, Fairview, Alta., Canada.

GOMEZ, Pamela Susan, b. 18 Aug. 1947. Promotional Consultant. Memberships: La. State Poetry Soc.; Evanston Art Ctr.; Pan Am. Coun. of Chicago; Art Inst., Chicago. Published works: Lyric Louisiana. Contbr. to: The Great Speckled Bird, Atlanta, Ga.; Citizens Educ. Prog. News Letter, Atlanta, Ga. Honours: Poem, Inner Dynamics, read from the pulpit by minister, a leader in Human Relations Field, 1968. Address: 2420 Grant St., Evanston, 5Ill. 60201, USA.

GOMEZ-COSTA, Arturo, b. 28 May 1895. Poet; Writer; Retired Insurance Executive. Education: Bus. Admin., Columbia Univ., N.Y. Personal details: son of Serafina Costa-Shaw, descendant of George Bernard Shaw. Positions held: Gen. Agt. for Puerto Rico, Liverpool & London, U.K., & Independence Indemnity Co. of Phila., U.S.A.; V.P., Companía Carrion, Inc., 20 yrs; Exec., Caribbean Dept., Great Am. Ins. Co. Memberships: Former Treas, Puerto Rico Inst. of Hispanic Culture; Fndn. Mbr. & Exec. Dir., Puerto Rico Acad. of Arts & Sci.; Hon., Mus. of Arts, Ponce; Soc. of Puerto Rican Authors; Puerto Rican Soc. of Writers. Published works: El Alcázar de Ariel, 1918; San Juan, Ciudad Fantástica de América, 1957; Puerto Rico Heroico, 1960; Presencia de Isabel la Católica en Puerto Rico, 1963; Canto a Ponce en 25 Estampas, 1965; Las Luces en Exasis, 1970. Contbr. to: El Mundo; El Imparcial; El Dia; Isla Literaria; Alma Latina; Puerto Rico Ilustrado; Revista de las Antillas; Mundo Hispanico; ABC; Revista Universitaria de Sevilla; Revista Arquero de Barcelona; La Nación; Revista Sur; Enciclopedia histórico-antológica de las más famosas obras en lengua castellana. Honours, awards: 1st pl., Puerto Rican Contest, 1913; 2 1sts., Puerto Rico Atheneum, 1918; 3rd, Int. Contest, Barcelona, Spain, 1959; 1st, La Perla theatre Centenary, Puerto Rico, 1964; Hon. Plaque, Cath. Univ. of Puerto Rico, 1970. Address: Teniente Matta, 60 Santa Teresita, Santurce, Puerto Rico 00913.

GOMRINGER, Eugen, b. 20 Jan. 1925. Cultural Relations Manager. Education: Studies of Political Science & History of Art in Bern & Rome. Married, 3 sons. Positions held: Sec. of Coll. for Design, Ulm, Germany, 1954-58; Art Dir., 1959-67; Mng. Dir. of Swiss Assn. of Art & Industry, 1962-67; Mgr. of Cultural Relations in Germany, 1967-. Member, Acad. of Arts, Berlin. Published works: (books of poetry) The Constellations, 1953; 33 Constellations, 1960; other books of poetry (Book of Hours), 1964 & '65; (first manifesto) From Verse to Constellation, 1954; Ed. of 'Max Bill', 1958; monograph about Josef Albers & another about Camille Graeser, 1968; (essay) Poetry as a Means of Environmental Design, 1969. Publisher of book series: Art & Environment, 1971-. Contbr. to var. newspapers. Address: 8672 Erkersreuth, Schloss, German Fed. Repub.

GONELLA, Aurora, b. 1 Oct. 1905. Poet. Married. Member, Poetry Soc. of Pa. Contbr. to: A Goodly Heritage, 1968; A Patrick Kavanagh Anthol., 1973; IWWP Anthol., 1973. Address: 912 Imperial Palm Dr., Largo, FL 33540, U.S.A.

GONZOLAS SILLS, Chiquita Lo Juana, b. 12 Dec. 1923. Writer and Artist. Positions held: Staff Writer, Saline County News. Memberships: World Poetry Soc. Intercontinental; Nat. Fed. of State Poetry Socs.; Illinois State Poetry Soc.; Internat. Platform Assoc.; Poet's Roundtable; Authors, Composers & Artists Soc.; Clover Internat. Poetry Soc. (life member); Ozark Writers & Artists Guild. Contbr. to: Saline County News; Marianna News; Ark. Democrat; Ark. Gazette; Clover Collection of Verse; Southwest Times Record; Poet's Roundtable Anthol.; South & West Poetry Anthol.; Grafic News; Oral Roberts Faith Mag.; True Story; Grit News; American Legion Mag.; Christian Home; Poetry Radio Programs (2); Lincoln Log; Poets; World of Poets. Recip. of numerous honours, awards, including: listing in Poetry Archives of USA; IWWP Anthol. (UK); certificates, etc. Address: Hacienda El Sombrero, 1423 So. Cedar St., Benton, AR 72015, USA.

GOODE, Cyril Everard, b. 5 Oct. 1907. Engineer. Positions held: wheat farming, W Australia; Miner; Engineering mainly in Power House positions, last 29 yrs. Memberships: currently on Comm., Int. PEN, Victoria Br.; VP, Bread & Cheese Club (writers); Mbr. of Comm., Fellowship of Writers. Published works: (poetry) The Grower of Golden Grain, 1932; Wattle in the Ranges, 1939; The Bridge Party at Boyanup, 1943; The Flame of Flesh, 1951; Hando with Bullocks, 1962; Horizontal Gothic, 1966; War Poems, 1967; Tale of Two Castles, 1969; (prose) Yarns of the Yilgarn, 1950; Stories of Strange Places, 1967; Vietnam Letters, 1968. Contbr. to: The Bulletin; Quadrant; Bohemia; The Kalgoorlie Miner; Poetry Mag.; Prism; The Southern Cross; Quaderni di Poesia, Editor of Kaleidoscope Quarterly, 1960. Composer of Folio f Folk Songs (words & music) 1966: kept literary diary w. daily entries over 40 yrs. Honours: Litchfield Prize for book of poetry, 1965; Silver Medal for Poetry, Rome, 1966; Hon. Litt.D. for services to literature, 1969. Address: GPO Box 707 F, Melbourne, Australia 3001.

GOODELL, Larry, b. 20 Jan. 1935. Poet. Education: Univ. of Southern Calif.; Univ. of New Mex. Positions held: Book Seller; Ed. & Publisher, Duende Press, 1964-; Ed. & Publisher, Fervent Valley, 1972-. Published works: Cycles, 1966; Sun Love Gypsy, 1966; Ometeotl, 1974. Contbr. to: Stooge; Caterpillar; Puerto del Sol; Fervent Valley; Oriental Blue Streak, etc. Address: Box 571, Placitas, NM 87043, U.S.A.

GOODING, Joan Beryl, b. 20 Apr. 1920. Freelance Writer; Student. Education: Hong Kong Univ. (Extra-Mural), 1959; Bangor Univ. (Extra-Mural), 1969-73; Flintshire Tech. Coll., 1973, '74. Divorced, 3 children. Positions held: WRAC Supvsr., Military Exchanges, 1948, '49; Admin. Asst., Office of Commnr. Gen. for South East Asia, Singapore, 1954; Confidential Asst., Dept. Commerce & Industry, Hong Kong, 1957-60. Memberships: Sec., Prestatyn & Dist. Writers' Circle, 1969-73. Contbr. to: Top Poets of 1968, 1968; Spring Anthol., 1969; Prestatyn Weekly; Rhyl Jrnl.; Cheshire Observer. Honours, awards: 3rd Prize, Dock Leaves Comp., Anglo-Welsh Review, 1968 & Hon. Mention,

1969. Address: 15 Bryn Melyd, Meliden, Prestatyn, N. Wales.

GOODMAN, Paul, b. 9 Sept. 1911. Teacher; Magazine Editor; Writer. Educ: B.A., C.C.N.Y., 1931; Ph.D., Univ. of Chgo., 1940. Married twice, three children. Positions held: Tchr., Manumit Schl. of Progressive Educ., Pauling, Black Mtn. Coll., N.Y. Univ., Sarah Lawrence Coll., Bronxville, Univ. of Chgo., Univ. of Wis., & Experimental Coll. of San Fran. State Coll; Former Ed., Complex mag.; Former Film Ed., Partisan Review; Former TV Critic, New Republic; Ed., Liberation Mag., 1960–. Published works: Stoplight, 1942; Pieces of Three (w. Meyer Liben & Edouard Roditi), 1942; Five Young American Poets (w. others), 1945; The Well of Bethlehem; Red Jacket, 1956; The Lordly Hudson: Collected Poems, 1962; Day and Other Poems, 1965; Hawkweed, 1967; North Percy, 1968; The Young Disciple, Faustina, and Jonah (play), 1965; Num. novels, short stories, essays. Contbr. to: Harper's; Commonweal; Esquire; Mademoiselle; Nation; Poetry; Playboy; (anthologies) A Little Treasury of American Poetry, 1948; Of Poetry and Power, 1964; New Modern Poetry, 1967. Recip., num. awards & fellowships.

GOODWYN, Margaret Sturgis, pen name **GOODWYN, Margaret,** b. 16 Jul. 1901. Writer. Education: Studied with Lizette Woodworth Reese; Alfred Dorn; Ralph Kinsey; Harry M. Meacham. Married Donald Lee Goodwyn; 2 d. Positions held: Freight Claim Investigator, Baltimore and Ohio R.R., 1918–32. Memberships: Poetry Soc. of Va.; Acad. of American Poets; C.A.A.A., also Sec. and Treas., Vice-Pres., Petersburg, Va. Chapter of C.A.A.A. Contbr. to: Kaleidograph; Florida Mag. of Verse; Lyric Virginia, Vol. II; Va. Fed. of Women's Clubs Anthol.; Pegasus in the Seventies; History of Poetry of Va. Awards: Kaleidograph, 195–; 11 State Prizes from Va. Fed. of Women's Clubs, 1952-72. Address: 789 David Dr., Arnold, MD 21012, USA.

GOONERATNE, Yasmine, b. 1936. English Lecturer. Educ: Bishop's Coll., Colombo, Ceylon. Positions held: Lectr., Engl., Univ. of Ceylon; Translator of French Poetry. Contbr. to: Journal of Commonwealth Literature; English; Thunapaha. Recip., Mary E. Woolley Research Fellowship. Address: English Dept., Univ. of Ceylon, Colombo, Ceylon.

GOOSSENS, Robert, pen name **GOSWIN, Rob,** b. 23 Mar. 1943. Teacher of Ethics & Dutch. Education: Royal Atheneum, Keerbergen, 1961; Schl. for Tchrs., Lier, Belgium, 1965. Married twice, 1 son by first marriage (Bryan). Currently tchng. Ethics & Dutch at schl. in Westerlo, Antwerp. Memberships: PEN Vlaanderen; V.V.L.; Redakteur Literai tjdschrift-Rimschi, (1969), Impuils, (1970-71), & Zenith, 1971-73; Int. Poetry Evening, Struga, Yugoslavia. Published works: (poetry) Satori voor de Blues in Jericho, 1968; De Trage Ontmaagding, 1968; De Bloem van Phil Bloom, 1969; Il Teken Ritueel, 1969; De Huid van Mechelen, 1970; Rapaille voor Robespierre, 1971; Robespierre, 1972; Rozenkrans, 1974; (novels) Vanitas, Vanitas, 1972; Tuberculose, 1974. Contbr. to: Nieuw Vlaams Tydschrift, De Vlaamse Gids, Dietsche Warande & Belfort, Morgen, Impuls, Kruispunt Sumier, Journal des Poetes, Rimschi, Belgium; Synthese, Yugoslavia: Nordlitt, Kentering, Bloknoot, Netherlands, etc. Honours, awards: Provinciale Poezieprijs Stad Herentals, 1971; Vermelding Poezieprijs Blanka Gyselen, 1972; Vermelding 3de Prijs Stijn Streuvels voor Proza, 1972; Provinciale Poezieprijs Stad Herentals, 1973; Prijs Tijdschrift 'Nieuwe Stemmen', 1973; Arkprijs van het Vrije Woord, 1973. Address: Wetstraat 20, 2000 Antwerp, Belgium.

GORDON, Giles Alexander Esme, b. 23 May 1940. Publisher. Education: Edinburgh Acad., UK. Married, Margaret Gordon, children's book illustrator, 2 s. Positions held: Advt. Mgr., Secker & Warburg; Ed., Hutchinson & Co. & Penguin Books; Ed. Dir., Victor Gollancz Ltd.; Mbr., Lit. Panel, Arts Coun. of GB;

Chmn., Soc. of Young Publrs. Mbr., Soc. of Authors. Published works: Two & Two Make One, 1966; Two Elegies, 1968; Eight Poems to Gareth, 1970. Contbr. to: Scotsman; Glasgow Herald; Irish Times; Outposts; Scottish Poetry, vols. 1-6; Winter Tales for Children; Blackwoods Mag.; BBC; Poetry Now, etc. Address: 9 St. Ann's Gdns., London NW5, UK.

GORDON, Guanetta Stewart. Writer; Poet. Education: Baker Univ., Baldwin City, Kansas; Univ. of Kansas, Lawrence, Kansas. Married, Lynell F. Gordon (Col., US Army); 1 s., 1 d. Positions held: Radio Dramatist, 1927-28, KMBC-KCMO; Radio Dramatist and Scriptwriter, 1929-1930; Freelance Writer, 1930-1973. Memberships: NLAPW, Nat. Rec. Secr., 1952-54, Nat. Insignia Chairman, 1954-56, Pres. Alexandria Branch, 1956-58, Nat. Registrar, 1962-64, Nat. 4th Vice Pres., 1964-66, Nat. Research Chairman, 1966-68, Nat 1st Vice Pres., 1970-72; Poetry Soc. of America; World Poetry Soc. Intercontinental; Midwest Fed. Chap. Poets; American Poetry League; Acad. of American Poets; Nat. Fed. of State Poetry Socs.; Poetry Soc. of Virginia; Poetry Soc. of Arizona; Kansas Authors Club; Sun City Poetry Soc.; Phoenix Poetry Soc. (Pres.) 1973). Published works: Songs Of The Wind, 1953; Under The Rainbow Arch, 1965; Petals From The Moon, 1971; Shadow Within The Flame, 1973. Contbr. to: American Album of Poetry; Golden Quill Anthol.; Avalon Anthol.; World's Fair Anthol.; Pegassian World Mosaic; Sat. Eve. Post; Farm Journal; The Pen Woman; Mod. Romances; Kansas City Star; Poet Intercontinental; Poetry Digest; American Bard; Kansas Authors Bulletin; World Poetry Journal; Midwest Chaparral; Bardic Echo; Sandcutter; Swordsman Review; American Poetry League Bulletin; Seydell Qtly.; Green World; Youth Instructor; Muse; Mod. American Sonnet; Poesy Book; Prairie Poet; United Poet; American Poet; also many others. Recip. numerous awards, including: Kansas Poetry of Year Award, 1966; and recent awards from World Poetry Soc. Intercontinental; Pegassian World Mosaic; Midwest Fed.; Poetry Soc. of Virginia; Poetry Soc. of Arizona; Kansas Authors; NLAPW; Nat. Fed. of State Poetry Socs., etc. Address: 12238 Riviera Dr., Sun City, AZ, USA.

GORDON, Marek Henryk, pen names **TEOFIL, & MAG,** b. 25 Apr. 1918. Journalist; Radio Commentator. Education: Drama & Art Schl.; Jrnlsts. Schl. Positions held: War Corres. during Warsaw uprising; Co-Fndr. of Polish Military Daily (Ostanie Wiadomosci) in Germany; Polish Daily, Chicago, U.S.A., 1947-50; Radio Commentator, Chicago Stn. WOPA, 1953–. Memberships: Polish Lit. Club, 1947-50; Mbrship. Comm., Int PEN, Am. Br. Published works: Cudzy Chleb (The Bread of Others), 1945; Wielka Gra (Big Game), 1948; Zabawki z Majoliki (Toys of Maiolica), 1951; Radiowe Igraszki (Radio Playthings), 1955; Muza Miasta (Muse of the City), 1957; Katedra (The Cathedral), 1964; Priest from the Border – Poem of Copernicus, 1973. Contbr. to var. Polish jrnls. in sev. countries. Lectures at Authors' Evenings in U.S.A. & Canada & has given readings at The Polish Nat. Mus. of Am. Honours, awards: First prize for Essay, Contest of Polish Daily, Argentina, 1962; Commemorative poem about Copernicus was reprinted in Congressional Record, 1973. Address: 3117 N. Kolmar, Chicago, IL 60641, U.S.A.

GORJAN, Zlatko, b. 15 July 1901. Literary Translator. Education: Univs. of Vienna & Zagreb. Positions held: Editl. Staff, Jrnls. 'Zagreber Tagblatt', 'Zagreber Morgenblatt', 'Belgrader Zeitung', 'Novosti', 1922-41; Corres., Prager Presse & Goetheaneum, Zurich & Neue Freie Presse, Vienna (concurrently); Editl. Staff, first Yugoslav Ency. 'Minerva', 1930-36; Mgr. of Publicity, Warner Bros., Zagreb, 1936-41; Asst. Mgr., Nat. Theatre in Zagreb & Ed. of the Theatre Review 'Pozornica', 1936-41; Ed., 'Matica Hrvatska', 'Zabavna biblioteka' & 'Znanje'; Fndr. & Ed. 'Kosmos', Belgrade, 1933-39; Disting. Lectr. & Guest Prof., Chico State Coll., Calif., U.S.A. Has travelled & lectured all over U.S.A., Japan & most European countries. Membership: Yugoslav PEN; Soc. of

Croatian Writers; Société des Auteurs Europeen; Fed. Internationale de Traducteurs; Pres., ibid, 1963; Pres., Jury for the int. translator prize 'Nathhorst', 1968. Published works: Pjesme, 1921; Fragmenti, 1921; Kronika bez Glavnog lica, 1955; Pjesme, 1933; Snomišljenja, 1959; Zabilješke za Pjesmu o Covjeku, 1957; Poems/Basne, 1966; Poems/Pjesme, 1967; Splendeur Dela Conscience, 1969; Da Sva Cudesa Budu Svima Znana, 1971; From St. Getor to Buddha, 1973. Contbr. to num. newspapers, mags. in var. countries. Translated num. books of prose & poetry. Recip., The Great Cross of Honour for Science & Art, Vienna, 1971. Address: Solovljeva 22,/IV, Zagreb, Yugoslavia.

GORST-WILLIAMS, Jessica Anthea, b. 12 Mar. 1948. Private Secretary to Member of Parliament; Editor of Enigma. Married to law student. Memberships: PEN Club; Kent & Sussex Poetry Soc.; London Writers' Circle. Contbr. to: Expression One; Orbis; Kent & Sussex Poetry Folio; Monday World. Has given lectures to var. schls. & colls. & compiled a programme & was interviewed on Radio Medway. Address: 18 Cornwall Gardens, London SW7, U.K.

GOSNELL, David Foote, b. 1 Feb. 1932. Buildings Management Specialist. Education: B.A., Principia Coll.; studied Jrnlsm., Northwestern Univ.; Public Admin., Geo. Wash. Univ. Positions held: worked for U.S. Govt. as Space Mgmt. Specialist in Wash. D.C.; Buildings Mgr. in Anchorage, Alaska & as U.S. Customhouse, N.Y.C.; currently Buildings Mgmt. Specialist w. GSA Regional Office. Memberships Past Treas. & V.P., Brooklyn Poetry Circle; Pres., ibid, 1972-74. Contbr. to: Christian Sci. Jrnl.; The Music Jrnl.; Christian Sci. Sentinal; The Anchorage (Alaska) News; Shore Christmas Anthol., 1974. Honours, awards: 1st prize, Christmas Writing Contest, Anchorage News, 1965; Brooklyn Poetry Circle Members Award, 1970, '71 & Critics Award, 1970, '71. Address: 12 Gales Rd., Edison, NJ 08817, U.S.A.

GOSNELL, Elizabeth Duke Tucker, pen name GOSNELL, Betty, b. 21 Apr. 1921. Housewife. Education: B.A., Hist., Duke Univ. Married to William Burton Gosnell. Positions held: Exec. Comm., Episc. Ch. of Transfiguration; Pres., Ark. Post Girl Scout Coun.; Treas., Ch. of Transfiguration; Pres., Sorosis Club (Federated Women); Bd. of Dirs., Drew Co. Hist. Assn.; Tchr., Creative Writing, MAD Camp, 1970; Ed., The Muse Poetry Column in Advance Moticellonian & The McGehee Times; Hostess, radio program Afterglow, KHBM AM/FM, Monticello, Ark. Memberships: Dir., State of Ark. World Poetry Soc. Intercontinental; Sec., South & West, Inc.; Chmn., S & W Poetry Workshop in Southeast Ark.; Poet's Roundtable (Nat. Fed. State Poetry Soc.); Authors, Artists & Composers Soc.; Diocesan Liturgical Commn., Ark.; UPLI; Drew Co. Rep. for Ark. Writers' Conf.; Poetry Soc. of America; Fellow, Internat. Poetry Soc. Author of The Poet Who Was a Painter of Souls, 1969. Contbr. to: Echoes of Faith Anthol.; Poet, India; South & West; Folio; Writers Notes & Quotes; Pancontinental premier Poets; Poets of Anglo America; Swordsman's Review; Llano Estacado; The Muse; Voices Int.; Discourses on Poetry, vol. 2; Ann Arbor Review; Ark. State Mag.; Encore; Cardinal Poetry Quarterly; Tulsa Poetry Quarterly; Images; Poems of Patriotism & Peace; Poetry Dial Anthol.; Contemporary Poets of Ark., etc. Recip. of various prizes & hons. for poetry. Address: 803 N Slemons, Monticello, AR 71655, USA.

GOTLIEB, Phyllis Fay, b. 25 May 1926. Writer. Educ: M.A., Univ. of Toronto, Canada. Married Calvin Gotlieb, Dir. of the Inst. of Computer Sci., Univ. of Toronto; Three children. Published works: Within the Zodiac, 1964; Ordinary, Moving, 1969; (novels) Sunburst, 1964; Why Should I Have All the Grief?, 1969. Contbr. to: Canadian Forum; Tamarack Review; (anthologies) Best Poems of 1958: The Borestone Mountain Poetry Awards, 1959; Poetry 62, 1961; First Five Years, 1962; Modern Canadian Verse, 1967. Address: 29 Ridgevale Dr., Toronto 392, Ontario, Canada.

GOTTARELLI, Maria, b. 27 April 1906. Writer. Education: Univ. Diploma in Teaching; Music Teacher. Personal Details: Noblewoman, descendant of the Counts Gottarelli of Imola. Published works: Armonie, 1939; Alba dei Vivi, 1953; Arco all'amore, 1954; Erba amara, 1959; Né giorno né notte, 1966; Cuori in siccità, 1972. Contbr. to newspapers: Il Resto del Carlino, Bologna; l'Avvenire d'Italia, Bologna; l'Arena, Verona; Il Nuovo Adige, Verona; Periodicals: Ausonia, Siena; Realtà, Naples; Misura, Bergamo; Centro studi critici, Treviso; Madre, Brescia; Esploriamo, Brescia; Il Nuovo Tempo, Naples; Il Bene, Milan. Honours, awards: Italian Acad. Prize, 1939; Pesaro City Prize, 1950; Livorno City Prize, 1951; Bismantova Prize, 1952; Eger Prize, 1953; Oriane Prize, Naples, 1954; Bologna Prize, 1957; Auditorium Prize, Rome, 1959; Award of Merit, Roberto Galli Prize, Bologna, 1972. Address: Piazza dei Martini 5/2, 40121 Bologna, Italy.

GOTTLIEB, Darcy, b. 13 March 1922. Poet and Teacher. Education: Hunter Coll. of the City Univ. of NY., M.A., 1961; Univ. of Wisconsin, Madison, 1945-46; Univ. of Calif., Berkeley, B.A., 1945. Married; one daughter. Positions held: Head, Engl. Dept. in private prep. school, NY, and Teacher of Engl., 1958-72; Asst. Editor at Mademoiselle mag., 1947-50. Membership: Poetry Soc. of America (one of judges for sev. annual awards: Christopher Morley, etc.). Published work: No Witness But Ourselves (book of poetry), 1973. Contbr. to: Mademoiselle; Ingenue; NY Times; The Diamond Anthol.; NY Times Book of Verse (anthol.). Recip. Dylan Thomas Award (Poetry Soc. of America), 1966. Address: 34-21 77 St., Jackson Heights, NY 11372, USA.

GOULET, Antoine, pen name GOLDEN, Anthony, b. 25 Dec. 1917. Reviewer of the weekly "Le Travailleur" (USA). Education: Seminary of Quebec. Memberships: Cercle de la Pensée et des Arts Francais (C.I.P.A.F.) (France), (Co-founder); Société des Poètes Canadiens-Francais. Published works: Jeux et Sortilèges, 1963; Archipel de mes Rêves (in preparation). Contbr. to: L'Action Catholique; Le Droit; Notre Temps; L'Appel; Poésie; Présence des Lettres et Des Arts; Art et Poésia; Points et Contrepoints; La Bohème, etc. Address: 1962 Rue Bonin, Sillery, Quebec 6, PQ, Canada.

GOURLAY, Elizabeth Wastfield (Babette), b. 10 March 1917. Writer; Poet; Playwright. Education: B.A., & Lib. Sci., McGill Univ., 1938, 1939; M.A., Univ. of B.C., 1968. Of British descent (both parents English-born). Married to Dr. Robert Humphrys Gourlay, F.R.C.S. (Canada), surgeon; 1 s. (Robert), 1 d. (Mary). Membership: League of Canadian Poets. Published works: Motions, Dreams & Aberrations, 1969. Contbr. to: (anthols.) Contemp. Poetry of B.C., 1970; Reaching Out, 1970; Forty Women Poets of Canada, 1971; (newspapers, journals): The Canadian Forum; The Fiddlehead; Inscape; Prism International; Quarry; The Far Point; Toronto Saturday Night; The Sun (News); Trace; West Coast Review; Atlantic Advocate. A full-length poetic drama, Andrea Del Sarto, given stage production (2 weeks), September, 1973, in Vancouver (New Play Centre), under auspices of Canada Council. Address: 6224 Carnarvon St., Vancouver 13, BC., Canada.

GOW, Patricia, b. 31 Dec. 1924. Instructor. Education: Grad., music, art & english, UCLA, U.S.A. Positions held: currently Instr., Douglas Co. Schls. Memberships: V.P., Ore. State Poetry Assn. Contbr. to the following anthols. & jrnls: Poesie Vivante Anthol., 1970; Human Voices Anthol., 1969; Unique Anthol., 1969; Chicago Tribune; The Oregonian; The Denver Post; The Medford Tribune; Quixote; West Coast Review; Human Voice Quarterly; Dragonfly; Concerning Poetry; Univ. of Portland Review; Poesie Vivante. Honours, awards: 1st, Ore. State Poetry Assn., 1963; 1st, Roseburg Writers Club, 1967. Address: Little River Rd., Glide, OR 97443, U.S.A.

GOWANS, Josephine Mhairi Oakley, b. 23 Mar. 1931. Astrologer. Member, Camden Poetry Grp., London. Contbr. to 'Slide into Poetry', Camden Poetry Grp. Mag. Address: Well Mount Cottage, Well Rd., London N.W.3, U.K.

GOY, Erwin, pen name **LYSOHORSKY, Ondra,** b. 6 July 1905. University Professor; Poet; Essayist; Prose-Writer; Translator of Poetry from French & German into Lachian & from Lachian, French, Slovac, Czech into German. Education: Ph.D., German Univ. of Prague, 1928; Sorbonne Univ., 1926, '38, '46; Univ. of Rome, 1930. Positions held: Prof., Grammar Schls., Kremnica, Bratislava, Trnava, Ostrava; Docent, HS of For. Langs., Moscow, USSR & Mil. HS of Red Army, WWII; Tchr., Kindergarten nurses, Czechoslovakia; Commercial Schl.; Prof., Grammar Schl.; Chair of Western Langs., Univ. of Bratislava, 1956-61; retired, 1961. Memberships: United Poets Laureate Int., World Poetry Soc. Intercontinental; Assn. des Amis de Romain Rolland, Paris; Assn. Francaise des Amis d'Albert Schweitzer, Paris; Arbeitsgruppe für das Geistige Werk Albert Schweitzers, Basle; Felibrige, Toulon; Hon. Mbr., Comm., Felibrige, Avignon; Int. Corresp., Soc. Coop. Poésie Vivante, Geneva; Suddeutscher Schriftstellerverband, Stuttgart; Hölderlin-Gesellschaft, Tübingen; Int. Comm., Eklitra; Assn. des ecrivains tchecoslovaques, Prague. Published works: (originals in Lachian) Spjewajuco Piasc (The Singing First), 1934; Hlos Hrudy (The Voice of the Soil), 1935; Wybrane Werse (Selected Poems), 1936; '37; Pesna o Matce (Song About the Mother), 1942; Zemlya Moya (My Country), 1942; Pesni o Solntse I Zemlye (Songs of the Sun & the Earth), 1945; Stichotvorenya (Poems), 1946; Aj Lasske Reeky Plynu do Mora (The Lachian Rivers Too Flow Into Sea), 1958; Brazdou K Vesmiru (Through the Furrow to the Universe), 1960; Gedichte (Poems), 1960; Danksagung (Thanksgiving), 1961; Poèmes Choisis (Selected Poems), 1962; Korom, Te Legy A Merce (Century, Be You the Measure), 1962; Mais La Vie est la plus Forte (But Life is Stronger), 1963; Jediny Pohar (The Unique Cup), 1964; Selected Poems, 1971; Works translated from Lachian into Russian, Slovak, Czech, German, Hungarian, French, Engl., Greek, Uzbek, Breton, en Bretagne en France, Provencal, en Provence en France, Portugais, Bulgarian. Contbr. to nearly 200 jrnls. & anthols., in all 6 continents, 1933–. These include: La Nouvelle Republique, France; Vers Univers, Netherlands; Literaturnu Ukraina, USSR; Cooperation, Switzerland; Athens Daily Post, Greece; Mlady svet, Czechoslovakia; Der Bund, Germany; London Mag., UK; Contemp. Lit. in Trans., Canada; Hundred Towers, A Czechoslovak Anthol., USA, 1946; Le Jrnl. des Poètes, Belgium; Poésie Vivante, Geneva; 1 Astrado, France; Tri Quarterly, USA; Chirimo, Rhodesia; Die Tat, Switzerland; Der Bund; Engramme; Die Horan; New Measure; Viewpoints; Contempory Review; Informer; DIB Mag., London; Poet; Poetry Australia, Sydney; Tribune, London; Poetry Chicago; Brennpunkte, Wien; Oasis; Pancontinental Premier Poets. Honours, awards: Granted Distinction of Plaquette Mbr., Ctrl. Comm. Nat. Front, Czechoslovakia, 1968. Refused on grounds of continued prohibition of publication of suppressed works in Czechoslovakia; UN Day, Philippines, UPLI, 1967; Hon. Officer for Eastern Europe, 1970; Hon. Life Fellow, I.B.A., England; Poems translated into Russian by B. Pasternak & into Engl., by W.H. Auden. Address: Mytna 37/VI, Bratislava, Czechoslovakia.

GRACE, Dorman John, pen name **GEE, Dee Jay,** b. 21 May 1904. Insurance & Travel Agent. Education: Mansfield State Normal School, 1921; Famous Writers Schl., 1967. Positions held: Tchr.; Office Clerk; Farmer; Columnist; Reporter & Editor; AAA Motor Club Mgr. & Ed., MOTOR TOPICS mag.; Chmbr. of Comm. Sec.; Hd., Grace Grp. of Fire & Casualty Ins. Cos.; Owner-Operator, D.J. Grace Ins. Agcy., 1928– & Lebanon Co. Travel Bureau, fnd. 1939; Asst. Ed., Mansfield State Normal Schl's paper, The Semaphore, 1920; Ed., Yrbook, The Carontewan, 1921; Ed., Hershey News, 1928; Poetry & Humor Columnist, Hershey Press, 1924-28, for Lancaster Intelligencer &

New Era, 1928, for Palm Advertiser, 1941. Published works: Is It Poetry? Well, It Rhymes (pamphlet), 1941; Grace Before Meals (book), 1969; All there Is (book), 1972. Contbr. to: Gallipolis (Ohio) Tribune; Lebanon Daily News; Palm Advertiser; Modern Images; Major Poets; Am. Poet; Prairie Poet; United Poets; Moon Age Poets; 70 Poets; Friendship Trails; Personal Poetry; Int. Hall of Fame Poets; Poet, India; Quaderni di Poesia, Rome; A Book of the Yr., 1972 (Poetry Soc. of Tex.), etc. Recip. num. poetry prizes & hons. from: Poetry Socs. of Pa., Tex., Va., N.C., Nat. Fed. of State Poetry Socs., Poets' Study Club of Terre Haute, Calif. Chaparral Poets, N.Y. Poetry Forum, & others. Address: P.O. Box 352, Ten West Main St., Palmyra, PA 17078, U.S.A.

GRAHAM, Courtenay P., b. 2 Jan. 1944. Poet; Photographer; Musician. Education: Long Island, Virginia, Wash. D.C., Italy & Spain. Memberships: Life Mbr., Acad. of Am. Poets; past mbr., Poetry Soc. of Va. Published works: (book of poems) IME, 1969; Poemstills from Moviearth, 1974. Contbr. to following anthols., jrnls., etc: Am. PEN, 1971; In Youth Anthol., 1972; Breakthrough Fictioneers, 1973; Second Assembling Anthol., 1971; Cavalier Daily Lit. Supplement, 1973: Jeffersonian Review, 1974; Boston Globe; UVM & Plume & Sword; Am. Poet. Poems read on WBAI-FM Radio (half hour show), 1972. Address: Box 5, Keswick, VA 22947, U.S.A.

GRAHAM, Henry, b. 1 Dec. 1930. Lecturer, Liverpool Polytechnic. Education: Liverpool Coll. of Art. Poetry Editor, Ambit (mag.), London. Published works: Soup City Zoo, 1968; Good Luck To You Kafka/You'll Need It Boss, 1969; Passport to Earth, 1971. Contbr. to anthols. in Italy, Spain, Germany, Norway, Holland, Argentina, USA and Canada. Contbr. to anthols in England: The Liverpool Scene; Love Love Love; British Poetry since 1945; Come on Everybody; P.E.N. Anthol., New Poems, 1971-1972; The house that Jack Built. Awards: £500 Arts Council award for Good Luck To You Kafka/You'll Need It Boss; £500 Arts Council award for Passport to Earth. Address: Flat 2, Bath House, Parkgate, Parkgate Parade, Wirral, Cheshire.

GRAHAM, Jeana Ardath, b. 20 Sept. 1914. Poetess; Text Writer. Education: B.M., Eastman Schl. of Music, Rochester, N.Y.; special studies, Berkeley Divinity Schl., Calif. Married Robert Graham, 5 sons. Positions held: Eng. Fac. Tchr., Rikkyo Jo Gakuin, Tokyo, Japan; Fac., St. Paul's Day Schl., Pomona, Calif.; Choral Dir., Schofield Chapel & Barber's Pt. Chapel; currently Min. of Music, Schofield Chapel. Memberships: Prairie Quill Club, Kansas; N.Y Poetry Forum; Clover Int. Poetry Assn. Published works: New Dawn, Calif. 1973, Wash. D.C., 1974. Texts for Choral Works, published by: Broadman Press, Abingdon Press, Canyon Press, Art Masters Studios, Belwin-Mills, Lorenz Publ. Co., Sacred Music Press, Choristers Guild, etc. (over 150 texts, inclng. texts for 28 cantatas). Contbr. to: Rochester Democrat Chronicle; Grit; Rosicrucian Anthroposophic Qtly.; Music Ministry, Abingdon Press. Address: Box 586, Waianae, HI 96792, U.S.A.

GRAHAM, Lola Amanda, pen name **GRAHAM, Lola Beall,** b. 12 Nov. 1896. Photographer; Poet. Education: Normal School (Teacher's Coll.). Married to Idaho rancher, 5 children. Positions held: Teacher, 1st, 2nd, 3rd grades in country schools. Memberships: Poetry Soc. of America; Ina Coolbrith Society (also hon. member); State Chaparral Poetry Soc.; Eugene Field Soc. (hon. member); Internat. Mark Twain Soc. (hon. member); Pres., Santa Cruz Chapter, Chaparral Poets. Contbr. to: Home News (Weekly) San Francisco Examiner; Oakland Tribune; Denver Post; Writer's Digest; Poet International; Nat. Parks Mag.; Santa Cruz Chaparral Prize Poems (book), 1973; also poems and pictures for calendars; Editor of poetry column, From The Cool Front (Mobile). Awards: Nat. Poetry Soc., June, 1971, also 1973; plus lesser and local prizes. Address: 225-93 Mt. Hermon Rd., Scotts Valley, CA 95066, USA.

GRAHAM, William Sidney, b. 19 Nov. 1918. Poet; Lecturer. Educ: Workers' Educational Assn. Coll., Newbattle Abbey, Scotland. Married. Positions held: Lectr., N.Y. Univ., U.S.A., 1947-48. Published works: Cage Without Grievance, 1942; The Seven Journeys, 1944; 2nd Poems, 1945; The White Threshold, 1949; The Nightfishing, 1955; Malcolm Mooney's Land, 1970; Penguin Modern Poets (w. others), 1970. Contbr. to: Poetry; Listener; New Statesman; (anthologies) Faber Book of Twentieth Century Verse, 1953; New Poets of England and America, 1957; Honour'd Shade, 1959; An Anthology of Modern Verse, 1961; Penguin Book of Contemporary Verse, 1962; Mid-Century, 1965; Modern Scottish Poetry, 1966; Longer Contemporary Poems, 1966; Oxford Book of Scottish Verse, 1966; A Book of Scottish Verse, 1967. Recip., Atlantic Award in Lit., 1947. Address: 4 Mountview Cottages, Madron, Penzance, Cornwall, England.

GRAINGER, Muriel A(rnott), b. 9 Apr. 1905. Journalist. Education: South Hampstead H.S. Positions held: Managing Ed. of a group of women's publications, Fleetway Publications (now I.P.C.) – retired. Membership: Soc. of Women Writers & Journalists. Published works: Music At Midnight, 1950; The Walled Garden, 1959; The Stranded Shell, 1973; 365 Bible Stories and Verses for Children, 1971. Contbr. to: Poetry Mag. (Canada); The Adelphi; Time & Tide; New English Weekly; Poetry Qtly.; English; Outposts; Gloucestershire Countryside; New Christian; Woman's Journal; Poetry Review; Manifold; Nine; Woman's Pictorial; Church of England Newspaper; Weekly Westminster; (anthols.): The Pattern of Poetry; Those Who Are Alive; People Are People; In Praise of London; Without Adam; Poetry Soc. Anthol., 1963 and 1969; Guildhall Anthol. for Verse Speakers; Here Be People; Greenwood Anthol.; Delight Upon Delight; A Show Of Hands; A Bouquet From Barnet., Incl. in HMV recording of The Pattern of Poetry; (Broadcast) BBC Schools, S. Africa. Address: 138 Hampstead Way, London NW11 7XJ, UK.

GRAMPOUND, Martin (Josiah Hepplethwaite), pen names ISSAC Awd & WORRIED OF BARNSLEY, b. 29 Feb. 1904. Poet. Positions held: Chmn., Worsborough Dale Unemployed Workers' Poetry Lovers' Fellowship, 1933-36; Co-Ed., Roots Mag., 1972-. Published works: Bread for the Workers, 1934; Poems on the Industrial Revolution, 1935; Coalmine Verses, 1947. Contbr. to: Hepplethwaite's Almanac; Barnsley Chronicle; Workers of the Thirties United Free Press Daily; Headland; Daily Herald; Ore; Roots. Address: c/o Roots, 30 Basegreen Ave., Sheffield S12 3FA, U.K.

GRANQVIST, Willy, b. 9 Aug. 1948. Writer. Education: studies in aesthetics, Univ. of Uppsala, 1970-71. Currently working with child programmes on a freelance basis at Swedish Radio. Published works: Grupp 73 (4 long poems), 1973. Contbr. to: Byggnadsarbetaren; Djurens Rätt; Expressen; Graal; Konflikt; Lyrikvännen; Ostersunds-Posten. Address: Cirkelvagen 4, 122 44 Enskede, Sweden.

GRANSDEN, Karl Watts, b. 1925. Teacher. Educ: Cambridge Univ., U.K. Positions held: Served, WWII; Asst. Keeper of Manuscripts, British Mus., London, 1951-57; Former Literary Ed., The Listener, ibid; Fac. Mbr., Engl. Dept., Warwick Univ., current. Published works: Any Day, 1960; (literary criticism) John Donne, 1954; E.M. Forster, 1962; Tennyson's "In Memoriam", 1964. Address: 2 Oppidans Rd., London N.W.3, U.K.

GRANT, Claude DeWitt, b. 20 Dec. 1944. Writer; Editor. Education: B.A., Hunter Coll., N.Y.C.; post grad. work, City Univ. of N.Y. Positions held: Asst. Musicologist, SESAC, Inc. (Music licensing co.); Copy Ed., McGraw-Hill, Publishing; Musicologist, Jazz Expert, Script Writer & Radio Announcer, Radio Stn. WQXR of the N.Y. Times; currently Music Ed., Essence Mag. & Music Critic, Players Mag. Published works: (pamphlet) Epitaph for My Self, 1972. Contbr. to: N.Y. Times; Essence Mag.; The Black Voice of Bronx Community Coll. Recip., Letter of Commendation from Dean Gloria Hobbs of Bronx Community Coll., 1972. Address: 1419 University Ave., Apt. 4C, Bronx, NY 10452, U.S.A.

GRANT, James Russell, b. 14 Dec. 1924. Physician. Education: Hamilton Acad., Scotland, 1930-41; Glasgow Univ., 1944-51; Inst. of Psychiatry, London, 1953-54. Married Olga Zarb, 1 son (Christopher). Positions held: Registrar, Maudsley Hosp., London; Psychiatrist, Govt. Hlth. Serv., Red Deer, Alta., Canada; Gen. Practitioner, Cromer St., London, U.K. Published works: Hyphens, 1958; Poems, 1959. Contbr. to: Prism Int.; Fiddlehead; Botteghe Oscure; Lines Review; Yes (Montreal); & to BBC & CBC. Address: 255 Creighton Ave., London N.2, U.K.

GRATTIDGE, Donald Arthur Phillip, b. 4 June 1933. Poet. Education: City of Bath Grammar Schl., U.K. Positions held: Clerk; Coal-Miner; Industrial Editor; Business Executive. Member, Pentameters Poetry Circle. Contbr. to: (anthols.) Poetry '71, 1971; Havens of the Muse, 1972; Pentameters Anthol. Address: 77a South Hill Park, Hampsted, London N.W.3, U.K.

GRAVE, Elsa, b. 17 Jan. 1918. Writer. Education: B.A. Divorced, 3 daughters. Memberships: Swedish Writers' Soc.; Swedish Drama Writers' Soc. Published works: 14 books of Poetry; 3 novels; approx. 10 plays for theatre & S.B.C. Radio. Contbr. to num. jrnls., etc. Honours, awards incl: Lit. Prize, Swedish Daily Post, 1956; The Bellman Prize, Swedish Academy, 1963; Evening Post Prize, 1958; The Nine Prize, 1968; The Ovralid Prize, 1973. Address: Halmstad 305 90, Sweden.

GRAVELLE, Barbara Ann, b. 30 July 1938. Writer; Teacher. Education: A.A., Va. Intermont Coll., Bristol, Va., 1958; studied at Univ. of N.C. & Univ. of Toledo, Ohio; B.S., Wayne State Univ., Detroit, Mich., 1970. Positions held: Taught Costume Design, Children's Theatre Workshop, Toledo, Ohio, 1962-65; Tchr., Detroit Public Schls., 1969-70; Tchr., Berkeley Schl. System, 1970-73; Poet-Tchr. for Poetry in the Schools, 1971-73; Program Co-ordinator, Intersection Ctr. for Religion & the Arts, 1973-. Published works: Keep Sake. Contbr. to: Moving Out; The New Orleans Review of Lit.; Freedom News; The Berkeley Barb; The Anthol. of Women Poets. Honours, awards: Am. Pen Women Award, Marion, N.C., 1956; 7 Lively Arts Awards, Hollywood, Fla. 1963; Jesse Stuart Award, Seven Mag., 1970. Address: 2922 Otis – C, Berkeley, CA 94703, U.S.A.

GRAVES, Charles, b. 31 Aug. 1892. Retired Journalist. Positions held: served on Editl. Staffs of The Leamington Spa Courier, The Glasgow Citizen, The Scotsman (Drama Critic during latter years); served on Scottish Comm. of Arts Coun. of G.B., 6 yrs. Memberships: Scottish Assn. for the Speaking of Verse, 1924-; served on Coun., ibid, & as Edinburgh Br. V.Chmn.; Pres., Scottish Arts Club, 1958, '59. Published works: Selected Poems of Pierre de Ronsard, 1924; The Bamboo Grove & Other Poems, 1925; The Wood of Time & Other Poems, 1938; Votive Sonnets, 1964; Lyrics of Pierre de Ronsard (transl.), 1967; Emblems of Love & War, 1970; Collected Poems, 1972. Contbr. to: The Weekly Westminster; The Spectator; Country Life; The Observer; The Scotsman; The Dublin Mag.; The Saltire Review; The Queen; The Fortnightly Review. Address: 34 Buckingham Terr., Edinburgh, EH4 3AF, U.K.

GRAVES, Robert Ranke, b. 1895. Writer, Poet. Education: St. John's Coll., Oxford; M.A., B.Litt. Positions held: w. Royal Welch Fusiliers, France; Prof. of Engl. Lit., Egyptian Univ., 1926; Clarke Lectr., Trinity Coll., Cambridge, 1954; Arthur Dehon Little Mem. Lectr., Mass. Inst. of Technol., USA, 1963; Prof. of Poetry, Univ. of Oxford, 1961-66. Published works: Over the Brazier, 1916; Goliath & David, 1916; Fairies & Fusiliers, 1917; The Treasure Box, 1919; Country Sentiment, 1920; The Pier Glass, 1921; Whipperginny, 1923; The Feather Bed, 1923; Mockbegger Hall, 1924;

Welchman's Hose, 1925; Poems 1914-1926; Poems, 1929; Poems 1926-30, 1931; Poems 1930-33; Collected Poems, 1938; No More Ghosts, Selected Poems, 1940; Poems 1938-45; 1946; On English Poetry, 1922; Lawrence & the Arabs, 1927; Goodbye to All That (autobiog.), 1929; But It Still Goes On, 1930; No Decency Left (w. Laura Riding), 1932; The Real David Copperfield, 1933; I, Claudius, 1934; Claudius the God, 1934; Antigua Penny Puce, 1936; T.E. Lawrence to his Biographers (w. Liddell Hart), 1939; Count Belisarius, 1938; Sergeant Lamb of the Ninth, 1940; The Long Week End–A Social History (w. Alan Hodge), 1940; Proceed, Sergeant Lamb, 1941; Wife to Mr. Milton, 1943; The Reader Over Your Shoulder (w. Alan Hodge), 1943; The Golden Fleece, 1944; King Jesus, 1946; The White Goddess, 1947; Collected Poems, 1948; Seven Days in New Crete, 1949; Watch the North Wind Rise, 1949; The Common Asphodel (Collected Essays on Poetry), 1949; The Golden Ass, Asclepius (transl.), 1949; The Isles of Unwisdom, 1949; Occupation–Writer, 1950; Poems and Satires, 1951; The Nazarene Gospel Restored (w. Joshua Podro), 1953; The Greek Myths, 1955; Homer's Daughter, 1955; The Crowning Privilege, 1955; Adam's Rib, 1955; Catacrok!, 1956; Alarcóns Infant with the Globe (transl.); George Sand's Winter in Majorca (transl.); Jesus In Rome (w. Joshua Podro), 1957; They Hanged My Saintly Billy, 1957; Suetonius's Twelve Caesar's (transl.); Lucan's Pharsalia (transl.); Steps, 1958; Collected Poems, 1959; The Penny Fiddle, 1960; More Poems, 1961; Oxford Addresses, 1962; The Anger of Achilles (transl. of Homer's Iliad); New Poems, 1962; Hebrew Myths–Genesis (w. Raphael Patai), 1964; Collected Short Stories, 1964; Man Does, Woman Is (poems), 1964; Mammon and the Black Goddess, 1964; Arrive At High Wood Hall, 1967; Love Re-spelt, 1965; Majorca Observed, 1965; Collected Poems, 1965; Colophon to Love Re-spelt, 1967; Poems 1965-68, 1968; Poetic Craft & Principle, 1967; The Rubaiyyat of Omar Khayaam (trans. w. Omar Ali-Shah), 1968; The Poor Boy Who followed His Star, 1968; The Crane Bug & Other Disputed Subjects, 1969; 5 pens in Hand, 1958; Food for Centaurs, 1960; Myths of Ancient Greece Retold for Young People, 1961; The Siege & Fall of Troy, 1962; (transl.) The Comedies of Terence, 1962; Seventeen Poems Missing, 1966; Poems About Love, 1965; Poems 1968-70; The Green-Sailed Vessel, 1971. Awards: Gold Medal, Nat. Poetry Soc. of Am., 1960; Hawthornden Prize, 1934; James Tait Black Mem. Prize, 1934; Stock Prize, 1939; Medal for Poetry, Olympics, Paris, 1924 & Mexico, 1968; Queens Medal in Poetry, 1968; Opened Int. Poets Conf., Budapest, Hungary, 1970. Address: c/o A.P. Watt & Son, 26-28 Bedford Row, London, WC1, UK.

GRAVES, Robert Steven, pen name **GRAVES, R. Steven,** b. 24 July 1951. Education: B.A. in Engl., Otterbein Coll., Westerville, Ohio, 1973. Positions other than student: Cook; Maintenance work; Painter; Janitor; Surveyor. Member of New Writers' Guild of Ohio, 1969-71; Quiz & Quill (Otterbein Coll.), Pres., 1972-73. Contbr. to: Clover Collection of Verse, 1969; Gato Poetry Anthology, 1970; Dream Shop, 1970, '71; Laureate-Best College Verse of 1970, 1970; Dance of the Muses, 1970; Hyacinths & Biscuits; J. Mark Press; The Shore Poetry Anthology; Yearbook of Modern Poetry; The American Poet, 1971; Twigs, 1973; Wind, 1973; Cardinal Poetry Quarterly, 1973; Pegasus, 1972. Awards: 2nd, Relig. Poetry, Quiz & Quill Poetry Contest, 1970; 1st, ibid, 1971; 2nd, Humorous verse, 1971. Address: 340 Longfellow Ave., Worthington, Ohio, 43085, USA.

GRAY, James Russell, b. 7 Sept. 1908. Accountant (Retired). Education: Eastern Okla. Coll., Wilburton, Okla. Positions held: Welfare Interviewer; Asst. Postmaster; Foreman in Ammunition Factory, WWII; Accountant. Memberships: Ozark Writers & Artists Guild; Poets' Roundtable of Ark. Contbr. to: Pen Mag.; Ladies' Home Jrnl.; Friendly Neighbors; Woman Mag.; Women's Circle; Tooele Transcript, Utah; The News, Hot Springs, Ark.; The Times, North Little Rock, Ark.; The Pacesetter, Benton, Ark.; The Siftings Herald,

Arkadelphia; The Southwest Times Record, Ft. Smith, Ark.; The Courier Index, Marianna, Ark. Honours, awards: Poet Laureate Award for best poetry in two Ark. newspapers for 1973. Address: 6913 Middleton St., Huntington Park, CA 90255, U.S.A.

GRAY, Kenneth Ian, b. 1 Apr. 1921. Teacher of Modern Languages. Education: Northern Univ. Positions held: Asst. Ed., Envoi; Contbng. Ed., The Songwriter (U.K.); Recorded & Published songwriter & composer. Memberships: Nottingham Writers Club; Nottingham & District Poetry Soc. Published works: Sonnets of Life & Love, 1965. Contbr. to: Scrip; Breakthru; Experiment; The Nottinghamshire Countryside; Poetry Nottingham; New Melody; Scribe; Manifold; Poetry Markets; Envoi; Chase; The Spring Anthol.; Laudamus Te; The London Anthol.; Poetry from the People, An Anthol. of Contemporary Poetry; Muse; Mentor; Bardic Echoes; Signal (USA); Message (Paris). Honours, awards: Past Winner, Nottingham Poetry Soc. Spring Poetry Contest; Past Winner, Cannock Chase Art's Fest. Poetry Contest; Manifold Appollo Award; The Songwriters Review, Song of the Yr. Contest, U.S.A.; Fellow, Int. Poetry Soc. Address: 23 Warren Ave., Sherwood, Nottingham NG5 1DF, U.K.

GRAY, Leonard Benjamin, b. 30 Sept. 1896. Minister of Religion. Education: Acadia Univ., NS, Canada; Andover Newton Theol. Schl., USA; Boston Univ.; Dartmouth Coll. Married Martha Evelyn Elder, 1956. Positions held: Congregational Min., Chs. in St. John, NB, Canada, & in E. Milton, Pittsfield, Dublin, Lebanon, Lynn, E. Douglas, & Berlin, USA; currently in relig. radio work, Mass. Coun. of Chs. Memberships: Ldr., Fireside Discussion Grp.; Great Books Grp. & Henry Thoreau Soc. of Am.; Moderator, E.S.P. Club, Lynn; Pres., Min. Fellowship; Pres., Ecumenical Min. Fellowship & Recreational Soc.; Poetry Forum, Gtr. Lynn; Boy Scouts of Am.; Rotary Club, etc. Contbr. to: Sonnets, 1939; Music in Miniature, 1940; N Am. Book of Verse, 1939; Christmas Lyrics, 1940; New Poems of Grace & Glory, 1944; Am. Poetry Old & New, 1965; Anthol. of NH Poetry, 1938; Am. Voices, 1939; Important Am. Poets & Song Writers, 1947; The Poetry Digest, 1942; Thanksgiving Anthol., 1967; Christmas Poems, 1969; Boston Globe; Boston Herald; Lynn Item; Lynn Sunday Post; Boston Transcript; Saugus Advertiser; Clinton Daily News; New Outlook; Am. Bard; Swordsman's Review; Cyclo-Flame; Emerson Jrnl.; Haiku Highlights; Creative Review; Jean's Jrnl.; Scimitar & Song; Driftwood; Versecraft, etc. Author, Coming to Grips With Life, 1971. Awards: Poet of the Month, Inky Trails, 1971; Prize for 'John Fitzgerald Kennedy', Am. Bard; 1969; 'On the Jericho Road', Kanona, NY, 1970; 'Abraham Lincoln', Creative Review, 1970; Prize for 'At the Birthplace of Robert Burns', Cyclo-Flame, 1970. Address: Morning Glory Bungalow, 17 Johnson Rd., Saugus, Mass. 01906, USA.

GRAY, Lynda Darneil, b. 17 Nov. 1945. Social Worker. Education: B.A., Psychol., Norfolk State Coll., Va.; M.S.W., Admin. & Planning, Grad. Schl. of Soc. Work, Va. C'wealth Univ., Richmond. Divorced, 1 daughter. Positions held: Claims Examiner w. N.J. Social Security Disability Determination Serv., 1966; Employment Counselor, Va. State Employment Serv., 1967-68; Psychiatric Soc. Work Cons., Balt. City Maternity & Infant Care Ctr., 1968-71; currently Sr. Cons., N.Y. City Dept. of Mental Hlth. & Retardation Serv. Memberships: N.Y. Poetry League; Poetry Soc. of Am.; Poetry Workshop. Address: 9 Parkside Ct., Brooklyn, NY 11225, USA.

GREBANIER, Bernard, b. 8 Mar. 1903. Writer. Education: B.A., CCNY, 1926; M.A., NY Univ., 1930; Ph.D., ibid, 1935. Positions held: Prof. of Engl., Brooklyn Coll., 1930-63; Prof. Emeritus of Engl., 1963–. Memberships: Poetry Soc. of America; PEN; Authors Guild; C.A.A.A. (1st Vice-Pres.; and Pres. of the NY Chapter). Published works: Fauns, Satyrs & A Few Sages, 1945; Mirrors of the Fire, 1946; The Other Love, 1957; The Angel in the Rock, 1971; The

Uninhibited Byron, 1971; Pegasus in the Seventies, (edited), 1973. Contbr. to: Ladies' Home Journal; Spirit; America; Catholic World; Motive; Univ. of Kansas City Review. Address: 215 W. 88th St., New York, NY 10024, USA.

GREEFF, Adele Montgomery Burcher, pen name **GREEFF, Adele,** b. 10 Dec. 1911. Writer; Painter; Business Woman. Education: Grad., Barnard Coll., NY.; Grad. study, Columbia Univ. School of Architecture, also Grad. Dept. of Engl.; study of poetry with Prof. Mark Van Doren and others. Married to Charles Alfred Greeff; 1 s. (Pieter). Positions held: Vice-Pres., Granbery Marache & Co., members NY Stock Exchange; Vice-Pres., Blair & Co. Inc., members of NY Stock Exchange. Memberships: Poetry Soc. of America; Authors' League of America; Artists' Equity Assoc. Published work: Love's Argument (collection of poems, with foreword by Mark Van Doren) publd. by The Macmillan Co., N.Y. Contbr. to newspapers, journals in USA and overseas. Address: Dune Rd., Quogue, Long Island, NY 11959, USA.

GREEN, Charles Price, b. 7 May 1897. Teacher. Education: A.B., Univ. of Okla., 1925; M.A., Univ. of Mich., 1927; Ph.D., Northwestern Univ., Evanston, Ill., 1948. Married Margaret Jane Smith, 3 children. Positions held: Tchr. of Speech, Okmulgee (Okla.) H.S., 1925-27; Instr. in Speech, Western Reserve Univ., Ohio, 1928-34; Chmn., Dept. of Speech, Univ. of Okla., 1934-44 & '45-56; Regents Prof. of Speech, 1964-, ret'd. Memberships: Lectr. & Rdr., Travers Newton Chautauqua, 1923-25; Past Pres., Okla. Speech Assn. & of the Ctrl. States Speech Assn.; Chmn. of the Study Comm. on Problems in Interpretation, a Comm. of the Speech Assn. of Am., 1948-50; V.P., Okla. Poetry Soc., 1971; Exec. V.P., ibid, 1972; Pres., 1974. Published works: Graduate Study in the Oral Interpretation of Literature, Southern Speech Jrnl., 1949; Lariat Laughter & Other Poems, 1970. Contbr. to: Red Earth Poetry Mag., Okla. City; Am. Weave; Am. Poetry Mag.; The Okla. Tchr.; Kaleidograph, A Nat. Mag. of Verse. Address: 809 College, Norman, OK 73069, U.S.A.

GREEN, F(rederick) Pratt, b. 2 Sept. 1903. Methodist Minister (retired). Education: Rydal School, Colwyn Bay; Didsbury Theological Coll. Memberships: Poetry Soc. of G.B. (member Editorial Bd. for 7 yrs.); Chairman, Norwich Writers' Circle; Member, East Anglian Writers' Assoc.; The Hymn Societies of G.B. and America. Published works: This Unlikely Earth, 1952; The Skating Parson, 1965; 26 Hymns, 1971. Contbr. to: The Listener; New Yorker; Time and Tide; Poetry Review; English; Outposts; Yorkshire Post; The Countryman; Methodist Recorder; Hibbert Journal; The Tablet; New Poems 1954, 1955, 1958, 1965; Best Poems, Borestone Mountain Award, 1960, 1968; Poems of Today (Fifth Series); Oxford Book of Twentieth Century English Verse, etc. Address: 96 Hillcrest Rd., Thorpe St. Andrew, Norwich, Norfolk NOR 8IS, UK.

GREEN, Galen, b. 30 Apr. 1949. Poet. Education: B.A. in Creative Writing & Literature, Wichita State Univ., 1972. Married Kate Schulte. Positions held: Stockboy; Folksinger; Custodian; Clerical Asst.; Lib. Asst.; Rsch. Corres. Published works: Apple Grunt, 1971. Guest Ed., Out of Sight, 1964. Contbr. to: Ark. River Review; Bones; Center (Woodstock); College Poetry Review Anthol.; Dragonfly; Florida Qtly.; Ghost Dance; Kans. Qtly.; The Little Mag.; Mikrokosmos; N.Y. Qtly.; Out of Sight; Pegasus Anthol.; Road Apple Review; The Sunflower; The Wichita Free Press; West Coast Review; Zahir. Address: 49 South 8th East, Apt. 4, Salt Lake City, UT 84102, U.S.A.

GREEN, Graham Martin, pen name **GRAY GREEN,** b. 17 Dec. 1952. Lecturer in English. Education: Leeds Univ. Memberships: Pres., Leeds Univ. Union Poetry Soc., 1973-74; Birmingham Poetry Ctr. Published works: Wordwood, 1970; Jokes for the Poet, 1971; Spoke, 1972; Dearth, 1972; Unmoons, 1974. Wrote &

directed 'Dearth', a poem/fact sequence on ecology, performed at the 1972 St. David's Arts Fest., the Workshop Theatre (Leeds), BBC Radio Leeds & the 1973 Sunday Times/N.U.S. Drama Festival. Contbr. to: The Moselean; Inklings; Hole; Manuscript; Viewpoints; Poetry & Audience, etc. Currently is leader of 'The Bard Band' & 'Travesty' (poetry/music/theatre grp.) Has read his own poems on BBC Radio Birmingham, BBC Radio Leeds, Radio Free London, Network 4 TV & BBC2 TV. Address: c/o 14 Smirrells Rd., Hall Green, Birmingham B28 OLB, Warwicks., U.K.

GREEN, James, pen name **GREEN, J.C.R.,** b. 19 Sept. 1949. Writer; Publisher. Education: John Neilson Institution, Paisley, Renfrewshire, Scotland; Coimbra Univ., Portugal. Positions held: Founder, Aquila Publishing Co. (1968); Director of Publications, Birmingham Poetry Centre, 1971; Editor, Muse Mag., 1971-72; Editor, Poetry News, 1971-72; Chairman, Birmingham Poetry Centre, 1971-72; Organiser, Birmingham & Midland Poetry Festival, 1972; Member, Birmingham & Midland Inst. Coun., Poetry Committee, 1972; Producer/Introducer "The Poets" BBC Radio Birmingham prog., 1972 onwards; Apptd. Chairman & Managing Director, Aquila Publishing Co. Ltd., 1972; Editor, Prospice mag., 1973; Editor, Assoc. of Little Presses Newsletter, 1973, also on committee of the Assoc.; Gen. Mgr., Indep. Book Distributors, 1974; Dir., Poetry Roundabout Ltd., 1974. Memberships: Poetry Soc. (UK); Chmn., Midlands Br., Writers Action Group; Birmingham & Midland Inst.; Birmingham, Poetry Centre; Poets Conference; Internat. Writers Union (US); Free Writers Congress (Brazil); Nat. Book League (UK). Published works: Go Dig Your Own Grave, 1968; Out of the Darkness, 1971; Lisbon Revisited, 1973; The Keeper of Flocks, 1973; Prospice One, 1973, and Prospice Two, 1974, both ed. with Martin Booth & Michael Edwards. Contbr. to: The Journal; The Observer; News Chronicle (N.Z.); Muse; Little Word Machine; Good Elf; The Scotsman; Gargantua; Exit; Missive; The Pigman; Farming World; Pentagram; Brisbane Courier Mail; Labor News; The Spectator (Canada); Busara; Esquire; Flying, etc. Address: 18 Atherstone Close, Shirley, Solihull, Warwicks. B90 1AU, UK.

GREEN, Judith Ann, b. 10 May 1945. Editor. Education: B.A., Univ. of Ariz., U.S.A., 1967; Grad work, Ariz. State Univ., 1967-. Positions held: Staff Writer, Editorial Asst., Photographer, Artist & Ed., First Nat. Bank of Ariz.; Staff Writer for CURRENT mag. & PULSE news digest, Ed., PULSE, Sr. Ed., External Publs., Salt River Proj.; Ed., Projection; Insight (a news digest to community thought leaders). Memberships: Ariz. Poetry Soc.; World Poetry Soc.; Fellow, Int. Poetry Soc. Published works: For Your Information (pamphlet); The Banker (mag.) & var. banking trade publs. Contbr. to: Sancutter; Apostrope; Poet. Address: 2666 E. Oakleaf Dr., Tempe, AZ 85281, U.S.A.

GREEN, Lewis, b. 14 July 1931. Insurance Official. Married, 2 children. Positions held: Accounts Clerk, 1945-58; Self-employed, 1958-61; Accounts Clerk, 1961-66; Civil Servant (Social Security), 1966-69; Insurance Official, 1969-. Memberships: Birmingham Poetry Ctr. (activities include monthly public readings with invited poets of some standing). Contbr. to Muse. Address: 17 Astbury Ave., Smethwick, Warley, Worcs., U.K.

GREEN, Lynn Hamilton, b. 18 Mar. 1954. Student. Education: currently a candidate for a B.A. at Millsaps Coll. Member, Millsaps Coll. Engl. Club. Published works: Earthwinds, 1972. Contbr. to: Millsaps Coll. 'Stylus', 1972; Poet, India, 1973. Recip., Hon. Mention, Nancy Thorp Meml. Contest, Hollins Coll., Roanoke, Va. Address: 154 Glenway, Jackson, MS 39216, U.S.A.

GREEN, Rose Basile, b. 19 Dec. 1914. Educator; Author; Critic. Education: B.A., Coll. of New Rochelle, N.Y., 1935; M.A., Columbia Univ., N.Y., 1941; Ph.D.,

Univ. of Pa., 1963. Married Raymond S. Green, 1 son, 1 daughter. Positions held: Tchr. of Engl., Italian, Torrington H.S., Conn., 1936-42; Assoc. Prof. of Engl., Registrar, Univ. of Tampa, Fla., 1942-43; Special Instr. of Engl., Temple Univ., Phila., Pa., 1953-57; Chmn., Full Prof. of Engl., Cabrini Coll., Radnor, Pa., 1957-70; Trustee, Phila. Free Lib., 1973–. Chmn. of Lit. Arts Comm., Phila. Art Alliance, 1972–. Published works: The Cabrinian Philosophy of Education, 1963; To Reason Why (sonnets), 1971; The Italian American Novel (lit. criticism), 1973; Primo Vino (sonnets), 1973; 76 For Philadelphia (sonnets), pending publ. Contbr. to: Azimuth (Fac. Jrnl.); The Italian Am. News; The Phila. Evening Bulletin. Address: Manor Rd., Route 2824, Philadelphia, PA 19128, U.S.A.

GREENBERG, Alvin, b. 10 May 1932. Teacher; Writer. Education: B.A., Univ. of Cinn., 1954; M.A., ibid, 1960; Ph.D., Univ. of Wash., 1964. Married, 3 children. Positions held: Instr., Univ. of Ky., 1963-65; Asst. Prof., Assoc. Prof., Prof., Macalester Coll., 1972–; Vis. Lectr. (Fulbright), Univ. of Kerala, India, 1966-67. Published works: The Metaphysical Giraffe, 1968; The House of the Would-Be Gardener, 1972; Dark Lands, 1973. Contbr. to: Am. Review; Antioch Review; Epoch; Poetry Northwest; Iowa Review; Seneca Review; Centennial Review; Ohio Review; Hiram Poetry Review; December; Perspective; Gnosis; Quartet; New Am. & Canadian Poetry; Dacotah Territory; The Little Mag. Recip., Nat. Endowment for the Arts Fellowship, 1972. Address: 3316 W. Owasso Blvd., St. Paul, MN 55112, U.S.A.

GREENE, Jonathan Edward, b. 19 Apr. 1943. Poet; Manager, University of Kentucky Press. Educ: B.A., Bard Coll., Annandale-on-Hudson. Divorced, two children. Positions held: Fndr., Gnomon Press Series, 1965; Designer & Asst. Production Mgr., Univ. of Ky. Press, 1967. Published works: The Reckoning, 1966; Instance, 1968; The Lapidary, 1969; A 17th Century Garner, 1969. Contbr. to: Lines; Unicorn Journal; Matter; Monks Pond; (anthologies) New Directions 20, 1968; American Literary Anthology 3, 1970. Address: 436 West Sixth St., Lexington, KY 40508, U.S.A.

GREENFIELD, Lois Jean, pen name SNOW, Jade, b. 24 May 1928. Homemaker; Freelance Writer. Married, 1 son (dec.), 2 daughters. Positions held: in Clerical & Advt. Dept., Radio Stn.; Advt. Dept. (Compositor) for newspaper; Securities Loan & Finance Co.; Sec. to States Atty.; Interview for S.D. State Employment Serv., etc. Memberships: Major Poets Chapt., Pierson Mettler Assocs. Published works: Sincerely Yours, 1972. Contbr. to: Ideals; Author/Poet; Best in Poetry; Am. Bard; Bardic Echoes; Speak Out; Reach Out; Major Poets; Poetry Parade; Homemaker Mag., Chevron Oil, etc. Honours, awards incl: Geo. Washington Medal of Hon. from Freedoms Fndn., Valley Forge, Pa. for patriotic poem, 1970. Address: 4119 Government Blvd., Mobile, AL 36609, U.S.A.

GREENHALGH, Margaret. Housewife. Memberships: Pres., Leyland Writers'; Preston Poets' Soc.; Preston Writers Circle; Lancashire Authors' Assn. Published works: A Lad fro' Cockermouth, book of poems published by The National Trust, 1970. Contbr. to: This England; The Lady; Child Education; Lancashire Evening Post; Oldham Chronicle; Lancashire Life; Ramblers' Assn. mag.; Lancashire Authors' Assn. mag. 'The Record'; Competitors' Jrnl.; 'The Shore'. Honours, awards incl: 2nd prize, Lancs. Authors' Assn. (Engl. verse), 1965; 1st prize, Preston Poets' Soc., 1963; Pomfret Cup., ibid, 1969; Edna Margaret Rose Bowl, 1969 (& 2nd prize 1972); 1st Prize, MacKenzie Trophy, 1966, '69, '71; Hons., Wharfdale Fest., 1973; 3rd prize, Leyland Writers', 1973. Address: Plover Scar, 224 Leyland Lane, Leyland, Preston PR5 3HH, Lancs., U.K.

GREGERSON, Doris, b. 23 Nov. 1923. Homemaker. Married Jim Gregerson, 1 son, 5 daughters. Positions held: Employee, Helmer Myre State Pk., Albert Lea, Minn., 1967–. Memberships: League of Minn. Poets; Midwest Fed. of Chaparral Poets. Contbr. to: Poetry

Parade; The Moccasin; The Best of Poetry, 1968; The Leatherleaf; The Minneapolis Argus. Recip., Hon. Mention, Midwest Fed. of Chaparral Poets, Spring 1970. Address: Rural Rte. 3, Box 34, Albert Lea, MN 56007, U.S.A.

GREGOR, Arthur, b. 18 Nov. 1923. Writer. Education: B.S., Newark Coll. of Engrng., 1945. Positions held: Sr. Ed., Trade Dept., The Macmillan Co., N.Y., 1962-70; Vis. Prof. in Poetry, Calif. State Univ., Hayward, 1972-73; Assoc. Prof., Hofstra Univ., 1974–. Memberships: PEN; Author's Guild. Published works: Octavian Shooting Targets, 1954; Declensions of a Refrain, 1957; Basic Movements, 1966; Figure in the Door, 1968; A Bed by the Sea, 1970; Selected Poems, 1971. Contbr. to: N.Y. Times; N.Y. Herald Tribune; The Chicago Tribune; The New Yorker; The Nation; The New Republic; Commentary; Commonweal; Harper's; Esquire; Poetry, etc. Recip., 1st appearance prize, Poetry Mag., 1948. Address: 49 Greenwich Ave., N.Y., NY 10014, U.S.A.

GREGORY, Georgina Elizabeth Anne, b. 21 June 1952. Education: Fashion & Textile Design, Salford Coll. of Technol., U.K., 1968-70. Contbr. to: Bogg; Gargantua; Moonshine; Yan, Tan, Tethera; Good Elf Interregnum; Your Friendly Faschist. Address: c/o 138 Mossway, Alkrington, Middleton, Manchester M24 1NT, U.K.

GREGORY, Horace V., b. 10 Apr. 1898. Professor Emeritus. Educ: Milwaukee Schl. of Fine Arts, 1913-16; B.A., Univ. of Wis., 1923. Married Marya Zaturenska, 1925; Two children. Positions held: Free-lance poet & critic, U.K. & U.S.A., until 1934; Tchr., Sarah Lawrence Coll., Bronxville, 1934-60; Prof. Emeritus, ibid, 1960–; Assoc. Ed., Tiger's Eye. Published works: Chelsea Rooming House, 1930; No Retreat, 1933; Wreath for Margery, 1933; Chorus for Survival, 1935; Poems, 1930-1940, 1941; Selected Poems, 1951; Medusa in Gramercy Park, 1961; Alphabet for Joanna: A Poem, 1963; Collected Poems, 1964; (verse translations) Poems by Catullus, 1931; The Metamorphoses by Ovid, 1958; Love Poems of Ovid, 1964; Num. literary criticisms; Ed. num. books. Contbr. to: New Republic; Nation; (anthologies) New Voices, 1928; New Poetry, 1932; Anthology of American Poetry, 1941; Twentieth Century American Poetry, 1944; Modern Verse in English, 1958; Atlantic Book of British and American Poetry, 1959; Erotic Poetry, 1963; Earth Is the Lord's, 1965. Recip., num. awards, fellowships. Address: Palisades, Rockland County, NY, U.S.A.

GREGORY, R(aymond) G(eorge), b. 6 Jan. 1928. Educator. Education: King's Coll., London Univ., 1949-52; Dip. in Drama, Inst. of Educ., Univ. of Newcastle, 1971-72. Married Pat, 3 children (Pat, Sue, Andrew). Positions held: Drama & Engl. Tchr., Fair Oak, Hants., 1953-57; Hd. of Engl., Wyvern Schl., Eastleigh, Hants., 1958-64; i/c Engl. Block, Sr. Sec. Schl., Kololo, Kampala, Uganda, 1965-67; Hd. of Drama, Grove Schl., Market Drayton, Shropshire, 1967-71; Mbr. of Word & Action (Dorset), 1972–. Memberships: Poetry Soc.; Fellow, Int. Poetry Soc.; One of Chesil Poets – based on Abbotsbury, Dorset. Published works: Imaginative Speech & Writing (w. R.D. James), 1966. Plays incl: Dreamer, 1962; Sex-Barrier, 1963; The Meek One, 1966; Trilogy – The Monster, 1959; The City, 1971; The Grot, 1971; Saxo, 1973. Poetry incls: Poems Between the Line & Hell, 1966-70; Proverbs of Hell, 1970; Poems Between Hell and the Circle, 1970-72; Through the Circle, 1972. Contbr. to: Ambit; Outposts; Workshop; Peace News; Anti-Apartheid News; Bogg, etc. Address: c/o Chesil Poets (Word & Action Dorset), 1 Back St., Abbotsbury, Nr. Weymouth, Dorset, U.K.

GREGORY, Robin Edward, b. 12 Feb. 1931. Lecturer; Editor; Writer. Education: B.A., Reading Univ., U.K. Married. Positions held: Educ. Officer, R.A.F.; Personnel Officer, LEO Computers; var. tchng. posts; Sr. Lectr., Matlock Coll. of Educ., 1962-68; Lectures for Nottingham Univ. & Open Univ. Memberships: Soc.

of Authors; Dir.-Gen., Int. Poetry Soc.; Dir.-Gen., Int. Writers Guild & Soc. of New Authors. Published works: Lebanese Pictures, 1973. Ed., 'Orbis' mag. of Int. Poetry Soc. Address: Rose House, Youlgrave, Bakewell, Derbyshire, U.K.

GREGORY, Violet L., b. 19 Jan. 1907. Writer; Poet; Housewife. Education: A.A., San Diego City Coll., U.S.A., 1966; B.A., Univ. of Calif., San Diego, 1972. Married 1) Allen Pruett, div., 1 son, 2) Walter Gregory, dec. Positions held: Corres., Grace Holmes Club Plan, 1949-53; Owner, Little Corner Store, Lyndhurst, N.J., 1953-55; Owner, Star Market, San Diego, Calif., 1956-58; Owner, Gregory Distributors, ibid, 1961-63. Memberships incl: Treas, 1962-64, Pres., 1970-72, Nat. League of Am. Pen Women, San Diego Br.; World Poetry Soc. Intercontinental, India; Fellow, Int. Poetry Soc. Published works: Mixed Bouquet, 1966; The Silver Link, 1969. Contbr. to num. mags., jrnls., anthols., reviews inclng: Let the Minds Create, 1961; Poetry Parade, 1963; Rhyme Time for The Very Young, 1964; Commemorative Anthol. (JFK), 1964; Haiku-Tanka, 1964; Florida Selected Poems, 1966 & 72; IWWP Anthol., 1972; Am. Bard; Bardic Echoes; Bitterroot; Cardinal Poetry Quarterly; Cyclotron; The Denver Post; Flame; Encore; Hartford Courant; Haiku Highlights; Ideals; Modern Images; The Oregonian; Orphic Lute; Poet (India); Prairie Poet; Scimitar & Song. Recip. many poetry prizes. Address: 1649 Pennsylvania Ave., San Diego, CA 92103, U.S.A.

GRESHAM, Ruby Flara, b. 1 Mar. 1909. Housewife; Poet. Education: High School and College. Married to G. Clark Gresham, County Commissioner of Wichita County, Texas. Two children: Joy Gresham Hagstrom, and Ronald C. Gresham. Member: Nat. Fed. of State Poetry Societies; Poetry Soc. of Texas; Wichita Falls Poetry Soc. (corresponding secretary), Chairman of Critic Judge Committee, current Literature Study Club secretary. Contrib. to: Burkburnett Star; Grit Magazine; Book(s) of the year (Poetry Soc. of Texas), 1969, 70, 72, 73. Texas State Poet Laureate, appointed by State Legislature, 1972-73; First place Nat. Fed. of State Poetry Societies, 1970; Numerous hon. mention awards, 1967-72; 33 Awards Poetry Soc. of Texas, including 15 first places, 1965-73; First place North and West Texas Contest, 1966. Address: Box 368, Burkburnett, Texas 76354, USA.

GREY, Robert Waters, b. 12 Oct. 1943. Poet-in-Residence; Instructor. Education: B.A., Brown Univ., 1965; special student, ibid, 1965-66; M.A., Univ. of Va., 1969. Married Lucinda Creswell Grey, 1 son. Positions held: w. Goodwill Industries; Emergency Ward, Mass. Gen. Hosp., Boston; Instr. in Engl., Poet-in-Res., Univ. of N.C., Charlotte, 1969–. Published works: Screaming in the Wind, pamphlet of poems, 1967; Cold Stone, to be published shortly. Co-Ed., Eleven Charlotte Poets, Spring 1971. Contbr. to: Cambridge Scene; Western Review; Human Voice; Southern Poetry Review; Carolina Jrnl.; Folio; Poet Lore; Poet; Quoin; Miss. Review; Ball State Univ. Forum; Wind; New Dawn Anthol.; Duchess House Review, etc. Honours, awards: Acad. of Am. Poets Prize for the Univ. of Va., 1969; 1st prize, N.C. Poets Contest, donated by The Miscellany, Davidson, N.C. Address: Box 345-C, Route 12, Charlotte, NC 28212, U.S.A.

GRIBBLE, Dorothy Rose. Actress-Manager & Speaker of Verse. Education: Wycombe Abbey; Univ. Coll., London, U.K. Positions held: Actress, Stage Mgr., West End, repertory, tours, children's theatre, TV; in Theatrical Mgmt., 1953–; Dir. of Prods., Plantagenet Productions & its associated Recorded Lib.; Dir. of Prods., Westridge Studio, Highclere. Published works: "And I Am A Doggerel Bard", 1973. Plays produced: Blood will Out or The Mistress of Malaponda; Will's Folly; The Friendly House (w. F. Howard Collier); The Pretty Chickens; & adaptations for two performers of Shakespeare's comedies, The Taming of the Shrew & Twelfth Night. Compiler of her recital anthol., A Pride of Writers. Address: Westridge, Highclere, Newbury, Berks., U.K.

GRICE, Deryck Connor, b. 3 Dec. 1948. Teacher. Education: Tchrs. Trng. Coll., Walsall, Staffs. Positions held: Wages Clerk; Lab. Asst. Memberships: Birmingham Poetry Soc.; Fndr., 'Pleck', grp. which perform music, poetry, dance, drama, etc. Published works: Child, a dialogue in verse, 1973. Contbr. to: Radio Times; var. progs. for BBC Leicester; var. coll. mags. Recip. award, Erimus Comp. Address: 2 Dingle Rd., Pedmore, Stourbridge, Worcs., U.K.

GRIER, E(Idon) B(rockwill), b. 13 Apr. 1917. Poet. Education: Private Schools in Montreal, Ottawa, Toronto. Positions held: A painter until 1950; Instr. in the Dept. of Architecture at McGill Univ.; Teacher of Drawing, Mural Painting and the Graphic Arts, Montreal Museum of Fine Arts. Has lived in Mexico and travelled extensively in Europe. Published works: A Morning from Scraps, 1955; Poems, 1956; The Ring of Ice, 1957; Manzillo and other Poems, 1958; A Friction of Lights, 1963; Pictures on the Skin, 1963; Selected Poems, 1971. Contbr. to: Adam; C.B.C.; The Canadian Forum; Delta; English Poetry in Quebec; The Fiddlehead; Fifteen Winds; How do I Love Thee; Made in Canada; New; Oxford Book of Mod. Canadian Verse; The Penguin Book of Canadian Verse; Poetry in our Times; Prism International, etc. Address: 6221 St. George's Place, West Vancouver, B.C., Canada.

GRIEVE, Christopher Murray, pen name **McDIARMID, Hugh,** b. 11 Aug. 1892. Writer, Poet. Education: Langholm Acad.; Edinburgh Univ. Positions held: Fndr. Mbr., Scottish Nationalist Party; Journalist. Published works: Annals of the Five Senses; Contemporary Scottish Studies; The Present Condition of Scottish Arts and Affairs; Scottish Scene; At the Sign of the Thistle; Scottish Eccentrics; The Handmaid of the Lord (a novel from the Spanish of Ramon Maria de Tenreiro); The Scottish Islands; Lucky Poet (autobiog.); Sangschaw; Penny Wheep; A Drunk Man Looks at the Thistle; To Circumjack Cencrastus; Stony Limits and other poems; First Hymn to Lenin and other poems; Second Hymn to Lenin and other poems; Cornish Herioc Song for Valda Trevlyn; The Birlinn of Clanrald (from the Gaelic of Alexander MacDonald); Direach; Speaking For Scotland; A Kist of Whistles; R.B. Cunninghame Graham, a Centenary Study; In Memoriam James Joyce; The Battle Continues; Three Hymns to Lenin; Burns Today and Tomorrow; Collected Poems 1920-61; The Kind of Poetry I Want; Scots Unbound; A Lap of Honour; A Clyack-Sheaf. Ed: Golden Treasury of Scottish Poetry. Contbr. to: Nation; Saltire Review; various Russian, Czech & Chinese jrnls. Honours: J.P. Angus; Hon. LL.D., Edinburgh. Address: Brownsbank, Biggar, Lanarkshire, U.K.

GRIFFITH EDWARDS, May (Victoria), pen name **GRIFFITH EDWARDS, May,** b. 24 May 1903. Freelance Writer. Education: Westcliff School, Weston-super-Mare; L.R.A.M. (piano); London Sch. of Journalism. Widow. Lecturer (on the sonnet) to poetry socs., writers' circles, and schools, 1970-73; Adjudicator (poetry) Isle of Wight Writers' Circle, and St. Cecilia Festival, Bournemouth, 1973; Lect. on traditional forms of poetry (incl. humorous verse), 1973-1974. Memberships: Fellow, Internat. Poetry Soc.; Member, Poetry Soc.; West Country Writers' Assoc. Published works: Many Coloured Glass, 1969; Heartscase, 1972. Contbr. to: Country Quest; Manifold; Sunday Companion; Christian Herald; Parnassian; Sign; Echo; Lansdowne Mag.; New Melody; Isle of Wight Mag. Awards incl.: Capetown Eisteddfod (S. Africa) 5 awards and 1 special prize, 1951; George Camp Prize, 1966; Anglo-Welsh Rev. Sonnet Prize, 1968; Isle of Wight Festival (poetry section) 6 awards, 1969; Bournemouth Music Festival (poetry section) 4 awards, 1973. Address: 27 Tollard Court, West Hill Rd., Bournemouth, Hants., UK.

GRIFFITHS, Brywllyn David, pen name **GRIFFITHS, Bryn,** Writer. Education: Coll. of Further Education, Swansea, U.K.; Harlech Coll., Harlech. Published works: The Mask of Pity, 1966; The Stones Remember, 1967; Scars, 1969; The Survivors, 1971:

Beast Hoods, 1972; Starboard Green, 1973; The Dark Convoys, 1973; Ed., Welsh Voices, an anthol. of Anglo-Welsh Poetry, 1967. Contbr. to: Mabon; Western Mail; Tribune; Westerly; Meanjin Review; English; Critical Quarterly; Blackfriars Mag.; Second Aeon; Poetry Review; Melbourne Herald; Outposts; Transatlantic Review; The Scotsman. Address: c/o J.M. Dent & Sons Ltd., Publishers, 26 Albemarle St., London W.1., U.K.

GRIFFITHS, Reginald, b. 6 May 1912. Photographer. Educ: Studied photography at London Polytechnic, U.K. Married, four children. Positions held: Served WWII; Self-employed photographer, current. Published works: Tugela and Other Poems, 1948; (novels) The Grey about the Flame, 1947; Children of Pride, 1959; This Day's Madness, 1960; Man of the River, 1968. Contbr. to: (anthologies) Modern Narrative Poetry, 1953; Poems of Spirit and Action, 1964; Turning World, 1967; Lines of Action, 1968. Address: 83 Church Square, Grahamstown, South Africa.

GRIFFITHS, Vivian Lawrnece, b. 26 Jan. 1935. Teacher. Education: Coleg Harlech, 1962-63; Bangor Univ. Coll., 1963-66; B.A.; Swansea Univ. Coll., 1966-67, Dip. in Education; Manchester Univ., 1971-72, Advanced Dip. Adult Education. Personal details: Merchant Seaman, 1950-58; Steel Erector, 1958-62. Married; 3 children. Positions held: Lecturer, Cardiff Coll. of Art, 1967-69; Teacher in Swansea, since 1969. Memberships: Poetry Soc. of America. Published works: Myths Of A Modern Mariner, 1967; Sinews From Salt, 1969; Stanzas One, 1970. Contbr. to: London Welshman; Anglo-Welsh Review; Planet. Address: 37 Samuel Cres., Gendros, Swansea, Wales, UK.

GRIGSON, Geoffrey, b. 2 Mar. 1905. Author. Education: Univ. of Oxford. Positions held: Editor, New Verse, 1933-39 (the mag. which published many of the early poems of Louis MacNeice, W.H. Auden, Dylan Thomas, etc.) Published works: Several Observations, 1939; Under the Cliff, 1943; The Isles of Scilly, 1946; Collected Poems, 1963; A Skull in Salop, 1967; Ingestion of Ice-Cream, 1969; Discoveries of Bones & Stones, 1971; Sad Grace of an Imperial Mongoose, 1972; Angles & Circles, 1974. Contbr. to: Penguin Poets 23, 1973; New Statesman; Listener; Poetry Chicago; Times Lit. Supplement; Spectator; Encounter. Recip., Duff Cooper Meml. Prize, (for Discoveries of Bones & Stones), 1972. Address: Broad Town Farm, Broad Town, Swindon, Wilts., U.K.

GRIMM, Edward, b. 2 Dec. 1931. Journalist. Education: B.A. (Cum Laude), City Coll. of NY., M.A., NY Univ. Married, 2 children. Manager of Publications for IBM World Trade Corp. Contbr. to: NY Herald-Tribune; The Nation; Occidental Review. Address: 137 Riverside Dr., New York, NY 10024, USA.

GRINBERG, Miguel, b. 18 Aug. 1937. Journalist. Education: Colegio Nacional No. 6 de Buenos Aires; British Lyceum of Culture; Buenos Aires Univ. Positions held: Sub-Editor, Arts, Panorama (Mag.), Buenos Aires, 1966-1970; Columnist, 2001 (Mag.), Buenos Aires, 1969–; Editor, Cine & Medios (Mag.), Buenos Aires, 1969-1971; Editor, Eco Contemporaneo (Mag.), Buenos Aires, 1961-1969; Editor, Contracultura (Mag.), Buenos Aires, 1970–; Disc Jockey, Radio Ciudad de Buenos Aires, 1972–. Published works: Cienagas, 1962, 1972; America Hora Cero, 1965; Opus New York, 1973; Lunes de Revolucion (in preparation). Contbr. to various journals in Brazil, Mexico, Spain, Argentina, USA, India, etc. Honour: Mencion de Honor, II Juegos Florales, Arequipa, Peru, 1968. Address: C.C. Central 1332, Capital Federal, Argentina.

GRONOWICZ, Antoni, b. 31 Jul. 1913. Poet; Playwright; Novelist. Education: Ph.D. Memberships: Dramatists Guild, Inc.; Authors Guild; P.E.N. American Center. Published works include: The Quiet Vengeance of Words (poetry), 1968; Polish Poems,

1972; An Orange Full of Dreams (novel), 1972; The Hookmen (novel), 1973; American Sextet (novel), 1974, etc. Contrib. to: The Activist; The American Citizen; Ariz. Quarterly; Arts in Society; Aspects Magazine; Ave Maria; Bitterroot; Cambridge Review; Cape Rock Qtly.; Churchman; Contemporary Review; DeKalb Lit. Journal; Druid Magazine; The Galley Sail Review; Graffiti Magazine; Human Voice Qtly.; The Idler; Ikarus Magazine; Jewish Currents; Jewish Forum; Laurel Review; The Lutheran; Manifold Qtly.; The Minnesota Review; Minority of One; Motive Magazine; N.M. Qtly.; News and Letters; New Voices; New Zealand Monthly; People's Voice; Phylon; Poet and Critic; Poetry Newsletters; Poetry Review; Quixote Magazine; The Rebel; Saturday Review; Showcase; Smoky Hill Review; Star Weekly, Step Ladder; United Church Herald, The Univ. of Kansas City Review; Voice of the Nation; Zeitgeist Magazine, etc. Address: 132 East 82 St., New York, N.Y. 10028, USA.

GROSS, Mary Elizabeth, b. 24 Aug. 1900. Teacher. Education: A.B., Ursinus Coll., Collegeville, Pa., 1923; A.M., Middlebury Coll., Vt., 1930. Positions held: Tchr. of Engl., West Phila. H.S., Phila., Pa., 1926-63; Lectr., Supvsr. of Student Tchrs. in Public Schls., Univ. of Pa., Phila., Jan-May, 1964. Memberships: Sec., Phila. Profl. Writers Club; Bd. Mbr., Phila. Regl. Writers Conf.; V.P., Sec., St. Petersburg, Fla., Ch. Drama Guild; Past Pres., St. Petersburg Writers Club, 1964–. Contbr. to: Am. Bard; Driftwood; Seydell Qtly.; Canadian Poetry Mag.; Kansas City Star; Messenger; Archer; Poetry Venture; Christian Sci. Monitor. Recip. var. poetry prizes. Address: Talisman Apts. No. 27, 2800 4th St. S., St. Petersburg, FL 33705, U.S.A.

GROSS, Ronald, b. 27 Nov. 1935. Poet & Writer. Currently Adjunct Prof. of Social Thought, N.Y. Univ. Published works: Pop Poems, 1969; A Handful of Concrete, 1970. Contbr. to: N.Y. Times; Book World; Harpers; Saturday Review, etc. Subject of ETV prog., The Poetry of Ronald Gross, produced at SUNY, Brockport, 1969 & of 30-page interview, Jrnl. of Popular Culture, 1971. Portfolio of poems illustrated by pop art paintings, Art News, 1971. Address: 17 Myrtle Dr., Great Neck, NY 11021, U.S.A.

GROSS, Walter, b. 12 Oct. 1924. Writer. Education: Univ. of Zurich. Freelance Writer since 1952. Memberships: Schweizer Autorengruppe/Gruppe Olten. Published works: Die Taube, poems, 1956; Botschaften noch im Staub, poems, 1957; Antworten, poems, 1964. Contbr. to: NZZ; Basler Nachrichten; Weltwoche; Gegenwart; Deutsche Zeitung; Hortulus; Akzente; Neue Deutsche Hefte; Spektrum; (anthols.) Transit (Suhrkamp); Widerspiel (Hanser); Jahresring (DVA/Stuttgart); Deutsche Gedlchte (Fischer). Contbr. to & broadcast on: Radio Zurich, Basel, Bern Süddeutscher, Rundfunk, Südwestfunk, Westdeutscher Rundfunk, Sender Freies Berlin, Hessischer Rundfunk, Radio Plzen, Radio Prag, Radio Usti nad Labem. Honours, awards: Stipendium d. Berlin-Stiftung des Bundesverbandes d. Deutschen Industrie, 1963; Hugo Jacoby-Preis, 1964; C.F. Meyer-Preis, 1966; Stipendium der Stiftung Pro Helvetia, 1967, etc. Address: Lärchenstr. 31, CH–8400 Winterthur, Switzerland.

GROVES, Dale Young, pen names **YOUNG, Dale; GROVES, Dale,** b. 28 Aug. 1915. Accountant. Education: Southern Methodist Univ.; Univ. of Houston; special courses at other univs. Positions held: Manager, Groves Oil Co.; Administrator, Crippled Childrens Hospital; Office Manager, The Oil Corp. (also the Corp. Sec.); Self-employed, Dale Y. Groves, Oil Production Accounting, etc. Memberships: Poetry Soc. of Texas; The Byliners of Corpus Christi (Pres., 1972-1973, 1973-1974); Texas Womens Press Assoc. (Vice-pres., South Texas Div.); Nat. Fed. of Press Women; Fine Arts Colony (member of the Bd. of Directors); South Texas Speech Assoc. (at various times Pres., Vice-Pres., Sec.). Published works: An Inch of Time, 1954; World of the Skyrocket, 1956. Contbr. to: Sat. Review; Texas Lit. Qtly.; Quicksilver Mag.; Flame; Different; American Weave, etc. Work also appears in sev. anthols. Recip. several poetry prizes (Southwest Writers Conf.; Internat. Avalon, etc.). Address: 310 Breezeway, Corpus Christi, TX 78404, USA.

GRUBB, David Herbert Watkins, b. 9 Feb. 1941. Educator. Education: St. George's Schl., Harpenden, Herts.; Culham Coll., Abingdon. Positions held: Hd. of Engl. Dept., Culverhay Comprehensive, Bath. Memberships: West Country Writers' Assn.; Poetry Panel, Dartington Hall Arts Comm.; Engl. Assn.; W.A.G. Published works: The Green Dancers, 1961; The Burial Tree, 1967; And Suddenly This, 1972; Frog, 1972; Caligula, 1973. Contbr. to: Tribune; Ambit; Platform; Second Aeon; Now; Samphire; Gargantua; Oasis; Encounter, etc. Honours, awards: Engl. Poetry Prize, 1972; Keats Prize Poems, 1972 & '73; PEN, 1973. Address: 21 Prospect Pl., Corsham, Wilts., U.K.

GRUBB, Frederick Stuart, b. 18 June 1932. Poet. Published works: Title Deeds: Poems, 1961; A Vision of Reality: Studies of Modern Poetry, 1965; September Sun, pamphlet, 1970. Contbr. to: New Poems 1971 & 1972 (PEN anthols.); Tribune; World Marxist Review; New Left Review; Le Provencal; La Marseillaise; L'Humanité; Labour Monthly; Aquarius; Listener; Pravda; Phoenix; Wave; Working Men's Coll. Jrnl.; Hampstead & Highgate Express; Tit Bits, etc. Address: The Attic, 243 Haverstock Hill, London NW3, U.K.

GRUBE, John Deen, b. 23 May 1930. Poet. Positions held: Jr. Ptnr., Toronto firm, Canada, 1959-64. Published works: Sunday Afternoon at the Toronto Art Gallery, 1966. Contbr. to: Canadian Forum; Fiddlehead.

GRUFFYDD, Peter, b. 12 Apr. 1935. Teacher; Free-lance Writer/Actor. Educ: B.A., Univ. of Wales, Bangor. Married, two children. Positions held: Nat. Serv., 1955-57; Lectr., Liberal Studies, Rochdale Coll. of Art, Lancashire, 1965-67; Actor, Welsh Theatre Co., 1967 & w. B.B.C. Wales TV, 1967; Free-lance Writer/Actor & Translator (Welsh to English), B.B.C., Wales. Published works: Triad (w. H. Webb & M. Stephens), 1963; The Cuckoo (dramatic poem), 1968; Articles of Literary Criticism. Contbr. to: Poetry Wales; Anglo-Welsh Review; Critical Quarterly; Observer; London Welshman; (anthologies) Welsh Voices, 1967; Poetry 69, 1969; Lilting House, 1969. Recip., E.C. Gregory Award, 1963. Address: East Sussex, U.K.

GUARDINO, Leonard J., pen names include **RAINGOUD, Ronald E., WALES, George Henry, HANSON, H.,** b. 22 May 1913. Printer; Poet. Married (wife dec.) Positions held: Boxer; Physical Culturist; Athletic Dir., YMCA; Printer; Layout Man & Ed., The Writer's Voice, 1958-64; Painter & Illustrator of books; Owner, Publisher & Ed., Guardino's Gazette. Contbr. of poems to num. mags. & jrnls. inclng: The Hollywood Herald; The Broward Tattler; Hollywood Sun; Miami Herald; Lauderdale Press; Dania News; N.Y. Jrnl.; Stars & Stripes; The Oregonian; The Tablet; The New Athenaeum; The Am. Courier; Rutland Herald; Hartford Jrnl.; N.Y. Herald Tribune; N.Y. Enquirer; Catholic Sun; The Italian News; Poets of Am. Mag.; Poets of Am. Anthol. Nightshade; Fireflower; Christian Writers Publ; Catholic Herald; The War Cry; Progress Mag.; Jr. World Mag.; The Am. Hebrew; Poetry Digest; Poet's Pick; The Villager; Green's Mag. Has also contributed short stories, jokes, puzzles to mags. Mystery stories published in: The Saint Detective Mag., 1953,55,56; Mystery Digest, 1958; Mike Shayne Mystery Mag., 1958; The Saint Mystery Mag., 1960; Mike Shayne, 1971. Recip. var. hons. Address: 789 Seneca Ave., Ridgewood, Brooklyn, NY 11227, U.S.A.

GUENTHER, Charles (John), b. 29 Apr. 1920. Librarian, Poet & Translator. Education: Harris Teachers Coll., St. Louis; St. Louis Univ.; B.A., Webster Coll., St. Louis. Married to Esther G. Klund, 1 s., 2 d. Positions held: Editorial assistant, St. Louis Star-Times, 1938; w. Social Security Commission of Mo., 1940; US Dept. of Labor, 1941-42; US War Dept., Corps of Engineers, 1942-43; USAF, 1943-72, and

Defense Mapping Agency Aerospace Center, 1972- as translator, historian, supervisory cartographer, librarian, etc. Reviewer, St. Louis Post-Dispatch, 1953-72; St. Louis Globe-Democrat, 1972-. Instructor, var. writers' confs., 1955-. Member, Poetry Soc. of America; Chairman, Bd. of Chancellors, St. Louis Poetry Center, 1965-72; VP, St. Louis Writers' Guild, 1958; Pres., ibid., 1959; VP, Mo. Writers' Guild, 1971-73; Pres., ibid., 1973-74; VP, Greater St. Louis Chapter, Special Libraries Assoc., 1968-69; Pres., ibid., 1969-70; VP for Mo., McKendree Writers' Assoc., 1964-66; Conference Director, ibid., 1969-73; hon. life member, ibid., 1973-. Hon. member, Bibliotheca Partenopea, Naples, Académie d'Alsace and various other European and Latin American literary societies. Assoc. member, Internat. American Inst. Pubs.: Modern Italian Poets, 1961; Paul Valery in English, 1970; Phrase/Paraphrase, 1970. Translator (with others) Selected Poems of Alain Bosquet, 1963. Contrib. to An Anthol. of Spanish Poetry, 1961; Modern European Poetry, 1966; The Sea and the Honeycomb, 1966; The French in the Mississippi Valley, 1965; From the Hungarian Revolution, 1966; The Missouri Poets, 1971; New Directions 20, 1968, etc. Contrib. to: Accent; Black Mountain Review; The Critic; Edge; Kenyon Review; The Literary Review; The Nation; Partisan Review; Minnesota Review; Poetry (Chicago); Quarterly Rev. of Literature; The Reporter; The Schooner, etc. Poetry editor of Weid: The Sensibility Revue, Homestead, Fla., 1973-75. Decorated Commander, Order of Merit of the Italian Republic, 1973; recip. The Shell Companies Foundation Grant, 1970; St. Louis Poetry Center translation prize, 1971, etc. Apptd. Commander, Order of St. George of Carinthia, 1958; M.Litt. (hon.) Agen (Lot-et-Garonne), France, 1957. Address: 2935 Russell Blvd., St. Louis, Mo. 63104, USA.

GUERRERO, Luis Beltrán, pen name **CANDIDO,** b. 11 Oct. 1914. Writer. Education: Doctor en Ciencias Politicas de la Universidad Central de Venezuela; Profesor en Letras de la Universidad de Buenos Aires. Married Enriqueta Fernández (Ribé), 2 sons, 1 daughter. Positions held: Writer for 'El Universal' newspaper, 1930-; Tchr. & Prof., Instituto Pedagógico & the Universidad Central; Sec., Universidad Central de Venezuela; Senator to Congress, 1969-74. Memberships: Indivíduo de Número de la Academia Venezolana de la Lengua; Indivíduo de Número de la Academia Nacional de la Historia; Miembro de la Asociación de Escritores de Venezuela. Published works: Secretos en Fuga, 1942; Posada del Angel, 1954; El Visitante, 1958; Tierra de Promisión, 1959; Poesía Electa, 1962. Contbr. to El Universal. Honours, awards: Premio Nacional de Literatura, 1970. Address: Prados del Este, Calle Amazona, Qta. El Cardón, Caracas, Venezuela.

GUEST, Barbara, b. 6 Sept. 1920. Writer. Education: B.A., Univ. of Calif. at Berkeley. Married to Trumbull Higgins. Positions held: Assoc. Ed., Art News, 1953-56. Mbr.: PEN. Published works: The Location Of Things, 1960; Poems, 1962; The Blue Stairs, 1968; I Ching, Poems and Lithographs (w. Sheila Isham), 1969; Moscow Mansions, 1973. Contbr. to: Partisan; Evergreen; Transatlantic; Paris Review; Poetry; Art & Lit.; City Lights Jrnl. Awards: Yaddo Fellowship, 1958. Address: 1148 Fifth Ave., New York, NY 10028, USA.

GUEST, Harry, b. 6 Oct. 1932. Lecturer. Educ: Malvern Coll.; B.A., Trinity Hall, Cambridge, U.K.; D.és L., the Sorbonne, France. Married, two children. Positions held: Hd., Modern Langs. Dept., Lancing Coll., Sussex, 1961-66; Lectr., Engl. Lit., Yokohama Nat. Univ., Japan, 1966-. Published works: Private View, 1962; A Different Darkness, 1964; Arrangements, 1968; The Cutting-Room, 1969; (translations) Beware of Pity, 1962; Trial of Strength (German Play), 1964. Contbr. to: Poetry Review; New Measure; Eigo Seinen; (anthologies) Best Poems of 1966: The Borestone Mountain Poetry Awards, 1967; Children of Albion, 1969; Penguin Book of Postwar British Verse, 1970.

GUEVARA, Juan G., b. 15 May 1944. Poet. Education: Tex. A & I Univ., Kingsville, Tex. Contbr. to El Grito, 1970, '71, '73. Address: P.O. Box 446, Benavides, TX 78341, U.S.A.

GUILLEVIC, Eugene, pen name **GUILLEVIC,** b. 5 Aug. 1907. Writer. Memberships: Union des Ecrivains; Societe des Gens de Lettres; PEN Club; Sacem; SACD; SDRM. Published works: Terraque, 1942; Executoire, 1947; Gagner, 1949; Carnac, 1951; Sphere, 1963; Avec, 1966; Ville, 1969; Paroi, 1970; Encoches, 1970; Inclus, 1973. Honours, awards: Aigle d'or du Festival du Livre de Nice, 1973. Address: 11 rue Emile Dubois, 75014, Paris, France.

GUILMAIN, Ray, pen names **ROSSEEUW & GUILMAIN, Ray, Jill,** Writer; Editor; Reporter. Education: Agrégation ès Lettres, Htes Ecoles Sciences Commerciales & Industriels. Married, 3 children. Head, Dir., A.S.B.L. Association Littéraire & Artistique "Poésie Vivante en Wallonie"; Approved by Ministère de la Culture Française & Education Nationale & Centre Culturel du Hainaut; Ed., Edition Arts & Littérature Caroloregiens. Published works: 'Revue Littéraire & Artistique', 'Anthologies', 'Recueils de Poésies' (french lang.), 'Nouvelles', 'Romans', 'Reportage'. Contbr. to some reviews & periodicals in France, Belgium, Sweden, U.S.A., Italy, etc. Recip. of approx. 40 literary prizes from France, Italy, Tunisia, etc. Address: 6 rue de la Côte, B 6090 Couillet, Belgium.

GUINNESS, Bryan Walter (Lord Moyne), pen name **GUINNESS, Bryan,** b. 27 Oct. 1905. Author; Director; Barrister at Law. Education: M.A., Mod. Langs., Oxford Univ., U.K. Married, 11 children. Positions held: Governor, Nat. Gall. of Ireland; Mbr., House of Lords, 1945–; V. Chmn., A. Guinness Son. & Co. Ltd.; Trustee, Guinness Housing Trust, London & Iveagh Housing Trust, Dublin; Pro-Chancellor, Trinity Coll., Dublin. Memberships: sometime Pres., sometime Chmn., Irish PEN; Irish Acad. of Letters; Fellow, Royal Soc. of Lit., London. Published works: Twenty three Poems, 1931; Under the Eyelid, 1935; Reflexions, 1947; Collected Poems, 1956; The Rose in the Tree, 1964; The Clock, 1973. Contbr. to: London Mercury; Irish Times; Sunday Times; Country Life; Poetry Review; Hisonica; The Adelphi; Harpers Bazaar; New English Weekly; Adam; The Listener; Oxford Book of Irish Verse; Penguin Book of Irish Verse. Address: Knockmaroon House, Castleknock, Co. Dublin, Ireland.

GULLANS, Charles B(ennett), b. 5 May 1929. Professor of Engl., Univ. of California, Los Angeles. Education: B.A., c.l., Univ. of Minnesota, 1948, M.A., ibid, 1951; Ph.D., Stanford Univ., 1956. Membership: Vice-Pres., Scottish Text Soc. (Edinburgh). Published works: Moral Poems, 1957; Arrivals and Departures, 1962. Contbr. to: Hudson Review; Southern Review; NY Times; Paris Review; Epoch; Spectrum; Coastlines; Yankee; Northerner; Western Poet; Poetry Northwest, etc. Awards: Stanford Poetry Fellowship, 1952-53; Fellow, Inst. of Creative Arts, Univ. of California, 1965-66. Address: UCLA., Dept. of Engl., Los Angeles, CA 90024, USA.

GUNERT, Johann, b. 9 June 1903. Poet; Writer; Professor. Married Barbara Furthner. Positions held: Tech. Employee, Tutor, Librarian, Newspaper Corres., Ed., 1921-27; entered Municipal Serv., 1927; Mil. serv. & P.O.W., 1941-46; joined Municipal Lib., Vienna, 1946; Lectr. in Modern Lit., etc. Memberships: Comm., Austrian PEN Club; Osterr. Schriftstellerverband (OSV); Pres., Grillparzer Gesellschaft; V.P., United Poets Laureate Int. for Europe; Dir., Austrian World Poetry Day; Presseklub Concordia; Société Européenne de Culture; Die Kogge; Rudolf Kassner-Ges.; Corres. Mbr., Wiener Secession; Hon. Mbr., Accademia Int. di Tavola rotonda, etc. Published works incl: Irdische Litanei, 1945; Das Leben des Malers Vincent van Gogh, 1949; Überall auf unsrer Erde, 1952; Aller Gesang dient dem Leben, 1956 & 62; Inschrift tragend und Gebild, 1958; Kassandra lacht,

1963; Es geschehen Zeichen, 1968; Austrian P.E.N. Club Bibliography, 1954, 59; Käthe Braun – Prager: Das himmlische Kartenhaus, 1965; Almanach der Stadt Wien, Lebendige Stadt (1-10), 1954-63 & many others. Contbr. to anthols. from Austria, Germany, France, Hungary, Spain, etc. & to var. mags. & jrnls. Honours, awards incl: Prize for Lit., City of Vienna, 1951; Govt. Prize for Lyric, 1956; Hon. Poet Laureate for Lyric of the United Poets Laureate Int.; Lit.D., 1967; Dr.h.c., 1969; Grand Prize for Poetry, City of Vienna, 1968. Address: 1130 Vienna (13), Feldkellergasse 30 a/9, Austria.

GUNN, Carroll David, b. 19 Dec. 1896. Retired (United States Postal Service). Education: Poetry Workshop of Chautauqua, N.Y., 10 yrs.; McKendree Writers' Workshop, Lebanon, Ill., 3 yrs. Memberships: Assoc. Mbr., Poet's Study Club, Terre Haute, Ind.; Wis. Fellowship of Poets; Charter Mbr. & for some yrs., Pres., Local Creative Writers' Forum. Published works: Custodian of the Covenant, 1971. Contbr. to: Poetry Annual, Rochester Fest. of Relig. Arts, N.Y.; War Cry, Salvation Army, Chicago; The Christian, St. Louis, Mo.; Anamils Mag., Boston, Mass.; La Salle, Peru, Daily News-Tribune, Ill.; Animals mag., Boston. Honours, awards: First prize, Laramore-Rader Poetry Grp., 1960; Hon. Mention, Rochester Fest. of Relig. Arts, 1950, '60, '61, '64 & Third prize, 1965. Address: 126 Gunn Ave., La Salle, IL, U.S.A.

GUNN, Richard M. 'Pek', pen name **'UNCLE PEK',** Poet; Columnist; Lecturer; Humorist & Publisher. Positions held: Exec. V.P., John T. Benson Publishing Co., Nashville, 1939-46; Premiere Coordinator for World Wide Pictures, 1954; Appointed by Gov. Frank G. Clement, Exec. Sec., Tenn. Alcoholism Commn., 1955; Apptd. by Gov. Clement, State Chmn., Inter-Am. Relations, 1956; Publicity Dir., Pasadena Coll.-Student Recruitment & raising living endowments, 1959-60; Lectr., Rural Philos., Federal Exec. Inst., Charlottsville, Va., 1970-71; Currently Poet-Philos. in Res., Cumberland Coll. & Writer in Res., Lees-McRae Coll. Writes weekly newspaper column "The Peekhole" devoted to nostalgic humor & carried by 32 newspapers. Memberships incl: ASCAP: Tenn. Poetry Soc.; Tenn. Folklore Soc.; Blue Ridge Crafts Assn.; Acad. of Am. Poets; Alpha Kappa Psi (life); Tenn. Educ. Assn. (life). Published works: Tumblin' Creek Tales (a composition of Folklore in humorous verse), 1963; The Peekhole (folklore in poetry & prose, 1974; var. greeting cards & prints of poetry. Recently recorded a record album of his humorous banquet speeches in verse & recorded 'Santa's Visit' in 1970. Honours, awards: Poet Laureate of Tenn., 1970; Apptd. by Gov. Winfield Dunn, State Chmn., Nat. Poetry Day, 1973. Address: 901 McClurkan Ave., Nashville, TN 37206, U.S.A.

GUNN, Thomson William, pen name **GUNN, Thom,** b. 29 Aug. 1929. Poet. Education: University Coll. Schl. & Trinity Coll., Cambridge Univ., U.K.; B.A. & M.A., Stanford Univ., Calif., U.S.A. Positions held: Engl. Tchr., Univ. of Calif., Berkeley, 1958-66; since 1966 has occasionally taught a term at other univs., namely Hayward, Princeton, Stanford & Berkeley. Published works: Fighting Terms, 1954; The Sense of Movement, 1957; My Sad Captains, 1961; Selected Poems (w. Ted Hughes), 1962; Positives (w. Ander Gunn), 1966; A Geography (pamphlet), 1966; Touch, 1967; The Garden of the Gods (pamphlet), 1968; Poems 1950-66, a Selection, 1969; The Explorers (pamphlet), 1969; The Fair in the Woods (pamphlet), 1969; Sunlight (pamphlet), 1969; Moly, 1971; Mandrakes, Songbook, To The Air, all pamphlets to be published 1973. Contbr. to: The Listener; Observer; Paris Review; Poetry; Spectator; New Statesman; London Mag.; Encounter; Sebastian Quill, etc. Address: 1216 Cole St., San Francisco, CA 94117, U.S.A.

GUPTA, Rohini, pen name, **ROHINI,** b. 26 Nov. 1953. Student. Education: Walsingham House Schl., Bombay; Cathedral & John Cannon Schl.; Presently studying (Senior) B.A., Elphinstone Coll., Bombay. Author of "My World of Fantasy" (a collection of 78

poems), 1965. Contbr. to: Children's World; Tapovan Prasad; Sunshine, etc. Awards: Nehru Award (Gold Medal) for collection of 26 poems, "Nature's Alphabet in Verse", Int. Children's Comp., 1968; W.P.S.I. Certificate of Merit, 1973. Address: Oceana, 214 Marine Dr., Bombay 400020, India.

GURNEY, Robert, b. 8 July 1907. Retired. Published works: Bardic Heritage, 1969. Address: c/o Messrs. Chatto & Windus Ltd., 40 William IV St., London W.C.2., U.K.

GUSTAFSON, Ralph Barker, b. 16 Aug. 1909. Poet; Editor; Music Critic. Education: M.A., Bishop's Univ., Lennoxville, Quebec, Canada; M.A., Oxford Univ., UK.; Hon. D.Litt., Mount Allison Univ. Married Elisabeth Renninger. Positions held: British Info. Servs., 1942-46; Music Critic, Canadian Broadcasting Corp., 1960-; Prof., Dept. of Engl. & Univ. Poet in Residence, Bishop's Univ., Canada, 1963-. Published Poetry: The Golden Chalice, 1935; Alfred the Great, 1937; Epithalamium in Time of War, 1941; Lyrics Unromantic, 1942; Flight into Darkness, 1944; Rivers Among Rocks, 1960; Rocky Mountain Poems, 1960; Sift in an Hourglass, 1966; Ixion's Wheel, 1969; Selected Poems, 1972; Theme & Variations for Sounding Brass, 1972; Fire on Stone, 1974; Summer Storm (Short Stories), 1974. Contbr. of poetry & short stories to the following anthols. & collections: Book of Canadian Poetry, 1957; Canadian Anthol., 1973; Oxford Book of Canadian Verse in English & French, 1966; Modern Canadian Verse, 1967; Best American Short Stories, 1948; Best American Short Stories, 1950; Book of Canadian Stories, 1962; Canadian Short Stories, 1960; Made in Canada; How Do I Love Thee. Editor of following: Anthology of Canadian Poetry, 1942; A Little Anthology of Canadian Poetry, 1942; Canadian Accent, 1944; The Penguin Book of Canadian Verse, 1958 & 1967. Author & Narrator, Nocturne: Prague 1968, & I Think of All Soft Limbs, works set to music by Richard Arnell, premiere, Bishop's Univ., 1970, & Canadian Broadcasting Corp., 1972. Awards: Canada Coun. Fellowship, 1960; Grant, Canada Coun., 1968; Arts Award, 1972. Address: PO Box 172, N. Hatley, PQ, Canada.

GUSTAFSON, Richard C., b. 10 Aug. 1933. Associate Professor of English. Education: A.B., Gonzaga Univ., 1955; M.A., Univ. of Kan., 1957; Ph.D., ibid, 1960. Positions held: Editor, Poet & Critic, 1964-. Contbr. to: Beloit Poetry Jrnl.; Colo. Qtly.; Kan. Mag.; Western Humanities Review; Epos; Descant; Midwest Qtly.; Perspective; New Orleans Review; Goliards; The Salt Creek Rdr.; College English; N.M. Qtly. Address: Dept. of Engl., Iowa State Univ., Ames, IA 50010, U.S.A.

GUSTAFSSON, Lars, b. 17 May 1936. Author. Education: D.Phil., Uppsala, Sweden, 1961; Philosophical studies in Uppsala & Oxford. Positions held: Ed. in Chief, BLM, 1966-72. Memberships: PEN; Corres. Mbr., Akademie der Wissenschaften und der Literatur, Mainz. Published works: (in Swedish) Ballongfararna, 1963; En förmiddag i Sverige, 1965; En resa till jordens medelpunkt, 1967; Bröderna Wright uppsöker Kitty Hawk, 1968; Kärleksförklaring till en sefardisk dam, 1971; Varma rum och kalla, 1972; Selections: En privatmans dikter, 1968; Fosterlandet under jorden, 1973; (in English) Selected Poems, transl. by Robin Fulton, 1972; (in German) Die Maschinen, transl. by Hans Magnus Enzensberger, 1966. Contbr. to: BLM; Lyrikvännen; Hvedekorn; Le Nouvel Observateur; Tworzsocz; Delos; Akzente; Micromegas; Neue Rundschau; The Lit. Review. Address: Blasbogatan 8, 722 15 Västeras, Sweden.

GUTHRIE, Ramon, b. 14 Jan. 1896. Poet. Education: LL.D., Univ. of Toulouse. Prof. Emeritus, Dartmouth Coll., Hanover, N.H., 1963-. Published works: Trobar Clus, 1923; Marcabrun, 1926; Parachute, 1927; A World Too Old, 1928; Graffiti, 1959; Asbestos Phoenix, 1968; Maximum Security Ward, 1970. Contbr. to: The New Yorker; Poetry; S4N; Carleton Miscellany; The Nation; The New Republic. Awards: Marjorie Peabody Waite Prize, 1969; National Endowment for the Arts,

1961. Address: Norwich, Vt., USA.

GUTTERIDGE, Donald George, b. 30 Sept. 1937. Teacher. Education: B.A., Univ. of Western Ont., Canada. Positions held: Tchr. of Engl., Ont. H.S.'s, 1960-67; Asst. Prof., Fac. of Educ., Univ. of Western Ont., 1968-. Member, League of Canadian Poets. Published works: Riel: A Poem for Voices, 1968 & 72; Perspectives, 1970; The Village Within, 1970; Death at Quebec, 1971; Saying Grace/An Elegy, 1972; Coppermine: The Quest for North, 1973. Contbr. to: Alphabet; Canadian Forum; The Fiddlehead; Edge; Quarry; West Coast Review; Adam (U.K.). Recip., The President's Medal, Univ. of Western Ont., 1972. Address: 114 Victoria St., London, Ont. N6A 2B5, Canada.

H

HAAVIKKO, Paavo Juhani, b. 25 Jan. 1931. Literary Director; Author. Married 1) Marja-Liisa Vartio, dec., 2) Ritva Rainio. Positions held: Lit. Dir., Otava Publishing Co., 1967-; Bd. Mbr., ibid, 1968-; Bd.Mbr., Yhtyneet Kuvalehdet Co., 1970-. Published works: Tiet etäisyyksiin (poems), 1951; Tuuliöinä (poems), 1953; Synnyinmaa (poems), 1955; Lehdet lehtiä (poems), 1958; Talvipalatsi (poems), 1959; Münchhausen, Nuket (two plays), 1960; Yksityisiä asioita (novel), 1960; Toinen taivas ja maa (novel), 1961; Vuodet (novel), 1962; Runot 1951-61 (poems), 1962; Lasi Claudius Civiliksen salaliittolaisten pöydällä (short stories), 1964; Puut, kaikki heidän vihreytensä (poems), 1966; Ylilääkäri (two plays), 1968; Neljätoista hallitsijaa (poems), 1970; Puhua, vastata, opettaa, (poems), 1972; Sulka (play), 1973; Runoja matkalta salmen yli (poems), 1973. Some of his novels, short stories & collections of poetry have been translated & published in other langs. Honours, awards: Pro Finlandia, Suomen Leijonan Ritarikunta; Dr. h.c., Helsinki Univ., 1969. Address: The Otava Publishing Co., Uudenmaankatu 8-12, SF-00120 Helsinki 12, Finland.

HABBYSHAW, Susan Larraine, b. 21 Apr. 1952. Contbr. to: var. issues, Texas Traveler, 1972; Saga (a small quarterly), 1972 & '73; Allied News (a Pennsylvania newsweekly), 1973. Address: 515 East Market St., Mercer, PA 16137, U.S.A.

HACKER, Marilyn, b. 27 Nov. 1942. Writer. Education: B.A., Wash. Sq. Coll., N.Y. Univ. Published works: The Terrible Children (pamphlet), 1967; Presentation Piece, 1974. Contbr. to: Ambit; Antaeus; Aphra; Aquarius; Arx; The Carleton Miscellany; City; Defiance; Epoch; The Little Mag.; London Mag.; ManRoot; The New Am. Review; Outposts; Poetry (Chicago); Poetry Northwest; Priapus; Quark; Samphire; The San Francisco Qtly.; Second Aeon; Stand; Strange Faeces; The Times Lit. Supplement; Workshop New Poetry; The World. Honours, awards: One of four poets selected for the Discovery '73 Award, Poetry Ctr., N.Y., 1973; 'Presentation Piece' chosen by Acad. of Am. Poets as the Lamont Poetry Selection for 1973. Address: 51 Paddington St., London, W.1., U.K.

HADFIELD, Charles Robert, b. 15 Feb. 1952. Student of French Literature, Russian, German, Italian; Social Worker. Education: Southampton Univ., 1971-. Memberships: Poetry Soc. Inc., London; Fndr. Ed. of 'P' mag. & its associated Poetry Workshop based at Southampton. Contbr. to: Hampshire Poets; Bogg; Lines; 'P'; Intergrad. Recip., Poetry Prize, Portsmouth Arts Fest., 1972. Address: 5 Seafields, Emsworth, Hants. P010 7MT, U.K.

HADLEY, Thomas Erle, (co-writer with wife, Arlene), born 20th September 1903. Registered Architect. Education: Grad., Archtl. Coll., Univ. of Mich., Ann Arbor, Mich., 1925. Positions held: Chief Archt., Fisher Body Div., Gen. Motors, 1929-48; Field Supt., Alaska Archt. & Engrg. Corp., Fairbanks, Alaska, 1951-63;

Project Supt., Bldg. Div. State of Mich., 1966–. Memberships: Mich. Poets; Peninsula Poets Anthol.; Hamilton Horticultural Soc., Ont., Canada; Nat. Audubon Soc.; Pres., Detroit Audubon Soc., 1944-45. Publications: Happy Valley, 1966. Contbr. to: Jessens Weekly, Alaska; Holly Advtsr., Mich. M.C. on following TV shows: Nature Trails, WWJ-TV, Detroit, 1953-56; Adventure Holiday, CKLW-TV, Windsor, Ont., Canada, 1957; Let's Get Around, WJR-TV, Flint, Mich., 1958. Mgr., Univ. of Mich. Hiawathan Wildlife Series, 1948-59; Lectr., Nat. Audubon Soc., 1945-59. Honours: Film made in collaboration with Walt Disney, Nature's Half Acre, won Lion of St. Mark Award, Venice, Italy, & Hollywood Oscar. Address: 306 S. Saginaw St., Holly, Mich. 48442, U.S.A.

HAESAERT, Clara, b. 9 Mar. 1924. Civil Servant, Min. of Dutch Culture, Brussels. Memberships: V.V.L. & PEN Club. Published works: De Overkant, 1953; Omgekeerde Volgorde, 1961; Onwaarschijnlijk Recht, 1967; Spel van Vraag en Aanbod, 1970. Contbr. to: De Meridiaan; Podium; Komma. Honours, awards: Basiel de Craene, 1952; Culturele Veertiendaagse Limburg, 1953. Address: Hertogenstraat 1, 1950 Kraainem, Belgium.

HAFEEZ, Abulasar Jallandhari Hilaale, pen name **HAFEEZ (Jallandhari),** b. 14 Jan. 1900. Poet & Author. Memberships: Fndr. & Life Mbr., Writers' Guild of Pakistan. Published works incl: (poetry) Naghmazar; Soz-o-Saz; Talkhaaba-e-Shireen; Shah nama-e-Islam (in 4 vols.); Bazm Nahin Razam; Charaaqh-e-Sahar; Git & Nazmen (4 books for children); Phool Maala (for children); Bahaar-Ke-Phool (for children); Hindustan Hamara (for children); Chiuntinama; Seventeen stories for children; (prose) Haft Paiker (short stories); Meyaari Afsane (short stories); Umr Ayyar (2 vols., for children); Intikhaab Hali. Ed. of var. monthlies & contbr. to jrnls. & periodicals. Honours, awards incl: Title of 'Hilati Imtiaz', Pakistan; Poet of Pakistan (wrote Nat. Anthem); title of 'Poet of Islam'; title 'Malikushoara (King of Poets), Tonk State; Shaire Islam, Bhohal State. Address: 74G Modeltown, Lahore, Pakistan.

HAFIZ, Abdulsalaam Hashim, b. 1929. Retired Civil Servant. Self Educated. Positions held: Sec., Committee for the Expansion of The Prophet's Mosque in Al-Medina; Police Department Official. Memberships: Modern Literature Soc., Cairo; The Blessed Valley Soc., Al-Medina. Published works: 10 volumes of Arabic poetry; sev. articles & research papers on history & religion; sev. short stories. Contbr. to all Saudi Arabian publications & some in other Arab countries. Recip., Ministry of Education Prize for Composition, 1964. Address: Al-Medina, Saudi Arabia.

HAFIZ, Ali, b. 1907. Journalist. Education: Tchng. Cert. from one of the Ulema of The Prophet's Mosque in Al-Medina. Positions held: Clerk in the Religious Courts, Al-Medina, then Chief Clerk; Mayor of Al-Medina; Fndr. of a school for nomadic children; Fndr. of Al-Medina Newspaper & it's Editor-in-Chief for 15 yrs. Memberships: Saudi Arabian Soc. for Belle Lettrists; Archaeol. Comm. of Riyadh Univ. Contbr. of Chapters in the History of Al-Medina, 1968 (408 pages); also to all Saudi Arabian newspapers as well as to the State Television Broadcasting network. Address: P.O.B. 1624, Jidda, Saudi Arabia.

HAGGITT, Eileen Maud, b. 12 Mar. 1929. Lecturer in English. Education: Municipal Trng. Coll., Kingston-upon-Hull, 1950-52; B.A., Open Univ., 1973. Married, 1 daughter. Positions held: Bank Clerk, 1945-47; Clerk, WAAF, 1947-48; Asst. Tchr., 1948-50; Student Tchr., 1950-52; Asst. Tchr., 1952-58; Hd. of Dept. of Engl., 1958-66; Deputy Hd., 1966-69; Lectr. in Engl., Boidesley Coll. of Educ., 1969–. Member, Birmingham Poetry Ctr. Contbr. to: New Poems (PEN), 1954; BBC Midland Poets; Midland Read, 1973; Time & Tide; Birmingham Post. Honours, awards: West Midlands Arts Assn. (Recommended), 1973; Keats Poetry Prize (Highly Commended), 1973. Address: 48 Torridon Croft, Birmingham B13 8RG, U.K.

HAGSTROM, Mary Joy, pen name **HAGSTROM, Joy Gresham,** b. 6 May 1933. Homemaker. Married to Clifford E. Hagstrom, 2 daughters, 1 son. Memberships: Internat. Poetry Soc. (Fellowship); Nat. Fed. of State Poetry Socs.; Poetry Soc. of Texas; Wichita Falls Poetry Soc. (Vice-Pres., Sec.). Contbr. to: Grit (newspaper); Burkburnett Informer Star; Wichita Falls Times. Recip. of numerous awards for poetry, and named Poet Laureate of the Texas Fed. of Women's Clubs, 1965-1966. Address: 506 Magnolia St., Burkburnett, TX 76354, USA.

HAHN, Hannelore, b. 9 Nov. 1926. Writer. Education: Black Mountain Coll., N.C., 1945-1947; Univ. of So. Calif., B.A., 1952. Born in Dresden, Germany, daughter of the late Consul, Dr. Arthur Hahn and Helene (Brach) Hahn. Positions held: Admin. Asst. to The Project on Recent Physics in the U.S., at the Am. Inst. of Physics, NY., 1962-1965; Exhibit. Co-Ordinator for US Information Agency, Wash., DC., for US Pavilion at EXPO '67, Montreal, Canada, 1965-1966; On Staff of NYC Parks, Recreation & Cultural Affairs Admin., 1966–; Director-Founder, The Phoenix House Poetry Workshops, Phoenix House Drug Rehabilitation Center, NYC., 1970–. Contbr. to: Internat. Who's Who in Poetry Anthol., 1972; NY Qtly.; Image; Poetry Roundtable; Charlie Mag., etc. Hons. and Awards: Guest Poet, NY Qtly., 1971; Hon. Mention Winner, Rego Award, 1972, NY Poetry Forum, also Spring Poet, 1970, Poet of the Month, April, 1973. Address: 1628 York Ave., New York, NY 10028, USA.

HAHN, Lola Elizabeth Fessenden, pen name, **HAHN, Lola E.,** b. 3 May 1914. Housewife; Musician; Pianist; Organist. Education: HS; Olivet Coll., Mich., 1 year; Marygrove Coll. Positions held: Piano Accompanist, W. Shore Symphony Orchestra, 1959-61; Asst. Organist, 1st Congregational Church, 1956-69; Bd., Trustees, ibid. Memberships: Poetry Soc. of Mich.; World Poetry Soc.; Fndr. Mbr., Acad. of Am. Poets; Hymn Soc. of Am.; Friends of Art, Muskegon; Pres., ibid, 2 yrs. Contbr. to: (jrnls.) Chicago Tribune; Poet; Muskegon Chronicle; Poet Lore; Peninsula Poets; PEO Record; Pilgrim Post; Church Schl. Worker; Muskegon Chmbr. of Comm. News; Am. Rose Soc. Annual Book; (anthols.) World Poetry Soc. Anthol.; American Mosaic, anthol. by Constance Henning. Honours, Awards: Nat. Level 1st place, for hymn (text & music), Nat. Stewardship Proj., United Ch. of Christ, 1964; 10th place, poem; 8th place for hymn (text & music), 1963; 1st place for hymn, State level; Spec. Award, World Poetry Soc., 1970; 2 awards, Mich. Poetry Soc., 1970; Awards, Peninsula Poets, 1970, 1973. Address: 2916 Roosevelt Rd., Muskegon, Mich., 49441, USA.

HAHN, Truce, b. 20 Mar. 1924. Housewife. Educated in Holland. Married, 3 children. Member, San Antonio Chapt., Poetry Soc. of Tex. Contbr. to The Free Press, 1972. Recip. several 1st, 2nd & 3rd prizes during years 1970-72. Address: 102 Shavano Dr., San Antonio, TX 78231, U.S.A.

HAINES, John Meade, Jr., pen name, **HAINES, John,** b. 29 June 1924. Author. Education: Am. Univ., Wash. DC, 1948-49; Hans Hofmann Schls. of Fine Art, NYC, 1950-52. Positions held: US Navy, Pacific area, 1943-46; US Navy Dept., 1949: Homesteader, Alaska, 1954-69; various skilled & unskilled jobs; Poet-in-residence, Univ. of Alaska, 1972-73. Publications: Winter News, poems, 1966; The Stone Harp, 1971; Twenty Poems, 1971; The Mirror, 1971; Selected Poems, 1973. Contbr. to: The Nation; Hudson Rev.; Unicorn Jrnl.; Kayak; San Francisco Rev.; Mass. Rev.; Oberlin Qtly.; Chicago Choice; The Critic; Tenn. Poetry Jrnl.; Roanoke Rev.; Alaska Rev.; The Strand; Chelsea; Poetry, Australia; Poetry, Chicago; Outsider; Tampa Poetry Rev.; Wormwood Rev.; Field; Carolina Qtly.; The Sixties; Lillabulero; Kayak; Choice; Changes; Southern Poetry Jrnl.; Dragonfly; Epoch; Hearse. Honours: Guggenheim Fellowship for Poetry, 1965-66; Nat. Coun. on the Arts Grant, 1967-68; Jennie Tane Award for Poetry, Mass. Review, 1964; Poet Laureate of Alaska, 1969. Address: 517 12th St., Pacific Grove, Calif. 93950, USA.

HAJEK, Louise, b. 14 Jan 1906. Homemaker. Education: Public GS; privately tutored. Widow; 3 s., 2 d. Memberships: Nat. League of American Pen Women (Chicago), Rec. Sec.; Pub. Rel. Chairman, Poetry Workshop Chairman; Woodawn Poets (poetry chairman); Poetry Forge; Kentucky Poetry Soc.; Poets & Patrons (Chicago). Published works: Remembered Music, 1971; One Candle, 1969. Contbr. to: Nat. Parent Teachers Mag.; Ladies Home Journal; Wilson Library Bulletin; The Writer; Scott Foresman Reader; Hallmark Treasure Books; The Lyric; Wings; Poet Lore; The Archer; South China Morning Post; San Francisco Chronicle; Chicago Tribune; NY Herald Tribune; Kansas City Star; Denver Post; Toronto Star; Washington Star; Oregonian Verse; Pen; The Instructor; The Friend; Canadian Messenger; The Grail; Chicago Jewish Forum; Adventure; Christian Advocate; Stories For Children; Wonder Time; etc. Awards: Deep South Writers Cont. Juv. Verse, 1st, 1961; Pen Women Nat. Peace Sonnet, 1st, 1966; Chicago Poets Internat. Sonnet Cont., 1st, 1961; Deep South Writers, Unpub. Book, 1st, 1965; Alexandria Br., NLAPW., Free Verse, 2nd prize, 1973; San Diego, 1st prize, Sonnet, NLAPW., 1973; Free Verse, Alexandria Br., NLAPW, 1973; Kentucky State Poetry Contest, 3rd prize, Haiku, 1973; Kentucky State Poetry Contest, 2nd prize, Sonnet, 1973; Arkansas Writers, Sonnet, 3rd Prize; Haiku, 1st. Address: 6701 S. Rockwell, Chicago, IL 60629, USA.

HALAKI, Theodore, b. 8 Sept. 1936. Poet; Author. Education: B.A. Engl., Hunter Coll. Positions held: worked mainly in advertising, 1961-67; Supervised the building of houses on Ibiza. Has written many poems, two novels. Currently working on a play in blank verse. Contbr. to: Encounter, 1973; Voices Int., 1973; Folio, 1973; Raven, 1973; Some Friends, 1973; North Am. Mentor, 1973; Ball State Univ. Forum, 1974; Expatriate Review, 1973; Caryatid, 1973; Perspective, 1973; Quality Am. Poetry (anthol.), 1973. Address: 319 West 92nd St., N.Y., NY 10025, U.S.A.

HALBERSTADT, John, b. 19 Sept. 1943. University Instructor. Education: B.A., N.Y. Univ., U.S.A., 1963; M.A., Univ. of Calif., Berkeley, 1965; M.Phil. and M.A., Yale Univ., 1972; Ph.D. cand., ibid. Positions held: Rdrship, Univ. of Calif., Berkeley, 1963-64; Instr., Western Mich. Univ., 1965-68, Rutgers Univ., Newark Br., 1969, Thames Valley State Tech. Coll., 1969-71; p/t Instr., Mohegan Community Coll., 1970-71; Asst. in Instrn., Yale, first semester, 1973; Tchng. Fellow, ibid, 2nd semester, 1973; Instr., Wichita State Univ., 1973–. Member, Associated Writing Progs. Published works incl: I'm In Love With Joanne Talsma (book of poems), 1971; Girlfriends (book of poems), to be published, 1974. Contbr. to num. reviews, jrnls. inclng: Mass. Review; Mulberry; The New Yale Grad.– Profl. Short stories, poems, criticism have appeared in: Papertexts; Perstare; The Trial Baloon; The Heights Daily News; The Violet; The Weekend Outdoor News, etc. Assoc. Ed., var. jrnls. Ed.-in-Chief, & Fndr., Bread, 1960. Recip. var. hons. inclng: Winner 'Best in Manhattan', N.Y. Univ. Prose Writer's Contest, 1959. Address: Engl. Dept., Wichita State Univ., Wichita, KS 67208, U.S.A.

HALBROOKS, Ruth Thomas, b. 4 Oct. 1914. Homemaker. Education: Dip., Christian Writers' Inst., 1967. Married Guy Cleveland Halbrooks, 1 son, 1 daughter. Positions held: Pres., 1948, '58, '64, '67, '72, Tchr., 1948-50, '63, Assoc. Tchr., 1953-58, '65, Assoc. Tchr., 1967-73, Baptist Sunday Schl.; Pres., 1962-64, V.P., 1964-65, Grp. Ldr., 1969-73, Woman's Missionary Union; Sec., 1957 & '60, V.P., 1959 & '61, PTA. Memberships: Anthol. Chmn., Awards Comm., Registration Comm., Ala. State Poetry Soc.; Prog. Comm., Sec. Pro Tempore, Birmingham Quill Club; Ala. Writers' Conclave; Woman's Club. Published works: Joy Springs (religious poetry), 1971; Look Out From The Mountain (poetry w. religious, nature & family background), 1974. Contbr. to: Ideals Mag.; The Sampler; Muse Messenger; The Informer; The Mustard Seed Anthol. Honours, awards: 1st prize for

relig. poem, Ala. Writers' Conclave, 1972; 1st prize for Christmas poem, The Birmingham Quill Club, 1972. Address: 1037 Hagwood Rd., Birmingham, AL 35235, U.S.A.

HALE, Paul V., b. 19 July 1921. Professor. Education: B.A., Canisius Coll., Buffalo, N.Y., 1950; M.A., Cornell Univ., Ithaca, N.Y., 1952; Ph.D., N.Y. Univ., 1962. Married Helena M. Menchini May, 1 daughter. Positions held: Engl. Dept., Niagara Univ., 1952-63; Prof. of Engl., State Univ. Coll., Buffalo, N.Y., 1963–; Dir., Siena Program, Siena, Italy, 1968-69 & '72-74. Published works: Martyrs Three (recording), 1968; Naked to the Wind, 1974. His radio play 'Erasmus in the Underworld' was one of six winners in the 1970 Golden Windmill Radio Drama Contest sponsored by RThe Lock Haven Review; Paedia. Address: 44 Burbank Terr., Buffalo, NY 14214, U.S.A.

HALL, Alice Elizabeth, pen name **HALL, Alice Clay.** Poet; Artist; Lecturer. Education: Pvte. Elem. Schls. in Va. and Colls. in Va., NC, Fla. & Tex. including: Blackstone Coll. for Girls, Va.; William & Mary Coll., Williamsburg, Va., Randolph-Macon, Longwood, Univ. of Fla. Trinity Univ. Memberships: Charter Mbr., Poetry Soc. of Va.; Organiser & First Pres., San Antonio Chapt., Poetry Soc. of Tex., 1968; Corresp. Sec. ibid, 1969; Avalon Worlds Arts Acad.; Permanent Int'l. Hostess, ibid; Nat. Soc. Arts & Letters; Ruth Taylor Fine Arts Ctr. Women's Comm. of Trinity Univ.; Council of Int'l. Relations; Inner Wheel of Rotary Int'l., etc. Publications: April-Hunger, 1958; Discernment (poem); Graduation Night (words & music); Illustration of Dedication Poem in Light From Other Stars (last book of poems of lilith Lorraine 1963–pub. before her death); Chaliced Atoms, 1972. Contbr. to: Avalon mags.; various anthols., 1940–; The Raven; Different; Avalon Golden Book; William & Mary Lit. Mag.; Southern Methodist; Pack of Fun; The Children's Friend; Blue Moon; Cyclo-Flame, 1967-68; Poetry Prevue, Summer 1969; Quintessence, 1968; La Grange Jrnl.; Poet. Recipient of many awards and recognitions including: Avalon Int'l. Poets' & Editors' Conf., 1957, '58; in recognition of this she was presented as Speaker, Trinity Univ., San Antonio, Tex.; Cert. for Personal Broadcast on Stn. WBUX, Doylestown, Pa., 1968; DIB Cert. of Merit, 1968; Fellow, Int. Biog. Assn., 1970; appeared on Artist & Celebrity Previews, IPA, 1965, etc. Address: 109 Saddletree Rd., San Antonio, Tex. 78231, USA.

HALL, Amanda Benjamin, b. 12 July 1890. Housewife. Education: Public and Private Schools, Norwich, Conn.; special courses in writing, NY Univ., Columbia, etc. Personal details: daughter of Joseph and Caroline Hall (Joseph Hall born in Huddersfield, Yorkshire, UK); married John Angell Brownell. Memberships: Poetry Soc. of America; The Women Poets of NY; The Pen and Brush (NY); Poetry Soc. of Virginia. Published works: The Little Red House in the Hollow, 1918; Blind Wisdom, 1920; The Heart's Justice, 1922; The Dancer in The Shrine, 1923; Afternoons in Eden, 1932; Cinnamon Saint, 1937; Honey out of Heaven, 1937; Unweave a Rainbow, 1942; Frosty Harp, 1954; The View from The Heart, 1964; The Blue Pigeon, 1973. Contbr. to: Yale Review; Queen's Qtly.; NY Tribune; New Yorker; Yankee; The Lyric; Poet Lore; Hartford Courant; The Oregonian; Imprints; Gourmet Mag. Awards include: Yrly. Prize, Poetry Soc. of America, 1923 (also later), Award, Poetry Soc. of Georgia; The Lyric, etc. Address: 542 Montauk Av., New London, CT, USA.

HALL, Blaine R., b. 18 Feb. 1921. General Insurance Business. Education: Coll., 3 yrs.; grad. of Alice Lloyd Jr. Coll., Pippa Passes, Ky. Positions held: Schl. Tchr., Floyd Co. Schls., 1941, '43, '45, '48; US Air Force, UK, 1943-45; Coal Miner, 1949-53; General Insurance Business, 1954–. Memberships: former Vice-Pres., Ky. Poetry Soc.; Eastern Ky. Poetry Soc. Author of From These Hills, 1968; Reflections and Moods, 1970. Contbr. to: (anthols.) Variety in Verse; A Burst of Trumpets; Contemporary Kentucky Poetry; Kentucky Harvest; Timeless Treasures. (Poetry Jrnls. & papers)

Herald Dispatch (poetry column), Huntington, W Va.; Ashland Daily Independent, Ashland, Ky.; Approaches, Elizabethtown, Ky.; South & West Int'l., Ft. Smith, Ark.; The American Bard, Hollywood, Calif. Honours; Kentucky State Poetry Soc., First Place, 1967; Kentucky Poetry Soc., Fourth Place, 1967; Cyclo-Flame, Sixth Place, 1968. Address: P.O. Box 508, Prestonsburg, Kentucky 41653, USA.

HALL, Donald, b. 20 Sept. 1928. Professor of English. Educ: B.A., Harvard Univ., 1951; B.Litt., Oxford Univ., U.K., 1953. Divorced, two children. Positions held: Worked w. Richard Wilbur, Theodore Morrison, John Ciardi & Archibald MacLeish, Harvard Univ., & w. Yvor Winters, Stanford Univ.; Poetry Ed., Paris Review, 1953-62; Mbr., Editorial Bd. of Poetry, Wesleyan Univ. Press, Middletown, 1958-64; Tchr., Univ. of Mich., 1957–; Prof. of Engl., ibid, current; Cons., Harper & Row Publrs., N.Y.C.; Gen. Ed., Series of portfolios combing poems and graphics, London Arts, Inc. Memberships: Jr. Fellow, Soc. of Fellows, Harvard Univ., 1954-57. Published works: Exiles and Marriages, 1955; A Roof of Tiger Lilies, 1964; The Alligator Bride: Poems New and Selected, 1969. Ed. of num. anthologies inclng. Man and Boy: An Anthology, 1968 & American Poetry: An Introductory Anthology, 1969. Honours, awards: Newdigate Prize for Poetry, 1952; Lamont Poetry Selection Prize, 1955; Guggenheim Fellowship, 1963; others. Address: 1715 South University, Ann Arbor, MI, U.S.A.

HALL, James B(yron), b. 21 July 1918. Author; Professor Literature. Education, B.A., Univ. of Iowa, 1947; M.A., ibid, 1948; Ph.D., 1953. Married Elizabeth Cushman Hall, 1946, 1 s., 4 d. Positions held: Instr., Cornell Univ., 1952-53: Asst. Prof., Engl., Univ. of Ore., 1954-57; Assoc. Prof., ibid, 1958-60; Prof., 1960-65; Prof., Dir., Writing Ctr., Univ. of Calif., Irvine, 1965-68; Prof. of Lit. & Provost of Coll. V., Univ. of Calif., Santa Cruz, 1969–; Cons. Ed., Doubleday & Co., 1962-67; Cultural Specialist, US Dept. of State, 1964: Advsry. Ed., The Northwest Review; Fndr., Dir., Summer Acad. of Contemporary Art, 1959-64. Memberships: Advsr., Contemporary Novelists & Short Story Writers of Engl. Lang. Proj., UK, 1970-71; Judge, Shelley Mem. Award, Poetry Soc. of Am., 1970-71; Fellow, Chapelbrook Fndn., 1967-68; Fellow, Inst. Creative Arts, 1967-68; PEN. Published work include: Not By the Door, 1954; The Short Story, 1956; TNT For Two, 1956; 15 x 3, 1957; Racers to the Sun, 1960, '61, '62, '64; Us He Devours, 1964; Realm of Fiction: 61 Short Stories, 1965, revised, 1970; Modern Culture & the Arts, 1967, revised, 1972; Mayo Sergeant, 1968, '71; The Hunt Within, 1973. Contbr. to: Experiment; Poetry, Chicago: Perspective: Olivet Quarterly; Western Review; Accent; Beloit Poetry Journal; Oregon Signatures; Sewanee Review; Poetry Northwest: Malahat Review; Kayak; Furioso; Epoch; Esquire; Harper's Bazaar; San Francisco Review: Gent Magazine; Carleton Miscellany; Virginia Quarterly Review; The Atlantic; Los Angeles Times; West Coast Review: Rediscoveries; Stories that Count; New Directions Anthols.; The Best American Short Stories, etc. Honours & Awards: Ohio Writer of Year, 1954; Rockefeller-Iowa Grant, 1955; 2nd, Va. Quarterly Review, 1967, etc. Address: Cardiff House, 1100 High St., Santa Cruz, Calif. 95060, USA.

HALL, John Clive, b. 12 Sept. 1920. Staff member of Encounter magazine. Education: Leighton Park, Reading; Orlei Coll., Oxford. Published works: Selected Poems (with Keith Douglas and Norman Nicholson), 1943; The Summer Dance (poems), 1951; The Burning Hare (poems), 1966; A House of Voices (poems), 1973; Edwin Muir (critical pamphlet), 1956. Address: c/o Chatto & Windus Ltd., 40 William IV St., London WC2, UK.

HALL, Keith Duane, Jr., b. 9 Sept. 1945. Writer; Actor. Education: B.A. in filmmaking, Univ. of Calif., L.A. Positions held: Film Reviewer for the Tustin News; Head Writer, The White Elephant Research Co.; Actor, sev. motion pictures. Contbr. to: All Time Favorite Poetry; Best in Poetry; Poet West; Child Life; Fun for

Middlers; The Instructor; Prim Aid; My Weekly Reader; Big Country; Grass Roots Forum; Carol. Address: 3001 A South Bradford Pl., Santa Ana, CA 92707, U.S.A.

HALL, Rodney, b. 11 Nov. 1935. Writer. Education: B.A., Univ. of Queensland. Poetry Editor, The Australian, 1967–; Poetry Advisor to Angus & Robertson, Ltd., 1973–. Member P.E.N. Publications: Penniless Till Doomsday, 1961; Statues & Lovers, 1962; Forty Beads on a Hangman's Rope, 1963; Eyewitness, 1967; The Autobiography of a Gorgon, 1968; The Law of Karma, 1968; Heaven, In a Way, 1970; A Soapbox Omnibus, 1973. Contrib. to: (Australia) The Age; Aspect; The Australian; Australian Letters; Australian Poetry; Balcony; The Bulletin; Galmahra; Makar; Meanjin Quarterly; The Melbourne Partisan; New Impulses in Australian Poetry; Overland; Poetry Australia; Prospect; Quadrant; Realist; Southerly; Sydney Morning Herald; The Term Review; Twentieth Century; Westerly. (U.K.) Outposts; Poetry Review. (U.S.A.) Ariel; The Literary Review; Spirit. (Argentina) Cormoran y Delfin. (France) Le Periscope. (West Germany) Aksente. (Malaysia) Dewan Sastra. (India) The Times of India. Recip. Creative Arts Fellowship, Australian Nat. Univ., 1968, 1969; Commonwealth Literary Fund Fellowship, 1970. Represented Australia as official delegate to India (1970) and Malaysia (1972). Address: P.O. Box 118, North Quay, Brisbane, Queensland, Australia.

HALL, Ruth Kennedy, b. 16 Sept. 1904. Teacher; Housewife; Freelance Writer. Education: Okla. State Teacher's Coll.; Univ. of Texas; Univ. of N.M. Married Richard P. Hall; 3 daughters. Memberships: N.M. Press Women (Treas., 2 yrs., Historian, 3 yrs.); Nat. Fed. of Press Women; N.M. State Poetry Soc.; Nat. Fed. of State Poetry Socs.; Nat. League of American Penwomen, Inc.; Acad. of American Poets; Mavericks (local workshop of prof. freelance writers; Chairman for sev. terms). Pubs. Prize Poems of Nat. Fed. of State Poetry Socs., 1969-70; Southwest issue of Poet (World Poetry Soc. Intercontinental), 1973. Contrib. to: Contemporary (Denver Post Supp.); Western Review; Southwest Heritage; The Press Woman; Message Mag.; Encore; Fellowship in Prayer; N.M. Mag. Awards: N.M. Press Women Writing Contest, 2nd place, 1964, and 1st place, Poetry, 1966; 1st place, Nat. Fed. of Press Women Sonnet Contest, 1967; 1st place, cash award, rhymed lyric, Nat. Fed. of State Poetry Socs., 1970; Hon. Mention, N.M. State Poetry Soc. Contest, and 2 hon. mentions in Nat. Fed. Contest, 1971; 1st prize, cash award, and on hon. mention in Major Poets Sonnet Contest: Cash Award Manardina Contest, 1972; Hon. Mention, Nat. Fed. of State Poetry Socs., 1973. Address: 1727 Chacoma Place, S.W., Albuquerque, N.M. 87104, USA.

HALLADAY, Geneva Rose, pen name, **HALLADAY, Geneva,** b. 27 Apr. 1926. Writer, Poet. Education: Montreat Coll.; Monmouth Coll.; B.A., ibid; Judson Coll. Positions held: Student Libn.; Tech., Photo Lab.; Tchr.; Pub. Schls.; Clerk; Tchr., adult courses. Writing for Publng., Carl Sandburg Coll., Galsburg, Ill.; Edit. Assoc., Writer's Digest. Memberships: Int. League of Children's Poets; Internat. Platform Assoc.; Internat. Poetry Soc.; former mbr., Am. Assoc. of Univ. Women; former Assoc., Christian Authors Guild; Monmouth Writers' Group. Publications: Twenty Poems For Children, 1968; Star Points, 1969; Projects in Writing For Publication, 1972. Contbr. to: (anthol.) Heart's Secrets, 1962; (jrnls.) Forum; Phylon; Midwest; Am. Bard; Denver Post; Highlights For Children; Purring In A Pocket; Pandora; Moody Monthly; Christian; Improvement Era; Home Life; Orphic Lute; Californian; Popular Dogs; Time of Singing; etc. Address: 818 N. A St., Monmouth, Ill. 61462, USA.

HALLSTROM, Karin Lyberg, pen name **LYBERG,** b. 31 Jan. 1907. Poet; Author. Education: Girls' Schl., Dress & Hatmaking, 1926-29; Practice of dressmaking, Paris, House Depuis-Magnin, 1930-31; trained by the Russian dancer, Tonja Ligovskaja-Grahm for the profession of dancer & pedagouge of Free Dance,

1931-35. Personal details: m. to Nils Hallström, Dentist, 1936, 3 s. Positions held: Hatmaker, 1931-32. Memberships: Sweden's Union of Authors; Soc. of New Idon; Int. Lit. Union. Published works: Minne, vad vill du mig? (Remebrance, what do you want of me?), 1944; Statyernas Leende (The Smile of the Statues), 1947; Spegelvänd (Picture in a Looking-glass), 1953. Contbr. to the following newspapers, reviews, mags. & anthols: Dagens Nyheter; Arbetaren; 40-tal.; Poesi; Prisma; Lyrikvännen; Vi; Folket i Bild; Dagens Dikt; Poeter pa Resa. Honours, awards, etc: Scholarship, from Aftonbladet & the Book-lottery, 1954; The Travelling Scholarship to Italy, from Sweden's Union of Authors, 1971. Address: Spanga Stationsplan 3, 16353 Spanga, Sweden.

HALPE, Ashley, b. 19 Nov. 1933. Professor of English; University Proctor. Educ: Univ. of Ceylon, Peradeniya, 1956; Ph.D., Univ. of Bristol, U.K., 1962. Married, two children. Positions held: Prof. of Engl. & Univ. Proctor, Univ. of Ceylon, 1965–. Exhibited paintings in London, Bristol & Colombo, Ceylon; Produces plays regularly inclng. The Zoo Story by Albee, The Father, Strindberg, & The Infernal Machine by Cocteau. Contbr. to: (anthologies) Poetry Peradeniya, 1958, '59, Young Commonwealth Poets '65, 1965; Commonwealth Poems of Today, 1967. Recip., Leigh Smith Prize for English, 1956. Address: Dept. of English, Univ. of Ceylon, Peradeniya, Ceylon.

HALPERN, Daniel, b. 11 Sept. 1945. Teacher; Poet; Translator; Editor. Education: M.F.A., Columbia Univ. Positions held: Instr., The New Schl. for Soc. Rsch.; Ed., Antaeus Mag.; Editor-in-Chief, The Ecco Press. Published works: Traveling on Credit, 1972; The Poems of Angela McCabe, 1973; The Midnight Caller, 1974; Songs of Mririda, 1974; The Whippet Ball, 1975. Contbr. to: The New Yorker; Harper's; Saturday Review; Esquire; The N.Y. Review of Books; Nation; New Directions Annual; Choice; The Humanist; Partisan Review; The Paris Review; Shenandoah; Perspective; Mademoiselle; Sumac; Antaeus; Malahat Review; N.Y. Qtly., etc. Honours, awards: Jessie Rehder Poetry Award, 1971; YMHA Discovery Award, 1971; Gt. Lakes Colls. Writers Award, 1973; Nat. Endowment for the Arts Fellowship, 1973. Address: 1 West 30th St., N.Y., NY 10001, U.S.A.

HAM, Barbra Allen, pen name **HAM, Barbra A.,** b. May 1952. Education: Grad., Paul A. Blazer H.S., 1969. Married to Philip Justice. Contbr. to: Internat. Who's Who in Poetry Anthol.; New Anthol. of Mod. Poetry; Off-Center newspaper, Univ. of KY. Community Coll., Ashland, KY. Address: 1104 Fern Ave., Lexington, KY 40504, USA.

HAMBLETON, Ronald, b. 1917. Writer. Positions held: Ed., Reading Mag., 1946; Radio and TV Writer, current. Published works: Unit of Five (w. others), 1944; Object and Event, 1953; (novels) Every Man Is An Island, 1959; There Goes MacGill, 1962. Contbr. to: Canadian Forum; (anthologies) Book of Canadian Poetry, 1948; Canadian Poetry in English, 1954; Penguin Book of Canadian Verse, 1958; Oxford Book of Canadian Verse, 1960.

HAMBURGER, Anne Ellen, pen name **BERESFORD, Anne,** b. 10 Sept. 1929. Drama Teacher. Education: Privately, and Central School of Speech Training and Dramatic Art. Married, 3 children. Has worked in the theatre and for BBC Radio. Positions held: Drama Teacher, Wimbledon H.S., 1969-1973; Drama Teacher, Arts Educational School, 1973–; Leader of Poetry Group, Cockpit Arts Workshop and Theatre, 1971-1973. Memberships: Poetry Soc.; Poetry Secretariat. Published works: Walking Without Moving, 1967; The Lair, 1968; Footsteps on Snow, 1972; Modern Fairy Tale (broadsheet), 1972; The Courtship, 1967. Contbr. to: The Scotsman; The Observer; Delta; Outposts; Kayak; Akzente; Boston Univ. Journal; Agenda, etc. Address: 34a Half Moon Lane, Herne Hill, London SE24, UK.

HAMBURGER, Michael (Peter Leopold), b. 22 Mar.

1924. Writer. Educ: Christ Ch., Oxford Univ., U.K. Positions held incl: Vis. Prof., SUNY, Buffalo, U.S.A., 1969; Vis. Fellow, Ctr. for Humanities, Wesleyan Univ., Conn., 1970; Vis. Prof., SUNY, Stony Brook, 1971, Univ. of Conn., Storrs, 1972; Regents Lectr., Univ. of Calif., San Diego, 1973. Memberships: Fellow, Royal Soc. Lit., 1972; Corres. Mbr., Deutsche Akadamie für Sprache und Dichtung, Darmstadt, 1973; Acad. of Arts, Berlin. Published works incl: (poetry) Flowering Cactus, 1950; Poems 1950-1951, 1952; The Dual Site, 1958; Weather and Season, 1963; Feeding the Chickadees, 1968; Penguin Modern Poets, w. A. Brownjohn & C. Tomlinson, 1969; Travelling, 1969; Travelling I-V, 1973; Ownerless Earth, 1973; Conversations with Charwomen, 1973; (translations) Poems of Hölderlin 1943, rev. eds., 1952, 1966; Modern German Poetry 1910-1960, w. C. Middleton, 1962; N. Sachs, Selected Poems, 1968; Paul Celan: Selected Poems, 1972. Contbr. to num. reviews & jrnls. inclng. Stand & Poetry. Honours, awards incl: Arts Coun. of Gt. Britain Translation Prize, 1969; Levinson Prize, Chgo., 1972. Address: 34A Half Moon Lane, London SE24 9HU, U.K.

HAMIDEI, Mehdi, b. 1914. Poet; University Professor. Education: Doctorate in Lit., Univ. of Tehran. Positions held: High Schl. Tchr.; Prof. in Lit., Coll., Univ. of Tehran; Chief of Saadi Literary Soc. in Tehran. Mehdi Hamidei is one of the famous poets of Iran who follows the classical style. Published works: 'Daryai-Gohar' selection of best persian poems; lyrics, in different editions; Research on poems of ancient poets and Arabic & Persian prose. Address: c/o Press Attache, Imperial Iranian Embassy, 16 Princes Gate, London S.W.7, U.K.

HAMILTON, Alfred Starr, b. 14 June 1914. Poet. Published works: The Poems of Alfred Starr Hamilton. Contbr. to: Epoch; Foxfire; The Archive; New American & Canadian Poetry; New Letters; Marks Pond; The Trojan Horse. Address: 41 S. Willow St., Montclair, NJ, U.S.A.

HAMILTON, Charles Granville, b. 18 July 1905. Clergyman; Teacher; Writer; Civic Leader. Education: A.B., Berea; M.A., Univ. of Miss.; B.D. & M.D. Columbia; Ph.D., Vanderbilt. Married Mary Elizabeth Casey Hamilton. Positions held: Rector, Mid South Field, 1928–; Quiet Hour Radio, 1942–; Democratic National Conventions, 1940-72; Floor Ldr., Miss. House of Representatives; Ed., Churchman, 1958–, & Crossroads, Jrnl. of Miss. Hist., Anglican Outlook; Chaplain Gen, Sons of Confederate Vetera. Published works: Our Brother Augustus, 1936; South, 1937; Mississippi I Love You, 1942; 48 in '48, 1955; Mississippi I Love You Still, 1974. Contbr. to: Aberdeen Examiner; Amory Advertiser; Ark. Gazette; Berea Alumnus; Birmingham News; Booneville Banner-Independent; Christian; Christian Century; Christian Observer; Jackson Clarion Ledger; Memphis Commercial Appeal; Memphis Press Scimitar; Sewanee Review, etc. & rep. in 41 anthols. Address: Meridian, Monroe & Maple, Aberdeen, MS 39730, U.S.A.

HAMILTON, Franklin W., b. 22 Nov. 1923. Teacher; Editor. Education: B.A. & M.A., Southern Ill. Univ.; M.S., Kan. State Univ., Emporia; Ed. D., Univ. of Kan. Married, 1 son, 1 daughter. Positions held: at Hiwassee Coll., Tenn.; Coll. of Emporia, Kan.; Ill. State Univ.; Univ. of Kan.; Mott Community Coll., Mich. Memberships: Nat. Coun. Tchr. Engl.; Thoreau Soc.; Mich. Coll. Engl. Tchrs. Assn.; Nat Wildlife Assn.; Soc. Am. Scholars. Published works: Leaf Scar (poetry), 1965; Thoreau On The Art Of Writing (Critical), 1967; Love Cry (poetry), 1970; Catch Me Only With Love (fiction-novel), 1973. Contbr. to: Scarb; Am. Bard; Poetry & Drama Mag.; Epos; Odyssey; Quicksilver; Prairie Poet; We Offer; Bitterroot; Manhattan Review; Envoi; Ore; Trace; Mich. State Quarterly; Pendulum; Ann Arbor Review; Intermission; Poetry Review & many others. Address: 423 South Franklin Ave., Flint, MI 48503, U.S.A.

HAMILTON, Ian, b. 24 Mar. 1938. Literary Journalist. Education: Keble Coll., Oxford Univ., UK. Positions held: Ed., The Review, 1962–; Asst. Ed., Times Lit. Supp., 1965–; Lectr., Poetry, Univ. of Hull, 1971-72. Publications: Pretending Not to Sleep, 1964; The Visit, 1970. Contbr. to: London Mag.; Paris Rev.; Agenda; New Statesman; Listener; Times Lit. Supp.; The Observer. Honours: E.C. Gregory Award, 1963. Address: Flat 6, 72 Westbourne Terrace, London, W2, UK.

HAMILTON, Leona, b. 3 Jan. 1915. Secretary. Married Dr. Homer Hamilton, 1. daughter. Memberships: Poetry Soc. of America; formerly member of Tyler Creative Writers' Club and served as Vice-Pres., 1957, and as Pres., 1958. Published works: Duel Before Dawn, 1960 (Duelo Antes del Amanecer, a selection from orig. book, in Spanish translation, 1960). Contbr. to: Chicago Lit. Times; Dallas News; Mainland Times; Valley Morning Star; Texas Parent-Teacher; Good Housekeeping Mag.; Catholic Home Journal; Baptist Home Life; Daily Meditation; (Anthologies:) Spring Anthol.; Diamond Anthol.; Young's Anthol.; New Orlando Anthol.; American Poetry League Anthol.; Avalon Anthol.; Trace Anthol.; Yearbook of Modern Poetry; Internat. Who's Who in Poetry Anthol., 1973; (poetry mags.): Manifold; Cardinal; South & West; Bitterroot; Poet (India); Imprints Qtly.; Flame; Voices Internat.; Epos; Trace; Seydell Qtly.; Green World; Fiddlehead; Poetry Digest; Lit. Calendar; Lynx; American Bard, etc. Recip. numerous awards for poetry (Avalon; Poet's Club of Chicago; Am. Poetry League; Odessa Coll. Writers' Roundup; Nat. League of Am. Pen Women, etc.). Address: 1784 Stanford, Brownsville, TX 78520, USA.

HAMILTON, M. Virginia, pen name **ADAIR, V.H.,** b. 28 Feb. 1913. University Professor. Education: B.A., Mount Holyoke Coll.; M.A., Radcliffe; T.A., Univ. of Wis., 1935-37; further grad. work, Univ. of Wash., Harvard, Claremont Grad. Schl. Married Douglass Adair, 2 sons, 1 daughter. Positions held: Instr. in Engl., Miss Fine's Schl., Coll. of Wm. & Mary, Pomona Coll., La. Verne Coll.; Asst., Assoc. & Full Prof., Calif. State Polytechnic Univ., 1957–. Member, Poetry Soc. of Am. Contbr. to: Christian Sci. Monitor; Atlantic; New Republic; Saturday Review; Poetry; Poetry Northwest; Poet Lore; N.Y. Qtly.; Mass. Review; Colo. Qtly.; Mich. Qtly.; Epos; Lyric; Wormwood; Snowy Egret; Janus-SCTH, etc. Honours, awards: 1st Prize, Katharine Irene Glascock, 1932 & '33; Special Category Prize, Poet Lore, 1972. Address: 489 West 6th, Claremont, CA 91711, U.S.A.

HAMMARBERG-AKESSON, Jarl, b. 22 Nov. 1940. Writer; Poet. Married Sonja Akesson, 1966. Published works: Bord, duka er, 1964; JA JA JA JA JA JA, 1966; järnvägar järnpiller järnplatar, 1968; Brev fran Jarl, 1970; Poemoj sen vortoj, 1971; (with Sonja Akesson) – Stralande dikter/nej sa fan heller, 1967; Kändis, 1969; Ha, vi är pa väg, 1972. Address: Ringarstigen 3, 161 52 Bromma, Sweden.

HAMMER, Lillian. Poet in 2 languages. Memberships: Charter Mbr., Lucia Trent Chapt., NPDC, Inc., 1969-70; Life Time Mbr., Int. Clover Poetry Assn.; Soc. of Literary Designates (Danae). Contbr. to the following anothols. & Jrnls: The Spring Anthol., 1968-69; American Poets, 1968; The New Poetry, 1967; Poets of America, Anthol., 1964-66; Prairie Press Books Anthol., 1969; Polished Pebbles, 1969; Pancontinental Premier Poets, 1971-72; Poet Int. Monthly, 1973; Selected Poems, 1972-73; Sweet Seventies Anthology, 1972; Int. Hall of Fame Books; Phoenix Fire, 1973; Outstanding Contemporary Poetry, 1972; Rufus; Yearbook of Mod. Poetry, 1971; Lyrics of Love, 1972; For All Your Wit, 1973; The Birth of Day, 1972; Flamingo; Writer's Voice; Robin; Major Poets; Mustang Review; Poetry Prevue; The Preserver; Sparkling Gems; Creative Review. Author, Waves of Fire. Honours: Merit in Poetry, Observance of Nat. Poetry Day; 1968; Hon. Mention Award for Original Work, Int. Poetry Comp., sponsored by Clover Collection of Verse, Wash. DC, 1969; Cert. of Recognition, Hon. Mention, Etta Josephine Mem. Award Contest, 1970. Address: 2820 Bronx Park E., Bronx, NY 10467, USA.

HAMMER, Louis Zelig, b. 27 Sept. 1931. University Teacher & Poet. Education: Norwich Free Acad.; B.A., Yale Univ., 1953; M.A., 1955; Ph.D., 1960. Positions held: Asst. Prof., Philos., Univ. of Southern Calif., 1960-64; Vis. Lectr., Hebrew Univ. of Jerusalem, Israel, 1964-65; Lectr., Wellesley Coll., 1965-66; Vis. Asst. Prof., Brandeis Univ., 1966-67; Assoc. Prof. of Philos., Rensselaer Polytechnic Inst., 1967–. Published works: Bone Planet, 1967. Contbr. to: San Francisco Review; The Sixties; Kayak; Epoch; Prairie Schooner; Tampa Poetry Review; South Fla. Poetry Jrnl.; Field. Address: Dept. of Philos., Rensselaer Polytechnic Inst., Troy, NY 12181, U.S.A.

HAMMOCK, Elizabeth Catherine, b. 13 Mar. 1927. Homemaker; Secretary; Entertainer. Education: Strayer's Bus. Coll. Married Earl G. Hammock, 1 son, 1 daughter. Positions held: Long Distance Operator, C. & P. Telephone Co. of Md.; Sec., Julian P. Friez Co.; currently Sec. for husband, Earl G. Hammock, Remodeling Co. Memberships incl: Comm. of One Hundred, Vincent G. Burns; Bd. Dirs., The Rainbow (Md's Poetry Mag.); Bd. Dirs., Annapolis Chapt., C.A.A.A.; Bd. Dirs., Md. Cultural Arts; Chairlady, Randallstown Div., Int. Culture & Poetry Soc., etc. Published works: Take My Feeble Self, 1972; My One Wish, 1973; Veterans of Old Fort Howard in News American, 1972. Contbr. to: The News American; The Community Times; The Jeffersonian; The Ridge Rider; The Rainbow; The Holy Family Bulletin, etc. Book reviewed in the Catholic Review. TV, WJZ, Channel 13, Arnold Zenker Show. Recip. var. hons. inclng: Poet of the Year, 1972 & 73; 1st prize, Madeline Mason Contest, 1972; Elizabeth Browning Award. Address: 3842 Terka Circle, Randallstown, MD 21133, U.S.A.

HAMMOND, Mac, b. 8 Feb. 1926. Professor of English. Education: B.A., Univ of the South, 1948; M.A., Harvard Univ., 1951; Ph.D., 1962. Positions held: Instr., Engl., Univ. of Va., 1956-58; Asst. Prof., Engl., Western Reserve Univ., 1960-63; Prof., Engl., SUNY, Buffalo, 1963–. Published works: The Horse Opera & Other Poems, 1966; Cold Turkey, 1969. Contbr. to: Partisan Review; Hudson Review; Sewanee Review; London Observer; Choice; Poetry (Chicago). Sewanee Review Fellow in Poetry, 1955-56. Address: 314 Highland Ave., Buffalo, New York, 14222 USA.

HANDLER, Frances Clark, pen name **CLARK, Frances Jamia,** b. 28 Feb. 1906, NH, USA. Teacher; Educator; Accountant; Author. Education: A.D., M.A., B.S., B.B.S., Litt.D.; Boston Univ.; Harvard; Courses in Real Estate & Property Management, TV, Creative Arts, etc. Married, Frank Stevenson Handler, Cdr., USN (retd). Positions held: Accountant with BBH and Co. (England – Brown Shipley); Accountant with Internal Revenue Service; Accountant with Republican Committee; President, Hotel Accountants Assoc.; presently – Secretary-Treasurer, Florida State Poetry Soc., Inc. (also Founder); Nat. Oirector, Nat. Poetry Day Comm. Inc.; Mbr.; Edit. & Advsry. Bd., Int. Who's Who in Poetry, UK.; Asst. to cabinet level off., Youth Affairs Dept., Wash. DC. Memberships include: Int. Platform Assoc.; Nat. League of Am. Penwomen; Fla. Arts Coun.; Membership Chmn., United Poets Laureate Int.; Charter Mbr., Smithsonian Inst.; Charter Mbr., Mus. of Natural Hist.; Life Mbr., Iowa & Nev. Poetry Socs.; NH, NJ, Va., Pa., W.Va., Tex., SD. Poetry Socs.; Charter Mbr. Audubon National Soc.; Charter Mbr. Museum of Science, Inc. (Fla.); Charter Mbr. National Travel Club; Member, Nat. Republican Club (Finance Committee); Charter Mbr. Third Century, USA (Bicentennial Celebration Com.). Published works: 3 hist. novels; Text Book on Poetry, 1970; Mem. Award Books (ed. and designer), annually since 1965; Governors Book, 1971; 200th Anniversary (Bicentennial) Commemorative Book; Selected Poems, annually since 1967; Book of Limericks; Int. Hall of Fame Poets Books, 1969-71; Ed. & Publr., Flamingo Mag., 1969-70; 9 Muses I and 9 Muses II,

1971; The Devastators; Nobel Goes to Heaven; Beyond the Silent River; Nurses Notes; Turns on the Spiral. Contrib. to more than 50 US newspapers and 25 mags. Honours, Awards: Over 100 awards and prizes including: Edwin Markham Award 1968; King Journalism Award 1972; Hon. Lt. Col. Aide-de-Camp, Ala. State Militia, 1973; Hon. Citizen, Montgomery, Ala., 1973. Address: 1110 N. Venetian Dr., Miami Beach, Fla. 33139, USA.

HANDLEY-TAYLOR, Geoffrey, b. 25 Apr. 1920. Bibliographer; Author. Positions held: Chmn., British Poetry-Drama Guild, 1948-1952; Publr., Leeds Univ. Poetry, 1949; Chmn., Gen. Coun., The Poetry Soc., UK, 1967-1968; Pres., Lancashire Authors' Assoc., 1969-1972. Published works: Ed., New Hyperion, 1950; Ed. Int. Who's Who in Poetry, 1959; Compiler, John Masefield, OM., The Queen's Poet Laureate, 1960; Co-Compiler, (w. Timothy d'Arch Smith) C. Day-Lewis, The Poet Laureate (a bibliography), 1969. Contbr. to many journals, newspapers, etc. incl. The Gryphon (Leeds Univ.); Lancashire Life; Ency. Britannica, etc. Honours, awards, etc.: numerous, incl. Fellow, Royal Soc. of Lit. Address: c/o National Liberal Club, Whitehall Place, London SW1, UK.

HANH, Nhat. Buddhist Monk; Writer of Poetry in Vietnamese and English. Published Works: Viet Nam Poems, 1967; Cry of Vietnam, 1968.

HAN JEN TSUN, pen name **LOMEN,** b. 20 Nov. 1928. Senior Technician & Fellow of Aviation. Education: Chinese Air Force Flying Schl.; FAA Training Ctr., USA. Married to Wang Jung-Chih, Poetess. Positions held: Profl. Footballer; Farm Mgr.; Libn.; Aircraft Accident Investigator; Ed., Lit. Mag.; Sr. Techn. & Former Fellow of Aviation Dev., CCAA. Memberships: Chief Ed., Blue Star Poetry; Supvsry. Bd., New Chinese Poetry; Bd. Dirs., Chinese Young Writers' Assn.; Poetry Judge, Chinese Mod. Poets, 1971; Hon. Mbr., United Poets Laureate Int. Published works: (poetry) Aurora, 1958; Undercurrent of Ninth Day, 1963; The Tower of Death, 1969; The Invisible Chair, 1971; (essays) The Tragic Mind of Modern Man & Modern Poet, 1964; Dilemma of the Modern Writer's Mind, 1968; Interview of a Poetic Mind, 1969; The Men Forever on Trial, 1971. Contbr. to: Anthol. of New Chinese Poetry, 1960; Poésie Chinoise, 1963; Anthol. of Mod. Chinese Poetry, 1970; Anthol. of Splendid Island, 1971; Anthol. of World Lit. Famous Works, 1972. Honours: Blue Star Prize, 1958; Prize, Assn. of Chinese Poets, 1958; Karta Award, UPLI, & Gold Medal from Pres. Marcos of Philippines, w. wife, as Distinguished Lit. Couple of China, 1966; Received Gold Medal, UPLI, for poem 'McKinley Fort', 1967; nominated w. wife, Disting. Lit. Couple of 1st World Congress of Poets, Philippines, 1969; Masters degree, 1972; Ph.D., 1973. Address: No. 6, Lane 388, Antung St., Taipei, Taiwan, Republic of China.

HANLEY, Evelyn Alice, pen name **HANLEY, Evelyn A.** College (Univ.) Teacher. Education: A.B., Brooklyn Coll.; A.M., Ph.D., NY Univ. Positions held: Instr. in Engl., Adelphi Coll., 1946-49; Lecturer, then Instr. in Engl., Hunter Coll. of C.U.N.Y., 1949-67, Asst. Prof., 1967-72; Assoc. Prof., since 1972. Memberships: Mod. Lang. Assoc. of America (Officer, Victorian Group); Poetry Soc. of America; Dickens Fellowship of NY; Dickens Fellowship of Philadelphia (Hon. Member). Published works: Six Sonnets, 1962; Poetic Profiles, 1962; Antiphony (book of Sonnets on Poets), 1963. Contbr. to: (anthols) Contemporary American Lyricists; World's Fair Anthol. of Verse; (mags.) The Raphaelite; The Windowan; The Univ. Review; La Lucerna; Italian Times Mag.; Ink Spot; The Buzfuz Bulletin (Dickens Journal); (poetry journals) The Poet's Scroll; Port o' Poets; Blue Moon; (newspapers) Paterson Morning Call; Long Island Press; The Envoy; Nightwatch; Hunter Coll. Eve. Newsletter; NY Daily News (2 poems to Pres. of the US., pub. 1969, 1973), etc. Awards: Parker Lloyd-Smith Prize in Poetry, 1954; Charles Dickens Commem. Medal (bronze), for work, including poem, on Dickens in his centennial year (1970), 1971; Cert. of Merit, DIB (London), 1973.

Address: 82-64 170 St., Jamaica, NY 11432. USA.

HANLIN, Katherine Hale, b. 7 Oct. 1907. Writer. Education: Howard Coll. (now Samford Univ.), Birmingham, Alabama. Married to William Arthur Hanlin, 1931 (dec. 1973); 1 d. Positions held: Newspaper Columnist, 6 yrs.; V.P. & Sec., Birmingham Gas Appliance Co., 1931-71. Memberships: Alabama State Poetry Soc. (Charter Mbr., past Gen. Sec., and past 1st Vice-Pres.); Birmingham Br., Nat. League Am. Pen Women; Birmingham Chapter of Nat. Arts & Letters; Alabama Writer's Conclave; The Quill Club of Birmingham (Pres.); Past Pres. (having held all other officer's positions) of The Woman's Club; Past Pres. and Organizer of Volunteer Progs. at both Baptist Medical Centers in Birmingham; Antique & Allied Arts Club; Ala. Bapt. Historical Soc.; Southern Baptist Historical Soc. Published works: 5 Historical brochures; Alabama Fed. of Women's Clubs Creative Writings of 1971 and of 1972; The Steeple Beckons, sesquicentennial hist. of First Baptist Church of Trussville, Ala., 1821-1971, 1973; Promise of the Bud (poetry), 1974. Contbr. to: The Congressional Record; The Eastern Sun; Ideals Mag.; 6 Ala. State Poetry Soc. anthols., etc. Awards or Honours from Alabama Fed. Women's Clubs; Quill Club of Birmingham; Ala. Writer's Conclave. Address: Route 5, Box 536, Hanlin Dr., Birmingham, AL 35235, USA.

HANNA, Thomas Philip, b. 19 Dec. 1940. Editor; Writer. Education: Tchng. Fellowship, State Univ. of N.Y. at Buffalo, 1964-65; B.A., Cornell Univ., 1964. Married Katharine Etha Sieverts, 1 son, 1 daughter. Positions held: Asst. Dir., Public Information, SUNY, Buffalo, 1965-66; Freelance Writer, Chipiona, Spain, 1966-69; Asst. Ed., Cornell Univ. Ithaca, N.Y., 1969-70; currently Ed., Human Ecology Forum, Cornell Univ.; Dir., Moveable Type Media Poetry, with support of N.Y. State Coun. on the Arts, 1970–. Published works: (anthol.) Quickly Aging Here, 1970; (videotape) Moveable Type, 1971; After The Flood, 1972; Agnes Flood Litany, 1974. Contbr. to: Epoch; New: Am. & Canadian Poetry; Kumquat; West Coast Review; Tenn. Poetry Jrnl.; Trojan Horse; Image. Honours, awards: Burns Poetry Prize, 1959; Morrison Poetry Prize, 1963. Address: 210 Eddy, Ithaca, NY 14850, U.S.A.

HANSBROUGH, Vivian Pearl, b. 27 June 1908. Freelance Writer. Education: B.A., Union Univ., Jackson, Tennessee, 1929; M.A., Univ. of Chicago, Illinois, 1933; Grad. study, Univ. of Missouri, Columbia, 1953-54. Married to Lewis D. Hansbrough; 2 children (David Lee and Nina Carol). Positions held: Teacher, Arkansas High Schools, 1928-53; Instr. in Journalism, Stephens Coll., Columbia, 1954-57; Home Editor, Missouri Farmer Mag., 1957-63; Librarian, Jefferson Jr. HS, Columbia, 1961-73. Memberships: Nat. League of American Pen Women; Missouri Writers' Guild. Published work: History of Greene County, Arkansas, 1946. Contbr. to: CS Monitor; Farm Journal; Christian Home; Roadrunner; Fun for Middlers; Whenever Whatever; Nursery Days; The Christian; Vital Christianity. Recip. of Awards from Missouri Writers' Guild, 1968, 1972. Address: 1840 Cliff Dr., Columbia, MO 65201, USA.

HANSON, Elayne June, pen name **HANSON, Elayne Clipper,** b. 4 June 1929. Accredited Record Technician. Education: Grad. Med. Sec., 1948; Accredited Record Techn. (A.R.T.), Am. Med. Record Assn., Chicago, Ill., 1972. Married Artis C. Hanson, 2 children. Positions held: Med. Sec. Dept. Hd., Midelfart Clinic, Eau Claire, Wis., 1948-50; Legal Sec., Bogue & Sanderson, Attys., Portage, 1950-54; Financial & Parish Sec., Bethlehem Lutheran Ch., Portage, 1955-65; Dir. of Med. Records, Divine Savior Hosp. & Nursing Home, Inc., Portage, 1965–. Memberships: Pres., Portage Writers' Workshop; Wis. Regl. Writers Assn.; Wis. Fellowship of Poets; Wis. Coun. for Writers. Published works: (book of poetry) So This Is Me, 1970. Contbr. to: New Poetry Out of Wis. (anthol.), 1969; Upstream-Downstream, Writers at the Portage (anthol.), 1972; Am. Jrnl. of Nursing;

Lutheran Digest; Grit; Portage Daily Register; Writers Showcase; Piggott Banner; Pleasant Views. Recip., Golden Crow Award, Portage Writers' Workshop Annual Contest, 1970. Address: 912 Cass St., Portage, WI 53901, U.S.A.

HANSON, Kenneth O., b. 24 Feb. 1922. College Professor. Education: B.A., Univ. of Idaho, Pocatello & Moscow, 1942; Grad., Chinese lang. & Engl. lit., 1946-54. Professor of Lit., Reed Coll., Portland, Ore., 1954–. Published works: 8 Poems (folio), 1958; The Distance Anywhere, 1966; Saronikos & Other Poems, 1970. Contbr. to: Accent; Botteghe Oscure; The New Yorker; The Nation; Poetry Northwest; Northwest Review; Transatlantic Review; Iowa Review; Sewanee Review; Kayak; Massachusetts Review; Accent Anthology, 1954; Oregon Signatures, 1960; Five Poets of the Pacific Northwest, 1964; Contemporary American Poets, 1969. Honours & Awards: Fulbright Fellowship, 1962; Bollingen Translation Grant, 1962; Rockefeller Grant, 1966-67; Lamont Award, Acad. of Am. Poets, 1966; Theodore Roethke Award, Poetry Northwest, 1964-65; Helen Bullis Award, 1970; Asia Soc. trans. commn., 1970. Address: Dept. of English, Reed Coll., Portland, Ore. 97202, USA.

HANSON, Pauline. Secretary; Assistant. Education: Boston Univ., 1 yr. Positions held: Res. Sec., Yaddo, 1950–; more recently, Asst. to the Executive Dir. at Yaddo. Published works: The Forever Young, 1948; The Forever Young & Other Poems, 1957; Across Countries of Anywhere, 1971. Contbr. to: Botteghe Oscure; Am. Poems & Drawings; Poetry Mag. Honours, awards: Award, Poetry Mag., 1965; Grant, Nat. Endowment for the Arts, 1972; Award, Nat. Inst. & Am. Acad. of Arts & Letters, 1972. Address: Yaddo, Saratoga Springs, NY 12866, U.S.A.

HARDER, Uffe, b. 29 Sept. 1930. Writer; Editor; Translator. Education: Grad. (French, English), Univ. of Copenhagen, 1957. Married to Maria Giacobbe, Italian writer. Positions held: Editor, Lit. Dept., Danmarks Radio; Editor, Louisiana Rev., pub. by the Louisiana Museum. Membership: Danish Acad., since 1973. Published works: Spraengte diger (poems), 1954; Udsigter (poems), 1960; Positioner (poems), 1964; Sort pa hvidt (poems), 1968; I disse dage (poems), 1971. Contbr. to various anthols. of poetry; also to newspapers, journals: Hvedekorn, Vindrosen (Denmark); Liberté (Canada); Plus (Belgium); Europa Letteraria (Italy); De Gids, Maatstaf (Holland); Komma (Sweden); Steps (Israel), etc. Awards: Louisiana-Prisen, 1961; The State Art-Foundations Stipendium (Denmark), 1967; Hon. Prize, Danish Translators Assoc., 1968. Address: Louisiana Museum, 3050 Humlebaek, Denmark.

HARDIN, Mary Frances, pen name **WILLIAMS, Kyle H.,** b. 21 Nov. 1926. Teacher. Education: B.A., Univ. of Texas at Austin M.A., Catholic Univ. of America; M.A., Univ. of Texas. Positions held: Tchr., Engl., Latin, Creative Writing, Jefferson HS, Edison HS, San Antonio Independent Schl. Dist., San Antonio, Texas; Tchr. Engl., San Antonio Coll.; currently, Tchr., (Engl., Latin) Brownsville HS, Texas. Memberships: Poetry Soc. of America; American Acad. of Poets; Poetry Soc. of Texas. Contrib. to: Scimitar & Song; Cardinal Poetry Qtly.; Comment; Eucharist; The Archer; U.S. Catholic, etc. Honours: Sonnets, SW Writers' Conf., 1950; Variance, Texas Poetry Soc., 1969. Address: 1814 W. Monroe, Brownsville, Texas 78520, USA.

HARDING, Donald E., pen names **PARRISH, Eugene; DAY, Donald; EDWARDS, Dan; EDWARDS, Donald Earl,** b. 7 Feb. 1916. Clerk. Education: Marion Bus. Coll., 1934-36; Kenyon Coll., Gambier, Ohio, 1956-60. Positions held: US Army, 1940-45; Book Store Owner, 1950-68. Memberships: American Amateur Press Assoc.; United Amateur Press. Published works: Who Walks With Dreams, 1947; A Sign to Solace, 1948; Cycles of the Season, 1949; Straw Hat, 1971; Applebough, 1972; The Shepherd Boy, 1973; Little Acorns, 1973; Pandora's Box, 1973; Little Twigs, 1973; Footprints of the Future, vol. 1. 1972, vol. 2.

1973. Contbr. to: NY Times; Time Mag.; NY Herald-Tribune; Different; Kaleidograph; Jean's Journal; Haiku Highlights; Janus-Scth; Encore; American Weave; Hartford Courant; Norfolk-Ledger Dispatch; Ohio State Journal; Columbus Citizen Journal; Yank of the Pacific; Bardic Echoes; American Bard; Prairie Wing; Silk Screen; Tumblin' Weed; La Grange Journal; North Carolina Folklore; Recip. of many book awards. Address: Ye Olde Western Inn, 19 N. State St., Elgin, IL 60120, USA.

HARDING, Gunnar, b. 11 June 1940. Poet; Editor; Poetry Critic; Translator. Education: Art Schl.; B.A. in Lit., Stockholm Univ., Sweden. Positions held: Chief Ed., FIBs Lyrikklubb, publishing house for poetry; Ed., Lyrikvannen, poetry mag., 1970–. Member, Swedish PEN Club. Published works: Lokomotivet som Frös Fast, 1967; Den svenske cyklistens sang, 1968; Blommor till James Dean, 1969; Ornen har landat, 1970; Apollinaires fantastiska liv, 1971; Skallgang, 1972; (books in English) Fabulous Life of Guillaume Apollinaire, 1970; They Killed Sitting Bull, 1973. Contbr. to: Evergreen Review; MPT; London Mag.; Ambit; var. Swedish lit. mags., etc. Address: Lidnersplan 16, 11253 Stockholm, Sweden.

HARDY, Dorothy, b. 12 May 1909. Freelance Writer. Married. Memberships: Lancs. Authors Assn.; Committee Mbr., Burnley & District Writers Circle; Mid Pennine Assn. for the Arts. Contbr. to: Anthol. of Yorkshire & Lancashire Verse & Prose, 1973; Writers' Review; Country Life; The Countryman; Lancashire Life; Country Quest; The Lady; Yorkshire Achievement; Woman's Weekly; The Christian; The Record; Gallery; Burnley Star; BBC Radio Blackburn. Honours, awards incl: 3rd pl., Batty Cup, Lancs. Authors' Assn., 1968 & 2nd pl., 1969; Maisie & Kenneth Eves Cup, Burnley Fest., 1967, '70, '71 (2 silver medals, 1970, '71); Josephine Hilton Cup (Writer of the Year), Burnley & District Writers' Circle, 1970, '72; Jean Stubbs Poetry Rose Bowl, ibid, 1973. Address: 4 Sawley Ave., Accrington, Lancs. BB5 6HE, U.K.

HARESNAPE, Geoffrey Laurence, b. 13 Jan. 1939. University Lecturer in English Literature. Education: B.A. & M.A., Univ. of Cape Town, S. Africa; postgrad. rsch. at Oxford Univ. Married Rosamund Lesley Deeble, 4 children. Positions held: Jr. Lectr., Rhodes Univ., Grahamstown, 1961; Lectr., Univ. of the Witwatersrand, Johannesburg, 1963-68; Sr. Lectr., Univ. of Cape Town, 1969–. Memberships: Exec. Comm. Mbr., PEN Ctr., Johannesburg, 1967-68; currently Comm. Mbr., PEN Ctr., Cape Town. Rep. in the following anthols: New South African Writing, 1965, 66, 67 & 68; Writing in South Africa To-day, 1967; The Penguin Book of South African Verse, 1968; Seismograph, 1970. Contbr. to: Contrast, Cape Town; New Coin, Grahamstown; The Purple Renoster, Jo'burg; New Nation, Pretoria; English Studies in Africa, Jo'burg; Izwi, Jo'burg; Workshop, London; The Cape Times. Poems broadcast by the S. African Broadcasting Corp. Recip., Prize, Engl. Assns. Poetry Comp., Cape Town Br., 1965. Address: Engl. Dept., Univ. of Cape Town, Groote Schuur, Rondebosch, Cape Province, S. Africa.

HAREVEN, Shulamith, b. 14 Feb. 1931. Writer, Columnist, Essayist, Translator. Education: Hebrew Univ., Jerusalem; Academy of Music. Married, with 2 children. Pubs. Yerushalaim Dorsanit, 1962; In the last Month, 1966; Separate Places, 1969; Reshut Netuna, 1970; A City of Many Days, 1972; Transl. classical & modern poetry, theatre et al, from English, French, Polish. Contrib. to: Keshet; Shdemot; Moznaim; Ha'aretz; Al Hamishmar; Davar; Ma'ariv; Ash-Sharq; Jerusalem Annual of Literature; Kol Israel Broadcasting Service; Galey Tzahal Br. Service; various anthologies, of Writers Ass., et al. Addresses: Publishers: Sifriat Poalim, Tel-Aviv, or Am Oved, Tel-Aviv, Israel.

HARKEY, Vada George, pen name **THE LASS,** b. 4 May 1910. Housewife. Married Charles R. Harkey, 2 daughters. Positions held: Bookkeeper; Store Clerk. Member, Poet's Roundtable of Ark., Little Rock. Contbr. to: Poet's Roundtable of Ark. Anthols., 1972-73; Perry Co. News; England Democrat, Ark.; Progressive Farmer, Memphis, Tenn.; Southwest Times Record, Ft. Smith, Ark.; Saline Co. Pacesetter, Benton, Ark. Honours, awards: 2nd pl. winner in short story contest, Grand Prairie Art Fest., Stuttgart, Ark., 1972; 2nd pl. winner in patterned poetry contest, Saline Co. Pacesetter Poets Forum, Benton, Ark., 1973. Address: Rte. 2, Box 19, England, AR 72046, U.S.A.

HARLAND, Frances Sabina, b. 13 Apr. 1920. Teacher of English. Education: Manchester Coll. of Domestic Economy. Married, 2 sons. Accredited Methodist Local Preacher, 1946. Memberships: Poetry Soc.; Lancs. Authors; Cumbrian Lit. Guild; Lancs. & Morecambe Poetry Circle. Published works: A Shell in my Hand, 1956. Contbr. to: Envoi; The Brompton Poets; Laudatum Te; Univ. of Lancaster Regional Bulletin; Slide into Poetry; Twixt Thee & Me. Recip., Premium Greenwood Prize, Poetry Review, 1953. Address: 333 Heysham Rd., Morecambe & Heysham, Lancs. LA3 2BP, U.K.

HARMON, William Ruth, b. 10 June 1938. Educator. Education: A.B., Univ. of Chicago, 1958; A.M., ibid, 1968; M.A., Univ. of N.C., 1968; Ph.D., Univ. of Cinn., 1970. Married Lynn Frances Chadwell, 1 son, 1 daughter. Positions held: w. U.S. Navy, 1960-67; Student, 1967-70; Instr., Univ. of N.C., Chapel Hill, 1970-71; Asst. Prof., ibid, 1971-72; Assoc. Prof., 1973-; Chmn. of Dept. of Engl., 1972-. Memberships: Acad. of Am. Poets; MLA; Poets Club, Chapel Hill, N.C.; A.H.S.C.Z. Published works: Treasury Holiday, 1970; Legion: Civic Choruses, 1973. Contbr. to: Carolina Qtly.; Antioch Review; Kayak; Hiram Poetry Jrnl.; San Francisco Review; Coastlines; Nimrod; Southern Poetry Review; St. Andrews Review. Honours, awards: Millard P. Binyon Award, 1958; John Billings Fiske Prize, 1958; Lamont Award, 1970. Address: Dept. of Engl., Univ. of N.C., Chapel Hill, NC 27514, U.S.A.

HARP, Sharon Kim, b. 18 Aug. 1949. Staff Psychologist. Education: B.A., Tex. Tech. Univ., 1970; M.A. in Clinical Psychol., ibid, 1973. Positions held: Staff Psychol., Big Spring State Hosp., Tex., 1973-. Memberships: past mbr., Poetry Club, Tex. Tech. Univ. & Tex. Poetry Soc. Contbr. to: Songs of Youth, 1967; Love Poems, 1967; Young America Sings, 1966. Address: 906 Birdwell Lane, Big Spring, TX 79720, U.S.A.

HARPER, Michael S(teven), b. 18 Mar. 1938. Professor, Poet. Education: B.A., M.A., Engl., Calif. State Univ., Los Angeles; M.A., Engl., Univ. of Iowa (Writers Workshop); postdoctoral fellow, Univ. of Ill. Married, 3 children. Positions held: taught at Contra Costa Coll., Reed C., Lewis and Clark C., Calif. State Univ. at Hayward, Univ. of Ill., Brown Univ. Published works: Dear John, Dear Coltrane, 1970; History Is Your Own Heartbeat, 1971; Song: I Want a Witness, 1972; History As Apple Tree, 1972; Debridement, 1973. Contbr. to: Mass. Review; Field; New Letters; Black World; Works in Progress; Poetry; Poetry Northwest; Southern Review; Carolina Qtly.; NY Times; SF Chronicle; LA Times; Kansas City Star; Chicago Sun-Times; Washington Post; Kayak; Essence; Works; Concerning Poetry; Blacks on Brown; Mundus Artium; Black Scholar; Burning Deck; Qtly. Review of Literature, etc. Awards: American Acad./Nat. Inst. of Arts & Letters, creative writing, Literature, 1972; Black Acad. of Arts & Letters, 1972, best book of poetry award. Address: Engl. Dept., Brown Univ., Providence, RI 02912, USA.

HARPER, Robert E., b. 15 Oct. 1908. Division Director. Education: Tulane Univ., New Orleans; A.B., Univ. of Ala., Tuscaloosa, Ala. Married, 2 sons (1 dec.) Positions held: Dir., Motion Pictures & Spec. Events, War Savings Staff, 1942; Asst. to Pres., Motion Picture Adv. Serv., 1942-44; Dir., Programs & Campaigns, Off.

of Def. Transportation, 1944-45; Dir., Advt. & Publicity, Nat. Assn. of Ice Industries, 1945-49; Pres., Nat. Business Pub., 1949-62; Dir., Office of Public Affairs Savings Bonds Div., U.S. Treasury, 1963-. Member, La. State Poetry Soc. Contbr. to: Descant; Apalachee; Am. Bard; Ariz. Medicine; Essence; Harford Courant; Jean's Jrnl.; Wash. Sun; Orphic Lute; Cardinal; Poetry Venture; Poet's Nook; Janus-SCTH, etc. Honours, awards: Hon. Mention, Gemstone Awards; Spec. Book, Quintessence; 1st pl., short poems, Scimitar & Song; Spec. Leaf, Inky Trails. Address: 3003 Van Ness St., N.W., Apt. W632, Wash. D.C. 20008, U.S.A.

HARR, Lorrain Ellis, pen names, **ELLIS, Lorraine; MUNDI, Dolores,** b. 31 October. Writer. Education: College classes in English, Literature, Languages, etc. Married; 2 s. (1 living). Memberships: Western World Haiku Soc. (Founder, and 1st Pres.); Haiku Soc. of America; Oregon State Poetry Assoc.; Williamette Writers; Calif. Fed. of Chaparral Poets. Contbr. to: Westward; Versecraft; Oregon Journal; The Press; Oregonian Verse; Denver Post; The Blue Print; Poetry Dial; Poetry Pendulum; Beloit Journal; Human Voice Qtly.; Hoosier Challenger; Janus/SCTH; Ascent; Haiku Highlights; Haiku Mag.; Modern Haiku; Haiku West; Haiku '64 (JAL); Tweed; Lunatic Fringe; The Ranger; East/West Journal; Macrobiotic Monthly; The Archer; Green World; Swordsman Review; KAKI (Persimmons) trans. into Japanese by Prof. Yagi; Ed., Dragonfly: a Qtly. of Haiku Highlights; Windless Orchard; Shorelines; Orphic Lute; Sidney Lanier Mem. of Tree Poems; Awards: Japan Air Lines Haiku Contest, 1964, Nat. Finalist; Black Ship Festival, Japan, Award, 1967; Deep South Artists & Writers, 1969 (Haiku article), 2nd Pl.; Modern Haiku vol. II, No. 3, Hon Men.; Vol. II, No. 2, Spec. Men.; Vol. III, No. 1, Hon. Men.; Vol. IV, No. 1, Outstanding Achievement Award; Ascent (MHCC) 1972, 1st Pl. for article on Haiku poetry; Haiku Mag., Vol. III, No. V., New Year's Contest, 1969, 3rd Pl.; Haiku West, Vol. 3, No. 2, Spec. Men., etc. Address: 4102 N.E. 130th Place, Portland, OR 97230, USA.

HARRELL, Irene Burk, pen names **AMOR, Amos & WAYLAN, Mildred,** b. 10 Mar. 1927. Author; Editor; Librarian. Education: B.A., Ohio State Univ., 1948; B.S. in L.S., Univ. of N.C., 1949; grad., Famous Writers Schl. Married Judge Allen W. Harrell, 6 children. Positions held: Libn., Westerville (Ohio) Public Lib., 1949-52, & Libn., Sociol., Lib. of Univ. N.C., 1952-53; Dir., Halifax Co. Lib., 1953-54; var. positions, C.L. Hardy Lib. Atlantic Christian Coll., 1958-64; Hd. Libn., ibid; An. Ed., Copy Ed. & Assignment Writer for Logos Int., Plainfield, N.J., 1970-. Published works: Prayerables: Meditations of a Homemaker, 1967; Good Marriages Grow: A Book for Wives, 1969; Lo, I Am With You, 1970; Ordinary Days with an Extraordinary God, Prayerables II, 1971; The Opposite Sex (w. A. Harrell), 1972; Security Blankets – Family Size, 1973; Muddy Sneakers & Other Family Hassles, 1974; The Windows of Heaven: Prayerables III, 1974. Contbr. to var. jrnls. Address: 408 Pearson St., Wilson, NC 27893, U.S.A.

HARRIS, Dorothy Dix, pen name, **HARRIS, Dorothy D.,** b. 20 Mar. 1904. Writer. Education: Judson Coll., Marion, Ala.; Univ. of Chicago. Personal details: m. to Chiles Harries (d.), Shakespearian Scholar & Hd. of Engl. Dept., Sidney Lanier HS; 4 d. Positions held: Dir., Christian Educ., Episcopal Ch. of the Ascension, Montgomery, Ala., 1939-53; Dir., Thornfield Private Schl., 1954-68. Memberships: Book Club for Poetry, Golden Quill Press; Ala. Poetry Soc.; Ala. Authors' Conclave. Published works: Lift th Wine Cup High, 1969; Plateau Pauses, 1970; Born to Dance, 1971. Contbr. to Alabama Sunday Magazine, The Montgomery Advertiser Newspaper. Recip., 1st Prize, Short Story and Poem, Ala. Writers Conclave, 1973. Address: Thornfield, Route 1, Box 304, Elmore, Alabama 36025, USA.

HARRIS, Marguerite, b. 5 July 1899. Poet. Published works: A Reconciling of Rivers, 1964; The Risk of the Vine, 1965; Ed., Letters from the World (anthology),

1969. Contbr. to: Yale Literary Review; Nation; Spero; (anthologies) Golden Year, 1960; A Garland for Dylan Thomas, 1963; Of Poem, 1966; East Side Scene, 1968. Recip., Edwin Markham Award for Poetry, 1966. Address: 165 West 91st St., New York, NY 10024, U.S.A.

HARRIS, Marie, b. 7 Nov. 1943. Poet. Education: Georgetown School of Foreign Service, 1963-63; Univ. of NC., 1966-67; Goddard Coll. (B.A.), 1969-71. Divorced, 2 s. Positions held: Teacher, East Hill School, Ithaca, NY.; Administrator of NY State Council on the Arts poetry-in-the-schools grant; Coordinator of Literature Progs., NH Commission on the Arts; Poetry Teacher, New Hampton School; Manchester Inst. of Art. Published works: Trio in Scarlet, 1969; Herbal, 1973. Contbr. to: (anthols.) Best Friends, 1972; Mountain Moving Day; (newspapers, journals) Yale Lit. Mag.; Folio; Lillabulero; Small Pond; The Smith; Foxfire; Earth's Daughters; Lamp in the Spine; Dragonfly; Epoch; Ohio Review; Southern Poetry Review; Granite; Shaman; New: American and Canadian Poetry; Trellis; Stooge; Arion's Dolphin. Address: R.F.D., Center Barnstead, NH 03225, USA.

HARRIS, Mary Imogene, b. 13 Sept. 1926. Teacher. Author. Education: B.A., Central State, Edmond, Okla.; M.A., Northwestern Univ., Evanston, Ill.; Ed.D., Univ. of Tulsa. Positions held: Tchr., Burley, Idaho; Tchr., Judson Coll., Marion, Ala.; Tchr., Tulsa Pub. Schools. Member: Tulsa Engl. Club; Speech Associations; sometime member, Tulsa Poetry Soc. Publications: Serenity, 1969; Ticklers and Tinglers, 1970; A Handbook of Speaking & Listening Activities for the Elementary School, 1971; Talks with God, 1973; They Faced the Cross, 1973; Nobody Would Believe It, 1973; A Walk in the Spirit, 1973. Contrib. to: Happy Times; Concordia; Southside Leader; Grit; The Spectrum; The Secret Place; Internat. Who's Who in Poetry Anthol., 1973. Address: Box 51367, Dawson Station, Tulsa, Okla. 74151, USA.

HARRIS, Max, b. 13 Apr. 1921. Publisher; Editor; Novelist; Poet. Education: St. Peter's Coll.; Univ. of Adelaide. Positions held: Fndr., Reed & Harris (publrs.); Ed., Angry Penguins (jrnl.); Co-Ed., Australian Letters (jrnl.); Broadcaster. Published works: The Vegetative Eye; The Coorong. Contbr. to: (anthol.) Modern Australian Verse, 1964. Address: 27 Park Rd., Kensington Park, South Australia.

HARRIS, T. Wilson, b. 24 Mar. 1921. Poet; Novelist; Critic. Educ: Queen's Coll., Georgetown, Guyana. Married. Positions held: Sr. Surveyor, Govt. of Guyana, 1955-58; Lived in U.K. since 1959: Deleg. Nat. Identity Conf., Commonwealth; UNESCO Symposium on Carribean Literatures, Cuba, 1968. Published works: Fetish, 1951; Eternity to Season, 1954; (novels), The Guiana Quartet: Palace of the Peacock, The Far Journey of Oudin, The Whole Armour, The Secret Ladder, 1960, '61, '62, '63; Heartland, 1964; The Eye of the Scarecrow, 1965; The Waiting Room, 1967; Tumatumari, 1968; Ascent to Omai, 1969; Tradition, The Writer and Society (literary criticism), 1967. Recip., Arts Coun. Award. Address: c/o Faber & Faber Ltd., 24 Russell Sq., London W.C.1, U.K.

HARRIS, William J., b. 12 Mar. 1942. Educator. Education: B.A., Central (Ohio) State Univ.; M.A., Stanford Univ.; Ph.D. (Engl. & Am. Lit.), ibid. Married. Positions held: Asst. Prof. of Am. Lit. & Creative Writing, Cornell Univ., 1972-. Published works: Hey Fella Would You Mind Holding This Piano A Moment, 1974. Contbr. to: Antioch Review; Beloit Poetry Jrnl.; Southern Poetry Review; New Campus Writing; Intro 2; Mad River Review; Plume & Sword; Lillabulero; Yardbird Rdr.; Nine Black Poets; Black Out Loud; New Black Voices; The Poetry of Black America, etc. Address: Dept. of Engl., Goldwin Smith Hall, Cornell Univ., Ithaca, NY 14850, U.S.A.

HARRISON, James Thomas, pen name **HARRISON, Jim,** b. 11 Dec. 1937. Writer. Education: M.A. Comp.

Lit., Mich. State Univ. Published works include: Plain Song, 1965; Locations, 1968; Outlayer & Ghazals, 1971. Contbr. to the following anthols., jrnls., mags., etc: Stony Brook; Sumac; Nation; Partisan Review; NY Times; Lillabulero; Spectrum; Poetry. Honours, awards: Nat. Endowment, 1967-68; Guggenheim Fellow, 1968-69; Two prizes, Am. Nat. Anthol. Address: RR1 Lake Leelanau, Mich. 49653, USA.

HARRISON, Joseph, pen name **CANDIDUS,** b. 19 Sept. 1907. Brush Worker. Memberships: Birmingham Poetry Circle; Yorks. Poets Assn.; Worcester Writers' Guild. Contbr. to: Anthol. of the Seasons, 1947: Autumn Anthol., 1969; 20th Century Poets, 1969; Poetry Int., 1970; Contemporary Poets, 1971; New Poetry 1971; Grand Anthol., 1971; Pulin Publications Jrnl., 1972; Broadcast, Birmingham Radio, Nov. 1972; Contemporary Poets, 1973; 'Shanghai', House of Harris. Address: 18 Ryefields Rd., Stoke Prior, Nr. Bromsgrove, Worcs., U.K.

HARRISON, Keith Edward, b. 29 Jan. 1932. Educator. Education: B.A., Univ. of Melbourne, Australia; M.A., Univ. of Iowa, U.S.A. Positions held: Tutor, Extra-Mural Dept., Univ. of London, 1961-63; Visiting Poet, Univ. of Iowa, 1966; Lectr. in Engl., York Univ., Toronto, Canada, 1967-68; Asst. Prof., Carleton Coll., 1968-. Memberships: Exec. Bd., Poets in Public, London, 1963-65; Hon. Mbr., ex officio, 1966-. Published works: Points in a Journey, 1966, '67; Two Variations on a Ground, 1967; Songs from the Drifting House, 1972. Contbr. to: The New Statesman; The Spectator; The Observer (London); The Atlantic Monthly; The N.Y. Times; Carleton Miscellany; Australian Poetry; The Scotsman; The Listener; The Toronto Telegram; New Poems (PEN), 1962; Best Poems, 1964; The Western Humanities Review; Quadrant, etc. Recip., Poetry Award from the Arts Coun. of G.B. for 'Songs from the Drifting House', 1972. Address: Hackberry Hollow, Rte. 1, Northfield, MN 55057, U.S.A.

HARRISON, Tony, b. 30 Apr. 1937. Poet. Education: Cross Flatts County Primary School, Leeds; Leeds Grammar School; University of Leeds. Married, 2 children (Jane and Max). Published works: Earthworks, 1964; Aikin Mata, 1966; Newcastle is Peru, 1969; The Loiners, 1970; Voortrekker, 1972; The Misanthrope (of Moliere), a new version, 1973. Contbr. to: Times Lit. Supp.; New Statesmen; Stand; Phoenix; Transatlantic Review; Planet; London Mag., etc. Awards: Northern Arts Fellowship in Poetry, 1967-1968; Cholmondeley Award for Poetry, 1969; UNESCO Fellowship in Poetry, 1969; Geoffrey Faber Mem Prize, 1972; Gregynog Fellowship, 1973-1974. Address: 9 The Grove, Gosforth, Newcastle upon Tyne, Northumberland NE3 1NE, UK.

HARROLD, William, b. 24 June 1936. University Professor. Education: B.A., Wake Forest Univ., 1959; M.A. (1961), Ph.D. (1967), Univ. of North Carolina. Positions held: Part-time Instr., Univ. of NC, Chapel Hill, 1962-65; Assoc. Prof. of Engl., Univ. of Wisconsin, Milwaukee, 1972-. Memberships: Avalon Poetry Soc.; Mod. Lang. Assoc.; Mod. Humanities Research Assoc.; Tennyson Soc.; Browning Soc. Published works: Beyond the Dream (poems), 1972; The Variance and the Unity: A Study of the Complementary Poems of Robert Browning, 1973. Contbr. to: Antioch Review; Sparrow; Grande Ronde Review; Midwest Qtly.; Discourse; Second Coming; Riverside Qtly.; Matrix; Poet Lore; Aylesford Review; Metanoia; Florida Qtly; South Carolina Review; The Fiddlehead; DeKalb Lit. Arts Journal; Snowy Egret; Scrip; Bitterroot; Barat Review; Suenos: Dreams; Modine Gunch; Forum; Folio; Florida Education Journal; Penumbra; Uptown Beat; The Liberator; Cardinal Poetry Qtly; Lit. Half-Yearly; This Book Has No Title (anthol); North American Mentor; Green Apple; Wisconsin Poetry Mag.; Lyrismos; Podium; Poetry Venture; Mustang; Flame; Bardic Echoes; Poetry Preview; Iota; Pyramid; Creative Review; Calif. Writer; Seydell Qtly.; Poetry Internat.; Orphic Lute; Haiku Highlights; The Angels; Scimitar & Song; Caravan; Harbor Lights; Ziggurat;

The Archer; Worksheet Directory; Poet's Bulletin; Encounter; The Guild; Bayshore Breeze; Encore Mag.; Prairie Poet; Poet; Fireflower; Ardentia Verba (anthol.); Cyclotron; Cyclo-Flame; Outstanding Contemp. Poetry (anthol.); Hoosier Challenger; Nutmegger; Enterprise; Spearman Publications; Fine Arts Discovery; Imprints Qtly.; American Poets; Writer's Notes & Quotes; The Crucible; Pop. Talisman Bulletin; Pull Here; Quaderni Di Poesi; Poetry Parade (anthol.); Yearbook of Mod. Writers (anthol.), etc. Recip. numerous awards and citations. Address: 1982 N. Prospect, Apt. 2A, Milwaukee, WI 53202, USA.

HARRY, J.S. Member, Poetry Soc. of Australia. Published works: The Deer Under The Skin, 1971. Contbr. to: The Australian; The Digger; Mok; Poetry Australia; Poetry Mag.; New Poetry; Poet's Choice, 1970, '71, '72, '73; Southerly; Spirit, U.S.A.; Twentieth Century; Vision; Westerly; (anthols.) Australian Poetry Now; We Took Their Orders and are Dead; Australian Poetry 1970, '71, '72, '73; This Land's Meaning; Paperback Poets' Anthol., 1974. Recip., Poetry Soc. Book Award, 1971. Address: c/o P.O. Box 184, Randwick, N.S.W., Australia 2031.

HARSENT, David, b. 9 Dec. 1942. Writer. Published works: Tonight's Lover, 1968; A Violent Country, 1969; Truce, 1973; After Dark, 1973. Contbr. to: Times Lit. Supp.; The Review; NY Times; Form; Agenda; Antaeus; New Statesman; Poetry Book Soc. Supplements. Recip. Arts Council Poetry Bursary, 1970-71; Cheltenham Festival Prize, 1968. Address: c/o Oxford Univ. Press, Ely House, 37 Dover St., London W1, UK.

HART, Paul Joseph, pen name **HART, Paul,** b. 6 Dec. 1949. Philosophy Research Student. Education: B.A., Univ. Coll., Bangor, U.K., 1972; M.A. in Philos., Univ. of Warwick, 1973; Darwin Coll., Univ. of Cambridge, 1973–. Poetry included in the following anthols: Doves For The Seventies, 1969; I Am A Sensation, 1971. Contbr. to: Radio Reviews: The Northern Drift & The Weekly World; Newspapers: Peace News; Mags: Second Aeon; Poetry Workshop; Breakthru; Viewpoints; Nemo. Address: 20 Shaw St., Glossop, Derbyshire SK13 8DW, U.K.

HARTFORD, Robert, b. 21 Mar. 1949. Farm Labourer. Education: Cokethorpe Coll. Contbr. to: Hampshire Poets; Second Aeon. Address: Woodfoot Farm, Auldgirth, Nr. Dumfries, U.K.

HARTLING, Peter, b. 13 Nov. 1933. Editor. Education: Gymnasium Nürtingen, 1946-52. Married Mechthild Maier, 4 children. Positions held: Ed., Deutsche Zeitung, Stuttgart & Köln, 1955-62; Ed. & Co-Publisher, Der Monat, Berlin, 1962-70; Chief Ed. & Mng. Dir., S. Fischer Verlag, Frankfurt, 1968–. Memberships: PEN; Akademie der Künste, Berlin; Akademie der Wissenschaften und Literatur, Mainz. Published works: Poeme und Songs, 1953; Yamins Stationen (poems), 1955, 65; Unter den Brunnen (poems), 1958; Spielgeist – Spiegelgeist, 1962; Bruchstücke (poems) w. 1 lith. by Raoul Ubac), 1964; Meine zwei Stimmen (poem w. 2 lithos. by Fritz Ruoff), 1966; Neue Gedichte, 1972. Contbr. to: Akzento; Merkur; Die Zeit; Süddeutsche Zeitung; Stuttgarter Zeitung; La Nouvelle Revue Francaise; Revue Svetovej Literatury, etc. Honours, awards: Kritiker-Preis, Berlin, 1965; Prix du meilleur livre etranger, Paris, 1966; Gerhart-Hauptmann-Preis, 1972. Address: 6083 Walldorf/Hessen, Finkenweg 1, German Fed. Repub.

HARTNETT, Michael J., b. 18 Sept. 1941. Poet. Married Rosemary Grantley, 1 son, 1 daughter. Positions held: Co-Ed., Arena, Dublin, 1963-65. Published works: Anatomy of a Cliché, 1968; The Hag of Beare, 1969; Selected Poems 1958-69, 1970; Tao, 1972; Gipsy Ballads (version of 'Romancero Gitano'), 1973; Collected Poems, 1974. Co-Ed. 'Choice' poetry anthol., 1973. Contbr. to: Poetry Ireland; Kilkenny Mag.; Arena; Hibernia; University Review; Irish Press; Irish Times; Soundings; N.Y. Times; Lace Curtain;

(anthols.) Penguin Book of Irish Verse; Sphere Book of Irish Verse; New Irish Writing Anthol.; Choice. Address: c/o Irish Times Ltd., Dublin 2, Eire.

HART-SMITH, William, b. 23 Nov. 1911. Poet. Positions held: Copywriter; Announcer, 2CH; Air Publicity Officer, ABC, Sydney; AIF, World War II. Published works: Columbus Goes West, 1943; Harvest, 1945; The Unceasing Ground, 1946; Christopher Columbus, 1948; On The Level, 1950; Poems of Discovery, 1959. Contbr. to: (anthol.) Modern Australian Verse, 1964. Address: c/o Angus & Robertson Ltd., 107 Elizabeth St., Melbourne, Australia.

HARVEY, Celia, pen name **HARVEY, Pippa.** Housewife. Married John Harvey, 1 son, 1 daughter. Memberships: Poetry Soc., London; Org., Wigan Br., Lancashire Poetry Assn.; Sec., Preston Poets' Soc.; Lancashire Authors' Assn.; Leyland Writers; Preston Poetry Workshop; Publicity Officer, Preston & District Arts Assn., etc. Contbr. to: Fleetwood Music & Arts Feest., 1972-73; The Record (Lancs. Authors' Assn.), 1973 & '74; Reflections (Preston Poets' Soc.); Preston Poetry Workshop Poetry Sheets, 1973; Preston Jrnl. Has read own works on Radio Blackburn. Has received awards for short story & poetry writing from: Lancashire Authors' Assn.; Leyland Writers; Preston Poets' Soc.; Fleetwood Arts Fest.; 'The Writer'. Address: 8 Whitefield Rd. East, Penwortham, Preston, Lancs., U.K.

HARVEY, Charles John Derrick, b. 2 July 1922. University Teacher. Education: B.A., Univ. of Natal, 1942; M.A., ibid, 1947. Positions held: Lectr. of Engl., Univs. of Witwatersrand & Stellenbosch; Sr. Engl. Lectr., Univ. of Natal; Prof. of Engl., Univs. of S. Africa & Stellenbosch. Engl. Ed. of bi-lingual lit. bi-monthly jrnl., 'Standpunte'. Published works: Afrikaans Poems with English Translations, 1962. Contbr. to: Standpunte; Contrast; Poets in Africa, anthol.; Vivid Verse, anthol. Address: 10 Binnekring Rd., Stellenbosch 7600, S. Africa.

HARVEY, Margie Ballard, b. 12 July 1910. Poet; Freelance Writer. Married Walter Frank Harvey. Memberships: Int. Clover Poetry Assn.; Poetry Soc. of Tex.; Hon. Mbr., The Laurel Publishers Int. Poetry Symposium; Orbis Int. Poetry Soc. Rep. in the following anthols: Am. Songbird, 1960; Bluebook of Am. Poetry, 1961; Treasures of Parnassus, 1962; Heart's Secrets, 1962; Fragments of Faith, 1963; Am. Poetry Old & New, 1965; A Burst of Trumpets, 1966; Golden Harvest, 1967; Clover Collection of Verse, Vol.3, 1970; Clover Collection of Verse, Vol.5, 1972; Yearbook of Modern Poetry, 1972; Lyrics of Love, 1972; Tower by the Sea, 1973; Poetry in Prayer, 1971. Contbr. to: The Southeast Star; The Kaufman Herald. Address: 205 Water St., Seagoville, TX 75159, U.S.A.

HARWOOD, Gwen, b. 8 June 1920. Poet. Secretary. Education: Brisbane Girls Grammar Schl., Australia. Married, 4 children. Positions held: Tchr.; Organist, All Saints Ch., Brisbane. Member, Aust. Soc. Authors. Published Works: Poems, 1963; Poems, Vol. II, 1968; Libretto, Fall of the House of Usher, 1965. Contbr. to: (anthol.) Modern Australian Verse, 1964; Meanjin Quarterly; Quadrant; Poetry Aust.; Spirit, US; Southerly; The Australian; The Age; Westerly; numerous anthols. Recip., Meanjin Poetry Prize, 1959, '60. Address: 89 Augusta Rd., Lenah Valley, Tas., Australia 7008.

HARWOOD, Lee, b. 6 June 1939. Poet. Education: B.A., Queen Mary Coll., Univ. of London, U.K., 1961. Positions held: Libn.; Bookshop Asst. & Mgr.; Forestry Worker; Writer-in-Res., Aegean Schl. of Fine Arts, Paros, Cyclades, Greece, 1971-72. Mbr., Poets Conf. Published works: Title Illegible, 1965; The Man with Blue Eyes, 1966; The White Room, 1968; The Beautiful Atlas, 1969; Landscapes, 1969; The Sinking Colony, 1970; Penguin Modern Poets, series, vol.19, w. Ashbery & Raworth, 1971; The First Poem, 1971; New Year, 1971; (anthols.) Children of Albion, 1969; British

Poetry since 1945, 1970; 23 Modern British Poets, 1971. Translations: Tristan Tzara – A poem sequence, 1969; Tristan Tzara – Destroyed Days, 1971. Contbr. to: Art & Lit.; Paris Review; London Mag.; Poetmeat; The World; Angel Hair; Ant's Forefoot;· Eleventh Finger; Collection; Iowa Review; The Boston Phoenix; Michigan Quarterly; The Tri-Quarterly; Fire Exit; Flame; Broadsheet; Big Venus, etc. Recip., Annual award, Poetry Fndn., N.Y., 1966. Address: c/o 9 Highfield Rd., Chertsey, Surrey KT16 8BU, U.K.

HASBROUCK, Patricia Marie, b. 26 Apr. 1953. Graphics Specialist. Education: Southern Meth. Univ. (majoring in Broadcasting & Music). Positions held: Graphics Specialist at WFAA–TV, Dallas, Channel 8, Vidifont & Teleprompt Operator, 1971–. Memberships: Int. Acad. of Poets; Acad. of Am. Poets; Poetry Soc. of Tex.; nominee for Platform Assn. of Am. Contbr. to: Richardson Daily News; Dallas Morning News; Nat. Anthol. of High School Poetry; Richland Jr. Coll. News; Southwest Tex. State Univ. Star. Honours, awards: 1st pl., Richardson H.S. Poetry Prize, 1970, & 2nd pl., 1971; had poems read in Richland Jr. Coll. Poetry Workshop, 1973. Address: 947 Blue Lake Circle, Richardson, TX 75080, U.S.A.

HASELOFF, Charles, b. 8 Dec. 1937. Education: Gymnasium, Germany, 1948-52; High School of Music and Art, N.Y.C., 1952-56; B.A. in Psychology, The City College of N.Y., 1968. Married to Barbara Knight; Children, one. Member, Committee of Small Magazine Publishers and Editors, U.S.A.; Andiron Club, N.Y.C. Pub. Ode to Susan, 1972. Contrib. to: Mulberry; Sun; New York Times; New York Quarterly; Equal Time: Bones; Connections; Toothpaste; Penumbra; Promethean; Endymion; Outcast. Publishes and edits Penumbra. Address: G.P.O. Hex Box 1501, New York, N.Y. 10001, U.S.A.

HASKALE, Hadassah, b. 3 May 1934. Poet; School Psychologist; Editor. Education: M.S., City Coll., N.Y., 1962; studied World Lit. w. Poet Leah Goldberg at Hebrew Univ., 1957; Writing Workshops at New Schl. for Soc. Rsch., N.Y. Positions held: Schl. Psychol., N.Y., San Francisco & Santa Fe; Ed., anthol. The End, 1965; Assoc. Ed. then Co-Ed., Illuminations Press, 1966-71; helped launch a little mag., 'Ally', 1973. Organised Poetry Readings & Workshops in Santa Fe, 1971 & 73. Published works: Message to and From the Universe, 1973. Contbr. to: The Red Clay Reader; Eureka; "i.e."; Deserted Times; Love Lights; Overflow; El Puerto del Sol; Sage; Illuminations;Pulse; Ally. Address: c/o Bar Dayan, 12 Rachel Hamishoreret, Jerusalem 96348, Israel.

HASSLER, Donald, b. 3 Jan. 1937. Teacher; Poet. Education: B.A., Williams Coll., 1959; M.A., Ph.D., Columbia Univ., 1967. Married w. 2 s. Positions held: Instr., Univ. of Montreal, Canada, 1961-65; Asst. Prof., Kent State Univ., USA, 1965-70; Assoc. Prof. ibid, 1971–. Member of Ohio Poets' Assn. Pub. On Weighing A Pound of Flesh, 1973. Contbr. to the following anthols. & jrnls: A Consort of Poets, 1969; Poets on the Platform, 1970; Read Out, Read In, 1971; American Weave; Ball State University Forum; Canadian Forum; Canadian Poetry; Descants; The Fiddlehead; Hiram Poetry Review; The Montreal Star; Podium; Polemic; The South Florida Poetry Journal; Spirit; Human Issue; Mélange. Address: 770 Marilyn Dr., Kent, Ohio 44240, USA.

HAUGE, Olav H., b. 18 Aug. 1908. Fruit Grower. Education: Horticultural Schl. Memberships: Norsk Forfatterforening; Norsk Maldyrkingslag. Published works: Glør i oska, 1946; Under bergfallet, 1951; Seint ròdar skog i djuvet, 1956; Pa ørnetuva, 1961; Dikt i utval, 1964; Dropar i austavind, 1966; Utanlandske dikt, 1967; Spør vinden, 1971; Dikt i samling, 1972. Contbr. to: Syn og Segn; Vinduet; The Lit. Review; Micromegas. Honours, awards: Norsk Kritikerlags Pris, 1961; Doblougprisen, 1969. Address: 5730 Ulvik i Hardanger, Norway.

HAUPT, Quita Ruth Moore, pen name **HAUPT, Quita**

Ruth M., b. 21 Aug. 1901. Poet. Education: Brooklyn Bus. Coll.; John Murray Anderson Schl. of Theatre & Dance; Pvte. Study. Married to James Haupt, dec. Positions held: Pvte, Sec., Shubael Douglas Malcolm, Gen. Mgr., Advtsg. Dept., Am. Express Co., 1919-22; Sec. & Girl Friday, Maj. Geo. Fielding Eliot, Free-lance Writer & War Correspondent, 1928; Sec., Sales Dept., Mgr., WEAF (later NBC), 1929. Memberships: Fla. State Poetry Soc., Inc., 1966-68; Charter Mbr., Ronald-Barze Poetry Group, 1967-73; Nat. League Am. Penwomen, 1968–; World Poetry Soc. Intercontinental, 1969–. Published works: Prayer for a Harbor, broadcast & publd. by NBC, 1936; Stardust on the Grass, What It Would Be Like, Keepers of the Key, all in Poet, 1969 & '70. Contbr. to: FSPS Selected Poems (3), 1966; & (9), 1967; Poet, 1967-72; FSPS (UPLI), Dr. Etta 1st Mem. Book, 1967; FSPS Limerick Book, 6 limericks, 1967. Honours: 1st Prize, Dr. Etta Josephean Murfey Mem. Contest, 1967; FSPS (UPLI) Poet-of-the-Yr.; World Poet Award, WPSI; 3rd Place, Conrad Aiken Prize Contest, Ga. Poetry Soc.; 1st Prize, NLAPW Poetry Contest, 1968. Address: 4641 Lacy Ave., Suitland, Maryland 20023, USA.

HAUSER, Jacob, b. 27 Dec. 1909. Retired Government Employee. Education: Brooklyn Coll., NY. Positions held: Employee of NY Post Office, 1930-61. Memberships: Poetry Soc. of Am.; International Platform Assoc.; International Poetry Soc. Publications: Dark Metropolis, 1931; Future Harvest, 1939; City Pastorals, 1943; Solo, The One Man Magazine of Poetry, 1946-67; Valentine for Venus, 1963; Walt Whitman, A Biography in Verse, 1966; The Olympians; The Traveller Returns, A Soliloquy of Hamlet; Greek Memoirs; Spring Stanzas; Charades of Earth; Key of Beauty; House of Dawn; Cast of Characters; The Story of Merlin, Part 1, The Childhood of Merlin; Part 2, The Wizard of Camelot. Contbr. to: Poetry of Chicago; Spirit; SW Rev.; Contemporary Verse; Chicago Tribune; NY Times; The Lyric; Sonnet Sequences; Radio programs, NY & Calif. Honours: Guggenheim Fellowship, Poetry, 1936; Interviews, NY Times, 1948, '63, regarding Solo; Time Mag., 1948. Address: 501 E. 21 St., Brooklyn, NY 11226, USA.

HAUSMAN, Gerald, b. 13 Oct. 1945. Teacher. Education: B.A., N.M. Highlands Univ. Married, 1 child. Positions held: Tchr., Windsor Mt. Schl., Lenox, Mass., 1968-72; Poet-in-Res., Pittsfield Schl. System, 1971–; Poet-in-Res., Central Conn. State Coll., 1973; Ed., Bookstore Press, Lenox, Mass. Published works: New Marlboro Stage, 1971; Circle Meadow, 1972; The Boy with the Sun Tree Bow, 1973. Contbr. to Contemporaries, Anthol. of Am. Poets, 1972; Berkshire Anthol. (Ed. & Contbr.) Address: New Marlboro Rd., Monterey, MA 01245, U.S.A.

HAVENNE, Edgard Emile Laurent, pen name **B2** (for technical articles), b. 30 Aug. 1919. Secretary, Defence Research Centre, ABC Establishment. Memberships: Cercle d'Art 'Les Peintres et l'Ardenne; V.P., ibid; Organist, choir-master & voluntary producer, Dramatic Club, Heer, until 1953. Published works: Aquarelles (poems), 1969; Commentaires (essays), 1970; Pêle-Mêle, images & poems, 1971. Contbr. to: La Dryade; Le Musée Gaumais; Vento Nuovo; Le Sanglier;·Syndic; SOB; La Chronique des Luxembourgeois; Publivire, etc. Honours, awards: Prix de la Ville de Bruxelles, 1970; Croix de Chevalier de l'Ordre de Léopold II, 1971; Palmes d'Or de l'Ordre de la Couronne, 1966. Address: CRD/EtABC, Oude Tuchthuisdreef, B–1800, Vilvoorde, Belgium.

HAVERSTOCK, Barbara (Babs) Jean, b. 15 Feb. 1944. Teacher. Memberships: Tex. Poetry Soc., 1969-72; Scribbler's Club, Houston, Tex., 1968-72. Contbr. to: 'Sound Off' Column, Houston Post; 'Viewpoints' Column, Houston Chronicle; T.L.C., 1962 & 63; Whetstone (S.H.S.U.), 1967; T.L.C. 'Expressions', 1964; Lone Star Lutheran; Footprints of the Future, 1972; Youth (record), 1972; Creative Urge, 1968-72. Address: 3402 Knoll Dr., Houston, TX 77055, U.S.A.

HAWKSWORTH, Marjorie, b. 16 Feb. 1922. Teacher

of English. Education: B.A., Barnard, 1941; grad. work, Univ. of Calif. at Santa Barbara. Widow of William D. Hawksworth, 4 children. Member, Poetry Soc. of Am. Contbr. to: Diamond Anthol., PSA, 1970; Nat. Poetry Anthol., 1970; Etc: A Jrnl. of Semantics; Thrust, vols. 24; Cardinal Qtly. Recip., First prize in poetry, Santa Barbara Annual Writers' Conf., 1966. Address: 2512 Selrose Ln., Santa Barbara, CA 93109, U.S.A.

HAY, George Campbell, pen name **DHEORSA, Maclain,** b. 8 Dec. 1915. Translator. Education: B.A. Classics, John Watson's, Edinburgh; Fettes College, Edinburgh; Corpus Christi College, Oxford. Positions held: Reviewer, The Scotsman; Scandinavian Buyer, Nat. Lib. of Scotland. Published works include: Fuaran Sléibh; Wind on Loch Fyne, 1948; O Na Ceiltur Airdenn, 1952. Contbr. to the following anthols., jrnls., mags., etc: The Scots Independent; Scotia; The Scotsman; Akros; Scottish International; Scottish Art and Letters; The Scots Magazine; The Scots Review; Gairm; An Gaidheal. Honours, awards: £750 Arts Council Bursary, 1971. Address: 6 Maxwell St., Edinburgh EH10 5HU, Scotland, UK.

HAYDEN, b. 4 Aug. 1913. Professor. Education: Wayne State Univ., Detroit; M.A., Univ. of Michigan, Ann Arbor, 1944. Taught at Univ. of Michigan, 1944-46, Fisk Univ., Nashville, Tenn.; Present position is Professor of English, Fisk Univ.; Visiting Professor, Univs. of Michigan, 1968, Louisville, Ky., 1969. Published Works: Heartshape in the Dust, 1940; The Lion & the Archer, 1948; A Ballad of Remembrance, 1962; Selected Poems, 1966; Ed., Kaleidoscope: Poems by American Negro Poets, 1967. Contbr. to: Poetry of the Negro, 1949; American Negro Poetry, 1963; Black Voices, 1968. Honours, Awards: Hopwood Award, 1938, 42; Rosenwald Fellowship, 1947; Ford Foundation Grant, 1954; Dakar (Senegal) World Festival of the Arts Grand Prize for Poetry, 1966. Address: 1804 Hermosa Street, Nashville, TN, USA.

HAYES, Ann Louise, b. 13 May 1924. University Teacher. Education: B.A., Stanford Univ., 1948; M.A., ibid, 1950. Widow of Frank A. Hayes. Positions held: Acting Inst., p/t, Stanford Univ., 1950; Tchng. Assoc., Indiana Univ., 1953-55; Instr., p/t, Coe Coll., 1955-57; Instr., Carnegie Inst. of Technol., 1957-60; Asst. Prof., ibid, 1960-65; Assoc. Prof., Carnegie Mellon Univ., 1965-74; Prof., 1974–. Member, The English Inst. Published works: For Sally Barnes, 1963; Amo Ergo Sum, Amo Ergo Est, 1969; The Dancer's Step, 1973. Rep. in following anthols: Poets of the Pacific, 2nd series, 1949; Laurel, Archaic, Rude, 1966; Cathedral Poets, I, 1966; Borestone Mountain Poetry Awards, 1969: Best Poems of 1968; In Honor of Austin Wright, 1972. Contbr. to: N.M. Qtly. Review; The Am. Scholar; The Va. Qtly. Review; The Southern Review, New Series; etc. Honours, awards: Irene Hardy Poetry Award, 1943; Clarence Urmy Poetry Prize, 1943, '47, '50; Ina Coolbrith Award, 1943; Hon. Mention, James D. Phelan Award in Poetry, 1947. Address: Dept. of Engl., Carnegie Mellon Univ., Pittsburgh, PA 15213, U.S.A.

HAYES, Charles Phillip, b. 3 Oct. 1949. Elementary School Teacher; Naturalist; presently co-authoring book on herbs. Education: Grad. with B.A. in Psychology, Univ. of Tampa, Fla.; Attended various NY State Univ. colleges; Kansas State Univ., to enter grad. school in Creative Writing; Student of Spanish poetry. Contbr. to: Palmer ublishers Anthol., 1971; Cardinal Qtly.; Idaho State Univ. Ecology Anthol., 1971; Poetry Review Qtly.; College Poetry Review; Univ. of S. Fla. Review; Ann Arbor Review; The Immanentists Anthol.: Art of the Superconscious, 1973; The Word. Awards: Finalist, Fla. Tech. Univ. Annual Poetry Contest, 1972. Address: c/o 158 Depew St., Peekskill, NY 10566,USA.

HAYES, Margaret F. (Frances), b. 29 Aug. 1900. Housewife and Writer. Education: Grad., Moreland Notre Dame, Watsonville, Calif. Creative Writing,

Hartnell Coll., Calif.; Cabrillo Coll.; Aptos. Positions held: Book-keeper; Sec. Memberships: Past Pres., Santa Cruz Chapt., Calif. Fed. of Chaparral Poets; Ina Coolbrith Poetry Circle, San Francisco, Calif., Arizona State Poetry Soc.; CSSI (Rome). Published work: Question The Wind (collection of poems), 1973. Contbr. to the following anthols., mags., newspapers, etc: Good Housekeeping Mag.; Writers Notes & Quotes; Calif. Herald; Santa Cruz Sentinel, Watsonville Register-Pajaronian & Calif. Fed. of Chaparral Poets Anthol., Sunburst (anthol. 4,1971); Ina Coolbrith Circle Anthol., 1971; Santa Cruz Chaparral Poets Anthol., 1973. Honours, awards, etc: 1st for Tanka, Chaparral State Contest, 1965; Lola Graham Award for sonnet, 1966; 1st for Portrait Poem, Forest Lawn & Alpha Chapt., SFCP, 1967; 1st Prize, Statewide Christmas poem contest; 1st for Free Verse, SC Chapt. CFCP annual contest; Grand Prize, 42nd Poets' Dinner Contest, 1968; Calif. Olympiad of Arts, 1st & trophy in sonnet; John Graham Mem. Award Grand Prize, Santa Cruz Chapt., CFCP annual contest, 1968 '70; Elias Lieberman Award, NY Poetry Forum Contest, 1970; 1st Prize for sonnet, 45th Annual Poets' Dinner, Berkeley, Calif., 1971; Calif. Writers' Club biennial contest, winner of poetry award; Scholarship to Calif. Poets' Conf., Mills Coll., Oakland, Calif. Address: 300 Hayes Rd., Watsonville, CA 95076, USA.

HAYMAN, Carol Bessent, b. 9 June 1927. Poet. Education: Grad. Beaufort HS, NC; Grad. Louisburg Coll., NC; attended East Carolina Univ. and ECU Camp Lejeune, NC Extension; Audited Black Mountain Coll. Creative Writing Class. Married to Dr. Louis D. Hayman, Jr., Cardiologist; 2 children. Positions held: Trustee, Louisburg Coll., NC, 1964-71; Lay Speaker, NC United Methodist Church; District Councilor, NC Medical Aux., 1971-74; NC Councillor to Southern Medical Assoc., 1969-73. Memberships: NLAPW (S.E. Regional Ed., The Pen Woman); World Poetry Soc.; Internat. Platform Assoc.; Acad. of American Poets; N.C. Poetry Soc. Inc. (Chmn., Mbrship. Comm., 2 yrs. & Student Cultivation "Poetry-in-the-Schools"); Published works: Keepsake, 1962; These Lovely Days, 1971 (reprint 1972); A Collection of Writings Published in the NC Christian Advocate, 1972. Contbr. to numerous anthols., newspapers, religious & poetry publs., etc. Recip. of several awards, N.C. & Fla. Poetry Contests, etc. Address: 406 Carmen Ave., Jacksonville, NC 28540, USA.

HAYS, H(offman) R., b. 1904. Drama Teacher. Education: B.A., Cornell Univ., Ithaca, N.Y.; M.A., Columbia Univ., N.Y.; Univ. of Liege, Belgium. Married Juliette Levine, 2 children. Positions Held: Acting Hd. of Drama Dept., Fairleigh Dickinson Univ., Rutherford, NJ, 1960-63; Co-ordinator of Drama Program, Southampton Coll., Long Island Univ., 1965-69. Published Works: Selected Poems, 1968; Novels: Stranger on the Highways, 1943; Lie down in the Darkness, 1944; The Takers of the City, 1946; The Envoys, 1955; Non-fiction works: From Ape to Angel, 1958; In the beginnings, 1963; The Dangerous Sex, 1964; Var. Translations incl: 12 Spanish American Poets, 1943; Selected Poems of Bertolt Brecht, 1959. Contbr. to: Losers, Weepers, 1969; Inside outer Space, 1970; Kayak, Chelsea Review, Tenn. Poetry Jrnl., Voyages. Address: Box 22, Baiting Hollow Road, East Hampton, NY 11937, USA.

HAYS, Janice, b. 27 Feb. 1929. Scholar-Teacher. Education: A.B., Univ. of Calif., Berkeley, 1968; M.A., ibid, 1970; Cand. Philos., 1972; Ph.D. due 1974. Married & divorced twice, 2 children. Positions held: Admin. Clerical positions, Univ. of Calif., 1964-66; Tchng. Asst., Engl., Univ. of Calif., Berkeley, 1970-71; Assoc. Instr. in Engl., ibid, 1972-74. Memberships: Hon. Mbr., Am. Acad. of Poets; MLA. Published works: New House – A Book of Women, 1972. Contbr. to: 1971 Yearbook of Poetry; Samisdat Review, 1974; Illuminations 6, summer 1972; The Gar I; Illuminations 7, 1972; Dryad 7/8, 1971; Beloit Poetry Jrnl., 1971; The Open Cell I:14; Illuminations 9; Dryad 5/6, 1969; Encore, 1970; Beloit Poetry Jrnl.; Ladies Home Jrnl., etc. Honours, awards:3rd prize, 1965, 1st prize, 1968, Calif. Collegiate Poetry Comp.; 3rd prize, Emily Chamberlain Cook Poetry Comp., Univ. of Calif., Berkeley, 1969, 72; Winner, Am. Acad. of Poets Comp., ibid, 1969, 71. Address: 63 Vicente Rd., Berkeley, CA 94705, U.S.A.

HAZAK, Yehiel, b. 25 Oct. 1936. Educator. Education: B.A., Hebrew Lit. & Bible; postgrad. Tchrs. Sem. Married twice, 4 daughters. Positions held: currently as Emissary of the Jewish Agency to 'Habonim' Youth Movement in the U.K. Member, Hebrew Writers' Assn., Israel. Published works: (books) Avnei Bazelet, 1961; Atha Al Panai, 1967; Behora Azuva, 1970; Veloh Hamelech, 1974. Contbr. to var. newspapers & mags. inclng: Davar; Maariv; Häärets; Lamerhav; Haboker; Keshet; Shdemot; Moznaim; Bakibuts; Eked; also to the colls. of the Hebrew Writers' Assn. & an international mag. which was dedicated to Israeli poetry. Rep. in Modern Hebrew Poetry, anthol. Address: Kibbutz Afiqim, Jordan Valley, Israel.

HAZARD, Geoffrey Edward, b. 8 Oct. 1934. Booksellers Assistant. Positions held: Clerk; Railwayman; Warehouseman; Booksellers Asst., etc. Published works: (pamphlet) Four Long Poems, 1970. Rep. in following anthols: Poems by Seven, 1959; Festival Poetry '65. 1965; Children of Albion, 1970; Children of Albion Revisited, 1974. Contbr. to: Mandrake; 'X' Mag.; Times Literary Supplement; The Lace Curtain; Outposts; The Holy Door; Poetry Ireland; Arena; New Helios; Simbolica; Sparrow Mag.; Flame; Ore; Combustion; The Outsider; John o'London's Weekly; New Departures; BBC Third Prog., etc. Address: c/o The Thurlestone Hotel, Thurlestone, Nr. Kingsbridge, S. Devon, U.K.

HAZELTON, Lucy Clare Elizabeth Schaeffer Reed, pen names **REED, Lucy; SHEPARD, Ellen; TERRY, D.E.** b. 9 Sept. 1929. Advertising/P.R. Manager; Copy Writer; Artist. Education: Schools at Webster Groves, Mo., St. Louis Univ. etc. Married, with 3 children: Terence G. Reed; Deborah Lucy Reed; Mrs. Ellen Reed Frisch. Member, Poetry Soc. of New Hampshire, 1967-68; St. Louis Poetry Center, since 1960; Editor Poetry Center Speaking, 1972-73; St. Louis Writer's Guild, since 1965. Pub. Pot Pourri, 1966. Contrib. to: Poetry Center Speaking, 1963, 64, 65, 66, 67, 68, 72, 73; New Hampshire Poetry Magazine, 1967; New Orleans Review, 1973. Awards: Hon. Mention Poetry, Wednesday Club, St. Louis, 1956-57, 1960-63; 1st place E. Oscar Thalinger Award for Verse Play (The Still Point), 1965; 2nd place Thalinger Award Verse Play (The River Laughs), 1966. Address: 668 Kirkshire, Kirkwood, Mo. 63122, USA.

HAZO, Samuel. Poet. Education: B.A., Univ. of Notre Dame; M.A., Duquesne Univ.; Ph.D., Univ. of Pittsburgh. Married, 1 s. Positions held: Tchr., Shady Side Acad.; Prof., Duquesne Univ.; Dir., Int. Poetry Forum. Published works; Discovery; The Quiet Wars; My Sons in God; Listen with the Eye; Blood Rights; Hart Crane, An Introduction; Seascript; Once for the Last Bandit. Contbr. to: The Atlantic; Harper's; Yale Review; Kenyon Review; Sewanee Review; Malahat Review; Minesota Review; Poetry Northwest; etc. Recip. of Man of the Year, 1961; National Book Award Finalist, 1973. Address: International Poetry Forum 4400 Forbes Ave., Carnegie Library, Pittsburgh, Pa. 15213, USA.

HEAD, Nancy, b. 6 Oct. 1917. Secretary. Education: Sec. Trng., Commercial Coll. Married. Positions held: Jr. Solicitor's Clerk, 1937-39; Aux. Territorial Serv., WWII, 1940-41; Office of the Minister Resident (Middle East) & Brit. Embassy, Cairo, 1942-45; Civil Servant, Cardiff & London, 1945-47. Contbr. to: Scrip; Hampshire Poets. Address: Dell Cottage, Bank, Lyndhurst, Hants. SO4 7FD, U.K.

HEANEY, Seamus, b. 13 Apr. 1939. Lecturer. Education: St. Columb's Coll., Derry; Queen's Univ., Belfast w. 1st class Hons. in English. Married w. 2 sons. Positions held: Tchr., Secondary Schl., 1962-63;

Lectr., St. Joseph's Coll. of Education, English, (ueen's Univ., Belfas Published works: Eleven Pomse Inglish, Queen's Univ., elfast, 19(6–. Published works: Eleven Poems 1965; Death of a Naturalist, 1966; A Lough Neagh Sequence, 1969; Door to the Dark, 1969. Contbr. to (Anthologies): Young Commonwealth Poets '65, 1965; Modern Poets, 1968; Voices, 196l; Penguin Book of Irish Verse, 1970; Faber Book of Irish Verse, 197C (Jrnls.): Phoenix; Listener; Irish Times. Honours: Eric Gregory Award, 1966; Cholmond Award, 1967; Geoffrey Faber Prize, j968; Somerset Maugham Award, 1968 Address: 16 Ashley Ave., Belfast 9, Northern Ireland.

HEASTER, Emmett Lawrence, b. 26 May 1897. Teacher & Farmer. Education: A.B., Alderson Broaddus Coll., Philippi, W. Va.; W. Va. Univ.; Perdue Univ.; Ohio Univ.; bus. course, Massey Bus. Coll., Richmond, Va. Positions held: Engl. Tchr., H.S.; Tchr., U.S. Govt., penal instn., Chillicothe, Ohio, 10 yrs.; Prin., small elem. schl. Memberships: Past V.P., Morgantown Poetry Soc.; W. Va. State Poetry Soc. Published works: Limericks & Lyrics from my Rhododendron Thicket, 1973. Contbr. to: Broaddus Coll. Anthol.; Echoes of West Va. Poetry Soc.; Poet, India; local newspapers. Recip. var. poetry prizes inclng: 1st prize, W.Va. State Limerick Contest, 1971; 3rd prize, Patriotic Song Writing Contest, 1972. Address: Route 7, Cliff House, Morgantown, WV 26505, U.S.A.

HEASTER, Georgia Golden, b. 12 Nov. 1903. Teacher. Education: Tchr. Trng., Alderson-Broaddus Coll.; A.B., West Va. Univ. Married Emmett Heaster, 3 sons, 1 daughter. Positions held: Tchr. in Barbour Co., Greenbrier Co. & Monongalia Co., W.Va. Memberships: Nat. Poetry Soc.; W.Va. Poetry Soc.; V.P., Morgantown Poetry Soc., 1973-74. Contbr. to: Echoes of the West Virginia Poetry Soc.; The Panorama Mag.; Scimiter & Song; Poet. Recip., 2nd prize, The Huntington Lyric Poetry Award of the W.Va. Poetry Soc., 1972. Address: Rte. 7, Cliff House, Morgantown, WV 26505, U.S.A.

HEATH-STUBBS, John Francis Alexander, b. 9 July 1918, London, UK. Writer & Lecturer. Education: 1st Class Hons., Engl., The Queen's Coll., Oxford Univ., UK, 1942. Positions held: Engl. Master, The Hall Schl., Hampstead, London, 1944-45; Edit. Asst., Hutchinson's publrs., 1945-46; Gregory Fellow in Poetry, Leeds Univ., 1952-55; Vis. Prof., Engl., Univ. of Alexandria, 1955-58; ibid, Univ. of Mich., USA, 1960-61; Lectr. in Engl., Coll. of St Mark & St. John, London, UK, 1963–. Memberships: Fellow, Royal Soc. of Lit.; Exec. Commn, Engl. Assoc.; Poetry Soc. Publications: (verse) Wounded Thammuz, 1942; Beauty & the Beast, 1943; The Divided Ways, 1946; The Charity of the Stars, 1950; The Swarming of the Bees, 1950; A Charm Against the Toothache, 1954; The Triumph of the Muse, 1958; The Blue-fly in his Head, 1962; Selected Poems, 1964; Satires & Epigrams, 1968; (drama) Helen in Egypt, & other Plays. 1959; (critism) the Darkling Plain, 1950; Charles Williams, 1955; (translns.) Hafiz of Shiraz, co-author, 1942; Selected Poetry & Prose of Giacomo Leopardi, co-author, 1967; Aphrodite's Garland, 1951; The Horn, 1969. Contbr. to: Times Lit. Supp.; Observer; Yorkshire Post; Scotsman; New Statesman; Time & Tide; The Listener; Tribune; Poetry London; Poetry Qtly.; Poetry Rev.; New Engl. Weekly; Outposts; Ambit; Agenda; Aquarius; Sobornost; Frontier; Nimbus; Stand, Poetry Review; translations; Nine; Penguin New Writing; New Writing & Daylight; Malahat Review; New Yorker; Two Rivers; X; Poetry Broadsheets, etc. Honours: Arts Coun. Award, 1965. Address: 35 Sutherland Place, London, W2, UK.

HECHT, b. 16 Jan. 1923. University Teacher. Education: B.A., Bard Coll., Annandale-on-Hudson, N.Y., 1944; M.A., Columbia Univ., N.Y., 1950. Divorced w. 2 sons. Positions held: Taught at Kenyon Coll. Gambier, Ohio, 1947, Univ. of Iowa, 1948, N.Y. Univ. 1949, Smith Coll., Northampton, Mass., 1956-59, Bard Coll., 1962-67, Univ. of Rochester, N.Y., 1967–.

Published works: A Summoning of Stones, 1954; The Seven Deadly Sins, 1958; The Hard Hours, 1968; Ed. w. John Hollander, Jiggery-Pokery: A Compendium of Double Dactyls, 1967. Contbr. to (Anthologies): A Little Treasury of Modern Poetry, 1950; A Little Treasury of World Poetry, 1952; New Pocket Anthology of American Poetry, 1955; Faber Book of Modern American Verse, 1956; New Poets of England & America, 1957,62; Poetry for Pleasure, 1960; Contemporary American Poetry, 1962; Poet's Choice, 1962; Modern Poets, 1963; American Lyric Poems, 1964; A Controversy of Poets, 1965; Poems on Poetry, 1965; Poems of our Moment, 1968; (Jrnls.): Hudson Review; N.Y. Review of Books; Quarterly Review of Literature; Transatlantic Review; Voices. Honours: Prix de Rome Fellowship, 1951; Guggenheim Fellowship, 1954,59; Hudson Review Fellowship, 1958; Ford Foundation Fellowship, 1960,68; Brandeis Univ. Creative Arts Award, 1965; Loines Award, 1968; Pulitzer Prize, 1968. Address: 240 East 82nd Street, N.Y., NY 10028, USA.

HEDIN, Mary Ann. Writer. Education: B.S., Univ. of Minn., U.S.A.; M.A., Univ. of Calif. Married Roger W. Hedin, M.D., 3 sons & 1 daughter. Positions held: Libn., Minn. Pub. Lib.; Prof. of Engl., Coll. of Marin, currently Mbr., Poetry Soc. of Am. Contbr. to: 'Places We Lost' in Best Am. Short Stories, 1966; Descant; Epos; South; Pacific Sun; S.D. Review; World Order; North Country Anvil; Chicago Tribune 'Poets Today'; South West Review; Independent Jrnl.; Scopcraeft; Perspective; Shenandoah; Foxfire; Southern Poetry Review; Arrows; Voice of the Poet; Peace & Pieces. Recip. prizes from Oakland Poets Dinner, 1964 & 65 & Poetry Soc. of Am., 1972. Address: 182 Oak Ave., San Anselmo, CA 94960, U.S.A.

HEDRICK, Addie Mae, b. 22 Aug. 1903. Poet. Married, Joseph A. Hedrick. Memberships: Nat. League of Am. Penwomen; World Poetry Soc. Intercontinental; Poetry Soc. of Tenn.; Ark. Authors, Composers & Artists. Publications: Sentient Dust, 1952; Mumbaloo & Other Poems, 1967; A Cup of Stars, 1969. Contbr. to: Radio-TV Mirror; Christian Science Monitor; Am. Courier; Lyric; Scimitar & Song; Kaleidograph; Sonnet Sequences; Bit O' Verse; Kansas City Poetry Mag.; Colo. Qtly.; Poetry Arkansia; Ark. State Mag., etc.; (anthol.) Golden Quill Anthology. Honours: Ark. Authors, Composers Annual awards, 1949, '55, '62; Poets Round-table, 1946; Country Voices, 1946; Poetry Day awards, 1953, '55, '58, '65; Fine Arts Festival of Ark. Fed. Clubs, 1957; State Fest. of Arts, 1965; Ark. Writer's Conf. awards for Sonnet, 1948, Dresbach Mem., 1967, Cinquain, 1968. Address: 1109 Weible, Pocahontas, Ark, 72455, USA.

HEFFERNA ff, Michael, b. 20 Dec. 1942. College Professor. Education: B.A., Univ. of Detroit, 1964; M.A., Univ. of Mass., 1967; Ph.D., ibid, 1970; Woodrow Wilson Scholar, 1964. Positions held: Instr. in Engl., Oakland Univ., Rochester, Mich., 1967-69; Asst. Prof., Engl., Kansas State Coll., Pittsburg, 1969–; Poetry Ed., The Midwest Qtly., 1970–. Published works: Booking Passage, 1973. Contbr. to: The Ark River Review (Wichita); The Chowder Review; Counter/Measures; Epoch; The Mass. Review; The New Newspaper of Wichita; Poetry (Chicago); Quabbin; Quixote; Shenandoah; Three Rivers Poetry Jrnl.; Voyages; Heartland: Poets of the Midwest, 2nd ed., 1975 (anthol.) Address: 401 W. Jefferson, Pittsburg, KS 66762, U.S.A.

HEFFERNAN, Thomas (Carroll, Jr.), b. 19 Aug. 1939. Teacher; Editor. Education: B.A., Boston Coll., 1961; M.A., Univ. of Manchester, U.K., 1963; Universitá per Stranieri, Perugia. Married Nancy Iler. Positions held: at Univ. of Manchester, 1964-65; Univ. of Bristol, 1965-66; Univ. of Hartford, 1967-70; N.C. State Univ., 1971-73; Poetry Cons., Tchr. in the 'Poetry in the Schls.' Prog., & Ed., N.C. Dept. of Public Instrn., Raleigh, N.C., 1973–; Poetry Sect., Vineyard Writers' Workshop, 1973–. Memberships: Mod. Lang. Assn.; The Renaissance Soc. of Am.; N.C. Poetry Soc.; New England Poetry Club; Poetry Soc. of Va. Published

works: Scenes from an Age, 1974. Ed., The Looseleaf Anthol., 1973–. Contbr. to: Botolphian; Stylus; Manchester Poetry 65; Southern Poetry Review; The Whole Thing; Saint Andrew's Review; The Vineyard Gazette. Honours, awards: Hon. Prize for Poetry awarded by the editors of The Whole Thing, 1973; The Dillard Award given for best poem read at Lynchburg Poetry Fest., Poetry Soc. of Va., 1973, etc. Address: 39 Range Rd., Boston, MA 02124, & 1020 Peace St., Raleigh, NC 27605, U.S.A.

HEGGELUND, Kjell, b. 16 Dec. 1932. Lecturer at the University of Oslo; Editor of Vinduet, 1970-74. Published works: Reisekretser, 1966; I min tid, 1967; Punkt.8, 1968. Contbr. to: Dagbladet; Vinduet; Profil. Honours, awards: Nygaards legat, Dagblad-prisen, 1968. Address: 1420 Svartskog, Norway.

HEIMBINDER, Barney A., b. 22 Jul. 1894. Printer and Publisher Bookkeeping Forms. Education: Public Schools, NYC. Married, Betty Lipstock; 2 children. Positions held: Served in U.S. Air Service, 1917-19; Pres., Redi-Record Payroll Systems, NYC and Valley Stream, NY. Memberships: Poetry Soc. of America (Reporter); Internat. Mark Twain Soc.; Eugene Field Soc.; American Polar Soc. Published work: White Conquest, An Epic of Antarctica, 1934. Contbr. to: (poems) Saturday Eve. Post; Voices; Poetry Qtly.; Interludies; NY Times, and various poetry anthols; (reviews) Times Lit. Supp.; Brooklyn Times; Poetry World; Berkeley Record; Wings, etc. Address: 501 Blue Heron Dr., Apt. 118–A, Hallandale, FL 33009, USA.

HEINBERG, Paul, b. 25 Aug. 1924. Prof. of Communication. Education: B.S., Columbia Univ., 1949; M.A., Tchrs. Coll., Columbia Univ., 1950; Ph.D., Univ. of Iowa, 1956. Married, 1 d. Positions held: Bomber Pilot, ETO, 1941-47; Instr., Speech & Drama, Tex. Women's Univ., 1950-52; Asst. Prof. of Speech, Okla. State Univ., 1952-57; Asst. Prof. of Speech & Dramatic Art, Univ. of Iowa, 1957-65; Assoc. Prof. & Prof. of Communication, Univ. of Hawaii, 1965–. Honours, Awards: 1st Prize, for play in dramatic verse, Calif. Olympiad of the Arts, 1964. Address: Dept. of Communication, 2560 Campus Rd., Rm. 131, Univ. of Hawaii, Honolulu, Hawaii 96822, USA.

HEISE, Hans-Jürgen, b. 6 July 1930. Employee of the Institute for World Economy at Kiel University. Married Annemarie Zornack. Positions held: Mbr., Editl. Comm., 'Sonntag', East Berlin; Reader in the Archives at the Inst. for World Econ., Kiel. Memberships: PEN (W. German Ctr.), 1972–. Published works incl: Poesie (Bilingual Italian-German selection of Heise poems), 1967; Ein bewohnbares Haus, Poems, 1968; Uhrenvergleich, Poems, 1971; Drehtür, Parables, 1972; Underseas Possessions, Selected Poems, 1972; Besitzungen in Untersee, Poems, 1973; Das Profil unter der Maske, Essays on Poetry & Painting, 1974. Contbr. to: (Germany) Die Neue Zeitung; Akzente; Humboldt; Merkur; Neue Deutsche Hefte; Neue Rundschau; Frankfurter Allgemeine, etc.; (U.K./U.S.A.) Stand; Lines Review; Oasis; Dimension; (Italy) Persona; Il Caffè; (Czechoslovakia) Svetová Literatura; (Norway) Vinduet; (Switz.) Die Tat; Spektrum. Honours, awards: Hon. Gift of the Andreas Gryphius Prize, 1973; Kiel Culture Prize, 1974. Address: Moltkestrasse 50A, 23 Kiel 1, German Fed. Repub.

HELLER, Michael David, b. 11 May 1937. Poet; Writer. Education: B.S. in Engrng., Rennselaer Polytechnic Inst.; course in philos., N.Y. Univ. Married, 1 child. Positions held: Chief Technical Writer, Norelco, 1963-65; Freelance Writer, 1965-67; Instr., N.Y. Univ., 1967–. Memberships: PEN; Poets & Writers. Published works: Accidental Center, 1972; Two Poems, 1970. Contbr. to: The Paris Review; The Nation; Chelsea; Sumac; Caterpillar; Extensions; Equal Time; The Park; The Young Am. Writers, 1967; Inside Outer Space, 1970; Open Poetry, 1973; Caterpillar Anthol., 1971, etc. Recip., Coffey Poetry Prize, New Schl. for Soc. Rsch., 1964. Address: P.O. Box 981, Stuyvesant Stn.,

N.Y., NY 10009, U.S.A.

HELLYER, Jill, b. 17 Apr. 1925. Writer. Education: Matric., N. Sydney Girls High Schl., Australia. Positions held: Exec. Sec., Australian Soc. of Authors, 1963-71. Member of Poetry Soc. of Australia. Author of The Exile, 1969. Contbr. to: Meanjin; Southerly; Westerly; Poetry Magazine; The Australian; Sydney Morning Herald; The Age; Overland: 20th Century. Honours: Grenfell Henry Lawson Award, 1963; Poetry Magazine Award, 1965. Address: 12 Yirra Rd., Mt. Colah, NSW, Australia 2079.

HELWIG, David Gordon, b. 5 Apr. 1938. University Lecturer. Education: Univ. of Toronto.; Univ. of Liverpool. Married w. 2 children. Positions held: Asst. Professor of English, Queen's Univ., Kingston, Ont. Published works: Figures in a Landscape, 1968; The Sign of the Gunman, 1969; The Streets of Summer (stories), 1969. Contbr. to: Quarry; Canadian Forum; Tamarack Review. Address: 73 Baiden Street, Kingston, Ont., Canada.

HEMPHILL, George, b. 15 May 1922. Professor of English. Education: A.B., Kenyon Coll., 1947; M.A., Univ. of Minn., 1948; Ph.D., ibid, 1954. Positions held: Instr. of Engl., Univ. of Conn., 1954-60; Asst. Prof., ibid, 1960-65; Assoc. Prof., 1965-69; Prof., 1969-. Chmn., Prosody Sect., MLA, 1962. Contbr. to: Fine Arts Magazine; Hika; Kenyon Review; Occum Ridge Review; Penny Paper; Perspective; Prairie Schooner; Shenandoah; Western Review; Yale Review. Address: Old Canterbury Rd., Hampton, Conn. 06247, USA.

HENDERSON, Archibald, b. 20 Dec. 1916. Professor of English. Education: A.B., Univ. of N.C., 1937; M.A., ibid, 1941; Ph.D., Columbia Univ., 1954. Married Helen White, 2 sons. Positions held: Engl. Instr., Auburn Univ., Ala., 1948-49 & Newcomb Coll., Tulane Univ., New Orleans, La., 1949-54; Asst. Prof., Engl., Univ. of Houston, 1954; Assoc. Prof., ibid, 1957; Prof., 1962-. Memberships: V.P., Houston Chapt, Poetry Soc. of Tex., 1961-63; Councillor, 1962-; Poetry Soc. of Am., 1964-. Published works: Omphale's Wheel, 1966; The Puzzled Picture, 1971. Contbr. to num. jrnls., mags., reviews. Recip., sev. Poetry Soc. of Tex. awards in annual competitions. Address: 8003 High Meadow, Houston, TX 77042, U.S.A.

HENDERSON, Bert, b. 8 Nov. 1908. Educator; Writer. Education: State Tchr. Coll., Troy, Ala.; Univ. of Ala. Positions held: H.S. Principal, & var. hotel work. Memberships: Poetry Soc. of Am.; Ala. Writers' Conclave; Poetry Soc. of Ala.; United Poets Laureate Int.; Writers' Guild. Published works: House of Paradoxes, 1941; Bright Armor, 1950; Blame Noah, 1953; Eternal Symphony, 1956; The Immortal Legions, 1966; The Ultimate Harvest, 1973. Contbr. to: The N.Y. Times; Am. Mercury; Southern Lit. Messenger; num. mags., etc. Edited poetry column for 3 yrs. Honours, awards: Int. Award, Poets Laureate Int. for book 'Immortal Legions'; Hon. Litt.D., Great China Arts Coll., World Univ. & Univ. of Asia; Poet Laureate of Ala., 1956-; Dip. of Merit, from Pres. of Poets Laureate Int.; num. prizes from Poetry Soc. of Ala. Address: 3938 Narrow Lane Rd., Montgomery, AL 36111, U.S.A.

HENDERSON, David, b. 1942. Actor; Fiction Writer; Poet. Education: Studied Writing, New Schl. of Social Research & Hunter Coll., NYC. Positions held: Ed., Umbra mag., N.Y.; Formerly poet-in-Residence, Free Southern Theatre. Member, Teacher's & Writer's Collaborative, Columbia Univ., N.Y. Published works: Felix of the Silent Forest, 1967. Contbr. to (Anthologies): New Negro Poets USA, 1964; Black Fire, 1968; New Black Poetry, 1969. (Jrnls.): 7th Street Quarterly; East Village Other; Umbra.

HENDERSON, Hamish, b. 11 Nov. 1919. Lecturer & Research Fellow. Education: Dulwich Coll., London; M.A., Downing Coll., Cambridge. Married w. 2 daughters. Positions held: Lecturer & Research Fellow, Schl. of Scottish Studies, Edinburgh Univ. Published works: Elegies for the Dead in Cyrenaica,

1948; Freedom Come-All-Ye (Chapbook), 1967; Ed., Ballads of World War II (Folksong collection), 1947. Contbr. to (Anthologies): Chatto Book of Modern Poetry, 1956; Poetry of War, 1965; Oxford Book of Scottish Verse, 1966; Modern Folk Ballads, 1966. Recip., Somerset Maughan Award, 1949.

HENDERSON, Mildred Inez (Rowan), pen name **HENDERSON, Mildred Rowan,** b. 28 Mar. 1918. Housewife. Education: Miss. Gulf Coast Jr. Coll., 1965-67. Married Niemann J. Henderson, 3 sons, 1 daughter. Positions held: Welder in Shipyard, 1944; Spinner in textile mill, 1947-50; Saleswoman, department store, 1955-60; w. Circulation Dept. of newspaper from 1963-66 & '69-70. Memberships: Sec., 1970-71, Pub.Chmn., 1971-72, Pres., 1972-73, Writers Unlimited, 1969-. Contbr. to: The Advance Monticellonian, Ark.; Legend, Westland, Mich.; Poet, Madras, India. Honours, awards: 3rd Narrative Poetry, Mid-South Poetry Fest., Memphis, Tn., 1972; Hon. Mention, Kenneth Lawrence Beaudoin Gemstone Award, 1970 & '72. Address: 907 Canal St., Pascagoula, MS 39567, U.S.A.

HENDERSON, Philip Prichard, b. 17 Feb. 1906. Author. Education: Bradfield Coll., UK. Married, 2 sons. Positions held: Co-Editor, British Book News, 1943-1946; Editor, Feature Articles, British Council, 1958-1963. Published works: First Poems, 1930; A Wind in the Sand, 1932. Contbr. to: Twentieth Cent. Poetry; Poems of Tomorrow; An Anthol. of Free Verse; The Poetry of Railways; Chorus: An Anthol. of Bird Poems; The Listener; Spectator; New Statesman; Poetry Review; The London Aphrodite; A Review of Engl. Literature; Twentieth Century; Art Qtly., etc. Address: 25 Christchurch Hill, London NW3, UK.

HENDERSON SMITH, Stephen Lane, b. 25 May 1919. Medical Practitioner. Education: Oxford Univ., U.K., 1937-42. Married with 5 children. Positions held: Medical Missionary, China, 1943-51 & The Congo, 1951-54; Huddersfield Gen. Prac., 1956-. Memberships: Treas., Yorks. Poets' Assn.; Poetry Soc.; Pennine Poets. Published works: Four Minutes, 1967; Snow Children, 1968; Beyond the City, 1971; Intimations, 1972. Contbr. to: Outposts; Envoi; Poetry East-West; Orbis; Expression One; Scrip; New Headland; Ludds Mill; Dalesman; Yorkshire Ridings; Pennine Platform; Lines. Honours, awards: 1st Prize, Wharfdale Comp., 1971 & 1st Prize, 1973; 1st Prize, Sunderland, 1970, 71 & 72. Address: Portland House, Lindley, Huddersfield HD3 4AL, U.K.

HENDRICKSON, Carol Follmuth, b. 8 Sept. 1920. Teacher. Education: Mason City Junior College; Univ. of Northern Iowa. Married Allen S. Hendrickson, 3 children. Positions held: served as Judge for H.S. & Grade schl. contest of Iowa Poetry Assn.; conducted Clinic & contests for Midwest Chaparral (Iowa Div.) Has appeared on panels & programs of poetry grps. Memberships: Am. Poetry League; United Amateur Press Assn.; Iowa Poetry Day Assn.; Iowa Poetry Assn.; Midwest Chaparral; North Iowa Writers. Published works: Bent Grass, 1967; One Hand Clapping, 1973; co-author, Song, 'Look Up Weary World', 1968 & co-publsr., paper, 'North Iowa Scribes', 1952-53. Contbr. to Candor; Midwest Chaparral; Am. Bard; Am. Courier; From Sea to Sea in Song Anthol.; Avalon Anthol., etc. Recip. num. poetry awards from Iowa Poetry Day Assn. & other poetry socs. Address: 118 21st St. S.E., Mason City, IA 50401, U.S.A.

HENDRIKS, Michel Arthur Lemière, pen name **HENDRIKS, A.L.,** b. 17 Apr. 1922. Writer. Education: Jamaica Coll.; Ottershaw Coll., U.K. Married Gisela Schiffer, 1 son, 4 daughters. Positions held: Asst. Mng. Dir., Arthur Hendriks Furniture Co. Ltd., 1940-50; Sales Mgr., Radio Jamaica Ltd., 1950-60; Gen. Mgr., Jamaica Broadcasting Corp., 1961-64; Exec. Dir. (Caribbean), Thomson Television Ltd., 1964-71; Freelance Writer, 1971-. Memberships: Past Pres., Int. PEN (Jamaica Ctr.); Past Chmn., Arts Coun. of Jamaica. Published works: On This Mountain, 1965;

These Green Islands, 1971; Muet, 1971. Contbr. to: Anglo-Welsh Review; Bim; Caret; Here Now; Honest Ulsterman; Christian Sci. Monitor; London Mag.; Phoenix; Outposts; New Headland; Workshop; Sunday Gleaner, etc. Address: Box 1360, Hamilton, Bermuda.

HENKES, Paul, b. 21 June 1898. Honorary Director of the Pedagogical Institute. Education: Univs. of Munich, Paris, Strasbourg, Montpellier, Bonn; D.ph. & lit. Married. Positions held: Prof.; Chmn. of the delegation of Luxembourg to the Cultural Treaty: The Netherlands-Luxembourg. Memberships: Chmn. of the Sect. Arts & Letters of the Institut Grand-Ducal; Chambre Syndicale des Arts et des Lettres. Published works: Olbaum und Schlehdorn, 1968; Das Bernsteinhorn, 1973. Contbr. to: Les Cahiers Luxembourgeois; Arts & Letters, Inst. Grand-Ducal, etc. Recip., Lit. Prize of the Govt. of Luxembourg, 1966. Address: 12 rue d'Orval, Luxembourg City, Grand Duchy of Luxembourg.

HENMARK, Kai, b. 23 Feb. 1932. Author & Critic. Education: M.A., Stockholm Univ., 1956. Positions held: Ed., Liberal monthly; Prog. Asst., BBC Swedish Broadcasting, 1956-57; work for Swedish radio & TV. Memberships: Swedish Soc. of Authors; Swedish PEN; Lyrikklubben; Förfallarförlaget (The Writers' Own Publishing Co.). Published works: Dikter i London, 1960; Säj farväl till de döda, 1961; Spott i ditt öga, 1963; Svenska Lyriker, 1963; I somnarens saliga dagar, 1966; Sangerna fran bergen, 1966; O min stackars buffel, 1967. Contbr. to: BLM; Ord och Bild; Tidskrift; Var Lösen; Lyrikvännen; Upptakt; Horisont, etc. Honours, awards: Gunnar Josephsons – stipendiet, 1972; Stipendietillägg (Författarfonden), 1972; Boklotteriet, 1962, 1967; Stockholms Stads Kulturst; pendium, 1965, 69. Address: Pokalvägen 3, S-11740, Stockholm, Sweden.

HENN, Thomas Rice, b. 10 Nov. 1901. University Teacher. Education: St. Catharine's Coll., Cambridge Univ., U.K., 1920-24. Positions held: War Service, 1939-45 (released 1945 as Brigadier, Gen. Staff, served in France, Italy, Middle East, etc.); Fellow, Praelector, Tutor, Sr. Tutor, Pres., St. Catharine's Coll., Cambridge Univ.; Univ. Lectr. in Engl., 1926-65; Rdr. in Anglo-Irish Lit., 1965-69; Chmn. of var. bodies inclng. Fac. Bd. of English, Fac. Bd. Architecture & Fine Arts. Memberships: Fellow, Royal Soc. of Lit.; Irish Acad. of Letters; Exec. Comm., Int. Assn. for the Study of Anglo-Irish Lit.; The English Assn. Published works: Selected Poems, 1958; Shoohing a Bat & Other Poems, 1964; Last Poems, in preparation; also 13 books. Contbr. to periodicals, etc. Honours, awards: CBE (Mil.); U.S. Legion of Merit (Mil.); Hon. Litt.D.; Hon. LL.D.; Seatonian Prize, Univ. of Cambridge, 1957, 63, 73. Address: 32 Millington Rd., Cambridge, U.K.

HENNING, Jean Maxine Oliver, b. 18 June 1918. Housewife; Teacher; Writer; Poet. Education: N. Central Coll., Naperville, Ill.; B.A., ibid. Married Harold W. Henning. Positions held: Sec., Norfolk Naval Base, 1942-43; Sec., British Consulate, 1943-44; Tchr., Norfolk Naval Base, 1944-45; Sec., Sears Roebuck, Chicago, Ill., 1946-47; Tchr., Chicago Schls., 1947-48; Tchr., Naperville, Ill., 1948-50. Memberships: Poets & Patrons, Chicago, Ill.; Off Campus Writers, Winnetka, Ill.; Childrens Reading Round Table, Chicago, Ill.; Avalon World Arts Acad.; Nat. League Am. Pen Women (Chicago Br.) Published works: Six Days to Swim (childrens biog.) Contbr. to: Child Life; Cyclotron; Cyclo-Flame; Bitterroot; Purring In A Pocket; Voices; Encounter; Nursery Days; Expressions. Honours, Awards: 1st pl., Ill. Fed. of Women's Clubs Writing Contest, 1968, 69; 2nd pl., poetry, Deep South Writers & Artists Contest, 1969 & 70. Address: Walnut Woods, Naperville, IL 60540, U.S.A.

HENRI, Adrian Maurice, b. 10 Apr. 1932. Lecturer, Writer, Vocalist. Education: B.A., Fine Art (Dunelm), King's Coll., Durham Univ., UK, 1955. Positions held:

Part-time Lectr., Manchester Coll. of Art & Design, 1964; Lectr., Liverpool Coll. of Art, 1964-68; Writer/Vocalist, with Liverpool Scene, a poetry & pop music group. Published works: The Liverpool Scene, 1967; The Mersey Sound, 1967; Tonight at Noon, 1968, USA, 1969; City, 1969; Autobiography: Poems, 1971. Contbr. to: Love Love Love, 1967; Holding Your Eight Hands, 1969; Pengium Modern Poets, No. 10. LP Gramophone Records: The Incredible New Liverpool Scene, 1967; Amazing Adventures of . . . 1968; Bread on the Night, 1969; (play) I Wonder, 1968. Address: 64 Canning St., Liverpool 8, UK.

HENRY, Fernand D.G.G., Pen name **DU GIVNA, Henry,** b. 18 May 1909. Electrician. Education: Accountancy Diploma. Memberships: S.A.B.A.M. (Société belge des droits d'Auteurs; Les Ecrivains Wallons, Brussels; Les Auteurs Wallons, Liège; Les Diciples de Jules Claskin, Liège; Société Littéraire et Culturelle (Le Cwerneu), etc. Contbr. to: Journal, La Meuse; Le Monde du Travail; Journal des Combattants; Journal des Invalides du Travail et de la Paix; Les Annuaires des Sociétés Littéraires; Falaises; L'Univers de la Poésie; Prométhée; de Fil en Aiguille. Honours, awards: Prix Joseph Durbuy, 1962; Prix des Auteurs Wallons, 1963, '65, '67, '69, '72; Societe Royale Ecrivains Wallons, & Les Diciples de Jules Claskin, 1968. Address: 57 Grand-Route, 4142 Ombret-Rausa, Prov. De Liege, Belgium.

HEPPENSTALL, (John) Rayner, b. 27 July 1911. Free-lance Writer. Education: Univ. of Leeds; B.A. (Hons., Modern Langs.), Univ. of Strasbourg, France. Married Margaret Harwood Edwards, 1 son, 1 daughter. Positions held: Schl. Tchr., 1934; Free-lance Writer, 1935-40; Served w. British Fores, 1940-45; Feature Writer, Producer, BBC, 1945-67; Free-lance Writer, 1967-. Published works (Novels): The Blaze of Noon, 1939; Saturnine, 1943 (revised as, The Greater Infortune, 1960); The Lesser Infortune, 1953; The Connecting Door, 1962; The Woodshed, 1962; The Shearers, 1969; (Verse): First Poems, 1935; Sebastian, 1937; Blind Men's Flowers are Green, 1940; Poems 1933-45, 1947; (Other): The Fourfold Tradition, 1961; The Intellectual Part, 1963; Portrait of the Artist as a Professional Man, 1969. Contbr. to (Anthologies): Penguin Book of Contemporary Verse, 1950; Faber Book of Twentieth Century Verse, 1965. Recip., Arts Council Prize, 1966. Address: 14c Ladbroke Terrace, London, W.11, UK.

HERBERT, Cecil, L., b. 1926. Poet. Educated in Trinidad. Contbr. to (Anthologies): Young Commonwealth Poets '65, 1965; Caribbean Voices, 1966; Caribbean Verse, 1967.

HERBERT, Moss, b. 21 Mar. 1914. Journalist. Education: Columbia Univ. Positions held: Feature Writer, newspapers, news service, magazines; Sports Ed. & Columnist, Los Angeles Examiner; Asst. Sports Ed. & Columnist, Los Angeles Herald-Examiner; TV Editor & Columnist, ibid. Memberships: Poetry Soc. of Am.; Int. Poetry Soc.; Los Angeles Press Club. Contbr. to: The Various Light, anthol. of modern poetry, 1964; The Golden Year Anthol., 1960; Int. Poetry Soc. Anthol., 1974; Lyric; Ariz. Qtly.; Coastlives; Am. Poet; Best Short Stories, 1952, '60, '61, '62, '64, '65, '66, '67. Holograph of poem in N.Y. Public Lib. Coll. Address: 1909 N. Normandoe, Los Angeles, CA 90027, U.S.A.

HEREFORD, Eula Frances, pen name **HEREFORD, Eula Shaw,** b. 4 Feb. 1900. Housewife; Part time Writer & Artist. Education: 10 yrs. in frontier 'One Room' country schl.; Tex. A. & I., 1 semester; corres. course in creative writing, The N.Y. Schl. of Writing, U.S.A. Widow. Memberships: Poetry Soc. of Tex. & its affiliate Acad. of Am. Poets; Fellow, IPS. Contbr. to: Land Mag.; Progressive Farmer; Rawls Inquirer; Blue Quail Column; Cycle-Flame Mag.; Singing Winds, etc. Honours, awards: First Prize & Critic's Award, Poetry Soc. of Tex. Contest, 1971; placed in num. poetry contests. Address: Box 261, Junction, TX 76849, U.S.A.

HERING, Helen D., b. 19 Mar. 1921. Merchant (partner in Clothing Store). Education: Grad. Marathon County Normal Sch.; Shepherd Sch. course in contesting and creative writing. Radio Singer, with sister, for 7 yrs., contest hobbyist, winner of many prizes; School teacher 5 yrs.; cashier bookkeeper, Employers Ins. Co., 7 yrs., etc. Memberships incl.: Wisconsin Reg. Writers Assoc. (vice-pres.); Wisconsin Fellowship of Poets; Council of Wisconsin Writers; Wausau Writers Club (Pres., Vice-Pres., Sec., Treas.). Editor, Rib Mountain Echoes (Anthol.), vol. 1, 1963, vol. 2, 1967; Poems Out of Wisconsin 111, WFOP Anthol. Contbr. to: Madison Capitol Times; Ideals; Milwaukee Journal; War Cry; St. Paul Pioneer Press; Grit; Birnamwood News; Lutheran Digest; Gwiazda Polarna; Granite Lutheran; Appleton Post Crescent; Melody of the Muse; Wisconsin History in Poetry. Awards incl.: 3rd prize, Wisconsin Reg. Writers Assoc. Ann. Jade Ring Contest, 1971; 2nd prize, Wisconsin Fellowship of Poets Semi-Annual Contest, 1967. Address: 521 Grant St., Wausau, WI 54401, USA.

HERMAN, Anne Elizabeth, pen name HERMAN, Betty, b. in London, UK. Housewife; Poet; Writer. Married; 8 s., 2 d. Memberships: Publicity, Ladies Sewing Circle Club, Rangely, Colo.; Historian, Angora Club, Rangely; Sec., Publicity, Chairman, Rangely Garden Club; Poetry Soc. of Denver, Colo., 1959-73; Special Mbr., Colo. Mothers' Comm., Denver, 1949-73; Outstanding Mother, 1949, '50, '51; Past Pres., Charter Mbr., Post 4663, Clifton Auxiliary, Clifton, Colo.; Le Petit Chapeau Passe, Grand Mesa Salon No. 343, Grand Junction, Colo.; Past Pres., Grand Junction, Women's Christian Temperance Union; ibid, 2nd Dist., WCTU of Colo.; Palisade Christian Church, 1939; Past Pres., Lincoln Post 50, Am. Legion Aux., Palisade, Colo.; Publicity Sec., Ladies Sewing Circle Club, Rangely & Angvia Club; Histn., Rangely Garden Club; Reporter, Rangely Mus. Soc. of Colo.; Rio Blanco Hist. Soc. of Colo., Meckner. Contbr. to: (anthols.) Of America We Sing, 1944; My Favorite Poems, 1944; Poetry Digest Anthol., 1945; Poetry Broadcast, 1946; Songs of the Free, 1947; Golden Harvest, 1971. (jrnls.) Rangely Times; WCTU Messenger, Boulder, Colo.; Auxiliary News; Denver Post; The Meeker Herald, The Colorado Columbine; Colorado West, etc. Honours: Prize for poem, Nat. Am. Legion Auxil., 1967; Poem for Hawaii, presented on scroll to Gvnr. Wm. F. Quinn, 1961; Poetry Soc. of Colorado, 1967 (Hon. Mention); Cert. of Merit, IWWP; Citation (1973), American Mother's Nat. Chapel. Address: P.O. Box 716, Rangely, CO 81648, USA.

HERMAN, Gordon Lee, b. 31 May 1931. Poet; Writer. Education: B.S., Ore. Coll., 1957; studied poetry at Univs. of Chicago & Washington. Married Violatte Grace Cheatham. Positions held: US Mil. Serv. Memberships: Poetry Soc. of Am.; Alpha Psi Omega; Theta Delta Phi. Published works: Night of Moons, 1967; Une Apdogie Pour la Guerre, 1966. Contbr. to num. jrnls., mags. especially the Industrial Worker organ of the Industrial Workers of the World. Address: Box 85, R.F.D.10, Spokane, WA 99204, U.S.A.

HERMAN, Ira H., pen name KORNEDEPLOV, Mitya, b. 13 June 1948. Novelist; Poet. Education: Univ. of Ky., Lexington; Marshall Univ., Huntington, W.Va.; Calif. State Coll., L.A.; UCLA. Published works: Fantasy fiction serial entitled 'Palapagos' in Space & Time mag., 1973-74; short story 'The Theorist', Golden Atom Publs.; var. short stories, essays, novels. Address: 915 W. 4th St., Huntington, WV 25701, U.S.A.

HERNANDEZ CRUZ, Victor, b. 6 Feb. 1949. Poet. Positions held: Guest Lectr., Univ. of Calif., Berkeley, 1969; Taught Creative Writing, San Francisco State Coll., 1969-70; Taught two semesters, Engl. Dept., Herbert H. Lehman Coll., N.Y.C., 1971. Published works: Papo Got His Gun, 1968; Snaps, 1969; Mainland, 1973. Contbr. to: Evergreen Review; Ramparts; The Rican; Black World; Confrontations; Mundus Artium; Umbra; N.Y. Review of Books. Address: P.O. Box 40148, San Francisco, CA 94140, U.S.A.

HERNDON, Brodie Strachan Jr., pen name HERNDON, Brodie, b. 24 Jan. 1901. Writer; Accountant. Education: Va. Commonwealth Univ.; Univ. of Richmond; Univ. of Va. Memberships: Former Pres., Poetry Soc. of Va.; Va. Writers Club; Acad. of Am. Poets; Poetry Soc. of Am. Published works: Time Clocks, 1973. Contbr. to: Saturday Review; Living Poetry; Poets' Chap Book; N.Y. Herald Tribune; The Lyric; Kaleidograph; Christian Science Monitor; Sonnet Sequences; Chicago Tribune Mag.; Voices; Va. Pilot; Am. Weave, etc. Recip. sev. awards, prizes & hons. Address: 4524 W. Seminary Ave., Richmond, VA 23227, U.S.A.

HERRICK, Helen Frost, b. 4 July 1933. Freelance Writer. Education: Schools in Atlanta, Georgia, Oakland & Los Angeles, Port Washington, NY, Chicago, Ill.; Teacher's Diploma in Piano & Guitar; primary training in lit., Palmer Inst. of Authorship. Positions held: Graphic Artist; Photographer; Publicity Writer (Radio-TV); Pianist; Editor & Silkscreen Publisher. Memberships: Vice-Pres., United Amateur Press Assoc. of America; Major Poets; CSSI; Internat. Platform Assoc.; Demming Chamber of Commerce. Published works: Scrapbook Poems, 1969; Of Earth & Spirit. Contbr. many anthols., journals, including: Outstanding Contemporary Poetry; The Birth of Day; The Soul Sings; Memories in Art; Grains of Sand; Yearbook of Modern Poetry; The Rufus; Angel Hour; Friendship Trails; Gato Anthol. Mag.; Singing Desert; Orphic Lute; Poetry Parade, Welcoming Door, etc. Honours, awards: numerous, including Writer of the Year Award from Nampa, Idaho, 1972; D.D. (h.c.) for "An Essay Against Reason", UCB., Calif., 1973. Address: P.O. Box 149, Portland, OR 97207, USA.

HERSCGBERGER, Ruth Margaret, b. 30 Jan. 1917. Poet; Playwright. Education: Univ. of Chgo.; Black Mountain Coll., N.C.; Univ. of Mich., Ann Arbor; Dramatic Workshop, New Schl. of Social Research, N.Y. Published works: A Way of Happening; (Plays): Adam's Rib; Edgar Allan Poe; A Ferocious Incident; Andrew Jackson. Contbr. to (Anthologies): A Little Treasury of American Poetry, 1948; 100 Modern Poems, 1949; A Little Treasury of Love Poems, 1950; A Little Treasury of Modern Poetry, 1950; Palgrave's Golden Treasury, 1953. Honours: Hopwood Award, 1941; Harriet Monroe Memorial Prize, 1953.

HERSCHEL, Sandi, b. 12 June 1933. Executive Sec. in psychiatric clinic. Education: HS grad., Erasmus Hall. Former member, Poetry Soc. of America. Contbr. to: Imprints Qtly.; New England Review; Cardinal Poetry Qtly.; Essence; Sclmltar & Song; Portal; Robin; American Bard; Laurel Rev.; Hartford Courant; The Symbolist; Ghost Dance; Sunday Denver Post; College English; Wisconsin Review; Painted Poetry Appreciation; Fine Arts Discovery; Voices Intl.; Folio; Hellcoal; Patterns; Quartet; Antigonish Rev.; Scopcraeft; Twigs; Wind; Shore Rev.; The Windless Orchard; Beyond Baroque; Sierra; Mustang Rev.; Sunstone Rev.; Major Poets; Gallery Series; The Second Coming; Hyperion; Junction; So. Carolina Rev.; Forum; Texas Qtly.; San Francisco, etc. Awards: Best Lyric Poem in Imprints Qtly., 1969; 2nd Place Award, Kentucky State Poetry Soc. Contest, 1970; Hon. Mention, NY Poetry Forum Contest; 3rd Place Award, Kentucky State Poetry Contest, 1971. Address: 295 West 11th St., New York, NY, 10014, USA.

HERSHON, Robert, b. 28 May 1936. Editor; Writer. Married Michaeleen, 2 children. Positions held: Co-Editor, Hanging Loose mag., 1966–. Published works: Swans Loving Bears Burning the Melting Deer, 1967; Atlantic Avenue, 1970; 4-Telling (w. others), 1971; Little Red Wagon Painted Blue, 1972; Grocery Lists, 1972. Contbr. to: Chicago Review; The Nation; Poetry Northwest; New Am. & Canadian Poetry; Minn. Review; Mass. Review; Hearse; Hierophant; Epoch; 31 New Am. Poets; Where Is Vietnam? Tri-Quarterly; New Letters; Antioch Review; Northeast, etc. Honours, awards: Elliot Harley Meml. Prize, Design Conceptualization Inst., 1972; Jarrett-Lourie Fndn., Ortiz y Schreiber Award, 1970. Address: 231 Wyckoff St., Brooklyn, NY 11217, U.S.A.

HERTZ, K(enneth) V(ictor), b. 3 May, 1945. Editor; Advertising Executive. Education: McGill Univ., Montreal. Positions held: Editor & Advertising Executive; Ed., Cataract Mag., Montreal, 1960-63. Published works: The Cracked Cellar, 1963; Poems, 1962-69; The Last Canadian Dreidle Maker (Midstream), Short Story, 1968; Eurethrea (fiction), 1969. Contbr. to (Anthologies): Poetry 64, 1963; English Poetry in Quebec, 1965; (Jrnls.): Canadian Forum; Pris International; Fiddlehead; Queen's Quarterly; Edge. Honours: Canadian Zionist Short Story Award; McGill Daily Fiction Award, 1966; Canada Council Grant, 1968. Address: 5385 Cumberland Ave., Montreal 29, P.Q., Canada.

HERTZ, Mary Cigoj, b. 25 Dec. 1914. Secretary; Housewife. Married, 3 children. Positions held: Sec. for lawyers, retired millionaire, exec. dir. of a home for delinquent girls and, currently, for editors of the Index to Religious Periodical Literature. Memberships: Ill. State Poetry Soc.; Poets & Patrons Club of Chicagoland. Published work: Kaleidoscope, 1970. Contbr. to: Chicagoland's Award-Winning Poetry for 1972, 1973; Kansas City Star; Int. Poetry Review; Sea to Sea in Song 1971; Voices of the Wind; Nat. Fed. of State Poetry Socs. Honours, awards: Poets & Patrons Annual Awards, 1968, '69, '70, '72, '73; World Atlas Book Prize, Writer's Digest. Address: 2700 W. Gregory St., Chicago, IL 60625, U.S.A.

HERTZ, Paweł, b. 29 Oct. 1918. Writer. Memberships: Editl. Bd., Rocznik Literacki; Bd. Mbr., PEN, Polish Ctr.; Union of Polish Writers. Published works: Nocna muzyka, 1935; Szarfa ciemności, 1937; Dwie podróze, 1946; Małe ody i treny, 1949; Nowy lirnik mazowiecki, 1953; Wiersze wybrane, 1955; Pieśni z rynku, 1957; Spiewnik podrózny i domowy, 1969. Contbr. to: Ateneum; Kamena; Kuźnica; Nowiny Literackie; Okolica Poetów; Skamander; Twórczość; Tygodnik Ilustrowany; Wiadomości Literackie; Zycie Literackie (Poznań); Zycie Literackie (Kraków); Tygodnik Powszechny. Honours, awards: Award, Alfred Jurzykowski Fndn., N.Y., 1972; Prize of PEN, Polish Ctr., 1972. Address: Nowy Swiat 33 m. 15, 00–029 Warsaw, Poland.

HERZBERG, Judith Frieda Lina, b. 4 Nov. 1934. Writer. Positions held: Writer for, & in cooperation with, The Dutch Inst. for Theatre Rsch. Memberships: Dutch Writers' Assn.; Rep., Amsterdam Arts Coun.; Mbr. of sev. juries in poetry & theatre. Published works: Zeepost, 1963; Beemdgras, 1968; Vliegen, 1970; Strijklicht, 1971; 27 Liefdesliedjes, 1971. Contbr. to: Handelsblad; Tirade; Hollands Maandblad; Poetry (Chicago); Barbarber; Sanat Dergisi (Turkey); Maatstaf, etc. Address: Vondelstraat 75A, Amsterdam, The Netherlands.

HESELTINE, Nigel, b. 1916. Economist; Political Adviser. Education: B.Sc., Econs., London Univ.; M.A., Trinity Coll., Dublin. Positions held: Farmer in Ireland & Tanzania; Worked for FAO(UN), mainly in Africa, 1950-65; Under-Secretary, Nat. Development & Planning, Zambia, 1965-68; Economic & Financial Adviser to the President of the Repub. Madagascar, 1968–. Published works: Violent Rain, 1938; The Four-Walled Dream, 1941; Fiction: Tales of the Squirearchy, 1949; The Mysterious Pregnancy, 1964; Other: Scarred Background: A Journey Through Alabnia, 1938; From Libyan Sands to Chad, 1959; Remaking Africa, 1961; Madagascar, 1970; Verse Translation: Selected Poems of Dafydd ap Gwilym, 1944. Honours: Chevalier de l'Ordre National Malagasy; Fellow, Royal Geographical Soc. Address: B.P. 3658, Tananarive, Madagascar.

HESELTON, Lette, pen name **BREWER, Jane,** b. 21 Mar. 1916. Writer. Married, 1 son & 1 daughter. Memberships: Yorks. Poets' Assn.; York Poetry Soc.

Published works: Wind in the Barley, 1968. Contbr. to: BBC Northern Drift; Country Life; East Riding Bystander; Intac; Yorkshire Post; Scarborough Evening News; var. anthols. Recip., First Prize, Yorkshire Poets' Assn., 1971. Address: 31 Red Scar Ln., Scarborough YO12 5RH, U.K.

HESKETH, Phoebe, b. 29 Jan. 1909. Writer. Education: Cheltenham Ladies' Coll., U.K. Married, 3 children. Positions held: Freelance articles & scriptwriting for the BBC in the 1940's; Woman's Page Ed., Bolton Evening News; Lectr., Women's Coll., Bolton; on panel, Poets Reading Poems, sponsored by the Arts Coun. Memberships: PEN; Fellow, Royal Soc. of Lit.; Soc. of Authors; London Poetry Secretariate; The Poetry Soc. Publshed works: Lean Forward, Spring! 1948; No Time for Cowards, 1952; Out of the Dark, 1954; Between Wheels & Stars, 1956; The Buttercup Children, 1958; Prayer for Sun, 1966; A Song of Sunlight (to be published shortly). Contbr. to: The Sunday Times; Times Lit. Supplement; The Observer; The New Statesman; The Spectator; The Listener; The Fortnightly Review; The Adelphi; Contemporary Review; Punch; English; The Poetry Review; Country Life; The Countryman; Time & Tide; John o'London's Weekly; Everybody's; Outposts; The Dublin Mag.; The Irish Times; also British Coun. Poetry Recordings, 1967. Recip., Greenwood Prize, The Poetry Soc., 1946 & 63. Address: Fisher House, Rivington, Horwich, Bolton BL6 7SL, Lancs., U.K.

HESLEP, Emma Leota Grider, b. 13 Dec. 1902. Educator. Education: Western Wash. State Coll., 1928; student, Univ. of Wash., 1952. Married, Charles Heslep. Positions held: Tchr., Garden City Schl., Elma, Wash., 1921-24; Prin., ibid, 1924-26, '28-31; Tchr., White Star Schl., Whites, Wash., 1931-36; Prin., ibid, 1936-41; Tchr., McCleary, Wash. Elem. Schl., 1944-57. Memberships: Grays Harbor Co. Bd. of Educ., 1959–; Leader, 4H Club, 1938-42; Committee-woman, Girl Scouts, USA, 1950-53; Leader, 1953-54; Bd. of Dirs., Mark E. Reed Hosp., 1958-60; Trustee, Grays Harbor Co. Lib., 1958-66; Mbr., Wash. Assoc. Co. Bds. Educ.; State Pres., ibid, 1963; Pres., Mark E. Reed Hosp. Aux., 1958-60; PTA; Wash. PTA; VFW Aux.; Past Pres., Daughters Union Vets.; NEA; Nat. Ret. Tchrs. Assoc.; Nat. Writers Club; Past Pres., Delta Kappa Gamma; Past Matron, Order Eastern Star. Published works: column, Truly Yours, McCleary (Wash.) Stimulator (newspaper), 10 yrs. What Manner of Love (poetry). Contbr. to: Sunshine Mag.; Nat. Mag. of Delta Kappa Gamma, 'I Am A Teacher Because'; 'A Town & Its People', 1968; McCleary's Second Growth & Bear Festival, From Timber to 'Tim Bear'. Address: Box 2, McCleary, WA 98557, USA.

HESS, Alice Leona, pen names **HESS, Alice Shoup, SHOUP, Si, MRS. J.M. Hess,** etc., b. 20 Apr. 1922. Homemaker & Freelance Writer. Education: Okla. State Univ.; Tulsa Univ. Positions held: Sunday Schl. Tchr.; sev. offices in Church Women's Soc.; Girl Scout Ldr.; PTA Pres.; Church Sec.; Tulsa Area Corres. for Southern Florist & Nurseryman; Sec.-Treas., Sunday Schl. Class; Children's Ch. Helper; Precinct V. Chmn. Memberships: Pres., Mother's Athletic Club; on Advisory Bd. for a city special election; Chmn., Tues. Writers; Okla. Writers Fed.; Sec., Book Review Club, etc. Contbr. to: Tulsa Tribune, 1954; Encore, 1971; Poetry of Our Times, 1971; Shore Poetry Anthol., 1971; Jean's Jrnl., 1971 & '72; Legend, 1972 & '73; Poet, 1973. Poetry read on Ark. radio stn., 1971 or '72. Honours, awards: 3rd prize, Jean's Jrnl., 1971; Book Award, Okla. Poetry Soc., 1972. Address: 620 Wilson, Sand Springs, OK 74063, U.S.A.

HEWETT, Dorothy Coade (Mrs. Merv Lilley), b. 21 May, 1923. Poet; Author; English Teacher. Education: B.A., Perth Coll., Univ. of Western Australia. Married Merv Lilley, w. 5 children. Positions held: Millworker, 1950-52; Advertising Copywriter, Sydney, 1956-58; Tutor in English, Univ. of Western Australia, 1964–. Published works: What about the People (w. Merv Lilley), 1962; The Hidden Journey, 1967; Late Night Bulletin, 1968; Windmill Country, 1968; Plays: This Old

Man Comes Rolling Home, 1968; Mrs. Porter & The Angel, 1969; Novel: Bobbin Up, 1959; Short Stories: Joey (Aust. Idiom), 1963; The Australians have a word for it, 1964; On the Terrace (Summer Tales Three), 1966; The Wire Fences of Jarrabin (Aliens in Their Land), 1968. Contbr. to (Anthologies): Brave Young Singers, 1938; Australian Poetry, 1946, 64, 68; An Overland Muster, 1965; (Jrnls.): Meanjin; Overland; Westerly; First Hearing; Quality Street; Poetry Australia. Honours: Australian Broadcasting Commission Nat. Poetry Prize, 1945, 65; Tom Collin's Prize for Australian Literature, 1963. Address: 89 Forrest Street, South Perth, 6151, W.A.

HEWITT, Geoff., b. 1 Sept. 1943. University Teacher. Education: B.A., Cornell Univ., Ithaca, N.Y.; John Hopkins Univ., Baltimore, Md.; M.F.A., Univ. of Iowa. Positions held: Formerly Teaching Fellow, John Hopkins Univ; Also taught, Coe Coll., Cedar Rapids, Iowa; Univ. of Iowa; Currently Tchr., Univ. of Hawaii, Honolulu. Published works: Poem & Other Poems, 1966; Waking Up Still Pickled; 1967; Ed., Quickly Aging Here: Some Poets of the 1970's, 1969; Other: Alfred Starr Hamilton: A Few Peoples' Poet (essay in The Trojan Horse), 1964; Introduction to Selected Poems of Alfred Starr Hamilton, 1969. Contbr. to (Anthologies): Best Poems of 1967: The Borestone Mountain Poetry Awards, 1968; (Jrnls.): Epoch; New; Foxfire; Choice. Honours: Acad. of American Poets Prize at Cornell, 1966; Grant from Co-ordinating Council of Literary Mags., for his little mag. of Poetry, Kumquat, 1967. Address: 29 Wayside Place, Montclair, N.J., USA.

HEWITT, John (Harold), b. 28 Oct. 1907. Museum Art Director; Editor. Education: Methodist Coll., Belfast; B.A., Queen's Univ., Belfast, 1930; M.A., ibid, 1951. Married Roberta Black. Positions held: Art Assistant, Deputy Dir., Belfast Museum & Art Gallery, 1930-57; Art Dir., Herbert Gallery & Museum, Coventry, 1957–; Assoc. Ed., Lagan, 1945-46; Ed., Arts in Ulster, 1951; Poetry Ed., Threshold, Belfast, 1957-61. Published works: Conacre, 1943; No Rebel Word, 1948; Tesserae, 1967; Collected Poems, 1932-67, 1968; The Day of the Corncrake, 1969; Ed., The Poems of William Allingham, 1967; Other: Coventry: The Tradition of Change & Continuity, 1966. Contbr. to (Anthologies): Poems of Tomorrow, 1935; 1000 Years of Irish Poetry, 1947; New Poems, 7 vols. from 1952-68; New Poets of Ireland, 1963; Mentor Book of Irish Poetry, 1965; Chorus, 1969; (Jrnls.): Irish Times; Listener. Honours: Fellow of the Museums Assn. Address: 5 Postbridge Rd., Coventry, Warwicks., UK.

HEY, Phillip Henry, b. 7 Apr. 1942. Assistant Professor of English. Education: B.A., Monmouth Coll., 1964; M.F.A., Univ. of Iowa Writers Workshop, 1966; Univ. of Wisconsin, 1968-69. Married. Positions held: Instr., Wisc. State Univ.; Asst. Prof. of Engl., Briar Cliff Coll. Guest Poet & Lectr. at: S.D.S.U. Fine Arts Fest.; Beuna Vista Coll.; Writers in the Schls. Prog., Iowa Arts Coun.; Writers on Tour program, Ill. Arts. Coun. Contbr. to: Young Anr. Poets, 1967; New Poetry Out of Wisconsin, 1968; I Love You All Day It Is That Simple, 1969; Eidolons, 1972; New Voices in American Poetry, 1973; Creamcheese Qtly.; Eclectic Irregular; Micromegas; Metaphrasis; Field; Hearse; Sequoia; Poetry Review; Shenandoah; Wisc. Review; Counterpoint; Arena, etc. Recip., Edwin H. Gardner Award, 1969. Address: 2805 Isabella, Sioux City, IA 51103, U.S.A.

HEYMAN, Jorj, b. 3 Aug. 1949. Poet. Published works: Target Practice, 1971; Ed., Publsr., Circular Causation, 1969, 70. Contbr. to: Raincoast Chronicles; Circular Causation; Blewointmentpress; Tish; Is; Georgia Straight; Capilano Review; Vigilante; This Magazine is for Workingmen; Runcible Spoon; Radio Free Rain Fores; Poem Company; Junk Mail, etc. Recip., Arts Bursary, Canada Coun., 1972. Address: Box 518, Sechelt, B.C., Canada.

HEYWOOD, James Philip, pen name HEYWOOD, Pip, b. 5 June 1951. Education: Bryanston School,

Blandford, Dorset; Marling Grammar School, Stroud, Glos.; Brighton Coll. of Education, 1971-1973. Member of the London Poetry Secretariat. Published work: Some Water Poetry from the Cutty Sark, 1972. Contbr. to: Resurgence; Contrasts; Scrip; Viewpoints. Award: First Prize, Stroud Festival Poetry Competition (Junior), 1969. Address: Viner's Wood, Wickstreet, Stroud, Glos. GL6 7QN, UK.

HEYWOOD, Terence. Education: M.A., Worcester Coll., Oxford Univ., U.K.; Uppsala Univ., Sweden. Memberships: Poetry Soc.; Poetry Workshop; former Mbr., Am. Poetry Soc.; Kent & Sussex Poetry Soc. Published works: approx. 10 poems in 'Background to Sweden', 1951; How Smoke Gets into the Air, 1951; Architectonic, 1954; Facing North (w. Edward Lowbury), 1960. Rep. in following anthols: Little Treasury, Modern Poetry; Oxford Book, S. African Verse; Commonwealth Poetry Today; Workshop Ox Poets, 20th C. Scandinavian Poets; S. African Schools Book/Verse. Contbr. to: Horizon; Encounter; Life & Letters; Outposts; English; New Statesman; Poetry Review; Oxford Mag.; Cambridge Review; New English Weekly; Platform; Poetry Chicago; N.Y. Herald Tribune; Christian Sci. Monitor; Am-Scandinavian Review; Prairie Schooner; Fiddlehead; Vou, Japan; Arena, N.Z.; Sydney Morning Herald, Australia; Splitter, W. Germany, & many more. Recip. var. poetry prizes. Address: 40 Egerton Gdns., London S.W.3, U.K.

HEYWORTH, Clifford, pen name BILL O' BOW'S, b. 25 June 1910. Retired Hotelier. Memberships: Corps Officer & Sec., St. John Ambulance Brigade, 1927-60; Gen. Sec., Lancashire Authors' Assn., 1956-60; Hon. Treas., Bacup Orchestral Soc., 1947-54. Published works: Nobbut a Thought from Lancashire, 1973. Contbr. to: A Rossendale Anthol.; Bacup Miscellany; Nowt so Queer as Others (by Joan Pomfret); Cotton Factory Times; The Rossendale Free Press; The Burnley Star; The Northern Daily Telegraph (now The Evening Telegraph). Recip., Scholes Trophy, Lancs. Authors' Assn., 1946; var. awards as a public speaker from such bodies as Rotary, Knights of Columbus. Address: c/o Mr. & Mrs. Derek Morgan, The Friendly Plaice, 231 Westminster Rd., Morecambe, Lancs. LA3 1EP, U.K.

HICKEY, Madelyn Eastlund, pen name EASTLUND, Madelyn, b. 13 July 1928. Administrative Assistant; Publisher & Editor. Positions held: Freelance Writer, 1959–; Publisher/Ed., Twigs, the mag. of Budding Talent, 1964-61 & Verdure Publs., 1969–; Dir., Long Island Lit. Agency; Instr., Fun with Poetry, Seminars for Armed Forces Writers League, L.I., 1968-72; Instr., Poetry Forms, Hicksville H.S. (Adult Ed.), 1969; Instr., Poetry Appreciation: What is Poetry?, Hicksville H.S., 1970; Instr., Seminars in Poetry, Oyster Bay, N.Y., 1971-72. Literary Column, Lyn's Literary Log, Writer's Exchange Mag., 1961 & Poetry Column, The Triumvate, Stewart Manor Mail, 1964-65. Member of num. poetry orgs. w. offices held in many. Published works: (Juvenile Picture Books co-authored w. Joseph V. Hickey) The Slowpoke Angel, 1970; Star Angels Christmas Tree, 1970; The Calico Cottage, 1969. Rep. in many anthols. inclng: Prairie Poet Anthol., 1965; Fantasia Anthol. of Contemporary Poets, 1966; From Sea to Sea in Song, 1968; Long Island Writers 1969 Anthol., 1969; Dance with Fireflies (haiku), 1970, & others. Contbr. to num. poetry mags., qtly., lit. & little mags., trade jrnls. newspapers. Recip., Trophy for dedicated service, A.F.W.L. Br. 11, 1967. Address: 9010 Tobias, No. 261, Panorama City, CA 91402, U.S.A.

HICKS, Alice, pen name HICKS, Betty Brown, b. 24 Nov. 1914. Homemaker. Education: DePauw Univ., Greencastle, Ind. Married to George W. Hicks, M.D., 1 s., 5 d. Positions held: Reporter, The Evening Star, Auburn, Ind., 1938-1940; Stringer, Fort Wayne, Ind., papers, 1936-1940. Memberships: South and West; The World Poetry Soc.; Poetry Soc. of Tennessee (Associate); Poetry Soc. of Texas; The Grand Bay Writers; formerly Writers Unlimited of Pascagoula,

1967-1973. (Originator of both Writers Unlimited and Grand Bay Writers). Published works: I Sing My Amazement, 1968; Lyrics From Cor Meum, 1969. Contbr. to: South and West; Voices Internat.; The Paper; Poet; Dragonfly; The Muse; Encore; Legend; The Mississippi Review; Yearbook of the Poetry Soc. of Texas. Honours and Awards incl: Moon Award, Poetry Soc. of Texas, 1970; Beaudoin Gemstone Awards, 1970, 1971; Award of Merit, Poetry Soc. of Ariz., 1971; Judge for The Poetry Soc. of Tenn., 1972, 1973; Read at Midsouth Poetry Festival, 1971 and 1973; Read at South and West Poetry Festival at Tulsa, 1972; Work incl. in Mississippi Poets (taped by Poetry Soc. of Tenn.), 1973. Address: P.O. Box 145, Grand Bay, AL 36541, USA.

HICKS, John Calvin, b. 10 Apr. 1902. Retired Highway Design Engineer. Positions held: Drug Clerk, 1923-24; Rural Schl. Tchr., Boone Co., Ark.; Profl. Photo Finisher, 1924-27; Chainman, Rodman, Draftsman, Office Engr., engrng. Auditor, & Design Engr., Ark. State Highway Dept., 1927-68. Memberships: Authors, Composers & Artists Soc. of Ark.; Pres., 2 terms & Sec., 2 terms, ibid; currently Youth Councilor of Jr. Chapt.; World Poetry Soc.; Poets' Roundtable of Ark.; Ozark Writers' Guild. Contbr. to: Poetry Arkansia (anthol.), 1964; Poets' Roundtable of Ark. (anthol.), 1966; Southwest Times Record; Ark. Gazette; North Little Rock Times; Advance Monticellian; Siftings Herald; Courier Index; Piggott Banner; Ark. Highways; Poet India; South & West; Voices Int.; Tulsa Poetry Qtly. & Creative Review, etc. Honours, awards: Lyric 1st pl., Mid-South Poetry Fest., Memphis, 1966; Haiku 3rd pl., Ark. Writers' Conf., Little Rock, 1970 & 1st pl., 1973; Haiku 1st pl., Ark. Poetry Fes., Little Rock, 1970. Address: 14 Fairfield Dr., North Little Rock, AR 72116, U.S.A.

HIDDEN, Norman Frederick. Editor & Publisher. Education: M.A., Brasenose Coll., Oxford Univ.; postgrad. work, Univ. of Mich., U.S.A. Positions held: Sr. Lectr. in Engl., Coll. of All Saints, London, U.K. Memberships: Chmn., Poetry Soc. of G.B. (Nat. Poetry Ctr.), 1968-71; Ed., Workshop New Poetry, 1967-; Fndr. & Dir., Workshop Press, 1970-; Exec. Comm., English Assn., 1968-; Gen. Coun., Nat. Book League, 1970-; Advisory Comm., English Speaking Bd., 1971-. Published works: These Images Claw, 1966; Say It Aloud, 1971; Dr. Kink & His Old Style Boarding Schl., 1973. Co-Ed., Nat. Anthol. of Student Poetry, 1968. Contbr. to: Poetry; Tribune; Outposts; Expression; Manifold; Poetry One; Envoi; Time Out; BBC Third Prog.; Child Educ.; Times Educl. Supplement; The Economist; Poetry Review; New Statesman, etc. Address: 2 Culham Ct., Granville Rd., London N4 4JB, U.K.

HIGGINS, Jean C., b. 27 Jan. 1932. Poet. Education: Charles Morris Price Schl. of Advtng. & Jrnlsm., Phila., Pa., U.S.A. Widow, 2 children. Memberships: Am. Mensa Ltd., Phila. Br.; Nat. Fed. of State Poetry Socs.; Pa. Poetry Soc.; Am. Poets' Fellowship Soc. Published works: Lindy, 1970; Rep. in The Spring Anthol., 1970 & The Clover Collection of Verse, 1969 & 70. Contbr. to var. little mags. Honours, awards: Best Short Poem, Haiku Highlights, 1969; Special Award for Lindy, Am. Poets' Fellowship Soc., 1970; Ariz. State Poetry Soc. Award (2nd Hon. Mention), Nat. Fed. of State Poetry Socs., 1972. Address: 267 Washington Ave., Phoenixville, PA.19460, U.S.A.

HIGGINS, Michael, pen name **MIHANGEL,** b. 17 Jan. 1948. Stock Correlator. Education: Lawrence Pk. Collegiate Inst., Toronto, Canada; private studies, Welsh Lang. (in assn. w. Dewi 'Sant, Toronto). Positions held: Co-Ed., Catalyst (w. Ian Young), 1969-71. Published works: Owlscript, 1971. Contbr. to: Poets of Canada (anthol.), 1969; The Male Muse (anthol.), 1973; Sixty Seven; Cyclops; Eye Opener Poetry Supplement; Canadian Poetry; Rapier; Acta Poetry Supplement; Acta Victoriana; Contemporary Lit. in Translation; The Globe & Mail Mag. Address: The Coopers, 132 Garforth St., Chadderton, nr. Oldham, Lancs. OL9 6RW, U.K.

HIGGINS, Richard Carter, pen name **HIGGINS, Dick,** b. 15 Mar. 1938. Writer & Publisher. Education: Yale Coll., Conn.; Columbia Univ. Schl. of Gen. Studies, N.Y.; Manhattan Schl. of Printing; musical studies w. John Cage, Henry Cowell, etc., 1957-59. Positions held: active in Happenings, 1958-, & Fluxus, 1961-; Fndr., Something Else Press, 1964; develops & names concept of Intermedia, Autumn, 1965; Tchr., Calif. Inst. of the Arts, 1970-71; Fndr., Unpublished Editions, 1973. Published works incl: (books) What Are Legends, 1960; Jefferson's Birthday/Postface, 1964; A Book About Love & War & Death, Canto One, 1965; Towards the 1970's, 1969; A Book About Love & War & Death, Cantos Two & Three, 1969; Pop Architektur (Ed. w. Wolf Vostell), 1969; Die Fabelhafte Getraume Von Taifun-Willi, 1969; Computers for the Arts, 1970; Die Fabelhafte Geträume von Taifun-Willi, 1970; Fantastic Architecture (Ed. e. Wolf Vostell), 1971; The Ladder to the Moon, 1973; For Eugene in Germany, 1973; Spring Game, 1974. var. booklets, graphics, multiples. Films incl: Men & Women & Bells, 1968; Scenario, 1968; Mysteries, 1969; Hank & Mary Without Apologies. Contbr. to many anthols. & mags. Address: P.O. Box 26, West Glover, VT 05875, U.S.A.

HIGGINSON, William J., b. 17 Dec. 1938. Published works: Twenty-Five Pieces of Now, 1968; Itadakimasu, 1971; thistle/brilliant/morning, 1973. Editor, From Here; Former Editor: Haiku Mag. Contbr. to: Byways; Crescent Review; Haiku Highlights; Haiku Mag.; Haiku Spotlight; Haiku West; Janus; Madrona; The Blue Print; The Haiku Anthol.; Modern Haiku, etc. Address: Box 2702, Paterson, NJ 07509, USA.

HIGHAM, Charles, b. 18 Feb. 1931. Poet. Positions held: Bookseller; Publr.'s Asst.; Book Critic, Sydney Morning Herald; Lit. Ed., Bulletin (jrnl.); Regents Prof., Univ. of Calif., USA; Official Histn., Time/Life Hist. of the Am. Films, 1971. Publications: A Distant Star, 1951; Spring and Death, 1953; The Earthbound and Other Poems, 1959; Noonday Country, 1966; The Voyage to Brindisi, 1969. Contbr. to: (anthol.) Modern Australian Verse, 1964; (jrnls.) NY Times; Hudson Review; Yale Review; London Mag.; Menjin Quadrant; North-West Review; Poetry Review; Times Lit. Supplement. Recip. Award, Poetry Soc. 1949. Address: c/o Angus & Robertson Ltd., 221 George St., Sydney, N.S.W., Australia.

HIGO, Aigboje, b. 22 June 1932. Publisher; Writer. Education: St. Andrew's Coll., Oyo, Nigeria; Univ. Coll., Ibadan, Nigeria; Univ. of Leeds, UK. Positions held: Sr. Engl. Master, St. Andrew's Coll., Oyo, Nigeria; Prin., Anglican Grammar Schl., Otuo, Nigeria; Mng. Dir., Heinemann Educ. Books (Nigeria) Ltd. Memberships: Exec. Comm., Mbari Artists & Writers Club, Ibadan, Nigeria. Contbr. to the following anthols. & jrnls: Horn; A Book of African Verse; Penguin Book of African Verse; Transition; Poetry & Audience. Awards: Prof. Mahood Poetry Prize, Univ. of Ibadan, 1958. Address: Heinemann Educational Books (Nigeria) Ltd., PMB 5205, Ibadan, Nigeria.

HILBERRY, Conrad, Arthur, b. 1 Mar. 1928. Teacher. Education: B.A., Oberlin Coll., 1949; Ph.D., Univ. of Wis., 1954. Married Marion Bailey, 1951, 3 daughters. Positions held: Instr.-Asst. Prof., DePauw Univ., 1954-61; Assoc. Prof. – Prof., Kalamazoo Coll., 1962-. Published works: Encounter on Burrows Hill, 1968; Rust, (forthcoming). Contbr. to: Antioch Review; Atlantic Monthly; Beloit Poetry Jrnl.; Carleton Miscellany; Christian Century; College English; Epoch; Field; Hiram Poetry Review; Mad River Review; N.Y. Times; New Yorker; Poem; Poetry Northwest; Saturday Review, etc. Recip., Eugene Saxton Award (Harpers Bros.), 1959 & Chapelbrook Fndn. Fellowship, 1971. Address: c/o Kalamazoo Coll., Kalamazoo, MI 49001, U.S.A.

HILL, Brian, b. May 1896. Publicist. Education: Merchant Taylors' School; Exhibitioner Wadham Coll., Oxford; C.A. (Glasgow). Grandson of George Birkbeck Hill, Johnsonian scholar. Positions held: Chartered Accountant, 1924-1932; Publicity journalist; Asst.

Publicity Manager, Gas Council, 1932-1962. Memberships: Soc. of Authors; Faculty of the History of Medicine and Pharmacy. Published works: Take All Colours, 1943; The Sheltering Tree, 1945; The Drunken Boat (translations Rimbaud), 1952; The Sky Above the Roof (translations Verlaine), 1957; Eight Poems, 1958; Fortune's Fool (translations Nerval), 1959; Gentle Enchanter (translations Gautier), 1960; The Enchanter, 1960; The Trophies (translations Heredia), 1962; Last Poems, 1969; Ganymede in Rome (translations Martial), 1971; An Eye for Ganymede (translations Martial), 1972. Contbr. to: Listener; New Statesman; Punch; Evening Standard; Everybody's Weekly; Country Life; Westminster Gazette; The Lady; Poetry Review; Observer; Ideal Home Mag.; The Gate, also in a number of anthols. Address: 2 Grove Rd., London NW2 5TB, UK.

HILL, Douglas Arthur, b. 6 Apr. 1935. Author. Education: B.A. (Hons.), Univ. of Sask., Canada; grad. schl., Univ. of Toronto, 2 yrs. Married, 1 son. Positions held: Ed., Aldus Books Ltd., London, 1962-64; Freelance Writer, 1964-71; Lit. Ed., Tribune, London, 1971–. Published works: (book) The Tourist (in preparation); over a dozen books of non-fiction prose. Contbr. to: Ambit; Akros; Encounter; Tribune; Poetry Review; BBC Third Prog.; Canadian Forum; Poesie Vivante; Adam Int. Review; Arts in Society; Poetry One; Poetmeat; Young British Poets, 1967; Poetry Dimension I, 1973, etc. Recip., Canada Coun. Arts Grant, 1968. Address: 16 Haslemere Rd., London N.8, U.K.

HILL, Geoffrey, b. 18 June 1932. University Lecturer. Education: Keble Coll., Oxford. Positions held: Lectr., Engl. Lit., Univ. of Leeds. Published works: (Poems), 1952; For the Unfallen, 1959; Preghiere, 1964; Penguin Modern Poets 8, 1966; King Log, 1968. Contbr. to various anthols. Honours, awards: Gregory Award for Poetry, 1961. Address: Leeds, UK.

HILL, Robert White, b. 17 Jan. 1941. University English Teacher. Education: A.B., Univ. of N.C., 1963; M.A., ibid, 1964; Ph.D., Univ. of Ill., 1972. Married Doris Davis, 2 sons. Positions held: Instr. of Engl., Converse Coll., 1964-65 & Clemson Univ., 1965-69; Asst. Prof. of Engl., Clemson Univ., 1971-74; Creator and host, Poetry Today weekly radio prog., S.C. Educl. Radio Network, 1972–. Memberships: MLA; Nat. Coun. of Tchrs. of Engl.; Soc. for the Study of Southern Lit. Published works: James Dickey: A Checklist & James Dickey: Comic Poet, in James Dickey: The Expansive Imagination, 1973; Sylvia Plath, cassette lecture, 1972. Ed., The S.C. Review, 1973–. Book reviews in South Atlantic Bulletin, 1967 & '68. Contbr. to: Red Clay Reader; Poem; Southern Poetry Review; Arlington Qtly.; New Writing in South Carolina, 1970. Recip., Anna Rena Blake Award, Erskine Coll., 1972. Address: c/o Dept. of Engl., Clemson Univ., Clemson, SC 29631, U.S.A.

HILL, Rudolph Nelson, b. 4 Apr. 1903. Lawyer, Judge. Education: B.A., Univ. of Okla., Norman, Okla., 1926. Positions held: Dpty. Ct. Clerk, Seminole Co., Okla.; Country Ct. Reporter, Seminole Co.; Municipal Judge, City of Wewoka, Okla. Memberships: Pres., Poetry Soc. of Okla., 3 terms; Fed. Writers of Okla.; Parliamentarian; United Poets Laureate Int. Publications: Red Ship Wings, 1928; Star of Peace on Trail of Cibola, 1954; Curtain Calls Before Curfew, 1962; Frontiers of Soonerland, 1965; From Country Lanes to Space Age Dawn, 1968. Contbr. to: (jrnls.) Christian Century; NY Times; Bethany Church-Guide; The Christian; Home Qtly.; Denver Post; Time of Singing; Kaleidograph; Westminster; Tulsa World; Daily Oklahoman; Blue Moon; Diplomat; Pen; Oregonian: (anthols.) Contemporary Am. Poets, 1929; Sparks Afar, 1936. Honours: 1st Prize, Poetry Soc. of Okla., 1967; 1st Prize (poetry), Fed. Writers of Okla., 1969; Appointed Poet Laureate of Okla., 1966; Nat. Recog. with 2nd Prize award, Elberta Clark Walker Nature Poetry Contest, 1940. Address: Box 1245, 1602 S. Okfuskee, Wewoka, Okla. 74884, USA.

HILLENIUS, Dirk, b. 29 May 1927. Biologist. Education: Univ. of Amsterdam. Married, 4 children. Positions held: Curator of Herpetology, Zoological Mus., Univ. of Amsterdam. Memberships: Maatschappy voor Letterkunde; Vereniging voor Letterkundigen; PEN. Published works: Tegen het Vegetarisme, 1961; Oefeningen voor het Derde Oog, 1965; Vit groeiende onwil om ooit nog ergens in veiligheid aan te komen, 1966; Het Romantisch Mechaniek, 1969. Contbr. to: Tirade; Hollands Maandblad; Propria Cures. Honours, awards: Poezie Prys, Amsterdam (Municipal), 1966. Address: Falckstraat 12, Amsterdam, The Netherlands.

HILLERT, Margaret, b. 22 Jan. 1920. Teacher. Education: Saginaw H.S.; A.A., Bay City Jun. Coll.; R.N., Univ. of Mich. School of Nursing; A.B...*, Wayne Univ. Coll. of Education, etc. Positions held: Registered Nurse, 3 yrs.; Teacher (primary), 25 yrs. Member: Detroit Women Writers; Poetry Soc. of Mich.; Internat. League of Children's Poets; Soc. of Children's Book Writers; Emily Dickinson Soc. Pubs. Farther Than Far, 1969; I Like to Live in the City, 1970; plus 14 juvenile books in print, with translations into Swedish, Danish, German, and Portuguese. Contrib. to: C.S. Monitor; The Lyric; The Horn Book; McCall's; Music Journal; Poet Lore; South and West; Western Humanities Review; American Legion; Pen; Ariz. Highways; Author & Journalist; Cat Fancy; Denver Post; Ellery Queen; Encyclopaedia Britannica; Missouri English Bulletin Year Book; Peninsula Poets; Poets of the Midwest, etc. Recip. various 1st. etc. prizes, Poetry Soc. of Mich., etc. Address: 4014 Phillips Ave., Berkley, Mich. 48072, USA.

HILTON, David, b. 20 Apr. 1938. English Professor. Education: B.A., San Jose State Univ., Calif.; M.A., Calif. State Univ. at Hayward; four yrs. doctoral work, Univ. of Wis. Published works: The Shot Goes In, 1969; Moving Day, 1969; The Man Upstairs, 1972. Contbr. to: Poetry; Chicago Review; Iowa Review; Poetry Northwest; New Letters; New American & Canadian Poetry; Hearse; Suction; Toothpaste; Search for Tomorrow; Gum; Abraxas; Iowa Defender; Foxfire; Quixote; Hanging Loose; Doones; Kumquat. Honours, awards: Borestone Award (Best Poems of 1968); twice 1st pl. winner, Univ. of Wis. Poetry Prize, 1969 & 70. Address: 225 Severn Ave., Annapolis, MD 21403, U.S.A.

HILTY, Peter Daniel, b. 16 July 1921. Professor of English. Education: M.A. & Ph.D., Univ. of Mo., U.S.A. Married, 1 son. Positions held: Instr. of Engl., Univ. of Mo. at Columbia; Prof. of Engl., Park Coll., Parkville, Mo.; Prof. of Engl., Southeast Mo. State Univ., Cape Girardeau, Mo. Memberships: Modern Lang. Soc.; Am. Name Soc. Published works: Shepherd's Calendar, forthcoming, 1974. Contbr. to: Saturday Evening Post; Cape Rock Jrnl.; Mo. Histl. Review; Discourse, etc. Address: 630 Bellevue, Cape Girardeau, MO 63701, U.S.A.

HINE, (William) Daryl, b. 24 Feb. 1936. Poet. Education: McGill Univ., Canada, 1954-58; Ph.D., Univ. of Chicago, USA, 1967. Positions held: Asst. Prof., Writing & Comparative Lit., Univ. of Chicago, 1967–; Ed., Poetry, a Mag. of Verse, Chicago, 1968–. Publications: Five Poems, 1954; The Carnal and the Crane, 1957; The Devil's Picture Book, 1960; The Wooden Horse, 1965; Minutes, 1968; The Homeric Hymns, 1972; In & Out, 1974. Contbr. to anthols. & jrnls. inclng: Poets of Our Moment; Poetry; The Atlantic; Cornhill; Harper's; New Republic; NY Rev. of Books; New Yorker; Hudson Rev.; Partisan Rev., Paris Rev., etc. Author of a novel, travel book, & several plays, incl. verse transln. of Euripides' Alcestis, prod. on Canadian Broadcasting Corp. & BBC 3. Honours: Various acad. hons., incl. Ingram Merrill Fndn. Grants; William Rainey Harper Fellowship; Canada Coun. Rockefeller Award. Address: Poetry, 1228 N. Dearborn Parkway, Chicago, IL 60610, USA.

HINEGARDNER, Verna Lee Linxwiler (Mrs.), born 2 Jan. 1919. Resource Technician. Positions held: Co-

Owner, Co-Mgr., with husband, ice-cream stores, La. & Miss. Sec., Alliance Rubber Co., Ark., 3 yrs.; currently Resource Technician., U.S. Forest Service, 15 yrs. Ouachita Nat. Forest, Hot Springs, Ark. Memberships: Poet's Roundtable of Ark.; Pres., Secretary, Treasurer, Hot Springs Br., ibid.; Ark. Artists, Authors & Composers. Publications: Magic Moments, 1966. Contbr. to: (jrnls.) Hot Springs News (Ed., poetry column, Poet's Partyline, past 6 yrs.); Am. Bard; Border; Angels; S.W. Times Record; Bardic Echoes; Sphynx Verse Reporter; Am. Haiku; Rhyme Time; Latchstrings; Poet's Forum; Muse; Poetry Dial; Homewood Herald; Just Singing; Poetry for Now; Science of Mind; Methodist Mature Yrs.; Unity; Poetry Rev.; (anthols.) Contemporary Poets of Ark; Golden Harvest Anthol.; Poems by Poet's Roundtable of Ark., 1967, 68, 69, 70, 71, 72, 73; S.W. Anthol.; Poetry Dial Anthol. Honours: Poet's Roundtable of Ark., Annual Contests, 3rd Place, 1967, 1st Place 1968; Second Place 1970; Fourth Place, 1972; Ark. Arts Fest., 1st, Free Verse, 2nd, Sonnet, 3rd illus. Lyric, 1969; Patriotic sonnet First Prize, 3rd prize illus. Nature Lyric, 1970; Love of Homeland Sonnet First Prize, 1971; 1st Place, Light Verse; 3rd Place Ecology Sonnet, 1972; Ark. Writer's Conference, 1st Prize, feature; 2nd Prize Shakespearean Sonnet; 3rd Prize, Inflexible Faith, 1973; Ark. Poetry Day 1st Prize; S.W. Times Record Award, 1972; Ark. Arts Festival 1st Prize Sonnet; 2nd Prize Light Verse, 1973; Ark. Poetry Day, 1st Prize, Illus. Trad. Verse, 1968. Address: 203 E. Vista Dr., Hot Springs, Ark. 71901, USA.

HIRSAL, Josef, b. 24 July 1920. Poet & Translator. Married. Positions held: Editor, Publishing House; Editor, Literary mag.; Independent Author. Published works: (vols. of poetry) Vedro stribra, 1940; Noclehys s klekánicí, 1942; Studené nebe, 1944; Matky, 1945; Soukromá galerie, 1965; JOB-BOJ (w. B. Grögerová), 1968. Translations of: Ch. Morgenstern; H. Heine; H.M. Enzensberger; H. Heissenbüttel; E.A. Poe; L. Góngora; F. Pessoa; G. Marino; L. Ariosto; Li Po; Chan San, etc. Contbr. to: Kritický mesícnik; Studenstký casopis; Mladá kultura; Ohnice; Kytice; Volné smery; Plamen; Slovenské pohlády; Die Sonde; ROT; Futura; etc. & num. anthols. Var. exhibitions of concrete & kinetic poetry in U.K., Germany, CSSR. Recip. translation prizes from publishing houses: Odeon, Prague, 1965; Mladá Fronta, Prague, 1965; Albatros, Prague, 1967; Odeon, Prague, 1968. Address: V horní stromce 6, 13000 Prague 3 – Vinohrady, Czechoslovakia.

HIRSCHMAN, Jack Aaron, pen name **JAH,** b. 13 Dec. 1933. Poet. Education: A.B., CCNY; A.M., Ph.D., Ind. Univ. Positions held: Tchr., Ind. Univ., 1955-59; ibid, Dartmouth Coll., 1959-61; Univ. of Calif. at Los Angeles, 1961-67. Published works: Fragments, 1953; A Correspondence of Americans, 1960; Two, (co-author) 1964; Interchange, 1964; Artaud Anthol., (ed.) 1965; Kline Sky, 1965; Yod, 1966; London Seen Directly, 1967; A Word in Your Season, (co-author) 1967; William Blake, 1967; Ltd., 1967; Jerusalem, 1967; Aleph Zaddik & Benoni, 1968; Shekinah, 1969; Black Alephs, 1969. Contbr. to: Open City, underground newspaper, LA; Free Press, ibid; Poetry Mag., Chicago; El Corno Emplumado, Mexico; Evergreen Rev., NY; Rupambara, India; Botteghe Oscure, Italy, etc. Address: 21 Quarterdeck St., Venice, Calif, USA.

HITCHCOCK, George, b. 2 June 1914. Poet. Education: B.A., Univ. of Ore. Positions held: Laborer; Smelterman; Carpenter; Steelwkr.; Mason; Cement Finisher; Gardener; Merchant Seaman; Actor; currently Lectr. in Lit., Univ. of Calif., Santa Cruz. Ed. & Publr., Kayak Books; Past Ed., San Francisco Review. Published works: Poems & Prints, 1962; Tactics of Survival, 1964; The Dolphin with A Revolver in its Teeth, 1967; A Ship of Bells, 1967; Losers Weepers–an Anthology of Found Poems, 1968; The Rococo Eye, 1970; Another Shore, 1971. Contbr. to num. reviews, mags., periodicals, etc. Address: 3965 Bonny Doon Rd., Santa Cruz, Calif. 95060, USA.

HOBSBAUM, Hannah, pen name **KELLY, Hannah,** b. 27 July 1937. Secretary. Education: Engl., Birkbeck Coll., Univ. of London; studied Violin, Trinity Coll. of Mus. Married Philip Hobsbaum, div. 1966. Positions held: Sec. & Rsch. Asst. to Philip Hobsbaum; currently Sec. to Dir. of Property Co.; Booklet Ed., Poets' Workshop. Memberships: Fndr. Mbr. & Hostess to The Group which published A Group Anthology (Oxford Univ. Press); Hostess to the Belfast Poets' Workshop; Fndr. Mbr. of Poets' Workshop, London; Camden Poetry Group. Author, Prelude, 1974. Contbr. to: Sceptre Press; Pink Peace; Wheels; Slide into Poetry (Camden Poetry Grp.). Address: 64 Lilyville Rd., London S.W.6, U.K.

HOBSBAUM, Philip, b. 29 June 1932. University Lecturer. Education: B.A., M.A., Downing Coll., Cambridge Univ., UK., 1952-1955; Ph.D., Univ. of Sheffield, 1968. Positions held: Lecturer in Engl., Queen's Univ., Belfast, 1962-1966; Lecturer in Engl. Lit., 1966-1972, Senior Lecturer in Engl. Lit., Univ. of Glasgow, 1972–. Published works: The Place's Fault and other poems, 1964; Snapshots, 1965; In Retreat and other poems, 1966; Coming Out Fighting, 1969; Some Lovely Glorious Nothing, 1969; Women and Animals, 1972; A Theory of Communication (criticism), 1970; A Reader's Guide to Charles Dickens, 1973; Editor, Anthols.: A Group Anthology (with Edward Lucie-Smith), 1963; Ten Elizabethan Poets, 1969. Contbr. to: Hudson Review; The Listener; Mod. Lang. Review; Encounter; Brit. Journal of Aesthetics; Brit. Journal of American Studies; Poetry Review, etc. Address: Dept. of Engl. Literature, Univ. of Glasgow, Glasgow, Scotland, UK.

HOBSON, Katherine Thayer, b. 11 Apr. 1889. Sculptor. Education: Univs. of Leipzig, Koenigsberg & Goetingen, Germany; Studied sculpture in Dresden, Paris & Athens; Harold Vinal's Poetry Workshop, N.Y. Memberships: Sec., Fine Arts Fed. of N.Y., 1952-69; Chmn. of Sculpture Sect., Nat. Assn. of Women Artists; Chmn. of Sculpture Sect., & Co-Chmn. of Poetry Grp., 1973, Pen & Brush; Poetry Soc. of Am.; Treas., N.Y. Women Poets. Contbr. to: Diamond Anthol., PSA; IWWP Anthol., 1972; Anthol. of Catholic Poetry Soc. of Am.; N.Y. Times; N.Y. Herald Tribune; Brooklyn Tablet; Charleston News & Courier; Stepladder; Kaleidegraph; Voices; Spirit; Scimitar & Song; The Westminster Mag.; Am. Weave; Poetry Digest, etc. Recip. var. prizes for sculpture. Address: 27 West 67th St., N. Y., NY 10023, U.S.A.

HO CHIH-HAO, b. 10 Jan. 1905. Professor. Education: Whampu Mil. Acad.; Army Infantry Schl.; The Army Coll.; Cmdr. & Gen. Staff Schl.; The Nat. Defence Coll. Positions held: Chief Committeeman of Civilian Mil. Trng. Comm. of Capital Nanking, 1934; Dir. of Dept. of Nat. Guards, Min. of Mil. Affairs, 1939; Dpty. C-in-C of Pacification H.Q. of Chekiang Province, ranking Lt. Gen., 1949; Chmn. of Designing Comm. of Gen. Political Warfare Dept., 1950; Sr. Mil. Staff of Pres. Office, 1964; Prof. of Coll. of Chinese Culture & Nat. Acad. of Arts, 1966–. Memberships: United Poets Laureate Int., 1964: Admin. Trustee, Chinese Writers & Artists Assn.; Fellow & Chmn., Assn. of Poets & Writers; Chmn., Chinese Nat. Dancing Assn. Published works: The Great Ambition; The Heroism; An Anthology of Chih-hao Ho's Poems & Folk Songs; A New Voval Music of The Republic of China; Suites of Chinese Folk Dancing; A History of Chinese Dancing; The General Study of Dancing; The Glory of The Sun & The Moon; The Spring Has Come Back on Earth. Contbr. to var. jrnls. Recip. num. honours & awards inclng: Academician of The China Acad., 1970; Laureate Poet (The Outstanding Chinese Poet), United Poets Laureate Int., 1965; 5 hon. doctorates. Address: 3, Lane 17, Chungshan South Rd., Taipei, Taiwan, Rep. of China.

HOCHMAN, Sandra (Mrs. Harvey Leve), b. 11 Sept. 1936. Poet. Married Harvey Leve w. one child. Published works: Voyage Home, 1960; Manhattan Pastures, 1963; The Vadeville Marriage, 1966; Loveletters from Asia, 1968. Contbr. to: Poetry;

Atlantic; Partisan Review; New Yorker; Harper's Bazaar. Recip., Yale Series of Younger Poets Award, 1963. Address: 180 East 79th Street, N.Y., NY, USA.

HOCKEY, Lawrence William, b. 12 June 1904. Schoolmaster (Ret'd). Education: B.A., Univ. Coll. of S. Wales & Monmouthshire, Cardiff, 1928; M.A., ibid, 1956. Married Phoebe Irene Lewis, 1 daughter (Sarah). Positions held: Sr. French Master, Hatherleigh Schl., Newport, Mon., 1928-59; Engl. Master, Hartridge H.S., Newport, 1959-69. Memberships: Fndr. Mbr. & on Comm., Gwent Poetry Soc.; Hon. Soc. of Cymmrodorion. Published works: The Undying Glory & Other Poems, 1939; Monmouthshire Poetry, 1949; W.H. Davies (biog.), 1971. Contbr. to: The South Wales Argus; The Anglo-Welsh Review; The Poetry Review; Poetry of To-day; English; The Western Mail; John o'London's Weekly; The Welsh Outlook; Great Thoughts; The Decachord; Comment; The Jongleur; The New Schoolmaster; This England; The Miami Herald, U.S.A.; Fiction Parade, U.S.A. & others. Has also written many articles dealing with poets & poetry. Recip., 1st Prize, Engl. Lyric, Eisteddfod of the Univ. of Wales, 1928. Address: 54 Beechwood Rd., Newport, Mon. NPT 8AH, U.K.

HODGES, Cyril, Former pseudonym: **Cyril Hughes,** b. 28 Feb. 1915. Industrial Manufacturer; Poet. Education: Studied Welsh Literature w. Dr. Cenydd Morus. Married w. 3 sons. Small-scale Industrial Manufacturer, 1948-. Published works: China Speaks, 1941; Seeing Voice: Welsh Heart, 1965. Contbr. to (Anthologies): For Those Who Are Alive, 1946; Modern Reading, 1947; (Jrnls.): Welsh Nation; Poetry Wales; Anglo-Welsh Review. Address: Smithies Avenue, Sully, Penarth, Glamorgan, Wales, UK.

HODGES, Frenchy Jolene, b. 18 Oct. 1940. Teacher. Education: B.S., Fort Valley State Coll., Georgia, 1964, with a major in English; M.A., in Afro-American Studies, with a concentration in Literature, Atlanta Univ., Georgia, 1973. Positions held: Teacher, Brooks Co. Bd. of Ed., Quitman, Ga., 1964-66 (English); Teacher, Detroit Pub. Schools, Michigan, 1966-present (Engl. and Social Studies) 1973 school term – Afro-American Lit. subject taught; Part-time Teacher, Univ. of Detroit Urban Studies Dept., 1968-69; Fall, 1973, teaching (part-time) African Literature. Memberships: African Image Makers' Workshop, Detroit (Founding Member); Detroit Teachers Council of Engl.; Concept East Theatre Poetry Readers Group. Published work: Black Wisdom, 1971. Contbr. to: Georgia Teachers and Educators Assoc. Herald; Concept East Black Theatre Arts Mag.; Phylon; Black World; Atlanta Daily World. Awards: Harold Jackmon Mem. Award, Atlanta Univ., March, 1973; A.D. Williams Elem. School Poetry Award, Atlanta, 13 Apr. 1973; Afro-American Studies Fellowship, Atlanta Univ., 1972-73. Address: 13725 LaSalle Blvd., Apt. 106, Detroit, MI 48238, USA.

HOEFLING, Susan Joan Brantweiner, b. 10 Nov. 1909. Poet; Writer. Education: City Schl. of Nursing, Cleveland, Ohio, 1929; Geneva Coll. Class of 1943; Graduated Nurses Aide, 1944. Licensed Practical Nurse, 1958. Married Charles W. Hoefling, 2 sons (1 dec.) Memberships: Fndr., Acad. of Am. Poets; Am. Poetry League; Fndr. & Charter Pres., Beaver Co. Chapt. of the Pa. Poetry Soc.; Chmn., Poetry Pa. Week; Special Corres., World Poetry Week; State Pres., Composers, Authors & Artists of Am., etc. Published works: 100 Pa. Poems, 1949; 100 Sesquicentennial Poems, 1950; For You – Dream Weaver Poems, 1949; For You – Melody of Life Poems, 1962; For You – Along the Avenue Poems, 1968; 400 Centennial Verse, 1968; Poems for Rotary Conventions & Confs., 1948-73; Verse for Reunions, 1973; Elegaic Poems; 100 Poems for Children (used in lectures); Topical & society verse; Centennial Theme Song, 1968; var. commercial verse, greeting card verses, dedication poems, poetry exhibits. Poetry read on Radio Stns. KDKA, WKST, WRYO, WJAS, WMBA, WBVP & WCAE. Contbr. to var. anthols., newspapers, jrnls. Honours, awards: Elegaic Poet, Poets Laureate

Int., 1966; Gold Medal, Pres. Marcos, & Medallion, Mayor of Manila; Hon. Dr. Humane Letters, 1969. Poet Laureate of Beaver Co., 1949-. Address: R.D. No. 2, Mercer Rd., Beaver Falls, PA, U.S.A.

HOEFT, Robert Dean, b. 21 Mar. 1932. Teacher. Education: A.A., Clark JC; B.A., Univ. of Wash.; M.S., Univ. of Ore. Married to Marjorie Hoeft, 1s., 1d. Positions held: Tchr. English, Blue Mountain Community Coll., Pendleton, Ore. Memberships: The Poetry Soc. of Am. Published works include: Handfuls of Day, Pocketfuls of Night, to be publ., 1972. Contbr. to the following anthols., jrnls., mags., etc: Northwest Review; Poetry Northwest; The Green World; The Druid; The Smith; The Lit; Fine Arts Discovery; Lyrismos; New England Review; Scimitar & Song; Uptown Beat; Voices International; Twigs; Quoin; The Symbolist; Hyacinths & Biscuits; Modern Images; Haiku Highlights; Goliards; Arcadian; The Christian Science Monitor; Northwest Poets; Poet Lore; Imprints Quarterly; Alive; Poetry Prevue. Address: 916 S.E. Byers Ave., Pendleton, Ore. 97801, USA.

HOFFMAN, Daniel (Gerard), b. 3 Apr. 1923. Professor of English. Education: A.B., Columbia Coll., N.Y., 1947; M.A., Columbia Univ., I Ph.D., ibid., 1956. Married Elizabeth McFarland w. 2 children. Positions held: Has taught at Columbia Univ., 1947, 1952-56; Rutgers Univ., New Brunswick, N.J., 1948-50; Temple Univ., Phila., 1950-52; Swarthmore Coll., Pa., 1957-66; Professor of English, Univ. of Pa., Phila., 1966–; Visiting Professor, Faculté des Lettres, Dijon, France, 1956-57; Fellow, Schl. of Letters, Ind. Univ., Bloomington, 1959; Univ. of Cinn., 1964; Yeats Studies Schl., Sligo, Ireland, 1965. Published works: An Armada of Thirty Whales, 1953; A Little Geste, 1960; The City of Satisfactions, 1963; Striking the Stones, 1968; Broken Laws, 1970; Literary Criticism: The Poetry of Stephen Crane, 1957; Form & Fable in American Fiction, 1961; Barbarous Knowledge: Myth in the Poetry of Yeats, Graves & Muir, 1967; Other: Paul Bunyan, 1952; Ed., The red Badge of Courage & other Stories, 1957; American Poetry & Poetics, 1962. Contbns. incl. (Anthologies): Pocket Book of Modern Verse, 1954; A Controversy of Poets, 1965; Possibilities of Poetry, 1969; (Jrnls.): Poetry; Hudson Review; Nation: Shenandoah; Encounter. Honours incl: The Yale Series of Younger Poets Award, 1954; The Ainsley Prize, 1957; Nat. Inst. of Arts & Letters Award, 1967. Address: c/o Dept. of English, Univ. of Pennsylvania, Phila., PA 19104, USA.

HOFFMAN, Jill, b. 3 Dec. 1938. College Teacher; Poet. Education: A.B., Bennington Coll., 1959; A.M., Columbia Univ., 1960; Ph.D., Cornell Univ., 1966. Positions held: Instr. of Engl., Women's Coll. of Univ. of N.C., 1960-61; Lectr. in Engl., Barnard Coll., 1965-66; Asst. Prof., Bard Coll., 1966-68; Asst. Prof., Columbia Univ., 1968-73; Asst. Prof., Brooklyn Coll. 1973. Published works: Mink Coat, 1973. Contbr. to: Qtly. Review of Lit.; New Yorker; New Republic; Chelsea; Kenyon Review; Some; Transatlantic Review; American Review; S.D. Review; Epoch; N.Y. Qtly.; Antioch Review; Antaeus; The Falcon; Chicago Review. Recip., Van Rensselaer Prize for Poetry, Columbia Univ., 1960. Address: Dept. of Engl., Brooklyn Coll., Brooklyn, N.Y., U.S.A.

HOFFMAN, Phoebe W., b. 3 Feb. 1894. Freelance Copy Editor. Education: Columbia Univ., 1932-36. Married J. Ogden Hoffman. Positions held: Asst. Ed., Women's Page, Philadelphia Evening Bull., 1919-20; Freelance Copy Ed., 1947-54. Memberships: Poetry Soc. of Am.; Fla. State Poetry Soc. Inc.; Poetry Soc. of Mich.; Calif. Fed. of Chaparral Poets; W. Va. Poetry Soc. Contbr. to: (anthols.) Anthol. of Mag. Verse, 1922; Cats in Verse, 1935; Home & Holiday Verse, 1935; P.S.A. Golden Yrs. Anthol., 1960; Poetry Soc. Selected Poems, 1966, '67, '68; (jrnls.) Contemporary Verse; Art World; Saturday Rev.; N.Y. Times; Prairie Poet; Am. Poet; Am. Bard; Vespers; Villager; Hartford Courant; New Hampshire Sunday News; Am. Poetry League Bull.; Scimitar & Song; The Oregonian; Denver Post, etc. Honours, awards: 3 prizes for poem, story &

play, Browning Soc. of Phila., 1917; 1st Prize, Ellen Askue Meml. Contest, Am. Bard, 1968; 1st Prize, Calif. Chaparral, 1968; Poet Laureate, Monterey Peninsula, Calif., 1970; 1st pl., Carl Sandburg Award, 1973, & many others. Address: 651 Sinex Ave., A-118, Pacific Grove, CA 93950, U.S.A.

HOFFMAN, William M., b. 12 Apr. 1939. Playwright; Poet; Director; Editor. Education: Grad., City Coll. of N.Y., 1960. Positions held: Drama Ed., Hill & Wang, 1961-68; Ed., New Am. Plays Series, ibid, 1968–; Lectr., Theatre Discussion Series, Eugene O'Neill Fndn., 1971; Lit. Adviser, Scripts Mag., 1971–; Artist-in-Res., The Changing Scene, Denver, 1972; & Lincoln Ctr. Student Prog., 1971-72; Vis. Lectr., Theatre Arts, Univ. of Mass., Boston, 1973. Memberships: Fellow, MacDowell Colony, 1971; ASCAP; Fndng. Mbr., N.Y. Theatre Strategy. Contbr. to: 31 New Am. Poets, 1970; Fine Frenzy, 1972; The Cloisters, 1968; Things; Hiram Poetry Review; Poetry Newsletter; Meat. Has written plays, poetry, song lyrics, motion picture & television scripts, play criticism. Edited three anthols. of plays. Has directed plays, motion pictures & television. Address: 199 Prince St., N.Y., NY 10012, U.S.A.

HOFMANN, Helen Lilian, pen name **SHAW, Helen,** b. 20 Feb. 1913. Writer; Poet; Editor. Education: B.A., Univ. of Canterbury, New Zealand. Married, 2 sons. Positions held: Ed., The Symposium, 'The Puritan & the Waif' (essays on the N.Z. novelist Frank Sargeson, 1954; Guest Ed., New Zealand Number Poet, 1968, Pacific Number Poet, 1972; Ed., 'The Letters of D'Arcy Cresswell', 1971. Memberships: PEN New Zealand Ctr.; World Poetry Soc. Intercontinental; Australian Soc. of Authors. Published works: Out of Dark (poems), 1968; Five Poems (poetry broadsheets), 1970; The Girl of the Gods, 1973; The Orange Tree; and other stories. Contbr. to: (anthols.) IWWP, 1972; Poetry New Zealand, 1971; Pancontinental Premier Poets, 1972; The First Flying Dragon Book of Poetry, 1971; The Spring Anthol. (Mitre), 1973; Gem Scent; (reviews, mags., jrnls.) Arena (N.Z.); Aylesford Review; Colloquium; Dialectic; Cardinal; Poet (India); Ocarina (India); The Aryan Path (India); Viewpoints; Expression; Ore; Quintessence; Poetry Nippon; South & West; Gong; Manifold; Scrip; The Fiddlehead; Outposts, etc. Honours, awards incl: Litt.D., Int. Acad. Ldrship, 1968; Disting. Serv. Cit., World Poetry Soc. Intercontinental, 1968 & 71; World Poet Award, ibid, 1972. Address: 42 Bassett Rd., Auckland 5, New Zealand.

HOGG, Robert Lawrence, b. 26 Mar. 1942, Edmonton, Alta, Canada. Professor of English. Education: B.A., Univ. of British Columbia, Canada, 1964; Grad. Studies, State Univ. of NY, at Buffalo, USA, 1965-68. Positions held: Fellowship, State Univ. of NY at Buffalo, 1965-68; Lectr., Carleton Univ., Ottawa, Canada, 1968-69; Asst. Prof., ibid, 1969-70. Member, League of Canadian Poets. Publications: The Connexions, 1966; Aries in Pisces Dream, 1969; Standing Back, 1971. Contbr. to: (anthols.) New Wave Canada, 1966; To Every Thing There is a Season, 1967; The Book of Mod. Canadian Verse, 1967; The Wind Has Wings, 1968; (jrnls.) Guppy Fancier's Qtly.; Island; Is; Mag. of Further Studies; Poetry Australia; RC Lion Sum; Tish; Wild Dog; Work; Blew Ointment; Change; New Student Rev.; Ant's Forefoot; Sum; Athanot; Imago; Georgia Straight; Presence; Collection. Address: Engl. Dept., Carleton Univ., Ottawa, Ont., Canada.

HOGGARD, James Martin, b. 21 June 1941. College Teacher. Education: B.A., Southern Meth. Univ., 1963; M.A., Univ. of Kansas, 1965. Married Bonnie Hubly, 2 children. Positions held: Reporter, Wichita Falls Record News; Instr., Midwestern Univ.; Asst. Prof., ibid; Assoc. Prof. Contbr. to: Back Door; Beyond Baroque; Bitterroot; The Blackbird Circle; Descant; The Fiddlehead; Forum; IWWP Anthol.; Kansas Mag.; Karamu; Miss. Review; Penny Poems from Midwestern Univ.; Pembroke Mag.; Poet (India); Poet & Critic; Poet Lore; The Rectangle; The Salt Creek Rdr.; South Fla. Poetry Jrnl.; West Coast Poetry Review;, etc. Honours, awards: David Russel Poetry Award, 1963; Univ. of Kansas Creative Writing Award, 1965; Carl Sandburg Lit. Fest. Awards, 1966; Midwestern Univ. Fine Arts Fest. Award, 1968; Hart Crane & Alice Crane Williams Meml. Fund Award, 1969. Address: Dept. of Engl., Midwestern Univ., Wichita Falls, TX 76308, U.S.A.

HOGGART, Richard, b. 24 Sept. 1918. Professor of English. Educ: M.A., Leeds Univ., U.K. Married Mary Holt France, 1942; 3 children. Positions held: Vis. Prof., Univ. of Rochester, U.S.A., 1956-57; Sr. Lectr., Engl., Univ. of Leicester, U.K., 1959-62; Prof., Engl., Birmingham Univ., 1962–; Dir., Ctr. for Contemporary Cultural Studies, 1964–. Memberships: Albemarle Comm. on Youth Servs., 1958-60; B.B.C. Gen. Advsry. Coun., 1959-60 & 1964–; Youth Serv. Dev. Coun., 1960-62; Gov., Royal Shakespeare Theatre; Gov., Birmingham Repertory Theatre. Published works: Auden, 1951; The Uses of Literacy, 1957; W.H. Auden, 1957; W.H. Auden–A Selection, 1961; The Critical Moment, 1964; The World in 1984, 1965; Speaking to Each Other, 1969. Address: Dept. of English, The University, Birmingham, U.K.

HOGNAS, Kurt Carl Alexander, b. 2 Feb. 1931. Language leacher. Education: B.A., Helsinki Univ., Finland, 1955; M.A., ibid, 1960. Positions held: Language Tchr. (Engl., German), Jakobstad, 1957-58, Björneborg (Pori), 1958-61, Kristinestad (Engl., German, Latin), 1961–. Member, Finland's Svenska Författarförening. Published works: (collections of poems) Början till liv, 1955; Vindvart, 1959; Glashus, 1972. Translated Italian poetry (Danilo Dolci) into Swedish. Contbr. to: Vasabladet; Horisont. Address: Sibeliusgatan 3, 64100 Kristinestad, Finland.

HOLBROOK, David, b. 9 Jan. 1923. Author. Education: City of Norwich Schl; Downing Coll., Cambridge. Married, 4 children. Positions held: Fellow, King's Coll., Cambridge, 1961-64; Coll. Lectr. in Engl., Jesus Coll., Cambridge, 1968-70; Writer-in-Res., Dartington Hall, 1971-73; Asst. Dir. of Engl. Studies, Downing Coll., Cambridge, 1973–. Has lectured in Am., Germany & Australia. Memberships: Writers' Action Grp.; Past Mbr., Soc. of Authors. Published works: Imaginings, 1961; Against the Cruel Frost, 1963; Object Relations, 1967; Old World, New World, 1969; num. books on English Tchng. Ed. many anthols. Contbr. to: Listener; Scotsman; Observer; New Statesman; The Human World; Outposts; Poetry Review; Encounter; The Use of English; Critical Qtly.; N.Y. Times, etc. Honours, awards: 'Imaginings' & 'Old World New World', Poetry Book Soc. Choice; Arts Coun. Writers' Grant, 1970; Prize, London Lit. Editions, Keats Meml. Comp., 1973. Address: Downing Coll., Cambridge Univ., Cambridge, U.K.

HOLDEN, Molly (Winifred), b. 7 Sep. 1927. Housewife. Education: B.A., Hons. Engl., 1948, King's Coll., Univ. of London, M.A., ibid., 1951. Published works: A Hill Like A Horse, 1963; The Bright Cloud, 1964; To Make Me Grieve, 1968; Air and Chill Earth, 1971. Contbr. to: Review of Engl. Literature; Outposts; Times Lit. Supp.; NY Times; Poetry Review; P.E.N. Poetry Anthols., etc. Awards include: Cholmondeley Award to Poets, 1972; Arts Council of G.B. Award, 1970. Address: 58 Willow Rd., Bromsgrove, Worcs., UK.

HOLENDER, Barbara D., (Mrs. H. William Holender). b. 15 Mar. 1927. Homemaker. Education: Cornell Univ., Univ. of Buffalo (now State Univ. of NY at Buffalo), B.A., 1948. Currently Instr. in Poetry, Dept. of Continuing Education, State Univ. of NY at Buffalo. Membership: Poetry Soc. of America. Contbr. to: (anthols): Diamond Anthol., 1971; NY Times Book of Verse, 1970; (newspapers, journals): NY Times; CS Monitor; Prairie Schooner; Ariz. Qtly.; Literary Review; Chicago Jewish Forum; Reconstructionist; Kansas City Star; Univ. Review (now New Letters); Music Journal; Clavier; Shakespeare Newsletter, etc. Address: 263 Brantwood Rd., Snyder, NY 14226, USA.

HOLLAND, Barbara A., pen name **HOLLAND, B. Adams,** b. 12 Jul. 1925. Freelance Researcher and Writer. Education: Baldwin School, 1943; Univ. of Pennsylvania, B.A., 1948, M.A., 1951. Niece of Leonie Adams. Positions held: Carl Marks & Co., brokerage house, 1962-1970; John C. Winston Co., lexicography, 1958-1961; Historical Services Inc., genealogy, 1957-1958; Writer's Digest, Critic, 1955-1957; G. & C. Merriam Co., 1951-1955. Member, New York Poets Cooperative, 1969-1972. Published works: Return in Sagittarius, 1965; A Game of Scraps, 1967. Contbr. to more than 650 little magazines, including: Bartlesby's Review; Greenfield Review; Granite; Man-Root; Carleton Miscellany; For Now; Antioch Review; Shenandoah; Beloit Poetry Qtly.; N.Y. Qtly.; Charas; Phoenix, etc. Awards include: Buder Award, 1972; Calliope Award, 1973. Address: 14 Morton St., Apt. 9, NY., NY 10014, USA.

HOLLAND, Priscilla, b. 3 Oct. 1915. Poet & Artist. Charter Mbr., Niles Writers Guild; Fellow, Orbis Mag. Contbr. to: Gangue, Niles Writers Guild Year Book, 1966; Gato, 1970; Dance of Muse, 1970; Golden Book Anthology, Orbis Mag. Recip., Literary Cert., Centro Studi e Scambi Int., 1972. Address: 1535 Estes Ave., Chicago, IL 60626, U.S.A.

HOLLANDER, John, b. 28 Oct. 1929. Poet; Teacher. Education: B.A., Columbia Univ., NY; M.A., ibid; Ph.D., Ind. Univ. Positions held: Jr. Fellow, Soc. of Fellows, Harvard; Lectr. in Engl., Connecticut Coll.; Instr., Yale Univ.; Asst. Prof., ibid; Assoc. Prof.; Prof. of English, Hunter Coll. Published works: A Crackling of Thorns, 1958; Movie-Going and Other Poems, 1962; Visions From the Ramble, 1965; Philomel, 1968; Types of Shape, 1969. Contbr. to: New Yorker; Partisan Review; Kenyon Review; Sewanee Review; Hudson Review; Southern Review; Poetry; Atlantic Monthly; Harper's Mag.; Encounter; New Statesman; Spectator; Listener; Book World, etc. Honours: Yale Younger Poets Award, 1958; Grant from Inst. of Arts & Letters, 1963. Address: 88 Central Park West, New York City, NY, 10023, USA.

HOLLIDAY, David, pen names **CUNNING, Alfred, SPEAKER, William** & others, b. 20 Aug. 1931. Poetry Editor; Postal Official. Married, 2 children. Positions held: Jt.Ed., DEUCE, 1957-61; on Editl.Bd., ENVOI, 1958-61; Central Ed., ibid, 1960-61; Ed., SCRIP, 1962-1973. Memberships: Brompton Poets, 1960-63; Poetry Soc., 1960-63. Published works: Pictures from an Exhibition, 1959; Compositions of Place, 1961; A Dusty Answer, 1973; co-operated in Six Chesterfield Poets, 1969. Contbr. to: Cornhill Review; Envoi; Expression One; Gob; Limbo; Medley; Manifold; New Christian; Catholic Herald; Outposts; New Voices Int.; Message; Betelgeuse; Poesie Vivante; Breakthru; Deuce; Paperway; Poetry & Audience; Tarasque; Thistle; Two Tone; Viewpoints; The Albemarle Book of Modern Verse, 1962; Poems of the Sixties, 1970. Address: 67 Hady Cres., Chesterfield, Derbyshire S41 OEB, U.K.

HOLLINGDRAKE, Sybil, b. 7 Sept. 1926. Lecturer. Education: B.A., Bristol Univ., 1947; Tchng. Cert., 1948; M.A., 1955; A.D.B., 1971. Positions held: Grammar Schl. Tchr.; Ency. Saleswoman; Lectr. for Extra Mural Dept. of Cardiff Univ.; Lectr. in Caerleon Coll. of Educ., etc. Memberships: Exec. Comm. Mbr., Drama Assn. of Wales; Monmouthshire Drama League; Comm. Mbr., Gwent Poetry Soc.; Guild of Welsh Playwrights; Newport Civil Defence Drama Soc.; Drama Bd. Assn. Published works: The Supertramp in Monmouthshire (a biog. of W.H. Davies), 1971, 2nd edn., 1973; God is my Mountain, one act verse play, 1961, '65, '72; Bakestones for a Pensioner, one act verse play, 1952; Charade with Percussion, one act verse play, 1963, '67; Dai Christmas, play in verse, 1972, '73. Contbr. to: Poetry Wales; Gwent Poetry Anthol.; Adam Int.; South Wales Argus; British Nylon Spinners Qtly. Honours, awards incl: Nonesuch Prize for Lit., Bristol Univ., 1955; Lord Howald de Walden All Britain Trophy, 1961; Guild of Welsh Playwrights Award, 1962; Monmouthshire Drama

League Playwriting Awards, 1960, '65. '69, '70, '71, & '72. Address: 51 Stockton Rd., Newport, Mon. NPT 7HJ, U.K.

HOLLINGER, Verna R., b. 25 Oct. 1908. Teacher & Library Clerk. Education: B.A. in Educ., Univ. of Ariz., 1931; postgrad. courses in writing craftsmanship, ibid. Divorced, 3 daughters. Positions held: Tchr.; Homemaker; Lib. Clerk. Memberships: Past Mbr., Writers' Workshop of Tucson; Past Recording & Corresponding Sec., Tucson Br., Ariz. State Poetry Soc. Contbr. to: Sing Naked Spirit Anthol., 1970; Poet Directory, 1973; Ariz. Daily Star; Familiar Poetry & Prose; Sandcutters Qtly.; Poet; Your Digest, etc. Honours, awards: 1st prize, Ariz. State Poetry Soc. Contest, 1931; 3rd prize, hon. mention, President's Contest, ibid, 1970; Hon. mention, Nat. Fed. of State Poetry Sos., 1970, 71, 72; 2nd & 3rd pl., Sandcutters, Autumn, 1971. Address: 4218 East Irving Circle, Tucson, AZ 85711, U.S.A.

HOLLIS, Barbara Coonley, b. 28 Jan. 1922. Librarian. Education: B.S., Bus. Admin., with grad. work in English, Sociology, Economics, Transportation, Univ. of Tennessee, Knoxville, 1949; Pre-Standard Cert., American Inst. of Banking, 1959. Positions held: Banker, Bangor Savings Bank, Bangor, Maine, 1949-61; Library Aide, Public Library of Brookline, Mass., 1961-62; Asst. to the Town Librarian, ibid, 1962–. Memberships: Poetry Fellowship of Maine; Pres. ibid, 1963-66; Sec., Correspondence School Poetry Rounds, 1966–; UPLI; Founder, Acad. of American Poets; 1st Vice Chancellor, Nat. Fed. of State Poetry Socs., 1964-66; Sec., ibid, 1966-68; Parliamentary & Protocol Chairman 1973, ibid; Louisiana State Poetry Soc.; Pine Tree Branch, Nat. League Am. Pen Women, 1967-70; Member-at-Large, ibid, 1972–; Poets' Study Club of Terre Haute; Indiana State Fed. of Poetry Clubs; Poetry Soc. of Michigan; Mass. State Poetry Soc.; American Inst. of Parliamentarians. Published work: Texture, 1966 (all proceeds to Mem. Scholarship Fund, Stonington, Maine, HS). Contbr. to: Island Ad-Vantages; Flamingo; Brookline Chronicle-Citizen; Poetry Fellowship of Maine, 2 anthols.; New Hampshire Sunday News; Laurel Leaves; Louisiana Anthol., 1973. Awards: Poetry Fellowship of Maine, 1st prize, 1965, 1968; 2nd prize, ibid, 1965, 1966, 1967; 3rd prize, 1961. Address: Box 473, Brookline, MA 02147, USA.

HOLLO, Anselm, b. 12 Apr. 1934. Poet and Teacher. Education: Helsinki Univ., Finland; Univ. of Tubingen, W. Germany. Married, Josephine Clare Wirkus, 3 children. Positions held: Various with BBC European Services, 1958-1966; Visiting Lecturer, Dept. of Engl., State Univ. of New York at Buffalo, NY., 1967; Assoc. Prof., Creative Writing Prog., Univ. of Iowa, 1968-1972; Visiting Prof., Writing Prog., Bowling Green State Univ., Ohio, 1973; Assoc. Prof. Dept. of Engl., Hobart and Wm. Smith Coll., Geneva, NY, 1973-1974. Published works: And It Is A Song, 1965; The Coherences, 1968; Maya: Works 1959-1969; Sensation: or, the book called Book, 1972; plus upwards of 15 chapbooks and pamphlets; Translations: Red Cats (poems by Yevtushenko, Voznesensky and Kirsanov), 1962; Some Poems by Paul Klee, 1963; Selected Poems by Andrei Voznesensky, 1964; Bertolt Brecht: Jungle of Cities (a play), 1966; Lars Gorling: 491 (a novel), 1966; Helsinki: Poems by Pentti Saarikoski, 1967; Paavo Haavikko: Selected Poems, 1968; In the Dark, Move Slowly: Poems by Tuomas Anhava, 1969; William Carlos Williams: Paterson, 1970; Thrymskvitha, 1970; Aleksandr Blok: The Twelve and Other Poems, 1971; Georg Buchner: Woyzeck (a play); Tom Raworth: Selected Poems, 1973; Tomaz Salamun: Nile (selected poems). Anthol. inclusions: Lyrik Aus Dieser Zeit (Poetry of Our Time), 1961, 1963, 1965; Jazz Poems (Ed.), 1963; Keine Zeit Fur Liebe: Moderne Deutsche Liebeslyrik (No Time for Love: Contemp. German Love Poems), 1964; Of Poetry and Power, 1964; "4", 1966; Modern European Poetry, 1966; Love Love Love, 1967; Eight Lines and Under, 1967; Uuden Runon Kauneimmat (The Finest of the New), 1967;

Evergreen Review Reader, 1968; Children of Albion: Poetry of the "Underground" in Britain, 1969; Poems from Poetry & Jazz in Concert, 1969; New Directions 21, 1969; British Poetry Since 1945, 1970; I Love You All Day: It Is That Simple, 1970; C'mon Everybody: Poetry of the Dance, 1971; 23 Modern British Poets, 1971; Sumac: An Active Anthology, 1973, Poetry of the Committed Individual, A Stand Anthology of Poetry, 1973, etc. Contbr. to numerous newspapers, journals, etc. Address: 112 Washington St., Geneva, NY., NY 14456, USA.

HOLLOWAY, Anthony John, b. 30 Apr. 1945. Architectural Assistant. Contbr. to: 20th Century Poetry, 1970; Flying Dragon First Book of Poetry, 1971; Hampshire Poets; Hampshire Telegraph. Address: 21 North Wallington, Fareham, Hants. PO16 8SN, U.K.

HOLLOWAY, Glenna, pen names ROSS, Glenn, GLENN, Rose, etc., b. 7 Feb. 1928. Artist. Education: Ward Belmont Coll., Nashville, Tenn. Married. Artist specializing in Enamels, Sculpture & Murals. Memberships: Poetry Soc. of Am.; Poetry Soc. of Tex.; Nat. League of Am. Pen Women; Bd. Trustees, Ga. Writers Assn. Contbr. to: Ga. Review; Christian Home; N.Y. Herald Tribune; The Baptist Student; Kans. City Star; Sacred Heart Messenger; The Pen Woman; PSA Diamond Anthol.; P.S. of Pa. Prize Poems of 1965; Rochester Fest. of Relig. Arts, 1967; Poet Lore; Music Ministry; P.S. of Ga. Winners, 1965; Christian Sci. Monitor; Panic Button; Denver Post. Honours, awards: Poetry Book Award, Ga. Writers Assn., 1968, '72; Chicago Poets & Patrons, 1st & 2nd, 1972, num other poetry awards. Address: 913 Bailey Rd., Naperville, IL 60540, U.S.A.

HOLLOWAY, John, b. 1 Aug. 1920. University Professor. Educ: New Coll., Oxford Univ.; D.Phil., Oxford, 1947; D.Litt., Aberdeen, 1954; Litt.D., Cambridge, 1969. Married, 2 c. Positions held: Lectr. in WW II; Temporary Lectr., Philos., New Coll., Oxford, 1945; Fellow, All Souls Coll., 1946-60; John Locke Scholar, 1947; Univ. Lectr., Engl., Aberdeen, 1949-54; Univ. Lectr., Engl., Cambridge Univ., 1954-66; Libn., 1964-66, Chmn., 1970, '71; Rdr., 1966-72; Prof., Mod. Engl., 1972–; Lecture Tours, Ceylon, India, Pakistan, 1958, & Middle E., 1965; Byron Prof., Univ. of Athens, 1961-63; Alexander White Prof., Chgo., 1965; Hinkley Prof., Johns Hopkins Univ., Balt., Md., 1972. Fellow, Royal Soc. of Lit. Published works: (verse) The Minute, 1956; The Fugue, 1960; The Landfallers, 1962; Wood and Windfall, 1965; New Poems, 1970; (prose) Language and Intelligence, 1951; The Victorian Sage, 1953; The Charted Mirror (essays), 1960; Poems of the Mid-Century, (Ed.), 1957; Selections from Shelley, (Ed.), 1960; Shakespeare's Tragedies, 1961; The Colours of Clarity (essays), 1964; The Lion Hunt, 1964; Widening Horizons in English Verse, 1966; Blake, The Lyric Poetry, 1968; contbr. to var. jrnls. Address: Queens' Coll., Cambridge Univ., Cambridge, U.K.

HOLLOWAY, (Sister) Marcella M(arie), b. 1 Dec. 1913. Professor of English Literature. Education: Ph.D., Catholic Univ. of America, 1947; Further study at Exeter Coll., Oxford, summer of 1963; Nat. Endowment of Humanities grant for study at Yale, summer of 1973. Positions held: Chairman, of Engl. Dept. at Avila Coll., Kansas City, Ho., 1948-63; Prof. of Engl. at Fontbonne Coll., St. Louis, Mo., since 1963, and director of the lit. mag., College. Member: Nat. League of American Penwomen; The G.M. Hopkins Soc., London. Contrib. to: The Liguorian; The Dawn Anthol.; Vol. 1, The Clover Anthol., 1972; The Ave Marie; The Eucharist; Internat. Who's Who in Poetry Anthol., 1972. Awards include: 1972 Internat. Clover Poetry Contest, 1st place; for verse drama, St. Louis Poetry Center (nat. contest), 1972. Address: Fontbonne Coll., St. Louis, Mo. 63105, USA.

HOLMAN, Ottilie, b. 1 Aug. 1949. Benefit Authorizer; Social Security Administration. Education: corres. course, Palmer Writers Schl. Positions held: Stenographer, Secretary, Benefit Authorizer, Social Security Administration. Former Mbr., The Fellowship of Profl. Poets. Contbr. to: Poetry Pageant; The Oregonian; Jean's Jrnl.; Yearbook of Modern Poetry, 1971; American Scenes; All-Time Favorite Poetry; Mary's Scrapbook of Poetry (4 poems); Outstanding Contemporary Poetry; Lyrics of Love; Outstanding Contemporary Poetry. Honours, awards: Cert. of Merit, J. Mark Press Org., 1970; Cert. of Mbrship, Fellowship of Profl. Poets, 1971. Address: 73–14 69 Ave., Middle Village, NY 11379, U.S.A.

HOLMAS, Stig, b. 25 Feb. 1946. Author. Positions held: Libn., Voss, 1971-73. Memberships: Norwegian Soc. of Authors; Norsk Forfattersentrum. Published works: (books of poetry) Vi er mange, 1970; Tenke pa i morgen, 1972. Contbr. to: Gruppe 68, 1968; Atte fra Bergen, 1969; Dagbladet; Bergens Arbeiderblad; Klassekampen; Röde Garde; Profil; Vinduet; BLM og Folket i Bild; var. anthols. Address: 5100 Isdalstö, Norway.

HOLMES, Elizabeth Anne, pen name, HOLMES, Liz, b. 25 Dec. 1945. Coypwriter, Advertising Agency. Education: Uplands School, Parkstone, Dorset; Brampton Down School, Folkestone, Kent; 2 yrs. at The New Coll. of Speech & Drama where gained London Univ. Dip. in Drama, and Dip. of The Internat. Phonetics Assoc. Positions held: Actress, 1966-68; P.A./Sec., 1969-70 (at The Daily Telegraph); 1970-72, P.A./Sec., at The Wallace Collection, London; 1972-73, Ball Sec., The English-Speaking Union; 1973–, Copywriter, Hilary Green & Ptnrs., Ltd. Memberships: The Writers' Workshop (Committee Member); Avator Poetry Group (London). Contbr. to: Reading Mercury; Expression Mag.; Tribune; Poets' Workshop Booklet (May, 1973); Wheels Mag. Recip. College Prize, The New Coll. of Speech & Drama, for poetry, 1966. Address: 13 Orchard Rd., Lewes, Sussex, UK.

HOLMES, Kate A. Retired from the United States Civil Service. Education: Jrnlsm., La. State Univ., Baton Rouge, La., 1950. Memberships: La. Poetry Soc., New Orleans; Friends of the Lib., New Orleans. Contbr. to: Scimitar & Song; Cyclo-Flame; Times-Picayune 'Deep in Dixie' stories, Dixie-Roto Mag.; 2 poems in 'Bought We This Freedom' (anthol.); Young's Anthol; 'Poets in the Sun'; poems in Lib. of Madras, India. Address: 2912 Prytania St., Apt. 7, New Orleans, LA 70115, U.S.A.

HOLMES, Mildred L(ouise), b. 8 Sep. 1920. Missionary. Education: B.A., Univ. of Wis., also degree in economics. Member, Wis. Fellowship of Poets. Contbr. to Immanuel Reformed Church Bulletins; Bulletin Bd., Milwaukee County Gen. Hospital, etc. Address: 2210 N. 42 St., Milwaukee, WI 53208, USA.

HOLMES, Theodore, b. 1928. University Teacher. Education: Princeton Univ., N.J. (B.A.), 1952; Ore. Univ., Eugene; Univ. of Iowa, Iowa City. Positions held: Has taught at Univ. of Iowa; Ore. Univ.; Harvard Univ., Cambridge, Mass. Published works: The Harvest & the Scythe, 1957; Ship on the Beach, 1965; An Upland Pasture: Poems, 1966. Contbr. to (Anthologies): A Controversy of Poets, 1965; (Jrnls.): Nation; Partisan Review; Poetry; Paris Review; Carleton Miscellany. Honours: Fulbright Fellowship, Oxford, 1963; Yaddo Fellowship, 1964-65.

HOLUB, Miroslav, b. 13 Sept. 1923. Physician; Scientific Worker; Immunologist. Education: Schl. of Med., Charles Univ., Prague, Czechoslovakia; Sci. Trng. & Ph.D., Inst. of Microbiol. Czech. Acad. of Scis., Prague. Married, 1 son. Positions held: Clin. Pathologist; Sci. Wkr. in Immunology. Memberships: PEN; Czechoslovak Writers Union, 1960-71; Union of Czech Scientific Workers, 1970-71; Bavarian Acad. of Arts. Published works: 11 books of poetry in Czech, 1958-71; 4 books of essays in Czech, 1963-72; (in English) Selected Poems, 1967; Although (poetry), 1971; (in German) Obwohl (poetry), 1969; Engel auf Rädern, (prose), 1967; Die Explodierende Metropole. (prose), 1967; 2 more books of translations in Polish & Hungarian. Contbr. to: Times Lit. Supplement;

Observer; London Mag.; Meanjin Quarterly; Mosaic; Landfall; Stand; New Zealand Monthly Review; Transatlantic Review; Ensemble & many other mags. in Europe, U.S., India & Japan. Recip., Publishers Awards, 1960, 63 & 69. Address: Inst. of Clinical & Experimental Med., Budejovicka 800, Prague 4, Czechoslovakia.

HOLZAPFEL, Rudi (Rudolf Patrick Holzapfel), Pseudonyms: **Rooan Hurkey, R. Patrick Ward,** b. 11 Dec., 1938. Teacher. Education: B.D., Trinity Coll., Dublin, 1961; M.A., ibid., 1964. Married Clara Mangan w. 3 children. Positions held: Deacon, Our Lady Queen of Peace Church, Dublin, 1962–; Geography Tchr., St. Phillip's Schl., Burley-in-Wharfedale, Yorks., 1967; Bibliography Tchr., Bradford Tech. Schl., Yorks., 1968–. Published works: Cast A Cold Eye, 1959; The Rain, The Moon, 1961; The Dark about Our Loves, 1962; Why Hitler is in Heaven, 1964; For Love of Ireland, 1967; Nollaig (w. Oliver Snoody), 1964; The Rebel Bloom, 1967; Other: Romances, 1960; The Leprechaun, 1963; Transubstantiations, 1963; Var. Political Pamphlets. Contbr. to (Anthologies): New Poets of Ireland, 1963; Ireland's Rebel Poets, 1967; Universities Poetry, 1968; Penguin Book of Irish Verse, 1970; (Jrnls.): Irish Stand; Ba'itah; Rebel; British League of Empire Loyalists Mag.; American Sword. Address: c/o Dept. of Italian, Univ. Coll., Galway, Ireland.

HOMAN, Agnes Ellen Jones, b. 3 Oct. 1909. Teacher. Education: Univ. of the State of N.Y., West Winfield, 1929, Oneonta, 1933; B.Ed., Univ. of Miami, 1955; studied Poetry at var. univs. Married Hilton S. Homan, 1 son, 3 daughters. Positions held: Tchr., Rural schls. in Herkimer Co., N.Y., 1929-33; Coral Gables Elem. Schl., 1945-46; Gulliver Schl., Coconut Grove, Fla., 1947-54; Hebrew Acad., Miami Beach, 1954-55; Coral Gables Elem. Schl., Fla., 1955–. Memberships: Acad. of Am. Poets; Laramore Rader Poetry Grp. (offices held: Chmn. of All Fla. Poetry Contest, 1966, Steering Comm., 1970, Chmn. & Rdr., World Poetry Day at the Coconut Grove Lib., 1970-74); Miami Poetry Grp., 1953-55. Published works: Dopey Duck Safety Book (in verse), 1952; Singing in the Sun, an anthol. of verse, 1964; Aunt Abbie, 1965. Record: Me (w. Alice Boyd Stockdale), 1960. Contbr. to: Y Drych; Folio; The Orbit; Christian Sci. Monitor; The Flame; Miami Daily News; Laramore Rader Poetry Yrbook, etc. Honours, awards: First Hon. Mention, La. Poetry Soc. Nat. Contest, for Sonnet, 1959; Monthly prizes, Laramore Rader Poetry Grp., 1968, '74, Yearly Prize, 1974; Stockdale Award, 1964; Alper Award, 1966; Pierce Award, 1973; Marjorie Stoneman Douglas Award, Univ. of Miami, 1961. Address: 3170 Gifford Ln., Coconut Grove, Miami, FL 33133, U.S.A.

HONG, Yoon Sook, pen name **YEO SA,** b. 19 Aug. 1925. College Lecturer; Poet. Education: Coll. of Educ., Seoul Nat. Univ., Korea. Married to Businessman, 1 s., 3 d. Positions held: Newspaper Reporter, 1947-49; HS Tchr., 1949-50; Coll. Lectr., 1970–. Memberships: Exec. Comm., Korean Ctr., Int. PEN; Exec. Comm., Korean Writers Assn. Published works: Yeo Sa Poetry, 1962; A Windmill, 1964; An Ornamentation, 1967; Sound of Clock in Dailiness, 1971; This City After Eden, 1967. Contbr. to: Modern Literature; Monthly Literature; Modern Poetry; Sindanga; Yeo Sung dang-A; Jubu Sang Hwal; Dari; Sam Teo; Dark Sea Sin moon; Catholic Shibo; Hanguk Weekly; Korea Journal; Chosum ilba; Dang-A ilba; Hanguk ilba; Jung ang ilba; Dai han ilba; Kyung Hyang Sinmoon. Address: 50-13 1-Ka, Chang-Ku, Chang Chung-Dong, Seoul, Korea.

HONIG, Edwin, b. 3 Sept. 1919. University Professor. Education: A.B., Univ. of Wisconsin, 1941; A.M., ibid, 1947; A.M. (ad eundem), Brown Univ., 1957. Positions held: Instr., Univ. of NM, 1948; Instr., Harvard Univ., 1949-52; Asst. Prof., ibid, 1952-57; Assoc. Prof., Brown Univ., 1957-60; Prof., ibid, 1960–; Chmn. Dept., 1967-68. Memberships: Authors Guild; Pen Club; Hon. Member of New England Poetry Club. Publications: Garcia Lorca, 1944; The Moral Circus, 1955; The

Gazabos, 41 Poems, 1959; new ed. 1961; The Making of Allegory, 1959; Poems for Charlotte, 1963; Survivals, 1964; Spring Journal, 1968; Four Springs, 1972; (translations) Calderon; Four Plays, 1961; Cervantes: Interludes, 1964; Selected Poems of Fernando Pessoa, 1971; Calisto and Melibea, 1972. Contbr. to: New York Times; New Republic; Nation; Poetry Mag.; Yankee; New Mexico Quarterly; Saturday Review; Kenyon Review; Sewanee Review; Shenondoah; Poetry; New Yorker; Va. Qtly. Review; Saturday Evening Post; Southwest Review, etc. Honours: Guggenheim Fellowship, 1948; ibid, 1962; Saturday Review Poetry Prize, 1956; New England Poetry Club Golden Rose, 1961; Am. Acad. of Arts & Letters, 1966; Amy Lowell Traveling Poetry Scholarship, 1968; R. I. Governor's Arts Award, 1970. Address: Dept. of English, Brown Univ., Providence, Rhode Island 02912, USA.

HOOFDAKKER, Rudi Rutger Hendrik van den, pen name **KOPLAND, Rutger,** b. 4 Aug. 1934. Psychiatrist. Education: Fac. of Med., Univ. of Groningen, 1951-59; Trng. & Sci. work in Neurophysiol., maily Electroencephalography, 1962-65; Trng. in Clincal Neurol., 1965-67; Trng. in Clin. Psych. & Psychotherapy, 1967-70. Married Dr. Ina Lamberts, 3 daughters. Positions held: Med. Officer, Army Psychotherapeutic Ctr., 1959-62; Rsch. Fellow, Dept. of Neurol., Univ. of Groningen, 1962-65; Registrar, Dept. of Clin. Neurol., ibid, 1965-67; Sr. Registrar, Dept. of Clin. Psychiatry, 1967-70; Cons. & Assoc. Prof., Dept. of Biological Psych., 1970–. Member, Vereniging van Letterkundigen. Published works: (poetry) Onder het vee, 1966; Het Orgeltje van yesterday, 1968; Alles op de fiets, 1970; Wie wat vindt heeft slecht gezocht, 1972; (prose) Het bolwerk van de beterweters, 1970. Contbr. of poetry & essays on poetry to var. jrnls. & reviews, also to radio & TV progs. Recip., Jan Campert Prize for 'Alles op de fiets', 1970. Address: Oude Boerenweg 13, Glimmen (Gr.), The Netherlands.

HOOLE, Margaret Mary, pen name, **GIBSON, M. Munro,** b. 10 Jan. 1921. Married, 1 daughter. Education: Convent of the Holy Child, Blackpool, U.K. Positions held: Sec., I.C.I. Salt Ltd., Winsford, 2 yrs.; Anti-Aircraft Battery (A.T.S.), 2 yrs.; Clerk, I.C.I. Winnington, Northwich, Ches., 2 yrs. Memberships: Fellow, Orbis Int. Poetry Soc.; Poetry Soc. of G.B.; Avalon Poetry Soc., U.S.A.; C.S.S.I., Italy; N.Y. Poetry Forum. Published works: Consider the Lilies, 1966; On the Still Air of Being, 1973. Contbr. to: Shropshire Mag.; Manifold; Breakthru; Candelabrum; Expression One; The Shore; Winsford Guardian; Cyclo-Flame, U.S.A.; Sunburst, U.S.A.; Writers Review; This England; Envoi; Scrip. Rep. in following anthols: Its World Makes the Love Go Round; Laudamus Te; Spring Anthol., 1972 & 73; Orbis Anthol., etc. Honours, awards: Caedmon Award, 1967; Lake Aske Meml. Award Cert, 1970; Otto Swan Awards, N.Y. Poetry Forum, 1972. Address: Thornley Villa, 213 Crook Ln., Winsford, Ches., U.K.

HOOPELL, Jane, b. 24 Aug. 1929. Journalist. Positions held: Sub-Editor; Fiction Editor; Freelance Sub-Editor. Memberships: Sec., Greenwich Poetry Soc., 1968-73; Camden Poets, 1972–. Contbr. to: Slide into Poetry (Camden Poets); Dumb Dumb (mag. of Greenwich Poetry Soc.); Centre 17 (mag. produced by Centre 17 Poetry Grp.); Keats Prize Poetry 73; York Poetry Prize (collected contbns.) Honours, awards: Runner-up, Keats Poetry Prize, 1973; Highly Commended, York Poetry Soc. Comp., 1972, Commended, 1971. Address: 52 Dallin Road, London SE18 3NU, U.K.

HOOPER, Hedley Colwill, pen name **HOOPER, Peter,** b. 19 May 1919. School Teacher. Education: B.A., Univ. of New Zealand, 1946. Positions held: Deputy Prin., Westland H.S., Hokitika, New Zealand, 1966–. Member, Thoreau Soc., U.S.A. Published works: A Map of Morning, 1964; Journey Towards an Elegy, 1969; A Pleasure of Friends (Ed.), 1970; The Mind of Bones, 1972; Earth Marriage, 1972. Contbr. to: N.Z.

Listener; N.Z. Jrnl. of Geology & Geophysics; N.Z. Broadcasting Corp.; Fragments; Argot; Arena; Mate; Meanjin Qtly.; Envoi; New Poet Mag.; John o'London's; Thoreau Jrnl.; Poet (India). Address: 13 Clough Rd., Paroa, Greymouth, New Zealand.

HOPE, Alex Derwent, b. 21 July 1907. University Teacher. Education: B.A., Sydney Univ., Australia, 1928; B.A., Oxford Univ., U.K., 1931. Married, 2 sons, 1 daughter. Positions held: Vocational Psychologist; School Tchr.; Lectr.; Prof. of Engl.; Library Fellow. Memberships: Past Pres., Australian Soc. of Authors; Australian Acad. of the Humanities. Published works: The Wandering Islands, 1956; Poems, 1960; Collected Poems, 1966; The Cave and the Spring, 1965, 1970; A Midsummer Eve's Dream, 1970; Dunciad Minor, 1970. Contbr. to num. mags., jrnls. & newspapers. Honours, awards: Australia-Britannica Award for Lit., 1965; Levinson Prize for Poetry, Chicago, 1969; Ingram Merrill Award for Lit., N.Y., 1969; O.B.E., 1972. Address: 66 Arthur Circle, Forrest, Canberra, SX ACT 2603, Australia.

HOPE, Francis, b. 1938. Journalist. Education: Eton Coll.; New Coll., Oxford (History). Positions held: Has worked for Encounter Mag.; Writes for The New Statesman Mag. Published work: Instead of a Poet & Other Poems, 1965. Contbr. to (Anthol.): New Lines 2, 1963. Fellow, All Soul's, Oxford.

HOPKINS, Hector Kenneth, b. 7 Dec. 1914. Author. Fellow, Royal Soc. of Lit. Published works: (poetry) Twelve Poems, 1937; Recent Poetry, 1937; New Sonnets, 1938; Six Sonnets, 1938; A Night Piece, 1943; Love & Elizabeth, 1944; Miscellany Poems, 1946; Songs & Sonnets, 1947; Poems on Several Occasions, 1948; To a Green Lizard Called Ramorino, 1949; To a Green Lizard, 1949; Apes & Elderberries, 1950; Poor Heretic, 1961; Foundlings & Fugitives, 1961; Forty-Two Poems, 1961; Collected Poems, 1935-65, 1965; Poems English & American, 1968; Slivers of Syntax, 1969; Bourbon & Branch, 1970; Kickshaws & Garnishings, 1970; American Poems & Others, 1970. Contbr. to approx. one hundred newspapers & mags. in U.K., U.S.A. & elsewhere. Address: Warren House, Southrepps, Norwich, NOR 35Y, U.K.

HOPKINSON, Allan Slade, b. 3 Nov. 1934. Public Relations Officer. Education: B.A., Univ. Coll. of the West Indies, Jamaica, 1955; Dip.Ed., ibid, 1956; Yale Univ. Drama Schl., New Haven, Conn., U.S.A., 1965-66. Married Freda Mae Campbell, 1 son, 1 daughter. Positions held: Tchr., Montego Bay H.S., Jamaica, 1956-58; Newspaper Ed., City Printery Ltd., Jamaica, Apr.-Dec., 1958; Info. Officer, P.R. Office, Jamaica Govt., 1959-61; Tchr., St. George's Coll., Trinidad, 1961-65; Lectr. in Engl., Univ. of Guyana, 1966-68; Tchr., St. George's Coll., Trinidad, 1968-73. Memberships: Artistic Dir., Caribbean Theatre Guild, Trinidad, 1970-73. Published works: The Four & Other Poems, 1954. Contbr. to: Focus (Jamaica); Bim (Barbados); Savacou (Jamaica); Commonwealth Poetry Today, U.K.; New Poems of the Commonwealth, U.K.; Caribbean Qtly., Jamaica; Breaklight, U.K.; Literary Half-Yrly., Univ. of Mysore, India. Address: c/o Jamaica Tourist Bd., Harbour St., Kingston, Jamaica, W.I.

HORAN, Leo, b. 12 Oct. 1891, Sioux City, Iowa, USA. Lawyer. Education: Master of Acct., pvte. commercial schls. in bus. admin. & fin.; LL.B., LaSalle Univ., Chicago, Ill., 1917. Married, Kate Gallaspy, 1923, 2 s. Positions held: Prin. Tchr., Live Oak Acad., Oxford, Miss., 1914-15; Ptnr., law firm, Water Valley; Assoc. Atty., War Dept., –1924; Atty., Jackson, 1924-37; w. Fed. Legal Serv., 1937-56. Memberships: Pres., Shreveport Writers Club, 1959-60; Past Mbr., La. Poetry Soc.; Miss. Poetry Soc.; Past Mbr., Am., State & Co., bar assns. Published works: The Kneeling Stranger & Other Poems, 1965; Beauty in a Breeze & Other Poems, 1971. Contbr. to: The Writer, Boston; The Commercial Appeal, Memphis; Miss. Poetry Jrnl.; Jrnl. of La. State Poetry Soc.; Author/Poet, etc.

Recip. sev. minor prizes. Address: PO Box 367, Decatur, Miss. 39327, USA.

HORDER, John Pearson (Peter), pen names **MEHER BABA, WONGLY GUERILLA POOH, WALLY,** b. 20 Nov. 1936. Male Model. Education: B.A., Selwyn Coll., Cambridge Univ., 1960; M.A., ibid, 1973. Positions held: Asst. Press Officer, Archbishop of Canterbury, 1961-62; Lit. Advisor, Constables, Publishers, 1964; Trustee, Ctr. for Bioenergy, Peckham, 1973; Model, Ugly Modelling Agency, 1973; Deputy Ed., 'Energy & Character', Jrnl. of Bioenergetic Rsch., 1974. Memberships: Chmn., Sufi Poetry Guild, Embodiment Comm., 1970; Chmn., Bioenergetic Therapists Poetry Assn., 1971; Chmn. w. John Bennett of Ctr. for Bioenergy Planning Comm. & Embodiment for Everyone, 1973; Chmn., Body Poetry Int. w. Gerda Boyesen & Mona Lisa Boyesen, 1974. Published works: The Child Walks Around its Own Grave, 1966; A Sense of Being, 1968, '69; Infinite Loving, 1973; Cecil & Baba, 1973; Baba, 1973; Potency & Aliveness in English Poets, 1974. Contbr. to var. jrnls., newspapers, mags. Honours, awards: Hafiz & Rumi Meml. Prizes for Meher Baba Poems, 1974; Pullitzer Prize for Meher Baba Poems, 1974. Address: c/o Ugly Enterprises Ltd., 6 Windmill St., London W.1., U.K.

HORN, Don Louis, b. 17 Jan. 1935. Physician (Pathologist). Education: B.S., Univ. of Miami, 1956; Grad., Cornell Univ. Med. Coll., 1960; Internship, Honolulu, Hawaii, 1 yr. Positions held: Asst. Prof. of Pathol., Louisiana State Schl. of Med., New Orleans, La., 1967; Assoc. Prof., ibid, 1969 & was appointed Surgical Pathologist, & for a time, Chief of Clinical Pathol., New Orleans V.A. Hosp.; currently Pathologist and Chief of Laboratories, The Medical Ctr. Hosp., Punta Gorda, Fla. Memberships: Org., New Orleans Poetry Forum; 2nd Pres., ibid, 1972-73. Contbr. to: New Orleans Poets Anthol., 1972; The Wisconsin Review, 1973; South & West, 1972; Poet India. Poetry Reading at Tulane Univ. Poetry Week, 1972. Poetry Forum Workshop conducted for La. State Univ., 1972. Address: 809 East Marion Ave., Punta Gorda, FL 33950, U.S.A.

HORN, Peter (Rudolph Gisella), pen name **SKELTON, Roger,** b. 7 Dec. 1934. Professor of German. Education: B.A., Witwatersrand, 1959; B.A. (Hons.), ibid, 1960; Ph.D., 1971. Positions held: Tchr.; Lectr.; Professor. Published works: Voices from the Gallows Tree, 1971. Contbr. to: Ophir; DeArte; New Coin; Wurm; Contrast; Sinn und Form; New Nation; Edge; Labris; Quinzena das Artes e Lettras; Unisa English Studies; The Poet; Expression One; Frontiers; Purple Renoster; The Classic; Workshop; IWWP Anthol. Address: Dept. of German Lang. & Lit., Univ. of Cape Town, Rondebosch, C.P., S. Africa.

HORNSTEIN, Patricia, pen name, **HUBBELL, Patricia,** b. 10 July 1928. Housewife. Education: B.A., Univ. of Conn., USA. Married, 1 d., 1 s. Positions held: Gen. Editl. Wk., Newtown Bee, Conn., & Westport Town Crier, Conn.; Horse and Dog Columnist, Bridgeport Post, Conn. Memberships: Authors Guild. Published works include: The Apple Vendor's Fair, 1963; 8 a.m. Shadows, 1965; Catch Me A Wind, 1968. Contbr. to the following jrnl.: NY Times. Address: RFD 1, Norton Road, Weston, Conn., USA.

HOROVITZ, Frances Margaret, b. 13 Feb. 1938. Teacher. Education: Hons. degree, English & Dramatics, Bristol Univ.; RADA; Married to Poet Michael Horovitz, 1 s. Published works include: Poems, 1967; The High Tower, 1970. Contbr. to the following anthols., jrnls., mags., etc.: Southern Review; Aylesford Review; Antigonish Review; Resurgence; Vortex; Adam International; Aquarius; Love, Love, Love; Inherited; New Departures; Children of Albion; Second Aeon; Prism. Address: c/o New Departures, 29 Colville Terrace, London, W11 2BU, UK.

HOROVITZ, Michael, b. 4 Apr. 1935. Poet; Reader; Editor. Education: Wm. Ellis Schl., Highgate, 1947-53;

Hons. degree, English Lang. & Lit., Brasenose Coll., Oxford. Personal details: Descended from Rabbis of Hungary, Germany, Poland & Bohemia; m. to Frances Horovitz, Poet. Positions held: Lectr., Univ. Maryland Overseas Program, 1961-64; Tutor, Royal Coll. of Art, other art schls.; Ed., New Departures, 1959-71. Published works include: Europa, 1962; Declaration, 1963; Nude Lines, 1964; Strangers, 1965; Poetry for the People, 1967; Bank Holiday, 1968; The Wolverhampton Wanderer, 1971; Children of Albion, 1969; Love Poems, 1971; Country Life, 1971. Contbr. to the following anthols., jrnls., mags., etc.: TLS; Tribune; Evergreen; City Lights; Review; NY Quarterly; Aylesford Review; Ukrainean Review; Akzente; Phantomas; Isis; Oxford Opinion; Granta; The Scotsman; Outposts; Oz; International Times; Ink; PEN News Poems, 1965; Western Daily Press; Manifold; Samphire; New Measure. Address: c/o Latimer Press, 4 Alwyne Villas, London N1, UK.

HOSKINS, Katherine de Montalant Lackey, pen name, **HOSKINS, Katherine,** b. 25 May 1909. Writer. Education: A.B., Smith Coll. Married, 1 d. Publications: A Penitential Primer, 1945; Villa Narcisse 1956; Out in the Open, 1959; Excursions, 1967. Contbr. to: Sewanee Review; Tiger's Eye; Yale Review; Partisan Review; Western Review; Poetry, Chicago; Wake. Honours: Brandeis Univ. Fine Arts Award, 1957; Guggenheim Fellowship, 1958. Address: Atheneum Publishers, 122 East 42nd St., New York, NY, USA.

HOUEDARD, Pierre Thomas Paul (dom Sylvester), pen names, **dsh; The Gloster Ode Construction Company,** b. 16 Feb. 1924. Profession: Benedictine Monk. Education: M.A., Jesus Coll., Oxford; Ph.L., S-Anselmo Coll., Rome, Italy. Published works include: Thalamussol 250364, 1964; Rock Sand Tide, 1964; Frog-Pond-Plop, 1965; Atom, 1965; Anthology/Chronology/& C of Concrete, 1965; Worm-Wood/Womb-Word 051165, 1966; Aesthetics of the Death Wish, 1966; To Catch a Whiteman by His Manifesto, 1967; Intro to Freewheel Catalog 090467, 1967; Brighton Festival Frog, 1967; Tantric Poems Perhaps, 1967; Book of 12 Mudras, 1967; A Book of Mazes Y Troytowns, 1967; Easter Frog Toy for Pesach-Skipover, 1967; Semaine Eucidienne, 1968; Poster for the Breakdown of Nations 4th World Conference, 1968; Gloster Wheel-ode for Kencox, 1969; A Snow Mouse En-Trance, 1969, December: Successful Cube Tranceplant in Honor of Chairman Mao, 1970; December: Ode to the Colonels, 1970; Auto-de-Chakra-Struction 090367, 1971; Ed. Glyn Pursglove, to be published 1972; many more. Num. visual poetry exhibs. in UK, USA, Canada, Spain, France, etc. Contbr. to num. anthols., jrnls., mags., etc., inclng: Il Compasso; Poesia Concreta; Experimentalni Poezie, Prague; Anthol. of Concrete Poetry, Chicago Review Anthol. of Concretism; Imaged Words & Worded Images; Antigonish Review; Approaches; Art & Artist; Beloit Poetry; Broadsheet; Ikon; Les Lettres. London Mag.; Notebook; Resurgence; Studio, etc. Address: Prinknash Abbey, Gloucester GL4 8EX, UK.

HOUGH, Graham Goulder, b. 14 Feb. 1908. Professor of English. Education: Univ. of Liverpool; Queen's Coll., Cambridge. Married Rosamund Oswell w. 1 son & 1 daughter; Married Ingeborg Neumann. Positions held: Lecturer in English, Rattley Coll., Singapore, 1930-50; Professor of English, Univ. of Malaya, 1946; Visiting Lecturer, John Hopkins Univ., Baltimore, Md., 1950; Visiting Professor, Cornell Univ., Ithaca, N.Y., 1958; Fellow, Christ's Coll., Cambridge, 1951–; Tutor, ibid., 1955-60; Praelector & Fellow, Darwin Coll., Cambridge, 1964–; Reader in English, Univ. of Cambridge, 1965-66; Professor, ibid., 1966–. Published works: Legends & Pastorals (verse), 1961; Literary Criticism: The Last Romantics, 1953, 67; The Dark Sun: A Study of D.H. Lawrence, 1956; Image & Experience, 1960; A Preface to the Faerie Queene, 1962; The Dream & the Task, 1963; An Essay on Criticism, 1966; Style & Stylistics, 1969; Other: Ed., Selected Poems of George Meredith, 1962; Orlando

Furioso, 1963; Poems of Samuel Taylor Coleridge, 1963. Honours: D.Litt., Malaya, 1955; Litt.D., Cambridge, 1961. Address: The White Cottage, Grantchester, Cambs.

HOUGHTON, Barbara Coan, b. 11 Aug. 1932. Registered Nurse; Homemaker. Education: B.S. in Nursing, Univ. of Pa.; M.A. in Public Hlth. Nursing, Univ. of Wash. Married, 3 children. Positions held: Staff Nurse, Multnomah Co. Hosp., Portland, Ore.; Staff Nurse, Mass. Hosp., Boston, Mass.; Head Nurse, Pa. Hosp., Phila. Member, Wis. Fellowship of Poets. Contbr. to: Dragma – mag. of Alpha Omicron Pi; Friends Jrnl.; McFarland Community Life. Address: 1723 Highway AB, McFarland, WI 53558, U.S.A.

HOWARD, Frances Minturn, Writer. Education: Friends School, NYC.; Art Students League; Nat. Academy. Memberships: Internat. P.E.N.; Poetry Soc. of America (Reg. Vice-Pres. for New England); Bd. Member, New England Poetry Club; Advisory Editor, Borestone Mountain Poetry Awards. Published works: All Keys Are Glass, 1950; Sleep Without Armor, 1953; Contbr. to anthols.: Man Answers Death; The Golden Year; 12th P.E.N. Anthol., New Poems; New Orlando Anthol.; Pergamon Press Anthol.; Women Poets of England and America. Poems also published in The New Yorker; Atlantic; Poetry; Va. Qtly. Review; Sat. Rev. of Literature; Antioch Review; Yankee; Southwest Review, etc. Awards include: 1000-dollars Award, Poetry Awards of California, for first book, All Keys Are Glass; New England Poetry Club Ann. Award of the Golden Rose, 1954; 1st and 2nd awards, Poetry Soc. of America, for best poem of year, 1963; 1st prize, 100gns. in internat. contest, 1963, sponsored (for Farmer's, Ltd.) by the North Side Arts Festival of Sydney, Australia; 1972, 300-dollars award for best poem of year from P.S.A., also Consuelo Ford Award of 200-dollars; also recip. of Kansas City Star Award for single poem. Address: 46 Mt. Vernon St., Boston, MA 02108, USA.

HOWARD, Richard, b. 1929. Journalist; Lexicographer & Translator of Contemporary French Literature. Education: Columbia Univ., N.Y.; Sorbonne, Paris. Positions held: Free-lance Translator & Lexicographer; Writer of Reviews & Criticism for Poetry Mag., Chgo. Published works: Quantities, 1962; Other: Second Growth : Studies in American Poetry since 1950, 1967; Alone with America: Studies in the Art of Poetry in the United States since World War II, 1969; Pre-eminent Victorians, 1969; Translations: Mobile, 1963; Force of Circumstance, 1965; The Poetics of Paul Valéry, 1966. Contbr. to: American Literary Anthology I, 1968. Recip., Guggenheim Grant, 1966-67.

HOWARD, Thelma L., b. 14 Mar. 1925. Teacher; Writer. Education: B.S. Psychology, M.L. Literature, Univ. of Pittsburgh; Georgetown Univ., Washington D.C. Sister of Byron Janis, concert pianist. Teaching positions in Pittsburgh, Pa., Wash. D.C., Miami, Fla. Memberships: Internat. Biog. Assoc.; Major Poets Chapter, Tremont, Ill.; Centro Studi e Scambi Internazionali. Pubs. Thoughts in Winter, 1973. Contbr. to: Pied Piper Press, 1973; Outstanding Contemp. Poetry, 1969; Modern Poetry, 1973; South and West, 1969; Kansas Kernels, 1972; Gato, 1970; Fine Arts, 1972; All Time Favorite Poetry, 1972. Awards include: Gato International Poetry Assoc., 1969; Clover International Poetry Assoc., 1973; Laurel Publishers, 1973. Address: 17800 Atlantic Blvd., Miami Beach, Fla. 33160, USA.

HOWE, Fanny, pen name **FIELD, Della,** b. 15 Oct. 1940. Teacher. Education: Stanford Univ., 2 yrs. Married Carl Senna, 3 children. Positions held: Clerk-Bookkeeper, Calif., 1960-63; Bookkeeper, Boston, 1963-64; Reader, N.Y., 1965-66; Tchr., Tufts Coll., Mass. Coun. for the Arts, Emerson Coll., 1968-73. Published works: West Coast Nurse, 1963; Vietnam Nurse, 1965; Forty Whacks, 1969; Eggs, 1970; Legacy of Lanshore, 1973; Radical Love, 1974. Contbr. to: The Atlantic Monthly; Ploughshares; Antaeus; Fire

Exit; Poetry. Honours, awards: MacDowell Colony Fellowship, 1965; Nat. Endowment for the Arts Award, 1969. Address: One Robeson St., Jamaica Plain, MA 02130, U.S.A.

HOWELL, Anthony, b. 20 Apr. 1945. Poet. Education: Royal Ballet Schl., London; Centre de la Danse Classique, Cannes, France. Mbr., Royal Ballet Co., London. Published works: Sergei de Diaghileff, 1968; Inside the Castle, 1969; Imruil: A Naturalized Version of his First Ode-Book, 1970; Other: Erotic Lyrics, 1970. Contbr. to: Poetry Review; Scotsman. Address: c/o Barrie & Rockliff, The Cresset Press, 2 Clements Inn, London, W.C.2, UK.

HOWES, Barbara, b. 1 May 1914. Poet; Anthologist; Housewife. Married William Jay Smith, 2 sons (David & Gregory). Education: B.A., Bennington Coll., U.S.A. Published works: The Undersea Farmer, 1948; In the Cold Country, 1954; Light & Dark, 1959; Looking up at Leaves, 1966; The Blue Garden, 1972. Ed. of the following anthols: 23 Modern Stories, 1963; From the Green Antilles, Writings from the Caribbean, 1966; From the Green Antilles, English Edn., 1967; From the Green Antilles, paper edn., England, 1970; The Sea-Green Horse w. Gregory Jay Smith, 1970; The Eye of the Heart, Short Stories from Latin America, 1973. Contbr. to: The N.Y. Times; The New Yorker; The New Republic; The Atlantic; Encounter; Stand; BIM; The Sewanee Review; The Yale Review; The Southern Review; The Mass. Review; Poetry Miscellany; Harper's Bazaar; Ladies Home Jrnl.; Le Petit Matin, etc. Honours, awards: Guggenheim Fellowship, 1955; Brandeis Univ. Creative Arts Poetry Grant, 1958; Award in Lit., Nat. Inst. of Arts & Letters, 1971; Annual Award, New England Poetry Club, 1973. Address: Brook House, North Pownal, VT 05260, U.S.A.

HOYEM, Andrew Lewison, b. 1 Dec. 1935. Printer. Education: B.A., Pomona Coll., Claremont, Calif. Married Judith Bordin Laws Hoyem. Positions held: Ptnr., Auerhahn Press, 1961-64; Owner, Andrew Hoyem, Printer, 1965-66; Ptnr., Grabhorn-Hoyem, 1966-73; Owner, Andrew Hoyem, Printer, 1973-. Published works: The Wake, 1963; The Music Room, 1965; Chimeras (transformation of Nerval's sonnet sequence), 1966; The Pearl (transl. from Middle Engl. w. John F. Crawford), 1967; Articles (poems 1960-67), 1969. Contbr. to: Now; Blue Grass; Prospect; Cow; Intransit; For Now; Poetry; Evergreen Review; Work; The World; Ambit; Sumac; San Francisco Chronicle, etc. Address: 4040 – 17th St., San Francisco, CA 94114, U.S.A.

HOYER, Mildred N., pen name **MERRITT, Si,** b. Brooklyn, NY. Poet, Freelance Writer, Assoc. Editor, Education: NY City Pub. Schools. Married to Nils Gunther Hoyer. Positions held: Pres., Noontime Group YWCA, 1946-1958; Committeewoman, Kings County Republican Com., 1947-1959; Vice Pres., Brooklyn Poetry Circle, 1959-1968, Pres., 1968-1972; Assoc. Critic, 1962-; Poetry Chairman and Dir. of Poetry Workshop, NYC Branch, Nat. League of Am. Pen Women, 1961-; Pres., Women Poets of N.Y., 1973-; Member, Poetry Soc. of Am.; Haiku Soc. of Am., etc. Published work: The Master Key, 1965. Contbr. to numerous newspapers and journals. Awards include: Louise Crittenden Mosely Award, 1955, 1957, 1958, 1959; Marie-Schroeder-Devrient Award, 1956, 1961; Anna Hempstead Branch Award, 1957, 1960; Ruth Mason Rice Award, 1959, 1971; BPC Ann. Book Award, 1963; Marie-Louise d'Esternaux Gold Medal, 1961; 2 Midwest Regional Awards, 1965; Edwin Markham Award, 1964; Citation, Rochester Festival Relig. Arts, 1966; BPC Gold Medal, 1968; Lady Beatrice Graham Award, 1968-1971; Citation, Nat. League of Am. Pen Women (1st pub. book), 1968; Haiku Highlights Book Award, 1970; World Poetry Day Award (Imprints Qtly.), 1969; Anne Lloyd Mem. (Women Poets of N.Y.), 1971; Citation (for 10yrs. service as dir. of its poetry workshop), Nat. League of Am. Pen Women, 1971; Citation, Brooklyn Poetry Circle (for 16 yrs. of outstanding service as an officer including 10yrs. service as Assoc. Critic), 1972.

Address: 352 85 St., Brooklyn, NY, USA.

HRISTIC, Jovan, b. 26 Aug. 1933. Publisher. Education: grad. in philos., Belgrade Univ. Married. Positions held: Theatre Critic of the monthly 'Književnost' (Literature); Sec., Yugoslav PEN, Belgrade Ctr., 1962-64. Memberships: AICTA (Association internationale des critiques de théâtre); PEN; SEC (Soc. européenne de culture). Published works: Dnevnik o Ulisu (A Diary on Ulysses), 1954; Pesme 1953-59, 1959; Aleksandrijska škola (Alexandrian School), 1963. Contbr. to: Književnost (Literature); Delo (Work); Neue Deutsche Literatur; Revue Svetova Literatura (Prague). Address: Skerlićeva 26, 11000 Belgrade, Yugoslavia.

HRUSKA, Elias Nicolas, pen name **HRUSKA-CORTES, Elias,** b. 7 July 1943. Professor of Ethnic Studies. Education: Grad., Univ. of Calif., Berkeley, 1970. Positions held: Painter; Tchr.; Faculty Advisor/Editor; Prof., San Jose, 2 yrs. Has been writing poetry for 5 yrs. Published works: This Side & Other Things, graphics by Rupert Garcia, & photographs by Alejandro Stuart, 1971 & 1972. Contbr. to: Yardbird; La Malcriada de Santa Clara; Berkeley Poets Commune Anthol.; Mundus Artium. Recip., Phelam Award, San Francisco Fndn. Address: 3541 Kirkwood Dr., San Jose, CA 95117, U.S.A.

HUBBELL, Lindley Williams, b. 3 Jun. 1901. Born in Hartford, Conn., USA. of English parentage; became Japanese citizen in 1960. Positions held: NY Pub. Library, 1925-46; Randall School, Hartford, Conn., 1946-53; Doshisha Univ., Kyoto, 1953-70; Mukogawa Univ., Nishinomiya, 1970-. Pubs. Dark Pavilion, 1927; The Tracing of a Portal, 1931; Winter-Burning, 1938; The Ninth Continent, 1947; Long Island Triptych, 1947; The Birth of the Diatom, 1949; Aki no Hi, 1962; Seventy Poems, 1962; Air Poem, 1967 (2nd ed. 1971); Autobiography, 1971; Atlantic Triptych, 1971; Lectures on Shakespeare, 1958; Shakespeare and Classic Drama, 1962; A note on the Shakespeare Apocrypha, 1966 (2nd ed. enlarged, 1972); Miscellany, 1972. Recip. Litt.D., Doshisha Univ., 1960. Address: Mukogawa Univ., 4–46 Ikebiraki, Nishinomiya, Japan.

HUBIN, Christian, b. 18 Sept. 1941. Professor. Educ: Licence, Philos. & Letters, Univ. of Liège. Memberships: Soc. of Men of Letters of France; Organising Comm., Int. Biennales of Poetry, Knokke, Belgium; Edit. Comm., Jrnl. des Poètes, Brussels; Charles Plisnier Fndn. Published works: Orphéon, 1962; Epitomé, 1962; Musique, 1963; Etudes Pour les Deux Mains, 1964; Soleils de Nuit, 1964; Messe Pour Une Fin du Monde, 1965; Prélude à une Apocalypse, 1966; Le Chant Décapite La Nuit, 1968; Terre Ultime, 1970; Traverse-Pierre, 1971; En Marge du Poème, 1972; Coma des Sourdes Veillées, 1973; Demeure Consumée, 1973; Alliages, 1974. Contbr. to: Carbone; Encres Vives; Odradek; Solaire; Sud; Dire; Haut-Pays; La Tour de Feu; Fantasmagie; Nouvelles à la Main; Espaces; Marginales; Le Jrnl. des Poètes; Marche Romane, etc. Honours, awards: Meridien Prize, 1964; Schmitz Prize, 1969; Flouquet Prize, 1970. Address: 49 Rue du Belvédère, 5000 Namur, Belgium.

HUCHEL, Peter, b. 3 Apr. 1903. Writer. Education: Univs. of Berlin, Freiburg, Vienna. Married Monica Huchel. Positions held: Tchr., Chief of Drama, Radio Producer & Artistic Dir., Berlin Radio, 1945-48; Chief Ed. of lit. jrnl., Sinn Und Form., 1949-62. Memberships incl: Gruppe 47, 1952; Société Européene de Culture, Venedig, 1958; COMES, Rome, 1961; PEN; Deutschen Akad. der Kunste, Berlin; Freien Akad. der Kunste, Hamburg; Deutschen Akad. fur Sprache u. Dichtung, Darmstadt. Published works: Gedichte, 1948; Gedichte, 1949; Chausseen Chausseen, 1963; Die Sternenreuse, 1925-47, 1967; Gezahlte Tage, 1972; Gedichte, 1973; & var. books publ. abroad. Contbr. to anthols., jrnls. & mags. in Germany, France, Czechoslovakia, U.K., U.S.A., Japan, etc. Recip. num. honours & awards inclng: Nat. prize of DDR, 1955; Johann-Heinrich-Merck-Prize, German Acad. for

Speech & Poetry, 1971; Austrian State Prize for European Lit., 1972; Arbeitsstipendium des Berliner Kunstpreises fur Literatur, 1972. Address: Botzenweg 51, D – 7813 Staufen im Breisgau, German Fed. Repub.

HUDDLE, David, b. 11 July 1942. University Teacher. Education: B.A., Univ. of Va., 1968; M.A., Hollins Coll., 1969; M.F.A., Columbia Univ., 1971. Positions held: Asst. Prof. of Engl., Univ. of Vt., 1971–. Contbr. to: Esquire; The Georgia Review; The Tex. Qtly.; The Carleton Miscellany; The Boston Phoenix. Address: Dept. of Engl. Univ. of Vt., Burlington, VT 05401, U.S.A.

HUDSON, Sylvia Constance, pen names, GOURRIET, Mel & Gray, Penelope, b. 15 Jan. 1928. Writer. Education: Abbot Typewriting Bur., Godalming, Surrey, U.K.; Evening Inst. & Tech. Coll.; Nat. Ext. Coll., Cambridge. Married, 3 daughters. Positions held: Asst. & Libn., W.H. Smith & Son, 1946; Sec. until 1953. Memberships: Soc. of Poets & Authors; Authors Analytical Soc.; The Poetry Soc.; Poem of the Month Club. Contbr. to: New Poetry, 1971; Quill Anthol.; Writers' Review Year Book, 1971; New Times Poetry, 1970; New Bond Anthol., 1970; Laudamus Te, 1967; Collected Poems Vol.2, 1968; The Muse; The Poets of Symbol, vols. 1 & 2; Success Christmas Anthols.; Ore; Writers Review; Manuscript; Quill; The Knaphill Publication. Recip. of var. prizes for poetry. 1973 Personal Poetry Broadcast, Washington D.C., U.S.A. Address: 54 Lansdown Close, St. John's, Woking, Surrey, U.K.

HUDSON, Thomas Cyril, b. 25 Aug. 1910. Engineering Estimator. Member, Isle of Wight Writers' Circle. Published works: Kairos, 1960. Contbr. to: Hampshire Poets; Humour Variety; The Boy's Own Paper; Southern Evening Echo. Honours, awards: 1st prize, I.O.W. Writers' Circle, 1971 & '72; The Margery Hume Cup, I.O.W. Musical Comp. Fest., 1972 & '73. Address: Wyvern, Newport Rd., Cowes, Isle of Wight, PO31 8PE, U.K.

HUDSPETH, Betty Sue, pen name HAMMELL, Andre, b. 3 Aug. 1923. Writer and Secretary. Education: Science Hill HS; Dunbarton Coll. of Holy Cross. Memberships: Académie D'Aquitaine, Maître-Es-Lettres, HC; Hon. Mbr.; Les Violetti Ricards & Normands; Mercante Del Tempio Dei Magnati Bibliofili, conferred by Min. of Pub. Instrn., Naples, Italy. Published works: Beauty Beyond Our Eyes, 1950; Leaves of Life, 1956; This Music, 1965. Contbr. to: Songs of the Free, 1947; Conquerors of Tomorrow, 1947; This Shall Endure, 1955; With No Secret Meaning, 1957; 7th Year Harvest, 1958; New Orlando Poetry Anthol.–This Singing Earth, 1958, '59; Prairie Wings; Different; Candor; Wildfire; Beat of Wings; Reflections; Driftwind; Commercial Appeal; Marches De France; Avalonian; Flame; Quicksilver; New Athenaeum. Awards: Le Mérite National Francais; Prix de L'Angérie Française, Concours Littéraire, Syndicat des Journalistes et Ecrivains; Ph.D. (hon.), Internat. Acad. Address: Temple Court, Apt. 9, 431 N.W. Third St., Miami, FL 33128, USA.

HUFANA, Alejandrino G., b. 22 Oct. 1926. University Teacher; Editor. Education: A.B., English, Univ. of Philippines, Quezon City, 1952; M.A., Comparative Lit., ibid., 1961; Special Studies in English Lit., Univ. of Calif., Berkeley, 1957-58; Currently studying for M.S. in Library Science, Columbia Univ., N.Y. Married Julita Quirning w. 4 daughters. Positions held: Asst. Prof. English & Comparative Lit., Univ. of the Philippines, 1964–; Managing Ed., Univ. of the Philippines Press, 1965-66. Mbr., Bd. of Judges, Palanca Memorial Awards in Literature (Chmn., Poetry Panel, 1968). Published works: 13 Kalisud, 1955; Sickle Season: Poems of a First Decade, 1948-59; Poro Point, An Anthology of Lives: Poems 1955-59, 1961; The Wife of Lot & New Poems, 1969. Contbr. to (Anthols.): A Doveglion Book of Philippine Poetry, 1962; Philippine Literature from Ancient Times to the Present, 1964; New Writing from the Philippines, 1966; (Jrnls.):

Diliman Review; Literary Review; Beloit Poetry Jrnl. Honours: Rockefeller Foundation Fellowship in Creative Writing (Poetry), Univ. of Calif., Berkeley, 1961-62; Repub. Cultural Heritage Award in Lit., 1965; Rockefeller Fellowship for study & Training in Librarianship, N.Y., 1968. Address: 54 Auxillary Rd., Area I, Univ. of the Philippines, Quezon City, Diliman, Philippines.

HUFF, Robert, b. 3 Apr. 1924. University Teacher. Education: A.B., Engl. Lit., Wayne State Univ., Detroit, Mich., 1949; A.M., Humanities, ibid., 1952. Married Sally Ann Huff w. 3 children. Positions held: Has taught at Wayne State Univ., 1950-52, 1957-58; Univ. of Ore., Eugene, 1952-53; Fresno State Coll., Calif., 1953-55; Ore. State Univ., Corvallis, 1955-57; Univ. of Delaware, Newark, 1960-64; Currently Assoc. Prof., Western Wash. State Coll., Bellingham. Published works: Colonel Johnson's Ride, 1959; The Course, 1966. Contbr. to (Anthols.): The Borestone Mountain Poetry Awards, 1958; Oregon Signatures, 1959; New Poets of England & America, 1962; Various Light, 1964; 19 Poetas de Hoy en Los Estados Unidos, 1966; Heartland, 1967; Contemporary American Poets, 1969; (Jrnls.): Harper's Mag.; Saturday Review; Nation; Atlantic; Voices; Northwest Review; Prairie Schooner; Paris Review; Kenyon Review. Recording of The Sound of Pacific Northwest Poetry, 1968. Hons. incl: Student Fellowship, Schl. of Letters, Ind. Univ., Bloomington, 1957; Writing Scholarship, Bread Loaf Writers Conference, Middlebury, Vt., 1961. Address: 2820 Eldridge Street, Bellingham, Wash. USA.

HUGHES, Dorothy (Berry), b. 17 Apr. 1910. Librarian. Education: B.A., Barnard Coll., Phi Beta Kappa; B.S., Columbia Univ. School of Library Service. Positions held: Asst. Librarian, Columbia Univ. Engineering Library; N.Y. Public Library. Member, Poetry Soc. of America. Pubs.: The Green Loving, 1953; The Great Victory Mosaic, 1971. Contrib. to: Poetry (Chicago); Mass. Review; American Scholar; Harper's; Chelsea; Univ. of Denver Qtly.; Chicago Tribune (Poets Today), etc. Recip. DeWitt Award (Poetry Soc. of America), 1969; Award from the Acad. of Arts and Letters and Inst. of Arts and Letters, 1973. Address: 740 West End Ave., New York, NY 10025, USA.

HUGHES, Glyn, b. 25 May 1935. Writer. Education: Regl. Coll. of Art, Manchester, 1953-57, '59-60; Qualified with N.D.D. & A.T.D., Univ. of Manchester. Positions held: Art Tchr., var. sec. schls. & Insts. of Further Educ. in Lancashire & Yorkshire, 1960-72. Published works: (poetry) The Stanedge Bull, pamphlet, 1968; Love on the Moor, pamphlet, 1969; Neighbours, (Macmillan) 1970; Rest the Poor Struggler, (Macmillan) 1972; Towards the Sun, pamphlet (poems & photographs), 1971; (prose) Northerners (a visionary-documentary account of the millstone grit area of the Pennines), (Gollancz) 1975. Contbr. to: Critical Survey; Sunday Times; Times Lit. Supplement; Granta; Malahat Review; Kenyon Review; Phoenix; New Statesman; Poetry Wales; Anglo-Welsh Review; Encounter; Michigan Qtly. Review; Tribune; Second Aeon; Wave; Contrasts. Rep. in following anthols: PEN New Poems 1967 & 1971-72 & 1972-73; Wise Wanton Womanly, 1967; The Young British Poets, 1971; reviews & articles to Tribune, 1973. Recip., Welsh Arts Coun. Young Poets Prize, 1969. Address: 28 Lower Millbank, Sowerby Bridge, Yorks. HX6 3ED, U.K.

HUGHES, Marjorie Ethel, pen name HUGHES, Margery Edwards, b. 14 Sept. 1913. Housewife; Writer. Married, 2 sons. Memberships: Am. Poetry League; United Amateur Press; Spafaswap Mag. Contbr. to: Lyrical Iowa, 1970; Am. Poetry League, 1972-73; Quid Nunc? 1973; Crum's Crumpets, 1973; United Amateur Press, 1973; Spafaswap, 1973; Times Republican newspaper, 1970. Recip., Hon. Mention, Times Republican, 1973. Address: R.R. no. 4, Marshalltown, IA 50158, U.S.A.

HUGHES, Ted, b. 1930. Writer. Poet. Education: Pembroke Coll., Cambridge Univ.; M.A. Published works: The Hawk In The Rain, 1957; Lupercal, 1960; Meet My Folks!, 1961; The Earth-Owl and Other Moon People, 1963; How The Whale Became, 1963; Nessie, the Mannerless Monster, 1964; Wodwo, 1967. Ed: Five American Poets, 1963; Selected Poems of Keith Douglas (w. intro. by Ted Hughes), 1964; Recklings, 1967; Scapegoats & Rabies, 1967; Poetry in the Making, 1967; The Iron Man, 1968; Crow, 1971; Eat Crow, 1971. Contbr. to: London Mag.; Encounter; Observer, New Statesman; Spectator; Vogue; Harper's Bazaar; Times Lit. Supplement; Atlantic; New Yorker; Partisan Review; Sewanee Review; etc. Awards: 1st Prize, Guinness Poetry Awards, 1958; John Simon Guggenheim Fellowship, 1959-60; Somerset Maugham Award, 1960; Hawthornden Prize, 1961. Address: c/o Faber & Faber Ltd., 3 Queen Square, London, UK.

HUGO, Richard Franklin, b. 21 Dec. 1923. University Lecturer. Education: B.A., M.A., Univ. of Wash., Seattle. Positions held: Mbr., Dept. of English, Univ. of Mont., Missoula (Visiting Lecturer & currently Assoc. Prof.), 1964–. Published works: The Run of Jacks, 1961; Five Poets of the Pacific, 1964; Death of the Kapowsin Tavern, 1965; Good Luck in Cracked Italian, 1969. Contbr. to (Anthols.): Of Poetry & Power, 1964; Poetry, 1968; Contemporary American Poets, 1969. Recip., Rockefeller Foundation Creative Writing Fellowship, 1967-68. Address: 643 East Front Street, Missoula, MT, USA.

HULL, William D., b. 13 Apr. 1918. University Professor. Education: B.A., Furman Univ., 1938; M.A., Univ. of Virginia, 1939; Ph.D., 1941. Positions held: Prof., Hostra Univ., 1946–; Fulbright Prof. in Am. Lit., Univ. of Ceylon, 1955-56; Univ. of Patna, 1959-60. Publications: Saul at Endor, 1954; Selected Poems: 1942-52, 1955; Dandy Brown, 1959; The Catullus of William Hull, 1960; The Other Side of Silence, 1964; The Mastery of Love, 1967; Visions of Handy Hopper I, 1970 & II, 1971; Collected Poems, 1942-68, 1971. Contbr. to: New York Review; New York Times; Approach; Arena; Beloit Poetry Jrnl.; Poetry; American Mercury; Arizona Quarterly; Calcutta Writers' Works Miscellany; Hofstra Review; Chicago Review; Intro U. of Kansas City Quarterly; Experiment; Johns Hopkins Review; Univ. of New Mexico Quarterly; Sewanee Review; Shennandoah Qtrly.; Westminster Mag. Address: 5 First Avenue, Merrick, New York 11566, USA.

HUME, Marguerite Frances, b. 28 Aug. 1921. Social Worker. Education: A.B., Sweet Briar Coll., Va., U.S.A., 1943; M.S., Univ. of Louisville, Ky.; Kent Schl. of Social Work, 1956. Positions held: P.R. & worked for radio & newspaper; Social Worker, Children's Hosp., Louisville, Ky.; Dir. of Soc. Service, Am. Red Cross, Louisville. Memberships: AAUW, Louisville Br.; Writers' Workshop; The Arts Club, Louisville, Ky.; Writers' Grp. Contbr. to 'Spots of Time', 1973. Recip., 1st Prize in Poetry, The Arts Club, Louisville, Ky., 1970. Address: 2218 Village Dr., Louisville, KY 40205, U.S.A.

HUMPHREY, James, b. 20 Feb. 1939. Poet & Teacher of Creative Writing. Positions held: (Academic year, 1972, 1973) Poet in residence South Braintree, Mass. Junior H.S.; Poet in residence Kennebunk, Maine H.S.; Poet in residence Grafton, Mass. Elem. School; Poet in residence Eastern Conn. State Coll., Willimantic, Conn. Published works: Argument for Love, 1970; The Visitor, 1972; An Homage: The End of Some More Land, 1972. 1 of 6 poets featured in Poets in the Schools, Conn. Commn. on the Arts. Awards include: Authors League Award, 1972; P.E.N. American Center Award, 1972; P.E.N. American Center Award, 1973. Address: 172 Pike Ave., Attleboro, MA 02703, USA.

HUMPHREY, Paul, pen name MORRISON, Edward, b. 14 Jan. 1915. Commercial Writer. Education: Univ. of Rochester, 1940. Married Dr. Eleanor N. Humphrey, 2 sons. Positions held: Tchr. & V.P., Penfield H.S., N.Y.; Tchr., Hist. & Engl., Univ. of Rochester, N.Y.; Dir.,

Educational Distribution & Rsch., F.E. Compton & Co., 1948, '59; Commercial Writer. Member, Rochester Poetry Soc., 1937–. Published works incl: Burnt Toast, or Slices at Life, light verse, 1968. Contbr. to var. newspapers & mags. Address: 2329 S. Union St., Spencerport, N.Y. 14559, U.S.A.

HUMPHREYS, Aletha. Poet; Former Teacher. Education: A.B., Sioux Falls Coll., S.D.; Ed.M., Boston Univ. Schl. of Educ., Mass., U.S.A.; grad. courses, Drake & Iowa Univs. Divorced, 1 son. Positions held: H.S. Tchr., 1943-57; H.S. Prin. & Dir., H.S. Vocal Music, WWII; Profl. singer in the 1920's. Memberships: Iowa Poetry Assn.; Des Moines Br.; Nat. League of Am. Pen Women; Pi Lambda Theta; Iowa Poetry Day Assn. Published works: As Planets Sing (coll. of poems), 1973; Two Prefaces for Lyrical Iowa, 1971 & 72. Contbr. to: Poets of the Midwest; Hawk & Whippoorwill; Flame; Cyclo-Flame; The Muse; English Jrnl., Midland Schls.; The Muse Anthol.; Oneota Review; Snowy Egret; Orphic Lute; Caravan; Green World; Cardinal; Scimitar & Song; Negro Digest; Quote; Pen; Baptist Ldr.; The Christian; Pen Women; The Sandcutters; The North Am. Mentor; Fire; Sleet & Candlelight; The Avalon Anthols.; Lyrical Iowa, 1956-73; poetry column, Rimes for the Times, Tama News-Herald, 1964-67. Recip. var. poetry prizes. Address: 106 South Church St., ToledpToledo, IA, U.S.A.

HUNT, Irvine, b. 27 Jan. 1930. Poet. Positions held: Former Foreign Desk Sub-Ed., Daily Telegraph, London; Mbr., British Film Inst. Lectr. Panel. Mbr., North-West Arts Assn. Poets-in-Schools scheme. Published works: The Worms are Growing Bolder, 1971, 3rd ed., 1973; Hippopotamud, poetry poster, 1972; Manlaff & Toewoman, 1973. Contbr. to: Cumbria; Umbrella; N.W. Evening Mail; N.W. Evening Star; Twixt Thee & Me (anthol.) Recitals at Edinburgh, Sheffield Fests., schls., colls. & theatres. Selections of poems broadcast by BBC. Address: The Old Cottage, Oxen Park, Ulverston, Lake District, U.K.

HUNT, Sam, b. 4 July 1946. Poet; Songwriter. Published works: Bracken Country, 1971; Bottle Creek, 1972; South into Winter, 1973; num. broadsheets. Has had var. readings & concerts (w. his rock band) in New Zealand. Contbr. to: Listener; Landfall; Cave; N.Z. Herald; num. New Zealand mags. & newspapers. Honours, awards: Young Poet of the Year, 1971. Address: Bottle Creek, Paremata, Wellington, New Zealand.

HUNT, Sylvia Inez, pen name HUNT, Inez Whitaker, b. 21 Aug. 1899. Lecturer; Writer; Teacher. Education: Northern Colo. Univ. Married Nelson V. Hunt, 1 daughter. Positions held: Campaign Sec., Am. Red Cross P.P. Chapt.; Tchr., Univ. of Colo., Colo. Springs Ctr. Memberships: Past Pres., Poetry Fellowship of Colo. Springs; Colo. Author's League; Nat. League of Am. Pen Women; Hon. Mbr., Delta Kappa Gamma & Phi Beta. Published works: Ghost Trails to Ghost Towns, 1958; High Country, 1962; Windows Through the Wall, 1956; 15 non-fiction books. Contbr. to: Poetry Forum (Denver Post); Poetry Corner (Colo. Springs Free Press); Golden Echo (Colo. Springs Evening Telegraph); Skylines (Annual Anthol.); var. newspaper columns, articles. Recip. over 50 nat. & local prizes & winner of 1st lecture on poetry award in Nat. Biennial Contest, Nat. League of Am. Pen Women, 1960. Winner of 1st pl. for Biographical & Sci. Non-fiction book, 1966. Address: 707 Prospect Pl., Manitou Springs, CO 80829, U.S.A.

HUNTER, Elsie Theresa, pen name HUNTER, Lorraine, b. 27 Nov. 1892. Retired Public Stenographer. Education: Night courses at UCLA. Widow of Virgil L. Hunter, 2 children. Positions held: Stenographer; Real Estate Broker; Self employed; Owner of three public stenographic offices in Los Angeles, Calif. & Beverly Hills. Memberships: Assoc., World Poetry Soc.; Ariz. State Poetry Soc. Published works: A Life Time of Poetry & Verse, 1964. Honours, awards: Has won first & 2nd prizes for her pencil portraits. Var sculptures & oil paintings. Address: 7201 Cottontail Run North, Scottsdale, AZ 85253, U.S.A.

HUNTER, Paul Curwood, b. 3 Apr. 1943. Writer. Education: B.A. in Engl. Lit., Univ. of Cinn., 1965; M.A. in Engl. Lit., ibid, 1966; Cand. in Philos., Univ. of Wash., 1969. Married, 2 children. Positions held: Tchng. & Rsch. Asst., then Pre-doctoral Instr., Univ. of Wash., 1966-70; Ed. & Publsr., Consumption mag., 1967-70; Co-owner of Bank Books, Bellingham, Wash., 1971; Transit Operator, Metro Transit, Seattle, 1972-74. Published works: Your House Is On Fire/And Your Children Are Gone, 1970. Contbr. to: Calif. Qtly.; Poetry (Chicago); Poetry Northwest; Dakotah Territory; Iowa Review; North Am. Review; The Quest; Epoch; Fiddlehead; Discourse, etc. Awards for poems in the Straus & Elliston Contest & the Lit. & Music Soc. Contest at the Univ. of Cinn., 1965-66; Two prize medallions, 1966 Neb. Wesleyan Contest; Awards, Acad. of Am. Poets Contest, 1967, '68, '69. Address: 4131 Greenwood Ave., N., Seattle, WA 98103, U.S.A.

HUNTER, Sarah Ann, b. 6 Feb. 1911. Housewife. Education: Elem. education to 16 yrs. of age, School for the Blind, Oldham. Memberships: Poetry Soc. (UK); Lancashire Authors' Assoc. Published works: Brittle Limbs and Other Poems, 1958; Lucille and Other Poems (including Lancs. dialect), 1967; The Beauty of the Opal (including Lancs. dialect), 1973. Contbr. to: (Braille periodicals) Skylark; Inspiration; (newspapers, journals) Teacher of the Blind; Oldham Chronicle; World Contact; Poetry Workshop (Dept. of Extra Mural Studies, Univ. of Manchester); Internat. Who's Who in Poetry Anthol., 1972. Awards: The Batty Cup, also 2nd Prize, Lancs. Authors' Assoc.; The Queensland Edwin Dickinson Literary Competition, Australia, prizes 2 1st-class, 1 2nd-class. Address: 186 Greenacres Rd., Oldham, Lancs. OL4 3EG, UK.

HUNTING, Constance, b. 15 Oct. 1925. Writer. Education: B.A., Brown Univ., 1947. Positions held: Tchr., Rockwood Park Schl., Boston, 1947-48, Purdue Univ., 1954-55 & Univ. of Me., Orono, 1969-. Published works: The Heron, 1960; After the Stravinsky Concert, 1969; Cimmerian, 1972. Contbr. to: Poetry; Western Humanities Review; Mass. Qtly.; Colo. Qtly.; Quartet; Sparrow; Christian Century; Fiddlehead; Discourse; Me. Times; Me. Sunday Telegram; N.Y. Times; Zahir. Recip., Disting. Author Award, Ind. Univ., 1970. Address: 76 Main St., Orono, ME 04473, U.S.A.

HUON, Ronan, b. 3 Aug. 1922. High School Teacher. Education: Licencié d'Anglais, Celtic langs, Univ. of Rennes. Positions held: currently Tchng. at the Lycee Brest; Ed., mag. 'Al Liamm' (also Publisher). Published works: (book of poetry) Evidon Va-Unan, 1955. (book of short stories) An Irin glas, (The Green Prunellas), 1966. Contbr. to: IL (Italian); (anthols.) Maor Nog Zingt Bretanje (Dutch); Poeti Bretoni Moderni (Italian); Defense de cracher par terre et de parler Breton (French); Al Liamm (poems & translations from Ondra Lysohorsky etc.). Address: 2 Venelle Poulbriquen, Brest, France.

HUSAIN, Adrian (Syed Akbar Husain), b. 9 Nov. 1942. Shirt Designer & Exporter. Education: B.A., New Coll., Oxford, 1963. Positions held: Established a Shirt Manufacturing plant in Karachi, 1968; Shirt Designer, Exporter, 1968-. Contbr. to (Anthol.): Pieces of Eight, 1969; (jrnls.): New Measure; Outposts. Recip., Guiness Poetry Competition 1st Prize, 1968. Address: 90 Mortlake Rd., Kew, Surrey, UK.

HUSSEIN, Nadir, b. 29 Sept., 1939. Business Manager; Free-lance Journalist & Broadcaster. Education: Univ. of the Philippines, Quezon City; Univ. of Neuchatel, Switzerland; Sorbonne, Paris. Positions held: Free-lance Journalist, 1962-69; Test Cricket Commentator, 1965-69; Gen. Manager, Constellation Advertising, 1966-67; Gen. Manager, Television Exhibition Corp., 1969-; Free-lance Broadcaster, Columnist & Scriptwriter. Contbr. to (Anthol.): Pieces of Eight, 1968; (Jrnls.): Vision. Address: c/o Isaac

Corp., Nadir House, McLeod Road, Karachi, Pakistan.

HUTCHINSON, Robert, b. 11 Apr. 1924. Editor. Education: A.B., Univ. of Kan., 1947; A:M., Middlebury Coll., 1950; Ph.D. cand., Columbia Univ. Positions held: Tchr., Mt. Hermon Schl. & Ala. Coll., 2 yrs.; Asst. Ed., Trade Dept., McGraw Hill Book Co., 1954-58; Sr. Ed., Dover Publs. Inc., N.Y., 1960-. Published works: Standing Still While Traffic Moved About Me, 1971; The Kitchen Dance, 1955; (Ed.) Poems of Anne Bradstreet, 1969; Poems of George Santayana, 1970; Contbr. to: The New Yorker Book of Poems, 1969; Springtime Two; Poetry Awards; Riverside Poetry, 1953; Poetry; The New Yorker; Saturday Review; The Atlantic; New Mexico Quarterly; Quarterly Review of Literature; Epoch; Accent; The American Scholar; PS; The N.Y. Times; Beloit Poetry Jrnl.; Riverside Poetry; The Expatriate Review; Univ. of Kan. City Review; Voices; Harper's Mag.; Southwest Review; Springtime Three; Western Review; Talisman; etc. Honours, awards: Saxton Trust Fellowship, Harper's; Short story Drugstore: Sunday Noon presented on TV Workshop, Omnibus, by Ford Fndn.; Elinor Frost Poetry Scholarship, 1950; DeVoto Fellowship, Bread Loaf Writers' Conf., 1963; Tuition Scholarship, New Schl. for Soc. Rsch., Writers' Sem.; Res. at Yaddo & MacDowell Colony. Address: 1437 First Ave., N.Y., NY 10021, U.S.A.

HUTCHINSON, (William Patrick Henry) Pearse, b. 16 Feb. 1927. Drama Critic; Translator. Education: Univ. Coll., Dublin; Salzburg Sem. in American Studies, Austria, Jan., 1952. Positions held: Crossword Checker, Sunday Press, Dublin, 1951-53; Barcelona, 1954-57, 1961-67; Translator, Int. Labour Org., Geneva, 1951-53; Sub-Editor, Dublin, 1953-54; Drama Critic, Radio Eireann, 1957-61; Telefis Eireann, 1968; Irish Rep., Spolet Poetry Festival, Italy, 1969. Published works: Tongue Without Hands, 1963; Faostin Bhachach, 1968; Expansions, 1969; Ed. & Trans., Josep Carner: Thirty Poems, 1962. Contbr. to (Anthols.): Faber Book of Contemporary Irish Verse, 1948; Dolmen Anthology of Irish Writing, 1962; New Poets of Ireland, 1963; Penguin Book of Irish Verse, 1970; (Jrnls.): Threshold; Lace Curtain; Kilkenny Mag.; Serra d'Or. Awarded Butler Family Awards Prize, 1969. Address: 179 Rathgar Rd., Dublin 6, Ireland.

HUTNER, Julie Sarah, pen names: (poetry) **HUTNER, Julie,** (plays) **CHERNO, Julie & WHITNEY, Leona,** Instructor of Voice & Speech; Artist. Education: Univ. of Miami, Fla.; Northwestern Univ., Ill.; studied w. Vivian Laramore Rader. Married Herbert H. Hutner, 1 son, 1 daughter. Positions held: Secretarial, Artists Agency, Legal Dept.; Speech Instr. & Creative Drama, N.Y.C. Acad. of Drama; Speech Dept., Bander Fashio Coll. Memberships: Vivian Laramore Rader Poetry Workshop, Miami; Huckleberry Mountain Workshop, Hendersonville, N.C.; Miami Poetry Grp. Contbr. to: Singing in the Sun, Anthol. of Poets, Fla., 1964; Poetry Digest; The Dynamo; The Writer; Miami Herald; The Times-News, Hendersonville; Writer's Digest, Boston; The Miami Hurricane; Northwestern Newsletter. Honours, awards incl: Judge's Prize, Vivian Laramore Rader Workshop, 1958, '60, '66; 1st prize for one-act verse play, produced Miami Beach, 1958; 1st prize for one-act poetic drama, produced N.Y.C. The Actors Rep. Theatre, 1963. Address: 210 – 172nd St., North Miami Beach, FL 33160, U.S.A.

HUTTO, Henry Hubert, b. 26 Aug. 1923. Episcopal Clergyman. Education: Del Mar Coll.; B.J., Univ. of Mo., 1943; M.Div., Va. Theol. Sem., 1955. Positions held: Newspaper Reporter & Editor; Episcopal Priest in Wyoming, Nevada & Calif. Published works: God of Quasars, & other poems, 1973. Contbr. to num. publs. in U.S.A., Canada & India. Address: 1501 West 30th St., Austin, TX 78703, U.S.A.

HWANG, Dong-Kyu, b. 9 Apr. 1938. University Professor. Education: B.A. & M.A., Engl. Lit., Seoul Nat. Univ., Korea; Dip., Engl. Studies, Edinburgh Univ., U.K., 1966-67. Positions held: Prof., Seoul Nat.

Univ., 1968–; Mbr., Int. Writing Prog., Iowa Univ., U.S.A., 1970-71. Memberships: Korean Lit. Assn.; The English Lit. Soc. of Korea. Published works: A Sunny Day, 1961; Elegies & Other Poems, 1964; Variations on the Kingship, 1968; Hot-River Journals, 1972. Contbr. to: Hyundae Munhak, monthly lit. mag.; Wolgan Munhak, lit. monthly; Dong-A Ilbo (The Far East Daily), etc. Recip., Hyundae Munhak Poetry Award, 1968. Address: c/o Seoul Nat. Univ., Seoul, Korea.

HYDERI, Shamsher Ali, b. 15 Sept. 1932. Editor. Education: Adib Alim (Sindhi Lang.); B.A., Sindhi Lit.; M.A., Sindhi Lit. Positions held: Asst., News Ed., Daily Hilal-e-Pakistan, Hyderabad, Sind, & Daily Khadim-e-Watan, 2 yrs.; Asst. Ed., Qtly. Mehraan, lit. jrnl. of the Sindhi Adabi Bd., Hyderabad Sind & Publ. Asst. to the Bd., 11 yrs.; Ed., Naeen Zindagi, Karachi, Govt. of Pakistan, 1966–. Memberships: Sec. Gen., Sindhi Adabi Sangat, 1955-66; Exec. Comm., Pakistan Writers Guild (Sindhi Sub-region), 3 yrs. Published works: Laata (Flame), coll. of poems, 1961; 9 German Love-Songs (poeticized & put into Sindhi music), 1965; The Origin of Free Verse in Sindhi Language, mongraph, 1964. Contbr. to var. jrnls., newspapers, mags. in India & Pakistan. Award for best book of Sindhi poetry for 1962 by Pakistan Writers Guild for editl. work on 'Akhyoon mengh Malhar', coll. of a popular Sindhi poet, Barda Sindhi. Address: Pakistan Publications, P.O. Box 183, Karachi, Pakistan.

HYER, Helen von Kolnitz, b. 30 Dec. 1896. Author; Museum Curator; Surgical Secretary; Education: Simmons Coll., Boston, Mass.; Bus. Schl., Charleston, SC. Personal details: father, Judge Geo. F. von Kolnitz of Austrian descent; m., Edward Allen Hyer, 1920, 4 d., 1 s. Positions held: Statn., War Savings Serv., Charleston, 1917-19; Curator of Pub. Instrn., Charleston Mus., SC & South Cardina Cultural Exhibit, 1919-23; Assoc. Curator, Educ., Kent Sci. Mus., Grand Rapids, Mich., 1929; Free-lance Writer, 1929-34; Statn., Dept. of State, The Capitol, Lansing, Mich., 1935-37; Mich. State Police HQ, ibid, 1937-38; Sec. to the Dir., Cranbrook Inst. of Sci., Bloomfield Hills, Mich., 1940-41; w. Post Engrs., Sullivan's Island, SC, 2½ years; Surg. Sec., Charleston, 1950-62; Retired. Memberships: Pres., 1971-72, Poetry Soc. of SC; Mich. Authors Assn.; Mich. Poetry Soc.; Poetry Soc. of Ga.; Poets Study Club. Terra Haute; Indians. Published works: Santee Songs, 1923; Wine Dark Sea, 1930; Danger Never Sleeps, 1971; 5 other books (juveniles & nature study supplementary readers). Contbr. to the following jrnls., mags., newspapers, etc: Poet Lore; Christian Science Monitor; Grand Rapids Herald; Grand Rapids Press; Charleston News & Courier; SC Mag.; Adventure Mag.; Poets Round Table; The Lyric West; Year Books; Poetry Soc. of SC; Poetry Soc. of Ga.; Peninsula Poets, Mich. Recip. of many honours. Address: 15-B Council St., Charleston, SC 29401, USA.

I

IDDON, Josephine, b. 26 Jan. 1926. Housewife. Married, 4 children. Memberships: Lancashire Authors Assn.; Preston Poets Soc.; Leyland Writers. Contbr. to: Lancashire Life; The Sun; Preston Poets, Reflections. Honours, awards: Pomfret Trophy, Preston Poets Soc., 2nd pl., 1971, 3rd pl., 1972; E.M. Rose Bowl (3rd prize), 1972; Pomfret Trophy, Lancashire Authors Assn. (3rd prize, dialect verse), 1973. Address: Ash Villa, Gill Lane, Longton, Nr. Preston, Lancs., U.K.

IDREES, Abdullah bin Abdulaziz, b. 1931. Cultural Affairs Official. Education: Licence, College of Sharia and Arabic Lang. Positions held: Technical Inspector, Religious Institutes, Ministry of Educ.; Dir., Technical Educ., ibid; Ed., 'Al-Da'wa' newspaper, Riyadh; currently Secretary General, Higher Council for Arts & Sciences. Member, Modern Literary League, Cairo. Has written sev. vols. of Arabic poetry. Contbr. to all

Saudi Arabian periodicals & to sev. in other Arab countries. Honours, awards: Prize, BBC Arabic Service; Prize, Voice of the Arabs Broadcasting Service, Cairo, 1956. Address: c/o Higher Council for Arts & Sciences, Ministry of Education, Riyadh, Saudi Arabia.

IGNATOW, David, b. 7 Feb. 1914. Teacher. Education: HS Grad., 1932. Married, Rose Graubert, artist & writer, 1 s., 1 d. Positions held: Co-Editor, Beloit Poetry Jrnl., 1949-59; Pres., Enterprise Bindery, Inc., 1955-62; Poetry Editor, The Nation, 1962-63; Poet in Residence, Univ. of Kentucky, 1965-66; ibid, Univ. of Kansas, 1966-67; Vassar Coll., 1967-68; Adjunct Prof., Columbia Univ., 1969–; Poet in Residence, York Coll., City Univ. of New York, Cons. Ed., Chelsea, 1968–; Advisory Mbr., Marquis Biographical Lib. Soc., 1969; Assoc. Ed., the Am. Poetry Review. Memberships: MLA; PEN; AAUP. Publications: Poems, 1948; The Gentle Weight Lifter, 1955; Say Pardon, 1962; Figures of the Human, 1964; Rescue the Dead, 1968; Earth Hard, 1968; Selected Poems, 1968; Collected Poems 1934-69, 1970; The Notebooks of David Ignatow, 1973. Contbr. to: Poetry, Chicago; Nation; Botteghe Oscure: Chelsea; Saturday Review of Lit.; New York Times; Perspective; Epoch; Antioch Review; Discovery 1; The Fifties; The Sixties; Kayak; Carleton Miscellany Midstream; Commentary; Golden Goose; Quarterly Review of Lit.; Beloit Poetry Jrnl.; New Mexico Quarterly; Yale Review; Chicago Tribune; Tenn. Poetry Jrnl.; Between Worlds; Chicago Jewish Forum; NO Poetry Jrnl.; Village Voice; Voices; American Poetry Mag.; Grist; Twelfth Street Quarterly; New Yorker; North American Review; Poetry Bag; Pogmoggan; Frostbite; IT; Choice; December; Floating World; Elizabeth; Some/Thing; Twice A Year; Cloud Marauder; Sou'wester; Arena; Simbolica; Stand; NY Qtly.; New World Writing; New Am. Review; Southern Review. Honours: Nat. Inst. of Arts & Letters Award, 1964; Guggenheim Fellowship, 1965; Shelley Mem. Award, 1966; Rockefeller Fndn. Grant, 1968; Nat. Endowment for the Arts, Wash. DC, 1969; Guggenheim Fellowship, 1973. Address: 17th St. & Gardiner Ave., East Hampton, New York, NY 11937, USA.

IGO, John N., Jr., b. 29 May 1927. Professor of English. Education, B.A., 1948, M.A., 1952, Trinity Univ., Texas. Positions held: Acquisitions Librarian, Trinity Univ., Instr. of Engl., ibid.; Prof. of Engl., San Antonio Coll. Membership: Sigma Tau Delta (life member). Published works: God of Gardens, 1962; Yanaguana, 1963; A Chamber Faust, 1964; The Tempted Monk: A Dance Poem, 1967; No Harbor, Else, 1972. Contbr. to: English-Spanish Review; Compass; The Rectangle; Quixote; Newman; Blue River Poetry Mag.; Scimitar and Song; La Prensa; Poetry Digest; Panache; American Weave; Poet Lore; Laurel Review; Descant; Nimrod; Ball State Forum; Poetry Parade; Haiku Highlights; Transatlantic; Dragonfly; Advent; Pan American Review; The Ranger; Trinitonian; San Antonio Eve. News. Awards: Creative Writing Award Plaque, Dallas Times Herald, 1947, 1964; Nat. Literature Award, Nat. Soc. of Arts and Letters, 1954; Chapbook Publication Award, Southwest Writers' Conference, 1962. Address: 12505 Woller Rd., San Santonio, TX 78228, USA.

ILLAKOWICZ, Kazimiera, b. 1890. Civil Servant (Foreign Office). Education: Cracow Univ. Memberships: Polish Lit. Soc.; PEN Club. Published works incl: L'Envolee d'Icare, 1912; Flambeaux, 1914; Les trois cordes, 1917; Les cantiques de la misère, 1917; Histoire du Prince La-Fi-Tchan, 1919; Les trois cordes/pages choisies, 1919; La mort du Phénix, 1922; Enfantines, 1923; Persécutions des chrétiens, 1924; La pêche, 1925; Les noms et leurs présages, 1925; La guirlande d'or, 1927; Du fond du coeur, 1928; Le miroir de la nuit, 1928; L'oiseau qui pleure, 1929; Les miroirs magiques, 1929; Perles et cendres, 1930; Don Carlos/traduction de Schiller, 1933; Vers gais, 1934; Ballades héroiques, 1934; Le rossignol lithuanien, 1936; Recueil de poésies sur le Maréchal 1912-35, 1936. Address: ul. Gajowa 4 m. 8, 60-815

Poznau, Poland.

IMANI PAMOJA, b. 3 Feb. 1947. Writer; Editor; Poet. Education: Bishop Coll., Dallas, Tex. Married, 2 children. Positions held: Freelance Writer; Co-Dir., Uhuru Family, 1971; Assoc. Ed., Today's Black World Mag., 1971; Contbng. Ed., Body & Soul Bazaar Mag.; Contbng. Ed., Black Scene Mag., 1973; Ed., Akini Isi Publishing Co., 1971; Dir., Akini Isi Inst., 1973. Memberships: Sec., Assn. of Advancing Artists & Writers, 1971; Southern Black Cultural Alliance, 1973; Poetry Soc. of Tex.; Chmn., Art & Cultural Enrichment Fndn.; Acad. of Am. Poets. Published works: Gittin Our Minds Together, 1971; Mama How Come, 1973; Sisters & Brothers Are We, 1973. Contbr. to: Dallas Express Newspaper; Keys Newspaper; Voices In Themselves, etc. & var. radio broadcasts. Address: c/o Akini Isi Publng. Co., P.O. Box 26057, Dallas, TX 75226, U.S.A.

INEZ, Colette, b. 23 June 1931. Poet. Education: Hunter Coll., NYC., B.A., Engl. Lit., 1961. Born in Belgium, of French parents. Positions held: Teacher in Fed. anti-poverty programs in ghetto schools, NY.; Adult education teacher, NY Univ.; HS Teacher, NYC Bd. of Education; Editorial positions with Le Figaro (NY office), Recreation Mag., and Internat. Theater Mag.; (currently) Teacher, poetry workshop, The New School, N.Y. Memberships: Poetry Soc. of America; Poetry Soc. (UK); Internat. Platform Assoc. Published works: The Woman Who Loved Worms and Other Poems, 1972. Contbr. to more than 80 U.S. and internat. journals, including: The Nation; Hudson Review; The New Republic; NY Times; Chicago Review; Prairie Schooner; Beloit Poetry Journal; Antioch Review; Poetry Northwest; Shenandoah; Minnesota Review; Anglo Welsh Review; Poetry Australia. Translations: French to English, including poetry of Jacques Dupin. Recordings: U.S. Library of Congress; Harvard Univ. Lamont Library. Awards: Great Lakes College Assoc. annual nat. book award, for The Woman Who Loved Worms, 1972; Reedy Mem. Award (nat. 1st prize winner, Poetry Soc. of America), 1972; Osgood Warren Award (nat. 1st prize winner, Poetry Soc. of New England), 1967; Nat. League of Pen Women Poetry Award, 1961; Rochester Festival of Arts Poetry Award, 1965. Address: 5 West 87 St., New York, NY 10024, USA.

INGALLS, Jeremy, b. 2 April 1911. Poet; Retired University Professor; Translator. Education: Tufts Univ.; Univ. of Chicago, B.A.; M.A.; Litt. D. Positions held: Asst. Prof. of Engl. Lit., Western Coll., 1941-43; Fellow Chinese Studies & Rsch. Assoc., Univ. of Chicago, 1944-48; Prof., Hd. of Dept. of Eng. & American Lit., Dir. of Asian Studies, Rockford Coll., 1950's; Rockefeller Fndn. Lectr., Am. Poetry; Ford Fndn. Fellowship, Asian Studies; Fulbright Prof. of American Lit., Japan, 1957-58. Memberships: Life Mbr., Poetry Soc. of America; Int. Acad. of Arts & Letters; New England Poetry Club; Poets Laureate Int. Published works: The Metaphysical Sword, 1941; Tahl, 1945; The Woman from the Island, 1958; These Islands Also, 1959. Contbr. to: Poetry; New Republic; Saturday Review; Accent; American Mercury; American Prefaces; Atlantic Monthly; Beloit Poetry Jrnl.; Chicago Review; Common Sense; Maryland Quarterly; Univ. of Kansas City Review; Western Review; Tuftonian; Christian Century; Literary Review; United Church Herald; Educational Forum; Poetry, India; Japan Today; Il Ponte, Italy; Japanese & Korean periodicals. Honours, Awards: Guggenheim Fellowship, Poetry, 1943; Am. Acad. of Arts & Letters Grant, 1944; Shelley Mem. Award, 1950; Lola Ridge Mem. Awards, 1951 & '52; Univ. of Ariz. Poetry Ctr. Lectrship., 1964; Epic Poet Laureate, UPLI, 1965; Steinman Fndn. Address: 6269 East Rosewood, Tucson, Arizona 85711, USA.

INGRAM, Charles Elden, b. 2 Oct. 1913 at Randolph, Utah, USA. Industrial Engineer. Education: B.A., Major Amer. & Engl. Lit., M.A., Major History, Univ. of Manila, P.I.; B.S., Major Indr. Engr., Univ. of Chattanooga, Tennessee. Positions held: Industrial

Engineer, Lockheed Aircraft Corp., Marietta, Georgia. Published works: Portal of Lyrics, 1945; Portal of Beauty, 1945; Portal of Poetry, 1947; Portal of Corona, 1963; Portal of Heaven, 1968; Songs of Mexico, 1969. Address: 19 Hillcrest Ave., Rossville, GA 30741, USA.

INGRAM, Maria, b. 25 May 1943. Manager & Partner of Spice & Herb Shop. Education: Winthrop Coll.; Baylor Univ.; Univ. of Fla.; Univ. of N.C.; B.A., Engl. & Drama, Pfeiffer Coll., Misenheimer, N.C., 1966. Positions held: Tchr., Lansing Community Coll., Mich. & Mich. Catholic Conf. Ctr., Lansing; Counselor with Neighborhood Youth Corps, Winston-Salem, N.C.; Poet-in-Res., N.C. Poetry in the Schools Prog. Memberships: N.C. Poetry Reading Circuit; N.C. Poetry in the Schls. Prog.; Sec.-Treas., The Tenth Muse, Winston-Salem. Published works: North Acre, 1973. Contbr. to: Carolina Qtly.; Red Clay Rdr.; Southern Poetry Review; Beloit Poetry Jrnl.; N.C. Folklore; Foxfire; N.C. Anvil; Arx; St. Andrews Qtly.; Univ. of Ala. Review. Recip., 2nd prize poetry, Southern Lit. Fest., 1966. Address: 125 Westview Dr., N.W., Winston-Salem, NC 27104, U.S.A.

INMAN, Loreta Lanona, b. 7 Dec. 1893. Housewife. Education: Upper Iowa Univ.; Business coll. Married, 1 son, 1 daughter. Positions held: Red Cross work, Bedford, Ind.; Billing Clerk, Eli Lillys, Indpls.; war work at Diamond Chain. Memberships: United Amateur Press Assn.; Am. Poetry League; Atlanta Writers Club. Published works: Just Thinking, 1955. Contbr. to: The Chicago Tribune; Charleston News & Courier; Brown Co. Democrat; Bloomington Evening World; Indpls. News; Indpls. Star; Montana Poetry Qtly.; The Am. Poet; Prairie Poet; From Sea to Sea in Song; Yearbook of Modern Poetry, 1971; Outstanding Contemporary Poetry, 1972 & '73; Awards Anthol., 1974. Recip. var. poetry hons. & awards inclng: Diploma di Benemerenza, Centro Studi e Scambi, 1969. Address: 2911 Pharr Court South, N.W., Apt. 913, Atlanta, GA 30305, U.S.A.

INMAN, Will, b. 4 May 1923. English Teacher; Writer. Education: A.B., Duke Univ., Durham, N.C. Married Barbara Ann Sherman. Positions held: Labor union org., 1948-50; Clerk, 1950-56; Lib. Clerk, Yale Club, N.Y. Univ., 1956-67; Artist-in-Res. (Poet), The Am. Univ., spring 1967; Instr., Engl. Dept., Montgomery Coll., Rockville, Md., 1969-73. Past Mbr., Poetry Soc. of Am. Published works: A River of Laughter, 1961; Lament & Psalm, 1960; I am the Snakehandler, 1960, 67; Honey in Hot Blood, 1962; 108 Verges unto Now, 1964; 108 Prayers for J. Edgar (selections), 1965; 108 Tales of a Po'Buckra, 1965; A Generation of Heights: Paths with Hoofs Ingrown, 1968, 69; Kauri 108, 1969. Contbr. to: Raleigh News & Observer; Epos; Mutiny; Fiddlehead; Wormwood Review; Umbra; Southwest Review; A Nosegay in Black; South & West; Bitterroot; Intrepid; Motive; Targets; Poet; Poet Lore; Phoebe; Challenge; N.Y. Herald Tribune; Writer's Forum; N.Y. Quarterly; Poets of North Carolina, 1963; Of Poetry & Power; Where is Vietnam; Poets for Peace; Mad Windows; Campfires of the Resistance; The East Side Scene; Washington Anthol. Vol. I; Only Humans with Songs to Sing. Address: 2551 West Mossman Road, Tucson, AZ 85706, U.S.A.

INSINGEL, Mark, b. 3 May 1935. Writer. Education: Nat. Schl. of Drama, 3 yrs.; French Lit., Sorbonne, Paris. Memberships: PEN Club, Flemish Ctr. Published works: (poetry) Drijfhout, 1963; Een kooi van licht, 1966; Perpetuum Mobile, 1969; Modellen, 1970; Posters, 1973; (novels) Een getergde jager, 1966; Spiegelingen, 1968. In English translation: Reflections; Signature 7. Contbr. to the main lit. reviews in the Netherlands. Recip., Biennal Prize of De Vlaamse Gids, 1970. Address: Ten Hole 5, B-9681 Nukerke, Belgium.

IQBAL, (Mian) Zafar, b. 27 Sept. 1932. Law Practitioner. Education: B.A.; LL.B. Memberships: Sec., Rotary Int., 1965-66; Sec., Bar Assn., 1961-62, '64-65; Fndr. Sec., Punjabi Majlis Lahore, 1957-58; Writers' Guild; Ed., Qtly. 'SAWERA', Lahore; Fndr.

Ed., Law Coll. mag. 'MIZAAN'. Resident Ed.-Columnist for 'Dhanak' monthly. Published works: (collections) Aab-e-Rawan, 1962; Gulaftab, 1966; Ratb-o-Yabis, 1970; Kukkar Kheh, 1974. Contbr. to: Daily Imroze; Daily Mashriq; Daily Nawa-i-Waqt; Qtly. Seep; Qtly. Sher-o-Hikmat, etc. Recip., 1st prize, Nat. Book Ctr., 1962. Address: 3-Iftikhar Shaheed Rd., Okara, Dist. Sahiwal, Pakistan.

IRBY, Kenneth, b. 18 Nov. 1936. Poet; Book Reviewer. Education: B.A., Univ. of Kansas, Lawrence, 1958; M.A., Harvard Univ., Cambridge, Mass., 1960; M.L.S., Univ. of Calif., Berkeley, 1968. Positions held: Former Reviewer of Books & Records, Kulchur Mag. (now defunct). Published works: The Roadrunner, 1964; Kansas-New Mexico, 1965; Movements/Sequences, 1965; The Flower of Having Passed Through Paradise in A Dream, 1968; Relation (Poems 1965-66), 1969. Contbr. to (Jrnls.): Matter; Caterpillar; Poetry; Paris Review. Address: 1614½A Russell, Berkeley, CA, USA.

IRELAN, Annislea, pen name **ANIKA,** b. 11 Mar. 1910. Teacher; Medical X-Ray Technologist; Writer. Education: Los Alamos Sci. Lab., N.M.; Univ. of Calif. Positions held: Teacher; Bookkeeper; Medical Technician; Artist; Writer. Memberships: Nat. Writers' Club, Denver, Colo.; Writers' Grp. in Los Alamos, N.M.; Canon City Writers' Club, Colo. & Poetry Club in Canon City. Contbr. to: The Muse; Advance Monticellonian; Poets Partyline; The News; Golden Echo; Nash Mag.; New Dawn Poetry Book II; Clover Publishing Co.; Shore Poetry Anthol., etc.; var. articles, stories. Several poems broadcast over KHBM AM-FM, Baker Broadcasting Co., Monticello, Ark. Honours, awards: Title 'Danae', Int Clover Poetry Assn. Address: 714 N. 15th St., Canon City, CO 81212, U.S.A.

IRELAND, Alan (Stuart), b. 23 Nov. 1940. Journalist. Education: Wennington Schl., Wetherby, Yorkshire, UK. Married, 1 d. Positions held: Sr. Sub-Ed. & Asst. News Ed., The Japan Times, Tokyo, 1963-. Memberships: Poets Soc. of Japan; Edit. Cons., Poetry Nippon, 1970-. Author of Implosion, 1968. Contbr. to: Critical Quarterly; Outposts; Quill; Expression One; Second Aeon; Sad Traffic; Amazing Grace; The Japan Times; The Japan Times Weekly; Poetry Nippon; The Study of Current English; Shinomura; An Asia Notebook; The American Bard; Orphic Lute; St. Andrews Review. Address: c/o Japan Times, 5-4 Shibaura 4-chome, Minato-Ku, Tokyo 108, Japan.

IRELAND, Kevin Mark, b. 18 July 1933. Poet. Published works: Face to Face, 1963; Educating the Body, 1968; Twentieth Century New Zealand Poetry, 1971; Elissaveta Bagryana (translation), 1971. Contbr. to: Landfall, Christchurch, NZ; Mate, Auckland; Arena, Wellington. Address: c/o Caxton Press, 119 Victoria St., Christchurch, New Zealand.

IRELAND, Thelma, b. 6 Sept. 1899. Retired Teacher. Education: Iowa State Coll.; Calif. State Coll.; Neb. Univ.; Columbia Univ., N.Y. Widow, 2 children. Positions held: Tchr., Creighton, Spencer & Bloomfield, Neb. & at Herlong, Calif. Memberships: P.E.O.; Hon. Mbr., Delta Kappa Gamma; Nev. Pen Women; Utah Poetry Soc.; Ariz. Poetry Soc.; State Bd. of Trustees, Nev. Histl. Soc. Published works: Home Work (poetry book). Contbr. to: Ladies Home Jrnl.; Instr.; Christian Herald; Sunset; Better Homes & Gardens; Nev. Mag.; Denver Post; Grit; Medford Tribune; Ensign; Calif. Farmer; Bard; Orphic Lute; Bardic Echoes; P.E.O. Record, etc. Honours, awards; M. of Humane Letters, Int. Acad. Award; 3rd pl., Encore, 1972, etc. Address: 25 Smithridge Pk., Reno, NV 89502, U.S.A.

IREMONGER, Valentin, b. 14 Feb. 1918. Diplomat. Education: Abbey Theatre Schl. of Acting, Dublin. Married w. 1 son & 4 daughters. Positions held: W. Abbey Theatre Co., Dublin, 1939-40; Gate Theatre, Dublin, 1942-44; Entered Irish Foreign Service, 1946;

Ambassador to Sweden, Norway & Finland, 1964-68; Ambassador to India, 1968-. Published works: On the Barricades, 1944; Reservations, 1950, 51; Other: Wrap up My Green Jacket (Play), 1947; Trans., The Hard Road to Klondike, 1962; An Irish Navvy, 1964; Ed. w. Robert Graecen, Contemporary Irish Poetry, 1949; Ed., Irish Short Stories, 1960. Contbr. to (Anthols.): 1000 Years of Irish Poetry, 1947; Contemporary Irish Poetry, 1949; Oxford Book of Irish Verse, 1958; New Poets of Ireland, 1963; (Jrnls.): Bell; Irish Times; Irish Writing; Envoy; Listener; Kenyon Review. Recip., A.E. Memorial Award, 1945. Address: Dept. of External Affairs, Dublin, Ireland.

IRVIN, Eric, b. 30 Nov. 1908. Journalist; Free-lance Writer. Married Margaret Irvin w. 2 daughters & 1 son. Positions held: Mbr., Editorial Staff, Sydney Morning Herald, 1962-. Published works: A Soldier's Miscellany, 1945; A Suit for Every Man, 1968; Other: (History) Place of Many Crows, 1953; Letters from the River, 1959; The Murrumbidgee Turf Club, 1960; Early Inland Agriculture, 1962. Contbr. to (Anthols.): Australia Weekend Book No. 1, 1942; Poets at War, 1944; Australian Poetry, 1946-48, 1951-53, 1968, 1969; A Book of Australian Verse, 1956; Poet's Range, 1961; Poetry in Australia II, 1964; (Jrnls.): Meanjin; The Age; Hemisphere; Poetry; Quadrant; Southerly; Sydney Morning Herald; Westerly; Var. Articles on the History of the Early Theatre in Australia. Address: 14 Osborn Rd., Normanhurst, Sydney, N.S.W., 2076, Australia.

IRVIN, Margaret Elizabeth (née Connolly), b. 12 Dec. 1916. Poet. Education: Holy Cross Coll., Woolahra. Married Eric Irvin w. 2 daughters & 1 son. Published works: The Rock & The Pool, 1967; Literary Criticism: Judith Wright's Dark Gift; The Poet's Dilemma, (both in Twentieth Century); The Subtle Country of my Heart in Poetry Mag. Contbr. to (Anthols.): Australian Poetry, 1953, 1955-57, 1959-61; Poetry in Australia II, 1964; Australian Poetry, 1965, 66, 67, 68; (Jrnls.): Southern Review; Meanjin; The Age; Westerly; Bulletin; Hemisphere; Southerly; Sydney Morning Herald; Australian. Recip., Commonwealth Literary Fund Grant, 1966. Address: 14 Osborn Rd., Normanhurst, Sydney, N.S.W. 2076, Australia.

IRWIN, Patricia Kathleen, pen names **PAGE, P.K. & CAPE, Judith,** b. 23 Nov. 1916. Writer & Artist. Education: studied art under Frank Schaeffer in Brazil & Charles Seliger in N.Y.; attended the Art Students' League & Pratt Graphics in N.Y. Married W. Arthur Irwin, 3 step-children. Positions held: Sales Clerk & Radio Actress in St. John, N.B.; Filing Clerk & Histl. Rschr. in Montreal; Co-Ed., Preview; Regl. Ed., B.C. Northern Review; Script Writer for Nat. Film Bd., 1946-50. One Man Exhibs: Picture Loan Soc., Toronto, 1960; Galeria de Arte Moderna, Mexico, 1962; Art Gall. of Gtr. Victoria, 1965; var. grp. exhibs. in Canada & Mex. Rep. in following colls: Nat. Gall. of Canada, Ottawa; Art Gall. of Toronto; Vancouver Art Gall.; Art Gall. of Gtr. Vic.; Univ. of Vic. Published works: The Sun & the Moon (novel), 1944; As Ten As Twenty (poems), 1946; The Metal & the Flower (poems), 1954; Cry Ararat! Poems New & Selected, 1967. Contbr. of poetry, short stories & articles to var. anthols., mags., reviews. Honours, awards: The Gov.-Gen's Award in Poetry, 1954; received as a Poet by the Academia Brazileira de Letras in Rio de Janeiro, 1959, etc. Address: 3260 Exeter Rd., Victoria, B.C., Canada V8R 6H6.

ISAAC, Charles Abraham, pen name **PETER PAN,** b. 7 Apr. 1922. Librarian. Education: Union Christian Coll., Alwaye (Travancore Univ.-), S. India. Positions held: served in R.I.A.F. (India Cmd.), 1942-46; worked as Forest Officer & Jrnlst. for short periods; Tchr., Sec. schl., Addis Ababa, Ethiopia, 1947-59 & simultaneously as Asst. Dir., The Am. Inst. in Addis Ababa (1948-58); Asst. Ed., Ethiopian Herald, 1955-58; P.R.O., for the Ethiopian Patriots' Assn., 1955-59; Libn., Wandsworth, U.K., 1960-65; Libn. in Lambeth, 1965-. Memberships: London Writer Circle; Int. PEN (Engl. Ctr.); Keats-Shelley Meml. Assn.; Poetry Soc.

(London). Published works: Indivisible India, 1947; Modern Ethiopia, 1956; Isaac's Telescopic Classification, 1969. Rep. in following: Longman's Miscellany: IV, 1947; Treasury of Modern Poets, 1971; World Poets, 1971; Anthology of Modern Verse, 1972. Contbr. to: United India; Onward; Ethiopian Herald; New Times & Ethiopian News; L'Ethiopie Contemporaine; Nippon Times; Thought; Vale Ch. News, London. Address: 292 Abercairn Rd., Streatham Vale, London SW16, U.K.

ISACKE, Peter Patrick, b. 17 Mar. 1952. Audit Clerk. Education: Brooklyn Tech. Coll., 1967-69; Sutton Coldfield Coll. of Further Educ., 1969-71; Birmingham Coll. of Dramatic Art. Positions held: Civil Servant, Dept. of Employment; Salesman, Debenhams Furniture Dept.; Asst. Libn. working in Shakespeare Lib. i/c. of theatre material, Birmingham Ref. Lib.; Currently Audit Clerk, Ruberg & Co. chartered accts. Memberships: Comm. i/c of Outdoor Activities & Readings, Birmingham Poetry Ctr.; formed The Sutton Coldfield Poetry Grp. in 1970; English Speaking Board. Editor of: Poems from Sutton Coldfield, 1972; More Poems from Sutton Coldfield, 1973. Address: 18 Chancellors Close, Edgbaston, Birmingham 15, U.K.

ITALIAANDER, Rolf, b. 20 Feb. 1913. Professor of Ethnology; Writer; Museum Founder. Education: var. European univs. Positions held: Explorer, Africa, over 30 yrs.; Vis. Prof., Inst. for European Studies, Univ. of Vienna, 1959; Univ. of Mich., U.S.A., 1961; Hope Coll., Mich., 1961; Kalamazoo Coll., 1961; Am. Negro Univs., 1962; Univ. de Bahia & Inst. Joaquim Nabuco, Recife, Brazil, 1967. Memberships incl: Co-Fndr., Free Acad. of Arts, Hamburg; Hon. Pres. & Fndr., German Translators Union. Published works incl: Die Neuen Manner Asiens, 1964; Immer wenn ich unterwegs bin, 1963; Konig Leopolds Kongo, 1964; Dappers Afrika 1668, 1964; The Challenge of Islam, 1964; Im Hamen des Herrn im Kongo, 1965; Die Friedensmacher, 1965; In der Palmwiesenschenke, 1966; Rassenkonflikte in der Welt, 1966; Frieden in der Welt – aber wie?, 1967; Heinrich Barth, 1967; Terra Dolorosa (Indoamerika), 1969; Weder Krankheit noch Verbrechen, 1969; Akzente eines Lebens, 1970; Kultur ohne Wirtschaftswunder, 1970; Albanien: Chinas Vorposten in Europa, 1970; Hallelujahs, 1969. Recip., Hans Henry Jahn Prize, 1964; Subj. of sev. biogs.; Ode Nat. de la République de Senegal. Address: Heilwigstr. 39, Hamburg 20, German Fed. Repub.

IVANCAN, Dubravko, b. 6 Mar. 1931. Writer. Education: grad. in philos., Zagreb Univ., 1954; postgrad. study, Münster/Westfal, 1959-61. Positions held: Librarian, 1955-59; currently Freelance Writer. Member, Društvo književnika Hrvatske, Zagreb. Published works: (vols. of poetry) Slobodna noć, 1957; Leptirova krila (haiku), 1964; Svjetlucanje, (haiku), 1966; Pjesma na putu, 1968; Uvijek iznova raste pjenušavo stablo bijelog vodoskoka, (haiku), 1968; Amor, 1971; Bijeli brod, 1971; More, 1974; (epic fable) Jaje harambaša, 1958. Contbr. to a variety of Yugoslav papers & periodicals. Address: Matije Ivanica 19, 41000 Zagreb, Yugoslavia.

IVANISEVIC, Drago, pen name **JORDAN, Albert,** b. 10 Feb. 1907, Trieste. Professor; Man of Letters; Painter. Education: Fac. of Letters, Belgrade; Univs. of Paris, Padua, Florence, Rome, Munich; Dr. of Letters, Padua, 1931; studied Theatre in Paris & Painting at la Grande Chaumière, Paris. Divorced. Positions held: Prof. & Dir. of var. schls. of dramatic art; Dramatist, Nat. Theatre of Croatia, Zagreb; Prof., Acad. of Dramatic Art, Zagreb; Dir. of Fest. of Dramatical Art. Memberships: Assn. of Croatian Writers; PEN, Zagreb Ctr.; COMES. Published works: Zemlja pod nogama, 1940; Dnevnik, 1957; Mali libar, 1959; Jubav, 1960; Srž, 1961; Poezija, 1964; Igra bogova ili pustinje ljubavi, 1967; Glasine, 1969; Vrelo vrelo bez prestanka, 1970; Od blata jabuka, 1971; Pismo mrtvoj ljubavi, 1973. Contbr. to: Republika, Zagreb; Mogućnosti, Split; Književnost, Belgrade; Dometi, Rijeka; Europa letteraria, Rome; Prospetti, Rome, etc. Honours, awards: Prix Goran, 1970; Prix Publique au

meilleur poète Yougoslave, 1972; Prix Marko Marulic, 1972. Address: Bogovićeva 1/VII, Zagreb, Yugoslavia.

IVASK, George, b. 1 Sept. 1907. Poet & Scholar. Education: Lic.iur, Univ. of Tyrtu, Estonia, 1932; Ph.D. in Slavic Langs. & Lits., Harvard Univ., U.S.A., 1954. Married Tamara Schmeling-Mezhak. Positions held: Asst. Prof., Univ. of Kans., 1957-60; Assoc. Prof., Univ. of Wash., 1960-68; Prof., Univ. of Vanderbilt, 1968; Prof., Univ. of Mass., Amerst, 1969–; Vis. Lectr. & pub. lectures at var. univs. inclng. Vis. Prof., Univ. of Freiburg i/Br., 1974. Memberships: MLAA; AATSEEL. Published works: (books of poetry in Russian) Severnyi Bereg (Northern Shore), 1938; Tsarskaia Osen' (Imperial Autumn), 1953; Khvala (Praising), 1967; Zolushka (Cinderella), 1970. Contbr. to: Sovremennye Zapiski; Put'; Novyi Zhurnal; Slavic Review; Russian Review; The Third Hour; Zeitschrift fuer Slavische Philologie; Vozrozhdenie, etc. Read own poetry at Int. Forum of Poetry, Austin, Tex., 1971. Address: Slavic Dept., Univ. of Mass., Amherst, MA 01002, U.S.A.

IVASK, Ivar (Vidrik), b. 17 Dec. 1927. Professor; Editor. Education: Univ. of Marburg, Germany, 1946-49; M.A., Univ. of Minn., U.S.A., 1950; Ph.D., ibid, 1953. Married Astride Ivaska. Positions held: Asst. Prof. of German, St. Olaf Coll., Northfield, Minn., 1952-54; Asst. Prof. & Acting Chmn., ibid, 1956-57; Assoc. Prof. & Dept. Chmn., 1958-63; Prof. & Dept. Chmn., 1964-66; Prof. of Mod. Langs. & Ed. of Books Abroad, int. lit. qtly., Univ. of Okla., Norman, 1967–. Memberships: Estonian PEN; MLA; AABS; AATG; Estonian Learned Soc. Published works: Tähtedetähendus (The Meaning of Stars), 1964; Päev astub kukesammul (Day Comes with a Rooster's Step), 1966; Gespieqelte Erde, 1967; Ajaloo aiad (The Gardens of History), 1970; Oktoober Oklahomas (October in Oklahoma), 1973. Contbr. to: Tulimuld; Mana; Jauna gaita; Cela zimes; Metmenys; Nootti; Origo; Der Bogen; Kaltio; Manuskripte; The Lit. Review; Books Abroad; Revista de Bellas Artes; El Urogallo; Varlik; Words; St. Olaf Alumnus; Die Presse. Recip., Henrik Visnapuu Prize awarded for Okttober Oklahomas, 1973. Address: Books Abroad, 401 West Brooks, Univ. of Okla., Norman, OK 73069, U.S.A.

IVENS, Michael William, b. 15 Mar. 1924. Director; Writer. Positions held: Dir., Fndn. for Business Responsibilities; Ed., Twentieth Century; Dir., Aims of Industry. Published works: Another Sky, 1963; Last Waltz, 1964; Private & Public, 1968. Contbr. to: New Statesman; Spectator; Twentieth Century; Outposts Rep. in following anthols: Oxford Book of Modern Verse, 1973; New Voices of the Commonwealth, 1968; Keats Anthologies, 1972/3; After A War Anthol., Australia, 1974. Borestone Award Anthol., 1957. Address: 13 Blenheim Terrace, London N.W.8., U.K.

IVERS, Nancy Marie, O.P., b. 15 June 1932. Teacher. Education: B.A., Siena Heights Coll., Adrian, Mich; M.A., Loyola Univ., Chicago, Ill.; postgrad. work at Univ. of Detroit, San Jose State Coll., Catholic Univ. of Am., Wash. D.C. Positions held: Tchr., grades 1–12, 23 yrs.; Activities Dir., Extended Care Facility, Dominican Hosp.; Birthright Volunteer. Assoc. Mbr., N.Y. Poetry Forum. Contbr. to: Desert Call mag.; Sedona Ariz. 'Waiting', summer 1973; Awakening, 1968 & Dominic's Commentary – ABM, 1968 (Dominican periodicals). Address: 108 High St., Santa Cruz, CA 95060, U.S.A.

IVES, Jacqueline Rose, pen name, **POINTER, Jacqueline,** b. 22 Nov. 1937. Housewife. Personal details: m. (1), to Edgar Mittelholzer, Guyanese novelist, 1960; dec., 1965; m. (2), to Philip Ives. Positions held: Asst. Rudolph Steiner School, 1958; mainly secretarial, 1958-60. Memberships: Panel of Eds., Envoi Mag.; Comm., Guildford Poetry Soc., br. of The Poetry Soc.(UK), 1967, 1968; CSSI. Publications: Nebuchadnezzar, and Other Poems, 1964; The Shadow Which the Soul Must Pass, 1969. Contbr. to the following anthols. and journals: Poetry from the

People; It's World that Makes the Love Go Round; Autumn Anthol.; Country Life; The Lady; Elizabethan; Breakthru; Envoi; Manifold; Christian Herald; Scrip; Pacifist; Peace News; Weyfarers; Overspill. Honours: Runner-up Prize, Short Story, The Observer, 1958; Guildford Poetry Soc. Competition, 1960; Schol. to Writers' Summer School, 1958. CSSI Award, 1971. Address: 40 Meadrow, Godalming, Surrey, UK.

J

JACK, Sheila Beryl, b. 26 Sept. 1918. Educator. Education: Derby Diocesan Trng. Coll. for Tchrs. Positions held: Tchr. of Engl. as Second Lang. in Wolverhampton; Wrockwardine Parish Councillor; Schl. Mgr.; Salop Co. Councillor. Member, Attingham Writers' Club. Published works: Thirty-Two Poems, 1962; Another Thirty-Two Poems, to be released shortly. Contbr. to: Shrewsbury Chronicle; Monday World. Address: Longacre, Wrockwardine, Nr. Telford, Shropshire, U.K.

JACKOWSKA, Nicki, b. 6 Aug. 1942. Writer. Education: full time course in Drama leading to Anea Acting Dip. Married Andrzej Jackowski, 1 daughter. Positions held: Regl. Co-ordinator for the South-West of England to the New Activities Comm. of the Arts Coun. of G.B. Member, Poetry Roundabout, 1972–. Ed., Fndr., Contbr. to Poetry St. Ives. Published works: Song for the Beginning of It (broadsheet), 1971; Today's Flower is White (broadsheet), 1972; Nightride (pamphlet), 1973; House of Effigies (broadsheet), 1973; The King Rises, (booklet), Second Aeon; My Master Comes & Goes, 1974. Contbr. to: Brighton & Hove Herald; Speech & Drama; Flourish; Aylesford Review; IWWP Anthol., 1972; Second Aeon; Prospice; Poet, etc. Many profl. readings of own work. Broadcast sev. times on Radio 3, Poetry Now. Honours, awards: Prizewinner, Stroud Fest., Guinness Int. Poetry Comp., 1972; Grant for Poetry, Soc. of Authors, 1973. Address: c/o The Nat. Westminster Bank, 40 Church St., Falmouth, Cornwall, U.K.

JACKSON, Alan, b. 6 Sept. 1938. Publisher. Education: Edinburgh Univ. Positions held: Labourer, Trainee Psych. Nurse, 1959-60; Sec., Scottish Comm. of 100, 1961-62; Fndr. & Dir., Kevin Press, 1965; Fndr. & Dir., Live Readings, Scotland, 1957. Published works: Underwater Wedding, 1961; Sixpenny Poems, 1962; Well Ye Ken Noo, 1963; All Fall Down, 1965; The Worstest Beast, 1967; Penguin Modern Poets 12, 1968; The Grim Wayfarer, 1969. Contbr. to various anthols. Address: 17 Cathcart Place, Edinburgh, 11, UK.

JACKSON, Lydia Octavia, b. 5 Mar. 1902. Homemaker & Poet. Education: Public schls. in N.D. Married Arthur F. Jackson, 1 daughter. Memberships: Publicity Chmn., Poetry Day, 1950; Treas., Grafton Schl. Dist., 1931-62; Treas., Walsh Co. Schl. Officers Assn., 1945-62; Am. Poets Fellowsp Soc.; World Poetry Day Assn.; Centro Studi e Scambi Int.; State Regent, Midwest Fed. Chaparral Poets, 1950-51; Nat. League Am. Pen Women; Am. Poetry League; Poetry Soc., London; Idaho Poets & Writers Guild; Order of Eastern Star; V.P., Riverside Womans Club, 1957-59. Published works: Rhymes For Every Season, 1943; Selected Poems, 1962; Pardon My Gaff, 1965. Compiled, Peace Garden of Verses, 1967. Contbr. of poems to over 200 mags., newspapers anthols., etc. Honours, awards: Nat. Writers Award, Farmers Union Educ. Dept., 1950; Bronze Medal, Centro Studi e Scambi Int., 1965; Silver Medal, ibid, 1967; Am. Poets Fellowship Poet Laureate V for 1972-73. Address: Rte. 2, Grafton, ND 58237, U.S.A.

JACKSON, Norman, b. 4 Mar. 1932. Journalist. Education: Hull Coll. of Art, UK; Hull Univ. Positions held: Vis. Fulbright Lectr., Univ. of Iowa, USA; Gulbenkian Fellow in Poetry, Univ. of Keele, UK. Published works: Beyond the Habit of Sense, 1968; 12 Poems, 1964; Faulkner, The Novelist Behind the Man,

1967. Contbr. to: Observer; Sunday Times; Am. Scholar; Reporter Mag.; New Yorker; Poetry Review; Sat. Review; Books & Bookmen; Tribune; BBC; Arena; Delta; Priapus. Honours, Awards: Fulbright Scholarship, 1967; Breadloaf Poetry Fellowship, 1967; Arts Coun. Grant, 1970; Yorks. Arts Assn. Grant to Writers, 1971. Address: 64 Auckland Ave., Cottingham Rd., Hull, Yorks., UK.

JACKSON, Peter, b. 1928. Government Official. Education: B.A., Engl. Lit., New Coll., Oxford. Positions held: Joined the Southern Rhodesian Native Affairs Dept., 1951; Exec. Officer, Capricorn Africa Soc., Zambia (formerly Northern Rhodesia), 1956. Contbr. to (Anthol.): A Book of South African Verse, 1959; (Jrnl.): London Mag.

JACKSON, Sue Settle, pen name **BROOKS, Sue Settle,** b. 16 Aug. 1900. Retired Secretary. Education: creative writing studies, Univ. of Louisville, Ky. Married Alvin Jackson, 1 daughter. Positions held: Sec., Western Ky. Coal Operators, Louisville; Ky. Coal Agency, 8 yrs. Memberships: Former Pres. & Sec., Austin Poetry Soc.; Councillor, Poetry Soc. of Tex.; twice Pres., Austin Kwill Klub; Nat. Fed. State Poetry Socs.; Acad. Am. Poets. Published works: (book of poetry) Tap Roots, 1974; var. stories & articles. Contbr. to: Cats Mag.; Baptist Standard; Anthol. of Am. Poetry, 1962-69; Avalon Anthol. of Tex. Poets, 1963; Anthol. of Ky. Poets; Pegasus; South & West; Flame; Cyclo-Flame, etc. Recip. var. poetry awards & hons. inclng: 1st Prize, Relig. Arts Fest., Rochester, N.Y.; Freedom Award, Freedom Fndn., Valley Forge, 1967; num. awards, Poetry Soc. of Tex. and Nat. Fedn. of State Poetry Socs. Address: 508 East 46th St., Austin, TX 78751, U.S.A.

JACKSON, William Hargadine, pen name **JACKSON, Wm. Dean,** b. 18 Aug. 1929. Teacher of Engl., Creative Writing, and Literature. Education: Georgetown Univ., Wash., DC; George Washington Univ., DC; The American Univ., Wash., DC, Bach. of Science in Literature, cum laude, 1970. Positions held: Poet in Residence, the Walden School, 1965-69; Director, Communications Dept., P.E.P., Skidmore Coll., Saratoga Springs, NY. Summers, 1968, 1969; Adjunct Instr., Dept. of Lit., Am. Univ., Wash. D.C., Fall 1969, Summer 1970; Full time Faculty, Dept. of Engl. and Philosophy, Montgomery Coll., Fall 1970 onwards. Memberships: The Washington Beat Poets; The Howard Univ. Poets; Assoc. Ed., Outcry Literary Qtly., Austin, Texas/Washington, DC. Contbr. to: The Archive Review; The Nat. Anthol. of College Poetry, 1955; Dasein: A Qtly. Journal of the Arts; Exordium; Outcry; The American Mag., etc. Awards: Selected for best sonnet, Nat. Anthol. of College Poetry, 1955. Address: Dept. of Engl. and Philosophy, Montgomery Coll., Rockville, MD 20850, USA.

JACOB, Paul, b. 27 Apr. 1940. Kerala, India. Journalist. Education: Christian Coll., Madras; St. Stephens Coll., Delhi. Positions held: Lit. Staff, The Century, a cultural-political weekly publd. by V.K. Krisha Menon; Copywriter, L.P.E. Aiyar's advt. firm; Asst. Ed., Entact. Mbr., Writer's Workshop, Calcutta, 1969; Alter Sonnets on Erotic Themes, 1970; Inlands in Sestina, 1971. Contbr. to: Homage to T.S. Eliot, 1965; Indian Poetry in English, 1970; Miscellany; Entact; Jr. Statesman; Thought; Engl., Madras. Read own poems on Delhi TV. Address: c/o Writers Workshop, 162/92 Lake Gardens, Calcutta 45, India.

JACOBS, Florence Burrill, pen name **LINCOLN, Anne,** b. 25 May 1898. Poet and Essayist. Married George B. Jacobs. Education: Skowhegan H.S., Valedictorian 1916 Courses, Farmington Normal, Colby Coll. Positions held: Grade School Teacher, 1916-1919, E. Madison; Sec. Farm Bureau, 1920-1923, Skowhegan; First Grade Teacher, Madison, 1924-1931. Memberships: Poetry Soc. of America; Nat. League of Am. Pen Women; Poetry Fellowship of Me., Chairman, Bd. of Review, over 30 yrs., vice-pres. sev. terms. Published works: Stones, 1932; Neighbors, 1949; Gentle Harvest, 1970; Colors of

Time, 1973. Contbr. New Yorker; N.Y. Times; Herald Tribune; Ladies' Home Journal; McCall's; Good Housekeeping; Sat. Eve. Post; Harper's Mag.; Rotarian; Woman's Day; Lyric Mag.; Poet Lore; Adventure; Yankee; Down East; Farm Journal, etc. Anthols.: Maine Lines; Sammy Kaye; Ted Malone. Also brochure published, The Poetry of Florence B. Jacobs (Westbrook College, 1969). Awards include: 200-dollar 1st prize, Nat. Fed. of State Poetry Socs., 1970; 100-dollar, Poetry Soc. of Texas, 1962; 100-dollar Nat. Life Conservation Soc., 1956; Lyric Mag., 2 50-dollar awards; 50-dollar Award, Univ. of Va., 1973; also 30 nat. awards (first), and many 2nd and 3rd place awards. Address: Skowhegan, Rt. 4, ME 04976, USA.

JACOBS, J.C., b. 31st Jan. 1945. Education: Smith Coll., Northampton, Mass.; B.A. in Classical Studies, Columbia Univ., N.Y., U.S.A. Published works: New American Poetry, Ed. Richard Monaco, published by McGraw-Hill, 1973; The Logic of Poetry, authors: Monaco & Briggs, published by McGraw-Hill, 1974. Address: 702 West End Ave., N.Y., NY, U.S.A.

JACOBSEN, Ethel Dorothy, pen name **JACOBSEN, Ethel Walker,** b. 12 May 1901. Writer. Education: Columbia Univ.; Monmouth Coll.; Famous Writers' Schl.; Writers' Workshops & Confs. Widow of Irvin Spencer Jacobsen, 3 stepsons. Memberships: V.P., Woman's Club of Asbury Park, N.J.; N.J. State Chmn., World Poetry Day; N.J. South Shore Rep., Int. Acad. of Poets; Int. Poets Shrine; Fla. Arts Coun.; Fla. League of Arts; Special Asst. to Nat. Dir., World Poetry Day Comm. Inc., Fla. & Nat. Poetry Day Comm. Inc.; Lakeland Dir., Fla. State Poetry Soc.; Dir., Lakeland Poetry Workshop; Hon. Rep., Centro Studi e Scambi Int.; United Poets Laureate Int., Philippines, & many others. Published works: Reaching to the Stars, 1969; Searching, 1973. Contbr. to: IWWP Anthol., 1972; Rainbow; Laurel Leaves; Bouquets of Poems; Selected Poems, Fla. State Poetry Soc.; Sun Herald, Fla.; Flamingo, Int. Hall of Fame Poets, Yearbook of Modern Poetry; Clover Coll. of Verse – Vol.5; From Sea to Sea in Song Anthols.; Poets of Am. Anthol., etc. Recip. many honours & awards inclng: Service Gold Medal, Nat. Poetry Day Comm., 1970; Dr. of Humane Letters, 1970; Award of Hon., United Poets Laureate, 1972. Address: 810 East Bella Vista, Apt. 203, Lakeland, FL 33801, U.S.A.

JACOBSEN, Rolf, b. 8 Mar. 1907. Author; Poet. Education: Univ. of Oslo, Norway, 1927-31. Positions held: Pressman inclng. 5 years as Editor; Bookshop Asst., 1950-60; Night Ed. in a daily newspaper, Hamar, 1960-71. Memberships: Den norske Forfatterforening (Norwegian Author org.), 1935–. Published works: (books of poems) Jord og jern, 1933; Vrimmel, 1935; Fjerntog, 1951; Hemmelig liv, 1954; Sommeren i Gresset, 1956; Brev til lyset, 1960; Stillheten efterpa, 1965; Headlines, 1969; Pass for dorene – dorene lukkes, 1972; Selected Poems, 1967; Collected Poems, 1973. Translation of poems (parts/anthols.) into 11 European langs. Honours, awards: Kritiker-prisen, Oslo, 1960; Riksmalsprisen, Oslo, 1965; Dobloug-Prisen, Stockholm (Svenska Akademin), 1968. Address: Skappels Gt 2, 2300 Hamer, Norway.

JACOBSON, Ethel, Poet. Education: N.Y. City Schls.; studied art, music. Married Louis John Jacobson, 2 daughters. Positions held: Freelance Writer; Book Reviewer; Speaker. Memberships: Dir., Calif. Writers' Guild; PEN Int.; Past V.P., L.A. Chapt.; Southern Calif. Womans Press Club; Chaparral Poets; Freedoms Fndn. Published works: Larks in my Hair, 1952; Mice in the Ink, 1955; I'll Go Quietly, 1966; Curious Cats, 1969; Who Me?, 1970; Diamonds For Your Jubilee, 1964; California, 1769-1969, 1969; The Cats of Seacliff Castle, 1971, 2nd edn., 1973. Contbr. to the following anthols., jrnls., mags., etc. Saturday Evening Post; Saturday Review; Atlantic; Ariz. Highways; Chatelaine; Christian Sci. Monitor; Family Weekly; Good Housekeeping; Gourmet; Ladies Home Jrnl.; Look; Times; Chicago Tribune; New Yorker; Sports Illustrated; Wall St. Jrnl.; St. Louis Post-Dispatch, St. Louis; over 6,000 contbns. have appeared in major markets in U.S., Canada, England. Honours, awards: Awards for I'll Go Quietly & Who Me?, Univ. of Calif. at Irvine, Friends of the Lib., 1967 & '70. Address: 108 Buena Vista, Fullerton, CA 92633, U.S.A.

JAECKLE, Erwin, b. 12 Aug. 1909. Editor. Education: Ph.D., Univ. of Zurich. Positions held: Publisher's Reader; Co-founder, Chief Editor, Swiss Independent Daily 'Die Tat', Zurich, 1943-71; Head of Lit. Editing, 1962–. Mbr., Zurich Town Council, 1942-50 & Swiss National Council, 1947-62. Memberships: PEN Club; Thomas Mann Soc.; Humboldt Soc.; Paracelsus Soc., etc. Published works incl: (poetry) Die Kelter des Herzens, 1943; Schattenlos, 1947; Gedichte aus allen Winden, (with a post-script on the modern lyric), 1956; Glück in Glas, (with a post-script on Time), 1957; Aber von Thymian duftet der Nonig, 1961; Das Himmlische Gelächter, 1962; Im Gitter der Stunden, 1963; Der Ochsenritt, 1967; Nachricht von den Fischen, 1969; Die Zungenwurzel ab., 1971; Das wachsende Gedicht, 1973; var. other works in many fields. Honours, awards incl: Chevalier de l'Ordre Militaire et Hospitalier de Saint-Lazare de Jérusalem; Grand Officier de Mérite; Ehrengaben des Kantons und der Stadt Zürich; Ehrengabe der Schweizerischen Schiller-Stiftung; Conrad Ferdinand Meyer-Preis für Lyrik, 1958. Address: Drusbergstrasse 113, CH-8053, Zurich, Switzerland.

JAFAREY, Ada, b. 22 Aug. 1924. Housewife. Married N.H. Jafarey, 2 sons, 1 daughter. Member, Pakistan Writers Guild. Published works: (colls. of poetry in Urdu) Main Saaz Dhoondhti Rahi (In Search of Expression), 1950; Shahr-e-Dard (Domain of Anguish), 1967. Contbr. to: Rooman; Savera; Funoon; Adab-e-Latif–Naya Daur; Auraq; Shahkar; Afkar; Naqoosh; Seep; Jang, Karachi & London. Recip., Adamji Prize for Lit. for best coll. of Urdu Poetry published in 1967. Address: I–50, F–6/3, Islamabad, Pakistan.

JAFFA, Aileen Raby, b. 26 Apr. 1900. Librarian. Education: A.B., Univ. of Calif. at Berkeley, 1922; Certificate, Univ. of Calif. School of Librarianship, Berkeley, 1928. Personal details: Daughter of Prof. Myer Edward Jeffa and Dr. Adele Solomons Jaffa; Married Milton Jerome Katzky, 1922, divorced, 1928; children: Lawrence Marvin; Joan Elizabeth (deceased). Positions held: Jr. Asst. Univ. of Calif Library, Berkeley, Agricultural Ref. Service, 1928-33; Agriculture Librarian, 1933-62; Head Agriculture Library, 1956-62. Memberships: NLAPW (Pres., Piedmont-Oakland Branch, 1970-72); Ina Coolbrist Circle (Pres., 1971-72); Editorial Committee, Ina Coolbrith Golden Circle, 1964-65, 1966-67, Golden Anniversary Anthol., 1969; San Francisco Browning Soc. (Artist Member); Calif. Writers' Club; Calif. Fed. of Chaparral Poets. Published works: Three Sonnets, 1939; Trondheims, 1960; Today, 1965; Word Out Of Time, 1965; Tiptoe To The Wind, 1967; Let The Star Shine, 1973; Spindrift of Thistle (not yet published). Contbr. to many journals, anthols., newspapers. Recip. sev. awards. Address: 1105 Wellesley Ave., Modesto, CA 95350, USA.

JAFFE, Daniel Freeman, pen name, **JAFFE, Dan,** b. 24 Jan. 1933. Prof. of English. Education: B.A., Rutgers Coll., 1954; M.A., Univ. of Mich., 1958. Positions held: Instr., Univ. of Neb.; Asst. Prof., Willamette Univ.; Assoc. Prof., Univ. of Mo., Kansas City. Published works include: Dan Freeman, 1967; The First Tuesday in November, 1971; All Cats Turn Grey When the Sun Goes Down (Libretto); The Forecast, & Hallelujah in a Hard Time, to be publ. Contbr. to the following anthols., jrnls., mags., etc: NY Times; Prairie Schooner; Mademoiselle; Ladies Home Jrnl.; Harrison St. Review; Saturday Review; Generation; Anthologist; Vortex; Kronos; Southwester; Focus Midwest; KC Star; Anderson Herald; The Reporter; The Screw; The Willa Cather Newsletter; Coll. English; Univ. of Kansas City Review; The Poetry Bag; The Salt Creek Reader. Honours, awards: Avery Hopwood Award, Univ. of Mich., 1958; 1st. & 2nd. Kansas City Star Award, 1965; Fellow of Breadloaf Writers Conf.,

1958. Address: 104 E 68th Terrace, Kansas City, Mo. 64113, USA.

JAFFE, Marie B., b. 26 April 1897. Teacher (retired). Grad. of Hunter College, N.Y.C. Member, Poetry Soc. of America; Composers, Authors & Artists of America. Pubs. Gut Yuntif, Gut Yohr; Ten for Posterity. Contrib. to: Poet Lore; Educational Forum; Chicago Jewish Forum; Spirit; Christian Science Monitor; Prairie Schooner; Poetry Review (London); Times Literary Supplement (London); Jewish Frontier. Address: 1388 Lexington Avenue, New York, N.Y., 10028, USA.

JAFFIN, David, b. 14 Sept. 1937. Historian. Education: B.A., M.A. & Ph.D., N.Y. Univ.; studying for the Ministry, Univ. of Tuebingen. Married, 2 sons. Published works: Conformed to Stone, 1968, 1970; Emptied Spaces, 1972; Opened (broadsheet), 1973; Late March (broadsheet), 1973; As One (forthcoming, 1974); In the Glass of Winter (forthcoming, 1974). Contbr. to: My Music Bent (anthol.); In Dark Mill Shadows (Univ. of Lancaster anthol.); English; The Contemporary Review; Ariel; The Poetry Review; Akros; The Decal Review; Forum; Elizabeth; The Anglo Welsh Review; Workshop New Poetry; Tribune; Poet (London); The Christian Century; The Cimarron Review; The Little Review; The Wis. Review; Poem; The Chelsea Review; Descant; Tagus; Samphire; Contrasts; Capella; Oasis; Hierophant; The Clare Market Review; Littack; The Chapman; The Dalhousie Review; Voices Int.; The Indian PEN; Enigma; Orbis; Second Aeon; St. Andrews Review; Galley Sail Review; Univ. of Portland Review; Open Places; Waves (Univ. of York, Canada).etc. Recip. num. academic hons. Address: c/o Abelard-Schuman Ltd., 450 Edgware Rd., London W2 1EG, U.K. or The Elizabeth Press, 103 Van Etten Blvd., New Rochelle, NY, U.S.A.

JAHNKE, Violette Louise (Mrs.) pen name **VIOLETTE,** born 19th June, 1922. Artist; Housewife. Education: B.S., Milwaukee State Tchrs. Coll. Memberships: Wis. Fellowship of Poets; Wis. Regional Writers Assoc.; Nat. League of Am. Pen Women; Assoc. Mbr., Poet's Study Club. Contbr. to: (anthols.) New Poetry Out of Wisconsin, 1969; Wisconsin History in Poetry, 1971. Writers' Notes & Quotes, 1966; Wis. Harvest Anthol., 1966; Wis. Poetry Anthol., 1969. (jrnls.) Karyn Mag.; Angel Hour Mag., 1966; Crawford Co. Courier, Ark.; Minneapolis Argus Poetry Corner; Lake Shore Penwoman Mag. Honours: 3rd Prize, Catherine Clark Award, Pa. Poetry Soc., 1966; 3rd Place Award, Wis. Regional Writers' Assoc., 1965; 1st Prize, Light Verse Div., Terre Haute Poets Study Club, 1969; Nat. Fed. Poetry Soc. 3rd prize, 1970; Hon. Mention, 5th prize, 1971; Ariz. State Poetry Soc. Contest, 1st Award, 1971; Poets Study Club, Members Contests, H.M., 1971, 1972. Address: 745 N. 3rd Ave., Cedarburg, Wis. 53012, U.S.A.

JAMES, Clifford Thomas, pen name **JAMES, Cliff,** b. 7 July 1943. School Teacher. Education: Tchrs. Trng. Coll., Swansea; Degree in Educ., Cardiff. Married, 2 children. Member, Poets Conf., G.B. Published works: Cadwgan To Keep A Song, 1970; included in 'Poems 72' anthol. by Welsh Arts Coun. of best poetry written in Wales during that year; stories included in 'The Old Man of the Mist & Other Stories, by Welsh Authors, 1974. Contbr. to: Second Aeon; Anglo-Welsh Review; London Welshman; Planet; Country Quest; Christian Sci. Monitor, etc. Address: 7 Sycamore Ct., Woodfieldside, Blackwood, Gwent, U.K.

JAMES, Eliott Dylan, b. 26 Sept. 1954. Writer. Member, N.Y. Poetry Forum. Published works: (books) Sky, 1970; From Under the Shade of Winter, 1972; Forgiving Blind Children, 1973; Three Seasons, 1974. Contbr. to: The Sumter News; The Guilfordian; Signature; Grit; Catalyst; Listen; Shore Anthol.; Poetry of Our Times; The Best in Poetry. Honours, awards: Poetry Day Poet, N.Y. Poetry Forum, Oct. 1971 & Apr. 1972. Address: The Summer Song Publishing Co., P.O. Box 10307, Atlanta, GA 30319, U.S.A.

JAMIESON, Peter, Pseudonym: **Shalder.** Editor; Poet (Shetland Dialect). Positions held: Fndr., The New Shetlander; Ed., 1947-57. Published works: Letters on Shetland, 1949. Contbr. to (Anthols.): Northern Lights, 1960; Scottish Poetry Two, Three & Four, 1967, 68, 69; (Jrnls.): Scotsman; Scottish Poetry.

JAMILA-RA, b. 31 Jan. 1945. Writer; Journalist; Film Critic. Education: A.A., Chicago City Jr. Coll., Ill.; A.B., Roosevelt Univ., Chicago; currently working for M.A. in Comparative Lit. at State Univ. of N.Y., Binghamton. Positions held: Film Critic-Reporter, Chicago Courier Newspaper, 1970; Creative Writing Tchr., Firman House, Chicago, 1971-72; Reporter, Chicago Daily Defender newspaper, 1972; Grad. Tchng. Asst. & Poet-in-Res., State Univ. of N.Y., Binghamton, 1973. Member, Nat. Assn. of Media Women. Published works: The Good Book, 1971. Contbr. to: Film Comment; Film News; Nommo; Jrnl. of Black Poetry; Take One; Negro Digest; To Gwen Brooks with Love; Chicago Daily Defender; Chicago Courier News; Chicago Reader News; Woodlawn Observer; Roosevelt Torch. Honours, awards: Winner, Chicago Poetry Fest., 1972. Address: P.O. Box 20155, Chicago, IL 60620, U.S.A.

JANDL, Ernst, b. 1 Aug. 1925. Teacher. Education: Dr. phil., Univ. of Vienna. Positions held: Tchr. at Grammar Schls. in Vienna; Tchr. at East Barnet Grammar Schl., England, 1952-53; Vis. Prof., German Dept., Univ. of Tex. at Austin, 1971. Memberships: Acad. of Arts, West Berlin; Forum Stadtpark, Graz, Austria; Exec. Comm., Grazer Autorenversammlung. Published works: Andere Augen, 1956; Lange Gedichte, 1964; Klare gerührt, 1964; Mai hart lieb zapfen eibe hold, 1965; Laut und Luise, 1966; Sprechblasen, 1968; Der künstliche Baum, 1970; Flöda and der schwan, 1970; Fünf Mann Menschen, 1971; Die Männer, 1973; Dingfest, 1973; Übung mit buben, 1973. Contbr. to: Neue Wege; Akzente; Dimension; Protokolle; Manuskripte; Ver Sacrum; Wort und Wahrheit; Wort in der Zeit; Literatur und Kritik; Neues Forum; Poor. Old. Tired. Horse.; Diskus, etc. Honours, awards: Hörspielpreis der Kriegsblinden, 1968. Address: Unt. Augartenstr. 1-3/1/19, A-1020 Vienna, Austria.

JANOWITZ, Abraham (Abe), b. 1 Jan. 1908. Retired Principal, Public School, and Retired Lecturer in Education, City Coll. of NY. Education: Bachelor of Social Science (1930); M.A. (1934), C.C.N.Y. Positions held: Teacher of English; Asst. Principal, Junior HS.; Principal, Public Elem. School and Lecturer (Coll.) in Education (concurrently). Assoc. Member, Poetry Soc. of America; Member, B.M.I. (Lyricist) Commercial recordings: Halleluyah Day (1953); The Old Red Barn (sung by Burl Ives) (1954); Tum-Bah-Lee, (1953). One of 4 judges in the Annual citywide Junior HS Poetry Contest, 1957-64. Contbr. to: The Instructor; Inst. for Retired Professionals Review; I.R.P. Newsletter; NY Principals Assoc. Publication, etc. Address: 163 Ocean Ave., Brooklyn, NY 11225, USA.

JANOWITZ, Phyllis, b. 3 Sept. 1940. Poet. Education: B.A., Queens Coll., N.Y.C.; M.F.A., Univ. of Mass., Amherst. Positions held: Instr., Mass. Bay Community Coll., Waltham, 1971; Tchr., Poets in the Schls. Prog., sponsored by Mass. Coun. of the Arts, 1972 & 73. Memberships: Phi Beta Kappa; New England Poetry Club. Published works: The Earth-Eaters, 1970. Contbr. to: Quest; Quabbin; Bantam Books; Intro I; The Nation; Bitterroot; Event; Esquire; Stony Lonesome; East Coast Anthol.; Radcliffe Qtly.; Univ. of Mass. Alumnus. Honours, awards: Fellow, Radcliffe Inst. in Poetry, 1971-72 & '72-73; Fellow, MacDowell Colony, summers 1972 & 73. Address: 33 Ivan St., Lexington, MA 02173, U.S.A.

JANTA, Alexander, b. 11 Dec. 1908. Poland. Writer; Book Dealer. Education: Lit. & Econs., Univ. of Poznan, Poland, 2 yrs.; Ecole de Jrnlism. & Ecole des Hautes Etudes Sociales, Paris, France. Positions held: For. Corres., Polish Press, mainly Far East; Asst. to

Pres. & Dir., 2 Fndns., USA; Lectr., Free-lance PR Mbr., Poetry Soc., NYC. Published works: 10 vols. of poetry in Polish, 1929–; Translator, Robert Frost & other Am. poets; Translator, The Hour of the Wild Duck, anthol. of Japanese poetry, 1967; Przestroga dla Wnukow (A Warning to Grandsons), 1971; Second Warnings, 1973. Contbr. to: Wiadomosci; NM Quarterly Review. Address: 88-28 43rd Ave., Elmhurst, NY 11373, USA.

JARMAN, Geraint, b. 17 Aug. 1950. Poet; Student. Education: Welsh Coll. of Music & Drama, Cardiff, UK. Married, Heather Jones, 1 d. Positions held: Factory Worker: Porter; Mbr. of Folksinging group. Fndng. Mbr., I No Walls Weekly Poetry Readings, Cardiff, 1968–; Actor; Free-lance Writer for TV. Published works: Burning the Hands of the Clock, 1967; Zutique, 1968; Eira Cariad (the Snow of Love), 1970. Contbr. to: Loudspeaker; Platform; Poetry Workshop; Riding West; Anglo-Welsh Review; NY; Enigma; Rumpus; Expression; Planet; Phoenix; Oyster; Taliesin; Y Genhinew; Y Faner; 2nd Aeon; Esra; Aeon; Tamerisk; Country Quest; Poetry Wales; London Welshman; Barn; Poet, India. Address: 67 Alfred St., 1 Roath Park, Cardiff, Wales, UK.

JARNAGIN, Margaret Fraser, b. 20 Aug. 1922. Housewife. Married Clifton W. Jarnagin, 3 sons (1 dec.) & 1 daughter. Memberships: Nat. Fed. of State Poetry Socs.; Wis. Fellowship of Poets; Wis. Regl. Writers' Assn. Contbr. to: New Poetry Out of Wis., 1969; Nat. Fed. of State Poetry Socs. Prize Poems, vol. III, 1971; Wis. History in Poetry, Nos. 1, 2 & 3, 1969, '70, '71; Life Today; Denver Post, Empire; Exposure; Muse; The Daily Tribune, Wis. Rapids. Honours, awards: First pl., The Jade Ring, Wis. Regl. Writers Assn., 1967 & also The Bard's Chair; First pl. Award, Nat. Fed. of State Poetry Socs., Rymed Poetry Category, 1968, etc. Address: 431 Fillmore Ave., Village of Port Edwards, WI 54469, U.S.A.

JARRETT, Emmett, b. 21 Feb. 1939. Poet. Education: B.A., Columbia Univ., N.Y.C.; M.Div. in progress, Gen. Theological Sem., N.Y.C. Married Carol Baum. Positions held: Prof. of Engl., Brit. Inst., Iraklion, Crete, 1966-67; Prof. of Hist., Engl. & Creative Writing, St. Ann's Schl., Brooklyn, N.Y., 1967-72; Tchrs. & Writers Collaborative, N.Y.C., 1972; Instr.-Poet, N.Y. State Poets in the Schls., 1972-1974. Memberships: Pres., Tallahassee Transcendentalist Soc., 1956-58; Fndr. & Co-Ed., Things (poetry mag.), 1964-66; Fndr. & Co-Ed., Hanging Loose (poetry mag.), 1966–. Published works: The Days, 1968; 4-Telling, 1971; Greek Feet, 1972; Getting into Another Head, 1974. Contbr. to: Tri-Qtly.; The Nation; Chicago Review; Hanging Loose; Things; New: Am. & Canadian Poetry; Northeast; Greenfield Review; Midwest Qtly. Review; All Previous Thought; Hearse; N.Y. Qtly.; Hierophant; Univ. of Tampa Poetry Review, etc. Honours, awards: La. Regl. Double Consonant Championship, 1951; Nat. Coun. on the Arts Prize, 1969. Address: 181 Amity St., Brooklyn, NY 11201, U.S.A.

JASPER, Catherine, b. 8 Apr. 1907. Piano Teacher. Education: Grad. of Beaver Falls HS; Garfield Business School; 10 yrs. private piano lessons. Positions held: Secretarial positions in various offices for 25 yrs.; currently, piano teacher. Memberships: Beaver County Branch of Pennsylvania Poetry Soc. (Corresponding Sec., 1973); Pennsylvania State Poetry Soc. Contbr. to: Selected Poems (Florida State Poetry Soc.), 1970; Prize Poems of Nat. Fed. of State Poetry Socs., 1971; Prize Poems of Penna. Poetry Soc., 1972-1973; Nor All Your Wit, 1973; Clover Collection of Verse, 1972; Beaver Falls News Tribune; Grit; Lyric; American Bard; Beaver County Times. Recip. of awards from Beaver County Branch of Pennsylvania Poetry Soc.; Vantage Press Poetry Contest; Calif. Fed. of Chap. Poets; Pennsylvania Poetry Soc.; Nat. Fed. of State Poetry Socs. Address: 1526 5th Ave., Beaver Falls, PA 15010, USA.

JASTRZEBSKI-GLINKA, Kristof Konstanty, pen name **GLINKA, Konstanty or K.G.,** b. 8 May 1946.

Education: Keble Coll., Oxford Univ. (Nat. Sci.); B.A. in Oriental Studies, ibid. Positions held: Dir./Producer of the National Theatre of Nepal, Kathmandu, summer 1969; Actor-Production Asst. in Jane Arden's 'The Other Side of the Underneath', 1971; Co-Dir. of 'Changes 72', Richard Demarco Galleries, Edinburgh, 1972. Memberships: Poetry Soc., Oxford; Pataphysical Soc., Oxford. Published works: Speak, 1965; Underground, 1966; Stranger Listen, 1971. Ed., No. 2, Flow Mag., Kathmandu, 1969 & No. 3, London, 1971; The Parish Newsletter, City of Camden, 1972-73. Contbr. to: The Polish Daily (London); Vasudha (Nepal); Flow Mag.; The Man Who Turned on the World, 1973; Drugs & Sexuality, 1973. Address: The Polytantrik, 60A Malden Rd., London N.W.5, U.K.

JAY, Peter Antony Charles, b. 24 May 1945. Publisher & Writer. Education: Lancing Coll., 1958-63 & Lincoln Coll., Oxford Univ., 1963-67 (Classics & Engl.) Positions held: Fndr. & Ed., New Measure (Poetry mag.), 1965-69; Fndr., Ed. & Publisher, Anvil Press Poetry, 1968–. Published works: Adonis & Venus, 1968; The Greek Anthology (Ed.), 1973; The Song of Songs (Tr.), 1974; The Still Unborn About the Dead: Selected poems of Nichita Stanescu (Tr. w. Petru Popescu), 1974; The Poems of Meleager (w. Peter Whigham), 1974. Contbr. to: Poetry Review; Agenda; London Mag.; Modern Poetry in Translation; Priapus; Oxford Mag. Recip., Newdigate Prize for Poetry, Oxford, 1965. Address: 69 King George St., London SE10 8PX, U.K.

JEFFARES, Alexander Norman, b. 11 Aug. 1920. University Professor; Author; Editor. Education: M.A. & Ph.D., Trinity Coll., Dublin; M.A. & D.Phil., Univ. of Oxford. Married Jeanne Agnes, 1 daughter. Positions held: Lectr. (Classics), Trinity Coll., Dublin, 1944-45; English Lector, Groningen Univ., Holland, 1947-49; Lectr. (Engl. Lit.), Univ. of Edinburgh, 1949-51; Jury Prof. (Engl. Lang. & Lit.), Univ. of Adelaide, 1951-57; Prof. of Engl. Lit., Univ. of Leeds, 1957-74; Prof. of Engl., Univ. of Stirling, 1974–. Memberships: Fellow, Royal Soc. of Lit.; Hon. Life Chmn., Int. Assn. for the Study of Anglo-Irish Lit.; Hon. Life Fellow, Assn. for Commonwealth Lit. & Lang. Study. Published works incl: Seven Centuries of Poetry, 1955, rev. '60; Disraeli's Sybil, 1957; The Scientific Background (w. M. Bryn Davies), 1958; Oliver Goldsmith, 1959; Language, Literature & Science, 1959; Oliver St. John Gogarty, 1961; The Poetry of W.B. Yeats, 1961; Poems of W.B. Yeats, 1962; Selected Poems of W.B. Yeats, 1962; A Goldsmith Selection, 1963; Cowper, 1963; Selected Prose of W.B. Yeats, 1964; Selected Plays of W.B. Yeats, 1964; Selected Criticism of W.B. Yeats, 1964; George Moore, 1965; In Excited Reverie: A Centenary Tribute to W.B. Yeats, co-ed., 1965; Selected Poetry & Prose of Whitman, 1965; Sheridan's The School for Scandal, 1966; Congreve's Love for Love, 1967; Fair Liberty was All His Cry: A Tercentenary Tribute to Jonathan Swift 1667-1743, 1967; A Commentary on the Collected Poems of W.B. Yeats, 1968; The Circus Animals, 1970; Farquhar's The Recruiting Officer, 1972; Restoration Drama, 4 vols., 1974. Address: c/o Dept. of Engl., Univ. of Stirling U.K.

JEFFERS, Florice Stripling. Book-keeper; Poetry & Short Story Writer. Education: Okla. Univ. courses. Married to F.G. Jeffers. Positions held: Book-keeper, Jeffers Oil & Drilling Co. Memberships: Poetry Soc. of Texas (Councillor); Wichita Falls Poetry Soc. (Pres.); Forum Writers, Wichita Falls (Pres.; Poetry Chairman); Nat. Fed. of Poetry Socs.; Acad. of American Poets (a Founder); Life Mbr., Current Literature Study Club, Burkburnett, Texas (Pres.). Contbr. to: Some Friends Mag.; Year Book of the Year; Quicksilver; Green World; South & West; Visions in Verse; Young's Anthol.; Dr. Heard's Anthol.; Ark. Anthol.; Tex. Club Women; Am. Haiku; Wichita Falls Daily Times & Record News; Burkburnett Star & News; Poetry Soc. of Texas Year Books; Reflections (Wichita Falls Poetry Soc. publication). Honours: Poet Laureate Awards, Tex. Fed. of Women, 1960, and Santa Rosa Dist. Fed. 1960; 1st & 2nd Place Award, Tex. Fed. Poetry, 1953;

1st Place, Short Story, Tex. Fed. Poetry, 1953; 4 1sts, Tex. Poetry Soc. 1964-68; Dee Walker Award, Quicksilver, 1955; Ian & Willie Davis Award, Poetry Soc. of Texas, 1969; Published 1970 Year Book, ibid; Rusk Co. Award, ibid, 1973; Purple Heart Award, 1972. Address: P.O. Box 638, 608 Meadow Dr., Burkburnett, TX 76354, USA.

JEFFRIES, Christie Frances, pen name **JEFFRIES, Christie,** b. 30 Jan. 1894. Retired College Professor. Education: B.S.; B.S. (Educ.), Central State Coll., Warrensburg, Mo., 1922; M.A. (English), Univ. of Mo., Columbia, 1925; Grad. work, Harvard, Cambridge, Mass.; Columbia Univ., NYC. Positions held: Instr., Pa. State Coll., Bloomsburg, 1926-29; Chmn., Dept. of Communication Arts, Paterson State Coll., Paterson, NJ, 1929-59. Memberships: Okla. Poetry Soc.; NJ State Pres., Nat. League of Am. Pen Women; Poetry Soc. of Am.; Pres., Paterson NJ Chaucer Guild, 1930; currently Charter Mbr., ibid; NJ Womens Press Club. Publications: Until This Moment, 1942. Contbr. to: numerous Anthols. including: The Golden Year; Breadloaf Anthology; The Diamond Year; (jrnls. & newspapers) NY Times; NY Sun; NY Herald Tribune; Wash. Star; Toronto Star-Weekly; Virginian Pilot; Kans. City Star; Farm Jrnl.; Saturday Evening Post; Household; Christian Century; Opinion; Am. Zionist; Ave Maria; Holland's; Spirit; Voices; NM Quarterly; Poetry Chapbook; Improvement Era; Boston Herald; Dallas News; Christian Sci. Monitor; Lit. Digest; Paterson, NJ Morning Call; Nature Mag.; Extension. Honours: Recipient of numerous poetry awards including: First Award, Annual Contest, Poetry Soc. of Am., New York, NY, 1964; Okla. Poetry Soc., 1968, '69, '70, '71; Lyric Award, Nat. Fed. of Poetry Socs., 1972; Sonnet Award, Ark. Writers, Little Rock, 1973; Ballad Prize, Nat. League of Am. Pen Women, 1970. Address: 719 North Morton, Okmulgee, Okla. 74447, USA.

JELLEMA, Roderick Hartigh, b. 11 Aug. 1927. Poet & Teacher. Education: B.A., Calvin; P.G. Dip. & Ph.D., Univ. of Edinburgh. Positions held: Instr., Univ. of Md., 1956; Asst. Prof., ibid, 1964; Assoc. Prof., 1967–; Vis. Lectr., Western Md. Coll., 1962; Dir., Annual Confs. on Poetry & the Nat. Conscience, Univ. of Md., 1968-72; Poet-in-the-Schools, Md. Arts Coun., 1971–; Co-Dir., Wash. Nat. Poetry Ctr., 1973. published works: Something Tugging the Line, 1974. Contbr. to: Beloit Poetry Jrnl.; New Republic; Poetry Northwest; Choice; Dryad; Field; Harvard Advocate; December; Motive; Rune; St. Andrews Review; So. Poetry Review; Mill Mountain Review; Wash. Star Sunday Mag., etc. Honours, awards: Prize for Poetry, Nat. Endowment for the Arts, 1968; Hart Crane Award, 1968; Yaddo Res. Fellowships, 1970, '71, '72, '73; Finalist, Int. Poetry Forum, U.S. Award, 1972; Md. Creative & Performing Arts Bd. Grants, 1968, '70, '72. Address: 5 Hill Top Rd., Silver Spring, MD 20910, U.S.A.

JENKINS, Jean R., b. 3 Aug. 1926. Professor of Speech and Drama. Education: B.A., M.A., Brigham Young Univ. Married 1952, Glen L. Jenkins who died in 1963. Memberships: Nat. Fed. of State Poetry Societies, Inc. – President, 1973-74; Secretary, 1968-70; Vice-President, 1971-72; Utah State Poetry Soc., Rec. Sec., Historian, 1972-74; American Assoc. of Univ. Women, Branch Pres., Sec.; Speech Communication Assoc.; Western Speech Assoc.; Thespian Nat. Honor Drama Soc.; Phi Kappa Phi; Theta Alpha Phi Drama Soc. (Branch Pres.); Beta Sigma Phi; White Key Honor Soc. Pubs.: The More for Loving, 1974. Contrib. to: McCall's; Prize Poems; South & West; Internat. Human Voice Qtly.; Sandcutter's; Poet; Poet Lore; Discourses; Sitemen/Brodhead Pubs.; Lyrics of Love. Recip. Second, Book Award, Poet of Year, Utah, 1972. Numerous other awards for poetry; Best Poem in South & West, Winter issue, 1972. Address: 452 West 800 South, Orem, Utah 84057, USA.

JENKINS, May Chalmers. Journalist. Education: M.A., Aberdeen Univ., U.K.; Dips. in Elocution. Positions held: Tchr.; Freelance Jrnlst. (Aberdeen jrnls.) Memberships: PEN; Soc. of Authors. Published works: Flitting, 1966. Contbr. to: The Scots Mag.; Life & Work; Aberdeen Univ. Review; Canadian Poetry Mag.; The Scotsman; The Glasgow Herald; Press & Journal. Address: 20 Bonnymuir Pl., Aberdeen AB2 4NL, U.K.

JENKINS, Nigel Philip, pen name **JENKINS, Philip,** b. 23 Feb. 1949. Student. Education: Queen's Univ., Belfast, 1967-69; Univ. of Nottingham, 1971–. Published works: View from a Strange Window, 1968; The Germ Layed Deviations, 1971; The Fantasy Childhood Reset, 1971; The Birth of Venus, 1973. Rep. in following anthols: The Wild Game of Sight, 1970; Typewriter Poems, 1972; Minimal Poetry, 1972; New Selections 1, 1973. Contbr. to: Belfast Telegraph; Interest; Crabgrass; Second Aeon; Poetry Wales; The Honest Ulsterman; Ore; Lon Chaney; Wilful Stranger; Albion; Joe Di Maggio; Accent; Time Out, etc. Address: Coed-Y-Rhyd, Tredegar, Mon. NP2 4LY, U.K.

JENNETT, Sean, b. 12 Nov. 1912. Author; Photographer; Designer. Married Irene Lumley w. 1 son & 1 daughter. Positions held: Formerly, Publisher, Printer, Advertising Agent. Published works: Always Adam, 1943; The Cloth of Flesh, 1945; Other: The Making of Books, 1951; Pioneers in Printing, 1958; The Sun & Old Stones: A Tour Through the Midi, 1961; The Young Photographer's Companion, 1962; Deserts of England; Ed., The Traveller's Guides, 1965. Contbr. to (Anthols.): Contemporary Irish Poetry, 1949; 1000 Years of Irish Poetry, 1953.

JENNI, Adolfo, b. 3 May 1911. University Professor. Education: Ph.D., Univ. of Bologna, 1934. Married Sabina Bürgi, 4 children. Positions held: Lector, Univ. of Berne, 1936; currently Professor Ordinarius of Italian Lang. & Lit., ibid. Memberships: PEN Club; Associazione Int. Studi Lingua e Lett. Italiana; Soc. of Italian Writers; Soc. of Swiss Writers; Accademia dell'Arcadia, Rome. Published works: Le bandiere di carta, 1943; Addio alla poesia, 1950; Recitativi, 1971; Le quattro stagioni, 1973. Contbr. to var. Italian & Swiss publs. Honours, awards: sev. Schiller prizes; Lugano prize; Veillon prize 1948; Premio Italia, 1969; Hon. Citizen of Lecco, Italy. Address: Blümlisalpstrasse 12, 3074 Muri/Berne, Switzerland.

JENNINGS, Elizabeth, b. 18 July 1926. Freelance Writer; Poet. Education: Hons. degree in Engl. lang. & lit., Oxford Univ., U.K. Positions held: Advertising Copywriter, 1 yr.; Public Libn., 8 yrs.; Publisher's Rdr., Chatto & Windus Ltd.; Freelance Writer. Mbr., Soc. of Authors. Published works: Poems, 1953; A Way of Looking, 1955; A Sense of the World, 1958; Song for a Birth or a Death, 1961; Recoveries, 1964; The Mind Has Mountains, 1966; The Secret Brother, 1967; Collected Poems, 1967; The Animals' Arrival, 1968; Lucidities, 1970; Relationships, 1972; Michelangelo's Sonnets (transl.), 1961. Contbr. to: The Spectator; The Listener; The New Statesman; London Mag.; Encounter; New Yorker; Vogue; Poetry Chicago; The N.Y. Times; The Times Lit. Supplement; Time & Tide; The Scotsman; Tribune; Observer; Sunday Times, etc. Honours, awards: Arts Coun. Prize, 1953; Somerset Maugham Award, 1956; Arts Coun. Prize, 1966; Richard Hillary Prize (shared), 1966; Arts Coun. Bursary, 1969 & 72. Address: 11 Fyfield Rd., Oxford OX2 6QE, U.K.

JENOFF, Marvyne Shael, b. 10 Mar. 1942. Teacher. Education: Grad., Manitoba Tchrs. Coll., 1960; B.A., Univ. of Manitoba, 1964; currently a student of Textile Design, Sheridan Coll., Mississauga, Ont. Married. Member, League of Canadian Poets. Published works: No Lingering Peace, 1972; The Spider & The Universe (under consideration). Contbr. to: The Fiddlehead Review; Canadian Forum; Alphabet; Volume '63; Creative Campus; The Tamarack Review. Honours, awards: c/o Holland, 12 Park St. E. No. 206, Port Credit, Ont., Canada L5G 1L5.

JENSEN, Jeffry Michael, b. 4 Apr. 1950. Graduate

Student. Education: B.A., La Verne Coll., 1972; currently working toward M.L.S., Univ. of So. Calif. Grad. Schl. Memberships: Pi Gamma Mu; Poetry Soc. of Am. Published works: The Temperament of Secrets, 1972. Contbr. to: Modern Images; Poetry of the Year; Jrnl. of Contemporary Poets. Address: 724 Camellia Dr., Covina, CA 91723, U.S.A.

JENSEN, Magny Landstad, b. 20 Nov. 1903. Housewife, Writer. Education: Grammar School in Norway. Married, 2 children, 3 grandchildren. Positions held: Editor Woman's Page, Norwegian News, Brooklyn, 1933-1957; Columnist, Morris County News, 1961-1965; American Editor, English Mag. Rainbow, 1967-1970; Memberships: Am. Poetry League, Apollo Chapter; Calif. Chaparall Poets, New Jersey Poetry Soc. Published works include: Testament of Love, 1964. Edited Norw. issue for Poet, India, 1965. Contbr. to: Am. Bard; Tempo; Vision & Tweed; Laurel Leaves; Rainbow; The Angels, Jean's Journal; Modern Images; Flame; Bardic Echoes; Kansas Kernels; Encore; Penman; Haiku Spotlight; Speak Out; Special Song; Greenup News; A.P.L. Bulletin, etc. Honours include: St. Olav Medal, Norway, 1953; U.P.L.I., 1963; Scand.-Am. Poet Laureate, ibid. (from Philippines), 1965; Winner, World Transl. Contest, ibid. 1967; George Washington Medal, Valley Forge Freedom Found, 1969; Dr. of Humane Letters (h.c.), Free Univ. of Asia, 1972; Recip. numerous poetry prizes and awards. Address: 2191 Harbor Blvd., Sp. 2, Costa Mesa, CA 92627, USA.

JEROME, Judson (Blair), b. 8 Feb. 1927. Prof. of Literature, and Writer. Education: M.A., Univ. of Chicago; Ph.D., Ohio State Univ. Married, 5 children. Positions held include: Prof. of Lit., Antioch Coll., 1953-1973. Publications include: Light in the West, 1963; The Ocean's Warning to the Skin Diver and other Love Poems, 1964; Serenade, 1965; Plays for an Imaginary Theater (poetic drama), 1969; The Poet and the Poem (essays), 1963; Poetry: Premeditated Art (text), 1968. Contbr. to: Harper's; Atlantic; Poetry; The Nation; Saturday Review; Southwest Review; Colo. Review; Partisan Review; Yale Review, etc. Awards include: Amy Lowell Poetry Travelling Scholarship, 1960-1961; William Carlos Williams Award in Fiction, 1963; Huntington Hartford Fellowship, 1956. Address: Downhill Farm, Hancock, MD. 21750, USA.

JESPERSEN, Mary Sperry, pen name, **JESPERSEN, Mary S.,** b. 5 Jan. 1902. Freelance Writer. Education: Coll. of Wooster, Ohio, 1920-23, B.A.; Biblical Seminary in NY, 1924-26; NY Univ. 1934-35, M.R.E., 1935. Positions held: Religious Ed. Director, Bradenton, Fla., 1926; N. Ala. Presbytery, 1927-31; Rel. Ed. & Social Worker, NYC Mission Soc., 1932-44; Service Manager, R.H. Macy & Co., 1945-46. Memberships: Avalon Poetry Soc.; World Poetry Soc. Intercontinental; South & West, Inc. Published works: Dream of Music, 1969; 1974: (The Mind of Jon Magnus; Wheels with Wings, and Shadow Dance, completed). Contbr. to: Cyclo-Flame, Cardinal Poetry Qtly.; Encore; Imprints Qtly.; Modern Images; Poet; Poet Anthols.; Quintessence; Quoin; Swordsman Review; Tulsa Poetry Qtly.; Voices Internat.; Internat. Who's Who in Poetry Anthol.; Wooster Coll. Alumni Monthly; Cat Anthol., 1969, etc. Address: 139-31 35th Ave., Flushing, NY 11354, USA.

JESTER, Ann Thompson, b. 22 Oct. 1931. Legal Secretary. Married, John Dallas Jester, 3 children. Published works: (books of poetry) Bouquets From My Heart, 1967; Stars of Destiny, 1972. Contbr. to: Courier-Tribune, Asheboro, N.C.; The Randolph Guide, Asheboro, N.C.; Sanford Herald, Sanford, N.C.; State Mag., Raleigh, N.C. Honours, awards: Hon. Mention, N.C. Poetry Soc. Conest, 1973; Cert. of Merit, N.C. Poetry Coun. Contest, 1973. Address: 361 Hawthorne Dr., Asheboro, NC 27203, U.S.A.

JESUS, Ramon de, pen name **VILLANEUVA, Jesus,** b. 25 Nov. 1914. Government Employee. Education: LL.B., Philippine Law Schl., 1948; M.B.A., Manila Ctrl. Univ., 1950. Married Amparo Moreno, 6 children.

Positions held: Capt. for Intelligence & Propaganda work in Western Luzon Guerrilla Forces, Zambales Mil. Dist., WWII; Chief, Complaints Sect., Bureau of Posts; Private Sec. to Congressman Ramon Magsaysay (later became Pres.); Chief, Rsch. & Publs. Div., Bureau of Census; Atty., Dept. of Comm.; Tech. Asst. to the Pres. of the Philippines; Asst. Dir. in the Ctrl. Bank of the Philippines. Memberships incl: College Editors' Alumni Assn.; Philippine Booklover's Soc. Fndr., Ed. or Assoc. Ed., var. publs. Contbr. to: Sunday Tribune Mag.; Philippine Free Press; Philippines Herald Mag.; Philippine Veterans Mag. (one-time Ed.), etc. Honours, awards incl: First Prize Winner, Nat. Essay Contest, Manila Post, 1947. Address: 36 Oxford, Cubao, Quezon City, Philippines.

JEWELL, Foster, b. 21 July 1893. Painter; Sculptor; Poet. Education: Chicago Art Inst.; studied in Europe for a year. Published works: Strato Lanes in Star Grass, 1959; Sand Waves, haiku, 1970; Beachcomber, haiku, 1971; Haiku Sketches, haiku, 1971; Mirage, haiku, 1972. Contbr. to: Am. Haiku; Haiku (Toronto); Haiku West; Haiku Highlights (now Dragonfly); Janus-SCTH, etc. Honours, awards: Awards for haiku, Nov., 1965, May, July, Nov., 1966, Apr., May & Oct., 1967, Jan. 1968, Am. Haiku; First Awards for haiku Vol. III, No. 3, Vol. 4, No. 1, Vol. 4, No. 2, Modern Haiku. Address: 1325 Cabrillo Ave., Apt. 12, Venice, CA 90291, U.S.A.

JEWELL, Rhoda de Long, b. 9 Feb. 1900. Editor; Composer; Teacher. Education: Univ. of N.D., U.S.A.; Columbia Ext., 4 yrs.; Champ Schl. of Art, San Diego. Positions held: Ed. & Publsr., poetry mags.; Fndr., Troubadour, 1929; Fndr., SCTH, 1964 (later enlarged to include Janus); Tchr., Piano. Published works: Seven Poems for Uranians (a pamphlet), 1929; Mother Goose's Lactsu, 1959; Moon In Splendor, 1959; Projections, 1967; "Wuthering Heights", 1967; The Lights, 1968. Contbr. to: Quoin In; Cyclo-Flame. Recip. var. awards & prizes. Address: 1325 Cabrillo Ave., Venice, CA 90291, U.S.A.

JOANS, Ted, b. 4 July 1928. Poet; Jazz Critic; Travel Writer. Education: B.A., Ind. Univ., 1951; New Schl. of Soc. Rsch., N.Y. & Brooklyn Coll., 1952-54. Has lectured on art in Europe. Published works: Mijn Zwarte Gedachten, 1970; A Black Manifesto of Jazz in Poetry & Prose, 1969-71; Black Flower Poems (in Dutch, Engl. & German), 1972; Black Pow Wow, Jazz Poems, 1969; Beat Poems, 1957; Funky Jazz Poems (poems & collages), 1958-59; All of T.J. & No More Poems, 1961; The Hipsters (collages & Prose), 1961; The Truth, 1968; Une Proposition pour un manifeste pouvoir noir, 1969; Afrodisia, 1970. Contbr. to var. anthols., mags., jrnls. Honours, awards: The Hadley Fellow Award as Poet-in-Res., Bennington Coll., U.S.A., 1973. Address: c/o Gunther Stuhlmann, 65 Irving Pl., NY, NY 10003, U.S.A.

JOFFE, Harold B., b. 26 Nov. 1931. Contractor. Education: Univ. of Md., College Pk. Positions held: Pres., Plaza Construction, 10 yrs. Memberships: Md. Poetry Soc.; Acad. of Am. Poets. Contbr. to: Harpers Mag.; Am. Bard; Dell Publs.; Sat. Evening Post Mag.; Ed., The Diamondbacks, Univ. of Md.; Baltimore Evening Sun. Address: 3739 Clarinth Rd., Baltimore, MD 21215, U.S.A.

JOHANNES, Poethen, b. 13 Sept. 1928. Writer. Education: University. Married, 1 daughter. Memberships: Verband Deutscher Schriftsteller, VS in Baden-Württemberg; Vorstandes und Delegierter; PEN, W. German Ctr. Published works: (books of poetry) Risse des Himmels, 1956; Stille im trockenen Dorn, 1958; Ankunft und Echo, 1961; Gedichte, 1963; Wohnstadt zwischen den Atemzügen, 1966; Im Namen der Trauer, 1969; Aus der unendlichen Kälte, 1970; Gedichte 1946-71, 1973. Contbr. to: Neue Rundschau; Akzente; Monat; L'Ephémère; Ateneu; Speichen; Engel der Geschichte; Frankfurter Allgemeine Zeitung; Deutsche Zeitung. Honours, awards: Hugo-Jacobi-Dichterpreis, 1959; Förderpreis der Stadt Köln, 1962; Fönderpreis zum Immermann-

Preis der Stadt Düsseldorf, 1967. Address: Zur Schillereiche 23, D – 7000 Stuttgart 1, German Fed. Repub.

JOHN, M.P., b. 29 Sept. 1911. Newspaper Editor, Education: Madras Univ., India. Positions held: Ed., New Times Observer (only English weekly in the Union Territory of Pondicherry); Dir. of Western Music, Pondicherry. Published works: Inner Space Voyages, 1973. Contbr. of one poem a week to the Weekly New Times Observer. Poems are being translated into French & Tamil & are being reproduced in other Indian Jrnls. Address: Ed., New Times Observer, P.B. 31, Pondicherry, S. India.

JOHNN-St.JOHNN, Allison Nichols. Writer; Poet; Editor; Critic; Literary Consultant; Composer (Classic and semi-classic). Education: Oberlin Coll., Ohio; Univ. of Chicago, Ill.; Columbia Univ., NY; degrees earned: A.B.; B.Sc.; M.A.; Ph.D. Positions held: Prof. Engl., French, Mathematics, Logic, Ill. Univ. Memberships: Acad. Leonardo Da Vinci (Rome); Cosmosynthesis League; Internat. Guild of Contemp. Bards (Australia); Overseas Regent for NY, New England and Canada; Internat. Poetry Soc. (UK). Published works include: The Soul of a Poet (3 vols.); The Fire Bird; Singing Echoes; Crystal Waters; Muffled Drums; Ashes and Sapphire; From Moulded Gold; Lights Out; (musical dramas) Time Tolls The Bell; The Seventh Isle; Editor, Singing Pens Anthol.; Ed., Brief Previews. Contbr. to many anthols., including: Modern American Poetry (4 vols.); American Lyric Poetry; American States Anthol.; Yearbook of Contemp. Poetry; The Largest Book of Poetry in The World, Nat. Poetry Ctr., NY World's Fair; Spring Anthol. (3 editions); Starlight Trail Anthol.; Poets of America Anthol.; Muse Anthol.; Golden Quill; Velvet Paws in Print; Wagging Tail; The Book of Golden Verse, and to many lit. mags. and journals, including: Vespers; By; Writer's Voice; American Bard; Wisconsin Poetry Mag.; Kaleidoscope (Australia); Swordsman Review; Ideals; Evangel, etc. Poetry broadcast over 3 nat. networks for 5 yrs.; Lights Out: poetic saga of WW2 broadcast over radio WQXR. Nominee, Nobel Prize in Lit., 1970. Recip. of many prizes, honors, awards (nat. and internat); large collection of work in Harris Special Collection, Brown Univ. Library, RI.; Member, Exec. Advisory Council of Nat. Register of Prominent Americans and Internat. Notables, etc. Address: Box 248, Radio City Station, New York, NY 10019, USA.

JOHNSON, B.S., b. 5 Feb. 1933. Poetry Editor. Education: B.A., King's Coll., London Univ. Married w. 2 Children. Positions held: Poetry Ed., Transatlantic Review, London, 1964–. Published works: Poems, 1964; Other: Travelling People, 1963; Albert Angelo, 1964; Trawl, 1966; The Unfortunates, 1969; Nonfiction: Statement Against Corpses, 1964; Street Children, 1964; Ed., The Evacuees, 1968; Film in Verse: You're Human Like the Rest of Them, 1967 (publ'd in New English Dramatists, 1970). Contbr. to (Anthols.): New Poems, 1962; Penguin Book of Animal Verse, 1965; Modern Folk Ballads, 1966. Hons: Gregory Award, 1962; The Somerset Maugham Award for Fiction, 1967; Grand Prix, Tours & Melbourne Int. Short Film Festivals, 1968; 1st Gregynog Fellow in Writing, Univ. of Wales, 1970. Address: 9 Dagmar Terrace, London, N.I. UK.

JOHNSON, Harold Leland, occasional pen name **JONSON, Hal,** b. 7 Oct. 1908. Retired. Positions held: Actor; Printer; Seaman; Photographer; Graphic Designer; Audio-Visual Technician; Exhibitor of designs, paintings, constructions (own). Memberships: Poetry Soc. of Am.; Calif. Writers' Club; Ina Coolbrith Circle. Published works: Lyrics for a Toccata & Fugue, verse play (booklet), 1968. Contbr. to: Calif. Highway Patrolman; Harlequin; San Franciscan; (anthols.) IWWP 1972, & York (England); Poetry Five & Poems from 21 Hands. Honours, awards: 1st pl., sonnet, CFCP, 1971; 1st pl., Creative Arts, 1970, etc. Address: 708 Inglewood Dr., Broderick, CA 95605, U.S.A.

JOHNSON, Jennifer Hilary, pen name **JOHNSON, Jenny,** b. 2 Nov. 1945. Education: Univ. of Keele, U.K., 1964-65; Eaton Hall Coll. of Educ., Nottingham, 1970-71. Positions held: Libn., 1965, Music Dept. Asst., 1966, Civil Servant, 1967, Insurance Officer, Bristol, 1969; Finance Officer, 1972, Clerk in Nat. Hlth. Serv., 1973, Nottingham. Memberships: Bristol Arts' Ctr., 1968–; Fndr. Mbr., Bristol Bach Choir, 1967-70; The Coffee Pot Club, 1968-69. Published works: Jetsam, 1970; Footfall (to be published soon). Contbr. to: The Poetry of the Circle in the Square; The Village Review, Essex; Contac, Doncaster; Ludd's Mill, Huddersfield; Bogg, Filey; Your Friendly Fascist. London; MAC, Ayrshire. Performed at Bristol Arts' Ctr. (translations of Lorca Verse), 1969. Readings of Poetry at The Midland Grp. Gall., Nottingham, 1973. Recip., award, BBC Limerick Comp., 1972. Address: 9 Gelligaled Road, Ystrad, Pentre, Glamorgan CF41 7RH, U.K.

JOHNSON, Kathryn, pen names **O'CONNOR, Bryn; O'NEALL, James Benjamin,** b. 7 Oct. 1943. Poet; Writer; Student. Education: N. Texas State Univ., Denton. Memberships: Poetry Soc. of Texas (Editor, bulletin); Poetry Soc. (UK). Contbr. to: Expression One; Poetry Soc. of Texas Anthol.; Some Friends; Poetry Journal. Recip. of awards from Poetry Soc. of Texas: Samply Award, 1970, 3rd place; Blake Johnson Peace Award, 1970, 3rd place; Panta Rei Prize (annual contest), 1971, 1st prize; Hoyt Mem. Award, 1972, 2nd place. Address: 1005 W. Hickory, Denton, TX 76201, USA.

JOHNSON, Louis, b. 27 Sept. 1924. Senior Lecturer, Dept. of Engl. and Mod. Languages. Education: Teachers' Tng. Coll., Wellington, NZ. Career divided almost equally between teaching and lit. pursuits (journalism, editing, broadcasting, television and freelance writing). Positions held: Journalist, various NZ newspapers, 1948-63; Editor, NZ Parent and Child (monthly), 1955-59; Editor, junior school journals, School Pub. Branch Dept. of Education, NZ., 1963-68; Officer in Charge, Bureau of Lit., Papua-New Guinea, 1968-69; Lecturer, Mitchell College of Advanced Education, Bathurst, NSW., since 1971. Published works: Sun Among the Ruins, 1951; Roughshod Among the Lilies, 1951; Poems Unpleasant (with others), 1952; Two Poems, 1956; The Dark Glass, 1955; New Worlds For Old, 1957; The Night Shift (with others), 1957; Bread and a Pension, 1964; Land Like A Lizard, New Guinea Poems, 1970; Endeavour's Wake, 1974; Editor, 12 vols. NZ Poetry Yearbook, 1951-64. Contbr. to: Arena; Angry Penguins; Poetry (Chicago); Poetry London; Outposts; Poetry Commonwealth; Nimrod; Coastlines; Borestone Mountain Poetry Awards (8 annual issues); Poetry Australia; The New Poetry; The Bulletin; NZ Listener; Yorkshire Post; Landfall; Numbers; NZ Herald; Auckland Star; Meanjin; Overland; New Orleans Poetry Journal; Epoch; Melbourne Age; The Australian; Sydney Morning Herald; Australian Poetry, 1972; New Guinea Qtly.; Comment; Education; Salient; Here & Now; Mate; Jindyworobak Anthol.; Penguin Book NZ Verse; Oxford Book of NZ Verse; London Mag., etc. Address: 210 Russell St., Bathurst, NSW 2795, Australia.

JOHNSON, Michael Henderson Flowers, b. 1 Apr. 1928. Physician. Education: St. Mary's Hosp. Med. Schl.; New Coll., Oxford; Goldsmith's Coll. of Art. Member, PEN. Published works: In Braver Sunlight, 1960. Contbr. to: Isis; Gemini; Outposts. Address: 77a Mount Nod Rd., Streatham, London S.W.16, U.K.

JOHNSON, Olive Elmyra Rachel, b. 27 Sept. 1893. State Registered Graduate Nurse. Education: Dip., Burlington Hosp. Schl. Nursing, 1919; Dip., Penn Coll. Acad., Oskaloosa, Ia., 1925; B.S. Educ., Univ. of Mich., Ann Arbor, 1940; Master's degree in Public Hlth., Univ. of Minn., 1950. Positions held: Surgical Supvsr., 1921-22; Supvsr., A.T.S.F. Hosp., Ft. Madison, Iowa, 1922-23; County P.H.N., Benton Co., Iowa, 1925-26; Schl. Nurse, Geneseo, Ill., 1927-33; Dist. Supt. State Dept. Hlth., Ill., 1936, '37; Dist. Supt. Nurse, State Dept. Hlth., Iowa, 1940, '49; Cons., Epidemiol. & Communicable Diseases, ibid, 1949-66.

Memberships incl: Dist. Rep., Iowa Poetry Day Assn.; World Poetry Soc. Intercontinental; Midwest Chaparral. Contbr. to: Midland Poetry Review, Shelbyville, Ind.; Am. Poet; Yearbook of Modern Poetry, anthol.; Poet; State Nurse's Bulletin; Public Hlth. Nurse's Jrnl.; Yearbook of the New Century Study Club, etc. Honours, awards incl: Elected to Mbrship, Sigma Iota Xi. Address: R.1, Montezuma, IA 50171, U.S.A.

JOHNSON, Roberta Orban Lamon, pen name **JOHNSON, Robin,** b. 25 Jan. 1924. Poet; Scholar. Education: B.A., Scripps Coll.; M.A., Philos., Univ. of Mich.; M.A., Engl., Univ. of Calif., Los Angeles; Ph.D., Engl., Univ. of Denver. Married Ronald Stafford Johnson, 2 daughters. Positions held: currently Lectr. in Creative Writing, Pepperdine Univ., Malibu, Calif. Member, Poetry Soc. of Am. Contbr. to: Qtly. Review of Lit.; Commonweal; The Mass. Review; Sat. Review; The Antioch Review; The Denver Qtly.; The Tex. Qtly.; Western Humanities Review; The Univ. Review; Poetry Northwest; N.M. Qtly.; Southern Poetry Review; Epoch; Trace; Fiddlehead; Concerning Poetry; Tempo; Colo.Qtly.; The Reporter; N.Y. Times; Am. Weave; Eclipse. Translator of Marie de France, in The Women Poets in English, 1972. Honours, awards: Women's Int. League for Peace & Freedom, for poem, 1966; Acad. of Am. Poets, for poems, 1970 & '71. Address: 361 Alma Real, Pacific Palisades, CA 90272, U.S.A.

JOHNSON, Ronald, b. 25 Nov. 1935. Poet. Education: B.A., Columbia Univ., 1960. Positions held: Writer-in-Res., Univ. of Ky., 1970. Published works include: A Line of Poetry, A Row of Trees, 1964; Sports & Divertissments, 1965; Assorted Jungles: Rousseau, 1966; Gorse/Goose/Rose, 1966; The Book of the Green Man, 1967; Sun Flowers (A Broadside), 1966; Io and The Ox-Eye Daisy, 1966; The Round Earth on Flat Paper, 1968; Reading 1 and Reading 2, 1968; Valley of the Many-Colored Grasses, 1969; Balloons for Moonless Nights, 1969; Sports & Divertissments, 1969; The Spirit Walks, the Rocks Will Talk, 1970; Songs of the Earth, 1971. Contbr. to the following anthols., jrnls., mags., etc: Poetry, Chicago; NY Times; Lugano Review; Tri-Quarterly; Coyote's Jrnl.; Stand; Columbia Review; Poor. Old. Tired. Horse; Solstice; The Ky. Review; Artes Hispanicas. Honours, awards: Boar's Head Prize, Columbia Univ., 1960; Inez Boulton Award, Poetry, Chicago, 1966; Nat. Endowment for the Arts Award, 1970. Address: 4566 18th St., San Francisco, CA 94119, U.S.A.

JOHNSON, Stella Gertrude, pen name **WORLEY, Stella,** b. 23 May 1910. Retired Federal Worker; Poet. Education: A.A., Sacramento City Coll.; Poetry, Univ. of Calif., Berkeley; Expository Writing, ibid. Married 1) Floyd P. Worley, dec., 1 son, 1 daughter, 2) Harold Leland Johnson. Memberships: Poetry Soc. of Am.; Calif. Writers' Club; Ina Coolbrith Circle. Work in prep: Windfeathers, illustrated book of Haiku. Contbr. to five anthols. inclng. The Diamond Anthol., 1971; many contbns. to newspapers & mags. Recip., twenty seven prizes in poetry contests, 1960-73. Address: 708 Inglewood Dr., Broderick, CA 95605, U.S.A.

JOHNSON, Stowers. Author; Art Collector. Education: St. Mark's Coll., London; B.A., Queen Mary Coll., Schl. of Slavonic Studies, London. Married Gwendolen Megan Jones, 1 son (Roderick). Positions held: Prin., Dagenham Lit. Inst., –1939; Headmaster, Aveley Schl., 1939-68; Ed., Anglo-Soviet Jrnl., 1966-68. Memberships: Fellow, Royal Soc. of Arts; Gen. Coun., The Poetry Soc., 1962-68; Hon. Treas., ibid, 1966-68; Hon. Treas., P.E.N., 1972-73; Nat. Coun., Nat. Book League, 1968–; V. Chmn., Soc. for Cultural Rels. w. U.S.S.R., 1966-67; Hon. Mbr., Turkmen Soc. of Writers, 1965; Chmn., Anglo-Turkish Cultural Comm., 1963-72. Published works: Branches Green & Branches Black (51 poems), 1944; London Saga, 1946; The Mundane Tree, 1947; Sonnets, They Say..., 1949; When Fountains Fall..., 1961. Contbr. to var. jrnls. & publs. & BBC progs., also Russian & Bulgarian poetry in translation. Presentation of Bulgarian Poetry in Translation at Foyles, 1965. Lectr. on Pencho Slaveikov (Nobel Prize ·winner elect) at the Nat. Theatre, Sofia & also at Triavna, Bulgaria, 1965 for the Centenary Celebrations. Address: Corbiere, 45 Rayleigh Rd., Hutton, Brentwood, Essex, U.K.

JOHNSON, Thomas Edward, Jr., b. 23 Feb. 1948. Writer. Education: B.S., Univ. of Tenn. Positions held: Instr. of Engl., Secondary Educ. in Memphis; Ed. & Publisher of Stinktree Jrnl. & Poetry Press. Literary Arts Advisor, Tenn. Arts Commn. Published works: Footholds (chapbook), 1973; Homing Signals (full length vol.), 1974. Contbr. to: Poetry (Chicago); N.Y. Qtly.; Iowa Review; The Nation; Ohio Review; Kayak; Southern Poetry Review; Ironwood; Lamp in the Spine; Chelsea; Hearse; Granite; Tenn. Poetry Jrnl.; West Coast Poetry Review; Dragonfly; Pebble; Antigonish Review; North Am. Review; Greenfield Review; Stone Drum Anthol., etc. Recip., Knickerbocker Poetry Prize, Univ. of Tenn., 1969. Address: P.O. Box 14762, Memphis, TN 38114, U.S.A.

JOHNSON, Violet C., b. 14 Oct. 1910. Office Clerk. Married, 1 daughter. Teacher of Juniors in Sunday Schl. & directs daily vacation Bible Schl. Church Treas. of non-denominational community church. Memberships: Pres., Aitkin Co. Democratic Farmer Labor Women's Club; V.P., Aitkin Golden Age Club; Midwest Chaparral Poets. Published works: Food for Thought, 1970; Walk into Spring, 1973. Contbr. to: Mpls. Argus; Rural Minn. News; The Farmer; Bible Friend; Midwest Chaparral; Mpls. Sun; Good Old Days; Wesleyan Methodist; Aitkin Independent Age. Was featured poet in the Mpls. Argus, 1972. Address: 117 Maryhill Manor, Aitkin, MN 56431, U.S.A.

JOHNSTON, George Benson, b. 7 Oct. 1913. Professor of English. Education: B.A., Univ. of Toronto, 1936; M.A., ibid., 1945; Univ. Coll., London, 1957. Married Jeanne McRae w. 3 sons & 3 daughters. Positions held: Asst. Prof., Engl., Mount Allinson Univ., Sackville, N.B., 1946-48; Mbr., Engl. Dept., Carleton Univ., Ottawa, 1950–; Currently Prof., ibid. Published works: The Cruising Auk, 1959; Home Free, 1966; Trans., The Saga of Gisli, 1963. Contbr. to (Anthols.): Blasted Pine, 1957; An Anthology of Poetry, 1961; Love Where the Nights are Long, 1962; Oxford Book of Canadian Verse, 1967; Penguin Book of Canadian Verse, 1967; Wind Has Wings, 1968.

JOHNSTON, George Burke, b. 8 Sept. 1907. College Professor. Education: B.A., Univ. of Ala., 1929; M.A., Columbia Univ., NY., 1930; Ph.D., ibid. 1943. Married to Mary Tabb Lancaster, 2 s., 2 d. Positions held: Instr. Va. Polytech. Inst., 1930-33; Instr. to Prof., Univ. of Ala., 1935-50; Dean of Arts and Scis., Va. Polytech. Inst. & State Univ., 1950-65; Miles Prof. of English, ibid, 1965–. Member, Poetry Soc. of Va. Pub. Reflections, 1965. Contrib. to: Wings; Lyric; Columbia Univ. Qtrly.; AAUP Bulletin; Radford Review; Phi Kappa Phi Journal; Poetry Digest; Southern Lit. Messenger; College English; Word Study; These Unmusical Days; Maelstrom; N.Y. Times; Washington Eve. Star; Kansas City Star; A Poetry Misc. by Univ. of Ala. Writers, 1938 and 1939; Internat. Who's Who in Poetry Anthol. Recip. Poetry Soc. of Va. awards: Whitney Mem. Prize, 1955; Keats Mem. Sonnet Prize, 1956, 1960, 1964; Helen Rushfeldt Duff Mem. Prize, 1970. Address: 804 Gracelyn Court, Blacksburg, Va. 24060, USA.

JOHNSTON, Lyman William, b. 8 Dec. 1916. Teacher. Education: B. Educ.; M. Educ. Married, 3 children. Positions held at: Clyde H.S., Ohio, 1949-51; Washington Jr. High, Port Huron, Mich., 1951-53; Cantrick Jr. High, Monroe, Mich., 1953-60; Forsythe Jr. High, Ann Arbor, Mich., 1960-67; Beach Middle Schl., Chelsea, Mich., 1967–. Memberships: Poetry Soc. of Mich.; World Poetry Soc. Intercontinental. Rep. in following anthols: Rainbow of Verse, 1965; The Singing Mariners, 1966; Third Annual Awards Contest, N.C. State Poetry Soc., 1968; Nat. Writers Club Awards, 1967, & '68; Author/Poet of Birmingham, Ala., 1971; Fla. State Poetry Soc. Awards, 1969 & '70;

Poets Study Club of Terre Haute, Ind., 1972; World Poetry Soc. Intercontinental, 'Premier Poets', 1972. Contbr. to: Southwest Times Record; Orphic Lute; Columbia Mag.; New Mag., Unity Ch.; Kansas Kernals Mag.; Flamingo; Poet. Recip. var. poetry awards, certs. or hon. mentions. Address: 323 Westwood, Ann Arbor, MI 48103, U.S.A.

JOKOSTRA, Peter, b. 5 May 1912. Writer. Education: Univ. studies in lit. & philos. Married, 2 daughters. Positions held: Farmer; Inspector of Schools; Editor. Memberships: PEN, German Ctr.; Verband deutscher Schriftsteller; Die Kogge. Published works: An der besonnten Mauer, 1958; Magische Strasse, 1960; Hinab zu den Sternen, 1961; Keine Zeit für Liebe? 1964; Die gewendete Haut, 1967. Contbr. to: Anthologie 56, Berlin; Merkur, Munich, 1960/61; Akzente, 1961; Jahresring, 1960/61, '64/65; Widerspiel, Deutsche Lyrik seit 1945, 1961; Lyrik aus dieser Zeit 1961/62, '63/64, '65/66; Contemporary German Poetry, Norfolk, 1962; La voix des poetes, 1966; 27 Gedichte interpretiert, 1972, etc. Honours, awards: Preis des Ministeriums für Kultur, 1956; Preis des Ministeriums für Kultur, 1958; Andreas Gryphius-Preis, 1965. Address: In der Mark 13, 5461 Kasbach/Rhein, German Fed. Repub.

JOLLY, Ralph M., b. 28 June 1940. Accountant. Education: B.A., Ouachita Univ., U.S.A., 1962. Married Linda Elder, 1 son (Vincent). Positions held: Acct., Blue Cross/Blue Shield of Tex., 1970–. Memberships: Tex. Soc. Cert. Public Accts. & local Dallas chapt. Has written poetry for 15 years & currently has a volume of assorted poems pending publication. Address: 12735 Cranberry Lane, No. 1024, Dallas, TX 75234, U.S.A.

JONAS, Ann. radio & TV name **HUBERT, Ann.** Poet; Former Radio & TV interviewer, Writer, Actor, & Producer. Education: Grad., Goodman Theatre, Chicago, Ill. Married, Walter H. Jonas. Positions held: Commentator, writer, actress, & producer, WMBH, Joplin, Mo.; Writer & actress, WJJD, Chicago, Ill.; Commentator, writer, actress & producer, WHAS, Louisville, Ky.; Interviewer & actress, WAVE, Louisville. Memberships: Poetry Soc. of Am; Fellow, Internat. Poetry Soc.; C.S.S.I. Hon. Rep.; Haiku Soc. of America. Published works: (anthols.) Dark Unsleeping Land, 1960; Deep Summer, 1963; Contemp. Ky. Poetry, 1, 1964, & 2, 1967; Ky. Harvest, 1968; (pamphlets) The Forge, 1962; Second Flight, 1968. Contbr. to: The Quest; The Colo. Quarterly; Midwest Quarterly; Carolina Quarterly; Midwestern Univ. Quarterly; Am. Haiku; Haiku West; The Worm Runner's Digest; Southern Humanities Review; Latitudes; Monks Pond; Bitterroot; Haiku (Canada); The Archer; Approach; Approaches; etc. A Review of Gen. Semantics. Honours: 1st Prize, Univ. of Louisville, 1962; 2nd Prize, Ky. State Poetry Soc. Haiku Contest, 1967; Resident, Yaddo writers retreat, Saratoga Springs, 1968; Finalist, Annual Poetry Contest, Poetry Soc. Am., 1970; Cecil Hemley Mem. Award, Poetry Soc. of America, 1972; Henry Rago Mem. Award, NY Poetry Forum, 1972; 1st Hon. Mention, Mayves Zantell Lyric Award, NY Poetry Forum, 1972; C.S.S.I. Dip. of Merit & Medal of Honor, 1972; Address: 2425 Ashwood Dr., Louisville, Ky. 40205, USA.

JONAS, George, b. 15 June 1935. Editor. Education: Lutheran Gymnazium, Liberal Arts Fac., Budapest; Studied Theatre & Film Arts w. F. Hont in Budapest. Married (separated), w. 1 Child. Positions held: Ed., Light Entertainment, Hungarian Broadcasting Corp., 1956; Script Ed., Can. Broadcasting Corp., 1962-68; Currently Chief Story Ed., ibid. Published works: The Absolute Smile, 1967; The Happy Hungry Man, 1970. Contbr. to (Anthols.): New Wave Canada, 1966; Penguin Book of Canadian Verse, 1967; Blasted Pine, 1967; Oxford Book of Canadian Verse, 1967; New Romans, 1968; Fifteen Winds, 1969; Thumbprints, 1969; Notes for a Native Land, 1969; (Jrnls.): Tamarack Review; Canadian Forum; Saturday Night; Prism International; Malahat Review; Quarry; Kayak. Recip., Can. Coun. Short Term Grant, 1968. Address:

c/o C.B.C., Box 500, Toronto, Ont., Canada.

JONAS, Gerald, b. 4 Oct. 1935. Writer. Education: Yale Univ., B.A., 1957; Pembroke Coll., Cambridge, UK., Henry Fellowship, 1957-58. Married to Susan Krieger; 2 d. (Sarah and Phoebe). Positions held: Reporter, Boston Herald, 1959-61; Writer, New Yorker Mag., since 1962. Published works: On Doing Good, 1971; Visceral Learning: Toward a Science of Self Control, 1973. Contbr. to: NY Times; Atlantic Monthly; Saturday Review; Spectator; The New Yorker; Nation; Poetry Northwest; Harper's. Recip. Nat. Media Award of the American Psychological Assoc., 1973. Address: 450 West End Ave., New York, NY 10024, USA.

JONES, Annette Kathleen. Actress. Education: studied Drama, Dancing, Singing. Contbr. to: Wheels; In Aid of Mental Health; 'Mum's Broadsheet'. Address: 24 Parliament Hill, London NW3, U.K.

JONES, Brian, b. 1938. Teacher. Married w. 2 Children. Published works: Poems, 1966; Family Album, 1968; Interior, 1969. Contbr. to (Anthol.): London Magazine Poems, 1966; (Jrnls.): London Mag.; Poetry Review.

JONES, Charles, b. 6 Feb. 1906. Writer. Married Delia Griffin, 1 daughter (Delia). Published works: Dose of Salts, 1957; Land of Song (satire), 1958; The Challenger, 1963; The Jingle, 1971. Contbr. to: Wales; Aryan Path; Y Faner (transl.); London Welsh; Lilliput; Western Mail; South Wales Echo; Daily Mirror; Daily Sketch; Daily Express; Herald of Wales; Merthyr Express; Irish Times; Scrip 10; Tribune; Spring Anthol. 1973 (Fudge); Adelphi; Time & Tide; John o'London; also many broadcasts on BBC TV & special recordings made for use in the U.S.A. by the Welsh BBC. Address: West Grove, Merthyr Tydfil, Glam., U.K.

JONES, David, b. 1 Nov. 1895. Painter; Poet. Education: Camberwell Schl. of Art, London; Westminster Schl. of Art, London. Positions held: One-Man Exhibition, 1944; Comprehensive Exhibition (Arts Council of Wales), Edinburgh & Tate Gallery, London, 1954-55. Published works: The Anathemata, 1952; The Tribune's Visitation, 1969; Other: In Parenthesis, 1937; Epoch & Artist, 1959. Recording of Anathemata & In Parenthesis. Contbr. to (Anthols.): Modern Welsh Poetry, 1944; Faber Book of Twentieth Century Verse, 1953; An Anthology of Modern Verse, 1961; Welsh Voices, 1967; Lilting House, 1969. Hons. incl: Hawthornden Prize, 1938; The Russell Loines Award for Poetry, Nat. Inst. of Arts & Letters, N.Y., 1954; The Harriet Monroe Memorial Prize, 1956; Arts Council Welsh Committee Award, 1960; City of London Midsummer Prize, 1968; Fellow of the Royal Soc. of Literature; D. Litt., Univ. of Wales, 1960; C.B.E., 1955.

JONES, Don, b. 11 Feb. 1938. Postal Clerk. Education: B.A., Univ. of Northern Colo., 1960; M.A., Johns Hopkins Univ., 1961; Univ. of Neb., 1962-66. Positions held: Caseworker, Baltimore Welfare Serv., U.S.A.; Tchr., Writer in Res., Trinitarian Coll., Univ. of Neb., Hastings Coll., Carleton Coll. & St. Olaf Coll.; Postal Clerk, US Post Office, Longmont, Colo., 1972–. Published works: Medical Aid & Other Poems, 1967; Nine Postal Poems, 1971; Miss Liberty, Meet Crazy Horse! 1972. Address: 1400 S. Collyer No. 193, Longmont, CO 80501, U.S.A.

JONES, Douglas Gordon, b. 1 Jan. 1929. Associate Professor. Education: B.A., McGill Univ., Montreal, 1952; M.A., Queen's Univ., Kingston, 1954. Positions held: Lectr., Royal Mil. Coll., Kingston, 1954-55; Asst. Prof., Ont. Agricl. Coll., 1955-61; Lectr., Bishop's Univ., 1961-63; Assoc. Prof., Université de Sherbrooke, 1963–. Memberships: Arts Advisory Panel, Canada Coun., 1971-74; The League of Canadian Poets. Published works: Frost on the Sun, 1957; The Sun is Axeman, 1961; Phrases from Orpheus, 1967; Ellipse No. 13, poems & French transl., 1974. Address: P.O. Box 356, N. Hatley, Quebec, JOB 2CO, Canada.

JONES, Evan, b. 1927. Education: Munro Coll., Jamaica. Published works (Not Poetry): Protector of the Indians, 1958; Trappers & Mountain Men, 1961; Var. Screenplays. Contbr. to (Anthols.): Young Commonwealth Poets '65, 1965; Modern Folk Ballads, 1966; Commonwealth Poets of Today, 1967; Sun's Eye, 1968.

JONES, Evan Lloyd, b. 20 Nov. 1931. Lecturer. Education: B.A. & M.A. in Hist., Univ. of Melbourne; A.M. in Engl., Stanford Univ., Calif., U.S.A. Married, 1 son, 3 daughters. Positions held: Tutor & Sr. Tutor in Hist., Univ. of Melbourne, 1955-58; Lectr. in Engl., Australian Nat. Univ., Canberra, 1960-63; Lectr. in Engl., Univ. of Melbourne, 1964; Sr. Lectr. in Engl., ibid, 1965-. Published works: Inside the Whale, 1960; Understandings, 1967; Recognitions, 1973, Rep. in many anthols. Contbr. to: The Literature of Australia (Australian Poetry since 1920), Ed. Geoffrey Dutton, 1964; Kenneth Mackenzie, 1969; Co-Ed., Poems of Kenneth Mackenzie, 1972. Address: Dept. of Engl., Univ. of Melbourne, Parkville, Vic., Australia 3052.

JONES, Glyn, b. 28 Feb. 1905. Former English Teacher of English. Education: St. Paul's Coll., Cheltenham. Married. Positions held: Formerly Tchr. of English, South Wales. Published works: Poems, 1939; The Dream of Jake Hopkins, 1954; Novels: The Valley, the City, the Village, 1956; The Learning Lark, 1960; The Island of Apples, 1965; Short Stories: The Blue Bed, 1937; The Water Music, 1944; Other: The Dragon Has Two Tongues (Essays), 1968; Trans. w. T.J. Morgan, The Saga of Llywarch the Old, 1955. Contbr. to (Anthols.): Modern Welsh Poetry, 1944; New Romantic Anthology, 1949; New British Poets, 1949; Poetry of the Present, 1949; Images of Tomorrow, 1953; Presenting Welsh Poetry, 1959; Colour of Saying, 1963; Welsh Voices, 1967; This World of Wales, 1968; Lilting House, 1969; (Jrnls.): Anglo-Welsh Review; Welsh Review; New Verse; Poetry London; Twentieth Century; Adelphi; Life & Letters; Today; Outposts; Poetry Quarterly; Wales; American Poetry Jrnl. Recip., Welsh Arts Coun. Award, 1968. Address: 158 Manor Way, Whitchurch, Cardiff, Wales.

JONES, Gretchen Page. Housewife. Education: HS, Haughton, La.; Centenary Coll., Shreveport, La., special courses in creative writing and painting; studied art at Southwestern Inst. of Arts, Shreveport. Married; 2 d. Memberships: Charter member, Shreveport Poetry Soc., 1935-1956, vice-president, 1950-56; Radio Chairman, Lowe-McDarlane American Legion Aux., 1944; current vice-pres., United Daughters of the Confederacy; Member, La. State Poetry Soc.; The Shreveport Writers Club; Shreveport Art Club; Hoover Water-Color Soc. Contbr. to: Good Housekeeping, Mag.; Holland's Mag.; American Women Poets, 1937; The White Heron, 1937; Red River Sand, 1940; The Singing Pines, 1949; Best Newspaper Poems, 1941; Shreveport Writers Club, Poets and Authors, 1972; New Voices in American Poetry, 1972; Internat. Who's Who in Poetry, 1972; Verse Craft; Kansas City Poetry Mag.; Talaria; Poetry Chapbook; The Green World; The Shreveport Journal; The Shreveport Times ("The Poets Corner"); Carmel Pine Cone; Kaleidograph; La. State Poetry Yearbook, 1972-73. Recip. of numerous poetry awards, including: 1st Place, Shreveport Writers Club Competition, 1969; awards from Deep South Writers Conference; 1st Pl., Interstate Art Competition, Panola Coll., Carthage, Tex., 1969; Award of Hon., Deep South Writers Conf., La. State Univ., New Orleans, 1972, etc. Address: 1624 Claiborne Ave., Shreveport, LA 71103, USA.

JONES, Helen Symons, pen name **JONES, H. Wendy,** b. 29 June 1906. Artist; Writer; Art Museum Director. Education: B.A., Mt. Holyoke, Mass., 1928; M.A., Columbia Tchrs. Coll., N.Y., 1944; var. grad. work. Positions held: Tchr., Oak Pk., Ill., 1928-30, Zion, Ill., 1936-37, Lake Forest, Ill., 1932-33; Recreation Dir., Georgetown, Wash. D.C., 1941-42 & Christodora House, N.Y.C.; Dir. of Int. Art Mus., Anchorage,

Alaska. Memberships: Ariz. State Poetry Soc., 1969-74; Alaska State Poetry Soc., 1962-74; League of Western Writers, 1968; Creative Writing Grp., Anchorage Womens Club. Published works: Man & the Mountain, 1962; Wendy's Windows, 1970. Contbr. to: Phoenix Fires; Sandcutters Mag.; Anchorage Times Newspaper; Wash. D.C. Post; Poet, etc. Recip. var. poetry prizes. Address: 3005 Wendy Way, Anchorage, AK 99503, U.S.A.

JONES, John Idris, b. 9 Mar. 1938. Managing Director, John Jones Cardiff Ltd. Education: B.A., Keele Univ., U.K., 1961; Cert. Educ., Leeds, 1963; M.A., Cornell Univ., U.S.A., 1965. Divorced, 1 son. Positions held: Schl. Tchr., London & Leeds; Grad. Asst., Schl. of Educ., Cornell Univ., 1964-65; Instr. in Engl., Northern Ill. Univ., DeKalb, 1965-66; Lectr. in Engl., Cardiff Coll. of Educ., U.K., 1967-73. Published works: Way Back to Ruthin, 1967; Barry Island & Other Poems, 1971. Contbr. to: Transatlantic Review; Twentieth Century, etc. Address: 41 Lochaber St., Cardiff, U.K.

JONES, LeRoi, b. 7 Oct. 1934. Editor. Education: B.A., Howard Univ., Wash. D.C., 1954. Married w. 4 Children. Positions held: Founded Black Arts Theatre, Harlem, NYC; Fac. Mbr., New Schl. for Social Research, N.Y.; Ed. w. Diane di Prima, Floating Bear, N.Y., 1961-63; Currently, Ed., Yugen Mag. & Totem Press, N.Y. Published works: Preface to a Twenty Volume Suicide Note, 1962; The Dead Lecturer, 1965; Black Art, 1966; Black Magic; Poetry 1961-67; Plays: Dutchman & Slave, 1965; The Baptism & The Toilet, 1967; Other: Blues People: Negro Music in America, 1965; The System of Dante's Hell, 1965; Home: Social Essays, 1968; Ed., The Moderns: An Anthology of New Writing in America, 1963; Ed. w. Larry Neal, Black Fire: An Anthology of Afro-American Writing, 1968. Contbr. to (Anthols.): New American Poetry, 1960; American Negro Poetry, 1963; New Negro Poets USA, 1964; Poets of Today, 1964; A Controversy of Poets, 1965; Kaleidoscope, 1967; Black Fire, 1968; (Jrnls.): Negro Digest; Jrnl. of Black Poetry. Hons: Whitney Fellowship, 1962-63; Guggenheim Fellowship, 1964-65; Var. Awards for his Plays & Productions. Address: Jihad Publications, Box 663, Newark, NJ, USA.

JONES, Margaret Alice Bartlett, b. 23 Oct. 1906. Retired Educational Administrator. Education: B.A., Univ. of Bristol, U.K., 1928; B.Sc. (Econ.), London, 1944; Barrister-at-Law, Middle Temple, London, 1951; Gwilyn Gibbon Fellow, Nuffield Coll., Oxford, 1953-54. Positions held: Head Tchr. of special & primary schls., 1929-42; Administrative work in education w. Gloucestershire L.E.A., 1942-56; Prin., St. Katherine's Coll. of Educ., 1956-65. Published works: Lake Vyrnwy & Other Poems, 1972. Contbr. to: Anglo-Welsh Review; Poetry Wales; Outposts; New Headland; Envoi; Scrip; Pink Peace; Muse; London Welshman; Weyfarers; Overspill; Viewpoints; Country Life; Scottish Field; Homes & Gardens; Country Quest; Shropshire Magazine; also to BBC (Midland Poets prog.) Address: 8 Mayfield Pk., Shrewsbury, U.K.

JONES, Peter Austin, b. 25 Apr. 1929. Publisher. Education: Read Classics & Engl., Oxford Univ. Positions held: on staff of Christ's Hosp., Horsham, Sussex, U.K.; Mng. Dir., Carcanet Press Ltd. Published works: Rain, 1969; Seagarden for Julius, 1970; The Peace & the Hook, 1972; Penguin Book of Imagist Poetry, 1972. Contbr. to sev. jrnls. & mags. Address: 266 Councillor Ln., Cheadle Hulme, Cheadle, Ches. SK8 5PN, U.K.

JONES, Phyllis Marjory, pen name **TRELAWNEY,** b. 12 Mar. 1923. Nurse. Memberships: Welsh Guild of Playwrights; Scribbler Soc. Hon. Ed. 'Newsletter', Coun. Protection Rural Wales. Published works: The Grass Has Not Yet Grown, 1971; Song of Gower, 1971; Sailboats & Mackerel, 1973. Contbr. to: Anglo-Welsh Review; Cornish Review; Cornish Nation; Country Quest; Occupational Health; Home & Country, etc. Honours, awards: Scribbler Awards, Poetry, 1970; Cornish Gorsedd Poetry Award, 1970; Best Novel of Literary Merit, Theodora Roscoe Award,

1970; var. prose awards. Address: Erw'n Grug, 61 Llannon Rd., Upper Tumble, Nr. Llanelli, Carms., U.K.

JONKLAAS, David, b. 1932. Business Man. Education: London Univ. Positions held: Formerly Vis. Lectr., Aquinas Univ. Coll.; Currently, Mbr., Firm of Carson Cumberbatch & Co. Ltd., Repub. of Srilanka. Contbr. to (Anthols.): Young Commonwealth Poets '65, 1965; New Voices of the Commonwealth, 1968.

JONSMOEN, Ola, pen names **OJO, OLE DOFTON, DOFTON, OL JONSA,** b. 9 July 1932. High School Teacher. Education: Tchrs. Trng. Coll.; studies of lit. & lang., Univ. of Oslo & abroad; Cand. philol. Married Unni-Lise, 3 children. Positions held: Farm Hand; Teacher. Memberships: Norwegian Soc. of Authors; Deputy to the Bd. of Literary Advisers; Norwegian Soc. of Critics. Published works: Dagen, vinden og hjartet, 1959; Humle Brumle, 1962; Omvegar, 1967; Jonas ved Amasonas, 1969; Celle, 1971; Den döde er död, (play), 1972; Om desse steinane tala, 1973. Contbr. to: Books Abroad; Dagbladet; Vinduet; Profil; Scandinavian Review; Syn og Segn. Rep. in following anthols: Ti unge; Nye navn i norsk kunst; Norsk lyrikk – Etterkrigstiden; Aschehougs litteraturutvalg; Norske dikt. Address: 2560 Alvdal, Norway.

JORDAN, Anna Maude, pen name, **JORDAN, Maude,** b. 12 June 1898. Retired Teacher. Education: Radford Coll, Radford, Va.; Wm. & Mary, Concord Colls. Married, Meth. Min. Positions held: former Tchr., Elem. & Public Schls. Memberships: Past Pres., Huntington Poetry Guild; W. Va. Poetry Soc.; Nat. Poetry Soc.; Huntington Woman's Club; Lib. Friends; Tri State Art Assn. Contbr. to: (Anthol.) W Va. Centennial Book of Poems, 1963; (Jrnls.) W Va. Hillybilly; Huntington Herald Dispatch; Huntington Advt. Honours, Awards: 1st Prize Award, Fed. of Womens Clubs, W Va., 1962; 1970; 1st prize, Lyric category, West Va. State Poetry Contest, 1972. Address: 3025 Wallace Circle, Huntington, W Va. USA.

JORDAN, Anne (Saunders), b. 27 June 1914. University Lecturer. Education: Newport News H.S., Va.; William and Mary Coll.; Univ. of Va. Widow, 3 sons. Positions held: Head, English Dept., Goochland H.S., Goochland, Va.; Member, English Faculty, Va. Commonwealth Univ., since 1965. Memberships include: Poetry Soc. of Va. (Sec.; Chairman of Contest Committee; Exec. Board); Richmond Writers' Workshop; Faculty Adv. to Writers' Forum, Va. Commonwealth U. Modern Lang. Assoc. Contbr. to: Oregonian Verse; Orphic Lute; The Hartford Courant; Proscript; Voices International; Folio Five; Bardic Echoes; The Beacon; Cardinal Poetry Qtly.; Richmond Times Dispatch; The Archer; The Creative Review; Dragonfly, A Quarterly for Haiku Highlights; Jean's Jrnl.; Best Poems of the Twentieth Century (anthol.); Notable American Poets (anthol.); Poetry of the Year (anthol.). Awards include: Edgar Allan Poe Lyric Prize, Va. Writers' Club, 1964; Internat. Poet's Shrine Lambert Castle N.J. Sonnet, 1964; Elizabethan Lyric Prize, Poetry Soc. of Va., 1966; Lynchburg Festival of Arts, Poets' Assembly Prize, 1965; Helen Rushfeldt Duff Shakespearean Sonnet Prize, Poetry Soc. of Va., 1969; Rochester Festival of Relig. Arts, Hon. Mention, 1970; Hon. Mentions and Commendations PSVA., 1964, 1966, 1969. Address: English Dept., Va. Commonwealth Univ., 901 West Franklin St., Richmond, VA. 23221, USA.

JORDAN, June Meyer, b. 9 July 1936. Poet; Teacher; Writer. Education: Univ. of Chicago. Married. Positions held: Tchr., English Fac., City Coll., City Univ. of NY, 1967–; currently Tchr., Sarah Lawrence Coll. Co-Dir., The Voice of the Children, creative writing workshop for Black & Puerto Rican teenagers, Brooklyn. Published works: Who Look at Me, 1969; Some Changes, 1970; Soulscript, 1971; His Own Where, 1971; The Voice of the Children, 1970; Dry Victories, 1972; New Days, 1973; I Love You, 1973; Fannie Lou Hamer, 1972. Contbr. to following anthols. & jrnls: Evergreen Review; Esquire; Nation; Mademoiselle; Urban Review; Am. Dialog; Liberator;

NY Times; New Black Poetry. Address: c/o Wendy Weil, The Julian Bach Literary Agency, 3 East 48 St., New York, NY 10017, USA.

JORDAN, Thornton Waddell, pen names **JORDAN, Troy & JORDAN, Khalid Walid Muhammad ibn,** b. 13 Nov. 1941. Historian; Poet; Writer; Lecturer; Researcher. Education: A.B., San Diego State Univ.; Trinity Univ.; grad. rsch. Fellow, Univ. of San Diego; var. other colls. Positions held: Calif. State Park Histn. I; V.P., Grad. Student Coun., Univ. of San Diego; V.P., Amadan Fed.; Assoc., Am. Mus. of Natural Hist.; Sec., Moslem Poets of Am.; Treas., Sec., Sargeant-at-Arms, Bulletin Ed., Toastmasters Int.; V.P., Grove Kenpo Club; Rep., San Diego State Univ. Islamic Studies Comm.; Bulletin Ed., So. Calif. Paleontological Soc., etc. Memberships incl: Centro Studi e Scambi; Accademia Internazionali Leonardo da Vinci; Int. Platform Assn; Cath. Poetry Soc. of Am.; Am. Assn. for State & Local Hist. Published works: No Slopmop, this!, 1968; The Vallecitos Stage, 1968; Derby's Dike, 1971; The Rifleman, 1971; Parting Mists, 1971; Interregnum, 1971; Gidget, 1971; Ode to a Brazilian Red-crested Cardinal, 1971; The Inner Germ, 1972; Life's Love, 1972; If You Would Be Immortal, 1972; Admonition, 1973; Lord of the Skies, 1973, etc. Contbr. to var. jrnls. Recip. num honours & awards inclng: Gold Medal, Islamic Poetry, 1968, '70; Jalal ad-Din Lyric Prize, 1969, '71; Moslem Poets of Am. Award, 1969-73; Serra Award, 1973. Address: 104 Jamul Ave., Chula Vista, CA 92011, U.S.A.

JORGENSEN, Ruth J., b. 31 July 1924. Housewife. Education: Brainerd Coll. Married Robert C. Jorgensen. Memberships: Midwest Fed. of Chaparral Poets, Mnpls., Minn. Contbr. to: Cappers Weekly; Evangelical Beacon; Women's Household; The Farmer; Christian Life; Midland Coop; Kitchen Klatter; The Bible Friend; Mnpls. Argus; Evangelical Free Ch. Bulletin; Farm Wife News, etc. Ed. of Malmo Moments, ch. newspaper. Recip. var. poetry awards & hon. mentions. Address: Star Rte., Isle, MN 56342, U.S.A.

JOSEPH, Michael Kennedy, b. 9 July 1914. Professor of English. Education: B.A., Auckland Univ. Coll., 1933; M.A., ibid., 1934; B.A., Merton Coll., Oxford, 1938; B.Litt., ibid., 1939; M.A., ibid., 1945. Married w. 5 Children. Positions held: Mbr., Fac. of Engl., Auckland Univ., 1946–; Currently, Prof., ibid. Published works: Imaginary Islands, 1950; The Living Countries, 1959; Other: I'll Soldier No More, 1958; A Pound of Saffron, 1962; The Hole in the Zero, 1967; Byron the Poet, 1964. Contbr. to (Anthols.): An Anthol. of New Zealand Verse, 1956; Penguin Book of New Zealand Verse, 1960; (Jrnls.): Landfall; New Zealand Listener; Poetry Yearbook. Recip., British Council Travel Award, 1962. Address: c/o Univ. of Auckland, New Zealand.

JOSEPH, Stephen M., b. 7 Jan. 1938. Writer; Teacher. Education: B.A., Ohio State Univ.; grad. work, Hunter Coll., N.Y. Married Barbara Randall, 1 daughter. Positions held: Tchr., N.Y. City Public Schls., 1960-69; Lectr., N.Y. Univ., 1969-70; Lectr., The Cooper Union, 1970-71; Cons., N.Y. State Coun. on the Arts, 1970–. Memberships: Tchrs. & Writers Collaborative, 1970-71; Cons., Poet-in-Res., Nat. Endowment on the Arts, 1973-74; Wyoming State Arts Coun.; St. Paul Arts Coun.; N.J. State Arts Coun.; N.Y. State Arts Coun. Editor, The Me Nobody Knows, 1969. Honours, awards: Obie Award for Best Off-Broadway Musical Play (The Me Nobody Knows), 1970; Runner-up, Antoinette Perry Award for Best Broadway Musical Play (The Me Nobody Knows), 1971. Address: Lanesboro Rd., Cheshire, MA 01225, U.S.A.

JOSHI, Umashankar, b. 21 July 1911. Teacher; Writer. Education: Gujarat Coll., Ahmedabad & Elphinstone Coll., Bombay; M.A., Bombay Univ. Married Jyotsna (dec.), 2 daughters. Positions held: Tchr., Gokalibai H.S., Vile-Parle, Bombay, 1937-39; Post Grad. Tchr., Vidya-Sabha, Ahmedabad, 1939-46; Prof. & Dir., Schl. of Lang. & Lit., Gujarat Univ., Ahmedabad, 1954-70; V. Chancellor, Gujarat Univ., 1966-72; Mbr. of Parliament, 1970–. Ed., Sanskriti monthly, 1947–.

Memberships incl: V.P., Indian PEN, 1973–; Pres., 1967-69 & Exec. Mbr., Gujarati Sahitya Parishad; Gen. Coun. & Exec. Bd., Sahitya Akademi, 1954-72. Presided over First All-India Poets' Conf., Calcutta, 1968. Published works: (poetry books) Vishua Shanti, 1931; Gangotri, 1934; Nisheeth, 1939; Prachina, 1944; Atithya, 1946; Vasant-Varsha, 1954; Mahaprasthan; Abhijna, 1967; publ. of var. poems in English translation. Contbr. to mags., jrnls. & anthols. Honours, awards: All-India Bharatiya Jnanpith Lit. Award for 1967 for book 'Nisheeth' (shared w. K.V. Puttappa); Two Gold Medals for Poetry, 1939, '47; Three Poetry Prizes, 1944, '69, '70. Address: 'Setu', 26 Sardar Patel Nagar, Ahmedabad 380006, India.

JOYCE, Brian Charles, pen name BORU, b. 19 Nov. 1951. Education: 3 yrs. Univ. of NSW, 1970-72, B.Com., transferred to B.A., 2nd yr., 1973. Poetry Co-ordinator, Aquarius Festival, 1973. Memberships: Poetry Soc. Univ. of NSW, 1972; Performing Poets of Nimbin, 1973. Published work: Meandering Paths, 1973. Contbr. to: Tweed; Saturday Club Book of Poetry; Tharunka; Grassleaves. Address: 140 McIntosh Rd., Dee Why, NSW 2099, Australia.

JOYCE, Robert Lee, b. 21 July 1907. Advertising Executive; Silk Screen Printer. Education: Ohio State Univ.; Columbus Coll. of Art & Design; B.S. in Educ., Otterbein Coll., 1969. Positions held: Engrng. Dept., Curtiss-Wright Corp.; Salesman, J.I. Holcomb Mfg. Co. & Southard Printing Co.; self employed as Joyce Advt., Westerville, Ohio. Memberships: W. Va. State Poetry Soc.; Ohio Verse Writers Guild; Chmn. designate for Nat. Contest, Nat. Fed. of State Poetry Socs., 1975. Contbr. to: Citizen-Jrnl.; Dream Shop; Ohio State Jrnl.; Sample Case; Indpls. News; Public Opinion, Westerville, Ohio; Sunday Gazette-Mail State Mag., etc. Recip. var. poetry awards from Nat. Fed. State Poetry Socs. & W. Va. State Poetry Soc. Address: 20 Lee Terrace, Westerville, OH 43081, U.S.A.

JOYCE, Trevor, b. 26 Oct. 1947. Editor. Positions held: Clerk w. Dublin Corp., 1967–; Ed. w. Michael Smith of The Lace Curtain, Dublin, 1969–. Published works: Sole Glum Trek, 1967; Watches, 1969. Contbr. to (Jrnls.): Hibernia; Dublin Mag. Address: 40 Rathlin Rd., Glasnevin, Dublin, 9, Ireland.

JUDSON, John Irvine, Jr., b. 9 Sept. 1930. Associate Professor. Education: A.B., Colby Coll.; Univ. of Maine; M.F.A., Univ. of Iowa. Married Joanne Carol Aker, 4 children. Positions held: Asst. Prof. of Engl., Univ. of Wis., La Crosse, 1965-67; Assoc. Prof., ibid, 1967–. Published works: Two From Where It Snows (w. J.S. Wade), 1964; Surreal Songs, 1969; Within Seasons, 1970; Finding Words in Winter, 1973; West of Burnam, South of Troy, verse play, 1974. Contbr. to over 200 mags. & periodicals inclng: Qtly. Review of Lit.; N.Y. Times; The Nation; The Southern Review; The Mass. Review; Kayak; Poetry Northwest; Shenandoah; Choice; The North Am. Review; N.Y. Qtly.; New Orleans Review; Cafe Solo; Apple; New Am. & Canadian Poetry. Honours, awards: Hart Crane Meml. Award, 1969; Wis. Writers Award for Within Seasons, 1971; Earplay Award for radio drama for West of Burnam, South of Troy, 1973. Address: c/o Engl. Dept., Univ. of Wis., La Crosse, WI 54601, U.S.A.

JUERGENSEN, Hans, b. 17 Dec. 1919. Professor; Writer; Poet. Education: B.A., Upsala Coll., E. Orange, NJ; Ph.D., Johns Hopkins Univ. Positions held: Jr. Instr., Johns Hopkins Univ.; Instr., Univ. of Kan., 1951-53; Chmn. of Engl., Quinnipiac Coll., Conn., 1953-61; Asst. Prof., Assoc. Prof., Prof. of Humanities, Univ. of S. Fla., 1961–. Memberships: Pres., Nat. Fed. of State Poetry Socs., 1968-70; Fndr., Am. Acad. of Poets; Poetry Soc. of Am.; Poetry Soc. of Mich.; Chmn., New Haven Poetry Soc., 1958-61; Chmn., Tampa Poetry Assoc., 1962-65; Chmn. of Poetry, New Haven Arts Festival, Conn., 1959, '60; American Writers Program (member); Internat. Poetry Soc. (Fellow). Published works: I Feed You From My Cup, 1958; In Need For Names, 1961; Existential Canon and Other Poems,

1965? Florida Montage, 1966; Sermons From The Ammunition Hatch Of The Ship Of Fools, 1968; Prom The Divide, 1969; Hebraic Modes, 1972; Points of Departure, 1974. Contbr. to following anthols. & jrnls: Where Is Vietnam?, 1967; Stars & Stripes Anthol., 1945; Poetry Americana, 1966; Golden Harvest, 1967; NY Times; NY Herald Tribune; PM; Piggott Banner; NY Times Mag.; Floridian; Essence; Quicksilver; Yale Lit. Mag.; Wormwood Review; Green World; Am. Weave; Bitterroot; Trace; Am. Judaism; Aufbau; Border; Apercu; Goliards; Voices Int.; Cardinal; Vagabond; Human Voice; Intermission; Outposts; Black Sun; Poet Lore; Afrasian; Revue Moderne; Now Save the Dead; The South Fla. Poetry Journal, etc. Awards: 1st Prize, Poetry Day, Fla., 1964; Fla. Poet of the Year, 1965-66; 2nd Prize, Stephen Vincent Benet Narrative Poetry Award, 1970; Award, Hart Crane, Alice Crane Williams Fndn., 1969. Address: 7815 Pine Hill Dr., Tampa, FL 33617, USA.

JUNKINS, Donald Arthur, b. 19 Dec. 1931. Writer; Professor. Education: B.A., Univ. of Mass., 1953; S.T.B., Boston Univ., 1956; S.T.M., ibid, 1957; A.M., 1959; Ph.D., 1963. Married Martha Edwards Luppold, 3 children. Positions held: Tchng. Fellow, Boston Univ., 1958-61; Asst. Prof., Emerson Coll., 1961-63; Asst. Prof., Calif. Univ. at Chico, 1963-66; Assoc. Prof., Univ. of Mass., 1966–. Member, Poetry Soc. of Am. Published works: The Sunfish & the Partridge, 1965; The Graves of Scotland Parish, 1968; Walden, 100 Years after Thoreau, 1968; And Sandpipers She Said, 1970. Contbr. to: The New Yorker; The Atlantic; Mass. Review; Beloit Poetry Jrnl.; Choice; Hungarian Lit. Review (Paris); Am. Lit. Anthol.2; The Berkshire Anthol.; Yankee; Va. Qtly.; Renaissane, etc. Honours, awards: Jennie Tane Award, Mass. Review, 1968; Nat. Endowment for the Arts Award, 1968; John Masefield Meml. Award, 1972. Address: Engl. Dept., Bartlett Hall, Univ. of Mass., Amherst, MA 01002, U.S.A.

JURGENSEN, Manfred, b. 26 Mar. 1940. Professor of German Literature. Education: B.A., Univ. of Melbourne, 1964; M.A., ibid, 1965; Ph.D., Univ. of Zurich, 1968. Married Marguerite Suzanne Bürki. Positions held: Tutor, Univ. of Melbourne, 1964; Sr. Tchng. Fellow, Monash Univ., 1965; Swiss Govt. Scholarship, Univ. of Zurich, 1966-68; Lectr., Univ. of Qld., 1968; Sr. Lectr., ibid, 1970; Rdr. & Prof. (Rsch.), 1971; Alexander von Humboldt Fellow, Univ. of Hanover, 1972-73; Ed., Qld. Studies in German Lang. & Lit.; Co-Ed., Seminar. Memberships: Poetry Soc. of Australia; Australian Fellowship of Writers. Published works: Stationen, 1968; Aufenthalte, 1969; Signs & Voices, 1973; Letters from the Suburbs, 1974; Heimkehr (poems in German), 1974; also 5 books of criticism. Contbr. to: Square Poets Anthol., 1971; The Australian; The Bulletin; Quadrant; Makar; Twentieth Century; Poetry Mag.; New Poetry; Australian Poetry, etc. Recip., Award, Lit. Bd. of the Australian Coun. for the Arts, 1973. Address: c/o Dept. of German, Univ. of Qld., Brisbane – St. Lucia, Qld. 4067, Australia.

JUSSAWALLA, Adil, b. 8 Apr. 1940. English Teacher. Education: A.A. Schl. of Archt., London; M.A., Univ. Coll., Oxford Univ., U.K. Married, 1 step daughter. Positions held: Tchr. of Engl., Int. Language Ctr., London, 4 yrs.; Tchr. of Engl. Lang. & Lit., St. Xavier's Coll., Bombay, 2 yrs. Published works: Land's End, book of poems, 1962. Rep. in following anthols: Young Commonwealth Poets '65, 1965; Modern Indo-Anglian Poetry; Young Poets of India, 1972; Indian Poetry in English, 1947-72, 1972; Contemporary Indian Poetry in English, 1973. Editor, New Writing in India, 1974. Contbr. to: Beloit Poetry Jrnl.; Carcanet; Poetry India; Illustrated Weekly of India; Quest. Address: Palm Springs, Cuffe Parade, Bombay 5, India.

JUSTICE, Donald, b. 12 Aug. 1925. Teacher. Education: B.A., Univ. of Miami; M.A., Univ. of N.C.; Ph.D., Univ. of Iowa. Positions held: Prof., Syracuse Univ.; Vis. Prof., Univ. of Calif., Irvine; Prof., Univ. of Iowa. Published works: The Summer Anniversaries, 1960; A Local Storm, pamphlet, 1963; Night Light, 1967; 16 Poems, pamphlet, 1970; From a Notebook, chapbook, 1972; Deptartures, 1973. Contbr. to: Poetry; New Yorker; Kayak; New Am. Review; Am. Poetry Review. Honours, awards: The Lamont Poetry Selection, 1959; The Inez Boulton Prize, Poetry, 1960; The Harriet Monroe Meml. Prize, Poetry, 1965; Fellow, Nat. Coun. on the Arts, 1967. Address: Dept. of Engl., Univ. of Iowa, Iowa City, IA 52242, U.S.A.

JWALA, Ravi Verma, pen name **JWALA,** b. 30 Oct. 1933. Poet; Journalist. Education: Grad., Univ. of Sangar, 1957. Positions held: Press Corres., Nagpur Times, Nagpur. Many times presided & conducted poet gatherings & participated in Kavi Gosthi prog. (a live broadcast arranged by AIR, 1973). Broadcasts regularly on All India Radio & special prog. was arranged for the reading of poems by Radio Moscow, 1972. Memberships: Adviser, Sankalp Lit. Soc.; Treas., Sanskratik Kala Mandir, Chhindwara; Sugam Manas Mandal. Published works: Mati Ka Moh, coll. of poems. Contbr. to var. newspapers & mags. Honours, awards: Honoured by Ajanta Prakashan Jabalpur, by awarding cit. of 'Sahitya Prabhakar'. Address: Nagpur Rd., Chhindwara, Madhya Pradesh (Bharat), India.

K

KABDEBO, Thomas George, b. 5 Feb. 1934. University Librarian. Education: Univ. of Budapest, Hungary; Univ. of Wales, UK; Univ. of London. Positions held: Temp. Asst. Libn., Univ. Coll., Cardiff; Asst. Libn., Univ. Coll., London; Libn., Univ. of Guyana, Georgetown, Guyana; Chief Librarian, City of London Polytechnic. Memberships: Fndr. & Pres., Univ. Coll. London Poetry Seminar, 1965-69; PEN; Brit. Rep., World Poetry Soc. Publications: Fortified Princescriptions, 1964; Attila Jozsef, 1966; Tribute to Gyula Jllyes. Ed., Poet, Hungarian number, 1967; Ed., Poet, Brit. number, Guyana number, 1969; Radnoti, 1971; Ed., Just for All That. (Poetry Annual in English & Hungarian), Twohearted, 1973; The Poetry of Hungary, 1974. Contbr. to: (anthol.) Univ. Coll. London Poetry, 1967 & '69; (jrnls.) ICA Bulletin; New Hungarian Quarterly; Image; Tribune; Poetry Singapore; Pi; Resurgence; Ana etcetera; Tool; Nemzetor; Irodalm; Ujsag etc. Honours: World Poetry Soc. Award & Distinguished Mbr.'s Citation, 1968. Address: School of Business Studies, 84 Moorgate, London EC2, UK.

KACHMAR, Jessie, b. 28 Mar. 1913. Teacher of English & Adult Education. Education: B.A., Univ. of Wash., 1935; grad. work, Creative Writing, Univ. of Minn., 1953, Loyola, 1959. Married, 1 daughter. Positions held: An Ed., Chicago Choice, 1961-62; Freelance Writer, 1962; Tchr., Adult Ed., part of Chicago Loop Coll. system; since 1963 also City Bd. of Educ. Tchr.; Consulting Ed., Gallery Series, 1967, '68, '70. Memberships: Nat. Writers' Sorority, 1953; Exec. Editl. Bd. and Comm., Poetry Seminar, Chicago, 1959-61. Contbr. to: Chicago Choice; Choice; Port Chicago Poets Anthol.; Your Only Hope Is Humor, Anthol.; Poetry Northwest; Poetry Dial, etc. Address: 7535 N. Rockwell, Chicago, IL 60645, U.S.A.

KAECH, René, b. 19 Apr. 1909. Physician; Specialist FMH in Psychiatry. Education: Dip. of Physician, Lausanne, 1935; M.D., Lausanne, 1938. Positions held: Chief, Psychiatric Clin. Corcelles-sur-Chavornay, Vaud, Switzerland; Ldr. of CIBA Pharmaceuticals Products, Lisbon & Rio de Janeiro. Memberships: Pres., PEN Club, Basle, 1964-68; Assn. of Swiss Writers, 1972-74; Pres. of Hon., Swiss Assn. of es., Med. Writers; Pres. World Union of Med. Writers; Comm., Basler Schriftsteller-Verein. Published works: Le Poète-Gueux, 1941; L'Epopée intérieure, 1944; Veuves et Veufs, 1966; var. translations of poems from Italian (Vittorio Locchi, Renato Valtecchi, Cesare Pavese, etc.) Poems published in many reviews, newspapers inclng: Poésie vivante; Chronique de l'Association suisse des Ecrivains médecins; Basler Nachrichten. Honours, awards: Gold Medal (Officer) Arts-Sciences-Lettres,

Paris, 1964; Gold Medal, Columbus Assn., Trieste, 1964; Silver Medal, Premi Letterari Giuliani, Milan, 1956. Address: Benkenstrasse 7, CH 4050 Basel, Switzerland.

KAHN, Hannah, b. 30 June 1911. Poet; Poetry Editor. Education: Grad., Fla. Atlantic Univ. Married, 2 sons, 1 daughter. Positions held: Poetry Review Ed., Miami Herald, 1958–. Memberships: Advisory Bd. for Affiliated Mbrships of Acad. of Am. Poets; Poetry Socs. of Am., Ga. & Va.; Past Pres., Laramore Rader Poetry Grp. Published works: Eve's Daughter, book of poems, 1963. Contbr. to: Am. Scholar; Harper's; Sat. Review; Southwest Review; Lit. Review; Prairie Schooner; Poem; Poetry; Ladies Home Jrnl.; N.Y. Times; var. anthols. & textbooks; Borestone Mountain Poetry Awards. Honours, awards: 1st prize, Jacksonville Coun. of the Arts, 1963; Conrad Aiken Award, 1960; 1st pl., Int. Sonnet Comp., Poetry Socs. of G.B. & Am., 1957; 2nd pl., annual award, Poetry Soc. of Am., 1970, etc. Address: 40 N.E. 69th St., Miami, FL 33138, U.S.A.

KAKUGAWA, Frances H., b. 22 Feb. 1936. Teacher; Curriculum Developer. Education: B.Educ., Univ. of Hawaii. Positions held: Teacher; Curriculum Developer for Literature Prog. for the State of Hawaii public schools. Published works: Sand Grains, 1970; White Ginger Blossom, 1971; Golden Spike, 1973. Contbr. to Mele publication: Haiku verses in Japanese & English. Address: 2649 Varsity Pl., Apt. 208, Honolulu, HI 96814, U.S.A.

KALICHMAN, Claire, pen name **CALLIAN, Selma,** b. 17 Mar. 1944. Painter. Education: Sorbonne, Paris; KoNiNkLi jk Lyceum, Gent, 1965. Memberships: Association des Ecrivains Belges de Langue Française; Arts, Sciences et Lettres de Paris. Published works: L'Arpège Chimérique, 1967. Recip., Silver Medal, Arts, Sciences et Lettres, 1970. Address: 24 Rozemarijnstraat, 9000 Gent, Belgium.

KALLMAN, Chester Simon, b. 7 Jan. 1921. Writer & Translator. Education: B.A., Brooklyn Coll., Univ. of Mich., U.S.A. Published works: (poetry) Storm at Castel Franco, 1956; Absent & Present, 1963; The Sense of Occasion, 1971. Honours, awards: Grant, Am. Acad. of Arts & Letters, 1953; Grant, Ingrim Merrill Fndn., 1964. Address: 3062 Kirchstetten, b. St. Pölten, N.O., Austria.

KALT, Jeannette, pen name **CHAPPELL, Jeannette,** b. 6 Apr. 1897. Author & Speaker. Married to William MacKenzie Kalt. Memberships: Chmn., Writers Sect., Pen & Brush, 1954; Frequently Co-chmn., Poetry Sect., ibid; Pres., Women Poets of NY, 1964-66; Poetry Soc. of Am.; Craftsman Grp.; Patron-Fndr., Acad. of Am. Poets; Poetry Soc. of Pa., Avalon; Reader of Prize Poems for the Women Poets of NY, 1972; Judge of Poetry Soc. of America James Joyce Award, 1973. Author of Destination Uncharted, 1963. Contbr. to: Anthol. of Marine Poems, 1956; The Golden Year (Poetry Soc. of Am.), 1960; The Golden Quill Anthol., 1956, '58, '66, '67, '68; Saturday Review; Quicksilver; Step Ladder; Voices; Am. Weave; C.S. Monitor; Westminster Mag.; Pegasus; Portland Oregonian; The Lyric; Am. Poetry Mag.; Variegation; Caravan; Fiddlehead; Caravel; Kaleidograph; NM Mag.; NY Herald Tribune; New Athenaeum; Cyclo-Flame; New Frontiers; Breakthrou; The Green World; Am. Haiku; Laurel Review; Hoosier Challenger; Seydell Quarterly; Golden Circle; South & West; Haiku Highlights; Imprints; Voices Int.; Swordsman Review; Haiku West; Tulsa Quarterly; Hartford Courant; Scimitar & Song; The Muse, etc. Address: 160 E. 72nd St., New York, NY 10021, USA.

KALTOVICH, Edith Lucia Rusconi, b. 13 Dec. 1925. Professor; Writer; Translator. Education: Univ. Nacional de Cordoba, Argentina; M.A., Mount Holyoke Coll., Mass., USA; Trenton State Coll.; NY Univ. Married, Samuel Kaltovich, schl. prin., 2 d. Positions held: Engl. Tchr., De Maria Coll., 1948-54; Engl. Tchr., Inst. de Intercambio Cultural Argentino

Norteamericano IICANA, US Info. Serv., 1950-54; Lang. Asst., Mt. Holyoke Coll., 1954-56; Asst. Inst., Duke Univ., 1955; Chmn., Spanish Dept., Westover Schl., 1956-58; Substitute Tchr., Florence Twp. & Burlington City Schls., 1958-67; Agt. Lit. & Art from Argentina & US, 1967-71; Instr., Spanish & Engl., Bordentown Mil. Inst., 1968-71; Tchr., Florence Mem. HS, Adult Schl., 1969-73; Bilingual Tchr., Ulysses S. Wiggins Schl., Camden, N.J., 1971-72, Carrol Robbins Schl., Trenton, 1972-74. Memberships include: NJ Poetry Soc.; Chmn., Lit. Grp., AAUW; Fed. of Univ. Women; Int. Platform Assn.; Mod. Poetry in Translation Ltd.; Soc. of Children's Book Writers; Democratic Club, Florence Twp.; Sociedad Argentina de Escritores, Cordoba; Sec. Mt. Holyoke Club; Circulation Mgr., Burlington Co. Art Guild; For. Lang. Tchr. Assn., NJ; PTA; Am. Poet Fellowship Soc. Published works include: Poems in Anthologies. New Sight, 1970; Fatso the Ghost (childrens poem), 1970; Someone a Little Strange, 1970; Deep Earth, 1970; Love makes Us Perfect, 1971; The Price of a Kiss, 1971; New & Better World of Poetry, 1971; A Glimpse at Edward Hopper, 1972; A Reminesance of Claude Monet, 1973; Mary Cassatt, An Angle of Reflection, 1973. Contributor to following magazines & newspapers: La Voz del Interior; El Gráfico; Burlington County Times, Trenton Times; Am. Voice; Poetry Soc. Intercontinental; Am. Poet; United Poets; Prairie Poet; Bouquets of Poems; Cardinal; Lincoln Log. Honours, Awards: A Majolica Ware, Burlington City Rotary Club, 1969; Named to Bd. of Educ. for Confraternity of Christian Doctrine by Bishop George Ahr, 1969; Gift of poetry books, Am. Poetry Fellowship Soc., 1970; Cert. of Merit, Accademia Leonardo Da Vinci, Rome, 1972; 2 Fellowships, 1973. Address: 129 Kinsmans Rd., Florence, NJ 08518, USA.

KALUGIN, David, b. 8 Mar. 1914. Postal Employee; Author; Poet. Positions held: US Army, 1943-46; Internat. Rep., Retail Wholesale Dept. Store Union, AFL-CIO, 1947-49; Pvte. Sec. to Pres., ibid, 1948; Labour Rep., 1949; Grocery Clerk, 1951-56; with NYC Post Office, 1957–. Memberships: Poetry Soc. of Am.; Internat. Platform Assoc.; Am. Legion; Assoc. of Jewish Postal Workers; Avalon Poetry Soc. Edit. Cons., Food Speciality Mag., 1966–. Publications: Tomorrow is So Far From Now, 1952; Naturally, 1953; For The Loneliest of Reasons, 1955; The Leaves Still Talk, 1959; The Tintinnabulations of Boos & Applause, 1964. Poetry & writing has been trans. into Japanese, Greek, Italian & German, & publd. in Australia, India, Canada & UK. Contbr. to: St. Louis Post-Dispatch; Aachener Nachrichten; Hamburger Echo; The Indian PEN; The Aryan Path; The Capitol Times; Poetry Pub. Letter; 21st Century; Colo. Quarterly; Cinzia; Die Kultur; Morning Star; The Cresset; Olivant; Epos; Flame; Trace; Am. Weave; Exile; Parnassus; Driftwind; Scimitar & Song; Russian Daily Morning News; Linden News; Approach; Creative Review; Candor; Avalon Anthol.; Cyclotron; Inferno; Quicksilver; Coercion Review; Kast (Japan); Wormwood Review; Neo; New Poetry Pamphlets; The Poet (Scotland); etc. Honours: mss. collected in David Kalugin Ms. Collection, Syracuse Univ., NY; Commendations in Armed Forces; some 350 US Post Office Citations & awards; 7th Consecutive year, Outstanding Suggestor, NYC PO. Address: 36-19 Bowne St., Flushing, NY 11354, USA.

KAMALA DAS, Madhavi Kutty, pen name **KUTTY, Madhavi,** b. 31 Mar. 1934. Writer. Positions held: Past Poetry Ed., Illustrated Weekly of India. Member, PEN. Published works: Summer in Calcutta (poems), 1965; Descendants (poems), 1968; The Old Playhouse (poems), 1973. Contbr. to: Poetry India; The Illustrated Weekly of India; Quest; Opinion; The Times of India; Caravan. Recip., The PEN's Asian Poetry Prize in 1963 (Manila). Address: Bank House, Backbay Reclamation, Bombay 20, India.

KAMALAKANTO, Mukherjee, pen name **KAMALAKANTO,** b. 14 Oct. 1913. Education: Calcutta Univ., India. Positions held: Tchr. of Sanskrit, English & History; Prof. of Engl.; Factory Exec. Memberships:

Hon. Mbr., W.P.S.I., 1969; Life Hon. Mbr., United Poets Laureate Int., 1970–. Contbr. to: The Poet; The Beacon Light; The New Times Observer; The Bombay Circle; The Mother India; The Laurel Leaves; IWWP Anthol. Title of 'Sacred Poet of India' conferred on him by U.P.L.I., 1970. Address: Shri Aurobindo Ashram, Pondicherry 2, 605002 India.

KANDEEL, Ahmad, b. 1913. Merchant. Education: Secondary Certificate. Published works: Twelve volumes of Arabic poetry. Contbr. to all publs. in the Western Province of Saudi Arabia. Recip., BBC Silver Cup, 1965. Address: P.O.B. 1267, Jidda, Saudi Arabia.

KANDEL, Lenore. Poet. Published works: A Passing Dragon – A Passing Dragon Seen Again – The Exquisite Navel, 1959; The Love Book, 1966; World Alchemy, 1968. Contbr. to (Anthols.): Best Poems of 1962: The Borestone Mountain Poetry Awards, 1963; Beatitude Anthology, 1965; Beat Anthologie, 1965; Evergreen Review Reader, 1968; (Jrnls.): Evergreen Review & many others. Address: c/o Donald Allen, 1815 Jones St., San Francisco, CA, 94109, USA.

KANE, Douglas V., b. 18 May 1903. Travel Consultant. Education: B.S., Coll. of the City of N.Y., 1923; grad. study at var. univs. Positions held: Sec., Portuguese Consulate Gen., San Francisco, Calif.; In Passenger Dept., Southern Pacific Co., San. Francisco & N.Y.C.; in Travel Dept., Am. Express Co., N.Y.C.; ret'd, but acting as Travel Cons. for Am. Express. Member, Poetry Soc. of Am. Published works: Heart's Wine, 1942; Westering, 1959; Dreaming of Seasons, 1971. Contbr. to: America; The Catholic World; The Lyric; N.Y. American; N.Y. Sun; N.Y. Times; Am. Poetry Jrnl.; Poetry Chap-Book; Saturday Review; Tudor City View; Kaleidograph; Westward; Wings; Voices; Simbolica; Portland Oregonian. Reading of his poetry recorded by American Airlines for 'Fun in Flight Program'. Address: Apt. 111, 905 West End Ave., N.Y., NY 10025, U.S.A.

KANGRO, Bernard, b. 18 Sept. 1910. Writer; Editor. Education: Mag. phil. in Lit., Univ. of Tartu, Estonia, 1938. Married Maria Wellner, 2 children. Positions held: Rsch. Fellow, Asst. & Lectr., Univ. of Tartu, Estonia, 1938-44; Lit. Adviser to the Vanemuine Theatre in Tartu, 1943-44; Dir. of the Estonian Writers' Cooperative, 1951–; Ed. & Publisher, Lit. periodical 'Tulimuld'. Memberships: PEN Club; Suomalaisen Kirjallisuuden Seura (Finland); Eesti Teaduslik Selts Rootsis (Sweden); Sveriges Författarförbund (Sweden). Published works: Sonetid, 1935; Vanad majad, 1937; Reheahi, 1939; Pőlenud puu, 1945; Pühapäev, 1946; Seitsmes öö, 1947; Tulease, 1949; Veebruar, 1951; Eikellegi maa, 1952; Suvihari, 1955; September, 1964; Varjumaa, 1966; Puud kőnnivad Kaugemale, 1969; Allikad silla juures, 1972; Ajatu mälestus, 1960; Vööramaa öhtu, 1967; Minu nägu, 1970; Earthbound, 1951; Flucht und Bleibe, 1954; Liekehtivä jälki, 1956. Contbr. to: Looming (Estonia); Vaba kodu (Germany); Tulimuld (Sweden); Vaba Eesti Sőna (USA); Estonian Daily (Sweden), etc. Honours, awards: H. Visnapuu Fund, 1964; REE Fund, 1967; EWC Fund, 1971. Address: Skördevägen 1, S-222 38 Lund, Sweden.

KANNADHASAN, b. 24 June 1927. Poet & Cine Lyricist. Education: Madras Univ., India. Positions held: Ed., Kannadhasan – devoted to poetry in Tamil & arts. Member, World Poetry Soc. Intercontinental. Writer of 4,000 lyrics, used in all Tamil films & sung by Tamils all over the world. Published works: Meaningful Hinduism; Pushpamalika, transl. into English. Contbr. to: Poet; Kadir; Ananda Vikatan; Dinamani, etc. Honours, awards: Nat. Integration Award from Pres. of India; Declared Poet Laureate of Tamil Nadu by W.P.S.I. Address: 16, Hensman Rd., T. Nagar, Madras 17, India.

KANTARIZIS, Sylvia, b. 9 Jan. 1936. Surrealist. Education: B.A., Cert.Ed., Bristol Univ., U.K.; M.A. & Ph.D., Univ. of Queensland, Australia. Married, 2 children. Positions held: Tchr. in Bristol, then London,

1958-62; Tutor in French, Univ. of Queensland, 1963-66; Post Grad. student, Univ. of Queensland, 1966-71; Surrealist, Contbr. to: The Australian; Poetry Mag. (Australia); New Poetry (Australia); Australian Letters; Southerly; Overland (Australia); Poetry Australia; Orbis; Ostrich (U.K.); Poet (India). Rep. in the following anthols: Australian Poetry Now, 1970; Laugh or Cry or Yawn, 1970. Jt. winner, Poetry Mag. Award, Australia, 1969 & Hon. Mention, 1970. Address: 14 Osborne Parc, Helston, Cornwall, U.K.

KAPLAN, Bernard Lawrence, b. 18 May 1944. Writer. Education: B.A., Antioch Coll., 1966; M.A., Yale Univ., 1970; M.F.A., Univ. of Iowa, 1970. Married 1) Claire Savit Bacha, 2) Jayne Hileman. Positions held: Fac. Mbr., Goddard Coll., Plainfield, Vt., 1971. Member, Authors Guild of Am. Published works: Prisoners of This World, 1970. Contbr. to: The Falcon; Ariel's Dolphin; Fiction International; currently Poetry Ed. of Fiction Int., N.Y. Address: 8 Reading Terr., Fair Lawn, NJ 07410, U.S.A.

KAPLAN, Milton, b. 6 Mar. 1910. University Professor. Education: B.S.S., Coll. of City of NY; M.A., Columbia Univ.; Ph.D., ibid. Positions held: English Tchr., Sec. Schls., NYC; Chmn., Dept. of English, George Washington High Schl.; Prof. of English, Tchrs. Coll., Columbia Univ. Memberships: Exec. Comm. Poetry Soc. of Am.; Modern Language Assoc.; Nat. Council of Tchrs. of English. Published works: Radio & Poetry, 1949; Co-ed., The World of Poetry, 1965; In a Time Between Wars, 1973. Contbr. to: New Yorker; Harper's Bazaar; Saturday Review; Commentary; Mag. of Verse; Am. Mercury; Partisan Review; Accent; Nation; New Republic; NY Times; Christian Sci. Monitor; Lyric; Prairie Schooner; Providence Jrnl.; Chicago Tribune Sunday Mag.; Saturday Evening Post. Address: 554 Summit Ave., Oradell, N.J., USA.

KARAN SINGH, Tiger, b. 9 Mar. 1931. Public Servant (Central Cabinet Minister). Education: M.A., & Ph.D., Delhi Univ., India. Married Yasho Rajya Lakshmi, 2 sons, 1 daughter. Positions held: Appointed Regent of Jammu & Kashmir, 1949; elected Sadar-i-Riyasat (Head of State) by Jammu & Kashmir Legislative Assembly, 1952; re-elected 1957 & 62; Gov., 1965-67; Union Min. for Tourism & Civil Aviation, 1967–; Past Chancellor, Banaras Hindu Univ. & Jammu & Kashmir Univ.; Portfolio of Hlth. & Family Planning, 1973; Sec., Jawaharlal Nehru Meml. Fund; Past Chmn., Ctrl. Sanskrit Bd.; Past Convenor, Nat. Comm. for the Sri Aurobindo Centenary; Chmn., Indian Bd. for Wild Life & Proj. Tiger; Hon. Major-Gen., Indian Army & Hon. Col. of its Jammu & Kashmir Regt. Memberships: Chmn., Selection Bd., Bharatiya Jnanpith, New Delhi; V.P., Nehru Meml. Mus. & Lib. Soc.; Sabhapati of Ramcharit Manas Chatuhshati Rashtriya Samiti; Pres., Dogra-Himachal Sanskriti Sangam; Life Trustee, India Int. Ctr., New Delhi, etc. Published works: Varied Rhythms, 1960; Shadow & Sunlight; Welcome the Moonrise; Prerana ke Morpankh (Hindi); 1970. Devotional songs in Sanskrit & Dogri broadcast by AIR. LP records of readings from Sri Aurobindo. Address: 3 Nyaya Marg, Chanakyapuri, New Delhi 110021, India.

KARIGER, Jean-Jacques, b. 3 Oct. 1925. Civil Servant; Writer. Married, 1 daughter. Positions held: Inspector of Financial Administration. Member, semi-literary, British-Luxembourg Soc. Active as a contbr. (introductions, lectures) to the Thomas Mann Bibliothek in Luxembourg City. Also occasional lectures for socs. (generally cultural). Published works: (Poetry w. special interest in natural sciences – in German) Leuchtender Kreis, 1962; Elemente, 1967; Akte, 1972. Contbr. to Luxembourg & German newspapers & reviews. Honours, awards: Subsidy by the Min. for Cultural Affairs, 1972 (for Akte). Address: 35a Nicholas Ries St., Luxembourg City, Grand Duchy of Luxembourg.

KARIUKI, Josiah Mwangi, b. 1931. College Principal. Education: Makerer Coll., Uganda; King's Coll., Cambridge. Positions held: Tchr., sev. yrs., Kangaru

Schl., Kenya; Currently, Principal, Inst. of Public Admin., Kenya. Published works: Mau Mau Detainee (non-fiction), 1964. Contbr. to (Anthols.): Modern Poetry from Africa, 1963; African Writing Today, 1967.

KARLEN, Arno, b. 7 May 1937. Writer & Editor. Education: B.A., Antioch Coll. Married, 2 children. Positions held: Articles Ed., Holiday Mag.; Assoc. Ed., Newsweek Mag.; Assoc. Prof. of Engl., Pa. State Univ.; Exec. Ed., Physicians World Mag. Member, Authors Guild. Contbr. to: Harpers; Saturday Review; Antioch Review; Northwest Review; Poetry Northwest; Jrnl. of General Education; Assembling, No. 1 & 3; Forum, Univ. of Tex.; Salmagundi. Address: 350 Bleecker St., N.Y., NY 10014, U.S.A.

KARLSTEDT, Karin Marie, pen name **SAARSEN, Karin,** b. 31 Dec. 1926. Teacher; Reporter; Publicist. Education: French Lyceum at Tallinn, Estonia, 1935-44; London Schl. of Jrnlsm., 1947-48; M.A., Univ. of Stockholm. Positions held: News Corres., Reuters News Agency, Stockholm Office, 1951-56; News Ed., Swedish Int. Press Bureau, 1962-63; Exec. Sec., Nobel Fndn., 1967-68; Pub. Rels. Ed. in Scandinavia, Unifrance Film, 1968-69; Schls. Admin., County of Stockholm, 1964-67 & '70–. Memberships: Int. PEN, London, 1966; The Estonian PEN, Stockholm, 1969; P.R. Sec., Assn. of Free Estonian Writers, Stockholm, 1967. Published works: The Conquerors (short stories in Estonian), 1967; (poetry booklets) Lizard on the Rock, 1961; On the Swaying Bridge, 1964; About a Happy Unhappy Love, (in Estonian), 1968; Lohengrin's Farewell (in Estonian), 1972. Contbr. to lit. mags. in W. Germany, Sweden, U.K., U.S.A. Recip., Prize for the best 'War poem' by Estonian Comm. in Flensburg, W. Germany, 1947. Address: Skyllbergsgatan 9, 5 tr, 124 45 Bandhagen, Sweden.

KASH, Marsha Elaine (Katzman), pen name, **ELAINE, Marsha,** b. 13 Nov. 1942. Executive/Administrative Secretary & Statistician. Education: HS grad. Married; 2 d.; divorced. Positions held: Reporter, county newspaper; Ad-copywriter, public service director, St. Louis radio station; Admin. Sec. to Director of Public Relations, Barnes Hospital, St. Louis; Statistician, Sec., etc. for an olive, pickle, cherry company. Memberships: Writers Guild of St. Louis; Life Seekers (publicity chairman, telephone chairman, writer on newspaper). Contbr. to: St. Louis Post Dispatch; St. Louis Jewish Light; Orphic Lute; The Piggott Banner; Voices Internat.; Reach Out; Modern Images; Second Coming; Jean's Journal; All Time Favorite Poetry; Special Song; New Dawn Publications; Creative Moment; Lake Superior Review; Grande Ronde Review; New Orlando Publications; Telephone; Shameless Hussy; The Gar; Gone Soft; Spafaswap; Apostrophe; Egg and One, etc. Award: Major Poets Book Award, Ecology Contest (July, 1973). Address: 1036 Rue La Chelle Walk, St. Louis, MO 63141, USA.

KASSAM, Yusuf O., b. 1943. Poet. Education: Grad., History & Engl., Makerere Univ. Coll., Kampala, Uganda. Contbr. to (Anthols.): Young Commonwealth Poets '65, 1965; New Voices of the Commonwealth, 1968; (jrnls.): Transition.

KASTE, Olav, b. 8 Oct. 1902. Teacher. Positions held: Tchr., Nordbygda Elementary Schl., Notodden. Memberships: The Norwegian Authorunion; The Artistunion. Published works: Let fade the Flowers, 1946; In the Shadow of Tearmount, 1955; And it Was Evening, 1950; In Morningdawn, 1958; And it was Morning, 1965; Ornament I, 1966; Ornament II, 1968. Contbr. to: Teledölen; Telen; Varden; Norsk Tidend; Dagbladet. Honours, awards: Artist Prize of the State, 1953, 56, 61, 65, 66 & 67; Prize of the Norwegian Authorunion, 1958; Prize of Nordahl Griegs Memory, 1964; The Norwegian Publisherunion, 1972; Norwegian Author & Translaterfond, 1972. Address: 3696 Orvella, Norway.

KASTEL, Daisylea Carl, pen name **KASTEL, Dee,** b. 30 Aug. 1919. Retired Vice-President, St. Michaels Marina, Inc. Married, Frederick Kastel. Education:

High School; Hood College; Creative Writing Course in Acad. of Arts, Easton, Md. Positions held: Vice-President, Anne Arundel Apts., Ten Oaks Manor; also St. Michaels Marina, Inc. Memberships: The Poet Laureate's Committee of One Hundred of Maryland; Bd. of Trustees, Enlightenment and Culture of the State of Md. Pubs. The Leprechaun in the Lighthouse, 1971; The Teardrop Fairy. Contrib. of poems to anthologies; In 1973 one of poems set to music for large-scale U.S. broadcasting. Contrib. also to: The Star Democrat, Easton, Md., Annapolis News; Balt. Sun; The Rainbow, etc. Recipient of numerous awards and honours, including: Emily Dickenson Award; Francis Scoot Key Award, etc. Address: Mt. Pleasant, St. Michaels, Md. 21663, USA.

KASTI, Abdulghani Mohammad, b. 1927. Newspaper Editor. Education: Higher Certificate from the Al-Sooltiya Schl., Mecca. Positions held: Asst. Dir., Accounts Dept., Municipality of Mecca; Ed., 'Al-Bilad' newspaper, Jidda. Published works: 'Ahzaan Qald' (volume of poetry). Address: Al-Bilad Corporation for Journalism & Publishing, Jidda, Saudi Arabia.

KATRAK, Kersy Dady, b. 8 Jan. 1936. Advertising Executive. Positions held: Dir., London Press Exchange; Mng. Dir., Mass Communications & Marketing Pvt. Ltd. Publications: A Journal of the Way, 1969; Diversions By The Wayside, 1969. Contbr. to: (anthols.) Poems From India; Young Commonwealth Poets, 1965; (jrnls.) Illustrated Weekly of India (Bombay); Opinion; Quest; Poetry India. Address: Bakhtawar, 9th Floor, opposite Colaba PO Bombay 5, India.

KATZ, Jonathan, b. 6 Dec. 1944. Arts Administrator; Teacher. Education: B.A., Brooklyn Coll., City Univ. of N.Y.; M.A., Purdue Univ.; A.B.D., Kent State Univ. Positions held: Tchng. Asst., Purdue Univ., 1965-67; Tchng. Fellowship, Kent State Univ., 1967-70; Asst. Prof. of Engl., Wichita State Univ., 1970-72; Community Dev. Co-ordinator, Kans. Arts Commn., 1972-73; Exec. Dir., ibid, 1973–. Memberships: COSMEP; CCLM; MLA. Editor (w. Arthur Vogelsang & A.G. Sobin) The Ark River Review, 1971–. Contbr. to: North Am. Review; The N.Y. Qtly.; The Midwest Qtly.; The Little Mag.; The Kan. Qtly.; The Wis. Review; Poetry Venture, etc. Honours, awards: Chosen to be Poet-in-Res. in 3 communities in Kansas in 1972 & '73 as part of the Poetry-in-the-Schools proj., co-sponsored by the Nat. Endowment for the Arts & the U.S. Office of Educ. Address: 348 North Ohio, Wichita, KS 67214, U.S.A.

KATZ, Menke, b. 12 April 1906, Lithuania. Poet; Teacher; Lecturer on Poetry, etc. Education: Columbia Univ.; Brooklyn Coll.; Univ. of Southern Calif. Married to Ruth (Rivke) Feldman; 1 s., 1 d. Positions held: Editor-in-Chief, Bitterrot, since 1962; previously Editor of "Mir" (Yiddish mag.) Memberships: Poetry Soc. of America; World Poetry Soc.; United Poets Laureate International. Published works (books of poetry in Yiddish): Three Sisters, 1932; Dawning Man, 1935; Burning Village, vol. 1 and 2, 1938; My Grandma Myrna, 1939; To Happier Days, 1941; The Simple Dream, 1947; Midday, 1954; (books of poetry in English) Land of Manna, 1965; Rockrose, 1969; Burning Village, 1972. Contbr. to: Atlantic Monthly; NY Times; Herald Tribune; Prairie Schooner; Epos; The Smith; Midwest Qtly.; Commentary; Poet & Critic; Poet (India); Thought (India); Poet Lore; Fiddlehead; Jewish Spectator; Chicago Jewish Forum; South & West; Manifold; Canadian Poetry; Bitterroot; NY Times Book of Verse, and many other anthols., numerous translations and forewords, etc. (in more than 50 languages). Honours: Pulitzer Prize Nominee, 1965, 1969, 1972; Stephen Vincent Benet Award, 1st Prize, 1969; Poet Lore Narrative Award, 1st Prize, 1967; Poet Lore, Descriptive Poem, 1st Prize, 1972. Address: Box 51, Blythebourne Station, Brooklyn, NY 11219, USA.

KATZMAN, Allen, b. 27 Apr. 1937. Author; Poet; Journalist. Education: B.A., Philos., City Coll. of N.Y.,

1958. Positions held: Fndr., Publsr., Ed., East Village Other (newspaper), 1965-72; Admnstr., 112 Greene Street Gallery, 1972-73; Adjunct Prof. of Media & Creative Writing, Jersey City State Coll., 1973–. Member, Poets & Writers. Published works: Poems from Oklahoma, 1962; The Bloodletting, 1963; The Comanche Cantos, 1964; The Immaculate, 1970. Contbr. to: The Nation; Yale Lit. Mag.; East Village Other; Straight Creek Jrnl.; Theo; Penumbra; Some; El Corno Emplumado; Center Mag.; The N.Y. Qtly., etc. Address: 112 Greene St., N.Y., NY 10012, U.S.A.

KAUFMAN, Bob Garnell, pen names, **KAUFMAN, Bob; BOMKAUF,** b. 18 April 1925. Poet. Personal details: born in New Orleans, Louisiana, USA, son of Martinique negress and German (Jewish) father; Creole background; father and 2 best friends drowned in Bayou; at age of 13 ran off to sea as cabin boy. Positions held: (to 1954) Cabin Boy, Merchant Seaman, Merchant Marine, USA, travelled world 9 times; caterer; and now poet. Published works: Second April, 1959; Abomunist Manifesto, 1959; Solitudes Crowded with Lonliness, 1964; The Golden Sardine, 1965; Does the Sect Mind Whisper, 1960; Bastard Angel, 1972; (anthols.): Points of Light, 1971; Understanding the New Black Poetry, 1972; Visions of America, 1973; New Black Voices, 1972; Making It New, 1973; Mark In Time, 1971; New Directions no. 17, 1961. Contbr. to many other publications, including: The Real Bohemians; City In All Directions; The Voice That is Great Within Us; New Black Poetry; Black American; Poetry of Black America. Honours, Awards: Contender for Guiness Poetry Award, UK, 1961 (included in their publication, Springtime Three); Ihr-long Nat. (US) TV show, "Coming From Bob Kaufman, Poet" produced on Education TV (NET) NYC., 1972, A Tribute to Bob Kaufman. Address: 102 Mono Ave., Fairfax, CA 94930, USA.

KAUFMAN, Shirley, b. 5 June 1923. Poet. Education: B.A., Univ. of Calif. at Los Angeles, 1944; M.A., State Univ. of Calif. at San Francisco, 1967. Married H.M. Daleski, 3 daughters. Positions held: Vis. Lectr., Univ. of Mass., Spring 1974. Member, Poetry Soc. of Am. Published works: The Floor Keeps Turning, 1970; Gold Country, 1973; A Canopy in the Desert, transl. from the Hebrew of the poems of Israeli poet Abba Kovner, 1973. Contbr. to: Am. Poetry Review; Arts in Society; The Atlantic Monthly; Chicago Tribune Mag.; Choice; European Judaism; Field; Harper's; The Iowa Review; Kayak; Mass. Review; The Nation; The New Yorker, etc. Honours, awards: 1st prize at San Francisco State Coll., Acad. of Am. Poets, 1964; U.S. Award of the Int. Poetry Forum, 1969; Assn. of Am. Univ. Presses Award for the Nat. Coun. on the Arts Selection in poetry, 1970. Address: 18 Neve Sha'anan St. Apt. 22, Jerusalem, Israel.

KAUFMANN, Walter, b. 1 Jul. 1921. Professor of Philosophy. Education: Grunewald Gymnasium, Berlin, Abitur 1938; Williams Coll., Mass., USA., B.A., 1941; Harvard Univ., M.A., 1942, Ph.D., 1947. Positions held: Dept. of Philosophy, Princeton Univ. since 1947, Prof. of Philosophy since 1962. Many visiting professorships, incl. Fulbright professorships at Heidelberg, 1955-56, and Jerusalem, 1962-63. Pubs. Cain and other poems, 1962 (enlarged ed. 1971); Goethe's Faust: a new (verse) trans., 1961; Twenty German Poets: Bilingual Edition, 1962; Nietzsche's The Gay Science, with a prelude in rhymes and an appendix of songs, trans., with commentary, 1974. Also author of sev. vols. of criticism and philosophy. Address: Dept. of Philosophy, Princeton Univ., Princeton, N.J. 08540, USA.

KAUKOVALTA, Kai-Kyösti Olavi, b. 25 Oct. 1950. Writer. Education: studies in cultural history at Abo Akademi, Swedish Univ. of Finland. Positions held: Vocalist for Jazz Band; Dramaturgist; Actor; Lectr. on Literature; Book Reviewer; Translator; Disc Jockey; Playwright. Memberships: Suomen näytelmäkirjailijoiden liitto (Finnish Playwrights' Assn.) V. Chmn., Luonais-Suomen kirjailijat (Southwestern

Finland's Writers' Soc.) Published works: Attentaatti (book of poetry), 1972; Maa tahrattu on 1973 (a play); Vapaan maailman laitamilla (a play), 1973; Huuto Ihmisestä (a play), 1971; Reunalla taivaan ja maan (a play), 1972; var. jazz & rock 'n roll songs. Contbr. to: The Middle Eye; Real Free Press; Los Angeles Free Press; var. Finnish publs. Honours, awards: Grants from the Finnish Min. of Educ.; some first prizes in Finnish young writers contests; Lit. Award, City of Tampere, Finland, April 1973. Address: Puolalanpuisto 3 as. 5, SF-20100 Turku 10, Finland.

KAUR, Prabhjot, b. July 1927. Poet. B.A., Khalsa Coll., Punjab Univ. Positions held: Assoc. Ed., Rajasthan Chronicle, Vice-Pres., Kendri Lekhak Sabha (Central Writers' Org.); Nat. Commn. for UNESCO; Editor, Vikendrit (Punjabi); Jt. Editor, Byword (English). Rajua Kavi (Poet Laureate), 1964–; Legislator, 1967–. Memberships: Int. PEN; Convenor, Delhi Br., Indian PEN; Soc. des Gens de Lettres, Paris; Soc. of French Poets; Pres., Punjabi Sahit Sabha (Punjab Literacy Soc.); Vice Pres., Kendri Lekhak Sabha; United Poets Laureate Int. Published works: Lat Lal Jot Jage, 1943; Palkan Ohle, 1945; Kuj Hore, 1945; Azal Ton, 1946; Kafle (operetta), 1947; Supne Sadhran, 1949; Chonvi Kavita, 1949; Do Rang, 1951; Pankheru, 1956; Shah Rah, 1957; Lala (Translation in Persian), 1958; Ban Kapasi, 1958; Ban Kapasi (in Urdu), 1958; Pahbi, 1962; Plateau (in English), 1966; Khari, 1967; Plateau (French), 1968; Vad-darshi Sheesha, 1973. Contbr. to: Indian Lit.; Thought; PEN Jrnl.; Indian Express; Arsee; Preetlate; Pritam Panj Darya; Punjabi Sahit; Jan Sahit; Kavita; Pagdandi; Nawan Sahit; Surtal; Hem Jyoti; Savera, London; Des Pardes; Fateh Weekly; Kundan Weekly; Ranjit Weekly; Kiena Weekly; Punjab Weekly; Sikh Review; Sportsman Weekly; Nat. Solidarity Weekly; Dharamyug; Femina. Honours: Sahitya Shiromani (Doyen of Lit.), 1964; Sahitya Akademi Award (Nat. Acad. Award), 1964-65; Rajya Kavi (Poet Laureate), Punjab, 1964–; Nominated to Punjab Legislative Council for contribution to Lit., 1966; Padmashri (Nat. Honour Title), 1967; Hon. Indian Poet Laureate, UPLI; Grand Prix de la Rose des Poètes Francais, Paris, 1968. Address: G–52 Lajpat Nagar, New Delhi 110024, India.

KAVADLO, Edith S., b. 28 Dec. 1917. Educator. Education: B.A., Hunter Coll., City of N.Y., 1941; M.S. in Educ. & Profl. Dip., Lib. Educ., 1962; M.L.S., 1968. Married, 3 daughters. Positions held: Tchr. of Lib., Bayside H.S., Queens, N.Y., 1959-67; Tchr. of Lib., Benjamin N. Cardozo H.S., Bayside, Queens, 1967–. Member, Poetry Soc. of Am. Contbr. to: High Points (mag. of schls. in N.Y.C.); Brooklyn Coll. Observer. Recip., 2nd prize in Annual Poetry Contest, 1936. Address: 140-01 69th Ave., Flushing, NY 11367, U.S.A.

KAVANAGH, P(atrick) J(oseph Gregory), b. 1931. Poet; Lecturer; Broadcaster. Education: Lycée Jaccard, Lausanne; M.A., ·Merton Coll., Oxford. Positions held: Sometime Lectr., Univ. of Indonesia, Java. Published works: A Soul for Sale, 1947; Come Dance With Kitty Stobling, 1960; One & One, 1959; On the Way to the Depot, 1967; About Time, 1970; The Perfect Stranger (autobiog.), 1966; The Great Hunger, 1967; A Song & Dance (Novel), 1968. Honours, awards: Richard Hillary Mem. P ize, 1966; Guardian Fiction Prize, 1969. Address: London, UK.

KAY, Ernest, pen names **RANDOM, Alan & LUDLOW, George.** Publisher; Editor; Author. Positions held: Managing Editor, London Evening News, 1954-59; Editor & Publisher, John O'London's Literary Weekly, 1959-63; Managing Editor, Time & Tide Magazine, London, England, 1964-66; Publisher & Hon. General Editor, Dictionary of International Biography, 1967–, International Who's Who in Poetry, 1969–. Memberships: World Poetry Society Intercontinental; Poetry Society of America; Royal Society of Arts (Life Fellow), London; Arts Theatre Club, London; National Arts Club, New York City. Published works: (books): History of London Transport, 1947; Great Men of Yorkshire, 1956; Isles of Flowers: The Story of the Isles of Scilly, 1956; Pragmatic Premier: An Intimate Portrait of Harold Wilson, 1967; The Wit of Harold Wilson, 1967. Contbr. to newspapers and periodicals throughout the world. Honours, awards: Gold Medal & Karta of Award, United Poets Laureate International, 1966; Hon. Life Member, Accademia di Filologia Classica, Milan, Italy, 1968; Ethiopian Gold Medal, 1971; Nom. Nobel Peace Prize, 1973. Address: 11 Madingley Road, Cambridge, U.K.

KAY, George Robertson, b. 29 Aug. 1924. Lecturer in Italian. Education: Schl., Shangai & Scotland; Univ. of London; Univ. of Edinburgh. Married to Peggy Ann Taylor, 1 d., 1 s. Positions held: Reporter, Falkirk Herald; Pvte., then Capt., Intelligence Corps; Language Tchr., Milan & Rome; Univ. Lectr., Glasgow. Memberships: Poetry Soc., Edinburgh Univ. Published works include: Four Part Song, 1949 (Co-author); Chant of Exiles, 1953. Contbr. to the following anthols., jrnls., mags., etc: Botteghe Oscure; Lines, Edinburgh; Scottish Poetry I. Address: Sunnylaw House, 1 Upper Glen Rd., Bridge of Allan, Stirling, Scotland, UK.

KEANE, Ellsworth McGranahan, Pseudonym (Musician), **Shake Keane,** b. 30 May, 1927. Jazz Musician. Education: London Univ. Married twice w. 2 children. Positions Held: Tchr., English & History, St. Vincent Grammar Schl. (West Indies), 1948-52; Contbr. to & Prod., BBC Carribean I Service, 1952-59; Jazz Soloist, Edelhagen Orch., WDR & Featured Recording Artist (Flügel Horn) w. Decca Records, London, 1965–. Published works: L'Oubli, 1950; Ixion, 1952; (Non-fiction): West Indianism in Poetry, 1952; Nature Poetry in the West Indies: The Religious Aspect, 1953. Contbr. to (Anthols.): Young Commonwealth Poets '65, 1965; Carribean Voices, 1966; Carribean Verse, 1967; (Jrnls.): Bim; Kyk-over-Al. Address: 5 Köln, Brusselstrasse 30, German Fed. Repub.

KEARNS, Lionel John, b. 16 Feb. 1937. Poet. Education: Univ. of British Columbia; School of Oriental & African Studies, London Univ. Published works: Songs of Circumstance, 1963; Listen George, 1965; Pointing, 1967; By The Light Of The Silvery McLune, Media Parables, Poems, Signs, Gestures and Assaults on the Interface, 1969. Recip. Canada Council Arts Grant, 1973. Address: c/o The English Dept., Simon Fraser Univ., Burnaby, BC., Canada.

KEARNS, Marguerite, b. 11 Oct. 1903. Church Organist & Teacher. Education: Oberlin Conservatory of Music; Baldwin Wallace Conservatory of Music. Married Cecil M. Burnett, 1 son. Positions held: Organist, Brecksville Ch. of Christ, Brecksville United Meth. Ch. & Independence United Meth. Ch. Memberships: Pres., Cleveland Chapt. of Poetry Soc. of Am.; State Pres., Ohio Poetry Soc. (4 terms); Bulletin Ed., ibid; Active mbr., Cleveland Chapt., Composers, Authors & Artists of Am.; Active mbr. & Prog. Chmn., The Fortnightly Musical Club of Cleveland. Contbr. to: What Women Should Know About the Breast Cancer Controversy (by George Crile, Jr., M.D.), 1973; The Cleveland Plain Dealer; The Cleveland Press; The Hondu Anvil Herald (Tex.); Dallas Daily Times Herald; The Heights Jrnl.; Listen My Children, Anthol. of Poems for Children, 1940; The North Am. Book of Verse, 1939; The Poetry Digest, 1942; Anthol. of Ohio Verse, 1946; Poet of India, & many others. Recip. many honours, awards inclng: 1st prize for lyric, Poetry Soc. of Am. Contest, 1939; 1st prize for song lyric, Ohio Poetry Day Contest, 1958, & for lyric, 1957; 2nd prize for free verse poem, 1971. She has set her poems to music and they have been performed on Fortnightly Coll. Poetry, 1946 & Composers, Authors & Artists, 1971 progs. Address: 9550 Brecksville Rd., Box 1, Brecksville, OH 44141, U.S.A.

KEATS, Eleanor B., b. 6 Aug. 1930. Poet; Teacher of Singing. Education: B.A., Cornell Univ., 1951; Juilliard Schl. of Music, 1952-53; Hamburg Hochschule für Musik, 1954-56; grad. work in Mus., Univ. of Minn.,

1958; Ecole Normale de Musique, Voice, 1956; var. poetry & writing workshops. Married, 3 children. Positions held: Editl. Asst., 'Nucleonics Mag.', 1951; Ed., Nat. Acad. of Scis., 1953; Tech. Writer, David Sarnoff Rsch. Labs, RCA, 1956; Freelance Writer, Editor, 1957-59; Coordinator, German Students Prog., Antioch Coll., 1959; Voice Tchr., Antioch Coll., 1966-74. Member, Poetry Socs. of Am. & England. Contbr. to: The Antioch Review; Humanist; Paris Tribune; Sojourner; Cornell Review; Maine Tower Anthol.; Wheels; St. Andrew's Review. Has given many multi-media performances of poetry, slides, movies & music at var. instns., colls. & univs. Has read her poetry over the Pacific Northwest Poets' Series, Seattle, Wash. & on the TV Arts Prog. 'Videoscope'. Address: 4785 Meredith Rd., Yellow Springs, OH 45387, U.S.A.

KEEFE, Mildred Jones, b. 14 Aug. 1896. Retired Educator. Education: Piano & Voice, New England Conservatory of Music; B.A., Educ., Boston Univ., 1934; M.A., ibid, 1936; Syracuse Univ.; Cinn. Univ.; Conservatory of Music, Smith Coll., Mass. Positions held: Pianist, Tchr., Boston, 1917-26; Dir., Relig. Educ., Cinn. & Syracuse, 1926-32; Asst. Prof. and Music Director, Fine Arts in Relig., Boston Univ., 1935-40; Dir., Drama & Speech, St. Mary's Coll., Md., 1943-45; Dir., Drama & Fine Arts, Greenbrier Coll., W.Va., 1945-71. Memberships: Nat. League Am. Pen Women; W.Va. Poetry Soc.; Founder & Pres., Creative Arts Council, Unitarian Church, Fairhaven, Mass., 1973-. Published works: Choric Interludes, 1942; Books for Libraries, 1969; White Beauty, 1956; The Quest of Light; Ed. & Fndr., Creative Arts Festival Brochures, 1955-68. Contbr. to: The Pen Women; Educational Horizons; Speech Jrnl.; Program Books; Brochures, Greenbrier Valley Creative Arts Fest.; Bulletin of Unitarian Meml. Ch., Mass. Honours, awards: Cit., W.Va. Creative Arts Fest., 1959; Medal of Hon., Centro Studi e Scambi, Int., 1971; 1st, W.Va. Fed. of Women's Clubs, 1971; Medal, Int. Who's Who in Community Serv., 1972. Address: 10 Pearl St., Mattapoisett, MA 02739, U.S.A.

KEEHN, Norman R., b. 15 Feb. 1947. House Painter. Contbr. to: Echoes of Faith (anthol.); Year Book of Modern Poetry (anthol.); Cyclo Flame; Poetry Parade; Oyez; Encore; Bardic Echoes; Haiku Highlights; Gato Mag. Address: 219 Elgin St., Thunder Bay 'P', Ont., Canada.

KEELER, Clinton Clarence, b. 14 Nov. 1919. Teacher; Editor; Chairman, Dept. of Engl., Okla. State Univ. Education: Ph.D., Univ. of Minnesota. Positions held: Teacher, Johns Hopkins Univ.; Univ. of Minnesota; Okla. State Univ. Memberships: Modern Poetry Assoo.; World Poetry Soc. Contbr. to: (anthols.) Poets of the Midwest, 1966; Thai Poets, 1968; Premier Poets. (journals etc.) Poet; Poetry Northwest; Southwest Review; New, American & Canadian Poetry; Poetry Australia; Calamus; Southern Humanities Review; Solstice; Blackbird Circle; Illinois Qtrly.; Midwest Qtrly., etc. Address: 4 Preston Pl., Stillwater, OK 74074, USA.

KEELEY, Edmund (LeRoy), b. 5 Feb. 1928. Professor of English & Creative Arts. Education: B.A., Princeton, 1949; D.Phil., Oxford, 1952. Positions held: Instr. in Engl., Brown Univ., 1952-53; Fulbright Lecturer, Salonika Univ., 1953-54; Instr., Asst. Prof., Assoc. Prof., Prof. of Engl. and Creative Arts, Princeton Univ., 1954-. Memberships: Modern Greek Studies Assoc. (Pres.); Authors Guild; P.E.N.; Mod. Language Assoc.; Comparative Literature Assoc. Published works: Six Poets of Modern Greece, 1960; George Seferis: Collected Poems, 1924-1955; 1967, 1969; C.P. Cavafy: Passions and Ancient Days, 1971; C.P. Cavafy: Selected Poems, 1972; Odysseus Elytis: The Axion Esti, 1974; C.P. Cavafy: Collected Poems, 1974. Contbr. to: Encounter; Times Lit. Supp.; NY Review of Books; Qtly. Review of Literature; Poetry; Partisan Review; Antaues; Transatlantic Review; Virginia Qtly. Review; The Charioteer; Shenandoah; Prairie Schooner; Beloit Poetry Journal; The Dutton Review; The Evergreen Review; Boundary 2; New Yorker; New

Letters; Accent; Western Humanities Review; Chicago Review, etc. Awards: Guinness Poetry Award (selection), 1962; Rome Prize, Am. Acad. of Arts & Letters, 1959; Guggenheim Fellowship, 1960, 1973; Finalist for Nat. Book Award in Translation, 1972; New Jersey Authors Award, 1968, 1970. Address: 185 Nassau St., Princeton, NJ 08540, USA.

KEESING, Nancy Florence, pen name, **KEESING, Nancy,** b. 7 Sept 1923. Writer. Education: Dip. of Soc. Studies, Sydney Univ., Australia. Married, A.M. Hertzberg, 2 children. Positions held: Clerk, Dept. of Navy, 1941-44; Soc. Worker, Royal Alexandra Hosp. for Children, 1947-51; Free-lance Ed. & Writer. Memberships: VP English Assoc., NSW Br.; Mgmt. Comm., Australian Soc. of Authors; currently ed., Aust. Author, jrnl. of Aust. Soc. Authors; PEN; Literature Board, Australian Council for the Arts. Publications: Imminent Summer, 1951; Three Men & Sydney, 1955; Showground Sketchbook, 1968. Contbr. to: Sydney Morning Herald; Meanjin; Southerly; Bulletin; Bridge; Aust. Broadcasting Commn.; numerous Anthols., etc. Address: c/o The Australian Soc. of Authors, 6th Floor, 252 George St., Sydney 2000, Australia.

KEGELS, Anne-Marie Adrienne, b. 26 Feb. 1912. Memberships: Acad ̄— ,̂ Luxembourgeoise; Membre du Conseil d'administration, ibid; Sociétaire de la Société des Gens de Lettres de France. Published works: Douze poèmes pour une Année, 1950; Rien que Vivre, 1953; Chants de la sourde Jole, 1955; Haute Vigne, 1962; Les Doigts Verts, 1967; Chants de la Présence, 1968; Lumière Adverse, 1970; Les Chemins sont en Feu, 1973. Contbr. to: Synthèses; La Revue Générale Belge; Le Thyrse; La Flûte Enchantée; Le Dryade; Marginales; Le Haut Pays; Poésie Présente; Le Journal des Poètes. Honours, awards: Prix Renée Vivien, Paris, 1953; Prix Gérard de Nerval, Paris, 1955; Prix Félix Denayer, Brussels, 1962; Prix Edmond Picard, Brussels, 1963; Prix Charles Van Lerberghe, Paris, 1968; Chevalier de l'Ordre de Léopold II. Address: Rue Michel Hamelius 65, B. 6700 Arlon, Belgium.

KEIN, Ernst, b. 27 Nov. 1928. Author. Education: Univ. of Vienna. Writer of stories, novels, radioplays & poems. Published works: Kein Buch, 1967; Wiener Panoptikum, 1970; Wiener Grottenbahn, 1972. Contbr. to: Neue Wege; Publikationen; Alpha; Manuskripte; Wort and Wahrheit; Wort in der Zeit; Literatur und kritik; Poetarium; Protokolle; Konfigurationen; Kurier; Neues Oesterreich; Neue Zeit; Stadt Wien; Neutralitaet. Honours, awards: Oesterreichischer Staatspreis, 1958; Preis der Stadt Wien, 1971. Address: Gablenzgasse 33, A–1150 Vienna, Austria.

KEITHLEY, George, b. 18 Jul. 1935. Writer. Education: Arlington Hts. H.S., Ill.; B.A., Duke Univ., Durham, N.C.; M.F.A., Univ. of Iowa; Stanford Univ., Calif. Married to Mary Zoe Keithley, 3 children. Instr.-Teaching Asst., Univ. of Iowa, 1958-1962; Since 1962 on staff of Chico State Univ., Calif.: Prof. of Engl., since 1973, Assoc. Prof. 1969-; Asst. Prof., 1965-; Instr., 1962-. Member, Poetry Soc. of America; Former Pres., Philological Assoc. of Central Calif., 1967-68, vice-president, 1966-67, Sec.-Treas., 1965-66. Pub.: The Donner Party, 1972. Contrib. to: numerous journals and other publications. Co-winner, Alice Faye di Castagnola Award, Poetry Soc. of America, 1973; Wrangler Award, Western Heritage Center, Okla. City, 1972; Joseph Henry Jackson Award, 1970. Address: 1302 Sunset Ave., Chico, Calif. 95926, USA.

KELEN, Stephen Kenneth, b. 12 Feb. 1956. Student. Education: Sydney Univ. Has held var. positions. Contbr. to: Poetry Australia; The Bulletin. Honours, awards: B.H.P. Poetry Prize for Writers 16-19 yrs., 1972; Farmers Poetry Prize for Australians under 18, 1973; Two B.H.P. Poetry Awards for Writers 16-19, 1973. Address: 1 Sussex Rd., St. Ives, N.S.W., Australia 2075.

KELL, Richard Alexander, b. 1 Nov. 1927. Teacher. Ecuation: Meth. Coll., Belfast, U.K.; Wesley Coll., Dublin, Ireland; Univ. of Dublin. Married Muriel Nairn, 4 children. Positions held: Lectr. I, Isleworth Polytech., 1960; Lectr. II, ibid, 1966; Sr. Lectr., Newcastle upon Tyne Polytech., 1970. Memberships: Critical Qtly. Soc.; Brit. Soc. of Aesthetics. Published works: Fantasy Poets 35, 1957; Control Tower, 1962; Differences, 1969. Contbr. to: BBC; The Bell; The Dubliner; Envoy; Icarus; Irish Press; Irish Times; Irish Writing; Listen, Hull; The Listener; London Mag.; New Statesman; Observer; Outposts; Poetry Ireland; Poetry Northwest; Poetry Qtly.; Rann; Time & Tide; World Review; Stand; var. anthols. Critical articles in: The Critical Qtly.; The Critical Survey; The Brit. Jrnl. of Aesthetics; The Dublin Mag.; Essays in Criticism. Address: 18 Rectory Grove, Gosforth, Newcastle upon Tyne, Northumberland NE3 1AL, U.K.

KELLER, Edith Light, pen name **HOUSTON, Logan,** b. 9 Jan. 1893. Teacher; Poet. Education: B.A., Park Coll., Wyoming Univ., Arizona Univ. Positions held: Teacher of HS Engl. and History, Cozad, Nebraska; HS Teacher, Crown King, Ariz.; Principal, Elem. Schools, Cave Creek and Yarnel, Ariz. Memberships: Youngtown Lit. Soc., and Scrblers (Pres.); Ariz. State Poetry Soc.; AAUW Creative Writing Group (Chairman); Phoenix Writer's Club; Penwomens' Soc., Phoenix. Published works: Rays of Light, 1970; Beatitude Pamphlet, 1970 and 1971. Contbr. to: Tacoma Times; World Poet; Ariz. State Poetry Anthols: Ballet on the Wind, Sing Naked Spirit; Sandcutters; Mid West Chaparral; Prairie Poet; United Poets; American Poet; Haiku West; Mod. Haiku; Mod. Images; Prairie Poet Anthol.; WPSI's Second Biennial Anthol., etc. Awards: Phoenix Writer's Club Poetry Contest, 1st place, 1970; 3rd prize Sandcutters, 1969; Mid West Chaparral Poetry, 3rd place, 1970; Phoenix Writers, 3rd place, 1973. Address: 1401 S. 7th Ave., No. 1F., Phoenix, AZ 85007, USA.

KELLER, Hans Peter, b. 11 Mar. 1915. Writer. Education: studied Philos. in Löwen & Cologne. Married Christel Sieburg, 1 daughter. Positions held: Lit. Tchr. in Publishers' Schl., Dusseldorf, etc. Member, PEN. Published works: (colls. of verse) Die wankende Stunde, 1958; Die nackten Fenster, 1960; Herbstauge, 1961; Auch gold rostet, 1962; Grundwasser, 1965; Panoptikum aus dem Augenwinkel, 1966; Stichwörter Flickwörter, 1969; Licht hinterm Schatten, 1970; Kauderwelsch, 1971; Transl. into English, French, Dutch, Spanish, Russian, Ukranian, Slovak & Arabic. Honours, awards: Ehrensold aus der Thomas-Mann-Stiftung, 1956; Heinrich-Droste-Preis, 1956; Förderpreis zum Jmmermann-Pre der Stadt Düsseldorf, 1958; Kogge-Literaturpreis, 1965. Address: Gartenstr. 2, 4046 Büttgen bei Neuss, German Fed. Repub.

KELLEY, Helen Joyce, pen name, **KELLEY, H.M.,** b. 22 Jan. 1941. Assistant Editor. Education: 2 yrs. Coll.; Oklahoma State Univ. Married; 1 child. Positions held: Asst. Editor, South & West, Inc., since 1970. Memberships: South & West, Inc.; Nat. Fed. of State Poetry Socs.; Oklahoma Poetry Soc.; American Acad. of Poets. Published work: Willow Child, 1970. Contbr. to: South & West; Bitterroot; Voices Internat.; Poetry East-West; St. Andrew's Review; Poetry Venture; Poetry Digest; Encore; Shore Poetry Anthol.; Jean's Journal; Poet (India), etc. Awards: several (Nat. Fed. of State Poetry Socs.; Poetry Soc. of Oklahoma; South & West Poet of the Year, 1972). Address: 19511 E 3rd., Tulsa, OK 74108, USA.

KELLY, Robert, b. 24 Sept. 1935. Editor; University Teacher. Education: City Coll. of N.Y. & Columbia Univ., N.Y. Married. Positions held: Has taught at Wagner Coll., Staten Island, N.Y.; Univ. of Buffalo, N.Y.; Tufts Univ., Medford, Mass.; Currently, Assoc. Prof. of Engl., Bard Coll., Annandale-on-Hudson, N.Y.; Ed., Chelsea Review, N.Y., 1958-60; Trobar, N.Y., 1960-64; Matter, Annandale-on-Hudson, 1963-; Contributing Ed., Caterpillar, N.Y., 1968. Published works: Armed Descent, 1961; Her Body Against Time,

1962; Roun Dances, 1964; Lunes, 1965; Lectiones, H:D: A Joining, 1967; Finding the Measure, 1968; Sonnets, 1967; Songs I-XXX, 1969; The Common Shore, Books I-V, 1969; Kali Yuga, 1970; Other: The Scorpions (Novel), 1967; Ed. w. Paris Leary, A Controversy of Poets: An Anthology of Contemporary American Poetry, 1965. Contbr. to (Anthols.): A Controversy of Poets, 1965; Poems Now, 1966; Young American Poets, 1968; (Jrnls.): Floating Bear; Noose; Sumac; Io; El Corno Emplumado; Big Venus. Hons: Fellow in Fiction, NYC Writers Conference, 1967. Address: c/o Bard Coll., Annandale-on-Hudson, New York, USA.

KEMPHER, Ruth Moon, b. 23 Jan. 1934. Writer; Student; Teacher. Education: Grad., Flagler Coll., B.A., 1972; Now enrolled at Emory Univ., in the Grad. School of Engl., Ph.D. program. Married, Joseph H. Kempher; now divorced. Published works: The White Guitar, 1967 (2nd edition, 1970); Carnival at Seaside, 1968; Porpoise in the Beer, 1970. Contbr. to: Aboveground Review; Ampersand; Apple; Argot; Bitterroot; Cafe Solo; Cardinal Poetry Qtly.; Carolina Qtly.; Children's Activities; Contempora; DeKalb Lit. Arts Journal; Delta Heritage; Dragonfly; Dust; Epos; Florida Education Journal; Florida Qtly.; Folio; Four Quarters; Gnosis; Goliards; Greenfield Review; Hiram Poetry Qtly.; Human Voice Qtly.; Imprints Qtly.; The Lamp in the Spine; McCall's; Maguey; Mikrokosmos; The Muse (Arkansas); The Muse (Washington); New Laurel Review; New Orleans Review; Oregonian Verse; Out of Sight; Poet (India); Poet Lore; Poetic License; Poetry Digest; Poetry Florida & Poetry Venture; Rain; Sat. Evening Post; The Small Pond; The Smith; Sonnet Sequences; South; South & West; Southern Poetry Review; South Florida Poetry Journal; South Florida Review; Trace; Tulsa Poetry Qtly.; TV Guide; US Lady; The Village Voice; Voices Internat.; Weid; Wormwood Review; The Writer; Zahir. Recip. of Steven Vincent Benet Prize (Poet Lore). Addresses: 1184 Willivee Dr., Decatur, GA 30033, USA, or P.O. Box 2224, St. Augustine, FL 32084, USA.

KENDALL, Alice B., b. 14 Apr. 1919. Housewife; Landscape Artist; Poet. Education: Vesper George Schl. of Art, Boston, Mass. Married, Kenneth K. Kendall Jr. Positions held: Poetry Ed. & Columnist, Writer's Rsch. Digest; Staff Writer, Feedback Jrnl. Memberships: Pres., Writer's Workshop of Orange Co., 1969, '70; Exec. Comm., ibid., 1968; Treas., 1971; Calif. Fed. of Chaparral Poets, 1970-71. Contbr. to: (anthols.) A Study in Crimson, 1969; Neo 2, 1968; Poems of Presidents & Your Townsmen, 1968; Echoes of Faith, 1970; Dance of the Muse, 1970; Anthol. of Am. Poetry, Book V, 1970; (jrnls.); The Pioneer; Gato; Phylis; BarbicBardic Echoes; Pixie Angel; Angel Hour; Breakthru; Feedback Jrnl.; Feline Defenders; Calif. Writer; Writer's Rsch. Digest, etc. Honours: 2nd Place, Poetry for Children, Pomona Valley Writer's Assoc., 1967; 1st & 2nd Place, Poetry Awards, Writer's Workshop of Orange Co; Writers Workshop Annual Award, 1969, '70; Hon. Mention, Chaparral Poets, 1970; SCAF Poets of 1969; Am. Poets Fellowship Soc., 1970. Address: 2105 W Forest Lane, Anaheim, Calif. 92804, USA.

KENDALL, Carlton, pen name **LADNEK, Odlaw,** b. 17 Aug. 1895. Businessman; Writer; Poet. Education: Univ. of Calif.; Yale Univ.; Harvard Univ.; Princeton Univ.; Columbia Univ.; Johns Hopkins Univ.; Oxford Univ.; Cambridge Univ. Positions held: Co. Dir.; Corres., League of Nations & U.N.; 2nd Lieut., U.S. Air Serv. Reserve. Member, Authors League of Am., N.Y.C. Contbr. to: (anthols.) Calif. Poets, 1932; Eminent Am. Poets, 1933; Christmas Lyrics, 1937; N.Am. Book of Verse, 1939; Spring Anthol., 1937, '41; (jrnls.) Chicago Tribune, Paris Edn.; Oakland Tribune; Wings; Westward; Overland; Occult Digest; Korea Review; Quintessen; Poetry Review, etc. Address: 1410 Jackson St., Oakland, CA 94612, U.S.A.

KENISON, Gloria, b. 14 Dec. 1910. Education: Pub. Schls., Newton, Mass.; Katharine Gibbs Schl. Personal details: Disabled. Positions held: Sec.,

Deloitte, Plender, Griffiths & Co., Boston, Mass.; Babson Inst.; Publr.'s Financial Bureau. Published works include: Contemporary American Poets, Paris. Contbr. to the following anthols., jrnls., mags., etc: The Wormwood Review; Pyramid; Premier; Spectrum; Experiment; The Green World; Umbra; Out of Sight; Action; King James Version; Talisman; Boston Herald; Hartford Courant. Address: 71 Union St., Millis, Mass. 02054, USA.

KENNEDY, Joseph, pen name **KENNEDY, X. J.,** b. 21 Aug. 1929. Teacher. Education: B.Sc., Seton Hall Univ.; M.A., Columbia Univ; Certificat litt., Univ. of Paris. Positions held: Instr. in Engl., Univ. of Michigan, 1960-62; Lecturer in Engl., Woman's Coll., Univ. of NC, 1962-63; Asst. Prof. of Engl., Tufts Univ., 1963-67, Assoc. Prof., 1967-73, Prof., 1973-. Memberships: P.E.N.; Authors Guild; John Barton Wolgamot Soc. Published works: Nude Descending a Staircase, 1961; Growing into Love, 1969; Bulsh, 1971; Breaking and Entering, 1971; Emily Dickinson in Southern California, 1973. Contbr. to: New Yorker; Poetry; Paris Review; Hudson Review; New Statesman; Atlantic; Harper's; Kayak; Hearse; Cornhill Mag.; Agenda, etc. Poetry Editor, The Paris Review, 1961-64; Editor and Publisher (with Dorothy M. Kennedy), Counter/Measures, 1971-. Awards: Avery and Jule Hopwood Awards, 1960; Lamont Award of Acad. of American Poets, 1961; Bess Hokin prize of Poetry Mag., 1961; Shelley Memorial award (co-recip. with Mary Oliver), 1970; Grant from Nat. Council Arts and Humanities, 1967-68; Guggenheim Fellow, 1973-74. Address: 4 Fern Way, Bedford, MA 01730, USA.

KENNEDY, Mary, Poet; Playwright. Education: St. Mary's, Augusta, Ga.; Columbia Univ., NYC. Mbrships: Govng. Bd., Poetry Soc. of Am.; Author's Guild; Author's League; Dramatist's Guild; Actor's Equity Assn.; Soc., Woman Geographers; The Craftsman Grp., ASCAP. Published works: I Am a Thought of You, adaptations of 9th Century Chinese Poems by Sie Thao, 1968; Ride into Morning, 1969; Behind the Day, 1972; (Forthcoming): The Bourrichon. Contbr. to: 9 Anthols.; (Jrnls.): Botteghe Oscure; Vogue; Confrontation; Voices; Ladies Home Jrnl.; McCalls; The Rhode Islander; Am. Weave; Good Housekeeping; Catholic World; Herald Tribune; Christian Science Monitor; P.E.N. Mag.; Saturday Review of Literature; Harper's Bazaar; Conning Tower; Am. Scholar; Num. Others. Hons: Wm. Rose Benet & Saturday Review of Literature Award, The DeWitt Lyric Award, (both from, Poetry Soc. of Am.); 5 Prizes, var. yrs., N.Y. Women Poets; Mark Twain Award; Nathan Haskell Dole Award, Lyric Mag.; Fellow, 3 times, MacDowell Colony. Address: Box 795, Church Street, Stockbridge, MA 01262, USA.

KENNELLY, Brendan, b. 17 Apr. 1936. Professor of English. Education: B.A., M.A. & Ph.D., Trinity Coll., Dublin, Ireland; Leeds Univ., Yorks. Married, 1 daughter. Positions held: Jr. Lectr. in Engl. Lit., Trinity Coll., Dublin, 1963-66; Lectr. in Engl. Lit., ibid, 1966-69; Assoc. Prof. of Engl., 1969-73; Vis. Prof. of Engl. (Cornell Prof. of Engl. Lit.), Swarthmore Coll., Pa., U.S.A., 1971-72; Prof. of Mod. Lit., Trinity Coll., Dublin, 1973-; Chmn., Engl. Dept., ibid, 1973-. Published works: Cast A Cold Eye, 1959; The Rain, the Moon, 1961; The Dark About Our Loves, 1962; Green Townlands, 1963; (all three with Rudi Hozapfel); Let Fall No Burning Leaf, 1963; My Dark Fathers, 1964; Up and At It, 1965; Collection One: Getting Up Early, 1966; Good Souls to Survive, 1967; Dream of a Black Fox, 1968; Selected Poems, 1969 (Am.edn., 1971); A Drinking Cup: Poems from the Irish, 1970; Bread, 1971; Love-Cry, 1972; Salvation, the Stranger, 1972. Ed., Penguin Book of Irish Verse, 1970. Contbr. to many mags., jrnls. & reviews inclng: Dublin Mag.; Arts in Ireland; Irish Times; N.Y. Times; Dubliner. Recip., A.E. Meml. Award, 1967. Address: Engl. Dept., 40, Trinity Coll., Dublin 2, Ireland.

KENNY, Herbert A., b. 22 Dec. 1912. Journalist. Education: A.B., Boston Coll. Married Teresa Flaherty, 3 children. Positions held: w. Boston Post, 1933-56;

Night City Ed., ibid, 1953-56; w. Boston Globe, 1956-; Ed. for the Arts, ibid, 1957-64; Book Ed., 1964-; Interviewer, The Poet Speaks, WGBH-FM Educl. Stn., 1971-73; Robert Frost Fellow in Poetry, Breadloaf Writers Conf., 1957. Memberships: New England Poetry Club; Poetry Soc. of Am.; Catholic Poetry Soc. Published works: Sonnets to the Virgin Mary (poetry), 1957; Twelve Birds (poetry), 1962; Suburban Man (poetry), 1963; Dear Dolphin, 1969; Alistare Owl, 1970; Cape Ann/Cape America, 1972; Literary Dublin, 1974. Contbr. to: The Cath. Ency.; Mass Review; Antioch Review; Saturday Review; Commonweal; National Review; N.Y. Times; America; Spirit; Four Winds, etc. Address: 804 Summer St., Manchester, MA 01944, U.S.A.

KENNY, Maurice, b. Aug. 1929. Writer. Education: Butler Unq. (B.A., 1955); also studied at St. Lawrence Univ., and NY Univ. Published works: The Hopeless Kill, 1956; Dead Letters Sent, 1958; With Love to Lesbia, 1958; And Grieve, Lesbia, 1960; Only As Far As Brooklyn, 1973. Contbr. to: Wetlands; Akwasasne Notes; The Gay Christian; The Straight Greek Journal; American Weave; Congress; The Green Thumb; Jefferson County Journal; Epos; Yeah!; Mendocino Robin; Kauri; Border; Bardic Echoes; The Muse; Explorer; Caravel; Abyss; Art Week; Holiday Mag.; Poet; San Juan Review; Mexican Qtly. Review; Mexican Life; Indianapolis News; Syracuse Post; Denver Post; The Oregonian; Durango Herald; NY Times; Bits & Pieces; Bitterroot; For Now; Merlin's Magic. Address: 62 Clark St., Brooklyn, NY 11201, USA.

KENWAY, Ian Michael, b. 13 May 1952. Undergraduate. Education: Price's School; Bristol Univ., U.K., 1970-71; Leeds Univ., 1971-. Positions held: Lab. Techn., Product Assessment Lab., Plessey Co., Titchfield; Ordination trng., Anglican Priesthood, 1971; currently reading Theology at Leeds Univ.; Treas., Fareham, Christian Youth Coun., 1969-70. Memberships: Gosport Writers Grp.; Lit. Soc. of Bristol Univ. Published works: Nine Poems, 1970; After the Subterfuge, 1969; Unde/Quo, 1970; The Persistence of Doubt, 1970, etc. Contbr. to: Hampshire Poets (11 times); Solent Arts Fest., 1970; Melchisedek (Leeds Theol. Dept.), 1972; Parish Mag. of St. Peter & St. Paul, Fareham, 1972. Recip., Lion Prize, 1968. Address: The Moorings, 6 Giles Close, Wickham Rd., Fareham, Hants., U.K.

KERIGAN, Florence, pen name **KERRY, Frances,** b. 4 Dec. 1896. Editor; Freelance Writer (retired). Education: HS grad. Positions held: Clerk; Editor; Sec. with social agency (now retired). Memberships: Professional Writers of Philadelphia (Pres., past Sec.); Penn Laurel Poets (Pres., past Sec.); Main Line Writers (Vice-Pres.); Philadelphia Writers' Conference (past Pres., Sec., Founder). Published works: 8 novels, and 1 book of non-fiction. Contbr. to: St. Nicholas, Youth's Companion; Spirit; Classmate; Forward, etc. Address: 128 Arnold Rd., Ardmore, PA 19003, USA.

KERLOGUE, Fiona Gordon, b. 4 Nov. 1951. Interior Designer. Education: Southampton Coll. of Art, U.K., 1969-70; Bedford Coll., Univ. of London, 1970-71. Positions held: Promotions Supvsr. in publishing co. in North Wales; Lib. work, Univ. of Southampton; Freelance Designer. Memberships: Poetry Soc.; Int. Poetry Soc.; Southern Arts Assn. Contbr. to: Spondee; Critical Quarterly Review; Hampshire Poets. Honours, awards: Malcolm Macdonald Essay Prize, 1966 & 67; 2nd Prize, Critical Quarterly Poetry Comp., 1970. Address: 14 River Green, Hamble, Hampshire, U.K.

KERN, William Bliem, Jr., pen name **KERN, W. Bliem,** b. 24 Nov. 1943. Book Designer. Education: B.A., Wilmington Coll., Ohio, 1967. Positions held: Dir. & Fndr., The Sound Poetry Workshop, 1971-74; Dir., Supernova Poetry Series, 1971-72; Dir., Spoken Word Poetry Series at American Art, 1972-73; Dir., Exchange Theatre Poetry Scene, 1973-74; Asst. to Art

Dir., Gregg & Community Coll. Div., McGraw-Hill Book Co., N.Y. Published works: MEDITATIONSMEDITATIONSMEDITATIONS, Selected Poems 1964-73, 1973. Contbr. to: Essais; M.E.A.L.; Friends Sem. Review; Clown War; The Minn. Review; The Third Assembling; Tooth Pick; Origins: A Living Anthol. of Transreal Expression. Has presented concerts of his poetry on radio stns. WBAI-FM (Pacifica), WKCR-FM (Columbia Univ.) & participated in a 2-hour colour prog. of exploration & conversation w. N.Y. poets, 'A for Art', channel A, N.Y.C. Also taped prog. Camera Three, Poems to Hear, Poems to See, CBS TV. Honours, awards: Hon. Mention, Wilmington Coll. Lit. Award, 1964, 2nd prize, 1965 & 1st prize, 1966; Poet Laureate, Wilmington Coll., 1966-67. Address: 309 W. 109th St., Apt. 2-K, N.Y., NY 10025, U.S.A.

KERSCHBAUMER, Luisa, b. 22 Jan. 1893. Physician; Surgeon; Psychiatrist. Education: Madchen Lyceum, Wien, Austria; Acad. Gymnasium; Vienna Wiener Univ. Personal details: Father a Coll. Professor. Positions held: M.D., Oral Surgeon, Milwaukee, Wis.; Asst. Physician, State School, Chippewa Falls, Wis.; St. Peter State Hospital, Minn.; Clarinda, Iowa State Hospital; Massillon State Hospital, Mental Sanitarium (City); Glenwood Sanitarium, St. Louis, Mo.; San., Peoria, Ill.; Hastings State/City School Physician, St. Louis, Mo.; Receiving Hospital, Youngstown, Ohio; Willard State Hospital, NY; now retired but working. Member of Medical Societies. Contbr. to anthol. and several mags., journals, etc., including: New Voices in American Poetry; Cyclo-Flame; Milwaukee Journal; Telegram (Elmira, NY), etc. Address: W. State Hospital, Willard, NY 14588, USA.

KERSHAW, Beulah Frances, pen name BEULAH, b. 9 Jan. 1919. Poet; Songwriter; Recording Artist; Musician. Educ: 20 yrs., pvte. music study. Positions held: Mgr., Al Lerry (Hickory Records) TV Radio; Mgr., Lucky Le Roy TV Records; Mgr., Russell Elliot Jr. TV Nightclubs; Music Tchr., Organ, Piano, Guitar, Accordion; Musical Therapist, Wilmar Restorem, & Shelter House, Endfield. Published works: Poems by Beulah, Vol. 1, 1968, Vol. 2, 1973; var. songs. Contbr. to: Songwriter Review; Vellez Music Mag., etc. Honours, awards: Award Lenin Moscow, World Wide Poetry Contest, Radio Moscow; 2 awards for 900 hrs. of volunteer serv. Address: Rte. 1, Crossville, IL 62827, U.S.A.

KERSHAW, Harvey, b. 20 Jan. 1908. Printer's Assistant. Memberships: Pres., Rochdale Edwin Waugh Dialect Soc., 1964–; Lancashire Authors' Assn. Published works: Lancashire Sings Again, 1958; Lancashire Sings Again – First Encore, 1963; also the author of a local history of Rochdale. Contbr. to: Lancashire Authors' The Record & Red Rose Mag.; Rochdale Observer. Honours, awards: L.A.A. Trophy 'Scholes Cup', 1957 & on five subsequent occasions, the last being in 1973; Recip., 'Pomfret' Trophy, ibid, 1958; Richard Holland Trophy, Edwin Waugh Soc., 1964, '65, '66, '67, '69 & '73; Angus-Butterworth Cup for outstanding work in the Lancashire Authors' Assn.; Guest of Hon., annual 'Boar's head Feast' of the Manchester Lit. Soc., 1972. Address: 11 Holmes St., College Rd., Rochdale OL12 6AQ, Lancs., U.K.

KERWICK, Susan Kathleen Mary Theresa, b. 17 Oct. 1951. Student. Education: currently Secretarial Student, East Warwickshire Coll. of Further Educ. Memberships: Young Conservative Assn., 1968–; Mbr., Exec. Coun., ibid, Rugby & past mbr. of the Area Coun. (W. Midlands); served on two Ward Comms. & Divl. Young Conservative Comm.; Hon. Sec., Conservative Political Ctr., Rugby, 1 yr.; Birmingham Poetry Ctr. Contbr. to: New Hall, schl. mag.; Michael Drayton Meml. Anthol. of Warwicks. Poets, 1971; The Golden Treasury of Poetry (Atlantic), 1972; The Rugby Advertiser; Poetry News, etc. Has appeared on BBC TV 'Open Door' series in connection with the Brum Poetry Ctr., 1973. Address: 281 Clifton Rd., Rugby, Warwicks., U.K.

KESHETH, Jacob Joshua, pen name KESHETH, Yeshurun, b. 29 Nov. 1893. Writer; Poet. Education: Univ. of Rome, Italy, 1920-21; Univ. of Berlin, 1921-23. Memberships: PEN Club; Delegate for Israel to XXXII PEN Congress, Oslo, 1964; Hebrew Writers' Assn. of Israel; AICA. Published works: 3 books of Lyrics & 14 books of essays in Hebrew, 1920-73. Translator of 30 books from English, French & German into Hebrew inclng: Le Livre de Mon Ami, by Anatole France; L'Ame Enchantee (9 vols.), by Romain Rolland; The Essays of Montaigne (selection); Pascal: Opuscules & Pensees (selection); The Varieties of Religious Experience, by William James; A History of Europe, by H.A.L. Fisher; Great Contemporaries, by Winston Churchill; Die Geschichten Jakobs: Jakob und seine Söhne, by Thomas Mann; Der Prozess; Erzählungen, by Franz Kafka; Historische Miniaturen, by A. Strirdberg; Martin Eden, by Jack London. Contbr. to: Davar; Haaretz; Maariv; Moznayim; Molad in Israel; Hadoar weekly in N.Y., U.S.A. & others. Recip. var. literary prizes & awards. Address: Givat Beth-Ha'Kerem 4, Jerusalem 96 268, Israel.

KESSLER, Jascha Frederick, b. 27 Nov. 1929. Professor of English. Education: B.A., Heights Coll. of Arts & Sci., N.Y. Univ., U.S.A., 1950; M.A., Univ...of Univ. of Mich., 1951; Ph.D., ibid, 1955. Positions held: Instr. in Engl., Univ. of Mich., 1952-54; Instr. of Engl., N.Y. Univ., 1954-55 & Hunter Coll., 1955-56; Curriculum Rsch. Dir., Harcourt, Brace & Co., 1956-57; Asst. Prof. of Engl., Hamilton Coll., 1957-61; Prof. of Engl., UCLA, 1961–. Memberships: Am. PEN; Am. Soc. of Composers, Authors, Publishers. Published works: Ed. & Intro., American Poems: A Contemporary Collection, 1964, 4th printing, 1973; Whatever Love Declares (poems), 1969; After the Armies have Passed (poems), 1970. Contbr. to: Poetry; Midstream; Encounter; Saturday Review; Kayak; Chelsea; Southwest Review; West Coast Poetry Review; Mich. Qtly. Review; Trace; UT Review; Malahat Review; The N.Y. Times; Epoch; N.Y. Herald Tribune; Prairie Schooner, etc. Honours, awards: Major Award in Poetry, The Hopwood Contests, 1952; Heptagaon Club of N.Y., 1954; Popular Panel Awards Prize, ASCAP, each yr. since 1965. Address: Engl. Dept., UCLA, Los Angeles, CA 90024, U.S.A.

KESSLER, Milton, b. 9 May 1930. Poet and Professor. Education: B.A., Univ. of Buffalo; M.A., Univ. of Washington. Married, Sonia Berer; 2 s., 1 d. Positions held: Lecturer, Engl., Queens Coll., City Univ. of NY, 1963-65; Assoc. Prof. of Engl., State Univ. of NY, Binghamton, NY., 1965 – ; Visiting Prof. of Engl., Univ. of the Negev, Beersheba, Israel, 1971-72; Co-Editor, Choice Magazine, a mag. of poetry and graphics. Published works: A Road Came Once, 1963; Called Home, 1967; Woodlawn North, 1970; Sailing Too Far, 1973. Contbr. to: Paris Review; The Nation; Transatlantic Review; Prism Internat.; Choice Mag.; Epoch; Epos; Chelsea Review; NY Times; Alcheringa. Awards: Robert Frost Fellowship in Poetry, Bread Loaf, 1961; Nat. Endowment for the Arts Grant (Poets in Concert), 1967; Yaddo Fellowships, 1965-1973; Edward MacDowell Foundation Fellowship, 1966; Distinguished Fellowship in Fine Arts, Research Foundation, State Univ. of NY, 1969. Address: 25 Lincoln Ave., Binghamton, NW 13905, USA.

KESTEMAN, Emile, pen name KESTEMAN, b. 6 July 1922. Scientific Adviser. Educ: Trng., Schl. for French Profs. Abroad. Married, 7 children. Positions held: Prof. of French, secondary level & Coll. level; Scientific Advsr., Inst. Supérieur Marie Haps; French Prof., Min. of For. Affairs. Memberships: Assn. of Belgian Writers; Permanences Poétiques, Brussels. Published works: Tentations, 1955; Et les Sarments bourgeonnent, 1958; Namestek, 1959; Tom Payot, 1968; New Earth Village, 1970; Les Amours, 1971; Distorsion, 1971; Relation brisée, 1972; Liturgie 73, 1973; Exorcismes, 1973; Holmead, 1973. Contbr. to: Belext; Peau de Serpent; Le Sacripant; Les Elytres du Hanneton; Phantomas; La Dernière Heure. Honours, Awards: Silver Medal, Arts, Scis., & Letters, Paris; Among 7 Best, Acad. Pictave, Poetry Competition,

1973. Address: 62 Avenue des Cerisiers, 1040 Brussels, Belgium.

KEY-ABERG, Sandro, b. 6 May 1922. Writer. Education: Univ. studies, Upsala, Stockholm, 1949-53; Fil. Kand. Married. Memberships: Bd. Mbr., Sveriges Forfattarforbund, 1965-71; Bd. Mbr., Litteraturfram jandet, 1965-; Bd. Mbr., Forfattarforlaget, 1968-71; Konsult, Forfattarcentrum, 1968. Published works: Ny Lyrik, 1947; Skramdas Lekar, 1950; Vattenträd, 1952; Bittergok, 1954; Barnet i Enklykan, 1957; Livets Cladje, 1960; Poetisk Lek, 1961; Livet en Stor Sak, 1963; Bildade Hanniskor, 1964; 1866-1966, 1966; En Stordikt Till Dk, 1968; Lovsanger, 1970; Uppslalsbok for Radvilla, 1970; Pa Sin Höjd, 1972. Contbr. to var. newspapers. Honours, awards: Svenska Dagbladets Lit. Prize, 1952; Abtis Lit. Prize, 1957; Kungastipendium, 1959; Fibis Lyrik Prize, 1962; Ferlinpriset, 1972; Carl Emil Englundspriset, 1972; Bellman Priset. Assress: Tegnerlunden 10, 11359 Stockholm, Sweden.

KEYSER, George Gustave, b. 19 Feb. 1910. Personnel Management Specialist, Dept. of Army (1940-71); Writer; Artist. Positions held: Classification Analyst, Off. Sec. of War, 1940-52; Personnel Mgmt. Specialist, Off. Dpty. Chief of Staff for Personnel, Dept. of Army, 1952-71; Retd. 1971. Memberships: Fndr., Contbr., Acad. Am. Poets; Poetry Soc. of America; CSSI; Internat. Poetry Soc. (UK); Dallas Mus. of Fine Arts; South & West Inc.; Poetry Soc. of Texas; World Poetry Soc.; Internat. Platform Assoc. Published works: Listen Softly, 1971. Author of approx. 500 poems in 90 journals and anthols., plus articles and artwork. Particularly interested in Japanese haiku and senryu. Contbr. to: Am. Bard; Am. Haiku; Am. Poet; Bardic Echoes; Bitterroot; Crystals Captive (anthol.); Georgia Mag.; Goliards; Haiku Highlights; Human Voice Qtly.; Orphic Lute; Poetry Dial; Scimitar & Song; South & West; Trace; Western Humanities Review; Poet & Critic; Modern Haiku; Haiku West; Haiku; NM Qtly.; Forum; Treasures of Parnassus (anthol.); Teaching Literature to Adolescents; Poetry (textbook); United Poet; Vision; Voices Int.; Wormwood Review; Writer's Notes & Quotes; The Windless Orchard; Dragonfly; Pancontinental Premier Poets (anthol.); Great American World Poets; Internat. Who's Who in Poetry Anthol., 1973, etc. Guest Editor for single issues of Am. Haiku & Green World; Consulting Editor, Dragonfly. Honours: Voice of the Year Award, Olivant Press, 1970; numerous cash and other prizes from many of the above listed journals, etc. Address: 4912 Gaston Ave., Apt. J, Dallas, TX 75214, USA.

KEYT, George, b. 1901. Painter; Poet. Education: Trinity Coll., Kandy, Repub. of Srilanka. Published works: Poems, 1936; The Darkness Disrobed, 1937; Image in Absence, 1937; Other: Trans., Gita Govinda: The Loves of Krishna & Radha, 1947; Ed., Poetry from the Singhalese, 1939. Exhibition of his Paintings, Peradeniya, Repub. of Srilanka, 1954.

KHAMEES, Abdulla bin, b. 1920. Educator & Lawyer. Education: Bachelor's degree from both the Sharia Coll. & The Coll. of Arabic Lang., Riyadh. Married. Positions held: Dir., Religious Inst. in Hofuf, Saudi Arabia; Dir., Coll. of Sharia & Arabic Lang., Riyadh; Dir. Gen., the Dir. for Islamic Legislation; Under Secretary, Ministry of Communications, Riyadh; Head, Riyadh Water Dept.; ret'd. Contbr. to most Saudi Arabian newspapers and mags. Honours, awards: Rep. Saudi Arabia three times at the Arab Poets' Convention; Received Medal from Fatah, the Palestinian Org.; Received Medal from the Tunisian Rep. for Poets. Address: 2 Jarir St., Malaz, Riyadh, Saudi Arabia.

KHAN, Ghani, pen names **GHANI & LEWANAE PALSAPI,** b. 1915. Chemical Engineer; Painter; Sculptor; Farmer. Education: College America, L.S.U.; Shantiniketan, India. Married, 1 son, 2 daughters. Positions held: Elected Mbr., Indian Legislative Assembly, 1945- to Partition of India. Memberships: V.P., Abasin Art Coun., 4 yrs. Published works: Da Panjre Chaghar; Palwashe; The Pathans, 1946. Contbr. to many newspapers, mags., jrnls., etc. Address: Ultmanzai, Charsadda, Peshawar, N.W.F.P. Pakistan.

KHERDIAN, David, b. 17 Dec. 1931. Poet; Editor. Education: B.S., Philos., Univ. of Wis., 1960. Positions held: US Army, Korea, 1952-54; Field Mgr., Crowell-Collier Publng. Co., 1951; Owner, The Sign of the Tiger Bookstore, 1962; Mgr., The Book House, 1963; Publr., The Giligia Press, 1967-72; Ed., Ararat, A Quarterly Mag., 1970-71; Poet-in-the-Schools, State of New Hampshire, 1971-72. Member, PEN. Published works: Six San Francisco Poets (prose), 1969; Eight Poems, 1969; On the Death of My Father & Other Poems, 1970; Down at the Santa Fe Depot: 20 Fresno Poets (co-ed.), 1970; Homage to Adana, 1970, 2nd ed., 1971; Looking Over Hills, 1972; Visions of America: by the Poets of Our Time (ed.), 1973; The Nonny Poems, 1974; Settling America: The Ethnic Expression of 14 American Poets (ed.) Contbr. to: The Nation; Evergreen Review; Ararat; Shoreline Ldr.; Marmara (Istanbul); Prairie Schooner; The Minn. Review; Cimarron Review; Racine Jrnl. Times; Fiddlehead, etc. Address: Malden Bridge, NY 12115, U.S.A.

KIDD, Virginia, b. 2 June 1921. Literary Agent; Writer & Editor. Education: Catonsville, Md. HS, 1938; Berlitz School of Languages, Baltimore, Maryland: French, Spanish, German, Italian, to 1940. Married (1st) Jack Emden, baritone; child: Karen Anne; Married (2nd) James Blish, writer; children: Asa Benjamin, deceased, Elisabeth, Benjamin; divorced (1963) for 2nd time. Positions held: Girl Friday, Peabody Book Store, Baltimore, Md.; Spanish-speaking Receptionist, Tucson, Ariz.; Music Librarian, Radio. Station WFBC, Greenville, S.C.; Ghost-Writer, Freelance Writer, NYC.; Literary Agent, Milford, Pennsylvania and NYC. Memberships: Vanguard Amateur Press Assoc. (founding member; served one year as official Tyrant). Co-Ed., w. Roger Elwood, Sving Worlds, all-original anthol. of ecological fiction, 1973-74. Contbr. to: Accent, 1952; Kirgo's; Mad River Review; Kinesis; Alchemy & Academe; Future City; Berserkers; Just Friends. Addresses: Box 278, Milford, PA 18337, USA, and Apt. 3A, One Sheridan Sq., New York, NY 10014, USA.

KIDD, Walter Evans, pen name **PENDLETON, Conrad,** b. 2 May 1915. University Instructor. Education: Univ. of Oregon, B.A., 1936; M.A., 1937; Univ. of Denver, Ph.D., 1945. Positions held: Portland, Oregon, HS teaching, 1939-45; Instructing in: Univ. of Nebraska, 1945-50; Stephen F. Austin State Univ., Texas, 1950-55; Fresno State Univ., Calif., 1955-58; Univ. of Houston, Texas, 1958-59; Univ. of Michigan, 1959-60; Stephen F. Austin State Univ., Texas, 1960-70; Lecturing, since 1970. Married, Nancy O. Pendleton. Memberships: Sigma Upsilon (Pres., of Univ. of Oregon chapter); Texas Poetry Soc. (regional rep.); Oregon Poetry Soc.; East Texas Writers (Chairman); Willamette Authors (Oregon); Three-Arts Club at Univ. of Oregon (Chairman). Published works: Slow Fire of Time, 1946; Time Turns West, 1951; West; Manhattan to Oregon, 1956; Oregon Odyssey of Wheels, 1973; Robert Frost: Yankee Classicist, 1963. Contbr. to: American Mercury; American Prefaces; American Weave; Antioch Review; Aphrodite; Beloit Poetry Journal; Catholic World; Commonweal; Cyclotron; Experiment; Cyclo-Flame; Forum; Frontier & Midland; Generation; The Green World; Kaleidograph; Kansas Mag.; The Lyric, NM Qtly.; New Republic; NY Times; NY Tribune; Poetry: A Mag. of Verse; Poetry Awards; Poet Lore; Portland Oregonian; Prairie Schooner; PS; Saturday Eve. Post; Snowy Egret; South & West Qtly.; Southwest Review; Texas Trends; Univ. Review; Va. Qtly.; Voices: A Journal of Verse, etc. Awards: George Sterling Lyric Prize, 1935; Southwest Grand Poetry Award, 1946; Texas Inst. of Letters Poetry Prize, 1969; 39 other poetry prizes . . . through mag. publication and writers' conferences. Address: 1325 S.E. Umatilla St., Portland, OR 97202, USA.

KIEFFER, Jane, b. 11 June 1901. Poet. Memberships: PEN Club Int.; Société des Gens de Lettres de France; Société des Poets Français. Published works: Chansons de la Sorciere, 1952; Forêts d'un Autre Monde; Jean des Brumes; Les Mains qui Flambert; Cette Sauvage Lumiere, 1962; Pour Ceux de la Nuit, 1964; Soleils des Grands Fonds, 1973. Contbr. to: Ariane Bételgeuse; Presence et Regards-Dire: Fenix; Monde et Vie, etc. Recip. var hons. & awards inclng: Livre d'or de la Poesie Française, 1971; Prix d'Academie Française; Prix des Gens de Lettres, 1971. Address: 15 rue Louis Ronquier, 92300 Levallas, France.

KIELY, Jerome, b. 23 May 1925. Catholic Priest. Education: Arts degree & theol. at Maynooth. Positions held: Lectr. in Scripture & Sermon Preparation, Carlow Coll., 1950-54; Tchr. of Engl. & Hist., Farranferris, 1954-67; Curate, Goleen, West Cork, 1967–. Published works: New Poets of Ireland, 1963; The Griffon Sings (coll.), 1966; Penguin Book of Irish Verse, 1970. Contbr. to: Adam; The Bell; Chanticleer; Dublin Mag.; Irish Times; Irish Writing; Irish Press; Kilkenny Mag.; Poetry Ireland; To-day. Recip., Adam Int. Prize, 1953. Address: Priest's House, Goleen, Co. Cork, Ireland.

KIESEL, Frédéric, b. 24 Feb. 1923. Journalist. Education: Docteur en Droit, UCL, 1947. Positions held: Lawyer, Arlon, Belgium, 1947-56; Journalist, (For. Policy Ed. & Lit. Critic), 'La Métropole', Antwerp, 1956-63, & at 'La Cité', Brussels, 1963–. Var cultural missions & lectures on poetry & culture in Lebanon, 1962, Syria, 1968, Canada, 1969, Poland, 1970 & Tunisia, 1973. Memberships: Coun., Jrnl. des Poètes, Brussels; l'Académie Luxembourgeoise. Published works: Poème pour la forêt, 1950; Ce que le jour m'avait donné, 1954; Elégies du temps et de l'été, 1961; Printemps-Orphée, 1962; Le Cadran solaire, 1964; Herbe sur le chemin, 1965; Paques sauvages, 1973. Essays on the poets: Albert Yande, 1955; Pierre Nothomb, 1965; Anna-Marie Kegels, 1973. Contbr. to var. jrnls. & reviews. Honours, awards: Prix Polak, Académie Royale, 1954; Prix 'Le Borée', Lille, 1962. Address: 48 Avenue des Jardins, 1030 Brussels, Belgium.

KILCHER-MARIOTT, Ruth Helen, b. 8 Mar. 1920. Freelance Writer; Poet. Education: Madchen gymnasium, Basle, Switzerland, 1930-38. Married twice, 8 children. Positions held: Chmn., Int. Rels., Nat. Fed. of Press Women, 1967; Pres., Alaska Press Women, 1968-70; Regl. Dir., ibid, 1968-71. Memberships: Charter Mbr., Poetry Soc. of Alaska; Poetry Soc. of N.M.; Poetry Soc. of NFSPS; Nat. Fed. of Press Women; Alaska Press Women. Ed., Pacific Northwest Poetry. Contbr. to: Anchorage Daily News; Neue Schweizer Bibliothek; Alaska Centennial Record Anthology; Stella Borealis; Poet; Haiku Drops; Orion; Unity; Alaska Mag.; Poet Anthol. Recip., First Silvertrophy, Alaska Legends Contest, 1969. Address: 2808 Monterey S.E., Albuquerque, NM 87106, U.S.A.

KILLINGWORTH, Gerald Charles, b. 24 June 1949. English Teacher. Education: Jesus Coll., Cambridge Univ., U,K. (Exhibitioner), 1968-71. Positions held: Ed., Poetry Jrnl. Tagus, 1972–; Engl. Corres., 'New Europe', published in Luxembourg. Published works: Collection of Poems, Autumn 1973. Contbr. to: New Europe; Vento Nuovo; Orbis; Tagus; Candelabrum; Naissance; Envoi; Headland; Scrip. Address: 6 New Road, Orton Waterville, Peterborough PE2 OEJ, U.K.

KIM, Jaihiun, b. 24 Jan. 1934. Professor of English, and Poet. Education: 1958, Hankuk U. of Foreign Studies, Seoul, Korea, B.A.; 1968 and 1969, Univ. of Massachusetts, USA, M.A., and M.F.A. Married; 1 d. Positions held: 1969-71, Asst. Prof. of Engl., Fort Valley State Coll.; 1971-72, Assoc. Prof. of Engl., Sacred Heart Coll. for Women; since 1972, Lecturer in Engl., Hankuk Univ. of Foreign Studies; Docksung Women's Coll. Memberships: The Korean PEN Centre; American Poets Fellowship Soc.; The Second World Congress of Poets (Floor Leader). Published

works: Detour, a book of Poems, 1972; A Pigsty Happiness, a book of Poems, 1973; Azaleas, 90 poems by Sowol Kim in Engl. version, 1973. Contbr. to: Kauri; United Poets; American Poets; Prairie Poets; Overflow; The Korea Times; Korea Herald; Korea Journal, etc. Recip. Best Poetry Selection Award, 1973, 2nd World Congress of Poets; Poetry Achievement Award, by Poetry of Our Times, 1970. Address: c/o The P.E.N. Centre, 163 Ankuk-dong, Chong-ro-ku, Seoul, Korea.

KIM, Kyung Sooh, pen name **MOCK YANG MIN,** b. 5 July 1925. Pastor. Education: Hankuck Theol. Sem., Seoul, Korea; Tex. Christian Univ., Fort Worth, Tex. Married Un Hi Cho, 3 daughters. Positions held: Prof., Ewha Womens Univ., Chaplain, Korean Navy; Pastor, Chang Hyung Presby. Ch. Member, Assn. of Modern Poets in Korea. Published works: (books of poems) The Flower & the Sea, 1954; Songs of the Creation, 1955; The Last Supper, 1956; The Mount of Olives & a Feast & a Loud Weeping, 1958; A Cloud & Arms, 1960; Kyung Sooh Kim's Selected Poems, The Spiritual Songs of Ancient Doors, 1969. Contbr. to var. mags. & newspapers. Address: 472-215 Suyudong Dobong-Ku, Seoul, Korea.

KIMBLE, Vesta Baker (Mrs.), b. 1900. Musician and Poet. Positions held: played in Frank Daugherty Orchestra; Program over Radio Station KFYO, Breckenridge, Tex.; Accompanist to violinist H.R. DeRoeck. Memberships: Vice-Pres., Breckenridge Poetry Soc.; Poetry Soc. of Texas. Fellow, Intercontinental Biographical Association, 1971. Publications: 75–poem book printed & copyrighted for gift purposes; also several booklets of poems. Poems printed in: Anthology of American Poetry; Ideals Mag.; America's Best Poems (Toronto, Canada); Breckenridge American Newspaper; Ideals Mag.; Defender Mag. etc. Donor of numerous poem cards to Sunday Schls. and Funeral Homes. Honours: Official Poet of Stephens Co. Hosp. Aux.; Plaque, Nat. Register of Prominent Americans, 1970; Plaque, Personalities of the South Award, 1971. Address: 701 West Hullum St., Breckenridge, Tex. 76024, USA.

KIMREY, Grace Evelyn Saunders, pen name, **KIMREY, Grace Saunders,** b. 3 Dec. 1910. Co-Proprietor of a Store; Reporter; Housewife. Married, Sam C. Kimrey. Positions held: Training Union Leader, WMU, 43 years; Sunday Schl. Tchr., 44 yrs.; Co-Proprietor, Roofing Bus; News Corres., Randolph Guide. Memberships: NC Poetry Soc.; UAPPA Chmn., Bureau of Critics; Burlington Writers; Int. Platform Assn.; Eastern Star; Former Mbr., Nat. Writers Club; NC Historical Soc.; Ramseur Book Club. Publications: Songs of Sunny Valley, 1954; Glimpses of Beauty, 1955; The Star of Hope, 1957; Spent Wrath, 1972; Of Heaven and of Earth, 1974. Contbr. to: (anthols.) UAPA–Young Anthol.; Stephenson Anthol.; Int. Who's Who Anthol.; Raleigh News & Observer; Biblical Recorder: Christian Advocate, NC; Randolph Guide; Greensboro Record; Asheville Citizen Times. Recip. of Poetry awards; Children's Story Awards; Feature Stories Awards. Address: PO Box 562, Ramseur, NC, USA.

KIM YANG-SHIK, pen name **CHO-EL,** b. 4 Jan. 1931. Poetess. Education: Grad., Dept. of Engl. Lit., Ewha Women's Univ., 1954. Married Ho-Sok Chae, 1 son, 1 daughter. Memberships: Korean Writers' Assn.; Korean Modern Poets' Assn. Published works: A Collection of Chŏng ŭp husa Kim Yang-Shik sijip (39 poems carved on wood & stone). Contbr. to: The Hankook Ilbo; The Tong A Ilbo; The Shin A Ilbo; Hyondae-Munhak; Wolgan-Munhak; Shi-Munhak; Yoryu-Munhak; Jubu-Senghwal; The Selection of Korean Modern Poetry. Recip., prize, The Literary Contest, The Monthly Literary Mag., Wolgan-Munhak. Address: 45–6 Heng Chon Dong, SodaeMoon-Ku, Seoul, Korea.

KINDS, Edmond, b. 11 Apr. 1907. Writer. Education: Cand. en philosophie et lettres, docteur en droit, Université de Bruxelles. Positions held: Writer;

Lawyer. Memberships: Int. PEN Club; Belgian Comm., Société des Auteurs et Compositeurs dramatiques. Published works: Jean Tardieu, on l'enigme d'exister, 1973; Ernest Delève, collection 'Poètes d'aujourd'hui', no. 213, 1973. Address: 224 Avenue Molière, 1060 Brussels, Belgium.

KINDS, LeVander (Rev. Dr.), b. 22 Mar. 1919. College Professor. Education: Cleveland Bible Coll.; A.B., Adelbert Coll. of Western Reserve Univ., Cleveland; M.A., Grad. Schl., ibid. Married to Marjorie Alethea Aderson, 1955, 2 children. Positions held: Prof. of Philos., Leland Coll., La., 1946-47; Prof. of Humanities, Tougaloo Coll., Miss., 1947-50; Prof. of Soc. Sci., Natchez Jr. Coll., Miss., 1950-64; Pres., ibid, 1964-68; Prof., Soc. Sci., Alcorn Coll., Miss., 1968-; Pastor, Mt. Heroden Bapt. Ch., Miss., 1960-. Memberships: Sponsor, Poetry Soc., Natchez Jr Coll.; Parnassus Soc. Published works: Reflections, 1946; The Otherwise Wise. Sermonairs, 1973. Contbr. to: The Natchez Times, 1953-56; Alcorn Coll. Lib. Exhibit, 1970. Recip. of Hon. D.D., Leland Coll., La. Address: PO Box 597, Natchez. Miss, 39120, USA.

KING, Francis Henry, b. 4 Mar. 1923. Author; Reviewer; Poet. Education: Balliol Coll., Oxford. Positions held: Served w. British Council in Italy, Greece, Egypt, Finland, Japan, 1949-65; Currently, Literary Advsr. to publishers, Macdonald & Co.; Regular Reviewer, Sunday Telegraph, London. Published works: Rod of Incantation, 1952; (Novels): The Dividing Stream, 1951; The Dark Glasses, 1954; The Widow, 1957; The Man on the Rock, 1957; The Custom House, 1961; The Last of the Pleasure Gardens, 1965; The Waves Behind the Boat, 1967; Short Stories: So Hurt & Humiliated, 1959 The Japanese Umbrella, 1964; The Brighton Belle, 1968; Other: Ed., Introducing Greece, 1961. Contbr. to (Anthols.): Penguin Book of Sick Verse, 1963; Terrible Rain, 1966; Poetry of the Forties, 1968. Hons: Somerset Maugham Award, 1952; The Katherine Mansfield Short Story Prize, 1965; Arts Council Bursary, 1966. Address: 17 Montpelier Villas, Brighton, Sussex, UK.

KING, Ruby Thompson, pen name, **KING, R.T.** Teacher of English. Education: A.B. and M.A.; Fla. State Univ.; Univ. of Ga. Married to Seaborn Laurence King. Positions held: Tchr., HS Engl., Glynn Co., Charlton, Lourdes, Brantley & Coffee Co. High Schls. Memberships: Organizer, Sponsor, Thespian Soc.; Prog. Chmn., Lit. Arts Soc.; Organizer & Sec., Poetry Soc.; AAUW; Int. Platform Assn.; Int. Comm., Centro Studi E. Scambi Int.; Register of Ga. Poets; Creative Writing, Poetry Div., The Fine Arts; Poetry Judge, Philharmonic Guild Assn. Contbr. to· Nat. Anthol. of Verse, 1968, '69; Am. Poetry Annual; Douglas Enterprise; Chicago Advocate; Wesleyan (Ga.) Advocate; Am. Poetry Press; Charlton Press; other leading daily newspapers in Ga. & Flo. Honours: Special Citation for inclusion in annual anthol. of Nat. Poetry Press, 1968, '69; num. press recognitions; TV and Radio comments, 1968, '69; Edit. Dedications for poems on Carl Sandburg, 1969. Address: PO Box 428, Douglas, Ga. 31533, USA.

KINNELL, Galway, b. 1 Feb. 1927. Poet-in-Residence. Education: A.B., Princeton Univ., N.J., 1948; M.A., Univ. of Rochester, N.Y., 1949; Fulbright Fellow in Paris, 1955-56. Married Inés Delgado w. 2 children. Positions held: Field Worker, Congress of Racial Equality, 1963; Tchr., Univ. of Grenoble, France; Poet-in-Residence, Juniata Coll., Huntingdon, Pa.; Univ. of Calif., Irvine, 1968-69. Published works: What a Kingdom it Was, 1960; Flower Herding on Mount Monadnock, 1964; Poems of Night, 1968; Body Rags, 1968; Other: Black Light, 1965; Trans., the Poems of François Villon, 1963 & On the Motion & Immobility of Douve, 1968. Contbr. to (Anthols.): New Poets by American Poets, 1953; Pocket Book of Modern Verse, 1954; New Poets of England & America, 1962; Poet's Choice, 1962; Modern Poets, 1963; Poems of Doubt & Belief, 1964; A Controversy of Poets, 1965; Poems on Poetry, 1965; (Jrnls.): Poetry; Nation; Sixties; &

Others. Hons: Guggenheim Fellowship, 1961-62; Longview Foundation Award, 1962; Nat. Inst. of Arts & Letters Grant, 1961; Rockefeller Foundation Grant, 1967-68; Brandeis Univ. Creative Arts Award, 1969; Amy Lowell Travelling Scholarship, 1969-70. Address: Sheffield, Vermont, USA.

KINSELLA, Mary D., pen name **DONOVAN, Maira,** b. 27 May 1906. Teacher; Librarian. Education: D'Youville Coll., Canisius, Buffalo, N.Y. Widow of Joseph Kinsella. Positions held: Tchr. of Engl. & Engl. Lit., Jr. & Sr. H.S., Buffalo, N.Y.; Libn., Ctr. Schl., Buffalo, N.Y. Memberships: Soc. of Children's Book Writers, Calif.; SOLA Lit. Assn. of Stamford, Conn.; United Amateur Press of Am.; Buffalo Poetry Soc. Published works: The Quiet Ones, book of short stories, 1970. Contbr. to: Buds of Promise, 1925; Sammy Kaye Sunday Serenade Radio Poetry Hour, 1940; Modern Maturity for Retired Persons, 1973; Speak Out, 1973-74; Jean's Jrnl., 1973-74; Poet's Nook, 1974; Buffalo Evening News, Reporter's Notebook, 1973. Honours, awards: Christopher Award, 1952; First Awards, sonnets & light verse, Jean's Jrnl., 1972, '73, '74. Address: 95 Warren Ave., West Seneca, NY 14224, U.S.A.

KINSELLA, Thomas, b. 4 May 1928. Poet; Civil Servant. Positions held: Exec. Off., Irish Land Commn.; Admin. Off., Dept. of Finance; Asst. Prin. Off., ibid; Writer in Residence, Southern III. Univ.; Prof. of English, ibid. Published works: Poems, 1950; Another September, 1958; Moralities, 1960; Downstream, 1962; Wormwood, 1966; Nightwalker, 1967; Nightwalker & Other Poems, 1968. Contbr. to: Encounter; Poetry Chicago; Irish Writing; Poetry Ireland; Irish Times; Listener; Shenandoah; Threshold; Kilkenny Mag.; Reporter; Atlantic Quarterly, etc. Honours: Choice of Poetry Soc., London, 1956; Guinness Poetry Award, 1958; Choice of Poetry Soc., 1962; Irish Arts Council Triennial Book Award, 1962; Denis Devlin Mem. Award, 1966; Poetry Soc. Choice, London, 1956, 1962. Address: Dept. of Engl., Southern III. Univ., Carbondale, III. 62901, USA.

KIRK, Preston Floyd, b. 1 Feb. 1945. Associate Editor. Education: B.A., Jrnlsm., Baylor Univ., Waco, Tex. Positions held: Reporter, The Baylor Lariat, Waco, Tex.; Reporter, The Galveston (Tex.) Daily News; Ed., The Lodestar, Bellmead, Tex.; Newsman, United Press Int., Houston; Assoc. Ed., Houston Bus. Jrnl. Memberships: Past Pres., Sigma Tau Delta; Past Area Coun., Poetry Soc. of Tex.; Acad. of Am. Poets; Houston Chapt., P.S.T.; Past Pres., Tex. Gulf Coast Chapt., Sigma Delta Chi, currently V.P. Tex. Assn., ibid. Contbr. to: The Bellmead News; The Avesta; The Phoenix, The Connally Caller; Pirates Jewels; The Chimes; The Baylor Lariat; The News Tribune; The Treasure Chest; Et Al; The Waco Citizen; Waco PST Anthol.; Houston Chronicle, etc. Address: 5314 Bingle Rd., Houston, TX 77018, U.S.A.

KIRKCONNELL, Watson, b. 16 May 1895. University Professor. Education: Queen's Univ., Kingston, Ont., Canada; Lincoln Coll., Oxford Univ., UK; M.A., Ph.D., D.Litt. Positions held: Prof., United Coll., McMaster Univ., Acadia Univ., Canada; Pres., Acadia Univ., 1948-64; Retired, 1964. Memberships: Nat. Pres., Canadian Authors Assn., 1942-44 & '56-58; Fellow, Royal Soc. of Canada, 1936-. Published works: European Elegies, 1928; The Tide of Life, 1930; The Eternal Quest, 1934; The Flying Bull & Other Tales, 1940; Centennial Tales & Selected Poems, 1965. Contbr. to: Canadian Forum; Warsaw Weekly; Saturday Night; Dalhousie Review; Canadian Poetry Magazine, etc. Honours & Awards: Kt. Cmdr., Order of the Icelandic Falcon; Kt. Officer, Order of Polonia Restituta; Medal of Hon., PEN, Hungary; Lorne Pierce Gold Medal in Lit., Royal Soc. of Canada; Nova Scotia Drama Trophy. Address: PO Box 460, Wolfville, Nova Scotia, Canada.

KIRKLAND, Margie, b. 3 Dec. 1927. Freelance Writer. Education: Grad. of Satterwhite Coll., Lufkin, Texas. attended writers' conferences and seminars at

Stephen F. Austin State Univ., Nacogdoches, Texas. Married; 1 s., 1 d. Memberships: Poetry Soc. of Texas (Area Councillor, and Pres., Pineywoods Chapter); Texas Press Women; Nat. Press Women; Avalon; Lufkin Story League (Member and Reporter). Published works: Profiles of East Texas, 1964; New-Kindled Fires, 1968. Contbr. to: Cyclo-Flame; Story Art; Quintessence; Writer's Notes & Quotes; Nutmegger; Echoes; Over the Ozarks; The Oregonian; South and West; Cats Mag.; Jean's Journal; The American Poet; The Lufkin News; The Angelina Star. Recip. sev. prizes, and hon. mentions, Writers' Conferences, Stephen F. Austin State Univ.; Cyclo-Flame Mag. citation, 1967; Cert. of Excellence, UPLI, 1968; for 3 yrs. hon. as resource worker in field of poetry, Lufkin Public Schools. Address: 411 Mantooth, Lufkin, TX 75901, USA.

KIRKUP, James, pen names **TSUYUKI, Shigeru, TERAHATA, Jun & ANDREW, James,** b. 23 Apr. 1923. Poet. Education: B.A., Double Hons., King's Coll., Durham, UK. Positions held: Gregory Fellow in Poetry, Leeds Univ., 1950-52; Vis. Poet, Bath Acad. of Art, 1953-56; Travelling Lectureship, Swedish Min. of Educ., 1956-57; Prof. of Engl. Lang. & Lit., Salamanca Univ., Spain, 1957-58; Prof. of Engl. Lit., Tohoku Univ., 1959-61; Vis. Prof. of Engl., Lit., Japan Woman's Univ., Tokyo; Poet-in-Res., Amherst Coll., Mass., USA, 1968-69; Prof., Dept. of Engl. Lit., Univ. of Nagoya, Japan. Memberships: Soc. of Authors; Royal Soc. of Lit. (Fellow). Published works include: The Cosmic Shape, 1947; The Drowned Sailor, 1948; The Creation, 1950; The Submerged Village, 1951; A Correct Compassion, 1952; A Spring Journey, 1954; Upon This Rock; The Dark Child; The Triumph of Harmony, 1955; The True Mystery of the Nativity; Ancestral Voices; The Radiance of Kings, 1956; The Descent into the Cave; The Only Child (Autobiography), 1957; The Peach Garden; Two Pigeons Flying High; Sorrows; Passions & Alarms, 1960; The True Mystery of the Passion; The Prodigal Son (poems' 1956-60); Those Horned Islands, 1962; The Love of Others, 1962; Tropic Temper, 1963; Refusal to Conform; Last & First Poems, 1963; The Heavenly Mandate, 1964; Japan Industrial, Vols. I & II, 1964-65; Tokyo, 1966; Bankok, 1967; Paper Windows: Poems from Japan, 1967; White Shadows, Black Shadows, 1970; The Body Servant: Poems of Exile, 1971; A Bewick Bestiary, 1971. Numerous transl. from French & German. Contbr. to the following anthols., jrnls., mags., etc.: Times Literary Supplement; New Statesman; Spectator; Listener; Poetry Review; Gasfitter's Gazette; The Queen; Sunday Times; New Yorker; NY Times, etc. Honours, awards: Atlantic Award in Lit., 1950; FRSL, 1962; Japan PEN Club Prize, 1965. Address: 5-13 Nakayama-Cho, Mizuhoku, Nagoya, Japan.

KIRSTINA, Väino Antero, b. 29 July 1936. Teacher. Education: B.A. (.kand.), Univ. of Helsinki, Finland, 1963. Married. Positions held: News Ed. & Translator at UPI, 1959-60; Ed., Finnish Broadcasting Co. (section of radio plays), 1965-67; Tchr. of Creative Writing, Univ. of Tampere, 1968-72. Memberships: PEN; Finnish Writers' Union; Pres., Union of Finnish Amateur Writers & Artists, 1972–. Published works: (poetry) Lakens, 1961; Hitast auringot, 1963; Puhetta, 1963; Luonnollinen tanssi, 1965; Pitkan tahtayksen LSD – suunnitelma, 1967; Talo inaalla, 1969; Saannostelty entanasia, 1973. Contbr. to Parnasso. Honours, awards: Prize, State of Finland, 1964; The Fellowship, ibid, 1970-73. Address: Tammelanpuistok 5-7 C 32, 33500 Tampere 50, Finland.

KISER, Thelma Scott, b. 25 Dec 1916. Chemist. Education: Transylvania Univ., Lexington, Ky.; Univ. Ky. Married, Alan Boyd Kiser. Positions held: Food Inspr., US Dept. of Agric.; Chemist, Univ. of Ky.; Ashland Oil & Refining Co. Memberships: Editor, Ky. State Poetry Soc.; Contest Chmn., 1966-71; Prog. Chmn., 1971; VP, 1970-71; Vice-Pres., Eastern Ky. Poetry Soc.; Organizer & Dir., Ky. Jr. Poets; Nat. Fed. of Poets; Co-Dir., Ky.-Brit. Pen Pal, Jr. Poets; Publisher, Ky. State Poetry Soc. Newsletter, Pegasus,

1966-69; Nat. League Am. Pen Women; Acad. Am. Poets; Org. & Curator, Ky. Poetry Mus. Lib. Contbr. to: Ashland Daily Independent; The Leader; Lookout; Approaches; Cyclo Flame; Contemporary Ky. Poetry; Ideals; Pegasus; Decision; 1st Flight; 2nd Flight; Poetry Pilot; Russell Times; Grayson Times–Jrnl.; Ky. Harvest; Ky. Writers Guild; Poetry Preview; Laudamus Te; Manifold; Beaches Ldr.; Cross Currents; Twigs; War Cry; CS Monitor; Saint; Angels; W-H Harvest; Prairie Poet; Poet (India); South & West. Honours: Commissioned Ky. Col. by Gvnr. of Ky. for contribution to Ky. poetry, 1967; Manifold's Atlantic Award, 1968; 2nd Place, Manifold's Relig. Poetry Comp., 1968; 3rd, Seven's Int. Jesse Stuart Contest, 1969; 3rd, Nat. Fed. Poetry Socs. 1968; Life Mbr., Ky. Poetry Soc., 1970; Jesse Stuart Award of Excellence, 1971. Address: 1508 Montgomery Ave., Ashland, KY 41101, USA.

KISNER, Jacob, pen names **KISNER, Jack,** & **SMALLWOOD, Jason,** b. 30 Apr. 1926. Poet; Editor; Writer. Education: Calvin Coolidge Coll.; Harvard Univ. Extension; Mass. State Univ.; Burdett Coll.; Cambridge Ctr. for Adult Educ.; Boston Mus. Fine Arts. Married, Gladys Kisner, 1 d. Positions held: Advtg., Boston American; Sunday Edit. Writer, Boston Globe; Local News Ed., Jewish Advocate; Fndr., Ed., Publr., Dorchester Herald; Trade Reporter, Fairchild News Serv.; Advertising Copywriter, Harold Cabot Advertising Agency; Sr. Proofreader, Recording & Statistical Corp.; Ed., Crossroads, Canada; Am. Ed., View, Canada; Research Director, N.Y. Bureau, Moneytree Publications; Memberships: Exec. Comm., Wilson MacDonald Poetry Soc., Canada; Discussion Moderator, Great Books Fndn.; Sec., Am.-European Friendship Assoc.; Am. Newspaper Guild; Nat. Geographic Soc.; Fndr., Acad. Am. Poets; Bd. of Directors, NY Poetry Forum; NYC Chmn., World Poetry Day Comm.; N.Y.C. Rep., Rochester World Poetry Day Comm.; Former Vice Pres., NY Poetry Forum. Publications: I Am Hephaestus, 1970; (plays) First Came Paula; Speak of the Devil; The Monkey's Tail; (TV plays) The Late Mr. Honeywell; A World Apart. Contbr. to: 1969 Anthol. of NY Poets; Poetry Prevue; Bachaet; Beyond Baroque; Cimarron Review; Tulsa Poetry Qtly.; Montrealer; Am. Rose; Boston Globe; Link; Kindergartner; Music for Primaries; Am. Baby; Advocate; Poetry Pageant; Worker's World; Boston Post; Dorchester Herald; Crossroads; Canada & Its Future; Am. Rose Soc. Calendar, 1970; Anthol. of Am. Poets, books X & XI; Coney Island Times; Escapade; Etcetera Review; Everett Leader-Herald; Fun Photography Mag.; Daily News-Record; Haiku Highlights; Henrietta Weekly Jrnl.; Highlights for Children; Looking Back; Manhattan East; Moneytree; Moneytree Cyclopedia; Mothers-to-be & Infant Care; Nat. Underground Press Illus.; NBC-TV Comedy Writers Develop. Project; NY Amsterdam News; NY Element; NY PM; Nursery Days; Orb (Fla.); Poetry Venture; Poetry Ventured Anthol.; Potpourri of Poetry, 1970: The Roaring Twenties; Shore Record; Speciality Salesman Mag.; SE Weekly Jrnl.; Town & Country; View (Canada); Williamsburg News; The Writer; Writers Digest; Young Musicians. Hons., Awards include: Gold Medal, Int. Poets Shrine, 1971; Special Citation Award, Poetry Pageant; World Peace Award, Kentucky State Poetry Soc.; Radio Award, WEFG, Virginia; Writers Digest Writing Contest Award, 1971; Best of Issue Award, Haiku Highlights, 1971; Henry Rago Mem. Award; Regina Forner Award; Mary Boyd Wagner Award; Robt. Martin Award; Eleanor Otto Award; Judge, NY Poetry Forum Fourth Annual Awards Contest; Bessie Wherry Noe Award, NY Poetry Forum, 1971. Address: 750 Park Ave., New York, NY 10021, USA.

KISSAM, Edward, b. 29 May 1943. Educator. Education: B.A. Philos., Princeton Univ.; postgrad. study, Magdalen Coll., Oxford; Ph.D., Comp. Lit., State Univ. of N.Y. at Buffalo. Married, 2 children. Positions held: Asst. Prof., San Francisco State Coll.; Asst. Prof., Senona State Coll.; Rsch. Asst., State Univ. of N.Y. at Buffalo; var. other positions. Published works: The Sham Flyers, 1969; Jerusalem & the People, 1970;

The Arabs, 1972; Flower & Song (Aztec transl. w. Michael Schmidt), 1974. Contbr. to: The Paris Review; The World; Bricoleur; Clear Creek; Poetry Review; New Measure; El Corno Emplarnado; Isthmus; Prairie Schooner; S.D. Review; Good Times; Free Poems: Virtue; Blake; Weed. Address: 6379 W. Dry Creek, Healdsburg, CA 95448, U.S.A.

KISTNER, Arthur Leroy, pen name **KISTNER, Art,** b. 26 Dec. 1933. Professor; Poet. Education: B.A., M.A., Ph.D., Univ. of Ill. Positions held: Asst., Univ. of Ill., 1960-62; Instr., ibid, 1962-63; Instr., Univ. of Del., 1963; Asst. Prof., Cornell Coll., 1964-68; Asst. Prof., Univ. of Colo., 1968-72; Assoc. Prof., ibid, 1972–. Contbr. to: Michigan's Voices; Nimrod; Caravan: Lyric; Muse; Discourse; Green World; Prairie Poet; Wormwood Review; Lynx; Southwest Times Record; Cyclotron; Renaissance; Kan. City Star; Gallery Sail; Golden Atom; Twigs; Kan. City Times; Hartford Courant; Dust; Midwest; Input; Archer; Am. Poet; Poet Lore; Poet & Critic; Hartford Times; Goliards; Angels; Orange Writer; Scrivener; Poetaster; Writers Notes & Quotes; The Goodly Co.; Jocaranda; Poetry Dial; Enterprise; Cardinal; Poetry Newsletter; Husk; Am. Weave; Plainsong; Gato; Folio; Encore; S. Fla. Poetry Jrnl.; Podium; Poetry Prevue; Sou'wester; Kan. Qtly. Address: 860 12th St., Boulder, CO 80302, U.S.A.

KITSCO, John Phillip, b. 12 Jan. 1947. Writer. Education: Alta. Coll., Edmonton, Canada; Univ. of Calgary. Positions held: Muralist in Ptnrship.; Sales Rep.; Adv. Ed. for newspaper; Dir., Heart of Alta. Art Gall.; Registrar, United Conservatory of Music; Writer, 'Kitsco on Art', Stettler Independent Newspaper. Memberships: Centro Studi e Scambi Int.; Guest Mbr., various Canadian Authors Meetings. Published works: Tears of Joy, 1969. Contbr. to: Orphic Lute; Muse; Guild; Ladies Delight; Jean's Jrnl.; Hoosier Challenger; Manifold; Nutmegger; Canadian Lights; Sunrise Sunset Silhouettes; Fireflower; Northwest Hobby-Go-Round; Villager; Poetry Prevue; Bay Shore Breeze; Tejas; Maganda; Kangaroo's Lining; Am. Bard; Edmonton Cultural Press; Viewpoints; Poet, India. Recip. various poetry awards. Address: Box 1622, Stettler, Alberta, Canada.

KITSON, ViYian Ian, b. 20 Dec. 1944. Freelance Journalist; Writer. Education: B.A., Univ. of Western Australia. Positions held: Co-Ed., Thrust lit. mag., 1965-68. Exec. Mbr., Fellowship of Australian Writers, W.A. Br., 1967-68. Contbr. to: Thrust; Westerly; Poetry Australia; New Poetry; Under 25 anthol., 1966. Address: 27 Albert St., Forest Lodge, Sydney, N.S.W., Australia 2037.

KIVIMAA, Arvi, b. 6 Sept. 1904. Poet; Essayist; Theatre Manager. Education: studied in Paris & in many foreign countries. Married 1) Hilkka Ahti, dec., 2) Kirsti Arnold, 1 son, 1 daughter. Positions held: Jrnlst. & Lit. Critic, 1922-32 & '34-37; Lectr. in Finnish, Univ. of Greisfswald, Germany, 1932-34; Gen. Dir., Tampereen Teatteri, 1937-40; Peoples Theatre, Helsinki, 1940-49; Dir. Gen., Nat. Theatre of Finland, 1950-74. Memberships: Chmn., Finnish PEN, 1936, '54-57; V. Chmn., Finnish Assn. of Writers, 1941-45; Hon. Mbr., Finnish Dramatists League & Finnish Actors League; Exec. Comm., Int. Theatre Inst., 1955-65; V.P., ibid, 1957-65; Pres., Finnish Theatre Union, 1957–. Published works: First Poems, 1925; Selected Poems, 1947; Passacaglia, 1950; Sydamen Levottomuus, 1954; Kerran Firenzessa, 1955; The Most Beautiful Poems (Selection), 1958; Sormus, 1959; Samothraken Nike, 1964; Prokonsuli ja Keisari, 1969; etc. Contbr. to many Finnish & foreign publs. Honours, awards: Twice recipient of Prize of the Finnish Lit. Soc.; Hon. Prize of Wihuris Fndn., 1964; Henrik Steffens Prize, Hamburg, 1971; Hon. Ph.D., Helsinki, 1973, etc. Address: Takojantie 1.L, 02130 Tapiola 3, Finland.

KIYOKAWA, Shoichi, b. 23 Feb. 1945. Poet. Published works: Proust & Lady Murasaki, Japan, 1963; John Cage, translation, Japan, 1971; Images, 1962. Contbr. to: Breakthrough Fictioneers, Anthol., U.S.A., 1973;

Yearbook, Anthol., U.S.A., 1973; N.Y. Qtly.; Poetry Review; Assembling; Ovum (Uruguay); Konglomerati. Recip., Prix de l'Ambassadeur de la France au Japon, 1963. Address: 239 Central Park West, N.Y., NY 10024, U.S.A.

KIZER, Carolyn Ashley, b. 10 Dec. 1925. Writer; Arts Administrator. Education: B.A., Sarah Lawrence Coll.; Grad. Fellowship, Columbia Univ.; Univ. of Wash. Married. Positions held: Fndr. & Ed., Poetry Northwest, 1959-66; Dir. of Literary Progs., Nat. Council on the Arts, 1966-69. Memberships: Former Dir., ALMA (Assoc. of Lit. Mags. of Am.); PEN; Author's League, USA; Acad. of Am. Poets; YMHA Poetry Ctrs. Published works: The Ungrateful Garden, 1962; Knock Upon Silence, 1965. Contbr. to following jrnls: Poetry (Chicago); New Yorker; Atlantic; Harper's; Partisan Review; Hudson Review; Kenyon Review; Sewanee Review; Paris Review; Transatlantic Review; Quarterly Review; New Republic; Nation; Observer (London); Spectator (London); Encounter; Prairie Schooner; Shenandoah; Contact; Choice; Epoch; Drama Survey; Northwest Review, etc. Address: c/o English Dept., Univ. of NC, Chapel Hill, NC, USA.

KLAHR, Myra, b. 16 Apr. 1933. Poet & Co-ordinator of New York State Poets-in-the-Schools Program. Education: B.A., Queens Coll., 1954; M.A., Queens Coll., 1960; poetry workshops with Kenneth Koch & Bill Berkson. Married Meyer Klahr, 4 children. Positions held: Tchr., Elem. Schl. Published works: The Waiting Room, 1972. Contbr. to: Small Pond; Sesheta; Unicorn. Recip., Dylan Thomas Poetry Award 1971. Address: 57 Old Farm Rd., Pleasantville, NY 10570, U.S.A.

KLAPPERT, Peter, b. 14 Nov. 1942. Poet; College Teacher. Education: B.A., Cornell Univ., 1964; M.A., Univ. of Iowa, 1967; M.F.A., Univ. of Iowa Writers' Workshop, 1968. Positions held: Instr., Rollins Coll., 1968-71; Briggs-Copeland Lectr. on Engl. & on Gen. Educ., Harvard Univ., 1971-74; Lectr., New Coll., Sarasota, Fla., summer 1972. Memberships: CEA; MLA. Published works: Lugging Vegetables to Nantucket, 1971. Contbr. to: The Nation; The Atlantic; The Trojan Horse; Epoch; Mill Mountain Review; Iowa Review; North Am. Review; Mass. Review; Poetry Venture; Greenfield Review; Armadillo; N.Y. Qtly.; The New Yorker; Epos; Middle Earth; Harper's; Beyond Baroque; New Am. Review; Arion's Dolphin; Iowa Defender; The Yale Lit., etc. Honours, awards: Yale Series of Younger Poets, 1970; Nat. Endowment for the Arts Award in Creative Writing, 1973; Residences at Yaddo, 1972 & '73 & The MacDowell Colony, 1973. Address: 9 Ellery St., Cambridge, MA 02138, U.S.A.

KLEIN, A(braham) M(oses), b. 14 Feb. 1909. Public Relations Executive. Education: B.A., McGill Univ., Montreal, Can., 1930; B.C.L., Univ. of Montreal, 1933. Married Bessie Koslov w. 3 children. Positions held: Began practising Law, 1933; Dir., Educ., Zionist Org. of Can., 1936-37; Former Ed., Canadian Zionist & Canadian Jewish Chronicle; Special Lectr. in Poetry, McGill Univ., 1946-47; Founder of Preview, First Statement, Northern Review (w. others); Currently, working Public Relations, Montreal. Published works: Hath Not a Jew, 1940; Poems, 1944; Hitleriad, 1944; The Rocking Chair & Other Poems, 1948; Other: The Second Scroll, 1951; Trans., Of Jewish Music, Ancient & Modern, 1952. Contbr. to (Anthols.): New Provinces, 1936; Canadian Poetry in English, 1954; Blasted Pine, 1957; Oxford Book of Canadian Verse, 1960; Penguin Book of Canadian Verse, 1967. (Jrnls.): Menorah Jrnl.; Canadian Forum. Hons: Edward Bland Fellowship Prize, 1947; Governor General's Medal, 1949; Literary Prize from Govt. of Province of Quebec, 1952; Lorne Pierce Gold Medal, 1957.

KLEMMACK, Lucille Eunice, b. 6 Nov. 1907. Housewife; Poet; Artist. Education: Univ. of Minn.; Mnpls. Coll. of Art; Walker Art Ctr., Mnpls. Married Raymond Klemmack. Positions held: Legal Sec., for Atty. John LaDue; Asst. to Editors of Northwest

Publishing Co., Mnpls.; Sec. to Minn. Gov. Theodore Christianson; Public Rep., Mnpls. Gas Co.; Office Mgr. for Archt. Gordon Tamblyn. Memberships: Dir., Midwest Chaparral (& past Vice Regl. Dir.) Minn. Chapt. Vice Regent, Midwest Fed. of Chaparral Poets (& past Treas.); Minn. Art Assn. Contbr. to: Midwest Chaparral (mag. of M.F.C.P.); Minneapolis Argus, etc. Honours, awards: Patron of Poetry, M.W. Chaparral, 1967; poem 'Fo Love of Minnesota', selected for Univ. of Minn's Poetry part of the 1958 Nat. Poetry Contest honouring Minnesota's Centennial; poem 'Be Still' awarded 1st pl. by Critics' Aw Popular vote, M.W. Chaparral, 1967. Address: 3447 So. Garf Minneapolis, MN 55408, U.S.A.

KLIMO, Jonathan, b. 3 Mar. 1942. Teacher. Education: A.B. & A.M., Brown Univ., R.I., 1972. Positions held: Tchr., major course in Creating Writing & courses in Engl. Comp., Phillips Andover Acad., summer session, 1971, '72; Poet, Poetry in Schls. Prog., R.I. State Coun. on Arts, 1970-71, '71-72; Poet, Poetry Writing Workshops in the Schls. Prog., Mass. Coun. on the Arts & Humanities, 1971-72, '73-74; Master Poet, N.J. State Coun. on Arts, 1973-74; Instr.-Poet, U.S. Manpower Dev. & Trng. Act, N.Y., 1973-74; Poet, Poets & Writers, Inc. & Poets-in-the-Schls. Prog., 1973-74; Adj. Prof., Rutgers Univ., New Brunswick, 1974. Chmn., Hellcoal Press (Ed. or Mng. Ed. of 11 Publs.), 1971-72. Chmn., Brown Lit. Bd., Brown Univ., 1971-72. Has given var. poetry readings at colls. & univs. Var. grp. & one-man art shows. Published works: Nineteen Poems, 1968; The Great Nebula in Orion, 1972; Prose Poetry (Ed.), 1972; Hellcoal Annual One, Two (Fndng. Ed.) Contbr. to var. periodicals & anthols. Honours, awards incl: 1st prize, Acad. of Am. Poets, 1970; 1st prize, Gilbert Stuart Prize in Art, 1972. Address: 1220 Washington St., Hoboken, N.J., U.S.A.

KLINGENSMITH, Don Joseph, b. 1 Apr. 1901. Radio Minister; Translator. Education: A.B., John Fletcher Coll., 1928; M.A., Okla. State Univ., 1941; B.D., Garrett Sem., 1946; Ph.D., Fla. State Christian Coll., 1969. Married Thelma Hyde, 1930, 1 s., 1 d. Positions held: Pt.-time Salesman, 1922-28; Pastor, Meth. Ch., 1928-53; Supt., Ponca Indian Meth. Mission, 1936-43; Mgr., Mandan Window Co., 1953-58; Mgr., Mandan Motors, 1958-62; Radio Min., The Word Today, 1962. Member of London Poetry Soc. Published works: The New Testament, Vol. I, according to Matthew, Mark, Luke–Acts in Everyday English, 1967, '68, '69; Victory Song of the People, 1971. Address: PO Box 122, Mandan, ND 58554, USA.

KLINKENBERG, Jean-Marie, pen name **ESOX,** b. 8 Oct. 1944. Assistant Professor. Education: Humanités Anciennes, Verviers, Belgium; studies of Philol. & Linguistics, Univs. of Liège, Belgium & Valladolid, Spain; Dr. in Romanic Philol. Married Claudine Dombret. Positions held: Asst. Prof., Univ. of Liège, Belgium. Memberships: Cercle Interfacultaire de Litterature, Liège, Belgium. Published works: Le Fantastique de l'Intellect, 1969; Rhétorique générale, 1970; Le jeu des figures chez Eluard, 1972; Style et archaïsme, 1973. Contbr. to: Ecritures; Jrnl. des Poètes; Degrés; L'eau Vive; Lettres Romanes; Le Français Moderne; Romanic Review; Bulletin de l'Académie; Le Jour; Communications; Amalgame; Hautes-Fagnes. Recip., Prix de l'Académie royale de langue et de littérature françaises de Belgique, 1969. Address: Residence Plein Vent, 349a rue St. Gilles, B 4000 Liège, Belgium.

KLIPPLE, Georgia Earnest, b. 19 Mar. 1915. Teacher. Education: M.A., Univ. of Texas at Austin; B.A., Mary Hardin-Baylor Coll., Belton, Texas; Del Mar Coll., and Univ. of Corpus Christi, Texas. Married to Philip A.Klipple; 1 d. (Karen). Positions held: Teacher at Zavala School, Austin, Texas; worked on newspaper, Corpus Christi Caller-Times; Teacher in Corpus Christi Public School; Teacher of Engl., in Del Mar Coll., Corpus Christi; Teaching Fellowship in Engl., at Univ. of Texas, Austin; Teacher in Burnet Public School, Texas; worked on newspaper, Burnet Bulletin.

Memberships: Austin Poetry Soc. (Pres.); Texas Poetry Soc.; Southwest Writers' Conference (Treas.); Corpus Christi Colony Writers (Pres.); Austin Kwill Klub; Sigma Tau Delta; Sigma Delta Pi; Royal Academia. Published work: Commencement Address (poems), 1973. Contbr. to: This Friendly Shore (anthol. of prize-winning poems), 1955; Nat. Poetry Anthol. 1957; Poetry Parade, 1963; Melody of the Muse, 1964; Mexican Life; Texas Observer; Texas Outlook; Burnet Bulletin; Corpus Christi Caller-Times; Corpus Christi News; Handbook of Texas. Awards: 1st Prize, Southwest Writers' Conference, 1954, 1955, 1956, 1957; 1st Prize, Colony Writers, 1953, 1954; 1st Prize, Austin Poetry Soc., 1968, 1969, 1970, 1971, 1972, 1973; 3rd Prize, Texas Poetry Soc., 1969; Book of poems, Commencement Address, published on a grant by Prairie Press, Charleston, Ill., 1973. Address: 3104 Beverly Rd., Austin, TX 78703, USA.

KNECHTEL, Cecily Lambert, pen name **LAMBERT, Cecily.** Lecturer. Education: B.A. & M.A., Columbia Univ., N.Y.C., U.S.A. Positions held: Tchr., Piano & Compositions, Julliard Schl. of Mus., N.Y., 1950-58; Lectr. in Writing & Engl. Lit., City Literary Inst., London, U.K., currently. Mbr., Poetry Soc., –1972. Published works: Greek Neighbours, 1971. Contbr. to: Poetry Review; Soup; Pink Peace; Envoi; Headland; Contemporary Review; Country Life; Glasgow Herald; Berkshire Mercury; Tribune; English, etc. Recip., Hon. Mention for poem 'Byron', Poetry Day, 1968. Address: 46 The Bishops Ave., London N2 OBA, U.K.

KNIGHT, Anne Katherine, pen name **KNIGHT, Katherine,** b. 8 July 1933. Home Economist. Education: Tchr. Trng. Course, Nat. Trng. Coll. of Domestic Subjects, 1954-57. Married, 1 daughter, 3 sons. Positions held: Jr. Reporter on local London paper; var. secretarial posts; Lib. Asst.; Tchr.; Home Economist; Housewife & Writer. Memberships: Poetry Soc., London; British Mensa. Contbr. to: Candelabrum; Contemporary Review; Expression One; Library Review; Mensa Jrnl.; Ore; Overspill; Pink Peace; Poetry Now (BBC); Scrip; Tribune. Recip., prize, Premium Comp. of the Poetry Soc., 1972. Address: 54 Woodside Ave., Highgate London N.6 4 ST, U.K.

KNIGHT, Etheridge, b. 1933. Poet. Published works: Poems from Prison, 1968. Contbr. to (Anthols.): For Malcom, 1967; Potere Negro, 1968; New Black Poetry, 1969; (Jrnls.): Negro Digest; Jrnl. of Black Poetry. Address: c/o Broadside Press, 12651 Old Mill Place, Detroit, MI, 48238, USA.

KNIGHT, (George) Wilson, b. 19 Sept. 1897. Professor. Education: M.A., St. Edmund Hall, Oxford Univ. Positions held: Served WWI, Middle E.; Master, Seaford House, Littlehampton, 1920 & St. Peter's, Seaford, 1921; St. Edmund Hall, 1922-23; Honour Schl. of Engl. Lang. & Lit., 1923; Master, Hawtreys, Westgate-on-Sea, 1923-25, & Dean Close Schl., Cheltenham, 1925-31; Chancellors' Prof. of Engl., Trinity Coll., Univ. of Toronto, Canada, 1931-40; Lectr., Jamaica, British Coun. & Coll. of W. Indies, 1951; Vis. Lectr., Univ. of Cape Town, S. Africa, 1952; Byron Fndn. Lecture, Univ. of Nottingham, 1953; Mbr., Delegation to Univ. of Munich, Germany, 1957; Clark Lectures, Cambridge, U.K., 1962; Festival Seminars, Stratford, Canada, 1963, '67; Lectr., Univ. of Chicago, 1963; Rdr. in Engl. Lit., Univ. of Leeds, 1946-56; Prof. of Engl. Lit., ibid, 1956-62; Emeritus; Hon. Fellow, St. Edmund Hall, Oxford, 1965. Produced & Acted in 'This Sceptered Isle', Westminster Theatre, London, 1941; Productions at Leeds Univ. of Agamemnon, Athalie, Timon of Athens, & performances of Timon, Lear, Othello & Shylock, 1946-60. BBC Talks & Readings on Shakespeare & Byron, 1963-64. Published works: Myth & Miracle, 1929; The Wheel of Fire, 1930; The Imperial Theme, 1931; The Shakespearian Tempest, 1932; The Christian Renaissance, 1933; Principles of Shakespearian Production, 1936; Atlantic Crossing, 1936; The Burning Oracle, 1939; This Sceptered Isle, 1940; The Starlit Dome, 1941; Chariot of Wrath, 1942; The Olive & The Sword, 1944; The Dynasty of Stowe,

1945; Hiroshima, 1946; The Crown of Life, 1947; Christ & Nietzsche, 1948; Lord Byron: Christian Virtues, 1952; Laureate of Peace, 1954; The Last of the Incas, 1954; The Mutual Flame, 1955; Lord Byron's Marriage, 1957; The Sovereign Flower, 1958; The Golden Labyrinth, 1962; Ibsen, 1962; Shakespearian Production, 1964; The Saturnian Quest, 1965; Byron & Shakespeare, 1966; Shakespeare & Religion, 1967; Poets of Action, 1967; Gold Dust (poems), 1968; Neglected Powers, 1971; Ed. & intro., Elysion by W.F. Jackson Knight, 1970. Contbr. to: John Masefield, OM, 1960; Times Lit. Supplement; Yorkshire Post; Review of Engl. Studies; Essays in Criticism; Twentieth Century, etc. Honours: Hon. Litt. D., Sheffield, 1967; Hon. D. Litt., Exeter, 1968; CBE, 1968; Fellow, Royal Soc. of Lit.; Fellow, Int. Inst. of Arts & Letters. Address: Caroline House, Streatham Rise, Exeter, Devon, U.K.

KNIGHT, Helen Jane Craigen, pen name **JANE,** b. 14 Oct. 1910. Apiarist. Education: Creative Writing Courses, Univ. of Wis.; Coll. Workshops & Seminars, ibid; Christian Writers Workshop, Green Lake, Wis. Married, 6 children. Memberships: Pres., Women's Aux. Wis. Honey Producers Assn.; Sec., Bible Church Missionary Soc., 25 yrs.; Corres. Sec., Wis. Regl. Writers Assn., 5 yrs.; Portage Writers Workshop; Wis. Fellowship of Poets; Nat. Fed. of State Poetry Socs. Contbr. to: Mnpls. Argus; Voice mag.; The Farmer; People-Places-Things; Showcase mag.; Portage Daily Register; Farm Wife mag.; Portage Writers, vol. 1, book 1; Am. Bee Jrnl. Address: Box 7, Dalton, WI 53926, U.S.A.

KNIGHT, Jeanne Enid, b. 6 Dec. 1923. Educator. Education: B.A., Hunter Coll., 1946; M.A., Columbia Univ., 1949. Married Reginald Caywood Knight, Architect (now dec'd); children: Jeanne Enid; Houghton Caywood; Eliot Holladay. Positions held: Instr., Engl., Wagner Coll., Staten Island, NY, 1946-51; Staff, Holy Trinity Day School, Maryland, 1967; Staff, St. Peter & Paul School, Florida, Spring 1968. Membership: Sigma Tau Delta. Contbr. to: The Islander (Anna Maria Island, Florida); Sarasota Herald Tribune; Echo Mag. (Hunter Coll.). Address: Box 47, Oxford, MS. 38655. USA.

KNIGHT, John. Poet. Published works incl: Straight Lines & Unicorns, 1960; Other Causes of Love, 1969. Contbr. to the following jrnls., mags. etc: Ambit; Delta, Paris; The Dublin Mag.; Enigma; The Listener; The Malahat Review; The Mass. Review; The New English Weekly; Outposts; Phoenix; Poetry, Chicago; Poetry & Audience; The Poetry Review; Solem; The Spectator; The Times Lit. Supplement; The Guinness Book of Poetry, 1960-61; Here Today; Let There Be God; New Poems, 1958, etc. Address: The Canyack, Bosorne, St. Just, Penzance, Cornwall, U.K.

KNODEL, Fern Evelyn Gay. Writer; Artist; Poet. Education: Profl. Writers' Coll., . Hollywood, Calif., studied voice & art, Wash. & Calif. Married to Henry Knodel. Memberships: former Pres., Poetry Scribes, Spokane, Wash.; Nat. League of Am. Pen Women; Am. Poetry League; Poets of the Pacific; United Poets Laureate Int. Contbr. to: Turquoise Lantern; Tacoma News Tribune; Albatross; Spokane Chronicle; Driftwind; Daily Meditation; Southland; Poetry Broadcast. Awards & Honours: Poet Laureate of Wash., 1948-49; Lilac Poet, 1959; Karta of Award & Gold Medal, United Poets Laureate Int., Embassy of Philippines, 1965; sev. awards from poetry socs. & jrnls. Address: 3006 Broadway, Huntington Pk., Calif. 90255, USA.

KNOEPFLE, John, b. 4 Feb. 1923. University Teacher. Education: Ph.B., Xavier Univ., Cinn., 1949; M.A., ibid., 1951; Ph.D., St. Louis Univ., 1967. Married Margaret Sower w. 4 children. Positions held: Lectr., Southern Ill. Univ., East St. Louis, 1957-61; Asst. Prof., Maryville Coll., St. Louis, 1963-66; Mbr. Fac., St. Louis Univ., 1966–; Assoc. Prof., ibid., 1969–. Published works: Rivers into Islands, 1965; After Gray Days &

Other Poems, 1969; Songs for Gail Guidry's Guitar, 1969; Trans., Twenty Poems of Cesar Vallejo, 1961. Contbr. to (Anthols.): From the Hungarian Revolution, 1966; Heartland, 1967. Hons: Fellow in Writing, Rockefeller Foundation, 1967-68. Address: 742 Trinity, Univ. City, MO 63130, USA.

KNOTT, William Kilborn, Pseudonyms, **Bill Knot (1940-66), Saint Geraud,** b. 17 Feb. 1940. Hospital Orderly. Published works: The Naomi Poems Book One: Corpse & Beans, 1968; Auto-Necrophilia, 1969. Contbr. to (Anthols.): Young American Poets, 1968. Address: 201 North Wells Street, Chicago, IL 60657, USA.

KNOWLES, Randall Eugene, b. 4 July 1947. Zoo Keeper. Positions held: Keeper of large carnivores at The Tulsa Zoo. Contbr. to Poet International, 1973. Address: 2638 N. Maplewood, Tulsa, OK, U.S.A.

KNOWLES, Susanne, b. 21 May 1911. Writer. Educated in Italy. Positions held: Sec. work, House of Commons, London, the Civil Service & the printing industry. Fellow, Int. PEN (London Ctr.) Published works: Birth of Venus & Other Poems, 1945; Mediterranean & Other Poems, 1962; Chorus: An Anthology of Bird Poems, 1969; The Sea-Bell & Other Poems, 1974. Contbr. to: Times Lit. Supplement; The Observer; The New Statesman; The Listener; Christian Sci. Monitor; Country Life; The Humanist; The Friend; The Inquirer; Poetry Review; Writing in England Today (anthol.), 1968 & other anthols. Address: 7 Glendower Rd., London SW14 8NY, U.K.

KNOX, Wilbur B., b. 25 Nov. 1912. Minister & Poet. Education: A.B., Johnson C. Smith Univ., 1946; B.D., Schl. of Theol., ibid, 1950. Positions held: Pastorates: Trinity Bapt. Ch., Rock Hill; First Washington Bapt. Ch., Lancaster, S.C.; Tchr. in Public Schls. in S.C. & Friendship Jr. Coll., Rock Hill. Co-Author, The Gold Medal Series of Contemporary Poets, 1950. Contbr. to: Best American Poems, 1967; Anthology of Poetry, 1949. Address: 307 W. Moore St., Rock Hill, SC 29730, U.S.A.

KOCH, James Harold, b. 5 Mar. 1926, Milwaukee, Wis. Writer. Education: B.A., Carleton Coll., Northfield, Min.; Woodrow Wilson Fellow, Princeton Univ. Positions held: w. Dun & Bradstreet, Inc., 1952-65; Credit Reporter, 1952-56; Dir. Mail Advt. Mgr., 1957-65; currently President, Aquarian Advtg. Assocs. Inc. Memberships: Poetry Soc. of Am.; Mensa. Contbr. to: NY Times; Wis. Poetry Mag.; Furioso; Western Review; Voix des Poètes; PSA Anthol., The Golden Year. Address: 1020 Park Ave., New York, NY 10028, USA.

KOCH, Kenneth, b. 27 Feb. 1925. Writer. Education: A.B., Harvard Univ., 1948; Ph.D., Columbia Univ., 1959. Positions held: Prof. of English & Comp. Lit., Columbia Univ. Published works incl: Poems, 1953; Ko, or a Season on Earth, 1959; Thank You & Other Poems, 1962; Bertha & Other Plays, 1966; The Pleasures of Peace, 1970; When the Sun Tries to Go On, 1970; Wishes, Lies and Dreams: Teaching Children to Write Poetry, 1970. Contbr. to the following anthols., jrnls., mags., etc: Poetry; Paris Review; Locus Solus; Art & Literature, etc. Honours, Awards: Harbison Award, Danforth Fndn., 1970; Guggenheim Fellowship, 1961; Fulbright Fellow, 1951. Address: Dept. of English, Columbia Univ., New York, NY 10027, USA.

KOEHLER, Stanley, b. 27 Mar. 1915. Teacher. Education: A.B., Princeton, 1936; M.A., ibid, 1938; Ph.D., 1942; M.A., Harvard Univ., 1937. Positions held: Instr. in Engl., Okla. State Univ., 1938-40; Instr. in Engl., Kan. Univ., 1946; Yale Univ., 1946-50; Vis. Prof., Amherst Coll., 1966-67; Prof. of Engl., Univ. of Mass., 1950. Memberships: Milton Soc. of Am.; MLA. Published works: A Curious Quire (co-author), 1962; 'The Perfect Destroyers', Mass. Review Signature Series of Poets No. 1, 1966; The Fact of Fall, 1969. Contbr. to: Yale Review; Sewanee Review; Poetry;

Mass. Review; Voices; New Am. Poets No. 2. Address: Dept. of Engl., Bartlett Hall, Univ. of Mass., Amherst, MA 01002, U.S.A.

KOERTGE, Ronald (Boyd), b. 22 Apr. 1940. Teacher. Education: Collinsville H.S.; U. of Ill., B.A.; U. of Ariz., M.A. Pubs.: Meat, 1973; The Father-Poems, 1973. Contrib. to: Wormwood Review; Sumac; Beloit Poetry Journal; Kansas Qtly.; Western Humanities Review; New College; L.A. Anthol. of Poets; The Living Underground; Trace; Occident; Pyramid; Bear, etc. Address: 55 Arlington Dr., Pasadena, Calif. 91105, U.S.A.

KOGAWA, Joy Nozomi, b. 6 June 1935. Education: HS. grad. 1953; various univ. courses, theology and music courses. Positions held: School Teacher; Teacher of Adults; Correspondence Writer, Prime Minister's Office. Membership: Canadian League of Poets. Published works: The Splintered Moon, 1967; (another book "A Choice of Dreams" forthcoming). Contbr. to: Forty Women Poets of Canada (anthol.), 1972; Poet (India); The Lit. Half Yearly (India); New Canadian & American Poetry; The Chicago Review; Alphabet; Edge; Canadian Forum; Fiddlehead; Chatelaine; Quarry; Queen's Qtly.; Prism Internat.; Other Voices; Anthology, C.B.C.; West Coast Review, etc. Awards: Saskatchewan Arts Bd. Scholarship, 1967; Canada Council Grant, 1969, 1973. Address: 185 4th Ave., Ottawa K15 2L5 Ontario, Canada.

KOLKER, (Sister) Delphine, pen name KOLKER, Eleanor, b. 12 Apr. College Professor. Education: B.S., Educ., Univ. of Dayton; M.A., Ph.D., Cath. Univ. of Am.; Postgrad., Univ. of Notre Dame, Ind.; New York Schl. of Writing. Personal details; Mbr. of Congregation of the Sisters of the Precious Blood. Positions held: Univ. of Dayton Ext., 1945-58; St. Joseph Coll., Rensselair, Ind., 1958-60; St. John Coll., 1960-71; currently Prof. of Engl. & Philos., ibid. Memberships: MLA; Shakespeare Assn.; American Catholic Philosophical Assoc.; Library of Ohio Writers. Author of Aspects & Attitudes, 1964. Contbr. to: Cat's Magazine; Pa. State Poetry Publ.; Ohio Poetry Day. Recip. of num. local & state comp. prizes. Address: St. John Coll., Cathedral Square, Cleveland, Ohio 44114, USA.

KOLLER, James, b. 30 May 1936. Poet. Education: B.A., North Central Coll., Naperville, Ill., 1958. Married, 3 children. Published works: Two Hands, poems, 1959-61, 1965; Brainard & Washington Street Poems, 1965; The Dogs & Other DarkWoods, 1966; Some Cows, Poems of Civilization & Domestic Life, 1966; I Went to See My True Love, 1967; California Poems, 1971; Messages, 1972. Contbr. to: Choice; Coyote's Jrnl.; The Floating Bear; The Paris Review; Out of Sight; Locus Solus; Poetry Review; The San Francisco Oracle; The Yale Review, etc. Recip., Nat. Endowment for the Arts Fellowship, 1973. Address: P.O. Box 629, Brunswick, ME 04011, U.S.A.

KOLTZ, Charles Ross, b. 9 June 1945. Poet. Education: Montclair State Coll., N.J., 1963-68; Creative Writing at Univ. of Ore., 1971 & Univ. of B.C., 1973. Contbr. to: Poetry of Our Times, 1973; Wascana Review, 1971; Prism Int., 1970 & '74; Wendigo, 1969; Fiddlehead, 1971 & '73; Quarry, 1971; Yearbook of Modern Poetry, 1971; Corduroy, 1973; Poet, 1970 & '71; Little Mother, 1969. Address: RR.1, Chapman Rd., Cobble Hill, B.C., Canada.

KOMEY, Ellis Ayitey, b. 1927. Editor. Education: Accra Acad. Positions held: Formerly Free-lance Journalist; Currently African Ed., Flamingo Mag. Published works: Ed. w. Ezekiel Mphahlele, Modern African Stories, 1964. Contbr. to (Anthols.): Voices of Ghana, 1958; Modern Poetry from Africa, 1963; Poems from Black Africa, 1963; (Jrnls.): Black Orpheus.

KONAN, Kakou, pen name NOKAN, Zégoua (Charles), b. 28 Dec. 1936. Professor. Education: Licencié en sociologie; Docteur en Philosophie.

Married, 3 children. Published works: Le Soleil Noir Point, récit, 1962; Violent Etait le Vent, roman, 1966; Les Malheurs de Chako, theatre, 1968; Abraha Pokan, theatre, suivi de la Voix Grave d'Ophinoi, poeme; La Traversee de la Nuit Dense ou Les Travailleurs Africainsen, France, theatre, suivi de Cris Rouge, 1972. Contbr. of var. articles to Jeune Afrique. Address: B.P. No. 103, Yamoussokro, Cote d'Ivoire.

KONICK, Marcus, b. 22 Oct. 1914. College Administrator & Professor of English. Education: B.S. in Educ., Temple Univ., 1936; M.A., Univ. of Pa., 1937; Ph.D., ibid, 1953. Married Evelyn Goldstein. Positions held: Lit. Sec. to Emily Solis-Cohen, 1936-40; Tchr. of Engl., Gillespie Jr. H.S., Philadelphia, 1941-44 & Northeast Sr. H.S., 1944-57; Hd. of Engl. & For. Lang. Depts., Edison Sr. H.S., Phila., 1957-60; Dir., Bureau of Instructional Materials & Services, Pa. Dept. of Public Instrn., 1960-66; Assoc. Prof. of Engl., Elizabethtown & Lebanon Vall. Colls., 1961-66; Dir., Div. of Humanities, Lock Haven State Coll., 1966-73; Dir., Academic Servs., Lock Haven State Coll., 1973-. Memberships: Pres., Pa. Coun. of Tchrs. of Engl., 1957-59; Nat. Coun. of Tchrs. of Engl.; Pa. Engl. Club. Published works: Land of Promise, 1937; Co-Ed., Tales in Verse, 1963; Ed., The Rubaiyat of Omar Khayyam by Edward Fitzgerald, 1967; currently working on Dramatic verse transl. of marriage grp. from Chaucer's Canterbury Tales. Address: 1214 N. Hillview St., Lock Haven, PA 17745, U.S.A.

KONNYU, Leslie, b. 28 Feb. 1914. Retired Geographer, Cartographer. Education: Elem. Tchrs. Dip., Baja, Hunary, 1933; Sec. Tchrs. Dip., Szeged, 1944; B. Mus. Educ., St. Louis Music & Arts Coll., U.S.A., 1954; Cartographers Dip., Defense Mapping Agency, St. Louis, 1957; M.A. in Geography, St. Louis Univ., 1968. Positions held: Elem. Tchr., Perecse-Jaszbereny, Hungary, 1936-42; Sec. Tchr., Nagykata H.S., 1942-44; Dir., Refugee Schl., Ampflwang, Austria, 1944-49; Church Organist, St. Peter's, Jefferson City, Mo., U.S.A., 1949-51; Lab. Techn., Schl. of Med., Wash. Univ., St. Louis, 1951-55; Cartographer, Defense Mapping Agency, St. Louis, 1955-73. Memberships incl: Int. PEN, N.Y., 1968; Mo. Writers' Guild, 1966; Treas., St. Louis Writers' Guild, 1968; Dir., St. Louis Poetry Ctr., 1972-; past mbr. var. Hungarian lit. assns. Published works: (Engl.) Bond of Beauty, 1959; Against the River, 1961; Collected Poems, 1968; (French) J'accuse mon Epoque, 1972; (German) Gedichte von Osterreich, 1965; (Hungarian) Tavaszi Uton, 1934; Sikoltas a Pusztan, 1935; Koltogeto alm aim Ravatalanal, 1938; Utszeli fak, 1943; Koratavasztol-Oszirozsakig, 1959; Szemben az arral, 1961; Idegenben, 1967; Osszegyujtott Versek, 1969. Contbr. to var. jrnls., reviews in U.S.A., Germany, Hungary. Honours, awards: Vas Gereben Lit. Award, 1938; Gardonyi Lit. Award, 1938. Cert. of Merit, D.I.B., 1971. Address: 5410 Kerth Rd., St. Louis, MO 63128, U.S.A.

KONONOWICZ, Józef Maciej, pen names HALIN, Maciej & MACIEJ, b. 1 Feb. 1912. Writer & Journalist. Education: Fac. of Arts, Univ. of Warsaw, Poland, 1934-39. Married Krystyna, 6 children. Positions held: Deputy Ed., lit. sect., Dziś i Jutre, weekly; Mgr., Słowo Powszechne, daily local office in Lódź; M.P. for Lódź in Seym/Parliament of Poland, 1957-61; Ed.-in-Chief of WTK weekly. Memberships: Pax, Publishing Inst.; Deputy Chmn. of Lódź Br. of Polish Writers Union, ZLP; Deputy Chmn. of Catholic Writers Club, Krag; PEN; Polish Jrnlsts. Assn. Published works: (poetry books) Stacje liryczne, 1951; W ramionach srebrnych rzek, 1953; W sitowiu niebieskim, 1957; Portret nieurojony, 1962; Rekonstrukcja biografii, 1967; (lyrical prose) Biskup Michał, 1968; (stories) Szyfr o ojczyźnie, 1971; (novel) Kilka imion miłości, 1973. Transl. of novels & poems from Byelorussian, etc. Contbr. to var. newspapers & jrnls. Recip., Lit. Award, Imienia Włodzimierza Pietrzaka, 1971. Address: ul. Mickiewicza 8 m.10, 90-444 Lodz, Poland.

KONRICK, Vera Bishop (Mrs.), b. 4 Mar. 1900. Writer; Poet; Artist. Memberships: Sec., Avalon World Arts

Acad., San Angelo, Tex., 1951-53; Nat. Councillor, ibid, 1953-55; Hon Life Mbr., 1952–; Nat. Vice-Pres. 1968–; Asst. Nat. Chmn., World Poetry Day, Philadelphia, Pa., 1963; State Chmn., La. Poetry Day, 1956-63; Western NY Chmn., Nat. Poetry Day Inc., 1963; Adv. Cons., Rochester Poetry Day, 1963–; Adv. Cons., Rochester World & Nat. Poetry Day, 1965–; Co-judge, Poetry Contest, Fed. of State Poetry Socs., Baton Rouge, La., 1966; Chmn., La., Composers, Authors & Artists of Am., 1953-57; Treas., Crescent City Chap., Nat. League of Am. Pen Women, 1953-55; Archivist Histn., ibid, 1955–; Chap. Pres., Sidney Lanier Chap., Avalon World Arts Acad., 1951-56; Nat. Poetry Soc.; Am. Poetry League; New Orleans World SF Gov. Publications: Moon Flame, 1953. Contbr. to: (anthols.) Eros, 1939; Fire, Sleet & Candlelight, 1961; Conquerors of Tomorrow, 1947; From Sea To Sea in Song, 1966; The Minds Create, 1961; Flame Annual, 1964, '65; To Each His Song, 1958; With No Secret Meaning, 1957; This Shall Endure, 1955; Nat. Poetry Day Anthol., 1965; Etta Josephean Murfey Mem. Book (anthol.), Nat. Poetry Day Committee, 1969; Internat. Who's Who in Poetry Anthol., 1972, etc. (jrnls.) Westminster Mag.; Starlanes; Golden Atom; Candor; Chromatones; Challenge; Cyclotron; Cyclo-Flame; Chimes; 'Different; Flame; Am. Poet; Verse Leaves; Prairie Poet; Nat. Penwoman; Mardi Gras Parade; Embers; Jackson Herald; Jean's Jrnl. Poems trans. into & publd. in French, Greek & Spanish, & read over La., Va. & Pa. radio stations. Honours: Poet Laureate, La. Poetry Day, 1953-54; Diploma, Radio Stations WBUX & WEFG-FM, 1967; Silver Medal & Diploma of Merit, Centro Studi e Scambi Internazionali, Rome, 1968; Bronze Medal, ibid, 1967; Diploma, Internat. Acad. of Leadership: Dr. of Lit. Leadership, the Philippines, 1968; Poet of the Month, Cahokia Herald & Dupo Trib., Ill., 1967, & many others. Address: c/o Golden Atom Publications, P.O. Box 1101, Rochester, NY 14603, USA.

KOONTS, J(ones) Calvin, b. 19 Sept. 1924. Educator. Education: A.B., Catawba Coll., Salisbury, N.C., 1945; M.A., Geo. Peabody Coll., Nashville, Tenn., 1949; Ph.D., ibid, 1958. Married, 1 son, 1 daughter. Positions held: Asst. to the Dir. of Student Tchng., Geo. Peabody Coll., 1951-52; Prof. of Educ. & Psychol., Erskine Coll., 1949-51; Hd., Dept. of Educ., ibid, 1953–; Tchr., Adult Educ., Abbeville Co. Community Ctr., 1955; Tchr. of the Univ. of S.C. ext. courses, 1955-56. Memberships: Sec.-Treas., Salisbury unit of the N.C. Educ. Assn., 1946-47; Liaison Rep., S.C., Am. Assn. of Colls. for Tchr. Educ.; Fndr., S.C. Assn. for Student Tchng.; Pres., ibid, 1955-56; NEA; S.C. State Coun. on Tchr. Educ.; S.C. Educ. Assn., Nat. Del. Assembly, Assn. of Tchr. Educrs., rep. S.C.; Fellow, Acad. of Am. Poets, etc. Published works: I'm Living in a Dream (song), 1947; Straws in the Wind, book of collected verse, 1968; Under the Umbrella, book of poetry. Editor, Green Leaves in January, 1972. Poems rep. in Nat. Poetry Anthol., 1957, 59, 60 & 62. Honours, awards: Algernon Sydney Sullivan Award, 1951; Holds Gov's appt. as Commnr. of Piedmont Tech. Educ. Ctr., Greenwood, S.C.; Winner, William Gilmore Simms Poetry Prize in S.C., 1973. Address: P.O. Box 163, Erskine Coll., Due West, SC 29639, U.S.A.

KOOSER, Ted, b. 25 Apr. 1939. Insurance Underwriter. Education: B.S., Iowa State Univ.; M.A. in Engl., Univ. of Neb., U.S.A. Published works: Official Entry Blank, 1969; Grass County, 1971; Twenty Poems, 1973. Contbr. to: Evergreen; The Lyric; Ga. Review; Rain; S. Fla. Poetry Journal; Univ. of Tampa Poetry Review; Prairie Schooner; Poet & Critic; Pebble; Rapport; Cottonwood Review; S.D. Review; Hearse; New; Am. & Canadian Poetry; Cafe Solo; Arke River Review; December; The Reporter; Stuffed Crocodile; Southern Poetry Review; The Little Review; Latitudes; Counter/Measures; Midwest Quarterly; Penny Poems from Midwestern Univ.; N.Am. Review; Scrip; Jean's Jrnl; Epos; Lyrics of Love; Dragonfly; Crazy Horse; Saltillo; The Salt Creek Reader, etc. Recip., John H. Vreeland Award, 1964. Address: 1720½ C. St.Lincoln, NB, U.S.A.

KOPETKA, Patricia Christine, pen name, **LATES, Patricia,** b. 27 Feb. 1952. Currently employed in the office of a major insurance co. Active Mbr., Laul Publishers Int. Poetry Symposium. Published works: Yearbook of Modern Poetry, 1971; Tower by the Sea, 1973; Shore Poetry Anthology, to be published 1973. Address: 1409 B Nottingham, Coram, NY 11727, U.S.A.

KOPPLER, Guinevere, pen name **KOPPLER, Vera & GORDON, Guinevere,** b. 16 Jan. 1914. Housewife. Married Leon F. Koppler, 5 children. Memberships: UAPA; Poet's Study Club of Terre Haute, Ind.; V.P., ibid, 1970-73; Contest Chmn., 1973-74; Libn., 1968-70; Ill. State Poetry Soc.; Ind. State Poetry Soc.; The Strugglers; The Brainstormers; The Ala. State Poetry Soc., 1972. Contbr. to: Grains of Sand anthol., 1971; Premier Poets anthol., 1970; Grit; Christian Home; Capper's Weekly; Inky Trails; Poet; Modern Haiku; Poet's Roundtable, etc. Published Lilacs, 1968; Wild Harvest, 1969; Little poems from a little mind (light verse), 1972. Recip., Hon. Mention, The Parody Prize, State Poetry Socs., 1973; Lillie Chaffin Award, Kentucky State Contest, 1973. Address: Rte.1, Box 243, Marshall, IL 62441, U.S.A.

KOPROWSKI, Jan, b. 10 Feb. 1918. Writer. Education: studies in philol., Univ. of Warsaw, 1937-39. Married, 3 sons. Positions held: Lit. Adviser, Teats Nowy, Lodz, 1953-64; Chief Ed., Kronika, Lodz, 1955-58 & Odgtosy, 1964-72; Ed., Literatura, Warsaw, 1972–. Memberships: Chmn., Foreign Sect., Polish Writers' Union; Polish PEN. Published works: (poetry) W tym Krajn, 1958; Studina przesztosci, 1961; Soze i Miskie, 1967; Nocne rodaliou rozmovy, 1974; (prose) Zidone Drzcwa – selection of stories, 1972; Wiezor u Cafe Raimund – stories, 1974; (essays) Z potudnia i potnocy, 1963; Drien pouszedin literatury, 1973; (translations) Peter Huchel – poems, 1967; Georg Trakl – poems, 1973. Contbr. to var. jrnls. Recip., Lit. Prize of the City of Lodz, 1966. Address: Dragonow 2, m 6, 00-467 Warsaw, Poland.

KOPS, Bernard, b. 28 Nov. 1926. Writer. Education: London Schls. Positions held: Docker; Chef; Door-to-door Salesman; Waiter; Liftman; Barrow-boy; Patient, Belmont Psych. Hosp., 1951; Resident Dramatist British Old Vic, 1959. Published works: Poems, 1955; Poems & Songs, 1958; An Anemone for Antigone, 1959; Erica, I Want to Read You Something, 1967; (novels) Awake for Mourning, 1958; Yes from No Man's Land, 1967; The Dissent of Dominick Shapiro, 1967; By the Waters of Whitechapel, 1970; (plays) David, It is Getting Dark, 1959; The Dream of Peter Mann, 1959; Four Plays, 1964; The Boy Who Wouldn't Play Jesus, 1965; (autobiog.) The World is a Wedding, 1964. Contbr. to various anthols. Address: 35 Canfield Gdns., London NW3, UK.

KORIYAMA, Naoshi, b. 3 Nov. 1926. Professor of English. Education: Kagoshima Normal Coll., 1941-47; Okinawa Foreign Language School, 1948-49; Univ. of New Mexico, 1950-51; NY State Coll. for Teachers at Albany, NY., 1951-54 (B.A., 1954). Married, I d., 2 s. Professor of English, Toyo Univ., since 1961. Membership: The Poets' Soc. of Japan. Published works: Coral Reefs, 1957; Plum Tree in Japan and Other Poems, 1959; Songs from Sagamihara, 1967; Chaucer Goes to Expo '70 (1), 1972; Chaucer Goes to Expo '70 (11), 1973. Contbr. to: CS Monitor; Poetry Nippon. Address: 2-chome-15-9, Yaei, Sagamihara-shi, Kanagawa-ken, Japan.

KORN, Rachel, b. 15 Jan. 1898. Poetess. Memberships: Int. PEN; World Poetry Soc.; Soviet Writers Union. Published works: The Village, 1928; Earth, 1935; Red Puppies, 1937; Home & Homelessness, 1948; Destiny, 1949; Beyond the Song, 1962; The Grace of Words, 1968; On the Edge of a Second, 1972. Contbr. to: The Poet; The Golden Chain, Israel; The Future, N.Y.; Sviva, N.Y. Honours, awards: Louis Lamed Prize, 1958; Chaim Greenburg Prize; Jewish Culture Prize; Kouner Meml. Poetry Award. 1969; H. Leivick Prize, 1972. Address: 21

Maplewood Ave., Montreal 153, Quebec, Canada.

KORNBLUM, Allan, b. 16 Feb. 1949. Poet, Printer. Education: NY Univ.; Univ. of Iowa; St. Mark's Poetry Project Workshops. Married. Positions held: US Post Office; Editor and Printer, Toothpaste Mag. & Press. Charter Member of Actualism. Pubs. Famous Americans, 1970; Tight Pants, 1971; The Salad Bushes, 1973. Contrib. to: Telephone; Gum; Oink; Milk Qtly.; Search for Tomorrow; Diana's Bimonthly; Sebastian Quill; NY Times; Candy; Penumbra; Asphalt, etc. Address: Box 546, West Branch, Iowa 52358, USA.

KOSTELANETZ, Richard, b. 14 May 1940. Writer; Lecturer. Education: A.B., Brown Univ., 1962; M.A., Columbia Univ., 1966; Fulbright Scholar, King's Coll., Univ. of London, 1964-65. Positions held: Writer, 1965-; Co-Fndr.-Compiler, Assembling (an annual); Contbng. Ed., Arts in Society, The Humanist, Lotta Poetica; var. lectures (including illuminated demonstrations of his poetry & fiction). Member, Am. PEN. Published works: Visual Language, 1970; In the Beginning, 1971; Accounting, 1972; Ad Infinitum, 1973; I Articulations, 1974. Contbr. to var. anthols., jrnls., mags. Honours, awards: Pulitzer Fellowship in Critical Writing, Columbia Univ., 1965; Guggenheim Fellowship, 1967-68. Address: c/o Assembling, P.O. Box 1967, Brooklyn, NY 11202, U.S.A.

KOTHARI, Madhu R., b. 16 Apr. 1939. Teacher. Education: M.A. Psychol. Positions held: Ed., lit. section in daily newspaper, 1968-72; Ed., Tantrum lit. monthly, 1968-. Memberships: Sec., experimental group, 1968; Chmn. & Fndr. Mbr., Daroon Daroon Grp. (Forgs' Voice), 1969. Published works: Chavine Thunki Doonchchu, 1964; Falananu Flowervase (poetic plays), 1968; Orbit, 1970; Sahityamon Manoyjanik Abhigam (criticism), 1973. Contbr. to: Samarpan; Navnit; Kesundon; Abhivykati; Kru, & other leading regional jrnls.; Century; Poet; Accent; Tornado. Recip., Govt. Award for the book of criticism on poetry. Address: Ed., Tantrum, Alphabet Schl., Kotecha Nagar, Rajkot 360001, India.

KOTOWICZ, Caroline Stefanec b. 26 July 1918. Poet Laureate, American Poets Fellowship Society. Married, Adam Kotowicz. Memberships: Sec. Treas., Arrowhead Poetry, Duluth, 1960-63; Am. Poets Fellowship Soc.; Am. Poets League; World Poetry Soc. Intercontinental; League of Minn. Poets; Ariz. State Poetry Soc.; Fla. Poetry State Soc., Inc.; Wis. Fellowship of Poets; Midwest Fed. of Chapparal Poets; Centro Studi e Scambi Internazionali, Italy; Accademia Internazionali Leonardo da Vinci, Rome. Contbr. to: (anthols.) Bread of Heartbeats, 1949; Anthol. of Am. Poetry, Bks. V, VI, VII, VIII, IX, X, XI 1963-71; Glow of Northern Lights Anthol., 1963; Haiku Anthol., 1966; The Soul & The Singer, 1968; Golden Harvest, 1967; New Poetry, 1967; Penpoint Serenade, 1947; La Poésie Contemporaine aux Etats-Unis (France), 1962; Bouquet of Poems (Italy), 1966-69; Burst of Trumpets, 1966; Todays Poets, Vol. 5, 1964; Fragments of Faith, 1963; Melody of the Muse, 1964; Rhyme Time, 1964; Versatility in Verse, 1965; Int. Hall of Fame Poets Anthol., 1968, '69, '70, '71; Sing Naked Spirit Anthol., 1970; Prairie Poet Anthol., 1970; New Voices in the Wind, 1969; Am. Poets Fellowship Soc. Anthol., 1967, '68, '69, '70, '71; The New Poetry Anthol.; 1967; 9 Muses Anthol., 1971 Pan Continental Premier Poets Anthol., 1970; New Poetry Out of Wisconsin, 1969; All Time Favourite Poetry Anthol., 1970; Mainstream American Poetry, 1966; Moon Age Poets, 1970; The Spring Anthology, London, 1968, '69, '70, '71; (jrnls.) Jean's Jrnl.; Stanza; Candor; Blue Moon; Flamingo; United Poets; Inky Trails; Duluth Herald & Trib., etc., etc. Honours: IV Poet Laureate, Am. Poets Fellowship Soc., 1969; Bronze, Silver & Gold Medals, Centro Studi e Scambi, Rome; Gold Medal, Accademia Internazionali Leonardo da Vinci, 1968, World Poet Award Winner, Magna cum Laude, 1970; 1st Place, I Am an American Contest, etc. Address: 215 Fairview Ave., S. Milwaukee, Wis. 53172, USA.

KOWALSKI, John J., b. 8 Oct. 1928. Teacher; Writer; Poet. Education: A.B., Emerson Coll., Boston, Mass.; Ed.M., Worcester State Coll., Mass. Married; 3 d. Position held: Engl. Teacher, Lyman Hall HS, Wallingford, Conn. Memberships: Acad. of American Poets (Founder in); Internat. Poetry Soc. (Fellow). Contbr. to: Chicago Tribune; English Journal; Denver Post; Dion; The Clearing House; American Forests; American Bard; Cyclo-Flame; Air Force Times; Hartford Courant; Voices Internat.; Imprints Qtly.; American Poet, etc. Address: 118 Algonquin Dr., Wallingford, CT 06492, USA.

KOZER, José, b. 28 Mar. 1940. Educator. Education: law studies, Havana Univ.; B.A., N.Y. Univ., 1965; M.A., Queens Coll., 1970; Ph.D. in progress. Positions held: Lectr. (w. Tenure), Queens Coll., N.Y., 1967-. Memberships: Phi Lambda Beta; Portuguese Honors Soc. Published works: Padres y otras profesiones, 1971; De Chepen a La Habana (published in conjunction with the work of Isaac Goldemberg, each poet with a separate individual title for his own poems, Kozer's being, Por la libre), 1972; Poemas de Guadalupe, 1973. Contbr. to: Boreal (Canada); Orfeo (Chile); Cormorán y Delfin (Argentina); Tulud, Papeles (Venezuela); Letras de ayer y de hoy, El caracol marino, El Corno Emplumado (Mexico); Norte (Holland); Artesa (Spain); Potpourri (Maine, USA), etc. Address: 123-35 82nd Road Apt. 2G, Kew Gdns., NY 11415, U.S.A.

KOZIKOWSKI, Edward, b. 13 Nov. 1891. Poet. Education: Polytechnic, Krakow & Warsaw. Positions held: Mgr., Lit. Theatre, Jeleniez Gorze, 1945-46; Reporter for monthly mag 'Slask', 1945-48; Mgr. in Lit. Theatre, Jeleniez Gorze, 1949-51; Dir.-Gen. of Fed. of Authors, 1952-64. Memberships: Fndr., Czartak, 1922-27; Gen. Sec. of Zarzadu Zwiazku Literatow Polskich, Warsaw, 1920-39; Life Mbr., Zwiazku Literatow Polskich, Warsaw, Polskiego Klubu Literatow PEN Club; Stowarzyszenia Autorow 'Zaiks'. Published works: Płomyk świecy, 1921; Tęsknota ramy okiennej, 1922; Antologia poezji murzyńskiej; przekłady wspólnie z Emilem Zegadłowiczem, 1923; Tęsknota ramy okiennej, wyd.II, 1924; Koniec Hortesji Europy, 1925; Wymarsz świerszczów, 1925; W towarzystwie wierzby, 1929; Pięciokłos, 1937; Mowa ludzka, 1951; Wertepami i gościńcem, 1967; oraz eseje i wspomnienia: O Jędrzeju Wowrze, snycerzu beskdzkim, 1957; Między prawdą a plotką, 1961; Więcej prawdy niz plotki, 1964; Portret Zegadłowicza bez ramy, 1966; Parandowski, 1967; Od Prusado Gojani czyńskiej, 1970; Lodz i pióro, 1972. Contbr. to many jrnls., mags., etc. Honours, awards: Candidate in 1938 for 'Wiadomosci Literackie' for his book 'Peciokles', 1937. Address: ul. 27 Stycznisa 32 m. 6, Katowice 40-026, Poland.

KOZIOL, Urszula, b. 20 June 1931. Editor. Education: studied Polish Philol., Univ. of Wrocław, 1950-53; M.A., ibid, 1964. Married. Positions held: Tchr., for sev. yrs.; Ed., lit. column for the student mag. Poglady, 1956-57; Dir., Wrocław Cultural Ctr., 1965-67; Lit. Ed., Odra mag., Wrocław, 1972-. Memberships: Polish Writers Union, 1963-; Chmn., Wrocław Br., ibid, 1971-; PEN, 1972-. Published works: (poetry books) Gumowe klocki, 1957; W rytmie korzeni, 1963; Smuga i promień, 1965; Lista obecności, 1967; Wiersze, 1969; W rytmie słońca, 1974; (prose vols.) Postoje pamieci, 1964; Ptaki dla mysti, 1971. Contbr. to: Odra; Twórczośe; Poezja; Kultura; Zycie Literackie; Literatura; Wspołczesność; Tygodnik Kulturalny. Honours, awards: PEN Award, 1963; The Władysław Broniewski Award, 1964; The Stanisław Piętak Award, 1965; The Wrocław Lit. Award, 1965; The Łódź Poetry Fest. Award for the Book of the Yr., 1968; The Kościelski Fndn. Award, Geneva, 1969; The Min. of Culture Award, 1971. Address: Redakcja Odry, Rynek-Ratusz 25, Wrocław, Poland.

KRAMER, Aaron, b. 13 Dec. 1921. Professor of English. Education: B.A., Brooklyn Coll., 1941; M.A., ibid, 1951; Ph.D., N.Y. Univ., 1966. Married Katherine Kolodny, 2 children. Positions held: Instr., Adelphi

Univ., 1961-63; Asst. Prof., ibid, 1963-66; Lectr., Queens Coll., 1966-68; Assoc. Prof., Dowling Coll., 1966-70; Prof., ibid, 1970–. Memberships: MLA; Keats-Shelley Assn., 1963-69; Poetry Soc. of Am., 1949-59 (Judge & Chmn. of Judges for var. awards; Chmn., Golden Anniversary Nominating Comm.); Assn. for Poetry Therapy, 1969–, etc. Published works: Another Fountain, 1940; Till the Grass is Ripe for Dancing, 1943; Seven Poets in Search of an Answer, 1944; Thru Our Guns, 1945; The Glass Mountain, 1946; The Thunder of the Grass, 1948; The Poetry & Prose of Heinrich Heine, 1948; The Golden Trumpet, 1949; Thru Every Window! 1950; Denmark Vesey, 1952; Roll the Forbidden Drums! 1954; Rosenfeld: The Teardrop Millionaire, 1955; A Ballad of August Bondi, 1955; Serenade: an L.P., 1957; The Tune of the Calliope, 1958; Moses, 1962; Goethe, Schiller, Heine: Songs & Ballads, 1963; Rumshinsky's Hat, 1964; Rilke: Visions of Christ, 1967; Henry At The Grating, 1968; Chelm, 1968; Poems by Abraham Reisen, 1971; On Freedom's Side, 1972; On the Way to Palermo, 1973. Contbr. to num. jrnls., reviews, newspapers. Recip. many honours & awards inclng: Los Altos Filmmaker's Fest., 2nd prize for Robert Feldman filming of poem, 1965; William E. Oliver Song Award, 1968; Va. Prize, Lyric Mag., 1969; Hart Crane Meml. Award, 1969. Address: Dept. of Engl., Dowling Coll., Oakdale, NY 11769, U.S.A.

KRAUS, Marcella, pen name **KRAUS, Marci,** b. 2 May 1917. Secretary. Positions held: Sec., Co. Supt. of Schls.; Commodities Foreman, Welfare Dept.; Exec. Sec., Am. Bridge (Div. of U.S. Steel Corp.); Sec., Investors Diversified Servs. (currently). Vice Regent, Midwest Fed. of Chaparral Poets. Contbr. to: Mnpls. Star Jrnl.: Mnpls. Argus; Mnpls. Sun Newspaper. Honours, awards: First Prize, Seminar, Midwest Fed. of Chaparral Poets, 1966; Has been placed First, Second or received Hon. Mention at every Poetry Seminar of Midwest Fed. of Chaparral Poets, 1966–. Address: 4220 – 3rd Ave. S., Minneapolis, MN 55409, U.S.A.

KRAUSE, Nina, b. 11 Aug. 1932. Housewife; Artist. Education: Liberal Arts degree, Bowling Green State Univ., 1954; var. post grad. educ. courses. Married Bill Krause, 1 s. 1 d. Positions held: w. Mail Order Catalog firm & in Advt. Agency, N.Y.; at Radio Stn., Schenectady; var. volunteer work at schl. Memberships: Poetry Soc. of Am.; Acad. of Am. Poets; Ky. State Poetry Soc. Contbr. to: Ky's 'Approaches'; Ohio's 'The Dream Shop'; the Louisville Art Workshop's 'Arts & Talents Fest. Digest, 1969'; Contemporary Ky. Poetry, 1967; 'Ten' (coll. of 10 Ky. poets). Recip. var. prizes. Address: 2410 Cross Hill Rd., Louisville, KY 40206, U.S.A.

KRAUSS, Mary, pen name **WINTER, Mary,** b. 10 May 1889. Homemaker. Educated: Art Inst., Chicago; Grad. Poetry courses, Columbia U., N.Y. (under Leonora Speyer). Married to Rev. Paul H. Krauss. Member, Poetry Soc. of America; Arts Club, Chicago; Life Member, Art Inst. of Chicago, and Antiquarian Society of Chicago. Pubs. The Archaic Smile, 1948; Tom Tiddlers Ground, 1961; Summer of the Heart, 1966. Contrib. to: Poems of Fifty Years (N.Y. Times Book), 1970. Recipient 3 Poetry Soc. prizes. Address: 5219 Woodhurst Blvd., Fort Wayne, Indiana 46807, USA.

KRAUSS, Ruth, b. 25 Jul. 1911. Writer. Married to Crockett Johnson. Memberships: The Authors League of America; PEN Internat. Published works: The Cantilever Rainbow, 1966; There's a little ambiguity over there among the bluebells, 1969; If Only, 1970; Under Twenty, 1971; This Breast Gothic, 1973. Contbr. to: The World; Telephone; Harper's; Wild Dog; Residu; Strange Faeces; Harper's Bazaar; Chelsea Review; Locus Solus, etc. Address: 24 Owenoke, Westport, CT 06880, USA.

KRKLEC, Gustav, b. 23 June 1899. Editor; Writer. Education: studied at Philos. Facs. in Vienna & Prague. Positions held: Chief Ed., Nolit Publishing House, Belgrade, 1929-33; Ed., Nakladni zavod Hrvatske, & Zora, publishing houses, Zagreb. Memberships: Yugoslav Acad. of Arts & Scis.; Pres., Matica Hrvatska (1950's); Assn. of Croatian Writers; PEN Club; Commita Europea degli scrittori; League of Yugoslav Writers, etc. Published works: Lirika, 1919; Srebrna Cesta, 1928; Ljubav Ptica, 1926; Izlet u Nebo, 1928; San Pod Brezom, 1940; Darovi za Bezimenu, 1942; Tamnica Vremena, 1944; Tri Poeme, 1949; Zubor Zivota, 1955; Izabrane Pjesme, 1962. Contbr. to most of the daily newspapers, lit. reviews, jrnls. in Yugoslavia. Honours, awards: Prize of Serbian Acad. of Scis., Belgrade for his book Ljubav Ptica; Prize of the Coun. for Culture of the People's Republic of Croatia for his book Tri Poeme; Prize of the Assn. of Croatian Writers for his book Zubor Zivota; Prize 'Zmajeva nagrada Matice Srpske', Novi Sad, for his book Izabrane Pjesme; Vladimir Nazor Prize for his life's work, 1969. Address: Gunduliceva 48, 41 000 Zagreb, Yugoslavia.

KRNJEVIC, Vuk, b. 6 May 1935. Television Film Editor. Educ: Fac. of Philol., Dept. of Yugoslav Lit., Univ. of Belgrade. Married. Positions held: Ed., lit. mag. 'Književne novine' & 'Odjek'; Ed. of TV progs., Belgrade TV. Memberships: Writers Assn. of Yugoslavia; Serbian PEN Club. Published works: Zaboravljanje kućnog reda, 1957; Dva brata uboga, 1959; Pejzaži mrtvih, 1962; Pjesme, 1966; Prividjenja gospodina Proteja, 1965; Ziva rana, 1971 – all colls. of poems. Rep. in following anthols: Posleratni srpski pesnici, 1972; Antologija savremenih jugoslovenskih pripovedača, 1965. Contbr. to: Delo; Savremenik; Izraz; Književne novine; Politika. Honours, awards: Poetry Award, The Writers' Assn. of Yugoslavia, 1965; Award for the best newspaper lit. review, 1971. Address: Bulevar Revolucije 225, 11000 Belgrade, Yugoslavia.

KROAH, Henrietta Augusta, b. 17 May 1917. Retired Civil Servant (Accountant). Education: Private Schools, NY. Born in Italy; Married to Mark E. Kroah; 2 s. Positions held: Accountant, Budget Analyst, Executive Sec. Memberships: Nat. Fed. of State Poetry Socs.; Pennsylvania Poetry Soc.; World Poetry Soc. Intercontinental. Contbr. to: Encore; American Bard; Prairie Poet; American Poet; United Poets; Poet (India); The Saint (now Poetry Preview); The Catalyst. Judge for Nat. and State Youth Poetry contests, 1971-73. Address: 92 Clairmont Ave., DeBary, FL 32713, USA.

KROHN, Herbert, b. 30 Nov. 1938. Poet; Physician; Musician. Education: degrees from N.Y. Univ. Positions held: Founded Poetry Proj. at Greenwich House Narcotics Treatment Ctr., N.Y.C. & Taught Workshop there, 1972-73. Contbr. to: Winning Hearts & Minds: War Poems of Vietnam Veterans (6 poems), 1972; The New Yorker; N.Y. Times; Partisan Review; The Nation; Columbia Forum; Defiance: A Radical Review; Evergreen Review; N.Y. Qtly. Recip., Dylan Thomas Poetry Prize of the New Schl., 1968. Address: 15 East 11 St., N.Y., NY 10003, U.S.A.

KROUWER, Margot. Artist; Poet; Poetry Reader. Married Henri Krouwer, 3 sons. Memberships: Poetry Soc. of Am.; Pa. Poetry Soc.; Centro Studi e Scambi Int. Contbr. to: SCAF Poets, 1968, '69; Cardinal Poetry Qtly., 1969, '70; Poetry Parade, 1969; Voices Int., 1969; Prize Poems Pa. Poetry Soc., 1970; New Voices in the Wind; Bitterroot; Ariz. Poetry Soc., 1971. Honours, awards: 2nd Prize, Edna Shoemaker Award, Pa. Poetry Soc.; Hon. Mention, Pa. Poetry Soc. & Nat. Fed. Assn. Poetry Soc., 1970; Hon. Mention, N.Y. Poetry Forum; Juried Entry Sharon Creative Arts Fndn., 1968, '69; num. awards in paintings, drawings. Address: 15 Rhynas Dr., Mount Vernon, NY 10522, U.S.A.

KRUGLICK, Lewis John, b. 4 Mar. 1942. Poet. Education: B.A., Univ. of Calif. at Los Angeles, 1962; M.A., San Fernando Valley State Coll., 1966; Doctoral work, Univ. of London (Birkbeck Coll.), 1966-68. Positions held: Poetry Ed., Eclipse, 1966; Lectr. in

Engl., San Fernando Valley State Coll., 1969-70. Published works: The Unknown Angel, 1970; A Letter From Brixton Prison, 1971. Contbr. to: Eclipse; Stolen Paper Review; Reflections; Tree. Has taped poetry readings for KPFK Radio, Los Angeles, 1972. Address: P.O. Box 307, Whitethorn, CA 95489, U.S.A.

KUBAM, Yadav Reddy, pen name, **NIKHILESWAR,** b. 11 Aug. 1938. Teacher. Education: Osmania Univ., Hyderabad, India. Positions held: Tchr. in Army; Clerk in Air Force; Sub-Ed.; Tchr. Memberships: Fin. Sec., Revolutionary Writers Assn., Andhra Pradesh. Contbr. to: Digambara Kavulu (Naked Poets), I, II, III, 1965-68; Andhra; Bharati, Srjana; Andhra Iyoti. Address: T.R.T. 46, Vidyanagar Colony, Hyderabad 500044, Andhra Pradesh, India.

KUBLY, Herbert Oswald, b. 26 Apr. 1915. Author; Educator. Education: B.A., Univ. of Wis. Memberships: Authors League of Am.; Nat. Sec., Dramatists Guild of Am., 1946-49; Coun. for Wis. Writers; Wis. Regl. Writers Assn.; Wis. Fellowship of Poets. Contbr. to: Hawk & Whippoorwill; Wis. Poetry Mag., etc. Recip., Nat. Book Award, for prose, 1956; Coun. for Wis. Writers, First Award, 1970. Address: Humanities Div., Univ. of Wis.-Parkside, Kenosha, WI 53140, U.S.A.

KUBOVY, Myriam, b. 11 June 1898. Writer. Education: HS. Born in Antwerp, Belgium. Married in Antwerp to Dr. A.L. Kubovy, Israeli Diplomatic Service (Ambassador to Prague; Warsaw; Argentine; Paraguay; Uruguay; Chile); 1 s., 1 d. From 1940-1948, resident in US. Published works: Monologues avec Dieu (French), 1957, (Spanish), 1958, (Hebrew), 1960, and 2nd edition, 1962; Climats (French); Wife of the Israeli Ambassador to Prague and Warsaw (prose), 1964; Israel en la nueva Sefarad, 1965. Contbr. to: Hatikwah; Pioneer Women's Journal (NY); Jewish Spectator (NY); Davar; Dvar Hapoeleth, etc. Address: 26 Ben Maimon Blvd., Jerusalem, Israel.

KUMAR, Shiv Kumar, b. 16 Aug. 1921. Professor. Education: M.A., Engl., Punjab Univ., 1943; Dip. in Jrnlsm., Punjab Univ., 1949; Ph.D., Cambridge Univ., 1956. Married, 1 son, 1 daughter. Positions held: Hd., Dept of Engl., Govt. Coll., Chandigarh (Punjab), 1953-57; Rdr. in Engl., Punjab Univ., 1957-59; Prof. & Chmn., Dept. of Engl., Osmania Univ., Hyderabad, 1959–; Dean, Fac. of Arts, ibid, 1971-73; Vis. Prof. of Engl., Cambridge Univ., 1961, Yale, 1962, Elmira Coll., 1967, Marshall Univ., 1968, Univ. of Northern Iowa, 1969, Drake Univ., 1971, Hofstra Univ., 1972; Govt. of Australia Cultural Award Visitor, 1971. Member, Indian PEN. Published works: Articulate Silences, 1970; Cobwebs in the Sun, 1974. Contbr. to: N.Y. Times; Ariel; Western Humanities Review; Midwest Poetry, 1972; The Cardinal Poetry Review; Pegasus; Westerly; Hemisphere; Meanjin; Little Review; The Times of India; The Australian; Poetry Eastwest; Int. Poetry Review; The Hindustan Standard, etc. Address: Dept. of Engl., Osmania Univ., Hyderabad 500007, A.P., India.

KUMIN, Maxine, b. 6 June 1925. Writer. Education: A.B., A.M., Radcliffe. Positions held: Instr., Tufts Univ., 1958-61; Lect. in Engl., Newton College, since 1971; Visiting Lect. in Engl., Univ. Mass., Amherst, 1972. Member: Poetry Soc. of America; Authors' Guild. Pubs.: Halfway, 1961; The Privilege, 1965; The Nightmare Factory, 1970; Up Country, 1972. Contrib. to: The New Yorker; The Atlantic; Harper's; Saturday Review; Poetry; The American Poetry Review; New Amer. Review, etc. Recip. Pulitzer Prize for Poetry, 1973; Eunice Tietjens Mem. Prize, Poetry Mag., 1972; Wm. Marion Reedy Award, Poetry Soc. of America, 1968; Lowell Mason Palmer Award, Poetry Soc. of America, 1960. Address: 40 Bradford Rd., Newton Highland, Mass. 02161, USA.

KUNENE, Mazisi, b. 1930. Author; Poet. Education: M.A., Natal Univ., Durban; Schl. of Oriental & African Studies, London Univ. Contbr. to (Anthols.): Modern Poetry from Africa, 1963; (Fiction): African Writing

Today, 1967, & Short Stories to Drum Mag. Recip., Bantu Literary Competition Award, 1956.

KUNITZ, Stanley J., b. 29 July 1905. Writer; Educator. Education: M.A., Harvard Univ. Positions held: Ed., Wilson Lib. Bull., 1928-42; served to Staff Sgt., US Army, 1943-45; Prof. of Lit., Bennington Coll., Vt., 1946-49; Dir., Seminar, Potsdam Summer Workshop in Creative Arts, 1949-53; Lectr. & Dir., Poetry Workshop, New Schl. for Soc. Rsch., NY, 1950-58; Dir., Poetry Workshop, The Poetry Ctr., NY, 1958-62; Lectr., Columbia Univ., 1963-66; Adjunct Prof., Grad. Schl. of Writing, Columbia, 1967–; Ed., Yale Series of Younger Poets, Yale Univ. Press, 1969–. Memberships: Nat. Inst. Arts & Letters. Published works: (poetry) Intellectual Things, 1930; Passport to the War, 1944; Selected Poems, 1958; (editions) Living Authors, 1931; Authors Today & Yesterday, 1933; Junior Book of Authors, 1934; British Authors of the XIX Century 1936; American Authors 1600-1900, 1938; XX Century Authors, 1942; British Authors Before 1800, 1952; XX Century Authors (1st Supplement), 1955; Poems of John Keats, 1964; European Authors 1000-1900, 1967. Honours: Garrison Medal for Poetry, 1926; Blumenthal Prize, 1941; Levinson Prize, 1956; Harriet Monroe Award, 1958; Pulitzer Prize for Poetry, 1959; Brandeis Creative Arts Poetry Medal, 1965; Hon. D.Litt., Clark Univ., 1961; Fellowship Award, Acad. of Am. Poets, 1968 & many others. Address: 157 W. 12th St., New York, NY 10011, USA.

KUPRIAN, Hermann Josef, pen names, **KUPRIAN, Hermann & MANN, Jan,** b. 12 Apr. 1920. Professor. Education: Humanist Grammar Schl.; Univ. of Vienna; Univ. of Zurich, Switz.; Univ. of Innsbruck, Austria; Dr. phil. Married Vilma Schmidt, 4 children. Positions held: Pres., Turmbund, Soc. for Lit. & Art, Innsbruck; Publr., Brennpunkte.; Ed., Publikation, Munich; Cultural Advsr. to the town of Landeck; Author; Playwright; Lyric Poet. Memberships: PEN, Vienna; Regensburg Grp. of Writers; Austrian Soc. of Authors, Vienna; Comm. Mbr., Vienna, Union of Austrian Writers; Knight of Yuste, Spain; Guild of Inn viertel; Lit. Union, Munich. Published works: The Little Shadow's Game (play), 1946, '65; In Front of the Windows, 1954; The Death of Orpheus, 1956, '60; The Flight (The Abduction from Europe), 1956; Humanitas, Festival Performance, 1958; The Blue Mirror, 1959 Solferino Festival Performance, 1959; The Big Shadow's Game (tragedy), 1960, '65; Ballads from the Golden Life (comedy), 1961; Western Melancholy, 1963; Seal Without End, 1969; Orphean Speeches, 1970; Flight & Game, four plays, 1970; Traumtexte (poems), 1970; Die Verschleierten, 1972; Lamasabathani, 1973; Der grosse Früchtebaum (poems), 1973. Contbr. to num. anthols., jrnls., newspapers inclng: The Barque Anthol., 1956, '63; Artists, Designers & Poets, 1960; German Students Cultural Almanach, 1964; Brennpunkte I, 1965; Housebook of Tirolean Poetry, 1965; Cycle Poetry of the Present, 1965; Brennpunkte I-VIII; Brennpunkte IX – Theoretische Grundlagen der Spirituellen Poesie, 1973; Brennpunkte X Analysen und Analekten zur Spirituellen Poesie, 1973; Alle Zeit ist nur geliehen – Solo prestamo es todo tiempo, Austrian-Spanish Anthol., W. Narciso Sanchez Morales; Creative Tirol; Encounters, 1969; Creative Tirol: Confessions, 1971; Europa Publikation. The conception of the rotative cause, appeared in Programme 'The Word in the Mountains X', 1971. Featured in many mags. & jrnls. Has written many radio plays. Honours, awards: Austrian Youth Culture Week Prize, 1953; Dramatist's Prize of the Town of Innsbruck, 1954; Silver Rose Lyric Poetry Award, Salzburg, 1969. Address: Hunoldstrasse 20/4, A6020, Innsbruck, Austria.

KURUP, Ammujavalli, b. 17 Mar. 1926. Education: Queen Mary's Coll., Madras; M.A., Madras Univ.; Schl. of Arts. Member, World Poetry Soc. Int. Published works: Moon-Lit Wishes & Other Poems, 1971. Contbr. to: The Madras Mail; My Mag.; Locks & Keys; The Presidencian; The Queen Mary's Coll. Mag.; The Animal Citizen; The Humanitarian, 1942-68; Poet.

Address: No. 9 First Main Rd., Kasturba Nagar, Adyar, Madras, India.

KURUP, Sankara, pen name **GI,** b. 3 June 1901. Retired Professor. Education: Vidwan Exam., Madras Univ., India. Positions held: Tchr., Govt. Service, 1921; Lectr., Coll., 1936; Retired as Prof. of Malayalam, Maharaja's Coll., Ernakulam; was Producer, All India Radio Trivandrum. Memberships: Pres., Samesta Kerala Sahitya Parishad, 1956-57; ibid, Kerala Sahitya Acad., 1966-68; Hon. Mbr., PEN; was Pres., Bharatiya Sahitya Parished; Mbr., Rajya Sabha, nominated by Pres. for 1968-72. Publications: Author of approx. forty pubs. of collected poems, essays & critical works including: Otakkuzhal and Patheyam. Contbr. to various Malayalam jrnls. and publs. in other Indian languages. Some poems translated into Russian & English. Editor, Kairali, Sahithya Parishath and Thilakam, literary publs. Honours: Sahitya Nipuna title, awarded by Sanskrita Coll. of Cochin; Kavitlakan, awarded by Maharaja of Cochin; First Award of Bharatiya Gnana Pita (highest literary award in India), 1965; Fellow, kerala Sahithya Akademi; Central Sahitya Acad. Nat. Award, 1963; Padma bhushan, conferred by Pres. of India; Soviet Land Nehru Award, 1967. Address: Bhadralayam, Monastry Rd., Cochin 11, Kerala, India.

KUSAN, Jakša, b. 11 July 1900. Writer. Education: Fac. of Economics, Zagreb. Positions held: Theatrical Mgr. for two yrs.; Tchr. in High Schl.; Ed. for Publishing House. Memberships: Lit. Soc. of Croatia; Matica Hrvatska (Croatian Cultural Soc.) Published works: Pjesme (poems), Sarajevo, 1925; Zemlja i Oblaci (Earth & Clouds), 1952. Contbr. to: Vijenac, Zagreb; Pregled, Sarajevo; Hrvatsko Kolo, Zagreb. Address: Drapšinov Trg 4, 41.000 Zagreb, Yugoslavia.

KUSAN, Vladislav, b. 3 May 1904. Writer; Poet; Essayist; Art Critic. Education: Studied at Univ., Zagreb, 1924-30 & at the same time practised music (piano) & painting. Visited sev. European capitals. Positions held: Artistic Ed., Hrvatska Revija, 1941-45. Memberships: Assn. of Croatian Writers, Zagreb; Assn. of Yugoslav Writers, Belgrade; PEN Club, Zagreb. Published works: Lišće Na Vjetru, 1932; Ponoćne Ispovijesti, 1937; Začarane Tmine, 1942; Izabrane Pjesme, 1964; Izabrana Djela, 1969. Contbr. to: Hrvatska prosvjeta; Hrvatska revija; Hrvatsko kolo; Književnik; Kolo; Forum. Address: Makančeva 2/III, 41000 Zagreb, Yugoslavia.

KUSNIEWICZ, Andrzej, b. 30 Nov. 1904. Poet & Novelist. Education: LL.B., Schl. of Pol. Scis. Married. Positions held: Diplomatic Serv., Foreign Office, 1936-50, Jrnlst., 1955-. Memberships: PEN Club; Polish Writers' Union. Published works: (poems) Give the Devil His Share, 1959; Private Time, 1962; (novels) Eroica, 1963; On the Road to Corinth, 1964; King of the Two Sicilies, 1970; Regions, 1971; State of Weightlessness, 1973. Contbr. to: Micsiecznik Literacki; Tworczosc; Polish Broadcasting, Warsaw. Honours, awards: First Prize of the Minister of Culture & Art, Poland, 1971 (Second Prize, 1965); The Alfred Jurzykowski Award, U.S.A., 1973. Address: Juliana Bruna 28 m. 57, 02-594 Warsaw, Poland.

KUTTNER, Brian Usherwood, b. 17 May 1949. Transport Administrator. Education: Univ. of Birmingham, 1968-70. Memberships: Fndr. & Mbr., Wordsmithy Experimental Poetry Unit; Fndr. & Chmn., Taliesin Poetry Discussion Grp.; Public Rels. Officer, Birmingham Poetry Ctr., 1973; Past Mbr., 'Tuppence' Soc., B'ham Univ. & Henry Dumolo's Poetry Grp. Contbr. to: Muse; Midland Read; Chronicle; Black Columbus. Recip., David Brester Cobb Essay Prize, B'ham Univ., 1970. Address: 119 Birmingham Rd., AlueChurch, Birmingham B48 7TD, U.K.

KYEI, Kojo Gyinaye, pen name **GYINAYE, Kojo,** b. 28 Aug. 1932. Architect. Education: B.Arch., Univ. of Kans., U.S.A., 1963; Dip., Imperial Coll. D.I.C., London, U.K., 1968. Married, 2 sons, 1 daughter. Positions held: Clerk, Audit Dept., Accra, 1953-54;

Clerk, Post & Telecommunications, 1955; Tchr., Govt. Boys' Schl., Rowe Rd., 1955-56; Advt. Clerk, Daily Graphic, 1956; Archt., P.W.D., 1963; Sr. Archt., ibid, 1971-. Member of Comm. of Enquiry into Affairs of Produce Buying Agency Ltd. Memberships: Pen & Paper Circle, 1969-70; Pres., Ghana Assn. of Writers, 1970-71; Nat. Assn. of Writers. Published works: The Lone Voice, coll. of poems, 1969; Kyekyekule & Other Poems for Children, 1972. Contbr. to: Poems from Black Africa, 1963; Messages – Poems from Ghana, 1971; Ghanaian Writing, 1973; Reading African Poetry; The Honey of Man; Kans. Mag.; Quil Mag.; Kans. Engr.; The Ghanaian Mag.; The Ghanaian Times, etc. Address: Architects' Br., Public Works Dept., P.O. Box 136, Accra, Ghana.

KYGER, Joanne Elizabeth, b. 19 Nov. 1934. Poet. Published works: The Tapestry & The Web, 1965; Joanne, 1970; Places to Go, 1970; Desecheo Notebook, 1971. Address: Box 42, Elm Rd., Bolinas, CA 94924, U.S.A.

KYLER, Inge Logenburg, b. 26 Jan. 1936. Housewife & Part time Librarian. Married Arthur J. Kyler, 3 children. Positions held: p/t Libn., Mason Co. Lib., 1973-; Admin. Aid, Ingham Co. Jury Bd., 1970-71. Memberships: Past V.P., Advsry. Comm., Lansing Poetry Club; Mich. State Poetry Soc.; Pa. State Poetry Soc. Published works: (brochure) The Wind & The Wood, 1961. Rep. in following anthols: Avalon Anthol., 1963; Poetry on Parade Anthol., 1963; Rymes for the Very Young, 1964; Guild Anthol., 1966; Poets of the Midwest, 1967; Spring Anthol., 1967; Poets on Parade Anthol., 1970; Prize Poems 1972; Prize Winning Poems of 1973. Contbr. to num. mags., newspapers, inclng: The Country Guide; Grit; Sault Ste. Marie Evening News; The Progress; Saline Co. News; Lansing State Jrnls.; Scimitar & Song; Poet, India; Am. Bard; Orphic Lute; Cyclotron; Bardic Echoes, etc. Has made personal poetry broadcasts (radio) & read poems in local schools, church groups, etc. Recip. of many poetry prizes & hon. mentions. Address: 2291 Park Lane, Holt, MI 48842, U.S.A.

L

LACEY, Thelma Harrison, b. 8 Aug. 1898. Poet; Writer of Fiction; Housewife. Education: B.A., N.E. Mo. State Univ., Kirksville; M.A., Educ., Univ. of Wash., Seattle. Married, 1 daughter. Positions held: Tchr. at: Wyaconda H.S., Perry H.S., Mo.; Franklin H.S. Seattle, Wash.; Willoughby H.S. Ohio; Physics & Educ., Kirksville State Tchrs. Coll., 2 summers; Asst. Prin. & Tchr., Jr. H.S., Kirksville, Mo. Memberships: Fndr. & 1st Pres., Parkersburg Chapt., W.Va. Poetry Soc.; Nat. Fed. of State Poetry Socs.; Past Pres., Aux. W.Va. Soc. of Osteopathic Med., Aux. Am. Osteopathic Assn., Local Y.W.C.A. & Women's Assn., First Un. Presbyn. Ch., Parkersburg, W.Va.; Past Treas., AAUW. Published works: Prayers & Poems, 1953; Here & There, 1958; Thoughts in Verse, 1969; (novel) Bruce Barrlett – Only Son, 1968. Contbr. to: Silver From the Moon, 1955; Bright Cargo, 1955; The Quintessence of Song, 1956; Rose Petals, 1956. Recip. var. poetry awards. Address: 1 Camden Pl., Parkersburg, WV, U.S.A.

LACHANCE, (Louis-Philippe) Bertrand, b. 26 Oct. 1948. Poet. Education: HS.; Coll. Editor of AIR, since 1971. Membership: Canadian League of Poets. Published works: Eyes Open, 1970; Tes Rivieres T'Attendent, 1971; Street Flesh, 1972; Cock Tales, 1973. Contbr. to: Dust; Vigilante; Georgia Straight; Manna; Fascist Court; Occupation Issue; Oil Slick Special; Poverty Issue; Open Picture Book; The Tantrik Special; Air 13; Canadian Contemporary Literature; Vancouver Province; Calgary Herald. Address: P.O. Box 8688 Station H., Vancouver 5, BC, Canada.

LA CLAUSTRA, Vera Berneicia (Derrick), b. 11 Apr. 1903. Retired Cosmetician. Married. Memberships:

Avalon World Arts Acad.; World Poetry Soc. Intercontinental; Calif. Fed. of Chaparral Poets; Am. Poetry League; Centro Studi e Scambi Int., Rome; Accademia Leonardo da Vinci; Mark Twain Soc. Published works: By The Cool Waters, 1953; The Purple Wheel, 1954; Gongs of Light, 1971. Contbr. to num. periodicals, anthols., inclng: Flame; Cyclo-Flame; Cyclotron; Poet (India); Am. Bard; Bitterroot; The Villager; Hoosier Challenger; Swordsman Anthol.; Young Publication anthols.; Spring Anthols., Mitre Press; Bouquets of Poems; Sea to Sea in Song; Avalon Anthols.; The Wash. Evening Star; Denver Post; Hartford Times; Hartford Courant; The Observer; The Dial; Desert Mag. Anthols.; Voices Int.; Versatility In Verse (anthol.), 1965; Sixty Seven Poets (anthol.), 1967; Great Am. Poets (Calif. 3.); Contemporary Poetry 1972; Anthology of Am. Poetry, 1963; Anthol. of Am. Poetry, 1966; Yearbook of Modern Poetry, 1971. Honours, awards incl: Cert. of Merit, Accademia Leonardo da Vinci, 1962, 68, 71; Cert. of Merit, Poet, India, 1970; Cert. of Merit for four poems read over radio stn. 1970-71. Address: 400 Perkins St., Apt. 209, Oakland, CA 94610, U.S.A.

LACROIX, Georgette, b. 6 Apr. 1921. Writer. Positions held: Radio Commentator, CHRC AM/FM, Quebec City, 1947-71; Art & Literature Commentator, L'Action Quebec (newspaper), 1971-72; currently Cultural Agent for the Min. of Cultural Affairs, Govt. of P.Q. Member, Société des Poètes Canadiens Francais, 1965-. Published works: Mortes Saisons, 1967; Entre Nous...Ce Pays, 1970; Le Creux de la Vague, 1972; Aussi Loin que Demain, 1973. Contbr. to Poesie; L'Action Quebec. Honours, awards: 2 prizes, La Société du Bon Parler Francais, Montreal, 1963 & '69; France-Quebec Prize for 'Entre Nous...Ce Pays', L'Association des Ecrivains de Langue Francaise, Paris, & the Min. of Cultural Affairs, Quebec, 1971; 2nd prize, Arts & Poésie de Touraine, France, 1972. Address: 694 rue St. Jean, Quebec City, P.Q., Canada.

LACY, Elsie Halsey, b. 31 July 1897. Teacher; Writer; Housewife. Married, 2 sons (1 dec.), 1 daughter. Positions held: Tchr.; Sunday Schl. Tchr. Memberships: Sec., Pen Womens Club; K.S.P.S.; Nat. Fed. State Poetry Socs.; Clover Poetry Assn.; World Poetry Assn.; Hon. Mbr., Int. Songwriters Union, etc. Published works: Kentucky Verseland, 1956; Characteristic Traits of Kentuckians, 1961; A Lacy Sampler, 1963; Voice of Appalachia, 1973; Poem Echoes, 1973; Thoughts Voiced in Poems, 1973. Contbr. to: New Voices in the Wind, anthol., 1969; Echoes, 1971; The Forever Bear, 1971; Mark Twain Jrnl.; Westminster Mag.; Greenup Co. News; The Journal Enquirer; Scimitar & Song, etc. Winner, W.Va. Poetry Soc. Contest, 1969, & other poetry awards. Address: Rt. 1, Box 241, Grassy Creek, KY 41435, U.S.A.

LA FOLLETTE, Melvin Walker, b. 7 Sept. 1930. Priest; Poet. Education: B.A., Univ. of Wash., Seattle; M.A., Univ. of Iowa; S.T.B. magna cum Laude, Berkeley Divinity Schl., New Haven, Conn., 1967. Married Alice Louise Simpson w. 2 Sons. Positions held: Asst. Prof. of English & Creative Writing, San Jose State Coll., Calif., 1961-63; Edith M. Clarke Lectr., Univ. of Kansas, Lawrence, 1965; Ordained to Priesthood of the Episcopal Ch., 1968; Currently, Assoc. Rector, St. Francis Episcopal Ch., San Jose. Published works: The Clever Body, 1959; Pentagonal, 1965. Contbr. to (Anthols.): New World Writing 5 & 11, 1954; New Poets of England & America, 1962; Oregon Signatures, 1959; America Listens to Literature, 1960; New Orlando Poetry Anthology, 1963; Best Poems of 1963 & 1965; The Borestone Mountain Poetry Awards, 1964; A Controversy of Poets, 1965; Cavalcade of Poems, 1965; The Charge of the Light Brigade & Other Story Poems, 1969; (jrnls.): Beloit Poetry Jrnl.; Poetry; Prairie Schooner; Prism; New York Times; New Yorker; Northwest Review; Time & Tide; Botteghe Oscure. Hons: New Poets of the Midwest Award (Beloit Poetry Jrnl. & Univ. of Chgo.), 1954; Yaddo Fellowship, 1963. Address: 1576 Tobias Drive, San Jose, CA 95118, USA.

LA GUMA, Alex, b. 1923. Poet. Published works: New Voices form S. Africa (w. others), 1963; Novels: A Walk in the Night, 1962; And a Threefold Cord, 1964. Contbr. to (short story): South African Writing Today, 1967. Delegate to African-Scandinavian Conference, 1967.

LAINE, Jarkko Aarre Juhani, b. 17 Mar. 1947. Writer. Married, 1 daughter. Positions held: Chief Sub-Ed., Parnasso (literary mag.) Member, Finnish Soc. of Authors. Published works: (poetry) Muovinen Buddha, 1967; Tulen ja jään sirkus, 1970; Niin se käy, 1971; Nauta lentää, 1973; (prose) Haamumaili, 1968; Niin kulki Kolumbus, 1969; Kuin ruumissaatto, 1970; Vampyyri eli miten Wilhelm Kojac kuoli kovat kaulassa, 1971; (plays) Virtasen Masa, 1972; Konstaapeli ja Suhonen, 1972; Kauniita unia, beibi! 1973; Mitä merkillistä metsässä, 1973. Has translated English lang. literature, inclng. works of Mark Twain, Richard Brautigan, Bob Dylan, James Leo Herlihy, into Finnish. Address: Temppelinkatu 3 C 3, 20810 Turku 81, Finland.

LAING, Bernard Kojo, b. 1 July 1946. Administrator. Education: M.A., Glasgow; Post-grad. Dip. in Public Admin., Ghana. Married, 6 children. Positions held: Prin., Eton Schls. & Colls., 1968-69; District Admin. Officer, Offinso, Ghana, 1969-72; District Admin. Officer, Obuasi, Ghana, 1972-. Pres., St. Ninians Lit. Soc. of Youth Fellowship, Glasgow, 1963-65. Co-Ed., 'Ringan', Scottish Youth Fellowship Lit. Mag., 1965-66. Contbr. to: Scottish Poetry 4, anthol., 1969; Lines Review No. 24 & 27, 1967; Scottish Int., 1968; GUM, 1967 & '68. Honours, awards: One of eight prizewinners of BBC 'Univ. Notebook' Poetry Comp. (winning poems broadcast), 1967. Address: Dist. Admin. Officer, Box 32, Obuasi-Ashanti, Ghana.

LAIRD, Antonia Bissell, pen name, **LAIRD, Antonia B.,** b. 8 Nov. 1932. Housewife. Education: Bennet Jr. Coll., Millbrook, NY. Personal details: Married to Walter J. Laird, Jr., Stockbroker; 5 s., 1 d. Poet Laureate of the State of Delaware, 1969-71. Membership: Nat. League of American Pen Women. Published works: Time Is Moonlight, 1968; A Quiet Voice, 1969; A Parasol of Leaves, 1973. Contbr. to: Ski Mag.; Ladies Home Journal; Gourmet; Delaware Today; Ideals; Major Poets; Garden Club of America Bulletin; Stowe Reporter; In Wyoming; Phila. Evening Bulletin. Honours, Awards: Statewide, Katherine King Johnson Mem. Poetry Contest, 1967; 1st Prize, Del. Scene Contest Poem, 1966; 2nd Prize; Major Poets Contest, 1971; 1st Prize, St. David's Writers' Conference for Poetry, 1971. Address: 719 Princeton Rd., Wilmington, DE 19807, USA.

LAL, P., b. 28 Aug. 1929, India. Professor of English. Education: B.A., St. Xavier's, Calcutta, 1950; M.A., Calcutta Univ., 1952. Married, 1 s., 1 d. Positions held: Prof., Engl., St. Xavier's Coll., Calcutta & Calcutta Univ.; Vis. Prof., Hofstra & Ill. Univs., USA, 1963, '68; Jawaharial Nehru Fellow, 1969-70; Ed., The Miscellany, book mag. Memberships: Sec., Poetry Grp., Calcutta, 1949-55; Sec., Writers Workshop, Calcutta. Published works: (translations) The Bhagavad Gita: The Golden Womb of the Sun; Isa Upanisad; Sanskrit Love Lyrics; The Dhammapada; Great Sanskrit Plays in Modern Translation; Some Sanskrit Poems; Premchand: His Life & Work; Premchand's Godan; The Mahabharata; The Farce of the Drunk Monk; Avyakta Upanisad; Mahanarayana & Brihadaranyaka Upanisads; An Annotated Mahabharata Bibliography; The Jap-ji; (Author) The Parrot's Death & Other Poems; Love's The First; 'Change' They Said; Draupadi & Jayadratha & Other Poems; The Art of the Essay; Yakshi From Didarganj & Other Poems; The Concept of an Indian Literature; (ed.) Modern Indian Poetry in English; T.S. Eliot: Homage From India; The First Workshop Story Anthol.; Modern Indo-Anglian Poetry: (in preparation) children's Tales from India; Ghalib's Love Poems; Critical & Other Essays; New Poems; Kalidasa's Vikrama & Urvasi; Creations & Transcreations. Contbr. to: The Rdr's Ency.; (jrnls.) Poetry (Chicago);

Atlantic Monthly; Outposts; Thought; The Lit. Half Yearly; Standard Mag.; Quest; (anthols.) Springtime; Span; Commonwealth Verse; Young Commonwealth Poets. Recip., Padma Shri, 1970. Address: 162/92 Lake Gdns., Calcutta 45, India.

LALIC, Ivan V., b. 8 June 1931. Writer. Education: M.A., Fac. of Law, Univ. of Zagreb. Married, 2 sons. Positions held: Ed., Radio Zagreb, 1956-61; Sec. Gen., Yugoslav Writers' Assn., 1961-64; Lector, 'Yugoslavia' Publsr., 1964-. Sec., Yugoslav PEN, Serbian Ctr. Published works: Bivši dečak, 1955; Vetrovito Proleće, 1956; Velika vrata mora, 1958; Melisa, 1959; Argonauti i druge pesme, 1961; Vreme, vatre, vrtovi, 1961; Cin, 1963; Krug, 1968; Izabrane i nove pesme, 1969; Fire Gardens, selected poems in Engl., 1970; A szerelem müvei, selected poems in Hungarian, 1971; Temps, feu, jardins, selected poems in French, 1973. Contbr. to var. lit. mags. & reviews in Yugoslavia & abroad. Honours, awards: The 'Zmaj' Prize, 1961; Grand Prize of the Yugoslav Radio for the verse play, Master Hanuš, 1964; The Nolit Prize, 1969. Address: Internacionalnih brigada 39, 11000 Belgrade, Yugoslavia.

LAM, Yan-Chiu, pen name **PHILIP Y.C. LAM,** b. 26 June 1916. Poet; Educator; Publisher. Education: Dip., Peiking Univ., China; B.A. & LL.B., Wen Hua Univ., China; M.A., The Rsch. Inst. of Wen Hua Univ.; L.H.D., The F.P. Episcopal Univ., England. Married, 3 sons, 1 daughter. Positions held: Mng. Dir. & Gen. Ed., Lam's Book Co., Canton, China, 1946; Prof., Wen Hua Univ., 1947; Mng. Dir. & Gen. Ed., Hon Sun Mag. Co., Hong Kong, 1950; Prof. of the Far East Coll., Hong Kong, 1953; Pres., Sun Lui Poetry Assn., 1955-; Prin., Confucius Hall Coll., 1960; Del. to the 3rd Asian Writers' Conf. of the H.K. Ctr., Nat. PEN, 1970; P.R.Dir., 2nd World Congress of Poets, 1973. Memberships: Dir., Chinese Ctr. of Hong Kong, Nat. PEN; Pres., Soc. for the Study of Religion & Culture; Dir. of Confucius Hall & The Confucian Acad. Published works: Screen, coll. of poems, 1940; A Collection of the Sun Lui Poems, 1956; Dun Yuet Chup, coll. of poems, 1970; The Way of Chinese Modern Poetry, 1971; The Principles of Poetry, 1973; The Kin Relationship Between Chinese & Poetry, 1973. Contbr. to var. mags., jrnls., newspapers. Address: Sun Lui Poetry Assn., 107 Sai Yeung Choi St., 9th Floor, Flat C, Kowloon, Hong Kong.

LAMANTIA, Philip, b. 23 Oct. 1927. Positions held: Asst. Ed., View Mag., N.Y., 1944. Published works: Erotic Poems, 1946; Ekstasis, 1959; Destroyed Works, 1962; Touch of the Marvelous, 1966; Selected Poems, 1943-66, 1967; Penguin Modern Poets 13, 1969; The Blood of the Air, 1970. Contbr. to (Anthols.): New American Poetry, 1960; Poesi degli Ultimi Americani, 1964; (Jrnls.): New Directions Annuals; View; VVV. Address: c/o City Lights Books, 261 Columbus Ave., San Francisco, CA 94133, USA.

LAMB, Elizabeth Searle, pen name **MITCHELL, K.L.,** b. 22 Jan. 1917. Free-lance Writer; Poet. Education: B.A., B. Mus., Univ. of Kan., 1939, '40. Married to F. Bruce Lamb. Memberships: Charter Mbr. The Haiku Soc. of America (pres., 1971); New York Women Poets (vice-pres., 1973); NYC Br., Nat. League of Am. Pen Women; Colo. Springs Poetry Fellowship. Co-author of (children's book) The Pelican Tree & Other Panama Adventures, 1953; also author of: Today and Every Day, 1970; Inside Me, Outside Me, 1974. Contbr. to: Haiku Anthol., 1968; SCAF Poets of 1967; A Treasury of Unity Poems, 1964; In Time of Need, 1964; Laudamus Te, Manifold, 1967; Best Broadcast Poems of 1967; Best Love Poems, 1962; Fragment of Faith, 1963; Rhyme Time for the Very Young, 1964; Award Winning Poems, 1964; Rochester Fest. of the Arts, 1967; Africana; Am. Bard; Am. Haiku; Americas; Aspire; Blueprint; Bravo; Christian Sci. Monitor; Poetry Forum; Encore; Green World; Haiku Highlights; Haiku W; Imprints Qtly.; Lyric; Nat. Poetry Letter; NY Herald Tribune; NY Pen Woman; Nutmegger; Poetry Dial; Poetry Digest; Renaissance; Saturday Evening Post; Scimitar & Song; S&W; Swordsman Rev.; Haiku;

Fiddlehead; Manifold; Poetry, Australia, etc. Widely publd. prose writer & song lyric writer. Honours: 2nd Place, Ruben Dario Mem. Poetry Contest, Pan Am. Union, 1967; 1st Prize, Unpubld. Collection of Poetry, Nat. League of Am. Pen Women Biennial, 1968; 1st Prize, Haiku Anthol. Award, 1968; 1st Place, Ruth Mason Rice Contest, 1966, '67, '72; 1st Place, Lady Beatrice Graham Peace Prize, 1965, '69; Anna Hempstead Br. Silver Medal, 1965; 1st Place, Triolet Contest, Int. League of Children's Poets, 1963; 1st Place, Nellie Burgett Miller Contest, Serious Verse, 1966; 1st Place, Dramatic Poem, Kan. Chaparral Poets, 1966; Trilinea, ibid, 1968; Cinquain Legacy Citation, 1969; num. other prizes. Address: 4 Wash. Sq. Village, NY, NY 10012, USA.

LAMB, Helen Keithley, b. 7 Sept. 1908, Des Moines, Iowa, USA. Poet. Education: B.A., Drake Univ., Des Moines. Married to Don Q. Lamb; 1 d., 2 s. Positions held: Actuarial Student, Bankers Life Ins., Co., Des Moines; Ptnr., Lambs' Ins. Serv., Manhattan, Kansas. Memberships: World Poetry Soc., Intercontinental; Kansas Authors Club. Contbr. to: Kansas Mag.; Kansas Qtly.; Poet; Kansas City Star; Denver Post; Caravan; American Bard; Kansas Kernels; Lyrics of Love, 1963; Fragments of Faith, 1970. Awards: Select Poem, magna cum Laude, World Poet Award, 1970; The Hayden Library Ariz. State Univ. Cert. of Appreciation & Thanks for Outstanding Contib. to Lit. & the American Mosaic Collect., 1970; Semi-finalist, Kan. City Star Nat. Poetry Contest, 1965; 1st Place, Kans. Authors Club Poetry Contest, 1961, 1962, 1969, 1971, 1973; 2nd, 1962, 1963, 1965, 1969, 1971, 1972. Address: 819 Humboldt St., Manhattan, KS 66502, USA.

LAMBERSY, Werner, b. 16 Nov. 1941. Advertising Executive. Education: Jesuites of St. Michel; Université libre de Bruxelles. Positions held: Pub. Rels., review Le Nouvelles a la Main. Memberships: Assn. of Belgian Writers; PEN Club of Belgium; Mbr. Organisateur des Biennales Mondiales de Poesie (Knokke). Published works: Caerulea, 1967; Radoub, 1968; A Cogne Mots, 1969; Haute Tension, 1970; Temps Festif, 1971; Silenciaire, 1972; Moments Dieses, 1973; Groupes de Resonances, 1973. Contbr. to var. lit. reviews & anthols. Recip., Premier prix du grenier aux chansons (jeunes poetes de Belgique). Address: 22 rue Aug. Snieders, 1030 Brussels, Belgium.

LAMMERS, (Sister) Monica, b. 12 Oct. 1916. Good Service Supervisor in Hospitals. Member, Upper Midwest Chaparrel Poets. Contbr. to: The Farmer; Minneapolis Argus; Core Bits. Reclp., Hon. Mention for Poetry, 1971. Address: 212 North Ash St., Crookston, MN 56716, U.S.A.

LAMMING, George, b. 1927. University Teacher. Broadcaster. Positions held: Schl. Tchr., Trinidad & Venezuela; Began Weekly Book Review; prog. for BBC West Indian Service, 1951; Mbr., Fac., Univ. of the West Indies, Kingston, Jamaica, 1968. Published works: (Novels) In the Castle of My Skin, 1953; The Emigrants, 1954; Of Age & Innocence, 1958; Season of Adventure, 1960; Essays: The Pleasures of Exile, 1960. Contbr. to: Young Commonwealth Poets '65, 1965; Caribbean Voices, 1966; Caribbean Literature, 1966; Caribbean Verse, 1967; Sun's Eye, 1968. Hons: Guggenheim Fellowship, 1954; Canada Council Fellowship; Somerset Maugham Award.

LAMONT, Corliss, b. 28 Mar. 1902. Author; Educator. Education: A.B., Harvard Coll., 1924; Grad. work, New Coll., Oxford Univ., U.K., 1924-25; Ph.D., Columbia Univ., U.S.A., 1932. Positions held: Instr., Philos., Columbii Coll., 1928-32; New Schl. for Soc. Rsch., 1940-42; Lectr., Columbia Schl. Gen. Studies, 1947-59. Memberships: V.P., Poetry Soc. of Am., 1973-. Published works: The Illusion of Immortality, 1935; Man Answers Death; An Anthology of Poetry (ed.), 1936; The Philosophy of Humanism, 1957; Freedom of Choice Affirmed, 1967; John Masl field Remembered, 19 -1; Lover's Credo, 1972. Address: 315 W 106 St..

New York, NY 10025, U.S.A.

LAMOREAUX, Velma, b. 27 March 1914. Proofreader and Cost Accountant for Commercial Printing Firm. Education: HS; Business Coll. Married; 2 d. Positions held: Practical Nurse during WW II; Manager, Drapery Dept. in Dept. Store; Proofreader and Cost Accountant for last 19 yrs. Memberships: United Amateur Press (Sec. Treas.); Judson Writers Conference, Judson Coll., Elgin, Illinois (Sec. and Newsletter publisher). Contbr. to: (books) Kansas Kernals, 1968-73; Lyrical Iowa, 1971-73; Yearbook of Mod. Poetry, 1971; The Fantasia Anthol. Series (Grains of Sand), 1971; Garland of Verse Anthol., 1971; Anthol. of Railroad Poems, 1971; A Sheaf of Sonnets, 1969; Phoenix, 1968; The Friendly Way, 1969, 1970, 1971, 1972; Poets on Parade, 1973; (mags., journals, etc.): Marshalltown Times Republican; Cappers Weekly; Kansas Kernels; The Friendly Way; Ideals; Haiku Highlights; Glowing Lanternes; Lyrical Iowa; Valley Center Index; Maize; Invictus; Golden Wedding Observance. Awards: Award of Merit, Judson Coll.; 2 Appreciation Awards. Address: P.O. Box 514, Marshalltown, IA 50158, USA.

LAMPORT, Felicia, b. 4 Jan. 1916. Writer. Education: B.A., Vassar Coll. Married to: Justice Benjamin Kaplan. Memberships: P.E.N.; Nat. Book Committee (Exec. Committee Member); Authors Guild (New England Rep.). Published works: Scrap Irony; Cultural Slag. Contbr. to: Atlantic Monthly; NY Times; Boston Globe; Harper's; New Yorker; Saturday Review; Life; Saturday Evening Post; Look; McCalls. Address: 2 Bond St., Cambridge, MA 02138, USA.

LAMPPA, William R., b. 11 Apr. 1928. Social Worker. Education: B.S., Univ. of Minn., 1955. Married to Shirley Lamppa; 2 s. (Jason and Clayton). Positions held: Control Tower Operator, USAF, 4 yrs.; School Teacher; Construction Worker; Laborer; Mineworker; Social Worker since 1958. Memberships: St. Paul Poets; Midwest Fed. of Chaparral Poets; N.H. Poetry Soc.; Mpls. Writers Workshop. Published works: The Crucial Point and Other Poems, 1971; In Familiar Fields With Old Friends, 1972; The Ancient Chariot and Other Poems, 1973. Contbr. to many journals, in which over 600 poems published. Also contbr. to numerous anthols. Awards: Small awards in various little journals; never enters contests. Address: 5119 Red Oak Dr., New Brighton, MN 55112, USA.

LAMPRILL, Paul, b. 18 March. Artist (Sculptor). Education: studied part A.C.I.I.; Tax Officer training; Dip. A.D. (Sculpt.) Cantuar. Co-Editor, "Sandwiches" magazine; Co-Director, Excello & Bollard Agency & Publishers; member of Pink Peace Road Show, readings and BBC broadcast, 1973. Memberships: Artists Union. Published works: An Evening With Chalice, 1972; Greatest Hits, 1973; Evironment: Writings for today (with others), 1973; E & B Special, 1973. Contbr. to: num. small mags., etc. Address: 77B New Dover Rd., Canterbury, Kent CT1 3DZ.

LAMPSON, Margaret Fraser, pen name (before marriage) **FRASER, Margaret Kimball,** b. 4 May 1900. Homemaker. Education: A.B., Barnard Coll., Columbia Univ., N.Y., 1927; Postgrad. studies, Univ. of Calif., Berkeley, 1933. Married Robin Lampson. Contbr. to: Poetry: a Mag. of Verse, Chgo.; The Lyric; College Verse; Am. Poetry Jrnl.; Carmel Pine Cone; Westward; Shards; N.Y. Herald-Tribune 'Books' Sect.; Oakland Tribune; Sacramento Bee, etc. Address: 190 W. Barrymore St., Stockton, CA 95204, U.S.A.

LAMPSON, Robin, b. 2 Feb. 1900. Writer. Education: Stanford Univ.; A.B., Univ. of Calif., Berkeley, 1932. Married Margaret Kimball Fraser. Positions held: Reporter, Santa Rosa Republican, 1916 & Sacramento Bee, 1917-18; Ed., Woodland Daily Mail, 1919; Philatelic Expert; Full time Writer, 1932–; Tchr., Poetry, Versification, Univ. of Calif., Berkeley, 5 yrs. Author in Res., Univ. of the Pacific, Stockton, Calif., 1971–. Memberships: Phi Beta Kappa; Hon. Life Mbr.,

Ina Coolbrith Circle, Berkeley & San Francisco. Published works: On Reaching Sixteen & Other Poems, 1916; Terza-Rima Sonnets, 1935; Laughter Out of the Ground, historical novel in verse, 1935; A Song of Pindar in Hades, 1935; A Vulcan Among the Argonauts, 1936; The Mending of a Continent, 1937; San Francisco Souvenir, 1938; Death Loses a Pair of Wings, historical novel in verse, 1939; The Man Who Gave the Golden Spike, 1969. Contbr. to: Scribner's; Forum & Century; San Francisco Examiner; San Francisco Bulletin; Prairie Schooner; Christian Sci. Monitor; Lit. Digest; Poetry World; The Best Poems of 1937; The Best Poems of 1938, etc. Honours, awards incl: Silver Medal, Commonwealth Club of Calif., for best book of poetry published in 1935, & in 1939 for his historical novel in verse, Death Loses a Pair of Wings. Address: 190 W. Barrymore St., Stockton, CA 95204, U.S.A.

LAND, Beatrice Marie, pen name **LAND, Beatrice M.,** b. 29 Dec. 1918. Homemaker; Head of Dept. of Sales for retail store. Education: Grad. with hons. from Princeton HS; Winner of a Scholarship from Draughns Coll. Married; 3 children. Positions held: Sunday School Teacher; Brownie Leader Sec. Childrens Work in Methodist Church; Missionary Sec. of Women's Soc, Vice-Pres. (3 terms) then Pres. of Women's Soc. of Christian Service, and life membership awarded for WSCS service in New Mexico Conference of United Methodist Women. Memberships: Garland Chapter, Poetry Soc. of Texas (Pres., recently re-elected for 3rd term), also Reporter to the State Soc.; Writers Workshop of Garland (Pres., also Vice-Pres., Sec., and Reporter). Contbr. to: Poetry, Classical & Contemporary, 1969; Book of the Year, 1973 (Poetry Soc. of Texas); Southwest Scene Mag.; Sunday Mag.; TV Times; Axe United Methodist; Garland Daily News; Dallas Times Herald; Dallas Morning News; Progressive Life, etc. Honours, Awards: In the Confederate Research Category, poem on display in Archives of Hillsboro Coll. in the Confed. Research Dept., 1971; Critics Award (PST), 1972; Harry Kovner Award, Nov. 11, 1972 (Ann. Awards · of PST); Citizenship Prize, Nov. 11, 1972 (Ann. Awards of PST); Naylor Award, Jan. 1973 (PST), and numerous local chapter awards. Address: 2609 Lakewood Dr., Garland, TX 75042, USA.

LANE, Gary Martin, b. 25 Mar. 1943. University Professor. Education: A.B., Oberlin Coll., 1964; Ph.D., Univ. of Mich., 1973. Twice married & divorced. Positions held: Poetry Instr., Muhlenberg Coll., 1969-72; Vis. Lectr., Poetry, Univ. of Mich., 1972-73; Asst. Prof., Poetry, Univ. of Miami, 1974–. Memberships: MLA; Poetry Soc. of Am. Published works: (criticism) A Concordance to the Poems of Theodore Roethke, 1972; A Concordance to the Poems of Hart Crane, 1972; A Concordance to the Poems of Marianne Moore, 1972; A Concordance to Personae: The Shorter Poems of Ezra Pound, 1972. Forthcoming: A Study of Cummings' Poems. Contbr. to: The Blackbird Circle; Arcade: Monmouth Review. Address: 2845 Bynan Dr., Ypsilanti, MI 48197, U.S.A.

LANE, Mary Louisa, pen name **LEE, Mariel,** b. 16 May 1894. Former Teacher. Education: Melbourne Tchrs. Coll., Australia; B.A., Melbourne Univ., 1917. Positions held: Hd. Tchr., Wal Wal Country Schl., 1915; Asst. Tchr., Beechworth, 1915, Traralgon, 1916, Nhill, 1917, Horsham H.S., 1918-19, Warracknabeal, 1919, Haven, 1920, Chewton, 1921, Renalla, 1921, Daylesford, 1922; Hd. Tchr., Bangerang, 1920-21. Memberships: Fellow, Australian Writers, Vic. Br.; Soc. of Women Writers, Vic.Br.; Catholic Readers & Writers' Soc.; Poetry Soc. of Australia. Contbr. to: Sydney Bulletin; Australian Woman's Mirror; Home Budget; New Triad; Sydney Morning Herald; Western Mail; Christian World; Poetry World (U.S.A.); Sydney Mail; House & Garden; Woman; Observer; Country Life; Liverpool Echo; The Countryman; Catholic Leader; This Australia; Poets of Australia, etc. Honours, awards: 2nd prize, Capt. Cook Bi-Centenary Poetry Comp., 1970; The W.A. & J.I. Henderson Meml. Prize, 1972; First in Nation-Wide Literary Services Poetry Comp.,

1973. Address: 65 McPherson St., Horsham, Vic.3400, Australia.

LANE, Millicent Elizabeth (Travis), pen name **LANE, M. Travis,** b. 23 Sept. 1934. Scholar; Critic; Poet. Education: B.A., Vassar, 1956; M.A., Cornell Univ., 1957; Ph.D., ibid, 1967. Positions held: Grad. Tchng. Fellow, Cornell Univ., 1958-59; P/t Instr., Univ. of New Brunswick, 1967-68; Hon. Rsch. Assoc., ibid, 1973-. Memberships: Phi Beta Kappa; League of Canadian Poets. Published works: Five Poets, 1960; An Inch or So of Garden, 1969; Poems 1968-72, 1973; a book length sequence of poems entitled Homecoming will be published by Fiddlehead mag. late 1973. Contbr. to: Southwest Review; Trail & Timberline; Vassar Review; Epoch; Fiddlehead; Canadian Forum; The Antigonish Review; The Atlantic Advocate; The Canadian Author & Bookman; Copperfield; Dalhousie Review. Address: 807 Windsor St., Fredericton, New Brunswick, Canada.

LANE, Patrick, b. 26 March 1939. Poet. Editor of Very Stone House In Transit. Published works: Letters From The Savage Mind, 1967; Sunflower Seeds, 1968; Separations, 1969; On The Street, 1970; Mountain Oysters, 1971; Hiway 401 Rhapsody, 1971; The Sun Has Begun To Eat The Mountain, 1972; Passing Into Storm, 1973; Beware The Months Of Fire, 1974. Contbr. to: almost all Canadian Poetry Mags.; American and English Journals and Mags., etc. Recip. York Univ. Poetry Award, 1971; Canada Council Awards, 1967, 1970, 1973. Address: R.R.3, Vernon, BC, Canada.

LANE, Pinkie Gordon, b. 13 Jan. 1923. College Professor. Education: B.A., Spelman Coll., Atlanta, Ga.; M.A., Atlanta Univ.; Ph.D., La. State Univ., Baton Rouge. Widow, 1 son. Positions held: H.S. Tchr., 1949-56; Coll. Prof., 1959-73 (currently Prof. of Engl., Southern Univ., Baton Rouge, La.). Memberships: Poetry Soc. of Am.; Nat. Fed. of State Poetry Socs.; Poetry Socs. of La. & Pa.; Nat. Writers Club. Published works: Wind Thoughts, coll. of poems, 1972; Discourses on Poetry: Prose & Poetry by Blacks, vol. VI, Ed., 1972; Poems by Blacks: an Anthol., vol. III, Ed., 1974. Contbr. to num. mags., anthols. inclng: Poet, India; Pembroke Mag.; South & West; Voices Int.; La. Review; Southern Review; Confrontation; Poems by Poets, vol. 1, 1973; Poems by Blacks, vols. I & II; Certain Days Are Islands; To Gwen With Love. Var. poetry readings at univs., schls., orgs. & has appeared on TV. Honours, awards incl: Cert. of Merit, Tulsa Poets, 1970; Works included in the Beinecke Rare Book & Ms. Lib. of Yale Univ. in the James Weldon Johnson Coll. of Negro Arts & Letters, 1972. Address: 2738 77th Ave., Baton Rouge, LA 70807, U.S.A.

LANGEROCK, Lydia, b. 20 July 1914. Education: studied history of music, harmony, piano. Married Robert Bosson. Positions held: Sec., Belgian Govt. in exil, London, 1940-41. Has lived in the Belgian Congo, 1942-60, Belgium, 1960-69, & Spin since 1969. Mbrships: PEN Club of Belgium; Société des Poètes Français, Paris; Assn. of Belgian Writers; Chevalier de l'Ordre International de la Renaissance des Arts et Lettres, Paris. Published works: (poetry) Tons Mineurs, 1935; Point d'Orgue, 1939; Gammes, 1950; Rapsodie, 1962; Les Ramiers de l'Aube, 1963; Orgues Océanes, 1964; Réponses d'Argile, 1965; La Quête de Plénitude, 1966; La Saison Végétale, 1971. Contbr. to: L'Etrave, Paris; Le Thyrse, Brussels; Le Journal des Poètes, Brussels; Bételgouse, Paris; (anthols.) J. Grassin, Paris; Revue Moderne, Paris, etc. Honours, awards: Premier Prix de poésie du Conseil Européen d'Art et Esthétique, Brussels, 1963; Médaille d'argent, ibid, 1969; Premier prix de poésie de la Ville d'Ouistreham Riva-Bella, France, 1964; Prix Jules Minne, Brussels, 1964; Prix Jeanne Marvig de l'Académie des Jeux Floraux de Toulouse, France, 1969; Laurier de Vermeil, ibid. Address: Urbanizacion Los Pinos, 83, Calpe, Province d'Alicante, Spain.

LANGFORD, Gary (Raymond), b. 21 Aug. 1947.

Teacher. Education: B.A., Hist. & Engl., Univ. of Canterbury, M.A.(Hons.) Hist. and Engl., Univ. of Canterbury; Diploma of Teaching, Christchurch Teachers Training Coll. Positions held: Co-Editor, Edge (Magazine), 1970-72; Poetry Editor, Canta, 1972; Reviewer, Christchurch Press; Editor, New Zealand Universities Literary Yearbook, 1973. Pubs.: The Family, 1973; Gut, 1973. Represented in the anthol. The Young New Zealand Poets, 1973. Contrib. to: Edge; Frontiers; Lipsync; The N.Z. Listener; Argot; N.Z. Monthly Review; Arena; N.Z. Earwig; The Southern Review; Poetry Australia; New Poetry; Expression; Westerly; Quadrant; Saturday Club Book of Poetry; Poet; Ark River Review; Focus Midwest; Archer; Scrip, etc. Recip. Vera Bladen Award for Poetry, 1971. Address: c/o M. Langford, 79 Kingsford St., Christchurch 6, New Zealand.

LANGLAND, Joseph Thomas, b. 16 Feb. 1917. Poet; Professor of English. Education: B.A. & M.A., Univ. of Iowa, 1940, '41; post grad. study, Univ. of Iowa, 1946-48; Fac. Fellowship, Harvard & Columbia Univs., 1953-54. Married, 2 sons, 1 daughter. Positions held: Tchr., one-room rural schl., Burroak, Ia, 1936-38; Instr., Dana Coll., Blair, Neb., 1941-42; Pvt. to Capt., Infantry & Mil. Govt., U.S. Army, 1942-46; p/t Instr., Univ. of Iowa, 1946-48; Asst. Assoc. Prof. Engl., Univ. of Wyoming, 1948-59; Assoc. to Full Prof., Univ. of Mass., Amherst, 1959-. Published works: (books) The Green Town, poems, 1956; The Short Story (co-ed.), 1956; Poet's Choice (co-ed.), 1962; A Little Homily, one long poem w. etchings, 1962; The Wheel of Summer, poems, 1963, '64; Songs, Lyrics & Half-Songs, poems, 1974; Adlai Stevenson, meml. poem & 2 ballads, 1973; Poetry From the Russian Underground (transl. w. others), 1973; Contemporary Poetry: 1945 to present, anthol., forthcoming. Contbr. to var. anthols., mags., newspapers, reviews. Has made var. poetry recordings. Honours, awards incl: Melville Cane Award (PSA), 1964; Nat. Coun. of Arts Grant in Poetry, 1966-67. Address: 16 Morgan Circle, Amherst, MA 01002, U.S.A.

LANGLEY, Eve Marin, b. 1 Sept. 1904. Poet; Novelist. Positions held: Libn., Auckland Public Lib., New Zealand. Memberships: Poetry Soc. of Australia, Sydney. Published works: The Pea Pickers; White Topee. Contbr. to: Sydney Bulletin; Womans Mirror; var. Auckland newspapers. Address: Inn Olympus, Clydebank Rd., Katoomba, N.S.W., Australia.

LANGTON, Daniel Joseph, b. 6 Sept. 1927. Teacher. Education: B.A., 1952, M.A., 1954, San Francisco State Coll.; Ph.D., 1970, Univ. of Calif. Positions held: Auditing Acct., Metropolitan Life Ins. Co., 1955-61; Teacher, San Rafael HS, 1963-67; Prof., Calif. State Univ., San Francisco, since 1967. Contbr. to: Nation; Coastlines; American Weave; Whetstone; Audience; New Orleans Poetry Journal; Odyssey; Mainstream; San Francisco Review; Extantis; Galley Sail; Beatitude; Penny Press; Paris Review; Dalhousie Review; San Francisco Examiner; Poetry; Approach; Mass. Review; Perspective; John O'London; Paris Tribune; Poetry Parade; Renaissance; Choice; Atlantic; Harvard Advocate; Carleton Miscellany; Open Places; Kayak; Sumac; Dryad; Saturday Review; Quixote; Colo. Review; Arlington Qtly.; Poetry Northwest; Colo. Qtly.; American Scholar; Folio; Carolina Qtly.; Red n White; Kilkenny Journal; Telegram; Vision; Northeast; Cottonwood Review; Antioch Review; Deserted Times; Southern Poetry Review; Dragonfly; Cimarron Review; Michigan Qtly. Review; White Elephant; Kansas Qtly.; Holy Doors; Spartan Poetry Review; Literary Review; Harvest; Gallimaufry; Anvil; Occident; Aisling. Awards: John O'London Prize, 1962; Browning Soc. Award, 1967; Hart Crane Mem. Award, 1970. Address: 1673 Oak St., San Francisco, CA 94117, USA.

LANSING, Gerrit Yates, b. 25 Feb. 1928. Education: B.A., Harvard Univ.; M.A., Columbia Univ. Pub: The Heavenly Tree Grows Downward, 1966. Contrib. to: Semicolon; Folder; Trobar; Set; Matter; Poems Now; A New Folder; Measure; Red Crow; Caterpillar; Anonym;

Wivenhoe Park Revue; A Controversy of Poets; Inside Outer Space; A Caterpillar Anthol., etc. Address: 302 Forbes St., Annapolis, Md. 21401, USA.

LANTAY, Patricia Joan Marx, pen name **MARX, Patricia,** b. 6 Mar. 1946. Poet; Editor. Education: Trinity Coll., 1964-66; Univ. of Ill., 1966-60; 4 Katherine Gibbs Schl., 1970; Hunter Coll., 1974. Married George C. Lantay, div., 2 daughters. Positions held: Sec.-Receptionist, Cushman & Wakefield, N.Y.C., 1966; Engl. Instr., Intext, Scranton, Pa., 1968-69; Ed. of St. Bartholomew's Review, N.Y.C., 1973-74. Memberships: Poetry Ctr., N.Y.C.; N.Y. Poetry Forum. Contbr. to: Green Leaf; The Record; Compass; St. Bartholomew's Review. Honours, awards: Anna Phillips Bolling Meml., 1964. Address: 333 East 43rd St., N.Y., NY 10017, U.S.A.

LANTIER, Nadine Marie Jez, pen name, **LANTIER, Nadine,** b. 26 Jan. 1922. Advertising Executive; Portrait Painter; Graphic Artist; Writer and Poet. Married to Lawrence Louis Lantier. Memberships: Fort Worth Poetry Soc.; Poetry Soc. of Texas; American Advertising Club, Fort Worth Chapter; Theta Sigma Phi; World Poetry Soc. Intercontinental; CSSI. Contbr. to anthols.: Treasures of Parnassus, 1962; Cavalcade of Poetry, 1963; Anthol. of American Poetry (Vols. 3, 4, 5, 6, 7, 8, (1961-66)); Bouquet of Poems, 1970. Recip. of sev. awards from CAAA; World Poetry Soc. Intercontinental; Internat. Who's Who in Poetry; World Acad. of Languages & Lit.; Inst. of Comparative Literature, etc. Address: 2312 Irwin, Ft. Worth, TX 76110, USA.

LANTZ, Ruth Cox, b. 11 Jan. 1914. Teacher; Writer; Artist. Education: A.B., Emory Univ., 1934; M.A., Mich. Univ., 1942; Yale Univ.; Pratt Inst. Married to John Edward Lantz, 1937; 2 s., 1 d. Positions held: Tchr., Druid Hills Schl., 1934-35; Instr., Speech, Vanderbilt Univ., 1946-52; Tchr., Speech, St. Mary's Acad., 1952; Instr., Relig. Educ., Interdenominational Theol. Ctr., 1960-69. Memberships: Dixie Coun. of Authors & Jrnlsts.; Ga. Writers' Assn.; Atlanta Writers' Club; Acad. Am. Poets. Contbr. to the following anthols. & jrnls: First 500 Poems from Georgia Magazine, 1964; Leaves of Life, 1964; Classmate; The Christian Home; Georgia Magazine; The Shepherdess. Awarded 1st Prize in poetry contest of The Atlanta Writers' Club, 1972. Address: 1040 Springdale Rd. NE, Atlanta, GA 30306, USA.

LA POINTE-HEATH, Beth, b. 1 June 1906. Retired Nurse; Writer; Graphoanalyst. Education: Ryrs Coll. of Nursing. Positions held: Tchr.; Musician; Linguist. Memberships: APL; Midwest Chaparral Poets; Int. Graphoanalysis Soc. Author, Time of Singing, 1966. Contbr. to: (anthols.) Golden Quill; From Sea to Sea in Song; These Are My Jewels; Poems of Am.; Am. Poets; Jewels on a Willow Tree; Melodies from a Jade Harp; New Voices; Ben Travato; Anthol. of Am. Poetry; Choice of the Angels; Rhyme Time for the Very Young; Purring in a Pocket; Versatility in Verse; (jrnls.) Author of Jrnlist.; Jr. Challenge; Scimitar & Song; Down Ink Lane; The Green World; Reflections; United Poets; Prairie Poet; Am. Poet; Midwest Chaparral; Writers Notes & Quotes; Jean's Jrnl.; Quarderno Di Poesia; Orphic Lute; Haiku Highlights; Haiku West; Am. Haiku; Haiku Canada; Nutmegger; Blue Print; Janus & SCTH; Peninsula Poets; Major Poets; Saint; Poetry Prevue; Muse; Am. Voice; World Poets; Mod. Haiku; Author/Poet; Brockton Enterprise, Mass.; NH Register & Jrnl.-Courier, Conn.; Poetry Highlights, Russell Time, Ky.; Poet's Corner, Altoona Mirror, Pa. Honours, Awards: Cert. of Merit, Accad. Leonardo Da Vinci, 1968; Personal Poetry Award, WHPI-AM Radio, 1968; ASFS Award, Major Poet, 1968; MFCP Award, 1970; Gr. Concepts Award, 1970; various small awards. Address: 13 Center Ave., East Haven, Conn. 06512, USA.

LARDAS, Konstantinos Nick, b. 3 Aug. 1927. Educator. Education: B.A., Univ. of Pitts., Pa., 1950; M.A., Columbia Univ., N.Y.C., 1951; Ph.D., Univ. of Mich., 1966. Married Sofia Lacios, 3 sons. Positions

held: Ptnr., industrial painting firm, 1950-60; Tchng. Fellow & Pre-Doctoral Instr., Univ. of Mich., 1962-66; Asst. & Assoc. Prof. of Engl., CCNY, 1966–. Memberships: Acad. of Am. Poets; Modern Greek Lang. Studies; Hon. Mbr., Phi Beta Kappa. Published works: And In Him, Too; In Us, Generation, 1964. Has translated many modern Greek poets, & the complete poems of Sappho. Contbr. to many jrnls., anthols., reviews. Honours, awards: Bain-Swigget Poetry Award for 1962, Univ. of Mich.; Borestone Mountain Poetry Awards, Best Poems for 1962 & 63; Rockefeller Fndn. Appreciation Grant, Univ. of Mich., 1963; Fulbright Student Grant to Greece, 1962; Phi Beta Kappa, reading of 'Commitments', Univ. of Pitts., 1968. Address: 68 Wakefield Ave., Yonkers, NY 10704, U.S.A.

LARKIN, Philip (Arthur), b. 9 Aug. 1922. University Librarian. Education: St. John's Coll., Oxford Univ., U.K., 1940-43. Positions held: var. lib. posts, 1943-55; Libn., Univ. of Hull, 1955–. Published works: The North Ship (poems), 1945, '66; Jill (novel), 1946, '64; A Girl in Winter (novel), 1947; The Less Deceived (poems), 1955; The Whitsun Weddings (poems), 1964; All What Jazz (essays), 1969; High Windows (poems), 1974. Contbr. to: The Spectator; New Statesman; Encounter; London Mag.; The Listener; Sunday Times; Observer; Oxford Book of 20th Century English Verse (Ed.), 1973. Honours, awards: The Queen's Gold Medal for Poetry, 1965; Arts Coun.'s Triennial Award for Poetry, 1965; Hon.D.Litt., Belfast, 1969, Leicester, 1970 & Warwick, 1973; Cholmondeley Poetry Award, 1973. Address: The Brynmor Jones Lib., The Univ., Hull, Yorks., U.K.

LARMON, (Mrs. Lawrence), b. 23 Apr. 1910. Teacher; Merchant; Homemaker. Education: Eau Clair, Wis., State Tchrs. Coll., 1931. Married, 1 son, 1 daughter. Positions held: Schl. Tchr.; operated Summer Market in vacation area; currently helps husband in General Store. Memberships: Wis. Fellowship of Poets; NFSPS; Sponsor & Judge two categories, The Fidelia Van Antwerp Ballad Award & the Agnes C. Brothers Significant Poetry Contest; Hd. of the State's Poetry III Robin. Contbr. to: Homecrofter; Milwaukee Jrnl.; Poems Out of Wis. III, 1967; The Periscope; New Poetry Out of Wis., 1969; Prize Poems of the Nat. Fed. of State Poetry Socs., 1966 & '72; Country Gentleman. Honours, awards incl: Jade Ring, Cash Award, State Bard's Chair, Wis. Regl. Writers, 1966; 2nd Prize, Lyrical Poetry, NFSPS, 1967; 1st Prize, Shakespearean Sonnet, ibid, 1972. Address: Star Route, Hannibal, WI 54439, U.S.A.

LARSEN, Carl, b. 28 Aug. 1934. Teamster. Education: El Camino Coll., Calif.; Actor's Studio, N.Y. Married three times, divorced twice. Positions held: Head Dispatcher, Freight co., 15 yrs. Member, Calliope Poetry Soc. Published works: (poetry pamphlets) Notes From a Machine Shop, 1956; The Journal of an Existentialist Villain, 1957; Arrows of Longing, 1958; The.Plot to Assassinate the Chase Manhattan Bank, 1962; The Naked And The Dead And The Sick And the Sad And The Sorry Meet Frankenstein, 1963; The Toad King, 1964; The Popular Mechanics Book of Poetry, 1966; (novels) Onan's Seed, 1960; The Book of Eric Hammerscoffer, 1964. Contbr. of over 400 poems to approx. 100 mags. Recip., Rosemary DeCamp Playwriting Award, 1953. Address: 243-16 130th Rd., Rosedale, NY 11422, U.S.A.

LARTER, Robert Oswald, pen name **LARTER, Bob,** 27 Sept. 1921. Gift Shop & Garden Centre Proprietor. Positions held: Farmer; Soldier; Sailor; Engineer; Oil Driller; Public Servant; Shop Owner. Memberships: Writers' Workshop, Adult Educ., Torquay, Hervey Bay, Qld. Address: P.O. Box 77, Pialba, Hervey Bay, Qld. 4655, Australia.

LASHLEY, Cliff, b. 21 Sept. 1935. Poet. Education: Univ. of the West Indies, Kingston; Univ. of Western Ont., London, Can.; Schl. of Librarianship, North Western Polytechnic, London, UK. Contbr. to (Anthol.): New Voices of the Commonwealth, 1968;

(Jrnls.) Black Orpheus; Bim; Folio; Jamaica Jrnl.; Outposts. Address: Apt. 1705, 322 Eglinton Court, Toronto 12, Ont., Canada.

LASSITER, Isaac Steele, b. 4 Jul. 1941. Engaged in Railroading. Education: HS., Campbell Coll., B.S. Married to Elsie Langston Bugg. Positions held: from 1966-71 Teacher in 3 public schools in Johnston County, NC.; 1971 commenced work for Norfolk Southern Railway Company. Membership: Internat. Platform Assoc.; N.C. Poetry Soc. Inc.; Major Poets Soc. Published work: The Owl's Nest Betrayal (poems), 1971. Contbr. to: (hardback anthols.) Echoes of Faith; Outstanding Contemporary Poetry; Yearbook of Modern Poetry; (softcover anthols.) Lyrics of Love; Anthol.-Winter 1961, vol. IV, (American Coll. Poetry Soc.), Anthol.-Summer, 1960, vol. 111. (mags.) The Lyricist, vol. 1, nos. 1 and 2; vol. III. Address: P.O. Box 552, Candor, NC 27229, USA.

LASZLO, Nagy, b. 17 July 1925. Poet. Education: 1 yr. at Acad. of Fine Arts.; 1 yr. at Fac. of Liberal Arts. Positions held: Artistic Ed. of lit. review, Elet es Irodalom, 1959–. Mbr., Comm. Bd., Assn. of Hungarian Writers. Published works: (in Hungarian) Pain Disappear! 1949; The Artilleryman & the Rye, 1951; Sabres & Zythers (trans. from the Bulgarian), 1953; The Bride of the Sun, 1954; Pleasuring Sunday, 1956; Selected Poems, 1944-56; Fair in Frosty May, 1957; Falcons' Blood, an anthology of Bulgarian folk-poetry, 1960; Hymn for Anytime, 1965; Facing the Sea, Poems, 1944-65, 1966; Wasp-king selected translations, 1958-68, from Engl., French, Spanish, Am., Bulgarian, Rumanian, Russian & Chinese poets, 1968; Sky & Earth, An Oratorio, 1972; Love of the Scorching Wind, Selected Poems, 1953-71, 1973; Hiding in Poem, 1973. Contbr. to: Uj iras; Kortars; Elet es Irodalom. Honours, awards: Jozsef Attila Prize, 1954; Kossuth Prize, 1966; Laureate of Gold Medal for Poetry, Int. Fest. of Poetry, Struga, Yugoslavia, 1968; Laureate of Gold Medal of Cyrill & Method, 1967. Address: III Arpad fejedelem utja 66, Budapest, Hungary.

LATTA, Ruth, b. 2 Dec. 1900. Education: Nursing School; A.B., M.S., Univ. of Rochester; 3 yr. fellowship in nutrition. Married. Positions held: Nurse; Asst. in Coll. Courses; Assoc. Prof. (chem.) etc. Memberships: Haiku Soc. of America; Western World Haiku Soc.; NY Poetry Forum; Michigan Poetry Soc.; W.Va. Poetry Soc.; Pennsylvania Poetry Soc.; Midwest Chaparral Poets; Avalon; World Poets; Idaho Poets, etc. Contbr. to more than 100 different sources, including Poet (India), and publications in UK, Australia, Canada, Japan, etc. Recip. of a variety of small awards. Address: P.O. Box 528, Carmel, NY 10512, USA.

LATTIMORE, Richmond, b. 6 May 1906. Professor (retired). Education: B.A., Dartmouth, 1926; M.A., Univ. of Illinois, 1927; B.A. (Oxon.), 1932; M.A., 1963; Ph.D., Univ. of Illinois, 1935; Rhodes Scholar, Indiana and Christ Church, 1929-32; Fellow, American Acad. in Rome, 1934-35. Married, Alice Bockstahler; 2 s. (Steven, and Alexander). Positions held: Asst., Classics, Engl., Univ. of Illinois, 1926-28; Asst. Prof., Wabash Coll., 1928-29; Asst. Philosophy, Univ. of Illinois, 1933-34; Asst. Prof. – Prof., Bryn Mawr Coll., 1935-71; Lieut., USNR., 1943-46. Memberships: Nat. Inst. of Arts & Letters; P.E.N.; Philadelphia Art Alliance. Published works: Poems, 1957; Sestina For a Far-Off Summer, 1962; The Stride of Time, 1966; Poems From Three Decades, 1972. Contbr. to: Accent; Antioch Review; Harper's; Hudson Review; Kenyon Review; Nation; New Republic; NY Times; New Yorker; Poetry (Chicago); Poetry Northwest; Qtly. Review of Literature; Saturday Review; Southern Review; Times Lit. Supp.; Virginia Qtly. Review. Address: 123 Locust Grove Rd., Rosemont, PA 19010, USA.

LAUBE, Clifford James, b. 28 Aug. 1891. Newspaper Editor. Married Dora E. Weber, 2 sons, 2 daughters. Positions held: Estab. w. father, Rico Weekly Item, 1907; Mbr., 21st Gen. Assembly, Colo. Legis., 1916-

17; Statehouse Reporter, Denver, Colo. Times & Rocky Mt. News, 1918-20; Asst. City Ed., Daily News, N.Y.C., 1921-28; Suburban Ed., N.Y. Times, 1930-42; Day Nat. News Ed., ibid, 1942-53; Poetry Ed., The Sign mag., Union City, N.J., 1945–, Queen of All Hearts mag., Bay Shore, N.Y., 1950–; Co Fndr., Assoc. Ed., Spirit poetry mag., 1934-69. Mbrships: Past Pres., Cath. Poetry Soc. of Am.; Poetry Soc. of Am. Published works: Crags, book of poems, 1938; The Triumph of the Cross, rendition in Engl. verse from the French Cantiques of St. Louis De Montfort, 1950 (rendition of 4 additl. cantiques completed 1974); Broken Crusts, 2nd book of poems, 1975. Contbr. to num. textbooks, anthols., jrnls., newspapers. Honours, awards: Elected to Gall. of Living Cath. Authors, Webster Groves, Mo., 1948; Recip., Cath. Poetry Soc. of Am's Gold Medal Award, 1959; Recip., three Hon.Litt. D. from var. colls. Address: 107-06 103rd Ave., Ozone Pk., NY 11417, U.S.A.

LAUGHLIN, James, b. 30 Oct. 1914. Commission Executive; Publisher; Poet. Education: A.B., Harvard Univ., Cambridge, Mass., 1939. Married Ann Clark w. 4 children. Positions held: Fndr.-Pres.-Ed., New Publishing Corp., N.Y., 1936–; Pres., Intercultural Publications, publisher of Perspectives, USA, 1956–; Chmn., Creative Writing Panel, Inst. for Int. Educ. Conf. on Arts Exchange; Dir., Goethe Bicentennial Foundation, 1949; Aspen Inst. of the Humanities, 1950; Mbr., US Nat. Commission for UNESCO, 1960-63; Trustee of the Allen-Chase Foundation; Co-Trustee, Thomas Merton Legacy Trust. Published works: Some Natural Things, 1945; A Small Book of Poems, 1948; Confidential Report & Other Poems, 1959; Pulsatilla, 1961; Die Haare auf Grossvaters Kopf, 1966; Quel che la Matita Scrive, 1970; The Pig, 1970; Other: Ed., New Directions in Prose & Poetry, vols. 1-22, 1937-70; A Wreath of Christmas Poems, 1942; A New Directions Reader, 1964. Contbr. to (Anthols.): War Poets, 1945; 100 Modern Poems, 1949; A Little Treasury of World Poetry, 1952; Exploring Poetry, 1955; Poetry for Pleasure, 1960; (jrnls.): Poetry; Stony Brook. Hons: Mbr., Am. Acad. of Arts & Sciences; Chevalier de la Legion d'Honneur; D. Litt., Hamilton Coll., Clinton, N.Y., 1969.

LaVALLEE, Susan Marie, b. 15 Nov. 1950. Writer. Education: Private School (12 yrs.); College (2 yrs.); Univ. of S. Calif. Memberships: Internat. Poetry Soc.; Lincoln Log Poetry Soc. Published works: Sea Shadow, 1972; Find Me, 1973. Contbr. to: Special Song; Tweed Mag.; Lincoln Log; Internat. Poetry Soc.; Quintessence; Verse in View; Southwest Breeze; Legend Mag.; Rio Hondo Lit. Mag. Awards: Special Song awarded a cash prize, Fall, 1972; The Editor Choice Poem; Special Song awarded a cash prize, Spring, 1972; Contest Winner. Address: 10440 Messina Dr., Whittier, CA 90603, USA.

LAWDER, Douglas Ward, b. 12 June 1934. Associate Professor. Education: Kenyon Coll., B.A., English; Univ. of Oregon, M.F.A. (with hons.). Positions held: Head, Dept. of Spanish, Wayland Acad., Beaver Dam, Wis.; Teaching Fellowship, Univ. of Oregon; Managing Editor, Northwest Review; Assoc. Editor, Northwest Folklore, 1964-67; Head, Dept. of Creative Writing, Earlham Coll., Richmond, Ind. Currently, Assoc. Prof. of Engl., Michigan State Univ. Published work: The Northwest Poets, 1970; Book of Poetry, 1974. Contbr. to: Chelsea Review; December; Descant; Lillabulero; The Nation; Northwest Review; Per/Se; Perspective; Poetry (Chicago); Poetry Review; Sumac; Wascana Review; West Coast Review; Southwest Review; Virginia Qtly. Review; NY Qtly.; Michigan Qtly. Review; Red Cedar Review; (translations) The Dragonfly; The Seventies. Awards: The Hunter Lit. Award (for poetry), 100-dollars, Univ. of Oregon, 1966, 1967; The Nat. Endowment for the Arts, 2,000-dollars Award, 1968; Danforth Foundation Grant, 1968; Michigan State Univ. summer writing grant, 1972, 1973. Address: 8604 E. Grand River Rd., Rt. 1, Box 250, Laingsburg, MI 48848, USA.

LAWNER, Lynne, b. 10 Apr. 1935. Poet; Writer;

Scholar. Education: B.A., Wellesley; Univ. of Cambridge (Henry Fellow at Newnham Coll.); Univ. of Rome; Columbia Univ.; Ph.D. Positions held: Directed translation projects for sev. publishing orgs., inclng. Ency. Britannica; Taught a seminar in Provençal Poetry at Univ. of Rome. Member, Phi Beta Kappa. Published works: (poetry) Wedding Night of a Nun, 1964; Triangle Dream, 1969; var. books & essays on other subjects. Contbr. to: Bottege Oscure; Atlantic Monthly; New World Writing; Best Poems of 1955 (Boreston Nat. Poetry Awards); Erotic Poetry, etc. Address: via del Governo Vecchio, 121, Rome 00186, Italy, & 531 Belmonte Park No., Dayton, Ohio, U.S.A.

LAWRANCE, William Scott, b. 9 July 1947. Poet. Education: B.A., Univ. of B.C., Canada, 1969; currently studying Tibetan Buddhism w. number of teachers. Positions held: Ed., Circular Causation, 1969-71; Assoo. Ed., Raincoast Chronicles, 1972–. Memberships: Canadian League of Poets. Published works: Apocolips, 1967; Should Stick to Carrying Water, 1971. Contbr. to: Circular Causation; Blew Ointment; Gronk; Ganglia; Haemoglobin Mail; Runcible Spoon; Raincoast Chronicles; Poet's Market; West Coast Seen; Georgia Straight; Synapse; Radio Free; Rain Forest. Address: General Delivery, Robert's Creek, B.C., Canada.

LAWRIN, Lura Dell, pen name **DELL, Nevada,** b. 14 Nov. 1917. Housewife. Married John Lawrin. Positions held: Model; Dress-Designer Apprentice; Bookbinder, Gulf Publishing Co.; Drugstore Clerk; Stockroom Clerk, Adel Precision Corp.; Dealer, The Old Las Vegas Club, Nev. Active in community affairs, school, church, civic activities. Treas., Nev. Poetry Soc., 1964-67. Contbr. to: Anthol. of Am. Poetry, Book V, 1963; Silver Strings (Nev. Poetry Soc. Anthol.), 1965; Am. Bard & Bard's Brighter Side, 1967; Las Vegas Sun; Morning Sun Scene; Las Vegas Review Jrnl.; The Nevadan, etc. Address: 7175 West Craig Rd., Las Vegas, NV 89108, U.S.A.

LAWSON, Adelaide Long, b. 28 Mar. 1902. Music Educator. Education: Artist's Dip. & Music Tchrs. Cert., 4 yr. courses at Blue Ridge Coll., New Windsor, Md. Married E. Everett Lawson. Memberships: Poetry Soc. of Am.; Past Pres., N. La. Br. of Nat. League of Am. Pen Women; Past Recording Sec., La. State Poetry Soc.; Nat. Fed. State Poetry Socs. Published works: Notes From Beauty's Lyre, book of poetry, 1949. Contbr. to: N.Y. Times; Chgo. Tribune; Denver Post; The Oregonian; Kaleidograph; Songs from Am. Hearts; Fla. Mag. of Verse; The Pen Woman; Folio; Bookfellow Poetry Annual; Am. Poetry Mag., etc. Honours, awards: First Prize for State of La. in Nat. Thanksgiving Assn. Poetry Contest, 1945; Mbr., Bd. Dirs., Deep South Writers & Artists Conf., 1969-74, etc. Address: 807 Auburn Ave., Monroe, LA 71201, U.S.A.

LAY, Norma (Marguerite), b. 13 Sept. 1904. Education: Grammar School & Secondary School, Elmira, NY; Elmira Free Acad.; A.B., Elmira Coll., NY; Teaching Cert. in Hygiene & Physical Education, Wellesley Coll., Mass. Memberships: Poetry Soc. of America; Cornell Univ. Library Assoc. Published work: Interval to Sun (poems), 1949. Contbr. to: Sat. Review of Literature; NY Times; NY Herald Tribune; Voices; CS Monitor; Trails; Epoch; Massachusetts Review; The Chirp; PSA Anthols. (twice); The Rochester (NY) Festival of Religious Arts booklets (twice). Address: 4163 2 Av. N., St. Petersburg, FL 33713, USA.

LAYTON, Irving (Peter), b. 12 Mar. 1912. Professor of Engl. Literature. Education: B.Sc.(Agr.), Macdonald Coll., 1939; M.A., Econ. and Political Sci., McGill Univ., 1946. Born in Rumania; arrived Canada, 1913. Married, 3 children. Positions held: Poet-in-Residence, Sir George Williams Univ.; Writer-in-Residence, Univ. of Guelph; Prof. of Engli. Lit., York Univ. Member, P.E.N. Pubs. Here And Now, 1945; Now Is The Place, 1948; The Black Huntsman, 1951; Cerberus (with Louis Dudek, Raymond Souster), 1952; Love The Conqueror Worm, 1953; In The Midst

Of My Fever, 1954; The Long Pea-Shooter, 1954; The Blue Propeller, 1955; The Cold Green Element, 1955; The Bull Calf And Other Poems, 1956; Music On A Kazoo, 1956; The Improved Binoculars, 1956; A Laughter In The Mind, 1958; A Red Carpet For The Sun, 1959; The Swinging Flesh, 1961; Balls For A One-Armed Juggler, 1963; The Laughing Rooster, 1964; Collected Poems, 1965; Periods Of The Moon, 1967; The Shattered Plinths, 1968; The Whole Bloody Bird, 1969; Selected Poems (edited by Wynne Francis), 1969; Nail Polish, 1971; The Collected Poems of Irving Layton, 1971; Engagements: The Prose of Irving Layton, 1972; Editor: Canadian Poems, 1850-1952 (with Louis Dudek), 1953; Love Where The Nights Are Long, 1962. Contrib. to Poetry (Chicago); Prism (International); Encounter; Queen's Qtly.; Black Mountain Review; Canadian Forum; Chicago Review, etc. Recip. Governor General's Medal, 1959; President's Medal for best poem of the year, awarded by Univ. of Western Ontario, 1959. Address: Winters College, York Univ., Downsview, Ont., Canada.

LAYTON, Winifred Heiskell, b. 12 Dec. 1917. Writer. Education: City Coll., Long Beach, Calif. Married, 2 s. Positions held: Ed. Staff, Long Beach Press-Telegram, Calif., 1937-50; Min. of Spiritual Sci. Church, I, 1939-45; Tchr. of Newswriting, 1946-48. Memberships: Nat. League of Am. Pen Women; Ore. Press Women; Ore. State Poetry Assn. (Ed. Qtly. Newsletter, 1966-71); Pro-Poets of Salem (Fndr., 1964). Published works include: In the Garden, 1938; Sermons In Bronze, 1940; 'Til Spring Comes, 1942; This Enchanting Earth, 1965. Contbr. to the following anthols., jrnls., mags., etc: Unity Publs.; Christian Sci. Monitor; Living Wilderness Mag.; The Grade Tchr.; Oregonian; Driftwood; The Lyric; Medford Mail Trib.; Spokane Chronicle; Kan. City Star; Am. Forests; Youth's Instr.; Encore; Author's Notes & Quotes; Hartford Courant; Los Angeles Times; The Muse; Am. Bard; Human Voice; Sr. Citizen, etc. Honours, awards: World's Fair Poetry Award, 1936; 3rd Prize Katherine Lyons Clark contest, Pa. Poetry Soc., 1961; 3rd Prize, Ore. State Poetry Assn. contest, 1961. Address: 2773 Florence Ave. NE, Salem, Ore. 97303, USA.

LAZARD, Naomi (nee Katz). Poet. Education: Studied graphics at Inst. of Design, poetry at John Logan's poetry workshop. Published works: Cry of the Peacocks, 1962: Contbr. to (Anthols.): Best Poems of 1966 & 1967: The Borestone Mountain Poetry Awards, 1967, 68; (Jrnls.): New Yorker; Michigan Quarterly Review. Recip., Poetry Soc. of America Devil's Advocate Award, 1969.

LAZARUS, A(rnold) L(eslie), b. 20 Feb. 1914. Professor of English; Poetry Editor. Education: B.A., Engl., Univ. of Mich.; M.A., UCLA. Positions held: Instr., Santa Monica Coll., Calif.; Lectr., LA State Coll.; Assoc. Prof., Univ. of Tex.; Prof., Purdue Univ. Memberships: Poetry Soc. of Am.; Phi Beta Kappa; Mod. Lang. Assoc.; CEA/Book-of-the-Month Club Writing Fellowships (judge); Indiana Arts Commission (judge); Wisconsin Arts Commission (judge). Author of Entertainments & Valedictions, 1970; A Suit of Four, 1973. Contbr. to: Saturday Review; New Republic; Quarterly Review of Literature; Prairie Schooner; The Commonweal; Christian Century; Dalhousie Review; Windsor Review; Massachusetts Review; Michigan Quarterly Review; Minnesota Review; Colorado Quarterly; Trace; Approach; Beloit Poetry Journal; Descant; Discourse; Cresset; William & Mary Review; Four Quarters; Etc.; English Journal; College English; Cea Critic; Literary Review; Northwest Review. Recip. of Ind. Sesquicentennial Poets Prize, 1969. Address: 340 Sylvia St., W Lafayette, Ind. 47906, USA.

LEACH, Norman Eugene, b. 20 Aug. 1938. Laboratory Technician. Positions held: w. U.S. Navy, 1957-61; Factory Worker, Calif.; Post Office Clerk, Calif.; Lab. Technician, Philco-Ford, Connersville, Ind. Poems have appeared in: Scimitar & Song; Denver Post; Grit Newspaper; News Examiner; church newspapers & on WIBC Radio in Indianapolis. Address: P.O. Box 96, Falmouth, IN 46127, U.S.A.

LEACH, Robert, b. 31 Jan. 1942. Director of Education Services. Education: Pembroke Coll., Cambridge, 1961-64, B.A. (Hons.), 1964; Univ. of Manchester, 1964-65, Cert. in Education. Married; 2 children. Positions held: Director of Education Services, Midlands Arts Centre, and Director, Cannon Hill Community Theatre. Published works: Left Luggage, 1967; A Tinker's Curse, 1971. Address: 17 Glenelg Mews, Beacon Rd., Walsall, Staffs., UK.

LEALE, B.C., b. 1 Sept. 1930. Bookseller. Education: Municipal Coll., Southend, U.K. Memberships: Fellow, Int. Poetry Soc.; The Poetry Soc. Contbr. to: Ambit; Breakthru; Clio; Expression; Extra Verse; A Group Anthology (O.U.P.); Iconolatre; The Listener; Manifold; Matrix; New Headland; New Poems 1963; The New York Times; Next Wave Poets 2; Next Wave Poets 3; Next Wave Poets 4; The Observer; Outposts; Phoenix; Platform; Poetry & Audience; A Review of English Literature; Samphire; Scrip; Second Aeon; The Spectator; The Spring Anthology 1969; The Spring Anthology 1973; The Times Literary Supplement; Twentieth Century; Viewpoints. Address: 1 Pine Walk, Hewarts Ln., Aldwick, Bognor Regis, Sussex, U.K.

LEARY, Olive C., b. 15 Dec. 1892. Housewife; Writer. Education: Mich. State Normal Coll., Ypsilanti, U.S.A. Married Charles D. Leary, 7 children (1 dec.) Memberships: Co-Fndr., Writers Guild of Hastings, Mich., serving as Pres., V.P. & Corres. Sec. during its first 7 yrs when it became Western Mich. Writers Guild; Poetry Soc. of Mich.; Nat. Fedn. of State Poetry Socs.; Acad. of Am. Poets. Contbr. to num. anthols., mags., jrnls. inclng: Contemporary Am. Women Poets, 1936; American Women Poets, 1937; Music Unheard; North American Book of Verse (5 vols.), 1939; Eros, 1939; Listen, My Children; Moments with Modern Poets; Muse of 1941; On the Horizon, 1941-42; Muse of 1943; Biographical Dictionary of Contemporary Poets; Am. Voice, 1942; New Am. Poetry, 1944; Rhyme Time for the Very Young, 1964; The Best Poems, 1968; Prize Poems of the Nat. Fed. of State Poetry Socs., 1969; Am. Bard; Am. Weave; Haiku Highlights; Lake Union Herald; More Fun; Peninsula Poets; Scimitar & Song; Sentinel; South & West; Beat of Wings; Better Verse; Denver Post; Hartford Courant; Christian Sci. Monitor; Tampa Tribune, etc. Recip. many poetry awards & prizes inclng. Citation and Silver Plate Medallion, P.R. Sec. Award, 7th Day Adventist Ch., Fla., 1973. Address: 205 Sixth St., Zephyrhills, FL 33599, U.S.A.

LEARY, Paris, b. 7 Jan. 1931. University Lecturer. Education: B.A., Centenary Coll., Shreveport, 1949; D Phil., St. Edmund Hall, Oxford, 1950. Positions held. Has taught at Univ. of Ky., Lexington; State Univ. of N.Y., New Platz; Fulbright Lectr., Univ. of Leicester, UK, 1964-65. Published works: Views of the Oxford Colleges, 1960; Other: A Rushing of Wings (play), 1960; The Innocent Curate (Novel), 1963; The Jack Sprat Cookbook, 1965; Ed. w. Robert Kelly, a Controversy of Poets: An Anthology of Contemporary American Poetry, 1965. Contbr. to (Anthols.): Best Poems of 1957 & 1963: The Borestone Mountain Poetry Awards, 1958; Oxford Poetry 1958, 1958; Today's Poets, 1964; A Controversy of Poets, 1965; (jrnls.): Perspective; Southwest Review; Chelsea Review; Hudson Review; New Yorker. Hons: Yaddo Fellowship, 1963; Bread Loaf Writer's Conf. Fellowship, 1963.

LEATH, Ida Belle, pen names, **LEATH, Mrs. John R. or I.B.L.,** b. 9 Sept. 1893. Educator. Education: Judson Coll., Marion, Ala.; Shorter Coll., Rome, Ga. Widow, 2 daughters. Positions held: Tchr., 39 yrs.; Hd. of Biol. Dept., Gadsden H.S., 35 yrs. Published works: Poems, 1968; Poems, 1969; Semi-Monthly Calendar w. Poems, Thoughts for The Day, & Prayers, 1970; Twelve Devotionals, 1971; The Missing Course in Education or Character Building, 1972; For Mothers – Provocative & Inspirational Poems w. Stories to Tell Children, 1972; Meditations & Prayers of the Twentieth Century, 1973. Poems: Twice Blest Teacher, 1962; Tis

Not, 1963; The Woodland Sanctuary, 1971; Love Unlimited, 1972. Address: 249 South Eighth St., Gadsden, AL 35901, U.S.A.

LEBO, Dell, b. 6 Aug. 1922. Clinical Psychologist. Education: B.A. cum laude, NY Univ., 1949; M.A., Fla. State Univ., 1951; Ph.D., ibid, 1956. Positions held: Assoc. Prof., Coll. of William & Mary, 1955-59; Pvte. Prac. & Cons., 1956-; Chief Psychol., Child Guidance Clinic, 1959-; Ed. or Book Review Ed., Fla. Psychol., 1959-; Lectr. in Indust. Psychol., Chmbr. of Comm., 1963-; Cons., Port-O-Let Co., 1970-; Cons., Dept. of Child Servs., 1970-. Memberships: Hon. Rep., Centro Studi e Scambi Internazionali; World Poetry Soc. Internat.; Preceptor, Arcane Order; Vice-Pres., Dylan Thomas Poetry Club; Foundation Fellow, Internat. Poetry Soc., 1973-. Publications: Poems & Verse, 1966; The Metaphysical Poems; The Three-Cornered Habit; Religion in the Poetry of Dell Lebo, 1969; Albo d'Oro del XXV Anniversario, 1970; A Two Factor Theory of Psychoanalytic Symbolism: In Prose & Verse; Imitations of Precariousness, 1973. Contbr. to: Psychology; Fla. Flambeau; Cyclotron; Quadernia di Poesia; Spring Anthols., 1967, '68, '69, '70; Best Broadcast Poetry, 1967, '70; Poet; An Internat. Monthly; Both Sides Now. Honours: Diploma di Benemeranza, 1967; Citation, Personal Poetry, WEFG-FM, 1967; World Poet Award for Serv. to Poetry, World Poets Soc., 1970. Address: 5340 Weller Ave., Jacksonville, Fla. 32211, USA.

LEBO, Elaine, b. 1. May 1926. Housewife. Education: B.A., N.Y. Univ., 1948; Teachers Cert., Fla. State Univ., 1951. Married, 1 child. Member: Dylan Thomas Poetry Club; Great Books Discussion Club. Contrib. to: Both Sides Now; Cyclotron; Quadernie di Poesia; Pet Fair; Spring Anthology, 1969 to 1972. Award: Best Broadcast Poetry. Address: 5340 Weller Ave., Jacksonville, Fla. 32211, USA.

LEBOIS, André, b. 27 May 1915. Professor of French Language & Literature. Education: Agrégé des Lettres; Docteur ès Lettres, Sorbonne, Paris, France, 1951. Positions held: French, Latin, Greek, Lycée de Nantes; Univ. of Algiers, 1952-56; Prof., French mod. & contemporary lang. & lit., Univ. of Toulouse, France, 1956-; Missions & Tchng. terms in Bonn, Germany, Portugal, Hungary, Japan, Cameroons, & Univ. of Calif. at Los Angeles, U.S.A. Memberships: V.P., Société des Poetes Français, Paris; Mainteneur Jeux Floraux, Toulouse, 1964-; Mbr. & Laureate, French Poets Soc., Paris, etc. Published works: Mythiques, 1944; Partage des Eaux, 1946; Poèmes 1939-64; Dame de mes Pensées, 13 sonnets funéraires, 1965; Gerbes sur le Parvis, 1968; Fabuleux Nerval, 1972; Dluon, transl. into French poetry. Author of books, monographs & prefaces on Alfred Jarry, Milosz, Franz Hellens, etc. Contbr. to var. mags., jrnls., reviews. Recip. sev. honours & awards inclng: Grand Prix de la Critique poétique, Soc. of French Poets, 1966. Address: Faculté des Lettres de Toulouse, Le Mirail, 31000, France.

LECKEY, Hugo McClelland, pen name **LECKEY, Hugo,** b. 8 July 1940. Writer. Education: A.B., Calif. State Univ. at Los Angeles, 1965; M.A., Brown Univ., R.I., 1967. Positions held: Instr., Bensalem Coll., Fordham Univ., 1967; Instr., Univ. of R.I., 1967-69; Dir., R.I. Gov's Schl. for Youth in the Arts, 1970-71; Exec. Dir., R.I. State Coun. on the Arts, 1970-72. Member, Lit. Panel, N.E.A. Published works: A Set for Edwin Honig, 1973; Grand Illusions, 1973. Contbr. to: Statement; LOS; The Rhode Islander; Herald Review. Address: 36 John St., Providence, R.I. 02906, U.S.A.

LECLERCQ, André, pen name **BERIMONT, Luc,** b. 16 Sept. 1915. Radio & Television Producer. Memberships: Pres., Assn. of Writers & Artists of Champagne; Pres., Assn. Guillaume Apollinaire; Acad. du Disque Français; Sociétaire aux Gens de Lettres; PEN; Soc. des Auteurs Dramatique, etc. Published works incl: (poetry) Domaine de la Nuit, 1940; Lyre à Feu, 1943; La Huche à Pain, 1944; Ballade de Hurlecoeur, 1946; La Brioche des Morts.

1948; Les Amants de Pleine Terre, 1949; Les Mots Germent la Nuit, 1951; Le Grand Viager (Hors-texte de Fernand Léger), 1954; L'Herbe à Tonnerre, 1958; Les Accrus, 1963; Un Feu Vivant, 1968; L'Evidence, Même, 1971; Demain la Veille, 1974; (other publs.) Les Loups de Malenfance, 1949, '62, '73; L'Office des Ténèbres, 1955; Le Carré de la Vitesse, 1958; Le Bois Castiau, 1964; Le Bruit des Amours et des Guerres, 1966 Les Ficelles, 1974 & others. Contbr. to var. mags., jrnls. Honours, awards: Prix Apollinaire, 1959; Prix Max Jacob, 1963; Prix Cazes, 1964; Grand Prix de la Société des Gens de Lettres pour l'ensemble de L'oeuvre, 1966; Chevalier des Arts et Lettres, 1964. Address: Home de la Forêt, Poigny-la-Forêt, 78120 Rambouillet, France.

LE CLERCQ, Guy, b. 15 Dec. 1928. Lighting Engineer. Education: College Saint-Michel, Brussels; Ecole Centrale des Arts et Metiers (E.C.A.M.), Brussels. Personal details: Son of Paul Le Clercq (lawyer) and Leonie Coupez. Positions held: (as engineer) A.C.E.C., Ruisbroek, Commercial Dept.; S.E.M., Brussels, Manager of an export service; Cogetric, Brussels, Manager of lighting dept.; Comeplan, Brussels, Managing Director. (as poet) Co-Editor, magazine "Jalons"; Co-Editor, Le Journal des Poetes. Memberships: Organizing Committee of the Biennales Internationales de Poesie; Mbr., Assoc. des Ecrivains Belges. Published works: Danses (poems), 1958; Chants de Terre (poems), 1961; Anthologie de la Troisieme Decade, 1963. Contbr. to: Jalons; Le Journal des Poetes. Award: Prix des Jeunesses Litteraires de Belgique, 1955. Address: Rue Cardinal Lavigerie 35, 1040 Brussels, Belgium.

LEE, Alfred Matthew, pen name, **LEE, Al,** b. 1 July 1938. Educator. Education: Yale Univ., B.A., 1960; Univ. of Iowa, M.F.A., 1963. Married to Johanna Karen Tobias; 1 s. Positions held: Secondary School Teacher, 1962-64; US Peace Corps, Ghana; Caseworker, 1965-67, Dept. of Social Services, NYC; Instr. of English, 1967-71, and since 1971 Asst. Prof. of English, Newark Coll. of Engineering. Membership: Modern Language Assoc. Published works: The Major Young Poets (anthol., selected and introduced), 1971; Time, 1974. Contbr. to: Poetry; The Iowa Review; The Yale Review; Partisan Review; Field; Decal, etc. Address: Dept. of Humanities, Newark Coll. of Engineering, 323 High St., Newark, NJ 07102, USA.

LEE, Amy Freeman (Mrs.), b. 3 Oct. 1914. Artist, Educator, Lecturer, Writer & Critic. Education: Univ. of Tex., Austin; Incarnate Word Coll.; Hon. ibid, 1965. Positions held: Art Critic, San Antonio Express, 1939-41; Art Critic, Radio Station KONO, San Antonio, 1947-50; Lectr. on Art, Humanities Dept., Trinity Univ., San Antonio, 1954-56; Lectr. on Art, San Antonio Art Inst., 1955-56; Lectr. on Art, Art Dept., Our Lady of the Lake Coll., San Antonio, 1969-70. Memberships: Participant, 50th Annual Exhib., Calif. Nat. Watercolor Soc. & Circuit Show, 1970-71; Pres., Friends of San Antonio Pub. Lib.; Judge, Young Pegasus Annual Children's Poetry Contest, ibid; Judge, Annual Book Design Award, Tex. Inst. of Letters, 1971; Judge, Annual Lit. Contest, Poetry Div., Robert E. Lee HS, San Antonio, Tex., 1973. Hon. Mbr., Eugene Field Soc.; Hon. Mbr., Internat. Mark Twain Soc.; Advisory Bd., Friends of the Seguin & Guadlupe C. Pub. Libs.; Member, Advisory Bd., Poetry Soc. of San Antonio, Tex., 1973. Adv. Bd., San Antonio Chap., Nat. Soc. of Arts & Letters; Poetry Soc. of Am.; Nat. Library Week–Tex. Citizens Comm.; Am. Soc. for Aesthetics, Cleveland, Ohio; Friends of Tex. Libs; Bd. Dirs., Coll. Community Creative Arts Ctr., San Antonio, Tex.; Bd. Mgrs., United Colls. of San Antonio; Chmn., Bd. of Dirs., Incarnate Word Coll., San Antonio; Bd. Dirs., Humane Soc. of the US, Wash. DC; Advsry. Coun., Voc. Educ. Dept., Alamo Heights, Indep. Schl. Dist., San Antonio; Advsry. Coun., Marquis Biog. Lib. Soc., Chicago; Exhib. Comm., Med. Schl., Univ. of Tex. at San Antonio; EAT (Experiments in Art & Technology); AAUP; Life, Am. Anti-Vivisection Soc., Phila.; Life, World Fed. for the Protection of Animals, Zurich, Switzerland; Defenders of Wildlife. Publications:

Remember Pearl Harbor, 1943; Reality is Becoming. Contbr. to: Am. Poetry Mag.; Tex. Quarterly; Mexico Quarterly Review, 1969; Eagle Nest Whistle Newspaper, San Antonio. Author of forward in art catalogues. Honours: Headliners Award, Fine Arts, Theta Sigma Phi, 1958; Chosen for inclusion, Univ. of Ky.'s Poetry Ms. Collection, Lexington, 1963; Elected Mbr., Tex. Philos. Soc., Austin. Address: 127 Canterbury -ill, San Antonio, TX 78209, USA.

LEE, Betty Merritt, pen names, **LEE, Betty M., AMPLE, Fanny, LEE, B.,** b. 10 June 1913. Homemaker; Registered Nurse; Poet; Freelance Writer. Education: Grad. HS, Milton, Iowa; Grad., St. Josephs Hospital, Keokuk, Iowa; Creative Writing, Lynwood HS, 1972. Married to Robert M. Lee; 2 children. Positions held: Private Duty Nurse; Staff Nurse in Polio School, Rancho Los Amigos, Downey; Charge Nurse, St. Francis Hospital, Lynwood, Calif. Membership: Major Poets Chapter (Mary Marks Tremont). Contbr. to: Cats Mag.; Yearbook of Modern Poetry, 1971; Outstanding Contemporary Poetry; Lyrics of Love, 1972; Nurses Journal. Recip. Certificate of Awards (Pierson Mettler Associates, 1972) 4 in all for Sonnet cont., Poets cont., Environment cont., Major Poets. Address: 11916 Bullis Rd., Lynwood, CA 90262, USA.

LEE, Christopher, b. 14 June 1913. Tutor in Art History & Literature. Education: B.A., History, Merton Coll., Oxford, 1937; M.A., ibid., 1946; M.A., King's Coll., Cambridge, 1954. Married Brenda Pool w. 2 children. Positions held: Sometime Staff Mbr., Arts Council of G.B.; Glyndebourne Opera & the British Council; Staff Tutor in Art History & Literature, Cambridge Univ. Bd. of Extra-Mural Studies. Published works: Poems, 1937; The Secret Field, 1940; Under the Sun, 1948; The Bright Cloud, 1961. Contbr. to (Anthols.): Poetry London X, 1944; New Poems, 1955; Albermarle Book of Modern Verse, 1962; Poetry of the Forties, 1968. Hons: French Govt. Scholarship, 1950; Italian Govt. Scholarship, 1952. Address: c/o King's Coll., Cambridge, UK.

LEE, Dennis Beynon, b. 31 Aug. 1939. Writer and Editor. Education: B.A. (1962), M.A. (1964), Univ. of Toronto. Married, 2 d. Positions held: Lecturer in Engl., Univ. of Toronto, 1962-66; Editor, House of Anansi Press, 1967-73; Lecturer in Engl., York Univ., 1972-73. Membership: League of Canadian Poets. Published works: Kingdom of Absence, 1967; Civil Elegies, 1968; Wiggle to the Laundromat, 1970; Civil Elegies and Other Poems, 1972. Contbr. to many Canadian periodicals. Recip. Governor-General's Award, 1973. Address: 118 Shaftesbury Av., Toronto M4T 1A5, Canada.

LEE, Harrison Edward, b. 29 Dec. 1922. Public Relations Director & Black History Professor. Education: B.A., Fort Valley State Coll., Ga.; M.A., Atlanta Uhiv., Ga.; Dr. of Letters, M.I. & Coll., Miss. Positions held: at Selma Univ., Ala.; Ala. Lutheran Acad. & Coll.; Ala. A. & M. Coll.; Rust Coll., Miss.; Lemoyne Coll., Tenn.; Bluefield State Coll., W.Va.; Jarvis Christian Coll., Tex.; M.V.S.C., Miss.; Prentiss Inst. Jr. Coll., Miss.; News Announcer, WKPO Radio Stn., Prentiss; Regular columnist, Prentiss Headlight. Published works: Poems for the Day, 1953; A Guide to Better Writing, 1957. Contbr. to: Birmingham World; Prentiss Headlight; Afro-Am.; Jackson Daily News; Clarion-Ledger. Address: P.O. Box 479, Prentiss, MS 39474, U.S.A.

LEE, Laurie, Writer. Education: Slad Village School (UK); Stroud Central School (UK). Memberships: P.E.N. Club (UK); Royal Soc. of Literature (Fellow); West Country Writers' Assoc. (Vice-Pres.). Published works: The Sun My Monument (poems), 1944; My Many-Coated Man (poems), 1955; The Bloom of Candles, (poems), 1947; A Rose For Winter (travel), 1955; Cider With Rosie (autobiography), 1959; Collected Poems, 1960; As I Walked Out One Midsummer Morning (autobiography), 1969. Contbr. to: The Listener; Horizon; Encounter; New Writing; London Magazine; The New Yorker Mag.; Harpers;

Vogue, etc. Awards include: M.B.E.; Wm. Foyle Poetry Prize, 1955; Poetry Soc. Prize, 1955; W.H. Smith Award for Literature, 1960. Address: 49 Elm Park Gardens, London SW10, UK.

LEE, Lawrence, b. 3 Jan. 1903. Professor Emeritus of Engl., and Writer. Education: Univ. of Virginia, B.S.; Harvard Univ., M.A., and study overseas. Positions held: Asst. Prof. French and Engl., Univ. of Va., 1930-41; Lecturer, French, NY Univ., Wash. Sq. Branch, summer 1949; Assoc. Prof. Engl., Univ. of Pittsburgh, 1949-53, and Prof. Engl., 1953-73. Ed., Va. Quarterly Review, 1940-1941, etc. Member, The Va. Poetry Soc. Pubs.: Summer Goes On, 1933; Monticello & Other Poems, 1937; Tomorrow Goodbye, 1937; The Tomb of Thomas Jefferson, 1940; Prometheus in Pittsburgh, 1952; The American as Faust, 1965; The Cretan Flute, 1968; The Voice of the Furies, 1969; La Dame a la Licorne, 1972; Cockcrow at Night, The Heroic Journey and 18 Other Stories, 1973; Between the Morning and the Evening Star (lyrics), 1973. Contrib. to: NY Times; NY Herald-Tribune; The Lyric; The Va. Qtly. Review; The Sewanee Review; Harper's; The Atlantic Monthly; The Pittsburgh Press; Scribner's Mag.; The Forum; QED Renaissance; Life & Letters (UK); The Classical World. Poetry translated into Greek for Greek Anthol., etc. Recip. The Virginia Prize, (The Lyric), Jan., 1971. Honour: The poem (The Cathedral) placed in incised slate with gold lettering in the stone of The Common Room, Univ. of Pittsburgh, Pennsylvia, 1973. Address: 510 Roslyn Place, Pittsburgh, Pa. 15232, USA.

LEE, Maria Berl, pen name (for German works only) **BERL-LEE, Maria,** b. 30 July 1924. Bilingual Writer & Poet (English & German). Education: early educ. in Austria, Switz., France, U.S.A.; B.A. in Engl., Nazareth Coll., Rochester, N.Y.; M.A. in Engl., Fordham Univ., N.Y.C. Married Ray E. Lee, Jr. Positions held: Translator & Interpreter, U.S. Embassy, Vienna, Austria, 1949-51; Georgetown Univ. Placement Office, Wash., U.S.A., 1951-53; John F. Fleming (Rosenbach) rare books, 1953-59; Jacobus F. Frank, Indonesian imports, 1965-69; Int. Inst. of Rural Reconstruction (mostly writing & editing), 1969–. Memberships: Nat. Writers Club; Ed., Verity Fair, Nazareth Coll., 1945-46; Asst. Ed., Gleaner, ibid, 1945-46; Kappa Gamma Pi. Published works: Schaumwein Aus Meinem Krug, 1974; Late Days in March, (novel), 1974; Ein Tag Der Uberraschungen, (play), 1967; Bombe Im Tor, (play), 1970. Contbr. to: Our Family (Canada); Timeless Treasures; A Burst of Trumpets; Yearbook of Mod. Poetry; Lyrics of Love; Poetry Parade 1968 & 69; Tempo (Canada) 1969 & 70; Best in Poetry 1970, 71, 73; Sapafaswap 1971, 72, 73; Reach Out 1972 & 73; Second Coming; Bitterroot; German-Am. Studies 1972 & 74; Osterreichisches aus Amerika, 1973; Shore Poetry & Dawn Anthols., etc. Recip. many hons. & awards inclng: Citation of Merit, Soc. for German – Am. Studies, 1973. Spafaswap, Editor's Pick Prize, 1971; Writer's Digest (short story prize), 1970; 1st prize for love poem, Tempo (Canada), 1970; Nat. Writers' Club, 4 prizes for poetry & short stories, 1967-73. Address: 68-46 Ingram St., Forest Hills, NY 11375, U.S.A.

LEE, Ting Hui, b. 5 May 1931. Educator. Education: M.A., Univ. of Singapore. Married Ho Ken Lin, 2 children. Positions held: Political Sec., Min. of Culture, Singapore, 1959; Deputy Dir., Political Study Ctr., 1964-71; Vis. Prof., Hist. Dept., Nanyang Univ., 1968-69; Vis. Prof., Dept. of Political Sci., Univ. of Western Ont., Canada, 1971-72; currently, Sr. Rsch. Assoc., Inst. of Southeast Asian Studies, Singapore. Memberships: Pres., Singapore Assn. of Writers; Pres., Island Soc. Published works: Selected Poems, 1966. Ed., Anthol. of Chinese Literature in Malaysia & Singapore, 8 vols., 1971. Contbr. to: Nanyang Siang Pau, Malaysia-Singapore; Sin Chew Jit Poh, Malaysia-Singapore; Island Literature, Singapore. Address: Inst. of Southeast Asian Studies, c/o Univ. of Singapore, Singapore.

LEED, Jacob, b. 26 Sept. 1924. Teacher. Education: Harvard Univ., U.S.A.; Univ. of Iowa; Univ. of Chicago.

Published works: Poems, 1966; Poet-Painter, 1967. Contbr. to: Poetry; Chicago Review; Nation; Black Mountain Review; Genesis West; Wild Dog; IO, etc. Address: 410 Stow St., Kent, OH 44240, U.S.A.

LEEDS, Morton Harold, b. 15 May 1921. Government Executive. Education: B.S.Sc., CCNY, 1944; M.A., Grad. Fac., The New Schl. for Soc. Rsch., 1948; Ph.D., ibid, 1950. Married to Ingrid Rheinstrom, 3 d. Positions held: Dept. of Housing & Urban Development, 1962-73; currently, Special Asst. to the Asst. Sec. for Housing Management, Wash., D.C. Fellow, Internat. Poetry Soc. Author of Jackstones, 1970. Contbr. to Vital Speeches; Cathedral Age; Cycles; Indianapolis Downtowner; Aging & Human Development; Social Work; American Journal of Nursing; Understanding Environmental Education; Journal of the Industrial Designers of America; Viltis; Woodwind. Address: 6219 Lone Oak Drive, Bethesda, Md. 20034, USA.

LEE GEOK LAN, b. 20 Nov. 1939. Teacher. Education: B.A., Univ. of Malaya, Kuala Lumpar. Positions held: Grad. Tchr., 1964-68; Grad. Tchr., The High Schl., Malacca, Malaysia. Contbr. to (Anthols.): Bunga Emas, 1964; A Private Landscape, 1967; (Jrnls.): Tenggara; Pelita.

LEEMING, Owen, b. 1 Aug. 1930. Playwright. Education: Music & Langs., Univ. of Canterbury, Christchurch, New Zealand, 1949-52; Musical Composition, Paris, France, 1954-55. Positions held: Radio Announcer, 1953-54; Talks Producer, BBC, 1956-62; TV Producer, NZBC, 1962-64; UNESCO Expert, 1965-66; Full-time Writer, 1967-71; UNESCO Cons., 1971-72; Full-time Writer, 1973–. Published works: Venus is Setting, 1972. Contbr. to: Guinness Book of Poetry, 1960; New Zealand Poetry, 1964; Recent Poetry in New Zealand, 1965; New Voices of the Commonwealth, 1968; London Magazine; Landfall; also to the BBC & NZBC. Recip., Katherine Mansfield Menton Fellowship, 1970. Address: Le Château, 13113 Lamanon, France.

LEENMANS, Margaretha, pen name **VASALIS, M.,** b. 13 Feb. 1909. Psychiatrist. Education: Medical studies, Leiden, 1927-34; Specialization, Santpoort, Amsterdam (Psychiatry), & also in Neurology. Married D. Fortuyn, 4 children (1 dec.) Positions held: Asst. Psych., Santpoort, 2½ yrs.; Sheep-shearing & psych. in S. Africa, 11 months; Asst. Neurol., Amsterdam, 2½ yrs.; Pvte. pract., 1941–; Child Guidance Clinic, Assen & Groningen, 1955–. Memberships: PEN; Netherlands Letterkunde. Published works: Ouerler (Thunderstorm), 1939; Parken Goestignen (poems), 1940; Vogel Phoenix, 1947; Vergesichter & Gesichten, 1957. Contbr. to var. jrnls. Honours, awards incl. Prize of the City of Amsterdam. Address: De Zulthe 10, Roden (Dr.), Netherlands.

LEE PENG JIN, pen names **TANG-SZE & NAM POH,** b. 4 July 1910. Reporter. Education: Kang Nam Univ., Shanghai, China. Positions held: Supvsr., Chung Hwa Hight Schl., Muar; Author; Reporter, Sin Chew Newspaper, Malaysia & Singapore. Pres., Nam Chou Poetry Club, South Malaysia. Published works: Chrysanthemum (prose), 1957; A Trip to the Country-Side (prose), 1958; The Dark Night, 1958; The Essays of EE TAT FOO, 1959; The Memoirs of EE TAT FOO, 1960; Durian, 1960; Morning Mist of Tanjong, 1959; Martyrs of Muar, 1942; Cemeteries, 1972; Kunlun Mountains & Hwang Ho Rivers, 1973; To Mourn Qu Yuan, 1973. Contbr. to: Sin Chew Newspaper, Malaysia & Singapore; Nanyang Newspaper, Singapore; Tong Nam Yik Poh, Thlail And; Sing Peng Yik Poh, Penang; Hong Kong Chinese newspaper. Recip., 1st prize & Gold Medal, Singapore Wong Kiong Banqueting House Poetry Contest, 1955. Address: No. 63, Jalan Haji Abu, Muar, Johore, West Malaysia.

LEE SU, pen names **LEE TSENG-CHUNG & LEE SU-YING,** b. 5 May 1910. Teacher; Writer; Librarian. Education: B.A., Lit., Yenching Univ., Peking, China, 1933; M.A., ibid, 1936. Widow of Tseng Te, 1 son, 3 daughters. Positions held: Tchr., Nan Wah Coll. & var.

other middle schls. in Meihsien, 1936-40; Ed. & Acting Chief of the Cultural Affairs Dept. of Women's Advisory Comm. of the New Life Movement, Chungking, China; Commnr. of Rsch. Bur., Min. of Soc. Affairs, Chungking; Tchr. & Libn., Pooi To Girls' Middle Schl., Kowloon, Hong Kong, 1951-53; Asst. Libn., New Asia Coll., Chinese Univ. of Hong Kong, 1956-67 (ret'd.) Member, Chinese PEN Ctr. of Hong Kong. Published works: (collected poems written in Chinese) Eden is Far Away, 1957; In Praise of Life, 1958; Street Corner, 1959; (collected essays) Some Wild Thoughts in Reading Poetry, 1969; (long essays) Criticism On the Poetesses In the Tang Dynasty, 1960; On the Great Poetess Lee Tsin Choa, 1962. Contbr. to var. mags. & periodicals. Honours, awards: Phi Tau Phi Scholastic Hon. Soc. Golden Key, 1933; Rsch. Fellow of Harvard-Yenching Inst., 1933-36; First Prize for Poetry Union Press, 1957. Address: 8B Belfran Rd., 1/F, Kowloon, Hong Kong.

LEE TZU PHENG, b. 13 May 1946. University Assistant. Education: B.A., Hons., English, Univ. of Singapore, 1968. Positions held: Teaching Asst., Dept. of English, Univ. of Singapore (while studying for M.A.), 1968–; Mbr., Editorial Committee of Poetry Singapore. Contbr. to (Anthols.): A Private Landscape, 1967; Seven Poets, 1969; (Jrnls.): Focus. Address: 1 Ascot Rise, Singapore 11.

LEGLER, Philip, b. 7 Mar. 1928. Professor of English. Education: B.A., Denison Univ., 1951; M.F.A., Univ. of Iowa, 1953. Married, 3 children. Positions held: Instr., Ohio Univ., 1953-56; Asst. Prof., Ctrl. Mo. State Coll., 1956-59; Asst. Prof., N.M. Highlands Univ., 1959-60; Asst. Prof., Ill. Wesleyan Univ., 1960-63; Asst. Prof. & Poet-in-Res., Sweet Briar Coll., 1963-66; Editl. Asst., N.M. Quarterly, 1966-68; Prof. of Engl., Northern Mich. Univ., 1968–. Published works: A Change of View, 1963; The Intruder, 1972. Contbr. to: Prairie Schooner; Poetry; N.M. Qtly.; The Western Review; Inscape; Poetry Northwest; Epos; Choice; Elizabeth; Southwest Review; N.Y. Times; Am. Scholar; Qtly. Review of Lit.; Counter/Measures. Honours, awards: Helen Wurlitzer Poetry Prize, N.M. Qtly., 1966; Poems in Best Poems of 1967 & 69. Address: Engl. Dept., Northern Mich. Univ., Marquette, MI, U.S.A.

LE GRANDE, II, W. Ames, b. 8 May 1931. Author, Anthologist. Education: Western Reserve Univ. Unmarried. Positions held: Director-General, The Nat. Faith Soc. Inc. of West Virginia, 1960-70. Memberships: The American Poets Fellowship Soc. (Nat. General Sec.); Internat. Poetry Advancement Assoc. Ltd. (Advisor and Member of the Board); Nat. Poetry Day Assoc. Published works: From The Embers Glow, 1952; Of Mortal Man, 1963. Forthcoming: The Wayward Leaves (novel). Contbr. to: Adventures in American Poetry, 1954; American Poetry Review, 1955; Poetry Digest; also some 2,000 poems published in various journals throughout the world. Awards: Hon. Dr. Letters, Berlin Memorial Univ; The American Poets Cup, 1952; 5,000-dollars Fellowship (1952), The American Poets Fellowship Soc. Corporation. Address: 4769 Sunset Dr., Westmorland, Huntington, WV 25704, USA.

LEHMANN, Geoffrey John, b. 28 June 1940. Solicitor. Education: Grad., Arts, Sydney Univ., 1960; ibid., Law, 1963. Positions held: Qualified as a Solicitor in 1963; Partner, C.R. Willcox & Lehmann, Sydney. Published works: The Ilex Tree, w. Les A. Murray, 1965; A Voyage of Lions, 1968. Contbr. to (Anthols.): Guinness Book of Poetry, 1960; Australian Poetry, 1962; Poetry in Australia II, 1964; Best Poems of 1963 & 1967: The Borestone Mountain Poetry Awards, 1964; A Book of Australian Verse, 1968; Vital Decade, 1968; (jrnls.): Australian Quadrant; Bulletin; Poetry Australia; Sydney Morning Herald; The Age; New York Times. Address: 8 Highfield Rd., Lindfield, N.S.W., Australia.

LEHMANN, John Frederick, b. 2 June 1907. Poet; Writer; Editor. Education: King's Scholar, Eton; Trinity Coll., Cambridge. Positions held: Ed., London Mag., from its foundation till 1961; Mng. Dir., John Lehmann

Ltd., from its fndn. till 1952; Fndr., Ed., New Writing & Orpheus; Ptnr., Gen. Mgr., Hogarth Press, 1938-46; Advisory Ed., The Geographical Mag., 1940-45; Ed. New Soundings, BBC 3rd Prog., 1952; Chmn., Edit. Advisory Panel, British Council, 1952-58; Pres., Alliance Francaise in Great Britain, 1955-63. Pres., Royal Lit. Fund. Memberships: Fellow, Royal Soc. of Lit. Published works: A Garden Revisited, 1931; The Noise of History, 1934; Prometheus and the Bolsheviks, 1937; Evil Was Abroad, 1938; Down River, 1939; New Writing in Europe, 1940; Forty Poems, 1942; The Sphere of Glass, 1944; Shelley in Italy, 1947; The Age of the Dragon, 1951; The Open Night, 1952; Edith Sitwell, 1952; The Whispering Gallery, 1955; I Am My Brother, 1960; Ancestors and Friends, 1962; Collected Poems, 1963; Christ the Hunter, 1965. Ed: Poems From New Writing, 1946; French Stories From New Writing, 1947; The Year's Work in Literature, 1949, '50; English Stories From New Writing, 1950; Pleasures of New Writing, 1952; The Chatto Book of Modern Poetry (w. C. Day Lewis), 1956; Modern French Stories, 1956; Italian Stories of Today, 1959; Selected Poems of Edith Sitwell, 1965. Honours, awards: CBE, 1964; Grand Officer, Etoile Noir; Officer, Legion of Honour, France; Officer, Order of Arts & Letters; Cmdr., Order of King George of the Hellenes. Address: 85 Cornwall Gardens, London, SW7, UK.

LEHNER, Peter, b. 23 Nov. 1922. Teacher. Education: studied at Univs. of Bern & Lausanne.; Dip. of Higher Studies. Married, 4 children. Positions held: Jrnlst.; Teacher. Memberships: Gruppe Olten; Berner Schriftstellerverein. Published works: Rot Grün, 1955; Asfalt im Zwielicht, 1956; Ausfallstrasse, 1959; Fase Kran, 1964; Ein bisschen miss im kredit, 1967/71; Sakralitäten blätterbuch, 1971; Wehrmännchens abschied, 1973; (prose) Angenommen, um o uhr lo, 1965; Was ist Das, Zerzählung, 1972. Contbr. to: Drehpunkt; TW; Vorwärts; National-Zeitung; Tages-Anzeiger; Beobachter; Das pult; Publikation. Honours, awards: Literaturpreis der Stadt Bern, 1960; Buchpreis (for 'Ein bisschen miss im kredit'), Stadt Bern, 1969; Literaturpreis des Kantons Bern, 1973. Address: Burgunderstr. 13, CH–3018, Bern, Switzerland.

LEIGH, Spencer, b. 1 Feb. 1945. Actuary. Education: Rydal School, Colwyn Bay, N. Wales. Position held: Actuary, Royal Insurance Group. Memberships: Southport Poetry Committee (Sec.); Crosby Arts Assoc. (Exec. Committee); Merseyside Poetry Festivals Committee (Committee member). Published works: Collage Two (with Richard Hill and Malcolm Barnes), 1972; Paul Simon: Now and Then, 1973. Contbr. to: Arts Alive Merseyside; Contrasts; Lancashire Life; Liverpool Echo; Roopvati. Recip. 1st Prize in Liverpool Echo Poetry Competition, 1970. Address: 8 Mersey Rd., Crosby, Liverpool, Lancs. L23 3AG, UK.

LEIGHTON, Nelda Una, b. 15 Mar. 1929. Housewife. Positions held: Proof Reader; Women's Army Corps; Nurse's Aide, etc. Member, The Rimers of Tucson. Contbr. to The Rimers Anthol. (50th yr.), 1973. Address: 2247 East 4th St., Tucson, AZ 85719, U.S.A.

LEIPER, Esther Mather, b. 18 Nov. 1946. Teacher. Education: B.A., Engl., Va. Commonwealth Univ., Richmond, U.S.A.; B.S., Educ., St. Joseph Coll., Overbrook, Pa.; studied under Wayne Lanter, James Hearst, Ulrich Troubetzkoi, Gertrude Curtler & Evelyn Bradford. Married Peter H. Estabrooks. Positions held: Mng.Ed., Image, a Jrnl. of creative ideas, 1966-68; Prog.Dir., Poetry Forum, Va. C'wealth Univ., 1967-70; Poetry Ed., The Richmond Review, 1969; Poetry Workshop Tchr., Our Lady of Angels Coll., 1972; Ldr., Howard Co. Writer's Workshop, 1973. Held one-man show in stitchery at Chadds Ford Pa. Bank Gall. Memberships: Ky. Poetry Soc.; N.Y. Poetry Soc. Contbr. to: Shenandoah; River City Review; Aye; Windless Orchards; Through Parable Streets, An Anthology of Richmond Poetry; Grande Ronde Review, etc. Honours, awards: 3rd Prize, Poetry

Parade, 1970; 1st Prize, Spectrum, 1969; lst Prize, S.C. Poetry Soc. for narrative Sandy Flash, Outlaw of Chester Co., 1971; 1st Prize, N.Y. Poetry Forum, Eleanor Otto Award, 1972, etc. Address: Waterstock, Cheyney, PA 19319, U.S.A.

LEIPPRANDT, Mary, b. 23 Apr. 1925. Writer; Composer; Musician. Married, 5 children. Positions held: Bookkeeper; Bank employee; Writer; Musician. Memberships: Int. Platform Assn.; A.S.C.A.P.; AGAC & Songwriters Hall of Fame. Published works: Lyrics for Michigan Water Winter Wonderland (song book), 1966. Regular contbr. to Progress-Advance, a weekly publication. Address: 3864 North Sturm, Pigeon, MI 48755, U.S.A.

LEISNER, Dorothy Roberts, pen name, **ROBERTS, Dorothy,** b. 6 July 1906. Writer. Education: schls. in England & Canada; Univ. of New Brunswick, 2 yrs. Married, 1 son, 1 daughter. Has held var. newspaper reporting jobs. Mbr., League of Canadian Poets. Published works: Songs for Swift Feet, 1928; Dazzle, 1957; In Star and Stalk, 1959; Twice to Flame, 1961; Extended, 1967; Notes on an Exhibit of Papers, 1967 (booklet). Contbr. to: The Hudson Review; The Yale Review; Queen's Quarterly; Dalhousie Review; Accent; New Orleans Poetry Jrnl.; The Fiddlehead; The Canadian Forum; The Northern Review; Delta; The Jrnl. of Gen. Educ.; The Lit. Review; Contact; Talisman. Address: 143 W. Park Ave., State Coll., PA 16801, U.S.A.

LEISTER, Lois, pen name **LEISTER, Lois Anderson,** b. 14 Oct. 1928. Housewife. Memberships: Poet Laureate's Comm. of 100; Int. Culture, Poetry & Efficiency Soc.; Am. Poets Fellowship Soc.; Avalon World Arts Acad. Contbr. to: Best in Poetry, 1969; Am. Poets Fellowship Anthol., 1969; Jean's Jrnl.; Cycloflame; Better Camping; United Poets; Am. Poets; Prairie Poets; Haiku Highlights; Modern Images. Recip. var. prizes for poetry, Jean's Jrnl., 1969-70 & citations for excellence from Cycloflame, Haiku Highlights, Imprints Qtly., Modern Images & Jean's Jrnl. Address: 4112 Ryon Rd., Upper Marlboro, MD 20870, U.S.A.

LEITER, Sharon, b. 12 Aug. 1942. Poet. Education: B.A., Brandeis Univ., Waltham, Mass., U.S.A.; M.A., Dept. of Slavic Langs. & Lit., Univ. of Mich., Ann Arbor. Memberships: Poetry Soc. of Am.; Phi Beta Kappa. Married Dr. Darryl Leiter, 1 daughter. Published works: The Lady & the Bailiff of Time, 1974. Contbr. to: Ararat; Cloud Marauder; Pyramid; Premiere; Cardinal Poetry Quarterly; Cyclo-Flame, etc. Translator of Russian Poetry – Russian Literary Triquarterly, 1973. Address: 2439 Stone Dr., Ann Arbor, MI 40105, U.S.A.

LEITZKE, Marcie, b. 4 Apr. 1927. Receptionist; Housewife. Education: Grad., Bus. Inst. of Milwaukee. Married Larry Leitzke, 6 children. Positions held: Traffic Mgr. for WTCH radio, Shawano; Receptionist, Shawano Community Hosp.; Antique business. Memberships: Corres. Sec., Nat. Fed. of State Poetry Socs.; Sec., Wis. Fellowship of Poets; Radio & Newspaper Ed., Shawano Area Writers. Contbr. to: New Poetry Out of Wisconsin, 1971; Poems Out of Wisconsin, 1969, III; Ideals, 1970; Wisconsin History in Poetry, I, II, III, 1969, '70, '71; Jean's Jrnl.; Life & Health Mag.; Appleton Post Crescent. Recip., 3rd prize, Wisconsin Fellowship of Poets, 1970. Address: R.2, Box 151, Bonduel, WI 54107, U.S.A.

LEM, Carol, b. 23 May 1944. English Teacher. Education: B.A. (Int. Rels.(, Univ. of So. Calif., 1963; M.A. (Engl.), Calif. State Univ., 1969. Positions held: Tutor O'seas, 1966; Clerk, L.A. Times, 1964-66; Tchr., Ramona Convent H.S., 1970-71; ESL Tchr., Speak-Easy Lang. Ctr., 1971-72; Tchr., L.A. Win Career Ctr., 1972–; Ed., Force of Opposites, 1973; Mbr. of Baido-Kai Musical Ensemble. Memberships: Pres., Democratic Club, Univ. So. Calif.; Calif. State Poetry Soc. Published works: (coll. of poetry) Searchings, 1972. Contbr. to: Rufus; Encore; Bitterroot; Meridians, An Anthol. of Modern Poetry, 1973; poem in preface of

book, Force of Opposites by Kenneth Charles, 1972. Recip. prize, New Voices in Am. Poetry Contest, 1973. Address: 1557 North Alexandria No. 19, Hollywood, CA 90027, U.S.A.

LE MAHIEU, Dennis Gene, b. 26 May 1947. Printer. Education: Grad. of Printing & Publishing, Lakeshore Tech. Inst., 1968. Married Mary Paegelow, 2 daughters. Contbr. to: J. Mark Press; Poetry of Our Times, 1970 & 71; Personal Poetry – Best Broadcast Poetry; vol. 2; Bachaet; Spafaswap; The Creative Review; Hyacinths & Biscuits; Jean's Jrnl.; New Voices In the Wind; Silk Screen; Over the Ozarks; New Dawn Publs.; Invictus; Pied Pieper Press; Shore Publng. Co.; Gems; Young Publs. Address: 1720 North Prospect, Milwaukee, WI 53202, U.S.A.

LEMASTER, J.R., b. 29 Mar. 1934. College Educator. Education: B.S., Defiance Coll., 1959; M.A., Bowling Green State Univ., 1962; Ph.D., ibid, 1970. Positions held: w. US Navy, 1951-55; Gen. Motors Corp., 1955-59; Stryker H.S., 1959-62; Defiance Coll., 1962–. Memberships: Ohio Poets Assn.; MLA; Midwest MLA; Ohioana Lib. Assn.; Poetry Soc. of Ky.; S. & W. Lit. Soc., etc. Published works: Certain Reconciliations (co-edited), 1972; Children of Adam, 1971; The Heart Is a Gypsy, 1967; Morning in the Sun (24 pp edited student poems), 1968; On Weighing a Pound of Flesh, (co-edited), 1973; Poets of the Midwest (420 pages edited poetry), 1966; Symposia Poets (co-edited), 1969; There Comes a Times (co-edited), 1971. Contbr. to: New Laurel Review; Pegasus; Bitterroot; South & West; Human Voice; Weid; Quartet, etc. Address: R.R.8, Defiance, OH 43512, U.S.A.

LEMIEUX LEVESQUE, Alice, b. 23 Sept. 1906. Writer. Education: Ursuline Convent, Quebec, Canada; Sorbonne, Paris, France, 1929. Positions held: Jrnlst.; Translator for the Quebec Govt., 1964-69. Memberships: La Societé des Poetes Canadiens-francais; Pres. for 5 yrs. in Quebec City, ibid; Canadian Authors Assn.; Historical Soc. of Quebec. Published works: Heures effeuillees, poems, 1927; Poemes, 1929; Silences, 1929; L'arbre du jour, 1964; Jardin d'octobre, 1972. Contbr. to: Poesie mag.; La Revue de l'Universite Laval; La Revue Moderne, etc. Honours, awards: David Prize for 'Poemes', Min. of Cultural Affairs, P.Q., 1929; Champlain Prize for 'Silences', 1929; Palmes academiques, French Govt., 1945. Address: St. Michel – Bellechasse, Province of Quebec, Canada.

LENGYEL, Cornel Adam, pen name **ADAM, Cornel,** b. 1 Jan. 1915, Conn., USA. Dramatic Poet; Teacher; Historian. Positions held: Mgr., Forty-Niner Theater, Georgetown, Calif., 1946-49; Lectr., Engl. Lit., Sacramento State Coll., Calif., 1962–; Vis. Lectr., Writer-in-residence, Hamline Univ., St. Paul, Minn., 1968-69; Guest Lectr., MIT, Cambridge, Mass., 1969; Translr. from Hungarian; Edit. Cons., US Dept. of Health, Educ. & Welfare. Memberships: Poetry Soc. of Am.; World Poetry Soc. Intercontinental; MLA; AAUP; Authors' Guild; PEN. Published works: (History) American Testament: The Story of a Promised Land, 1956; Four Days in July, 1958; I, Benedict Arnold: The Anatomy of Treason, 1960; Presidents of the USA, 1961; Ethan Allan & the Green Mountain Boys, 1961; The Declaration of Independence, 1969; (poetry) Thirty Pieces, 1933; First Psalms, 1950; Fifty Poems, 1965; Four Dozen Songs, 1970; The Lookout's Letter, 1971; (plays) The World's My Village, 1935; Jonah Fugitive, 1936; The Giant's Trap, 1938; The Atom Clock, 1951; Eden, Inc., 1954, revised edit., Omega, 1963; Will of Stratford, 1964; Three Plays, 1964; (essays) The Creative Self, 1971. Contbr. to: The Golden Year, 1960; Interpretation In Our Time, 1966; The Britannica Library of Great American Writing, 1961; The Menorah Treasury, 1964; Poet Lore; The Coast; The Argonaut; Saturday Rev.; Menorah Jrnl.; Poet; Int. Monthly, etc. Honours: 1st Prize, Maritime Poetry Award, 1945; 1st Prize, Poetry Soc. of Va., 1950; 1st Prize, Maxwell Anderson Award, 1951; Huntington Hartford Fellowship, 1951, '63; MacDowell Colony Fellowship, 1967; Ossabaw Island Fndn.

Fellowship, 1968; Alice Fay di Castagnola Award, Poetry Soc. of Am., 1971; Internat. Who's Who in Poetry Award, 1972-73. Address: dam's Acres West, Georgetown, CA 95634, USA.

LENNON, Florence Becker, b. 20 Feb. 1895. Freelance Writer; Teacher; Formerly Radio M.C. Education: B.S., Columbia Univ., 1925; M.A., U. of Colo., 1947; Dip., Trng. Schl. for Montessori Tchrs., 1921. Married 1) Samuel Becker, 2) John Lennon, 2 daughters. Positions held: Psychiatric Social Wkr., Jewish Big Sisters; Directress, Montessori Schl., Bronx Day Nursery, 1916–; Freelance Writer; Conducted Enjoyment of Poetry Prog., Radio Stn. WEVD, N.Y., 1956-64; Directress, Jarrow Montessori Schl., Boulder, 1964; Tchr. of Poetry as a Performing Art in var. schls. in Boulder, 1969–. Memberships: Poetry Soc. of Am.; New England Poetry Club; Authors Guild; Denver Womans Press Club; O'seas Press Club, etc. Published works: Farewell to Walden (sonnet sequence), 1939; Victoria Through the Looking-Glass, the Life of Lewis Carroll, 1945 (republished under var. titles); Forty Years in the Wilderness, 1961. Rep. in following anthols: Am. Caravan, 1927; May Days, 1925; Bread Loaf Anthol., 1939; Thomas Moult's Best Poems of 1937; Poetry of the Am. Negro, 1970; Diamond Anthol. of the Poetry Soc. of Am., 1971, etc. Contbr. to var. mags. & newspapers. Wrote a prose column, then poetry column in Town & Country Review, Boulder, 1968-71. Recip. var. honours, & awards inclng: Fellowship, Macdowell Artists Colony, 1962; Huntington Hartford Fndn., 1962. Address: 1074 Rose Hill Dr., Boulder, CO 80302, U.S.A.

LENNON, John Winston, b. 9 Oct. 1940. Musician; Vocalist; Author; Composer. Educ: Liverpool Coll. of Art, U.K. Married Yoko Ono, 1969. Positions held: Ex-Beatle; Lengthy career composing songs, touring the world giving concerts. Published works: John Lennon in His Own Write, 1964; A Spaniard In the Works, 1965; (songs w. Paul Mccartney) Love Me Do; Please, Please Me; She Loves You; Can't Buy Me Love; All My Loving; Ticket To Ride; All You Need is Love; Penny Lane; Hey Jude; Get Back; Revolution; Yesterday; I Want to Hold Your Hand; Strawberry Fields Forever; etc. Honours, awards: O.B.E., 1965; Grammy Awards (w. other Beatles). Address: 105 Bank St., New York, NY 10014, U.S.A.

LeNOIR, Ivy Anita (Darensbourg), pen name LeNOIR, **Ivy Anita,** b. 27 Feb. 1894. Teacher. Education: Elem., Grade School, and HS in Public Schools, and Guillaume Coll.; Teacher-Training, 2 yrs., New Orleans Univ.; Philos. & French Lit., 2 yrs. (evening) St. Louis Univ., Mo. Positions held: 1 yr. Principal, Estherwood Elem., Acadia Parish, La.; 8 yrs. Teacher of 7th & 8th Grades, Beauregard Parish Training, De Ridder, La.; 10 yrs. Prin. of Gretna Elem., La.; 6 yrs. Teacher of Reading & French, Catholic Schools, St. Louis, Mo. Memberships: Secretaire de la Correspondance du Cercle Francis de St. Louis, Mo.; Poetry Soc. of Texas (4 yrs.); Houston Chapter, Poetry Soc. of Texas (4 yrs.); Nat. Fed. State Poetry Socs. (4 yrs.); Acad. of American Poets (3 yrs.); Ethel Ransom Art & Lit. Club (4 yrs.). Published work: Sursum Corda (Lift Up Your Hearts), 1973. Contbr. to: Louisiana Weekly; Pittsburgh Courier; St. Louis Post Dispatch; St. Louis Argus; Forward Times (Houston). Awards: 2 First Prizes, Houston Chapter Poetry Festival, 1970; 1 Hon. Mention, Houston Poetry Festival, 1970; 1 Certificate Award of Honor, Deep South Writers & Artists Conference, 1970; 1 Popular Award, Texas State Poetry Soc., 1972; 1 Hon. Mention, Houston Chapter Festival, 1973. Address: 266 Owens Ave., Houston, TX 77029, USA.

LEON, Valerie, b. 19 Apr. 1940. 5 children. Sec., Birmingham Poetry Ctr., 3 yrs. Contbr. to: Muse, two, three & four; Gargantua; Point Three; Birmingham Mail; Ver Poets Voices. Address: 158 Long Nuke Rd., Northfield, Birmingham 31, U.K.

LEONARD, Maurice, b. 27 July 1939. Scriptwriter.

Education: Guildhall Schl. of Music & Drama. Writer of Thames T.V. 'This is Your Life' and var. radio shows for Radio Oxford, Radio Medway & Radio London. Published works: The Open Door, An anthol. of poems collated & edited by Maurice Leonard, containing sev. of his poems. Contbr. to: Nova; Tit-Bits; Destiny. Honours, awards: Gold Medal with honours, for poetry, L.A.M.D.A., 1972; Silver Medal, ibid, 1971 & Bronze, 1970. Address: 3 Alexandra Ave., London S.W.11, U.K.

LEONARD, Tom, b. 22 Aug. 1944. Clerk. Education: Glasgow Univ., U.K. Married, 1 child. Positions held: Civil Servant; Proof-Rdr.; Clerk; Post Office Wkr. Published works: Six Glasgow Poems, 1969; A Priest Came on at Merkland Street, 1970; Poems, 1973. Contbr. to: Akros; Scottish Int.; Aquarius; Scottish Poetry 5; Scottish Poetry 6. Recip., Scottish Arts Coun. Award, 1971. Address: 56 Eldon St., Glasgow G3 6NJ, U.K.

LEONG, Russell C(harles), b. 7 Sept. 1950. Student. Education: Commodore Stockton Grammar School; Marina Jr. HS; Lowell HS; San Francisco State Coll., B.A., Social Science. Third-generation Chinese-American, born and raised in San Francisco Chinatown. Published work: Threads (Asian-American Authors) (ed. Kai-yu Hsu). Address: 1020 Stockton, San Francisco, CA 94108, USA.

LEPAGE, Jacques, b. 9 Oct. 1909. Writer. Married, 2 children. Published works: (poetry) Mosaïque, 1937; Vigiles, 1958; Rivages d'Eau, 1963; Cardiogrammes, 1966; Les Yeux déchirés, 1968; Le Déluge, 1969; Approximation, 1971; Intégrité, 1972; Ostréiculture, 1973; Non Lieu, 1973; (essays) Emilie, 1956; Entretien avec André Verdet, 1963; Présence et devenir d'une poésie au Québec, 1970; Annuaire de l'Avant-Garde d'Agentzia, 1971; René Daumal, 1971; Inter Art Agentzia, 1972. TV Film, Yellow now Gallery, 1971. Contbr. var. articles to Le Monde; Esprit; les Lettres Françaises; Sud; Le Journal des Poètes; Entretiens; Poésie 1, etc. Address: Ch. du Bois de Boulogne, 06200 Nice, France.

LePAN, Douglas Valentine, b. 25 May 1914. University College Principal. Education: B.A., Univ. Coll., Univ. of Toronto; M.A., Merton Coll., Oxford. Positions held: Instructor & Tutor in Engl. Literature, Harvard Univ., Cambridge, Mass., 1938-41; Can. Dept. of External Affairs, 1945; 1st Sec., Staff of the Can. High Commissioner in London, 1945-48; Dept. of External Affairs, Ottawa, 1941-51; Counsellor & Late Minister Counsellor, Can. Embassy, Wash. D.C., 1951-55; Sec. & Dir. Rsch., Royal Commission on Canada's Economic Prospects (Gordon Commission), 1955-58; Asst. Under-Sec. of State for External affairs, 1958-59; Prof., Engl. Lit., Queen's Univ., Kingston, Ont., 1959-64; Prin., Univ. Coll., Univ. of Toronto, 1964–. Published Works: The Wounded Prince & Other Poems, 1948; The Net & the Sword, 1953; The Deserter (Novel), 1964. Hons: Guggenheim Fellowship, 1948-49; Gov. General's Award for Poetry, 1953, for Fiction, 1964. Address: Univ. Coll., Univ. of Toronto, Toronto 5, Ont., Canada.

LEPIK, Kalju, b. 7 Oct. 1920. Poet; Writer. Education: Studied literature & philology at the Univs. of Tartu (1942-43) & Stockholm. Published works incl: (vols. of verse) Nägu koduaknas (A Face in the Home Window), 1946; Mängumees (The Fiddler), 1948; Kerjused treppidel (Beggars on the Stairs), 1949; Merepõhi (Sea Bottom), 1951; Muinasjutt Tiigrimaast (A Tale of Tigerland), 1955; Kivimurd (Stone Quarry), 1958; Kollased nõmmed (Yellow Heaths), 1965; Marmorpagulane (The Marble Refugee), 1968; Verepõld (Fields of Blood), 1973; a selection from previous volumes, Ronk on laululind (The Raven is a Singing Bird), 1961; Tõrvapõletaja poja õpetussõnad (Maxims of the Charcoal Burner's Son), 1950; Vilemees (The Piper), 1958; Kantat för flöjt och änglakör (Cantata for Flutes & Angelic Choirs), 1955. Transl. of his verse have appeared in Swedish, German, English, Finnish, Latvian, Italian, French &

Lithuanian periodicals. Address: Skebokvarnsvägen 334, II, S–124 34 Bandhagen, Sweden.

LEPORE, Dominick Jsmes, b. 1 July 1911. Teacher; Poet. Education: A.B., Holy Cross Coll.; M.A., Univ. of Conn.; Georgetown Univ.; Univ. of Hartford. Positions held: w. US Govt., 1935-45, '50-55; w. pvte. inds., 1945-50; Tchr., 1955–. Memberships: Poetry Soc. of Am.; Cath. Poetry Soc. of Am.; Nat. Council of Tchrs. of Engl.; Mod. Lang. Assoc. of Am.; Authors League of Am. Publications: The Praise and the Praised, 1955; Within His Walls, 1968. Contbr. to: Ariz. Quarterly; NM Quarterly; Prairie Schooner; Cape Rock Jrnl.; Experiment; Compass; Green World; Conn. Engl. Jrnl.; Hartford Times; NY Herald Tribune; Bloomsburg Press; Folio; Talaria; etc. Address: 4 Mitchell Dr., Enfield, Conn. 06082, USA.

LEPSON, Ruth Rosalind, b. 15 Feb. 1949. Poet; Teacher; Editorial Assistant. Education: B.A. in Engl. Lit., Univ. of Pa., Phila., 1970; M.A. in Creative Writing, Boston Univ., 1972. Positions held: Tchr. & Substitute in Headstart – Get Set Program in Phila., 1970-71; Taught poetry workshops at Project, Inc., 1973 & privately; Poet/Tchr. for Mass. Coun. on the Arts & Humanities (gives poetry workshops in the public schls.), 1972–; Editl. Asst., Boston Univ. Jrnl., 1973–; Freelance Writer. Contbr. to: Maio, 1973; Women Poems, 1973; The Boston Phoenix, 1973; Zahir, 1973; Boston After Dark, 1972; Read It, 1970; Sev. articles. Address: 1802 Mass. Ave., Apt. 22, Cambridge, MA 02140, U.S.A.

LERNER, Laurence David, b. 12 Dec. 1925. University Teacher. Education: B.A., Univ. of Cape Town, 1944; M.A., ibid, 1945; B.A., Pembroke Coll., Cambridge Univ., 1949. Married Natalie Winch, 4 sons. Positions held: Taught at var. univs. in G.B. & Northern Ireland, Africa, France, Germany & U.S.A.; Prof. of Engl., Univ. of Sussex, (on Fac. since 1962). Published works: (books) Domestic Interior, 1959; The Directions of Memory, 1964; Selves, 1969; The Englishmen, 1959; A Free Man, 1968; The Truest Poetry, 1960; The Truthtellers, 1967; The Uses of Nostalgia, 1972; (pamphlets) Fantasy Press Poets (Oxford), 1955; Spleen, 1966. Contbr. to: New Statesman; Spectator; Listener; Encounter; London Mag.; Times Lit. Supplement; Harpers Mag.; Sunday Times; Outposts; Listen; Wave, etc. Frequent appearances on BBC poetry programmes. Recip. prizes, Hampstead Arts Fest. & the Camden Fest. Address: 232 New Church Rd., Hove, Sussex, U.K.

LESLIE, Kenneth, b. 1 Nov. 1892. Magazine Publisher. Education: B.A., Dalhousie; Colgate Theological Seminary; M.A., Univ. of Nebraska; Harvard Univ., work towards Ph.D. Positions held: Farmer; Teacher; Preacher; Editor and, always, poet. Pubs.: Such A Din; Lowlands Low; By Stubborn Stars; Windward Rock; The Poems of Kenneth Leslie; O'Mally to the Reds and Other Poems of Kenneth Leslie; Songs of Nova Scotia; The Protestant Digest; The New Christian and The New Man. Contrib. to: Literary Digest, NY Times, etc. Recip. Governor General's Award for Poetry, 1938. Address: Pine Haven Estates, Box 5001, Armdale, Nova Scotia.

LEVENDOSKY, Charles (Leonard), b. 4 July 1936. Poet-Teacher. Education: B.S. (Physics), 1958, B.A. (Mathematics), 1960, Univ. of Oklahoma; M.A. (Education), 1963, NY Univ.; Grad. Studies in Philosophy, Univ. of Oklahoma, 1961, Univ. of Hawaii, 1960. Positions held: Grad. Assistantship, Univ. of Oklahoma, 1960-61; Teacher, US Virgin Islands, 1963-65; Instr., Engl. (as a second language), Kyoto Univ., 1965-66; Tutor, Private Schools in NYC, 1966-67; Instr. in Engl., NY Univ., 1967-70; Asst. Prof. of Engl., NY Univ., 1970-71; Poet-in-Residence: NY; NJ; Georgia; Wyoming, 1971-74. Membership: P.E.N. Published works: perimeters, 1970; small town america, 1974; Breakthrough Fictioneers (edited by Richard Kostelanetz), 1972; perimeters (produced as a multimedia dramatization at Center of Creative & Performing Arts, State Univ. of NY at Buffalo, & at

Cubiculo Theatre in NYC, 1972); From Hell To Breakfast (collab. with composer & choreographer), staged 1972; Death's Red Flower: an audio concrete poem for 2 voices & synthesizer, perf. 1973. Contbr. to: El Corno Emplumado; Elizabeth Press; NY Qtly.; DeKalb Lit. Arts Journal; Survivor's Manual; The Casper Star-Tribune; TV FACTS; Parnassus: Poetry in Review; Measure. Recip. Teacher of the Year Award, 1965, US Virgin Islands; nominated Great Teacher Award; 1971, NY Univ. Address: c/o Mrs. George Jaeger, 5811 Liebig Ave., New York, NY 10471, USA.

LEVENSON, Christopher Rene, b. 13 Feb. 1934. University Teacher. Education: Downing Coll., Cambridge Univ., UK, 1954-57; Univ. of Iowa, USA, 1964-68. Positions held: Tchr., Int. Quaker Schl. Eerde, Ommen, Netherlands; Lectr. in Engl., Univ. of Münster, Germany; Tchr., Mangotsfield Tech. HS, Bristol, UK; Instr., Engl., Univ. of Iowa, Iowa City, USA; Asst. Prof., Engl., Carleton Univ., Ottawa, Canada. Memberships: Soc. of Authors. Publications: In Transit, 1959 (part of New Poets 1959, three-pot collection); Cairns, 1969. Contbr. to: Listener; New Statesman; Transatlantic Rev.; Texas Qtly.; Malahat Rev.; London Mag.; Critical Qtly.; Ambit; New Campus Writing, 7; Best Poems of 1966; Outposts; Spectator; Encounter; Delta; New Poems, 1965; English; Univs. Poetry, 4; N.Am. Rev.; Poetry Mag., Australia; Commonwealth Poets of Today, BBC & CBC Radio. Honours: Eric Gregory Trust Fund Award, 1960. Address: Dept. of Engl., Carleton Univ., Ottawa 1, Ontario, Canada.

LEVERTOFF, Denise, pen name **LEVERTOV, Denise,** b. 24 Oct. 1923, Ilford, Essex, UK. Poet. Education: Private; Ballet Studies. Married to Mitchell Goodman, 1947, 1 child. Positions held: Assoc. Scholar, Radcliffe Inst. for Independent Study, USA, 1964-65; Vis. Lectr., Drew Univ., 1965-66; Writer in res., CCNY; 1965-66; Vis. Lectr., Vassar Coll., 1966-67; Poetry Ed., Nation, 1961 & '63-65; Initiator, Writers & Artists' Protest Against the War in Vietnam, 1965. Published works: The Double Image, 1946; Here & Now, 1957; Overland to the Islands, 1958; With Eyes at the Back of our Heads, 1959; The Jacob's Ladder, 1961; O Taste & See, 1964; The Sorrow Dance, 1967; Cold Spring & Other Poems, 1968. Contbr. to: The New American Poetry; Contemporary American Poetry; Poet's Choice; Today's Poets; Poets of Today; New Poets of England & America. Honours & Awards: Bess Hopkins Prize, 1959; Longview Award, 1960; Guggenheim Fellowship, 1962; Inez Boulton Prize, 1964; Nat. Inst. of Arts & Letters Grant, 1965; Morton Dauwen Zabel Mem. Prize, 1965. Address: c/o New Directions Publishing Corp., 333 Sixth Ave., New York, NY 10014, USA.

LEVI, Adele Frances, b. 11 Sept. 1908, d. 28 June 1972. Social Services Worker; Writer. Education: B.A., Univ. of Calif., Berkeley, U.S.A.; var. post grad. studies. Positions held: Tchr., under-privileged children, 4 yrs.; worked on Fed. Writers Proj., 2 yrs.; Social Wkr., San Francisco Dept. of Social Servs., 1943; Supvsr., Div. for the Totally Disabled, ibid, 1965-71. Memberships: Poetry Soc. of Am.; Activists, San Francisco. Contbr. to: (anthols.) The Golden Year, Poetry Soc. of Am., 1960; The Diamond Anthol., PSA, 1971; Accent on Barlow, anthol. of Activist poetry, 1962; (newspapers) N.Y. Times; San Francisco Chronicle; (mags.) Pacific Spectator; New Mexico Quarterly; Perspective; Variegation, etc. Recip. var. poetry prizes. Address: c/o Mrs. Grace S. Dilley, Executrix, Estate of Adele Levi, 1399 Queens Rd., Berkeley, . CA 94708, U.S.A.

LEVI, Peter, b. 16 May 1931. Priest. Published works: The Gravel Ponds, 1960; Water, Rock & Sand, 1962; Penguin Yevtushenko, transls., 1962; The Shearwaters, 1965; Fresh Water, Sea Water, 1965; Pancakes for the Queen of Babylon, 1968; Ruined Abbeys, 1968. Contbr. to: New Statesman; Kenyon Rev.; Encounter; London Mag.; Times Lit. Supp.; Agenda. Honours, awards: The Gravel Ponds, Poetry Book Soc. Choice. Address: Campion Hall, Oxford,

UK.

LEVINE, (Albert) Norman, b. 1924. Author; Poet. Education: McGill Univ., Montreal, Can. Positions held: Resident Writer, Univ. of New Brunswick, Fredericton, Can., 1965–. Published works: The Tight-Rope Walker, 1950; Other: The Angled Road (Novel), 1952; Canada Made Me, 1958; One Way Ticket, 1961; Ed., Canadian Winter's Tales, 1968. Contbr. to (Anthols.): Penguin Book of Canadian Verse, 1958; Oxford Book of Canadian Verse, 1960.

LEVINE, Philip, b. 10 Jan. 1928. Poet. Education: B.A. & M.A., Wayne Univ., Detroit; M.F.A., Iowa. Married, 3 sons. Positions held: Tchr., Calif. State Univ., Fresno. Published works: On The Edge, 1963; Not This Pig, 1968; Thistles (pamphlet), 1970; 5 Detroits (pamphlet), 1970; Pili's Wall, 1971; Red Dust, 1971; They Feed The Lion, 1972. Contbr. to: New Yorker; Harper's; Atlantic; Encounter; N.Y. Review of Books; Kayak; Hudson Review; Paris Review; Am. Poetry Review; Poetry; Stand; New Canadian & Am. Poetry; The Am. Review; Anteus; Zilch; Naked Poetry; Poet's Choice; Sumac, etc. Honours, awards: Joseph Henry Jackson Award, 1961; Chaplebrook Fndn. Award, 1968; Frank O'Hara Meml. Award, Poetry Mag., 1972; Acad. of Am. Arts & Letters Award, 1973; Guggenheim Fellowship, 1973. Address: 4549 N. Van Ness, Fresno, CA 93704, U.S.A.

LEWIN, Leopold, b. 28 July 1910. Poet; Poetry Translator. Education: grad., Law Dept., Univ. of Warsaw, 1931; grad., Higher Schl. of Jrnlsm., Warsaw, 1931. Positions held: Co-Ed., Warsaw Press Agency Warszawska Informacja Prasowa', 1937-39; Lit. Ed., Polish Socialist Party's Daily 'Robotnik', 1946-48; Lit. Ed. of weekly 'Kultura', 1963-71. Memberships: Sec. Gen., Polish Writers' Union, 1948-50; Mbr., Ctrl. Bd & Presidium, ibid, 1960-72; Chmn., Foreign Comm., 1968-72; Presidium, Societé Européenne de Culture, Poland; PEN Club; Dpty. Ed.-in-Chief, Literatura na świecie. Published works incl: (colls. of poems) Kora pisana, 1933; Sen zimowy, 1934; Sny o powrocie, 1948; Zolnierska droga, 1953; Poezje wybrane, 1956; Na mojej ziemi, 1966; Wybor wierszy, 1968; Wyznania, 1969, etc.; (colls. of poetical transl.) Rainer Maria Rilke, Poezje, 1939; 'Poerje wybrane', Mikolaj Niekrasow, 1951; Schiller, Ballady, 1962; Nikoloz Barataszwili, Slowik i miecz, 1973, etc. Contbr. to many jrnls., mag., reviews. Honours, awards: Poetry Prize of the Min. of Defence; num. prizes in poetry comps. Address: Nowy Swiat 25/3, 00-029 Warsaw, Poland.

LEWIS, Miriam Schwenk, b. 2 Feb. 1904. Research Librarian (until retirement). Education: Phil. Girl's H.S.; A.B., Bryn Mawr Coll.; M.A., Univ. of Wisconsin; also grad. Lutheran School of Christian Education. Currently, Chairman, Library Committee, New Century Guild. Contrib. to: Phil. Inquirer; Printers' Ink; Country Gentleman; American Bard; Southwest Breeze; Episcopal Recorder; Angel Hour; Better Verse; Lutheran Lyrics (anthol.); St. Paul's Journal; Penna. Poets (anthol.); Poetry Parade (anthol.), etc. Address: 5721 Moris St., Apt. 544, Philadelphia, Pa 19144, USA.

LEWIS, Pamela Rozalia, pen name LEWIS, Pamela, b. 4 Mar. 1929. Occupational Therapist. Education: London Schl. of Occupational Therapy, 1949-52. Married, 3 children. Published works: One Mile From the Centre (pamphlet), 1971. Contbr. to: Workshop; Cornhill; ICA Mag.; Samphire; Poetry Review; English; Poet; Int. Monthly; Encounter; Gonster & Gong – both Nottingham Univ. publs.; var. other little mags. Also Contbr. to BBC Schls. progs., BBC 3 Poetry Now & BBC 4. Rep. in following anthols: Shapes & Creatures; Impetus. Address: 3 Third Ave., Sherwood Rise, Nottingham NG7 6JH, U.K.

LEWIS, Ruth A., b. 22 Mar. 1911. Housewife. Married, 3 children. Memberships: Poetry Soc. of Mich.; Writers Grp. of Muskegon & former Chmn. of Writers; active in Methodist Church, office of Pres. Published works: Trial Flight, 1971. Contbr. to: Muskegon Chronicle; Ravenna Times; Bardic Echoes; Christian Herald. Recip., award for 'Michigan' from radio stn. WEFG-FM. Address: 1705 Oak Park Ave., Muskegon, MI 49442, U.S.A.

LEWIS-SMITH, Anne Elizabeth, pen names McGREGOR, A.E. & McCORMICK, A.E.,** b. 14 Apr. 1925. Poet; Journalist. Married, 1 son, 2 daughters. Positions held: Edited, 1st WRNS Mag.; Ed. of Envoi; Engl. Chmn., World Poetry Day; Chmn., Poetry Day, London, 1967, 70; On Steering Comm., East of England Arts Coun., 1969; Ed. of Aerostat (the British Balloon & Airship Club's mag.) Membership: London Press Club; P.E.N.; Poetry Soc.; Hon. Rep., Studi e Scambi Int.; Nat. Book League; Comm., Brit. Balloon & Airship Club. Published works: The Seventh Bridge, 1963; The Begining, 1964; Flesh & Flowers (3 edns.), 1967; Dandelicn Flavour, 1970. Contbr. to over 30 poetry mags. & many newspapers & jrnls. Rep. in over 14 anthols. & in 8 ref. books. Honours, awards: Medal of Hon., Studi e Scambi Int., 1970; 1st Prize, Leicester Fest., 1967. Address: Primrose Cottage, Peppard Common, Henley on Thames, Oxon., U.K.

LE WITT, Jan, b. 3 Apr. 1907. Artist-Painter. Member of Exec. Coun., Société Européenne de Culture, Venice & PEN. Published works: 'From the Artist's Notebooks', a selection of poems and aphorisms contained in monograph Jan Le Witt, by Sir Herbert Read, Jean Cassou & John Smith, preface by Pierre Emmanuel de l'Academie Française, London, 1971, Paris 1972, N.Y. 1973. Contbr. to: Poetry Review, London; Expression, London; Adam Int. Review, London; Comprendre, Venice; Malahat Review, Vic., Canada. Address: 117 Ladbroke Rd., Holland Park, London W11 3PR, U.K.

L'HEURLIEUX, John Clarke, b. 26 Oct. 1934. Priest; Resident Writer. Education: Nat. Acad. of Theatre Arts, 1952; Coll. of the Holy Cross, Worcester, Mass., 1952-54; B.A., Boston Coll., Chestnut Hill, Mass., 1959; M.A., Philosophy, ibid., 1960, M.A., Engl., ibid., 1963; Harvard Univ., Cambridge, Mass. Positions held: Entered Soc. of Jesus, 1954; Ordained a Priest, 1966; Writer in Residence, Georgetown Univ., Wash. D.C., 1965; Regis Coll., Weston, Mass., 1970. Published works: Quick as Dandelions, 1964; Rubrics for a Revolution, 1967; One Eye and a Measuring Rod, 1968; No Place for Hiding, 1970; Other: Picnic in Babylon: A Priest's Jrnl., 1967. Contbr. to (Anthol.): Young American Poets, 1968.

LIDDY, James, b. 1 June 1934. Writer. Education: M.A., Univ. Coll., Dublin; Barrister-at-Law, Kings Inns, Dublin. Positions held: Vis. Poet at: San Francisco State Coll., 1967-68; Lewis & Clark Coll., 1970; Denison Univ., 1971, 72; Univ. of Wis., Parkside, 1972-73. Published works: Blue Mountain, poems, 1968; A Life of Stephen Dedalus, 1969; A Munster Song of Love & War, 1970; Homage to Patrick Kavanagh, criticism, 1972. Contbr. of poems to: Choice; N.Y. Times; Tuatara; The Dolmen Miscellany of Irish Writing; Funge Broadsheet; Neptune's Kingdom; Poetry Ireland, etc. Ed. of: Arena, 1963-65; Nine Queen Bees, 1970-72; Pleiades, 1972–. Address: Coolgreany, Gorey, Co. Wexford, Ireland.

LIE, Arvid Torgeir, b. 18 Aug. 1938. Author. Education: Univ. of Oslo, Norway. Mbr., The Norwegian Writers' Union. Published works: (poetry books) Under fugleus vengjekross, 1967; Snovinter, 1968; 'Fra eit halvt liv', 1969; 'Skrive og tenke', 1971; 'Sol og Sekund', 1973. Contbr. to: Dagbladet (newspaper); Vinduet (review); Syn og Segn (review). Address: Dr. Kobros Vei 4, 1474 Nordbyhagen, Norway.

LIE, Tove, b. 20 Mar. 1942. Secretary. Education: Schl. of Commerce; Florist educ. Mbr., Den Norske Forfatterforening. Published works: Øyeblikk, 1967; Syrinx, 1970; Verden er Goliath, 1971; Lotus, 1972; Speil dine øyne, 1973. Contbr. to: Aftenposten; Morgenbladet; Dagbladet; Libra. Recip., prize, Cappelen Publsrs. for contbn. to 'Gruppe 67'. Address: 3525 Hallingby, Norway.

LIEBERMAN, Laurence, b. 16 Feb. 1935. Professor of English. Education: B.A. in Engl., Univ. of Mich., 1956; M.A. in Engl., Univ. of Mich., 1958; 2 yrs. grad. study in Engl., Univ. of Calif. at Berkeley, 1958-60. Positions held: Instr. in Engl., Orange Coast Coll., Calif., 1960-64; Assoc. Prof. of Engl., Coll. of the Virgin Islands, 1964-68; Prof. of Engl., Univ. of Ill., Urbana, 1968-; Poetry Reviewership, Yale Review, 1970-; Poetry Editor, Univ. of Ill. Press, 1971-. Pubs. The Unblinding (poems), 1968; The Osprey Suicides (poems), 1973; The Achievement of James Dickey (criticism), 1969. Contrib. to: The New Yorker; Atlantic Monthly; Harper's; Poetry; Hudson Review; Yale Review; Paris Review; Saturday Review; The Nation; New Republic; Qtly. Rev. of Literature; Audience Mag.; Beloit Poetry Journal; Poetry Northwest; Shenandoah; (anthols.): A Controversy of Poets; The Contemp. American Poets; Comtemp. Poetry in America. Awarded Fellowships to Yaddo in poetry writing, 1963, 1967, 1971; Ann. Award from Nat. Endowment for the Arts, 1969; Assoc. Fellowship to Center for Advanced Study, Univ. of Ill. – creative writing grant to travel in Japan for 1 year (Sept. 1971 to Sept. 1972). Address: English Dept., Univ. of Illinois, Urbana, Ill. 61801, USA.

LIEBKNECHT, Henrietta, b. 9 Nov. 1897. Author. Education: Clark Bus. Coll., Louisville, Ky.; Acctng., Covington Evening Classes; Evening Lang. Classes, Young Mens' Christian Assn., Louisville. Positions held: Ed., Women's & Children's Sect., L & N Mag., Louisville; Ed., Speaker & Contbng. Author, Louisville Poetry Club; Contbng. Author, Ky. Writers' Guild, Cinn. Ohio & Poet, India, also to Nat. Fed. of State Poetry Socs., Dodgeville, Wis.; currently Circulation Mgr., Pegasus Mag., Louisville. Memberships: Ky. State Poetry Soc.; World Poetry Soc. Intercontinental; Lousville Poetry Club; Nat. Fed. State Poetry Socs. Published works: Childhood's Sweet Enchantment, 1965; Telling It Like It Is (under ps. Daniel Wallace-White), 1973. Contbr. to many mags., jrnls. inclng: Poetry Digest, N.Y.; Poet; Ky. Writers' Guild; Message of the East; Sunshine Mag.; Neb. Farming; Am. Farming. Recip. num. honours & awards inclng: Jesse Stuart Award of Excellence, Ky. State Poetry Soc., 1974. Address: 2126 Village Dr., Apt. 6, Louisville, KY 40205, U.S.A.

LIFSHIN, Lyn (Diane). Poet. Education: B.A., Syracuse Univ.; M.A., Univ. of Vermont; grad. work at Brandeis Univ.; State Univ. of N.Y. at Albany; Bread Loaf. Pubs.: Lady Lyn, 1972; Why Is The House Dissolving, 1968; Black Apples, 1971; Leaves and Night Things, 1971; Femina 2, 1970; Tentacles, 1972; Moving by Touch, 1972; Museum, 1972; Merchurochrome Sun Poems, 1972; I'd Be Jeanne Moreau, 197?; Audley End, 1973; The Old House on the Croton, 1973; All the Women Poets I Liked Didn't Have Their Fathers, 1973; Collected and Selected Poems, 1974, etc. Contrib. to magazines and numerous anthols. Recip. Yaddo Fellowship, 1970, 1972; Hart Crane Mem. Award, 1970; Bread Loaf Scholar, 1971; MacDowell Fellowship, 1973. Address: 2142 Apple Tree Lane, Niskayuna, NY 12309, USA.

LIM SUNG SOOK, Maria, b. 19 Jan. 1933. Housewife. Education: Grad., Kong-Joo Coll. of Educ. (study of Korean Lit.) Married, 1 daughter. Memberships: Korean Lit. Assn.; Korean Poets Assn.; Cheong-mi Club; PEN Club, Korean Br. Published works: (amatory poems) Remain works for a long time. Rep. in following anthols: 'A Court of Melancholia'; 'Flower'; Cheong-mi Anthol., I, II, III. Contbr. to: Modern Lit.; Modern Poetry; The Monthly Lit.; Lit. of Poetry. Pvte. Address: 146 Sansung Dong, Kong Joo UP, Choong Nam, Korea. Official Address: K.P.O. Box 444, Seoul, Korea.

LINDABURY, Richard Vliet, b. 5 Sept. 1900. Editor. Education: A.B., Princeton, 1921; M.A., ibid, 1923; Ph.D., 1930. Married Alice Ballantine Young, 1 son, 2 daughters. Positions held: Instr. (Engl.), Princeton Univ.; Social Sci. Analyst, O.S.S.; Assoc. Ed., Collier's Ency.; Ed. Writer & Poetry Ed., N.Y. Herald Tribune; Ed., Proceedings of the N.J. Histl. Soc.; Assoc. Prof.,

Fairleigh Dickinson Univ. Memberships: Pres., The Poetry Soc. of Am., 1963, 1973-; Pres., Princeton Community Players, 1940-41; Pres., Archaeological Soc. of Princeton, 1959-62. Contbr. to: Scribner's Mag.; N.Y. Herald Tribune. Address: Millstone River Apts., Princeton, NJ 08540, U.S.A.

LINDEN, George W(illiam), b. 18 Aug. 1928. Professor, Philosophy. Education: Spring, 1948, Augustana Coll.; 1948-51, Univ. of Missouri, A.B., Engl./Philosophy (1951); 1952-54, Univ. of Ill., M.A., Philosophy (1954); 1954-56, ibid., Ph.D., Philosophy (1956). Divorced, 1973, 4 d. Positions held: 1952-56, Univ. of Ill., Grad. Asst. & Teaching Fellow; 1956-62, North Texas State Coll., Asst. & Assoc. Professor, 1962-68, Southern Ill. Univ., Edwardsville, Assoc. Prof., and since 1968, Professor; Judge, St. Louis Poetry Contest, 1973; Judge, McKendree Writer's Conference, 1971. Published work: Reflections on the Screen, 1971. Contbr. to: Personalist; AAUP Bulletin; Saturday Review; Trace; The Fair; Scimitar & Song; Sou'wester; The Back Door. Address: Dept. of Philosophy, Southern Ill. Univ., Edwardsville, IL 62025, USA.

LINDER, (Alfhild) Marianne, b. 7 July 1919. Author; Lyric; Poet; Teacher; Reciter; Freelance Translator. Education: Fil. kand. (B.A.), Univ. of Stockholm, 1947; Deanery Examination of German, Univ. of Innsbruck, Austria, 1967; Cert., Culture Pedagogical Inst., Stockholm, 1973. Married Lennart Wiechel. Positions held: Instr., Brevskolan, Kooperative Förbundet, 1941-42; Asst. Ed.-in-Chief, the jrnl. 'Idé', 1942-46; Youth Ldr., St. Görans Hemgard & Stockholms Stadsmission, 1946-51; Publishing Sect., Sveriges Radio, 1948; Schl. Sec., Studieförbundet Medborgarskolan, Stockholm, 1949-50; at Nobel Lib., Swedish Acad., Stockholm, 1951-56; Org. & Ldr. of study circles, lit. & artistic progs., etc., 1947-; Puppet theatre performer & introduced into Sweden the Italian 'Trebbo Poetico'. Memberships incl: a Fndr., Active Mbr., Hon. Mbr., Sec. 1958- & Pres. (Sweden) 1971-, Literary Union; Assn. of Swedish Authors, Sect. of Lit. Translators, 1971-; Writers' Ctr., Sweden, 1969-; Strindberg Soc., 1969-; a Fndr., Active Mbr., Mbr. of Rep. Comm., 1952-57, Working Team for Swedish Dramatic/Scenic Art. Published works: Brunnarna, 1950; De röda lutorna, 1951; Chonchet, Djävulen och Döden, 1954; Dockspelet och 'Chonchet, Djävulen och Döden (pamphlet), 1954; Ros och bröd, 1965; Ed. anthol., Studiegrupp Poesi 67; Sju rosor senare, 1969. Contbr. to publs. in Sweden, Germany & Hungary. Honours, awards incl: 1st Int. Poetry Prize, Lit. Union, 1968; Italy Travel Award, 1971; Award of Fredrik Ström Commemoration Fund, 1973. Address: Heleneborgsgatan 50, III, S-117 32 Stockholm, Sweden.

LINDERMAN, Linda Lee, b. 6 Mar. 1949. Operator of Ty-Tape Editor. Education: Henry Ford Community Coll., 1967-68. Married. Positions held: Clerk, Solventol Chemical Prods., 1966; Stenographer-Sec., Olsten's Temp. Help Agency, 1967-69; Operator of Ty-Tape Editor, Sec., Stenographer, Kelsey-Hayes Co., 1969-74. Mbr., Laurel Publishers Int. Poetry Symposium, 1973. Published works: Invisibly True, 1971; Escaping, 1971; Pictures of You and Me, 'Escaping', 1971; Crossing the Bridge of Love, 1973. Recip., Cert. of Merit, The Laurel Publishers Int. Poetry Symposium, 1973. Address: 22335 Columbia, Dearborn, MI 48124, U.S.A.

LINDGREN, Kaj August, b. 20 Aug. 1908. Lecturer. Educ: Matriculation, 1928; Fil.kand., 1934; Fil.mag. 1934; Study trips to Sweden, 1944-45 & Denmark, 1947. Married Elna Linnea Stromberg, 2 sons. Positions held: Prin., Eastern Nyland's Peoples' Coll., Perna Fishing Schl., 1938-53; Lectr., Mother Tongue, Munksnäs Swedish Coed. Schl., 1953-71; w. Helsingfors Swedish Hosp. Inst., 1954-; Swedish Div., Veterinary Med. Coll., Helsingfors, 1957-63; Evening Classes, var. Swedish Schls., 1972-; Tchr., Corres. Inst. Kansanvalistusseuran Kirjeopisto (Finnish), 1972-. Memberships: V.P., Friday Assn., Literary

Student Assn., 1931-38; Finland's Swedish Author Assn. Published works: Ett blad år vänt, 1935; Trä-Orgel, 1937; Brevbtill mitt hjärta, 1939; Stig fram vart land, 1943; Tall i storm, 1944; I Bagens tid, 1948; Ed., Antologin Dikterna om Finlands Kamp, 1940; Contbr., Antologin Finlands Natur i Dikt Och Konst, 1945; 2 hymns, Finland's Swedish Hymnbook; Cantatas, Perna Ch., Borga Town, etc. Contbr. to: Nya Argus; Wiborgs Nyheter; Nya Pressen; Finsk Tidskrift; Vasabladet; Hufvudstadsbladet; Literary Prog., Finnish Radio. Address: Bredviksvägen 14 A 8, 00330 Helsingfors 33, Finland.

LINDGREN, Sören Gotthard, b. 13 Mar. 1935. Journalist. Education: Philosophical & sociological studies at the Univ. of Helsinki, Finland, 1957-60. Married 1) Berit Klatt, 2) Kerstin Kall. Positions held: Ed. of literature & art at Nya Pressen, Helsinki, 1960-64; Freelance Jrnlst. in Sweden, 1965–. Member, Finland's Svenska Författareförening. Published works: Ornament, 1954; De tolv, 1957; Exil, 1958; Abals död, 1959; Politiska dikter, 1969. Contbr. to: Nya Argus; Dagens Nyheter; Horisont; Hufvudstadsbladet. Address: Melonvägen 31, S-170 10 Ekerö, Sweden.

LINDSLEY, Mary Frances. University Professor (retired). Education: A.B., Hunter Coll., NYC; M.A., Columbia Univ., NYC.; Dr. of Humane Letters (h.c.), Free Univ. of Asia, Karachi; Dr. of Liberal Arts (h.c.), Gt. China Arts Coll., World Univ., Hong Kong. Positions held: Instr., Asst. Prof., Assoc. Prof., Hunter College of the City Univ. of NY. Memberships: Eastern Centre, Poetry Soc. of London; Poetry Soc. of America; NY Poetry Forum; Calif. Fed. of Chaparral Poets (vice-pres. of the Orpheus Chapter, and Sec. of the Apollo Chapter); Accademia Leonardo da Vinci; UPLI; Baker Street Irregulars; Praed Street Irregulars; Dickens Fellowship; Intercontinental Biographical Association (Fellow). Published works: Uncensored Letter, 1949; Grand Tour, 1952; Promenade, 1965; Pomp & Circumstance, 1966; Selected Poems, 1967; Pax Romana, 1967; Otma, 1968; Rosaria, 1969; The Workday of Pierre Toussaint, 1970; Circe and the Unicorn, 1971; The Masquers, 1972; One Life, 1973; Co-Author w. husband Dr. I.L. Jaffee, Beyond Baker Street, 1973. Contbr. to: North American Review; Catholic World, Poet; Interracial Review; Pontine Dossier, etc. Awards: Bronze Medal (1965), Silver Medal (1966) Accademia Leonardo da Vinci; Pres. Marcos Medal, Philippines, 1968; Golden Laurel Wreath, Philippines, 1969; 1st Prize, Apollo Chapt. Poetry Contest, 1971; 1st Prize for Sonnet, Calif. Olympiad of Arts, 1972; 1st Prize for Theme Poem, CFCP Convention at Sacramento, 1973; Elected to Hall of Fame, Hunter Coll., CUNY, 1974, etc. Address: 13361 El Dorado, Apt., 201H, Seal Beach, CA 90740, USA.

LINDQUIST, Ray, b. 6 May 1941. Clergyman. Education: Pomona Coll., 1959-63; Princeton Theological Sem., 1963-67. Positions held: Pastor, Covington United Presbyterian Ch., nr. Pavilion, N.Y., 1967–. Published works: By-Products, 1972. Contbr. to: Epos; New Am. & Canadian Poetry; Lyric; West End. Address: Craig Rd., Pavilion, NY 14525, U.S.A.

LINDSAY, John Maurice, pen name **BROCK, Gavin,** b. 21 July 1918. Director of the Scottish Civic Trust. Education: Glasgow Acad., Scotland, UK, 1926-36; Royal Scottish Acad. of Music, 1936-39. Married to Aileen Joyce Lindsay, 1 s., 3 d. Positions held: Drama Critic, Scottish Daily Mail, Edinburgh, 1946-47; Music Critic, Bulletin, Glasgow, 1946-60; Free-lance Broadcaster, BBC, Glasgow, 1946-61; Prog. Controller, Border TV, Carlisle, 1961-62; Prod. Controller, ibid, 1962-64; Features Exec. & Sr. Interviewer, 1964; Dir., The Scottish Civic Trust, 1967–. Memberships: Hon. Publs. Sec., Saltire Soc., Edinburgh, 1948-52; Scottish PEN. Published works: (poetry) Perhaps Tomorrow, 1941; Predicament, 1942; No Crown for Laughter, 1943; The Enemies of Love, 1946; Hurlygush, 1948; At the Wood's Edge, 1950; Ode for St. Andrew's Night & Other Poems, 1951; The Exiled Heart, 1957; Snow Warning, 1962;

One Later Day, 1964; This Business of Living, 1969; Comings & Goings, 1971; (editor) Poetry Scotland, 1-4, 1943-49; Modern Scottish Poetry; An Anthol. of the Scottish Renaissance, 1946, '66; A Book of Scottish Verse, 1968; Scottish Poetry 1-4, 1966, '67, '68, '69; John Davidson: A Selection of his Poems, 1959; (prose) num. works, incl. Robert Burns: the Man: his work: the Legend, 1954, '68; The Burns Encyclopedia, 1959, '69; Portrait of Glasgow, 1972. Contbr. to: The Listener; Spectator; Tribune; Poetry Rev.; Poetry London; Life & Letters; Glasgow Herald; Scotsman; Lines; Scottish Int.; Akros; Scottish Field, etc. Honours: Rockefeller Atlantic Award, 1946. Address: 11 Gt. Western Terr., Glasgow, W2, Scotland, UK.

LINDSLEY, Mary F. Retired University Professor. Education: A.B., Hunter Coll., City Univ., N.Y.; M.A., Columbia Univ. Married Dr. Irving Lincoln Jaffee. Positions held: Instr., Asst. Prof. & Assoc. Prof., Engl. Dept., Hunter Coll., City Univ., N.Y. Memberships: Sec., Apollo Chapt., Calif. Fed. of Chaparral Poets; V.P., Orpheus Chapt., ibid.; Accademia Leonardo da Vinci; United Poets Laureate Int.; World Poetry Soc.; Poetry Soc. of Am.; N.Y. Poetry Forum; Eastern Ctr., Poetry Soc. of England; Dickens Fellowship. Published works: Uncensored Letter, 1949; Grand Tour, 1952; Promenade, 1965; Pomp & Circumstance, 1966; Selected Poems, 1967; Pax Romana, 1967; Otma, 1968; Rosaria, 1969; The Workday of Pierre Toussaint, 1970; Circe & the Unicorn, 1971; The Masquers, 1972; One Life, 1973; (book of short stories) Beyond Baker Street, w. husband Dr. Irving L. Jaffee, 1973. Contbr. to: Praed St. Jrnl.; The Younger Poets; The Stream of Engl. Poetry; N.Am. Review; Catholic World; Interracial Review; Spring Anthol.; Poet; Laurel Leaves. Honours, awards: Hon. Mbr., Int. Mark Twain Soc., 1949; Bronze Medal, Accademia Leonardo da Vinci, 1965; Silver Medal, ibid, 1966; Golden Laurel Wreath, UPLI, 1968; Pres. Marcos Medal, ibid, 1968; Dr. of Humane Letters, Free Univ. of Asia, Karachi, Pakistan, 1969; Dr. of Liberal Arts, Gt. China Arts Coll., World Univ., Hong Kong, 1973; Order of Merit, World Doctorship, ibid, 1973; Poets Championship Medal, Chinese Poetry Soc., Taiwan, 1973; Hunter Coll. Hall of Fame, CUNY, 1974. Address: 13361 El Dorado, 201H, Seal Beach, CA 90740, U.S.A.

LINEBARGER, James Morris, b. 6 Jul. 1934. Teacher. Education: A.B., Columbia Coll., 1956; M.A., Columbia Univ., 1957; Ph.D., Emory Univ., 1963. Married Lillian Tillery; 2 s. Positions held: Instr. and Asst. Prof. of Engl., Ga. Tech, 1957-62; Asst. Prof. 1963-65, Assoc. Prof. 1965-70, Prof. 1970–, at North Texas State Univ. Member: Poetry Soc. of America; Poetry Soc. of Texas; Modern Lang. Assoc.; Conference of Coll. Teachers of Engl. Pubs: Five Kinds (poetry); John Berryman (prose) a study of the poet. Contrib. to: Southwest Review; Southern Humanities Review; Laurel Review; Pebble; Encore; Quartet; Cimarron Review; Arlington Qtly.; Descant; Notes & Queries. Address: Route 1, Argyle, Texas 76226, USA.

LINER, Amon George, Jr. Library Assistant. Education: B.A. (Engl.), Kenyon Coll., 1963; M.A. (Drama), Univ. of N.C. at Chapel Hill, 1965. Published works: Marstower (book), 1972. Contbr. to: 11 Charlotte Poets Anthol., 1972; Anvil; Crucible; Folio; Foxfire; Carolina Qtly.; Quixote; Red Clay Rdr. Address: 67 Maxwell Rd., Chapel Hill, NC 27514, U.S.A.

LINK, S. Gordden, pen name, **LINK, Gordden,** b. 9 Apr. 1907. Writer in Residence & Professor of Humanities. Education: B.S., NY Univ., 1929; A.M., 1930; M.Ed., Harvard Univ., 1932; Ph.D., Geo. Peabody Coll. for Tchrs. Grad. Schl., 1938; Fellow, Higher Educ., Yale Univ., 1931; Fellow, Oriental Lit. & Art, Columbia Univ., 1935. Married, Dr. Mae M. Link, Space Med. Histn. Positions held: Prof., Poetics, Limestone Coll., 1930-34; Instr., Engl., Dir., Dramatics & Ext. Lectr., Drama, Geo. Peabody Coll. for Tchrs., 1934-38; Dir., Jrnlism., Grad. Schl. & Prof., Engl., Oglethorpe Univ., 1938-39; Vis. Prof., Civilization &

Prof., Engl., Summer Schl., St. Lawrence Univ., 1939-40; Prof., Engl. & Comparative Lit., Drury Coll., 1940-41; US Army, N Africa, Middle East, India, Burma, China & Philippines, 1942-47; Dir., McCoy Coll. Writing Workshop, Johns Hopkins Univ., 1947-51; Lectr., Mod. Poetry, Dunbarton Coll., 1951-52; Br. Dir., Cmd. & Gen. Staff Dept., USAR Schl., Ft. Myer, Va. & Ft. Geo. G. Meade, Md. (Summers), 1953-61; Poet in Res. & Chmn., Humanities Div., Anne Arundel Community Coll., 1962-64; Poet in Res. & Prof., Engl., ibid, 1964-66; Writer in Res., Southeastern Univ., 1966–; Dir., Liberal Arts, ibid, 1967-71; Dir., Dellbrook-Shenandoah Coll. Writers Conf., 1969. Memberships: Pres. Elect., Ctr. for Adv. Studies, Riverton, Va., 1971; Poetry Soc. Am.; Poetry Soc. Va.; Baker St. Irregulars. Published works: Jt. Author, Christ in the Breadline, 1932, '33; A Dozen Years After: A Peace Poem, 1937; Three Poems for Now: A Book of Verse, 1953, '58; Apocalypse, 1955; Quartet from the Golden year, 1961. Contributor to: Adventure; Ainslee's; Asia; The Christian; Christian Century; Contemporary Verse; Forum; Globe; Golden Book; Household Mag.; Engl. Jrnl.; Kaleidoscope; NY Times; Poetry; Plain Talk; Poetry of Today; Poetry Review; Saturday Review; Theatre Arts; Vision; Voices; Arena; New Zealand Quarterly; 21 anthols. Honours, awards: Lola Ridge Award for Poetry of Social Significance, Poetry Soc. Am.; 1948; Nat. Awards, Poetry Soc. Va., 1956, '58; James Joyce Award, Poetry Soc. Am., 1971. Address: Southeastern Univ., 1736 G St. NW, Washington DC 20006, USA.

LINTON, Virginia, b. 19 Aug. 1913. Poet. Education: Bucknell Univ., Lewisburg, Pa. Married Wallace R. Linton, 1 daughter. Positions held: Mkt. Rsch., Young & Rubicam & Curtis Publng. Co. Memberships: Poetry Soc. Ga.; Poetry Soc. Am. Contbr. to: Sat. Evening Post; Ladies Home Jrnl.; Christian Sci. Monitor; The Islander; N.Y. Times; Year Book, Poetry Soc. Ga.; Savannah Sun. Mag.; Chicago Tribune Mag.; Today's Poets; NY Times Book of Verse; Poetry Soc. of Ga. Anthol. of Verse; The London Daily Telegraph Mag.; The Southern Poetry Review, Columbia, S.C. Honours, awards: Award for best poem, Poetry Soc. Ga., 1970; Guinness Int., Stroud, U.K., 1972; Furman Univ., Columbia, S.C., 1972; Poetry Soc. of Ga., 1972. Address: 712 Green Heron Rd., Hilton Head Island, SC 29928, U.S.A.

LINZE, Georges, b. 12 lfar. 1900. Writer. Memberships: V.P., Assn. of Belgian Writers; Corres. Mbr., Luxembourg Acad.; Int. Acad. of French Culture. Published works: (poetry) Poème de la Patience de l'Univers; Manifestes Poétiques; Poème de l'Etrange Prison; Poème d'aujourd'hui; Poème des bonheurs Insolites; Poème de la Grande Invention; Poème de la Paix Incroyable; Poème de la ville survolée par les Rêves; (novels) Les Dimanches; Les Enfants bombardés; Sébastien, etc. Contbr. to: Le Soir, Brussels; Marginales; La Dryade; Vérités, etc. Honours, awards: Prix Denayer, French Acad. of Belgium; Prix du Reportage. René Jauniaux; Prix Marcel Loumaye; Prix René Lyr; Prix des Amitiés françaises (for the novel Le Père et le Fils ou les Secrets). Address: 98 rue Xhovémont, Liège 4000, Belgium.

LINZE, Jacques-Gérard, b. 10 Sept. 1925. Advertising Manager. Education: LL.D.; Musical Studies (piano). Married, 2 sons. Positions held: Jazz pianist, Am. Army & civil ballrooms, 1944-45; Barrister, 1949-51; Adviser in legal matters, 1951-52 (all Liège, Belgium); Adviser in legal matters, personnel manager, Leopoldville & Brussels, 1952-55; Advertising Mgr., Brussels, 1956–. Memberships: French PEN Club (Belgium section); Association des Ecrivains Belges, Groupe du Roman. Published works: Confidentiel, 1960; Trois tombeaux, 1963; Passé midi, 1974. Contbr. to: Marginales, Brussels; Le Bayou, Houston, U.S.A.; Flammes vives, Paris; Université, Liège; Le cocotier, Liège; Lettres nouvelles, Liège; La Dryade, Virton (Belgium); La Tour de Babel, Malines (Belgium). Recip., Prix Emile Polak, l'Académie Royale de Langue et Littérature françaises, Brussels, 1960.

Address: Rue Melpomène 24 C, B-1080, Brussels, Belgium.

LIPPENS, Louis, b. 21 June 1932. Man of Letters; Essayist; Poet. Education: Indusl. & Commercial Schl., Tourcoing. Married Geneviève Rémory, 1 son, 1 daughter. Positions held: Dir., 'Elan Poetique Litteraire et Pacifiste', 1955–. Memberships: Int. Leonardo da Vinci Acad., Italy; Int. Poetry Biennale, Knokke, Belgium; Pres., Cultural Exchanges, Assn. Linselloise des échanges internationaux. Published works incl: (colls. of poems) Ecrit à l'Aube, 1955; Interdit aux militaires, 1957; Lippens de poche, 1961; D'Hiroshima à Mururoa, 1968; (essays) Face aux dangers nucléaires, 1963 (preface Dr. Schweitzer); Face à la Paix en péril, 1965 (preface Raoul Follereau); Face au racisme, 1967 (preface Martin Luther King); Face à la Peine de mort, 1968 (preface Jean Rostand); Face au nationalisme, 1970 (preface Alfred Kastler); Face à l'argent (preface Bernard Clavel), 1972; Face aux pollutions (preface Alain Bombard), 1974. Var. translations, records. Contbr. to over 100 jrnls., mags., anthols. Honours, awards: Prix Martin Luther King, 1969; Prix Fraternité Humaine, 1971, etc. Address: 31 rue Foch, 59126 Linselles, France.

LIPSITZ, Lou, b. 29 Oct. 1938. University Teacher. Education: B.A., Univ. of Chgo., 1957; M.A., Yale Univ., New Haven, Conn., 1959; Ph.D., ibid., 1964. Married w. 2 children. Positions held: Reporter for Daily Standard, Celina, Ohio, 1957-58; Instructor, Univ. of Conn., Storrs, 1961-64; Assoc. Prof. of Political Science, Univ. of N.C., Chapel Hill, 1964–. Published works: Cold Water, 1967; Other: Work Life & Political Attitudes, 1964; Political Consensus (Ency. of the Social Sciences), 1968; Ed., American Politics: Behaviour & Controversy, 1967. Contbr. to (Anthols.): Eight Poems of Germany & America, 1967; Young American Poets, 1968; (Jrnls.): Kayak; Lillabulero; Chelsea Review; Quarterly Review of Literature. Recip., Nat. Foundation for the Arts Fellowship, 1968-69. Address: 416 Westwood Drive, Chapel Hill, NC, USA.

LIPTON, Helen Laura Duberstein, pen name **DUBERSTEIN, Helen**, b. 3 June 1926. Poet; Playwright. Education: B.S. Educ., CCNY, U.S.A., 1947. Married Victor Lipton, 2 daughters (Jacqueline & Irene). Mbr., Dramatists Guild. Published works: Succubus/Incubus, 1970; The Human Dimension, 1970. Contbr. to: The Outsider; Liberation; Confrontation; Ingenue; Assembling; For Now; Gnosis; Ghostdance; Zahir; WIN; Shantih. Address: Westbeth, 463 West St., 904 D, N.Y., NY 10014, U.S.A.

LISOWSKI, Joseph, b. 17 Sept. 1944. Teacher. Education: B.S., B.A., Acctng., Duquesne Univ., 1966; M.A., Engl., ibid, 1968; Ph.D., Engl., State Univ. of N.Y., 1974. Positions held: Tchr. of Engl., St. Mary's H.S., Sharpsburg, Pa., 1966-67 & Engl. & Geometry, Ctrl. Cath. H.S., Pittsburgh, Pa., 1967-69; Instr. of Engl., Duquesne Univ., Pittsburgh, 1968-69; N.D.E.A. Fellow, State Univ. of N.Y., 1969-71; Tchr. of Engl., Cath. Ctrl. H.S., Binghamton, N.Y., 1971-74. Contbr. to: The Archer; Boundary 2; Brown's Window; Cardinal Poetry Qtly.; Clarendon; Medicine Jug; Poetry Eastwest; Quoin; Spectrum; Tangent; Twigs; Wind; Silence; Yearbook of Mod. Poetry. Address: 55 Park Terr. Pl., Binghamton, NY 13903, U.S.A.

LITT, Iris, b. 18 Mar. 1928. Advertising & Magazine Writer. Education: B.A., Ohio State Univ.; Exchange Student, Universidad de las Americas, Mexico City. Widow of Gilbert Burris, 2 sons. Positions held: Advt. Copywriter, Benton & Bowles; Norman, Craig & Kummel, etc.; Ed. & Columnist, The Writer, Boston; Editl. Writer, Compact, Mademoiselle; Ed., Magazine Mgmt. Co.; Free-lance Writer of mag. articles; currently p/t Advt. Copywriter, ACR Advt. (Br. of Ted Bates). Memberships: Poetry Soc. of Am.; Copy Club of N.Y. Contbr. to: Kaleidograph; Cronos; Literature; Poetry Chapbook; Compact; Scholastic; Atlantic Monthly. Recip., Atlantic Monthly Award for Coll.

Poetry, 1947. Address: Garden Apt., 252 West 11th St., N.Y., NY 10014, U.S.A.

LITTLE, Geraldine Clinton, b. 20 Sept. 1928. Freelance Writer; Teacher; Musician. Education: B.A. in Engl. Lit., Goddard Coll., Plainfield, VT., and currently working on Master's degree in Engl. Born in Portstewart, Ireland; Married; 3 s. Positions held: Exec. Private Sec.; Professional Singer; Teacher. Memberships: Leaves of Grass Chapter, NJ Poetry Soc. (Pres.); Authors' Guild of America. Contbr. to: The Haiku Anthol.: Engl. Lang. Haiku by Contemp. American and Canadian Poets, 1974; Bitterroot; The Connecticut Critic; Speak Out; Modern Images; Jack & Jill; The Christian Herald; The Congregationalist; The Journal of the Speech Assoc. of NJ.; 4 NJ State Anthols.; Cats Mag.; Phila. Sunday Bulletin Mag.; Best in Poetry; Jean's Journal Christmas Anthol., 1973; Modern Haiku; Dragonfly; Haiku/West; Haiku; Byways; Tweed. Awards: 3 prizes in 1972 Nat. Fed. of State Poetry Socs., Inc., Contest (1 first, and 2 hon. mentions); 2 1st prizes, NJ Poetry Soc. Contests; 3rd prize, Poets' Study Club of Indiana Contest; many prizes in contests around the country; 74th in Writer's Digest 1971 Contest. Address: 519 Jacksonville Rd., Mt. Holly, NJ 08060, USA.

LITTLE, Larry Douglas, b. 13 Apr. 1948. Bookseller. Education: B.A. in Creative Writing, Purdue Univ., West Lafayette, Ind. Member, South & West, Inc. Contbr. to: Poet's Pulse; Sunshine. Address: 1024 25th St., Bedford, IN 47421, U.S.A.

LITTLEWOOD, Francis Desmond, occasional pen name **HAYES, Thornton,** b. 25 Sept. 1905. Solicitor & Town Clerk. Education: King's Coll., London. Positions held: var. local govt. appts., the last being Town Clerk of Cheltenham, & also Sec. to the Cheltenham Festival Company. Memberships: Chmn., Cheltenham Fest. of Lit., 1969–; West Country Writers' Assn. & Hon. Sec., 1966-72. Published works: The Law of Municipal & Public Entertainment; var. articles, mainly concerned with literary and Festival administration. Address: 5 Ryeworth Rd., Charlton Kings, Cheltenham GL52 6LG, Glos., U.K.

LITVINOFF, Emanuel, b. 1915. Television Playwright. Published works: Conscripts: A Symphonic Declaration, 1941; The Untried Soldier, 1942; A Crown for Cain, 1948; Other: The Last European, 1959; The Man Next Door, 1968. Contbr. to (Anthols.): New Treasury of War Poetry, 1943; War Poets, 1945; A Treasury of Jewish Poetry, 1957; A Garland for Dylan Thomas, 1963; I Burn for England, 1966; Poetry of the Forties, 1968.

LITWINKO, Anthony John (Jr.), b. 9 May 1944. Poet & Writer. Education: B.A., W.Va. Univ., 1966; M.A., Univ. of Pa., 1967. Positions held: Instr., then Lectr. in Engl., Bryn Mawr Coll., 1970-73; Poet in Res., Pa. Poetry in the Schools Proj., Fall-Winter, 1973-74. Contbr. to: Pa. Review; New Poets 1970; Shenandoah; New Am. Review; Mill Mountain Review; Poetry Newsletter; Three Rivers Poetry Jrnl. Honours, awards: Waiteman Barbe Poetry Prize, 1966; Acad. of Am. Poets Prize, 1969 & 1970; Pa. Poetry Series Award, 1971. Address: 117 Anderson Rd., Todd Estates, Newark, DE 19711, U.S.A.

LIU, Stephen Shu-Ning, b. 16 Mar. 1930. Educator. Education: Dip. in Chinese Lit., Nanking Univ.; B.A. in Engl. Lit., Wayland Coll.; M.A. in Engl. Lit., Univ. of Tex.; Ph.D. in Engl. Lit., Univ. of N.D. Married, 1 daughter. Positions held: Instr. of Engl., Northern Montana Coll., 1966-69; Asst. Prof. of Engl., ibid, 1969-70; Asst. Prof. of Engl., Clark Community Coll., 1973–. Contbr. to: College English; S.D. Review; N.D. Qtly.; Western Humanities Review; Southern Humanities Review; Mich. Qtly. Review; Poetry Australia; Beloit Poetry; Prairie Schooner; Forgotten Pages in Am. Lit., anthol.; Ga. Review; Prism Int.; Poet Lore; Ill. Qtly.; Christian Sci. Monitor; etc. Address: Engl. Dept., Clark Co. Community Coll., Las Vegas, NV 89101, U.S.A.

LIVELY, William Earle, b. 23 Apr. 1918. Author. Personal details: Disabled veteran of World War II; owner of a 25-acre farm. Memberships: Internat. Clover Poetry Assoc. (life member). Contbr. to: Poet Mag.; Author/Poet; South West Breeze; Tempo; Literary Amateur; Internat. Clover Poetry Assoc.; Grains of Sand (anthol.); Timeless Treasure (anthol.); Clover Collection of Verse (anthol.); Golden Anthol. of Poetry; Hospitalized Veterans Writing Project. Winner of several prizes, hon. mentions. Address: RFD 3, Box 166, Sparta, IL 62286, USA.

LIVESAY, Dorothy (Mrs. D.C. Macnair), b. 12 Oct. 1909. University Teacher. Education: B.A., Univ. of Toronto, 1931; Diplome d'Etudes Supérieures, Sorbonne, Paris, 1932; M.A., Educ., Univ. of British Columbia, Vancouver, 1966; Studied at London Inst. of Educ. & UNESCO, Paris, 1959. Married Duncan Macnair w. 2 children. Positions held: UNESCO Engl. Specialist, N. Rhodesia, 1959-63; Lectr., Creative Writing, Univ. of B.C., 1965-66; Writer-in-Residence, Univ. of New Brunswick, Fredericton, 1966-68; Currently, Assoc. Prof., Dept. of Engl., Univ. of Alta., Edmonton. Published works incl: Signpost, 1932; Day & Night, 1944; Poems for People, 1947; Call My People Home, 1950; The Colour of God's Face, 1965; Plainsongs, 1969; Other: The Sculpture of Poetry (Can. Literature), 1965; A Prairie Sampler (Mosaic), 1970; Ed., The Collected Poems of Raymond Knister, 1949. Contbr. to (Anthols.): Canadian Anthology, 1956; Penguin Book of Canadian Verse, 1958; Oxford Book of Canadian Verse, 1965; Commonwealth Poems of Today, 1967; Poets Between the Wars, 1967; Modern Canadian Verse, 1967; (jrnls.): Outposts; Adam; Canadian Forum; Prism International; Queen's Quarterly; Fiddlehead; Poetry Australia. Hons: Gov. General's Medal for Poetry, 1944, 47; Royal Soc. Lorne Pierce Medal for Lit., 1947; 2 Can. Coun. Awards for study in Engl. Teaching. Address: POB 425, Sechelt, B.C., Canada.

LIVINGSTON, Myra Cohn, b. 17 Aug. 1926. Author; Teacher; Lecturer. Education: B.A., Sarah Lawrence Coll., 1948. Married Richard Roland Livingston, 3 children. Positions held: Tchr. & Lectr. in many places in U.S.A.; currently Poet in Res., Beverly Hills Unified Schl. Dist.; Lectr. for Univ. of Calif. Ext., 5 Campuses; Tchr., UCLA Ext. on Poetry for Children & Creative Writing with Children. Memberships: Tex. Inst. of Letters; Southern Calif. Coun. of Lit. for Children & Young People (formerly 1st V.P.); Authors' Guild; PEN. Published works: Whispers & Other Poems, 1958; Wide Awake & Other Poems, 1959; I'm Hiding, 1961; See What I Found, 1962; I Talk to Elephants, 1962; I'm Not Me, 1963; Happy Birthday, 1964; The Moon and a Star & Other Poems, 1965; I'm Waiting, 1966; Old Mrs. Twindlytart & Other Rhymes, 1967; A Tune Beyond Us (ed.), 1968; A Crazy Flight & Other Poems, 1969; Speak Roughly to Your Little Boy (Ed.), 1971; The Malibu & Other Poems, 1972; Listen, Children, Listen (Ed.), 1972; What a Wonderful Bird the Frog Are (Ed.), 1973; When You Are Alone/It Leaves You Capone: An Approach to Creative Writing with Children, 1973; The Poems of Lewis Carroll (Ed.), 1973. Recip. var. awards. Address: 9308 Readcrest Dr., Beverly Hills, CA 90210, U.S.A.

LIVINGSTONE, Douglas (James), b. 5 Jan. 1932. Bacteriologist. Published works: The Skull in the Mud, 1960; Sjambok & Other Poems from Africa, 1964; Poems (w. Kinsella & Sexton), 1968; Eyes Closed Against the Sun, 1970; The Sea My Winding Sheet (verse play) & Other Poems, 1970. Contbr. to: The London Magazine; Encounter; Listener; New Statesman; Weekend Observer; Outposts; Poetry Review; New Coin (S Africa); Contrast; The Purple Renoster; Rhodesian Poetry; Chirimo (Rhodesia); The Southern Review (USA); The Bulletin (Australia); New Nation (S Africa); Two Tone, (Rhodesia); Poet (India); English. Awards: 1st Prize, Guinness Poetry Comp., Cheltenham Festival, UK, 1965; Cholmondeley Award, 1970. Address: c/o CSIR, PO Box 1, Congella, Natal, South Africa.

LLEWELLYN, David William Alun, b. 17 Apr. 1903. Barrister. Education: M.A., LL.B., St. John's Coll., Cambridge Univ.; Lincolns Inn. Positions held: Attached to Geneva Secretariat, League of Nations, 1936-39; Legal Adviser, Egyptian Govt., Montreux Capitulations Conf. & Reviser of Treaty at Geneva, 1937; Sec., Ctrl. Valuation Bd., Coal Nationalisation, 1947-49. Memberships: Pres., Sunday Tramps (philos. soc. founded by Leslie Stephen), 1951-; Treas. & Councillor, Poetry Soc. of G.B., 1950-62; Pres., Hardwicke Soc. (Bar), 1953; Pres., Union Soc. (Bar), 1935; Authors Club; PEN. Published works: Ballads & Songs, 1921; St. Francis, 1923. Rep. in following anthols: Oxford Book of Spoken Verse, 1957; Modern Lyrical Verse, 1958; Best Poems of Year 1960, 1961; Pattern of Poetry, 1963 (HMV Recording); Lib. of Congress (Wash.) Lit. Recordings, 1966, '68; etc. Contbr. to: Anglo-Welsh Review, 1962-; Aryan Path, 1964-; Punch, 1949-53; Poetry Review; Chambers Jrnl.; Time & Tide; Observer; Sunday Times; London Welshman, etc. Recip., Chancellor's Gold Medal, Cambridge Univ. Address: 52 Silchester Pk., Glenageary, Dun Laoghaire, Co. Dublin, Ireland.

LLEWELLYN-WILLIAMS, Hilary Maria Beatrice Helen, b. 27 Sept. 1951. Library Assistant. Education: B.A., Southampton Univ., 1973. Married. Memberships: The Poetry Soc., London; Hampshire Poets; Southampton Poetry Circle. Contbr. to: The Cornishman; Scoop (Lit. mag. for schls.); The Muse; Dorking Advertiser; Audio-Visual Developments (Oxford) Ltd.; Stroud Fest. Publ., 1971; Surrey Life; Hampshire Poets; 'P' Poetry Mag. Poem 'Green' in publ. & on L.P. record, Audio-Visual Devs. Ltd., 1967. Honours, awards: 1st Prize for 'Waking to Rainsmell', Guildford Fest., 1969; County Prize for 'Hero', Brooke Bond Nat. Schls. Comp., 1969; 2nd Prize for 'Rex Futurus', Guinness Int. Poetry Comp., Stroud Fest., 1971. Address: 114 Gordon Ave., Southampton, SO2 1DA, U.K.

LLOYD, Cecil Robert, pen name **BYRD, Lloyd,** b. 14 Sept. 1927. Cultural Research Analyst; Poet; Actor. Education: Univ. of Minn., 1944-51; Univ. of N.M. Positions held: Photo-Optical Tech., Field Measurements Br., White Sands Missile Range, 1952-57; Photographer, Harvard Peabody Mus. of Arch. & Ethnol., Nat. Geol. Soc. Jt. Field Expeditions, Hell Gap, Wyoming, 1960-63; Cultural Rsch. Analyst, Albuquerque Model Cities Prog., 1969-70. Member, Poetry Soc. of Am., 1964. Contbr. to: The N.M. Independent; Fervent Valley; Encanto Mag.; The N.M. Qtly.; The Fiddlehead; De Paul Lit. Mag.; The Caliche Co. Rendering Works; The Diamond Anthol., etc. Address: 424 Jefferson Ave., N.E., Apt. 2, Albuquerque, NM 87108, U.S.A.

LLOYD, David Dilsworth Talbott, b. 9 May 1930. Teacher. Education: B.A., Montclair State Tchrs. Coll., 1952; M.A., Univ. of Mich., 1957. Married Martha C. Walker, 5 children. Positions held: Tchng. Fellowships, Univ. of Mich., 1955-57; Drama Coach, Olivet Coll., Mich., 1957-59; Prof. of Engl. & Communications, Glassboro State Coll., N.J., 1959-. Memberships: Pres., Leaves of Grass Poetry Soc., 1971-72; N.J. Poetry Soc.; V.P., ibid, 1970-72; Bd. Mbr., 1970-72; N.J. State Coun. on the Arts – Poet in the Classroom Workshops in N.J., 1970-73. Published works: The Circle, a book of Haiku & Inkings, 1974. Contbr. to: Doubleday Anchor Anthol. of Am. Haiku Poets, 1974; Dragonfly; Haiku West; Modern Haiku; Haiku Mag.; Janus & SCTH; The Windless Orchard; Tweed; Byways; Boston Times; N.J. Poetry Soc. Anthols., etc. Recip. var. poetry awards inclng: Am. Poets Fellowship Award, Modern Haiku, 1971. Address: 2 Washington Ave., Pitman, NJ 08071, U.S.A.

LLOYD, Susan Jacqueline, pen name **JAMES, Susan,** b. 22 Aug. 1946. Research Assistant. Education: External hons. degree in hist., London Univ., 1973. Married Ivor Lloyd. Positions held: Personal Asst. to Dir. of an Engrng. Industry, 1967-69; Rsch. Asst. of Hist. Proj. & on Med. Proj.. 1969-73. Memberships:

Oxford Poetry Grp.; Oxford Writers' Circle; Critical Quarterly Soc. Contbr. to: Ver Poets; Critical Quarterly; Isis (Oxford Univ. Mag.) Recip., 3rd prize, Stroud Fest., 1966. Address: The Briars, Gadden Hill, Finstock, Oxford OX7 3DW, U.K.

LLYWELYN-WILLIAMS, Alun, b. 27 Aug. 1913. Director of Extra Mural Studies. Education: Univ., Coll., Cardiff, U.K. Married, 2 daughters. Positions held: Jr. Libn., Nat. Lib. of Wales, Aberystwyth; Announcer & Talks Producer, BBC, Cardiff, London & Bangor; Dir. of Extra Mural Studies, Univ. Coll. of North Wales, Bangor, 1948-. Mbr., Yr Academi Gymreig (The Welsh Acad.) Published works: Cerddi (poems) 1944; Pont y Caniedydd, 1956. Contbr. to: The Oxford Book of Welsh Verse; The Penguin Book of Welsh Verse; Cerddi Heddiw, & Cerddi '70, '71, '72, '73; Poetry Wales; Lleufer; Taliesin; (Tir Newydd); y Faner; (y Llenor); y Traethodydd. Transl. of poems into Engl. have appeared in The Western Mail; Life & Letters; A History of Welsh Lit.; Introducing Welsh Poetry. Address: Pen-y-Lan, 55 Ffordd Belmont, Bangor, Caernarvonshire, U.K.

LOCHHEAD, Douglas Grant, b. 25 Mar. 1922. Librarian. Education: B.A., McGill Univ., Montreal, 1943; M.A., Univ. of Toronto, 1947; B.L.S., McGill Univ., Montreal, 1951. Positions held: Univ. Libn., Dalhousie Univ., Halifax, N.S., 1953-60; Dir. of Libs., York Univ., Toronto, & Asst. Prof. of Engl., 1960-63; Libn., Massey Coll., Univ. of Toronto, 1963-; Special Lectr., Dept. of Engl., Univ. Coll. & Grad. Dept. of Engl., Univ. of Toronto, 1965-; Prof. of Engl., ibid; Assoc. Instr., Fac. of Lib. Sci., Univ. of Toronto, etc. Memberships incl: V.Chmn., League of Canadian Poets, 5 yrs.; Pres., Bibliographical Soc. of Canada, 1974-76. Published works: The Heart is Fire, poems, 1959; It Is All Around, poems, 1960; Poems in Folio, No. 1, 1959, No. 2, 1963; Poet Talking, 1964; A & B & C &: an Alphabet, 1969; Millwood Road Poems, 1970. Contbr. to: Canadian Forum; Canadian Poetry; Contemporary Verse; Dalhousie Review; Descant; Queen's Qtly.; Saturday Night; White Pelican. Address: Massey Coll. Lib., 4 Devonshire Pl., Toronto, Ont. M5S 2E1, Canada.

LOCKE, Duane. College Professor. Education: Ph.D., Univ. of Fla., specializing in lit. of Engl. Renaissance. Positions held: Poet in Res., Univ. of Tampa; Prof. of Engl.; Ed., UT Review. Published works: (poetry books) From the Bottom of the Sea, 1968; Inland Oceans, 1968; Dead Cities, 1969; Light Bulbs' Lengthened Eyelashes & Storks' Nests, 1969; Rainbow Under Boards, 1969; The Submerged Fern In the Waistline of Solitude, 1972. Rep. in following anthols: Southern Writing in the Sixties: Poetry, 1967; Christmas 1968: 14 Poets, 1968; The Living nderground: An Anthol. of Contemporary Am. Poetry, 1969; Am. Univ. Poets, Madras, India; Poesia Mundo, Buenos Aires, Argentina; New Generation: Poetry, 1971; Assembling the Madhouse: A Collection of Eight Poets, 1972. Contbr. of poems to num. mags., jrnls. inclng: Nimrod; The Writer's Voice; Etchings; Wormwood Review; Bitterroot; Poetmeat; Am. Poet; South & West. Address: 2716 Jefferson St., Tampa, FL 33602, U.S.A.

LOCKLIN, Gerald Ivan, b. 17 Feb. 1941. Associate Professor of English. Education: B.A., John Fisher Coll., Rochester, N.Y.; Ph.D., Univ. of Ariz., Tucson. Positions held: Assoc. Prof. of Engl., Calif. State Univ. at Long Beach. Published works: Sunset Beach, 1967; The Toad Poems, 1970; Poop, & Other Poems, 1972; Son of Poop, 1973; Loced In (short stories), 1973; Toad's Europe (poems), 1973. Contbr. of over 200 poems to periodicals (mainly the Wormwood Review). Recip., Wormwood Award for 'Poop', 1972. Address: c/o Dept. of Engl., CSULB, Long Beach, CA 90840, U.S.A.

LOCKWOOD, Sarah (Peple), b. 14 Jul. 1921. Poet and Platform Reader. Education: St. Catherine's School, Richmond, Va.; Randle Ayrton's Coll. of Drama, Stratford-on-Avon and The Old Vic Dramatic School,

London, UK. Married to Frank Lockwood; 1 d. Positions held: Toured with repertory company and undertook film work in UK; On Staff of the Dellbrook-Shenandoah College Writers' Conference, 1971-. Memberships: Composers, Authors & Artists of America, Inc.; Poetry Soc. of America; The Poetry Soc. (UK); The Internat. Poetry Soc.; Acad. of American Poets; The Poetry Soc. of Virginia. Published works: New Lyrics, 1972; Pegasus In The Seventies (Co-Editor with Bernard Grebanier and Anne Marx), an anthol., 1973. Contbr. to: Poetry Of Today; The Lyric; Poet Lore. Awards: Poetry Soc. of America, Christopher Morley Mem. Award, 1971; Two prizes, Poetry Soc. of Virginia, 1970-71; Three prizes, The Lyric, 1968-73; Irene Leach Sonnet prize, 1970; The Mason Sonnet Award, Composers, Authors and Artists of America, Inc., 1973; First Prize, "Narrative Poem" Award, Poet Lore, 1972. Address: 5101 Wythe Ave., Richmond, VA 23226, USA.

LODGE, Edith Bennett, pen name LODGE, Edith, b. 17 Nov. 1908. Writer. Education: Oberlin Coll., Ohio, B.A., 1929; Old Dominion Univ., Norfolk, Va., M.A., 1970. Married, Dr. George Townsend Lodge, Prof. Psychology, Old Dominion Univ., 1 s., 1 d. Positions held: Library Asst., Teacher's Coll., NYC, 1944-45; Library Asst., Duke Univ. Library, Durham, NC., 1955-58; Lecturer in Engl., Old Dominion Univ., 1970-. Memberships: Poetry Soc. of America; Poetry Soc. of Va.; Acad. of American Poets. Published works: Song of the Hill, 1964. Contbr. to: (anthols.) The Golden Year, 1960; PSA Diamond Anthol., 1971; (journals and newspapers) Arrows in the Air; Kaleidograph; American Haiku; NY Times; Saturday Review; Christian Century; Presbyterian Survey; Carmel Pine Cone; Portland Oregonian; Lantern; Imprints Qtly.; American Bard; Lyric; Pulpit; Poet Lore, etc. Awards: Irene Leache Memorial First Prize for a sonnet, 1964, and for a lyric, 1965. Address: 1329 Oak Park Ave., Norfolk, VA 23503, USA.

LOEWINSOHN, Ron(ald) William, b. 15 Dec. 1937. Academic Teacher. Education: A.B., Univ. of Calif., Berkeley, 1967. Married w. 2 sons. Positions held: Taught Poetry workshops, San Francisco State Coll., 1960-61; Centre for Adult Educ., Cambridge, Mass., 1968; Grad. Student, Teaching Fellow, Harvard Univ., Cambridge, 1967-. Published works: Watermelons, 1959; The World of the Lie, 1963; Against the Silences to Come, 1965; L'Autre, 1967; Lying Together, Turning the Head & Shifting the Weight, The Produce District & Other Places, Moving-A Spring Poem, 1967; The Sea, Around Us, 1968; The Step, 1968; Meat Air: Poems 1957-69. Contbr. to (Anthols.): New American Poetry, 1960; Junge Amerikanische Lyrik, 1961; Beat, 1962; Poeisa degli Ultimi Americani, 1964; New Writing in the USA, 1967; Uvöltés: A Beat Nemzédekröl, 1967; (jrnls): Poetry; Tri-Quarterly; Capitalist Bloodsucker; Open Space; Yugen; R.C. Lion. Hons: Poets Foundation Award, 1963; Am. Acad. of Poets' Irving Stone Award, 1966; Woodrow Wilson Graduate Fellowship, 1967-68.

LOGAN, Dixie, b. 19 Oct. 1907. Nurse. Married Neil Logan. Contbr. to: Leavenworth Echo; Pageant of Poetry. Address: 202 Commercial St., Leavenworth, WA 98826, U.S.A.

LOGAN, John Burton, b. 23 Jan. 1923. Professor of English. Education: B.A., Zoology, Coe Coll., Cedar Rapids, Iowa, 1943; M.A., Engl., Univ. of Iowa, Iowa City, 1949; Georgetown Univ., Wash. D.C. Married w. 9 children. Positions held: Tutor, St. John's Coll., Annapolis Md., 1947-51; Assoc. Prof., The Gen. Prog., Univ. of Notre Dame, Ind., 1951-63; Vis. Prof., Dept. of Engl., Univ. of Wash., Seattle, 1965; San Francisco State Univ., 1965-66; Prof. of Engl., State Univ. of N.Y., Buffalo, 1966-; Ed., Choice Poetry Mag., Chgo. Published works: Cycle for Mother Cabrini, 1955; Ghosts of the Heart, 1960; Spring of the Thief, 1963; The Zig-Zag Walk, 1969; Other (fiction): The Bishop's Suite, 1966; The Last Class, 1958; The Loss, 1962; The Panic Round, 1965; (Criticism): Dylan Thomas & the Ark of Art, 1961; The Organ Grinder & the

Cockatoo: Poetry of E.E. Cummings, 1961; Psychological Motifs in Melville's Pierre, 1967. Contbr. to (Anthols.): New Poets of England & America, 1962; American Poetry, 1964; A Book of Love Poems, 1965; New Modern Poetry, 1967; Contemporary American Poets, 1969; (Jrnls.): Sewanee Review; Poetry; Minnesota Review. Hons: Ind. Schl. of Letters Fellowship, 1965; 69; Miles Modern Poetry Award, 1967; Rockefeller Grant, 1968. Address: Dept. of Engl., State Univ. of N.Y., Buffalo, N.Y., USA.

LOGUE, Christopher. b. 23 Nov. 1926. Poet. Published works: Wand & Quadrant, 1953; The Weakdream Sonnets, 1955; Devil, Maggot and Son, 1956; Songs, 1959; She Sings, He Sings, 1957; A Song for Kathleen, 1958; The Song of the Dead Soldier, 1959; Songs from the Lily-White Boys, 1960; Selection from a Correspondence Between an Irishman & A Rat, 1966; Christopher Logue's ABC, 1966; Pax, 1967; New Numbers, 1969. Red Bird (w. music by Tony Kinsey, gramophone record). Address: c/o Jonathan Cape, Ltd., 30 Bedford Sq., London, WC1, UK.

LOIR, Germaine, b. 15 July 1925. Librarian. Education: B.A., Brooklyn Coll.; B.L.S., Pratt Inst. Lib. Schl.; M.A., Columbia Univ.; student of Mark Van Doren & Joseph Wood Krutch. Widow of William John Cattani. Positions held: Fac. Mbr., Columbia Univ., Brooklyn Coll., N.Y. Univ., Univ. of Miami, Fla.; Dir. of Rsch. for Collier's Encyclopedia. Memberships: Poetry Soc. of Am.; Composers, Authors & Artists of Am.; Nat. Mbrship. Chmn. for Lit., ibid & V.P. of the local N.Y.C. Chapt. Contbr. to: English Literature & its Backgrounds (textbook-anthol.), 1949; Pegasus in the Seventies, anthol., 1973, etc. Address: 588 West End Ave., Apt. 12 C, N.Y., NY 10024, U.S.A.

LONG, Beatrice Powell, pen names LONG, Bee Bacherig & POWELL, Patsy, b. 8 Oct. 1907. General Insurance Broker; Retired Secretary. Education: Miss. Womens Coll., Hattiesburg; Bowling Green, Ky., Bus. Univ.; Univ. of Tenn. Married Benjamin J. Long. Positions held: Sec., Cashier, Bookkeeper, Credit Mgr., Pvte. Sec., Ins. Broker. Memberships: Past Pres., Memphis Chapt., Credit Women Int.; Former Hostess Chmn., Libn., Recording Sec., Poetry Soc. of Tenn.; Poets' Roundtable of Ark.; Acad. of Am. Poets; Centro Studi e Scambi; Int., Rome; World Poetry Soc. Intercontinental, India. Published works: Reflections 1964; Where Treasures Lie, 1967; author, Memphis Meml. (Stadium) Plaque, commemorating men of WW I, WWII & the Korean War. Contbr. to: Candor; Spirit; Haiku Highlights; Am. Poets; Prairie Poets; United Poets; Jean's Jrnl.; Am. Poetry League Bulletin. Rep. in following anthols: Haiku Highlights Easter Anthol.; Bouquet of Poems (Italy); The Spring Anthol., London, 1969-73; The Clover Collection of Verse, Wash., 1973; Greenhouse Anthol., 1962-69; Am. Poets Anthol., 1965-67; Poems by Poets Roundtable of Ark., 1968-69, etc. Poems broadcast over WBUX & WNAK (pa) & WKNO (Tn), 1973. Recip. var. awards inclng: 1st Prize 1973 Haiku, Am. Fed. of Poets. Address: 103 Eastland Dr., Memphis, TN 38111, U.S.A.

LONG, Sara Louise, b. 4 Sept. 1907. Retired Teacher. Education: B.S., East Tex. State Univ.; Univ. of Tex.; Midwestern Univ. Positions held: Tchr., Commerce, Tex., 5 yrs.; Tchr., Megargel, Tex., 2 yrs.; Tchr., Wichita Falls, Tex., 23 yrs. Memberships: Councillor, Poetry Soc. of Tex.; Past Pres., The Wichita Falls Poetry Soc. (also served as V.P., Treas. & Sec.); Beta Rho Chapt., Delta Kappa Gamma. Published works: (book of poetry) Sundial, 1946. Contbr. to: A Book of the Year, 1953 & '74; Reflections (anthol.), 1971; The Dallas Morning News; Wildfire Mag.; Kaleidograph Mag.; Westminster Mag.; Wichita Falls Record News & Times, etc. Honours, awards incl: The Campbell Couplet Prize Award, Poetry Soc. of Tex., 1953; The Garland Chapter Award, ibid, 1973. Address: 1814 Dayton, Wichita Falls, TX 76301, U.S.A.

LONGCORE, Randall James, b. 19 Feb. 1936. Lecturer in Natural Science & Mathematics.

Education: B.S. (Maths.), Univ. of Mich., Ann Arbor, 1957; M.S. (Maths.), ibid, 1959; A.M. (Hist. of Sci.), Harvard Univ., 1965; Ph.D. (Hist. & Philos. of Sci.), Indiana Univ., Bloomington, pending. Positions held: Assoc. Ed. for Waves: A Tri-Annual York Univ. Mag., York Univ. (one of the founding editors). Member, Poetry Soc. of Mich. Contbr. to: The Woods-Runner, Lake Superior State Coll., Mich.; Peninsula Poets, Poetry Soc. of Mich.; Balloon, Atkinson Coll., York Univ.; Waves: A Tri Annual York Univ. Mag. Address: Atkinson Coll., York Univ., 4700 Keele St., Downsview, Ont., Canada M3J 2R7.

LONGLAND, Jean Rogers, b. 11 Jan. 1913. Librarian; Freelance Poetic Translator. Education: A.B., Wheaton Coll., Mass., 1934; S.B., Simmons Coll., 1935; courses at Boston Univ., Columbia Univ., N.Y. Univ. Positions held: First Cataloguer, The Hispanic Soc. of Am., N.Y., 1936-46; Curator of Portuguese Books, ibid, 1946-53; Curator of the Library, 1953–. Guest Lectr., Cooper Hill Writers Conf., 1970 & City Univ. of N.Y., 1973; Chmn., Panel of poetic transl. at the annual conven. of the Am. Translators Assn., 1971. Memberships: PEN; Poetry Soc. of Am.; Authors Guild; Hispanic Soc. of Am.; Charter Mbr., Phi Lambda Beta; Am. Translators Assn.; Am. Portuguese Soc., etc. Published works: Selections from Contemporary Portuguese Poetry, 1966; Ed., Poetic Translation: A Panel Discussion, 1972. Contracted by the Acad. of Am. Poets to make literal translations of modern Brazilian poetry for the use of Am. poets in preparing its anthol. edited by Elizabeth Bishop & Emanuel Brasil, 1968-71. Has undertaken num. translations & is a contbr. to var. jrnls. Honours, awards incl: 2nd prize, Translation Award, Poet Lore, 1970; Portugal Prize, Int. Poetry Assn. & the Portuguese Govt., 1973. Address: 490 West End Ave., N.Y., NY 10024, U.S.A.

LONGLEY, Michael, b. 27 July, 1939. English Teacher. Education: Trinity Coll., Dublin. Married Edna Longley w. 1 daughter. Positions held: Tchr. of Engl., Royal Belfast Academical Inst., 1964–. Published works: Ten Poems, 1965; Three Regional Voices, 1968; Secret Marriages, 1968; No Continuing City, 1969. Contbr. to (Anthols.): Young Commonwealth Poets '65, 1965; Commonwealth Poems of Today, 1967; Penguin Book of Irish Verse, 1970; Faber Book of Irish Verse, 1970; (Jrnls.): Irish Times; Dublin Mag.; Northern Review; Encounter; Listener; New Statesman. Recip., Eric Gregory Award for Poetry, 1965. Address: 18 Hillside Park, Stranmillis, Belfast 9, Northern Ireland.

LONN, Oystein, b. 12 Apr. 1936. Author. Member, Norwegian Soc. of Authors. Published works: Prosesjonen (short stories), 1966; Kontinentene (novel), 1967; Arkeologene (novel), 1971; Historie (short stories), 1973. Contbr. to: The Literary Review, 1968; Neue Deutsche Hefte, 1967; Vinduet, 1973. Address: 4670 Hornnes, Norway.

LOOTEN, Emmanuel, b. 6 Nov. 1908. Writer. Educ: Univ. of Lille, France. Memberships incl: Sec., Acad. Septentrionale, 1959; PEN Club Int.; Syndicate of Literary Critics; Int. Assn. of Literary Critics; Mbr., num. confs., etc. Published works incl: Flamme, 1942; Masque de Cristal, 1944; Sortilèges, suivie de La Légende de Godelieve; La Saga de Lug Hallewijn, 1950; Sangs Bruts, 1952; Cellule de l'Indifferenza; Oiw, 1956; Khaim, 1960; Hai Kai, 1960; Liturgies Flamandes; Exil Intérieur; Gwen Fydd; Flandre à Coeur; Le Chaos Sensible; num. films & records. Honours, awards incl: Grand Prix des Lettres; Prix Verlaine; Prix Int. de la Genèse; Gold Laurel, Int. Ctr. of Esthetic Studies, Turin, Italy; Grand Prix Demedts, Marnix Ring, Courtrai. Address: La Capitainerie, 06 Golfe-Juan, France.

LOPEZ, Alonzo, b. 29 Nov. 1949. Poet. Education: Inst. of Am. Indian Arts, Santa Fe, N.M., 4 yrs.; Yale Univ., New Haven, 1 yr.; Wesleyan Univ., Middletown, Conn., 4 yrs. Published works: Whispering Wind, 1972; Songs of a Young Hunter, 1972; Sound of a Distant Drum, 1972. Contbr. to: Craft Horizons, 1966;

Ariz. Highways, 1966; Writers Reader (pamphlet), 1966-68; S.D. Review, 1969; Youth (pamphlet), 1969; Dance with Indian Children (Ctr. for the Arts of Indian Am.), 1972; Akwasasne Notes, 1972; Sun Tracks (Amerind Lit. Qtly.), 1972; Learn with Indian Children, 1972. Honours, awards: 1st prize, Scottsdale Nat. Indian Arts & Crafts Exhib., Ariz., 1966 & 2nd prize, 1967; Patricia Benton Poetry Award, 1966; Hon. Mention, Vincent Price Poetry Awards, 1968. Address: P.O. Box 464, Sells, AZ 85634, U.S.A.

LOPEZ ANGLADA, Luis, b. 13 Sept. 1919. Military Officer. Educ: Univ. of Valladolid; Mil. Studies, Infantry Acad., Zaragoza. Married. Positions held: Served in León, Canary Islands & Madrid; Chief, Army Press Off.; Chief, Cultural Ext. for Youth, 1958-62; Sec., Madrid Athenaeum, 1968-70. Memberships: Spanish-Am. Acad., Cádiz; Acad. of Bellas Artes Purisima Concepcion, Valladolid; Int. Soc. of Literary Critics. Published works incl: (poetry) Impaciencias, 1943; Indicios de la rosa, 1945; Al par de tu sendero, 1946; Destino de la espada, 1947; Continuo mensaje, 1948; La vida conquistada, 1952; Dorada canción, 1954; Elegías del Capitán, 1955; Aventura, 1956; Contemplación de España, 1961; Antología, 1962; Ayer han florecido los papeles donde escribí tu nombre, 1964; Sonetos a Ceuta, 1964; Plaza partida, 1965; Poemas americanos, 1966; Arte de amar, 1967; Escrito para la esperanza, 1968; En los brazoa del mar, 1969; Los amantes, 1972; La areana y los sueños, 1972; (prose) Panorama poético español, 1965; Caminos de la poesía española, 1967; El Duque de Rivas, 1972; Antología de poetas gaditanos del siglo XX, 1972. Contbr. to var. anthols. & mags. Honours, awards: Nat. Prize for Lit., 1961; Prizes, Ceuta & Amantes de Teruel, etc. Address: Calle de Aviación Española 5, Madrid 3, Spain.

LOPEZ DE VICTORIA, María, pen name **LOMAR, Martha,** b. 8 Feb. 1893. Journalist; Housewife. Positions held: Tchr., Public Schl.; Designer; Editor (reviews); Journalist. Memberships: Bd. Dirs., Sociedad Puertorriqueña de Periodistas y Escritores; Sociedad Roerick; Hon. Mbr., Sociedad de Graduadas de La Universidad de Puerto Rico; Bd. Dirs., Sociedad de Escritores de Puerto Rico; Am. Int. Acad., etc. Published works: Silabario de Espuma (poems), 1931; Vejez Sonora (poems), 1931; Por Aquí Pasa un Hombre (poems), 1939; La Canción de la Hora (poems), 1959; Trujillo y Yo (prose), 1959; Seis Cuentos Tristes (prose), 1969. Contbr. to: El Imparcial; El Mundo; El Día; La Correspondencia de Puerto Rico; Puerto Rico Ilustrado; Alma Latina; Artes y Letras; Isla, etc. Address: 1133 S.E. 18th St., Caparra Terr., Puerto Rico 00921.

LORD, Gigi. Poet; Social Worker. Education: B.S. & M.A., N.Y. Univ.; grad. study, Columbia Univ., Schl. of Soc. Work. Positions held: Supvsr. in tchng. & training of students & Soc. Wkr. in individual & grp. casework; Rehabilitation work w. displaced persons in Europe; Rsch. work w. battered children. Memberships: Poetry Socs. of Am., England & Pa.; Acad. of Am. Poets. Published works: (book) Toppling After Itself, 1969. Contbr. to: Beloit Poetry Jrnl.; Carleton Miscellany; Fiddlehead; Boston Phoenix; Wis. Review. Honours, awards: 1st pl. Award for 'Toppling After Itself', Nat. Fed. of State Poetry Socs., 1968; Premium Award, Poetry Soc. of England, 1969/70; Henry Rago Award, N.Y. Poetry Forum, 1973. Address: 55 – East 21st St., Brooklyn, NY 11226, U.S.A.

LORD, Vera. Housewife. Education: HS; An Honour Grad. of Business Coll.; Univ. Extension Night Courses, 2 yrs.; sev. art courses, etc. Married to Albert Leonard Lord. Positions held: Sessional stenographer during term of Ont. Parliamentary Session, 1 yr., also other positions in accounting etc., Bank head office, etc. Memberships: Hospital Auxiliary. Former memberships include: Women's Canadian Club; Art Gall. of Toronto; N. Toronto Horticultural Soc.; Women's Anglican Church organization (Exec. member for sev. yrs.); Canadian Opera Guild (1960 donor membership), etc. Contbr. to: (anthols.)

American Poetry, Old and New, 1965; A Burst of Trumpets, 1966; Yearbook of Modern Poetry, 1971; Anthol. of American Poetry, Book X, 1970, Book X1, 1971; also poems and articles (1965-67) to Parish Newsletter (St. Philip's Anglican Church, Weston, Ont.). Address: Apt. 1210, 236 Dixon Rd., Weston, Ont., M9P 2M3, Canada.

LORDE, Audre Geraldin, pen name **DOMINI, Rey,** b. 18 Feb. 1934. Poet. Education: B.A., Hunter Coll., 1959; M.S., Columbia Univ., 1960; Univ. of Mex. Positions held: Asst. Prof. Engl., John Jay Coll. of Criminal Justice, 1970–; Lectr., City Coll. & Lehman Coll.; Poet-in-Res., Tougaloo Coll., Jackson, Miss. Member, Harlem Writers Guild. Published works: The First Cities, 1968; Cables to Rage, 1970; From A Land Where Other People Live, 1973. Contbr. to: Mass. Review; Transatlantic Review; Women: A Jrnl. of Liberation; Aphra; Freedom Ways; Jrnl. of Black Poetry; Black World; Fits; Parasite; Venture Mag.; PEN Jrnl.; Works; Liberation; Harlem Writer's Qtly. Honours, awards: Nat. Endowment to the Arts Grant, 1968; Creative Artist Public Service Grant, 1972. Address: 207 St. Pauls Ave., Staten Island, NY 10304, U.S.A.

LORENZ, Lincoln, b. 17 Jan. 1895. Writer. Education: A.B., Harvard Univ., U.S.A.; A.M., ibid; Ph.D., Stanford Univ. Positions held: Instr. in Engl., Univ. of Wis., Univ. of Tex., Univ. of Calif., L.A.; Lectr. in Engl., Western Md. Coll.; Prof. of Engl. & Hd. of Dept., High Point Coll. Mbr., Poetry Soc. of Am. Published works: (books) Fall of Apollo: Lost Art & Wisdom of Poetry, 1972; Quest at Dawn, with Preface 'Values in Poetry', 1960; The Admiral & the Empress, 1952; John Paul Jones: Fighter for Freedom & Glory, 1943; The Life of Sidney Lanier, 1935. Address: 2811 Robin Hood Dr., Greensboro, NC 27408, U.S.A.

LORIES, Robert, pen name **TREZEL,** b. 17 Apr. 1925. University Professor. Education: Sc.D. (Physical Chemistry). Positions held: Prof., Univ. of Louvain. Memberships: Association des Ecrivains Belges; Scriptores Catholici. Published works: Citordines, 1953; Les Oiseaux et les Ombres, 1957; Ciels (Prix Max Rose), 1958; Arriere – Pays, 1963; La Faveur des Sources, 1967. Contbr. to: La Revue Nouvelle; Les Cahiers Jean Tousseul; Le Thyrse; La Voix des Poètes; Anthologie de la Dernière Décade; A Quarter Century of Poetry from Belgium, 1970. Recip., Prix Max Rose, 1958. Address: 35 Chaussee de Renaix, Tournai, Belgium.

LORING, Nancy, b. 13 May 1906. Musician; Teacher; Christian Science Practitioner. Education: Winsor School, Boston, Mass.; A.B., Radcliffe Coll., Cambridge, Mass.; Mt. Holyoke Coll.; Gerald Moore (UK), etc. Positions held: Director of Music, Sunset Hill School, Kansas City, Mo., 1932-39; Mt. Holyoke, 1940-41; Director of Choral Music, Concord Acad., Concord; Voice and Music Teacher, 1942-60; Since 1960, CS practitioner. Contbr. to: CS Monitor; CS Journal; CS Sentinel, etc. Address: Box 1157, Duxbury, MA 02332, USA.

LOSSE, Arlyle Mansfield, b. 15 Apr. 1917. Librarian. Education: B.S., Milwaukee State Tchrs. Coll.; M.S. Lib.Sci., Univ. of Wis., Madison. Positions held: Asst., Ref. Dept., Mead Public Lib., Sheboygan, Wis.; Libn., Milwaukee Public Lib. System. Memberships: Art Libraries Society/North America; Acad. of Am. Poets; Nat. League of Am. Pen Women; Wis. Fellowship of Poets. Contbr. to anthols., mags., newspapers inclng: Listen, My Children, 1940; Poems for Mother, 1940; Father, 1957; Northern Spring, 1956; Poems out of Wisconsin, 1961; Poems Out of Wisconsin III, 1967; New Poetry out of Wisconsin, 1969; Wisconsin History in Poetry, books 1-3, 1969-71; The Spring Anthol., 1968-73; Yearbook of Mod. Poetry, 1972; IWWP Anthol., 1972; Poetry of Our Times, 1971; All-Time Favorite Poetry, 1972; Am. Scenes, 1972; Best in Poetry, 1973; Christmas, 1973; Seydell Quarterly; Wis. Poetry Mag.; Cyclo Flame Mag.; Haiku Highlights; ALA Bulletin. Honours, awards: Gold Pin, Milwaukee State

Tchrs. Coll., 1938; Prize for best mod. poem, Nat. Fed. State Poetry Socs., 1964. Address: 4124 W. Fond du Lac Ave., No. 6, Milwaukee, WI 53216, U.S.A.

LOVE, Alice, Hellena Lowery Jezeski, pen name **LOVE, Alice H.,** b. 19 May 1917. Housewife; Painter. Contbr. to: Major Poets, 1972; Pied Piper Press, 1971; David Ross Personal Poetry; Youngs Publs.; Poet Lore; Milwaukee Sentinal; N.Y. Times; Red Book; Pocohontas Sentinal; Chicago Times; Denver Times; Oregonian, Portland; Arkansas Democrat, etc. Address: Ray Ave., Green City, MO 63545, U.S.A.

LOVEL, Isabel Evelyn, b. 24 Oct. 1902. Housewife; School Teacher; Freelance Artist. Education: B.A. in Educ. & B.A. in Art, Southeastern La. Univ., Hammond. Married 1) Harry A. Hatch, div., 2) Walter R. Lovel, dec. Positions held: Schl. Tchr., Careywood, Idaho, 1921-22 & Kellogg, 1922-23; Riveter, Boeing Aircraft Co., Seattle, 1942-45; Newspaper work, Hammond Vindicator, 1953-56; Newspaper Artist, The Sun, Hammond, La., 1956-58; Schl. Tchr., ABC Schl., Hammond, 1969-70. Memberships: La. State Poetry Soc., 1953– (1st V.P. in 1970, to complete husband's term); Nat. League of Am. Pen Women, 1965–. Contbr. to: Lyric Louisiana, 1960, '65, '70; LSPS Yearbooks, sev. yrs.; Portland Oregonian; Columbia Anthol.; The Hammond Vindicator; The Sun; The Daily Star; The Northern Idaho News. Honours, awards: 5th pl., Deep South Writers & Artists Conf. Nat. Contest, 1967; 2nd pl. tie, LSPS Contest, free verse, & 2nd pl., inspirational poem, 1957. Address: 608 West Colorado Ave., Hammond, LA 70401, U.S.A.

LOVELL, Cleoral A. (Mrs. Edward J. Lovell), b. 4 Feb. 1918. Editor, Poet, Writer, Public Relations Worker. Positions held: P.R., St. Joseph's Hosp., Elmira, NY., 1966; Ed., monthly Bulletin, ibid. Memberships: Pres., Elmira Writers Group, 1957-58; Chmn., NY State Poetry Day, 1957-60; Internat. Platform Assoc.; Eastern Centre, Poetry Soc. of England; Am. Poets Fellowship Soc.; Ill. State Poetry; World Poets Resource Ctr., Inc. Published work: Unicorn in the Wilderness (poetry), 1973. Contbr. to: Canadian Home Jrnl.; Seydell Quarterly; Flame; Am. Bard; Rural New Yorker; Home Chat (London); Wash. Evening Star; Boston Globe; Denver Post; Oregonian; Hartford Courant; Ariz. Highways; Elmira Sunday Telegram; Wis. Poetry Mag.; Poetry Digest; Talent; & many anthols. Honours: 2nd Place, Triad Contest, 1957; 1st & 2nd Place, Latona Contest, 1958; 1st Place, Daphnis Contest, 1959; 2nd Place, Snow Poem Contest, 1962; 14th Place, Am. Poetry League Annual Contest, 1963; Winner, William Souers Memorial Contest, Ill. State Poetry Soc., Spring, 1973; Hon. mention, Annual Internat. Platform Assoc. Poetry Contest, Aug., 1972; accepted gift from Kingdom of Saudi Arabia to Int. Who's Who in Poetry, 2nd World Congress of Poets, 1973. Address: 1147 River Rd., Elmira, NY 14903, USA.

LOVIN, Judith Elizabeth Olive, pen name **SMALDON, Judith Elizabeth,** b. 21 Aug. 1943 in Paignton, Devon, UK. Housewife and College Student. Education: Grad. of Ursuline Acad., Galveston, Texas; currently attending the Coll. of the Mainland (the Arts) in Texas City, Texas. Permanent resident in US, but a citizen of UK. Married to John Henry Lovin. Contbr. to: Nat. HS Poetry Anthol., 1963; Baptist Standard; Hilda Butler Farr's Column; The Angels; Choice of the Angels; Karyn; Angel Hour; Internat. Who's Who in Poetry Anthol., 1972-73; Internat. Clover Poetry Anthol., 1973. Awards: 1st place, Catholic Daughters of America contest, 1963; 2nd place, Readers Choice, The Angels, 1965; Cert. of life membership, Clover Internat. Poetry Assoc., 1973; 1st & 2nd place, College of Mainland Poetry Contest, 1973. Address: P.O. Box B., League City, TX 77573, USA.

LOWBURY, Edward Joseph Lister, b. 6 Dec. 1913. Research Bacteriologist; Poet; Writer. Education: St. Pauls School, London; Scholar of Univ. Coll., Oxford; London Hospital Medical Coll.; B.A. (Hons. Physiology), 1936; B.M., B.Ch., 1939; M.A. (Oxon.),

1940; D.M. (1957); F.R.C.Path. (1964); M.R.C.P. (elected 1972). Married to Alison Young (d. of the late Canon Andrew Young, the poet), 3 d. Positions held: Member of the Scientific Staff of the Medical Research Council, since 1947; Bacteriologist to the Industrial Injuries & Burns Research Unit at Birmingham Accident Hospital; Hon. Director of the Hospital Infection Research Lab., since 1964. Membership: Poetry Soc. (UK). Published works: (poetry) Fire, 1934; Port Meadow, 1936; Crossing the Line, 1947; Metamorphoses, 1958; Facing North (w. T. Heywood), 1960; Time for Sale, 1961; New Poems, 1965; Daylight Astronomy, 1968; Figures of Eight, 1969; Green Magic: Poems for Children, 1972; Two Confessions, 1973; The Night Watchman, 1974; (criticism & biog.) Thomas Campion: Poet, Composer, Physician (with T. Salter & A. Young), 1970. Contbr. to: New Statesman; Times Lit. Supp.; Encounter; London Mag.; NY Times; Southern Review; Sunday Times; Critical Qtly.; Review of Engl. Lit.; Ariel; Cambridge Review; Nat. Review; Time & Tide; Birmingham Post; Wave; Penguin New Writing; Western Mail; Extra Verse; Compass; New Engl. Weekly; Palgrave's Golden Treasury (1964); A Map of Modern Verse; Guinness Book of Poetry (1960), etc. Honours: Newdigate Prize (Oxford), 1934; Matthew Arnold Mem. Prize (Oxford), 1937; John Keats Memorial Lecturer (London), 1973. Address: c/o Chatto & Windus Ltd., 42 William IV St., London WC2, UK.

LOWELL, Robert T.S., b. 1 Mar. 1917. Poet. Education: Kenyon Coll., Ohio; Harvard Univ. Published works: Land of Unlikeness, 1944; Lord Weary's Castle, 1946; Poems 1938-49, 1950; The Mills of the Kavanaughs, 1951; Life Studies, 1959; Imitations, 1961; The Old Glory, 1964; For The Union Dead, 1964; Near The Ocean, 1967; The Voyage & Other Versions of Poems by Baudelaire, 1968; Notebooks, 1967-68, 1969. Plays: The Old Glory: Endecott & the Red Cross; My Kinsman, Major Molyneux; Benito Cerano. Awards: Guggenheim Fellow, 1947; Pulitzer Prize, 1947; Am. Acad. of Arts & Letters Prize, 1947; Guinness Poetry Prize, 1959; Nat. Book Award, 1960; Bollingen Translation Prize, 1962. Address: c/o Faber & Faber, Ltd., 3 Queen Square, London, UK.

LOWEN, Marilyn, pen names **MARYAM; FLETCHER, Marilyn Lowen,** b. 1 Nov. 1944. Poet; Mother. Education: Bennington Coll.; Colorado Coll.; Wayne State Univ.; B.A., 1973, Goddard Coll.; Prof. dance study under Holm, Rodgers, Nikolais, Meehan, Dance Theater Workshop of NY; Poetry study under Umbra Soc. of Poets. Positions held: Dance teacher, Michigan, NY, 1958-72; Teacher and Administrator of Early Childhood Education Progs., Mississippi, 1965-68. Published work: How We Smelled and Why, 1968. Contbr. to: (anthols.) Campfires of the Resistance, 1971; The New Women, 1970; Sisterhood is Powerful, 1970; (newspapers, journals) Other Scenes; Liberated Guardian; Rat Newspaper; Off Our Backs; Reflections; Feelings; Free Palestine; Toward Revolutionary Art. Address: 243 East Broadway, Apt. 5F, New York, NY 10002, USA.

LOWENFELS, Walter, b. 10 May 1897. Poet. Memberships: PEN; Authors Guild; Poetry Soc. of Am. Published works incl: (poetry) Episodes & Epistles, 1925; Finale of Seem, 1929; Apollinaire, 1930; Elegy for D.H. Lawrence, 1932; The Suicide, 1932; Sonnets of Love & Liberty, 1955; American Voices, 1959; Song of Peace, 1959; Some Deaths, 1964; Land of Roseberries, 1965; Translations from Scorpius, 1966; Thou Shalt Not Overkill, 1968; Found Poems & Others, 1973; (play) U.S.A. With Music, 1930; (prose) To An Imaginary Daughter, 1964; The Life of Fraenkel's Death (w. Howard McCord), 1970; Robert Gover's The Portable Walter, 1968; The Poetry of My Politics, 1969; The Revolution is to be Human, 1973. Ed. of: Walt Whitman's Civil War, 1960; Selections from Leaves of Grass, 1961; Poets of Today: A New Am. Anthol., 1964; Where is Vietnam? Am. Poets Respond, 1967; New Jazz Poets, 1967; In the Time of Revolution:

Poems from our Third World, 1969; The Writing on the Wall: Protest Poems, Whitman To Today, 1969; The Tenderest Lover: Whitman's Erotic Poetry, 1970; From the Belly of the Shark, 1973. Address: Boulder Dr., Peekskill, NY 10566, U.S.A.

LOWENSTEIN, Tom, occasional pen name **SAMUEL, Gutkin,** b. 15 Aug. 1941. Teacher. Education: B.A., Queens' Coll., Cambridge Univ., 1965; Cert. Ed., Univ. of Leicester, 1967. Positions held: Taught at South Hackney Schl., London, U.K., 1967-71; & at Northwestern Univ., Evanston, Ill., U.S.A., 1971-74. Published works: Our After-fate (poems), 1971; Eskimo Songs from Canada & Greenland (translations), 1973; I'll Make Me a World, anthol. in Six vols., 1974; Mrs. Owl & the Field Marshall, poems, 1974. Contbr. to: Poetry Review; The Scotsman; Tribune; Paris Review; Chicago Review; The World; Telephone; The Chelsea Review; Egg; Aspen Leaves; Miss. Valley Review; Out of Sight; Chicago Express; European Judaism; Calif. Qtly.; Second Aeon. Address: Dept. of Engl., Northwestern Univ., Evanston, IL 60201, U.S.A. or Queens' Coll., Cambridge, U.K.

LOWRY, Betty, b. 24 July 1927. Writer. Education: A.B., Univ. of Calif., Berkeley, 1948. Married Ritchie Peter Lowry, 2 children. Positions held: Freelance Writer, 1947–; Copywriter to copy chief & account exec., Abbott Kimball Co. (Advt.), San Francisco, 1948-50; Dir., Young Homemaker Div., Jackson Furniture Co., Oakland, Calif., 1950-52; Columnist, 'Family Travel' City Desk Features, N.Y., 1966-73. Memberships: New England Poetry Club; Pres., Wellesley Chapt., Nat. League of Am. Pen Women; Sec., Boston Chapt., Women in Communications, Inc. Contbr. to: Christian Sci. Monitor; Yankee; Calif. Crossroads; The Pen Woman; The Christian; Its Own Excuse; Author & Jrnlst.; Living; The Villager; Ohio Motorist; AAUW Jrnl.; Cats; America, etc. Honours, awards: 1st pl. nat., AAUW, 1964; 4th pl. nat., Writers' Digest, 1966; 2nd pl. nat., AAUW, 1963. Address: 79 Moore Rd., Wayland, MA 01778, U.S.A.

LUBBE, Catherine Case, b. 24 Sept. 1898. Instructor; Poet. Education: Columbia Conservatory of Music & Dramatic Art; Northern Ill. Univ.; Lyceum Arts Schl. Married, John A. Lubbe. Positions held: Instr., Pub. & Pvte. Schls. of Ill. Memberships: Corresponding Sec., Poetry Soc. of Tex., 1952-56; Dir. & active on many commns., ibid, 1957–; 3rd Vice-Pres., Nat. Fed. State Poetry Socs., Inc., 1968-72, 2nd Vice-Pres., 1972-73, 1st Vice-Pres., 1973–; Sponsorship Chairman, 1972-74; Registrar, Nat. Convention, ibid, 1965; Apptd. Administrator of Whitney & Vaida Stewart Montgomery (Kaleidograph Publishers) Literary Estate, 1972. United Poets Laureate Internat.; La. State Poetry Soc.; Vachel Lindsay Assn.; Fndr., Acad. of Am. Poets; Avalon World Arts Acad.; Hon. Mbr., Eugene Field Soc. of Authors & Journalists; Charter mbr., Quill Club, Colo. Springs. Contbr. to: Dallas Morning News; New Orleans Times; Colo. Springs Gazette Telegraph; Williamsport Daily Sun; Interludes; Ave Maria; Attic Salt; Kaleidograph; Scimitar & Song; Cyclotron; South & West; Child Welfare; Books of the Year, Poetry Soc. of Tex.; Surf, Stars & Stone; Poets of Am.; Avalon Anthol. of Tex. Poets; Moon in the Steeple; Avalon Anthol., 1962; The White Heron; Hawk & Whippoorwill Recalled; Encore; Progressive Life; Laurel Leaves; Poems by Poets, 1973; Louisiana State Poetry Soc. Anthol., 1972-73 & many others. Honours: Gold Medal for La., NY World's Fair Poetry Day, 1940; Poetry Soc. of Tex. Awards, including: Song Lyric, 1954, '57, & Nyogen Senzaki Mem. Haiku Award, 1966; Old South Prize, 1971, Edsel Ford Memorial Award, 1971, Purple Heart Award, 1971. UN Day Leadership Award, Philippine Assoc. of Drs. in Law, Internat. Acad. of Leadership & United Poets Laureate Internat., 1967; Decretum, Gold Medal, UPLI, 1968; LPD, Int. Acad. Ldrship., 1969; LHD, Free Univ. of Asia, 1970. Address: 419 Clermont Ave., Dallas, TX 75223, USA.

LUBBE, John Andrew, b. 10 Jan. 1896. Retired

Government Official. Education: Nat. Bus. Coll., Mnpls., Minn. Married Catherine Case Lubbe, 2 sons. Positions held: U.S. Forest Serv., 1918-42; Regl. Admin. Officer, Office of Defense Transportation, WWII, Tex., La., Okla., N.M., 1942-46; Exec. positions in Finance & Budget Divs., U.S. Veterans Admin., 1947-58. Memberships: Poetry Soc. of Tex., 1958–; Treas., ibid, 1962-68; served on Finance, Annual Awards, Awards Dinner, Editl. (Book of the Yr.), Yrbook Sales Chmn., 1962–; Nat. Fed. State Poetry Socs., 1965–. Donor, John A. Lubbe Annual Award, Poetry Soc. Tex., 1960–. Donor, Lubbe Annual Award, Nat. Fed. State Poetry Socs., 1971–. Honours, awards: Cited, 35 yrs. serv., Am. Red Cross, 1956, 40 yrs. serv., U.S. Govt., 1958, & serv., Poetry Soc. of Tex., 1969; Title of Treas. Emeritus, ibid, 1970, Life Mbrship., 1974. Address: 419 Clermont Ave., Dallas, TX 75223, U.S.A.

LUCAS, Georgia Briggs. Investments Manager. Education: Univ. of Tex. Memberships: Acad. of Am. Poets; Nat. League of Am. Pen Women; Women in Communications; Poetry Soc. of Tex.; Austin Poetry Soc.; Past Pres., Kwill Klub; Nat. Writers Club. Published works: Prelude (book of poetry). Contbr. to: The Christian Advocate; Dallas News; The Pen Woman; Tex. Lit. Quarterly; This Friendly Shore; The College Book of Verse; Go; Drug Topics; The News; The Messenger; We The People; The Bright Scrawl; Poetry Digest; Poets of the Lone Star State; Visions in Verse; 1886 Gazette, etc. Recip. of prizes from Poetry Socs. of Tex. & Austin. Address: 1801 Lavaca Apt.7C, Austin, TX 78701, U.S.A.

LUCAS, John, b. 26 June 1937. University Teacher. Education: 1st class degree in philos. & Engl. lit., Univ. of Reading, 1959; Ph.D., 1965. Married Pauline van Meeteren, 1 son, 1 daughter. Positions held: Asst. Lectr., Univ. of Reading, 1961-64; Lectr., Univ. of Nottingham, 1964-70; Vis. Prof. of Engl., Univs. of Maryland & Ind., U.S.A., 1967-68; Sr. Lectr., Univ. of Nottingham, U.K., 1970–. Memberships: Adviser, Young Writers Assn.; Lit. Panel, Arts Assn. Published works: About Nottingham, 1971; A Brief Bestiary, 1972; Chinese Sequence, 1972; For Louis Armstrong, 1972. Contbr. to: Tribune, Transatlantic Review; N.Y. Times; Phoenix; Ambit; Poetry Workshop; Voyages; Dryad; Scrip; Spectator; Orbis; Tamesis; Calvert Review; Western Humanities Review; Prairie Schooner; New Chapter; Unicorn, etc. Address: 19 Devonshire Ave., Beeston, Notts., U.K.

LUCIE-SMITH, (John) Edward (McKenzie), b. 27 Feb. 1933. Free-lance Writer, Broadcaster, Journalist. Education: B.A., Merton Coll., Oxford Univ., UK, 1951-54. Positions held: Advertising, 10 yrs. Memberships: Fellow, Royal Soc. of Lit. Publications: Fantasy Pamphlet No. 25, 1954; A Tropical Childhood, 1961; Confessions & Histories, 1964; Penguin Modern Poets, No. 6 (co-author), 1964; Jazz for the NUF, 1965; Borrowed Emblems, 1967; Towards Silence, 1968; More Beasts for Guillaume Apollinaire, portfolio, 1968; Egyptian Ode, 1969; (translns.) Jonah, by Jean-Paul de Dadelsen, 1967; Five Great Odes, by Paul Claudel, 1967. Contbr. to: (anthols.) A Group Anthol., 1963; The Penguin Book of Elizabethan Verse, 1965; The Liverpool Scene, 1967; (Ed.) The Penguin Book of Satirical Verse, 1967; Holding Your Eight Hands: A Book of SF Verse, 1969, '70; Penguin Book of Elizabethan Verse, 1967; the Liverpool Scene, 1967; British Poetry Since 1945, 1970; A Primer of Experimental Verse 1870-1922, 1971; (jrnls.) Audience; Beloit Poetry Jrnl.; Critical Qtly.; Delta; Departure; Encounter; Flame; Isis; Listener; London Mag.; Meanjin; New Statesman; Outposts; Poetry Rev.; San Francisco Rev.; Shenandoah; Spectator; Sunday Times; Time & Tide; Umbrella; Sussex Outlook; Tribune; Union; Vortex; Western Mail; Times Lit. Supp.; Univ. of Kansas City Rev.; NY Times Supp.; Transatlantic Rev.; Arts in Society; Bulletin; ICA Bull.; Chirimo; Liberté; Posésie Vivante; Poetry India; Priapus; Slovenske Poh'lady; Southern Rev.; Modern Poetry in Transln.; Spindrift; New Yorker. Honours: John Llewellyn Rhys Mem. Prize, 1961; Arts Coun.

Award, 1961. Address: 24 Sydney St., London, SW3, UK.

LUCY, Sean, b. 12 Mar. 1931. Professor of Modern English. Education: B.A., Univ. Coll., Cork, Ireland, 1952; M.A., ibid, 1957. Married, 5 children. Positions held: Sr. Engl. Master, Prior Park, Bath, 1957-61; Asst. Lectr. in Engl., Univ. Coll., Cork, 1961-67; Prof. of Modern Engl., ibid, 1967–. Memberships: Chmn., Cork Conference, Subcomm. of the Int. Assn. for the Study of Anglo Irish Lit., 1973. Published works: T.S. Eliot & the Idea of Tradition (criticism), 1960; Ed. & Contbr., Irish Poets in English (criticism), 1973; Love Poems of the Irish (anthol.), 1967, reprinted 1973; Five Irish Poets (anthol.), 1970. Contbr. to: Dublin Mag.; Poetry Ireland; Irish Writings; New Irish Writing; Irish Times; Irish Press; Irish Independent; Kilkenny Mag.; The Tablet; Unicorn; Ariel; The Atlantic Monthly; The Hudson Review; Soundings; Radio Eireann, etc. Recip., Irish Arts Coun. Prize, 1954. Address: Dept. of Engl., Univ. Coll., Cork, Ireland.

LUECKE, Jane-Marie, b. 24 Apr. 1924. Teacher. Education: B.A., Benedictine Heights Coll., 1948; M.A., Marquette Univ., 1956; Ph.D., Notre Dame Univ., 1964. Positions held: Tchr., Engl. & Jrnlsm., H.S., 10 yrs.; Dir. of Pub. Rels Prog.; Dean & Asst. Prof. of Engl., Coll., 5 yrs.; Prof. of Engl., Okla. State Univ., 8 yrs. Memberships: Benedictine Order of Cath. Sisters; Fellow, Int. Poetry Soc., U.K. Published works: The Meter & Rhythm of Beowulf. Contbr. to: Spirit, 1964; Cimarron Review, 1967-71; Adam Among the Television Trees, 1971. Address: Dept. of Engl., Okla State Univ., Stillwater, OK 74074, U.S.A.

LUNDE, David Eric, b. 14 Oct. 1941. Teacher: Associate Professor of English. Education: Aramco Sr. Staff School, Abqaiq and Dhahran, Saudi Arabia, until 1956; Grant HS, Portland, Oregon, 1956-57; Mt. Hermon School for Boys, Northfield, Mass., 1957-59; Knox Coll., Galesburgh, Ill., 1959-63, B.A.; Univ. of Iowa, Iowa City, Iowa, 1963-67, M.F.A. Personal details: US citizen, b. in Berkeley California. Parents: John and Alice Lunde. Spent childhood in Saudi Arabia. Managing Editor, Drama & Theatre, 1968-71; Poetry Editor, The Riverside Qtly., 1968–; Co-Editor, The Basilisk Press, 1970–. Positions held: Instr. of Engl., State University of NY Coll. at Fredonia, 1967-69; Asst. Prof., 1969-72, Assoc. Prof., since 1972, SUNY at Fredonia. Memberships: Science Fiction Writers of America, and Science Fiction Writers of America Speakers' Bureau. Publishgd works: Ironic Holidays, 1965; Les Papillons, 1967; Sludge Gulper 1, 1971. Contbr. to: Abbey; Ann Arbor Review; Antigonish Review; Ark River Review; Baby John; Bachaet; The Back Door; Beloit Poetry Journal; Beyond Baroque; Bones; Cafe Solo; Colo. State Review; Concerning Poetry; Connections; December; Edge; Fredonian; The Fredonia Statement; FROM/the other side of silence; Grecourt Review; Hearse; Intrepid; Invisible City; Iowa Review; Jam Today; Just Friends, Kansas City Star; Karamu; La Huerta; Micromegas; Motive; New Worlds; North American Review; Northwest Passage; Open Places; Our Original Sins; Poetry Now; Poetry Northwest; The Quest; Rapport; Riverside Qtly.; Road Apple Review; Search For Tomorrow; Seneca Review; Tampa Poetry Review; Tri Qtly.; West Coast Review; Wind. Awards: Old Gold Fellowship in Writing, Univ. of Iowa, 1966-67; Acad. of American Poets Prize, Univ. of Iowa, 1967; Faculty Research Fellowship, State Univ. of NY, 1969, 1970, 1974; Yaddo Residence Foundation, August, 1972. Address: 1179 Central Ave., Dunkirk, NY 14048, USA.

LUNN, Hilda Beatrice Ellen, pen name **LUNN, Sally,** b. 12 May 1919. Justice of the Peace. Married, 1 son (Martin). Positions held: Legal Sec., Grey's Inn, London; served w. WAAF, 1940, commissioned, 1942; p/t Court Official, 1968-73; Appointed Magistrate, 1973. Memberships: Solihull Writers Workshop; Lit. Sect., Solihull Soc. of Arts; Ver Poets (St. Albans); Poets Vigilantes. Published works: Smashing Against the Air, 1971; O Pussy My Love, 1972; What a

Beautiful Pussy You Are, 1973; To Pet a Leo. Contbr. to: Norfolk News; Glasgow Herald; Solihull News; Ver Poets Broadsheet; Cat Lovers Jrnl.; Radio Birmingham; Norfolk Mag.; Animal Forum, & var. small cat mags. Recip., 2nd Prize, Battle of Britain mag., 1968. Address: 56 Stoneleigh Rd., Solihull, Warwickshire, U.K.

LURIE, Hannah Ross, occasional pen name **STARR FISH,** b. 8 Nov. 1934. Poet. Education: Rosemont Coll.; var. courses in Art Ctrs. Positions held: Publsr., co-operative effort w. NOW; Creator, Writer & Ed. of weekly poetry column 'City Lights' publd. by The Drummer Newspaper, Phila., Pa.; Creator, Writer & Ed. of weekly poetry column 'Delicate Dreams of Summer' publd. by The Beachcomber Newspaper, Long Beach Is., N.J.; Creator & participant, 'Women in Sciences' prog., Franklin Inst., Phila., Pa.; Speaker, Publicity, P.R., Nat. org. for Women; Publicity, P.R., UNICEF; Cook, Housekeeper, Childcare, 15 yrs.; Advt. Mgr., Philadelphia Gear Works; Tech. Publ. Ed., Gen. Electric Missiles; Art, Promotion, Brochures, Reuben H. Donnelley Corp.; Copywriter, Asst. Personnel Mgr., etc., var. dept. stores, advt. agencies, bus., camps, stores. Member, Pa. Poetry Soc. Author, The Edge of an Era, 1973. Contbr. to: Beachcomber; The Drummer; Women Speaking Jrnl.; Nat. Org. of Women Newsletter; The Rotarian; Above Ground Review; Times Jrnl. Mag.; Take One; Grit; Tri County News; Sunday Denver Post Mag.; Phila. Tribune; Velvet Glove; Am. Bard; Ampersand, etc. Recip. var. hons. & awards. Address: 23 Derwen Rd., Bala Cynwyd, PA 19004, U.S.A.

LUSCHEI, Glenna Berry, b. 11 Feb. 1934. Editor. Education: Stephens Coll.; grad., Univ. of Neb.; granted fellowship to study the influence of Ruben Dario in Chile, Santiago, 1957; Iowa Writers' Workshop; M.A., Engl., Univ. of Neb., 1960. Married Martin Luschei, 4 children. Positions held: Editl. Asst. to Karl Shapiro, 1956; Tchng. Asst., Univ. of Neb., 1957; Tchr., Greengates Schl., Mexico City, 1960; Tchr., Jr. H.S., Nueva Granada Schl., Bogota, Colombia, 1964; Poetry Workshop for Economic Opportunity Commn., San Luis Obispo, Calif., 1972–. Memberships: Phi Beta Kappa; Chi Delta Phi. Published works: Carta al Norte Columbia, (bilingual vol. of poems), 1967; The Mama Who Couldn't Stop Yelling, (play), 1969; Back Into My Body, (book of verse), 1973; Ed., Cafe Solo, 1969– & of the Solo Press, 1968–. Contbr. to: Anthol. of Southwestern Verse; 'But is it Poetry?'; Dacotah Territory; Dragonflys; N.M. Qtly.; Prairie Schooner; etc. Recip. var. awards inclng: Poetry Ctr. Discovery Award, WMHA, N.Y.C., 1973; D.H. Lawrence Fellowship & Cabin, San Cristobal, N.M., June '73-Aug. '73; Appt. to the Lit. Panel, Nat. Endowment for the Arts, 1973. Address: The Solo Press, 1209 Drake Circle, San Luis Obispo, CA 93401, U.S.A.

LUSTGARTEN, Celia Sophie, b. 24 Oct. 1941. Advertising Copywriter. Education: New Schl. for Soc. Rsch.; City Coll.; Brooklyn Coll. Positions held: Sec., 1959-64; Advertising Copywriter, Arkwright Mdsing Corp., 1964-65, Kleins Dept. Store, 1965-67, B. Altman & Co., 1967-73. Contbr. to: Yearbook of Modern Poetry, 1971; Love Poems, 1972; Poetry Annual, 1972. Address: c/o P.J. Meade, 126 E. 73 St., N.Y., NY 10021, U.S.A.

LuTOUR, Lou, b. St. Louis, Mo., U.S.A. Poet-Evangelist; Educator; Broadcaster; Columnist. Educ: B.A., Harris Tchrs. Coll., St. Louis, Mo.; M.F.A., Douglas Univ., ibid; M.Ed., Special Educ., Tchrs. Coll., N.Y.C.; Doct., Religious Educ. Positions held: Community Rels. Coord., PS 83, Manhattan, 1964-68; Dir., Poetry Therapy Workshop, Sci. of Living Inst., N.Y.C.; Dir., Communications, Community Schl. Dist. 5, N.Y.C. Bd. of Educ.; Chancellor, 2nd World Cong. of Poets, Taipei, Taiwan; Fndr., Pres., World Poets Resource Ctr., Inc.; Advsry. Comm., Int. Who's Who in Poetry, 1969–. Memberships: World Cong. of Docts.; Life Fellow, Royal Soc. of Arts, U.K.; World Cong. of Poets; Nat. Guild of Career Women; Nat. Coun. Negro

Women; Am. Poets Fellowship Soc.; AAUW; IPA; NAACP; Chmn., Eastern Ctr., (USA) Poetry Soc. of London, 1967–. Published works incl: The Power & The Glory (poems) 1967; I Dreamed a Dream (dedicated to Martin Luther King), 1968; Treasure House, 1970; Poetic Verses In Honor of Our Lady of Lourdes. Honours, awards incl: Laurel Wreath, United Poets Laureate Int., 1967; APFS Gold Cup, 1968; Rep., Int. Who's Who in Poetry, World Cong. of Poets & 1st Int. Cong. of Docts., Manila, Philippines, 1969; Int. Hon. Poet Laureate, World Cong. of Poets & Plaque, Gold Medallion & Gold Medal Awards; Int. Award of Hon., World Inst. of Drs.; World Poets' Trophy, Pakistan, 1972; UN Day Award; Recip., num. hon. degrees. Address: 1270 5th Ave., N.Y., NY 10029, U.S.A.

LUX, Yolanda Attianese, pen name **YOLANDA.** Writer. Membership: Staten Island Poetry Soc. Published works: Staten Island Poetry Anthol., 1966-67, 1973. Contbr. to: Staten Island Advance. Address: 18 Hudson St., Stapleton, Staten Island, NY 10304, USA.

LU YU, pen name **CHI HSIEN,** b. 27 Apr. 1913. Professor. Education: Soochow Arts Coll. Positions held: Deputy Hd., Chinese Del. to the First WCP, Manila, Philippines, 1969; Del., 3rd Asian Writers' Conf., Taipei, 1970; Del., 37th PEN Congress, Seoul, Korea, 1970; Hon. V.P., 2nd WCP Arrangement Comm., Taipei, 1973; Ed., Modern Poetry, 10 yrs. Mbrships: Chinese Poetry Soc.; Int PEN, Chinese Ctr.; 2nd World Congress of Poets. Published works: The Youth Who Picks Stars; Drinker; Coconut Tree (vol. A-E); Chi Hsien's Essays on Poetry. Contbr. to mags. & newspapers in Shanghai, Hongkong, Taiwan, etc. over the past 45 yrs. Honours, awars: Pres. F. Marcos Medal as Outstanding Chinese Poet, Manila, Philippines, 1969. Address: 4 Chi Nan Rd., Sec. 2, Taipei, Taiwan, Rep. of China.

LYALL, Charles Leslie, pen name **WITSEND, Dipso,** b. 10 June 1919. Horticulturist. Education: Charterhouse; Worcester Coll., Oxford Univ. Memberships: Former Hon. Treas., Petersfield Lit. Soc.; currently Press Officer, ibid. Published works: Poems From a Padded Cell (in prep.). Contbr. to: Country Life; Punch; Poetry; Scrip; Oyster, etc. Recip., minor prizes, Keats Memorial Award, 1972 & '73. Address: Meadowleigh, Weston Road, Petersfield, Hampshire, U.K.

LYBECK, (Carl Mikael) Sebastian, b. 3 Aug. 1929, Finland. Poet. Educ: Abo Acad., 1947-49; Mil. Acad., Helsingfors, 1949-51; Jrnlsm. Educ., 1951-52; Sales Educ., Michelin, 1952-53; Univ. of Helsingfors, 1953-54. Married Berthe Ruud, 1958. Positions held incl. var. posts in different trades, fisherman, steelworker, troubadour, etc. Spent 5 yrs. in Norway, 3 yrs. in Denmark, & in Sweden, 1967–. Memberships: Swedish Authors' Assn.; The Authors' Ctr. in Finland, Sweden & Norway; Friedrich-Bödecker-Kreis e.V., Hannover, Germany; Die europäische Autorenvereinigung "Die Kogge", Minden, Germany; Finland's Swedish Authors' Soc.; Authors' Club, Gothenburg. Published works incl: I tornet, 1951; Fagel över sju floder, 1956; Jorden har alltid sitt ljus, 1958; Dikter fran Lofoten, 1961; Liten stad vid havet, 1963; Mitt i den nordiska idyllen, 1972; Vierendelen, (Netherlands), 1965; Det upplysta manlammet, 1958; Med andra ögon, 1968; En diktare är ingen sockersäck, 1968. Contbr. to: Radio/TV in Finland, Sweden, Norway, W. Germany; Dagens Nyheter, Svenska Dagbladet, Ord och Bild (Sweden); Dagbladet, Aftenposten, Vinduet (Norway); Hufvudstadsbladet, Nya Pressen, Horisont (Finland); Hvedekorn (Denmark); etc. Honours, awards incl: The Swedish State's Gt. Schlrship., 2 yrs., 1971-72; City of Gothenburg's Gt. Schlrship., 1973; Schlrships., Finnish State, Finnish Educ. Dept., & Swedish Authors Fund; Prize, Längmanska Culture Fund, 1966, & Der Deutsche Jugendbuchpreis, 1959. Address: Morgonbrisvägen 2 C, S-451 00 Uddevalla, Sweden.

LYDIC, Frank Aylsworth, b. 22 Jan. 1909. River Man.

Education: Elem., Dist. 60, Frontier Co., Neb., 1916-23; HS, Farnmam, Neb., 1923-27; Grad. Kearney State Coll., 1927-31, B.F.A. in Ed., 1931 Grad. Study. Univ. of S. Calif., San Francisco State, Humboldt State, and Sacramento State Colls. Married, Florence Meadows; 3 children (1 decd.). Positions held: Teacher at schools in various parts of Calif., for 19 years, period 1931-1956. Returned to the life of merchant seaman, which he had followed during and for period after World War II. Since that time has followed the work of either merchant seaman, or river man in inland rivers of US. Memberships: Ill. State Poetry Soc.; Nebraska Writers' Guild. Published works: Desert Lure and Other Verse, 1971; 2nd Ed., 1972; Rhymes of a River Man, 1973. Contbr. to: Oakland Tribune; Honolulu Star Bulletin; Los Angeles Saturday Night; Westward; Fletcher's Farming; The N.M.U. Pilot; Writers' Notes and Quotes; Desert Mag.; Harbor Lights; Orphic Lute; Creative Review; (anthols.) Best New Love Poems of 1963; Versatility in Verse; Anthol. of American Poetry, vols. V, VI, VII, VIII; The Golden Quill Anthol., 1966, 1967; 1971 Medley of Poetry; Outstanding Contemporary Poetry, 1972 & 1973; 73 Poets, Ill. St. Poetry Soc. and others. Address: General Delivery, Joliet, IL 60431, USA.

LYLE, Rob(ert Francis Xavier), b. 1920. Education: R.C.M., London, 1937-39. Published works: Guitar, 1951; Saudades, 1953; Halcyon, 1953; Lunar Corn, 1956; Heroic Elegies, 1957; Poems from Limbo, 1960; Other: Mistral, 1953.

LYLES, Donald R., b. 11 Apr. 1946. Columnist & Freelance Writer. Education: U.S. Army Artillery & Missile Schl., Ft. Sill, Okla.; Prairie View A & M Coll., Tex., 2½ yrs. Positions held: Columnist, National Afro-American & The Houston Informer; Columnist & Rep., Frontier News; Columnist, Adv. Salesman & Rep., Songwriter (Ireland); Columnist, Bronze Thrills Mag., 1972-74. Memberships: Am. Poetry League; Life (Danae) Mbr., Clover Int. Poetry Assn.; Fellow, Acad. of Am. Poets; former mbr., Am. Poets Fellowship Soc. & Ill. State Poetry Soc. Contbr. to: Summertime; Man..When Born of Fire; The Prairie Poet Coll.; Am. Poet; United Poets; The 1971 Shore Poetry Anthol.; The 1972 Shore Poetry Anthol.; The Strand Book of Modern Verse; 73 Poets Anthol.; From Sea to Sea In Song; Los Angeles Sentinel; The Mich. Chronicle; The Journal-Enquirer, Ky., etc. Recip., Cert. of Merit, Am. Poets Fellowship Soc. Address: 2675 S. Arlington Ave., No. 4, Los Angeles, CA 90018, U.S.A.

LYMAN, Irene Vera Ponting, pen names **HARRINGTON, Ann & FAREYSTONE, Elizabeth.** Novelist. Memberships: Fndr. Mbr., Int. Poetry Soc.; West Country Writers Assn.; Soc. of Authors; Romantic Novelists Assn. Has published var. novels. Contbr. to: Northampton Co. Mag.; Radio Eireann; Cats; Wellingborough News. Address: Plas Meudon, Maenporth Rd.. Mawnan, Falmouth, Cornwall, U.K.

LYNES, Ruth C., pen name **BOLEN, J. Carpenter,** b. 21 Jan. 1946. Musician; Instructor of Music. Education: B.A. (in music education), Seattle Pacific Coll., Washington; M.F.A. (in vocal performance), Univ. of Minnesota, Minneapolis. Positions held: Director of Music, Goodridge Public Schools, Minn., 1967-70; Vocal Instr., Univ. Baptist Church Scholarship Prog. (Minneapolis), 1971-72; Minnesota Opera Company, Minneapolis, 1972; Instr. of Music, Northwestern Coll., Roseville, Minn., 1972 to present. Contbr. to: Essence; Maelstrom; Cardinal; Bitterroot; The Villager; The Dance of the Muse (anthol.). Address: 902 East 26th St., Minneapolis, MN 55404, USA.

LYON, Mabelle A., b. 12 June 1904. Housewife; Author; Editor. Married, Edward Hamilton Lyon; 1 d. Positions held: Legal Sec.; Asst. Mgr., St. Louis Restaurant; Ins. Office Sec. Memberships: World Poetry Soc. Intercontinental (State Dir.), also Chancellor since 1970, and re-elected for a further term of 3 yrs.); Rep., CSSI, 1967–; Pres., Phoenix Branch, Nat. League Am. Pen Women, 1968-70; Pres.,

Ariz. State Poetry Soc., 1966-68; Avalon; American Poetry League (Pres., 1971-73); Nat. Fed. State Poetry Socs.; U.P.L.I.; Internat. Poetry Soc. (UK); Poetry Soc. of Texas. Editor of anthols.: Jewels on a Willow Tree, 1966; Melodies From A Jade Harp, 1968; Ballet on the Wind, 1969; Sing Naked Spirit, 1970; Sea to Sea in Song (APL anthol.), 1971, 1972; Editor, Poet; Editor, The American Poetry League Bulletin, 1970-73. Co-Author, Road Runner, 1971. Contbr. to: Am. Haiku; Haiku West; Haiku, Toronto; Haiku Spotlight; Quadernia di Poesia; Cyclo-Flame; Am. Poet; Prairie Poet; United Poets; Denver Post; Nutmegger; The Spring Anthol., 1969; Images; Tulsa Qtly.; Poetry Okla.; Poetry Dial; Science of Mind; Am. Poetry League Bulletin; Swordsman Review; The Sandcutters; Am. Bard; This Day; The Pen Woman; Encore; Premier Poets, 1970; Driftwood East; Educational Forum; Tweed (Australia); Bitterroot. Honours: Gold Cup, Am. Poets Fellowship Soc., 1968; 1st Prize, Phoenix Writers Club contest, 1969; 1st Prizes, Nat. Haiku Contests, Fed. of Chap. Poets, 1967, 1968; World Poetry Soc., Disting. Serv. Citation, Magna cum Laude, 1970; Dr. of Literature (h.c.), L'Universite Libre (Asie), 1972; Dip. from World Acad. of Langs. and Lit., deg. of Hon. Pres., Sao Paulo, Brazil, 1972; Dip. Two Thousand Women of Achievement; Dip. of Merit as World Poetry Leader from Committee of Arts & Culture, 1971 Constitutional Convention, Republic of The Philippines, Dec. 31, 1972; and numerous other awards, also prizes for poems entered in nat. and local contests. Address: 8801 N. 17th Ave., Phoenix, AZ 85021, USA.

LYSONS, William Dennis, pen name **LYSONS, Dennis,** b. 28 Aug. 1944. Welder. Married twice. Positions held: Underground Pipe Fitter in Coal Mine, 7 yrs.; Welder. Memberships: Fndr., Lancs. Poetry Assn., 1968; Fndr., Wigan Poets Soc., 1969. Has read his poetry in clubs, pubs & libraries & on radio. Has appeared on TV & was subject of film made by the BBC. Contbr. to: Warrington Guardian; Lancs. Evening Post; St. Helens Reporter, etc. Recip., Sir Arthur Markham Meml. Prize, 1968. Address: 18 Sycamore Ave., Goldborne, Nr. Warrington, Lancs., U.K.

LYTTLE, Cosíma Lucille Venet, pen name, **KOZ or KOZ VENET,** b. 17 Jan. 1948. Homemaker. Mother. Education: Emory Univ., Atlanta, Ga., 1965-66; Computer & Bus. Skills Inst., Chicago, Ill., 1967-68. Married to pollution control engr., 1 s. Positions held: Part-time Tax Return Checker, IRS, Atlanta, 1966; Sec. to Dean, Emory Law Schl., 1966; Clerk, Specialty Food Shop & Delicatessen, Chicago, 1967; World Field Rsch. Corresp., 1967–; Cost Acct., Home Office Retail Credit Co., Atlanta, 1968-69. Memberships: Quill & Scroll Lit. Soc.; Order of the Boofus. Pubs. Excerpts from Tomorrow, 1970; The Welcome Wagon is a Tumbrel, 1971; (in progress) The Calculus of Yesterdays. Contbr. to: Perspectus; Haiku Highlights; Chicago Tribune; Rambler; Palladian; Arrow. Honours: Best Haiku, Haiku Highlights, 1967. Address: 1468-A Druid Valley Drive NE., Atlanta, Ga. 30329, USA.

M

MacADAMS, Lewis Perry, b. 12 Oct. 1944. Poet. Education: Princeton Univ., N.J.; Univ. of Buffalo, N.Y. Married Phoebe MacAdams. Positions held: Formerly Switchman on the S. Pacific Railroad; Currently assoc. w. Pacific High Recording Co. Published works: City Money, 1966; Water Charms, 1968. Contbr. to (Anthols.): Young American Poets, 1968; Sparklers, 1969; (jrnls.): Paris Review; Mother; Mag. of Further Studies; Other: Where the Girls are: A Guide to Eastern Women's Colls., 1966. Recip., Poets Foundation Award, 1967. Address: 5233 Lobello Drive, Dallas, TX, USA.

McAFEE, James Thomas, pen name **McAFEE, Thomas.** b. 13 May 1928. Professor of English.

Education: A.B., Univ. of Mo., 1949; M.A., ibid, 1950; Ph.D., 1952. Positions held: Instr., 1945-49, Asst. Prof., 1950-64, Assoc. Prof., 1964-67, Prof., 1967-, Univ. of Mo. Memberships: Authors' League; Authors' Guild. Published works: Poems & Stories (book), 1960; I'll Be Home Late Tonight (book of poems), 1967; Four Poets (anthol. edited by Charles Willig), 1967; Rover Youngblood (novel), 1969. Contbr. to num. mags. & reviews inclng: Western Review; Modern Short Stories; Contempora; Midwestern Univ. Qtly.; Open Places; Harrison Street Review; The Scope of Satire; West Coast Review; The Denver Qtly.; Inscape; Colo. Qtly.; Carleton Miscellany; Kan. City Times. Honours, awards: 'Rover Youngblood' nominated for Pulitzer Prize & William Faulkner Award; Recip. Award, Nat. Coun. on the Arts for story 'Lady of the World'. Address: Engl. Dept., 217 A & S Bldg., Univ. of Mo., Columbia, MO 65201, U.S.A.

MACAINSH, Noel Leslie, b. 15 June 1926. University Lecturer. Education: Univs. of Melbourne, Australia & Munich, W. Germany; M.A.; Ph.D.; Dip. Pub. Admin. (Melb.); A.M.I.E. Aust.; A.M.I.R.E.E. Aust. Positions held: served w. RAAF; Chartered Communications Engr., C'wealth Govt. Author of book on art, critical essays, translations & reviews. Has given num. public lectures & participated in public poetry readings at the Victorian State Art Gall. & elsewhere. Contbr. to: Meanjin Quarterly; Quadrant; Southerly; Westerly; Overland; The Bulletin; Poetry Australia; Australian Letters; The Sydney Morning Herald; Melbourne Age; Australian; The Int. Lit. Annual; The Penguin Book of Australian Verse; Commonwealth Poets; New Voices of the Commonwealth; On Native Grounds; Overland Muster; Australian Poetry, 1957, 58, 59, 61, 62, 63, 64, 65, 68, 69, 71, 72; Verse in Australia, etc. Address: James Cook Univ., Townsville, Queensland, Australia 4810.

McALLISTER, Bill, b. 28 Dec. 1945. Teacher. Education: B.A., Delta State Coll., Cleveland, Miss.; grad. work, ibid & The Univ. of Miss., Oxford, Miss. Married Janice. Positions held: Tchr., Ocean Springs, Miss., City Schls.; Tchr., Powtotoc, Miss., City Schls.; Tchr., New Albany, Miss., City Schls. Founding Mbr. & Past Pres., Delta State Lit. Soc. Contbr. to 'Poet'. Address: 810 Oxford Rd., New Albany, MS 38652, U.S.A.

McALLISTER, Claire, b. 25 Nov. 1934. Poet. Education: Sorbonne, Paris; Trinity Coll., Dublin, Ireland. Married John Chanler White, 1 daughter. Positions held: Robert Frost Fellow, Vt., 1960. Past Mbr., Irish Georgian Soc., Ireland. Published works: Arms of Light, 1964. Contbr. to: Twentieth Century Am. Poetry, 1963; Encyclopedia di Cultura Moderna, 1959; Pocket Book of Am. Verse; Partisan Review; Botteghe Oscura; Atlantic Monthly; Envoy (Dublin); Mass. Review; The Month (London); Poetry London – New York; PEN Anthol.; Poetry Ireland; Points (Paris); The Dublin Mag.; Sumac; The N.Y. Qtly.; Kenyon Review; Commonweal; Prairie Schooner; The Lit. Review, etc. Honours, awards: Yaddo Fellowship, 1961; 1st prize for Street Ballad commemorating 50th anniversary of Irish Rebellion, 1966. Address: 2055 Robinson Rd., Grand Rapids, MI 49506, U.S.A.

MacARTHUR, Bessie Jane Bird, b. 6 Feb. 1889. Poet. Education: Charlotte Sq. Instn., Edinburgh; Dip. in Music Tchng.; L.R.A.M. piano. Married, 3 sons (2 dec.), 1 daughter. Mbr., PEN, 1927-. Published works: The Starry Venture, 1934; Scots Poems, 1938; Last Leave, 1943; From Daer Water, 1962; And Time Moves On, 1972. Rep. in following anthols: Scottish Verse 1851-1951; Oxford Book of Scottish Verse; Book of the Feill. Poems included in Schools Curriculum for Western Isles. Contbr. to: Scotsman; Glasgow Herald; Chambers Jrnl.; New Alliance; Celtic Monthly; Life & Work (Edinburgh); Burns Chronicle. Address: 4 Glencairn Cres., Edinburgh EH12 5BS, U.K.

MCAULEY, James J., b. 8 Jan. 1936. Associate Professor; Poet. Education: B.A., Univ. Coll., Dublin, 1962; M.F.A., Univ. of Ark., 1971. Married twice, 3 sons by first marriage (James, Anthony, Kevin); 2 sons by second marriage to Almut Nierentz (Owen & Rory). Positions held: Clerk & Jrnlst., Electricity Supply Bd., Dublin, 1954-66; Grad. Asst., Engl. Dept., Univ. of Ark., U.S.A., 1966-68; Asst. Prof. of Engl., Lycoming Coll., Pa., 1968-70; Asst. Prof. of Engl., Eastern Wash. State Coll., 1970-72; Assoc. Prof., ibid, 1972-73. Memberships: Chmn., Contemp. Lit. Sect., NEMLA, 1969; Panel Mbr., SAMLA, 1971; Trustee, Spokane Allied Arts Coun., 1972-75; Coll. Engl. Assn., 1973-74. Published works: Observations, 1960; A New Address, 1965; Draft Balance Sheet, 1970; Home & Away, 1973. Contbr. to: Kilkenny Mag.; Poetry Ireland; Irish Times; University Review; Arena; Hibernia; Confluence; Ark. Traveler; Nimrod; Preview; Lycoming Review; Poetry Northwest; New Irish Writing; Love Poems of the Irish, etc. Honours, awards: Most Outstanding New Prof., Lycoming Coll., 1969; Fellowship in Creative Writing, Nat. Endowment for the Arts, 1972. Address: Dept. of Engl., Eastern Wash. State Coll., Cheney, WA 99004, U.S.A.

McAULEY, James Philip, b. 12 Oct. 1917. Professor of English. Education: M.A., Sydney Univ., Australia; Dip. Ed., ibid. Positions held: Smith Lectr. in Govt., Australian Schl. of Pacific Admin., 1946-60; Rdr. in Poetry, Univ. of Tas., 1960; Prof. of Engl., ibid, 1960-. Mbr., Coun., Aust. Soc. of Authors. Published works: Under Aldebaran, 1946; A Vision of Ceremony, 1956; The Six Days of Creation, 1963; Selected Poems, 1963; Captain Quiros, 1964; Surprises of the Sun, 1969; Collected Poems 1936-70, 1971. Contbr. to: Encounter; Australian Letters; Sidney Bulletin; Meanjin Quarterly; Quadrant; Australian Poetry; Solidarity, Manila. Address: Univ. of Tasmania, Box 252c, GPO, Hobart, Tas. Australia.

McBEATH, Lida W., b. 21 Feb. 1913. Scientific & Technical Writer; Editor, U.S. Forest Products Laboratory. Education: B.A., Univ. of Wis. Positions held: Freelance Writer; Ed., Univ. of Wis. Press; Ed., Wis. Farm Bureau Fed. Member, Wis. Fellowship of Poets. Contbr. to: Hawk and Whippoorwill Recalled, Wis. Fellowship of Poets, & CHIPS, employee publ. of U.S. Forest Products Lab. Address: 10 Calumet Circle, Madison, WI 53705, U.S.A.

MacBETH, George Mann, b. 1932. Poet. Educ: New Coll., Oxford Univ., U.K. m. Elizabeth Browell Robson, 1955. Positions held: joined BBC, 1955; Prod., Overseas Talks Dept., 1957; Prod., Talks Dept., 1958; Ed., Poet's Voice, 1958-65, New Comment, 1959-64, & Poetry Now, 1965-. Published works: (poems) A Form of Words, 1954; The Broken Places, 1963; A Doomsday Book, 1965; The Colour of Blood, 1967; The Night of Stones, 1968; A War Quartet, 1969; The Burning Cone, 1970; Collected Poems 1958-1970, 1971; The Orlando Poems, 1971; Shrapnel, 1972; (prose poems) My Scotland, 1973; (anthols.) The Penguin Book of Sick Verse, 1963; Penguin Modern Poets VI (w. J. Clemo & E. Lucie-Smith), 1964; The Penguin Book of Animal Verse, 1965; Poetry, 1900-1965 (w. notes), 1967; The Penguin Book of Victorian Verse, 1968; The Falling Splendour, 1970; (children's book) Jonah & the Lord, 1969. Recip., Sir Geoffrey Faber Mem. Award, jointly, 1964. Address: c/o BBC, Broadcasting House, London W.1, U.K.

McBROOM, Ruby Cureington, pen name **CUREINGTON, Ruby,** b. 21 Dec. 1918. Housewife. Education: Attended La. State Normal Coll., Natchitoches, La. Widow of Haskell L. McBroom, 1 son, 2 daughters. Positions held: Asst. Postmaster, Zenoria, La., 1942-52. Memberships: La. State Poetry Soc. Contbr. to The Jena Times, Jena, La. Honours, awards: Gertrude B. Saucier Humorous Award, La. State Poetry Soc. Spring Fest., 1971; 3rd pl., Renee Viosea Religious Award & in May Lacassagne Humorous Award, La. State Poetry Soc. Spring Fest., 1973. Address: Rte.1, Box 81, Trout, LA 71371, U.S.A.

McBURNETT, Leila Mae, b. 13 Aug. 1901. Field Representative. Education: var. Pub. Rels & Sales courses. Widow, 2 children. Positions held: Hostess &

Field Rep. for Advertisers, local business, insurance, cosmetic sales. Memberships: Poets Roundtable; Am. Business Womens Assn.; Nat. Womens Club; PTA. Contbr. to: Cumberland Presbyn.; Missionary Messenger; North Little Rock Times; Spectator. Address: 4820 Alpha St., N. Little Rock, AR 72117, U.S.A.

McCAFFERY, Steve, b. 21 Jan. 1947. Managing Editor. Education: B.A., Hull Univ., U.K., 1968; M.A., York Univ., Toronto, Canada, 1969. Positions held: Contributing Ed., Open Letter (Literary Review); Co-Ed., Gronk; Ed., Anonbeyond Press; Mng. Ed., The Canadian Who's Who. Memberships: League of Canadian Poets; Co-Fndr., Toronto Rsch. Grp.; The Four Horsemen (a collaborative 4-man sound poetry group). Published works: Carnival (1st section), 1969; Transitions to the Beast, 1970; Maps a different Landscape, 1971; Groundplans for a Speaking City, 1971; Carnival – 1st Panel 1967-70, 1973; 'Ow's Waif', 1973; co-author, Collbrations, 1973. Anthologies: Three Concrete Poets, 1970; The Cosmic Chef, 1970; New Direction in Canadian Poetry, 1971; I am a Sensation, 1972; (record) Canadada (w. The Four Horsemen), 1972. Visual Poetry exhib. at: Univ. of Alta.; Exhib. of Canadian Concrete Poetry, 1970; 'Microsophicus' Avelles Gall., B.C., 1971; Staedlijk Mus., Amsterdam; Uruguay; Germany; U.S.A. Has toured Canada w. The Four Horsemen reading & conducting poetry workshops. Contbr. to: Canadian Forum; White Pelican; Blewointment; Gronk; Dust; Poet's Eye, etc. Address: 52 Claxton Blvd., Toronto, Canada.

MacCAIG, Norman, b. 14 Nov. 1910. Reader in Poetry. Education: Degree in Classics, Univ. of Edinburgh, U.K. Married, 2 children. Positions held: Schoolmaster, Edinburgh schls.; Fellowship in Creative Writing, Univ. of Edinburgh, 1967-69; Lectr. in Engl. Studies, Univ. of Stirling, 1970-72; Rdr. in Poetry, Univ. of Stirling, 1972. Fellow, Royal Soc. Lit. Published works incl: Far Cry, 1943; The Inward Eye, 1946; Riding Lights, 1955; The Sinai Sort, 1957; A Common Grace, 1960; A Round of Applause, 1962; Surroundings, 1966; Measures, 1965; Rings On A Tree, 1968; A Man in My Position, 1969; Contemporary Scottish Verse; Selected Poems, 1971; The White Bird, 1973. Contbr. to: The Spectator; The New Statesman; The Observer; Encounter; Poetry (Chicago); The Listener; Lines Review; The Guardian; Agenda; The Glasgow Herald, etc. Recip., 4 Arts Coun. Awards & 1 Soc. of Authors Award. Address: 7 Leamington Terr., Edinburgh, U.K.

McCALL, Margaret Dole, pen names **DOLE, Margaret Aliona & DEANE, Mark Anderson,** b. 26 Jan. 1891. Writer. Memberships: Poetry Soc. of Am.; Sec., N.Y. Women Poets, 24 yrs.; Sec., Craftsman Grp., 15 yrs. Contbr. to: Riding in the Rain (anthol.); The Boston Transcript; Boston Post; N.Y. Herald Tribune; The Lyric, etc. Recip. var. poetry prizes. Address: 525 West 238th St., Apt. K2, Riverdale, Bronx, NY 10463, U.S.A.

McCALLUM, Righton Hodgkin, b. 7 July 1942. Librarian. Education: A.B., Converse Coll., Spartanburg, S.C.; Lib. Sci., Univ. of Ga. Married Brown McCallum, Jr. Positions held: Engl. Tchr., Atlanta & Waycross, Ga.; Libn., Peace Coll., Raleigh, N.C., St. Timothy's Schl. & Hale H.S.; Freelance Writer. Memberships: Treas., N.C. Poetry Soc., 1969–; Am. Acad. of Poets; Poetry Coun. of N.C.; Nat. Fed. of State Poetry Socs.; Longview Writers Grp.; N.C. Folklore Soc. Contbr. to: Gleanings; Raleigh News & Observer; Waycross Jrnl. Herald; Better Camping Mag.; The Ga. Mag.; Pieces; DeKalb Lit. Arts Jrnl.; Wildlife; Award Winning Poems. Recip. var. prizes, N.C. Poetry Soc., 1969. Address: 24 Warwick Pl., Asheville, NC 28804, U.S.A.

McCANN, Andrew Joseph, Jr., b. 1 Feb. 1929. Personnel Officer (retired). Education: HS Dip., Wm. Penn Charter School, 1947; B.A., Univ. of Pennsylvania, 1951; Dip., American Foundation of Dramatic Arts, 1958. Personal details: Married to Mary Jane Bones; 1. son (Michael Kevin Andrew). Member of MENSA; D.A.V., K. of C. Positions held: Radio Announcer, Producer, WIFI, Philadelphia, 1960-67; Personnel Advisor, Phila. Nav. Shipyard, 1961-67; Singing Teacher, since 1960. Memberships: United Amateur Press. Published work: Bright Labyrinths. Contbr. to: Suburban Life, North; Bucks County Life; Panorama; Valley Views of Ohio; Veteran's Voices; Willow Grove Guide; Roslyn Life; The Unsung (anthol.); Yearbook of Modern Poetry, 1972; Outstanding Contemp. Poetry (anthol.); Lyrics of Love (anthol.); Troll (anthol.); Poetry of Our Time, 1973 (anthol.); Spafaswap (mag.); United Amateur Press Pubs.; Jean's Journal. Recip. Poet of the Year Award (Poetry of Our Time), 1973; 1st Prizes "Veteran's Voices", 1967, Poetry and Short Stories, 1968. Address: 1241 Johnston Ave., Roslyn, PA 19001, USA.

McCARTHY, Bryan Eugene, b. 3 Mar. 1930. Teacher. Education: B.Sc., Physics, Imperial Coll. of Science & Technology, London, 1951. Married w. 2 children. Positions held: Worked as Radar Technician, Mid-Canada Line, 1956; Reporter on the Prince George Citizen; Var. other jobs; Taught for var. periods, Herzliah High Schl., Montreal, 1960–. Published works: Smoking the City, 1965; Other: Trans., The Singing Cells, 1970. Contbr. to (Anthols.): To Every Thing There Is a Season, 1967; (Jrnls.): Canadian Forum; Tamarack Review; Evidence; West Coast Review; Prism; Bloody Horse; Moment. Recip., Canada Council Arts Scholarship, 1966-67. Address: 1218 Greene Ave., Montreal, Quebec, Canada.

McCARTHY, Cavan, b. 1 Apr. 1943. Librarian; Founding Editor. Education: B.A., Hons., Russian, Leeds Univ., 1965; Leeds Schl. of Librarianship. Positions held: Coll. of Technol., 1967; Asst. Librarian (Slavonic subject specialist), Brotherton Library, Univ. of Leeds, 1967–; Fndr. & Ed., Tlaloc, a mag. of concrete poetry. Assoc. of the Library Assn. Contbr. to (Anthols.): Anthology of Concrete Poetry, 1967; Experimental Ni Poezie, 1967; Once Again, 1968; (Jrnls.): New York Times; East Village Other. Address: BCM/Cavan, London, W.C.1., UK.

McCARTHY, Eugene Joseph, b. 29 Mar. 1916. American politician. Education: B.A., St. John's Univ., Collegeville, Minn.; M.A., Univ. of Minn., 1939. Positions held: Tchr., Soc. Sci., Minn. Sec. Schls.; Novitiate, St. John's, 9 mths.; Prof., Econs. & Educ., St. John's Univ., Collegeville, Minn.; Civilian Tech. Asst., War Dept., Military Intelligence Div.; Acting Chmn., Sociol. Dept., St. Thamas Coll., St. Paul, Minn.; Mbr., US House of Reps. (4th Minn. Dist.) 1948-58; Senator for Minnesota, 1958–; Democratic Presidential electional candidate, 1968. Published works: Frontiers in American Democracy. Author of poetry and contbr. to various nat. jrnls. Honours include: Cardinal Newman Award, 1955; Hon. LL.D., St Louis Univ., 1955. Address: 2103 Inglehart Ave., St. Paul, Minn.; Senate Office, Bldg., Washington 25, DC, USA.

McCARTNEY, Dorothy Wilson. Housewife; Poet. Education: A.B., Pa. State Univ., 1934; M.A., Engl. Lit. & Mus., Cornell Univ., 1943. Married John R. McCartney. Positions held: Tchr., H.S. & Elem. Schl.; Music Libn., Cornell Univ.; Asst. Libn., Francis Harvey Green Lib., W. Chester State Coll., Pa.; Pianist, Gilbert & Sullivan prodns.; Music Arranger, Accompanist, revised silent movies. Memberships incl: Pres., Writers' Club, Wilmington, Del.; Am. Poetry League; Am. Poets Fellowship Soc.; Fndr., Acad. of Am. Poets; Fellow, Int. Poetry Soc.; Hon. Rep., Centro Studi e Scambi Int.; Poetry Socs. of Pa., N.C., Md., Mass., Tex., Alaska; Chester Co. Art Assn.; AAUW. Published works: Lemmus Lemmus & Other Poems, 1973. Contbr. to: (anthols.) 1st State Writers, Wilmington, 1951; NC Poetry Soc. Award Winning Poems, 1966, '68, '69, '72; Bay Leaves (NC Poetry Coun.), 1968; Am. Poetry League Bulletin, 1968; Badge of Promise, 1968; The Am. Poet, 1968; From Sea to Sea in Songs;

Festival Poets, 1969; Friendship Trail, 1970; The Sandcutters, 1971; Red Horse Hill; Moon-age Poets; Yearbook of Mod. Poetry; Lyrics of Love; NFSPS Prize Poems, 1969, '72; Haiku Drops from the Great Dipper; Oriole; Pa. Poetry Soc. Prize Poems, 1968, '69, '71, '73; Sixty-Eight Poets; Prairie Poet Anthol., 1970; Selected Poems, Fla. State Poetry Soc., 1968; A Patrick Cavanaugh Anthol.; Golden Eagle Anthol.; (jrnls.) Prairie Poet; Mod. Haiku; Dragonfly; Poet Lore; The Progressive Teacher; The Brandywine Bugle & many others. Recip. num. awards & prizes inclng: 7 first prizes (4 gold cups); 8 second prizes; 10 third prizes; 18 hon. mentions; 1 congressional award, etc. Address: Box 34, Westtown, PA 19395, U.S.A.

MACARTNEY, Frederick Thomas Bennett, pen name **MACARTNEY, Frederick T.,** b. 27 Sept. 1887. Author. Married Mavis Murray Walker. Positions held: Univ. Ext. Lectr., 1933-34; C'wealth Lit. Fund Lectr., 1940-49; Pres., Fellowship of Australian Writers, Victoria, 1945-49. Life Mbr., Fellowship of Australian Writers. Published works: Dewed Petals, 1912; Earthen Vessels, 1913; Commercium, 1917; In Wartime, 1918; Poems, 1920; Something for Tokens, 1922; A Sweep of Lute Strings, 1929; Hardlight, 1933; Preferences, 1941; Ode of Our Times, 1944; Gaily the Troubadour, 1946; Tripod for Homeward Incense, 1947; Selected Poems, 1961. Contbr. to: Bulletin; Birth; Meanjin; Verse; Australian Poetry. Recip., C'wealth Lit. Fund Fellowship, 1954. Address: 66 Stanley St., Black Rock, Victoria 3193, Australia.

McCARTY, Raymond M., pen name, **McCARTY, Raymond,** b. 27 July 1908. Attorney; Poet; Retired Civil Serv. Employee. Education: LL.B., Southern Law Univ., Memphis, Tenn. Positions held: Licensed Atty., Tenn., 1948–; Chief, Planning & Control Br., Real Estate Div., Memphis Dist., Corps of Engrs., US Army, 1953-72. Memberships: 1st Pres., Poetry Soc. of Tenn., 1953-54; Dir. & Treas., 1954-58; Dir. & Parliamentarian, 1969-71; Parliamentarian, 1972-74; World Poetry Soc. Intercontinental; Avalon World Arts Acad.; Ala. Writers' Conclave; Ala. State Poetry Soc. Published work: Harp In a Strange Land, 1973. Contbr. to (newspapers) Springfield, Mo. Leader-Press; The Commercial Appeal (Memphis); Ohio State Journal; (anthols.) Conquerors of Tomorrow, 1947; Songs From American Hearts, 1948; Caravane de la Paix (Belgium), 1950; The Avalonian, 1952; This Too Shall Endure, 1955; One Hundred Poems, Poetry Soc. of Tenn., 1956; Poetry Soc. Tenn. Yearbook, 1959; Warriors of Eternity, 1963; Lyrics of Love, 1963; Fragments of Faith, 1963; Avalon Annual, 1964; Memorabilia, 1965; Avalon Annual, 1966; Yearbook of Mod. Poetry, 1971; Internat. Who's Who in Poetry, 1972; (journals) Winged Word; Eoimitar & Song, Driftwind; Kaleidograph; Different; Singing Quill; Blue Moon; Florida Mag. of Verse; Composers & Authors Mag.; Maine Universalist; Hippocrene; Silver Star; Wildfire; Wings; New Athenaeum; Chap. Writer; Chromatones; Folio; The Searchlight; Clarion; Poet's Reed; American Weave; Flatbush Mag.; SW Mo. State Coll. Bulletin; The Emancipator; Flame; Cyclotron; Green World; Writer's Voice; Lyric; American Bard; Candor Mag.; Quintessence; Quoin; Poet; Old Hickory Review; Tenn. Voices. Honours, Awards: Winner numerous contests; staff & cash awards; Gemstone Awards; prize brochures; book prizes; readers' vote prizes; Countess d'Esternaux Gold Medal Award, 1950; Becky Ridge Prize, 1950; Gould Prize, 1950; Award for essay, Ala. Writers' Conclave, 1969; 1st Prize; Ala. Writers' Conclave for poems, 1969 & 1973; "Select Poem Magnum Cum Laude" Disting. Serv. Citation, World Poetry Soc. Intercontinental, 1969-70. Address: 1247 Colonial Rd., Memphis, TN 38117, USA.

McCAULEY, Carole Mae Spearin, b. 18 Apr. 1939. Writer-Editor. Education: A.B., Antioch Coll., Yellow Springs, Ohio; Certs. in French Lit. & Lang., Univs. of Montpellier & Besançon, France; Fiction Writing Workshops, The New Schl., N.Y.C.; German Lit. Courses, Manhattanville Coll., Purchase, N.Y. Positions held: Editl. Asst., Popular Sci. Monthly Mag.,

N.Y.C.; Market Report Ed., Columbus, Ohio Citizen-Jrnl. (newspaper); Medical News Writer, NIH Record (U.S. Govt.), Bethesda, Md.; Sec. Work, Antioch Coll.; Religious News Writer & Ed., Grailville Community Coll., Loveland, Ohio; Real Estate Sales Work, Scarsdale, N.Y.; currently Freelance Writer & Assoc. Ed., Panache, lit. mag., Princeton, N.J. Memberships: NESPA. Published works: Six Portraits (poetry book), 1973; Computers & Creativity, (book), 1974; Happenthing in Travel On (novel), awaiting publication. Rep. in following anthols: In Youth, 1972; Breakthrough Fictioneers, 1973; Women: Omen, 1971; Women, 1973. Contbr. to var. jrnls. Has done much work w. computer to achieve design poetry & prose, completed by machine programming. Recip. 3 lit. awards for essay & fiction. Address: 23 Buena Vista Dr., Greenwich, CT 06830, U.S.A.

McCLEERY, Edna, pen name, **HULL, Edna,** b. 18 Feb. 1925. Housewife and Poet. Education: Belfast Shorthand Inst. & School of Commerce, UK. Married James A. McCleery. Positions held: Admiralty, N. Ireland, WWII; Sec. to Prof. of Surgery in leading northern univ., England. Memberships: Internat. Poetry Soc. (Fellow); Lancs. Authors' Assoc.; Poetry Soc. (UK); Inst. of Contemp. Arts, London. Novel ('Ladder of Knives') in prep. Contbr. to: Ormskirk Advertiser (features); W. Lancs. Agric. Advertiser (features); Ulster Gazette (column, Strictly Feminine); Mourne Observer; Mid-Ulster Observer; Liverpool Weekly News; The Record (L.A.A.); Down Recorder (N. Ireland); Mail Star (Halifax Nova Scotia); Internat. Who's Who in Poetry Anthol. Awards: Author's Badge, Lancs. Authors' Assoc.; Cert. of Merit (and contributor) to Internat. Who's Who in Poetry Anthol. Address: Edendariff, 45 Granville Park, Aughton, Nr. Ormskirk, Lancs. L39 5DT, UK.

McCLINTOCK, Michael Windsor, pen name **RESIN,** b. 31 Mar. 1950. Student. Education: B.A., Occidental Coll. Positions held: Ed.-in-Chief, Franklin Press, 1968; Asst. Ed., Haiku Highlights mag., 1969-72; Ed., The Bi-Monthly Awards, 1970-72; Assoc. Ed., Modern Haiku mag., 1970–. Memberships: Phi Beta Kappa; Awards Comm. Mbr., Haiku Soc. of Am., 1973; Affiliate Mbr., Acad. of Am. Poets; Calif. State Poetry Soc.; Area Rep. for L.A., Western World Haiku Soc.; Greek Theatre Assn. Published works: Light Run, 1971; work in progress: Thief: Dairy Notes; Complete Poems of Resin; Arcturus Rising. Contbr. to: The Haiku Anthol.; Haiku Highlights; South & West Qtly.; Modern Haiku; Haiku Mag.; Tweed, Australia; Byways, U.K., etc. Honours, awards: R.H. Blyth Award, Haiku West, 1970; Eminent Mention (best of issue award), Modern Haiku, vol. III, No.3, 1972; Argonaut Award for Best Novel, Occidental Coll., 1971; Best New Haiku Poet, Haiku Mag., vol.4, No.1, 1970. Address: 560 Meridian Terr., L.A., CA 90042, U.S.A.

McCLOSKEY, Mark, b. 1 Feb. 1938. University Teacher. Education: B.A., Iona Coll., New Rochelle, N.Y.; M.A., Ohio Univ., Athens. Married w. 2 children. Positions held: Asst. Ed., Ohio Univ. Press, 1964-66; Asst. Prof. of Engl., State Univ. of N.Y., Cortland. Published works: Goodbye, But Listen: Poems, 1968; Other: The Latin Poetry of George Herbert: A Bilingual Edition, 1965. Contbr. to (Anthols.): Best Poems of 1961 & 1962: The Borestone Mountain Poetry Awards, 1962; (Jrnl.): Poetry. Recip., Faculty Fellowships in Creative Writing from the Rsch. Foundation of the State Univ. of N.Y. Address: State Univ. of N.Y., Cortland, N.Y., 13045, USA.

McCLUNEY, Miriam, b. 20 Dec. 1935. Teacher. Education: B.A., Univ. of N.M., U.S.A., 1957; M.A., Tex. Christian Univ., 1961; postgrad. study, Univ. of Colo. Positions held: Tchr., Univ. of Colo., 1961-62; Tchr., Cumbres Jr. H.S., Los Alamos, N.M., 1967-73; Tchr., Albuquerque Acad., N.M., 1973–. Memberships: N.M. State Poetry Soc.; Nat. Assn. of State Poetry Socs.; Assn. for Poetry Therapy. Contbr. to: Yearbook of Modern Poetry; Sunspots; A Collection of Poetry for Today; Nat. Anthol. of Poetry by Tchrs.; Encore Mag.; The Sunstone Review; Poetry

Venture. Recip., Hon. Mention, N.M. State Poetry Contest, 1971 & 73 & 3rd pl., 1972. Address: 9108 Atkinson, N.E., Albuquerque, NM 87112, U.S.A.

McCLURE, Michael, b. 20 Oct. 1932. Poet. Married w. 1 child. Published works: Passage, 1956; Peyote Poem, 1958; For Artaud, 1959; Hymns to St. Geryon & Other Poems, 1959; Dark Brown, 1967; Ghost Tantras, 1964: Thirteen Mad Sonnets, 1964; Poisoned Wheat, 1966; Love Lion Book, 1966; The Sermons of Jean Harlow & the Curses of Billy the Kid, 1968; Little Odes and the Raptors, 1969; Plays: The Beard, 1965; The Blossom or Billy the Kid, 1967; Other: Meat Science Essays, 1963; Freewheelin' Frank, Secretary of the Angels, 1967; Ed. w. others, Journal for the Protection of All Beings No. 1., 1961. Contbr. to (Anthols.): New American Poetry, 1960; Beat Scene, 1960; Poets of Today, 1964; A Controversy of Poets, 1965; New Writing in the USA, 1967; War Poems, 1968; (Jrnls.): Nation; Evergreen Review; Chicago Review; Poetry; Big Table; San Francisco Earthquake; City Lights Journal; Black Mountain Review; Origin.

McCOIN, Joseph Young, Jr., pen name **McCOIN, Mac,** b. 14 June 1946. Sec.-Treas., MWM Industries Inc. Education: Baylor School, Chattanooga, TN.; Bradley HS, Cleveland, TN.; Univ. of Chattanooga; Univ. of Tennessee Coll. of Law; City of London Coll.; The Hague Acad. of Internat. Law. Married. Contbr. to: Univ. Chattanooga Echo; Power; Springs of Wisdom (Tenn. Wesleyan); Anthol. of Modern Am. Poets. Address: 443 Worth St., NW., Cleveland, TN 37311, USA.

McCONNELL, Howell A., b. 8 Dec. 1935. Government Analyst. Education: B.A., Hist., Villanova Univ., Pa. Positions held: Fndr., Past Pres., Templeton Knolls Civic Assn.; Co-Fndr., Community of Reconciliation (Ecumenical Rel. Community). Mbr., Maryland State Poetry Soc. Published works: Flame & Mist, 1967; Unsung Vol. II, 1964; Soul & The Singer, 1968; Golden Harvest, 1967; Versatility in Verse, 1965. Contbr. to: Love & Laughter Column, Wash. Post; Higginson Jrnl. of Am. Poetry; The Am. Poet, 1967-69. Address: 6110 Longfellow St., East Riverdale, MD 20840, U.S.A.

McCORMICK, Geraldine Dixon, pen name **McCORMICK, Jeri,** b. 31 Mar. 1934. Writer. Education: B.S. in Ed., Tchrs. Coll., Univ. of Cinn., Ohio, 1955; M.S. in Ed., Univ. of Pitts., Pa., 1972. Married. Positions held: Elem. Tchr.; Gen. Office Wkr.; Subs. Tchr.; Copyediting & Proofreading. Recording Sec., Wis. Fellowship of Poets. Contbr. to: Hawk & Whippoorwill Recalled. Address: 4810 S. Hill Dr., Madison, WI 53705, U.S.A.

McCORMICK, Mary Thelma, pen name, **McCORMICK, Mary,** b. 24 Feb. 1908. Clerk and Secretary (retired). Education: Schools in Indiana, Ohio, and Alabama; commercial course in Alabama; training in journalism; studied poetry. Married Dennis Joseph McCormick, 1952 (dec. 1958). Positions held: Stenographer; Book-Keeper; Clerk in auditing dept., New Orleans, La., and Houston, Texas; Mechanic helper, US Air Base, Mobile; Tech. Order Clerk, US Air Base, Mobile; work in Air Force Base Civil Service. Memberships: Avalon World Arts Acad.; The Pensters (a Mobile Writers Group); Alabama Poetry Soc. (served on Reading & Evaluation Committee); Education Committee, State Soc. affil. with Nat. Organization; American Mosaic; Ariz. State Univ. Published works: Fourteen Poems, 1967; Harp on the Willow Tree, 1970. Contbr. to many newspapers, journals, mags., anthols. Recip. various citations, awards from Orphic Lute; CSSI; Avalon; Bishop Carpenter, etc. Address: 3205 Riverside Dr., Mobile, AL 36605, USA.

McCOY, Mary Maurine, pen name, **McCOY, Billie,** b. 25 April. Housewife. Education: B.A. (in Education), Indiana Univ. Married; 1 s. Memberships: Ind. Univ. Alumni Assn.; Internat. Clover Poetry Assoc.; Nat. News Registry; Nat. Fed. of State Poetry Socs., Inc.; Tennessee Women's Press and Authors' Assoc.;

Poetry Soc. of Tennessee; Wabash Valley Press Club; Free-Lance Press Club. Published works: Anthol. of Southeastern Poets, 1971; 1972 Yearbook of Modern Poetry; Clover Collection of Verse, 1973; The Bunny Who Wanted to Fly, 1973. Contbr. to: Children's Day; American Legion Mag.; Look; The Oriole News; Ideals Poetry Mag.; Tapesqueal Mag.; Author & Poet: New Frontier News; Grit; Knoxville News-Sentinel; Indianapolis Star; Linn's; Owen County Leader; Sevier County News-Record; The Mountain Visitor; The Gatlinburg Press; Signs Of His Coming. Awards: Writers' Digest Poetry Contest, 1963; Christus Gardens Poetry Competition, Grand Nat. Winner, 1968; Clover Internat. Poetry Soc. (Danae Award Cert.), 1973. Address: Route 4, Thurman Addition, Sevierville, TN 37862, USA.

McCRACKEN, Rachel, b. 15 Aug. 1927. Poet. Education: Rio Grande Coll., Ohio, U.S.A. Mbr., Editl.Bd., Tangent Poetry Quarterly. Published works: (Anthologies) Best American Poems, 1969; All-Time Favorite Poetry, 1969; Yearbook of Modern Poetry, 1971; (Book) Strange Music in Strange Places (forthcoming). Contbr. to: Adult Tchr.; Bachaet; Bardic Echoes; Bitterroot; The Bubbler; Cardinal Poetry Quarterly; The Catholic World; Cottonwood Review; Creative Review; Explorer; Green Apple; Ideals; Imprints Quarterly; The Living Church; Mustang Review; The Plain Dealer; Poet Lore; Tangent; Twigs; Wind. Has personal poetry radio prog. on WEFG Stereo, Winchester, Va. Honours, awards: Book Award, Am. Poetry Fellowship Soc., 1969; Cert. of Achievement Award, J. Mark Press, 1969; Cert. of Merit Award, ibid, 1969; Cert. Award for Poetry of superior broadcast quality, WEFG Stereo & WHPL – AM. Address: 4207 Redfern Rd., Parma, OH 44134, U.S.A.

McCUAIG, Ronald, b. 1908. Poet. Positions held: Radio Journalist, 'Wireless Weekly' & ABC Weekly; Journalist, Smith's Weekly; ibid, Sydney Morning Herald; Mbr., Lit. Staff, Bulletin; Mbr., Staff, Australian Commonwealth News & Info. Bur., Canberra, 1961–. Published works: Vaudeville, 1938; The Wanton Goldfish, 1941; Tales Out Of Bed, 1944; Quod Ronald McCuaig, 1946; The Ballad of Bloodthirsty Bessie and Other Poems, 1961. Address: c/o Angus & Robertson Ltd., 107 Elizabeth St., Melbourne, Australia.

McCULLOCH, Dewey Allen, b. 17 July 1942. Freelance Writer. Positions held: Pres., Trauma Studio Card Co. Published works: Winter Garden, 1970; Dark Country, 1972. Contbr. to: Dance of the Muse (anthol.), 1969; Yearbook of Modern Poetry (anthol.), 1971; Outstanding Contemporary Poetry (anthol.), 1972; Voices Int.; Haiku Highlights; Modern Haiku; Jean's Jrnl.; Bachaet; The Muse, etc. Recip. var. poetry awards. Address: P.O. Box 111, Royal Oak, MI 48068, U.S.A.

McCURTAIN, Lucile V., b. 17 Apr. 1894. Writer. Education: B.A., Mt. Holyoke Coll.; post grad. in Engl., Univ. of Calif. at Berkeley. Married. Positions held: Tchr. of Creative Writing under the Adult Educ. Prog. in Berkeley & Richmond, Calif. Memberships: Poetry Soc. of Am.; Composers, Authors & Artists of Am.; Calif. Writers' Club; Nat. League of Am. Pen Women; Vergilian Soc. of Am. Published works: The After-Image, 1946; High Moment, 1958; Thresholds of Awareness, 1966. Contbr. to: The Muse; Poet Lore; The Educational Forum; World Affairs; Progressive Farmer; Scimitar & Song; Poetry; The Musician; Christian Sci. Monitor; Ariz. Highways; The Am. Bard; Seydell Qtly.; The Seattle Post-Intelligencer, etc. Recip. sev. awards from Calif. Writers' Club & Ina Coolbrith Circle; Translation Prize & Award, Poet Lore, 1971. Address: 2808 N.W. 91 St., Seattle, WA 98117, U.S.A.

McDANIEL, David Earl, b. 7 Nov. 1906. Vocalist; Transportation Specialist. Education: State Normal Schl. (now the San Jose State Univ.), Calif. Positions held: Lib. Asst., Santa Clara Co. Lib.; Radio Artist, KQW – now KCBS, & KEEN, San Jose, Calif.; Soloist for var. churches; Traffic Specialist for Security Transportation & General Electric APED, San Jose; ret'd 1971; currently tchng. Poetry & Creative Writing at his studio-home, Writers' Workshop & Poets' Corner, and San Jose State Univ.; Lib. Commnr. for San Jose Public Lib. Memberships: Bd. Mbr., Ina Coolbrith Circle, San Francisco; Robert Frost Chapt., Calif. Fed. Chaparral Poets; Am. Poetry League; World Poetry Soc. Int.; Edwin Markham Poetry Soc., San Jose; Calif. Lib. Assn.; Western World Haiku Soc., Portland, Ore.; Peninsula Br., Calif. Writers Club. Contbr. to: Ina Coolbrith Anthol., 1973; Santa Cruz Chaparral Poets, 1973; Shore Poetry Anthol., 1971; Pancontinental Premier Poets, 1971-72; Am. Poetry League Bulletin; Desert Mag.; Driftwind; Haiku West; Janus-SCTH; Modern Haiku; Pacifica; Poet; Westward; Newsletter, Calif. Fed. of Chaparral Poets. Address: Writers' Workshop & Poets' Corner, 1939 The Alameda, San Jose, CA 95126, U.S.A.

McDANIEL, Esther C., pen name **McDANIEL, Esther Koerner,** b. 18 Nov. 1906. Poet; Freelance Writer. Education: Lockyear's Bu. Coll., Evansville, Ind., U.S.A., 1926. Married William R. McDaniel, 1 son (dec.) Positions held: Private, & Law Sec., Evansville, Ind., 1926-29; Hospitality Hostess & Food Columnist, Supermarkets, Alaska, 1956-68; Guest Poet & Food Commentator, TV, Radio & Clubs, Alaska, 1964-67; Poet & Freelance Writer, Alaska, Ark. & Ore., 1964–. Memberships: Nat. League of Am. Pen Women; World Poetry Soc.; Poetry Soc. of Alaska; Ozark Writers Guild; South & West, Inc.; Poetry Soc. of Tex. (Assoc.); Ore. State Poetry Soc. Published works: Rainbow To The Storms, 1964; Contbr. to: 100 Years of Alaskan Poetry, 1965; Haiku Drops from the Great Dipper, 1973; Portland Oregonian; Anchorage News; Anchorage Times; Pen Points; Flame Annual; Am. Bard; Alaska Review; Stella Borealis; Discourses on Poetry; Modern Images; Alaska Centennial Record; Miss. Poetry Jrnl.; Poet (India); Phoenix Fires (Mosaic). First Prize Awards from the following: Poetry Soc. of Alaska, 1964; Nat. League Am. Pen Woman, Colo., 1965; South & West, Ark., 1966; Miss. Fest. of Arts, 1968, 69, 70; Writer's Unlimited, 1971, 72; Calif. Fed. of Chaparral Poets, 1968; Deep South Writers Conf., La., 1969, 71; Ozark Writers' Guild, 1969, 71; Southwest Conf., 1969; Ark. Writers Conf., 1970, 73. Address: 850 Hillview Dr., Ashland, OR 97520, U.S.A.

McDONALD, Ellis Atkisson, b. 7 Dec. 1912. Homemaker. Married George E. McDonald. Positions held: var. inclng. Sec. to a Doctor; Bookkeeper; Internal Revenue Serv. Clerk. Memberships: Poetry Soc. of Va.; Pa. Poetry Soc.; Nat. Fed. of State Poetry Socs. Published works: Green Leaves, 1959. Contbr. to: Univ. of Kans. City Review, Ga. Mag.; The Wash. Post; Bride's Mag.; Ga. Review; N.Y. Herald Tribune; Wings; Carolina Qtly.; The Country Poet; Christian Advocate; Golden Atom; Charleston Evening Post; Dallas Morning News, etc. Recip. many prizes from Atlanta Writers' Club, & sev. from other state poetry socs. Address: 4117 Ashford Dunwoody Rd. N.E., Atlanta, GA 30319, U.S.A

McDONALD, Ian Archie, b. 18 Apr. 1933. Company Executive. Education: B.A. & M.A., Cambridge Univ., U.K., 1951-55. Positions held: Sec., Bookers Grp. Comm., Georgetown, Guyana, 1955-59; Co. Sec., Bookers Sugar Estates Ltd., ibid, 1959-64; Admin. Sec., 1964-72; Admin. Dir., Bookers Sugar Estates Ltd., Georgetown, 1972–, also Chmn., Demerara Sugar Terminals, Dir., Bookers Shipping (Dem) Ltd., Demerara Foundry & Guyana Sugar Prod. Assn. Ltd. Memberships: Comm., Nat. Pub. Lib. Comm., Georgetown; Fellow, Royal Soc. of Lit., 1970. Published works: The Hummingbird Tree (novel), 1969; Pot-o-Rice Horowitz's House of Solace (short story), 1968. Contbr. to BIM (poems); Pembroke Mag.; Savacou. Recip., Winifred Holtby prize for the best regional novel, Royal Soc. of Lit., 1969. Address: c/o Bookers Sugar Estates Ltd., 22 Church St., Georgetown, Guyana.

MACDONALD, Joan, b. 12 July 1920. Housewife;

Social Worker. Education: Social Studies Cert., Portsmouth Tech. Coll., 1963. Married Rear Admiral Roderick MacDonald, C.B.E., 3 sons. Positions held: M.T.C. Ambulance Driver, 1940; Plotter in W. Africa & S. Africa (Civilian), 1942; Admiralty Plotter (TACO), 1943-44; Voluntary Welfare Visitor for WRVS & for Le Court Cheshire Home. Member, Petersfield Lit. Soc., 1965. Published works: Shadows & Reality, 1962. Contbr. to: Cruelty, Spring Anthol., 1960; var. local newspapers. Address: Spinner's Ash, Tilmore, Petersfield, Hants, U.K.

McDONALD, Nancy May, pen name **McDONALD, Nan,** b. 25 Dec. 1921. Editor. Education: B.A., Univ. of Sydney, Australia. Positions held: Publr's. Ed., Angus & Robertson Ltd., Sydney. Member of Poetry Soc. of Australia. Published works: Pacific Sea, 1947; The Lonely Fire, 1954; The Lighthouse, 1959; Selected Poems, 1969; Australian Poetry (ed.), 1953. Contbr. to: The Bulletin; Southerly; Quadrant; Poetry Magazine; Penguin Book of Australian Verse, 1958; Modern Austalian Verse, 1964. Recip. of Grace Levin Prize, 1948. Address: 24 Yates Ave., Mount Keira, NSW, Australia 2500.

McDONALD, Roger, b. 23 June 1941. Publisher's Editor. Education: B.A., Sydney Univ., Australia. Married, 1 daughter. Positions held: Educl. Producer, Australian Broadcasting Commn.; Lit. Ed., Univ. of Queensland Press. Published works: Citizens of Mist, 1968; The First Paperback Poets Anthology (Ed.), 1974. Contbr. to: The Australian; The Age; Poetry Australia; Poet's Choice, etc. Address: P.O. Box 42, St. Lucia, Queensland, Australia.

McDOWELL, Edward Allison, III, b. 17 Sept. 1927. College Professor. Education: B.A., Furman Univ., 1949; M.A., Vanderbilt Univ., 1951; B.D., Yale Univ., 1954. Married; 6 children. Positions held: Asst. Prof., Stetson Univ., 1954-56; Instr., Stephens Coll., 1957-59; Asst. Prof to Prof., Philosophy, Montgomery Coll., 1960-74. Contbr. to: In Context; Georgia Review; Impetus; Yearbook of Modern Poetry; Poems from the Capitol; Forum; Southern Poetry Review. Address: Montgomery Coll., Rockville, MD 20850, USA.

McELROY, Colleen Elizabeth Johnson, b. 30 Oct. 1935. Writer; Teacher. Education: B.S., Kansas State Univ., 1958; M.A., ibid, 1963; Ph.D., Univ. of Wash., 1973. Married David F. McElroy, 2 children. Positions held: Cons., Office of Econ. Opportunity, Proj. Upward Bound, 1967-69; Asst. Prof., Western Wash. State Coll., 1966-73; Instr., Cross-cultural Approaches to Communication – in cooperation w. projects in the Dept. of Educ., WWSC, 1970-71; Lang. Arts Cons , Ctrl. Region Seattle Public Schls., 1972-73; Predoctoral Lectr., Univ. of Wash. Dept. of Engl., 1972-73; Asst. Prof., Univ. of Wash., 1973–, etc. Memberships incl: United Black Artists Lit. Guild, Seattle; Am. Speech & Hearing Assn. Published works: (poetry book) The Mules Done Long Since Gone; (textbook) Speech & Lang. Dev. of the Preschool Schild, 1972; (films) Tracy Gains Language & Introduction to Clinical Practicum. Contbr. to: Poetry Pilot; S.D. Review; Northwest Review; Essence; Choice; Sojourner Collective; Kansas Speech Jrnl.; Wormwood Review, etc. Recip., Carnation Tchng. Incentive Award, 1973. Address: 2200 N.E. 75th, Seattle, WA 98115, U.S.A.

McELWAIN, Daniel Bernard, Jr., b. 26 Aug. 1924. Equipment Specialist. Education: Grad. w. Dip. in Aircraft Design, Acad. of Aeronautics, 1947; Attended Fairleigh Dickinson Univ., N.J., 1954-65; Indl. Coll. of the Armed Forces, 1972-73. Married Palma Dorothy Kammerl, 5 children. Positions held: Commnd. 2nd Lt., USAF, 1950; Aircraft Engine Instr., 1954-56; Market Analyst, Physicist, Techn., 1956-60; Owner of Iron Shop, 1960-61; active duty, USAF, 1961-62; Mathematical Engr., 1962-65; Math. Instr. & Stress Analyst Consulting Engr., 1966-68; Writer of Job Resumes (Interviewer, Counselor) & Printer, 1963-73; currently Equipment Specialist, Pentagon, Wash. D.C. & Lt. Col., USAF Res. Memberships: N.J. Poetry Soc.;

Past V.P., Delaware Valley Poetry Chapt. Contbr. to: The Soul & The Singer, 1970; International Anthol., 1973. Address: 2132 Lawrenceville Rd., Trenton, NJ 08638, U.S.A.

McELVANY, Nancy, b. 10 Nov. 1973. Housewife. Published works: The Soul Sings by New Dawn, 1973; Birth of Day, 1972; Echoes of Faith, 1970. Contbr. to: Spencer Book's Poetry Parade; Jean's Jrnl.; Shore Poetry Anthol.; Yearbook of Modern Poetry; Grains of Sand; Poetry Column, Poetry of the Southwest. Address: 504 Smith St., Clute, TX 77531, U.S.A.

MACENTEE, Seán (John Francis), pen name **KEERAN, Laurence,** b. 22 Aug. 1889. Government Minister. Education: St. Malachy's Coll., Belfast; Belfast Municipal Coll. of Technol. Married Margaret Browne, 1 son, 2 daughters. Positions held: Cons. Engr. & Patent Agent, 1917-32; Mbr., Nat. Exec. Comm., of Irish Volunteers & Irish Republican Army, 1917-21; Min. for Finance, 1932-39 & '51-54; Min. for Industry & Commerce, 1939-41; Min. for Local Govt., 1947-48; Deputy Prime Minister of Ireland, 1959-65; Min. for Hlth. in the Govt. of Ireland, 1957-65; Min. for Soc. Welfare, 1958-61; Former Tanaiste; Mbr., Coun. of State, 1968; T.D., South Monaghan, 1919-21, Monaghan, 1921-22; Dublin Co., 1927-37, Dublin Townships, 1937-48, & Dublin South (East), 1948–; Co. Dir. Mbr., PEN, Dublin. Published works: Poems, 1918; Episode at Easter, 1966. Contbr. to: Irish Review; Irish News; The Observer. Honours, awards: Kt. Grand Cross, 1st Class of Order of Pius, 1916; Medal w. Bar, 1918 & '21; Hon. LL.D., Nat. Univ. of Ireland. Address: Montrose, Trimleston Ave., Booterstown, Co. Dublin, Ireland.

MACEWEN, Gwendolyn (Margaret), b. 1 Sept. 1941. Writer; Poet; Novelist. Published works: The Rising Fire, 1963; A Breakfast For Barbarians, 1966; The Shadow Maker, 1969; The Armies Of The Moon, 1972; Julian The Magician, 1963; King of Egypt, King of Dreams, 1972; (short stories) Noman, 1973. Contbr. to the main literary magazines and journals in Canada. Awards: The Borestone Mountain Poetry Award, 1964; The Governor General's Award, 1970; The A.J.M. Smith Award, 1973; also recip. of several Canada Council Grants, both for prose and poetry. Address: c/o MacMillan Publishers, 70 Bond St., Toronto, Ont., Canada.

McEWEN, Jean, b. 14 Dec. 1923. Artist; Painter. Has written two unpublished books: Le Temps des Pays Vastes, 1972 & Adagio d'un printemps a venis, 1973. Contbr. to: Gant du Ciel; La Nouvelle Relère; Amerique Française; Le quartier Latin. Address: 580 Davaar, Montreal 153, Canada.

McFADDEN, David, b. 11 Oct. 1940. Writer. Mbr., League of Canadian Poets. Published works: The Poem Poem, 1966; The Saladmaker, 1967; Letters from the Earth to the Earth, 1968; The Ova Yogas, 1969. Contbr. to: Ant's Forefoot; Fiddlehead; Quarry; Weed; Bust; Is; Talon; Hyphid; Canadian Forum; Wormwood Review; Tish; Tamarack Review; Ann Arbor Review; Little Mother; Work; Pot Pourri; New Wave Canada; The Enchanted Land; The Wind Has Wings; Thumbprints; Imago; Pliego; Open Letter; From A Window. Honours: Canada Council Arts Bursaries, 1968, '69. Address: 86 Garside Ave. N., Hamilton 27, Ont., Canada.

McFADDEN, Roy, b. 14 Nov. 1921. Lawyer. Education: Queen's Univ., Belfast. Married w. 5 children. Positions held: Co-Ed., Rann, an Ulster Quarterly of Poetry, 1948-53; Currently in practice as Lawyer. Published works: Russian Summer, 1941; Three New Poets, 1942; Swords & Ploughshares, 1943; Flowers for a Lady, 1945; The Heart's Townland, 1947; Elegy for the Dead of the Princess Victoria, 1952. Contbr. to (Anthols.): 1000 years of Irish Poetry, 1947; Contemporary Irish Poetry, 1949; Oxford Book of Irish Verse, 1958; Mentor Book of Irish Poetry, 1965; Love Poems of the Irish, 1967; Penguin Book of Irish Verse, 1970. Address: White Thorn, Shrewsbury Gardens,

Belfast, Northern Ireland.

McFARLANE, Basil Clare, b. 23 Apr. 1922. Journalist; Broadcaster. Education: Jamaica Coll.; Jamaica Schl. of Arts & Crafts, 1952. Married 3 times, five sons. Positions held: w. RAF in Britain during WWII. Published works: Jacob & the Angel & Other Poems, 1952. His verse has been published in Britain, U.S.A., Germany, Nigeria, Guyana, as well as the West Indies. Contbr. to: Public Opinion; West Indian Review; Life & Letters (London Mercury); Phylon; Mag. of Atlanta Univ.; BIM; Caribbean Qtly.; Kykoveral; Focus; Black Orpheus; Sunday Gleaner; London Mag.; Jamaica Jrnl.; Now. Address: c/o Inst. of Jamaica, Kingston, Jamaica, W.I.

McGAUGHEY, Florence Helen, b. 1 Mar. 1904. Professor of English. Education: A.B., De Pauw Univ., Greencastle, Ind., U.S.A., 1926; A.M., Middlebury Coll., Vt., 1932; grad. work at sev. univs. Positions held: Tchr. of H.S. Engl., Kentland, Cloverdale, Plymouth & Greencastle, Ind.; Prof. of Engl., Ind. State Univ., Terre Haute, 1946-70. Memberships incl: Nat Arts Club, N.Y.C.; Nat. League of Am. Pen Women; Hon. Rep., Centro Studi e Scambi Int., Rome; Fellow, Int. Poetry Soc., U.K.; Acad. of Am. Poets; Hon.Mbr., Eugene Field & Mark Twain Socs. Published works: (books) Wind Across the Night, 1938; Music in the Wind, 1941; Spring is a Blue Kite, 1946; Reaching for the Spring, 1958; Selected Poems (Rome), 1961; Shadows (Rome), 1965; Petals from a Plum Tree, 1967. Ms., opera libretto, The Dispossessed in hands of Composer, Jon J. Polifrone. Contbr. to many mags. jrnls. etc., inclng: Christian Sci. Monitor; Portland Oregonian; N.Y. Sun; Chicago Tribune; Home Life; Am. Bard; Am. Weave. Recip. many hons. & awards inclng: 1st Prize, ballad, Nat. League Am. Pen Women, 1948; 1st Prize, Am. Weave, 1961; Prize Award Accademia Int. Leonardo da Vinci. Address: 136 South 25th St., Terre Haute, IN 47803, U.S.A.

McGAUGHEY, Kathryn Elizabeth, b. 3 Feb. 1918. Apartment Manager & Housewife. Married, 7 children. Positions held: num. offices in 'We Write' (a local writers org.), 1968-72; Tchr., poetry courses, Jefferson Co. Adult Educ., 1969-72; Treas., Poetry Soc. of Colo., 1971-73. Published works: Treasures, 1966; Little Red Chair, 1966; Gift of Laughter, 1972; Jefferson Co. Histl. pamphlet for Jefferson Ave. United Meth. Ch., 1973. Contbr. to: Denver Post; Jefferson Co. Sentinel; Grit; Protestant Herald; Callaway Courier; Farm Wife News; Carpenter; Roaring Twenties; Good Old Days; The Rotarian; Colorado West; Colorado Mag. Recip., 2nd prize, Denver Writers Workshop, 1972. Address: 4561 Kipling St. Apt. 12, Wheat Ridge, CO 80033, U.S.A.

MacGAVIN, Elizabeth Louise Cushing, pen name, **MacGAVIN, Elizabeth Cushing,** b. 20 Feb. 1938. Poet. Education: St. Mary's Acad., Los Angeles, 1954; Anglo-American HS, Kifissia, Greece, 1955; Redlands HS, Calif., 1962; San Bernardino Valley Coll., A.A. in Liberal Arts, 1972; and currently studying Comparative Literature, Univ. of Calif., Riverside (Dean's Honor List). Married to Robert R. MacGavin; 5 children. Memberships: Calif. Fed. of Chaparral Poets (Awards Chairman); CSSI; World Poetry Soc. Intercontinental; American Poetry League; Nat. League of American Pen Women, Inc.; Arrowhead Allied Arts Council (Arts Director). Published works: The Open Meadow, 1971; Sweet and Bitter, 1971. Contbr. to: Poet; Modern Haiku; The Archer; Major Poets; American Poetry League Bulletin; Epos; Prospect; Phineas; Yearbook of American Poetry; New Voices in the Wind; The Soul and the Singer; Outstanding Contemporary Poetry; Voices International. Awards: Hon. Mention, Ina Coolbrith Mem. Contest, 1972; 2nd Prize and Hon. Mention, Twin Counties Press Club's Poetry Contest, 1970; C.F.C.P. John Stephen McGroarty Pilgrimage & Nat. Poetry Day reading, 1970. Address: 22755 Scott St., Colton, CA 92324, USA.

McGILLEY, (Sister) Mary Janet, pen name **RYAN,**

Teresa, b. 4 Dec. 1924. College President. Education: B.A., St. Mary Coll.; M.A., Boston Coll.; Ph.D., Fordham Univ.; Post grad. studies, Univ. of Notre Dame; Columbia Univ. Entered Sisters of Charity of Leavenworth, 1946. Positions held: Teacher, Hayden HS., Topeka, Ks.; Teacher, Central HS, Billings, Mont.; English faculty, St. Mary Coll., Leavenworth, Ks., and since, 1964, President. Memberships: Catholic Poetry Soc. of America; Delta Epsilon Sigma. Contbr. to: University Review; Commonweal; Kansas Qtly.; Four Quarters; Western Humanities Review; Spirit; Catholic World; Delta Epsilon Sigma Bulletin; Sponsa Regis; New Mexico Qtly., etc. Address: St. Mary Coll., Leavenworth, KS 66048, USA.

McGINLEY, Phyllis (Mrs. Charles L. Hayden), b. 21 Mar. 1905. Author; Poet. Education: Univ. of Utah, Salt Lake City; Univ. of Calif., Berkeley. Married Charles L. Hayden w. 2 children. Positions held: Formerly Schl. Tchr., Utah & N.Y.; Worked for an Advertising Agency; Former Staff Writer, Town & Country, N.Y. Mbrships: Advsry. Bd., The American Scholar, Wash., D.C.; Nat. Inst. of Arts & Letters. Published works incl: One More Manhattan, 1934; Husbands are Difficult, 1941; Stones from a Glass House, 1946; Times Three: Selected Verse, 1960; Mince Pie & Mistletoe, 1961; Wonderful Time, 1966; Other: Province of the Heart, 1959; A Girl & Her Room, 1963; Ed., Wonders & Surprises, 1968. Contbr. to (Anthols.): Poems for a Machine Age, 1941; A New Treasury of War Poetry, 1943; Faber Book of Modern American Verse, 1956; Poetry for Pleasure, 1960; Poems & Poets, 1965; This Land is Mine, 1965; (Jrnls.): New Yorker; Reader's Digest; Ladies' Home Jrnl.; Vogue. Recip., Num. Hons. 60 Beach Ave., Larchmont, N.Y., 10538, USA.

McGOUGH, Roger, b. 9 Nov. 1937. Poet. Education: St. Mary's Coll., Liverpool, U.K.; Hull Univ. Published works: Frinck, Summer with Monika, 1967; Watchwords, 1969; After the Merrymaking, 1971; Gig, 1973. Contbr. to: Penguin Modern Poets No. 10; Oxford Book of Twentieth Century English Verse. Address: c/o Hope Leresche & Steele, 11 Jubilee Pl., Chelsea, London SW3 3TE, U.K.

McGOVERN, Robert, b. 2 Dec. 1927. Poet; Professor. Education: B.A. & M.A., Univ. of Minn.; Ph.D., Engl., Case Western Reserve Univ.; pre-doctoral study at Univ. of London. Married, 4 children. Positions held: Asst. Prof., Engl., Radford Coll., Va., 1957-65; Prof. of Engl. & Creative Writing, Ashland Coll., Ohio, 1965–. Co-Ed., The Ashland Poetry Press; Co-Dir., Ohio Poets' Assn. Published works: A Feast of Flesh & Other Occasions, 1971; The Way of the Cross in time of Revolt, 1971. Co-Ed. of 17 collections & anthols. of pootry, 1060-74. Contbr. to: The Nation; The Christian Century; Laural Review; Spirit; Hiram Poetry Review; Fine Arts Discovery; The Cresset; Kans. Qtly.; Midwestern Univ. Qtly.; num. anthols., etc. Address: R.D.4, Box 131, Ashland, OH 44805, U.S.A.

McGRATH, Thomas M., b. 20 Nov. 1916. Editor; Associate Professor. Education: B.A., Engl., Univ. of N.D., Grand Forks, 1939; M.A., Engl., La. State Univ., Baton Rouge, 1940; Rhodes Scholar, New Coll., Oxford, 1947-48. Positions held: Formerly Univ. Tchr. & Script-writer during the 1950's; Asst. Ed., California Quarterly; Ed., Crazy Horse, Fargo, N.D.; Sometime Assoc. Prof. of Engl., N.D. State Univ., Fargo. Published works: Three Young Poets, 1940; The Dialectics of Love, 1944; A Garland of Practical Poesie, 1949; A Witness to the Times, 1953; Letter to an Imaginary Friend, 1962, Vols. I & II, 1970; Other: About Clouds, 1955; The Gates of Ivory, The Gates of Horn, 1956; The Beautiful Things, 1958. Contbr. to (Anthols.): Poetry for Pleasure, 1960: New Poets of England & America, 1962; Poets of Today, 1964; Heartland, 1967: Where is Vietnam, 1967; (jrnls.): Kayak; Sixties; Poetry. Hons: Swallow Book Award, 1955; Amy Lowell Travelling Poetry Scholarship, 1965-66; Guggenheim Fellowship in Poetry, 1968; Address: 51 Seventh Ave. South, N.Y., NY 10014, USA.

MACGREGOR-HASTIE, Roy Alasdhair Niall, b. 28 Mar. 1929. Author. Education: Royal Mil. Acad., Sandhurst; Univs. of Manchester & Surrey; B.A., M.F.A., dr. univ. Married Mariagrazia Dallago, 2 sons. Positions held: Foreign Corres., United Press Int. & London Express Features, 1953-58, '60-64; Ed., Staff Writer, This Week prog., 1958-59; Sr. Lectr. in Engl. & Comp. Lit., Coll. of Educ., Inst. of Educ., Univ. of Hull, 1965–. Memberships: Poetry Soc., London; Int. Poetry Soc.; Sec., The British Assn. for Romanian Studies. Published works: Poems Lyrical & Empirical, 1953; The Mirror to the Mind, 1954; Interim Statement, 1962; Anthol. of Romanian Poetry (UNESCO), 1969; Eleven Elegies (Stanescu), 1970; Frames (Sorescu), 1971; The Last Romantic (UNESCO – Eminescu), 1972; Sweet Swan of Humberside, 1974. Contbr. to: Int. PEN Anthol., 1975; most lit. mags. & the world's press (as Foreign Corres.); BBC; ABC; SABC; NZBC. Honours, awards: Florence Garland, Arthur Lyon Meml., 1945; BARS Prize (verse transl.), 1970, '71, '74. Address: Savage Club, 86 St. James St., London SW1, U.K.

MACHUGA, John Allen, b. 21 Mar. 1947. Educator; Freelance Media Script Writer. Education: A.A., Macomb Community Coll., Warren, Mich., 1967; B.S., Wayne State Univ., Detroit, 1971; var. postgrad. work. Positions held: Ed., Macomb College's newspaper 'Sporadic', 1966-67; Dir. of P.R., ESP-TV, Wayne State Univ.; Hd. of Educational TV Dept., Bishop Gallagher H.S., 1972–. Memberships: ASCAP; Mbr., Nat. Poets of Am.; Nat. Assn. of Educl. Broadcasters; Poetry Soc. of Mich. Wrote, & Asst. Produce, an expmtl. screenplay entitled 'A Nation in Exile', telecast, Detroit, Chicago & San Francisco area, 1971. Contbr. to: Am. Poet; Bardic Echoes; Archer; Peninsular Poets; Encounter; (anthols.) A Year in Modern Poetry; Lyrics of Love. Produced two half-hour TV progs. dealing w. modern poetry, 'Ins and Outs of Love' & 'Poets to the People', 1972. Address: 14763 Lydia, East Detroit, MI 48021, U.S.A.

McHUGH, Terence, pen name **LEPRECHAUN,** b. 17 Mar. 1905. Married. Positions held: Ptnr., Jackson Stops & Staff, Land Agents, London & Provinces, 1930-73. Member, Cheltenham Poetry Soc. Published works: (books of poems) Love, Life & Laughter, 1970; Poems of a Countryman, 1972; Red Skies at Eventide, 1973. Contbr. to: The Field (London); The Wilts & Glos Standard (Cirencester); The Estate Times (London); The Shooting Times; Western Daily Press (Bristol); ITV TV. Address: Waterfowl Sanctuary, Baunton Fields, Nr. Cirencester, Glos., U.K.

McINNIS, Blanche Warren Page, b. 31 Aug. 1919. Writer. Education: B.A., Engl., Univ. of Tex., Austin, 1941; Incarnate Word Coll., San Antonio; grad. work, Jrnlsm., Univ. of Wis., Madison. Married Ernest Charles McInnis, 1 son, 1 daughter. Positions held: Mathematician, U.S. Govt.; USO Chmn., San Antonio, Tex.; Jr. H.S. Instr.; Sec.-Treas., Charles McInnis Inc. Memberships: Pres., Pan Hellenic Soc., San Antonio; Social Chmn., & Circle Ldr., St. Andrew's Ch., Wellesley, Mass.; Kappa Kappa Gamma; Wellesley Writers Workshop; Custodian of Poems, Poetry Soc. of San Antonio, Tex. Contbr. to: The Green World; The Villager; Poetry Soc. of San Antonio, Tex. Mag. Honours, awards: Awards for serious & humorous poems, Mass. Fed. of Women's Clubs, 1964; Memorial poem written for St. Andrew's Ch., 1965 & for Girl Scouts of Am. Address: 500 South Vandiver, San Antonio, TX 78209, U.S.A.

McINTOSH, (Alexander) Sandy, b. 18 Nov. 1947. Music School Director. Education: B.A., Long Island Univ., Southampton, 1970; M.F.A., Columbia Univ. Schl. of Arts, 1973. Positions held: Reporter, Southampton Summer Day, 1969; Ed., Survivor's Manual, lit. jrnl., 1969–; Taxi Driver, 1973; Mng. Dir., E. McIntosh Schl. of Music, 1973–. Published works: Earth Works, 1970; Which Way to the Egress? 1974; The Beginning of the Bed was Before the War, 1971 (privately printed & distributed). Contbr. to: Chelsea; Kayak; The Nation; Venice Krak; Unmuzzled Ox; Some; Noise; Saltillo; The Windmill, etc. Honours, awards: 1st pl., Southampton Poetry Prize, 1969;

Grant, Nat. Endowment for the Arts (Lit.) for 'Survivor's Manual', 1972; Poet-in-Res., Wantagh, Merrick & Hewlett Public Schls., 1973–. Address: 3 January Walk, Long Beach, NY 11561, U.S.A.

McINTOSH, Elaine Virginia, b. 30 Jan. 1924. Biochemist-Nutritionist. Education: B.A., Augustana Coll., Sioux Falls, S.D.; M.A., Univ. of S.D., Vermillion; Ph.D., Iowa State Univ., Ames. Married Thomas H. McIntosh, 3 sons. Positions held: Asst. Prof., Chem., Sioux Falls Coll., S.D., 1945-48; Rsch. Fellow, Univ. of S.D., 1948-49; Instr., Iowa State Univ., 1949-54; Rsch. Assoc., Univ. of Ill., 1954-55; Rsch. Assoc., Iowa State Univ., 1955-62; Asst. Prof., Univ. of Wis., Green Bay, 1968-72; Assoc. Prof., ibid, 1972–. Memberships: Green Bay Writers' Club; Wis. Fellowship of Poets; Wis. Regl. Writers; Nat. Fed. of State Poetry Socs., Inc., U.S.A. Contbr. to: two children's books of poetry, published by S.D. Dept. of Public Instn., 1936 & '37; Waubay H.S. newspaper; Lyrical Iowa; Pasque Petals; 1949 Anthol. of Poetry Digest; Green Bay Press Gazette. Address: Coll. of Human Biol., Univ. of Wis.-Green Bay, WI 54302, U.S.A.

McINTYRE, Wade, b. 26 Mar. 1949. Freelance Writer. Education: Grad., La. State Univ. (Jrnlsm. & Creative Writing), 1971. Positions held: Freelance Writer; Copywriter; currently New Orleans Mgr., The Waterways Jrnl. Mag. Contbr. to: Poet, India, 1973. Honours, awards: 1st pl. in Poetry Div., La. Coll. Writers' Soc., 1971 & 1st pl. in Short Story Div. Address: c/o Amos B. McIntyre, 3344 Gerlando Dr., Baton Rouge, LA 70814, U.S.A.

MACKAY, Florence Ruth, pen name **GILBERT, Ruth,** b. 26 Mar. 1917. Poet. Education: Grad., Otago Schl. of Physiotherapy, Dunedin, New Zealand. Married, 4 children. Positions held: Physiotherapist at var. N.Z. Hosps. until 1945. Memberships: Past Pres., PEN Int. (N.Z. Ctr.); Past Pres., N.Z. Women Writers Soc. Published works: Lazarus & Other Poems, 1949; The Sunlit Hour, 1955; The Luthier, 1966. Contbr. to var. anthols. in U.K. & N.Z.; also to the BBC, NZBC & the N.Z. Listener. Recip., Jessie Mackay Memorial Award for Poetry, 1950, '51, '66. Address: 83 Donald St., Karori, Wellington, New Zealand.

MacKAY, Louis Alexander, pen name **SMALACOMBE, John,** b. 27 Feb. 1901. Retired Educator. Education: M.A., Univ. of Toronto, Canada, 1925; M.A., Balliol Coll., Oxford Univ., 1948. Positions held: Instr.-Asst. Prof., Univ. of Toronto, 1928-41; Assoc. Prof., Univ. of B.C., 1941-48; Prof., Univ. of Calif., 1948–. Memberships: Hon. Pres., Univ. Coll. Lit. & Athletic Soc., Toronto, Canada, 1938-40; San Francisco Browning Soc., 1954. Published works: Vipers Bugloss, 1938; The Ill-Tempered Lover, 1948; Arethusa, 1968. Contbr. to: Canadian Forum; Toronto Saturday Night; Poetry; Outposts; Northern Review; Poetry Commonweal; Contemporary Verse. Address: 36 Ardmore Rd., Kensington, CA 94707, U.S.A.

McKEE, Mel, b. 22 June 1934. Teacher; Publisher; Editor. Education: B.A., Tenn. Temple Coll.; M.A., Univ. of Ga. Positions held: Aviation Boatswain, U.S. Naval Air Force; on Fac., DeKalb Coll., Clarkston, Ga., 10 yrs.; Ed. & Publsr., This Issue & DeKalb Lit. Arts Jrnl. Contbr. to over 30 mags. & anthols. Honours, awards: First Prize for Book Manuscript of Poetry, Ga. Writers Assn. Inc. for 'Of Hell & Wonder', 1974. Address: Box 15558, Emory Stn., Atlanta, GA 30333, U.S.A.

McKEE, Ruby McKinley, b. 8 Apr. 1897. Housewife. Education: North Tex. State Univ., Denton, Tex.; Certs. of Tchng. Married W. Ervin McKee, 5 children. Mbr., Poetry Soc. of Tex., 8 yrs.; Councilor, ibid, sev. yrs. Book, Stepping Stones Down Life's Pathway, to be published soon. Contbr. of poems to: The Bulletin, Brookfield, Mo.; The La Grange Jrnl.; Gainesville Daily Register; Visions in Verse. Address: Rte.1, Box 80, Gainesville, TX 76240, U.S.A.

McKENNON, Joyce Hilton, b. 7 Feb. 1932. Freelance Writer. Education: Coll. of The Ozarks (2 yrs.) Clarksville, Ark.; Long Beach Jr. Coll., Calif.; Univ. of Tulsa, Okla. Married to C.H. McKennon; 2 children. Positions held: Reporter, Tulsa City/County Civil Defense Mag.; Asst. Editor, Forum House Publishing Co., Atlanta; Freelance Writer. Memberships: Tulsa Night Writers (various offices; member 15 yrs.); Okla. Writers Fed.; Ga. Writers Assoc.; Scribe Tribe, Atlanta. Published work: Yearbook of Modern Poetry, 1971. Contbr. to: Ark. Gazette; Twigs; The Bixby Bulletin; The Broken Arrow Ledger; Words on the Wind; Blue River Anthol., etc. Awards: Clara Lester Award for Excellence, 1968; Night Writer Woman of the Year, 1967; Post Award, 2nd prize for poetry manuscript (Brush Strokes), prizes for short-stories, children's book, and sci. fiction book, Ga. Writers Assn., 1973. Address: 2710 South 75th East Avenue, Tulsa, OK 74129, USA.

McKENZIE, Lillian Crawford, b. 15 June 1905. Housewife; Club Woman. Education: Wesleyan Coll., Macon, Ga.; studied Art at Art Students League, N.Y. Married Dr. Norton McKenzie. Positions held: On Bd. of The Dade Co. Med. Aux., The Children's Theatre, The Miami Music Club, The United Daughters of Confederacy, Nat. League of Am. Pen Women (Miami Br.) Mbr., Laramore Rader Poetry Club. Published works: Dear Mama & Papa. Contbr. to var. poetry mags. Address: 3120 Brickell Ave., Miami, FL, U.S.A.

McKEOWN, Thomas S., pen name **McKEOWN, Tom,** b. 29 Sept. 1937. Educator. Education: B.A., Univ. of Mich., 1961; M.A., ibid, 1962. Positions held with: Alpena Coll., 1962-64; Univ. of Wis., Oshkosh, 1964-68; Stephens Coll., 1968-74. Published works: (books) The Luminous Revolver, 1973; Driving to Santa Fe, 1974; The House of Water, 1974. Contbr. to: The New Yorker; The Sat. Review; The Atlantic Monthly; Harper's Mag.; The Nation; Commonweal; The N.Y. Times; The Harvard Advocate; The Chicago Tribune; The Kan. City Star, etc. Honours, awards: Avery Hopwood Award for Poetry, Univ. of Mich., 1968; Res. Grant, Wulitzer Fndn., Taos, N.M., 1972 & Yaddo Colony, N.Y., 1973. Address: P.O. Box 82, Pentwater, MI 49449, U.S.A.

McKERNAN, John Joseph, b. 11 May 1942. College English Teacher. Education: B.A., Univ. of Omaha, 1965; M.A., Univ. of Ark., 1967; M.F.A., Columbia Univ., 1971. Positions held: Prof. of Engl., Marshall Univ., 1967; Ed. of the Little Review Press, 1968–. Books in Manuscript: Translations of Vergers & Les Quatrième Valasien of Rainer Maria Rilke; Translation of Arthur Rimbaud's Le Bateau Ivre; Translations of Odes & Epodes of Horace; Edition of The Collected Art & Music Criticism of Ezra Pound; Original Poetry 'The Father Poems'. Contbr. of poems, translations, reviews & articles to many jrnls. inclng: Field; Beloit Poetry Jrnl.; Prairie Schooner; Little Review; Chelsea; The Smith; National Review; Antaeus; The Salt Creek Reader; The Goddard Jrnl.; Grain of Sand; Sparrow; Gnosis; Occident. Address: Dept. of Engl., Marshall Univ., Huntington, WV 25701, U.S.A.

McKERROW, Marjorie-Jean, b. 17 Nov. 1918. Hairdresser; Beauty Culturist; Modern Artist. Co-Ed., Moonaboola Quill, the official organ of the Hervey Bay (Qld.) Writers Workshop, under the auspices of the Qld. Adult Educ. Dept. Has had two exhibs. of Modern Art. Contbr. to: Kyabam Press; Moonaboola Quill. Has written poems to be used in scripts for John & Sue Erbacher Documentary films. Recip. 26 art prizes. Address: Ahimsa House, 655 Esplanade, Urangan, Qld., Australia 4658.

MACKIE, Albert David, b. 1904. Journalist. Education: Edinburgh Univ. Married w. 1 son & 2 daughters. Positions held: Ed., Edinburgh Evening Dispatch, 1946-54; Scottish News Ed., Picture Post, 1955; Feature Writer, Scottish Daily Express, 1956; Sometime Journalist in Kingston, Jamaica. Published works: Poems in two Tongues, 1928; Sing a Sang o Scotland, 1944; The Book of Macnib, 1960; (Plays):

Gentle Like Dove, 1953; The Hogmanay Story, Festival City, Hame, Sheena and MacHattie's Hotel; Other: Edinburgh, 1951; The Hearts, 1959; Scottish Pageantry, 1967. Contbr. to (Anthols.): Honour'd Shade, 1959; Modern Scottish Poetry, 1966; Oxford Book of Scottish Verse, 1966. Address: 27 Blackford Avenue, Edinburgh, Scotland.

McKINLEY, Hugh, b. 18 Feb. 1924. Poet & Critic. Positions held: Farmer; Opera-singer; Salesman; Mgr.; Accountant; Public Acct.; Tchr.; Lectr.; currently Lit. Ed., Athens Daily Post. Memberships: Fellow, Int. Poetry Soc.; PEN Club, Dublin Ctr.; Editl. Bd., Orbis, U.K.; Editl. Bd., Bitterroot, U.S.A.; Editl. Bd., Ocarina, India; European Ed/Parnassian Jurist, Poet, India; Assoc. Ed., Envoi, U.K.; Association Lecomte du Nouy, France. Translator, w. Ewald Osers, Lydia Pasternak & W.H. Auden, Selected Poems, by Ondra Lysohorsky, 1971. Contbr. to: Athens Daily Post; Nea Estia; The New Zealand Tablet; Dublin Mag.; Poesie Vivante; Bitterroot; Chicago Tribune; Poet Lore; Anglo-Welsh Review; Country Life; Writers' Review; Breakthru; London Mag.; Ariel; Orbis; Two Tone; Laurel Leaves; N. Am. Mentor; Fireflowers, & others. Recip. var. hons. & awards inclng: Pres. Marcos Medal, United Poets Laureate Int., 1967; Litt.D., l'Universite Libre (Asia), 1973. Address: Filaka, Syros, Greece.

McKINNON, Barry Benjamin, b. 13 Oct. 1944. Teacher. Education: B.A., Sir George Williams Univ., Montreal; M.A., Univ. of B.C., Vancouver. Married Joy McKinnon, 1 daughter. Positions held: var. jobs as Musician, Social Worker, etc.; Tchr., Coll. of New Caledonia, Prince George, B.C., 5 yrs. Ed. & Publsr., Caledonia Writing Series. Published works: Three Poems, 1966; The Golden Daybreak Hair, 1967; The Carcassess of Spring, 1971; Carbon Copies, 1971; Lust Lodge, 1973; Stamp Collection, 1973; I Wanted to Say Something, 1973. Contbr. to: White Pelican; Ga. Straight; Intercourse; Vigilante; Canadian Forum; Prism 66; Anvil; West Coast Seen, etc. Recip., Best Poem Award, Prism (Sir Geo. Williams Univ.), 1967. Address: 1420 Gorse St., Prince George, B.C., Canada V2L 1G3.

McKINSTRY, Charles Earl, b. 24 Jan. 1951. Electronic Technician. Grad., Elec. Techn., Tarrant Co. Jr. Coll., 1973. Memberships: Pres., Sam Houston Poetry Club, 1968-69; Pres., Arlington Poetry Soc., 1969-71; Dallas Poetry Soc., 1969-73. Contbr. to: 'Prints', Sam Houston Book of Poetry, 1969; Poems by Blacks, vol. II, 1972. Address: 742 Manning Rd., Grand Prairie, TX 75050, U.S.A.

MoKUEN, Rod, b. 29 Apr. 1933. Oakland, Calif., USA. Poet; Composer; Concert Artist. Positions held: Laborer; Cowherder; Lumberjack; Radio Disc Jockey; Newspaper Columnist; Scriptwriter, Psychol. Warfare, Korean War; Song Composer, 1953; Concert Tours, USA, UK, Austria, Australia, Japan & New Zealand; Narrator, Say Goodbye, NBC documentary by David Wolper, 1971; Dir., Chuck, feature film, 1971; Pres., Stanyan Records, Discus Records, New Gramophone Soc., Mr. Kelly Productions, Montcalm Corp., Stanyan Books, Cheval Books & Rod McKuen Enterprises; VP, Tamarack Books; Dir., Animal Concern; Bd. Dir., Am. Nat. Theatre of Ballet & Am. Humane Soc.; Bd. Gov., Nat. Acad. of Recording Arts & Scis. Memberships: ASCAP; Writer's Guild; AFTRA; AGVA. Published works include: And Autumn Come, 1954; Stanyan Street & Other Sorrows, 1954; Listen to the Warm, 1967; Caught in the Quiet, 1970; With Love, 1970; Twelve Years of Christmas, 1968; Lonesome Cities, 1968; The World of Rod McKuen, 1968; In Someone's Shadow, 1969; Fields of Wonder, 1971; Pastorale, 1971. Song Compositions include: The World I Used to Know; If You Go Away (w. Jacques Brel); Love's Been Good to Me; Ally, Ally, Oxen Free; I Think of You; Two, Ten, Six, Eighteen; Rusting in the Rain; Seasons in the Sun; Jean (from the film, The Prime of Miss Jean Brodie); I'll Catch the Sun; The Single Man; We; Pastures Green; One by One; Kaleidoscope; A Cat Named Sloopy; Trashy; Everybody's Rich But Us; The

Ivy That Clings To The Wall; The Beautiful Strangers; The Ever-Constant Sea. Film Scores include: Joanna; Me, Natalie; Scandalous John; A Boy Named Charlie Brown; The Loner; Come To Your Senses; Wild Flowers. Musical Compositions include: Symphony 1; Concerto for Four Harpsichords & Orchestra; Concerto for Guitar & Orchestra. Honours, awards: 3 books in one year in Publisher Weekly's best-seller list, 1968; Acad. Award Nomination, Golden Globe Award from Nomination, Golden Globe Award from Hollywood Foreign Press Assn., Grammy Nomination, all for 'Jean', 1970; 3 Grammy Nominations for 'A Boy Named Charlie Brown' for record album & for Best Talk Album, Home to the Sea, 1971. Address: c/o Random House Inc., 201 E 50th St., New York, NY 10022, USA.

MACLAREN, Hamish, b. 7 Mar. 1901. Publisher's Commission Representative. Education: Royal Naval Co., Dartmouth, Devon. Widower w. 1 daughter. Positions held: Poetry Ed., Spectator, 1928-36; Scotland Representative, Laurence Book Co. Ltd. in the 1950's; Publisher's Commission Agent. Published works: Sailor with Banjo, 1930; Other: Cockalorum; Writings in the Summer Season 1936, 1936; Ed., Private Opinions of a British Bluejacket, 1929. Contbr. to (Anthols.): Modern Scottish Poetry, 1966; (Jrnls.): Spectator; Observer; New Statesman; English Review. Recip., Grants from Royal Literary Fund & Soc. of Authors.

McLAUGHLIN, Emma Jeanetta Seiders, pen name **McLAUGHLIN, Emma S.,** b. 19 Oct. 1911. Homemaker; Poet; Freelance Writer. Married W. Kenneth McLaughlin, 1 son, 1 daughter. Positions held: Stenographer, Plant Dept., Bell Telephone Co. of Pa.; Tchr. in church related day schls: Stevens Meml. Methodist; Camp Hill Presby. & Christ Presby. Memberships: Harrisburg Chapt., Pa. Poetry Soc.; Nat. Fed. of State Poetry Socs.; World Poetry Soc. Intercontinental; Centro Studi e Scambi Int.; Am. Poetry League. Published works: Shining Fearless Flying Proud, 1967. Contbr. to: The Christian Sci. Monitor; Presby. Life; Contbng. Ed., Fellowship in Prayer; Poet Lore; Bitterroot; South & West; Voices Int, etc. Recip. var. poetry awards & prizes inclng: 1st Prize, Louise Louis Award, 1972 & Sylvia Argow Award, 1972, N.Y. Poetry Forum. Address: 1304 Carlisle Rd., Camp Hill, PA 17011, U.S.A.

McLAUGHLIN, Laurence Leclair, pen name **TROUBADOUR, Ernest,** b. 19 May 1924. Biological Illustrator and Lettering Artist. Education: Univ. of Miami., Fla. (no degree) Engl.; California State Univ. at Hayward, Calif., B.S. in Scientific Illustration; Univ. of Calif. at Berkeley, post grad. work. Married, 2 d., 1 s. Memberships: Miami Poetry Society, Fla. (Pres., 3 yrs.); Only Judge in Nat. Pen Women's Annual Poetry Contest, 1960. Published works: Poetry MENSA, An Internat. Anthol. of Poetry, 1966; An Anthol. of American Poetry, 1970. Contbr. to: Miami Daily News; Scimitar & Song; College Publication, Hayward, Calif.; Intelligencer, San Francisco, etc. Address: 710 E. 22nd St., Oakland, CA 94606, USA.

McLAUGHLIN, William DeWitt, pen name **McLAUGHLIN, William,** b. 26 Aug. 1918. Schoolteacher. Education: B.A., Western Reserve Univ., Cleveland, Ohio, 1948; M.A., Univ. of Wis., Madison, 1950. Currently tchng. in public schl. of a Cleveland suburb. Member, Ohio Poets Assn. Contbr. to: Ariel; Concerning Poetry; The English Record; Counter/Measures; Beloit Poetry Jrnl.; Cape Rock Jrnl.; Coll. Engl. (Wesleyan Univ.); Colo. Qtly.; Cottonwood; Epoch; DeKalb Lit. Arts Jrnl.; Epos; The Davidson Miscellany; Folio; Forum; Hearse; Kans. Qtly.; Laurel Review; The Little Mag.; The Malahat Review; Midwest Qtly.; New Am. Review; Poetry Cleveland; Poetry Northwest; Poetry Venture; Queen's Qtly.; Red Clay Rdr.; Satire Newsletter; Scopcraeft; The Small Pond; Southern Humanities Review; Southern Poetry Review; Sou'Wester. Address: 20865 Chagrin Blvd., Cleveland, OH 44122,

U.S.A.

MacLEISH, Archibald, b. 7 May 1892. Poet. Education: Yale Univ.; Harvard Univ.; B.A.; LL.B.; M.A.; Litt. D. Positions held: Libn. of Congress, 1939-44; Dir., Office of Facts & Figures, 1941-42; Asst. Dir., Office of War Info., 1942; Asst. Sec. of State, 1944-45, resigned; Chmn., US Del., UNESCO, 1945; Dpty. Chmn., ibid, 1946; US Mbr., Exec. Bd., UNESCO, 1946-47; Boylston Prof., Harvard Univ., 1949-62; Simpson Lectr., Amherst Coll., 1964-67. Memberships: Pres., Am. Acad. of Arts & Letters, 1953-56. Published works: The Happy Marriage, 1924; The Pot of Earth, 1925; Nobodaddy, 1925; Streets in the Moon, 1926; The Hamlet of A. MacLeish, 1928; New Found Land, 1930; Conquistador, 1932; Union Pacific (Ballet), 1934; Panic (play), 1935; Public Speech, 1936; The Fall of the City (radio verse play), 1937; The Land of the Free, 1938; Air Raid (radio verse play), 1938; America Was Promises, 1939; The Irresponsibles, 1940; The American Cause, 1940; A Time To Speak, 1941; A Time to Act, 1943; The American Story, 1944; Act·Five and Other Poems, 1948; Freedom Is The Right To Choose, 1951; Collected Poems, 1952; This Music Crept By Me Upon The Waters (verse play), 1953; Songs for Eve, 1954; J.B. (play), 1958; Poetry and Experience, 1961; The Eleanor Roosevelt Story, 1965; The Collected Poems of Archibald MacLeish, 1962; No. 4 S.E., 1961; No. 30 S.E., 1963; Herakles, 1967; 'The Wild Old Wicked Man', 1968; A Continuing Journey, 1968. Awards & Honours: Pulitzer Poetry Prize, 1932, '53; Pulitzer Drama Prize, 1958; Cmdr., Legion of Honour, France; Cmdr., Order of the Sun of Peru. Address: Conway, Mass. 01341, U.S.A.

McLELLAN, Joyce Anne, pen name **MARRIOTT, Anne,** b. 5 Nov. 1913. Writer. Education: summer courses in creative writing, Univ. of B.C., 1942, '56. Married Gerald McLellan, 3 children. Positions held: Casual scriptwriter for Canadian Broadcasting Corp. (school broadcasts), 1942-44; Script Writer, Nat. Film Bd., 1945-49; Women's Ed., Prince George Citizen, 1950-54. Chmn., Adjudication Comm., North Vancouver Community Arts Council, 1971-72. Published works: The Wind Our Enemy, 1939; Calling Adventurers! 1941; Salt Marsh, 1942; Sandstone & Other Poems, 1945; Countries, 1971. Contbr. to: Canadian Forum; Sat. Night; Poet; Fiddlehead; Prism Int.; Poetry; Oregonian; Contemporary Verse; N.Y. Times; num. anthols., etc. Recip., Gov-Gens. Award for Poetry, 1942. Address: 3645 Sykes Rd., North Vancouver, V7K 2A6, B.C., Canada.

McLELLAN, Robert, b. 28 Jan. 1907. Playwright. Education: Bearsden Acad.; Glasgow Univ. Married Kathleen Heys, 1 son, 1 daughter. Memberships: Chmn., Scottish Sub-Comm., League of Dramatists, 1951-61; Chmn., Scottish Sub-Comm., Soc. of Authors, 1961-64; Scottish Soc. of Playwrights. Published works: The Carlin Moth, 1946; Sweet Largie Bay, 1956; Island Burn, 1965. Contbr. to: The Scotsman; Poetry Scotland; Scottish Art & Letters. Recip., Scottish Arts Coun. Poetry Prize, 1956. Address: High Corrie, Isle of Arran, KA27 8JB, U.K.

McLEOD, Joseph Bertram, b. 21 Oct. 1929. Teacher. Education: McMaster, Hamilton (Bachelor's degree); Toronto (Grad., Education). Married: 2 children. Membership: League of Canadian Poets; Published works: I Am An Indian; Conversations With Maria. Contbr. to: Canadian Forum; Quarry; Fiddlehead; Inscape, Edge; N.A. Literary Review; Four Quarters; North; Bitterroot; Quixote; Poet & Critic; Poetry Australia; Poetry Florida; Cardinal; Trace, etc. Address: The Elms, RR 1, Omemee, Ont., Canada.

MACLEOD, Joseph Todd Gordon, pen name **DRINAN, Adam,** b. 24 Apr. 1903. Broadcaster; Theatrical Director. Education: Balliol Coll., Oxford Univ., U.K.; Inner Temple, London. Married 1) Kit MacGregor Davis, d. 2) Maria Teresa Foschini, 1 son, 1 daughter. Positions held: Sole Dir., Festival Theatre, Cambridge,

1933-36; Announcer, B.B.C., 1938-45; Mng. Dir., Scottish Nat. Film Studios, 1946-47. Mbr., P.E.N., sev. yrs. Published works: The Ecliptic, 1930; Foray of Centaurs, 1931; The Cove, 1940; Men of the Rocks, 1942; Ghosts of the Strath, 1943; Women of the Happy Island, 1944; The Passage of the Torch, 1951; Script from Norway, 1953; An Old Olive Tree, 1971. Contbr. to: Cherwell; Oxford Outlook; Criterion; This Quarter (Paris); Poetry (Chicago); Festival Theatre Review; New Verse; Life & Letters; Horizon; Poets of Tomorrow; Maryland Quarterly; Adam; Scottish Poetry, etc. Recip., Scottish Arts Coun. Award for 'An Old Olive Tree', 1972. Address: Via delle Ballodole 9/7, Trespiano, Firenze 50139, Italy.

MACLEOD, Norman Wicklund, b. 1 Oct. 1906. Professor; Novelist; Poet; Editor. Education: B.A., Univ. of N.M., Albuquerque, 1930; M.A., Tchrs. Coll., Columbia Univ., N.Y.C., 1936; var. grad. work. Positions incl: Instr. & Asst. Dir. of Poetry Ctr., San Fran. State Coll., 1954-55; Engl. Tchr., H.S.'s, 1958-62; Chmn., Engl. Dept., Chowchilla Union H.S., Calif., 1962-63; Hd., Engl. Dept., Higher Inst. of Langs. & Hd. of Unified Engl. Dept., Univ. of Baghdad, Iraq, 1963-64; Asst. Prof., Chadron State Coll., Neb., 1964-65; Asst. Prof. of Engl., Savannah State Coll., Ga., 1966-67; Assoc. Prof. Engl., Dir. of Creative Writing Prog. & Ed., Pembroke Mag., Pembroke State Univ., N.C., 1969-; var. public welfare appts. Published works: (vols. of poetry) Pure as Nowhere, 1952; A Man in Midpassage, 1947; We Thank You all the Time, 1941; Thanksgiving Before November, 1936; Horizons of Death, 1934; (novels) The Bitter Roots, 1941; You Get What You Ask For, 1939. Ed. of var. Am. & other mags. Contbr. to: Esquire; Poetry (Chicago); Common Sense; Scribner's Mag.; Sewanee Review; N.Y. Herald Tribune, etc. Work in Progress: The Whaling Christ & Other Poems; I Never Lost Anything in Istanbul, a lit. autobiog. Recip., Horace Gregory Award for 1972. Address: P.O. Box 756, Pembroke, NC 28372, U.S.A.

MAC LOW, Jackson, b. 12 Sept. 1922. Poetry Editor; Teacher. Education: A.A., Univ. of Chgo., 1939-43; A.B., cum laude in Greek, Brooklyn Coll., N.Y., 1955-58. Married Iris Lezak w. 2 children. Positions held: Freelance Tchr. of music & engl., Ed. & trans., 1950-66; Ref. Book Ed., Funk & Wagnalls, 1957-58, 1961-62; Unicorn Books, 1958-59; Copy Ed., Alfred A. Knopf, 1965-66; Instructor, Am. Lang. Inst., N.Y. Univ., 1966; Mbr., Editorial Staff, Resistance (Why) mag., 1945; Poetry Ed., 1950-54; Poetry Ed., Win Mag., NYC, 1966. Published works: The Pronouns – A Collection of 40 Dances – For the Dancers – 6 February – 22 March 1964, 1964; August Light Poems, 1967; 22 Light Poems, 1968; 23rd Light Poem/7th Poem for Larry Eigner, 1969; Stanzas for Iris Lezak, 1970; Other: The Marrying Maiden: A Play of Changes, 1960; The Twin Plays: Port-au-Prince and Adams County Illinois, 1966; Questions and Answers ... A Topical Play, 1963; Verdurous Sanguinaria, 1967. Contbr. to (Anthols.): Chicago Review Anthology, 1959; Seventh Street, 1961; An Anthology, 1963; A Controversy of Poets, 1965; Happenings, 1965; An Anthology of Concrete Poetry, 1967; (Jrnls.): Caterpillar; Win; Hudson Review; Nation; New Mexico Quarterly; Now. Address: 1764 Popham Ave., Bronx, N.Y., 10453, USA.

McMAHON, Bryan T(homas), pen names **CATHBAD, Sean** & **DANGER, A.,** b. 27 Sept. 1950. Poet. Education: B.A., Oakland Univ., Rochester, Mich. Positions held: Dir., Fndr. & Playwright, Electric Warning Theatre, 1970; Dir. & Playwright for The Macomb Co. Community Theatre, 1971; Instr. of Expository Writing, Oakland Univ., 1970-71; Poet-in-Res., State of Mich., 1972; For. Corres. & currently Special Writer for The Detroit News. Memberships: PEN Int.; Miles Modern Poetry Comm.; Creative Writing Progs., Wash. D.C., part of Nat. Endowment for the Arts; Fndr. & First Pres., The Acad., Detroit. Published works: Kontuse (a concrete poem & anthol.), 1971; Kree (selected book of verse, illustrated), 1972; In Search of the Hound, (essay),

1972; The Vachel Lindsey Memorial Drugstore Band (studio tape of jazz & poetry, distributed to schls. & radio), 1973. Contbr. to: Poetry East/West; Mich. Hot Apples; Poetry Americana; Amaranthus; Alley; Le Penseur, etc. Honours, awards: Anibal Meml. Award for Foreign Travel Expenses, 1971; Santa Fe Contemporary Arts Award, 1971. Address: 14680 Spring Garden, Detroit, MI 48215, U.S.A.

MACMILLAN, Ellen Rogers, b. 27 Nov. 1902. Homemaker. Education: Univ. of Wash., Seattle, over 3 yrs.; sev. Community Coll. Interest Courses in Lit. & Mineral.; Corres. Course Cert., Newspaper Inst. of Am. Married John R. MacMillan, 3 children. Positions held: w. Skaguay Daily Alaskan; Taught schl., Ruby, Alaska & in Skaguay; Special program radio broadcasting from local stn.; Mgr., Book Store (within the Stationery & Office Supply Store where she previously worked). Memberships: World Poetry Soc. Intercontinental; local Lib. Bd. Contbr. to Poet Int. Address: 304 Madison St., Ketchikan, AK 99901, U.S.A.

MACNAB, Roy (Martin), b. 17 Sept. 1923. Former Diplomatist. Education: M.A., Jesus Coll., Oxford Univ. Married, 2 children. Positions held: Cultural Attaché, South African High Commn., London, 1955-59; Counsellor, South African Embassy, Paris, 1959-67; London Dir., South Africa Fndn., 1968-. Memberships: Poetry Soc., England; Fellow, Royal Soc. of Arts. Published works: Testament of a South African, 1947; The Man of Grass & Other Poems, 1960; Ed., Poets in South Africa, 1958; Ed., Towards the Sun – a miscellany, 1950; Ed., Oxford Poetry, 1947. Contbr. to: Oxford Book of South African Verse, 1959; Penguin Book of South African Verse, 1969; New Poems 1961; The Spectator; Poetry Review; Outposts; BBC & SABC, etc. Address: c/o The Travellers' Club, London SW1, U.K.

McNABB, Linda Lee, b. 28 Aug. 1947. Freelance Writer; Substitute School Tchr. Education: Grad. w. degree in Jrnlsm., Univ. of Houston. Positions held: Tchr., Houston Independent Schl. Dist.; Clerk, Gulf Oil Co., U.S. Member, Quill & Scroll Club. Contbr. to: Poetry of Our Times, 1970; Merlin's Magic, 1970; Bardic Echoes, 1973; Bachaet, 1970; Poetry Preview, 1970; Yearbook of Modern Poetry, 1971; Dance of the Muse, 1970; Northwest News. Address: 5217 Rose St., Houston, TX 77007, U.S.A.

McNAIL, Eddie Gathings, b. 28 Nov. 1905. Teacher of English in High School. Education: Univ. of Mississippi, Oxford, 1927, B.A.; Univ. of Texas, Austin; A. & I. Univ., Kingsville, 1948, M.A. Personal details: daughter of Dr. James Covington Gathings (who practised medicine for 40 yrs. at Aberdeen, Mississippi) and Lavinia Prewett Gathings. Positions held: Teacher of English in HS, for 29 yrs. ("Best Teacher of the Year", 1967); Past Regent, of Lt. Thomas Barlow Chapter, NSDAR, 1967-68; Past Matron, Eastern Star, No. 732, 1937-38; Past Pres., Cultural Club, 1964-65; Pres., Rio Grande Valley Poetry Soc., 1971-72; Member, Texas Poetry Soc., 1973-74; Pres., Rio Grande Valley Fed. of Women's Clubs, 1973-75; Chairman of Admin. Bd. of First United Methodist Church of La Feria, 1973. Published work: The Silver Cord (poems), 1971. Contbr. to: La Feria News; The Valley Morning Star; The Harlingen Press; The San Benito News. Address: Box 164, La Feria, TX 78559, USA.

MACNAIR, Dorothy, see **LIVESAY, Dorothy.**

McNAIR, Marguerite, b. 21 Aug. 1900. Supreme Court Reporter. Education: Bus. Coll.; summer schl. painting courses at Mt. Allison Univ., Sackville, N.B.; painting course at Univ. of N.B.; creative writing at Univ. of N.B., Fredericton. Positions held: Sec. to Atty. Gen.; Supreme Ct. Reporter, Govt. of N.B. Memberships: Canadian Soc. for Educ. Through Art (rep. Canadian Socs. in Tokyo 1964 at Int. Conf.); Int. Folk Music Soc.; North East & Maine Folklore Soc.;

Past Pres., Fredericton Soc. of Artists; Past Pres., The Fredericton Art Club. Published works: Lilacs & Other Poems, 1968. Rep. in following anthols: Anthology of Maritime Poetry; Nova Scotia Book of Verse, 1953; Book of Verse, Alta., 1955. Contbr. to: The Spur, N.Y.; The Daily Gleaner, Fredericton; The Atlantic Advocate, Fredericton; The St. Stephen Courier, N.B. Address: 'Low Eaves', Churchill Row, Fredericton, N.B., Canada.

McNAMARA, Eugene Joseph, b. 18 Mar. 1930. Poet; University Professor. Education: B.A., DePaul Univ.; M.A., ibid; Ph.D., Northwestern Univ. Married Margaret Lindstrom, 5 children. Positions held: Instr., Univ. of Ill., 1955-59; Prof., Univ. of Windsor, 1959-; Ed. & Co-Fndr., Mainline, a little mag. of poetry, 1968-; Ed. & Fndr., Univ. of Windsor Review, 1965-. Member, League of Canadian Poets. Published works: For the Mean Time, 1965; 21 x 3 (w. Gasparini & Farmiloe), 1967; Outerings, 1970; Love Scenes, 1970; Dillinger Poems, 1971; Hard Words, 1972; Passages & Other Poems, 1972. Contbr. to: Quarry; Queens Quarterly; Tex. Quarterly; Malahat Review; Prism Int.; Fiddlehead; Edge; Wascana Review, etc. Recip., Hart Crane & Alice Crane Williams Meml. Prize, 1969. Address: c/o Engl. Dept., Univ. of Windsor, Windsor, Ont., Canada.

MACNAMARA, Michael Raymond Harley, b. 5 Jan. 1925. University Lecturer (Philosophy). Education: M.A., D. Litt. et Phil. Married, 2 sons. Positions held: Sr. Lectr. in Philos., Univ. of S. Africa. Contbr. to: De Arte (S. Africa); Edge (Canada); Expression One (U.K.); Labris (Belgium); New Coin Poetry, New Nation, Ophir, Purple Renoster & Unisa English Studies (all S. Africa); Poet (India); Workshop (U.K.). Address: Philos. Dept., Univ. of S. Africa, P.O. Box 392, Pretoria, S. Africa.

McNEIL, Florence Anne, b. 8 May 1937. Educator. Education: B.A. & M.A., Univ. of B.C., Canada. Married. Positions held: Instr., Western Wash. State Coll.; Asst. Prof., Univ. of Calgary; Asst. Prof., Educ. Dept., Univ. of B.C. Member, League of Canadian Poets. Published works: A Silent Green Sky, 1967; Walhachin, 1972; Rim of the Park, 1972; Ghost Towns, to be published 1975. Contbr. to most Canadian periodicals & some Am. (inclng. Queen's Qtly., Canadian Forum, Prism Int., Alaska Review, Malahat Review, West Coast Review, Quarry). Honours, awards: Prize for Poetry, MacMillan Co. of Canada Ltd., 1965; Theo Kaerner Creative Writing Award, 1960. Address: 5330 Wallace Dr., Delta, B.C., Canada.

McNEIL, Neil, b. 20 Apr. 1940. Community Worker – Social Development. Education: Ruskin Coll., Oxford Univ., U.K.; Dip. Econ. Pol. Married, 2 children. Positions held: Draughtsman, Clydeside Shipbuilding, – 1964; Student, 1964-66; Regl. Sec., TOC H, 1966-68; Youth & Community Serv., West Lothian, 1968-70; Community Dev., Milton Keynes, 1970-73; Environmental Off., Glasgow, 1973-. Memberships: Glasgow Ballad Club; Poets Vigilante; Fellow, Int. Poetry Soc.; Fndr., Poetry Workshop One (Milton Keynes); Co-Fndr., Rannoch Gillamoor Poets; Co-Fndr., Strath Mag.; Co-Ed., Strath; British Amateur Press Assn. Published works: (pamphlets) Diadema, 1962; Clydesmoke, 1970; Poems (short version), 1964; Poems, 1960-1970; Branwen, 1972. Contbr. to: Orbis; Greenock Telegraph; Scotsman; Coracle; New Epoch; New Forum; Poembag; Chapman; Radix; Strath; You Name It; 1st Anthology International Poetry Society. Address: 76 Hawthorn Rd., Abronhill, Cumbernauld, Glasgow G67 3LY, U.K.

McNEILL, Wayne, b. 24 Aug. 1953. Student. Education: currently studying at the Univ. of Toronto. Published works: Shells, 1973; Pantomime, 1974. Contbr. to: Suntan mag.; Boston, U.S.A.; Stuffed Crocodile mag., Ont.; Quarry mag., Ont. Address: 74 Barrymore Rd., Scarborough, Ont. M1J 1W6, Canada.

McNICHOL, Vera Luella, pen name **SUNSHINE,** b. 30

Apr. 1910. Nurse. Education: Nursing, Listowel & Peterboro Hosps., Canada, 6 yrs. Married John McNichol. Published works: From Manger to Glory, 1964; Little Drops of Water, 1962; Bible Stories in Verse (2 vols.); Reflections of Sunshine, 1955; Sunshine & Afterglow, 1956; This & That, 1970; Smiling Through Tears, autobiog., vol. I, 1970, vol. II, 1972 (vols. III & IV at publishers); Reveries of a Pioneer – Perth County, 1967; Townships (7 books), 1967. Address: Box 106, Millbank, Ont., Canada N0K 1LO.

McNITT, Gale, b. 5 Mar. 1921. Homemaker. Married Gordon McNitt, 2 sons, 2 daughters. Member, Cycloflame Poetry Fellowship. Contbr. to: Young Publishing Co.; Cardinal Poetry Qtly.; The Muse; Jeans Jrnl.; Pied Piper Press; Best in Poetry; Bardic Echoes; Poetry of Our Times; Haiku Highlights; Major Poets Fellowship; Imprints Qtly.; Encore; Cycloflame; The Poets Guild. Honours, awards: Hon. Mention, Major Poets Environmental Contest, 1972; Citation, Cycloflame, 1973; Poet of the Year Award, Poetry of Our Time, 1973; Hon. Mention, poem in Jean's Jrnl. Contest, 1974. Address: c/o FAA, Fire Island, AK 99695, U.S.A.

McNUTT, Effie Curtis, b. 15 Dec. 1906. Teacher (ret'd.); Housewife; Poet. Education: A.B. & M.A., Northeastern State Coll., Tahlequah, Okla. Married Oliver Benjamin McNutt. Positions held: Tchr., Ala., Okla. & Calif. Memberships: Reading & Evaluation Comm., Ala. State Poetry Soc.; World Poetry Soc. Intercontinental; Am. Poetry League; Poetry Soc. of Tex.; Nat. Writers Club; Int. Poetry Soc., U.K.; Int. Platform Assn.; Tahlequah Chapt. No. 148, O.E.S.; Order of the White Shrine of Jerusalem, Muskogee, Okla. Published works: A Spark of Deity, 1957; Ambrosial Wines, 1960. Contbr. to: The Okla. Tchr., 1936; New Voices in Poetry (anthol.), 1950; Florence Times-Tri-Cities Daily, 1971; The Decatur Daily, 1969-73; Poet (India); Am. Poetry League Bulletin; Nat. Fed. of State Poetry Socs. Yearbook, 1972, etc. Honours, awards: West Va. Poetry Soc. Award (3rd), 1972; Hon. Mention, Beaudoin Gemstone Award – Mystic, 1972. Address: Rte. 3, Box 184, Danville, AL 35619, U.S.A.

McNUTT, Joan Sturhahn, pen name **STURHAHN, Joan,** b. 23 Sept. 1930. Art Historian & Writer; Public Relations Counselor. Education: B.A., Univ. of Miami, Fla., U.S.A.; M.A., Art Hist., ibid. Divorced, 1 son. Positions held: Sec., Nat. Airlines, Inc.; Miami Rep., Director's Grp., Inc., N.Y.; Publicity Dir., Miami Art Ctr.; Dir., 3008 Gall., Miami; Gen. Staff Mbr., Lowe Art Mus., Univ. of Miami; self employed. Memberships: Phi Kappa Phi; Epsilon Tau Lambda; Kappa Pi; AAUP. Contbr. to: (art criticism) Lowe Art Mus. Quarterly; Village Post Mag.; (poetry) Bitterroot; Cyclotron; Cyclo-Flame; Fernandina Beach News-Leader; Hartford Courant. Var. short drama scripts for TV. Address: 7721 A.S.W. 56th Ave., Miami, FL 33143, U.S.A.

MACPHERSON, Jean Jay, pen name **MACPHERSON, Jay,** b. 13 June 1931. Professor of English. Education: B.A., Carleton Coll., Ottawa, 1951; B.L.S., McGill Univ., 1955; M.A., Univ. of Toronto, 1955; Ph.D., ibid, 1964. Positions held: p/t Tchr., Victoria Coll., Univ. of Toronto, 1954-57; Full time Tchr., ibid, 1957–. Published works: (Pamphlets) Nineteen Poems, 1952; O Earth Return, 1954; (book) The Boatman, 1957. Contbr. to: Canadian Forum; Contemporary Verse; The Fiddlehead; Alphabet; Poetry (Chicago). Honours, awards: Gvnr.-Gen's Award, 1958; Levinson Prize for Poetry, 1958. Address: Dept. of Engl., Victoria Coll., Univ. of Toronto, Toronto 5, Canada.

McQUILKIN, Frank, b. 17 Sept. 1936. Teacher & Writer. Education: B.A., St. Norbert Coll., West DePere, Wis., 1959; M.A., San Francisco State Univ., 1969. Positions held: Asst. Prof. of Engl., Rutgers Univ., Camden, N.J., 1970–. Bd. Dirs., Philadelphia Writers Conf. Published works: Think Black: An Introduction to Black Political Power (non-fiction

book), 1970; Vercingetorix (opera libretto), 1973. Contbr. to: Epos; Christian Century; Catholic World; America; Descant; Motive; Ball State Univ. Forum; Foxfire; Pacific Sun; Cloud Marauder; Above Ground Review; Folio; Road Apple Review; Southern Humanities Review; Forum. Recip. Rutgers Univ. Rsch. Coun. Grant for completion of the opera Vercingetorix. Address: 253 South 16th St., Philadelphia, PA 19103, U.S.A.

McRAE, John, b. 14 Dec. 1949. Educator. Education: B.A., Columbia Univ., 1973; M.A. cand., Hist., Harvard Univ., 1974. Positions held: Former Pres., Choreodrama Int. Inc., 1967-69; Creative Writing Instr., Manna House Workshop, 1969; Cons. to City Planning Commn., 1970; Human Resources Cons. to H.R.A. Div. of Social Services of N.Y., 1970; Pres., 5X Publishing Co., 1971; H.S. Instr., Black Studies Bd. of Educ., N.Y., 1972-73. Published works: Ghetto 68, 1968; 360 Degrees of Blackness Coming at You, 1971; We Be Word Sorcerers, 1973; Islam & the Rebirth of Black Civilization in America, Vol. 1, 1974. Recip., Lyricists & Music Award, N.Y. Schl. of Mus., 1965. Address: 86 College St., Amherst, MA 01012, U.S.A.

McREYNOLDS, Douglas John Brooke, b. 5 June 1946. Instructor of English. Education: B.A., Univ. of Mo., 1967; M.A. (Engl.), Univ. of Mo., 1969. Married Carol Susan Ghio, 1 son (Roland). Positions held: Instr. of Engl., East Carolina Univ., Greenville, N.C. Memberships: South Atlantic Modern Lang. Assn.; East Carolina Poetry Forum. Published works: Tar River Poets: The Douglas McReynolds Issue, 1974. Contbr. to: The Poetry Bag; Workshop: New Poetry; Miscellany; Mark Twain Jrnl.; Tar River Poets; Wake; Crucible. Recip., Literary Prizes from Stephens Coll., 1969, Atlantic Christian Coll., 1972 & Wake Forest Poetry Contest, 1972; Sam Ragan Poetry Award, 1973. Address: Dept. of Engl., East Carolina Univ., Box 2707, Greenville, NC 27834, U.S.A.

McREYNOLDS, Ronald W(eldon), b. 26 Jan. 1934. Professor of English. Education: B.A., Miami Univ., Ohio, 1955, M.A., Engl., ibid. 1956; Ph.D., Engl., Univ. of Texas, 1959. Positions held: Instr. in Engl., Belleville, Michigan, 1956-57; Prof. of Engl., Central Missouri State Univ., Warrensburg, Missouri, since 1959. Published works: A Time Between and Other Poems, 1967; The Poet's Poetry, 1970; The Missouri Poets (anthol.), 1971. Contbr. to: The Kansas City Star-Times; Per Se; The Ball State Forum; Caravan; Seminar; The University Bulletin; Deep Channel Packet, etc. Address: High Field, RR 5, Warrensburg, MO 64093, USA.

McROBBIE, Kenneth Alan, b. 6 Feb. 1929. Professor of History; Editor. Education: Univs. of Liverpool & Toronto. Married w. 1 daughter. Positions held: Prof. of History, Univ. of Man., Winnipeg; Ed., Mosaic, A quarterly Jrnl., Winnipeg. Published works: Jupiter C: 4 Poems for the Missile Age, 1958; Eyes Without a Face, 1960; Trans., The Selected Poems of Ferenc Juhasz, 1970. Contbr. to (Anthols): Poetry 62, 1961; Poetry of Mid-Century, 1940-60; The Plough and the Pen, Writings from Hungary, 1930-56; Penguin Book of Modern Verse Translation, 1966; Arion 2, 1969; (Jrnls): Candian Forum; Poetry; Far Point. Hons: Felicia Hemans Medal for Lyrical Poetry, Liverpool Univ., 1952; "Pro Litteris Hangaricis" Medal, Hungary, 1968. Address: 6 Cornell Drive, Fort Richmond, Winnipeg 19, Man., Canada.

MacSWEENEY, Barry, b. 17 July 1948. Editor; Director. Education: Harlow Tech. Coll. Positions held: Formerly Reporter & Arts Feature Writer, Var. weekly & daily newspapers; Currently; Dir., Blacksuede Boot Press & Ed., The Black Suede Boot Poetry Mag. Published works: The Boy from the Green Cabaret Tells of His Mother, 1967; The Last Bud, 1969; Joint Effort, 1970; Our Mutual Scarlet Boulevard, 1970. Contbr. to (Jrnls.): Curiously Strong; The Anona Wynn; Resuscitator; English Intelligencer; Flame; Asylum 2; Stand; Grosseteste Review; Blue Pig.

Recip., Poetry Prize, Stand Mag. Address: 35 The Drive, Denton Burn, Newcastle-upon-Tyne 5, Northumberland, UK.

McWHORTER, Bright Jasper, pen names, **McWHORTER, Bright; JASPER, Bright,** b. 9 July 1911. Doctor of Physical Medicine (semi-retired). Education: McWhorter HS.; Lost Creek HS; Pennsylvania Coll. of Chiropractic, full degree D.C. 1945 after Physical Therapy diplomate 1937 Nat. Coll. of Chicago, Ill. Extended to a Doctorate from Lincoln Coll. of Indianapolis, Ind. & D.C. March 1945 where received N.M.D.(doctor of medicine and of physical therapy). Married. Practiced Acupuncture in 1930's, Huntington, WV 2 yrs.; Physical Medicine, Clarksburg WV. 1940's, until called to WWII, 1942; In charge of a hospital Physical Therapy dept. (served 3 yrs. approx.); returned to Clarksburg; then practiced in Nashville, Tennessee, as a licensed Physician, 1 yr; nearing retirement, has an office at McWhorter, WV. Memberships: Internat. Clover Poetry Assoc. (life membership, Danae); Major Poets Chapter, Pierson Mettler Associates; ISPS of the Illinois State Poetry Soc.; CSSI (Rome); ASCAP. Published works: Christmas Cards, 1973, 1974. Contbr. to: Orion; Lincoln Log; Poet Series (Illinois State Poetry Soc.); West Virginia Hillbilly; Paul Salyers Syndicated Poetry Column, Olive Hill Times; Young Publications; Poetry Review (Brooklyn); World Poets; Outstanding Contemporary Anthols.; Spencer Books; Poetry Parade; New Dawn Publications (2 anthols.); Fireflower; Poetry Pageant Mag.; Clover Assoc. Anthols. Awards: 1973 Award of Major Poets; Gold certificate, 5 certificates of award, 1973, Major Poets Chapter; Certificate Award of Paul Salyers; Sarah Churchill Award (of her book of poems) by Poetry Parade Mag., also Clover Poetry Assoc. certificates. Address: Box 19, Rt. 1, Walkersville, WV 26447, USA.

MADER, Miroslav, pen name **SLAVKO,** b. 1 July 1929. Journalist. Education: Degree, Philos., Zagreb Univ. Member, Yugoslav Lit. Soc. Published works: (books of poetry) Rakršče vjetra (The Crossroads of Wind); Mislim na sunce (I think of the Sun); Utaman (In Vain); U čovjeku (In Man); Antene riječi (Antenas of Words); Zelene Lenije (The Green Park Lenije); Izabrane pjesme (The Choice of Poems); (Dramas) Covjek koga nema (TV play); Junaci (Radio play). Contbr. to: Republika; Forum; Mogućnosti; Revija; Enciklopedia moderna; Krugovi; Književnik, etc. Honours, awards: The Lit. Prize of the Yr. for the book, The Choice of Poems, 1969; Prize of mag. 'Revia' for Poems, 1971. Address: The Radio-Televizia of Zagreb, Jurišićeva 4/IV, 41000 Zagreb, Yugoslavia.

MADGE, Charles Henry, b. 10 Oct. 1912. Former Professor of Sociology; Commission Executive; Poet. Education: Magdalene Coll., Cambridge. Was married Kathleen Raine w. 1 son & 1 daughter, now married Inez Pearn. Positions held: Social Dev. Off., Stevenage, 1947-50; Prof. of Sociology, Univ. of Birmingham, 1950-70; Mbr., UN Technical Assistance Mission, Thailand, 1953-54; India, 1957-58; Southeast Asia, 1959-60; Ldr., Mission to Ghana, UN Econ. Commission for Africa, 1963. Published works: The Disappearing Castle, 1937; The Father Found, 1941; Other: Mass Observation (w. T. Harrisson), 1937; War-Time Pattern of Saving & Spending, 1943; Industry after the War: Who is Going to Run It?, 1943; Society in the Mind, 1964; Ed., Var. Books. Contbr. to (Anthols.): Oxford Book of Modern Verse, 1936; Modern Poet, 1938; Faber Book of Modern Verse, 1945; Penguin Book of Contemporary Verse, 1950; A Book of South African Verse, 1959; Commonwealth Poems of Today, 1967. Address: 17 Valentine Rd., Birmingham 14, UK.

MADGETT, Naomi Long, b. 5 July 1923, Norfolk, Va. Professor of English. Education: B.A., Engl., Va. State Coll., 1945; M.Ed., Engl., Wayne State Univ., 1955; Univ. of Detroit & Wayne State Univ. Personal details: daughter of Clarence M. Long, Bapt. Min., & Maude Hilton Long; Divorced, 1 d; Married, Leonard P.

Andrews, Sr. Positions held: Staff Writer, The Mich. Chronicle; Serv. Rep., Mich. Bell Telephone Co.; Tchr., Engl., Northwestern HS, Detroit, Mich.; Lectr., Engl., Univ. of Mich., Ann Arbor; Assoc. Prof., Eastern Mich. Univ., and now Professor of English. Memberships: Nat. Writers Club; Poetry Soc. of Mich.; Detroit Women Writers. Published works include: Songs To A Phantom Nightingale, 1941; One & The Many, 1956; Star By Star, 1965, '70; Textbook, Success in Language & Literature (w. C. Tincher & H.B. Maloney), 1967; Pink Ladies in the Afternoon, 1972. Contbr. to the following anthols., jrnls., etc: The Poetry of the Negro, 1746-1949, 1949; American Literature By Negro Authors, 1950; Beyond The Blues, 1962; Afro-Amerikaanse Poezie, 1964; New Negro Poets, 1964; Ik Ben De Nieuwe Neger, 1965; Kaleidoscope, 1967; Les Noirs Américains, 1967; Mirror of Men's Minds, II, 1967; Literature for Listening: An Oral Interpreter's Anthology, 1968; Ten, 1968; Black Voices, 1968; L'Idea Deglie Antenati, 1968; Black Poetry, 1969; Mich. Signatures, 1969; Black American Literature: Poetry, 1969; Tomorrow Won't Wait, 1969; Black America, Yesterday & Today, 1969; The Harlem Renaissance & Beyond, 1969; Poems To Enjoy, 1970; Poems To Remember, 1970; Right On, 1970; Soulscript, 1970; Britain America, 1970; Black Insights, 1971; The Black Poets, 1971; A Broadside Treasury, 1971; New Black Voices, 1972; The Comp Box, 1972; Composition & Literary Form, 1972; Modern & Contemp. Afro-American Poetry, 1972; Afro-American Writing, 1972; The Poetry of Black America, 1973; Within You, Without You, 1973; Love Has Many Faces, 1973; On Freedom's Side, 1972; World of Challenge, 1972; New Black Voices, 1972; Face the Whirlwind, 1973; Am. Negro Poetry (rev. ed.), 1974. Cavalcade: Negro American Writing From 1760 To The Present, 1971; Oral Interpretation, 1971; Poetry of the Negro, 1746-1970, 1971; Promise of America: Breaking & Building, 1971; Up Against The Wall, Mother..., 1971; The Freelance; Poet; Engl. Jrnl.; Poetry Broadsides; Ebony; Phylon; Negro Digest; Mich. Challenge; Freedom ways; Poetry Digest; American Pen; Jrnl. of Black Poetry; Negro History Bulletin; Poetry News-Letter; The Free Lance; Blue River Poetry Mag.; Mo. Schl. Jrnl.; Detroit News; Mich. Chronicle; The Norwester; Va. Statesman, etc. Honours, awards: Poetry Award, Nat. Writers Club, 1955. Address: 16886 Inverness Ave., Detroit, MI 48221, USA.

MADHAVAN, A., b. 9 Oct. 1933. Diplomat. Education: M.A., Economics, Loyola Coll., Madras, India; B.A., Modern History, Trinity Coll., Cambridge. Married w. 1 son. Positions held: Joined Indian Foreign Service, 1956; 1st Sec., Indian Embassy, Peking, China, 1968–. Published works: Poems, 1968; Contbr. to (Anthol.): New Poems, 1958; (Jrnl.): Illustrated Weekly of India. Address: c/o Ministry of External Affairs, New Delhi, India.

MAGNER, James Edmund, Jr., b. 16 Mar. 1928. Professor of English. Education: B.A., Duquesne Univ., 1957; M.A., Univ. of Pittsburgh, 1961; Ph.D., Univ. of Pitts., 1966. Divorced, 4 children. Positions held: Sergeant, U.S. Infantry, Korean War; Seminarian, Passionist Order of The Roman Catholic Faith, 1951-56; Tchr. of Engl., South Hill Catholic H.S., 1957-61; Instr. of Engl., John Carroll Univ., 1962-65; Asst. Prof., ibid, 1965-68; Assoc. Prof., 1968–. Memberships: AAUP; MLA; NCTE; Ohio Poets Assn. Published works: Toiler of the Sea, 1965; Although There Is The Night, 1968; Gethsemane, 1969; John Crowe Ranson: Critical Principles & Preoccupations, 1971; The Dark Is Closest To The Moon, 1973. Contbr. to: College English; Mediterranean Review; The Hiram Poetry Review; The Christian Century; The New England Review; Bitterroot; Spirit; Tangent; Fine Arts; FreeLance, etc. & many anthols. Recip., George E. Grauel Meml. Fellowship for research & writing. Address: Engl. Dept., John Carroll Univ., Cleveland, OH 44118, U.S.A.

MAGORIAN, James, b. 24 Apr. 1942. Writer.

Education: B.S., Univ. of Neb., 1965; M.S., Ill. State Univ., 1969; Harvard Univ.; Oxford Univ. Published works: (books) Almost Noon, 1969; Ambushes & Apologies, 1970; The Garden of Epicurus, 1971; The Last Reel of the Late Movie, 1972; Distances, 1972; Mandrake Root Beer, 1973. Contbr. to: North Am. Mentor; Kans. Qtly.; Legend; Ararat; Driftwood; Orphic Lute; Montana Arts; Reach Out; Bardic Echoes; The Beggar's Bowl; Poet; Tejas; The Montebello Jrnl.; Rufus; Quintessence; Express; Driftwood East; Invictus; Midwest Chaparral; Green's Mag.; Essence; Modern Images; Hoosier Challenger; Encore; Special Song. Address: 1006 Madison Ave., Helena, MT 59601, U.S.A.

MAH, Chonggi Laurence, b. 17 Jan. 1939. Physician and University Professor. Education: Pre-Med. Dept., Seoul, Korea; Yonsei Med. School, Seoul, Korea, M.D.; Seoul Nat. Univ., Korea, M.Sc. Positions held: Assist. Prof., Dept. of Radiology and Dept. of Pediatrics, Medical Coll. of Ohio, USA; Chief, Nuclear Medicine Section, Medical Coll. of Ohio. Memberships: Korean Literary Academy; Korean Poets Soc.; Korean Modern Poets Assoc. Published works (poetry): Quiet Triumph, 1960: Second Winter, 1965; Trio No. 1, 1968; Trio No. 2, 1972; Translated and published in Engl., Oriental Modern Poetry. Contbr. to: Monthly Modern Literature; Modern Poetry; Literature and Thought; Monthly Poetry; Dong-A Ilbo; Chosun Ilbo; Korea Newspaper, and others. Recip. Yonsei Literary Awards, 1962. Address: Dept. of Radiology, Medical Coll. of Ohio, P.O. Box 6190, Toledo, OH 43614, USA.

MAHAPATRA, Jayanta, b. 22 Oct. 1928. Reader in Physics. Education: Ravenshaw Coll., Cuttack, India; 1st class Master's degree in Physics, Sci. Coll., Patna. Positions held: Coll. Tchr., 20 yrs. Mbr., World Poetry Soc. Intercontinental, 1971. Published works: Close the Sky, Ten by ten, 1971; Svayamvara & Other Poems, 1971; Countermeasures: Poems translated from Oriya, 1973. Contbr. to: (U.K.) The Critical Quarterly; The Times Lit. Supplement; Candelabrum; (Canada) The Malahat Review; Queen's Quarterly; (Australia) Meanjin Quarterly; (N.Z.) Edge; (India) Quest; Illustrated Weekly; (U.S.A.) Chicago Review; Nimrod; Miss. Review; N.Y. Quarterly & others. Recip. 2nd Prize, IWWP Contest, London, 1970. Address: Tinkonia Bagicha, Cuttack 753 001, Orissa, India.

MAHAPATRA, Sitakant, b. 17 Sept. 1937. Indian Civil Servant. Education: B.A.(Hons.) Utkal Univ.; M.A., Allahabad Univ.; Dip. Overseas Dev. Studies, Cambridge Univ., UK. Married; 3 d., 1 s. Positions held: Teacher, Post-Grad. Dept. of Political Science, Utkal Univ., 1959-61; Joined the I.A.S. in 1961 (topping the All India List): Charge Officer, Settlement, 1964-65; Sub-Collector, Bargarh, 1965-66; Dy. Sec., Revenue & Excise, 1966-68; District Magistrate, Sundargarh, 1968; Dy. Sec., Works & Transport Dept., 1969; Dy. Sec., Planning & Coord. Dept., 1969-70; District Magistrate, Mayurbhanj, 1970-72; Jt. Sec.,

Planning & Coord. Dept., 1972; Sec. to the Chief Minister, Orissa, 1972-73; Sec., Health & Family Planning Dept., since March, 1973. Memberships: Orissa Sahitya Akademi; Language Advisory Committee of Central Sahitya Akademi; Language Advisory Committee of Bharatiya Jnanpith; Founder-Member, All Orissa Writers' Conference; Founder-Member, Harmony; Member, Indian P.E.N. Published works: Four anthols. of poems in Oriya, "Dipti O' Dyuti", "Ashtapadi", "Sabdar Akash", "Samudra: Samudra"; three anthols. of poems in English translation: Quiet Violence; Old Man in Summer; The Other Silence. Three anthols. of tribal poetry, edited with introduction: The Empty Distance Carries...(Munda Oroan poetry); The Wooden Sword (Munda poetry); Staying is No-Where (Kondh Paraja poetry). Contbr. to: Indian Literature; Indian Writing Today; The Illus. Weekly of India; Indian & Foreign Review; Thought; Poetry India; Literary Studies; Dialogue India; Dialogue Calcutta; Caravan; Poetry East West; Bhubaneswar Review; Dhara; Adam International; Samikshya; Ocarina; Helicon; Vägartha; Byword. Recip. Visuva Milan Award for Poetry, 1971; Orissa Sahitya Akademi Award for Poetry, 1971. Address: Sec. to the Government of Orissa, Health & Family Planning Dept., Bhubaneswar 751001, Orissa, India.

MAHON, Derek, b. 23 Nov. 1941. Writer. Education: Grad., Trinity Coll., Dublin, 1965. Married. Published works: Night-Crossing, 1968; Lives, 1972. Contbr. to: The Listener; Encounter; Times Lit. Supplement; The Dublin Mag.; The Honest Ulsterman. Honours, awards: Gregory Award, 1965; Arts Coun. Bursary, 1972. Address: 9F Observatory Gdns., London W.8, U.K.

MAHONEY, John J., b. 21 Jan. 1944. Educator. Education: B.A. & M.A., postgrad. studies, with work done at Drexel Univ., Glassboro State Coll., LaSalle Coll. & Ball State Univ. Married. Positions held: Hd. of Engl. Dept. at Saint Augustine Prep., Richland, N.J., 1970; Humanities Chmn., ibid, 1971; Dir., all Catholic Engl. Depts. in South Hersey, 1973. Formed student film group: Short Films For Long Hairs, & produced three films that have been reviewed at a series of colls. Memberships: N.J. Poetry Soc.; Am. Poets Fellowship Soc.; S.J. Poetry Soc.; V.P., Am. Lit. Soc.; Int. Platform Assn. Published works: Interludes (coll. of mod. verse); Symphony of Seasons (coll. of poems & inkings), 1971. Rep. in following anthols: Anthol. of the Year, 1969; World Spring Anthol., 1971, 72 & 73; An Anthol. of Am. Poetry, 1971; Nat. Poetry Press; Dance of the Muse; Yearbook of Mod. Poetry, 1971; haiku in small mags. in U.S.A. & Canada. Recip. var. awards inclng: Cash Award & Nat. Third Prize for poem 'Tricycle', published in Poetry Parade's Nat. Mag. Contest for the Yr.; Outstanding Lit. Achievement for sonnets from the Am. Fellowship. Address: Tuckahoe Rd., Milmay, NJ 08340, U.S.A.

MAHR, Allan David, pen name **MAHR, David,** b. 7 Jan. 1910. U.S. Postal Clerk. Education: var. article & short story writing studies, St. Louis Univ. & Mo. Univ. Extension. Married, 5 sons, 3 daughters. Positions held: Postal Clerk, U.S., 34 yrs. Memberships: McKendree Writers; St. Louis Poetry Ctr.; Avalon Writers; Tex. & Ariz. Poetry Socs.; Ac-Escambi. Contbr. to: Belleville News Democrat; Southwest Times Jrnl.; Cyclo-Flame; Ariz. Poetry Soc. Anthols. 'Ballet on the Wind & Naked Spirit'; Anthol. of Am. Poets; Quaderni di Poesia-e Scambi, Italy, etc. Recip. var. hons. inclng: Hon. Mention, St. Louis Poetry Ctr. Has poems in the Winston Churchill Meml. Lib., Kennedy Meml. Lib., L.B. Johnson Meml. Lib. & The Truman and Tom Dooley Room at Notre Dame. Address: 4838 Cote Brilliante, St. Louis, MO 63113, U.S.A.

MAIDEN, Jennifer Margaret, b. 7 Apr. 1949. Student. Education: currently studying at Macquarie Univ., N.S.W., Australia. Memberships: Australian Poetry Soc.; Australian Labour Party. Contbr. to: New Poetry;

MAGOWAN, Robin, b. 4 Sept. 1936. Poet. Education: B.A., Harvard Univ., U.S.A.; M.A., Columbia Univ.; Ph.D., Comp. Lit., Yale Univ. Positions held: Tchr., Univ. of Wash., 1962-65; Tchr., Univ. of Calif., Berkeley, 1965-70. Published works: Voyages (kayak), 1968; trans. H. Michaux 'Ecuador', 1969; Persian Notes; Drums & Melodeons. Contbr. to: Ante; Assembling; Choice; Cloud Marauder; Far Point; Field; Edge; Kayak; Noise; Partisan Review; Perspective; Poetry; Poetry Northwest; Rune; Sweet Thief. Recip., Far Point Judges Prize, 1970. Address: 2100 Washington St., San Francisco, CA, U.S.A.

MAGUIRE, Francis, b. 5 Oct. 1911. Writer. Education: A.B., Boston Coll., 1933; M.A., Harvard Univ. Mbr., Poetry Soc. of Am. Published works: Journey with Music, 1949. Contbr. to: America; Canadian Poetry; Catholic Worker; Daily Word; The Lyric; N.Y. Times; The Sign; Spirit; Tulsa Poetry Quarterly. Address: 21 Clinton St., N.Y., NY 10002, U.S.A.

Poetry Australia; Meanjin; Free Poetry; The Australian (newspaper); Southern Review; Westerly; Sydney Morning Herald; Arena (Macquarie Univ.); Poetry Eastwest; New Poetry from Australia. Address: Box 4, 514 High St., Penrith, N.S.W. 2750, Australia.

MAILER, Norman, b. 31 Jan. 1923. Writer. Education: S.B., Harvard Univ., 1943. Published works: Death for the Ladies (and other Disasters), 1961. Author of many prose & non-fiction works, including: Naked and the Dead; An American Dream, 1964; Cannibals & Christians, 1966; Why Are We in Vietnam, 1962; The Armies of the Night, 1968; Miami & the Siege of Chicago, 1968; Moonshot, 1969; Of a Fire on the Moon, 1970. Honours, awards: Nat. Book Award, 1969; Pulitzer Prize, non-fiction, 1969. Address: c/o Charles Runber, 19 W 44th St., New York, NY 10036, USA.

MAINES, Rachel Pearl, b. 8 July 1950. Needlework Historian. Education: B.A., Univ. of Pitts., 1971. Married Christopher A. Cooper. Positions held: Clerical Asst., Univ. of Tex. at Austin Libs., 1967-69; Clerical Asst., Univ. of Pitts. Libs., 1970; Lib. Clerk, Classics Dept., Univ. of Pitts., 1970-73; Ref. Asst., Univ. of Pittsburgh, Hillman Lib., 1972-. Memberships: N.O.W. Task Force on Women in the Arts; Nat. Coordinator of Fund-raising & Grant Support. Contbr. to: Cloud Marauder; Hanging Loose; Occident; Best in Poetry for 1968; The Windless Orchard; Riata; The Shore Review Yearbook of Modern Poetry, 1971. Address: 5660 Beacon St., Pittsburgh, PA 15217, U.S.A.

MAINONE, Robert Franklin, b. 11 Feb. 1929. Naturalist. Education: B.S., Mich. State Univ., 1951; B.S.F., ibid, 1952; M.S., 1959. Married Carolyn Bothwell. Positions held: Interpretive Ecologist, MSU's Kellogg Bird Sanctuary, 1967-; Naturalist, Kalamazoo Nature Ctr., 1961-66; Jr. Curator, Detroit Zoological Pk., 1960-61; Ranger, Naturalist, Everglades & Rocky Mountain Nat. Pks., 1957 & 58; Weather Observer, USAF, 1953-56. Memberships: Poetry Soc. of Mich.; Nat. Fed. of State Poetry Socs. Published works: An American Naturalists' Haiku, 1964; Parnassus Flowers, 1965; Where Waves Were, 1966; This Boundless Mist, 1968; Shadows, 1971. Contbr. to: Art Around Town, Tokyo; Art & Artists, Detroit; Haiku '64, Japan Air Lines; Peninsula Poets, Mich.; Poet, Madras, India. Address: Rte. 3, Box 485, Delton, MI 49046, U.S.A.

MAINOR, Rayfer Earl'e, b. 25 Mar. 1950. Youth Counselor. Education: Langston Univ., Okla.; Paul Quinn Coll., Waco, Tex.; B A.; Inst. of Theatre Arts, Jefferson City, Mo., summer 1969; currently working on Master's degree, San Fernando State Univ. & UCLA, Calif. Positions held: Youth Counselor, State of Calif. Dept. of Youth Authority (Corrections); served as Poet-in-Res., Paul Quinn Coll., Waco, Tex., 1970-71. Memberships: V.P., Langston Univ. Lit. Soc.; United Poets Laureate Int.; World Poetry Soc. Int.; Int. Clover Poetry Assn.; Nat. Network of Poets, Milwaukee, Wis.; L.A. Municipal Arts Dept. Published works: Poems by Rayfer Earl'e Mainor, 1969; In Preview: A Book of Poetry, Prose & Free Verse by Rayfer E. Mainor, 1974. Rep. in following anthols: New Voices in Am. Poetry, 1973; Clover Coll. of Verse, 1974; New Dawn Poetry Anthol., 1974; Poets of Seventy-Four, 1974; Poetry of the Yr. Anthol., 1974; Sweet Seventies Anthol., 1974; Starlight Poetry Anthol., 1974. Contbr. to many poetry jrnls., mags. & newspapers. Honours, awards: The Melvin B. Tolson Award, 1969; Awarded title of Poet Laureate, for outstanding works in the fields of poetry & contbns. to humanity, by Town Council of Langston, Okla., 1969. Address: c/o P.O. Box 37158, Los Angeles, CA 90037, U.S.A.

MAJOR, Clarence, b. 31 Dec. 1936. Poet and Writer of Fiction. Positions held: Lecturer in Creative Writing, Sarah Lawrence Coll. Memberships: Authors League; P.E.N. Published works: The New Black Poetry, 1969;

All Night Visitors, 1969; Swallow The Lake, 1970; Dictionary of Afro-American Slang, 1970; Private Line, 1971; Symptoms & Madness, 1971; The Cotton Club, 1972; No, 1973; The Dark And Feeling, 1974; Slaveship & Relationship, 1974; Scat, 1974; the syncopated cake walk, 1974. Contbr. to many newspapers and journals. Awards: Nat. Council of the Arts Prize, 1970: New York Cultural Foundation Grant, 1971. Address: c/o William Morris Agency Inc 1350 Ave. of the Americas, New York, NY 10019, USA.

MAKAR, Boshra, b. 23 Sept. 1928. Professor of Mathematics. Education: Cairo Univ., B.Sc., 1947, M.Sc., 1952, Ph.D. in Mathematics, 1955. Married; 2 s. Positions held: Cairo Univ., Egypt, all ranks to Assoc. Prof., 1948-65; American Univ. of Beirut, Lebanon, Visiting Assoc. Prof., 1965; Michigan Tech. Univ., Assoc. Prof., 1966; St. Peter's Coll., Prof., since 1966. Memberships: Poetry Soc. (UK) (life); Internat. Poetry Society (Fellow); Internat. Platform Assoc.; American Assoc. for the Advancement of Science; NY Acad. of Science, and NJ Acad. of Science; American Mathematical Soc., and Mathematical Assoc. of America; Internat. Speaker Network; Soc. for Industrial and Applied Mathematics; American Assoc. for Univ. Prof.; Intercontinental Biographical Assoc. Published work: The Theory of Coordinates, Part 1. Awards: Special Award, 1972, Distinguished Award, 1973, Poetry Soc. of London (Eastern Centre). Address: 110 Glenwood Ave., Apt. 402, Jersey City, NJ 07306, USA.

MAKAR, Nadia, b. 7 Oct. 1938. Educator. Education: B.A. in Chem., Physics, Maths. & French, St. Peter's Coll., 1969; grad work, Hope Coll. & Brown Univ. Married Dr. Boshra Makar, 2 sons (Ralph & Roger). Positions held: Tchr. of Chemistry, 1970-72; Chmn. of Sci. Dept., 1972-. Memberships: Life Mbr., Eastern Ctr. of the Poetry Soc. of London; Bd. Dirs., World Poets' Resource Ctr. & Chmn. of Jr. Poets in the Int. Verse Speaking Fest., Int. Platform Assn.; AAAS; N.Y. & N.J. Acads. of Sci.; Nat. Sci. Tchr. Assn.; Nat. Sci. Supvsr. Assn. Honours, awards: Special Award, Poetry Soc. of London (Eastern Crt.), 1972 & 73; Disting. Award Winner, Poetry Soc. of London, 1973; Nat. Winner of the Outstanding Educator of the Year Award, 1973. Address: 110 Glenwood Ave., Apt. 402, Jersey City, NJ 07306, U.S.A.

MAKKAI, Adam, b. 16 Dec. 1935. Professor of Linguistics. Education: Univ. of Budapest, Hungary; Harvard Univ., U.S.A.; B.A., Yale Univ., 1958; M.A. Gen. Linguistics, ibid, 1962; Ph.D., Gen. Linguistics, 1965. Married Valerie June Becker, 1 daughter. Positions held: Lectr. in Russian, Univ. of Hawaii, 1959-60; Lectr. in German, ibid, 1960; Lectr. in Russian, Yale Univ., 1962-63; Asst. Prof. of Linguistics, Univ. of Malaya, 1963-64; Post doctoral Rsch. Fellow, The Rand Corp., 1965-66; Asst. Prof. of Russian, Occidental Coll., 1966-67; Asst. Prof. of Engl. & Linguistics, Calif. State Coll., Long Beach; Asst. Prof. of Linguistics, Univ. of Ill., Chicago Circle, 1967-69; Assoc. Prof., ibid, 1970-74; Prof., 1974-. Memberships: PEN in Exile, Am. Br., 1970-; Fndr. & Pres., Zoltán Kodály Hungarian Lit. Soc. of Chgo. Published works: Szomj és ecet (Thirst & Vinegar) coll. poems 1952-66; K2 = 13 collected poems, 1967-70; The Poetry of Hungary: An Anthology of Hungarian Poetry in Translation from the 13th Century to the Present, co-ed., in press. Contbr. to var. Hungarian jrnls. in the West & to var. Am. jrnls. Address: 360 MacLaren Ln., Lake Bluff, IL 60044, U.S.A.

MALANGA, Gerard, pen name FARFALLA, Angelica, b. 20 Mar. 1943. Film-maker; Photographer. Education: Univ. of Cinn. Schl. of Applied Arts; New Schl. for Soc. Rsch.; Wagner Coll. Positions held: Assoc. to Andy Warhol; Sec. to Virgil Thomson, composer. Published works: 3 Poems for Benedetta Barzini, 1967; Prelude to International Velvet Debutante, 1967; Screen Tests/A Diary, 1967; The Last Benedetta Poems, 1969; Cristina's World, 1970; Selbsportrat Eines Dichters, 1970; 10 Poems for 10

Poets, 1970; The Blue Book, 1970; Beatle Calendar, 1970; Chic Death, 1970. Contbr. to: Poetry; Angel Hair; The New Yorker; Rolling Stone; Partisan Review; The Paris Review; Evergreen Review; Aspen; Tri-Quarterly; Fuck You; Tamarack Review; Nuovi Argomenti; Nadada; Film Culture; The Ant's Forefoot; Silo; New York Herald Tribune; The Herald; Sumac; The World; Tish. Honours & Awards: Stanley Corprew Paul Peace Prize, Poetry Soc. of Va., 1961; Robert Lee Strauss Poetry Prize, Univ. of Cinn., 1961; Williams Poetry Prize, Cinn. Lit. & Musical Soc., 1961; The 1st Gotham Book Mart Avant-Garde Poetry Prize, NY Writers Conf., 1961; Dylan Thomas Mem. Poetry Prize, New Schl. for Soc. Rsch., 1962; Comm. on Poetry Form Grant, 1968; Am. Film Inst. Grant, 1969; Nat. Inst. of Arts & Letters Grant, 1969 & '71; Carnegie Fund for Writers, 1969; Friends of New Cinema Grant, 1971. Address: PO Box 1811, FDR Stn., New York, NY 10022, USA.

MALEK, John Francis, II, pen name DOUGLAS, John Cameron, b. 29 May 1950. Writer; Editor. Education: grad., Western Wash. State Coll., Bellingham, Wash., 1972. Published works: Edited & self published, Window, 1969 & Aberdeen River Poetry Review, 1971-72. Contbr. to: Gato, 1969; Jeopardy, 1970; Best College Verse of 1970; New Voices in the Wind (anthol.), 1970; Anthol. of Modern Poetry, 1971; Madison Broadside Review, 1971; College Verse (Nat. Poetry Press Anthol.), 1971; IWWP, 1972. Address: 1734 South 305th Pl., Federal Way, WA 98002, U.S.A.

MALIK, Abdul Jamil, pen name JAMIL MALIK, b. 12 Aug. 1928. Poet; Writer; Associate Professor. Married, 1 son, 2 daughters. Memberships: Progressive Writers Assn. of Pakistan, 1947-54; Mbr., Ctrl. Comm., ibid, 1952-54; Pakistan Writers Guild, 1958–; Mbr., Ctrl. & Provincial Exec. Comms., ibid, 1964-74. Published works: Sarw-e-Charagan (a coll. of 'Ghazals'), 1957; Talu-e-Fardah (coll. of poems), 1962; Nadeem ki Shairi (criticism on the thought, art & life of Ahmad Nadeem Qasmi), 1973. Contbr. to: Naqoosh; Fanoon; Sawera; Imroz; Adbe-Latif; Naya Daur; Saqi, etc. Address: N/222 Piracha St., Rawalpindi, Pakistan.

MALIK, Keshav, b. 5 Nov. 1934. Editor; Journalist. Education: B.A.; Columbia Univ., N.Y.C., U.S.A. Married Usha Malik. Positions held: Personal Asst. to the late Prime Minister Nehru; Lit. Ed., Thought, Delhi; Art Critic, the Hindustan Times; Ed., Indian Lit. of Sahitya Akademi. Memberships: Sahitya Akademi; Art Soc., Delhi. Published works: Lake Surface & other poems, 1959, 2nd ed 1960; Rippled Shado, 1960, 2nd ed 1961; More Poems, 1971. Contbr. to: Quest; Thought; Poet; Indian Lit.; Mini-mag.; Indian Express; Illustrated Weekly; Opinion; Adam Int. Review; Botteghe Oscure; Lit. Review, U.S.A.; Bitter Root; Australian Poetry Anthol., etc. Address: c/o Indian Literature, Sahitya Akademi, Rabindra Bhavan, Feroze Shah Rd., New Delhi 1, India.

MALLALIEU, Herbert B., b. 1914. Associate Editor. Married w. 1 child. Positions held: Has worked in a Shipping Office & on Provincial Newspapers; Assoc. Ed., Twentieth Century, London. Published works: Poets of Tomorrow (w. others), 1939; Letter in Wartime & Other Poems, 1940. Contbr. to (Anthols.): War Poets, 1945; Poetry of the War, 1965; I Burn for England, 1966; (Jrnls.): Listener; Twentieth Century; Poetry.

MALLAMO, Margaret. Artist. Education: studied religion, creative writing & painting. Married with children. Charter Mbr., Ariz. State Poetry Soc. Published a small book of philosophical thoughts in 1940. Contbr. of poetry to: Verdure; Sandcutter; Your Digest; Creative Newsletter; Science of Mind; Poet; sev. anthols. Address: 350 N. Scherbell Rd., Scherbell Apt. 40, Tucson, AZ 85705, U.S.A.

MALONE, Kirby Smith, III, b. 6 July 1954. College Student. Education: Writers' Workshop, Oglethorpe Univ. (by the Dixie Coun. of Authors & Jrnlsts.), 1971; Oglethorpe Univ., 1972-73; Antioch Coll. Poetry Workshop, Ilchester, Md., 1973. Positions held: Student Poet Laureate, Oglethorpe Univ., Atlanta, Ga., 1972-73. Contbr. to: Knight Light (lit. mag. of Briarcliff H.S., Atlanta); Southern Recorder (campus newspaper of Oglethorpe Univ.); Atlanta Journal; Aurora (lit. mag. of Agnes Scott Coll., Atlanta); Ga. Poets' Anthol. (Dekalb Lit. Arts Jrnl.). Honours, awards: 1st prize & 1st runner-up, Annual Poetry Day Contest, sponsored by Atlanta Br. of The Nat. League of Am. Pen Women, 1972. Address: 1908 Jacolyn Pl. N.E., Atlanta, GA 30329, U.S.A.

MALONE, Marvin H(erbert), pen names BOOK, M.K.; SYPHER, A.; LEE, P.H., b. 2 Apr. 1930. Professor of Pharmacology. Education: B.S., Univ. of Nebr., 1951; M.S. (Physiology & Pharmacology), ibid., 1953; Ph.D. (Pharmacology), ibid., 1958. Married, Shirley Ruth Cane; 2 children. Positions held: Grad. Asst., Univ. of Nebr., 1951-53; 1956-58; Rsch. Asst., E.R. Squibb Inst. Med. Resch., 1953-56; Asst. Prof., Univ. New Mexico, 1958-60; Assoc. Prof., Univ. Conn., 1960-69; Prof., Univ. of the Pacific, 1969–. Memberships: Delian-Union Lit. Soc.; Editor: The Wormwood Review, 1961–. Published works: Two Over Twice Equals Sixteen, 1958; One Over Twice Equals Eight, 1958; Conversation Peece, 1959; Bucolics & Cheromanics, 1963; Hippo et Hip Poet, 1967. Contbr. to: Scholastic; Hearse; Trace; New Improved; Poor Old Tired Horse; Ole; Premier; Fiddlehead; Brand X; rongWrong; Poet; Galley Sail Review; Outcast; Wormwood Review; Schist; California Librarian; Sun; Poesie Vivante. Recip. Cert. of Merit, National Scholastic Writing Awards, 1947. Address: 722 Bedford Rd., Stockton, CA 95204, USA.

MALOUF, George Joseph David, pen name MALOUF, David, b. 20 Mar. 1934. University Lecturer. Education: Brisbane Grammar Schl., Queensland, Australia; Univ. of Queensland. Positions held: Sr. Tutor in Engl., Univ. of Sydney; Advisory Ed., Poetry, Angus & Robertson, Publishers; Mbr. of the Australian Literature Bd., Australian Coun. for the Arts, 1973. Published works: Four Poets, 1962; Bicycle & other Poems, 1970. Contbr. to: Meanjin; Southerly; Overland; The Australian; Sydney Morning Herald. Address: 3/37 Walton Cres., Abbotsford, Sydney, N.S.W., Australia.

MALOY, Miriam (Craig), b. 25 Oct. 1908. Librarian (retired). Education: B.A., 1930, Univ. of Calif., Berkeley (with hons. in Anthro.), also Cert. in Librarianship (1931); additional study in US History and Verse Writing, Stanislaus State Coll., and Calif. State Univ., San Jose. Positions held: Junior Librarian, Univ. of Calif., Berkeley, 1931-38; Supervising Catalog Librarian, Calif. State Library, 1938-43; Head Cataloger, Humboldt State Coll., 1950-60; Head of Tech. Services and Asst. Librarian, Stanislaus State Coll., 1960-68. Memberships: Calif. Fed. of Chaparral Poets (Pres., Santa Cruz Chapter, 1973-74); Ina Coolbrith Circle (life member); Pennsylvania Poetry Soc.; Calif. State Poetry Soc. Contbr. to: Cats Mag.; Denver Post; Haiku Highlights; Jean's Journal; Explosion; Poet Lore; Worm Runner's Digest; Cardinal Poetry Qtly.; Harlequin Press; Horn Book Mag.; AAUW Journal; Pacifica; Sundaz; Santa Cruz Sentinel; Viking; Ina Coolbrith Circle Anthol., 1971; Santa Cruz Chaparral Poets (anthol.), 1973; The Sandcutters. Awards: 1st Prizes: Calif. Fed. of Chaparral Poets, 1971, 1973, Calif. State Poetry Soc., 1971, North Carolina Poetry Soc. Carl Sandburg Award, 1972; Greatest Merit: Am. Assoc. of Univ. Women's Nat. Writing Project, 1970; 2nd Prizes: Ina Coolbrith Circle, 1970; Unitarian Art Festival, Sacramento, 1970; Valley Writers' Council, 1970; Poets Round Table of Arkansas, 1970; Nat. Fed. of State Poetry Socs., 1972; Calif. State Poetry Soc., 1972; Sevenelle Contest, 1972; North Carolina Poetry Soc. Ogden Nash Awards, 1973; 3rd Prize: Pennsylvania Poetry Soc. Edna Shoemaker Awards, 1973. Address: 107 Farley Dr., Aptos, CA 95003, USA.

MAMMANA, Louise Carmela, pen name MAMMANA, Camille Louise, b. 2 Mar. 1918. Housewife. Married

Frank Mammana, 2 daughters. Positions held: Supvsr. for Miller Art Greeting Cards, 1942-44; w. Street & Smith Publsng. House, 1944-47; Artist; Sculptor. Member, N.Y. Poetry Forum. Contbr. to: Clover Coll. of Verse, 1968; The Soul & the Singer, 1969. Honoured for Poetry on Pres. John F. Kennedy, 1970. Address: 336 Farview Ave., Paramus, NJ 07652, U.S.A.

MAMMATT, Doreen Rosalie, pen name, **Morisot, Simone,** b. 21 Jan. 1947. Freelance Artist & Designer. Education: North Lindsey Technical Coll.; Lincoln Coll. of Art; London Art Coll. (Correspondence Course). Positions held: Horse-stable girl; Asst. to vet. surgeon. Membership: Internat. Poetry Soc. (Fellow). Contbr. to: Viewpoints; Orbis; Platform; Spring Anthol., 1967, 1968, 1969; Lincolnshire Life; Internat. Poetry Mag. Anthol. Orbis. Recip. 2nd Prize, Poetry Day (held at L.S.E.), 1967. Address: 22 Ferriby Rd., Ashby, Scunthorpe, Lincs., UK.

MANCHAM, James Richard Marie, b. 11 Aug. 1939. Chief Minister of the Seychelles. Education: Seychelles Coll.; Middle Temple, London, U.K.; Faculte de Droit, Paris, France. Positions held: Barrister-at-Law, Supreme Court of Seychelles, 1963-65; Pres. & Ldr. of Seychelles Democratic Party, 1965-70; Chief Minister, Seychelles, 1970-. Fellow, Royal Soc. of Arts. Published works: Reflections & Echoes of Seychelles. Contbr. to: Seychelles Weekly; Seychelles Bulletin; Le Mauricien; Playboy Mag. Address: Office of the Chief Minister, P.O. Box 217, Mahé, Seychelles.

MANDEL, Eli(as Wolf), b. 1922. Professor of English. Education: Univ. of Saskatchewan, Saskatoon; Univ. of Toronto. Positions held: Past Mbr., currently Prof., Engl. Dept., Univ. of Alberta. Published works: Trio, 1954; Fuseli Poems, 1960; Black & Secret Man, 1964; An Idiot Joy, 1964; Other: Ed. w. Jean-Guy Pilon, Poetry 62, 1961. Contbr. to (Anthols.): Blasted Pine, 1957; Penguin Book of Canadian Verse, 1958; Oxford Book of Canadian Verse, 1960; (jrnls.): Tamarack Review; Canadian Forum; Queen's Quarterly; Fiddlehead. Address: c/o Dept. of Engl., Univ. of Alberta, Edmonton, Alberta, Canada.

MANGOLD, Christoph, b. 17 Mar. 1939. Journalist. Education: University. Married, 2 sons. Positions held: Freelance Jrnlst. for newspapers in Switzerland & Germany; Lectr. for Radio & Publishing cos.; Ed., National-Zeitung, Basle. Memberships: Gruppe Olten (Swiss Authors Grp.); PEN. Published works: Manöver (novel), 1962; Seis's Drum (poems), 1968; Konzert für Papagei and Schifferklavier (novel), 1969; Christoph Mangold's ·Agenda (short stories), 1970. In preparation: Regerupfeifer (poems) & Kon und der Orange September (novel). Contbr. to: National-Zeitung, Basel; Die Welt, Hamburg; Frankfurter Allgemeine Zeitung; Spektrum, Zurich; Reformatio, Bern; Neue Zürcher Zeitung. Honours, awards: Stiftung Pro Helvetia, 1970; Basler Literaturkredit, 1967. Address: Dammerkirchstrasse 34, SH-4056 Basle, Switzerland.

MANICKAM, T. Sambasiva, pen names **MANI, CHENNAI Sa MANIYARASAN,** b. 16 Mar. 1931. Teacher. Education: M.A., Tamil lang. & lit., Madras Univ., India; M.Litt. (Annamalai); Certs. in Linguistics. Positions held: Tutor in Tamil, Presidency Coll., Madras, 1955-57; Lectr. in Tamil, Osmania Univ., Hyderabad, 1957-66; Rdr. in Tamil, ibid, 1966-. Memberships: Fndr. & Patron of Bharthiya Tharmizh Sangam & Kural Neri Manram of Secunderabad; served as Jt. Sec., Tamil Lakkiya (Lit.) Sangam Secunderabad. Published works: Poetic Rain, 1963; sev. poems published in leading jrnls. of Tamil Nadu, Ceylon & Hyderabad. Contbr. to: Poonthamizh (organ of Bharathiya Thamizh Sangam Secunderabad; Tamizhtthenral (organ of Trimulgherry); Tamizh Sangam; Poet WPSI, 1973. Honours, awards: Shawl & Felicitation Address, Bharathiya Thamizh Sangam, 1965; World Poetry Soc. Int. Award, 1973. Address: Venkat Rao Colong, 136 Prenderghast Rd., Secunderabad 500005, India.

MANIFOLD, John Streeter, b. 21 Apr. 1915. Writer; Adult Education Lecturer. Education: Jesus Coll., Cambridge Univ., U.K. Married Katharine Hopwood, dec., 2 children. Memberships: Fellowship of Australian Writers; Pres., Qld Br., ibid, 1959. Published works: The Death of Ned Kelly & Other Ballads, 1941; Selected Verse, 1947; Nightmares & Sunhorses, 1961; Op.8: Poems 1961-69, 1971; also prose works on muoic & theatre. Contbr. to: (U.K.) Life & Letters Today; Poetry & the People; Tribune; The Listener; Our Time; New English Weekly; (U.S.A.) Harper's; Harper's Bazaar; Poetry; The Am. Scholar; The Nation; Masses & Mainstream; (Australia) Publicist; Poetry-Australia; Overland; Realist; Australian Poetry (annual); Queensland Guardian; (Hong Kong) Eastern Horizon; & many others. Address: 361 Wynnum North Rd., Wynnum, Qld 4178, Australia.

MANN, Leonard, b. 15 Nov. 1895. Poet. Education: LL.B., Univ. of Melbourne, Aust. Married Florence Eileen Archer w. 2 children. Published works: The Plumed Voice, 1938; Poems from the Mask, 1941; The Delectable Mountains, 1944; Elegiac and Other Poems, 1957; Novels: Flesh in Armour, 1932; Human Drift, 1935; A Murder, 1937; Mountain Flat, 1940; The Go-Getter, 1942; Andrea Caslin, 1959; Venus Half-Caste, 1963. Contbr. to (Anthols.): Australasian Anthology, 1946; Modern Australian, 1946. Hons: Aust. Literary Soc. Crouch Award for Poetry, 1941; Grace Leven Award for Poetry, 1957; 2 Aust. Literary Soc. Awards for fiction. Address: Greenthorpe Road, Olinda, Victoria, 3788, Australia.

MANSFIELD, Margery, pen names **SWETT, Margery & MANSFIELD, Margery Swett,** b. 6 June 1895. Writer. Education: New Schl. & Joseph Medill Schl. of Jrnlsm.; Univ. of N.Y. State. Married 1) Jay Van Everen, dec., 2) Kelly Janes. Positions held: Asst. Woman's Ed., Chicago Herald; Assoc. Ed., Fashion Art; Bus. Mgr., Poetry (Chicago); Sec., Poetry Soc. of Am. Memberships: Poetry Soc. of Am.; Authors Guild of Am.; Catholic Poetry Soc. of Am.; Poetry Socs. of the States of Tex., Va., & Ga. Published works: Workers in Fire, 1937; A Berkshire Settler, 1961. Contbr. to num. mags., newspapers inclng: Atlantic Monthly; Harpers Mag.; Sat. Review; N.Y. Herald Tribune; N.Y. Sun; N.Y. Examiner; Christian Sci. Monitor; Poetry Soc. of Am. Anthols.; Commonweal, etc. Recip. var. poetry prizes. Address: Box 338 Monterey, MA 01245, U.S.A.

MANWARING, Randle, b. 3 May 1912. Business Executive; Poet. Education: London Univ., U.K. Positions held: Wing Cmdr, RAF, 1940-46; w. C.E. Heath & Co. Ltd., Lloyds Ins. Brokers, 1956-71; currently Vice-Chmn., Midland Bank Ins. Servs. Memberships: Poetry Soc.; Poetry Workshop; Council Mbr., Corp. of Ins. Brokers, 1965-71; Vice-Chmn., 1969-71; Pres., Soc. of Pension Consultants. Published works: Posies Once Mine, 1951; Satires & Salvation, 1960; Slave to No Sect, 1966; Under The Magnolia Tree, 1967. Contbr. to: Outposts; Poetry Review; Scrip; John o'London's; Oxford Mag.; Sussex Life; Tribune; Muse; We Offer; Expression; Layman; New Christian; Medley; Limbo (Canada); The Field; Aylesford Review; St. Martin's Review; Transition; How to Read An English Poem (anthol.), Japan; New Poems (anthol. PEN), 1954. Address: High Paddock, Rodmell, Lewes, Sussex, U.K.

MAO, Tse-tung, b. 26 Dec. 1893. Teacher; Politician; Writer; Poet. Education: First Tchrs. Trng. Schl., Hunan. Positions held: w. Revolutionary Army, 1911-12; Lib. Asst., Peking Univ., Co-fndr., New Citizen's Soc. & Evening Class Tchr., 1918; Tchr., Hsiu-yeh Primary Schl., Changsha, 1919; Dir., Primary Schl. Sect., First Tchrs. Trng. Schl., 1921-22; Fndr. Mbr., Chinese Communist Party, 1921; Fndr., Hunan Br., Socialist Youth Corps; Chmn., Assn. of Trade Unions of Hunan, 1922; Sec., Propaganda Dept., Kuomintang, 1925; Chief, Peasant Dept., Chinese Communist Party, 1926; Sec., Front Comm., 1927-28; Chmn., All-China Peasants Union, 1927; Chmn., Spec.

Comm. Chingkangshan Base Area, 1928; estab. Kiangsi Prov. Soviet Govt., 1930; Chmn., Nat. Soviet Govt., 1930; led 'Long March' thro' Kweichow to Yenan after defeat of Red Army, 1934-35; Chmn., Ctrl. Comm. & Politburo, Communist Party, 1943–; defeated Kuomintang thro' Mainland of China, 1945-49; Chmn., Ctrl. People's Govt., Repub. of China, 1949-54; People's Repub. of China, 1954-58; Ex-officio Chmn., Nat. Defence Coun.; Hon. Chmn., Chinese People's Polit. Consultative Conf., 1949–; Chmn., Constit. Drafting Comm., 1953; Initiator, the following compaigns: Hundred Flowers, 1956, Great Leap Forward, 1959 & the Great Proletarian Cultural Rev., 1965. Published works include: The Great Union of the People, 1919; An Analysis of the Classes in Chinese Society, 1926; Report on the Peasant Movement in Hunan, 1927; Strategic Problems of China's Revolutionary War, 1936; Selected Works of Mao Tse-tung, 4 vols., 1937; On The Protracted War, 1938; Problems of War and Strategy, 1938; Let Politics Take Command, 1958; 37 Poems of President Mao; President Mao's Poetry; essays, etc. Address: Office of the Chairman, Communist Party of China, Peking, China.

MAPLES, Phyllis Lorraine Buehrens, b. 11 Aug. 1918. Homemaker. Married, 6 children. Memberships: Pres., Women's Fellowship, Moravian Ch.; Past Pres. & Treas. & currently V.P., Door Co. Writers; Sec., Sturgeon Bay Home & Garden Club, 1973-74; Sec., Bd. of Elders, Moravian Ch., 1972-74; Publicity Chmn., Ch. Women United, 1972-74; Wis. Fellowship of Poets; Wis. Regl. Writers Assn.; Wis. Press Women. Contbr. to: Wis. Hist. in Poetry, 1969; Think, Jrnl. of Moravian Ch. Women; Door Co. Advocate; Shore Poetry Anthol.; Native Lumber, anthol., 1974. Address: 438 N. Fifth Pl., Sturgeon Bay, WI 54235, U.S.A.

MARCHAND, Marie-Rose (Rosine), pen name **PACORA, Madou,** b. 8 Sept. 1900. Retired Nurse; Poet. Memberships: Soc. of Men of Letters of France; Soc. of French Poets; French Ballad Acad.; Syndicate of Periodical Jrnlsts.; Fndg. Mbr., Friends of Jean Giono; Fndg. Mbr., Citizens of the World; Violet Legion; Writers of Champagne. Published works incl: Le Mors aux dents, 1967; Pétales d'Automne, 1968; Le Pain Blanc, 1969; Les Murs on du Salpêtre, 1970; Petite Lumière, 1971; Les Contes de Regain, 1972. Contbr. of poems & prose to num. anthols. & literary & medical publs. Honours, awards, incl: Silver Medal of Public Hlth., 1939; Silver Medal, Swimming & Lifesaving, 1939; Silver Medal, Arts, Scis. & Letters, 1970; Bronze Medal, Int. Arts & Letters, 1971; Silver Medal, Public Encouragement, 1972; Prize, Acad. Française, 1973. Address: Montagny-Sainte-Félicité, 60950 Ermenonville, France.

MARCHESINI, Ida, b. 22 Mar. 1909. Poet. Education: Dip., piano, La Regia Acc. Filarmonica (Bologna). Memberships: Acad. Leonardo da Vinci; Lauro Accademico; Accademico Tiberina; Accademico Inter. Burchgardt; Accademico '500'; Accademico Am. Institute; Counsellor, Univ. of Canada; Free World Acad,; Accademico 'Gentium Popolorum Progressio'; Acc. Teatina; Legion d'oro ed altre. Published works: Quà e là, 1952; Un giorno un altro giorno, 1957; La nonna racconta, 1957; La tortura libera l'anima; Le voci; La proprietà, 1963; Quaderni di poesie, Centro studi inter. 'Frammenti', 1966; Acqua di fonte, 1967; Il canto mio, 1969; Per te, 1972. Contbr. to: La Sonda; Il Dialogo; Il mondo libero, etc. Recip. var. awards for poetry; Gold & Silver Medals. Address: 9 San Giovanni alle murate, 47011 Castrocaro Terme, Forli, Italy.

MARCUS, Adrianne, b. 7 Mar. 1935. Writer; Teacher. Education: A.B., San Francisco State Coll., 1955; M.A., ibid, 1963. Positions held: Newspaper Columnist, Pacific Sun, 1967-69 & intermittently afterwards; Pt-time Instr., Coll. of Marin, 1968–; Pt.-time Instr., Indian Valley Colls., 1973–. Member, Poetry Soc. of Am. Published works: The Moon is a Marrying Eye, 1972. Contbr. to: Mark in Time, anthol.; Peace & Pieces, anthol.; The Diamond Anthol., PSA; Pacific Sun; Shenandoah; Chgo. Tribune; Calif. Living; Motive; Black Box; Descant; Road Apple Review; Southern Poetry Review; Atlantic Monthly; The Nation; N.M. Qtly.; Wis. Review; The Smith; Epoch; Choice; S.D. Review; Tenn. Poetry Jrnl.; Forum, etc. Honours, awards: Borestone Mt. Poetry Awards, 1968 & '71; Grant, Nat. Endowment for the Arts & Humanities, 1968. Address: 79 Twin Oaks, San Rafael, CA 94901, U.S.A.

MARCUS, Mordecai, b. 18 Jan. 1925. Professor of English. Education: B.A., Brooklyn Coll., 1949; M.A., N.Y. Univ., 1950; Ph.D., Univ. of Kansas, 1958. Married, 1 son, 1 daughter. Positions held: Taught at Rutgers Univ., Univ. of Kans., Purdue Univ.; currently Prof. at Univ. of Nebraska-Lincoln. Published works: Five Minutes to Noon (pamphlet), 1971. Contbr. to: Aegis; Arion's Dolphin; Ark River Review; Casaba Poetry Review; Country Bumpkin; Epos; Falcon; Fuse; Greenfield Review; Icarus; The Lamp in the Spine; Mill Mountain Review; North Stone Review; Pebble; Prairie Schooner; Quarry; Wind, etc. Address: Dept. of Engl., Univ. of Nebraska-Lincoln, Lincoln, NB 68508, U.S.A.

MARCUS, Morton Jay, b. 10 Sept. 1936. Poet; Teacher. Education: B.A., State Univ. of Iowa, U.S.A.; M.A., Stanford Univ. Positions held: Engl. Instr., Cabrillo Coll., Aptos, Calif. Published works: Origins, 1969; Where the Oceans Cover Us, 1972; The Santa Cruz Mt. Poems, 1972. Contbr. to: The Nation; The Quarterly Review of Lit.; The Chicago Review; Poetry Northwest; Kayak; Epoch; Choice; Chelsea; December; The North American Review; The Minn. Review; Motive; the Colo. State Review; Hearse; the Iowa Review; Crazy Horse; & over 40 others. Rep. in over 25 anthols. inclng: Best Poems of 1966; The Young American Poets; The New American Poets; First Voices; Poetry: A Fine Frenzy. Runner-up for the Joseph Henry Jackson Award, 1972. Address: 266A Cliff Ct., Aptos, CA 95003, U.S.A.

MAREK, Benita Louise, pen name, **MARK, Benita Marek,** b. 31 Aug. 1915. Educator and Poet. Education: Central School; Brenham HS; St. Paul's Lutheran & St. Peter's Episcopal Church Schools; Washington County Jr. Coll.; Texas Woman's Univ.; Southwest Texas State Univ. Positions held: Teacher, Kuykendal School, 1938-40; Union Grove Pulaski School, 1940-45 (Teacher & Prin.); Hd. Soc. Sc. Dept., Brenham HS, Texas, 1947; Teacher Alamo Elem. School, Texas, 1947-50; Private School Yukan, Kathleen, 1953-54, 1957-60; Parochial Episcopal, 1945, Austin, 1948-55, Brenham. Memberships: Heartland Poetry Chapter, Brenham; The Poetry Soc. of Texas; Southern Methodist Univ., Dallas, Texas; Acad. of American Poets. Published works: History of Brenham Public Schools, 1932; Masterpieces of the World, 1938. Contbr. to: Poetry Soc. of Texas; Heartland Poetry Chapter; San Jacinto Dist. of Texas Fed. Women's Club of the Gen. Fed. Women's Club of USA.: Internat. Who's Who in Poetry. Recip. of awards, including Poetry Soc. of Texas Leap Yr. Award, 1972, etc. Address: 506 West Alamo Ave., Brenham, TX 77833, USA.

MARGOLIS, William J. (Julius), pen names **BIMGO & WILL FRIAR,** b. 13 Aug. 1927. Poet. Education: Univ. of Fla., Tallahassee; Ill. Inst. of Technol., Chicago; Roosevelt Univ., Chicago. Widower. Positions held: Ed. & Publsr., Miscellaneous Man, 1954-59; Co-Ed. & Co-Fndr., Beatitude, 1959; Ed. & Publsr., Mendicant, 1961; Ed. of renascent Miscellaneous Man, 1968; Ed. & Publsr., Mendicant Editions, 1958–. Published works: (books) The Anteroom of Hell, poems, 1957; The Little Love of Our Yearning, poems, 1960, '62; KPFK 'Folio' (pamphlet), 1968. Hosted a series of 'Every Other Saturday Night Poetry Readings', in conjunction with publishing Miscellaneous Man, mid 1950's; Read own poetry in coffee houses & bars in San Francisco's North Beach, 1958-59; Var. Public Readings in 'Venice West', Los Angeles, 1960-61, 1965– & over the radio. Contbr. to num. jrnls., mags., anthols., etc. Address: 4618 Prospect Ave., Los Angeles, CA 90027, U.S.A.

MARIAH, Paul, b. 3 June 1937. Poet. Mental Health Therapist. Education: B.S., Southern Ill. Univ., 1959; M.A., San Fran. State Coll., 1969. Positions held: Chmn., Poetry & Writing Workshop, Soc. for Individual Rights, San Fran., 1967–; Org., Cosmep, conf. of small mags., eds. & publrs., 1968; Poetry Ed., Van Guard Mag., 1967-68; Poetry Ed., Vector Mag., 1968-69; Sec. to Kay Boyle & Robert Duncan, 1968-69; Co-org., Read-in, San Fran. State Coll., 1968; Asst. Ed., Gollards Mag., 1968; Fndr. & Co-Ed., ManRoot Mag., 1969–; Tchng. Asst., Engl., San Fran. State Coll., 1969-70; Proj. Scheduler, Rsch. Asst., Kinsey Study of deviant socialization, Inst. for Sex Rsch., Ind. Univ., 1969–. Memberships: Fndg. Charter, Phi Sigma Kappa; Southern Ill. Univ., 1957; Fndng. Task Force on Homosexuality, San Fran. Mental Hlth. Assn.; Symposium on Homosexuality, San Fran. State Coll. Published works: Diana (a folio of 16 poems), 1968; Personae Non Gratae, 1971; Love Poems to an Army Deserter Who Is In Jail (pamphlet). Contbr. to: (anthol.) The Male Muse; (anthol.) Love Today; Chelsea Review; West End; New Canadian & American Poetry; Motive; Calif. Quarterly; Defiance; ManRoot; Descant; Fiddlehead; Envoi; The Liberal Context; Wormwood Review; The Idler; Edge of Canada; The Ladder; Gay Sunshine; Love Today; A New Exploration, 1972. 20 Minute Documentary for Ind. Univ. etc. Recip. Arx Poet Award, Arx Fndn., 1970. Address: ManRoot, Box 982, South San Francisco, CA 94080, U.S.A.

MARIANOWICZ, Antoni, b. 4 Jan. 1924. Writer. Education: Diplomatic & Consular Schl., Warsaw, 1945. Positions held: Corres., Polish Press Agency, Brussels, 1945; Ed. 'Polska Dzisiejsza', Brussels, 1946-47; Attaché at the Polish Legation, Brussels, 1947-48; Ed. 'Przeglad Miedzynarodowy', Warsaw, 1948-49; Ed. 'Szpilki', Warsaw, 1949–. Memberships: Pres., Sect. of Satirists, Polish Writers' Union; Polish PEN. Published works: more than 20 vols. of poetry, satire & poetry for children; many translations from Engl. & Am. poetry: Alice in Wonderland, 1955, '57, '69; A.A. Milne's Poetry for Children, 1957; English Light Verse, 1958, '74. Collected poems in: Satyry, 1954; Plamy na Sloneczku, 1957; Bawim sie w rymy, 1974, etc. Contbr. to var. jrnls. Honours, awards: Prize of the Polish Min. of Culture & Arts & Polish Writers' Union, 1952; 4 prizes of Polish Radio & TV, 1960, '61, '65, '69. Address: Sniadeckich 1/15 m. 17, 00-654 Warsaw, Poland.

MARINELLI, Josette, b. 29 June 1927. Barrister; Professor. Licenciée ès Lettres et en Droit, Univ. of Geneva. Published works: Au fil de l'Heure (poems), 1950; L'Enterrement, 1952; Eté, (poems), 1969; Printemps, suivi de Pour Antigone, 1970, Printemps, Pour Antigone, Eté, 1972; Pour l'Espagne, précédé de Roses, suivi de Prière pour un Vendredi-Saint (poems), 1972. Collaborator, Séquences, Grassin, Paris & Club des Poètes, Paris. Address: 69 rue de Saint-Jean, 1202 Geneva, Switzerland.

MARISSEL, André, b. 5 Mar. 1928. Critic & Art Advisor. Education: French classic studies; Invited by Harvard Univ., 1967. Memberships: Syndicat des Ecrivains; Syndicat des Critiques Littéraires. Published works: (poetry books) Le Poete Responsable; L'Homme et L'Abime; Les Moissons de L'Orage; L'Arbre de L'Avenir; L'Envoutement Perpetuel; Nouvelle Parabole; Cicatrices; Choix de Poems; Sauve des Eaux; (essays) Jean Rousselot, 1960-73; Cinq Poetes; Poetes Vivants. Contbr. to: Esprit; Iô; Marginales; Jrnl. des Poetes; Ariane; Laudes; L'Envers et L'Endroit; Entretiens; Reforme; Horizons Protestants; Paix et Liberte; Nouvelles Litteraires; French Review (N.Y.) Honours, awards: Prix Unimuse, 1954; Prix Saint-Pol-Roux, 1959; Prix Ronsard, 1963; Prix Louise-Labe, 1964. Address: 14 rue de la Fraternité, 93130 Noisy-le-Sec, France.

MARKHAM, Beulah Belle, pen name **MARKHAM, Beulah Raines,** b. 1 Jan 1900. Housewife. Education: East Central State Coll., Ada, Okla., U.S.A. Widow of Talmage M. Markham, 2 sons. Positions held: Sewing Tchr., Lighthouse for the Blind, Houston, Tex.; Rdr. to Blind Student, Univ. of Houston, under State Commn. for Blind, Tex. Memberships: Pres., Artists, Composers & Authors; V.P., 1 yr. & Pres., 1½ yrs., Poetry Soc. of Tex., Houston Chap.; Corpus Christi Tex. Story League; Pasadena Lit. Club; Caddo Okla. Music. & Lit. Club. Published works: Build Thee More Stately Mansions (book of poems), 1972. Contbr. to: Bryan Co. Star, 1970-72; Wildfire; Home Life Mag.; Houston Press; Amarillo Times; Church Times-Houston; Am. Bard. Address: P.O. Box 274, Caddo, OK 74729, U.S.A.

MARKHAM, Muriel (Elizabeth) b. 17 Feb. 1911. Married, 1 s., 3 d. Member, Oregon State Poetry Association (for sev. years Secretary, and currently Historian). Contbr. to: The Sunday Oregonian; Driftwood; Medford Mail Tribune; Lincoln City News Guard; Cyclo-Flame; The Guild; Swordsman's Review; Am. Bard; Poet Lore; Oregon Journal; United Poets; American Poet; Clover Book; Creative Review; Redmond Spokesman; Tulsa Poetry Quarterly; Farmland, etc. Awards: 3rd Place, Annual Contest (Oct. 1970), Oregon State Poetry Association. Address: Route 3, Box 1350, Boring, OR. 97009, USA.

MARKLEY, Francis Xavier, b. 25 May 1919. Administrator. Education: B.A., U.S. Armed Forces Coll., 1947; var. corres. courses; Grad., Famous Writers Schl., 1973. Married Ann Teresa Garofalo, 1 son, 1 daughter. Positions held: Master Sergeant, U.S. Army, 1941-59; Medical Records Supvsr., The Johns Hopkins Hosp., 1964-68; Adminstr., Erection Dept., Strescon Industries Inc., 1968–. Memberships: Am. Poets Fellowship Soc., 1972; Major Poets Chapter-Pierson-Mettler Assocs., 1972; World Congress of Poets, 1973; Maryland Poetry Soc., 1970. Published works: Nature's Wonder, 1973. Contbr. to: The Lion; Songs of the Free State Bards; The Rainbow; Yearbook of Modern Poetry, 1971; Lyrics of Love, 1972; The John Fitzgerald Kennedy Meml. Lib., 1966; The Dr. Martin Luther King Jr. Meml. Lib., 1968, etc. Recip., 1st Prize, Major Poets Chapter, 1973; 40 Hon. Mention Awards. Address: 1313 Stevens Ave., Arbutus, MD 21227, U.S.A.

MARKS, Aline Musyl, b. 14 Apr. 1920. Educator. Education: N.Y. Univ. Positions held: Newspaper Reporter; Tchr. of Engl. & Art Mbr., Pa. Poetry Soc. Published works: Trace, 1967; Lyrics of Love, 1963. Contbr. to: Davis Anthology of Newspaper Verse, America Speaks, 1942; The Muse of 1943; Pa. Poetry Soc., 1968; Poet Lore; Bitterroot; Angel Hour; The Dekalb Lit. Arts Jrnl.; The Wormwood Review, Storrs, Conn.; Malestrom, Christiansburg, Va. Honours, awards: Pa. Poetry Soc., 1968; Poetry Soc. of Ga. Prize, 1962. Address: 68 Comly Rd., Lincoln Pk., NJ 07035, U.S.A.

MARKS-HIGHWATER, Jamake, pen names **MARKS, J. & MARKS-HIGHWATER, J.,** b. 14 Feb. 1942. Writer. Education: A.A., Univ. of Montana, 1956; B.A., UCLA, 1957; M.A., Univ. of Chicago, 1959; Ph.D., ibid, 1962. Positions held: Dir., Contemporary Theatre; collaborated with Karlheinz Stockhausen on theatre work 'Memesis'; Feature Writer successively for Los Angeles Free Press, Crawdaddy, Fusion, Chicago Tribune, N.Y. Times, Stereo Review, Playboy, Vogue Mag., etc. Memberships: Dramatist Guild; Am. League of Authors. Published works: Rock & Other Four Letter Words, 1968; Motion, Image & Form, 1969; Fodor's Europe Under 25, 1972, '73, '74; Mick Jagger, The Singer Not the Song, 1974. Contbr. to: Life; Look; Vogue; Cosmopolitan; Fusion; Crawdaddy; L.A. Free Press; Saturday Review; N.Y. Philharmonic Prog.; Harper's Bazaar; Performance; Chicago Tribune; San Francisco Chronicle; N.Y. Times; Penthouse; Gallery, etc. Recip., N.Y. Art Directors' Award for the design of Rock & Other Four Letter Words. Address: c/o Alfred Hart, Fox Chase Agency, 60 East 42nd St., N.Y., NY 10036, U.S.A.

MARLATT, Daphne (Buckle), b. 11 July 1942. Writer. Education: B.A., Univ. of B.C., Vancouver, 1964; M.A.,

Indiana Univ., Bloomington, 1968. Divorced, 1 son. Positions held: Engl. Instr., Napa Jr. Coll., Calif., summer 1968, Capilano Jr. Coll., Vancouver, fall 1968, Vancouver City Coll., S.P.D., spring 1972; currently tchng. Engl. at Capilano Coll. Ex. Mbr., League of Canadian Poets. Published works: Frames: of a Story, 1968; Leaf Leaf/s, 1969; Rings, 1971; Vancouver Poems, 1972. Contbr. to var. mags. & anthols. inclng: Iron; Imago; Origin; Open Letter; Tish; Evidence; The Story So Far; The Gist of Origin: an Anthol.; New Wave Canada. Honours, awards: Canada Coun. Grants, 1969-70, spring 1971, summer 1973. Address: 2749 A, West Third Ave., Vancouver 8, B.C., Canada.

MARLEY, Anne Augusta Bonner, pen name, **RENNOB, Enna,** b. 10 Jan. 1884. Musician; Composer; Poet; Writer. Education: B.Mus., Inst. of Musical Art, Wash. DC; Chicago Musical Coll.; Juilliard Schl. of Music. Married, Gen. James P. Marley, US Army (dec. 1952). Memberships: Poetry Soc. Tex.; Hon. Life, Austin Poetry Soc.; DC Br., Nat. League Am. pen Women Inc.; Friday Morning Music Club, Wash. DC; Pres., Harmony Club, Austin; Austin Colony Chapt., DAR. Published Works: Heart-Acres & Other Poems, 1958; Wings & Other Poems, 1971. Contributor to: Tulsa Mag. of Poetry; Wash. Evening Star; Hartford Courant; Hartford Times; Christian Sci. Monitor; Blue Moon; Talaria; The Lantern; Quicksilver; Driftwood; Notebook; Bozart Westminster; Visions; Poetry Caravan; Reflections; Panama Star & Herald; The Luling Signal; Tampa Fla. Tribune; Farm Jrnl. & Farmers Wife; Christian Sci. Sentinal; Christian Sci. Jrnl.; World Fair Anthol. of Verse; Music in Minature; Wash. Vistas; NLAPW Anthol.; The Pen Woman; United Songs of Am.; This Friendly Shore; NRTA Mag.; Austin Poetry Soc. Contest Winners, 1955; The Link; Lookout; Austin Statesman; Blue Quill Poets; Sr. Citizen; Wash. DC The Seydell Quarterly of Verse; DAR Mag.; Badge of Promise Anthol.; Melodies From A Jade Harp Anthol.; Prairie Poet Anthol.; Bapt. Standard; Le Traveleur, Canada; South & West Poetry Mag.; Eastern Star Mag., etc. Winner, numerous 1st Prizes in Nat. Contests in music, poetry & stories. Address: 504 B. Bellevue Place, Austin 5, Tex. 78705, USA.

MARMOLYA, Gary Allen, b. 29 Mar. 1948. Medical Student. Education: Washington Univ., St. Louis, Mo.; Case Western Reserve Univ., Cleveland, Ohio. Positions held: Hospital Stock Man; Dept. Store Clerk; Rsch., Neuropsychology; Stock-Man, Drug Store, etc. Contbr. to: United Poets Mag.; Images; Major Poetry; Prairie Poet; Year Book of Modern Poetry (anthol.); Lyrics of Love (anthol.) Freelance writer for Am. Greetings Corp. Address: 3305 Nelson Park, Rocky River, OH 44116, U.S.A.

MAROEVIC, Tonko, b. 22 Oct. 1941. University Assistant. Education: Grad., Fac. of Arts & Scis., comp. lit. & hist. of art; working on Doctorate at same Fac.; var. study courses in Italy. Positions held: Asst., Dept. of Middle Ages; Asst., Inst. for Rsch. & Documentation of Modern Art. Member, Soc. of Croation Writers. Published works: (books of poems) Primjeri, 1965; Slijepo Oko, 1969. Has published many criticisms of Art & Lit., also essays. Contbr. to: Forum; Kolo; Razlog; Mogućnosti; Telegram; Slobodna Dalmacija; Vidik; Die Brücke; La Battana; Mlada tvorba; Les Cahiers de la grive; Poesie Croate d'aujourdhui. Also to the book 'Polje Moguéeg, 1969. Address: Marjanovićev prilaz 1, 41020, Zagreb, Yugoslavia.

MARR, Phillip L(loyd), b. 16 Mar. 1937. English Teacher; Librarian. Education: Assoc. of Arts, Odessa Coll., Texas; B.A.; Texas Western Coll., El Paso; M.A. (Engl.), Univ. of Texas at El Paso; (currently working on Ph.D.(Engl. Lit.). Married; 3 children. Served 4 yrs. US Navy, 1957-60. Positions held: Teacher, St. Pius X School, 1964-66; Ref. Librarian, El Paso Pub. Library, 1966-67; Teacher/Librarian, San Elizario HS, 1967 to present. Memberships: Poetry Soc. of Texas; Delta Psi Omega Drama Fraternity. Contbr. to: Writer Mag.; Ankh Review; Nat. Poetry Press Anthol.; Internat.

Who's Who in Poetry Anthol.; Library Journal (regular book reviewer). Address: 1119 Prescott, El Paso, TX 79915, USA.

MARR, William Wei-Yi, b. 3 Sept. 1936. Nuclear Engineer. Education: B.Sc., Mech. Engrng., Taipei Inst. of Technol., Taiwan, 1957; M.Sc., Mech. Engrng., Marquette Univ., U.S.A., 1963; Ph.D., Nuclear Engrng., Univ. of Wis., 1969. Married, 2 sons. Positions held: Asst. Engr., Taiwan Sugar Corp., 1959-61; Sr. Engrng. Analyst, Alli-Chalmers Mfg. Co., Milwaukee, Wis., 1963-67; Nuclear Engr., Argonne Nat. Lab., Argonne, Ill., 1969-. Member, Li (Bamboo Hat) Poetry Soc., Taiwan. Published works: Chansons, 1971 (Engl. transl. of the young Chinese poet Pai Chiu's work). Contbr. to: Li Poetry Mag., 1964-; Yearbook of Modern Poetry, 1971; Melody of the Muse, 1973; Modern Chinese Poetry (colls of Japanese translations of modern Chinese poetry), 1970; The City, Tokyo, 1970. Address: 737 Ridgeview St., Downers Grove, IL 60515, U.S.A.

MARSCH, Lucy-Leone, b. 13 Oct. 1912. Writer. Education: Lutheran Bible Coll., Mnpls., Minn. Memberships: League of Minn. Poets, 1939; Charter Mbr., Midwest Fed. of Chaparral Poets, 1941-; Hon. Mbr., Poets' Haven, L.A., Calif., 1963-. Published works: A Thousand Rainbows, a coll. of early verse; White Wine, Petrarchan sonnets; Grapes of Thorns, based on biblical stories; Out of the Darkness; The Way of Escape; The Wine Cup; Harps Upon the Willows. Rep. in following anthols: Davis' Anthol. of Newspaper verse, 1941; Minn. Skyline, 1944; From the Valleys to the Mountains, 1945; Am. Poets' Best, 1962; Poets' Haven Anthols., 1962, '65, '70; Young's Yrbook of Modern Poetry, 1971; Pied Piper Press Anthol., Outstanding Contemporary Poetry, 1972. Contbr. to: The Am. Bard; The Moccasin; Scimitar & Song; Sonnet Sequences, etc. Poems read over var. radio stns. in Calif. & Minn. Recip., var. hons. Address: Rte. 4, Box 213, Jesse Glen Farm, Alexandria, MN 56308, U.S.A.

MARSHALL, Inez Mildred, pen name **MARSHALL, Inez.** Poet; Writer. Married James F. Marshall, Jr. (decd) 1 d. Positions held: Secretary-stenographer, Swift and Co.; Sec. for Manager, Travelers Ins. Co.; Bookkeeper, Western Auto Co.; Civil Service, US Gov.; Trust Dept., Frost Nat. Bank, San Antonio, Texas; Writer on staff of Stallings Publishing Co., San Antonio, Texas. Memberships: American Poetry League; (formerly) San Antonio Chapter, C.A.A.A. (Corresponding Sec., Historian, Recording Sec.), also Reading Club, Navasota, Texas (Treas., then Vice-Pres.). Published works: Dream Patterns, 1949 (also 2nd edition). Contbr. to: Seek; Ideals; Different; New Horizons; Avalaff; Montana Poetry Qtly.; Seydell Qtly.; American Poetry Mag.; Candor; Blue Moon; Home Life; Christian Home; Kansas City Poetry Mag.; The Friend; Composers & Authors of America; also produced (and sold) greeting card verse for several companies. Awards: 1st Prize, Different (Conquest of Space mag.); other prizes Different (mag.), and various poetry mags. Address: 6442 Ave. A., New Orleans, LA 70124, USA.

MARSHALL, Jack, b. 1937. Married Kathleen Fraser. Published works: The Darkest Continent, 1967. Contbr. to (Anthols.): Of Poetry & Power, 1964; Young American Poets, 1968; (Jrnls.): New Yorker; Hudson Review; Harpers; Kayak.

MARSHALL, Lenore G., b. 7 Sept. 1899. Writer; Poet. Education: B.A., Barnard Coll., 1919. Married James Marshall, 1919. Positions held: Lit. Ed., Cape & Smith, 1929-32; Exec. Bd., Post World War Coun., 1943; Co-fndr., Bd. Dirs., Nat. Comm. for Sane Nuclear Policy, 1957; Co-chmn., Prog. policy Comm., Exec. Bd., Am. Ctr.; Co-chmn., Comm. for Nuclear Responsibility, 1971. Memberships: Women's Int. League for Peace & Freedom; Authors League; Poetry Soc. Am.; Pen & Brush Club; PEN; Soc. of Friends. Published works: Only the Fear, 1935; Hall of Mirrors, 1937; No Boundary, 1943; Other Knowledge, 1957; The Hill is

Level, 1959; Latest Will, 1969. Contbr. to: Poetry; The New Yorker; Saturday Review; Partisan Review; Scribners; The New Republic; The Modern Quarterly; The American Scholar; Books; Poetry Northwest; Living Wilderness. Address: 30 W 54th St., New York, NY 10019, USA.

MARSHALL, Thomas Archibald, pen name **MARSHALL, Tom,** b. 9 Apr. 1938. University Professor of English. Education: B.A., Hist., Queen's Univ., Kingston, Ont., Canada; M.A., Engl., ibid. Positions held: Instr., Lectr., Asst. Prof., Assoc. Prof., Dept. of Engl., Queen's Univ. Mbr., League of Canadian Poets. Published works: The Beast With Three Backs, 1965; The Silences of Fire, 1969; Magic Water, 1971; The Earth-Book, 1974. Contbr. to: Quarry; Queen's Quarterly; Tamarack Review; Canadian Forum; Alphabet; Saturday Night; Tuatara; Southern Review (Australia). Address: Dept. of Engl., Queen's Univ., Kingston, Ont., Canada.

MARSHFIELD, Alan Edwin Charles, b. 5 June 1933. Teacher. Education: Portsmouth Coll. of Technol., 1954-55; King's Coll., London, 1955-58. Positions held: Hd. of Engl. Dept., Edgware Comprehensive Schl. Published works: Centaurs, 1970; Mistress, 1972; Dragonfly, 1972; Vox Dei, 1973; The Moonstone, 1973; The Blood Rules, 1974. Contbr. to: The Cambridge Review; The Listener; The New Statesman; Outposts; Oyster; Paperway; Stardock; The Transatlantic Review; Tribune; The Kenyon Review; Littak; New Measure; Oasis; Phoenix; The Times Lit. Supplement; Pink Peace; Resident Poet; Encounters (RKP); The Greek Anthol., etc. Poems broadcast on BBC progs: The Poet's Voice; Poetry Today; The Five Seasons; and on Dial-a-Poem. Address: 54 Montrose Ave., Edgware, Middx. HA8 0DW, U.K.

MARTIN, Adele Lee, pen name **STERLING,** b. 9 Sept. 1920. Homemaker; Religious Worker; Singer; Poet; Writer; Former Teacher. Education: Pvte. Instrn., Fine Arts, Voice, Drama, Poetry, & Speech; special courses in Child Psychol., Bible Study courses & Workshops for Tchrs. in Christian Educ. Married Russell Martin, 3 children. Positions held: Garden Therapy Chmn. for Gulfport Garden Club at VA Hosp. for Mental Patients, 5 yrs.; Past Pres., ibid; Speaker in charge, 19th Annual Spring Pilgrimage, Gulfport, Miss. area Garden Clubs; Dist. Dir. of Workshops for Tchrs. in Christian Educ. of Children; Soloist for Gulfport, Miss. Womens Club; Tchr. Dir., Children's Choirs; Dir. of Dramas for Children; Dir., Youth Work; Sec., Christian Educ.; Acting Dir. of Christian Educ.; Dist. Dir. of Christian Educ. for Children; Tchr., Christian Ldrship Trng. Sohl. Memberships: Volunteer Dir., News Media for Miss. Heart Assn., Harrison Co., 3 yrs.; Helped conduct Pilot prog., ibid; Charter Mbr., Wis. Fellowship of Poets; 1st Music Chmn., ibid; Vol. Organiser, Classes, Am. Red Cross, 2 yrs.; Hon. Rep., Centro Studi e Scambi; Acad. of Am. Poets. Contbr. to: Bouquet of Poems, Rome, 1968-73; Capital Times of Madison; Tomah Jrnl.; Dixie Guide, Miss. Honours, awards: Dip. of Merit & Medal of Hon., Centro Studi e Scambi, 1969; Dip. of Merit, ibid, 1972, etc. Address: 401 Second St., Gulfport, MS 39501, U.S.A.

MARTIN, Albert Anthony, pen name **'THE CAJUN POET',** b. 28 Oct. 1898. Retired Scenic Artist. Member, La. State Poetry Soc. Published works: (booklets) The Years Astray, 1964; Golden Memories, 1973; Among My Verses, 1972; Song of the Old South, 1973; Life on the Farm – in the Good Old Days, 1973; October Leaves, 1971; Tender Moments, 1972; Acadian Tales, 1971. Contbr. of articles to the Lafayette Daily Advertiser. Address: P.O. Box 2082, Lafayette, LA 70501, U.S.A.

MARTIN, Connie Gay Lakey, b. 16 Mar. 1951. Housewife. Education: Deep Creek HS, Chesapeake, Va. Married, 1 s. Positions held: Manifolder, Dunn & Bradstreet, 1969; Receptionist, Dawkins Construction Co.; Radio & TV., Christian Broadcasting Network, Inc.,-1970; Teller, Home Fed. Savings & Loan, 1973.

Contbr. to: Bachaet; The American Bard; Prairie Poet; Yearbook of Mod. Poetry (1971). Address: Rt. 2, Box L22, Orangeburg, SC 29115, USA.

MARTIN, David, b. 1915. Poet, Novelist. Positions held: Republican Med. Corps, Spanish Civil War; Journalist, UK & Europe; Social Rschr. Published works: Battlefields and Girls, 1942; The Shepherd and the Hunter (play), 1946; Tiger Bay (novel), 1946; The Shoes Men Walk In (stories), 1947; The Stones of Bombay (novel), 1949; From Life, 1953; Poems 1938-58, 1958; Spiegel the Cat, 1961; The Young Wife (novel), 1962. Contbr. to: (anthol.) Modern Australian Verse, 1964. Address: c/o Angus & Robertson Ltd., 107 Elizabeth St., Melbourne, Australia.

MARTIN, Dom, b. 1950. Poet; Writer; Artist. Positions held: Profl. Cartoonist contbng. cartoons to 6 mags., 1969-71. One Man Show w. 60 exhibits, Menezes Braganza Hall, 1969; 30 paintings in the Basilica of Bom Jesus, Old Goa. Paintings incl: the 'Stations of the Cross'; life-size pictorial biog. of St. Francis Xavier. Works awaiting publication: In Touch With West, 1970; A Bouquet of Thoughts; A Bouquet of Feelings; Love; Silent Thoughts; My Maiden Fair; My Thoughts of Thee; Death; Regret; To my Sister; To a Leaf in the Wind; To Freedom; To Resurrection; Death at Trigger; On Truths of Life, etc. Address: Alto de Porvorim, Bardez, Goa 403501, India.

MARTIN, Ellen, b. 18 Jul. 1942. Freelance Writer and Editor. Education: Grammar School; HS; Christian Writer's Inst. Positions held: Brooklyn, NY Director, American Poets Fellowship Soc., 1964, 1965; Poetry Editor, Mizpah Messenger, 1964, 1965, 1966; Poetry Editor, Coney Island Times, and Williamsburg News, 1970, 1971; Poetry Editor, The Shore Record, 1972, 1973; Poetry Editor, Town and Country Newspaper, 1972, 1973. Memberships: American Poets Fellowship, C.A.A.A.; NY Poetry Forum; American Platform Assoc.; Poetry Soc. of Texas. Published work: Faith Walks With Me, 1965. Contbr. to: Ideals; Coney Island Times; Williamsburg News; Town and Country; C.A.A.; The Angels; The Marian; Mizpah Messenger; Tooele Transcript; The Mountaineer Herald; Daily Mirror; Brooklyn Times; Grass Roots; American Bard; Faraway Places; Bethlehem Globe Times; La Voice Italiano; Irish Echo; My Weekly Bible Reader; The Roadrunner; The Gospel Herald; Angel Hour; The Nutmegger; Daily Siftings Herald; The News; Spencer Publishing Company, D.C. Cook Publishing Company. Address: P.O. Box 1035, F.D.R.Sta., New York, NY 10022, USA.

MARTIN, Gloria Ann, b. 19 Mar. 1937. Poet; Freelance Writer. Married Larry E. Martin, 1 son. Positions held: Acquisitions Sec., Coll. of Wm. & Mary Lib., Williamsburg, Va., 1959-61; Exec. Med. Sec., Dept. of Internal Med., Creighton Univ. Schl. of Med., Omaha, Neb., 1961-66; 2nd V.P., Iowa Poetry Assoc., 1972-; Poetry Judge for United Amateur Press, 1970-71, 72-73; Past TAC Chmn.; Iowa Selections Off. for Am. Mosaic, 1973-; Past Lanterne Contest Sponsor & Judge; Speaker. Memberships incl: World Poetry Soc. Int.; Iowa Poetry Assn.; Fellow, Int. Poetry Soc.; Am. Poetry League; Haiku Soc. of Am.; Toastmistress Club; N.M. Poetry Soc.; Nat. Fedn. of State Poetry Socs. Published works: Velvet Pillows of Perfume, 1971; Ed., Glowing Lanternes, 1969-. Contbr. to num. mags., jrnls., anthols. inclng: Skating Mag.; Modern Haiku; Haiku West; Sunshine Mag.; Annals of Iowa; Congressional Record; Lyrical Iowa; Tweed; Ideals; Grit; Poet; Orbis; Bitterroot; Times Repub. Newspaper; Cyclo-Flame; M.F.C.P.; From Sea to Sea in Song Anthol.; Am. Bard; Am. Poetry League Bulletin; Poets' Guild; Shore Poetry Anthol.; Encore; Fellowship in Prayer; Fur & Feathers; I.P.D.A.; Premier Poets Anthol.; Prairie Poet & var. radio stns. & newspapers. Recip. of over 100 hons. & prizes inclng: Int. Poets' Shrine Rondeau Contest, 1971; Monica Boyce's Chain Lanterne Contest, 1971; Tenn. Poetry Soc. Poet Laureate Award Category, 1972. Address: 829-26th Ave., Council Bluffs, IA 51501, U.S.A.

MARTIN, James Lawrence, b. 14 Jan. 1948. Writer; Graduate Student in Theology & Literature. Education: B.A., Colby Coll., Waterville, Me., 1970; Th.M., Boston Univ. Schl. of Theol., 1973; Ph.D., Boston Univ. Grad. Schl., 1976; Univ. of Edinburgh Divinity Schl., 1971-72. Positions held: Grad. Student, 1970–; Student Chaplain, Mass. Gen. Hosp. & Boston Univ. Hosp., 1973; Ordained United Methodist Minister (Deacon), 1973. Published works: A Reunion & Other Poems, 1974; Ten American Poets, 1974. Contbr. to: Poetry (Chicago); New Am. Review; Esquire; Harper's; The Christian Century; The Poetry Miscellany; Boston Univ. Jrnl., etc. Honours, awards: N.Y. YMHA-Poetry Ctr's. Discovery 72 prize; Maine State Arts & Humanities Prize in Poetry, 1970. Address: 311 Swanee Dr., North Dighton, MA 02764, U.S.A.

MARTIN, Lillis Oneida, pen name **LEE, Oneida,** b. 9 Apr. 1923. Secretary. Education: Draughon's Bus. Coll.; Memphis State Univ. (night classes). Positions held: Poet Laureate of Radio Station WMQM, Memphis, Tenn. Memberships: The Poetry Soc. of Tenn.; Order of Eastern Star of Tenn., Normal Chapt. No. 295. Contbr. to: Commercial Appeal Greenhouse, 1969; TOPS Club Mag., 1972; Victor Freeman Acrostic Contest, 1970; Essay Contest on The Cardinal Principles of Americanism, Ladies Aux., VFW of the United States, 1941. Honours, awards: Hon. Mention, Book Award, Victor Freeman Acrostic Contest, 1970; VFW Essay, Bronze Medal for 1st pl. in Dist., Silver Medal for 2nd pl. in State of Tenn., 1941. Address: 3784 Douglass Ave., Memphis, TN 38111, U.S.A.

MARTIN, Marjorie, b. 18 Jul. 1942. Freelance Writer and Editor. Education: Grammar School; HS; Newspaper Inst. of America; Christian Writer's Institute. Positions held: Brooklyn Director, American Poets Fellowship, 1964, 1965; Poetry Editor, Mizpah Messenger, 1964, 1965, 1966; Poetry Editor, Coney Island Times, and The Williamsburg News, 1970, 1971; Poetry Editor, The Shore Record, 1972, 1973; Poetry Editor, Town and Country Newspaper, 1972, 1973. Memberships: American Poets Fellowship; C.A.A.A.; NY Poetry Forum; American Platform Assoc.; Poetry Soc. of Texas. Published works: A Friend Asked Me and Other Poems, 1964; The Span of Dreams, 1969. Contbr. to: Coney Island Times; Williamsburg News; Town and Country; Climb; The Friend; Story Friends; C.A.A.; The Angels; The Marian; Mizpah Messenger; Tooele Transcript; The Mountaineer Herald; Daily Mirror; Brooklyn Times; Grass Roots; American Bard; Ideals; Faraway Places; Bethlehem Globe Gimes; La Voice Italiano; Irish Echo; The Texas Clarion; My Weekly Bible Reader; The Gospel Herald; Angel Hour; The Nutmegger; Daily Siftings Herald; The News; Spencer Publishing Company. Recip. 3rd Prize, Spencer Book Publishers, 1968. Address: P.O. Box 1035, F.D.R. Sta., New York, NY 10022, U.S.A.

MARTIN, Robert James, b. 11 Oct. 1896. Freelance Writer. Education: High School; Grammar School. Married; 2 d. Asst. Director, American Poets Fellowship Soc., Brooklyn, NY Chapter, 1964, 1965. Membership: NY Poetry Forum. Published work: A Firm Purpose, 1964. Contbr. to: The Irish Echo; Coney Island Times; The Gospel Herald; Williamsburgh News; Shore Record; Brooklyn Times; Town and Country; Mizpah Messenger; Daily Record; The News; Nutmegger; Angel Hour; The Angels; The Marian; The Mountaineer Herald; Altoona Mirror. Address: P.O. Box 1035, F.D.R. Sta., New York, NY 10022, USA.

MARTIN, Rodger Clayton, b. 2 Feb. 1948. Teacher. Education: B.S. Ed., Millersville State Coll.; grad. work at Univ. of Mass., Millersville State. Positions held: Tchr. of Engl., Narragansett Regl. Schl. Dist., Mass., 1972. Memberships: Worcester Co. Poetry Assn.; Pa. Poetry Soc.; Mass. Poetry Soc. Contbr. to: Lancaster Independent Press; Quill; Muse; George St. Carnival; Mo. English Bulletin; Worcester Review. Honours, awards: Worcester Co. Poetry Contest, 1973. Address: 84½ Main St., Peterborough, NH 03458, U.S.A.

MARTINSON, David Keith, b. 13 May 1946. Poet. Education: B.A., Moorhead State Coll., 1968; grad. studies in lit. & hist. at Moorhead State Coll. & N. Dakota State Univ., 1968-72. Positions held: Res. Poet, Stillwater Schl., 1972–; Poet in the Schls., St. Paul Coun. of Arts & Scis., 1971-72; Poet in Res., N. Dakota Arts Coun., 1970-71. Published works: Nineteen Sections From A Twenty Acre Poem, 1973; Three Pages, 1971; Moon of Many Bird Tails, ed., 1973; Whispering Pariah, in press. Contbr. to: The Nation; The N.Y. Qtly.; The Lamp in the Spine; Dakota Territory; Cafe Solo; Beggar's Bowl; Skopcraeft; Poets of the Red River; Imagination 71; Steelhead; Time & Place, etc. Address: Marine-on-St. Croix, MN 55047, U.S.A.

MARTY, Sid, b. 20 June 1944. Park Warden. Education: B.A., Sir. Geo. Williams Univ., Montreal, 1967. Positions held: Folk Singer; Park Warden, Mountain Nat. Parks, 1966–. Published works: (book) Headwaters, 1973; (pamphlets) The Dream Horseman, 1969; The Tumbleweed Harvest, 1973. Rep. in following anthols: Soundings, 1970; Storm Warning, 1971; The Speaking Earth, 1973; Sights & Sounds, 1973; Toboggans & Turtlenecks, 1973; Marked By The Wild, 1973. Recip., Canada Coun. Grant, Govt. of Canada, 1971. Address: Box 1755, Banff, Alta., Canada.

MARX, Anne, b. Bleicherode am Harz, Germany. Poet; Author; Lecturer. Education: Eleonoren Gymnasium, Worms am Rhein, Germany; Med. Schls., Univs. of Heidelberg & Berlin; var. colls. in the U.S.A. Married Frederick E. Marx. Memberships: Poetry Soc. of Am.; Officer, Exec. Bd., ibid, 1965-70; V.P., 1971-72; Nat. Assn. of Am. Pen Women; Pres., Westchester Co. Br., ibid, 1962-64; N. Atlantic Regl. Chmn., 1964-66; Nat. Letters Bd., 1972-74; Poetry Soc. of Pa.; Acad. of Am. Poets; Nat. Fed. of State Poetry Socs.; Poetry Soc. of G.B.; Fac., Writers Conf., Iona Coll., New Rochelle, 1964, '65, '70; Guest Poet, Writers V Conf., Fairleigh Dickinson Univ., 1962, '63; NYC Writers Conf., Fellowship, Wagner Coll., 1965; State of Maine Writers Conf.; N.H. Writers Conf.; Prin. Spkr., Ark. Writers Conf. & South & West Conventions, 1967, '70, '71, '72; Chmn., Coun. for the Arts in Westchester Inc., Poetry Div., 1970; Guest Critic, Poetry Soc. of Am. Workshop, 1970-71; Fac., The Bronxville Adult Schl., 1972-73; Hon. Mbr., South & West Inc.; Rep. at Large, Ed. of New S & W Titles, 1972–; Composers, Artists & Authors of Am. (Poetry Ed.), 1973-74; Co.Ed., Memoir Anthol., ibid, 1973; Annual Spkr. & Workshop Ldr.; N.Y. Poetry Forum; Dir., poetry series, (The Bridge of Poetry), Donnell Lib. Ctr., N.Y. Pub. Lib., 1970-74. Many published works. Honours, awards incl: Poetry Soc. of Am. Fellowship to Fairleigh Dickinson Univ. Writers Conf., 1964; Fellowship to N.Y. Writers Conf., Wagner Coll., 1965; Greenwood Prize, Poetry Soc. of G.B., 1966; Am. Weave Chapbook Award, 1960; South & West Publication Award, 1965; Biennial Book Award, Nat. League of Am. Pen Women, 1966; Nat. Sonnet Contest of Chicago, 1959, '68; Annual Braithwaite Contest, 1960; Prizes, Poetry Soc. of Am., 1960, '61, '64, '72; Prizes, Nat. Fed. of State Poetry Socs., 1962, '65, '66; Ivan Franko Meml. Comp., 1966; Atlantic Award, Manifold Mag., 1967; Annual Prizes, Poetry Soc. of Pa., 1961, '62, '64, '65, '66, '67, '69, '70, '71, '72, '73; Countess d'Esternaux Gold Medal, 1965; C.B. Keysner Meml. Award, 1970; Mason Sonnet Award, 1970, '71, '72; N.Y. Poetry Forum awards; Cecil Hemley Mem. Award, Poetry Soc. of Am., 1974. Address: 315 The Colony, Hartsdale, NY 10530, U.S.A.

MAS, Joan, b. 30 June 1926. Freelance Writer; Poet; Sculptor. Widow of Ramon Mas. Positions held: Contbng. Ed. for Australia, "Ocarina", India. Author, Isis in Search (poetry), 1967. Contbr. to: Spirit (America); Quest (India); Poet Int.; The Sydney Morning Herald; The Age; The Bulletin; Meanjin; Southerly; Twentieth Century; Australian Letters; Hemisphere; Australian Poetry (anthol.); var. lit. quarterlies & newspapers. Recip., Special Award by The Cultural Literary Fund. Address: 10 Osborn Rd.,

Normanburst, N.S.W., Australia 2076.

MASIYE, Agrippa Viane, b. 8 Oct. 1931. African Book Centre Manager & Director; Former Teacher. Married, 4 sons, 3 daughters. Positions held: Sch ol Tchr., 1950-66 (Headmaster for 12 yrs.); Ndebele Editl. Officer, Rhodesia Lit Lit, 1967-68; Editl. Officer, Daystar Publs., Bulawayo, 1969-70; Educational Advisor, African Book Ctr (Pvt) Ltd, Bulawayo; Mgr. & Dir., ibid. Memberships: V.Chmn., Shona & Ndebele Writers' Assn.; PEN Int., Rhodesia Ctr.; Editl. Staff, Good Words (Church publ.). Contbr. to: Kusile Mbongi Zohlanga, anthol. of Ndebele poetry; Ugqozi Lwezimbongi, anthol. of Ndebele poetry; Ihawu, Daystar Publ.; Two Tone; Rhodesia Broadcasting Corp. Address: P.O. Box 2020, Bulawayo, Rhodesia.

MASLEN, Elizabeth (nee Thomas), b. 18 Sept. 1935. English Lecturer. Education: B.A., 1st class Hons., Westfield Coll., Univ. of London, 1957; Dip., Comparative Philol., 1959. Married w. 3 sons & 1 daughter. Positions held: Lectr., Engl. Dept., Westfield Coll., London, 1959-61; Part-time Lectr., Univ. of Warsaw, 1961-63; Lectr., Engl. Dept., Univ. of Singapore. Contbr. to Poetry Singapore; Focus; Poetry Australia. Address: c/o English Dept., Univ. of Singapore, Bukit Timah, Singapore.

MASON, John Frederick (Jack), born 16th May, 1940. Commercial Artist. Education: B.A., Fine Arts, Tyler Schl., Temple Univ., Philadelphia, Pa. Memberships: Contemp. Poets of S. Jersey Poetry Forum; Rosicrucian; C.S.S.I. (Italy). Pub. 16 poems (pamphlet), 1973 (Italy). Contbr. to: High Schl. Poetry; Young America Sings; Tyler Schl. of Art Folio; Stylus Lit. Mag. (Temple Univ.); Am. & Canadian Poetry, no. 9, 1969; Podium. Address: Box 462, Shore Rd., 3rd Ave., Cape May Ct. House, N.J. 08210, U.S.A.

MASON, Madeline. Poet; Author; Critic; Lecturer. Education: Private schls., special studies, U.S.A. & U.K.; music composition w. Ernest Bloch; piano w. Rudolph Ganz & Alex Siloti; literature w. Arthur Symons; sci. w. Sir Oliver Lodge. Married Malcolm McKesson. Positions held: Lectrs. & Readings & Recordings for the Audio-Visual Dept. of the Bd. of Educ. of the City of N.Y.; Poet-in-Res., Shenandoah Coll., Winchester, Va., & Dellbrook Ctr. for Adv. Studies, Riverton, Va.; Lectures & readings throughout the U.S.A., U.K. & France; Co-Fndr. & Co-Dir. (w. Geo. Abbe), New England Writers' Conf., Suffield, Mass., 1956; Dir., Poetry Workshop, Rudolph Steiner Seminars in the Arts, 1960-66. Memberships: V.P., Poetry Soc. of Am.; PEN (London & N.Y.); Pen & Brush; Nat. League of Am. Pen Women; Nat. Poetry Chmn., ibid, 1958-60; Composers, Authors & Artists of Am.; Nat. V.P., N.Y. State Pres., Nat. Poetry Chmn.; ibid; Ldr., Poetry Workshop, Poetry Soc. of Am.; Authors' League. PUBLISHED WORKS: (poems) Hill Fragments, w. foreword by Arthur Symons, 1932; The Cage of Years, 1949; At the Ninth Hour: a Sonnet Sequence in a New Form, 1958; Sonnets in a New Form, 1971; (prose) Riding for Texas, 1936, London, 1938 (under Ps. Tyler Mason); (transl.) Le Prophete, 1928 (transl. into French of Gibran's 'The Prophet'). Contbr. to: Ladies Home Jrnl.; Forum; Century; Harper's Bazaar; N.Y. Times; N.Y. Herald-Tribune; Coronet; Bookman; John O' London's; Christian Sci. Monitor, etc. Honours, awards: Diamond Jubilee Award of Distinction in Poetry, Nat. League of Am. Pen Women, 1958; Award of Distinction, Composers, Authors & Artists of Am., 1960; Edna St. Vincent Millay Award for her invention of the Mason Sonnet, 1968; International Who's Who in Poetry Awards, 1st Prize, $1000, 1974; num. other awards & prizes. Address: (Nov.-May) Hotel Seville, 22 East 29, N.Y.C., NY 10016, (May-Nov.) 'Casa Benita', Onteora Club, Tannersville, NY 12485, U.S.A.

MASON, (Sister) M. Albertina, C.D.P., pen names **ALBERTINA, M.; ALBERTINA, Sister M., C.D.P.**, b. 9 Oct. 1904. Librarian-Teacher (English). Education: NY Public Schools; Acad. Notre Dame of Providence HS;

Villa Madonna Coll.; Xavier Univ.; Catholic Univ. of America. Positions held: Teacher, Grade school, Corpus Christi, Newport, 1931-44; HS Lexington, 1945-63; Ashland Holy Family High, 1963-68; Covington Latin School, 1969, and Our Lad of Providence Acad. for past 4 years (Librarian and Teacher). Memberships: Co-Founder, Eastern Kentucky Poetry Soc., first Pres.; Kentucky State Poetry Soc. Bd. member; Ohio Poetry Day; Nat. Fed. of State Poetry Socs.; Nat. Council of Teachers of Engl.; World Poetry Internat.; Acad. of American Poets. More than 300 poems published in anthols., mags., including: Invitation to the City, 1957; Nat. Anthol. of Teachers' Poetry, 1965; Kentucky Harvest, 1967; The Forever Bear, 1971; First Flight, and Second Flight (edited); America; Commonweal; Ave Maria; Sacred Heart Messenger; St. Anthony Mess.; Music Journal; Musart; Sign; Extension; Queen; Waif's Messenger; Catholic World; Poet; Approaches; Human Voice Qtly.; Cardinal Qtly.; South & West; Writers' Notes & Quotes; Canzoni; World of Poetry; Pegasus; hansel; Off-Center, and many others. Awards: 1st Prize Religious Poet-yPoetry 1972 Ohio Poetry; 2nd Prize in Kentucky Religious Poetry, 1972; Hon. Men. Bible Poetry; Hon. Men. Humorous Poetry – at NFSPS 1972; 1st Prize Humorous Poetry, Ky. State, 1973; Ohio 1st Prize (patriotic); Many other minor prizes and hon. mentions; Judged La. Poets Mem. Contest, 1973. Address: Our Lady of Providence Academy, Sixth & Linden Ave., Newport, KY 41071, USA.

MASON, Ronald Alison Ketts, b. 10 Jan. 1905. Writer. Education: Classics, Auckland Univ. Coll., New Zealand. Positions held: Tchr., 1923-32; Co. Sec., 1933-35; Pub. Works Foreman, 1936-39; Ed., weekly publ., 1940-42; Asst. Union Sec. & Ed., jrnl., Challenge, 1943-54; Landscape Gardener, 1955-62. Memberships: Fndn. Mbr. & Officer, People's Theatre & News Theatre Groups; Fndn. Mbr. & Officer, Auckland Burns Soc.; Hon., Dunedin Burns Club. Published works: The Beggar, 1924: Penny Broadsheet, 1925; No New Thing: Poems 1924-29, 1934; End of Day, 1936; This Dark Will Lighten: Selected Poems, 1941; Collected Poems, 1962; Strait is the Gate, 1963. Contbr. to major anthols. Author, numerous lit., hist. & pol. articles. Honours, Awards: Robert Burns Fellowship, Otago Univ., 1962; Jessie Mackay Mem. Prize, 1963. Address: 24 Tennyson House, Auckland 9, New Zealand.

MASON, Wauneta Hackleman, pen name **MASON, Val**, b. 7 Jan. 1915. Secretary. Education: Grad., Fairmont Schl. of Nursing; Cert. in Jrnlsm. (NIA). Married, 1 son. Positions held: w. General Motors, 10 yrs.; Registered Med. Asst., Lab. Techn., Salt River Proj. (as Sec.), 1957–. Memberships: Pres., Ariz. State Poetry Soc., 2 yrs.; Mbrship. Chmn., 2 yrs., currently Nat. Treas., Nat. Fed. of State Poetry Socs.; Mbr., Nat. Elections Bd., Br. Pres., Phoenix Br., Nat. League of Am. Pen Women; Ariz. State Pres., ibid; Nat. Music Bd.; Phoenix Writers Club. Published works: Soliloquies in Verse, 1965; Living Lines (byline in Phoenix Gazette), 1969-72. Contbr. to: Poet; Am. Poet; United Poet; Am. Bard; Am. Poetry League; Am. Poetry Fellowship Soc.; Creativity Newsletter; Current News; Cyclo Flame; Encore; Haiku (Canada); Modern Haiku; Modern Images; Prairie Poet; (anthols.) Sea to Sea in Song; Ballet on the Wind; Sing, Naked Spirit; Melodies From A Jade Harp; Mitre Press Anthol.; Prairie Poet Anthol.; Dance of the Muse, etc. Recip., var. honours & awards inclng: Mother of the Yr. (Church), 1969; Woman of the Year, Phoenix Bus. & Profl. Women's Clubs, 1972; Pen Women's Nat. Awards, 1971, 72, 73; Poet Laureate of BPW; Cert. of Merit, Am. Poets Fellowship Soc. Address: 5532 West Monterosa, Phoenix, AZ 85031, U.S.A.

MASSEY, Reginald. Poet. Education: B.A., Punjab Univ.; M.A., Agra Univ.; Delhi & Lille Univs. Positions held: Official Indian Delegate, Poetry Conf. of the Commonwealth Arts Festival, 1965. Published works: The Splintered Mirror, 1960; Other: Indian Dances: Their History & Growth, 1967. Contbr. to (Anthols.): An

Anthology of Commonwealth Verse, 1963; Commonwealth Poems of Today, 1967; (Jrnls.): Illustrated Weekly of India; Indian P.E.N.; Thought; Dancing Times; Films & Filming; Guardian; History Today; New Statesman; Tribune; Music & Musicians; Musical Times.

MASSINGHAM, Harold William, b. 25 Oct. 1932. Poet; Author. Education: Mexborough Grammar School, Yorks.; Manchester Univ., Lancs. Married; 3 s., 1 d. Sometime Schoolteacher; now part-time tutor, Poetry Workshop, Manchester Univ. Extramural. Membership: Orbis. Published works: Black Bull Guarding Apples, 1965; Creation, 1968; The Magician, 1969; Storm, 1970; The Pennine Way, 1971; Snow-Dream, 1971; Frost-Gods, 1971. Contbr. to: (journals) Caret; Contrasts; Critical Qtly.; Encounter; Listener; London Mag.; Malahat Review; Manchester Univ. Poetry; New Statesman; New Yorker Mag.; Observer; Outposts; Platform; Poem of the Month Club; Phoenix; Times Lit. Supp. Broadcasts Third Programme. (anthols.): Shouts and Murmurs, 1962-63; Penguin Book of Animal Verse, 1965; London Mag. Poems, 1966; Poems of Protest, 1966; A Flock of Words, 1969; Breakthrough, 1970; P.E.N. New Poems, 1973; New British Poetry, Antaeus 12; Poetry Book Soc. Supplement, 1971. Recip. Guinness Poetry Prize, 1962; Arts Council of GB Award, 1965; Cholmondeley Award, 1968. Address: 29 Moorland Rd., Manchester, Lancs. M20 OBB, UK.

MASTERS, Gale, b. 24 Nov. 1955. Student. Education: Syracuse Univ., N.Y. Past Ed., Yonkers H.S. Lit. Mag. 'Prism'. Contbr. to Prism, 1972 & '73. Honours, awards: 3rd Prize, Greenburgh Poetry Contest, 1973. Address: 9 Saratoga Ave., Yonkers, NY 10705, U.S.A.

MASTERS, Marcia Lee (Schmid). Poetry Editor. Education: Univ. of Chicago; Northwestern Univ. Widow, 2 daughters. Positions held: Poetry Ed. of Chicago Tribune. Memberships: Poetry Soc. of Am.; Soc. of Midland Authors. Published works: (poems) Intent on Earth, 1965. Contbr. to: Poetry Mag.; N.Y. Qtly.; Voices; Sat. Review of Lit. Honours, awards: Co-Winner of Di Castagnola Award for her 2nd book of poems in progress, 1970; Poetry Award, Midland Authors, 1969 & Friends of Literature, 1959. Address: Chicago Tribune Mag., 435 N. Mich., Chicago, IL, U.S.A.

MATCHETT, William H., b. 5 Mar. 1923. Professor of English; Editor. Education: B.A., Swarthmore Coll., Pa., 1949; M.A., Harvard Univ., Cambridge, Mass., 1957; Ph.D., ibid., 1957. Married Judith Wright w. 3 children. Positions held: Teaching Fellow, Harvard Univ., 1953-54; Mbr., Engl. Dept., Univ. of Wash., Seattle, 1954–; Prof. of Engl., ibid., 1966–; Mbr., Editorial Bd., Poetry Northwest, Seattle, 1961-66; Ed., Modern Language Quarterly, 1963–. Published works: Water Ouzel and Other Poems, 1955; Other: Poetry: From Statement to Meaning (w. Jerome Beatty), 1965; The Phoenix and the Turtle: Shakespeare's Poem & Chester's "Loues Martyr", 1965; Ed., The Life and Death of King John, 1966. Contbr. to (Anthols.): Poetry Awards 1951, 1951; New Poets of England and America, 1957; A Way of Knowing, 1959; Poet's Choice, 1962; Great Occasions, 1968; Contemporary American Poets, 1969; New Yorker Book of Poems, 1969; (jrnls.): New Yorker; Saturday Review; Harper's Mag.; Furioso; Poetry Northwest; Shenandoah. Address: Dept. of Engl., Univ. of Wash., Seattle, Washington 98105, USA.

MATERA, (Brother) Richard (Anthony), F.S.C., b. 23 June 1948. Teacher. Education: B.A., Catholic Univ. of America, Wash., D.C., 1971. Positions held: Entered relig. order, Brothers of the Christian Schools (Christian Brothers); Acting Librarian, De La Salle College, June 1970–May, 1971; Teacher, St. Bernard Boys' H.S., Uncasville, Conn., 1971-72; Teacher of Spanish, La Salle Acad., Providence, R.I., since 1972. Member: Internat. Platform Assoc.; American Council on the Teaching of For. Lang.; American Assoc. of Teachers of Spanish and Portuguese. Contbr. to:

Spirit; The Best College Verse, etc. Address: 612 Academy Ave., Providence, R.I. 02908, USA.

MATHEW, Ray, b. 14 Apr. 1929. Poet; Critic. Positions held: Tchr., small schls., NSW; Clerk; Lectr.; Barman. Published works: With Cypress Pine, 1951; Song and Dance, 1956; South of the Equator, 1961; A Bohemian Affair, 1961; A Spring Song, 1961; Miles Franklin (criticism), 1963. Contbr. to: (anthol.) Modern Australian Verse, 1964. Address: c/o Angus & Robertson Ltd., 107 Elizabeth St., Melbourne, Australia.

MATHEWS, Antoinette Mary, pen names **MATHEWS, A. & MATHEWS, Toni,** b. 19 May 1946. Information Specialist for the Wisconsin Information Service. Education: Engl. major, Univ. of Wis., Milwaukee. Contbr. to: British Spring Anthol., 1968; Yearbook of Modern Poetry, 1971 & '74; Kaleidoscope; Social Dev. Commn. News; The Madison Free Press; Quixote, Madison, etc. Address: 2443 A. North Bremen, Milwaukee, WI 53212, U.S.A.

MATHEWS, Richard Barrett, b. 16 Nov. 1944. College Professor; Poet. Education: B.A., Univ. of Fla., 1966; Hon. Woodrow Wilson Fellow & NDEA Fellowship, Univ. of Va., Charlottesville, 1967; Rotary Fellowship for Int. Understanding to Univ. of Heidelberg, Germany, 1968-69; Ph.D., Univ. of Va., 1973. Positions held: Asst. to the Publsr., The Beach News, Jacksonville Beach, Fla.; Ed., The Beaches Leader, Fla.; Reporter, The Florida Times-Union, Jacksonville; Desk-Asst. Trainee, ABC TV, N.Y.C.; Fndng.Ed., Florida Quarterly, Univ. of Fla., Gainesville; Ed.-Publsr., Konglomerati Press, Gulfport, Fla., 1971–; Asst. Prof. of Lit., Eckerd Coll., St. Petersburg. Memberships incl: Phi Beta Kappa; MLA; Fndng. Mbr., Comm. of Small Mag. Editors & Publishers, South. Published works: A Mummery, 1971. Contbr. to: Adam Among the Television Trees, 1971; Poetry Ventured, 1972; Assembling; Poet Lore; Southern Poetry Review, etc. Honours, awards: Acad. of Am. Poets Prize, Univ. of Va., 1968; STORY Honor Publ. Award, 1968 & 2nd Prize for Poetry, 1969; 1st prize, Lyric Coll. Poetry Contest, 1967. Address: 5719 29th Ave. South, Gulfport, FL 33707, U.S.A.

MATHIAS, Roland Glyn, b. 4 Sept. 1915. Editor; Lecturer; Freelance Writer. Education: B.A., Oxford Univ., 1936; B.Litt., ibid, 1939; M.A., 1944. Married Mary Hawes, 3 children (Glyn, Mary, Ceinwen). Positions held: Headmaster, Pembroke Grammar Schl., 1948-58, The Herbert Strutt Schl., Belper, Derbyshire, 1958-64, King Edward's Five Ways Schl., B'ham, 1964-69; Freelance Writer, 1969–; Ed., The Anglo-Welsh Review, 1961–. Memberships: Poets Conf.; The Powys Soc.; Pres., South & Mid-Wales Writers Assn. Published works: Break in Harvest, 1947; The Roses of Tretower, 1952; The Flooded Valley, 1960; Absalom in the Tree, 1971. Contbr. to: The Listener; Poetry Chicago; Wales; The Welsh Review; Akros; Spirit (U.S.A.); The Anglo-Welsh Review; Poetry Wales; Planet; Poetry London; Life & Letters Today. Recip., Welsh Arts Coun. Prize, 1972. Address: Deffrobani, Maescelyn, Brecon LD3 7NL, U.K.

MATSON, Clive, b. 13 Mar. 1941. Poet. Education: Univ. of Chgo., 1 yr. Positions held: Dir., Taxi Unlimited (a producers' collective in Berkeley, Calif.) Member, Berkeley Poets Cooperative. Published works: Mainline to the Heart, 1966; Space Age, 1969; Heroin, 1972. Contbr. to: (colls.) Loves, Etc.; For Bill Butler; In a Time of Revolution; The Eastside Scene; Thunderbolts of Peace & Liberation; 31 New American Poets; Lung Socket; Lancaster Art Festival Poems; num. small mag. contbns. inclng. Hanging Loose; For Now; In New York; Intrepid; The Floating Bear; Berkeley Poets Cooperative. Address: P.O. Box 2191, Stn. A., Berkeley, CA 94702, U.S.A.

MATTEI, Olga Elena, b. 24 June 1933. Press, Radio & TV Commentator in Colombia, S.A.; Model. Education: Fac. of Philos. & Letters, Univ. Pontificia Bolivariana;

Fac. of Fine Art, ibid. Married Justo Arosemena, div. 1971, 5 children. Mbr., Instituto de Integracion Cultural, Medellin. Published works: Silabas de Arena, 1962; Pentafonia, 1964; La Voz de Olga Elena Mattei (record), 1966. Has given over 120 Poetry Recitals in Colombia, Puerto Rico, Spain & U.S.A. Contbr. to: El Espectador; El Tiempo; El Siglo; El Colombiano; El Coreo; El Diario; El Pais; Occidente; Letras Nacionales & many other mags. & newspapers in Puerto Rico, Panama, Venezuela, Nicaragua & Colombia. Premio Nacional de Poesia Guillermo Valencia. Address: Apartado Aereo 10-29, Medellin, Colombia, S.A.

MATTELAER, Eugène-Marie, b. 26 July 1911; Doctor of Dental Surgery. Education: Univ. of Louvain. Married, five children. Positions held: Past Chmn. of the Doctors Stomatologists (Belgium); Hon. Burgomaster of the town Knokke-Heist. Memberships: Rotary Int.; Orde van de Prince; Chr. Vlaams Kunstenaarsverbond (Belgium); Stedelijke Kultuurraad Knoffe; Centro Studi e Scambi Int.; SABAM. Published works: Terugblik (poems), 1966; Kring des Levens (poems), 1969; Liber Amicorum, 1970; a new vol. of verse is due for publ. in Aug. 1974; many sci. publs. Contbr. to: Vlaanderen (periodical, Dutch lang.); Brugs Handelsblad. Recip., Golden Medal of Culture. Address: Binnenhof 16, B.8300 Knokke, Belgium.

MATTHEWS, Courtland Wade, b. 14 Dec. 1897. Freelance Writer; Editor; Photographer. Memberships: Poetry Soc. of Am.; Ore. State Poetry Assn. Published works: Aleutian Interval, 1949; To the Little Wabash, 1970. Contbr. to: Alaska Review; Chicago Tribune Mag. (Today's Poets); Christian Sci. Monitor; Midwest Qtly.; N.Y. Times; The Oregonian; Sat. Evening Post; Sat. Review; Univ. of Portland (Ore.) Review. Address: 3425 N.E. 32nd Ave., Portland, OR 97212, U.S.A.

MATTHEWS, J(ohn) H(erbert), b. 11 Sept. 1930. Professor of French. Education: B.A., Wales, UK, 1949; B.A., 1951; Doct., Univ. of Montpellier, France, 1955. Positions held: Univ. Tchr., UK, 1955-63; USA, 1963–; Prof., French, Syracuse Univ., NY, USA, 1965–; Ed., Symposium, quarterly jrnl. on mod. for. lits., 1965–. Memberships: Int. Comm., Centro Studi e Scambi Int.; Edit. Bd., Books Abroad; Edit. Bd., Studies in Romance Languages, Univ. of Ky. & Dada/Surrealism; U.S. Corres., Phases (Paris), Sud (Marseilles), & Gradiva (Brussels). Published works: Surrealist Poetry in France, 1969; André Breton, 1967; Surrealism & the Novel, 1966; An Anthology of French Surrealist Poetry, 1966; An Introduction to Surrealism, 1965; Péret's Score, 1965; Surrealism & Film, 1971; Theatre in Dada and Surrealism, 1973. Address: 123 Pine Ridge Rd., Fayetteville, NY 13066, USA.

MATTHEWS, Paul Michael Forster, b. 29 Sept. 1944. Educator. Education: Sussex Univ., 1963-66; Emerson Coll., 1967-69. Positions held: Ed., '11th Finger' w. Paul Evans; In process of building up a Writing Course at Emerson Coll., Sussex. Published works: No Other Sun, 1969; To Interpret Love, 1970; Descriptions & Other Poems, 1971; Footnotes, 1971; 8 Inkblots & Poems, 1972; Belladonna, 1973. Contbr. to: Poetry Review; C'mon Everybody; Children of Albion; Michigan Quarterly Review; Oasis; Resurgence; 2nd Aeon; Curtains; Platform; Black Eggs; Move; Poetmeat; Target; Ver Poets Voices; Anthology of Little Mag. Poets; Tlaloc; 11th Finger; The English Intelligencer; New Measure; Driftwood Quarterly; Thunderbolts for Peace; Iconalatre; Contrast; Imprint; For Bill Butler; Earthship; One; Turpin; Gargantua; Muse; The Golden Blade; The Kings Langley Mus. Soc. Newsletter. Address: c/o Sandford House, Sandford-on-Thames, Oxford, U.K.

MATTHEWS, William, b. 11 Nov. 1942. College Teacher. Education: B.A., Yale Univ., 1965; M.A., Univ. of NC at Chapel Hill, 1966. Positions held: Instr. in Engl., Wells Coll., 1968-69; Asst. Prof. in Engl., Cornell Univ., 1969-73; Poet-in-Residence, Emerson

Coll., 1973-74. Published works: Broken Syllables, 1969; Ruining The New Road, 1970; The Cloud, 1971; Sleek for the Long Flight, 1972; An Oar in the Old Water, 1973. Contbr. to: Poetry; Poetry Northwest; The Nation; The New Republic; kayak; Tennessee Poetry Journal; Chelsea; Apple; Granite; Ironwood; Qtly. Review of Literature; Greensboro (NC) Daily News; Southern Poetry Review; Ohio Review; Epoch, etc. Address: 393 High Plain Rd., Andover, MA 01810, USA.

MATTHEWS, William Procter, b. 11 Nov. 1942. College Teacher. Education: B.A., Yale Univ., 1965; M.A., Univ. of Chapel Hill at N.C., 1966. Positions held: Instr., Dept. of Engl., Wells Coll., 1968-69; Asst. Prof., Dept. of Engl., Cornell Univ., 1969–; Poet-in-Res., Emerson Coll., 1973-74. Published works: Broken Syllables, 1969; Ruining The New Road, 1970; The Cloud, 1971; Sleek for the Long Flight, 1972; An Oar in the Old Water, 1973. Contbr. to: Atlantic Monthly; Poetry; New Am. Review; The Nation; The New Republic; Poetry Northwest; Tenn. Poetry Jrnl.; Kayak; Field; Southern Poetry Review; Granite; Epoch; Qtly. Review of Lit.; Sewanee Review; Carolina Qtly.; Ironwood; New Am. & Canadian Poetry, etc. Address: 393 High Plain Rd., Andover, MA 01810, U.S.A.

MATTHIAS, John, b. 5 Sept. 1941. Professor of English. Education: B.A., Ohio State Univ., 1963; M.A., Stanford Univ., 1966; grad. study, Univ. of London, 1966-67. Positions held: Assoc. Prof., Univ. of Notre Dame, Dept. of Engl. Memberships: London Poetry Secretariat; Gtr. London Arts Assn.; Poets & Writers Prog.; N.Y. State Coun. on the Arts; Prog. of Poetry Readings; Ill. Arts Coun. Published works: Bucyrus, 1971; Other Poems, 1971; 23 Modern British Poets, 1971; TriQuarterly 21: Contemporary British Poetry, 1971; Herman's Poems, 1973; Turns, 1974. Contbr. to: Poetry; Partisan Review; Encounter; Poetry Review; Poetry Nation; Second Aeon; N.Y. Qtly.; Antioch Review; The Nation; Center; Tri-Qtly.; Sou'wester; Prism Int.; Ambit; Solstice; New Orleans Review; Hiram Poetry Review; Prairie Schooner; The Lit. Review; Heartland II; Experiments in Prose. Honours, awards: Woodrow Wilson Fellowship, 1963; Fullbright Fellowship, 1966; Tri-Qtly. Schumaker Prize for Poetry, 1972. Address: Dept. of Engl., Univ. of Notre Dame, Notre Dame, IN 46556, U.S.A.

MATTHYSSEN, Joannes Michael, pen name MARIJNEN, Joannes, b. 20 Apr. 1902. Bank Director. Memberships: PEN Club (Mgmt. Flemish Ctr.), Brussels; Vereniging Vlaamse Letterkundigen, Brussels; Treas., Van Ostaijen-Genootschap, Antwerp; Die Kogge, Minden, Germany. Published works: Vluchtende Verten, 1961; Amerika-Impressies, 1962; Kosmos, 1962; Stemmen, 1963; Voices, 1963; Spiralen, 1964; Kontinenten, 1965; Diagonaal, 1966; Spektraal, 1967; Voix, 1968; Intermezzo, 1969; Integraal, 1971; Universum, 1972; Fataal, 1972; Aspekten, 1972; Horizonten, 1973. Contbr. to: Nieuw Vlaams Tijdschrift; Nieuwe Stemmen; Leievaart; Het Kahier X; De Tafelronde; Espaces; Elan; Spectator; De Gentenaar; The Lit. Review. Honours, awards: Prize for Poetry, Vierde Jong-Nederlandse Literaire Dagen, Landegem & the Province of Antwerp, 1965; United Poets Laureate Int., Philippines, 1969; Kt. Order of Leopold I; Officer Order of the Crown; Officer Order of Leopold I; Cmdr. Order of the Crown. Address: Cederlaan 4, B-2610 Wilrijk (Antwerp), Belgium.

MATTLIN, Norma R., pen name by former marriage, KEATING, Norma, b. 23 Nov. 1901. Poet; Writer; Author. Education: privately & N.Y. City Coll. ext. courses. Positions held: V.P., The Nat. Soc. of Music, N.Y.C; Co-owner of Shore Music Co., N.J.; V.P., 'Blue Note', Asbury Park, N.J. Memberships: Poetry Soc. of Am., N.Y.C. (served twice as Judge). Published works: Giants & Dwarfs (poetry coll.), 1946; Songs of a Salammander, 1949. Contbr. to: The Am. Review; N.Y. Herald Tribune; N.Y. Times, etc. Has written own column in newspapers, N.Y.C. & N.J. Honours, awards: Gold Medal, Pres. Marcos of the Philippines &

Dr. Yuzon, Pres. of the United Poets Laureate; other awards from UPLI & Sovereign Order of Alfred The Great; Dr. of Humane Letters, Int. Acad. S.O.A.G. Address: 297 Fairfield Rd., R.D. 2, Freehold, NJ 07728, U.S.A.

MATULLA, Oskar, b. 4 Nov. 1900. Artist; Writer; Professor. Education: Art Schl., Acad. of Fine Arts, Tech. H.S. Univ., all Vienna, Austria. Married, 1 son, 1 daughter. Positions held: Art Tchr. in High Schls.; Freelance Artist & Writer. Memberships: V.P., Wiener Secession, 1956–; Fndr. Mbr., Donauwaldgruppe, Lower Bavaria; Artists Union of Salzburg & Vienna New Town; Artists Guild of Esslingen & Neckar. Published works: Die Alte Schanze, (novel) 1936; Canaletto reist durch das Land, (novel) 1936; Wo ist Alaxandra, (radio play) 1971; Kunst im Bezirk Bruck an der Leitha, 1954; Die Wiener Secession, 1962; Betrachtungen zur modernen Kunst, 1967; Druckgraphik der Wiener Secession, 1972; Architektur in landwirtschaftlicher Landschaft, 1971. Contbr. to var. jrnls. Honours, awards incl: Radio Prize, Min. of Work & Social Affairs, the E. German Cultural Coun. in Bonn, 1970; Culture Prize of the Lower Austria Dist., 1963. Address: A 1220 Vienna, Loewenzahngasse 17a, Austria.

MAUER, Grace (Bapst), b. 10 Sept. 1903. Education: Batavia, Ill., H.S.; No. Ill., State Teachers Coll. Married John W. Mauer. Children: Lt. Col. John C. Mauer (ret.), Ronald J. Mauer; 5 grandchildren. Columnist for Knox County News. Memberships: Nat. League of American Penwomen (Fla. State Sec., Gainesville Branch Pres.; Knoxville, Tenn., Branch Pres., Sec., Workshop Chairman, etc.); Tenn. Women's Press and Authors Club; American Poetry League; American Poets Fellowship Soc. Contrib. to: D.C. Cook Publishing Co.; Southern Churchman; Christian Advocate; Extension Mag.; Tropical Homes & Gardening; Christian Home; Knoxville News-Sentinel; American Poetry-League Bulletin; Breckenridge News; Our Dumb Animals; War Cry, etc. Recip. Prizes (sev. yrs.) in contests sponsored by Knoxville Branch, N.L.A.P.W. Address: 7005 Gainesborough Dr., Knoxville, Tenn., USA.

MAUNULA, Allan Arthur, b. 24 Sept. 1924. Education: 2 yrs. Agric.; 2 yrs. Jrnlism.; Flight Trng. & Sales courses. Divorced, 4 children. Realtor. Positions held: Estate Agent; Grading Contractor; Income Tax Officer; Heavy Equipment Operator; Farmer. Memberships: Pres., Tierra del Sol Writer's Club; Dir. of Awards, Midwest Federation of Chaparral Poets; League of Minnesota Poets; Tierra del Sol Writer's Club; San Diego Poets Assn. Contbr. to: (anthols.) Heart's Secrets, 1962; Rhyme Time for the Very Young, 1964; (jrnls.) Argus; The Chaparral; Farmer; Moccasin; Moose Lake Star Gazette; Duluth News Tribune; CBS Radio Network. Honours: 2nd prize, Leonara Clawson Stryker Contest, 1963; 1st prize, Nell Mabey Contest, 1961; 3rd prize, ibid, 1961. Address: 8835 La Mesa Blvd., Apt. L, La Mesa, Calif. 92041, USA.

MAYER, Frederick Joseph, b. 16 Sept. 1950. Journalist; Graduate Student. Education: B.A., Calif. State Univ., Sacramento; currently completing M.A. in Hist. Positions held: p/t Instr. of Classes, 'Libertarianism' & 'Egypt & Christianity'; Political Ed. at a local radio station & host of the program 'The Arts with Frederick'. Memberships: Fndr., Chmn., Rho-Xi Chapt., Phi Alpha Theta; Histn., Sec., Pres., local Blue Key Ldrship. & Hon. Soc.; Fndr. of local chapt. of Pi Sigma Alpha; appointed to the State's Nat. Selective Serv. System Bd.; former Mbr., United Amateur Press; Centro Studi e Scambi Int.; Am. Poets Fellowship Soc. Rep. in following anthols: Anthol. of Contemporary Poets, 1969; Golden Anthol. of Poetry, 1970; Voice of Am., 1970; A Melange of Poetry, 1972; Anthol. of Calif. Poets, 1973; Grains of Sand; Dawn; Echoes of Faith, etc. Contbr. to var. poetry mags. Honours, awards: 3rd Prize, Humorous Div., Chaparal Poets of Calif., 1967. Address: 1622 N Street, Apt. 302, Sacramento, CA 95814, U.S.A.

MAYER, Parm, Pseudonyms: **Michael Martin, Carol Paget,** b. 3 Feb. 1915. Resident Writer; Professor. Education: A.B., Olivet Coll., Mich.; M.A., Univ. of Mich., Ann Arbor. Married w. 2 sons. Positions held: Resident Writer & Professor, Northwood Inst., Midland, Mich., 1959–. Contbr. to (Anthols.): Heartland, 1967; New Orlando Anthology, 1968; New Generation of Poets, 1969; (jrnls.): Antioch Review; Chicago Review; Literary Review; Prairie Schooner; Prism; Epoch; Northwest Review. Address: 804 River Ave., Alma, MI 48801, USA.

MAYES, Edythe Beam, b. 9 May 1902. Writer. Education: Lenoir Rhyne Coll.; Juilliard Schl. of Mus., 5½ yrs.; studied Opera in Paris with Count Trabadello & Jereki, & in Milan with Cortesi; studied Dancing with Ned Wayburn, 5 yrs.; studied Writing, Columbia Univ., 2 yrs.; grad. student of Writing, N.Y. Univ., 1962–. Married. Positions held: w. N.Y. Times; i/c Foreign Dept., MacFadden Publs. Helped husband to raise millions of dollars for colls. & univs. in Am. Memberships: World Poetry Soc. Intercontinental; Am. Poetry League; Avalon; Major Poets Chapt.; Am. Poets Fellowship Soc.; United Amateur Press; S.C. Poetry Soc.; Life Mbr., DAV; Life Danae Mbr., Clover Int. Poetry Assn. Published works: Washington – God's Workshop, 1973; Gift, 1973. Contbr. to: Wash. Times Herald; Staten Is. Advance; Poet; Cyclo-Flame; Inky Trails; Scimitar & Song; Major Poets; Prairie Poets; Voices Int.; Jean's Jrnl.; Orphic Lute; Action; Those That Cared; Crum's Crumpets; Sweet Seventies Anthol., 1972-73; Clover Coll. of Verse, 1972-73; Fellowship Poetry Book, 1973, etc. Honours, awards incl: Poem of Yr. Award, 1970; Writer of Yr. Award, 1971; Poet of the Month, Inky Trails, Sept. 1972; Special Award for poem in Trilogy, 1973. Cover Poet, 3 times, Scimitar and Song; Cert. of Merit for Disting. Serv. to Poetry, Short Story, Essay, and Novel. Address: 358 Clark Ave., Staten Is., NY 10306, U.S.A.

MAYFIELD, Gordon Earl, b. 28 Feb. 1947. Poet. Education: B.Sc. in Educ., Millersville State Coll., Pa., 1968; corres. course, Newspaper Inst. of Am., 1970. Positions held: Engl. Tchr.; U.S. Marine Corps, 1969-71; Lib. Desk Clerk; Student Corrector of Themepapers for Engl. Instr.; Proofreader; Poet, etc. Member, Keysner Chapt., Pa. Poetry Soc. Contbr. to: Lancaster Sunday News; The Shopping News of Ephrata, Pa.; The Globe newspaper, Lejeune, N.C.; The Window, newsletter of local Lutheran Church; The Adak Sun, Alaskan newspaper; The Ephrata Review; The Atlantic; Redbook; Psychic. Address: R.D.3, Ephrata, PA 17522, U.S.A.

MAYNARD, Don, b. 19 June 1937. Poet. Education: Univ. of Queensland. Positions held: Tchr., Geelong Grammar Schl.; Edit. Staff, Publr., Melbourne; Prog. Orgr., British Coun., London, 1965; Freelance Ed. & Literary Advsr., Angus & Robertson, Sydney, 1967–. Contbr. to: Four Poets, 1962; Modern Australian Verse, 1964. Address: c/o Angus & Robertson, 107 Elizabeth St., Melbourne, Australia.

MAYNE, Seymour, b. 18 May 1944. Writer; Teacher. Education: B.A. (Hons.), McGill Univ.; M.A., Univ. of B.C.; Ph.D., ibid. Positions held: Lectr., Univ. of B.C.; Asst. Prof., Univ. of Ottawa; Mng. Ed., Very Stone House; Ed., Ingluvin Publs. Memberships: League of Canadian Poets; Canadian Artists' Representation. Published works: That Monocycle the Moon, 1964; Tiptoeing on the Mount, 1965; From the Portals of Mouseholes, 1966; I Am Still the Boy, 1967; Earseed, 1969; Anewd, 1969; Manimals, 1969; The Gigolo Teaspoon, 1969; Ticklish Ticlicorice, 1969; Mutetations, 1969; Mouth, 1970; For Stems of Light, 1971, '74; Face, 1971. Editor: Collected Poems of Red Lane (w. Patrick Lane), 1968; Forty Women Poets of Canada (w. Dorothy Livesay), 1971; Engagements: The Prose of Irving Layton, 1972. Translation: Genealogy of Instruments by Jerzy Harasymowicz, from the Polish (w. Catherine Leach), 1974. Contbr. to: The Canadian Forum; The Fiddlehead; Tamarack Review; Prism Int.; Quarry; Canadian Lit.; Arts

Canada; Ingluvin; Jewish Dialog, etc. Honours, awards: Chester MacNaughten First Prize for Poetry, 1962; Canada Coun. Arts Bursary, 1969; Canada Coun. Arts Grant, 1973. Address: Dept. of Engl., Univ. of Ottawa, Ottawa K1N 6N5, Canada.

MAYO, E(dward) L(eslie), b. 26 July 1904, Boston, Mass., USA. Teacher of English Literature. Education: B.A., magna cum laude, Univ. of Minn., 1932; M.A., 1936. Married, Myra Margaret Buchanan Morton, 1936, 1 s., 2 d. Positions held: Tchr., ND State Coll.; Univ. of Minn.; Phillips Acad., Andover; Amherst Coll.; Prof., Engl., Drake Univ., 1947–. Published works: The Diver, 1947; The Center is Everywhere, 1955; Summer Unbound, 1958; a pamphlet of poems, 1954; Selected Poems, 1973. Contbr. to: 15 anthols. inclng. The Contemporary Am. Poets; (jrnls.) Poetry Chicago; Poetry Northwest; Epoch; Northwest Review; Nation; NY Times; London Times; New Statesman. Honours, awards: Payne Prize, Univ. of Minn., 1932; Blumenthal Prize, Poetry Chicago, 1942; Amy Lowell Poetry Travelling Fellowship, 1953, '54; Hon.LL.D., Iowa Wesleyan Univ., 1960. Address: 1532 24th St., Des Moines, Iowa 50311, USA.

MAYROCKER, Friederike, b. 20 Dec. 1924. Teacher. Education: Tchng. Cert. of the Austrian Bd. of Educ. Positions held: Tchr. at Secondary Schls. in Vienna; Freelance Writer, 1969–; Artist in Res. in West Berlin (DAAD-Berlin-programme), 1973. Memberships: Acad. of Arts, W. Berlin; Forum Stadtpark, Graz, Austria; Grazer Autorenversammlung. Published works: (books) Larifari, 1956; Metaphorisch, 1965; Texte, 1966; Tod durch Musen, 1966; Sägespäne für mein Herzbluten, 1967; Minimonsters Traumlexikon, 1968; Fantom Fan, 1971; Fünf Mann Menschen, 1971; Sinclair Sofokles der Baby-Saurier (children's book), 1971; Metaphysisches Theater, 1972; Je ein umwölkter gipfel, 1973; Blaue Erleuchtungen. Erste Gedichte, 1973; Augen wie Schaljapin, 1973. Contbr. to: Plan, 1945, 46; Neue Wege; Akzente; Dimension; Protokolle; manuskripte; Ver Sacrum; Wort und Wahreit; Wort in der Zeit; Literatur und Kritik; Neues Forum; Diskus, etc. Recip., Hörspielpreis den Kriegsblinden, 1968. Address: Zentagasse 16/40, A-1050 Vienna, Austria.

MAZANI, Eric Charles Fambai, pen name **EMARS,** b. 15 Aug. 1948. School Teacher. Education: St. Peter's Mandea and Mutanda Govt. School; Bernard Mizeki Coll., Marandellas; Primary Teacher's Higher, Coll. of Christ the King. Married, 2 d. Positions held: Editor of T.T. Coll. Mag.; Publicity Sec., H.S. Sports Assoc. Membership: Chirimo of Rhodesia. Contbr. to: Bernard Mizeki Coll. Mag.; Daramombe T.T. Coll. Mag.; Poetry in Rhodesia; Poesie Vivante. Awards: Chirimo, 1969. Address: St. Mary's Schl., Chingwaro, P.O. Box 35, Mrewa, Rhodesia.

MAZOBERE, Crispin Christopher Godzo, b. 3 Jan. 1926. Minister of the Gospel. Education: Tchrs. Dip., Waddilove Tchr. Trng. Schl., Rhodesia, 1943; Dip. in Youth Work, Westhill Coll., B'ham Univ., U.K., 1962; S.T.B., Boston Univ., U.S.A., 1968; M.A., ibid, 1969; Ph.D., 1972. Positions held: Min., St. Mark Congl. Ch. (UCC), Boston, Mass.; Prof., Epworth Theol. Coll., Salisbury, Rhodesia; Capl., Nyatsime Coll., Salisbury; Circuit Min., Leicester North Methodist Circuit, U.K.; Chmn., Shona All Africa Sunday Schl. Curric. Comm.; Chmn., Salisbury Christian Action Grp. Memberships: World Poetry Soc. Intercontinental; Rhodesia Rep. for African Authors' Conf., Pretoria, S. Africa, 1961, to World Youth Conf., U.K., 1962, to World Conf. on Sunday Schl. & Christian Educ., Zurich, 1964, etc. Published works: Manzwi Makuru Orutendo Rwedu (Great Words of Our Faith); Ndakada Musikana (I Love the Girl), 1957; Doro Kudya (on Problems of Alcoholism), 1964; Utshwala Yikudla, 1970; A Theological Word Book (w. H.L. DeWolf), 1964; Racial Conflict in Rhodesia, 1974. Contbr. to many newspapers, jrnls. Published a dozen poems with the World Poetry Intercontinental, published in India & the U.S.A. Recip. many hons. & awards inclng: Order of Ghandi Award of Hon., Poet of Mankind, 1971; Acad.

Ondra Lysohorsky, Poet of World Brotherhood, 1971; La Legion d'Honneur Victor Hugo, Grand Prix de Poésie, 1971. Address: 722 Commonwealth Ave., Apt. 14, Boston, MA 02215, U.S.A.

MBITI, John Samuel, b. 30 Nov. 1931. Clergyman; University Professor. Education: B.A., Makerere (from London Univ.), 1953; A.B., Barrington Coll., U.S.A., 1956; Th.B., ibid, 1957; Ph.D., Cambridge 1963; L.H.D. (Hon.), Barrington, 1973. Married, 1 son, 1 daughter. Positions held: William Paton Vis. Lectr., Selly Oak Coll., Birmingham, U.K., 1959-60; Parish Curate, St. Michael's Ch., St. Albans, U.K., 1963-64; Lectr. in New Testament & African Religions, Makerere Univ., Kampala, Uganda, 1964–; Vis. Lectr., Univ. of Hamburg, W. Germany, 1966-67; Prof. & Hd. of Dept. of Relig. Studies & Philos., Makerere Univ., Uganda, 1968-74; Fosdick Vis. Prof., Union Theol. Sem., N.Y.C., U.S.A., 1972-73; Dir., the Ecumenical Inst. of the World Coun. of Chs., Geneva, 1974–. Published works: Der Wanderer von Land zu Land, 1963; Poems of Nature & Faith, 1969. Contbr. to Transition. Address: The Ecumenical Inst., World Coun. of Chs., Château de Bossey, 1298 Celigny, Switzerland.

MEAD, Matthew, b. 12 Sept. 1924. Poet. Former Ed., Satis. Publications: A Poem in Nine Parts, 1960; Identities, 1964; Kleinigkeiten, 1966; Identities & Other Poems, 1967; The Administration of Things, 1969; (translations from German, w. Ruth Mead) Shadow Land, Johannes Bobrowski, 1966; Generation, Heinz Winfried Sabais, 1967; some poems, O The Chimneys, Nelly Sachs, 1967; Generation & Other Poems, Heinz Winfried Sabais, 1968; Amfortiade & Other Poems, Max Holzer, 1968; Selected Poems, Horst Bienek, 1969; Selected Poems of Elisabeth Borchers, 1969; most poems in The Seeker, Nelly Sachs, 1970; Penguin Mod. European Poets, Selected Poems of Johannes Bobrowski & Horst Bienek, 1971. Contbr. to: Delta; Descant; Epos; Galley Sail Review; Mica; Nat. Review; Neue Zürcher Zeitung; Nomad; Orange St. Jrnl.; Peacock; Phoenix; Poet & Critic; New Measure; Times Lit. Supplement; Mademoiselle; New Yorker; Dimension; Stand; Agenda; Am. Weave; Grosseteste Review; Poetry Review; Sum; Contemp. Lit. in Translation; Mundus Artium; Nation; The Sixties. Address: c/o Anvil Press, 69 King George St., London SE10, UK.

MEDLOCK, Julius Lester, b. 7 Nov. 1894. Poet; Author; Educator; Rancher. Education: B.S., Okla. State Univ., 1925; M.A. Educ., Univ. of Okla., 1937. Widower of Alma Wendt. Positions held: Tchr. in Okla. schls: Center, 1921-22; El Reno, 1923-24; McAlester, 1925-27; Pauls Valley, 1937-38; Poteau, 1938-41; Instr., Okla. Industrial Coll. Diversified Occupations, Weatherford, 1941; Elmore City H.S., 1946-50. Memberships incl: Life Fellow, Int. Inst. Arts & Letters; Am. Poets Fellowship Soc.; Okla. Writers Assn.; Pres., Poetry Soc. of Okla., 1958-60; Avalon World Arts Acad. Published works: Stray Hearts, 1956; Threads of Flame, 1960; When Swallows Fly Home, 1962; Fragments of Forever, 1964; Trumpets in Eden, 1966; Pearls & Tears, Australian & N.Z. Poetry, 1967; Tryst With the Stars, 1972; Winds in the Willows, 1974; Tomorrow is Forever, 1975. Contbr. to num. newspapers, mags., anthols. etc. Honours, awards incl: Merit Award, Okla. Writers Assn., 1963. Address: Rte. 1, Box 227, Pauls Valley, OK 73075, U.S.A.

MEDNICK, Murray, b. 24 Aug 1939. Playwright; Poet. Education: Brooklyn Coll., N.Y. Published works (Plays): Sand in The New Underground Theatre, 1968; Keystone's The Hawk, 1968; The Hunter, 1969; Five Plays by Murray Mednick, 1971. Contbr. to (Jrnls.): Transatlantic Review; Evergreen Hons: Nat. Foundation of the Arts Poetry Award, 1967; Rockefeller Grant, 1968-69. Address: c/o Carolyn Jenks, Literary Agent, 191 Ninth Ave., N.Y., NY 10011, USA.

MEEHAN, Mary Taft Hitchings, pen names **HITCHINGS. Mary T., MEEHAN, Mary H.,** b. 6 May

1911. Writer; Poet; Public Relations Woman; Moderator. Married Howard W. Meehan. Education: B.A., Case Western Reserve Univ.; Dip., Sorbonne.; Dip., Univ. of Nancy. Positions held: Soc.Serv. Staff Sec., Psych. Hosp.; Soc. Wkr., Dept. of Welfare; Employment Interviewer. Contbr. to: (anthols.) Am. Women Poets, 1937; World's Fair Anthol., 1938; I.W.W.P. Anthol., 1973; (jrnls.) Driftwind; Gato. Address: General Delivery (P.O. Box Pending) White Plains, NY 10602, U.S.A.

MEEK, Jay, b. 23 Aug. 1937. Teacher; Writer. Education: B.A., Univ. of Mich.; M.A., Syracuse Univ. Married Martha George, 1 daughter. Positions held: Instr., Grand Valley State Coll.; Asst. Prof., Colby Coll.; Vis. Lectr., Syracuse Univ. Contbr. to: Agni Review; Antioch Review; Apple; Beloit Poetry Jrnl.; Carleton Miscellany; The Fault; Field; The Iowa Review; Malahat Review; The Mass Review; The Nation; The N.Y. Qtly.; The North Am. Review; Poetry Northwest; Prairie Schooner; Road Apple Review; Salmagundi; The Seneca Review, etc. Honours, awards: Ford Humanities Rsch. Grant, 1969; Borestone Mountain Poetry Awards, 1972; Nat. Endowment for the Arts Grant, 1973. Address: 201 Seeley Rd., F-6, Syracuse, NY 13224, U.S.A.

MEHREN, Stein, b. 16 May 1935. Author. Education: Zoology, Chemistry, Philosophy, Hist. of Religion, studies in Cambridge, Munich, Oslo. Member, Den Norske Forfattenforening. Published works: one drama, one novel, two books of essays, two books of myths, one satire, eight books of poetry. Honours, awards: Kritikerprisen, 1963; Norsk Kulturfond, 1966; Norsk Kulturrod, 1969; Onskedikt prisen, 1968; Doublongs AErespris, 1971; Aschehougprisen, 1973; State Stipend, 1964–. Address: Ullevalsveien 60, Oslo 4, Norway.

MEIER, Gerhard Werner, b. 20 June 1917. Poet. Married, 3 children. Positions held: Designer, 33 yrs. Memberships: Berner Schriftstellerverein; Gruppe Olten. Published works: Das Gras grünt, poems, 1964; Im Schatten der Sonnenblumen, poems, 1967; Kübelpalmen träumen von Oasen, prose & poetry, 1969; Es regnet in meinem Dorf, prose & poetry, 1971; Einige Häuser nebenan, poems, 1973. Contbr. to: Neue Zürcher Zeitung; Die Tat; National-Zeitung; Der Bund; Schweizer Monatshefte; Reformatio; Spektrum, etc. Honours, awards: Literaturpreis des Kantons Bern, 1964, '68 & '71; Preis der Schweizerischen Schillerstiftung, 1970; Werkauftrag der Pro Helvetia, 1970. Address: Lehnweg 17, CH-4704 Niederbipp BE, Switzerland.

MEIER, Herbert, b. 29 Aug. 1928. Freelance Writer. Education: Univs. of Basel, Vienna, Fribourg; Dr. phil. Mbr., Schweizer Schriftsteller der Gruppe Olten. Published works: (poetry) Siebengestirn (anthol.), 1956; Sequenzen (anthol.), 1969; Gli Spaziali (text for music of Wladimir Vogel), 1971. Contbr. to Neue Zürcher newspaper. Honours, awards: Bremer Literature prize; Arts prize of the Lions Club, Basel; C–F Meyer Prize. Address: Mühlehalde 21, CH–8032, Zurich, Switzerland.

MEINKE, Peter, b. 29 Dec. 1932. Professor; Writer. Education: A.B., Hamilton Coll., N.Y., 1955; M.A., Univ. of Mich., 1961; Ph.D., Univ. of Minn., 1965. Married Jeanne Clark, 4 children. Positions held: Army, 1955-57; H.S. Tchr., Mountain Lakes H.S., N.J., 1958-60; Asst. Prof. of Engl., Hamline Univ., 1961-66; Prof. of Lit., Eckerd Coll., (formerly Fla. Presbyn. Coll.), 1966–. Member, Directory of Am. Poets. Published works: (children's poetry) The Legend of Larry the Lizard, 1968; Very Seldom Animals, 1970; (criticism) Howard Nemerov, 1969; (poetry) 4 pamphlets, published 1965, '66, '68, '73; (book) Lines from Neuchatel & Other Poems, 1974. Contbr. to: New Republic; Antioch Review; N.Y. Qtly.; Motive; New Orleans Review; Christian Century; Red Clay Reader; Epos; Mass. Review; (anthols) Best Poems of 1963, '70; Poems One Line & Longer; Poetry of Baseball, etc. Honours, awards incl: 1st. prize, Olivet Nat.

Sonnet Comp., 1964, 2nd prize, ibid, '66 & '67; 3rd prize, '70; Younger Humanists Summer Grant in Children's Lit., 1970. Address: Dir., Writing Workshop, Eckerd Coll., St. Petersburg, FL 33733, U.S.A.

MEIR, Mira, b. 21 May 1932. Teacher; Editor. Education: B.A., Lit. & Hebrew Lang., Tel Aviv Univ. Married Dan Meir, 4 children. Positions held: H.S. Tchr.; Ed. of children's publications, Sifriat Poalim. Memberships: Israel Org. of Writers; Irgun Sofrei Hakibbutz Artz (Org. of Kibbutzartzi Writers). Published works: Lo Hakol, 1967; Baaretz Hahey Mitahat Lamayim, 1970; Ma Osim Dagim Bageshem? (for children), 1970; Ani Dhev Letzayar, (for children), 1973. Contbr. to: Al Hamishmar; Keshet; Moznayim; Maariv. Recip., For Ani Ohev Letzavar – Rabinovitch Prize, 1973. Address: Kibbutz Nahshon, D.N. Shimshon, Israel.

MELENDEZ, Jesús Papoleto, b. 13 June 1950. Poet; Playwright. Education: City Coll. of N.Y., 1970-71; Hunter Coll., N.Y., 1971-72. Married, 1 son. Positions held: Conducted Creative Writing Workshops, taught English to high schl. students, & other subject, Fieldston Schl. Upward Bound Prog., N.Y.; Conducted Creative Writing Workshops for the Teachers' & Writers' Collaborative. Has read poetry & lectured at var. univs. & colls. Published works: (vols. of poetry) Casting Long Shadows, 1970; Have You Seen Liberation, 1971; Street Poetry & Other Poems, 1972; (plays) The Junkies Stole the Clock, 1973; Jacinto. My Name is Jacinto, 1973; The Silent Words of Love (currently rewriting his 1967 version). Rep. in following anthols: Talkin About Us, 1970; Grito: A Collection of Angry Voices, 1973. Contbr. to: Hanging Loose; The Herald; The Rican Jrnl.; Latin N.Y., etc. Has appeared on TV & contbd. to radio broadcasts. Address: 1420 College Ave., Apt. 5-G, Bronx, NY 10456, U.S.A.

MELHEM, D.H. Poet. Education: B.A., N.Y. Univ.; M.A., The City Coll. of the City Univ. of N.Y., 1971; Ph.D. cand., City Univ. of N.Y. 2 children. Positions held: Editor; Tchr., The City Coll. of N.Y., 1971. Memberships: Phi Beta Kappa; Sigma Delta Omicron; MLA; Acad. of Am. Poets; N.Y. Poets' Cooperative; Calliope. Published works: Notes on 94th Street, 1972. Articles on poetics: Ivan Fónagy & Paul Delbouille: Sonority Structures in Poetic Language, 1973; The Poetics of Charles Olson, 1974. Contbr. to: The Nation; Confrontation; For Now; Promethean; Gnosis; Bitterroot; Light; Rune; var. other mags. & anthols. in U.S.A. & abroad. Recip., Macey Seymour Award. Address: 250 West 94th St., N.Y., NY 10025, U.S.A.

MELODY, Rose, b. 14 June 1922. Homemaker; Writer. Education: Ill. State Normal Coll., 2 yrs. Married G.L. Melody, 3 sons (1 dec.), 1 daughter. Positions held: Elem. Schl. Tchr., Ill.; Newspaper work, Jasper, Ala.; Columnist, Birmingham, Ala.; Receptionist, Chiropractic Clinic (currently). Memberships: Pres., Univ. Poetry Club of Fayetteville, Ark., 1970-72; 3rd V.P., N.W. Ark. Br. of Nat. League of Am. Penwomen. Contbr. to: Voices Int.; Southwest Ark. Times; The Lyric; South & West Inc.; Birmingham Sunday Mag. Original poetry column in Catholic Week, B'ham, Ala., 1956-68. Recip. var. awards from Poetry Day Contests, Tex. Poetry Contests, Ark. Writers Conf., etc. Address: 1917 Woodland, Fayetteville, AR 72701, USA.

MELTZER, David, b. 17 Feb. 1937. Poet. Married, 3 d. Positions held: Ed., Maya Books, 1969-71; Ed., Tree Books, 1971–; Co-Director, The New World, 1971–. Memberships: Sci. Fiction Writers of Am. Published works include: Poems, 1957; Ragas, 1959; The Clown, 1959; The Process, 1965; The Dark Continent, 1967; Yesod, 1970; Greenspeech, 1970; Luna, 1971; Knots, 1971. Contbr. to the following anthols., jrnls., mags., etc: Akzente; Outburst; Semina; Yale Lit. Review; Caterpillar; Yugen; White Dove Review; Beatitude; Coyote's Jrnl.; Kulchur; The Outsider; Antaeus; Davka; Matrix; Measure; Tractor: LA Free Press; Big Table; Renaissance; Floating Bear; Signal; Notes from the Underground; Poetry Review; The New Am.

Poetry; Junge Amerikanische Lyrik; On the Mesa, etc. Address: PO Box 365, Bolinas, Calif. 94924, USA.

MEMMO, Paul Eugene, Jr., b. 25 May 1918. Author, Poet, Professor. Education: B.A., Fordham Coll., NYC; M.S., Columbia Grad. Schl. of Journalism, 1940; Ph.D., Engl. & Comparative Studies, Columbia Univ. Positions held: Sgt.-Major, Battle of the Bulge; Sec., Promotion Dept., NY Daily News, 1940-41; Asst. to Architect, Searsdale, NY, 1041 4C, Insti., & subsequently Assoc. Prof. & Dir. of Engl. & Comparative Studies, Fordham Univ., NY. Memberships: Cath. Poetry Soc. of Am.; Renaissance Poetry Soc. of Am.; Fndr., NY Chapter, ibid; MLA; Dante Soc., Cambridge, Mass.; Shakespeare Assoc. of America. Publications: Giordano Bruno's The Heroic Frenzies (adaptation into Engl. verse & prose of Dagli Eroici Furori by Giordano Bruno), 1964; 3 sonnets by Michelangelo, 1961; (forthcoming) Michelangelo: Odyssey of a Spirit. Contbr. to: Spirit; NY Herald Tribune; New Mexico Quarterly. Address: 52 Holmes Ave., Hartsdale, NY 10350, USA.

MENKE, William Vernon, b. 28 Apr. 1952. Student. Education: B.A., Oakland City Coll., Ind., 1973; currently working towards M.A., Ind. State Univ., Terre Haute. Positions held: Dir. of Audio Visual, Oakland City Coll., 1970-73; Grad. Asst. in Coll. of Arts & Scis., Ind. State Univ., Terre Haute, Ind., 1974–. Memberships: N.Y. Poetry Forum; Shore Nat. Network of Poetry Soc. Contbr. to: Nat. Anthol. of Coll. Poetry, 1973; Pegasus Anthol. of Poetry, 1973; 1974 Shore Anthol. of Poetry; Poets of 1974 Poetry Anthol.; O.C. Collegian. Address: 814 West Fourth St., Bicknell, IN 47512, U.S.A.

MENKITI, Ifeanyi Anthony, b. 24 Aug. 1940. Teacher; Writer. Education: B.A., Pomona Coll., Claremont, Calif.; M.S., Columbia Univ., N.Y.; M.A., N.Y. Univ. Positions held: Tchng. Fellow, Harvard Univ., Cambridge, Mass., 1971-73; Lectured in African Lit., Univ. of Mass., Boston, 1972 & at Univ. of Hartford, Conn., 1972; currently Instr. in Philos., Wellesley Coll., Mass. Published works: Affirmations, 1971. Contbr. to: Contemporary African Lit., 1972; The Word is Here: Poetry from Africa, 1973; Open Poetry, 1973; New Letters; Shantih; Sewanee Review; Southwest Review; Bitterroot; Chelsea; Boston Review of the Arts; Biafra Review; Sumac; Transition; Evergreen Review, etc. Has read poetry at schls., univs., etc. Address: 18 St. Stephen's Rd., Onitsha, E.C.S., Nigeria.

MENON, Kavungal Gangadhara, pen name **K.G.,** b. 1 Feb. 1922. Consulting Engineer & Architect. Education: Maharaja's Coll., Cochin, Kerala, India Married Dr. Chandra Valli, 1 son, 1 daughter. Member, Instn. of Engrs., India (M.I.E:). Published works: Vichara Dhara (Flow of Thoughts), vol. 1 (vol. 2 in process of being published). Ed. & Publisher of Anveshanam, a Malayalam Monthly Mag. (lit.). Contbr. to: Ocarina; Poetry of India; Contemporary Lit. Address: Jayasree, No. 3, 1st St., Jayalakshmipurem, Madras 600034, India.

MENON, R. Rabindranath, pen names, **MENON, R.R., RABINDRANATH, R.,** b. 13 June 1927. Officer of the Indian Administrative Service. Education: Grad. in Chemistry; Post grad. in Metallurgical Engrng.; B.S.; D.I.I.Sc. (Met. Eng.) Married, 2 sons, 1 daughter. Positions held: Income-tax Officer; Collector & District Magistrate; Dir. of Evaluation; Controller of Civil Supplies; Dir. of Treasuries; Mng. Dir. of var. Public Sector Undertakings; Jt.-Sec. to Govt. Chmn., Marine Products Export Promotion Coun.; Chmn., Coir Bd., 1951–. Memberships: Fellow, Inst. of Auditors & Accts.; Indian Inst. of Metals; Hon. Mbr., United Poet Laureate Int. Published works: Ode to Parted Love & Other Poems, 1958; Dasavatara & Other Poems, 1967; Seventy Seven, 1971; Straws in the Wind, 1973; Gananjali (a selection of Malayalam poems), 1973; Poems in var. jrnls. Contbr. to: Poetry; Poet; South & West; Cyclo-flame; The Angels; Literary Half-Yearly; Triveni; Adam & Eve; Poetry East West; Caravan.

Honours, awards: Gold Medal & Poet Laureate Crown, UPLI, Univ. of Manila, 1971; Litt. D., Univ. of Asia. Address: Coir Bd., Coir House, Cochin-16, India.

MENUSY, Yedidia, pen name **MENUSY, Didi,** b. 9 May 1928. Journalist. Education: B.A. in Lit. & Philos. Married, 2 daughters. Positions held: U.N. Corres. in Far East, 1955; Foreign Corres., Africa, 1959, Australia, 1967, South Am., 1972; Regular Columns in 'Yediouth Aharonot' (evening paper), 1962–. Member, Assn. of Composers & Writers. Published works: Songs of Genesis, 1950; Leave Without a Pass, 1951; Morning's Gift, 1953; 101 Limericks, 1958; Crown of Omens, 1961; The Situation is Deadly But Not Serious, 1969. Contbr. to var. lit. mags. in Israel. Address: 131 Hayarkon St., Tel Aviv 63453, Israel.

MERCADO, Simon A(Ivarez), pen names, **DIWALAAN; MAKAHIYA; ELIAS; IYO, Dahil Sa,** b. 28 Oct. 1892 in Penaranda, Province of Nueva Ecija, Philippines. Attorney & Counselor-at-Law. Education: Grad., Manila Inst., 1921; Grad. HS. of Univ. of Manila, 1926; Assoc. of Arts, Prep. Law course, Univ. of Manila, 1928, and Bach. of Laws, Univ. of Manila Law Coll., 1932; Passed Bar Examinations, 1939. Married (1st) Lorenza R. Francisco; 3 children; following decease of 1st wife, married Eulalia S. Gregorio; 6 children. Positions held: Customs Examiner, 1936-45; Chief Appraiser, Iloilo Customhouse, 1945-50; Supervising Customs Examiner, Oct., 1950-Dec. 1950; Sr. Atty., 1951-52; Asst. Investigator, 1952-53; Chief, Law Div., 1953-55; Chief Legal Counsel, 1955-66; Manila Port Service (Chief Legal Counsel, 1956-57); Chairman, Bd. of Examiners for Customs Brokers, Feb. 1955. Memberships: Vice-Pres., Parnaso, a lit. soc.; Mbr., Bd. of Directors, Taliba ng Inang Wika, a lit. soc.; Mbr. of the 4 best selected poets (Cuarteto) of the Ilaw at Panitik, a lit. soc. Published works: Kuwintas Ng Alaala (collection of 153 poems, 45 of which won prizes), 1945. Contbr. to: The Ang Mithi; Taliba; Tribune; Mabuhay & Pagkakaisa; The Liwayway; Sinag-Tala; Hiwaga; Ilang-Ilang & Tagumpay. Awards and honours: numerous prizes and awards. Address: 2586-B Misericordia St., Sta. Cruz, Manila, Philippines.

MEREDITH, William, b. 9 Jan. 1919. Professor of English. Education: A.B., Princeton Univ., 1940.; H.L.D., honoris causa, Carnegie-Mellon Univ., 1972. Positions held: Instr. and Woodrow Wilson Fellow, Princeton Univ., 1946-50; Asst. Prof. of Engl., Univ. of Hawaii, 1950-51; Lect., Asst. Prof., Assoc. Prof., Prof. of Engl., Connecticut College, 1955–. Chancellor, Acad. of American Poets, 1963–; Member, Nat. Inst. of Arts & Letters, 1969–. Pubs.: Love Letter from an Impossible Land, 1044; Ships and Other Figures, 1948; The Open Sea and Other Poems, 1958; The Wreck of the Thresher and Other Poems, 1964; Earth Walk: New & Selected Poems, 1970; Trans: Alcools, by Guillaume Apollinaire, 1964; Editor: Shelley, 1962. Contrib. to: Poetry; Hudson Review; Va. Quarterly; New Yorker; Saturday Review; Shenandoah; Partisan Review; Ironwood; New York Review, NY Times Book Review, etc. Awards: Harriet Monroe Prize, Poetry Mag., 1944; Loines Award, American Acad. of Arts & Letters, 1967; Van Wyck Brooks Award, 1971. Address: Connecticut Coll., New London, Conn. 06320, USA.

MERRETT, Cyril Vincent, b. 4 Jan. 1902. Schoolmaster. Education: Pembroke Coll., Oxford Univ., 1920-24; M.A. Oxon., F.I.L. Positions held: Classics Master, Priory Schl., Shrewsbury, & at King Edward VI G.S. Morpeth; Assistant de langue Anglaise, Lycée du Parc, Lyon; Classics Master, Simon Langton Schl., Canterbury; Sr. Classics Master, Queen Mary's Schl., Walsall, 1929-63. Member, West Country Writers' Assn. Published works: A verse transl. of Virgil's Sixth Aeneid, 1936. Contbr. to: The Countryman; Pegasus; The Field; The A.M.A.; This England; The Animals' Defender; Acta Diurna (Latin verse); BBC Midland Poets prog. Honours, awards: 2 prizes in the Glos. Poetry Comp. of the Cheltenham Fest. of Contemporary Lit., 1953;

Prize in the Keats Prize Poems Comp., 1973. Address: 7 Glencairn Ct., Lansdown Rd., Cheltenham GL51 6QN, U.K.

MERRIAM, Virginia A., b. 11 Mar. 1906. Homemaker. Married Halsey Merriam, 1 son. Memberships: W. Va. Poetry & local Soc.; Corres. Sec., Parkersburg Chapt., ibid, 4 yrs.; Former Mbrship Chmn. & later Sec., local AARP; Past County Grange Officer; currently Prog. Chmn., local Parkersburg AARP, etc. Contbr. to: Echoes of the W. Va. Poetry Soc., 1971; Poet Int., 1972; Lyrics of Love, 1972; Gems of the Hills; Melody of the Muse, 1973; Senior Citizens local monthly Newsletter, etc. Recip., Ribbon, L.K.R. Nature Festival, 1971, '72 & '73, & other poetry awards. Address: 1018 Lake View Dr., Parkersburg, WV 26101, U.S.A.

MERRIFIELD, Annabelle, b. 27 June 1883. Poet. Educ: Ashland Coll., Ohio. m. Albert Wilson Merrifield, 3 d. Memberships: Poetry Soc. of Am.; Poetry Soc., London, U.K.; World Poetry Day Assn.; Am. Poetry League; Am. Bard. Published works: The Grace Notes, 1952; Whitely Straightening, 1967. Honours, awards incl: var. poetry awards & some 1st nat. awards. Address: 5301 W. 1st Ave., Lakewood, CO 80226, U.S.A.

MERRIFIELD, Gladys, b. 16 Apr. 1907. Retired Editor. Education: B.A., Univ. of Calif. at Berkeley, 1928; grad. year, Columbia Univ., N.Y.C., 1928-29. Daughter, Gail Merrifield, is Asst. to Prod. Joseph Papp, N.Y. Shakespeare Festival Theatre. Positions held: Ed. & staff writer on Family Circle Mag., N.Y.C., 1950-71. Member, Poetry Soc. of Am. Published works: Sonnets Under a Roof, 1927. Contbr. to: Wings; Westward; The Lyric West; Univ. of Calif. Chronicle; The Lit. Review; Poet Lore; Palms; Yankee Mag. Honours, awards: Emily Chamberlain Cook Prize for Undergraduate Poetry, 1927; Hon. Mention, Witter Bynner Prize, 1928; Robert Browning Prize (Calif.), 1947; James D. Phelan Fellowship in Lit., 1935-36. Address: 339 West 20th St., N.Y., NY 10011, U.S.A.

MERRILL, James, b. 3 Mar. 1926. Poet. Education: B.A., Amherst Coll., Mass. 1947. Published works: The Black Swan, 1946; Short Stories, 1954; The Country of a Thousand Years of Peace, 1959; Water Street, 1962; Nights & Days, 1966; The Thousand and Second Night, 1966; The Fire Screen, 1969; Other: The Immortal Husband, 1956; The Bait, 1960; The Seraglio, 1957; The Diblos Notebook, 1965. Contbr. to (Anthols.): Penguin Book of Modern American Verse, 1954; Modern American Poetry, 1955; New Poets of England and America, 1962; Contemporary American Poetry, 1962; Modern Poets, 1963; Poems on Poetry, 1965; Poems of Our Moment, 1968; (Jrnls.): Hudson Review; Poetry. Hons incl: Oscar Blumenthal Prize, 1945; The Levinson Prize, 1949; The Nat. Book Award, 1967. Address: 107 Water Street, Stonington, CT, USA.

MERWIN, William S., b. 30 Sept. 1927. Poet & Translator. Education: A.B., Engl. Lit. Positions held: Pvte. Tutor; Poetry Ed., The Nation, 1961. Published works include: The Carrier of Ladders, 1970; The Lice, 1967; The Moving Target, 1963; The Drunk in the Furnace, 1960; Green With Beasts, 1956; The Dancing Bears, 1954; A Mask for Janus, 1952; (translations) Transparence of the World, 1969; Voices, 1969; Products of the Perfected Civilization, 1969; Selected Translations, 1948-68; The Song of Roland, 1963; Lazarillo De Tormes, 1962; The Satires of Perseus, 1960; Spanish Ballads, 1960; The Poem of the Cid, 1959; (prose) The Miner's Pale Children, 1970. Contbr. to the following anthols., jrnls., mags., etc.: The New Yorker; Poetry; Kayak; Hudson Review; Lillabulero; The Atlantic Monthly; Tri-Quarterly; Evergreen Review; Quarterly Review of Lit.; NY Review of Books. Honours, awards: Pulitzer Prize, 1971; Nomination, Nat. Book Award in Poetry, 1970; Translation Prize, PEN, 1969, & sev. others. Address: c/o Atheneum publrs., 122 E. 42nd St., New York, NY 10017, USA.

MESCHEDE, Beverly Ann, b. 20 Nov. 1950. Grants Coordinator. Education: Grad., Bellarmine Coll., Louisville, Ky., 1972; grad. study, Univ. of Edinburgh, U.K., 1972. Positions held: Asst., Bellarmine Coll. (Grants Rsch.), 1971-72; Asst. to Gen. Mgr. & Credit Mgr., Cooke Pontiac Co., Louisville, 1972-73; Grants Co-ordinator, King Educational Ctr., Nazareth, Ky., 1973-. Memberships: South & West, Inc.; Assoc. Mbr., Poetry Soc. of Tenn. Contbr. to: Nat. Anthol. of College Poetry; South & West; Pegasus, 1972; Ed., lit. & photographic mag. 'Keenings', Spring 1972. Address: P.O. Box 2, Nazareth, KY 40048, U.S.A.

MEUDT, Edna Kritz (Mrs.), b. 14 Sept. 1906. Homemaker; Writer; Teacher. Education: Acad. of the Sacred Heart, Edgewood, Madison, Wisconsin. Positions held: Teaching Staff, Rhinelander School of the Arts, since 1964; Continuing Staff, The Valley Studio; Judge & Moderator, Poetry, Wis. HS.; Supvsr., Workshops, Colls. in Idaho, La., W.Va., etc. Memberships: Comm., Chmn., Creative Writing, Wis. Arts Foundation & Council; Charter Mbr. and Former Bd. Mbr., Wis. Regional Writers' Assoc.; Charter Mbr., 1st Sec. & Pres., 2 terms, Wis. Fellowship of Poets; State Chairman, Nat. Poetry Day, 1958-; Pres., Nat. Fed. State Poetry Socs., Inc.; Vice-Pres., NLAPW; Vice-Pres., Am. Poetry League; Acad. of Sciences, Arts & Letters; Internat. Poetry Soc., UK (Hon. U.S. Edit. Adviser). Published works: Round River Canticle, 1960; No Strange Land, 1964; No One Sings Face Down, 1969; Valley of the Hackmatacks (novel); The Ineluctable Sea. Contbr. to numerous journals, mags., etc. Awards: numerous, including The Governor's Award for Creativity in the Arts, 1971. Address: Route 3, Dodgeville, WI 53533, USA.

MEYER, Emma Voorhees, b. 8 Aug. 1892. College Teacher (ret'd). Education: grad., Eastern Ky. Normal (now Eastern Ky. State Univ.), 1914; Univ. of Ky.; grad., Franklin Coll., Ind., 1920; Univ. of Toulouse, France; Master's degree, Columbia Univ., 1927. Widow, Dr. Leland W. Meyer, histn. Positions held: Elem. Schl. Tchr., Sparta, Owen Co., Ky.; Monticello H.S.; Franklin Coll., Ind.; Engl. Tchr., Georgetown Coll., Ky.; Acting Hd. of Hist. Dept., ibid, 6 yrs. Memberships: Ky. State Poetry Soc.; World Poetry Soc.; Chi Delta Phi; past Mbr. & Ky. State Pres., League of Am. Pen Women, etc. Published works: (books of poetry) First & Last Defense; Children Keep His Image Whole. Contbr. to var. mags., jrnls., newspapers, inclng: Poetry; Best Poems; DAR mag. Recip., Jeff Davis Award, Tex. State Poetry Soc. Address: 1979 Prince Albert Dr., Riverside, CA 92507, U.S.A.

MEYER, Vivian M., b. 22 Nov. 1915. Poetry Editor; Student (Eng. major). Education: A.A. Co. College of Morris; Grad. Famous Writers School. Married; 1 daughter. Positions held: Chem. Lab. Tech, 1942-60; Poetry Ed. and newspaper columnist, Morris Co. News, 1960-67; Limericks Ed., Swordsman Review, 1966-71; Poetry Ed., Boonton Times-Bulletin, 1966-; N.J. Council on the Arts Poet-in-Residence Prog., Jan. & Feb. 1973. Founder and Pres., New Jersey Poetry Soc. Pubs. Ed. Star Borne, 1970; Co-ed, Catch a Falling Star, 1966; Cosmic Cadence, 1971; Unripe Fruit, 1973. Contrib. to: Cyclo-Flame; Writers' Notes and Quotes; American Bard; Jean's Journal; Haiku Highlights; World Poetry Day Magazine; The Promethean; Swordsman Review; Rainbow Magazine; Grit; Union Gospel Press; From Sea to Sea in Song; American Poetry League Bulletin, etc. Also Radio interviews: WMTR; WDHA; WRAN. Personal poetry broadcasts: WDUX. Awards: 2nd, N.J. Coll. Press Assoc., 1969; 1st, Nature of Man Award, N.J. Poetry Soc., 1968; 1st, Love Sonnet Award, N.J. Poetry Soc., 1969; 1st, Freeman Award, Golden Anniversary American Bard, 1969; Poet of the Year, Rainbow Magazine, London, 1968. Address: 6 Park Ave., Mine Hill, Dover, NJ 07801, USA.

MEYERSON, Edward L., b. 14 Sept. 1904. Credit Analyst; Accountant; Poet. Education: Crane Tech. HS; Northwestern Univ.; Loyola Univ., Chicago, Ill.;

New Schl. for Social Rsch. Positions held: Acct. & Credit Analyst; Lectr., City Coll., NYC; Lectr., Henry George Schl. of Social Sci.; Asst. Ed., South & West Books. Memberships: World Poetry Soc.; Poetry Soc. of Am.; South & West; Acad. of Am. Poets; NY Poetry Forum; Caravan House of NY. Publications: Parcae, 1934; Flying Dust, 1937; The Seed Is Man, 1967; Chameleon, 1970. Contbr. to: NY Times; Herald Tribune; Bitterroot; Imprints; Cardinal; Am. Bard; South & West; Voices Int.; Tulsa Poetry Quarterly; Bardic Echoes; Orlando Anthol.; Poetry Dial Anthol.; The Diamond Anthol. (Poetry Soc. of America); Internat. Who's Who in Poetry Anthol.; Oceanology: an introduction, 1973; Quoin; Cyclo-Flame. Awards: 1st Prize, Poetry Contest, Voices Int., 1968; 1st Prize, South & West Pestival, 1969, 2nd Prize, 1972. Address: (Apt. 106), 1414 San Carlos Ave., San Carlos, Calif. 94070, USA.

MEZEY, Robert, b. 28 Feb. 1935. Writer. Education: Kenyon Coll.; Iowa Univ.; Stanford Univ. Positions held: Tchr., Memphis State Univ.; Western Reserve Univ.; Beaver Coll.; Buffalo; Franklin & Marshall Coll., Pa.; Fresno State Coll., Calif.; Assoc. Prof., Univ. of Utah, since 1973. Published works: The Lovemaker, 1961; White Blossoms, 1965; The Mercy of Sorrow, 1966; Favors, 1968; The Door Standing Open, 1970; A Book of Dying, 1970. Contbr. to: Poetry; New Yorker; Kayak; Contact; Stand; Paris Review; Chicago Tribune; Harper's; Botteghe Oscure; Nuove Presza; Partisan Review; Hearse; Liberation; Trans-pacific; Rat, etc. Honours: Lamont Poetry Award, 1960; Stanford Writing Fellowship, 1960-1;1960-61; Ingram Merrill Award, 1973. Address: Univ. of Utah, Salt Lake City, Utah, USA.

MHO, Youn Sook, pen name YOUNG WOON, b. 5 Mar. 1910. Poetess. Education: B.A. in Lit., Dept. of Engl. Lit., Ewha Womens Univ.; studied Engl. Lit. at the Kyung Sung Univ. Married, 1 daughter. Positions held: V.P., the Korean P.E.N.; Pres., Korea Modern Poets' Assn.; Advisor, Korea Women Writers' Soc.; Mbr., Nat. Assembly; Chmn., Organizing Comm. for the 2nd Symposium on the Arts in Asia. Memberships: Korea Acad. of Arts; Korean Writers' Assn.; Korean Modern Poets' Assn.; Korean Women Writers' Soc.; PEN. Published works: (poems) Land of Morning Calm, 1932; A Jade Hair Pin, 1945; Ren's Elegy, 1948; Wind & Waves, 1953; Pathetic Scene, 1962; Natural Features, 1970; At the Lake-side, 1973; (essays) The World I Saw, 1949; Vineyard, 1949; Note of a Wife, 1958; A Love Song of Cloud, 1963; To a Youth, 'Young', 1963; Tears in Smile, 1967; Reminiscence, 1968. Contbr. of poems, essays & articles to almost all major newspapers in Korea, & many monthly mags. & other periodicals. Honours, awards: Cit. of Merit for Cultural Serv. by Ewha Womens Univ., 1961; Prize for Lit., Korea Acad. of Arts, 1963; Order of Civil Merit, Moran Medal, 1970. Address: 131 Hwayang-dong, Songdong-gu, Seoul, Korea.

MICHAEL, Hjalmar Fridolf Martin, pen name 'St M', b. 6 Nov. 1898. Clergyman. Education: M. Philos., Academi of Abo, 1924; Theol. studies, sacrimin. cand., pastor, 1934; Pastoral exam., 1938; Clergyman in Abo, Wasa, Helsinki. Positions held: Jrnlst., Abo, Stockholm, Wiborg; Clergyman in Pargas, Vasa, Helsinki (Helsingfors), Liljendal, Lovisa, Abo; Tchr. of Religion. Memberships: Soc. of Swedish Authors in Finland; The Ctr. of Finnish & Swedish Authors in Finland; The Swedish Reform Union, Stockholm; Int. Order of Odd Fellows. Published works: Modern gudstro (Modern faith), 1948; Glorious is the Earth, 1950; Stoft och himmel (Dust & Heaven), 1956; Sang och sanning (Song & Truth) poems, 1958; Den nya jorden (The New Earth), 1960; Sanningen i en ny tid (The truth in a new Time), 1964; Mänskligheten vid skiljevägen (The Mankind at the Cross-Road), 1967; Var stora nya varld-vart-han? (Our Grand New World-Whiter?) pamphlet, 1970. Contbr. to var. jrnls. Recip. author's prize, 1938. Address: Slottsgatan 37 A 7 Abo (Turku), Finland.

MICHAELSON, Louis W., pen name MICHAELSON,

Michael, b. 27 Mar. 1917. Educator. Education: M.A., Univ. of Iowa; Ph.D., Univ. of Denver, Colo. Positions held: Newspaperman, N.Y.C., Seattle, Wash., United Press & Associated Press, 1950-56; Coll. Tchr., Ariz. State; at Idaho Univ., 1956-58; Asst. Prof., Engl., Colo. State Univ., 1958-. Member, Phi Beta Kappa. Published works: (poetry books) New Shoes on an Old Man, 1968; Songs of my Divided Self, 1970; Everyone Revisited, 1974. Contbr. to: N.Y. Times; Sat. Review; Esquire; Saturday Evening Post; Antioch Review; Prairie Schooner; Colo. Qtly., etc. Address: English Dept., Colo. State Univ., Ft. Collins, CO 80521, U.S.A.

MICHAEL-TITUS, Constantin, b. 4 Aug. 1925. School Master. Education: studied Law & Philos., Univs. of Bucharest & Paris; Tchrs. Dip., Exeter Univ., U.K.; M.A., Nottingham Univ.; Docteur (Lettres) w. mention 'Très Honorable', Univ. of Toulouse. Married Nora Mary Goodchild. Positions held: Ed. of Panopticum, press serv., Paris, 1950-52; Foreign corres. for var. newspapers in Europe, 1952-57; School Master, U.K., 1957-; Permanent Corres. in U.K. for 'Bulletin Européen' of Rome, 1967-72; Vis. Prof. at a Canadian Univ., 1963-64; Ed., The Reminder, political newsletter, 1971-. Memberships: Società Accademica Romena, Rome; Académie des Poètes de Rhodanie 'L'Ile des Poètes'; Delegate in U.K. for the Fndn. 'Convergence Occidentale', Lisbon, etc. Published works: Mal Du Ciel, 1964; Cri Muet, 1965; Agenda D'Exil, 1970. Contbr. to var. periodicals in France & Romania. Honours, awards: Prix Bardet de l'Académie Française, 1965; Prix 'Jeanne Evian' d'Honneur, de l'Académie Rhodanienne. Address: 44 Howard Rd., Upminster RM14 F, U.K.

MICHELET, Marcel, b. 25 Sept. 1906. Catholic Priest. Educ: Licence ès lettres, Paris; Doct., Philos. & Theol., Rome; Spanish studies, Palma Majorca. Positions held: Prof., Philos., Relig., Greek, Latin, French, & Spanish; Currently, Chap., Inst. St. Joseph, Monthey. Memberships: Swiss Soc. of Writers; Pres. Valaisanne Soc. of Writers; Alsace Acad.; Acad. Int. de Lutèce, Paris, etc. Published works: Trois Couronnes de Roses, 1940; Les Sentiers de Broceliande, 1942; Les Chants intérieurs, 1944; Madeleine, 1949; Accords et Dissonances, 1962; Psaumes, 1956; La Colporteuse, 1965; O Toi qui m'as blessée, 1968; Le Lotus parfumé, 1970; Ma Maison, in prep. Contbr. to: Treize étoiles; Les Alpes; Civitas; Les Echos de Saint-Maurice; Poésie Vivante, Geneva, etc. Honours, awards incl: Medal of French Lang., Acad. Française, 1959; 3 prizes, ibid; 1st Prize, Int. Acad. of Poetical Exchange, 1969; Grand Prize, Acad. of Lutèce, 1970; Gold Medal, ibid, 1973. Address: Rue Dufays, 1870 Monthey, Switzerland.

MICHIE, James, b. 1927. Publishing Director. Education: Trinity Coll., Oxford. Positions held: Ed. & Lectr. for London Univ.; Dir., Bodley Head Publishers, London. Published works: Possible Laughter, 1959; Trans., The Odes of Horace, 1963. Contbr. to (Anthols.): Comic and Curious Verse, 1952; New Poets of England and America, 1962; Guinness Book of Poetry, 1962; New Lines 2; (jrnls.): New Yorker; Harper's; Listener; Times Literary Supplement.

MICKELSEN, Maud Donnelly, b. 4 Jan. 1893. Housewife. Education: HS, 1910; Syracuse Univ., B.A., Cum Laude, 1916; 1 yr. (with husband), at Auburn Theological Seminary, 1918-19. Married to the Rev. G. H. Mickelsen, 1918; 1 s. (John Kenneth), 1 d. (Alice). Positions held: Teacher, Engl. and Biology, Newark, NY HS.; Pres., Council of Church Women, Tonawanda; Pres., Church Women United, Phelps Area; Chaplain, D.A.R. in Trumansburg, NY.; Children's Sec., Buffalo Presbyterial, etc. Memberships: Ithaca Poetry Soc., NY.; Galley Slaves, INK, Geneva, NY (Pres., Sec., Historian); The Academe, North Tonawanda, NY (Sec.); Theta Chi Beta, Hon. Biblical Soc. at Syracuse Univ. Published works: Broken Strings, 1939; A Lighted Torch, 1972. Contbr. to: Rochester Democrat & Chronicle; Outreach; Newark Courier Gazette; Women & Missions; The Rotarian; Blue Moon; Chapel Bell;

American Bard; Jean's Journal; Haiku Highlights; Tonawanda News; American Agriculturist; Penny-a-Thought; Purring in a Pocket; Ithaca Writer's Anthol.; Galley Slaves, INK; Caravan to Christmas (anthol.); Words (anthol.); Inspirational Anthol.; Three Poems set to Music (The Easter Symphony, Christmas Symbols, and Why Weepest Thou?). Address: 11 Ontario St., Phelps, NY 14532, USA.

MICKWITZ, Johan, b. 29 June 1937. Journalist. Education: Univ. of Helsinki, 1957-62; Universität der Wien, 1958. Married 1) Berit Ylander, div., 2) Margaretha Roschier-Holmberg, 3 children. Positions held: News Sec., Finnish News Agency, 1960-65; News Reporter, Finnish Broadcasting Corp, 1965-66; News Editor, Finnish News Agency, 1966-. Memberships: Finlands Svenska Författareförening, 1962-; Sec., ibid, 1964-65; Helsingin Kirjailijat, 1969-; Sec., ibid, 1969-70. Published works: (poetry) Vassvinter, 1961; Sandsten, 1962; Uppgörelse, 1964; Fröken Ur ville intekomma, 1968; (other books) Oktober, 1959; Nattvinge, 1963; Aret ingenting hände, 1972. Contbr. to: Hufvudstadsbladet; Horisont; FBT. Honours, awards: State Scholarship, 1969 & '73; Helsinki Award, 1970. Address: Fabriksgatan 21 A 19, Helsinki 15, Finland.

MIDDLETON, Christopher, b. 10 June 1926. University Teacher. Education: Merton Coll., Univ. of Oxford, U.K. Positions held: Engl. Lektor, Zürich Univ., Switzerland; Asst. Lectr., King's Coll., London Univ.; Lectr., King's Coll., London Univ.; Sr. Lectr., ibid; Prof., Univ. of Tex. at Austin, U.S.A. Extraordinary Mbr., West German Acad. of Arts. Published works: Torse 3, 1962; Nonsequences/Selfpoems, 1965; Our Flowers & Nice Bones, 1969; The Fossil Fish, 1970; Wie wir Grossmutter zum Markt bringen (tran. into German), 1970; Briefcase History, 1972. Recip., Sir Geoffrey Faber Meml. Prize, 1963. Address: c/o Dept. of Germanic Langs., Univ. of Tex., Austin, TX 78746, U.S.A.

MIDDLETON, Kathleen (Maud), b. 9 Apr. 1923. Secretary. Education: Sec. Coll., in Oxfordshire. Membership: Oxford Writers Circle. Published work: Spring Song (book of childrens' poetry), 1960. Contbr. to: Berkshire Mercury (18 poems between 1970-73); WEN 3; This England. Address: 41 Alice Smith Sq., Littlemore, Oxford, UK.

MIDDLETON, Laura Mary, pen name, **MIDDLETON, Laura,** b. 27 Apr. 1952. Educator. Education: Liverpool Univ., U.K. Currently Teacher of History & Geography. Fellow, Int. Poetry Soc., 1973. Contbr. to: Roots; The Writer; Southern Arts Literary Review; Contact 5; Int. Poetry Soc. Anthol., 1973; also to Radio I & Radio II. Address: The Flat, 9 Tarbock Rd., Huyton, Liverpool 36, U.K.

MIEZAN-BOGNINI, Joseph, b. 18 Sept. 1936. Professor. Educ: Double CAP, Tech. Coll., Abidjan; Projecteur, Profl. Schl. of Indl. Design, Paris; CAECET; Tech. Teaching Dip.; Inst. of Superior Tech. Studies, Paris. Married, 3 children. Positions held: Dpty. Chief of Serv., Construction Permits, Min. of Construction & Urbanism, 1965-68; Dir. of Studies, Ctrl. Serv. for Org. & Methods, Min. of Pub. Function, 1970-72; Dir. of Studies, Dir. of Pedagogic Rsch. & Exams., Min. of Tech. Instrn. & Profl. Dev. Memberships incl: Soc. of Men of Letters; Ivory Assn. of Men of Letters; Pres., Nat. Fedn. of Theatre, Ivory Coast. Published works: Ce Dur Appel de l'Espoir, 1961; Herbe Féconde, 1973; Tafie (theatre); sev. works in prep. Named Chevalier, Order of Agricl. Merit, Dahomey. Address: Direction de la Recherche Pédagogique et des Examens, Min. de l'Enseignement Technique et de la Formation Professionnelle, Abidjan, Ivory Coast.

MIFKA, Ljerka, b. 22 Mar. 1943. Professional Writer. Education: Grad., comp. lit. & Italian lang., Univ. of Zagreb, 1966. Published works: Piramida, (Razlog, Zagreb), 1970; Eseji, (Mladost, Zagreb), 1970. Contbr.

to: Telegram; Mladost; Polja; Ifjusag; Uj simposion; Kolo; Republika; Forum; Vidici; Vidik; Encyclopedia Moderna; Kamov; Danas; Dubrovnik. Honours, awards: Prize of newspaper 'Mladost', 1962 & '65; Prize 'A.B. Simić'. Address: Krajiška 27/1, 41000 Zagreb, Yugoslavia.

MIGNAULT, Euna Maxine Hoyden, pen names **RUSSELL, Euna & RUSSELL-MIGNAULT, Euna,** b. 27 Nov. 1898. Osteopathic Physician. Education: Mass. Osteopathic Coll., 4 yrs; var. courses in writing & art. Married twice. Memberships: Yankee Scribblers, Manchester, Mass. (Sec.-Treas., 3 yrs., V.P., 3 yrs.); Formed Houtherson Writers' Grp., Salem, 1968 & served as Pres., 1968-; Fellowship of Profl. Poets, N.Y., etc. Published works: My Sampler 1st Poetry Book, 1965; Looking Sunword, 1968; They Touched My Life (autobiog.), 1969; Kindling & Embers (poetry), 1968; Soundings, 1971; The Soaring Eagle, 1973. Contbr. to: Pendulum; Kans. Kernal; Inky Trails; Major Poets Am.; Angel Hour; Express Mag.; Poetry Review; World Poets; sev. anthols., etc. Honours, awards incl: 3 book awards; Poet of the Month, Inky Trails, July 1972. Address: 33 Federal St., Beverly, MA 01915, USA.

MIHALY, Ladányi, b. 12 Feb. 1934. Poet. Education: studied Hungarian Lang. & Hist., Univ. of Budapest. Married, 4 children. Memberships: Hungarian Writer's Assn.; Hungarian PEN Club. Published works: (all books) Az út kezdete, 1959; Oklök és tenyerek, 1961; Mint a madarak, 1963; Utánad kószálok, 1965; Dobszóló, 1967; A túloldalon, 1969; Elhettem volna gyönyörüen, 1970; Kedvesebb hazát, 1971; Kitépett tollú szél, 1974; Se csillaga, se holdja, 1974. Contbr. to: Népszava; Magyar Hirlap; Népszabadság; Elöre; Elet es Irodalom; Utunk; A hét; Jelenkor; Alföld; Napjaink; Uj Iras; Kortárs; Tiszatáj; Látóhatár, etc. Recip., Jozsef Attila Prize. Address: 1365 Budapest 5, Pf.717, Hungary.

MILANI, Elvezia, b. 20 Nov. 1925. Educator. Educ: Univ. of Pavia, Italy. Positions held: Tchr., var. schls. Published works incl: Il campo del tuo riso, 1958; Ore del mio tempo, 1959; Orda di pena, 1961. Contbr. to: La Gostra; Lettere Nueve; Parnaso; La Zagora. Honours, awards incl: 2nd Prize, Poetry, Ostia Lido, 1972; 2nd Prize, Poetry, Pellegrini Edizioni, ibid, 1973; Gestoldi Award, 1960. Address: Gallerie Mansoni 3, Pavia, Italy.

MILES, Geraldine, b. 8 Apr. 1920. Writer. Married. Religious Education Tchr. for 33 yrs. in F.B.C.; Councillor & has own Personal Ministry; Pro Tem Pianist, Pacos Dist. Memberships: Treas. & Chap., Poetry Soc. & Acad. of Am. Poets; Chaplain, Creative Writers' Club, Odessa, Tex.; Poetry Soc. of Tex.; Nat. Fed. of State Poetry Socs.; Grp. Capt., Sunday Schl., 1st Bapt. Ch. Contbr. to: Baptist Standard; Poetry Corner 1973; many anthols. & newspapers. Honours, awards: Cit. & Mbrship of C.S.S.I., Rome, Italy; Cit. in Music, 1969; Cit. in Lit., 1969; Hon. Mention in Creative Writing, Tex. Independence Contest, 1973. Address: 2701 N. Hancock, Odessa, TX 79760, U.S.A.

MILES, Joel Eugene, pen name **THRODE, Gith,** b. 16 Dec. 1907. Artist; Poet. Education: Univ. of Neb., 1 yr. Married, 4 children. Published works: (children's book) Bibbsy the Bug, 1937. Published 'Edgewater Firecracker' newspaper for over a year. Contbr. of one poem each Sunday to the Edgewater United Methodist Church Bulletin, 1972-. Address: 2510½ Fenton, Edgewater, CO 80214, U.S.A.

MILES, Josephine, b. 11 June 1911. Educator; Poet. Education: B.A., UCLA, 1932; M.A., Univ. of Calif., Berkeley, 1934; Ph.D., ibid, 1938; Lit.D., Mills Coll., 1965. Positions held: Mbr., Fac., Dept. of Engl., Univ. of Calif., Berkeley, 1940-; Prof. of Engl., ibid, 1952-73; Univ. Prof. of Engl., 1973-. Mbrships: Am. Acad. of Arts & Scis.; MLA; Phi Beta Kappa; Chi Delta Phi. Published works: Lines at Intersection, 1939; Poems on Several Occasions, 1941; Local Measures, 1946; The Vocabulary of Poetry (3 studies), 1946; The

Continuity of English Poetic Language, 1951; Prefabrications, 1955; Eras & Modes in English Poetry, 1957, '64; Renaissance, Eighteenth Century & Modern Language in Poetry, 1960; Poems, 1930-60, 1960; House & Home (verse play), 1961; Emerson, 1964; Style & Proportion: Language of Prose & Poetry, 1967; Civil Poems, 1966; Kinds of Affection: Poems, 1967; Poetry and Change, 1974; To All Appearances: Poems New and Selected, 1974. Recording, Today's Poets Voll. II. Co-ed: Criticism: Foundations of Mod. Judgement, 1948; Idea & Experiment, 1950-54; Ed: The Poem, 1959; The Ways of the Poem, 1961, rev. ed., 1972; Classic Essays in English, 1961, '65. Contbr. to num. jrnls., mags., anthols. Honours, awards: Shelley Award, 1935; Blumenthal Award; Nat. Inst. of Arts & Letters Award, 1956; Endowment for Arts & Letters, 1967. Address: 2275 Virginia St., Berkeley, CA, U.S.A.

MILICEVIC, Nikola, b. 27 Nov. 1922. Poet; Critic; Translator. Education: B.A., Fac. of Arts, Zagreb Univ., 1952; Ph.D., ibid, 1965. Married, 1 daughter. Positions held: Lang. Ed. & Sr. Ed. of var. jrnls. & newspapers, 1948-55; Fac. of Arts, Yugoslav Lit. Dept., Zagreb Univ., 1955-. Translator of poetry from Spanish, Portuguese, Italian & Latin. Memberships: Yugoslav Writers' Assn.; V.P., Croatian Writers' Soc. Published works: (poetry) Zlatna grana, 1952; Pod ravnodusnim zvijezdama, 1953; Obećanja zute zore, 1956; Snijeg i crna ptica, 1964; Prah zemaljski, 1974; (translations) Antologija novije spajolske poezije, 1959; Novija hispanoamericka poezija, 1962; Latinska poezija, 1964; Zlatna knjiga spanjolske poezije, 1972. Contbr. to: Krugovi; Republika; Forum; Mogućnosti; Knjizevnost. Honours, awards: City of Zagreb Award for the vol. of transl. 'New Hispano-Am. Poetry', 1963; Vladimir Nazor Award for Anthol. of Spanish Poetry, 1973. Address: Ulica 8, maja 81, 41000 Zagreb, Yugoslavia.

MILLER, Brown, b. 9 Oct. 1943. Instructor of English. Education: Univ. of Calif. at Berkeley, 1961; B.A., San Francisco State Univ., 1966; M.A., ibid, 1967. Married twice, 4 children. Positions held: Engl. Instr., City Coll. of San Francisco, 1967-. Published works: Fertilized Brains, 1968; Whiskeytown Iron Mountain Triptych, 1968; Autopsies & Family Ghosts, 1968; Thirty-Three Phases of the Fatal Stroboscope, 1968; The World is Coming, 1969; Waters & Shadows, 1969. Contbr. to: Dust; Trace; The Lampeter Muse; Second Aeon; Pyramid; Boss; New Am. & Canadian Poetry; Meatball; The Runcible Spoon, etc. Recip. grant for poem 'Terminal Waiting' included in The Am. Lit. Anthol., 1969. Address: 501 Foerster St., San Francisco, CA 94127, U.S.A.

MILLER, Cecilia Parsons, b. 15 July 1909. Poet. Education: Arts degree, Hillsdale Coll., Mich., U.S.A., 1932. Married H. Lionel Miller, 4 adopted children. Positions held: Community volunteer work & Ed., Church Women United News, 1962-; Mbr., Radio Panel, Coun. of Ch., Gr. Harrisburg, 1962-; Harrisburg Arts Coun., Comm. Chmn., By Laws & Mbrship Sec., 1970-72; V.P., 1972-73; Pres., 1973-74. Memberships incl: 1st Pres., var. other offices, Nat. Fed. of State Poetry Socs.; 2nd Pres., Pa. Poetry Soc., 1957-61; Trustee, ibid, 1965-69, var. other offs.; South and West; Am. Poetry League; Poetry Soc. of Mich.; Published works: Not Less Content, 1960; Peculiar Honors, 1962; To March to Terrible Music, 1966; Stand At The Edge, 1970; Space Where Once A Husband Stood, 1972. Contbr. to over 60 anthols., 70 mags., 30 newspapers inclng: South & West; Voices Int.; Imprints Qtly.; Christian Sci. Monitor; Cyclo-Flame; Hartford Times; Hartford Courant; Am. Bard. Recip. var. poetry hons. & awards inclng: 2nd pl., Nat. Fed. State Poetry Socs., 1961, Hon. Mention Grand Prix, 1966, 2nd pl., 1966, 71, 72; Carl Sandburg Award, N.C., 1971; Carlisle (Pa.) Award, 1971. Address: 264 Walton St., Lemoyne, PA 17043, U.S.A.

MILLER, Edmund Charles, III, b. 18 July 1943. College Teacher. Education: B.A., CW Post Coll., 1965; M.A., The Ohio State Univ., 1969; Ph.D., The State Univ. of N.Y. at Stony Brook, 1974. Positions held: Tchr. of Engl. & Creative Writing, The Ohio State Univ., Rockhurst Coll., Newark Coll. of Engrng., State Univ. of N.Y. at Stony Brook. Memberships: MLA; Coll. Engl. Assn.; North East MLA; Nat. Coun. of Tchrs. of Engl.; Coun. on Coll. Composition & Communication. Published works: F--- A---: A Book of Poems, 1973; The Nadine Poems, 1973. Contbr. to: The Wis. Review; Concepts; The World; Haiku Spotlight; Hey Ladyl; Tangonto; Aspect; Oonfrontation, Halku Mag.; Abbey; Haiku Highlights; The Higginson Jrnl. of Poetry; The Mo. Engl. Bulletin; Jean's Jrnl.; The Little Review; The Escutcheon; Soundings. Honours, awards: Rhetoric Prize, College Engl., 1969; Special Mention in Season Word Contest, Haiku Mag. for Jan. 1970. Address: 2386 Ryer Ave. 4E, The Bronx, NY 10458, U.S.A.

MILLER, Eleanora Liljegren, b. 17 Nov. 1916. Freelance Writer. Education: B.A., Augustana Coll., Rock Is., Ill.; Grad. Schl., Univ. of Iowa. Married Forest Miller. Positions held: Tchr. of Engl. & Speech; Freelance News Corres. & Writer; Ed. & Writer of FOR FRONT, publ. of The Fndn. for Freedom & Democracy in Community Life, Inc. Memberships: Past Iowa State Pres., Nat. League of Am. Pen Women; Past Pres., Des Moines Br., ibid; Currently State Pres., Iowa Poetry Assn.; Nat. Fed. of Press Women, Iowa. Contbr. to: Lyrical Iowa; Northwest Ark. Times; The Friendly World; Saga – of Augustana Coll.; Cat's Mag.; Des Moines Register & Tribune; For Front; Iowa Poetry Day Assn.; The Gowrie News. Honours, awards: First pl. & Reserve Champion, Contest of Times Republican Newspaper, Marshalltown, Iowa, 1973; First pl., Lyric Div., Nat. Contest, NLAPW, 1972; 3rd pl. & hon. mention, Lyrical Iowa, etc. Address: 208 South Church St., Leon, IA, U.S.A.

MILLER, Heather (Ross), b. 15 Sept. 1939. Teacher; Writer. Education: B.A., Univ. of N.C., Greensboro, 1961; M.F.A., ibid, 1969; postgrad. studies, Appalachian State Univ., Birbeck Coll., London, 1973. Married Clyde H. Miller, 2 children. Positions held: Lectr. in Engl. & Writing, Pfeiffer Coll., 1965-66; Instr. in Engl., Southeastern Community Coll., 1969-72; Cons. in Writing, N.C. Dept. of Public Instrn., 1972-73; Asst. Prof., Stanly Tech. Inst. & Pfeiffer Coll., 1974. Memberships: N.C. Writers Conf.; Tenth Muse, Inc.; Poets & Writers Inc.; Teachers & Writers Collaborative. Published works: The Edge of the Woods (novel), 1964; Tenants of the House (novel), 1966; The Wind Southerly (poetry), 1967; Gone a Hundred Miles (novel), 1968; Horse Horse Tyger Tyger (poetry), 1973, (two novels transl. into French). Contbr. to: Vogue; Am. Scholar; N.Y. Times; N.Y. Times Book of Verse, etc. Honours, awards: The Oscar Arnold Young Meml. Cup, 1968; Sir. Walter Raleigh Cup, 1966; recip., two writing fellowships from the Nat. Endowment for the Arts & Humanities, 1968-69, '73-74. Address: 40 Elm St., Box 685, Badin, NC 28009, U.S.A.

MILLER, Henry Lionel, pen name MILLER, Lion, b. 4 May 1908. Writer, Director of Motion Pictures. Education: Hillsdale Coll., Mich. Positions held: Adv. Agency, Mansfield, Ohio; Adv. Westinghouse; Sound Pictures Corp., Cleveland, Ohio; Sales trng. & promotion, Gen. Electric, Cleveland, Ohio & Bridgeport, Conn.; Civilian Tech. w. Navy, WWII; Loucks & Norling, N.Y.C.; Prodn. Mgr., Willard Pictures, N.Y.C.; Motion Picture Studio, Penn State Coll., later Univ., 5 yrs.; Studio Dir., Michener & O'Connor; Motion Picture Unit, C'wealth of Pa. Highway Dept. Memberships: Pres., Harrisburg Manuscript Club, 1958-59; Contest Chmn., ibid, 1972-74; Pa. Poetry Soc., Harrisburg Chapt., then Keysner Poets Chapt.; Nat. Fed. of State Poetry Socs.; Arts Fest. Comm., 1968, Pub. Rels. Chmn., 1972-74, Harrisburg Arts Coun. Contbr. to: Starlanes; Okla. Poetry 1968; Signet; Encore; Cyclo-flame; Harrisburg Evening News; A Goodly Heritage, historical anthol.; The Christian Sci. Monitor. Recip. many awards for films. Address: 264 Walton St., Lemoyne, PA 17043, U.S.A.

MILLER, Jessie Ruhl, pen name **KENT, Julia Ann,** b. 20 Aug. 1909. Piano Teacher. Education: Dickinson Coll.; Cumberland Valley State Tchrs. Coll.; Sherwood Music Schl. Married to blast furnace engr., 4 s., 1 d. Memberships: Past Pres., Harrisburg Manuscript Club; Treas., Pa. Poetry Soc.; Nat. Poetry Soc.; Carlisle Poetry Grp.; Terre Haute Study Club; World Poetry Day. Contbr. to: World Poetry Day Anthol.; Pa. Prize Poems, 1971, '72; John F. Kennedy Commemorative Anthol.; Velvet Paws in Print; Stepping Stones to Faith; Pa. Hist. Anthol. (A Goodly Heritage); 1st Prize, Portrait category, Pa. Prize poems, 1973; Time of Singing; Pa. Prize Poems, 1963, '65, '66, '67, '69, '70. Honours, Awards: 1st Prize, Pa. Sonnet, 1965; 1st Prize, Pa. Hist. Contest, 1967; 1st Prize, Light Verse, 1968; 1st Prize, World Poetry Day, Tuanartsa, 1968, '69; 1st Prize, Chaparral Tanka, 1970; many 2nd prizes & hon. mentions; 1st prize, Phila. Writers Conference, 1971. Address: 670 W Louther St., Carlisle, Pa. 17013, USA.

MILLER, Jim Wayne, b. 21st Oct. 1936. Professor; Poet. Education: B.A., Berea Coll.; Ph.D., Vanderbilt Univ. Positions held: Assoc. Prof. of German, Western Ky. Univ., Bowling Green, and since 1970, Prof., also Graduate Director, Dept. For. Langs., since 1971; Visiting Prof., Summer Term, Berea Coll., 1973, and Consultant, Appalachian Studies Workshop, 1973. Mbr: Poetry Soc. of Am.; Ky. State Poetry Soc. Publications: Copperhead Cane, 1964; The More Things Change The More They Stay The Same (ballads), 1971; Dialogue With a Dead Man (poems), 1973. Contbr. to: Writer; Ga. Review; Mod. Philology; Laurel Review; Approaches; Mountain Life & Work; Ky. Folklore Record; Appalachian Review; Am. Weave; Southern Humanities Review; Southern Poetry Review; Green River Review; Buffalo; Wind, etc. Awards: Alice Lloyd Mem. Prize for Appalachian Poetry, 1967. Address: 1512 Eastland, Bowling Green, Kentucky 42101, USA.

MILLER, John L., b. 16 July 1941. Member, Leonardo da Vinci Acad. of Arts & Letters, Rome, Italy. Contbr. to: U.S.C. Lit. Mag. 'The Mystic Spring'; Buchaet; Reach Out; Arcadian; Personal poetry broadcasts. Recip., 2 certs. of Broadcast Quality, Personal Poetry Broadcasts, D.C. Address: 135 Barcelona, Camarillo, CA 93010, U.S.A.

MILLER, Martha Agnes Allen, pen name **MILLER, Agnes Allen,** b. 22 Sept. 1905. Teaching & Educational Administrator. Education: A.B., So. Meth. Univ.; M.Ed., Univ. of Md.; grad. work at var. univs. Married Hiram Austin Miller, 1 son. Positions held: Classroom Tchr. in Mer Rough H.S. & Monroe City Schls (H.S., Jr. H.S., & Elem. Schls.); Prin., Sallie Humble Elem. Schl., Monroe; Cons. in Elem. Sci., La. State Dept. of Educ.; Mbr., Gov's. Comm. on Tchng. of Sci. Memberships: Local Pres., State Treas., Nat. League of Am. Pen Women; State V.P., La. State Poetry Soc.; Bd. Mbr., Deep South Writers & Artists Conf.; Am. Poetry Soc. Contbr. to: Ideals; Church Schl.; Prayers in Poetry; Good News; The Christian; Daily Meditation; Explore; Am. Red Cross Jrnl.; Lyric Louisiana, etc. Honours, awards: Alpha Delta Kappa Scholarship for work for children. Address: 311 Lakeside Dr., Monroe, LA 71201, U.S.A.

MILLER, Maxine McCray, b. 27 Jul. 1911. Homemaker. Education: Nat. Honor Soc. Member, Beaumont High School; Alpha Iota Sorority Member Speedway Business Coll.; Night courses in Journalism, Gettysburg Coll. Positions held: Private Sec.; Co-owner, Food Business. Former Member, Avalon; Penna. Poetry Soc.; Contest Chairman, Penna. Poetry Soc.; Editor-in-chief of School Yearbook. Contrib. to: Ideals; Prize Poems of Penna., Poetry Soc.; World Poetry Mag.; Flame Annual; Cyclotron; Evening News; Patriot News; Years Alive Anthol.; Cardinal Poetry Qtly.; Daily Meditations; Messenger; Green World Mag.; Scimitar & Song; American Songbird Anthol.; Poetry Digest; Nat.Fed.Prize Poems; Spencer's Anthol.; Poetry Parade; Poet; Starlanes; Moore's Outstanding

Contemp. Poetry; Young's Yearbook of Modern Poetry, etc. Numerous poetry awards, including: Texas Poetry Workshop Contest, 1966; Abbie Frank Smith Memorial, 1965; Best Sonnet Contest PPS-1964-65; Margaret Deland Memorial 1965; Chandler's Memorial, 1963; A.B. Carter Peace Award, 1967; Lucia Clark Markham, 1968; Lan & Willie Davis Award, 1967; Nat.Fed. of Poetry Socs. Grand Prix, 1966; C. Sterling Clifton Award Contest, 1967; Margaret Deland Mem. 1969; Col. Henry W. Shoemaker Mem. 1968; La. State Poetry Soc. 1966, etc. Address: 410 Bonnymead Ave., Harrisburg, Pa. 17111, USA.

MILLER, Mona. Poet; Freelance Writer; Acting Accountant. Education: Dip., Royal Acad. of Mus., Royal Soc. of Arts (Hons. in Drawing) & Nat. Assn. of Tchrs. of Dancing. Married, 2 children. Positions held: Dancer; Tchr. of Dancing; Company Sec.; Personnel Officer; Freelance Writer (short stories, articles); currently Acting Accountant. Memberships: Chmn., London Writer Circle Poetry Grp.; Fellow, Int. Poetry Soc.; Poets Vigilantes; Expression One; Outposts; Weyfarers; Sean Dorman Manuscript Soc.; Envoi; Success; Quintessence (USA); Ore; Richmond Poetry Grp., Surrey. First coll. of poems to be published in 1974. Contbr. to: Cork Weekly Examiner; Competitors Jrnl.; Rainbow; Tonic; Symbol; Success; Quill; Gateway; Maximag; Expression One; Writing Published; Purpose (USA); Penman Mag.; PV Publs.; (anthols.) Versewise; Symbol Poets; Success; Nucleus 2; Int. Poetry Soc., 1973. Honours, awards: 9 First, 5 Seconds, 3 Thirds, 4 Fourths, Cork Weekly Examiner, 1970-72; 7 First, 5 Runners-up, Competitors Jrnl., 1969-73; 2 Thirds, Success Mag., 1973. Recorded, Studio One (Hosp. patients), 1969 & London Radio 2, 1972-73. Address: 30 Carmichael Ct., Barnes, London SW13 OHA, U.K.

MILLER, Orville Crowder, b. 16 August 1897. Educator; Clergyman; Poet; Editor; Executive. Education: B.A., Ind. Univ.; M.A., Univ. of Mich.; Litt.D., Free Univ. of Asia; Postgrad., Univ. of Wis.; Columbia Univ. Positions held: Educator, Univ. of Pacific, Univ. of Mich., Vanderbilt Univ., Purdue Univ., 1917-45; local Clergyman or State Stewardship Evangelist, Tenn., Ind., Ill., 1942-63; Exec., Delora Quality Homes, 1963–; Pancontinental Exec. Chancellor & Am. Hemisphere Ed., Poet, World Poetry Soc. Intercontinental, 1968-71; VP & Pancontinental Ed., ibid, 1971–; Chancellor for the Americas, Cosmosynthesis League; Hon. Poet Laureate-Ed. United Poets Laureate Int.; Hon. Rep., Centro Studi e Scambi Int.; Corres., Acad. Leonardo da Vinci & Poesie Vivante; Cornucopia Columnist, Poets Corner; Pancontinental Poets Press; American Poetry League; American Mosaic Poets; Arizona State Poetry Soc.; Nat. Fedn. of State Poetry Socs., and others in USA. Life Fellow, Royal Soc. of Arts; Past Nat. VP & Province Gov., Tau Kappa Alpha; Fndr., Ind. Univ. Chapt., Theta Alpha Phi. Most recent Published Works: (ed.) Abraham Lincoln, A Biographic Trilogy in Sonnet Sequence, 3 vols. (688pp., 473 continuity Petrarchan sonnets w. extensive illus., annotations & indices; received awards from 4 continents), 1965; Treasured Legacy, 1966; Light Uplift Loaves, 1969; (ed.) Pancontinental Premier Poets, 1970; Nurture Poems, 1971. Works in progress (as author): Selected Poems; (as editor): World Anthol. of Contemporary Poets. Contbr. of poems, poetry articles, reviews & forewords in num. books, jrnls. & anthols. in every continent, including: Laurel Leaves (UPLI); Quaderni di Poesia (CSSI); Stathmi (Greece); Pancontinental Premier Poets; The Statesmen (India); The Rhodesian Herald (Rhodesia), etc. Honours incl: Int. Gold Medallion & Laurel Wreath, Philippine Pres. Marcos; Karta of Award as Hon. Poet Laureate-Ed. & Disting. Lyric Poet, United Poets Laureate Int.; Disting. Serv. Citation as Ed., Am. Univ. Poets, World Poetry Soc. Intercontinental; Leonardo da Vinci Award for sonnet, Tree of Paradise; Gold Medal, UPLI Intercontinental Poet Laureate-Ldr.; Award, Int. Acad. of Ldrship.; Citation, Am. Poetry League; num. lesser medals & awards. Address: 7 Montclair Rd., Urbana, IL 61801, USA.

MILLER, Peter, b. 1920. Published works: Meditation at Noon, 1958; A Shifting Pattern, 1962; Trans., Alain Grandbois: Selected Poems with Translations, 1964. Contbr. to (Jrnls.): Fiddlehead; Delta; Canadian Forum; Canadian Author; Bookman.

MILLER, Robert J., b. 12 June 1918. Litterateur. Education: A.A., Hendrix Coll., 1939; B.Sc. in Educ., State Coll. of Ark. 1941. Member The Am. Poets Fellowship Soc. Published works: Freely Remembered, 1972; Rustique, 1947; Weird Balk (a pamphlet), 1964. Rep. in following anthols: Poetry Parade, 1963; Melody of the Muse, 1964, '73; Versatility in Verse, 1965; The Soul & The Singer, 1968; New Voices in the Wind, 1969; Dance of the Muse, 1970; Yearbook of Modern Poetry, 1971; Outstanding Contemporary Poetry, 1972 & '73; A Burst of Trumpets, 1966; Lyric Moderns, 1940; Am. Lyric Poetry, 1935. Contbr. to: Poetry; Opaque Clouds; United Poets; The Am. Poet, etc. Honours, awards incl: Res., MacDowell Colony, Peterborough, N.H., Spring 1941. Address: Highway 60, Plainview, AR 72857, U.S.A.

MILLER, Roger Dale, pen name **HOUSTON, Erin,** b. 16 Jan. 1945. Factory Worker. Memberships: Ky. State Poetry Soc.; The Tennessean's Gold Star Club. Contbr. to: Anthol. of Am. Poetry, Books 8, 10, 11, 1966, '70, '71, respectively; Poetry Parade, 1967, '68, '69; Golden Harvest, 1967; Am. Poetry, Old & New, 1965; Yrbook of Modern Poetry, 1971; Stewart-Houston Times; Community News; Clarksville Leaf-Chronicle; Grit; Hyacinths & Biscuits; The Tennessean; Reader's Digest; Nashville Banner; Sat. Evening Post, etc. Honours, awards: Annual Mentor Poetry Award, (2), 1966; The Tennessean's Gold Star Club, 1969; Ky. State Poetry Soc. Award, 1970; Radio Stn. WEFG-FM, 1971 & WHPL-AM, 1972, Winchester, Va.; Major Poets Chapt. Award (2), 1973. Address: 918 N. 14th St., Nashville, TN 37206, U.S.A.

MILLER, Vassar (Morrison), b. 19 July 1924. Teacher of Creative Writing. Education: B.S., Univ. of Houston. Tex., 1947; M.A., ibid, 1952. Positions held: Instructor in Creative Writing, St. John's Schl., Houston, 1964–. Published works: Adam's Footprint, 1956; Wage War on Silence, 1960; My Bones Being Wiser, 1963; Onions & Roses, 1968. Contbr. to (Anthols.): New Poets of England and America, 1957; Poet's Choice, 1962; A Poetry Sampler, 1962; Poems of Doubt and Belief, 1964; Today's Poets, 1964; A Controversy of Poets, 1965; (Jrnls.): New York Times; Paris Review; Transatlantic Review; New Orleans Poetry Jrnl. Recip., Tex. Inst. of Letters Award, 1956, 60 & 63. Address: 1651 Harold Street, Houston, TX 77006, USA.

MILLETT, John, b. 3 Feb. 1928. Solicitor. Education: LL.B., Sydney Univ. Married Marion Moss, 2 children. Published works: Calendar Adam, 1971; The Silences, 1973; Love Tree of the Coomera, 1974. Contbr. to: Meanjin; Sydney Morning Herald; The Australian; Poet's Choice, 1972, '73, '74; Ear of the Wheatfield; Poetry Mag.; New Poetry; Poetry Australia; 20th Century; Makar; Fiddlehead; Poetry East-West. Address: Riverlands, Upper Coomera, Qld. 4210, Australia.

MILLS, Louise Ellen, b. 10 Sept. 1900. Retired U.S. Government Employee. Positions held: Switchboard Operator, Supvsr., S.W. Bell Telephone Co., 3 yrs.; Operator, Supvsry. Work & Chief Operator, Brooks A.F.B. Member, San Antonio Chapt., State Poetry Soc. of Tex. Has had two songs published. Contbr. to: Song Writers & Poets of Am., anthol., 1945. Recip. poetry awards from San Antonio Chapt., Poetry Soc. of Tex., 1971. Address: P.O. Box 383, Devine, TX 78016, U.S.A.

MILLS, Martha, b. 13 Sept. 1922. Assembler. Education: Springfield Public Grade and HS. Married to Louis Mills. Past Pres., The Unique Matronettes (social club); Sec. for Springfield Deanery Council of Catholic Women. Memberships: Ill. Poetry Soc.; Smithsonian Inst. Published work: Various Verses, 1971; Contbr. to: Ill. State Register; Springfield Voice; Sangame Leader; Shore Anthol.; Sangamon State Univ. for poetry for Black Awareness Week. Honours awarded: Ill. State Centennial (Black History), Feb. 1972, from Ill. State Library. Address: 2821 Piper Rd., Springfield, IL 62707, USA.

MILLWARD, Eric (Geoffrey William), b. 12 March 1935. Airline Steward. Memberships: County Sec., Conservation Soc., Sussex Br.; Poetry Ed., Towards Survival; Fellow, Int. Poetry Soc. Published works: A Child in the Park, 1969. Contbr. to: John o'London's; BBC; The Listener; Poetry Review; The Friend; The Montreal Star; Spastics News; New Poems, 1965 (PEN); Tribune; Towards Survival; The Poet's Sphere (Anthol.); Active Anthologies (IV); The Golden Bird (Anthol.); This Astonishing Planet (Anthol.); S. African Broadcasting Co.; Contemporary Poets. Address: Hope Cottage, 67 Hillside, Horsham, Sussex, U.K.

MILLWARD, Pamela (nee Huth), Pseudonym, Perspicacity Midling (detective novels), b. 24 Feb. 1937. Author; Poet. Education: North Central Coll., Naperville, Ill. Married w. 1 child. Published works: The Route of the Phoebe Snow, 1966; Once and for All, 1969; (Novel): Mother: A Novel of the Revolution, 1969. Contbr. to (Jrnls.): San Francisco Oracle; Coyote Jrnl.; Wild Dog. Recip., Nat. Arts Commission Grant, 1968. Address: P.O. Box 1360, Jackson, Wyo., 83001, USA.

MILNE, (Charles) Ewart, b. 25 May 1903. Poet. Education: Nuns Cross Schl., Ashford, Wicklow; Christ Ch. Cathedral Grammar Schl., Dublin. Published works: Forty North Fifty West; Letter From Ireland; Listen Mangan; Jubilo; Boding Day; Diamond Cut Diamond; Elegy For A Lost Submarine; Galion; Life Arboreal; Once More To Tourney; A Garland For The Green, 1962: Time Stopped, 1967. Contbr. to: Irish Times; New Statesman; Dublin Mag.; Poetry, Chicago; Johns Hopkins Review; The Bell; Irish Writing; London Mag.; New Irish Poets; 1000 Years of Irish Poetry; Faber Book of Children's Verse; Poetry Now; Penguin Book of Curious & Comic Verse; Poems From New Writing. Address: 46 De Parys Ave., Bedford, U.K.

MILTON, John R., b. 24 May 1924. Teacher; Editor. Education: B.A. & M.A., Univ. of Minn.; Ph.D., Univ. of Denver. Married, 1 daughter. Positions held: Instr. in Engl. & Philos., Augsburg Coll., Minn.; Assoc. Prof. to Prof. & Chmn., Engl. Dept., Jamestown Coll., N.D.; Prof. of Engl. & Chmn. of the Dept., Univ. of S.D.; resigned Chairmanship to become Editor, South Dakota Review & Dir. of Creative Writing. Memberships: Affil., Acad. of Am. Poets; Delta Phi Lambda. Published works: The Loving Hawk, 1962; Western Plains, 1964; The Tree of Bones, 1965; This Lonely House, 1968; The Tree of Bones & Other Poems, 1973; also writes fiction & lit. criticism. Contbr. to: Northwest Review; Kan. Qtly.; DeKalb Lit. Jrnl.; Taos News; Poetry North; Poet; N.M. Qtly.; The Chicago Review, etc. Address: 630 Thomas, Vermillion, SD 57069, U.S.A.

MINER, Caroline Eyring, b. 14 Dec. 1907, Colonia, Juarez, Mexico. Teacher (retired). Education: A.B., Brigham Young Univ., 1929; M.S., Utah State Univ., 1943; Grad. work, Univs. of Calif., Hawaii, Alaska & Utah. Married to Glen B. Miner, 1931, 8 children. Memberships: Utah Poetry Soc.; Reynolds Club; Nat. Am. Poetry Soc.; State & Salt Lake City Pres., VP, Sec., Nat. League Am. Pen Women. Published works: Earthbound No Longer; There's Always Mother; Utah American Pen Women in Review, 1972. Contbr. to: Improvement Era; Relief Society Magazines; Alentour; Oregonian; Deseret News. Awards: Christmas Poem, Deseret News, 1952, '59; Eliza R. Snow Contest, Relief Society Magazine, 2 yrs.; Utah Poetry Soc., 1971. Address: 2429 Kensington Ave., Salt Lake City, Utah 84108, USA.

MINER, Virginia Scott, pen names, **KIPLINGER,**

David, THATCHER, Amelia, WILCOX, Hannah Sims, HOOSIER HANNAH, HOSSIER HANK & MINER, Scott, b. 9 Aug. 1901. Retired Teacher; Free-lance Writer. Education: B.A., Northwestern Univ.; Grad. Work, Univ. of Chicago, Univ. of Mo., Univ. of Kan.; Okla. State Univ., Kan. City Univ., etc. Married, D.H. Miner. Positions held: Tchr., Latin & Engl., Morris, Ill. HS; Tchr., Music & Engl., Marissa Twp. HS; Tchr., Engl. & Libn., Pembroke Co. Day Schl., Kan. City, Mo., 24 yrs.; Retd. as Hd. Engl. Dept., ibid, 1967. Memberships: Past Mbr., Poetry Soc. Am.; Diversifiers, Kan. City. Published works: Many-Angel River, 1938; The Slender Screen, 1967. Contbr. to: Over 30 anthols. & textbooks inclng: Poetry Soc. Am. Anthol., 1946, Golden Spurs, 1962, & Shining Bridges, 1965, '70; (jrnls.) Irish Digest; Women & Beauty; Sat. Review; Atlantic; Univ. Review; Lit. Quarterlies of Univs. of Colo., NM, Ariz., Seton Hall, Kan., Northwestern, etc.; NY Times; Kan. City Star; NY Herald Tribune; Christian Sci. Monitor; Ladies He Jrnl.; Sat. Eve. Post; Good Housekeeping; McCalls; Engl. Jrnl.; Nat. Parent Tchr.; Columbia; Wash. DC Star; Wash. DC Post; Poetry World; Author & Jrnlist.; Ave Maria; Portal; Classmate; Am. Mercury, etc. Honours, Awards: Annual Free Verse Prize, Kan. City Univ.; Rdr. of own poems on Am. Poets Series, 1968; Dir., Poetry Workshop, Univ. of Kan. Writers Conf., 1957-58; One of 6 Midwest poets sent by Kan. Cultural Arts Commn. to appear in HS's & Community Colls., SW Kan., 1971. Address: 3949 Oak St., Kansas City, Mo. 64111, USA.

MINOR, Pearl (Jeffords), b. 15 Jan. 1903. Retired Librarian. Education: B.A., & M.A., Univ. of Iowa; M.A., Library Science, Drexel Univ.; Writers Workshop (a grad. course leading to MFA degree), Univ. of Iowa, 1966-1968, and 1971-. Married Loyal Leonard Minor. Positions held: Engl. Teacher, Norway, Iowa HS., 1924-1926; Canton S.D. HS., 1926-1929; Waukon, Ia., HS & Jun.Coll., 1930-1931; Teacher, Edith McCurdy Mission School, Santa Cruz, NM., 1933-1935; Engl. Teacher, Van Meter, Iowa, HS., 1935-1937; Librarian, Mason City, Iowa, Pub. Library (rural extension), 1938-1941; Librarian, Mason City, Iowa, HS & Jun. Coll., 1945-1966 (also Teacher part-time). Memberships: Iowa Poetry Assoc. (past pres., member of the Board, editor HS contest); Midwest Fed. of Chaparral Poets (treasurer, one of three on board of governors); Nat.League of Am. Pen Women (treasurer, Iowa City Branch); has also held many other offices in past. Contbr. to: Mason City Globe-Gazette; Christian Century; Different; Flame; Cyclo-Flame; The Muse; The Lyric; Epos; American Bard; Cape Rock Quarterly; Bitterroot; Candor; Midwest Chaparral Mag.; Caravan; Wisconsin Poetry Mag.; Lyrical Iowa; Midwest Poetry Review; New Orlando Anthol.; Writers Notes & Quotes; Scimitar & Song; New Atheneum; Yearbook of Mod. Poetry; Avalon Anthol.; Nat. Poetry Anthol.; Sea to Sea in Song; Boulders & Flints; Cyclotron; Poets of the Midwest; Cats Mag.; The Morning Press (Bloomsburg, Pa.), etc. Awards: Lyrical Iowa (Iowa Poetry Assoc.) 1956 Hon. Mention; 1963, 3rd prize main contest; 1968, Members only award; 1967, Hon. Mention; 1969, 2nd prize main contest; 1970, Members only award; 1971, 3rd prize main contest, etc. Address: 411 E. Market St., 304A, Iowa City, IA. 52240, USA.

MINTZ, Martha Annie, pen name **MINTZ, Mattie,** b. 6 Apr. 1916. Writer. Widow of James Mintz, 5 children. Contbr. to: Amateur Writers Jrnl.; Electrical Workers Jrnl.; Springfield Daily News; West Side Story (weekly newspaper); Yearbook of Modern Poetry. Honours, awards: 1st pl., Poetry Contest at Christis Gardens, Gatlinburg, Tenn., 1968. Address: 3962 Greenleaf Ave., Knoxville, TN 37919, U.S.A.

MINTZ, Ruth Finer, b. 25 Nov. 1919. Poet; Translator; Editor. Education: B.Hebrew Letters, Jewish Theol. Sem. of Am.; M.A., Engl. Lit., Univ. of Calif.; studied at Oxford Univ., U.K. & Hebrew Univ., Jerusalem. Married Prof. Yale Mintz, 1 son, 2 daughters. Memberships: Poetry Soc. of Am.; PEN Israel. Published works: Modern Hebrew Poetry – bilingual

(anthol. Ed. & transl. by Ruth Finer Mintz), 1967, '68; The Darkening Green (poems), 1965; Traveler Through Time, (poems), 1970. Contbr. to: Antioch Review; The Beloit Poetry Jrnl.; Poetry, Chicago; The Prairie Schooner; Poetry Northwest; Midstream; Ariel (Jerusalem); The Jerusalem Post; Carmelite (Haifa); Lamerhav (Tel Aviv); Encounter (UK); The Poet (India); N.Y. Times; Los Angeles Times, etc. Honours, awards: Florence Kovner Award for Poetry, Jewish Book Coun. of Am., 1966; Jewish Book Coun. of Am., for poetry, 1971; Hayiim Greenberg Award for Lit., 1973. Address: Neve Granot, Block 3 Entr. 5, Jerusalem, Israel & 10765 Cushdon Ave., Los Angeles, CA, U.S.A.

MISRA, R.A., b. 31 Dec. 1909 in U.P., India. University Professor (Emeritus). Education: Canning Coll.; Lucknow Univ., B.A., 1929, M.A., 1931, Ph.D., 1953. Positions held: Lecturer-cum-Fellow in Engl., Lucknow Univ., 1931-32; Prof. of Engl., Bareilly Coll., Bareilly (Agra Univ.), 1932-57; Head of Post-grad. Dept. of Engl., Bareilly Coll. (Agra Univ.), 1957-72; Dean of Faculty of Arts, Agra Univ., 1964-67; Mbr.; Senate, Exec. Council & Academic Council, Agra Univ., 1964-70; twice elected as Mbr. of the Court, Lucknow Univ.; Ex-Mbr. Exec. Committee, Indian Council for Engl. Studies; Ex-Mbr. Research Degree Committee, Agra Univ.; Guiding Doctoral Research in Engl. of seven Ph.D. students of the Agra Univ. at present; after retirement in 1972 awarded Univ. Grants Commission award of Professorship (Emeritus) of Engl. at Bareilly Coll.; Paper-setter & Examiner of a score of Indian Univs., and of sev. Public Service Commissions, including the Union Public Service Commission. Published work: Life's Fantasia (poems in English), with a foreword by Edmund Blunden; Gibbon's Autobiography (edited); Arnold's Sohrab & Rustum (edited); Standards of Life; 36 research papers & articles, etc. Address: 105-B Civil Lines, Bareilly, U.P., India.

MITCALFE, Barry, b. 31 Mar. 1930. Writer. Positions held: Former Lectr. in Polynesian Studies, Wellington Tchrs. Coll. & Chmn., Polynesian Inst.; Chmn. of the Peace Media Org.; Fndr. of Comm. on Vietnam, N.Z.; Former Nat. Exec. Mbr., PEN, N.Z. Sailed to Mururoa against French nuclear weapons. Published works: Thirty Poems, 1960; Poetry of the Maori, 1961; Writing, 1969; Maori Song, 1974. Contbr. to var. periodicals in Australia & New Zealand. Address: Private Bag, Tauranga, New Zealand.

MITCHELL, Adrian, b. 24 Oct. 1932. Writer. Positions held: Reporter, Oxford Mail; Reporter, Evening Standard: Pop Record Columnist, Daily Mail; Instr., Writers' Workshop, State Univ. of Iowa; TV Columnist, The Sun; TV Columnist, Sunday Times; Pop Record Columnist, Woman's Mirror; Columnist, Peace News; Edit. Bd., The Black Dwarf. Memberships: Poetry In Motion. Published works: Jazz Poems, 1963; Love Love Love, 1967; Children of Albion, 1969. Fantasy Poets No. 24, 1955; Poems, 1964; Peace Is Milk, 1966; Out Loud, 1968. Contbr. to: Black Dwarf; Peace News; Challenge; Sanity; East Village Other; New Yorker; New Departures; Flourish; Evening Standard; ICA Bulletin; Int. Times; London Mag.; Labour Monthly; Manchester Independent; New British Poetry; New Gambit; New Statesman; People's World; Poetry Review; Priapus; Resistance; Times Lit. Supplement; Sunday Times; Solidarity; Topolski's Chronicle; Transatlantic Review; Tribune; Underdog; Underground; Circuit; Wholly Communion; Animals' Friend; Cruse; Delta; Isis; Stand; Int. Socialism; Trio; New Writing; Kenyon Review; Viva Che; Chants Pour Le Vietnam; Ord Om Vietnam; etc. Awards & Honours: Gregory Award for Poetry, 1961; Granada Fellow, Univ. of Lancaster, 1967-69. Address: c/o Jonathan Cape Ltd., 30 Bedford Sq., London WC2, UK.

MITCHELL, (Sister) Elaine, O.P., pen name **MICHAUD, E.G.,** b. 25 Mar. 1920. Dietitian and Braille Instructor. Education: A.B., Theology Cert., Aquinas Coll., Grand Rapids; Dietary Cert., Int. Food Rsch. Ctr., Boston; Braille Instrn., Assn. for the Blind.

Positions held: Primary Teacher; Elementary Teacher; Certified Dietitian; Braille Instructor. Memberships: Intercontinental Biog. Assoc.; I.P.A.; Nat. Writer's Club; etc. Pubs: Love Has Many Voices, 1973. Contrib. to: Nat. Anthol. for Teachers & Librarians; Intercontinental Poetry Anthol.; Nat. Poetry Press, etc. Awards include: 1st place, Essay Contest opposing pornography, 1970; 1st place C.D.A. contest, etc. Address: 2025 E. Fulton, Grand Rapids, Mich., 40603, USA.

MITCHELL, Hugh Powers, b. 9 Nov. 1934. Social Worker. Education: B.A., Rollins Coll., 1958; M.A., N.Y. Univ., 1964; M.Soc. Work, State Univ. of N.Y., 1974; Rsch. Student, London Schl. of Econs. (Barnett Fellow), 1966-67. Married Barbara Hargate, 2 children. Positions held: Tchng. positions, 1958-64; Admnstrn. posts, 1965-69; Social work counseling, 1969–. Member, Rochester Poetry Soc., N.Y. Published works: Dream Tigers, 1963; Spirals, 1964; Recessional, 1969. Contbr. to: Best Poems of 1963; var. Univ. jrnls. & local pamphlets. Address: 147 Hillside Ave., Rochester, NY 14610, U.S.A.

MITCHELL, James Alvin, b. 28 Aug. 1920. Dentist; Poet; Scouter; Farmer; Cattleman. Education: B.A., Westminster Coll., Fulton, Mo.; D.D.S., Wash. Univ. Schl. of Dentistry, St. Louis, Mo.; M.S., Georgetown Univ. Positions held: Student Instr., Coll.; Sunday Schl. Tchr.; Supt., Ch. Schl.; Elder, Opelousas Presbyn. Ch.; Bd., Review, Eagle Scouts of St. Landry Parish. Memberships: La. Cattlemen's Assn.; Mo. Dental Bd.; Am. Dental Assn.; La. Dental Assn.; State Treas., La. State Poetry Soc.; W.Va. Poetry Soc.; Deep South Writers & Artists Conf.; Acad. Am. Poets. Published works: Heart to Heart Verse, 1967. Contbr. to: Lyric La.; Opelousas Daily World; La. State Poetry Soc. Yearbook, 1967-69; Swordsman Review; New Orleans Times Picayune; Poet Lore. Honours, awards: Winner, 250th Anniversary of New Orleans Contest, 1968; La. State prizes, 1968. Address: 448 South Union St., Opelousas, LA 70570, U.S.A.

MITCHELL, Robby Koons, b. 2 Apr. 1916. Housewife; Bookkeeper; Housing Manager; Poet Laureate of Texas. Education: N. Tex. State Univ.; Univ. of Tex. Married Dr. Glenn Mitchell, 4 children. Positions held: Timekeeper, N. Am. Aviation, 1943-45; Saleslady, Neiman-Marcus, 1945-47; Bookkeeper & Receptionist, Mitchell Clinic, 1947-52; Mgr., Shaunlyn Homes, 1963-70. Memberships: Pres., Mockingbird Chap. & Councillor, Poetry Soc. of Tex., 1969-70; Past Pres., En Ami Lit. Club, 1950-51; Dir., Xi Eta Eta Chap., Beta Sigma Phi; Acad. Am. Poets. Publications: Mockingbird's Song in the Night, 1956; Fire & Frost, 1963; And Burn my Brand, 1970. Contbr. to: Victoria Advocate; Dallas Times Herald; Stars & Stripes; McKinney Examiner; The Penny-Saver; McKinney Courier-Gazette; A Tex. Sampler; World's Fair Anthol.; Radio KVOO & KMAE; McKinney H.S. Yearbook, 1970, etc. Honours: Winner, Dist. Fed. Women's Club Contest, 1967; 2nd Humorous Poetry Contest, Mockingbird Chapt., 1970; 3rd, Hist. Poetry Contest, Mockingbird Chapt., 1971; Appointed Poet Laureate of Tex., 1970-71. Address: 405 N. Waddill, McKinney, Tex. 75069, USA.

MITCHELL, Roger, b. 8 Feb. 1935. Teacher. Education: A.B., Harvard Coll., 1957; M.A., Univ. of Colo., 1961; Ph.D., Manchester Univ., 1963. Positions held: Instr. & Asst. Prof., Univ. of Wis., 1963-68; Asst. Prof. & Assoc. Prof., Marquette Univ., 1968–; Ed., The Minn. Review, 1973–. Published works: Another Time (w. Sy Kahn), 1968; Reading the News, 1969; Letters from Siberia & Other Poems, 1971; In a Meantime, 1971; Edges, 1973. Contbr. to: New Republic; Colo. Qtly.; Nation; Beloit Poetry Jrnl.; Minn. Review; Chicago Tribune; Carleton Miscellany; Trace; Times Lit. Supplement; Tribune, etc. Honours, awards: Abby M. Copps Award, 1971; Poetry Award, Coun. for Wis. Writers, 1972; Midland Poetry Award, 1972; Borestone Mt. Awards, Best Poems of 1972, 1973. Address: 3129 N. Shepard, Milwaukee, WI 53211, U.S.A.

MIX, Amelia Evans, b. 29 Nov. 1912. Homemaker; Poet. Education: Columbia Coll. & Univ. of Mo. Married Alva L. Mix, 1 son, 3 daughters. Positions held: Private Tchr. in Speech & Dramatics; Sec. Memberships: Kan. City Br., Nat. League Am. Penwomen; Am. Poetry League; Mo. Writers Guild; Pres., Boonville Creative Writers. Published works: Scarlet Leaves (book of poems), 1970. Contbr. to: Moonage Poets anthol., 1970, Yearbook of Modern Poetry, 1971; Golden Anthol. of Poetry, 1971; Oregonian; Kan. City Star; Ideals; The Ch. Schl.; Christian Home; Cameron News Observer; Cameron Citizen; The Christian Bethany Guide; Creativity Newsletter; DeKalb County Heritage; Cyclo-flame; Bardic Echoes; Modern Images; Author-Poet; Scimitar and Song; Farmland; Farm Wife News; Jean's Jrnl.; Tejas; Creative Review; Am. Poetry League bulletin; S.W. Times Record; Springfield Daily News; Capper Weekly; Science of Mind; Quoin, etc. Honours, awards incl: 1st pl., Creativity Newsletter sweepstakes, 1967-70; 4 firsts, currently running 2nd pl.; 3rd pl., Mo. Fed. Clubs, 1971; 1st in Etheree, 3rd in Shakespearean Sonnet, 3rd in Poem for Child, 29th Annual Ark. Writers' Conf., 1973. Address: Harris Street Rd., Cameron, MO 64429, U.S.A.

MIZER, Raymond Everett, pen name **MIZER, Ray,** b. 29 Sept. 1918. University Professor. Education: B.A., Muskingum Coll., New Concord, Ohio, 1940; M.A., Ohio State Univ., Columbus, 1947; Ph.D., ibid, 1952. Positions held: Farmer; Jr. H.S. Prin.; U.S. Army, WWII; Instr. in Engl. & Communications, Grinnell Coll., Ia., 1947-50; Grad. study, Ohio State Univ., 1950-52; Prof. of Engl., DePauw Univ., Greencastle, Ind., 1952–; summer schl. of p/t tchng. at Albion (Bay View, Mich. Br.) & Butler Univ. Member, Ind. Coll. Engl. Assn.; Former Mbr., AAUP & MLA. Contbr. to: Indiana Sesquicentennial Poets, 1967; Motive; Kaleidoscope; College English; Carolina Qtly.; Am. Bard; Western Poet; Beloit Poetry Jrnl.; Flame; Fiddlehead; Am. Weave; Envoi; Epos; Sun; Kansas Mag.; Chatelaine; Quicksilver; Poetry Digest; Prairie Poet, etc. Honours, awards: Prize, State Contest, sponsored by Ind. Coll. Engl. Assn. & Ind. Sesquicentennial Commn., 1967; Nat. Fndn. for the Arts Award under Am. Lit. Anthol. Prog., 1969; A relig. drama 'Unto the Least of These' won nat. comp. sponsored by Gen. Bd. of Lay Activities of the Meth. Ch., 1967. Address: 711 Highridge Ave., Greencastle, IN 46135, U.S.A.

MOAT, John, b. 11 Sept. 1936. Writer; Poet. Education: Exeter Coll., Oxford Univ., UK. Married to Antoinette Moat, 2 children. Co-Founder of The Arvon Fndn. Published works: 6d per annum (poems), 1966; Heorot (novel), 1968; A Standard of Verse, 1969; Thunder of Grass (poems), 1970. Honours: Francis Steloff Fiction Award, 1967. Address: c/o A.D. Peters & Co., 10 Buckingham St., London, WC2, UK.

MOBLEY, Grace Fox. Housewife; Artist; Poet. Education: N. Tex. Tchrs. Univ.; Poetry studies w. poet Glen Coffield. Married to E. Lexter Mobley. Positions held: Tchr., 2 yrs.; Cashier, Tex. Bank; Auditor, Tex. Legislature, 5 sessions; Ch. Organist, 10 yrs.; Sang w. San Antonio Civic Opera. Memberships: Fla. State Poetry Soc., Inc.; Sarasota Music Club; World Poetry Soc. Intercontinental; various offices, Nat. League Am. Pen Women. Contbr. to: Selected Book of Poems, Fla. State Poetry Soc., 1967; Poet Intercontinental, 1969 & '70; United Poets Laureate Int., 1967 & '68; Creative Newsletter, 1968; Flamingo, 1969; International Hall of Fame Poets (4 poems), 1970; Nine Muses (11 poems), 1971. Awards: Cert. of Recognition, Nat. Poetry Day Comm., Inc., 1970; Merit Citation for Excellence of Poetry Form, Fla. State Poetry Soc., 1970; various prizes in other poetry contests. Address: 1767 Baywood Dr., Sarasota, Fla. 33581, USA.

MODAYIL, Anna Sujatha, b. 24 May 1934. Teacher and Social Worker. Education: M.A., English Literature, Univs. of Delhi and Bangalore; Post-Grad. degree in Social Work, Univ. of Edinburgh, Scotland, UK. Personal details: Father (Samuel Mathai), Vice-

Chancellor of Kerala Univ. Married: George Modayil, Orthopaedic Surgeon; 1 s. (Arjun). Positions held: Social work in UK and India; also teaching in India; Was one of 4 selected from India for Internat. Social Work Prog. at Minneapolis, 1969. Memberships: P.E.N. India; Abhinaya (Theatre-Poetry Group, Bangalore, Founder-Member). Published works: Crucifixions, 1970; We, The Unreconciled, 1972. Contbr. to: Gray Book (issue on "Indian Woman as Creative Artist"); Illus. Weekly of India (poetry page); Quest; Howard McCord's "Young Poets of India"; The Poet; Indian & Foreign News Review; P. Lal's Anthology, Modern Indian Poetry in English, 1969; Pritish Nandy's anthology, Indian Poetry in English-1947-1972, 1972; PEN Special Poetry Number, 1973; Dialogue India. Address: 49 Cunningham Rd., Bangalore 560052, India.

MODISANE, (William) Bloke, b. 25 Aug. 1923. Writer; Actor; Broadcaster. Divorced w. 1 child. Published works (other): The Dignity of Begging, (West African Review), 1962; The Situation, (the Reporter), 1964; Why I Ran Away, (Anthology), 1960; Sorry, No Coloureds, (Twentieth Century), 1962; Blame Me on History, 1963. Contbr. to (Anthols.): Modern Poetry from Africa, 1963; Poems from Black Africa, 1963. Address: 32A Chalcot Square, London, N.W.1., UK.

MOFFETT, Judith Lynne, b. 30 Aug. 1942. Educator. Education: B.A., Hanover Coll., 1964; M.A. (Engl.), Colo. State Univ., 1966; M.A. (Am. Civilization), Univ. of Pa., 1970; Ph.D. (Am. Civilization), ibid, 1971. Positions held: Asst. Prof. of Engl., Behrend Coll. of the Pa. State Univ., 1971–. Contbr. to: Contemporaries: Twenty-Eight New Am. Poets (anthol.); Poetry; Ga. Review; Minn. Review; Lyric; Contempora; Shaman; Southern Poetry Review. Honours, awards: Eunice Tietjens Meml. Award, Poetry Mag., 1973; Chosen to record a tape of poems & transl. for the Lib. of Congress archives. Address: Behrend Coll., Station Rd., Erie, PA 16510, USA.

MOFFITT, John, b. 27 June 1908. Writer; Poet; Editor. Education: A.B., Princeton Univ.; Composition, Curtis Inst. of Music; graduate, ibid, 1932. Positions held: Monastic Probationer, NY Ctr., Ramakrishna Order, 1933-35; Tchr., Spring Farm Schl., New Hope, Pa. 1935-36; Pvte. Tutor, 1936-39; Monastic Probationer, Ramakrishna Order, 1939-49; Novice, ibid, 1949-59; Monk, ibid, 1959-63; became a Roman Catholic, 1963; Copy Ed., 'America' Mag. (Nat. Cath. Review), 1963-70; Poetry Ed., ibid, 1963–. Publications: Engl. trans., the poems & hymns in Gospel of Sri Ramakrishna, 1942; This Narrow World, 1958; The Living Seed, 1962; Adam's Choice, 1967; Escape of the Leopard, 1974. Contbr. to: Atlantic; Antioch Review; Chelsea Review; Mod. Age; Noonday; Jubilee; Granta (Cambridge); Sat. Review; Springtime 2; Sewanee Review; Kenyon Review; New Yorker; Quixote; Prairie Schooner; Poetry Review; Va. Quarterly Review; Voices; Barat Review; America; Commonweal; Wormwood; Prism; Approach. Awarded 1 of 10 prizes in National Anthem Contest, USA, 1929. Address: Rocklands, Gordonsville, Va. 22942, USA.

MOGUL, Ebrahim, b. 1 Mar. 1918. Painter; Sculptor. Education: Nat. Dip. in Design, Camberwell Schl. of Art, London, U.K.: Ecole Nat. Supérieure des Beaux-Arts, Paris, France. Translator of poems of medieval Indian poet Bhartrihari into French, & a booklet currently in print which is illustrated with own original engravings. Illustrator of Deluxe publications. Address: 32 rue des Noirettes, CH 1227, Geneva, Switzerland.

MOHAMAD HAJI SALLEH, b. 26 Mar. 1942. English Tutor. Education: English Grad., Univ. of Singapore; Currently studying for M.A., Univ. of Malaya, Kuala Lumpur. Positions held: Tutor, Dept. of Engl., Univ. of Malaya, Kuala Lumpur. Published works: Since the Rain, 1970. Contbr. to (Anthols.): Commonwealth Poems of Today, 1967; Seven Malaysian and Singapore Poets, 1969; (Jrnls.): Poetry Singapore; Focus; Tenggara; Meanjin. Recip., Asia Foundation

Grant, 1969. Address: English Dept., Univ. of Malaya, Kuala Lumpur, Malaysia.

MOHAMMED, Faqir, pen name **GRACEFIELD, Robert H.,** b. 25 Dec. 1919. Editor; Civil Servant. Education: Wesleyan Collegiate H.S.; Maharaja's Coll. of Mysore Univ. Personal details: Related to the dynasty of His Majesty Martyr Sultan Tipoo, & son of Capt. Mohammed Ismail, Officer Cmndg. The Mysore Horse Regt. & War Recruiting Officer, WWI. Positions held: Cadet in Indian Army before WWII; Hon. Editor, Book-reviewer, Poetry Critic, 'Message' Weekly, New Delhi; Head of pooled Typists' Br., Indian Railways. Memberships: Life Mbr., The Cosmosynthesis League, Vic., Australia; Ex. Mbr., Royal Asiatic Soc. of Bengal. Published works: (book under ps. Robert H. Gracefield) Emotional Voice, 1938. Contbr. to: Rhythm (Calcutta); Wedding-Bells (New Delhi); The Lit. Half-Yearly; Caravan; Mysindia; Deccan-Herald Daily; Students Star; Message; Wayfarer-Gazette; Fact & Faith; Poetry-Hour-Annual (San Diego, Calif.); Bardic Echoes (Mich.); Stockwell Anthols. of Christmas Festival of Britain. Recip., Poetry premium prize from Wayfarer-Gazette, Somerset, U.K., 1949. Address: 3341 Eidgah Main Rd., Mysore 1, India.

MOHAN, K.E., b. 15 July 1934. Chief Engineer; Businessman. Education: Dip. in Civil Engrng. Positions held: former Civil Engr., Ctrl. P.W.D. Govt. of India; currently Chief Engr. & Ptnr., K.K. Ethirajulu Bhagavathar & Sons, undertaking Govt. contracts. Memberships: Lions Club of Kodambakkam – Lions Int.; Dir., Poets Workshop, Madras; Sec.-Gen., 2nd All India Poets Meet, Madras. Published works: Time; T.S. Eliot Identified – Four Quarters. Contbr. to: Poet; Tapovan Prasad. Address: K.K. Ethirajulu Bhagavathar & Sons, No. 5, Giriappa Road, Madras 600017, India.

MOKASHI-PUNEKAR, b. 8 May 1928. University Teacher. Education: K.E.B's Art Coll.; M.A., Karnatak Coll., Dharwar, 1953; Ph.D., ibid., 1965. Married w. 5 children. Positions held: Asst. Ed., Jayakarnatak, 1950-51; Music Critic, The Times of India, Bombay, 1965-67; Lectr. in Engl., Lingaraj Coll., Belgaum, India, 1954-56; Kishinchand Chellaram Coll., Bombay, India, 1956-61; Indian Inst. of Technol., Bombay, 1961-69; Asst. Prof., ibid., 1969–; Prin., Sri Poornaprajna Coll., Udipi, India, 1967-68. Published works: The Captive, 1965; The Pretender, 1967; Trans., The Cycle of Seasons, 1966; Other: The Later Phase in the Development of W.B. Yeats, 1966; P. Lal: An Appreciation, 1968. Contbr. to (Jrnls.): Illustrated Weekly of India; Times of India; Writers Workshop Miscellany. Address: Dept. of Humanities, Indian Inst. of Technology, Powai, Bombay 76, India.

MOLAND, Ruby Louise, b. 20 Sept. 1918. School Teacher; Poet; Housewife. Education: Normal Tchng. Cert.; Piano & Voice Studies. Married, 4 daughters. Positions held: Schl. Tchr., 4 yrs. Memberships: Am. Poets Fellowship Soc.; Eastern Ctr., Poetry Soc. of London; I.B.A. Published works: Spiritual Ways, 1973. Contbr. to: Independence 'News, Kans., 1970; The Valley Advertiser, N.Y., 1970; Poetry Preview, 1966 & '71; Poetry Parade, 1967-69; The Best in Poetry, 1968 & '69; Tejas, 1967-73; Guild, 1968-72; Canadian Lights, 1968; The Coast Guard, Shelburne; Major Poets; World Poets. Honours, awards: Three hon. cert. awards in Major Poets Contests, plus one Book Award for Free Verse Contest. Address: Box 417 Shelburne, N.S., Canada.

MOLL, Ernest George, b. 1900. Professor Emeritus of English. Education: Concordia Coll., Adelaide, Aust.; Harvard Univ., Cambridge, Mass. (M.A.) Positions held: Prof. of English, Univ. of Ore., Eugene, 1928-66; Prof. Emeritus; Exchange Lectr., Sydney Tchrs. Coll., 1939-40. Published works: Sedge Fire, 1927; Native Moments, 1931; Blue Intervals, 1935; Cut from Mulga, 1940; Beware the Cuckoo, 1947; The Lifted Spear, 1953; The Rainbow Serpent, 1962. Contbr. to (Anthols.): An Anthology of Australian Verse, 1952; A Book of Australian Verse, 1956; Boomerang Book of

Australian Poetry, 1956; New Land, New Language, 1957; Penguin Book of Australian Verse, 1958; Australian Poets Speak, 1961; Poetry in Australia II, 1964. Address: c/o Univ. of Oregon, Eugene, OR, USA.

MOLLET, Marette, b. 24 May 1940. Instructor. Education: B.S. in Educ. (Art & Engl.); M.A. in Art. Positions held: Art Instr., Lincoln Univ. Three one-man shows in painting & graphics. Memberships: N.Y. Poetry Forum; W.Va. Poetry Soc.; NFSPS. Honours, awards: E.A.R. Award for Characterization, 1973; Josephine Spinner Meml. Award, 1974. Address: Box 226, Lincoln Univ., Jefferson City, MO 65101, U.S.A.

MOLLOY, Martha Bankhead, b. 31 Dec. 1916. Art Teacher. Education: B.S., Home Econs. Educ.; Tchrs. Cert. in Art & Home Econs. Married Daniel Wilson Molloy, 1 son. Positions held: Tchr. of Art & Home Econs. at high schls. & colls., 10 yrs. Memberships: Exec. Bd. (twice), Ala. Writers' Conclave; Exec. Bd., Centro Studi e Scambi Int.; Ala. Chmn., World Poetry Day; Regent, Chaparral Poets, S.E.; Nat. League of Am. Pen Women; Am. Poetry League. Contbr. to num. anthols., newspapers, mags., jrnls. in U.S.A., France, U.K., Italy, Belgium, Canada, inclng: Anthol. of Am. Poetry; Modern Am. Muse; Fragments of Faith; Literary Gold; Blue Book of Am. Poetry; Bouquets of Poems; Wis. Poetry Mag.; Am. Poetry League Bulletin; Am. Bard; Midwest Chaparral; The Muse; Orphic Lute; Seydell Qtly.; Prairie Poet Anthol.; From Sea to Sea in Song, etc. Honours, awards incl: U.S. Congressional Cit. for Lit., 1962; Relig. poetry exhib. at Lambert Castle, the Int. Poets' Shrine, 1964; Medal of Hon. for Lit., Centro Studi e Scambi Int., 1966; Book dedication, ibid, 1973; Hon. doctorate. Address: 505 Vernon St., P.O. Box 304, Sulligent, AL 35586, U.S.A.

MOLOFSKY, Merle, b. 8 July 1942. College Teacher. Education: B.A., Brooklyn Coll., 1969; M.F.A., Columbia Univ. Schl. of the Arts, 1971. Positions held: Tchr., Tchrs. & Writers Collaborative w. P.S.75, Manhattan (tchng. creative writing), 1971; Adjunct Lectr., Brooklyn Coll. Adult Educ., 1971–; Lectr., Medgar Evers Coll., CUNY, 1971–. Member, MLA. Published works: 'Koolaid', 2 ode act plays, presented at TYC Forum, Lincoln Ctr., 1971. Short story published in Storefront. Address: c/o MedgEvers Coll., 317 Clermont Ave., Brooklyn, N.Y., U.S.A.

MO LO-FU, pen name **LO FU,** b. 11 May 1928. Editor. Education: Nat. Hunan Univ.; B.A., Tamkang Coll. of Arts & Scis. Married Chen Chung-Fong, 1 daughter, 1 son. Positions held: Navy Officer w. rank of Commander (ret'd); Chief Ed., the Epoch Poetry Quarterly. Memberships: Chinese Poets' Club, Taipei; Exec. Bd., Young Writers Assn. of China; United Poets Laureate Int., Manila; Centro Studi e Scambi Int., Italy. Published works: The Spiritual River, 1958; Death in the Stone-Cell, 1964; Poems of Beyond, 1967; A River Without Banks, 1970; The Mirror of a Poet (critical essays on poetry), 1969. Contbr. to: Epoch Poetry Quarterly; Young Lit. Monthly; Modern Lit. Monthly; Lit. Quarterly; Modern Chinese Poetry (trans. & selected by Wai-lin Yip); A Comprehensive Anthol. of Modern Chinese Lit. (co-ed.); Anthol. of Chinese Lit. Vol. 2 (ed. by Cyril Birch); Trace (Calif.); Northwest Review (Ore.); Contemporary Chinese Poetry from Taiwan (trans. & selected by A.J. Palandri). Honours, awards: 1st Prize, Chinese Poets Club, 1959; Disting. Poet Award, United Poets Laureate Int., 1970. Address: Wu-hsin St. Lane 239, No.54-2, Taipei, Taiwan.

MOMADAY, N. Scott, b. 27 Feb. 1934. Professor of English & Comparative Literature. Education: A.B., Univ. of N.M., 1958; A.M., Stanford Univ., 1960; Ph.D., ibid, 1963. Positions held: Asst. Prof. of Engl., Univ. of Calif., Santa Barbara, 1963-67; Assoc. Prof. of Engl., ibid, 1967-69; Prof. of Engl. & Comparative Lit., Univ. of Calif., Berkeley, 1969-72; Vis. Disting. Prof. of the Humanities, N.M. State Univ., 1972-73; Prof. of Engl. & Comparative Lit., Stanford Univ., 1973–; Vis. Lectr., State Univ. of Moscow, USSR, spring 1974. Published

works: Angle of Geese & Other Poems, 1974. Contbr. to: N.M. Qtly.; Sequoia; Southern Review. Address: Dept. of Engl., Stanford Univ., Stanford, CA 94305, U.S.A.

MONACO, Richard, b. 23 Apr. 1940. Writer. Education: Columbia Univ. Positions held: Asst. to the Dirs., Grp. for Contemporary Music, Columbia Univ.; Curator of Music, Columbia Univ.; Fiction & Poetry Ed., The Univ. Review; Assoc. Publisher & Ed., N.Y. Poetry; Co-Producer, N.Y. Poetry (WBAI-Radio); Tchr., Poetry Course, New Schl. for Soc. Rsch. Mbr., The Int. Poetry Soc. Published works: New American Poetry, 1973; The Logic of Poetry, 1974. Contbr. to: Prairie Schooner; The Univ. Review; N.Y. Poetry; Int. Poetry Soc. Anthol., 1974, etc. Address: 702 West End Ave., New York, NY 10025, U.S.A.

MONAHAN, James Henry Francis, b. 16 Dec. 1912. Broadcasting Administrator. Education: Christ Church, Oxford. Married Merle Park w. 6 children. Positions held: Critic & Reporter, Manchester Guardian, 1937-39; Admin., BBC, 1945–; Controller, European Services, 1952–. Published works: Far from the Land, 1944; After Battle, 1948; Other: Fonteyn: A Study of the Ballerina in her Setting, 1957; Ed., Before I Sleep...The Last Days of Dr. Tom Dooley, 1961. Contbr. to (Anthols.): Poetry of the Forties, 1968; (Jrnls.): Fortnightly; Listener; Nineteenth Century and After; Time and Tide. Hons: C.B.E., 1962.

MONDALE, Ruth Caroline, b. 26 Dec. 1908. Secretary; Newspaper Reporter. Education: Bus. Coll. Married Clifford T. Mondale. Positions held: Secretarial, news reporting, ch. organist & offices in the following orgs: Meth. Ch.; Nat. Fed. of Women's Clubs; Am. Guild of Organists; Am. Legion Aux.; United Meth. Women; League of Women Voters; Public Lib. Bd.; PTA; League of Minn. Poets (Clipping Chmn.); Midwest Fed. of Chaparral Poets (Treas. for 11 yrs.); Polio & Cancer Drives. Contbr. to: Midwest Chaparral; The Moccasin; Seydell Qtly.; Candor; Am. Poetry League; Yrbook Chaparral Writer; Mnpls. Sunday Tribune; Rochester Post Bulletin; Pine Island Record; The Am. Poets Speak, 1957, etc. Address: Box 336, Pine Island, MN, U.S.A.

MONILAWS, Ora Olivine, b. 3 Oct. 1909. Housewife. Positions held: V.P., Mothers Club in Oyster Bay, N.Y., 1935; Youth Grp. Dir., Syosset, 1944-46; Girl Scout, Brownie Ldr., 1940-50's; Pioneer Girls Club Guide, 1952-61; Comm. Chmn., ibid, 1962-67; Pioneer Girls Camp Bd., 1963-69; Pres., Missionary Soc. Memberships: Life Mbr., Int. Clover Poetry Assn.; Soc. of Designates, Wash. D.C. (with the title 'Danae'); Treas., Long Island Writers. Contbr. to: Verdure Mag., 1969-73; L.I. Writers Anthol.; Ideals; Clover Int.; Lib. Book, Poetry Soc.; Oyster Bay Guardian; Syosset Advance; Syosset Tribune; Kingsport Times, var. anthols., etc. Recip., Danae Award, 1969. Address: 54 Humphrey Dr., Syosset, NY 11791, U.S.A.

MONIRUZZAMAN, Mohammad, b. 15 Aug. 1936. University Professor; Poet; Writer; Broadcaster. Education: B.A., 1958, M.A., 1959, Ph.D., 1969, Univ. of Dacca; Rsch., SOAS, Univ. of London, 1969-70. Married Rashida Zaman, 1 son, 1 daughter. Positions held: Sunday Mag. Ed., Daily Millat, Dacca, 1957-58; Fellow, Rsch. Scholar, 1959-62, Lectr., Sr. Lectr., Asst. Prof., 1962-72, Assoc. Prof., 1972–, Dept. of Bengali, Univ. of Dacca, Bangladesh. Memberships incl: Fndr.-Pres., Gen. Ed., Poetry Bangladesh; Fellow, Royal Asiatic Soc., London; British Mus. Soc., London; Life Mbr., Bangla Acad., Dacca; Life Mbr., Asiatic Soc. of Bangladesh, Dacca; Pres., Natya Acad.; Pres., Bangladesh Sukanta Acad., Dacca; Bd. of Secs., Bangladesh U.N. Assn., Dacca; Dir., Int. Serv., Rotary Club of Dacca-North. Published works: Durlava Din (The Rare Day), 1961; Shankito Alok (The Frightened Light), 1968; Bipanna Bishad (The Distressed Sorrow), 1968; Anirvan, 1968; Sukh Asukh Sangsoy, 1973; Sadandi Udbed, 1973; Poems, 1967, 2nd ed., 1972. Has written over 1000 lyrics for Radio, TV, Films & Records. Poems translated into Engl.,

French, Russian, Hindi, Urdu & Japanese. Contbr. to var. jrnls. & newspapers. Recip., Bangla Acad. Award for Poetry, Dacca, 1972. Address: Dept. of Bengali, Univ. of Dacca, Dacca-2, Bangladesh.

MONTAG, Tom, b. 31 Aug. 1947. Freelance Researcher & Writer. Education: B.A., Dominican Coll., 1972. Married, 1 d. Positions held: Editor/publisher, Monday Morning Press, 1971–; Bugle-American poetry editor, Dec. 1971–; Editor, Margins: a review of little mags. & small press books, Aug. 1972–. Published works: Wooden Nickel, 1972; Twelve Poems, 1972; Measures, 1972; To Leave/This Place, 1972; Making Hay, 1973. Contbr. to: Wisconsin Review; Road Apple Review; Modine Gunch; Mojo Navigator(e); Harpoon; Bugle-American; The Mag.; Erratica; Sorts, etc. Address: 2912 N. Hackett, Milwaukee, WI 53211, USA.

MONTAGUE, John, b. 28 Feb. 1929. University Teacher. Education: B.A., Engl. & History, Univ. Coll. Dublin, 1949; M.A., ibid., 1952; Fulbright Scholar, Yale Univ., New Haven, Conn.; M.F.A., State Univ. of Iowa, Iowa City, 1955. Married Madelaine de Brauer. Positions Held: Worked for State Tourist Board, Dublin, 1956-61; Tchr., Poetry Workshop, Univ. of Calif., Berkeley, Spring 1964, 65; Univ. Coll., Dublin, Spring & Summer, 1967, Spring 1968; Currently, Tchr., Experimental Univ. of Vincennes. Published works: Forms of Exile, 1958; Poisoned Lands, 1961; Patriotic Suite, 1966; A Chosen Light, 1967; The Bread God, 1969; Other: Death of a Chieftain & Other Stories, 1964; Ed., The Dolmen Miscellany of Irish Writing, 1962; Ed., The Faber Book of Irish Verse, 1970. Contbr. to (Anthols.): Six Irish Poets, 1962; Mentor Book of Irish Poetry, 1965; New Modern Poetry, 1967; Modern British Poetry, 1969; (Jrnls.): Dublin Mag.; Irish Times; London Magazine; Encounter; Listener; New Statesman; Spectator; Agenda; Critical Quarterly; Les Lettres Nouvelles; Le Monde; Paris Review; Atlantic. Hons: May Morton Memorial Prize, 1960; Mbr., Irish Acad. of Letters. Address: 11 Rue Daguerre, Paris 14, France.

MONTEITH, Lionel, b. 6 Aug. 1921. Psychotherapist & Minister of Religion. Education: New Coll., London, U.K.; Univ. of London. Positions held: Chartered Surveyor's Pupil, 1939; Ed., Poetry Commonwealth, 1948-53; Min., W. Kensington Congl. Ch., 1957-64; Min., Christ Ch. & Upton Chapel, 1964-68; Chap., St. Mary Abbotts Hosp., 1959-64; Profl. Psychotherapy prac., 1959–; Dir., Lincoln Meml. Clinic, 1966–; Fndr., Christian Psychotheraphy Fndn., 1967–. Fellow, Int. PEN. Contbr. to: (U.K.) Outposts; Poetry Quarterly; Poetry Review; Poetry (Jrnl. of the Brit. Poetry Assn.); The Gate Int. Review; Prospect; Phoenix; Verse; (U.S.A.) Interim; Line; Poets Log Book; Variegation; The Poetry Book Mag.; The Contemporary Review of Poetry; (Argentina) English Folios; (Br. C'wealth) Thunderbird; Arena; Southerly; Trek, etc. Address: The Lincoln Tower, 77 Westminster Bridge Rd., London SE1 7HS, U.K.

MONTGOMERIE, William, b. 30 May 1904. Retired Lecturer. Education: M.A., Glasgow Univ., UK; Ph.D., Edinburgh Univ. Published works: Via, 1933; Squared Circle, 1934; A Selection of Three Poems, 1966. Contbr. to: BBC; New Poets British; The Modern Scot; Life & Letters Today; The Adelphi; New Poems; Poetry Scotland; Modern Scottish Poetry; The Saltire Review; Tape Recording, Harvard Univ., USA. Address: 11 Castle Terrace, Broughty Ferry, Dundee DD5 2EG, UK.

MONTGOMERY, Louise Moss, b. 22 Oct. 1892. Poet; Retired Teacher. Education: B.A. & M.A., Univ. of Miss.; UCLA; Columbia Univ. Positions held: Tchr., German & French, Delta State Coll., Cleveland, Miss.; Tchr., Spanish & Hist., Lausanne Schl. of Girls, Memphis, Tenn. Memberships: Past Pres., Northern Half, State of Miss. Poetry Soc.; Org. Pres., Delta Br.; Nat. League of Am. Pen Women; Poet Laureate, Miss. Soc., DAR. Published Works: Village Vignettes, 1949; Pharthon. Contbr. to: Christian Herald; Progressive

Farmer; Greenhouse, Memphis Tenn. Commercial Appeal & Press; Scimitar; poetry column, Clarksdale Miss. Press Register. Proclaimed Poet Laureate of Miss. Apr. 1973, by Gov. William Waller. Recip., numerous poetry awards. Address: 434 W 2nd St., Clarksdale, Miss., USA.

MONTGOMERY, Stuart, b. 1940. Publisher. Education: Univ. Coll., London. Married Deirdre Montgomery w 2 daughters. Positions held: Fndr., Fulcrum Press, London, 1965; Fndr., Assn. of Little Presses. Published works: Circe, 1969. Contbr. to (Jrnls.): Ambit; Matter.

MONTIS, Costas, b. 18 Feb. 1914. Civil Servant. Education: LL.B., Pol.Sci. & Econs., Athens Univ. Married, 4 children. Positions held: Jrnlst.; Lectr.; Ed. of lit. mags.; Fndr. of the first profl. theatre in Cyprus; Sec.-Gen. of the Chamber of Comm.; Dir. of Tourism.; Sr. Officer, Min. of Commerce & Industry, Cyprus. Memberships: V.P., Cyprus Lit. Soc.; V.P., Cyprus Assn. of Theatrical Writers. Published works: (all publd. in Greek) Me metro ke hois metro, 1934; Minima, 1946; Songs of Humble Life, 1954; Moments, 1958; Supplement to Moments, 1960; Poetry of Costas Montis, 1962; Letter to Mother, 1965; To an Unknown Human Being, 1968; From Beloved Cyprus, 1969; Nicosia, the.., 1970; Second Letter to Mother, 1972; Ke tot'en inalii Kypro, 1974. Three books transl. into English. Contbr. to many lit. mags. & newspapers in Greece & Cyprus. Honours, awards: First State Poetry Prize, Cyprus, 1969; Grand State Prize for his contbn. to Greek Literature, Cyprus, 1973. Address: P.O. Box 4040, Nicosia, Cyprus.

MOONEY, Alfred Leland, b. 26 Mar. 1907. Retired English Teacher. Education: B.S., Clarion State Coll., 1931; Grad., Adjutant Gen's Schl., 1943; post grad. work, Univ. of Pitts., U.S.A. Positions held: Tchr., Engl., Barnett Township H.S., 1927-30; Tchr., Engl., Duquesne H.S., 1931-67; Army Serv., 1942-46. Mbr., Pa. Poetry Soc. Published works: Eagle Feather, 1927; American Schoolboy, 1960. Contbr. to: N.Y. Times; N.Y. Herald-Tribune; Christian Sci. Monitor; Chicago Tribune; Wash. Evening Star; Denver Post; Indianapolis News; Rochester Democrat & Chronicle; Harrisburg Evening News; Rutland Herald; Hartford Times; Hartford Courant; Altoona Mirror; English Jrnl.; Wings; Kaleidograph; The Fiddlehead; The Lyric; Am. Bard; Am. Letters; Experiment; Epos; Prairie Poet; Poetry Caravan; Starlanes; The Elbeetee; The Lone Indian; The Old-Timer; The Am. Evangelist; Youth; The Fan; The Lone Scout, etc. Recip. of over 60 prizes awarded 1928 to present inclng. 3 Schumaker Prizes for best poem on Pa. Hist. Address: P.O. Box 28, Lamartine, PA 16375, U.S.A.

MOORE, Honor, b. 28 Oct. 1945. Poet; Writer. Education: B.A., Radcliffe Coll., 1967; Yale Schl. of Drama, 2 yrs. Positions held: Dir., Poetry Series, Manhattan Theatre Club, N.Y.C.; Produced 'The Nest', a play off-Broadway at the Mercury Theatre, N.Y.C., 1970. Contbr. to: American Review, No. 19, 1974; Women: The New Voice, Anthol., 1974; Sunbury, 1974; Litchfield Hills, 1974; Nova, 1971; Liberation, 1970; Leviathan, 1970. Address: 238 W. 22 St., N.Y., NY 10011, U.S.A.

MOORE, John E., b. 17 May 1913. College Teacher. Education: B.A., Univ. of Mich., 1936; M.A., ibid, 1937. Positions held: Engl. Instr., Penn. State, 1937-39; Engl. Instr., Western Mich. Univ., 1939-42; Instr. to Prof., Engl., Univ. of Mont., 1942-72 (ret'd). Member, World Poetry Soc. Published works: By Selkirk's Lake & Other Poems, 1972. Contbr. to: Epoch; Commonweal; Poetry Northwest; Poet. Recip., Major Hopwood Award in Poetry, Univ. of Mich., 1936. Address: 314 Connell Ave., Missoula, MT 59801, U.S.A.

MOORE, John Travers, b. 24 Aug. 1908. Poet; Author. Education: LL.B., Univ. of Dayton. Admitted to Ohio State Bar & U.S. Fed. Bar, 1933. Positions held: Prac. of Law, 1933-40; Mng. Ed., Plane Facts, official tech.

publ. of Air Service Command, 1941-45; Ed., var. publs., 1945-50; Full time Writer, 1951–. Published works: (poetry) A Child's Book of Psalms, 1946; Near Centerville, 1950; Poems, 1955; God's Wonderful World, 1964; My Prayer (as John Tripp); When You Walk Out in Spring, 1965; Cinnamon Seed, 1967; Town & Countryside Poems, 1968; There's Motion Everywhere, 1970; Poems: On Writing Poetry, 1971; Certainly, Carrie, Cut the Cake, 1971; We Are Like Wine, 1972; All Along the Way, 1973; (prose) Sing-Along Sary, 1951; Cincinnati Parks, 1953; Little Saints, 1953; Big Saints, 1954; Mod. Crusaders, 1957; The Three Tripps, 1959; On Cherry Tree Hill, 1960; The Story of Silent Night, 1965; The Little Band & the Inaugural Parade, 1968; Pepito's Speech at the United Nations, 1971. Contbr. to var. jrnls., anthols., etc. Address: 525 Ehringhaus St., Hendersonville, NC 28739, U.S.A.

MOORE, Joyce Inman, b. 29 Oct. 1927. Housewife & Poet. Education: Shoals High Schl., Ind., 1947. Published Midwest Caller from Apr. 1968 to Nov. 1970. Memberships: Ind. State Fed. of Poetry Clubs (Treas., 1971); Nat. Fed. of State Poetry Socs., Inc.; Nat. Amateur Press Assn.; United Amateur Press (Past VP); Gem State Writer's Guild, Idaho; Terre Haute Poets' Study Club, Ind. Published works include: Restful Hours of Poetry, 1964; Reflective Harvest, 1966; Lyric Legacy, 1968. Contbr. to the following anthols., jrnls., mags., etc: The Schoals News; Mason Co. Democrat; The Sumner Press; Johnson City Press-Chronicle; Midwest Caller; Quid Nunc; Lit. Newsette; Ashland Independent; Long Island Kernel; Grit; Pathway Press; Dell Publs.; Columbia Mag.; Ideals Publishing Co. Honours, awards: Trophy, First Place, Ind. State Fed. of Poetry Clubs, 1970; 1st Place Award Certificate, Nat. Amateur Press Assn., 1971; Outstanding Achievement in Writing, GSWG, 1967; Poet Laureate Award, UAPA, 1968; 1st place conventional poetry section award, 4th Trans-Atlantic competition, 1971; 1st place, 5th Trans-Atlantic competition, 1972; 2nd place also, and 1st place, patterned poetry section. Address: 119 E. Reel Ave., Vincennes, Ind. 47591, USA.

MOORE, Leona Pearl, pen name **MOORE, Leona Goodwin,** b. 18 July 1911. Housewife; Poet; Writer. Married Loyd A. Moore, 1 son, 1 daughter (dec.) Positions held: Sales Clerk; Sunday Schl. Tchr.; Sec.; Tex. Licensed Insurance Agent; Sales Rep., etc. Memberships incl: Life Mbr., Poetry Soc. of Tex. & Womens Soc. of Christian Serv. (Meth.); Pres. & Fndr. of Garland Chapt., Poetry Soc. of Tex., 1970-71, Second V.P. i/c Poetry Day (local) Observance, 1971; Nat. Fed. of State Poetry Socs.; Acad. of Am. Poets; Troao., Southwest Writers, Dallas, Tex., 1973-74; Chmn., Annual Awards Comm., ibid, 1973; Woodman of the World; Int. Platform Assn. Published works: Out of My Loss; The Golden Years; 'A Mothers Meditation', News, Views & Interviews, official paper of Meth. Youth Fellowship, 1949. Recip. num. honours & awards inclng: Quatrain Prize, Poetry Soc. of Tex., 1952; World Citizenship Prize, ibid Annual Awards, 1971; First Hon. Mention, New Year Contest, P.S.T., 1972; Selected for appearance on Ten Top Poets prog., 1973. Has donated var. awards to Poetry Soc. of Tex. Address: 3013 Browne Dr., Garland, TX 95041, U.S.A.

MOORE, Lucia, pen names **MOORE, Lane; GOLTRA, L.,** b. 8 Feb. 1887. Artist; Historian; Author. Education: B.A., Univ. of Oregon; studied Short Story under Mrs. Jacques Futrelle; Corres. in Short Story, Columbia Univ.; Famous Writer's School grad., 1968. Married, Dr. Harvard C. Moore, US Army Medical Corps (1915-45), retired with rank of Colonel. Positions held: Past Pres., Soroptimist Club, Eugene; Member Bd., Oregon Historical Soc.; Member (for 6 yrs.) Bd. of Oregon State Poetry Assoc.; Pres., Oregon Lewis & Clark Chapter, D.A.R.; Nat. League, American Pen Women, Past Pres., Eugene, Oregon Branch, Past Pres., Eugene Unit; also Past State Pres., NLAPW; Sec. Treas., Eugene Branch; Hon. Member, Int. Soroptimists. Memberships: Western Writers of America; NLAPW; Oregon State Poetry Assoc. Contbr. to: CS Monitor; American Bard; Okla. Today; Oregonian Verse; The Christian; Westways; Church Management; Hearthstone; The Muse. Awards: 1st prize, best poem, Oregon State Poetry Assoc., and 3 times winner (in same) for best humorous verse; 1st, Roseburg Writers Club; Gertrude Atherton Cup for short story (poetry), San Francisco BR Nat. League APW. Address: 65 West 30th Ave. Eugene, OR 97405, USA.

MOORE, Marianne Craig, b. 15 Nov. 1887. Writer. Education: Metzger Inst., Carlisle, Pa., 1896-1905; A.B., Bryn Mawr, 1909; Carlisle Commercial Coll., 1910; Litt.D., Wilson Coll., 1949; ibid, Mt. Holyoke Coll., 1950; Univ. of Rochester, 1951; Dickinson Coll., 1952; Long Island Univ., 1953; L.H.D., Smith Coll., 1950, Pratt Inst., 1958, Pace Coll., 1964; Litt.D., Douglas Coll., Rutgers Univ., 1955, Goucher Coll., 1960. Positions held: Tchr., Carlisle US Indian Schl., 1911-15; Vis. Lectr., Bryn Mawr Coll., 1953; Asst., NY Pub. Lib., 1921-25; Acting Ed., The Dial, 1925-29. Memberships: Nat. Inst. Arts & Letters; Am. Acad. Arts & Letters. Published works: Poems, 1921; Observations, 1924; Selected Poems, 1935; The Pangolin & Other Verse, 1936; What Are Years, 1941; Nevertheless, 1944; Collected Poems, 1951; The Fables of La Fontaine (trans.), 1954; Predilictions, 1955; Like a Bulwark, 1956; O To Be A Dragon, 1969; A Marianne Moore Reader, 1961; The Absentee (play), 1962; Three Tales From Perrault Retold, 1964; The Artic Ox, 1964. Contbr. of criticism & verse to mags. Honours: Dial Award, 1924; Helen Haire Levinson Prize, 1933; Ernest Hartsock Mem. Prize, 1935; Shelley Mem. Award, 1940; Contemp. Poetry's Patrons' Prize, 1944; Harriet Monroe Poetry Award, 1944; Guggenheim Mem. Fellowship, 1945; Nat. Inst. of Arts & Letters Award, 1946; Bollingen Prize, poetry, Yale Univ. Lib., 1951; Nat. Book Award, 1951; Pulitzer Prize, poetry, 1951; M. Carey Thomas Award, 1953; Nat. Inst. Arts & Letters Gold Medal for Poetry, 1953; Gold Medal, Poetry Soc. of Am., 1960 Nat. Medal For Literature, 1968. Address: 35 W 9th St., New York, NY 10011, USA.

MOORE, Mary Jane, b. 13 Jan. 1922. Homemaker; Writer. Education: HS Grad.; Creative Writing and Journalism Studies. Married, Lester Moore; 2 s., 2 d. Memberships: American Poets Fellowship Soc.; Poetry Soc. of Texas; Newspaper Inst. of America; Avalon Poets. Published works: Stillness and Simplicity (poems), 1967; Heir To A Pair of Boots (awaiting publication). Contbr. to: American Bard; Major Poets; Cyclo-Flame; Poetry Forum; Jrnl. Press, New Athens, Ill.; United Poets; Am. Poet; Prairie Poet; Poetry Soc. of Texas Yearbook, 1972; Internat. Who's Who In Poetry Anthol., 1972, etc. Awards: The Spiritual Direction Award; Poetry Soc. of Texas Yearbook, 1972 (at banquet, Dallas, Nov. 11, 1972); Citation for poems, Cyclo-Flame; Pegasus Award Cert., Cahokia Herald, Ill., etc. Address: 6025 Broadmoor, Corpus Christi, TX 78413, USA.

MOORE, Nicholas, b. 1918. Editor. Poet. Positions held: Has Edited, Poetry London & Seven. Published Works: The Island and the Cattle, 1941; A Wish in Season, 1941; The Cabaret, The Dancer, The Gentleman, 1942; The Glass Tower, 1944; Three Walls, 1944; Recollections of the Gala; Selected Poems, 1943-48, 1950; Other: The Tall Bearded Iris, 1956; Ed. w. others, The Fortune Anthology, 1942; Ed., The P.L. Book of Modern American Short Stories, 1945; Ed. w. Douglas Newton, Atlantic Anthology, 1945. Contbr. to (Anthols.): New Road, 1944; New Writing and Daylight, 1945; Little Reviews Anthology, 1946; (Jrnls.): Poetry; Adam; Poetry Review; Perspective; Changing World; Prairie Schooner; Furioso; English Folios; Million. Hons: Patrons Prize, Contemporary Poetry, 1945; Harriet Monroe Memorial Prize, Poetry, Chicago, 1947.

MOORE, Pamela, b. 28 March 1903. Social Worker. Education: Grad, 1920, Girls' Latin School, Boston; A.B., Radcliffe Coll., 1924; Special Study, Sorbonne,

1924-25; MSW Univ. of Washington, 1949. Married; 1 s. Positions held: In theatre for 9 yrs., followed with 30 yrs. in social work. Prior to retirement, Director, Soc. Service, Harborview Medical Center, Seattle. Contbr. to: Poets' Guild Anthol., 1972; Asian Student; Imprints Qtly.; Bulletin (King County Medical Soc.); My Weekly; Tail-Wagger; Young Crusader; Quoin; Friendship Ferry; Hyacinths & Biscuits; Scimitar & Song; Plume & Sword; Nutmegger; Haiku Highlights; Puget Soundings; Wanderlust; Poetry Digest; Caravel; Orphic Lute; Denver Post; Hartford Courant; Tacoma News Trib.; Radcliffe Qtly.; Swift Annual; Coins Mag.; Portland Press Herald; Social Work; Nat. Rehab. Journal; Survey Midmonthly. Honours: Proceedings, 8th Annual Conference of CAPP (Conf. for the Advancement of Private Practice in Social Work); Prize, Haiku, Thoreau Journal Qtly., July, 1973. Address: P.O. Box 49, University Station, Seattle, WA 98105, USA.

MOORE, Reginald Charles Arthur, b. 8 Aug. 1930. Journalist; Travel Writer. Education: Grammar Schl., Cambridgeshire; RAF Apprenticeship, St. Athan, S. Wales. Married, 1 daughter. Positions held: RAF Sgt./Navigator, 5 yrs.; Proof Rdr. & Reporter, Christchurch Press, New Zealand; Sports Reporter, Cambridge News; General Reporter, Crawley, Sussex; Berlitz English Tchr., Versailles, France; Proof Reader, Brighton; Freelance Jrnlst., 1968–. Published works: Sentiments, 1967; Free Spirits of the Pyrenees, 1971; Where the Mountains Meet the Sea, 1974. Contbr. to: Viewpoints; Rainbow; Headland; PEN (The Best in Poetry), 1968, etc. Address: 3 Cliff Gardens, Seaford, Sussex, U.K.

MOORE, Richard, b. 25 Sept. 1927. Poet. Education: B.A., Yale Univ., 1950; M.A., Trinity Coll., Hartford, Conn. Positions held: Lectr., Humanities, New England Conservatory of Music, Boston, Mass. Member, PEN. Published works: A Question of Survival, 1971; Word From the Hills, 1972. Contbr. to: The New Yorker; The Atlantic Monthly; Harper's Mag.; Sat. Review; The Reporter; Mademoiselle; The Listener; The Nation; Am. Scholar; Denver Qtly.; New Orleans Review; Ga. Review; Southern Review; Poetry; Modern Occasions; Countermeasures; The Hollins Critic; Mill Mountain Review; Transatlantic Review; Tuatara; Va. Qtly. Review; Poetry Northwest; Perspective; Sewanee Review; Salmagundi. Address: 81 Clark St., Belmont, MA 02178, U.S.A.

MOORE, T. Inglis, b. 28th Sept. 1901. Poet. Education: St. Paul's Coll., Univ. of Sydney; B.A., ibid; B.A., M.A., Univ. of Oxford. Positions held: Assoc. Prof., Univ. of the Philippines, 1927-30; Lectr., Adult Educ., Australia, 1931; Writer, Sydney Morning Herald; Dpty. Asst. Dir., Army Educ. Serv., WWII; Assoc. Prof., Australian Nat. Univ. Published works: Adagio In Blue, 1938; Emu Parade, 1941; Bayonet and Grass, 1957; We're Going Through (radio verse play), 1945; Six Australian Poets (criticism), 1942. Ed: Selected Poems of Henry Kendall, 1957. Contbr. to: (anthol.) Modern Australian Verse, 1964. Address: 79 Dominion Circuit, Canberra, A.C.T., Australia.

MOORE, Wanda Allen, b. 8 Dec. 1909. Retired Social Worker. Education: Drama major, Univ. of Wash., Seattle, Wash., U.S.A. Positions held: Soc. Wkr., State Dept. of Public Assistance, Seattle; Asst. Ed., Experiment Press, Seattle (simultaneously); Regl. Rep., The Poets' Guild (Idaho publ.); Poetry Ed., Japan Forum (Tokyo). Memberships: Avalon World Arts Acad., U.S.A.; The Scotian Pen Guild, N.S., Canada. Published works: Before Every Star, 1968; So Speaks the Dream, 1967. Contbr. to num. anthols., jrnls., mags., etc. inclng: (Canada) Can. Author & Bookman; Can. Forum; Can. Lights; Can. Poetry; Fiddlehead; Fireflower; Friendship Ferry; Haiku Mag.; Innovator; Inscape; Maritime Bapt.; Temp; Young Can.; Chatelaine; Alta. Poetry Yearbook, 1971 & 72; Idella; Pegasus; Salt; Fur & Feathers; (U.K.) Envoi; Expression One; Manifold; New Melody; Ore; Scip; Rainbow; The Thistle; Writer's Review; (Italy) Albo d'Oro; (Japan) Let's have a Chat; Japan Forum;

(U.S.A.) The Am. Evangelist; Bardic Echoes; Cyclo-Flame; Durango-Cortez Herald; Encore; Guardino Gazette; Hoosier Challenger; Harbor Lights; Imprints Quarterly; Legend; The Messenger; The Poets' Guild; The Union Jack; Accent; Am. Bard; Am. Courier; Am. Poet; Hartford Courant; N.Y. Herald Tribune; Scimitar & Song; These are My Jewels; New Melody; Melody of the Muse; Muse Anthol., 1963; Best Poems of 1960; Avalon Anthols., 1957, 59-63. Recip. many hons. & awards. Address: R.R.1 loco, B.C., Canada.

MORAES, Dom(inic Frank), b. 1938. Poet; Novelist; Writer. Education: Jesus Coll., Oxford Univ. Published works: A Beginning, 1958; Gone Away, 1960; Poems, 1960; Crooked Mile, 1964; The Brass Serpent (transl. of Hebrew poems), 1964; Kicking Horse, 1965; Kangaroo Summer, 1965; Gone Away: An Indian Journal, 1960; John Nobody, 1965; Poems 1955-65, 1966; My Son's Father, 1968. Contbr. to: Atlantic Monthly; Botteghe Oscure; Encounter; London Mag.; Listener; New Statesman; Observer. Address: c/o William Heinemann Ltd., 15-16 Queen St., Mayfair, London W1, UK.

MORDEN, Veatrice (Buck), pen name **MORDEN, Veatrice Victoria,** b. 16 Dec. 1899. Company Executive. Executrix, Leigh Emerson Morden Estate; related to Queen Victoria through grandfather, Frederick Simon. Positions held: President, owner and operator of Morden Oil Co., and of real estate holdings. Memberships: Nat. Fed. of State Poetry Socs.; Acad. of American Poets; Poetry Soc. of Michigan; Lansing Poetry Club. Published works: Reaching for the Stars (poems), 1974; Spring and Lilacs (a musicale), 1974. Contbr. to: Penninsula Poets; Evergreen Echos; Lansing State Journal; and has 20 songs registered in Library of Congress. Awarded Internat. Who's Who in Poetry Cert. of Merit, 1971. Address: 535 Townsend St., Lansing, MI 48933, USA.

MORENO, Virginia (nee Reyes), Pseudonym, **Pile,** b. 24 Apr. 1935. University Teacher. Education: B.Ph., M.A., Engl. Lit., Univ. of Philippines, Diliman, Rizal; Univ. of Kansas, Lawrence. Positions held: Mbr., Fac., Univ. of the Philippines, 1958–; Asst. Prof., Humanities, ibid., 1964–. Published works: Batik Maker and Other Poems, 1969; (Play), Straw Patriot: A Tragedy in Five Scenes, 1967. Contbr. to (Anthols.): New Writing from the Philippines, 1966; (Jrnls.): Sunday Times Mag.; Manila Chronicle; Literary Apprentice; Literature East and West; Beloit Poetry Journal; Literary Review; Encounter. Hons: Rockefeller Foundation Fellowship for Creative Writing, 1954; Fellowship, Breadloaf Writers Conf., Vermont, 1954; Mbr., 1st Philippine cultural mission representing Filipino poets to India & the Repub. of China, 1962. Address: 2457 Juan Luna, Tondo, Manila, Philippines.

MOREN VESAAS, Halldis, b. 18 Nov. 1907. Writer. Education: language studies, Tchrs. Schl. Married Tarjei Vesaas, dec. Memberships: Riksteatrets direction, 20 yrs.; Forfatterforeningens litteraere rad; Norsk Kulturrad, etc. Published works: (poetry) Harpe og Dolk, 1929; Morgonen, 1930; Strender, 1933; Lykkelege hender, 1936; Tung tids tale, 1945; Treet, 1949; I ein annan skog, 1955; (prose) 3 children's books, the novel Hildegunn, 1943, a biography Sven Moren og heimen hans, 1951, a book on Greek Mythology entitled Gudefjellet, 1970. Contbr. to: (newspapers) Dagbladet; Norsk Tidend; (periodicals) Vinduet; Syn og Segn. Recip., The Swedish-Norwegian Prize Dobloug-prisen; sev. prizes for translations, Racine, Shakespeare. Address: 3890 Ytre Vinje.Jac.Aallsgt. 9B, Oslo 3, Norway.

MOREY, Frederick L., b. 16 Apr. 1924. Professor of English (assoc. rank), District of Columbia Teachers Coll. Education: A.B., Ashland Coll., 1955; M.A., Univ. of Maryland, 1966; Ph.D., Howard Univ., 1970. Positions held: Sunday school teacher, Foundry Methodist Church, Washington, DC.; Organiser of three local poetry workshops in Maryland and D.C.;

Election judge, Brentwood, MD (1960's); Pres., Brentwood Garden Club, 1962. Memberships: Nat. Fed. of State Poetry Socs. (Vice Pres., 1972–); Maryland S.P.S. (Pres., 1971-72); Member, Mod. Language Assoc. Published works: Dickinsonic and Other Poems, 1972; Emily Dickinson Bulletin (since 1968); Higginson Journal of Poetry (since 1971). Contbr. to: Oberlin Yeoman; Poesy; Markham Review; Thought; Papers of the Bibliog. Soc. of America. Honours awarded, etc.: Feature on his journals, Baltimore Sunday Sun (27 May 1973); Passing mention, NY Times (22 May 1973); Hon. guest, Emily Dickinson stamp ceremonies, Amherst, Mass., (20-22 Aug., 1971). Address: Emily Dickinson Bulletin, 4508 38th St., Brentwood, MD 20722, USA.

MORGAN, Edwin (George), b. 27 Apr. 1920. University Teacher. Education: Glasgow Univ., U.K. Positions held: Asst. in Engl., Glasgow Univ., 1947-50; Lectr. in Engl., ibid, 1950-65; Sr. Lectr., 1965-71; Rdr., 1971–. Published works: The Vision of Cathkin Braes, 1952; Beowulf, 1952; The Cape of Good Hope, 1955; Poems from Eugenio Montale, 1959; Sovpoems, 1961; (Ed.) Collins Albatross Book of Longer Poems, 1963; Starryveldt, 1965; Emergent Poems, 1967; The Second Life, 1968; Gnomes, 1968; Proverbfolder, 1969; Twelve Songs, 1970; The Horseman's Word, 1970; (trans. Weöres in) Sándor Weöres & Ferenc Juhász, Selected Poems, 1970; Wi the Haill Voice, 1972; Instamatic Poems, 1972; Glasgow Sonnets, 1972; From Glasgow to Saturn, 1973; The Whittrick, 1973. Contbr. to: Akros; Lines Review; Scottish Int.; Listener; Times Lit. Supplement; New Statesman; Ambit; Stand; Second Aeon; Sunday Times. Honours, awards: Cholmondeley Award, 1968; Scottish Arts Coun. Publn. Award, 1968; Mem. Medal of Magyar PEN, 1972. Address: 19 Whittingehame Ct., Glasgow G12 0BG, U.K.

MORGAN, Frederick, b. 25 Apr. 1922. Writer; Editor. Education: A.B., Princeton Univ., 1943. Married Paula Deitz. Positions held: Co-Fndr., The Hudson Review, 1948; Ed., ibid, 1948–. Editor & contbr. to sev. anthols. Memberships: Acad. of Am. Poets; PEN. Published works: (coll. of poetry) A Book of Change, 1972. Contbr. to: The Hudson Review; The New Yorker; Art Int.; The Kenyon Review; The N.Y. Times; The Maine Times; The Sewanee Review; Commonweal; The Nation; The Southern Review; Encounter; Kayak; The Mich. Qtly. Review; Poetry Northwest; Tex. Qtly.; Christianity & Crisis; The New Republic; Poetry; The Am. Scholar. Nat. Book Award Nominee, 1973. Address: 65 East 55 St., N.Y., NY 10022, U.S.A.

MORGAN, Joan Elizabeth, b. 21 Apr. 1945. Artist; Composer; Writer. Education: Liberal Arts, Okaloosa-Walton Jr. Coll., Valparaiso, Fla.; de Burgos Schl. of Art, Georgetown, Wash. D.C.; summer study prog., Humanities, Rome, Florence (Italy), Geneva (Switzerland), Paris (France) & London (UK), sponsored by Am. Int. Acad., Salt Lake City, Utah. Positions held: Pharmacist's Asst., Montgomery, Ala. & Ft. Walton Beach, Fla. Member, Int. Platform Assn. Published works: Isles of Thought, 1966; Merchant of Memory, 1973. Contbr. to The Soul & The Singer (anthol.), 1968. Address: 3 Miller St., Ft. Walton Beach, FL 32548, U.S.A.

MORGAN, Pete, b. 7 June 1939. Writer. Positions held: Commnd. in Army (Infantry), 1959, resigned 1963; worked in advertising & jrnlsm., –1969. Member, Poetry Soc. Published works: A Big Hat or What? 1968; Loss of Two Anchors, 1970; Poetry: Introduction 2, 1972; Poems for Shortie, 1973; The Grey Mare Being the Better Steed, 1973. Contbr. to: Akros; Ambit; Capella (Dublin); Lines Review; New Statesman; Poetry (Chicago); Poetry Review; Second Aeon; The Scotsman; Scottish Int.; Solstice (Cambridge); Spirit (N.J.), etc. Broadcasts: BBC Radio, 1, 2, 3 & 4; BBC TV; ITV. Honours, awards: Writers Bursary, Scottish Arts Coun., 1970; Arts Coun. of G.B. Award, 1973. Address: c/o David Higham Assocs., 5/8 Lower John St., Golden Sq., London W1R 4HA, U.K.

MORGAN, Robert, b. 17 Apr. 1922. Schoolmaster, Head of Remedial Dept., in Comprehensive School. Education: Penrhiwceiber Sec. School, Glamorgan, Wales; Glamorgan Tech. Coll.; Fircroft Coll., Birmingham, UK; The Coll. of Education, Bognor Regis, Sussex; Univ. of Southampton, Hants. Married, 2 d. Membership: Soc. of Authors. Published works: The Night's Prison (50 poems & verse-play), 1967; Poems & Extracts, 1968; On The Banks Of The Cynon, 1973; Keepsake Poems, 1973. Contbr. to: Anglo Welsh Review; Blackfriars Review; BBC; Dublin Review; Hibbert Journal; London Welshman; Poetry Wales; Panache; Planet; Poetry India; Hampshire Poets; Review of Internat. Eng. Lit.; Review of Eng. Lit.; Southern Arts Mag.; The Use of English; Transatlantic Review; The New Statesman; Tribune; Workshop New Poetry; Welsh Voices, etc. Address: 44 Martin Ave., Denmead, Portsmouth, Hants. PO7 6NS, UK.

MORGAN, Robert Ray, b. 3 Oct. 1944. University Teacher. Education: B.A., Univ. of N.C., Chapel Hill, 1965; M.F.A., Univ. of N.C., Greensboro, 1968. Positions held: Instr. in Engl., Salem Coll., Winston-Salem, N.C., 1968-69; Farmer & Writer, Hendersonville, N.C., 1969-71; Lectr. & currently Prof., Cornell Univ., Ithaca, N.Y., 1971–. Published works: Zirconia Poems, 1969; The Voice in the Crosshairs, 1971; Red Owl, 1972. Contbr. to: Lillabulero; Am. Scholar; The Nation; Southern Poetry Review; The Am. Review; Epoch; Greensboro Review; New Direction; Choice; Little Mag.; Granite; N.C. Folklore Jrnl.; Sumac, etc. Recip., Grant, Nat. Endowment for the Arts for writing poetry, 1968. Address: RD4 Comfort Rd., Ithaca, NY 14850, U.S.A.

MORINA d'AGIRA, Domenico Maria, pen name **MORINA, Mimmo,** b. 4 Aug. 1933. Journalist; Consultant in Public Relations; Translator. Education: LL.D., Univ. Positions held: Lawyer; Teacher of Italian; Publicist; Journalist; Poet; Dir., New Europe, Case Postale 212, Luxembourg. Membership: Int. Assoc. of Poetry, Rome, Italy. Published works: I Want To Pay Myself, 1955; Le Fragole, 1964; Psyche, 1967; Sei Tu La Terra, 1970; De Slinger, 1973; C'est Toi La Terre, 1973; Contrappunto, 1974; European Contemporary Poetry (record, recited by Tun Deutsch), 1968. Contbr. to: Luxemburger Wort; Il giornale dei Poeti; Silarus; La Parola del Popolo; Alla Bottega; La Fiera Letteraria; Echi d'Italia; România Literara. Awards: Nat. Poetry Prize, Nicola Scarano, 1968; Culture Prize, Presidency of Cabinet Coun., Italian Republic, 1969. Address: 32 rte. de Kehlen, Mamer, Luxembourg.

MORNE, (Signe) Barbro, b. 6 Feb. 1903. Library Amanuensis. Educ: Matriculation; Lib. Course. Positions held: Lib. Amanuensis, Helsingfors Town Lib. Memberships: Finland's Swedish Author Assn. Published works: (poetry) Tystnadens spar, 1923; Bild och syn, 1927; Dikter, 1933; Trädet i vinternatten, 1942; Jag bands av arets tider, 1948; Läggspel (prose), 1950; Vingar, skuggor, segel, 1951; Namnlös ort, 1953; Skymningsrummet, 1956; Den du är, 1959; (storybook) Garden som försvann, 1946; Filips resa runt jorden, 1948; Dikter i urval, 1970; (play) Aventyr i Florios land, performed by Swedish Theatre, Helsingors & Stockholm's Radio. Contbr. to: Vi; Nya Argus; Lucifer & other Christmas publs.; Story; Horisont; Hufvudstadsbladet. Honours, awards: Literary Nat. Prize, 1927; Prize, Langmanska Fund; Grant, Finland's Swedish Author Assn. Address: Grankulla, Finland.

MORPURGO, John De, b. 3 Jan. 1923. Company Executive. Education: 1st Class Hons., Oriental Langs., King's Coll., Cambridge, 1948. Mbr., Workshop Two. Publications: XXX Poems, 1969. Contbr. to: Janus, Paris; Workshop, UK. Address: 27B Hampstead Hill Gardens, London NW3, UK.

MORRIS, Bernard Newth, pen name **MORRIS, Bernie,** b. 11 Nov. 1919. Ordained Minister; U.S. Navy Chaplain; Administrative Director of an Older American Volunteer Program. Education: A.B.,

Eastern Baptists Coll.; S.T.B. & S.T.M., Temple Univ. Schl. of Theol. Married Lorraine W. Weiderhold, 1 son, 3 daughters. Positions held: Min., Bapt. Churches, Passic, N.J. & Glenolden, Pa.; Chaplain, U.S. Navy, 8 yrs.; Min., 1st Bapt. Ch., Schenectady, N.Y. & Pine City, N.Y.; Dir., Older Americans Volunteer Prog., Watkins Glen, N.Y. Memberships: Major Poets of Am.; Avon Soc.; Writers Guild; The Kiwanis Club – Poet of Grp.; Trustee, Capital Area Bapt. Soc.; Pres., Bapt. Retirement Ctr. Published works: (books) Harmony of Words, 1965; Harmony of Truth, 1972; Harmony of Sermons, 1973; Harmony of Hope, 1974. Contbr. to: Schenectady Gazette; Schenectady Union Star; Albany Times Union; Dimension; New Dawn Publs.; Elmira Star Gazette; Watkins Review, & num. articles & poems in sev. newspapers & anthols. & for many groups professionally & privately. Recip., Nat. Musical Award, 1937 & '38. Address: Box 202, R.D. 1, Rock Stream, NY 14878, U.S.A.

MORRIS, James Cliftonne, b. 18 Dec. 1920. English Instructor. Education: B.S., Columbia Univ., 1949; M.A., ibid, 1950; studied poetry writing under late Leonora Speyer, Columbia Univ., 4 yrs. Married Gladys Reynolds. Positions held: Jr. H.S. Tchr. in capacity of Dept. Chmn. for the past 18 yrs.; Evening Tchr., Queensborough Community Coll., N.Y.C., in Black Lit. & Composition Writing; Has lectured on the nature of poetry, short stories & Engl. tchng. essay techniques, N.Y.C. Selected to rep. N.Y.C. Bd. of Educ., Jr. H.S. Div., on Engl. tchng., ABC TV Spotlight, 1971. Memberships: Exec. Bd., N.Y.C. Assn. of Tchrs. of Engl. (Jr. H.S. Div.), 5 yrs.; Poets & Writers Inc.; Black Poets Speaking; Int. Clover Poetry Assn., etc. Published works: Cleopatra, & Other Poems, 1955; From A Tin Mouth God to His Brass-Eared Subjects, 1966. Contbr. to: The Phylon Qtly.; Negro Digest; Black World; Black Poetry for All Americans; Nat. Poetry Anthol.; Shore Poetry Anthol.; Poetry Parade; Outstanding Contemporary Poetry; Buffalo Courier Express; Fragments of Faith, etc. Honours, awards incl: Poetry selected to be read on Christmas Day, BBC, London, 1963; Poem Selected among TV CBS, Spotlights on Black Verse, 'Beyond the Blues', 1967; Sonnet Award, Major Poets Award, 1972. Address: 174-31, 126 Ave., Springfield Gdns., NY 11434, U.S.A.

MORRIS, John Nelson, b. 18 June 1931. Teacher of English Literature. Education: A.B., Hamilton Coll., 1953; A.M., Columbia Univ., 1956; Ph.D., ibid, 1964. Married, 3 children. Positions held: Instr., Univ. of Del., 1956-58; Lectr., Instr., Asst. Prof., Columbia Univ., 1958-67; Assoc. Prof., Prof., Wash. Univ., 1967–. Published works: Versions of the Self (criticism), 1966; Green Business, 1970. Address: Poetry; New Yorker; Sewanee Review; Harper's; Hudson Review; New Republic, etc. Address: Dept. of Engl., Wash. Univ., St. Louis, MO 63130, U.S.A.

MORRIS, Linda Marlene (Cochrane), pen name **COCHRANE, Micky,** b. 12 July 1950. Student. Education: B.A., Carson Newman Coll., 1973; currently PFC, U.S. Army. Memberships: World Poetry Soc.; Hypatian Lit. Soc.; Calliopian Lit. Soc.; Pres., Allusion. Published works: Introspection – a trip inward, 1973. Contbr. to: Poet; Pegasus; Annual Anthol. of Coll. Poetry; Allusion; Chiarosaro; Hypatian Lit. Review; White County News; Standard Banner; RBA-70 Poetry Review. Address: 2911 Pharr Ct., Apt. 1538, Atlanta, GA 30305, U.S.A.

MORRIS, Mervyn, b. 1937. University Warden. Education: Univ. of the West Indies, Kingston; Rhodes Scholar, St. Edmund Hall, Oxford. Positions held: Formerly Asst. Registrar, Univ. of the West Indies & Senior English Master, Munro Coll.; Warden, Taylor Hall, Univ. of the West Indies, 1966–. Published works: Other: Feeling, Affection, Respect (Essays), 1963. Contbr. to (Anthols.): Independence Anthology of Jamaican Literature, 1962; Young Commonwealth Poets, '65, 1965; Caribbean Literature, 1966. Address: Taylor Hall, Univ. of the West Indies, Mona, Kingston 7, Jamaica.

MORRIS, Michael Spence Lowdell, pen name **MORRIS, Michael,** b. 31 Jan. 1940. Research Scholar and Author. Education: South African Coll. School; South African Police Coll.; Union Coll.; Univ. of South Africa. Positions held: Currently, Research Scholar of Conflict in Southern Africa; former Member S.A. Police (Internal & Border Service); Founder & Editor, S.A. Poetry Journal, Poetry South. Memberships: Poetry Soc. of S. Africa; Poetry Soc. of Rhodesia. Published works: (poetry) The Only Peace is Death, 1972; Requiem, 1971; Phoenix, 1971; Redfive, 1969; Now That I'm Dead, 1968; Dreams of War, 1967; A Passion For Home, 1966; The Sweetness and the Sadness, 1964; (other subjects) Terrorism, 1971; Fuzzversus, 1973; Chimurenga, 1974. Contbr. to: New Coin; New Nation; Two Tone; The Cape Times, etc. Honours: Best Student of Year, S.A. Police Coll. (Premier's Award), 1968. Address: P.O. Box 1464, Cape Town, Republic of South Africa.

MORRIS, Richard, b. 26 Feb. 1909. Actor-Producer; Writer; Poet. Education: Wesley Coll., Dublin, Ireland. Positions held: Dir. & Producer, Richard Prestwick Repertory Co., 1935-36; Dir. & Prod. Shakespearean Co. Plays & Music in Air-Raid Shelters; Pres., Sheen Players DS, 1943-55; Verse Recitals, Kingsway Hall, 1947-48; Drama Instr., Borough of Willesden, London; Dir., New London Theatre Group, 1947-55; Dir., New Torch Theatre, London, 1951-55; Dir., Groupe Richard Morris, Geneva, Switzerland; Presenter of world's only 1 Actor–10 voice version of Hamlet, Royal Festival Hall, London; Theatre de la Cour St. Pierre, Athenee, Geneva, & in Dublin, Zurich, Brussels, Paris, Antwerp, Louvain, The Hague, Rotterdam, Amsterdam, etc.; Lectr. on Shelley, Keats, Byron, Donne, etc., Royal Festival Hall, London, 1956-60; Fndng. Pres., Les Treateuax Libres, 1967; Creator & Prod., 'One-Man Beatnik', contemporary revue w. verse, 1970. Memberships: Former Organizing Sec., Shaw Soc., London; Former Comm. Mbr., John O'Londons Lit. Circle; Pres., Geneva Arts Club; Cons. Mbr., Cartel des Théâtres de Geneve; Pres., Assoc. des Amis du Museé d'Instruments Anciens de Musique. Publications: Cocktails With the Captain; Norfolk Island (1 act plays); Considered Trifles, 1967; Desarmer ou Mourir, 1969; Poor Byron (biog.) & lyrics, sonnets, short stories & playlets. Honours: Winner, Poetry Recital, London Civil Defence Contest, 1944. Address: 'Riverrun', 1295 Tannay, Switzerland.

MORRIS, Stephen, b. 14 Aug. 1937. Senior Lecturer. Education: Univ. Coll., Cardiff, U.K.; Leicester Univ.; Moseley Art Schl.; Fircroft Coll.; Marieborgs Coll., Sweden. Married, 3 children. Positions held: Asst. Lectr., Mansfield Coll.; Lectr., Wolverhampton Coll. of Art; Sr. Lectr., Fac. of Art, Wolverhampton Polytechnic. Member, Poets Conf. Published works: Alien Poets, 1965; Wanted, 1968; Doubts & Memories, 1969; Penny Farthing Madness, 1969; Born Under Leo, 1971; The Revolutionary, 1972; The Kingfisher Catcher, 1974. Contbr. to: The Guardian; The Sunday Times; The Observer; Time Out; Rolling Stone; Daily Mirror; Tribune; Peace News; Second Aeon; S.B. Gazette; Poetry India; Int. Times. One Man Exhibs: Wolverhampton Art Gall. (Visual Poetry), 1972; New Lane Gall., Bradford (Visual Poetry), 1972; Focus Gall., Nottingham (Visual Poetry & Paintings), 1973; Blackfriars Gall., Boston, Lincs. (Visual Poetry & Paintings), 1973; Exe Gall., Exeter (Visual Poetry & Paintings), 1974; Warwick Gall., Warwick (Visual Poetry & Paintings), 1974. Address: 17 Tavistock Ave., Mapperley Pk., Nottingham, U.K.

MORRIS, William E(dward), b. 11 Sept. 1913. Journalist. Education: Westport Tech. Coll.; Victoria Univ., Wellington, N.Z. Positions held: Editor-Manager, Country Weekly, 1933-38; Acting Manager, Millar's Timber & Trading Co. (Overseas) for N.Z., 1948; Branch Manager, B.O.P. Times, 1957-68, and Librarian, Historical Writer, B.O.P. Times, since 1968. Memberships: World Poetry Soc. (Intercontinental), Oceanian Editor; Foundation Fellow, Internat. Poetry Soc.; Poetry Soc. of Japan; Poetry Book Society (UK); N.Z. Poetry Soc.; Convener, Tauranga Poetry Group;

P.E.N. International (N.Z. Centre). Published works: N.Z. Poetry Broadsheets, 1970; The Silent Touches of Time ('poems'), 1971; Te Awanui; The Story of a Canoe, 1973; Alchemy of Time, 1973; Children of Zero and Other Poems, 1974; Premier Poets (Anthol.), 1971-72; Poet (Pacific Edition), 1971. Contbr. to: Bay of Plenty Times; NZ Monthly Review; Arena; Poetry Nippon; Northland; Poet, etc. Tape-recorded poetry for American Internat. Poetry programme. Address: 50 Harvey St., Tauranga, Bay of Plenty, NZ.

MORRISON, Madison, b. 28 June 1940. Teacher. Education: B.A., Yale Univ., 1961; A.M., Harvard Univ., 1962; Ph.D., ibid, 1969. Contbr. to: Beyond Baroque; Center; Diana's Bimonthly; The Little Review; The World. Address: 520 West Eufaula St., Norman, OK 73069, U.S.A.

MOSER, Norman, b. 15 Oct. 1931. Editor. Education: B.A., San Francisco State Coll., 1961; M.A., ibid, 1966; grad. work, Univ. of Wash. & Univ. of B.C. Positions held: Co-Publisher, Staff-writer, Bay Window (later, Bay Area Arts Review), 1957-59; Theatre-Films Ed.-Critic, Activities Mag.; Fndng. Ed., Illuminations, 1965-73; Contbng. Ed., Grande Ronde Review, 1971-; Staff Ed.-Writer, The Gar, 1972-73. Memberships: Coordinating Coun. of Lit. Mags.; Cooperative of Small Press Eds. & Publishers; Underground Press Syndicate (now, APS: Alternative PS). Published works: (collections) Jumpsongs, 1973; A Shaman's Songbook, 1974; Open Season, 1974-75. Rep. in following anthols: A Decade of Poems: Southern Poetry Review Anthol., 1968; N.C. Poetry/1970, 1970; The Living Underground, 1973; Waiting at the Washington St. Bookshop, 1973. Contbr. to many mags., reviews, etc. Honours, awards: Transfer Poetry Contributor's Prize, San Francisco State, 1959; Illuminations Prize, 1966 & Grants, 1967 & '70; PEN Gen. Grant. Address: Box 4793, Austin, TX 78765, U.S.A.

MOSES, Brian George, b. 18 June 1950. Teacher. Education: Kingston Polytechnic, Kingston-upon-Thames, U.K.; Tchng. Cert., Eastbourne Coll. of Educ. Positions held: Exec. Officer, Dept. of Environment, Surbiton, 1960-70; Student Tchr., 1971-74. Memberships: Chmn., Treas., Malenka Arts Soc., Eastbourne Coll. of Educ.; Co-Ed., Malenka Arts Mag.; Co-Ed., Radix Poetry Mag. (Poets Vigilantes); Poet Vigilantes. Published works: Look to the Scars (pamphlet) poems by Brian Moses & Greg Venables, 1973. Contbr. to: Malenka; Envoi; Pink Peace; Scrip; Contac; Radix; Nucleus; Lines; Time Machine; Attila; Outburst (anthol.); Colleges Poetry (anthol.) Address: 44 Finsbury Rd., Ramsgate, Kent CT11 7NN, U.K.

MOSHER, Betty Joan Knight, b. 12 Feb. 1913. Housewife. Memberships: United Amateur Press; Gem State Writers' Guild. Contbr. to: Nampa Press & to contests with awards in the Writing Guilds. Honours, awards: 1st pl., British Amateur Press Assn., 1970. Address: Meridian, Idaho 83642, U.S.A.

MOSHIRI, Fereidiun, b. 1932. Poet. Education: Technical education in the field of Posts & Telegraphs. Positions held: Employee, Ministry of Posts & Telegraphs. F. Moshiri is a well-known Iranian poet who has published collections of verse. Address: c/o Press Attache, Imperial Iranian Embassy, 16 Princes Gate, London S.W.7, U.K.

MOSS, Howard, b. 22 Jan. 1922. Writer. Education: Univ. of Wisconsin, B.A., 1943; Grad. work at Columbia Univ. toward M.A. (not completed). Positions held: Instr. of Engl., Vassar Coll., 1944-46; Poetry editor, The New Yorker Mag., 1948-. Memberships: P.E.N.; The Authors' Guild; The Nat. Inst. of Arts & Letters. Published works: (poems) The Wound & the Weather, 1946; The Toy Fair, 1954; A Swimmer in the Air, 1957; A Winter Come, A Summer Gone, 1960; Finding Them Lost, 1965; Second Nature, 1968; Selected Poems, 1971; (criticism) The Magic Lantern of Marcel Proust, 1962; Writing Against Time, 1969. Edited with an introduction: Keats, 1959; The

Nonsense Poems of Edward Lear, 1964; The Poet's Story, 1973. Contbr. to: The New Yorker; The Nation; The New Republic; The NY Qtly.; The Chicago Review; Botteghe Oscure; Harper's; Harper's Bazaar; Poetry; Poetry London-New York; The Poetry Review; The Maryland Poetry Review; Briarcliff Qtly.; Commentary; Antaeus, etc. Awards: Award in poetry, Poetry Mag., 1946; Award in creative writing, Nat. Inst. of Arts & Letters, 1968; Ingraham-Merrill Foundation Grant, 1972; Nat. Book Award In poetry, 1972. Address: 27 West 10th St., New York, NY 10011, USA.

MOSS, Stanley, b. 21 June 1925. Private Art Dealer & Poet. Education: Trinity Coll., Hartford, Conn.; Yale Univ., New Haven. Married Dr. Jane Z. Moss. Mbr., PEN. Published works: The Wrong Angel, 1966; The Wrong Angel & New Poems, 1969. Contbr. to Poetry; Antaeus; New Yorker; The Nation; The New Republic; Encounter; Book Week; The Observer; Poetry Northwest; Quarterly Review of Lit.; Sewanee Review; Transatlantic Review; Tri-Quarterly. Ed., Bottegre Oscure. Contbr. & former poetry ed., The New Am. Review. Recip., Rockefeller Fellowship, 1967-68. Address: 241 Central Park West, N.Y., NY 10024, U.S.A.

MOTT, Michael Charles Alston, b. 8 Dec. 1930. Lecturer. Education: Oriel Coll., Oxford Univ., U.K.; Ctrl. Schl. of Arts, London; Law Schl. of the Law Soc., London; B.A., London Univ. Married Margaret Watt, twin daughters. Positions held: Contbr. & Editl. Advisor to The Oldebourne Ency. of the Arts & to The Ency. of the Arts; Vis. Lectr. in Engl., Kenyon Coll., Ohio, U.S.A., 1966-70; Vis. Prof. in Engl., SUNY, Buffalo, summer 1968 & Sir Geo. Williams Univ., Montreal, summer, 1970 & '74; Vis. Lectr. in Engl. & Writer-in-Res., Emory Univ., 1970-. Poetry Ed., The Kenyon Review, 1967-70, etc. Var public lectrs., reading of own poems & papers at lit. confs. Published works: (poetry colls.) The Cost of Living, 1957; The Tales of Idiots & New Exile, 1961; A Book of Pictures, 1962; Quipus, 1974; (novels) The Notebooks of Susan Berry, 1962; Helmet & Wasps, 1964; (children's novels) Master Entrick, 1962; The Blind Cross, 1968; (short fiction) A Cage to Keep Secrets, 1970; Three Prose Portraits, 1970. Contbr. of poems to mags., reviews, anthols. & articles & reviews to newspapers & mags.; TV & radio broadcasts. Address: The English Dept., Emory Univ., Atlanta, GA 30322, U.S.A.

MOUAT, Kit, b. 1 March 1920. Writer, Poet, Author, Journalist, Bookseller. Married, 1 s. Memberships: Writers' Guild of Great Britain; The Poetry Soc. (1939-1940). Published work: Time Smoulders and Other Poems, 1971. Contbr. to: Poetry Today; The Norseman; Tribune; The Freethinker; The Humanist; Breakthru; Viewpoints; Scrip; Headland; Croydon Advertiser; The New Shetlander; The Progressive World. Address: Mercers, Cuckfield, Sussex RH1 75JU, UK.

MOULT, Thomas. Poet; Critic; Editor; Novelist; Lecturer. Positions held: Assoc. with late Charles E.B. Russell, Heyrod St. Lads Club, Manchester, in Borstal & convict prison work; Assoc. with H. Wood & C.E. Heald in boy's club work in Manchester & London; Mus. Critic, Manchester Guardian & Manchester City News; Art & Drama Critic, The Athenaeum, The English Review, etc.; Lit. Ed. & Advisory Sports Ed., Sunday Referee; Fndr., Voices (Mag. of the Arts), 1919; Chmn., Edit. Bd., The Poetry Review, 1952-62. Pres., The Poetry Soc., 1952-61. Published works: (poetry) Down Here The Hawthorn, 1921; Brown Earth (choral poem), 1922; Willow Pattern (cricket poems) 1936; I Love England; (novels) Snow Over Elden, 1920; The Comely Lass, 1928; Sally Go Round The Moon (for children), 1931; Saturday Night, 1931; (autobiog.) All-Sports Special!; Wind in The Trees; (criticism) Barrie, 1928; Mary Webb, a biography & a criticism, 1932; W.H. Davies, 1934; Bat & Ball; A New Book of Cricket, 1935; Robin of Sherwood (radio play), 1937; The Great Partnership: Hirst & Rhodes; Derbyshire in Prose & Verse, 1929. Editor: Mod. Writers & Playwrights series of Critical Biogs., 1929;

The Best Poems of 1922 & then Best Poems, annually, to 1943; Forty Years in My Bookshop, 1923; Cenotaph, 1923; Poems From Books, 1927; Playing for England, by Jack Hobbs, 1931; Sport's Great Stories, 1931; Master Showman, 1937; Down North: by Tony Onraet, Canadian Trapper, 1942; Cricket is My Life, by Len Hutton, 1949, etc. Contbr. to numerous jrnls., including: Daily Telegraph; Guardian; Liverpool Post; Fortnightly Review; Yale Review; Quarterly Review; Sunday Times; Observer. Address: Essex, UK.

MOWER, Gail Patricia Devine, b. 3 May 1945. Dental Assistant. Education: Grad., Lynn Classical H.S., 1963; currently enrolled in study of Creative Writing; also studying music & piano w. Annette Dollard of Lynn. Married, 1 son. Member, N.Y. Poetry Forum. Currently working on completion of first book of poetry. Contbr. to: The North Shore's Sunday Post; Yankee Mag.; Lifespring, etc. Address: 12 Sachem St., Lynn, MA 01902, USA.

MOZOLA, Michael John, b. 31 Jan. 1950. Hospital Business Management. Education: St. Basil's Coll. Sem., Stamford, Conn., 1967-69; B.A., St. Paul's Coll., Wash. D.C., 1971. Positions held: Account Analyst, Patient Services, Henry Ford Hosp., Detroit; Asst. Supvsr., Patient Services, ibid; Supvsr., Admitting & Discharge. Memberships: Am. Civil Liberties Union; Nat. Democratic Party. Contbr. to: Atom Mind; Encounter; The New Star, Catholic News Weekly; Cardinal Poetry Qtly.; Poetry Prevue; Pegasus, Coll. Poetry Anthol.; College Poetry Review; America Sings. Address: 31910 Dolly Madison Dr., Apt. G, Madison Heights, MI 48071, U.S.A.

MTSHALI, Oswald Mbuyiseni, pen name, **SPARKS, Joseph,** b. 17 Jan. 1940. Messenger; Poet. Education: Dip., Short Story Writing; Univ. of S Africa. Married, Margaret Mtshali. Contbr. to: Sounds of a Cowhide Drum; The Classic; The Purple Renoster; Ophir; Critique; New Coin; D'Arte; Unisa Enlg. Studies; Drum; Sunday Times; The Star; Golden City; Post Sunday Tribune; Pretoria News; Daily News; Daily Graphic; NY Times; Compiler of material for Black & Blue, poetry & jazz revue; Interviews on BBC, SABC & Canadian Broadcast Corp. Address: 40 Renoster Books, 1a 5th St., Victoria, Johannesburg, South Africa.

MUDIE, Ian, b. 1 Mar. 1911. Poet. Education: Scotch Coll., Adelaide. Positions held: Farmhand; Journalist; Mgr., Real Estate Agcy.; Ed., Rigby's Ltd. (Publrs.), Adelaide. Published works: Poems 1934-44, 1945; The North-bound Rider, 1963. Contbr. to: (anthol.) Modern Australian Verse, 1964. Honours: W.J. Mem. Prize, 1943; Commonwealth Literary Fund Fellowship, 1946; Grace Leven Prize, 1963. Address: 8 Bristol St., Glenelg South, S. Australia, Australia 5045.

MUHRINGER, Doris Agathe Annemarie, b. 18 Sept. 1920. Freelance Writer. Studied at University. Mbrships: PEN Club; Osterr. Schriftstellerverband; Verband deutscher Schriftsteller; Verband deutschsprachiger Ubersetzer; Podium. Published works: Gedichte I, 1957; Wald und Wiese, 1960; Dorf und Stadt, 1960; Das Märchen von den Sandmännlein, Bilderbuch, 1961; Gedichte II, 1969; Gedichte III, 1974. Contbr. to num. jrnls. inclng: Neue Wege; Literatur u. Kritik; Die Presse; Akzente; Dimension (USA); Rumanian Literara; Neutralität; anthols. in many langs. inclng. Poezia Austriacá moderná. Honours, awards: Georg Trakl Preis, 1954; Förderungspreis d. Stadt Wien, 1961; Boga Tinti Preis f. Lyrik, 1972; etc. Address: Goldeggasse 1, A-1040 Vienna, Austria.

MUKHERJEE, Sujit, b. 21 Aug. 1930. Publishers' Editor. Education: M.A. & Ph.D. in English & Am. Lit. Positions held: Lectr. in Engl., Patna Univ.; Rdr. in Engl., Univ. of Poona; currently Chief Publisher, Orient Longman Lit. Memberships: Indian Assn. for English Studies; Indian Assn. for Am. Studies. Translator of modern Bengali poetry into English inclng: Bewitching Veil (by Manindra Ray), 1968. Contbr. to: Kavita (Calcutta); Mahfil (Chicago); Books Abroad (Eugene,

Ore.); Poetry India (Bombay); Indian Writing Today (Bombay). Address: 3/5 Asaf Ali Rd., New Delhi 100 001, India.

MUKHOPADHYAY, Durgadas, pen names **D'CRUZ ALVIN AJATASHATRU,** b. 4 Oct. 1946. Educator. Education: B.A., Presidency Coll., Calcutta; M.A., Delhi Schl. of Economics. Positions held: Fac. Mbr., Dept. of Econs., Delhi Univ., 1970–. Memberships: Fndr.-Pres., Minimax Soc.; Ed., Minimax; The PEN; Avant Garde Poets Grp., Calcutta. Published works: New & Selected Poems (Bengali), 1966; written four plays in English & Bengali; Produced & acted in a dozen plays; Composed music on own lyrics for plays. Forthcoming publs: Modern Images, Forgotten Melodies, 1973; Poems of Sukanta Bhattacharya, transl. from Bengali, 1973; Lesser Known Poems of Tagore, transl. from Bengali, 1974. Organised the first ever audio-visual enactment of Poetry, New Delhi; Organised Poetry workshops, workshops in photography. Recited poetry over Calcutta, Delhi, Jaipur stns. of All India Radio & TV. Contbr. to Anthologies of Modern Bengali Poets, 1967 & var. jrnls. Address: K–5/8 Model Town, Delhi-110009, India.

MULLER, André, b. 19 June 1925. Publisher. Education: Lycée Kléber, Strasbourg; Faculté de Droit, Strasbourg; Docteur en Droit; Laureat de la faculte de droit de Strasbourg. Married Marie-Louise Kuderlé, 2 children. Positions held: Fndr., 1948, & Pres.Dir.Gen., Inst. de Documentation Juridique et Fiscale; Dir., la Documentation Organique. Memberships: Soc. of Poets & Artists of France; Soc. of Writers of Alsace & Lorraine. Published works: Les vaisseaux brûlés, Editions Saint-Germain des Prés, 1972. Contbr. to: Les Poètes de France, 1970; Peau de Serpent; Vento Nuovo. Recip., 2nd Prize, Poètes de l'Est, 1969. Address: 17 rue René Schickelé, Strasbourg, France and 25 avenue Pierre Ier de Sorbie, Paris, France.

MULLINS-JOHNSON, Helene, (MULLINS, Helene), b. 12 July 1899. Writer. Married Linne Johnson. Memberships: Poetry Soc. of Am.; Acad. of Am. Poets; Composers, Artists & Authors of Am. Published works: Paulus Fy (novel in collaboration), 1924; Earthbound (poems), 1929; Convent Girl (novel), 1930; Balm in Gilead (poems), 1930; Streams from the Source (poems), 1938; The Mirrored Walls (poems), 1970. Contbr. to: N.Y. World; N.Y. Times; N.Y. Evening Sun; Am. Scholar; Am. Mercury; Commonweal; Scribner's Mag.; Harper's Mag.; Ladies Home Jrnl.; Ga. Review; Lit. Review; New Yorker; Yale Review; Jewish Forum; The Nation; Montreal Star, etc. Rep. in following anthols: L.A.G. Strong; Thomas Moult; Modern Religious Poems; The Diamond Anthol., 1971; The Music Makers, 1945; New Yorker Anthol. of Verse, 1935. Address: 16 West 16th St., N.Y., NY 10011, U.S.A.

MUNDAY, Katharine Amy, b. 3 Mar. 1903. Poet. Hon. Sec., Salisbury Poetry Circle, 1933–. Published works: Collection of Poems, 1973. Contbr. to: Poetry Review; Women in Council; The Window (anthol.); Circle Poets (anthol.). Address: 56 Bouverie Ave., Salisbury SP2 8DX, U.K.

MUNDELL, William Daniel, b. 30 Dec. 1913. Developer; Writer. Education: Middlebury Coll.; U.S.M.C. Service Schls. at Grove City Coll. & Corpus Christi Radar Schl.; Marlboro Coll. Positions held: Self employed Carpenter & Building Contractor; Maintenance Foreman for Vt. State Highway Dept.; Auditor, Town of Newfane; Justice of the Peace; Selectman, Town of Newfane; Asst. Ed., Poet Lore mag. Memberships: Poetry Soc. of Am.; Poetry Soc. of Vt. Published works: Hill Journey, 1970, 2nd printing 1973; Plowman's Earth, 1973. Contbr. to: Poetry (Chicago); Poet Lore; The Atlantic; Am. Forests; Life; The New Yorker; Sat. Review of Lit.; The Ladies Home Jrnl.; The Saxonian; The Vermonter; Yankee; The Diamond Anthol.; New Yorker Book of Poems; N.Y. Times; N.Y. Herald Tribune, etc. Recip., The Stephen

Vincent Benet Narrative Poetry Award, Poet Lore. Address: So. Newfane, VT 05351, U.S.A.

MUNHEIM, Peter, b. 6 Jan. 1891. Writer. Memberships: Den Norske Forfatterforening. Published works: Einsemd-songar, 1925; Nye dikt, 1933; Atlantiske dikt, 1942; Vinterblomstring, 1965; Ein vandrar, 1967; Kveldspel, 1970. Contbr. to: Morgenbladet; Bergens Tidende; Gula Tidend (nowopaporo); Janus; Horisont, Ergo (periodicals). Honours, awards: Abetment, Norsk Forfatterfond. Address: 5633 Mundheim, Hardanger, Norway.

MUNN, Harold Warner, b. 5 Nov. 1903. Office Manager; Writer. Positions held: Asst. Mgr., F.W. Woolworth Co.; Office Mgr., Stoker Lad Heating Co. Memberships: Tacoma Writers' Club; Northwest Writers' Conf.; Int. Soc.; Protection of Mustangs & Burros; Washington Poets Assn.; Ed., Tacoma Writers' Club Newsletter, 1966, '67, '68. Work pending: The Banner of Joan, coll. of poems on the life of St. Joan. Contbr. to: Athol Daily News; Weird Tales; Driftwind from the North Hills; Weirdbook; The Muse; Nutmegger; Personal Poetry; The Tahoman; Washington Verse; WHOA; WT-50; Charas; Whispers; Singing San Juan; Puget Sound Review; Ideals; Moonbroth; Down Remembrance Lane; Written Word Anthols.; Durang-Cortez Herald. Address: 5019 No. Vassault, Tacoma, WA 98407, U.S.A.

MUNN, Harry Victor, b. 15 Oct. 1910. Retired Clerk. Widower. Positions held: Cost Clerk, 1928-39; Accounts Clerk & Cashier (Electricity), 1939-48; Consumers Accounts & Connections Clerk i/c of Section, 1948-68. Memberships: Poetry Soc. of G.B., 1959-64; Fndr.-Fellow, Int. Poetry Soc., 1973; Wey Poets, Guildford, 1973. Published works: The Blue Angel (book of poems), 1963. Contbr. to: Angling, 1967; Malenka; Scrip; Weyfarers; Radix; Envoi; Eastbourne Gazette & Herald; Mag. of S.E. Electricity Bd., etc. Honours, awards: Cert. of Merit, The Writer Short Story Contest, 1964; Highly Commended, Authors Analytical Services Poetry Comp., 1965; Highly Commended for Poem, Poetry Day 1967; 3rd Prize, Alice H. Bartlett Competition, 1962; var. other poetry prizes. Address: 26a Belmore Rd., Eastbourne, Sussex BN22 8AY, U.K.

MUNROE, Elizabeth Grenelle, pen name **GRENELLE, Lisa,** b. 22 Jan. 1910. Instructor. Married 1) Henry L. Abbott, dec., 2) David Munroe, dec., 2 sons, 1 daughter. Positions held: By-lined Daily Columnist syndicated by King Features; Freelance Writer, articles, short stories & poetry; Market Researcher; Real Estate Broker; Instr. for poetry & writing workshops under the Bd. of Educ. in N.Y.C. & surburban areas; Instr., Creative Writing, Cooper Union. Memberships: Gov. Bd., Poetry Soc. of Am., 1962-64 & '72-74; Pres., Manhattan Br., Nat. League of Am. Penwomen, 1953-61; Pen & Brush, 10 yrs., Chmn., Poetry Sect., 4 yrs. Published works: This Day is Ours, 1946; Selections, 1951; No Light Evaded, 1957; Self is the Stranger, 1963; No Scheduled Flight, 1973. Contbr. to: Poetry Soc. Anthol. Golden Yr., 1960 & Diamond Yr., 1971; August Derleth Anthol., Fire & Sleet & Candlelight; N.Y. Times; N.Y. Herald Tribune; Chicago Herald Tribune; Denver Post; Yankee; Voices; Prairie Schooner, etc. Recip., Gustav Davidson Meml. Sonnet Award, Poetry Soc. of Am. Address: 140 East 92nd St., N.Y., NY 10028, U.S.A.

MUNSHOWER, Susan Scott, b. 13 July 1942. Student. Education: B.S., Pa. State Univ., 1964; currently completing M.A. degree in Art Hist., ibid. Positions held: Art Instr., Phoenixville Area H.S., Pa.; Art Instr., J.E. Smith Elem. Schl., Newark, Del.; Art Instr., Emmaus Jr. H.S., Pa. Memberships: Am. Poetry Soc.; World Poetry Soc.; Treas., Alpha Delta Kappa. Contbr. to: Pivot Mag.; Poet; Am. Poetry Soc. Jrnl.; Outstanding Contemporary Poetry; Yearbook of Modern Poetry, 1972. Address: Apt. 209, 458 East Coll. Avenue, State Coll., PA, U.S.A.

MURALIDHAR, Advikolanu, b. 3 Oct. 1929. Shipping Company Employee. Education: M.A. (Engl. Lit.); Art Appreciation course, Siddardh Coll., Bombay Univ. Memberships: Convener of the Free Verse Writers' Conf., a writers' workshop at Hyderabad (Andhra Pradesh), India; Navya Sahiti Samiti, Hyderabad; Andhra Vishva Sahiti, Hyderabad; All India Telugu Writers' Conf.; Jignasa Samiti, Hyderabad; Andhra Mahasabha, Bombay. Published works: Bhinna Dhruvaalu (Poles apart), 1962; translated Tagore's Gitanjali & Gardener, 1961; Chain of Tears; Song on the Lips; Fright of Night & Other Poems; That Which Is Not. Editor & Translator of anthol. of modern Telugu short stories, into English, 1968. Contbr. to var. jrnls. & has broadcast poetry on All India Radio, Hyderabad. Recip., Poetry Prize, All India Radio Comp., 1960. Address: 46/10 Ashok Kunj, J.B. Nagar, Andheri East, Bombay 59, India.

MURDOCK, Patricia Alice, b. 30 Mar. 1920. Poet. Education: St. Joseph's Acad., North Bay, Ont., Canada. Married Don Murdock, 6 children. Mbr., Wilson Macdonald Poetry Soc., Toronto. Contbr. to: N.Y. Anthol. of Verse, 1938; H.S. Yearbook; Canadian Reg.; J.F.K. Lib., U.S.A.; Carmens Jrnl.; The Miraculous Medal; St. Joseph's Alumnae Publs.; Oshawa Times; World Poetry Day Publs., Rochester; Sudbury, Ont., paper; Ottawa newspaper; Toronto Daily Star; I.W.W.P. Anthol., 1972, 1973; I.B.A. Yearbook, 1973. Recip. var. hons. Address: 1140 Mary St. N., Apt. 309, Oshawa, Ont. L1G 5HI, Canada.

MURPHY, Joseph Francis, b. 14 June 1917. Hotelman. Education: Brighton Acad., Island Pond, Vt.; Warren Harding H.S., Bridgeport, Conn. Exec. Bd. Mbr., Poetry Soc. of Am. Published works: Night Visions, 1971; Black Diamonds, 1973. Contbr. to: New Yorker; Sat. Review; N.Y. Times; N.Y. Herald Tribune; Mass. Review; Yankee; Wall St. Jrnl.; The Lyric; Essence; Voices; The Sign; Poet Lore; The Hartford Courant; Promenade; The Poetry Chap Book, etc. Honours, awards: The Reynolds Lyric Prize, 1967; The New England Prize, 1968; The Roberts Memorial Prize, 1970. Address: 287 East 18th St., Brooklyn, NY 11226, U.S.A.

MURPHY, Mary Elizabeth, pen name **MURPHY, Marybeth Magnenat,** b. 17 Feb. 1916. Clerical Worker. Education: Ctrl. Bus. Coll., Kans. City; Univ. of Kansas City. Positions held: Advertising, Kans. City Post & Kans. City Jrnl., 1935-42; Clerk, N. Am. Modification Ctr., Kans. City, 1942-45; Clerk & Clerk Typist, V.A.; Corps of Engrs. & Weather Bur., 1946-65. Memberships: Libn., Kans. City Br., Nat. League Am. Pen Women, 1972-74. Published works: In Everything Given Thanks, 1955, 2nd printing, 1960. Contbr. to: Kans. City Star; Vets' Gazette; Portland Oregonian; Mark Twain Qtly.; New Verse Mag.; Candor; Wednesday Mag.; Midland Poetry Review; The Arizonian; Songs of the Free (anthol.) etc. Recip. var. awards. inclng. 3rd pl. & money, free verse, K.C. Br., Nat. League of Am. Pen Women Contest, 1972. Address: 3948 Oak, Kansas City, MO 64111, U.S.A.

MURPHY, Redmond Dwyer, b. 23 Apr. 1910. Teacher. Education: Marist Brothers schls. Positions held: Tchr., Engl., various schls., NSW, Victoria & S Australia; Engl. Master, Marist Brother High Schl., Eastwood, NSW. Memberships: Poetry Soc., Australia. Published works include: Speak to Strangers, 1961; Sixth Finger, forthcoming. Contbr. to the following anthols., jrnls., mags., etc: Mod. Australian Verse, 1964; Australia Writes, 1953; Penguin Book of Australian Verse, 1958; Verse in Australia, 1961; Poetry in Australia, 1964; Australian Poetry, 1954, 1956-57, 1960-61, 1964-65, 1968, 1971; Sydney Morning Herald; The Bull.; The Cath. Weekly; Poetry Mag. Address: Marist Brothers' High Schl., 54 Hillview Rd., Eastwood, NSW, Australia 2122.

MURPHY, Richard, b. 6 Aug. 1927. Writer; Poetry Lecturer. Education: M.A., Magdalene Coll., Oxford. 1 daughter. Positions held: Writer-in-Residence, Univ. of Va., Charlottesville, 1965; Vis. Fellow, Reading Univ., Berks., 1968; Compton Lectr. in Poetry, Univ. of Hull,

1969. Published works: The Archaeology of Love, 1955; Sailing to an Island, 1963; Penguin Modern Poets 7 (w. others), 1965; The Battle of Aughrim, 1968 (recorded). Contbr. to (Anthols.): Poetry Now, 1956; English Love Poems, 1957; New Poets of Ireland, 1963; Faber Book of Twentieth Century Verse, 1965; Love Poems of the Irish, 1967; New Modern Poetry, 1967. Hons: AE Memorial Award for Poetry, 1951; Guinness Award, 1962; Arts Council of Great Britain Bursary, 1967; Fellow, Royal Soc. of Literature, 1968. Address: Cleggan, County Galway, Repub. of Ireland.

MURRAY, Gloria Geller, b. 7 Jan. 1943. Housewife. Married, 2 children. Contbr. to: Yearbook of Modern Poetry, 1971-72; Writers Notes & Quotes, 1961; The Writer Mag., 1962 & '65; December, Face, 1963; Caravan Poetry Mag., 1961; Bardic Echoes, 1970, '72; The Quill, 1962. Recip. var. hons. Address: 206 E. 4th St., Deer Park, L.I., NY 11729, U.S.A.

MURRAY, (Ies(lie) A(Ilan), b. 17 Oct. 1938. Translator; Poet. Education: Univ. of Sydney. Married Valerie Gina Maria Morelli w. 2 children. Positions held: Trans., Aust. Nat. Univ., Canberra, 1963-67. Published works: The Ilex Tree, 1965; The Weatherboard Cathedral, 1969; Trans., Introduction to the Principles of Phonological Description, 1968. Contbr. to (Anthols.): Australian Poetry, 1963-68; Young Commonwealth Poets '65, 1965; A Book of Australian Verse, 1968; New Impulses in Australian Poetry, 1968; Poetry in Australia II, 1969; (Jrnls.): The Age and the Meanjin; Sydney Morning Herald; Australian Poetry Australia; Poetry; Quadrant; Southerly; Outposts. Hons: Grace Leven Prize for Poetry, 1965; Australian Commonwealth Literary Fund Fellowship, 1968; Australian Council for the Arts grant, 1970. Address: 7 Giles Street, Kingston, Canberra, A.C.T. 2604, Australia.

MURRAY, Rona Jean, b. 10 Feb. 1924. University Teacher. Education: Mills Coll., Oakland, Calif., 1941-44; Univ. of B.C. at Victoria Coll., Victoria, B.C., 1960-61: B.A.; Univ. of B.C., Vancouver, 1963-65: M.A.; Univ. of Kent at Canterbury, 1966-67: Ph.D. granted 1972. Married to Walter Dexter; 3 children by prev. marriage. Positions held: 1961-62, Victoria Coll., Victoria, Special Instr. in History Dept.; 1963-65, Teaching Asst. in Engl. and Creative Writing at U.B.C., Vancouver, B.C.; 1966-67, Lecturer in Engl. Dept., U.B.C., Vancouver; 1968-73, Lecturer at Selkirk Coll., Castlegar, B.C. Membership: League of Canadian Poets. Published works: Blue Duck's Feather and Eagledown (one act verse play); The Enchanted Adder, 1965; The Power of the Dog, 1968. Forthcoming: Ootischenia; Selected Poems. Contbr. to: (anthols.) A Canadian Anthol.; Commonwealth Poetry; Contemp. Poets of British Columbia; 40 Women Poets of Canada; (journals): Canadian Poetry; Voices; Alphabet; Prism International; Canadian Forum; Fiddlehead; Alaska Review; Envoy; Poet; Blackfish Review; Vanguard; Outposts. Also to BBC and CBC for broadcasting. Awards: 1958 BC Centennial One Act Play Award (verse play); 1964 MacMillan of Canada Creative Writing Award (U.B.C., Vancouver); 1965 Norma Epstein Nat. Award for Creative Writing (Toronto); 1971, three-act verse play (One, Two, Three, Alary) chosen to be performed at Renaissance '71, Toronto. Address: R.R.1, South Slocan, B.C., Canada.

MUSARIRA, Edgar, b. 13 July 1938. Teacher. Education: currently studying for B.A. (Ext.), London Univ. Married, 3 children. Positions held: Schl. Staff Sec.; Asst. in running schl's Young Writers Club. Member PEN Rhodesia. Contbr. to: Two-Tone; London Mag.; Illustrated News Rhodesia; Rhodesia Poetry. Address: Highfield Secondary Schl., P.O. Box DH19, Highfield, Rhodesia.

MUSGRAVE, Susan, pen name DICKINSON, Emily, b. 12 Mar. 1903. Volkswagen Mechanic. Memberships: League of Canadian Poets; Poetry Secretariat, London, U.K. Published works: Kung, 1973; Gullband thought Measles was a Happy Ending (forthcoming);

Songs of the Sea-Witch, 1970; Mindscapes (w. others), 1971; Skuld, 1971; Entrance of the Celebrant, 1972; Equinox, 1973; Grave-Dirt & Selected Strawberries, 1973; (Anthologies) Contemp. Poetry of B.C., Vol. 1 & 2; Contemp. Fiction of B.C.; 40 Women Poets of Canada; Cloud Nine: Vancouver Island Poems; Solo Flight. Contbr. to: Blackfish; Capilano Review; Canadian Forum; Edge; The Far Point; Fiddlehead; The Malahat Review; Manna; Northern Journey; Prism Int.; Quarry; Tamarack Review & other newspapers & mags. in U.S.A. & U.K. Poems have been broadcast on CBC & the BBC 3rd prog. Recip., Canada Coun. Travel Grant, 1969-70 & Arts Bursay, 1972-73. Address: Box 26, Tlell, Queen Charlotte Is., B.C., Canada.

MUSGRAVE, Susan, pen name WINDSOR, Elizabeth, b. 7 Jan. 1922. Farrier. Memberships: League of Canadian Poets; London Poetry Secretariat; Poetry Soc. (London). Published works: Songs of the Sea-Witch, 1970; Mindscapes, 1971; Skuld (pamphlet), 1971; Entrance of the Celebrant, 1972; Birthstone (pamphlet), 1972; Equinox (pamphlet), 1973; Kung (pamphlet), 1973; Grave-Dirt & Selected Strawberries, 1973; Gullband Thought Measles was a Happy Ending, forthcoming. Contbr. to: Malahat Review; Poetry Review; N.Y. Times; Second Aeon; Tamarack Review; Prism Int.; West Coast Poetry Review. Honours, awards: Canada Coun. Travel Grant, 1969-70; Canada Coun. Arts Bursary, 1972-73. Address: 2931 Seaview Rd., Victoria, B.C., Canada.

MUSGROVE, Virginia Margaret, pen name, RENALDO, Kathryn, b. 21 Jan. 1915. Poet. Education: Oceanside-Carlsbad Coll., Calif.; San Diego State Univ.; Palmer Writer's School, Minn., etc. Married; 1 d. Positions held: Chairman, Bldg. Committee, Humane Soc., also publicity, finance, membership, youth recruitment, shelter, etc. committees; Senior Social Worker, Navy Relief Soc., Camp Pendelton, Calif. Memberships: Haiku Soc. of Am.; Int. Poetry Inst., Inc.; Western World Haiku Soc.; American Poets Fellowship Soc.; Internat. Platform Assoc. Published works: Raindrop In A Dust Pool, 1972; Sonnets and Poems, 1972; To Color The Echo, 1973. Contbr. to: NY Times Book Review; Springfield Daily News; San Diego Union; Arkansas County Courier; Gazette (Utah); Words With Wings; Green World; Quintessence; The Guild; Haiku West; Los Angeles Times; Prairie Poet; Cardinal; Angel Hour; The Writer; American Poets; United Poets; The Muse; Worksheet Directory; Quoin; Haiku West; Haiku Highlights; Modern Haiku; Dragonfly; Voice of The Voiceless; Cat's Mag.; Internat. Who's Who in Poetry Anthol., 1973; Jean's Journal; These are My Jewels (anthol.); Yule Log Anthol.; Christmas Anthol.; Baltimore NewsNews-Post; Vista Press, etc. Recip. of many awards, hon. mentions including Haiku; Angel Hour; Pixie Award, etc. Meritorious Award for volunteer social welfare service (5 yrs.) at Camp Pendelton, US Marine Base, Calif. Address: Rt. 2, Box 198, Hartville, MO 65667, USA.

MUSKE, Carol, b. 17 Dec. 1945. Poet; Writer. Education: M.A. in Creative Writing, San Francisco State Coll., 1970. Positions held: Poetry & Proj. Dir., Poetry in the Prisons Prog., Riker's Island; Tchr., Poetry in Prisons Proj.; Asst. Ed., Antaeus Lit. Mag. Published works: Salad Days. Contbr. to: The Nation; Esquire; N.Y. Qtly.; Goddard Jrnl.; Elima; The Little Mag.; Village Voice; MS.; Review; Antaeus; San Francisco Qtly.;Tenth Muse. Poetry Readings at: New Schl., April 1973; Vassar Coll., Apr. 1974; WBAI Radio, Mar. 1974. Honours, awards: Dylan Thomas Poetry Award, New Schl. for Soc. Rsch., N.Y.C., 1973; Finalist, CAPS Prog., 1973-74. Address: 1 W. 30th St. PHA, N.Y., NY 10001, U.S.A.

MUTEL, Claude, b. 12 May 1939. Teacher. Education: Baccalaureat de Philosophie. Mbr., Academie Poetique de Provence. Published works: (books) Chansons et rêves, 1960; La seule musique, 1964; Les Jardins d'exil, 1973; (records of poetry) Choix de poemes, 1966 & '68 (Academie du Disque de Poesie);

(reviews) Les Nouveaux Cahiers de Jeunesse; Flammes Vives,; Profils Poetiques des Pays Latins; Art et Poesie; (anthologies) Anthologie des Poètes de l'Enseignement, 1958, 59, 60, 61; Choix de Poèmes d'aujourd'hui, 1971. Honours, awards: Silver Medal, 4th Jeu des Troubadours, 1965; Albert Samain Prize, 1967; Diplôme d'Honneur, Société Libre de Poesie, 1968; Rose d'Honneur, L'Ile des Poetes, 1969. Address: 9 rue de Chaâlis, Thorigny, 77400 Lagny, France.

MUTIGA, Josiah G. Kenyan, b. 1940. Business Man. Education: Makerere Univ. Coll., Kampala, Uganda (B.A.), 1964. Married w. 2 children. Positions held: Formerly, Dist. Off., Kenya; Currently, Working for a Commercial Firm in Thika. Contbr. to (Anthols.): Origin East Africa, 1965; African-English Literature, 1965; Young Commonwealth Poets '65, 1965; Drum Beat, 1967; (Jrnls.): Transition.

N

NABOKOV, Vladimir, pen names **SIRIN, V.; SHISHKOV, Vasiliy,** b. 23 Apr. 1899. Writer. Education: Tenishev School, St. Petersburg, Russia; Cambridge Univ. (Trinity College), U.K., B.A., 1922. Married to Vera Slonim; one son: Dmitri. Lecturer, Wellesley College, USA., 1941-48; Research Fellow in Entomology, Museum of Comparative Zoology, Harvard, 1942-48; Prof. of Russian Lit., Cornell Univ., 1948-59. Pubs. (in Russian) Gorniy Put' (The Empyrean Way), 1923; Grozd' (The Cluster), 1923; Vozvrashchenie Chorba (Chorb's Return), a collection of poems and stories, 1930; Stihotvoreniya (poems), 1952; (in English): Poems, USA, 1959, Eng. 1961; Poems and Problems (a collection of poems and chess problems), USA and Eng. 1970. Contrib. to: The New Yorker; The Atlantic Monthly, and numerous Russian emigre periodicals. Address: c/o Weidenfeld & Nicolson Ltd., 11 St. John's Hill, London SW11 1XA, UK.

NACHANT, Mary Frances Grant, pen name, **NACHANT, Frances Grant,** b. 19 October. Music Teacher; Lecturer; Poet; Freelance Writer. Education: Univ. of Washington, School of Music; Dr. Dip. in Lit. Married; 1 s., 2 d. Positions held: Music Teacher, Seattle, 1929-55. Memberships: Pres., San Diego Br.; Nat. League, Am. Pen Women, 1968-70; Past Pres., Western League of Writers; Poet Laureate Rep., Southwestern Rep. of Internat. Poets Shrine, Vice Pres. Torrey Pines Chap., Calif. Fed. of Chaparral Poets; Assoc. Chairman, American Congress of Poets; Member of Pacific Northwest Internat.; Avalon World Arts Acad.; World Poetry Soc. Intercontinental; UPLI; Internat. Platform Assoc.; American Poets Fellowship Soc.; Florida State Poetry Soc.; Seattle Poetry Club; San Diego Poets Assoc.; Nat. Music Educators. Published work: Song of Peace, 1969; Contbr. to: (Anthols): J.F. Kennedy Commemorative Anthol., 1964; 100 Yrs. of Alaskan Poetry, 1966; Haiku & Tanka, 1964; Christmas Anthol., 1965; Etta Josephine Murfey Mem. Anthol., 1967, 1968; Internat. Hall of Fame, 1968, 1969; Scambi Internat., 1968; Showcase, 1968; Golden Quill, 1969, 1970; Wagging Tales, 1969; Selected Poems, 1967, 1969; Nine Muses, 1971, 1972; Spring Anthol., 1971. World Premier Poets, 1973; Internat. Who's Who in Poetry, 1973; (Journals) The Saint; Message; Sharing; Nat. Cath. Press Syndicate; Amer. Bard; Orphic Lute; The Archer; Poet Lore; Flamingo; Swordsman Review; The Lyric; Ideals; American Poets; Prairie Poets; Lets Have a Chat (Tokyo); The Muse; Haiku Highlights; Gold Star; Cyclotron; Oregonian; South & West; Seattle Times; Denver Post; Alaska Weekly; Saturday Review; Cyclo-Flame; San Francisco – Oakland Bull.; Windless Orchard; Tweed; Hyacinths & Biscuits; Caravel; Poets Forum, Kansas Chronicle; Poet-India; Laurel Leaves; Internat. Poetry Review; Pen Women. Awards: 1st book prize, Arkansas Writers Con. Nat. contest, 1966; 1st prize Torrey Pines Chap., Cal. Poets, 1966, 1967, 1968; Crowned Peace Poet Laureate, World Congress

of Poets, UPLI, 1969; Citation & Medal for Song of Peace from Dr. A. Yuzon, Pres., UPLI.; Medal of Distinction & Inter. Dip. of Hon., Internat. Acad. of Leadership, 1969; 1st prize, Seattle Times, 1948; 3rd Prize, San Diego Br., Nat. League Am. Pen Women, 1965; Sonnet Award, NLAPW, 1967; Medal from Dr. Henry Picola, Pres., Internat. Poets Shrine, 1971; D.H.L. Dip., Internat. Acad., Sov. Order of Alfred the Great, Hull (UK), 1969; 2 1st, 1 2nd prize, and Hon. Mention, 1972; 1st, 2nd, & 3rd, P.W. 1973; Dip. from Acad. Leonardo da Vinci, Rome, 1972; Citation from Cal. Fed. of Poets, and Florida State. Address: 3043 32nd St., San Diego, CA 92104, USA.

NADERPUR, Nader, b. 1929. Poet. Education: Grad. in French Lit., Paris. Positions held: Employee of the Fine Arts Department; Mbr., Iran-Italy Cultural Soc.; Iranian Delegate to International Persian Lit. Congress, Tashkent, 1968. Is reputed to be one of the renowned modern Iranian poets and has written a number of poetical works as well as var. articles about Persian verse. Address: c/o Press Attache, Imperial Iranian Embassy, 16 Princes Gate, London S.W.7, U.K.

NAGARAJAN, R., pen names, **LEO; ARUN; DIANA, O.G.,** b. 13 April 1946. Hydrogeologist. Education: Annamalai Univ., Annamalai Nagar, B.Sc., M.Sc. Positions held: Geological Asst. in P.W.D. Government of Madras, 1967-68; Jr., Hydrologist, Groundwater Div., Trichy, 1968-1970; Sr. Scientific Asst., I.H.D., C.S.I.R., New Delhi, since 1970. Published work: Vistas Old and New (poems), 1969. Contbr. to: Annamalai Students' Weekly, 1962-65; Poet. Awards include: Distinguished Service Citation of World Poetry Soc. Intercontinental, 1973. Address: Internat. Hydrological Decade Unit, Council of Scientific & Industrial Research, Rafi Marg, New Delhi 1, India.

NAGAYAMA, Mokuo, b 14 Dec. 1929. School Teacher. Education: Doshisha Coll. of Foreign Affairs, 1950. Married, 2 children. Positions held: Translator, Liaison Office, Kobe Custom House, 1951-53; School Tchr., 1953–. Memberships: Poets' Soc. of Japan; Japan Poets Club; Int. Poetry Soc. Contbr. to: Poetry Nippon; Japan Poets Club Anthol.; The Poet; World Anthol. of Contemporary Poets. Address: 1168 Ouchi, Kurashiki, Okayama Pref., Japan.

NAGEL, Chester Scott, b. 14 Jan. 1899. Retired Statistician & Educator. Education: Geneva Coll., 1920; Univs. of Maine & Md. Positions held: Tchr. in var. Elem. & H.S's, 1920-30; Schl. Admnstr., 1930-37; Statistician & Analyst, State of Pa., 1937-68. Memberships: Pa. Poetry Soc.; Harrisburg Manuscript Club; Pres., Harrisburg Chapt. of Pa., 1972–. Contbr. to: Beaver Falls, Pa. Review; Harrisburg Evening News; Encore; A Goodly Heritage, anthol. Address: 200 Verbeke St., Harrisburg, PA 17102, U.S.A.

NAHAS, Joseph K(amil), b. 22 Mar. 1896. Education: St. Johns Acad.; Am. Univ.; A.M. Philos. Married Marian Davenport, dec., 4 children. Positions held: (formerly) Asst. Ed., Almuhajer; Contbng. Ed., AsSayeh; Asst. Ed., Al Nisr; Personnel Mgr., Wentworth Mfg. Co.; Gen. Supt., Whitehouse Mfg. Co.; Pres., Whitehouse Uniforms Inc.; Bd. Chmn., Arkapparel, Inc.; Pres., Ozark Textile Corp.; Fndr. & Chmn., The Joseph Nahas Co. Memberships: Nat. Rehabilitation Assn.; Southern Artists Assn.; Exec. Bd., Ark. Poets' Roundtable; Authors, Composers, & Artists of Ark.; Smithsonian Inst.; Int. Platform Assn. Published works: Philosophy of Healthy Business Relations; (poetry) Musing Through Life; Seventy Eight & Still Musing; (philos.) Observations & Reflections; A Sideroad Chapel. Num. articles on industry. Poems & essays published in sev. anthols. Address: P.O. Box 87, Lake Hamilton, AR 71951, U.S.A.

NAHEED, Kishwar, b. 3rd Feb. 1940. Government Official. Education: Master of Economics, Punjab Univ., Pakistan. Positions held: Asst. Dir., Public Rels.,

Dept. of Local Govt., Punjab; Feature Writer in the Min. of Information; Res. Dir., Pakistan Nat. Ctr. Published works: Lab-e-Goya (The Lips Which Can Speak), 1969; Be-nam Musafat (Un-named Journey), 1971; Gadhey na Bajai Bansri (The Donkey Played the Mute), poems for children, 1971. Contbr. to: Naqoosh; Fanoon; Adab-e-Lateef; Adbi Duneya; Tehreerin; Seep; Naqash; Afqar; Saqi; Auraq; Akhbar-i-Khawateen; Jang; Imroze; Musawaat; Mashraq; Denak, etc. Honours, awards: Best Poet Nat. Award for 1965, awarded in 1966 by Tareekhi Majlis; Adam Jee Lit. Award for 1969. Address: Res. Dir., Pakistan Nat. Ctr., Room No. 210, Al-Falah, Lahore, Pakistan.

NAHOR, Aliza, b. 3 Oct. 1915. Painter; Teacher; Poet. Education: Hebrew Univ., Jerusalem. Mbr., Assn. of Hebrew Writers in Israel. Published works: (in Hebrew) The Irmes Courtyard, 1965; The Shape of the Wind, 1968; The Labyrinth of the Rose, 1970; Closed Bell, 1973; (in French) La Cours Interieure. Contbr. to most Hebrew dailies in Israel & to var. lit. reviews. Recip., 1st Prize, AKUM (Soc. for the Protection of the Writer, Composer & Editor), 1965. Address: P.O.B. 574, Eilat, Israel.

NAKAGAWA, Atsuo, pen name NAKAGAWA, Onsey, b. 10 Apr. 1927. Assistant Professor of English. Education: Nanzan Univ., Engl. Dept. (graduated, 1953). Married, 1 s., 1 d. Positions held: Asst. Prof., Gifu Coll. of Economics, since 1969. Founder and Editor, Poetry Nippon. Membership: The Poets' Soc. of Japan (Founder and Secretary). Published work: Stepping Stones of Faith (anthol.), 1967. Contbr. to: Poetry Nippon; The Japan Christian Qty.; Poet, etc. Address: 5-11 Nagaike-cho, Showa-ku, Nagoya 466, Japan.

NAMJOSHI, Suniti Manohar, b. 20 Apr. 1941. Civil Servant; Student. Education: M.A., Univ. of Poona, India, 1963; M.S., Univ. of Mo., USA, 1969; Working on Ph.D., McGill Univ., Canada. Positions held: Lectr., Engl. Litt., Fergusson Coll., Poona, India, 1963-64; Officer, India Admin. Serv., 1964-69; Rsch. Asst., Univ. of Mo., USA, 1968-69; Tchng. Asst., McGill Univ., Canada, 1969-71; Student, 1970-. Published works include: Poems, 1967; Poems of Govindagrai (transl.; Co-author), 1968; Cyclone Pakistan, 1971. Contbr. to the following anthols., jrnls., mags., etc: Poetry, India; Poetry Singapore; Writers Workshop Miscellany; Transition. Address: Writers Workshop, 162/92 Lake Gdns., Calcutta 45, India.

NANDY, Pritish, b. 15 Jan. 1947. Poet; Editor; Translator. Positions held: with Publicity Dept., Internat. bus. firm of Calcutta; Fndr., Ed. & Publisher, Dialogue Calcutta (Monthly Poetry Anthols.); Fndr. & Ed., Indian Poetry Review, 1969-. Mbr., Writers Workshop, Calcutta. Published works: Of Gods & Olives, 1967; On Either Side of Arrogance, 1968; I Hand You in Turn My Nebbuk Wreath, 1968; Rites For a Plebian Statue, 1969; Myths From a Burning Wing, 1969; Masks to be Interpreted in Terms of Messages, 1969; From the Outer Bank of the Brahmaputra, 1969; Madness is the Second Stroke, 1969; The Poetry of Pritish Nandy, 1973. Ed: Selected Poems of Subhas Mukhopadhyay; Selected Poems of Samar Sen; Selected Poems of Agyeya; Selected Poems of Parvez Shahedi, etc. Translr., The Meghnad-Bahd Kavya of Michael Madhusuadhan Datta. Contbr. to: Trace; Opinion; Thought; Hiram Poetry Review; El Corno Emplumado; Dialogue Calcutta; The Miscellany; Abyss; Mahfil; Quest; Los Huevos del Plata; Tulsa Poetry Quarterly; Poltergeist; Rupambara; Pyramid; This And...; New Indian Writings. Poetry From India, etc., etc. Address: 5 Pearl Rd., Park Circus, Calcutta 17, India.

NATACHEE, Allan, pen names PINONGO, Avaisa, MALAKA, APIPO, ISAPU, b. 16 July 1924. Poet; Writer & Translator of Mikeo – traditional poems, songs & legends. Positions held: Govt. Clerk, 1946-47; Wood Machinist, 1948-67; Poet & Translator, 1968-. Memberships: Hon. Mbr., United Poets Laureate Int., Quezon City, Philippines. Published works incl: Only

Oceania, 1952. Contbr. to: Pacific Islands Monthly Mag.; Post-Courier, Port Moresby; 'The Last Unknown' by Gavin Souter; Australian Territories; Papua New Guinea Writing; Words of Paradise Book; UPLI, etc. Honours, awards: Karta of Award, Disting. Poet of Papua, UPLI, 1966; Award of Hon., Premier Poet of Papua, ibid, 1967; Decretum, Poet in Res. of Papua, 1970. Address: Univ. of Papua New Guinea, Ctr. for Creative Arts, P.O. Box 5098 Boroko C.D., Port Moresby, Papua New Guinea.

NATHAN, Edward Leonard, pen name NATHAN, Leonard, b. 8 Nov. 1924. University Professor. Education: Georgia Tech., 1934-44; Univ. of Calif., Los Angeles, 1946-47; B.A. summa cum laude, Univ. of Calif., Berkeley, 1950; M.A., 1952; Ph.D., 1960. Married to Carol Gretchen Nash; 1 s., 2 d. Positions held: Instr., Modesto (Calif.) Jr. Coll., 1954-59; Prof. dept. of rhetoric, Univ. of Calif., Berkeley, 1960-, dept. chairman, 1968-72. Published works: Western Reaches, 1958; The Glad and Sorry Seasons, 1963; The Matchmaker's Lament, 1967; The Day the Perfect Speakers Left, 1969; Flight Plan, 1971; Confessions of a Matchmaker (record), 1972. Contbr. to: Poetry; Qtly. Review of Literature; Perspective; Shenandoah; The New Yorker; The New Republic; The Nation; Commentary; Antaeus; Antioch Review; Beloit Poetry Journal; Chelsea; Chicago Tribune Mag.; Chicago Review; Discovery No. 5; December; Encounter; Epoch; Kenyon Review; Literary Review; Massachusetts Review; The NY Times; Northwest Review; Prairie Schooner; Ramparts; Tennessee Poetry Journal; Voices; Western Review. Recip. Phelan Award, 1958; Longview Foundation award, 1961; Creative Arts Fellowship, 1961-62; American Inst. of Indian Studies Fellowship, 1966-67; Nat. Inst. of Arts and Letters Award in Creative Literature, 1972; Creative Arts Fellowship, 1973-74. Address: 1135 Fresno Ave., Berkeley, CA 94707, USA.

NATHAN, Norman, b. 15 Nov. 1915. Professor of English. Education: B.A., N.Y. Univ., 1936; M.A., ibid, 1938; Ph.D., 1947. Married, 3 daughters. Positions held: Motion & Time Study Engr., Western Electric; Tutor, Instr., City Coll. of N.Y.; Lectr., Rutgers Univ.; Asst. Prof., Assoc. Prof. & Full Prof. of Engl., Syracuse Univ., Utica Coll.; Prof. of Engl., Fla. Atlantic Univ.; Vis. Prof. at: Coll. of the Virgin Is., Univ. of Mo. at Kansas City, Nevada Southern. Published works: Though Night Remains, 1959; Judging Poetry, 1961. Contbr. to: N.Y. Times; Sat. Review; Sat. Evening Post; N.Y. Herald Tribune; Ladies' Home Jrnl.; Western Humanities Review; Wascana Qtly.; The Fiddlehead; So. Humanities Review; Fla. Qtly.; Canadian Forum; Prairie Schooner; Christian Sci. Monitor; N.M. Qtly., etc. Address: 1189 S.W. Tamarind Way, Boca Raton, FL 33432, U.S.A.

NATHAN, Robert, b. 2 Jan. 1894. Author. Education: Exeter Univ.; Harvard Univ. Personal details: Descendant of Gershom Seixas, Rabbi officiating at George Washington induction as Pres. of Us. Married Joan Boniface Winnifrith. Memberships: VP, Nat. Inst. of Arts & Letters; Pres., Am. Centre PEN; Chancellor and Honorary Fellow, Acad. Am. Poets; Writers Guild of Am.; Dramatists Guild. Published works: Youth Grows Old, 1922; A Cedar Box, 1929; A Winter Tide, 1940; Dunkirk, 1942; The Darkening Meadows, 1945; Selected Poems, 1935; Morning in Iowa, 1944; The Green Leaf, 1950; The Married Man, 1962; Evening Song, 1973. Contbr. to: The Century Magazine; Scribeners; Harper's; Atlantic Monthly; The New Yorker; Saturday Review. Address: 1240 N Doheny Dr., Los Angeles, Calif. 90069, USA.

NATHANIEL, Arthur S., b. 14 Feb. 1905. Chartered Accountant. Education: M.A. & B.L., Madras Univ.; F.C.A., Fellow of the Inst. of Chartered Accts. of India. Married Selina Devanayagam, 5 children. Positions held: Dpty. Registrar of Co-operative Socs., Madras State; Post Grad. Prof. of Commerce, Mar Ivanios Coll., Trivandrum. Member, World Poetry Soc., Intercontinental. Published works: Virgin Bouquet (in 7 books containing 181 pieces). Contbr. to: The Poet;

Voice of Youth; Student Movement Review; My Magazine. Recip., 1st prize, Voice of Youth, All Travancore Comp., 1925. Address: Diamond Cottage, Charachira, Trivandrum 695003 S India.

NAUDE, Adèle (nee da Fonseca Wollheim), b. 14 Aug. 1910. Free-lance Journalist; Scriptwriter for Radio. Education: B.A., Univ. of Cape Town. Widow of D.F. Hugo Naudé, w. 1 daughter. Positions held: Formerly Ed., num. Womens' Jrnls.; Currently, Free-lance Journalist & Radio Scriptwriter. Published works: Pity the Spring, 1953; No Longer at Ease, 1956; Only a Setting Forth, 1965; Other: Strooihoed en Sonbril, 1965; Tousandale aan my Voete, 1968. Contbr. to: (Anthols.): Poets in South Africa, 1958; Oxford Book of South African Verse, 1959; Poet Sings, 1959; An Anthology of Commonwealth Verse, 1963; New South African Writing, 1964; Vivid Verse II, 1967; Penguin Book of South African Verse, 1968; (Jrnls.): Contrast; Standpunte. Address: c/o Colonial Orphan Chamber & Trust Co., 4 Church Square, Cape Town, South Africa.

NAUMAN, Frances I., pen name **WOLF, Frances,** b. 20 Apr. 1914. Administrative Secretary, Automobile Club of Southern California. Education: Univ. of Calif. Ext., San Francisco, 1938; Berkeley Bapt. Divinity Schl., 1938; Univ. of Wash., Seattle, 1942-43; A.A., Pueblo Jr. Coll., 1945; Univ. of Calif., Berkeley, 1954, '55; UCLA, 1963-65, etc. Married St. Elmo Harry Nauman, div., 1 son, 1 daughter. Positions held: Corres., E.R. Moore Co., 1963-65; Sec. to Pres., Financial Indemnity Co., 1965-66; Sec. to Pres. & others, Cecil Saydah Towel Co., 1966-67; Sec. to Bd. of Grievance, Comm. of Bus Drivers of SCRTD, 1967. Memberships incl: Am. Inst. of Fine Arts; Am. Poetry League; Sec. of Bd., Calif. Fed. of Chaparral Poets, 1965; Poetry Prize Chmn., ibid, 1963; Ina Coolbrith Circle; Sec., Manuscript Club of L.A., 1967-68; Pres., ibid, 1971-73; Prog. Chmn., 1973-74; Writers Socs. in Phoenix, Ariz. & Seattle., Wash. Has been illustrating & printing original Christmas cards for over 30 yrs. Contbr. to num. mags., jrnls., reviews, anthols. inclng: Baptist Beacon, St. Paul, Minn.; Baptist Builder, Berkeley, Calif.; Oakland Tribune; Ariz. Highways; Poet's Haven Anthol.; Am. Bard; Am. Poetry League Bulletin; Portraits of Christmas anthol.; Yearbook of Modern Poetry; The Seeds of Thoughts, etc. Recip. sev. hons. & awards. Has given many performances of original poetry since 1965. Has had three one-woman art shows & participated in sev. grp. exhibs. Address: 1100 South Ninth St., Alhambra, CA 91801, U.S.A.

NAZAR, Qayyum, b. 7 Mar. 1914. Professor. Education: Forman Christian Coll.; Dyal Singh Coll.; Oriental Coll., Lahore, M.A., Punjab Univ. Positions held: Divl. Acct. in var. Pub. Works Dept. of Punjab (Brit. India), 1938-49; Lectr. in Urdu Lang. & Lit., Govt. Coll., Lyallpur, 1950-51; Asst. Prof., Govt. Coll. Lahore, 1951-67; Prof., 1961-67; Res. Dir., Pakistan Nat. Ctr., Lahore, 1967-69; Subject Specialist (Urdu & Punjabi), West Pakistan Text Book Bd., 1970-71; Chmn., Punjabi Dept., Punjab Univ., 1971-73. Memberships: Halqa Arbab-i-Zauq, Lahore (Sec.-Gen., 1953-58); V.P., Majlis-i-Iqbal, 1952-64; Pakistan Writers Guild; Pres., Translator Soc., Govt. Coll., Lahore, 1960-65; Exec. Comm., Majlis-i-Tara'i-i-Adab, 1967-; Exec. Comm., Bazm-i-Iqbal, 1970-. Published works: (in Urdu) Qindeel, poems, 1945; Pawan Jhakole, songs, 1947; Sawaid, poems, 1952; Aida, opera, 1956; Hamsafeer, verse plays, 1962; Zinda Hai Lahore, war songs, 1967; Ghazleen, lyrics, 1973; (in Punjabi) Punjabi Prosady, 1959; Tun Tey Main, lyrics, 1974. Ed. or Jt. Ed. var. publs. Recip., Abdi Dunya Best Poetry Prize, 1938; UNESCO Fellowship to Europe, 1956-57. Address: 42 Ghulam Nabi Colony, Samanabad, Lahore, Pakistan.

NDU, Pol Nnamuzikam, b. 14 Nov. 1940. University Professor. Education: B.A., Univ. of Nigeria, 1965; M.A., State Univ. of N.Y., 1972; Ph.D. Engl., 1974. Married, 2 children. Positions held: Asst. Lectr., Engl., Univ. of Nigeria, Nsukka, 1966-70; Lectr., Engl., ibid, 1970-71; Asst. Prof., Black Studies Dept., State Univ.

of N.Y., Buffalo, 1972-74. Memberships: Am. Acad. of Political & Soc. Sci. Published works: Golgotha, 1971; Songs for Seers, 1974; From the Lighthouse, 1974. Contbr. to: Africa Report; Modern Poetry from Africa; Ufahamu; Times Lit. Supplement; Presence Africaine; Abbia; Okike; Nigeria Mag.; Black Orpheus; New Canadian & Am. Poetry; The New African; Young Commonwealth Poets '65; New Voices of the Commonwealth, etc. Honours, awards: The Am. Peace Corps Poetry Prize, 1963; Aggrey Fellow, SUNY, Buffalo, 1971-72. Address: Dept. of Engl., State Univ. of N.Y., Buffalo, NY 14214, U.S.A.

NEAL, Arnethia Murdock, pen names **TRUMPET BREWSTER & JAMILA YAMINAH,** b. 10 Apr. 1952. Student. Education: currently attending The Virginia Coll. for A.A. degree. Past Mbr., United Amateur Press Assn. Contbr. to: Shore Poetry Anthol., 1972; United Amateur Press, 1971; The Virginia Coll. 'Blaze', 1973; Worldbook of Modern Poetry. Address: 1204 Eighth St., Lynchburg, VA 24504, U.S.A.

NEALE, (Edna) Dorothea, b. 22 Aug. 1902 in Baltimore, Maryland, USA. Poet & Writer; Executive Director, The NY Poetry Forum, Inc. Education: Piano study (over 10 yrs.); Philadelphia School of Expression & Dramatic Art; Univ. of Maryland (Engl. Major); Univ. of Baltimore (Journalism); Writing Courses at NY Univ.; Writing Courses & Public Relations, New School for Social Research, NYC. Married 3 times; 2 s., 1 d. Positions held: Taught piano; held real estate licence; dramatic coach; conducted own studio of music & dramatics & two little theatre groups in Baltimore, Md.; Wrote and directed "Childrens' Playshop" on Radio Station WBAL in Baltimore; recent yrs. employed front desk of Hotel Berkshire in Manhattan; now giving full time to the NY Poetry Forum, and own writing (2 books of poetry in preparation). Memberships: NY Poetry Forum, Inc. (Founder, Exec. Director & Pres.); World Poetry Day (Hon. life member); World Poetry Soc. Intercontinental; Brooklyn Poetry Circle. Published works: Maryland Poets; Crown Anthol.; Paeber Anthol.; Paeber Christmas Anthol.; Eminent Poets; Eros, An Anthol. of Love Poems; Contemporary American Women Poets; The Brooklyn Poetry Circle Silver Anniversary Anthol.; 1969 Anthol. of New York Poets. Contbr. to: Interludes; American Poets; The Open Window; Pendulum; World Poetry Day Mag. 1970; "Poetry Personalities" Flatbush Mag.; Martin's Garden of Poets; Williamsburgh News; Coney Island Times; wrote monthly column "Fact & Fancy" in Taff Talk. Awards: United Poets Laureate Internat. Gold Medal (Gift of Pres. Marcos), 1969 (1st World Congress of Poets, Manila, Philippines); Hon. Life Membership. World Poetry Day, 1971. Address. 221 East 28th St., Apt. 17, New York, NY 10016, USA.

NEAME, Alan John, b. 24 Jan. 1924. Literary Consultant. Education: M.A., Modern Languages, Wadham Coll., Oxford. Positions held: Hd., Modern Language Dept., Cheltenham Coll., 1948-52; Lectr. in English, Univ. of Baghdad, Iraq, 1952-56; Consultant, Int. Commission for the Use of Engl. in the Roman Liturgy, 1967-. Published works: (Novels), The Adventures of Maud Noakes, 1959; Maud Noakes, 1965. Other: Stanley's Diaries, 1961; Jerusalem Bible, 1966; The Happening at Lourdes, 1967; Var. Translations. Contbr. to (Anthols.): New Poems, 1957; (Jrnls.): Poetry; Aylesford Review. Recip., Bess Hokin Prize from Poetry, Chgo., 1958. Address: Fisher Street, Nr. Faversham, Kent, UK.

NEDROW, Ella L., pen name **NEDROW, Ella Castle,** b. 30 May 1903. Housewife and Poet. Education: HS., Owosso, Mich., 1908-21; Courses at MSU E. Lansing, Mich., in Engl., Poetry, in 1942-43; Attended LBU, 1942-43. Positions held: Played piano in music trio for theatre in Durand, Mich., 1920-35; Receptionist for State Civil Service Dept., 1942-54; In restaurant business from 1954-65. Memberships: Lansing Poetry Club, since 1942; Lansing Poetry Soc. (Pres., 1950-52; 1967-69); Poetry Soc. of Michigan, since 1965; Nat. Fed. of Poetry Socs., since 1965. Published works:

Fragments, 1965; A Handful of Stars. Contbr. to: American Bard; Bardic Echoes; The Guild; Voices Internat.; Cyclo-Flame; United Amateur Press (guest editor at times); Birch and Bittersweet; Perennials; Jean's Journal; State Journal; Detroit News; Detroit Times; Ideals, etc. Awards: Ariz. State Univ. Award, 1966; "Personal Poetry" Award, Maryland Broadcasting System, 1967; Poet Laureate, 1971, from United Amateur Press. Address: 136 Linden Blvd., Mason, MI 48854, USA.

NEGALHA, Jonas, b. 26 Apr. 1933. Poet; Philosopher; Critic; Novelist; Painter; Historian; Professor; Anthropologist, etc. Education: has received approx. 30 degrees from Universities and Academies from var. parts of the world. Positions held: Jrnlst.; Prof. of Portuguese Lit., Faculdade de Filosofia, Ciencias & Letras de Sao Jose dos Campos, Brazil; Prof. of Brazilian Culture, Faculdade de Filosofia de Sao Bernardo do Campo; Prof. of Romanic Philol. & Esthetics & Hist. of Art, ibid; Prof. of Anthropol., Fac. of Econ., Sao Caetano do Sul; Conferencist, Univ. Humboldt of Berlin; Assoc. Ed. 'Angel Hour', U.S.A.; Asst. Ed. 'Ocarina', etc. Member of num. assns. & acads. inclng: Regent of Latin Am., World Poetry Soc.; Councillor, Botisava Inst. for Buddhology, S. Viet Nam; Pres. in Brazil, La Federation Internationale des Corps Savants de Recherches. Has written num. profl. & sci. communications & works, as well as translations of poetry, philos., econ., etc. His many poetic works have been translated into dozens of langs. Has received num. hons. & awards inclng: Gold Medal from Pres. Marcos of the Philippines, 1967; Chevalier of the Sovereign Order of St. John of Jerusalem, 1972; Comendador de la Soberana Orden de la Corona Asteca, Mexico, 1972; Titular Bishop of Disha, 1972; Nom. for Nobel Prize in Lit., 1971 & for Nobel Peace Prize, 1974; Dip. of Exemplary Citizen of the World, UN Day, 1967. Address: Caixa Postal 7244, Sao Paulo 01000, Brazil.

NEGREPONDIS, Yiannis, b. 6 Dec. 1930. Writer; Poet; Playwright. Education: Lit. & Archeol. studies, Univ. of Athens. Married. Mbr., Nat. Soc. of Greek Writers. Published works: Letters of Love, 1956; Faces & Places, 1958; Bloodstained, 1960; Donations, 1963; Enclosed, 1965; Iphigenia, 1967; Bourini, a play; The Matchmaker, a play. Translator of Aeschylus, Sophodes, Euripides & Aristophanis. Contbr. to lit. mags. inclng: Nea Estia; Epitheorissi Technis. Many of his poems have been set to music by Mikis Theodorakis. Address: 3 Thopombou St., Pagrati, Athens, Greece.

NEIGHBOURS, Frances Brandon. Freelance Writer; Director of Poets Tape Exchange. Married 1) Horace Stuart Taylor (dec.), 2) L. Robert Crouse. Memberships: Poetry Soc. of Va.; Pa. Poetry Soc.; Am. Poetry League; Fndr. & Dir. of Poets Tape Exchange; Ky. State Poetry Soc. Published works: (poetry books) Blue Candles, 1942; Bright Coin, 1944; Verses & illustrations for original line of greeting cards in black & white & by special order in oil color, 1961-63; I Took A Thousand Steps, lyrics of gospel song published in sheet music, 1966; Let's Make Fun of It, taped article on humorous poetry w. original poems, 1970. Contbr. to: Am. Bard; Modern Haiku; Haiku West; Dragonfly/Haiku Highlights; Haiku Mag.; Janus SCTH; The Christian; Cats Mag.; Am. Poetry League Bulletin; Together Mag.; Pegasus; The Golden Anniversary Anthol., Poetry Soc. of Va., 1974; var. other State Poetry Soc. Yearbooks & anthols. & contbns. to newspapers. Honours, awards incl: First Prize (tie) The Mason Sonnet Contest, Poetry Soc. of Va., 1969; Hon. Mention, ibid, 1970; First Pl., The Lucy B. McIntire Meml. Prize, Poetry Soc. Ga., 1971; First Prize, Blanche Whiting Keysner Meml. Award, Pa. Poetry Soc., 1973; Hon. Mention, Cash Award, Wash. Poets Assn. Int. Haiku Contest, 1973; 1st Pl., Lucia Markham sonnet contest, Ky. State Poetry Soc., 1971; 2nd Pl., Edna Shoemaker Award, Pa. Poetry Soc., 1973. Address: 109 Twin Oak Dr., Lynchburg, VA 24502, U.S.A.

NELSON, Doris Starr, pen name **NELSON, Starr,** b. 10 Dec. 1913. Writer. Education: Ithaca Conserv. of Music, 3 yrs. Widow of Arthur E. Nelson. Memberships: Poetry Soc. of Am.; MacDowell Colony Fellows. Published works: Song of Summer, 1939; Heavenly Body (prize vol. of poems publd. by the League to Support Poetry), 1942; The Myth in the Vein, 1961. Contbr. to: Sat. Review; Voices; Yankee; Fantasy & Science Fiction; many other poetry mags., quarterlies & anthols. Also contbr. of reviews of poetry to mags. & quarterlies. Recip. League to Support Poetry publ. prize, 1942; Num. Poetry Soc. of Am. monthly prizes. Address: 145-A Heritage Village, Southbury, CT 06488, U.S.A.

NELSON, Harry William, b. 9 June 1908. Poet; Author; Artist; Teacher. Education: Brown Univ., 1926-28; Yale Univ., 1931-33, A.B. cum laude; Post Grad.: Univ. of New Hampshire, 1939; Univ. of Connecticut, 1950-51; Lafayette Univ., 1951. Positions held: Teacher, Robert E. Fitch Sr. HS, Groton, Connecticut, 1934-64. Memberships: Poetry Soc. of America; Chi Delta Theta (Nat. Hon. Lit. Soc., Yale Chapter); New London Art Students League (pres., 1965-68); Living Heritage Guild of Groton (pres., 1965-67); Nat. Fed. of State Poetry Socs.; Pennsylvania Poetry Soc.; Essex Art Assoc. (artist member); Mystic Art Assoc. (artist member). Artist: one-man shows and group shows. Published works: Startled Flight, 1930; Impelling Reminiscence, 1940 (Leitner Award); Ours is the Work, 1942; The Years of the Whirlwind, 1943; The Moon is Near, 1944; Never to Forget This, 1944; The Fever in the Drum, 1945; From Moon-Filled Sky, 1947; Look to the Horizon Within, 1948; The Winter Tree, 1972 (Suffield Award); Not of This Star Dust, 1973. Contbr. to many mags., journals, etc. Awards: Leander Leitner Award, Am. Lit. Assoc., 1940; Cora Smith Gould Mem. Award, Am. Lit. Assoc., 1946; Monday Prize, Poetry Soc. of Georgia, 1969; Suffield (Conn.) Conference Poetry Award, 1971. Address: 213 Pleasant Valley Rd., Groton, CT 06340, USA.

NELSON, Sharon H., b. 2 Jan. 1948. Writer. Education: B.A. Hons. Hist. & Philosophy of Religion, B.A. Hons. Engl., 1970, Sir George Willlams Univ., Montreal, Quebec. Published works: Delta Quarterback 6, Poems, 1970; A Broken Vessel, 1972; Sayings of My Fathers, 1972; seawreck, 1973. Contbr. to: Critical Qtly.; Duel, European Judaism; Tree; Poetry Review; Adam; Montreal Star. Address: 5618 Eldridge Ave., Montreal 268, Quebec, Canada.

NELSON, Stanley, b. 9 June 1933. Writer; Editor. Education: B.A., Univ. of Vt., 1957. Married Betty Jean Nelson, 2 daughters. Positions held: Reporter, Burlington Vt. Daily News, 1957-58; Tchr. of Retarded Children, Schl. System in Hackensack, N.J., 1958-59; Mutual funds rep., Investors Planning Corp., N.Y.C., 1958-62; Sr. Writer, Medica Materia, N.Y.C., 1962-63; Asst. News Ed., Medical World News, N.Y.C., 1963-65; Sr. Writer, Image, N.Y.C., 1965-66; Sr. Ed., Hospital Practice, N.Y.C., 1966-69; Freelance Medical writer for Consultant, Drug Therapy, Chronic Disease Mgmt., Visual Concepts & var. physicians, 1969-. Co-Chmn., N.Y. Drama Concept. Published works: The Passion of Tammuz (book), 1959; Idlewild (book), 1970, 2nd edn., 1971; The Brooklyn Book of the Dead (book), 1972. Contbr. to: Beloit Poetry Jrnl.; Kan. Qtly.; The Smith; For Now; Gnosis; Back Door; Folio; Tri-Quarterly; New Am. & Canadian Poetry; Poetry Review, etc. Recip., Thomas Wolfe Poetry Award, 1961. Address: 372 Pacific St., Brooklyn, NY 11217, U.S.A.

NELSON, Vera Joyce, b. 22 Jul. 1903. Housewife. Education: Behnke-Walker Business College, 1922-24; BS degree in Humanities, Portland State Univ., 1957. Married to C.A. Nelson; 1 daughter, 3 grandchildren. Member: Poetry Soc. of America; World Poetry Soc. Intercontinental; Served as President of Verseweavers, 1949 and 1955. Pubs. Webs from an Old Loom, 1952; Moccasin Prints West, 1955; Contribs. include: Mirror Northwest; Wisconsin Review; Lyric; Creative Review; Modern Images; Human Voice; Driftwood; Voices International; South and West. Anthologies: Internat. Who's Who, 1972; Modern Poets; Dance of the Muse; Grace Jordan's Idaho Reader; Poetry By the Sea; Poet International – Great American World Poets; Glen Coffield's Anthology of Poetry; Fabric of Song, vol. 1 and 2. Awards include: Voices International 1970, 1st; Willamette Writers 1972, 1st. Address: 5558 S. E. Aldercrest Lane, Milwaukee, Oregon 97222, USA.

NEMEROV, Howard, b. 1 Mar. 1920. Professor of English. Education: A.B., Harvard Univ., Cambridge, Mass., 1941. Married w. 3 children. Positions held: Assoc. Ed., Furioso, 1946-51; Taught at var. Colls., 1948-69; Vis. Lectr., Engl., Univ. of Minn., Minneapolis, 1958-59; Writer-in-Residence, Hollins Coll., Va., 1962-64; Consultant in Poetry, Library of Congress, 1963-64; Prof. of Engl., Wash. Univ., St. Louis, 1969. Published works: The Image and the Law, 1947; Guide to the Ruins, 1950; The Salt Garden, 1955; Mirrors and Windows, 1958; New and Selected Poems, 1960; The Next Room of the Dream: Poems and Two Plays, 1962; The Blue Swallows, 1967; The Winter Lightning: Selected Poems, 1968; (Novels), The Melodramatists, 1949; Federigo; or, The Powere of Love, 1954; The Homecoming Game, 1957; A Commodity of Dreams and Other Stories, 1959; (Other): Poetry and Fiction: Essays, 1963; Journal of the Fictive Life, 1965; Ed., Poets on Poetry, 1965. Contbr. to (Anthols.): War Poets, 1945; Penguin Book of Modern American Verse, 1954; Fifteen Modern American Poets, 1956; New Poets of England and America, 1957; Contemporary American Poetry, 1962; Poet's Choice, 1962; Poetry in English, 1963; A Controversy of Poets, 1965; Faber Book of Modern Verse, 1965; Poems on Poetry, 1965; This Land is Mine, 1965. Num. Hons. incl: Kenyon Review Fellowship in Fiction, 1955; Blumenthal Prize from Poetry, Chgo., 1958; Virginia Quarterly Review Short Story Prize, 1958; Theodore Roethke Memorial Award, 1968; Guggenheim Fellowship, 1968-69. Address: Engl. Dept., Wash. Univ., St. Louis, MO 63130, USA.

NENCKA, Helen. Writer; Artist. Education: postgrad. study at Milwaukee Ext. in philos., art & langs., 4 yrs. Married. Positions held: Sec. to Pres. of Underwriters Casualty Co.; own Radio Prog., Reminiscence in Rhyme, a fifteen minute Program of prose & poetry, 2 yrs.; Ran, w. husband, The Alpine Retreat restaurant. Memberships: Nat. League of Am. Pen Women; Histn. of Lake Shore Br., ibid, 14 yrs.; Int. Platform Assn.; Nat. Writers Club; Coun. for Wis. Writers, etc. Published works: Island Seed, 1954, 2nd end., 1969; To My Love, 1959; The Christmas Tree Story, 1965. Contbr. to: North Austin Review; Hartford Times Press; Ideals Mag.; Pen Woman Mag.; var. anthols. Her poetry column 'Tender Conscience' appears weekly in the Times-Press, Hartford, Wis. Honours, awards incl: Nominated for Nat. Histn. of the Am. Pen Women, 1973; var. hon. mentions. Address: 1400 Friess Lake Rd., Hubertus, WI 53033, U.S.A.

NERUDA, Pablo, pen name of REYES Y BASOALTO, Ricardo Eliezer Neftali, b. 1904. Poet. Education: Institute Pedagógica, Santiago, Chile. Positions held: Chilean Consul, Rangoon, Burma, 1927; Consul, Colombo, Ceylon, 1929; Consul, Batavia, Java, 1930; Consul successively at Buenos Aires, Siam, Cambodia, Anam, & Madrid, 1930's; Wkr. w. Spanish refugees, Paris, 1939; at Chilean Embassy, Mexico City, Mexico, 1939-41; Consul, 1941-44; Elected Mbr., Chilean Senate; Opposed Pres. Videla, charged him w. selling out to the USA, which charge was brought before the Chilean Supreme Ct. where Videla's position was upheld; Neruda left for Mexico; Travelling in Italy, France, USSR, & China; returned to Chile, 1953; Mbr., World Peace Coun., 1950–; Pres., Chilean Writers' Union, 1959–. Published works: La Canción de la fiesta, 1921; Crepusculario, 1923; Veinte Poemas de amor y una canción desesperada, 1924; Tentativa del hombre infinito, 1926; Prosas de Pablo Neruda, 1926; El Habitante y su esperanza, 1926; Anillos (w. Tomas Logo), 1926; El Hondero entusiasta–1923-24, 1933; Residencia en la tierra (2

vols.), 1933, '35; Cantos materiales, 1935; España en el corazón–Himno a las glorias del pueblo en la guerra 1936-37, first published at the battlefront by Spanish Republic soldiers; Neruda entre nosotros, 1939; Las Furias y las penas, 1939; Un Canto para Bolivar, 1941; Presencia de Garcia Lorca, 1943; Cantos de Pablo Neruda, 1943; Nuevo Canto de amor a Stalingrado, 1943; Pablo Neruda–Sus mejores Versos, 1943; Selección, 1943; O Partido Comunista e a liberdade de cilacao (w. Pedro Pomar & Jorge Amado), 1946; Carta a Mexico, 1947; Tercera Residencia, 1935-45, 1947; Viajes al corazón de Quevedo y por las costas del mundo, 1947; Alturos de Macchu Picchu, 1948; Que despierte el leñador, 1948; Himno y regreso, 1948; Pablo Neruda acusa, 1948; Gonzalez Videla, el Lavale la América Latina, 1949; Dulce Patria, 1949; Poesias completas, 1951; Poemas, 1952; Cuando de Chile, 1952; Poesia politica (2 vols.), 1953; Todo el amor, 1953; Odas elementales (3 vols.), 1954, '56, '57; Las Uvas y el viento, 1954; Los Versos más populares, 1954; Regreso la sirena, 1954; Viajes, 1955; Los mejores Versos de Pablo Neruda, 1956; Oda a la tipografía, 1956; Antología, 1957; Tercer Libro de las odas, 1957; Estravagario, 1958; Discurso al Alimon sobre Ruben Dario (w. Frederico Garcia Lorca); Todo lleva tu nombre, 1959; Odas–Al libro, a las Américas, a la luz, 1959; Navegaciones y regresus, 1959; Cien Sonetos de amor, 1959; Algunas Odas, 1959; Toros, 1960; Canción de gesta, 1960; Las Piedras de Chile, 1961; Los primeros Versos de amor, 1961; Cantos ceremoniales, 1961; Cuba, los obispos, 1962; La Insepulta de Paita, 1962; Oceana, 1962; Pable Neruda y Nicanor Parra–Discursos (w. Nicanor Parra), 1962; Poema con grabado (w. Toral), 1962; Plenos poderes Buenos Aires, 1962; Los Versos del capitán–Poemas de amor, 1963; Memorial de Isla Negra, 1964; Canción de gesta, 1964; Colección Residencia en la tierra–Obra poética (10 vols.), 1947-48; Canto general, 1950; Obras completas, 1957. Translations of Neruda's work: Residence on Earth, and Other Poems (transl. by Angel Flores), 1946; Residence on Earth (transl. by Clayton Eshleman), 1962; The Heights of Macchu Picchu (transl. by Nathaniel Tarn), 1967; Peace For Twilights To Come! (transl. by Jayant Bhatt), 1950; Elementary Odes (transl. by Carlos Lozano), 1961; Selected Poems by Pablo Neruda (transl. by Angel Flores), 1944; Let The Rail Splitter Awake, and Other Poems, 1950; Selected Poems (transl. by Ben Belitt), 1961; Bestiary/Bestiario (transl. by Elsa Neuberger, w. woodcuts by Antonio Frasconi), 1965; Twenty Poems of Pablo Neruda (transl. by Robert Bly & James Wright), 1966. Translations by Neruda: The Daughters of Albion, and The Mental Traveller, by William Blake, 1935; Shakespeare's Romeo and Juliet. Contbr. to: Poetry, Chicago; Enoounter; etc. Awards & Honours: Int. Peace Prize, 1950; Lenin Peace Prize, 1953; Hon. Mbr., Chile Univ.; Hon. Mbr., Harvard Univ.; Hon. D.Litt., Oxford Univ.; Nat. Prize of Lit., Chile; Nobel Prize for Literature, 1971. Address: Union de Escritores Chilenos, Santiago, Chile.

NEWCOMBE, Rosemarie, b. 27 Nov. 1938. Student. Education: currently working for B.A. in Lit. Divorced, 4 sons. Positions held: Telephone Operator; Advertising Copy Writer; German Lang. Instr. Published works: Dear John, 1971. Contbr. to Poets of the Capital (anthol.). Address: 1769A Russell Rd., Ottawa, Ont., Canada K1G ON1.

NEWLIN, Margaret Rudd, b. 27 Feb. 1925. Writer; Painter. Educ: B.A., Bryn Mawr Coll.; Ph.D., Reading Univ. Married Nicholas Newlin, 4 sons. Positions held: Admissions, Bryn Mawr Coll., U.S.A.; Tchr., ibid & Harcum Jr. Coll.; Tchr., Wash. Coll. Memberships: Poetry Soc. of Am.; Poetry Soc., London, U.K. Published works: Divided Image (study of Blake and Yeats), 1953, reprint 1971; Organized Innocence: The Story of Blake's Prophetic Books, 1956, reprint, 1973; The Fragile Immigrants, 1971; Day of Sirens, 1973. Contbr. to: Tamesis; The Bryn Mawr Bulletin; Stroud Festival Poems; SCAF Poets, 1968; Poet Lore; Manifold; The Poetry Soc. of Am. Anthol., 1971; The Southern Review. Honours, awards: K.F. Gerould

Award, 1947; Sharon Creative Art Fndn. Award, 1968; Greenwood Award, Poetry Soc. of London, 1969, '71, etc. Address: Shipley Farm, Secane, PA 19018, U.S.A.

NEWLOVE, John Herbert, b. 13 June 1938, Regina, Sask., Canada. Writer. Positions held: Currently Sr. Ed., McClelland & Stewart Ltd., Toronto; Lectr., Rdr., Univ. of B.C., Simon Fraser Univ., Dalhousie Univ., Nova Scotia Coll. of Art, Vancouver Schl. of Art, Univ. of Ariz., USA, Seattle Pub. Lib., Carleton Univ., Waterloo Univ., etc. Published works: Moving in Alone, 1965; Black Night Window, 1968; The Cave, 1970; Lies, 1972; (chapbooks, pamphlets, etc.) Grave Sirs, 1962; Elephants, Mothers & Others, 1963; Notebook Pages, 1966; What They Say, 1967, '68; 7 Disasters, 3 Theses, Welcome Home, Click, 1971. Contbr. to the following anthols., mags., etc: Poetry '64, 1964; Commonwealth Poems of Today, 1967; The Oxford Book of Modern Canadian Verse, 1967; The Revised Penguin Book of Canadian Verse, 1967; A Century of Canadian Literature, 1967; The New Romans, 1968; New Voices of the Commonwealth, 1968; Fifteen Winds, 1969; Notes for a Native Land, 1969; Thumbprints, 1969; Made In Canada, 1970; Contemporary Poetry of BC, 1970; Canadian Writing Today, 1970; How Do I Love Thee, 1970; Generation Now, 1970; Quest, 1970; Look Through a Diamond, 1971; 15 Canadian Poets, 1971; Poems for Voices, 1971; I Am A Sensation, 1971; CHQM-FM, CBC, BBC radios; The Dalhousie Review; Fiddlehead; Is; The Canadian Forum; The Tamarack Review; The Malahat Review; Prism Int.; New American & Canadian Poetry; Potpourri; The Pan American Review; Wild Dog; The Wivenhoe Park Review; Collection; Tzarad; Outposts; Envoi; El Corno Emplumado; Parva; Poetry Australia; Poetry, Madras; Les Lettres Nouvelles; Literara Romania; & many others. Honours & Awards: Canada Coun. Grants, 1966, '67, '69, '70; Koerner Fndn., Vancouver, 1964; Deep Springs Coll. Arts Award, Calif., 1969. Address: Editorial Dept., McClelland & Stewart Ltd., 25 Hollinger Rd., Toronto 374, Ont. Canada.

NEWMAN, Paul Baker, b. 12 May 1919. College Professor. Education: B.S. (Physics), Univ. of Chicago, 1940; M.F.A., Univ. of Iowa, 1951; Ph.D. (Engl.), Univ. of Chicago, 1958. Married; 3 children. Positions held: Lecturer in Engl., Univ. of Puerto Rico, 1956-58; Asst. Prof., Kansas State Univ., 1959-62; Assoc. Prof., Queens Coll., Charlotte, NC., 1963-67, and Prof. of Engl., since 1967. Works Published: The Cheetah and the Fountain, 1968; Dust of the Sun, 1969; The Ladder of Love, 1970. Contbr. to: Antioch Review; Chicago Review; Poetry; Virginia Qtly. Review; Mass. Review; Carleton Miscellany; Lit. Review; Ariz. Qtly.; Kansas Qtly.; Southern Poetry Review; Carolina Qtly.; Western Humanities Review; Univ. Review; Red Clay Reader; Christian Century; Coll. English; English Record; English Journal; Minnesota Review; Northeast; Shenandoah; Hiram Poetry Review; Prairie Schooner; UT Review; St. Andrews Review; Southwest Review; South Carolina Review; Chelsea; Smith; Dryad; Four Quarters; South; South Dakota Review. Awards: William Billings Fiske Award in Poetry, Univ. of Chicago, 1955; Roanoke-Chowan Award, N.C. Lit. and Hist. Assoc., 1968; Crucible Award, Atlantic-Christian Coll., 1970; Roanoke-Chowan Award, 1971. Address: 2215 Hassell Pl., Charlotte, NC 28209, USA.

NEWTON, Cosette Faust, b. 18 July 1889. Museum Owner; Author; Lecturer. Education: Ph.D., Harvard; J.D., Chicago; J.S.D., New York; LL.D., Branch of Univ. of Chicago; M.D., Baylor Univ., M.S.-part of M.D., at Univ. of Chicago. Personal details: Mother's family home in Houston, Texas, also a school for girls, now a museum, called the Noble House. Positions held: Former Dean of Women; writer; lecturer; owner (with husband) of museums. Memberships: Texas Poetry Soc.; Nat. Poetry Soc.; American Pen Women at large; Nat. Pen Women; also member of sororities, national and Texas (social, literary, hon. oratorical). Published works: The Rainbow-Hued Trail, 1932; Around The World In Rhyme, 1939; Dark Interval,

1941; War-Blown, 1941; Relatives in Rhyme At Christmas Time, 1938; Songs For Singers, 1942; The Great American "Accident", 1951; MacArthur's Hour, 1951. Contbr. to: Corpus Christi Chronicle; Raven's Roost; The Kaleidograph Press; The Exposition Press; The Southwester; Crown Publications; Poetry Digest. Awards: Songs For Singers, Avon House, 1942; also other prizes. Address: 2217 Cedar Springs, Dallas, TX 75201, USA.

NEWTON, Violette (Mrs. W.L.). Poet. Education: Lamar Coll., Beaumont, Tex. Memberships: Councillor, Beaumont Area, & Pres., Beaumont Chap., Poetry Soc. of Tex.; Pres., Beaumont Writers Club; Past Prog. Chmn., ibid; La. State Poetry Soc.; Poetry Soc. of Am. Publications: Moses in Texas, 1967; The Proxy, 1973. Contbr. to: Am. Bard; Am. Weave; Ariz. Highways; Ball State Forum; Bitterroot; Book of the Year; Caravan; Cyclotron; Cycloflame; Desert; Doubleday's Loves, Etc.; Empire; Experimentalist; Flame; Golden Circle; Green World; Imprints; Letters from the World; Life; Lyric La.; Manifold; Mod. Maturity; Modernalia; Mustang Review; New Athenaeum; Orphic Lute; Poem; Poesy; Poet; Poetaster; Poet Lore; Poetry Digest; Quicksilver; Scimitar & Song; Voices; Writers Notes & Quotes. Recip. of numerous poetry awards & hons. Poet Laureate of Texas, 1973. Address: 3230 Ashwood Lane, Beaumont, Texas 77703, USA.

NGIAM, Tong-Fatt, b. 11 Jan. 1917. Civil Servant; Author; Educator. Education: London Chmbr. of Commerce Certs., Cambridge Schl. Cert., etc. Positions held: Tchr., Singapore, 1937-39; Staff Mbr., Overseas Chinese Banking Corp., Singapore, 1939-42; Clerk, Interpreter, Nippon Kazima Gumi Ltd., 1942-45; Ex ec. Officer, Ministry of Defence (Army Dept.), 1945-63; Attached to Ministry of Pub. Bldng. & Works, Far East, 1964-70; w. Dept. of Environment, Far East, 1970-. Publications: A Collection of Poems, 1937; Inspirational Essays, 1946; My Prayer, 1939; The Sowers, 1940; When She is Away, 1940. Contbr. to: The Student; The Youth; The Studies-in-English Mag.; Singapore Standard. Address: 36, Ean Kiam Place, Singapore 15.

NIATUM, Duane, b. 13 Feb. 1938. Teacher. Education: B.A., Univ. of Wash., 1969; M.A., The Johns Hopkins Univ., 1972. Positions held: Tchr., Writing Seminars, Johns Hopkins Univ., 1 yr.; currently editing a program for Native American Authors at Harper & Row. Published works: After the Death of an Elder Klallam, 1970; A Cycle for the Woman in the Field, a chapbook, 1973; Taos Pueblo & Other Poems, a chapbook, 1973; Ascending Red Cedar Moon, 1974. Contbr. to jrnls., mags., reviews inclng: Prairie Schooner; The Wis. Review; Scimitar & Song; The Seattle Times; Prospero's Cell; Prism Int.; Cimarron Review; N.Y. Qtly. Has read poetry at colls., schls., univs. etc. Honours, awards incl: Marie K. Dearborn Lit. Award, Seattle Music & Art Fndn., 1968; 2nd Prize, Ben Hur Lampman Award, Ore. State Poetry Assn. & The Oregonian, 1968; one of seven authors of Wash. to win a Gov's Award for 1971. Address: c/o Harper & Row, Publishers, 10 East 53rd St., N.Y., NY 10022, U.S.A.

NICHOL, Barrie Phillip (bp Nichol), b. 30 Sept. 1944. Poet. Education: Univ. of B.C., Can. Positions held: Formerly Schl. Tchr.; Co-Ed., grOnk, Toronto. Published works: Cycles Etc., 1965; Konfessions of an Elizabethan Fan Dancer, 1967; bp, 1967; Var. Poetry pamphlets Town, 1966; Fodder Folder, 1966; Portrait of David, 1966; The Birth of O, 1966; Last Poem with You in Mind, 1967; Dada Lama, 1968; Scraptures: var. sequences, 1965-67. Contbr. to (Anthols.): Concrete Poetry, Britain, Canada, United States, 1966; New Wave Canada, 1966; Anthology of Concrete Poetry, 1967; Concrete Poetry, 1969; (Jrnls.): Quarry; Talon. Recip., 2 short-term Grants, Canada Council. Address: c/o The Village Bookstore, 29 Gerrard Street West, Toronto, Canada.

NICHOLAS, Clifford, b. 6 June 1928. Teacher.

Education: Culham Coll., Oxfordshire. Memberships: Poets Conference; Yorks. Poets Assn.; Birmingham Poetry Ctr.; W.A.G.G. Published works: Eye of My Belly, 1972; To Walsingham at Easter, 1973. Contbr. to: BBC Midland Poets, Radio 4; BBC Northern Drift, Radio 3; BBC Northern Valentine, Radio 3; many small mags. Address: 60A Wootton Rd., King's Lynn, Norfolk, U.K.

NICHOLAS, Michael R(umpanos), b. 7 Jan. 1941, Mobile, AL, USA. Student/Teacher; Poet. Education: Los Angeles City Coll., Russian language, 1959-63; UCLA, Slavic languages, 1963-65; B.A., Univ. of Hawaii, Linguistics, 1966-68; M.A., UCLA, Linguistics, 1969-70 Grad. Student. Positions held: Hospital kitchen and laundry worker, Inglewood, 1959-62; Clerk, Los Angeles, 1965; Russian Calligrapher, Univ. of Hawaii, East-West Center Library, Honolulu, 1966-68; Special Instr., Linguistics, UCLA, 1968-69; Research Consultant, Southwest Reg. Lab. (SWRL) Inglewood, 1969-70; Teaching Asst., UCLA, Linguistics Dept. academic yr. 1969-70; Assoc. Instr., Merrill Coll., Univ. of Calif., Santa Cruz, 1971, 1972; Community Organizer, Community Action Prog. of Santa Cruz, 1971-72. Memberships: World Poetry Soc. Intercontinental; Alpha Mu Gamma. Published works: Watermelons into Wine, 1968; Races and Crossroads – A Poem about Hawaii, 1968 (unpublished); Basic Russian Vocabulary List for teaching Machines, 1967; The Speech of Young Black Children in Los Angeles, (with others), 1971. Contbr. to: Mele; Poetry Parade; Prisma; Kapa; Poet; Journal of Black Poetry; Young Hawaii Mag.; The New Black Poetry; Poetry Singapore; American Voice; Major Poets; USA Last Chance. Recip. Youth Poetry Award, Honolulu, 1968; Hon. Mention for trans. of V. Mayakovski's "Black and White", 1967. Address: 312 Otis St., Santa Cruz, CA 95060, USA.

NICHOLL, Louise Townsend. Free-lance Writer & Editor. Education: B.A., Smith Coll., Northampton, Mass. Positions held: Reporter, N.Y. Evening Post; Assoc. Ed., E.P. Dutton & Co., N.Y.; Freelance Ed. & Writer, 1956–; Fndr. Ed., The Measure: A Journal of Poetry. Published works: Water & Light, 1939; Dawn in Snow, 1941; Life is the Flesh, 1947; Explicit Flowers, 1952; Collected Poems, 1953; Curious Quotient, 1956; The World's One Clock, 1959; The Blood That is Language, 1967; Other: The Blossom Print, 1938. Contbr. to (Anthols.): Poetry Society of America Anthology, 1946; New Poems by American Poets, 1953; Imagination's Other Place, 1955; Poet's Gold, 1956; Untune the Sky, 1957; Golden Year, 1960; Earth is the Lord's, 1965. Recip., Acad. of American Poets Fellowship, 1954.

NICHOLSON, Nicole N., pen name **NICOLE,** b. 7 June 1942. Typist. Education: 2½ yrs. Coll. Contbr. to: Internat. Who's Who in Poetry Anthol., 1972; Ball State Univ. Forum; Beyond Baroque; Ante; New Renaissance; New Orleans Review; The Smith; Wisconsin Review; Haiku Highlights; Jean's Journal; Anthol. of American Poetry, X, XI; New Orlando Anthol.; Brass Ring; Antigonish Review; Cinquefoil; Matrix; The Oregonian. Award: 3rd prize, IWWP Contest, 1970-71. Address: 5353 E. Morada, Stockton, CA 95205, USA.

NICHOLSON, Norman Cornthwaite, b. 8 Jan. 1914. Author. Fellow, Royal Soc. of Lit., U.K. Published works: Selected Poems (w. Keith Douglas & John Hall), 1942; Five Rivers, 1946; Rock Face, 1948; The Pot Geranium, 1954; Selected Poems, 1966; A Local Habitation, 1972. Contbr. to: Poetry London; Poetry Chicago; Times Lit. Supplement; New Statesman; Time & Tide; Tribune; London Mag.; Stand; Phoenix, etc. Honours, awards: Heinemann Prize, 1945; Cholmondeley Award, 1967; Grant from Northern Arts, 1969; Soc. of Authors Travelling Award, 1972. Address: 14 St. George's Terr., Millom, Cumberland, U.K.

NICOL, Davidson Sylvester Hector Willoughby, pen name **NICOL, Abioseh,** b. 14 Sept. 1924. Diplomat; Physician & Educator. Education: 1st class hons. in Nat. Scis., Univ. of Cambridge; Hon. Fellow of Christ's Coll., Cambridge. Positions held: V. Chancellor, Univ. of Sierra Leone, 1960-68; Permanent Rep. of Sierra Leone & Ambassador to the U.N., 1968-71; Ambassador to Sweden, Norway & Denmark, 1971-72; High Commnr. to the U.K. of Sierra Leone, 1971-72; Under Sec.-Gen., U.N., 1972–. Member., PEN Club, U.K. Contbr. to: An African Treasury selected by Langston Hughes, 1960; Poems from Black Africa, Ed. Langston Hughes, 1963; Commonwealth Book of Poetry; BBC Broadcasts, 1945-60; Jrnl. of Royal African Soc., 1948; Contemporary African Literature, 1972; Africa: Tradition & Change; Africa is Thunder & Wonder, 1972. Honours, awards: Hon. D.Litt., Davis & Elkins Coll., W. Va., U.S.A. & Hon. LL.D., Leeds Univ., U.K.; Hon. D.Sc., Newcastle Upon Tyne, U.K. & Kalamazoo Coll., Mich., U.S.A.; Margaret Wrong Meml. Prize & Medal for lit. in Africa, 1952; C.M.G., Grand Cmdr., Order of the Rokel, Sierra Leone. Address: c/o Oxford Cambridge Univ. Club, Pall Mall, London S.W.9, U.K.

NIE, Hannu Pertti, b. 29 June 1929. Education: Tchrs. Trng. Coll., Helsinki, 1948-51. Married Nelly Myllärinen, 3 sons, 1 daughter. Positions held: Master of Kaukas Public Schl. in 1951–; Lectr. of Chinese Lit., Univ. of Hkää, Helsinki, 1972–; Lectr. of Chinese Lit., Univ. of Turku, 1974. Memberships: The Finnish Soc. of Authors; Assn. of Finnish Translators. Published works: Kivikausi, 1956; Uurnat, 1958; Päivät kin nuolet, 1961; Silmissä maailman maisemat, 1964; Rautaportista tulevat etelätuuli ja pohjoistuuli, 1968; Niin kiire tässä elämässä, 1972; Näinä päivinä (a festive poem), 1969; translations from the Chinese: Suuri tuuli, 1960; Jadepuu, 1963; Syksyn ääni, 1966; Virralla, 1970; Mao Tse-tung: Runot (Poems of Mao Tse-tung), 1973. Christmas Poem for radio & TV, Finnish Broadcasting Corp., 1965. Three fantasies over Vivaldi's 'Winter', Finnish TV, 1968. Contbr. to var. jrnls. Recip. many prizes for translating & writing inclng: Prize of Finnish State for Authors, 1965 & for Translators, 1971; Hyvinkää Prize, 1971. Address: SF–05510 Päivärinta, Finland.

NIEMOJOWSKI, Jerzy Klosowski, b. 8 Dec. 1918. Writer. Education: Dept. of Laws, Jagiellonian Univ. of Cracow, Poland; Dept. of Econs., Univ. of London, U.K.; Schl. of Foreign Trade & Port Administration, London. Memberships: Int. P.E.N.; Polish Writers' Union; Int. Fed. of Free Jrnlsts. Published works: (in Polish) With Eagles Embroidered, a tragedy, 1945; The Most Costly Poem, 1945; The Pupils, 1956; Concerto for Female Voice, 1960; Epigrammata, 1963; Dance Order of Indygowlosa, 1970; Appassionata, 1971; (translations into Polish) Persona & Canto of Ezra Pound, 1960; Evocations, an Anthology of Latin-Am. Poetry, 1968. Contbr. to: Dialog; Horyzonty; Kultura; Literatura na swiecie; Miesiecznik literacki; Odra; Poezja; Tematy; Tworczosc; Wiadomosci; Zycie literackie & many others. Address: 64 Sumatra Rd., Hampstead, London NW6, U.K.

NIENSTAEDT, Marjorie, b. 9 Apr. 1923. Homemaker. Education: B.S., Univ. of Mich.; M.S., Yale Univ. Married, 6 children. Positions held: Rsch. Asst. in Horticulture, Mich. State Univ.; Fellowship in Genetics, Conn. Agricl. Expmt. Stn., New Haven. Memberships: Former V.P., Rhinelander Rustic Writers; past V.P., Rhinelander Br., AAUW; Bd. Dirs., Wis. Regional Writers Assn., 1972-74; Wis. Fellowship of Poets. Published works: The Christmas Haiku, 1969 (for reading or presentation as a pageant – has been performed 23 times in Wis. & Hiroshima, Japan); A Fiesta for Giovanni, 1971 (story or pageant with tape). Contbr. to: The Angels; Martin Luther King Anthol.; New Poetry Out of Wis. Anthol. Honours, awards: 1st prize for poetry, State writing proj. of Wis. AAUW, 1968; 1st pl. dramatic sketch (script in haiku & verse), 1969; Hon. Mentions for Short Stories, Wis. Regl. Writers Assn., 1972 & 73. Address: 809 Dorr Ave., Rhinelander, WI 54501, U.S.A.

NIKHILESWAR, b. 11 Aug. 1938. Teacher. Education:

B.A.; B.Ed. Memberships: Gen. Sec., Revolutionary Writers' Assn., A.P., 1972-73; Exec. Mbr., ibid. Published works: Digambara Kavntu, poetry; Mandutunna Taram, poetry; Godala venuka, jail memoirs. Contbr. to var. jrnls. in Telugu. Address: 46 Vidyanagar Colony, Hyderabad 500044, A.P., India.

NIKOLAI, Lorraine C., b. 20 Feb. 1910. Sales Lady. Education: H.S.; Dale Carnegie course for Public Speaking. Married Jacob J. Nickolai, 2 daughters. Positions held: former Sales Rep., Avon Co.; currently Sales Lady for Industrial Aid for the Blind, Milwaukee, Wis. Memberships: Chmn., Queen of Peace Grp., St. Michael's Parrish, seven consecutive yrs.; Sec., North Ctrl. Tech. Inst. Homemakers Club; Treas., Key Project, ibid; Wausau Writers Club, 22 yrs.; Int. Platform Assn., Cleveland, Ohio; Rib. Mt. Echoes; New World Poets & Bouquet of Roses; Quaderni de poesia; Centro Studi e Scambi Int.; Mondo; Award Chmn. for Cancer Drive & for Multiple Sclerosis Annual Drive; Reg. Writers Assn. Inc.; var. other church, civic & fraternal orgs. Published works: Rib Mt. Echoes, vol. I, 1963, vol. II, 1967; Rainbow Magic, 1966. Contbr. to: New World Poets; Bouquet of Roses; Quaderni de Poesia; Wausau Daily Record Herald, 1973; Times Review Catholic Diocesan Paper, 1973, etc. Address: 701 Humboldt Ave., Wausau, WI 54401, U.S.A.

NILES, Gwendolyn Arilla, b. 11 Mar. 1914. English & Literature Instructor. Education: B.S., Eastern Mich. Univ., Ypsilanti, Mich., 1940; M.A., Univ. of Mich., Ann Arbor, 1946; study at Columbia Univ., N.Y. & Stanford Univ., Calif. Positions held: H.S. Engl. Tchr., Pickford, Mich., 1941-43; H.S. Engl. Tchr., Plymouth, Mich., 1943-47; Engl. Tchr., Lake Mich. Coll., Benton Harbor, Mich., 1947-73. Memberships: Pres., Mich. State Poetry Soc., 1960-64; Chmn. of Creative Writing Grp., AAUW, Benton Harbor, Br.; Co-Chmn. & Co.Fndr., Southwest Mich. Writers Soc.; Sec., Twin Cities Arts Coun., 1974. Published works: A Changing Sky, 1945; The Singing of the Days, 1963; The Silence of the Rose, 1970. Contbr. to: Oregonian Verse; Portland Oregonian; Lyric; Kaleidograph; Versecraft; Christian Sci. Monitor; Poetry Digest; Am. Poet, etc. Honours, awards incl: 1st prize, Contest, Mich. State Poetry Soc., 1955 & '65; 1st prize for Christmas poem, Archer, 1955; Humorous Verse Award, Flame Mag., 1962; 1st prize, sonnet, Mich. State Poetry Soc. & another for serious quatrain, 1973. Address: 706 Pipestone, Benton Harbor, MI, U.S.A.

NIMS, John Frederick, b. 20 Nov. 1913. Professor of English & Comparative Literature. Education: Ph.D., Univ. of Chicago, 1945. Married, 4 children. Positions held: var. Professorships etc. at: Univ. of Notre Dame, Univ. of Toronto, Bocconi Univ. (Milan), Univ. of Florence, Univ. of Madrid, Univ. of Ill., Harvard Univ., Univ. of Fla. Published works: The Iron Pastoral, 1947; A Fountain in Kentucky, 1950; The Poems of St. John of the Cross, 1959, rev. 1968; Knowledge of the Evening, 1960; Of Flesh & Bone, 1967; Sappho to Valéry: Poems in Translation, 1971; Western Wind (a book about Poetry), 1974. Honours, awards: Harriet Monroe Meml. Award, 1942; Guarantors' Prize, 1943; Levinson Prize, 1944; Fulbright Award, 1952, '53; Smith-Mundt Award, 1958 '59; Nat. Fndn. Arts & Humanities Grant, 1967; Creative Writing Award, Am. Acad. of Arts & Letters, 1968. Address: Dept. of Engl., Univ. of Fla., Gainesville, FL 32601, U.S.A.

NIXON, Colin Harry, b. 9 Mar. 1939. Executive Officer, Department of Employment. Education: Dip. in Sociol., London Univ., 1968. Married Betty Morgan, 1 daughter. Memberships: Richmond Poetry Grp., 1970-; Editl. Bd., Orbis, 1972-. Contbr. to: Next Wave Poets, 1-1969, 2-1970, 3-1971, 4-1972; Civil Service Poetry, 1969, '70, '73; Swing Back Anthol.; Univ. Coll. Anthol., 1973; Tribune; Outposts; Samphire; Dublin Mag.; Tracks; Bogg; New Christian; Christian Century; Scrip; Orbis; New Headland; Expression One; Centre 17; Oasis; Voice; Chapman; Global Tapestry; Poetry Australia; Platform; Village Review; Parnassian; Glass Onion; Pink Peace, etc. Address: 72 Barmouth Rd., Wandsworth Common, London SW18 2DS, U.K.

NOBOA, Julio, Jr., b. 9 May 1949. Teacher. Education: Music major at Lane Tech. H.S.; B.A., Anthropol. at Univ. of Ill. at Chicago Circle. Positions held: Salesman; Teacher; Statistical Clerk; Personnel Specialist; Bilingual-Bicultural Tchr.; Literary Ed., Jrnl. of Contemporary Puerto Rican Thought. Contbr. to: The Rican, Jrnl. of Contemporary Puerto Rican Thought; Scott Foresman Reading Systems, anthol.; Book II of Variations: A Contemporary Literature Prog. Address: 2123 N. Point St., Chicago, IL 60647, U.S.A.

NOCHMAN, Lois, K., b. 5 Nov. 1924. Instructor of English. Education: A.B., Engl., 1946, A.M., Engl. Lang. & Lit., 1949, Univ. of Michigan. Married to Harold I. Pitchford Jr., 1944 (div. 1949); 2 children; Married to Marvin A. Nochman, 1953; 1 s. Positions held: Teacher, Adult ed., Honolulu, Hawaii, 1947; Ypsilanti HS., 1951-52; Special Instr. of Engl., Wayne State Univ., Detroit, 1953-54; Teacher, Instr. of Engl., Highland Park (Mich.) College, 1950-51, and since 1954. Contbr. to: Reflections, 1971; World Order, 1968; Midland Poetry Review, 1952 (under Lois Pitchford); Songs of the Open Road, 1952 (under Lois Pitchford); Ladies'Home Journal, 1952 (under Lois Pitchford); The Baha'i World, Vol. X11, 1954. Invited to give poetry reading at McGregor Public Library, Highland Park, Mich., Sept. 21, 1972. Address: 25227 Parkwood, Huntington Woods, MI 48070, USA.

NOE, Bessie Wherry, b. 27 Aug. 1904. Poet; Publicist; Lecturer; Patron of the Arts. Education: Indiana Univ. of Pennsylvania; NY Univ; Columbia Univ., Teachers Coll. Married, Ralph Wilson Noé (dec'd); 2 s. Positions held: Teacher, Vandergrift, Pa., Public Schools; Bentley School, Horace Mann, Alexander Robertson, NYC, (Private); NYC Public Schools; Columnist, Atlantis (Greek newspaper, in Engl. section); Lecturer, Women's Clubs (literary subjects). Memberships: Past Pres. Mark Twain Assoc. of NY; Archivist-Historian & Publicist; Treas. NY Poetry Forum; Life Member, Poetry Soc. of America; C.A.A.A.; Past Treas. NY Br.; Acad. of Am. Poets, Founder; Patron & Book Comm. Fifty Amer. Artists; Life Mem. Nat. Assoc. of Am. Composers & Conductors; Charter mem., Edwin Markham Soc.; Patron & Publicist, Broadway Grand Opera Assoc.; Grand Rapids Bards; Mem. New York Hist. Soc.; Mem. Eastern Centre, Poetry Soc. of London & World Poets Resource Center; World Poetry Soc. Intercontinental; Coordinator, World Poetry Day Luncheon for WPSI, 1973. Contbr. to: Riverdale News; Riverdale Press; Raleigh News & Observer; Beaufort News; Everywoman's Mag.; Atlantis; Riverdale Presbyt. Ch. Bulletin; Music Journal; Farnelle Anthol. on Perfume, in Poetry. Awards: Gold Medal, Int. Poets' Shrine, 1966; Qtr. Century Award, Mark Twain Assoc. of NY; Gold Medal Award, Mark Twain Assoc. of NY, 1973; Citation from World Poets' Resource Center, Inc., 1973, Citation as Donor of Award, NY Poetry Forum, 1972; Hon. Mention, Maurice Farnelle Award, 1973. Address: 226 Naples Terr., Bronx, New York, NY 10463, USA.

NOLAN, Pat "Rocky", pen names, DIABLO, Martian; PEEPER, Peter; REVERB, Max; PHIL, Phil, b. 3 Sept. 1943. Poet; Novelist. Education: St. Patrick's, Trois Reviere, Que., Canada; PS 10, Oakland, Ca.; Benteley High, Livonia, Mich.; Wayne State Univ., Detroit, Mich.; New School for Social Research, NYC; Duke Univ., Durham, N.C.; Univ. of Kansas, Lawrence, Kansas; Univ. of Mexico City, Mexico City; Sonoma State Coll, Ca. Divorced; 1 s. Positions held: Editor, In My Mind (poetry mag.), 1961; Editor, Anchor's Aweigh (poetry mag.), 1962-65; Editor, Polygon Press, poetry publishers, 1965-69; Editor, The End (poetry mag.), 1970-73; presently Poetry Consultant to the Russian River Writer's Conference, Inc. Memberships: Fellowship of American Poetry (Sec.); Translators Anonymous; The Shakespearian Sonnet Soc. (hon. member); The Russian River Writer's Conference (Poetry Consultant); Zen Psycho-Phallic Inst. (Translator). Published works: The Big Heart, 1959; Spain In My Ear, 1963; After Kublai Kahn, 1965; Liner Notes For An Album Entitled The Rolling Stones Sing Jack Spicer, 1967; Rock Me/Roll Me Vast Fatality,

1970; Bob Hope In A Buick, 1971; Our Fashion Plate, 1972; The Chinese Quartet, 1973. Contbr. to: Adventures In Poetry; Blue Suede Shoes; Hollow Orange; Z; Toothpick; Paper Pudding; Open Hand; Telephone; Corduroy; Baloney Street; The Paris Review; The World; Rolling Stone; 49 South; Roy Rogers; Strange Faeces; Silver; Tarzan of The Apes; Dog Bite; The Brand New Testament; Ladies Home Jungle. Recip. The Poets Foundation Award, 1972; The Doris Green Award, 1973. Address: Box 798, Monte Rio, CA 95462, USA.

NOLAND, Mary Ruth, b. 8 Jan. 1919. Artist. Education: Ariz. State Univ., Tempe, Ariz., 1950. Married Robert I. Noland. Positions held: Has demonstrated art in Galls., stores & NLAPW regl.-Albuquerque, N.M., 1971; Rdr., Ariz. State Dept. of Public Instrn. Statewide Poetry Contest, 1969 & Judge 1970. One-woman shows: Capitol Bank City, Nashville, Tenn., 1965; Parthenon Gall., ibid, 1966; David Lipscomb Coll., 1967; WSM Color TV, 1967; Parthenon Gall., 1967; Rhodes Gall., Phoenix, Ariz., 1968; Goldwaters, ibid, 1968; Univ. of Ariz., Tucson, 1968; Big Boy Restaurant, Phoenix, 1969. Rep. in permanent pvte. colls. throughout U.S.A., Holland, Italy, U.K., Thailand. Memberships incl: Nat. Art Bd., Nat. League of Am. Penwomen, 1972-74; Phoenix Histn. & Press Book, 1972-74; Nat. Art Assn. Comm. Bienniel, 1968-70; State Sec., 1970-72 & Phoenix Art Chmn., 1968-70; World Org. China Painter, 1973-74; Histn., Ariz. State Poetry Soc., 1969-70; Recording Sec., 1970. Rep. in following anthols: Ballet on the Wind, 1969; Prairie Poet, 1970; 70 Poets Anthol., 1970; Echoes of Faith, 1970; Moon Age Poets, 1970; Bouquet of Poems, Italy, 1971; The Spring Anthol., 1971; Vol. II Anthol. Am. Poets, 1971; Yearbook of Modern Poetry, 1971, etc. Contbr. to var. mags. & jrnls. Poetry read over many radio stns. Recip. num. prizes, hons., ribbons & trophy. Address: 4211 E. Roma, Phoenix, AZ 85018, U.S.A.

NOLAND, Patricia Hampton. Writer. Education: Univ. of Houston, Texas. Memberships: Internat. Poetry Inst., Inc., (Founder and Pres.); Houston Chapter, Poetry Soc. of Texas (Vice Pres.; Prog. Chairman (1969-70)). Published works: Poems, 1969. Contbr. to: Times Picayune; Buffalo Courier Express; Houston Chronicle; Houston Post; Idaho Statesman; Gulf Coast Gardner; Jackson Daily News. Awards: Hon. Dr. Leadership in Poetry (Internat. Acad. of Leadership, Quezon City, Philippines), 1969; Named Hon. Internat. Poet Laureate by UPLI, Philippines, 1969; recip. many small prizes for poetry. Address: P.O.Box 52454, Houston, TX 77052, USA.

NOLL, Lou Barker, pen name **NOLL, Bink,** b. 15 Apr. 1927. Professor of English. Education: A.B., Princeton Univ., 1948; M.A., The Johns Hopkins Univ., 1950; Ph.D., Univ. of Colo., 1956. Divorced, 3 children. Positions held: Instr. & Asst. Prof., Dartmouth Coll., 1954-61; Fulbright Lectr., Univ. of Zaragoza, Spain, 1960-61; Asst., Assoc. & Full Prof., Beloit Coll., 1961– & Poet-in-Res., 1968–; Sr. Fellow in Humanities, Princeton Univ., 1967-68. Published works: The Center of the Circle, 1962; The Feast, 1967. Contbr. to: Poetry; The New Yorker; Atlantic; Yale Review; Va. Qtly. Review; Beloit Poetry Jrnl., etc. Address: 805 Church St., Beloit, WI 53511, U.S.A.

NOLTE, Juanita H., b. 7 June 1913. Writer. Education: Coll. of Commerce, Wheeling, W.Va. Married George M. Nolte. Positions held: Wrote radio scripts for var. radio stns.; Continuity Dir., WBZE, Wheeling; Produced Commercials; Interviewed personalities in connection w. radio. Memberships: var. offices in Wheeling Poetry Soc.; Corres. Sec., W.Va. Poetry Soc., 4 yrs. Rep. in following anthols: The Spring Anthol., 1961; Modern Am. Muse, 1961; UAPA Poetry Anthol., 1964; Echoes of Faith, 1970; Echoes of the W.Va. Poetry Soc., 1971. Contbr. to: Ideals; Our Pets; Hyacinths & Biscuits, etc. Poetry Ed., W.Va. Register for sev. yrs. Has judged yearly contests for diocese of W.Va. Elem. & H.S., sponsored by Court Carroll No. 299, Cath. Daughters of Am., 1955-74. Recip. var.

poetry prizes. Address: Apt. 303, River View Towers, 601 Main St., Wheeling, WV 26003, U.S.A.

NORMANTON, John, b. 1918. Painter; Works in the Textile Trade. Education: Bradford Technical Coll., Yorks. Published works: The Window Game, 1968. Contbr. to (Anthols.): London Magazine Poems, 1966; (Jrnls.): Adelphi; London Mag.; Prospects.

NORRIS, Leslie, b. 21 May 1921. Writer. Education: Coventry Trng. Coll.; Univ. of Southampton. Married. Positions held: Tchr., Grass Royal Schl., Yeovil, 1948-52; Dpty. Hd. Tchr., Southdown Schl., Bath, 1952-55; Hd. Tchr., Aldingbourne Schl., Sussex, 1956-58; Prin. Lectr. in Degree Studies, The Coll. of Educ., Bognor Regis, 1958-73. Memberships: The Poetry Soc.; The Soc. of Authors; Yr Academi Cymreig; Chmn., Lit. Panel, The Southern Arts Assn. Published works: The Tongue of Beauty, 1941; Poems, 1944; The Loud Winter, 1967; Finding Gold, 1967; Ransoms, 1970; Mountains Polecats Pheasants, 1974. Contbr. to: The Atlantic Monthly; The Anglo-Welsh Review; The New Yorker; The Poetry Review; The Listener; Workshop; Poetry Wales; Poetry North-West; Planet; Transatlantic The Review; The London Mag.; Priapus; The Observer; Stand; English; The London Welshman; The N.Y. Times; The Poet (India), etc. Honours, awards: Welsh Arts Coun. Award, 1969; British Arts Coun. Award, 1969; The Alice Hunt Bartlett Prize, Poetry Soc. Award, 1972; Vis. Poet at The Univ. of Wash., Seattle, 1973; Fellow, Royal Soc. of Lit., 1974. Address: Plas Nant, Northfields Lane, Aldingbourne, Chichester, Sussex, U.K.

NORSE, Harold George, b. 6 July 1916. Poet. Education: B.A., Brooklyn Coll., 1938; M.A., NY Univ., 1951. Positions held: Ballet Dancer; WPA Archives; Sheet metal Wkr., Maritime Commn.; Coll. Instr.; Mag. Ed.; Publr. Asst.; Film-dubber, Italy; Tutor of Engl., Europe, & various other. Published works include: The Undersea Mountain, 1953; The Roman Sonnets of GG Belli (transls. & adaptns.), 1960, 1972; The Dancing Beasts, 1962; Karma Circuit, 1966; Olé Mag. (H. Norse Issue), 1966. Contbr. to the following anthols., jrnls., mags., etc: Penguin Mod. Poets 13, 1969; Accent; Accent Anthol.; Between Worlds; Botteghe Obscure; Commentary; Kenyon Review; Paris Review; Sewanee Review; Saturday Review; Poetry, Chicago; Hudson Review; Evergreen Review; Big Table; Two Cities; Cosmos; Klactoveedsedsteen; Art News; NM Quarterly; Quarterly Review of Lit.; New Directions Anthol.; New World Writing; The Nation; Ladies Home Jrnl.; Olé, Los Angeles Free Press; Folder The Outsider; Residue; El Corno Emplumado, etc. Honours, awards: Poetry Grant, Rome–NY Fndn., 1962; Invitation to record work, Lib. of Congress Archive. Address: c/o Herman, 29B Guy Place, San Francisco, Calif. 94105, USA.

NORTH, Eleanor Beryl, b. 6 July 1898. College Professor; Poet. Education: M.A., Pa. State Univ.; Harvard Univ.; Cambridge, Oxford & London Univs., UK. Positions held: Prof. of Lit., Juniata Coll.; Youngstown Univ., & Berry Coll.; Visiting Prof. of Shakespeare & Poetry; Sponsor of 'Literary Pilgrimages' (annually) for small groups of students, summers. Memberships: AAUP; Daughters of the Am. Revolution; Colonial Dames; AAUW; Delta Kappa Gamma; Cons., Int. Poetry Soc.; Am. Poetry League; Sigma Tau Delta; Poetry Soc. of Aesthetics; United Poets; Vice-Pres., Internat. Poets Shrine; Accademia Internazionali Leonardo da Vinci; Authors' League; Royal Order of Bookfellows; Poetry Guild; Centro Studi E Scambi Internazionali, Shelley-Keats Assoc.; Shakespeare Fndn.; Poetry Soc. Publications: Break of Dawn, 1928; Fall o' Dew, 1936; Grace Notes, 1953; My Heart Sings, 1969. High Tide (poetry), 1973. Contbr. to: Sea to Sea in Song; Delta Kappa Gamma Mag.; Poetry (Australia); Filigree (UK); Ch. Advocate; Am. Poet. Prairie Poet; United Poets; Nat. Anthol.; Year Alive; Quadernia di Poesia; Garden Gateways; Ch. Window; Manifold; Ga. Mag.; Nat. Educ. Assoc. Mag.; Am. Poetry League Mag. Honours: Poem inscribed on bronze plaque, Berry Coll., unveiled,

1967; Lit. Rsch. Grant, 1963, 1966; Philos. Scholarship, Harvard Univ., 1942; Medal of hon., Accademia Internazionali, 1968; Citation, 2000 Women of Achievement; Award of Merit, Nat. Register of Prominent Ams.; Award of Merit; Who's Who of Am. Women; Citation, Who's Who in the East, etc. Address: 204 E Hamilton Ave., Apt. 14, State Coll., Pa. 16801, USA.

NORTHE, James Neill, b. 1894. Singer; Pianist; Lecturer; Composer; Reader; Teacher; Reviewer; Dealer in rare & out of print books; Poet. Education: St. Louis Coll.; Chaffey Jr. Coll. Memberships: Poetry Soc. of Am.; Hon Life Mbr., Oklahoma State Writers; etc. Ed., Silhouettes, Warp & Woof (newspaper column), & Seven. Sponsor, Davis Annual Contest & Jesse Stuart Contest. Published works: History of Ontario; California; Mata Hari; Confalon; It Dawneth in the East; Though Sunsets Die; Fires of a Tropic Moon; etc. Trans. into Italian, Spanish, Chinese, Japanese, French. Ed., anthols: Threads & Shadows; Land of Gold. Contbr. to: Lit. Digest; Sunset; Lit. Review; Charleston Evening Post; The Christian; L.A. Saturday Night; Man; N.Y. Am.; Pasadena Star News; CS Monitor; Author & Jrnlst.; La Fiera Lettretaria (Italy); Seydell Qtly. (Belgium); etc. Recip. many hons. Address: A Pointe Northe Bookstore, 21½ N. Harvey, Terminal Arcade, Oklahoma City, OK 73102, U.S.A.

NOTT, Kathleen Cecilia. Author; Poet; Philosopher; Critic. Education: Mary Datchelor Girls' Schl., London; King's Coll., London Univ.; Oxford Univ. Positions held: Pres., Progressive League; Ed., Pen-Unesco Bull. of Selected Books. Memberships: Engl. Centre, Pen (VP). Published works include: Lands-scapes & Departures, 1947; Poems from the North, 1956; Creatures & Emblems, 1961; 4 novels & 2 lit. philos. wrks.; Co-author of sev. books. Contbr. to the following jrnls. & mags: Observer; New Statesman; BBC. Honours, awards: Arts Coun. Bursary, 1968. Address: 6 Newlands Rd., Horsham, Sussex, UK.

NOVAK, Ladislav, b. 4 Aug. 1925. Professor; Writer; Painter. Education: Charles' Univ., Prague, Czechoslovakia. Memberships: Prague Grp. of Expmtl. Poetry, 1961-64; Artistic Movement, PHASES, Paris, 1965-72. Published works: Pocta Jacksonu Pollockovi, Prague, 1966; Závraté, Prague, 1968; Textamenty, Brno, 1968; Gedichte für Bewegte Rezitation, Berlin, 1970. Frequent Expositions in Prague (Spálova Gaerie), 1965, '69, '70, Paris (Les Mains Libres), 1971 & Milan (Schwarz), 1974. Contbr. to: An Anthology of Concrete Poetry, 1967; Concrete Poetry: A World View, 1968; Spatialisme et Poésie Concrete, 1968; MPT 5 (Czech), 1969; Aktuelle Kunst in Osteuropa, 1971; Phases, Paris, 1966-72. Address: Nezvalova 44, 67401 Třebič, Czechoslovakia.

NOVAK, Michael Paul, b. 6 July 1935. Professor of English. Education: A.B. (Engl.), Cath. Univ., 1957; MFA (Engl.), Univ. of Iowa, 1962. Married to J. Callanan, 1958, 1 d., 1 s. Positions held: Instr. of Engl., Ill. State Univ., 1962-63; Assoc. Prof. of Engl., St. Mary Coll., 1963–; Chairman, Dept. of Engl., 1972–. Mbr., Mod. Lang. Assoc. Pub.: The Leavenworth Poems, 1972. Contbr. to: Hudson Review; Kenyon Review; Malahat Review; Denver Quarterly; Perspective; Colo. Quarterly; Western Humanities Review; Midwest Quarterly; Poetry Bag; Descant; Nimrod; SD Quarterly; Kans. Quarterly; Mad River Review; Four Quarters; Southwester; Fine Arts Discovery; Poem; Nat. Cath. Reporter. Honours: Harcourt, Brace & World Fellowship, Writers' Conf., 1966; Kan. City Star Award, 1969, '70. Address: St. Mary Coll., Leavenworth, Kans. 66048, USA.

NOVAK, Robert Lee, b. 4 Sept. 1933. Assistant Prof. of English. Education: A.B., Wabash Coll.; Univ. of Indiana; M.A.; Ph.D., Univ. of Oklahoma. Editor, The Windless Orchard. Member: Creators, Ft. Wayne. Pubs.: High Afternoon, 1971; The Woman in the Red Skirt, 1971; At the Splinter House, 1971. Contrib. to: Baby John; Happiness Holding Tank; Westigan Review; Stoney Lonesome; Crazy Horse, etc.

Address: Engl. Dept., Purdue Univ., Ft. Wayne, Ind. 46805, USA.

NOWLAN, Alden, b. 25 Jan. 1933. Writer. Positions held: News Editor, The Telegraph-Journal, St. John, N.B., 1963-68; Writer in residence, Univ. of New Brunswick, since 1968. Pubs.: Between Tears and Laughter, 1967; The Mysterious Naked Man, 1969; Playing the Jesus Game, 1970; Miracle at Indian River, 1968; Various Persons Named Kevin O'Brien, 1973. Contrib. to: Reader's Digest; The Realist; Maclean's; Saturday Night, etc. Recip. Governor-General's Award for Poetry, 1967; Guggenheim Fellow in Poetry, 1967; Hon. Dr. of Letters, Univ. of N.B., 1971. Address: Dept. of Engl., Univ. of New Brunswick, Fredericton, N.B., Canada.

NOYES, Stanley Tinning, pen name, **NOYES, Stanley,** b. 7 Apr. 1924. College Teacher; Writer. Education: Univ. of Calif., Berkeley, A.B., 1950, M.A., 1951. Personal details: Married to Nancy Black; 3 children (Frank, Charles, Julie). Positions held: U.C., Berkeley, Extension Div., Instr., fall 1954, spring, 1955; Calif. Coll. of Arts & Crafts, Oakland, Asst. Prof. of Humanities and Dean of Men, fall 1954, through spring 1961; Coll. of Santa Fe, New Mexico, Lecturer in Humanities, spring 1965 through fall 1971; Program Coordinator, Poetry-in-the-Schools project, Santa Fe, fall 1972 to present; Poetry Editor, New Mexico mag., March 1973 to present. Published works: No Flowers for a Clown (novel), 1961; Shadowbox (novel), 1970; The Truchas County War (novel in preparation); Faces and Spirits, (poems) 1974. Contbr. to: Poems Southwest (anthol), 1968; Poets on Street Corners (anthol), 1969; (short stories) Berkeley Review; Alfred Hitchcock's Mystery Mag.; Coastlines; (poetry) Carmel Pinecone; Janus; Le Goeland; Variegation; San Francisco Review; The Galley Sail Review; dust; Voices Internat.; NM Qtly.; SUR; Quetzal; The NM Review & Legislative Journal; The Desert Review; The Sunstone Review; Sumac; Trace; Steelhead; Pembroke Mag.; Puerto del Sol; Goat's Head. Address: 634 East Garcia, Santa Fe, NM 87501, USA.

NUNN, Marie Downs, b. 23 May 1905. Writer; Poet. Education: A.B. in Engl., San Jose State Univ.; Grad. of Heald's Business Coll.; Grad. work at Univ. of Calif., at Berkeley (Poetry & Prose). Widow; 1 s. Positions held: Sec., US Civil Service, with Air Corps; Freelance writer and poet; Former Editor of Airy Views. Memberships: World Poetry Soc. Intercontinental; Intercontinental Biographical Assoc. (life fellow); Nat. Writers Club; NLAPW; American Assoc. of Univ. Women; Pacific Northwest Writers; Calif. Writers; Calif. Olympiad of the Arts; Calif. Fed. of Chaparral Poets (Santa Cruz & Robt. Frost Chapters); Ina Coolbrith Circle (Calif. Poetry group honoring 1st Calif. Poet Laureate); Edwin Markham Poetry Soc.; Valley Writers; Smithsonian Inst. (Wash., DC.); The Museum Soc. of San Francisco; Montalvo Assoc. (Art Center); Order of Eastern Star; Genealogical Soc. of Santa Cruz County (charter member); Napa Study Club; Rutherford Grange; Spring Valley Farm Bureau; Santa Cruz Camera Club; Seamaster's Club; Lady Sabena Club, etc. Past Pres. and Sec. of several clubs. Published work: Rumbling Wagon Wheels (fiction). Contbr. to: (anthols.) Shore Anthol., 1971; Santa Cruz Chaparral Poets, 1973; Ina Coolbrith Anthol., 1973. Contbr. to mags., journals: Poet; Janus; Modern Haiku; Haiku Highlights; Dragonfly; Good Deeder; Mount Hermon Log; Swordsman; Pacifica Mag. Awards: Prize, Santa Cruz Chap. Poets for Christmas Poem, 1971; Honored with membership in Relic Accumulators (Calif.) for work done in field of antiques (prose writing and speaking engagements on same subject). Other hons. in field of prose writing, 1969, 1970 for newspaper features, etc. Address: 362 Horizon Way, Pacifica, CA 94044, USA.

NUSBAUM, Willene Hinson, b. 30 June 1915. Postal Clerk (19 yrs.). Education: HS Grad., Chanute HS, Kansas, 1933. Married to Max Nusbaum. Positions held: Asst. Editor, Modern Haiku, 1969; Editor, Student Section, Modern Haiku, 1970; Book Reviewer,

Modern Haiku, Haiku West, and Jean's Journal. Memberships: World Poetry Soc. (Rep.); CSSI (Rep.); American Haiku Soc.; Idaho Poets & Writers Guild; Kansas Authors Club; Midwest Chaparral; Internat. Platform Assoc., etc. Published work: These I Love, 1967 (2nd printing, 1971). Contbr. to many anthols., journals, etc. Awards: Numerous, including hon. mentions and prizes from: Poet Mag., Haiku West, Am. Poetry Fellowship Soc., Haiku, Password (TV Prog.), NI APW, Poets Guild, Internat. Platform Assoc. Poetry read on radio and TV. Address: P.O. Box 141, Bern, KS 66408, USA.

NUTTALL, Jeff, b. 8 July 1933. College Lecturer. Education: Bath Acad. of Art. Positions held: Painter; Comic-strip Writer; Trumpeter; Pianist; Editor; Script Writer, The People Show; Ed., My Own Mag.; Tchr., Art Depts., Sec. Schls.; Lectr., Fundamental Studies Dept., Bradford Coll. of Art; Lectr., Fine Arts, Leeds Coll. of Art. Published works: The Limbless Virtuoso, 1963; Songs Sacred & Secular, 1964; Poems I Want to Forget, 1965; Journals, 1968; Penguin Modern Poets, 12; Poems 1963-69, 1970; (fiction) The Case of Isabel & the Bleeding Foetus, 1966; Come Back Sweet Prince, 1966; Mr. Watkins Got Drunk & Had to be Carried Home, 1968; Oscar Christ & the Immaculate Conception, 1968; Pig, 1969; (soc. crit.) Bomb Culture, 1968. Address: 461 Huddersfield Rd., Wyke, Bradford, Yorkshire, UK.

NYE, Robert, b. 15 Mar. 1939. Writer. Positions held: Poetry Ed., The Scotsman, 1967–; Poetry Critic, The Times, 1971–. Published works: Juvenilia 1, 1961; Juvenilia 2, 1963; Darker Ends, 1969; Sir Walter Ralegh, 1972; William Barnes, 1972; Swinburne, 1973. Contbr. to: Times Lit. Supplement; London Mag.; Encounter; Atlantic Monthly; Critical Quarterly; Observer; Listener; Am. Review; New Statesman; Spectator; Art & Literature; The Tablet, etc. Rep. in var. anthols. inclng: The Young British Poets, 1971. Honours, awards: James Kennaway Meml. Award, 1970; Scottish Arts Coun. Publ. Award, 1970; Scottish Arts Coun. Bursaries, 1970 & 73; Gregory Award, 1963. Address: c/o Calder & Boyars, 18 Brewer St., London W2, U.K.

NYE, Sarah Litsey, pen name, **LITSEY, Sarah,** b. 23 June 1901. Teacher. Education: Sargent Schl. of Phys. Educ., Cambridge, Mass. Personal details: Daughter of Edwin Carlile Litsey, Poet Laureate of Ky.; married. Positions held: Inst., Mary Baldwin Schl., Staunton, Va.; Inst., Atherton HS, Louisville, Ky.; Inst., Famous Writers Schl., Westport, Conn.; Freelance writer. Memberships: PEN Int.; NY Women Poets; (past mbr.) Poetry Soc. Am.; Louisville Arts Club; VP, Conn. Br. Penwomen. Published works: Legend, 1936; For the Lonely, 1937; The Oldest April, 1957. Contbr. to: Scribners; Sat. Eve. Post; Good Housekeeping; NY Times; NY Herald Tribune; Christian Sci. Monitor; Contemporary Verse; Voices; The Lyric; Poetry Digest; Kaleidescope; Commonweal; Poetry World, etc. Honours, Awards: 1st Prize, NY Women Poets, 1958, '59; 1st Prize, Poetry Soc. Am., 1940; 1st Prize, Shards, 1937, '38; 1st Prize, Ted Malone's Radio Contest, 1937; 1st Prize, Poetry World, 1935; 1st Prize, Pa. Poetry Soc., 1959, etc. Address: RFD 2, West Redding, Conn. 06896, USA.

NYGARDSHAUG, Gert, b. 22 Mar. 1946. Teacher in Philosophy & Sociology. Education: Univ. of Oslo, Norway. Positions held: Writer, Friheten (Communist Newspaper), 1968-71; The Authors' Rep., Solidarity Comm. for Vietnam's Leadership, 1972. Memberships: Den Norske Forfatterforening (The Norwegian Authors Union); Norsk Litteraturkritikerlag (Union of Literature Critics). Published works: Impulser, (poetry), 1966; Paxion, (poetry), 1971. Contbr. to: Dagbladet; Østlendingen; Klassekampen; Profil; Friheten; Pax; Fjell-Ljom; Universitas. Address: Vallervn 128, 1346 Gjettum, Norway.

O

OAKES, Philip, b. 31 Jan. 1928. Journalist. Education: Royal School, Wolverhampton; Darwen Grammar School. Personal details: Married: Stella Fleming; 1 s. (Toby), 1 d. (Susan). Positions held: Arts columnist, The Sunday Times; and formerly Critic/Columnist, Evening Standard, Sunday Telegraph, etc. Published works: Unlucky Jonah, 1933, In the Affirmative, 1968; Exactly What We Want, 1965; The God Botherers, 1969; Experiment at Proto (novel), 1973; Married/Singular (poems), 1973. Contbr. to: London Mag.; New Statesman; Transatlantic Review; Spectator; The Listener; The Sunday Times; Times Lit. Supp.; Nova; also broadcast on BBC TV and Radio. Address: Pinnock Farm House, Pluckley, Kent, UK.

OBRESTAD, Tor, b. 12 Feb. 1938. Poet. Published works: Kollisjon (Collision), 1966; Vart daglige brød (Our daily bread), 1968; Den norske løve, (The Norwegian Lion), 1970; Sauda og Shanghai, 1973. Poets translated into Norwegian: William Blake, 1967; Ho Chi Minh, 1969; Heberto Padilla, 1970; Mao Tsetung, 1971; Robert Bly, 1972. Contbr. to: Dagbladet, Oslo; Vinduet, Oslo; Profil, Oslo; Syn og Segn, Oslo. Recip., Norwegian Debut-Prize, 1967. Address: Vestbyveien 23a, Oslo 9, Norway.

O'BRIEN, Katharine (Elizabeth), b. 10 Apr. 1901. Educator. Education: A.B., Bates Coll., A.M., Cornell Univ., Ph.D., Brown Univ., Sc.D.Ed. Hon., Univ. of Maine; L.H.D. Hon., Bowdoin Coll. Positions held: Chairman, mathematics dept., Coll. of New Rochelle; Head, mathematics dept., Deering HS.; Lecturer in mathematics, Univ. of Maine, Portland campus; Lecturer in mathematics, Brown Univ., Summer Sessions. Memberships: Phi Beta Kappa; Sigma Xi; NY Acad. of Sciences; Mathematical Assoc. of America; Poetry Soc. of America; Internat. Platform Assoc. Published works: Excavation and other verse, 1967; Sequences (Mathematics Enrichment Series), 1966; also Contbr. to: (anthols.) The Golden Year, 1960; The Phoenix Nest, 1960; The Diamond Anthol., 1971; (textbook) ASTC Mathematics, Book 3, 1970; (newspapers and journals) Saturday Review; CS Monitor; NY Herald Tribune; Ladies' Home Journal; Harper's; Poet (India); Poetry Chap-Book; Survey; Rotarian; Boston Herald; Scientific Monthly; Scripta Mathematica; Bulletin of the American Mathematical Society; American Mathematical Monthly; Mathematics Mag.; Mathematics Teacher; Science; NY Theater Program. Address: 130 Hartley St., Portland, ME 04103, USA.

OCHESTER, Edwin Frank, pen name, **OCHESTER, Ed,** b. 15 Sept. 1939. Educator; Farmer. Education: B.A., Cornell Univ.; M.A., Harvard Univ.; Univ. of Wis. Positions held: Instr., Univ. of Fla., 1967-70; Instr., Univ. of Pitts., 1970–. Published works: Dancing on the Edges of Knives, 1973; The Third Express, 1973; The Great Bourgeois Bus Company, 1969; We Like It Here, 1967. Contbr. to: The New Republic; Chicago Review; The Colo. Quarterly; Poetry Northwest; Prairie Schooner; West Coast Review; Centennial Review; Wormwood Review; Beloit Poetry Jrnl.; TransPacific; Transition; Cafe Solo; Three Rivers Poetry Jrnl., etc. Recip., The Devins Award, 1973. Address: RD1, Box 174, Shelocta, PA 15774, U.S.A.

OCKERSE, Thomas, b. 12 Apr. 1940. Associate Professor of Graphic Design; Artist; Poet. Education: B.F.A., Ohio State Univ., 1963; M.F.A., Yale Univ., 1965. Positions held: Sr. Designer, Fogleman Assocs., Morristown, N.J., 1965-67; Asst. Prof., Ind. Univ., Bloomington, Ind., 1967-71; Assoc. Prof. (Dept. Hd.), Rhode Is. Schl. of Design, Providence, 1971–; Ed.-Publr., Tom Ockerse Editions. Published works: System SP-VI, 1968; Stamps-TO, 1968; Six (poems), 1968; The A-Z Book, 1969; T.O.P., 1970; Pray for Peace, 1971; Space Trunk Alphabet, 1971; The Visual Hist. of Numbers, 1972. Contbr. to: Tafelronde (Belgium); Subvers (Netherlands); The Courier Jrnl. & Times, Louisville, Ky.; Third Assembling; Breakthru in

Fiction; In Youth, etc. Address: 37 Woodbury St., Providence, RI 02906, U.S.A.

O'CONNELL, Richard (James), b. 25 Oct. 1928. Poet; Educator. Education: B.S. in Educ., Temple Univ., 1956; M.A., Johns Hopkins Univ., 1957. Positions held: Instr. in Engl., Temple Univ., 1957-61; Asst. Prof. of Engl., ibid, 1961-69; Assoc. Prof. of Engl., ibid, 1969-; Guest Lectr. in Poetry, Dept. of Writing Seminars, Johns Hopkins Univ., 1961-; Ed., Poetry Newsletter & Atlantis Editions. Memberships: MLA; Lit. Fellowship of Phila.; Associated Writing Programs. Published works: From an Interior Silence, 1961; Cries of Flesh & Stone, 1962; Pith & Vinegar (anthol. edited by William Cole), 1969; Of Poetry & Power (J.F.K. anthol.); Brazilian Happenings, 1966; Terrane, 1967; Open Poetry (anthol. edited by Ronald Gross & George Quasha), 1973. Contbr. to: The Paris Review; The New Yorker; The Atlantic Monthly; Qtly. Review of Lit.; Evergreen Review; The Tex. Qtly.; The Southern Humanities Review, etc. Honours, awards: Twice Fulbright Lectr. in Am. Lit., Rio de Janeiro, Univ. of Brazil, 1960 & in Pamplona, Spain at the Univ. of Navarre, 1962-63; Contemporary Poetry Prize, 1972. Address: 4910 North 12th St., Philadelphia, PA 19141, U.S.A.

O'CONNOR, Fleann Patrick, b. 13 Feb. 1944. Academic; Actor; Editor. Education: B.A., Engl. Lit. & Lang. Positions held: A debating Tour of US (40 Univs.), sponsored by the Inst. of Int. Educ., N.Y.; Mbr., Abbey Schl. of Acting, 1965-66; Actor, Kinuara Castle, County Galway, 1966; Reviews Ed., The Dublin Mag., 1968-; Research Student, St. Catherine's Coll., Cambridge, 1969-. Contbr. to (Jrnls.): Dublin Mag.; Irish Times; Icarus; Broadsheet. Address: 5 Fitswilliam Square, Dublin 2, Repub. of Ireland.

O'CONNOR, Marie Philip Constant Bancroft. Writer. Married twice, 9 children. Mbr., Soc. of Authors. Published works: Selected Poems, 1968. Contbr. to: Penguin Poets, 1974; New Verse; Zoot; Century Verse; Life & Letters; Poetry London & num. anthols. Address: Clair de Lune, rue Jeanne d'Arc, 62930 Wimereux, France.

O'CONNOR, Patrick Joseph, pen name **PADRAIC FIACC,** b. 15 Apr. 1924. Poet. Education: St. Joseph's Seraphic Seminary, Calicoon, N.Y. State, U.S.A. Married, 1 daughter. Member, The Poetry Soc. Published works: By the Black Stream, 1969; Odour of Blood, 1973. Rep. in following anthols: New Irish Poets, 1948; Penguin Book of Irish Verse, 1971; Sphere Book of Modern Irish Poetry, 1972; Choice, 1973; 10 Irish Poets, 1974. Contbr. to: The Irish Times; The Irish Independant; New Irish Writing; Poetry Ireland; Hibernia; Era; The Honest Ulsterman; Words; Irish Bookman; Capuchin Annual; Northern Ireland BBC, etc. Recip., George Russell (AE) Meml. Prize for vol. of poems 'Woe to the Boy', 1957. Address: 43 Farmley Pk., Glengormley, New Town Abbey, Co. Antrim, U.K.

O'CONNOR, Philip, b. 1916. Scriptwriter for BBC Third Programme. Education: Mature Student at Tchrs. Training Coll. Married w. 6 children. Positions held: Ed., Seven (own Mag.); Has worked in a Continental Telephone Exchange & in a Library; Prose Writer & Scriptwriter for BBC Third Prog., 1950-. Published works: Selected Poems, 1936-1966, 1968; Other: Memoirs of a Public Baby, 1958; Steiner's Tour, 1960; The Lower View, 1960; Living in Croesor, 1962; Vagrancy, 1963; Journal (Ed. by John Berger), 1969. Contbr. to (Anthols.): A Little Treasury of Modern Poetry, 1946; Penguin Book of Comic and Curious Verse, 1952; Poetry of the Thirties, 1964.

O'CONNOR, Robert Patrick, pen name **PATRICK, Robert,** b. 27 Sept. 1937. Playwright. Education: Eastern N.M. Univ. Memberships: N.Y. Theatre Strategy; Playwrights Cooperative; Actors Studio West. Contbr. to: Things (Columbia Univ.); M.E.A.L. (Hunter Coll.); Calliope (Univ. of Ga.); El Portal (Eastern N.M. Univ.); Cineaste (N.Y.C.) Address: 3426

Winslow Dr., Los Angeles, CA 90026, U.S.A.

ØDEGARD, Knut, b. 6 Nov. 1945. Author; Poet. Education: Examen artium, 1965; Examen philosophicum, 1965; studies in theology & langs. Lit. Critic, Aftenposten, 1968-. Memberships: Norwegian Soc. of Authors, 1968-; Bd. Mbr., ibid, 1970-72; Norwegian Soc. of Critics, 1969-; Bd. Mbr., ibid, 1970-; European Soc. of Culture, 1973; Norwegian Authors Ctr., 1968. Published works: (books) Drøymaren, vandraren og kjelda, poems, 1967; Konsert i eit kvitt hus, poems, 1968; I pensjonatet, poems, 1970; Det mørke regnet, poems, 1972; Hljómleikari Hvítu húsi (selected poems in Icelandic transl.), 1973. Translations: Regn i mai, Einar Bragi's (Icel.) poems, 1973; Det ma bli lys, Sandor Petöfi's (Hung.) poems, 1973; Gyula Illyes, poems, 1974; Modern Poetry from the Faroes, 1974. Contbr. to: Aftenposten; Dagbladet; Syn og Segn; Ergo; Vinduet; Minervas Kvartalskrift; Svenska Dagbladet; Réttur; Samvinnan, etc. Recip. Scholarship, Norwegian State (artists), 1972. Address: Anders Rørholts v. 2, 3100 Tønsberg, Norway.

ODEI, Larbi Ernest, b. 10 Oct. 1939. Journalist. Education: Dip. in Jrnlsm. Positions held: Reporter; Sr. Reporter; Regl. Rep. Address: Graphic Corp., P.O. Box 425, Cape Coast, Ghana.

ODEN, Gloria Catherine, b. 30 Oct. 1923. Writer. Education: B.A., Howard Univ., 1944; J.D., ibid, 1948; postgrad. work in Am. Studies. Positions held: House Ed. for the Am. Jrnl. of Physics, 1961-66 (published by the Am. Inst. of Physics); Sr. Ed., Inst. of Electric & Electronic Engrs., 1966-67; Supvsr. for all mathematics & sci. books published by Appleton-Century-Crofts, 1967-68; First, Sr. Ed. for mathematics & sci. books, college dept., later Proj. Dir. for Lang. Arts Books, schl. dept., Holt, Rinehart & Winston, 1968-71. Published works: The Naked Frame, 1952. Contbr. to num. mags., jrnls., anthols. inclng: Quicksilver; The Canadian Forum; The Writer's Voice; The Muse; Poetry Digest; The Wormwood Review; Epos; Oak Leaves; Am. Negro Poetry; New Negro Poets: USA, 1964; Beyond the Angry Black, 1966; Invitation to Poetry; Modern & Contemporary Afro-Am. Poetry, 1972; The Poetry of Black America, 1973. Honours, awards incl: Fellowship to Yaddo, Saratoga Springs, N.Y., 1956; Breadloaf Writers Scholarship, 1960. Address: Univ. of Maryland Baltimore County, 5401 Wilkens Ave., Baltimore, MD 21228, U.S.A.

ODIORNE, Maggie Jean, Housewife. Education: Grad., American River Coll., Sacramento, Calif., Engl. Major; Minor in Psychology; currently enrolled, Univ. of Calif., Sacramento. Married to Robert Theodore Odiorne, Jr.; 1 s. Positions held: Sec. to HS principal; Civilian Requirements Officer, Brookley Air Force Base; Tutored Engl. at American Riber Coll., Sacramento, Published work: Alpha To Now (collection of poems), 1973. Contbr. to: Light and Life Press; Modus Operandi; Mary's Scrapbook; Home Base; Faraway Places; The Showcase; Joy in Faith; Literary Newsette; Telescope; Birth of Day Anthol.; Grains of Sand Anthol.; Resident and Staff Physician Mag., etc. Awards: Winner of "Inky Trails" poem of the month contests for Apr. 1970 and May 1971; Winner of "Encoze" American Mosaic Awards, Unusual Events in History, Feb., 1973, etc. Address: 4142 Tyrone Way, Carmichael, CA 95608, USA.

OERKE, Andrew Halvor, b. 4 Oct. 1932. Development Officer; Poet. Education: B.A. & M.A., Baylor Univ.; grad. work at Free Univ. of Berlin, Mex. City Coll., Univ. of Tex., State Univ. of Iowa. Positions held: Instr., Bemidji State Univ.; Educ. Mgr., Look Mag.; Poet-in-Res., Saint Andrews Coll.; Peace Corps Dir.; Malawi & Jamaica; Cons., Smithsonian Instn.; I Dev. Officer, Data Use & Access Labs. Published works: Speak Then of Love, 1973; Many Voices, 1974. Contbr. to: The New Yorker; Mademoiselle; Poetry; The Listener; The Mich. Qtly.; The N.Y. Herald Tribune; Epoch; The Carleton Miscellany; Christian

Century; Univ. of Windsor Review; Beloit Poetry Jrnl.; The Washingtonian; The New Republic, etc. Address: 2949 Macomb St., N.W., Wash. DC 20008, U.S.A.

OFFEN, Yehuda, b. 4 April 1922. Journalist. Memberships: Hebrew Writers' Organization; ACUM (Soc. d'Auteurs, Compositeurs et Editeurs de Musique); World Poetry Soc. Published works: L'Lo L'An, 1961; Har Vakhol, 1963; Shirim Lirfua (trans.), 1965, Lo Agadal Khoref, 1969. Contbr. to: most Israeli newspapers and periodicals, and to: Poet (anthol.); Ocarina (anthol.), etc. Honours: ACUM Lit. Prize, 1960. Address: 8 Gazit St., Tel-Aviv 69271, Israel.

OFFERLE, Mildred Gladys, b. 3 Jan. 1912. Teacher. Education: Dip., Duluth Tchrs. Coll., 1932; Dip., Famous Writers Course, 1963; B.S., Mankato State Coll., 1966. Married Martin A. Offerle, 1 daughter. Positions held: Tchr., Rural Mapleton, 1932-33, Barnum, Minn., 1933-38, Madelia, Minn., 1964–. Memberships: World Poetry Soc.; Centro Studi e Scambi; Am. Poetry League; League of Minn. Poets; Hon. Rep., CSESI; Minn. Rep., WPI. Published works: Crystal Wells (poetry), 1950; The Long Cry (fiction), 1960; Moods & Thoughts (poetry), 1970. Contbr. to: Yearbook of Modern Poetry; Sea to Sea in Song; Great Am. World Poets, 1973; Quaderni di Poesia; United Poets; Prairie Poets; Am. Bard; Portland Oregonian; Hartford Courant, etc. Recip., Miller Pettingill Meml. Award, 1950. Address: 105 Third St., S.W., Madelia, MN 56062, U.S.A.

O'GORMAN. Published works: The Night of the Hammer, 1959; Adam Before His Mirror, 1961; The Buzzard and the Peacock, 1964; The Harvester's Vase, 1968. Contbr. to (Anthols.): Poetry for Pleasure, 1960; Twentieth Century American Poetry, 1963; (Jrnls.): Nation; Columbia University Forum.

O'GRADY, Desmond James Bernard, b. 27 Aug. 1935. Teacher of English Literature. Education: Sacred Heart Coll. (Jesuit), Limerick, Ireland; Cistercian Coll. Roscrea, Co. Tipperary, Ireland; M.A., Harvard Univ., U.S.A. Positions held: Tchr., Roxbury Latin Schl., & Harvard, 1962-64; Tchr., O'seas Schl. of Rome, 1965–; Sr. Engl. Master, St. Georges Schl., Rome, Italy, 1968-72. Member, Community of European Writers. Published works: Chords & Orchestrations, (poems), 1956; Reilly, poems, 1961; Professor Kelleher & the Chatles River, 1964; Separazioni, poems with Italian translations, 1965; The Dark Edge of Europe, poems, 1967; Off Licence, poems transl. from Italian, Irish, Armenian, 1967; The Dying Gaul, 1969; Hellas, poem, 1971; Separations, 1973; Sing Me Creation, 1974. Contbr. to mags., jrnls., anthol., etc. Recordings: Harvard Poetry Room; BBC Princeton; Radio Eireann. Address: via Catalana 1/A, Rome, Italy.

OHAIMID, Nasser Sulaiman, b. 1930. Businessman. Education: Secondary. Has published one volume of poetry. Address: c/o Higher Council for Arts & SCIENCES, Ministry of Education, Riyadh, Saudi Arabia.

O'HANDLEY, Robert Gerard, pen name **O'HANDLEY, Robert,** b. 31 Jan. 1946. Broadcast Engineer. Education: Grad. of Announcer Training Studios; Production Dept. and Engineer Dept, 1973; Grad., Power Mem. Acad., 1964. Positions held: Teller, Loeb Rhoades and Co.; Specialist, 4th Class, US Army; Paying Teller, Fed. Reserve Bank. Memberships: Eastern Centre, Poetry Soc. of London; World Poet's Resource Centre (Chairman, Panel of Readers; Member, Bd. of Directors). Contbr. to: Yearbook of Mod. Poetry, 1971; Mod. Contemporary Poetry; Poetry Prevue. Awards: Special Award, 1st, 2nd, 3rd, 4th Annual Poetry Festival. Address: 635 56 St., Brooklyn, NY 11220, USA.

OHARA, Miyao, b. 23 Jan. 1905. Professor. Education: Grad., Engl. Lit. Dept., Hiroshima Univ.; Litt.D., 1964. Positions held: Prof. of Wakayama Med. Coll., 1939; Prof. of Hiroshima Women's Coll., 1945:

Prof. of the Hiroshima Inst. of Technol., 1963. Memberships: V.P., Hiroshima Poets' Assn.; Chief Ed., Hiroshima Letter; Japan Modern Poetry Soc. Published works: Ed., Hiroshima Poets, 1930; The Songs of Hiroshima (in Japanese & Engl.), 1930; The Prelude (pamphlet), 1925-60; The Poems of Atomic Bomb (Edited – Japanese), 1970; The Songs of Hiroshima (in Japanese & English), 1971. Contbr. to: The Japan Modern Poetry; Ocarina. Address: Kansuiyen, Miyake Itsukaichi-machi, Hiroshima 738, Japan.

OKAI, John. Poet. Education: M.A. (Litt.), Gorky Literary Inst., Moscow, 1967; Univ. of Ghana, Accra; Univ. of London. Published works: Flowerfall, 1969. Contbr. to (Anthols.): New Voices of the Commonwealth, 1968; (Jrnls.): New American Review; Atlantic; Outposts; Okyeame; Black Orpheus. Recip., Royal Soc. of Arts Fellowship, 1968.

OKARA, Gabriel Imomotimi Gbaingbain, b. 24 Apr. 1921. Public Servant. Education: Govt. Coll., Umuahia, 1935-40; Northwestern Univ., Ill., U.S.A., 1959-60. Married three times, div. twice, 3 children (inclng. 1 stepson). Positions held: Asst. Publicity Off., Min. of Info., 1955-59; Publicity Off., Information Off., 1960-62; Prin. Information Off., 1962-71; Gen. Mgr., Rivers State Newspaper Corp., 1971-73; Gen Mgr., Rivers State Broadcasting Corp., 1973–. Member, PEN. Published works: The Voice (novel), 1964. Contbr. to: Black Orpheus; udume. Recip., Silver Cup, Nigeria Fest. of the Arts, 1953. Address: P.M.B. 5170, Port Harcourt, Nigeria.

ØKLAND, Einar, b. 17 Jan. 1940. Freelance Writer. Education: Univ. of Oslo, Norway, 1965. Married. Positions held: Clinical Psychologist, Rønvik Hosp., Bodø, 1965-66; Dir. of Norsk Forfattersentrum (Norwegian Writers' Ctr.), 1973–. Memberships: Norwegian Soc. of Writers (Den norske Forfatterforening); Norwegian Soc. of Playwrights (Norske drmatikeres forbund); Norwegian Soc. of Lit. Critics (Norsk Kritikerlag). Published works incl: Ein gul dag (A Yellow Day), 1963; Mandragora (mandrak (Mandrake Root), 1966; Vandreduene (The Passenger Doves), 1968; Gullalder (A Golden Age), 1972; Du er sa rar (You're so cute), 1973. Contbr. to: Dagbladet; Dag og Tid; Apropos; Vinduet; Syn og Segn; Samtiden; Fossegrimen; Profil; Hvedekorn (Danish); Ta' (Danish). Rep. in many anthols. Address: c/o Det Norske Samlaget, Trondheimsveien 15 B, Oslo 5, Norway.

OK NALL, b. 12 July 1926. Government Officer. Education: Master of Law. Married Nhéa Seng Im, 1 son, 3 daughters. Positions held: Civil servant in Income Taxes Serv.; Customs Officer; Chief of Cabinet & Dir. of Political Affairs at the Prime Minister's Office; Gov. Chief of Province of Kratié; Dir. of Information; Dir. of Daily French newspaper 'Le Courrier Phnompenhois'; Govt. Delegate of administrative region. Poems published daily in 'Le Courrier Phnompenhois', 1971-72, some of which collected into two booklets called 'Political Poems', 1971-72. Honours, awards: Plaque, Trophies, Medal at the end of Second World Congress of Poets, Taipei, Taiwan, 1973. Address: c/o Ministry of Interior Phnom-Penh, Khmer Republic, (Cambodia).

OKOPENKO, Andreas, b. 15 Mar. 1930. Writer. Education: studied Chemistry, Univ. of Vienna, Austria. Positions held: Cost Controller, Parsons & Whittemore Paper Mill, Austria; Freelance Writer, 1968–. Memberships: Grazer Autorenversammlung (Second Austrian PEN Club). Published works: Grüner November, 1957; Seltsame Tage, 1963; Warum sind die Latrinen so traurig?, 1969; Orte wechselnden Unbehagens, 1971. Recip., Austrian State Prize for Stories, 1968, & other awards. Address: Autokaderstrasse 3/3/7, A-1210 Vienna, Austria.

OLAGUER, Valdemar O., b. 5 Apr. 1922. Associate Professor. Education: A.B., Ateneo de Manila Univ.; M.A., San Francisco State Coll., Calif.; Loyola Univ.,

Chgo.; Univ. of Notre Dame, Ind.; Stanford Univ., Calif. Married Aurora G. Alvarez w. 3 sons. Positions held: Instructor in Engl., Univ. of the East, Manila, 1958-64; Instructor in Engl. & Humaniaties, Mapua Inst. of Technol., Manila, 1959-60; Instructor in Engl., De La Salle Coll., Manila, 1962-64; Asst. Prof. of Engl., Ateneo de Manila Univ., 1964-66; Assoc. Prof., ibid., 1966–. Contbr. to (Anthols.): New World Writing 17, 1960; Equinox I, 1965; Asian P.E.N. Anthology, 1966; Horizons East, 1967; (Jrnls.): Beloit Poetry Jrnl.; Weekly Graphic; Weekly Women's Mag.; Weekly Nation. Address: Dept. of Engl., Ateneo de Manila Univ., P.O. Box 154, Manila, Philippines.

OLD COYOTE, Elnora A. (Stenersen), pen name OLD COYOTE, Sally, b. 6 Mar. 1922. Associate Professor of Education. Education: Dip., Eastern Montana Coll. at Billings, 1941; B.S., Botany, Mont. State Univ., Bozeman, 1950; M.S. Educ., Ecology, ibid, 1957; Ed.D., Harvard Univ. at Cambridge, 1966. Married John M. Old Coyote, 1 son, 1 daughter. Positions held: Rural Elem. Tchr., Jr. H.S.; Tchr.; 1st Grade Tchr.; Instr., Asst. Prof., Assoc. Prof., Dept. Elem. Educ., Mont. State Univ.; Curric. Dir., Title VII Bilingual Ed., Schl. Dist. 17H, Hardin, Mont. State & local Writers' Chmn., Montana Inst. of Arts. Published works: For Me, For You, 1956; When Comes Tomorrow, 1961; The Death of John Bozeman & Other Montana Poems, 1964; Sang It All His Life, 1965; Seed In The Soil, 1968; Seedlings, 1972. Contbr. to: IWWP Anthol., 1973; Portland Oregonian; Denver Post; MIA Qtly.; Mont. Arts Mag.; Absaraka. Honours, awards: 3rd pl., Mary Clapp Meml. Poetry Contest, 1969-70; Award, IWWP Contest, 1972-73; winner, var. times, Mont. Inst. of Arts Poetry Contests. Address: Box 415, Crow Agency, MT 59022, U.S.A.

OLDERVIK, Anbjørg Pauline, b. 10 July 1918. Teacher. Education: Tchr's Schl. Positions held: Tchr. for children & youth with mental handicap. Published works: Lytt (poems), 1967; I Dette Element (poems), 1969; Nattog (poems), 1970; Menneske (inner autobiography in a lyrical way), 1971; Et Ord Om Hap (poems), 1972. Contbr. to: Aftenposten; Dagbladet; Kvinner og Klaer; Vinduet. Address: Ole Bulls gt. IIa, Oslo 4, Norway.

OLIVER, Mary, b. 10 Sept. 1935. Poet. I Education: Vassar Coll., 1956-57; Ohio State Univ., 1955-56. Member, Poetry Soc. of Am. Published works: No Voyage & Other Poems, 1963 (enlarged edn. 1965); The River Styx, Ohio & Other Poems, 1972. Contbr. to: Am. Scholar; Am. Weave; Antioch Review; Chgo. Review; Chgo. Tribune; Commonweal; Lit. Review; Minn. Review; New Republic; N.Y. Times; Prairie Schooner; War/Peace Report; Harper's Bazaar; Harper's Mag.; The Listener; Mademoiselle; Outposts; Swanee Review; The Spectator; Va. Qtly. Review, etc. Honours, awards: 1st Prize Award, Poetry Soc. of Am., 1963; Alice Fay di Castagnola Award, 1973; Shelley Meml. Award, 1972; Creative Writing Grant from Nat. Endowment for the Arts, 1972, & 73. Address: Box 338, Provincetown, MA 02657, U.S.A.

OLIVER, W(illiam) H(osking), b. 14 May. Professor of History. Education: M.A., Victoria Univ., Wellington, N. Zealand.; Ph.D., Oxford Univ. Positions held: Mbr., History Dept., Univ. of Canterbury, Christchurch; Victoria Univ., Wellington; Ed., Comment Mag., Wellington; Prof. of History, Massey Univ. of Manawatu, Palmerston North, New Zealand; Currently, History Chair, Victoria Univ., Wellington, N. Zealand. Published works: Fire Without Phoenix: Poems 1946-54; Other: Poetry in New Zealand, 1960; The Story of New Zealand, 1963. Contbr. to (Anthols.): New Zealand Poetry Yearbook, 1951; An Anthology of New Zealand Verse, 1956; Penguin Book of New Zealand Verse, 1960; Recent Poetry in New Zealand, 1965; (jrnls.): New Zealand Listener; Numbers; Landfall; Oxford Poetry.

OLSON, Charles (John), b. 27 Dec. 1910. Educator; Poet. Education: Wesleyan Univ., Middletown, Conn.; Yale Univ., New Haven, Conn.; B.A., M.A., Harvard Univ., Cambridge, Mass. (1932, 33). Positions held: Taught at Harvard, 1936-39; Instructor & Rector, Black Mountain Coll., N.C., 1951-56. Published works incl: To Corrado Cagli, 1947; Letter for Melville, 1951; In Cold Hell, in Thicket, 1953; The Maximus Poems, 1-10, 1953, 11-12, 1956; Projective Verse, 1959; The Maximus Poems, 1960; Selected Writings, 1967; Other: Call Me Ishmael: A Study of Melville, 1967; Apollonius of Tyana, 1951; The Mayan Letters (Ed. by Robert Creeley), 1968; Anecdotes of the Late War, 1955; A Bibliography on America for Ed Dorn, 1964; The Human Universe & Other Essays, 1964. Contbr. to (Anthols.): New American Poetry, 1960; A Controversy of Poets, 1965; Lincoln and the Poets, 1965; New Writing in the USA, 1967; (Jrnls.): Black Mountain Review; Big Table; Poetry; Evergreen Review; Poetry New York; Yugen; Kulchur; Partisan Review; Origin; Wild Dog. Hons: 2 Guggenheim Awards; WennerGren Foundation Grant to study Mayan hieroglyphics; Oscar Blumenthal-Charles Leviton Prize of Poetry, Chgo., 1965.

OLSON, Elder (James), b. 9 Mar. 1909. University Educator; Professor of English. Education: B.A., Univ. of Chgo., 1934; M.A., ibid., 1935; Ph.D., ibid., 1938. Married Geraldine Louise Hays w. 4 children. Positions held: Tchr., Armour Inst. of Technol., Chgo., Ill., 1935-38; Mbr., Fac., Univ. of Chgo., 1936–; Prof. of Engl., ibid., 1953–; Vis. Lectr. num. Univs. in US & Abroad. Published works: Thing of Sorrow, 1934; The Cock of Heaven, 1940; The Scarecrow Christ, 1954; Poems & Plays 1948-1958; Collected Poems, 1963; Literary Criticism: General Prosody, Rhythmic, Metric, Harmonics, 1938; Critics and Criticism (w. others), 1952; The Poetry of Dylan Thomas, 1954; Tragedy and the Theory of Drama, 1961; Other: Ed., American Lyric Poems: From Colonial Days to tle Present, 1964; Aristotle's "Poetics" and English Literature, 1965. Contbr. to (Anthols.): New Poetry, 1932; New Pocket Anthology of American Poetry, 1955; A Poetry Sampler, 1962; Poetry in English, 1963; Modern Religious Poems, 1964. Hons. incl: Friends of Literature Award, 1935; Eunice Tietjens Memorial Award, 1953; Poetry Society of America Award, 1954; Univ. of Chgo's Quantrell Award, 1966. Address: Dept. of English, Univ. of Chicago, Chicago, IL 60637, USA.

OLSON, Marie A., b. 8 July 1890. Registered Nurse. Education: Grad. from a Class A Hospital in Mnpls., Minn. Positions held: served the U.S. Govt. for 30 yrs. in three Veterans' Hospitals (Night Supvsr.) Assoc. Mbr., N.Y. Poetry Forum. Address: 881 – 7th Ave., Carnegie Hall Studio 1106, N.Y., NY 10019, U.S.A.

OLSON, Robert Glen Kennith Leif, pen name GRENEFORST, Leif, b. 11 Aug. 1917. Architectural & Aeronautical Designer. Education: 11 Diplomas from univs., colls., trade schls. 6 children. Positions held: Production Manager; Cadet-Pilot; Radio-Operator; Instr.-Observer; Chief-Draftsman; Aeronautical Designer; Stonemason; Contractor; Architectural Designer; Consultant; Fndr., The Poets' Pulse. Memberships: Am. Acad. of Poets; Writers' & Artists' Guild. Published works: The Poets' Pulse, vol. 1, 1973; A P O San Francisco, 1973; A Crock of China, 1974. Contbr. to: Springfield Daily News; Tulsa Daily World; South & West; Voices Int.; Laurels; The Am. Bard; The Cardinal; The Muse; Sat. Evening Post, etc. Honours, awards: 1st Award Winner, Book Award Publication, Ozark Writers' Guild, 1968 & Nat. Veteran's Writers, Humorous, 1969. Address: The Poets' Pulse, Box 584, Tulsa, OK 74119, U.S.A.

O'MALLEY, (Sister) Emanuela, b. 23 Jul. 1914. College Teacher of Engl. and Creative Writing. Education: Workshops in Fiction and Poetry Writing, Iowa Univ.; Studies in Afro-American Literature, De Paul, Chicago; M.A. in Lit. and Creative Writing, Syracuse Univ., NY. Position held: Engl. Dept., Marymount Coll., Salina, Kansas. Memberships: Kansas Authors Club (State Pres.); Midwest Chaparral Poets (Poet of the Year, 1972-73). Contbr. to: Educational mags., articles on poetry writing; Poetry in nat. mags. and lit. reviews. Address: Marymount

Coll., Salina, KS 67401, USA.

OMAR MOHAMMAD NOOR, b. 24 Oct. 1941. Teacher of English. Education: Malayan Tchrs. Coll. Positions held: Tchr. of Engl., Malay, Sec. Schl. Contbr. to: Anthology of Malaysian in English, 1966; (Jrnls.): Focus; Tenggara; Poetry Singapore.

ONDAATJE, Michael, b. 12 Sept. 1943, Ceylon. Writer; Teacher Currently tchng. Engl. at Glendon Coll., York Univ., Canada. Published works: The Dainty Monsters, 1967; The Man with 7 Toes, 1969; The Collected Works of Billy the Kid, 1970; (Ed.) The Broken Ark: A Book of Beasts, 1971. Contbr. to various Canadian magazines. Recip. of Gov.-Gen.'s Award for Poetry, 1970. Address: English Dept., Glendon Coll., York Univ., 2275 Bayview Ave., Toronto, Ont., Canada.

O'NEAL, Opal Jane Langston, b. 19 Sept. 1919. Store Manager. Education: Basic Psychol., Henderson State Coll., Arkadelphia, Ark. Married Benjamin H. O'Neal, 2 sons, 1 daughter. Positions held: Departmental Mgr., Chain Store; Mgr. of local Gift Shop. Memberships: Hot Springs Br., Ark. Poets Roundtable; Nat. Fed. of Poets; Assoc. Mbr., Poetry Soc. of Tenn.; Ark. Authors, Composers & Artists; V.P., Hot Springs Br., Poets Roundtable, 1970-71; Pres., ibid, 1971-72; currently Pres. Contbr. to: Arkansas Poets Anthology, 1968-72; Ark. Democrat Sunday Mag.; Baptist Trumpet; Poets Partyline; Hot Springs News. Honours, awards: 1st pl. for Free Verse, Ark, Arts Fest., 1970; 1st pl. for Children's Verse, Nat. Poetry Day, 1970; 2nd pl. for Children's Verse, Writers' Conf., 1968; 2nd pl. Sonnet, Nat. Poetry Day, 1972; 3rd pl. Annual Anthol. Award, 1973; 1st pl., Minority Group Award, Mid-South Conf., 1973. Address: 421 Dell, Hot Springs, AR 71901, U.S.A.

O'NEIL, Terrence (William), pen name, **O'NEIL, Terrence,** b. 31 Mar. 1928. Journalist. Education: Churchfield H.S., Coventry; Tech. Coll., Coventry, Warwickshire. Since 1969 has appeared in poetry recitals in USA., Canada, Spain, Italy, France, Ireland and UK. Founder and Director of Productions, Dumasian Theatre Group, 1956-1959; Instr., I.L.E.A., 1965-1968; Drama Adviser, Jewish Brady Clubs and Settlement, London, 1966-1968, and currently journalist with Press Assoc. Ltd., London. Memberships include: Talisman Theatre, Kenilworth; Barbican Poetry Club, London. Published works include: Christmas Countdown, 1969; Fragments and Splinters, 1971. Contbr. to: Internat. Who's Who in Poetry Anthol., 1972; Coventry Eve. Telegraph; Islington Gazette; Brighton Argus; Canadian Poetry Mag.; Village Voice, NY. Address: 9 Claremont Close, London N1 9LT, UK.

O'NEILL, Luis, pen names, **MISTRAL; BRADOMIN,** b. 12 Oct. 1888. Librarian. Education: Univ. of Puerto Rico; Pratt Inst., Brooklyn, NY. Positions held: Under Librarian, Insular Library of Puerto Rico, 1912-16; Carnegie Library of P.R., 1916-19; Director, Carnegie Library of P.R., 1919-1955; retired 1955. Librarian, Library of the Sociedad Puertorriquena de Escritores, 1955-71. Memberships: Soc. Puertorriquena de Escritores (Pres., Library Committee); Asociacion Interamericana de Escritores; Ateneo Puertorriqueno (ex-Pres. Seccion Recreativa); Asociacion Bibliotecaria de Puerto Rico (Pres.). Published work: Arca de Recuerdos (poems), 1955. Contbr. to: Puerto Rico Ilustrado; Alma Latina; Prensa Literaria; Escuela; Los Catorce; American Literary cents; Il Mondo Libero; Ecos de Provincia; La Verdad. Honours & Awards: Laureated at Poetical Contest, Ateneo Puertorriqueno, 1951; Rep. for P.R. at 1st Internat. Congress of Librarians & Bibliographers, Rome, Italy, 1929; Degree in Philosophy (h.c.), Acad. Filosofica de Psicomentesofia, Buenos Aires, Argentina, 1957; Hon. Member, Sociedad de Bibliotecarios de Puerto Rico, 1968, and others. Address: 123 O'Neill St., Hato Rey, PR 00918, USA.

O'NEILL, Seamus, b. 10 May 1910. Professor.

Education: B.A.; M.A.; Queen's Univ., Belfast; Nat. Univ., Dublin; Innsbruck, etc. Married, 4 children. Positions held: Prof. of Irish Hist., Carysfort Coll. of Educ. Memberships: V.Chmn., PEN, Dublin; Consultative Comm. of Irish Historians. Published works: Danta, 1947; Danta do Phaisti, 1949; Iomramh an Ousel, 1950; Colmcille, 1963. Contbr. to: Comhar; An Iris; Radio Eireann; WGB-FM; Abbey Theatre Prog.; Radio na Gaeltachta; Irish Press; Peacock Theatre Poetry Readings, Harvard Univ. Poetry Readings; EMI recordings; Nuavearsaiocht, etc. Has written var. plays & novels. Address: 25 Glenart Ave., Blackrock, County Dublin, Ireland.

OOI BOO ENG, b. 16 Feb. 1936. Lecturer in English. Education: Tchrs. Trng. Coll. Cert., Malaysia; B.A. Hons. in Engl., Univ. of Durham, U.K.; M.Litt., Univ. of Newcastle upon Tyne. Married, 1 son, 1 daughter. Positions held: Schl. Tchr., 5 yrs.; Asst. Lectr. in Engl., Univ. of Malaya, 3 yrs.; currently Lectr. in Engl., ibid. Contbr. to: Poet, Madras; Westerly, Western Australia; Southern Review, Adelaide; Lidra, Dept. of Engl., Univ. of Malaya. Address: Dept. of Engl., Univ. of Malaya, Kuala Lumpur, Malaysia.

OPPEN, George, b. 24 Apr. 1908. Writer. Published works: Discrete Series, 1934; The Materials, 1962; This in Which, 1965; Facsimile Reprint, 1966; Of Being Numerous, 1968; Seascape, Needle's Eye; Collected Poems. Contbr. to the following anthols., jrnls., mags., etc: Active Anthol.; Objectivist Anthol.; Poetry; Hound & Horn; San Francisco Review; Mass. Review; New Yorker; The Nation, etc. Honours, awards: Pulitzer Prize, 1969. Address: c/o New Directions Publng. Corp., 333 Sixth Ave., New York, NY 10014, U.S.A.

OPPENHEIM, Eva, pen name **MIODOWNIK, Eva,** b. 27 July 1933. Free lance writer. Education: B.A., Queens Coll., CUNY, 1955; grad. work, Schl. of the Arts, Columbia Univ., 1971-72; Poetry Workshops at New Schl., N.Y., 1959-60, '63-64. Married Alan Oppenheim, 2 daughters. Positions held: Asst. to Publicity Dir., McGraw-Hill Book Co., N.Y.C., 1960-65; Asst. to Publicity Dir., Basic Books, N.Y., 1964-65; Asst. to Publicity Dir., David McKay Book Co., N.Y., 1957-64; Publicity Writer, Columbia Pictures, London, 1956-57. Member, Poetry Soc. of Am. Contbr. to: New Voices 4, 1960; New Voices '64; The Little Mag.; Odds & Ends; Baby Care; Bard. Has read poetry over radio stn. WBAI & poetry readings at Unit Theatre & at Spring Lake Park. Recip., Third Prize, Writers' Derby, McGraw-Hill Book Co., 1962. Address: 245 West 107th St., N.Y., NY 10025, U.S.A.

OPPENHEIMER, Christine Backus, pen name **OPPENHEIMER, C.B.,** b. 9 July 1920. Poet; Antique Dealer; Poetry Instructor & Reader. Education: B.A., UCLA, U.S.A., 1942; Calif. Tchng. Cert., ibid. Married Max B. Oppenheimer, Jr. Positions held: H.S. Tchr. of Engl., 1943-46; Housewife, 1946–; Voluntary Community Wkr.; Private Instr. or Critic in Poetry (by corres. or appt.) Memberships: Iowa City Br., League of Am. Pen Women; Wis. Fellowship of Poets; Avalon Int.; Iowa Poetry Day Assoc.; World Poetry Day Assoc.; Poetry Soc. of Australia; Comm., Centro Studi e Scambi Int.; United Poets Laureate Int.; Calif. Olympiad of the Arts; Int. Platform Assn. Chautauqua Poets; Cleveland Art Mus.; Fndr.-Mbr., Acad. of Am. Poets. Published works: Building the Bridge, 1964; 2 books of poetry in progress. Contbr. to: N.Y. Times; Oregonian; Cyclo-Flame; Mass. Review; Poet; Laurel Leaves; The Muse; N.Am. Mentor; The Green World; Writings 1968; Bitterroot; Swordsman Review; Abyss; Cardinal Qtly.; Am. Bard; The Lyric; Poet Lore, etc. Honours, awards: var. 1st prizes & Hon. Mentions, State & Poetry Soc. Contests, 1962–; Bronze & Silver Medals, Centro Studi e Scambi Int., Italy, 1965, '67; Gold Medal, Pres. Marcos of Philippines, 1968; 1st prize & Laurel Wreath, Calif. Olympiad of Arts, 1968; 1st prize, Wis. Fest. of Arts, 1968. Address: 10 Lowell Pl., Fredonia, NY 14063, U.S.A.

OPPENHEIMER, Joel L(ester), pen name, **AQUARIUS,** b. 18 Feb. 1930. Poet. Education: Public

Schools, Yonkers, NY.; Cornell Univ.; Univ. of Chicago; Black Mountain Coll. Married. Positions held: Director, The Poetry Project, St. Mark's Church in the Bowery, 1966-68; Director, Teachers & Writers Collaborative, 1968-69; Poet-in-residence, City Coll. City Univ. of NY, 1969 to present. Membership: Authors Guild. Published works: The Dutiful Son, 1956; The Love Bit, 1960; In Time, 1969; On Occasion, 1973; The Great American Desert (play), 1963; The Wrong Season (non-fiction), 1973. Contbr. to: Village Voice; Poetry Chicago; Paris Review; The Nation; Origin; Black Mountain Review; The World; Grosseteste Review; Yugen; Neon; Evergreen Review, etc. Awarded Grant, NY State Council on the Arts, 1971. Address: 463 West St., New York, NY 10014, USA.

OPPITZ, René Charles, pen name **MARINE, J.-J.,** b. 4 July 1904. Journalist. Education: studied Ancient Humanities in Geneva & at l'Athenee Royal de Bruxelles; LL.D., Free Univ. of Brussels, 1930; Mil Schl., 1932. Married, 5 children. Positions held: Ed., 1940-45, & Editl. Sec., 1946-55, 'Pourquoi Pas', weekly; Ed. in Chief, 'L'Informateur-Midi', daily, 1945-46; Freelance Ed., 'Bonne Soirée', weekly, 1956-73. Memberships: Assn. of Belgian Writers of the French Lang.; Association Générale de la Presse; S.A.B.A.M. Published works: (poems & poems & prose) Visions des jours heureus, 1923; Chuchotements, 1923; Fétus et hautes ondes, 1925; Les Etapes lucides, 1928; (essays) Coup droit, 1927; Optimisme clairvoyant, 1930; Louis Dumont-Wilden, l'oeuvre, l'homme, le sage, 1955; Entretiens avec mon dentiste, 1963; (novels) Le Joyeux Messie, 1942; Daniel et Nicole, 1945; (for children) Sortilèges, 1947; Martine en exil (with Colette Oppitz), 1943; other books under pseudonym. Contbr. to var. lit. reviews. Choreographical corres. for Belgium, 'Saisons de la Danse', Paris. Honours, awards: Médaille Commémorative de la Guerre 1940-45, 1946; Médaille de la Résistance, 1949; Médaille du Volontaire de Guerre-Combattant, 1969. Address: Ave. Ducpétiaux 147A, B-1060, Brussels, Belgium.

ORLAND, Ya'acov, b. 14 July 1914. Poet; Dramatist; Translator. Education: Hebrew Univ., Jerusalem; London Univ.; Royal Acad. of Dramatic Arts, London, U.K. Married Bat-el Axelrod, 1 son, 1 daughter. Memberships: Hebrew Writers Assn., Israel; Israel P.E.N. Ctr. Published works: Tree in the Wind; Poems of a Vulture & a Dove; Leaves of Autumn; Poems from the Land of Uz; The Toy House; The Nameless City; Play the Harp; Songs of Once Upon a Time (words & music); translations from English & Am. poets & 52 classical & modern plays. Contbr. to most of the lit. mags. & jrnls. in Israel. Recip., Lamdan Prize for Lit., Israel, 1963. Address: 79 Moriah Ave., Haifa, Israel.

ORLOVITZ, Gil, b. 1918. Poet. Married w. 3 children. Published works: Concerning Man, 1947; Keep to your Belly, 1952; The Diary of Dr. Eric Zeno, 1953; The Diary of Alexander Patience, 1958; The Papers of Professor Bold, 1958; Selected Poems, 1960; The Art of the Sonnet, 1961; Couldn't Say, Might be Love, 1969; Other: The Story of Erica Keith and Other Stories, Poems and a Play, 1957; Milkbottle H, 1967; Ice Never F, 1970; Ed., Award Avant-Garde Reader, 1965. Contbr. to (Anthols.): Today's Poets, 1964; (Jrnls.): Beloit Poetry Jrnl.; San Francisco Review; Inferno; Poetry; Poetry New York; Pegasus; Trace; Quarterly Review of Literature. Address: 924 West End Ave., N.Y., NY 10025, USA.

ORLOVSKY, Peter, b. 8 July 1933. Poet. Education: San Francisco Jr. Coll. Positions held: Var. jobs incl., Ambulance Attendant, Farmer's Help, Mental Hospital Attendant. Contbr. to (Anthols.): Beat Scene, 1960; New American Poetry, 196C; Beatitude Anthology, 1965; (Jrnls.): Yugen; Outsider.

ORMOND, John, b. 1923. Documentary Film-Maker. Positions held: Staff Writer, Picture Post, 1945-49; Documentary Film-Maker, BBC, 1955–. Published works: Indications, 1943. Contbr. to (Anthols.):

Modern Welsh Poetry, 1944; Images of Tomorrow, 1953; Lilting House, 1969. (Jrnls.): Poetry Wales.

ORR, Richard Wayne, pen name **RIK,** b. 15 Apr. 1948. Writer. Education: B.A., East Carolina Univ., Greenville, N.C.; Univ. of Heidelberg; M.A., Univ. of Tulsa, Okla. Contbr. to: The Rebel; Poet. Address: 1606 Tieman Dr., Glen Burnie, MD 21061, U.S.A.

ORVIL, Ernst Richard, b. 12 Apr. 1898. Author; Poet. Member, PEN, Oslo. Published works: Bölgeslag, 1940; Kommer du tilmeg, 1947; Sol over stupene, 1951; Syngende sommer, 1953; Slórene faller, 1955; Lisbet, 1959; Flyktige dager, 1959; Farende ar, 1962; Kontakt, 1964; Jdyller, 1967; Brekasjer, 1970; Dikt i utvalg, 1971; Nok sagt, 1972; Contbr. to: Aftenposten, Oslo; Dagbladet, Oslo; Ord och Bild, Stockholm. Address: Vibes Gt. 21, 3 Oslo, Norway.

OSBORNE, Charles, b. 24 Nov. 1927. Literary Director. Positions held: Asst. Ed., The London Mag., 1957-66; Asst. Literary Dir., The Arts Council of G.B. Published works: Swansong, 1968; Other: Kafka, 1967; Fifty Works of English Literature We could do Without, 1967; Complete Operas of Verdi, 1970; Ned Kelly, 1970; Ed., Australian Stories of Today, 1961; Opera 66, 1966; Australia and New Zealand: A Handbook, 1970. Contbr. to (Anthols.): Australian Poetry, 1951; A Book of Australian Verse, 1956; Australian Writing Today, 1968; (jrnls.): Bulletin; London Magazine: New Statesman; Spectator; Observer; Sunday Times. Address: 84 Prince of Wales Mansions, London, S.W.11, UK.

OSERS, Ewald, b. 13 May 1917. Member BBC Senior Staff. Education: Charles Univ., Prague; Univ. of London. Personal details: Married; 1 s., 1 d. Positions held: various, in BBC Monitoring Service, now Assistant Head of Dept. Memberships: Inst. of Linguists (Fellow; also member of Council since 1973); Translators' Guild (Vice-Chairman, 1973); Translators Assoc. (Vice-Chairman, 1970, Chairman, 1971); Soc. of Authors; Internat. P.E.N.; Internat. Poetry Soc.; Poetry Soc. (UK); Poetry Book Soc. Published works: Modern Czech Poetry, 1945; Three Czech Poets, 1970; Selected Poems by Ondra Lysohorsky, 1971; Underseas Possessions & Other Poems by Hans-Jurgen Heise, 1972; With The Volume Turned Down & Other Poems by Reiner Kunze, 1973; The Aztec Calendar & Other Poems by Antonin Bartusek, 1974. Contbr. to: (translations) Stand; London Mag.; Modern Poetry in Translation; Contemporary Literature in Translation; Outposts; Oasis; Partisan Review; The Malahat; Times Literary Supplement; Observer; CS Monitor; Poetry/Australia; The Poet; Lines Review; Dimension; Index; Informer; Poesie Vivante; Prism Internat.; Twentieth Century; Universitas, and others. Own poems in Outposts; Orbis; Workshop New Poetry; own poems in translation to Die Horen. Recip. of Schlegel-Tieck Translation Prize, 1971. Address: 33 Reades Lane, Sonning Common, Reading RG4 9LL, UK.

OSHIMA, Shotaro, b. 28 Sept. 1899. Emeritus Professor of English Literature. Education: Grad., Waseda Univ., 1923; Merton Coll., Oxford, U.K., 1936-39. Personal details: friend of W.B. Yeats & Douglas Hyde. Positions held: Dir., Japan Poets' Club; Pres., Yeats Soc. of Japan; Ex-Pres., Japan-Ireland Friendship Soc.; PEN; Nippon Bungeika Kyokai; Advsry. Bd., Yeats Studies: An International Journal; Advsry. Coun., Int. Assn. for Study of Anglo-Irish Lit. Published works incl: W.B. Yeats: A Study, 1927; Studies in English Prose & Verse, 1935; Poems: Among Shapes & Shadows (in Engl.), 1939; Poetic Imagination in English Literature, 1953; Collected Poems of Yeats (Japanese transl.), 1958; Yeats, the Man & the Poet, 1961; W.B. Yeats & Japan (in Engl.), 1965; Poems: Journeys & Scenes (in Engl.), 1968; Poems (in Engl.), 1973. Contbr. to: Eigo Seinen (The Rising Generation); Gendai Shisen (The Select Modern Poems); Shikai (The Poetry World). Articles: Yeats & the Japanese Theatre, 1965; Jack B. Yeats, 1971; Synge in Japan, 1971. Address: 34-4, 3 chome,

Nishisugamo, Toshima-ku, Tokyo, Japan.

OSNER, Dorothy Faye, b. 20 Dec. 1913. Writer; Housewife. Married Raymond Osner, 1 daughter. Memberships: Wis. Fellowship of Poets; Portage Writers Workshop (Histn. for two yrs.); Regional Writers of Wis. Contbr. to: Upstream, Downstream – Writers at the Portage, 1972; Portage Daily Register; Appleton Post Crescent; Grit; Denver Post; Am. Jrnl of Nursing; Baptist Ldr. Address: 823 W. Conant St., Portage, WI 53901, U.S.A.

OSTRIKER, Alicia, b. 11 Nov. 1937. English Professor. Education: B.A., Brandeis Univ.; M.A. & Ph.D., Univ. of Wis., U.S.A. Married J.P. Ostriker, 3 children. Positions held: Asst. Prof., Rutgers Univ., 1965-68; Assoc. Prof., ibid, 1968–. Published works: Songs, 1969; Once More Out of Darkness, 1971. Contbr. to: Sewanee Review; Shenandoah Review; New Mexico Quarterly; Carleton Miscellany; Quarterly Review of Lit.; Smith; Vagabond; Arts in Society; Counter Measures; Womens' Studies. Address: Engl. Dept., Rutgers Univ., New Brunswick, N.J., U.S.A.

OSTROFF, Anthony J., pen name **ALEXANDER, A.J.,** b. 9 Nov. 1923. Teacher; Writer. Education: B.S., Northwestern Univ., U.S.A., 1946; M.A., Univ. of Mich., 1949; post grad., Sorbonne & Univ. of Grenoble, France, 1950-51. Married Miriam Virginia Border, 1 son (Nicholas). Positions held: Prof. of Rhetoric & Lit., Univ. of Calif. at Berkeley, 1949-69; Vis.Prof. of Engl., Univ. of Buffalo, 1958 & Vassar Coll., 1959; V.P., Acad. Affairs & Dean of Fac., Lewis & Clark Coll., 1969-71; Prof. of Engl., ibid, 1971–. Published works: 3 Self Evaluations (w. others), 1953; Imperatives, 1962; Contemporary Poet as Artist & Critic (ed.), 1964. Contbr. to: Accent; Atlantic Monthly; Am. Review; Berkeley Review; Beloit Poetry Jrnl.; Chicago Review; Chicago Tribune; Epoch; Epos; Esquire; Golden Goose; Harper's Bazaar; Harper's Magazine; Hudson Review; New Yorker; N.Y. Times; Paris Review; Perspective; Poetry; Quarterly Review of Lit.; Recurrence; Shenandoah, etc. Honours, awards: Borestone Mountain Poetry Award, 1957; Litt.D., Westminster Coll., 1971 & others. Address: 4647 S.W. Dosch Rd., Portland, OR 97201, U.S.A.

OSTROMECKI, Bogdan Michał, b. 12 July 1911. Writer; Poet; Translator. Education: Fac. of Law, Univ. of Warsaw. Married, 1 s. Positions held: Ed. of Poetry prog., Polish Radio Broadcasting, Warsaw. Memberships: Union of Polish Writers; Polish PEN Ctr. Published works: (poetry books) Popiół Niepodległy, 1947; Muzyka nad Młynowem, 1952; Wędrowcy czasu, 1958; Wieza z ziarnek maku, 1960; Ptaki u słonych źródeł, 1965; Znak planety, 1968; Wybór wierszy, 1972; (essays) Lirnioy, trubadurzy i tyrteje, 1973; Laury i piołuny, 1974. Transl.: Jules Laforgues – Poems (French), 1972. Contbr. to: Tygodnik Warszawski; Tygodnik Powszechny; Kultura; Zycie Literackie; Poezja, etc. Honours, awards: Prize, Włodzimierza Pietrzaka, 1972; Prize of Polish Poetry Fest., Lodz, 1973. Address: ul.J.Dabrowskiego 54 m. 1, 02-561 Warsaw, Poland.

O'SULLIVAN, Vincent Gerard, b. 28 Sept. 1937. University Teacher; Editor. Education: M.A., Univ. of Auckland, 1959; B.Litt., Lincoln Coll. Oxford, 1962. Married. Positions held: Formerly Lectr., Victoria Univ., Wellington, N.Z.; Currently, Sr. Lectr., Waikato Univ., Hamilton; Ed., Comment, Wellington, 1963-66. Published works: Our Burning Time, 1965; Revenanats, 1969; Zealand Verse, 1970. Contbr. to (Anthols.): Best Poems of 1960 & 1963: The Borestone Mountain Poetry Awards, 1961; Universities Poetry, 1963; New Zealand Poetry Yearbook, 1964; Oxford Book of New Zealand Verse, 1970; (Jrnls.): Landfall; Poetry Australia. Hons: Commonwealth Scholarship, 1960; Macmillan Brown Poetry Prize, 1961; Jessie Mackay Award, 1965; Farmer's Poetry Prize, Sydney, 1967. Address: Pukeroro, R.D.3, Hamilton, New Zealand.

OSWALD, Ernest John, b. 20 Jan. 1943. Hospital Worker; Poetry Editor. Education: A.A.S., Bus. Mgmt., Bronx Community Coll., 1967; B.A., Engl. Lit., Fordham Univ., 1973. Positions held: Dept. Mgr., E.J. Korvette Stores, N.Y.C., 1967-68; Production Clerk, Fawcett Publs., N.Y., 1969-73; Poetry Ed., Heirs Mag., San Francisco, Calif., 1973–. Member, N.Y. Poetry Forum, 1972-73. Contbr. to: N.Y. Qtly.; Lake Superior Review; Imprints Qtly.; The Small Pond; Folio; El Viento; Bachaet; Roagh Qut; Point Mag.; Nomad Mag., Caryatid; The Monthly; Second Coming; The Shore Poetry Anthol.; Eastern Poetry; Major Poets; Quality Am. Poetry, Book I. Address: 128 Laguna St., San Francisco, CA 94102, U.S.A.

OTTO, Eleanor. Writer; Musician. Education: A.B., Univ. of Rochester; M.A., Columbia Univ.; Opera, The Juilliard Schl.; The Manhattan Schl. of Mus.; The Colo. Coll., Colo. Springs. Positions held: Tchr. of Adults, Bd. of Educ., N.Y.C., 1956-72. Memberships: Am. Soc. of Composers, Authors & Publishers; Composers, Authors & Artists of Am.; Hon.Mbr., Int. Mark Twain Soc., St. Louis, Mo.; Int. Platform Assn.; N.Y. Poetry Forum; Am. Guild of Musical Arts. Published works: Winged Rhapsodies (poems), 1953; To the Stars (poems), 1966; Newville Clipper & Morar's Studio (plays), 1967; I Want Victory (a play w. songs), 1967; Forsythia (song for voice & piano, words & music), 1967; The Brass Instruments of the Orchestra, 1967; How to Start (booklet), 1969; Moon Ring (an epic poem), 1968; Apollo (Eagle on the Moon), 1969. Rep. in anthols. inclng: Yearbook of Contemporary Poetry, 1971; Lyrics of Love, 1972; Outstanding Contemporary Poetry, 1972; The Soul Sings, 1973. Recip. awards & grants. Address: 850 Amsterdam Ave., Apt. 10–D, N.Y., NY 10025, U.S.A.

OUGHTON, Edith, pen name **FRISBY, Katie,** b. 19 Apr. 1922. Clerical Worker. Contbr. to: Tates Quarterly, 1964-65; Headland, 1969; Spring Anthol., 1973; Competitors Jrnl.; Woman. Address: 59 Linton Ave., Boreham Wood, Herts. WD6 4RB, U.K.

OUTRAM, Richard Daley, b. 9 Apr. 1930. Poet. Education: B.A., Univ. of Toronto, Can. Married. Positions held: Worked for 2 yrs. in London w. BBC. Published works: Eight Poems, 1959; Exsultate, Jubilate, 1966. Contbr. to: Poetry. Address: c/o 6 South Drive, Rosedale, Toronto 5, Ont., Canada.

OVADIA, Jacques, b. 1 Aug. 1919. Journalist. Education: Baccalauréat. Married twice, 1 son. Positions held: w. Foreign Legion; Journalist. Published works: Chameurs rationnées (poetry), 1963; Elie Cohen, l'espion de Damas, 1967. Honours, awards: 1st prize, Italian review, 'Tutti gli nomini', 1964. Address: 33 Arlosorov St., Ramat-Gan, Israel.

OVERMYER, Janet Elaine, b. 25 July 1931. Educator. Education: B.A. & M.A., Ohio State Univ., Columbus, Ohio, U.S.A. Positions held: Instr., Dept. of Engl., Ohio State Univ. Contbr. to: Trace; Red Clay Reader; Quoin; Haiku Highlights (now Dragonfly); Jean's Jrnl.; Cycloflame; The Archer; In Montana, etc. Address: 544 Melrose Ave., Columbus, OH 43202, U.S.A.

OWEN, Guy, b. 24 Feb. 1925. Novelist; Educator. Education: B.A., M.A., & Ph.D., Univ. of N.C., Chapel Hill. Married, 2 sons. Positions held: Taught & served as Writer-in Res. at the following: Univ. of N.C.; Elon Coll.; Stetson Univ.; Davidson Coll.; Univ. of N.C. at Greensboro; currently Prof. of Engl., N.C. State Univ. Mbr., N.C. Poetry Soc. Published works: The White Stallion & Other Poems; Cape Fral & Other Poems; Ed., Southern Poetry Review (1958-73); Co-Ed., Southern Poetry Today, 1974. Contbr. to: Saturday Review; South; Miss. Review; Poetry, etc. Address: Dept. of Engl., N.C. State Univ., Raleigh, NC 27607, U.S.A.

OWEN, Thomas, b. 22 July 1910. Author & Poet. Education: LL.D. Memberships: Assn. of Belgian Writers; Int. Assn. of Art Critics; Free Acad. Published works: La Cave aux Crapauds; Cérémonial Nocturne; La Truie; Pitié pour des ombres; Le Jeu Secret; Le

Livre Interdix; Les Espalard; Portrait d'une Dame de qualité; Hotel Meublé. Contbr. to: Le Phare; Fiction; Fantasmagie; Temps Mlés; Metropole; Matin; Flandre Liberale, etc. Address: 74 Ave. Eugene Demolder, 1030 Brussels, Belgium.

OWENS, Rochelle, b. 2 Apr. 1936. Playwright; Poet. Married to George D. Economou. Memberships: Dramatists Guild; N.Y. Theatre Strategy; Womens Theatre Coun. Published works: Not Be Essence That Cannot Be, 1961; Salt & Core, 1968; I am The Babe of Joseph Stalin's Daughter, 1971; The Joe 82 Creation Poems, 1973; Selected Poems, 1973; Futz & What Came After (plays), 1968; The Karl Marx Play & Others, 1973. Contbr. to: The Nation; El Corno Emplumado; The N.Y. Qtly.; Partisan Review; The Unmuzzled Ox; Chicago Review; Southern Poetry Review; The Paris Review, etc. Honours, awards: Obie Best Play; Obie Disting. Playwrighting, 1968; N.Y. Drama Critics Circle Award; Guggenheim Fellow, 1972; Yale–ABC Fellow, 1969; Creative Artists Pub. Serv. Grant, 1973. Address: 606 West 116 St., N.Y., NY 10027, U.S.A.

OXLEY, William, b. 29 Apr. 1939. Poet; Chartered Accountant. Education: Private and Commercial Schools. Married; 2 children. Positions held: Office boy; Merchant Banker; Publisher, The Ember Press; Editor of poetry mags.: (Littack; Laissez Faire; New Headland); Associate Editor, The Village Review; Orbis. Published works: Dark Structures & Other Poems, 1967; New Workings, 1969; Passages From Time, 1971; The Icon Poems, 1972; Opera Vetera, 1973; Mirrors of the Sea, 1974. Contbr. of poems to: NY Times; Encounter; Delta; The Anglo-Welsh Review; The Dublin Mag.; Tribune; Workshop; Samphire; Akros; Platform; Priapus; Here Now; Expression One; Outposts. Contbr. of prose to: Stand; Poetry Review; Gong; Expression One; Pink Peace; Centre 17, and other mags. Has given readings of poetry at Nat. Book League; Poetry Soc.; City Lit. Inst.; Cheltenham Poetry Soc., 'Lamb & Flag', etc. Address: 27 Brook Rd., Epping, Essex, UK.

OZÓG, Jan Bolestaw, pen names **SOL, JAN WOS & JAN ZDEB,** b. 1 Mar. 1913. Writer; Poet. Education: M.A., Jagellonian Univ., Krakow, Poland. Positions held: Tchr. of College, 1944-51. Memberships: PEN Club; Union of Polish Writers. Published works: (poetry) Wyjazd wnuka, 1937; Arkusz poetycki, 1938; Ogieri makalagwa, 1939; Kraj, 1945; Jej Wielki Woz, 1947; Swiatla planow, 1953; Do logdu dobrejnadziei, 1956; Wiersze wybrane, 1957; Zielony wiatr, 1958; Panimtodoi, 1959; Gdzie powoj Wota, 1961; Wdzien gdy noc, 1963; Dzikie joiblkoi, 1964; Poezje wybrane, 1965; Ucieczkoi, 1965; Jemiota, 1966; Spokoj, 1967; Mury, 1968; Koilectwoi, 1968; Ziemia wielkanocna, 1969; Poezje wybrane, 1970; Oko, 1971; Wyspa Boirbarus, 1973; Poezje wybrane, 1973; (prose) Scigani, 1956; Kuloi, 1958; Chustka, 1959; Odstepcoi, 1962; Popiot mirtowy, 1963; Braciol, 1969; Kiedy ptaki odleciaty, 1969; Cienie ziemi, 1970; Wybor opowiodoin, 1972. Contbr. to most important Polish lit. reviews. Honours, awards: Prize of the Min. of Arts & Culture, 1967; The Lit. Prize of the City of Rzeszow, 1957. Address: ul. Krupniczoi 22, 31-123 Krakow, Poland.

P

PACE, Patsy Edwina Clark, b. 4 June 1929. Teacher; Poet. Education: B.A., Blue Mountain Coll., 1949; M.A., Univ. of Miss., 1950; M.Lib.Sci., Univ. of Miss., 1967. Married William M. Pace, 1 son, 1 daughter. Positions held: Tchr., Univ. H.S., Oxford, Miss., 1950-51; Instr., Univ. of Miss. Ext. Schls., 1951-52; Tchr. & Libn., Aberdeen H.S., Miss., 1952-64; Instr., Miss. State Coll. for Women, Columbus, Miss., 1965-68; Instr., Itawamba Jr. Coll., Amory, Miss. Ctr., 1972 & '73 summer sessions. Memberships: Miss. Poetry Soc.; Miss. Folklore Soc.; Northeast Miss. Histl. Soc. Rep. in following anthols.: Nat. Poetry Anthol. for Colls. &

Univs., 1949; Lyric Mississippi, 1955; Nat. Poetry Anthol., 1954 & '55. Contbr. to: Progressive Farmer; Conn. Lit. Review; Scimitar & Song; Poetry Digest; Midland Poetry Review; The Commercial Appeal; Miss. Poetry Jrnl.; Amateur Notes & Quotes. Address: P.O. Box 112, Woodland Rd., Aberdeen, MS 39730, U.S.A.

PACHE, Jean, b. 4 Mar. 1933. Teacher. Education: Licence-ès-Lettres, Univ. of Lausanne. Divorced, 2 sons, 1 daughter. Positions held: currently Teacher of French Lit., Gymnase de Lausanne; Editor of a Literary Series (Editions l'Aire, Lausanne) and a lit. chronicle for "24 Heures". Memberships: PEN Club; Association des Ecrivains de Langue française; Association des Ecrivains vaudois; Association internationale des Critiques littéraires. Published works: Les Fenêtres simultanées, poems, 1955; Poèmes de l'Autre, poems, 1960; Analogies, poems, 1958-61, 1966; Repères, poems 1962-66, 1969; Ritnel, poems 1966-69, 1971; Anachroniques, récit (notes marginales 1962-72), 1973. Contbr. to: Les Cahiers du Sud; La Nouvelle Revue Française; DU; La Revue de Belles-Lettres (Ed. i/c 1959-62); Pays du Lac (editorial comm. 1953-55); Gazette de Lausanne; 24 Heures (regularly since 1967). Honours, awards: Prix Follope de Poésie, Univ. of Lausanne, 1959; Prix de la Fondation Schiller, 1967. Address: 16 Ave. du Servan, CH-1006 Lausanne, Switzerland.

PACHECO, Henricus Luis, pen name **PACHECO, Henry L.,** b. 27 July 1947. Journalist; Editorial Specialist; English Literature Instructor. Education: B.A. & M.A. in Engl. Lit., Univ. of Wyoming, Laramie. Position held: Reporter, Wyoming State Tribune, & USMC; Communications Cons., San Diego Model Cities Prog.; Grad. Asst., Engl. Dept., Univ. of Wyoming; Dir., UW Ethnic Cultural Media Ctr.; Mgr., Editl. Servs., Fleetwood Corp. Memberships: Sigma Delta Chi; Marine Corps Combat Correspondents Assn.; Chicano Tchrs. of Engl. Published works: The Kindred/La Familia, 1972. Contbr. to: Alkahest; Workshop Writing; Flora Y Canto; Poets West; Sunstone Review; N.M. Mag. Recip., Harcourt World & Brace Poetry Fellowship, 1968. Address: Box 3681, Laramie, WY 82070, U.S.A.

PACK, Robert, b. 19 May 1929. Teacher; Editor. Education: B.A., Dartmouth Coll., Hanover, N.H., 1951; M.A., Columbia Univ., N.Y., 1953. Married Patricia Powell. Positions held: Former Tchr., Barnard Coll., N.Y.; Middlebury Coll., Vt.; The Poetry Workshop of the New Schl. for Social Research, N.Y.; Bread Loaf Writer's Conf., Vt.; Ed., Discovery. Published works: The Irony of Joy, 1955; A Stranger's Privilege, 1959; Guarded by Women, 1963; Selected Poems, 1965; Other: Wallace Stevens, 1958; How to Catch a Crocodile, 1964; Ed. w. var. Others, New Poets of England and America, 1957; New Poets of England and America, Second Selection, 1962; Poems of Doubt and Belief: An Anthology of Modern Religious Poetry, 1964; Short Stories, 1967. Contbr. to (Anthols.): New Pocket Anthology of American Verse, 1955; New Poets of England and America, 1957; Erotic Poetry, 1963; Poems of Doubt and Belief, 1964; A Controversy of Poets, 1965; (jrnls.): New Yorker; Paris Review. Hons: Fulbright Fellowship, 1956-57; Nat. Inst. of Arts and Letters Award, 1957.

PADGETT, Ron, Pseudonyms: **Tom Veitch, Harlan Dangerfield,** b. 17 June 1942. Poetry Teacher. Education: A.B., Columbia Coll., N.Y., 1964; Fulbright Fellow, Paris, 1965-66. Married w. 1 son. Positions held: Tchr., Poetry Workshop, St. Mark's in-the-Bowery, N.Y., 1968. Published works: In Advance of the Broken Arm, 1964; Bean Spasms, 1967; Tone Arm, 1967; Great Balls of Fire, 1969; Trans., The Poet Assassinated, 1968; Ed. w. David Shapiro, Sparklers: An Anthology of New York Poets, 1969. Contbr. to (Anthols.): Young American Poets, 1968; Contemporary American Poetry, 1970; (Jrnls.): Paris Review; Angel Hair; World; Adventures in Poetry; "C" Mag. Hons: Boar's Head Poetry Prize, Columbia Univ., N.Y., 1964; George E. Woodberry Award, ibid., 1964;

Gotham Book Mart Avant-Garde Poetry Prize, 1964; Poets Foundation Grant, 1965,68. Address: 342 East 13th Street, N.Y., NY 10003, USA.

PAGE, Maura June Ann, pen name **OLBRECHTS, Maura,** b. 15 Dec. 1940. Housewife; Freelance Journalist. Married, 3 children. Positions held: County Court Officer, Yeovil County Court & High Court of Justice, 1958-61. Member, Portsmouth Poetry Soc. Contbr. to: Writers' Review Short Story & Poetry Year Book, 1971; Hampshire Poets No. 13; The Cornish Review; The Writers' Review; var. small poetry mags. Honours, awards: Cert. of Merit, Writers' Review Lit. Comp. Poetry, 1969 & Book Prize. Address: 16 Queen Mary Road, Portchester, Fareham, Hampshire, U.K.

PAGE, Sarah Geneva, pen names **PAGE, S. Geneva, PAGE, Geneva,** b. 9 Aug. 1913. Radio Continuity Director. Married, Raymond J. Page, 2 s. Positions held: Newspaper Reporter; Poetry Column Ed.; Radio Advertising Copywriter; Radio Continuity Director. Memberships: Pres., Poetry Soc. of Mich.; Member, Nat. Fed. of State Poetry Socs.; Battle Creek Creative Writers' United Arts Council Coordinator and past president; Lansing Poetry Club, Mich.; Ariz. State Poetry Soc. Published works: Poetry Digest Anthol., 1942; Peninsula Poets Anthol., 1959; Ballet on the Wind (anthol.), 1969. Contbr. to: Poet; Christian Herald; Christian Advocate; Bardic Echoes; Creative Review; Peninsula Poets, Qtly.; Metropolitan Mag.; Muskegon Chronical; Record & News; Enquirer & News, also numerous church and other publications. Poetry Prizes and Awards incl.: 1st place, 1972, ASPS (Ala.) Nat. Poetry Contest; 1st place, Battle Creek Creative Writers (Mich.) Poetry Contest, 1973; 2nd place, RAXPO Poetry Contest (Mich., religious), 1970. Address: 256 Burr St., Battle Creek, MI 49015, USA.

PAIN, Margaret, b. 27 March 1922. Company Secretary. Education: Private School; Business College; Adult Education; Private Study. Currently director of R. Pain & Sons Ltd., (Builders and Engineers), UK.; Associate Editor, Envoi. Memberships: Committee Member, Guildford Centre of the Poetry Soc.; Fellow, Internat. Poetry Soc.; Member, Poets Conference; Poet's Vigilantes; Wey Poets. Published work: Walking to Eleusis, 1967. Contbr. to: Country Life; Country Quest; Surrey Life; Breakthru; Envoi; Expression One; Outposts; Overspill; Poetry Eastwest (US); Radix; Scrip; Viewpoints; Weyfarers; Workshop; (Anthols.): 1st Flying Dragon Book of Poetry; Nature Poetry 3; The Spring Anthol., 1973; Internat. Who's Who in Poetry Anthol., 1973; (forthcoming) IPS Anthol. Translation, by Agnes Sotiracopoulou-Skina in: Nea Estia (Athens), and in: Smyrna (Athens). Address: Ardnardeen, Danes Hill, Woking, Surrey GU22 7HQ, UK.

PAINTER, Charlotte. Writer. Education: M.A., Stanford Univ. Positions held: Lectr. at Stanford Univ. & Univ. of Calif. at Berkeley & Santa Cruz. Published works: (books) Who Made the Lamb, 1966; Confession from the Malaga Madhouse, 1971. Contbr. to: Place Mag.; Yardbird. Address: 372 – 63rd St., Oakland, CA 94618, U.S.A.

PAINTON, Ivan Emory, pen name, **ZARELLIO, Florian,** b. 7 Aug. 1909. Artist; Poet; Art Instructor; Lapidary; Painter. Education: Northwest State Coll., Alva, Oklahoma; Oklahoma Baptist Univ., Shawnee, Oklahoma; Ph.D., Colorado Christian Coll. 2 yrs. private art instruction under late Albert E. von Strode; Creator and originator of Rock Art, oil portraits of the actual interior of rocks. Married to Mildred Overstreet; 3 d. Exhibitions: Travelling art shows in USA and Europe; special guest artist exhibits at 1-man shows (more than 40), including Nat. Show in Washington, DC, Internat. Show in Washington, DC, Oklahoma City, Phoenix, Arizona; Wichita; Kansas; and Lincoln, Nebraska, etc. Memberships: CSSI and Internat. Acad. Leonardo da Vinci, Rome (membership committee); Artists Equity Assoc.; Artists of North America; Art Inst. of Chicago; IPA; American Fed. of

Mineralogical Socs.; Neihardt Foundation, Nebraska; Nat. Fed. of State Poetry Socs.; American Poets Fellowship; Oklahoma State Poetry Soc.; Oklahoma Authors of the Oklahoma Dept. of Libraries. Published works: Reflections From The Inner Room, 1969, 1971; The Ballad Of Old Pogue, 1969; Whispers In The Night, 1971. Contbr. to: D.I.B. Mag., 1970; Internat. Who's Who in Poetry Anthol., etc. Address: Studio of Fine Arts, Orion, Fairview, OK 73737, USA.

PAISLEY, Miriam Rose, b. 8 Jan. 1920. Freelance Secretary; Poet; Playwright. Education: Eastern HS Grad.; YMCA Business Coll. Grad.; Famous Writers School (Corres. Course) Cert. of Completion, 1973 (fiction writing). Married to John Calvin Paisley; 1 s. (Ronald William Bounds). Positions held: Sec., Johns Hopkins Univ., 1947-51; Publ., Balt. City Pub. Schools, 1962-68; Radio-TV. Dept., ibid., 1968-70; Northwood-Appold United Meth. Ch., Balt., 1970-72; Able Temporaries, 1972–; Dir., Actress, Religious Drama Grp., Mt. Vernon Pl. United Meth. Ch.; Past Dir., Balt. Mt. Vernon Players, 1963-68. Memberships: Maryland State Poetry Soc. (Recording Sec.); Nat. Fed. of State Poetry Socs., Inc.; DANAE (life membership), Clover Poetry Assoc., Soc. of Lit. Designates, Wash., DC. Published works: The Literary Urge, 1966, 1969. Plays performed: Saddlebag to Satellite (author), 1970; From Riches to Religion (author), 1972. Contbr. to: The Co-Ed. Triangle, 1947-48; Sad, Sad America, 1967; Gato Mag., 1969; Patterson HS Clipper, 1969; The Clover Book of Poetry – Collection of Verse, Vol. III; Dance of the Muse, 1970; Yearbook of Modern Poetry, 1971; The Oriole – Md. State Poetry Soc., Vol. 1, 2, 4 (1971-73); The Best of Gato, 1971; Internat. Who's Who in Poetry Anthol., 1973. Awards: Hon. Mention, Clover Int. Poetry Assoc. Contest, 1969; Hon. Mention, Int. Who's Who in Poetry Anthol. Contest, 1971. Address: 1525 East 35th St., Baltimore, MD 21218, USA.

PALEN, Jennie M. Certified Public Accountant; Writer; Poet; Poetry Critic. Education: B.Sc., N.Y. Univ., U.S.A. Positions held: Report Reviewer, Principal, Haskins & Sells, 1918-49; Acct., Ed., Researcher, Lectr. in Acctcy., Ghost Writer, 1950–; Instr. in Acctcy., Baruch Coll., 1957-62; Sr. Ed., Prentice-Hall, 1963-66. Mbrships incl: Pres., Pen & Brush, 1970-72; Poetry Soc. of Am.; Am. Inst. of CPAs; Pres., Am. Womens Soc. of CPAs, 1946-47; Chmn. & mbr. sev. comms., N.Y. State Soc. of CPAs; Nat. Advsry. Coun., Nat. League of Am. Pen Women, 1956-58; Poetry Ed., ibid, 1962-64; Dir., Women's Press Club of N.Y., 1965-67; Pres., Brooklyn Poetry Circle, 1959-65. Published works: Moon Over Manhattan, 1949; Report Writing for Accountants, 1955; Good Morning, Sweet Prince, 1957; Stranger, Let Me Speak, 1964; Vol. I, Encyclopedia of Accounting Forms & Reports, 1964; Ed., Contbr., Compiler, Ency. of Auditing Techniques, 2 vols., 1966. Contbr. to num. newspapers, jrnls., mags. inclng: The Fiddlehead (Canada); The Forum; Pegasus; N.Y. CPA Jrnl.; Sat. Evening Post; Good Housekeeping; N.Y. Herald Tribune; Toronto Star Weekly; Best Articles & Stories; Denver Post; Am. Bard; The Poetry Review (London); Wall St. Jrnl., etc. Rep. in num. anthols. inclng: Poetry Soc. of Am. Golden Yr. & Diamond Anthols.; The Various Light; IWWP; Golden Quill (10); John F. Kennedy Meml.; Nat. League of Am. Pen Women. Poems have been read on TV & radio. Recip. num. poetry prizes. Address: 26 East Tenth St., N.Y., NY 10003, U.S.A.

PALMA, Margaret Tanghe, pen name **PALMA, Peggy,** b. 3 Apr. 1924. Social Worker. Education: Temple Univ. Evening Schl. Married, 3 sons. Positions held: Tchr. at Teen-Age Charm Clinic for Girls; social work w. boys at Glen-Mills Boys' Reformatory, Pa., & in Seattle, Wash.; Radio advice Prog. for Youth people. Memberships: Sec., Pa. Poetry Soc.; Dela. Country Arts & Crafts; Writers' Club of Dela. Co.; Phila Art Mus.; Mbr. & Tchr., Phila. Int. House (Foreign students), etc. Published works: Silhouettes & Shadows, book of poems, 1971. Contbr. to: Reader's Digest; Springfield Press; Seattle Times; Phila.

Evening Bulletin; many women's mag., etc. Honours, awards incl: 1st Award, Lit. Div., Dela. Co. Fed. of Women's Clubs, 1969, '70; many other awards, ibid & from NFSPS & Phila. Writers Club. Address: 913 – S, 47th St., Philadelphia, PA 19143, U.S.A.

PALMATEER, Robert Donald, b. 19 Apr. 1946. Freelance Writer; Educator. Education: Univ. of Ore., Eugene, 4 yrs. Married, 2 children. Positions held: worked in sev. political campaigns, as Speech Writer, P.R. Dir., etc.; Founded & Advised Kapaa Student Writers' Workshop, org. on Kauai of student writers, while teaching high schl. & adult educ. classes. Published works: Rituals, 1974. Contbr. to: English Jrnl.; Cardinal Poetry Review; Zahir; Encore; Scopcraeft; Overflow; Oregonian Verse; Medford (ore.) Mail Tribune; The Last Cookie; All Time Favorite Poetry; Poetry Review; Poetry Parade; Mandates. Honours, awards: 5th prize, Spenser Book Co's Third Annual Poetry Contest, 1969; 1st Prize, World Poetry Day, Rochester, N.Y., Contest; Wilson MacDonald Poetry Soc. Award, Toronto, 1969. Address: P.O. Box 505, Kapaa, Kauai, HI 96746, U.S.A.

PALMER, Ida Catherine, b. 12 Apr. 1913. Secretary; Teacher. Education: B.A., Dickinson Coll., Carlisle, Pa., 1933; Bloomsburg State Tchrs. Coll., 1 yr.; Susquehanna Univ., 2 summers; attended Univ. of Southwestern La., Lafayette. Married John Charles Palmer, 3 children. Positions held: Sec./Auditor, Byers & Dunn; Tchr. of Engl. & Typing, Business Methods, Caraopolis H.S., Pa.; Nursery Schl. Music Tchr. & Subs. Tchr., Lafayette, La.; Sec., Evangeline Area Guidance Ctr., Lafayette, La.; Sec. & Records Custodian, Acadiana Mental Hlth. Ctr. Mbrships: La. State Poetry Soc.; Zeta Tau Alpha; DAR. Contbr. to: La. State Poetry Soc. Book of the Yr., 1970-71; Bachaet, 1971; The Lykens Standard, Address: 602 Lafayette St., Lafayette, LA 70501, U.S.A.

PALMER, Michael, b. 11 May 1943. Poet. Education: B.A., Harvard Coll., 1965; M.A., Harvard Univ., 1967. Published works: Plan of the City of O, 1971; Blake's Newton, 1972; C's Songs, 1973; The Circular Gates, 1974. Contbr. to: Joglars; Sumac; Friendly Local Press; Paris Review; Grosseteste Review; The World; Caterpillar; Spectrum; This; One; Open Reading; Fire Exit; Tens; Sesheta; Buttons; Sparrow; Ear in a Wheatfield; Occident; Imago; Boston Eagle, etc. Address: 17 Beaver St., San Francisco, CA 94114, U.S.A.

PALMER, Pamela Lynn, pen name **PALMER, Lynn,** b. 29 May 1951. Graduate Teaching Assistant. Education: B.A. & M.A., Stephen F. Austin State Univ. Positions held: Grad. Tchng. Asst., Stephen F. Austin State Univ. & Tex. A & M Univ. Memberships: Life Mbr., Poetry Soc. of Tex.; Int. Poetry Inst.; Tex. Folklore Soc. Published works: Rain is for Dreaming, 1968. Contbr. to: The Houston Chronicle; The Bellaire Texan; Encore; Am. Forests; Jean's Jrnl. Honours, awards: 3rd prize, Deep South Writers & Artists Conf., 1969, Piney Woods Writers Conf., 1969 & Hemisfair Pan Am. Award, 1968; 1st prize, Ecology Contest, Int. Poetry Inst., 1971. Address: 5235 Lymbar, Houston, TX 77035, U.S.A.

PANDIT, Raghunath Vishnu, pen name **RAVI,** b. 6 Apr. 1917. Author. Education: B.A., Univ. of Poona, India. Married Sushama, 1 son. Positions held: Press Photographer; Press Corres. & Ed. (Marathi); Judge, Min. of Educ., UNESCO Awards, 1969; Mbr., Advisory Bd., Kala Acad., 1970-71. Memberships: World Poetry Soc. Int.; Konkani Bhasha Pracharini Sabha; Advisor, Lit. Guild of India (N.Y.); FIBA. Published works: 8 colls. of poems in Konkani lang.; 5 colls. of poems in Engl. translation (of the present poet) by Thomas Gay; Rashmia (coll. of poems of the present poet in Kannada); Zaisa Aaya Vaisa Gaaya (coll. of poems in Hindi). Contbr. to num. mags. jrnls., etc. inclng: Poet; The Illustrated Weekly of India; Rashtramat; Sadhana; Nav Hind Times; O Globo; Goa Today; IWWP Anthol.; Patriotic Songs of the World; Rizal Leaves; Maharashtra Times; Sanyukta Karnatak; Bharati; Hind

Praja; Indian Sociologist; Konkani Schl. Books. Honours, awards: U.N. Day Gold Medal, Philippines, 1967; Dr. Leadership in Poetry, Int. Acad. of Leadership; Ph.D., Acad. of Philos., U.S.A.; Litt.D., World Acad. of Langs. & Lit., Brazil, etc. Address: Block No.12, 2nd Fl., Bambolkar's Bldg., Fontainhas, Panaji, Goa, India.

PANOWICH, Gertrude Moessner, b. 21 Dec. 1927. English Instructor. Education: Univ. of Colorado; Kent State Univ.; Sul Ross, 1962, B.A.; Univ. of Texas, 1967, M.A., and work on Ph.D., Univ. of Texas in progress. Positions held: Prof. of Engl., Southwestern Univ., Georgetown, Texas. Membership: Poetry Soc. of Texas. Published work: Abstractions, 1962. Contbr. to: Cyclotron; Writers' Notes; Internat. Who's Who in Poetry. Recip. of numerous poetry awards; Internat. Who's Who in Poetry, 1973. Address: 5621 Shoal Creek Blvd., Austin, TX 78756, USA.

PANT, Gauri, b. 28 Aug. 1920. Freelance Writer; Housewife. Education: privately & at Sir J.J. Schl. of Arts, Bombay, India. Married, twin sons. Memberships: P.E.N.; World Poetry Soc. Int. Published works: Weeping Season, 1971; Voodoo, 1972; Staircase-17, due for release 1973; Happenings, an autobiographical jrnl. in English under publication. Contbr. to: Poetry India; Poetry East West; Poet; Quest; Levant; Thought; Enact; PEN Jrnl.; Hindustan Standard; Ladies Study Grp. Jrnl.; The Jrnl. of Indian Writing in English; Sunday Standard. Has broadcast her poems for All India Radio & on TV. Recip. var. hons. Address: 21 Metcalfe House, Delhi–6, India.

PAPPAS, Neva J. (Flansburg), pen name **JAY, Neva,** b. 1 Feb. 1917. News Copywriter; Poetry Editor and Columnist. Education: Diploma in Costume Designing, Woodbury Coll., Calif.; Special Courses in Painting, Univ. of Michigan. Positions held: 25 yrs. with Dry Cleaners; 6 yrs. newspaper; Copywriter and Typist, Thayer News (Thayer, Mo.); Poetry Editor and Columnist, Salem (Ark.) Headlight; Freelance Writer, 1970-73. Membership: Arkansas Poet's Roundtable. Published works: Light Lines and Rhymes, 1967. Contbr. to: Fire Flower; Cyclo-Flame; Manifold; Over the Ozarks; A Place for Poets; Latchstrings; Rhyme & Reason; Penman; Words with Wings; Swordsman Review; Poetry Parade (vols. 1-14); Ardentia Verba; Ben Travato; Best in Poetry 1968-69; All Time Favorites 1969; Ark. Poetry 1968; Contemp. Poets of Arkansas 1969; Anthol. of American Poetry (vols. 7-11); Poems of Presidents and Your Townsmen 1967; Poets of Arkansas Roundtable 1972; Birth of Day 1972; Shore Anthol. 1972; Internat. Who's Who in Poetry Anthol., 1973; Better Thoughts, 1970; articles in Horoscope Guide (mag.); American Astrology (mag.); School and Community (Mo.); Writer's Digest; Calif. Writer's Mag.; Featured in Afterglow – radio station Monticello, Ark., and on WHPL Winchester, Va. Awards: 2nd place, Poetry Parade, 1968 (vol. 7); Hon. Mention, North American Mentor, 1967; Poet Laureate of Penman, 1967; Highly Commended, Internat. Who's Who in Poetry, 1972-73; 3rd Poem of the Reverend, 1972 (Ark. Poets Roundtable, Nat. Poetry Day). Address: Rt. 1, Box C29, Mammoth Spring, AR 72554, USA.

PAQUIN, Helen Grace, b. 6 Mar. 1933. Housewife. Published works: Humorously Yours, 1971; The Ding-Dong Doosey, 1972. Contbr. to: Mary's Scrapbook; Gato; Poetry Parade; Prairie Poet; United Poet; Bachaet; Am. Poet; 70 Poets; Poetry Club; Royal Publishing Co.; Moon Age Poet; Orphic Lute; Poetry Prevue; Creative Urge; Written Word; Echoes of Faith; Guild; Little Gray House; Friends & Hobbies; Inky Trails; Major Poets; World Poets; Am. Voice; Echoes of Love; Friendly Way; Ogdensburg Jrnl.; The Wise Shopper; Scimitar & Song; Bouquet of Poems; New & Better World Anthol.; Fla. Notes; Coney Island Times; Trilogy; Tower by the Sea; Birth of Am.; Invictus; Town & Country; Clover Coll. of Verse, etc. Honours, awards: 12 merit certs. from 1969-73; Award for winning 3rd pl. in 6th Trans Atlantic Comp. 'Novella' contest, 1973. Address: Rt. 2, Lisbon, N.Y. 13658,

U.S.A.

PARADIS, Suzanne, b. 27 Oct. 1936. Writer. Married, 2 children. Memberships: Académie Canadienne-française; P.E.N. Int.; Société des Auteurs et compositeurs; Association des compositeurs, auteurs et éditeurs du Canada. Published works: Les Enfants continuels, 1959; A temps le bonheur, 1960; La Chasse aux autres, 1961; La Malebête, 1962; Pour les enfants des morts, 1964; Le visage offensé, 1966; L'oeuvre de pierre, 1968; Pour voir les plectrophanes naitre, 1970; Il y eut un matin, 1972; La voie sauvage, 1973. Honours, awards: Prix de la Province de Québec, 1963; Prix Camille-Roy, 1961; Prix France-Québec, 1965; Prix du Maurier, 1970. Address: 1324 rue Saint-Jacques, Ancienne-Lorette, Quebec, Canada.

PARHAM, Robert Randall, b. 21 Apr. 1943. College Teacher. Education: B.A., Belmont Coll.; M.S., Fla. State Univ. Married Dorothy Ann Van Hook Parham, 1 son, 1 daughter. Positions held: Tchr., public schls., Fla., 1965-69; Engl. Instr., Francis Marion Coll., Florence, S.C., 1970-74. Published works: Shadows & Resurrections (chapbook), 1974. Contbr. to: The Malahat Review; Ariz. Qtly.; Trace; The Goddard Jrnl.; Spectrum; Spirit; The S.D. Review; Kans. Qtly.; Southern Humanities Review; Twigs; Wind; Wis. Poetry Mag.; Mustang Review; Karamu; Discourse; Forum, etc. Honours, awards: 1st prize, William Gilmore Simms Prize, 1971; place, Writers Digest Writing Contest, 1970. Address: P.O. Box 4140, Florence, SC 29501, U.S.A.

PARINI, Jay Lee, b. 2 Apr. 1948. University Teacher. Education: B.A. (with Hons.) (1970), Lafayette Coll., Pa.; B.Phil. (1973), Univ. of St. Andrews, Scotland. (Ph.D., expected, 1974). Positions held: Fellow of St. Salvator's Coll., Univ. of St. Andrews, 1972-74. Memberships: Pres., Poetry Soc. of St. Andrews, 1971-73; Poetry Soc. (UK). Published works: Singing in Time, 1972; A Garden of Earthly Delights, 1974. Contbr. to: Aien; Echoes; Umbrella. Has given many poetry readings in colleges in America and GB. Award: The MacKnight Black Poetry & Literature Award, 1970. Address: 149 South Rebecca Av., Scranton, PA 18504, USA.

PARK, Michael, b. 18 Dec. 1941. Radio Technician in Civil Service. Married, 1 son, 1 daughter. Positions held: served in Royal Signals, 10 yrs.; TV Service Engr., 1 yr.; Radio Techn. in Civil Service; Co-Fndr., Rannoch Gillamoor Poets; Co-Ed., Strath Mag. Memberships: Fndr. Fellow, Int. Poetry Soc.; Area Rep., Poets Vigilantes; Bletchley Writers Soc.; Yorks. Dialect Soc.; Yorks. Poets Assn.; Penman Club; 'Success'. Published works: Broad Acres, 1972; Just Afooar Dawn, 1972; Collected Poems I & II, 1972; Alpha to Omega, 1972. Contbr. to: Yorks. Dialect Soc. Summer Bulletin & Transactions; Radix; All People are Poets Anthol.; Strath; Yorks. Achievement; Bletchley Gazette. Awarded Fellowship of Int. Poetry Soc., 1972. Address: 1 Buttermere Close, Bletchley, Milton Keynes MK2 3DG, U.K.

PARKER, Bonnie Elizabeth, pen name **McCONNELL, Bonnie,** b. 20 Sept. 1929. Writer; Publisher; Editor. Education: Wayne State Univ., 2 yrs.; Ph.D., Colorado Christian Coll., 1973. Widow, 2 daughters. Positions held: Book Reviewer for Scrivener, Tempo & Legend; Contest Judge for poetry contests, int. & state. Memberships: State Pres., Composers, Authors & Artists of Am.; Mich. Poetry Soc.; N.H. Poetry Soc.; Ariz. State Poetry Soc.; Poets' Guild; Versewriters' Guild of Ohio; Catholic Poetry Soc. Published works: Dark Tigers of My Tongue, 1957; Season of the Golden Dragon, 1960; Leopard on a Topaz Leash, 1963; A Pride of Lion-Noons, 1964; Seed of the Wild Stallion, 1969; Morning of the Unicorn, 1972. Contbr. to: N.Y. Herald Tribune; N.Y. Times; Christian Sci. Monitor; McCall's; Ladies Home Jrnl.; Spirit; Detroit News; Denver Post; Good Housekeeping; South & West; Voices Int.; Flame; The Lyric; Fiddlehead; Am. Mentor, etc. & approx. 50 anthols. & Radio & TV

Readings. Honours, awards incl: The Writers Digest Annual Creative Writing Contest Awards, 1971, '72; Cert., Community Ldrs. of Am., 1970. Address: 39213 Gloucester, Westland, MI 48185, U.S.A.

PARKER, Derek, b. 27 May 1932. Editor; Free-lance Journalist. Married Julia L. Parker. Positions held: Local Weekly & Nat. Daily Journalism, in TV & as a Freelance Literary & Radio Journalist; Ed., Poetry Review, 1966–. Published works: The Fall of Phaethon & Other Poems, 1954; Company of Two, 1954; Other: Byron and his World, 1968; Astrology?, 1970; Ed. w. Selected Letters of Edith Sitwell, 1970. Contbr. to (Anthols.): Peninsula: An Anthology of Verse from the West Country, 1957; Best Poems of 1965: The Borestone Mountain Poetry Awards, 1966. Address: 37 Campden Hill, London W.11, UK.

PARKER, (James) Stewart, b. 20 Oct. 1941. University Teacher. Education: B.A., Queen's Univ., Belfast, 1963; M.A., ibid., 1966. Married Kate Ireland. Positions held: Instructor, Dept. of Engl., Hamilton Coll., Clinton, N.Y., 1964-67; Instructor, Dept. of Engl., Cornell Univ., Ithaca, N.Y., 1967-69. Published works: The Casualty's Meditation, 1965; Maw, 1967. Contbr. to (Anthols.): Young Commonwealth Poets '65, 1965; Penguin Book of Postwar British Verse, 1970. Address: c/o 74 Hillsborough Drive, Belfast 6, Northern Ireland.

PARKER, Kay Grayman, b. 20 Sept. 1912. Businesswoman. Education: B.A., Mt. Mary Coll., Milwaukee, Wis. Married Allen F. Parker. Positions held: Employed by Ill. Bell Telephone Co., 1937–; worked in Commercial, Marketing, P.R. & Personnel Depts.; currently composes letters for the Pres. of the Company. Memberships: Past Pres., The New World Poets' Club; Past Workshop Dir., Poets & Patrons; Farr Horizons Poetry Club; Chicago Poets Club. Contbr. to var. newspapers, mags., anthols. inclng: Gold Star Family Album; Haiku Highlights; Am. Poetry League; New World Poets Anthol. of Poems; From Sea to Sea in Song; Playboy; Jean's Jrnl.; Chicago Daily News; Hallmark Treasury of Verse. Recip. var. poetry awards & hons. inclng: 1st pl. in Lullabye & H.M. in Dramatic Monologue catergories, Poets & Patrons, 1973. Address: 7061 N. Kedzie Ave., Apt. 912, Chicago, IL 60645, U.S.A.

PARKER, Lois W., b. 15 Sept. 1921. Assistant Professor of English. Education: B.A., M.A., Sul Ross Coll., Alpine, Tex.; Grad. study, Univ. of Okla., Univ. of Ariz.; Ph.D., Southern Ill. Univ., Carbondale. Positions held: Instr., Engl., Sul Ross State Coll.; Asst. Prof. of Engl., Southwestern Univ., Georgetown, Tex. Memberships: Acad. of Am. Poets; MLA; AAUP; Poetry Soc. of Tex. Contbr. to: Sage; Stride; Cardinal Poetry Quarterly; Timeless Treasures; Living Lyrics; The N.Am. Mentor; Poetry, Classical & Contemp. Honours, awards: Cert. of Merit, N.Am. Mentor Poetry Award, 1967. Address: Atholea, 403 Elm St., Georgetown, TX 78626, U.S.A.

PARKER, Mabel, pen name **PHILOMELA,** b. Winsford, Cheshire. Education: Sir John Deane's Grammar School, Northwich, Cheshire; The Hiatt Ladies' Coll., Wellington, Salop.; London Schl. of Jrnlsm. Ltd. (Poetry Sect.). Memberships: Poetry Soc. (UK); Nat. Book League; Friend of the Keats-Shelley Memorial Assoc. Published works: Moods and Modulations, 1961. Contbr. to: The Spring Anthol., Mitre Press, (1965 to 1973); Poetry Review; Outposts; Envoi; Expression One; John O'London's; Church Times; The Pilot, etc. Recip. of Poetry Soc. Premium Prize, 1957. Address: Hilbre, Chester Rd., Over, Winsford, Cheshire CW7 2NG, UK.

PARKES, Frank (Francis Ernest Kobina Parkes), b. 1932. Editor; Press Attaché. Education: Adisadel Coll., Ghana. Positions held: Formerly Clerk in the Deeds Registry; Reporter, Daily Graphic; Ed., Monitor & Eagle; Press Attaché, Min. of Information, Ghana. Contbr. to (Anthols.): Voices of Ghana, 1958; African Voices, 1960; An African Treasury, 1961; Poems from

Black Africa, 1963; A Book of African Verse, 1964; Young Commonwealth Poets, '65, 1965; West African Verse, 1967. Hons: Pres., Ghana Soc. of Writers.

PARKINSON, Thomas Francis, b. 24 Feb. 1920. Professor of English. Education: B.A. & M.A., Univ. of Calif., Berkeley; Ph.D., ibid, 1948. Married Ariel Parkinson, 2 daughters. Positions held: on staff, Univ. of Calif., Berkeley, 1948–; Full Prof., ibid, 1960–; Vis. Prof., Wesleyan Univ., 1951-52; Fulbright Prof., Univs. of Bordeaux, Toulouse, Frankfurt, 1953-54; Prof., Yeats Summer Schl., 1965 & 68; Fulbright Prof., Univs. of Grenoble & Nice, 1965-66; Vis. Prof. & Hon. Fellow, St. Peter's Coll., Oxford, 1969; Vis. Prof., Univ. of York, 1970. Memberships: Comm., Small Press Mags. & Editors; Lit. Panel, Nat. Endowment for the Arts. Published works: Letter to a Young Lady, 1947; Men, Women, Vines, 1959; Thanatos, 1965; Homage to Jack Spicer, 1970; Protect the Earth, 1971; What the Blind Man Saw, 1973; Forgeries, 1974; The Canters of T.P., 1974. Contbr. to: Colo. Review; Ark; Contour; Formalist; Horizon; Nation; Now; Encounter; Prairie Schooner; Mass. Review; Critical Review, etc. Honours, awards: Guggenheim Fellow, 1957-58; Fellow, Inst. of Creative Art, 1963-64. Address: Dept. of Engl., Univ. of Calif., Berkeley, CA 94720, U.S.A.

PARKKINEN, Pekka Kustaa, b. 4 June 1940. Writer & Poet. Member, The Finnish Authors' Soc. Published works: The Moon is Still Glowing (novel), 1965; If I Loved My Country (poetry), 1967; The Shell (novel), 1969; So It Is (poetry), 1970; Little Rider (novel), 1971; The Town Called Lotto (poetry), 1972; One Winter It Then Happened Something (novel), 1972; The Tree Who Waves The Winds (poetry), 1973. Contbr. to: Parnasso (Finland); Le Monde (France); Arion (Hungary); A Capital (Portugal); Union (Cuba); Cormorán y delfín (Argentina); Literary Review (USA); Sassafras (W. Germany), etc. Address: c/o Weilin & Göös, Töölönkatu 10, 00100 Helsinki 10, Finland.

PARKS, Rena Ferguson, b. 17 Jan. 1888. Adult Educator. Education: Univ. of Ore., Ore. State Univ. & Univ. of Pa., U.S.A. Widow. Positions held: Tchr., Creative Writing, 7 yrs.; Educ. Cons., City Bureau of Hlth., 11 yrs.; workshop serv. for Portland Verseweavers Soc.; Assoc. Ed., The Country Bard, N.J., 4 yrs.; Assoc. Ed., Driftwood mag., Ore., 11 yrs Mbr., Ore. State Poetry Assn. Published works: The Changing Land, (37 poems), 1966; Furrows in the Sun (51 poems), 1972; Miniature Profiles (31 poems), 1972. Contbr. to num. mags. inclng: Driftwood Mag.; Portland Oregonian Verse; Univ. of Portland Review; Review Moderne; Paris; South & West; Medford Mail Tribune; Ore. Jrnl.; The Country Bard. Recip. var. awards. Address: 709 S.W. Clay, Apt. 15, Portland, OR 97201, U.S.A.

PARMEE, Frederick Cecil, b. 25 Jan. 1916. Deputy Principal, Primary School, New Zealand Education Service. Education: St. Ignatius Coll., London; Cooper Hill Trng. Coll. for Tchrs., Egham, Surrey, U.K. Married, 2 children. Positions held: Lectr. in Poetry to Writers' Clubs, Trng. Colls. & Higher Educ. Ctrs.; Exec. Educ. positions in U.K., Africa & N.Z. Memberships: Centro Studi e Scambi Int.; Vis. Poet to Student Art Fest., Victoria Univ., Wellington, N.Z.; Judge, N.Z. National Poetry Comp., run by Penwomens Club & sponsored by Rothman's Sport & Cultural Fndn. Published works: The Road, 1964; pamphlets of poems published in 1970, '71, & '72. Edited Penpoint 4 for 1968. Has had sev. readings of own work in Auckland, Wellington & other places in N.Z. One of New Zealand's first concretist poets. Contbr. to: N.Z. Listener; N.Z. Farmer; Poet Int.; Poetry Australia; Canadian Poetry; Argot; N.Z. Monthly Review, etc. Address: The Red House, 140 Beach Rd., Oneraki, Northland, New Zealand.

PARR, Michael Harry, b. 14 Apr. 1927. Proofreader. Married, 2 sons. Published works: The Green Fig Tree, 1965. Contbr. to the following anthols., jrnls. mags., etc: Yale Review; N.Y. Times; Canadian Forum; The Fiddlehead; N.Y. Times Book Review; Folio; Lit.

Review; Canadian Poetry. Address: 10 Clifford Ct., Scarborough, Ont., Canada M1R 3L3.

PARRISH, Edna Kendall, b. 21 Dec. 1916. Housewife. Education: studied poetry w. Vivian Laramore Rader at Barry Coll., Fla., 1961-63; studied w. Gilbert Maxwell, 1970-74. Married 1) James C. Murray, div., 1 son, 2 daughters, 2) Stephen Parrish II, 2 sons, 1 daughter. Memberships: Acad. of Am. Poets; Affil. Mbr., Laramore Rader Poetry Grp.; Chmn. of the All Fla. Poetry Contest (Irving Zieman Award), ibid, 1964, '67-70; Chmn. of Special Monthly Awards, 1974; Histn., The Miami Poetry Grp., 1953-55. Work in progress: Uneven Stiches, coll. of selected poetry. Contbr. to: Singing in the Sun, anthol., 1964; The Laramore Rader Poetry Grp. Yrbook; Orbit; Gtr. Miami Poetry Fest.; The Miami Beach Reporter; Guardino's Gazette. Honours, awards: Helen Knaus Meml. Award, 1972, '73; Chosen to read on World Poetry Day Prog., Coconut Grove Lib., Miami, Fla., 1970, '71, '72, '73. Address: 6520 S.W. 72 Ct., Miami, FL 33143, U.S.A.

PARRISH, Jemima Buchanan, pen name **PARRISH, Buchanan,** b. 23 Jul. 1906. Artist; Writer; Poet. Education: Graduate, Public HS. Married A. Leonard Parrish (retired banker); 1 s. (David Buchanan, artist). Memberships: Nat. League of Am. Pen Women (State Art Chairman, 1968-70, 1973-74); Acad. of Am. Poets; Ala. Writers Conclave; Ala. Poetry Soc.; Quill Club (various offices held). Contbr. to: (Anthols.) Testament of Faith, 1942; New American Poetry, 1945; The Samplers (Ala. State Poetry Soc. ann. publication), 1970, 1971, 1973; Internat. Who's Who in Poetry Anthol. Address: 1426 24th St., NO., Birmingham, AL. 35234, USA.

PARSONS, Geoffrey Charles, pen name, **PARSONS, Geoffrey C.,** b. 12 Jan. 1945. Male Nursing Sister (General, Psychiatric, Geriatric). Education: Dip. in Writing, 1971; Gen. Nursing Certificate, 1970; Psychiatric Nursing Certificate, 1972; Geriatric Nursing Certificate, 1973. Personal details: born Belmont, Australia; travelled to more than 60 countries and islands; appeared in Haydn's "The Creation" (as part of Festival of London). Membership: Victorian Fellowship of Australian Writers. Contbr. to following anthols.: 20th Century Poets, 1970; New Poets 71, 1970; The World of Verse, 1971; New Poetry, 1971; All People Are Poets, 1972; The Strand Book of Modern Verse, 1973. Contbr. to: Snap; Tone Vale Hospital Mag.; Sensibility; Poetry Forum. Awards: Poem of the month, Sensibility Mag., 1970; "Grace Darling and the Farne Islands" permanent display, Grace Darling Museum, Bamburgh, UK, 1972. Address: 91 Old Main Rd., Belmont North, NSW, Australia.

PARTHASARATHY, R., b. 20 Aug. 1934. Publishing Editor. Education: B.A. & M.A., Engl. Lit., Bombay Univ., India, 1957 & '59; Postgrad. Dip. in Engl. Studies, Leeds Univ., U.K., 1964; Brit. Council Scholar, Leeds Univ., 1963-64. Married Shobhan Koppikar, 1969. Positions held: Lectr. in Engl. Lit., Ismail Yusuf Coll., Bombay, 1959-62; Lectr. in Engl. Lit., Mithibai Coll., Bombay, 1962-63 & '64-65; Lectr. in Engl. Lang. Tchng., The British Council, Bombay, 1965-66; Asst. Prof. of Engl. Lit., Presidency Coll., Madras, 1966-67; Lectr. in Engl. Lit., The South Indian Educ. Society's Coll., Bombay, 1967-71. Member, The PEN, All-India Ctr., Bombay. Co-Ed., Poetry from Leeds, 1968. Contbr. to num. mags., jrnls., anthols. inclng: Commonwealth Poems of Today, 1967; Encounter; The Illustrated Weekly of India; Indian Foreign Review; Jrnl. of Indian Writing in English; London Mag.; Mahfil; New Voices of the Commonwealth, 1968; New Writing from India, 1973; Pergamon Poets 9: Poetry from India, 1971; Poetry India; Quest; A Review of Engl. Lit.; Times Lit. Supplement; Times of India; Young Commonwealth Poets '65. Recip., Ulka Poetry Prize, sponsored by Poetry India, 1966. Address: Oxford Univ. Press, Oxford House, Mount Rd., P.B. 1079, Madras 600006, India.

PARVIN, Betty, b. Oct. 1917. Housewife; Poet.

Education: Heathfield House Convent; Further Education in Art, History, Engl. Lit., Musical Appreciation, Geology. Married; 1 s. Positions held: Sec., Nottingham Poetry Soc., 1965-71, and Vice-Chairman, since 1972; (currently) Member Advisory Panel (Literature), East Midlands Arts Assoc. Memberships: Poetry Soc. (UK); Leicester Poetry Soc. (Committee Member); Nottingham Poetry Soc. (Vice-Chairman)' Nottingham Writers' Club: East Midlands Arts Assoc. (Member, Advisory Panel). Published works: A Stone My Star, 1961; The Bird With The Luck, 1968; Sketchbook From Mercia, 1968; Guernsey's Gift, 1972. Contbr. to: Chicago Tribune; Punch; Western Mail; Nottingham Journal; Notts. Weekly Guardian; Guernsey Press; Poetry Nottingham; Poetry Review; Outposts Poetry Qtly.; Scrip Poetry Qtly.; Expression One; Workshop Poetry Qtly.; Envoi; Country Life; Countryman; Good Housekeeping; The Lady; Tagus; Manifold; The Beacon (Braille); Notts. Countryside; Mofussil; Lincs. Life; The Listener; New Statesman; Leics. Univ. Papers; Courier; Laurels; Converse; Gong; This England; Poetry East/West; New Writing; Orbis; Platform; Literature & Arts; BBC. Home, Third, Nottingham, Leicester; (anthols.): P.E.N.; Borestone Mountain Awards; Without Adam; Look Through A Diamond; Evans Book of Children's Verse; Lines & Levels; Poetry Nottingham; Harvest; Laudamus Te; York Festival Anthol. Recip. Albert Ralph Korn Award (USA); Manifold Century Scholarship, 1968; Lake Aske Memorial Award (3 times); Highly Commended York, Stroud, Nottingham. Address: ''Bamboo'', Bunny Hill Top, Costock, Nr. Loughborough, Leics. LE12 6UX, UK.

PASEK, Catherine (Mya) Louise Kern, pen name **PASEK, Mya Kern,** b. 30 Apr. 1910. Homemaker; Bookkeeper. Married Milo D. Pasek. Positions held: Clerk; Dental Asst.; Bookkeeper. Memberships: St. Louis Writers Guild; Fellow, Int. Poetry Soc., U.K.; Charter Mbr., Metro East Br., Nat. League of Am. Pen Women, Cahokia, Ill.; associated w. St. Louis Poetry Ctr. Published works: Eye Sea (pending publ.) Contbr. to: Cycloflame; Image; Phoenix Fires; Am. Mosaic; Lyrics of Love; St. Louis Post-Dispatch; St. Audubon Bulletin; Cahokia Herald; Dupo Herald; New Athens Press, etc. Recip., Wednesday Club of St. Louis, Mo. Award of Merit, 1969 & '70. Address: 7805 Utica Dr., St. Louis, MO 63133, U.S.A.

PASLEY, Mary Beth, pen name **PASLEY, Beth,** b. 6 Jan. 1943. Housewife & Mother to 1 son. Positions held: Telephone Chmn., Odessa Chapt., Poetry Soc. of Tex., U.S.A. Memberships: Odessa Chapt., Poetry Soc. of Tex. Contbr. to the following Anthologies: Anthology of American Poetry, 1969, 70, 71; Poetry Classical & Modern, 1971; Poetry Classical & Contemporary, 1969; The Odessa Chapter Anthology, 1972; Encore Winter, 1970. Honours, awards: Cert. of Recognition, Odessa Fine Arts Comm., 1969; Cert. of Merit, IWWP, 1971; Clover Club Award, 1971; Winner, Odessa World Poetry Day, 1971. Address: 3205 Bellaire, Odessa, TX 79761, U.S.A.

PASSAVANT, Elise, b. Oct. 1912. Musician. Education: Private Schools. Born in New South Wales; reared in Co. Cork, Ireland. Positions held: Director of Ladies Orchestra; Organiser of Lewes Poetry Group (3 years); Director, The Mask Theatre, 1939. Membership: Poetry Soc. Published works: Desert Places, 1964; Baraka, 1973. Contbr. to: Tribune; Poetry Review; Cornhill; Country Life; Sussex Life; Transatlantic Review; Good Reading; Poetry Ireland; Poesie Vivante, etc. Poetry prize: Premium Competition Award (No. 61), Poetry Review, 1965; P.E.N. Anthology, 1965. Address: 31 Caburn Cres., Lewes, Sussex, UK.

PASSEL, Anne, pen name **WONDERS, Anne,** b. 12 Sept. 1918. Professor. Education: B.A., cum laude, 1940, Mt. Holyoke Coll.; M.A., 1964, Ph.D., 1967, Univ. of the Pacific. Married; 2 s. Positions held: Editor and feature writer: book publishers, magazines, and newspapers, 1940-54; Advertising and public relations, 1955-62; Asst. Prof., Univ. of the Pacific, 1967-68; Assoc. Prof., Fresno State Coll., Bakersfield, 1969-70; Prof., Calif. State Coll., Bakersfield, since 1970. Memberships: American Pen Women; Blackstick (pres.). Published works: Poems 68 (1968); The Learning Poets (ed.) (1972); Poems 74 (in preparation). Contbr. to: Collage; College Verse; Press (Bronxville); Mirror; Mt. Holyoke Monthly; Mandorla; The Beginning; Reporter; Villager, Recip. MacFarland Award, 1940. Address: Engl. Dept., Calif. State Coll. Bakersfield, Bakersfield, CA 93309, USA.

PASSMORE, J(eremy) M(aurice), b. 6 Oct. 1937. Journalist. Education: Nautical Coll., Pangbourne, Berkshire, 1951-55; Obtained a Second Mate's Certificate, 1959; School of Oriental & African Studies, Univ. of London, 1968-71, B.A. (in Japanese); M.R.I.N. (Member, Royal Inst. of Navigation). Contbr. to: Vortex; Contemp. Poets of 1969; Asahi Evening News; The World of Verse; Gems of Mod. British Poetry, Vols. 2 & 3; Poetry Universal (Collection Two); Not Dedicated to the Public. Address: 7 Ranelagh Gardens, Stamford Brook Ave., London W6, UK.

PASTAN, Linda, b. 27 May 1932. Poet. Education: B.A., Radcliffe Coll., 1954; M.A., Brandeis Univ., 1957. Married Dr. Ira Pastan, 3 children. Memberships: Poetry Soc. of Am.; Acad. of Am. Poets. Published works: A Perfect Circle of Sun, 1971. Contbr. to: Harpers; Esquire; The Nation; N.Y. Times; Am. Scholar; Sewanee Review; Shenandoah; Field; Sumac; Chelsea; Chicago Tribune; Radcliffe Qtly.; Voyages; Dryad; Qtly. Review of Lit. Honours, awards: Dylan Thomas Poetry Award of Mademoiselle Mag., 1955; Fellowship, Nat. Endowment for Arts, 1972. Address: 11710 Beall Mt. Rd., Potomac, MD 20854, U.S.A.

PATAKI, Heidi, b. 2 Nov. 1940. Editor; Literary Critic. Education: studied slavistic philos. & hist. of arts at Univ. of Vienna, Austria. Married Friedrick Geyrhofer. Member, Grazer Autoren Versammlung. Published works: Schlagzeilen, 1968. Contbr. to: Akzente; Das Pult; Der Bogen; Die Presse; Eroffnungen; Labris; Literatur und Kritik; Lyrische Hefte; Neues Forum; Neue Dege; Torn; Manuskripte, etc. Honours, awards: Literatur preis des Wiener Kunstfonds, 1966; Theodor Korner Preis, 1969; Staatsstipendium fur Literatur, 1973. Address: Traungasse 7/22, A-1030 Vienna, Austria.

PATEL, Gieve, b. 18 Aug. 1940. Medical Officer. Education: M.B., B.S., Bombay Univ. Married. Positions held: Currently, Medical Officer in Charge, Primary Health Centre, Primary Health Centre, Sanjan, District Bulsar, Gujerat. Published works: Poems, 1966. Contbr. to (Anthols.): Young Commonwealth Poets '65, 1965; New Voices of the Commonwealth, 1968; (Jrnls.): Poetry India. Address: J-15, Cusrow Baug, Fort, Bombay 1, India.

PATER, Elias, Pseudonym for **John Friedman,** Religious name, **Father Elias,** b. 16 Mar. 1916. Priest; Teacher of Theology. Education: Studied to be a Physician, Univ. of Cape Town, 1938; Studied for Priesthood, UK, 1946; Studied Discalced Carmelite Order, Ireland, 1947; Theology, France, 1948; Ordained, Avignon, France, 1953. Positions held: Mbr., Stella Maris Monastery, Haifa, Israel, 1954–; Currently, Mbr. of Staff, Int. Coll. of Theology, Stella Maris, Israel. Published works: In Praise of Night, 1969; Other: The Redemption of Israel, 1947; Trans., The Diocese of the Latin Patriarchiate of Jerusalem, 1963. Contbr. to (Jrnls.): New Coin; New Nation; Cape Times. Address: Stella Maris Monastery, P.O. Box 9047, Haifa, Israel.

PATERSON, Allister Ian Hughes, pen names **PATERSON, A.I.H. & PATERSON, Alistair,** b. 28 Feb. 1929. Naval Officer; Teacher. Education: Christchurch Teachers Coll., New Zealand, 1948-49; Victoria Univ. Coll., 1951-53; Auckland Univ., 1970-72; B.A., Univ. of New Zealand; Dip. Ed., Univ. of Auckland; Dip. Tchng., ANZIM. Married, 5 children. Positions held: Instr. Off.,

Royal New Zealand Navy, 1954–; currently Sr. Instr. Off., HMNZS Philomel, w. rank of Lt.-Cmdr.; Naval Liaison Off. to the Royal Akarana Yacht Club, 1970–. Memberships: Chmn., N. Shore Br., N.Z. Workers' Educ. Assn.; Co-organiser, N.Z. Workers Educ Assn. Seminar on Aspects of N.Z. Lit., 1969; Reviewer on the Reviewing Panel of N.Z. Bookworld, 1973; Fndr./Org., North Shore Winter Poetry Readings, 1971; Ed., MATE, a N.Z. Lit. periodical, 1973–; Org., Manuwera Fest. Poetry Reading, 1971 Published works: Caves in the Hills, Selected Poems, 1965; Birds Flying, Selected Poems, 1973. Contbr. to: Arena; Argot; Best Poems 1971; Experiment; After a War (An Anthol. of War Poetry), 1973; The N.Z. Listener; The N.Z. Poetry Yearbook; Poetry New Zealand; Poetry Australia; Poet (India); Orpheus, etc. Recip., 1st Prize, N.Z. Penwomen's Club Nat. Poetry Contest, 1968. Address: 16 Totara Grove, Northcote, Auckland, New Zealand.

PATHAK, Jayant, b. 20 Oct. 1920. Educator. Education: M.A., Gujarati & Sanskrit; Ph.D., Modern Gujarati Poetry. Positions held: Prof. of Gujarati Lang. & Lit., M.T.B. Arts Coll., Surat, 1953–; Dir., Chunilal Gandhi Rsch. Inst., Surat, 1965–. Memberships: PEN India; Exec. Comm. & Sec., Gujarati Sahitya Parishad, Ahmedabad; Exec. Comm., Narmad Sahitya Sabha, Surat. Published works: (colls. of poetry) Marmara, 1953, 2nd ed., 1957; Samketa, 1960; Vismaya, 1963; Sarga, 1969. Contbr. to: Kavita; Kavi-loka; Kumar; Sanskriti; Buddhi-Prakash; Samarpan; Vishva-manau. Honours, awards: Kumar Medal, 1957; State Govt. Prize for Marmara, 1957; State Govt. Prize for Sarga, 1969. Address: 23 Kadambpalli, Nanpura, Surat 1, Gujarat, India.

PATRICK, J(ohnstone) G(illespie), pen name **FORWARD, Luke,** b. 24 Oct. 1918. Clergyman. Education: Cliff Coll., Sheffield, UK., and Spurgeon's Theol. Coll., London; UK. Born in the Burgh of Buckhaven & Methil, Fifeshire, Scotland; Married, Irene Alice Austick; children: Hamish John, Philippa Susan, Gavin Keith, and Simon Blaise. Positions held: pastorates in London, UK., St. Peter Port, Channel Islands; Ontario, Canada; Pittsburgh, PA., USA., and presently Senior Minister of the First Presbyterian Church of St. Louis, MO. Memberships: Life F.R.S.A.; Fellow, Philosophical Soc., UK. Published works: Above the Thorn and Other Poems, 1957; Under the Mistletoe and Other Poems, 1969; The Rainbow and the Resurrection (poetry and prose), 1962. Work also appears in anthols.: The Treasury of the Christian World, 1953; The Book of Immortality, 1954; A Treasury of Poems for Worship and Devotion, 1959; The Minister's Manual, 1960, 1969, 1970, 1972, 1973; Holy, Holy Land, 1969; Best Sermons, 1959; Images of Faith, 1963. Contbr. to: The British Weekly; Canadian Poetry Mag.; Canadian Nature; The Christian Century; Daily Telegraph (UK.); The Christian World; John O'London's Weekly; NY Herald Tribune; NY Times Mag.; Poetry of Today (UK.); The Tablet (UK.); The Weekly Scotsman; Transactions of the Brontë Soc.; American Poetry Digest; English (UK.). Award: Literary Prix D'honneur of the Eisteddfod in Poetry and Essay, St. Peter Port, Guernsey, Channel Islands, 1948 and 1949. Address: 7920 Teasdale Court, University City, St. Louis, MO 63130, USA.

PATTEN, Brian, b. 7 Feb. 1946. Poet. Published works: Little Johnny's Confession, 1967, 1969; Penguin Modern Poets No. 10, 1967; Notes to the Hurrying Man, 1969, 1971; The Elephant & The Flower (collection of childrens stories), 1970; When You Wake Tomorrow, 1971; The Irrelevant Song, 1971; Jumping Mouse (adaptation of an American Indian tale), 1972; The Unreliable Nightingale, 1973. Contbr. to: Vogue; The Sunday Times; The Observer; Poetry Review; Transatlantic Review; Peace News; various overseas magazines and journals, etc. Recip. The Eric Gregory Award, 1967. Address: c/o Allen and Unwin, Publishers, 40 Museum St., London WC1, UK.

PATTERSON, Samuel White, b. 25 Dec. 1883. Professor of Education & English. Education: A.B.,

City Coll. of the State Univ. of N.Y., U.S.A., 1903; M.A., Columbia Univ., N.Y., 1910; Master's Dip. in Educ., Columbia Univ., 1910; M.A., N.Y. Univ., 1912; Ph.D., ibid, 1913. Positions held incl: Instr. of Engl., Columbia Univ., N.Y.; Prof. of Educ., Hunter Coll., State Univ. of N.Y.; Lectr. on Am. Hist.; Ldr., Young Men's Bible Class & Club; Instr., Wellesley Sum. Conf.; Mbr. Staff of Sanitary Corps, U.S. Dept. of War (Surg.-Gen's. Off.); Chmn., War Activities Comm. of Hunter Coll. Memberships: World Cong. of Poets; Poetry Soc. of Am., N.Y.; N.Y. Chapt., Am. Red Cross; Acting Dir., Evening Sessions, Hunter Coll. Published works: The Spirit of the Am. Revolution as Revealed in the Poetry of the Period; Horatio Gates (Biog.); Famous Men & Places in the History of N.Y.C.; Hunter College: 85 Years of Service; Teaching the Child to Road; Old Chelsea & St. Peter's Church; Over There to Over Here (written for U.S. War Dept.); The History of Religious Influences at Harvard Univ.; Knight-Errant of Liberty (Biog. of Maj. Gen. Charles Lee); The Good Samaritan & His Friends (in prep.) etc. Edited: Coleridge: Rise of Ancient Mariner; Gregory: Spreading the News; Hale: Man Without a Country, & others. Address: 300 Old Hook Rd., Westwood, NJ 07675, U.S.A.

PAUKER, John, b. 26 Jan. 1920. Writer; Poet; Playwright; Fashioner of Fiction; Translator; Editor. Education: Yale Univ., 1938-42; Columbia Univ., summers 1940-41. Positions held: Ed., Fieldston News, 1937-38; Chmn. & Ed., Yale Lit. Mag., 1939-40 & 1940-41; Mng. Ed., Furioso, 1947-50; Mbr., Editl. Bd., ibid, 1950-53; Advisory Ed., Voyages, 1967–. Memberships: Elizabethan Club; Chi Delta Theta Hon. Lit. Soc.; Poetry Soc. of Am. Published works: (books) A Poetry of Our Time, 1972; Excellency, 1968; Yoked by Violence, 1949; (pamphlets) Poems (Iran), 1970; Poems (India), 1970. Contbr. to num. mags. periodicals inclng: N.Y. Qtly.; New Republic; Beloit Poetry Jrnl.; Prairie Schooner; Denver Qtly.; Hollins Critic; North Am. Review; Poet Lore; Voices Int.; Berita Haryan (Malaysia); Topic (Lebanon), etc. Has presented var. recitals of own poetry in U.S.A. & abroad. Honours, awards: William Holland Fndn. Award for Disting. Book of Poetry, 1968; Award from Nat. Endowment for the Arts, 1969. Address: 3006 Porter St. N.W., Washington, D.C. 20008, U.S.A.

PAUL, Elizabeth Virginia, b. 9 Jan. 1909. Housewife. Education: High School. Editor and publisher of journal, The Spinners. Memberships: A.A.P.A.; U.A.P.P.A. (member Bd. of Directors). Contbr. to: Worcester Gazette; Laurel Mag.; St. Louis Globe; Cape Girardeau newspaper; Vantage Press, etc. Recip. Certificate from Laurel publishers; Certificate, Internat. Who's Who in Poetry, 1970. Address: 300 High St., Winchendon, MA 01475, USA.

PAUL, Sukrita, b. 10 Nov. 1949. Researcher in Fiction. Education: M.A., Engl. Lit., currently working for Ph.D., on Marathwada Univ. Fellowship. Positions held: Lecturer in Engl., for 2 yrs. at Government College, Aurangabad. Shortly to publish first collection of poems. Contbr. to: Indian and Foreign Review; Thought; Accent; Poet. Address: c/o Principal Joginder Paul, S.B.E.S. Coll. of Arts, Aurangabad (Dn.), Aurangabad, Maharashtra, India.

PAULIN, Dorothy Margaret, b. 3 Feb. 1904. Writer; ex-editor; ex-farmer. Education: Edinburgh Univ., M.A., B. Com. Widow; 1 d. Positions held: Editor, Gallovidian Annual, 1926-36; Editor (poetry section), Poetry Review, 1941-43; Editor, Scottish Home & Country, 1947-51; Liaison Officer, Dept. of Agriculture, 1942-47. Currently: Chairman, local Preservation Society; Member, Council, Assoc. for Preservation of Rural Scotland; Member, Council, Soil Association; Member, Scottish P.E.N. Published works: Country Gold, 1936; The Wan Water, 1939; Solway Tide, 1952; Springtime by Loch Ken and Other Poems, 1958. Contbr. to: Scotsman; Poetry Review; Chambers Journal; Edinburgh Eve. Dispatch; Country Life; Soil Association Magazine. Address: Drumrash, Parton, Castle Douglas, Kirkcudbrightshire, Scotland, UK.

PAUST, Marian, b. 5 Feb. 1908. Housewife; Farm Manager; Freelance Poet. Education: Univ. of Wis. Married, 4 daughters. Positions held: Sec.-Guard, V.P., Pres., P.E.O.; Sec. to Bd. & on Bd. Dirs., Richland Co. Bank. Memberships: Nat. League of Am. Pen Women, 1954–; State Histn., Wis. Fellowship of Poets (has held var. other offs.); Anthol. Editl. Bd., ibid, 1960; State Poetry Chmn., Wis. Regl. Writers Assn., 1949–; Acad. of Am. Poets, 1960–; Wis. Acad. of Scis., Arts & Letters, 1956–; Nat. Contest Chmn., Nat. Fed. of State Poetry Socs., 1963; Midwest Chaparral Poets, 1957–. Published works: Honey to be Savored, 1968; Everybody Beats a Drum, 1970; One Hundred Years, brochure, 1956. Rep. in following anthols: New Poetry Out of Wis.; Holy Holy Land; Northern Spring; Poems Out of Wis., vol. 2 & 3; Wis. Harvest; Anthol. of Am. Poetry, vol. 4; Wis. Lore; Am. Lyricists; Varied Verses; IWWP Anthol. Contbr. to: P.E.O. Record; Ideals; Blue Moon; Arabian World; Midwest Chaparral; Wis. Tales & Trails; Folio; Farm Jrnl.; Wis. State Jrnl.; Madison Capital Times; Republican Observer; Richland Democrat, etc. Honours, awards: State Poetry Contest Awards, 1952, 53, 54, 55, 56 & 59; Bard's Chair, 1956 & 59; Annual State Writers Cup Award, 1960. Address: Rte. 4, Double M Ranch, Richland Ctr., WI 53581, U.S.A.

PAVLOVIC, Miodrag, b. 28 Nov. 1928. Writer; Editor; Educator. Education: Medical degree, Belgrade, 1954. Positions held: Practised med., 1955-59; Ed., Prosveta Publishing House, Belgrade; Univ. Tchr. from time to time; Dir., Nat. Theatre, Belgrade, 1960-61. V.P., Serbian PEN, 1966-71. Published works: (books of poetry) 87 pesama, 1952; Stub sećanja, 1953; Oktave, 1956; Mleko iskoni, 1963; Sobowtory, 1964; Gedichte, 1968; Velika Skitija, 1969; Nova Skitija, 1970; Hododarje, 1971; La Voix sous la Pierre, 1970; Svetli i tamni praznici, 1971; Karanici, 1972; Početak básne, 1973; Velika Skitija i druge pesme, 1972. Num. publs. of poems in lit. mags in Yugoslavia & abroad. Recip. sev. nat. & int. prizes. Address: ul. 29 Novembra 95, stan 30, Belgrade, Yugoslavia.

PAYNE, Basil. Poet; Writer; Lecturer. Positions held: Extensive Radio & TV work for Radio Telefis Eireann as Guest Ed., Presenter & Scriptwriter (progs. incl. culture & the arts, theatre, films, current affairs & children's and adult educ.); Regular lecturer on modern Irish & Am Poetry, drama & fiction to the Engl. Lang. Inst., the Nat. Assn. of Drama for Young People, the Belfast Arts Fest. (Queens Univ.), Municipal Gall. of Mod. Art (Dublin), Irish PEN, etc.; Poet-in-Res., Glassboro State Coll., N.J., U.S.A., 1974–. Has edited, scripted & presented critical studies of Am. & Irish writers in Radio Telefis Eireann Adult Educ. series on novels, poetry & short stories; var. educl. & gen. TV & radio broadcasts in Canada & U.S.A. Published works: Sunlight on a Square (coll. of poems), 1962; Elegy for the Western World (transl. of long narrative poem from the German of Hans Carossa), 1965; Love in the Afternoon (coll. of poems), 1971; Voyage a Deux (poems in French transl.), 1974; Another Kind of Optimism (coll. of poems), 1974. Rep. in var. anthols. & contbr. to mags., jrnls. & newspapers. Twice recipient of the Guinness Poetry Prize, Cheltenham Fest., U.K. Address: Cortona, 137 Rathfarnham Rd., Dublin 14, Ireland.

PAYNE, Malcolm Roger, b. 3 Mar. 1927. School Teacher. Education: Leeds Univ. Positions held: Tchr., Arts & Philos., Rudolf Steiner Schl.; Soldier; Tchr. (specialist in Anthroposophy); Freelance Writer; Tchr. to Autistic & ESN, Rudolf Steiner Schl. Memberships: London Writer Circle; Int. Poetry Soc.; Advt. & P.R. Mgr., Orbis; Fndr., Poet's Vigilantes; Fndr., P.V. Press & P.V. Publications; Ed., Nucleus, Radix & P.V. Newsletter. Published works: Colours, 1969; Presentation, 1969; Centifrugal, 1970; Mucidenious & Onion Skin, 1971; Crossbar, 1972; Tyle, 1973. Contbr. to: Kent & Sussex Courier; Sussex Express; Men's Own; Envoi; Expression One; Weyfarers; Malenka; Orbis; Nucleus; Radix; Pink Peace; Purple Smoke; Zig; Handsel; Monument; Apag; Yes; Out There; New; Erotic; Splurdge; Bondi

Bag; Petite; Pis; Da Capo; Coram, etc. Honours, awards: Fndr. Fellowship, Int. Poetry Soc. Address: 4 Wealden Cl., Crowborough, Sussex, U.K.

p'BITEK, Okot, b. 1931. Teacher. Education: King's Coll., Budo; B.Litt., Oxford Univ., 1963; Studied Law, Aberystwyth Univ., Wales. Positions held: Schl. Tchr. nr. Gulu. Published works: Lak tar miyo kinyero wo lobo?, 1953; The Song of Lawino, 1966. Contbr. to (Anthols.): Modern Poetry from Africa, 1963.

PEARCE, Bessie Belle, pen name **PEARCE, Bess Browning,** b. 17 Aug. 1897. Education: B.A., Okla. Univ., Norman, U.S.A.; grad. study, Geo. Peabody Coll., Nashville, Tenn. & Tchrs. Coll., Canyon, Tex. Positions held: Elem. Tchr., Porum, Okla., 1918; H.S. Tchr., Thomas, Okla., 1921-23 & Electra, Tex., 1936-53. Memberships: World Poetry Soc. Intercontinental; Am. Poetry League; Poetry Soc. of Tex.; Pres., Waco Chapt., ibid. Published works: Unto A Land (prose), 1968. Contbr. to: Am. Poetry League 'From Sea to Sea in Song' Anthol., 1969, 70, 71, 72; A Book of the Yr., The Poetry Soc. of Tex., 1973. Honours, awards: First Award, Poetry Soc. of Tex. 'A Book of the Yr.', 1973. Address: 2700 Cumberland, Waco, TX 76707, U.S.A.

PEARCE, Brian Louis, b. 4 June 1933. Librarian; Poet; Local Historian; Editor. Married, 1 daughter. Positions held incl: Tutor-Libn., Twickenham Coll. of Technol., 1966–; Examiner, Lib. Assn., 1964-70. Mbr. of many orgs. inclng: sometime mbr., P.E.N., Poetry Soc., Poets Conf. Workshop; Fndr. Mbr., New Richmond Poetry Group; Mbr., Org. Comm., Poetry Day, 1967; Ed., Expression (now Expression One), 1965-67; Ed., Quarto Poets Series, 1973–. Published works incl: The Eagle & the Swan, a play in 3 acts, 1966; The Argonauts & other poems, 1970; The Art of Eric Ratcliffe, an appreciation, 1970; Requiem for the Sixties, 1971; Ed., Twickenham Eyot, anthol., 1973. Contbr. to num. jrnls., mags. & anthols. inclng: Enigma; Envoi; Expression Poetry Quarterly; The Guardian; Headland; Message; Outposts; Platform; Poésie Vivante; Poetry Review; Scrip; Tribune. Hons. incl: F.L.A., 1961; 5th-6th pl., Poetry Soc. One-Act verse play contest, 1964. Address: 72 Heathfield South, Twickenham, Middx. TW2 7SS, U.K.

PEARCE, Carol Ann, pen name **BREL, Jennifer.** Writer. Education: B.A. in drama, Clarke Coll., Dubuque, Iowa; M.A. in theatre and playwriting, Villanova Univ., Pa. Currently Asst. Editor of Show Magazine, NYC, and engaged in freelance feature writing. Membership: Poetry Soc. of America. Contbr. to: North American Mentor; Crossroads; Young America Sings; Circus Mag. Awards: Poetry Soc. of America Annual Devil's Advocate Award, 1971; 2nd prize and Hon. Mention, North American Mentor's annual awards, 1968 and 1969; Langston Hughes Poetry Award of NYC., 1970. Address: 155 E. 52nd St., Apt. 8–F, New York, NY 10023, USA.

PEARCE, Ellen, b. 28 Aug. 1946. Poet. Education: B.A., Engl., Lake Erie Coll., Painesville, Ohio. Published works: Life in (very) minor Works, 1968. Address: 145 Neperan Road, Tarrytown, N.Y., 10591, USA.

PEARCE, Thomas Matthews, b. 22 May 1902. Educator. Education: B.A., Univ. of Montana, 1923; M.A., Univ. of Pittsburgh, 1925; Ph.D., ibid, 1930; post grad. summer study, Univ. of Calif., 1928; Univ. of Chicago, 1930. Positions held: Instr., Univ. of Pitts., 1923-27; Asst. Prof., Univ. of N.M., 1927-30; Assoc. Prof., ibid, 1930-40; Prof., 1940-64; Prof. Emeritus, 1964–. Memberships: Chancellor & Mbr., N.M. Poetry Soc.; Acad. of Poets, N.Y.C. Published works: Monograph on the poet Alice Corbin Henderson, 1969; Chapter on 'Poetry' in Southwest Heritage, A Literary History with Bibliography, 1972. Contbr. to: N.M. Poetry Soc. Anthol., 1974; Encore; A Qtly. of Verse & Poetic Arts; Poet; South & West; The Gtr. Llano Estacado Southwest Heritage. Address: Dept. of Engl., Humanities Bldg., Univ. of N.M., Albuquerque, NM 87131, U.S.A.

PEARSON, Alan, b. 17 Dec. 1930. Public Relations Speechwriter. Education: var. schls., Sheffield, U.K. Positions held: w. Nat. Film Bd., Canada; Canadian Nat. Railway; Canadian Industries Ltd. Mbr., League of Canadian Poets. Published works: 14 poems, Delta Press, Montreal, 1969. Contbr. to: Canadian Forum; Delta (Canada); Moment (Canada); Adam International (UK); Delta (Cambridge); Poetry Review (UK); Canadian Radio, & sev. small mags. Recip., $2,500 Engl. Lang. Poetry Prize awarded by the Quebec Dept. of Cultural Affairs, 1969 & also Canada Coun. grant. Address: 3850 Hampton Ave., Montreal 261, Quebec, Canada.

PEASLEE, David Thomas, b. 22 Sept. 1945. Rancher. Education: B.S., Educ., Southwestern Univ., Georgetown, Tex. Memberships: Pres. & Fndr., Southwestern Univ. Poetry Soc.; Virginia Poetry Soc.; Acad. of Am. Poets; Int. Platform Assn., Wash. D.C. Contbr. to: New Poetry, 1971; Annual Anthol. of Coll. Poetry, 1971. Address: Rt. 3, Box 177P, Georgetown, TX 78626, U.S.A.

PECK, John, b. 13 Jan. 1941. Teacher. Education: B.A., Allegheny Coll.; Ph.D., Stanford Univ. Positions held: Instr. of Engl., Princeton Univ.; Vis. Lectr. in Writing, ibid. Published works: Shagbark, 1972. Contbr. to: Hudson Review; New Yorker; Antaeus; Poetry Chicago; Salmagundi; Southern Review; New Am. Review; Qtly. Review of Lit.; Modern Poetry in Translation. Address: 118 Jefferson Rd., Princeton, NJ 08540, U.S.A.

PEGGE, Cecil Denis, b. 7 Dec. 1902. Author. Education: Magdalene Coll., Cambridge Univ. Has written reviews & articles, & given lectures on poetry. Has also given readings of his own poetry & been an adjudicator of poetry, e.g. Crabbe Meml. Poetry Prize. Memberships: Authors Soc., U.K.; Poetry Soc., U.K. Published works: Obsidian, 1934; The Fire, 1943; The Flying Bird, 1955; Tribute, 1966. Contbr. to: The Jongleur; The Cambridge Review; The Cambridge Writer Circle Mag.; The Poetry Review; Scrip; Expression One; Envoi; The Sun (Las Palmas); Poetry (Australia); Fear No More, anthol. & also to The BBC Midland Poets prog. Address: c/o Barclays Bank Ltd., Benet St., Cambridge, U.K.

PELLEY, Ruth, pen name **PHILOTHEA,** b. 28 June 1913. Homemaker; Secretary. Education: Business coll.; courses in lit., poetry writing & appreciation; public speaking courses. Married George P. Pelley, 2 sons, 1 daughter. Positions held: Sec. to the Chief of Police, Peabody, Mass. Memberships: Catholic Poetry Soc. of Am.; Sec., Libn., North Shore Poets' Forum of Mass.; N.H. Poetry Soc. Contbr. to: Boston Pilot; Lynn Item; Lynn Sunday Post; Peabody Times; Salem News; Boston Globe; Carmelite; Working Boy; Eschata; Penman; Bardic Echoes; Atmosphere; N.H. Poetry Soc. Newsletter; Town Crier, etc. Address: 4 Griffin Rd., Peabody, MA 01960, U.S.A.

PELOSI, Helen Priscilla, pen names, **DUNBAR, Helen; SCOTT, Elena,** b. 9 July 1912. Homemaker; Writer. Education: Primary & Sec. Schools in New England; Grad. of Mass. General Hospital School of Nursing, Boston, Mass. Married to Col. M.C. US Army (retired); 4 children. Positions held: Private Duty Nursing; Operating Room Nurse, Mass. Gen. Hospital and Columbia Hospital for Women, Washington, DC.; Catechetical School Principal and Teacher in US and Europe; Drama Director, American Youth Assoc. of American Students in Germany. Memberships: Asst. Editor, Driftwood East; NY Poetry Forum, Inc.; American Poets Fellowship Society, Illinois; Laurel Publishers Poetry Symposium; Poetry Fellowship of Maine; Rhode Island Writer's Guild; United Amateur Press of USA. Contbr. to: Ideals; Kansas Kernels; Driftwood East; Mod. Haiku; Tower By The Sea; Memories in Art; Bardic Echoes; Reach Out; Invictus; Hyacinths & Biscuits; Inky Trails; United Amateur Press papers; Battersean; Quid Nunc?; Tumblin Weeds; Britches & Braids; Vivo Sentio; Robbins Song; Modus Operandi; Cranston Herald (RI); Journal-

Enquirer (Ky.); The American Poets Fellowship Soc.; Olive Hill Times (Ky.); Understanding. Awards: Poem of the year award, Inky Trails, 1972; 1st, 4th Prize (with cash prizes) for top awards, plus 6 hon. certs., special categories; Cert. of Appreciation for outstanding poetry, Quid Nunc?, 1972; Olive Hill Times Hon. Cert., (2), 1973; Box Top Poetry Contest, Cranston Herald, 4th Prize, 1972; Cert. of Merit, Hon. Award, Laurel Publishers Internat. Poetry Symposium, 1973; Cert. of Merit, American Poets Fellowship Soc., 1973. Address: Peace Cove, 281 Gordon Lake Blvd., Warwick, RI 02886, USA.

PENDEXTER, Hugh, III. Teacher. Education: A.B., Bowdoin Coll.; M.A., Northwestern Univ.; Ph.D., Univ. of Pa. Married, 2 children. Positions held at Armstrong Coll. Memberships: Poetry Soc. of Tex.; Ga. Poetry Soc. Published works: The Pantessey, 1962; A Prosody, 1968; Sacred Poems, 1971. Recip., Curtal Sonnet Award & John A. Lubbe Award, Poetry Soc. of Tex., 1973. Address: Armstrong Coll., Savannah, GA 31406, U.S.A.

PENN, Emily Josephine, pen name **ELVESMERE ROSE,** Poet. Education: Bd. of Education's Cert. for Elem. Schl. Tchrs., Royal Normal Coll. for the Visually Handicapped, Upper Norwood, London, S.E.; L.R.A.M. in Music; 1st class Cert., Corres. course in Poetry, Hadley Schl., Winnetka, U.S.A. Positions held: Tchr. of Piano, Singing & Theory; Gave talks on music & other subjects, with pupils illustrating with poetry & music, Tarleton Church Schl. Memberships: Lancs. Authors' Assn.; Preston Poets Soc. Contbr. to: The Sunday Companion; Progress & The Beacon (two Braille mags.); Northern Anthols., edited by Joan Pomfrett. Honours, awards incl: 1st Prize, Olive Scott Comp. run by the R.N.I.B., 1965; Second Prize, ibid, 1967; Third Prize, 1969 & '71; 2nd Prize, Louis Braille Centenary Comp. run by R.N.I.B [& Third Prize in that organised by the Am. Braille mag. 'The Jewish Review'; a number of Firsts, Seconds & Thirds in Brisbane Fest. of Music & Poetry; Third Prize, Colne Fest. of Music & Arts, 1973; The Batty Cup, Lancs. Authors Assn., 1962 & '63 & a Third Prize, 1967; The Pomfrett Cup, Preston Poets, 1971 & '72; McKenzie Cup, 1973, etc. Address: Hertford House, 104 Hesketh Lane, Tarleton, Preston PR4 6AQ, U.K.

PENNIMAN, Gwendolen Brooks, pen names also **PENNIMAN, Gwen & PENNIMAN, Gwendolen B.** Writer; Poet; Author; Editor; Drama Director; Previously Dramatic Actress. Address: 22100 Mt. Eden Road, Saratoga, CA 95070, U.S.A.

PENNINGTON, Lee, b. 1 May 1939. Teacher; Poet; Writer. Education: B.A., Engl., Berea Coll., 1962; M.A., Engl., Univ. of Iowa, 1965; Baldwin-Wallace Coll.; San Diego State Coll.; Univ. of Ky. Married to Joy Pennington. Positions held: Farmer, 1945-59; News Writer, Portsmouth Times; Ashland Daily Indep.; Huntington Herald Dispatch, Greenup News, 1956-58; Treasurer's Office, Berea Coll., 1959; Asst. to Engl. Instr., ibid, 1959-60; Hd. News Bur. Writer, Berea Coll., 1960-61; Publicity Writer, Coun. of Southern Mountains, 1961-62; Instr. of Engl., Newburgh Free Acad., NY, 1962-64; Mgr., Bingham Trio, Gatlinburg, Tenn., summer 1963; Chmn., Engl. Dept., SE Community Coll., Cumberland, Ky., 1965-67; Created 1st Writing of Fiction & Writing of Poetry Classes, publishing 4 books of student verse, ibid; Instr., Upward Bound, Cumberland, 1966; Instr. of Engl., Jefferson Community Coll., Louisville, Ky., 1967-; Poetry Instr., Jesse Stuart Creative Writing Workshop, Murray State Univ., 1969-71. Memberships: MLA; Bd. Mbr., Ky. State Poetry Soc.; Eastern Ky. Poetry Soc.; Idaho Poets & Writers Guild; Avalon Int.; Centro Studi e Scambi Internazionali; United Amateur Press Assn.; Am. Poetry Soc.; United Poetry Soc.; Ky. Writers' Guild; World Poetry Soc. Intercontinental; Southern Rep., Pixie Angel, Calif. & Cardinal Poetry Quarterly, Ill. Contbng. Ed., W Hollow Harvest, a Ky. Review. Poetry Readings & Folksong Concerts, Colls. & Univs., Eastern U.S., on record, & on Voice of Am. Radio. Published works: Scenes From a Southern Road,

1969; Bloody Bones & Bloody Harlan; (plays) The Porch, 1962; The Spirit of Poor Fork, 1966; Appalachia, My Sorrow, 1971; Hornet Wings (poetry); Songs of Bloody Harlan (in prep.); Run on Seven Gravels (novel); Wind & Foxes (short stories), 1969; The Dark Hills of Jesse Stuart (criticism), 1967; April Poems, 1971; Wildflower . . . Poems for Joy, 1970. Contbr. to over 100 mags. & anthols., inclng: Trace; The Angels; New York Herald Tribune; Author & Journalist; Mountain Life & Work; Sing Out!; Am. Bard; Alaska Review; Bardic Echoes; Orphic Lute; Seed Ole; Caravel; United Poet; Freelance Flame; Calif. Writer; Cardinal; Experiment; Prairie Poet; Kauri; Laurel Review, etc. Recip. of num. writing & poetry hons., inclng: Ky. State Poetry Award, 1967; Angel Award, 1967; Pixie Award, 1968; Merit Award, NY State Poetry Soc., 1968; Poet Laureate, Angels Publs., 1971; Magna Cum Laude, World Poetry Soc. Intercontinental, 1970. Address: 12105 Old Shelbyville Rd., Middletown, Ky. 40243, USA.

PERCIVAL, J(ohn), b. 16 Sept. 1931. Poet; Artist; Playwright; Composer. Positions held: Collaborator in Art Distribution, Art Ashram, Stockholm, Sweden. Memberships: FIBs Lyrikklubb, Stockholm; Författarförlaget, Gothenburg. Published works: in English: Words (poetry & prose), 1966; Crosswords (prose poem), 1968; Text from the Void (prose poem), 1972; Time Plays (plays & poems) in preparation; in Swedish: Text ur Tomheten, 1966; Horisontstaden (novel), 1966; Vagabond-eposet, 1966; Horisontessäer (essays & poetry), 1969; Min vän Hedningen (short stories), 1969; Tema pa Tiden (opus magnum), 1971; Fyra diktcykler (Poetry by Nelly Sachs in Swedish interpretation), 1970; Brev fran en hedning till den röde Konungens dotter (letters), 1974; En världsluffares syn pa tingen (diary), 1974; Människoriket (plays), 1974. Address: c/o Art Distribution, Rindögatan 34, S – 115 35 Stockholm, Sweden.

PERKINS, Margaret, b. 8 Aug. 1926. Teacher; Lecturer. Education: Sheffield Coll. of Educ., U.K.; F.C.G.; F.V.C.M.; A.N.E.A.; A.L.C.M. (Speech & Drama). Married, 1 daughter. Positions held: Examiner for Oral Engl., London Univ. Memberships: Chmn., Yorkshire Poets Assn., 1970–; Regional Rep., The Wheel of Yoga, 1973; Yorkshire Regional Rep., Communications Guild, 1973; Sheffield Authors Club; Pennine Poets; English Speaking Bd. Published works: Fog by Night, 1966; Omega to Alpha, 1968; Speech Mastery in 15 Lessons, 1970; Yoga for Womens Lib, 1972; Ed., Yorkshire Poets', '71 & '72. Contbr. to: It's World that Makes the Love Go Round; Spring Anthols., 1968, '69; Int. Who's Who in Poetry Anthol.; 1st Int. Poetry Soc. Anthol. Poetry for Peace; Poetry for the City; Halifax Evening Courier; Platform; Pennine Platform; Halifax Theatre Club Mag.; Midland Poets; Headland; Orbis Anthol.; Animal Defender; Gargantua; Ore; Expression; Tribune; Breakthru; Informer; The Star (Sheffield). Address: 64 Broomgrove Rd., Sheffield S10 2NA, Yorks., U.K.

PERKINS, Michael, b. 3 Nov. 1942. Professional Writer. Education: B.A., Ohio Univ. (Athens), 1963; Grad. work, New School for Social Research, and Coll. of the City of NY, 1966. Married, Renie McCune, painter; children 3. Positions held: Caseworker for NYC Dept. of Social Services; Remedial Teacher, NYC Bd. of Education; Narcotic Parole Officer for NY State Narcotic Addiction Commission; Editor-in-chief, Tompkins Square Press, and Croton Press Ltd. Published works: The Blue Woman, 1966; Shorter Poems, 1968; When I Alone and Loveless Walk, 1970. Contbr. to: The Nation; NY Qtly.; Choice; The Little Mag. Address: c/o Harold M. Wit, Allen and Co., 30 Broad St., New York, NY 10004, USA.

PERKOFF, Stuart Z., b. 29 July 1930. Poet; Painter; Sculptor. Published works: The Suicide Room, 1957. Contbr. to (Anthols.): New American Poetry, 1960; Seeds of Liberation, 1965.

PERLMAN, John Niels, b. 13 May 1946. Poet.

Education: B.A., Ohio State Univ., Columbus, Ohio, 1969. Married, 1 daughter. Positions held: Poet-in-Res., Wyoming Community Coll.; Tchr. of Poetry Writing, Ohio State Univ.; Tchr., Poets-in-the-Schools Program. Published works: Kachina, 1971; Three Years Rings, 1972; Dinner, 1974. Contbr. to: Grosseteste Review; Origin; Elizabeth; First Issue: Expatriate Review; Survivors Manual; Mouth; Bartloby'o Review; Tuatara, Shuttle, Escutcheon; Margins; DeKalb Lit. Jrnl. Honours, awards: Acad. of Am. Poets Prize, 1969; Vanderwater Poetry Prize, 1969. Address: 71 Strawberry Hill Ave. No. 1002, Stamford, CT 06902, U.S.A.

PERREAULT, John, b. 26 Aug. 1937. Editorial Associate; Art Critic; Seminar Organiser & Teacher. Positions held: Ed. Assoc., Art News, N.Y.; Regular Art Critic, The Village Voice, N.Y.; Conducts, Art Sem., Schl. of Visual Arts, N.Y. Published works: Camouflage, 1966; Luck, 1969. Contbr. to (Anthols.): Young American Poets, 1968; American Anthology I, 1968; Young American Writers, 1968; (jrnls.): Paris Review; Angel Hair; World; 0 to 9. Hons: Dylan Thomas Award, N.Y., 1960; Poets Foundation Award, 1963 & 1967; Nat. Council of the Arts Award, 1967. Address: 105 West 27th Street, N.Y., NY 10001, USA.

PERRI, Joseph G., b. 4 July 1907, Aiello Calabro, Italy. Professional Engineer; Scientist. Education: Art Schl., Catanzaro, Italy, 1921-27; Military Schl., Spoleto, 1930; Wagner Inst. of Music, 1931-33; B.C.E., Brooklyn Polytech. Inst., NY, USA, 1937; M.C.E., ibid, 1939; Sc.D., NY Univ., 1948; Dr. Engrng. Sci., Univ. of Rome, Italy, 1956. Positions held: Asst. Chief Engr., M.W. Kellogg Co., NY, 1941-49; Chief Engr., Praeger Maguire, 1950-52; Staff Tech. Cons., Vitro Corp. of Am., 1953-54; Chief Engr., Ross & Co., 1955; Rsch., Univ. of Rome, Italy, 1955-56; Staff Tech. Cons., Vitro, ibid, 1958-59; Staff Tech. Cons., Burns & Roe, Inc., USA, 1960-66; Staff Tech. Cons., Parsons, Brinckeroff, Quade, Douglas, 1957; Proj. Mgr. & Staff Cons., The Ralph Parson/Parsons Jurden Corp., 1968; Proj. Co-ord., Staff Cons., Walter Kidde Inc., 1969-70; Cons. Engr., 1971–. Memberships include: Fellow, Am. Soc. Civil Engrs.; AAAS; Int. Platform Assn.; Am. Acad. Pol. Sci.; Past, Calabria Letteraria, Italy. Published works: A Splurge of Green, 1952; You Were His Toy, 1953; Sweetly, 1953; Di Dio Siam L'azione, 1958; Light of My Soul, 1968; (Lyrics) Aflame; A Kiss from You Baby; Dream All Night of Me; Life is Short; Many Years; Babble, Babble, Say!; Don't Kiss a Girl in the...; Dreams Were True; Cry no More; Bambina Spensierata; Danzar, Danzar...; Moderna Gioventu'; Non Dir di No; Fiore. Contbr. to engrng. jrnls. Honours & Awards: Granted design & execution of marble Altar & Mural, Chapel of Civil Hosp., Cosenza, Italy, 1962; Special Personal Blessing from Pope Pius XII for hymn composed for Cath. Action, 1958. Address: 60 E 12th St., Apt. 2-D, New York, NY 10003, USA.

PERRICONE, Elvira, b. 10 Oct. 1905. Educator. Memberships incl: Centro Studi e Scambi Int.; Acad. Leonardo da Vinci; Acad. Tiberina; Union of Gold Legion. Published works incl: Felicita. Contbr. to: Quaderni di poesia; IV & V Codice di poesia; La poésie italienne de la femme et de l'enfant; Poesiaitaliana contemporanea-Relations latines. Honours, awards incl: Dip. of Hon., IX Festival of Italian Poetry, Paris; Dip. of Hon. for Felicita, Naples, 1967. Address: Via Monte Pertica 13/21, 16162 Genova-Bolzaneto, Italy.

PERRIER, Anne, b. 16 June 1922. Married J. Hutter, 2 sons. Writer. Education: Baccalaureat, Lausanne. Memberships: PEN Int.; Société des Ecrivains Vaudois. Published works: Selon la nuit, 1952; Pour un Vitrail, 1955; Le Voyage, 1958; Le Petit Pré, 1960; Le Temps est mort, 1967; Lettres Perdues, 1971. Contbr. to: Revue Nova et Vetera, Geneva; Revue Recontre, Lausanne; Revue La Traverse, Paris; Revue Ecriture, Lausanne. Honours, awards: Prix Schiller, 1958; Prix Rambert, 1971. Address: Pont Bessières 1, 1005 Lausanne, Switzerland.

PERRY, Carolyn Oliver, b. 18 Oct. 1917. Teacher. Education: B.S., English and education, N. Tex. Univ., Denton, 1939; M.A.', English, ibid, 1952; post grad. studies in English, Univ. of Houston (1 yr.); short story and poetry study, Fine Arts Colony, Corpus Christi, Texas. Married to Weldon R. Perry, 1937. Positions held: English Teacher, Henderson, Texas, 1942-54; Galena Park HS, 1954-61; Chairman of English Dept., South Houston HS, Pasadena, 1961-69; Instr. in English, San Jacinto Coll., Pasadena, 1961, 1968, 1969-. Memberships: Houston Chapt., PST, and Poetry Soc. of Texas, 1954-; Houston Chapt.: 2nd VP., Prog. Chmn., 1962-63; 1st VP., contest Chmn., 1964-65; Pres., 1966-67. PST State Councillor, 1968-; as mbr. of Poetry Soc. of Texas has undertaken following: Lectr., Piney Woods Writers' Conf., Nacogdoches, Stephen F. Austin State Univ., 1965-66-67; Conductor of Poetry Workshops for Galena Park Independent School Dis., Houston Chapter, PST; Scribblers' Club, Houston; Beaumont English Teachers at Lamar Tech. Coll.; sponsor and critic judge for poetry contests on state and local levels; founder of San Jacinto Chapt., Poetry Soc. of Texas; Faculty founder & sponsor for Pasadena Friends, Library Annual Poetry Contest for HS and intermed. school students, 1967; Nat. Council of Teachers of English; Houston Area Coun. for TE; Coll. Comp. & Communication SRCE; TJEC; Charter Member, Theta Sigma Chapt., Delta Kappa Gamma; past pres., 1968-70; Charter Member, DAR, Jane Long Chapter; First United Methodist Church, Pasadena. Contbr. to: Poesy; Sphinx; Texas Methodist. Honours: Cert. of Award for outstanding service to poetry, UPLI, 1965; Life Membership, Pin and Plaque, for outstanding community service in poetry for HS students, Nat. Congress of PTA, 1960. Address: 2205 Locklaine Dr., Pasadena, TX 77502, USA.

PERRY, Elizabeth Handley, b. 3 Aug. 1909. Personnel Officer. Education: St. Mary of the Pines Notre Dame Acad.; Visitation Convent Virginia Intermont Coll. Widow, 1 son. Positions held: Statistician, Unemployment Compensation Bd., Wash. D.C.; Industrial Analyst for War Production Bd., Wash. D.C.; Marketing Specialist, Wash. D.C.; Personnel Officer, U.S. Dept. of State, Office of Foreign Liquidation in Shanghai, Manila, then Guam; Personnel Officer for Army-Air Force, Guam; Industrial Relations Officer, U.S. Naval Air Stn., Guam & Admin. Officer, U.S. Naval Ship Repair Facility, ret'd 1968. Member, United Poets Int. Published works: Verses for Children Book 1, 1966; Verses for Children Book 2, 1968; Ribbons & Ribs, 1968; Verses for Children, Combination Books 1 & 2, 1969; This? That?? Other??? (in press). Contbr. to: Guam Recorder; Pacific Daily News; Guam Daily News. Honours, awards: Disting. Lady of the Muses, Second World Congress of Poets, Taipei, Taiwan, 1973; Poet Laureate of Guam, United Poets Laureate Int. Address: P.O. Box 3722, Agana, Guam 96810.

PERRY, Etta May Kenyon, pen name **PERRY, Kay,** b. 23 Mar. 1902. Freelance Writer. Education: Munson Secretarial; Creative Writing, Palo Alto, Calif. Married, 2 daughters. Positions held: Sec.; Office Mgr.; Insurance Analyst; Independent Acct.; Shopping Serv., Shanghai; Oriental Art & Art Needlework Shops; Amanuensis Stanford Univ. Memberships: Pres., Santa Cruz Chapt., Calif. Fed. of Chaparral Poets; Ina Coolbrith Circle; Pa., Ky., Ind., Calif. State Poetry Socs.; Nat. Fed. State Poetry Socs.; DAR; Bus. & Profl. Women, etc. Produced the book 'Santa Cruz Chaparral Poets', 1973. Contbr. to: Santa Cruz Chaparral Poets; Ina Coolbrith Circle Anthols.; Fla. Selected Poems; Santa Cruz Sentinal; Am. Weekly; Saline Co. News; Personal Poetry, WEFG Stereo, Va., etc. Recip. many awards inclng: Ruth Comfort Mitchell Award, Calif. Olympiad of the Arts, 1972; Valley Writers Conf. Trophy, 1972. Address: 225-114 Mt. Hermon Rd., Scotts Valley, CA 95066, U.S.A.

PERRY, Grace, b. 26 Jan. 1927; Medical Practitioner; Poet; Editor. Education: M.B., B.S., Sydney Univ., Australia, 1951. Married Dr. Harry Kronenberg, 3 children. Positions held: Ed., Poetry Mag., 1962-64;

Ed., Poetry Australia, 1964-; Fndr. & Dir., South Head Press, 1964; Fndr., Biennial WRITE IN, 1963; Fnded. & Conducted the Summer Creative Writing Schls. for the Arts Coun. of Australia, 1967-71; also published short stories in Westerly, Overland, Sunday Mail & on the BBC. Published works: Red Scarf; Frozen Section; Two Houses; Black Swans at Berrima, 1972. Contbr. to: The Age; Australian Broadcasting Commn.; The Australian Bulletin; Cimarron (U.S.A.); Hemisphere; The Listener (N.Z.); Poetry Australia; Poetry East West (U.S.A.); Quadrant; South Florida Poetry Jrnl.; Sydney Morning Herald; Twentieth Century. Anthologies: Australian Poetry; The Penguin Book of Aust. Verse; New Australian Poetry, 1973; Best Poems of 1971. Address: Poetry Australia, Five Dock, N.S.W. 2046, Australia.

PERRY, Ronald Peter Lee, b. 29 Jan. 1932. Univ. of Miami, Fla., 1952; M.A., ibid., 1954. Positions held: Instructor in Cryptography, US Army, 1954-56; Gen. Sec., Engineering Firm, Vientiane, Laos, 1957-59; Advertising & Public Relations Manager, Outboard Marine Int., Nassau, 1960-69. Published works: The Fire Nursery, 1956; The Rock Harbor, 1959; The Pipe Smokers, 1959; Voyages from Troy, 1962. Contbr. to (Anthols.): New Poets of England & America, 1962; Gloria Victis, 1966; From the Hungarian Revolution, 1966; Southern Writing in the Sixties, 1967; (Jrnls.): Hudson Review; Epoch; Quarterly Review of Literature. Recip., Creative Writing Fellowship in Poetry, State Univ. of Iowa, Iowa City, 1956. Address: P.O. Box 711, Nassau, Bahamas.

PETER, Lily. Writer; Farmer. Education: B.S., Memphis State Univ.; M.A., Vanderbilt Univ.; grad. study, Univ. of Chicago, Columbia Univ.; music study, Chicago Musical Coll. & Juilliard Schl. of Mus., N.Y. Positions held: Tchr.; Writer; Owner & Operator of two plantations in the Arkansas Delta country; Owner of two cotton gins; Bd. Dirs., Moravian Music Fndn.; Ark. State Festival of Arts; Southern Cotton Ginners Assn. Memberships: Poets' Roundtable of Arkansas; Nat. League of Am. Pen Women; The Acad. of Am. Poets; The Nat. Soc. of Arts & Letters; Ark. Cmposers, Authors & Artists Soc.; Nat. Coun., Metropolitan Opera Assn.; Poetry Socs. of Tenn., Tex. & Ga. Poet Laureate of Ark. Published works: The Green Linen of Summer, 1964; The Great Riding, 1966; The Sea Dream of the Mississippi, 1973; var. feature articles on hist., music, art & poetry. Contbr. to: Am. Poetry Mag.; Baltimore Sune; N.Y. Times-Herald; Southwest Review; Kaleidograph; Agora; Am. Bard; Nashville Tennessean; Am. Weave; Delta Review; Ark. Gazette; Westminster Mag.; Am. Indian Mag.; Ark. Democrat; Twin City Tribune, etc. Recip. num. honours & awards inclng: Allard Gold Cup, 1961; Ark. Composers, Authors & Artists Soc. Gold Cup, 1965; Hon. L.H.D., Moravian Coll., Bethlehem, Pa., 1965; Kenneth Beaudoin Gemstone Award, 1967 & '71; Poetry Soc. of Okla. Gold Cup, 1967. Address: Rte. 2, Box 69, Marvell, AR 72366, U.S.A.

PETERS, Frank, b. 14 Sept. 1927. Paint Chemist. Married, 2 children. Positions held: House Painter; Paint Technician; Paint Chemist; currently Chief Chemist, Conchemco Inc., L.A. Div. Member, Poetry Soc. of Am., 1963-. Contbr. to Poetry Soc. of Am. Diamond Anthol. Address: 1470 Millar Dr., Glendale, CA 91206, U.S.A.

PETERS, Lenrie Wilfred Leopold, b. 1 Sept. 1932. Surgeon. Education: Trinity Coll., Cambridge Univ., UK; Med. Schl., Univ. Coll. Hosp., London. Positions held: House Surg.; Registrationsip: Specialist Surg. Published works: Poems, 1964; The Second Round (novel), 1965; Satellites, 1967; Katchikali, 1971. Contbr. to: Black Orpheus; Transatlantic Review; Prism; Outposts; many anthols. Address: 34 Howitt Close, Howitt Road, London N.W.3, U.K.

PETERS, Robert, pen name **BRIDGE, John,** b. 20 Oct. 1924. Poet; Professor of English. Education: B.A., M.A. & Ph.D., Univ. of Wis., 1946-52. Positions held: Tchng. positions at Univ. of Wis., Univ. of Idaho,

Boston Univ., Ohio Wesleyan Univ., Wayne State Univ., Univ. of Calif., Riverside, UCLA, Univ. of Calif., Irvine; currently Prof. of Engl. & Comparative Lit. Memberships: Poetry Soc. of Am.; Calif. State Poetry Soc.; MLA. Published works: Songs for a Son, 1967; Pioneers of Modern Poetry (w. G. Hitchcock), 1967; The Sow's Head & Other Poems, 1969; In the English Lake District, 1973; Byron Exhumed, 1973; Cool Zebras of Light, 1974. Contbr. to: New Measure; Invisible City; Prairie Schooner; Hearse; Wormwood Review; Ante; Minn. Review; N.Am. Review; Choice; Chelsea, etc. Address: 433 Locust St., Laguna Beach, CA 92651, U.S.A.

PETERSEN, Donald, b. 11 Nov. 1928. University Teacher. Education: B.A., Carleton Coll., Northfield, Minn., 1950; Indiana Univ., Bloomington; Univ. of Iowa, Iowa City, M.F.A., 1952. Married Jeanne Ahrens w. 4 children. Positions held: Tchr., Univ. of Iowa, 1954-56; SUNY, 1956–; Asst. Ed., Western Review, Denver, Colo. 1950-55. Published works: The Spectral Boy, 1964. Contbr. to (Anthols.): Midland, 1961; New Poets of England and America, 1962; (Jrnls.): Poetry; Paris Review. Address: SUNY, Oneonta, N.Y., USA.

PETERSON, Freddie Phelps, pen name HANSON, **Freddie Phelps,** b. 8 Jan. 1908. Teacher; Author; Poet. Education: B.A., Univ. of Calif., 1926; M.A., Ariz. State Univ., 1956; world travel work for Ph.D. in Social Studies, 1960-70. Married 1) Philip Hanson, dec., 2 sons, 2) Elmer Herbert Peterson. Positions held: Tchr., Wilson Schl., Phoenix, Ariz., 1928-29; Tchr., Japanese Relocation Authority, Rivers (Sacaton), Ariz., 1943-44; U.S. Post Office, Phoenix, Ariz., 1945-52; Tchr., Wash. Schl. Dist., Phoenix, 1952-73, ret'd. Memberships incl: Past Pres., Bus. & Profl. Women; Nat. Fed. of Poetry Socs.; Phoenix & Tucson Br., Ariz. Poetry Soc.; Nat. Assn. of Retd. Persons; Past Pres., Phoenix Writers Club, De Molay Mothers Club, & Wash. Womans Club; Ariz. Pioneer Histl. Soc.; Dons Club; Ladies Oriental Shrine; Nat. Tchrs. Retirement Assn.; Nat., Ariz. & Maricopa Co. Educl. Assns.; Pi Gamma Mu; Kappa Delta Pi. Published works: Book of Poems, Westward, Whoa!, State song, Copper State, 1973. Contbr. to: Ariz. Highways Mag.; Md. Soc. of Poets; Calif. Capers; Milwaukee Sweet Talk; N.C. Fun & Fantasy; Ballet on the Wind, 1969; Sing Naked Spirit, 1970; Readers Digest; Unity; Science of Mind; Ariz. Republic; Apache Co. Observer, etc. Honours, awards: Winner, Nat. League of Am. Penwomen Contest w. poem 'Cattails', 1943, and others. Address: 1402 West Ajo Way, Sp. 64, Tucson, AZ 85713, U.S.A.

PETERSON, Robert, b. 2 June 1924. Poet. Education: B.A., Univ. of Calif., 1947; M.A., San Francisco State Coll., 1958. Positions held: Hotel Manager; Magazine Editor; Tchr.; Writer-in-Res., Reed Coll., Portland, Ore., 1969-71, etc. Published works: Home for the Night, 1962; The Binnacle, 1967; Wondering Where You Are, 1969; Vietnam Blues (anthol. of Protest Poems, ed. & published), 1965. Rep. in following anthols: Focus On Rebellion, 1962; A Poetry Reading Against the Vietnam War, 1966; Where is Vietnam? 1967; New Am. & Canadian Poets, 1971; Peace & Pieces Anthol., 1973, etc. Contbr. to: Mica; Migrant; Combustion; Choice; Genesis West; Ohio Review; The Nation, etc. Honours, awards: Nat. Fndn. on the Arts Grant in Poetry, 1966; Amy Lowell Traveling Fellowship, 1972-73. Address: P.O. Box 401, Ranchos de Taos, NM 87557, U.S.A.

PETRIE, Paul James, b. 1 July 1928. Professor of English Literature. Education: B.A., Wayne State Univ., 1950; M.A., ibid, 1951; Ph.D., State Univ. of Iowa, 1957. Married Sylvia Spencer, 3 children (Philip, Emily & Lisa). Positions held: Assoc. Prof., Peru State Coll., 1958-59; Instr., ibid; Asst. Prof., Assoc. Prof., Prof., Univ. of Rhode Is., 1959–. Published works: Confessions of a Non-Conformist, 1963; The Race With Time & The Devil, 1965; From Under The Hill of Night, 1969; The Idol, 1973. Contbr. to: Antioch Review; Atlantic Monthly; Carleton Miscellany; Colo. Quarterly; Commonweal; Epoch; Iowa Review; Mass. Review; Mich. Quarterly; Minn. Review; Nation; New

Republic; New Yorker; N.Y. Times; North Am. Review; Outposts; Poetry; Prairie Schooner, etc. Address: 66 Dendron Rd., Peacedale, R.I. 02879, U.S.A.

PETROCELLI, Marie F., b. 8 July 1921. Attorney at Law. Education: Columbia Univ., 1943; St. John's Schl. of Commerce; grad., St. John's Law Schl., 1950. Positions held: Ed., Bulletin for Long Island Chapter Columbiettes, 1960 72. Former Mbr., Catholic Poetry Soc. of Am. Contbr. to: Brooklyn Tablet; former Daily Mirror. Address: 965 39th St., Brooklyn, NY 11219, U.S.A.

PETRY, C(linton) B(rowning), pen names, **BROWNING, Peter; ASPIRA,** b. 28 Apr. 1921. Publisher. Positions held: Publisher, Clover Publishing Co.; Founder, Clover Internat. Poetry Assoc.; Founder Nat. Supply Assoc.; Founder, Peter Browning Products, Aspirall Products. Membership: Internat. Clover Poetry Assoc. Address: 210 Fifth Ave., New York, NY 10010, USA.

PETRY, Evelyn M., Executive Editor. Education: UK; France; USA. Exec. Editor, Clover Internat. Poetry Assoc. Memberships: Internat. Clover Poetry Assoc.; Florida State Poetry Soc.; Nat. Poetry Day Committee Inc.; Poetry Soc. of S. Carolina. Published works: (Editor) The Clover Collection of Verse, Vol. 1, 1968; Vol. 2, 1969; Vol. 3, 1970; Vol. 4, 1971; Vol. 5, 1972, etc. Address: 210 Fifth Ave., New York, NY 10010, USA.

PETTIT, Marjorie, b. 5 Feb. 1922. Office Accountant. Education: Univ. of Wis., Stevens Point; grad. work in Jrnlsm., Univ. of Wis., Madison. Positions held: H.S. Engl. Tchr., sev. yrs.; Office Acctng., Univ. of Wis., Dept. of Hist., Madison. Memberships: Wis. Fellowship of Poets; Asst. Ed. 'Muse Letter', ibid, 1971-74, also Regl. V.P., So. Dist., 1973-74; Displays Chmn., Nat. Conven., Edgewood Coll., 1971; Wis. Regl. Writers' Assn.; Sigma Tau Delta. Contbr. to: The Clover Coll. of Verse; Hawk & Whippoorwill Recalled; Stevens Point Daily Jrnl.; Milwaukee Jrnl.; St. Paul's Meth. Ch. Bulletin. Lyrics & Music for an original children's play, prod. in Madison, Wis. under auspices of Village Playhouse Drama Grp. Honours, awards: 1st pl., Wis. Fellowship of Poets Contest, 1970, etc. Address: 2243 Woodview Ct., Apt. 18, Madison, WI 53713, U.S.A.

PETTIT, Stephen Lewis Ingham, b. 25 Feb. 1921. Retired Company Director; Writer; Poet. Education: Wykeham House Schl., Worthing, Sussex, U.K.; Brighton Coll.; RAF Coll., Cranwell. Positions held: Pilot, RAF Vol. Reserve, based Heliopolis, Cairo, Egypt; Company Dir. Memberships: V.P., Poetry Soc. of Cheltenham; Poetry Soc., London; Royal Inst. of Philos. Published works: The Peregrine Instant, 1967; In The Deserts of Time, 1969; Anthol. of the Wye Valley, 1971; Arthur, King of the Britons, 1971; For a Moment of Time, 1971. Contbr. to: Poesie Vivante, Geneva; Quill; Breakthru; Platform; The Pilot; Contrasts; Pause; Mofussil; Paperway/Oyster; Dean Forest Guardian; Anglo-Welsh Review; Scrip; Expression One; Rainbow; Viewpoints; Envoi; Manuscript; (anthols.) The Spring Anthol., 1969; Top Poets of 1968; Viewpoints Anthol., 1968; Poesie Vivante Co-op. Anthol., 1970; Honours, awards: Sovereign's Commendation for Valuable Service in the Air, 1945; Cert. of Merit, B'ham Fest., 1969, Rainbow Satirical Verse Comp., 1968 & Rainbow Winter Poems Comp., 1968-69. Address: Ballaglass Farmhouse, Maughold, Nr. Ramsey, I.O.M., U.K.

PETTIWARD, Daniel, b. 7 Nov. 1913. Journalist & Critic. Education: Eton Coll.; 2nd class hons. degree in Politics, Economics & Philos., Univ. Coll., Oxford Univ. Positions held: R.A.S.C., WWII; Freelance Jrnlst.; Illustrator & Cartoonist: Stage & TV Actor; Drama Critic, Southern Evening Echo, 1963–. Member, West Country Writers' Assn. Published works: (book of verse) Truly Rural, 1939. Contbr. to: Punch; Wall St. Jrnl.; The Argosy; var. anthols. Address: 48A The Close, Salisbury, Wilts. SP1 2EL, U.K.

PETTY, William Henry, b. 7 Sept. 1921. County Education Officer. Education: M.A., Peterhouse, Cambridge Univ., U.K.; B.Sc., Univ. of London. Married, 2 daughters, 1 son. Positions held: var. educl. posts in the North & West Ridings of Yorks. & in London, 1946-64; Dpty. Co. Educ. Off. of Kent, 1964-73; Co. Educ. Off. of Kent, 1973-. Memberships: Poetry Soc.; English Assn. Published works: No Bold Comfort, 1957; Conquest, 1967. Contbr. to many mags. & anthols. inclng: Ambit; Chequer; Delta; English; Envoi; John o' Londons; Northern Echo; Outposts; The Poet; The Poetry Review; Poetry & Audience; A Review of English Lit.; Scrip; Poetry East-West; Official Architecture & Planning; Telegraph & Argus; Sunday Times; Transatlantic; Truth; Yorkshire Life; Twentieth Century; Yorkshire Post; Zebra, & to the BBC; PEN Anthols.; New Poems, 1954, 65, 67 & 70; Northern Aspect; Stroud Fest. Prog., 1973; New Poems (Dock Leaves); York Poetry; Poetry from 21 Hands. Recip. Prize, Cheltenham Fest. of Lit., 1968 & Camden Fest. of Music & the Arts, 1969. Address: Godfrey House, Hollingbourne, Nr. Maidstone, Kent, U.K.

PEZHMAN, Bakhtiyari Hossein, b. 1899. Poet. Positions held: w. Ministry of Posts & Telegraphs, ret'd 1960. Published works: History of Post & Telegraph; transl. of 'Fidelity of Women' by Benjamin Constant & var. other books from French into Persian; Ed. of 'Diwane Hafez'; a number of poetical works, the most important being 'Khashak' (Straw). Address: c/o Press Attache, Imperial Iranian Embassy, 16 Princes Gate, London S.W.7, U.K.

PFANOVA, Dora, b. 30 Oct. 1897. Professor; Educator; Writer; (ret'd). Education: Dept. of Psychol. & Special Philos., Romanistic French & German, Univ. of Philos. & Arts, Zagreb. Positions held: Prof. of French & German, Gymnasium; Referee of Educ. (The Libn. of the Min. of Culture & Educ.), also worked on Croatian Ency.; Scientific work; Sec. of Historical & Archaeol. Mus.; Prof. in Gymnasium. Memberships: Soc. of Croatian Writers, -1945; Soc. of Writers of Croatia, 1945-. Published works: Dreams & Their Causes; Anticipation & Telepathy & Their Conditions; Poems I, (140 pgs.), 1932; Poems II, (166 pgs. inclng. essay as intro.), 1938. Contbr. to: Književni Jug; Jugoslavenska žena; Savremenik; Njiva; Vijenac; Hrvatska revija; Slobodna Tribuna; Jutarnji list; Književni novine; 7 Dana; Hrvatski dnevnik; Srpski književni glasnik; Zivot i rad; Volja; Budućnost - Sarajevo; Narodno jedinstvo; Glas naroda; Venac-Beograd; Slovenski jug, etc. Address: Jabukovac 7, 41000 Zagreb, Yugoslavia.

PHILIPS, Charlotte (Evelyn), b. 9 June 1921. Housewife. Education: HS., and 2 yrs. Bible School. Member, Ithaca Poetry and Writers Group. Contbr. to: Elmira Telegram; Democrat and Chronicle; Coney Island Times; Newark Courier Gazette; The Piggotte Banner; Newfield News; American Poet; Prairie Poet; United Poets; Jean's Journal; Haiku Highlights; American Haiku; Orphic Lute; The Lyric; American Bard; The Nutmegger; Torn Out of Time (Anthol.); These Are My Jewels (Anthol.); The Swordsman Review, etc. Address: 1294 Elmira Rd., Newfield, NY 14867, USA.

PHILLIPS, Douglas, b. 11 Feb. 1929. Lecturer. Education: B.A., Wadham Coll., Oxford Univ., UK. Positions held: Journalist, 1953-62; Schl. Tchr., 1962-66; Coll. Lectr., 1966-. Author of Merlin's Town & Other Poems, 1965. Contbr. to: Poetry Wales; Anglo-Welsh Review; Western Mail; Welsh Nation; Transatlantic Review; Texas Quarterly; Delta; Poetry & Audience; Poetry Manchester. Address: 3 Norman Crescent, Ilkeston, Derbyshire, UK.

PHILLIPS, Michael Joseph, b. 2 Mar. 1937. Poet. Education: B.A., Wabash Coll., Ind., 1959; Univs. of Edinburgh & Paris; M.A., ibid, Univ., Bloomington, 1964; Ph.D., ibid, 1971; Oxford Univ., U.K.; Harvard & N.Y. Univs. Positions held: Prac. Tchr., Oxford Univ. (Travel Study Int), 1969; Lectr., Univ. of Wis.,

Milwaukee, 1970, '71; Substitute Tchr., Indianapolis Pub. Schls., 1972; Tchr., Free Univ. of Indianapolis, 1973. Published works: The Concrete Book, 1971; Concrete Sonnets, 1973; 8 Page Poems, 1971. Contbr. to var. mags., jrnls., newspapers, anthols. inclng: Abbey; Am. Poets; Bouquets of Poems; Haiku Highlights; Jean's Jrnl.; Prairie Poets; United Poets; America Sings; Anthol. Two.; Encounter; Golden Harvest; Imaged Words & Worded Images; Pegasus; Poezie in Fusie; This Book has no Title, & many others. Address: Colony Apts., 2012 A.W. 76th St., Indianapolis, IN 46260, U.S.A.

PHILLIPS, Robert Schaeffer, b. 2 Feb. 1938. Writer. Education: B.A., Syracuse Univ.; M.A., ibid. Married Judith Bloomingdale, 1 son (Graham). Positions held: Book Review Ed., Modern Poetry Studies. Memberships: PEN; Authors' Guild; Authors' League of Am. Published works: 8 ⅔, '_fl*¾ ffl More, 1961; Inner Weather, 1966; Moonstruck, 1973 (anthol.); A Case of Knives (forthcoming); Land of Lost Content (stories), 1970; Aspects of Alice (anthol.), 1971; The Confessional Poets (essays), 1973; Denton Welch (criticism), 1974. Contbr. to: Encounter; Poetry (Chicago); N.Y. Quarterly; Mass. Review; Choice; Manhattan Review; S.D. Review; Carleton Miscellany; N.M. Quarterly; Modern Poetry Studies; Windsor Review; Voices; Descant; Discourse; Galley Sail Review; N. Am. Review, etc. Address: Cross River Rd., Katonah, NY 10536, U.S.A.

PHILOMBE, René, b. 1930. Writer; Editor. Married, 1 child. Positions held: Sec., Tribunal Coutumier de Saa, 1947-49; Police Insp.; Dir., 2 revolutionary newspapers, La Voix du Citoyen & Bëbëla-Ebug, 1959-62; Pres., Les Comédies du Peuple theatrical troup. Memberships: Fndg. Mbr., Sec.-Gen., Nat. Assn. of Cameroon Poets & Writers; Assn. of Writers in French Lang.; Int. Corres., Poésie Vivante; Cameroon Rep., Acad. of Poetry Records. Published works: La Passerelle Divine, 1960; Au Premier Président de la République Camerounaise, 1960; Lettres de ma Cambuse; Hallalis et Chansons Nègres; Sola ma Chérie; Un Sorcier Blanc à Zangali, etc. Contbr. to: Revue Abbia; Effort Camerounais; Le Cameroun Littéraire; Emergences; Arts et Poésie; Ozila; African Arts; Poésie Vivante; Croissance des Jeunes Nations; Le Monde. Honours, awards: 1st Prize, Cameroon Poetry in French Lang., Soc. of Poets & Artists of France, 1965; 1st Prize, French Classical Poetry, 1966; Silver Medal, Int. Ctr. of French Arts & Thought, 1966; Mottart Prize, Acad. Française, 1965; El Hadj Ahmadou Ahidjo literary & artistic prize. Address: B.P. 2180, Yaoundé-Messa, Cameroon, Africa.

PICKARD, Thomas Mariner, pen name **PICKARD, Tom,** b. 7 Jan. 1946. Writer. Positions held: Co-Fndr. & Co-Org., Morden Tower Poetry Readings in Newcastle. Published works: (poetry) High on the Walls, 1967; The Order of Chance, 1970; Dancing Under Fire, 1973; (semi-autobiographical fiction) Guttersnipe, 1971. Contbr. to: Stand; London Mag.; Poetry (Chicago); Poetry Review; Hawaii Review; Second Aeon; City Lights Jrnl.; The Seventies; 20th Century; Lip; Contact; Brown Window, etc. Has toured the U.S.A. three times, reading from his published work. Currently is working on long project documenting aspects of tyneside working class work & life with film makers & photographer, & has been commnd. by BBC to write 30 min. TV play. Recip., Arts Coun. Bursary, 1969 & '73. Address: 2 Hubert Terr., Gateshead, Co. Durham NE8 2HE, U.K.

PICKARD, William Priestley, pen name **PICKARD, Bill,** b. 9 Mar. 1931. Personnel & Welfare Work (Graduate of the Inst. of Personnel Management). Education: Mercers' School, London EC1.; Matric. in London Univ., 1947; Clifton Theological Coll., Bristol; Bristol Polytechnic (Management School); Redland Coll. of Education, Bristol. Positions held: Internat. Sugar Salesman; Deacon and Priest, Church of England; Teaching; Personnel & Welfare Work; Director of Literature, Bristol Arts Centre since 1966.

Memberships: Poetry Soc. (UK); Poets' Conference. Editor, The Circle in the Square (mag. of Bristol Arts Centre); Co-Editor and Contbr. to 600 Years of Bristol Poetry, 1973. Published works: All Systems Stop, 1968; Hardware & Software, 1969; Everything By Starts, 1970, 2nd Ed., 1971, Rev'd Ed., 1972, 4th Ed., 1973. Contbr. to: The House that Jack Built, 1973; Doves for the 70's, 1970 and 1972; People Within, 1973; Tribune· The Listener; Sunday Times; Ecology; Xenia 1 and 2; Opus 1; 15 editions of The Circle in the Square; also BBC Radio and TV., and ITV. Address: Bristol Arts Centre, 4/5 King Square, Bristol BS2 8JG, UK.

PICKER, Elizabeth E., pen names **PICKER, Eliza; HANEY, Elizabeth,** b. 25 Apr. 1929. Secretary. Education: B.A., Ursinus Coll., 1950; Grad. work, State Univ. of NY.; Drexel Univ. Married, now divorced; 5 children. Positions held, include: Work on a Vermont dairy farm; case history worker in a mental asylum; vegetable sorter in frozen food factory; library clerk; librarian; teacher; secretary, YMCA of Phila. and vicinity. Memberships include: Catholic Poetry Soc., New Jersey Poetry Soc.; Clover Internat. Poetry Soc.; American Poets Fellowship Soc. Published works: City of Man & All that Jazz, 1964; Since the Beginning and Other Poems, 1966; Pieces of Identity, 1974. Contbr. to: The Haddon Gazette; Feathers from the Aerie; The Geographic Platinum Falcon; Poetic Licence. Poetry readings at Ursinus College; The Far Corners Coffeehouse; Glassboro State College Coffeehouse. Winner of the Clover Internat. Poetry Award, 1969, Hon. Mention for poem, Taurus. Address: 36 Jefferson Ave., Haddonfield, NJ. 08033, USA.

PICKTHALL, Edith Gwendoline, b. 30 Dec. 1893. Retired Nurse. Education: Queen Charlotte's Hosp., London. Positions held: Sec., Liverpool, 1916-32; Nurse, London & Bournemouth, 1933-38; Nurse, Cornwall, 1938-58. Assoc. Ed., Envoi, 1965–. Published works: In Time of Need, 1960; Wonder, 1961; The Quest for Peace, 1963; The Choice is Mine, 1969. Contbr. to: The Dorset Year Book, 1961-62; The Lady; Message; Outposts; Envoi. Address: St. Mylor Vicarage, Mylor, Falmouth, Cornwall, U.K.

PICKUP, Beth Walmsley, num. pen names. Writer. Education: Bolton Technical Coll. Married w. children. Positions held: Press Corres., Women's Inst.; Treas., ibid. Memberships: Lancs. Authors' Assn.; Preston Poets' Soc.; Leyland Writers' Soc.; Regnear Student, Swanwick Writers' Summer Schl. Contbr. to: Eadon's Press; Enterprize Fndn.; Gerrard's Publications of Lancashire Prise & Verse; IPC; Lancs. Authors' Assns. 'Red Rose' mag. & 'Record'; Preston's 1972 Guild Year Publication 'Reflections'; Oldham Chronicle Mag. Sect.; The Lady; Radio 4; Radio Blackburn. Honours, awards: 2nd prize in Prose Sect., L.A.A., 1964; ever winner of Preston Poets' MacKenzie Trophy, 1965 (& in 1969); rst Winner, Brown Cup for Engl. Prose & 3rd prize in same sect., L.A.A., 1965; First Award in Preston Writers' Article Sect. & 2nd Prize in L.A.A. Dialect Verse, 1966; Winner, Batty Cup for Engl. Verse, L.A.A., 1967; 3rd prize, Engl. Prose Sect., ibid, 1968; 3rd Prize, President's Cup for Engl. Verse, Preston Poets', 1969; 3rd Prize, Engl. Verse, Sect., L.A.A., 1969 & '70; 4th Prize, Short Story Sect., ibid, 1971. Address: Innisfree, School Lane, Euxton, Chorley PR7 6JL, Lancs., U.K.

PICOLA, Henry, b. 6 Sept. 1913. Teacher; Editor; Poet. Education: Rutgers Univ., Univ. of Miami. Positions held: Prof. of Poetry, Amado M. Yuzon Shrine of Poetry; Poetry Fndr., Cons., Int. Poets' Shrine; Ed., Vespers Poetry Mag., 1934-59; Ed., Int. Poetry Review, 1961–; Lit. Ed., Ill Nuova Italiano-Americano; Ed., Miller Books, Alhambra, Calif. Memberships: Pres., Int. Acad. of Poets; Pres., Am. Poets Congress; Poetry Soc. London; Evec Bd., Manuscript Club, LA; Poetry Soc. of Southern Calif.; Calif. Fed. of Chaparral Poets; Liaison Mbr., World Poetry Soc. Intercontinental. Published works: Looking To Harvest and Other Poems, 1934. Ed., Contemporary Women Poets, 1970. Contbr. to: Int.

Poetry Review; Poetry Review, UK; Am. Bard; Versecraft; Atlanta Jrnl.; NY Times; Paterson Call; Hartford Times; Special poems for John J. Leedy's M.D. pamphlet, Poetry Therapy, 1959; Contemporary Poets; Peterson Evening News; NJ Poets; Expression; Am. Weave; Sonnet Sequences; Laurel Leaves; Sonnet Poet Laureate; Am. Poetry League Bull.; Annual Anthol.; Writers Digest; Seydell Quarterly. Honours, Awards. Oliver Cup Award, South & West, 1964; Am. Poets Cup, 1970-71; Cash Prize, Appalachian Anthol. of Poetry. Address: 6050 Fountain Ave., Hollywood, Calif. 90028, USA.

PIDOUX, Edmond, b. 25 Oct. 1908. Professor. Education: studies in Belgium & Switzerland (Lausanne); Licence ès Lettres. Positions held: Prof., Morges & Lausanne (Gymnasium; Normal Schl. for Tchrs.); Lectr. in Diction, Fac. of Theol., Lausanne. Memberships: Soc. of Swiss Writers; Agregate Mbr., Soc. of Poets & Artists of France; V.P., Soc. romande des auteurs dramatiques; V.P., Assn. des ecrivains vaudois. Published works: La Chambre Haute, 1941; Charmes pour la Male Heure, 1964; Sur ma natte, je prie (African poems), 1964; Bois d'Ebene, (pub. book & record), 1965; Je lance ma joie vers le ciel (African poems), 1969; Africaines, 1967; Passage de la Ligne, 1967; De David à Jonas, 1969; 400 texts for different editors of music & for composers; main poetical collaborator for the new hymnbook Psautier Romand & occasionally for the int. Cantate Domino; num. poems broadcast by Radio Suisse romande. Honours, awards: Prize, Assn. des Ecrivains Vaudois, 1960; Prix international de l'Expression francaise, Ctr. d'Art National Francais, 1963; 1st & 2nd Prize, Soc. des Poetes et Artistes de France, 1966; Prix de l'Association des Chanteurs vaudois, 1971. Address: 7 Chemin du Moléson, 1012 Lausanne, Switzerland.

PIECH, Paul Peter, b. 11 Feb. 1920, in Brooklyn, NY, USA. Artist; Designer. Education: Cooper Union School of Art, NY, USA; Chelsea School of Art, London, UK. Positions held: Art Director, Dorlands Internat. Advertising Agency, NY; Columbia Records, Conn., USA; W.S. Crawfords Advertising Agency, London, UK; Service Advertising Agency, London, UK; Lecturer in Graphics, London School of Printing and Middlesex Polytechnic, UK. Memberships: Soc. of Typographic Designers (Fellow); Typographic Centre; Internat. Poetry Soc. Established, 1959, the Taurus Press of Willow Dene, publishing numerous books of poetry, including own poetry. Graphic works extensively exhibited and included in collections of Museum of Mod. Art, USA; Seattle Museum of Art, USA; Philadelphia Museum of Art, USA; Brooklyn Museum of Art, USA; Florida State Univ., USA, Library of Congress, USA, etc. Address: 2 Willow Dene, Bushey Heath, Herts. WD2 1PS, UK.

PIECHAL, Marian, pen names **STALOWY, Andrzej & OSCIEN, Zygmunt,** b. 24 Aug. 1905. Poet; Satirist; Essayist. Education: Ph.D. Positions held: Hd. of Lit. Dept. of Polish Radio in Oddziału Lódzkiego ZLP; Ed., Osnowa, monthly mag.; Deputy Ed., Poezja, Monthly mag.; Ed., Miesięcznika Literackiego. Memberships: Life Mbr., Związku Literatów Polskich; PEN. Published works: (poetry) Krzyk z miasta, 1929; Elegie calopalne, 1931; Garść popiołu, 1932; Srebrna waga, 1936; Raj na ziemi, 1947; Wybór poezji, 1952; Nowa wiosna, 1954; Ognie, 1958; Wiersze, 1958; Miasto nadziei, 1964; Miara ostateczna, 1965; Punkt oparcia, 1965; Być, 1969; Poezje wybrane, 1970; Garść popiołu (edycja bibliofilska), 1970; Poezje, 1973; also essays, satire, etc. Contbr. to lit. jrnls. Honours, awards incl: Krzyz Oficerski Orderu Odrodzenia Polski, 1965; Medal Zasługi dla Obronności Kraju, 1967; Państwowa Nagroda Literacka, 1968; Zasłużony Działacz Kultury, 1969. Address: ul. Krakowskie Przedmiescie 87/89 m. 18, 00-079 Warsaw, Poland.

PIERCE, Maylen Newby, b. 13 Mar. 1901. Homemaker; Lecturer; Writer. Education: A.B., Sweet Briar Coll., Va., 1922; grad. work, Univ. of Miami, Dade Community Coll., & Am. Univ., Wash. D.C. Divorced, 3 sons. Memberships: Nat. League Am. Penwomen;

Pres., Laramore Rader Poetry Club; Past Pres., AAUW; Past Pres., Chapt. K. of P.E.O.; Past Pres., Women's Assn. Presbyn. Ch.; Org. Bd., Crippled Children's Hosp.; Youth Ctr. of Coral Gables, Fla.; D.A.R.; Colonial Dames XVII Century; Jamestowne Soc.; Poetry Soc. of Ga.; Poetry Soc. of Va.; Am. Acad. of Poets. Published works: Kathryn Maule (biog.), 1973; Word Weavers, 1972; Mind Ravels & Heart Frays (poems), 1973. Contbr. to: Singing in the Sun (anthol.), 1967; Author-Poet Anthol., 1973; Ideals; Guide Posts; Crewe Chronicle; Thom Hendricks Publications. Recip., Laramore Rader Poetry Grp. Awards. Address: 300 Mendoza Ave., Coral Gables, FL 33134, U.S.A.

PIERCY, Marge, b. 31 March 1936. Writer. Education: B.A., Univ. of Michigan; M.A., Northwestern Univ. Membership: Authors Guild. Published works: To Be Of Use, 1973; 4-Telling (with 3 other poets, R. Hershon, E. Jarrett, and D. Lourie), 1971; Hard Loving, 1969; Breaking Camp, 1968, and (novels): Small Changes, 1973; Dance The Eagle To Sleep, 1970; Going Down Fast, 1969. Contbr. to: Hearse; Up from Under; Off Our Backs; Massachusetts Review; Leviathan; Minnesota Review; Epoch; Epos; New; Poltergeist; Clown War; Carleton Miscellany; Anon; Periodical Lunch; Motive; Premiere; Berkeley Tribe; The Fifth Estate; New Left Notes; CAW!; Earth's Daughters; Now; Pyramid; Apple; Liberation News Service; KPFA Folio; Rough Times; Transatlantic Review; Moving Out; Aphra; Reflections; December; Prairie Schooner; 100 Flowers; Free Women; The Rat; Poems of the People; Georgia Straight; Harrison Street Review; Whirlwind; University of Tampa Poetry Review; The Liberated Guardian; Shenandoah; Everywoman; Southern Poetry Review; Second Wave; Gidra; American Dialog; Spark, Williamette Bridge; The Patriot; Equal Time; Some; Unmuzzled Ox; Nevermind; Street Cries; Aye; Good Times; Hard Times; Lamp in the Spine; Mosaic, etc. Address: Box 943, Wellfleet, MA 02667, USA.

PIERRE, Georges, b. 20 Feb. 1916. Reporter. Memberships: PEN Int., Belgian French-speaking Ctr.; Assn. of Belgian Writers; Association Royale des Ecrivains Wallons; Fondation Charles Plisnier. Published works: Le Bal des Ombres, 1965; Les Analogues, 1966; De Haute Peine, 1967; Le Dit du Provisoire, 1971; Ces Mots de Cendre, 1971. Address: Rue Vautier 34, 1040 Brussels, Belgium.

PIGG, Arthur Carnes, pen name **JOSEPH,** b. 1 May 1948. Student. Education: Univ. of Tenn., Knoxville, 1966-71. Memberships: N.Y. Poetry Forum; Shore Poetry Assn.; U.T. Poetry Club, 1967-68; Knoxville Rejects, 1968-70, '71; Co-Chmn., U.T. Sci. Fiction-Fantasy Soc., 1970-71. Contbr. to: Nat. Anthol. of High Schl. Poetry, Spring 1966; Best Poets of the Twentieth Century, 1974; Jrnl. of Contemporary Poets; Expressive Arts Review. Address: P.O. Box 8597, U.T. Station, Knoxville, TN 37916, U.S.A.

PILLIN, William, b. 3 Dec. 1910. Pottery Craftsman. Education: North-Western Univ., Evanston, Ill. Married Polia Pillin s. 1 son. Positions held: For Past 22 yrs. has operated his own pottery studio. Published works: Poems, 1939; Theory of Silence, 1949; Dance Without Shoes, 1956; Passage After Midnight, 1958; Pavanne for a Fading Memory, 1963. Contbr. to (Anthols.): Eight American Poets, 1952; Exile, 1957; Poetry Los Angeles, 1958; Prismatic Voices, 1958; Poets of Today, 1964; (Jrnls.): Poetry; Nation; Kayak; Illuminations; Galley Sail Review; New Mexico Quarterly; Coastlines; Prairie Schooner; Literary Review; Poetry Northwest. Address: 4913 Melrose Ave., Los Angeles, CA 90029, USA.

PILON, Jean-Guy, b. 12 Nov. 1930. Head of Arts Broadcasting of Radio-Canada. Education: Licence en droit, Université de Montréal, 1954. Positions held: Dir., "LIBERTE" review; Lit. Dir., Editions "L'ACTUELLE". Memberships: Sec. Gen., Rencontre québécoise internationale des Ecrivains; Société royale du Canada; Jury, Grand Prix international de Poésie, Prix Canada-Belgique. Published works incl: La Fiancée du Matin, poèmes, 1953; Les Cloîtres de l'Eté, poems (w. René Char), 1955; L'Homme et le Jour, poems, 1957; La Mouette et le Large, poems, 1960; Recours au Pays, poems, 1961; Pour saluer une ville, poems, 1963; Comme eau retenue, poems, 1969; Saisons pour la Continuelle, poems, 1969; Silences pour une souveraine, poems, 1972. Honours, awards: Prix de poésie du Québec (Prix David), 1956; Prix Louise Labé, 1969; Prix France-Canada, 1969; Prix van Lerberghe, 1969; Prix du Gouverneur-général du Canada, 1970. Address: 5724 Chemin de la Cote Saint Antoine, Montreal, Que., Canada.

PINO, Nino, b. 17 Sept. 1909. Educ: Med. & Vet. Studies; Grad., 1930; Pol. Sci. Studies, Univ. of Perugia, Italy. Positions held incl: Fndr., 1st Sec., Casa del Popolo (Peoples' Home), in his own region, 1944, Vicesindaco, 1946; Sec., Italian Anti-Fascist Ctr., 1945; Hon. Pres., Popular Democratic Front, Messina, 1947; Dpty., Nat. Parliament, 1948-63; Mbr., num. parliamentary commns. inclng. Agric., Forestry & Alimentation Commn., Pub. Instrn. & Fine Arts Commn., & Protection of Landscape & Artistic & Cultural Heritage Commn.; Docent, Prof., Inst. Dir., Fac. of Vet. Med., Univ. of Messina. Mbr., num. profl. orgs. Published works incl: Sciami di sparse parole, 1939; Altalene, 1951; Sul dialetto siciliano, 1955; Mminuzzàgghi, 1956; Due conferenze, 1957; L'epopea di Gagarin, 1963; Tre profili, 1963; Procedimento penale contro Dante Alighieri ed altri, 1965-66; Moli protesi, 1966; Tifo sportivo e suoi effetti, 1935; Dalla tribuna parlamentare, 1948-63; Discorsi attorno al pesce, 1965; Eugenetica e progresso, 1967. Recip., num. hons. Address: Via Operaia 102, 98051 Barcellona di Sicilia, Messina, Italy.

PINTER, Harold, b. 10 Oct. 1930. Playwrite. Member, Drama Panel, Arts Coun. of GB. Published works: The Room & The Dumb Waiter, 1960; The Birthday Party, 1960; The Caretaker, 1960; A Slight Ache, 1961; The Collection & The Lover, 1963; The Homecoming, 1965; The Tea Party & The Basement, 1967; Mac, 1968; Landscape, 1968; Landscape & Silence, 1969; Poems, 1968; Five Screenplays, 1970; The Caretaker; The Servant; The Pumpkin Eater; Accident; The Quiller Memorandum; The Go-Between; Ed., (jointly) New Poems, 1967; A PEN Anthology, 1967. Honours, awards: Evening Standard Drama Award, 1961; The Newspaper Guild of NY Award, 1962; The Italia Prize, 1963; CBE, 1966. Address: 7 Hanover Terrace, Regents Park, London, NW1, UK.

PIRZADA, Dastgir Zaheer, pen name **ZAHEER KASHMIRI,** b. 21 Aug. 1920. Journalist; Poet. Positions held: Ed., Savera Monthly, Lahore, 1948-49; Column Writer, Daily Ehsan, Lahore, 1954; Ed., Daily Halaat, Lahore, 1963; Column Writer, Daily Nawa-i-Waqat, Lahore, 1969-70; Column Writer, Daily Mussawat, Lahore, 1972–. Past Mbr., Progressive Writers' Assn., India, Ctrl. Organising Comm. of Pakistan, Exec. Comm. of Halqa-e-Arbab-e-Zauq, Lahore. Published works: Azmat-e-Adam (coll. of poems); Taghazzul (coll. of Ghazals); Selected Poetry of 1948 (anthol.) Contbr. to: Adabi Dunya; Adab-e-Latif; Savaira; Shahrah; Afkaar; Naya Adab; Naqoosh; Fanoon; Seep; Jaiza; Daily Nawa-i-Waqat; Daily Imroze; Daily Mussawat; Weekly Nusrat; Weekly Qandeel. Recip., Adamji Award for best poem of the Yr., 1963. Address: 9 Beadon Rd., Lahore, Pakistan.

PISTELLA, Domenic J., b. 1 Nov. 1914. Catholic Clergyman. Education: Ph.B.; Th.B.; M.S. in Educ.; Ph.D. (Classics). Positions held: Tchr. at var. levels, H.S. & Coll., Italy & U.S.A., 1937-65. Memberships: World Acad. of Art & Professions, Rome, Italy, 1950; Am. Poetry Soc., U.S.A.; Am. Soc. of Latin Tchrs.; Am. Assn. of Univ. Profs. Published works: Juvenilia, Rome, 1937; Meditazioni, Rome, 1940; Piccolo Canto, Rome, 1950; Crowning of a Queen, N.Y., U.S.A., 1954. Contbr. to: Avvenire, Rome; Osservatore, Rome; Regina, Rome; Echo, N.Y. Honours, awards: Premio delle Vittorie, 1950. Address: 448 E. 116th St., N.Y., NY 10029, U.S.A.

PITCHES, Douglas Owen, b. 6 Mar. 1930. Teacher. Education: Bognor Regis Tchr. Trng. Coll., U.K. Published works: Poems, 1965; Prayer to the Virgin Mary, 1965. Contbr. to: Breakthru; Scrip; Outposts; Manifold; Riding West; Tribune; Expression; Laudamus Te (Manifold Religious Anthol.); Mitre Press Spring Anthols.; It's World that makes the Love go Round, (Corgi anthol.); Man (Harrap Schl. anthl.); Responding (Ginn U.S.A. II.C. series). Address. 14 Linkway, Westham, Pevensey, Sussex BN24 5JB, U.K.

PITCHFORD, Kenneth S(amuel), b. 24 Jan. 1931. Free-lance Editor. Education: B.A., summa cum laude, Univ. of Minn., Minneapolis, 1952; Fulbright Fellow, Oxford Univ.; M.A., N.Y. Univ., 1959. Married Robin Morgan. Positions held: Tchr., N.Y. Univ., 1958-62; Poetry Workshop, The New Schl. for Social Rsch., N.Y., 1960; Assoc. Ed., The New Int. Yearbook, N.Y., 1960-66; Currently Free-lance Ed., N.Y. Published works: The Blizzard Ape: Poems, 1958; A Suite of Angels and Other Poems, 1967; Other: The Brothers (New World Writing), 1963; Longhairs are Dangerous (Village Voice), 1968. Contbr. to (Anthols.): Oxford Poetry 1957, 1958; Selected Poems of Wierzynski in English Adaptations, 1959; Poems by Seven, 1959; Erotic Poetry, 1963; Best Poems of 1963: The Borestone Mountain Poetry Awards, 1964; Various Light, 1964; A Controversy of Poets, 1965; (Jrnls.): Chicago Review; Kenyon Review; Listener; New Statesman; New York Times Book Review; New Yorker; Transatlantic Review. Recip., Eugene Lee-Hamilton Award for Poetry, Oxford-Cambridge, 1957. Address: 109 Third Ave., N.Y., NY 10003, USA.

PITTER, Ruth, b. 7 Nov. 1897. Poet. Published works: First Poems, 1920; First and Second Poems, 1927; Persephone in Hades, 1931; A Mad Lady's Garland, 1934; The Rude Potato, 1941; The Bridge, 1945; Pitter on Cats, 1946; Urania, 1951; The Ermine, 1953; Still by Choice, 1966. Awards: Hawthornden Prize, 1937; Heinemann Award, 1954; Queen's Medal for Poetry, 1955. Address: The Hawthorns, Chilton Road, Long Credon, Aylesbury, Bucks., U.K.

PIZER, Marjorie, b. 3 Apr. 1920. Psychotherapist; Editor; Researcher into Australian Poetry. Education: B.A., Melbourne. Memberships: PEN Int.; Fellowship of Australian Writers; Australian Soc. of Authors. Published works: Thou & I, 1967; To Life, 1969; Tides Flow, 1972. Contbr. to: Melbourne Univ. Mag.; The Bridge (Sydney); The Jewish Herald (Melbourne); Newsletter of the Assn. of Humanistic Psychol. Address: 6 Oaks Ave., Cremorne, Sydney, Australia 2090.

PLA, Josefina, b. 9 Nov. 1909. Professor. Positions held: Prof., var. municipal schls. of dramatics, dance; Int. Inst. of Pub. Relations; Cath. Univ. of the Assumption. Memberships: Hispanoamericana Acad. Ruben Dario; Acad. of Spanish Lang. Published works incl: El Precio de los Sueños, 1934; La Raiz y La Aurora, 1960; Rostros en el Agua, 1963; Invención de la Muerte, 1964; Satélites Oscuros, 1967; El Polvo Enamorado, 1968; Poesia Paraguaya, Anthol., 1963. Contbr. to: Sur; Vers; Poesie Vivante; Humboldt; Cuadernos Hispanoamericanos; Alcor, etc. Address: Estados Unidos, 1120 Asunción, Paraguay.

PLAISTED, Edward R., b. 7 Oct. 1908. Retired Pianist, Organist & Piano Tuner. Education: Western Pa. Schl. for the Blind; Home courses in psychol., Lib. of Congress. Married Alverta Plaisted, 1 son. Memberships: V.P., Butler Poetry Soc.; Pa. Poetry Soc.; Poets Tape Exchange. Contbr. to anthol. 'Prickle of a Thistle', Butler Poetry Soc., 1969; Janus SCTH; Dragonfly; Haiku Highlights; Haiku West; Prize Poems (Pa. Poetry Soc.) Has given var. public poetry readings & lectures. Honours, awards: 1st Prize, Pa. Poetry Soc. Free Verse Contest, 1963; 2nd Prize, Pa. Poetry Soc. Contest, Sonnet, 1964; 1st Prize, Poets Tape Exchange Contest, 1968 & 2nd Prize 1968 & '69; 1st Prize, Mason Sonnet Contest, PTE Contest, 1970; 1st Prize, PTE, 1971 Annual Contest; 13 ribbons for State & local awards; 1st Prize, Haiku Contest, 1972;

1st Prize for Haiku published in Haiku Highlights/Dragonfly, Jan. Feb., 1973; Poem 'Music' chosen for publication in Butler Symphony Concert, 1974. Address: 78 Old Plank Rd., Butler, PA 16001, U.S.A.

PLANZ, Allen, b. 2 Jan. 1937. Poet. Education: M.A., N.Y. Univ., 1961. Positions held: Licensed Capt., Charterboat Amor Fati; Lectr., Chapman Coll., Montauk, N.Y.; Press Sec., East Hampton Democratic Party; Poetry Ed., The Nation, 1969-72; Dir., St. Marks Poetry Proj., 1965-68; Instr., N.Y. Univ., Queens Coll. Member, Acad. of Am. Poets. Published works: Studsong, 1965; Four Poets/Four Poets, 1967; Poor White & Other Poems, 1966; A Night for Rioting, 1969; Wild-Craft, 1974. Contbr. to: The Nation; Poetry; Choice; Chicago Review; Survival Manual; Streets; N.M. Qtly.; Chelsea; Wild Dog; Am. Poetry Review; Kayak; Mass. Review; (anthols.) America, A Prophecy, 1974; Poets of Today, 1969; Where is Vietnam, 1968. Honours, awards: N.Y. Poetry Ctr., Comp. for Younger Poets, 1966; Hart Crane Meml. Prize, 1967, '69. Address: 463 West St., N.Y., NY 10014, U.S.A.

PLATT, Eugene Robert, pen name, **PLATT, Eugene,** b. 20 Feb. 1939. Poet. Education: B.A., Univ. of South Carolina, 1964; Dip. in Anglo-Irish Literature, Trinity Coll., Dublin, 1970; M.A., Clarion State Coll., Pennsylvania, 1973. Positions held: U.S. Fed. Civil Service, 1964-69; Clarion State Coll., Office of Student Affairs, 1970-73. Memberships: Poetry Soc. of South Carolina; Pennsylvania Poetry Soc. Published works: Coffee & Solace, 1970; Six of One/Half Dozen of the Other, 1971; Allegheny Reveries, 1972; A Patrick Kavanagh Anthol., 1973; An Original Sin and other poems, 1974; An Outer Banks Anthol., 1974. Address: 355-1 Pennell Circle, Tallahassee, FL 32304, USA.

PLATTHY, Jeno, b. 13 Aug. 1920. Classical Scholar. Education: Peter Pazmany Univ., Budapest, 1939-42; Jozsef Ferencz Univ., Kolozsvar, 1943-44; The Catholic Univ. of Am., Wash. D.C., 1963-65. Divorced. Positions held: Lectr., Univs. of Japan, Korea, Rep. of China, The Philippines & South Vietnam, 1956-59; Sec., Int. Inst. of Boston, Mass., 1959-62; Trustees for Harvard Univ., Washington, D.C., 1962-; Ed.-in-Chief, Monumenta Classica Perennia, N.Y., 1967-. Memberships: Int. PEN Club, N.Y.; New England Poetry Club (Harvard Univ. Fac. Club); Chmn., Org. Comm. for the Third World Congress of Poets, 1976. Published works: Tavasz, 1948; From Budapest to Tokyo, 1957; Summer Flowers, 1960; Autumn Dances, 1963; Bamboo, Opera in Three Acts (Libretto & Music), 1965; Ts'au mou (Poems in Chinese transl.), 1066; Sources on the Earliest Greek Libraries with the Testimonia, 1968; Winter Tunes, 1974. Contbr. to: The Boston Globe; Info (Tokyo); Nemzetor (Vienna); Hirunk (Wash.D.C.). Honours, awards: Dist. Poetry Award & Poet Laureate of the U.S., Second World Congress of Poets, 1973. Address: 4409 Brandywine St., N.W., Washington, D.C. 20016, U.S.A.

PLOETZ, Richard Grant, b. 27 July 1939. Playwright. Education: B.A., State Univ. of N.Y. at Albany; Yale Schl. of Drama. Married Julia Lebentvitt. Positions held: Safety & Progress Inspector, U.S. Army Corps of Engrs.; H.S. Tchr., Unalaska Schl., Alaska; Schl. Bus Driver, Waterbury, Vt.; Security Guard, New Haven, Conn. Contbr. to: Pivot; Primer; Truck 12. Honours, awards: John Golden Fellow, Yale Schl. of Drama, 1970-71; Creative Writing Grant from Vt. Coun. on the Arts, 1972-73. Address: 35 Cottage St., New Haven, CT 06511, U.S.A.

PLUMLY, Stanley, b. 23 May 1939. University Professor. Education: B.A., Wilmington Coll.; M.A., Ohio Univ. Positions held at: Louisiana State Univ., 1968-70; Ohio Univ., 1970-. Published works: In the Outer Dark, 1970; How the Plains Indians Got Horses, 1973; The Sleep-Horse, 1973; Giraffe, 1974. Contbr. to: Iowa Review; Kenyon Review; Lillabulero; The Nation; New Am. Review; New Letters; New Yorker; N.Y. Times; North Am. Review; Northwest Review; Ohio Review; Partisan Review; Poetry Northwest; Qtly.

Review of Lit.; Salmagundi; Shenandoah; Southern Review; Strivers' Row; Sumac; Va. Qtly. Review. Honours, awards: Delmore Schwartz Meml. Award, 1973; John Simon Guggenheim Meml. Fndn. Award, 1973-74. Address: Dept. of Engl., Ohio Univ., Athens, OH 45701, U.S.A.

PLUMPP, Sterling Dominic, b. 30 Jan. 1940. Teacher. Education: Sumner Hill Grammar School, 1948-55; Holy Ghost Grammar School, 1955-56; Grad. Holy Ghost HS (as Valedictorian), 1960; St. Benedict's Coll., Atchison, Kansas, 1960-63; (Army Service, 1964-68); Roosevelt Univ., 1966-68, grad. B.A. in psychology (Roosevelt Grad. School in Psychology, 1969-71). Positions held: Clerk, Chaico Main Post Office, 1962-69; Counsellor, North Park Coll., 1969-71; Instr. in Engl. Dept., Univ. of Illinois, Chicago Circle, 1971-73; Instr. in the Black Studies Prog. at the Univ. of Illinois at Chicago Circle, 1973-74. Memberships: Urban Gateways' Young Writers Workshop (Director, 1972-74); OBAC Writers' Workshop (1969-72); Third World Press (Editor, 1970-74); Black Books Bulletin (Managing Editor, 1971, 1972). Published works: Portable Soul, 1969; Half Black, Half Blacker, 1970; Black Rituals, 1972; Muslim Men (a broadside), 1972. Contbr. to: Black Liberator; Black World Mag.; Black Expression; Journal of Black Poetry; The Covenant Companion; Black Books' Bulletin; Savage. Honours, Awards: Guest Speaker, Convocation at Kennedy-King Coll., 1973; Guest Artist, Second Annual Black Writers Conference, Univ. of Pittsburgh, 1973; Featured Poet, Chicago Poetry Festival, 1972. Address: 1401 E. 55th St., Apt. 816-N, Chicago, IL 60637, USA.

PLYMELL, Charles Douglas, b. 26 Apr. 1935. Poet. Education: M.A., Johns Hopkins Univ., Baltimore. Married Pamela Beach w. 1 daughter. Positions held: Has done a variety of jobs incl., farm & ranch work, truck driver, railroad worker, printer; formerly ed., Now Now. Published works: Apocalypse Rose, 1966; Neon Poems, 1970; Cherokee, 1970. Contbr. to (Jrnls.): City Lights Jrnl.; Poetry; Hudson Review; Evergreen Review; Paris Review; Long Hair; El Corno Emplumado. Address: c/o City Lights, 261 Columbus Ave., San Francisco, CA, USA.

PODOKSIK, David, pen name OPALOV, Leonard, b. 2 Feb. 1904. Married, 1 son. Mbr., Am. Poetry League. Contbr. to: Christian Science Monitor; Hartford Courant; Paul's Poetry Corner; City News; Messenger; Wind; South-West; Times Record; Denver Post; Invisible City; Bitterroot; The Old Red Kimono; Folio; Quixote; Journal 31; El Viento; Poetry Venture Gems; Poet Lore; The Penny Dreadful; Quvin. Honours, awards: 2nd Prize, Poet Lore, 1972; Descriptive Poem Awards, 1973; Poet Lore Translation Award, 1972. Address: 140-10 Alcott Pl., Bronx, NY 10475, U.S.A.

POE, Marian Gloyd McNabb, pen name POE, Marian M.,** b. 25 Oct. 1933. Educator; Writer. Education: B.A., North Tex. State Univ., Denton, Tex. Married Ralph D. Poe. Positions held: Tchr. & Substitute Tchr. in pub. schls.; Pvte. Tutor. Memberships: Verse Writers Guild of Ohio; V.P., Shreveport Writers Club, 1972-73; Acting Pres., ibid, 1973; Pres., 1973-74; Chmn. of Bureau of Critics, Nat. Amateur Press Assn., 1972-73; Co-Ed., The Blue Print (a quarterly publication of Haiku poetry), 1967-70. Published works: (Anthologies) Poetry Dial Anthology, 1968; Our Best to You, 1968; The Shreveport Writers Club Anthol. of Poets & Authors, 1972. Contbr. to: Columbus Dispatch; U.S. Lady; Mustang Review; Reach Out; The Windless Orchard; Piggot Banner; Haiku West; American Haiku; Nutmegger; The Blue Print; Dream Shop; Haiku Mag.; Modern Haiku; Dragon Fly, etc. Recip. poetry awards inclng: Best Haiku in issue, Haiku Highlights, 1968. Address: Rte. 2, Box 336B, Haughton, LA 71037, U.S.A.

POGONOWSKA-OPLUSTIL, Anna, pen name POGONOWSKA,** b. 7 Jan. 1922. Writer. Education: Grad., Polish Philol., Univ. of Lodz, 1950. Married, 2 children. Memberships: Polish PEN, Warsaw; Polish

Writers Union. Published works: Wezly (The Knots), 1948; Przemiany (The Transformations), 1951; Kregi (The Circles), 1958; Urzeczywistnienie (The Realisation), 1958; Gaszcze (The Thickets), 1961; Mlodosc Okupacyjna (War-Time Youth), 1961; Zbroja (The Armour), 1965; Ceremonial (The Ceremonial), 1969; Wizerunek (The Effigy), 1973; Wiersze Wybrane (Selected Poems), 1973. Contbr. to: Odrodzenie; Kuznica; Tworczosc; Pokolenie Tygodnik Powszechny; Kronika; Zycie Literackie; Odra; Miesiecznik Literacki; Wiez; Poezja; Wspolczesnosc; Literatura. Address: Argentynska 9M 24, 03952 Warsaw, Poland.

POLAMERI, Veikko Olavi, b. 11 Feb. 1946. University Lecturer. Positions held: Ed.-in-Chief, Manifesti, 1968; Lectr. of Hist. of Japanese Lit., Univ. of Helsinki, 1973. Memberships: Finnish Writers' Union; Finnish Soc. of Translators; Nippon-Finland Bungaku Kyōkai. Published works: '365', 1967; Veden ääni, 1968; Kevään kuolleet lehdet, 1970; Nyt kun en kysy sinum mieltäsi maailma, 1971. Contbr. to: Parnasso; Aika; Aikalainen; Suomen Kuvalehti; Ryhmä 66 (anthol.), 1966. Exhibition of concrete poetry 'Runoa ja grafiikkaa', 1967. Honours, awards: J.H. Erkko Prize, 1968; Kalevala Soc. Prize, 1971. Address: Uudenmaankatu 27 B 11, 00120 Helsinki 12, Finland.

POLLAK, Felix, b. 11 Nov. 1909. Librarian. Education: Dr. jur., Univ. of Vienna; A.M.L.S., Univ. of Michigan; B.S.L.S., Univ. of Buffalo, NY. Personal details: Born in Vienna, Austria, came to USA in 1938; married to Sara Allen. Positions held: Reader's Adviser, Buffalo Public Library; Curator of Special Collections, Northwestern Univ. Library, Evanston, Ill.; Curator of Rare Books, Univ. of Wisconsin, Madison (currently); Poetry Ed., Arts in Society, 1973-. Published works: (poetry collections) The Castle and the Flaw, 1963 (5th printing 1972); Say When, 1969 (3rd printing 1971); Ginkgo, 1973; (poetry anthols.) 28 Poets, 1964; Of Poem, 1965; Best Poems of 1965 (1966); Where is Vietnam?, 1966; The Writing on the Wall, 1969; New Poetry out of Wisconsin, 1969; Man (Poetry Series No. 6), 1970; My Music Bent, 1973; One-Line-Poem Anthol., 1972; Open Poetry, 1973; (prose anthols.) Perspectives on Pornography, 1970; Freedom and Culture, 1970; Contbr. to magazines: Approach; Ariz. Qtly.; Beloit Poetry Journal; Between Worlds; Blue Guitar; The Carleton Miscellany; Chelsea; Chicago Review; Choice; Coastlines; Combustion; Commonweal; Compass Review; El Corno Emplumado; December; Delta (Montreal); Elizabeth; Epoch; Gallery; Hearse; Hiram Poetry Review; Kayak; The Mass. Review; The Minnesota Review; New Orleans Poetry Journal; Northeast; Northwest Review; Outposts; Pebble; Perspective; Poetry Northwest; Prairie Schooner; Quartet; San Francisco Review; Shenandoah; Southwest Review; Sparrow; Sumac; Talisman; Trace; Triquarterly; Two Cities; Voices; Western Humanities Review; Whetstone; The Wormwood Review; Catalogue of Small Press Publications; Library Journal; Manas; Poetry Public, etc. Address: 3907 Winnemac Ave., Madison, WI 53711, USA.

POLLAK, Seweryn, var. pen names, b. 10 Jan. 1907. Critic; Poet; Poetry Translator. Education: M.A. in Polish Philol., Warsaw Univ. Positions held: Mbr., Editl. Bd., weekly 'Kuźnica', Lodz, Poland; Dept. Hd. of Russian Lit., weekly 'Nowa Kultura', Warsaw; Cons. for Poetry in Publishing House 'Czytelnik', Warsaw; Ed. in Chief, qtly. 'Opinia', Warsaw. Memberships: Pres. & V.P., Regl. Grp. in Lodz, Assn. of Polish Writers; Pres. & V.P., Club of Poets, Warsaw; Presidium, Polish PEN. Published works: An Hour of Life, 1946; Bullet & Word, 1952; Selder poems & translations, 1954; Net mesh, 1960; Permeation, 1965; Name of a Star, in print. Transl. & Ed., poetry transl. of: A. Puszkin, A. Blok, A. Achmatowej, B. Pasternak, M. Tsvetaevą, W. Majakowski, O. Mandelsztam, A. Bieły, etc. Contbr. to many lit. jrnls. Honours, awards: Award of the lit. mag. 'Okolica Poetów', 1937; State Prize – 3rd Class, 1955; Award of Polish PEN Club, 1967. Address: Iwicka 8a m.12, 00-735 Warsaw, Poland.

POLTTILA-TURTIAINEN, Brita Aleksandra Elinor, b. 27 Oct. 1920. Author. Education: M.A., Univ. of Helsinki, Finland. Married. Memberships: Finnish Soc. of Authors; Soc. of Writers & Artists KIILA; Assn. of Finnish Translators; Eino Leino Soc. Published works: Katson tästä, 1963; Tapahtumista, 1966; Surua seuraa ilo, 1971; Nazim Hikmet, 1972. Translations of Selected Poems of Bertolt Brecht, 1964. Contbr. to var. anthols. Address: Siilitie 1 K, 00800 Helsinki 80, Finland.

POMEROY, Marnie, b. 29 Mar. 1932. Editor of the Ladysmith Press. Education: A.B., Sarah Lawrence Coll., Bronxville, N.Y. Married Sean Haldane, 2 daughters. Published works: A Calendar for Dinah, 1966; Soft Jobs & Miracles, 1969; For Us Living, 1970; The Speck, 1972. Contbr. to: New World Writing No. 14; Int. Lit. Annual No. 2; Poetry Supplement – Poetry Book Soc., Christmas 1959; The London Mag., Nov. 1957; Antioch Review, Fall 1961. Address: The Ladysmith Press, Ladysmith, Quebec JOX 2AO, Canada.

POMEROY, Ralph, b. 12 Oct. 1926. Painter; Poet. Education: Art Inst., Chgo.; Univ. of Ill., Urbana; Univ. of Chgo. Positions held: Has worked as Magazine Ed.; Art Gallery Dir., Stage Manager, Bartender. Published works: Still and Movies, 1961; In the Financial District, 1968. Contbr. to (Anthols.): A Controversy of Poets, 1965; (Jrnls.): New Yorker; Paris Review; Quarterly Review of Literature; San Francisco Review; London Magazine; Times Literary Supplement. Recip., Yaddo Fellowship, 1955.

POPHAM, Hugh, b. 15 May 1920. Author. Education: Repton Schl., 1934-38; CCC Coll., Cambridge, 1938-40. Positions held: Fleet Air Arm Pilot, 1940-46. Memberships: Int. PEN; Soc. of Authors. Publications: Against the Lightning, 1944; The Journey & the Dream, 1945; To The Unborn Greetings, 1946. Honours, Awards: The Bodley Head Poetry Prize, John Lane, 1944. Address: Thatchways, Inlands Lane, Nutbourne, Chichester, Sussex, UK.

PORTER, Bernard Harden, pen name **PORTER, Bern,** b. 14 Feb. 1911. Poet. Education: B.S., Colby Coll., Waterville, Maine, 1932; Sc.M., Brown Univ., Providence, R.I., 1933; D.Sc., Inst. of Advance Thinking, Calais, Maine, 1959. Positions held: Founder, Director, Chairman of the Board, Emeritius, Bern Porter Books, Bern Porter, Inc., Inst. of Advanced Thinking. Memberships: Phi Beta Kappa, USA; Internat. Poetry Soc. UK. Published works: Doldrums, 1941; Waterfight, 1941; Aphasia, 1961; Day Notes For Mother, 1964; Native Alphabet, 1964; scda 19, 1969; The Wastemaker, 1972; Found Poems, 1972; 89 Offenses, 1972; Manhattan Telephone Book, 1973; The Very, Very Dead, 1973; The Books of Dos, 1973. Contbr. to: Kuam; Bezige Bij Nieuws; Circle, Berkeley; Edition Et; Leaves Fall; Quest; Encuentro; Fullwingspan; Rocket; Ego Ist; Kyeame; Elam; ICA Bulletin; Jazz News; El Corno Emplumado; Ed 912; Assembling, 0 to 9; Walton Press; Bern Porter Books; Broadside; Encentro Sao Paulo; Abyss; Wormwood Review; Poetry Southwest; Island. Awards: The Fenway Prize, 1959; Houghton-Lantern Award, 1964. Address: Box 209, Belfast, ME 04915, USA.

PORTER, Grace Ann, pen name **PORTER, Grace Kelly,** b. 21 Sept. 1904. Retired Secretary. Education: Tchrs. Coll., 2 yrs.; Commercial Coll., 1 yr. Married Ralph D. Porter, 1 daughter (Patricia). Positions held: Elem. Tchr., S.D., U.S.A., 4 yrs.; Legal Sec., 25 yrs. Memberships: Camellia Br. of Calif. Fed. of Chaparral Poets. Published works: Pamphlet entitled Rose Petals containing 27 poems in press; poem 'Angel Tears', 1973. Contbr. to: Dakota Farmer, Aberdeen, S.D.; Argus Leader, Sioux Falls, S.D. Recip. 1st prize for humorous poem, Camellia Br. of Calif. Fed. of Chaparral Poets, 1972 & 2nd prize for serious poetry, 1972. Address: 5884 Callister Ave., Sacramento, CA 95819, U.S.A.

PORTER, Hal, b. 16 Feb. 1911. Writer. Positions held: Schoolmaster, 1927-52; Librarian, 1952-61. Published works: The Hexagon, 1956; Elijah's Ravens, 1968; (Plays), The Tower, 1963; (Novels), A Handful of Pennies, 1958; The Tilted Cross, 1961; Other: Short Stories, 1942; A Bachelor's Children, 1962; The Cats of Venice, 1965; The Watcher on the Cast-Iron Balcony, 1963; The Paper Chase, 1966; Australian Stars of Stage and Screen, 1965; The Actors: An Image of the New Japan, 1968. Contbr. to (Anthols.): Australian Poetry, 1954-57; A Book of Australian Verse, 1956; Penguin Book of Australian Verse, 1958; Poetry in Australia II, 1964; Animal Anthology, 1968; (Jrnls.): The Age; Bulletin; Sydney Morning Herald. Hons: Commonwealth Literary Fund Fellowship, 1956, 60, 64, 68; Encyclopaedia Britannica Award, 1967. Address: Glen Avon, Garvoc, Victoria 3275, Australia.

PORTER, Hamish Sinclair, b. 14 July 1952. Solicitor. Education: The Leys Schl., Cambridge; Southampton Univ. Contbr. to: Hampshire Poets; Broadsheet; 'P'. Address: 73 Beaumont Rd., Cambridge, U.K.

PORTER, Jenny Lind, b. 3 Sept. 1927, Ft. Worth, Tex. Educator; Poet. Education: B.A., M.A., Tex. Christian Univ.; Ph.D., Univ. of Tex., 1955; further study, ibid. Positions held: Instr., Engl., Univ. of Tenn., 1958-59; Asst. Prof. of Engl., W Tex. State Univ., 1959-61; Asst. Prof., Southwest Tex. State Univ., 1961-64; Currently Hd. of Engl. Dept. Huston-Tillotson Coll., Austin. Memberships: Poetry Soc. of Am., 1954–; Poetry Soc. of Tex.; Hon., Poetry Soc. of Austin; United Poets Laureate Int.; World Poetry Soc. Published works: The Lantern of Diogenes, 1954; Azle & the Attic Room, 1957; The Witch Poesy, 1960; On the Trellis of Memory, A Psychic Journey into Pre-History (w. Elithe Hamilton Kirkland), 1971. Contbr. to: John Fitzgerald Kennedy, 1964; The Personalist; Prairie Schooner; The Classical Journal; The New York Times; Fiddlehead; Seventeen; The Ladies Home Journal; This is TCU; Wings; The Congressional Record; Texas in Color; PSA Golden Year Anthol., 1960; Surf, Stars & Stones, 1961; Laurel Leaves; Poetry Soc. of Texas Yearbook; The Articulate Woman; Folio. Honours & Awards: Poet Laureate of Tex., 1964, '65; One of ten Outstanding Women of Austin, 1964; One of ten Women of Achievement, Tex., AAUW, 1967; Gold Medal, Pres. Marcos of Philippines, 1970; Alice Fay di Castagnola Award, Poetry Soc. of Am., 1970; named to edit an issue of Poet by Dr. Srinivas of India. Address: 1713 Wethersfield Rd., Austin, Tex. 78703, USA.

PORTER, Peter, b. 16 Feb. 1929. Poet. Positions held: Newspaper Cadet Reporter; Wholesale Warehouseman; Clerk; Bookshop Asst.; Advtng. Copywriter, etc. Published works: Once Bitten Twice Bitten, 1961; Poems Ancient & Modern, 1964; A Porter Folio, 1969. Contbr. to: Mod. Australian Verse, 1964; Young Commonwealth Poets '65, 1965; New Poetry, 1966; Poetry, 1900-65; Penguin Book of Satirical Verse, 1967, & all major periodicals in UK. Address: 42 Cleveland Sq., London W2, U.K.

POST, Marie J. (Tuinstra), pen name **POST, Marie J.,** b. 8 Feb. 1919. Writer. Education: A.B., Calvin Coll., Grand Rapids, Mich., U.S.A. Married R. Jack Post. Positions held: Tchr.; Conference Director. Memberships: V.P., Bards; Pres., Pen Queens; Sec., Conf. Dir., Fine Arts Fellowship. Author, I Had Never Visited an Artist Before, 1973. Contbr. to: Banner; Chr. Home & Schl.; Chr. Educator's Jrnl.; Peninsula Poets; Hallmark; Ideals; For the Time Being; Glory Mag.; Haiku West; Grand Rapids Press (daily feature poem); Bardic Echoes; Church Herald; Christianity Today; Dyer Ives Voices. Has had 4,000 poems published. Honours, awards: Grand Rapids 1st Prize, 1967; Dyer Ives Hon. Mention, 1972; Dyer Ives 2nd pl., 1973. Address: 2105 E. Shiawassee Dr., S.E., Grand Rapids, MI 49506, U.S.A.

POTTS, Paul Hugh Patrick Howard, b. 17 July 1911. Book Reviewer. Published works: Instead of a Sonnet, 1944; Other: Dante Called You Beatrice, 1960; To Keep a Promise, 1969. Contbr. to (Anthols.): New

British Poets, 1949; Faber Book of Twentieth Century Verse, 1953; New Poems, 1965; Children of Albion, 1969; (Jrnls.): Arena. Address: 4 Cruickshank Street, Percy Circus, London, W.C.1, UK.

POULIN, Alfred Maurice, pen name **POULIN, A., Jr.,** b. 14 March 1938. Teacher. Education: B.A., St. Francis Coll., 1960; M.A., Loyola Univ., 1962; M.F.A., Univ. of Iowa, 1968. Positions held: Asst. Prof. of Engl., St. Francis Coll., 1962-64; Lecturer, Univ. of Maryland, European Div., 1965; Instr. in Engl., Univ. of New Hampshire, 1965-66; Asst. Prof. of Engl., Chairman, Div. of the Humanities, and Asst. to the Pres., St. Francis Coll., 1968-71; Director, The Writer's Forum, Planning Faculty, The Alternate Coll., and Assoc. Prof. of Engl., State Univ. of NY at Brockport, 1971 to present. Memberships: P.E.N.; Poetry Soc. of America; Rochester Poetry Soc. Published works: In Advent, 1972; The Widow's Taboo: Poems after the Catawba, 1974; Editor, Contemporary American Poetry, 1971. Contbr. to: Alcheringa; The Atlantic Monthly; American Poetry Review; Blackbird Circle; The Carleton Miscellany; Chicago Review; The Commonweal; College English; Crazy Horse; December; Esquire; Four Quarters; Journal of Popular Culture; Kayak; Kenyon Review; New American Review; New Directions; New Letters; North American Review; Poetry Northwest; Shenandoah; Stone Drum; Striver's Row; Voyages, etc. Recip. Fellowship, State Univ. of NY Research Foundation, 1972, 1973. Address: 92 Park Ave., Brockport, NY 14420, USA.

POULSEN, Ezra James, b. 26 Dec. 1889. Educator; Writer-Publisher. Education: B.A., Brigham Young Univ., 1917. Married Elsie Sullivan, 5 children (3 dec.) Positions held: served as traveling missionary in Va., Ch. of Jesus Christ of Latter-day Saints, 1910-12; Prin., Elem. & Jr. H.S., Garden City, Utah, 1917-19; Prin. Juab Latter-day Saints religious sem., 1919-22; Hd. of Engl. Dept., Nephi H.S., 1922-23; Hd. Engl. Dept., Granite H.S., Salt Lake City, 1924-43; on Editl. staff, Salt Lake Telegram, 1945-47; Assoc. Ed., Intermountain Horseman, 1948-49; estab. Granite Publishing Co., 1950. Memberships: Utah Acad. of Sci., Arts & Letters; Utah Poetry Soc.; Fellow, Int. Inst. of Arts & Letters. Published works: Songs for the Toilers, 1922; Poems in Various Moods, 1935; A Star Has Fallen, 1965; (prose) Versatile Pioneer, 1958; Robert Price, 1962 & others. Contbr. to var. mags. & anthols. Address: 587 First Ave., Salt Lake City, UT 84103, U.S.A.

POULTER, Scott Larry, b. 27 Oct. 1943. Freelance Writer; Student. Currently studying at The Univ. of Wis., Milwaukee. Divorced, 3 daughters. Positions held: Ed., Impact Mag.; Am. Ed., Tweed (Australia) Mag.; Co-Chmn., Speak Out Literary Assn.; Co-Chmn., IMPACT. Memberships: Poetry Soc. of Am.; The Haiku Soc. of Am.; The Acad. of Am. Poets; The Wis. Fellowship of Poets; The Wis. Regl. Writers Assn. Published works: The Glass Partition, 1972; In the Tall Grass, 1974; A Collection of Time, 1974. Rep. in following anthols: Postmortem; Outstanding Contemporary Poetry; Yearbook of Modern Poetry; Contemporary Am. Love Scene. Contbr. to: Epos; The Lyric; Poetry Venture; Tweed; Sunstone Review; Encore; Voices Int.; Haiku Mag.; Haiku West; Bitterroot, etc. Gives lectures, readings & recitals. Recip. var. honours & awards inclng: Winner, Coun. for Wis. Writers Award for the best book of poetry by a Wis. poet, 1973. Address: 1714 South 7th St., Milwaukee, WI 53204, U.S.A.

POUNDS, Kara Esther, pen name **POUNDS, Kara McFadden,** b. 11 July 1895. Writer of stories, poems, books. Memberships: Pres., Runnels Co. Poetry Soc.; V.P., Writers Club; var. positions in Beaumont Writers & Poetry Clubs; currently Councillor, Garland Chapt., Poetry Soc. of Tex.; Judge, Poetry Dept., Abilene Writers Guild, 1974, etc. Contbr. to: Abilene Reporter News; Oklahoma; Western Trails; Ark. Ranch Romances; Poet; Scimitar & Song; Note Book; Dallas Morning News; Progressive Farmer, etc. Recip. many poetry honours & awards inclng: 2nd hon. mention,

John Williams Andrews Stephen Vincent Benet Award, Poet Lore, 1970; Donald Roy Ditto, Metal Sculpture Prize, Odessa Poetry Soc., 1970. Address: 4118 Sweetbriar, Garland, TX 75042, U.S.A.

POWELL, Brian Sharples, b. 25 May 1934. Teacher; Lecturer; Writer; Traveller. Education: M.A., McGill Univ., Canada; Dip. Ed., Oxford Univ.; D.B.A., London Univ. Positions held: Asst. Headmaster, Lower Canada Coll., Montreal; Headmaster, Shaunigan Lake Schl., B.C.; Cons. in Engl., Protestant Schl. Bd. of Gtr. Montreal. Exec., Canadian Engl. Tchrs. Assn. International rep. for Canada of skiing, golf & cross-country running. Published works: English Through Poetry Writing, 1967; Making Poetry, 1973. Address: 38 Church Hill, Montreal 217, P.Q., Canada.

POWELL, Craig, b. 16 Nov. 1940. Psychiatrist. Education: Sydney Univ., 1964. Positions held: Med. Officer, Parramatta Psych. Ctre. Published works: I Learn By Going, 1968; A Different Kind of Breathing, 1966. Contbr. to: Poetry Australia; 20th Century; Meanjin; Quadrant; Southerly; New Impulses in Australian Poetry; Sydney Morning Herald; Encounter, London; Prairie Schooner; Best Poems of 1967; Spirit. Honours: Poetry Mag. Award, 1964; Henry Lawson Festival Prize for Verse, 1969. Address: c/o Parramatta Psych. Ctr., 5 Fleet St., Parramatta, Sydney, NSW, Australia 2150.

POWELL, Jane (Guard), b. 2 April 1912, in Jerome, Idaho, USA. Nurse. Education: Rupert HS. Married, 1 s., 1 d. Memberships: Colorado Poetry Soc. (on Hospitality Committee); Midwest Chaparral Poets; Gem State Writers Guild. Contbr. to: Haiku Highlights, 1966, 1967, 1968, 1969, 1970; The Guild (Idaho), 1967, 1968, 1969, 1970; Midwest Chaparral, 1967, 1968, 1969; Poets Bulletin; Golden Harvest Anthology (Colo. Poetry Soc.), 1971; Am. Jrnl. of Nursing, A Nurses Prayer, Apr., 1967. Recip. 2nd Prize, Poetry Soc. of Colo., Haiku contest, Autumn 1970. Address: 41 Grove St., Denver, CO 80219, USA.

POWELL, John Enoch, b. 16 June 1912. Former Member of Parliament. Education: Trinity Coll., Cambridge Univ. Positions held: Fellow, Trinity Coll., Cambridge, 1934-38; Prof. of Greek, Sydney Univ., 1937-39; Financial Sec. to H.M. Treasury, 1957-58; Minister of Health, 1960-63. Published works: First Poems, 1936; Casting Off, 1938; Dancer's End, 1951; The Wedding Gift, 1951. Address: 33 S. Eaton Place, London, S.W.1. U.K.

POWELL, Pansye Hawkins, b. 7 July 1902. Retired Teacher. Education: A.B., Mo. Univ., U.S.A., 1926; A.M., ibid, 1942; grad. study at Univs. of Utah & Wyoming & Rutgers Univ. Divorced, 1 son. Positions held: Tchr., Mo. H.S's, 1921-25, Ill. H.S's, 1926-29, Salt Lake City H.S., 1942-60, Pa. H.S's, 1960-68. Memberships: Sec., Utah State Poetry Soc.; Pa. State Poetry Soc.; Am. Poetry League; Nat. League of Am. Pen Women; Treas., Salt Lake City Br., ibid; Utah League of Writers. Published works: Deep Roots, 1968. Contbr. to num. jrnls. inclng: Portland Oregonian; Denver Post; Washington Post; Mayflower Log; Phila. Bulletin; The Improvement Era; Wall St. Jrnl. Recip. 5 awards for poetry, 1973. Address: 919 South 1500 East St., Salt Lake City, UT 84105, U.S.A.

POWELL, Tinnie Byrd, b. 10 Mar. 1902. Homemaker; Retired Teacher. Education: N. Tex. State Tchrs. Coll., Denton, Tex., U.S.A. Married S. Ballard Powell, dec., 1 son (Young). Memberships: Poetry Soc. of Tex., 23 yrs.; Study Club (has held all offices). Published works: Kitchen Dreamer, 1951; Indian Summer, 1958. Honours, awards: 1st Prize, Fed. Club Dist., 1941. Address: 814 5E 1st, Wilson, OK 73463, U.S.A.

PRAETORIUS, Cecilia W., b. 22 Sept. 1912. Secretary. Education: HS; 2 yr. Spanish; Corrs. course in Journalism. Twice married; 3 d., 1 s. Positions held: Sec. to Director, Div. of Nursing, Charity Hospital of La. at New Orleans; Pres., Gentilly Terrace Chapter 990, American Assoc. of Retired Persons; Sec., Hazel

Place Social Club. Memberships: Nat. Platform Assoc.; Nat. Poetry Soc. Published work: Fantasy and Emotion, 1972. Contbr. to: Internat. Who's Who in Poetry Anthol., 1972; Poetry Pageant; Poetry Parade; Gato Mag.; Western Girl Mag. Awarded Desk Calendar (Poetry Pageant, 1969 – The Tryst). Address: 9029 Camille Dr., New Orleans, LA 70123, USA.

PRANCHU, Joseph Kalarickal, pen name **JAYADEVA,** b. 5 Mar. 1930. Civil Servant; Accountant. Education: B.Sc., Univ. of Kerala, India. Married, 1 son, 1 daughter. Memberships: Fndr. Sec., New Writers Grp., New Delhi, India, 1958-60; Fndr. Mbr., Youth Cultural Grp., New Delhi, 1958-62; Poetry Soc., London. Published works: Notes on the Era & Other Poems, 1973. Contbr. to: Caravan, New Delhi; Labour World, New Delhi; Visala Keralam, Bombay; Poet, Madras; Kerala Kaumudhi, Trivandrum; Illustrated Weekly of India; Century, New Delhi. Address: Kalarickal House, P.O. Udayamperoor, Via, Tripunittura, Kerala State, India.

PRATT, Thursa A. Teacher of Cosmetology (retired), Licensed Cosmetologist. Education: Univ. of Cincinnati; Advanced studies in Cosmetology at Chicago, NY, Detroit; West Va. Wesleyan Coll. Mission Studies; Poetry Workshops, St. Petersburg, Fla. Married, Walter E. Pratt. Positions held: Member, W.Va. Bd. of Missions of United Methodist Church; Accredited Judge and Consulting Rosarian, American Rose Society; Sec., Colonial Dist. of A.R.S.; Nat. Council Flower Show Judge; Teacher, Moler System Coll., Cincinnati, Ohio; Teacher, Nat. School of Cosmeticians, Marinello System, Cin.; Owner and Teacher, Pratt School of Advanced Hairdressing. Memberships: Internat. Platform Assoc.; West Va. Poetry Soc. (Pres., since 1971); Nat. Fed. of State Poetry Socs.; Acad. of American Poets; World Poetry Soc.; American Poetry League; C.S.S.I.; Poetry Soc. of Texas; Louisiana State Poetry Soc.; Kentucky State Poetry Soc.; Parkersburg Women's Club (past Chm., Literature and Fine Arts). Contbr. to: Encore; Poets' Crossroads; American Poet; Prairie Poet; United Poets; Poet, Internat. Monthly; New Poetry; American Poetry League Anthol.; From Sea to Sea in Song Anthol.; Kentucky State Poetry Soc. Anthol.; Louisiana State Poetry Soc. Year Book; Gems From The Hills; Echoes of West Va. Poetry Soc. Anthol. Awards: W.Va. Fed. of Women's Clubs, 1968; Louisiana State Poetry Soc., 1st prize, 1969; Dowager Queen Award, 1st prizes, 1963, 1964, 1965. Address: 1625 Oak St., Parkersburg, WV 26101, USA.

PRATT, William Crouch, Jr., b. 5 Oct. 1927. Professor of English. Education: Tchng. Fellow, Engl., Vanderbilt Univ., 1952-53; Instr. of Engl., ibid, 1955-57; Instr. of Engl., Miami Univ., 1957-59; Asst. Prof. of Engl., ibid, 1959-64; Assoc. Prof. & Dir. of Freshman Engl., 1964-69; Prof. of Engl., 1968–. Advisor, Ohio Poetry Circuit, 1964–. Published works: The Imagist Poem: Modern Poetry in Miniature, 1963; The Fugitive Poets: Modern Southern Poetry in Perspective, 1965. Contbr. to: Transl., Ten Poems of Rainer Maria Rilke, Sewanee Review, 1966; Transl., Twelve Poems of Rainer Maria Rilke, Colo. Qtly., 1972; (article) Imagism: A Retrospect Sixty Years Later, in Words,' 1973; Images of the Ohio Valley (poems), in Words, 1973. Honours, awards: 'The Carousel' transl. from Rilke by Wm. Pratt, reprinted in High Schl. Lit. Textbook, 1969. Address: 212 Oakhill Dr., Oxford, OH 45056, U.S.A.

PREMONT, Henri, b. 8 July 1933. Business Executive. Positions held: Pres., First Int. Org. of Welcome, 1964-68. Memberships: PEN Club of Belgium; Association Royale des Ecrivains Wallons. Published works: Makes Known in French Unknown Writers From Latin America, such as Carlos Esteban, Veloz Maggiolo, Gonzalves Dias. Contbr. to: L'Avant-Scène (No. 339 & 444); Horizons du Fantastique (No. 23); 'B' Revue (No. 9). Recip., Prize of the Concours Culturel de Braine-l'Alleud, 1967. Address: 26 Ave. Léon Jourez, B1420 Braine-l'Alleud, Belgium.

PRESS, John Bryant, b. 11 Jan. 1920. British Council Officer. Education: Corpus Christi Coll., Cambridge Univ., 1938-40, '45-46. Married, 1 son, 1 daughter. Positions held: var. posts for British Council in Athens, Salonika, Madras, Cambridge, London, Paris. Fellow, Royal Soc. of Lit. Published works: Uncertainties, 1956; Guy Fawkes Night, 1959. Contbr. to: Times Lit. Supplement; Encounter; Vogue; Listener; Transatlantic Review; Southern Review; N Y Times; Sunday Times. Recip., Poetry Prize, Cheltenham Fest., 1959. Address: c/o British Coun. Personnel Records, 65 Davies St., London W1Y 2AA, U.K.

PRICE, E. Curmie, b. 17 Feb. 1940. University Lecturer. Education: B.A., Wilmington Coll.; M.A., Ohio Univ.; M.A. in Am. Studies, Yale Univ.; grad. work in Theol. & Lit., The Univ. of Chicago. Positions held: Instr. in Engl., Ohio Univ.; Asst. Prof. & Dir. of Afro-American Studies Prog. in the Coll. of Ethnic Studies, Western Wash. State Coll.; Lectr. in the Engl. Dept., Western Wash. State Coll.; Tchng. Fellow, Yale Univ. Published works: The State of the Union, 1970. Contbr. to: Black World; Concerning Poetry; The Jrnl. of Black Poetry; Earlham Review; The Malahat Review; Prism Int.; The Denver Qtly.; Jeopardy; The Far Point; Canadian Forum; Pembroke Mag.; Window; Pebble; Page, etc. Honours, awards: Kent Fellow, Danforth Fndn.; Farmington Fellow, Yale Univ. Address: 5841 Blackstone St., No. 3A, Chicago, IL, U.S.A.

PRICE, Frances Brown, b. 21 Feb. 1895. Teacher of English. Education: B.A., Oberlin Coll., Ohio, 1914-18; M.A., Ohio State Univ., 1949; Sorbonne Univ., Paris, France, 1927; Columbia Univ., N.Y.; Univ. of Wis. Positions held: Tchr., Maths & Sci., H.S. Connellsville, Pa.; Tchr., Engl. Lit., Composition & Jrnlsm., Steele H.S., Dayton, Ohio; Am. & Engl. Lit., Comp., Roosevelt H.S.; Chmn. of Counselling; Asst. Prin. Memberships incl: Poetry Socs. of Tex. & Ohio; Charlotte Emerson Lit. Soc., Franklin, Ind.; United Poets Laureate Int.; Avalon; Nat. League of Am. Pen Women, Inc.; V.P., Indpls. Chapt., ibid; Ind. State Fed. of Poetry Clubs; Treas., Columbus Poetry Club, Ind.; Nat. Poetry Coun.; Acad. of Am. Poets; World Poetry Soc. Published works: Blue Flame, 84 poems, 1967. Guest Ed., Poet, India, May 1972. Contbr. to num. mags., anthols. etc. inclng: The Oregonian; Poet Lore; Voices Int.; Bitterroot; Lyric; Prize Poems, Nat. Fed. State Poetry Socs., 1965, '66, '67; The Quiet Time, Dayton Poets' Round Table, 1965; Ind. Sesquicentennial Poets, 1967; Flame Annual; Am. Bard. Recip. var. hons. & awards inclng: Poet Laureate of Ind., 1966; Dist. Serv. Cit., World Poetry Soc., 1971. Address: 1070 W. Jefferson St., Franklin, IN 46131, U.S.A.

PRICE, Jonathan Reeve, b. 19 Oct. 1941. Poet. Education: B.A., Harvard Univ., 1963; D.F.A., Yale Univ., 1968. Positions held: Asst. Prof., Dept. of Engl., N.Y. Univ. 1968-70; Writer, N.Y., 1970–. Published works: Ice Cream Cone, 1968. Contbr. to: Fiddlehead; Twentieth Century; Yale Alumni Mag.; Harper's Mag.; Transatlantic Review. Exhibits of concrete poetry: Dartmouth Coll., 1969; Jewish Mus., 1970; N.Y. Univ., 1970; Cooper Union, 1970; Avant Garde Festivals, 1972, '73; Alphabet in the Spectrum of the Rainbow (1 man show), West Broadway Gallery, 1974. Address: Newell Farm, Main St., West Newbury, MA, U.S.A.

PRICE, Ken, pen name, **RHYS, Elwy,** b. 24 July 1924. Poet. Education: Correspondence Course, English Literature, Ruskin Coll., Oxford; Lytham Coll. of Further Education; Burton Coll. (W.E.A.). Positions held: Decorator, Baker, Fair Ground Boxer, Clerk, Student Teacher, Holiday Camp Foreman, Bank Messenger, Foundry Worker, Postman, Kitchen Porter, Warehouseman, Lift Attendant, College Cleaner, Freelance Writer. Memberships: Preston New Left Lit. Soc. (former Pres.); Apocalyptic Lit. Soc., and Poetry Soc. (UK.) (former member). Currently member: Internat. Poetry Soc.; The Poetry Vigilantes; Preston Poetry Workshop. Published works: Anachronisms, 1968; Taken from Time 1968; Stolen from Time, 1969; Poems (broadsheet), 1967;

Not Major Yet – But, 1967. Contbr. to: Headlands; Poetry Workshop; Writers World; Blackburnian; Glass Onion; Firebird; Phoenix; Viewpoints; Breakthru; Writers Journal; Quill; Poetry Advertiser; Controversy; Planet; Poetry Vigilantes; Viewpoint Anthol., 1968; Success Anthol., 1973. Address: 29 Parker St., Preston, Lancs. PR2 2AH, UK.

PRICE, Lucie, pen name **LOCKE, Lucie,** b. 22 Feb. 1904. Housewife; Artist; Poet. Positions held: Taught art to individual pupils, & in classes during WWII. Memberships: Centro Studi e Scambi Int.; Nat. Fed. of State Poetry Socs.; The Poetry Soc. of Tex.; Writers Workshop (Corpus Christi & vicinity). Published works: Naturally Yours, Texas, 1949; Seize the Ring, 1973. Contbr. to: Navy News; Discovery; Flame; Cyclotron; Cyclo-flame; You in Corpus Christi; Quaderni di Poesi, Rome, 1968, 72; The Mitre Press Anthol., 1967; To Tell of Tex., 1952 (anthol.); This Friendly Shore, 1955 (anthol.); To Each His Song, Sing Loud for Loveliness, With No Secret Meaning, This Shall Endure, (Avalon Anthols.) Recip. var. awards. Address: 401 Southern St., Corpus Christi, TX 78404, U.S.A.

PRIGOGINE, Hélène, b. 31 Dec. 1921. Critic. Married to architect, Robert Courtois. Published works: Sang Lointain, Aux nouveaux Horizons, Paris, 1953; Ici commence un autre temps, Seghers, Paris, 1968; Ponts suspendus, G.L.M., Paris (avec eau-forte en couleurs de J. Miro), 1965. Regular contbr. of critical articles to Syntheses-Bruxelles & poems to Journal des poetes, Bruxelles, 1973. Address: Ave. A. Huysmans 179, B–1050, Brussels, Belgium.

PRIMUS, Jane Davis, b. 31 May 1924. Homemaker Service Administrator. Education: B.S., Iowa State Univ. Positions held: Home Economics Tchr.; Home Economist, Field Extension, Iowa State Univ.; Homemaker Service Administrator. Memberships: Iowa Poetry Assn.; Iowa Poetry Day Assn. Published works: Through The Window, 1973. Contbr. to: Voices Int.; Lyrical Iowa; Iowa Poetry Day Brochure; Hardin Co. Index, Eldora, Iowa; Marshalltown Times Republican; PEO Record; Osage Weekly; IWWP. Recip. 1st pl., Iowa Poetry Assn. (Lyrical Iowa), 1963 & 3rd pl., 1971. Address: Steamboat Rock, IA 50672, U.S.A.

PRINCE, Frank Templeton, b. 13 Sept. 1912. University Teacher. Education: Christian Brothers Coll., Kimberley, S. Africa; Balliol Coll., Oxford Univ., U.K.; Princeton Univ., U.S.A. Married Pauline Elizabeth Rush, 2 daughters. Positions held: Asst. Sec., Study Groups Dept., Chatham House, 1937-40; Army Intelligence, 1941-46; Lectr. in Engl., Univ. Coll., Southampton, 1946-57; Prof. of Engl., Univ. of Southampton, 1957–; Vis. Fellow, All Souls Coll., Oxford Univ., 1968-69; Clark Lectr., Univ. of Cambridge, 1972-73. Published works: Poems, 1938; Soldiers Bathing, 1953; The Doors of Stone, 1964; Memoirs in Oxford, 1970; Penguin Modern Poets 20, 1972. Contbr. to: The Criterion; The Listener; Daylight & New Writing; The Observer; Poetry Review. Address: 32 Brookvale Rd., Southampton SO2 1QR, U.K.

PRINS, Sonja, b. 14 Aug. 1912. Poet. Educated in Holland, U.S.A., Canada, U.K. & Switzerland. Positions held: Staff Sec. in a publsng. house; Sec. in a lawyer's office; Editl. Sec. of the monthly 'De Nieuwe Stem'. Memberships: Vereniging van Letterkundigen, Vakbond van Schrijvers; Maatschappij der Nederlandse Letterkunde. Published works: Proeve in Strategie (Experiment in Strategy), under ps. Wanda Koopman, 1933; Brood en Rozen (Bread & Roses), 1953; Het geschonden aangezicht (Face of the Earth), 1955; Nieuwe proeve in Strategie (New Experiment in Strategy), 1957; Het boek van de Cineast (A narrative and descriptive poem), 1965; Notities (Notes), 1973. Fndr., Dir. & Ed., w. others, of tri-lingual lit. qtly. 'Front'. Contbr. to var. lit. jrnls. Address: Eikenlaan 6, Baarle – Nassau (NB), Netherlands.

PRIYAMBADA, Sujata (formerly Miss Panigrahi), b. 12 June 1940. Writer; Social Worker. Memberships: United Poets Laureate Int.; Cultural Sec., Poets' India; Dir., Poets' Home. Published works: Pratham Kavita (Oriya); Urvasi (Gujarati); Urvasi (- Oriya); Urvasi (Assamese); Hiroshimar Kavya (Assamese); Pagoda Deshar Kavya (Assamese). Contbr. to num. jrnls. & mags. in the following langs: Asamiya; Bengali; Gujarati; Hindi; Ho (Adivasi); Kannad; Kashmiri; Konkani; Malayalam; Marathi; Oriya; Punjabi; Sindhi; Tamil; Telugu; Urdu; Bahasa Indonesia; Ceylonese; Chinese; English; French; German; Italian; Korean; Nepalese; Portuguese; Slovak; Swedish; Tibetan; Vietnamese. Honours, awards: Greatness & Leadership Award, Nat. Comm. of the U.N. Day, Philippines, 1970; Dip. of Merit, Comm. on Arts & Culture, 1971 Constitutional Conven., Rep. of Philippines, 1973. Address: Pallee Nivas, P.O. Raruan, 757035 Dist. Mayurbhanj, Orissa, India.

PROCTOR, Dorothea Hardy. Housewife; Painter; Sculptor; Poet. Education: Univ. of Tulsa, museums & Master teachers. Positions held: Publicity, Writer's Club on Campus, Tuesday Writers; Public Relations, Nat. Lit. Conventions & Poetry Mag. etc. Memberships: Poetry Soc. of Oklahoma; Oklahoma Fedn. & Nat. Fedn. of Tuesday Writers; South & West, Inc.; Poet Laureate Int.; World Congress of Poets, etc. Published works: Listening for Absolutes, 1968; Poems/Sculpture; The Delight Of Being. Contbr. to many mags. and journals, etc. Honours: Best Book Award for The Delight of Being, Nat. Conven.; Hon. Doct., Andorra. Address: 1542 E. 34 St., Tulsa, OK 74105, USA.

PROKOSCH, Frederic, b. 17 May 1908. Author. Education: Ph.D., Yale Univ., New Haven, Conn., 1933; M.A., King's Coll., Cambridge. Positions Held: Instructor in Engl., Yale Univ., 1932-34; Vis. Lectr., Univ. of Rome, 1950-51; Cultural Attaché, American Legation, Stockholm, 1943-45. Published works: The Assassins, 1936; The Carnival, 1938; Death at Sea, 1940; Chosen Poems, 1944; Trans., Some Poems of Hölderlin, 1943; Love Sonnets of Louise Labé, 1947; Novels incl: Night of the Poor, 1939; The Skies of Europe, 1942; Age of Thunder, 1945; The Idols of the Cave, 1946; A Tale for Midnight, 1955; The Seven Sisters, 1963; The Wreck of the Cassandra, 1966.

PROUR, Octave, b. 24 Aug. 1918. Physician. Education: M.D.; Docteur en sciences économiques; Docteur en sciences juridiques; Licencié en philosophie; Licencié en chimie. Memberships: PEN Club of France; Syndicat des Journalistes et Ecrivains; Union Mondiale des Ecrivains-Medécins. Published works: (poetry) Poémes pour la silence de la nuit, 1941; Un mot à dire, 1969; Autre destin, 1970; Vie inédite, 1971; Le quatrième cycle, 1973; La découverte de l'homme, 1973; (essays) Retour à la poésie (2 vol. art & poetry), 1973; La description de l'homme (2 vol. art & poetry), 1973; La Cité Florissante, 1973; La voie moyenne, 1973; (anthols.) L'Univers de la poésie, 1968-73; Florilège sur un thème éternel, 1971; Thèmes préférés de poètes, 1973; Méridiens Poétiques, 1974; Dictionnaire de poétes francophones, 1974. Dir., review 'Prométhée' (lit. mag.). Contbr. to var. jrnls. Honours, awards: Grand Prix de Poésie de la ville Ouistreham Riva-Bella, 1968; Premier Prix de poésie du Golfe du Morbihan, 1967; Prix la Libellule d'or, 1968; Médaille de bronze de la Haute Acad. Int. de Lutèce à Paris, & Belgium, 1968. Address: 2 rue Juliette Dodu, 75010, Paris, France.

PROUTY, Morton Dennison, Jr., b. 18 Mar. 1918. Company Executive. Education: B.S., Univ. of Ill., 1939; grad. work, Northwestern Univ., 1947. Positions held: Audit Staff, Arthur Andersen & Co., Chicago, 1939-41, '45-49; Asst. Treas., Alabama-Tennessee Natural Gas Co. (gas pipelines), Florence, Ala., 1949-50; Treas., Asst. Sec., ibid, 1950-54; Sec., 1954–; V.P., 1961–. Memberships: Treas., Ala. State Poetry Soc., 1968-69 & '69-70; Pres., ibid, 1972-73 & '73-74.

Published works: Sparks On The Wind, 1961; Footsteps On The Mountain, 1969. Contbr. to: Good Housekeeping; Friends Jrnl.; Church Mgmt.; The Churchman; Scimitar & Song; The War Cry; Florence Times; Presbyterian Survey; The Sampler. Address: 921 Olive St., Florence, AL 35630, U.S.A.

PRULLANSKY, Raquel Jodorowsky, pen name **JODOROWSKY, Raquel,** b. 9 June 1927. Chile. Poet. Education: Music & Archaeol. Positions held: Specialist in old books; Libn. Published works: Extravio, 1945; Aposento y Epoca, 1952; Dimensión de los Dias, 1949, '52; La ciudad Incle mente, 1954; En la pared de los sueños alguien llama, 1955; En sentido inverso, 1962; Togen, 1964; Alniko y Kemita, 1965. Contbr. to the following newspapers; El Tiempo, Bogotá, Colombia; Excelsior, Mexico; El Mercurio de Santiago de Chile; Open Letter, Canada; Mele, Univ. of Hawaii; Mundus Artium, Ohio Univ.; Warning Water, Berkeley; La Nueva Sangre, NY; Imagenes, Caracas, Venezuela; Zone Franca, ibid; The Plumed Horn, Mexico; Cormorán y Delfin, Buenos Aires. Address: Almirante Guisse 2367 (Lince), Lima, Peru.

PRYNNE, J.H., b. 24 June 1936. Published works: Force of Circumstance and Other Poems, 1962; Kitchen Poems, 1968; Day Light Songs, 1968; Aristeas, 1968; The White Stones, 1969; Fire Lizard, 1970; Brass, 1971; Into The Day, 1972; A Night Square, 1973.

PUCKETT, Claire Medlin, b. 5 Feb. 1897. Educator. Education: B.A., Sul Ross Univ., Alpine, Tex.; M.A., Tex. Arts & Inds., Univ., Kingsville, Tex. Widow of Hal Henslee Puckett, M.D., 2 sons. Positions held: Speech Tchr. in Wolfe City & Henderson H.S's in Tex.; Elem. Schl. Tchr. in Celeste, Alice, Rosenberg & other Tex. towns. Memberships: Former Counsellor in the Poetry Soc. of Tex.; former Mbr. of Border Poets, Kingsville, Tex.; Houston Chapt., Poetry Soc. of Tex.; Former Mbr., Delta Kappa Gamma. Rep. in following anthols: The Silver Spur, 1942; Cenizo Spray, 1947; Yucca Trail, 1951; Cactus Tongues, 1955; This Friendly Shore, 1955. Contbr. to: The Delta Kappa Gamma Bulletin; Southwest Review, Southern Meth. Univ. Lit. Mag.; Sul Ross Univ., The Sage, lit. mag.; Boulder & Flints, Writers Workshop, Denver Univ.; Year Book Poetry Soc. of Tex.; Dallas News; Kaleidograph, Mag. of Poetry. Address: 1611 Houston St., Rosenberg, TX 77471, U.S.A.

PUDNEY, John, b. 19 Jan. 1909. Writer. Positions held: Producer, Writer, Staff of BBC, 1934-37; Corres., News Chronicle, 1937-41; Served in RAF, 1941-45; Book Critic, Daily Express, 1947-48; Literary Ed., News Review, 1948-50; Dir., Putnams, Publrs., 1953-63. Published Works incl: (verse) Ten Summers, 1944; Selected Poems, 1945; Sixpenny Songs, 1953; Spandrels, 1969; Take This Orange, 1971; Selected Poems 1967-1973; (novels) Jacobson's Ladder, 1938; Estuary, 1947; Shuffley Wanderers, 1949; The Accomplice, 1950; Hero of a Summer's Day, 1951; The Net, 1952; A Ring for Luck, 1953; Trespass in the Sun, 1957; Thin Air, 1961; The Long Time Growing Up, 1971; (non-fiction) The Green Grass Grew All Round, 1942; Who Only England Know, 1943; World Still There, 1945; Six Great Aviators, 1955; Home and Away (autobiographical), 1960; A Pride of Unicorns, 1960; The Golden Age of Steam, 1966; Suez, De Lesseps' Canal, 1968; Crossing London's River, 1972; Brunel and His World, 1974. (film scripts) Blue Peter, 1955; Mission of Fear, 1966; The Little Giant, musical play, 1972. Contbr. to: Ambit; 20th Century; Transatlantic; New Statesman; New Yorker. Address: 4 Macartney House, Chesterfield Walk, Greenwich Pk., London SE10 8HJ, U.K.

PUEBLA, Alvaro de, b. 12 Oct. 1931. Translator and Simultaneous Interpreter. Education: French Baccalaureat; Indl. Engrng. & Phys., Univ. of Buenos Aires. Positions held: Argentine Commercial Attache in the USSR, 1954; Freelance Interpreter, 1959-66; UN Official, 1967. Membership: Assoc. Internat. Poesie Vivante (Geneva); Société Genevoise des Ecrivains.

Published works: Amor de Hippie, 1970; A Don Juan Carlos, 1971; La Tortuga del Bósforo, 1972; Pochades 1972-73, 1973. Contbr. to: Poesie Vivante; Poesie Sonore; Boreal. Address: Case 47, 1212 Grand Lancy, Switzerland.

PUECHNER, Ray, pen names **HADDO, Oliver, VICTOR, Charles B. & TIGER, Jack,** b. 12 Aug. 1935. Literary Agent; Writer. Education; B.S. in Math & Hist., Marquette Univ. Positions held: Publisher, Milwaukee Lit. Times, 1961; Gen. Ed., Chicago Lit. Times, 1961-62; Gen. Ed., Literary Times, 1962-66. Memberships: Coun. for Wis. Writers; Sci. Fiction Writers of Am.; Wis. Regl. Writers Assn. Contbr. to: Wormwood Review; Kauri; The Gadfly; Spectroscope; Cardinal Poetry Qtly. Address: 2625 N. 36th St., Milwaukee, WI 53210, U.S.A.

PUMPHREY, Jean, b. 3 Dec. 1931. Writer; Teacher. Education: B.A., Denison Univ., Granville, Ohio; M.A. Engl. Lit., Calif. State Univ., San Francisco (formerly called San Francisco State Coll.). Positions held: Teacher, Crystal Springs School for Girls, Hillsborough, C.A.; Engl. Instr., Coll. of San Mateo, CA. Memberships: Internat. Poetry Soc. (Fellow); Member, Franco-Calliopean Soc. (a lit. hon. soc., Denison Univ.). Contbr. to: I.W.W.P., 1972-73; A Parade of Lines, 1971; ManRoot, 1971; Buttons, 1972; Coll. English, Feb., 1973. Honour: poem "San Miguel" (published), highly commended by IWWP, 1972. Address: Engl. Div., Coll. of San Mateo, San Mateo, CA 94402, USA.

PURDY, A(lfred) W(ellington), b. 30 Dec. 1918. Poet. Married w. 1 son. Positions held: num. jobs; Attended the Commonwealth Conf. of the Arts, Cardiff, 1965. Published works: The Enchanted Echo, 1944; Pressed on Sand, 1955; Emu, Remember!, 1957; The Crafte So Longe to Lerne, 1959; Poems for All the Annettes, 1962; The Blur in Between, 1963; The Cariboo Horses, 1965; North of Summer, 1967; Poems for All the Annettes, 1968; Wild Grape Wine, 1968; Criticism: Leonard Cohen (Canadian Literature), 1965; West of Summer: New Poets from the West Coast (Tamarack Review), 1967; Ed., The New Romans: Candid Canadian Opinions of the United States, 1968; Fifteen Winds, 1969. Contbr. to (Anthols.): Canadian Poetry in English, 1954; Poetry 62, 1961; Modern Canadian Verse, 1967; Penguin Book of Canadian Verse, 1967; Best Poems of 1968: The Borestone Mountain Poetry Awards, 1969; (Jrnls.): Canadian Poetry; Canadian Forum; Tamarack Review: Fiddlehead; Delta; Queen's Quarterly Hons: President's Medal, Univ. of Western Ont., 1964; Gov. Gen's. Award for Poetry, 1966; Canada Council Sr. Literary Fellowship, 1968-69. Address: Rural Route 1, Ameliasburgh, Ont., Canada.

PURDY, James, b. 17 July 1923. Writer. Published works: The Running Sun, 1971; Sunshine is an Only Child, 1973. Address: c/o Jonathan Cape, Ltd., 30 Bedford Sq., London, U.K.

PURI, Kailash, b. 17 Apr. 1926. Editor. Education: B.A., Punjab, India. Married, 1 son, 2 daughters. Ed., Roopvati Int. in English & Punjabi. Memberships: Merseyside Poetry Fest.; Crosby Writers' Assn. Published works: Bibni (Black Beauty), 1966; Lahuda Safar (Travels of a drop of Blood), 1970; Angiari (Burning Coal), 1973; Teesri Akh (Third Eye), 1974. Contbr. to: Arsi; Preet Lari; Subhagwati; Roopvati; Shere-e Punjabi Weekly; Sandesh Weekly; Panjab Times Weekly. Address: 36 Merrilock Rd., Blundellsands, Liverpool 23, U.K.

PURNELL, Kathryn Isobel, b. 14 Sept. 1911. Short story Writer; Lecturer. Education: Canadian public schls. & Melbourne Univ. Married, 2 daughters. Memberships: Australian Soc. of Authors; Int. PEN; Soc. of Women Writers; Fellowship of Australian Writers. Contbr. to: 20th Century; Expression; Education Mag.; Poetry Mag.; Tweed Qtly.; Spectrum; Two-Tone; Poets of Australia, 1972; PEN (Australia) Workshop '72. Honours, awards: Prize for Poetry, Soc. of Women Writers (Australia), 1972; Bunbury

Arts Fest. Award, 1973. Address: 30 Currajong Ave., Camberwell, Victoria 3124, Australia.

PURSLOW, Duncan John Marshall, b. 27 Feb. 1947. Teacher. Education: B.A. (Hons.), Univ. of Birmingham, 1971. Memberships: Poetry Soc. of London; Birmingham Poetry Soc.; Birmingham & Midland Inst. Published works: Pisces: Twenty Poems, 1971. Contbr. to: Outsider of Cambridge, 1972; Golden Eagle & Regency Anthols. Address: 19 St. Michael's Rd., Claverdon, Warwicks. CV35 8NT, U.K.

PY, Albert, b. 9 Apr. 1923. University Professor. Education: Lic., Univ. of Geneva; Dr. of Letters, ibid. Married, 4 children. Published works: La Nult sur la ville, 1956; Les Mythes grecs dans la poésie de Victor Hugo, 1963; L'Homme rouge et son ombre cheval, 1966; Illuminations de Rimbaud, 1967; De l'amour et du comportement lyrique chez André Breton, 1967; Ronsard, 1972; Pietà, 1973. Recip., Prix des écrivains genevois offert par la Ville de Genève, 1966. Address: Chemin de l'Ancien-Tir 6, CH 1252 Meinier, Geneva, Switzerland.

Q

QUASIMODO, Salvadore, b. 20 Aug. 1901. Poet. Education: Rome Polytechnic. Positions held: Asst. Ed., Tempo, 1938-40; Drama Critic, ibid; Prof. of Italian Lit., Giuseppe Verdi Conservatory, Milan, 1941–. Published works: Acque e terre, 1930; Oboe Sommerso, 1932; Odore di Eucalyptus ed altri versi, 1933; Erato e Apollion, 1936; Poesie, 1938; Ed è subito sera, 1942; Giorno dopo giorno, 1946; La vita non e sogno, 1949; Billy Budd (libretto), 1949; Il falso e vero verde, 1953; La terra impareggiabile (collected verse), 1958; Tutte le Poesie; Il Poeta e il politico e altri saggi; Dare e avere (Poems 1959-66), 1966. Translations of his work have appeared in Argentina, Australia, Belgium, Brazil, Czechoslovakia, France, Germany, Great Britain, Rumania, Spain, Sweden, USA, USSR, & Yugoslavia. Translations by Quasimodo: Romeo and Juliet; Othello; Richard III; The Tempest; Poesie scelte di E.E. Cummings; Edipo Re, Sophocles; Elettra, Sophocles; Le Coefore, Aeschylus; Carmina, Catullus; Il Tartufo, Molière; Il Diore della Antologia Palatina. Contbr. to: Solario; Circoli; L'Italia Letteraria; Il Frontespizio; Letteratura; Primato; Gazzetta del Popolo; etc. Awards: Nobel Prize for Lit., 1959.

QUENEAU, Raymond, b. 21 Feb. 1903. Poet; Writer. Education: Univ. of Paris. Positions held: Dir., Ed., Encyclopédie de la Pléiade, 1955–. Mbr., Académie Goncourt, 1951–. Published works: le Chiendent, 1933; Gueule de pierre, 1934; les Derniers Jours, 1936; Odile, 1937; Un rude hiver, 1939; les Temps mêlées, 1941; Pierrot mon ami, 1942; Loin de Rueil, 1945; Exercices de style, 1947; Saint-Glinglin, 1948; Petite cosmogonie portative, 1950; Bâton; Chiffres et Lettres; Si tu t'imagines, 1952; le Dimanche de la vie, 1952; Zazie dans le métro (filmed), 1960; Cent mille milliards de poèmes, 1961; les Oeuvres complètes de Sally Mara, 1962; Bords, 1963; le Chien à la mandoline, 1964; les Fleurs bleues, 1965; Une histoire modèle, 1966; Autobus S, 1966; Courir les rues, 1967; Battre la campagne; le Vol d'Icare, 1968. Filmscripts: Monsieur Ripois, 1953; la Mort en ce jardin, 1956; Un couple, 1960; le Dimanche de la vie, 1967. Address: c/o Gallimard, 5 rue Sebastien-Bottin, Paris, France.

QUENNELL, Peter, b. 9 Mar. 1905. University Professor. Education: Balliol Coll., Oxford. Positions held: Prof., Engl. Lang. & Lit., Tokyo Bunrika Daigaku, 1930-31; Ed., The Cornhill Mag., 1944-51; Ed., History Today, London, 1951–. Published works include: Poems, 1926; Inscription on a Fountain Head, 1929; Baudelaire & the Symbolists, 1929; The Phoenix-Kind, 1929; Aspects of Seventeenth Century Verse, 1933; Sympathy & Other Stories, 1933; Byron: The Years of Fame, 1935; Caroline of England, 1939; Byron in Italy, 1941; Four Portraits, 1945; John Ruskin: The Portrait of a Prophet, 1949; The Singular Preference, 1952;

Hogarth's Progress, 1955; The Sign of the Fish, 1960; Shakespeare: The Poet & His Background, 1963; Alexander Pope; The Education of Genius, 1688-1728, 1968; Ed., Mayhew's Characters, 1967. Address: c/o History Today, Bracken House, 10 Cannon St., London EC4, UK.

QUINN, Catherine Schroeder, pen names, **SCHROEDER, Catherine M.; MORELAND, Catherine S.,** b. 17 July 1932. Investor and Business Manager. Education: Acad. of the Holy Cross, Washington, DC.; Strayer Coll., Washington, DC.; Kinyon School of Business, New Bedford, Massachusetts. Married; 1 s., 1 d.; 2nd marriage, 1972. Positions held: Legal Sec., Washington, DC.; Sec. in Maryland State Senate; Aux. Volunteer, Nevada & NY Hospitals; Active in civic, church, and political affairs; Claims Rep. for Insurance Co.; Distributor of original oil paintings (owned Consolidated Arts of Poughkeepsie, NY); Notary Pub., Md., 1961-68. Memberships: Maryland State Poetry Soc. (Treas., 1966, 1967); The Key Key School (Member of Bd.); formerly, with the Annapolis Chorus (Charter member in Md.); Poughkeepsie Community Chorus, NY (3 years, singer with). Contbr. to: Nat. HS Anthol., 1951; Evening Capital Newspaper, etc. Address: Shaw Mansion Hill, Waterbury Center, VT 05677, USA.

QUINOT, Raymond, b. 12 Feb. 1920. Educator. Positions held: Dept. Hd., Pub. Instrn. Memberships: Fndr.-Sec., then Pres., Jeunesses litteraires de Belgique; Dir., Les Etoiles review; Admin., Assoc. des Ecrivains Belges; Admin., Biennales internat. de Poesie; Admin., Amicale des Ecrivains Combattants; Admin., Jrnl. des Poetes; Sec., Commn. Radio de la Sabam; PEN Club francaise de Belgique. Published works: L'Age d'Or, 1944; La IXe Croisade, 1945; La Lampe d'Aladin, 1948; Ciel Bleu, 1952; Les Aventures de Jaune et Jaunette, 1955; Blues, 1955; Manifeste de la Poesie du XXe Siecle, 1955; Chansons de Bruxelles, 1956; Le Fruit defendu, 1957; Enfants non Admis, 1957; Un agreable Passe-temps, 1958; Choisissez votre Planete, 1959; Le Fond de la Bouteille, 1962; Soleils, 1963; Made in USA; Le Diable dans le Benitier; Le petit Ange; Futur I; L'An 40 et l'An 60; Improvisation sur . . . Contbr. to: Jalons 48; Anthol. poetique de l'Exposition, 1958; Troisieme Decade; La Tour de Babel; Le Thyrse; La Quinzaine litteraire; Letras da Marginales; Le Jrnl. des Poets; Nos Lettres; Cahier Jean Tousseul; Le Cyclope; Revue generale Belge; Les Cahiers des Midis; La Peau de Serpent; L'Essai; La Nouvelle Gazette; Signor Si; Scarabee; Seydell Quarterly; Vlan; Le Soir; La Derniere Heure; (Italy) Un secolo di Poesia Belga; Cinzia; Il Giornale dei Poeti; (France) Prisme; La Revue neuve; Marches de France; Flammes Vives; Elan; (Canada) Le Courrier de Montmagny; Amerique francaise; (Brazil) Novo Mundo; Letras da Provincia; Stikhi Belgiiskikh Poetov (Russia); Revue Transjurane (Switzerland); L'Echo du Katanga (Congo); La Seve (Mauritius); Le Bayou (USA); L'Ile des Rats (Spain); Le Jrnl. de Tanger; Le Phare de Tunis et d'Alger; A vos de Sao Tome (Portugal); ALA (Argentina); SB Gazette (USA); Le Matin d'Haiti; Times of Cyprus, etc. Honours: Medaille d'or Arts, Sciences et Lettres, 1966; Merite Civique Francais, 1965; Prix Interfrance (poetry), 1955; Prix Interfrance (Poetry essay), 1963; Prix Davaine, l'Acad. Francaise, 1967; Prix Ernest Renan, 1967, & others. Address: Le Bel-Air, 76 ave. du Onze Novembre, Brussels 4, Belgium.

QUIST, Susan, b. 10 Sept. 1944. Education: Univ. of Pittsburgh; Univ. of Cincinnati. Positions held: Sunday Schl. Tchr.; Nursery Schl. Tchr.; Photographer; Film Maker; Secretary; etc. Published works: Indecent Exposure, 1974. Contbr. to: Oinkl; Pendulum; Speculum; Sojourner; 13th Moon. Recip., Poetry Prize, Univ. of Cinn., 1967. Address: Box 335, Cherry Valley, NY 13320, U.S.A.

R

RAAB, Lawrence, b. 8 May 1946. Teacher. Education: B.A., Middlebury Coll., 1968; M.A., Syracuse Univ., 1972. Married. Currently Jr. Fellow, Univ. of Mich. Soc. of Fellows. Published works: Mysteries of the Horizon, 1972. Contbr. to: Poetry; The Atlantic Monthly; The Am. Scholar; Shenandoah; Poetry Northwest; Denver Qtly.; Antioch Review; The N.Y. Qtly., Arion, Encounter; Kayak; Pebble; Southern Poetry Review; The New Orleans Review; Prairie Schooner; The Mag. of Fantasy & Science Fiction; Voyages; The Quest; Poetry Miscellany; The Berkshire Anthol.; Best Poems of 1969. Honours, awards: Book-of-the-Month Club Creative Writing Grant & Fulbright Grant, 1968; Cornelia Carhart Ward Fellowship, Syracuse, 1972; Acad. of Am. Poets Award, 1972; Nat. Endowment for the Arts Creative Writing Grant, 1972. Address: 39 Ann Dr., Pittsfield, MA 01201, U.S.A.

RABORG, Jr., Frederick Ashton, pen name **KERN, Canyon,** b. 10 Apr. 1934, Richmond, Virginia, USA. Writer and Journalist. Education: B.A. in Engl., Calif. State Coll., Bakersfield, with grad. studies in lit. criticism and children's lit. Married to Eileen Mary; 6 children. Positions held: Drama reviewer, The Bakersfield Californian; book reviewer and columnist, The Bakersfield News-Bulletin; editor for Pantry, a lit. monthly (now defunct); liaison editor, The Oildale News; Instr., Bakersfield Coll.; Sergeant Major, US Army, 1953-55. Memberships: World Poetry Soc.; Poetry Soc. of Tex.; Int. Platform Assn.; Poetry Soc. of America; Authors Guild, Inc.; Authors League of America, Inc.; Kentucky State Poetry Soc.; Kern County Writers Group (organised, but group since disbanded). Published works: Why Should the Devil Have All the Good Tunes?, 1972; The Other Side of the Island, a poetic play, produced by the Bakersfield Theatre Guild, 1973, and Kern County Drama Festival, 1973; 2 vols. of poetry in progress: Any Wail the Wind Decides Is Right; Faces on the Arena Floor. Contbr. to: Best in Poetry; Cyclo-Flame; Driftwood East; Patterns; The Statesman; The Poet's Guild; Quoin; The Archer; Bakersfield Californian; BC Arts; Cardinal Poetry Qtly.; Christian Living; Gospel Carrier; Grit; North American Voice of Fatima; Oildale News; Our Navy; Personal Poetry Broadcasts; Valley Views; Westways; Writers Notes & Quotes. Awards: 1st Prize, Class Internat. Intercollegiate Writing Competition, 1969-70. Military Awards: Cert. of Achievement, 25th Inf. Div. Korea; American Spirit Honor Medal from Citizens Committee for the Army, Navy and Air Force; 1st Prize, Guideposts Mag. Writers Workshop, 1973. Address: P.O. Box 2385, Bakersfield, CA 93303, USA.

RAFAT, Taufiq, b. 25 Oct. 1927. Factory Manager. Education: Muslim Univ., Aligarh. Married w. 5 children. Positions held: Bank Trainee, 1951; Minor Official, Oil Co., 1953-56; Insurance Salesman, 1957-60; Manager, Family-owned Sports Goods Factory, Sialkot, 1961-. Contbr. to (Anthols.): Span, 1958; First Voices, 1965; Young Commonwealth Poets '65, 1965; Commonwealth Poems of Today, 1967; New Voices of the Commonwealth, 1968; (Jrnls.): Vision; Eastern Horizon; Prairie Schooner; Beloit Poetry Jrnl.; Antioch Review. Address: c/o Hazir & Co., Kutchery Rd., Sialkot, West Pakistan.

RAGHAVAN, Srinath, b. 28 Nov. 1955. Student. Education: currently studying for B.A. in Engl. Lit. Member, World Poetry Soc. Intercontinental. Published works: A Book of Verses – 'Torch Bearers', in print. Contbr. to: Poet & other int. jrnls. Represented 'Vidya Mandir' in sev. comps. & received awards. Address: 2/B Cathedral Rd., Madras 600086, India.

RAHIKAINEN, Kalevi Ferdinand, b. 3 Apr. 1927. Author. Married Pirkko Kokko, 2 children. Positions held: Sailor; Painter; Editor; Critic, etc. Memberships: Author & Artists Group, Kiila ry; The Finnish Writers' Union. Published works: Hyvää huomenta, 1958; Kuin maa, 1958; Aurinko on vielä nuori (novel), 1962; Vaiti minussa, 1962; Kaikki se (novel), 1966; Paikka maassa, 1969; Asiakirja, 1970; Pois päin, 1972; Ekalogia, 1973; Minä, Urho ja Mao (novel), 1973. Contbr. to Parnasso; Tilanne; Aikalainen. Rep. in following anthols: Kiila 30, 1966; Poezija finljandija (Moscow), 1962. Address: Postipuuntie 5, 02600 Leppävaara, Finland.

RAHMANI, Nosrat, b. 1933. Poet; Writer. Education: Grad., Lit., Tehran Univ. Positions held: Literary Columnist, Tehran mago.; Poot; Novelist. Address: c/o Press Attache, Imperial Iranian Embassy, 16 Princes Gate, London S.W.7, U.K.

RAINE, Kathleen (Jessie), b. 14 June 1908. Poet. Education: Girton Coll., Cambridge. Published works: Stone and Flower, 1943; Living in Time, 1946; The Pythoness, 1949; The Year One, 1952; Selected Poems, 1952; Collected Poems, 1956; William Blake and Traditional Mythology (Andrew Mellon Lectures, 1962), 1963; The Hollow Hill & Other Poems, 1960-64; Six Dreams & Other Poems, 1968; Ninfa Revisited, 1968; Penguin Modern Poets, 1970. Address: c/o Hamish Hamilton Ltd., 90 Great Russell St., London WC1, UK.

RAINER, Dachine, b. 13 Jan. 1921. Poet; Writer. Education: B.A., M.A., Hunter Coll., N.Y. Widow w. 1 daughter. Positions held: Formerly Ed., Retort Mag., The Wasp, Bearsville, N.Y. (now defunct). Published works: Outside Time, 1947; Other: The Uncomfortable Inn, 1961; Ed. w. Holley Cantine, Prison Etiquette, 1950. Contbr. to (Anthols.): New Directions 13, 1951; New Poems by American Poets, 1953; Faber Book of Modern American Verse, 1956; (Jrnls.): American Scholar; Commentary; Nation; Liberation; New World Writing; Saturday Review of Literature; Quarterly Review of Literature; Paris Review; Poetry London-New York. Hons: Woodstock Foundation Grant for Poetry, 1957. Address: Dwelly, Edenbridge, Kent, UK.

RAJAB, Diyauddin, b. 1916. Lawyer. Education: Higher Certificate from The Prophet's Mosque, Al-Medina. Positions held: Judge in Medina; a Legal Counselor to the Municipality of Al-Medina & to the Dept. of Religious Endowments; Mbr., Advisory Council of Mecca. Published works: var. publs. in Law, Belles Lettres & Social History. Contbr. to the publs. in the Western Province of Saudi Arabia. Address: King Abdulaziz St., Diyauddin Rajab, Legal Cons., Al-Ahli Bank Bldg., No. 2, 9th Floor, Jidda, Saudi Arabia.

RAJAN, Tilottama, b. 1 Feb. 1951. Academic. Education: B.A., Trinity Coll., Univ. of Toronto, 1972; M.A., Univ. of Toronto, 1973; currently doing work towards Ph.D., Univ. of Toronto. Published works: Myth In A Metal Mirror, 1967. Contbr. to: Outposts; Manifold; English; New Voices of the Commonwealth; Workshop; Writers Workshop (Calcutta); Hindustan Times Mag. (Delhi); Mahjil (Chicago); Arion (Univ. of Tex.); Modern Indian Poetry in English. Address: 478 Regent St., London 24, Ont., Canada N54 4H4

RAJANI, Mom Chao (Prince) Chand. Pen names: **CHAND, TAN/EMCEE/SRI,** and **PRAMUANMARK, P. na,** b. 21 Jul. 1910. Retired Civil Servant, Writer, Poet. Education in UK: Dulwich Coll.; Gonville & Caius Coll., Cambridge; M.A. (Cantab.); Hon. Ph.D., Free Univ. of Asia, Karachi, Pakistan. Positions held: Govt. Serv, Min. of Finance, Bangkok, Siam. Memberships: Poet Laureate of the Orient, World Poetry Soc.; Hon. Poet Laureate, U.P.L.I. Author of numerous poems, especially in the Thai Kloang stanza form, which he also used in English. Addresses: Chiengmai Univ., or 17 Hasdisevi Rd., Chiengmai, Thailand.

RAJIVA, Stanley Frederick, Pseudonym, **F.R. Stanley,** b. 3 Mar. 1932. Professor of English. Education: B.A., Hons., Engl., Madras Christian Coll., Tambaram, India; M.A., ibid., 1952; M.A., Engl., Univ. of Wisconsin, Madison, 1964; Ph.D., Engl., ibid., (Danforth Fellow), 1967. Married w. 1 daughter. Positions held: Formerly, Mbr., Engl. Fac., Wisconsin State Univ., Whitewater; Mbr., Engl. Fac., Madras Christian Coll., 1958–; Currently, Prof. of Engl., ibid. Married w. 1 daughter.

Published works: The Permanent Element, 1968; Criticism: The Artist as Pornographer (literary Half-yearly), 1963; The Empathetic Vision (Literary Half-Yearly), 1968; The Singular Person (Literary Criterion), 1968; Ed. w. others, India Today, 1967. Contbr. to (Anthols.): Modern Indo-Anglian Poetry, 1960; (Jrnls.): Illustrated Weekly of India; Quest; Thought; Miscellany; Literary Half-Yearly. Address: Dept. of Engl., Madras Christian Coll., Tambaram, Madras-59, India.

RAKOSI, Carl, Pseudonym for **Callman Rawley,** b. 6 Nov. 1903. Psychotherapist in Private Practice. Education: Univ. of Wisconsin, Madison; Univ. of Pa., Phila.; Univ. of Chgo.; Univ. of Texas, Austin (degrees in Engl., Psychol., social work). Married Leah Jaffe w. 1 son, 1 daughter. Positions held: Exec. Dir., Jewish Family & Children's Service, Minn., 1945-68; Private Practice of Psychotherapy, Minn., 1955–. Published works: Selected Poems, 1941; Two Poems, 1942; Amulet, 1967. Contbr. to (Anthols.): American Caravan, 1927; An "Objectivists" Anthology, 1932; Modern Things, 1934; American Literary Anthology 3, 1970; Inside Outer Space, 1970; (Jrnls.): Paris Review; Nation: Caterpillar; Chelsea; Massachusetts Review; Quarterly Review; Sumac. Address: 4451 Colifax Avenue South, Minneapolis, Minnesota 55409, USA.

RALL, Fran, b. 8 Apr. 1974. Homemaker. Education: Ore. State Univ., 2½ yrs. Married, 2 children. Positions held: Ldr. in Great Books Prog. for Children, 3 yrs.; work in Int. Wives, a group to help students' wives from other countries adjust to the U.S.A., 7 yrs. Memberships: Wis. Fellowship of Poets, Wis.; Nat. Fed. of State Poetry Socs. Contbr. to Oxford Review, U.K. Address: 135 N. Prospect, Madison, WI 53705, U.S.A.

RALSTON, Sonia Murray Scott, pen name **RALSTON, S. Scott,** b. 17 Dec. 1921. Freelance Writer; Housewife. Married Edward Ralston, 3 sons. Contbr. to: West Chester Daily Local News; The Episcopalian Mag.; Philadelphia Bulletin; Modern Woman; Delaware Poets. Address: Chadds Ford, PA, U.S.A.

RAMANUJAN, A.K., b. 16 Mar. 1929. University Teacher. Education: B.A. Hons. & M.A., Univ. of Mysore, India, 1949-50; Ph.D., Linguistics, Ind. Univ., USA, 1963. Positions held: Lectr., Engl., SN Coll., Quilon, Thiagarajar Coll., Madurai, Lingaraj Coll., Belgaum, & MS Univ., Baroda, India, 1950-58; Asst. Prof., Univ. of Chicago, USA, 1962; Assoc. Prof., ibid, 1966; Prof. of Dravidian Studies & Ling., 1968–. Published works: The Striders, 1966; Fifteen Tamil Poems, 1965; The Interior Landscape, 1967; No Lotus in the Navel, 1969. Contbr. to: Quest; Thought; Illustrated Weekly of India; Atlantic Monthly; Poetry (Chicago); Poetry (India); Poetry NW; Best Poems of 1961; Young Commonwealth Poets; New Voices of the Commonwealth. Honours: Poetry Soc. Recommendation for The Striders, 1966; Tamil Writers Assoc. Gold Medal for The Interior Landscape, 1969. Address: Foster Hall, Univ. of Chicago. 1130 E 59th St., Chicago 60637, Ill., USA.

RAMEL, May Leone, b. 16 Apr. 1895. Housewife. Education: A.B., Trinity Univ., San Antonio, Tex., 1912; grad. work, Southern Meth. Univ., Dallas, 1923; Grad. Schl., Columbia Univ., N.Y.C., 1941-42 (under Mark Van Doran); var. writers' confs. in U.S.A. Married. Positions held: Former Tchr. of Latin. Memberships: Literary Societies, Ratio Maonion; Poetry Soc. of Am.; Poetry Soc. of Tex.; var. offices inclng. Pres., Poetry Soc. of Dallas & Houston, Tex.; Pres. of var. Lit. Clubs in Dallas & Houston; DAR. Published works: Dawn Wind. Contbr. to: Dallas News; Houston Chronicle; Southern Lit. Messenger, etc. Honours, awards: Tex. Poetry Soc. Critics' Award, 1945; var. awards from Houston Pen Women & Dallas Pen Women; Good Housekeeping Award at Gunnison Univ. in Colo. Address: Judson Park, 23600 Marine View Dr. South, Seattle, WA 98188, U.S.A.

RAMIREZ, Francisco M., pen name, **ZERI, F.** Mar. b.

23 Jan. 1896. Teacher & Lecturer. Education: HS., 1909-1913; Grad. with hons. as class poet, Philippine Normal School, Manila, 1913-1916; at various Univs., U.P., Journalism and Education, P.L.S.(Law) (2 gold medals), N.U. (elem. education); Isabela Colleges (Grad. School), M.A. Personal details: 1st marriage; 1 s., 4 d. (2 dec'd); 2nd marriage; 5 s. Positions held: Government Service, 1916-20; City Schools in Manila, 1920-27; Provincial Government Service, Isabela, 1927-45; Guerilla Capt. during Japanese Occupation, 1943-45; Teacher, in Isabela Colls., 1947-51; Bd. Member, Isabela, 1951-54; Dept. of Justice, 1954-55; Provincial Investigator & District Census Supervisor, 1955-62; Dean of Men and Principal, Isabela Colls., 1962-72. Memberships: Philippine Deleg., World Congress of Poets, Manila, 1969; Literary Soc. headed by the late Salazar, 1916 (formerly), and, in 1922, member of soc. founded by Fernando Maramag, Editor. Contbr. of articles, poems, and stories to: The Tribune; The Herald; The Independent. Also translated into English the Spanish History of the Philippines by Teodora Kalaw. Address: Cauayan, Isabela, Philippines.

RAMIREZ de ARELLANO, Olga, b. 17 Aug. 1910. Writer & Poet. Education: Goucher Coll., Balt.; Univ. of Puerto Rico, 1936. Memberships: Pres., Mu Iota Alpha; Puerto Rican Athenaeum; Puerto Rican Soc. of Writers; Soc. of Puerto Rican Authors; Puerto Rican Athenaeum of NY; Poetry Workshop, Univ. of Puerto Rico. Published works: Cauce Hondo, 1947; Rosal Fecundo, 1962; Tierra Diafanidad, 1962; Te Entrego, Amor, 1962; A La Lux Flamboyan, 1962; Mar de Poesia, 1963; Dos Veces Retoño, 1965; Orbe, 1966; Cada Ola, 1966; Eschucha Mi Alma, 1966; Diario de Montana, 1967; En Mis Ojos Verás, 1968; Cundaamor, 1969; Traigo un Ramillete, 1971. Contbr. to: Institute of Culture Mag.; El Mundo; Atenea; Alma Latina; El Dis; Ala; Horizontes; Isla Literaria; Arts & Science Acad. Bulletin; La Torre; Escuela; Angela Luisa; Bohemia; El Imparcial; Daily Egyptian. Honours & Awards: Hon. mention, Puerto Rican Athenaeum, 1963; 1st Prize, Civic Club, 1964; Dip., Spanish Am. Poets of NY, 1965; 1st Prize, Athenaeum & Civic Club, 1967; 1st Puerto Rican Award, 1968. Address: Box 820, Mayaguez, Puerto Rico.

RAMSEY, Jarold, b. 1 Sept. 1937. College Teacher. Education: B.A., Univ. of Ore., 1959; Ph.D., Univ. of Wash., 1966. Married Dorothy Quinn, 1 son, 2 daughters. Positions held: Instr. in Engl., Univ. of Wash., 1963-65; Instr. in Engl., Univ. of Rochester, 1965-66; Asst. Prof. of Engl., ibid, 1966-71; Assoc. Prof. of Engl., 1971–. Published works: Love in an Earthquake, 1973; The Space Between Us, 1970; Coyote Was Going There, 1975; The Lodge of Shadows (cantata, in collaboration w. Samuel Adler, composer), 1974. Contbr. to: Atlantic; The Nation; Poetry Northwest; Shenandoah; Qtly. Review of Lit.; Northwest Review; West Coast Review; Open Spaces; Crazy Horse; Lillabulero; Coll. English; Prairie Schooner; New Orleans Review; Fiddlehead; Poet & Critic; Ohio Review, etc. Honours, awards: Prize Poem, Poet & Critic, 1967; 'Love in an Earthquake' chosen for Borestone Mt. Prize Volume, Best Poems of 1972, nominated for Nat. Book Award, 1973 & awarded the Lillian Fairchild Prize, 1973. Address: c/o Engl. Dept., Univ. of Rochester, Rochester, NY 14627, U.S.A.

RAMSEY, Paul, b. 26 Nov. 1924. Poet; Teacher. Education: B.A., Univ. of Chattanooga; M.A., Univ. of N.C.; Ph.D., Univ. of Minn., 1956. Married Bets Ramsey, 4 children. Positions held: Univ. of Ala., Elmira Coll., Raymond Coll.; Univ. of the South, Univ. of Chattanooga (became Univ. of Tenn., Chattanooga). Memberships: Dir., Tenn. Poetry Circuit; Judge, Poetry Soc. of Am.; Acad. of Am. Poets; The Milton Soc. Published works: Triptych (w. others), 1964; In An Ordinary Place, 1965; A Window for New York, 1968; The Doors, 1968; (criticism) The Lively & the Just, 1962; The Art of John Dryden, 1969. Over 200 poems in num. periodicals & anthols. inclng: America; The Anglo-Welsh Review; Factotom; Four

Quarters; Hudson Review; Poetry; Quarterly Review of Literature; Southern Poetry Review; Transatlantic Review; Yankee; Southern Writing in the Sixties; Poetry Brief. Honours, awards: 1st Prize for Poetry, Rochester Fest. of Religious Arts, 1966; 1st Prize, for The Naming of Adam, Beaudoin Gem Stone Awards, 1967; Roberts Meml. Prize for Lyric, 1972. Address: Poet-in-Res., Univ. of Tenn., Chattanooga, TN 37401, U.S.A.

RANAIVO, Flavien, b. 13 May 1914. Director of Information & Broadcasting. Education: Tananarive, Madagascar & Paris, France. Positions held: Official, Post & Telecommunication Service, Madagascar; w. info. office, 35 yrs.; currently Dir., Info., Radio & TV. Published works: L'ombre et le vent, 1947; Mes Chansons de toujours, 1955; Retour au bercail, 1963. Contbr. to Revue de Madagascar. Awards: Grand Prix Lit., Madagascar, 1955; Grand Prix Lit., Akbaraly, 1965; Carlier Monceau Award, 1969. Address: Directeur de l'Information et de la Radio Télévision, Tananarive, Madagascar.

RANDALL, Dudley (Felker), b. 14 Jan. 1914. Librarian. Education: B.A., Wayne Univ., 1949; M.A.L.S., Univ. of Mich., 1951. Married Vivian Spencer, 1957. Positions held: Libn., Lincoln Univ., Mo., 1951-54; Libn., Morgan State Coll., 1954-56; Lib., Wayne Co. Lib., 1956-69; Libn., Univ. of Detroit, 1969–; Poet in Res., ibid, 1969–. Published works: Poem Counterpoem, 1966; For Malcolm (Ed.), 1967; Cities Burning, 1968; Black Poetry (Ed.), 1969; Love You, 1970; More To Remember, 1971; The Black Poets, 1971; After the Killing, 1973. Contbr. to: Midwest Jrnl.; Black World; Peninsula Poets; Essence. Recip., Tompkins Award, 1962 & 66. Address: 12651 Old Mill Pl., Detroit, MI 48238, U.S.A.

RANDALL, Julia (Mrs Julia Sawyer), b. 15 June 1923. Associate Professor of English. Education: A.B., Bennington Coll., Vt., 1945; M.A., Johns Hopkins Univ., Baltimore, 1950. Positions held: Asst. Prof., Hollins Coll., Va.; Assoc. Prof., Engl., ibid., 1966–. Published works: The Solstice Tree, 1952; Mimic August, 1960; The Puritan Carpenter, 1965; Adam's Dream, 1969. Contbr. to (Anthols.): Poesia Americana del Dopoguerra, 1958; Hollins Poets, 1967; Poetry Southeast, 1968; (Jrnls.): Sewanee Review; Tennessee Poetry Jrnl.; Southern Poetry Review; Hollins Critic. Hons: Sewanee Review Fellowship in Poetry, 1957-58; National Foundation on the Arts & Humanities Grant, 1966-67; Nat. Inst. of Arts & Letters Grant, 1968-69. Address: Hollins Coll., VA 24020, USA.

RANDALL, Margaret, b. 6 Dec. 1936. Writer. Education: Univ. of N.M., Albuquerque, 1 yr. Positions held: Sec.; Tchr.; Translator; currently working as a Writer for the Social Scis. Publishing House of the Cuban Book Inst. Published works: (poetry) Giant of Tears, 1959; Ecstasy is a Number, 1961; Small Sounds from the Bass Fiddle, 1964; Songs of the Glass, 1964; October, 1965; 25 Stages of my Spine, 1967; Water I Slip into at Night, 1968; Part of the Solution, 1973; (essays) The Hippies: Sigh of Crisis, 1968; The Women, 1970; Cuban Women Now, 1972; Women in the Rev., 1973; (transl. & essay) This Great People has said 'Enough and has Begun to Move', 1973. Contbr. to var. jrnls., mags. Judge for Poetry Category, Casa de las Americas lit. contest, 1970. Delegate to the Cultural Congress in Havana, 1968. Address: Apartado Postal 13-546, Mexico 13, D.F., Mexico.

RANDRIAMAROZAKA, b. 5 Feb. 1919. Journalist; Critic; Poet. Education: Bachelier ès Lettres, law studies towards licence, Univ. of Tananarive; Dip., Int. Inst. of Journalism, Berlin. Married, 5 children. Positions held: Jrnlst., Min. of Info., 1964–; Dir., Bulletin de Madagascar, 1965–; Chroniqueur d'Arts de la Revue de Madagascar, 1965-72; Chef de la Division Internationale à la Direction de la Press, 1973. Memberships incl: Union of Poets & Writers in Madagascar; Hon. Mbr., Centro Studi e Scambi Int., Rome; Assn. of French lang. Writers, Paris, etc.

Published works: A Toute Volée, 1972; Des Poèmes; (essays) Les Proverbes des Ancêtres, 1973; Quelques centres d'intéret dans Bina, 1973; Un roman pas comme les autres, 1973, etc. Contbr. to var. reviews, jrnls. Honours, awards: Prix Fredy Rajaofera, 1969; Chevalier de l'Ordre National; Chevalier du Mérite de Madagascar. Address: Division Internationale (Direction de la Presse du Ministere de l'Information), Tananarive, Malagasy Republic.

RANGACHARI, Asoori Vilangadu, b. 7 Dec. 1921. Teacher. Education: B.A., Madras Univ., 1940; B.Tchng., ibid, 1949. Married V. Sengamalam, 1 son, 3 daughters. Delegate to All India Poets Meet, World Poetry Soc., Madras. Contbr. to Poet. Recip., Ripon Gold Medal for Proficiency in English, Madras Christian Coll., Tambaram, Madras, 1940. Address: 14 Muthukrishnan St., Kondithope, Madras 1, India.

RANIVILLE, Francis Oliver, b. 19 Oct. 1920. Businessman; Table Tennis Player; Hymnologist; Poet. Memberships: Bards of Grand Rapids; Former Treas. & Chap., 8 yrs.; Past Mbr., Brooklyn Lit. Soc.; N.Y. Poetry Forum, Inc.; Life Mbr., Hymn Soc. of Am. & London Poetry Soc.; Runner up, Sr. Men's Singles Consolation, U.S. Nat. Open Table Tennis, 1966; Centro Studi e Scambi, Rome, Italy. Contbr. to: Sonnet Sequences; Challenger; Bardic Echoes; Haiku West; Poetry Prevue; Haiku Highlights; New Angle Hour; Table Tennis Topics; Banner; 20th Century Hymns; Poet; Bouquet of Poems. Composer of hymns, Lord of All Nations & God's Loving Heart At Christmas. Honours, awards incl: U.N. Day Award of Hon. for Bible Hymns, United Poets Laureate, 1969; M. Relig. Lit., Karachi, Pakistan, 1969; Hymnol., m.c.l., World Poetry Award, 1969; Wm. Noble Haiku Award, Bardic Echoes, 1968; Book Award, Bardic Echoes & Poetry Prevue, 1970; 1st Prize, Brooklyn Lit. Soc., 1970; Bardic Echoes Cinquain Award, 1972; Guest of Hon., N.Y. Poetry Forum Spring Fest., 1973; Hon. Mention, Nat. Sylvia Argow Sonnet Award Contest, 1972; Hon. Dr. Lib. Arts, World Univ., Kowloon, Hong Kong, 1972; Hon. Dr. Var. Arts; Invited to 2nd World Congress of Poets, Taipei, Taiwan & also to the World Poetry Day, N.Y., 1973. Currently serving on Staff as Libn. to read Poetry, Kent Community Hosp. Address: P.O. Box 1524, Grand Rapids, MI 49501, U.S.A.

RANKIN, Jane (Mina Jane Rankin), b. 4 Apr. 1910. Poet. Education: Coe Coll.; B.A., Northern Iowa Univ.; Drake Univ.; Univ. of Calif. Married Russell Lowell Rankin. Positions held: Rdr., Dramatic Coach, Des Moines, Ia.; Tchr., Dramatics; Tchr., Engl. & Hist., Westlake Schl. for Girls, L.A.; Critic, Judge, Dramatic contests. Memberships: Acad. of Am. Poets; Calif. Fed. of Chaparral Poets; Pres., Santa Cruz Chapt., ibid; Fla. State Poetry Soc.; Pa. State Poetry Soc.; Ina Coolbrith Circle; Poets' Study Club of Terre Haute, Ind.; Friday Shakespeare Club; AAUW; Ams. of Royal Descent; DAR; Magna Charta Dames; State Histn., Soc. of Mayflower Descendents; Huguenot Soc.; DAC; Centro Studi e Scambi Int.; Acad. Int. Leonardo da Vinci; Ariz. Fed. Poetry Socs.; Fed. of Womens Clubs; Channel Cities Women's Forum. Published works: Shoshone Princess, histl. narrative. Contbr. to num. anthols., jrnls. mags. etc. inclng: Hall of Fame Poets; Sunburst Anthol.; Coolbrith Anthol.; Bouquets of Poems; IWWP Anthol.; Poet (India); Orphic Lute; Phoenix Fires; Nat. Anthol. of Am. Poetry; Selected Poems, Fla. State Poetry Soc., sev. yrs.; Top Poets of the Yr., 1968, '70; Inky Trails; Am. Bard. Recipe. num. hons. & awards inclng: 1st Prize, Utah State Award, Nat. Fed. State Poetry Socs., 1971; 1st Prize, Modern, W.Va. State Poetry Soc., 1972; Albo D'Oro Cert. of Merit, Accademia L. da Vinci, Rome. Address: 21 East Valerio, Santa Barbara, CA 93101, U.S.A.

RANSOM, John Crowe, b. 30 Apr. 1888. Poet; Writer. Education: Vanderbilt Univ.; Christ Church, Oxford; B.A. Positions held: Prof. of Engl., Vanderbilt Univ., 1927-37; Carnegie Prof. of Poetry, Kenyon Coll., 1937-58; Ed., Kenyon Review, 1931-32. Published works: Poems About God, 1919; Grace After Meat, 1924; Chills and Fever, 1924; Two Gentlemen In Bonds,

1927; God Without Thunder, 1930; World's Body, 1938; New Criticism, 1941; Poetics, 1942; Selected Poems, 1945; Selected Poems By John Crowe Ransom, 1963. Awards: Guggenheim Fellowship, 1931-32; Bollingen Award, 1951; Russell Loines Award, Nat. Acad. of Arts & Letters, 1951. Address: c/o Alfred A. Knopf, Inc., 501 Madison Ave., New York, NY 10022, USA.

RAPIN, Simone, b. 16 June 1901. Actress; Singer; Poet; Writer; Producer; Professor of Dramatic Art. Education: Baccalauréat ès lettres, & Maître ès sciences, Lausanne, Switzerland Théâtre Vieux-Colombier, Paris, France. Positions held: Actress, Theatre of Jouvet, Kommisarjevski, etc., Paris, France; Singer of title roles in classical opera, inclng: Armide, Alceste, Iphigénie; Lectr., H.S. & Alliances françaises, U.S.A., France, Switzerland; Producer of plays, pvte. schl. of dramatic art. Memberships: Ile des Poétes, Lyon, France; Fdr., Prix Simone Rapin de Théâtre Poétique; V.P., Geneva Arts Club, 1963–. Published works: Une Jeune Fille juive, 1955; L'Année de l'Amour, 1957; Le Ciel de l'Instant, 1957; Ce que Terre dit, 1959; Hommage á Ramuz, 1960; Mon Lac, 1962; Une Nuit dans Chillon, 1962, '65; (novel) L'Enfant victorieux, 1965; La Symphonie du Partir, 1957; Méditations Orientales en occident, 1969; Petits Albums de voyage; (plays) La Trève de Dieu; L'Oeil du Temps; L'Anneau jeté dans le Fleuve; La Journée a plus de 24 heures; La Pêche du Matin; Petite Galerie Marcel Proust, Cette France, & Mon Italie (all three received special prize of Acad. Berrichonue). Contbr. to: Masques et Visages; Art et Poésie; Cahiers Luxembourgeois; Poésie Vivante; Points et Contre Points; La Thyrse; L'Essai; Messager catholique Romand (as Protestant guest). Honours, awards: Prix Interfrance de Poésie classique, 1957; Prix International des Poètes de France, 1960; Prix Portugal, Society of journalists & writers of all Latin countries, 1964; Prix Paul Chevassus, Académie Rhodanienne des Lettres, 1965; Inclusion in Larousse Dict. of Poetry, 1968; Award, Inst. Acad. of Naples, 1973-74. Address: 16 Boulevard des Philosophes, 1205, Geneva, Switzerland.

RAPOPORT, Janis Beth, b. 22 June 1946. Publishing Consultant & Writer. Education: B.A., Philos., Univ. of Toronto, 1967. Married, 3 children. Positions held: Hostess at EXPO '67, Montreal, 1967; Editl. Asst., Which? Mag., U.K., 1968-69; Asst. Ed., Paul Hamlyn, U.K., 1969; Ed., Bellhaven House (Canadian Subsid. of H.E.B.), 1970-72; Publishing Cons. & Freelance Ed., 1972–; on Editl. Staff of Tamarack Review, 1970–. Memberships: League of Poets; Writers' Union of Canada; Exec. Mbr. responsible for organising courses, workshops & seminars relating to and for people employed in the publishing industry, Book Promotion & Editl. Club. Published works: Within the Whirling Moment, 1967; Foothills, 1973; Jeremy's Dream, 1974. Contbr. to: Canadian Forum; Quarry; Tamarack Review; Tabloid; Out of Sight; SF: Inventing the Future (anthol.); Process; The Far Point; Stuffed Crocodile. Address: 36 Tarbert Rd., Willowdale, Ont., Canada M2M 2Y2.

RASA, Risto Olavi, b. 29 Apr. 1954. Student. Education: currently studying librarianship at the Univ. of Tampere, Finland. Member, The Finnish Soc. of Authors. Published works: Metsän seinä on vain vihreä ovi, 1971; Kulkurivarpunen, 1973. Contbr. to Parnasso. Honours, awards: Otavan Kirjasäätiö, 1972; Etelä-Pohjanmaan Kulttuurirahasto, 1973. Address: Koulukatu 15 A 9, 65100 Vaasa 10, Finland.

RASHEED, Mohammad Hashim, b. 1928. Educational Supervisor. Education: Higher Certificate, Religious Institute, Medina. Positions held: many positions in the field of Education; currently Educl. Supvsr., Al-Medina Educl. Distr. Published works: "Wara' As-Sihaab" (a coll. of poetry). Contbr. to all Saudi Arabian dailies and weeklies. Recip., Tunisian Poetry Medal, Second Class. Address: c/o Al-Medina Educational District Office, Al-Medina, Saudi Arabia.

RATCLIFFE, Eric Hallam, b. 8 Aug. 1918. Information Scientist. Education: Birkbeck Coll., London Univ. Positions held: Expmtl. Off., Nat. Physical Lab., Teddington; Higher Sci. Off., Water Pollution Rsch. Lab., Stevenage. Memberships: Inst. of Info. Scientists; Royal Inst. of Pub. Hlth. & Hygiene; Assoc., Royal Soc. of Hlth.; Assoc., Inst. of Hlth. Educ.; Companion of Inst. of Sci. & Technical Communicators; Companion, Druid Order of G.B.; Fndr. Mbr., Teddington, Barnet, Stevenage & Whitton Poetry Socs.; Ed., Ore Mag. & Mgr., Ore Publs.; Ex Foreign Ed., Wis. Poetry Mag.; Fndr. Ed., Expression (One); Org., Youthful Voices Children's Poetry Comps., Teddington, 1962 & Stevenage, 1968. Published works: The Visitation, 1952; Little Pagan, 1955; The Ragnarok Rocket Bomb, 1957; Transitions, 1957; The Chronicle of the Green Man, 1960; Mist on My Eyes, 1961; Gleanings for a Daughter of Aeolus, 1968; Leo Poems, 1972; Warrior of the Icenian Queen, 1973. Contbr. to var. mags. & jrnls. inclng: Outposts; Envoi; Am. Bard; Fiddlehead; The Druid; New Poems 1960 (anthol.) Honours, awards: Braithwaite Award, U.S.A., 1959; Silver Medal, Richmond, Twickenham Fest., 1964; Civil Serv. Regl. Prize for Further Educ., 1971. Address: 7 The Towers, Stevenage, Herts. SG1 1HE, U.K.

RATNER, Rochelle, b. 2 Dec. 1948. Poet. Education: New Schl. for Soc. Rsch. Positions held: Book Review Ed., East Village Other, 1969-72; Co-Ed., Survivor's Manual (poetry mag.), 1971–. Mbr., Coordinating Coun. of Lit. Mags. Published works: False Trees, (book), 1973; A Birthday of Waters, (book), 1971; Variations on a Theme in Blue, 1971. Contbr. to: The Nation; The Minn. Review; Antaeus; Carleton Miscellany; Shenandoah; The N.Y. Quarterly; Sumac; Prism (Canada); Quickly Aging Here (anthol.); Loves, Etc. (anthol.); Ironwood; Epoch; Some Feminist Poets (anthol.); Lines Review (Scotland), etc. Address: 50 Spring St., Apt. 2, New York, NY 10012, U.S.A.

RATTRAY, David, b. 17 Feb. 1936. Poet; Writer & Editor. Education: B.A., Dartmouth Coll., 1957; Diplôme d'Etudes Supérieures des Langues Classiques (D.E.S.), Sorbonne, 1959; Harvard Univ., 1965. Married Lin Fisher, 1 daughter (Mary). Positions held: Solar Energy Supvsr., Int. Trade Fair, Saloniki, Greece, 1957; Reviewer of Am. books for Gallimard, Paris, 1966; Assoc. Ed., Am. Heritage Publishing Co., N.Y.C., 1966-71; Freelance Translator for int. patent attorneys, specializing in German & French patents, 1967–; Assoc. Ed., Reader's Digest Gen. Books, N.Y.C., editing a thesaurus, 1973–, etc. Member, Linguistic Soc. of Am. Published works: Artaud Anthology (poetic transl.), edited by Jack Hirschman, 1965. Currently writing a novel. Contbr. to: The Alhambra (Newsweek Books); Between Worlds; City Lights Jrnl.; Gnomon; Hip Pocket Poems; Horizon; Insect Trust Gazette; Intrepid; Meal; Nation. Has given many poetry readings at colls., churches & community ctrs. Narrations for two films: Nossa Terra by Mario Marret and A Nine O'clock Movie by Don Snyder. Honours, awards: Dartmouth Coll. Prize for Lit., 1957; Harvard Monthly Prize, 1959; Residence at Yaddo, 1960. Address: c/o Reader's Digest Gen. Books, 380 Madison Ave., N.Y., NY 10017, U.S.A.

RAUHALA, Niilo Pekka, b. 10 July 1936. Clergyman. Education: B.D., Helsinki Univ., 1963. Member, Finnish Soc. of Authors, 1970–. Published works: This Is Where Summer Ends, 1967; The River Is Flowing, Not Moving, 1969; I Listen To The Voice of My Heart, 1971; Between Snow and the Sun, 1973. Contbr. to: Parnasso; Kotimaa; Päivämies, & var. religious publs. Address: 94 200 Kemi 20, Karihaara, Finland.

RAUSCH, Marilyn L., b. 18 June 1947. Teacher. Education: Viterbo Coll., La Crosse, Wis., 2 yrs.; B.A., Univ. of Iowa; postgrad., ibid; studied under George Starbuck, Anselm Hollo, Robert Bell at Writing Workshop. Positions held: Tchr., Creative Writing, Prairie Coll. Community, Cedar Rapids, Iowa, 8 weeks; Tchr., Jr.-Sr. Lit. Courses, St. Mary's, Clinton, Iowa, 2 yrs.; Currently Hd. of Engl. Dept. & Speech-Debate

Coach, Mt. Pleasant, Iowa. Contbr. to: sev. issues of Touchstone, lit. quarterly, Viterbo Coll. & Poetry Anthology, 1961-65. Recip. var. awards from local groups. Address: 105 S. Jackson, Mount Pleasant, IA 52641, U.S.A.

RAVIKOVITCH, Dahlia, b. 17 Nov. 1936. Poet Education: Hebrew Univ., Jerusalem. Positions held: Teacher; Translator; Free-lance Journalist. Memberships: Hebrew Assoc. of Writers, Israel. Published works: Love of An Orange, 1959; Hard Winter, 1964; The Third Book, 1969. Contbr. to numerous jrnls. Honours: The Shlonsky Prize, 1965. Address: 4 Mordecai St., Tel-Ganim, Ramat-Gan, Israel.

RAWLEY, Callman, pen name **Rakosi, Carl,** b. 6 Nov. 1903. Psychotherapist & Social Worker. Education: B.A., Univ. of Wis.; M.A., ibid; M.S.W., Univ. of Pa. Married to Leah Rawley, 1 s., 1 d. Positions held: Lectr. in Poetry, Grad. Schl. of Educ., Univ. of Minn. Exec. Dir., Jewish Family & Children's Serv., Mpls. Published works include: Ere-Voice, 1971; Amulet, 1967; Selected Poems, 1940; Two Poems, 1933. Contbr. to the following anthols., jrnls., mags., etc: The Little Review; Hound & Horn; Ezra Pound's Exile; Transition; Poetry; Contemporary Lit., The Iowa Review; Grosseteste Review; Jrnl. of the Otto Rank Assn.; The Minn. Review; Chelsea; The Paris Review; The Nation; Quarterly Review; Sumac; The Mass. Review; Caterpillar; Stony Brook; Midstream; The Park; Pagany; Westminster Mag.; The Windsor Quarterly; Contact, etc. Honours, awards: Nat. Endowment tfor the Arts Award, 1970; Writer-in-Res.; Univ. of Wis., 1969-70. Address: 4451 S Copfax Ave., Minneapolis, Minn. 55409, USA.

RAWLINS, Winifred Kate, b. 20 Jan. 1907. Positions held: Public speaker for the peace movement; Hd. Res., Adult Center for study & contemplation; Dir., hostel for Jewish Refugees; currently Dir. of a home for the elderly. Published works: Winter Solstice, 1952; Before No High Altars, 1955; Fire Within, 1959; Russian Pictures, 1960; Dreaming is Now, 1963; The Small Land, 1966; Man is a Tender Plant, 1969. Contbr. to: Christian Sci. Monitor; Approach; Inward Light, Wash. D.C.; Friends Jrnl., Phila.; Christian Century, Chicago & many daily newspapers & other periodicals. Selected for 'Best Poems of 1964', Borestone Mountain Poetry Awards, Calif. All books & some manuscripts in the perm. coll. of Am. poetry, Temple Univ. Lib., Phila. Address: 505 Glenwood Ave., Moylan, PA 19065, U.S.A.

RAWLINSON, Gloria, b. 1 Oct. 1918. Poet. Published works: Gloria's Book, 1933; The Perfume Vendor, 1935; Poems, 1936; The Islands Where I Was Born, 1955; Of Clouds and Pebbles, 1963; Other: Ed., Jindyworobak Anthology, 1951; Houses by the Sea and Later Poems of Robin Hyde, 1952. Contbr. to (Anthols.): Australian and New Zealand Verse, 1950; Penguin Book of New Zealand Verse, 1960; Commonwealth Poems of Today, 1967; New Voices of the Commonwealth, 1968; (Jrnls.): Poetry Yearbook; New Zealand Listener; Arena. Address: 76 Market Road, Epsom, Auckland 3, New Zealand.

RAWORTH, Thomas Moore, b. 19 July 1938. Writer. Education: St. Joseph's Acad., Blackheath, London; M.A., Univ. of Essex. Married Valarie Murphy, 5 children. Positions held: Owner, Matrix Press, 1959-64; Jt.-Owner, Goliard Press, 1965-67; Res. Poet, Univ. of Essex, 1969-70; Fiction Instr., Bowling Green State Univ., Ohio, U.S.A., 1972-73; Poet-in-Res., N.E. Ill. Univ., Chicago, Ill., 1973-74. Member, PEN. Published works: The Relation Ship, 1966; Haiku, 1968; The Big Green Day, 1968; Lion Lion, 1970; Moving, 1971; Tracking, 1972; Pleasant Butter, 1972; Back to Nature, 1972; An Interesting Picture of Ohio, 1972; Here, 1972; From the Hungarian, 1972; Act, 1973; The Mask, 1974. Contbr. to over 100 mags., jrnls., etc. Honours, awards: The Alice Hunt Bartlett Prize, 1969/70; Cholmondeley Award, 1972. Address: c/o Raworth, 8 Avondale Rd., Welling, Kent, U.K.

RAY, David Eugene, b. 20 May 1932. Poet; Teacher; Editor. Education: B.A., Univ. of Chicago, 1952; M.A., ibid, 1957. Married, 4 children. Positions held: Instr. in Engl., Cornell Univ., 1960-64; Asst. Prof. in Humanities, Reed Coll., 1964-66; Lectr., Writers' Workshop, Univ. of Iowa, 1969-70; Vis. Prof., Bowling Green Univ., 1970-71; Assoc. Prof. & Ed. of New Letters, Univ. of Mo., Kansas City, 1971-. Editor: The Chicago Review Anthol 1959: From the Hungarian Revolution, 1966; Co-Ed., A Poetry Reading Against the Vietnam War, 1966 & Richard Wright: Impressions & Perspectives, 1973. Published works: X-Rays, 1965; Dragging The Main, 1968; A Hill in Oklahoma, 1972. Contbr. to: The Atlantic Monthly; Ambit; Black Swamp; New Am. Review; Poetry; Antioch Review; The Nation; Qtly. Review of Lit., & many others. Has lectured or read his poems at many colls. & univs. Recip., Woursell Fndn. Fellowship, Univ. of Vienna, 1966-70. Address: 5517 Crestwood Dr., Kansas City, MO 64110, U.S.A.

RAY, Pramod Ranjan, b. 30 June 1945. Teacher. Education: M.A. in Saskrit. Positions held: Rsch. Fellow, Ctr. of Adv. Study in Sanskrit, Univ. of Poona; Lectr. in Sanskrit, Nayagarh Coll.; Lectr. in Sanskrit, Utkal Univ., Bhubaneswar; Lectr. in Sanskrit, Govt. Evening Coll., Sambalpur. Memberships: Pres., Ekamra Sahitya Samsad (Bhubaneswar); Jt. Sec., All Orissa Sanskrit Conf. (Sambalpur); Jayadera Samskrit Parisad (Bhubaneswar); ASALC. Published works: The River's Song & Other Poems (in press). Contbr. to: Yatri; Swarajya; The Poet. Address: Govt. Evening Coll., Sambalpur, Orissa, India.

RAYAPROL, Marthandam Srinivas, b. 25 Oct. 1925. Government Employee. Education: Benares Hindu Univ.; B.A., Maths., M.S., Civil Eng., Stanford Univ., Calif. Married Rajeswari w. 3 daughters. Positions held: 17 yrs. as a Civil Eng., assoc. w. num. Hydroelectric & Building Projects in India; Currently, Employed by Gov. of Andhra Pradesh; Former Ed., East & West, Secunderabad. Published Verse: Bones and Distances, 1968. Contbr. to (Anthols.): Modern Telugu Poetry, 1956; Modern Indian Poetry, 1958; Modern Indo-Anglian Poetry, 1959; (Jrnls.): Illustrated Weekly of India; Writers Workshop; Miscellany; Poetry. Address: Anupama, 6-4-481/2 Krishnanagar, Secunderabad 3, Andhra Pradesh, India.

RAYBIN, Alexander Louis, b. 12 Dec. 1945. Poet. Contbr. to: 31 New American Poets, 1972; Hanging Loose; Great Society; San Francisco Earthquake; Beatitudes; Bitterroot Qtly. Address: 2709 Woolsey St., Berkeley, CA, U.S.A.

RAYNOR, Vera, b. 24 Nov. 1937. Poet; Dance Therapist. Education: Boston Conservatory of Dance, 1952-54; Univ. of Wis., Madison, 1960-63. Positions held: Dir., The Environmental Dance Grp.; Coordinator, Dance Happenings in the Parks; Fndr., Ed., Publisher & Printer of Patterns, a mag. of art & poetry; Dance Therapist, Troy Hills Nursing Home; Poet-in-Res., N.J. State Coun. on the Arts. Memberships: N.J. Poetry Soc.; Dance Therapy Assn.; Morris County Art Assn.; Am. Dance Guild. Contbr. to Patterns, a mag. of poetry & art. Address: 2 Whaleback Waddy, Denville, NJ 07834, U.S.A.

REANEY, James (Crerar), b. 1 Sept. 1926. Teacher. Education: Elmhurst Pub. School; Stratford Collegiate; Univ. of Toronto. Married; 2 children. Positions held: Teacher, English Dept., Univ. of Manitoba, 1949-60; English Dept., Univ. of Western Ontario, 1960-. Published works: Red Heart, 1949; Suit of Nettles, 1958; Killdeer & Other Plays, 1962; Dance of Death At London, Ontario, 1964; Masks of Childhood, 1972; Listen to the Wind, 1972; Colours in the Dark, 1970; Selected Poems, 1972; Alphabet, the iconography of the imagination (edited, 1960-70). Contbr. to: Northern Review; Canadian Forum; Contemporary Verse; Tamarack Review; Poetry (Chicago); Atlantic Monthly. Recip. Governor General's Award, 1962. Address: Engl. Dept., Univ. of Western Ontario, London, Ont., Canada.

REBANO, (Lt.-Col.) Luis, b. 19 June 1901. Public Health Nurse. Education: Newspaper Inst. Am.; Mil. & Aviation Engrng., Dayton Schl. of Aviation; Rockefeller Fndn. Fellow, Univ. of the Philippines. Married, 2 s. Positions held: USAFFE Cmdr., WWII; Ed., RPC, Am. Embassy, Philippines. Memberships: Poetry Lovers Soc., Philippines; Asst. Sec., United Poets Laureate Int. Author, One Way to Write Poetry. Contbr. to: World Poetry Soc. Intercontinental, 1969; Laurel Leaves, 1969; Anthol. of Universal Poetry, Brazil. Honours, Awards: Poet-Author Meritissimus & DLL; D. Ldrship. in Philos., World Inst. of Drs., 1971; Poet-Investor Meritissimus Int. Acad. of Ldrship. & Inst. of Pub. Opinion, 1967. Listed various ref. works. Address: 32 Gladiola St. Roxas Dist., Quezon City, Philippines.

REBER, Clara Belle Smith, pen name REBER, Clara Smith. Homemaker; Poet; Writer. Education: Knoxville Bus. Coll. Married John H. Reber. Positions held: Personnel & Engrng. Dept., Tenn. Valley Authority, 1933-44; Freelance Writer & Poet; Corres., Kingsport Times-News, 1966-73. Memberships: State Pres. for Tenn., Nat. League of Am. Pen Women, 1968-70; World Poetry Soc. Intercontinental; Tenn. Women's Press & Authors Assn.; Tenn. Poetry Soc.; Am. Poetry League, etc. Published works: Life's Musicale, 1941; Blue Haze, 1944; Tapestry of Time, 1968, 2nd issue, 1969; Contbr. to num. religious & home mags., Am. Poetry League bulletins & anthologies. Personal Poetry Column in Weekly newspaper in 1960's; Num. newspaper & poetry publs. Fed. Women's State & local progs. in Pa. & Tenn. Radio Progs: WPSI 'Poet'. Recip. var. poetry awards. Address: Rt. 6, Box 169, Church Hill, TN 37642, U.S.A.

REBERT, M. Charles, b. 10 May 1920. Teacher; Writer (Poet). Education: Western Md. Coll., Westminster; grad. work at York Coll. of Pa.; Penn State Univ.; Western Md. Coll.; Shippensburg Coll. Positions held: Statistical Economist, Atlantic Richfield Oil Co., Philadelphia, Pa., 1947-60; w. Littlestown H.S., Pa., 1960-. Memberships: Fellow, Int. Poetry Soc.; World Poetry Soc.; Pa. Poetry Soc.; Pa. Schl. Press; V.P., York-Adams Press Assn.; Pa. State Tchrs. Assn.; V.P., Littlestown Tchrs. Assn. Published works: (books) Shadow Prints, 1958; I Remember, 1964; Like Sudden Roses, 1967; Waiting for the Red Light, 1965; An Armistice of Flesh, 1967; The Glass Scene, 1973. Contbng. Ed., Time of Singing, Judson Coll. Contbr. to var. jrnls., mags., anthols., newspapers inlng: N.Y. Herald Tribune; Hartford Courant; Am. Bard; Descant; Golden Quill Anthol. Recip. var. hons. & awards inclng: Vagabond First Award, Germany, 1968; Cit. of Merit, Int. Poetry Soc., 1969; Medal of Hon., Centro Studi e Scambi Int., 1967. Address: 140 Meade Ave., Hanover, PA 17331, U.S.A.

RECCHIA, Kitty Parsons, pen name, PARSONS, Kitty. Writer & Artist. Education: Grad., Cathedral School of St. Mary, Garden City, NY; Special Study, Pratt Inst., NY; NY Acad. of Dramatic Art; Teachers' Coll., Columbia Univ.; Boston Univ.; Chicago Univ. Married to Richard Recchia, sculptor. Positions held: Chairman, State of Maine Writers' Conference, 1965-68; On board, Rockport Art Assoc., holding various positions, 1936-60; Literary Chairman, Boston Branch, NLAPW, 1965-67, Membership Chairman, 1968-70. Memberships: Boston Authors' Club; NLAPW; American Poetry League; Vermont League of Writers; Poetry Socs. of Penn., Virginia, Kentucky, and New Hampshire; League of Vermont Writers. Published works: Dogtown Common, 1936; Buccaneer Ballads, 1944; Gloucester Sea Ballads, 1946; As the Wind Blows, 1951; Ancestral Timber, 1957; Down to Earth, 1964; Up and Down and Roundabout, 1967; Your Husband or Mine, 1970. Contbr. to: Lyric; American Weave; CS Monitor; NY Times; Times (London); Parents' Mag.; Christian Herald; Boston Eve. Transcript; Boston Globe; Boston Herald; Washington Star; Saturday Eve. Post; Saturday Review; Wall St. Journal; Poetry Digest; Poet; American Poetry League Bulletin; NH Poetry Soc. Newsletter; Penn. Poetry Soc. Prize Poems;

Voices Internat.; Rotarian; Child Life; Wee Wisdom; Children's Playmate; The Villager; Glamour; Atlanta Times, and many anthols. Awards: numerous including: Cert. of Excellence, Poetry Book Contest, Tulsa, 1969; various NLAPW awards; 2nd Prize, Nat. Contest, Alabama, 1972; 2nd Prize, N. Carolina Poetry Soc., 1972; Hon. mentions, Kentucky Poetry Soc., 1972; other awards NH Poetry Soc., Poets Study Club, Terre Haute, Deep South Writers Conference, etc. Address: Box 27, Rockport, MA 01966, USA.

REDDY, V. Madhusudan, b. 20 June 1926. University Professor. Education: B.Sc. (Physics, Chemistry, Maths.); M.A. (Engl. Lit.); M.A. (1st Div. Philos.); Ph.D. Positions held: Fulbright Prof. of Philos., Monmouth Coll., Ill., U.S.A., 1969; Gen. Sec., Sri Aurobindo Darshan, a non-profit, cultural org. & Dir., Inst. of Human Study, a post-grad. rsch. & study ctr., Hyderabad, India; Prof. & Hd. of Dept. of Philos., Osmania Univ., Hyderabad. Published works: Sapphires of Solitude (poems), 1961; Towards Eternity, 1973; Sri Aurobindo's Philosophy of Evolution, 1966; Avatarhood & Human Evolution, 1972; Mankind on the March, 1972; Values & Value Theories, 1973, etc. Address: Dept. of Philos., Osmania Univ., Hyderabad 500007, India.

REDFEARN, Christopher Martin, b. 30 Nov. 1927. Unemployed; Ex-Pottery & Glassware Retailer. Education: Manchester Univ., U.K. Positions held: Clerical posts with Pastures Hospital, Mickleover & Derby Corp. Memberships: Fellow, Int. Poetry Soc.; Comm. Mbr., Derby Poetry Soc.; Exec. Comm. Mbr., Derby & Dist. Arts Assn. Address: Bromley House, 26 Becher St., Derby DE3 8NN, U.K.

REDGROVE, Peter, b. 1932. Poet; Writer. Education: Taunton Schl., Somerset, U.K.; Open & State Schlr., Queen's Coll., Cambridge Univ. Positions held: Fndr.-Ed., Lit. mag., Delta; Sci. Jrnlst. & Ed., 1954-61; Vis. Poet, Buffalo Univ., N.Y., U.S.A. (Fulbright Award), 1961; Gregory Fellow in Poetry, Leeds Univ., 1962-65; Freelance, 1965-66; Res. Poet, Falmouth Schl. of Art, Cornwall, 1966-; Prof. of Engl., Colgate Univ., N.Y., 1974-75. Published works: (poetry) The Collector & Other Poems, 1960; The Nature of Cold Weather & Other Poems, 1961; At The White Monument & Other Poems, 1963; The Force & Other Poems, 1966; The Sermon (a performance for TV), 1966; The God-Trap, 1966; The Old White Man, 1969; Work in Progress, 1969; The Mother, The Daughter & the Sighing Bridge, 1970; The Shirt, The Skull & the Grape, 1970; Love's Journeys: A Selection, 1971; The Bedside Clock, 1971; Dr. Faust's Sea-Spiral Spirit & Other Poems, 1972; Three Pieces for Voices, 1972; The Hermaphrodite Album (w. Penelope Shuttle), 1973; Selected Poems 1954-74, etc. (novels) In the Country of the Skin, 1972 & 73; In the Country of the Skin: the Radio Script, 1973; The Terrors of Dr. Treviles (w. Penelope Shuttle), 1974. Ed. of following anthols: Poets' Playground, 1963; Universities Poetry 7, 1965; New Poems, 1967: A PEN Anthol., 1967, etc. Has broadcast frequently for the BBC since 1956. Has also appeared & written for TV. Recip. var. honours & awards inclng. 3 major Arts Coun. Awards; Guardian Fiction Prize for poem-novel, 1973. Address: c/o Routledge & Kegan Paul Ltd., Broadway House, 68-74 Carter Ln., London EC4V 5EL, U.K.

REDKNAP, Ellen Edith Hannah, pen name COLLINS, Ellen E.H.,** b. 15 Apr. 1906. Retired Secretary. Positions held: Shorthand Typist, 1924-32; Shorthand Typist, Heston Airport, 1932-40; i/c Editl. Corres., Picture Post, then on staff, Lilliput, 1932-40. Memberships: Fndr. Mbr., Whitton Poetry Group (now New Richmond Poetry Grp.); Editl. Bd., Envoi Poetry Mag. Published works: Poems of Earth, Sea & Sky, 1959; More Poems of Earth, Sea & Sky, 1960; Impressions, 1961; Poems for all Seasons, 1961; Astrology & other Poems, 1961; The Flowers of Marathon, 1965; Strange Altars, 1973. Has also written books & short stories under var. pseudonyms about flying & space travel. Contbr. to: The Poetry Review; Envoi; New Poet; Scrip; Manifold; Druid; Ore;

Homes & Gardens; Expression One; Candelabrum; Centre 17; Berkshire Mercury; John o'London's; Evening Mail, Hounslow; Spring Anthols.; Collected Poems; Schl. Anthols.; Laudamus Te; IWWP Anthol., 1973; The Shore. Recip., Bronze Medal, Twickenham & Richmond Mus. Fest., 1964 & 65. Address: 56 Worton Way, Isleworth, Middx., U.K.

REDMOND, Eugene Benjiman, b. 1 Dec. 1937. Teacher; Writer. Education: Public Schools, East St. Louis, Illinois; B.A., Engl., Southern Ill. Univ., 1964; M.A., Engl. Lit., Washington Univ. 1966. Positions held: Asst. Editor, East St. Louis Beacon newspaper, 1961-62; various editorial positions in ALESTLE, SIU student newspaper, 1962-64, and Editor-in-Chief, 1963-64; Assoc. Editor, East St. Louis Eve. Voice, 1962-63; Publicist & Proposal Writer, Human Development Corporation, St. Louis, Missouri, 1964 (Summer); Co-founder and editor, East St. Louis Monitor newspaper, and holder of various editorial positions (1963-69), including Exec. Editor; Director, Project Head Start: Grace Hill Settlement House, St. Louis, 1965-66; Southern Ill. Univ., 1966-69, Teacher-Counselor (1966-67) and Director of Language Workshops and Poet-in-Residence (1968-69), Experiment in Higher Education; Writer-in-Residence, Oberlin Coll., 1969-70; Prof. of Engl. and Poet-in-Residence, Calif. State Univ., Sacramento, 1970–; Visiting Writer-in-Residence, Southern Univ., Baton Rouge, Louisiana, 1971 and 1972 (Summers); Editorial Director, Black Anthol. Project, 1972–. Memberships: World Poetry Soc.; CSSI; Black River Writers (Publisher, Founder); Intercontinental Biographical Assoc. Published works: A Tale of Two Toms, 1968; A Tale of Time and Toilet Tissue, 1969; Sides of the River: A Mini-Anthol. of Black Writings (Editor), 1969; Sentry of the Four Golden Pillars, 1970; River of Bones and Flesh and Blood, 1971; Songs from an Afro/Phone, 1972; Consider Loneliness as These Things, 1973; In a Time of Rain and Desire, 1973; Poetry for My People (co-editor), 1970; Ark of Bones and Other Stories (by the late Henry Dumas) (co-editor), 1970. Contbr. to: Journal of Black Poetry; Black World; World Mag.; Poet; Internat. Qtly.; Reflections; Freelance; Confrontation; Black Orpheus; East St. Louis Monitor; Black Liberator; Oberlin Review; The Activist; The Commuter; St. Louis Sentinel; The Hornet; The ALESTLE; The Nickel Review; Tambourine; Sides of the River; The New Black Poetry; Today's Negro Voices; The Poetry of Black America; New Black Voices; Poems by Blacks, vols. 1, 2, 3; Words Among America; Understanding the New Black Poetry; Open Poetry; Third World Anthol.; Poetry Cleveland; Black Poets & Vietnam. Awards: 1963, Award for Writing & Creative Community Leadership ("Outstanding Collegian of the Year"), Pro-Eight Social-Civic Club, East St. Louis, Ill.; 1965, 1st Prize for Poetry, Annual Festival of Arts Poetry Contest (Washington Univ.); 1966, 2nd Prize, Annual Norma Lowery Poetry Contest; 1966, 1st Prize, Annual Freelance Mag. Poetry Contest; 1968. Hon Mention, Annual Wednesday Club Senior Orig. Verse Contest; 1972, Merit Award for Creative Writing and Community Leadership (The Community School, East St. Louis, Ill). Address: 610 Howe Ave., 39, Sacramento, CA 95825, USA.

REED, Henry, b. 22 Feb. 1914. Free-lance Journalist, Broadcaster & Radio Scriptwriter. Education: M.A., Univ. of Birmingham. Positions held: Tchr. & Free-lance Journalist, 1937-41; Worked at Foreign Office, 1942-45; Engaged in Broadcasting, Journalism & Writing Radio Scripts. Published works: A Map of Verona, 1946; Other: The Novel since 1939; Trans., Perdu & His Father, 1954; Trans., Three Plays, 1957. Contbr. to (Anthols.): Penguin Book of Contemporary Verse, 1950; An Anthology of Contemporary Verse, 1953; Faber Book of Modern Verse, 1960; An Anthology of Modern Verse, 1961; Poetry of the Thirties, 1964; Poetry of the Forties, 1968. Address: c/o Jonathan Cape Ltd., 30 Bedford Square, London, W.C.1, UK.

REED, Ishmael, b. 22 Feb. 1938. Writer. Memberships:

Authors' Guild of Am.; PEN. Published works: (novels) The Freelance Pallbearers, 1967; Yellow Back Radio Broke-Down, 1969; Mumbo-Jumbo, 1972; Conjure, 1972; Chattanooga, 1973; The Last Days of Louisiana Red, 1974. Nominated for two Nat. Book Awards, 1973. Address: Reed, Cannon & Johnson Communications Co., 2140 Shattuck Ave., Room 311, Berkeley, CA 94704, U.S.A.

REED, John Robert, b. 24 Jan. 1938. University Professor. Education: B.A. in Music and English, Univ. of Minn. at Duluth; Ph.D., in Engl., Univ. of Rochester, NY. Positions held: Instr., Univ. of Cincinnati, 1962-64; Asst. Prof., Univ. of Connecticut, 1964-65; Asst. Prof., Wayne State Univ., 1965-68; Visiting Fellow & Lecturer, Univ. of Warwick, 1966-67; Assoc. Prof., 1968-71, and since 1971, Prof., Wayne State Univ. Memberships: Mod. Language Assoc.; Midwest Mod. Language Assoc.; The Dickens Soc.; The Tennyson Soc. Published work: Hercules, 1973. Contbr. to: Poetry; Prairie Schooner; Epos; Spirit; Modern Poetry Studies; The Univ. of Windsor Review; Contempora; Prologue; Bitterroot; The Fiddlehead; Southern Humanities Review; Works. Address: Dept. of Engl., Wayne State Univ., Detroit, MI 48202, USA.

REED, Robert Rentoul, b. 16 Nov. 1911. Professor of English. Education: Harvard Coll., 1930-32, 33-34; A.B., Pomona Coll., 1937; Ph.D., Columbia Univ., 1950. Positions held: Tchr., Ariz. ranch schls., 1936-40; U.S. Coast Guard, 1942-45; Tchr., N.Y. Univ., 1947-50; Pa. State Univ., 1950–. Memberships: Renaissance Soc. of Am.; Shakespeare Assn. of Am. Published works incl: Young April, 1937; East of Hatteras, 1969. Contbr. to: Wings; Prairie Schooner; The Muse; Scimitar & Song; Fiddlehead, etc. Address: 144 Burrowes Bldg., University Park, PA, U.S.A.

REES, Alun William, b. 25 Sept. 1937. Journalist. Educ: Univ. Coll., Cardiff, Wales; Sheffield Univ., Yorkshire. Positions held: Ed. Bd., Envoi, Cheltenham, 1962-63; Sports Writer, Sunday Telegraph, London, 1966-68; Features Sub-Ed., TV Times; Soccer Corres., Sunday Telegraph. Published works: My Name Is Legend, 1962. Contbr. to: Scrip; Manifold; Icarus; Medley; Tribune; London Welshman; Poetry Wales; Arrows; Elegreba; Envoi; (anthologies) Poetry from Sheffield, 1960; Healing of the Nations, 1965; Crucible Anthology of Modern Poetry, 1965; Lilting House, 1969. Address: 21 Royal Ave., Tonbridge, Kent, U.K.

REEVE, Franklin D., b. 18 Sept. 1928. Writer. Education: A.B., Princeton; Ph.D., Columbia Univ. Positions held: Adjunct Prof. of Letters, Wesleyan Univ. & Vis. Lectr. in Engl., Yale Univ. Memberships: Int. PEN; Connecticut Acad. of Arts & Scis. Published works: The Stone Island, 1964; Six Poems, 1964; In the Silent Stones, 1968; The Blue Cat, 1972. Contbr. to: The Am. Scholar; The Beloit Poetry Jrnl.; Burning Deck; Focus/Midwest; Folio; The Hudson Review; The Kenyon Review; The Little Mag.; Occident; The N.Y. Herald Tribune; Poetry; The New Yorker; Shenandoah; The Western Review; Wind; The Tin Drum. Recip., Award in Lit., Nat. Inst. of Arts & Letters, 1970. Address: Higganum, Connecticut, U.S.A.

REEVES, James, b. 1 July 1909. Freelance Author; Editor; Broadcaster. Education: M.A., Cambridge Univ., U.K. Married Mary Phillips, 1 son, 1 daughter. Positions held: Schl. Master & Lectr., Tchrs. Trng. Colls., 1933-52. Published works: (poetry) The Natural Need, 1936; The Imprisoned Sea, 1949; The Password & Other Poems, 1952; The Talking Skull, 1958; Collected Poems, 1929-59, 1960; The Questioning River, 1964; Selected Poems, 1967; Homage to Trumbull Stickney (w. S. Haldane), 1968; Subsong; (children's poetry) The Wandering Moon, 1950; The Blackbird in the Lilac, 1952; Prefabulous Animiles, 1957; Ragged Robin, 1961; Hurdy-Gurdy, 1961; The Merry-Go-Round (ed.), 1955; The Story of Jackie Thimble, 1965; Free Verse, 1968; One's None, 1968; (children's prose) Pigeons & Princesses, 1956; Sailor Rumbelow & Britannia, 1962; The Strange Light; Titus in Trouble (co-author), 1959; Mulbridge Manor, 1958;

English Fables & Fairy Stories, 1954; Fables from Aesop, 1961; Exploits of Don Quixote, 1959; A Golden Land (ed.), 1958; A First Bible, 1962; Three Tell Tales, 1964; Primrose & the Winter Witch, 1964; The Pillar-Box Thieves, 1965; The Road to a Kingdom, 1965; The Secret Shoemakers & Other Stories, 1966; The Cold Flame, 1967; Rhyming Will, 1967; The Trojan Horse, 1968; The Christmas Book, 1968; (drama) Mulcaster Market, 1951; The King Who Took Sunshine, 1954; A Health to John Patch, A Ballad Opera, 1957; (educl.) The Critical Sense, 1956; Teaching Poetry, 1958; The Quality of Education (co-ed.), 1947; A Short History of English Poetry, 1961, '64; Understanding Poetry, 1965; The War, 1939-45 (co-author), 1960, '67; A New Canon of English Poetry (co-author), 1967. Ed. & Selector, 12 vols. in The Poetry Bookshelf Series (Heinemann), 1951–. Ed: The Idiom of the People, 1959; The Everlasting Circle, 1960; Georgian Poetry, 1962; The Modern Poets World, 1935; Great English Essays, 1961; The Bible in Brief, 1954; The Cassell Book of English Poetry, 1965. Editions: Gulliver's Travels, 1955; The Unicorn Stephen Leacock, 1960; Dialogue & Drama (w. N. Culpan), 1950, etc. Anthols: The Poets World, 1948; Orpheus, Bk. I 1950, Bk. II 1952; Heinemann's Jr. Poetry Series, Bks. I-IV, 1954; The Rhyming River, IV Bks., 1959; The Speaking Oak, 1951; The Writers Way, 1948. Contbr. to: Encounter; New Statesman; Nation; Listener; Tribune; Scotsman; Spectator. Address: Flints, Rotten Row, Lewes, Sussex, U.K.

REGE, Purushottama Shivarâma, pen names **CHAMPA, Suhrid & KATTHAK, Roop,** b. 2 Aug. 1910. Teacher. Education: B.A., 1931; B.Sc. (Econ.), 1934. Married Sarita, 3 children. Positions held: Lectr. in Econs., Sydenham Coll., Bombay, 1938-46; Prof. of Econs. of Transport, ibid, 1946-58; Prin., Ismail Yusuf Coll., Bombay, 1958-62, Elphinstone Coll., 1962-69 & Chowgule Coll., Margao, Goa, 1969-71. Memberships: Life Mbr., Mumbai Marâthi Sâhitya Sangh, Bombay; Pres., Marâthi Sâhitya Sammelan, Wardha, 1969; Writers Comm., Indian Coun. of Nat. Integration. Published works: Sadhanâ, 1931; Fulorâ, 1937; Himasek, 1943; Dolâ, 1950; Gandharekhâ, 1953; Pushkalâ, 1959; Dusrâ Pakshi, 1966; Svânandabodh, 1970; Priyâl, 1972; Chhândasi (critical essays), 1962; also var. short stories, plays & novels. Contbr. to: Chhand; Satyakathâ; Mouj; Poetry India; Atlantic Monthly & others. Honours, awards: Mumbai Mârathi Sahitya Sangh Award, 1943; Five Mahârashtra State Awards. Address: 3/13 Prakash Soc.; off Juhu Rd., Bombay 400 054, India.

REGELSON, Abraham, pen name **BEN-HANAGAR, Sidrophel,** b. 19 Oct. 1896. Writer; Hebrew Poet. Married with children. Positions held: Tchr. & Libn., Hebrew Schls. in N.Y.C., U.S.A. & Cleveland, Ohio; on staff of daily 'Davar', Tel Aviv, Israel, 1934-36; Translator & Ed., 'Am Oved' publishing house, Tel-Aviv, 1949-50; on staff of daily 'Al Hamishmar', Tel-Aviv, 1951-59; also writes for Yiddish & Anglo-Jewish publs. Memberships: Chmn., Hebrew Poetry Soc. of Am.; Hebrew Writers' Assn. of Israel; Org., Hevel Philopoesia, Tel-Aviv. Published works: Cayin ve Hevel (Cain & Abel) a Poem, 1932; El HaAyin Venivca (Non-Being Cleft) poems, 1943; Israel's Sweetest Singer, Yehudeh Halevi, inclng. a new translation of 'Love of Zion', 1943; Ed., Rivon Catan, 1944; Haquqoth Otiyatayich, poems, 1964; Shiratayim, two poems, 1973. Contbr. to: Davar; Al Hamishmar; Hadoar; Moznayim; Orot; Di Goldens Keyt. Recip., Brenner Prize, Tel-Aviv, 1964 & Bialik Prize, 1973. Address: Rechov Hapninim 18, N'Veh Ephraim 60986, Israel.

REID, Alastair, b. 22 Mar. 1926. Writer; Translator. Education: M.A., Univ. of St. Andrews, U.K. Divorced, 1 son (Jasper). Positions held: Sarah Lawrence Coll., 1950-55; Vis. Prof., Antioch Coll., 1969-70. Mbr., The Poetry Soc. Published works: To Lighten My House, 1953; Oddments Inklings Omens Moments, 1959 & 61; Passwords, 1963 & 65; Weathering, forthcoming 1974. Translations of the poetry of Pablo Neruda, Jorge Luis Borges, Judas Roquiń, Jorge Guillen & other Latin

Am. poets. Contbr. to: The New Yorker; The Atlantic Monthly; Encounter; The Listener; Poetry, etc. Staff Writer, The New Yorker Mag., 1959–. Recip., Guggenheim Fellowships, 1955-56 & 1956-57. Address: c/o John Wolfers, 3 Regent Sq., London W.C.1, U.K.

REIDY, Maurice Joseph Reidy, b. 14 Jan. 1922. Farmer. First breeder of T.B. winners under I.R.R. in Co-Kerry. Bred horses to win over 100 races. Published works: Poetry & script book 'The Kerry Piper', 1973; second collection contains 22 poems & 22 poems of script, 1973. Poems with Atlantic Press & The Kerryman. Recip., Special Cert., Atlantic Press. 1973. Address: The Little Stud, Cordal Castleisland, Co. Kerry, Ireland.

REIN, Karl Carolus Hilding Gabriel, pen name **REIN, Carolus,** b. 14 May 1935. Author. Education: candidate in humanistic scis., Univ. of Helsinki, Finland, 1966; M.A., Abo Akademi, 1970. Positions held: Proof Rdr., Hufvudstadsbladet & Nya Pressen, 1958-59; Probationer, Lib. of Abo Akademi, 1966-67; Auditor, Lib. of Uppsala Univ., 1967. Member, Finland's Svenska Författareförening. Published works: (colls. of poems) Färd genom verkligheter, 1954; Syskon till ingen, 1955; Dansens yta, 1956; Varsvart, 1958; Seende, 1960; Världen ar endast du, 1963; Det obesegrades röst, 1967; Vagbrytningar, 1971. Contbr. to: Nya Argus; Finsk Tidskrift; Lucifer; Documenta; Parnasso, etc. Recip., extra scholarship of Svenska Litteratursällskapet i Finland 1959 & a part of the Lybeck Prize, as it is called, 1968. Address: c/o Mrs. Hillevi Rein, Kopingsvagen 25 B, Grankulla, Finland.

REISS, Alvin, b. 31 Oct. 1932. Writer. Education: Univ. of Ore. & Southern Ore. Coll. Married Audrey Spencer, 2 daughters. Positions held: Office Mgr. for Union Pacific Railroad & Denver & Rio Grande Western Railroad, Medford, Ore., 1955-61; Announcer for KBOY-FM Radio, Medford, Ore., 1961-66; Announcer & FM Prog. Dir., KBOY, 1966-69; News Dir. for KYJC Radio, Medford, 1969-73; Staff Writer for Maîl Tribune (film & drama reviewer & news writer), 1969–. Member, Poetry Soc. of Am. Contbr. to: Christian Sci. Monitor; McCall's; Oregonian Verse; Mail Tribune; Diamond Anthol. of Poetry Soc. of Am.; Univ. of Ore. Alumni Mag. Have published short stories, written features & drama reviews for United Press Int. & features for Ottaway News Serv. Honours, awards: 1st Award for TV Drama, B'ham, Ala. Fest. of Arts, 1963 & 4th Award, 1964; Winner, Western States playwriting comp., Eugene, Ore., 1965; John Masefield Meml. Award, Poetry Soc. of Am., 1970. Address: P.O. Box 597, Jacksonville, OR 97530, U.S.A.

REISS, James, b. 11 July 1941. English Professor. Education: B.A., Univ. of Chicago, U.S.A., 1963; M.A., ibid, 1964. Positions held: Tchng. Asst., Univ. of Calif., Davis, 1964-65; Instr. in Engl., Miami Univ., Ohio, 1965-69; Asst. Prof. of Engl., ibid, 1969-73; Assoc. Prof. of Engl., 1973–. Memberships: Poetry Soc. of Am.; Ohio Poets Assn. Published works: 12 at Miami University, 1969; Self-Interviews, 1970 & 72; The Breathers, 1974. Contbr. to: Saturday Review; The New Yorker; New American Review; The New Republic; Va. Quarterly Review; Antaeus; Antioch Review; Prairie Schooner; The N.Y. Times; The Lit. Review; Mich. Quarterly Review; University Review; New Letters, etc. Regular Poetry Critic for the Cleveland Plain Dealer. Honours, awards: 1st Prize, Acad. of Am. Poets Contest, Univ. of Chicago, 1960 & 62. Address: 110 N. University Ave., Oxford, OH 45056, U.S.A.

REISS, Lionel S., b. 29 Jan. 1894. Painter; Etcher; Teacher. Education: Educl. Alliance; Art Students League; Nat. Acad. of Design. Married Frances Grossel, 1 son. Positions held: Designer & illustrator for var. newspapers, periodicals & publishers; Art Dir., Goldwyn Pictures Corp.; Art Dir., Hanf-Metzger Agency. Member, Poetry Soc. of Am. Published works: My Models Were Jews, 1938; New Lights & Old

Shadows, 1954; Illustrated: A Golden Treasury of Jewish Literature, 1937; The Complete Poetic Works of Chaim Nachman Bialik, 1948. Contbr. to var. mags. Artistic works exhibited at var. art insts. & museums & in permanent colls at: Brooklyn Mus., N.Y.; J.T.S.A.; Columbia Univ.; Sinai Ctr., Chicago; Jewish Mus., N.Y.; Tel-Aviv Mus.; 100 portrait drawings, anthropological studies of the Jewish Type, Houghton Lib., Harvard Univ., etc. Recip. var. honours & awards Address: 370 Central Park West, N.Y., NY 10025, U.S.A.

REITER, Thomas, b. 7 Mar. 1940. Associate Professor of English. Education: B.A., Loras Coll., Dubuque, Iowa; M.A., Univ. of Va.; Ph.D., Univ. of Mass. Positions held: Instr. of Engl., Siena Coll.; Asst. Prof. of Engl., Monmouth Coll.; Assoc. Prof., ibid. Mbr., Poetry Soc. of Am. Var. poetry readings at: Smith Coll.; Hollins Coll.; Upsala Coll.; Marietta Coll.; Univ. of So. Miss. Contbr. to: Approach; Choice; Cimarron Review; Colorado Quarterly; Commonweal; Critic; Discourse; Kansas Quarterly; Mill Mountain Review; Minnesota Review; Mississippi Review; Perspective; Poetry Northwest; S.D. Review; Southwest Review; Sparrow; Trace; Prism Int. Honours, prizes: Gerard Manley Hopkins Poetry Prize, 1961; Acad. of Am. Poets Prize, 1963; Dir. of Poetry Workshop, Inst. for Tchrs. of Creative Writing, Univ. of So. Miss., 1972. Address: 105 Sycamore St., Neptune, NJ 07753, U.S.A.

REKOLA, Mirkka Elina, b. 26 June 1931. Writer; Poet; Critic. Member, Suomen Kirjailijaliitto (Soc. of Finnish Writers). Published works: Vedessä Palaa (It is Burning in the Water), 1954; Tunnit (The Hours), 1957; Syksy Muuttaa Linnut (Autumn Changes the Birds), 1961; Ilo ja Epäsymmetria (Joy & Asymmetry), 1965; Anna päivän olla kaikki (Let the Day be all), 1968; Muistikirja (The Notebook), 1969; Minä rakastan sinua, minä sanon sen kaikille (I Love You, I'll say it to everybody), 1972. Contbr. to Parnasso. Recip., Finnish State Awards for Writers, 1965, 68, 72. Address: Huvilakatu 20–22 A10, 00150 Helsinki 15, Finland.

RENAUD, Alix, b. 30 Aug. 1945. Actor; Writer. Education: Clovis Bonhomme Coll., Port-au-Prince, Haiti; Nat. Acad. of Dramatic Art, Haiti, 3 yrs.; Ecole ABC de Paris, France (corres.); currently studying Linguistics at Université Laval, Quebec City, Canada. Positions held: Translator; currently in Information; Lit. Critic, Quebec newspaper. Former member of var. lit. assns. Published works: Careme (book of poems), 1972. Contbr. to: L'Information médicale et paramédicale, Montreal, 1972 & '73; L'Amitié par la plume (review of Club des Intellectuels Français), 1969 & '70. Collaborated on following anthols: Anthologie Poésie Vivante, No. 3, Geneva, 1971; Anthologie des Poètes et Prosateurs Francophones de l'Amérique Septentrionale, Vol. II, Chicago, 1971. Recip., Diplôme d'Honneur, Société des Ecrivains des Provinces Françaises, Bordeaux, France, 1970. Address: 2620 Chemin Ste-Foy, Apt. 28, Quebec 10e, P.Q., Canada.

RENDLEMAN, Danny Lee, b. 25 Nov. 1945. Poet; Free-lance Writer & Artist. Education: Ctrl. Mich. Univ., 1963-68; Univ. of Mich., 1968-74; B.G.S. Degree. Married Alice Mae Sanford, 1 son. Positions held: Drugstore Clerk; Switchboard Operator; Warehouse Mgr.; Advt. Artist & Copywriter; Bookstore Asst. Mgr.; Mag. Ed.; Security Guard; Freelance Artist & Writer; Poet. Memberships: The Welch Fndn. for Talented Student; Sigma Tau Delta; Corres. Sec., Petition Ed., Newsletter Ed., Pledge Treas., Sigma Chi. Published works: Signals To The Blind, 1971. Contbr. to: Salt Lick; The Little Mag.; New: Am. & Canadian Poetry; Motive; Hearse; Epoch; Carolina Qtly.; Folio; Zahir; Wis. Review, etc. Honours, awards: Univ. of Mich. Poetry Prizes, 1968, '69; Mott Community Coll. Poetry Award, 1970; William Lockwood Reading Grant, 1972, '74. Address: 213 West Taylor, Flint, MI 48505, U.S.A.

RENIERS, Annie, b. 14 May 1941. University Professor. Education: studied German lang. & Philos., Univ. of Brussels, Belgium. Married Paul Philippot, 1 child. Positions held: Prof. of Hist. of Contemporary Art Aesthetics, Univ. of Brussels. Published works: Het Ogenblik, 1964; Gelijktijdigheid, 1967; Tussenruimten, 1969; A contre-gré, 1970; Demain à Canaan/Morgen in Kanaän, 1971; Le jour obscur/Wonen een Feest, 1972; Encentriques, 1070, Van verte tot verte, 1973. Contbr. to De Vlaamse Gids, Brussels. Address: 102 Avenue Coghen, 1180 Brussels, Belgium, & 11, via degli Zingari, 00184 Rome, Italy.

RENNER, Bruce, b. 8 Oct. 1944. Poet. Education: B.S., Univ. of Wisconsin, 1970; M.F.A., Columbia Univ., 1972. Published works: Six Poems, 1972; Poetry 1967, 1967 (w. Dan Rose); The Water Under The Zoo (unpublished). Contbr. to: Arts in Society; Choice; Esquire; First Issue; Jeopardy; The Minn. Review; Prairie Schooner; Shenandoah; Worksheet. Recip., Grant from the Ariadne Fndn., New Haven, Conn., 1972. Address: 3114 N. Bartlett, Milwaukee, WI 53211, U.S.A.

REPLANSKY, Naomi, b. 23 May 1918. Poet. Education: B.A., Univ. of Calif., Los Angeles, 1956. Published works: Ring Song, Scribner's, 1952. Contbr. to: Choice (Chicago); San Francisco Review; Agenda (London); Poetry Pilot; The Nation (New York); Lamp in the Spine; Dacotah Territory (Moorhead, Minn.), etc. Rep. in following anthols: Poets in America; International; Pick Me Up; Poems One Line or Longer; No More Masks, etc. Nominated for Nat. Book Award in Poetry, 1952. Address: 146 West 76th St., N.Y., NY 10023, U.S.A.

REXROTH, Kenneth, b. 22 Dec. 1905. Author. Education: Chicago Art Inst.; New Schl. of Soc. Rsch.; Art Students' League. Positions held: Reporter, Chicago papers, 8 yrs.; Columnist for San Francisco Examiner; currently Columnist for San Francisco Mag. & Wis the San Francisco Bay Guardian; Poet-in-Res., Univ. of Wis., Milwaukee & Juniata Coll. Has lectured at var. univs.; Weekly book-reviewer on KPFA Radio, Berkeley, KPFK, Los Angeles, WBAI, N.Y.C. for over 20 yrs. Many TV shows, nightclub & jazz room appearances. Has had var. one man art shows. Published works: (poetry books) In What Hour; The Phoenix & The Tortoise; The Art of Worldly Wisdom; The Signature of All Things; The Dragon And The Unicorn; Thou Shalt Not Kill; In Defense of the Earth; The Homestead Called Damascus; Natural Numbers: New & Selected Poems; The Heart's Garden: The Garden's Heart; Collected Shorter Poems; Collected Longer Poems. (plays) Beyond The Mountains; var. translations & criticism. Honours, awards incl: Two Commonwealth Medals; Shelley Meml. Award, PSA; 2 Guggenheim Fellowships. Address: 1401 E. Pepper Lane, Santa Barbara, CA 93108, U.S.A.

REYBURN, Morris, b. 15 Sept. 1899. Retired. Education: courses in Lit. & Poetry at N.Y. Univ., New Schl. of Soc. Rsch., CCNY. Married, 2 sons. Positions held: Salesman in Bloomingdale's Dept. Store, 1922; Stock Merchandising Dept., Am. Lithograph Co., 1925; U.S. Post Office, 1926-61; Cashier's Dept., Bache & Co., Wall St. Brokerage, 1961-70. Memberships: Corres. Sec., N.Y. Poetry Forum; Brooklyn Poetry Circle; Treas., Greenwich Village Poetry Soc. Published works: Dreams Beyond Wings, 1970. Rep. in sev. anthols. inclng: This Will Endure, 1955; To Each His Song, 1958; Muse Anthol., 1962; Am. Poetry New & Old, 1965; Poets of Am., 1961-62; Haiku Anthol., 1973. Contbr. to: Am. Bard; Seydell Qtly.; Flame mag.; Poetry Digest. etc. Honours, awards: Annual Gold Medal Award, Int. Poetry Review, 1963; Book of Poems by John Keats, Brooklyn Poetry Circle, 1965, etc. Address: 3442 Fenton Ave., Bronx, NY 10469, U.S.A.

REYNOLDS, Tim, b. 18 July 1936. Teacher & Translator. Education: Antioch Coll.; B.A., Univ. of Wis.; M.A., Tufts Coll. Published works incl: Ryoanji,

1964; Halflife, 1964; Catfish Goodbye, 1968; Slocum, 1968; Que, 1971; Peace (transl. of Aristophanes, staged in N.Y. 1967-68); The Women Poem, 1973. Honours, awards: Rockefeller Grant, 1969. Address: Leamington House, Coxwell Rd., Faringdon, Berks., U.K.

REZMERSKI, John Calvin, b. 15 Jan. 1942. Teacher. Education: B.A., Gannon Coll., 1963; M.A., John Carroll Univ., 1965; grad. study at Univ. of Kansas. Married Mary K. Naegle, 3 children. Positions held: Tchng. Assoc., John Carroll Univ., 1963-65; Asst. Instr., Univ. of Kans., 1965-67; Asst. Prof. of Engl., Gustavus Adolphus Coll., 1967-73; currently Assoc. Prof. of Engl., ibid. Published work: Held for Questioning, 1969. Contbr. to: Kansas Write-In; National Catholic Reporter; Sumac; Hanging Loose; S.D. Review; Chelsea; Dacotah Territory; New Letters; Steelhead; Ghost Dance; Road Apple Review; Humor Is Our Only Hope: Some Public Poems; 1972 Minn. Poetry Anthol.; 1973 Minn. Poetry Anthol.; Northeast; Poetry Northwest; New: American & Canadian Poetry; Carroll Qtly. Honours, awards: Devins Award, 1969; Fellowship, Nat. Endowment for the Arts, 1973. Address: Gustavus Adolphus Coll., St. Peter, MN 56082, U.S.A.

REZNIKOFF, Charles, b. 31 Aug. 1894. Writer. Education: Schl. of Jrnlsm., Univ. of Mo., 1910-11; LL.B., Law Schl., N.Y. Univ., 1915; admitted to the Bar of the State of N.Y., 1916. Married Marie Syrkin. Published works: Rhythms, 1918; Rhythms II, 1919; Poems, 1920; Uriel Acosta: A Play and a Fourth Group of Verse, 1921; Chatterton, The Black Death, & Meriwether Lewis, Three Plays, 1922; Coral & Captive Israel, Two Plays, 1923; Five Groups of Verse, 1927; Nine Plays, 1927; Jerusalem the Golden, 1934; In Memoriam: 1933, 1934; Separate Way, 1936; Going To and Fro and Walking Up and Down, 1941; Inscriptions: 1944-5 6, 1959; By the Waters of Manhattan: Selected Verse, 1962; Testimony: The United States 1885-90, 1965. Recip., Morton Dauwen Zabel Award for Poetry, Nat. Inst. of Arts & Letters, 1971. Address: 180 W. End Ave., Apt. 22F, N.Y., NY 10023, U.S.A.

RHYS, Keidrych, b. 26 Dec. 1915. Poet; Writer; Editor. Positions held: Army (London Welsh AA), 1939-45; Fndr., Ed., Wales (jrnl.) 1937-60; Helped found, Poetry London, 1938-55; w. Min. of Info., London, 1943-44; PR Cons., various orgs., 1950-54; Welsh Columnist, 'The People', 1954-60; Ed., Colofn y Bardd; London Ed., Poetry London-New York, 1956-60. Memberships: Vice-Pres., Int. Music Festival & Eisteddfod; Chmn., Friends of Wales Soc.; Vice-Pres., Carmarthen Arts Club. Published works: The Van Pool and Other Poems, 1941; Ed., Poems From The Forces, 1942; Ed., More Poems From the Forces, 1943; Ed., Modern Welsh Poetry, 1945; Angry Prayers, 1952; The Expatriates, 1954; Ed., Wales, 1969. Contbr. to: New Writing; Wales; New Statesman; Time & Tide; Listener; Horizon; Times Lit. Supplement; Poetry, Chicago; Partisan Review; Life & Letters; Spectator; Poetry London; Tribune; Our Time; The People; New Wales, etc. Honours, Awards: Welsh Arts Coun. Award, 1969; Boreston Mountain Poetry, Best Poems of 1967; Jr. dedication, w. Vernon Watkins to Anthol. of Welsh Poetry 1917-1967. Address: 40 Heath St., Hampstead, London, NW3, UK.

RIBALOW, Meir Zvi, b. 3 Sept. 1948. Theatrical Director; Production Associate, NY Shakespeare Festival. Education: Phillips Exeter Acad., 1962-66, received Classical dip. in 1966; Princeton Univ., 1966-70, B.A. as Univ. Scholar in 1970. Positions held: Teacher of Engl., Lawrenceville School, 1970-71 (NJ.); Theatrical Producer, Director, Actor, 1971-72; Production Assoc., NY Shakespeare Festival, 1972 onwards. Contbr. to: The Literary Review; The Nassau Lit.; The Notice; The Nassau Review; The Pendulum. Has given poetry readings at various univs., high schools, groups, including Princeton Univ., Fairleigh Dickinson Univ., Rider Coll., and others, 1969-70, under auspices of Nat. Endowment for the Humanities, and NJ Council for the Arts. Address: 108

E. 86th St., New York, NY 10028, USA.

RIBERA CHEVREMONT, Evaristo, b. 16 Feb. 1896. Poet. Education: B.A., Mistica El Escorial, Spain. Married. Positions held: Lectr., Univ. of Puerto Rico, Rio Piedras; Res. Poet, ibid. Memberships: Corres. Mbr., Real Academia Española; Instituto de Cultura Puertorriqueña; Instituto de Artes y Ciencias, etc. Published works: (poetry) La hora del Orifice, 1918; El Templo de los Alabastros, 1921; Los Almendros del Paseo de Covadonga, 1928; Pajarera, 1929; Color, 1938; Tonos y Formas, 1943; La Naturaleza en Color – Ensayo, 1943; Barro, 1945; Tierra y Sombra, 1942; El Niño de Arcilla (novel), 1947; Verbo, 1950; Antologia Poetica, 1950; La Lama Pensativa, 1955; Inefable Orilla, 1961; El Semblante, 1964; Memorial de Arena, 1962; Punto Final, 1963; Principio de Canto, 1965; Nueva Antologia, 1966; Canto de Mi Tierra, 1971. Contbr. to var. jrnls. & reviews. Honours, awards incl: Premio a 'Inefable Orilla', Instituto de Literatura, 1961; Premios a Canto de Mi Tierra, ibid, 1972. Address: Vieques 1117, Condado, Santurce, Puerto Rico.

RICE, Clovita, b. 17 Jul. 1929. Teacher of Spanish and English. Education: B.A., Univ. of Ark.; M.S.E., Ark. State Univ. Positions held: Grad. Asst. in Engl., Ark. State Univ., 1963, 1964, 1965; Teacher of Spanish and Engl. at Wilbur D. Mills HS, Little Rock, since 1969; Editor, Voices International, a literary qtly., since 1969. Memberships: South and West, Inc., (Bd. Member); Poetry Soc. of America; N.L.A.P.W.; Poets Roundtable of Ark.; South and West Poetry Workshop in central Ark. (Chairman). Published works: Blow out the Sun, (poems), 1967; Red Balloons for the Major (poems), 1969. Contbr. to: Discourses on Poetry, vol. 4, 1969 (symposia paper entitled: Psyche & Mystique of the Mid-South Woman Poet); South and West; Tulsa Poetry Qtly.; Denver Post; Commercial Appeal; Ark. Gazette; Poet (India); Am. Poets, 1966; Contemp. Poets of Ark., 1969; Ferment; Poetry Dial; Poetry Pendulum; Singing Mariners; Voices Int.; Writer's Notes & Quotes; Modern Images; Apercu; Arrow; Words with Wings; Lincoln Reader; Saint; Creative Review; Memorabilia; Poems of Patriotism and Peace; Human Voice; Muse; Stepping Stones to Faith; Poetry Dial Anthol.; Reverie; CS Monitor. Awards: Named "Poet of the Present" in Ark., Oct., 1969; Recip. South and West Silver Award for contribs. towards poetry, Oct., 1969. Address: 6804 Cloverdale Dr., Little Rock, AR 72209, USA.

RICE, John, pen name **ALLAN, Jonathan,** b. 12 Mar. 1948. Printer. Education: St. Michaels Coll., Ayrshire; Army Schl. of Langs. Positions held: Ed., 'Pink Peace', arts mag. Chmn., Folkestone Poetry Circle. Published works: Poems, 1971; Folk of the Green Cloak, 1971; Bringing Rain from Cyprus, 1972; Junta, 1973. Contbr. to: She; Samphire; Aquarius; New Headland; Littack; Pink Peace. Address: Mumbles, 93 Biggins Wood Rd., Folkestone, Kent CT19 4NH, U.K.

RICE, William J., b. 7 July 1900. Publications: Poems (illus. from paintings by Jeanne Elsa Rice), 1965; desultory pamphlets, 1961-69. Address: 99 South 6th St., Brooklyn, NY 11211, USA.

RICH, Adrienne, b. 16 May 1929. English Lecturer. Educ: A.B., Radcliffe Coll., Cambridge, Mass., 1951. m. Alfred H. Conrad, 1953, 3s. Positions held: Lectr., Engl., Swarthmore Coll., Pa., 1966-68; Adjunct Prof., Writing, Grad. Schl. of the Arts, Columbia Univ., 1967-69; Lectr., Engl., SEEK Prog., C.C.N.Y., 1968-. Published works: A Change of World, 1951; The Diamond Cutters, 1955; Snapshots of a Daughter-in-Law, 1963; Necessities of Life, 1966; Selected Poems, 1967; Leaflets, 1969. Contbr. to: Nation; Hudson Review; Harper's; N.Y. Review of Books; New Republic; Quarterly Review of Literature; Poetry; (anthologies) New Poets of England and America, 1957; Contemporary American Poetry, 1962; A Controversy of Poets, 1965; Poems of Our Moment, 1968. Honours, awards: Guggenheim Fellowship, 1952-53 & 1961-62; Am. Inst. of Arts & Letters Award for Poetry, 1960; Bollingen Fndn. Commn., 1962;

D.Litt., Wheaton Coll., Norton, Mass., 1967.

RICH, Elaine Sommers, b. 8 Feb. 1926. Teacher. Education: B.A., Goshen Coll., Ind., 1947; M.A., Mich. State Univ., 1950. Married Dr. Ronald L. Rich, 4 children. Positions held: Tchr. of Engl. & Speech, Goshen Coll., Bethel Coll., Kans. & Int. Christian Univ. Memberships: World Poetry Soc.; ICU Poetry Club; Newton (Kans.) Creative Writers. Contbr. to: Christian Living; Mennonite Life; Gospel Herald; The Mennonite; Christian Century; Japan Christian Qtly. Address: House 348, I.C.U., 10-3 Osawa, 3-chome, Mitaka, Tokyo 181, Japan.

RICH, Vera, b. 24 Apr. 1936. Writer; Translator. Education: St. Hilda's Coll., Oxford Univ.; Bedford Coll., London. Positions held: Ed. of Manifold Review of Poetry & the Arts, 1962-69. Memberships: Poetry Soc.; Poetry Soc. of Am.; PEN. Published works: Outlines, 1960; Portents & Images, 1963; Heritage of Dreams, 1964; Song out of Darkness (transl. of the poetry of Taras Shevchenko), 1961; Lesya-Ukrainka, poems (transl.), 1968; Like Water, Like Fire, an anthol. of Byelorussian poetry (transl.), 1971; Ivan Franko, poems, (transl.), 1974. Contbr. to: John o'London's; Envoi; Unicorn; Manifold; Scrip; Reading Mercury; Icarus; Old Palace; Orcadian; The New Shetlander; South & West; N. Am. Mentor; Fla. Educ.; Wis. Poetry; Bardic Echoes; Voices Int.; Original Works; Bitterroot; (anthols. inclng.) Without Adam; Healing of the Nations; Doves for the '70's; Pa. Prize Poems; Sonnetarium; Laudamus Te, etc. Honours, awards incl: Sara Teasdale Award, 1965; 1st Prize Edna Shoemaker Award & 2nd Prize C.S. Clifton Award, Pa. Poetry Soc., 1966; 1st Prize, N. Am. Mentor Annual Contest, 1967. Address: 99 Vera Ave., Grange Pk., London N.21 1RN, U.K.

RICHARD, Hughes, b. 12 July 1934. Writer. Positions held: varied career until 1957; Tchr., 1957-59; Sec.-Gen. 'Prix Rencontre', Paris & assisted with Rencontre publications; Freelance Writer, 1967–. Published works: Le Soleil délivré, 1961; La Ballade pour parler d'adolescence, 1962; La Vie lente, 1965; La Saison Haute, 1971. Contbr. to: Poésie vivante, Geneva; Journal de Genève; Gazette de Lausanne; La Tribune de Lausanne; Sur Parole, Delémont; Actes de la Société jurassienne d'Emulation, Porrentruy; Cahier de l'alliance culturelle romande, Geneva; Marginales, Brussels; Le Thyrse, Brussels; Les Lettres Nouvelles, Paris; Commune Mesure, Paris; Anthologie jurassienne, 1965; Jura, 1971, etc. Honours, awards: Prix des jeunes de l'Emulation jurassienne, 1960; Prix littéraire du Canton de Berne, 1965 & '71; Bourse Pro Helvetia, 1966; Prix du Rotary Club, 1972; Prix Auguste Bachelin de littérature, 1973. Address: Case postale no. 1, 2000 Neuchaâtel 4, Switzerland.

RICHARDS, Ivor Armstrong, b. 26 Feb. 1893. University Professor. Educ: B.A., Clifton Coll., Cambridge, U.K., 1914; M.A., Magdalene Coll., ibid, 1918. m. Dorothy Eleanor Pilley. Positions held: Lectr., Engl., Cambridge, 1919; Fellow, Magdalene Coll., 1925; Vis. Prof., Tsing Hua Univ., Peking, China, 1929-30; Vis. Lectr., Harvard Univ., U.S.A., 1931, Univ. Lectr., 1939, Univ. Prof., 1943-63, Prof. Emeritus, 1963–. Published works: Goodbye Earth and Other Poems, 1958; The Screens and Other Poems, 1959; (verse plays) Tomorrow Morning, Faustus! An Infernal Comedy, 1962; Why So, Socrates?, 1964; (literary criticism) The Meaning of Meaning (w. C.K. Ogden), 1923; Principles of Literary Criticism, 1924; Practical Criticism, 1929; Speculative Instruments, 1955. Contbr. to: Times Literary Supplement; (anthologies) Poets and the Past, 1959; Poetry for Pleasure, 1960; Garlands for Christmas, 1965. Honours, awards: Russell Loines Award for Poetry, 1962; Emerson-Thoreau Medal, 1970; Hon. Fellow, Magdalene Coll., Cambridge, 1964. Address: Magdalene Coll., Cambridge, U.K.

RICHARDS, Mark, b. 2 Mar. 1922. Teacher. Education: B.A., Auckland Univ., New Zealand. Published works: Solomon Grundy & Other Poems,

1958; Go Back, Lazarus, 1964; Jericho Road, 1967; The Ballad of Drunken Bay, 1970; Long Weekend, 1973. Plays in verse produced and broadcast by the N.Z.B.S: Odysseus; A Burnt Child; Ecce Homo; The Premier's New Missile; Starfall; Alpha & Omega; A Comprehensive Cover, & var. short pieces & talk series. Recip., 1st prize, Cheltenham Fest. Poetry Comp., 1960. Address: 41 Norwood Rd., Bayswater, Auckland, New Zealand.

RICHARDSON, Bonita M., b. 19 Mar. 1932. Calligraphy Teacher; Freelance Writer of Art. Education: Geo. Fox Coll., Newberg, Ore.; Reed Coll., Portland; Portland Mus. Art Schl.; Clackamas Comm. Coll., Ore. City; var. poetry workshops & courses. Married Donald Richardson, 6 children. Positions held: Tchrs. Aide, N. Clackamas Co. & Poetland Schl. Dist. No. 1; Freelance Writer; Calligraphy Tchr., Damascus Pioneer Craft Schl., Ore. Memberships: N.Y. Poetry Forum; Pacific Northwest Writers' Conf.; Ore. State Poetry Assn.; Mt. Hood Poetry Circle. Contbr. to: Christian Sci. Monitor; Modern Bridge; Quinto Lingo; Dawn; St. Andrew's Review; Children's Friend; The Oregonian; Enterprise Courier. Recip., var. hons. & awards. Address: Rte. 1, Box 289 G, Colton, OR 97017, U.S.A.

RICHARDSON, Dana Dimitri, b. 11 Apr. 1953. University Student. Education: Université du Nouveau Monde, Switzerland, 1971; currently at Univ. of Pa., Philadelphia. Positions held: Taught Creative Writing to prisoners in the City of Philadelphia; Basketball Coach for L.I., N.Y. Leagues. Member, Penn Review, Univ. of Pa. Contbr. to: Yearbook of Modern Poetry, 1971; Lyrics of Love, 1972; Melody of the Muse, 1973; Voices Int.; Friends; Jean's Jrnl.; Straight; Cardinal; Tejas; The Symbolist; Modern Images; Scrutinize; J & C Transcripts Anthol.; The Malverne Times. Honours, awards: The Malvern Lib, Young Poets Recognition, 1973. Address: 7 Winfield Pl., Malverne, NY 11565, U.S.A.

RICHARDSON, Dimitra, b. 26 Mar. 1929. Educator; Poet; Writer; Lecturer. Education: B.A., Hunter Coll., N.Y., 1950; M.A., Stanford Univ., Calif., 1951; grad. studies in Philos., Long Beach Acad., Calif., 1954. Married, 3 sons. Positions held: Greek & French Tutor, 1946– (privately); Tchr. of Art Hist. & Greek & Roman Mythol., 1970; Tchr. of Art Hist. & Greek Drama, 1971-72; Lectr., Comparative Mythol., Hofstra Univ., 1973. Memberships incl: Treas., L.I. Writers, 3 yrs.; Centro Studi e Scambi Int.; Byzantine Fellowship; Int. Platform Soc. Rep. in following anthols: L.I. Writers, 1969; Contemporary Am. Love Scene, 1971; Lyrics of Love, 1972; Melody of the Muse, 1973; These Are My Jewels, 1969-73, etc. Contbr. to: Malverne Herald; Malverne Times; Major Poets; Jean's Jrnl.; Am. Bard; Haiku Highlights, etc. Recip. many poetry contest awards inclng: Long Island Writers, 1969, '70, '71, '72, '73. Address: 7 Winfield Pl., Malverne, NY 11565, U.S.A.

RICHARDSON, Dorothy Lee, b. 13 Aug. 1900. Poet. Education: Univ. of Pa., Bus. Schl., Harvard Ext., 1967; Harvard-Radcliffe Seminars on Writing & Performance of Poetry given by Ruth Whitman, 1970-71, 72-73. Married Arthur H. Richardson. Memberships: Exec. Comm., Poetry Soc. of Am.; New England Poetry Soc.; Mass. State Poetry Soc.; Acad. of Am. Poets. Published works: Signs at My Finger Ends, 1962. Contbr. to: N.Y. Times; N.Y. Herald Tribune; Sat. Review; Va. Quarterly Review; St. Louis Post Dispatch; Christian Sci. Monitor; Kan. City Star; Chicago Tribune Sunday Mag.; Am. Scholar; Atlantic Monthly; Poet Lore; Poetry; Rotarian; 7 anthols., etc. Honours, awards: IWWP 1st Prize, 1970; 1 Poetry Soc. of Am. Annual Award, 1972 & 2 monthly Awards, 1971, 72; 1st Prize, Clement Hoyt Ballad Award, Tex. Poetry Soc., 1972; Ala. State Poetry Soc. Award, 1971; Evans Spencer Wall Meml. Award, Nat. Fed. State Poetry Socs., 1973; Joseph Martin Long Award, Tex. Poetry Soc., 1973, & many more. Address: 9 Washington Ave., Cambridge, MA 02140, U.S.A.

RICHARDSON, Margaret O(nrust), b. 14 Jul. 1923. Homemaker. Education: High School, and adult courses in religion, writing, and art. Positions held: Governess; Sales Clerk, IBM Operator, Office Worker. Founder and President, The Daly City Creative Writers Group. Contbr. to: The American Poet; Caravan; Orphic Lute; Reflections Press; Penman; Pen; The Ladder; Prairie Poet; The Muse; Angel Hour: Crawford County Courier; Hoosier Challenger; Angel Flyer; Aloha to Hawaii; Young Pub. Anthol.; Bay Shore Breeze; Spencer Book Co.; Williamsburg News; Coney Island Times; S.F. Territorial News; Jeans Journal; Merlins Magic; Poets Bulletin; Harbor Lights; Modern Maturity; County Living Projects; The Angels; The Guild; Phylis; Author-Poet; Sunrise, Sunset & Silhouette; Poetry Club; Karyn; Mizpah Messenger; Ladies Delight; Graphomania; Oakland Tribune; Los Angeles Weekly; Pixie Angel; Bardic Echoes; Quoin; Clover, etc. Awards: Best Light Verse Book Award, 1967; Pixie Awards, 1967, 1969; Award for Poetry Anthol. Title, 1968; Certificate Award, 1968; 3 Book Awards, 1969; Record Award, 1969; 2 Book Awards, 1970; Book Award, 1971; Continuous Hon. Mentions, etc. Address: 243 Lakeshire Dr., Daly City, CA 94015, USA.

RICHARDSON, Marion Jane. Born 4 Nov. Secretary; Actress (retired). Education: studied piano, voice & drama; Journalism at Hunter Coll., and spec. classes in Spanish and poetry. Married; 2 d. Positions held: Sec.; Asst. Credit Mgr. & Hd. Corres., MO Dept., 5th Ave. Store, NYC; Actress, off-Broadway & summer stock. Memberships: Haiku Soc. of America; Acad. of American Poets; NY Poetry Forum; World Poetry Soc. Intercontinental; London Poetry Soc. (World Poets' Resource Center); Internat. Clover Poetry Soc.; United Amateur Press; Internat. Poetry Soc. (UK). Published works: From these Years, 1968; Images, 1968; Moments, 1969; A Merry Christmas, 1972. Contbr. to: Bay Shore Breeze & Pacific Breeze (anthol.); Angel Publications; Phylis; Mustang Review; Jean's Journal; Poetry Preview; The Blue Print; World Poetry Soc. Intercontinental; Fellowship in Prayer; Unity Mag.; Friendly Way; Haiku Highlights; Dragonfly HH; Modern Haiku; Haiku; Haiku West; Kansas Kernels; Robin's Song; Tumble Weeds; Poets Guild; Nutmegger Anthol.; Thom Henricks Author/Poet and Anthols.; Ruddy Haiku Hunt; Driftwood East; Sand Pebbles; Mimeorays; Poets on Parade; Ideals; Quintessence; Gems; Shore Review; Star Journal of NJ; Olive Hill Times (Ky.); Valley Centre, etc. Recip. various awards, including: Haiku; Int. Clover Soc.; hon. mentions, etc. Address: 320 E. 42nd St., Apt. 208, New York, NY 10017, USA.

RICHARDSON, Vincent Phipps, b. 9 July 1921. Clerical & Administrative Worker. Education: Pvte., secondary & commercial schls. Positions held: Trade Union Wkr., Clerical & Administrative Wkrs.' Union; Active in Labour Party; Twice Parliamentary Candidate, ibid; Lay Preacher, Meth. Church. Memberships: UN Assn.; York Poetry Soc.; Yorkshire Poet's Assn. Contbr. to the following anthols., jrnls., mags., etc: Tribune; Peace News; Viewpoints; Envoi; New Expression; Headland; Scrip; Yorkshire Poets Anthol., 1971; Ludd's Mill; Somethings; Breakthru; Pause; BBC, etc. Honours, awards: 1st Prize, Envoi Poetry Competition, 1971. Address: Brockett Willows, Daw Lane, Appleton Roebuck, York, UK.

RICHEBOEUF, Suzanne, pen name **RICQ, Anne,** b. 4 Sept. 1922. Secretary. Married, 2 daughters, 1 deceased. Memberships: Soc. of Letters of Saintonge & Aunis; Int. Soc. of Arts & Letters; Cultural Assn. of the Violet Legion; Acad. of Classical Poets of France. Published works: Le Printemps et l'Eté puis l'Automne, 1964; Troublante Afrique, 1972. Contbr. to: Revue de la S.L.S.A.; L'Etrave; La Légion Violette; La Coupe d'Ambroisie. Honours, awards: Hon. Mention, Competition for Ambroisie Cup, 1970; Chevalier, Int. Order of Renaissance of Arts & Letters, 1967; Chevalier, Order of Poetic Merit, Acad. of Classical Poets of France, 1971; Medal & Prize, Religious Inspiration, S.L.A., 1971; 1st Prize for Sonnet, ibid,

1971, etc. Address: B.P. 20498, Abidjan, Ivory Coast, W. Africa.

RICHFORD, Frederick George, b. 11 Dec. 1907. Professor, Poet. Education: Univ. of London. Positions held: Sr. Engl. Lectr. & Acting Prin., Coll. of Engl., St. Leonard's-on-Sea; Reviewer, Ore (jrnl.); Reviewer, Outposts (jrnl.). Memberships: Engl. Assoc.; Soc. of Authors; Int. PEN; Fellow, Royal Soc. of Arts. Published works: Mythology & Religion In English Epic Poetry, forthcoming. Contbr. to: Spring Anthol., 1964. Address: c/o Outposts Quarterly Poetry Mag., 209 E Dulwich Grove, London SE22, UK.

RICKER, Vivian, b. 24 Oct. 1898. Poet; Lawyer. Education: Rice Univ. & Houston Law Schl.; Admitted to The Tex. Bar, 1930. Memberships: Past Pres., Elizabeth Baldwin Lit. Soc. Alumnae, Rice Univ.; Poetry Soc. of Tex.; Past Pres., Houston Chap., Poetry Soc. of Tex. Published works: The Divided Heart, 1971. Contbr. to: The Christian Sci. Monitor; The Lyric; The Christian Family; The Lamp; The Am. Bard; Holland's mag.; Kaleidograph; The Ave Maria; The Westminster Mag.; Yearbooks of the Poetry Soc. of Tex. & others. Recip. 44 cash prizes, Poetry Soc. of Tex., Awards, Writers Unlimited of Miss.; Prizes, Nat. Fed. of State Poetry Socs. Address: 3736 Jardin, Houston, TX 77005, U.S.A.

RICKETTS, Elizabeth Page Mayer, pen name **RICKETTS, Elizabeth,** b. 6 Mar. 1919. Secondary School Teacher. Education: B.A., Coll. of Educ., Fla. Atlantic Univ., Boca-Raton, Fla., 1969; Miami-Dade Jr. Coll.; Univ. of Miami, Coral Gables; Fla. State Univ., Tallahassee, Fla. Married Emery Ricketts, Jr., div., 2 sons, 2 daughters. Positions held: Proof Rdr., Westchester Publrs., White Plains, N.Y., 1960-61; V.P., Freight Traffic Advisors, Miami, Fla., 1962-65; Lab. Techn., Univ. of Miami, Coral Gables, Fla., 1965-66; Sub. Tchr., Dade Co. Bd., Pub. Instr., 1967-69; Tchr., Engl., Miami Sr. H.S., ibid, Pub. Instr., 1969–; Sponsor, Creative Writing Club of Miami Sr. H.S., printers, publrs. & writers of Insight mag., 1972 & '73, Tchr. of Creative Media, inclng. Radio & TV prodn., etc., 1973 '74. Memberships: Poetry Soc. of Am.; Poetry Soc. of Ga.; Laramore-Rader Poetry Grp., Miami, Fla.; Acad. of Am. Poets. Contbr. to: Fla. Poets, 1940; Singing in the Sun, 1964; Ladies' Home Jrnl.; Miami Daily News; Miami Sun; N.Y. Times; Fla. Flambeau FSU; Falcon MDJC Yearbook; The Village Post; Personnel & Guidance Jrnl.; Quill & Scroll; Veritas; Univ. of Miami Staff mag. Honours, awards etc: 3rd prize, Serious Poetry, Int. Contest, SE Conf., Nat. League of Am. Pen Women, 1961; 1st Prize, Laramore-Rader Contest, Poem in mem. of Joseph Auslander, Una Voce Pura, 1965; 1st Prize, Poem in mem. of Dr. Fay Lucille Corey, 1966; Annual Award, 1967. Address: 1435 S.W. 127 Court, Miami, FL 33144, U.S.A.

RICKS, Margaret Mary, b. 29 Aug. 1912. Housewife. Married, five children. Memberships: Int. Poetry Soc.; Ohio Poetry Soc.; Past Pres., Akron Br., Ohio Poetry Day Assn. Published works: Halcyon & Fury, 1963; Stage Magician, 1966. Contbr. to: Am. Weave; Am. Bard; Columbus Dispatch; Columbus Citizen; Christian Sci. Monitor; Denver Post; Adult Tchr.; Epos; Encore; Green World; Haiku Highlights; Cats Mag.; Kauri; Small Pond; West Richfield News & Calendar; U.S. Lady; The Villager; Prairie Schooner; Prairie Poet; Poet Lore; Lyric; 59 Ohio Poets; Poetry Cleveland, etc. Honours, awards: Nat. Fed. State Poetry Socs. Grand Prize & Villanelle, 1973; Ohio Lyric Gold Cup, 1973. Address: 624 Cove Blvd., Akron, OH 44319, U.S.A.

RICKWORD, J. Edgell, b. 22 Oct. 1898. Editor. Positions held: Ed., Calendar of Mod. Letters, 1925-27; Assoc. Ed., Left Review, 1934-38; Ed., Our Time, 1944-47. Published works: Behind the Eyes, 1921; Invocations to Angels, 1928; Twittingpan and Some Others, 1931; Collected Poems, 1947. Contbr. to: (anthologies) Comic and Curious Verse, 1952; Faber Book of Twentieth Century Verse, 1953; Chatto Book of Modern Poetry, 1956. Recip., Arts Coun. Award,

1966. Address: c/o E. & J. Stevens, 2 Prospect Rd., London N.W.2, U.K.

RIDDELL, Alan Thomas Cockburn, b. 16 Apr. 1927. Journalist. Education: M.A., Edinburgh Univ. Positions held: Staff work on sev. papers in Britain & Australia inclng. Scotsman, Daily Telegraph, Sydney Morning Herald; currently p/t features sub-ed. & occasional theatre & book reviewer for Daily & Sunday Telegraphs; Fndr., Scottish lit. qtly. 'Lines Review', 1952; Ed., ibid, 1952-55 & '62-67. Member, Poetry Soc. Published works: (books) Beneath the Summer, 1952; Majorcan Interlude, 1960; The Stopped Landscape, 1968; Eclipse, 1972. Rep. in many anthols. & contbr. to jrnls., reviews, newspapers. Participant in var. grp. shows of concrete & visual poetry. One-man show at New 57 Gallery, Edinburgh, 1971. Honours, awards: Hon. Mention, BBC Scottish Coronation Yr. Poetry Comp., 1953; Heinemann Prize, Australian Book Week, 1956; Scottish Arts Coun. Poetry Prize, 1968. Address: c/o Clydesdale Bank, 198 Piccadilly, London W.1, U.K.

RIDDELL, Elizabeth, b. 21 March 1909. Poet; Editor. Married to E.N. Greatorex. Positions held: Journalist, Smith's Weekly & Sydney Sunday Sun, 1930; Ed., Nat. Woman's Mag. Published works: The Untrammelled, 1940; Poems, 1948; Forbears, 1961. Contbr. to: Mod. Australian Verse, 1964. Address: c/o Angus & Robertson Ltd., 89 Castlereagh St., Sydney, Australia.

RIDDELL, Mary Ellen, b. 20 Dec. 1897. Poet and Writer. Education: Corres. Courses & Evening School. Positions held: Steno., Ctrl. Pa. Lib. Co.; US Rubber Co.; Fleck-Marshall Co.; Hd., Steno. Dept., Smith Prtg. Co.; Sec. to Exec. V.P., Susque-Trust Co.; Sec. to Hd. of Investment Dept., Lycoming Trust Co.; Exec. Legal Sec., Furst, McCormick, Muir & Lynn; Corporate Sec., Dir. & Registered Rep., Haven Securities, Inc.; Registered Rep., Waddell & Read, Inc., Investment Counselor. Memberships: Internat. Poetry Soc. (Fellow); Pa. Poetry Soc.; Creative Writers Forum of Williamsport. Published works: Thoughts in the Night, 1965. Contbr. to sev. anthols. including: Internat. Who's Who in Poetry Anthol., 1972. (magazine contbr.) Mature Years. Honours: 1st Prize & 3 Hon. Mentions, Greater Williamsport Community Arts Festival, 1961. Address: 1100 Market St., Williamsport, PA 17701, USA.

RIDING, Laura, b. 16 Jan. 1901. Poet, Writer. Education: Cornell Univ. Married to Schuyler B. Jackson. Positions held: Hon. Mbr., The Fugitives (group of Southern Am. Poets); Ed., Epilogue; operated Seiz in Press with Robert Graves; has renounced poetry as humanly inadequate & has sought a more direct linguistic approach to the handling of truth; working with her husband on a definitional project concerning this search for a more direct linguistic approach. Published works: The Close Chaplet, 1926; Contemporaries and Snobs, 1927; Survey of Modernist Poetry (w. Robert Graves), 1927; Anarchism Is Not Enough, 1928; Experts Are Puzzled, 1930; Progress of Stories, 1935; A Trojan Ending, 1937; Collected Poems, 1938; The Left Heresy (w. Harry Kemp), 1939; Lives of Wives, 1939; (Ed.) The World and Outselves, 1938. Contbr. to: Art & Lit.; Chelsea; Civilta Delle Macchine; The Telling. Address: Box 35, Wabasso, FL 32970, U.S.A.

RIDLER, Anne Barbara, b. 30 July 1912. Poet; Writer. Published works: (poetry) Poems, 1939; A Dream Observed, 1941; The Nine Bright Shiners, 1943; The Golden Bird, 1951; A Matter of Life & Death, 1959; Selected Poems, 1961; Some Time After, 1972; (plays) Cain, 1943; The Shadow Factory: A Nativity Play, 1946; Henry Bly & Other Plays, 1950; The Trial of Thomas Cranmer, 1956; Who Is My Neighbour? 1963. Editor: A Little Book of Modern Verse, 1941; Best Ghost Stories, 1945; Supplement to Faber Book of Modern Verse, 1951; The Image of the City & Other Essays by Charles Williams, 1958; Shakespeare Criticism 1935-60, 1963; Poems of James Thomson, 1963; Thomas Traherne, 1966. Contbr. to: Delta;

Seven; The Listener; The Times Lit. Supplement; Purpose; Horizon; New Writing; The New Statesman; The Critical Qtly.; The Sunday Times; The New Yorker; The N.Y. Times; Poetry (Chicago); Poetry, London. Address: 14 Stanley Rd., Oxford, U.K.

RIEDER, Violette, b. 9 Feb. 1890. Poet. Education: Collège de Chartres. Positions held: Tchr., Paris, 1929-50. Mbr., la Société des poètes français. Published works: les Rythmes du silence, 1926; Départs, 1928; Ciels, 1932; les Fiancés, 1934; Secret des vergers, 1938; Présages, 1949; Ex-Voto, 1953; Limonaire, 1954; Surgeons, 1958; Tracé sur l'onde, 1964; Rêver dans l'isle, 1965. Honours & Awards: Officier des Palmes académiques; Lauréate du Prix Alfred de Vigny, 1949; Prix Paul Verlaine, 1964.

RIEMER, Ruby, b. 18 Aug. 1924. College Teacher (Philosophy). Education: B.A., Temple Univ., Phila. Pa., U.S.A.; M.A., Boston Univ., Mass. Married Neal Riemer, 3 sons. Positions held: Instr. (Philos.), Pa. State Univ.; Lectr., Univ. of Wis.; Instr., Essex. Co. Coll., Newark, N.J. Contbr. to: The N.Y. Times; The Nation; Poet Lore; Poetry Out of Wisconsin (Anthol.); Festschrift for Helen Adolf (Anthol.); Cheshire; Pivot; Focus. Address: Village Road, Green Village, NJ 07935, U.S.A.

RIFKIN, Stephen, b. 30 Apr. 1939. Teacher. Education: B.A., Brooklyn Coll., N.Y., 1960; grad. work in Engl., ibid. Positions held: Sec. Schl. Tchr. of Engl. in the N.Y.C. Schl. System (Jr. & Sr. H.S.) Member, Poetry Soc. of Am. Contbr. to: Landscapes; Latitudes; Poet Lore. Address: 194-02 A, 64 Circle, Apt. 2C, Fresh Meadows, NY 11365, U.S.A.

RIGGS, Dionis, pen name **RIGGS, Dionis Coffin,** b. 6 Aug. 1898. Teacher. Education: N.J. State Teachers' Coll.; Special Courses, Columbia Univ., and NY Univ. Married, Dr. Sidney N. Riggs, educator and illustrator; 3 d. Positions held: Teacher, rural school in NJ; Teacher, Lyndhurst, NJ; Adult education: History & Literature of Martha's Vineyard, M.V. Regional HS. Memberships: New England Poetry Club; Poetry Soc. of America; Acad. of American Poets; Poetry Soc. of Virginia; Martha's Vineyard Poetry Group. Published works: (Biog.) From Off Island, 1940 (USA), and as Martha's Vineyard (UK); Martha's Vineyard, Poems by 4 Vineyard poets, 1965; Sea Born Island, poems, 1969. Contbr. to: Good Housekeeping; Ladies' Home Journal; McCalls'; Yankee; American Weave; Antioch Review; Minnesota Review; CS Monitor; Kansas City Star; NY Herald-Tribune; NY Times; Saturday Evening Post; The Nation; Vineyard Gazette. Recip. Narrative Poetry Prize, Poet Lore, 1967; Hon. Mention, Stephen Vincent Benet Award, 1972; Hon. Mention, Lynchburg, Virginia, Poetry Festival, 1973. Address: West Tisbury, Martha's Vineyard, MA 02575, USA.

RIGHTMIRE, Charles Paul, b. 13 Aug. 1935. Sunday Editor. Education: Univ. of Montana, 1952-54; Eastern Montana Coll., Billings, 1964-70; B.A., Engl. Positions held: U.S. Air Force, 1955-59; Bill Collector, Mountain Bell, May-Sept., 1959; Reporter, Billings Gazette, 1959-60, Livingston Enterprise, 1960-61; Reporter & var. positions, Billings Gazette, 1961– (currently Sunday Ed.) Contbr. to: Denver Post Poetry Forum; Church Musician. Address: 2227 Spruce St., Billings, MT 59101, U.S.A.

RIGHTON, Marian Castle, pen name **EMERSON, Ethelyn,** b. 30 June 1910. Housewife; Writer. Widow. Memberships: W.C.T.U.; Nat. Writers Club, Denver. Published works: (anthologies) Poetry Parade No.4, 1967; All Time Favorite Poetry, 1970. Contbr. to: Northern Messenger; The Adventurer (Toronto); Sherbrooke Daily Record; Link & Visitor; Reflections; The Christian (Mo.); S.S. World; Christian Home; Congregationalist; Treasure; Family Herald; Harbor Lights; Author/Poet; Wildfire Poetry mag.; Purpose; Poetry Prevue, etc. Recip., var. poetry prizes. Address: 326 Denison St. W., Granby, Que. J2G 4E4, Canada.

RILEY, Cyril Leslie, pen name **REILLY, Michael,** b. 18 Jan. 1922. Antiquarian Book Seller. Positions held: RAF; Chief Electrician in the Theatre; own business. Memberships: A.M. Inst. B.E.; past Mbr., Poetry Soc. & Soc. of Authors; Admnstr., Int. Soc. of Lit.; Correspondante à l'Etranger, Academie Française de la Poesie, France; Centre Int. d'Etudes Poetiques, Belgium. Published works: The Garden Sleeps, 1968; The Gypsy Maid, 1969; Consciousness, 1970; Life Dust, 1971; Into the Void, 1973. Contbr. to: anthols., 1969-73; The Dalesman; Telegraph & Argus; Craven Herald; BBC 2 & local radio stations; Academie Francaise de la Poesie Jrnl.; Acad. Am. Poets. Honours, awards: Medal Poetiques par Excellence, France, 1972; Hon. Ph.D., Paris, France, 1972. Address: 109 Main St., Burley in Wharfedale, Yorks., U.K.

RINALDI, Nicholas Michael, b. 2 Apr. 1934. College Professor. Education: A.B., Shrub Oak, 1957; M.A., Fordham Univ., 1960; Ph.D., ibid, 1963. Married Jacqueline Blanche Tellier, 4 children (Christina, Paul, Stephen, David). Positions held: Tchng. positions at Fordham, St. John's, CUNY, Columbia, Univ. of Conn.; currently Prof., Engl. Dept., Fairfield Univ. Memberships: Poetry Soc. of Am.; NESPA. Contbr. to: New American Review; Epoch; Prairie Schooner; Thought; Descant; Southern Poetry Review; Carolina Quarterly; New England Review; Poem; Beyond Baroque; This Issue; Goliards. Recip., Fellowships, Ind. Univ. Writers Conf. & Colo. Univ. Writers Conf., 1969. Address: Fairfield Univ., Fairfield, CT, U.S.A.

RING, Israel, b. 22 Dec. 1922. Teacher. Published works: David & Joab (play), 1952; Poems of Diamond, 1962; Understanding Poetry (research w. translations), 1965; The Right of Being Morning Time (poems), 1967; Poems of Theodor Storm (transl.), 1970; The Kibbutz & the Future (research), 1971; Ilona Barne'ah (novel). Contbr. to: Al-Hamishmar; Hedim; Keshel; Orlogin. Recip., prize, for 'The Kibbutz & the Future'. Address: Kibbutz Ein-Hamifratz 25210, Israel.

RINGBOM, Marten Eric Jonas, b. 14 June 1934. Lecturer. Education: M.A., Univ. of Helsinki, 1958; Lic.Phil., ibid, 1963; Postgrad. studies, Oxford Univ., 1958-59. Married Christina E. Sucksdorff, 2 children. Positions held: Jrnlst., newspaper Hufvudstadsbladet, 1957-60; Rsch. Asst., State Commn. for Hymanistic Studies, 1962-67; Asst. Lectr. in Ethics, Univ. of Helsinki, 1967–. Memberships: Sec., Finland's Svenska Författareförening, 1960-65; Vi.Chmn., ibid, 1968–; Chmn., Ctr. Org. for Lit. Work, 1973–; Finnish PEN Club. Published works: (poetry) Begrip (Understand), 1961; Den flerdimensionella människan (The Multidimensional Man),· 1969; (transl. & commentary) Aristoteles, Den nikomachiska etiken, 1967; Finlands svenska författareförening, 1919-69; Författarens villkor i Norden, 1973. Address: Brunnsgatan 10 A, SF-06100 Borga, Finland.

RIOFF, Suzanne Berger, b. 5 Apr. 1944. Writer; Teacher. Education: B.A., Northwestern Univ., 1966; M.A., Johns Hopkins Univ., 1969; grad. course in Poetry Therapy, Ind. Univ. Positions held: Instr. of Engl., Mass. Bay Community Coll., 1969-74; Poetry Workshops for Mass. Coun. on the Arts, 1970-74; Instr. of Engl., Boston Univ., 1974. Contbr. to: The New Yorker; Antaeus; Women/Poems; If You Want; Cimarron Review; Phoenix; No More Masks; Aspen Review; Hellcoal Press; Perspective; Arion's Dolphin; Boston Univ. Mag. Readings at Harvard Advocate, Colgate Univ., Harvard Univ. Recip., Prize in Creative Writing, Northwestern Univ., Evanston, Ill., 1966. Address: 61 Frost St., Cambridge, MA 02140, U.S.A.

RIPPLINGER, Yvette J., b. 3 Apr. 1922. UN Secretariat (permanent member). Education: Secondary, and sep. studies at The Sorbonne, Paris; Columbia Univ.; NYC Coll.; NY Univ. for Engl., writing, literature and arts. Positions held: Admin. of training progs. for developing countries officials, UN Inst. for Training and Research (UNITAR), NY. Memberships: Catholic Poetry Soc.; Poetry Soc. of America (since 1962).

RITCHIE, Elisavietta Artamonoff, pen name, **RITCHIE, Elisavietta,** Writer; Poet; Translator; Instructor in French. Education: B.A., Univ. of Calif., U.S.A.; Cornell Univ.; Sorbonne, Paris, France; Am. Univ., Wash. D.C. Married Lyell Hale Ritchie, 3 children. Positions held: Poet-in-Res., Va. Commn. for the Arts at Olde Creek Elem. Schl., Fairfax, 1972 & Oakton Elem. Schl., Va., 1973; John Eaton Schl., 1973-74; Grad. Tchng. Fellow & Lectr., Am. Univ., Wash. D.C. Memberships: Poetry Soc. of Am.; Ga. Poetry Soc. Published works: Timbot, 1970; Translation of Aleksandr Blok's The Twelve, 1969; Readings in the French-Speaking World, 2 vols., 1969; Tightening the Circle Over Eel Country, 1974. Articles, stories, poems, reviews, translations from var. langs. for govt. & pvte. clients, 1955–. Anthols. in which poems appear: The Diamond Anthol.; Adam Among the Television Trees; Washington Poets; New Generation Poetry; Fiftieth Anniversary Anthology of the Ga. Poetry Soc.; Four Dumb Broads, etc. Contbr. to: N.Y. Times; Christian Sci. Monitor; Wash. Post; Wash. Star; Paris Tribune; Chicago Tribune; Art. Int.; Voyages; Mass. Review; So. Poetry Review; New Republic; Denver Quarterly; Discovery; Bitterroot; DeKalb Lit. Arts Jrnl. & many others. Invited to record for Lib. of Congress series, Contemporary American Poets. Has given poetry readings at many colls., schls. & univs. & at Rio de Janeiro, Brazil under USIS auspices. Honours, awards incl: Marion Reedy Award, Poetry Soc. of Am., 1973. Address: 3207 Macomb NW, Wash. DC 20008, U.S.A.

RIVERA, Tomás, b. 22 Dec. 1935. Professor of Literature. Education: B.S. in Ed., Southwest Tex. State Univ., 1958; M.Ed., ibid, 1964; M.A., Univ. of Okla., 1969; Ph.D., ibid, 1969. Positions held: Instr., Southwest Tex. Jr. Coll., 1965-66; Grad. Asst., Univ. of Okla., 1966-68; Instr., ibid, & Asst. Dir., Spanish Studies Prog. in Madrid, 1968-69; Assoc. Prof. of Spanish, Sam Houston State Univ., 1969-71; Full Prof. of Spanish Lit., Dir., Div. of For. Langs., Lits. & Linguistics, Coll. of Humanities, Univ. of Tex. at San Antonio, 1971-73; currently Prof. & Assoc. Dean, Coll. of Multidisciplinary Studies, ibid. Memberships incl: Phi Theta Kappa; Sigma Delta Pi; Bd. Dirs., Editl. Bd., MICTLA Publs., 1971–; Editl. Bd., El magazin, San Antonio, 1972–; Bd. Dirs., Pan Am. Student Forum, 1965. Published works: (poetry) 'Me lo enterraron' Original Works. A Foreign Language Qtly., 1967; 'Poetry' El grito, 1969; 'Young Voices' Songs & Dreams, 1972; 'Ten Poems' Chicano Literature: An Anthology, 1973; 'Seven Poems' El espejo/The Mirror, 1972; 'The Child', 'Young Voices', 'When Love To Be', Revista Chicana-Riqueña, Vol. 1, 1973; Always & Other Poems, 1973; var. short stories & lit. criticism. Honours, awards incl: Nat. Quinto Sol Lit. Award, 1971. Address: 5912 Trone Trail, San Antonio, TX 78238, U.S.A.

ROACH, Eric M. Teacher; Writer. Positions held: Feature Writer, Evening News, Trinidad, W. Indies. Contbr. to: Bim; Caribbean Quarterly; (anthologies) Young Commonwealth Poets '65, 1965; Caribbean Voices, 1966; Caribbean Literature, 1966; New Voices of the Commonwealth, 1968.

ROBB, Wallace Havelock, b. 19 May 1888. Poet. Positions held: Office Clerk, Canadian Bronze Co.; Estab. & Pres., Canuck Supply Ltd., 10 yrs. Mbr., Kingston Histl. Soc. Published works incl: Thunderbird, 1949; Tecumtha, 1958; Kayonakonte, 1961; Hail Canada, 1966; The Quill & the Candle, 1927; The Door of Dawn, 1937; The Tyrian Quill, 1969. Leading columnist for Canadian Countryman for 22 yrs. Syndicated wild-life stories to many Canadian newspapers. Var. articles & poems in Toronto Globe & Mail. Monthly for Canadian Red Cross Junior & Canadian Outdoors, etc. Honours, awards: Robed in the tyrian, St. Catharines, Ont., 1955; Adopted by blood rite by Mohawks of the Kente & made Great White Eagle & Pine Tree Chief of the Iroquois, 1948. Address: Abbey Dawn, R.R.1., Kingston, Ont. K7L 4V1, Canada.

ROBBINS, Julie, pen name, **JULIE OF COLORADO SPRINGS.** Registered Nurse. Education: Crawford W. Long School of Nursing; B.A. in Arts & Sciences, Univ. of Colorado. Positions held: Private duty, Calif., Texas, Colorado; currently medical and surgical staff duty in Government Hospital, Colorado. Memberships: Pen Woman; Pikes Peak Poetry Soc.; Colorado State Poetry Soc.; World Poetry Soc. Intercontinental. Published work: Poetry and Peanut Butter, 1970. Contbr. to: Colo. Spring Gazette; Colo. Springs Sun; Tempo; The Angels; Pegasus; Nova Scotia; Encore; The Muse; Voices Internat.; Cyclo-Flame; Orphic Lute; Modern Images; Quoin; Jean's Journal; Denver Post; Beaumont Daily Record; Clackamas County News; Capper's Weekly; South & West; Yearbook of Mod. Poetry; Bardic Echoes; J. Mark Press; Friendship Ferry; Verdure Publications; Pikes Peak Skylines Anthol.; Hyacinths and Biscuits; Valley Views; The Paper; Poets' Guild; Outstanding Contemporary Poetry (anthol.); Quintessence; Mississippi Review; The Log; Southwest Heritage, and others. Recip. American Poetry Fellowship Soc. Award, 1970; Major Poets Anthol. Award, 1971; Hon. Mention, Pikes Peak Poetry Fellowship, May, 1972; Moon Age Poets Anthol., Book Award, 1971; Great Ideas Anthol., Hon. Mention; Work used on radio WEFG Virginia and on Afterglow Poetry Program in Arkansas; (Two Thousand Women of Achievement, 1972 listing), etc. Address: 105 Everett Dr., Colorado Springs, CO 80911, USA.

ROBBINS, Martin, b. 10 July 1931. Writer; Teacher. Education: B.A., Univ. of Colo.; M.A., State Univ. of Iowa; Ph.D., Brandeis Univ. Positions held: Sr. Fulbright-Hayes Lectureship in Am. Lit., Nat. Univ. of Buenos Aires, Argentina; currently teaching writing courses at Harvard Univ. & Boston Coll. Is a trained concert singer (baritone) & appears from time to time in oratorio, in progs. of Elizabethan songs, Lieder & Am. Hist. through songs & readings from lit. Memberships: Poetry Soc. of Am.; V.P., New England Poetry Club, 1 yr. Published works: A Refrain of Roses, 1965; A Reply to the Headlines: Poems 1965-70. Rep. in following anthols: Sprints & Distances, 1965; Messages, 1973. Contbr. to: N.Y. Times; N.Y. Herald Tribune; Chicago Tribune; Colo. Qtly.; San Francisco Review; Voices; Fiddlehead; The Jewish Spectator; World Federalist, etc. Address: 17 Pond St., Jamaica Plain, MA 02130, U.S.A.

ROBERSON, Charles Edwin, pen name **ROBERSON, Ed.,** b. 26 Dec. 1939. Educator. Education: B.A., Univ. of Pittsburgh. Positions held: Rsch. Asst., Limnology, Univ. of Pitts.; Advt. Mgr., Aspen Corp.; Tankman, Pittsburgh Zoological Soc. Aquazoo; Artist, Film Graphics Corp.; Lectr., Community Coll. of Allegheny County.; Instr., Engl., Univ. of Pitts. Member of U.S. El Sangay Mountain Climbing Expedition to Peruvian & Ecuadorian Andes, rep. the Explorers Club of Pittsburgh, 1963. Published works: When Thy King Is A Boy, 1970. Contbr. to: (anthols.) Third World Voices; Heart Blows: Black Veils; The Poetry of Black Am.; New Black Voices; The Poetry of The Negro; New Directions: 22; May We Speak; (mags., jrnls.) Atlantic Monthly; Beloit Poetry Jrnl.; Black Lines: Jrnl. of Black Studies; Detroit Artists' Workshop: Work/3. Recip., Grand Prize Atlantic Monthly, 1962. Address: 542 Elm St., P.O. Box 142, East Millstone, NJ 08873, U.S.A.

ROBERTS, Carol A. (Ann), b. 5 Mar. 1933. Teacher. Education: B.S. in Ed., Shippensburg State Coll.; M.A. in Engl., Middlebury Coll., Vt.; M.S. in Educ., Temple Univ., Phila. Positions held: Elem. Tchr., Harrisburg, Pa., 1955-59 & Ctrl. Dauphin Schl. Dist., 1960-63; Asst. Prof. of Engl., Shippensburg Coll., 1963-66; Elem. Tchr., Ctrl. Dauphin Schl. Dist., 1966-73; Elem. Lang. Arts. Comm., 1970-73. Memberships: Nat. Fed. of State Poetry Socs.; Mbrship Chmn., Pa. Poetry Soc., 1971; V.P., Keysner Poets of Harrisburg, 1972-

73 & Pres., 1973-74; Kappa Delta Pi; South & West Inc. Published works: A Nebish named Lovable, 1971. Contbr. to: South & West; Quadernia di Poesi; Time of Singing; NFSPS Prize Poems; Poet India (Northeast edn); Poetic License; Pa. Poetry Soc's Prize Poems; Shippensburg State Coll. Review; John F. Kennedy Meml. Anthol.; Timeless Treasures; A Goodly Heritage; The Written Word Anthol.; Poems of Patriotism & Peace. Honours, awards. South & West Book Publ. Awards, 1971; Convention Gemstone Award (NFSPS Convention), 1972, etc. Address: 308 Arbys Rd., Harrisburg, PA 17109, U.S.A.

ROBERTS, Dorothy (Mrs. A.R. Leisner). Poet. Education: Univ. of New Brunswick, Fredericton, Canada. Married w. 2 children. Positions held: Formerly Worked as a Journalist. Published works: Dazzle, 1957; In Star and Stalk, 1959; Twice to Flame, 1961; Extended, 1967. Contbr. to (Anthols.): Best Poems of 1955, 56, 57: The Borestone Mountain Poetry Awards, 1956; Book of Canadian Poetry, 1957; A Canadian Anthology, 1961; Enchanted Land, 1967; (Jrnls.): Hudson Review; Canadian Forum; Fiddlehead; Queen's Quarterly; Dalhousie Review; Delta; Yale Review; Jrnl. of General Education. Address: 143 West Park Avenue, State Coll., PA 16801, USA.

ROBERTS, Edna, pen names, **HILTON, Josephine; FINLAY, Michael; OWEN, Richard; EDDY, Roberta.** (also 'Ghost' Writer), b. 3 Nov. 1912. Journalist. Education: 2 yrs. at village school, and privately thereafter. Married; 1 s. Positions held: Nelson Leader, 12 yrs.; Mansfield Reporter; Yorkshire Eve. News; News Chronicle; BBC The Window-Guideposts. Memberships: Burnley and Dist. Writers Circle (Pres., and founder member); Lancashire Authors' Assoc.; Yorkshire Poets Assoc.; Mid Pennine Assoc. for the Arts. Contbr. to more than 250 mags. (worldwide), with prizewinning poems included in 5 anthols. (and many poems broadcast); The Way of Life; John O'London's; The Writer; The Lady; Poetry; Methodist Mag.; Dalesman; Country Quest; Yorkshire Post; Yorkshire Achievement; The Window; Woman's Weekly; Good Housekeeping; The Friend; Lancashire Life; Christian Herald; Gallery; Eve. Star; Burnley Express; Nelson Leader; Mansfield Reporter; Eve. Telegraph; The Christian; Writer's Review; Red Rose Mag., etc. Awards: Batty Cup; Writer of the Year Award; Simon Award, 1969 (all Lancs. Authors' Assoc.). Total awards since 1969: 3 rose bowls, 5 cups, 1 statue, 2 silver medals, 2 bronze medals, 13 1st prizes, 10 2nd prizes, and 27 3rd prizes in various literary competitions, drama festivals, etc. Address: 22 Reedley Gr., Reedley, Nr Burnley, Lancs. BB10 2LA, UK.

ROBERTS, Fay Ingram, pen name **INGRAM, Gloria,** b. 18 Jan. 1907. Civil Service Clerk. Education: Tex. Tech. Univ., Lubbock, Tex. Married, Paul James Roberts. Positions held: Tchr., Rural Schls. of W. Tex.; Civil Service Clerk. Memberships: Poetry Soc. of Tex. Publications: In White Starlight, 1962. Contbr. to: Internat. Who's Who in Poetry Anthol. Address: 2912 Hubby Ave., Waco, TX. 76707, USA.

ROBERTS, Kathryn L., b. 29 June 1914. Foster Parent for Mentally & Physically Handicapped Babies (Ret'd.) Education: A.A., Univ. of Minn. Married, 1 son, 1 daughter. Positions held: Foster Parent for Physically & Mentally Handicapped Babies, 8 yrs.; Employee, Department Store, 4 yrs.; Foster Home for Older Women of Welfare, 4 yrs. Memberships: Sec., Mnpls. Poetry Soc.; League of Minn. Poets, & Midwest Chaparral. Contbr. to: Durango Herald Democrat; Colorado Sun; Mocassin, Minn. State Poetry mag. Address: 4732 Blansdell Ave. South, Minneapolis, MN 55409, U.S.A.

ROBERTS, Lotus Lorraine, pen name **ROBERTS, Lotus Knowlton,** b. 19 Sept. 1907. Library Assistant; Proof Reader. Married Charles B. Roberts, dec., 1 daughter (Carol). Positions held: Lib. Asst., Pottsville, Pa., 1925-33; Proof Rdr., Telegraph Press, Harrisburg,

Pa. until retirement (22 yrs.) Memberships: Harrisburg Chapt. of the Pa. Poetry Soc.; Treas. & Contest Chmn., Keysner Poets Chapt., ibid; Nat. Fed. of State Poetry Socs.; Harrisburg Manuscript Club; South & West Lit. Soc. International; St. Petersburg Poetry Soc.; Am. Poetry League. Contbr. to: Evening News, Harrisburg, Pa.; Poetic License; Kennedy Meml. Anthol.; A Burst of Trumpets Anthol.; Timeless Treasures Anthol.; Poems of Patriotism & Peace Anthol.; Stepping Stones to Faith Anthol.; From Sea to Sea in Song; Quaderni di Poesie, etc. Recip., Virginia Burley Miller Meml. Award, Keysner Poets, 1973. Address: 308 Arby's Rd., Harrisburg, PA 17109, U.S.A.

ROBERTS, Lynette, b. 4 July 1909 in Buenos Aires. Poet and Author. Education: Bournemouth HS; Constance Spry (and horticultural diplomas). Published works: Poems, 1944 (2nd impression, 1945); Village Dialect, 1944; Gods With Stainless Ears, 1951; The Endeavour (novel), 1954. Contbr. to: (anthols.) New Directions, 1949; New British Poets, 1948-49; Poetry in Wartime; Modern Welsh Poetry, 1944; Celtic Anthol.; plus 5 others; (newspapers, journals) La Nacion (Argentine); Life & Letters; Times Lit. Supp.; The Field; South Wales Post; Horizon; Listener; New Statesman and Nation; The World Review; Departure; Penguin New Writing; Here and Now; Poetry London; Now; Poetry Quarterly; Time & Tide; Poetry and Poverty; Wales; The Welsh Review; Dublin Mag.; Fantasy; Furioso; New Directions; Poetry Chicago; Voices; Briarcliff Qtly. (Canada); Epoch; Quarto; Agonia; also various scripts & work broadcast; poetry readings at Oxford Univ.; Inst. of Contemp. Arts; East End Music Assoc.; Ethical Church; "Poetry & Plays in Pubs", etc. Address: 99 Lamas St., Carmarthen, Carmarthenshire, South Wales, UK.

ROBERTS, Percival R., Jr., pen name **ROBERTS, Percy,** b. 4 Apr. 1910. Author; Writer; Lecturer. Education: Univ. of Delaware, 3 yrs. Positions held: Lab. Asst. at Biochemical Rsch. Fndn. in Newark, Del.; Lab. Asst., Chemical Engrng. Dept., Univ. of Del.; Shift Chemist, Dupont Co. pigments plant, Newport; Sawmill Operator, power chain saw sales & service. Ed. & Publsr., The Poetry Press, 1934-36. Hon. Mbr., United Poets Laureate Int., 1967. Published works: Minor Prelude, 1966; Flowers From The Ghetto, 1968; Monadelphous, 1970; My Side of the Street, 1974. Contbr. to: Bozart & Contemporary Verse; Blue Moon; Versemaker; Southern Lit. Review; Popular Poetry; Flue Dust; The Poet's Corner; Galley Three; Random Shots; Davis Anthol. of Newspaper Verse; The Am. Bard; Nat. Poetry Day Comm. for reading his poetry over the Voice of Am. radio; South & West; Poet, etc. Honours, awards: Page Poet (w. son) Winter 1969 issue of Am. Bard. Address: 47 East Cleveland Ave., Newark, DE 19711, U.S.A.

ROBERTS, Percival Rudolph III, b. 2 Nov. 1935. Art Educator; Administrator; Poet. Education: A.B., M.A., Univ. of Del.; Ed.D., Ill. State Univ.; Litt.D., Free Univ., Asia. Married Mary Jane McVaugh, 2 daughters. Positions held: US Naval Off.; Ops. Off., USS Portunus (ARC-1); Art Instr., Del. Art Ctr., Univ. of Del., 1960-65; Lectr. in Art, Ill. State Univ., 1965-68; First Artist in Res., Wm. Penn Meml. Mus., Pa., 1972; currently Chmn., Dept. of Art, Bloomsburg State Coll., Pa.; 9th Poet Laureate, State of Del. Memberships: Pres., Del. Assn. for Art Educ., 1964-65; Kappa Alpha; Kappa Delta Pi; Omicron Delta Kappa; Pres., Del. Poetry Soc., 1963-64; Acad. of Am. Poets; United Poets Laureate Int.; World Poetry Soc., Inc.; Hon. Rep., Nat. Poetry Day Comm.; Chmn., Eastern Region, Higher Educ., Div. NAEA, 1969-73; Acad. Am. Poets; Poetry Soc., U.K.; Pa. Art Educ. Assn.; Mid-states Artists Assn. Published works: Arches, 1962; Profiles of Delaware's Past Poets Laureate, 1964; Word Echoes, 1966; Centaurian Flight, 1968; Out, Out, Brief Candle, 1968; Red Sky in the Morning, 1974. Ed., mid Atlantic issue, Poet. Poetry Ed., Normal News, Ill.; Newark & Newcastle Weeklies; Palimpsest; Focus on Poetry. Eastern Rep: Cardinal Poetry Qtly.; Bitterroot; South &

West; Voices Int. Contbr. to: Poetry Review; Laurel Leaves; Am. Bard; Guild; S. & W. Rainbow; Hull House; Angels; Haiku Highlights; Poet, India; Major Poets; Fiddlehead; Human Voice; Venture, etc. Honours, awards: $500 Ship Award, Nat. Art Educ. Assn. Conf., Phila., 1965; $250 1st Profl. Educator's Award, DSEA, 1965; Am. Poets Gold Cup Award, Am. Poets Fellowship Soc.; Karta, Gold Medal, UPLI, 1967. Address: Dept. of Art, Bloomsburg State Coll., Bloomsburg, PA 17815, U.S.A.

ROBERTS, Sheila Valeria, b. 25 May 1937. English Lecturer. Education: M.A., Univ. of South Africa; Ph.D. student, Univ. of Cape Town. Positions held: Various typing jobs while studying; worked for the South African Institute of Race Relations while completing M.A. degree, and gave evening lectures to Black students. Contbr. to: Ophir; New Nation; Izwi; Contrast (8 short stories). Awarded a drama prize in competition held by the Foundation for Art and Theatre, Cape Town, 1973. Address: 6 Ipanema, Ringwood Road, Pretoria. Republic of South Africa.

ROBERTS JONES, Sally, b. 30 Nov. 1935. Librarian. Education: B.A., Univ. Coll. of N. Wales, Bangor; A.L.A., Schl. of Librarianship, North Western Polytechnic, Camden Town. Married, 2 sons. Positions held: Lib. Asst, Essex County Libs., 1960-65; Asst., Ref. Lib., London Borough of Havering, 1965-67; Ref. Libn., Borough of Port Talbot, 1967-70. Memberships: Sec./Treas., Yr Academi Gymreig (Engl. Lang. Sect.); Pres., Port Talbot Writers' Circle; Port Talbot Lit. Grp. Published works: Turning Away, 1969. Contbr. to following anthols., reviews, mags: Welsh Voices, 1967; The Lilting House, 1969; Young Commonwealth Poets '65, 1965; Poems '69, 1969; Poems '70, 1970; Tribune; The Poetry Review; Ambit; Extra Verse; Prism; The Welsh Nation; The Anglo-Welsh Review; Poetry Wales; Decal; Country Quest; Poetry 1; Dawn; Portal. Honours, awards: Plaque, Univ. of Wales Inter Coll. Eisteddfod, 1959; Welsh Arts Coun. Prize, 1969. Address: 3 Crown St., Port Talbot, Glamorgan, U.K.

ROBERTSON, Edith Anne, b. 10 Jan. 1883. Educ.: Girls High School, Glasgow. m. Prof. J.A. Robertson (dec.) w. 3 ds. Published works: Pilgrimage and Battle, 1917; He Is Become My Song, 1930; Collected Ballads and Poems in the Scots Tongue, 1968; Forest Voices and Other Poems in English, 1969; (verse translations): Poems of War, 1955; Poems, 1968. Contbr. to: Scotsman; Listener. Awards: Poetry prizes at Burns Centenary and for poems in the Scotsman and the Listener. Address: Scales, Grantchester, Cambridge, U.K.

ROBERTSON, Marnelle Haynes, b. 15 May 1912. Retired Teacher. Education: B.A., Univ. of Ark. at Monticello; Creative Writing at Phillips Community Coll. Married Edward Robertson, 3 children. Positions held: Classroom Tchr. in rural schls., 1929-39; Engl. Tchr., Marianna, Ark., 1950-72. Memberships: Poetry Soc. of Am.; Pres., E. Ctrl. Br., Poets' Roundtable of Ark.; South & West; Int. Poetry Soc.; Pres., Woman's Self Culture Club; Pres., Delta Kappa Gamma; Pres., Scribblers' Club. Ed., poetry column, 'Just Singing', Courier-Index; Ed. of sev. jr. high poetry colls. Contbr. to anthols., mags., newspapers inclng: The Lyric; South & West; Am. Bard; Ozarks Mountaineer; Haiku Highlights; Ark, Educ. Assn. Jrnl.; Sawdust & Tomatoes, 1944; Poems by Poets Roundtable of Ark., 1949, '50, '69-73; Contemporary Poets of Ark., 1971; Poems by Poets, 1973; Ark. Democrat; Ark. Gazette; Courier-Index; Southwest Times Record. Recip. sev. awards inclng: Best of issue Award, The Lyric, 1972. Address: 124 West Main St., Marianna, AR 72360, U.S.A.

ROBERTSON, Olive Hope, pen name **ROBERTSON, Olive,** b. 28 Aug. 1909. Retired Medical Practitioner; Senator. Education: Delta Collegiate Inst., Hamilton, Ont., Canada; Edinburgh Univ., U.K. Married J.H.G. Robertson, F.R.C.S., 3 sons. Positions held: Councillor, Bulawayo City Coun., Rhodesia, 1946-53;

Pres., Fed. of Women's Insts. of So. Rhodesia, 1956-57; V. Chmn., Rhodesia Assn. for the Prevention of Tuberculosis, 1958-59; Pres., Assn. of Univ. Women of Rhodesia, 1961-63; Councillor, Salisbury City Coun., 1961-69; Deputy Mayor, 1967-68; Senator, Parliament of Rhodesia, 1970–. Memberships: Chmn., Poetry Soc. of Rhodesia, 1973; formerly, Salisbury Poetry Soc.; Editl. Bd., Two Tone (a Quarterly of Rhodesian Poetry): Chmn., ibid, 1970-73; Salisbury Arts Coun. (rep. Two Tone & the Rhodesia Poetry Soc.), etc. Published works: The Mighty Turtle & Other Poems, 1966. Anthologies: New South Africa Writing, Nos. 2 & 3, 1967 & 68; Longman's Anthols., Book Three, Poems about People & Places, 1966, Book Five, This is Poetry, 1966, Book Six, Poems for a Wider World, 1971; Poetry in Rhodesia, 1968. Contbr. to var. newspapers, poetry reviews & work has appeared in all vols. of Two Tone, 1964–. Honours, awards: Sonnet Prize, South African Eisteddfod, 1958 & 60; Lyric Prize, ibid, 1960; Fed. of Women's Insts. Lit. Award, 1963; M.B.E., 1956. Address: 5 St. Breock Cl., Mt. Pleasant, Salisbury, Rhodesia.

ROBERTSON, Pauline Durrett, b. 17 Apr. 1922. Writer; Teacher; Homemaker. Education: Amarillo Coll., Tex., U.S.A. Married Roy L. Robertson, 10 children. Positions held: Org., Amarillo Cerebral Palsy Treatment Ctr.; Pres., Amarillo Child Care Assn.; Tchr. of Poetry, Amarillo Coll. Community Classroom; Lectr. on Poetry. Subject of NBC documentary, Story of a Family, 1960. Memberships: Pres., Panhandle Pen Women, 1972-73; Charter Mbr., Hi-Plains Chapt., Poetry Soc. of Tex.; Nat. Writers Club; Girl Scout Ldr. & Coun.; Dir., Camp Friendship (for underprivileged children); Fndn. Comm., Opportunity House (for teenagers in trouble). Contbr. to: Christian Herald; Together; Bethany Guide; Hearthstone; Guideposts; Vision; Home Life; Poetry Soc. of Tex. Yrbook; The Christian; World Call; Protestant Ch. Builders; Amarillo Globe Times; Family Digest; Amarillo Coll. Ranger; La Airosa; Boys & Girls; Christian Courier; The Disciple. Honours, awards: Conquistadores Award, 1st pl., Int. Exposition Hemisfair, 1968; 1st prize, Annual poetry contest, Panhandle Pen Women, 1969 & 72; 2nd prize, ibid, 1970 & 71; Nat. Fed. of State Poetry Socs. Humor Award, 3rd, 1973, etc. Address: 124 Wayside Dr., Amarillo, TX 79106, U.S.A.

ROBERTSON, Peter, pen name **ROBERTSON, Pete,** b. 3 Nov. 1951. Clerk. Education: various primary schools in Edinburgh and Arbroath; private boarding school in Suffolk, and 2 yrs. at Southampton Coll. of Tech., studying engineering. Positions held: Cost Clerk; Local Government Clerk; Journalist; Photographer's Asst.; now working in a Building Soc.; also freelance writer. Membership: Movement founded by Tammo De Jongh, which issues its own publications. Published works: Oink, a collection of poems, illustrations and ephemera, 1970; Love, Death, and the man behind the garden wall, a collection of love poems, 1973-74. Contbr. to: Sixth Dimension; Good Elf; Frendz; MAC; Gargantua; Something to Say; Bogg; Headland; Jade; Albino; IT. Address: 11 Lanehouse Rocks Rd., Weymouth, Dorset.

ROBEY, Timothy Lester Townsend, pen name **TOWNSEND, Timothy,** b. 9 May 1934. Teacher of Chemistry. Education: B.Sc., Imperial Coll., Univ. of London; A.R.C.S. Positions held: Rsch. Off., Paint Rsch. Stn.; Tchr. of Chem., Blackpool Grammar Schl. Memberships: English Assn.; Lancashire Authors' Assn.; Preston Writers' Soc.; Preston Poets' Soc.; Hon. Treas., Cleveleys Poetry Circle, 1971–; Fellow, Int. Poetry Soc. Published works: Within the Sphere, 1970. Contbr. to: The Dublin Mag.; Lancashire Life; Envoi; Towards Survival; Quill; Scrip; Lines; Centre 17; The Shore; Viewpoints; Black Columbus. Recip., Pomfret Cup, Preston Poets' Soc., 1973. Address: 648 North Dr., Cleveleys, Nr. Blackpool, Lancs. FY5 2QD, U.K.

ROBINETTE, Vivien Lucile. Author; Poet; Musician. Education: Public Schools. Married, James F.

Robinette. Membership: California Fed. of Chaparral Poets. Published works: Down Catnip Trail, 1955; Orchestra of Storm, 1955; Poems, 1956; Wind In The Night, 1964; Three Famous Cats, 1969; We Moved to California, 1951; Mr. Tipps, 1956; Four Paws, 1973; Now In November, 1973. Contbr. to: Best Poems of 1956; The American Poets Speak, 1958; Anthol. of American Poetry Vol. II, 1960, Vol. IV., 1962; Prairie Poet Anthol., 1961; American Poetry Review, 1955; Today's Poets, 1964; The American Bard, Ariz. Highways; Poetry Digest; Prairie Poet; Poesy Book; The Country Poet; Scimitar & Song; The American Courier; The Creative Writer; American Poetry Mag.; The Caxton Review; Cats Mag.; Voice of The Voiceless; Bayshore Breeze. Address: 2021 Primrose Ave., South Pasadena, CA 91030, USA.

ROBINS, Natalie, b. 20 June 1938. Poet. Education: B.A., Mary Washington Coll., Fredericksburg, Va., 1960. Married Christopher Lehmann-Haupt, 1 daughter. Positions held: Tchr., Poets-in-the-Schools Prog. sponsored by Poets & Writers, Inc. & the N.Y. State Coun. on the Arts, 1970–. Published works: Wild Lace, 1960; My Father Spoke of His Riches, 1966; The Peas Belong on the Eye Level, 1972; School Pieces, 1975. Contbr. to: Poetry (Chicago); The New Republic; The Nation; Open Places; Chelsea Review; Burning Deck; Redbook Mag. Address: 627 West 247th St., Bronx, NY 10471, U.S.A.

ROBINSEN, C.H., b. 24 Dec. 1895. Administrative Officer; Cowboy. Education: Valparaiso Univ., Ind. Positions held: Admin. Officer, Railway Mail Serv.; Tchr. in Elem. Schls., 15 yrs.; Cowboy on var. ranches. Published works: Moments of Memory, 1970. Contbr. to: The Woman's Companion; Woman's Comfort; Dutch Kitchen; Household; Friendly Way; Poet, India. Address: 524 North First, Aberdeen, S.D., U.S.A.

ROBINSON, Dorothy Anderson, b. 30 May 1924. Librarian. Education: B.A., Mich. State Univ., 1948; M.S. in L.S., Univ. of Ky., 1954. Positions held: at Michigan public schls., 1948-53; Walnut Hills H.S., Cinn., Ohio, 1954-57; Ky. Wesleyan Coll., 1957-59; Fairmont State Coll., W. Va., 1963-64; Marion Co. Schls., W. Va., 1959-60, 1969-70. Member, Fairmont Poetry Soc., W. Va. Contbr. to: Unity; W. Va. Garden News; The West Virginian (newspaper); Poetic License, St. Petersburg, Fla.; Nat. Poetry Anthol.; Echoes of The West Virginia Poetry Soc., 1971. Address: 5949 15th Ave. South, Gulfport, FL 33707, U.S.A.

ROBINSON, Forrest, b. 4 Nov. 1931. University Professor. Education: A.B., Miami Univ., Oxford, Ohio; M.A., ibid; Ph.D., Ohio Univ.; special studioo, Univ. of Iowa & Breadloaf Grad. Schl. of Engl. Positions held: at Miami Univ.; Ohio Univ.; Heidelberg Coll.; Western Ill. Univ. Contbr. to: Prism Int.; Kan. Qtly.; Denver Post; Folio; The Christian Century; Am. Weave; Miss. Valley Review; Encore; Faith & Art. Recip., Award, from Gwendolyn Brooks for work-in-progress in the field of poetry at Ind. Univ. Writers' Conf., 1971. Address: Dept. of Engl., Western Ill. Univ., Macomb, IL 61455, U.S.A.

ROBINSON, Roland Edward, pen name **THE BASTARD FROM THE BUSH,** b. 14 June 1912. Author. Positions held: Mbr. first pro-Ballet Co.; Ballet Critic; lived with Aborigines, gathered material for seven books of mythology; Lectr., Poetry Recitals for Adult Educ. Dept., etc. Pres., Poetry Soc. of Australia, 10 yrs. Published works: Legend & Dreaming, 1952; The Feathered Serpent, 1956; Blackfeller-Whitefeller, 1958; Man who sold his Dreaming, 1960; Aboriginal Myths & Legends, 1966; Australian Aboriginal in Colour, 1968; Wandjina, 1968; The Drift of Things, 1973; Grass-tree Spears, 1944; Language of Sand, 1948; Tumult of the Swans, 1952; Deep Well, 1960; Grendel, 1968; Altjiringa, 1970; Selected Poems, 1972. Contbr. to: Meanjin Qtly.; Sydney Morning Herald; The Australian; Australian Poetry Anthol., etc. Honours, awards: Grace Levin Award, 1952; 4 C'wealth Lit. Fellowships, etc. Address: 115 Sunshine

Parade, Sunshine, N.S.W. 2264, Australia.

ROBLES, Mireya. Professor of Hispanic Literature at Briarcliff College, Briarcliff Manor, New York. Education: B.A., M.A. & Ph.D. cand., SUNY, Albany. Published works: Petits Poemes, in French transl., 1969; Tiempo artesano, 1973. Contbr. of poems, short stories & articles on lit. criticism in lit. mags., anthols., jrnls. in sev. countries inclng: Nuevos narradores cubanos, anthol.; Voces de manana, anthol.; Poet (India); Norte (Holland); Latina, Letras de ayer y de hoy, Xilote, Cuadernos americanos, El rehilete, Et Caetera, Tlaxcala cultural (Mexico); S.A.L.A.C., Cormoran y delfin (Argentina); Trimestre bibliografico, Cuervo international, La nueva sangre, Resumen de los profesionales, Envios, Nueva generacion, Star-West, S-B Gazette, Revista del Municipio de Guantanamo, Briarcliff Lit. Refiew (USA); Il giornale dei poeti (Italy); Esparavel, Esquirla, Arco, (Colombia), etc. Recip. 9 int. awards inclng: Hon. Mention for the trilogy entitled 'Tres poemas', awarded by Xilote, Mex., 1970; First prize for book of poems 'Tiempo Artesano', awarded by the Iberoamerican Poets & Writers Guild of N.Y., 1971. Address: Birch Brook Manor, 87 So. Highland Ave., Apt. B-25, Ossining, NY 10562, U.S.A.

ROBSON, Ernest, b. 24 Dec. 1902. Experimental-Multi-Media Poet. Education: HS, Chicago, Ill.; Amherst Coll., A.B. (student of Robert Frost); Pratt Inst. Bkly. Chemistry School; Chemistry & City Coll. of NYC. Married; 1 s. Positions held: Newspaper Reporter; HS Teacher; Messenger Boy; Advertising Exec.; Industrial Worker; Pres., NY State fur-trapper's cooperative; Analytic Chemist; Red Cross AFD in Pacific; Detergent Chemist; Director, Lehigh Valley Amateur Astronomy Soc.; Council of Astronomic League of America; Teacher graphic symbols of creative language (mini-course) psychology dept. of Albright Coll., Reading, PA. Membership: The Authors Guild, Inc., NYC. Published works: The Wind Listens (Anthol. of Contemp. Poetry), 1952; The Orchestra of the Language, 1959; Transwhichics, 1970; Poster Poem Portfolio, 1973. Contbr. to: NY Tribune; Amherst Student Mag.; Modern Engl. & American Poetry; Saturday Review; Astronomic League Bulletin; Proceedings of Int. Union of Amateur Astronomers; Polish Acad. of Science Mag., Urania. Award: Transwhichics won award (1970) of Am. Inst. of Graphic Arts, NYC. Address: Box 105, Parker Ford, PA 19457, USA.

ROBSON, Jeremy, b. 5 Sept. 1939. Education: Haberdashers' Aske's Shcl.; Regent St. Polytechn. Coll. Married to Carole Robson, twin d. Positions held: Ed., Aldus Books; Chief Ed., Vallentine, Mitchell, Publrs.; Poetry Critic, Tribune. Published works include: Thirty Three Poems, 1964; In Focus, 1971. Contbr. to the following anthols., jrnls., mags., etc: Corgi Mod. Poets in Focus, 1971; Poems from Poetry & Jazz in Concert, 1969; The Young British Poets, 1970; Encounter; New Statesman; London Mag.; Adam Int.; Poetry Review; 20th Century; Northwest Review, etc. Address: 37 Briardale Gdns., London NW3, UK.

ROBSON, Peter, b. 5 Nov. 1937. Teacher. Education: Scarborough HS, UK. Positions held: Master, Marton Hall Schl., Bridlington, 1962-70; currently Master, Cundall Manor Schl., York. Author of Between the Laughing Fields, 1966. Contbr. to: Outposts; Tribune; Poet, India; Aylesford Review; Breakthru; The Northern Drift, BBC. Address: 31 Red Scar Lane, Scarborough, Yorkshire, UK.

ROCHE, Lila Nalder, b. 1 Apr. 1906. Artist; Poet. Education: B.A., Literature, Washington State Univ.; Chicago Art Inst. Married, Alphonse V. Roche. Membership: Rimers (Tucson, Arizona). Contbr. to: Rimers Yearbook, 1973; etc. Address: 421 N. Sawtelle, Tucson, AZ 85716, USA.

ROCHE, Paul, b. 25 Sept. 1928. Poet; Translator. Education: Ushaw Coll., Durham; Ph.B., & Ph.L.,

Gregorian Univ., Rome, Italy. Positions held: Instr., Smith Coll., Northampton, Mass., 1957-59; Bollington Fndn. Fellow, 1959; Poet-in-Residence, Emory & Henry Coll., Va., 1969; Vice-Pres., London Appreciation Soc. Memberships: Poetry Soc. (UK); Poetry Soc. of Am. Published works: The Rat & the Convent Dove, 1952; O Pale Galilean, 1954; The Oedipus Plays of Sophocles, 1958; The Orestes Plays of Aeschylus, 1962; Prometheus Bound, 1962; Vessel of Dishonour, 1964; The Love-Songs of Sappho, 1964; The Rank Obstinacy of Things, 1962; All Things Considered, 1966; To Tell The Truth, 1967; Three Plays by Plautus, 1968. Contbr. to: The New Yorker; Encounter; London Mag.; Harper's Bazaar; The Listener; Saturday Review; NY Herald Trib.; New World Writing, etc. Recordings: Lamond Lib., Harvard; Univ. of Chicago Lib.; Spoken Word Inc. Frequent appearances on Radio & TV, USA & UK; Film: Oedipus the King (translated by P. Roche), 1968. Readings & Lectrs. Throughout USA & UK. Honours: Co-winner, Castagnola Award, 1965; Co-winner, 1st Alice Hunt Bartlett Award, 1966. Address: The Stables, The Street, Aldermaston, Berks., UK.

RODAS, Virginia, b. 24 Apr. 1932. Writer & Journalist. Education: Literary studies. Positions held: Jrnlst.; Editl. Sec. Memberships: Cultural Am. Org.; United Artists, etc. Published works: Petals (poems), 1964; There Will Be One Day ... And Other Poems, 1968; Century XXI Brother, 1971; My Natal Grece's Emotions (prose), in prep. Has written plays, novels, stories, & her works have been translated into English, Greek, Italian, Portuguese. Contbr. to newspapers & mags. in Argentina, Brazil, Uruguay, Chile, Colombia, U.S.A., Spain, India. Address: C. Correo No. 6, Haedo, Buenos Aires, Argentina.

RODENBOUGH, Jeannette Green, pen name **RODENBOUGH, Jean,** b. 18 Sept. 1933. Teacher; Writer. Education: B.A., Randolph-Macon Woman's Coll., Lynchburg, Va., 1955; M.A., Univ. of N.C., Greensboro, 1973. Married, 4 children. Positions held: Instr. in Engl., Rockingham Community Coll., 1969-71; Tchr. of Engl., Oak Ridge Acad., Spring, 1973; Participant in N.C. Poetry-in-the-Schools Prog., 1972, '73 & N.C. Arts Coun. Readings, 1971, '72; currently serving on Town Bd. of Aldermen, Memberships: Corres. Sec., N.C. Poetry Soc., Inc., 1969-72; 2nd V.P., ibid, 1972-73; Chmn., Poetry Workshop, Greensboro Writers, 1969-73; Rockingham Co. Fine Arts Fest. Assn., 1969– (currently Pres.) Published works: If I Were A Ghost (illustrated children's poem in book form), 1972. Contbr. to: Southern Pines Pilot; The Messenger; Crucible; Coraddi; Poet Lore; Sunburst Anthol.; S.C. Review; Higginson Jrnl. of Poetry; N.C. Poetry Soc.'s Award Winning Poems; The Wake Weekly. Recip., many poetry honours & awards inclng. sev. from N.C. Poetry Soc. Address: P.O. Box 46, Madison, NC 27025, U.S.A.

RODGERS, Carolyn M. Teacher; Writer. Education: Univ. of Ill., 1960-61; Wilson Jr. Coll., 1961-62; Roosevelt Univ., 1962-66. Positions held: Grp. Wkr., Social Studies, Language Arts Instr. to H.S. dropouts, 1966-68; Columbia Coll., 1968; Summer Afro-Am. Lit. Tchr., Univ. of Wash., 1969-70; Writer-in-Res., Albany State Coll., 1971; Afro-Am. Arts Lit. Instr., Ind. Univ. 1973–. Memberships: Gwendolyn Brooks Writers' Workshop; OBAC. (Fndng. Mbr.) Published works: Paper Soul, 1968; Songs of a Blackbird, 1969; (broadsides) Now Ain't That Love, For. H.W. Fuller, & Poem for Flip Wilson, 2 Love Rags; Testimony: How I Got Ovah, 1974. Contbr. to var. mags., anthols., jrnls. Honours, awards: First Conrad Kent Rivers Award, 1969; Soc. of Midland Authors Poet Laureate Award, 1970; Nat. Endowment of the Arts Award, 1970. Address: 5954 S. Bishop St., Chicago, IL 60615, U.S.A.

RODITI, Edouard Herbert, b. 6 June 1910. Interpreter; Journalist; Lecturer. Educ.: Elstree School, Hertfordshire; Charterhouse, London; Balliol Coll., Oxford; B.A., Univ. of Chicago, 1938; Univ. of Calif., Berkeley. Published works (poetry): Pieces of Three,

1942; Poems 1928-1948, 1949; New Hieroglyphic Tales, 1968; (other): Oscar Wilde, 1947; Wrote the introduction to As a Man Grows Older, by Italo Svevo, 1949; Dialogues on Art, 1960; De L'Homosexualité, 1962; contbr. to: (anthology): New Directions 21, 1969. Address: 8 rue Gregoire de Tours, Paris 6, France; 8 Calle Ribbi Mordejai Bengio, Tangier, Morocco.

RODRIGUEZ, Judith, b. 13 Feb. 1936. Lecturer in English Literature. Education: B.A., Univ. of Queensland, Australia, 1957; Victoria Univ. Coll., Wellington, N.Z.; M.A., Girton Coll., Cambridge Univ., U.K. Married Fabio Rodríguez, 4 children. Positions held: School Tchr., Toowoomba, Queensland; Lectr. in Engl., Dept. of External Studies, Univ. of Queensland, Philippa Fawcett Coll. of Educ., London, Univ. of the West Indies, St. Mary's Coll. of Educ., Twickenham, Middx., U.K., La Trobe Univ. Regularly conducts Poetry workshops for the Coun. of Adult Educ. in Melbourne. Memberships: Australian Soc. of Authors; Victorian Fellowship of Australian Writers. Published works: A Question of Ignorance (15 poems) in Four Poets, 1962; Nu-Plastik Fanfare Red, 1973. Contbr. to: The Age; The Australian; Australian Letters; Granta (Cambridge, U.K.); Makar; North; Overland; Poetry Australia; Poetry Mag.; Quadrant; Westerly, etc. Recip., 1 yr. Fellowship, Arts Coun. of Australia, 1974. Address: 2 Rill St., Heidelberg, Vic. 3084, Australia.

ROE, Christopher John, b. 2 Feb. 1940. Composer. Education: Royal Acad. of Music, 1958-62. Married 1) Sandra Morris, div., 2) Jenny Mackie, 2 sons. Positions held: Dir. of Music, Royal Grammar Schl. of King Edward VI, Guildford, 1961-63; Dir. of Music, Highbury Tech. Coll., Portsmouth, 1969-71; Lectr., Isle of Wight Tech. Coll., 1973–. Contbr. to Hampshire Poets. Honours, awards: London Bach Soc.'s C'wealth Award, 1962; Manson Bequest, R.A.M., 1962. Address: Holme Vale, Shimpling, Diss, Norfolk, U.K.

ROEBUCK, John Athey, b. 22 June 1920. Executive; Author; Group Staff Personnel Officer. Education: private tuition followed by attendance at Taylor Univ., U.S.A. Personal details: g.-g.-g.-g.-grandson of Dr. John Roebuck, Fndr. of Carron Co., 1718-1794; g.-g.-nephew of Rt. Hon. John A. Roebuck, P.C., Q.C., M.P., 1802-1879; g.-g.-nephew of Florence Nightingale, O.M. Family motto 'Free'. Positions held: U.K. Agent, Corres. & Int. Comm. Chmn., Pen-Prints Inc., 1952–; Engrng. Admin., nationalised int.; Dir. (U.K.), Curry Electronics (U.S.A.); Mgmt. Services Exec., into grp. of cos., 1965–. Memberships: Fellow, Royal Soc. of Arts, London, 1950; Assoc. Mbr., fac., Taylor Univ., 1953; Assoc. Mbr., Inst. of Personnel Mgmt.; Philosophical Soc. of England, 1953; Fndr., Chmn., The Arts Club, S. Elmsall, 1950; Int. Coun. of Ldrs. & Scholars, 1969; Arts Theatre Club, London, 1965; Editl. & Advisory Bd., Int. Who's Who in Poetry. Published works: The Life Mind Man; E. Tenebris Lux; Philosophy For Everyman; Accepted Principles of Planned Maintenance in Industry; The Roebuck Story (in collab. w. cousin, The Hon. A.N. Roebuck, Q.C.) Honours, awards: Ph.D., Taylor Univ., U.S.A., 1951; M.Ph.S. of Engl., 1953; Int. Award of Hon., 1st Int. Congress of Drs., 1969. Address: 'Inglenook', Stockingate, S. Kirkby, Pontefract, Yorks., U.K.

ROGERS, Ida Rice, b. 27 Aug. 1910. Educator. Education: B.A., Hendrix Coll., Conway, Ark.; M.A., Univ. of Ark., Fayetteville; post grad. work at Leyden Univ., Netherlands & in Criminal Justice & Police Sci., Univ. of Ark., Little Rock. Married 1) John Rice, dec., 3 children, 2) Geo. P. Rogers, dec. Positions held: Tchr. of Arts & Crafts, N. Little Rock Boys' Club, 30 yrs.; Americanisation Classes to foreign born, State Dept.; Taught in Med. Corps, U.S. Army, WWII; set up Occupational Therapy Room in Base Hosp., Camp Robinson, ibid; Chmn. of Fine Arts, Little Rock Univ., 1957-69; Tchr. of Tchr. Educ. & Advanced Crafts. Memberships: Ark. Poets Round Table; Prog. Chmn., Authors, Composers & Artists Assn.; Art. Chmn., Nat.

Soc. of Arts & Letters, 5 yrs.; Art Chmn., Nat. League of Am. Pen Women, etc. Published works: Thoughts of the Wanderer, book of poems, 1971; composed & recorded two songs, 1973; var. articles on Art Hist. & has exhibited in Italy, Portugal & U.S.A. Contbr. to: Benton Co. News; Centro Studi e Scambi, Rome; N. Little Rock Times. Address: 2409 W. 16th St., N. Little Rock, AR 72114, U.S.A.

ROGERS, Mary Bernadette, pen name **ROGERS, Mary Bee,** b. 23 Jan. 1922. Housewife. Education: Univ. of Louisville (w. special emphasis on Creative Writing). Married Jack Rogers, 3 sons, 1 daughter. Memberships: Pres., Louisville Writers Club, 8 yrs.; Ky. State Poetry Soc.; Louisville Arts Club. Published works: Tapestry House, 1972. Contbr. to: Approaches; Twigs; Pegasus; The Muse; Wind; Encore. Anthologies: The Forever Bear; Echoes of Faith; Spots of Time. Honours, awards: Prize, Nat. Writers Digest Contest, 1971; 1st Pl., Lyric Poetry, Ky. State Poetry Soc., 1972; Award of Excellence from Jesse Stuart, 1972; 2nd Pl. Poetry, Louisville Arts Club, 1972. Address: 3323 Nanz Ave., Louisville, KY 40207, U.S.A.

ROGGEMAN, Willem Maurits, b. 9 July 1935. Journalist. Education: Univ. of Ghent. Positions held: Lit. Critic, Het Laatste Nieuws (leading Flemish newspaper), 1959–; Ed., lit. reviews, De Vlaamse Gids & Kentering. Memberships: Bd. Mbr., Fndn. for Translations of Dutch Lit. in Amsterdam; Sec., Flemish PEN Ctr.; Maatschappij der Nederlandse Letteren in Leiden (Holland); Bd. Mbr., Poetry Int. in Rotterdam (yearly festival). Published works: Rhapsody in Blue, 1957; Een (hinder) paalwoning, 1958; De revolte der standbeelden, 1960; Bij wijze van schrijven, 1960; Baudelaire verliefd, 1963; Incunabel, 1964; Het orakel van New York City, 1969; Gedichten 57-70, 1972; L'ombre d'un doute, 1972; Vijftig na 50, 1973; Een gefilmde droom, 1973; Sneeuwblindheid, 1974. Contbr. to: Het Laatste Nieuws; De Vlaamse Gids; Kentering; Nieuw Vlaams Tijdschrift; Dietsche Warande en Belfort; Yang; Revolver, etc. Honours, awards: Poetry Prize of De Nevelvlek in Antwerp, 1956; Dirk Martensprize in Aalst, 1963 & '64. Address: Diksmuidelaan 40, 1000 Brussels, Belgium.

ROHEN, Edward, pen name **CONNORS, Bruton,** b. 10 Feb. 1931. Art Teacher. Education: Cardiff Coll. of Art, 1947-52. Positions held: at Ladysmith Jr. Sr. H.S., B.C., Canada, 1956-57; Saint Bonaventure's Schl., 1958-73; Ilford County H.S., 1973–. Memberships: one time mbr., Poets Soc. of Japan; Academician, Centro Cultural, Literário e Artístico de 'O Jornal de Felgeiras', Portugal. Published works: Nightpriest (poetry), 1965; Bruised Concourse (pamphlet), 1973. Contbr. prose to: Tracks; Earthship; Joe Dimaggio; Corridor; Straight. Poetry & Prose to: Twentieth Century; Anglo-Welsh Review; Viewpoints; New Irish Writing; Somethings; Pause; Gong; Naissance; Mabon; Here Now; Argot (N.Z.); Dodo; Iron Flute; Nepam; New Expression; Ludd's Mill; Caret; Vole; Edge (N.Z.); Oasis. Poetry also in num. mags. & anthols. inclng: It's World that makes the Love go Round; Doves for the Seventies; La Rosa Blanca (Argentina); Sunburst (USA); Tweed (Australia); Poetry Workshop; Poet (India). Address: 57 Kinfauns Rd., Goodmayes, Ilford, Essex 1G3 9QH, U.K.

ROKEAH, David, b. 22 July 1916. Engineer; Writer; Poet. Published works: Bagesher Hayeud (Bridge of Destiny), 1939; Yamim Ashenim (Smoky Days), 1941; Moadey Erge (Seasons of Yearning), 1954; Arar Aley Shaham (Juniper on Granite), 1958; Keyno Shel Yam (Blades of the Sea), 1963; Mikaitz El Kaitz (From Summer to Summer), 1964; Shahar Laheleh (Dawn of the Wanderer), 1965; Eynaim Basela (Eyes in the Rock), 1967; Vlo Ba Yom Aher (No Other Day), 1969. Translations of his work: (German) Poesie (bilingual Hebrew/German), 1962; Von Sommer Zu Sommer, 1965; Ijara (Bilingual Hebrew/German), 1969; (Engl.) Eyes In The Rock, 1968 & '69; (French) Les Yeux Dans Le Rocher, 1968. Contbr. to: (German) Neue Zuercher Zeitung, Switzerland; Du, Switzerland; Neue Rundschau, W Germany; Merkur, W Germany;

(French) Esprit, Paris; Preuves, Paris; La Nouvelle Revue Française, Paris; Gazette de Lausanne, Switzerland; (Engl.) Times Lit. Supplement, London; New Statesman, London; Agenda, London; Transatlantic Review, London; Paris Review, Paris/New York; Quarterly Review of Lit., USA; Tri-Quarterly, USA; Poetry, Chicago, USA; (Arabic) Lit. Supplements of Arabic newspapers in Israel. Address: POB 178, Tel Aviv, Israel.

ROLLINS, Leighton, Professor. Educ: Summer Classes, Oxford Univ., U.K., 1925; Grad., Bown Univ., U.S.A., 1926. m. Catherine Joralemon, 1944, 1 s., 1 d. Positions held: Dir., Rollins Theatre Schl., 1929-50, Mt. Desert Playhouse, Bar Harbor, Me., 1931-34, Lenox, Mass. Theatre, 1947-49, Original Palm Beach, Fla. Playhouse, 1929-30; Lectr., Drama, W. Colston Leigh, Inc., N.Y.C., 1929-64; Fndg. Chmn., Santa Barbara Symph. Orch., 1952; Organizing Chmn., Dev., Am. Field Serv., 1951-53; V.P., Dev., W. Experiment in Int. Living, 1953-55; Dir., ibid, 1954-61; Dir., Pacific Coast Festival & Inst., Santa Barbara, Calif., 1951-; Exec. Dir., Lobero Theatre, Santa Barbara, 1951-; Educl. Counsellor, Acad. World Studies; Dir., Cultural Affairs Inst., Santa Barbara; Advsr., Drama Affiliates, Univ. of Calif.; Vis. Lectr., Hamlin Schl., San Fran., 1973; Lectr., Adult Educ., Santa Barbara, 1970-. Memberships: Steering Comm., Youth Theatre, 1974; Comm., Planned Parenthood; Pres., Engl. Speaking Union, 1964-; New England Poetry Club; Vice Chmn., Friends of Santa Barbara Pub. Lib., 1970-. Published works: Disasters of War, 1938; Adaptation of Hippolytus, 1963. Ed., Beacons Burn Again, 1938. Address: Box 5181, Santa Barbara, CA 93108, U.S.A.

ROLLS, Eric Charles, b. 25 Apr. 1923. Author; Farmer & Grazier. Married Joan Stephenson, 3 children. Owner of farming properties, first at Boggabri & now at Baradine (north-west of N.S.W.) Memberships: Australian Soc. of Authors; Poetry Soc. of Australia. Published works: Sheaf Tosser, 1967; New Guinea Mosaic, 1973; also three works in prose. Contbr. to: The Bulletin; Sydney Morning Herald; Poetry Australia; Poetry Mag.; Westerly; Southerly, & many anthols. Honours, awards: Henry Lawson Fest. Awards, 1964 & 68; David Myer Trust Award for Poetry, 1968; Commonwealth Lit. Fund Scholarships, 1968 & 69; Cook Centenary Award for prose, 1970. Address: Cumberdeen, Baradine, N.S.W. 2858, Australia.

ROMANO, Emily, b. 28 Dec. 1924. Homemaker. Education: Boonton HS. Married. Memberships: New Jersey Poetry Soc.; Avalon; Western World Haiku Soc.; World Poetry Day; Internat. Poetry Soc.; World Poetry Soc.; The Nat. Fed. of State Poetry Socs. Contbr. to: American Poet; Bardic Echoes; Cycloflame; Chicago Jewish Forum; Dragonfly; A Qtly. of Haiku Highlights; Fireflower; Haiku Highlights; Haiku West; The Highlander; Holiday; Ideals; First Internat. Poetry Soc. Anthol.; Legend; Missouri English Haiku; Modern Haiku; Methodist Missile; Morris County News; New World Haiku; Nutmegger; New Jersey Poetry Soc. Anthol.; Poet; Poetidings; Rainbow; Scimitar & Song; Special Song; Southwest Breeze; Swordsman Review; Times-Bulletin; Verdure; Western World Haiku Soc. Newsletter; Winged urposes; Young Pub.'s Anthols., and others. Awards: numerous from World Poetry Day; NJ Poetry Soc.; Pennsylvania Poetry Socs.; Rainbow; Nat. Fed. of State Poetry Socs.; Utah State (Award); Haiku; Dragonfly, etc. Address: 230 Madison St., Boonton, NJ 07005, USA.

ROMANO, Liboria Elizabeth, pen name (in earlier years), LIB RO, b. 17 Jul. 1899. Freelance Writer, and Tutor in English. Education: B.A., cum laude, M.A., Hunter Coll., NYC, 1955, 1958; D.Phil., Litt., Inst. of Arts and Crafts, 1959. Married, Dominic Romano; 3 s. Positions held: Editor, Manhattan Pen Women; Assoc. Ed., Musings, and, The Writers' Voice; Insurance Broker; Writer of poems, essays, book reviews, newspaper columns; translator from Italian; Tutor. Memberships: NLAPW Auditor, 1950-52; Pres.,

Manhattan Branch, NLAPW, 1948-50, 1960-1966, Poetry Soc. of America; World Poetry Soc. Intercontinental; Hon. Member, Fla. Nat. Poetry Soc.; American Assoc. Univ. Women; Hon. Rep., C.S.S.I.; Hon. Life Member, World Poets' Resource Center and Eastern Centre, Poetry Soc. of England; Pa. Poetry Soc.; Hunter Coll. Alumni Assoc. Published works: Tangent Moods, 1952; Venus For A Crown, 1959; Content To Observe, 1964; Transl. A Child's Dream of Music, 1961; Coney Island and Other New Poems, 1970. Contbr. to: (anthols.) Golden Year, Poetry Soc. Amer., 1960; Nat. League of Amer. Pen Wm., 1951; Davis Newspaper Verse, 1940-41; Fire & Sleet & Candlelight, 1961; Spring Anthol., 1963-1972; (newspapers, journals) NY Herald Tribune; Ital. News; So. W. Times-Record; Poet (India); So. W. Lit. Qtly.; Encore; Imprints Qtly.; Seydell Qtly.; Sphinx Verse Reporter; Am. Bard; Prairie Poet; Mendocino Robin; Creative Rev.; Piggott Banner; The Messenger; Pen Wm., Manhattan Pen Wm.; Pa. Prize Poems; Skylines, etc. Awards: Theresa Hotchner Mem. Prize for poetry; Blanche Lewy JoŒph Mem. Prize for Lit., and Dante Alighieri Soc. Medal, Hunter Coll., 1955; N. Atlantic Reg. Prize, NLAPW, 1953; Flat Nat. Poetry Soc. prize for song lyric, 1959; 3rd prize ann. trans. award (from Fr.) Poet Lore, 1969; NLAPW Biennial Prizes (2), 1956; Hon. Mention, Amer. Assoc. Univ. Wm., 1957-58, Nat. Writers' Project; Special Award, 1971 World Poets Res. Center. Address: 1455 81st St., Brooklyn, NY 11228, USA.

ROMBOUTS, Tony, b. 7 Feb. 1941. Editor. Married Maris Bayar. Positions held: Ed., lit. mag. 'Hoos' (monthly), 1961; Publsr. & Ed., lit. mag. 'Stuip' (quarterly), 1961-71; Ed. mag. 'Proces' (fortnightly), 1965; Publsr. & Ed. mag. 'Muze-n-Express' (monthly), 1966; Ed., lit. mag. 'TNT' (quarterly), 1965-67; Hd. of publsng. co. 'Contramine', specialising in publishing poetry; connected w. the office of the harbour master of Antwerp. Chmn., Poetry Soc. 'Contramine', Antwerp. Published works: Bergen kristal, 1962; Stella Magnola, 1963; Het koudvuur der aarde, 1966; De vrouw van waas, 1967; De feodale verzen, 1974. Contbr. to: Slnteze; Hoos; Doorbraak; Stuip; De Tafelronde; Het Kahier; Sumier; Baal; Proces; Otzdos. Poetry trans. into French, German & Croatian. Address: Alfred Coolsstraat nr. 2, 2020 Antwerp, Belgium.

ROMERO SERRANO, Marina, b. 5 Feb. 1908. Professor of Romance Languages & Literature (Emeritus). Education: HS, Inst. Escuela; B.A., Normal School of Guadalajara, Spain, 1931; Grad., Studies in Education, Smith Coll., Northampton, Mass, USA, 1935-36, and Mills Coll., Calif., USA, 1936-37 (M.A., Mills Coll., 1936); Studies towards Ph.D. at Middlebury Coll., Vermont, and Rutgers Univ., New Brunswick, NJ, USA. Positions held: HS Teacher at Inst. Escuela, Madrid, Spain, 1933-35; Asst. in Lit. & Education, Mills Coll., 1936-37; Director of the Spanish House at Douglass Coll., Rutgers Univ., New Brunswick, NJ, 1938-55; Instr., Asst. Prof., Assoc. Prof., Prof., Douglass Coll., Rutgers Univ., 1938-70. Membership: Asociacion de Escritores y Artistas, Spain. Published works: Poemas ''A'', 1935; Nostalgia de manana, 1942; Presencia del recuerdo, 1952; Midas. Poema de amor, 1954; Paisaje y literatura de Espana; Antologia de la Generacion del 98, 1957; Sin agua, el mar, 1961; Alegrias: Poemas para ninos, 1973. Contbr. to many publications, journals, etc. Awards: 2nd in list of honour of the Comision Catolica Espanola de la Infancia, 1973, for book: Alegrias: poemas para ninos. Address: Paseo de la Habana 134 C - Atico G, Madrid, 16 Spain.

ROMIG, Edna Davis, b. 16 Jan. 1889. Retired Professor of English Language. Education: B.A., DePauw Univ., 1911; M.A., Univ. of Wis., 1924. Married Albert S. Romig, 1 son. Positions held: Instr., Univ. of Colo., 1921-22; Asst. Prof., ibid, 1922-31; Assoc. Prof., 1931-56. Member of many socs. Published works: (books) Blue Hills, 1930; Lincoln Remembers, 1930; Marse Lee, 1930; The Torch Undimmed, 1931; Sketches & Overtones, 1936; An

Amherst Garden, 1938; The Heart Affirming, 1939; These Are The Fields, 1955; Flash of Wings, 1967; num. poems & articles in var. mags., etc. Recip., Univ. of Colo. Writing Fellowship, 1955. Address: 100 Inca Parkway, Boulder, CO 80303, U.S.A.

RONCH, Isaac Elhanan, b. 5 Sept. 1899. Writer; Teacher. of Yiddish. Married, 1 son. Positions held: Schl. Tchr. Chicago 1919-24: Instr. ,Jewish Workers Univ., 1926-34; Lectr., Art Theatre, N.Y., 1931-34; Nat. Sec., Jewish Music Alliance, 1952-62; Ed., Undzer Fraind Monthly, 1931-35. Memberships: Pres., Jewish Writers Union, N.Y., 1930-34; Pres., Jewish Writers Club, L.A., 1965-67. Published works: Six volumes of Yiddish Poetry; 3 vols. of Prose; The Awakening of Motek, novel, 1953; Jewish Youth at War, 1947; The World of Marc Chagall (reminiscence), 1968; Selected Poems, 1961; In the Desert, 2nd ed., poems, 1970. Contbr. to: Am. in Yiddish Poetry; Jewish Currents, monthly, N.Y.; Canadian Jewish Outlook; Jewish Qtly., London; Morning Freiheit, N.Y.; Chicago Jewish Forum; Free Israel; Naie Presse, Paris, etc. Address: 152 So. Sycamore Ave., Los Angeles, CA 90036, U.S.A.

RONEY, Alice Lorraine (Mann), b. 6 Dec. 1926. Homemaker. Education: B.A., UCLA, 1950. Married Robert Kenneth Roney, 1 son, 1 daughter. Positions held: Tech. Writer, Hughes Aircraft Co., 1949-52; Corres. Sec., Ebell Juniors, The Ebell of L.A., 1958-59; Chmn., Ebell Jr. Blind Recording, 1959-63 (Organized this grp. of volunteers to record textbooks for visually-handicapped students from Jr. H.S. through Coll.); Libn., St. Augustine by-the-Sea Episcopal Day Schl., 1961-68; Mbr., Schl. Bd., St. Augustine's Day Schl., 1964-67; Corres. Sec., Assistance League of Santa Monica, 1966-68; Altar Guild Directress, St. Augustine by-the-Sea Episcopal Ch., 1969-71; Pres., P.E.O. Chapt. QB (Calif.), 1969-71; Treas., Episcopal Churchwomen, L.A., 1970-73; Cottey Coll. Area Chmn., Calif. State Chapt., P.E.O., 1972-74; V.P., Inglewood Reciprocity P.E.O., 1973-74. Mbr., sev. poetry socs. & Int. Platform Assn. Published works: Those Treasured Moments, 1972. Contbr. to: Yearbook of Modern Poetry, 1971; Lyrics of Love, 1972; Premier Poets Anthol., 1972; Outstanding Contemporary Poetry, 1972 & '73; Melody of the Muse, 1973; Poet; Major Poets; United Poets, etc. Recip. hon. mention in poetry contests. Address: 1105 Georgina Ave., Santa Monica, CA 90402, U.S.A.

ROOK, Alan, b. 31 Oct. 1909. Company Director. Education: Oxford Univ., U.K. Fellow, Royal Soc. of Lit. Published works: Songs from a Cherry Tree, 1938; Soldiers, This Solidude, 1942; These Are My Comrades, 1943; We Who Are Fortunate, 1945; Not as a Refuge, 1948; Diary of an English Vineyard, 1972. Contbr. to: Bolero; Poetry Review; The Listener; Kingdom Come; Poetry (London); Poetry (Chicago); Bugle Blast; Modern Reading; New English Weekly; Now; Poetry Quarterly; Poetry Review; Tribune; Wartime Harvest; John o'London's; Life & Letters Today; Times Lit. Supplement; & many anthols., mags., periodicals in the U.K., U.S.A. & Middle East. Address: Stragglethorpe Hall, Lincoln, U.K.

ROOK, Douglas Lee, b. 9 May 1924. Candy Manufacturer. Education: B.A., Hobart & William Smith Coll., Geneva, N.Y. Positions held: Pres., Sarah Coventry Jewelry firm, Newark, N.Y.; Exec. V.P., Empire Crafts (china & silver); Pres., More Candy Co., Rochester, N.Y. Memberships: Rochester Poetry Soc.; Co-Ed., Anthol. 'Touchstone', 1971, 72; Centro Studi e Scambi Int. Contbr. to: Swordsman Review; Touchstone; Haiku Highlights; Rochester Democrat & Chronicle. Recip., Haiku of the Year Award, 1966. Address: 126 Williams St., Newark, NY 14513, U.S.A.

ROOK, Pearl Lucille, pen names: **ROOK, Pearl Newton; SCRIBNER, Lucille,** b. 26 March 1923. Poet. Married to Douglas L. Rook. Positions held: Music Teacher, 1945; Ed., Poet's Corner, Newark Courier Gazette, 1966–; Society Ed., ibid 1967-1968; Poetry Ed., Rochester Democrat & Chronicle, 1973–.

Memberships: Nat. League of Am. Pen Women; Rochester Poetry Soc., Recording Sec. ibid 1970-72; Co-Ed. of Rochester Poetry Soc's anthol. Touchstone, 1970-71-72; Avalon; Nat. Fed. State Poetry Socs.; CSSI, Hon. Rep., 1970-73, Comitato Internazionale, 1973. Published work: Shifting Sands, 1971. Contbr. to: Am. Poets; The Angles; Bay Shore Breeze, Bitterroot; Cardinal; Cyclo-Flame; Encore; Haiku Highlights; Imprints Qtly.; Jean's Journal, NII Sunday News; Quintessence; Quoin; Rochester Democrat & Chronicle; Swordsman Review; Tangent; United Poets; Williamsburg New; Coney Island Times; Quaderni Di Poesia; Pacific Breeze Anthol.; 67 Poets; Touchstone. Awards: 3rd place, Space thoughts contest, Haiku Highlights, 1966; Cert. of Excellence, Tulsa Poetry Qtly. Book Brochure Contest, 1969. Address: 126 Williams St., Newark, NY 14513, USA.

ROOT, William Pitt, b. 28 Dec. 1941. Writer. Education: B.A., Univ. of Wash., 1965; M.F.A., Univ. of N.C., 1967; postgrad. study, Stanford Univ., 1968. Positions held: Instr., Slippery Rock State Coll., 1967; Asst. Prof., Mich. State Univ., 1968; Session Ldr., Mid Peninsula Free Univ., 1968-70; Vis. Writer-in-Res., Amherst Coll., 1971, etc. Published works: Striking the Dark Air for Music, 1973; The Storm & Other Poems, 1969. Contbr. to: The Nation; New Yorker; Poetry; The Atlantic; Sewanee; Hudson; Yankee; Lillabulero; Prairie Schooner; Poetry Northwest; Va. Qtly.; Mass. Review; Radical Therapist; Free Family Notes, etc. Honours, awards: Grants in Writing, Rockefeller Fndn., 1970, Guggenheim Fndn., 1971 & Nat. Endowment of the Arts, 1973; 1st prize, Acad. of Am. Poets Coll. Writing Contest, 1967, etc. Address: c/o Harry Ford, Atheneum Publishers, 122 E. 42nd St., N.Y., NY 10017, U.S.A.

ROPER, Neil C(ampbell O(mmanney), b. 9 June 1941. Translator. Education: Malvern Coll., Worcs.; Perugia Univ., Umbria, Italy (1965); Geneva School of Interpreters, Switzerland (1968-70). Son of Capt. N.E.G. Roper, D.S.O., RN (retd). Positions held: Translator, Int. Antiques Fair, Florence, Italy, 1965; Tchr., Brit. Inst., ibid 1965. Memberships: Founder Fellow, Internat. Poetry Soc.; Sometime Member, Internat. Committee, C.S.S.I.; Associate, Inst. of Linguists. Published works: Tides of Destiny, 1971; (forthcoming) In Search of Silence. Contbr. to Anthols.: Gardens of Within, 1970; Bouquets of Poems, 1972; Gems of British Poetry, 1971. Awards: Monde Mers, awarded Grand Prix d'Edition in Belgium, 1971; Diploma di Benemerenza awarded for poem, 1972; Cert. of Merit awarded for short stories by The Writer, 1972. Address: c/o Glebe House, East Meon, Petersfield, Hants., UK.

ROQUEMORE, Lois Evelyn Masterson, b. 14 July 1903. Teacher. Education: Baylor Coll. Acad., Belton, Texas; Univ. of New Mexico, Albuquerque, NM., 3 yrs.; A.B. Summa Cum Laude, and M.A., Highlands Univ., Las Vegas, NM. Married, Judson Carl Roquemore; 1 s., 1 d. Positions held: Teacher, San Jon, NM; Logan, and Waterflow, NM; 16 yrs. in Farmington, City schools, NM.; NM Highlands Univ.; Las Vegas City schools; 14 yrs. El Paso City schools, Texas. Memberships: NLAPW (Pres., Las Vegas Chapter); Manuscript Club of El Paso (Pres.); Texas Press Women (Treas., El Paso, District 1); El Paso Writer's League (Sec.); El Paso Historical Society; Page 7, College Writer's Club (Sec.). Contbr. to: Good Housekeeping; Poet; Ideals; Cyclo-Flame; Pen Woman; The Guild; Archer; American Bard; Orphic Lute; Jean's Journal; Wisconsin Poetry; Hoosier Challenger; Bachaet; Modern Images; Quintessence; Sparkling Gems; American Voices; Am. Poet; Prairie Poet; Mary's Scrapbook; Author & Poet; United Poet; The Triangle of Sigma Sigma Sigma; New Mexico Mag.; Wick; Wonder Time; Children's Friend; Nursery Days; Internat. Who's Who in Poetry Anthol., etc. Awards: 1969, David Ross's Personal Poetry Broadcast, Poems on Astronauts; 1973, Chosen Woman of the Week by Station K.R.O.D., El Paso; 1971, 2nd Prize, Donald R. Ditto 300-dollar Award, Poetry Soc. of Texas; 1969-1973, 1st prizes in El Paso

Manuscript Club contest; 1970-1971, 1st prizes in El Paso Writer's League contest; 1971, 1st prize in Odessa, Texas, contest for relig. poetry; Song chosen by Sigma Sigma Sigma Nat. sorority for song of year, 1965; also many other prizes and awards. Address: 1401 Randolph, El Paso, TX 79902, USA.

ROS, Eva Voncile Livandais, b. 20 Mar. 1932. Teacher Aide. Education: currently taking coll. courses through Tougaloo Coll. toward degree specializing in Early Childhood Educ. Married Pol Mikel Ros, Jr., 3 children. Memberships: served. on South Miss. Fest. of Arts Comm., representing Girl Scouts as Chmn. of Exhibits, 1970, Chmn. of a Poetry Reading for Writers' Unlimited, & Chmn. of a Pre-School Art Exhib. for 2 yrs., 1972 & '73; Rep. Writers' Unlimited on Advisory Comm. relating to the Arts & the Community for Jackson Co. Jr. Coll.; has held positions as Treas., V.P. & Pres. of Writers' Unlimited; served 4 yrs. as Chmn. of Pascagoula Girl Scouts. Contbr. to: Advance Monticellonian; Legend Poetry Mag.; Gautier Independant, Miss. Honours, awards: Hon. Mention, Expmtl. Poetry Award, So. Miss. Fest. of Arts Lit. Comp., 1970; Magic Dragon Award for poem on Fantasy, local Writers' Club, 1970; One of 15 nominees in 1968 for the Outstanding Citizen's Award given by Pascagoula Bus. & Profl. Womens Club. Address: 3020 Frederic St., Pascagoula, MS 39567, U.S.A.

ROSBERG, Rose, b. 29 Sept. 1916. Librarian. Education: B.A. & M.L.S. Positions held: 1st Asst., NY Pub. Lib.; Lib. Asst., High Schl. of Music & Art; Tchr. of Lib., George Washington High Schl. Published works include: Trips-Without LSD and Other Poems, 1969. Contbr. to the following anthols., jrnls., mags., etc: Book Club for Poetry Anthol., 1956; Golden Quill Anthol., 1959 & 1967; The Various Light, 1964; Emily Dickinson: Letters from the World, 1970; Caravel; Carolina Quarterly; Engl. Jrnl.; Fiddlehead; Kan. Quarterly; Limbo; Lit. East & West; Midwest Quarterly; Moonlight Review; NY Times; Poetry East West; Prairie Schooner; Quarterly Review of Lit.; Southern Poetry Review; Sparrow; Womwood Review, etc. Address: 880 W 181st St., New York, NY 10033, USA.

ROSE, Elinor Kiess, pen name, ROSE, Elinor K. Feature Writer. Lecturer. Education: A.B., Hillsdale Coll. Married, Dana Rose, 3 s. Positions held: Staff, Oakland Univ. Writer's Conf., 1962-70; Staff, Writer's Conf., Carnegie Lib., Pitts.; Judge, Scholastic Writing Award, 1958-; Lectr. on writing at colls.; Speaker, Poetry Progs. Memberships: Poetry Soc. Mich.; Detroit Women Writers. Published works: Relax Chum, 1954; Sugar & Spice, 1959; Rhyme & Reason, 1967. Author of over 6000 poems publd. in daily syndicated feature. Contbr. to the following mags: Rdr's Digest; Good Housekeeping; McCall's; Christian Herald; Sat. Eve. Post; Quote; The Writer; Writer's Digest; Penninsula Poets. Honours, Awards: Writer of the Year, Detroit Women Writers, 1959; Achievement Award, Hillsdale Coll., 1955; Achievement Award, Nat. Convention, Kappa Kappa Gamma, 1968. Address: 25560 Dundee Rd., Royal Oak, Mich. 48070, USA.

ROSE, Elizabeth, b. 25 July 1904. Housewife. Widow, 2 sons. Member, Poetry Soc. of Am. Contbr. to: N.Y. Herald Tribune; Am. Weave; Lakeville (Conn.) Jrnl.; Bulletin of the Garden Club of Am.; The Diamond Anthol., Poetry Soc. of Am.; St. Margaret's Qtly.; SCAF Poets 1969. Address: R.D. 3, Box 140, Great Barrington, MA 01230, U.S.A.

ROSE, Harriet Ellen. Author. Education: Hofstra Univ. & Univ. of Iowa, U.S.A. Memberships: Nat. Poetry Soc., U.K.; Poet's Conf., U.K. Contbr. to: Workshop New Poets; Akros; New Headland; Candelabrum; Wheels; Centre 17; Littack; U.T. Review, U.S.A.; Weid, U.S.A.; Pink Peace; Poetry Australia. Address: 53 Blenheim Gdns., London N.W.2, U.K. & c/o Anne Rose, 520 Cedarwood Dr., Cedarhurst, NY 11516, U.S.A.

ROSE, Nancy A., b. 6 May 1934. Freelance Writer.

Education: many writing seminars & workshops. Positions held: Chmn., Institutional Writing Prog., Wis. Penal Instns., 1972-. Memberships: Dir., Wis. Regl. Writers Assn., 1972-; Dir., Wis. Fellowship of Poets, 1973-; Dir., Scripters Manuscript Reading Grp., 1972-; Green Bay Writers Club; Nat. Fed. of State Poetry Socs. Contbr. to: Warner Press; Nazarene Publng. House; Light & Life Press; Free Meth. Press; Am. Bapt. Bd. of Educ.; Story Friends; Junior Trails; Fun for Middlers; Christian Home; Wis. Hist. in Poetry, 1970; The Spirit; Ideal Publs.; New Poetry Out of Wis., 1971; Perspectives; The Alligator; Hawk & Whippoorwill Recalled, 1974. Honours, awards incl: 1st & 2nd pl., Trophy Poem Contest, Wis. Fellowship of Poets, 1973. Address: 215 Oak Hill Dr., Green Bay, WI 54301, U.S.A.

ROSELIEP, Raymond, b. 11 Aug. 1917. Clergyman; Poet; Critic. Education: B.A., Loras Coll., Dubuque, Iowa, 1939; Theol. Coll., Catholic Univ. of Am., 1939-43; M.A., Cath. Univ. of Am., 1948; Ph.D., Univ. of Notre Dame, 1954. Positions held: Ordained Roman Cath. Priest, Archdiocese of Dubuque, 1943; Asst. Pastor, Gilbertville, Iowa, 1943-45; Mng. Ed., The Witness, Dubuque, 1945-46; Prof., Engl., Loras Coll., Dubuque, 1946-66; Resident Chaplain, Holy Family Hall, Mt. St. Francis, Dubuque, 1966-. Memberships: Poetry Soc. of Am.; Modern Poetry Assoc.; Modern Lang. Assoc.; Nat. Coun. Tchrs. of Engl.; Cath. Press Assoc.; Cath. Poetry Soc. of Am. Published works: (poems) The Linen Bands, 1961; The Small Rain, 1963; Love Makes the Air Light, 1965. Contbr. to: 2 dozen poetry anthols., various eds.; (jrnls.) Poetry; The Nation; Time; Chicago Rev.; Modern Age; Prairie Schooner; Minn. Rev.; Mass. Rev.; Poetry NW; Ga. Rev.; Lit. Rev.; NY Times; Choice; Univ. of Kan. Rev.; Colo. Qtly.; Shenandoah; Yankee; Beloit Poetry Jrnl.; Arts in Soc.; Commonweal; Tablet, UK; Dubliner; Indian PEN, India; Blackfriars, Cambridge, UK; Canadian Poetry Mag.; Aylesford Rev., UK Honours: 3rd Prize, Carolina Qtly., 1962; Poet-in-Residence, Georgetown Univ., Wash., DC, 1964; 3rd Prize, Writer's Digest, 1968; Kenneth F. Montgomery Poetry Award, 1968; 1st Hons., Leigh Hanes Mem. Poetry Contest, Poetry Soc. of Va., 1968; 3rd Prize, Yankee, 1970. Address: Holy Family Hall, 3340 Windsor Extension, Dubuque, Iowa 52001, USA.

ROSENBAUM, Sylvia, b. 16 Aug. 1928. Housewife. Education: City Coll., 2 years; studied oil painting, sculpture & acting. Married, 1 s. Positions held: Artist; Former Sec., Insurance Co. Memberships: Fla. State Poetry Soc.; Am. Poets Fellowship Soc.; Poets' Study Club of Terre Haute. Published works: Ribbons, 1972. Contbr. to the following anthols., jrnls., newspapers, etc: Dance of the Muse, 1970; Gato Anthol., 1971; Gato Mag., 1970; United Poets, 1970; Am. Voice, 1970 & '71; Am. Poets Anthol., 1971; The Am. Poet, 1970; Poetry of Our Times, 1970; The Best in Poetry, 1970; WEFG Radio Stn., 1970; Shore Poetry Anthol., 1971; Collage of Emily (in prep.). Honours, awards: Gato Nat. Trophy, 1970; 2nd Prize, World Poems Contest, 1971; Certs. of Achievement, J. Mark Press, 1970; Cert. of Recog., Fla. State Poetry Soc., 1971; Cert., Personal Poetry, 1970; 1st Prize, Nat. Fdn. of State Poetry Socs. Address: 10 Heritage Court, Valley Stream, N.Y., 11581, USA.

ROSENBERG, David, b. 1 Aug. 1943. Poet; Editor; Teacher. Education: B.A., Univ. of Mich., 1964; M.A., Syracuse Univ., 1966; Ph.D. cand., Univ. of Essex, U.K. Positions held: Lectr., York Univ., Toronto, 1966-70; Ed., McClelland & Stewart, Toronto; Editl. Assoc., Coach House Press, Toronto; Ed., The Ant's Forefoot, Toronto, Wivenhoe Pk. & N.Y.; Poet in Res., Ctrl. Conn. State Coll., 1972; Vis. Poet, Poet-in-the-Classroom Progs., N.J. State Coun. on the Arts, & N.Y. State Arts Coun.; Poet-in-Res., Westchester Arts Coun., N.Y.; Educl. Cons. in Poetry, Fairleigh Dickinson Univ., 1973; Adjunct Asst. Prof., LaGuardia Community Coll., 1973-. Published works: Excellent Articles of Japan (photography & conceptual art), 1969; (poetry books) Disappearing Horses, 1969; Headlights, 1970; Night School, 1970; Paris & London,

1971; A Star in My Hair, 1971; Leavin' America, 1972; Frontal Nudity, 1972; The Necessity of Poetry, 1973; Some Psalms, 1973. Contbr. to: The Paris Review & num. other in England, Canada & the U.S.A. Honours, awards: Hopwood Award, 1964; Syracuse Creative Writing Fellowship, 1965; Canada Coun. Grants, 1969 & 71. Address: 29 St. Mark's Pl., N.Y., NY, U.S.A.

ROSENBERG, Sydell. Freelance Writer. Education: B.A. Brooklyn Coll., M.A., Hunter Coll., NYC. Married, 2 c. Positions held: Editorial Asst., Universal Publishing & Distributing Corp.; Copy Editor, Harper & Row; Substitute in Secondary Schools; Tchr., Engl. as 2nd Lang., etc. Memberships: Japan Society; Haiku Soc. of America; C.E.P.I. Published works: I Love You All Day/it is that simple (Modern Marriage Poems), 1970; The Haiku Anthol: Engl. Language Haiku by Contemp. American & Canadian Poets, 1974. Contbr. to: Marriage: The Mag. for Husband and Wife; Modern Haiku; New World Haiku; M.E.A.L., etc. Awards: 1972, Environment Contest, Hon. Mention; Poets Tape Exchange, 3rd Prize, 1972. Address: 141-30 Pershing Cres., Jamaica, NY 11435, USA.

ROSENBERGER, Francis Coleman, b. 22 Mar. 1915. Attorney-at-Law. Education: Univ. of Va.; J.D., Geo. Wash. Univ. Positions held: Book Reviewer for Richmond Times-Dispatch, 1938-40, Wash. Post, 1940-43, N.Y. Herald Tribune Book Review, 1945-62 & Wash. Star, 1967-71; Occasional Reviewer for N.Y. Times Book Review & Va. Qtly. Review, etc.; Adviser, U.S. Delegs. to Intergovernmental Confs., Geneva, 1955, '56 & Vienna, 1973. Published works: (books) The Virginia Poems, 1943; XII Poems, 1946; Ed., American Sampler: A Selection of New Poetry, 1951. Rep. in following anthols: The Best Poems of 1942; The Best Poems of 1943; American Writing, 1944; Cross Section, 1945; Cross Section, 1947; New Poets, 1948, etc. Contbr. to var. jrnls., reviews inclng: Poetry (Chicago); Poetry Qtly. (London); Voices; Am. Prefaces. Honours, awards: Univ. of Va. Poetry Award, 1936; Nat. Poetry Ctr. Award, N.Y. World's Fair, 1939. Address: 6809 Melrose Dr., McLean, VA 22101, U.S.A.

ROSENBLATT, Joseph, b. 26 Dec. 1933. Writer & Editor of Jewish Dialog. Married Faye Smith, 1 son (Eliot). Positions held: Instr., Artist's Workshop; Three Schls.; York Univ. summerschool. Mbr., League of Canadian Poetry. Published works: (Books) Voyage of the Mood, 1962; L.S.D. Leacock, 1966; Winter of the Luna Moth, 1968; The Bumblebee Dithyramb, 1972; (anthologies) Enchanted Forest, 1967; Oxford Book of Canadian Verse, 1968; Fourteen Winds, 1970; Bookstore Anthology, 1971; How do I Love Thee, 1971; Nobody But Yourself, 1972; anthol. published by MacMillan of Canada, 1973. Contbr. to: The Nation; Canadian Forum; Prism; Impulse; Quarry; Exile; Chelsea; Toronto Telegram. Honours, awards: Canada Coun., 1967 & 69; Ont. Arts Coun., 1972. Address: 136A Walmer Rd., Toronto M5R 2X9, Ont., Canada.

ROSENBLUM, Martin Jack, b. 19 Aug. 1946. College Lecturer. Education: B.A., Univ. of Wis., Madison, 1969; M.A., ibid, 1971; Ph.D. Candidate, ibid, Milwaukee. Married. Positions held: Rsch. Asst., Engl. Dept., Univ. of Wis., Milwaukee, 1970-71; Lectr., ibid, 1971-72, '73-; Dir., Div. of Continuing Educ., Marquette Univ., Milwaukee, Wis., summer '72, etc. Memberships: COSMEP, 1970-; Midwest Poetry Reading Circuit; Poetry Workshop Dir., Albatross Press & The Union Lit. Comm., Univ. of Wis., Madison, 1970; Rep., Madison writers & publishers at poetry conf., ibid, 1970. Ed. & Contbng. Ed. for var. publs. Published works: Bright Blue Coats, 1970; First Words The Moon Sings Near Drowning, 1970; Settling Attention & Other Poems, 1970; Albatross One (an anthol. of poems from Madison, Wis.), 1970; Father For My Prayer, 1971; Home, 1971; Sequence 50 from The Werewolf Sequence, 1971; On, 1972; Brewing: 20 Milwaukee Poets (anthol.), 1972; The Werewolf Sequence, a poem in 100 Sequences, 1974. Recip. var. hons. inclng. Hon. Mention for poem 'The Logs',

Acad. of Poets comp., 1971. Address: 3016 W. Michigan St., Milwaukee, WI 53208, U.S.A.

ROSENBURG, Robert Kemper, b. 10 June 1920. Poet; Editor-Publisher. Education: writing seminars, The Johns Hopkins Univ. Positions held: Ed., Linden Press, Balt., Md., 1960-. Published works: Music & its Environment, 1949; Shelomo (poems), 1955; Choruses for Morning (poems), 1963; 12 Studies After Rodin, (poems), 1960, Reflections From the White Room (poems), 1970; Dreams & Responsibilities (poems), 1974. Editor: Broken Death; Outside the Four Walls of Everything; In Need of Names; Populations of the Heart; Lyrics of Three Women; (anthol.) Confessions & Experiments; Beyond the Square: A Tribute to Elliott Coleman. Contbr. to: The Charles Street Jrnl.; Poet Lore; Orange Street Review, etc. Honours, awards: Nat. League of Crippled Children & Adults Cit., 1951; Award, N.Y. Design Club for book design, 1971. Address: 3601 Greenway, Baltimore, MD 21218, U.S.A.

ROSENFELD, Judith, pen name **HEMSCHEMEYER, Judith,** b. 7 Aug. 1935. Teacher of Creative Writing. Education: M.A., Univ. of Wis. Positions held: Copy Editor, Time Inc., 2 yrs.; currently Assoc. Instr. of Engl., Univ. of Utah. Published works: I Remember The Room Was Filled With Light, 1973. Contbr. to: Kenyon Review; The Hudson Review; The Carleton Miscellany; Southwest Review; The Beloit Poetry Jrnl.; The Western Humanities Review. Address: 803 Fourth Ave., Salt Lake City, UT 84103, U.S.A.

ROSENFIELD, Patricia Alanah, pen name **ALANAH, Patricia,** b. 6 June 1925. Teacher. Education: A.S., Newton Jr. Coll., 1967; B.S., Boston Univ., 1972. 2 s. Positions held: Dir., Learning Lab., Newton Jr. Coll., 1967-69; Asst to Dir., Harvard-Newton Summer Prog., Harvard Grad. Schl. of Educ., 1971. Memberships: New England Poetry Club; NY Poetry Forum; Ky. State Poetry Soc. Published works include: Cat in the Mirror, 1970. Contbr. to the following anthols., Jrnls., mags., etc: Observations; The Gryphon; Author/Poet; Haiku Highlights; Quoin; The New Angel Hour; Approaches; Review Mec; Phylon; Cardinal Poetry Quarterly; Pyramid; Ubulum; The Spring Anthol.; Fire Flower; New Mag. Honours, awards: Hon. Mention, Writers' Digest Nat. Poetry Contest, 1969; 1st Hon. Mention, Ky. State Poetry Soc., 1968; Mary F. Lindsey Award, NY Poetry Forum, 1969. Address: 42 Wessex Rd., Newton, Mass. 02159, USA.

ROSENSAFT, Menachem Zwi, b. 1 May 1948. Writer & Teacher. Education: B.A. & M.A., The Johns Hopkins Univ., Balt., Md. Married Jean Bloch. Positions held: Adjunct Lectr., Dept. of Jewish Studies, City Coll. of N.Y., 1972-. Member, Phi Beta Kappa. Published works: Fragments, Past & Future, 1968. Contbr. to: Midstream; Jewish Heritage; The Jewish Spectator; Beyond the Square (a Tribute to Elliott Coleman, published in Balt., Md., 1972); The Asahi Evening News (Japan); The Jewish Qtly., London. Address: 179 East 70th St., N.Y., NY 10021, U.S.A.

ROSENTHAL, Helene, b. 2 Apr. 1922. Educator. Education: B.A., Univ. of B.C., Canada, 1969. Married, 2 children. Positions held: Freelance photography & commercial art, sev. yrs.; Photographer, R.C.A.F., 2 yrs.; Engl. Tchr., Univ. of B.C., 2 yrs. Mbr., League of Canadian Poets. Published works: Peace is an Unknown Continent, 1968; A Shape of Fire, 1972; Listen to the Old Mother, 1973; (anthologies) Poets Market, 1968; West Coast Seen, 1969; Contemporary Poetry of British Columbia, 1970; 40 Women Poets of Canada, 1971. Contbr. to: The Canadian Forum; West Coast Review; Prism Int.; Talon; The Fiddlehead; Vancouver Life; Canadian Jewish Outlook; Edge; Ubyssey; Vanguard; var. publs. in U.S.A. Honours, awards: Macmillan Co. of Canada Prize for Creative Writing, 1967; Vancouver Centennial Comm. Runner-up Prize for Poetry, 1967; 1st Prize & Hon. Mention, Arts Undergrad. Soc. Poetry Contest, 1967. Address: 4218 W. 13th Ave., Vancouver 8, B.C., Canada.

ROSENTHAL, Macha Louis, b. 14 Mar. 1917. Professor of English. Education: B.A., Univ. of Chicago, 1937; M.A., ibid, 1938; Ph.D., N.Y. Univ. 1949. Married Victoria Himmelstein, 2 sons, 1 daughter. Positions held: Instr., Mich. State Univ., 1939-45; N.Y. Univ., 1945–; Poetry Ed., The Nation, 1956-61, The Humanist, 1970–, Present Tense, 1973–. Memberships: PEN; MLA. Published works: co-author, Exploring Poetry, 1955, '73; The Modern Poets: A Critical Introduction, 1960; A Primer of Ezra Pound, 1960; Blue Boy on Skates: Poems, 1964; The New Poets: Am. & British Poetry since World War II, 1967; Beyond Power: New Poems, 1969; The View from the Peacock's Tail: Poems, 1972; Randall Jarrell, 1972. Editor: Selected Poems & Two Plays of William Butler Yeats, 1962; The William Carlos Williams Reader, 1966; The New Modern Poetry: An Anthol. of Am. & Brit. Poetry since WWII, 1967, '69; 100 Postwar Poems, Brit. & Am., 1968; co-ed., Chief Modern Poets of Brit. & Am., 1970. Contr. to var. mags., newspapers, jrnls. Honours, awards: Am. Coun. of Learned Societies Fellow, 1942, 1950-51; Guggenheim Fellow, 1960-61, '64-65. Address: Dept. of Engl., N.Y. Univ., 19 University Pl., N.Y., NY 10003, U.S.A.

ROSEVEARE, Ursula Stella Catherine, b. 26 Oct. 1914. Education: King's Coll., London Univ., 1932-34; Schl. of Slavonic & East European Studies, 1932-34. Positions held: Editl. Staff, Illustrated London News, 1935; Min. of Info., Foreign Publicity Directorate, 1939-41; U.S. Army, SOS, ETO, 1943-45; Tchng. appts. in Cheltenham, 1946, Gloucester, 1946-59, Coventry, 1959-63; Sr. Lectr., Dept. of Engl., Trent Park Coll. of Educ., 1963–. Memberships: Advisory Coun., BBC (Midland Region), 1946-52; PEN, 1966–; West Country Writers' Assn., 1951–; Press Club; Univ. Womens Club. Contr. to var. jrnls. & mags. Address: Flat 4, The Abbey's, 15 Abbey Hill, Kenilworth Warwicks, U.K.

ROSKOLENKO, Harry, pen names, **ROSS, Colin & LYNN, Ross K.,** b. 21 Sept. 1907. Author; Poet; Novelist; Journalist; Critic. Positions held: Drawbridge Operator; Law Clerk; Seaman; 2nd Officer, S. Pacific, WWII. Mbr., Authors League, NY. Published works: Sequence on Violence, 1938; I Went into the Country, 1940; A Second Summary, 1944; Notes From A Journey & Other Poems, 1947; Paris Poems, 1950; American Civilization, 1971; (travel) Poet on a Scooter, 1958; White Man Go, 1962; (novels) Black is a Man, 1953; Lan-Lan, 1962; (autobiography) When I Was Last On Cherry Street, 1965; The Terrorized, 1968; The Time That Was Then, 1971. Contr. to: Poetry Chicago; Chelsea Review; Antioch Review; Meanjin, Quadrant; Midstream, etc. Address: c/o Clyne, 697 East 219 St., Bronx, NY 10467, USA.

ROSOCHACKI, Daniel, b. 5 Oct. 1942. Writer. Education: B.A., Mich. State Univ., 1965; M.A., Mich. State Univ., 1968. Positions held: Asst. Instr., Mich. State Univ.; Ed., Mich. State Univ. Press; Furniture & Cabinet Maker; Fulltime Writer. Memberships: Mich. Coun. of the Arts (involved in Poet visits to schls. & conduct workshops under the auspices of the council). Published works: Book Three, 1972; currently preparing a new manuscript of poems & completing a novel, Walking the Dog, for possible publication in early 1975. Contr. to: Red Cedar Review (Editing & contbng.); Sumac Mag.; Diesel Mag., etc. Recip., First Prize, Lawson Writing Contest sponsored by Mich. State Univ. Address: 215 High St., Northport, MI 49670, U.S.A.

ROSS, Alan, b. 6 Apr. 1922. Writer; Editor; Publisher. Education: St. John's, Oxford. Positions held: Staff, The Observer, 1950–; Ed., London Mag., 1961–; Dir., Alan Ross Ltd. (Publishers). Published works: Poems 1942-67, 1967; South to Sardinia, 1957. Contr. to: New Statesman; New Yorker; Times Lit. Supplement; London Mag.; Encounter; Spectator. Honours: Rockefeller Atlantic Award for Lit., 1949. Address: Clayton Manor, Hassocks, Sussex, UK.

ROSS, David, b. 7 July 1896. Radio Broadcaster; Announcer. Education: courses at sev. colls. Pioneered in the reading of good poetry on radio. Poetry readings at colls. & the Lib. of Congress. Memberships: former V.P., Poetry Soc. of Am.; Mbr. of the Bd., Hon. Mbr. Ex Officio, Fellow, ibid. Published works: Poet's Gold, anthol. of poetry to be read aloud; Illustrated Treasury of Poetry for Children. Contbr. to: Atlantic Monthly; The Lyric; Polemic; The Nation; New Republic; Partisan Review. Honours, awards: Reynolds Lyric Award, 1957; Samuel De Witt Lyric Award, 1966; Christopher Morley Award, 1969. Address: 829 Park Ave., N.Y., NY 10021, U.S.A.

ROSSETTI, Reto Mario, b. 11 Apr. 1909, Biasca, Switzerland. Lecturer in Education. Education: Edinburgh D.A. & M.A., 1930. Positions held: Hd. of Dept. of Art Educ., Bristol, 1958-68; Lectr. in Educ., Bristol Univ., 1968-74. Memberships: Esperanto Acad., 1967–; Fndr. & Mbr., La Skota Skolo, Scottish Schl. of Esperanto Poetry, successor to La Budapeŝta Skolo, 1947–. Published works: (books) Oazo, La Laguna, 1952; Angla Antologio, Rotterdam, 1957; Pinta Krajono, La Laguna, 1959; La Tragedio de Otelo, 1960; (critical study) A Crux & No Crux, in Shakespeare Qtly., 1962; Publd. lecture at Int. Summer Univ., La Kimraj artfestoj (The Welsh eisteddfodau), 1948. Contbr. to: Esperanto Antologio Poemoj, 1887-1957, 1958; Literatura Mondo, Budapest; Norda Prismo, Stockholm; Nica Revuo, Nice; Revuo Esperanto, London & Rotterdam; Suda Stelo, Zagreb; Revuo Orienta, Tokyo. Recip., awards in the yearly Belar ă Konkurso and other int. poetry competitions. Address: 120 Cromwell Rd., Bristol 6, UK.

ROSSINI, Sarah Lois, pen name **McNEAR, Elizabeth,** b. 15 Sept. 1928. Teacher. Education: Cert., Famous Writers Schl., New Haven, Conn., 1967; Grad., Univ. of Ark., 1974. Married Francis Rossini, 6 children. Memberships: V.P., St. Mary's Home Schl. Soc.; Alpha Chi; Poet's Roundtable of Ark. Recip., Novice Award, 1973. Address: Star Rte.1, Box 44, Lake Village, AR 71653, U.S.A.

ROTH, Paul B., b. 6 Apr. 1949. Poet. Education: Univ. of Tampa, Fla.; Geo. Wash. Univ., Wash. D.C.; Goddard Coll., Plainfield, Vt. Positions held: Asst. Ed., Univ. of Tampa Poetry Review; Tchr. of Creative Writing to Children between the grades 4 & 6 (Program funded by the Nat. Endowment for the Arts). Published works: After the Grape, 1969; Basements of Tears, 1973. Contbr. to: U.T. Review; Ann Arbor Review; Patterns; Ghost Dance; Cardinal; Zahir; Epoch; Immanentist Anthol.; Mantras: Immanentist Anthol.; New Generation Poets Anthol. Address: 310 Bradford Pkwy., Syracuse, NY 13224, U.S.A.

ROTHENBERG, Jerome, b. 11 Dec. 1931. Poet. Education: B.A., City Coll. of N.Y., U.S.A., 1952; M.A., Univ. of Mich., 1953. Positions held: Instr., City Coll. of N.Y., 1960; Lectr. in Engl., Mannes Coll. of Mus., N.Y., 1961-70; Regents Prof., Univ. of Calif. at San Diego, 1971; Vis. Lectr. in Anthropol., New Schl. for Soc. Rsch., N.Y., 1971-72; Freelance Poet & Writer, 1972–. Memberships: PEN Am. Ctr.; Bd. Dirs., New Means Fndn.; Bd. Dirs., The Performance Union. Published works incl: Conversations (poems), 1968; Technicians of the Sacred: a Range of Poetries from Africa, America, Asia & Oceania, 1968; The Book of Hours & Constellations, or Gomringer by Rothenberg, 1968; Sightings & Red Easy A Color, 1968; Poems 1964-67, 1968; The 17 Horse-Songs of Frank Mitchell: Nos. X-XIII, 1970; A Book of Testimony (poems), 1971; Poems for the Game of Silence (selected poems), 1971; Esther K. Comes to America (poems), 1973; Shaking the Pumpkin (anthol. of Am. Indian poetry), 1972; America a Prophecy, 1973; Seneca Jrnl. 1: A Poem of Beaver, 1973; Poland/1931 (complete), 1974 (also performed in N.Y., San Diego & London as a mixed media event), 1968-71; (theater) Broadway adaptation, The Deputy, by Rolf Hochhuth, 1964, etc. Contbr. to num. anthols., mags., reviews, jrnls. Var. recordings. Recip., Longview Fndn. Award for Poetry,

1960 & Wenner-Gren Fndn. grantin-aid, 1968. Address: 600 W. 163 St., N.Y., NY 10032, U.S.A.

ROUNTREE, Thomas, J., b. 22 July 1927. University Professor. Education: B.A., Troy State Univ., Ala.; M.A., Univ. of Ala.; Ph.D., Tulane Univ. Positions held: USN & US Army; Tchr., Univs. of La., Tex. & Ala.; Currently Chmn., Dept. of Engl., Univ. of S. Ala., Mobile. Memberships: MLA; South Atlantic Mod. Lang. Assn.; The Wordsworth Circle, The Rydal Mount Summer Schl. Assn.; Soc. for Study of Southern Lit. Contbr. to: American Haiku; Cats Magazine; The DeKalb Literary Arts Journal; Journal of American Folklore; Scimitar & Song; Twigs Magazine. Address: Box U-342, Univ. of South Alabama, Mobile, Ala. 36688, USA.

ROUSSELOT, Jean, b. 27 Oct. 1913. Writer. Currently Literary Dir. of two publishing houses. Memberships: Pres. of Hon., Union of Profl. Writers; Pres., Société des Gens de Lettres de France; Dir. of Comm., Nat. Comm. of Writers; PEN Int., etc. Published works incl: Poèmes, 1934; Le Goût du Pain, 1937; Le Sang du Ciel, 1944; Il n'y a pas d'exil, 1954; Maille à partir, 1961; Hors d'eau, 1968; A qui parle de vie, 1972; Du même, même, 1973. Cons., Jean Rousselot, book by André Marissel, in the series "Poètes d'aujourd'hui". Contbr. to: Les Cahiers du Sud; Mercure de France; Jrnl. des Poètes; Poésie 43; Sud, Création; Les Cahiers du Nord; Les Nouvelles littéraires; Les Lettres Françaises & var. poetry reviews in the U.S.A., Spain, Italy, Hungary, Yugoslavia, Switzerland, Holland; Denmark. Honours, awards: Prix International Syracuse, 1954; Prix Apollinaire, 1958; Grand Prix de Poésie de la Ville de Paris, 1969; Grand Prix de l'Académie Française, 1973, etc. Address: 90 rue de Saint Nom, L'Etang La Ville 78, France.

ROUTIER, Simone, b. 4 Mar. 1901. Poet. Education: Normal Schl. of Tchng., Laval Univ., Quebec, Canada; Course of Phonetics, Sorbonne, Paris, France, 1930; Philos., Dominican Inst., Ottawa, Canada, 1940-41; Novice, Dominican Contemplative Cloister, Berthierville, PQ, 10 months. Married, J.F. Drouin, 1958. Positions held: Map Designer. Canadian Archives, Paris, France, 1930-40; Asst. Archivist, Ottawa, Canada, 1940-50; Press Attache, Canadian Embassy, Brussels, Belgium, 1950-54; Press Attache & Vice Consul, Canadian Consulate, Boston, Mass., USA, 1954-58. Memberships: Poets Soc., Quebec, 1929-71; Poets Soc., France, 1932-40; Soc. of Canadian Writers, 1929-69; French Canadian Acad., 1947-; Acad. Bernichonne, France, 1960. Published works: L'Immortel Adolescent, 1929, '30; Ceux qui seront aimés, 1930; Paris-Amour-Deauville, 1932; Les Tentations, 1934; Adieu Paris, 1941; Les Psaumes de Jardin Clos, 1947; Le Long Voyage (Je te francerai), 1949. Contbr. to the following newspapers & jrnls: Le Soleil; L'Eversement; Le Droit; La Tribune; La Presse; La Patré; L'aison: Poésie (Quebec); Poésie (Paris); La Bouteille à la mer; La Revue Dominicaine; Le Journal des Poétes; Le Plare; 1943, etc. Honours, Awards: Prix David, 1929; Lt. Gov's Medal, 1930; Médaille des Jonx de Languedoc, France, 1934. Address: 11730 Tolhurst St., Montréal 357, PQ, Canada.

ROWBOTHAM, David, b. 27 Aug. 1924. Poet; Critic; Lecturer. Education: Toowoomba Grammar Schl.; State Tchrs'. Coll.; Queensland & Sydney Univs. Positions held: with RAAF, SW Pacific, WWII; Lit. & Theatre Critic, Brisbane Courier-Mail, 1955-; Lectr., Commonwealth Lit. Fund, sev. Aust. Univs & Queensland. Published works: Ploughman & Poet, 1954; Inland, 1958; All The Room, 1963; Town & Cities, 1956; The Man in the Jungle (novel), 1964. Contbr. to: Mod. Australian Verse, 1964. Address: 38 Nelson St. Coorparoo, Brisbane, Queensland, Australia

ROWE, Tony (Clara), pen name **ROWE, Tony.** Masseuse (I.S.T.M.), retired. Education: Private; Training for ISTM Cert., King Edward VII School for Massage and Remedial Exercises, Royal Infirmary, Cardiff. Positions held: Masseuse, Netley Military Hospital; Bangour Military/War Hospital, near Edinburgh; Red Cross Clinic, Cardiff; Private Practice, Cardiff. Memberships: English Assoc.; Cardiff Writer Circle. Published works: Before Abraham (collection of poems), 1971; also novel, and one-act plays. Contbr. to: Hibbert Journal; Envoi; Country Quest; Ore; Scrip; Expression One; The New Shetlander; The Inquirer. Address: Flat 8, Druidstone House, Druidstone Rd., St. Mellons, Mon., UK.

ROWLAND, John Russell, b. 10 Feb. 1925. Diplomat. Education: Univ. of Sydney, Australia. Positions held: entered Australian Dept. of For. Affairs, 1944; served London, 1948-49, Canberra, 1949-52, Saigon, 1952-54, Washington, 1955-57, London, 1957-59, Canberra, 1959-65; Ambassador to the U.S.S.R., 1965-68; High Commnr. to Malaysia, 1969-72; Ambassador to Austria, 1972-. Published works: The Feast of Ancestors, 1965; Snow, 1971; annual anthols. of Australian verse, 'Australian Poetry'. Contbr. to var. newspapers & periodicals inclng: Sydney Morning Herald; The Australian; The Bulletin; Meanjin Qtly.; Southerly. Recip., 2nd prize, Sydney Morning Herald Comp., 1951. Address: c/o Dept. of Foreign Affairs, Canberra, A.C.T., Australia.

ROWLAND DU PUY, Gertrude, pen name **ROWLAND, Gertrude D.,** b. 29 July 1902. Freelance Writer. Education: courses in Creative Writing at Adult night schls. & at Univ. of Pa., Penn State, La Salle Coll., etc. Married Joseph Ritterhouse Rowland, 1 son, 2 daughters. Positions held: Bd., Abington Meml. Hosp., 25 yrs.; currently Assoc. Mbr., ibid; var. volunteer work w. Jr. League & on Bd. of Day Nursery for black children. Memberships: Pres., Phila. Br., Nat. League Am. Penwomen, 1960-62; V.P., 2 terms & on Bd. for 10 yrs., ibid; Bd., Phila. Regl. Writers Conf., 1951-61; On Bd., St. David's Christian Writers Conf., 1947-62. Published works: (book of poetry) Hours Bright As Leaves, 1965. Contbr. to var. jrnls. Honours, awards incl: 1st prize, Nat. League Am. Pen Women, Phila., Br., Annual Comp., 1960, and article, 1974. Address: 1454 Marshall Rd., Meadowbrook, PA 19046, U.S.A.

ROWSE, A(lfred) L(eslie), b. 4 Dec. 1903. Writer; Historian; Poet. Education: St. Austell, Cornwall; Christ Church, Oxford Univ. Positions held: Fellow, All Souls Coll., Oxford Univ. Memberships: Fellow, Brit. Acad.; Fellow, Royal Soc. of Lit.; Pres., English Assn. Published works: Poems of a Decade, 1941; Poems Chiefly Cornish, 1944; Poems of Deliverance; 1946; Poems Partly American, 1959; Poems of Cornwall & America, 1967; Strange Encounter: Poems, 1972. Contbr. to: The Spectator; Books and Bookmen; The Sunday Telegraph; Poetry Review. Address: All Souls Coll., Oxford Univ., U.K.

ROYCE, Catherine Purdy, b. 11 Nov. 1948. Instructor of Dance. Education: B.A., Wesleyan Univ., 1972. Positions held: currently working on a special proj. in dance at Wesleyan Univ. Contbr. to: Tin Drum; Ad Lit; Pot Pourri. Recip., Conn. Student Poet, 1972. Address: Old Campus Rd., Andover, MA, U.S.A.

RUBADIR, David, b. 19 July 1930. Lecturer. Educ: King's Coll., Kampala, Uganda; B.A., Makerere Univ. Coll., Kampala; Dip. Ed., Bristol Univ., U.K.; M.A. King's Coll., Cambridge, U.K. Positions held: Malawi Ambassador to U.S.A. & UN, 1964-65; Lectr., Engl. Lit., Makerere Univ. Coll., Uganda, 1965-. Published works: No Bride Price (novel). Contbr. to: Transition; Pen Point; Zuka; East African Journal; (anthologies) Darkness and Light, 1958; Modern Poetry from Africa, 1963; Poems from Black Africa, 1963; A Book of African Verse, 1964; Young Commonwealth Poets '65, 1965; Zuka I & II, 1968; Poetry from Africa, 1970. Recip., Margaret Graham Poetry Prize, 1956. Address: c/o Engl. Dept., Makerere Univ. Coll., Kampala, Uganda.

RUBIN, Jean, b. 6 Jan. 1928. Instructor in English. Education: M.A., 1957, Columbia Univ.; B.A., 1948, Smith Coll. Positions held: Instr. in Engl., The Maryland Inst., Coll. of Art. Baltimore, Maryland, since

1962; prior positions: Bookseller; Radio Programmer and Reader (at KPFA, Radio Pacifica, Berkeley, Calif.); Public Relations Assistant; Secretary; Freelance Writer; Re-Writer of Encyclopedia articles; Ghost Writer, etc. Contbr. to: Zero; Osmose; Poetry New York; Le Bayou; Riverside Poetry II; Quixote; The Notre Dame English Journal; Contact; The Paper. Award: Co-Winner, Robert Frost Award (Poetry Soc. of America), Jan., 1963. Address: 1529 Bolton St., Baltimore, MD, USA.

RUBIN, Larry Jerome, b. 14 Feb. 1930. Professor of English. Education: B.A. (1951), M.A. (1952), Ph.D. (1956), Emory Univ., Atlanta, Georgia. Positions held: Instr. of English, Georgia Tech., Atlanta, 1956-58, continuing Asst. Prof. of Engl., 1958-65, Assoc. Prof. of Engl., 1965-73, and since 1973, Prof. of Engl. Membership: Poetry Soc. of America. Published works: The World's Old Way, 1963; Lanced in Light, 1967. Contbr. to: The New Yorker; Harper's Mag.; Saturday Review; Poetry (Chicago); The Nation; Yale Review; Kenyon Review; Sewanee Review; Virginia Qtly. Review; Qtly. Review of Literature; Tri-Qtly.; Chicago Review; Antioch Review; Southern Review; New American Review; Denver Qtly.; Carleton Miscellany, and many others. Awards: Reynolds Lyric Award, Poetry Soc. of America, 1961; Literary Achievement Award, Ga. Writers Assoc., 1963; Sidney Lanier Award, Oglethorpe Univ., 1964; John Holmes Memorial Award, Poetry Soc. of New Hampshire, 1965; Ga. Poet of the Year Award, Dixie Council of Authors, 1967; Kansas City Star Award, 1969; Annual Award, Poetry Soc. of America, 1973. Address: Box 15014, Emory Univ., Atlanta, GA 30333, USA.

RUBIN, Riva Regina, former pen name **LADOR, Riva,** b. 11 Jan. 1932. Freelance Translator. Education: Hebrew Tchrs. Seminar, Johannesburg, S. Africa, 1951. Married Harold Rubin, 2 sons (Adam & Ezra). Positions held: Tchr., Hebrew Nursery Schls., Johannesburg, S. Africa, 1953-60; Asst. Ed., I.C.E.P., Israel, 1968-70; Reviewer for Hebrew Book Review, 1970-73. Mbr., Hebrew Writers Assn., Israel. Published works: The Poet Killers, 1969. Public readings of own poetry at Writers House; Community Ctrs.; Radio; Town Halls; Nat. Poetry Ctr. (London) 1973. Contbr. to: Purple Renoster, 1958-69; Writing in S.A. Today, 1967; Poet Lore, U.S.A., 1969; Yom Hashirah, 1970; Lit. supplements, Israeli Press, 1969-73; Poet (India), 1971; Bagvulam, anthol., 1970; Hebrew Book Review (every quarter from 1970-73). Recip., PEN Short Story Prize (S.A.), 1960. Address: 55 David Hamelech St., Herzlia B, Israel.

RUBY, Kathryn, b. 27 Sept. 1947. Reviewer and Technical Writer. Education: B.A. in Engl. Lit., New York Univ., 1969; M.A. in Engl. Lit., ibid, 1972. Positions held: Co-Ed. & Contbr. to Women the New Voice: An Anthol. of Feminist Poetry, 1974. Book Reviewer, Metropolitan Review; Dance Reviewer, Dance Scope Mag. Member, Modern Language Assn. of Am. Contbr. to: Earth's Daughters; Metropolitan Review; Washington Sq. Review; The Destruction of Philadelphia; Off Our Backs; Margins. Address: 55 Downing St., Apt. 8, N.Y., NY 10014, U.S.A.

RUDBERG, Gertrude Jones, pen names, **LYNDS, Clara, FROST, Diana & WENTWORTH, Nina,** b. 17 June 1909. Beautician. Positions held: Owner of Beauty Shop for 30 yrs.; Dir. of Activities in Nursing Home for past 6 yrs. Contbr. to: Ideals Mag.; Lym Daily Item; Lym Sunday Post; Saugas Advertiser; Boston Globe; Manchester Jrnl., N.H.; United Ch. Women Mag. Has received letters of recognition from Presidents Eisenhower, Kennedy, Johnson, Nixon & many well known people including Dr. Albert Schweitzer about whom she has written poems. Address: 32 Hawthorne St., Lym, MA, U.S.A.

RUDD, Margaret Thomas, b. 15 Dec. 1907. Educator; Author. Education: B.A., Univ. of Richmond, Va., 1929; M.A., Columbia Univ., 1937; summer sessions grad., La Sorbonne & Univ. of Mex. Positions held: Tchr., Spanish & French, Stuart Hall, Staunton, Va.;

Ed., household organ, Dugan Bakery, Brooklyn, N.Y.; Ed., Va. State Hlth. Bulletin; Tchr. & Dean, Blackstone Jr. Coll., Blackstone, Va.; Spanish Tchr., Stephens Jr. Coll., Columbia, Mo.; Asst. Prof., Assoc. Prof. & Chmn., Modern For. Lang. Dept., Univ. of Richmond, Va. Memberships: Nat. League of Am. Pen Women, Inc.; Va. Poetry Soc.; The Va. Writers Club; World Poetry Soc. Intercontinental; Am. Poetry League. Published works: co-author, Nuestros Vecinos Mexicanos, 1945; The Lone Heretic (biog. of Unamuno), 1963; (co-author) ... And Three Small Fishes, original poems, 1974. Contbr. to: Moon Age Poets, 1970; Am. Poetry League; original poems & transl. of poems from Spanish to English frequently appear in Poet. Honours, awards: Hon. Mention, Poetry Contest, Alexandria Br., Nat. League of Am. Pen Women, 1972. Address: 2013 Franklin Ave., McLean, VA 22101, U.S.A.

RUDD, Peggy Ray, b. 23 June 1933. Teacher. Education: B.S., Hardin Simmons Univ., Abilene, Tex.; McMurry Coll., Abilene; Laman State Coll., Beaumont, Tex.; SW Mo. State Coll., Springfield, Mo.; Grad. Study, Drury Coll., Springfield. Married to Lucian Rudd, 2 children. Positions held: Elem. Tchr., Ft. Worth, Tex., Neosha, Mo., Springfield, Mo., Waterloo, Iowa & Odessa, Tex. Memberships: Nat. Educ. Assn.; Tex. State Tchrs. Assn; Odessa Classroom Tchrs. Assn.; Belmont Bapt. Church (Dir., Coll. Work); Tex. Poetry Soc. Odessa Poetry Soc.; Kappa Kappa Iota. Published works include: Christmas At Burleson, 1969; The Day Before, 1968. Contbr. to the following jrnls: Abilene Reporter News; Merkel Mail. Honours, awards: 3rd Place, Tex Poetry Celebration, Odessa, Tex., 1968. Address: 2810 Cambridge, Odessa, Tex. 79761, USA.

RUDMAN, Mark, b. 11 Dec. 1948. Poet; Translator. Education: B.A., New Schl., 1970; M.F.A., Grad. Schl. of the Arts, Columbia Univ., 1973. Positions held: Tchng. children to write in public schls., Writer's Collaborative & Poets & Writers; currently translating Russian & Ukranian Poetry, primarily Pasternak & Bohdan Antonych. In collaboration w. Stanley Kunitz & three other poets, has translated the selected poems of the Ukranian poet Ivan Drach, 'Orchard Lamps'. Poems will appear in forthcoming anthols. produced by Harcourt Brace & the Acad. of Am. Poets. Contbr. to: Atlantic Monthly; Harper's; Modern Occasions; Shenandoah; Columbia Forum; The Northwest Review; The Calif. Qtly.; Granite; The Minn. Review; ILM Jrnl.; Folio; Tractor; The Little Mag.; Icarus; Poetry, etc. Honours, awards: Acad. of Am. Poets Prize, Columbia, 1972; The Hackney Prize, 1973. Address: 2 Tudor City Pl., N.Y., NY, U.S.A.

RUDOLF, Anthony, b. 6 Sept. 1942. Translator; Editor. Education: B.A. Married. Positions held: various; currently – translator. Member, General Council, Poetry Soc. Published works: Selected Poems of Yves Bonnefoy (trans.), 1968; Manifold Circle (poems), 1971; M.P.T. French Anthol. (editor), 1973; Poems & Prose of A. Tvardovsky (trans.), 1973; Poems of E. Vinokourov (trans.), 1973/74. Contbr. to: Transatlantic Review; Modern Poetry in Translation, etc. Awards: Scott-Moncrieff Award of Soc. of Authors (runner-up), for best French translation of 1968. Address: 1 Primrose Gardens, London NW3 4UJ, UK.

RUEBNER, Tuwia, b. 30 Jan. 1924. Lecturer. Education: mainly autodidact. Married; 3 children. Memberships: Hebrew Writers Assoc.; Hugo von Hofmannsthal Gesellschaft; Soc. of World Poetry; PEN Club. Published works: Haesh Ba'even, 1957; Shirim Limtzo Et, 1961; Kol Od, 1967; Mishirej T. Ruebner, 1970; Ejn Lehashiv, 1971. Contbr. to: numerous journals, publications. Awards: Anna Frank, 1960–; Acum, 1967. Address: Kibbutz Merchavia, Israel.

RUEHM, Gerhard, b. 12 Feb. 1930. Writer. Positions held: Prof., Acad. for Arts, Hamburg. Published works incl: Die wiener Gruppe, 1967; Fenster/Texte, 1955-66, 1968; Knochenspielzeug – Märchen und Fabeln,

1970; Gesammelte Gedichte und Visuelle Texte, 1970; Charles Baudelaire – die Reise nach Cythera, 1971; Die Frösche und andere Texte, 1971; Ophelia und die Wörter/Gesammelte Theaterstücke 1954-71, 1972; Mann und Frau, 1972; Ergebnisse des Ersten Berliner Dichter-workshops, 1972/Achleitner, Brus, Roth, Rühm, Wiener, 1973; Wahnsinn – Litaneien, 1973, & many other. Records incl: Ophelia und Die Wörter, ein Hörspiel, 1973. Films: Ophelia und die Wörter, 1960/70; Witz, 1971. Contbr. to many German & int. anthols. & mags. Address: Offenbacherstr. 8, 1 West Berlin 33, German Fed. Repub.

RUIZ, Nora Beatriz Ousset, b. 23 Jan. 1918. Teacher. Education: Maestra-Maestrade Musica; Positions held: Engl. Sec., IICANA, 6 yrs.; Tchr., Nat. Schl. 177, Argentina; Tchr., Adult Educ., FC Gral Belgrana, Nat. Min. of Educ., Cordoba. Mbr., Soc. of Argentine Writers, Cordoba. Author, Mas Alla, (beginning reader for adults), 1966 & many poems. Recip., prize for Mas Alla, Buenos Aires. Address: Montevideo 1275-Cordoba, Argentina.

RUKEYSER, Muriel, b. 15 Dec. 1913. Poet; Writer; Teacher. Education: Fieldston Schl.; Vassar Coll. 1 s. Positions held: Bookshop & office jobs; Reporter, theatre mag. Memberships: Nat. Inst. of Arts & Letters. Published works include: Theory of Flight, 1935; US 1, 1938; A Turning Wind, 1939; Beast in View, 1942; Wake Island, 1943; The Green Wave, 1947; One Life, 1955; Body of Waking, 1958; Waterlily Fire, 1962; Selected Poems, 1951; Elegies, 1951; Soul & Body of John Brown, 1942; The Speed of Darkness, 1968; The Outer Banks, 1969; 29 Poems, 1971; Breaking Open, 1973. Contbr. to the following anthols., jrnls., mags., etc.: Poetry Review; Transatlantic; Antaeus; Poetry; NY Quarterly; Observer; Nation; New Republic; Kenyon Review; Atlantic Monthly; New Yorker; Ikon; Sat. Review; Chelsea; New Directions Annual; Life & Letters; Today; Liberation; Unicorn Folders; Evergreens; Tri-Quarterly; Tomorrow; Discovery, etc. Honours, awards: Guggenheim Fellowship, Harriet Monroe Prize, 1942, '43; Nat. Inst. Award, 1942; Swedish Acad., Translation Award, 1968. Address: c/o Monica McCall, 1301 Ave. of the Americas, N.Y.C., NY., USA.

RUMAKER, Michael, b. 5 Mar. 1932. Lecturer. Education: B.A., Black Mountain Coll., N.C.; M.F.A., Columbia Univ., N.Y.C. Positions held: Lectr., The New Schl. for Soc. Rsch.; Lectr. & Writer-in-Res., City Coll. of N.Y., Univ. of Buffalo, Cobbleskill Coll., N.Y. Member, Am. P.E.N. Published works: The Other Side of the Night; The Use of the Unconscious in Writing (essay). Contbr. to: The Nation; The Floating Bear; Evergreen Review; Poeti Americani (anthol.); The Black Mountain Review; Measure; Wild Dog; From the Belly of the Shark (anthol.) Address: 112 River Rd., Grand View-on-Hudson, NY 10960, U.S.A.

RUSSELL, David Seager, b. 12 June 1940. Teacher; Journalist. Education: Univ. of Durham, U.K., 1959-62. Positions held: Freelance work, Mid-Century Authors, 1965-66; Lectr. in Liberal Studies, Guildford Co. Tech. Coll., 1967-68; Tech. Publng., 1969-; Sub-Ed., British Safety Coun., currently. Memberships: Org., Poetry Workshop, Notting Hill Arts & Community Ctr.; Org., Live Poetry Reading Grp., The Grove Spirit. Published works: Exacting Modality of the World Web, 1970; A Chip off the Old Block, 1973. Contbr. to Cread Poetry Poster. Address: 8 MacGregor Rd., London W.11, U.K.

RUSSELL, Norman H., b. 28 Nov. 1921. University Dean. Education: Ph.D., Univ. of Minn., 1951. Positions held: (past) Prof. of Biol., Grinnell Coll.; Buena Vista Coll.; Ariz. State Univ.; Rutgers Univ.; (current) Dean, School of Maths. and Science, Central State Univ., Edmond, Okla. Published works: Indian Thoughts: The Small Songs of God, 1972; The Hunt, 1973; At The Zoo, 1969. Contbr. to: 200 journals, including – South Dakota Review; Prism Internat.; Virginia Qtly. Review; Poet Lore; Nimrod; Crazy Horse, etc. Awards: 500-dollars Award, US Nat. Arts &

Humanities Foundation, 1970; Poet Lore, 50-dollars award, 1970. Address: School of Maths. and Science, Central State Univ., Edmond, OK 73034, USA.

RUSSELL, Richard Michael Friend, pen name **RUSSELL, Dick,** b. 30 May 1944. Computer Consultant. Education: William Penn Comprehensive School, London. Married to Heather Hill. Positions held: Tech. Officer, I.E.A. (UNESCO), Columbia Univ., NY.; Consultant to: Codgwiok Musoum, Oambridgc; Greater London Council; British Railways, London; King County Medical Corp., Seattle. Membership: London Poetry Secretariat. Published Work: Wolfprints, 1971. Contbr. to: 2nd Aeon; Chapman; Poetry Review; Malenka; Workshop New Poetry; Aesop; Hexham Courant; Say It Aloud (Hutchinson Anthol.). Recip. Arts Council of GB grant in aid, 1971. Address: c/o Workshop Press Ltd., 2 Culham Court, Granville Rd., London N4 4JB, UK.

RUSSELL, Sydney King, b. 29 Nov. 1897. Poet; Composer of Music. Education: Univ. of Calif., 1919. Married, 4 children. Positions held: Guest Ed., Voices; Ed., Poetry Chapbook; Libn., 4 Arts Lib., Palm Beach, Fla. Memberships: Poetry Soc. of Am.; ASCAP. Published works: The Changing Flame, 1922; Pilgrimages, 1925; The Golden Snare, 1927; Lost Warrior, 1931; Bright Avowal, 1937; Proud Universe, 1943; Songs for America, 1943; Selected Poems, 1949; The Listening Year, 1953; Give the Heart Rein, 1955; Clock & Bottle, 1959; Thursday is All Things, 1960; A Poet's Notebook, 1960; Cock Eyed Mother Goose, 1960; Lend Me Your Laughter, 1963; The Wind Said, 1963; Hello Doctor, 1963; Comfort Her With Mink, 1964; Whistler's Mother, 1965; This is Where We Came In, 1966; Nobody Knocks, 1967; Year of the Dove, 1968; Dog Catcher's Daughter, 1969; Songs for America, etc. Contbr. to var. jrnls. & anthols. Recip., Lyric Award, 1967. Address: 124 Brazilian Ave., Palm Beach, FL, U.S.A.

RUSSO, Albert, pen name **ROVIN, Alex,** b. 26 Feb. 1943. Writer & Language Teacher. Education: Humanités modernes, Athénée Royal d'Usumbura, Ruanda, Urundi 1960; Diplôme de Rhétorique, 1963; B.Sc. in Gen. Bus. Admin., N.Y. Univ.; Dip., German Lang. & Culture, Heidelberg, 1964. Positions held: Mag. Dir. in an export firm, Italy, 1964-71; Stage Mgr. at RTL (Radio Luxembourg), 1972; Language Tchr. at Linguaphone, 1973–. Memberships: PEN Club of Belgium; Fichier International de poésie, Geneva. Published works: Incandescences, 1970; Eclats de malachite, 1971; La Pointe du diable (novel/prose poetry); Une adolescence en Urundi (in preparation). Contbr. to: Tribune Poetique, Belgium. Recip., Prix de Poesie Regain, 1971. Address: 247 Ave. Winston Churchill, 1180 Brussels, Belgium.

RUTHERFORD, Michael Andrew, b. 22 Dec. 1946. Librarian; Teacher of Creative Writing. Education: B.A., SUNY at Albany, N.Y., 1970; M.L.S., 1973. Positions held: Libn. & Tchr., Albany Pub. Lib., 1969–; Albany area co-ordinator for the Poetry-in-the-Schools prog.; Chief Ed., Conspiracy Press, Albany. Published works: Lesbia-Catullus, (book of Latin translations), 1972; Meat Is My Business, (coll. of poems), 1973. Contbr. to: Knickebocker News; Times Union; Dial-a-Poem (Albany). Honours, awards: Lovenheim Poetry Award, State Univ. of N.Y., Albany, 1968. Address: 450 Western Ave., Albany, NY 12203, U.S.A.

RUTSALA, Vern, b. 5 Feb. 1934. Teacher. Education: B.A., Reed Coll., 1956; M.F.A., Univ. of Iowa, 1960. Positions held: Instr., Lewis & Clark Coll., 1961-64; Asst. Prof., ibid, 1964-69; Assoc. Prof., Lewis & Clark, 1969–; Vis. Prof., Univ. of Minn., 1968-69. Published works include: The Window, 1964; Small Songs, 1969; The Harmful State, 1971. Contbr. to the following anthols., jrnls., mags., etc: Poetry; The New Yorker; The New Republic; The Nation; New Am. Review; Paris Review; Esquire; Southern Review; Poetry NW; Kayak; Iowa Review; Epoch; NW Review; Mass. Review; Tex. Qtly.; Qtly. Review of Lit.; Minn. Review;

Colo. Review; N Am. Review; Chicago Review; Choice of the Seventies, etc. Address: Dept. of Engl., Lewis & Clark Coll., Portland, Ore. 97219, USA.

RUTSKY, Lester, b. 23 May 1924. Manager. Education: Violin & theory, Christadora House, N.Y.C., 4 yrs. Married. Positions held: Co-Mgr. of a Firm that supplies the Garment Industries; Composer; Author; Published & licensed through A.S.C.A.P. Memberships: Am. Poetry League; Poetry Soc. of Mich.; Ill. State Poetry Soc.; Centro Studi e Scambi Int., Rome, Italy; Poets' Study Club of Terre Haute, Ind. Contbr. to: La Grange Jrl., Tex.; Greenup News, Ky.; Cahokia Herald, Ill.; Cycloflame; Bardic Echoes; The Am. Poet; The Am. Bard; Bitterroot; Encore Mag.; Peninsula Poets; Inky Trails; Orphic Lute; Cardinal Poetry Mag.; Modern Images; Moon Age Poets, etc. Recip. num. poetry awards inclng. approx. 40 places or awards in 40 contests during 1972-73. Address: 2930 W. 5th St., Brooklyn, NY 11224, U.S.A.

RUTTEN, Mathieu Jacques Henri, pen names **BERKELAAR, Willy, LAMBERTUS & DEUGD VERHEUT,** b. 18 Apr. 1906. University Professor. Education: Agrégé de l'Enseignement Supérieur, Univ. of Liège, Belgium. Positions held: Asst., Chargé de cours, Professeur ordinaire, Prof. of Dutch Lit., Univ. of Liège, Belgium. Memberships: Maatschappij der Nederlandse Letterkunde Leiden; Zuidnederlandse Maatschappij voor Taal – en Letterkunde en Geschiedenis, Brussels. Published works: Pijnen der Stilte, De Doedelzak, 1929; Okarina, Wij, Stemmen van Jongeren, 1929; Altengrabow, De Bladen voor de Poëzie, 1941; Met de Tong gezegd, Colibrant, 1972; Nederlandse Dichtkunst van Kloos tot Claus, 1957; Nederlandse Dichtkunst Achterberg en Burssens voorbij, 1967; Karel van de Woestijne, 5 studies, 1934, 43, 59, 70, 72. Contbr. to: De Kunstgids; Pan; De Vlaamse Gids; Klaverendrie; The Debating; De Tijdspiegel; De Nieuwe Gaalgidd; Spiegel der Letteren; Forum der Letteren. Honours, awards: Prix des Amis de l'Université de Liège, 1935; Prijs der literaire Kritiek van de Vlaamse Provincies, 1934-36; Prijs van het Comité Hendrik van Veldeke, 1945. Address: quai de l'Ourthe 15, Liège, Belgium.

RYAN, Doreen McMahon, b. 30 Apr. 1917. Housewife. Education: A.B., St. Louis Univ., Fontbonne Coll., St. Louis, 1936; Master's degree, Emory Univ., Atlanta, Ga., 1937. Married John Savage Ryan, 1 son. Positions held: Pvte. Sec., 1937; Acctng. Dept., 1939; P.R.O., U.S.N., 1942; Trng. & Personnel then Admin., Rich's Dept. Store, Atlanta, Ga., 1946. Memberships: Poetry Assoc., AAUW, Evansville, Ind.; Vivian Laramore-Rader Poetry Grp., Miami, Fla. Contbr. to Anthol. of the Laramore-Rader Poetry Grp. Address: 1035 N.E. 96th St., Miami Shores, FL 33138, U.S.A.

RYAN, Florence Holmes (Mrs. John E. Ryan), born 10th April 1913. Personnel Director; Librarian. Education: A.B., Univ. of Tenn., U.S.A., 1934; Lib. Sci. courses, Peabody Coll. Positions held: Libn., Brownsville, Tenn. High Schl., 1934-40; ibid, Benton Township (Ill) High Schl., 1940-41; Personnel, Procter & Gamble Def. Corp., 1941-45; Personnel Dir., Cain-Sloan Co., Nashville, 1945-47; currently Libn., Hutchison Schl., Lower Schl. Memberships: Past Mbrship. Chmn., Nat. League Am. Pen Women; Poetry Soc. of Tenn.; Manuscript Club. Contbr. to: International Anthol., 1959; Memphis Tenn. Anthol., 1968; Memphis Poems by Memphis Poets, 1969; One Hundred Poems, Tenn. Poetry Soc.; Yearbooks, ibid. (jrnls.) Human Voice Quarterly; South & West; Voices Int.; Flame; Poet Lore; Encore; Roanoke Review; Old Hickory Review; Oregonian; Poetry Dial; Driftwind; Prelude; Scimitar & Song; Poetry Digest; The Link; Wilson Bulletin; Archer; Christian Home; Home Life; Baby Talk; Western Family; Modern Baby; Hartford Courant; Seydell; Survey. Recipient of poetry awards including: K.L. Beaudoin Gem Stone Awards; Tenn. Poetry Soc. Contest and Mid-South Poetry Festival Awards; Clara Laster Agcy. Award, 1972. Address: 2162 Lochlevin, Memphis, Tennessee, 38138, U.S.A.

RYAN, Richard, b. 11 Dec. 1946. Teacher. Education: B.A., Univ. Coll., Dublin, Eire, 1967; M.A., ibid, 1971. Positions held: Vis. Poet, Coll. of St. Thomas, St. Paul, Minn., USA, 1970-71. Published works include: Ledges, 1970; My Lai, 1970 (pamphlet). Contbr. to the following anthols., jrnls., mags., etc: The Faber Book of Verse; Poetry Introductions: Z; Irish Times; Irish Press; The Spectator; The Malahat Review, etc. Address: 16 Pembroke Pk., Dublin 4, Repub. of Ireland.

RYE, Anthony Francis, b. 24 Sept. 1904. Author & Artist. Married Constance Colclough, 1 son, 1 daughter. Positions held: Process Engraver w. Emery Walker's Ltd., Upper Mall, Hammersmith, 1927-33. Memberships: PEN; Soc. of Authors; Authors' Club; West Country Writers' Assn. Published works: The Inn of the Birds, 1947; To a Modern Hero, 1957; Poems from Selborne, 1972; (prose) Gilbert White & His Selborne, 1970. Contbr. of a Ghost Story to each of two colls. edited by James Turner, The Fourth Ghost Book, 1965 & The Unlikely Ghosts, 1967. Contbr. to: Dublin Mag.; Country Life; Countrygoer; Farmer & Stockbreeder; Out of Doors; Everybody's; Observer; Listener; Irish Times; Coming Events; Far & Wide; Modern Reading; Art News & Review; Hampshire Chronicle; Collected Poems Series Three; British Council Arts in Britain Series; Poetry 1945-50; We Offer; Selborne Mag.; BBC Long March of Everyman; BBC Interludes, etc. Address: Sparrow's Hanger, Selborne, Alton, Hants., U.K.

RYMKIEWICZ, Alexander, b. 13 Apr. 1913. Poet. Education: LL.M., Stefan Batory Univ., Wilno. Positions held: Govt. Official at Supply & Trade Min. in Warsaw, 1945-47; Mgr. in the Chief Comm. of the Union of Polish Writers, 1947-49; Lit. Ed. of the weekly 'Radio i Swiat', 1949-52; Mbr. of the Editl. Comm. of the monthly 'Poezja', 1972-. Memberships: Chief Comm. of Auditors, Union of Polish Writers, 1935-; Chief Comm., Polish PEN, 1971-. Published works incl: Promień dla artysty, poems, 1965; Czarny zając, poems for children, 1967; Dziki powój, poems, 1968; Selected Poems, 1970; Gadanie baranie, poems for children, 1970; Slepi drwale, poems, 1971; Selected Poems, 1971; Polskie drzewa, poems, 1972; Olsztyński wrzos, selected poems, 1974, etc. Sev. dramatic works for children & youth, performed in theatre & on radio & TV. Translations of sev. libretti & num. poems Hungarian, Bulgarian, Czech & Slovakian. Contbr. of poems & translations to num. reviews periodicals & anthols. Honours, awards incl: Best vol. of poetry for 'Dziki powoj', Nat. Fest. of Poetry, Lódz, 1969; Knight Cross of the Order of Poland's Revival. Address: ul.Karlowicza 1/7 m 131, 02-501 Warsaw, Poland.

S

SAALBACH, Robert P., b. 13 July 1913. College Teacher. Education: B.A., Univ. of Pitts., Pa., 1934; M.A., Univ. of Chicago, Ill., 1939; Ph.D., Univ. of Wash., Seattle, 1951. Married Anna Louise Pavluska, 2 children. Positions held: Instr. in Engl., Pa. State Univ., 1940-41; Circulation-Promotion, Pitts. Post Gazette, 1941-42; Instr., Carnegie Tech., Pittsburgh, Pa., 1942-44; U.S. Maritime Serv., 1944-47; Instr., Univ. of Idaho, Moscow, 1947-49; Grad. Asst. & Acting Instr., Univ. of Wash., Seattle, 1949-52; Asst. Prof. of Engl., S. Dakota Schl. of Mines, Rapid City, 1952-55; Prof. & Hd., Dept. of Engl., Scottsbluff (Neb.) Coll., 1955-58; Asst. Prof., Ark. State Univ., Jonesboro, 1958-59; Asst., Assoc. & Prof. of Engl., Ind. State Univ., Terre Haute, 1959-. Memberships: World Poetry Soc., 1971-; Poets Club, Ind. State Univ., 1959-64. Published works: Sixteen on Trial, 1969. Contbr. to: Poet; Pied Pipings, Associator. Address: 1301 Royce Ave., Terre Haute, IN 47802, U.S.A.

SAARITSA, Pentti Juhani, b. 29 Dec. 1941. Writer; Translator. Education: studies in modern lit., Univ. of Helsinki, Finland. Positions held: CULTURAL Ed. with different newspapers, 1964-67; Vis. Lectr., Theatre High Schl. of Helsinki (Dramaturgy), 1971; Vis. Lectr., Univ. of Turku (Latin-Am. Lit.), 1972. Memberships: The Finnish Writers Union; Int. PEN Club; The Finnish Translators Assn.; The Eino Leino Soc.; Union of Finnish Critics. Published works: (poetry) Pakenevat merkit, 1965; Huomenna muistan paremmin, 1966; Varmuus kerrallaan, 1967; En osaa seisahtaa, 1969; Jäsenkirjan lisälehdet, 1971; Syksyn Runot, 1973; (play) Kaamos, performed in 1973. Contbr. to: Tiedonantaja; Horisont; Parnasso; Ylioppilaslehti; BLM (Sweden); Stockholms Tidningen (Sweden); Elöször Magyarul (anthol. – Hungary); Vsesvit (USSR, Georgia); Union (Cuba); Cormorán y Delfín (Argentina). Recip., Poetry Prize, 1971 & Translators Prize, 1969 of the State of Finland. Address: Kapteenink. 7 C 56, Helsinki 14, Finland.

SABATIER, Robert, b. 17 Aug. 1923. Poet, Novelist, Critic. Positions held: Dir., 'La Cassette' (lit. review), 1947-50; Dir., Press Serv. & Publicity, Presses universitaires de France, 1951-64; Lit. Dir., Editions Albin Michel, 1965–. Memberships: PEN Club Int.; Syndicat des Ecrivains; Comité du Syndicat des critiques littéraires; Syndicat des journalistes; Jury, Prix Combat; Jury, Grand prix de la critique littéraire; Jury, Prix de L'Edition critique; Jury, Prix de l'humour noir. Published works: Alain et le Nègre, 1953; le Marchand de sable, 1954; le Goût de la cendre, 1955; les Fêtes solaires, 1955; Boulevard, 1957; Canard au Sang, 1958; Saint-Vincent-de-Paul, Dédicace d'un navire, 1959; la Sainte Farce, 1960; l'Etat princier, 1961; la Mort du figuier, 1962; Dessin sur trottoir, les Poisons délectables, 1965; le Chinois d'Afrique, 1966, Dictionnaire de la Mort, 1967; les Châteaux de millions d'années, 1969; Les Fêtes Solaires. Contbr. to: Arts; le Figaro littéraire; la Revue de Paris; etc. Awards: Prix Guillaume Apollinaire, 1954; Prix Antonin Artaud; Prix de Paris, 1956; Grand Prix du Roman des Gens de Lettres, 1957; Prix Richelieu, 1959. Address: 23 rue Fantin-Latour, Paris, 16me, France.

SABLJAK, Tomislav, b. 15 Feb. 1934. Assistant at the Institute for Literature & Theatre. Education: Gymnasium & Univ. of Zagreb (degree in literature). Positions held: Lit. Critic, Daily & Weekly newspapers; Ed., Lit. Mag.; Jrnlst.; Profl. Writer & Asst., Inst. for Lit. & Theatre, Theatrology Dept., Yugoslav Acad. of Sci. & Art, 1969–. Memberships: Assn. of Writers of Croatia (Yugoslavia); Assn. of Translators; PEN Club; Pagwash Assn.; Int. Assn. of Lit. Critics, Paris. Published works: (books of poetry) Nemiri tijela (Uneasiness of Body), 1955; Situacije (Situations), 1960; i Krvavo prijestolje (Bloody Throne), 1972. Contbr. to num. jrnls., mags., periodicals, newspapers. Recip., 2nd Award, 'Young Culture', Belgrade, 1954. Address: Moše Pijade 57, 41.000 Zagreb, Yugoslavia.

SACHS, Arieh, b. 24 Mar. 1932. Poet. Education: M.A.(Philosophy), Johns Hopkins Univ. 1955; Studied at the Sorbonne, 1956-7; Studied at Cambridge Univ., 1958-60; Ph.D., Hebrew Univ. 1962. Served in Israel's Army as officer and paratrooper, 1948-52; Student 1952-60; Lecturer 1960-73; Theatre Director, 1966-73. Currently Professor (English Lit. and History of Theatre) at Hebrew Univ.; Chairman, Theatre Dept., Hebrew Univ, since 1971. Member, Arts Council of Israel. Pubs. Ze Haya Yoffi (poetry), 1973; Passionate Intelligence, Reason and Imagination in the Work of Samuel Johnson, 1967; The English Grotesque, 1969; Contrib. to: Paris Kiosk; Yaad; Yochani; Haaretz; Massa; Akshav; Siman Kria, etc. Address: Dept. of English, Hebrew University, – Jerusalem, Israel.

SACKETT, Samuel J., b. 23 Jan. 1928. Teacher. Education: A.B. (1948), M.A. (1949), Univ. of Redlands; Ph.D. (1956) Univ. of Calif. at Los Angeles. Positions held: Instr. in Engl., Hastings Coll., 1949-51; Asst. Prof. of Engl., Fort Hays Kansas State Coll., 1954-57; Assoc. Prof., ibid. 1957-65; Professor, ibid. since 1965. Contbr. to: Antioch Review; Kansas Mag.; Western Humanities Review; Arts & Society; American Weave; Smoky Hill Review; The Archer; College

English. Address: Box 386, Hays, KS 67601, USA.

SADEH, Pinhas, b. 17 June 1929. Author. Published works include: Life as a Parable, 1966; Masah Dumah, 1951; Hachaim Kemashal, 1958, '68; Mot Avimelech, 1969; Book of Poems (with translations), 1970; The Journey, 1971. Contbr. to the following publications: Commentary, NY; Le Thyrse, Brussels; Ha'aretz, Israel; Molad; Jedioth, etc. Translated into & printed in French, Arabic, Hungarian, etc. Address: 3 Yehonathan St., Ramat-gan, Israel.

SAFFORD, Veronica Joan, b. 19 Dec. 1920. Writer; Housewife. Education: Worcester (Mass.) Schools. Married, 2 s., 2 d. Positions held: Gen. office clerk; Western Union Teleg. Operator; receptionist; secretary; bookkeeper; poet; reporter; freelance writer. Memberships: Worcester (Mass.) Poetry Soc. (Founder and 1st Prs. and Sec.); Salvation Army; Red Cross; Girl Scouts; Fresh Air Fund; Poetry Soc. of New Hampshire; Republican Woman's Club. Contbr. to: Argus-Champion Newport, N.H.; Granite State Gazette, N.H.; Keene Sentinel, N.H.; N.H. Poetry Soc. Mag., Concord, N.H.; Md. Independent News, Md.; Worcester Eve. Gazette; Tri-Town Times; Barre Gazette; Brockton Daily News; Ideal Mag.; Manchester Union Leader (NH); American Anthology of Verse; We, the People (yearbook); Food For Thought; poems read over radio: WKOX (Framingham), WOTW (NH), also Toronto (Canada); WPTR (Albany, NY), also Nome (Alaska), etc. Address: 32 Severance St., Claremont, NH 03743, USA.

SAGEN, Rolf, b. 21 Dec. 1940. Psychologist. Education: Univ. of Oslo, Norway. Member of Den Norske Forfatterforening. Published works: (books) Dörklinker (poetry), 1968; Kvengedal (collage), 1970; Morgonmannen held utstilling (novel), 1971. Contbr. to: Dagbladet, Oslo; Profil, Oslo; Syn og Segn, Oslo; Dag og Tid, Oslo; Ny Verd, N.Y. Recip., Vesaasprisen, 1968. Address: Sykkylven, Norway.

SAHA, Prosanta Kumar, pen name **SAHA, P.K.,** b. 4 Dec. 1932. Writer; Teacher of Literature and Linguistics. Education: B.A., Univ. of Calcutta, 1956; M.A., Oberlin Coll., Ohio, 1957; Ph.D., Western Reserve Univ., Cleveland, Ohio, 1966. Married, Frances Saha, 1 s., 1 d. Positions held: Teacher, Hawken School, Cleveland, 1957-62; Instr., Engl., Case Inst. of Technol., 1962-64; Assoc. Prof., Engl. & Lings., Case Western Reserve Univ., 1966–, and Chairman, Lings. and Undergrad. Humanities Programs. Memberships: Writers Workshop, Calcutta; Style; Cleveland Poetry Group. Published works: Poems From the Fifties, 1965; Collected Poems, 1974. Contbr. to: American Weave; Span; Modern Indo-Anglian Poetry; An Anthol. of Commonwealth Verse; Echoes of Experience; Thought; Illus. Weekly of India; Quest; Mod. Indian Poetry in English; The Golden Treasury of Indo-Anglian Poetry; Caravan; Internat. Who's Who in Poetry Anthol. Honours, Awards: Caravan Poetry Competition, 1954; Carl F. Wittke Award, 1971. Address: Crawford Hall, Room 414, Case Western Reserve Univ., Cleveland, OH 44106, USA.

SAHA, Subhas Chandra, b. 6 Feb. 1946. Businessman. Education: St. Xavier's Coll., Calcutta; M.A., Calcutta Univ., India; Bus. Mgmt. Course, Indian Inst. of Soc. Welfare & Bus. Mgmt., Calcutta; Law Course, Calcutta Univ. Member, Writers Workshop, Calcutta. Published works: The Unseen Bird, 1971; The Under World, 1972; Modern Indo-Anglian Love Poetry, 1971; Insights, 1972; Down the Silent Night World, 1973; The Other Side, 1973. Contbr. to: The Illustrated Weekly of India, Bombay; Thought, Delhi; Caravan, New Delhi; The Junior Statesman, Calcutta; The Miscellany, Calcutta; Poet, Madras; Literary Half-Yrly, Mysore; Indian Literature, New Delhi; Hindusthan Standard, Calcutta. Address: 43/B Nandaram Sen St., Calcutta 700005, India.

SAHAI, Hari Prakash, b. 14 Oct. 1937. Teacher.

Education: M.A. Engl., Vikram Univ., Ujjain, India, 1963; B.Ed. (C.I.E.), Delhi Univ., 1970; M.Phil. (Educ.), Meerut Univ., 1971; Sahityaratna, Hindi Sahitya Sammelan, Prayag (Allahabad), 1958; Cert. in Yoga, Vishwayatan Yogashram, Katra Vaishnavi Devi, 1969; var. other courses. Married Shrimati Usha Sahai, 2 sons, 1 daughter. Positions held: Lectr. in Engl., 1963–. Memberships: Indian Assn. for English Studies, Delhi; Sec., New Horizons, Meerut Univ., 1970-71; Sahityarchan, Lalitpur; Pratibha, Jhansi; Maitra Club, Kailas, Agra. Poems in Hindi have been broadcast by Yuva-Vani, Delhi, 1970. Published & edited a mag. for students, Pipasa, 1959. Contbr. to: Poet; Vikas; Memtech; Pipasa; Pankaj; Rashmi-Rekha. Recip., Disting. Serv. Cit., World Poetry Soc., 1973. Address: N.A.S. College, Meerut (U.P.), India.

SAHAKIAN, Lucille, b. 1 July 1894. Teacher; Poet; Housewife. Education: Ind. Univ.; St. Mary's Univ. Married to J. Sahakian. Positions held: Tchr., Ind. rural Schls.; Tchr., Fairmount Grade Schl. & High Schl., Ind.; Subst. Tchr., Indianapolis Schls. Memberships: Pres., Lady Aberdeen Artist Chap., Ind. Univ. Women's Club, 1933-38; Internat. Travel Study Club; Pres., San Antonio Ms. Club; Pres., San Antonio Chap., Composers, Authors & Artists of Am.; Nat. Auditor, ibid; Tex. State Pres.; Am. Poetry League; Poet Laureate, Alpha Omicron Alpha Nat. Sorority; Tex. Bakers Dozen; Eastern Star (Writer). Published works include: Vivian at College, 1942; War & Romance, 1944; A Heart Speaks, 1948; Stars From a Texas Sky, 1956; Faith Treasures, 1961; Starlight, 1963; Bonds of Friendship, 1964; A Calendar of Thoughts, 1966; A Star's Delight, 1969; Christmas Joy, 1962; The Brightest Star, 1970. Co-author, Seek (book of prayers), 1961. Forthcoming publications: Hearts Aflame (novel); Rainbow of Romance (poems); Star of Hope (poems & essays). Contbr. to the following anthols., jrnls., mags., etc: Miami News; Indianapolis News; San Antonio Express; San Antonio Light; San Antonio Mag.; Laurel Leaves; Tex. Wildfire Mag.; Baker's Dozen Mag.; The Triangle; Alpha Omicron Alpha Mag.; Hoosier Challenger; Blue Moon; Candor; Am. Poetry League; CAAA Mag.; The Gleaner; Sea to Sea in Song. Honours: 1st Prize, Tex. Author's Day, 1951; 2nd Prize, Corner Stone Contest, 1961; Selective Serv. Award, 1941; Hoosier Poet Chap. named in her honour, 1957; Hobby Festival Award, Ft. Sam Houston; 1st Prize, Tex. Poetry Day, 1971, etc. Address: 223 Hillwood Dr., San Antonio, TX 78213, USA.

ST. FRANCIS, Carol Herring, b. 28 Nov. 1937. Magazine Editor. Education: B.F.A., Ohio Univ.; art study, Nurnberg, Germany; grad. work in Creative Writing, Murray State Univ., Ky. & Bowling Green Univ., Ohio. Positions held: Tchr., H.S. Art; Ed. of a womans mag.; Ed. of a state mag. Memberships: Ky. State Poetry Soc.; World Poetry Soc. Contbr. to: Third Summer anthol., 1971; Wind, 1972; Poet, 1972; Woman's mag., 1973. Address: 1858 A Coventry Lane, Columbus, OH 43227, U.S.A.

ST. JACQUES, Elizabeth (Joyce) (Gloria), b. 9 Apr. 1939. Freelance Writer. Education: Elem., Iroquois Falls, Ontario, Canada; St. Mary's Acad., North Bay, Ontario (1 yr.); HS: Grade Eleven, Iroquois Falls; Ontario Corres. Course: Hons. Student, Grade 12 English; HS Hons. in Commercial. Personal details: Married to Rene (Ray) St. Jacques; 2 s. (Rene Jr.); (Delmer). Positions held: Invoice Typist, 1955-56; Druggist Asst., 1956, until marriage in 1957. Memberships: U.A.P. (Vice-Pres., 1973-74; Historian, 1972-73; Laureate Judge of Misc. Prose, 1972-73); Trans-Atlantic Competition Judge, Patterned Poetry, 1973-74; Internat. Clover Poetry Assoc. (Life member); Carter County Poetry Soc., Kansas; Scotian Guild, Canada; Comments Editor for Pegasus & Amber, 1972-74; Poetry Judge in various poetry contests. Published work: Diary of Thoughts, 1967 (poetry). Contbr. to: Modern Maturity; Capper's Weekly; Cyclo-Flame; Modern Images; Focus; Quintessence; Kansas Kernals; Inky Trails; Angel Hour; Author/Poet; Bardic Echoes; Verdure; Legend;

Further & Feathers; The Battersean; Modus Operandi; AWJ; Pegasus; Amber; Other Voices; Fireflower; Tempo; Elves Mailbox; Hyacinth & Biscuits; Robbins Song; Friendship Ferry; Quid Nunc ?; Idella; Le Livre de...; Texas Traveler; Home Base; Pacific Sun; Atlantic Review; Durango-Cortez Herald; Olive Hill Times; View Mag. Newspaper; Timmins Press; The Enterprise; Northern News; Sault Star; Abitibi Mag. Awards: 2nd Place, Trans-Atlantic Competition, Conventional Poetry, 1973; 1st Place, Carter Co. Poetry Soc. Easter Poem, 1973; 1st Place, UAPA Poetry Contest about Music, 1972; Sylvia Martin Award for Outstanding Writing, 1972; Poet of the Month, Inky Trails, 1971; Poem of the Year, Editor's Award, 1970; Golden Prize Award, 1973; 2nd Place in Remembrance Contest, 1970; Inky Trails contest, 1971; Outstanding Writing Award, 1971; H.M. in Alberta Poetry Contest, etc. Address: 406 Elizabeth St., Sault Ste. Marie, Ontario P6B 3H4, Canada.

ST. JOHN, Bruce Carlisle, b. 24 Dec. 1923. University Lecturer. Education: B.A., London Univ., U.K., 1953; M.A., Toronto, Canada, 1964. Married twice, 2 children from 2nd marriage. Positions held: Tchr., St. Giles' Boys' Schl., 1942-44; Tchr., Combermere Schl., 1944-64; Lectr. in Spanish, Univ. of West Indies, 1964–; V. Dean, Fac. of Arts & Gen. Studies, 1962–. Contbr. to: Bim; Savacou; Contact; Contrast; Tapia; New Writing; Greenfield Review; Manna; Revista de Letras. Recip., Bussa Award, 1973. Address: P.O. Box 64, G.P.O. Bridgetown, Barbados, W.I.

SALA, Florence Sarah, b. 7 Apr. 1905. Housewife. Education: Hillyer Coll. Married V. James Sala. Memberships: Sec., Poetry League Workshop, Hartford, Conn.; Pioneer Valley Scripters, Springfield, Mass. Contbr. to: (anthol.) A World of Light, Poetry League Workshop; (jrnls.) Hartford Courant; Hartford Times; W. Hartford News; Meriden Record; Vermont Horse & Bridle Trail Bull.; Hoof Prints; New Haven INFO.; Wethersfield Post. Honours, awards: 2nd prize, Prof. G.D. Saul, Univ. of Conn. Address: 398 Middletown Ave., Wethersfield, CT 06109, U.S.A.

SALEH, Dennis, b. 8 Dec. 1942. Poet; Professor. Education: B.A., Psychol., Calif. State Univ., Fresno, 1964; Grad. study, ibid, & Univ. of Ariz.; M.F.A., Creative Writing, Univ. of Calif., Irvine, 1968. Married, 1 son, 1 daughter. Positions held: Lectr., Univ. of Calif., Riverside, 1968-69, Univ. of Calif., Santa Cruz, 1969-71, Calif. State Univ., San Diego, 1972-73, Calif. State Univ., Fresno, 1973–. Published works: A Guide to Familiar American Incest (poems), 1972; Just What The Country Needs, Another Poetry Anthology, (co-ed.), 1971. Contbr. to: (anthols.) Messages; Sources; New Am. & Canadian Poetry; Down at the Santa Fe Depot, etc.; (periodicals) Poetry; Shenandoah; Iowa Review; Choice; Beloit Poetry Jrnl.; Carleton Miscellany; Kayak; Mass. Review; North Am. Review, etc. Address: c/o Wm. B. Saleh, 3935 North Angus, Fresno, CA 93726, U.S.A.

SALINGER, Herman, b. 23 Dec. 1905. Professor of German Literature. Education: A.B., Princeton Univ., 1927; M.A., Stanford Univ., 1929; German, Univs. of Berlin & Cologne, Germany, 1929-31; Ph.D., Yale Univ., USA, 1937; Postdoc. studies in Comparative Lit., Univ. of Wis., 1951, '52, '53. Positions held: Asst. Instr., Stanford Univ., 1927-29; Instr., Princeton Univ., 1932-35; Instr., Univ. of Wis., 1937-42; Asst. Prof., Univ. of Kan. City, 1946-47; Assoc. Prof., Grinnell Coll., 1947-50; Prof., 1950-55; Prof., German, Duke Univ., 1955–; Chmn. of Dept., 1956-70. Mbr., Poetry Soc. Published works: Angel of Our Thirst, 1951; A Sigh is the Sword, 1963; (translations) 20th Century German Verse, 1952; Germany: A Winter Tale, Heinrich Heine, 1944; Ballad of the Buried Life, Rudolf Hagelstange, 1962; Poems Against Death, Karl Krolow, 1969. Contbr. to the following jrnls: Voices; Poetry (Chicago); Beloit Poetry Jrnl.; Sat. Review; Elizabeth; NM Quarterly; Books Abroad; Poet Lore; Lyrica Germanica; Prairie Schooner; Univ. of Kan. City Review; Cafe Solo; Dimension. Honours, Awards: Badge of Hon., 1st Prize, 1942; Roakoke-Chowan

Poetry Award, 1963. Address: 3444 Rugby Road, Hope Valley, Durham, NC 27707, USA.

SALISBURY, Ralph, b. 24 Jan. 1926. University Teacher. Education: M.F.A., Univ. of Iowa. Married 1) Joyce Hurlbert, 2 sons, 2) Ingrid Wendt, 1 daughter. Positions held: Prof., Tex. A & M Coll., 1951-54; Prof., Drake Univ., 1954-60; Prof., Univ. of Ore., 1960-. Published works: Ghost Grapefruit & Other Poems, 1972. Contbr. to: Transatlantic Review; New Yorker; Poetry (Chicago); Perspective; Epoch; Prism Int.; Poetry Northwest; West Coast Review; December; Southwest Review; Mass. Review; Goodly Co.; New Letters; Clearance; Beyond Baroque; Dragonfly; Backwash; Minn. Review; Seizure; Tribune; Outposts; Hearse; Confrontation; The Smith; Quixote; Colo. Qtly.; Forum; Quartet; Evidence; Jeopardy. Honours, awards: Univ. of Ore. Grad. Fac. Creative Award, 1966 & '62; Chapelbrook Award, 1966. Address: Engl. Dept., Univ. of Ore., Eugene, OR 97403, U.S.A.

SALKEY, Andrew, b. 30 Jan. 1928. Freelance Radio Journalist (BBC Overseas). Education: B.A. English, London Univ., U.K. Published works: Jamaica, a long poem, 1973. Recip., Thomas Helmore Poetry Prize, 1955. Address: Flat 8, Windsor Ct., Moscow Rd., London W.2, U.K.

SALOMON, Isidore Lawrence, b. 10 Dec. 1899. Teacher & Lecturer. Education: B.A., City Coll., NY, 1923; M.S., ibid, 1924. Conductor, courses in Art of Tchg. Poetry; Chmn., Poetry Readings, NY Pub. Libs. Memberships: MacDowell Assoc.; Acad. of Am. Poets; PEN American Center; James Joyce Soc. (Chr. Mbr.). Published works include: Unit & Universe, 1959; (transls.) Carlo Betocchi: Poems, 1964; Dino Campana: Orphic Songs, 1968; Alfredo de Palchi: Sessions With My Analyst, 1971; Mario Luzi: In the Dark Body of Metamorphosis, 1974. Contbr. to the following anthols., jrnls., mags., etc: The Sat. Review; The New Yorker; Tri-Quarterly; NY Times; Va. Quarterly Review; The Mass. Review; Mich. Quarterly; The Arlington Review; Common Ground; Trinity Coll. Review; Phoenix Nest; Dublin Mag.; Contemporary Poetry; Herald Trib.; The American; Am. Mercury; Am. Schol.; Tomorrow; Spirit; Minn. Review; Poetry NW, etc. Honours, awards: Award, Nat. Coun. on the Arts, 1966; Gold Medal, Marradi, Italy, 1968; Award, Nat. Endowment for the Humanities, 1970, also grant in linguistics, 1971. Address: 12 Stuyvesant Oval, New York, NY 10009, USA.

SALSMAN, Lillian Viola, b. 10 Dec. 1899. Educator; Administrator. Education: A.B., Boston Univ., 1921; R.N., New England Deaconess Hosp., Boston, Mass., 1925; M.A., Tchrs. Coll., Columbia Univ., 1935; Grad. in Psych. Nursing, McLean Hosp. Schl., Mass., 1936; Ph.D., Grad. Schl. Arts & Scis., NY Univ., 1964. Positions held: Instr. in Nursing, New England Deaconess Hosp., 1925-26; Dir. of Nursing Educ., ibid, 1926-28; Matron, Ellen Mitchell Mem. Hosp., Moulmein, Burma, 1928-34; Dir. of Nursing, Ring Sanatorium, Mass., USA, 1936-38; Dir. of Nursing, Hastings State Hosp., Ingleside, Neb., 1938-43; Dir. of US Cadet Nursing, Army Nursing Corps, 1943-45; Dir. of Nursing Servs., NY State Dept., Mental Hygiene, Albany, 1946-68; Retired. Memberships: Internat. Platform Assoc.; Eastern Centre of The Poetry Soc. of London, and World Poets' Resource Center, Inc. Contbr. to: The Beacon; Zion's Advocate. Address: 1 Elm St., Marblehead, MA 01945, USA.

SAMPLEY, Arthur M(cCullough), b. 9 Jan. 1903. Professor of English (retired). Education: B.A.(1923), M.A.(1925), Ph.D.(1930), Univ. of Texas; B.S. in L.S. (1947), Columbia Univ. Married (1930) Vera Almon, who died 1954; Married (1961) Mrs. Eva Joy McGuffin, who died 1968. Stepchildren: Horace McGuffin and Mrs. Ann Barton. Tutor of English, Univ. of Texas, 1923-25; Instructor, 1925-28, Assoc. Prof., Louisiana State Normal Coll., 1930-31; Prof., Sul Ross State Coll., 1931-35; Prof., North Texas State Univ., 1935-72; retired 1972. Member: Poetry Soc. of America, Vice-Pres. for the South; Texas Inst. of Letters, Pres.,

1942, 1952, 1953; Poetry Soc. of Texas, Pres., 1951. Pubs.: This Is Our Time, 1943; Of the Strong and the Fleet, 1947; Furrow with Blackbirds, 1951; Selected Poems 1937-1971, 1971. Contrib. to: Antioch Review; Arlington Quarterly; Arizona Quarterly; Borestone Mountain Poetry Awards; Christian Century; Cimarron Review; Georgia Review; Kenyon Review; Literary Review; New Mexico Quarterly; Lyric; New York Times; Prairie Schooner; Saturday Evening Post; Saturday Review; Southwest Review; Southern Humanities Review; Virginia Quarterly Review. Recipient Texas Inst. of Letters Award for best book of poems by a Texan, 1947, 1951, 1971; Co-winner, Lola Ridge Award, Poetry Soc. of America, 1948, 1951; Edwin Markham Award, Poetry Soc. of America, 1964, 1965; James Joyce Award, Poetry Soc. of America, 1969. Address: Box 5263, N. T. Station, Denton, Texas 76203, USA.

SANCHEZ, Ricardo, b. 29 Mar. 1941. Chicano Cultural Consultant; Lecturer; Writer; Publisher. Education: Ford Fndn. Grad. Fellow, Union Grad. Schl., Antioch Coll., Ohio. Married Maria Teresa Silva, 1 son, 1 daughter. Positions held: Rsch. Dir., Proj. Machos, El Paso, Tex., 1969; Staff Writer, Tchr., Schl. of Educ., Univ. of Mass., 1970; Dir., Interstate Itinerant Migrant Hlth. Prog., Colo. Migrant Coun., Denver, 1970-71; Vis. Prof., Acad. de la Nueva Raza, Dixon, N.M.; Writer/Cons., TTT Prog. & UTEP; Mng. Ed., Mictla Publs., El Paso; Reporter, Afro Am. Newspapers; Ed.-at-Large, La Luz Mag., Denver; Counseling Supvsr., Trinity OIC, El Paso, 1972; Comm. Staff Cons., Soc. Work Tchng. Ctr., N.M. State Univ., Las Cruces, 1973. Memberships: Writers & Poets, N.Y., 1973; Dir., S.W. Poets Conf., 1969-73; Consortium of Chicano Writers, 1970-73; Escritores por la Raza, 1971-73; Estoque y Pluma, 1972-73; Am. PEN. Published works: Canto y Grito Mi Liberacion, 1971, '73; We Are Chicanos, 1973; Obras, 1971; Los Cuatro, 1970; Points of Departure, 1972; El Cuaderno, 1973; La Luz, 1973; Mano a Mano, 1971. Wrote, produced, filmed: Cantos de Aztlán; Chicanos in Transition; Vitalidad the Fifth Horseman. Contbr. to sev. mags. & jrnls. inclng: Nosotros Mag., El Paso; Magazin, San Antonio; La Luz, Denver; Richmond Chronicle; El Grito del Sur; The Yesca & Yucca Review. Recip., George A. Miller Fellowship, Univ. of Ill., Urbana – Champaign, 1973-74. Address: 7845 Lilac Way, No. 103, El Paso, TX 79915, U.S.A.

SANDBURG, Helga, b. 24 Nov. 1918. Writer. Education: Mich. State Coll., U.S.A., 1939-40; Univ. of Chicago, 1940-. Positions held: Sec., to Carl Sandburg; Dairy Goat Breeder (w. mother) & Personal Sec. to father, 1944-51; Sec. to Manuscripts Div. & for The Keeper of the Collections, Lib. of Congress, Wash. D.C., 1952-56; Admin. Asst. for the Papers of Woodrow Wilson, Woodrow Wilson Fndn., N.Y., 1958-59; Lectr., W. Colston Leigh Lectr. Bur., N.Y., 1960-64; for Bureau of Cultural & Educl. Affairs, State Dept., Wash., 1961; Ind. Lectr., 1964-. Memberships incl: The Author's Guild; Poetry Soc. of Am. Published works incl: (novels) The Wheel of Earth, 1958; Measure my Love, 1959; The Owl's Roost, 1962; The Wizard's Child, 1967; (non-fiction) Sweet Music, A Book of Family Reminiscence & Song, 1963; Above & Below (w. George Crile, Jr.), 1969; (poetry) The Unicorns, 1965; To a New Husband, 1970; var. other young adult novels, children's books, short stories, poems & articles. Recip. var. prizes & awards. Address: 2060 Kent Rd., Cleveland Heights, OH 44106, U.S.A.

SANDELIN, Peter, b. 30 May 1930. Author. Education: Helsingfors Univ. (Drawing), 1954-55; studied in Italy, 1953 & 59. Married Nina Parland, 2 children. Held exhibition of paintings, 1957. Memberships: Comm., Finlands Svenska Författareförening, 1973; Helsingin Kirjailijat-Helsingfors Författare. Published works: (books of poems) Ur svalans loggbok, 1951; De Lysande och de döda, 1953; Etyder, 1957; Stunder av ljus, 1960; Hemma i universum, 1962; En vanlig solig dag, 1965; Minuter pa jorden, 1968; Fageln i Stenmuren (a lyrical diary), 1970; Tyst stiger havet,

1971; Var det du? 1973. Contbr. to: Horisont; Parnasso; Nya Argus; Hufvudstadsbladet; Swedish Art Review 'Paletten', 1964-66; lit. reviews in newspapers & mags., etc. Honours, awards: Finnish State Prize, 1961 & 66; Prizes from Svenska litteratursällskapet, 1961, 66, 69 & 72; Prize for Konstsamfundet, 1971. Address: Ulfsbyvagen 19 a B, 00350 Helsingfors 35, Finland.

SANDERS, Ed, b. 17 Aug. 1939. Editor; Publisher; Professor. Educ: B.A., N.Y. Univ. Positions held: Ed. & Publr., Fuck You: A Magazine of the Arts & Dick, N.Y.C., 1962–; Prof., Free Univ., N.Y.C., 1965–; Owner, Peace Eye Book Store, 1965–. Published works: Poems from Jail, 1963; The Toe-Queen Poems, 1964; Banana: An Anthology of Banana-Erotic Poems, 1965; The Complete Sex Poems of Ed Sanders, 1965; Peace Eye, 1965; King Lord – Queen Freak, 1966. Contbr. to: New Writing in the U.S.A. (anthology), 1967.

SANDERS, Edith M. (Mrs. Oliver C. Sanders), born 5th March 1896. Housewife & Poet. Education: Univ. of Wis. Memberships: Regional Writers Bd., Univ. of Wis.; Regional Pres., Wis. Fellowship of Poets; Pres., ibid.; Vice-Pres., Bapt. Women of Wis.; Educ. Sec., ibid.; Mbr., Bd. of Mgrs., & Exec. Comm., Wis. Bapt. Conv.; Dramatic Rdr., Mus-e-Hes, Laguna Hills; Masonic Aux. Study Group, Laguna Hills, Calif.; Ebell, Laguna Hills; Heritage Group, Laguna Hills; Art League Bd., Janesville, Wis.; Publicity Chmn., ibid.; Bd., MacDowell Club, Janesville; Pres., United Ch. Women, Janesville. Publications: Gems of Inspiration, Asst. Ed., Wis. Anthol. Contbr. to: Janesville Daily Gazette; Albion Jrnl., Mich.; Woman's Missionary Mag., Pittsburgh; Secret Place. Address: 2087 (E) Ronda Granada, Laguna Hills., Calif. 92653, USA.

SANDERS, Mary Alberta, pen name **SANDERS, Sandi,** b. 3 Apr. 1912. Private Secretary. Education: Univs. of Toledo, Ohio & U.S.C., Los Angeles. Positions held: Police Sec. in Oregon; Law Sec. in Ore. & Ohio; Govt. Sec. in Nev. Contbr. to: The Oregonian; The Boulder City News; The Review-Journal, Las Vegas; The News Bee, Toledo; The Los Angeles Times; The Christian Sci. Monitor, Boston. Address: 631 Calif. St., Boulder City, NV 89005, U.S.A.

SANDOVAL, Roberto L., pen name **SANDOVAL, Sandy Roberto,** b. 13 Nov. 1950. Poet. Education: B.S. in Physics; currently doing grad. work in Engl. Positions held: Techn., Nat. Accelerator Lab., Batavia, Ill., 1973; Poet in Poetry-in-the-Schools Prog., Nat. Endowment of the Arts, Jan. '73. Contbr. to: Sunstone Review, Santa Fe, N.M.; N.M. Mag., Santa Fe; Puerto del Sol., Las Cruces, N.M.; (anthols.) From the Belly of the Shark, 1973; Come to Power, 1974. Address: 137 Romero St., Santa Fe, NM 87501, U.S.A.

SANDS-SMITH, Eleanor, pen name, **SANDS, Eleanor,** b. 26 June 1906. Teacher and Poetry Editor. Education: Pennsylvania State Univ.; Bloomsburg State Teachers' Coll.; Marywood Coll., Pennsylvania, etc. Married, Ranald Leary Smith (deceased); 1 s., 2 d. Positions held: Poetry Editor, Morning Press, 1942-72; Editor, Unicorn (mag. of poetry), for 30 yrs.; Consultant and Ms. Reviewer, Falmouth Publishing Co., 1950-52; Consultant to Creative Expression Prog. Bloomfield, New Jersey, 1930-42. Memberships: (in earlier years) Poetry Soc. of America; Pennsylvania Poetry Soc.; Leigh Hunt Group; Scribblers (Montclair, NJ). Contbr. to: St. Martin's Summer, 1951; Everywhere Is Here and Lonesome, 1958; Anthol. of Poetry Soc. of America, 1950; Prize Poems, Poetry So. of Pennsylvania, 1968, 1969; NY Times; CS Monitor; St. Louis Post Dispatch; Chicago Daily News; Newark Eve. News; NY Herald Tribune; Poetry Chap Book; The Lyric; Voices; Saturday Review; The Morning Press; Trails; Unicorn; Kaleidograph; The Abbey Qtly. (Dublin). Awards: C. Sterling Clifton Award, 1968, and Katherine Lyons Clark Award, 1969, Pennsylvania Poetry Soc.; Henry Shoemaker Award, 1950, Pennsylvania Folk Lore Soc.; also others. Address: Red House W., Market St., Benton, PA

17814, USA.

SANDY, Stephen, b. 2 Aug. 1934. Professor. Educ: A.B., Yale Univ.; Ph.D., Harvard Univ. Positions held: Instr., Engl., Harvard Univ., 1963-67; Vis. Asst. Prof., Brown Univ., Providence, R.I., 1968-69; Prof., Engl., Bennington Coll., Vt., current. Published works: Caroms, 1960; Mary Baldwin, 1962; Stresses in the Peaceable Kingdom, 1967; Japanese Room, 1969. Contbr. to: Atlantic; Poetry; Kayak; New Yorker; (anthologies) Best Poems of 1961: The Borestone Mountain Poetry Awards, 1962; A Controversy of Poets, 1965; New Yorker Book of Poems, 1969; City, 1970. Address: Bennington Coll., Bennington, VT, U.S.A.

SANER, Reginald, pen name **SANER, Reg,** b. 30 Dec. 1932. Teacher of Literature. Education: B.A., St. Norbert Coll., 1954; M.A., Univ. of Ill., 1955; Ph.D., ibid, 1962. Married, 2 children. Positions held: Freelance Photographer; Grad. Student; Teacher. Member, Poetry Soc. of Am. Works to be published: Stoning the River. Contbr. to: Poetry (Chicago); The N.Y. Qtly.; Works; Perspective; Prairie Schooner; The Malahat Review; Greenfield Review; Stone Drum; Ohio Review; Midwest Qtly.; Carleton Miscellany; Ill. Qtly.; Kansas Qtly.; Green River Review; Small Pond; Colo. Qtly.; Southern Poetry Review; Poet & Critic; West Coast Review; Epoch; Antigonish Review, etc. Honours, awards: Best Poem Award, Poet & Critic, 1970; Borestone Mt. Poetry Awards: Best Poems of 1973. Address: Dept. of Engl., Univ. of Colo., Boulder, CO 80302, U.S.A.

SAN JUAN, Epifanio S., b. 29 Dec. 1938. Associate Professor. Educ: A.B., Univ. of Philippines, Manila; A.M., & Ph.D., Harvard Univ., U.S.A. Positions held: Former Asst. Prof., Engl., Univ. of Calif., Davis; Former Prof., Engl. & Comparative Lit., Univ. of Philippines; Assoc. Prof., Engl., Univ. of Conn., U.S.A., 1967–. Published works: Godkissing Carrion: Selected Poems 1954-64, 1964; The Exorcism and Other Poems, 1967; Maliwalu: Poems in Filipino, 1969. Contbr. to: Literary Apprentice; Beloit Poetry Journal; New Writing from the Philippines (anthology), 1966. Honours, awards: Rockefeller Fellowship, 1963-65; Palanca Mem. Award for Poetry, 1965. Address: Star Rte., Mansfield Depot, CT 06251, U.S.A.

SANMARK, Kurt Olof, b. 22 July 1927. Department Manager. Education: Chemical Exam., 1948 & Maths. studies, Univ. of Abo Akademi, Turku. Married Meeri Sihvola, 5 children. Positions held: Statist, Fennia Insurance Co., 1951-55 & at Svensk-Finland, 1955-62; Department Re-insurance Mgr., Svensk-Finland, 1962–; Critic of Lit. in Borgabladet, 1956-57, Hufvudstadsbladet, 1957–, & in Nya Argus. Memberships: Soc. of Swedish Authors in Finland, 1954; Mbr., Exec. Comm., ibid 1960-64, 67–; Union of Finnish Critics; Finnish PEN Club. Published works: Människas ansikte, 1952; Vind av stoft, 1955; Blott Du, 1960; OSV, 1964; Obundna Texter, 1973. Contbr. to: Hufvudstadsbladet, Julen, 1956; Progress, Aikalainen, Finland; Ord och Bild, Sweden; Hvedekorn; Digte for en daler, Denmark; Rot, W. Germany, 1965; Artes Hispanias/Hispanic Arts, U.S.A., 1968. Address: Prästgatan 14, 06100 Borga, Finland.

SANNER, Alice M., b. 31 Oct. 1913. Business Executive; Editor. Education: Grad., Dubuque Senior HS. Positions held: Rockford Machine Tool Co., Rockford, Ill., 1942, advertising manager; Greenlee Bros. & Co., 1972, advertising manager; Editor, Hot Chips mag., 1951; Editor, Greenleaves, Greenleaf, 1972. Published work: One Flower One Sun One Hour, 1957. Address: 122 North Chicago Ave., Rockford, IL 61107, USA.

SANSOM, Clive Henry, b. 21 June 1910. Author. Education: Speech Inst., London; Phonetics Dept., Univ. Coll., London. Married Ruth Large. Positions held: Examiner in the Art of Spoken Lang., Univ. of London; Examiner in Speech & Drama, London Acad. of Music & Dramatic Art (LAMDA); Supvsr. of Speech

Educ., Tasmania. Memberships: Poetry Soc.; English Assn. Published works: The Unfailing Spring (w. intro by Walter de la Mare), 1942; The Witnesses (poems), 1951; The Cathedral, 1957; The World of Poetry, 1959; Dorset Village, 1962; The Golden Unicorn: verse for children, 1965; Return to Magic, 1969. Contbr. to: The Listener; English; N.Y. Times; Cornhill Mag.; The Countryman; Observer. Honours, awards: Prize for long poem in Fest. of Britain, Arts Coun. of G.B., 1951; M.B.E. for services to lit. & educ., 1972. Address: c/o David Higham Assocs. Ltd., 5-8 Lower John St., Golden Sq., London W1R 4HA, U.K.

SANTALIZ, Pedro, pen names **PITU & PEDRITO,** b. 28 May 1938. Actor; Theatrical Director; Writer; Conductor of Acting Workshops for the Young. Education: B.A. (Humanities), Univ. of Puerto Rico, 1962. Positions held: Dir. & Conceiver of the El Nuevo Teatro Pobre de América Inc. of Puerto Rico, in the City of N.Y. Published works: Cemí en el palacio de Járlem (Puerto Rico Ritual Stone in the Palace of Harlem), book of poems in Spanish, 1970. Contbr. to: Guajana of Puerto Rico. Address: Goddard-Riverside Community Ctr., 161 W. 87th St., N.Y., NY 10024, U.S.A.

SANTHI, S., b. 28 Dec. 1934. Civil Servant. Educ: M.A., Loyola Coll., Madras Univ., India. Positions held: Off., Special Duty Planning Dept., Govt. of Mysore, 1960-61; Under-Sec., Min. of Home Affairs, New Delhi, India, 1962-65; Dpty. Sec., Food, Civil Supplies & Labour Dept., Bangalore, 1966–. Published works: Lamplight in the Sun, 1967; Whispers near a Niagara, 1969. Contbr. to: Deccan Herald; Modern Indian Poetry in English (anthology), 1969. Address: Govt. of Mysore, Bangalore, India.

SANTOS, Bienvenido N., b. 22 Mar 1911. University Dean; Vice-President. m. Beatriz N. Santos, 1s., 3d. Positions held: Former Pres., Legazpi Coll.; Dean & VP, Univ. of Nueva Caceres, Naga City, Philippines, current; Fulbright Exchange Prof., Engl., Univ. of Iowa, U.S.A., 1966–. Published works: The Wounded Stag, 1956; (fiction) You Lovely People, 1955; Brother My Brother, 1960; Villa Magdalena, 1965; The Volcano, 1965. Contbr. to: Free Press; Graphic; Chronicle Magazine; Philippine Studies; Solidarity; New Writing from the Philippines (anthology), 1966. Honours, awards: Rockefeller Fellowship. 1958-60; Guggenheim Fellowship, 1960-61; Rep. Cultural Heritage Award in Lit., 1965. Address: P.O. Box 578, Iowa City, IA 52240, U.S.A.

SANTOS, Emmanuel Tiu, pen names **SANTOS, Noli, & SANTOS, E.T.,** b. 26 Jan. 1938. Lawyer; Banker; Author; Businessman. Education: A.A., Univ. of Philippines, 1956; A.B., ibid, 1959; LL.B., 1960. Married Carmelita Soriente-Santos, 1 son, 1 daughter. Positions held: Mgr., Corp. Sec. & Legal Counsel, Cabanatuan City Dev. Bank, 1961-66; Corp. Sec. & Legal Counsel, ibid, 1966-73; Instr., Pol. Sci., Banking & Finance & Bus. Laws, Philippine Wesleyan Coll., Cabanatuan City, 1963-66; Ptnr., Santos, Santos & Assocs. Law Office, 1966-73; Asst. V.P., Mfrs. Bank & Trust Co., 1968-73; Dir. & Asst. Corp. Sec., ibid, 1973; Pres., E.T. Santos Realty Co., 1969-71; Del. to the 1971 Constitutional Convention, Rep. of Philippines; On var. legal comms. & counsel or cons. to many corps. Published works: The Philippine Business Laws, 1969; Love Poems (pamphlet), 1960; Love That Silly Girl (poem turned into music), 1967. Lit. Ed., The Philippine Collegian Golden Jubilee Lit. Review, 1958. Contbr. to var. newspapers & jrnls. Honours, awards incl: Cit., Comm. on Arts & Culture, Constitutional Conven., Rep. of Philippines, 1972. Address: Cabanatuan City, Philippines.

SARABHAI, Bharatidevi, b. 31 July 1912. Writer; Theatre Centre President; Educator. Education: grad., Engl. & Sanskrit, Bombay Univ., 1933; grad., Oxford Univ., 1936. Positions held: Prin., Shreyas Arts & Sci. Coll., Ahmedabad, India; Prof., Post-Grad. Inst. of Indian Culture & Rsch. (B.J. Inst. of Learning & Rsch.), Ahmedabad; Pres., Theatre Ctr., India, affiliated to ITI

of UNESCO, 1960; Pres., Ahmedabad Theatre Ctr., affiliated to Theatre Ctr., India; Hon. Sec., Gujarat Univ. Commn. appointed by Govt. of Bombay, 1945-47. Memberships: Gujarat Sahitya Sabha, Ahmedabad; Indian PEN; Gujarat Vidya Sabha, Ahmedabad. Published works: The Well of the People, a poetic drama, 1942 (2 edns.); Two Women, an Indian social drama, 1952 (produced at The Excelsior Theatre, Bombay, 1940 & at the Kenya Nat. Theatre, Nairobi, 1952); Gujarati Plays: Be Nari & Ghar Lakhoti, 1956. Contbr. to: London Mercury; India; Art & Culture; Our India; Behar Herald; New Horizon, etc. Awarded 2nd Bombay State Prize for Gujarati Plays in 1956 for 'Be Nari'. Address: The Retreat, Shahibag, Ahmedabad 380004, India.

SARAZIN-HEIDET, Gaby, b. 2 Sept. 1927. Teacher. Memberships: Société des Gens de Lettres de France; Société des Poètes Français; Société des Ecrivains de Provinces Françaises; Haute Académie Internationale de Lutèce; Société des Ecrivains d'Alsace et de Lorraine; Académie d'Alsace; Académie d'Arts, Sciences, Lettres; Regional Delegate, Société des Poètes et Artistes de France, etc. Published works: Vagabondages avec ma muses, poems, 1959; Fleurs des Muses, with record choice of poems, 1967; Terre de demain, record, 1969; Le Chant de ma terre, poems; Sous le signe de la Croix, poems. Contbr. to lit. jrnls. & reviews. Honours, awards incl: Chevalier des Palmes Académiques, 1973; Officier de l'O.I. de la Renaissance des Arts et Lettres, 1973; Médaille d'Argent d'Arts, Sciences, Lettres, 1971; Grand Prix International de Poésie de l'Halaf, 1972; Prix Foulque d'Anjou, Prix de la Ville d'Antibes, 1973. Address: 21 Rue de Madagascar, 90000 Belfort, France.

SARGENT, Genevieve, pen name, **GINGER.** Engineering Technician; Freelance Writer & Poet; Editor. Education: Grad. (with highest distinction) Phoenix Coll., 1969; additional credits from: Indiana State Univ. Extension; Ariz. State Univ.; Univ. of Calif., Riverside (Phoenix Program); Univ. of Santa Clara., Calif. Personal details: Born in Taylorville, Illinois, USA; mother of Jeffrey J. Sargent. Positions held: Engineering Technician, 9 yrs. Editorships: The Other Poetry Book (anthol.), Northwoods Press, 1974; Orbis (edit. cons.), 1973–; The Sandcutters, 1971, 1972, 1973; Founder & First Editor, Silhouette, 1965-66; Editorial Asst., Drum, 1965. Memberships: Internat. Poetry Soc., UK (Fellow, also U.S. Rep., 1974–); World Poetry Soc. Intercontinental; CSSI; Ariz. State Poetry Soc. (Editor, 1971, 1972, 1973; Nat. Poetry Contest Chairman, 1970); Phoenix Poetry Soc. (Pres., 1971); Internat. Clover Poetry Assoc. (Life Member); American Poetry League (Sec.-Treas., 1974, 1975, 1976); American Mosaic Foundation for Creativity Education; Nat. Fed. of State Poetry Socs.; Acad. of American Poets; Nat. Writers' Club (member, 1969-70); Phoenix Coll. Writers' Club (member, 1968-69). Contbr. to many journals and anthols. including: Contact, 1967; Ballet on the Wind, 1969; Sing, Naked Spirit, 1970; Internat. Poetry Soc. Anthol., 1973; Tantrum (India); Poet (India); Apostrophe; The Ferret; The Sandcutters; Silhouette; Drum; Chicago Daily News; Phoenix Fires, etc. Honours & Awards: numerous prizes, hon. mention, etc. NFSPS; Ariz. State Poetry Soc.; Nat. Writers' Club; CSSI, etc. Address: P.O. Box 15092, Phoenix, AZ 85060, USA.

SARHAN, Hussain, b. 1914. Retired Civil Servant. Positions held: var. positions, the last being Chief of the Government Printing House in Mecca. Published works: 'Wings Without Feathers'. Contbr. to all the newspapers published in the Western Province of Saudi Arabia. Address: Mu'abidah, Mecca, Saudi Arabia.

SARMA, Gunturu Seshendra (G. Seshendra Sarma), b. 20 Oct. 1927. Government Official. Education: grad., Andhra Univ.; studied Law, Madras Univ.; Scholar of Sanskrit. Married Rajkumari Saheba Indira Devi Dhanrajgir. Positions held: Govt. Official, The Municipal Admin. Dept., Andhra Pradesh. Memberships: The Andhra Pradesh Sahitya Akad.;

V.P., The Indian Languages Forum. Published works: Sohrab (long poem), 1951; Ritughosh (long poem), 1963; Pakshulu (coll. of short poems), 1968; Sheshajyotsana (coll. of prose poems), 1972; Meghdoot (Engl. transl. of The Sanskrit Classic in collab. w. Indira Devi Dhanrajgir): Baudelaire (prose poems of the French poet Baudelaire transl. into Telugu), 1973; Mande Suryudu (coll. of poems); Champoo Vinodini (humorous poems), 1968; (play) Mabbullo Darbaru, 1968; (short stories) Vihwala, coll. of short stories, 1968; var. lit. criticism, essays & studies. Contbr. to var. mags., jrnls., newspapers. Address: Gyan Bagh Palace, Goshamahal, Hyderabad 12, A.P., India.

SARMA, S.R., b. 22 July 1909. Medical Practitioner. Education: Grad. in Chemistry & in Medicine & Surg. (M.B.B.S.), Madras Univ., India. Served in WWII with 8th Army in Africa, Italy, Greece & Middle East; In Command of a C.C.J. w. rank of Lt. Col., 1945-46. Member, World Poetry Soc. Intercontinental. Published works: The Way of all Flesh (poem), 1973; The Deluded Soul, (poem), 1973. Recip., 2nd verse Award, Lit. Comp., Land Forces Greece, Athens, 1945. Address: 129/1 Arcot Rd., Madras 26, India 600026.

SAROYAN, Aram, b. 25 Sep. 1943. Writer. Education: Trinity H.S. in Manhattan; attended (briefly) Univ. of Chicago; N.Y. Univ., and Columbia Univ. No degrees. Edited and published Lines Magazine and Lines Books, 1964-67. Pubs. Aram Saroyan, 1968; Pages, 1969; Words & Photographs, 1970; Cloth, An Electric Novel, 1971; The Rest, 1971; Poems, 1972. Contrib. to: The Nation; Poetry: A Magazine of Verse; The Paris Review; The Chicago Review; Art and Literature; Lines; C. Magazine; 0 to 9; Joglars; Angel Hair; Adventures in Poetry. Awarded: Nat. Endowment for the Arts Award for Poetry, 1967 and 1968. Address: Box 1, Elm Rd., Bolinas, California 94924, USA.

SARTON, May, b. 3 May 1912. Lecturer. Educ: Inst. Belge de Culture Française, Brussels. Positions held: Script Writer, Overseas Film Unit, N.Y., 1941-42; Tchr. & Lectr., Harvard Univ., Univs. of Chgo., Kan., Iowa; Colo. State Coll., Beloit Coll., Wellesley Coll., Lindenwood Coll. Published works: Encounter in April, 1936; Inner Landscape, 1939; The Lion and the Rose, 1948; The Land of Silence, 1953; In Time Like Air, 1958; Cloud Stone Sun Vine, 1961; As Does New Hampshire and Other Poems, 1967; (novels) The Single Hound, 1938; The Bridge of Years, 1946; Shadow of a Man, 1950; Faithful Are the Wounds, 1955; The Fur Person, 1957; The Small Room, 1961; Miss Pickthorn and Mr. Hare, 1967; The Poet and The Donkey, 1969. Contbr. to: (anthologies) A New Treasury of War Poetry, 1943; New Poems by American Poets, 1957; Modern Love Poems, 1961; Modern Religious Poems, 1964; Earth Is the Lord's, 1965. Honours, awards: Edward Bland Mem. Prize, 1945; Reynolds Lyric Prize, 1953; Lucy Martin Donnelly Fellowship, 1953-54; Guggenheim Fellowship, 1954; Hopkins Poetry Fest. Award, 1961; Litt. D., Russell Sage Coll., N.Y.

SATISH, Uma Shankar, pen name SATISH, b. 11 May 1937. Teacher of Linguistics. Education: M.A. (Hindi), Agra Univ., India, 1962; M.A. (Linguistics), ibid, 1966; Ph.D. (Linguistics), Delhi Univ. Positions held: Jrnlst., local paper of DehraDun, U.P.; Script Writer, All India Radio, New Delhi; U.G.C. Rsch. Fellow, Delhi Univ.; Asst. Ed., 'Sahitya Sandesh' Hindi Jrnl.; Rsch. Fellow, E.R.C., Univ. of the State of N.Y., Albany, U.S.A.; Lectr. in Ctrl. Inst. of Hindi, Delhi (at present). Published works: (in Garhwali) Garh Geetika, 1955; Raimasi, 1956; Khuder, 1957; Jikuri Boulali, 1958; (in Hindi) Himshila Pighli, 1971. Contbr. to: Karm Bhumi (Garhwal); Gramya (Lucknow); Saptahik Hindustan (New Delhi); Nav-Bharat Times (New Delhi); Hindustan (New Delhi); Nandan (New Delhi); Kadambini (New Delhi); Uttrakhand (Rishikesh); Van Gaurd (DehraDun). Recip., Gold Medal, All India Garhwal Sabha, Dehra Dun, U.P., 1957. Address: Central Inst. of Hindi, K118, Hauz Khas, New Delhi 110016, India.

SAUL, George Brandon, b. 1 Nov. 1901. Writer. Education: Univ. of Pennsylvania: A.B., 1923; A.M., 1930; Ph.D., 1932. Twice married: to Dorothy M. Ayers (ob. 1937) and Eileen S. Lewis; son. George Brandon, 2nd, by first marriage, son and daughter, Michael Brandon and Barbara Brigid Brandon (Mrs. John M.C. Townsend, Jr.) by second. Asst. in English, Univ. of Pennsylvania, 1922-23; Harrison Scholar in English, 1930-31; Research awards, Univ. of Conn., 1967 and 1970. Positions held: Univ. of Pa., 1922-23; Clerk, Indemnity Ins. Co. of No. America, Philadelphia, 1923-24; Faculty, Univ. of Conn., 1924-72; retired as Prof. Emeritus of English, 1972; Contrib. Ed., Journal of Irish Literature, 1972-. Member, Poetry Soc. of America. Pubs: The Cup of Sand, 1923; Bronze Woman, 1930; Unimagined Rose, 1937; Only Necessity.., 1941; Selected Lyrics, 1947; October Sheaf, 1951; Hound and Unicorn: Collected Verse – Lyrical, Narrative and Dramatic, 1969; Candlelight Rhymes for Early-to-Beds, 1970; A Touch of Acid, 1971; Postscript to Hound and Unicorn, 1971; Skeleton's Progress, 1971. Contrib. to: Contemporary Verse; The Measure; The Phila. Public Ledger Lit. Review; New York Herald Tribune Books; The Carillon; General Magazine...(Univ. of Pa.); Contemporary Poetry; Queen's Quarterly; Arizona Quarterly; College English; Poet Lore; N.Y. Public Library Bulletin; Dublin Magazine, etc. Awards received from: Contemporary Verse; The Lyric; Poet Lore. Address: Owls' Watch, 136 Moulton Road, Storrs, Conn. 06268, USA.

SAUNDERS, Patricia Anne, pen name JOYNER, Anne, b. 6 Sept. 1931. Housewife & Foster Parent. Married Richard Saunders, 7 children. Memberships: V.P., Alpha Rho Gamma, 1948; Pres., ibid, 1949; 2nd V.P., United Amateur Press Assn., 1973-74; Wis. Fellowship of Poets; Am. Amateur Press Assn. Published works: White Poppies, 1974. Contbr. to: Soucier; Calico Patches; Here & There; State Street; Paul's Poetry, Olive Hill Times; Quid Nunc; Lancaster Gazette; Badger Herald; Pacific Greenery; Review & Herald; Tweed; Ellisonian Echoes; Amateur Writers' Jrnl. Columnist for Ore. Observer, 1964, '65. Honours, awards incl: 1st Pl., United Amateur Press Assn., 1973; The Golden Prize Award, Mar. 1973. Address: Route 3, Irish Lane, Madison, WI 53711, U.S.A.

SAUNDERS, Robert Crombie, b. 23 Apr. 1914. Editor; Schoolmaster. Educ: Glasgow Univ., Scotland. Positions held: Ed., Scottish Art and Letters, Glasgow, 1944-48; Ed., Scottish Angler, 1948-54; Asst. Ed., Forward, 1951-56. Published works: The Year's Green Edge, 1955; Ed., Selected Poems of Hugh MacDiarmid, 1944; Ed., Ploy, 1945. Contbr. to: Saltire Review; Scots Review; Poetry Scotland; Britain Today; Modern Reading; Poetry London; (anthologies) Honour'd Shade, 1959; Modern Scottish Poetry, 1966; Oxford Book of Scottish Verse, 1966.

SAUNDERS, Thomas, b. 21 Feb. 1909. Literary Editor. Educ: B.A., Univ. of Manitoba, Winnipeg, Canada, 1935; D.D., United Coll., Winnipeg, 1959. m. Janet Agnes Clark, 1940, 3s. Positions held: Former Min., United Church of Canada; Literary Ed., Winnipeg Free Press, 1960-. Published works: Scrub Oak, 1949; Horizontal World, 1951; Something of a Young World's Dying, 1958; The Devil and Cal McCabe, 1960; Red River of the North, 1969. Contbr. to: Poetry 62 (anthology), 1961. Address: 527 Oxford St., Winnipeg, Manitoba, Canada.

SAUNDERS, Walter Gerard, b. 15 July 1930. Lecturer in English. Education: B.A., Univ. of S. Africa, 1959; Honours B.A. (Engl.), 1962. Married Gloria Ehrich, 3 children. Positions held: var. tchng. posts in private & govt. schls. in S. Africa & Rhodesia; Lectr. in Engl., Univ. of S. Africa, Pretoria, 1963–; Co-Ed., Ophir Poetry Mag., 1967–. Contbr. of poetry & drama to: Ophir; Wurm; New Coin; De Arte 1; Unisa English Studies; Poet (India); Workshop 6 (London); Purple Renoster; New Nation. Address: Dept. Engl., UNISA, Box 392, Pretoria, S. Africa.

SAUTER, Rudolf Helmut, b. 9 May 1895. Artist;

Painter. Education: Harrow School. Fellow, International P.E.N. Published works: Songs in Captivity, 1921; Four Hungers, 1946; Crie du Coeur, 1968; A Soothing Wind, 1969; Erda – The Trial of Man, 1972; The Fifth Hunger (a poetic drama completed 1973); Grotesques & Realities (a series of pamphlets); Galsworthy The Man (a biographical study), 1967. Poems spoken on BBC (Midland poets) & individual poems have appeared from time to time in var. jrnls. Illustrations to: Awakening; The Manaton Edition of the works of John Galsworthy. Address: Fort William, Butterrow, Stroud, Glos. GL5 2LR, U.K.

SAVAGE, Frances Higginson, b. 1 Jan. 1898. Writer; Painter. Education: A.B., Bryn Mawr Coll.; Art Students League, N.Y.C. Married, 2 daughters. Positions held: Instr. in Engl., Bryn Mawr Coll.; Pres., N.Y. Women Poets. Memberships: Poetry Soc. of Am.; Hon. Mbr., Pen & Brush Club, N.Y.C. Published works: Bread & Honey, 1939; A Pinch of Salt, 1941; Winter Nocturne, 1964; Postscript to Spring, 1968. Contbr. to: The New Yorker; Voices; The Atlantic; The University Review; Yankee; The N.Y. Times; The N.Y. Herald Tribune; Sat. Evening Post; Ladies Home Jrnl.; The Lyric; Spirit; Educl. Forum, etc. & sev. anthols. Honours, awards: Annual Award, The Lyric, 1945 & '66; New England Prize, The Lyric, 1965; Love Prize, Poetry Soc. of Ga., 1967; The Green World Prize, 1965. Address: 150 Brewster Rd., Scarsdale, NY 10583, U.S.A.

SAVE VITOLO, Lina. Teacher of English Language & Literature. Education: Degree in Engl. Lang. & Lit.; Cert. of Attendance & Examination in Lang., Phonetics, Lit. & Instns., Univ. of Cambridge, U.K., 1937. Positions held: Former Tchr. of Engl. in State schls. Memberships incl: Assoc. Mbr. (Academician) Accademia Tiberina, Rome; The Legion d'Oro Union; Hon. Mbr., Acad. Class 'Nobel', Acad. of Sci. Letters & Arts.; Hon. Mbr., Accademia di Santa Brigida di Svezia, & actively collaborated w. many cultural ctrs. & on juries of lit. comps., etc. Published works: Meditazioni – Aneliti, lyrics; Inghilterra Dagli Albi Confini, 1960. Contbr. to num. anthols., newspapers, reviews, inclng: Il Duemilista, Palermo; Italscambi, Ivrea; Omnia, Rome; Antologia di Poeti Nuovi; Antologia Poetica de la Famiglia Italiana; Arte Poesia Narrativa Turismo Stampa Storia; Gli Amici di Talento; Modern Italian Art & Lit.; Poet (India). Recip. num. honours & awards inclng. Degree of Counsellor in Literature, awarded by the Nat. Univ. of the Dominion of Canada, 1972. Address: Via Belvedere 98, 80127 Naples, Italy.

SAVORY, Teo. Press Editor. Educ: Royal Coll. of Music, London, U.K.; Conservatoire, Paris, France. Positions held: Script Reader & Producer, Am. Nat. Theatre & Acad., N.Y.C.; Ed., Unicorn Press, Santa Barbara, Calif., current. Published works: Traveler's Palm: A Poetry Sequence, 1967; Snow Vole: A Poetry Sequence, 1968; (novels) The Landscape of Dreams, 1960; The Single Secret, 1961; A Penny for the Guy, 1964; (translations) Corbière, 1967; Supervielle, 1967; Prévert, 1967; Jammes, 1967; Michaux, 1967; Guillevic, 1968. Contbr. to: Approach; Sixties; Unicorn Journal; Dimension; Prairie Schooner. Address: R.F.D. 1, Housatonic, MA, U.S.A.

SAWA, Yūki, b. 13 Jan. 1945. Poet. Education: B.A., Doshisha Univ., Kyoto, Japan, 1968; M.A., Kansai Univ., Osaka, forthcoming. Member, Haibungaku-kai (Learned Soc. of Haiku). Published works: Anthology of Modern Japanese Poetry (w. Edith Marcombe Shiffert), 1972; Chieko, a chapbook of poetry translations (w. E. Shiffert), 1973. Contbr. of original poems to Midwest Qtly. Translations in: Southern Review; Literature East West; Northwest Review; Trans Pacific; Mundus Artium, Puget Soundings. Address: 37 Mizukuchi-cho, Shimogamo, Sakyo-ku, Kyoto, Japan.

SAWAI, Atsuhiro, b. 9 Feb. 1939. University Lecturer. Education: grad., Kyoto Univ. (majored in Engl. & Am. Lit.) Positions held: Corres. Ed., TransPacific; Ed.,

English & Am. Lit.; Lectr., Kyoto Univ. of Industry. Published works: (collected poems) Seishum no Ma (Devil of Adolescence), 1967; Kagami (The Mirror), 1973. Contbr. to: The Kyoto News; Shi to Hihyo (Poetry & Criticism); Hon no Techo (Pocketbook for Books); Engl. & Am. Lit.; TransPacific. Address: 1013 Nishijin Danchi, Horikawa Imadegawa, Kamigyo-ku, Kyoto, 602 Japan.

SAXON, Elizabeth Ann, b. 12 Apr. 1943. Civil Servant. Education: B.A., Univ. Coll. of Swansea; Dip. Ed., ibid; currently completing M.Sc. Econ. Thesis, Univ. Coll. of Wales, Aberystwyth. Memberships: The Scribbler; Poetry Soc. Published works: Here Be Dragons, 1973; Poems, w. Della Fish, 1965. Contbr. to: New Statesman; Tribune; Hampshire Poets; Meridian; Human World; Platform; Anglo-Welsh Review; Church News; Dial-a-Poem; Welsh Arts Coun., 1973. Recip., Main Engl. lang. poetry prize, Univ. of Wales Eisteddford, 1973. Address: 384 Cromwell Lane, Burton Green, Kenilworth, Warwicks., U.K.

SAYE, Edward Lee, Jr., b. 14 Aug. 1940. Educator. Education: B.A., Univ. of Md., 1965; M.Ed., Ga. State Univ., 1970. Married, Susan Hutchinson Saye, 1 d. Positions held: Dental Lab. Technician, USAF; HS Tchr.; Asst. to Dean, Schl. of Educ., Ga. State Univ. Member, Sci. Fiction Writers Am. Contributor to: Haiku Highlights, 1969, '70; Creative Review, 1968, '70; Jean's Jrnl., 1971; Janus-SCTH, 1971. Recip., Book Award for Haiku, Haiku Highlights, 1969. Address: 1739-B North Decatur Rd., N.E., Atlanta, Ga. 30307, USA.

SAYED, Ahmed Shah Bokhari, pen name **BOKHARI, Ustad,** b. 16 Jan. 1930. Lecturer. Education: B.A. & M.A., Sind Univ., Pakistan. Positions held: Lectr. in Sindhi, Govt. Coll., Dadu, Sind. Memberships: Writers Guild, W. Pakistan; Jamiat u Sshuaza Sind (Pakistan); Writers Panel, Textbook Bd., Hyderabad Sind. Published works: Geet Asanja, Jeet Asanjee; Barana Bol. Contbr. to: Mehran; Nain Zindagi; Sohni; Ibrat, etc. Recip. cash prizes from West Pakistan Writers Guild & Sindhology, Sind Univ. Address: Government Coll., Dadu, Sind, Pakistan.

SAYEED, Bano Tahira, b. 9 Nov. 1922. Journalist; Radio Artist; Writer. Education: Grad., Univ. of Lucknow, India; Dip. in Jrnlsm., Univ. of Tehran, Iran; studied French, German, Turkish & Arabic in var. instns. in the Middle Eastern countries; study tour of the U.K., European & some communist countries. Married. Positions held: V.P., Students Union, ALBORZ Am. Coll., Tehran, 1940; Libn., Pasteur Inst., Tehran, 1941-43; Tchr. in Engl., Noor Baksh Schl., Tehran, 1943-44; Announcer & i/c Urdu Sect., Tehran Radio, 1943-46; Pres., Army lit. & var. lit. & welfare socs. in India, 1947-66; Prin., Kindergarten Shcl. & p/t Artist, All India Radio, 1966–. Memberships: Sec., Mahfil-e-Khwateen; Engl. Poetry Soc.; Indo Iranian Soc.; Bazm-e-Saadi; Urdu Majlis. Published works: Bano-e-Misr (short stories in Persian), 1943; Hadya-e-Tahira (devotional poems in Urdu), 1957; Berg-e-Sabz (coll. of poems in Urdu), 1963; Arpana (Telugu transl. of self Urdu poems), 1966; Ashyan Hamara (coll. of Urdu patriotic poems), 1973; Gul-e-Khonchikan (Urdu poems); Mahikte Biyaban (Urdu poems & lyrics); Sapnou-ke-Mahfil (Short stories in Urdu); Beneath the Bough (Engl. poems) under publ. Contbr. to var. jrnls., newspapers & periodicals. Recip. many honours, inclng: Honoured by Iranian Govt., 1944, 61 & 72; Award, Sahitya Acad., 1959; Award for Berg-e-Sabz, 1963; Award & Hon. 'SANMANAM', Min. of Cultural Affairs, 1966; World Poetry Soc. Award, 1973. Address: 'Green View', Shantinagar, Hyderabad 500028, Andhra Pradesh, India.

SAYLOR, Neville Swaim, b. 2 Sept. 1922. Teacher. Education: B.A., Ouachita Bapt. Coll., 1944; M.S.E., Henderson State Coll., 1969. Widow of Earney Saylor, 5 children. Positions held: Lab. Techn., Memphis, Tenn.; Agricl. Ext. Serv. Lab. Techn.; Tchr., Morrilton, Ark., Sparkman, Ark. & Arkadelphia H.S. Memberships: Poets Roundtable of Ark.; Int. Comm.,

Centro Studi e Scambi Int. Published works: (poetry book) The New Genesis; (poetry pamphlets) Saylor's Songs. Writes column in Southern Standard Newspaper & Daily Siftings Herald Newspaper. Contbr. to: Moon Age Poets; Prairie Poets; Poets Roundtable of Ark.; Poetry Dial Anthol.; Modern Images; Encore; Ark. Gazette, etc. Recip. var. poetry hons. & awards inclng. 1st pl., Choya Award, Poetry Day Celebrations, 1973. Address: 1838 Center St., Arkadelphia, AR, U.S.A.

SAYYAR, Othman bin, b. 1928. Educational Inspector. Education: Licence, Sharia Coll., Saudi Arabia. Positions held: Educator & Employee of the Ministry of Education, in Educational Inspection. Contbr. to Al-Jazira Newspaper. Address: c/o Higher Council for Science, Literature & Arts, Ministry of Education, Riyadh, Saudi Arabia.

SCANNELL, Vernon, b. 23 Jan. 1922. Writer. Education: Leeds Univ. Married, with 5 children. Fellow, Royal Soc. of Literature. Published works: A Mortal Pitch, 1957; The Masks of Love, 1960; A Sense of Danger, 1962; Walking Wounded, 1965; Epithets of War, 1969; Mastering the Craft, 1970; Company of Women, 1971; Selected Poems, 1971; The Winter Man, 1973. Contbr. to: Ambit; Encounter; Cornhill; London Mag.; New Statesman; The Listener; Times Lit. Supp.; Sunday Times; The Observer; Transatlantic Review; Poetry Review, etc. Recip. The Heinemann Award for Literature, 1960. Address: Folly Cottage, Nether Compton, Sherborne, Dorset DT9 4QG, UK.

SCANTLAN, Samuel William, pen name **LEUMAS, Wm. S.,** b. 24 Feb. 1901. Minister of the Gospel. Education: B.D., Okla. Baptist Univ., Shawnee, Okla; D.D., ibid, 1957; writing courses, Okla. Univ., Norman, Okla. Married. Positions held: Pastor of sev. churches; Sec. of Dept. of Missions for Okla. Convention, 25 yrs.; currently Pres., Bapt. Gen. Convention of Okla. Memberships: Poetry Soc. of Okla.; Okla Writers; Southern Bapt. Histl. Soc.; Okla Baptist Histl. Soc. Published works: Andrew Potter – Baptist Builder (a biog.), 1955; Through God's Revolving Doors (book of poems), 1964; T.B. Lackey – The Man And an Epoch (a biog.), 1972. Contbr. to: Bapt. Messenger of Okla.; The Davis News; The Crawford Mirror; Daily Oklahomian; Poetry Soc. Mag., etc. Recip. var. poetry hons. Address: 402 South Sixth St., Davis, OK 73030, U.S.A.

SCARBROUGH, George (Addison), b. 20 Oct. 1915. College Professor of English. Education: B.A., Lincoln Mem. Univ., Harrogate, Tennessee; M.A., Univ. of Tennessee, Knoxville; 2 yrs. on Lit. Fellowship, Univ. of the South, Sewanee, Tennessee; Study at Iowa State Univ., Iowa City; Colorado Mountain Coll., Glenwood Springs, Colorado. Positions held: Has taught for 18 yrs. in the secondary schools and colleges of USA. Published works: Tellico Blue, 1949; The Course Is Upward, 1951; Summer So-Called, 1956; Tennessee Tones, 1941 (pamphlet). On literary staff of The Chattanooga Times. Contbr. to 11 anthols. Contbr. to journals, newspapers, including: Polk County News; Chattanooga Times; Progressive Farmer; Versecraft; Driftwind; Sewanee Review; Atlantic; Harper's; New Republic; NY Times; Poetry (Chicago); Voices; New Orleans Poetry Journal; Poetry Dial; Southern Fireside; Qtly. Review of Literature; Monument; Georgia Medical Journal; Saturday Review of Literature; Houston Post; Chicago Review; Southwest Review; Minnesota Qtly.; Hearse; Wind; Appalachian Journal; Spirit, etc. Recip. Borestone Mountain Award, 1961; Lit. Fellowship to Univ. of South, Sewanee, Tennessee, 1941; Mary Rugeley Ferguson Poetry Award, Sewanee Review, 1964; "Summer So-Called" selected by NY Times as one of the best books of the year, 1956; Class Poet, Lincoln Mem. Univ., 1947. Address: 100 Darwin Lane, Oak Ridge, TN 37830, USA.

SCARFE, Francis, b. 18 Sept. 1911. British Institute Director. Education: Univs. of Durham & Cambridge, UK; Univ. of Paris, France. Positions held: Lectr., Univ. of Glasgow, UK; Lt.-Col., Royal Airforce Educ. Corps.; Prof. of French, Univ. of London; Dir., British Inst., Paris, France. Fellow, Royal Soc. of Lit. Published works: Buscapes, 1940; 40 Poems & Ballads, 1941; Underworlds, 1950. Contbr. to: 20th Century Verse; Contemporary Poetry & Prose; Poetry London; Poetry Chicago; Poetry Scotland; Horizon; The Listener; Kingdom Come. Recip. of OBE. Address: British Institute in Paris, 6 rue de la Sorbonne, Paris 5, France.

SCARPHOUT, Ria, b. 31 Jan. 1930. Art School Teacher. Education: Inst. for Journalists, Belgium; Royal Conservatory of Brussels. Positions held: Freelance Jrnlst., Belgian radio & TV; Tchr., Schls. of Art. Memberships: Assn. of Flemish Authors; Int. PEN Club; Die Kogge, Germany. Published works: Boven de Tuinen, 1959; Gordel en Sluier, 1961; var. novels & short stories. Honours, awards: Prize, Young-Dutch Lit. Days, 1958; Prize, Province West-Vlaanderen for Poetry, 1960; Aragoniaprize, 1961; Prize, Review Nieuwe Stemmen, 1962; First pl., Referendum van de Vlaamse Letterkundigen, 1963; Recip., twice, Prize of the Gen. Dir., Nat. Co. of Belgian Railways, 1965 & 66. Address: Domeindreef 10, 8200 Brugge-Sint-Michiels, Belgium.

SCEARS, Lucie, b. 10 July 1928. Poet. Education: HS; Jr. Coll.; self-educated. Positions held: Soda Fountain Clerk; Asst. to Libns.; Bank Bookkeeper; Civil Serv. Typist-Clerk; Part-time Clerk, mineral-lapidary store. Contbr. to the following anthols., jrnls., mags., etc: Yearbook of modern Poetry (pending), 1971; Dance of The Muse (pending), 1970; Anthols., Gato Publs. (pending), 1971, '72. Contbr. to: The Swordsman Review; Driftwood (Lit. Mag.); Gato Mag. Address: Apt. 3, 22328 S. Garden Ave., Hayward, Calif. 94541, USA.

SCELZA, Gennaro, b. 28 July 1933. Elementary School Teacher. Memberships: Acad. Int. Leonardo da Vinci, Rome; Hon. Mbr., Acad. Int. G. Leopardi, Rome; Centro Studi e Scambi Int., Rome; Soc. of Authors & Editors, Music Sect., Rome. Contbr. to anthols: Poeti Nuovi, 1961; Quaderni di Poesia, 1961; Le Langhe, 1965; Quaderni di Poesia, 1970; La Mamma Nel Canto Dei Poeti Contemporanei, Vols. III & IV, 1968, '70; Silloge Conviviale, Vol. II, 1970; Il Padre Nel Canto Dei Poeti Contemporanei, Vol. II, 1969; Autori Da Ricordare, 1971; Selected Passages from International Authors, 1971; Poets & Poems, 1972; Poeti e poesie, 1973. Contbr. to: Omnia, Rome; Le aquile, Rome. Honours, awards: Citation, Int. Poetry Contest, Centro Studi e Scambi Int., 1960; Citation, Nat. Poetry Reporting Contest, 1971. Address: Via Capo di Mezzo 17/A, 84040 Angellara di Vallo (SA), Italy.

SCHAEFER, Oda (Oda Lange), b. 21 Dec. 1900. Writer; Poet; Journalist. Education: Schl. of Arts. Member, P.E.N. Published works: Gedichte & Balladen, die Windharfe, 1939; Irdisches Gelei, 1946; Grasmelodie, 1959; Der grüne Ton, 1973. Contbr. to: Frankfurter Zeitung; Neue Zeitung; Die Zeit; Stuttgarter Zeitung; Rheinische Post; etc. Honours, awards incl: Prize, Academy of Science & Lit., Mainz, 1950; Hon. Award, Bavarian Acad. of Fine Arts, 1952; Förderpreis, Literature, Munich, 1959; Hon. Award, Andreas Gryphius Prize, Esslingen, 1968; Literaturpreis der Gesellschaft zur Förderung des Schrifttums, 1970. Address: Züricherstr. 104, D8 Munich 71, German Fed. Republic.

SCHAEFFER, Susan Fromberg, b. 25 Mar. 1941. College Professor. Education: B.A., 1961, M.A., 1963, Ph.D., 1966, Univ. of Chicago. Positions held: Instr., Assistant Prof., Associate Prof. Published works: The Witch and the Weather Report (poetry), 1972; Falling (novel), 1973; Anya (novel), 1974; Granite Lady (poetry), 1974. Contbr. to: The Spectator; New Statesman; Encounter; American Scholar; Kayak; Seneca Review; Texas Qtly.; Delta; Sceptre Press; Poetry; Partisan Review; Esquire; Mademoiselle; Beloit Poetry Journal; Chelsea; Chicago Review; Iowa

Review; Carleton Miscellany; Chicago Tribune; Invisible City; Armadillo; Workshop, Florida Qtly.; Yale Lit. Mag.; NY Qtly.; Shenandoah; New Orleans Review; Prism Internat.; Fiddlehead; Far Point; Canadian Forum; Occident; Meanjin Qtly.; Cave; Edge; Mirror Northwest, etc. Address: Brooklyn Coll., Dept. of Engl., Bedford Ave. & Ave. H, Brooklyn, NY, USA.

SCHECHTER, Ruth Lisa. Poet; Teacher; Lecturer; Poetry Therapist. Education: N.Y., Univ., Boston Univ., The New School of Social Science; Certified N.Y. Bd. of Education, Teacher: Creative Writing. Consulting Poetry Therapist, Odyssey House, a nationwide rehab. center for drug abuse. Previously: Admin. Asst. Montefiore Hospital and Albert Einstein Coll. of Medicine, Dept. of Surgery; Free Lance: Editorial Asst. Currently guest editor at Barlenmir House, N.Y.C. Member: Poetry Soc. of America; Poetry Forum; Vermont Writers' League; Bronx Council on the Arts; American Poetry Therapists. Pubs. Near the Wall of Lion Shadows, 1969, 1970; Movable Parts, 1970; Suddenly Thunder, 1972; Night Theater, 1973. Alan, Carlos, Theresa, a 2-act play perf. off Broadway, NYC. Contrib. to: Forum Magazine; Beloit Poetry Journal; Prairie Schooner; Southwest Review; Red Clay Reader; American Dialogue; N.Y. Quarterly; Dasein; Wagner Lit. Magazine; Chicago Tribune; The Cooperator, etc.; Anthologies: We Mainline Dreams; In the Belly of the Shark; Rising Tides; Poets for Peace; The Writing on the Wall; Poetry Healer, etc. Honours: Poet-in-Residence, Mundelein Coll., Chicago; Scholar, Wagner Writers' Conf.; Fellowships: MacDowell Colony, 1963 and 1970; The Abby Smith Award, Texas (prize); Book Mss., accepted for Special Collection of Women's Achievements at Mundelein Coll. Learning Resource Center; Chairman, Poetry-Literature, Bronx Council on the Arts; N.Y. State Council on the Arts (Grant), 1973. Address: 9 Van Cortlandt Place, Croton-on-Hudson, N.Y., USA.

SCHERMAN, Richard L., b. 12 Aug. 1942. Architectural Designer. Education: B.A. in Archt., Univ. of Ill. Schl. of Archt., U.S.A. Positions held: Archtl. Designer (self employed), Pueblo, W. Colo.; currently Archtl. Designer in Nashville, Tenn. Member, World Poetry Soc., Phoenix, Ariz. Contbr. to: Legend Mag., Mich.; Poets Guild, Idaho; Hyacynths & Biscuits, Calif.; Atlantic Monthly, N.J. & Mass. Address: 801 Bradford Ave., Apt. B., Nashville, TN 37204, U.S.A.

SCHEVILL, James, b. 10 June 1920. Poet; Playwright & Professor of English. Education: B.S., Harvard Univ., 1942. Positions held: Writer, reviews & articles, var. newspapers; Tchr., Univ. of Calif. Ext. Div. & in the Humanites Dept., Calif. Coll. of Arts & Crafts, 1950-59; & in Engl. Dept., San Fran. State Coll., 1959-67; Dir., The Poetry Ctr., San Fran., 1961-67; currently Prof. of Engl., Brown Univ., Providence, R.I. Published works incl: Twelve stage, radio & TV plays produced throughout U.S.A., Canada, U.K. & Europe; The American Fantasies (poems), 1951; The Right to Greet (poems), 1956; The Roaring Market & the Silent Tomb (biog.), 1956; Selected Poems: 1945-59, 1959; The Bloody Tenet, verse play, 1956; The Black President; Voices of Mass & Capital A, 1961; This Is Not True, one-act opera libretto, 1963; The Stalingrad Elegies (dramatic poem), 1965; Lovecraft's Follies, play, 1969; The Ushers, expmtl. play, 1971; Breakout: In Search of New Theatrical Environments, 1973; The Buddhist Car and Other Characters (poems), 1973. Poems, plays & articles in many mags. & anthols. published in U.S.A., U.K., Europe & Japan. Has given many readings of his poems & plays in secondary schls., colls., univs. & community groups throughout the U.S.A. & England. Recip. num. prizes & awards. Address: Engl. Dept., Brown Univ., Providence, RI 02912, U.S.A.

SCHIFF, Medad, b. 25 Aug. 1917. Writer. Education: B.Com., London School of Economics, UK. Membership: Hebrew Writers Union. Contbr. to: Commentary; BBC; Hebrew publs. in Israel. Address: 9 Yad Shalom St., Ramat Gan, Israel.

SCHIRMBECK, Heinrich Wilhelm, b. 23 Feb. 1915. Novelist; Essayist; Scientific Author; Public Lecturer; Editor; Bookseller. Married 1) Ursula Possekel, div., 4 children, 2) Evelyne Rossberg, div., 1 daughter. Positions held: Publicity Mgr., Akademische Verlagsgesellschaft Athenaion, Potsdam, 1938-39, of the Ullstein-Verlag, Berlin, 1939, of the Frankfurter Zeitung, Frankfurt a/m, 1939-40; Ed., Schwäbische Zeitung, Leutkirch, 1946-50; Freelance Writer, Columnist, 1950–. Memberships incl: Deutsche Akademie für Sprache und Dichtung, Darmstadt, 1969–; Akademie der Wissenschaften und der Literatur, Mainz, 1964–; PEN, 1958–. Published works: Die Fechtbrüder, symbolic-poetical tales, 1944; Gefährliche Täuschungen, poetic novel, 1947; Das Spiegellabyrinth, magic tales, 1948; Argert dich dein rechtes Auge, symbolic sci. novel, 1957, Engl. edn., 1960, Am. edn., 1961; Der junge Leutnant Nikolai, lyric-poetic sci. novel, 1958, 2nd edn., 1969; Die Nacht vor dem Duell, magic tales, 1964; Die Formel und die Sinnlichkeit – Bausteine zu einer Poetik im Atomzeitalter, essays, 1964; Aurora, lyric tales, 1968; Träume und Kristalle, phantastic tales, 1968; Tänze und Ekstasen, poetic tales, 1973. Honours, awards: Grosser Literaturpreis der Akademie der Wissenschaften und der Literatur, Mainz, 1951; Fördererpreis zum Immermann-Preis für Dichtung der Stadt Düsseldorf, 1962. Address: 13 Park Rosenhoehe, D-61 Darmstadt, German Fed. Repub.

SCHISGAL, Murray, b. 25 Nov. 1926. Playwright. Education: Brooklyn Conservatory of Mus.; L.I. Univ.; LL.B., Brooklyn Law Schl., 1953; B.A., New Schl. for Soc. Rsch., 1959. Married Reene Schapiro, 2 children. Positions held: Musician, 1947-50; practised law, 1953-55; taught private & public schls., 1955-59; full time writer, 1960–. Published works: (plays) The Typists & The Tiger, 1960, '63; Ducks & Lovers, 1961, '72; Knit One, Purl Two, 1963; Luv, 1964, '65; Windows, 1965, included in Fragments, Windows & Other Plays, 1965; Fragments, produced Off-Broadway, 1967, with The Basement, included in publ.; Memorial Day, 1968; Jimmy Shine, 1968, '69; The Chinese & Dr. Fish, 1970. Screenplay: The Tiger Makes Out, 1967. Original TV play: The Love Song of Barney Kempinski, 1966. Recip. Vernon Rice Award & Outer Circle Award, 1963. Address: 275 Central Park West, N.Y., NY, U.S.A.

SCHJEDAHL, Peter. Poet. Educ: Carleton Coll., Northfield, Minn. Positions held: Co-Fndr., Mother Magazine, N.Y.C. Published works: White Country, 1968. Contbr. to: New York Times; Village Voice; Art News; Young American Poets (anthology), 1968.

SCHLOSS, David, b. 2 Jan. 1944. College Professor of English. Education: Columbia Univ., 1960-61; Univ. of So. Calif., 1961-62; B.A., Brooklyn Coll., CUNY, 1965; M.F.A., Univ. of Iowa, 1967. Married Penelope Davis. Positions held: Film Ed., summer 1964; Rsch. Asst. to Poets, Univ. of Iowa, 1966-67; Instr., 'Writing Poetry', Ency. Britannica course, summer 1967; Grad. Tchng. Fellow, Univ. of Iowa, 1967-68; Instr., Univ. of Cinn., 1968-72; Asst. Prof., ibid, 1972–. Mbr., Ohio Poets' Assn., 1971–. Published works: The Beloved, 1972. Contbr. to: Best Poems of 1972 (Borestone Mt. Poetry Awards); Poetry; The Am. Poetry Review; Ohio Review; Lamp In The Spine; The Strong Voice, I & II: The Iowa Review; The North Am. Review, etc. Honours, awards incl: Winner, Donald Whitelide Award, Brooklyn Coll., 1965; Winner, Leonard Hecht Poetry Explanation Contest, Brooklyn Coll., 1967; Dept. of Engl. Poetry Prize, Brooklyn Coll., 1963. Address: 3427 Whitfield Ave., Cinn., OH 45220, U.S.A.

SCHMIDT, Eberhard, b. 7 Oct. 1937. Meteorological Official. Education: Studied philos., Psychol. at University. Married, 1 daughter. Positions held: Mechanic; Soldier; Painter; Jrnlst.; Lectr. (Reader); Official, German Meteorological Serv. Memberships: Verband deutscher Schriftsteller; Literarische Union; Interessengemeinschaft deutschsprachiger Autoren; V.Chmn., Arbeitsgemeinschaft junger Publizisten. Published works: Inselleben, 1973; Durch Die Wildnis,

1973; Zwanzigmal Lyrik, 1973; Texte Durch Drei (w. others), 1974; Maske & Spiegel, 1974; Absichten, 1974. Contbr. to: Unio; Blätter für Lyrik und Kurz Prosa; Das Literarische Wort; Epitaph; var. anthols. Address: Hohenzollernstrasse 143, D-54 Koblenz, German Fed. Repub.

SCHMIDT, Michael Norton, Publisher. Education: Harvard Univ.; B.A., Oxford Univ., 1971. Positions held: Gulbenkian Fellow of Poetry, Manchester Poetry Ctr. Published works: Bedlam & the Oakwood, 1969; Desert of the Lions, 1972; British Poetry Since 1960 (Ed., critical anthol.) Contbr. to: Poetry (USA); Hudson Review (USA); Listener; New Statesman; Critical Qtly.; Poetry Nation; Stand; Caret, etc. Address: Carcanet Press Ltd., 266 Councillor Ln., Cheadle Hulme, Cheadle, Ches. SK8 5PN, U.K.

SCHMIDT, Thomas Victor, pen name **SCHMIDT, Tom,** b. 5 Apr. 1939. Teacher; Musician. Education: B.A., San Francisco State Coll., Calif., U.S.A., 1961; M.A. Engl., ibid, 1964. Positions held: Instr. of Engl., Am. River Coll., Sacramento, 1965-73; Woodwinds, The Greater Carmichael Traveling Street Band, 1966–. Contbr. to: New American & Canadian Poetry (anthol.), 1971; Antioch Review; Chelsea; Field; Hanging Loose; Modern Poetry in Translation (London); Poetry Review (Tampa); Steps: Journal of The Free University of Berkeley; Transatlantic Review (fiction); Works. Honours, awards: James T. Phelan Award for Short Fiction, 1970; Hon. Mention, James T. Phelan Award for Poetry, 1970. Address: 8036 California Ave., Fair Oaks, CA 95628, U.S.A.

SCHMITZ, Dennis, b. 11 Aug. 1937. Teacher. Education: B.A., Loras Coll., 1959; M.A., Univ. of Chicago, 1961. Married, 5 children. Positions held: at Ill. Inst. of Technol., 1961-62; Univ. of Wis., Milwaukee, 1962-66; Calif. State Univ., Sacramento, 1966–. Published works: We Weep For Our Strangeness, 1969; Double Exposures, 1971; (tape) The Poetry of Dennis Schmitz, 1971. Contbr. to: Audience; Antaeus; Arts in Society; Chicago Review; Choice; Critic; December; Epoch; Hudson Review; Iowa Review; The Nation; Field; Ironwood; Poetry Northwest, etc. Honours, awards: Discovery Award, Poetry Ctr., N.Y.C., 1968; First Book Comp., Big Table Books, Follett Publishing Co., 1969. Address: c/o English Dept., Calif. State Univ., 6000 Jay St., Sacramento, CA, U.S.A.

SCHMULLER, Aaron, b. 27 May 1910. Poet & Translator. Education; City College, NY; Mainly self-educated. Positions held: variously, Delivery Boy; Store Clerk; Laundry Worker; Dishwasher; Section Hd., large mail-order house; Glove-worker; Store Mgr.; Small Businessman. Memberships: Poetry Soc. Am.; Am. Poetry League. Publications: Man in the Mirror (poems), 1945; Moments of Meditation (poems & translations), 1953; Treblinka Grass (translations), 1957; Crossing the Borderland (poems, prose poems & translations), 1959; Legend of his Lyre (poems & translations), 1960; Tokens of Devotion (poems), 1960; While man Exists (poems & translations); Triumphalis (poems & translations), 1973; In preparation: Poetical Soliloquies (poems & translations). Translator of many outstanding Jewish poets into English. Contbr. to: (jrnls.) The Humanist; Poet Lore; Lit. Rev., Fairleigh Dickinson Univ.; Phylon, Atlanta Univ. Rev.; Judaism Qtly.; Opinion; Jewish Horizon; Jewish Day; Am. Bard; Flame; Cyclotron; Cyclo-Flame; Human Voice Qtly.; Wisc. Poetry Mag.; Kaleidoscope; Pegasus; Wildlife; The Poet; Driftwood; The Searchlight; Poets of Am. Mag.; Hearth Songs Jrnl.; Am. Hebrew; The Crisis; Chinese Nationalist Daily; Opportunity; Quote; The Answer; Pioneer Woman; Jewish Spectator; Candor; The Muse Mag.; Poesy Book; Prairie Poet Mag.; Poetry Digest; Am. Bard; Sonnet Sequences; Writers Voice; Literary Corner; Am. Poetry League Bull., etc.; (anthols.) Avalon Anthols.; Am. Poetry League Anthols.; Songs From Am. Hearts; The Golden Year, Poetry Soc. of Am.; New Orlando Anthol.; Determined Dust Anthol.; Exploring Anthol.; Guild Anthol.; Spring Anthol.; Muse

Anthol. (co-ed.); Singing Muse Anthol. (co-ed.), etc. Address: 9227 Kaufman Place, Brooklyn, NY 11236, USA.

SCHNEID, Miriam, b. 1 Jan. 1924. School Consultant. Education: Tchr. Sem. & Hebrew Univ., Jerusalem; currently doctoral cand. in Hebrew Lit. Married Prof. Dr. Otto Schneid, 2 sons. Positions held: Tchr. of H.S., Tchrs. Coll., Post grad. classes in ancient & modern Hebrew lit. Published works: Roman be Mikhtavim (novel), 1949; Ad Tom (poetry), 1959; Shirey Stav (poetry), 1968; Sheath Ratzon (poetry), 1973. Contbr. to: Moznayim; Davar; Haaretz; Hadoar; Bitzaron, etc. Recip., First prize for poetry awarded by the Israel Assn. of Authors & Composers, 1957. Address: 48 Laurelcrest Ave., Downsview, Ont. M3H 2A4, Canada.

SCHNEIDER, Dorothy Fay, pen name **SCHNEIDER, Dolli,** b. 16 May 1932. Professional Writer & Executive Secretary. Education: Engl. Lit. & Creative Writing at coll. Divorced, 1 son. Positions held: Private Sec., St. Mark's Lutheran Ch., Dubuque, Iowa, 1954-56; Sec.-Clerk, Agric. Stabilization & Conservation Comm., U.S. Govt., 1961-63; Records Clerk, Ariz. State Univ., Tempe, Ariz., 1969-72; Specialized Clerk, Salt River Proj., Tempe, Ariz., 1972–. Memberships incl: Am. Soc. of Composers, Authors & Publishers; Nat. League of Am. Pen Women. Contbr. to: Quaderni di Poesia, 1968; Poetry Parade, vols. 8, 9, 10, 11, 12, 13, 14, 1968 & '69; Mustang Review, vols. 1, 2, 4, & 5, 1967, '68, '69; The Am. Poet, 1970; Prairie Poet, 1970; The Sandcutters, 1973; Encore, 1970; The Southwest Times Record, Ft. Smith, Ark.; The Times, North Little Rock; The Muse; Personal poetry, WHPLAM, Wash. D.C., etc. Producer of own weekly poetry prog. 'Poetry of the People', radio stn. KMCR-FM, Phoenix. Honours, awards incl: 3rd pl. for Percussion, Trans-Atlantic Comp., Brit. Amateur Press Assn., 1968; 1st pl., Palette, Paints, Brush & Transition, The Sandcutters, Spring, 1973. Address: 707 West Colter St., Apt. 104, Phoenix, AZ 85013, U.S.A.

SCHOEBERLEIN, Marion, b. 28 Feb. 1937. Secretary. Education: B.A., De Paul Univ. Published works: 2 books of poetry, 1962, 1963. Contrib. to: Atlantic Monthly; Good Housekeeping; Ladies Home Jrnl.; The Elmhurst Press; N.Y. Times, etc. Awarded: 2nd prize, Christian Poets Contest, 1969, etc. Address: 114 E. Columbia, Elmhurst, Ill. 60126, USA.

SCHOECK, Richard J., b. 10 Oct. 1920. Scholar; Univ. Professor; Director in Research Library. Education: M.A., and Ph.D., Princeton Univ. Married 1945; 3 children. Presently: Director of Research Activities, Folger Shakespeare Library; Director, Folger Inst. of Renaissance & 18th-c. Studies; Adjunct Prof. of English, Univ. of Maryland. Author of more than 100 articles & papers, 200 reviews, etc. Contrib. also to: Kaleidograph; Queen's Review; Dalhousie Review; Spirit; Poetry Review (London), etc. Address: Folger Shakespeare Library, 201 E. Capitol St., Washington, DC 20003, USA.

SCHOENE, Mary Patricia, pen names **MOREAU, Lucie; MOREAU, Lucette,** b. 9 Apr. 1919. Secretary. Education: B.S. in Engl. (with Fine Arts Minor), and M.A. in Engl., Washington Univ., St. Louis, Mo.; special courses in Art and Public Relations; art course at Corcoran School of Art, Washington, DC. Positions held: currently employed as secretary in a bank; from 1949-1961 engaged in public relations (director of public relations in a bank); instr. in Engl. at local college for girls. Memberships: Poetry Center of Greater St. Louis (Recording Sec., also handling publicity); Avalon Acad. of Poets; Int. Poetry Soc. Author, Move Among Stars, book of space poetry, 1974. Contbr. to: St. Louis Mag.; Poetry Center Speaking; Cyclo-Flame; Moreana, etc. Awards: 3rd Prize, Poetry Center, for verse play, 1964; Hon. Mention, NY Poetry Forum, for poem, 1971; Hon. Mention, NY Poetry Forum, for 2 poems, 1972. Address: 7451 Jenwood, St. Louis, MO 63136, USA.

SCHOLES, Olive. Teacher (retired). Taught for 41 yrs.

in Oldham, London, Paris, Coventry. Memberships (formerly): The Quill Club, 1908; The Poetry Soc. London, 1918; Oldham Poetry Soc. (Sec. until 1927); Poetry Discussion Groups based on Wireless BBC Talks (Coventry) (Leader, 1929). Published work: Poems for and about Children, 1912. Contbr. to: Nash's; Chambers's Journal; The Queen; Home Chat; Woman's Friend; Woman's Own; Woman's Companion; St. George's Mag.; The Empire Review; The Lady: Great Thoughts; The Field; Country Life; Christian Science Periodicals-Journal, Sentinel; The Golden Hour Book of Verse; Royal Leamington Spa Courier; Coventry Evening Telegraph, and many others. Address: Treblok, St. Mawes, Truro, Cornwall TR2 5BH, UK.

SCHOTT, Webster, b. 8 Sept. 1927. Business Executive. Education: B. Jrnlsm., Univ. of Mo., Columbia, 1948. Married, 3 children. Positions held: Advt. Writer, St. Louis, Mo., 1948 & Kansas City, Mo., 1949-59; Ed., Hallmark Cards, Inc., Kans. City, 1959; V.P. & Ed. in Chief, ibid, 1969; V.P. & Ptnr., April House, Inc., 1972; Lit. Ed., Focus Midwest, 1959-65. Member, Lit. Advisory Comm., Nat. Endowment for the Arts, Wash. D.C. Published works: Editor: Poetry for Pleasure, 1961; American Christmas, 1969; Imaginations, by William Carlos Williams, 1970. Contbr. to: New Republic; The Nation; LIFE; Sat. Review; Time; N.Y. Times; Wash. Post; Prairie Schooner; Milwaukee Jrnl., etc. Address: Lake Quivira, Kansas City, KS 66106, U.S.A.

SCHRADER, Dorothy Cole, b. 22 Mar. 1905. Homemaker. Married, 2 daughters. Positions held: Office Helper; Telephone Operator; Retail Saleslady. Memberships: Org., Pres. & Sec., local Writers Club; Wis. Regl. Writers' Assn.; W. Va. Poetry Soc.; Wis. Fellowship of Poets; Midwest Chaparral Writers' Grp. Contbr. to following anthols., mags: Poems Out of Wisconsin, 1951 & 63; Poems Out of Wisconsin III, 1967; Yearbook of Modern Poetry, 1972; Echoes of Faith, 1970; Prize Poems of Nat. Fed. State Poetry Socs., 1965, '66; Wis. Hist. in Poetry, book 1 1969, book 2 1970, book 3 1972; Madison Capital Times; Evansville Review; Edgerton Reporter; Sun Prairie Star; Ideals; Chaparral Midwest; Minn. Mpls. Argus; var. small poetry mags. Honours, award: 1st prize, Wis. Regl. Writers Assn., 1964; 2nd prize, Nat. Fed. State Poetry Socs., 1965; 1st prize, ibid, 1966; 3rd prize, W. Va. Poetry Soc., 1972. Address: Rte. 1, Box 249, Evansville, WI 53536, U.S.A.

SCHRAMM, Richard, b. 10 Feb. 1934. Professor of English. Education: B.Sc., 1955; M.A., Ohio Univ., 1960; Ph.D., Duke Univ., 1964. Married, 1 son. Positions held: Instr. in Maths., Capital Univ.; Instr. in Engl., Ohio Univ.; Instr. in Engl., Univ. of N.C. at Chapel Hill; Asst. Prof., Assoc. Prof., Prof. of Engl., Calif. State Univ. at Northridge; Prof. of Engl., Univ. of Utah. Published works: Rooted in Silence, 1972. Contbr. to: The New Yorker; Poetry; The Southern Review; Qtly. Review of Lit.; The Iowa Review; Shenandoah; Poetry Northwest; The Southern Poetry Review; The Mass. Review; Western Humanities Review; Antaeus; The Am. Poetry Review, etc. Address: Dept. of Engl., Univ. of Utah, Salt Lake City, UT 84112, U.S.A.

SCHRECK, Jyri Matti, b. 16 Dec. 1927. Freelance Writer & Theatreman. Education: degree of mag. phil. (M.A.), Helsinki Univ., Finland, 1951; Theatre studies in Helsinki. Married & divorced three times, 3 children. Positions held: Officer, publishing firm OTAVA, Helsinki, 1952-64; Theatre Producer, Nat. Theatre, Helsinki, 1964-68; Theatre Producer, City Theatre of Helsinki, 1968-73. Memberships: Finnish Soc. of Authors (SKL), 1959-; Soc. Eino Leino, 1959-; Soc. Aleksis Kivi, 1959-. Published works: Lumi (The Snow), 1959; Päiviä, sateita (Days, Rains), 1962; Leijan ilma vihreää (The Air of Kite is Green), 1966; Mustan perhosen aika (The Time of the Black Butterfly), 1970; Muuttopäivät (Moving Days), 1973. Contbr. to: Parnasso (Finnish lit. periodical); Log (German lit. periodical). Honours, awards: Prize,

Kordelin Fndn., 1963; Prize, City of Helsinki, 1966; Prize, Finnish Soc. of Authors, 1971. Address: Messeniuksenkatu 3 B 14, Helsinki 25, Finland.

SCHREIBER, Ron, b. 25 Jan. 1934. Teacher. Education: B.A., Wesleyan Univ., 1955; M.A. (1959), Ph.D. (1967), Columbia Univ. Positions held: Lecturer & Preceptor in Engl., Columbia Univ., 1959-65; Instr. in Engl., Rutgers Univ., Newark, 1960-61; Asst. Prof. of Engl., Univ. of Massachuootto, Boston, 1965 to present. Published works: 31 New American Poets (Editor (and intro.)), 1966; Living Space (poems), 1972. Contbr. to: Hanging Loose; New: American & Canadian Poetry; Hierophant; Poems of the People; Wormwood Review; Mainline; The Shore Review; Tide; Salt Lick; Poetry Review; Hearse; The Falcon; Quetzal; Berkeley Poets Cooperative Mag.; West Coast Review; Happiness Holding Tank; Stuffed Crocodile; Minnesota Review; Pyramid; Boston after Dark (weekly paper); Southern Poetry Review; Perspective; Out of Sight; Mississippi Review; Fag Rag; Silver; Abraxas; Some; Ab Intra; Toucan; Northeast; Sun Tan; Road Apple Review; Wind; the goodly co; Hyperion; Pebble; Measure; Gay Sunshine. Address: 15 Westwood Rd., Somerville, MA 02143, USA.

SCHROEDER, Andreas Peter, b. 26 Nov. 1946. Freelance Writer; Journalist; Editor. Education: B.A. (Comp. Lit.), Univ. of B.C., Canada; M.A. (Creative Writing), ibid. Positions held: Asst. Ed., Prism Int., 1967; Co-Fndr.-Co-Ed., Contemporary Literature in Translation, 1969-; Ed., Poetry Canada, 1971; Editl. Bd. Mbr., Canadian Fiction Mag., 1971-; Dir., British Columbia Film Co-op, 1972. Memberships: League of Canadian Poets; Canadian Writers' Union; Young Writers' of America. Published works: The Ozone Minotaur, 1969; File of Uncertainties, 1971; Universe (Concrete), 1971; The Late Man, 1972. Contbr. to: Prism Int.; Contemporary Lit. in Translation; Malahat Review; Fiddlehead Review; Mundus Artium; Arts Canada; Trace; Occident; Riverside Qtly.; Canadian Literature; Expression; The Minn. Review; New Orleans Review; Canadian Fiction Mag., & many others. Honours, awards: Canada Council Grants, 1968, (arts Bursary) 1969, (arts Bursary) 1971 & 1973; Woodward Meml. Prize for Poetry, 1970; Nat. Film Bd. Grant, 1971. Address: P.O. Box 3127, Mission City, B.C., Canada.

SCHROETER, Heinrich, b. 23 Mar. 1917. Editor. Married. Positions held: Ed., German newspapers, 1948-65; Ed., Deutsche Presseagentur, Frankfurt am Main, 1965-. Memberships: Verband Deutscher Schriftsteller; Literarische Union. Published works: Katharsis, 1973; Von Neujahr bis Silvester, 1974; Liebeslyrik, 1974. Contbr. to lyric poetry & prose to many newspapers, lit. reviews, mags., anthols. & popular sci. publs. Address: Lilienthalstr. 7, 6236 Eschborn/Ts., German Fed. Repub.

SCHUCHAT, Simon, b. 21 Jul. 1954. Student. Chairman, Midwest Conference, Internat. Metabolist Movement. Pubs: Svelte, 1971; Blue Skies, 1973; Ravioli Red, 1973; Contrib. to: Asphalt; Buffalo Stamps; Chicago; Hanging Loose; Voyages; Woodwind; Milk Quarterly; Toothpick; Toothpaste; Search for Tomorrow; Chicago Literary Review; Doones; Baloney Street; Fervent Valley; Strange Faeces; Genesis; Grasp; Suction; Telephone; Trilby. Hon. Mention, Junior Div., Scholastic Magazine, 1969. Address: c/o Schuchat, 36 Quinoy Street, Chevy Chase, Maryland 20015, USA.

SCHUCK, Marjorie Massey, b. 9 Oct. 1921. Publisher; Editor; Lecturer. Education: Acad. degree, Collegiate Schl. for Girls, Richmond, Va., 1941; Univ. of Minn., 1941-43; New Schl., N.Y.C., 1948; N.Y. Univ., 1952, 1954-55. Married 1) Ernest George Metcalfe, div., 2) Franz Schuck, dec. Positions held: V.P., Poetry Chmn., Lectr., Fla. Suncoast Writers' Confs. Corp. (sponsored by Univ. of S. Fla.), 1973-; Fndr., Owner & Pres., Valkyrie Press, Inc., Fla.; Co-Fndr., Co-Ed., Publisher, Poetry Venture, 1968-69 & Ed. & Publsr.,

1969–; Co-Ed., Publsr., The Poetry Venture Qtly. Essays, vol. 1, Nos. 1-4, 1968-69, vol. 2, Nos. 1-4, 1970-71; Cons., Trade pubs. & annual reports, etc. Memberships incl: Coord. Coun. of Literary Mags., N.Y.C.; Acad. of Am. Poets; COSMEP; Int. Platform Assn. Contbr. to var. newspapers, mags. & anthols. Ed., Poetry Ventured: Four Yrs. of PV's Best Poetry, 1972. Var. lectures, speeches & workshops before local & state grps., clubs, schls., colls. & univs., & poetry readings on radio & TV. Recip., var. hons. & awards. Address: 8245 26th Ave. North, St. Petersburg, FL 33710, U.S.A.

SCHUETTE, Margarete, b. 12 Aug. 1924. High School Counselor, and College English Teacher. Education: Grad., Harlandale HS, 1941; Assoc. in Arts, Texas Lutheran Coll., 1943; B.A. (Engl. major), Univ. of Texas, 1945; M.A. (Engl. major) Univ. of Northern Colorado, 1949; additional grad. work, Our Lady of the Lake Coll., San Antonio, Texas, 1963-65. Positions held: HS Engl. Teacher, 1945-63, Sidney Lanier HS, San Antonio, Texas; Head, Engl. Dept., 1963-67, Highlands HS, San Antonio, Texas, also Counselor; Engl. Teacher in the part-time and evening div., San Antonio Coll., 1967 to present. Memberships: American Poetry League; Texas Poetry Soc.; San Antonio Poetry Soc.; Writer's Group of American Assoc. of Univ. Women. Contbr. to: Nat. Assoc. of High School Poetry Anthol.; Nat. Poetry Anthol. by Librarian and Teachers in the Schools and Colleges; The Southern Lutheran, 1973; San Antonio Poetry Soc. Mag. Recip. sev. prizes and hon. mention, San Antonio Poetry Soc. Address: 723 Kayton Ave., San Antonio, TX 78210, USA.

SCHUFF, Karen Elizabeth, b. 1 June 1937. Housewife; Clerk; Typist; Poet. Memberships: World Poetry Soc. Intercontinental; Danae; Poetry Soc. of Mich.; NJ Poetry Soc.; Eastern Ctr., Poetry Soc. London; Acad. Am. Poets; Idaho Poets' & Writers' Guild; Am. Poets Fellowship Soc.; Am. Poetry League; Armed Forces Writers' League; United Amateur Press of Am. Published works: Barefoot Philosopher, 1968; Come, Take My Hand, 1968; Of Rhythm & Cake, 1970. Contbr. to the following anthols., jrnls., newspaper & mags: Am. Bard; Orion; Bardic Echoes; Penman; Best in Poetry; Poet; Hoosier Challenger; Major Poetry; Images; W Seneca Press, NY; Am. Poet; Archer; Boonton Times, NJ; Friendship Trails anthol.; The Guild; Kans. Kernels; Poetry Prevue; Peninsula Poet; Poetry Parade; Quoin; Encore; Prairie Poet; United Poets; Orphic Lute; Angels; Quintessence; Swordsman Review; SCTH; Jean's Jrnl.; Angel Hour; Writer's Notes & Quotes; Muse; Grass Roots; Bay Shore Breeze; Haiku Highlights; Badge of Promise Anthol.; Poetaster; Country Living Projects Mag.; Bell's Letters; Poet's Bull.; Nutmegger; Harbor Lights; The Saint; Karyn; Phylis; Poetry Parade; Pixyanna; New Jrnl.; NJ; Creative Hodgepodge; New Poetry Anthol.; These are my Jewels Anthol.; In Quietness & Confidence Anthol.; Tajas; Written Word Anthol.; Ladies' Delight Mag.; Sunrise Sunset Silhouette; Encore; Selected Poems 1967; Author/Poet; Manse of the Muses; Lit. Newsette; Focus on Poetry; Normal News, NJ; Russell Times, Ky.; Country World; Major Poets; Pixie Angel; Piggott Times, Ark.; Glendale News Press, Calif.; Am. Poetry League Bull.; Watts Star Review, Calif.; Mother & Homemaker Mag.; United Poets; Express Mag.; United Amateur Press Publ.; Inky Trails; Mod. Images; Quorum of Cats Anthol.; 68 Poets Anthol.; 1969 Prairie Poet Anthol.; APFS 1969 Anthol.; Friendship Trails; NJ Poetry Soc. Anthol.; Verdure; Poetry Pagent; Polished Pebbles Anthol.; Royal Publng. Co. Anthol.; Happy Landing Collection; New Engl. Homestead; Golden Quill Press Anthols.; Tempo; All Time Favorites Anthol.; Bouquet of Poems, Italy; Flamingo; Spring Anthol. 1970; New Voices in the Wind Anthol.; Moon Age Poets Anthol.; Cyclo Flame; Am. Evangelist & Ajayer; 1970 Poets Anthol.; Fireflower; Home Base, Canada; Mary's Scrapbook of Poetry; Robbin's Song; Valley Advertiser, Calif.; Tumblin' Weeds; From Sea to Sea in Song; Poets on Parade Anthol.; 1970 Anthol. of Poets in N Ctrl. States; Yearbook of Mod. Poetry 1971; Mod.

Haiku. Recip. of various poetry awards & hons. Address: 15310 Windemere, Southgate, Mich 48195, USA.

SCHULMAN, Grace, Poetry Editor; Assistant Professor of English. Education: B.S., Am. Univ.; M.A., N.Y. Univ.; Ph.D., ibid, 1971. Positions held: Jrnlst. for var. mags. & newspapers, –1963; Grad. Asst., N.Y. Univ.; currently Asst. Prof., Baruch Coll., CUNY; Poetry Ed., The Nation. Memberships: Poetry Soc. of Am.; Graduate English Assn. (NYU), Steering Comm. Published works: Burn Down the Icons, 1971. Ed., Ezra Pound, a Collection of Criticism, 1974. Contbr. to: Poetry; Poetry Northwest; The Nation; Antaeus; Hudson Review; Am. Poetry Review; For Now; Shenandoah; New Orleans Review; Qtly. Review of Lit. Honours, awards: Fellowships to Yaddo, MacDowell Colony, Karolyi Fndn., 1973. Address: No. 14F, One University Pl., N.Y., NY 10003, U.S.A.

SCHULTE, Rainer, b. 8 July 1937. Professor of International Literature. Education: Lit. studies in Germany, France, Spain, Italy, S.Am.; Masterclass for Piano, Darmstadt. Positions held: Dir., Comparative Lit. Prog. & Translation Workshop, Ohio Univ., 1965–; Ed.-in-Chief, Mundus Artium: A Journal of Int. Lit. & the Arts. Published works: The Suicide at the Pinao (book of poems), 1969. Contbr. to: Trace; Prism Int.; Southern Humanities Review; Ante; The Archer; Dimension; Books Abroad; Mundus Artium; Contemporary Literature in Translation; Zona Franca. Address: 34 Cross St., The Plains, OH 45780, U.S.A.

SCHULTE NORDHOLT, Jan Willem, b. 12 Sept. 1920. Professor of American History at Leiden University. Education: Gymnasium at Zwolle; studied History at Amsterdam Univ. Memberships: Maatschappj van Letterkunde; PEN. Published works: Levend Landschap, 1950; Tijd Voor Eeuwigheid, 1953; Het Eenvoudig Gezaaide, 1959; Een Lichaam Van Aarde en Licht, 1961; Het Weefsel Gods, 1965; Hymns, Latin & Greek (transl.), 1967; Contrafacten, 1974. Contbr. to: Maatstaf; Ontmoeting; Wending. Honours, awards: V.D. Hoogt Prijs, 1952; Poëzie Prijs Gemeente Amsterdam, 1962. Address: Groot Hoefijzerlaan 32A, Wassenaar, The Netherlands.

SCHULZ, Günter, b. 20 Dec. 1946. Education: Theology studies; Rumania; Linguistics & psychology studies in West Berlin. Published works: Rezensierte Gedichte, 1971. Contbr. to: Akzente; Neue Literatur (Rumania); (anthologies) Grenzgänge; Wir Kinder von Marx und Coca Cola. Address: Menzelstr. 8, 1 Berlin 41, German Fed. Repub.

SCHUMACHER, Priscilla Farrington (Mrs.), born 15th February 1911. Art Teacher; Housewife; Poet. Education: Colby Coll., Waterville, Me.; Art Schls., Boston, Mass., & Chester Springs, Pa. Positions held: Art Tchr., Local Pub. & Parochial Schls., 1933-45, 1964-69. Memberships: Chmn., Project Comm., Poetry Fellowship of Me.; Ariz. State Poetry Soc.; Fla. State Poetry Soc.; Nat. Fed. Soc. of Poets. Contbr. to: Me. Sunday Telegram; Poet (India); The Hudson Review; N.H. Profiles; Cats; Jean's Jrnl.; De Paul Lit. Mag.; Mod. Images; The Angels; Chapbooks 9, 10, & 11, Me. Writers Conf.; Prairie Poet; Swordsman Review; The Sandcutters; Am. Mosaic, etc. Recip. of various poetry awards. Address: 56 Mayflower Hill Dr., Waterville, Me. 04901, U.S.A.

SCHUMANN, Werner Otto Gustav, b. 2 Oct. 1898. Writer. Educ: Trained as Jrnlst. & Dramatic Producer; Univ. study, Theatre Faculty, Halle. Positions held: Art critic; Editor, Braunschweig & Hanover, since 1945. Memberships: P.E.N.; Founder, Verband deutscher Schriftsteller (Niedersachsen); Hon. Mbr., German Writers' Union, Lower Saxony. Published works incl: Die Tat, 1963; Ergriffenheit, 1934; Die Liebenden, Andacht & Beschwörung, 1953; Licht & Schatten, 1963; Unsterblicher Kabarett, 1948; Gärten Gassen Grotten, 1968; Niedersachsen-Porträt eines Landes, 1965; Künstler-Monographien, 1966/67. Contbr. to: Die Tat, Zurich; Frankfurter Rundschau; Die Feder;

Welt der Arbeit; Der Literat; Radio Bremen; Neue Westfälische; etc. Recip. var. hons. Address: Karl-Kraut-Strasse 6, 3 Hanover, German Federal Republic.

SCHURING, William John, b. 8 Dec. 1921. Puppeteer; Television Assistant. Education: New Schl. for Social Rsch. (Dramatic Workshop), N.Y.C. Positions held: Dir., The Glen Rock Puppeteers, N.J.; Sec., Frederick A. Praeger, Publishers, N Y C ; Sec , Frederick Fell, Publishers, N.Y.C.; Legal Sec., Leon, Weill & Mahoney, N.Y.C.; Dir., Bill Schuring's Marionettes, N.Y.C.; Sales Asst., WNEW-TV (Channel 5), N.Y.C. Memberships: The Shelley Soc., N.Y.C.; The N.Y. Poetry Forum; The Mark Twain Assn., N.Y.C. Contbr. to: Jrnl. of Religious Educ. Recip., First Prize (Caesar DeWitt Meml. Prize) in Fine Arts, Ridgewood H.S., 1941. Address: 252 West 10th St., N.Y., NY 10014, U.S.A.

SCHUYLER, James Marcus, b. 9 Nov. 1923. Fiction Writer; Poet. Educ: Bethany Coll., W.Va. Positions held: Staff Mbr., Mus. of Mod. Art, N.Y.C. Published works: Salute, 1960; May 24th or So, 1966; Freely Espousing, 1969; Alfred and Guinevere (fiction), 1958; A Nest of Ninnies (w. John Ashbery) (novel), 1969. Contbr. to: New American Poetry (anthology), 1960. Address: 49 S. Main St., Southampton, NY 11968, U.S.A.

SCHWARTZ, Barry, b. 15 Oct. 1942. Educator/Author. Education: B.E., Chem.Engrng., Pratt Inst.; M.A., Humanities, N.Y. Univ.; Grad. work, Humanities, ibid; Ph.D. cand., Union Grad. Schl., Antioch. Positions held: Planner, Arts & Humanities, UCLA Extension; Asst. Prof., Communication Arts & Skills, N.Y. Community Coll.; Instr. in Humanities, Pratt Inst. Memberships: Clover Poetry Soc.; Authors' Guild; The Humanist Ctr. Published works: Prisoners of Their Passions, 1972; The Voyeur of Our Time, 1974. Contbr. to: Discourse: a Review of the Liberal Arts; Trace; Tangent; Creative Review; Cardinal Poetry Qtly.; Original Works; Mondine Grunch; Spectrum; Poetry Parade; The Archer; Quintessence; Encore; Fireflower; Graffiti; Haiku Highlights; The Saint; Cycloflame; Poetry Newsletter; Bardic Echoes. Honours, awards: 1st Prize, Poetry Parade No. 10 & 2nd Prize, No. 9; Prattler Award, 1968. Address: Arts & Humanities, UCLA Ext., Los Angeles, CA 90024, U.S.A.

SCHWARTZ, Loretta Jean, b. 28 Sept. 1943. Poet; Freelance Writer; College Teacher. Education: B.A., Engl., Seattle Univ., 1969; M.A., Engl., Univ. of N.M., 1971; coursework completed for Ph.D. at Ind. Univ., 1972. Married, 2 daughters. Positions held: Instr. in Engl., Community Coll. of Phila., 1973–; Book Reviewer, Phila. Inquirer, 1973–; Lectr. in Engl., St. Joseph's Coll., 1974. Memberships: MLA; Phila. Poetry Ctr.; Phila. Poetry Comm.; N.Y. Poetry Forum; Women Scholars in the Mod. Langs. Published works: Set Free, (under consideration). Contbr. to: Spring Fragments, Seattle Univ. Press; Phila. Poets Anthol.; The Thin Dime Poems, Vol.1 & 2; Temple Univ. Poetry Newsletter; Atlantis Edns. Publs.; Phila. Inquirer. Address: 210 Locust St., 20B, Phila., PA 19106, U.S.A.

SCHWEBELL, Gertrude C., b. Diller, Neb., U.S.A. Writer & Translator. Educated in Germany. Married John R. Schwebell. Memberships: Recording Sec., The Pen & Brush, N.Y.; Query, N.Y.; Asia Soc.; Japan Soc., Goethe House. Published works: Ed. & Transl., Where Magic Reigns, 1957 & 73; Transl., Contemporary German Poetry, 1964, '66; Transl., New Places-Neue Orte (selected poems by William Carlos Williams, 1966; Huldigung für Mistress Bradstreet (rendered into German verse from original by John Berryman), 1967; Die Geburt Des Modernen Japan, history, Karl Rauch Verlag, 1970; Undine (adapted from the German story by F. de la Motte Fouqué, 1971. Contbr. to: Ency. of World Lit. in the 20th Century, 3 vols., 1967, 69, 70; New Standard Ency., Yearbooks, 1966,67,68,69,70,71,72. Has contbd. English & German poems to num. periodicals in the U.S.A.,

Canada, Germany & Japan & to many anthols. in U.S.A. & Germany inclng: The Fiddlehead, Canada; Accent, Poet Lore, Epos, The N.Y. Times, The Wash. Post, The Oregonian, The Hartford Courant, Atlas, The Orphic Lute, Poetry, U.S.A.; Carolinum, Göttingen & Die Horen, Hannover, Germany; Asahi Evening News, Tokyo, Japan. Short stories & articles have appeared in U.S.A. & Germany. Recip., Pen & Brush Poetry Awards, 1969, 71 & 73. Address: 549 Riverside Dr., 4-G, New York, NY 10027, U.S.A.

SCHWERNER, Armand, b. 11 May 1927. Poet. Education: B.S. & M.A., Columbia Univ. Married Doloris Holmes, 2 children. Positions held: Prof. of Engl., Staten Is. Community Coll. of the City Univ. of N.Y. Member, PEN. Published works: The Lightfall, 1963; (if personal), 1968; The Tablets, I-VIII, 1968; Seaweed, 1969; The Tablets I-XV, 1971. Rep. in many anthols. inclng: Shaking the Pumpkin, 1972; Breakthrough Fictioneers; The New Open Poetry, 1973; Love, etc., 1973; From the Belly of the Shark, 1973; America a Prophecy, a New Map of its Poetries from Origins to the Present, 1974; Asian-American Heritage, 1974. Contbr. to var. mags. inclng: The Nation; San Francisco Review; Am. Poetry Review; Beloit Poetry Review; Accent. Honours, awards: Fac. Rsch. Fellowship, SUNY, 1970 & '72, CUNY, 1971; Creative Artists Public Serv. Prog., N.Y. State Coun. on the Arts, 1973; Nat. Endowment for the Arts Creative Writing Fellowship, 1973. Address: 30 Catlin Ave., Staten Is., NY 10304, U.S.A.

SCOBIE, Stephen Arthurs Cross, b. 31 Dec. 1943. Prof. of English. Education: M.A. (with 1st cl. hons.), Univ. of St. Andrews, Scotland, 1965; Ph.D., Univ. of B.C., Canada, 1969. Born in Carnoustie Scotland, resident in Canada since 1965. Married to Sharon Maureen McHale. Position held: Asst. Prof., Univ. of Alberta, Edmonton, since 1969. Membership: League of Canadian Poets (Vice-Chairman). Published works: Babylondromat, 1967; In The Silence of the Year, 1971 (reprinted 1973); Stone Poems, 1973; The Rooms We Are (in press); The Birken Tree, 1973. Contbr. to: Quarry; Far Point; Prism International; Antigonish Review; Fiddlehead; White Pelican; Gronk; Blew Ointment, etc. Address: 13 Merryvale Cres., Sherwood Park, Alberta T8A 0N4, Canada.

SCOTT, Alexander, b. 28 Nov. 1920. Hd., Dept. of Scottish Lit. Education: M.A., Aberdeen Acad., Aberdeen Univ., 1947. Married, 2 s. Positions held: Ed., N.–E. Review, 1945-46; Co-Ed., Scots Review, 1950-51; Fndng. Ed., Saltire Review, 1954-57; Gen. Ed., The Scottish Lib., 1968–. Memberships: Univs. Comm. on Scottish Lit. (Sec.); Assn. for Scottish Lit., Studies (Mbr., Coun. & Publs. Comm.). Published works include: Prometheus 48, 1948; The Latest in Elegies, 1949; Selected Poems, 1950; Untrue Thomas, 1952; Mouth Music, 1954; Cantrips, 1968; Greek Fire, 1971. Also Author of: Still Life: William Soutar, 1958. Contbr. to the following anthols., jrnls., mags., etc: Agenda; Akros; Catalyst; Chapman; Lines Review; Scotia; Scottish Int.; Scottish Poetry; The Glasgow Herald; The Scotsman; BBC, etc. Honours, awards: 2 Festival of Britain awards, 1951; Scottish Arts Coun. Award, 1968. Address: 5 Doune Gdns., Glasgow NW, Scotland, UK.

SCOTT, Dennis Courtney, b. 16 Dec. 1939. Teacher. Education: B.A., Univ. of West Indies, 1970; Dip. in Drama in Educ., Univ. of Newcastle upon Tyne, 1973. Married, 1 son. Published works: Uncle Time, 1973. Rep. in following anthols: Focus, 1960; The Sun's Eye, 1968; Caribbean Voices, vol. II, 1970; Anthol. of W.I. Poems, 1971; Breaklight, 1971; Bite-in (stages 2, 3), 1972; W.I. Poetry, 1971; Young Commonwealth Poets, 1965. Contbr. to: Caribbean Qtly.; Sunday Gleaner; Public Opinion; Jamaica Jrnl.; London Mag. (U.K.); East India Review. Recip., Int. Poetry Forum Award (Uncle Time), 1973. Address: 14 Charlton Dr., Kingston 8, Jamaica, W.I.

SCOTT, Francis Reginald, b. 1 Aug. 1899. Poet and Professor of Law. Education: B.A., Bishop's Coll.,

Lennoxville, Quebec, Canada, 1919; Rhodes Scholar, B.A., Magdalen Coll., Oxford, U.K., 1922; B.Litt., ibid, 1923; B.C.L., McGill Univ., Montreal, 1927. Married Marian Dale, 1 son. Positions held: Called to the Bar of Quebec, 1927; Tchr., Law Fac., McGill Univ., 1928; Prof., ibid, 1934; Dean, 1961-64; Guggenheim Fellow, 1940; UN Tech. Asst. Res. Rep. to Burma, 1952. Memberships & Editorships: Co-Ed., McGill Fortnightly Review, 1925-27; The Can. Mercury, 1928; Can. Forum, 1936-39; Preview, 1942-45; Northern Review, 1945-47; Chmn., Can. Writers' Conf., 1955; League of Can. Poets. Published works: Overture, 1945; Events & Signals, 1954; The Eye of the Needle, 1957; Translations from St. Denys Garneau & Anne Hébert, 1962; Signature, 1964; Selected Poems, 1966; Trouvailles (found poems), 1967; The Dance Is One, 1973. Co-Ed., New Provinces: Poems of Several Authors, 1936; The Blasted Pine, 1957, 2nd edn., 1967. Contbr. to var. anthols., jrnls., mags. Honours, awards: Guarantors Prize, Poetry, Chicago, 1944; Lorne Pierce Medal, Royal Soc. of Canada, 1964; Molson Award, Canada Coun., 1967. Address: 451 Clarke Ave., Montreal, Canada H3Y 3C5.

SCOTT, Janis Marie, b. 17 Mar. 1939. Professor. Education: B.A., Univ. of Ark., 1969; M.A., Univ. of Miss., 1971; Ph.D., ibid, 1973. Divorced, 3 sons. Positions held: Instr. of Engl., Univ. of Miss., 1970-73; Asst. Prof. of Engl., Gordon Coll., Barnesville, Ga., 1973-. Contbr. to Images. Address: Box 436, Roberta, GA 31078, U.S.A.

SCOTT, Jean Mary, b. 14 May 1919. Widow, 3 children. Positions held: Asst. Ed., Spectrum Literary Mag. Memberships: Asst. Treas. & V.P., Fellowship of Aust. Writers, Qld.; Qld. Writers Workshop. Contbr. to Poets of Australia, 1972, '73, '74; Australian Broadcasting Commn. Friendship Book, 1970; Qld. Writers Workshop Publications; Australian Broadcasting Commn. Hospital Hour. Honours, awards: Shared Xavier Award for children's novel, 1968; Special Award, Capt. Cook Centenary Hymn, Qld. Govt. Address: 38 Aston St., Toowong, Brisbane 4066, Australia.

SCOTT, Johnie Harold, b. 8 May 1946. Essayist; Poet. Educ: Harvard Coll.; Stanford Univ. Memberships: Watts Writers Workshop, 1965. Contbr. to: Black on Black; Sequoia; Antioch Review; Negro Digest; (anthologies) From the Ashes, 1967; New Black Poetry, 1969; We Come as Liberators, 1970. Recip., Westminster Writers Workshop Award for Poetry, 1965. Address: 2000 Cooley Ave., Number 24, East Palo Alto, CA, U.S.A.

SCOTT, Margaret Helen, b. 26 Dec. 1898. Librarian. Education: B.A., Univ. of Wis., 1921; grad. work, Univ. of Calif., 2 yrs.; M.A., Univ. of Chicago, 1943. Positions held: H.S. Tchr. of Engl. & Hist., 1923-25, '26-29, '35; Employed by Am. Missionary Assn. of the United Church of Christ (Congregational) at Marion, Ala., 1 yr., Talladega Coll., Ala., 23 yrs., Tougaloo, Miss., 1 yr.; currently i/c County Histl. Room of Brewer Lib., Richland Ctr., Wis. Memberships: Wis. Regl. Writers' Assn.; Wis. Fellowship of Poets. Contbr. to: Nat. Poetry Anthol., 1960, '61, '62, '63, '64, '71; Modern Maturity; Time for Singing; Before the Shadow; The Mycophile; Trinity News; six books published by Youngs Publs.; Minneapolis Argus. Address: 220 South Ira St., Richland Ctr., WI 53581, U.S.A.

SCOTT, Mina Morris, b. 14 Nov. 1899. Teacher; Housewife. Education: Ind. State Tchrs. Coll., Adult Ext. Courses, Purdue Univ. & Ind. Univ. Memberships: Fndr. & Pres., Columbus, Ind. Poetry Club, 1944; Pres., 20 yrs., Study Dir., 25 yrs., ibid; V.P., Ind. State Fed. of Poetry Clubs, 1946; Poet Laureate, ibid, 1950; Nat. Assn. of Poetry Socs.; Past Pres., Azalia Home Study Club; Nat. League Am. Pen Women; Nat. Fed. of State Poetry Socs. Published works: Turquoise & Silver, 1940; The Silver Birch, 1950; On Silver Sandals, 1965. Contbr. to: Indpls. News; Ideals Magazine; Hoosier Farmer; Desert Mag.; Poetry Mag.; Bulletin of Nat. Assn. of Watch & Clock Collectors, etc. Recip.

many contest awards. Address: 1302 California St., Columbus, IN 47201, U.S.A.

SCOTT, Thomas McLaughlin, pen name, SCOTT, Tom, b. 6 June 1918. Writer. Education: M.A. Hons. & Ph.D., Univ. of Edinburgh, UK. Married, Heather Fretwell, 1 s., 2 d. Mbr., Soc. of Authors. Published works: (poems) Seeven Poems o Maister Francis Villon, 1953; An Ode til New Jerusalem, 1956; The Ship & Other Poems, 1963; At the Shrine o the Unkent Sodger, 1968; (prose) Dunbar: A Critical Exposition of the Poems, 1966; Fergusson: A Study of the Poems; A Critical History of Scottish Literature; (children) Tales of King Robert the Bruce, 1969; Poetry of the Scots; Scottish Folk Stories. Editor: Oxford Book of Scottish Verse (w. J. MacQueen), 1966; Late Medieval Scots Poetry, 1967; Penguin Book of Scottish Verse. Gen. Ed., Scottish Literature Series, Pergamon Press. Contbr. to the following jrnls. & newspapers: Poetry London; Poetry Quarterly; Poetry Scotland; Poetry (Chicago); New Statesman; Tribune; The Tablet; Encounter; London Mag.; Botteghe Oscure; New World Writing; Twentieth Century; Lines Review; Saltire Review; Agenda; Nine; The Scotsman; Times Lit. Supplement; Listener; Arkos; Glasgow Herald; Wind & The Rain; Poetry Review; Catalyst; Gambit, etc. Honours: Atlantic Award, 1950. Address: 59 The Promenade, Edinburgh 15, Scotland, UK.

SCOTT, Vera Evelyn, pen names, SALLY; AUSTEN, Vera, b. 2 Nov. 1908. Buyer, Dept. Store (retired). Education: HS, also specialised courses in salesmanship, etc. Married to Ray O. Scott; 1 d. Positions held: Salesgirl, Montgomery Ward, Mansfield, Ohio; Salesgirl, Maxwell's, Mansfield, Ohio; Dept. Manager, Zanes's, Mansfield, Ohio; Manager, Ross Rug; Buyer, Scattergoods. Memberships: Verse Writers Guild of Ohio; Ohio Poetry Soc.; American Pen Women; Internat. Platform Assoc.; Ohio Poetry Day Assoc.; Poet's Tape Exchange. Published works: Birth of Wings, 1965; V. and E. Seasoning, 1968. Contbr. to: (anthols.) American Poets, 1966; This Way Of Life; Farm Journal, 1971; Moon Age Poets, 1970; Badge Of Promise, 1968; Poetry Parade, 1963; Our Best To You, 1968; VWG 73, 1973, etc., (mags., etc.) Wooster Daily Record; Columbus Dispatch; Columbus Citizens Journal; Readers Digest; Poetry Preview, and many others. Recip. of various poetry awards. Address: Hathaway Rd., Rt. 3, Bellville, OH 44813, USA.

SCOVEL, Myra, b. 11 Aug. 1905. Free-lance Writer; Poet. Education: Grad., Syracuse Univ. Schl. of Nursing; Postgrad., Columbia Univ. Married, Dr. Frederick Gilman Scovel, 6 children. Positions held: Med. Missionary, China & India, 1930-59; Special Assignments Writer, Ed., Off. of Communication, United Presby. COEMAR, 1959-68; Children's Ed., Friendship Press, 1968. Memberships: former Pres., NYC Br., Nat. League Am. Pen Women; Poetry Soc. Am.; Rochester, NY Poetry Soc. Published Works: 7 books of prose; 6 juveniles; 4 books of poetry. Contributor to: Am. Weave; Caravan; Imprints Quarterly; Kaleidograph; NY Herald Tribune; Spirit; The Lyric; The Villager; Time of Singing (anthol.); Today; The Christian Century; Poet Lore; Int. Who's Who in Poetry Anthol., 1973; Diamond Anthol. Poetry Soc. of America. Recip., 2nd Prize, Biennial Contest, Nat. League of Am. Pen Women, 1970. Address: 37 Farley Dr., Stony Point, NY 10980, USA.

SCOVELL, Edith Jay. Poet. Educ: Somerville Coll., Oxford, U.K. m. Charles Elton. Published works: Shadows of Chrysanthemums, 1944; The Midsummer Meadow, 1946; The River Steamer, 1956. Contbr. to: Botteghe Oscure; Highway; Listener; London Magazine; New Statesman; Penguin New Writing; New World Writing; (anthologies) Penguin Book of Contemporary Verse, 1950; A Little Treasury of British Poetry, 1951; An Anthology of Contemporary Verse, 1953; An Anthology of Modern Verse, 1961; Faber Book of Modern Verse, 1965.

SCULLY, James, b. 23 Feb. 1937. Educator. Education: B.A., Univ. of Conn., 1959; Ph.D., ibid,

1964. Married Arlene Steeves, 2 children. Positions held: Instr., Rutgers Univ., 1963-64; Asst. Prof., later Assoc. Prof., Univ. of Conn., 1964-; Tchr., Hartford St. Acad., Spring 1969; Vis. Assoc. Prof., Univ. of Mass., Spring 1973. Published works: The Marches, 1967; co-author, Communications, 1970; Avenue of the Americas, 1971. Ed: Modern Poetics, 1965; Modern Poets on Modern Poetry, 1966. Contbr. to: Leviathan; Poetry; The New Yorker; The Far Point; The Penny Paper; The Mass. Review; Equal Time; Occam Ridge Review; Inner Tooth; The Critical Qtly., etc. Honours, awards: Lamont Poetry Award, 1967; Contributors' Prize, 1969; Jennie Taine Meml. Award; Guggenheim Fellowship, 1973-74. Address: 1000 Warrenville Rd., Mansfield Ctr., CT 06250, U.S.A.

SEAGER, Ralph William, b. 3 Nov. 1911. Teacher; Lecturer; Poet. Education: Penn Yan Acad., 1928; Univ. of Calif., Berkeley, 1950-51; Studied w. R.P.T. Coffin, Pulitzer Poet, 1954. Married, Ruth Lovejoy, 3 s. Positions held: US Post Office, 1938-68; Poet & Lectr., 1950-; Asst. Prof., Engl., Keuka Coll., Keuka Park, NY, 1960-. Memberships: Poetry Soc. of Am.; Dir., Poetry Workshops (summer), St. David's Writers' Conf.; Judson Coll. Creative Arts Conf.; Green Lake Writers' & Editors' Conf., Wis.; Cooper Hill Writer's Conf., E. Dover, Vt. Listed in sev. ref. works. Published works: (verse) Songs From a Willow Whistle, 1956; Beyond the Green Gate, 1958; Christmas Chimes in Rhyme, 1962; Cup, Flagon & Fountain, 1965; A Choice of Dreams, 1970; (prose) The Sound of an Echo, 1963. Co-author, Correspondence Course in Writing Poetry, Christian Authors' Guild. Contbr. to the following newspapers & jrnls: Sat. Evening Post; Ladies' Home Jrnl.; McCalls'; Good Housekeeping; NY Times; NY Herald Trib.; Together; Ideals; Christian Living; The Lyric; Yankee; Am. Weave; Writer's Digest; NY Engl. jrnl.; KC Star; Christian Herald; Oregonian; etc. Honours: Publishers Award for Beyond the Green Gate, 1958; Litt.D., Keuka Coll., 1970. Address: 311 Keuka St., Penn Yan, NY 14527, USA.

SEALS, William Harold, pen name **SWEET WILLIAM,** b. 23 Oct. 1932. Business Manager. Education: course in short story & poetry writing, corres. course, Univ. of Calif. at Berkeley; tech. writing course, Tech. Publs. Inst. Positions held: Mgr. of Dry Cleaners, Restaurant & Beauty Salon. Memberships: United Amateur Press; The Am. Poets Fellowship Soc. Published works: (book of poetry) Doing My Thing, 1970; (pamphlet) The World Will Never End, 1968. Contbr. to: Star Review; L.A. Sentinal; L.A. Herald Dispatch; Angel Hour; Author & Poet. Recip., 'Brotherhood & Peace Award', Angel Hour, 1969. Address: 769 E. Theodore, Banning, CA 92220, U.S.A.

SEAMONDS, Gainal Tucker, b. 4 July 1912. Free-lance Writer; Housewife;Housewife. Education: Grad., Eastern Schl. for Dental Assts., 1934; Currently, studying Engl. Lit., Douglass Coll., Rutgers Univ., New Brunswick, N.J. Married, Weldon L. Seamonds, 1939, 1 s., 1 d. Positions held: Clerk, Employees Liability Assurance Co., Boston, Mass., 1930-33; Hostess, Admitting Off., McLean Hosp., Waverly, 1934-41; Volunteer, Rsch. Lab., Mass. Eye & Ear Hosp., Boston. Memberships: Agnes Carr Writers Club, Boston; Poetry Soc., NH; Ed., The Churchlight, publ. of Belmont United Meth. Ch., 1964-70. Contributor to: The Writer; Pen; Christian Living; Cyclo-Flame; Fireflower; Vision; Hearthstone; (anthols.) Badge of Promise, 1968; Anthol. of Am. Poetry, 1970; articles, Belmont Citizen, Boston Herald & Belmont Herald. Honours, Awards: 1st Prize, adult fiction, Agnes Carr Writers Club, 1969; 1st Hon. Mention, serious poetry & 2nd Hon. Mention, humourous verse, Agnes Carr Writers Club, 1969. Address: 23 Birchview Dr., So., Piscataway, N.J. 08854, USA.

SEBASTIAN, Proceso, pen names **PELINEGRO, 'CESO',** b. 26 Jan. 1892. Lawyer. Education: AB, Coll. of Liberal Arts, 1914, & LL.B., Coll. of Law, Univ. of the Philippines, 1915. Positions held: Senator of the Philippines, 1944-47; Hd., Phil. Delegation to UNESCO Conf., & a Vice-Pres. during 1st Gen. Assembly, 1946,

'49, '50, '51; Envoy Extraordinary & Min. Plenipotentiary to Nanking, China, 1948-; Envoy Extraord., with personal rank of Ambassador, to Rome, Italy, 1949-51; Amb. to Paris, France, Brussels, Belgium, Hague, Holland, 1951-52; ibid, Djakarta, Indonesia, 1952-54; Ret. from diplomatic service as Dean of Diplomatic Corps, Indonesia, 1954; Dean, Francisco Law Coll., & Law Prof., 1955-57; Elected Councillor, Quezon City, Phil., 1959-67. Memberships: Pres., Umiloko, Assoc. of Ilokano writers & poets; United Poets Laureate Int. Published works: Isu Daytat Claveria? Ili Nakayanakak (That is Claveria, my native town), 1909; Salaknibantay Toy Dagatayo (Safeguard Our Heritage), 1943; Siak Ilokanoak (I am an Ilokano), 1949; Maudi A Pakada Ni, Dr. Jose Rizal, Rev. 1960. Honours: Numerious awards, decorations, citations from foreign govts, civic clubs & other organizations, incl. Cavaliere Magistrale, Sov. Mil. Order of Malta; Knight Cmndr., Order of Rizal; Pres. Emeritus, Phil.-Italian Assoc.; Grande Ufficiale, Order of Merit, Italy, etc. Address: 77-79 Don A. Roces Ave., Quezon City, Philippines.

SEBENTHALL, Roberta Elizabeth, pen names **KRUGER, Paul & DAVIS, Harry,** b. 6 Jan. 1917. Writer. Publications: Acquainted with a Chance of Bobcats, 1969; Voyages to the Inland Sea, 1973. Contrib. to: Western Humanities Review; Perspective; Kenyon Review; Mass. Review; Epoch; Colo. Quarterly; Beloit Journal; Human Voice; St. Andrew's Review; N.Y. Times; Poetry Northwest. Recip. of National Endowment for the Arts Discovery Award Grant, 1970. Address: 104 Thompson St., Mount Horeb, Wis. 53572, USA.

SEDAM, Malcolm, b. 17 Aug. 1921. Professor of English. Education: B.A., M.A., Ball State Univ. Positions held: 3 yrs., Fighter Pilot, USAF.; 15 yrs., Private Business; 3 yrs., Instr., Ball State Univ.; 6 yrs., Engl. Prof., Miami Univ. Memberships: Ohio Poets Assoc.; World Poetry Soc. (India). Published works: Between Wars, 1967; The Twentieth Mission (play), 1969; The Man in Motion, 1971. Contbr. to: Per Se; Dimensions; Quartet; English Journal; Forum, etc. Awards: 1962, Erwin Shoemaker Poetry Award; 1967, Indiana Sesquicentennial Poets Award. Address: 4200 University Blvd., Middletown, OH 45042, USA.

SEE, Margielea Stonestreet, pen name **MALLORY-BECK,** b. 10 Nov. 1911. Teacher; Counsellor (ret'd). Education: B.A., W.Va. Inst. of Technol., 1938; grad. studies at var. univs. Positions held: Tchr., Elem. Schl., 4 yrs., Adult Blind, 1944-72, travelling in three large counties to teach clients in their homes, preparing them for rehabilitation or for community orientation. Thirty-two years of service to Blind children, adults & their families. Memberships incl: World Poetry Soc.; Poets Tape Exchange, 1965-; W.Va. State Poetry Soc.; Md. Poet Laureate's Comm.; Nat. Poetry Day Comm.; Am. Poetry League; Composers, Authors & Artists; Co. Fndr., Poetry Day in Md.; AAUW; Ky. State Poetry Soc. Published works: Dawn Whispers, 1934-35; Noon Shouts, 1970; The Banner Floats On, 1971; Hymns to Him at Christmas, 1972; Drama In The Dark, in prep.; Mady (poetry & hist. biog, in prep.) Contbr. to: Echoes of W.Va. Poetry Soc. Anthol.; From Sea to Sea in Song; Bouquet of Poems; W.Va. Heritage Ency.; Songs of the Free State Bards; Am. Poet; Prairie Poet; Poetry Digest; United Poets; Avalon Dispatches; Scimitar & Song, etc. Recip. var. honours & awards inclng: Nat. Poetry Day Gold Medal for Md., 1970; Cert. of Merit, Centro Studi e Scambi Int., & Acad. Leonardo Da Vinci. Address: 508 Forster Ave., Cumberland, MD 21502, U.S.A.

SEESE, Ethel Thelma Gray, pen name, **SEESE, Ethel Gray,** b. 13 Sept. 1903. X-Ray Technician. Education: Grad., Meade Co. HS, Brandenburg, Ky.; X-Ray and Lab. training; Night classes, Wayne State Univ., Detroit, Michigan. Married twice; divorced twice; 4 children. Positions held: Teacher, grade school, 1923; Drs. Matrin and McNeil, 1935 & 1936; Wyandotte Gen. Hosp. 1937; Dr. Sylvester Ford, 1937-41; Bohn Brass & Aluminium Co., 1942; Detroit Dept. of Health at

Herman Keifer Hosp. and Maybury San, 1943-69. Memberships: Poetry Soc. of Michigan (sometime Vice-Pres.); Ky. State Poetry Soc.; Detroit Women Writers. Published works: Ten (anthol.) (2 editions); The Psychic Hinge, 1974. Contbr. to: Peninsula Poets; South & West; Wind; Human Voice; Anthol. of Kentucky poets, 1967, 1974; Legend; Luddington News; Approaches; Phoenix Fires; Pasque Petals. Awards from Lansing Poetry Club; Michigan State Poetry Soc., etc. Address: P.O. Box 224, Lake Ann, MI 49650, USA.

SEFERIADES, George, pen name **SEFERIS, George,** b. 29 Feb. 1900. Poet, Diplomat. Positions held: entered Greek For. Serv., 1926; Acting Consul-Gen., London, 1931-34; Consul, Albania, 1936; Hd., For. Press Serv., Athens, 1938-41; w. Free Greek Govt. in Crete, S. Africa, the Middle East & Italy, 1941-44; Prin., Chef de Cabinet, & Private Sec. of Regent Archbishop Damaskinos, 1945-46; Counsellor, Embassy, Ankara, 1948-50; Min. Counsellor, London, 1951-52; Ambassador to Lebanon & Min. to Syria, Iraq & Jordan, 1953-56; Ambassador of Greece to the Court of St. James, 1957-62. Published works: Strophi, 1931; Sterna, 1932; Mythistorema, 1935; Gymnopedia, 1936; Book of Exercises, 1940; Log Book I, 1940; Essays, 1944; Cyprus, 1953; Log Book III, 1955; Collected Poems, 1963; On The Greek Style, 1966. Translations of his work include: The King of Asine & Other Poems, 1948; Poems (transl. by Rex Warner), 1960; Seferis (in French), 1945; Poèmes (in French), 1963; Poesie (in Italian), 1963; Poesie (in German), 1962; Dikter (in Swedish), 1963. Honours & awards: Nobel Prize for Lit., 1963; Grand Officier, Order of George I & Order of Phoenix; Hon. Litt. D., Cambridge, 1960; Hon. D. Litt., Oxford, 1964.

SEGAL, Helen (Gertrude), b. 5 Sept. 1929. Shorthand-typist. Education: B.A., Univ. of the Witwatersrand; Eng. Hons., Univ. of South Africa. Married to Mark Segal; 3 sons: Steven, Martin, Robert. Contrib. to: Internat. Who's Who in Poetry Anthol., 1973; Seismograph; New S.A. Writing; New Coin; New Nation; Contrast; Wurm; UNISA English Studies; De Arte; Ophir; Purple Renoster, etc. Address: 7 Dunbar St., Yeoville, Johannesburg, S. Africa.

SEGUN, Mabel. Editor; Freelance Broadcaster. Educ: Univ. Coll., Ibadan, Nigeria. Positions held: Ed., Hansard, Western Nigeria Parliament; Ed., Modern Woman, Lagos; Freelance Broadcaster & Journalist. Published works: My Father's Daughter (novel), 1965. Contbr. to: Black Orpheus; New Voices of the Commonwealth (anthology), 1968.

SEIDEL, Frederick, b. 19 Feb. 1936. Writer. Education: A.B., Harvard Coll., 1957. Positions held: Paris Ed., The Paris Review; Lectr. in Engl., Rutgers Univ. Published works: Final Solutions, 1963. Contbr. to: Atlantic Monthly; Evergreen Review; Hudson Review; The Listener; The N.Y. Review of Books; The Paris Review; Partisan Review; var. anthols. Recip., Nat. Coun. of the Arts Award, 1965. Address: Random House, 201 E. 50th St., N.Y., NY, U.S.A.

SEIDMAN, Hugh, b. 1 Aug. 1940. Poet, Teacher. Education: B.S., Polytechnic Inst. of Brooklyn; M.S., Univ. of Minnesota; M.F.A., Columbia Univ. Positions held: Visiting poet, Branford Coll. of Yale Univ. (fall term 1971, spring term, 1973); Poet-in-residence, City Univ. of N.Y. (City Coll.), (spring term 1972 to present). Member: American P.E.N. Pubs. Collecting Evidence, 1970; Blood Lord, 1974. Contrib. to: Atlantic; Columbia Review; Chelsea; Harper's; Minnesota Review; Nation; New American Review; N.Y. Quarterly; Poetry; Seneca Review; Yale Literary Magazine; 100 American Poems, etc. Awards include: Yale Series of Younger Poets Prize, 1969; Poetry grant, Nat. Endowment For the Arts, 1970; Poetry grant, N.Y. State Council On The Arts, 1971; Nat. Endowment for the Arts Creative Writing Fellowship, 1972-73. Address: 463 West St., New York, NY 10014, USA.

SEIFERT, Jaroslav, b. 23 Sept. 1901. Journalist; Poet. Education: Primary & Secondary Schl., Prague, Czechoslovakia. Memberships: Pres., Union of Czech. Writers, 1968-69. Published works: City in Tears, 1921; Nothing but Love, 1923; On the Waves TSF, 1925; Nightingale sings wrong, 1926; Stars above the Garden of Paradise, 1929; Post Pigeon, 1929; Apple from the Lap, 1933; Hands of Venus, 1936; Song to the Rotary Press, 1936; Farewell Spring, 1937; Eight Days, 1937; Autumn in Bohemia, 1937; Switch out the Lights, 1938; Bozena Necová's Fan, 1940; Pantomimes About Love, 1940; Hand & Flame, 1943; Bridge of Stone, 1944; Helmet full of Earth, 1945; Nine Rondeaux, 1945; Mozart in Prague, 1946; Skirt of Angels, 1947; Until it does not rain on our Coffin, 1948; A Poor Painter went to the World, 1949; Greeting to Frantisek Halas, 1949; Song about Viktorka, 1950; The Mother, 1954; The Boy & the Stars, 1956; Concert on the Island, 1965; Halley's Comet, 1967; The Casting of the Bells, 1967; The Pest's Column, in press. Contbr. to: Red Right; The Devetsil; Reflektor; Nová scéna; Pestré kvety; Rannì noviny; Národnì práce; Práce; Kytice; Tvorba; Avantgarda; Host; Pasmo; Red; Plán; Odeon; Kvart; Rozhledy po literature; Lidové noviny, etc. Honours: State Prize, 1936, Poet of the Nation, 1966. Address: U Ladronky 23, Prague 6, Brevnov, Czechoslovakia.

SELBY, Bernard Allen, Jr., pen names (for prose writings) **WARDD, Robert & WADD, Roberta,** b. 21 Feb. 1935. Clinical Chemist. Education: B.Sc., Suffolk Univ., Boston, Mass., 1963; grad. work at var. univs. Positions held: w. Thiokol Chemical Corp., Elkton, Md., 1958-59; Engrng. Techn., Brown Univ., Providence, R.I., 1963-64; Toxicologist, Ind. Univ., Indpls., Ind., 1964-66; Chemist, City of Philadelphia, Pa., 1966-69; Registered Medical Chemist (ASCP), Bryn Mawr Hosp., Pa., 1969–. Memberships: R.I. Writers Guild; R.I. Writers' Acad.; Penn Laurel Poets, Phila.; Les Amis de la Poesie Française, P.Q., Canada. Published works: Life, Death & Other Considerations, 1964; Things – Natural, Unnatural & Otherwise, 1968; Thoughts, Dreams & Other Images, 1969; And I Shall Live Forever, 1972; Shadows, 1975. Contbr. to: Nat. Anthol. of Coll. Poetry, 1960 & '61; The Mark, 1963; currently an Ed., Intellectualist. Has given var. poetry readings in Conn., R.I., New Brunswick, Quebec & Pa. Honours, awards: Youth Hope of the Yr. Award, R.I. Writers Guild, 1964 & Clifford M. Eddy Meml. Award, 1969; Scholarship Award to attend Phila. Writers Conf., Penn Laurel Poets, 1972; Plaque for transl., Les Amis de la Poesie Française, 1972. Address: 108 Charles Dr. (M-1), Bryn Mawr, PA 19010, U.S.A.

SELJOUK, Mehdi Ali, b. 12 July 1935. Poet; Fiction & Non-Fiction Writer, Explorer. Education: M.A., LL.B., plus dips. in Comp. Religion, Social Philosophy, Theol., History & Jrnlsm. Activities: Explorations in Western Himalayas; Language studies & explorations in jungles of Asia, Central & S America; US State Dept. & Fulbright Fellow; Asia Fndn. Travelling Grant; Philosophy Fellowship; Macdowell Assoc. Fellow Huntington Hartford Fndn. Fellow; Fellow, Yaddo Artists & Writers Colony. Fellow & Mbr., of following: Royal Soc. of Arts, London, UK; Royal Asiatic Soc., London; Royal Geog. Soc., London; Royal Commonwealth Soc., London; elected Mbr., Royal Central Asian Soc., London; Fndr., Acad. Am. Poets, NY; Poetry Soc. of Am. Published works: MY Goddess: An Epic; Corpses; Gloria Mundi; Pleasures of Valhalla; Rendezvous With God. Contbr. to sev. jrnls. Honours: Karachi Univ. Dept. of English Gold Medal; Pres. of Pakistan Special Prize for Poetry; UPLI Gold Medal awarded by Pres. Marcos of Philippines; Gold Medal, Int. Studies Ctr., Rome, Italy. Address: PO Box 665, Hollywood, Calif. 90028, USA.

SELLIN, Eric, b. 7 Nov. 1933. Professor. Education: Univ. of Pennsylvania – Romance Languages: B.A. (1955); M.A. (1958), Ph.D. (1965). Positions held: Asst. Instr. of French, Univ. of Pennsylvania, 1955-60; Lecteur in American Lit., Univ. of Bordeaux, 1956-57; Instr. in French, Clark Univ., 1958-59; Lecturer in Creative Writing, Dept. of Engl., Univ. of Pennsylvania,

1960-62; Instructor/Prof. of French, Temple Univ., 1962-; Lecturer, American Lit., Univ. of Algiers, 1968-69. (Chairman, Dept. of French & Italian, 1970-73); (Senior Fellow, Nat. Endowment for the Humanities, 1973-74). Published works: Night Voyage, 1964; Trees at First Light and Other Poems, 1973; Borne kilométrique, 1973; Tanker Poems, 1973. Contbr. to: New World Writing; NY Times; Journal des Poètes; Cahiers du Sud; BLM; Chelsea, Massachusetts Review; The Literary Review; Solstice; Cape Rock Journal, and some fifty others. Awards: Borestone Mountain Poetry Awards, 1954; Cape Rock Journal Annual Prize Poet, 1971. Address: 312 Kent Rd., Bala-Cynwyd, PA 19004, USA.

SELMAN, Elsie E., pen name **TAYLOR, Selman,** b. 5 June 1919. Bookshop Manageress. Married, 2 sons. Positions held: Civil Servant (Clerical Officer); Bookshop Manageress at Bristol Polytechnic. Memberships: Past Mbr., St. Augustine's Lit. & Debating Soc.; West Country Writers' Assn. Published works: (detective novels) The Marshmead Murders, 1969; Murder Grows Roots, 1970; currently compiling a book of children's poems. Contbr. to: Pulse; She; The Lady; New Christian; The Sign; Church News; Contact; Portishead Post; Bristol Evening Post. Address: 1 Bayham Rd., Knowle, Bristol BS4 2EA, U.K.

SELVINSKY, Ilya Lvovich, b. 1899. Poet; Dramatist. Education: Moscow Univ. Positions held: Docker; Fisherman; Wkr., Canning Factory; Actor; Swimming & Wrestling Instr.; Dir., Theatre Section, Eupatoria Revolutionary Comm.; Envoy for fur exports, Kirgizia, 1932; Mbr. of D.Y. Schmidt's Polar expedition in ice-breaker 'Chelyuskin', 1933-34; Battalion Commissar, & subsequently Lieut.-Col., Crimean front, Caucasian front, 2nd Baltic front, 1941-45; Tchr., Lit. Inst., 1936-62. Published works: (poetry) Rekordy (Records); Tikhookeanskiye Stikhi (Pacific Poems); Krym-Kavkaz-Kuban (Crimea-Caucasus-Kuban); O Vremeni, O Sudbakh (Time and Destiny); (plays) Komandarm 2; Pao-Pao; Umka–Bely Medved (Umka the White Bear); Rytsar Ioann (John the Knight); Orla na Pleche Nosyashchi (The Man With An Eagle On His Shoulder); Chelovyek Svyshe Svoyei Sudby (A Man Greater Than His Destiny); etc. Honours: Order of the Patriotic War; Order of the Red Star; Order of the Red Banner of Labour. Address: c/o Union of Soviet Writers, Vorovsky Street 52, Moscow, USSR.

SEN, Bubli(Dipali), b. 9 Apr. 1949. Marketing Executive. Education: Loreto House, Calcutta; Presidency Coll., Calcutta, B.A., Economics; M.B.A., Indian Inst. of Management, Calcutta (1972). Positions held: 1971, Summer, Trainee in Personnel Dept. of Rallis India Limited, Bombay; Management Trainee, G.E.C. of India Limited from July, 1972, and currently undertaking research (marketing research) in Bombay, with Lintas India Limited. Membership: Writers Workshop, Calcutta. Contbr. to: Modern Indian Poetry in English: an Anthology, 1969; The Miscellany (Writers Workshop); Journal of the Ladies' Study Circle. Address: 24 Satchidananda Chambers, 7 Jawarlal Nehru Rd., Calcutta 13, India.

SEN, Pradip, b. 9 Sept. 1926. Business Executive. Education: Calcutta Univ., India. Married, 2 sons, 1 daughter. Positions held: Dir., Mackinnon MacKenzie & Co. Ltd. (a subsid. of the P & O Grp., London, Shipping), Bombay. Memberships: Fndr. Mbr., Writers' Workshop, Calcutta; PEN, India. Published works: And Then The Sun, book of poems, 1960, 2nd edn. w. additional poems, 1968. Contbr. to: Modern Indo-Anglian Poetry, an anthol., 1959; An Anthol. of C'wealth Verse, 1963; New Voices of the C'wealth, 1968; C'wealth Poems of Today, 1967; Illustrated Weekly of India; Writers Workshop Miscellany, etc. Address: 43 Hill Park, Pawai Rd., Malabar Hill, Bombay 6, India.

SEN, Shukdeb, b. 7 Sept. 1943. Biologist; Educator. Education: B.Sc. (Hons.), Calcutta Univ., 1965; M.Sc. (Botany), 1967; M.S. (Biol.), Atlanta Univ., 1969; Ph.D.,

ibid, 1975. Married, 1 son. Positions held: Ed., Kalantak, 1967 & Spectrum, 1969-70; Asst. Prof. of Biol., Friendship Coll., Rock Hill, S.C., 1969-73. Memberships: World Poetry Soc. Intercontinental; Jagari; Fndr. Mbr., Kalantak. Ed. of SANKALAN – A Coll. of short stories in Bengali written by the late Bhudeb Sen, 1967. Contbr. to: Poet; Sunspots; Jagari; Kalantak; Ashabari; Spectrum; Presidency Coll. annual mag., etc. Address: Biol. Dept., Atlanta Univ., Atlanta, GA 30314, U.S.A.

SENGHOR, (President) Leopold Sedar, b. 9 Oct. 1906. President of Senegal Republic. Educ: Lycée de Dakar, Senegal; Lycée Louis le Grand, Paris, France; Paris Univ. Positions held: Tchr., Descartes Lycée, Tours, 1935-44; Tchr., Lycée Marcelin Berthelot, Paris, 1944-48; Mbr., Constituent Assemblies, 1945-46; Dpty. from Senegal to Nat. Assembly, France, 1946-58; Prof., Ecole Nat. de la France d'Outre-Mer, 1948-58; Sec. of State, Présidence du Conseil, 1955-56; Mbr., Consultative Assembly, Coun. of Europe; Pres., Fed. Assembly, Mali Fedn. of Senegal & Sudan, 1959-60; Pres., Senegal Rep., 1960–; Minister of Defence, 1968–. Published works: Langage et poésie négro-africaine, 1954; L'Apport de la poésie nègre, 1953; Esthéthique négro-africain, 1956; (poems) Chants d'ombres, 1945; Hosties noires, 1948; Chants pour Naëtt, 1949; Ethiopiques, 1956; Nocturnes, 1961. Honours, awards: Dag Hammarskjöld Prize, 1965; Peace Prize of German Book Trade. Address: Office of the President, Dakar, Senegal, West Africa.

SENNA, Carl, b. 13 Apr. 1944. Writer; Editor. Education: Boston Univ. Coll. of Liberal Arts, 1962-67; Columbia Univ. Grad. Schl. of the Arts, 1967-69. Positions held: Lectr., Tufts Univ., Medford, Mass., 1968-69; Writer-in-Res., Northeastern Univ., Boston 1969; Lectr., Univ. of Mass., Boston, 1969-73. Published works: Parachute Shop Blues & Other Poems of New Orleans, 1972; The Fallacy of I.Q, Ed., 1973. Contbr. to: Ploughshares; Boston Phoenix. Address: Suite 801, 755 Boylston St., Boston, MA 02116, U.S.A.

SENNETT, Gerti H., b. 28 Feb. 1919. Accountant. Education: Univ. of Wis. Ext.; Univ. of Calif. at L.A.; Vocational & Tech. Inst. Married Robert I. Sennett, 1 daughter, 1 stepson. Positions held: Co-Ptnr. in pvte. prac., tax. & acctng. firm; Financial Dir., Menominee Co. Community Action Prog.; Payroll Co-ordinator for lumber & forest products firm; Acctng. Dept. of TV & motion picture Producers; Owner & Operator of restaurant/Credit & collection cos. Memberships: Nat. Fed. of State Poetry Socs.; Wis. Fellowship of Poets; Wis. Regl. Writers Inc.; Shawano Area Writers Chairperson, 1972-73, '74; Editor, 1974. Corres., Wis. Regl. Writer qtly. mag. Contbr. to: New Poetry Out of Wisconsin, 1969; Shawano Area Writers Anthols., 1968, '69, '71, '74; Native Lumber-Friends of Art, 1974; Hawk & Whippoorwill, 1973; Poet, 1973; Shawano Evening Ldr., etc. Recip. var. poetry awards & hons. inclng: 1st pl., Wis. Fellowship of Poets Trophy Contest, 1971; 1st, Contest, Friends of Art, Neville Mus., 1973. Address: Wolfedge, Star Rte., Keshena, WI 54135, U.S.A.

SEPEHRI, Sohrab, b. 1928. Painter; Poet. Education: Grad., Fac. of Fine Arts, Tehran, 1953; Grad., Lithography, Fine Arts Schl., Paris; Studied wood carving in Japan. Group Exhibitions: Venice Biennial & Tehran Biennial, 1960; Iran Painters Work Exhib., Israel; Sao Paulo World Biennial; Iran Art Exhib., Le Havre; Grp. Exhib. in Burgese Gall., 1965. One man exhib. at Burgese Gall. Published works: (colls. of poems) The Sun Earthquake; Green Volume. Address: c/o Press Attache, Imperial Iranian Embassy, 16 Princes Gate, London S.W.7, U.K.

SERGEANT, Howard, b. 6 May 1914. Senior Lecturer & Department Head. Education: The Coll. of Commerce, Hull, U.K. Married Jean Crabtree. Positions held: Company Sec., Chief Acct., Jordan & Sons Ltd., 1949-54; Company Sec., Chief Acct., E. Austin & Sons (London) Ltd., 1954-63; Lectr.,

Norwood Tech. Coll., 1963-65; Sr. Lectr./Dpty. Hd., Wandsworth Tech. Coll., 1965-68; Sr. Lectr., Brooklands Tech. Coll., 1969-72; Hd., Dept. of Mgmt., ibid, 1972-. Memberships: Int. PEN; The English Assn.; The Soc. of Authors; The Poetry Soc.; Universities' Poetry. Published works: (poetry) The Leavening Air, 1946; The Headlands, 1954; (criticism) The Cumberland Wordsworth, 1950; Tradition in the Making of Modern Poetry, 1952; A Critical Survey of South African Poetry, 1958; has also compiled selections from the poetry of Milton, 1953 & from Milton & Wordsworth, 1970. Ed. of many anthols. inclng: Commonwealth Poems of Today, 1967; New Voices of the Commonwealth, 1968; Poems from Hospital, 1968; Poetry from Africa, 1968; Poetry from Australia, 1969; Poetry from India, 1970; Evans Book of Children's Verse, 1972; African Voices, 1973; Ed. for British C'wealth on Bd. of Borestone Poetry Awards & Fndr./Ed., Outposts. Contbr. to many jrnls., mags., reviews & newspapers. Address: 72 Burwood Rd., Walton-on-Thames, Surrey, U.K.

SESKIN, Jane Rosenblum, b. 8 May 1944. Freelance Writer; Educational Consultant. Education: B.A., N.Y. Univ.; M.A., Bank St. Coll. of Educ. Positions held: Elem. Schl. Tchr., 7 yrs.; Educl. Cons.; Instr., N.Y. Univ., Lang. Arts & Reading; Freelance Writer & Novelist; Book Reviewer. Memberships: N.Y. Poetry Forum; Philadelphia's Writers Conf. Published works: Living Single, book, 1974; Getting It All Together, book, 1974. Contbr. to: Creative Review; Best In Poetry; Chicago Daily News. Recip., Clover Poetry Award, 1973. Address: 60 E. 12th St., N.Y., NY 10003, U.S.A.

SETTERBERG, Ruth Elizabeth. Educator. Education: B.A., Macalester Coll., St. Paul, Minn.; M.A., Univ. of Minn., Mpls.; Ph.D., Boston Univ., Mass.; Tchrs. Cert, Am. Acad. of Dramatic Art, N.Y.; Adv. study, Harvard and Columbia. Positions held: Hd. of Engl. Dept. & Instr. of Engl. Lit., Little Falls H.S., Minn.; Dir. of Drama & Instr. in Engl. Lit., Mpls. Pub. Schls.; Asst. Prof. in Engl. Lit., Boston Univ., Mass. Memberships: Poetry Soc. of Am.; Pres., Boston Br., Nat. League of Am. Pen Women; V.P., Boston Manuscript Club; Pres., Engl. Div., Minn. Educ. Assn.; Coll. Engl. Assn.; Coll. Sect. of the Nat. Coun. of Tchrs. of Engl.; Coll. Engl. Assn. of New England; Pi Phi Epsilon; Delta Kappa Gamma. Contbr. to: Poet Lore; The Univ. Review; The Univ. of Kans. City Review; Voices; The Oregonian; Kaleidograph; Scimitar & Song; Hartford Daily Times; The Muse; Bardic Echoes; The Pen Woman; Special Song; Modern Images; Versecraft, etc. Honours, awards: 2nd prize in Annual Award for Subjective Poetry, Poet Lore, 1966; 1st prize, Boston Br. of Nat. League of Am. Pen Women, 1969; Prize, Manuscript Club of Boston, 1972; Cert. of Merit, Pa. Poetry Soc., 1974. Address: 770 Boylston St., Boston, MA 02199, U.S.A.

SETTERLIND, Bo Alf Ingemar, b. 24 Aug. 1923. Poet. Education: Matric. exam, Vasteras, 1944. Memberships: Swedish PEN Club; Swedish Union of Authors. Published works: Moon Cradle, 1948; Journey within Yourself, 1949; Letters, 1950; The Heaven of Poets, 1950; The Heart & the Traffic, 1951; Poems from San Michele, 1954; The Poet & the Society, 1954; The Girl & the Hind, 1955; Hovering Over the Panic, 1956; I Have Two Souls, 1957; Via The Emptiness, 1958; The Transfigured Flower, 1959; A Few Words to Embroider on Silk, 1961; It Becomes Lighter, 1961; Stranger on the Beach, 1964; The Moment of Your Falling, 1965; Report on the Wax Works Show of Madame Tussaud, 1967; The Wisdom of Nefertiti, 1968; The Picture of the Denier, 1969; Mary & the Child, 1970; Eyes of Ash, 1970; Poems from Gotland, 1971; Behold the Man, 1971; Heaven Has Landed, 1971; The Land in the Highest, 1972; Poems, 1947-52, 1954; My Tongue, 1963; From Night to Nightingale, Love Poems, 1967; The Cross & the Star, Poems of Confession, 1969; There is a Joy, 1971; Poet in Peru, 1973; Poems, 1948-72, 1973; The Heart-Robbery & other Songs, 1973; On This Speck of Dust, 1974. Contbr. to sev. publs. Recip. num. awards.

Address: Ekegarden 152 00, Strangnas, Sweden.

SETTLE, Patricia Claire Peters, pen names **PETERS, Patricia & SETTLE, Claire,** b. 14 Jan. 1944. Systems Analyst; Teacher. Education: B.A., Skidmore Coll., 1965; M.F.A., Univ. of N.C., 1968; additional studies at Columbia Univ., N.Y. Univ. & The New Schl. Div., 1 child. Positions held: Hematology Techn., 1958-65; Tchng. Asst., The Univ. of N.C., 1966-68; Instr., Western Carolina Univ., 1968-69; Taught poetry writing in Title III Prog. in Appalachia, summer, 1968; currently Systems Analyst for Garan, Inc. Member, Poetry Soc. of Am. Completed Ms., Poems for Joanna & John. Contbr. to: The Sewanee Review; So. Poetry Review; The Greensboro Review; Greensboro Reader; Brown Bag; Intro No. 1. Honours, awards: Am. Acad. of Poets prize, 1967 & hon. mentions, 1965 & '68. Address: 55 Morton St., Apt. 4L, N.Y., NY 10014, U.S.A.

SEWELL, Margaret Elizabeth, b. 9 Mar. 1919. University Professor of English. Education: B.A., Cambridge Univ., 1942; M.A., ibid, 1945; Ph.D., 1949. Positions held: Vis. Prof. of Engl., Fordham Univ., 1954-55 & '58-59; Vis. Mershon Lectr., Ohio State Univ., 1958; Vis. Prof. of Engl., Bennett Coll., Greensboro, N.C., 1960-61 & Calif. State Coll. at Los Angeles, 1962, '66; Prof. of Engl., Tougaloo Coll., Miss., 1963-64 & Fordham Univ., 1967-69; Disting. Vis. Prof. of Poetry, Ctrl. Wash. State Coll., Ellensburg, Wash., 1970; Prof. of Engl., Hunter Coll., CUNY, 1971-. Member PEN Int. Published works: Poems 1947-61, 1963; Signs & Cities, 1968. Contbr. to: Aylesford Review; Cambridge Review; Tablet; Pylon; Thought; Commonweal; Antigonish Review. Address: c/o Harold Ober Assoc. Inc., 40 E. 49 St., N.Y., NY 10017, U.S.A.

SEXTON, Anne, b. 9 Nov. 1928. Poet. Lectr., Creative Writing, Boston Univ. Fellow, Royal Soc. of Lit. Published works: To Bedlam & Part Way Back, 1960; All My Pretty Ones, 1962; Live or Die, 1966; Love Poems, 1969; Selected Poems, 1964; transformations. Contbr. to: The Hudson Review; New Yorker; Harper's; Yale Review; Hudson Review; Sat. Review; Poetry; Sewanee Review; Encounter; Partisan Review; Poetry USA; Critical Quarterly, UK. Honours, Awards: Radcliffe Inst. for Creative Writing, 1961-63; Am. Acad. Arts & Letters Travelling Fellowship, 1963-64; Ford Fndn. Resident Poet for Plays, 1965; Lit. Mag. Travel Award, 1966; Pulitzer Prize, 1967; Phi Beta Kappa, Harvard, 1968; Redcliffe Guggenheim Grant, 1969-70; D.Litt., Tufts Univ., 1970; Regis Coll., 1971. Address: 14 Black Oak Rd., Weston, Mass. 02193, USA.

SEYMOUR, A(rthur) J(ames), b. 12 Jan. 1914. Public Relations. Education: Queen's Coll., Georgetown, Guyana. Married; 3 s., 3 d. Positions held: 1954, Chief Information Officer, Govt. of British Guiana; 1962, Development Officer (Information & Cultural Collaboration), Caribbean Organisation; 1965, Community Relations Officer, Demerara Bauxite Co.; 1973, Cultural Relations Adviser, Ministry of Information & Culture, Guyana. Membership: British Guiana Centre of PEN (Pres., 1960). Published works: Verse, 1937; More Poems, 1940; Over Guiana Clouds, 1944; Sun's in my blood, 1945; The Guyana Book, 1948; Leaves from the Trees, 1951; Selected Poems, 1965; Monologue, 1968; Patterns, 1970; Black Song, 1971; I, Anancy, 1971; Passport, 1972; Song to Man, 1973. Editor, Kykoveral, 1945-61. Contbr. to: Bim; Savacou, etc. Awarded the Golden Arrow of Achievement by the Republic of Guyana (A.A.) for services to literature and the arts, 1970. Address: 23 North Rd., Bourda, Georgetown, Guyana.

SEYMOUR, Rosemary Yolande Levinge, b. 16 June 1919. Teacher. Education: M.A. (Auckland), New Zealand Univ. Positions held: Jr. Asst., Engl. Dept., Auckland Univ., New Zealand; Tutor, Sociology Dept., Waikato Univ. Published works: The Man From Mars, 1964. Address: 37 Bretton Terrace, Hillcrest, Hamilton, New Zealand.

SEYMOUR, William Kean, b. 27 Sept. 1887. Author; Poet; Journalist; Lecturer. Education: King's Coll., London, 1912-14. Memberships: VP Poetry Soc. of England, 1947-; Mbr. Gen. Council, ibid, 1948-69; Chmn., 1961-64; Pres., Guildford Ctr., 1961-; Hon. Treas., PEN Engl. Ctr., 1932-37; Nat. Council, Nat. Book League, 1936-68; Comm., The West Country Writers' Assoc., 1965-; Lib. & Art Comm., Nat. Liberal Club, London, 1965-; Fellow, Royal Soc. of Lit. Published works: The Street of Dreams, 1914; To Verhaeren: 23 Poems, 1917; Swords & Flutes, 1919; Caesar Remembers, 1929; Time Stands, 1935; Collected Poems, 1946; Burns in to English, 1954; The First Childermas (verse-play), 1959; (parodies) A Jackdaw in Georgia, 1925; Parrot Pie, 1927; Chinese Crackers, 1938; (criticism) Jonathan Swift: The Enigma of a Genius, 1967. Co-ed: The Pattern of Poetry, 1963; Happy Christmas, 1969. Ed: A Miscellany of Poetry, 1919; Ditto, 1920-22. Contbr. to: Daily News; Daily Herald; Outposts; John O'London's; Mercury; Observer; New Age; To-Day; Poetry Review; Contemp. Review; Sunday Times; Good Housekeeping; Country Life; The Sackbut; Pall Mall Mag.; GK's Weekly; NY Times; The Scotsman; Decachord; Week–End Review; Wheels; Shorter Lyrics; Best Poems Series; Treasury of Living Poets, & other jrnls. & anthols. in UK, US, & Canada. Honours: Philippines Pres. Gold Medal for Poetry as Distinguished Anglo-Irish Poet, 1968; Elected Dr. of Lit. (hon. causa), Free Univ. of Asia, Karachi, 1968. Address: White Cottage, Old Alresford, Hants., UK.

SEYMOUR-SMITH, Martin, b. 24 Apr. 1928. Writer. Education: Highgate School; St. Edmund Hall, Oxford, M.A. Positions held: Teacher, 1951-59; Freelance writer and critic, 1959-; Poetry Editor, Truth, 1955-57; Poetry Editor, The Scotsman, 1963-67. Membership: Writers' Action Group; Authors' Soc. Published works: Poems (with Rex Taylor, Terence Hards), 1952; Fantasy Press Pamphlet No.10, 1953; All Devils Fading, 1954; Tea With Miss Stockport, 1963; Reminiscences of Norma, 1971; Guide to World Literature; Poets Through Their Letters, etc. Contbr. to: Daily Telegraph; Sunday Telegraph; Encounter; Listener; Spectator; New Statesman; Times Lit. Supp.; Truth; New Yorker; Financial Times; Observer; Time and Tide; Listen; Birmingham Post; Scotsman; Encyclopaedia of World Literature; Cassell's Encyclopaedia of World Literature; Midcentury Authors; Contemporary Poets of the English Language, etc. Address: 36 Holliers Hill, Bexhill-on-Sea, Sussex TN40 2DD, UK.

SHABTAI, Aharon, b. 11 Apr. 1939. University Tutor. Education: Grad., Greek & Philos., Jerusalem, 1966; Sorbonne, Paris, France, 2 yrs. Married, 1 daughter. Positions held: Tutor, Greek Lit., Hebrew Univ., Jerusalem, 1971-. Mbr., Hebrew Writers Assn. in Israel. Published works: Gabriel Preil, a selection of his poems & a study of his poetry, 1965; Hadar Hamorim (The Teachers' Room), poems in Hebrew, 1966; Kibbutz, poems in Hebrew, 1973; currently writing a cycle of poems: The Domestic Poem. Contbr. to: Haaretz Lit. Supplement; Syman Kria Quarterly; Ahshav Quarterly. Address: 7 Yishay St., Abu-Tor, Jerusalem, Israel.

SHAFER, Elizabeth Jane, b. 18 Jan. 1924. Writer. Education: Colo. Coll., 1946. Positions held: Advertising Staff, Colo. Springs News, 1944; Continuity Writer, KVOR, 1944-46; Staff Writer, Suhre & Assocs., 1955-57; Colo. Ed., Western Advertising, LA, 1958-59; Colo. Springs Reporter, Fairchild Publs., NYC, 1959-70; Reporter, Relig-News Serv., 1961; & USIA, Wash. DC, 1970-. Memberships: Pres., Pikes Peaks Br., Nat. League Am. Pen Women, 1958-60; Sec., ibid., 1954-58; Mkt. Chmn., 1961-; Colo. Authors League; Dir., Colo. Springs Workshop, Poetry Soc. of Colo., 1966-; Pres., Colo. Springs Poetry Fellowship, 1960-62. Mbr., Edit. Comm., Skylines, 1959-63. Contbr. to the following anthols., jrnls. & newspapers: McCall's; CS Monitor; Carleton Miscellany; NM Quarterly; Poet Lore; Am. Bard; Improvement Era; Christian; Westways; Denver Post; In Wyo.; Capper's Weekly; Vision; Children's Friend; HiCall; Encore;

Alaska Guide; Relig. Arts Festival Best Poems, 1963; Sharon Creative Arts Festival Poets of 1966 & '67; New; War Cry; Ariz. Highways; Caravel; Snowy Egret; Pen Woman; Venture; Understanding; Flower & Feather; Kan. City Poetry Mag.; Portland Oregonian; Pa. Prize Poets, 1963; Skylines, 1959-; Golden Harvest Anthol., 1971; Int. Who's Who in Poetry Anthol., 1973, etc. Honours, Awards: Pan Am. Poetry Prize, 1960; Lee-Huff Pegasus Prize, Colo. Springs Poetry Fellowship, 1962; Sylvia Pezoldt Nat. Mem. Award, Shakespearean Sonnet, 1966 & 2nd Prize, Chicago Sonnet Contest, 1967; Nat. League Am. Pen Women Sonnet Award, 1968; 1st Prize, International Shakespearean Sonnet Contest, 1971; Colo. Authors League Tophand Award, 1971, 1973, & many awards in nat., state & regional contests. Address: 215 N. Custer Ave., Colo. Springs, Colo. 80903, USA.

SHAFER, Mabel Hadessa Hall, pen name **HALL, Hadessa,** b. 2 Mar. 1906. Rural School Teacher, Life Insurance Underwriter, Naturopathic Technician. Education: NY State Tchrs. Training; Insurance, Mutual Life Ins. Co., NY. Married, George I. Shafer. Positions held: Rural Schl. Tchr.; Life Ins. Underwriter; Naturopath. Technician for husband, George I. Shafer, ND, 14 yrs. Memberships: Div. Chmn., Buffalo Philharmonic Soc.; Chmn., Displaced Persons Proj., St. Mathias Episcopal Churchwomen, E. Aurora, NY, after WWII; Lead Soprano, various Episc. Choirs & HS, until 1949; Publicity Chmn., Tucson, Ariz. Chapt., Christian Women's Club of Am.; Ariz. State Poetry Soc. Contbr. to the following anthols. & jrnls: Ballet on the Wind, Ariz. State Poetry Soc. Anthol., 1969; Sing Naked Spirit; Swordsman Review; Ariz. Daily Citizen (religious articles); Int. Who's Who in Poetry Anthol., 1973. Address: 2663 N Norris Ave., Tucson, Ariz. 85719, USA.

SHAFFER, Olive C(harlotte), b. 13 July 1896. Elementary School Teacher. Education: Elem. School; (Acad.) HS; B.A., Shepherd Coll., Shepherdstown, W.Va.; M.A., West Virginia Univ. Positions held: Teacher in one-room schools; teacher in graded schools; Principal of Elem. School. Memberships: Major Poets, Chapter Pierson Mettler Associates. Contbr. to anthols.: Poetry Digest Anthol., 1945; Who's Who in Poetry in America, 1945; Book of Modern Poetry, 1941; Poets of America, 1941 (1942); Of America We Sing, 1944; Poetry Broadcast, 1946; The Muse of 1943; From Sea to Sea In Song, 1971, 1972; Lyrics For Song Hits, 1942; Yearbook of Modern Poetry, 1971; Internat. Who's Who in Poetry Anthol., 1972. Journal contributions: Poet; A Collection of Verses (Delta Kappa Gamma Soc.); Grant County Press, Petersburg, W Va ; The Mountain Ripple (HS paper); Shepherd College paper, etc. Awards: Certs. of Merit, 1971, 1973. Address: 127 Mt. View St., Petersburg, WV 26847, USA.

SHAH, Idries, b. 16 June 1924. Writer; Philosopher. Positions held: Dir. of Studies, Inst. for Cultural Rsch., London, U.K., 1966-. Memberships: Fellow, Royal Soc. Arts; Fellow, Royal Econ. Soc.; PEN; Soc. of Authors; Authors Club, London; Folklore Soc.; Brit. Assn. for Adv. of Sci.; Royal Humane Soc. Published works: Wisdom of the Idiots; Caravan of Dreams; Tales of the Dervishes; The Sufis; Special Problems in the Study of Sufi Ideas; Oriental Magic; Destination Mecca; Exploits of Nasrudin; Pleasantries of Nasrudin; The Way of the Sufi; The Book of the Book; Reflections; The Dermis Probe; Thinkers of the East; Textos Sufis, etc. Many translations of Eastern poets. Honours, awards: Dermis Probe, Outstanding Film of the Yr., London & N.Y. Film Festivals, 1965; Paradise of Song, Classic Story Choice, Nova, 1970; The Way of the Sufi & Reflections, Outstanding Books of the Yr., BBC, 1968; Six First Prizes, Buenos Aires (UNESCO Int. Book Yr.), 1972; Vis. Prof., Univ. of Geneva, 1972-73; Dipl. of Hon., Int. Community Serv., 1973; Subject of a Volume of Studies in Honour of Idries Shah (Sufi Studies East & West) by 24 world poets, orientalists & scholars, Jonathan Cape, 1974. Address: c/o Jonathan Cape Ltd., 30 Bedford Sq., London, WC1B 3EL, U.K.

SHAH, Rammanlal Vadilal, b. 14 Feb. 1904. Author; Poet; Philosopher; Occultist; Palmist. Publications: Pourings of Struggling Soul; Message of S'akuntala; Wife; Reality of Life; Message of Shrimad-Bhagvad-Gita. Address: No. 5 Jain Society, Opp. Akhada, Ellisbridge, Ahmedabad 380006, Gujarat State, India.

SHAHRIAR, Mohammad-Hossein, b. 1906. Poet. Education: Studied Medicine at Tehran Univ. for 5 yrs.; Studied Persian Literature & Poetry. Positions held: Civil Servant, 1931–; Employee, Notary Public Dept. of Neishabur; Employee, Agricultural Bank, 1935; Hon. Prof., Fac. of Literature, Tabriz Univ., 1968. Mohammad Shahriar is considered to be one of the most famous contemporary Iranian poets. Four volumes of his poems were printed in 1969 and his book of poems was published in five volumes. Var. poems in Turkish. Address: c/o Press Attache, Imperial Iranian Embassy, 16 Princes Gate, London S.W.7, U.K.

SHAIN, Richard Arthur, pen name SHAIN, Rick, b. 18 Mar. 1948. Psychologist; Teaching Associate. Education: B.A., Queens Coll., 1969; M.A., Temple Univ., 1972. Positions held: Program Coordinator, Work Study Unit, Camp Lymelight, 1968-70; Tchr.-Coordinator, Dept. of Special Educ., Mount Vernon Public Schls., 1969-70; Rsch. Asst., Temple Univ., 1970-71; Admin. Asst., Developmental Rsch. Lab., 1971-73; Tchng. Assoc., Temple Univ., Dept. of Psychol., 1973–. Memberships: World Poetry Soc.; Centro Studi e Scambi Int.; Int. Platform Assn.; Nat. Writers Club. Contbr. to: Chicago Tribune; Poet (India); Spring Anthol. (London); Quaderni di Poesia (Italy); Voices Int.; Cardinal Poetry Qtly.; Anthol. of Am. Poetry, etc. Honours, awards incl: Medal of Hon., Centro Studi e Scambi Int., 1972; Commemorative Medal, Int. Who's Who in Community Affairs, 1973. Address: 1300 West Columbia Ave., Philadelphia, PA 19122, U.S.A.

SHALEV-TOREN, Puah, b. 29 Mar. 1930. Poet; Translator. Education: M.A., Hebrew Univ., Jerusalem, Israel, 1952. Married Haim Toren, 1952. Mbr., Hebrew Writers Assn., Israel. Published works: Verses From the Folds of my Fan, 1956, 61, 65; My Heart Waketh, 1964, 68. Translator of Rabindranath Tagore into Hebrew – Stray Birds, Lover's Gift, Crossing, Tales of Women, Set Me as a Seal, Wing of Death, Fireflies & The Herald of Spring. Honours, awards: Miss Jerusalem, 1954; Klausner Prize, 1957. Address: 19 Shmaryahu Lewin St., Jerusalem, Israel.

SHALOM, Shin, b. 28 Dec. 1904. Poet & Author. Education: Mizrahi Tchrs. Sem., Jerusalem, 1922-25; Univ. Erlangen, 1930, '31. Positions held: Tchr., Galilee, 1927-28, Hedera, 1938-39; Freelance Author, 1940–; Chmn. of the Hebrew Writers Assn. in Israel, 1962-66, 1968-70; Pres., ibid, 1973–. Published works: (in Hebrew) The Collected Works in eleven volumes, 1973; (in English) Storm over Galilee, 1967; On Ben Peleh, 1963. Contbr. to: Davar; Moznaim; Jedioth Achronot; Bitzaron; Karmelit. Honours, awards: Bialik Prize, 1941; Tschernichovski Prize for Hebrew Translation of the Sonnets of Shakespeare, 1945; Brenner Prize, 1949; Ruppin Prize, 1956; Ramat Gan Prize, 1963; Prime Minister's Prize, 1971; Israel Prize, 1973. Received the Keys of Newark, N.J., U.S.A., 1950 & became Hon. Citizen of Haifa, 1961. Address: P.O. Box 6095, Haifa, Israel.

SHAMLU, Ahmad, pen name BAMDAD, b. 1930. Poet. Education: Grad. in Lit., Tehran Univ. Positions held: In charge of Bamshad, 'Ashna', & 'Ettela' at Honari', 'Book of the Week' (from Kayhan Org.), etc. Has published collections of poems. Address: c/o Press Attache, Imperial Iranian Embassy, 16 Princes Gate, London S.W.7, U.K.

SHAPCOTT, Thomas William, b. 21 Mar. 1935. Public Accountant; Author. Education: Ipswich Grammar School; Univ. of Queensland (B.A., 1967). Married; 4 children. Member of the Literature Board, Australian Council for the Arts. Published works: Time on Fire (verse), 1961; The Mankind Thing (verse), 1964; Sonnets 1960/3, 1964; A Taste of Salt Water (Verse), 1967; Focus on Charles Blackman (art monograph), 1967; New Impulses in Australian Poetry (editor, with Rodney Hall), 1968; Inwards to the Sun (verse), 1969; Fingers at Alr (verse), 1970; Australian Poetry Now (editor), 1970; Begin With Walking (verse), 1972. Contbr. to: NY Times; NY Qtly.; Outposts; Bulletin; Sydney Morning Herald; The Age (Melbourne); The Australian; Southerly; Westerly; Meanjin; Quadrant, etc. Awards: Grace Leven Prize (for Time on Fire, 1961); Sidney Meyer Charity Trust Award, 1967 (for A Taste of Salt Water), 1969 (for Inwards to the Sun); Sir Thomas White Mem. Prize, 1967 (for A Taste of Salt Water); Churchill Fellowship, 1972 (to USA and England). Address: P.O. Box 91, Ipswich, Queensland, Australia.

SHAPIRO, David Joel, b. 2 Jan. 1947. Poet. Educ: B.A., Columbia Univ.; Kellett Fellow, Clare Coll., Cambridge, U.K., current. Published works: January: A Book of Poems, 1965; Poems from Deal, 1969; Ed., Sparklers: An Anthology of New York Poets, 1969. Contbr. to: Poetry; Nation; Paris Review; (anthologies) Young American Writers, 1968; Poems of Our Moment, 1968; Possibilities of Poetry, 1969. Honours, awards: Gotham Book Mart Avant-Garde Poetry Award, 1962; N.Y. Poets Fndn. Award, 1965; Robert Frost Fellowship, 1965; Merrill Fndn. Fellowship, 1966; Book-of-the-Month Club Fellowship, 1968. Address: 132 Sagamore Rd., Millburn, NJ, U.S.A.

SHAPIRO, Harvey, b. 27 Jan. 1924. Journalist. Educ: B.A., Yale Univ., 1947; M.A., Columbia Univ., 1948. m. Edna Lewis Kaufman, 1953, 2s. Positions held: Served, U.S.A.F., WWII; Instr., Engl., Cornell Univ., 1949-52; Staff Mbr., Commentary, N.Y.C., 1955-56, The New Yorker, 1956-57, The N.Y. Times Mag., 1957–. Published works: The Eye, 1953; The Book and Other Poems, 1955; Mountain Fire, Thornbush, 1961; Battle Report, 1966. Contbr. to: Nation; Chelsea Review; Harper's; Midstream; Poetry; Quarterly Review of Literature; (anthologies) New Directions 16, 1957; How Does a Poems Mean?, 1959; Midtream Reader, 1960; Breakthrough, 1964; Of Poetry and Power, 1964; New Yorker Book of Poems, 1969; Decade, 1969. Honours, awards: Y.M.H.A. Poetry Ctr. Introductions Award, 1952; Bard Coll. Creative Writing Fellowship, 1951-52; Rockefeller Fndn. Award in Poetry, 1967. Address: 264 Hicks St., Brooklyn, NY, U.S.A.

SHAPIRO, Karl Jay, b. 10 Nov. 1913. Poet. Education: Johns Hopkins Univ. Positions held: w. US Army, 1941-45; Cons. in Poetry, Lib. of Congress, 1946-47; Assoc. Prof., Johns Hopkins Univ., 1947-50; Ed., Poetry, Chicago, 1950-55; Prof., Univ. of Neb., 1956-66; Prof., Univ. of Ill. at Chicago Circle, 1966–; Ed., Prairie Schooner, 1956-63. Published works: Poems, 1935; Person, Place and Thing, 1942; The Place of Love, 1942; V-Letter and Other Poems, 1944; Essay on Rime, 1945; Trial of a Poet, 1947; Bibliography of Modern Prosody, 1948; Poems 42-53, 1953; Beyond Criticism, 1953; Poems of a Jew, 1958; The Bourgeois Poet, 1964. Ed: Am. Poetry Anthol., 1960. Honours & awards: Jeanette S. Davis Prize, 1942; Levinson Prize, 1943; Contemporary Poetry Prize, 1943; Am. Acad. of Arts & Letters Grant, 1944; Pulitzer Prize for Poetry, 1945; Shelley Mem. Prize, 1945; Guggenheim Fellowship, 1945-46, '53-54; Fellow in Am. Letters, Lib. of Congress; Hon. D.H.L., Wayne State Univ. Address: c/o Random House, Inc., 457 Madison Ave., New York, NY 10022, USA.

SHARMAN, Gopal, b. 19 Aug. 1935. Theatre Director; Critic. Educ: B.A., Univ. of Lucknow, India. Positions held: Critic, Performing Arts, The Indian Express, Delhi, 1960-66; Critic, The Sunday Standard, ibid, 1960-66; Dir., Ramayana Theatre, 1967–; Critic, The Times, London, U.K. Published works: Full Circle, 1969. Contbr. to: Illustrated Weekly of India; Sunday Standard. Recip., Homi Bhabha Fellowship for Poetry & Drama, 1968. Address: 11-B Irwin Rd., New Delhi, 1, India.

SHARP, Saundra Pearl, b. 21 Dec. 1942. Actress; Singer. Education: B.S., Music, w. special cert. in Radio-TV prodn., Bowling Green State Univ., Ohio, 1964; Mbr., John O. Killens Writers Workshop, Columbia Univ., N.Y., 1971–. Positions held: Copywriter for TV Guide, nat. publ., 1964-65; Entered field of profl. theatre, 1965–. Published works: From the Windows of My Mind, 1970; In the Midst of Change, 1972. Rep. in following anthols: We Speak as Liberators, 1970; The Magic of Black Poetry, 1972; A Rock Against the Wind, 1974. Contbr. to Black Creation & Black Digest. Poems performed by N.Y.C. Theatre cos. Al Fann Theatrical Ensemble, Afro-Am. Studio & Bed-Stuy Theatre Co. Address: c/o Victoria Lucas Assocs., 1414 Sixth Ave., 15th Fl., N.Y., NY 10019, U.S.A.

SHARP-CARTER, Marjorie Elizabeth, pen names **SHARP, Margery, ST.CLAIRE, Dorothy & CARTER, Marjori S.,** b. 30 Mar. 1916. Associate Editor; Poet; Artist; Music Composer; Lyricist. Education: Grad., Fawcett Coll. of Fine Arts, N.J.; courses in poetry, M.B. Dickson, Hd. of Engl. Lit., Valparaiso Univ.; ext. course in poetry technique, Univ. of Calif., Los Angeles. Married Rexford Wordsworth Sharp. Positions held: Decorative Designer, L. Bamberger, N.J.; Artist, Pictorial Review Mag., N.Y.C.; Designer in advt., Javan Mfg. Co. (also Writer), N.Y.; Co-Ed., Am. Bard; Designed covers for var. mags.; Ed., Personality Portraits and Word Portraits in the Bard, 1948-73. Memberships incl: Past Pres., Hollywood Br., Nat. League of Am. Penwomen; Calif. State Fed. of Chaparral Poets. Contbr. to: Poets' Haven Anthols.; From Sea to Sea in Song; The Poets' Guild Anthol.; Poet, India; The Torch; Am. Poetry League; The Am. Bard; The Archer; The Poets' Guild; Int. Poetry Review; Ideals Mag.; Fellowship in Prayer; United Poets; Desert Sun; Canzoni; Am. Poet, & many others. Recip. var. honours & awards inclng: Am. Pen Women Plaque of Hon., 1967; Hon. Doctorate in Arts & Letters, The Free Univ., 1970; Gold Medal and plaque award for most 1st prizes in poetry & music, Int. Poets' Shrine, 1971. Address: 2692 McCarn Rd., Palm Springs, CA 92262, U.S.A.

SHARPE, Ruth (Collier), b. 6 Aug. 1897. Writer. Education: Music (voice & Drama & Metaphysics; Painting (oil). piano); riting (first in poetry, then in prose); Married to Richard Sharpe. Memberships: Pen & Brush, NYC. Published works: Poets on Parade, 1939; The Song of the Paramahamsa & Other Poems, 1940; When Falcon From the Wrist, 1949; Tristram of Lyonesse Novel but containing many poems), 1949; Important American Poets & Song Writers, 1949; The Poetry Digest Anthology, 1950; Mid Century Anthology, 1950. Contbr. to: American Weave (poetry monthly mag.); Composers & Artists of America. Honours, awards, etc: Prize for Tristram's Song, Poets on Parade, Watchtower Books, 1939; Olcott Fndn. Award for The Song of Paramahamsa, 1940; 1st Prize for grp. of poems in Important Am. Poets, etc., Valiant House, NY; Prize for When Falcon From the Wrist, Mid Century Anthol., 1950. Address: El Morya, 956 West Point Rd., Lake Oswego, Ore. 97034, USA.

SHATTUCK, Roger Whitney, b. 20 Aug. 1923. Author. Education: B.A., Yale Univ., 1947; Soc. of Fellows, Harvard Univ., 1950-53. Positions held: Film Information Officer, UNESCO, 1947-48; Asst. Ed., Harcourt Brace & Co., 1948-49; Instr. of French, Harvard Univ., 1953-56; Asst. Prof. to Prof. of French & Engl., Univ. of Tex., 1956-71; Commonwealth Prof. of French, Univ. of Va., 1974–. Memberships: V.P., Poets' Theater, Cambridge, Mass., 1950-53; Tex. Inst. of Letters; Am. PEN. Published works: Translator, Ed., Selected Writings of Guillaume Apollinaire, 1950; Half Tame, 1964, 2nd ed., 1968. Contbr. to: Poetry (Chicago); Chimera; Qtly. Review of Lit.; Hudson Review; Audience; Prairie Schooner; Botteghe Oscure; Tex. Qtly.; Truck. Address: RFD 1, Lincoln via Bristol, VT 05443, U.S.A.

SHAUGHNESSY, Timothy, b. 21 Feb. 1947. Teacher of English Language & Literature. Education: B.A.,

Ariz. State Univ., 1970; M.A., Northern Ariz. Univ., 1971. Married. Positions held: Bookseller, B. Dalton Bookstore, Phoenix, Ariz.; Engl. Tchr., Chinle Public Schls., Ariz.; Engl. Tchr., Tombstone H.S., Ariz. Contbr. to: Poet; College Poetry Review; Pegasus; Pine Knots; Catalyst: 1970. Address: Box 52, Tombstone, AZ 85638, U.S.A.

SHAVER, Helen Ruth Manning, pen name, **SHAVER, Helen Ruth,** Teacher. Education: Grad., Quinton HS, Oklahoma; B.S. in Education, Arkansas State Teachers Coll., Conway, Arkansas, 1947; M.Ed., Univ. of Oklahoma, Norman, 1949. Married, Jess Shaver; 2 children (James Larry and Mary Ruth). Positions held: Music Teacher, Mayflower, Arkansas, 1947-48; Director of Public School Music, Conway, Arkansas, 1949-52; Music Instr., Arkansas State Coll., Conway, 1949-52; Engl. Instr., Searcy HS, Arkansas, 1952-53; Engl. Instr., Wetumpka HS, Alabama, 1953-55; Engl. Instr., Robert E. Lee HS, Montgomery, Alabama, 1955-58; Engl. and Psychology Instr., Georgetown Coll., Kentucky, 1958-59; Engl. Instr., Huntington Beach HS, Calif., 1959-62; Engl. Instr., Downey Sr. HS, Calif., 1963-1968: 1970– (present position); Supervisor of Reading Clinic, Downey Sr. HS, 1968-70. Published work: Green Lace, 1969. Contbr. to: Los Angeles Herald-Examiner; Independent Press-Telegram (Long Beach); The Forty-Niner (Calif. State Coll.). Address: 122 Granada Ave., Long Beach, CA 90803, USA.

SHAVIT, Yehuda, b. 13 Aug. 1923. Social Worker; Author. Published works: Suddenly in the Mirror Upside-down, 1970; To See Black With Love, 1972. Contbr. to var. lit. supplements, mags. etc. Address: 7 Harcabi St., Jaol-Elihu, Tel-Aviv, Israel.

SHAW, Izola E., pen name **CALBRE, Zo,** b. 1 Oct. 1921. Housewife (divorced). Positions held: Sunday Schl. Tchr.; Missionary League Ldr. Member, Am. Poetry League, Phoenix City. Poems have been read on Shut-In Prog. on WEEC radio. Address: P.O. Box 151, Bryn Mawr, CA 92318, U.S.A.

SHAW, Richard O., b. 25 Nov. 1930. Lecturer. Education: B.A., St. Mary's Coll.; DePaul Univ.; M.A., A.B.D., Univ. of Minn. Married, 2 children. Positions held: Tchr., St. Mel HS, Chgo.; Cryptanalyst, Army Security Agcy., Japan, Korea, & Nat. Security Agcy., Wash. DC; Co-ord., Sunday Progs., Walker Art Ctr., Mpls.; Asst. Ed., Student Writing for Study, Univ. of Minn.; Lectr., Co-ord., Creative Writing Prog., ibid; Assoc. Prof., Chmn., Div. of Liberal Arts, Mpls. Coll. of Art & Design; Playwright, Children's Theatre Co., Mpls. Memberships: Ithunn Apple Occasional Poets Colletive; Black Flag Poets; Nat. Fndn. for Endowment of Arts & Letters; Acad. Am. Poets; Associated Writing Progs.; VP; Pres., Delta Phi Lambda; MLA. Author of Without a Clever Title, 1968. Contbr. to: American Weave; Black Flag; Bottega Review; Changes; Creative Review; Ivory Tower; Japan; Theme & Variation; Just Friends; Lincoln Herald; Minneapolis Star; Minnesota Daily; Minnesota Review; North Stone Review; Odyssey; Open Places; Plainsong; Poetry Review; Readings Towards Composition; Region; Renascence; Voices Int.; Stuff; Syzygy; Review IV; Ventures; Ronald Regan; Waukesha Freeman; Am. Flyer; Kademi; Toward Composition; Breakthrough Fictioneers. Address: Minneapolis Coll. of Art & Design, 133 E. 25th St., Mpls., MN 55404, USA.

SHEAFF, Ardeana, pen name **SHEAFF, Ardeana Hamlin,** b. 1 Aug. 1945. Homemaker. Married Gerald C. Sheaff, 2 sons. Active in community affairs. Contbr. to: Tweed; Legend; Special Song. Address: Box 265, Patten, ME 04765, U.S.A.

SHEILS, Linda Jean, b. 11 Feb. 1940. Housewife; Teacher. Education: Wilmington Coll., Ohio, U.S.A. Married, 1 son. Positions held: Girls' Swimming Instr., Middletown YWCA & sev. camps; 7th Grade Tchr. of Engl. & Am. Hist., Babbitt, Minn., 1962-63; Ldr. of an inter faith Bible study group, Two Harbors. Memberships: League of Minn. Poets; Ariz. State Poetry Soc.; Arrowhead Poetry Soc., Duluth. Contbr.

to: The Moccasin; The Sandcutters; The Essais; Duluth News Tribune; Two Harbors Chronicle & Times Newspaper; The Middletown Jrnl.; Ferment; Al Ramz; Seed. Recip. awards from Arrowhead Poetry Soc., 1972 & Winner, The Sandcutters Comp. with poem 'Beth Becomes', 1973. Address: 313 3rd Ave., Two Harbors, MN 55616, U.S.A.

SHELLEY, Eugenia E., b. 5 June 1919. Civil Servant. Education: A.B., Hunter Coll., 1940. Positions held: Supvsng. Investigator, Finance Administration, N.Y.C. Memberships: Poetry Soc. of Am.: N.Y. Poetry Forum; NYPF Delegate to 2nd World Congress of Poets, Taipei, Taiwan, 1973; Calliope; Composers, Authors & Artists of Am. Contbr. to: New Orlando Poetry Anthol., vol. 3; La Poésie Contemporaine aux Etats-Unis; Vespers; Newsletter, Am. Humanist Assn.; Composers, Authors & Artists of Am. Mag. Honours, awards: 1st Prize, serious poetry, Suffield, Conn. Writer-Reader Conf., 1960; 2nd Prize, traditional poetry, CAAA Nat. Contest, 1967; 1st Prize, Expmtl. poetry, ibid; Sylvia Argow Sonnet Award in Nat. Contest of N.Y. Poetry Forum, 1971; Award for poetry submitted to 2nd World Congress of Poets, 1973; Muse of Poetry, 2nd World Cong. of Poets, Taipei, Taiwan, 1973. Var. poetry readings in N.Y.C. Address: 101 Lafayette Ave., Brooklyn, NY 11217, U.S.A.

SHELTON, Richard, b. 24 June 1933. Writer. Education: B.A., Abilene Christian Coll., 1958; M.A., Univ. of Ariz., 1960. Married Lois Bruce, 1 son. Positions held: Instr., Univ. of Ariz., 1960-64; Dir., Univ. of Ariz. Poetry Ctr., 1964-65; Asst. Prof., Univ. of Ariz., 1968-73; Assoc. Prof., ibid, 1973-. Member, Univ. of Ariz. Poetry Ctr., 1961-71. Published works: Journal of Return, 1969; The Tattooed Desert, 1971; The Heroes of Our Time, 1972; Of All the Dirty Words, 1972; Calendar, 1972; Among the Stones, 1973. Contbr. to: Poetry; The New Yorker; Chicago Tribune Mag.; Antaeus; N.Y. Qtly.; The Am. Scholar; Inscape; Lillabulero; Sumac; Poetry Northwest; North Am. Review; Ohio Review; Falcon; Trace, etc. Honours, awards: U.S. Award, Int. Poetry Forum, 1970; 1st Award, Borestone Mt. Poetry Awards, 1972 (Best Poems of 1971). Address: Dept. of Engl., Univ. of Ariz., Tucson, AZ 85721, U.S.A.

SHEPHERD, Barbara Lilian, pen name LISLE, Lilia, b. 20 Dec. 1926. Physiotherapist. Education: Middlesex Hosp. Schl. of Physiotherapy. Married, 1 daughter. Positions held: Physiotherapist at the following hospitals: Edgware Gen. Hosp., 1947-48; Royal Berks. Hosp., 1948-50; Addington Hosp., Durban, S. Africa, 1950-52; Inst. of Royal Therapy, London, 1952-53. Private pract: Johannesburg, S. Africa, 1955, Durban, 1955; Salisbury, Rhodesia, 1955-57 & currently Umtali, Rhodesia. Contbr. to: Personality (S. Africa); Mustard Seed (Rhodesia); Highway (Rhodesia); Poet; Mitre Press Spring Anthol.; World Poetry Soc. Anthol. Address: Box 350, Umtali, Rhodesia.

SHEPHERD, Nan, b. 11 Feb. 1893. Lecturer in English Literature. Education: M.A., Aberdeen Univ. Positions held: Lectr., Aberdeen Coll. of Educ.; Ed., Aberdeen Univ. Review. Published works: In The Cairngorms, 1934. Recip., Hon. LL.D., Aberdeen Univ. Address: 503 N. Deeside Rd., Cults, Aberdeen, U.K., AB1 9ES.

SHERIFF, Bat-Sheva, b. 28 June 1937. Teacher. Education: B.A., Lit.; M.A., Philos. Married w. 2 s. Positions held: Tchr.; Writer; Radio-Critic. Memberships: Hebrew Writing Assn., Israel; Israeli Govt. Arts Culture Coun., 1971-74. Published works: Poetry, 1961; Not All the Rivers, 1969. Contbr. to: Maarive; Haaretz; Yediot-Acharonot; Lamerhave; Davar; Moznaim; Poetry. Honours: Guest of Günter Grass, Akademi der Kunste, Berlin, 1968. Address: 28 Haavodah St., Tel-Aviv, Israel.

SHERLOCK, (Sir) Philip Manderson. University Administrator. Educ: London Univ., U.K. Positions held: Former Sec., Inst. of Jamaica, London; Educ. Off., Jamaica Welfare Ltd.; Dir., Extra-Mural Studies, Univ. Coll. of W. Indies; Chmn., Bd. of Govs., St.

Andrew's H.S. & Calabar H.S., W. Indies; Vice Prin., Univ. Coll. of W. Indies; Hd., Univ. of W. Indies, St. Augustine Br., Trinidad; Pro Vice Chancellor, Univ. of W. Indies, Kingston, 1962-63; Vice Chancellor, ibid, 1963-69; Sec.-Gen., Assn. of Carribean Univs. & Rsch. Insts., 1969-. Published works: The New Age Poetry Books, 1932; Anancy Stories (w. Arthur J. Newman), 1936; The West Indies, 1950; Anansi, the Spider Man, 1956; West Indian Story, 1960; Three Finger Jack's Treasure, 1961; This Is Jamaica, 1968; Iguana's Tail, 1969. Recip., K.B.E., 1967. Address: Assn. of Carribean Univs. & Rsch. Insts., 25 Hope Rd., Kingston 10, Jamaica, West Indies.

SHERMAN, Ingrid, b. 25 June 1919. Counselor; Educator; Lecturer; Author; Poet; Naturopath; Composer. Education: N.D., Anglo-Am. Inst. of Drugless therapy, UK; D.O., ibid; Pss.D., Sci. of truth Inst., Cinn., Ohio, USA. Married, Morris Sherman, 2 s. Positions held: Sec., Reifenberg & Cie., Textiles, Germany, 1935-38; ibid, Renson & Stafford, Textiles, UK, 1939-40; Pvte. Sec., Gen. Stamp Co., Postage Stamps, USA, 1941-44; Owner, Sherman Novelties, 1944-58; Pvte. Sec. to Jan Kiepura & Marta Eggerth, famous opera singers, 1958-62; Owner, Couns., Fndr., Peace of Mind Studio, 1962-; Tchr., langs., commercial subjs., art, music, etc., Bd. of Educ., 1963-. Memberships: Fndr., Westchester Philo-Cultural Soc.; Dist. Dir., Assoc. of Soc. Psychol.; Poetry Ed., Jrnl. of Soc. Psychol. Int.; Corresp. Accademia Internazionale Leonardo Da Vinci, Italy; Hon. Rep., Studi E Scambi Internazionali, Italy; Liaison Comm., Robert Louis Stevenson Soc.; Co-Fndr., Acad. of Am. Poets; World Poetry Soc. Intercontinental; Poetry Soc., UK; Patron, Coll. of Natural Therapeutics, Ceylon; and many others. Publications: (booklets with poems) Thoughts for You, 1963; For Your Reading Pleasure, 1966; Face to Face with Nature, 1966, '69; Gems from Above, 1966; Ripples of Wisdom, 1966; Poems that Speak of Love, 1966; Prayer Poems that Heal, 1966, '67; Philosophical Titbits, 1967; Radiations for Self-Help, 1967; Strange Patterns (Idiosyncracies), 1967; Let Thy Heart Sing, 1967; As I Recall It, 1969; Natural Remedies for Better Health; The Spiritual Life & works of Dr. Ingrid Sherman. Contbr. to: (jrnls.) Herald Statesman; Home News & Times; Laurel Leaves; Rainbow; Enterprise; Seydell Qtly.; Quaderni di Poesia; Author/Poet; Jean's Jrnl. of Poems; Prairie Poet; Scimitar & Song; Orion; Nutmegger; Poets Bull.; Grace; Health & Longevity; Poet; 'Bama Writer; Bay Shore B Breeze; Calamus; Ellisonian Echoes; Explorer; The Joy Bearer; Hoosier Challenge; Orphic Lute; Penman Mag.; Rays; RNL Hobbies; On Wings of Song; Voices in the Valley; Writers Notes & Quotes; Bell's Letters; Angls. Mag.; Poetry Club; Tree Bees; Spencer Book Co.; Fantasia; Leos Pen Friends; Ozark Gardens; Westchester Philocultural Newsletter; Food for Thot; Michigamme Review; Bouquet of Roses; Inky Trails Bull.; Quintessence. (anthols.) Fantasia Anthol. Cont. Poetry; Today's Poets; Anthol. of Am. Poetry; From Sea to Sea in Song; Prairie Poet; These Are My Jewels; Royal Publg. Co. Anthol. of Am. Poetry; Poetry Parade, etc. Over 500 poems publd. altogether. Poems read on Personal Poetry, Pa. & Va. Honours: Numerous awards, incl. Hon. Poet Laureate & 1st Lady of Poetry Therapy, UPLI, 1967; Poet-of-the-Month, Inky Trails, 1968; Poetry Therapist in Residence, Int. Poetry Shrine, Hollywood, Calif., 1969; ND, Coll. of Natural Therapeutics, Ceylon; Ph.D., Int. Univ. of India; DD. Universal Life Ch. Inc., Ariz.; DPTh., Ind. Univ. of India; D. Hum., Sovereign Order of Alfred the Great; D. Litt., ibid; D. Lib. A., Great China Arts Coll.; LP recordings of poetry read by film stars, & TV & radio readings. Address: 102 Courter Ave., Yonkers, NY 10705. USA.

SHERMAN, Joseph (Howard), b. 4 Aug. 1945. Lecturer in English Literature. Education: B.A., Univ. of New Brunswick, Canada, 1968; M.A., ibid, 1970. Married Ann Riseley, 1 daughter (Rebekah). Positions held: Charge d'enseignement (Lectr.), Dept. of Engl., College Saint-Louis-Maillet, 1970-73; Prof. Adjoint (Asst. Prof.), ibid, 1973-. Mbr., League of Canadian

Poets. Published works: +1 (student anthol.); ... or perish (anthol.); Birthday: a collection of 21 poems, 1969; Ninety Seasons (anthol.), 1974; Chaim the Slaughterer (poems), 1974. Contbr. to: The Fiddlehead; The Atlantic Advocate; Salt; Intercourse; Poet (India); The Beloit Poetry Jrnl. (U.S.A.); Floorboards; First Encounter; The Brunswickan; Porcépic; Waves; Voices Down East; also CBC (radio). Recip., Bliss Carman Meml. Poetry Scholarship, 1968. Address: 17-A Cyr St., Edmundston, New Brunswick, Canada.

SHERMAN, Susan, b. 10 July 1939. Author. Education: B.A., Engl., Philos., Univ. of Calif.; M.A., Philos., Hunter Coll. Positions held: Freelance Writer; Ed., Ikon Mag., 1966-69; Tchr., Mannes Coll. of Mus., 1967; Tchr., Creative Writing Workshops & courses on Modern Philos. at Free Univ. & Alternate Univ.; Poetry Ed., Village Voice, 1968-69; Guest Lectr., Indiana State Writers Conf.; Ran IKON Bookstore, a cultural bookstore which presented weekly poetry readings, music events, etc. Memberships: Poets & Writers; Poets-in-the-Schools. Published works: With Anger/With Love: Selections, Prose & Poems (1963-72), 1974; Shango de Ima, transl. of Cuban Yoruba play, 1971; Areas of Silence, selected poems, 1963. Contbr. to: The Eastside Scene, 1972; Poetry (Chicago); The Nation; The Judson Review; The Eastside Scene; Fire; Opium; The Wormwood Review, etc. Recip., Emily Chamberlein Cook Poetry Award (Univ. of Calif. Poetry Prize), 1959-60. Address: 305 E. 6 St. No.3, N.Y., NY 10003, U.S.A.

SHERRATT, Evelyn, b. 31 Jan. 1908. Housewife. Memberships: Comm. Mbr., Fellowship of Australian Writers, 4 yrs.; N. Coast Lit. Soc.; Redcliffe Music & Arts Soc.; Redcliffe Art Contest Soc. Wrote 'The Seeds' & a children's operetta 'The Discontented Flowers', both of which were produced on half hour progs. for Christian TV, 1962. Contbr. to: Redcliffe Writing II, 1973; Poet's Corner in 'Sandgate Echo' (was regular contbr.); Endeavour, Jrnl. of the N. Coast Lit. Soc.; The Bulletin, of Fellowship of Australian Writers, Redcliffe Br. Honours, awards: Bronze Medal for poem 'The Golden Years', at the Qld. Industries Fair, 1968; 1st Prize for a lyric poem suitable for setting to music, 1971; 1st Prize for a one act play, F.A.W., 1971, etc. Address: Wandana, 25 Whytecliffe Parade, Woody Point, Redcliffe, Qld. 4019, Australia.

SHERRY, Helen Luster, pen name **LUSTER, Helen,** b. 17 Mar. 1913. Writer of Poetry. Education: A.B., Univ. of Ill., U.S.A.; Chicago Art Inst., 1 yr. Positions held: Poetry Advisor on staff of 'Trace', 1965-67; Dir., Los Angeles Poetry Ctr., 1968-69; Recent association with 'The Venice Poetry Company' putting on mixed media happenings at 'The Other Side', Venice, Calif., 1971; Dir. of Poets Workshop, San Rafael, 1972-73. Dir. & Fndr., Los Angeles Poetry Ctr. Published works: A Watcher from that Moment (with 'Circle Built In'), 1968; 'I(EE), Book I, In Pisces', 1971; 'I(EE), Book II, The Yellow Christmas', 1971; 'I(EE), Book III, Bell's Book', 1973; Book IV, 'The House of Di', 1974. Contbr. to: The Humanist; The New Athenaeum; Spectroscope; Cyclotron; South & West; The Fiddlehead; Grande Ronde Review; Perspectives; Confrontation; Ante; Second Coming, etc. Address: 330 Paloma Ave., San Rafael, CA 94901, U.S.A.

SHERRY, Ruth Forbes, b. 14 Nov. 1883. Writer. Education: Vassar; Stanford; Sorbonne, France. Married to Ralph H. Sherry. Positions held: Opera Reporter, Music News; Real Estate Bus.; F.A. Sherry & Co.; Lecturer. Memberships: Pen & Brush, NY; Poetry Soc. of Am.; Press Club, Los Angeles; Am. Pen Women; Poets of the Pacific; Centro Studi E Scambi, Rome; Poets Laureate Int.; Ina Coolbrith Circle, Calif.; Poetry Soc. of Southern Calif.; Calif. Writers Club; Poetry Soc., UK; Soc. of Arts & Letters. Published works: Hourglass in the Mojave, 1942; Lament & Prophecy, 1943; Chart for Voyage, 1943; Imperishable Gene, 1958; Mojave Motives, 1958; Prismatic Voices, 1963; Partisan, 1964; Seize on Tragic Time, dramatic poem staged 3 times, 1964; Human Voices, 1965;

Mojave (1000 dollar Olivant Award), 1966, & 3 further eds.; Of Time & The Dry Heart, 1968. Works transl. into Greek, Japanese, French. Voice tapes, radio Exhibitions, readings & progs. 6 concerts reading with Electronic Music; Song lyrics; Symphonic Composition for Earth Mother, by Floris Hudnall; Chorale, Requiem for a Soldier, by Michael Higgins; Over 100 conversations in Contemporary Poetry. Contbr. to: About 60 USA & foreign anthols.; (jrnls.) Fiddlehead; Epos; Prairie Schooner; Poet Lore; Lyric; Outposts; Humanist; Flame; Poetry Digest; S&W; Wisc. Poetry Jrnl., etc. about 200 in all. Honours: Fellowship, Intercontinental Soc., 1969; Contemporary Poets Int. Hall of Fame, for Mojave, 1969; 2 1sts, Poetry Soc. of Am.; Tom Paine Soc.; Poetry Soc. of Southern Calif.; Bronze, Silver & Gold Medals, CSSI; Gold Medal & Laureate of Youth, UPLI; Orange Co. Authors Award, 1967, & many others. Address: 145 Cedar Way, Apt. 4, Laguna Beach, Calif. 92651, USA.

SHERWIN, Judith Johnson, b. 3 Oct. 1936. Writer. Education: Diller-Quaile Music Schl., 1947-52; Julliard Music Schl., 1952-53; Studied music comp. w. Suzanne Bloch & Bernard Wagenaar; Radcliffe Coll., 1954-55; NA, cun luade, Barnard Coll., 1958; Columbia Univ. Grad. Schl., 1958-59. Married, James T. Sherwin, int. master in chess, 2 d. Memberships: PEN; Poetry Soc. Am.; Authors. Guild. Published works: Uranium Poems, 1969; The Life of Riot, 1970. Contbr. to the following jrnls: Atlantic Monthly; Beloit Poetry Jrnl., Fiddlehead; Lit. Review; Mademoiselle; Poetry; Poetry Northwest; Prairie Schooner; Quest; Sewanee Review; Southwest Review; Anon; Ante; Imprints; Sparrow; Acad. Am. Poets pamphlet of prize winning poems; Barnard Alumnae Mag.; Le Bayou; Canadian Poetry Mag.; New Engl. Review; Poetry Digest; Poets for Peace Pamphlet; South & West; Southern Poetry Review; Yale Alumni Mag.; Dalton Alumnae Mag.; Lumenn; Mass. Review; Va. Quarterly Review. Honours, Awards: Van Rennselaer Prize for Lyric Poetry, 1957; Amy Loveman Poetry Prize & Acad. of Am. Poets Prize, 1958; Poetry Soc. Am. Fellowship, 1964; Yale Series of Younger Poets Award, 1968; Finalist, NY Philharmonic Young Composers Award, 1947; Finalist, Stanley Drama Award, 1960; NY Radcliffe Club Scholarship, 1954-55; Woodrow Wilson Nat. Fellowship, 1958-59; Rose Fellowship in Fiction, Aspen Writers Workshop, 1967; Yaddo, 1964. Address: 490 Ave. Reine Astrid, Kraainem 1950, Belgium.

SHERWIN, Richard Elliott, b. 21 Aug. 1933. Senior Lecturer in English and American Literature. Education: B.A., U.C.L.A.; M.A., Ph.D., Yale Univ. Married; 1 s., 2 d. Positions held: Chairman, Dept. of English, Bar Ilan Univ., Ramat Gan, Israel; Visiting Prof. of Engl., U.C.L.A. Membership: World Poetry Soc. Contbr. to following, journals, mags., newspapers, etc.: (poems) Ragnarok (Tel Aviv Univ. Overseas Prog.); Reconstructionist (NY); Poet (India); Egeret (NY); Beloit Poetry Journal; Poet & Critic; Encounter; Jerusalem Post Supp.; Image (Hebrew Univ.); B'Gvulam (Tel Aviv); The Literary Review; (reviews) Nineteenth Century Fiction; Bikoret V'Parshanut (Bar Ilan Univ.); Supplement; The Jerusalem Post. Address: 97 Rh. Shlomo Hamelech, Herzliyah, Israel.

SHIBASAKI, Sosuke, pen name **CIVASAQUI, José,** b. 2 Jan. 1916. Literary Executive. Education: Yokohama Ctrl. Army Educ. Prog. Schl., H.Q. Eighth Army; studied poetry w. Edmund Blunden, 1948-50. Married Setsuko Hirose, 2 sons, 1 daughter. Positions held: on Literary staff, Toshiba E.M.I., 1955-. Memberships: Councillor, Japanese Soc. of Rights of Authors & Composers; Mng. Dir., Japan Authors & Composers' Union; Mng. Dir., Japan League of Poets; Mng. Dir., Japan Lyric Translators' Soc.; Poets' Soc. of Japan; The Shakespeare Soc. of Japan; The Lang. Lab. Assn. of Japan. Published works: In His Bosom, 1950; In Thy Grace, 1971. Contbr. to: The Nippon Times; The Mainichi; Come Come Club, monthly mag.; The Study of Current English; New Age; Poetry Nippon; Kings

Records; Children's Songs from Japan. Address: Honcho 2-12-11, Ikebukuro, Toshima-ku, Tokyo 170, Japan.

SHIBLES, Warren, b. 10 July 1933. Educator; Chairman of Department. Education: B.A., Univ. of Conn., U.S.A., 1958; M.A., Univ. of Colo., 1963; Ind. Univ., 1963-66. Married Patricia Pell, 3 children. Positions held: Instr. in Philos., N. Tex. State Univ., Spring 1966; Lectr. in Philos., Parsons Coll., Summer 1966-Fall 1967; Asst. Prof. of Philos. & Chmn. of Dept., Univ. of Wis., Whitewater, 1967-. Memberships: Poetry Soc. of Am.; AAUP; Am. Philos. Assn. Published works: Philosophical Pictures, 1969, rev. 1971; Wittgenstein, Language & Philos., 1969 (1971); Models of Ancient Greek Philos., 1971; An Analysis of Metaphor, 1971; Metaphor: An Annotated Bibliography, 1971; Essays on Metaphor, 1971; Emotions, 1973; Death: An Interdisciplinary Analysis, 1973. Contbr. of articles to many profl. jrnls. inclng: Philosophy and Phenomenological Research; Communication; Am. Rationalist; Sophia; So. Jrnl. of Philos.; six poems published since 1966 in var. poetry jrnls. Var. profl. papers read at philosophical meetings. Address: RR3, Whitewater, WI 53190, U.S.A.

SHIELDS, Milford E., b. 29 Oct. 1898. Retired Farmer; Motion Picture Projectionist. Positions held: Poet Laureate of Colo., 1954-; 1st Poet Laureate, Int. Platform Assn., 1970; Exec. VP, United Poets Laureate Int., 1963-; Guest Ed., World Poetry Day No. of Poet, 1970. Memberships: Royal Order of Scotland; For. Assoc., Acad. Francaise de la Poesie; Past Pres., Am. Lit. Assn.; Pres. Emeritus, Poets of the Pacific Inc.; Life Fellow, FIAL; Hon. Mbr., Int. Acad. Jain Wisdom & Culture – Centro Studi E Scambi Int. Published works: Colorado & Other Poems; Burning Weeds & Other Poems; Dirty Face; Static Land (prose); Engine 315; Poems of Int. Goodwill, 5 vols.; Poem, 'Korea Flaming High' in forward to Pres. Syngman Rhee's book of same title; Poem, 'Dr. Sun Yat-sen,' only poem by for. contbr., in Dr. Sun Yat-sen Centennial Anthol., 4 vols.; Poem, 'Africanism' in forward to Dictionary of African Biog. Contributor to: Congressional Record (18 poems); Denver Post; Manila Times; Times of Vietnam; Korean Republic; Kambuja; Tanganyika Standard; Arrow; Voice of Ahinsa; Dairio de Centro America, Guatemala; Les Etudes Poetiques, Paris; Poet, India; Am. Bard; Midwest Chaparral, etc. Honours: Litt. LD, Int. Acad. of Ldrship.; Ph.D., Free Univ. of Asia; LAD, Great China Arts Coll.; Hon. Worlds Poet Laureate of Peace w. Gold Medal & Laurel Wreath from Pres. Macapagal, 1965; Pres. Marcos Gold Medal for efforts on behalf of world peace, 1966; Bronze, Silver & Gold Medals & Certs., Centro Studi E Scambi; Humanist Award, AMORC, Rosecrusian, 1963; Diploma of Merit (the first awarded) by Committee on Arts & Culture of the 1971 Constitutional Convention, Repub. of the Philippines. etc. Address: PO Box 1217, Durango, Colo. 81301, USA.

SHIFFERT, Edith Marion, pen name **SHIFFERT, Edith Marcombe,** b. 19 Jan. 1916. Professor of English. Education: Univ. of Wash., U.S.A. Positions held: Tchr., Kyoto, Japan, 1963– at Doshisha Univ., Kyoto Univ. & Kyoto Seika Coll. Published works: In Open Woods, 1961; For a Return to Kona, 1964; The Kyoto Years, 1971; Anthology of Modern Japanese Poetry, translations (w. Yūki Sawa), 1971; Chieko, translations (w. Yūki Sawa), 1973. Forthcoming: Hermit, Lover, Cat; When a Bird Rests & Other Tanka by Taeko Takaori, translations, 1974; Buson, translations of Haiku. Contbr. to: Lit. Review; Mass. Review; Ariz. Quarterly; Botteghe Oscura; Canadian Forum; Christian Sci. Monitor; Kyoto Seika Engl. Papers; Lit. East & West; Malahat Review; Prism; Beliot; Poetry Nippon, etc. Rep. in following Anthols: The Women Poets in English, 1973; The New York Times Book of Verse, 1970; Japan, Theme & Variations, 1959. On editl. staff of following: Poetry Northwest & East-West Review (formerly); Kyoto Seika English Papers; Poetry Nippon. Address: Kyoto Seika Coll., Iwakura-Kino,

Sakyo-ku, Kyoto, Japan 606.

SHILLON, Shmuel, pen name **SHATTAL, Shmuel,** b. 13 Apr., 1913. Construction Engineer; Translator; Poet. Education: Hebrew HS, Pinsk, White Russia; Fac. of Civil Engrng., Technion, Israel Inst. of Technol., Haifa. Positions held: Engr., Israel. Memberships: Hebrew Writers Assoc., Israel; Assoc. Mbr., Young Poetry Salon 'Eked', Tel-Aviv. Published works: The White Thread, 1960; Stone's Strings, 1964; Fire and Ice–Selected Poems of Robert Frost (translation) 1969; Selected Poems of Heinrich Heine (Co-Author, transl.), 1965; Selected Poems of Boris Pasternak (Co-Author, transl.), 1961. Contbr. to: Moznayim; Haaretz; Lamerhav (long extracts from his translation of Under Milkwood by Dylan Thomas); Davar; Eked. Address: 3 Moser St., Tel-Aviv. Israel.

SHIMAOKA, Akira, pen name, **SIMAOKA, Sin,** b. 8 March 1932. Editor and Writer. Education: Grad., Meiji Univ., Tokyo, 1955. Married; 1 d. Membership: Japanese Modern Poets Soc. Published works: Sanran (Lay Eggs), 1970; Poet Mitsuharu Kaneko, 1973. Contbr. to: Mugen (Infinity); Rekitei (Successive Ways). Address: 8-3-11 Tamagawagakuen, Machidashi, Tokyo, Japan.

SHIN, Dong-Jib, b. 5 Mar. 1924. Professor of English. Education: B.A., Seoul Nat. Univ., Korea, 1951; Grad. Schl., Ind. Univ., Bloomington, USA, 1 yr. Married to Jung-Souk Kim, 1s., 2 d. Positions held: Prof. of Engl., Young-Man Univ., Taegu, Korea, 1955-68; Prof. of Engl., Keimyung Christian Coll., 1969-. Memberships: Korean PEN; Korean Poets Assn.; Korean Writers Assn. Published works: Lyric Exiled, 1954; The Second Prelude, 1958; The Water of Contradiction, 1963; Boiling Vowels, 1965; An Empty Cola Bottle, 1968; A Man of Dawn, 1970; The Return Home, 1971; Sending Sign, 1973. Contbr. to: Shigaku, 1967; Chinese Li-Poetry Mag., 1971; Modern Literature; Poetic Literature; Modern Poetics; Monthly Literature. Awards: Free Lit. Prize, 1955; Kyung-pook Cultural Prize, 1961; Korean PEN Prize, 1969. Address: Residence No. 6, Keimyung Christian Coll., Taegu, Korea.

SHINDO SUZUKI, Chizu, pen name **CHIZU SUZUKI,** b. 17 Aug. 1941. Landowner. Education: Am. Schl. in Japan; Art Dept., Nihon Univ. Married Tsuneshi Suzuki. Published works: The Expected (English), 1957; At The End of Secret (Japanese), 1971; The Shield of Flora (Japanese), 1973. Contbr. to: The Fire; The Wind; The Modern Esprit; The Mita Criticism. Address: I-31-16 Denenchofu, Otaku, Tokyo, Japan.

SHINGLETON, Peter, b. 14 Sept. 1945. Poet. Education: Mainly self-educated. Writes poetry only for the sense of art & not for commerce. Publications: Own poems publd. in private mags. Address: 242 Iffley Rd., Oxford, UK.

SHINKEL, Grace Ruth, born 16 Jul. 1904. Nurse. Education: 1 year college; several sessions night school diverse studies. Married to L.F. Shinkel. Positions held, include: Singer; Choir Director; Sewing Instructor; Political Secretary – County Commissioner; School Vice-Pres.; Pres., P.T.A.; Nurse. Memberships: Nat. League of Am. Penwomen (secretary, treasurer); 6 writers' groups; Rimers; Arizona State Poetry Soc.; Intimates; numerous other poetry societies. Contrib. to: Waif; Your Digest; Prairie Poet; The Sand Cutters; From Sea to Sea in Song; Midwest Chaparral; The American Poet; Year of the Poet; American Song Bird. Award Blue Ribbon, Art Festival, 1965. Address: 2701 Winchester Vista, Tucson, Arizona 85713, USA.

SHIVELY, Ruth Webber, b. 7th Nov. 1915. Education: Assoc. of Arts, George Washington Univ., Washington, DC.; working towards B.A. degree, Univ. of Dallas, Irving, Texas. Married to Herb Shively; 1 s., 1 d. Positions held: Secretarial positions for a number of yrs., including 10 yrs. in US Civil Service, Washington, DC., also 4 yrs. in direct sales. Memberships: Nat. Fed.

of State Poetry Socs.; Poetry Soc. of Texas (Councillor for Irving, since 1967); Southwest Writers (Dallas). Contbr. to: NY Times; South & West Mag.; Christianity Today; Modern Maturity; Different Mag.; Spring Anthol., 1968; Cats Mag.; Dallas Times Herald; Tampa Morning Tribune; Texas Baptist Standard. Awards: Nat. Fed. of State Poetry Socs.: 1968, 1st, Modern; 1969, 1st Modern, and 1st, Daisy E. Tennant; 1973, 1st, Emily Dickinson Bulletin; and 2nd, Tucson Poetry Soc.; Poetry Soc. of Texas (Annual Awards): 1967, 1st, Aline B. Carter Peace; 1969 1st Lena B. Morton Human Relations; 1972, 1st Nora E. Johnson Inner-Space; Poetry Soc. of Texas (Monthly Critics Award: 1st, Oct., 1965, Mar., 1971; Mar., 1972; PST: 9 other awards less than 10-dollars, 1967 to Jul. 1973; Southwest Writers (Dallas) 1st & 2nd Poetry Prizes (Annual), June, 1973. Address: 718 West Lynn Dr., Irving, TX 75062, USA.

SHLOMO, Vinner, b. 28 Sept. 1937. Maths Teacher. Education: Ph.D., Maths, Hebrew Univ., Jerusalem, Israel. Positions held: Tchr., Maths Dept., Hebrew Univ., Jerusalem. Memberships: The Soc. of Hebrew Writers in Israel. Published works: Only For Few Hours (book of poems). Contbr. to: Amot; Moznaim; Keshet; Davvar. Address: Even Ezra 19, Jerusalem, Israel.

SHOEMAKER, Brant, b. 10 Oct. 1924. Professor of English and Humanities; Poetry Studio Director. Education: A.B. with Hons., Univ. of Pennsylvania, 1951; M.A., Univ. of Connecticut, 1953; Ph.D. prelim. exam., Univ. of Pennsylvania, 1955; Certified Poetry Therapist, 1972. Positions held: USMC, 1942-46; Teaching Fellow, Univ. of Conn., 1951-53; ibid, Univ. of Pa., 1954; Instr., Fenn Coll., 1955-58; Prof., Pa. State Univ., 1958–; Dir., Ogontz Poetry Studio. Memberships: Poetry Soc. of America; Member, Internat. Committee, C.S.S.I. Published works, Taps, 1958; Taps & Other Poems, 1959; The Peacock Lady, 1962; Philadelphia Poems, 1967; Primary Structurist Poems, 1968; Cross of Flowers, 1968; Krishna Impaled, 1969; Our Own Angels, 1972. Copyrights 1971 – (Plays): General Albanos and the Rebel (1-Act) presented by Wyncote Players, 1972; Room 205 (1-Act) presented by Theatre Workshop at Pa. State Univ., 1972; Croquet; and The Credit Card Man. Many drama reviews published in Inscape (Pa.) and Curtain Call (NY). Contbr. to: American Weave; Gen. Mag. & Historical Chronicle, Univ. of Pa.; PSEN; Pa. Gazette; Phila. Tribune; Pivot; Suburban Life North; Per/Se; Inscape; Outposts; CS Monitor; Sound of Language textbooks; Quaderni di Poesia. (Anthols.) Living Lyrics; Poesie Contemporaine des Americains; Poets of the Seventies; Diamond Anthol., 1971. Many poems read on TV in Phila.; Poetry Seminar on Radio, WUHY-FM, Phila., 1972. Director, Pilot Program, "Poets in the Elem. Schools", Pa.D.E.1973. Honours: Elected Fellow, Duke Univ. Lib. in recognition of poetry, 1967; 3rd Poetry Competition, Fleetwood Music & Arts Festival, UK, 1972. Address: Box 15, Ogontz Campus, Pa. State Univ., Abington, PA 19001, USA.

SHORE, Henry, b. 20 Mar. 1911. Medical Practitioner. Education: Vienna Univ.; London Univ. Married. Positions held: Colonial Medical Serv., 1951-61; Medical Officer of Health (currently). Member, Birmingham Poetry Soc. Published works: The Roundabout, 1972; The Nomad, 1973. Contbr. to: Pulse; Midland Read; Breakthru; BBC (Poetry Today). Address: The Cedars, 15 Knights Hill, Aldridge, Nr. Walsall, Staffs. WS9 0TG, U.K.

SHORT, Billy Young, b. 21 Dec. 1926. Ft. Worth, Tex. Art Director. Education: B.A., Tex. Christian Univ.; N Tex. State Univ., Denton, 1950. Positions held: Asst. Dir., Neiman Marcus, 1952; Art Dir., A. Harris & Co.; Dallas; Art Dir., Harpers Bazaar, NY, 1956. Memberships: Veterans Voice; Waco Poetry Soc., Tex. Contbr. to: New Yorker; Antiques Mag.; Harpers Bazaar; Poetry; Veterans Voice. Awards: Tex. State Poetry Soc., 1971; Veteran Hosp. Comp., 1971. Address: 3304 S. Third St., Waco, Texas 76706, USA.

SHORT, Lucille Doughton, b. 23 July 1903. Educator

& Lecturer. Education: A.B., Ohio Wesleyan; S.B. Ed. & A.M. in Engl., Boston Univ.; grad. work at var. univs. Widow of Edward Preston Short. Positions held: Engl. & Latin Tchr., Vermont Coll., Montpelier; weekly Radio Prog.; Tchr., Margaret Hall Schl., Verseilles, Ky. & at Midway Jr. Coll., Ky.; Tchr., Radford Schl. for Girls, El Paso, Tex.; Tchr., St. Mary's Schl. for Girls, Spanish and Speech Instr., Sewanee, Tenn.; Tchr., Shelby Co. System, Tenn. Memberships: Athenaeum Lit. Soc.; Pres., 1965-66 & Prog. Chmn., 1973-74, Poetry Soc. of Tenn.; Acad. of Am. Poets; N.Y. Browning Soc.; Pearl S. Buck Book Club; Tenn. Women's Press and Authors' Club; Am. Classical League; World Poetry Soc. Intercontinental; Int. Poetry Soc.; Alpha Delta Kappa; Kappa Beta Pi, etc. Published works: Brownings Theory of Life; Syllabus for Teaching Foreign Languages; Foreign Languages as a Way to Peace; Classical Mythology in World Literature; Reading – an Art. Contbr. to: Paul Flowers' column, "Greenhouse"; Poet, India; Premier Poets Anthol.; Teachers' Yearly Anthol. Address: 207 South Marne St., Memphis, TN 38111, U.S.A.

SHORT, Marcia, b. 15 June 1888. Former School Teacher; Writer. Education: Victoria Univ., Wellington, New Zealand. Positions held: Dir. of Chatauqua; Beauty Consultant; Lecturer; Actress (amateur & profl. stage); Writer of poetry, articles & short stories. Memberships: Hon. Mbr., N.Y. Poetry Forum; Past Mbr., Mark Twain Soc., N.Y.; Dickens Soc., N.Y.; Parnassus Club, N.Y. Published works: Selected Poems, 1970. Poems have been set to music by 15 Engl. & Am. Composers (8 publs. of these as songs & chorales). Contbr. to: Houston Post; Open Window; The Preserver; Auckland Weekly. Her poems have been used in radio & TV progs in N.Y. & recently 'Hymn for the United Nations' was narrated with a background of orchestral music especially composed for it. Honours, awards: Prize for humorous poetry & hon. mention for song lyric & sacred poem, N.Y. Poetry Forum, 1972. Address: 93 Waipapa Rd., Hataitai, Wellington 3, New Zealand.

SHRIRA, Shoshana, pen names SH.SHANI, SH-SH-SH, SHOSHANA SH., SH.BARON, b. 10 Mar. 1917. Writer; Journalist; Translator; Editor. Education: B.A., Inst. of Educ., King's Coll., London Univ., U.K. Married Ariel Kohn, 1 daughter (Eilat). Positions held: Mbr. of Staff, Daily Haboker. Memberships: Hebrew Writers Assn., Israel; Past Mbr. of Coun., ibid; World P.E.N. Club; Former Mbr., Journalists' Assn.; Akum. Societe d'auteurs, compositeurs et editeurs de Musique en Israel. Published works: The Grin River Short Stories, 1947; Bread of the Beloved (novel), 1957; The Gates of Gaza (novel), 1960; Thanks to the Fig Trees (short stories), 1971; For Whom For Whom For Whom, 1972. Lit. & theatre criticism in most dailies in Israel. Translations incl: Jane Austen's Pride & Prejudice. Contbr. to: Gilionoth; Moznaim; Kneset; Hharetz; Masa; Davar; Lamenhav, etc. Honours, awards: The Kessel Prize of Hebrew and Yiddish Lit. of the Mexican Jewry, 1958; The Usishkin Prize of Lit., Jerusalem, 1960. Address: 9 Bezalel St., Tel-Aviv, Israel.

SHRIVER, Donna Newcomer, pen name, LAYTON, Jean, b. 17 June 1931. Piano Teacher; Homemaker. Education: B.M., Stetson Univ. Married to Dr. George Shriver; 4 children (Becky, Bonnie, Laurie, David). Memberships: North Carolina Poetry Soc. (Member State Bd.); Georgia Poetry Soc. Contbr. to various poetry journals, and mags., etc. Recip. various poetry prizes, North Carolina Poetry Soc., Charlotte Writers' Club. Address: 120 Lee St., Statesboro, GA 30458, USA.

SHTERN, Adele, b. 9 Jul. 1947. Artist at Advertising Studio. Education: B.A. (Major in Fine Arts), Sir George Williams Univ., Montreal, 1968; Studied sculpture, painting, drawing, silk screen printing, photography and design. Contbr. to: Viewpoints (Manchester, UK); Poet (India). Address: 6741 Baily Rd., Montreal 266, Quebec, Canada.

SHTERN, Israel Hirsh, pen name YAIR, Ish, b. 25th

June 1914. Professor, Poet. Education: Wilno Jewish Technicum; B.Sc., Sir George Williams Univ.; M.A., NY Univ.; M.Sc., McGill Univ.; Ph.D., ibid. Positions held: Tchr., Vice-Prin., Jewish Peretz Schls.; Lectr., Sir George Williams Univ.; Lectr., Asst. Prof., McGill Univ.; Assoc. Prof., Loyola Coll. Memberships: United Poets Laureate Int.; World Poetry Soc. Intercontinental; Hon. Rep., Centro Studi E Scambi Internazionali; Canadian Poetry Soc.; Montreal Jewish Writers Union. Int. Corr., Poésie Vivante. Publications: Fables, 1967; Out Of The Burning Bush, 1968. Contbr. to: Poet; Breakthru; Viewpoints; Envoi; Platform; Firebird; Gem Scent; Expression; Expression One; Second Aeon; Poésie Vivante; Quaderni Di Poesia; Poet, India; Laurel Leaves; Kauri; Bitterroot; Yiddisher Kemfer; Zein; Zukunft; Undzer Aygen Vinkel; Bnai Yiddish; Elipse; Eagle. Recip. of num. honours & awards. Address: 6741 Baily Rd., Montreal 266, Québec, Canada.

SHUCARD, Alan Robert, b. 2 Dec. 1935. Professor of Literature. Education: A.B., Union Coll., Schenectady, N.Y., 1957; M.A., Univ. of Conn., 1963; Ph.D., Univ. of Ariz., 1971. Married Maureen O'Higgins, 1 daughter. Positions held: Engl. Instr., Univ. of B.C., 1965-70; Asst. Prof. of Engl., Univ. of Wis.-Parkside, 1970-73; Assoc. Prof., ibid, 1973–. Published works: The Gorgon Bag, 1970; The Louse on the Head of a Yawning Lord, 1972. Contbr. to: Beloit Poetry Jrnl.; Jabberwocky; Idol. Address: Div. of Humanistic Studies, Univ. of Wis.-Parkside, Wood Rd., Kenosha, WI 53140, U.S.A.

SHUFORD, Cecil Eugene, pen name **SHUFORD, Gene,** b. 21 Feb. 1907. Educator. Education: B.A., Univ. of Ark., 1928; M.S.J., Northwestern Univ., 1929; Univ. of Wis., summer 1941. Married Catherine Brooks, 3 children. Positions held: Reporter, Fayetteville (Ark.) Daily Democrat, 1926-28; Instr., Jrnlsm., Alabama Polytechnic Inst., Auburn, Ala., 1929-30; Instr., Engl., Univ. of Ark., 1934-36; Asst. Prof. & Publicity Dir., Trinity Univ., Tex., 1936-37; Publicity Dir., Instr. to Asst. Prof., North Tex. State Univ., 1937-42; Dir./Chmn., Jrnlsm., ibid, 1945–; Prof., 1959. Memberships: Poetry Soc. of Am.; Tex. Inst. of Letters; Poetry Soc. of Tex. Published works: The Red Bull & Other Poems, 1964; Selected Poems 1933-71, 1972. Rep. in following anthols: Southwest Writers Anthol., 1967; North Am. Book of Verse, 1939; The Golden Yr. Anthol. (1910-60); The Diamond Anthol., 1971. Contbr. to var. mags., jrnls. Honours, awards incl: Tex. Inst. of Letters Voertman Award (for Selected Poems, 1933-71), 1973. Address: 2910 East McKinney, Denton, TX 76201, U.S.A.

SHUMWAY, Mary Louise, b. 21 Aug. 1926. Professor of English; Writer. Education: A.B., Univ. of Chicago, 1957; M.A., San Francisco State Coll., 1965; Ph.D., Univ. of Denver, 1971. Positions held: Instr., Engl. & Anthropol., Geo. Williams Coll.; Coordinator of Undergraduate Studies, Dean of Women, Instr., Humanities Dept., San Francisco Art Inst.; Prof. of Engl., Univ. of Wis., Stevens Point. Published works: Song of the Archer & Other Poems, 1964; Headlands, 1972; Mindar & the Gandy Dancer, pending; Time, & Other Birds (scheduled for publication 1974). Contbr. to: Chicago Review; Motive; Christian Scholar; Modern Age; Beloit Poetry Jrnl.; Prairie Schooner; Transfer; Arts in Society, etc. Honours, awards incl: Acad. of Am. Poets Prize, 1965 & '69; Robert Frost Fellowship in Poetry, Bread Load, 1969; MacDowell Fellow, The MacDowell Colony, 1973. Address: Dept. of Engl., Univ. of Wis.-SP, Stevens Point, WI 54481, U.S.A.

SHUTTLE, Penelope Diane, b. 12 May 1947. Writer. Member, Writers Action Grp. Published works: An Excusable Vengeance, 1967; Nostalgia Neurosis & Other Poems, 1968; All the Usual Hours of Sleeping, 1969; Branch, 1971; Jesusa, 1972; The Hermaphrodite Album, 1973. Forthcoming: Wailing Monkey Embracing a Tree (novel), 1973; Rainsplitter in the Zodiac Garden (novel); Candle-Poems, 1973; Photographs of Persephone, poems, 1973; The

Candlemas Notebook, poems 1970-73; The Village of the Giant, (novel); The Terrors of Dr. Treviles (novel w. Peter Redgrove). Contbr. to: The Poetry Review; Poet; Wave; Second Aeon; Transatlantic Review; The Scotsman, & many others. Has broadcast on BBC Radio 3, on Poetry Now. Honours, awards: Arts Coun. Awards, 1969 & '72; Greenwood Poetry Prize, 1972. Address: c/o 20 Glebe Rd., Staines, Middx., U.K.

SIANO, Mary Martha, b. 23 Feb. 1924. Freelance Writer. Memberships: N.J. Poetry Soc.; Pa. Poetry Soc.; Tex. Poetry Soc.; Am. Poets Fellowship; Pierson Mettler Assocs.; Soc. of Children's Book Writers; Songwriters' Cooperative. Contbr. to: Yearbook of Modern Poetry, 1971-73; Through the Years, 1972; Melody of the Muse, 1973; N.J. Poetry Soc. Anthol., 1972; Outstanding Contemporary Poetry, 1972; Prairie Poet, 1973; Major Poets, 1972; The Am. Poet, 1973; Lyrics of Love, 1972; United Poets, 1973; Shore Poetry Anthol., 1973; United Poets, 1973, etc. Honours, awards incl: Cert. of Award, Major Poets Chapter, 1973; Hon. Cert., Soc. of Children's Book Writers, 1973; Cert. of Lifetime Mbrship, Int. Poetry Assn., Title of 'Danae', 1973. Address: 37 Shore Haven Park Rd., Hazlet, NJ 07730, U.S.A.

SIBLY, John, b. 30 Apr. 1920. Teacher. Education: M.A., St. John's, Cambridge Univ., 1945; Dip. Ed.; Bristol Univ., 1946. Positions held: Lectr., Makerere Univ.; Engl. Master, Dudley Grammar Schl.; Sr. Lectr., Birmingham Polytechnic. Member, Poetry Soc. Published works: Death of William Rufus, 1948; Sinfonia Elizabethana, 1956; Winter Doomset, 1965. Contbr. to: Windmill; Poetry Review; Fantasma; BBC Midland Poets, Third Programme. Address: 62 Halesowen Rd., Halesowen, Worcs. B62 9BA, U.K.

SIBUG, Brigido B., pen names **FLORO, Ruben & WATER-LILY,** b. 8 Oct. 1898. Journalist; Town Mayor; Businessman. Education: A.A.; A.B.; B.S.E.; LL.B. Positions held: Town Mayor; Sec., Comms. held by former Senator Yulo, Philippine Senate; Former Ed., Manila Social; Former Ed., Noventa y Seis & Emangabiran Impartial; 1st Poet Laureate of Pampanga, Philippines. Memberships: Acad. Hispanica de Filipinas; Akademya ng Wikang Pilipine; Acad. Pampanguena. Contbr. to various jrnls. in Engl., Spanish & Pampango. Address: 29 A. Bonifacio St., San Juan, Rizal, Philippines.

SIEBRASSE, Glen, b. 5 Nov. 1939. Publisher. Positions held: Co-ed., Yes Magazine, 1956-60, '64-67; Mng. Ed., Delta Canada Press, 1965–. Memberships: Treas., Independent Publrs. Assn., 1971–; Canadian League of Poets. Published works: The Regeneration of an Athlete, 1965; Man unman, 1968; Jerusalem, 1971; Editor, The Vanderbilt Poetry Review (Canadian Issue), 1972. Contbr. to the following anthols., mags., newspapers: McGill Daily; Montreal Herald; Best Poems, 1969; Unicorn Folio; Canadian Broadcasting Corp.; Maganda Radio; Blue Guitar; Canadian Forum; Canadian Poetry Magazine; Dalhousie Review; Delta; Edge; Evidence; Fiddlehead; Forge; Jaw Breaker; McGill Daily Review; Prism; Prism International; Quarry; Queen's Quarterly; Tamarack Review; Yes. Honours & Awards: Concours Lit. du Quebec, 1965; Canada Coun. Bursary, 1966; Scholarship, Quebec, 1968; Pres.'s Medal, Univ. of Western Ont., 1970; Canada Coun. Bursary, 1970; Scholarship, Quebec, 1971. Address: 351 Gerald St., Lasalle H8P 2A4, Quebec, Canada.

SIEGEL, Eli, b. 16 Aug. 1902. Poet; Founder & Teacher, Aesthetic Realism. Education: Baltimore City Coll., 1919. Published works include: Hot Afternoons Have Been in Montana: Poems, 1957; Hail, American Development, 1968. Contbr. to the following anthols., jrnls., mags., etc: Blues; Commentary; Hound & Horn; Poetry; The Nation; New Rep.; Times Lit. Suppl., London; Poor Old Tired Horse; Lit. Reveiw; Iowa Review; NY Quarterly, etc. Honours, awards: The Nation Poetry Prize, 1925; Nomination, Nat. Book Award, 1958. Address: c/o Definition Press, 39 Grove St., New York, NY 10014, USA.

SIGOGO, Ndabezinhle S., b. 2 June 1932. Journalist. Married. Positions held: Tchr.; Clerk for Govt. Dept.; currently Jrnlst. Memberships: PEN Int.; Chmn., Ndebele & Shana Writers' Assn. Published works: Imbongi Zalamhla Layizolo, 1959; Poems from An Africa, 1962; Kusile Mbongi Zohlanga, 1969; Uggozi Lwezimbongi, 1973. Contbr. to: The African Parade, 1958; Chirimo, 1968 & 69; Profile of Rhodesian Poets, 1969; The Voice of Black Africa, 1970; Rhodesia Calls, 1971. Address: Mambo Press, Box 2329, Bulawayo, Rhodesia.

SIKTANC, Karel, b. 10 July 1928. Writer. Education: Tchrs. Trng. Inst.; Charles Univ. Fac. of Pedagogy, Prague. Positions held: Ed., Czechoslovak Radio, 1950-60; Ed. of Czech lit., then Chief Ed. of the publishing house 'Mladá fronta', Prague, 1960-70; Freelance Writer, 1970–. Memberships: Czech Writers' Union, 1958 until its abolition; PEN. Published works: (books of poetry) Tobě živote, 1951; Pochodeň jara, 1954; Vlnobití, 1956; Žížeň, 1959; Heinovské noci, 1960; Patetická, 1961; Nebožka smrt, 1963; Paměť, selection, 1964; Artéská studna, 1964; Zařikávání živých, 1966; Město jménem Praha, 1966; Slepá láska, selection, 1968; Adam a Eva, 1968; Horoskopy, 1969. Translated: Slepa lubov; Makedonska kniga, 1970; Adam i Eva, 1971; (prose) Mariášky, 1970. Contbr. to var. lit. jrnls. Translations published in var. reviews & jrnls. in Yugoslavia, Hungary, Poland, Switz., Sweden, West Germany. Honours, awards: Prizes awarded for Heinovské noci, 1960 & Artéská studně, 1964 by Mladá fronta Publishing House; Prizes Awarded for Zařikávání živých, 1966 & Adam a Eva, 1968 by Ceskoslovenský spisovatel Publishing House. Address: Simackova 12, 170 00 Prague 7, Czechoslovakia.

SILK, Dennis Peter, b. 10 July 1928. Lecturer; Editor; Writer. Education: London Univ. Positions held: Publisher's Reader, John Lane, The Bodley Head; Lectr. in Puppet Theatre, Inst. of Fine & Performing Arts, Hebrew Univ. of Jerusalem. Published works: A Face of Stone, 1964; 'Now' (w. others), 1964; Retrievements: A Jerusalem Anthology, 1968. Contbr. to: Times Literary Supplement; N.Y. Times; Encounter; Midstream; Get That; Panorama moderner Lyrik; New Directions; Springtime; Jewish Quarterly & many Hebrew mags. Recip., Howard Fndn. Fellowship, Brown Univ., 1966-67. Address: P.O. Box 8103, Jerusalem, Israel.

SILKIN, Jon, b. 2 Dec. 1930. Writer. Education: Wycliffe and Dulwich Colls.; B.A.(Hons.), Leeds Univ. Positions held: Engl. Teacher; Founder, Editor, Stand (lit. journal); Visiting Lecturer, Denison Univ., Ohio, USA; Teacher, Writers' Workshop, Univ. of Iowa, 1968-69. Memberships: W.A.G.; Soc. of Authors. Published works: The Peaceable Kingdom, 1954; The Two Freedoms, 1958; The Re-ordering of the Stones, 1961; Nature With Man, 1965; Penguin Modern Poets 7 (with Murphy & Tarn), 1965; Poems New and Selected, 1966; Killhope Wheel, 1971; Amana Grass, 1971; Poets of the First World War (criticism), 1972; Poetry of the Committed Individual, 1973; The Principle of Water, 1974. Contbr. to: Stand; Times Lit. Supp.; New Statesman; Iowa Review; Poetry (Chicago), etc. Awards: Gregory Fellowship in Poetry, Leeds Univ., 1958-60; Beck Chair, Denison Univ., 1965; Geoffrey Faber Mem. Prize, 1966. Address: 58 Queens Rd., Newcastle on Tyne NE2 2PR, UK.

SILKO, Leslie Marmon, b. 5 Mar. 1948. Poet & Story Teller. Education: B.A., Univ. of New Mex., Albuquerque, 1969. Married John Silko, 2 sons. Positions held: Engl. Instr., Navajo Community Coll., Chinle, Ariz., 1972-73. Memberships: Phi Beta Kappa (Alpha Chapt.). Published works: The Man To Send Rainclouds: Contemporary Fiction by American Indians, 1974; Stories Southwest, 1973. Contbr. to: The Chicago Review; The Southern Review; The Northwest Review; Quetzal. Recip., Discovery Grant, Nat. Endowment for the Arts, 1970. Address: P.O. Box 652, Ketchikan, AK 99901, U.S.A.

SILLIMAN, Ronald Glenn, pen name **SILLIMAN, Ron,** b. 5 Aug. 1946. Writer; Organizer. Education: Merritt Coll.; San Francisco State Coll.; Univ. of Calif., at Berkeley. Married, 1965-70. Since 1972, Organizer for the Committee for Prisoner Humanity and Justice; Lobbyist for the Committee of 2600; Editorial Asst. for Mecca Publications, San Francisco. Membership: Coalition of Activist Writers. Published works: Moon in the 7th House, 1968; 3 Syntactic Fictions for Dennis Schmitz, 1969; Crow, 1971; Mohawk, 1973; nox, 1974. Contbr. to: Poetry; Chicago Review; Tri-Qtly. Review; Southern Review; Poetry Northwest; Caterpillar; This; El Corno Emplumado; Roy Rodgers; PF Flyer; Tuatara; Diana's BiMonthly; Shirt; Shelter; Silver; Grist; Beatitude; Occident; Arts in Society; American Weave; Nexus; Hollow Orange; CPHJ Newsletter; The Outlaw; City; L; Search for Tomorrow; Trace; Strange Faeces; Kauri; Bitterroot; Avalanche. Recip. Hart Crane & Alice Crane Williams Award, 1968; Joan Lee Yang Award, 1970, 1971. Address: 235 Missouri, San Francisco, CA 94107, USA.

SILLITOE, Alan, b. 4 Mar. 1928. Writer. Education: Schooling up to 14 yrs. Position held: Literary Adviser, W. H. Allen and Co. Ltd., Publishers. Membership: Soc. of Authors. Published works: Without Beer Or Bread, 1957; The Rats and Other Poems, 1960; A Falling Out Of Love and Other Poems, 1964; Love in the Environs of Voronezh, 1968; Shaman (poems), 1968; Barbarians and other poems, 1973. Contbr. to: New Statesman; Outposts; Transatlantic Review; Twentieth Century; New Yorker; Southern Review; Shenandoah Review; Encounter; Wave; Vanderbilt Poetry Review. Address: 21 The Street, Wittersham, Kent, UK.

SILVERMAN, Linda Parker, b. 23 Dec. 1942. Teacher; Freelance Editor. Education: B.S. in Educ., Northwestern Univ., 1965; M.A. in Engl. in progress, Univ. of Mich. Positions held: Program Asst., Office of Student Services, Univ. of Mich., Ann Arbor; Instr., Creative Writing, Ann Arbor 'Y'; Tchng. Asst. to Prof. Donald Hall, Dept. of Engl., Univ. of Mich. Contbr. to: Chelsea (N.Y.); Michigan Daily; Ann Arbor Review; Anon; Instant Coffee; Heartland. Honours, awards: 1st prize, Hopwood Award, Major Div., Poetry, Univ. of Mich., 1972, etc. Address: 2422 Laurelwood Circle, Ann Arbor, MI 48104, U.S.A.

SILVERS, Vicki, b. 22 Jan. 1941. Housewife. Positions held: Tchr. of Creative Writing for Children; Tchr. of Adult Educ. Prog. of Creative Writing, Brentwood H.S's Adult Educ. Prog. Published works: Sing a Song of Sound (children's book); Poetry published throughout U.S.A. & abroad; Haiku Poetry published & booklet of poetry. Contbr. to newspapers & mags. Recip., N.Y. State Merit in Poetry Cert., 1968; Hon. Mention Cert. for poem, Clover Coll. of Verse, 1969. Address: 60 Noble St., Brentwood, L.I., NY 11717, U.S.A.

SIMMONS, Dorothy Mary Murrell, b. 31 Aug. 1906. Poet. Memberships: Suffolk Poetry Soc.; Essex Poetry & Prose Soc. Contbr. to: A Suffolk Garland for the Queen (Suffolk Poetry Soc. Anthol.); The Field; Country Life; Good Housekeeping; Homes & Gardens; The Lady; Norfolk Mag.; East Anglian Mag.; Chambers Jrnl.; The Sign; Samphire; BBC Poetry from East Anglia. Awards: 1st Prize, Suffolk Poetry Soc. Crabbe Competition; 1st Prize, Essex Poetry & Prose Soc. Competition, 1966. Address: Salix, Haughley, Stowmarket, Suffolk, UK.

SIMMONS, James Stewart Alexander, b. 14 Feb. 1933. Teacher. Education: B.A. Engl., Leeds Univ., 1958. Married, 5 children. Positions held: Engl. Tchr., Friends' Schl., Lisburn; Lectr., Engl., Ahmadu Bello Univ., Nigeria; Engl. Lectr., New Univ. of Ulster, Coleraine, N. Ireland. Published works: Ballad of a Marriage, 1967; Late But in Earnest, 1967; Ten Poems, 1968; In the Wilderness, 1969; No Ties, 1970; Energy to Burn, 1971; No Land is Waste, Dr. Eliot, 1972; The Long Summer Still to Come, 1973. Contbr. to: Encounter; The Honest Ulsterman; Hibernia; The Irish

Times; The New Statesman; Paris Review; Listener; Spectator; Counter Measures; Caret; Phoenix; The Irish Press; The Belfast Telegraph; Scottish Int.; Atlantis; Transatlantic Review; Fortnight; Acorn; Capella; Everyman. Recip., Gregory Award, 1962. Address: 15 Kerr St., Portrush, N. Ireland.

SIMMONS, Margaret A., pen name "A", b. 14 Aug. 1940. Harpist; Co-Owner, Buckabest Publications. Education: B.A., 1969; M.A., 1971 & '73. Married, 2 sons. Positions held: Ed., Mgr., Pendragon Press; Libn., Rare Books, St. Patrick's Sem.; French Tchr., Woodside Priory; Cons. to Redwood City Arts Coun. Memberships: Welsh-Am. Lit. Soc.; Caughey Fellowship. Published works: Buckabest, 1973, '74; Unicorn, 1973; Cymru, 1973; In Search of Castles, 1972; Ed., Memoires of Diane Miller, 1965. Contbr. to: The Conch Shell; The Looking Glass; The Wheel, etc. Recip., The Fulton Legion of Am. Poets Award 'Oasis Prize' for most promising Bay Area Poetess. Address: 247 Fulton St., Palo Alto, CA 94301, U.S.A.

SIMMS, Colin, b. 15 June 1939. Naturalist. Editor, York Poetry (mag. and booklet series), and sometime Chairman, York Poetry Soc. Published works: Cleveland Acknowledged, 1971; Pomes and Other Fruit, 1971; Working Seams, 1972; Adders and Other Worms, 1972; Bear Skull or Before America, 1972; Birches and Other Striplings, 1973; (other works in progress); (Long poems): 1900 Worn for York, 1971; 2,000 Syllables for York, 1973; Modesty or Swaledale Summer, 1973 (others in progress). Contbr. to: Dalesman; York and County; Nature; Yorkshire Poets, 1971 and 1972; Yorkshire Gazette and Herald; Pennine Platform; Headland; New Headland; The York Consumer; Poetry Review; York Poetry; Here Now; Roots; The Sandcutters; and broadcasts BBC Radio, Leeds, and KRAR, Seattle. Awarded: Joe Skipsey Award for 1972 (by Sid Chaplin), 1973. Address: Llyn Buckler Studio, Bessie Surtees' House, Sandhill, Newcastle upon Tyne, UK.

SIMON, Hélène, b. 25 Mar. 1914. Author. Memberships: Acad. Internationale Leonardo da Vinci, Rome, Italy; Acad. Rhodanienne de Poésie, Lyon (Rhône), France; Acad. des Poètes de la mer, Rouen (Seine-Maritime); Haute Acad. Litt. et Artistique de France. Author of poetry, novels, tales and dramas including: Anthology Collections published by Editions de la Revue Moderne, Paris, France; Union culturelle de France: Editions subervie (Rodez). Contbr. to: Revue Indépendante (Syndicat des Journalistes et Ecrivains), Paris; L'Amitié par la plume (Club des Intellectuels Francais), Paris; Vent Noureau, Seix (Ariége); Idées pour tous, Nîmes (Gard); Cahiers de Poésie, 1970; Poèms d'ici et d'ailleurs, 1970; Acad. de Disquede Poésie, 1970. Honours: (prizes) Union culturelle de France, Paris, 1962, '65; Vent Nouveau, Seix, 1962, Acad. des Poètes de la mer, Rouen, 1967; Medal, Ville de Rouen, 1967; Diploma, Laurier Acad. Leonardo de Vinci, 1968. Address: 21 rue Championnet, 75, Paris 18e, France.

SIMON, István, b. 16 Sept. 1926. Writer; Literature Professor. Married, 2 children. Positions held: Journalist, 1952-55; Ed. of Uj Hang (lit. review), 1955-56; Ed. of Kortárs (lit. review), 1963-71. Memberships: Hungarian PEN Club; Union of Hungarian Writers. Published works: Egyre magasabban, 1944; Tanu vagyok, 1950; Hajnali la kodalmasok, 1952; Erlelö napok, 1954; Nem elég, 1955; Felhö árnyéka, 1955; Pacsirtaszó, 1958; Februári-szivarvány, 1959; Almafák, 1962; Gyümölcsoltó, 1964; Veröfény, 1968; Forró egöv Alatt, 1969; Gyalogutról a Világba, 1970; Orök körben, 1973; A Magyar Irodalom, 1973. Contbr. to: Kortárs; Uj Irás; Elet Es Irodalom; Europe; L'Esprit; New Hungarian Qtly.; Novi Mir; Innostrannaia Literatura. Honours, awards: Kossuth Prize, 1955; József Attila Prize, 1952, '54, '67. Address: Wallenberg U.7, Budapest XIII, Hungary.

SIMON, John Oliver, b. 21 Apr. 1942. Poet. Education: Swarthmore Coll., 1960-64; Univ. of Calif., Berkeley,

1964-66. Married Jan Manzanita, 2 daughters. Positions held: Yellow Cab, Oakland, 1966 & 67; U.S. Post Office, 1967-68; People's Printer, Noh Directions Press, 1968-70; Edited Aldebaran Review, 1967-; Org., People's Community Schl., 1969-73; has been working with Poetry in the Schools program, 1972-. Published works: Roads to Dawn Lake, 1968; Adventures of the Floating Rabbi, 1968; Cat Poem, 1969; Dancing Bear, 1969; The Woodchuck Who Lives on Top of Mt. Ritter, 1970; A Ten Days Journey from Badwater to Lone Pine, 1971; Animal, 1973; Living in the Boneyard, 1973. Contbr. to: (anthols.) Contemporaries; New American & Canadian Poetry; Campfires of the Resistance; Mark in Time; In Youth; Poems Read in the Spirit of Peace & Gladness, & var. mags., reviews etc. Address: 2209 California, Berkeley, CA 94703, U.S.A.

SIMON, Dr. Lorena (Samuel), b. 16 Jan. 1897. Author; Teacher; Lecturer. Education: Kidd Key Coll. & Conservatory, 1913-14; Grad., St. Joseph's Acad., Sherman, Tex., 1915; Dip., Sherwood Music Schl., 1941; Hon. Litt. L.D.; Hon. H.L.D. Married, Samuel C. Simon. Positions held: Author; Tchr., Violin & Piano; Poet Laureate; Composer & Publr. of Songs; Lecturer; Director; Adjudicator. Memberships: Edit. & Advsry. Bd., Int. Who's Who in Poetry; Crowned Hon. Int. Catholic Poet Laureate (life appt.), chosen by United Poets Laureate Int. to succeed late Cardinal Spellman, 1968; Judge, Int. Poetry Contest, World Congress of Poets, Manila, Philippines, 1969; Nat. & Tex. Press Women's Assocs.; Charter Mbr., Nat. Guild of Piano Tchrs.; Nat. & Tex. Music Tchrs. Assoc.; Pres., Writers Club, Port Arthur, Tex.; Poetry Soc. of Tex.; Am. Poetry League, etc. Publications: The Golden Key, 1958; From My Heart, 1959; Children's Story Hour, 1960; Golden Memories, in press. Composer of songs & carols widely performed. Contbr. to: (anthols.) Today's Poets, 1965; Anthol. of Am. Poetry, 1962; From Sea to Sea in Song; Bouquet of Poems, etc. (jrnls.) NY Times; Laurel Leaves; Am. Poetry League Mag.; Houston Post; Tex. Music Educator; Tex. Observer; Music Leader; Nat. Guild Piano Guild Notes; Beaumont Enterprise; Port Arthur News; Austin Statesman; Am. Music Tchrs., etc. Honours: numerous honours & awards, incl. Poet Laureate, State of Tex., 1961; Resolutions from Senate of Tex. & from Tex. House of Reps. for outstanding work in lit. & music around the world, 1967; Children's Story Hour, 1st Place Winner, Nat. Fed. Press Women's Annual Writers' Contest, 1961-62; From My Heart, 1st Place Winner, Annual Poetry Writers' Contest, Tex. Press Women's Assoc., 1961; Golden Key, Book of the Week, NY Times, 1959; Bronze, Silver & Gold medals, Centro Studi E Scambi Internazionali; Gold Laurel Wreath, Gold medal, Karta of Award, UPLI, etc. Address: 411 5th Ave., Port Arthur, Tex. 77640, USA.

SIMON, Sally Lee Taylor, b. 14 Aug. 1919. Poet & Writer. Education: Barry Coll.; studied poetry w. V. Laramore Rader courses for 3 yrs., Univ. of Miami. Divorced, 6 children. Memberships: Laramore Rader Poetry Grp.; V. Laramore Rader Poet Laureate of Fla. Contbr. to: Miami Herald; Eye Dr. Mag. Address: Apt. B.204, Banyon Bay Apt., 750 N.E. 64th St., Miami, FL 33138, U.S.A.

SIMONOV, Konstantin Mikhailovich, pen name of KIRILL, b. 28 Nov. 1915. Poet; Dramatist; Novelist. Education: Maxim Gorky Lit. Inst., Moscow. Positions held: War Correspondent, Red Star; ibid., Pravda; Dpty. to Supreme Soviet, 1946-54; Ed., Literaturnaya gazeta (jrnl.), 1950-53; Ed., Novy Mir (jrnl.), 1946-50, '54-58. Published works: (poetry) Real Men, 1938; Ice Blood Battle, 1938; Pavel Cherny, 1938; A Son of an Artilleryman, 1942; Friends and Enemies, 1948; Selected Poems, 1960; Three Note Books, 1964; Selected Poems, 1964; (plays) A Story of Love, 1940; Fellow From Our Town, 1942; The Russians, 1942; Russian Question, 1946; Alien Shadow, 1949; The Fourth, 1962; (novels) Days and Nights, 1944; Comrades in Arms, 1953; Those Alive and Those Dead, 1959; Over there, where were once..., 1964; Soldiers Are Not Born, 1964; From Lopatin's Notes,

1965. Awards; 6 state prizes.

SIMONS, Maxine, b. 16 July 1939. Medical Receptionist; Secretary. Education: Phoenix Coll., Ariz. Memberships: Poetry Soc. of Tex.; V.P., Garland Chapt., ibid, 1971; Reporter for newspapers, Garland Chapt., 1970. Recip. awards from Garland Chapt., Poetry Soc. of Tex. Address: 700 W. Ave. G., Garland, TX, U.S.A.

SIMPSON, Barbara Flanagan, b. 23 Feb. 1920. Secretary; Artist; Writer. Education: A.B., Florence State Univ., Ala., 1963; postgrad., Christian Educ., Presbyn. Schl. of Christian Educ., Richmond, Va., 1967-68; Penland Schl. of Crafts, Penland, N.C. Divorced, 2 children. Positions held: Area Corres., B'ham Post Herald; Substitute Tchr., City of Florence; Sec., Dept. of Art, Florence State Univ. Memberships: Sigma Tau Delta; Charter Mbr., Ala. State Poetry Soc.; Comms. for Designing Emblem, 1970 & for editing yearly publ. 'The Sampler', 1971; Ala. Writers Conclave. Contbr. to: The Rectangle; The Sampler; Florence Times; Tri Cities Daily; The Messenger. Honours, awards: 2nd prize, Poetry Contest, The Messenger, 1970; Hon. Mention, Ala. State Poetry Soc. Student Contest, 1973. Address: North Lane Apts. B., Box 420-B, Rte. 3, Florence, AL 35630, U.S.A.

SIMPSON, Edith Eva, b. 17 Feb. 1902. Accounting Clerk (Rtd.). Education: High Schl., Twinsburg, Ohio, USA, 1920. Married to Edmund Simpson (divorced). Positions held: Clerk, US Fed. Civil Serv., 1951-63. Memberships: Int. Clover Poetry Assn., Wash., DC (Life mbr.). Contbr. to the following anthols., jrnls., mags., etc: Poetry Parade, 1966. 1968; Penman Anthol., 1966-68; Shore Anthol., 1971; Grit; Angel Hour; Spafaswap Mag.; J. Mark Press Anthol., 1971; Am. Scenes, 1972; Notable Am. Poets, 1973; Best Poets of the Twentieth Century Anthol., 1973; SW Breeze Poetry Mag.; Int. Who's Who in Poetry Anthol., 1973. Honours, awards: 2nd Prize, 1st & 3rd. Hon. Mention, San Diego Poet's Assn. Contest, 1970; 3rd Prize, Int. Clover Poetry Competition, 1971; Cert. of Merit, 4th Hon. Mention for Mod. Lyric, Nat. Fedn. of States Poetry Socs. Contest, 1972; 3rd Prize, Light Verse, San Diego Poet's Assn. Contest, 1971; 3rd Prize, Int. Jesse Stuart Contest, Okla., 1973. Address: 630 'F' St., San Diego, Calif. 92101, USA.

SIMPSON, Joan Murray, b. 16 Dec. 1918. Writer; Poet. Positions held: w. Latin American Serv., BBC; Poetry Reader, Home Serv., BBC. Memberships: Poetry Soc.; PEN Club. Published works: Driving At Night, 1968. Contbr. to following anthols. & jrnls: Without Adam, 1968; My Kind Of Verse; The Pattern of Poetry; The Healing of the Nations; See Through A Diamond; Laudamus Te; Outposts; Poetry Review; English; The Lady; Tablet; Manifold; Priapus; Envoi; etc. Awards: Gold Medal, Poetry Soc. Address: 60 Highfield Ave., London, NW.11, UK.

SIMPSON, Louis, b. 27 Mar. 1923. Writer. Education: B.S., Columbia Univ. N.Y., U.S.A., 1948; A.M., ibid, 1950; Ph.D., 1959. Married 1) Jeanne C. Rogers, 1 son, div.; 2) Dorothy M. Roochvarg, 2 children. Positions held: Assoc. Ed., Bobbs-Merrill Publishing Co., N.Y.C., 1950-55; Tchr., Columbia Univ., N.Y., 1955-59; Tchr. (Prof. of Engl.), Univ. of Calif., Berkeley, 1959-67; Prof. of Engl., State Univ. of N.Y., Stony Brook, 1967-. Fellowships: Am. Acad. in Rome; John Simon Guggenheim Meml. Fndn. Published works: The Arrivistes, Poems 1940-49, 1949; Good News of Death & Other Poems, 1955; A Dream of Governors, 1959; At the End of the Open Road, 1963; Selected Poems, 1965; Adventures of the Letter I, 1971. Contbr. to num. jrnls., mags. etc. inclng: Hudson Review; Paris Review; Harper's Mag.; The New Yorker; New Statesman; London Mag.; Times Lit. Supplement; Critical Quarterly. Honours, awards: Hudson Review Fellow in Poetry, 1957; Prix de Rome, 1957; Disting. Serv. Award, Schl. of Gen. Studies, Columbia Univ., 1960; Edna St. Vincent Millay Award, 1960; Pulitzer Prize for Poetry, 1964; Columbia Univ.

Award for Excellence, 1965. Address: P.O. Box 91, Port Jefferson, NY 11777, U.S.A.

SIMPSON, Matt, b. 13 May 1936. Lecturer. Education: Fitzwilliam House, Cambridge, U.K., 1955-58; Liverpool Univ., 1958-59. Married German Actress, Monika Weydert, 2 children. Positions held: Sr. Lectr. in Engl., Coll. of Educ. Memberships: Merseyside Poetry Festivals Comm.; Poets Conf. Published works: Letters to Berlin, 1971; A Skye Sequence, 1972; Collage One, 1972. Contbr. to: The Listener; Phoenix; Second Aeon; Oasis; Outposts; Caret; Contrasts; The Village Review; Lines; Country Quest; Arts Alive Merseyside, Liverpool; Envoi; Gemini; Granta; Delta; Sphinx; Torch; Universities Poetry; The Anglo-Welsh Review; (anthols.) Poetry from Cambridge, 1954-58; Roll the Union On, 1973. Numerous poetry readings inclng: Philharmonic Hall, Liverpool; Warwick Univ. & weekend confs. at Oxford, Bowness, Manchester, etc. Address: 29 Boundary Dr., Liverpool L25 OQB, U.K.

SIMPSON, Minerva Maloon, b. 19 Apr. 1876. Housewife and Poet. Education: Public Schools of East Machias, Maine; Grad. from Washington Acad. (East Machias) in 1895 (class poet). Married, Dr. George E. Simpson in 1901; 3 d. Published works: Songs from the Sky, 1947; Poems, 1968. Contbr. to: Poet; Pegasus; Poets of America (anthol.), 1940; Spirit of America (anthol.), 1943; Post War Anthol., 1947; Quinsnickett Book of Verse; Cranston Herald; Valley News (East Machias, Maine). Awards: 1st Prize, Annual Arts Festival, Cranston, R.I., 1965; Hon. Membership, World Poetry Soc., 1971. Address: Danielson Pike, Scituate, RI 02857, USA.

SIMPSON, Ronald Albert, b. 1 Feb. 1929. Lecturer; Poet. Trnd. Primary Tchrs. Cert., Melbourne Tchrs. Coll., Australia; Assoc., Royal Melbourne Inst. of Technol. Married, 2 children. Positions held: Primary Tchr., Aust. & UK; Sec. Tchr., Aust.; Sub-Ed., Publs. Dept., Educ. Dept.; Lectr. & Hd., Painting Dept., Caulfield Inst. of Technol. Memberships: Aust. Soc. of Authors; Poetry Ed., The Bull., 1963-65; Poetry Ed. & Reviewer, The Age, 1969-. Published works: The Walk Along the Beach, 1960; This Real Pompeii, 1964; After the Assassination, 1968; (forthcoming) Diver. Contbr. to: Meanjin; Observer; Poetry Chicago; The Australian; Aust. Poetry (anthols.); Sidney Morning Herald, etc. Address: 29 Omama Rd., Murrumbeena, Melbourne, Australia 3163.

SIMPSON, Rubye Lucille Tennyson, b. 9 July 1924. Accountant. Memberships: Rep., World Poetry Soc.; Sec., Tenn. Poetry Soc., 1966-67 & 68-69; Treas., ibid, 1969-70; Recording Sec., 1973-74; Am. Poets Fellowship; Poets Roundtable of Ark., Okla. State Poetry Soc.; Marquis Lib. Soc.; Cherokee Nat. Hist. Soc.; Tenn. Hist. Soc. Published works: Diamonds on a Chain (poetry), 1965. Contbr. to: Tenn. Poetry Soc. Book of the Year, 1965-73 (now Tenn. Voices); Todays Poets; Selected Poems 1966; Greenhouse; Memphis Poems by Memphis Poets, Sesquicentennial Anthol., 1969; Home Life, 1973; Commercial Appeal; Bolivar Bulletin-Times; North Little Rock Times; The Guild; Haiku Highlights; Am. Poet, etc. Honours, awards: var. awards, Mid-South Poetry Fests., 1966-71; Sonnet-Poets Roundtable of Ark., 1967; Edgar Lee Masters Centennial Award, 1969; var. awards, Tenn. Poetry Soc., 1966-73. Address: 935 Newell Rd., Memphis, TN 38111, U.S.A.

SINCLAIR, Bennie Lee, b. 15 Apr. 1939. Writer. Education: B.A., Furman Univ., 1961. Married Don Lewis. Positions held: Poet-in-the-Schools, sponsored by the Nat. Endowment for the Arts & S.C. Arts Commn., 1972-73, '73-74; var. poetry readings & workshops. Published works: Little Chicago Suite, 1971; The Conditions, 1971, '72, '73. Contbr. to: Foxfire; The S.C. Review; Furman Studies; Aim; The Human Voice; Prize Poems; The New Janitor's Nose; Poet Lore; The Yearbook of the Poetry Soc. of S.C.; The Landrum Leader. Honours, awards: Katherine Lyons Clark Free Verse Award, Pa. Poetry Soc., 1969; Shakespearian Sonnet Award, Poets Club of Chicago,

1969; Charleston News & Courier Award, Poetry Soc. of S.C., 1970; Stephen Vincent Benet Narrative Poem Award, Poet Lore, 1970; Poetry Award, Ky. State Poetry Soc., 1970; S.C. Poets Award, S.C. Review, 1972. Address: P.O. Box 278, Campobello, SC 29322, U.S.A.

SINCLAIR, Keith, b. 5 Dec. 1922. Professor of History. Education: M.A., Ph.D., N.Z.; Litt.D. Positions held: Lectr. in Hist., Univ. of Auckland, 1947; Prof. of Hist., ibid, 1962–. Memberships: PEN; Chmn., N.Z. Authors Fund Advisory Comm. Published works: Songs For A Summer, 1950; Strangers or Beasts, 1954; A Time to Embrace, 1963; The Firewheel Tree, 1973. Contbr. to: A Book of New Zealand Verse, 1923-50; A Charlatan's Mosaic: New Zealand; An Anthol. of C'wealth Verse; Arts in N.Z. Yearbook; Australian Letters; Comment; Edge; Here & Now; Jindyworobat Anthol.; Kiwi; Landfall; Meanjin Qtly.; N.Z. Listener; N.Z. Poetry Yearbook; Numbers; Poetry Yearbook; Southerly, etc. Address: Dept. of Hist., Univ. of Auckland, Private Bay, Auckland, New Zealand.

SINGER, Elsie S., pen name **SINGER, Elsie,** b. 25 Aug. 1910. Retired Court Reporter, Civil Servant. Married to Perry Singer (now deceased). Secretary, Poetry Society of Georgia, 1950 and 1951, and member (for 30 years). Contrib. to: The Chicago Jewish Forum; Spring Anthology (Mitre Press), 1967; Cyclotron; Christian Science Monitor; Good Housekeeping; McCall's; Home & Gardens; Yankee. Recipient various monthly awards Poetry Soc. of Georgia. Address: P.O. Box 807, Orleans, Mass., 02653, USA.

SINGER, Sarah (Beth), b. 4 Jul. 1915. Writer, Teacher. Education: B.A., NY Univ.; Post-grad., New School for Social Research. Married to Leon E. Singer; 2 children. Positions held: Teacher of Creative Writing, and Poetry. Memberships: Poetry Soc. of America; Nat. League of Am. Penwomen, Long Island Branch (Poetry Chairman). Published work: Magic Casements, 1956. Contbr. to: NY Times; Commentary; Voices; Lyric; New Mexico Qtly.; McCall's; Yankee; Chicago Jewish Forum; Fiddlehead; Quicksilver; Talking Book; Poet Lore; Imprints Qtly.; Poetry Digest; Penwomen; Village Gazette; Flower & Feather; Bitterroot; CS Monitor; Rochester Democrat and Chronicle; Voices Internat; Golden Quill Anthols., 1966, 1967, 1968, 1969, 1970, 1971. Poetry Prizes, etc.: Magic Casements recorded by The John Milton Soc., 1957; 1st Prize, Poetry Contest, Manhattan Br., Nat. League of Am. Penwomen, 1960; 2nd Prize, Confederacy Centennial Poetry Contest, Poetry Soc. of Virginia, 1964; 3rd Prize, Stephen Vincent Benet Narrative Poetry Contest, Poetry Lore, 1968; World Poetry Day Award and Prize for best trad. poem, Imprints Qtly., 1969; 1st Prize, Stephen Vincent Benet Narrative Poetry Contest, Poet Lore, 1971; James Joyce Award, Poetry Soc. of America, 1972; Consuelo Ford Mem. Award, Poetry Soc. of America, 1973. Address: 38 Stephan Marc Lane, New Hyde Park, NY 11040, USA.

SINGERLING, Vivian Melissa (Drake), b. 20 Mar. 1911. Education: Home Study Course in Writing, Writers' Inst., Newspaper Inst. of Am., 1967. Married, 1 son, 1 daughter. Var. volunteer services. Memberships: Past Sec. & Past Pres., Belvidere Soroptimist Club, Soroptimist Fed. of the Americas; Treas., Musconetcong Chapt. of the N.J. Poetry Soc.; World Poetry Soc. Intercontinental; Am. Poets Fellowship Soc.; Speak Out Lit. Assn. Contbr. to: Our Pets Anthol., 1967; Pet Prose & Poems, anthol., 1966; New Voices in the Wind, 1969; The Soul & The Singer, 1968; Moon Age Poets, 1970; Star Borne; Cosmic Cadence; 1972 N.J. Poetry Soc. Anthol.; Unripe Fruits; Poet; The Am. Poet; Swordsman Review; Speak Out; The Miami Times, etc. Honours, awards: Cert. of Merit, The Am. Poets Fellowship Soc., 1973; 3rd Prize in Lanterne Form Contest, N.J. Poetry Soc., 1973. Address: R.D. Box 29, Belvidere, N.J. 07823, U.S.A.

SINGH, Gopal, b. 29 Nov. 1917. Poet; Writer;

Diplomat; Translator. Education: M.A., Ph.D., Punjab Univ., Lahore, India. Positions held: Prof., Engl. Lit., Univ Coll., 1938-46; Migrated to India, 1946; Ed., Publr., The Liberator, weekly Engl. lang. jrnl., 1946-50; Writer, 1950–; Nominated by Pres. of India to India's Parliament as a distinguished man of letters, 6 yr. term, 1962; Lectr., Broadcaster, radio & TV, all over world; Jury Service, various prize comms., Govt. & other cultural bodies; Indian Ambassador, Bulgaria, 1970–. Memberships: Sponsor, World Congress on Religion & Peace; Past Chmn., Tibetan Industrial Rehabilitation Soc.; Past Chmn., Punjabi Writers' Union; ibid, Punjabi Writers' Co-op. Publg. House; Gvng. Coun., Indian Coun. for Cult. Relations; Fellow, Punjab Univ. Senate; Indian Inst. for Higher Studies, Simla; Gvng. Coun., Indian Inst. of Scis., Bangalore; Past mbr., Central Advsry. Bd. for Educ., New Delhi; Gvng. Coun., Christian Bd. for Higher Educ. (only non-Christian mbr.); Central Govt. Films Consultative Comm.; Chmn., Indian Coun. for Human Rights. Published works: Two early vols. of verse, 1942, 1950; History of Punjabi Literature; Romanticism in Punjabi Poetry; Adi Granth as Literature; Maya te Brahm (God & Illusion: short stories); Principles of Literary Criticism; Free-Verse Engl. Transl. of The Sikh Scripture, Shriguru Granth Sahib, 4 vols., 1960-62; Anhad Nad (Punjabi verse), 1964, also transl. by author into Engl.; The Man Who Never Died, long poem in Engl., a mystic reinterpretation of Jesus & His philos., with foreword by the Pope, to be publd., UK; Two Ciogs: Guru Nanak; Guru Gobind Singh, publd. in 14 langs.; The Religion of the Sikhs; A History of the Sikh People. Contbr. to: BBC (humerous sketches); All India Radio; various Indian daily newspapers (articles on social & political affairs); Illustrated Weekly of India (short stories), etc. Honours, Awards: Much critical acclaim for transl. of Sikh Scripture; Numerous prizes, gold medals, citations, from govts., lit. & cult. organizations. Address: Ambassador of India, Sofia, Bulgaria.

SINGH, Gurvir Inder, pen name, **BULBUL,** b. 22 March 1942. Painter. Education: Senior Cambridge, from the Lawrence School, Sanawar, India; B.A.(Hons.) in History, Delhi Univ., India; M.A. in History, Kansas State Univ., USA. Positions held: Sales & Marketing Manager, Lever's, 1964-70; Group Head, Lintas, 1970-72. Memberships: Phi Alpha Theta, nat. scholastic history, honorary, USA, 1963; All-India Scholarship holder (history), 1958-61, Univ. of Delhi. Published works: Not Seriously, 1964 (essays & poems); Faraway, 1970 (painting and poetry); OM is, 1971 (prose-verse); Mud poems, 1973 (poetry); Windblown 1973 (painting and poetry). Contbr. to: Sainik Samachar; Illustrated Weekly of India; Poetry India; Junior Statesman; Quest; Dialogue; Ocarina; Debonair; (poetry readings in Bombay, Delhi, Kabul, Tehran, Athens, Rome, Paris, London). Address: A-3 Beach House Park, Gandhigram Rd., Juhu, Bombay 400 054, India.

SINGH, Narenderpal, b. 17 Oct. 1924. Army Officer. Education: B.A., Sikh Nat. Coll., Punjab Univ. Positions held: Military Attaché, Embassy of India, Kabul, Afghanistan, 1956-59; Dpty. Mil. Sec. to Pres. of India, 1962-66; Mil. Attaché, Embassy of India, Paris, France, 1966-69; Commandant, Cent Ordnance Depot, Poona; Rank of Brigadier; Editor, Byword (English); Jt. Editor, Vikendrit (Punjabi). Memberships: Int. PEN; Poetry Soc. of Am.; Indian PEN; Société des Gens de Letteres, Paris; Société des Poétes françaises, Paris; Punjabi Sahit Sabha; United Poets Laureate Int., Manila, Philippines. Published works: about 35 books, incl. 6 collections of poems: Agami Wehan, 1948; Kil Te Kame, 1957; Tira Jal, 1957; Aman de Rah, 1957; Gleanings from the Masters, 1965; Chants Spitituels de Sikhs (transl. into French), 1968; Chanan Khara Kinare, 1968; Light Stands Aside, 1969; Tapu, 1969; Vikendrit, 1971; On the Crest of Time, 1971; Love in Nagaland, 1972; Paris de Portrait, 1972; Sir Dije kan na Kije, 1973. Contbr. to: Indian Lit.; PEN Jrnl.; Sikh Rev.; Spokesman; Arsee; Panj Darya; Punjabi Sahit; Jan Sahit; Surtal; Hem Joyti; Savera, London, UK; Des Pardes, London;

Sanjhi Dunyan; Fateh Weekly; Ranjit Weekly; Kirna Weekly; Illustrated Weekly of India; Femina; Eve's Weekly. Honours: Dr. of Literacy Leadership, Int. Acad. of Leadership, Manila, 1967; Grande Medaille d'Or de la Ville de Paris, 1968; Robe of Honour by the govt. of Punjab for being Doyen of Litterateurs; Hon. Mbr., Punjabi Univ. Senate. Address: G-52 Lajpat Nagar, New Delhi 110024, India.

SINGH, Nirupama, b. 20 Feb. 1950. Poet. Education: American School, Kabur, Afghanistan; Inst. des Etudes Science Politiques, Paris; Panjab Univ., Chandigarh, India. Daughter of Brigadier Narenderpal Singh and Prabhjot Kaur. Married to J.P. Singh, grandson of Mr. Hukam Singh, Speaker, Parliament of India. Positions held: Asst. Editor, Byword (English); Vikendrit (Punjabi); Sec., Lajpat Social Welfare Board. Member: Indian P.E.N.; Soc. des Gens de Lettres, Paris. Pub.: Upturned Shoe, 1972. Contrib. to: Spokesman; National Solidarity; Illustrated Weekly of India; Femina; The Poet; The Indian P.E.N.: Punjab Mail, etc. Address: 6a Ring Rd., Lajpat Nagar III, New Delhi, India.

SIPFLE, Louise Adele Hinners, b. 20 Aug. 1909. Housewife & Poet. Education: B.S., Ill. Wesleyan Univ., Bloomington, 1931. Married Karl E. Sipfle. Memberships: Pres., Friends of Wheaton Pub. Lib., Ill., 1963-65; Sec., Friends of Am. Writers, Chicago, 1968-70; Charter Mbr., Dupage Co. Poetry Club, Ill.; Poets & Patrons, Chicago. Contrib. to: Chicago Tribune; Selected Poems, Fla. State Poetry Soc., 1966; Haiku Highlights; Jean's Jrnl.; United Poets; Am. Poet; Prairie Poet; Progressive Woman; The Rotarian. Honours, awards: var. 1st prizes, 10th Dist., Ill. Fed. of Women's Clubs contests, 1968-69; 2-1st Prizes, Poets & Patrons of Chicago, 1971; 1st Prize, Nat. League of Am. Pen Women, Chicago Br., 1973. Address: 19W074 Ave. Barbizon, N., Oak Brook, IL 60521, U.S.A.

SISSON, Charles Hubert, pen name SISSON, C.H., b. 22 Apr. 1914. Writer. Education: Univs. of Bristol, Berlin, Freiburg, and Paris. Positions held: War-time service in the ranks (army) mainly in India; Simon Senior Research Fellow (Manchester Univ.); senior administrative posts in the Civil Service for some years. Published works: Versions and Perversions of Heine, 1955; The London Zoo, 1961; Numbers, 1965; Catullus, 1966; The Discarnation, 1967; Metamorphoses, 1968; Roman Poems, 1968; In the Trojan Ditch, 1974. Contrib. to: New English Weekly; Scotsman; Dublin Mag.; Anthos; Holy Door; X; Two Rivers; Agenda; Aquarius; Other Voices; Poetry Nation; Critical Qtly.; Botteghe Oscure. Address: Moorfield Cottage, The Hill, Langport, Somerset, UK.

SITARAMAYYA, Kolar Bhaskarapandit, b. 17 Apr. 1926. Postgraduate Professor of English. Education: B.A., St. Joseph's Coll., Bangalore, India, 1947; M.A., Presidency Coll., Madras, 1950. Positions held: Sr. Telugu Pandit, St. Aloysius H.S., Bangalore, 1947-48; Lectr. in Engl., Annamalai Univ., Annamalainagar, 1950-71; Postgrad. Prof. of Engl., Scott Christian Coll., Nagercoil, 1971–. Memberships: Hon. Mbr., United Poets Laureate Int., Philippines; Reg. Mbr., Am. Studies Rsch. Ctr., Hyderabad. Contbr. to many mags., jrnls., quarterlies in U.S.A., Australia, Philippines, S. Africa & India inclng: Am. Bard; The Saint; The Angel Hour; Vision Quarterly; Laurel Leaves; Poet, Madras; Vedanta Kesari; Ocarina; Visvabharati, Shantiniketan; The Call Divine, Bombay; Mother India, Pondicherry. Honours, awards, incl: UPLI Pres. Mancos Gold Medal, 1963. Dr. of Lit. Ldrship, Int. Acad. of Ldrship, 1967; Winner's Award for Translation of Jose Rizal's Postrer Adios, 1968. Attended Second World Congress of Poets at Taipei, Taiwan, 1973. Address: Scott Christian Coll., Nagercoil, Kanyakumari (Cape Comorin), S. India.

SITO, Jerzy S., b. 8 Nov. 1934. Writer. Education: Structural Engrng., London. Positions held: Foreign Ed., 'Współczesność', arsaw, 1960-66; Lit. Dir., 'Teatr Zeromskiego', Kielce, 1962-63; Lit. Dir., 'Teatr Klasyczny', Warsaw, 1963-65; Lit. Dir., 'Teatr Powszechny', Warsaw, 1966-69; Lit. Dir., 'Teatr Narodowy' (Nat. Theatre), Warsaw, 1969-74. Memberships: Polish Writers' Union; PEN Club; V.P., Polish Dramatic-Writers' Club. Published works: Wiozę Swój Czas Na Ośle, 1958; Zdjęcie z Koła, 1960; Smierć i Miłość, 1963; Ucieczka do Egiptu, 1964; Pasja i Potępienie Doktora Fausta, 1973; Wiersze Dawne i Nowe, 1974; (2 vols. of essays on poetry & drama) W Pierwszej i Trzeciej Osobie, 1967; Szekspir na Dzisiaj, 1971. Co-edited a 3-vol. anthol. of 'Poets of the English Language', 1964, '71. Var. translations from Metaphysical Poets, Shakespeare & Marlowe. Contbr. to jrnls. in Paris, London, Warsaw & Cracow. Honours, awards: Poznań Poetry Award (Best Debut of 1958); Marian Kister Award for transl. of Engl. poetry, N.Y., 1968. Address: UL. Czeska 16, Warsaw 03-902, Poland.

SITWELL, Phronsie Irene (Mrs. H.C. FitzRoy Sitwell), pen names, **COLE, Florence; TOURNIER, Ann Catherine,** b. 1 April 1907. Educator; Owner & Manager of historic properties in Lynchburg and Bedford, Virginia. Education: Mary Washington Coll., B.S., 1927; Columbia Univ., M.A., 1952; NY Univ. (candidate for Ph.D., 1940-41, work not completed on dissertation). Positions held: Teacher in Secondary Schools and Colleges, 1927-72. Memberships: Writers Club of Va.; Poetry Soc. of Va.; Acad. of American Poets; Poetry Soc. of Bedford, Va., (served as co-founder & Pres., 1961-62, 1970-71); NLAPW, Lynchburg Branch; Mod. Language Assoc. (NY). Contbr. to: Social Science Qtly.; New Castle Record; NY State Education Journal; Dist. of Columbia Education Assoc. Bulletin; Bedford Bulletin Democrat. Recip. of several awards for poetry. Address: Three Otters Estate, RFD 2, Box 15, Bedford, VA 24523, USA.

SITWELL, (Sir) Sacheverell, b. 1897. Poet; Writer. Education: Eton Coll.; Balliol Coll., Oxford. Positions held: High Sheriff of Northamptonshire, 1948-49. Published works: Southern Baroque Art, 1924; All Summer In A Day, 1926; The Gothick North, 1929; Life of Liszt, 1936; Dance of the Quick and the Dead, 1936; Conversation Pieces, 1936; La Vie Parisienne, 1937; Narrative Pictures, 1937; Roumanian Journey, 1938; Old Fashioned Flowers, 1939; Mauretania, 1939; Poltergeists, 1940; Sacred and Profane Love, 1940; Valse de Fleurs, 1941; Primitive Scenes and Festivals, 1942; The Homing of the Winds, 1942; Splendours and Miseries, 1943; British Architects and Craftsmen, 1945; The Hunters and the Hunted, 1947; The Netherlands, 1948; Selected Poems, 1948; Morning, Noon, and Night in London, 1948; Spain, 1950; Cupid and the Jacaranda, 1952; Truffle Hunt With Sacheverell Sitwell, 1953; Portugal and Madeira, 1954; Denmark, 1956; Arabesque and Honeycomb, 1957; Malta, 1958; Bridge of the Brocade Sash, 1959; Journey to the Ends of Time–Vol. 1, Lost in the Dark Wood, 1959; Golden Wall and Mirador, 1961; The Red Chapels of Banteai Srei, 1962; Monks, Nuns and Monasteries, 1965; The People's Palace; Doctor Conne and Gargantua; The Hundred and One Harlequins; Actor Rehearsing and Other Poems; Dance of the Quick & the Dead; The Thirteenth Caesar; Canons of Giant Art; Touching the Orient; Trio; Collected Poems; Southern Baroque Revisited, 1967. Honours, awards: Freedom of the City of Lima, Peru. Address: Weston Hall, Towcester, Northamptonshire, UK.

SJOSTRAND, Osten Sigvard, b. 16 June 1925. Poet; Translator; Editor; Contbr. to Swedish Broadcasting Corp. Positions held: Lit. Jrnlst.; Co-Ed., Utsikt; Ed., sev. anthols., lit. reviews. Memberships: Svenska Författarförbundet; The Writers' Union; Union of Swedish Dramatists; Union of the Swedish Translators; PEN. Published works incl: Dikter mellan midnatt och gryning, 1954; Främmande mörker, främmande ljus, 1955; Dikter 1949-55, 1958; Hemlöshet och hem, 1958; I vattumannens tecken, 1967; Ensamma stjärnor, en gemensan horisont, 1970; Drömmen är ingen fasad, 1971; (essays) Ande och verklighet, 1954; Världen skapas varje dag, 1960; Fransk lyrik, 1969 (transl. & Ed.); Yves Bonnefoy, Dikter, 1971 (transl. & Ed.); Gästabudet, 1962; (textbook for opera); Fantasins nödvändighet, 1971; The Hidden Music, 1974, & many transl. Contbr. to many anthols., jrnls., mags. Recip. of sev. honours, awards inclng: Bellmanpriset, Royal Swedish Acad., 1967. Address: Bergsgatan 12, 150 30 Mariefred, Sweden.

SKAWRON, Virginia, pen name, **NOBLE, Virginia,** b. 22 Jan. 1909. Sales Lady. Education: Self educated; Evening College, etc. Personal details: born at Blountstown, Florida, USA, of English and Irish parents. Positions held: Clerk and Switchboard Operator at Tampa Internat. Bank, Tampa, Florida; Sales Lady, Sacramento, Calif. Memberships: Sacramento Poetry Soc. (1 yr. Pres., 3 yrs. Sec. & Treas.); Nat. Fed. of State Poetry Socs., Inc.; California State Poetry Soc.; California Fed. of Chaparral Poets (El Camino Chapter, Sacramento). Inventor of poetry form – 'the Sevenelle'. Contbr. to: Jacksonville (Florida) Beach Journal; Jacksonville Journal; Nat. Reporter; Sacramento Union; American Bard; Swordsman Review; 2 anthols. (Swordsman Publishing Co.); Yearbook of Mod. Poetry, 1972; Dunnellon Sun (Florida). Recip. of sev. awards and hon. mentions (Sacramento Poetry Soc.; St. John's Annual Poetry Contest; Ina Coolbrith Poetry Contest; Calif. Fed. of Chap. Poets; Major Poets, etc.). Address: 1406 57th St., Sacramento, CA 95819, USA.

SKEETER, Sharyn Jeanne, b. 12 July 1945. Writer; Editor; Teacher. Education: B.A., City Coll. of N.Y., 1966; Grad. work in Lit., City Coll. Grad. Schl. Positions held: Tchr., N.Y. City Public Schls., 1966-69; Fiction/Poetry/Book Review Ed., Essence Mag., 1970–. Memberships: Authors' League; American Society of Magazine Editors; Fellow, Int. Poetry Soc. Contbr. to: Essence; Dues; Works; Black Creation; Keeping the Faith; The Thirteenth Moon. Address: Box 4442, Grand Ctrl. Stn., N.Y., NY 10017, U.S.A.

SKELTON, Robin, b. 12 Oct. 1925. Author & University Professor. Education: Christs Coll., Cambridge Univ., U.K., 1934-44; Univ. of Leeds, 1947-51. Married Sylvia Mary Jarrett, 1 son, 2 daughters. Positions held: Asst. Lectr. in Engl. Lang. & Lit., Univ. of Manchester, 1951-53; Lectr., ibid, 1953-63; Assoc. Prof. of Engl., Univ. of Victoria, B.C., Canada, 1963-66; Prof., ibid, 1966–; Chmn., Dept. of Creative Writing, 1973–. Memberships: Authors Soc.; PEN; League of Canadian Poets. Published works incl: Inscriptions, 1967; Because of This, 1968; Selected Poems 1947-67, 1968; An Irish Album, 1969; Georges Zuk: Selected Verse, 1969; Answers, 1969; The Hunting Dark, 1971; Two Hundred Poems from the Greek Anthol., 1971; Remembering Synge, 1971; The Hold of Our Hands, 1968; A Different Mountain, 1971; A Private Speech, 1971; Three for Herself, 1972; Musebook, 1972; A Christmas Poem, 1972; Country Songs, 1973; (criticism) The Writings of J.M. Synge, 1971; The Practice of Poetry, 1971; J.M. Synge, 1972; (biog.) John Ruskin: The Final Years, 1955; J.M. Synge & His World, 1971. Contbr. to num. anthols., periodicals, reviews. Honours, awards: Fellow, Royal Soc. Lit., 1966. Address: Dept of Creative Writing, Univ. of Victoria, Victoria, B.C., Canada.

SKIBA, Henry Patrick, pen name **WALENTY, Ryk,** b. 1 June 1931. Clerk-Typist. Education: Jrnlsm., Charles Morris Price Schl. of Philadelphia. Positions held: Staff mbr., Columbia Univ. Scholastic Press Assn. Conf., 1960-63; French Forms Ed., The Swordsman Review, 1966–, & Book Review Ed., ibid, 1967–. Memberships: Pres., Calif. Fed. of Chaparral Poets, 1965-67; Pres., Franklin's Junto Writers, 1960-61; V.P., Profl. Writers Club. of Phila., 1962-63; Treas., ibid, 1960-61; Sec.-Treas., Penn Laurel Poets of Phila., 1960-61; Sec., Phila. Catholic Poetry Soc., 1957-58; Bd. Mbr., Phila. Regl. Writers Conf., 1958-60; Recording Sec., ibid, 1959-60; Prog. Chmn., Poetry Forum, 1964; Pa. Poetry Soc.; Robert W. Service Chapt. of C.F.C.P. & Poets' Haven. Contbr. to: Am. Courier; Sonnet Sequences;

Starlanes; Poesy Book; The Spokesman; Am. Weave; Am. Bard; Wanderlust; Italian-Am. Herald, etc. Var. transl. from the Polish in jrnls. Address: 2812 St. George St., Los Angeles, CA 90027, U.S.A.

SKIBBE, Loretta Jean, b. 18 Nov. 1931. Education: Norwood Park Elem.; Wm. Howard Taft HS; Wright Coll. Positions held: The Chicago Daily News, TV. and Movie reviews, advertising copywriter; Public Relations Rep., Delton Corp. Memberships: U.P.L.I.; Internat. Culture, Poetry & Efficiency Soc.; Maryland State Poetry Soc. Published work: Poetry for The Thinking Woman. Contbr. to: Songs of the Free State Bards; Wm. Randolph Hearst Newspapers; Baltimore Sun; Baltimore Scene Mag.; Baltimore Jewish Times; The Jefferson Newspaper. Honour: Maryland Citizens Acting Poet Laureate, 1967. Address: 1 Chiara Ct., Towson, MD 21204, U.S.A.

SKINA, Agnes, pen name **SOTIRAKOPOULOU, Agnes,** b. 4 Nov. 1920. Writer. Education: Dip. in French Lit. Memberships: Greek Writers Soc.; Correspondante etrangere pour les ecrivains professionels de France; United Poets Laureate Int.; World Poetry Soc. Intercontinental. Published works: A Lonely Woman; The Lost Game; Seal on the Breast. Translations: French Poets Anthol.; The Wanted to Die of Love; From Land of Mana; The Revolution of 1911; But Life is the Strongest, etc. Contbr. to: Cahiers du Sud & Lettres Francaises (France); Marches de France (Belgium); Bitterroot (N.Y.); Nea Estia, Revue of Art, New Age & Iolkos (Greece) etc. Recip., Gold Medal & AWard as Lyric Poet, United Poets Laureate, Philippines. Address: 8 Stilponos St., 502 Athens, Greece.

SKINNER, Knute, b. 25 Apr. 1929. Poet. Education: A.B., Colo. State Coll., 1952; M.A., Middlebury Coll., 1954; Ph.D., Univ. of Iowa, 1958. Positions held: Instr. of Engl., Univ. of Iowa, 1955-56, '57-58, '60-61; Asst. Prof. of Engl., Okla. Coll. for Women, 1961-62; Lectr. in Engl., Western Wash. State Coll., 1962-71; Assoc. Prof. of Engl., ibid, 1971-73; Prof. of Engl., ibid, 1973–. Memberships: Poetry Soc. of Am.; Washington Poets Assn.; MLA. Published works: Stranger With A Watch, 1965; A Close Sky Over Killaspuglonane, 1968; In Dinosaur Country, 1969; The Sorcerers: A Laotian Tale, 1972. Rep. in many anthols. inclng: The New Orlando Poetry Anthol., vol. 3, 1967; Laudamus Te: A Cycle of Poems to the Praise & the Glory of God, 1967; An Introduction to Poetry, 1971; New Generation: Poetry Anthol., 1971; The Diamond Anthol., 1971; Our Only Hope is Humor: Some Public Poems, 1972; Poetry: An Introduction Through Writing, 1973; Messages, 1973. Contbr. to num. jrnls., mags., reviews & newspapers. Recip., Huntington Hartford Fndn. Fellowship, 1961. Address: 2600 Hampton Pl., Bellingham, WA 98225, U.S.A.

SKLAREW, Myra. Poet; Teacher. Married Bruce H. Sklarew, 1 son, 1 daughter. Currently involved in the translation of Macedonian poetry for an anthology & the writing of poems to be set to music in the tradition of the medieval Hebrew poetry which has been incorporated into the prayer books in use today. Poetry recorded for the Lib. of Congress Contemporary Poet's Series. Tchr. of Creative Writing, Am. Univ. in Wash., D.C. Mbr., Poetry Soc. of Am. & Acad. of Am. Poets. Contbr. to: 5 New Poets; Wash. Star Newspaper; N.Y. Times; Southern Poetry Review; Poet Lore; The Jerusalem Post; Al Hamishmar (transl. into Hebrew); Voyages; The Carolina Quarterly; Dryad; Arion's Dolphin; U.J.A. World; Response; Charles St. Jrnl.; Premiere; The Johns Hopkins Magazine; P.S.A. Diamond Anthol.; Nimrod; Lit. Annual 1972; Tufts Criterion; Edge. Poetry readings at: Trinity Coll., D.C.; Tel Aviv, Israel; Dunbarton Coll., D.C.; Montgomery Coll., Md.; Folger Shakespeare Lib., D.C.; Nat. Org. for Women, O. St. Theatre, D.C.; FM Radio, Balt.; The Johns Hopkins Univ.; Smithsonian Instn., D.C.; Tennessee Poetry Circuit (4 colls.); WETA TV. Co-Winner, Poetry Soc. of Ams. di Castagnola Award, 1972; Finalist, Discovery '72 program, Poetry Ctr., N.Y. Address: 6615 Hillmead

Rd., Bethesda, MD 20034, U.S.A.

SKONECZNY, Stanisław, b. 25 Feb. 1910. Forrestry Official. Education: Radom Univ., 1930; Szkely Rolniczej in Zynewicach pod Slonimion; Szkoly Glownej Gospodarstwa Wiejskiego, Warsaw. Memberships: Zwiazku Literatow Polskich; PEN Club. Published works: Słońce za murem, 1931; Słowa inne, 1937; Ziemia była szeroka, 1938; Nio milknie pieśń, 1939; Z lasu, 1946; Wierni ziemi, 1947; Pleban z Chedla, 1950; Wiersze wybrane, 1951; Kostka Napierski, 1951; Jak galäż, 1955; Obraz świata, 1957; Ptak pod chmurą, 1959; Wizje, 1961; Ureki, 1962; Koło, 1963; Zaklęcie, 1964; Pod wielkim wozem, 1965; Poezje wybrane, 1966; Istnienie, 1968; Powietrze, 1970; Objawienia, 1970; Lad, 1972; Zywieły, 1974. Contbr. to var. lit. jrnls. Honours, awards: Ziemi Krakewskiej Prize for Writing, 1950; Polonia Restituta, for 40 yrs. achievement/discovery in his profession, 1971. Address: ul. Krupnicza 22 m. 8, 31-123 Krakow, Poland.

SKRENTNY, Roger, b. 27 Aug. 1947. Writer. Education: B.A., Engl., Univ. of Wis., Milwaukee; M.A., Universidad de las Americas, Puebla, Mex. Positions held: Studio Engr.; Riding Instr.; Script Writer; Lectr. in Engl., etc. Memberships: Co-Dir., The Third Coast Poetry Ctr., Co. Mbr., Theater X; Plastik Fantastik Great Soc. Traveling Troop. Published works: I'd Rather Throw Bricks or Something Different for the Man Who Drinks Martinis, 1971. Contbr. to: Amalgamated Holding Co.; Freek Poetry; Tempest; Roots Forming; Here's a Few More; Workshop Writing; Interrobang; Suenos; Mex. Qtly.; Minn. Review; Chelsea; Stations; This Book Has No Title; New Poetry Out of Wisconsin. Honours, awards: Manuscript Award, Univ. of Colo. Writers' Conf., 1970; Hon. Mention, Hirham Poetry Award, Acad. of Am. Poets, 1968 & '69. Address: 2411 N. Oakland Ave., Milwaukee, WI 53211, U.S.A.

SKRZYNECKI, Peter Michael, b. 6 Apr. 1945. School Teacher. Education: St. Patrick's Coll., Strathfield; Sydney Teachers' Coll.; Univ. of New England, Armidale. Polish-Ukrainian descent, came to Australia in 1949. Taught in north west and Northern Rivers districts of NSW. in one-teacher schools; currently teacher in Sydney. Has also written radio scripts for the Australian Broadcasting Commission. Published works: There, Behind the Lids, 1970; Head-Waters, 1972. Contbr. to: The Age; The Australian; The Catholic Weekly; Hemisphere; Issue; Makar; Meanjin Qtly.; New Poetry; Poetry Australia; Poetry Mag.; Quadrant; Sydney Morning Herald; Southerly; The Aust. Broadcasting Commission; (anthols.) Australian Poetry (1969-73); Australian Poetry Now; The Penguin Book of Aust. Verse; Best Poems of 1970; We Took Their Orders & Are Dead; A Survey of Aust. Verse; Contemp. Aust/American Poetry; A Book of Aust. Verse. Awarded prize for poem "Randolph Stow" in the Captain Cook Bi-Centenary Literary Competition, 1970, sponsored by the Gov. of NSW. Address: 96 McClelland St., Chester Hill, NSW 2162, Australia.

SKVOR, Jiři Jan, pen name **JAVOR, Pavel,** b. 24 June 1916. Professor. Education: Fac. of Law, Charles Univ., Prague, 1935-39; Fac. of Letters, Université de Montreal, 1955-60; LL.D., Prague, Czechoslovakia, 1945; M.A., Montreal, Canada, 1956; Ph.D., ibid, 1960. Positions held: Sec. of Czech Cultural Coun., Prague, 1939-43; Ed. in Chief, 1945-48; Deputy Mbr. of House of Commons, Prague, 1946-48; Ed., Radio Canada Int.; Prof., Université de Montreal. Memberships: Int. PEN, Ctr. for Writers in Exile; V.P., Czech Soc. of Arts & Scis., N.Y., 1968-72; Canadian Assn. of Slavists, 1955–; V.P., Promethean Soc. of Canada, 1964-72. Published works: (poetry) Zlatokop, 1941; Vítr v krovech, 1941; Mladý čas, 1941; Modré studánky, 1944; Pozdrav domu, 1951; Chudá sklizeň, 1953; Daleký hlas, 1953; Nad plamenem píseň, 1955; Hořké verše, 1958; Kouř z Ithaky, 1960; Nedosněno-nedomilováno, 1964; Země křížovaná, 1970; (novels) Kus života těžkého, 1967; Vzkříšení Jana Horna, 1974. Contbr. to: Editions Rencontres, Paris; Univ. of

Toronto Qtly.; Czech Lit. Abroad, Stockholm; Pen in Exile, London; Books Abroad, Univ. of Okla.; Tribune, Chicago; Poetae in Exilio, Stockholm; Czechoslovakia Past & Present, 1969; Proměny Metamorphoses, N.Y. Honours, awards: Lit. Fndn., Czech Acad. of Arts & Scis., Prague, 1944; Czech Christian Acad., Rome, 1952; Czech Cultural Coun. Abroad, Stockholm, 1954; Editions Rencontres, Paris, 1953. Address: 3523 Oxford Ave., Montreal, P.Q. H4A 2X9 Canada.

SLADEK, John, pen names **NOONE, Willard, KNYE, Cassandra & BOET, Bugs,** b. 31 June 1937. Writer of fiction & non-fiction. Positions held: Draftsman; Engrng. Asst.; Technical Writer. Memberships: Delta Phi Lambda, Univ. of Minn., U.S.A. Contbr. to: Region, 1963; Ronald Reagan: The Magazine of Poetry, 1970; Strange Faces, 1971; Just Friends, 1971; New Worlds Mag., 1968 & 70; Frendz, 1972; Holding Your Eight Hands, (anthol), 1969; Man in the Poetic Mode, (anthol.), 1970. Address: c/o A.P. Watt & Son (Literary Agents), 26-28 Bedford Row, London W.C.1, U.K.

SLATER, Lydia Elizabeth, pen name **SLATER, Lydia Pasternak,** b. 21 Mar. 1902. Biochemist; Writer; Poet; Translator; Performer at Poetry Recitals. Education: Univ. of Moscow, U.S.S.R.; Dr. phil., Berlin, Germany. Married, 4 children. Positions held: Asst. at K.W.J. für Biochemie in Berlin; Rsch. Asst., in Forschungsoustalt für Psychiatrie, Chem. Dept., Munich. Memberships: World Poetry Soc. Intercontinental; Fndr. Fellow, Int. Poetry Soc. Published works: Poems by Boris Pasternak, (translations), 1958, '59; Pasternak, Fifty Poems, (translations), 1963, '69, '72; Before Sunrise, (poems), 1971, '73; Eighteen Contemporary Russian Poems, (translations), 1973. Two small records: B. Pasternak, poems, 1960, '61. Two tapes: The Poetry of B. Pasternak, 1973 (Sussex Tapes) & Pasternak, Brother & Sister, 1973. Contbr. to: Times Lit. Supplement; Oxford Mail; Isis; Scotsman; John o'London's; N.Y. Herald; Spring Anthol.; Poesie Vivante; Hungarian Poetry in translation; Expression; First Int. Poetry Soc. Anthol., etc. Address: 20 Park Town, Oxford OX2 6SH, U.K.

SLATER, Stuart, b. 6 Sept. 1934. University Teacher. Education: Univ. of Otago; Victoria Univ. of Wellington; B.Sc. (N.Z.); B.A. (Hons.) Victoria. Positions held: Rsch. Officer, Dept. of Educ. (Govt.); Sr. Lectr., Dept. of Psychol., Victoria Univ. of Wellington, N.Z. Published works: Dawns & Trumpets, 1962. Contbr. to: A Review of English Literature; The Listener (BBC); Landfall; Monthly Review; The Listener (N.Z.); Poetry Yearbook. Recip., 1st prize, North Shore Lit. Comp., 1962. Address: c/o Dept. of Psychol., Victoria Univ. of Wellington, Private Bag, Wellington, New Zealand.

SLATTERY, Bradley, pen name **LEE, Brad,** b. 19 Dec. 1917. Freelance Writer. Education: M.A., Sociology, New School of Social Research, NYC.; B.S. Econ., NY Univ. Married, 1 d. Positions held: Instr., Pace Coll., NYC.; Instr., Stevens Inst. of Tech., Hoboken, NJ.; also tennis coach. Memberships: The Nat. Writers Club, Metrop. NY Chapter (Pres., 1963-64; Prog. Chairman, 1961-70); Nat. Writers Club, Denver, Colo., since 1951; Mystery Writers of America, since 1966. Contbr. to: Poetry Parade (anthol.), 1963; Melody of the Muse (anthol.), 1964; Golden Harvest (anthol.), 1967; Yearbook of Modern Poetry (anthol.), 1971; Outstanding Contemp. Poetry (anthol.), 1972, etc. Address: Box 8, Forest Hills, NY 11375, USA.

SLAVITT, David Rytman, pen name **SUTTON, Henry,** b. 23 Mar. 1935. Writer. Education: B.A., Yale Univ., 1956; M.A., Columbia Univ., 1957. Positions held: Assoc. Ed., Newsweek, 1958-65. Published works: Suits for the Dead, 1961; The Carnivore, 1965; Day Sailing, 1969; The Eclogues of Virgil, 1971; Child's Play, 1972; The Eclogues & the Georgics of Virgil, 1972. Contbr. to: Kenyon Review; Yale Review; Sewanee Review; New Republic; Southern Review; Georgia Review, etc. Address: 44 Coolidge Ave., Cambridge, MA 02138, U.S.A.

SLAVOV, George, b. 15 Aug. 1932. Journalist. Education: Engl. Philol., Sofia State Univ., 1956. Positions held: Freelance Translator of poetry & prose in Bulgarian, 1950-66; Sr. Evaluator (of cultural, ideological & foreign policy matters), East European Rsch. & Analysis Dept., Radio Free Europe in Munich, the F.R.G., 1967-. Memberships: PEN Club, Writers in Exile, Am. Br., 1970-; U.S. Newspaper Guild, 1968-; West German Jrnlsts. Union, 1967-; Former Mbr., Belles-Lettres Translators' Assn. of the Bulgarian Writers' Union. Published works: I Am America, Too, 1962; Walt Whitman, Leaves of Grass, 1966 (both books are verse transl. into Bulgarian). Contbr. to: Radio Sofia, Bulgaria; Literaturen Front; Narodna Kultura; Literaturni Novini; Vecherni Novini; Septemvri; Plamak; var. other newspapers & publs. Recip., Best Poetry Translation Award for 1966 (for Walt Whitman). Address: Osterwaldstr. 73/W.81, 8 Munich 40, German Fed. Repub.

SLAVUTYCH, Yar, b. 11 Jan. 1918. University Professor. Education: Dip., Pedagogic Inst., Zaporizja, Ukraine, 1940; M.A., Univ. of Pa., U.S.A., 1954; Ph.D., ibid, 1955. Married Elwira Cybar, 2 children. Positions held: Sr. Coll. Instr., Ukrainian, U.S. Army Lang. Schl., 1955-60; Asst. Prof., Slavic Langs. & Lit., Univ. of Alta, Edmonton, Canada, 1960-65; Assoc. Prof., ibid, 1966-. Memberships: Ukrainian Writers' Assn., Slovo, N.Y.; Shevchenko Sci. Soc., Toronto; Ukrainian Free Acad. of Scis., Winnipeg. Published works: Spivaje kolos, 1945; Homin vikiv, 1946; Pravdonostsi, 1948; Spraha, 1950; Spiegel und Erneuerung (co-transl. w. V. Derzavyn), 1949; Oaza, 1960; Majestat, 1962; The Muse in Prison, 1956; Oasis (transl. by Morse Manly), 1959; John Keats Selected Poems Translated into Ukrainian, 1958; Zavojovnyky prerij, 1968; Don'ka bez imeny, narrative poems, 1952; Trofeji, collected poems, 1963; Mudroshchi mandriv, 1972. Contbr. to: Arka, Munich; Zahrava; Augsburg, MUR; Novidni; Porohy; Vyzvol'nyj shliakh; Slovo I-V; Pivnichne siajvo, I-V; Svoboda; Canadian Literature; Suchasnist', etc. Honours, awards: Poetry Prize, America, 1951; Hon. mention, Ukrainian Lit. Comp., Chicago, 1970. Address: 72 Westbrook Dr., Edmonton, Alta., Canada.

SLESINSKI, Judith, pen name **SLESINSKI, Judy.** Editor; Printer. (Special Song Press). Married John Slesinski, 3 children. Memberships: Milford Letters Comm. (Div. of the Fine Arts Comm.); Poetry Comm., Arts Fest., New Haven, 1971; Ldr., discussion on Poetic Creativity at Fest; New England Poetry Club; Centro Studi e Scambi Int.; Kentucky State Poetry Soc.; Acad. of Am. Poets; Poets Study Club of Terre Haute, etc. Published works: On Keeping Humble, 1973. Contbr. to: Orphic Lute; Tweed; Poets Round-Table; Verse in View; The Olive Hill Times; Haiku Highlights; The Jrnl.-Enquirer; The Bridgeport Sunday Post; Jean's Jrnl.; Bardic Echoes; Vista; Inky Trails; Omen, etc. Recip., Tweed Book Award, 1973. Address: Box 74, Woodmont Stn., Milford, CT 06460, U.S.A.

SLESSOR, Kenneth, b. 27 Mar. 1901. Editor. Positions held: Reporter, The Sun, Sydney, Australia, 1920; Staff, Smith's Weekly, Sydney, 1927, Assoc. Ed., 1936, Ed., 1938; Ed.-in-Chief, Smith's Newspapers, 1939; Ldr. Writer & Lit. Ed., The Sun, 1944-57; Ed., Southerly, 1956-61; Ldr. Writer, Daily Telegraph, Sydney, current. Published works: Thief of the Moon, 1924; Earth Visitors, 1926; Darlinghurst Nights, 1931; Cuckooz Contrey, 1932; Five Bells, 1939; One Hundred Poems, 1919-1939, 1943; Poems, 1962; Ed., Australian Poetry, 1945; Co.-Ed., The Penguin Book of Australian Verse, 1958. Contbr. to: Meanjin; Bulletin; Sydney Morning Herald; (anthologies) Australian Poetry, 1957; An Anthology of Australian Verse, 1952; Boomerang Book of Australian Poetry, 1956; A Book of Australian Verse, 1968; Penguin Book of Australian Verse, 1958. Recip., O.B.E. Address: 712 Pacific Hwy., Chatswood, Sydney, N.S.W., Australia.

SLETTEN, Madra Rix Oliver, pen names **OLIVER, Rix Madra, OLIVER, M.R., OLIVER, Madra Imogene &**

OLIVER, Emogene. Public School Teacher. Education: Oberlin Coll., Ohio; B. in Schl. Music, Univ. of Mich.; New England Conserv. of Music; Univ. of Wis.; M.A., Claremont Calif. Grad. Schl. Positions held: Schl. Music & Engl. Tchr., Milwaukee, Madison, Richland Ctr., Wis., & Mich., Ont., Calif., Belvidere, Ill.; Var. recitals; Pvte. music tchng. in voice & keyboard; Soloist. Memberships: ASCAP; Wis. Fellowship of Poets; Acad. of Am. Poets; Milwaukee Book Club. Published works: Seven Songs for Youth, 1963. Contbr. to: Poems Out of Wis., anthol., Vol. III, 1967; Wis. Hist. in Poetry, Vol. II & III, 1970, '71; Calif. Am. Bard; Upland Calif. Co. News; Lafayette Co. News; Quaderni di Poesia; Diamond Bar Times, etc. Honours, awards: Cert. of Merit, Quaderni di Poesia, 1972; Anniversary Issue, ibid, 1973; Front Cover Page, Mich. Bardic Echoes, 1973. Address: 112 W. Madison St., Belvidere, IL 61008, U.S.A.

SLIWINSKI, Wincenty Piotr, b. 18 Jan. 1915, Plock, Poland. Poet; Painter; Graphic Artist; Constructor of Violins; Metal Worker. Education: Tchrs. Sem., Plock, 1930-36; Univ. & Engrng. Coll., Warsaw, 1936-39; Acad. of Fine Arts, Warsaw, 1948. Married to Eugenia Dwigubska, art histn., 1945. Positions held: Collector, Polish Folk Art now in Mus. of Folk Sculpture, Warsaw, Municipal Mus. in Toruń, Ethnog. Mus. in Lódź, Municipal Mus. in Bytom, Mus. of Sci. Soc. in Plock, Diocesan Mus., ibid, 1931-37; Archaeol. excavations, Mus. of Sci. Study & Univ. of Wilno, 1931-39; One-man Exhib. of Paintings, Plock, 1936; Constructor of Violins, 1940-46; Painter & Graphic Artist, num. exhibs. in Poland, USA, Australia, Italy, Canada, West Germany, Monaco & Reconstructor of archtl. monuments, 1946-; Poet, Painter, Graphic Artist, 1965-. Memberships: Deleg., Accad. Int. Leonardo da Vinci; Deleg., Centro Studi E Scambi Int.; Hon. Accad. Int. Tommaso Campanella; Deleg., La Haute Acad. Int. de Lutece; Arts, Scis., Lettres, France; Int. Arts Guild, Monaco; Assn. Int. des Arts Plastiques, France; Union of Polish Plastic Artists, Warsaw. Author of The Violin Mezzosopran & an Instrument Strengthening the Sound of the Violin, 1942. Honours & Awards: Town of Plock, 1946; Dip. & Medal, Centro Studi E Scambi Int., 1969; Dip. & Medal, Accad. Int. Leonardo da Vinci, 1969; Dip. of Hon., La Haute Acad. Int. de Lutece, 1970; Silver Medal, Accad. Int. Tommaso Campanella, 1970; Prize, Piccole Enciclopedia delle Arti, 1970; Dip. & Silver Medal, Arts, Scis., Lettres, 1971. Address: 4/78 Tatrzańska St., Warsaw, Poland.

SLOAN, Clara Helen, b. 25 June 1916. Housewife. Married William H. Sloan. Memberships: Am. Poets Fellowship Soc.; Int. Writers Fellowship; Int. Comm., Centro Studi e Scambi Int.; Ill. Poetry Soc. Published works: With the Wild Oak (22 poems), 1969; Links in the Chain, and Lands Alive (forthcoming). Rep. in following anthols: Pacific Breeze, 1966; Seventh Year Harvest, 1958; Heart of Angels, 1967; New Poetry, 1967; Shower of Angels, 1968; Heavenly Angels, 1971; Poetry Pageant Vol. 1, 1970; Poetry Pageant, Vol. II, 1970; Echoes of Faith, 1970. Contbr. to: Columbus Sunday Citizen; Ashland Times Gazette; Boston Post; Hartford Times; Hartford Courant; Prairie Poet; Am. Poet; Echoes; Lincoln Log, etc. Recip. var. prizes & awards inclng: Book Award, Hoosier Challenger, 1958; Fifth Prize, Poetry Pageant Contest, 1970; Dip., Centro Studi e Scambi, 1972. Address: 128 Lee Ave., Ashland, OH 44805, U.S.A.

SLOBODNIK, Wlodzimierz, b. 19 Sept. 1900. Poet. Education: Univ. of Warsaw. Married. Memberships: Poets' Group 'Kwadryga', 1927-36; Union of Polish Writers. Published works: Prayer for a Word, 1927; Fiddler's Shadow, 1929; Walk on the Side of Vistula, 1931; To The Memory of My Mother, 1937; Poetry (1922-1935), 1936; Evening's Unquietude, 1937; House in Forgana, 1946; Collected Poetry, 1948; Lights on the Road, 1950; New Poetry, 1952; Sonnets on Vit Stwosz, 1954; Everday's Language, 1956; Imaginary Travels, 1957; The Weight of Earth, 1959; Stony Shadow, 1960; In the Shadow of a Mermaid & a Willow, 1963; Letters from Paris, 1964; Song for Goodnight, 1965; Rose of the Light, 1967; Selected

Poems, 1971; Colours Collecting, 1973; satirical poems, children's poetry, poetry translations. Contbr. to: Skamander, 1927-28; Wiadomosci Literackie, 1925-28; Kwadryga, 1927-36; Nowa Kultura, 1945-; Kultura; Zyeie Literackie; Poezja, etc. Honours, awards: Order Polonia Restituta, 1953; Award of City of Lodz for complete works, 1956. Address: Tamka 34 A, m. 10, 00355 Warsaw, Poland.

SMALLWOOD, Vivian, b. 7 Nov. 1912. Bank Vault Custodian and Customer Service. Education: Grad. Murphy HS, Mobile, Alabama; Huffstetler Business Coll.; Certificates, American Inst. of Banking. Chairman of the Board, Chickasaw Public Library. Positions held: Bank bookkeeper, then Vault Custodian, American Nat. Bank & Trust Co. of Mobile, Alabama. Memberships: Alabama State Poetry Soc.; Alabama Writers' Conclave; and Pensters. Published work: Window to the South, 1972. Contbr. to: Poet; Poetry World; The Sampler; A.F.W.C. Creative Writings, 1971, 1972; Prize Poems (Nat. Fed. State Poetry Socs., 1972, 1973); The Florence Times; Fairhope Courier; Baldwin Times; Mobile Register. Awards: Nat. Fed. of State Poetry Socs., the Grand Prize, 1972, 2nd place in Lubbe Award, 1972, and 3rd place 1973; 2nd place, Ariz. State Poetry Soc. Award, 1973, hon. mention, Evans S. Wall Memorial Award, 1973, 3rd prize, Kate Heanue Mem. Award, 1971; 1st place, lyric contest, Alabama Writers' Conclave, and 2nd place in another category, 1972; 1st place sonnet and 2nd place lyric in Alabama State Poetry Soc., 1971; Four 1st prizes in Alabama Fed. of Women's Clubs Creative Writing Contest, 1972, and three 1st prizes in the AFWC, 1971. Address: 302 6th St., Chickasaw, AL 36611, USA.

SMET, Joachim Frederick, b. 9 Oct. 1915. Carmelite Priest, Poet. Education: B.L.S., Univ. of Chicago; M.A., Cath. Univ. of Am.; H.E.D., Gregorian Univ., Rome. Positions held: Mbr., Inst. for Carmelite Studies, Italy; Ed.; Carmelus (jrnl.), 1954-. Mbr.: Cath. Poetry Soc. of Am. Contbr. Spirit; America; The Poets Rosary; Drink from the Rock. Address: Via Sforza Pallavicini, 19,00193 Rome, Italy.

SMETHURST, Jennifer, b. 4 June 1950. Bank Clerk. Treas., Blackpool Writers' Circle. Contbr. to: Blackpool Evening Gazette; Competitors Jrnl.; The Shore; Arnold H.S. Mag. Recip., Competitors Jrnl. Poetry Prize, 1973. Address: 328 Bispham Rd., Bispham, Blackpool, Lancs., U.K.

SMITH, A.J.M., b. 8 Nov. 1902. University Professor; Critic; Editor; Poet. Education: McGill Univ., Canada, B.Sc., 1925, M.A., 1926; Edinburgh Univ., Ph.D., 1931. Born in Montreal of English parentage. Married; 1 s. Positions held: Prof. of Engl., Michigan State Univ., from 1936 until retirement, 1972. Visiting Prof: Univ. of Toronto; Univ. of British Columbia; Queen's Univ.; Dalhousie Univ.; Sir George Williams Univ.; McGill Univ. Membership: League of Canadian Poets. Published works: News of the Phoenix, 1943; A Sort of Ecstasy, 1954; Collected Poems, 1962; Poems, New & Collected, 1967; Editor: New Provinces (with F.R. Scott), 1936; The Book of Canadian Poetry, 1943, 1948, 1957; Seven Centuries of Verse, 1947, 1957, 1967; The Blasted Pine (with F.R. Scott), 1957, 1967; The Oxford Book of Canadian Verse, 1960; Mod. Canadian Verse, 1967; Towards a View of Canadian Letters: Selected Critical Essays 1928-1971, 1973; The Colonial Century and The Canadian Century, vols. I and II, The Book of Canadian Prose, 1973. Contbr. to: The Adelphi; The Bermondsey Book; The London Aphrodite; New Verse; Contemp. Poetry and Prose; The Dial; The Nation; The Measure; Poetry; The Rocking Horse; The Hound & Horn; NY Times; The Canadian Forum; Queen's Qtly.; Northern Review. Awards: Harriet Monroe Prize, Poetry (Chicago), 1941; Governor General's Medal for Poetry, 1943; Royal Soc. of Canada Medal for Literature, 1966; Hon. degrees from McGill Univ., Queen's Univ., Dalhousie Univ., Bishop's Univ., Canada. Address: 640 Bailey St., East Lansing, MI 48823, USA.

SMITH, Alan Frederick, b. 26 June 1935. Lecturer; Freelance Writer. Education: M.A., Selwyn Coll., Cambridge Univ.; Dip. in Educ., Oxford Univ. Positions held: Tutor, Art Therapy, Withymead Ctr., Exeter; Tchr., Greater London Authority; Lectr., Wolverhampton Coll. of Art; Engl. Lang. & Lit. Tutor, Anglo-Continental Schl. of Engl. Memberships: Fellow, Salzburg Seminars in Am. Lit., 1966; Ctr. for Contemporary Cultural Studies, Birmingham Univ., 1965-66. Published works: London & Meander, 1973; Animal, Vegetable & Mineral, a compendium of English idiom & metaphor for students of the language (in progress). Contbr. to: London Atmospheres, anthol. Poetry readings at Hampstead Pentameters Poetry Soc. & at Oxford & Birmingham. Address: 36 Westgate Rd., Lytham St. Annes, Lancs., U.K.

SMITH, Bertie Reece, b. 16 Nov. 1913. Senior Reviewer, Retail Credit Company. Education: Grad. Central HS, Charlotte, NC; Grad., Ideal Business Coll., Charlotte; Queens Coll., Charlotte. Married, Reginald Lowell Smith, 2 s. Memberships: NC Poetry Soc. (past Treasurer); American Acad. of Poets. Published works: Lace & Pig Iron, 1931; A Time for Poetry, 1966. Address: 1012 Keystone Court, Charlotte, NC 28210, USA.

SMITH, Chard Powers, b. 1 Nov. 1894, Watertown, N.Y., U.S.A. Freelance Writer. Education: B.A., Yale Coll., 1916; LL.B., Harvard Law Schl., 1921; Oxford Univ. Summer Schl., U.K., 1921; M.A., Columbia Univ., U.S.A., 1949. Married 3 times, 2 children. Positions held: Law Prac., Habbell, Taylor, Goodwin & Moser, Rochester, N.Y., 1921-22; Freelance Writer, 1922-; Pres., P.T.A., Cornwall, Conn.; Trial Justice, ibid; Trustee, Friends Sem., N.Y. Memberships: Chmn., Min. and Coun., Friends Meeting, Albany and Bennington, Vt.; Elizabethan Club, Yale Univ.; Corporate, MacDowell Assn.; Poetry Soc. of Am.; PEN. Published works: Along the Wind, 1925; Lost Address, 1928; Hamilton, a Poetic Drama, 1930; The Quest of Pan, 1930; Prelude to Man, 1936; Poets of the Twenties, 1967. Contbr. to: Poetry Mag.; Contemporary Verse; The Reviewer; Harper's Mag.; The Virginia Quarterly; Scribner's Mag. Address: Arlington, VT 05250, U.S.A.

SMITH, C.U., pen name CROWBATE, Ophelia Mae, b. 29 July 1901. Waitress. Married three times, 7 children (2 dec.) Memberships: UAPA; UAP; Pacific Northwest Writers; ASCAP; Poetry Soc. of S.C.; Wash. Pioneers Assn. Published works: If the Shoe Fits Wear It, 1962; Through Hell in a Hand Basket, 1963; Hello, Hello! Partyline, 1965; The Morning & the Evening, 1967; Ramrod, 1970; Smitty's Short, 1972. Writes poetry sheet each month called 'Ramrod or The Facts of Life. Contbr. to: Inky Trails; The Seattle Times; Poets on Parade; American Poets, 1966; Sixty Seven Poets, 1967; Poetry Parade; The Birth of Day, 1972; Echoes of Faith; Golden Hours, 1972; Year Book of Modern Poetry, 1971; Lyrics of Love, 1972; Modern Haiku; 73 Poets Anthol., 1973, etc. Recip. var. hons. & awards inclng: 3rd pl., Short Story, Trans Atlantic Comp., 1973; Lone Indian Eagle Feather Award, 1973; Lone Indian Fellowship Cert. of Hon.; Award of Merit (Ramrod page), UAPA, 1972-73; var. personal poetry broadcasts. Address: P.O. Box 10636 Winslow, Bainbridge Is., WA 98110, U.S.A.

SMITH, Delphia Frazier, b. 24 Apr. 1921. Poet; Writer; Artist; Musician; Speaker; Collector; Sculptress; Wood Carver. Education: Dip., U.S. Schl. of Mus.; Dip., Newspaper Inst. of Am.; var. other courses. Married, 2 daughters. Memberships: Int. Platform Assn.; Poets Congress; The Smithsonian Assocs.; Intercontinental Biog. Assn.; Advisory Bd., Am. Security Coun.; Rep., World Poetry Soc., Centro Studi e Scambi Int.; Fndr.-Fellow, Int. Poetry Soc.; Patron, Subscriber, Exhibiting Mbr., Nat. Carvers Mus.; Newspaper Inst. of Am.; Soc. of Lit. Designates; The Collectors Guild, etc. Published works incl: Along Life's Way, 1961; So Swift the Night, 1972; Profiles & Footprints, 1972; Tapestry of Life, 1972; Winged Thoughts, 1972; Daffodils in the Snow, 1972; Bright

Remnants, 1972; Splintered Prisms, 1972; Ribbons of Thought, 1973; Patches & Ruffles, 1973; Award Winning Poems, 1973; Voice of the Wind, 1973; Voice of the Dove; To Catch A Dream; Brocade and Denim; Author of 15 books used in schls. & colls. & placed in archives; Works included in many nat. & int. anthols. Contbr. to num. jrnls. & mags. inclng: Ideals; Bardic Echoes; Tempo; Major Poets; Modern Images; Int. Poetry Review; Japan Forum; Southwest Times Record; Premier Poets; American Narrative. Appears regularly on TV for interviews, readings, speaking & exhibiting art & books. Recip. of num. honours & awards inclng: Gold Medal & Cert. of Hon., Leonardo Da Vinci Acad., 1972; Janie Spellmon Award, Japan Forum, 1971 & 72; Disting. Serv. Citation Award, World Poetry Soc.; Medal, Centro di Cultura, Taranto, anthol. poetry contest. Address: 202 9th St., Mammoth Spring, AR 72554, U.S.A.

SMITH, Dorothy Anita, b. 2 Apr. 1927. Assoc. Professor of Engl. Literature. Education: B.S., Fordham Univ., NY.; M.A., Ph.D., St. John's Univ., NY. Positions held: Chairman, Dept. of Engl., also Div. of Humanities. Memberships: Mod. Language Assoc.; Coll. Engl. Assoc.; Nat. Council of Teachers of Engl. Published work: R.S. Thomas: The Poet As Querulous, 1970. Recip. 1st Prize on local, state, and national level, CDA Poetry Contest, 1956. Address: Dominican Coll., Blauvelt, NY 10913, USA.

SMITH, Florence Thelma, pen name **DRAYTON, Florence Smith,** b. 24 Sept. 1911. Clerical Worker. Education: courses at Morgan State Coll. Positions held: Clerical Wkr., 1957–. Memberships: Int. Platform Assn.; N.Y. Poetry Forum. Published works: Me and My Shadow, poetry, 1972. Contbr. to: The Balt. Afro-Am.; An Anthol. of Poetry; a monthly o'seas publ. Address: 3425 Liberty Heights Ave., Balt., MD 21215, USA.

SMITH, Harriet Fullen, b. 12 Sept. 1906. Author; Educator. Education: A.B., Univ. of S. Calif., 1926; M.A., ibid, 1927; grad. studies in Educ., 1926-33; summer sessions in Educ., Columbia Univ., 1929; Workshops in Poetry, UCLA, also lecture series in Art, 1960-70. Widow of M. Lewis Elden Smith, 4 children. Positions held: Fellow & Faculty Asst. in Orientation, Univ. of S.C., 1926-30; Instr. & Dean of Women, Compton Jr. Coll., 1930-36. Recording Sec., The Poetry Soc. of Southern Calif. Published works: Raphael & Consuelo (w. Florence C. Means), 1929; My Shadow Self (poetry), 1931; Your Life as a Citizen, 1952, rev. edn., 1961, new edn., 1967. Contbr. to: the Jrnl. of The Blaisdell Inst., 1974; Am. Women Poets 1937; var. mags. & periodicals. Recip. var. hons. inclng. Two poems among 20 best poems of the yr., Poetry Soc. of S. Calif. Critic's Meeting, 1971. Address: 315 Muirfield Rd., Los Angeles, CA 90020, U.S.A.

SMITH, Helen C., b. 7 June 1903. Freelance Writer. Education: Univ. of Calif., Los Angeles; post grad., Christian Coll.; B.S., M.S., Ph.D., D.D. Ordained to Ministry, Christian Church as Christian Writer. Married Charles Harmon Smith, 3 children. Positions held: Instr., primary grades, 1922-23; Legal, 1933-72; Writer, 1949-73. Memberships incl: Life Mbr. & Hon. Life Mbr. of Bd. Dirs., Wis. Regl. Writers Assn.; Life Mbr., Coun. for Wis. Writers; Wis. Acad. of Scis., Arts & Letters; Wis. Fellowship of Poets; Life Mbr., Am. Lit. Assn.; Nat. League of Am. Pen Women; AAUW; Sustaining Mbr., Phi Beta Kappa; Hon. Life Mbr., United Poets Laureate; Pres., Evansville Writers Club, 1973, etc. Published works: (poetry books) From the Countryside; Stars in My Eyes; Windfalls; Chiaroscura; Applesauce; Mirrors of Faith; But Not Yet, 1973; (fiction – juvenile) Laughing Child, Books I, II & III; (fiction – adults) Off the Record; Concepts; Weeping Wijlows; Called Back. Contbr. to num. mags., jrnls., anthols. & newspapers. Recip. num. honours & awards inclng: Elected Poet Laureate, Am.-Visayan, 1967; Awarded Laurel Wreath, UPLI & Gold Medal from Pre. Marcos, 1967; Elected to Contemporary Poets Int. Hall of Fame, 1969; 1st Award, Fleetwood

Mus. & Arts Fes., U.K., 1972. Address: 409 Lincoln St., Evansville, WI 53536, U.S.A.

SMITH, Iain Crichton, b. 1 Jan. 1928. Teacher. Education: Hons. degree in Engl., Aberdeen Univ. Positions held: Tchr., Oban H.S. Argyll. Fellow, Royal Lit. Soc. Published works: Thistles & Roses, 1961; The Law & the Grace, 1965; From Bourgeois Land, 1969; Selected Poems, 1970; Love Poems & Elegies, 1972. Contbr. to: The Spectator; New Statesman; Scottish Int.; Times Lit. Supplement; Times Review; New Saltire; The Tablet; The Scotsman; The Glasgow Herald, etc. Recip., 4 Scottish Arts Coun. Awards & PEN Prize for Poetry. Address: 42 Combie St., Oban, Argyll, U.K.

SMITH, Janet McQueen, b. 13 Apr. 1917. Housewife; Ex Schoolteacher. Education: Qld. Tchrs. Coll. Married, 3 sons, 1 daughter. Positions held: Schoolteacher; Ed. of Commonwealth Church Youth Mag., 7 yrs. Member, Qld. Writers' Workshop. Contbr. to: Poets of Australia, 1972, '73; Toowoomba Carnival of Flowers Brochure, 1974; The Australian Womens' Mirror; The Toowoomba Chronicle; The Australian Evangel; Scope; Yukana. Honours, awards: 2nd Prize, Qld. Eisteddfod, 1968; 1st Prize, ibid, 1969; 2nd Prize, 1973; Christmas Poem Award, Scope Mag., 1973. Address: 39 Alford St., Toowoomba, Qld., Australia 4350.

SMITH, Jared, b. 24 Mar. 1950. Tutor. Education: B.A., N.Y. Univ., 1973; M.A., ibid, 1974. Positions held: Tchr. of Creative Writing, N.M. Schl. System, 1968-69; Tutor, N.Y. Univ's Reading Inst., 1971-73. Member, Poetry Soc. of Ga. Contbr. to: N.Y. Qtly.; The Remington Review; Gnosis; The Lamp In The Spine; Buffalo; Wind; The Grande Ronde Review; The Smith; Bridge; Sumus. A quarter of his first book, Traveler's Notebook, published as part of anthol. of major young poets, 1974. Address: 9 Bursley Pl., White Plains, NY 10605, U.S.A.

SMITH, Jo Ann Selig, b. 6 Aug. 1934. Housewife; Artist; Poet. Education: Henderson State Tchrs. Coll., Arkadelphia, Ark., 2 yrs. Married Billy Jack Smith, 3 children. Positions held: Asst. Libn., Garland Co. Lib., 1952-53; 2nd Grade Tchr., Cutter Morning Star Schl., Hot Springs, Ark., 1954-56. Memberships: Pres., Demoiselle Federated Womens Clubs, 1964-66; Pres. of Coun., Hot Springs Federated Womens Clubs, 1970-72; Pres., Garland Co. Drug Abuse Educ. Assn., 1971-72; Ark. Poets Roundtable, Hot Springs Br. Contbr. to: Ark. Poets Roundtable Anthol., 1970-74; Lyrics of Love, 1973; Melody of the Muse, 1974; Am. Bard; Poets Party Line; Poets Forum, etc. Honours, awards incl: Winner, Ark. Fest. of Arts, Illustrated Poetry (1st pl. Award), 1972; 2nd pl., ibid, 1973. Address: 111 Suburban Dr., Hot Springs, AR 71901, U.S.A.

SMITH, John, pen name **SMITH, C. Busby,** b. 5 Apr. 1924. Editor; Poet. Positions held: Mng. Dir., Christy & Moore Ltd., Lit. Agts., London, U.K.; Ed., Poetry Review, London, 1962-65. Published works: Gates of Beauty and Death, 1948; The Dark Side of Love, 1952; The Birth of Venus, 1954; Excursus in Autumn, 1958; A Letter to Lao Tze, 1961; A Discreet Immorality, 1965; The Mask of Glory (verse play), 1956. Ed., The Pattern of Poetry (w. W. Kean Seymour), 1963; My Kind of Love, 1965; Twentieth Century Love Poems, 1969. Contbr. to: (anthologies) New Poems, 1954; Mavericks, 1957. Recip., Adam Int. Poetry Prize, 1953. Address: 52a Floral St., Covent Garden, London W.C.2, U.K.

SMITH, Ken, b. 4 Dec. 1938. Poet. Knaresborough & Hull Grammar Schls.; B.A., Leeds Univ. Published works include: Eleven Poems, 1963 (pamphlet); The Pity, 1967; Academic Board Poems, 1968 (pamphlet); Arc Pamphlets 4 & 5, 1969; Work, Distances/Poems, 1972. Contbr. to the following anthols., jrnls., mags., etc: Poésie Vivante; Stand; Trib.; Transformation; Poetry NW; Pebble; New Statesman; The Listener; 20th Century; Sou'Wester; Mich. Qtly.; Shenandoah;

NW Review; Tenn. Poetry Jrnl.; Trace; Hanging Loose; Mojo Navigatore; Kayak; Nimrod; Minn. Review; The Nation; The Smith Stone Review: Lotus; Qtly. Review of Lit. Prism; Agenda; Phases; Brumes Blondes; Transatlantic; Poetry Review, London. Honours, Awards: Commendation, Cheltenham Festival, 1963; Gregory Award, 1967. Address: 418 Franklin, Slippery Rock, Pa. 16057, USA.

SMITH, Latta Conway, pen name SMITH, Latta C., b. 5 Dec. 1899. Education: Fourth Dist. Agricultural School; Presbyterian Synodical Coll., Ala. Membership: NC Poetry Soc. Published work: Songs of a Young Heart (poems), 1958. Contbr. to: The Monroe Journal; The American Legion Mag. Address: 411 West Windsor St., Monroe, NC 28110, USA.

SMITH, Maggie, pen name SMITH, Maggie Aldridge, b. 19 Oct. 1913. Teacher; Homemaker. Education: Univ. of Mo., Kans. City, 2 Yrs. Married Melvin Smith. Positions held: Schl. Tchr., Greenwood, Shawnee, Kans., 1941-49; Schl. Bd. Dir., Greenwood, Shawnee, 1950-57; Pres., Railway Mail Aux., Kans. City, 1954-56; Ed., 'Pioneer' Qtly. for Ark. Histl. Soc. Memberships: Pres., Benton Co., Ark., Histl. Soc.; 1967-69; Pres., Benton Co., Ark., Bapt. Women; Poets Roundtable of Ark.; Dir., Siloam Springs Writers Workshop; Ozark Artists & Writers Guild. Published works: Siloam Souvenir, 1968; The Lines in Pleasant Places, 1973; Glowing with Lois, (poetry of Lois Snelling w. biog. written by Maggie Smith), 1974. Contbr. to: Ark. Gazette; Ark. Bapt.; Southwest Times Record; Interstate News; Herald & Democrat; Benton Co. Observer; Southern Standard; Siloam Souvenir; The Builder; Ark. Poets Anthol.; Contemporary Poets of Ark.; Ozarks Mountaineer. Honours, awards: Lyric Award, 1968; Hon. Mention, Book of Poetry, Okla. Poetry Soc., 1970; C.T. Davis Meml. Award, 1973; 2nd in Children's Verse, 1973. Address: 109 N. Madison, Siloam Springs, AR 72761, U.S.A.

SMITH, Margery, b. 21 Mar. 1916. Teacher; Poet. Education: Charlotte Mason Coll., Ambleside, Westmoreland; Cert., PNEU Tchr. Positions held: Abbey Guide, Newstead Abbey, 1940-42; Tchr., Iraq Petroleum Co., Iraq, 1950-53; Bd. Mbr., Manifold Jrnl., 1965-; Org., Portfolio of Story & Verse (PNEU), 1964-; Mbr., Exec. Coun., Charlotte Mason Coll. Assn., 1971-; currently edits L'Umile Pianta for Charlotte Mason Coll. Assn. Memberships: Poetry Soc., U.K., 1938-; Gen. Coun., 1967-; Poetry Soc. of Am.; Co-Fndr., Hon. Sec. & Treas., Nottingham Poetry Soc., 1941; Fellow, Int. Poetry Soc. Published works: In Our Time, 1941; Still In My Hand, 1964. Contbr. to: (anthols.) Poems of This War, 1947; Verse of Valour; Mitre, 1907; Kentucky Harvest, 1067; Anthol. of Contemp. Northern Poetry; Poetry of the Sixties; Laudamus Te; Without Adam; (jrnls.) Poetry Review; Outposts; The Glass; Manifold; Anglo-Welsh Review; Envoi; Mentor; South & West; PNEU Jrnl.; Nottingham Evening News; Ashland Daily Independent, Ky.; Bardic Echoes; Scrip; Saint; Pink Peace. Honours, awards: Poetry Review Premium Prizes, 1939, '40; South & West, Roxana Webb 1st Pantograph, 1967; Lucia Markham Sonnet Comp., 1st prize, 1968; Anglo-Welsh Sonnet Comp., 1st Prize, 1968; Manifold Sonnet Comp., 1st Prize, 1969; var. fest. contbns. Address: 12 Springfield Cres., Horsham, Sussex, RH12 2PP, U.K.

SMITH, M.G. Lecturer. Educ: Jamaica Coll., W. Indies; Univ. Coll., London, U.K. Positions held: Lectr., Univ. of the W. Indies, Kingston, 1952-61; Prof., Anthropol., Univ. of Calif., U.S.A. Contbr. to: Focus; (anthologies) Caribbean Literature, 1966; Caribbean Verse, 1967.

SMITH, Michael, b. 1 Sept. 1942. Teacher; Editor; Poet. Educ: B.A. & H. Dip., Univ. Coll., Dublin, Ireland. Positions held: Tchr., Latin & Engl., St. Paul's Coll., Raheny, Dublin, 1966-; Ed., New Irish Poets Series, New Writers Press, Dublin; Ed., The Lace Curtain, ibid. Published works: With the Woodnymphs, 1968: Dedications, 1968; Homage to James Thompson (B.V.) at Portobello, 1969. Contbr. to: St. Stephens

Magazine; Arena; Holy Door; Poetry Ireland; University Review; Kilkenny Magazine. Address: 19 Warrenmount Place, SCR, Dublin 8, Ireland.

SMITH, Phillip Hoseason, b. 26 Apr. 1912. Retired Public Servant; Book Reviewer. Education: Th.L.; A.C.T.; A.S.A. Positions held: Holy Orders in Ch. of England; Report Writer, Filing Clerk, Bus. Admin, S.A. Govt. Public Service, etc.; Book Reviewer for S.A. Public Service Paper. Contbr. to: Transition, anthol. of profl. Australian writers; Poet Lore (U.S.A.); Poetry Australia; Vision; Expression Australasia; Optimist; Am. Forests (USA); Eirigh (Ireland); P.S.A. Review; Riverlander. Honours, awards: Commendation, Capt. Cook Bicentenary, N.S.W., 1970. Address: 3 Raymel Cres., Campbelltown, S.A., Australia 5074.

SMITH, Robert Denis, pen name DIE-HARD, b. 25 Apr. 1931. Electrical Labourer. Married, 2 sons. Positions held: w. Middlesex Regt., 1949, served in Hong Kong, Korea, Austria; w. Dungeness Power Station, 1973. Memberships: Poetry Soc.; London Writers' Circle; Chmn., Cinque Port Poets Soc., Greatstone, Romney Marsh, Kent. Published works: Fragmentations of Thoughts, 1969; Poems of Romney Marsh, 1971; Poems of Kent (in process of publ.). Contbr. to: Envoi; Outposts; Amazing Grace; Grapevine; Lydd Parish Mag.; Kent Messenger; Rider; Folkstone Herald. Address: Palm Beach, 17 Seaview Rd., Greatstone, Kent, U.K.

SMITH, Sydney Bernard, b. 4 Aug. 1936. Poet. Education: Oxford; McDavid's Coll. Married, 1 s. Positions held: Schl. Master, Clongowes, 1961-68; Memberships: Int. Writing Prog., Univ. of Iowa, 1968-70. Published works include: Girl With Violin, 1968. Contbr. to the following anthols., jrnls., mags., etc: Poetry, Ireland; Irish Times; Kilkenny Mag.; Everyman; Arena; Holy Door; Hayden Murphy's Broadsheet; Irish Press; Dublin Mag.; Irish Ind.; Aquarius; Iowa Review; Iowa State Liquor Store; Radio Eireann. Address: Inishbofin, County Galway, Rep. of Ireland.

SMITH, Sydney Goodsir, b. 26 Oct. 1915. Freelancer. Education: Edinburgh & Oxford Univs. Positions held: Tchr.; Broadcaster; Jrnlst. Published works: Kynd Kittock's Land, 1965; 15 Poems & a Play, 1969; The Vision of the Prodigal Son, 1960; Figs & Thistles, 1959; Under the Eildon Tree, 1948; So Late Into the Night, 1953; The Deevil's Waltz, 1946; Gowdspink in Reekie, 1974. Contbr. to: Times Lit. Supplement; New Statesman & Nation; Botteghe Oscure; Hudson Review; Poetry (Chicago); Nine; Saltire Review; Lines Review; Scottish Int.; The Scotsman; Ariel; Aquarius; Akros; Encounter. Honours, awards: Rockefeller Atlantic Award, 1946; Festival of Britain Scots Poetry Prize, 1951; Poetry (Chicago) Award, 1956; Scottish Arts Coun. Award, 1972. Address: 25 Drummond Pl., Edinburgh 3, U.K.

SMITH, Vivian Brian, b. 3 June 1933. Lecturer in English, Univ. of Sydney. Education: Univs. of Tasmania and Sydney. Married; 3 children. Positions held: Lecturer in French, Univ. of Tasmania, 1956-67; Lecturer in Engl., Univ. of Sydney, 1968-. Published works: The Other Meaning, 1956; An Island South, 1967. Contbr. to: Australian Poetry; Southerly, and most Aust. lit. journals and newspapers. Address: 19 McLeod St., Mosman, NSW., Australia 2088.

SMITH, William Jay, b. 22 Apr. 1918. Author & Teacher. Education: B.A., Wash. Univ., U.S.A., 1939; M.A., ibid, 1941; grad. work at Columbia Univ., Oxford Univ., Univ. of Florence. Married Sonja Haussmann, 2 sons by former marriage, 1 stepson. Positions held: Asst., French Dept., Wash. Univ., 1939-41; Instr., Engl. & French, Columbia Univ., 1946-47; Instr., Engl., Williams Coll., 1951; Poet in Res. & Engl. Lectr., ibid, 1959-64; Elected to Vt. House of Reps., 1960-62; Poetry Reviewer, Harper's, 1961-64; Writer in Res., Hollins Coll., Va., 1965-66; Poet in Res. & Engl. Lectr., Williams Coll., 1966-67; Prof. of Engl., Hollins Coll., 1967-68; Cons. in Poetry, Lib. of Congress, 1968-70; Prof. of Engl., Hollins Coll., 1970-; Hon. Cons. in Am.

Letters, Lib. of Congress, 1970–. Memberships: Acad. of Am. Poets, 1969; Am. Rhodes Scholars; PEN; Authors Guild; Authors League. Published works incl: Poems, 1947; Celebration at Dark, 1950; Poems 1947-57, 1957; The Tin Can & Other Poems, 1966; New & Selected Poems, 1970; (criticism) The Spectra Hoax, 1960; The Streaks of the Tulip, Selected Criticism, 1973; (transl.) Poems of a Multimillionaire by Valery Larbaud, 1955; Selected Writings of Jules Laforgue, 1956, 1972; Ed. of var. anthols. & colls. Has written more than a dozen books for children & has translated poems, essays & articles. Recip. var. hons. inclng: Loines Award, Nat. Inst. Arts & Letters, 1972; Dr. Lit., New England Coll., 1973. Address: Upper Bryant Rd., West Cummington, MA 01265, U.S.A.

SMITHGALL, Elizabeth, b. 10 May 1902. Teacher. Education: B.S., Tchrs. Coll., Columbia Univ., 1929; M.A., ibid, 1934; post. grad. study at var. univs., 1939-70. Positions held: Tchr., Public Schls., Lancaster, Pa., 1923-50; Supvsr. of Student Tchng., General Beadle State Coll., 1950-52; Wis. State Coll., 1952-53; Plymouth State Coll., 1955-56; Tchr., Thomas Jefferson Schl., Levittown, Pa., 1957-69; Tchr., St. Michael Schl., Levittown, 1969–. Memberships: Nat. League of Am. Pen Women; Pa. Poetry Soc. Contbr. to: The Explorer; Grade Tchr.; Lancaster mag.; Midwest Chaparral; N.H. Educator; The Pen Woman; Seydell Qtly.; Prairie Poets II. Recip., Cert. of Recognition, Fla. State Poetry Soc. Address: 66 Huckleberry Ln., Levittown, PA 19055, U.S.A.

SMITHYMAN, Kendrick, b. 9 Oct. 1922. Senior Tutor. Educ: Seddon Mem. Tech. Coll., Auckland, N.Z.; Auckland Tchrs. Coll.; Auckland Univ. Coll. m. Mary Stanley Smithyman, 3s. Positions held: Served, Royal N.Z. Air Force, WWII; Primary Schl. Tchr., 1946-63; Sr. Tutor, Dept. of Engl., Univ. of Auckland, current; Vis. Fellow, Commonwealth Lit., Univ. of Leeds, U.K., 1969. Published works: Seven Sonnets, 1946; The Blind Mountain, 1951; The Gay Trapeze, 1955; The Night Shift: Poems on Aspects of Love (w. others), 1957; Inheritance, 1962; Flying to Palmerston, 1968. Contbr. to: (anthologies) A Book of New Zealand Verse, 1951; New Zealand Poetry Yearbook, 1951-54; An Anthology of New Zealand Verse, 1956; Penguin Book of New Zealand Verse, 1966; Recent Poetry in New Zealand, 1965; Commonwealth Poems of Today, 1967. Address: Dept. of Engl., Univ. of Auckland, Auckland, New Zealand.

SMITHYMAN, Mary Isobel, b. 15 May 1919. Teacher. Educ: Auckland Tchrs. Coll., N.Z.; B.A., Univ. of Auckland. m. Kendrick Smithyman, 3s. Published works: Starveling Year, 1953. Contbr. to: (anthologies) New Zealand Poetry Yearbook, 1951; An Anthology of New Zealand Verse, 1956. Recip., Jessie Mackay Prize for Poetry. Address: 78 Nile Rd., Milford, Auckland 9, New Zealand.

SMUUL, Johannes, b. 18 Feb. 1922. Poet. Published works: Grim Youth, 1946; Son of Storm, 1947; Team of Chaps of Yarvesuu, 1948; Estonian Poem, 1949; Poems, 1951; I Am A Member Of The Komsomol, 1953; The Ice Book, 1956; Atlantic Ocean, 1956; Murka the Sailor, 1961; The Sea of Japan, 1963; Sea Songs, 1963; The Wild Captain, 1964; Colonel's Widow, 1966. Honours & awards: State Prize, 1951; Lenin Prize, 1961; Merited Writer of Estonia SSR. Address: c/o Union of Estonian Writers, Tallinn, Estonian SSR, USSR.

SNEAD, Helen Olsen, b. 27 Aug. 1897. Housewife; Poet. Married, 1 son, 1 daughter. Positions held: Bookkeeper, Hazard-Gould Cos., San Diego, Calif., 1917-20; Sec. & Bookkeeper, Snead-Payne Co., Lynchburg, Va., 1935-40. Memberships: V.P., Poetry Soc. of Va.; Sec. Treas., Nat. League of Am. Pen Women, Lynchburg, Va. Br.; Treas., The Poetry Workshop of The Lynchburg Women's Club, 1961-73; Va. Writers Club; The Poets Tape Exchange; The Acad. of Am. Poets. Published works: My Kinsmen: All Danes, 1961; Standing Here, 1971. Contbr. to: Poetry Ventured (anthol.), 1972; Garden Gossip; Amherst

New Era Progress; The Garden Club of Va. Jrnl., 1955-73; Poet Lore, 1967; Haiku Highlights, 1969-72; Dragonfly, 1973; Lynchburg, 1971-73; Haiku Mag., 1971; Mod. Haiku, 1971-73; Haiku West, 1972-73; Tweed, Australia, 1972, etc. Recip. var. awards inclng: 1st pl., serious profl. verse, Va. Fed. of Women's Clubs, 1963, 67, 68, 73. Address: 3000 Rivermont Ave., Apt. 2, Lynchburg, VA 24503, U.S.A.

SNEYD, Steve, b. 20 Mar. 1941. Advertising Copywriter. Education: B.Sc., Chem., 1960; Dip. in Marketing, 1971. Memberships: Co-ordinator, Ludd's Mill Poetry Publishing Co-operative; Sec., Inner Circle Poetry/Media Grp.; Poets Conf.; Assn. of Little Presses. Published works: Coute Preis, 1969; Icarus Landing, 1971; Out of Sight 37, 1973. Contbr. to: Poetmeat; Breakthru; Rejected Verses; Eruption; Origins & Diversions; Stanza; Wolverhampton Workshop; Mailbag; Pact; Cogito; Informer; Socialist Viewpoints; Bogg; Albion; Zahir; Gargantua; Leaves; Mallorn; Confrontation; Good Elf; Iron Flute; Sol; Sanity; Following You; Oasis (Lincoln); Wilful Stranger; Here Now; Swing Back; Ostrich Lines; Moonshine; Headland; Turpin; Purple Smoke; Ore; New Headland; Sonnet; Hope; Grope Again; Reynard; Iron; Radix; Abbey; Clare Market; Sunken Rag, etc. Recip., Trend '67 Prize for Socialist Poetry, 1967. Address: 4 Nowell Pl., Almondbury, Huddersfield HD5 8PB, Yorks., U.K.

SNIKERE, Velta, pen names WILSON, Velta Snikere & SNIKERE, Velta, b. 25 Dec. 1920. Poet; Dancer; Teacher of Yoga. Education: Philos., Univ. of Riga; Modern Ballet; Indian Dancing; M.C.S.P. Memberships: Int. PEN, English Ctr., Latvian Ctr., and PEN in Exile; Latvian Press Soc.; Latvian Nat. Coun.; British League for European Freedom; Wheel of Yoga. Published works: Three Authors, 1950; Continued Divination, 1960; Invocation, 1967. Translation: God Thy Earth is Aflame. Contbr. to: Daugava; Cela Zimes; Jauna Gaita; Tilts; Arena; Jrnl. of PEN; Londonas avize; Latvija; Laiks; Yoga Educl. Supplement; Yoga and Hlth., etc. Address: 46 Crouch Hall Rd., London N8 8HJ, U.K.

SNODGRASS, William DeWitt, b. 5 Jan. 1926. Poet. Education: State Univ. of Iowa; B.A.; M.A.; M.F.A. Positions held: Instr., Engl. Dept., Cornell Univ., 1955-57; Istr., Univ. of Rochester, 1957-58; Prof., Engl. Dept., Wayne State Univ., 1959–; Ldr., Poetry Workshop, Morehead, Ky., 1955. Published works: Heart's Needle, 1951. Awards: Pulitzer Prize for Poetry, 1960. Address: R.D.1, Erieville, NY 13061, U.S.A.

SNOW, Alfred Herbert, pen name SNOW, A.H., b. 20 July 1910. Educator. Education: King's Coll., London; Inst. of Educ., London. Married, 2 sons. Positions held: Editl. Panel, Envoi. Memberships: Poetry Soc. of G.B.; Havering Poetry Soc. (Poetry One). Contbr. to: Envoi; Scrip; Breakthru; Workshop; Poetry One; Carnival Poems; Poems 1973 (Ver Poets); BBC Poetry Now. Honours, awards: Prize Poem, Envoi, 1968, 69 & Workshop, 1972. Address: 86 Marshalls Dr., Romford, Essex RM1 4JS, U.K.

SNYDER, Gary, b. 8 May 1930. Poet. Education: B.A., Reed Coll., 1951; Ind. Univ., 1951; Univ. of Calif., Berkeley, 1953-56. Published works include: Riprap, 1959; Myths & Texts, 1960; The Firing, 1964; Nanao Knows, 1964; Hop, Skip and Jump, 1964; Six Sections from Mountains and Rivers Without End, 1965; A Range of Poems, 1966; The Back Country, 1967; Earth House Hold, 1969. Contbr. to the following anthols., jrnls., mags., etc: Janus; Evergreen Review; Black Mtn. Review; Yugen; Chicago Review; Jabberwock; San Francisco Review; Big Table; Poems from the Floating World; Origin; Kulchur; Jrnl. for the Protection of All Beings; Nation; City Lights; Yale Lit. Mag.; Beloit Poetry Jrnl.; Poetry Recip. of various grants. Address: c/o New Directions Publishing Corp., 333 Sixth Ave., New York, NY 10014, USA.

SNYDER, Kirtland Alan, b. 3 July 1948. Secondary School English Teacher. Education: B.A., St. Michael's Coll., 1966-70; M.Ed., Univ. of Hartford, 1971-73; M.A., Trinity Coll., 1971-73. Positions held: Engl. Tchr., Bloomfield H.S., Bloomfield, Conn., 1971; Tchr. Corps, Hartford, Conn., 1971-73; Engl. Tchr., Hall H.S., West Hartford, 1973-. Member, Poetry Soc. of Am. Contbr. to: The Hartford Courant; The N.Y. Sunday News; Foreword; Hog River Review; Aspen Leaves. Honours, awards: 1st prize, Town of Greenburg Poetry Contest, Westchester Community Coll., 1972; 2nd prize, Hog River Review Poetry Contest, 1971. Address: Turkey Hill Apts. No. 102, East Granby, CT 06026, U.S.A.

SOBILOFF, Hyman (Hy) Jordan, b. 16 Dec. 1912. Businessman. Education: Univ. of Ariz., 1929-32; Boston Univ., 1932-33; NY Univ., 1943-44; LL.D., Fla. Southern Coll., Lakeland. Currently Chmn. of the Bd. & Dir. of following: Larchfield Corp., NY; Marshall-Wells Internat., Nassau, Bahamas; Johnson Stores, Inc., Raleigh, NC; Auto-Lec Stores, Inc., New Orleans, La. Published works: When Children Played as Kings & Queens, 1948; Dinosaurs & Violins, 1954; In the Deepest Aquarium, 1959; Breathing of First Things, 1963. Films: Montauk, 1959; Central Park, 1960; Speak to Me Child, 1962; Market to Market, 1968. Recordings: Library of Congress poetry readings, 1956, 1960; Breathing of First Things/Speak to me child, Gryphon Records, 1963. Contbr. to following anthols. & jrnls: New Pocket Anthol. of Am. Verse, 1955; Silver Treas. of Light Verse, 1957; 20th Century Am. Poetry, 1963; Anthol. of Am. Verse, 1966; Poetry for Pleasure, 1960; Poetry From Hidden Springs, 1962; Poetry (Chicago); The Hudson Review; Mutiny; The Literary Review; The Salty Thumb; Nassau Magazine; The Minn. Review. Honours: Awarded citation of Excellence, color photography, 1st Boston Internat. Film Festival, Cambridge, Mass., for Montauk, 1959; Central Park selected as US entry, Film Festivals, Venice & Edinburgh, 1960. Address: 67 E 77th St., New York, NY 10021, USA.

SODERHJELM, Ulf Stefan, b. 21 July 1934. Scientific Collaborator for Sandoz Ltd., Basle. Education: Agronomist, Helsingfors Univ. Married, 2 children. Member, Soc. of Swedish Authors in Finland. Published works: Sval Fristad, 1956; Hög Sjö och Marviol, 1962; Angslycka, 1971. Contbr. to Femina, Sweden (Love Poem of the Week), 1972. Address: Björkkulla, 07930 Pernä, Finland.

SOJCHER, Jacques, b. 8 Sept. 1939. Professor. Education: Lit. & Philos., Univ. of Brussels. Positions held: Prof., (Aesthetics), Univ. of Brussels. Memberships: Comm. of Resolution, Cahiers internationaux de symbolisme; le Journal des Poètes. Published works: La démarche poétique, 1969; La question et le sens, Esthétique de Nietzsche, 1972; & many articles. Contbr. to: Critique; Les Lettres Nouvelles; La Quinzaine Littéraire; Cahiers internationaux de symbolisme; Revue internationale de philosophie; Courrier due centre international d'études poétiques; Le Journal des Poètes; Phantomas; Degrés; Gradiva, etc. Recip., Prix Léopold Rosy (Triennal prize of essay from Academie Royale de Langue et de Litterature Française de Belgique). Address: 10 rue du Magistrat, 1050 Brussels, Belgium.

SOKIRA, (Sister) Mary Lucina, R.S.M., b. 1 May 1927. Teacher. Education: B. Ed., Medaille Coll., Buffalo, N.Y.; currently working on Master's at Nazareth Coll., Rochester, N.Y. Member, Poetry Soc. of Am. Contbr. to: Hornbook; N.Y. Times; Music Jrnl.; Sisters Today; Christian Century; This Issue. Address: Mount Mercy Convent, 625 Abbott Rd., Buffalo, NY 14220, U.S.A.

SOLECKI, Thomas Alexander, b. 15 Mar. 1945. Brooklyn, N.Y. Laborer. Educ: P.S. 31; J.H.S. 126; Queens Aviation H.S.; John W. Brown Schl. Ship. Positions held: Foundry Worker; Restaurant Owner; Rail Road Worker. Contbr. to: Polish American World; Jean's Jrnl.; Speak Out Mag.; Lunatic Fringe; Poetry

Scrap Book; The Archer; Special Song. Address: 40-20 70 St., Woodside, NY 11377, U.S.A.

SOLJAN, Antun, b. 1 Dec. 1932. Poet; Novelist; Playwright. Education: Engl. Lang. & Lit., Univ. of Zagreb. Positions held: Ed. of 'Krugovi' (The Circle), 1955-58; Ed. of 'Književnik 'The Writer', 1959-61; Sec. of the Croatian Writers' Union, 1961-63; Pres. of the Croatian PEN Club, 1970-73. Published works: (poetry) On the Edge of the World, 1956; Out of Focus, 1959; Gazelle & Other Poems, 1970; Selected & New Poems, 1974; (novels) The Traitors, 1961; A Short Excursion, 1965; The Port, 1974; (short stories) The Special Envoys, 1957; Ten short-stories for My Generation, 1966; (plays) The Hill, 1966; Galileo's Ascension, 1968; Diocletians Palace, 1969; Mototor & Trampeste, 1974; many translations, especially of Engl. & Am. poetry. Contbr. to var. European & Am. mags. Address: Draškovičeva 12, Zagreb, Yugoslavia.

SOLOUKHIN, Vladimir Alexeyevich, b. 1924. Poet, Novelist. Education: Maxim Gorky Inst. of Lit. Published works: (poetry) Rain In The Steppe, 1953; Saxifrage; Steamlets on the Asphalt, 1959; Tale of the Steppes, 1960; How To Drink The Sun, 1961; Postcards from Vietnam, 1962; (novels) Birth of Zernograd, 1955; The Goldmine, 1956; Beyond the Blue Seas, 1957; The Drop of Dew, 1963; A Lyrical Story, 1964; Mother – Stepmother; The Loaf of Bread, 1965; Don't Seek Shelter from the Rain (Poems), 1967. Honours, awards: Order of Red Banner of Labour. Address: c/o Union of Soviet Writers, Moscow Br., Moscow, USSR.

SOLVIN, Lois Lorene Chinn, pen name **SOLVIN, Lois C.,** b. 2 Apr. 1918. Secretary & Record Room Supervisor. Married & div. twice. Positions held: For past 24 yrs. w. exception of 1959-62, has worked for soc. serv. agencies: City Welfare Dept. (City Workhouse); Jefferson Co. Welfare Dept. & now the Metropolitan Soc. Serv. Dept. (City & Co. combined Depts.) Memberships: Int. Poetry Soc.; Ky. State Poetry Soc.; Int. Conf. of Black Writers; Ky. Br. of Nat. League of Am. Pen Women. Published works: Forecast, 1971; Now & Then, to be published. Contbr. to: Wind; Modern Images; The Guild; Valley Views; Fireflower; The Poets Guild; Author/Poet; The Olive Hill Times; Black Writers News; Encore; Salem Headlight; Tejas; Friendly Way; Inky Trails; Grains of Sand (anthol.); Forever Bear (anthol.); Southwest Breeze; Poetry Corner; Fragments of Faith (anthol.); Sweat & Sneakers (anthol.); Nelson's Mag.; Hyacinths & Biscuits; Poets Forum; Poetry Club Mag.; Orphic Lute; Sparkling Gems; Angel Hour; Saline Co. News; Courier-Jrnl.; West Louisville Star; United Poets; Jean's Jrnl.; The Angelo; Yank; The Am. Poet; Prairie Poet. Recip., Hon. Mention for Appalachian Daughter, KSPS, 1972. Address: 213 Downs Ln., Louisville, KY 40214, U.S.A.

SOMMER, Richard Jerome, b. 27 Aug. 1934. University Teacher. Education: B.A., Univ. of Minn., U.S.A., 1956; A.M. in Engl., Harvard Univ., 1957; Ph.D. in Engl., ibid, 1962. Positions held: Asst. Prof. of Engl., Sir Geo. Williams Univ., 1962; Assoc. Prof. of Engl., ibid, 1967-. Memberships: Phi Beta Kappa; Lambda Alpha Psi (Univ. of Minn.); MLA until 1967. Published works: Homage to Mr. MacMullin, 1969; Blue Sky Notebook, 1973. Contbr. to: Prism (Montreal); Canadian Dimension; Canadian Forum; Duel; Anthol.; The Far Point; West Coast Review; Edge; Epoch; Antioch Review; Tamarack Review; Harvard Advocate; Field; Yes; The Ninth Circle, etc. Recip., Acad. of Am. Poets prize, Harvard Univ., 1958. Address: 3757 Draper Ave., Montreal 261, Quebec, Canada.

SONNE, Jørgen, b. 15 Oct. 1925. Poet. Education: M.A., Hist., 1951. Married, 2 children. Positions held: Tchr., 1951-1967; Lectr., Copenhagen Univ., 1971. Memberships: Bd. of Danish Authors' Assn.; Authors' Union (Co-Fndr.). Published works include: 8 Collections of Poems, 1950, 1951 & 1964, 1952, 1954, 1960, 1963; Choice 1950-65, 1965, 1972; Novel, 1971;

Essays, 1972; Num. transls. Contbr. to the following publications: Politiken; Vildtlvede; Hvedekorn; Perspektiv; Vindrosen; Selvsyn. Ed. of series, The Peoples' Poetry. Honours, awards: Benzon, 1963; Drachmann, 1964; Life-time State Grant, 1965. Address: Gl. Kongeve, 101A, 1850 V Copenhagen, Denmark.

SONNE DIPOKO, Mbella, b. 28 Feb. 1936. Writer. Education: Fac. of Law & Econ. Scis., Paris Univ., 1962-65. Positions held: Accounts Clerk, Cameroon Dev. Corp., Tiko, 1956-57; News Reporter, Nigerian Broadcasting Corp., Lagos, 1958-60; Translator, Writer, etc. Published works: Poetry for Boys & Girls, 1955; Black & White in Love, 1972; All the Harvest For All, 1974. Contbr. to: United Asia; Presence Africaine; Quest; Transition; Black Orpheus; The Monparnasse Review; BBC. Address: c/o Heinemann Educl. Books, 48 Charles St., London W.1, U.K.

SONNEVI, Sven Göran Manne, b. 3 Oct. 1939. Writer. Education: Fil.kand., Univ. of Lund, Sweden, 1963. Memberships: Swedish Union of Authors. Published works: Outfort, 1961; Abstrakta dikter, 1963; Ingrepp-modeller, 1965; Och nu! 1967; Det gäller oss, 1969; Det Maste Ga, 1970; Det oauslutade spraket, 1972; Dikter 1959-1973, 1974. Foreign editions: On the War, 1968; Et maintenant, 1970. Translator of Ezra Pound, Paul Celan, Hans Magnus Enzensberger, & Robert Bly. Honours, awards: BLM Prize, 1968; Carl-Emil Englund Prize, 1971; Aftonbladets Lit. Prize, 1972. Address: c/o Albert Bonniers Förlag, Sveavägen 56, Stockholm, Sweden.

SOP, Nikola, b. 19 Aug. 1904. Poet; Teacher. Education: Roman Law, Zagreb Univ., 2 yrs.; Grad., Comp. Lit. & Latin, Belgrade Univ., 1931. Married. Positions held: Freelance Writer; Sec. Schl. Tchr.; w. Croatian Bibliographical Inst., Zagreb, 1943; Ed., Zora Publishing House, Zagreb, 1947; Sci. Contributing Mbr., Yugoslav Acad. of Sci. & Art (worked on the transl. of mediaeval Croatian writers, Ivan Cesmički, Ignjat Gjurgjevic, Juraj Sižgorić (Latinists). Memberships: Belgrade Writers' Union, 1928–; mbr., PEN; Croatian Writers' Union. Published works: Pjesme siromašnog sina, 1927; Nokturno, 1928; Isus i moja sjena, 1934; Knjiga o Horaciju, 1935; Od ranih do kasnih pijetlova, poems, 1939; Za kasnim stolom, poems, 1943; Tajanstvena prela, lyric prose, 1943; Kućice u svemiru i Svemirski pohodi, two poems, 1957; Astralije, poems, 1961; Poezija, poetry, 1966; Bosnian Trilogy, 1968; Pohodi, poems, 1972. Contbr. to var. jrnls. Honours, awards: The Great Lit. Reward 'Cvijeta Zuzorić', Belgrade, 1934; Anthony Prize, Zagreb, 1944; The Great State Prize for Poetry 'Vladimir Nazor', Zagreb, 1971; The First Radio Drama Prize, Zagreb, 1968. Address: Voćarska 90, 41000 Zagreb, Croatia, Yugoslavia.

SOR, Daniel, pen name JACQUEMIN, Jean, b. 26 Sept. 1923. Journalist. Education: Licences de Lettres et de droit. Married, 2 children. Positions held: Pres., Syndicat of Journalists & Writers; Redacteur en chef et Directeur de Pa Revue independante. Published works: Quelques vers pour toi, 1942; Les Chagrins, 1952 & rep. in num. anthologies. Contbr. to: Lettres et Poesie; L'Interforain; Revue Independante; L'homme libre, etc. Recip., Grand Prix Baudelaire, Paris, 1971. Address: 27 Villa des Lilas, 75019, Paris, France.

SORESCU, Marin, b. 29 Feb. 1936, Bulzesti, Rumania. Writer. Education: Fac. of Philology, Univ. of Jassy, Rumania. Married. Positions held: Ed., Viata studentească; Ed., Luceafărul; Chief Ed., Animafilm Studio. Memberships: Union of Rumanian Writers; Société des Auteurs dramatiques de France. Published works: Alone among poets, 1964; Poems, 1966; Death of the Clock, 1967; Don Quixote's Youth, 1968; Where are we Running To? 1967; Cough, 1970; Frames, 1972; Soul, good to everything, 1973; Theory of Influence Spheres, 1969; Sleeplessness; Jonah, 1968; Nerves do Exist, 1968; A Wing & a Leg, 1970. Contbr. to: Times; Le Monde; Encounter; Mosaic; România literară; Luceafărul. Honours, awards: Prize,

Union of Writers in Rumania, 1966 & 68; Prize, Rumanian Acad., 1971; Prize, Italian Review 'Il Dramma', 1970. Address: Str. Gr. Alexandrescu nr. 43, Sectorul 1, Bucharest, Rumania.

SORRELLS, Helen, b. 1 Jan. 1908. Writer. Education: B.Sc., Jrnlsm., Kan. State Univ., Manhattan, 1931; Poetry workshops at UCLA & Calif. State Univ., Northridge, Calif., 1961-65. Married, 2 daughters. Positions held: Newspaper Reporter, 1926-27; Radio Script Writer, 1934-40 in Kan. City, Mo. Memberships: Poetry Soc. of Am.; Calif. Writers Guild; Theta Sigma Phi. Published works: Seeds as They Fall, poems, 1971. Contbr. to: Esquire Mag.; The Reporter; The Ariz. Quarterly; The Beloit Poetry Jrnl.; The Carleton Miscellany; The Chicago Tribune Mag.; Coastlines; The Colo. Quarterly; Commonweal; The Fiddlehead; Fine Arts Discovery; The Mass. Review; The Mich. Quarterly Review; The New Orleans Review; The North American Review; Perspective; Poetry Northwest; Prairie Schooner; Shenandoah; Southern Poetry Review; Trace; The Univ. Review; The Western Humanities Review; Denver Quarterly Review; Concerning Poetry; Yankee; The Women Poets in English (anthol), 1973; The Borestone Mountain Awards for 1967 (anthol.) Honours, awards: Ariz. Quarterly Best Poem of Yr. Award, 1968; Cecil Hemley Meml. Award, Poetry Soc. of Am., 1973; Creative Writing Grant, Nat. Endowment for the Arts, 1973. Address: 221 Tranquillo Rd., Pacific Palisades, CA 90272, U.S.A.

SORRENTINO, Gilbert, b. 27 Apr. 1929. Editor. Educ: Brooklyn Coll., N.Y. Positions held: Ed., Grove Press, N.Y.C., 1965–. Published works: The Darkness Surrounds Us, 1960; Black and White, 1964; The Perfect Fiction, 1968; The Sky Changes (novel), 1966; Jack Spicer: Language as Image (criticism), 1966. Contbr. to: Poetry; (anthologies) New American Poetry, 1960; Poesia Americana del 1900, 1963; Poems Now, 1966; New Writing in the U.S.A., 1967. Address: 541 E. 13th St., N.Y., NY, U.S.A.

SOTOLA, Jiří, b. 28 May 1924. Writer. Education: Acad. of Dramatic Arts, Prague. Positions held: Actor, Producer, Theatre, 1948-52; Ed., Chief Ed., weekly Lit. Mag., 1964, '67; Chief Sec., Writers Union of Czechoslovakia, 1964-67. Member, PEN. Published works: Náhrobni´ kámen (The Tombstone), 1946; Cas dovršený (The Time Completed), 1946; Za život (For the Life), 1955; Cerveny květ (The Red Flower), 1955; Svět náš vezdejší (Give Us This Day Our Daily World), 1957; Venuše z Melu (Venus from Melos), 1959; Bylo to v Evropě (It Was In Europe), 1960; Hvězda Ypsilon (The Star Y), 1962; Poste Restante, 1963; Co a jak (What & How?), 1964; Podzimníček (The Autumn Variationen), 1967. Address: Hradčanské nám. 1, Prague 1, Czechoslovakia.

SOTO-RAMOS, Julio, b. 20 Apr. 1903. Writer; Poet; Publicist. Education: HS and Military Courses. Positions held: US Customs Patrol Inspector; Prohibition Agent, US Treasury Dept.; ibid, Investigator; US Army Officer, Puerto Rico and Trinidad, WW 11; Inspector, Alcohol & Tobacco Tax Div., Internal Revenue Service, US Treasury Dept. (Retired 196). Received Albert Gallatin Award. Memberships: Internat. Pontzen Acad. for Letters, Sciences & Arts, Naples, Italy (Academician); (Hon.) Comité Cultural Argentino; (Hon.) Parnasilo Castellano, Madrid, Spain; (Hon.) Casa do Poeta A. Garibaldi, Felgueiras, Portugal. Published works: Cortina de Suenos (Curtain of Dreams), 1923; Relicario AZul (Blue Shrine), 1933; Soledades en Sol (Sunny Solitude), 1952; Trapecio (Trapeze), 1955. Contbr. to: Puerto Rico Ilustrado; El Carnaval; Gráfico de Puerto Rico; El Diluvio; Alma Latina; Alma Popular; El Mundo; El Imparcial; La Tijera Literaria, Madrid, Spain; Rumbos, Barcelona, Spain; El Nuevo Día; La Voz de Cayey. Awards: Dip. of Merit and Gold Pen, Towards The Glory of Internat. Pontzen Acad., 1967; Dip. of Merit and laurel crown, The Universal Song of Internat. Pontzen Acad., 1969; Plaque of his home town (Coamo), 22 Jan. 1960. Address: 429 Salvador

Brau, Floral Park, Hato Rey, PR 00917, USA.

SOUDERS, Bruce Chester, b. 27 Dec. 1920. Clergyman; Educator. Education: A.B., Lebanon Valley Coll., Annville, Pa., 1944; M. Div., United Theol. Sem., Dayton, Ohio, 1947; M.A., Columbia Univ., 1953. Married Patricia Marie Bartels, 1 son. Positions held: Instr. in Engl., Lebanon Valley Coll., 1947-49; Pastor, Neidig Meml. United Methodist Ch., Oberlin, Pa., 1949-57; Dir. of Public Rels., & Instr. in Engl., Philos. & Religion, Lebanon Valley Coll., 1957-66; Chmn. of Engl. Dept. (1966-72) & Chmn. of Arts & Scis. Fac. (1972-), Shenandoah Coll., Winchester, Va. Memberships: Poetry Soc. of Am.; Poetry Soc. of Va.; Advisor, Winchester Poetry Workshop; Participant, Dellbrook-Shenandoah Coll. Writers' Conf., 1969-. Contbr. to: Winchester Star, Va.; The Telescope-Messenger; Our Home; Together; Southern Humanities Review; Va. Poetry Soc.'s Golden Anniversary Anthol.; Poetry Digest Anthol.; Nat. Poetry Anthol. Address: Rte. 6, Box 233, Winchester, VA 22601, U.S.A.

SOUPAULT, Philippe, b. 2 Aug. 1897. Poet; Writer. Education: Bachelier es lettres, Bachelier en droit, Sorbonne, Paris. Married, 2 children. Positions held: formerly Prof., Swarthmore Coll., Pa., U.S.A.; associated w. the early Surrealists. Published works incl: (poetry) Les Champs Magnétiques, 1921; Westwego, 1922; Georgia, 1929; Poésies Complètes, 1937; L'arme secrète; Message de l'île déserte, 1948; Chansons, 1950; Sans phrases, 1953; Poemes et poesies 1917, 1973; (novels) Le Bon apôtre, 1923; Les frères Durandeau, 1925; En Joue! 1926; Le Coeur d'or, 1927; Le Nègre, 1929; Les Moribonds, 1934; (biog. studies) Henri Rousseau; Charles Baudelaire; Paolo Uccello, 1928; William Blake, 1929; Lautréamont, 1931; Souvenirs de James Joyce, 1943; (plays) Rendez-vous! 1957; La nuit du temps, 1962; (essays) Profils Perdus, 1963; Eugène Labiche, 1964; Vous m'oublierez; Alibis, 1972; Le 6 me coup de minuit, 1973, etc. Honours, awards: Strassburger Prize, 1932; Prix Italia, 1958, '63; Grand Prix de la Société des Gens de Lettres, 1973. Address: 11 rue Chaney, Paris XVIe, France.

SOUSTER, R(aymond) H(olmes), pen name **HOLMES, Raymond; HOLMES, John** (fiction only), b. 15 Jan. 1921. Bank Clerk. Education: Univ. of Toronto Schools; Humberside Collegiate Inst., Toronto, Canada. Married. Positions held: Bank Clerk, 1939-40, and 1945 onwards; Equipment Asst., RCAF., 1941-45. Memberships: League of Canadian Poets (former Chairman and Vice-Chairman). Published works: When We Are Young, 1946; Go To Sleep, World, 1947; City Hall Street, 1951, Cerberus (with Dudok and Layton), 1952; Selected Poems, 1956; Place of Meeting, 1962; A Local Pride, 1962; The Colour of the Times, 1964; Ten Elephants On Yonge Street, 1965; As Is, 1967; Lost & Found, 1968; So Far So Good, 1969; The Years, 1971; Selected Poems, 1972; The Colour Of the Times and Ten Elephants On Yonge Street (combined volume), 1973; Change-Up, 1974; Triple Header, 1974. Awards: Governor-General's Award For Poetry in English, 1964; President's Medal of Univ. of Western Ontario, 1967; Centennial Medal, 1967. Address: 39 Baby Point Rd., Toronto M6S 2G2, Canada.

SOYINKA, Wole, b. 13 July 1934. Writer; University Professor. Education: B.A. Engl., Univ. of Leeds, U.K. Married w. children. Currently Prof. in Drama, Univ. of Ife, Nigeria. Mbr., London Poetry Secretariat. Published works: Idanre, 1967; A Shuttle in the Crypt, 1968, '72. Contbr. to: Transitions; Encounter; Black Orpheus; New Statesman; Times Lit. Supplement; Presence Africaine, etc. Address: c/o London Poetry Secretariat, Garrick House, 27 Southampton St., London WC2E 7JL, U.K.

SPACKS, Barry, b. 21 Feb. 1931. Poet & Novelist. Education: B.A., Univ. of Pa., 1952; M.A., Ind. Univ., 1956; Pembroke Coll., Cambridge Univ. (on Fulbright Fellowship), 1956-57. Married, 1 daughter. Positions

held: Asst. Prof., Engl., Univ. of Fla., Gainesville, Fla., 1957-59; Instr. to Prof., MIT, 1960-. Published works: The Company of Children, 1969 & Something Human, 1972 (both poems); Orphans, 1972 & The Sophomore, 1968 (both novels). Contbr. to: Poetry; New Yorker; Atlantic; Harper's; Yale Review; Sewanee Review, etc. Recip., St. Botolph's Arts Award, 1971. Address: 16 Abbott St., Wellesley, MA 02181, U.S.A.

SPAIN, Jane Spalding, b. 13 Sept. 1901. Teacher. Education: B.S., Kansas State Tchrs. Coll., 1927; Chicago Art Inst.; Kans. City Art Inst.; Univ. of Ariz. Positions held: Rural schl. tchng. for six yrs. in Missouri hills, Colo. ranch area & Kansas prairies; Sec. tchng. for 36 yrs., last 33 yrs. being in Tucson public schls. in the southwestern desert of the U.S.A.; Private studio in collab. with a sculptor & a craftsman; Taught private painting lessons before returning to public schl. tchng. Memberships: World Poetry Soc. Intercontinental; Nat. Fed. of State Poetry Socs.; Recording Sec. for State, V.P. & Pres. of local affil., Ariz. State Poetry Soc.; Life Mbr., Clover Int. Poetry Assn.; Mbr., Int. Toastmistress Clubs, etc. Rep. in following anthols: Sing Naked Spirit, 1970; Premier Poets, 1972; The Clover Collection of Verse, 1973. Contbr. to: The Harp; Sonnet Sequences; The Thalia of Pi Delta Theta; Poet, etc. Honours, awards incl: Woman of Yr., Am. Business Women's Assn., 1966; seven first prizes in monthly contests of Ariz. State Poetry Soc. Address: 2012 W. Calle Placida, Tucson, AZ 85705, U.S.A.

SPARK, Muriel Sarah. Writer. Fellow, Royal Soc. of Lit., 1963. Positions held: worked in Political Intelligence, Dept. of For. Office, WWII; Gen. Sec., Poetry Soc., London; Ed., the Poetry Review, 1947-49. Published works: The Fanfarlo & Other Verse, 1952; (critical & biog.) Tribute to Wordsworth, 1950; Selected Poems of Emily Bronte, 1952; Child of Light: A Reassessment of Mary Shelley, 1951; John Masefield, 1953; Emily Bronte: Her Life & Work (co-author), 1953; The Bronte Letters, 1954; Letters of John Henry Newman, 1957; (fiction) The Comforters, 1957; Robinson, 1958; The Go-Away Bird, 1958; Momento Mori, 1959, adapted for stage by Eleanor Perry, 1964; The Bachelors, 1960; Voices at Play, 1961; The Prime of Miss Jean Brodie, 1961; The Girls of Slender Means, 1963; The Mandelbaum Gate, 1965; Collected Stories I, 1967; Collected Poems I, 1967; The Public Image, 1968; The Very Fine Clock (for children), 1969; The Driver's Seat, 1970; Not to Disturb, 1971; The Hot House by the East River, 1973; (play) Doctors of Philosophy, 1963; Not to Disturb, 1971. Honours, awards: Italia Prize for Dramatic Radio, The Ballad of Peckham Rye, 1962; O.B.E. Address: c/o Macmillan & Co. Ltd., 4 Little Essex St., London WC2, U.K.

SPARKS, Hypatia Katharine, pen name **SPARKS, Katharine.** Housewife. Education: London Central School. Daughter of Oxford bookseller who was also founder of English Language Club (London), 1919, and founder of magazine, English. Comm. and Ed., Oxford City Writers' Club, 1957; Comm. and Ed., Gosport Writers' Club, 1968-69 (and currently member); Founder/Editor, magazine: Hampshire Poets, 1969, and currently. Contbr. to: Envoi; Scrip; Breakthru, and subsidiaries: (Poetry of the Left; Poetry of the People); Manifold; CS Monitor; Viewpoints; Winchester Poets; Internat. Who's Who in Poetry Anthol.; On The House (anthol); Oxford Times; Hampshire Telegraph; Morning Star. Broadcasts on BBC Radio Solent Progs. Awards: Trophy and 1st Prize N.U.M. Eisteddfod, S. Wales, 1967, English Poem; Trophy and 1st Prize, Hants. Fed. Community Centres, Poetry Section, 1969; 2nd Place, ibid. 1968; Month's Prize, John O'London, poetry, 1961; Month's Prize, Reading Mercury, 1963. Address: 7 Leep Lane, Alverstoke, Gosport, Hants. PO12 2BE, UK.

SPARROW, Louise Winslow Kidder, b. 1 Jan. 1884. Sculptor. Education: var. studies in Europe. Widow of Capt. H.G. Sparrow, U.S.N., 1 son, Maj.-Gen. USA, (Retd.). Positions held: Self employed Sculptor;

Writer; Ed. of Translations, Star Dust, Jrnl. of Poetry, 3 yrs. Memberships: Boston Authors Club; Vice Sec., Dante Alighieri Soc. of Boston, Mass.; Sec. Coterie Française, Wash. D.C.; Fellow, Royal Soc. of Arts, etc. Published works incl: A Handful of Lyrics, 1970; Narrative Poems, 1970; Spiced Herbs & Rose Petals, 1971; Violets & Mimosa, 1971; Espic of the Sea, 1971; Tales Retold at Twilight, 1972; Evening Carillon, 1972; Autumn Snowflakes, 1973; Rocking Chair Verses, 1973. Contbr. to: Poet Lore; Boston Evening Transcript; Wash. Post; Am. Bard; Bardic Echoes; Major Poets; Stardust; var. anthols., etc. Recip. var. hons. Address: 6200 Oregon Ave. N.W., Wash. D.C. 20015, U.S.A.

SPARSHOTT, Francis (Edward), b. 19 May 1926. Professor of Philosophy. Education: M.A., Corpus Christi Coll., Oxford Univ., 1950. Positions held: Prof. of Philos., Victoria Coll., Univ. of Toronto, Canada, 1964–. Mbr., Exec. Comm., League of Canadian Poets, 1970-74. Published works: A Divided Voice, 1965; A Cardboard Garage, 1969. Contbr. to: Canadian Forum; Canadian Poetry; Catalyst; Descant; Fiddlehead; Literary Mag.; The Nation; New; Pan; Poet (India); Poetry (Chicago); Saturday Night; Tamarack Review; West Coast Review; Alphabet. Recip., President's Medal, Univ. of Western Ont., 1959. Address: 50 Crescentwood Rd., Scarborough, Ont. M1N 1E4, Canada.

SPAZIANI, Maria Luisa, b. 7 Dec. 1924. Professor. Education: Liceo Classico, Univ. of Turin, Italy; Scholarship from Sorbonne Univ., Paris, 1953, '54; Int. Seminar, Harvard Univ., Boston, Mass., 1955. Positions held: Responsible for TV & Radio services, 1957–; Prof., Messina Univ., (German Lit.), 1964-66, (French Lit.), 1966–; Univ. of Palermo, Italy, 1973–. Memberships: PEN Club; Soroptimist Club; Associazione Internazionale Critici Letterari; Sindacato Scrittori; Associazione Nazionale Giornalisti; Accademia Peloritana. Published works: Primavera a Parigi, 1954; Le acque del Sabato, 1954; Luna Lombarda, 1959; Il Gong, 1962; Utilità della memoria, 1966; L'occhio del ciclone, 1970; Da Stello a Chatterton, 1971; Ronsard fra gli astri della Pléiade, 1972. Contbr. to: Paragone, L'Approdo (Florence); Tempo Presente, Terzo Programma, La Fiera Litteraria (Rome); Forum Italicum, The Literary Review (USA). Honours, awards: Premio Viareggio, 1950; Premio Lerici, 1957; Int. Byron Award, 1960; Premio Costantino Nigra, 1962; Premio Firenze, 1962; Gran Premio Saint-Vincent, 1962; Premio Carducci, 1966; Premio Cittadella, 1970; Premio Trieste, 1970. Address: Via del Babuino 68, 00187 Rome, Italy.

SPEAR, Charles. Lecturer. Positions held: Former Tchr. & Journalist; Lectr., Engl., Univ. of Canterbury, Christchurch, N.Z., current. Published works: Twopence Coloured, 1951. Contbr. to: Landfall; Arachne; (anthologies) A Book of New Zealand Verse, 1951; New Zealand Poetry Yearbook, 1953; An Anthology of New Zealand Verse, 1956. Address: Dept. of Engl., Univ. of Canterbury, Christchurch, New Zealand.

SPEARS, Woodridge, b. 22 Jan. 1913. Educator. Education: Transylvania Univ., Lexington, Ky., U.S.A., 1931-32; A.B., Morehead State Univ., Ky., 1935; A.M., Univ. of Ky., Lexington, 1947; Ph.D., ibid, 1953. Married Mary Evalena Gilbert, 2 sons, 1 daughter (Philip, Richard & Sandra). Positions held: Tchr. & Asst. Prin., pub. schls. of Greenup Co., Ky.; Grad. Asst. & Instr., Univ. of Ky.; Assoc. Prof. & Prof. of Engl., Georgetown Coll., Ky. Memberships: Phi Bet Kappa; Nat. Coun. Tchrs. of Engl.; Conf. on Communications; AAUP; Poetry Soc. of Am.; Ky. State Poetry Soc.; Ky. Coun. Tchrs. of Engl.; Scott Co. Histl. Soc.; Sigma Tau Delta. Published works: The Feudalist, 1956; The Poetic Dramas of Cale Young Rice, 1947; Elizabeth Madox Roberts: A Biographical & Critical Study, 1953; River Island, 1963. Contbr. to: P.S.A. Anthol., The Golden Year, 1960; P.S.A. Diamond Anthol., 1970; The Lyric; Poetry: A Mag. of Verse; Voices, etc. Prose & Verse in mags. since 1936.

Address: Coll. Stn., Georgetown Coll., Georgetown, KY 40324, U.S.A.

SPEER, Mildred Crabtree, b. 19 Dec. 1905. Writer. Married, John E. Speer. Positions held: Taught in primary schools of Texas for 6 yrs., clerical worker in Texas Agricultural Office for 2 yrs. Memberships Poetry Soc. of Texas; High Plains Chapter of the Poetry Soc. of Texas (membership chairman); Panhandle Pen Women (president for 2 yrs. in the 1950's). Contbr. to: CS Monitor; Kansas City Star; Time of Singing; The Amarillo Citizen (113 poems in this weekly newspaper); The Progressive Farmer; Snowy Egret; Denver Post; Grit; Trunks, Ltd.; Modern Maturity; Eternity; Christian Home; 1973 Poetry of the Year; War Cry; Capper's Weekly; Union Gospel Press; Humpty Dumpty's Mag.; Progressive Life; The Friend; Good Housekeeping; Explore. Awards: 1973, Nat. Fed. of State Poetry Socs., Inc. Poetry Soc. of Texas Award: First; C. Hoyt Memorial Award: 1st Hon. Mention, 1973, Nat. Fed. of State Poetry Socs., Inc. Address: Rt. 1, Box 217, Amarillo, TX 79106, USA.

SPEER, Robert Louis, b. 8 Oct. 1903. Investment Broker (retired). Education: Grad. school system, Fort Smith, Ark.; student, Univ. of Ark.; Grad. with Bach. of Journalism degree, Univ. of Missouri at Columbia, 1927. Married, Rachel Lucille Davis, 2 d. (1 decd). Positions held: Newspaper reporter and editor, 17 yrs.; Advertising manager, sev. daily newspapers; Investment broker, 20 yrs. Membership: Poets Roundtable of Ark. Publications: The Sounder; The Lyric; Modern Images; Contemp. Poets of Ark,; Southwestern Poets; US Congressional Record; 1 book, co-authored with Betty Bell Sanders, 1973. Also contbr. to: Southwest Times Record; Kansas Kernels, etc. 715 North 14 St., Fort Smith, AR, USA.

SPELLMAN, Alfred B., b. 7 Aug. 1934. Writer. Educ: Howard Univ., Wash. D.C., Howard Law Schl. Positions held: Mgr., Bookshop, Greenwich Vill., N.Y.C.; Producer, Series of verse plays for radio; Mus. Ed., Kulchur Magazine; Writer, Record Reviews for Jazz Mags.; Writer-in-Residence, Morehouse Coll., Atlanta, Ga., current. Published works: The Beautiful Day and Others, 1964. Contbr. to: (anthologies) New Negro Poets, 1964; New Black Poetry, 1969.

SPELLMON, Fronzell Lincoln, pen name, **ORLEY, Van L.,** b. 12 Feb. 1925. Education: B.A., B.S., Dip. of Art; D.D. (h.c.) Church Universal Brotherhood, Hollywood, California; Grad. of Butera School of Fine Arts, Boston, Mass.; Bishop Coll., Dallas, Texas. Positions held: State Chairman of American Art; Nat. Director of American Art; Chairman, Art, Louisiana Education Assoc.; Founder-Director, Ark-La-Tex. Artt Assoc.; Poetry Editor, Let's Have A Chat Mag. (Tokyo, Japan). Memberships: World Poet; American Poets Fellowship Soc.; Japan Forum (American Poetry Editor and Advisor). Published works: Tips for the Beginning Poet. Contbr. to: Link; The Aquarist; Hoosier Challenger; Road Between (Armed Forces Writers' League Book Project in Japan); World Messenger; Anthol. of Texas Poets; American Poetry League Journal; Jean's Journal; Times; The Indianapolis Recorder; The Informer; Denver Blade; Calif. Tribune; Bardic Echoes; World Poet; The Poet (India); The Soul Sings; American Poet, and many others. Awards: Pres. Eisenhower Award, People-to-People (work in Asia in Poetry and Literature); Geo. Washington Honor Medal, 1969, etc. Address: 6530 Monterey St., San Antonio, TX 78237, USA.

SPENCER, Sylvia. Writer; Businesswoman. Education: studied painting, Paris. Married Theodore S. Ruggles. Positions held: Former Head of Sylvia Spencer Assocs., Pub. Rels. Cons., serving clients in Arts, Govt. & also UNICEF; Mbr., President's Comm. on Employment of the Handicapped, Wash. D.C.; Chmn., Council of Trustees, Proj. Earning Power, Wash D.C.; Mbr., Comm. to Save Carnegie Hall, & other civic comms. in N.Y.C. Memberships: Poetry Soc. of Am.; Acad. of Am. Poets; Cons. to N.Y.C. H.S. Poetry Contest for past 4 yrs. Contbr. to: Up From the

Earth, anthol. of Garden Poetry; Contbng. Ed., Am. Authors, 1690-1900; Sat. Review of Lit., Two Cities Review, etc. Address: 24 Bank Lane, Essex, CT 06426, U.S.A.

SPENDER, Stephen (Harold), b. 28 Feb. 1909. Poet, Writer. Education: Univ. Coll., Oxford. Positions held: Co-Ed., Horizon (jrnl.), 1939-41; Fireman, NFS, 1941-44; Counsellor, Section of Letters, UNESCO, 1947; Elliston Chair of Poetry, Univ. of Cincinnati, 1953; Beckman Prof., Univ. of Calif., 1959; Co-Ed., Encounter, 1953-66; Corresponding Ed., ibid, 1966-67; Vis. Lectr., Northwestern Univ., Ill., 1963; Cons. in Poetry in Engl., Lib. of Congress, Wash., 1965-; Fellow, Inst. of Adv. Studies, Wesleyan Univ., Middletown, Conn., 1967; Prof., Engl. Lit., University Coll., London, 1970-. Published works: Twenty Poems; Poems; The Destructive Element; Vienna; The Burning Cactus, 1936; Forward from Liberalism, 1937; Trial of a Judge; Poems for Spain, 1939; The Still Centre, 1939; The Backward Son, 1940; Ruins and Visions, 1941; Life and the Poet, 1942; Citizens in War and After, 1945; Poems of Dedication, 1946; European Witness, 1946; The Edge of Being, 1949; World Within World (autobiog.), 1951; Learning Laughter, 1952; The Creative Element, 1953; Collected Poems, 1954; The Making of a Poem, 1955; Engaged in Writing, 1958; The Struggle of the Modern, 1963; Nine Experiments - Being Poems Written at the Age of Eighteen, 1964; Selected Poems, 1965; The Year of the Young Rebels, 1969; The Generous Days, 1971. Translation: Ernst Toller's Pastor Hall, 1939; Schiller's Mary Stuart, 1958. Contbr. to: (anthol.) The God That Failed; (jrnls.) Encounter; Horizon. Honours, awards: CBE; Hon. D.Litt., Montpelier Univ. Address: 15 Loudoun Rd., London, NW8, UK.

SPICER, Marcella, pen name, **SPICER, Marcy,** b. 31 Oct. 1920. Freelance Writer; Medical Technologist (retired); Housewife. Education: Mt. Mary Coll., Milwaukee, Wisc.; St. Mary's Hospital, Madison, Wis.; Wisconsin Conservatory of Music, Milwaukee; Univ. of Wisconsin Extension Courses (writing and art). Married, Melville Spicer; 4 s., 1 d. Positions held: Medical Technologist, St. Anthony's Hospital, Rockford, Ill.; Medical Technologist, for Dr. G. J. Schweitzer, Milwaukee; Medical Technologist, Beaver-Dam, Wis. Currently Feature Writer, Portage Daily Register, Portage, Wis.; Church Organist. Memberships: Wisconsin Fellowship of Poets; Illinois State Poetry Soc.; American Poets Fellowship Soc.; Midwest Chaparral Poets; Wisconsin Regional Writers; Council for Wisconsin Writers (past committe member); Portage Writers Workshop (past pres., and publicity chairman). Contbr. to anthologies: New Poetry Out Of Wisconsin; Yearbook of Modern Poetry; Outstanding Contemporary Poetry, 1972, 1973; Upstream, Downstream, etc. Contbr. to journals, mags.: Jean's Journal; Haiku Highlights; Modern Haiku; Janus-SCTH: Spafaswap; Inky Trails; Prairie Poet; American Poet; United Poet; Poetry Dial of The Piggott Banner; Denver Post; Nutmegger; Writer's Showcase; Tooele Transcript; Midwest Chaparral; American Journal of Nursing; Appleton Post-Crescent; Columbus Citizen's Journal; The Farmer; The Waifs' Messenger; Minneapolis Argus; Creativity Newsletter, etc. Recip. numerous prizes from poetry mags., Illinois State Poetry Soc.; Friends of The Arts, etc. Address: Shore Acres, Pardeeville, WI 53954, USA.

SPIESS, Robert, b. 16 Oct. 1921. Canoeist. Education: B.S. & M.S., Univ. of Wisconsin. Position held: Poetry Ed., Am. Haiku; Assoc. Ed., Modern Haiku. Published works: The Heron's Legs, 1966; The Turtle's Ears, 1971; Five Caribbean Haibun, 1972. Contbr. to: Am. Haiku; Am. Poetry Mag.; Beloit Poetry Jrnl.; Christian Sci. Monitor; Epos; Haiku; The Haiku Anthol.; Haiku '64 (Japan Air Lines); Haiku West; The Humanist; Modern Haiku; Poems Out of Wisconsin; Wisconsin Trails; Travel Mag. Recip., Nyogen Senzaki Meml. Award, 1964. Address: 916 Castle Pl., Madison, WI 53703, U.S.A.

SPILLEBEEN, Willy, b. 30 Dec. 1932. Professor. Education: studies in Greek & Latin; Aggregate of Lit. Positions held: Prof. of Languages (Dutch & French), technical school. Member, Dietsche Waraude en Belfort (lit. review), etc. Published works: De Spiraal (The Spiral), 1959; Naar Dieper Water (Into Deeper Water), 1962; Emmanuel Looten, de Franse Vlaming (E.L., the French Flemish), 1963 - an essay & translations of poems of the poet E. Looten; Groei-Pijn (Growth-Pain), 1966; De maanvis (The moon fish), 1966; De Krabben (The Crabs), 1967; De Sfinks op de belt (The Sfinks on the Rubish Dump), 1969; Een zevengesternte (Of Seven Stars), 1967; Steen des aanstoots (A stone of scandal), 1971; Een Teken van leven (A Sign of Life, collected poems 1959-73), 1973; Drie Drempelvrees (Threshold fear, three long novels), 1973, etc. Contbr. to var. jrnls. Honours, awards: Prize of the Flemish Poetry days, 1965; Prizes of the Province West-Vlaanderen for poetry in 1965, for essay in 1965, 66 & 72, for roman in 1967. Address: Sluizenkaai 47, Menen, Belgium.

SPILLEMAECKERS, Werner Lodewijk, b. 3 Dec. 1936. Clerk at the Court of First Instance, Antwerp. Education: Public Schl. (Atheneum) in Antwerp - Greek, Latin studies. Memberships: PEN Club, Flanders Ctr.; Assn. of Flemish Authors; Chancellor, Pink Poets; Paul van Ostaijen Assn. Published works: Ik ben Berlijn, 1961; Tekst in tekst asbest, 1964; Fuga Magister, 1970. Contbr. to: Atomika, 1954; Mandragora, 1954; Athenea, 1955-57; Frontaal, 1959; Artisjok, 1968; Avenue, 1973. Address: Molenstraat 57, B-2000 Antwerp, Belgium.

SPINDLER, Emily, b. 10 Sept. 1938. English Teacher. Education: B.S. in Sec. Educ., 1960. Married, 1 daughter. Positions held: Tchr., Milwaukee, Wis.; Dir. of Horsemanship, Girls' Camp; Camp Dir., ibid. Sec., Kokomo Poetry Circle, 1973-74. Contbr. to: Good Housekeeping Mag.; The Christian Home; Catalyst; The Friend; Primary Treasure; Ideals. Honours, awards: 2nd pl. & 1st Hon. Mention, Kokomo Poetry Circle Contest, 1972. Address: 1418 W. Jefferson St., Kokomo, IN 46901, U.S.A.

SPINGARN, Lawrence Perry (Perreira), b. 11 Jul. 1917. Professor of English Literature. Education: B.S., with Engl. Honors, Bowdoin Coll., 1940; M.A. in Engl., Univ. of Michigan, 1948. Married to Sylvia Wainhouse. Positions held: Special Consultant, Library of Congress, 1941-43; Freelance Editor and Writer, 1943-48; Instr. in Engl., Pomona Coll., 1948-49; Instr. in Engl., Univ. of Calif., 1949-51; 1954-57; Prof. of Engl., Valley Coll., 1959-. Memberships: Internat. Inst. of Arts and Letters (Switzerland); Poetry Soc. of America; Poetry Soc. (UK); Authors Club (London); Authors League (NY); P.E.N.; Calif. State Poetry Soc. Published works: Rococo Summer & Other Poems, 1947; The Lost River (poems), 1951; Letters from Exile (poems), 1961; Madame Bidet & Other Fixtures (poems), 1968; Freeway Problems - and Others (poems), 1970. Anthols.: Poetry Awards, 1949; The Golden Year, 1960; The New Yorker Book of Poems, 1969. Contbr. to: Harper's Mag.; Kenyon Review; Mass. Review; Modern Age; New England Qtly.; New Yorker; NY Times; Paris Review; Poetry; Poetry Review (UK); Qtly. Review of Literature; Saturday Review; Southern Review; Southwest Review; Transatlantic Review; Twentieth Century (UK); Univ. Review; Yale Review. Recip. Poetry Soc. of America, Annual Prize, 1953. Address: c/o Perivale Press, 13830 Erwin St., Van Nuys, CA 91401, USA.

SPIRO, Leon, b. 5 Dec. 1912. Publications Director. Positions held: Dir., Star West Publs. Memberships: Ina Coolbrith Circle of Calif.; Chevalier de l'ordre Celtique, Paris, France; Academico Benemerito, Portugal; Life Mbr., Etudes Psycologique, France. Corres., The Journal, B'ham, U.K.; Assoc. Ed., Elan, France; Contbng. Ed., Momento, Buenos Aires, Argentina. Contbr. to over 600 periodicals w. transl. in 9 langs. Contbns. incl: Now; Littack; New Headlands; Ina Coolbrith Anthol.; Peace & Bread Anthol.; Synopse; Marin Scope; Enterprise Jrnl.; Gargantua;

Xilote; El Mundo, etc. Recip., Segualazione d'onore, Centro Piemontese di Cultura, 1973. Address: Star West of Am. Lib., P.O. Box 731, Sausalito, CA 94965, U.S.A.

SPIVACK, Kathleen Romola Drucker, b. 22 Sept. 1938. Writer. Education: B.A., Oberlin Coll., 1959; M.A., Boston Univ., 1963. Married, 2 children. Positions held: Fellow, Radcliffe Inst. for Independent Study, 1969-72; Tchr., Through Poets-in-the-Schls. Prog., Mass. Coun. on Arts, 1971-72; Tchr., Adv. Poetry Workshop, 1971-74. Published works: Flying Inland, Doubleday & Co, N.Y., 1973; The Jane Poems, Doubleday & Co. N.Y., to be published fall 1974. Contbr. to: The New Yorker; Harpers; The Atlantic Monthly; Poetry; Encounter; Boston Phoenix; Antaeus; The Antioch Review; Arions Dolphin; Sumac; Old West Review; Esquire; Peacefeelers; Women Poems I & II; The Nation; N.Y. Qtly.; Best Poems of 1971, Borestone Mt. Press, & others. Recip., Fellowship, the Writing of Poetry, Radcliffe Inst. for Independent Study, 1969-72. Address: 53 Spruce St., Watertown, MA 02172, U.S.A.

SPRACKLEN, Myrtle Lilly, pen names **ARCHER, Myrtle & ANDERSON, Marlene,** b. 14 June 1926. Freelance Writer. Married, 1 son. Memberships: Pres., Eden Writers; Dir., Calif. Writers' Club, 1972-74; Pen Women. Contbr. to: Conquest; Progress; Children's Friend; Time of Singing; Family Digest; Our Sunday Visitor; Health Culture; Mendocino Robin; Mature Years, insight & outlook; Haiku Highlights; Explorer Mag.; Westways; Negro Hist. Bulletin; Bardic Echoes; Sausolito-Belvedere Gazette; Pen Women; The Angels; Hartford Courant; Carmel Pine Cone; Honolulu; Dance of the Muses; Gall. Series IV; Grit; Yearbook of Modern Poetry; The Christian; Ski Mag.; Marriage; the Mag. for Husband & Wife; Messenger; North Little Rock Times; Better Camping; Outstanding Contemporary Poetry Anthol.; Cyclo-Flame. Has had prose published in var. mags. Recip., 1st Hon. Mention, Nat. League of Am. Pen Women Contest, 1971. Address: 21172 Aspen Ave., Castro Valley, CA 94546, U.S.A.

SPRATLING, Neil Robert, b. 7 Aug. 1945. Poet. Memberships: Ver Poets, St. Albans; Folio Soc. Published works: Three Poems, 1964; Weather of Stars, vols. 1 & 2, 1966 & 68; Dawn Poetry, 1973. Contbr. to: Origins-Diversions; Minus One; Iconolatre; How; St. Albans Abbey Mag.; Envoi; Writers' Forum Prog.; The Holy Door; St. Andrews Parish News; Manifold; Scrip; Second Aeon; Lyric; Haiku; The Blue Print; Ver Poets Broadsheet; Katawakes; Global Tapestry; Envoi; Gold Elf; Free Poets; All In, wallstickers; Iron Flute; Hertfordshire Countryside; Voices; Liberation; Gargantua; Headland, etc. Winner of Watford Music Fest. Poetry Comp., 1968. Address: 110 Hempstead Rd., Watford, Herts. WD1 3LA, U.K.

SPURR, Rita. Writer; Poet; Lecturer. Education: B.A. (Econs. Hons.), Univ. of Manchester, U.K. Positions held: Deptl. Dir., Czech Refugee Trust; Editl. Info. Serv., UNRRA; Lectr. & Org. of Educ. & Drama to H.M. Forces; Editl. positions w. publishing houses & jrnls.; Festivals Adjudicator. Memberships: Chmn., Camden Poetry Grp.; Fndn. Mbr., Int. Poetry Soc.; Poetry Soc. of G.B. (formerly Gen. Coun.); Hon. Poetry Advisor, Writers' Guild & Metropolitan Sec.; Editl. & Advsry. Bd., Dict. of Int. Biog. & Int. Who's Who in Poetry; Lancashire Authors Assn.; Ver Poets; Nottingham Poetry Soc. Published works: Footprint in Snow (poems), 1954; 'Slide Into Poetry' Ed: Camden Poetry Grps. book of 'Visual Poems' published 1973. Poetry published in many anthols. in G.B. & overseas; read & spoken in Poetry progs. & Festivals inclng. Edinburgh. Play in verse for children, performed 1966. L.P. Record 'Poems & Stories for Children', Plantagenet Prodns., 1968. Contbr. to: Poetry Review; 'This England'; Anglo-Welsh Review; Orbis; Country Life; 'Lancs Record'; Regional Journals; IWWP, etc. Recip., occasional lit. awards inclng. 'acta diurna' Manifold, 1966 & Dip. from The World Who's Who of Women, 1973. Address: Flat 4, 7 Netherhall Gdns.,

Hampstead, London NW3 5RN, U.K.

SQUIRES, Radcliffe, b. 23 May 1917. Professor of English. Education: A.B., Univ. of Utah, U.S.A.; A.M., Univ. of Chicago; Ph.D., Harvard Univ. Positions held: Instr., Dartmouth Coll., 1946-48; Prof. of Engl., Univ. of Mich., 1952–; Ed., Michigan Quarterly Review. Mbr., Writers & Dramatists Guild of Am. Published works: Cornar, 1940; Where the Compass Spins, 1951; Fingers of Hermes, 1965; Light Under Islands, 1967; Daedalus, 1968; Waiting in the Bone, 1973. Contbr. to: N.Y. Times; Chicago Tribune Sunday Mag.; Accent; Poetry; Sewanee Review; Southern Review; Nation; New Republic; Voices; Chicago Review; Mich. Quarterly Review; Western Review; Western Humanities Review. Recip., John Billings Fiske Prize, Univ. of Chicago, 1947 & Young Poets Prize, Voices mag., 1948. Address: 7270 Warren Rd., Ann Arbor, MI 48105, U.S.A.

SRABIAN HERALD, Leon, b. Jan. 1892. Newspaper Man. Education: Wis. Univ., Madison. Memberships: The Authors' Guild, Inc.; Poetry Soc. of Am. Published works: This Waking Hour, poems, 1925; Pagany, poems; The World Tomorrow, poems, 1924. Contbr. to: Poetry (Chicago); The Dial mag.; This Quarter, Paris; Double Dealer, New Orleans; Detroit News; Am. Poetry Mag.; Back to Nature; Am. Review; The Commonweal; The Nation; Ararat Qtly. Featured in 'The Dream & the Deal', published in 1973 (Fed. Writers Proj.) Has submitted all his works to the Memorial Lib. of Wis. State Univ., Madison. Address: 419 West 17th St., N.Y., NY 10011, U.S.A.

SRECKO, Diana. Pensioner. Education: Economics Schl. Married. Positions held: Cultural Referent, Community of Split; Instr. of var. amateur assns., administration; Sec., Dir., Historic Archive; Fndr. & Ed., lit. review 'Književni Jadran' & Library of that edn.; Promoter, Branch 'Matica Hrvatska' for Town of Split & the Ed. of the publication 'Mogućnosti' & 'Biblioteka suvremenih pisaca' (The Library of Contemporary Writers); First Pres. of the Coun. of the Library 'Vidik' in Split (& printing estab. 'Marko Marulić). Member, Assn. of Croatian Writers & Assn. of Yugoslav Writers, 1955–. Published works: (books of poetry) Miris srca i krvi (The Scent of the Heart & the Blood), 1931; Osviti i tišine (The Daybreak & the Silence), 1953; Nitko u svijetu nije sam (Nobody in the World is Alone), 1955; Opsjedanje (The Siege, poem), 1962; Okus ljeta (The Summer Taste), 1963; 28 Pjesama o Trpnji (28 Poems About Suffering), 1967; Iskustvo mora (The Experience of the Sea), 1969; Vriježi tla (The Roots of the Native Soil), 1971. Contbr. to many jrnls., reviews, newspapers, mags. & radio. Address: Hektorovićeva 4, 58000 Split, Yugoslavia.

SREENIVOS, Prathivadi Bhayankaram, pen names **PIBBSS, ESPY BEE, M.M. Lover; MADHU VANDU, S. PRIYA BHAASHI & many others,** b. 22 Sept. 1930. Singer. Education: B.Comm., Andhra Univ.; Hindi Visharad degree, Dakshina Bharath Hindi Prachar Sabha. Positions held: Play-back Singer in Kannada, Tamil, Telugu, Hindi, Malayalam, Tulu, Sinhalese, Bengali, Sourashtra, etc. (language films). Memberships: Hon. Pres., Diamonds & Kala Priya (cultural orgs.); Madras Film Fans Assn.; Cine Musicians Union; Cine Technicians Union; Punjab Assn.; World Poetry Soc. Int., etc. Published works: Man has set his foot on Moon (poem), released extended play record through Columbia, India. Contbr. to: Poet; Free India; Movieland; Amudha Surabi; Balanandam; Ittihad; Sawan, etc. Honours, awards: titles of 'Amuthakkural Isai Arasan' & 'Gana Samrat' given consecutively by Indian Inst. of Technol., Madras & Sri Kalahasti Temple. Address: 'Shree Mandir', 310/A, Second Cross St., West C.I.T. Nagar, Madras 600 035, India.

SRINIVAS, Krishna, pen name, **KESRI,** b. 26 Jul. 1913. Editor and Publisher. Education: B.A., Madras Univ.; Litt.D., Free Univ. of Asia, Karachi; Ph.D., Acad. of Philosophy, USA; D. Arts, World Acad. of Languages & Literature, S. Paulo, Brazil. Positions held: War Propaganda, All India Radio, New Delhi; Editor, Ajanta and other monthlies; Currently Editor, Poet, Internat. Monthly. Memberships: World Poetry Soc. Intercontinental (Pres. & Founder); UPLI, Philippines; Internat. Culture Acad., Rome; Cosmo Synthesis League, Melbourne; Am. Poets Fellowship Soc. NY (Director for India). Published works: Dance of Dust, 1947; Wheel, 1965; He Walks the Earth (translated into 30 languages), 1967; Music of the Soul, 1969; Nirvana, 1970; Everest, 1971. Contbr. to: Voices Internat.; Poet; Laurel Leaves; 2nd Aeon, UK; Wendigo, Canada; Malta News; South & West USA. Honours: Gold Medal from Philippines Pres. & named Outstanding Indian Poet; Elected to Internat. Hall of Fame, Manila; Crowned with laurel wreath as Poet Laureate Leader UPLI; Named Internat. Poet Laureate, by Mayor of Yonkers, NY, 1971; Nominated for Nobel Prize in Lit., 1968, by Poets Laureate in over 100 countries; Convened All India Poets Meet, 1973; World Poets Meet, NY, 1973, etc. Address: 20A Venkatesan St., Madras 17, India.

SRINIVAS, Talwar Sampath, pen name, **SHEPHERD, Erle,** b. 15 Dec. 1945. Student, Writer. Education: B.A. Hons. Positions held: Guest Ed., Chinese Issue of Poet, Intercontinental monthly jrnl. Memberships: World Poetry Soc., Ill. Published works: Passionate Persuasion, novel in modern poetry, 1963; Lasting Memory, poems, 1964; She Knows Me Not, poems, 1965; Poems – at Santiniketan, 1969; Unknown Pleasure, selected poems, 1969. Contbr. to: Poet, monthly. Address: 16 1st Cross St., W CIT, Madras 35, India.

SRINIVASARAJAGOPALAN, Thirunarayanan, pen names **AMBI, RAHULAN, NIRAJ,** b. 15 Apr. 1928. Office Assistant. Education: Arts grad., Madras Univ., India. Memberships: V.P., Tamil Vasagar Sangam; participant, All India Poets' Meet, Madras, 1973; Poetry Workshop, Madras. Contbr. to: Poet; Ocarina; Youthfare. Address: 2 Raju Naicken St., Madras 600033, India.

SRINIVASARAO, Srirangam, pen name **SRI SRI,** b. 2 Jan. 1910. Writer for films. Education: B.A. (Zoology & Botany) Madras Coll. Married, 1 son, 4 daughters. Memberships: Pres., Andhra Pradesh Writers Assn.; PEN India; Sahitya Akad. Published works: Complete Works (up to 1970). Honours, awards: Nehru Award, 1966; Sahitya Akad. Award, 1972. Address: 11 Canal Bank Rd., R.A. Puram, Madras 28, India.

STADLER, Jeanne Zilla, b. 4 June 1906, Urbana, Ill., USA. Piano Accompanist. Education: Temple Univ.; Creative Writing, Univ. of Pa. Positions held: Sec., Elkan-Vogal Music Publishers (now w. Theo. Presser Co.); Piano Accompanist, privately & at the Lankenau Schl. (& for public functions); Sec.; Westtown, Pa. Quaker Schl.; Sec. & Piano Accompanist, Phila. Bd. of Public Educ. (ret'd.) Memberships: Corres. Sec., Penn Laurel Poets, Phila.; Pa. Poetry Soc.; Nat. Fed. of State Poetry Socs.; World Poetry Day. Contbr. to: The Music Jrnl.; The Miquon Schl. Reading Primer; Center City Philadelphian Mag.; Numismatic Scrapbook. Honours, awards: 2nd Prize, Tuanortsa Contest, World Poetry Day Bulletin, 1966; Cert. of Merit, Evan Spencer Wall Contest, Nat. Fed. of State Poetry Socs., 1972. Address: 1900 Rittenhouse Sq., 17C, Philadelphia, PA 19103, U.S.A.

STAFFORD, Mabel E., pen name **ELCY, Mabel.** Educator. Education: A.B., Kansas Univ. Positions held: H.S. Tchr. of Engl. & Dramatics, 20 yrs.; Interviewer; Realtor. Memberships: Nat. League of Am. Pen Women; State Judge of Poetry, Kansas Authors; Midwest Chaparral; Writers Group; Fla. State Poetry Soc. Contbr. to: Poet, India; Flamingo; K.A.C. Recip. awards from Fla. State Poetry Soc. Address: 3016 Harvard Rd., Lawrence, KS, U.S.A.

STAFFORD, William E., b. 17 Jan. 1914. College Teacher. Education: B.A. & M.A., Univ. of Kansas; Ph.D., Univ. of Iowa. Married, 4 children. Positions held: Tchr., Lit. & Writing, Lewis & Clark Coll.; then Manchester (Ind.) Coll.; San Jose State, Calif.; Lewis & Clark Coll. Published works: (poetry colls.) West of Your City, 1960; Traveling Through the Dark, 1962; The Rescued Year, 1966; Allegiances, 1970; Someday, Maybe, 1973. Contbr. to: Atlantic; Poetry; Harper's; Encounter; New Republic; Nation; Hudson Review; Saturday Review; Va. Qtly.; Kenyon Review; Poetry; Poetry Northwest; Poetry Australia; Granta; Stand; Malahat Review; New Yorker; Northwest Review; The Critical Qtly.; Field; N.Y. Qtly.; Granite; N.M. Qtly.; The Literary Half-Yearly, etc. Honours, awards: Nat. Book Award, 1962; Shelley Meml. Award, 1965; Poetry Cons. at The Lib. of Congress, 1970. Address: c/o Dept. of Engl., Lewis & Clark Coll., Portland, OR 97219, U.S.A.

STAHL, Virginia McDaniel, pen name **STAHL, Virginia,** b. 20 July 1914. Real Estate Salesl4dy. Education: B.S., Educ., Kent State Univ., Ohio. Married, Harvey John Stahl; 3 children. Appalachian poet and artist; Pres., Monroe County Art Guild, 1972-73. Positions held: Elem. Teacher; Employment Counselor; Real Estate Saleslady. Memberships: Ohio Verse Writers Guild; West Virginia State Poetry Soc.; American Poets Fellowship Soc.; CSSI.; Major Poets Nat. Chapter; World Poets. Published works: Few for the Many, 1966; Splashes from an Ohio Pump, 1971; Appalachian Apples, 1972; Fireflies in the Fog, 1973; Inspirational Poetry, 1973. Contbr. to: Monroe County Beacon; Akron Beacon Journal; American Poets; United Poets; Prairie Poets; World Poet; Major Poet; Albo D'Ore; Timeless Treasures; Medina County Gazette; Martins Ferry Times-Leader; Nat. Retired Teacher Journal; Burst of Trumpets; Moon Age Poets; Outstanding Contemporary Poetry; Internat. Who's Who in Poetry Anthol. Awards: Dogwood Medal from Freedoms Foundation, Valley Forge, 1965; 1st Prize (relig. poetry), 1972, West Virginia State Poetry Soc.; Certs. of Merit, 1972, 1973 from CSSI, Rome. Address: Rte. 1, Woodsfield, OH 43793, USA.

STALEY, Ronald Christopher, pen names: **DARLON, Christopher; McCONNELL, Evelyn,** b. 19 June 1915. Author and Playwright. Education: Dip., Advertising Management; Intermed. Certificate, Advertising Assoc. Married. Positions held: Professional script-writer and composer, 1936-1954; Advt. Dept., local newspapers, 1954-67; Sales Promotion Dept., Automation Co., 1967-1969; Author and Playwright, 1969–. Memberships: Poetry Soc. of Great Britain; Fellow, Internat. Poetry Soc.; New Poetry Workshop, London. Published works: Honor Est A Nilo (booklet-length poem of the Battle of the River Nile), 1973; Wings for Victory, 1943. Contbr. to: The Performer; Quintessence; Viewpoints; Expression One; Breakthru; Love Poetry No. 4.; The Journal Enquirer; The Olive Hill Times; The Rufus; 20th Cent. Poets, 1972; Poetry Galaxy; Scrip; Merlin's Magic; Poetry Nippon; Internat. Who's Who in Poetry Anthol (1973). Awards: Certificate of Merit (1972), Internat. Who's Who in Poetry; Runner-up in British Amateur Drama Association's Nat. Playwriting Competition, 1973. Address: Durham Cheshire Home, Murray House, St. Cuthbert's Rd., Blackhill, Co. Durham, UK.

STALLWORTHY, Jon Howie, b. 18 Jan. 1935. Author & Publisher. Education: B.A., Magdalen Coll., Oxford, 1958; B.Litt., ibid, 1961. Married, 3 children. Positions held: w. The Oxfordshire & Buckinghamshire Light Infantry & 'the Royal West African Frontier Force, 1953-55; Ed., Oxford Univ. Press, London, 1959-71; Vis. Fellow, All Souls Coll., Oxford, 1971-72; Ed., Clarendon Press, Oxford, 1972–. Bd. Mbr., Poetry Book Soc. Ltd. Published works: (poetry) The Earthly Paradise, 1958; The Astronomy of Love, 1961; Out of bounds, 1963; The Almond Tree, 1967; A Day in the City, 1967; Root & Branch, 1969; Positives, 1969; A Dinner of Herbs, 1971; (critical books) Between the Lines/W.B. Yeats's Poetry in the Making, 1963; Vision & Revision in Yeats's Last Poems, 1969; Ed., Yeats: Last Poems & Plays, 1968. Translations: The Twelve & Other Poems by Alexander Blok, 1970; Five Centuries of Polish Poetry (w. Jerzy Peterkiewicz & Burns Singer). Ed. w. Alan Brownjohn & Seamus Heaney, the P.E.N. Anthol. NEW Poems, 1970/71; Ed., The

Penguin Book of Love Poetry, 1973. Contbr. to: Agenda; Critical Quarterly; London Mag.; Times Lit. Supplement. Recip., Newdigate Prize for Poetry, 1958. Address: The Mill House, Wolvercote, Oxford, U.K.

STANCU, Zaharia, b. 5 Oct. 1902. Poet; Novelist. Education: Univ. of Bucharest. Positions held: Ed., Azi (jrnl.), 1932-40; Ed., Lumea Româneasca (Romanian World), 1937-39; Ed., Gazeta Literara (jrnl.), 1954-62; Gen. Mgr., I.L. Caragiale Nat. Theatre, Bucharest, 1946-52, '58–; Chmn., Writers' Union of Socialist Repub. of Romania, 1966–; Mbr., Acad. of Socialist Repub. of Romania, 1955–. Published works include: (poetry) Simple Poems, 1928; Whites, 1937; The Golden Bell, 1939; The Red Tree, 1940; The Years of Smoke, 1944; Whispering Song, 1970; Works-Poems, 1971; (novels) Typhoon, 1937; Barefoot, 1948; The Mastiffs, 1952; The Flowers of the Earth, 1954; Roots Are Bitter (5 vols.), 1958-59; A Gamble With Death, 1962; The Mad Forest, 1964; How Dearly I Loved You, 1968; Shatra, 1968; The Wind & The Rain, 3 vols., 1969; (essays) The Century of the Underdog, 1946; Salt is Sweet, 1955; Bull Necks, 1955; For the People of Tandirea; Viata Romaneasca; Axi, etc. Honours, awards: Poetry Prize, 1971, & others. Address: Str. Helesteulvi No. 30A, Bucharest, Roumania.

STANFORD, Ann. Writer. Education: B.A., Stanford Univ.; M.A., Ph.D., Univ. of Calif., Los Angeles. Married, 4 children. Positions held: Prof. of Engl., Calif. State Univ., Northridge, Calif., since 1962. Memberships: Poetry Soc. of America (West Coast vice-pres., since 1971); P.E.N. Published works: The Descent: Poems, 1970; The Weathercock, 1966; Magellan: A Poem to be Read by Several Voices, 1958; The White Bird, 1949; In Narrow Bound, 1943; The Bhagavad Gita: A New Verse Translation, 1970: The Women Poets in English: An Anthology, 1972 (Editor). Contbr. to: New Yorker; Southern Review: Mass. Review; Poetry, Sewanee Review; NM Qtly. Review; Atlantic; Recurrence; Variegation; New Republic; Va. Qtly. Review; Epoch; Talisman, etc. Awards: Nat. Inst. of Arts and Letters, (Award in Literature), American Acad. of Arts & Letters, 1972; Shelley Mem. Award, Poetry Soc. of America, 1969; 1st Prize, Borestone Mountain Poetry Awards, Best Poems of 1960; Silver Medal for Poetry, Commonwealth Club of California. Address: 9550 Oak Pass Rd., Beverly Hills, CA 90210, USA.

STANFORD, Derek, pen name **CHARLES, Timothy,** b. 11 Oct. 1918. Poet; Critic: Reviewer; Teacher; Editor. Married: Margaret Holdsworth. Positions held: Tchr. of Engl. Lit. & Hist. of Art, Girls' Public Schl., 5 yrs.; Tchr. of classes on modern poetry, the modern novel & poetry writing, City Lit. Inst., Holborn, 1956–; Poetry Critic, Books & Bookmen, 1967–; Editl. Cons. to Orbis Mag. Memberships: Fellow, Royal Soc. of Lit., 1956-60; Hon. Fellow, Int. Poetry Soc. Published works incl: (studies in the field of modern poetry) The Freedom of Poetry: Studies in Contemporary Verse, 1947; Movements in English Poetry, 1900-1958, 1959; (critical books) Christopher Fry: An Appreciation, 1951; Christopher Fry Album, 1952; John Betjeman: a Study, 1961; Muriel Spark: a Biog. & Critical Study, 1963; Dylan Thomas: a Lit. Study, 1964; (studies & critical edns. of 19th century writers) Emily Bronte: Her Life & Work, in collab. w. Muriel Spark, 1953; Ann Bronte: Her Life & Work, in collab. w. Ada Harrison, 1959. Has published a number of critical anthols. concerned w. the latter half of the Victorian era inclng. Critics of the Nineties: J. Baker, 1970 & Witticisms of Oscar Wilde, 1971. Has contributed to var. anthols. & jrnls. Address: c/o National Westminster Bank, Hurdis House, Broadstreet, Seaford, Sussex, U.K.

STANFORD, Donald Elwin, pen name **STANFORD, Don,** b. 7 Feb. 1913. Professor of English; Editor. Education: A.B., Stanford Univ., 1933; M.A., Harvard Univ., 1934; Ph.D., Stanford Univ., 1953. Married Maryanna Peterson, 1953. Positions held: Engl. Instr., Colo., Dartmouth & Univ. of Neb.; Instr. to Prof. of Engl., La. State Univ., Baton Rouge, 1949–; Ed., The Soutern Review, 1963; Vis. Assoc. Prof., Duke Univ.,

1961-62. Memberships: PEN; MLA. Published works: New England Earth, 1941; The Traveler, 1955; Ed., The Poems of Edward Taylor, 1960; Edward Taylor, 1972. Rep. in following anthols: Ten Introductions, 1934; Trial Balances, 1934; Twelve Poets of the Pacific, 193/; Laurel, Archaic, Rude, 1966. Contbr. to: Poetry; Hound & Horn; The Magazine; The Harvard Advocate; New Republic; Commonweal; Talisman; Duke Univ. Archive. Honours, awards: Guggenheim Fellowship, 1959-60; Nat. Endowment for the Humanities Grant, summer, 1972; Disting. Fac. Fellowship, La. State Univ., 1973-74. Address: Dept. of Engl., La. State Univ., Baton Rouge, LA 70803, U.S.A.

STANLEY, George. Student; Poet. Educ: B.A., San. Pran. State Coll., 1969; Studying for M.A., current. Published works: The Love Root, 1958; Tete Rouge/Pony Express Riders, 1963; Flowers, 1965; Beyond Love, 1968. Address: 1822 Bush St., San Francisco, CA 94109, U.S.A.

STAPLETON, (K.) Laurence, b. 20 Nov. 1911. Teacher & Writer. Education A.B., Smith Coll., 1932; Univ. of London, 1932-33. Positions held: Examiner, Mass. Public Employment Serv., 1933-34; Instr. in Engl., Bryn Mawr Coll., 1934-38; Asst. Prof., ibid, 1938-42; Assoc. Prof., 1942-48; Prof. of Engl. & Political Theory, 1948-64; Chmn., Dept. of Engl., 1954-65; Mary E. Garrett Prof. of Engl., 1964–. Memberships: English Assn. (London); Thoreau Soc.; Renaissance Soc. of Am. Published works: Yushin's Log & Other Poems, 1969. Contbr. to: Sequence; The Title; Counterpoint; Quixote; Bryn Mawr-Haverford Review; Mass. Review. Recip., Creative Writing Fellowship Award, Nat. Endowment for the Arts (U.S.A.). Address: 229 N. Roberts Rd., Bryn Mawr, PA 19010, U.S.A.

STARBUCK, George, b. 15 June 1931. Poet; Professor of Literature. Published works: Bone Thoughts, 1960; White Paper, 1966; Elegy in a Country Church Yard, 1973. Contbr. to New Yorker, etc. Recip., Prix de Rome & Guggenheim Fellowship. Address: English Dept., Boston Univ., Boston, MA, U.S.A.

STARK, Bradford, b. 27 May 1948. Urban Planner. Education: B.A., City Coll. of N.Y., 1969; M.Sc., Urban Planning, Columbia Univ., 1972. Positions held: num. planning positions with public & private agencies, 1969–; Lectr. (off Campus Coll./State Univ. of N.Y. at Binghamton 1972–) poetry workshop; Vis. Poet, N.Y. State Coun. of the Arts, Poets in the Schls. prog., 1973–. Published works: An Unlikely But Noble Kingdom, 1974. Contbr. to: Caterpillar; Choice; For Now; Promethean; Gnosis; The World; Endymion; Transition; The Mysterious Barricades; Mulch; Lip & Anduril. Address: 57 Kneeland Ave., Binghamton, NY 13905, U.S.A.

STARLING, Lirrel (Elsie May Gardella), b. 25 Apr. 1909. Journalist; Columnist. Positions held: Legal secretarial work; Typist; Reporter; Columnist. Memberships: Past Mbr., Calif. Fed. Chaparral Poets, Am. Poetry Soc. & Stockton Poetry Soc.; currently Mbr., Ina Coolbrith Circle; Nat. Poetry Day Comm.; Donor, Acad. of Am. Poets. Published works incl: Music in Miniature, 1940's; Motifs; White Foxes; Lady of Icon. Contbr. to num. mags., jrnls., newspapers, anthols. inclng: America Speaks, World War II Anthol., 1940's; Am. Poetry Old & New Anthol., 1960's; Golden Circle Anthols., 1960's & '70's. Honours, awards incl: Marie Schroeder-Devrient Silver Medal circa 1949; Special Gold Medal from Countess D'Esternaux, for outstanding poem on brotherhood, 1950's. Address: San Andreas, via Gold Strike Route, CA 95249, U.S.A.

STARR, Billie Joe, pen names **STARR, B.J., STARR, BILL & STARR, Saguaro,** b. 28 Dec. 1945. Teacher & Construction Laborer. Education: B.A. & M.A., Engl., Univ. of Ark., Little Rock. Positions held: U.S. Marine Corps; H.S. Engl. Tchr.; Construction Laborer & Carpenter's Helper. Contbr. to: Cimarron Review; Thoreau Jrnl. Qtly.; Southern Poetry Review; Poet; Encore; Westways; Am. Opinion; Village; Best in

Poetry, 1969; The DeKalb Lit. Arts Jrnl.; Colo. State Review; The Denver Post Poetry Forum; New Am. & Canadian Poetry; Black Creation; The Smith; Four Quarters; Suenos: Dreams; The New Review; Mount to the Stars!; Motive; The Southern Review; Prairie Schooner; Perspective; The Iowa Review. Address: 2024 Durwood Rd., Little Rock, AR 72207, U.S.A.

STARR, Nathan Comfort, b. 29 Mar. 1896. Professor of English Literature. Education: A.B., A.M. & Ph.D., Harvard Univ., U.S.A.; B.A. & M.A., Oxford Univ. (Christ Church), U.K. Positions held: Asst., Tutor & Instr. in Engl., Harvard & Radcliffe, 1921-29; subsequent professorial posts at Colgate, St. John's (Annapolis), Williams, Mollins & Univ. of Fla. (ret'd 1963 as Emeritus Prof. of Engl. & Humanities); Vis. Prof., Hamilton Coll.; Fulbright Lectr. in Japan; sometime mbr. of tchng. staff, New Schl. for Soc. Rsch., N.Y.C. Member, Poetry Soc. of Winter Pk., Fla. Published works: Long Yesterday & Other Poems, 1972. Contbr. to: Fla. Mag. of Verse; Southern Lit. Messenger; Miami Daily News; N.Y. Herald-Tribune; Life; Harvard Alumni Bulletin; Yankee; Unicorn, Japan: Theme & Variations (Tokyo 1959) includes the sonnet 'Momijigari'. Recip., Litt.D., h.c., Mollins Coll., 1949 & var. prizes from Poetry Soc. of Winter Pk. Address: 333 E. 68th St., N.Y., NY 10021, U.S.A.

STASSAERT, Lucienne, b. 10 Jan. 1936. Writer. Married, 2 children. Memberships: PEN Club; Vereniging van Vlaamse Letterkundigen; Voorsitster Vereniging Vlaamse Toneelauseurs. Published works: Fossiel, 1968; Het dagelykse feest, 1970; M de Klok van de mochine tikt een meus, 1973. Contbr. to: Labris; Stuip; Revolver; Yang; Nieuw Vlaams; Tydschrift; De Vlaamse Cjids; Dietsche Warande en Belfort; Kentering; Betoel; Impuls; Die Sonde; Contre. Address: Ballaerstraat 39, 2000 Antwerp, Belgium.

STAVAUX, Michel, b. 6 May 1948. Civil Servant. Education: Docteur en droit; Licencié en droit européen. Married w. children. Positions held: Mbr. of the Cabinet of Monsieur A. Coppé, Mbr. of the Commn. of the European Community; Asst. to the Dpty. Financial Controller of the Commn. of the European Community. Memberships: PEN Club Int.; Assn. of Belgian Writers. Published works: D'outre moi-même, poèmes, 1962; Les roses crucifiees, poèmes, 1963; Cheval d'Ivoire, poèmes, 1964; Les Coctus que la mer rejettera demain, poèmes, 1969; La promenade rue voliere, poèmes, 1971. Contbr. to: Le journal des poètes; Le Figaro litteraire; Les lettres francaises; Les nouvelles littéraires, etc. Recip., Polak prize, Royal Acad. of French Lang. & Lit. of Belgium, 1973. Address: 33c Avenue du Paepedelle, 1160 Brussels, Belgium.

STAYT, Michael John, b. 25 Apr. 1941. Insurance Superintendent. Education: var. Grammar Schls., U.K. Married, 2 children. Positions held: w. Eagle Star Grp., Reading, Slough, Harrow & London; Br. Life Supt., ibid, Cardiff; Ed., anthols. publd. by Flying Dragon Publs., U.K. Memberships: Fellow, Int. Poetry Soc.; Mng. Ed., Flying Dragon Publs. Published works: Inspired By Love, 1968; Prayer for Happiness, 1970; Straight into my Daydreams, 1973. Rep. in following anthols: Nature Poetry 2, 1969; Poetry for the City & Machine Age 2, 1969; Love Poetry 3, 1970; Nature Poetry 3, 1971; Love Poetry 4, 1972; The First Flying Dragon Book of Poetry, 1971; The Flying Dragon Hymn Sheet No. 1, 1972; Chosen Poets of 1969, 1969; Golden Eagle Treasury, 1970; Next Wave Poets 1, 1969, 2 1970, 3 1971, 4 1972; The Twelve Days of Christmas, 1970; The Christmas Anthol., 1969; Poetry Today, 1970; Gardens of Within, 1970; IWWP, 1972. Contbr. to: Breakthru; Headland; Leisure; Muse; Parnassus; Star; Viewpoints; Expression One. Address: Boromir, 6 Corbett Rd., Llandough, Penarth, Glam. CF6 1QX, U.K.

STEAD, Christian Karlson, b. 17 Oct. 1932. Professor of English. Education: M.A., Univ. of Auckland, New Zealand, 1956; Ph.D., Univ. of Bristol, UK, 1960. Married, 3 children. Positions held: Lectr. in Engl.,

Univ. of New England, NSW, Australia, 1956-57; Michael Hiatt Baker Schl., Univ. of Bristol, UK, 1957-59; Lectr. in Engl., Univ. of Auckland, NZ, 1959-61; Sr. Lectr., ibid, 1962-64; Assoc. Prof., 1964-68; Prof., 1969-. Memberships: PEN. Published works include: Whether the Will is Free, poems, 1964; new book of poems in prep; The New Poetic Yeats to Eliot, 1964, '67; World's Classics New Zealand Short Stories, 2nd series, 1966; Smith's Dream, 1971 (novel). Contbr. to the following anthols., jrnls., mags., etc. Landfall; NZ Listener; Mate; Meanjin; Poetry Australia; The Bull.; Arena; London Mag.; New Statesman; Univs. Poetry; Critical Qtly.; Punch. Honours, awards: 1st prize, Univ. Poetry Award, Borestone Mountain Poetry Awards, USA, 1955; Landfall Readers' Award for best poem publd. in 15 yrs. of publ.; Winn., Manson Mentor Fellowship, 1972. Address: Engl. Dept., Univ. of Auckland, Auckland 1, NZ.

STEADMON, Jerry Donald, b. 20 Apr. 1937. Associate Professor. Education: Grad. theol., Baptist Bible Coll., 1959; B.S.E., Southwest Mo. State Coll., 1963; M.A., Eastern N.M. Univ., 1965. Divorced, 3 children. Positions held: Assoc. Prof. of Engl., Eastern New Mex. Univ. Memberships: Int. Poetry Soc.; former Mbr., N.M. Poetry Soc. Contbr. to: Encore; Orion; Poetic License; Best in Poetry; Arrows; Mustang Review; Pembroke Mag.; Llano Estacado Heritage; Sou'wester; Quetzal; Folio; Rendezvous; Creative Moment; The Greater Llano Estacado Southwest Heritage; Cardinal Poetry Qtly.; Thunderbird; Southwest Heritage. Honours, awards: 3rd pl., Cloverleaf Int. Poetry Anthol. Comp., 1971. Address: Eastern New Mex. Univ., Portales, NM 88130, U.S.A.

STEANE, Nina, artistic name **CARROLL, Nina.** Freelance Artist; Writer. Education: Cheltenham Ladies Coll.; St. Anne's, Oxford Univ.; p/t Ruskin Schl. of Art. Married, 1 son, 2 daughters. Positions held: Tutor, Dept. of Adult Educ., Leicester Univ., 1967-. Memberships: Poets Conf.; Chmn., Kettering Three Arts Club; Sec., Kettering Poets. Edited & published series, ALL IN wallstickers from 1967-, 17 issues to date. Contbr. to: Priapus; Muse; Mofussil; Poetry & Audience (prizewinner 1969 & runner up Poets Award 1971); Workshop; Radio Liecester; Poetry Now; BBC, etc. Address: 31 Headlands, Kettering, Northants, U.K.

STECK, Harriet Mildred Fisk, pen name, **STECK, Mille Fisk,** b. 4 Dec. 1903. Retired Elementary Principal. Education: Kansas, Emporia State Teachers Coll.; Colorado (Boulder) State Univ.; Kansas (Wichita) State Univ. Positions held: Elementary Teacher, 7 yrs. in Caldwell, Kansas; 17 yrs. as Elem. Principal in Wichita, Kansas. Memberships: 20th Century Club (member since 1959), and its Creative Writing (poems and plays, etc.) and Drama Chairman for sev. years. Published works: Fireside Reflections (poetry), 1968; Uncle Sam's Girl Friends (play), 1970; Kansas Kernels. Contbr. to: Wichita Light; Wellington News, Kansas, etc. Address: 4006 E. Gilbert St. & Bluff, Wichita, KS 67218, USA.

STEIN, Beverley Walden, b. 25 Sept. 1924. Secretary. Education: Tex. State Coll. for Women, Denton, 2 yrs.; Univ. of Houston; Cert. of Bus. Arts, Metropolitan Bus. Coll. Positions held: Hearing Stenographer, Mbr., Bd. of Special Inquiry, U.S. Dept. of Justice, Immigration & Naturalization Services, 1943-53; Exec. Sec., Galveston Chmbr. of Comm.; Registrar, Bay Area Coun., Boy Scouts of Am.; on staff of Galveston 'The Letter Shop' & currently Sec. to the firm of E.S. Levy & Co., Clothier, Galveston Is., Tex. Memberships: Alpha Lamba Delta; World Poetry Soc.; Friends of the Rosenberg Lib., Galveston, Tex. Published works: (coll. of poems) Watercolours from my Father's Studio, 1973; (pamphlet) Let's License Our Drinkers, pending. Ed., A Splinter's Width of Light, by Elizabeth Jane Baxter, 1965. Contbr. to: The Spring Anthols., 1966-73; Poetry Parade; Poet; Galveston Histl. Soc. Address: 1628 Avenue H (Ball), Galveston, TX 77550, U.S.A.

STEINBERGH, Judith W., b. 18 Oct. 1943. Poet; Teacher of Poetry Writing. Education: B.A. in Econs., Wellesley Coll., Mass. Married Alex Steinbergh, 1 daughter. Positions held: Mgr. of Economic Rsch. Dept., McKinsey & Co., 1965-71; Poetry Tchr. for E. Cleveland Public Schls. & Cleveland Heights H.S., 1971-72; Educational Dir., Calliope Childrens Theatre, Brookline, Mass., 1972; Poetry Tchr. for Poets-in-the-Schools Prog., Mass., 1972-73. Member, Ohio Poets' Assn., 1970-72. Published works: Marshmallow Worlds (book of poems & photographs about children), 1972. Contbr. to: Boston Globe Sunday Mag.; Detroit Free Press; The Am. Weave; Consumption; Freelance; Small Pond; Scopcraft; Poetry Venture; Ab Intra, etc. Rep. in following anthols: New Voices in the Wind; Poetry Cleveland; Read-Out. Ten poems written into a song cycle by Dr. Victor Babin & premiered at Aspen Music Festival, summer '73. Address: 34 Park St., Brookline, MA 02146, U.S.A.

STEINGESSER, Martin, b. 21 Feb. 1937. Writer. Education: B.A., Hofstra Univ., 1959. Positions held: News Writer, News Bureau of N.Y. Univ., 1969–; Reporter &/or Ed., Doubleday & Co., Inc., Newsday, United Press Int. & The Am. Banker. Memberships: Pi Delta Epsilon. Contbr. to: The Tenth Muse, an anthol. of eight poets, 1973; The N.Y. Times; The Nation; Evergreen Review; N.Y. State Jrnl. of Medicine; Holiday Mag.; The Remington Review; Shaman; Two Charlies Mag.; New: Am. & Canadian Poetry; The Expatriate Review; Granite; The Mediterranean Review; The Smith; Confrontation; New Measure; Unicorn Folio; Trace; Christian Sci. Monitor; The Hartford Courant; The Harvard Advocate; The Grecourt Review. Poetry readings at: The Donnell Br. of the N.Y. Public Lib.; The Cubiculo; The Mercer Arts Ctr.; N.Y. Univ., N.Y.C.; Middlebury Coll., Vt.; Vassar Coll., Poughkeepsie, N.Y. Recip., 5th pl., Writer's Digest Creative Writing Contest (poetry), 1972. Address: 16 East 8th St., No. 1-R, N.Y., NY 10009, U.S.A.

STEINHAUER, Lillian R., b. 4 Apr. 1910. Educator. Education: Bachelor's degree, N.Y. Univ.; Master's degree in Guidance & Personnel Administration, ibid. Married, 2 daughters. Positions held: Hd. Tchr. & Supvsr. on City Park Projects, 1930's; Shipfitter at Todd Shipyard, WWII; Tchr., 1950's; Acting Asst. to Prin. & Coordinator of Teaching Engl. as a Second Lang., 1960's. Memberships: Assoc. Mbr., Poetry Soc. of Am.; N.Y. Poetry Forum; Treas., Mark Twain Assn. of N.Y.; Shelley Soc. of N.Y.; Pi Lambda Theta; Kappa Delta Pi. Published works: Poems, 1961. Contbr. to: Nat. Poetry Anthol., 1964. Honours, awards: Festival Poet, N.Y. Poetry Forum, 1973. Address: 175 Adams St., Brooklyn, NY 11201, U.S.A.

STEINMETZ, Jean-Luc, b. 30 Sept. 1940. Profession: Assistant Instructor. Education: Aggregate, Classical Lit., 1967. Married, 2 children. Positions held: Asst. Instr., Faculty of Lit., Rennes, France. Published works include: Le Clair et le Lointain, 1967; L'Echo Traversé 1969; Marques/Mage, forthcoming. Contbr. to the following anthols., jrnls., mags., etc: Promesse; Le Journal des Poètes; Sud; Le Pont de l'Epée; Quaternaire; TXT (Co-Fndr., 1969); l'Année Balzacienne; RHLF; Les Annales de Bretagne, etc. Address: 9 Rue de Brest, Rennes 35, France.

STENNEVIN, Raymond, b. 20 May 1927. Industrial Designer. Education: Diplôme de chef-monteur-dépanneur Radio-E.P.S. Paris. Positions incl: Radio Trouble Shooter; Chef monteur dépanneur Radio; Industrial Designer. Memberships incl: Fellow, Higher Int. Acad. of Lutèce; Agregate Mbr., Soc. of Poets & Artists of France; Active Mbr., French Intellectuels Club. Contbr. to: l'Anthologie Poétique, 1971; Visions, poems (preface by the author, illustrations by Antonio Castillo); Collection Arpèges, 1972; 'En Souvenir de Toi' (radio drama entered in ORTF comp.) 1973. Honours, awards: 1st Dip. of Hon., SPAF Comp., 1970, '71, '72, & '73. Address: 37 bis Rue Viala, 69003, Lyon, France.

STEPANCHEV, Stephen, b. 30 Jan. 1915. English Professor. Educ: A.B., Univ. of Chgo., 1937; M.A., ibid, 1938; Ph.D., N.Y. Univ., 1950. Positions held: Served, U.S. Army, 1941-45; Tchr., Purdue Univ., Lafayette, Ind., 1938-41; Tchr., N.Y. Univ., 1946-48; Prof., Engl., Queens Coll., Flushing, N.Y., 1949–. Published works: Three Priests in April, 1956; Spring in the Harbor, 1967; A Man Running in the Rain, 1969. Contbr. to: Poetry; Nation; Extensions; Massachusetts Review; Sewanee Review; (anthologies) War Poets, 1945; An Anthology of French Poetry, 1958; An Anthology of German Poetry, 1960; An Anthology of Spanish Poetry, 1961; American Literary Anthology 2, 1969. Honours, awards: Soc. of Midland Authors Prize, 1937; Nat. Coun. on the Arts Award, 1968. Address: Engl. Dept., Queens Coll., Flushing, NY 11367, U.S.A.

STEPHAN, Ruth, b. 21 Jan. 1910. Poet; Historial Novelist; Film Producer. Education: Northwestern Univ., U.S.A., 1927-29. Positions held: Hd. of Lib. Book Comm., Lib. of Int. Rels., Chicago, Ill., 1937-43; Ed., The Tiger's Eye, a mag. on arts & letters, N.Y.C., 1947-50; Editl. Bd., MANKIND, New Delhi, India, 1962–. Memberships: PEN; Author's Guild; Fndr. & Bd. Mbr., Univ. of Ariz. Poetry Ctr.; Ruth Stephan Poetry Ctr., Univ. of Tex. Published works: (poetry) Prelude to Poetry, 1946; Various Poems, 1963; Poems for Nothing, 1973; (novels) The Flight, 1956; My Crown, My Love, 1960. Ed. & Transl., The Little Anthol. of Peruvian Poetry, 1948; The Singing Mountaineers – Songs & Tales of the Quechua People, 1957. Guest Ed., Black Americans 5/70. Producer & Writer of documentary film, ZEN IN RYOKO-IN, 1971. Ed. & writer of introductions – Record Albums: The Spoken Anthol. of Am. Lit.; Part I The Nineteenth Century, Centro Documentazione Foniche, Rome, Italy 1959; Vol. I The Nineteenth Century (Am. ed.), 1963; Vol. II The Twentieth Century, 1965. Contbr. to var. mags. Recip. var. hons. inclng: Award of Hon., Lib. of Int. Rels., 1940; Best Novel Award, Friends of Lit., 1957; Dr. of Letters, Univ. of Ariz., 1972; Fellow, Int. Poetry Soc., U.K. Address: Stone Legend, Khakum Wood, Greenwich, CT 06830, U.S.A.

STEPHEN, Sidney James, pen name **STEPHEN, Sid,** b. 28 July 1942. Officer, Canadian Forces. Education: B.A., Univ. of Alta., 1971. Married Carol Friesen, 2 children. Member, The League of Canadian Poets. Published works: Air, 1971. Contbr. to: 39 Below: Anthology, 1972; Canadian Forum; Black Moss; Another Poetry Mag.; Blewointment; Merry Devil of Edmonton; White Pelican; Fiddlehead; Copperfield. Recip., Edmonton Jrnl. Annual Poetry Award, 1970. Address: Box 542, Shilo, Manitoba, Canada.

STEPHENS, Alan, b. 19 Dec. 1925. Teacher. Educ: Univ. of Colo, Boulder; Univ. of Denver; Ph.D., Univ. of Missouri, Columbia; Stanford Univ. m. Frances Stephens, 3s. Positions held: Fac. Mbr., Engl. Dept., Univ. of Calif., Santa Barbara, 1959–. Published works: The Sum, 1958; Between Matter and Principle, 1963; The Heat Lightning, 1967; Tree Meditation and Others, 1970. Address: 326 Canon Dr., Santa Barbara, CA 93105, U.S.A.

STEPHENS, Diana, b. 1 July 1955. Poet. Education: Student, Southwestern-at-Memphis, Tenn., U.S.A. Editor of Tennessee Voices Bulletin, monthly newsletter of Poetry Soc. of Tennessee, 1973-74. Member, Poetry Soc. of Tenn., AAAS & Zero Population Growth, Inc. Contbr. to: Voices Int.; Modern Images; Valley Views; South & West; Old Hickory Review; Encore; (anthols.) Poems by Poets; Tenn. Voices Anthol-Yearbook; Sweat & Sneakers Sports Poetry; Memphis Mosaics; Columbia Univ. Press Anthol. of Best High School Writing. Address: 64 N. Yates Rd., Memphis, TN 38117, U.S.A.

STEPHENS, Meic, b. 23 July 1938. Editor; Director; Poet. Educ: B.A., Univ. Coll. of Wales, Aberystwyth & Bangor, Wales; Dip., Univ. of Rennes, France. m. Ruth Wynn Meredith, 1965; 3d. Positions held: French Master, Ebbw Vale Grammar Schl., 1962-66; Journalist, Western Mail, Cardiff, Wales, 1966-67;

Fndr. & Ed., Poetry Wales, Ed. (w. others), current; Asst. Dir., Welsh Arts Coun., 1967–. Published works: Triad (w. others), 1963; Ed., The Lilting House: An Anthology of Anglo-Welsh Poetry, 1917-67 (w. John Stuart Williams), 1969; Ed., Writers of Wales (w. R. Brinley Jones), 1970. Contbr. to: Poetry Wales; Anglo-Welsh Review; Y Faner; (anthologies) Welsh Voices, 1967; This World of Wales, 1968. Address: Twynyrodyn, Clos Bryn Deri, Rhiwbeina, Cardiff, Wales, U.K.

STEPHENS, Rosemary, pen name (for fiction only) **CARSWELL, Leslie,** b. 4 Dec. 1934. Freelance Writer. Education: Ph.D. in English, Univ. of Mississippi, 1971; M.A. in English, Univ. of Mississippi; B.A., Magna Cum Laude, Memphis State Univ. Married to Dr. Harold W. Stephens (Professor of Mathematics), one daughter: Diana Patricia. Pres., Poetry Soc. of Tennessee, 1972-74; Pres., Tennessee Woman's Press and Authors Club, 1973-75; Member, Modern Language Assoc.; Soc. for the Study of Southern Literature; Nat. League of American Pen Women. Contrib. to: Discourses on Poetry; Poem, Cape Rock Journal; Mississippi Review; Epos; South and West; Voices International; WEID; Human Voice; Hiram Poetry Review; Tennessee Voices; Southeast U.S. Poets Edition of POET; Anthologies: Dance of the Muse; Yearbook of Modern Poetry; Poems by Poets; Memphis Poems by Memphis Poets, and others. Recipient of South and West Award for Distinguished Poetry, 1970; Honoured: One of Four Outstanding Poets in United States, Cape Rock Journal, 1970; First Prize for Modern Poetry, Nat. League of American Pen Women, 1972. Address: 64 N. Yates Rd., Memphis, Tenn. 38117. USA.

STERN, Eugenia Louise, b. 17 Feb. 1953. Volunteer Worker. Contbr. to: Sage (Joaquin Miller H.S.); The Thorn (Episcopal Diocesan Youth paper); PAN. Address: 435 Georgina Ave., Santa Monica, CA 90402, U.S.A.

STERNLICHT, Sanford, b. 20 Sept. 1931. University Professor. Education: B.S., State Univ. of N.Y., U.S.A., 1953; M.A., Colgate Univ., 1955; Ph.D., Syracuse Univ., 1962. Married Dorothy Hilkert, 2 sons. Positions held: Instr., State Univ. of N.Y. at Oswego, 1959-60; Asst. Prof., ibid, 1960-62; Prof., 1962–; Prof. & Chmn., Dept. of Theatre, ibid. Memberships: Poetry Soc. of Am.; MLA. Published works: Gull's Way, 1962; Love in Pompeii, 1967. Contbr. of over 300 poems to: N.Y. Times; Herald Tribune; New Mexico Quarterly; Sat. Evening Post; Southwest Review; Poetry, London; Canadian Forum, etc. Honours, awards: Writer Mag. New Poets Award, 1960; Poetry Soc. of Am. Fellow, 1965. Address: 87 Sheldon Ave., Oswego, NY 13126, U.S.A.

STEVENS, Holly, b. 10 Aug. 1924. Author; Editor; Business Manager, The Yale Review. Education: Vassar Coll.; Univ. of Conn. Married twice, div., 1 son. Positions held: Fire Underwriter, Aetna Life Affil. Cos., Hartford, Conn., 1942-46; Purchasing Asst., Trinity Coll., Hartford, Conn., 1955-64; Sec., Yale Univ., 1966-68; Advt. Mgr., The Yale Review, 1968-69; Bus. Mgr. ibid, 1969–. Memberships: Fndr. & Dir., New England Poetry Circuit, 1963-68; Fndr. & Dir. of Conn. Poetry Circuit, 1968-72; Selection Comm., ibid, 1972–; Fndng. Mbr., Trinity Coll. Poetry Ctr., Hartford, Conn.; The English Inst.; Fellow, Timothy Dwight Coll., Yale Univ., etc. Published works: Ed: Letters of Wallace Stevens, 1966, '67; The Palm at the End of the Mind: Selected Poems & a Play by Wallace Stevens, 1971. Contbr. to The Southern Review. Honours, awards: Ingram Merrill Fndn. Grantee, 1964 & supplemental grant, 1965; Sr. Fellow, Nat. Endowment for the Humanities, 1972-73. Address: c/o The Yale Review, 1902A Yale Stn., New Haven, CT 06520, U.S.A.

STEVENS, Jean, pen name **STEVENS, Jean-Edouard,** b. 3 Nov. 1922. Manager/Announcer, Belgian Broadcasting, Brussels. Studied at the Univ. of Brussels, Belgium. Member, Association des Ecrivains belges de langue française. Published works: L'automme est sur la mer, poèmes, 1957; Le temps de la terre, poèmes, 1968; La planète folle, poèmes (in preparation). Contbr. to anthol. 'Des Poètes Chantent l'amour', 1973. Address: Place Flagey 21, 1050 Brussels, Belgium.

STEVENS, Peter, b. 17 Nov. 1927. University Professor. Education: B.A., Univ. of Nottingham, UK; M.A., McMaster Univ., Hamilton, Ontario, Canada; Ph.D., Univ. of Saskatchewan. Positions held: Manchester Educ. Comm.; Lectr., McMaster Univ.; Hd., Engl. Dept., Hillfield Coll., Hamilton, Ont.; Asst. Prof., Univ. of Saskatchewan; Assoc. Prof., Univ. of Windsor, Ont. Memberships: League of Canadian Poets. Published works incl: Nothing But Spoons, 1969; A Few Myths, 1971; Process, Tape, Canadian Broadcasting Corp., 1971. Contbr. to: Canadian Forum (Poetry Ed.); Fiddlehead; Prism Int.; Alphabet; Edge; Quarry; W Coast Rev.; Vol. 65; Yes; Talon; Trace; Poet & Critic; Human Voice Qtly.; Queen's Qtly.; Wascana Rev.; Malahat Rev.; Univ. Rev.; Kansas; Hartwick Rev.; Far Point; Cottonwood Rev.; Outposts; Quest; Poetry Australia; Univ. of Windsor Rev.; Wisc. State Rev., etc. Address–: 2055 Richmond St., Windsor 15, Ont., Canada.

STEVENSON, Anne Katharine, b. 3 Jan. 1933. Freelance Writer; Teacher. Education: B.A., Univ. of Mich., U.S.A., 1954; M.A., ibid, 1961. Married three times, 3 children (2 sons & 1 daughter). Positions held: Tchr. of Engl., Lillesden Schl., Kent, U.K.; Advt Mgr., A. & C. Black, publishers, London; Tchr. of Engl., Westminster Schl., Atlanta, Ga., U.S.A. & The Cambridge Schl. of Weston, Mass.; Tutor, Extra Mural Dept., Univ. of Glasgow, U.K.; Fellow in Creative Writing, Univ. of Dundee, 1973-74. Memberships: Poetry Soc. of Am., 1973; Fellow, Radcliffe Inst. of Harvard, 1970-71. Published works: Living in America, 1965; Elizabeth Bishop (criticism), 1966; Reversals, 1969; Selected Poems, 1974; Correspondences, 1974. Contbr. to: Generation; Wave; Encounter; The London Mag.; Open Places; Outposts; The Scotsman; Phoenix; The Mass. Review; The Mich. Quarterly Review; Saturday Review; Lines Review; Scottish Int.; Glasgow Herald; Paris Review; Poetry (Chicago); Analecta, also BBC Broadcasts. Recip., Hopwood Awards, Univ. of Mich., 1952, 53 & 54. Address: 156 Wilton St., Glasgow G20 6BS, U.K.

STEVENSON, James Patrick, pen name **TOMOS RADYR,** b. 17 Mar. 1910. Anglican Priest. Education: St. Catherine's Coll., Oxford Univ., U.K.; Lausanne Univ. Married Leila Mary Flack, div., 2 sons, 1 daughter. Positions held: British Army Chaplain, 1939-55; Australian Church, 1955–; Protector of Natives, 1957-59; Corres., Le Monde, 1969–. Memberships: Athenaeum, London; Australian Soc. of Authors. Published works: Crisanzio (collected poems), 1948; Religion & Leadership, 1948; Contbr. to Poems from Italy, 1945. Contbr. to: New Statesman; Spectator; Guardian; Poetry Review; Poetry Today; Royal Army Chaplains Dept. Jrnl.; var. Australian papers. Address: 16 Osburn Ave., North Balwyn 3104, Australia.

STEVENSON, Mabel Brollier, pen name, **STEVENSON, Mabel B.,** b. 4 May 1916. Writer; Lecturer. Education: Dip., Capital Univ., Columbus, Ohio, 1937; B.S. Education, Ashland Coll., Ohio, 1952; Dip., Famous Writer's School, Westport, Connecticut, 1967. Married to Van L. Stevenson; 1 step-son. Positions held: School Teacher from Sept. 1937 until retirement in 1967 (with 1 yr. leave to teach seminar for teachers). Memberships: Nat. Retired Teachers Assoc.; Internat. Clover Poetry Assoc. (life member); Soc. of Literary Designates; CSSI, !nternat. Platform Assoc. Recorded songs: "Faith is Always the Answer", 1971; My Wonderful Lord, 1972. Contbr. to: Clover Collection of verse (various vols.); Gato Anthol. (various editions); Columbus Dispatch, and others. Awards: 3rd prize, 1971, Clover Internat. Poetry Competition; recip. title of Danae, 1969. Address: 188 W. Raleigh Ave., Mansfield, OH 44907, USA.

STEVENSON, Mary Blanche (Mrs. Arthur L.), pen name, **STEVENSON, Mary B.,** b. 29 June 1889, in Chattanooga, Tennessee, USA. Housewife; Poet. Education: Honor Grad., Petersburg, Virginia, HS; Methodist Training School, Nashville, Tennessee; Summer Schools, Farmville, Va. Teachers' Coll. and Univ. of Virginia: Married Arthur L. Stevenson, Methodist Minister; 3 children. Positions held: Airplane Spotter; Red Cross Canteen Work; Chairman, Education Committee, Salem, Va. Woman's Club; Sunday School Teacher; Officer, Woman's Missionary Soc.; Judge, annual contest, American Poetry League; Rep. for Georgia, World Poetry Day Assoc.; Chairman, Poetry Group, Atlanta Writers Club; Mbr. Bd. of Directors, Atlanta Authors Guild, etc. Memberships: Brit. & American Poetry Soc. (past); Atlanta Writers Club; World Poetry Day Assoc.; Poetry Soc. of Georgia; Poetry Soc. of Arizona; Atlanta Authors Guild; Laramore-Rader Poetry Group; Poetry Soc. of Va.; Published works: Clusters From My Vineyard, 1942; The Vineyard Bears Again, 1945; Latchkeys to the Heart, 1955; Where Wonder Treads, 1960. Contbr. to many anthols., journals, newspapers. Recip. of many prizes, awards, etc. Address: 225 West French Broad Av., Brevard, NC 28712, USA.

STEWART, Douglas Alexander, b. 6 May 1913. Poet. Education: Victoria Univ. Coll., New Zealand. Positions held: Lit. Ed., The Bulletin, Sydney, Australia, 1939-59; Lit. Advsr., Angus & Robertson Ltd., publrs., 1959-. Memberships: Advsry. Bd., Commonwealth Lit. Fund. Published works: (poems) Green Lions, 1936; The White Cry, 1939; Elegy for an Airman, 1940; Sonnets to the Unknown Soldier, 1941; The Dosser in Springtime, 1946; Glencoe, 1947; Sun Orchids, 1952; The Birdsville Track, 1955; Rutherford, 1962; Selected Poems, 1963; Collected Poems, 1936-67, 1967; (verse plays) Ned Kelly, 1943; The Fire on the Snow, & The Golden Lover, 1944; Shipwreck, 1947; (criticism) The Flesh & the Spirit, 1948; (short stories) A Girl With Red Hair, 1944; (reminiscences) The Seven Rivers, 1966. Contbr. to: Bulletin; Southerly; Meanjin Qtly.; Overland. Honours: Encyclopaedia Britannica Humanities Award, 1968. Address: 2 Banool Ave., St. Ives, N.S.W., Australia 2075.

STEWART, Harold Frederick, b. 14 Dec. 1916. Poet. Published works incl: Phoenix Wings, 1948; Orpheus, 1956; A Net of Fireflies (transl. & essay), 1960; A Chime of Windbells (transl. & essay), 1969. Contbr. to: Mod. Australian Verse, 1964, & others. Address: Hotel Shirakuso, Higashisenouchicho 29 Kitashirakawa, Sakyo-ku, Kyoto, Japan.

STEWART, Ora Pate, b. 23 Aug. 1910. Author; Poet; Composer; Program Lecturer. Education: Brigham Young Univ.; Univ. of Utah. Married, Col. Robert W. Stewart. Positions held: Mus. Tchr., Rock Springs, Wyo., 1930-31; Missionary to Eastern US, 1931-33, & UK, 1969-71; Tchr., LI Conservatory of Music, 1933-34; Mus. Tchr., Wyo., 1934-35; Fndr., Sweetwater Conservatory of Music, Rock Springs; Radio Writer & Lectr. for many stations; Numerous ch. positions, Ch. of Jesus Christ of LDS; Lectr., Nat. Artist & Lectr. Serv., 1953-; Member, Nat. Music Bd., NLAPW, 1972-74. Memberships: World Poetry Soc.; Poetry Soc. of Am.; Pres., Hollywood Br., Nat. League Am. Pen Women, 1968-70; Am. Soc. Composers, Authors & Publishers; State Pres., Young Women's Mutual Improvement Assn., 1967-68; Poetry Soc. of Tex.; Ariz. State Poetry Soc.; San Joaquin Writers & Artists; Utah Poets; League of Utah Writers; Speaker-in-Residence, Annual Chautauqua, 1973, also at Annual Round-Up, League of Utah Writers, 1973, and Mid-Administration Congress, NLAPW, 1973. Publications: Tours Through the Sunset Land, 1934; Radio Lectures, 1934; Intimations, 1939; Pages from the Book of Eve, 1946; God Planted a Tree, 1947; Gleanings, 1948 (now 7th Ed.); I Talk About My Children, 1948; Branches Over The Wall, 1950; A Letter To My Son, 1951; Treasures Unearthed, 1953; We Believe, 1954; A Letter to my Daughter, 1956; This Word of Wisdom, 1958; Dear Land of Home, 1960;

From Where I Stood, 1960; Brown Leaves Turning, 1953 (now 3rd Ed.); Mopey the Mop, 1955; Buttermilk & Bran, 1964; West Wind Song, 1964 (now 4th Ed.); Tender Apples, 1965; The Singing Kings, 1969; The Brightness of Hope, -1969; The Quenchless Flame, 1969. Published songs include: What Was That Song, 1969; Be Humble, 1970; Brotherhood of Man, 1970 (1st place UK 1970 Folksong Festival); Song of Love, 1965; Crossing the Bar, 1964; Blessed Are the Meek, 1972; Mother Song, 1973; Claim Thou My Heart, 1941; The Battle Line of Home, 1943; To A Child (adopted as official anthem of the Nat. Young Women's Council, 1969), 1964; A Tree Stood Tall, 1967; Golden Promise, 1968; As Stars Together, Let Us Sing, 1969. Honours: Nat. Winner, 'Moment of Truth', Nat. League Am. Pen Women, 1964; Gold Medal, Internat. Poets' Shrine, 1969, 1st Place, Engl. Folk Song Festival, 1970; Magna Cum Laude, World Poetry Soc., 1970; 1st Place, short story, USA, 1970, & numerous state & regional awards; Nat. Best Writing of Non-Fiction, Book, 1972, NLAPW; Hon. Doctorate, Univ. of Free Asia, 1972. Address: 383 East, 1980 North, Provo, UT 84601, USA.

STEWART, Vincent, b. 13 May 1939. Educator. Education: Tulane Univ., 1957-59; B.A. & M.A., Stephen F. Austin State Univ., 1959-62; Univ. of Iowa (Poetry Workshop), 1962-64. Positions held: Writer-in-Res., Northeast Mo. State Coll., 1964-66; Instr. of Engl., Va. Polytechnic Inst. & State Univ., 1966-68; Assoc. Prof. of Engl., Lock Haven State Coll., 1968-. Memberships: Nat. Coun. of Tchrs. of English; Pa. Associated Writing Progs.; Canadian Assn. of Commonwealth Lang. & Lit. Studies. Published works: Words for the Builder, 1966; Small Deceits, 1968; Three Dimensions of Poetry: An Introduction, 1969. Contbr. to: Hudson Review; Appalachian Review; Laurel Review; Voices; Lock Haven Review; Re: Arts & Letters; Poetry Florida and Maelstrom; Blue Guitar; Wanderlust; New Athenaeum; Orphic Lute; Charlatan Dawn; Northwest Challenge. Recip., Karle Wilson Baker Poetry Award, 1961. Address: 401 South Main St., Jersey Shore, PA 17740, U.S.A.

STIEF, Willie Gay Morgan (Mrs. Frank David Stief), pen name O'PENYON, Anne, b. 15 Mar. 1918. Teacher. Education: A.B., A.M., Birmingham Southern Coll.; Grad. work at the Univ. of Alabama. Positions held: Teacher, Walker County Schools; Birmingham City Schools; Wheeler Business Coll., Teacher of business subjects on Alabama Educational TV.; Currently teaching English at Banks HS and the American Inst. of Banking in Birmingham, Alabama. Memberships: Ala. Writers Conference; Ala. State Poetry Soc. Published regular column in Birmingham Education Assoc. Journal, 1968-1972. Contbr. to: The Mountain Eagle; The Birmingham News; Trade Mag.; Birmingham Ed. Assoc. Journal. Awarded 2nd place prize commemorating Alabama's 150 yrs. (1969). Address: 203 West Linwood Dr., Homewood, Birmingham, AL 35209, USA.

STIEHL, Harry Charles Christopher, pen name KREUZ, Hieronymo, b. 29 Jan. 1927. Editor & Professor. Education: B.A., Univ. of Tex., 1947; M.A., Univ. of Calif., 1949; Ph.D., Univ. of Tex., 1969. Positions held: Translator, USAF Intelligence, 1950-51; Lab. Dir., Mexico, 1952-56; Book Ed., San Francisco, 1957-58; Prof., Univ. of San Francisco, 1958-61; Ed., Ramparts, 1961-69; Prof., San Diego State Univ., 1969-. Published works incl: Destinies, 1956; The Farrells of Sea Vineyard, 1963; Talleyrand's Ghost at the Funeral of JFK, 1966; The Irish Angst, 1969; The Marine Graveyard on Point Loma, 1971; Pictures For An Ossuary, 1972; Soliloquy Art, 1972; A Prussian Garden in Texas, 1973. Contbr. to num. anthols., jrnls., mags. inclng: America; Reflections; The Nation. Honours, awards: Selected for Best Poems of 1964, Borestone Mtn. Poetry Awards. Address: 3834 Goldfinch, San Diego, CA 92103, U.S.A.

STIFF, JoAnn M., b. 13 July 1933. Homemaker. Married Richard D. Stiff, 5 children (Steven, Richard,

Brian, Christine, Melanie). Memberships: Treas., Eau Claire Writers Club; Midwest Fed. of Chapparal Poets. Published works: Ideals, 1966; America, My Country, 1970. Contbr. to: Minneapolis Argus; Lenten Devotions, 1972 & 73. Recip., 1st pl., 1971, 3rd pl., 1972 & 5th pl., 1973, Midwest Fed. of Chapparal Poets Seminars. Address: 805 Bauer Ave., Eau Claire, WI 54701, U.S.A.

STILL, James, b. 16 July 1906. Librarian; Teacher; Writer. Education: A.B., M.A., B.S., Litt.D. Positions held: Staff, Hindman Settlement Schl.; Assoc. Prof., Morehead State Univ.; Vis. Prof., Ohio Univ.; Vis. Prof., Berea Coll.; Lectr., Univ. of N.C. Published works: Hounds on the Mountain, 1937, rev. 1967; River of Earth (novel); On Troublesome Creek (short stories); Way Down Yonder on Troublesome Creek (juvenile). Contbr. to: Atlantic Monthly; The Yale Review; Va. Quarterly Review; Poetry: A Magazine of Verse; The Nation; The New Republic; Saturday Evening Post; Saturday Review of Lit.; Sewanee Review; Mountain Life & Work, etc. Recip. var. awards. Address: Wolfpen Creek, Mallie, KY 41836, U.S.A.

STIP, Kees, pen name **TRIJNTJE FOP,** b. 25 Aug. 1913. Freelance Author. Education: Litt. class. cand. (B.A.), Univ. of Utrecht. Married, 5 children. Memberships: Vereniging van Letterkundigen; Maatschappij der Nederlandse Letterkunde; Beroepsvereniging van Nederlandse Filmers. Published works: Dieuwertje Diekema, 1945; Vijf variaties op een misverstand, 1946; Dierkundige dichtoefeningen, 1952; Beestachtigheden, 1956; Vis à Vis, 1962; Zoo Zoo, 1964; De Peperbek, 1967. Contbr. to almost all publs. in the Netherlands. Address: Het Nieuwe Schelver 10, Diepenheim, The Netherlands.

STIPCEVIC, Augustin, b. 28 July 1912. Writer. Education: studied Law at Univ. Published works: Nemirne vode (Restless Waters), 1937; Mladost u kolima (Youth in the Cart), 1939; Sunce u ćeliji (Sun in the Cell), 1939; Pjesme (Poems), 1955; Zapaljena truba (Burning Trumpet), 1961; Na tragu svih stvari (On the Track of all Things), 1971, etc. Contbr. to: Savremenik, Zagreb; Mogućnosti, Split; Republika, Zagreb; Književnik, Belgrade; Književne novine, Belgrade, etc. Honours, awards: Društvo književnika Hrvatske, 1960. Address: Bijenička 52, Zagreb, Yugoslavia.

STOCK, Robert Paul, b. St. Paul, Minn., 30 June 1923. Professional Writer of Programmed Instruction. Married, with 5 children. Has worked as jazz musician; translator; teacher; writer of literary criticism. Published work: Covenants, 1967. Contbr. to: Poetry (Chicago); Yale Review; NY Times; Qtly. Review of Literature; Minnesota Review; Wisconsin Review; South Dakota Review; Poetry Northwest; Poetry London; Beatitude Anthol.; Borestone Mountain Anthol.; Antaeus; The Expatriate Review; San Francisco Bark, etc. Address: 7704 Third Ave., Brooklyn, New York, NY 11209, USA.

STODGHILL, Pat, b. 1 Feb. 1935. Teacher. Education: B.S., North Tex. State Univ., 1956; M.A., Univ. of Tex. at Austin, 1958. Married Donald R. Stodghill, 1 son, 1 daughter. Positions held: Tchr., Dallas Independant Schl. Dist., 1957-65. Memberships: Dir., Monthly Contest Chmn.; Annual Awards Banquet Chmn.; Extension Chmn.; Poetry Soc. of Tex. Contbr. to: A Book of The Year, The Poetry Soc. of Tex., 1966, '68, '70, '71, '72, '73, '74; Prize Poems, Nat. Fed. of State Poetry Socs. 1971, '73. Recip. num. awards from the Poetry Soc. of Tex. inclng: Nora Elmore Johnson Meml. Award, 1973; David Atamian Meml. Award, 1973; Ida Paramore Bard Meml. Award, 1973. Recip., 1st pl. in the following Nat. Fed. of State Poetry Socs. Contest: The Manningham Award, 1971 & The Utah State Award, 1973. Address: 1424 Highland Rd., Dallas, TX 75218, U.S.A.

STOLZAR, Betsy H., b. 17 Apr. 1912, in Cleveland, Ohio, USA. Housewife. Education: HS; Sacred Heart Acad., Louisville, Ky.; Ward Belmont Jr. Coll., Nashville, Tenn., 1931-32; Univ. of Louisville, Ky., 1933-34; later attended business school. Personal details: Divorced 1st husband, and married Irwin H. Stolzar, M.D. Positions held: Wartime appt. in Louisville Post Office, 1942; Receptionist & Stenographer, Reynolds Aluminium Plant, Louisville, Ky., 1943-45; Sec. to Director of Public Relations, Louisville Courier-Journal & Times, 1945-49. Memberships: Poetry Soc. of Texas; Longview & East Texas Poetry Soc. (past pres.). Published work: A Fair Share (poems), 1970. Contbr. to: The Longview News & Journal (poetry column); Woman's World Weekly; Tisdell Anthol. of Poetry, Classical & Contemporary; American Bard; Blue Moon; The Arizonian; Candor; Virgin Isle Hotel News; Chromatones; The Writer Mag. Awards: Cash Prize, Longview News Contest, 1955, 1956; Hon. Mention in Anne Hamilton's Column in The Writer, 1956; Special Comment from Editor of The Bard on sonnet, 1957. Address: P.O. Box 887, Longview, TX 75601, USA.

STONE, Alfred Wheeler, b. 24 Apr. 1887. Clergyman. Education: A.B., Bowdoin Coll., 1910; S.T.B., Bangor & Andover Theol. Sems., 1916; post grad. study in Lit., Harvard Univ., 1914-16; Harvard Divinity Schl. Positions held: Assoc. Min., Eliot Congl. Ch., Newton, Mass., 1914-16; Min., West Concord Union Ch., Mass., 1916-36; Interim Preaching, Gtr. Boston Area & Lecturing, featuring 'The Living Emerson, His Message for Today', 1936-49; Min., Prospect Hill Congl. Ch., 1949–, etc. Memberships: Poetry Soc. of London; World Poets Resource Ctr., N.Y. Published works: As the Spirit Blows, 1971. Contbr. to: The Congregationalist; Advance; The Boston Herald; The Prospect Hill Messenger, etc. Honours, awards: D.Rel.A. (Order of Merit, World Doctorate), Great China Coll. (World Univ.), 1973; First Hon. Mention, Carl Sandburg Poetry Contest, IPA, Wash. D.C., 1973. Address: 78 Marion Rd., Watertown, MA 02172, U.S.A.

STONE, Henry, b. 8 Feb. 1908. Lawyer. Education: Pub. School in NYC.; Univ. of Pennsylvania, 1929, B.A.; Columbia Law School, 1932, LL.B. Married, 2 s. Positions held: Worked with NY State Legislature in 1939 as draftsman of NY Public Housing Law of 1939; Corporal in Army of the U.S. Membership: Poetry Soc. of America. Contbr. to: Ladies Home Journal; Good Housekeeping; Beloit Poetry Journal; Transcript; gnosis; Legend, etc. Address: 120 Broadway (Suite 1825), New York, NY 10005, USA.

STONE, Idella Purnell, pen name **PURNELL, Idella,** b. 1 Apr. 1901. Writer. Education: Univ. of Calif., Berkeley, 1922. Married R. Stone. Positions held: Fndr., Ed., Publsr., poetry mag. 'Palnes', 1923-30; Sec., Am. Consulate, 1922-24; Org. & Dean of First Summer Session of Univ. of Guadalajara, Mex., 1931; Creative Writing Course, First Congl. Ch. 'Schl. for Living', 1937; Freelance Writer. Memberships: a Fndr., The Verse Guild, Univ. of Calif.; Poetry Soc. of Am.; Science Fiction Writers Assn. Rep. in many anthols. inclng: Modern Am. Contemporary Verse; Northwest Anthol., 1929; Am. Scrap Book, 1930; The Best Poems of 1924, '25, '26, '27, '28, '29; Northeast Anthol., 1930; The Golden Echo. Contbr. to num. mags., jrnls., newspapers inclng: N.Y. Leader; N.Y. Post; L.A. Times; N.Y. Herald Tribune; Christian Sci. Monitor; El Informador, Guadalajara; The Lyric West; Poetry; Voices; The Lit. Digest; Double Dealer; Good Housekeeping; Harper's Bazaar; The Nation; Sat. Evening Post. Recip. var. hons. & awards. Address: 321 E. Grandview Ave., Sierra Madra, CA 91024, U.S.A.

STONEHAM, Gillian Elizabeth, b. 18 May 1932. Psychiatric Social Worker. Education: Soc. Studies, Edinburgh Univ., Scotland, UK, 1962-64; Cert, in Psych. Soc. Wrk., Manchester Univ., 1964-65. Positions held: Shorthand-Typist, Oxford & London, 1953-62; Psych. Soc. Wrkr., St. Clements Hosp., London, 1965-67; Rsch. Psych., Soc. Wrkr., Inst. of Psych., 1967-68; Psych. Soc. Wrkr., Brixton Child Guidance Unit, 1968–. Memberships: Past Mbr.,

Poetry Soc., UK; Past Mbr., Oxford Writers Circle. Published works: When That April, poems, 1960. Contbr. to the following anthols., jrnls., & radio progs: Outposts; Botteghe Oscure; Poetry Rev.; Envoi; Oxford Mag.; Isis; Deuce; Short Story & Poetry Year Book, 1969; New Poems, PEN, 1954; Midland Poets, BBC. Address: 86 Sandfield Rd., Headington, Oxford, Oxon., UK.

STOPPLE, Libby (Elizabeth Carrie), b. 7 July 1910. Retired Nurse; Poet; Composer. Education: Degree in Nursing, Sanatorium, Tex. Positions held: on Nursing Staff, Woodlawn Hosp., Dallas, Tex. (i/c large ward, many years). Memberships: past Off., Poetry Soc. of Am.; Poetry Soc. of Tex.; Affiliate, Acad. Am. Poets; Nat. Fed. of State Poetry Socs.; Former Mbr., 'Saturdays', London, U.K. Published works: Red Metal, 1952; Never Touch a Lilac, 1959; No Other Word, 1960; Singer in the Side, 1969; Peppermints, 1970. Rep. in following anthols: Golden Quill, 1958. Golden Year, 1960; Various Light, 1964. Poems appear in following books, fly leaf: For Abe Lincoln, in The Philosophy of Abraham Lincoln, by Dr. William Barringer; Springtime Child, in Dr. Chas Muses book, Consciousness & Reality. Contbr. to many newspapers & mags. inclng. poem in 'Modern Maturity', 1973. Composer, folk singer & poet whose songs & lyrics & poems are on permanent display in de Grummond Coll., Univ. of So. Miss. Lib. Recip. var. awards. Poem, Death of a Morning, used in 10th Annual Mem. Serv. to late John F. Kennedy, 1973. Address: 2512 Welborn, Dallas, TX 75219, U.S.A.

STOREY, Edward, b. 28 Feb. 1930. Writer. Member of Literature Panel, Eastern Arts Assoc., Cambridge. Published works: A Year to Come (verse), 1954; North Bank Night (verse), 1969, reprinted 1970; A Portrait of the Fen Country (prose), 1970, reprinted 1971; A Man in Winter (verse), 1971; Four Seasons in Three Countries (prose), 1974. Contbr. to: Anglo-Welsh Review; Ariel; Critical Qtly.; The Countryman; Blackwoods Mag.; The Listener; NY Times; New Statesman; Outposts; Priapus; Scrip; 7 Themes in Modern Verse; The Tin Whistle; Poetry Makers, and various anthols. Awards: 1st Prize English Poetry Soc. Festival Competition, 1969; £25 prize-winner in Keats Memorial Prize Competition, 1973. Address: 18 Eastfield Grove, Peterborough PE1 4BB, UK.

STOUT (Mrs. J. Bruce) Dorothy L., pen names, **BENNETT, Valerie; REED, Kelly,** b. 8 June 1916. Research Scholar. Education: Scarritt Coll., Nashville, Tennessee; Univ. of Oklahoma. Married; 4 children. Positions held: Coordinator of Campus Religious Activities, Staff of Dean of Students, Univ. of Oklahoma. Memberships: State Fed. of Oklahoma Writers., Oklahoma City Chapter (Vice-Pres., Corresponding Sec., and member of Board, 1949 to present); Poetry Soc. of Oklahoma and its affiliate the Nat. Soc. Published works: The Magnificent Present, 1970; A Man of Character, 1971; A Hint of Jade, 1974. Contbr. to: Poetry Soc. of Oklahoma anthols.; The Daily Oklahoman; Motive Mag. (Nashville); American Bard; Hollywood, Calif. Poetry Parade; Words on the Wind Column (Okla. newspaper). Honours: Presentation of selected readings at Nat. Fed. of Poetry Socs. of America, 1970; Holograph poems in N.F.P.S.A. Archives at Provo, Utah, and Tempe, Arizona. Address: 2518 N.W. 67, Oklahoma City, OK 73116, USA.

STOUTENBURG, Adrien Pearl, pen name **KENDALL, Lace,** b. 1 Dec. 1916. Free-lance writer of books for young readers, fiction, folk tales, conservation, & biographies. Positions held: Clerical Worker; Typist; Asst., X-ray Lab.; County Libn.; Newspaper Reporter; Ed., Juvenile Book Firm. Mbr., Authors Guild. Published works: Heroes, Advise Us, 1964; Short History of the Fur Trade, 1969; Engl. edit., 1970. Contbr. to: New Yorker; Yale Review; Nation; Southwest Review; Epoch; Accent; Shenandoah; Northwest Review; Kayak; Saturday Review; Prairie Schooner; Poetry Northwest; Commonweal, etc. Honours, Awards: Michael Sloan Award, Poetry Soc.

of Am., 1962; Edwin Markham Award, ibid, 1962; Lamont Poetry Selection, Acad. of Am. Poets, for best 1st volume, Heroes, Advise Us, 1964; Commonwealth Club of Calif. Silver Medal for Short Hist. of the Fur Trade, 1969, etc. Address: PO Box 291, Lagunitas, Calif. 94938, USA.

STOW, (Julian) Randolph, b. 28 Nov. 1935. Writer. Education: Guildford Grammar School, Western Australia; Univ. of Western Australia (B.A., 1956). Positions held: Tutor in Engl., Univ. of Adelaide, 1957; Cadet Patrol Officer, Papua-New Guinea, 1959; Lecturer in Engl., Univ. of Leeds, 1962; Lecturer in Engl., Univ. of Western Australia, 1963-64; Harkness Fellow, USA., 1964-66; Lecturer in Engl. and Fellow in Commonwealth Lit., Leeds, 1968-69. Published works: Act One, 1957; Outrider, 1962; A Counterfeit Silence: Selected Poems, 1969; Eight Songs For A Mad King (music-theatre work, music by Peter Maxwell Davies), 1969. Address: c/o Richard Scott Simon Ltd., 36 Wellington St., London WC2E 7BD, UK.

STRACHAN, Terence, b. 2 Jan. 1933. Teacher. Education: Mus.B., Manchester Univ.; B.Sc.(Econ.), London Univ.; A.R.M.C.M. (Royal Manchester Coll. of Mus.) Married, 2 children. Has published 70 poems from 1968-73. Contbr. to: Viewpoints; Scrip; Anglo-Welsh Review; Expression One; Cyffro; Good Elf; Critical Review; Naissance; Breakthru; Vis Viva; Orbis; New Expression; Somethings; Gong; Poetry & Audience; Bogg; London Welshman; Platform, etc. Address: 17 St. Mary's Close, The Grove, Merthyr Tydfil, Glamorgan, U.K.

STRAND, Betsy Denker, b. 8 Apr. 1940. Housewife. Education: Kalamazoo College; Univ. of Ill.; Northwestern Univ. Married Richard Strand, 3 children. Positions held: Column Writer, Dodgeville Chronicle. Memberships: Wis. Fellowship of Poets; Upland Writers. Contbr. to: Poet; Hawk and Whippoorwill Recalled; Muse Letter of Wis. Fellowship of Poets. Honours, awards: Best Senyra (tied for 1st), Rhinelander Schl. of the Arts, 1973. Address: 306 W. Clarence, Dodgeville, WI 53533, U.S.A.

STRAND, Mark, b. 11 Apr. 1934. Professor. Educ: B.A., Antioch Coll., Yellow Springs, Ohio; B.F.A., Yale Univ.; M.A., Univ. of Iowa. m. Antonia Ratensky, 1d. Positions held: Fulbright Lectr., Univ. of Brazil, Rio de Janeiro, Brazil, 1965-66; Vis. Prof., Univ. of Wash., U.S.A., 1968; Adjunct Assoc. Prof., Columbia Univ., 1969; Vis. Prof., Yale Univ., 1969. Published works: Sleeping with One Eye Open, 1964; Reasons for Moving, 1968; Ed., The Contemporary American Poets, 1969. Contbr. to: New Yorker; New York Review of Books; (anthologies) Poems of Our Moment, 1968; Young American Poets, 1968. Honours, awards: Cook Prize, 1959; Bergin Prize, 1959; Fulbright Schlrship. to Italy, 1960-61; Ingram Merrill Fellowship, 1966; Nat. Coun. for the Arts Award, 1967-68. Address: 35 W. 92nd St., N.Y., NY 10025, U.S.A.

STRATE, May, Writer; Poet. Married Clarence Leroy Strate. Positions held: Radio Script Writer; Freelance Prose Writer; Poet; from 1935-55 wrote radio scripts dramatizing the service prog. of veteran & civic orgs. Gave num. talks for schools, churches, veterans' & civic orgs. Held offices in Am. Legion Aux. at unit, county, dist. & state level. Served 6 yrs. as Americanism Chmn., Am. Legion Aux. unit, 4 yrs. Americanism Chmn. of Iowa Dept. of the Am. Legion Aux. Wrote & directed prod. of patriotic pageant for the Am. Legion Aux. Jrs.; wrote & directed pageant for Order of the Eastern star & wrote religious pageant for United Protestant observance of World Day of Prayer. Edited THE BOMB, an Am. Legion Aux. publ., 1944 & '45. Published works: The Tree That Talks With God, 1967. Contbr. to: (prose) Am. Legion Mag.; Iowa Legionnaire; This Day; feature articles in War Cry; num. southern & mid-western newspapers; (poetry) Mason City (Ia.) Globe Gazette; Am. Bard; Orphic Lute; num. poetry columns. Honours, awards: Geo. Wash. Medal, Freedoms Fndn., 1953; Voted Poet of the Present, Poets' Roundtable of Ark., 1971; var. 1st pl. awards, Ark. Writers, Poets' Roundtable of Ark., Ozark Authors & Artists Guild, & many others. Address: 116 Suburban Dr., Hot Springs, AR 71901, U.S.A.

STRAW, Lewis, b. 17 Oct. 1884. Coal Miner; Labour Party Political Agent. Widower, 2 sons, 2 daughters. Positions held: Coal Miner, 19 yrs.; Insurance Agent & Labour Party Sec. & Agent, 14 yrs.; semi-skilled worker, Rolls-Royce, Derby. Memberships: Derby Poetry Soc. (has served on comm.); Fellow, Int. Poetry Soc. & Mbr. of mid-Derbyshire Br. Contbr. to: Derby Poetry Soc. Annual Poetry Coll.; Derbyshire Countryside; BBC Midland Poets Prog.; John O'London's; Here Now; Derby Local Radio (poems & short stories broadcast Autumn & Christmas 1971), etc. Recip. var. poetry awards. Address: 22 Station Rd., Mickleover, Derby PE3 5GH, U.K.

STREHLOW, Loretta Jean, b. 14 Jan. 1933. Housewife; Freelance Writer. Education: Univ. of Wis., Madison, 2 yrs. Married Roland Strehlow, 1 son. Positions held: Creative Writing Instr. of Adult Classes. Memberships: Bd. Mbr. & Past Sec., Coun. for Wis. Writers; Wis. Regl. Writers' Assn.; Regl. V.P., Fellowship of Wis. Poets; Fictioneers; By-Liners. Contbr. to: Creative Wis.; Together mag.; Mnpls. Argus; Hawk & Whippoorwill; 1971 Prize Poem Anthol. of the Nat. Fed. of State Poetry Socs., Inc. Honours, awards: 1st pl., Jade Ring Winner, Wis. Regl. Writers' Assn., 1970; Bard's Chair, 1970; 1st pl., NFSPS Yearly Contests, Evans Spencer Wall Meml. Award, 1971; 2nd Pl., ibid, Gabriel Light Verse Award, 1971; Hon. Mention, W.Va. Contest, 1971; 1st Hon. Mention, The Manningham Award, 1972. Address: 312 W. Brentwood Ln., Glendale, WI 53217, U.S.A.

STREMICH, Norma Florence, pen names, **WHEELER, Norma Jones; CRUE, Norma Jones; HANSEN, Norma Jones; STREMICH, Norma Jones,** b. 25 June 1914. Poet; Composer; Editor; Proofreader; Freelance Writer. Education: Western HS.; YMCA Coll. Secretarial Science; Polytechnic Inst., Journalism and Public Relations, etc. Married, Charles Peter Stremich; 3 children. Positions held: The Sunpapers, A.S. Abell Co., Copyholder; The Service Composition Co., Proofreader; Freelance Writer. Memberships: CAAA, Inc. (Member, Bd. of Directors, 1973-75); Golden Key Class of the Otterbein Memorial (Pres., 1971-73); Baltimore Chapter, CAAA (Pres.); Maryland State Pres., CAAA; Sec. to Poet Laureate, Maryland, since 1965; Sec. to Committee of 100; Maryland State Poetry Soc. (charter member); Asst. Editor, Stanz Mag., 1941-43; Nat. Soc. of Poetry, Inc. (vice pres., 1941); Soc. of American Poets (Baltimore), since 1940. Published works: By Candlelight, 1948; The Boneyard Dance (an operetta), 1966; The Glory Flag Forever, 1972. Contbr. to: Rainbow; Baltimore News-Post; Maryland Gazette; Brooklyn News; The Songs of the Free State Bards, etc. Awards: Francis Scott Key Award, 1970; 3rd prize for Mason sonnet, 1970; 1st prize for Sonnet to Spring, 1970; Maria Brisbane Croker Award, 1971, 1972. The Lizette Woodworth Reese Award, 1969; Mason Sonnet, 1st Prize, 1970; Emily Dickinson Award, 1972, also 3rd Prize, Mason Sonnet Poem; Cert. of Commendation, NY Poet's Press, 1940. Address: 3827 Roland Ave., Baltimore, MD 21211, USA.

STRINGER, David Allan, pen name **BLUNDEN, David,** b. 13 Aug. 1944. Gardener. Education: currently, course in Film/Theatre & TV, Bradford Regional Coll. of Art & Technol. Poetry readings over past six years in pubs, cafes, schls., colls. mainly in the North of England & Midlands & also ran poetry clubs in Leeds & Manchester; Exhibiting Painter & playwrite (radio & film scripts). Has researched & printed works of unknown nineteenth century poets & is currently engaged in translating the French works of African poets. Memberships: Yorks. Poets' Assn.; Fellow, Int. Poetry Soc.; Assn. of Little Presses. Published works: New Songs for an Old North (pamphlet), 1965; By Fires & Waters (booklet), 1966; In the Land of the

Gorsedd Bard & Ballad of Fowey, (booklet), 1973; England, Drumflowers & Sunsongs, (pamphlet), 1973; Ecstacies & Excorcisms, (book), 1974. Co-Ed., North Eastern Artists Directory. Contbr. to; Second Aeon; Cornish Review; Phoenix; Int. Poetry Soc. Anthol.; Ludd's Mill; Platform; Global Tapestry; Roots; Ostrich; Hapt; Breakthrough; Firebird; Albion. Address: c/o The Bookshop, Univ. Annexe, 153 Woodhouse Ln., Leeds 2, Yorks., U.K.

STRMEN, Karol, b. 9 Apr. 1921. Poet; Translator; Educator. Education: grad. studies at the Slovak Univ. in Bratislava, Czechoslovakia; Ph.D., Case Western Univ., Cleveland, Ohio, 1966. Positions held: Bd. Mbr., Instituto Slovacco (Cleveland – Rome); Bd. Mbr., Slovak Writers & Artists Assn. Memberships: Société Paul Claudel; PEN Club, Writers in Exile Sect. Published works incl: Vyzinok zivota (Partial Harvest), poems, 1943; Strieborna legenda (The Silver Legend), poems, 1949; Cakaju nivy jar (The Meadows Await the Spring), poems, 1964; Znamenie Ryby (The Sign of the Fish), 1969. Translations: Dante, Novy zivot (Vita nova), 1942; Rainer Maria Rilke, Obraz na vazach (Vasenbild), an anthol., 1942; Novy zakon (The New Testament), 1954; Dante, Peklo (Inferno), 1965; Paul Claudel, Dobre slovo (A Kind Word), an anthol., 1968; Rainer Maria Rilke, Stvorversia z Valais, Ruze, Obloky (Les Quatrains valaisans, Les Roses, Les Fenêtres), 1972; Navstevy (Visits), an anthol. of world poetry, vol. 2, 1972. In prep: Petrarch, an anthol. Contbr. to: Most, qtly. for Slovak Culture; Slovenske pohlady, Bratislava. Honours, awards: Chevalier dans l'ordre des Palmes Academiques. Address: The Cleveland State Univ., Cleveland, OH 44115, U.S.A.

STROH, Ruth Kathryn, pen names **APRIL, Ruth & ALLEN, Mary,** b. 9 Apr. 1927. Teacher; Artist; Musician. Education: State Tchrs. Coll.; Johns Hopkins Univ., U.S.A. Positions held: Elem. Tchr., 1949-55; Freelance Writer, 1955-63; H.S. Substitute Tchr., 1963-73. Mbr., Soc. of Am. Poets. Published works: Bluephony – The Blue Book of Verse, 1966. Contbr. to: Va. Wildlife; Am. Rose Mag.; Christian Publications; Pen Mag. Honours, awards: Gold Medal, Soc. of Am. Poets, Baltimore, Md., 1957; many prizes from Writers Unlimited, Int. Poetry Lit. Comp. Address: 600 Sherwood Rd., Cockeysville, MD 21030, U.S.A.

STROIK, Kathy Bremmer, b. 26 Oct. 1946. Domestic Engineer. Education: Eau Claire State Univ., Wis., 1 yr Married Thomas F. Stroik, 2 children. Member, Wis. Fellowship of Poets. Address: Box 5, Amherst Junction, WI 54407, U.S.A.

STROM, Carl-Erik, b. 25 July 1938. Decorator. Education: Middle Schl., autodidact as Writer. Member., Soc. of Swedish Authors in Finland. Published works: Tre (with Börje Ahlö & Dan Sundell), 1968; I Molnmuseet, 1971. Address: Thurmansallen 4 B 10, 02700 Grankulla, Finland.

STROMSTED (Stabell), Finn (Chr), b. 9 June 1925. Author. Education: Examen artium, engelsk-linjen; Art Schl. (S.H.K.S.). Married, 2 children. Memberships: Den Norske Forfatterforening; Norsk Forfattersenter; Norske grafikere; U.K.S. (Young Artists Soc.). Published works: Angelicafloyten, 1956; Bidevind, 1961; Meridianer, 1967; Ferdaskrin, 1969; Susquehanna Blues, 1971; Noe Gront I Melkeveien, 1973; Nakkul & Lainit (Lappic adventures, selected, w. Prof. Quigstad & Prof. Manker). Contbr. to: Dagbladet; Arbeiderbladet; Aftenposten; Scandinavian Review; Vinduet; Samtiden; Minerva; Syn og Segn; Forfatteren. Honours, awards: Reisestipendium, Italy; Statens tre-arige arbeidsstipend, 6 yrs.; Oppholdsstp., 1 month; Mads Nygaards Legat (Aschehoug forlag); Statens 3-arige arbeids-stip. Address: Kalvosund, Staubo 4920, Norway.

STRONG, Eithne, b. 28 Feb. 1923. Journalist; Student. Educ: Trinity Coll., Dublin, Ireland, current. m. Rupert Strong, 9 children. Published works: Songs of Living, 1961. Contbr. to: An Glor; Comhar. Address: 17 Eaton Sq., Monkstown, Dublin, Ireland.

STRONG, Julia Hurd, b. 14 Aug. 1908. Poet. Education: Grad., Rice Univ. Married T.A. Strong, 1 daughter. Memberships: Poetry Soc. of Am.; Pres., Owen Wister Lit. Soc. Alumnae of Rice Univ.; Councillor, Poetry Soc. of Tex.; Past Pres., Houston Chapt., Poetry Soc. of Tex.; San Jacinto Chapt., ibid; many other cultural & histl. socs. Published works: Postlude to Mendelssohn, 1964. Contbr. to: The Sat. Evening Post; Good Housekeeping; Christian Sci. Monitor; Catholic Home Jrnl.; The N.E.A. Jrnl.; The Christian Home; The Houston Press; Highlights for Children; Children's Activities; The Golden Year Anthol., Poetry Soc. of Am. & num. other anthols. such as Treasured Memories (Our Baby) & From Little to Big, 1972. Honours, awards: Between 1953 & 73 won 39 first pl. awards in the annual contests of the Poetry Soc. of Tex.; recip., prizes in contests of Poetry Soc. of Ga., Poetry Soc. of N.C., Poets Roundtable of Ark., etc. Address: 3740 Rice Blvd., Houston, TX 77005, U.S.A.

STRONG, Rupert, b. 10 May 1911. Psychoanalyst. Education: Westminster School; Trinity Coll., Dublin. Published works: Jonathan of Birkenhead and Other Poems, 1953; From Inner Fires, 1962; Poems of The Ordinary, 1967; The Challenger, 1968. Contbr. to: Surge; Pulse; Tidings; Runa Press Poetry Quartos; Hayden Murphy's Broadsheet; New Ireland Arts Lab. publications; Dublin Mag.; Faith & Freedom. Address: 17 Eaton Sq., Monkstown, Dublin, Ireland.

STRUGHOLD, Mary Webb, b. 12 July 1914. Poet. Education: Coll. of Indl. Arts, Denton, Tex.; San Antonio Coll. Married 1) Terry Dalehite, 3 daughters, 2) Dr. Hubertus Strughold. Positions held: worked for U.S. Air Force, 23 years, during which time was a Public Information Specialist & Writer for 17 yrs. Wrote many articles on aircraft, engines, aerospace ground equipment & accessories, nuclear projects, engrng., etc. while carrying out assignment at Kelly AFB. Memberships: Poetry Soc. of San Antonio; Am. League of Poetry; Chmn., Courtesy Comm., Poetry Soc. of San Antonio; Histn., Kelly Mgmt. Club; Sec., San Antonio Chapt., Am. Inst. of Astronautical & Aeronautical Scis. Contbr. to: Poetry Soc. of San Antonio Mag. Honours, awards: 2nd prize for poem 'My Lonely River' & 1st prize for poem 'Thanksgiving Meditation', Poetry Soc. of San Antonio, 1972. Address: 202 East Mayfield, San Antonio, TX 78214, U.S.A.

STRUTHERS, Dorothy M., pen name **MAIZE, Zea**, b. 10 Apr. 1900. Teacher; Librarian. Education: B.A., Eastern Ill Univ.; grad. work, Univ. of Mich., Northwestern Univ. & Univ. of Ill. Married Robert D. Struthers. Positions held: Tchr. of Elem. Schls., Jr. H.S's, H.S. & H.S. Libn., 30 yrs.; ret'd 1960; Bible Tchr., 45 yrs. Memberships: Pres., V.P., Treas., Mattoon Br. of Nat. League of Am. Pen Women; V.P., Phoenix Writers' Club; Ariz. State Poetry Soc.; Am. Poets Fellowship Soc.; Am. Poetry League; Centro Studi e Scambi Int.; Ill. State Poetry Soc.; World Poetry Soc. Intercontinental; Major Poets. Contbr. to: (anthols.) From Sea to Sea in Song, 1966, '67, '68, '69, '70, '72; Melodies From a Jade Harp, 1968; Jewels on a Willow Tree, 1966; Stepping Stones to Faith, 1967; Sing Naked Spirit, 1970; Prize Poems of Nat. Fed. of State Poetry Socs., 1972, etc.; (mag., jrnls.) Prairie Poet; Am. Bard; Haiku Highlights; The Poet; Denver Post, etc. Recip. var. poetry hons. & awards inclng: Merit Cit., Dr. Etta Josephean Murfey Mem-anth, United Poets Laureate Int., 1967; 1st pl., Nat. Fed. of State Poetry Socs., 1972. Address: Box 182, Humboldt, IL 61931, U.S.A.

STRYK, Lucien, b. 7 Apr. 1924. Teacher. Education: B.A., Ind. Univ.; MFA, Univ. of Iowa. Married, 2 children; Positions held: Prof., Engl., Northern Ill. Univ.; Vis. Lectr., Japan; Lectr., Writers Confs., Ill., Ky. & Minn.; Gives numerous poetry readings & talks. Published works: Taproot, 1953; The Trespasser, 1956; Co-Author, Zen: Poems, Prayers, Sermons, Anecdotes, Interviews, 1965; Notes for a Guidebook, 1965; Ed., Heartland: Poets of the Midwest, 1967; Ed.,

World of Buddha, 1969; The Pit & Other Poems, 1969; Co-Translator, Afterimages: Zen Poems of Shinkichi Takahashi, 1971. Contbr. of poems, translations & essays to numerous periodicals & anthols. Honours, Awards: Jt. Recip., 1st Prize, Chicago Daily News, New Chicago Poem Competition; Isaac Rosenbaum Poetry Award, Voices; Nat. Translation Ctr. Grants w. Takashi Ikemoto; New Poetry Series Award; Grove Press Fellowship; Antioch Writing Seminar; Worksheet Collection, Lockwood Mem. Lib., Univ. of Buffalo; Manuscrip Collection, Moger Mem. Lib. Boston Univ.; Asia Soc. Grant, Yale Univ.; Ford Fndn. Fac. Fellowship, Univ. of Chicago; Excellence in Tchng. Award, Northern Ill. Univ.; Fulbright Lectrship., Iran. Address: c/o Doubleday & Co., 277 Park Ave., New York, NY 10017, USA.

STUART, Alice Vandockum, b. 16 Dec. 1899. Poet. Education: Somerville Coll., Oxford Univ., U.K. Positions held: Tchr. of Engl., Schls. in England & Scotland; Examiner in Postal Censorship, 1940-41; Tchr. of Engl. to foreign students, 1941-45; Tutor in Engl. Poetry, Edinburgh Coll. of Speech & Drama, 1945-48. Memberships: Soc. of Authors; Scottish Ctr. Int. PEN; Scottish Assn. for the Speaking of Verse; Hon. Mbr., Soc. of Tchrs. of Speech & Drama; V.P., Edinburgh Musical Fest. Assn. Published works: The Far Calling, 1944; The Dark Tarn, 1953; The Door Between, 1963; The Unquiet Tide, 1971; David Gray the Poet of the Luggie, 1961; Selected Poems, Plantaganet Prods. Recorded Lib., 1969. Contbr. to: Burns Chronicle; Country Life; Chambers' Jrnl.; The Cornhill; The Contemp. Review; The Fortnightly; Glasgow Herald: Hibbert Jrnl.; Life & Work; New Athenian Broadsheet; Poetry Review; Punch; Scottish Prizewinning Poems 1957-58; Scotland's Mag.; The Scotsman; The Scots Review; The Scottish Field; The Stewarts; The Tablet; & the anthol. The Oxford Book of Scottish Verse, 1966. Recip., Lilian Bowes Lyon Award, Poetry Soc., 1955 & Premium Award, 1966. Address: 57 Newington Rd., Edinburgh EH9 1QW, U.K.

STUART, Dabney, b. 4 Nov. 1937. University Professor. Education: A.B., Davidson Coll., N.C., U.S.A., 1960; A.M., Harvard Univ., Cambridge, Mass., 1962. Married, 2 sons. Positions held: Instr. in Engl., Coll. of Wm. & Mary, Williamsburg, Va., 1961-65; Instr. in Engl., Wash. & Lee Univ., Lexington, Va., 1965-66; Asst. Prof. of Engl., ibid, 1966-68; Vis. Prof. of Engl., Middlebury Coll., Middlebury, Vt., 1968-69; Assoc. Prof., Wash. & Lee Univ., 1969–; Poetry Ed. of Shenandoah, 1966–. Memberships: AAUP; Authors Guild of Am. Published works: The Diving Bell, 1966; A Particular Place, 1969; Modern Poets in Focus, vol. 3, 1972. Rep. in sev. anthols. inclng: Of Poetry & Power, 1964; Southern Writing in the Sixties, 1967; Southern Poetry Review: A Decade of Poems, 1969; Best Poems of 1968, vol. 21; N.Y. Times Book of Verse, 1970; The New Yorker Book of Poems, 1969; The Diamond Anthology, 1971; Contemporary Poetry in Am., 1973. Contbr. to: The New Yorker; The Southwest Review; Red Clay Reader; Am. Review; Ohio Review; Pebble; Southern Poetry Review; Jeopardy; N.Y. Times, etc. Honours, awards: Howard Willett Rsch. Prize, Coll. of Wm. & Mary, 1963; Dylan Thomas Prize, PSA, 1964, etc. Address: 331 Enfield Rd., Lexington, VA 24450, U.S.A.

STUART, Jesse Hilton, b. 8 Aug. 1907. Teacher; Lecturer; Farmer; Writer. Education: B.A., Lincoln Meml. Univ., 1929; grad. work, Vanderbilt Univ., 1931-32. Positions held: Tchr., Greenup Co. Schls., 1929–; H.S. Tchr.; Greenup Co. H.S., Prin., later Supt., Greenup City Schl., until 1937; Portsmouth H.S., Ohio, 1938-39; Univ. of Indiana, 1940; summers at Morehead State Coll., 1947, 48, 49; Prin., McKell H.S., 1956-57; Univ. of Nev., 1959; Am. Univ. in Cairo, 1960-61; worked for the USIS, Right Arm of State Dept. in Dual Professions, Tchng. & Creative Writing, in Egypt, Greece, Lebanon, Iran, W. Pakistan, Bangladesh, The Philippines, Taiwan & Korea. Member, W.Va. & Ky. Poetry Socs. Published works: Harvest of Youth, 1930; Man with a Bull-Tongue Plow, 703 sonnets,

1934; Album of Destiny, 1944; Kentucky Is My Land, 1952; Hold April, 1962. Contbr. to approx. 400 mags. in U.S.A. & abroad. Honours, awards incl: Poet Laureate of Ky., 1954; Acad. of Am. Poets Award, 1961. Address: W-Hollow, Greenup, KY 41144, U.S.A.

STUBBE, Anne, b. 13 Mar. 1911. Housewife. Education: Univ. of Wis. Co. Ctr., Schl. of Arts, Rhinelander, Wis. Married Ervin Stubbe, 3 children. Positions held: Treas. & Sec., Wis. Valley Art Assn. of Wausau, Wis. Memberships: Bd. Dirs., Wis. Regl. Writers Assn.; Chmn., Jadering Contest Comm., ibid; Chmn., Poetry Contest, Wausau Fest. of Arts, –1973. Rep. in following anthols: Wis. Harvest, 1967; Wis. Fellowship of Poets, nos. II & III, 1968 & 69; num. smaller anthols. Contbr. to: Mnpls. Argus; Green Bay Press-Gazette; Jeans Jrnl.; Encore; Haiku Highlights; Janus; Prairie Poet, etc. Honours, awards: 1st pl., Jade Ring Poetry Contest, 1965; 2nd pl., Nat. Fellowship of Poets; Limerick Contest, 1967; 3rd pl., Poetry, ibid, 1970, etc. Address: 905 So. 6th Ave., Wausau, WI 54401, U.S.A.

STUDEBAKER, William Vern, b. 21 May 1947. Educator. Education: B.A., Hist., Idaho State Univ., 1970; M.A., Engl., ibid, 1971; Ethel E. Redfield Academic Scholarship, Spring 1970. Married Judy K. Infanger, 1 daughter. Positions held: Tchng. Assoc., Idaho State Univ., 1970-71; Instr. of Engl., Coll. of Southern Idaho, 1972–. Member, World Poetry Soc. Intercontinental. Published works: Earthday Broadsheet, 'I am God', 1970. Contbr. to: Iota; Rendezvous; Trukin' Home; Dragonfly; Poet; Ecolit. Address: 451 5th Avenue North, Twin Falls, ID 83301, U.S.A.

STUMP, Doris Joyce, pen name **CORTI, Doris,** b. 29 Dec. 1928. Housewife. Education: Havering Coll. of Further Educ. (night schl.) Married, 2 sons. Positions held: Sec. to a Buyer in City firm of Importers; worked for Merchant Bankers; currently p/t Sec., Brentwood. Memberships: Former Asst. Sec., Brentwood Writers' Circle; London Writers' Circle & Poetry Group. Published works: (book of poems) Shutters of the Mind, 1971. Contbr. to: Viewpoints Mag.; Hambros Merchant Bankers Mag.; Brentwood Gazette; St. Thomas Church Mag.; Cinque Port Poets, 1974. Address: 4 Gerrard Cres., Brentwood, Essex, U.K.

STURMER, Wava Regina, b. 2 Oct. 1929. Author. Education: Jakobstads samlyceum; Vasa Handelsinstitut. Married Ake J.F. Stürmer, 2 children (Ditte & Petra). Memberships: Chmn., Svenska Osterbottens Litteraturförening; Bd. Mbr., Finlands Dramatikerförbund. Published works: (books of poetry) Bevingad vardag, 1955; Därför att ljuset, 1967; Det är ett helvete att mala himlar, 1970; Möta en människa, 1973. Contbr. to: Vasabladet, Horisont, Nya Argus & Parnasso, Finland; Ord och Bild, Sweden. Address: Pedersespl. 12, 68 620 Jakobstad 2, Finland.

STYLE, Colin Thomas Elliot, b. 3 Aug. 1937. Marketing & Market Research Manager. Education: Rhodes Univ., Grahamstown. Married, 1 daughter. Positions held: Exec. Off., Dept. Labour, Rsch. & Statistics, Rhodesian Govt., 1960-63; Market Rsch. Officer, Lever Bros. (Rhodesia) Ltd., 1963-67; Marketing & Market Rsch. Mgr., Commercial Television Ltd., 1968–. Co-Ed., Chirimo, int. jrnl. of the Humanities. Co-Producer, 'Rhodesian Poets', (recording of readings of Rhodesian Poetry). Editl. Cons. Contemporary Poets of the Engl. Lang. Memberships: Chmn., Poetry Soc. of Rhodesia, 1972; PEN. Rep. in following anthols: Poetry in Rhodesia – 75 Years, 1968; Beneath a Rhodesian Sky, 1972. Contbr. to var. periodicals inclng: Outposts; The Contemporary Review; The Cornhill; Stand; Poesie Vivante; Contrast; New Nation; Standpunte; The Christian Science Monitor; Poetry Australia; Dalhousie Review. Honours, awards: Rhodian Poetry Prize, 1956; New Nation's Poet of the Month, Jan. 1969. Address: P.O. Box A 294, Avondale, Salisbury, Rhodesia.

SUDRABKAIN, Ian Karlovich, b. 1894. Poet. Positions held: Mbr., Central Comm., Latvian CP; Dpty., USSR Supreme Soviet. Published works: Lantern To The Wind, 1942; Food For The Road, 1944; Family of Brothers, 1947; Swallows Return, 1951; Collected Works (5 vols.), 1959-60. Awards: State Prizewinner, 1948; People's Poet of the Latvian SSR; Order of Lenin. Address: c/o Writers' Union of Latvia, Riga, Latvia, USSR.

SUKNASKI, Andrew, b. 31 July 1942. Poet. Education: studied at Univ. of Victoria, Univ. of B.C., Notre Dame Univ. of Nelson, & Simon Fraser Univ., all Canada; studied Fine Arts at Kootenay Schl. of Art, Nelson & at Schl. of Art & Design, Montreal Mus. of Fine Arts; Dip. in Fine Arts, Kootenay Schl. of Art. Currently Ed. of two small presses & mags: Anak Press & Elfin Plot, dealing with expmtl. poetry; also Sundog Press & Sundog, dealing with straight poetry. Published works: The Shadow of Eden Once, 1970; Circles, 1970; In Mind of Xrossroads of Mythologies, 1971; Rose Way in the East, 1972; Old Mill, 1972; The Nightwatchman, 1972; The Zen Pilgrimage, 1972; Y The Evolution into Ruenz, 1972; Four Parts Sand (w. others), 1972; Wood Mountain Poems, 1973; Suicide Notes, Book One, 1973; Phillip Well, 1973; Leaving, 1974; These Fragments I've Gathered for Ezra, 1974; On First Looking Down from Lion's Gate Bridge, 1974. Contbr. to var. poetry mags. Concrete Poetry has appeared at: EXPO 1969 in Buenos Aires; EXPO Internacional de Proposiciones a Realizar, Buenos Aires, 1971 & Exposicion Exhaustiva de la Nueva Poesia/Galeria U, Montevideo, Feb-Mar., 1972. Address: Wood Mountain, Sask., Canada.

SULLIVAN, Nancy. Teacher. Education: B.A., Hunter Coll.; M.A., Univ. of R.I.; Ph.D., Univ. of Conn. Positions held: Member, Dept. of Engl., Brown Univ., 1955-62; Dept. of Engl., Rhode Island College, 1962–. Published works: The History of the World as Pictures (poems), 1965; Perspective and the Poetic Process, 1969; Body English, 1972. Contbr. to many American magazines. Recip. Devins Award for Poetry, 1965. Address: Hillsdale Rd., West Kingston, RI 02892, USA.

SULLIVAN, Patricia Ann, b. 21 Jan. 1949. Secretary. Positions held: Filing Clerk, 1967; Acctg. Clerk, 1967-69; Bookkeeping & Acctg. Clerk, 1969-73; Bookkeeping & Acctg. Clerk & Sec. to Treas., a Savings & Loan, 1973–. Memberships: Poetry & Patrons in Chicago; Ill. State Poetry Soc. Contbr. to: Am. Poet; Prairie Poet; United Poet. Recip., 1st Prize in 'Dramatic Monologue', Poets & Patrons Contest in Chicago, 1973. Address: 832 So. Cuyler Ave., Oak Park, IL 60304, U.S.A.

SUMMERS, Henry Forbes, pen name **SUMMERS, Hal,** b. 18 Aug. 1911. Retired Government Official. Education: Trinity Coll., Oxford Univ., U.K. Married Rosemary Roberts, 2 sons, 1 daughter. Positions held: Under Sec., Min. of Housing & Local Govt. & Dept. of the Environment, London, 1955-71. Mbr., PEN. Published works: Smoke After Flame, 1944; Hinterland, 1947; Poems in Pamphlet, 1951. Contbr. to The Listener, 1942-63. Address: Folly Fields, Linden Gardens, Tunbridge Wells, Kent TN2 5QU, U.K.

SUMMERS, Hollis Spurgeon, Jr., b. 21 June 1916. Teacher of English. Education: A.B., Georgetown Coll., Ky., U.S.A., 1937; M.A., Breadloaf Schl. of Engl. Middlebury Coll., Vt., 1943; Ph.D., State Univ. of Iowa, 1949. Positions held: Tchr. of Engl., Holmes H.S., Covington, Ky.; Georgetown Coll., Ky. & Univ. of Ky. at Lexington; currently at Ohio Univ., Athens. Memberships: Poetry Soc. of Am.; Am. Assn. of Poetry; MLA. Published works: The Walks Near Athens, 1959; Someone Else, Sixteen Poems About Other Children, 1962; Seven Occasions, 1965; The Peddler & Other Domestic Matters, 1967; Sit Opposite Each Other, 1970; Start From Home, 1972; also author of five novels & ed. of three colls.; Short Story coll., 1973. Contbr. to: Poetry; The Antioch Review; Ky Writing; The Va. Quarterly Review; The Beloit Poetry Jrnl.; The New Orleans Poetry Jrnl.; Epos;

Promenade; Accent; Views; The Sewanee Review; Saturday Review; N.Y. Herald Tribune; The Am. Scholar; Prairie Schooner; The Humanist; N.M. Quarterly, etc. Honours, awards: Hon. LL.D., Georgetown Coll.; Sat. Review's Poetry Award, 1957; Danforth Lectr. in Poetry at var. univs. & colls. Address: 181 N. Congress St., Athens, OH 45701, U.S.A.

SUMMERS, John Arthur Campbell, b. 27 Dec. 1916. Bookseller. Education: 2 terms, Otago Univ., New Zealand. Positions held: Farm Hand; Taxi Office; Builder's Labourer; Window Cleaner; Sub Ed.; Religious Jrnl.; Shop Asst., Bookshop; Own Business, 1958–. Published works: Seven for Strings, 1967; Letters to Joe, 1967; Hymns E 6 O.E., Strictly for the Words, 1974. Contbr. to: N.Z. Listener; Argot; Comment; Poet; Frontiers; Dispute; Edge; Poetry N.Z. (a Bienniel N.Z. Anthol.); Meanjin, Australia; Karaki, Canada; Second Coming; etc. Runner up for Wellington Fest. Prize, 1973. Address: John Summers Bookshop, 119 Manchester St., Christchurch, New Zealand.

SUNDARESAN, Ramamurthy, pen names **SUNDARESAN, R. & SUNDAR, R.,** b. 18 Aug. 1935. Radio Newsreel Assistant. Education: B.A., 1955. Positions held: Asst. in Annamalai Univ., S. India, 1956-62; Reporter for Indian Express, 1962-64: P.A. to Mgr. of a Madras firm, 1965-68; Newsreel Asst., All India Radio, Madras, 1968–. Memberships: Srinvasa Sastri Inst. of Pub. Affairs; World Poetry Soc. Intercontinental; Poetry Workshop, Madras; Toastmasters Club, Madras; Youth Forum, Madras. Contbr. of articles to: Mysindia, 1962; Sunday Standard, 1963; Newsman, 1970, '71 & '72; Yuva Bharati, 1973; Student Telegraph, 1962, '63 & '64. Published a pamphlet on Mr. Kamaraj, 1967. Contbr. of poems to: Poet; Mirror; Youthfare; Yuva Bharati. Has broadcast poems from All India Radio, Madras sev. times. Participant, All-India Poets Meet, Madras, 1973. Address: 30 Sundararajan St., Abhiramapuram, Madras 600018, India.

SUOMI, Maila Annikki, b. 9 June 1931. Freelance Author. Education: The Finnish Normal Lyzeum for Girls, Helsinki, 1951; studied folklore, psychology, genetics, Univ. of Helsinki, Finland. Married Kaarlo Olavi Suomi, 2 children (Riiko & Karolus). Member, The Finnish Soc. of Authors. Published works: Klassilliset tunteet (The Classical Feelings), 1957; Jeesuksen kylä (The Village of Jesus), 1958; Arvo (The Value), 1959; Ilmaa (Ear), 1960; Kaikuu (It's Echoing), 1960; Valta (The Power), 1962; Virheitä (Errors), 1965; Tarina tappelusta (Tale about a Fight), 1969; Muistista (About Remembering), 1972. Contbr. to: Parnasso; The Finnish Lit. Rdr.; Uuden runon kauneimmat, anthol., 1968; Suomen lyriikkaa tanään (Lyrics in Finland Today, Finnish-Swedish), 1969; The Lit. Review, N.J., U.S.A., 1970. Recip., Prize of State, Finland, 1973. Address: Haapasaarentie 2 C 1, 00960 Helsinki 96, Finland.

SURE, Ethel, b. 29 May 1905. Retired Businesswoman. Married Prof. Barnett Sure, 1 daughter, Charmian. Memberships: Altrusa Int., Inc.; Pres., twice, ibid; Nat. League of Am. Penwomen; League of Women Voters; Poetry Soc. of Tex.; Past Pres., Ark. Writers & Artists; Past Bd. Mbr., Bus. & Profl. Women, Houston, Tex. Collected, edited & sold book "Ozarks Folk Literature" to Pageant Press, N.Y.C. Contbr. to following: Handsel, Lexington, Ky.; Poet Int., India; Encore, N.M.; Cycloflame, Tex.; Poems From the Hills, 1971; Poetry Dial, Ark.; N.M. Mag., Albuquerque; Better Verse, Mont.; Skylines poetry mag.; Bozart-Westminster, Ga.; Prospect; Poetry Soc. Yr. Book, 1970; Ballet on the Wind (book), 1970; Sing Naked Spirit (book), 1971; Southwest Heritage (collaborated w. Dr. T. M. Pearce & Mabel Mason), 1972; The Villager, N.Y.C.; Dance Mag., N.Y.; Gen. Motors nat. trade publ.; Progressive Farmer mag.; Rexall Drug "Hometown" mag.; Phoenix Fires, Ariz.; Tulsa World newspaper; Ark. Gazette; Ark. Democrat; Kan. City Star; Boston Transcript; W. L.A.

Indep., Calif. Address: 844 W. Osborn Rd., Phoenix, AZ 85013, U.S.A.

SURKOV, Alexei Alexandrovich, b. 1899. Poet. Education: Inst. of Red Profs., Moscow. Positions held: Alternative Mbr., Central Comm., CPSU, 1956; 1st Sec., Writers' Union of the USSR, til 1959; Sec., ibid., 1959–; Pres., USSR-Great Britain Soc., 1958–; Dpty., USSR Supreme Soviet. Published works: Let's Sing, 1930; Peace to the World, 1950; Moscow Is At Our Backs; Flame Beats In The Small Stove; Victory!; Collected Works (2 vols.), 1954, '59; Songs of Mankind; Bullet Is Frightened By Brave Man, 1964; The Voice of Time, 1965; Relay Race of Friendship, 1968. Awards: State Prizewinner, 1946, '51; Order of Lenin; Red Banner; Red Star; Badge of Honour; Hero of Socialist Labour; Gold Medal 'Hammer & Sickle'. Address: cSUSTER, Gerald, b. 2 Aug. 1951. Undergraduate. Education: Trinity Hall., Cambridge Univ., 1970–. Memberships: Sec.-Chmn., The Scribblers Club; Dir., The Meber Film Grp.; C.U. Engl. Club. Contbr. to: The Scribblers Mag. (poetry & articles); The Cholmleian; The Flying Dragon Book of Poetry, 1972. Address: 25B Frognal, London NW3, U.K.

SUSTER, Gerald, b. 2 Aug. 1951. Undergraduate. Education: Trinity Hall., Cambridge Univ., 1970–. Memberships: Sec.-Chmn., The Scribblers Club; Dir., The Meber Film Grp.; C.U. Engl. Club. Contbr. to: The Scribblers Mag. (poetry & articles); The Cholmleian; The Flying Dragon Book of Poetry, 1972. Address: 25B Frognal, London NW3, U.K.

SUTCLIFFE, Pavella Dolores, pen name **PLOUGHMAN, Nina.** Secretary & Freelance Writer. Education: Ladies Coll., Harrogate; Medical studies in Sheffield & Doncaster. Married, 1 son, 1 daughter. Positions held: Hospital Staff; Sec. in Air Ministry; Liaison Officer, RAF-USAAF. Memberships: Lancashire Authors' Assn.; Hon. Sec., Preston Poets' Soc., 1960-71; Former Mbr., Preston Writers' Circle & Cleveleys Poets' Circle; Social Sec., Preesall W.I.; Sec., Ladies' Forum, Preesall U.R. Church. Contbr. to: Reflections, Preston Poets' Soc., 1972; 'Twixt Thee & Me', 1973; poems in var. edns. of poems published by Preston Poets' Soc.; local papers; BBC; Sunday Companion; My Weekly; Homes & Gardens, etc. Honours, awards: Four awards, Preston Poets' Soc. Annual Comps., 1965-73; First Prize for Poetry, Preston Writers' Circle, 1968; First Prize for Short Story & Second Prize for Poetry, ibid, 1969. Address: Sea Winds, 22 Lune View, Knott End On Sea, Fylde Coast, Lancs. FY6 0AG, U.K.

SUTHERLAND, Robert Garioch, pen name, **GARIOCH, Robert,** b. 9 May 1909. Retired School Teacher. Education: 3rd class hons. Engl., Univ. of Edinburgh. Published works: 17 Poems for 6d, 1940; Chuckles on the Cairn, 1949; The Masque of Edinburgh, 1954; George Buchanan's 'Gepbthah' & 'The Baptist' translated in Scots, 1959; Selected Poems, 1966; The Big Music, 1971; Doktor Faust in Rose Street, 1973. Address: 4 Nelson Street, Edinburgh 3, U.K.

SUTTON, David John, b. 19 May 1944. Computer Programmer. Education: M.A., Anglo-Saxon, Corpus Christi, Cambridge Univ., UK. Married, 1 s. Published works: Out on a Limb, 1969. Address: 93 Blagrove Drive, Wokingham, Berks., UK.

SUTTON, Louise Weibert, b. 22 Apr. 1920. Homemaker. Poetry Judge for var. publs., 1958–. Memberships: Nat. Amateur Press Assn.; Past Poetry Adviser for sev. small poetry mags. Published works: Through Lens Of Poetry, 1968; Songs From the April Hills, 1969; The Voice of Verse, 1969; A Pen of Stars, 1970; The Emerald Quill, 1970; A treasure of Poetry (pending). Contbr. to: Ideals Publs.; Cats Mag.; Canadian Pet Mag.; Gospel Trumpet; Jean's Jrnl. of Poetry; Tower Press Publs.; Reflections; NAPA Publs.; Northwest Farmer (Songs From The Fields); Kindness Club Columns (Canada); Gems of Faith; The Evangel;

local newspapers. Honours, awards: 3rd pl., Nat. Religious Poetry Award, 1967; NAPA & UAPAA Awards for outstanding poetry, 1968; Lone Indian, Eagle-Feather Awards for poetry, 1960-68, etc. Address: 203 S. Bosse Ave., Evansville, IN 47712, U.S.A.

SUTTON, Peter John, b. 1 Aug. 1942. Teacher. Education: Bretton Hall Coll. of Educ. Positions held: Chmn., Producer, Actor, Retford Little Theatre; Teacher. Memberships: Comm. Mbr., Retford Music Club; Treas., Retford Amateur Music Group; Sec. Retford Poetry Group; Nottingham Poetry Soc.; Poetry Soc., London; Life Mbr., Engl. Speaking Bd.; Labour Party; Retford & Dist. Hist. & Archaeol. Soc.; Robin Hood Theatre, Averham, Notts.; Nottingham Playhouse Club; UN Assoc.; British Drama League; Nat. Assoc. of Tchrs. of Engl.; Soc. of Tchrs. of Speech & Drama. Address: 119, Northfield Way, Hallcroft, Retford, Notts.

SUTZKEVER, Abraham, b. 15 July 1913. Editor. Married, 2 daughters. Positions held: Ed., 'Di Goldene Keyt'. Memberships: PEN Club; Assn. of Yiddish Writers, Israel; Israel Soc. of Editors of Periodicals. Published works: Lider, 1937; Valdiks, 1940; Di Festung, 1945; Lider fun Getto, 1946; Yidishe gass, 1948; Geheynishtot, 1948; In Fayerwoogn, 1952; Sibir, 1953; Ode tzu der Taib, 1955; In Uidber Sinai, 1957; Oazis, 1960; Gaystike erd, 1961; Poetishe werk, 1-2 vol., 1963; Lider fun Jam Hanioves, 1968; Firkantike Oisies an Mofsim, 1968; Tzaitike Perinuer, 1970; Di Fidlroizn, 1974. 'Sibir', poem transl. from the Yiddish, UNESCO, 1961. Contbr. to: Di Goldene Keyt Qtly. Honours, awards: J. Manpor Prize; J. Firhosuan Prize; Prize of Jewish Congress; Kessel Prize, Mexico; Prize of the 'Petite Parisienne'. Address: St. Moshe Sharet 20, Tel Aviv, Israel.

SUU, Thai Thi, pen name, **Mông Tuyêt Thât Tiêu muôi,** b. 19 Jan. 1914. Landlady. Education: Sec. Ed. Grad. Widow of Dong Ho (poet). Positions held in field of publishing. Membership: V.N. PEN Club. Published works: Forest Parfum, 1939; Spring Parfum; The Way to Hatien (novel), 1960; Miss Ai Co Story, 1961; Under the Moon (historical), 1969; Tender Chrysanthemum (poetry), 1974. Contbr. to: Bach Khoa; Van Hoc; Van; Van Hoa Tap San. Awards: Tu Luc Van Doan, 1939. Address: 328 Nguyen Minh Chieu, Saigon, Sth. Vietnam.

SVERDRUP, Harald Ulrik, b. 29 May 1923. Writer. Education: Oslo Univ., Norway; Wadham Coll., Oxford. Positions held: w. RAF, 1944-45; Sailor; Tchr.; Film Operator; Jrnlst.; Mbr. of Spitsbergen Expedition. Memberships: Assoc. Mbr. of Lit. Coun., Den Norske Forfatterforening; Norsk Forfattersentrum; Kunstnerforeningen. Published works: (books of poetry) Drøm og drift, 1948; Evig byggende Babel, 1949; Han finner sin elskede, 1953; Syngende natt, 1955; Sankt Elms ild, 1958; Snurrebassen (nonsense verse), 1958; Isbjørnfantasi, 1961; Sang til solen, 1964; Hvem er du (selected poems), 1966; Farlig vind, 1969; Fredløse ord, 1971; Kjaerlighet (selected love poems), 1973. Transl. into Norwegian: Selection of Dylan Thomas poems & his Portrait of the Artist as a Young Dog; Maxwell Anderson's Winterset; James Baldwin's The Fire Next Time. Contbr. to: Dagbladet; Arbeiderbladet; Aftenposten; Nationen; Bergens Tidende; Vinduet; The Lit. Review; Ord och Bild, etc. Recip., Norwegian Critic's Prize, 1958 & other awards. Address: 3160 Stokke, Norway.

SWAIM, Alice Mackenzie, b. 5 June 1911. Writer; Contest Judge; Critic. Education: Chatham Coll., Pitts., Pa., U.S.A.; Wilson Coll., Chambersburg, Pa.; pvte. writing instruction. Married William T. Swaim, 2 daughters. Positions held: Columnist, Cornucopia, 1953-55; Poetry Critic, Nat. Writers' Club, 1953-55; Columnist, Carlisle Evening Sentinel, 1956-70; Tejas Mag., 1968-70; Book Reviewer, Am. Poetry League, 1964–; Poetry Therapy Nat. Cons., 1970-73. Memberships: 1st V.P., Am. Poetry League,1964-70; P. R. Dir. for U.S., 2nd World Congress of Poets, 1973;

United Poets Laureate Int.; World Poetry Soc.; Poetry Soc. of Am.; Studi e Scambi Int.; Nat. Writers Club; Book Club for Poetry, U.K.; Acad. of Am. Poets; Pa. & N.H. Poetry Socs.; Poetry Therapy Assn.; N.Y. Poetry Forum; Idaho Writers' Guild; Calif. Chaparral; Avalon, etc. Published works: Up to the Stars, 1954; Let the Deep Song Rise, 1952; Sunshine in a Thimble, 1958; Poetry Calendar, 1960; Crickets are Crying Autumn, 1960; The Gentle Dragon, 1962; Pensylvania Profile, 1966; Scented Honeysuckle Days, 1966; Here on the Threshold, 1966; Beneath a Dancing Star, 1968; Beyond my Catnip Garden, 1970; many brochures. Contbr. to over 400 mags., jrnls., periodicals, newspapers etc. Recip. num. prizes for poetry & medals. Address: 322 N. 2nd St., Apt. 1606, Harrisburg, PA 17101, U.S.A.

SWAN, Jon. Editorial Staff. Educ: B.A., Oberlin Coll., Ohio. Positions held: Tchr., Boston Univ.; Mbr., Ed. Staff, The New Yorker, N.Y.C., 1956–. Published works: Journeys and Return: Poems, 1960. Contbr. to: American Scholar; Prairie Schooner; London Magazine; ·Poems and Poets (anthology), 1965. Address: c/o The New Yorker, 25 W. 43rd St., N.Y., NY 10036, U.S.A.

SWANK, Ann Dashner, pen name **SWANK, Ann Heffner,** b. 5 Dec. 1931. Housewife. Education: B.S., Okla. State Univ., 1953. Married David Swank, 1 son, 1 daughter. Member of Okla. Designer Craftsman (wall hangings & 3 dimensional weavings). Contbr. to Poet; Oklahoma Today. Address: 909 Timberdell Rd., Norman, OK 73069, U.S.A.

SWANN, Brian, b. 13 Aug. 1940. Assistant Professor. Education; Fndn. Scholar, Double 1st Engl. Tripos., Queens' Coll., Cambridge Univ., U.K.; Ph:D., Princeton Univ.; Proctor Fellow. Positions held: Asst. Mgr., Manchester Grammar Schl.; Instr.-Lectr., Asst. Prof., Princeton Univ., U.S.A.; Instr., Rutgers Univ.; Univ. of Ariz.; Univ. of Mass.; Asst. Prof., Humanities, The Cooper Union, N.Y.C., 1972-73. Mbr., Exec. Bd., PSA. Published works: The Collected Poems of Lucio Piccolo (co-ed. & translator), 1972; transl., Italian, Spanish, Rumanian, Old Norse Anglo-Saxon. Contbr. to: Poetry; Yale Review; Quarterly Review of Lit.; Beloit Poetry Jrnl.; Va. Quarterly Review; Prairie Schooner; Commonweal; N.Y. Times; N.Y. Quarterly; Univ. Review; Malahat Review; Lit. Review; Roanoke Review; Salmagundi; Aim; Southern Poetry Review; Southwest Review; Western Review; Western Humanities Review; Antaeus; Univ. Poetry 4; Granta; Delta; The Cambridge Review; New Directions Annual; Measure; The Nation; Boundary 2; Modern Poetry in Translation; Granite; The Little Mag.; Tex. Quarterly; Modern Poetry Studies; The Humanist; Partisan Review; Forum Italian; Chelsea; Voyages; etc. Address: 739 Washington St., N.Y., NY 10014, U.S.A.

SWANSON, Beda Elisabeth, b. 24 Mar. 1897. Housewife; Poet; Amateur Artist. Education: Bus. Coll.; Special Coll. Corres. Course; Ldrship. Trng. Courses. Married William Benjamin Swanson, 1 daughter. Positions held: Off. Sec. – Bookkeeper; Sunday Schl. Tchr.; Cradle Roll Supt.; Sunday Schl. Children's Prog. Dir. Memberships: Am. Poetry Fellowship Soc.; Iowa Poetry Day Assn.; Iowa Poetry Assn.; Centro Studi e Scambi, Italy; The Int. Poetry Soc. (England); Major Poets Chapt., PMA. Published works: Whispered Tones, 1970. Contbr. to: Davenport Daily Times; Davenport Times-Democrat; Jean's Jrnl.; Lyrical Iowa; Easter & Christmas Anthologies J.J.; Prairie Poet; Am. Poet; United Poets; Annual Brochure of Poems; Quaderni Di Poesia, Italy; N. Am. Mentor Mag.; The Central News; Young Pub. Echoes of Faith; Yearbook of Modern Poetry; Outstanding Contemporary Poetry 1972 & 73; Major Poets; I.W.W.P. Anthol. Honours, awards: Iowa Poet of Year, IPDA, 1969 & var. certs. of merit & hon. mentions, book prizes, etc. Address: 2113 Highland Ave., Davenport, IA 52803, U.S.A.

SWARD, Robert Stuart, pen name **DR. SOFT,** b. 23 June 1933. Writer; Teacher; Publisher & Editor.

Education: B.A., Univ. of Ill., 1956; M.A., Univ. of Iowa, U.S.A., 1958; post grad. work, Univ. of Bristol, U.K. & at Middlebury Coll., Vt., U.S.A. Divorced, 4 children (Cheryl, Barbara, Michael, Hannah). Positions held: Instr. in Engl., Conn. Coll., New London, 1958-59; & at Cornell Univ., Ithaca, N.Y., 1962-64; Writer-in-Res., Univ. of Iowa Writers' Workshop, 1967; Poet-in-Res., Aspen Writers' Workshop, Aspen, Colo., 1967; Asst. Prof. of Engl., Vis. Poet-in-Res., Univ. of Victoria, B.C., Canada, 1969-73; Ed. & Publisher of Soft Press, 1970-. Memberships: Phi Beta Kappa; Modern Poetry Assn.; League of Canadian Poets; COSMEP. Published works: Advertisements, 1958; Uncle Dog & Other Poems, 1962; Kissing the Dancer & Other Poems, 1964; Thousand-Year-Old Fiancée, 1965; Hannah's Cartoon, 1970; Quorum-Noah, w. Mike Doyle, 1970; Songs From the Jurassic Shales, 1971; Gift, 1971; Horgbortom Stringbottom, I am Yours, You are History, 1970; Poems: New & Selected (1957-73); Half a Life's History, 1973; The Jurassic Shales, A Narrative. Contbr. to num. jrnls., mags. & anthols. Honours, awards: Dylan Thomas Meml. Award, 1958; Guggenheim Fellowship for Poetry, 1964-65; D.H. Lawrence Fellowship, Univ. of N.M., 1966; Fulbright Fellowship for study in U.K., 1960-61; Canada Council grant, 1973. Address: c/o Soft Press, 1050 Saint David St., Victoria, B.C., V8S 4Y8, Canada.

SWEARINGEN, Annette Wildman, b. 21 May 1897. St. Paul, Mo. Minister; Teacher; Writer. Education: Jr. Coll., Kan. City Univ.; Metaphysicis, Unity Schl. of Christianity, Lee's Summit; Tchrs. degree; Ordained Min. Personal details: m. (1) Mitchell Soutee, 1 s.; m. (2) Dick Swearingen, 1967. Positions held: Student Tchr., Unity Schl. of Christianity, Lee's Summit, Mo., 1925; Licensed Tchr., 1947; Ordained Min., 1966; Co-Fndr., Unity Northeast Ch., Kan. City, 1963; Min. of Educ., Unity Valley Ch., Hemet, Calif., 1967-. Memberships: Kan. City Westport Br., Nat. League Am. Pen Women, 1952-70; Pres., ibid, 1956-58; Hemet Calif. Br., 1971-; Mo. State Pres., NLAPW, 1958-60; Ed., Kan. City Westport News, 1957-60; The Nat. Fed. Press Women, Inc., 1958; Hon., Mark Twain Soc.; Mo. Writers Guild, 1958; Kan. City Quill Club, 1957; Unity Alumni Assn., 1934. Published works: Mosaic of Living, 1951; Sonnettones, 1951; Moments of Mood, 1952; Of Heart & Home, 1956. Contbr. to: The Kansas City Star; Johnson County Herald; St. Charles Daily Banner News; The News & Courier; Kansas City Poetry Magazine; Recommended Poems for the Elementary Grades by Forrest E. Wolverton; Our Reading Heritage, Exploring Life; Wednesday Magazine, Scimitar & Song; Midland Poetry Review; Chromatones; Blue River Press; Renaissance; American Courier; Blue Moon; The American Bard. Honours & Awards: Cert. of Recognition, Hist. Record Assn., Ky., 1959; Annette Wildman Hon. Award, Kan. City Westport Br., NLAPW, 1961-64; Guest Ed., Kan. City Poetry Mag., 1953. Address: 25124 Yale St., Hemet, Calif. 92343, USA.

SWENSON, May, b. 28 May 1919. Poet. Education: B.A., Utah State Univ. Positions held: Ed., New Directions Press, N.Y.C.; Writer-in-Res. for limited periods at the following univs: Purdue Univ., Univ. of N.C., Univ. of Lethbridge, Canada, Utah State Univ., Univ. of Calif. at Riverside. Memberships: Nat. Inst. of Arts & Letters; PEN Am. Ctr. Published works: Another Animal: Poems, 1954; A Cage of Spines, 1958; To Mix With Time, New & Selected Poems, 1963; Poems to Solve, 1966; Half Sun Half Sleep, 1967; Iconographs, 1970; More Poems to Solve, 1971; transl. from Swedish, Windows & Stones, Selected Poems by Tomas Transtromer, 1972. Contbr. to num. jrnls. & mags. inclng: Accent; Antaeus; Arts in Soc.; Atlantic Monthly; Bard; Contact; Chicago Tribune; Dallas Times-Herald; Dialogue; The Elements; Epoch; First State; Folio; Harper's Bazaar; The Herald Tribune; Mademoiselle; The Nation; New Am. Review; N.Y. Times Sunday Book Review; The New Yorker; Paris Review; N.Y. Quarterly; N.Y. Times; Survival. Recip. many honours, awards, prizes inclng: Nat. Inst. Arts & Letters Grant, 1960; Ford Fndn. Poet/Playwrite Grant, 1964; Borestone Mountain Poetry Awards, 1967 & 68.

Address: 73 The Boulevard, Sea Cliff, Long Island, NY 11579, U.S.A.

SWICK, Ila Elizabeth Rose, pen name **ROSE, Ila Elizabeth,** b. 10 Jan. 1897. Musician; Teacher; Homemaker. Married Brice Swick, 1 son, 1 daughter. Positions held: Tchr. of Dramatic Art; Tchr. in Fla. pvte. schl. Memberships: Lansing Poetry Club, 35 yrs.; Pres., ibid, 2 yrs.; Mich. Poetry Assn.; Civic Players Guild; Hon. Mbr., Delta Phi, Beta Sigma Phi. Published works: As the Spool Unwinds (183 poems), 1965; currently working on 2nd book to be called 'Mood Moments'. Contbr. to: Lansing State Jrnl.; Detroit Free Press; Pompano Beach Sun; Christian Sci. Jrnl.; Am. Bard; Avalon Press; Peninsula Poets; Country Poet, etc. Recip. var. poetry awards inclng: Nat. & Int. Award for Christmas Poem, Beta Sigma Phi, 1955. Address: 1914 Walnut St., Holt, MI 48842, U.S.A.

SYKES, Ruth, pen name **SYKES, Ruth Welch,** b. 14 Dec. 1929. Saleswoman. Education: Bus. Coll.; Northeast La. Univ. Widow, 3 sons, 1 daughter. Positions held: Sales, Field Enterprises, World Bank. Memberships: La. State Poetry Soc.; Past Matron, Order of Eastern Star. Contbr. to: Lyrics of Love, 1972; Ideals; Readers Digest; Helicon. Address: 1905 Richard Dr., Monroe, LA 71201, U.S.A.

SYLVESTRE, Jean Guy, b. 17 May 1918. Author; Librarian. Education: B.A., Univ. of Ottawa, 1939; B.Ph., 1940; M.A., 1942. Married Françoise Poitevin, 3 children. Positions held: Translator, Dept. Sec. of State, 1942-44; Ed., Wartime Info. Bd., 1944-45; Asst. Pvte. Sec. to Min. of Justice, 1945-47; Pvte. Sec. to Sec. of State for External Affairs, 1947-48; Pvte. Sec. to Prime Minister, 1948-50; Admin. Off., Dept. of Resources & Dev., 1950-53; Asst. Libn., Lib. of Parliament, 1953-56; Assoc. Libn. of Parliament, 1956-68; National Libn., 1968-. Memberships: Fellow, Royal Soc. of Canada, 1952-; Pres., ibid, 1973-74; Acad. Canadienne française, 1965-; Société des Ecrivains canadiens; Dir., Canadian Writers Fndn.; Pres., ibid, 1960-61; Mbr. of many lit. juries & Chmn. of the Gov. General's Lit. Awards, 1960-62; Org. of the World Poetry Conf., Expo 1967; Past Chmn., Canada Coun. Comm. on Aid-to-Publication. Published works: Situation de la poésie canadienne, 1941; Anthologie de la poésie canadienne-française, 1943, '58, '64, '66, '68; Poètes catholiques de la France contemporaine, 1944; Sondages, 1945; Impressions de théâtre, 1950; Panorama des lettres canadiennes-françaises, 1964; Canadian Writers, 1964; Literature in French Canada, 1967; A Century of Canadian Literature, 1967. Contbr. to learned mags. & encys. Canadian Advsr. to the Funk & Wagnalls Ency. Honours, awards: Hon. D.L.S., 1969 & D.Litt., 1970; Commandeur de l'Ordre du Bien Public. Address: 1870 Rideau Garden Dr., Ottawa K1S 1G6, Canada.

SYMES, Colin Timothy, b. 25 Apr. 1945. Teacher. Education: B.Educ., Univ. of Southampton, U.K., 1972. Married Frances Mealin. Positions held: Poet; Teacher. Member, Poetry Soc. of Australia. Published works: Poettree, supplement to Earthship, Series I, 1970. Contbr. to: Katawakes; Earthship; Curtains; Ear in a Wheatfield; New Poetry (Australia); Etymspheres. Address: 177-39 Abbotsford Rd., Homebush, N.S.W., Australia 2140.

SYMONS, Julian, b. 30 May 1912. Freelance Writer. Positions held: Publr. & Ed., Twentieth Century Verse, London, U.K., 1937-39; Freelance Writer, 1947-; Fiction Reviewer, Sunday Times, current. Published works: Confusions about X, 1938; The Second Man, 1944; (novels) The Colour of Murder, 1957; The Progress of a Crime, 1960; (other) Charles Dickens, 1951; Thomas Carlyle, 1952; Horatio Bottomley, 1955; The Thirties, 1960; Buller's Campaign, 1963; England's Pride, 1965; Crime and Detection, 1966; Critical Occasions, 1966; Ed., Anthology of War Poetry, 1942. Contbr. to: (anthologies) Poems from the Forces, 1941; War Poets, 1945; A Little Treasury of Modern Poetry, 1947; Poetry of the Thirties, 1964. Honours, awards: British Crime Writers Assn. Award,

1957; Mystery Writers of Am. Award, 1960, '66. Address: 37 Albert Bridge Rd., London S.W.11, U.K.

SZABO, Béla, pen name **CSEPELI SZABO BELA,** b. 14 May 1924. Editor; Poet; Writer. Education: Univ. of Arts 'Eötvös Loránd'. Married Maria Nagy, 1 son, 1 daughter. Positions held: Metal worker & Machine Tool Smith, Csepel Iron Works, –1948; Reporter & Ed., var. newspapers; currently Ed. of the lit. review 'Magyar Papir'. Memberships: Sec.; Nat. Assn. of Hungarian Newsmen, 1951-52; Assn. of Hungarian Writers; PEN. Published works: (colls. of poetry) Revolutionary from Rebel, 1951; Far Way, 1956; On the World's Boundary, 1959; Son of the Earth, 1960; Turbulent Times, 1966; Don't Bother, Atlas, 1973; (novels) Romance on the Danube Bank, 1962; Whirlwind, 1965; Ed. of biographies & anthols. 'Sparks of Csepel', 1970 & 'The Word of Letters', 1973. Contbr. to var. newspapers & reviews in Hungary & abroad. Honours, awards: Poetry Prize, Nat. Lit. Comp., 1955; József Attila Prize, 1958; 1st Prize in Poetry, Nat. Youth Lit. Comp., 1971. Address: Tárház u. 50, 1213 Budapest XXI, Hungary.

SZENTKERESZTY, Elizabeth (Baroness), pen names, **DE ZAGON, Elizabeth & ZAGONI, Erzsébet,** b 30 May 1905. Editor; Translator; Press Reader. Education: Baccalaureate, Budapest; Social Sci., London; Budapest Univ. Married, 1 d., 2 s. Positions held: Probation Officer, Juvenile Court; Int. Red Cross; Press Rdr., British Legation, Budapest; Ed., Caractère et Culture de l'Europe, Europe Cultural Fndn., Amsterdam, The Netherlands. Works to be published: l'Europe des Poètes, transl. Contbr. to the following anthols., jrnls., mags., etc.; Hĭd (The Bridge); Uj Idök (New Times); various Belgian Newspapers. Address: 42 Av. Arnold Delvaux, Brussels 1180, Belgium.

SZERLIP, Barbara Leslie, b. 28 Nov. 1949. Editor. Education: Univ. of Miami; Univ. of Calif., Santa Barbara. Positions held: Asst. Tech. Dir., Summer Stock Theater, N.Y.; Instr. in Hatha Yoga, Kirtan Mantras at Sivananda Ashram, Val Morin, Quebec, Canada; Ed., Tractor, mag. of poetry, prose, translations, San Francisco. Published works: Teopantiahuac, 1971; Four Young Women: Poems, 1973; Bear Dancing, 1974. Contbr. to: Peace & Pieces Anthol., 1973; Three Rivers; Heirs; Another Poetry Mag. (Toronto); Tractor; N.Y. Qtly.; Spectrum; Four Dog Mountain Songs; Posibilidades (Mex. City); The Nexus; The North Stone Review. Recip., CCLM Grant for the continued publication of Tractor, Nat. Endowment for the Arts, 1973. Address: 508 Twin Oaks Rd., Union, NJ 07083, U.S.A.

T

TABENKIN, Moshe, b. 15 May 1917, Kibbutz Kinneret, Israel. Educator. Education: Hebrew Univ. of Jerusalem; Inst. of Educ., London, UK. Positions held: Hd. Instr., Youth Ldrs. Dept., Histadrut Working Youth; Chief Edu. Officer, Northern Front, Israel War of Indep., 1948-49; Hd. Master, Ein-Harod (Meuchad) Schl. & Tchr., Hebrew Lit.; Lectr., Ef-Al (Kibbutz Hameuchad Educ. Ctr.); Lectr., Educ., Oranim Tchrs. Trng. Coll. of the Kibbutzim; Chmn., Educ. & Cultural Comm., Kibbutz Hameuchad. Memberships: Ctrl. Comm., Israel Labour Party; Israel Writers Assn. Published works: Sefer Shirim (Book of Poems), 1949; Od Shirim (More Poems), 1971; Hashetach she mi'ever Lawadi (The Place Beyond the Valley), play, 1948; Uri Guri ve Shuri (4 childrens stories), 1959. Contbr. to: Mibifnim; lit. supplements of Lamerhav, Davar & Al Hamishmar; also anthols. Address: Kibbutz Ein-Harod, (Meuchad), Israel.

TABLIGAN, Nicator Filemon, b. 20 Mar. 1920. College Teacher & Writer. Education: studied for the gospel ministry after H.S.; A.B. & M.A., Silliman Univ., Dumaguete, Philippines. Positions held: Elem. Tchr.; Evangelist; Newspaperman; Religious Ed.; Pastor-at-Large; College Tchr. Assoc. Mbr., United Poets

Laureate Int. Contbr. to: Philippines Free Press; Philippine Christian Advance; Crusader Mag.; Sunday Times Mag. (Manila, Philippines); Saturday Herald (Philippines Herald, Manila, Philippines); This Week Mag. (Manila Chronicle); Manugbantala Herald, (Iloilo City, Philippines); Sands & Coral (Silliman Univ.); Laurel Leaves (United Poets Laureate). Address: Kabankalan, Negros Ocidental, Philippines.

TADLOCK, Lila Clementa, pen name **TADLOCK, Lila Swindell,** b. 13 Jan. 1903. School Teacher. Education: B.S. & M.S., East Tex. State Univ.; studied violin, 8 yrs. Married W.L. Tadlock. Positions held: Tchr., Elem. Schls., Fannin Co., 1922-42; Schl. Supt., 1942-43; Math Tchr., Bells H.S. & N. Fannin H.S., 1943-46; Engl. Tchr., Gober H.S., 1946-54; Prin., Lannius, 1954-68; Primary Tchr., Wisdom, 1968-69. Memberships: Poetry Soc. of Tex., 1946–; Nat. Writers' Club; Poets' Study Club, Terre Haute, Ind.; V.P., Bonham Women's Club; Past Pres. & V.P., Triple L Club; Nat. Retired Tchrs. Assn. Contbr. to: (anthols.) Visions in Verse, 1968; Contemporary Poets, 1969. Song lyrics: 'Forever Yours'; 'It Was Too Late'; 'Angels Unaware'; 'To the Class of Twenty One'. Recip., Humorous Prize, 1954; Woman of Woodcraft Award, Woodmen of the World, 1971. Address: Box 334, Franklin & Denison Ave., Bonham, TX 75418, U.S.A.

TAGLIABUE, John, b. 1 July 1923. Poet; College Teacher. Education: B.A., Columbia Univ., N.Y.C., U.S.A., 1944; M.A., ibid, 1945; Fulbright student, Univ. of Pisa, 1950-52. Married Grace Ten Eyck, 2 children (Francesca & Dina). Positions held: Tchr., Am. Univ. of Beirut, State Coll. of Wash., Alfred Univ., N.Y., Univ. of Pisa, Italy, Tokyo Univ., & Tokyo Joshi Daigaku & Tsuda Daigaku, Japan; currently Prof. of Engl. Lit. Bates Coll., Me; also summer courses in poetry at Int. Inst. in Madrid, Univ. of Natal, Brazil & at Bennett Coll., N.C. Has given poetry readings in U.S.A., Brazil, Spain, Italy, Greece, Japan. Published works: Poems (selection of 150 poems written between 1941 & 58), 1959; A Japanese Jrnl., 1966 & 69; The Buddha Uproar, 1967 & 70; The Doorless Door, 1970; Selections from A Shakespeare Notebook, 1973. Rep. in anthols. publ. by Knopf, Basic Books, Crowell, Pacific Books, Scott Foresman, Lippincott, Doubleday, Macmillan. Contbr. to: The Atlantic Monthly; The Chicago Review; Columbia Univ. Forum; Chelsea; First Stage; The Greenfield Review; The Hudson Review; Harpers; Kayak; Ktaadn; Literature East & West; The Mass. Review; The Nation; N.Y. Quarterly; Northeast; The Northwest Review; The Prairie Schooner; Poetry Northwest; Poet Lore; Shenandoah; The Seneaca Review; The Transatlantic Review, etc. Address: 59 Webster St., Lewiston, ME 04240, U.S.A.

TAIT, Elizabeth, pen name **TAIT, Elizabeth Leeds,** b. 1 Aug. 1906. Insurance Executive. Education: Grad., Temple Univ. Schl. of Educ. Positions held: Ptnr. of Henry H. Leeds Ins. Agency, 1935-73; Acting Prin. & Chmn., Rancocas Friends Schl., 1948–. Memberships: Leaves of Grass Chapt. of the N.J. Poetry Soc.; Quaker Poets, a South Jersey Poetry Soc. Contbr. to the 1972 N.J. Poetry Soc. Anthol. Recip., 1st Prize, Sonnet Contest, N.J. Poetry Soc., 1972. Address: 45 East Main St., Rancocas, NJ 08073, U.S.A.

TAIT (Rev.) Tommy, b. 22 June 1906. Minister of Religion. Home Teacher of the Blind. Education: Edinburgh Univ., Scotland, UK. Positions held: Parish Minister, Church of Scotland. Published works: Rev. Tommy Tait's Quarterly, subscription publ. Address: The Manse, Rendall, Orkney, Scotland, UK.

TAKAHASHI, Shohachiro, b. 9 Mar. 1933. Memberships: Vou, Avangarde Artists' Club, Tokyo; Lotta Poetica, Italy. Published works: (poetry) Oiseaux, 1968; Vent, 1968; Ombre, 1968; Terre d'eau terre de feu, 1969; Domaine de 1972. Contbr. to: Liberté, Montreal; Approches, Paris; An Int. Anthol. of Advanced Poetry, Milan; Once Again, N.Y.; Agentzia, Paris; Asa, Tokyo; Letter & Image, N.Y.; Mec, Milan; Lotta Poetica, Brescia, etc. Address: 4 chome, 19-3

Takamatsu, Morioka 020-01, Japan.

TAKAORI, Taeko, b. 1 Jan. 1915. Poet. Education: Sacred Heart Womens Coll., Tokyo, Japan. Positions held: Tanka Critic, Maimchi Newspaper; associated with sev. tanka book publishers. Pres., Kyoto Kajin Kyokai (Kyoto Tanka Grp.). Published works: Busoge, 1963; Are Gawa, 1968; Eenu-tae Kashu, 1946; When a Bird Rests (transl.), 1974; North Cape, 1974. Contbr. to: Southern Review Anthol. of Modern Japanese Poetry, 1972; num. Japanese lang. mags. & newspapers. Address: 5 Ginkakugi Mae, Sakyo-ku, Kyoto, Japan.

TAKATS, Gyula, b. 4 Feb. 1911. Museum Director. Education: Philos., hist. of art, geol. & hist., Univ. of Pecs, Hungary. Positions held: Tchr., Kaposvár, 1935-49; Dir., Rippl-Rónai Mus., Kaposvár, 1949-; Dir., Museums of Somogy Co. Memberships: Magyar Irók Szövetsége; PEN Club. Published works: Kut, 1935; Kakuk a dombon, 1937; Május, 1939; Családfa helyett, 1941; Hold és hárs, 1943; se ég föld, 1947; Vizitükör, 1955; Az emberekhez, 1955; Rozsava lett róka, 1958; Mézöntö, 1958; Virágok Virága, 1961; Képek és versek útjain, 1961; Evek Madarak, 1965; A Tündérhal és a háló, 1968; Villámok mêrtana, 1968; Egy kertre emlékezvue, 1971. Contbr. to: Hyugat; Valasz, Kelet Népe; Napkelet; Sersunk; Jelenkor; Kortárs; Uj Irás Elet és Irodalom Vigalia; Eletünk; Népszava; Magyar Hirlap; Nök Lapja; Csillag; Uj Hang; Magyar Csillag; Dunĕntul; Magyarok; Puszatak; Népe, etc. Honours, Awards: Baumgarten dij, 1941; József Atila-dij, 1960; Kaposvár Varosnagydija, 1971; Munka Erdemrend Arany-lokozata, 1971. Address: Kovacs S. Gy-u-952, Kaposvár, Hungary.

TALBOT, Norman Clare, b. 14 Sept. 1936. University Lecturer. Educ: Hatfield Coll., Durham Univ., U.K., 1956-59; Ph.D., Leeds Univ., 1962. Married Jean Margaret Perkins. Positions held: Lectr. in Engl., Newcastle Univ. Coll. of Univ. of N.S.A., Australia, 1962-69; Sr. Lectr., ibid (under new name of Univ. of Newcastle), 1969-73; Assoc. Prof., 1973–; Rsch. Fellow, Am. Coun. of Learned Socs., Yale Univ., U.S.A., 1967-68. Published works: The Seafolding of Harri Jones, 1965; Poems for a Female Universe, 1968; Son of a Female Universe, 1971; The Fishing Boy (w. plates by John Montefiore), 1973; also tapes of poetry (w. interviews) held by Yale Univ. Younger Poets Series & Canadian Broadcasting Corp. Ed. of following anthols: XI Hunter Valley Poets VII, Hunter Valley Poets, 1973; Australian Poets (in Spanish). Rep. in following anthols: Australian Poetry, 1965-73, annually; Australian Poetry Now; Penguin Book of Australian Verse; Vietnam Postscript, We took their orders & are dead; The Vital Decade; etc. Contbr. to: The Australian; Australian Highway; Balcony; Meanjin; Nimrod; Overland; Poetry Australian; Quadrant; The Realist; The Fiddlehead; Outposts; Nation (N.Y.); Yale Lit. Mag. & to BBC radio, etc. Recip., Gregory Award for Poetry, 1965. Address: Dept. of Engl., Univ. of Newcastle, NSW 2308, Australia.

TALLMAN, Albert, b. 21 Jul. 1902. Businessman (retired). Education: HS; Extension Courses, Univ. of California. Memberships: World Poetry Soc.; C.S.S.I.; Acad. Leonardo da Vinci; Avalon Internat. Poetry Soc.; South & West Lit. Assoc.; Fellow, Internat. Poetry Soc. (UK). Published works: Weeds, 1967; The End of the Cycle, 1967; Pebbles, 1969; Plus & Minus, 1972. Contbr. to: Voices Internat.; American Voice; Bitterroot; Bardic Echoes; Cardinal Poetry Qtly.; Quaderni di Poesia; Cyclo-Flame; Encore; Southwest Times Record; Sunstone Review; Sunburst; South & West; The Spring Anthol. (London); Poet; Ocarina; The North American Mentor; Moon Age Poets Anthol.; Legend; The Golden Quill Anthol.; Internat. Who's Who in Poetry Anthol. Awards: World Poetry Soc. Disting. Service Citation, Magna Cum Laude, 1970; The Hart Crane & Alice Crane Williams Mem. Fund, 1969; Acad. Leonardo da Vinci Cert. of Merit, 1971; North American Mentor Cert. of Merit, 1972. Address: 709 Nevada Ave., San Mateo, CA 94402, USA.

TAMMINGA, Douwe Annes, b. 22 Nov. 1909. Scientific Cooperator. Education: Seminary for Tchrs.; Certs. for Tchr. of Sec. Instrn. Married, 1 son (dec.) Positions held: Social Worker, 1935-42; Tchr., Sec. Schl., 1942-63; Scientific Cooperator, Fryske Akademy, 1963–. Memberships: Int. PEN, Netherlands Ctr.; Maatschappij Nederlandse Letterkunde; Frysk Skriuwersboun. Published works: (poetry) Brandaris, 1938; Balladen en Lieten, 1942; It Griene Jier, 1943; Nije Gedichten, 1945; Leksums, 1945; Balladen, 1956; Floedmerk, 1965; In memoriam, 1968; Dagen fan heil, 1973; Tsien Psalmen, 1973. Contbr. to var. jrnls. Recip., Gysbert Japicx priis, 1957. Address: Ds. Visserleane 4, Ysbrechtum (post Snits/Sneck), Friesland, Netherlands.

TANNY, Shlomo, pen name, **ALOMIN, S.,** b. 27 Nov. 1919. Poet; Journalist. Personal details: Descendant of Rabbi Elimelech, a fndr. of Hassidic Movement in Poland. Positions held: Hd., Educ. Info Dept., Israel Labour Fed. Memberships: Bd. Dirs., Soc. of Authors & Composers; Israel Writers Assn. Published works: 6 books of poetry, latest: Selected Poems, 1970; 4 books for children; 2 records for children; book of war of independence, 1948-49. Contbr. to daily periodicals. Address: 9 Derech Haifa Rd., Tel Aviv, Israel.

TAN PAI, Joshua, pen name **TIRA, J.,** b. 2 July 1914. Journalist. Positions held: Ed., Haaretz Daily newspaper, Jerusalem. V. Chmn., Writers Assn. in Israel. Published works: From Alpha to Omega, poems, 1937; Variations on the Spring, poems, 1941; Songs of Darkness & Light, poems, 1942; All the Men, poems, 1951; Souls in my Grasp, poems, 1973; Anthol. of Engl. & Am. Poetry, transld. into Hebrew, 1967; Dictionnaire Francais-Hebrew, 1966; Trans. into Hebrew from Baudelaire, Rimbaud, Valery, Shakespeare (sonnets), Chekhov, Balzac, Maupassant, etc. Contbr. to: Haarets; Davar; Moznaym; Gilyonoth; Tourim; Hed Jerushalaim. Recip., Prime Minister's Award for Lit., 1971. Address: Flat No. 14, Bldg. 1, Kiryath Wolfshon, Jerusalem, Israel.

TARARO, Muhammed Siddique (s/o KHAMISOKHAN), pen name **SARWECH SUJAWALI,** b. 14 Mar. 1937. Civil Servant. Memberships: Gen. Sec. 'Sindhi Adabi Sangat', Sujawel Town; mbr. of all Sindhi lit. socs. Published works: Alyoon Akhyoon, Anbhawar (in Sindhi lang.), 1972. Contbr. to: Hilal-e-Pakistan; Ibrat; Mehran; Ilhadem-e-Watan; Azad; Mazooi; Adyoon; etc. Recip. cash prize awarded by Pakistan Writers' Guild. Address: P.O. Sujawel, Dist. II, Ihatta, Sindh, Pakistan.

TARLOW, Idell Rose, pen names **IDELL, AYA, ARAYA, IDELL TARLOW,** b. 14 Aug. 1932. Secretary; Astrologer. Married three times. Positions held: Toured S.F. reading poetry in the 1950's; Playwrite; worked in offices; Ed., Anthol. of works for women (in 3 vols); worked in photolab, etc. Published works: Poems for Selected People, 1961; Epomene, 1963; Marks of Asha, 1963; Zen Love Poems, 1967. Contbr. to: Semina; Coastlines; Miscellaneous Man; Tree; Eidolons. Ed. & Contbr. to Matrix: For She of the New Aeon. Address: Box 4218, N. Hollywood, CA 19607, U.S.A.

TARN, Nathaniel, b. 30 June 1928. University Professor. Education: B.A., Cambridge Univ., 1948; M.A., 1952; Cert. C.F.R.E., Sorbonne & Ecole des hautes Etudes, Paris; M.A., Univ. of Chgo., 1952; Ph.D., 1957; London Schl. of Econs. & Schl. of Oriental & African Studies, Univ. of London. Positions held: Anthropol., Guatemala & Burma; Lectr., Univs. of Chgo. & London; Lectr., many countries, 1952-67; Gen. Ed., Cape Editions, London & Dir., Cape Goliard Ltd., London, 1967-69; Vis. Prof., SUNY, Buffalo & Princeton Univ., 1969-70. Published works include: Old Savage/Young City, 1964; Penguin Modern Poets 7, 1966; Where Babylon Ends, 1968; The Beautiful Contradictions, 1969; October, 1969; Contbr. & Ed., various publs. Honours, Awards: Guinness Prize for

Poetry, 1963. Address: c/o Talese, Random House, 210 E 50th St., New York, NY, USA.

TARNAWSKY (Tarnavs'kyj), George (Jurij), b. 3 Feb. 1934. Electrical Engineer; Computer Systems Designer. Education: B.S., Elec. Engrng., Newark Coll. of Engrng., Newark, N.J., U.S.A. Positions held: Employed by IBM Corp. (worked on automatic lang. translation & other computer-linguistics proj.); Lit. Ed., Horyzonty, Ukrainian-Am. Student Mag., 1961-62; Co-Ed., Novi poeziji, Ukrainian avant-garde poetry jrnl., 1959–; Co-Fndr., ibid. Memberships: Co-Fndr., N'jujorks'ka hrupa (The N.Y. Grp.), avant-garde grp. of Ukrainian poets; Slovo, Ukrainian Writers' Assn.; PEN. Published works: Zhyttja v misti, 1956; Popoludni v Pokipsi, 1960; Idealizovana biohrafija, 1964; Spomyny, 1964; Bez Espaniji, 1969; Poeziji pro nishcho i inshi poeziji na cju samu temu, collected poems inclng. Pisni je-je, Ankety, Vyno i ropa & Poeziji pro nishcho, 1970. Contbr. to var. Ukrainian, Am., Engl., German, Polish, Canadian & Portuguese jrnls. Address: IBM Corp., Yorktown Heights, N.Y., U.S.A.

TARTOUE, Cassie Eugenia, pen name DIXSON, Cassie Eugenia, b. 9 June 1931. Secretary; Cuisinere; Writer; Poet; Housewife. Education: Northwestern Coll., Alva, Oklahoma; Panhandle A. & M. Coll., Goodwell, Oklahoma, studied journalism and humanities. Married to Pierre Tartoué, an artist. Positions held: Sec. to Prof. of Agric., Panhandle A. & M. Coll.; Wolfe Advertising Co., Oklahoma City; Oklahoma League for the Blind; Standard Life Ins. Co., 6 yrs.; Hardford Ins. Co., 6 yrs.; Cuisinere at A.T.O. House, U. of I. Memberships: Oklahoma Poetry Soc.; Idaho Poets' & Writers' Guild; Catholic Poetry Soc. of America. Published works: One Small Candle, 1968; Souvenir, 1968; Fragments, 1971; Old Crystal – New Wine, 1972; Gypsy Shadows, 1972; Palette & Palate (novelty cookbook), 1972. Contbr. to: The Maryknoll Book of Treasures, 1968; Ideals; Catholic Digest; Our Sunday Visitor; Idaho Farmer; Oklahoma Today; Daily Oklahoman; Oregonian; Northwest Mag.; The Christian; Good Old Days Mag.; Harper County Journal; American Bard; Midwest Chaparral; Guild Qtly.; The Muse; Seconds Sanctified; Bardic Echoes; The Swordsman Review; Quaderni Di Poesia, etc. Awards: 1st Place, Editor's and Critics Choice, Midwest Chaparral, 1968; Angel Award, Nomination to membership in the Internat. Platform Assoc., etc. Address: Apt. 311, Hotel Moscow, Moscow, ID 83843, USA.

TATE, Allen, b. 19 Nov. 1899. Poet & Critic. Education: B.A., Vanderbilt Univ., 1922. Positions held: Poet-in-Res., Princeton Univ., 1939-42; Ed., The Sewanee Review, 1944-46; Regents Prof. of Engl., Univ. of Minn., 1951-68; Fulbright Prof., Univ. of Rome, 1953-54; Univs. of Oxford & Leeds, 1958-59. Memberships: Pres., Nat. Inst. of Arts & Letters, 1968; Am. Acad. of Arts & Letters, 1964–; Chancellor, Acad. of Am. Poets, 1968–. Published works incl: Mr. Pope & Other Poems, 1928; Reactionary Essays on Poetry & Ideas, 1936; Selected Poems, 1937; The Winter Sea (poems) 1944; The Hovering Fly (essays), 1949; Poems: 1922-47, 1948; The Forlorn Demon, 1954; Essays of Four Decades, 1969; The Swimmers & Other Selected Poems, 1971. Contbr. to var. reviews & jrnls. Honours, awards: Bollingen Prize for Poetry, 1956; Brandeis Medal Award, 1962; Medaglio d'Oro, Società di Dante Alighieri, Florence, 1962; Award, Acad. of Am. Poets, 1963. Address: Running Knob Hollow Rd., Sewanee, TN 37375, U.S.A.

TATE, James Vincent, b. 8 Dec. 1943. Poet. Education: B.A., Kans. State Coll. of Pittsburg, 1965; Univ. of Mo., Kans. City; M.F.A., Univ. of Iowa, 1967. Married Liselotte Jonsson. Positions held: Asst. Instr., Univ. of Iowa, 1965-67; Vis. Lectr., Univ. of Calif. at Berkeley, 1967-68; Asst. Prof., Columbia Univ., 1969-71; Asst. Prof., Emerson Coll., 1970-71; Asst. Prof., Univ. of Mass., 1971–. Published works: (books) The Lost Pilot, 1967; Notes of Woe, 1968; The Torches, 1968; Row With Your Hair, 1969; Shepherds of the

Mist, 1969; The Oblivion Ha-Ha, 1970; Are You Ready Mary Baker Eddy? (w. Bill Knott), 1970; Hints to Pilgrims, 1971; Absences, 1972; var. pamphlets & broadsheets. Contbr. to num. mags. & jrnls. Honours, awards: Yale Series of Younger Poets Award, 1966; Nat. Lit. Anthol. Award, 1968, '69; Phi Beta Kappa Poet of the Year, Brown Univ., 1972. Address: County Rd., Deerfield, MA 01342, U.S.A.

TAUSS, Margaret Leah, b. 30 July 1929. Editorial Assistant. Education: B.A., Hunter Coll., N.Y., 1956. Married & divorced. Positions held: Copywriter, 1956; Editl. Asst. on Super Market Merchandising mag., 1957-62 (also Travel mag. & Florists Exchange mag.); Caseworker, 1965; Directory Compiler, 1966-68; Freelance Book Review Writer, 1969; Census Enumerator, 1970; Market Rsch. Survey Interviewer & other proj. duties, 1970-73. Memberships: Greenwich Village Poetry Soc.; N.Y. Poetry Forum. Contbr. to: Mitre Press Spring Anthol., 1966; The New Orlando Poetry Anthol., vol. 3, 1968; Vespers; La Voce Italiana, etc. Recip., Annual Gold Medal, Int. Acad. of Poets, 1966. Has read own poetry on TV & radio. Address: 414 West 121 St., Apt. 47, New York, NY 10027, U.S.A.

TAVALLALI, Freidun, b. 1919. Poet; Archaeologist. Education: Grad., Archaeol., Univ. of Tehran. Positions held: Employee, Dept. of Archaeol.; Officer, & responsible for Exploration in var. parts of the country, Dept. of Archaeol.; Head of Fars Dept. of Archaeol. Wrote poems in classical style until 1942, when he started writing modern poetry under the influence of Nima Yushidj. He developed his own style which gained him recognition & his poems and translation of his poems have given him a world-wide reputation. Published works incl: Altafasil (free style, a social comment in Sadi Golestan's style); Raha (a coll. of poems); var. archaeol. articles. Address: c/o Press Attache, Imperial Iranian Embassy, 16 Princes Gate, London S.W.7, U.K.

TAVEL, Ronald, b. 17 May 1941. Writer. Education: M.A., Univ. of Wyoming. Positions held: Playwright-in-Res. of: Play-House of the Ridiculous, N.Y.C., 1965-67, The Actors Studio, N.Y.C., 1972 & The Theatre of the Lost Continent, N.Y.C., 1971-73; Lit. Advisor for Scripts Mag., 1971-72; Lectr. for the N.Y. State Coun. on the Arts, 1968–. Fndng. Mbr., N.Y. Theatre Strategy. Published works: (pamphlet) The Cuban & Other Poems, 1959. Contbr. to: The Lyric; Writing at Wyoming; Chicago Review; Wormwood; Tri-Quarterly; Graffiti; ...You, a Mag. of the Arts; Poets at Le Metro; News of The Am. Place Theatre; Orville Stoeber Songs (dust jacket). Winner of The Lyric poetry contest for 'Virginia Woolf', 1955. Address: 1095 E. 53rd St., Brooklyn, NY 11234, U.S.A.

TAVIN, Balbina Ostrowiak, b. 6 Oct. 1932. Writer; Poet; Translator; Housewife. Education: Brooklyn Coll., N.Y.; Newspaper Inst. of Am.; Nassau Community Coll. Ext. Married Sol Tavin, 2 sons. Positions held: Clerk-typist & Bus. Machine Operator; Science Teacher, High School; Staff, Riverrun lit. mag. of Brooklyn Coll. Memberships: Nat. League of Am. Pen Women; United Poets Laureate Int.; World Poetry Soc. Int.; Treas., Brooklyn Lit. Soc. Contbr. to the following anthols., jrnls. & newspapers: Am. Coll. Poetry Soc., 1958; Nat. Poetry Assn., 1958; Am. Poetry League, 1966; Altoona Mirror; Am. Zionist; Angels; Anubis; Author/Poet; Bell's Letters; Bitterroot; Bohemia Poblana, Mexico; Canzoni; Coney Island Times; Cycloflame; Down Ink Lane; Echoes; Encore; Fine Arts Discovery; Guild; Haiku Highlights; Haiku W.; Harbor Lights; Hoosier Challenger; Jean's Jrnl.; Ladies Delight; La Voce Italiana; Mod. Images; Nutmegger; Penman; Piggott Banner; Poetry Prevue; Scrivener; SCTH; Russell Times; Swordsman Rev.; Fireflower; Riverrun; Talisman; Williamsburg News, etc. Honours, awards: 1st prize, Talisman Contest, 1967; Hon. Mention, John Masefield Narrative Poem Comp., Manifold, U.K., 1968; UN Day Award of Hon., Philippines, 1968; Award of Merit, Eastern N.Y. Poetry Day Comm., 1968; Award of Merit, J. Mark Press.

Address: 2449 E. 63rd St., Brooklyn, NY 11234, U.S.A.

TAYLOR, Alexander Douglas, b. 8 July 1931. Teacher. Education: B.A., Skidmore Coll., U.S.A.; M.A. & Ph.D., Univ. of Conn. Married Patricia Louise Busher, 3 children (Susan, Anne, Peter). Positions held: Tchr., Queensbury Public Schl., Glens Falls, N.Y.; Sales Rep., Eastern Corp., N.Y., N.Y.; Tchr., Univ. High Schl., Storrs, Conn.; Asst. Prof., Eastern Conn. State Coll. Contbr. to: Botteghe Oscure; Contemporary Literature in Translation; The Far Point; Fiddlehead; Ladies Home Jrnl.; The Malahat Review; N.Y. Times;, Prism Int.; Penny Paper; West Coast Review; The Wormwood Review. Address: 321 Jackson St., Willimantic, CT 06226, U.S.A.

TAYLOR, Andrew McDonald, b. 19 Mar. 1940. English Lecturer. Educ: B.A., Melbourne Univ., Australia. Positions held: Engl. Tchr., British Inst., Rome, Italy; Temporary Lectr., Engl., Univ. of Melbourne, Australia, 1969–. Contbr. to: Meanjin; Overland; Twentieth Century; Poetry Magazine; New Impulses in Australian Poetry (anthology), 1968. Recip., Lockie Fellowship, 1965-68. Address: Fitzroy, Victoria, Australia.

TAYLOR, Brian Dormer, b. 17 Sept. 1946. Lecturer in Law. Education: Leverhulme Entrance Scholar, London Schl. of Econs., Univ. of London. Positions held: Lectr. in Govt., Kingston Coll. of Further Educ.; Lectr. in Law, City of Leicester Polytechnic. Memberships: Leicester Writers' Club; Lic., Guildhall Schl. of Mus. & Drama. Rep. in 'Its World That Makes The Love Go Round' (anthol.), 1968. Contbr. to: Breakthru; Expression; Morley Mag.; Riding West. Honours, awards: Assoc. & Gold Medallist, London Acad. of Music & Dramatic Art; Commended, Open Poetry Comp., Long Eaton Fest. of Music & the Arts, 1973. Address: Bod Awel, Gors Ave., Holyhead, Anglesey LL65 1PB, U.K.

TAYLOR, Eleanor Ross, b. 30 June 1920. Housewife; Poet. Married Peter Taylor. Published works: Wilderness of Ladies, 1960; Welcome Eumenides, 1972. Contbr. to: Poetry Mag.; Kenyon Review; Sewanee Review; Accent; Greensboro Review. Recip., Award in Poetry, Nat. Inst. of Arts & Letters, 1967. Address: Rt. 1, Box 240, Earlysville, VA 22936, U.S.A.

TAYLOR, Florence Marie, Writer. Education: Butler Univ. Positions held: Personnel work, Diamond Chain Co., Indianapolis; Corres., Universal Trade Press Syndicate, N.Y.C., 1944-56; Corres., Fairchild's Publications, 1950's. Memberships: 1st V.P., Ind. Fed. of Poetry Clubs, 1940; Story-A-Month Club, 1940-42; Ind. Br., Nat. League of Am. Pen Women, 1943–; Ind. Fed. of Womens Press Clubs, 1956–; Nat. Fed. of Womens Press Clubs. Published works: Night of Stars, 1956. Contbr. to: Denver Post; Grit; N.Y. Times; Bethany Ch. Guide; N.Y. Jrnl. American; Sunday Digest; Think; The Wash. D.C. Star; The Progressive Farmer; The Oregonian; The Christian Family; Indianapolis Star; Indianapolis News; Indianapolis Times; Ind. Poetry Soc. Mag.; Ind. Poetry Soc. Anthol., etc. Honours, awards incl: 3 prizes from Ind. Fed. of Poetry Clubs; Poet Laureate of The Ind. Fed. of Poetry Clubs, 1945-46. Address: 219 E. Eleventh St., Indianapolis, IN, U.S.A.

TAYLOR, Gloria Lee, Artist & Library Associate. Currently a student at Sangamon State Univ., Springfield, Ill. Divorced, 3 daughters. Positions held: Children's Libn., State Lib.; Lib. Assoc. & Artist in Res., ibid. Memberships: The Casbah Poetry Club, Chicago, Ill.; Famous Int. Poetry Club, San Francisco. Published works: Dreams for Sale, 1953. Contbr. to: Vicksburg Evening Post; Chicago Defender; San Francisco Chronicle; Ill. State Register & Jrnl. Recip., The Mark Twain Medal for Outstanding Contribution to Literature, 1952-53. Address: 1128 East Adams St., Springfield, IL 62703, U.S.A.

TAYLOR, Henry (Splawn), b. 21 June 1942. Teacher. Education: B.A. in Engl., Univ. of Va., 1965; M.A. in Writing & Criticism, Hollins Coll., 1966. Married 1) Sarah Bean, div., 2) Frances Carney, 1 son. Positions held: Instr. in Engl., Roanoke Coll., 1966-68; Asst. Prof. of Engl., Univ. of Utah, 1968-71; Assoc. Prof. of Lit., The Am. Univ., Wash. D.C., 1971–. Memberships: MLA; S. Atlantic MLA; Poetry Soc. of Va. Published works: The Horse Show at Midnight, 1966; Breakings, 1971; An Afternoon of Pocket Billiards, 1974; The Children of Herakles, transl. from Euripides, scheduled for publication 1974 or '75. Contbr. to num. mags. etc. inclng: Poetry Northwest; N.Y. Qtly.; Western Humanities Review; Tenn. Poetry Journal; Cimarron Review; Folio; Book Week; The N.M. Qtly.; Shenandoah; Plume & Sword; The Ga. Review; Stylus; Encounter. Honours, awards: Acad. of Am. Poets Prize, Univ. of Va., 1962 & '64; Utah State Inst. of Fine Arts Award for Poetry, 1969 & '71. Address: 6931 Hector Rd., McLean, VA 22101, U.S.A.

TAYLOR, John Alfred, pen names **DUPIN, August; WARD, Charles,** b. 12 Sept. 1931. College Professor. Education: B.A., Univ. of Missouri, 1953; M.A. (1957), Ph.D. (1959), Univ. of Iowa. Personal details: Married to Dorothy Vance Taylor; 3 stepchildren. Positions held: Teaching Assistantship, Univ. of Iowa; Instructorship, Univ. of New Hampshire; Asst. Prof., Rice Univ.; Asst. Prof., Buffalo State Coll., NY.; Asst. and Assoc. Professorships, Washington & Jefferson Coll. Published works: The Soap Duckets, 1965; Portfolio 3: Twelve Poems by John Taylor, 1971. Contbr. to: December; Midwest Qtly.; Perspective; Colorado Qtly.; New Mexico Qtly.; Chicago Review; Arlington Qtly.; Virginia Qtly. Review; Cottonwood Review; Carleton Miscellany; Denver Qtly.; NY Qtly.; A Legend; Trace; Back Door; Mutiny; Arizona Qtly.; Wormwood Review; The Western Poet; Beloit Poetry Journal; South Dakota Review; Midwestern Univ. Qtly.; Concerning Poetry; Poetry Northwest; Paris Review; Kenyon Review; Southwest Review; Massachusetts Review; Kayak; Crazy Horse; Colorado State Review; Transpacific; Alternatives; Kansas City Times; Verb; XAOE; United Church Herald; Forum; Janus; Mandala; Univ. Review; Xanadu; American Weave. Poems reprinted in Best Poems of 1968, 1970, 1971; (Borestone Mountain Poetry Awards Volume) Pacific Books. Address: 395 North Wade Ave., Washington, PA 15301, USA.

TAYLOR, Margaret. Educator; Poet; Artist. Education: Grad., State Tchrs. Coll., Clarion, Pa. Married Lynn A. Taylor. Positions held: Tchr.; Choir Soloist, Madrigal Music Club; H.S. Basket-ball Coach; Play Dir.; Silversmith; Artist; Sunday-School Tchr.; Girl Scout Ldr.; Golfer. Member, World Poetry Soc. Intercontinental. Published works: An Artist's Rondel, 1969; Caravan, 1973. Contbr. to: Builders; State Button Bulletin; Am. Mosaic; The Written Word Anthol.; Young Publications Selected Poems; Sing Naked Spirit; Evening News, Ctrl. Pa., etc. Honours, awards: Chandler Award, World Poetry Day, 1967; Paul A.W. Wallace Award, NFSPS, 1969; Marvin Davis Winsett Original Form, ibid, 1969; Gertrude Soucier Hist. Award, 1969. Address: R.D.1, Box 157, Terra Alta, WV 26764, U.S.A.

TAYLOR, Mary Ola, pen name **TAYLOR, May Ola,** b. 10 Apr. 1880. Housewife. Education: Navasota HS, Texas; Sam Houston Teacher's Coll., Huntsville, Texas; Baylor Univ., Waco, Texas. Married to Walter T. Taylor. Positions held: Member of Coun. on Organisation and Public Relations, 1938. Memberships: Key Women of America (Hon. Life Member, 1938); Poetry Soc. of Texas (Hon. Life Member, 1968); Internat. Platform Assoc., 1971; Shakespeare Club (Org. and first Pres.); Fed. Clubs of Texas. Published works: Greater Anthol. of Verse, 1936; Anthol. of American Poetry, Book IV, 1962; Visions in Verse, 1967; Poetry Soc. of Texas Book of the Year, 1968; Life's Meditations, 1958. Texas History of Poetry (unpublished). Contbr. to: Progressive Farmer; Christian Herald; Navasota Examiner, etc.,

etc. Address: 167 Oak Dr., Lake Jackson, TX 77566, USA.

TCHERNINE, Odette, Author; Journalist; Poet. Positions held: Sub-Ed., news-feature agency & trade paper; London Edit. Staff, Hearst Grp., U.K.; Brit. Corres., Am. Weekly, –1963; Freelance & Outside Corres., nat & country newspapers & jrnls.; Engl. & French Poetry Readings, BBC-TV; Expo Sussex 68 Fest., 1968; Lecturing in Am. Univs., 1974. Memberships: Fellow, Royal Geographical Soc.; Press Club; Fndr. Mbr., the late Women's Press Club; Hon. Sec., Hon. Libn., formerly U.K. Fndr., Young Poets Grp.; Advsr., poetry & prose, publrs. & young people. Published works: (prose) Explorers & Travellers Tales, 1958, '63; The Snowman & Company, 1961: Spain, 1963; Explorers Remember, 1967, '68; The Yeti, 1970 (pub. U.S.A. under title 'In Pursuit of Abominable Snowman', 1971); Pamphlet of early poems, 1956. Contbr. to: (anthols) Pattern of Poetry (also recorded by EMI), 1963; My Kind of Verse, 1965; Poetry Soc.'s Tchrs. Anthols., 1966-68; Gallery, (Methuen), 1967; Without Adam, 1968; also many contbns. to newspapers & jrnls. Address: c/o The Royal Geographical Soc., Kensington Gore, London SW7, U.K.

TEEL, Knowles Witcher, b. 14 Mar. 1906. Retired Educator. Education: B.A. in Educ.; M.A. in Educ. & Speech. Married. Positions held: Tchr., Lake Victor, Tex., 1 yr., Florence, Tex., 3 yrs., Mathis, Tex., 1 yr. & Bandera, Tex., 38 yrs. Memberships: Poetry Soc. of Tex.; San Antonio Br., ibid; Local Pres., Delta Kappa Gamma; NEA; Tex. Educ. Assn.; Pres., local Tchr. Assn., sev. yrs.; Worthy Matron, Order of Eastern Star, 2 yrs.; Current Pres., Hill Co. Ret'd Tchr. Assn. Published works: group of poems in Wings Over Chaos; group of poems in Old Guard; Lift The Latch, 1973; Come In, 1973. Contbr. of poems to: Tex. Outlook (Tex. Tchr. Mag.); Mercury Mag., Lincoln, 1972; & in var. poetry mags. & local Bandera paper. Honours, awards: Poet Laureate, Chapt. 643, Order of the Eastern Star, 1973. Address: Box 174, Bandera, TX 78003, U.S.A.

TELEMAQUE, Harold Milton, b. 20 Aug. 1909. Educator. Education: Govt. Tchrs. 'n Coll., W. Indies; Engl. Lit., London Univ., UK; Dip. in Educ. Admin., UK; Cert. in Educ. Testing, ibid. Married, 1 s. Positions held: Prin., Fyzabad Intermediate Schl., Trinidad; Inspector of Schls., Sr. Inspector of Schls. & Schls. Supvsr., I & II, ibid. Memberships: Pres., Lit. League of Trinidad & Tobago; Pres., Schls. Supvsrs.' Assn.; Pres., St. Patrick's Lions Club; Writers' Soc.; Readers & Writers' Guild, Trinidad; Pres., Apax Lit. & Debating Assn.; Pres., St. Patrick Co. Lit. Assn. Published works: Burnt Bush, 1940; Scarlet, 1953. Contbr. to: The Teachers' Herald; The Beacon; Bim; Kykoveral; Caribbean Voices; Caribbean Verses; Trinidad Anthology; Caribbean Federal Supplement; American Anthology; European Anthologies (Sweden, Germany, Russia, Czechoslovakia); Bite iln Anthology; West Indian periodicals. Recip. of BBC Pulitzer Prize as leading W. Indian Poet, 1947, '48. Address: Bungalow 11 (Bel Air), No. 22 Rd., Crest Camp, Fyzabad, Trinidad, West Indies.

TENE, Benjamin, b. 10 Dec. 1914. Editor. Married, 1 son & 1 daughter. Positions held: Editor, Michmar L'Iladim. Memberships: Assn. of the Hebrew Writers in Israel; P.E.N. club. Published works: Mehora, 1939; Massa Begalil, 1949; Beheret Hadwai, 1945; Tmolin Al Hasaf, 1947; Hazamir, 1963; Shirim Upoemot, 1967; Ktsir Hapele (for children), 1957; Mizmor Lehag (for children), 1973. Recip., Alfred Jurzykowski Fndn. Award, 1970. Address: Karni 8, 69 025 Tel-Aviv, Israel.

TENNANT, Daisy Mae Elmore, b. 27 Aug. 1910. Poet. Education: Univ. of Tex., 1930; Odessa, Tex. Evening Coll.; Rutherford Bus. Coll., 1967. Married Tracy W. Tennant (div.), 2 daughters. Positions held: p/t Sec. to Chmn. Bd., Chief Exec. Off., Office Mgr., Ormand Inds. Inc., Odessa, Tex., 1955-64; Dallas, 1964–;

Office Mgr., Main Lafrentz & Co.; Poetry Workshop Ldr., Odessa Evening Coll., 1957-59; Poetry Chmn., Odessa Coll. Writer's Roundup, 1957-63; Special Adv. Comm. Servs., Womens Dept., Tex. Bank & Trust Co., Dallas, 1966–. Memberships: Poetry Soc. Am.; Nat. Fed. State Poetry Socs.; affiliate, Acad. Am. Poets; Poetry Soc. Tex. (Rec. Sec., 1968–, Chmn., Tex. Poet's Meml. Coll., Baylor Coll., 1966–, Prog. Chmn., 1967–; Treas., 1969); Pres., Writer's Workshop, Odessa, 1961-62; V.P., Shakespeare Club, Odessa Coll., 1962; Avalon World Arts Acad.; Vachel Lindsay Assn., etc. Judge, var. poetry contests. Published works: (books of verse) Shifting Sands, 1954; Miss Fitts & Miss Cellany, 1960. Contbr. to: (anthols.) Anthol. of Am. Poetry, 1959; Avalon Anthols., 1962; Nat. Fed. Anthol., 1968, etc. & also to newspapers, mags., radio, TV. Honours, awards: Hadra Meml. Award, 1965; Chapbook Award, 1963; Globe Peace Award, 1966; Lyric Award, 1966; Grand Prix Award, Nat. Fed. State Poetry Socs., 1966; Hurley Meml. Award, 1967, etc. Address: 7131 Casa Loma St., Dallas, TX, U.S.A.

TESSLER, Yvonne Ferree Fair, b. 25 July 1934. Writer. Education: Radcliffe Coll., 1952-53; Univ. of Denver, 1955-56. Married Gary S. Tessler, 3 sons. Positions held: Sec., Mental Hlth. Div., Colo. State Dept. of Public Hlth.; Co–Owner, Talent a la Carte & Stage a la Carte. Memberships: Poetry Soc. of Am.; South & West Lit. Assn.; Screen Actors Guild; Am. Fed. of TV & Radio Artists; Colo. Communicators Assn.; Writers Roundtable. Contbr. to: Poems by Poets, Vol. I, 1973, & Vol. II, 1974; Community Mental Health; The Denver Post; Red-Axe. Address: 637 South Corona, Denver, CO 80209, U.S.A.

TEUFEL, Dolores E., b. 11 June 1921. Executive Secretary (retired). Education: Grad. from Lewistown HS, Lewistown, Pa.; Grad. from Central Pa. Business Coll., Harrisburg, Pa. Married, Donald H. Teufel; 6 children. Writes editorials and articles; also artist (has had several one-man shows of paintings). Position held: Executive Sec., Fed. Government, 20 yrs. Memberships: Harrisburg Chapter, Pennsylvania Poetry Soc., Inc.; Pennsylvania Poetry Soc., Inc.; Nat. Fed. of State Poetry Socs., Inc.; Poet's Study Club of Terre Haute, Ill.; American Poetry League. Published works: Collected Poems, 1963; Reflections, 1967; Soft Sound of Beauty, 1968; Star Gazers, 1969; Footprints on the Moon, 1971; Let Freedom Ring, 1973. Contbr. to: Eve. News & Patriot; Altoona Mirror; The Sentinel; Daily News; Spring Creek Church of the Brethren Messenger; American Poetry League Bulletin; The Swordsman Review; Pennsylvania Poetry Soc., Inc. Newsletter. Awards: 2nd Prize, Wisconsin Award, Nat. Fed. of State Poetry Socs., Inc., 1973; 1st Hon. Mention, Winter Contest, Indiana State Poetry Contest, 1973; 2nd Hon. Mention, Estella Mayer MacBride Mem. Award, Pennsylvania Poetry Soc., Inc., 1973; Hon. Mention, Sans Souci Award and Hon. Mention, The Edna Groff Diehl Mem. Award, Pennsylvania Poetry Soc., Inc., 1971, etc. Address: 322 Meadow Lane, Hershey, PA 17033, USA.

THACKRAY, Brian, b. 22 Feb. 1947. Retail Manager. Education: Liverpool Coll. of Commerce, U.K., 1966-68; B.A., Univ. of Guelph, Ont., Canada, 1970-72. Married Judith Price, twin-daughters. Positions held: Acctg. Clerk, Asst. Serv. Mgr. (Automobile), 1968; Acct., 1968-70; Asst. Lectr. in Film, Univ. of Guelph, 1972-73; Ont. Area Mgr. for Retail Chain of Craft & Jewellery Boutiques, 1973–. Member, League of Canadian Poets. Published works: The Bent Wire & Other Poems, 1972; Three Fires Down, an anthol., 1974; Poem, anthol., 1974. Contbr. to: Alive; Canadian Author & Bookman; Grub; Inscape; The Ontarion; Queen's Qtly. Et in Arcadia id (a fine art multi-media proj. on the spacetime continuum exhibited in 1972 at the Univ. of Guelph & the West Surrey Coll. of Art, Surrey, U.K.) Recorded for BBC Radio. Verse play 'The Pawns' produced at Univ. of Guelph, 1973. Recip., 1st winner of Univ. of Guelph Students' Fed. Lit. Comp., 1972. Address: 16 Towering Heights Blvd.,

Suite 202, St. Catharines, Ont., Canada.

THADDEUS, Janice, b. 20 Jul. 1933. College Professor. Education: B.A., Barnard, 1955; Ph.D., Columbia Univ., 1965. Married; 1 s., 1 d. Positions held: Teaching at Barnard Coll., 1956–. Membership: Poetry Soc. of America. Contbr. to: Atlantic; Beloit Poetry Journal; Michigan Qtly. Review; The Quest; The Golden Year; Internat. Who's Who in Poetry Anthol., 1972. Address: 606 West 116 St., New York, NY 10027, USA.

THALAND, Rijn, b. 27 Mar. 1914. Author & Editor. Educ: studied var. subjects at Univ., 1931-36. Positions held: Dramatic Producer, Production Assistant, 1936; Editor, Theatre, Music & Lit. Critic, 1937-42; Soldier, 1943-45; Publisher's Reader, 1946-51; Chief Editor of periodicals, Editor & Author num. works, since 1952. Published works incl: Die Regina, poems, 1967; Der Grosse Bruder, 1968; Vogelmenschen und Meilergötter, 1969; Wie wird neue Sprache wirklich? 1971. Contbr. to: Rostocker Anzeiger; Niedersächsische Tageszeitung; Würzburger Wolksblatt; Die Weltliteratur; Die Schöne Literatur; Die Feder, Address: c/o Edition Oliva, Postfach 309, D 7547 Wildbad, German Fed. Republic.

THANGAPPA, Mathanapandian Lenin, pen name **THANGAPPA, M.L.,** b. 8 Mar. 1934. Educator. Education: B.A. Econs., 1954; B. degree in Tchng., 1957; M. degree in Tamil Lit., 1962. Married, 4 children. Positions held: H.S. Tchr., H.S. in Pondicherry, 1957-68; Tutor in Tagore Arts Coll., Pondicherry, 1968-71; Asst. Prof. in Tamil, ibid, 1971–. Memberships: former Mbr., Tamil Writers Assn., Madras. Published works: Hues & Harmonies From An Ancient Land, 1970 (trans. into Engl.), 1970; I Sing, 1973; booklet of children's verses in Tamil, 1973. Contbr. to: Vanambadi; Thenmozhi; Thenaruvi; Kavignan; Kaikatti; Cyclo-Flame, U.S.A.; Poet, Madras; New Times Observer, Pondicherry; Modern Rationalist, Madras. Honours, awards: Medal, Tamil Writers Assn., 1957; Prize for trans. of Tamil poem, 1965, 1st pl., trans. comp., 1972. Address: Avval Nagar, Pondicherry 8, India.

THEIS, 'Ed' Edmund G., pen names **AEON, AESONIUS, PUBLIUS II, Jr., etc.,** b. 14 Sept. 1927. Poet; Philosopher. Education: Luxembourg 'Gymnase'; Free Univ. of Brussels; Sorbonne, Paris; Univ. of Chicago; Univ. of Colo. Contbr. to: Poetry (Chicago); The Atlantic; The Colo. Quarterly; Ladies' Home Jrnl.; Veterans' Voices. Has written hundreds of poems, sev. plays, essays & 'The Book of Aton'. Address: Unit 8, VA Hosp., Ft. Lyon, CO 81038, U.S.A.

THEROUX, Paul, b. 10 Apr. 1941. English Lecturer; Novelist. m. Anne Castle Theroux, 1s. Positions held: Tchr., Soche Hill Coll., Malawi; Tchr., Makerere Univ., Uganda; Lectr., Engl., Univ. of Singapore, 1968–. Published works: (novels) Waldo, 1968; Fong and the Indians, 1968; Girls at Play, 1969. Contbr. to: Transition; Black Orpheus; Transatlantic Review; Evergreen Review; Malahat; Drum Beat (anthology), 1967. Address: Dept. of English, Univ. of Singapore, Singapore 10.

THERSON-COFIE, Larweh, b. 8 Sept. 1943. Journalist. Education: Universal Coll., Somanya, Ghana; Ghana Inst. of Jrnlsm., Accra. Positions held: Staff Reporter, Daily Graphic, 1967; Sr. Reporter, ibid, 1971. Memberships: Nat. Assn. of Writers, Ghana; Past Sec., Ghana Assn. of Writers, 1969-71; Mbr., Rsch. Bd., ibid. Contbr. to: African Voices (anthol. of poems by Africans), 1974; The Voice of Black Africa, in press; BBC; Ghana Broadcasting Corp. Address: Editl. Dept., Daily Graphic, P.O. Box 742, Accra, Ghana, W. Africa.

THEVOZ, Jacqueline, pen name also **BELSEN, Patricia,** b. 29 Apr. 1926. Ballet Teacher & Journalist. Education: studied Pol. Sci. at University; Acad. of Music & Ballet. Married, 2 daughters. Positions held:

Writer; Choreographer; Composer of Music; Head Mistress of Ballet Schl.; Music & Rhythmic Tchr.; Jrnlst. & Traveller. Memberships incl: Société Suisse des Ecrivains; Société Fribourgeoise des Ecrivains; Société des Ecrivains Vaudois; Société Suisse de Pédagogie musicale; Fndr., Centre de chorégraphie musicale & the Mouvement pour le retour à l'ancienne liturgie catholique. Published works: (poetry) Mon Grand Voyage autour du monde, 1966; Raison vagabonde, 1959; Le Cheval, 1972; La Danse, 1972; La Fête des Mères (record); var. other publs. Contbr. to: Revue de Belles-Lettres; Revue indépendante; Présence Humaine; Revue Moderne; Art et Poésie, etc. Honours, awards: Prix Folloppe de la Faculté des Lettres de Lausanne, 1949; 1er Prix au Joutes poétiques de la Société des Poètes et Artistes de France, 1968; Prix d'honneur de l'Ile des Poètes; Prix Michael-Titus; Prix 'Perspectives'; Prix Regain; Médaille Honoré Broutelle; Mention honorable de la Société toulousaine Arts et Lettres; Médaille de bronze de la Ville de Valenciennes, 1972; Médaille d'Or & Médaille d'honneur de l'Académie Internationale de Lutèce, Paris, 1973, etc. Address: 23 Avenue de Collonges, 1004 Lausanne, Switzerland.

THIBAUDEAU, Colleen, b. 29 Dec. 1925. Housewife. Education: B.A., Univ. Coll., Univ. of Toronto, 1948; M.A., ibid, 1949. Married James Reaney. Positions held: Promotion Dept., McClelland & Stewart; Teaching Asst. in Angers, France; p/t Govt. Census Jobs; p/t Canadiana bookstore. Member, local Poets' Workshop. Published works: Lozeges, Poems in the Shapes of Things; Air 3, 20 poems, 1971; Air 14, 15, 16. Contbr. to: Canadian Forum; Contemporary Verse; Northern Review; Poetry (Chicago); Alphabet: Here & Now; (anthols.) Made in Canada; The Wind Has Wings. Address: 276 Huron St., London N6A-2J9, Ont., Canada.

THIBEAU, John G., pen name **THIBEAU, Jack,** b. 14 Jan. 1941. Writer. Published works: The Saint & the Football Players, 1968; Conversation with Apollinaire, 1972; Los Cines, 1973. 'The Saint & Football Players' produced for theatre by Mabou Mines, Lamama etc., N.Y.C., 1973. Contbr. to: Rolling Stone Mag.; San Francisco Mag.; Wild Dog.; The Daily Planet; Focus/Media Textbook; Ploughshares; Nexus. Address: 11 Royce Rd., Newton Ctr., MA, U.S.A.

THIELE, Colin Milton, b. 16 Nov. 1920. Teacher. Education: B.A., Univ. of Adelaide, Australia; Adelaide Tchrs. Coll. Positions held: Tchr.; Lectr. in Engl., then, Sr. Lectr. & Vice-Prin., Wattle Pk. Tchrs. Coll., 1957-65; Prin., ibid, 1965–. Memberships: Fellowship of Australian Writers (Pres., S. Australia); Engl. Tchrs. Assn. (Pres.); Australian Soc. of Authors (Coun. mbr.); Adelaide Festival of Arts (Mbr. Lit. Comm.). Published works include: Progress to Denial, 1945; Splinters and Shards, 1945; The Golden Lightning, 1951; Man in A Landscape, 1960; Gloop the Gloomy Bunyip, 1962; In Charcoal and Conté, 1966; Selected Verse, 1970; Gloop the Bunyip, 1970. Contbr. to the following anthols., jrnls., mags., etc: Jindyworobak Anthol., 1953 (Ed.); Favourite Australian Stories, 1963 (Ed.); Meanjin; Poetry Mag.; Canadian Poetry Mag.; Overland; Australian Letters; The Bull.; Australian Book Review, & many others. Also author of num. radio verse plays, etc. Honours, awards: Miles Poetry Prize, 1944; Jubilee Radio Prize for Verse Play, 1951; Grace Leven Poetry Prize, 1961. Address: 24 Woodhouse Crescent, Wattle Park, S Australia, 5066.

THIERRY, Marie-Paule, b. 30 Sept. 1923. Education: l'Ecole Normale des Soeurs de Notre-Dame, Bastogne. Married Jean Roisin, 2 sons. Memberships: Societe des Gens de Lettres de France; Association des Ecrivains Belges; Scriptores Catholici; Association des Ecrivains Wallons. Published works: Poemes du Bord de l'Eau, 1954; Les Primejoies, 1957; Chere Solitude, 1969; La Maison de Toile, 1971. Contbr. to: Femmes d'Aujourd'hui; Annette; Cahiers de l'Union des Ecrivains Vosgiens. Honours, awards: Prix Blaise Cendrars, for 'Chere Solitude', 1969; Prix

H.-J Proumen, l'Académie Internationale de Culture Française, 1970; Prix des Poètes Belges for 'La Maison de Toile', 1970. Address: Avenue des Noisetiers, 28, 1170 Brussels, Belgium.

THIERY, Herman, pen name **DAISNE, Johan,** b. 2 Sept. 1912. Librarian. Educ: Econ. Scis. & Slavic Langs., Univ. of Ghent, Belgium. Positions held incl: Prof., Germanic Langs.; Chief Libn., Ghent. Memberships: PEN Club; Royal Flemish Acad. of Lang. & Lit.; Admin. Coun., Royal Film Archive, Belgium. Published works in Dutch incl: collections of poetry since 1935; (Novels) L'escalier de pierre et de nuages; L'Homme au crâne rasé; Baratzeartea; Les Dentelles de Montmirail; (theatre) L'épée de Tristan; var. books on the cinema. Contbr. to var. newspapers & revues. Honours, awards: Prize, City of Ghent, 1944; Die Kogge Int. Prize, Germany, 1967; Belgian State Prize, 1946, 1960; Royal Flemish Acad. Prize, 1957, 1958. Address: Ottogracht 2, B-9000 Ghent, Belgium.

THIRY, Marcel, b. 13 Mar. 1897. Poet; Writer. Education: Univ. of Liège. Published works: (poetry) Toi qui pâlis au nom de Vancouver, 1924; Plongeantes Proues, 1925; L'Enfant Prodigue, 1927; Statue de la Fatigue, 1934; La Mer de la Tranquillité, 1938; Ages, 1950; Poésie, 1958; Vie Poésie, 1961; Le Pestin d'Attente 1963; (prose) Marchands, 1937; Echec au Temps, 1945; La Belgique pendant la Guerre, 1947; Juste, 1953; Simul, 1957; Comme si, 1959; Le grand Possible, 1960; Le Tour du monde en guerre, 1965; Nondum Jam Non, 1966. Awards: Prix Verhaeren, 1926; Prix triennal de Poésie, 1935; Grand Prix Quinquennal de Poésie, 1958, Prix Bernheim, 1963; Grand Prix quinquennal de Littérature, 1965.

THOMAE, Betty Jane, b. 9 Sept. 1920. Legal Secretary. Education: Franklin Univ. Married & divorced twice, 1 son, 1 daughter. Memberships: Poetry Soc. of Mich.; CSSI, Rome; Int. Clover Poetry Assn.; Marquis Biographical Lib. Soc. Published works: (pamphlets) Stand Still, 1969; Collected Sonnets, 1969; (book) Roses & Thorns, 1970. Rep. in num. anthols. inclng: Fragments of Faith; Poetry Parade; Modern Am. Lyrics; Lyrics of Love; Spring Anthols.; From Sea to Sea in Song; Prairie Poet Anthol.; Poetry Pageant; IWWP Anthol. Contbr. to: The Am. Bard; The Muse; The Am. Poet; Jean's Jrnl.; Flame; Scimitar & Song; Am. Poetry League Bulletin; Prairie Poet; Am. Poetry Mag.; Scintilla; Poet, etc. Honours, awards: Medal of Hon., CSSI, Rome, 1969; Cit., World Poetry Soc., 1970; Danae, Int. Clover Poetry Assn.; Advisory Mbr., Marquis Biographical Lib. Assn. Address: 1008 Hardesty Pl. West, Columbus, OH 43204, U.S.A.

THOMAS, D(onald) M(ichael), b. 27 Jan. 1935. Lecturer. Education: New Coll., Oxford Univ., U.K. Positions held: Sr. Lectr. in Engl., Hereford Coll. of Educ. Published works: Personal & Possessive (pamphlet), 1964; Two Voices, 1968; Logan Stone, 1971; Ed., The Granite Kingdom, 1970; The Shaft (pamphlet), 1973. Contbr. to: Penguin Modern Poets, 1968; Encounter; London Mag.; Times Lit. Supplement; Critical Quarterly; Poetry (Chicago); New Letters; Denver Quarterly; Transatlantic Review; N.Y. Times; Spectator; Observer; Meanjin; Listener; New Worlds; Cornish Review. Honours, awards: Richard Hilary Prize, 1960; Bard of the Cornish Gorseth, 1973. Address: 10 Greyfriars Ave., Hereford, U.K.

THOMAS, Gilbert Oliver, b. 10 July 1891. Author & Literary Journalist. Education: Loeys Schl., Cambridge. Positions held: Edit. Staff, Chapman & Hall Ltd., Publrs., 1910-14 & Swarthmore Press, 1919-21; Ed., The Ventures, 1919-21. Memberships: Poetry Soc.; Engl. Assn. Published works include: Birds of Passage, 1912; The Wayside Altar, 1913; The Voice of Peace, 1914; The Further Goal, 1915; Towards the Dawn, 1918; Poems 1912-19, 1920; Mary of Huntingdon, 1928; The Inner Shrine, 1942; Selected Poems, 1952; Later Poems, 1960; Collected Poems, 1969. Contbr. to num. leading UK & USA anthols., & to

the following jrnls: Observer; Sunday Times; Punch English; NY Times; NY Herald Trib., etc. Address: Woodthorpe, Ipplegen, Newton Abbot, Devon, UK.

THOMAS, Henri, b. 7 Dec. 1912. Poet; Novelist Education: Strasbourg Univ. Positions held: Tchr., til 1939; Forces, 1940-47; Prog. Asst., French Section BBC, 1947-58; Lectr., Brandeis Univ., Mass., USA, 1956-60; Ed., German Dept., Editions Gallimard, Paris 1960-. Published works: (poetry) Travaux d'aveugle 1941; Signe de vie, 1944; le Monde absent, 1947; Nu désordre, 1950; (novels) Le Seau à Charbon, 1940; le Precepteur, 1942; la Vie ensemble, 1945; le Porte-a-faux, 1948; le Déserteur, 1951; la Nuit de Londres 1956; John Perkins, 1960; la Dernière Année, 1960; le Promontoire, 1961; la Chasse aux trésors, 1961; Sous le lien du temps, 1963; le Parjure, 1964; la Relique 1969. Awards & Honours: Prix Sainte-Beuve, 1956 Prix Medicis, 1960; Prix Femina, 1961; Chevalier, Légion d'honneur. Address: c/o Editions Gallimard, 5 rue Sebastien-Bottin, Paris 7me, France.

THOMAS, Jessie Leah, pen name, **THOMAS, Jessie Brown,** b. 8 Dec. 1893. Mortician (retired). Education: Grad., Floydada HS, Floyd Co., Texas, 1910; West Texas Teacher's Coll., 1910; Central Nazarene Univ., 1912; Creative Writing Courses, Oklahoma Univ. (Norman), 1945-47; Arkansas Univ., 1948; Feather & Feather ARTU, Houston, 1949; Univ. of Houston, Business Adm., 1951; Texas Woman's Univ. (Bible and Art), 1962-63. Widow of James M. Thomas; 1 s., 1 d. Memberships: Poetry Soc. of Texas (life member, councillor, donor of prizes, and acting judge); Wichita Falls, Texas, Poetry Soc. (pres., 1945); Wichita Falls, Texas, Woman's Forum Writer's Dept. (pres., 1946-47); University City Poetry Club, Fayetteville, Ark. (co-founder and councillor, 1948); Houston Chapter, Texas Poetry Soc. (co-founder and councillor, 1949, also vice-president); Modern Writers Club, Wichita Falls, Texas (pres.); Wichita Falls Poetry Soc. (pres.); Shakespeare Club, Denton, Texas (poet laureate, reporter, name on club "Honor Roll"); Poet Laureate, Texas Fed. Woman's Club, 1968-69, for State, and 3 times Poet Laureate in Pioneer District, 1966, 1967, 1968. Published works: Poems of Precious Memories, 1942; Dove at the Window, 1943. Contbr. to: Poetry Soc. of Texas Yearbook, 1946, 1948, 1950, 1951, 1954, 1958, 1960, 1963, 1972, 1973; New Mexico Mag. (for 15 yrs.); Baptist Standard Mag.; Pictorial New Mexico; Kaleidograph; Texas Outlook; Methodist Pub. House; Different; Hemisphere; Nevada Mag.; Progressive Farmer; Casket and Sunnyside. Recip. of many honours, and apptd. to Texas Governor's Fine Arts Committee, 1968, etc. Address: 1134 Frame St., Denton, TX 76201, USA.

THOMAS, Jill Penelope, b. 11 July 1938. District Nurse. Married, 2 daughters. Memberships: Fndr. Fellow, Int. Poetry Soc.; Attingham Writers' Grp.; Critical Qtly. Soc. Contbr. to: MacMillan's Educational Tapes; Educational Productions Ltd.; The Nursing Mirror; Orbis; Country Quest; The Dark Horse. Address: 'Haydock', New Works, Telford, Shropshire TF6 5BS, U.K.

THOMAS, Peter Derek, pen name **PEDEREK, Simon,** b. 11 May 1928. College Professor. Education: Magdalen Coll., Oxford Univ., UK, 1947-50; Hampshire Drama Schl., 1955-56. Positions held: Sr. Engl. Master & Headmaster, UK, 1954-57; ibid, Opoku Ware, Ghana, 1958-60; Lectr. in English, Univ. of Nigeria, 1960-65; Visiting Lectr. in English, Univ. of Utah, USA, 1965-68; Jr. Fellow, Mackinac Coll., Mich., 1968-69; Humanities Prof., Lake Superior State Coll., Mich., 1969-. Memberships: Poetry Soc. of Am.; World Poetry Soc.; Poetry Soc. of Mich.; Int. Poetry Assn. Cleveland, Ohio; Am. Poets Fellowship Soc. Charleston, Ill. Ed., The Woods-runner, LSSC. Publications: Poems from Nigeria, 1967; Ashanti Blood, 1969; The Iron Gates, Polyphonic Poem in XIII parts, 1970-71; Isis Speaks, 1971; The Alien City, 1971; Of Dreams & Bullets, 1971; Revealer of Secrets, 1972; A Handful of Bright Days, 1972; Sun Bells, 1973.

Contbr. to: Capuchin Annual; Review of English Lit.; Insight; Nigeria Mag.; Literary Review; Quest; Chicago Tribune; African Arts; Western Humanities Review; Conch, Paris; Quoin; Cardinal Poetry Quarterly; Hiram Poetry Quarterly; DeKalb Jrnl. of Lit. Arts; Voices Int.; Angels. Honours, awards: Utah State Inst. of Fine Arts Poetry Prize, 1967; NFSPS Certs. of Excellence, 1967 & '68; Poems From Nigeria nominated to World Poetry Soc. Archives, 1968-69, & num. others. Address: Humanities Dept., Lake Superior State Coll., Sault Ste. Marie, Mich. 49783, USA.

THOMAS, (Rev.) Ronald Stuart. Poet; Priest. Education: Univ. of Wales; B.A.; St. Michael's Coll., Llandaff. Positions held: Ordained deacon, 1936; Priest, 1937; Curate of Chirk, 1936-40; Curate of Hanmer, in charge of Talarn Green, 1940-42; Rector of Manafon, 1942-54; Vicar of St. Michael's Eglwysfach, diocese of St. David's, 1954-. Published works: Stones of the Field, 1947; Poems 1942-54, 1955; Song At The Year's Turning, 1955; Poetry For Supper, 1958; Tares, 1961; Bread Of . Truth, 1963; Words of the Poet, 1964; Pietà, 1966; Not That He Brought Flowers. Honours, Awards: Heinemann Award, Royal Soc. of Lit., 1956; Sovereign's Gold Medal For Poetry, 1964; Welsh Arts Coun. Award for Poetry, 1967-68. Address: St. Michael's, Eglwysfach, Cardiganshire, Wales.

THOMAS, Stanley Joseph, b. 10 Aug. 1932. Businessman. Education: Princeton Univ. Married, 3 daughters. Currently self employed businessman (printing allied profession). Memberships: Walthamstow Poetry Soc.; Richmond Poetry Soc.; Cockpit Theatre Workshop Grp., etc. Published works: Hawk & Handsaw, 1971; Dream Sequence, 1972. Contbr. to: Goswellian; Candelabrum; Somethings; Quill; Scrip; Samphire; Anglo-Welsh Review; Expression One; Good Elf; Gong; Informer; Viewpoints; Bogg; Platform; Contrasts; Shore; Gargantua; Poetry One; Wheels; Promontory; Vole; Poets & Poetry; New Headland; Ember Press; Lines; Centre 17; Poet Tree Centaur; The Village Review; Pink Peace; Poet; Littack. Address: 115 Old St., London EC1V 9JR, U.K.

THOMAS, Stelleta Marie Angel, pen name, THOMAS, Stelleta Angel, b. 10 April 1910. Secretary; Engineer; Sales; Inspector. Education: HS; 2½ yrs. College. Memberships: Texas Poetry Soc., Dallas; Fort Worth Branch (Sec., and Publicity); Internat. Poetry Soc. Contbr. to: Wee-Wisdom; Halton News; N.Side News; Fort Worth Press; Westminster Mag.; Texas Parents Mag.; Quicksilver; 4 Anthols.; Spring Fiesta; Baylor Coll. (special publication), etc. Awards: Commendation, Westminster Mag.; 3rd Prize, Texas Poetry Soc., etc. Address: 3705 Tulsaw Way, Apt. E., Fort Worth, TX 76107, USA.

THOMAS, William Stephen, b. 5 Sept. 1909. Museum Director. Education: A.B., Harvard Coll., Cambridge, Mass., 1932; var. grad. course; Apprentice Course in Museum Admin., Newark Mus., N.J., 1934. Positions held: Accompanied sci. expeds. for botany, biol., etc. to var. Ctrl. & South Am. countries; Volunteer Asst., U.S. Ranger-Naturalist (Guide-Lectr.) Glacier Nat. Park, Mont., summers, 1931, '32, '33; Admin. Staff (Asst. Registrar), Metropolitan Mus. of Art, N.Y., 1934-36; Dir. of Educ., Acad. of Natural Scis., Phila., Pa., 1936-39; Dir., Rochester Mus. of Arts & Scis., 1946-68; Lectr. & Cons. to Museums in many countries, 1949-67. Memberships: Editl. Bd., Harvard Advocate, 1932, '33; Co-Ed., The Gleam, Rochester Poetry Soc., 1960-61; Lit. Discussion Grp. Mbr., The Fortnightly Club, Rochester, N.Y., 1948-; Sec., ibid, 1952-73; Century Assn., N.Y.C., 1966-; V.P., Arts Coun. of Rochester, Exec. Coun., 1971-. Published works: Lie Quiet Soul, pamphlet, 1947. Contbr. to: The Dutchman Yearbook; Harvard Advocate; Coll. Verse anthol.; N.Y. Herald Tribune, etc. Recip. var. hons. Address: 988 Park Ave., Rochester, NY 14610, U.S.A.

THOMPSON, Amanda Meade, pen name **THOMPSON, Amanda Meade Brewer,** b. 18 Oct. 1903.

Educator (retired). Education: A.B., Marshall Univ., Huntington, W.Va. Married Jay Vernon Thompson. Positions held: Tchr. in Mingo Co. Educational System; Prin., Mingo Co. Schl. System. Memberships: Fndr. & Pres., Appalachian Poetry Guild; 2nd V.P., W. Va. Poetry Soc.; World Poetry Soc.; Johnson Co. Poetry Soc., Prestonsburg, Ky.; Ky. Poetry Soc., Lexington. Published works: Romantic West Virginia, 1963; I Sing of Appalachia, 1967, 2nd printing, 1972; Ballad of Rose Anna McCoy, 1961. Contbr. to: Appalachian Poets, vols. I-X, 1950-73; Williamson Daily News, W.Va.; Huntington Herald Dispatch; Ashland Independent, Ky.; Greenup News, Ky.; W.Va. DAR News, Charleston; Alta Vista Jrnl., Va.; World Poets, India; Seydell Qtly., Brussels, Belgium; Ideals, Milwaukee, Wis. Poetry Ed. of the 'Poetry Page', W.Va. Schl. Jrnl., 1966-73; Poetry Ed. of the 'Poetry Corner', Williamson Daily News, W.Va., 1950-73. Honours, awards incl: Recip., Best Tchr. Cert, NBC, 1941; Decoration of Chivalry Medal, Odd Fellows Lodge, 1946; Medal, Valley Forge Freedoms Fndn., 1963. Address: Box 365, Kermit, WV 25674, U.S.A.

THOMPSON, David E., pen name HOMPSON, Davi Det, b. 7 Aug. 1939. University Instructor. Education: B.A., Anderson Coll., Ind.; M.F.A., Ind. Univ., Bloomington. Positions held: Grad. Tchng. Asst., Ind. Univ.; Asst. Prof., Herron Schl. of Art, Ind. Univ., Indianapolis; Artist-in-Res., Va. C'wealth Univ., Richmond, Va. Published works: Disassemblage, 1966; Blue Light Containment, 1966; S553 Study Manual, 1967; White Table Cloth, 1969; Everyday Friendship Postcards, 1969; There's Music in My Soles! 1970; Letter Packet, 1972; NNa, 1973. Contbr. to: Pulls, Rolls & Folds, 1966; Koan, 1967; Notebook, 1970; Space Atlas, 1971; This Book is a Movie, 1971; Assembling II, III, & IV, 1971-73; Art Work, No Commercial Value, 9 Ozs, 1972; Breakthrough Fictioneers, 1973; In Youth, 1972; De Tafelronde, 1973; Fluxshoe, 1973; Pferscha 2, 1973. Address: 2824 Monument Ave., Richmond, VA 23221, U.S.A.

THOMPSON, Esther Lee, b. 7 Apr. 1919. Freelance Writer. Education: Eve. classes, Southern Methodist Univ., 1972, and Tarrant County Jr. Coll., 1973; Sec. course, Texas Business Coll.; Drama & Playwriting, Dallas Theater Center, and Journalism with Newspaper Inst. of America. Married, now widowed. Positions held: Insurance Underwriter, Universal Life Ins. Co.; Feature Writer for Dallas Star Post, and Bronze Texan Newspapers; Assoc. Editor of Good Publishing Co.; Hat Designer; Public Speaker. Memberships: Poetry Soc. of Texas; Nat. Fed. of State Poetry Socs.; Internat. Platform Assoc. (past member); Florence B. Brooks and Leola Gray Lit. and Art Club (Chairman of Poetry & Short Story Division). Contbr. to: Dallas Star Post; Bronze Texan; Fort Worth Press; Poet Lore; Poetry Soc. of Texas Book of the Year. Recip. John C. Klein Award from the Newspaper Inst. of America, 1968; Popular Prize, Poetry Soc. of Texas, 1971, and Eva Welles Wangsgaard Lyric Award, 1973. Address: 200 South Chandler Dr., Fort Worth, TX 76111, USA.

THOMPSON, Fannie Lee, pen name THOMPSON, Fannie Lee McCondiehie, b. 6 Feb. 1891. Teacher. Education: Cert. of Hon. for Jr. H.S. Tchng.; D.H.L., London Inst. for Applied Rsch. Married W.W. Thompson. Positions held: Classroom Tchr.; Prin.; TV Progs. Memberships: Ala. State Poetry Soc., 1968-; Retired Tchrs. Assn.; Int. Platform Assn. Published works: Presentation for Children, 1960; var. articles for Thom Henrich Publs., -1972. Contbr. to: The Sampler; Easter Anthol., 1971; Anthol. of Southeastern Poets, 1971; Garland of Verse, 1971; Wilcox Progressive Era; Anthol. of Ala. Poets, 1967; Birmingham Post; Birmingham News; Western Sun; Ala. Writer, etc. Address: 308 – 4th Court West, Birmingham, AL 35204, U.S.A.

THOMPSON, Jessie Grace Cowan (Mrs. E.L.), pen name **GAYE, Jay,** b. 11 Dec. 1891. Speech and Drama Teacher (retired). Education: Grad., School of

Speech, Northwestern Univ., 1917; B.A., Chadron State Coll., 1939. Positions held: Teacher, Elem. grades, Lenox, Iowa, 1910-15; Speech & Physical Education Teacher, Chadron State Normal, now Chadron State Coll., Neb.; Speech & Drama (replacement), ibid, 1954. Memberships: Neb. State Pres., Nat. League of Am. Pen Women, Inc., 1964-66; State Pres., Neb. Pharmaceutical Auxiliary, 1949-50; Worthy Matron, Ivy Leaf Chap., Order of the Eastern Star, 1928; Pres., Chapter BL, PEO Sisterhood; ibid, Daughters of American Revolution; Chadron Culture Club; Writing Octette. Published work: The Photo-Birthday Book, 1954. Contbr. to: To Each His Own, Avalon Anthol., 1958; Today the Stars, Avalon Anthol., 1960; The Muse Anthol., 1962; Midwest Chaparral; Modernalia; Scimitar & Song; Seydell Qtly.; American Bard; New Athenaeum; Pen Woman; Alliance Daily Times-Herald; Radio broadcasts. Honours: Poet Laureate, Midwest Fed. of Chaparral Poets for Neb., 1957-60. Address: 120 East 10th St., Chadron, NB 69337, USA.

THOMPSON, John, b. 1907. Broadcaster. Education: Melbourne Univ. Positions held: with Aust. Broadcasting Co., 1939–; with AIF, WWII; ABC War Corres., Java. Published works: I Hate & I Love, 1963; Hubbub in Java (prose); On Lips of Living Men (prose), & 3 other books of Poetry. Co-ed., Penguin Book of Mod. Australian Verse. Contbr. to: Mod. Australian Verse, 1964. Address: c/o Angus & Robertson Ltd., 89 Castlereagh St., Sydney, Australia.

THOMPSON, Kent, b. 3 Feb. 1936. Associate Professor of English. Education: B.A., Engl. & Philos., Hanover Coll., Ind., U.S.A., 1957; M.A., State Univ. of Iowa, 1962; Ph.D., Univ. of Wales, U.K., 1965. Married Michaele, 2 sons (Kevin & David). Positions held: Instr., Ripon Coll., Wis., U.S.A., 1961-63; Asst. Prof., Colo. Women's Coll., Denver, Colo., 1965-66; Asst. Prof., later Assoc. Prof., Univ. of New Brunswick, Canada, 1966–. Mbr., League of Canadian Poets. Published works: Hard Explanations, 1968; sev. short stories; radio plays. Contbr. to: Canada First (anthol.); Queen's Quarterly; Canadian Forum; The Far Point; Quarry; West Coast Review; New Canadian & American Poetry; Floorboards; Salt; The Fiddlehead; var. CBC anthol. broadcasts. Address: Dept. of Engl., Univ. of New Brunswick, Fredericton, New Brunswick, Canada.

THOMPSON, Robert Bruce, b. 28 Oct. 1920. Industrial Chemist. Education: Univ. of Auckland; Tchr. Trng. Coll., Auckland. Positions held: Soldier; Tchr.; Indl. Chemist. Memberships: PEN Int., N.Z. Section; N.Z. Rep., Poetry Mag., Australia. Published works: Cast on the Doting Sea, 1955. Contbr. to: Arena; Poetry East-West; Poetry Australia; Poetry Mag. (Australia); Outposts; Bengali Lit.; Mate; Experiment; Poet (India); Frontiers; Ubulum (Oxford); N.Z. Monthly Review; New Voices of the Commonwealth; N.Z. Poetry Yearbook. Co-Fndr. & Ed., Image, 1958-61; Ed., 13 N.Z. Poets, 1952. Address: P.O. Box 79, Kawatawa, Bay of Islands, Northland, New Zealand.

THORBURN, James Alexander, b. 24 Aug. 1923. English Teacher. Education: B.A., Ohio State Univ., 1949; M.A., ibid., 1951. Positions held: Surveyor, Field Artillery, World War II; Surveyor, Internat. Boundary & Water Commn., US & Mexico; Hd., Engl. Dept., Sheridan Rural Agric. Schl., Mich.; Instr. in Engl., Univ. of Mo., Columbia; Instr. in Engl., Monmouth Coll., Ill.; Instr. of Engl., Tex. Western Coll.; Instr. of Engl., & in charge, Engl. Prog., Univ. of Mo. in St. Louis; Instr. in Engl., La. State Univ., 1961-70; Asst. Prof. Engl., Southeastern La. Univ., 1970–. Memberships: Avalon World Arts Assoc.; Experiment Group (formerly); Mod. Poetry Assoc. (formerly); Am. Name Soc.; Phi Kappa Phi; Nat. Council Tchrs. of Engl.; Conf. on Coll. Composition & Communication; Am. Assoc. Univ. Profs. Book Review Ed., Experiment: An Internat. Review. Contbr. to: (anthols.) Avalon Anthol., 1959-63; Nat. Poetry Anthol., 1960; The Spring Anthol., 1967-69; The Prairie Poet Anthol.,

1961; Ardentia Verba, 1967; Laudamus Te, 1967; Poetry Dial Anthol., 1968; Jacob Hofstadter (verplay), Experiment Theatre Anthol., 1, 1959; (jrnls.) Am. Weave; New Athenaeum; The Prairie Poet; Simbolica; Poetry Digest; Cape Rock Quarterly; Coll. Composition & Communication; Cats Mag.; Cyclotron; Cyclo-Flame; Flame; The Church Schl.; The Piggott (Ark.); Banner; Discourse; Home Life; NH Sunday News; Per/Se; Haiku Highlights; Writer's Digest; Cardinal Poetry Quarterly; Voices Internat.; Encore; Am. Haiku; Haiku (Canada); Poet Lore; Laurel Review. Translator of sev. Old Portuguese & Old Provencal lyrics into mod. Engl. verse, & of Beowulf into mod. Engl. verse. Honours: Citations for Merit, Flame, 1960, Cyclotron, 1965, & Flame Annual, 1966; 1st Prize, Category of Sacrements, Manifold Relig. Poetry Competition, 1966-67, & others. Address: Box 739, Engl. Dept., Southeastern La. Univ., Hammond, LA 70401, USA.

THORNOCK, Wanda Wilcox, b. 3 Mar. 1917. Poet. Education: Montpelier H.S.; Washington School of Art, Washington D.C., etc. Married to Royal A. Thornock; 1 s., 2 d. Member, Int. Platform Assoc.; Gem State Writers Guild (sometime Chairman). Pub. Relief Soc. pamphlet of the Church of Jesus Christ of Latterday Saints, 1972-73; The Idaho Egg pamphlet. Contrib. to: The Poets Corner of the Idaho Free Press, and News Tribune; The Era. Some material used on radio and TV. Awards: 3rd place, Gem State Writers Guild poetry contest, 1971, 1972; Award, Lathem Found. World Wide Art Contest; 1st Place, Idaho Egg Co. Poetry Contest; Prize, Relief Soc. Poetry Contest, Ch. of Jesus Christ of Latterday Saints. Address: 608 19th Ave. North, Nampa, Idaho 83651, USA.

THUMBOO, Edwin Nadason, b. 22 Nov. 1933. University Teacher. Education: B.A., Univ. of Malaya, Singapore, 1953-57; Ph.D., 1970. Married, 1 s., 1 d. Positions held: with Civil Service, 1957-66. Editor, Poetry Singapore, & Singapore/Malaysia issue, Poet (Madras); Lectr., Univ. of Singapore, 1966–; Gen. Ed., Mod. SE Asia Authors Series, Oxford Univ. Press. Mbr., Assn. Commonwealth Lit. & Lang. Studies. Published works: Rib of Earth, 1956; Seven Poets (ed.). Contbr. to: London Magazine; Meanjin; Outpost; Poetry Australia; Poetry Singapore; Poet (Madras); Solidarity; Southern Review; Transition; Tenggara; Wascana Review. Address: Engl. Dept., Univ. of Singapore, Bukit Timah Rd., Singapore 10.

THURMAN, Judith, b. 28 Oct. 1946. Writer. Education: B.A., Brandeis Univ., Waltham, Mass., U.S.A. Positions held: Lectr. in Engl. as a Second Lang., Brooklyn Coll.; Interpreter, U.S. Dept. of State. Published works: Putting My Coat On, 1972; Contbr. to The New York Times, Shenandoah, MS. Address: 141 Sullivan St., N.Y., NY 10012, U.S.A.

THURSTON, Mona Jane, pen name, VAN DUYN Mona, b. 9 May 1921. Writer; Teacher; Editor. Education: M.A., Univ. of Iowa; Hon. D.Litt., Wash. Univ., St. Louis, Mo.; Positions held: Instr. in Engl., Univ. of Iowa & Univ. of Louisville; Lectr. in Engl., Wash. Univ. Published works include: Valentines to the Wide World; A Time of Bees; To See, To Take. Contbr. to the following anthols., jrnls., mags., etc: The New Am. Review; The New Yorker; The New Republic; The Southern Review; Poetry; The Kenyon Review; Pebble; Poetry Northwest; Kayak, etc. Recip. of num. honours & awards, inclng: Borestone Mtn. Awards, 1968; Bollingen Prize in Poetry, 1971; Nat. Book Award in Poetry, 1971. Address: 7505 Teardale Ave., St. Louis, Mo., USA.

THWAITE, Anthony (Simon), b. 23 June 1930. Poet; Freelance Writer. Education: M.A., Oxford Univ. Positions held: Vis. Lectr. in Engl. Lit., Tokyo Univ., 1955-57; BBC Producer (radio), 1957-62; Lit. Ed., The Listener, 1962-65; Asst. Prof. of Engl., Univ. of Libya, 1965-67; Lit. Ed., New Statesman, 1968-72; Co-Ed., Encounter. Published works: Home Truths, 1957; The Owl in the Tree, 1963; Penguin Book of Japanese

Verse (co-ed.), 1964; The Stones of Emptiness, 1967; Inscriptions, 1973; New Confessions, 1974. Contbr. to: Encounter; Listener; London Mag.; New Statesman; Observer; Spectator; Sunday Times; Times Lit. Supplement. Recip., Richard Hillary Meml. Prize (for The Stones of Emptiness), 1968. Address: The Mill House, Low Tharston, Norfolk NOR 7OW, U.K.

THWAITES, Michael Rayner, b. 30 May 1915. Education: Geelong Grammar Schl.; Trinity Coll., Melbourne Univ.; New Coll., Oxford Univ.; Rhodes Scholar for Victoria for 1937; B.A., Melbourne; B.Litt., Oxon.; M.A., Oxon. Positions held: R.N.V.R., 1939-45; Lectr. in Engl. Dept., Melbourne Univ., 1947-49; Australian Commonwealth Service, 1950-71; Asst. Parliamentary Libn., Parliamentary Lib., Canberra, 1971–. Poetry Convenor for Canberra Arts Coun., 1974. Published works: Milton Blind, 1935; The Jervis Bay & Other Poems, 1942; Poems of War & Peace, 1968, '70. Contbr. to: The Age; Quadrant; Meanjin; Southerly; The Australian; Australian Poetry; Poetry in Australia; The Times. Honours, awards: Newdigate Prize, Oxford, 1938; King's Medal for Poetry, 1940. Address: The Parliamentary Lib., Parliament House, Canberra, A.C.T., Australia.

TIANG, Seng-yong, pen name, **LI, Lin,** b. 2 Sept. 1941. Teacher, Editor, Poet, Writer. Education: B.A., Nat. Chengchi Univ., Taipei, Taiwan. Positions held: Sec., Catering Servs. Staff & Workers' Trade Union, Singapore, 1963; Ed.-in-Chief, Evergreen Monthly, 1963; ibid., Laureate Engl. Mag., Taipei, 1965-66; ibid., Compass Engl. Mag., Taipei, 1966-67; Tchr., Nat. Chengchi Univ., Taipei. Memberships: United Poets Laureate Int.; Fndr., Ed.-in-Chief, Constellation Poetry Soc., Taipei. Published works: Our Songs, 1962; Unique Sound in December, 1966; Nights In Our Hands, 1969; The Roses, 1963; Love Song At The West Coast, 1961. Contbr. to: Constellation Poetry Quarterly, Taipei; Chung-wah Daily News; Sin Chew Daily News, Singapore; Intellectual Monthly, Taipei; Epoch Poetry Quarterly, Taipei; Laureate; Compass; Pioneer; Chinese New Poetry Mag. Address: 2, Lane 333, Antung St., Taipei, Taiwan, Repub. of China.

TIEMPO, Edith Lopez, b. 22 Apr. 1919. Professor of English. Educ: B.S.E., Silliman Univ., Dumaguete City, Philippines, 1947; M.A., Univ. of Iowa, U.S.A., 1949; Ph.D., Univ. of Denver, 1958. m. E.K. Tiempo, 2 children. Positions held: Prof., Engl., Silliman Univ., Philippines, 1961–; Chmn., Engl. Dept., ibid, current; Vis. Prof., Engl., Western Mich. Univ., Kalamazoo, 1963-64, '65-66; Vis. Prof., Wartburg Coll., Waverly, Iowa, 1964-65. Published works: The Tracks of Babylon and Other Poems, 1966; Abide, Joshua and O to: Poetry; Beloit Poetry Journal; (anthologies) Six Philippine Poets, 1954; Midland, 1961; Poems from XV Languages, 1964; New Writing from the Philippines, 1966. Honours, awards: Rockefeller Fndn. Grant, 1949-50; Palanca Award for Poetry, 1967. Address: Silliman Univ., Dumaguete City, Philippines.

TIFFT, Ellen, b. 28 June 1917. Writer. Education: Elmira Coll. Married Bela Tifft, 3 sons. Member, Poetry Soc. of Am. Published works: Door In A Wall, 1966, reprinted 1968; The Kissed Cold Kite, 1968; The Carnival Woods (w. Emily K. Harris), 1972; The Live-Long Day. A videotape of her work, accompanied by a Music Group, was made at Mansfield State Coll., 1972. Contbr. to: The New Yorker; The Christian Sci. Monitor; The Sat. Evening Post; The Transatlantic Review; The Wormwood Review; Lillabulero; Pyramid; Tle Wormwood Review; The Anglo-Welsh Review; Kaleidoscope; Abraxas 5 Anthol.; Poetry; Voices; The Poetry Book Mag.; Premiere; Yes; Chicago Tribune Mag.; Charas; Everywoman's; Accent; Poetry New York; Quicksilver; Haiku Highlights; Jean's Jrnl.; etc. Winner of Poetry Book Mag. Annual Award, 1950. Address: Crane Rd., East Hill, Elmire, NY 14901, U.S.A.

TIKHONOV, Nikolai Semyonovich, b. 1896. Poet, Novelist. Positions held: Del., Paris Conf. for the Defence of Culture, 1935; Chmn., Soviet Peace Comm., 1950; Chmn., Comm. for Lit. & the Arts, Lenin Prize Comm.; Dpty., USSR Supreme Soviet. Published works: (poetry) The Horde; Mead, 1922; Poems of Kakhetia, 1935; Friend's Shadow, 1935; Kirov Is With Us, 1941; Year Of Fire, 1942; Poems of Yugoslavia, 1947; Georgian Spring; Two Streams, 1951; At the Second World Congress of Supporters of Peace, 1961; May Morning, 1961; Poems, 1961; The Morning of Peace, 1962. Also sev. novels. Awards: State Prizes, 1942, '49, '52; Int. Lenin Peace Prize, 1958; Hero of Socialist Labour; Order of Lenin. Address: c/o Writers' Union of the USSR, 52 Vorovsky St., Moscow, USSR.

TIKKANEN, Jarmo Juhani, pen name **TIKKANEN, Juhani,** b. 12 Aug. 1945. Radio Operator. Education: Cert. of Proficiency in Radiotelegraphy, 2nd class, Admin. of the Posts & Telegraphs in Finland, 1968. Married, twin sons. Positions held: Sailor, 1962-67; Radio Officer, sev. merchant vessels, 1968–. Memberships: Finnish Soc. of Authors; The Writers in Southwest Finland (one of the Founders). Published works: Vapaus (Freedom), poems, 1966; Huoneessa, jossa on ovi (Inside the room, which has a door), poems, 1967; Sininen Delfiini (Blue Dolphin), poems, 1970; Sulle on sanoma täällä (You've got a message here), poems, 1972. Address: Pahaniemenkatu 77, sf 20200 Turku 20, Finland.

TILDEN, Lorraine Henrietta Frederick, pen names **GRANT, Mary, HENRIETTA, MATHEWS, Lorraine, WINDSOR, Betty,** b. 16 May 1912. Educator. Education: A.A., Ill. State Univ.; B.A., U.C.L.A.; M.A., Claremont Grad. School; Doctoral studies: UCLA, UC Riverside, and Univ. of Redlands. Other coll. work at De Paul Univ., Univ. of Ill., Washington Univ., Univ. of Wisconsin, Cornell Univ., Whittier Coll., San Francisco State Univ., Universidad de la Habana (Cuba), Universidad de Madrid (Spain), Universidad de Guanajuato (Mexico); Field studies in Italy and Greece, 1971. Married, Wesley R. Tilden. Positions held: Teacher, The English School, Habana, Cuba, 1937-41; Lecturer In Spanish, Scripps Coll., 1950-52, (and Claremont Men's Coll., 1959-61); Instr., Mt. San Antonio Coll., 1954-60; Asst. Prof., Chaffey Coll., 1954-56; Teaching Fellow, Univ. of Calif. at Los Angeles, 1956-57; Assoc. Prof. in Humanities, Upland Coll., 1962-65; Teacher of Spanish and World Mythology, Glendora HS, 1967-73. Memberships: Vachel Lindsay Assoc.; Asociación Panamericana de Escritores y Artistas. Published works: All Hallow's Eve, 1928; Why, I'm in Love, 1933; Ballads from a Benzedrine Binge, 1947; Cats! Cats! Cats!!!, 1948; Modernism in the Poetry of José Asunción Silva (dissertation), 1954. Contbr. to: Ill. State Journal; Ill. State Register; The Senator; The Vidette; The Atlantic; Hispania; National Printer Journalist. Awards: Special recognition for excellence in poetic composition HS and Coll. years, 1925-32. Address: 351 Oakdale Dr., Claremont, CA 91711, USA.

TILLER, Terence Rogers, b. 19 Sept. 1916. University Lecturer. Education: B.A., Jesus Coll., Cambridge, 1937; M.A., 1940. Positions held: Rsch. Scholar & Dir. of Studies, Cambridge Univ., 1937-39; Univ. Lectr., Medieval Hist., Cambrdige, 1939; Lectr., Engl. Hist. & Lit., Fuad I Univ., Cairo, Egypt, 1939-46; w. BBC, 1946; Writer-Producer, Features Dept., 1946-65; Radio Drama Dept., 1965–. Published works: Poems, 1941; The Inward Animal, 1943; Unarm, Eros, 1947; Reading A Medal, 1957; Notes for a Myth, 1968; (verse plays) The Death of a Friend, 1949; Lilith, 1950; The Tower of Hunger, 1952; Ed., Transltr., Conbr., various publs. Honours, awards: Chancellor's Medal for English Verse, Cambrdige, 1936. Address: Roehampton, London, UK.

TILLEY, Eugene D., b. 22 Sept. 1913. Farmer. Education: Agric. Coll., 2 years; Palmer Inst. of Authorship. Personal details: Scots, Engl. & German ancestry; 5 children. Positions held: Farm-Owner; Rank of Sgt., WWII Air Force. Memberships: Ark.

Artists & Writers Soc.; Ark. Poets' Roundtable; Co-host & Workshop Critic, Ark. Writers' Conference, 1973. Published works: (Pamphlets) One Dozen Poems, 1965; Big Shot Farmer, 1965; The Deer Slayer, 1966; The Dyke Walker, 1970; (Poetry) The Minutes of the Years, 1972; (Recording) Tears On A White Carnation, 1965. Contbr. to the following anthols., jrnls., newspapers, etc: Anthol. of Am. Poetry; Poetry Parade; Poetry Pageant Vol. 1, Voices International; The Daily Oklahoman; The Memphis Commercial Appeal; The Ark. Farmer; The Saint's Herald; Saline Co. News; Southern Standard; Hot Springs News, Ark.; The Salem Headlight, Ark.; The Wynne Progress, Ark.; The Modern News, Harrisburg, Ark. Honours, awards, etc: 3rd Prize, Poetry Parade, book II, 1969; 3rd Prize, Anthol. of Am. Poetry, book 9, 1969. Address: Route 1, Box 5, Fisher, Ark. 72429, USA.

TILLINGHAST, Richard, born 25th November, 1940. University Professor. Education: A.B., Univ. of the South; A.M., Harvard Univ. Positions held: Asst. Prof., Univ. of Calif. Publications: Sleep Watch, 1969. Contbr. to: Atlantic Monthly; Boston Review; Carolina Quarterly; Fire Exit; Ga. Review; Harper's Mag.; Harvard Advocate; Island; New Left Review; New Republic; Partisan Review; Poetry; San Francisco Oracle; Sewanee Review; Shenandoah; Southern Review; Sumac; Tenn. Poetry Jrnl.; Yale Review. Address: Garden of Allah, 112 Edison Ave., Corte Madera, Calif., USA.

TILLION, Diana, pen name **TILLION, Diana Rystbaek,** b. 1 June 1928. Artist; Sculptor. Education: var. courses, Univ. of Neb. & Univ. of Alaska. Married Clement Vincent Tillion, 2 sons, 2 daughters. Memberships: V. Chmn., Alaska State Coun. on the Arts; State Pres., Nat. League of Am. Penwomen; Member at Large, Poetry Soc. of Alaska. Published works: (book) Alaska in Haiku (w. David Hoopes), 1972. Contbr. to: Int. Poets Review; Anchorage Daily Times; Jewels From a Willow (Anthol. of Am. Haiku); One Hundred Yrs. of Poetry. Honours, awards: Hon. Mention (Top Ten), Alaska Poetry Soc., 1964; Int. Poets' Review Award, 1967. Address: Ismailof Island, Homer, AK 99603, U.S.A.

TING, Simon, b. 19 Jan. 1925. Prof. of Philosophy and concurrently Director, Inst. of Chinese Culture, Philippine Christian Coll.; Minister, United Church of Manila; Guidance Supervisor, Hope Christian High School. Education: A.A., Arellano, 1946; A.B., Cornell, 1948; M.A., Oberlin, 1950; D.Phil., Oxford; M.Div., Vanderbilt; Summer, Paris, 1956; Munich & Marburg, 1956. Commentator, First Int. Conf. of Historians, 1960; Member, Translation Committee, Philippino Bible House, 1959-69; Translation consultant, Bible Socs. of Hong Kong & Taiwan, 1964; Sec., Philippine Chinese Hist. Assoc., 1968-70; Treas., NECCOS, Boy Scouts of the Philippines, 1968–; Member, Comm. on Christian Literature and Education, Nat. Council of Churches in the Philippines, 1964–; Vice Chairman, Committee on Cultural Affairs, Chinese Lit. Club, Manila, 1968-70; Director, Philosophical Assoc. of the Philippines, 1973. Pubs. Selected Short Stories from Chinese Classical Literature, 1946; Fifty Stories of Worship Value, 1948; Children of Light, 1956; Song of Songs, 1960. Contrib. to: Unitas; Ching Feng; Church & Community. Awards: First Prize for Academic treatises, Chiang Kai Shek Cultural Foundation, 1967; Commendation, Chinese Cultural Renaissance Council, 1968; Class A Citation of Merit, Commissioner of Overseas Affairs, Republic of China, 1970; Citation of Merit, Dept. of Educ., Republic of the Philippines, 1971. Address: Institute of Chinese Culture, Philippine Christian Coll., P.O. Box 907, Manila, Philippines.

TIPTON, David (John), b. 28 Apr. 1934. Published works: Poems in Transit, 1960; City of Kings, 1967; Peru The New Poetry (trans.), 1970; The Spider hangs too far from the ground (trans.), 1970; Millstone Grit, 1972; Common Grave (trans.), 1973; A Sword in the air (prose) (forthcoming). Contbr. to: London Mag.;

Stand; Ambit; Second Aeon; Transatlantic Review; Poetry Review; Poetry (Chicago); Beloit Poetry Journal, etc. Recip., Arts Coun. grant, 1974. Address: 157 Sharrow Vale Rd., Sheffield 11, Yorks., UK.

TOCZEK, Nicholas, pen name **TOCZEK, Nick,** b. 20 Sept. 1950. Poet. Education: Hons. degree in Indl. Metallurgy, Birmingham Univ., U.K., 1972. Positions held: Ed. & Fndr., 'Black Columbus' poetry mag. of Birmingham Univ., 1970-72; Ed. & Fndr. 'The Little Word Machine', a poetry mag., 1972–; Co-Ed., 'Midland Read', West Midlands Arts Assn. Poetry Publ., 1973; Dir., New Schl. of Living Poetry, 1973–. Memberships: Nat. Poetry Secretariat; London Poetry Secretariat. Published works: Because the Evenings, 1972; Mosaic, 1973; Chronology, 1974; Book of Collected Poems, to be published 1974. Contbr. to num. mags., newspapers, anthols. & school text books inclng: The Sunday Times; Samphire; Pink Peace; Playboy; BBC TV; BBC Radio Leeds; BBC Radio Birmingham; Poetry One/Two; Black Columbus; Worse Verse; Dodo; Little Word Machine; Yorkshire Poets '72, etc. Has given a number of readings on Radio & over 300 readings around the country in univs., pubs, colls., schls., art ctrs. & art festivals. Recip., 2nd Prize, Dudley Fest. Poetry Comp., 1972. Address: 103 Moorhead Ln., Shipley, Yorks., U.K.

TODD, Margaret Burr, b. 18 June 1902. Writer of prose & poetry. Education: Grad., Adelphi Coll., 1922; grad. work at N.Y. Univ. & Coll. of the City of N.Y. Married Charles Davis Todd. Memberships: Chmn., Nat. Poetry Day Comm., Me., 1958; Nat. League of Am. Pen omen, Me. Br.; Br. Pres. & formerly State Pres., ibid. Published works: Beautiful Harpswill, 1958. Contbr. to: Chapbooks; Me. Writers Conf., 1960–. Recip., Freedoms Fndn. Award for poem 'I Sing of Home', 1958. Address: Orr's Island, ME, U.S.A.

TODD, Ruthven, b. 14 June 1914. Novelist; Poet. Published works: Until Now, 1942; The Acreage of the Heart, 1943; The Planet in My Hand, 1946; A Mantelpiece of Shells, 1954; Garland for the Winter Solstice, 1962; (novels) Over the Mountain, 1946; The Lost Traveller, 1969; Tracks in the Snow (essays), 1947; Ed., Life of William Blake, by Alexander Gilchrist, 1942. Contbr. to: (anthologies) An Anthology of Contemporary Verse, 1953; Poetry of the Thirties, 1964; Modern Scottish Poetry, 1966; A Book of Scottish Verse, 1967. Honours, awards: Nat. Acad. of Arts & Letters Award, 1954; Guggenheim Fellowship, 1960 & '67; Chapelbrook Fellowship, 1968-69. Address: Ca'n Bielo, Galilea, Majorca, Spain.

TOLENTINO, Guillermo E., pen name, **BATANG ELIAS,** b. 24 July 1890. Sculptor. Education: HS; U.P. School of Fine Arts, followed by studies in USA and Italy. Positions held: Teacher in Fine Arts (Sculpture) as Asst. Instr., Instr., Asst. Prof., Prof., Director; apptd. Professor Emeritus and Director when, in 1955, concluding 29 yrs. of service. Memberships: Diwang Tagalog; Taniw., etc. Published work: Last Farewell. Contbr. to other publications. Address: 2012 Retiro St., Sampalok, Manila, Philippines.

TOMICIC, Zlatko, pen name **CROAT, Aurel,** b. 26 May 1930. Writer; Poet. Education: Univ. of Zagreb. (Dept. of Comparative Lit. & German lang. & lit.), 3 yrs. Married Ana Tomičić, 1 son. Positions held: Jrnlst.; Ed. of sev. newspapers & lit. mags.; Freelance Writer. Memberships: Pres., Soc. of Free Writers 'TIN'; PEN Club; Soc. of Writers of Croatia; Union of Writers of Yugoslavia; Union of European Writers. Published works: Vode pod ledinom, 1955; Cetvrtoga ne razumijem, 1955; Dosegnuti ja, 1956; Nema blaga nad slobodom, 1956; Bučni faun, 1960; Balada uspravnog čovjeka, 1964; Revolucionarni kalendar, 1965; Traženje Bivstva, 1969; Zir, 1968; Hrvatsko more, 1969; Bogumilsko groblje, 1968; Križni put, 1966. Contbr. to num. newspapers, mags., periodicals, reviews in Yugoslavia & abroad. Address: Moščenićka 12, 41000 Zagreb, Yugoslavia.

TOMLIN, Eugene Edward, pen name **TOMLIN, Gene,** b. 23 Jan. 1926. Minister; Teacher of English. Education: B.A., Howard Payne Coll., 1950; M.Ed., Stephen F. Austin State Univ., Nacogdoches, Tex., 1960. Married Pauline Cox, 2 sons. Positions held: Asst. Pastor & Youth Dir., First Bapt. Ch., Rusk, Tex.; Pastor at: Old Palestine Bapt. Ch., Alto, Tex.; Camp Ground Bapt. Ch., Alto; Forest Bapt. Ch.; Reklaw Bapt. Ch.; Lone Oak Bapt. Ch., Rusk; Lily Grove Bapt. Ch., Nacogdoches; Martinsville, Bapt. Ch.; Tchr.-Prin., Bulah Elem. Schl., Rusk & Douglass Schl., Tex.; Tchr., Nacogdoches H.S. Memberships: Poetry Soc. of Tex.; Pineywoods Chapt., ibid; Palestine Poetry Soc.; East Tex. Writers' Assn.; Tex. Jr. Engl. Comm.; Tex. Coun. of Tchrs. of Engl.; Tex. State Tchrs. Assn.; Int. Platform Assn.; Pres., Nacogdoches Art League, 1972-73. Published works: Whispering Pines, 1971; Ed., Listen/Hear, 1972. Contbr. to: Orphic Lute; Vista; Am. Bard; Cyclo-Flame; Nat. Poetry Anthol., 1969-70; Inky Trails; Tex. Traveler; Redland Herald; Foxfire, etc. Recip., Cit. by Tex. Coun. Tchrs. of Engl. at Authors Luncheon, 1973. Winner of monthly contest, Inky Trails. Address: 2912 Swann Dr., Nacogdoches, TX 75961, U.S.A.

TOMLINSON, Charles, b. 8 Jan. 1927. Reader in English Poetry. Education: Queens' Coll., Cambridge Univ., 1945-48; Royal Holloway Coll., 1952-54; Bedford Coll., 1955-56. Positions held: Schl. Tchr. in London, 1948-51; Sec. to Author & Critic, Percy Lubbock in Italy, 1951-52; Extra mural lecturing, Univ. of London, 1954-55; Lectr. & finally Rdr., Univ. of Bristol, 1956–; Vis. Prof., Univ. of N.M., U.S.A., 1962-63 & O'Connor Prof., Colgate Univ., 1968. Published works: Relations & Contraries, 1951; The Necklace, 1955, rev. 1966; Seeing is Believing, 1958; Versions from Tyutchev (w. H. Gifford), 1960; A Peopled Landscape, 1963; Castilian Ilexes – Versions from Machado (w. H. Gifford), 1963; Poems: a selection, 1964; American Scenes, 1966; The Way of a World, 1969; America West Southwest, 1970; Ten Versions from Trilce (w. H. Gifford), 1970; Renga (w. Paz, Roubaud, Sanguineti), 1971; Written on Water, 1972. Contbr. to: Agenda; Encounter; Form; Hudson Review; Jrnl. of Creative Behaviour; Listener; London Mag.; Poetry Chicago; Stand; Sunday Times; Times Lit. Supplement. Honours, awards: Levinson Prize, Poetry Chicago, 1960; Union League Civic & Arts Fndn. Prize, 1962; Inez Boulton Prize, 1964; Frank O'Hara Prize, 1968. Address: Dept. of Engl., Univ. of Bristol, 40 Berkeley Sq., Bristol 8, U.K.

TONG, Raymond, b. 20 Aug. 1922. Officer of The British Council (currently Area Officer, Bristol). Education: London Univ., B.Sc. (Econ.) Hons. Married to Mariana Apergis. Positions held: Principal, Government Teacher Training Coll., Ibadan, Nigeria; Director, British Inst., Cordoba, Argentina; Director, Centre of Engl. Studies, Baghdad, Iraq; Area Officer, Bristol (The British Council). Memberships: Poetry Soc. (UK) (life member); English Assoc.; West Country Writers' Assoc. Published works (poetry): Today the Sun, 1947; Angry Decade, 1950; Fabled City, 1960; African Helicon (poetry anthol., editor), 1955, 2nd ed. (8th impression), 1974. Contbr. to: The Adelphi; A Review of Engl. Literature; The Fortnightly; Contemporary Review; Poetry Review; Ariel; The Dublin Mag.; Outposts; Time and Tide; English; John O'London's Weekly; Wormwood Review; Meanjin; Bim; Arena; African Affairs; Eve. Standard, etc. (anthols.) Modern Lyrical Verse; This Day and Age; Conflict and Compassion; Theme and Variations; I Burn for England; Air Force Poetry. Address: c/o Personnel Records, The British Council, 65 Davies St., London W1Y 2AA, UK.

TONKS, Rosemary. Novelist; Poet. Published works: Notes on Cafes and Bedrooms, 1963; Iliad of Broken Sentences, 1967; (novels) Opium Fogs, 1963; The Bloater, 1968; Businessmen as Lovers, 1969; (children's books) On Wooden Wings: The Adventures of Webster, 1948; Wild Sea Goose, 1951. Contbr. to: Observer; New Statesman; Encounter; Listener; Adam; Ambit; Flourish; Poetry Review; London

Magazine; (anthologies) Best Poems of 59 1959: The Borestone Mountain Poetry Awards, 1960; A Standard of Verse, 1969; Penguin Book of Postwar British Verse, 1970; An Anthology of Contemporary Poetry, 1970. Address: 46 Downshire Hill, London N.W.3, U.K.

TONOGBANUA, Francisco G., b. 1 Dec. 1900. College Professor & Dean of Graduate Studies (Emeritus). EDUCATION: A.A., Univ. of the Philippines, 1924; Ph.B., ibid, 1926; B.S.E., 1928; M.A., Univ. of Wis., 1930; Ph.D., Univ. of Santo Tomas, 1950. Positions held: Prin., var. H.S.'s, 1934-38; Gen. Supvsr. of Measurements & Rsch., Bus. of Educ., 1938-41; Prof. of Engl. & Sec., IAS, Far Eastern Univ., 1946-66; Dean of Grad. Studies, Golden Gate Coll., 1966-73; Cons. on Engl., Chiang Kai Shek Coll., 1967-73; Prof. of Grad. Studies, Univ. of the City of Manila, 1967-68, etc. Memberships incl: V.P., Philippine Writers Assn.; 1926-28; One of 15 Fndrs., U.P. Writers Club, 1927; Life Mbr., Sigma Delta Chi.; Bd. Editors, Philippine Historical Bulletin, 1965-66; World Poetry Dir. for the Philippines, 1959–; Published works: Verse Trilogy: Fallen Leaves, 1951, Green Leaves, 1954 & Brown Leaves, 1965; Forty-One Christmases, 1959, '65; A Stone, A Leaf, A Door, 1962; Sonnets (125), 1964, '66; My God, My Mercy, 1967, '72. Contbr. to jrnls., newspapers, etc. Honours, awards incl: UPLI Award of Title of Hon. Poet Laureate of the Cursillo Movement in the Philippines w. Pres. Carlos P. Gardia Gold Laurel Wreath & Justice Eulogio Serrano Gold Medal, 1967; two hon. doctorates. Address: 32 Ragang St., Barrio Manresa, Quezon City, Rep. of the Philippines.

TOPPE, Georgia Joyce, b. 13 Mar. 1942. Teacher. Education: B.Mus., Ind. Univ.; M.A., ibid. Married James A Toppe, 1 son, 2 daughters (Nicolle, Michele & Mark). Positions held: Tchr. of Engl., Highland H.S., Anderson, Ind. Contbr. to: Poet; I.W.W.P. Anthol., 1972. Recip., Fndrs. Award, Ind. Univ. Writers Conf., 1965. Address: RR 1, Box 72 D, Middletown, IN 47356, U.S.A.

TORGERSEN, Eric, b. 6 Oct. 1943. University Professor of English. Education: Half Hollow Hills HS, Huntington, NY, 1960; A.B., German Lit., Cornell Univ., 1964; M.F.A., Univ. of Iowa Writers' Workshop, 1969. Positions held: Lecturer, Haile Selassie 1 Univ., Addis Ababa, Ethopia; Graduate Teaching Asst., Univ. of Iowa; Instr. of Engl., Quincy Coll., Illinois; Asst. Prof. of Engl., Central Michigan Univ., Mt. Pleasant, Michigan. Membership: Mod. Lang. Assoc. Published work: The Carpenter, 1969; At War with Friends, 1972. Contbr. to: Epoch; Poetry Northwest; Poetry Review (Univ. of Tampa, Florida); Perspective; Poetry Bag; Kayak; Foxfire; Ann Arbor Review; Lillabulero; Choice; Field; Greenfield Review; Doones; Cimarron Review; Salt Lick; Hearse; Crazy Horse; Kamadhenu; Back Door; Some; Happiness Holding Tank; The Lamp in the Spine; Abraxas; New Letters; Frankfurter Rundschau. Address: Dept. of Engl., Central Michigan Univ., Mt. Pleasant, MI 48858, USA.

TORODE, Mary R. Artist Model. Education: Dip., Chenier Bus. Coll., Beaumont, Tex.; B.A., Engl. & Lit.; Dip. for Export-Import Traffic Mgr. inclng. French & Spanish diplomatic correspondence & translations. Positions held: Bookkeeper; Accountant; Office Manager; Storekeeper 1st Class, US Navy; Documents & Corres., Translation, Foreign Trade Sec.; Lectr. for Theosophical Soc. of Am. Memberships: Chmn., Writers' Workshop, Northwestern Univ., Chicago, 4 yrs.; Treas., Iota Sigma Epsilon; Treas., Poets' Club of Chicago; Chmn., Int. Sonnet Contest, PCC. Contbr. to: South & West; Human Voice; Bardic Echoes; Fire Flower; Prairie Poet; Bouquet of Poems; New World; Voices Int.; Encore; Quintessence; Colo. Qtly.; Poet Lore, etc. Recip. 1st Prize for Nature Poem & First Hon. Mentions for Shakespearean Sonnet & also Haiku by Poets & Patrons; Chicago Liaison for Two Tone Qtly., University of Rhodesia. Address: 1541 N. Avers Ave., Chicago, IL 60651, U.S.A.

TORREGIAN, Sotère, b. 25 June 1941. Poet.

Education: classes in Greek Metaphysics, Coll. of Rutgers Univ., Newark, N.J., 1961-62. Positions held: Book store clerk; Asst. to Dr. St. Claire Drake in the Dept. of Anthropol. at Stanford Univ., Calif. Memberships: affil. with Surrealist Grp. of Painters & Poets in France; affil. with N.Y. Grp. of Poets. Published works: The Wounded Mattress, poems, 1965; The Golden Palomino Bites the Clock, 1967; Song For Woman (a poem), 1966; The Age of Gold (inclng. The Age of Gold, poems 1968-70, expanded version of Song for Woman & The Sex Life of Arshille Gorky); Kulchur, in prep.; A Nestorian Monument in Cathay (prose) in prep. Contbr. to: Art & Literature, Lausanne, Switz.; Paris Review, France; The World Poetry Jrnl.; Chicago Review, etc. Recip. Frank O'Hara Award, Poet's Fndn., 1968. Address: 2405 Alpine Rd., Menlo Park, CA 94025, U.S.A.

TORRES, Emmanuel, b. 29 Apr. 1932. Professor of Lit., at Ateneo Univ. Education: A.B., in Education, Ateneo Univ., 1954; M.A., in Engl., State Univ. of Iowa, 1957; Fulbright/Smith-Mundt Scholarship, 1955-57. Positions held: Editor-in-Chief, Philippines International, 1957-58; Vice-Pres., Art Assoc. of the Philippines, 1964-65; Curator, Ateneo Univ. Art Gallery, since 1960; Commissioner-General, Philippine participation in the 32nd Venice Biennale, 1964. Member, Iowa Writers Workshop in Poetry, 1955-57. Published works: Angels and Fugitives, 1966; Shapes of Silence, 1972. Contbr. to: Philippines Free Press; Signatures (Manila); Philippine Studies; St. Louis Journal (Baguio City); The Asia Mag.; Asia-Philippines Leader; Botteghe Oscure; Beloit Poetry Journal; Poetry (Chicago). Recip. Carlos Palanca Mem. Lit. Awards: 1964 (2nd prize, for group of poems), 1965 (2nd prize, for group of poems); 1966, (1st prize, for Angels & Fugitives); 1968 (3rd prize, for group of poems). Address: 125-D Kamuning Rd., Quezon City, Philippines.

TORRES BODET, Jaime, b. 17 Apr. 1902. Poet, Novelist, Diplomat. Education: Univ. of Mexico. Positions held: Hd., Dept. of Libs., Secretariat of Public Educ., 1922-24; Prof., Univ. of Mexico, 1924-28; Sec., Legation, Spain, 1929-31; Chargé d'Affaires, Holland, 1932; Sec., Legation, France, 1932-34; Sec., Embassy, Buenos Aires, 1934; 1st Sec., Legation, Paris, 1935; Chief, Diplomatic Dept., Min. of For. Affairs, 1936-37; Chargé d'Addaires, Brussels, 1938-40; Under Sec. for For. Affairs, 1940-45; Min. of Educ., 1945-46; Min. of For. Rels., 1946-48; Dir.-Gen., UNESCO, 1948-52; Ambassador to France, 1954-58; Sec. for Educ., Mexico, 1958-64. Published works: (poetry) Fervor, 1918; Canciones, 1922; Nuevas Canciones, 1923; Los Días, 1923; La Casa, 1923; Pomas, 1924; Biombo, 1925; Destierro, 1930; Cripta, 1937; Sonetos, 1949; Sin Tregua, 1957; Trébol de Cuatro Hojas, 1958. Also sev. novels.

TOULSON, Shirley, b. 20 May 1924. Editor; Poet. Educ: Univ. of London, U.K. Positions held: Former Freelance Journalist; Features Ed., The Teacher, 1967–. Published works: Shadows in an Orchard, 1960; Circumcision's Not Such a Bad Thing After All, 1970. Contbr. to: Listener; Ambit; Outposts; Tribune; (anthologies) A Group Anthology, 1963; Poems Understood, 1966; Hazard, 1966. Address: 63 Denmark Rd., Wimbledon, London S.W.19, U.K.

TOURE, Askia Muhammad, b. 13 Oct. 1938. Poet-Essayist; Social Activist; Editor. Positions held: Lectr., African Studies, San Francisco State Coll., 1967-68; currently Lectr. in African & African-Am. Hist. & Culture, Manhattan Community Coll., N.Y., Amherst Coll., Mass. & Bronx Community Coll., N.Y.; Ed., Umbra lit. jrnl., 1963; Editl. Staff, Liberator mag., 1964-66; Editl. staff, Black America, Afro-Am. political jrnl., 1964-66; Ed., Black Dialogue, 1967-69; currently, Ed.-at-Large, Jrnl. of Black Poetry; Ed., The Western Sunrise, newspaper of the Afro-Am. Orthodox Muslim Community, 1970-73. Memberships: John Oliver Killens Writers Workshop, Columbia Univ.; former mbr., Umbra Writers' Workshop. Published works: Ju Ju, 1969; Songhai! 1972. Contbr. to: Freedomways;

Black World; Black Dialogue; Mainstream; Soulbook; (anthols.) Black Fire; The Poetry of the Negro; Black Spirits, etc. Honours, awards: Poet of the Year, Liberator mag., 1965. Address: 161 W. 95th St., Apt. 2-R, N.Y., NY 10025, U.S.A.

TOURISON, Martha Downey, b. 26 Feb. 1887. Housewife. Education: Rawlings Inst., Charlottesville, Va. Past member, Penwomen. Published works: (book of poetry) In the Sunlight of Remembrance. Contbr. to: Life Mag.; Time of Singing; Educational Forum; Ideals Mag. Address: 7013 Ardleigh St., Philadelphia, PA 19119, U.S.A.

TOURNEBIZE, Jean-Marie, b. 25 Mar. 1945. Physical Education Instructor; Poet. Memberships: Pres., Higher Lit. & Artistic Acad. of French; Hon. Mbr., Int. Acad. of Poetic Exchange, Switzerland; ibid, Artistic & Poetry Club of France Guiana; Assoc. Poesie Vivante en Wallonie, Belgium; Soc. of Arts & Letters of Cote d'Azur; mbr. of 30 other French & foreign socs. Published works: Propos; Esquisses; Symboles; Un Peu de Bonheur. Contbr. to: (Anthol.) Poemes d'Ici et d'Ailleurs, Vols. I & II. Numerous jrnls. in France & in following countries: Belgium, Germany; Italy; Canada; USA; Argentina; Spain; Portugal; Morocco; Algeria. Has also appeared at several poetry readings in France & Belgium & Int. radio broadcasts. Honours: Knight, Int. Order of the Renaissance of Letters & Arts; Cultural & Philanthropic Order of France; Ordre de la Pemarie d'Olt; Merite de la Poesie; Palme d'argent de l'Encouragement Public; Merite Guyanaie; Cro-Argent Couronne Lauriers, Ministère de la Prévoyance Sociale, Belgique; Officier, Merite Poetique; Commandeur de Medulicus. Recip. of over 150 poetry awards & prizes. Address: 41 Bis Rue du General De Gaulle, 60 Nogent, Oise, France.

TOWEY, Augustine Denis, b. 30 June 1937. Professor of English & Theatre; Religious Brother. Education: B.A., M.A., St. John Univ., NY; Univ. of Birmingham, UK; Ph.D., N.Y. Univ. (1973). Positions held: Instr., St. John's Univ.; Prof., Niagara Univ.; Dir., Theatre Prog., Chmn., Arts Festival, ibid; on sev. performing arts bds. Plays produced: Catch a Fallen Star, 1961; Mission from Folleville, 1960; Ashgrove, 1964. Contbr. to: Commonweal Mag.; Aquila; Talon. Address: Niagara Univ., NY 14109, USA.

TOWLE, Tony, b. 13 June 1939, Manhattan, NY. Poet. Education: Georgetown Univ., 1957; NY Univ., 1962; Columbia Univ., 1963; New Schl. for Soc. Rsch., 1963. Currently Sec., Universal Limited Art Editions since 1964. Published works: Poems, 1966; After Dinner We Take a Drive into the Night, 1968; North, 1970. Contbr. to: 'C' Magazine; Mother; Art & Literature; The Paris Review; Lines; The New Yorker; The World; Adventures in Poetry; Angel Hair; Penumbra; Extensions; Toothpaste. Awards: Gotham Book Mart Avant-Garde Poetry Prize, Wagner Coll. Writers' Conf., 1963; Poets Fndn. Award, 1964, '66; Frank O'Hara Award, 1970. Address: 100 Sullivan St., New York, NY 10012, USA.

TOWNSEND, Joan, pen name **POMFRET, Joan,** b. 23 May 1913. Writer (freelance) and Housewife. Education: Darwen Grammar School; The Park School, Preston. Married to Douglas C. Townsend, J.P., F.R.I.B.A. Memberships: Fellow, Royal Soc. of Arts; Lancashire Authors' Association (Deputy-Chairman), 1952–. Published works: Rhymes of the War, 1940; The Admiralty Regrets, 1941; Coastal Command, 1942; Second Officer, 1944; Merchant Navy Man, 1946; Rhymes of a Country Housewife, 1956; Poems, 1963; The Old Peel Line, 1972. Editor of Anthols.: Summat From Home, 1964; Lancashire Evergreens, 1969; Nowt So Queer, 1969; 'Twixt Thee And Me, 1973. Contbr. to: BBC Northern programmes; Radio Blackburn; The Dalesman; The Isle of Man Times; Lancashire Life; Clitheroe Advertiser; Accrington Observer; Blackburn Times; Lancashire Eve. Telegraph; The Record; The Lady, etc. Awards: Recip. of annual Poetry Awards, Lancs. Authors' Assoc: The Batty Cup (Engl. Verse), 1937, 1938, 1940,

1942, 1946, 1947, 1948, 1952, 1953, 1959, 1972, and recip. of Simon Award, 1972; Writer of the Year Award, 1972. Shared 4th Prize, Internat. Who's Who in Poetry 1,000-dollar Awards for 1972. Address: Stoops Farm, Great Harwood, Blackburn, Lancs., UK.

TOYNBEE, Philip, b. 25 June 1916. Novelist; Editor. m. Frances Genevieve Smith, 1950, 1s., 4d. Positions held: Ed., Birmingham Town Crier, 1938-39; Served, Intelligence Corps, 1940-42; Employed w. Min. of Econ. Welfare, 1942-45; Lit. Ed., Contact Publs., 1945-46; Mbr., Ed. Staff, The Observer, London, 1950-. Published works: Pantaloon, 1961; Two Brothers, 1964; A Learned City, 1966; Views from a Lake, 1968; (novels) The Savage Days, 1937; School in Private, 1941; The Barricades, 1943; Tea with Mrs. Goodman, 1947; The Garden to the Sea, 1953; Ed., Fearful Choice:A Debate on Nuclear Policy, 1958. Address: The Barn House, Brockweir, Nr. Chepstow, Monmouthshire, U.K.

TRACY, Neil, b. 31 Aug. 1905. Teacher. Education: B.A., 1928, M.A., 1929, Bishops Univ. Married, Dorothy Ida Gentry. Positions held: Dist. Rep., Canadian Nat. Inst. for the Blind, 1940-67; Lecturer, Sherbooke Univ., 1962-73. Membership: Internat. Platform Assoc. Published works: The Rain it Raineth, 1936; Shapes of Clay, 1968; Voiceline, 1970. Recip. 2nd Prize, Jewish Braille Inst. of Am., Int. Competition. Address: P.O. Box 274, Lennoxville, JOB 120, PQ, Canada.

TRACY, Pauline Aloise, pen names **GAY, Ellen, & TRACY, Aloise,** b. 20 Nov. 1914. Poet; Author; Teacher (retired). Education: B. Ed., Eastern Ill., Univ., 1937; Grad. Art classes, ibid & Univ. of Mo.; Writers Workshop(s), Ill., NC & NM. Married, James Richard Tracy, 1946 (deceased 1972). Positions held: Teacher, Wiley Brick Elem. School, 1937-38; Tracy Elementary School, 1938-46. Member: American Poetry League; American Poets Fellowship Soc. (Hon. life); New World Poets Club; Egypt Branch (Chaplain), Nat. League of American Pen Women; Ill. State Poetry Soc. (charter member); Ill. Woman's Press Assoc.; Ill. Pen Women; Friends of the Library; Nat. Fed. of Press Women. Pubs. His Handiwork, 1954; Memory Is A Poet, 1964; The Silken Web, 1965; A Merry Heart, 1966; In Two Or Three Tomorrows, 1968; All Flesh Is Grass, 1971; Beyond The Edge, 1973. Contrib. to: Chicago Tribune; Boston Post; Home Life; Bridgeport Leader; Prairie Poet; American Poet; Poet (India); Seydell Quarterly (Belgium); Major Poets; The Christian; Upward; Ideals; Ill. St. Poetry Soc. Newsletter; American Poetry League Bulletin; Economist Newspapers; Grit; New World, etc. Anthologies: Spring Anthology; Golden Quill; From Sea to Sea in Song; Silver Laurels; Blue River Press Publications, etc. Addresses: 447 Chestnut Street, Bridgeport, Ill., 62417, USA, and (Winter): Box 382, Gulf Shores, Ala. 36542, USA.

TRAINER, Clyde Vernon, pen name **DIX, Lee,** b. 24 Apr. 1914. Poet. Past Mbr., Int. Platform Soc. Contbr. to: IWWP, 1972; America Versonified, 1973; Charlotte Republican-Tribune; The Express Mag.; Hyacinths & Biscuits; The Pink Elephant; The Lowell Ledger & Suburban Life. Address: 4026 Causeway Dr., Lowell, MI 49331, U.S.A.

TRANBARGER, Ossie Elmo, b. 6 April 1914. Nurse. Education: Coll. hrs. in Creative Writing, Journalism, Literature, Mass Commucations. Married to Jack Tranbarger. Memberships: NLAPW (Kansas State Pres.; Coffeyville Branch Pres.); Midwest Fed. Chaparral Poets (Past Kansas State Regent); Kansas Authors (Past Pres., 3rd Dist.); World Poetry Soc.; UPLI; South & West, Inc.; Ozark Writers & Artists Guild; Int. Poets Shrine; Internat. Clover Poetry Assoc.; Flint Hills Round-Up Pen; Verdigris Valley Writers; Patron, Arts Independence Museum; Patron, Kansas Kernels; Patron, Voices Internat, and others. Guest Editor, Midwest Edition of Poet (India). Contbr. to many poetry journals, mags., etc. Recip. of numerous awards and honours, including: L.P.D.,

Acad. of Leadership, Philippines; D.H.L., Univ. of Asia; citations, recognitions, certificates, prizes from sev. societies, publishers, NLAPW, UPLI, WPSI, Ariz. State Univ., Haiku, etc. Address: 619 West Main St., Independence, KS 67301, USA.

TRANSTROMER, Tomas G., b. 15 Apr. 1931. Psychologist; Writer. Education: Univ. of Stockholm, Sweden, 1951-56. Married, 2 children. Positions held: Psychologist, Psycho-technical Inst., Stockholm, 1957-60; ibid, Rextuna (Institution for delinquent youth), 1960-66; Pa-radet, Vasteras (Occupational Psychol.), 1966-. Memberships: PEN; Swedish Soc. of Writers. Published works: 17 Dikter, 1954; Hemligheter pa vägen, 1958; Den halvfärdiga himlen, 1962; Klanger och spar, 1966; Kvartett, 1967; Mörkerseende, 1970. Contbr. to: Ord & Bild; BLM; Literary Review; Böckernas Värld; Akzente; Malahat Review; Granite; Transition; Kayak; Adam; Lines; New Directions; Looming; Dzefas Diena, etc. Honours: Aftonbladets Litteraturpris, 1958; Bellmanspriset, 1966; Int. Poetry Forum Swedish Award, 1971. Address: Infanterigatan 144, Västeras, Sweden.

TRANTER, John Ernest, b. 29 Apr. 1943. Education: B.A., Sydney Univ., 1970. Editor. Positions held: Various jobs, inclng. Wages Clerk, Art Gallery Asst., Lepidopterist & Student. Memberships: Poetry Australia (Ed.). Published works include: Parallax, 1970; Free Grass, 1968; Epigrams, 1970; Red Movie, 1971-72. Contbr. to the following anthols., jrnls., mags., etc: The Australian; Bulletin; Poetry Australia; Poetry Mag.; Arna; Meanjin; Southern Review; Southerly; Balcony; Forum; Free Poetry; Pluralist; Transit; Twentieth Century; Uphill. Address: c/o Flat 2, 100 Muston St., Mosman, NSW 2088, Australia.

TRASK, Sherwood, b. 5 Feb. 1890. Teacher, Historian, Poet. Education: Dartmouth Coll.; Post-Grad., Harvard Univ. Positions held: Soc. Wkr., Tchr., South End Settlement House, Boston, Mass.; Investigator of local industries, Mass. State Bd. of Labour; Civilian Dir. of Field Work, War Dept. Commn. of Training Camp Activities, WWI; Tchr., Mod. Schl., NJ; Tchr., Organic Schl., Fairhope Single Tax Colony, Ala.; Tchr., Pioneer of 'school-on-wheels' (peripatetic schl.), Walden Schl., NYC, 1927-55; Retd., 1955. Published works: From the Furnace of the Sun–The Negro in America, A Revue of the Race (drama); The Interweaving Poetry of American History, The Near Frontiers, 1967. Contbr. to: Best Poems of 1927 (Ed., L.A.G. Strong); Liberator; Chapbook (Ed., Harold Monro); Poetry (Ed., Harriet Monroe); New Criterion (Ed., T.S. Eliot); Voices (Ed., Harold Vinal); The World Tomorrow; Pagany; Panorama (Ed., Isaac Goldberg); Hound & Horn; Atlantic; Scribner's. Mss. in Beinecke Rare Book & Ms. Lib., which houses principal rare book & ms. collections of Yale Univ. Address: Congregational House, Apt. 406, 2855 Gulf to Bay Blvd., Clearwater, Fla. 33515, USA.

TRAWICK, Leonard M., b. 4 July 1933. Professor of English. Education: B.A., Univ. of the South, Sewanee, Tenn.; M.A., Univ. of Chicago; Ph.D., Harvard Univ. Positions held: Asst. Prof. of Engl., Columbia Univ., N.Y., 1961-69; Assoc. Prof. & Prof. of Engl., The Cleveland State Univ., 1969-. Published works: Beast Forms, 1971 (emblem poems, illustrated by himself). Contbr. to: Antioch Review; Sewanee Review; Everyman; Dark Tower; Greensboro Review; Poetry Cleveland. Address: Dept. of Engl., The Cleveland State Univ., Cleveland, OH 44115, U.S.A.

TREFETHEN, Florence, b. 18 Sept. 1921. Editor. Education: A.B., Bryn Mawr Coll.; M.Litt. (Cantab.). Married, Lloyd MacGregor Trefethen; children: Gwyned; Lloyd Nicholas. Positions held: Instr. in Engl., Tufts Univ., 1958-66; Lect. in Engl., Northeastern Univ., 1967-69; Lect. in Engl., The Radcliffe Inst., 1969-70; 1972-73; Freelance Editor, 1967-. Memberships: Poetry Soc. of America; New England Poetry Club (Board Member). Published work: Writing a Poem, 1970. Contbr. to: Harper's; Poetry; NY Times; Poetry Northwest; Poetry Australia;

468 INTERNATIONAL WHO'S WHO IN POETRY

Counter/Measures. Columnist, The Poet's Workshop, in The Writer (bi-monthly), since 1966. Award: Annual Lyric Prize, New England Poetry Club, 1971. Address: 23 Barberry Rd., Lexington, MA 02173, USA.

TREININ, Avner, b. 14 Feb. 1928. Professor of Physical Chemistry. Education: Ph.D., Hebrew Univ., Jerusalem, Israel, 1958; Postdoc. Studies, Cambrdige Univ., UK, 1958-59. Married, 2 d. Positions held: Asst. Hebrew Univ., 1954; Instr., ibid, 1956; Lectr., 1959; Sr. Lectr., 1963; Assoc. Prof., 1965; Prof., 1971–; Vis. Prof., Brandis Univ., USA, 1962-68. Mbr., Hebrews Writers Assn. Published works: Hyssop of the Wall, 1957; Mount & Olives, 1969. Contbr. to the following periodicals & newspapers: Massa (Lamerchav); Haaretz; Al-Hamishmar; Davar; Maariv; Golionoth; Mollad. Recip., Millo Prize, Club of Writers & Artists, Tel-Aviv, 1970. Address: Dept. of Phys. Chem., Hebrew Univ., Jerusalem, Israel.

TREJOS, Carlota, b. 5 July 1920. Teacher. Education: Calif. Credentialled Tchr. of Creative Writing & Jrnlsm. Married Jose Mario Trejos, 1 son. Memberships: Pres., Calif. Fed. of Chaparral Poets, Apollo Chap.; World Poetry Soc. Intercontinental; Comitato Internazionali, Centro Studi & Scambi Int.; Int. Platform Assn. Published works: Variegated Verse, 1973. Contbr. to: Am. Bard; Archer; Bachaet; Modern Images; Poet India; Am. Scenes; Poets Nook Springfield News; Meridan Connecticut News; Ozark Mountaineer; Bouquet of Poems (Italy); Simbolica; (anthols.) Poetry Parade; The Muse; Soul & the Singer; Yearbook of Modern Poetry; Lyrics of Love; Birth of Day; Outstanding Contemporary Poetry. Recip., Cert. of Merit, Am. Poets Fellowship Soc., 1973. Address: 22503 Meyler St. No. 33, Torrance, CA 90502, U.S.A.

TREMAYNE, Sydney (Durward), b. 15 Mar. 1912. Published works: For Whom there is no Spring, 1946; Time and the Wind, 1948; The Hardest Freedom, 1951; The Rock and the Bird, 1955; The Swans of Berwick, 1962; The Turning Sky, 1969; Selected and New Poems, 1973. Contbr. to numerous magazines, journals, etc. Recip. Scottish Arts Council award, 1970. Address: Blawan Orchard, Westerham Hill, Kent, UK.

TREMBLAY, William Andrew, pen name **TREMBLAY, Bill,** b. 9 June 1940. Poet-Teacher. Education: A.B. (Engl. & Philos.), Clark Univ., Worcester, Mass., 1962; M.A. in Am. Lit., ibid, 1969; M.F.A. in Creative Writing (Poetry), Univ. of Mass., 1972. Positions held: Engl. Tchr., sev. High Schls. in Southbridge, Sutton & Sturbridge, Mass.; Taught at Leciester Jr. Coll., 3 yrs.; Tchr., Univ. of Mass.; currently Asst. Prof. in Engl., Colo. State Univ. Published works: A Time for Breaking (pamphlet), 1970; Crying in the Cheap Seats, 1971. Contbr. to: Mass. Review; Chicago Review; Occum Ridge Review; Cafe Solo; Tulsa Poetry Qtly.; Zahir; The Lamp in the Spine; Lynx; Helicon; Clark Review, etc. Recip., 1st prize, Hoyt Poetry Award, 1961 & '62. Address: 827 LeMay Ave., Ft. Collins, CO 80521, U.S.A.

TREMBLE, Stella Craft (Mrs.). Housewife; Editor; Poet. Education: Eastern Ill. Univ.; Hon. D. Litt., Free Univ. of Asia, Pakistan. Positions held: Ed., Am. Poet; Ed., Prairie Poet; Ed., United Poets; Ed., Am. Poetry League Bulletin. Memberships: Nat. League of Am. Pen Women; Pres., Am. Poets Fellowship Soc., 1965–; Pres., Am. poetry League. Published works: The Silver Chain, 1953; Thorns and Thistledown, 1954; Wind in the Road, 1957; Crystal Prism, 1958; Loom and Lyre, 1961; Telescope of Time, 1962; Happy Holidays, 1963; Songs of the Prairie, 1964; In His Day, 1966; Goodbye, Little Country School, 1966; Bells of Autumn, 1967; From Isles of Silence, 1968; Broken Arcs, 1969; Paths to Parnarsas, 1969. Ed. of: Prairie Poet Anthol., 1961, '65; Am. Poets (Anthol.), 1966, '67, '68; From Sea To Sea In Song (Anthol.), 1965, '68. Awards: George Washington gold medal, '66, 67 Freedom Fndn., Valley Forge, 1962; Gold Cup, Am. Poets Fellowship Soc., 1964-65; Book of the Year Award, Am. Poets

Fellowship Soc., 1958; 1st Place Awards, Nat. Fed. of Press Women; Hon. Poet Laureate of World Greatness & Leadership, from Dr. Yuzon, Philippines; Gold Medal, from the President of the Philippines. Address: 830 7th St., Charleston Ill. 61920, USA.

TRIBE, David Harold, b. 17 Dec. 1931. Writer; Broadcaster. Education: Univ. of Queensland, Australia. Positions held: Ed., Trophine; Edit. & Advt. Staff, Time & Tide; Tchr.; PR Officer to Impresario. Lectr.; Ed., Freethinker; Lectr. in Lib. Studies & Jrnlsm. Memberships: London Poetry Secretariat; Soc. of Authors; Poetry Soc.; Poets' Workshop; Poets' Conf. Published works include: Why Are We Here?, 1965; Figure in a Japanese Landscape, 1971. Contbr. to the following anthols., jrnls., mags., etc: BBC Third Prog. & Radio 3; Twentieth Century; Tribune; Punch; Manifold; Aquarius; Poetry 1; Poetry 2; Inquirer; Outposts; New Statesman; Quarry, Canada; Ophir (SA); Wurm (SA); Doves for the Seventies; Sunday Times. Address: 10 New Row, London WC2, UK.

TRIEM, Eve, b. 2 Nov. 1902. Poet; Lecturer. Education: Univ. of Calif., Berkeley; Greek, Univ. of Dubuque; Univ. of Wash. Married, Paul Ellsworth Triem, 1 s., 1 d. Positions held: Dir., Poetry Workshops, YWCA, Seattle, Wash.; Lectr., nationally on poetry. Mbr. Poetry Soc. Am. Published works: Parade of Doves, 1946; Poems, 1965; Heliodora, Translations from the Greek Anthol., 1967-68; Selected Poems, 1974. Contbr. to: E.E. Cummings (monograph), 1969; Yale Review; Nation; Botteghe Oscure; Poetry Chicago; Am. Scholar; Mass. Review; Poetry Northwest; Dalhousie Review; Quarterly Review of Lit.; Prairie Schooner; Southwest Review; Human Voice Mag.; Beloit Poetry Jrnl.; Voices; Yankee; Galaxy; Providence Review; NY Times; Kavita. Honours, Awards: Charlotte Arthur Awards, 1937, '38; Carmel Pine Cone Prize, Nat. Inst. of Arts & Letters, 1966; League to Support Poetry Award, 1946; Grant, Authors League, 1967; Nat. Endowment for the Arts, Wash. DC, grant, 1967-68; Hart Crane & Alice Crane Williams Mem. Fund, 1969. Address: 911 Alder St., Apt. 790, Seattle, Washington 98104, USA.

TRIM, Douglas, b. 13 Jan. 1910. Statistician & Office Manager. Education: Collège de St. Jean Berchmann, Antwerp, Belgium. Married twice, div. once & now a widower, 1 son & 1 daughter. Positions held: Builder's Clerk; Timekeeper; Storekeeper; Carpenter's Mate; Plumber's Mate; Painter; Market Gardener; Greyhound Trnr.; Profl. Portrait & Landscape Photographer; Publisher of Greetings Cards & Calendars; RAF Photographer during WWII; Freelance Writer; Company Sec. & Dir. of a Market Gardeners Assn.; Records Officer in the Heavy Chemicals Ind.; Market Researcher in the Pharmaceutical Ind.; Site Clerk on the building of the M6 Motorway; Prodn. Planner in Textiles; Statistician for a machine tools concern; Dealer in foreign stamps, etc. Member, Manchester Poetry Soc. Published works: The Reality of Stars (poetry), 1973. Contbr. to: Chambers Jrnl.; Irish Woman's Jrnl.; Creation (Ireland); English; Here & Now; The Jongleur; Poetry Workshop; New Poets Mag. Address: 9 Cromer Ave., Manchester M20 9DU, U.K.

TRIPP, John, b. 22 July 1927. Information Officer. Educ: Dip., Morley Coll., London, U.K. Positions held: News Rschr. & Sub-Ed., B.B.C., London, 1951-58; Press Off., Indonesian Embassy, London, 1958-67; Info. Off., Central Off. of Info., London, 1967–. Published works: Diesel to Yesterday, 1966; The Loss of Ancestry, 1969. Contbr. to: Poetry Wales; London Welshman; Tribune; (anthologies) Young Commonwealth Poets, '65; Welsh Voices, 1967; Lilting House, 1969. Address: c/o 1c Aberdeen Place, London N.W.8, U.K.

TRIPP, Lena Elvina. Retired Teacher. Education: A.B., Univ. of Wash.; M.A., Univ. of Calif. Widow of Elmer Tripp. Positions held: First Grade Tchr., Plymouth, Calif., ret'd 1969. Memberships: United Amateur Press; Ky. State Poetry Soc.; Int. Clover

Poetry Assn.; Am. Poets Fellowship Soc.; Centro Studi e Scambi Int.; The Laurel Publishers Int. Poetry Symposium. Published works: Verses, 1968; More Verses, 1970; The Broken Tree, 1971; Those Pets of Mine, 1971; Christmas, 1971; Two Years Old, 1972; Words Are Wonderful, 1972; Autumn Leaves, 1973. Contbr. to num. jrnls., anthols. mags. inclng: United Poets; The Am. Poet; Jean's Jrnl.; Prairie Poet; The Muse; Quintessence; Author/Poet; Hoosier Challenger; The Christian; Orphic Lute; Verdure; Quaderni di Poesia; The Best in Poetry Anthols., 1968 & '70; Christmas Anthols., 1969, '71, '72; Garland of Verse Anthol., 1971. Recip. of num. prizes from Creativity Newsletter & others. Address: Box 124, Plymouth, CA 95669, U.S.A.

TROLLIET, Gilbert, b. 13 June 1910. Writer; Translator; Journalist. Education: Univ. Educ., Geneva, Switzerland; Neuchâtel & Paris, France. Positions held: Ed., First Nat. Film Co., Paris & N.Y. World; Union Europeenne de Radiodiffusion, Geneva, Switzerland; Dir., Presence lit. review. Memberships: Pen Club Int.; European Cultural Soc., Venice, Italy; European Community of Writers, Rome; Swiss Soc. of Writers. Published works: Cadran, 1930; Petite Apocalypse, 1931; Eclaircies, 1932; La Vie Extreme, 1932; Itineraire de la Mort, 1933; Vingt Poemes de Juin, 1934; Nouveau Monde, 1934; Unisson, 1936; Paysages Confidentiels, 1938; Poemes Mineurs, 1939; Deux Odes, 1940; La Bonne Fortune, 1942; Offrandes, 1944; Fallait-il, 1945; L'Inespere, 1949; La Balle au Bond, 1950; La Colline, 1955; Prends Garde au Jour, 1962; Laconiques, 1966; Avec la Rose, 1967; Fabliaux, 1969; Le Fleuve et l'etre, 1968; Douze textuels; Fabliaux; Autoscopie, 1969; L'Ancolie, 1971. Contbr. to: (anthols.) Le Fleuve et l'Etre, 1968; (jrnls.) Le Mercure de France; La Table Ronde; Preuves; Les Nouvelles Litteraires; Betelgeuse; La Nef (Paris); Le Thyrse; Jrnl. des Poetes; Syntheses (Brussels); Presence; Suisse Romande; Suisse Contemporaine; Jrnl. de Genève; Gazette de Lausanne; Lettres, etc. Honours, awards: Grand Prix de Littérature Rhodanienne, 1949; Prix Romand de Poésie, 1934; Prix Guillaume-Apollinaire, 1957; Prix Van Lerberghe, 1961; Prix de la Fondation Schiller, 1968; Prix Int. des Amities Francaises, 1970 Address: 29 quai des Bergues, 1201 Geneva, Switzerland.

TROLLOPE-CAGLE, Vivian Jewel, pen names **CAGLE, Billie Trollope & ONE-MINUS-ONE.** Poet. Positions held: Charter Mbr., 1st Sec.-Treas., & On Bd. Dirs., 1962-69, Nev. Poetry Soc.; 2-yr Judge, 1968-69 Nat. Contests, Am. Poetry League; Am. Rep., Poetry Soc. of Aust., 1969; Northwest Rep., Int. Poets Shrine, 1969-72; Las Vegas, Nev. Rep., Centro Studi e Scambi Int., Rome, 1969; Advsr., 2nd World Congress of Poets, Taiwan, 1973. Memberships incl: Life Mbr., Poetry Soc. of Am.; Fndr., Acad. of Am. Poets; United Poets Laureate; Int. Platform Assn. Rep. in the following anthols: Echoes of Faith (Young Publs.); Utah Sings, Vol. IV; Am. Poetry League from Sea to Sea in Song, 1962-69; Silver Strings; Nat. Fed. State Poetry Socs. 1968 Prize Winning Poems; Diamond Anthol., Poetry Soc. Am., 1971; IWWP Anthol., 1972; Poet India: SW Poets of the USA, 1973; South & West: Poems by Poets, 1973. Contbr. of approx. 400 poems to newspapers & mags. inclng: Oakland Tribune; Salt Lake Tribune; Las Vegas Sun; Boulder City News; Ariz. Highways; The Children's Friend; Am. Bard; Laurel Leaves, Philippines; Poetry (Australia); Poet (India). Recip. many poetry hons. & awards inclng: Decretum & Hon. Poet Laureateship, UPLI, Manila Univ., Cert. of Hon. on U.N. Day, Philippines, Hon. Doctorate, Lit. Ldrship, Int. Acad. Ldrship, 1967; Gold Laurel Wreath from Past Pres. (RP) Carlos P. Garcia, 1968; Hon. Dr. of Mod. Humanities, Free Univ., Pakistan, 1973. Address: 4211 W. Baxter Pl., Las Vegas, NV 89107, U.S.A.

TRONI, Armando, b. 6 July 1911. Writer; Economist; International Organiser. Education: Sc.D. (Econ. & Co.), Univ. of Palermo, Italy; 1933-37. Positions held: Rsch. Analyst, PWB, JICA, USNOB, 1944-45; Insp. of Plays & High Commr. of Sicily, 1944-46; Sec.-Gen.,

Centro Studi E Scambi Internazionali; Co-Dir., Mondo, Int. Monthly Bulletin of Cultural Inf.; Comm. Mbr. & Organiser, 15 Int. Congresses & Meetings in various countries. Memberships: Hon. Corresp., Royal Acad. of Cordoba, Spain; Acad. Chablaisienne; Acad. de Sciences, Lettres et Beaux Arts de Dijon, France; Hon., Int. Comm. for Unity & Universality of Culture, Italy; World Cultural Council, Germany; Comite Cultural, Argentino; Hon. Prof., St. Andrew's Ecumenical Univ. Intercollegiate, London, UK. Published works: I Colloqui col tempo, 1935; Palestina, 1937; La Cambiale, 1939; Bologna, 1940; Il Canale di Suez, 1941; L'Insulindia, 1942; Le Filippine, 1942; Storia del Giappone, 1942; Dante et Mahome, 1948; La Nuova Turchia, 1953; Il Canale di Cortinto, 1954; Un Verso arabo nella Divina Commedia, 1957; Radio e TV in Giappone, 1958; Le Theatre Moderne Turc, 1962. Contbr. to: Le Forze Armate; Rivista Marittima; Rivistadelle Colonie; Yamato-ci; La Vie del Mondo; Universo; etc. Honours: Gold Medal, Literary Assoc., Genoa, Italy; ibid, Comm. for the Valorization of Econ. Resources of Greece; Lateran Cross; Premio della Cultura della Presidenza del Consiglio dei Ministri. Address: Centro Studi E Scambi Internazionali Via Corrado Sefre 7 Rome, Italy.

TROTT, Rosemary Clifford, pen name **TROTT, R.C.,** b. 8 Mar. 1914. Author; Poet; Columnist; Lecturer on Poetry. Education: Columbia Univ. Schl. of Jrnlsm., 1945; Continuing Educ. Div., Univ. of Me. & Gorham State Coll., 1965. Married James E. Trott, 1 son, 1 daughter. Positions held: Feature Writer, Portland Evening News, 1930 (wrote Buyers' Guide Column); Town Reporter & Feature Writer, Gannett Publs., 1942-46; Columnist & Feature Writer, Brunswick Record, Me., 1942-47; Radio Copywriter, W.P.O.R. Radio, 1948-49; News Reporter, W.L.O.B. radio, 1957; Radio Copywriter, W.L.O.B., 1972; Staff Mbr., Writer, Dealerscope Mag., 1969–; Columnist, Freeport Post, 1972–, etc. Memberships incl: Poetry Soc. of N.H.; Sec., Poetry Fellowship of Me., 1948-50; Pres., 1950 & intermittently since, Me. Poetry Day Assn.; Elected Hon. Life Pres., ibid, 1972; Am. Poetry League (Judge in sev. contests); United Poets Laureate Int. (Poet Laureate of Nature, 1966); Pres., Pine Tree Br., Nat. League of Am. Pen Women, 1960-62; served as Sec. & Publicity Chmn. & Mbrship. Chmn., ibid, 1968; Co-hostess, Washington Biennial Banquet, also Poetry Banquet Chmn., Nat. Poetry Chmn., etc.; Fndr., Me. Poetry Week, 1950, legis. 1957; Fndr.; Am. Poetry Sunday, 1969; Dir. & Sec., Womens State Relief Corps. Published works: Maine Christmas, 1945; Sea Mist & Balsam, 1958; Blue Through Tears, by Wind & Water, 1971; Path of Roses, edited 'From One Bright Spark', 1959; Freeport, Cradle of Ships, 1973. On Editl. Bds. of 'Maine Indians, In Story & Legend', 'Maine Islands', & 'As Maine Writes'. Contbr. to num. anthols., jrnls., mags., newspapers. Recip. num. hons. & awards inclng: Gold Medal from Pres. Marcos & Laurel Wreath from Dr. Yuzon, UPLI, 1966; Award from U.N. for Ldrship in Poetry, 1967; 1st Prize (World Prize), World Poetry Day, 1967; Judge of sev. comps.; Dr. of Lit., UPLI; 23 Governor's proclamations for Me. Poetry Week. Invited Spkr., World Congress of Poets, Manila, Philippines, 1969. Address: Blueberry Hill, Freeport, ME 04032, U.S.A.

TROUPP, Lotte, pen name **ZURNDORFER, Lotte,** b. 26 July 1929. Lecturer in English. Education: St. Hugh's Coll., Oxford Univ., UK; Sorbonne Univ., France. Married to Henry Troupp, neurosurgeon, 2 d. Positions held: Publs. Officer, Shirley Inst., Manchester, UK, 1951-53; Assistante, Rouen Lycée, France, 1953-55; Tchr., Inst. des Hautes Etudes d'Interpretariat, Univ. of Paris, France, 1954-55; Lectr., Svenska Handelshögskola, Helsinki, Finland, 1955-56; Lectr., Univ. of Helsinki, 1956–. Published works: Fantasy Press Pamphlet, 1952; Poems, 1960. Contbr. to: Oxford Poetry No. 9, 1951; Oxford Univ. Broadsheets & other mags.; The Guinness Book of Poetry, 1960-61; Truth; Methuen Anthology of Modern Verse, 1940-60. Recip. of Poetry Soc. Prize, Oxford Univ., 1950. Address: Myötäle 5, Mankans, Esbo, Finland.

TROWER, Peter (Gerard), pen name **PETRO,** b. 25 Aug. 1930. Assoc. Editor. Education: H.S., and Vancouver School of Art. Positions held: Logger, 1949-56; Smelterworker, 1956-58; Logger, 1963-65; Surveyor, 1966-68; Logger, 1970-71; Writer & Editor, 1972– (Assoc. Ed., Raincoast Chronicles and Harbour Publishing); freelance writer & poet. Pubs. Moving Through The Mystery, 1969; Between the Sky and the Splinters, 1973; Kites & Cartwheels (Anthol.), 1972; Listen (Anthol.), 1972; West Coast Seen (Anthol.), 1970; Contemporary Verse in B.C. (Anthol.), 1973. Contrib. to: Raincoast Chronicles; Poetry (Chicago); Poetry Australia; Blew Ointment; New Society; Saturday; Internat. Times. Recip. Borestone Mountain Poetry Award, 1967. Address: Box 193, Gibsons, B.C., Canada.

TRUCHINSKI, Joyce Ailene, b. 8 Nov. 1923. Homemaker. Education: Dale's Tech. Schl.; Univ. of St. Louis, Mo.; Western Union Multiplex Op. Schl. Married Edward Truchinski, 4 children. Positions held: Civilian Instr., U.S.A.A.F., 1940's; Western Union Telegraph Multiplex Operator; var. other positions. Memberships: Vice Regent & Awards Dir., Midwest Fed. of Chaparral Poets; Saint Paul Poets, Minn.; Minn. League of Poets. Contbr. to: Gnostica Bulletin; The Sun Newspaper. Address: 6913 52nd Ave. N., Crystal, MN 55428, U.S.A.

TRUESDALE, (Calvin) William, b. 27 Mar. 1929. Publisher; Teacher. Education: B.A. Univ. of Wash., Seattle, 1951; Ph.D., ibid, 1957. Married, 3 children. Positions held: Instr., Univ. of N.M., 1954-55; Asst. Prof., Va. Military Inst., 1956-62; Asst. Prof., Macalester Coll., 1962-67; Lectr., New Schl. for Soc. Rsch., 1973-74; Ed./Publisher, New Rivers Press, 1967– & The Minnesota Review, 1971-73. Memberships: Coordinating Coun. of Lit. Mags. (has been on sev. grants bds.); COSMEP; Pres., The Print Ctr., Inc., 1972–. Published works: In the Country of a Deer's Eye, 1966; The Loss of Rivers, 1967; Moonshots, 1968; The Master of Knives, 1971; Plastic Father, 1971; Cold Harbors, 1973; transl. w. Charles Simic, Fire Gardens, The Selected Poems of Ivan V. Lalic, 1971. Contbr. to: Inscape; Shenandoah; Second Coming; Broadway Boogie; Minn. Review; Va. Qtly. Review; New Edinburgh Review; Borestone Mt. Awards Anthol., etc. Address: New Rivers Press, P.O. Box 578, Cathedral Station, N.Y., NY 10025, U.S.A.

TRUMPOWER, Mabel Gertrude, b. 19 April 1896. Artist; Poet. Positions held: Worked for artist, Edward R. Sitzman, Indianapolis; Teacher, Commercial Art, Landscape, Myer Booth Coll., Chicago. Memberships: Peninsular Poets Club; Vets. of World War One; Am. Legion, Reed City, Mich., etc. Publlshed work. My Favourite Poems, 1944. Contbr. to: Am. Legion Auxillaire of Michigan; Veterans of World War One News; Songs reproduced on radio, etc. Address: 715 E. Chase Rd., RR No. 3, Evart, MI 49631, USA.

TRYPANIS, Constantine Athanasius, b. 22 Jan. 1909. University Professor. Education: Univs. of Athens, Berlin & Munich; D.Litt. (Oxford); D. Phil. (Athens); M.A. Oxford. Married Aliki Macris, 1 daughter. Positions held: Lectr. in Classics, Univ. of Athens, 1940-47; Prof. of Medieval & Modern Greek, Univ. of Oxford, 1947-67; Univ. Prof. of Classics, Univ. of Chicago, 1967–. Memberships: Patron, Oxford Poetry Soc.; Poetry Panel, Arts Coun. of G.B., 1965-67; Fellow, Royal Soc. of Lit., 1958. Published works: Tartessos, 1945; Pedasus, 1955; The Stones of Troy, 1956; The Cocks of Hades, 1958; Pompeian Dog, 1964; Grooves in the Wind, 1962; The Elegies of a Glass Adonis, 1967; The Glass Adonis, 1973. Contrib. to: Times Lit. Supplement; Spectator; Encounter; Listen; Stand; Truth; Departure; Botteghe Oscure; Oxford Mag.; Stapledon Mag.; Gemini; 3rd prog. BBC: New Yorker, etc. Recip., Heinemann Prize (for The Cocks of Hades), Royal Soc. of Lit. The Stones of Troy & The Cocks of Hades were made 'Choices' of the Poetry Soc. Address: 5825 South Dorchester Ave., Chicago, IL 60637, U.S.A.

TSCHUMI, Raymond, b. 27 Nov. 1924. Professor of English Literature. Education: Brown Univ.; Dr. ès lettres, Geneva Univ., Switzerland, 1951. Married w. 3 children. Positions held: Docent, Geneva Univ., 1951; Jrnlst., Translator, Poet, Traveller, etc., until 1953; Extraordinary Prof., Engl. & Am., St. Gallen Univ., 1956; Prof., 1959; Dean, 1963-64. Memberships: Comm., Swiss PEN; Inst. Jurassien of Sci., Letters, & Arts; Soc. of Swiss Writers; Soc. des écrivains neuchâtelois et jurassiens. Published works: L'Arche, 1950; Regards voraces, 1952; Renouveau, 1953; Concert d'Ouvertures, 1968. Contbr. to: Revue de Suisse; Présence; Anhembi; La Chouette aveugle; Journal de Genève; Anthologie jurassienne; Petite anthologie de la poésie jurassienne vivante; L'Impartial; Journal du Jura; Pour l'Art; Profil littéraire de la France; Journal de la société suisse des instituteurs. Address: Flurhofstrasse 88, 9000 St. Gallen, Switzerland.

TSCHUMPERLIN, Marie Dolores Ann, b. 27 Mar. 1945. Telephone Representative. Education: Sacred Heart School, Salinas, Calif.; Palma HS, Salinas; Hartnell Jr. Coll., Salinas. Membership: Literary Guild of America. Contbr. to: Poetry of the Year; Catholic Theatre; Jean's Journal; The Best in Poetry; Gato; Poetry Pageant; Poetry Parade. Award: Cert. of Merit from J. Mark Press, 1970. Address: P.O. Box 277, Coyote, CA 95013, USA.

TULL, George Francis, b. 21 Oct. 1920. Tutor. Education: London Univ. Extra-mural studies; studying for B.A., Open Univ., 1971–. Positions held: Corres. Tutor, Schl. of Poetry, Guernsey, 1972–. Memberships: World Poetry Soc. Intercontinental; Hellenic Writers' Club, Athens; Catholic Poetry Soc. Published works: The Quiet Ways, 1969; Poet's Eye on London, 1972; var. prose works. Contbr. to: Reading Evening Post; The Tablet; Aylesford Review; The Cat; The Ark; Ozark Gardens (USA); Sussex Life; Catholic Standard (Ireland); Poet, etc. Address: 148 Gander Green Lane, W. Sutton, Surrey, UK.

TULLETT, Denis John, pen names **SUTTON, John, MELMOTH,** b. 20 Mar. 1928. Poet. Mbr., 20th Century Writers Guild. Published works: Fifty For Tradition, 1953; Stones Out, 1958; None Over the Eight, 1968. Contbr. to the following jrnls. & anthols: Proof; Scrip; Expression; Accent; Viewpoints; Manifold; Orbis; Manuscript; Fireflower; Laudamus té; Quill; Poetry Workshop; Orb; Lincolnshire Writers; All People Are Poets; Regency Press; Cathay Books; Lincolnshire Echo; London Anthol. Honours, Awards: 1st Prize, Reading Literary Festival, 1953-55; Lincoln Lit. & Music Festival, 1965 & '67; Silver Medal, Richmond-Upon-Thames Lit. Festival, 1967. Address: 63 Harewood Crescent, N Hykeham, Lincoln, UK.

TUNC, Seyfettin, b. 5 Mar. 1940. Restaurant Manager. Married, 2 s. Memberships: Writers' Club, Liverpool. Book of Poetry published in Turkey, 1968. Address: 6 Oban Rd., Anfield, Liverpool 4, UK.

TUNSTALL, Velma Barrett, pen name, **TUNSTALL, Shana Barrett,** b. 11 Aug. 1914, Vidette, Ark., USA. Housewife. Education: self-educated. Personal details: grandfather, county judge; Engl., Scottish & Irish descent. Memberships: Internat. Platform Assoc.; Calif. State Poetry Soc.; Calif. Fed. of Chap. Poets. Published works: Shadows On My Soul, 1971. Contbr. to: Better Thoughts Anthol., 1970; Anthol. of Am. Poetry, 1971; Internat. Who's Who in Poetry, 1972-73 Edition; Daily Quill; Salem Headlight (poetry & articles), 1970-71; Shore; Dawn; Quality American Poetry; El Viento; CQ; Springfield Daily News (Mo.). Award: Hall of Fame, West Plains, Mo. (for literary achievements). Address: 928 Third Place, Upland, CA 91786, USA.

TURCO, Lewis Putnam, b. 2 May 1934. Writer; Teacher. Education: B.A., Univ. of Conn., 1959; M.A., Univ. of Iowa, 1962. Married Jean Cate Houdlette, 2 children. Positions held: Instr. of Engl., Univ. of Conn., 1959, & Cleveland State Univ., 1960-64 (Fndr. & 1st

Dir., C.S.U. Poetry Ctr., 1961-64); Asst. Prof. of Engl., Hillsdale Coll., 1964-65; SUNY Coll., Oswego, 1965-; Prof., ibid, 1970– (Dir., Prog. in Writing Arts). Published works: First Poems, 1960; The Sketches, 1962; Awaken, Bells Falling, 1968; The Inhabitant, 1970; Pocoangelini: A Fantography & Other Poems, 1971; The Weed Garden, 1973; The Book of Forms: A Handbook of Poetics, 1968; Poetry: An Introduction Through Writing, 1973. Contbr. to: Atlantic; New Yorker; New Republic; Nation; Commonweal; Poetry; Sewanee Review; Kenyon Review; Tri-Qtly.; N.Y. Qtly.; Saturday Review; Modern Poetry Studies; Iowa Review; Poetry Northwest; Johns Hopkins Mag.; Mich. Qtly. Review; Carleton Miscellany; Antioch Review; Am. Scholar; N.Y. Times Mag.; Mass. Review; N.Am. Review; Southern Review, etc. Recip. var. hons. & awards inclng: Helen Bullis Prize, Poetry Northwest, 1972; Borestone Mountain Poetry Awards, Best Poems of 1965 & 71. Address: 54 W. 8th St., Oswego, NY 13126, U.S.A.

TURKAY, Osman (Mustafa) b. 16 Feb. 1927. Journalist (Editor & Columnist). Education: Schl. of Mod. Langs., Regent St. Polytechnic, London; London Univ. Positions held: Asst. Ed., Daily Hürsöz & Columnist, 1951-53; London Corres., Bozkurt, 1953-58; Ed. & Ldr. Writer, Bozkurt; Mbr., Cyprus Consultative Assembly, 1959-61; Freelance Jrnlst. & Ed. of Vatan; Sec.-Gen., Cyprus Turkish Assn., London, 1970–. Memberships: Int. PEN, London Ctr.; Fellow Fndr., Int. Poetry Soc., U.K.; Nat. Union of Jrnlsts., Ctrl. London Br.; Centro Studi e Scambi Int., Rome. Published works: 7 Telli (Septet), 1959; Uyurgezer (Somnambulist), 1969; Beethoven de Aydinliğa Uyanmak, 1970; Evrenin Düşümde Gezgin, 1971; Kiyamet Günü Gözlemcileri, 1973; Selected Poems of T.S. Eliot, 1965; Complete Poetry of T.S. Eliot (transl. into Turkish), 1973; Towards the Light (transl. from Turkish into Engl.), 1971; O World Stop Revolving (transl. into Engl.), 1972; Selected Poems of Pablo Neruda (transl. into Turkish), 1974. Contbr. to var. jrnls., mags. & to radio progs. Personal Poetry broadcasts in the U.S.A. Honours, awards: 'Uyurgezer (Somnambulist)' chosen as one of the best books of poems & included in 100 Best Books of Poems by Turkish PEN. Address: 22 Avenue Mansions, Finchley Rd., London N.W.3, U.K.

TURMEAU, Constance Evelyn, pen name **COLETTE,** b. 24 Aug. 1906. Housewife. Married, 1 son, 1 daughter. Memberships: Chmn., Brentwood Writer's Circle, 1971-73; Fellow, Int. Poetry Soc. Contbr. to: Billericay Standard Recorder; Manifold; Viewpoints; The Guide; Brentwood Gazette. Honours, awards: 1st prize, Brentwood Writers' Circle Comp., 1973; Highly commended, sev. comps., Manifold. Address: Domani, 31 Myln Meadow, Stock, Ingatestone, Essex, U.K.

TURNBULL, Gael Lundin, b. 7 Apr. 1928. Poet; General Practitioner. Published works: A Trampoline: Poems 1952-64, 1968; Scantlings: Poems 1964-69, 1970; Finger Cymbals, 1971. Address: Bridge House, Cradley, Malvern, Worcs. WR13 5NN, U.K.

TURNER, Alberta Tucker, b. 22 Oct. 1919. Poet; Professor of English. Education: A.B., Hunter Coll., N.Y.C., U.S.A., 1940; M.A., Wellesley Coll., 1941; Ph.D., Ohio State Univ., 1946. Married W. Arthur Turner, 1 daughter, 1 son. Positions held: Lectr. in Engl., Oberlin Coll., 1947-69; Lectr., Asst. Prof., Assoc. Prof. of Engl., Cleveland State Univ., 1969–; Dir., Cleveland State Univ. Poetry Ctr., 1964–; Assoc. Ed., Field: Contemporary Poetry & Poetics, 1970–. Memberships: Acad. of Am. Poets; Milton Soc. of Am.; Ohio Poets Assn.; Midwest MLA. Published works: North, 1970; Need, 1971; Learning to Count, 1974. Contbr. to: Atlantic; Antioch Review; Beloit Poetry Jrnl.; Approach; Poetry & Audience; Harper's Mass. Review; Shenandoah; Canadian Forum; Malahat Review; The Far Point; Stand; Midwest Quarterly; Prairie Schooner; Quarterly Review; Poetry Northwest; Univ. of Kan. City Review, etc. Honours, awards: one of six runners-up, U.S. Award, Int. Poetry

Forum, Univ. of Pitts. Press, 1974. Address: Dept. of Engl., Cleveland State Univ., Euclid at 24 St., Cleveland, OH 44115, U.S.A.

TURNER, Bessye Tobias, b. 10 Oct. 1917. Assistant Professor of English & Speech. Education: A.B., Engl., Rust Coll., 1939; M.A., Engl., Columbia Univ., 1954, M.A., Speech, ibid, 1964; Further Study, Speech, Theatre, Speech Pathol., Columbia Univ. Positions held: Engl. Tchr., Burglund HS, 1939-44; IRS, Bronx, NY, 1945-49; Engl. Tchr. & Drama Coach, Alexander HS, 1950-55; Asst. Prof., Engl., & Dir. of Theatre, Alcorn A & M Col., 1955-62; Asst. Prof., Engl. & Speech, Southern Univ., La., 1962-63; Asst. Prof., Tex. Southern Univ., 1964-67; Asst. Prof., Miss. Valley State Coll., 1968–. Memberships: Chmn., Creative & Performing Arts; Centro Studi e Scambi Int.; Advsr.; Marquis Biographical Lib.; Fellow-Fndr., Int. Poetry Soc.; The National Historical Soc., Smithsonian Instit. Pubs: La Librae: An Anthology of Poetry for Living, 1969; Peace and Love, Quaderni Di Poesia, 1972. Contrib. to: Quaderni Di Poesia; Albo D'Ore del XXV Anniversario, 1971; Enterprise Journal; Miss. Teachers Journal; Alcorn Alumni Bulletin; Poetry Parade, 1967-68. Honours & Awards: Cert. of Achievement, Hon. Mention, Coll. Arts Poetry Contest, 1967; Int. Exhib., Centro Studi e Scambi Int., 1971, '72; DIB Cert. of Merit, 1973; Cert. Nat. Assoc. of Prominent Americans & Internat. Notables, 1973-75; Cert. of Merit, Who's Who of American Women, 1974-75; Cert. of Merit: World Who's Who of Women, 1973; IBA Yearbook, 1972; CSSI Yearbook, 1973. Address: 829 Wall Street, McComb, Mississippi 39648, USA.

TURNER, James Ernest, b. 16 Jan. 1909. Author. Education: Queen's Coll., Oxford, 1927-31. Married Lucie Alice Porter. Memberships: Mark Twain Soc., U.S.A.; West Country Writers Assn.; Crime Writers' Assn. Published works: Pastoral, 1943; The Alien Wood, 1945; The Hollow Vale, 1947; The Interior Diagram, 1960; The Accident & Other Poems, 1963. Contbr. to: Times Lit. Supplement; The Listener; Contemporary Review; Cornish Review; Borestone Mountain Poetry; Poetry Review. Address: Parsonville, St. Teath, Bodmin, Cornwall.

TURNER, Marjorie Ethel, b. 9 Sept. 1916. Clerk; Secretary. Positions held: Clerical Officer, Civil Service, 1934-47; War Serv. VAD, 1943-45; p/t Sec. work, 1967–. Member, Wolverhampton Poetry Grp., 1972–. Address: 84 Wynn Rd., Wolverhampton WV4 4AN, Staffs., U.K.

TURNER, Mary Ann (Mrs. Howard G.), born 22nd September 1922. Freelance Writer. Education: studied art, Ariz. State Univ. Positions held: Juvenile Writer, 1954–. Memberships: Nat. League of Am. Pen Women; Treas., Ariz. State Poetry Soc.; Co-ed., Sandcutters, quarterly bulletin, ibid; Ariz. Assoc. of Univ. Women Creative Writing Club. Contbr. to: Ballet on the Wind Anthology, 1969; Echoes of Faith, 1970; Sing, Naked Spirit, 1970; The World of Language, Book 1, Teacher's Edition, 1970. The Children's Friend; Our Little Messenger; Story World; The Little Folks; 'Til Eight Stories; Our Little Friend; Teen Talk; Progressive Tchr.; Boys & Girls; Wee Wisdom; Instructor; Canadian Red Cross Jr.; Child Life; Ideals; Purring in a Pocket; Methodist Publishing House; Highlights for Children; Swordsman's Review; Stories; Grade Tchr.; Children's Playmate: Sandcutters; Monte Vista Schl. News & Views; Pen Woman; Am. Mosaic; (Anthol.) Ballet On The Wind Anthol., 1969. Honours: tied 1st Place, Ariz. State Poetry Soc. Nat. for On The Wings of a Butterfly, 1969: 3rd Place, Pennsylvania Poetry Soc. National, 1972; Two awards, World Poetry Day Contest, 1968. Address: 3624 E. Weldon, Phoenix, Ariz. 85018, U.S.A.

TURNER, Myron, b. 22 May 1935. Professor of Engl.; Education: B.A., City Coll. of NY 1956; M.A., Rutgers Univ., 1958; Ph.D., Univ. of Wash., 1965. Positions held: Asst. Prof. of Engl., Whitman Coll.; Assoc. Prof. of Engl., Univ. of Manitoba, Winnipeg, Canada; Ed., The Far Point, mag. of poetry & criticism. Published works include: Things That Fly, forthcoming. Contbr. to the following anthols., jrnls., mags, etc.; Atlantic Monthly; Contact; Accent; Minn. Review; Prism; Yale Review; Canadian Dimension; Quest; Canadian Forum; Lit. Review; Mich. Qtly; Mass. Review; Omphalos; Made in Canada: New Poetry of the 70's; Poetry NW; Malahat Review; Little Mag.; Dreadnought; Poet, etc. Address: Dept. of Engl., Univ. of Manitoba, Winnipeg 19, Manitoba, Canada.

TURNER, Raymond, b. 28 Mar. 1920. Local Government Officer. Education: Westcliff HS, Essex, 1931-38; London School of Economics (London Univ.), 1938-40, 1945-46: B.Sc.(Econ.), D.P.A. Married; 2 s. Positions held: Kent County Council, 1946-49; Middlesex County Council, 1949-50; Derbyshire County Council, 1950-57; Staffordshire County Council, 1957-73. Memberships: Wolverhampton (W.E.A.) Poetry Group; British Humanist Assoc. Published works: Flies in Amber, 1971; The Garden of Cain, 1973. Contbr. to: Viewpoints; Breakthru; Scrip; Express and Star (Wolverhampton); Poetry of the 70's; Spring Anthol.; and has broadcast on Radio Birmingham. Address: 84 Wynn Rd., Wolverhampton, Staffs. WV4 4AN, UK.

TURNER, William Price, b. 14 Aug. 1927. Novelist; Book Reviewer. Positions held: Gregory Fellow, Poetry, Leeds Univ., 1960-62; Tutor, Creative Writing, Swarthmore Adult Educ. Ctr., 1963-65. Published works: First Offence, 1955; The Rudiment of an Eye, 1956; The Flying Corset, 1962; Fables from Life, 1966; Baldy Bane, 1967; More Fables from Life, 1969; The Moral Rocking Horse, 1970. Contbr. to: Ariel; Artisan; Arena; Akros; Cleveland Press; Departure; Dubliner; Elizabeth; Envoi; Flame; Glasgow Herald; Honest Ulsterman; The Lady; Lines Review; Listen; Nova; Orient West; Outposts; Peace News; Pegasus; Phoenix; Poet; Poetry; Poetry Chicago; Poetry & Audience; Poetry Review; Prairie Schooner; Quicksilver; Saltire Review; Sat. Review; Scotsman; Samphire; Stand; Twentieth Century; Tribune; Times Lit. Supplement; Vagabond. Honours, awards: Brit. Poetry Assn. Poetry Prize, 1953; Gregory Fellowship in Poetry, 1960; Envoi Mag. Poetry Prize, 1969; Scottish Arts Coun. Publ. Award, 1970. Address: 8 Methley Terrace, Chapel Allerton, Leeds LS7 3NL, UK.

TURTIAINEN, Arvo Albin, b. 16 Sept. 1904. Author. Education: Inst. of Soc. Scis., Helsinki, Finland. Married. Positions held: Dental Techn., 1924-31; Jrnlst., 1933-39; Freelance Author, 1939-. Memberships: Hon. Mbr., Finnish Soc. of Authors; Soc. of Writers & Artists Kiila; Eino Leino Soc.; Assn. of Finnish Translators. Published works: First coll. of poems, 1936; 11 other colls. & 2 works of prose. Translations: Edgar Lee Masters, Spoon River Anthology; Walt Whitman, Leaves of Grass; Wladimir Majakovsky, Cloud in Trousers; Wladimir Iljits Lenin; Scandinavian, German & other poetry. Contbr. to num. Finnish & Finnish-Swedish publs. & for. country mags. & anthols. Honours, awards: Prize of The State (Translators Prize) 1956, 63, 71; Aleksis Kivi Prize, 1962; Eino Leino Prize, 1972; Hon. Ph.D., Univ. of Helsinki, 1973. Address: Siilitie 1 K. 00800 Helsinki 80, Finland.

TUSIANI, Joseph, b. 14 Jan. 1924. University Professor. Education: Ph.D., Univ. of Naples; Litt.D., Coll. of Mount Saint Vincent. Positions held: Prof. of Italian Lit., Coll. of Mount Saint Vincent, 1948-71; Prof. of Romance Langs., Herbert H. Lehman Coll. of the City Univ. of New York, 1971-. Memberships: V.P., Poetry Soc. of Am.; Dir., Catholic Poetry Soc. of Am.; PEN. Published works: Rind and All, 1962; The Fifth Season, 1965; The Complete Poems of Michelangelo, 1960; The Poems of Machiavelli, 1963; Boccaccio's Nymphs of Fiesole, 1971; Tasso's Jerusalem Delivered, 1971; Italian Poets of the Renaissance, 1971; The Age of Dante, 1973; From Marino to Marinetti, 1973. Contbr. to: Spirit; The Poetry Review (London): Audience; The New York Times; The New Yorker; La Voix des Poetes (Paris); The Lit. Review; The Catholic World; Herald Tribune, etc. Honours,

awards: The Greenwood Prize, 1956; The Di Castagnola Award, 1968; The Spirit Gold Medal, 1969; Knighted by the Italian Govt., 1973. Address: 553 E. 188th St., Bronx, NY 10458, U.S.A.

TUSON, (Mrs.) Sheila Irene Mary (Atchison), pen name **MRS. LAUREL BROWN,** b. 15 Nov. 1911. Nurse. Author of Autumn Leaves, 1967. Contbr. to: Envoi; New Poets Mag.; Bedsitter Mag.; Modern Poets; Cork Weekly Examiner; Scrip; New Melody; Quill; Limbo; Yukoner; Breakthru; Phoenix; Rainbow; Manifold; Symbol; Share; Taits Qtly.; Tonic; Writers Review; Foreward; Midnight Sun Qtly. Address: Flat 9, Beechwood House, Bartley, Hants., U.K.

TUWHARE, Hone. Poet. Published works: No Ordinary Sun, 1964. Contbr. to: Landfall; (anthologies) New Zealand Poetry Yearbook, 1957-62; A Book of New Zealand, 1964.

TVEIT, Jon, b. 19 Sept. 1910. Teacher. Memberships: The Norwegian Authors Assn.; One World Assn.; The Peoples Against War. Published works: The Three Hands (novel), 1936; The Virgin With the Dark Lamp (novel), 1953; Return of the Sun in the Night (novel), 1956; In the Land of Life (novel), 1959; Insels of Light (poems), 1967; To an Unknown Morning (novel), 1972; Glomshilderslatten (novel – Gula Tidend); var. poems & short stories. Contbr. to Bergens Tidende; Verdens Gang; Dagbladet. Address: 5648 Holmefjord, Norway.

TWICHELL, Penelope Chase, pen name **TWICHELL, Chase,** b. 20 Aug. 1950. Student. Education: B.A. (Hons.), Trinity Coll., Conn., 1973; currently working on a Master's Degree; studying in a formal writing program. Contbr. to: The Walrus; Changes; The Trinity Review. Honours, awards: 1st prize, John Curtis Underwood Meml. Prize in Poetry, Trinity Coll., 1972 & 2nd prize, 1973. Has read poetry at colls. in the State of Connecticut. Address: c/o Charles Twichell, 820 Hartford Turnpike, Hamden, CT 06517, U.S.A.

TWIEG, B.J., Writer. Education: B.A., SUNY at Binghamton, N.Y., 1972; credits towards M.A., Coll. at Cortland, N.Y. Positions held: Sec., Denver, Colo.; Freelance Author. Memberships: Poetry Soc. of Colo.; Past Mbr., Am. Poetry League. Contbr. to: Quarry (short story) (Canada); The Singing Pens (anthol.); Confrontation (short story); The Am. Scandinavian Review; Kaleidograph; Quicksilver; Fiddlehead (Canada); The Lantern; Am. Bard; Blue Moon; Pegasus; Simbolica; Flame; Am. Poetry Mag.; Whimsy; The Writers Jrnl., etc. Recip. var. awards inclng: 1st Prize for sonnet, Lillian Evert's column, The Writer's Jrnl.; Student Writing Award, SUNY at Binghamton, 1972; Schlrship. for high potential to attend Breadloaf Writers Conf., short story category, summer 1972. Address: 95 Oak St., Binghamton, N.Y., U.S.A.

TWITE, Irene, b. 22 July 1920. Shop Assistant (S.H. Bookselling). Widow. Memberships: Yorkshire Poets Assn.; Fellow, Int. Poetry Soc. Contbr. to: Competitors Jrnl.; Cork Weekly Examiner; Viewpoints Mag.; Success Writers Mag.; Garden News; Yorkshire Poets '72; Poem, Alabama, U.S.A.; Intak, V.P.A. Jrnl.; The Osgoldcross Poetry Review; Pennine Platform. Recip., 3rd prize, Yorkshire Poets Comp., 1971. Address: 34 Warminster Cres., Sheffield S8 9NW, U.K.

TYNNI-HAAVIO, Aale Maria, pen name **TYNNI, Aale,** b. 3 Oct. 1913. Writer. Education: M.A., Univ. of Helsinki, 1936. Married 1) Kauko Antero Pirinen, div. 2) Martti Henrikki Haavio, 3 children. Positions held: Tchr. of Finnish; Literary Critic. Memberships: V.P., Finnish-Irish Soc.; Exec. Comm. & V.P., Finnish Writers' Assn.; Chmn., Literal Sect., Alfred Kordelin Fndn.; Pres., Minna Canth Soc. Published works: (poetry) Kynttilänsydän, 1938; Vesilintu, 1940; Lähde ja matkamies, 1943; Lehtimaja, 1946; Soiva Metsä, 1947; Ylitse vuoren lasisen, 1949; Tuntematon puu, 1952; Torni virrassa, 1954; Kootut runot (collected Poems), 1955; Valitut runot (Selected Poems), 1958; Yhdeksän kaupunkia, 1958; Maailmanteatteri, 1961;

Balladeja ja romansseja, 1967; Pidä rastaan laulusta kiinni, 1969. Translations & editions: Tuhat laulujen vuotta (Thousand Years of Songs, Anthol. of Western Poetry), 1957; Henrik Ibsen: Brand 1947, re-transl., 1963; Tulisen järjen aika (Time of Fiery Reason, Ten Modern French Poets), 1962; William Shakespeare: Sonetit, 1965; William Butler Yeats: Runoja, 1966. Ed. & transl. books for children. Honours, awards: Gold Medal, Art Comp. of the Olympic Games, London, 1948; Gold Medal, Italian Foreign Office; Giacomo Leopardi Medal of Milan. Address: Kauppiaankatu 7 A 19, Helsinki 16, Finland.

U

UHRMAN, Celia, b. 14 May 1927. Spanish Teacher; Artist; Poet. Education: B.A., Brooklyn Coll., 1948; M.A., ibid, 1953; Tchrs. Coll., Columbia Univ., 1961; Admin. & Supvsn. Course, CUNY, 1966; Brooklyn Mus. Art Schl., 1956-57. Positions held: Tchr., NY City Schl. System, 1948–; Self-employed artist & writer, 1958–. Exhibitions include: (solo) Leffert Jr. HS, Brooklyn; (2 man) Flatbush Chmbr. of Comm., Brooklyn, NY; Conn. Chmbr. of Comm., New London, Conn.; Lazarre Lodge, Old Saybrook, Conn.; (Grp.) Smithsonian, Wash. DC; Carnegie Endowment Int. Ctr., NY; Brooklyn Mus.; Springfield Mus. of Fine Arts, Mass.; Old Mystic Art Ctr., Conn.; Palacio de la Virreina, Barcelona, Spain; Lyman Allyn Mus., New London, Conn.; YWCA, Brooklyn; United Fed. of Tchrs. Art Exhibs., NY; Premier Salon Int., Charleroi, Belgium: Premi Int. Dibuix-Joan Miro, Barcelona, Spain: Palme D'Or Beaux-Arts Exhib., Monaco, Monte-Carlo; 'Perspective 68' Monaco, Monte-Carlo, Americana Hotel, NY Rep. in permanent collects. Memberships: Hon. Rep., Centro Studi E Scambi Internazionali; Int. Exec. Comm.; Commandeur Mbr., Int. Art Guild (Arts & Letters); Rep-at-Large, The World Poetry Soc. Intercontinental; IPA; Guest of Hon., Brooklyn Coll. Alumni Assn., 1964. Published works: Poetic Ponderance, 1969; A Pause for Poetry, 1970; Poetic Love Fancies, 1970; A Pause for Poetry for Children, 1973. Contbr. to the following anthols., jrnls., newspapers, etc: Quaderni di Poesia; Flatbush Life; Coney Island Times; Williamsburg News; Poet; Talent Mag.; Poet Mag.; all Courier Life Publs.; CSSI's 25th Anniversary pamphlet. Film, part 4, 'Ten Seconds to Air', Div. of Gen. Educ., NY Univ., 1958. Honours, Awards, etc: Dip. & Medal, CSSI, 1969; Freedoms Fndn. Award, Geo. Wash. Medal of Hon., 1964; Dip. d'Honneur, Palme D'Or Des Beaux-Arts Exhib., Monaco, Monte-Carlo, 1969; Cert., Personnal Poetry, WEF6 Stereo, 1970; Litt.D., World Acad. of Langs. & Lit., 1973; Ph.D., Acad. of Philos., 1973. Address: 1655 Flatbush Ave., Apt. C 2010, Brooklyn, NY 11210, USA.

UHRMAN, Esther, b. 7 July 1921. Civil Servant; Artist; Writer. Education: Traphagen Schl of Fashion, 1955; Currently studying for A.A.S., NYC Community Coll. Positions held: Full Charge Book-keeper, 1939-54; Commercial Artist, Trade Mag. Writer & Advt. Prod., 1954-59; Civil Servant, NY State, 1959–; Artist, Writer, 1959–. 2 man shows: Shows sponsored by Flatbush Chmbr. of Comm. & Conn. Chmbr. of Comm. New London; Lazarre Lodge, Old Saybrook & gall. showings. Grp. Exhibs. incl: Smithsonian, Wash. DC; Carnegie Endowment Int. Ctr., NYC; Traphagen Schl. of Fashion, Springfield Mus. of Fine Arts, Mass.; Old Mystic Art Ctr., Conn.; Palacio de la Virreina, Barcelona, Spain; Lyman Allyn Mus., New London, Conn.; YWCA, Brooklyn, Conn.; Premier Salon Int., Charleroi, Belgium; Premi Int. Dibuix-Joan Miro, Barcelona. Paintings in well-known collections throughout the world. Memberships: Cmdr. Mbr., Int. Arts Guild; Centro Studi E Scambi. Author, Gypsy Logic, 1970. Contbr. to: Quarderni di Poesia; Flatbush Life; Courier Life Publs.; Spook. Honours, Awards incl: CSSI Cert. for inclusion in XXV Anniversary Ed., 1970; Silver Medal (Olympic) designs for Verso Mexico, 1968; Cert. for stamp designs for 1968 Olympics; Dip. d'Honneur, Palme D'Or des Beaux Arts Exhibs., Monaco, Monte Carlo, 1969; 5 NY State Merit Awards,

1964-66. Address: Apt. C2010, 1655 Flatbush Ave., Brooklyn, NY 11210, USA.

UNANGST, Florence Beck, b. 31 Dec. 1911. Secretary, Van Heusen Co. Education: Bogota Grammar; Bogota High; Newspaper Inst. of America; Personal details: Widow; 3 d. Positions held: Reporter; Butcher; Secretary; Beautician; Editor and Publisher; Information Clerk; NY Delegate of World Poetry Soc.; Pres., Brooklyn Lit. Soc.; Editor & Publisher, Poetry Prevue. Memberships: Poetry Soc. (UK) Eastern Centre (Membership Chairman); Assoc. Poetry Therapy (Membership Chairman & Editorial Ed.); Grand Rapids Bards; NY Poetry Forum; Danae. Published works: Mainly Laughter, 1964; Mainly Quatrainly, 1965; Love & Stuff, 1966; Searching Soul, 1967; Past and Present, 1967: Lines and Points, 1967; Mellowing Years, 1970; Memos to Myself, 1972. Contbr. to: Expression; Bard; Am. Bard; Bardic Echoes; Quintessence; Poesy Book; Poet's Packet; Enterprise; Canadian Lights; Bay Shore Breeze; Nutmegger; Jean's Jrnl.; Haiku Highlights; Echoes; The Saint; Poetry Prevue; Orphic Lute; Kans. Kernels; Am. Poet; United Poet; Prairie Poet; Express; Angel Hour; Angels; Cardinal Poetry Quarterly; Fellowship in Prayer; Phoenix; Poet; The Guild; Hoosier Challenger; Harbor Lights; Imprints Quarterly; Inky Trails; Karyn; Sunrise Sunset; Silhouette; Merlin's Magic; Midwest Chaparral: Mo. Chaparral Poetry Anthol; Muse; Pendulum; Poetry Club; Quoin; Scimitar & Song; Tejas; Driftwood; Tempo; Seydell Quarterly; Bell's Letters; Down Ink Lane; Midnightsun Quarterly; Fireflower; Vespers; Poet's Bull.; Mizpah Messenger; Life & Letters; Popular Poetry; Writers' Notes & Quotes; Bitterroot; NY Jrnl. Am.; New Jrnl.; Brooklyn Times; Place for Poets; Far Horizons; Words With Wings; Poetry Pendulum: Poetry Dial; Focus on Poetry; Shades of Thought; Stardust & Dreams; Images; Rythmic Bard Beats; Author/Poet; Peninsula Poets; Angel Michael; The Guild; Golden Circle; Rubia's Scrapbook; Good Old Days; GTA Digest; Fla. Notes; Friendly Way; Versecraft; Verdure; Laurel Leaves; (anthols.) Rainbow of Verse; Harvest of Holidays; Ben Travato; Ardentia Verba; Written Word, 1,2,3,4,5, & 6; Cornwall Anthol; Heart's Secrets: Treasures of Parnassus; Poetry Unlimited; Choice of Angels; Mainstream of Am. Poetry; Rhyme Time; New Poetry; Pacific Breeze; Dr. Etta Josephean Murfey Award Book, 1968, & many other jrnls. newspapers & anthols. Also Guardino's Journal; Driftwood East; Paul's Poetry Corner. Honours: Cert. of Merit, Penman, 1965; Angel Award, 1968; Mentor Cert. of Merit, 1966; Special Merit Award, Clover Poetry Comp., 1969; Red Rose Award from Add Enchantment & many others. Also Hon. Doc. Humane Lit. (Internat. Acad. Hull, UK, 1971); Hon. Doc. Lib. Arts, Great China Arts Coll., 1972. Address: 88 Church Ave., Brooklyn, NY 11218, USA.

UNGERER, Kathryn D(avis), b. 13 Nov. 1946. Poet. Education: Pa. Acad. of Fine Arts; Univ. of Pa.; Barnard Coll.; Columbia Univ.; Goddard Coll. Positions held: Instr., Community Coll. of Vt.; Master Poet, Vt. Coun. on the Arts. Contbr. to: Atlantic Monthly; Antioch Review; Iowa Review; Goddard Jrnl.; Fiction Int.; Strivers Row. Honours, awards: Nancy Thorpe Prize, 1963; Amy Loveman Award, 1967. Address: Box 101, East Calais, VT 05650, U.S.A.

UNTERECKER, John E., b. 14 Dec. 1922. Writer; Teacher. Education: B.A., Middlebury Coll., 1944; M.A., Columbia Univ., 1948; Ph.D., ibid, 1956. Positions held: Radio Announcer, WBNY, Buffalo, N.Y., 1944-45; Actor, off-Broadway & Summer Stock, also TV & Radio, 1944-50; Researcher, Office of War Information, 1945-46; Lectr., City Coll. of N.Y., 1946-56; Asst. Prof., Columbia Univ., 1956-59; Assoc. Prof., 1959-64; Prof., 1964-73; Vis. Prof., Univ. of Hawaii, 1969, Univ. of Tex., 1974; Prof., Univ. of Hawaii, 1974–. Published works: The Dreaming Zoo, book length poem for children, 1964; Stone (poetry book), 1974; Dance Sequence (poetry book), 1974-75; The Persons & the Objects in the Room (poetry book), 1974-75; special issue of Voyages (vol. IV, No. 1 & 2) devoted to his poetry, 1971. Contbr. to num. jrnls., reviews, etc. Address: Dept. of Engl., Univ. of Hawaii, Honolulu, HI, U.S.A.

UNTERMEYER, Louis, b. 1 Oct. 1885. Writer, Poet, Editor. Positions held: Contbng. Ed., The Masses & The Liberator; Publs. Ed., Office of War Info., & Ed., Armed Services Editions, 1939-45; Lectr., various univs., USA; Cultural Ed., Decca Records, 1945-58; Cons. in Poetry, Lib. of Congress, 1961-63. Published works: Challenge, 1914; Roast Leviathan, 1923; Moses, 1928; Food and Drink, 1932; Rainbow in the Sky, 1935; Heinrich Heine–Paradox and Poet (2 vols.), 1937; Play In Poetry, 1937; The Wonderful Adventures of Paul Bunyan, 1945; The Inner Sanctum–Walt Whitman, 1949; The Magic Circle, 1952; Makers of the Modern World, 1955; Lives of the Poets, 1959; Long Feud–Selected Poems, 1962; Labyrinth of Love, 1965; Bygones–An Autobiography, 1965. Ed., numerous anthols., including: The Book of Living Verse, 1932; Modern American Poetry; Modern British Poetry; A Treasury of Great Poems, 1942; A Treasury of Laughter, 1946; The Best Humor of 1949-50, '50-51, '51-52; A Treasury of Ribaldry, 1956; The Golden Treasury of Poetry for Young People, 1959; Collins Albatross Book of Verse, 1962; An Uninhibited Treasury of Erotic Poetry, 1963; The Letters of Robert Frost to Louis Untermeyer, 1963; The World's Great Stories, 1964; The Pursuit of Poetry. Contbr. to: Yale Review; Saturday Review; etc. Awards: Gold Medal, Poetry Soc. of Am. Address: Great Hill Rd., Newton, Conn. 06470, USA.

UPDIKE, John (Hoyer), b. 18 Mar. 1932. Free-lance Writer. Education: A.B., Harvard Coll., Cambridge, Mass., U.S.A., 1954; Ruskin Schl. of Drawing & Fine Arts, Oxford, UK. Positions held: Staff Reporters, The New Yorker Mag., 1955-57; currently, Free-lance Writer. Mbr., Nat. Inst. Art & Letters. Published works: The Carpentered Hen & Other Tame Creatures, 1958; Hoping for a Hoopoe, 1959; Telephone Poles, 1963; Midpoint & Other Poems, 1969; (novels) The Poorhouse Fair, 1959; Rabbit, Run, 1961; The Centaur, 1963; Of the Farm, 1965; Couples, 1968; (short stories) The Same Door, 1962; Pigeon Feathers, 1962; The Music School, 1966. Contbr., various anthols. Honours, awards: Rosenthal Award, 1959; Nat. Book Award, 1962. Address: 26 East St., Ipswich, Mass., USA.

UPTON, David Laurence, b. 23 May 1950. Freelance Graphic Designer. Education: Schl. of Art, Sutton Coldfield, U.K., 1967-69; Dip. A.D. Graphic Design, Polytechnic, Wolverhampton, 1969-72. Positions held: Antiquarian Book Cataloguer, Frank Hammond (Booksellers); Lib. Asst., Southgate Circus Lib.; Freelance. Graphic Design work (concurrent). Memberships: Poetry Soc.; Poets Pub. (Unity Theatre) Reading Grp. Published works: Small Poems, 1973. Contbr. to: The Jrnl.; Global Tapestry; Bogg; Ore; Sandwiches; Workshop; Pod (Poets Pub. Mag.), etc. Is currently revising a book on the legend of King Arthur. Address: 20 Cremorne Rd., Sutton Coldfield, Warks. B75 5AH, U.K.

UPTON, Lawrence John, pen name **IRVING, Henry & UPTON, Lawrence,** b. 20 Feb. 1949. Writer. Positions held: Contracts Clerk, -1972; Writer, 1972-. Memberships: Owner, Good Elf Reading Grp.; Co-Org., The BBC Poets; The Poetry Soc.; Birmingham Poetry Ctr.; Hon. Mbr., Redditch Poetry Soc.; Poetry Roundabout Performance Grp.; Poets Conf.; Assn. of Little Mags.; Sec. & Exhibs. Org., Assn. of Little Presses of G.B. Published works: From Waters, 1969; Glancing Back, 1969; Nineteen Attempts, 1971; Trying to Keep Upright, 1972; A Chant, 1972; The Unsuccessful Candidate, 1972; Strange Tales for Strange Children, 1972; How to Make Money, 1973; The Life & Times of Thermo S Pylae, 1973; Cheap Thrill (w. Paul Becker), 1973. Contbr. to num. jrnls., mags. inclng: The Jrnl.; Poetry Workshop; Viewpoints; Candelabrum; The Iron Flute; Gargantua. Ed., Good Elf Mag.; Ed., Visst Mag.; Co-Ed., Zerone Mag.; Co-Ed., Round Up Mag.; Runs Good Elf Publs. & manages Coarsecrash Press. Has read all over U.K. as mbr. of

grps. & as lone performer. Address: c/o 18 Clairview Rd., Streatham, London SW16, U.K.

URABE, Shigeo, b. 22 Jan. 1929. High School Teacher. Education: Grad., Waseda Univ., Tokyo, Japan. Married, 1 s. 1 d. Positions held: Ed., Japan Forum, a quarterly for prose & poetry, 1962-. Mbr., Japan Forum. Address: 50 Okado-machi, Hachioji-shi, Tokyo, Japan.

URDANG, Constance Henriette. Housewife. Education: A.B., Smith Coll.; M.F.A., Univ. of Iowa. Married Donald Finkel, 3 children. Member, Women's Int. League for Peace & Freedom. Published works: Charades & Celebrations, 1965; Natural History, (a prose work of the imagination), 1969. Contbr. to: Accent; Am. Poetry Review; Antaeus; Arts in Society; Burning Deck; Carleton Miscellany; Chicago Review; Chelsea; Contact; Counter/Measures; Epoch; Focus Midwest; Harpers; New Am. Review; The New Republic; Poetry; Poetry Northwest; Perspective; Paris Review; Pebble; Qtly. Review of Lit.; Red Clay Qtly.; Sojourner; Tex. Qtly. Address: 6943 Columbia Pl., St. Louis, MO 63130, U.S.A.

URISTA HEREDIA, Alberto Baltazar, pen name **ALURISTA,** b. 8 Aug. 1947. Professor; Organizer; Writer. Education: B.A. in Psychol., San Diego State Univ. Positions held: Group Counselor, 1965-67; Psychiatric Technician, 1967-68; Instr./Lectr., 1968-; Xicano Studies Ctr., Dir., 1971-72. Published works: El Espejo: Selected Chicano Literature, 1969; Chicano Arts, 1972; Floricanto en Aztlán, 1971; El Ombligo en Aztlán, 1971; Nationchild Plumaroja, 1972; Aztlán: An Anthology of Mexican American Literature, 1972; Literatura Chicana: Texto y Contexto, 1972; Tula y Tonan, 1973. Contbr. to: El Grito; El Gallo; La Verdad; La Gente; El Pocho Che; Voices of the Ghetto; El Universal; Casa de las Americas; Inside the Beast; Sunrise; San Diego Free Press; Mester; Hispámerica, etc. Address: 1329 Grove, San Diego, CA 92102, U.S.A.

URSILLO, Margaret Cecelia, b. Feb. 1920. Home Maker; Writer. Married, 3 sons, 3 daughters. Positions held: Clerk. Memberships: World Poetry Soc. Intercontinental; Am. Poetry League; Int. Platform Assn.; Am. Montessori Soc. Contbr. to: Bouquets of Poems, 1973; Poet, 1971; From Sea To Sea In Song, 1968-69; Prairie Poet; Am. Poet; Year Book of Modern Poetry, 1972; Times Review; United Poets, etc. Address: 84 Franklin St., Haworth, NJ 07641, U.S.A.

UU, David, b. 1948. Poet. Married. Positions held: Fndr., Fleye Press, Toronto, 1966; Co-Fndr., first & only Canadian concrete poetry periodical, 1967; Organizer, Canada's first int. exhib. of concrete poetry, 'Brazilia 73', Vancouver, 1968 & a similar show called 'Microprosophus' at Avelles Gall., Vancouver, 1971; currently Ed. of art periodical Lodgistiks & the Canadian Ed. & Corres. for the Italian monthly art review, Lotta Poetica; Exec. & Artistic Dir., Isle of Avalon Soc., 1970-, Member, Image Bank; Co-Fndr. & Coordinator of the Divine Order of the Lodge. Published works: (books) Poems, 1966; Gideon Music, 1967; Touch, 1967; Pamplemousse, 1967; Motion/Pictures, 1969; Before the Golden Dawn, 1971; Aurora Hyperborealis, 1971; Cheoptics, 1974; Antedeluvian Rush, 1974; Violet Pilot Lights (children's book), 1974. Rep. in many anthols. inclng: An Evening of Concrete, 1970 (Winner, Gov.-Gen's Award for Poetry 1971); New Directions in Canadian Poetry, 1970; The Next Poets, 1971; Canadian West Coast Hermetics, 1973; Living Artists of the North West, 1974. Participant in many exhibs. of concrete poetry; also theatre & Poetry dance. Recip., Canada Coun. Grant for Writing, 1967 & 68; Canada Coun. Arts Bursary 1968 & 72; Ont. Arts Coun. Award, 1974. Address: Box 40, Shannonville, Ontario, KOK 3AO, Canada.

V

VAISH, Yogi Nandan, b. 31 Dec. 1932. Author. Education: M.A. (Eng.Lit.). Memberships: Soc. of Authors; London Writer Circle. Published works: New Year's Day (verse play, in 3 acts), 1968; Funeral March (in press). Contbr. to: The Hibbert Journal; The Literary Half-Yearly; Poet; Thought; The Century; Human Events; Internat. Pen-Friend; Expression One; Cork Weekly Examiner. Recip. First Prize, awarded by Cork Weekly Examiner, 26 Apr. 1973. Address: H. No. 14/14 Palamal St., Aligarh (U.P.), India.

VAKY, James Russell, pen name **LINDEN, Ronald,** b. 3 Nov. 1911. Teacher of Piano & English. Education: B.A., Univ. of Ill.; pvte. Organ study w. the late Dr. Ernest B. Douglas; art study at Corcoran Schl. of Art, Wash. D.C., 1955-56. Positions held: Instr., Page Mil. Acad., L.A., 1942-43 & '44-45; Pianist w. Barker Unit, Red Cross, 1945-46; Mgr., Lansburgh's Book Dept., 1961-62; Mgr., Four Corners Bookshop, Wash. D.C., 1962-63. Memberships: Federal Poets, Wash. D.C., 1959-64; Vachel Lindsay Assn., Springfield, Ill.; Pres., Pegasus Soc., 1968-70; Life Mbr., Int. Clover Poetry Assn., Wash. D.C. Published works: (book) Selected Sonnets, 1973. Rep. in following anthols: Modern Am. Lyrics; Clover Anthol.; Poets of the Midwest; North Am. Mentor Anthol. Contbr. to: Greek Star; Hartford Courant; News Gazette; Wash. Post; Cyclotron; Hoosier Jrnl., etc. Recip. 4th prize, North Am. Mentor, Winter, 1964, & other poetry prizes. Address: 1505 35th Ave., Rock Island, IL 61201, U.S.A.

VALLIS, Valentine Thomas, pen name **VALLIS, Val.,** b. 1 Aug. 1916. Lecturer. Education: Rockhampton HS; Univ. of Queensland, 1946-50; Univ. of London (Birkbeck Coll.), Ph.D., 1953-55. Positions held: Clerk in a Town Council office, 1935-41; War Service in New Guinea and Australia, 1941-46; Student at Univ. of Queensland on Commonwealth Govt. Training Scheme, 1946-50; Appointed to Staff, Univ. of Queensland (in Philosophy), 1950, later transferred to Dept. of Engl., and still there, as Reader. Published works: Songs of the East Coast, 1947; Dark Wind Blowing, 1961. Contbr. to: The Bulletin (Sydney), 1944-62; Meanjin; Poetry; poems also broadcast on A.B.C. Address: c/o Dept. of Engl., Univ. of Queensland, St. Lucia, Brisbane, Queensland 4067, Australia.

Van BRUNT, Howell Lloyd, pen name **Van BRUNT, H.L.,** b. 18 July 1936. Freelance Writer. Education: Alan Hancock College (Assoc. in Arts), 1956. Born in Tulsa, Oklahoma. Former associate book review editor, Saturday Review. Published works: Uncertainties, 1968; Indian Territory & Other Poems, 1974. Contbr. to: Arlington Qtly.; NY Qtly.; New Orleans Review; Southwest Review; South Dakota Review; Cimarron Review; Meanjin Qtly.; West Coast Review; Literary Review; Southern Humanities Review; Hearse; Quartet; December; Red Clay Reader; NY Times; The Arts in Ireland; (anthol.) The Living Underground. Address: 53 Leroy St., New York, NY 10014, USA.

VANDALL, Donna Mae Whitewing, pen name **WHITEWING,** b. 3 May 1943. Educator; Artist; Writer of Prose, Poetry, Plays. Education: post grad. work, Inst. of Am. Ind. Arts, Santa Fe, N.M., 2 yrs.; currently at Univ. of Neb., Omaha. Positions held: Sec./Receptionist; Grocery Clerk; Motel Maid; Substitute Day Care Tchr.; Instr. of Theatre & Drama; Tchr. Aide. Published works: Whispering Wind, 1970. Contbr. to: school newspapers & booklets, 1960-70; U.S.A. Qtly., 1968; The New Indian, 1968; schl. records & publs. at Inst. of Am. Ind. Arts, 1962-73; var. mags. Honours, awards: 1st pl., Vincent Price Creative Writing Award, 1963 & 2nd pl., 1964; 1st pl., Scottsdale Nat. Indian Creative Writing, 1971. Address: P.O. Box 365, Winnebago, NB 68071, U.S.A.

VAN DEN HEUVEL, Cor, b. 6 Mar. 1931. Poet. Education: B.A. in Engl. Lit., Univ. of New Hampshire, 1957; M.A. in Engl. Lit., N.Y. Univ., 1968. Mbr., Haiku Soc. of Am. Published works: sun in skull, 1961; a bag of marbles, 1962; the window-washer's pail, 1963; E07, 1964; BaNG, 1966; water in a stone depression, 1969. Edited The Haiku Anthology: English Language Haiku by Contemporary Am. & Canadian Poets, 1974. Contbr. to: Haiku Mag.; Haiku West. Address: 11th Fl., 444 Madison Ave., N.Y., NY 10022, U.S.A.

VAN DORE, Wade, b. 12 Dec. 1899. Motel Owner-Operator; Writer. Education: Bollitat Music Schl., Detroit, Mich. (studied harmony, musical hist. & piano), 1919-21; studied poetry w. Robert Frost. Positions held: Operator of First Youth Hostel, Northfield, Mass., 1939-41; Poet-in-Res., Marlboro Coll., 1950; Dir., St. Petersburg Poetry Assn., 1969; Trustee, Thoreau Lyceum, 1969-; Co-Fndr., V.P., Thoreau Fellowship, Inc., 1969-; currently Poetry Ed. for Thoreau Jrnl. Qtly. Memberships: Poetry Soc. of Am.; Wilderness Soc.; Natural Resources Coun. of Me.; Thoreau Lyceum; Thoreau Fellowship, Inc. Published works: Far Lake, 1930; Verse With a Vengeance, 1961. Contbr. to: London Mercury; Atlantic; New Yorker; New Republic; N.Y. Herald Tribune; Christian Sci. Monitor; Nature; Living Wilderness; Writers' Digest; Detroit Free Press; Detroit News; Household; Dearborn Independent; Inland Seas; Clearwater Sun; Churchman; Thoreau Jrnl. Qtly.; The Circle. Recip., Alice Fay di Castagnola Award, 1969. Address: 62 Somerset St., Clearwater Beach, FL 33515, U.S.A.

VAN EPPS, Lynnette Marie, b. 20 Sept. 1951. Artist and Poet. Contbr. to: Internat. Who's Who in Poetry Anthol.; San Jose Red Eye; Modern Poetry Anthol.; Thot; El Gato, etc. Address: 2222 Glenwood Dr., Scotts Valley, CA 95066, USA.

VAN HEERDEN, Ernst, b. 20 Mar. 1916. Professor of Afrikaans. Education: B.A., Univ. of Stellenbosch, SA; D.Litt. & Phil., Univ. of Ghent, Belgium. Positions held: Lectr., Univ. of Stellenbosch, SA, 1945-59; Sr. Lectr., Univ. of Witwatersrand, Johannesburg; Rdr. in Poetics, ibid; Prof. of Afrikaans. Memberships: Maatschappij voor Nederlandse Letterkunde, Leyden, Holland; SA Acad. of Sci. & Arts. Published works include: Weerlose Uur, 1942; Verklaarde Nag, 1946; Die Sewe Vrese, 1951; Die Bevrijding, 1952; Reisiger, 1953; Koraal van die Dood, 1956; Die Klop, 1961; Op Die Mespunt, 1963; Anderkant Besit, 1966. Contbr. to the following publs: Standpunte, SA; Nieuw Vlaams Tijdschrift, Brussels, Belgium. Honours, awards: Silver Medal, Olympic Games Arts Festival, 1948; Hertzog Prize for Afrikaans Poetry, SA Acad., Pretoria, 1962. Address: Witwatersrand Univ., Jan Smuts Ave., Johannesburg, SA.

VAN HOOREBEECK, Albert, b. 7 Mar. 1915. Chief of Lecturers Dept., Sabena. Married Bodaer Augusta, 3 children. Positions held: Jrnlst., Periodical Press. Memberships: Societe des Orateurs et Conferenciers (Paris), 1939; Association des Conferenciers de Belgique, 1946; PEN Int.; Assn. of Belgian Writers; Association des Journalistes Professionnels Belges de l'Aeronautique et de l'Astronautique. Published works: Sur Terre, Sur Mer et dans les Airs, 1950; Epopee de l'Atlantique Nord, 1961; Paysan des Escales (poem) 1962; Histoire des Tours du Monde Aeriens, 1969; Cinquante Ans d'Aviation Belge, 1966, 69, 73; La Conquete de l'Air (Chronology 2nd vol.), 1967; Messerschmitt, Ingenieur du Ciel (Transl. from Dutch), 1967; Nord Atlantic Fluge (in German), 1968; Vijftig Jaar Luchtvaart (in Dutch), 1966, 68, 70, 73; L'Homme a la Conquete de l'Espace, 1971. Contbr. to var. aviation jrnls. & encys. Honours, awards: Officier d'Academie (France), 1951; Prix d'Histoire de L'Aero Club of France, 1962; Prix de la Presse Aeronautique Belge, 1973; Chevalier de l'Ordre de Leopold II & de la Couronne; Mbr., Histl. Commn., Aero. Club of France; Médaille de Vermeil, Arts, Scis., Lettres. Address: Ave. Vincent van Gogh 15, 1140 Brussels, Belgium.

VAN ITALLIE, Jean-Claude, b. 25 May 1936. Playwright. Education: Deerfield Acad.; B.A., Harvard Univ., 1958. Published works: The Serpent, 1969.

Address: 463 West St., Apt. H724, N.Y., NY 10014, U.S.A.

VAN ITTERBEEK, Eugene Rene, b. 21 Jan. 1934. Government Official. Education: D.Lit. & LL.D. Positions held: Master, French Lang. & Lit., Tchrs. Sem., Hasselt, Belgium, 1959-69; Official, Belgian Min. of Culture, Brussels & Advsr., Cabinet Prime Min., 1969-. Memberships: Adj. Sec.-Gen., Int. Biennial, Knokke; PEN; Flemish Lit. Soc.; Maatschappj der Nederlande Letteren, Leiden; Belgian Commn., UNESCO. Published works: Hedendagse Franse Letterkunde (Contemporary French Literature), 1964; Spreken en zwygen (Word & Silence), 1965; Socialisme et poesie chez Charles Peguy, 1966; Actuelen, 1968; Tekens van leren (Signs of Life), 1969; A Quarter Century of Poetry in Flanders, 1970. Contbr. to: Le Monde; De Haagse Courant; De Standaard, Brussels; Ed. in Chief, Kultersleven & many other Flemish periodicals. Address: Rerum Novarumlaan 35, Kessel-Lo, Belgium.

VANNIER, Angele, b. 12 Aug. 1917. Broadcasting Producer. Education: B.A. Memberships: Société des Gens de Lettres; SACEM; SDRM. Songes de la Lumière et de la Brume, 1947; Arbre a Feu, 1950; Avec la Permission de Dieu, 1953; A Hauteur d'Ange, 1956; Choix de Poèmes, 1963; Le Sang des Nuits, 1966. Contbr. to: Le Goëland; Le Journal des Poétes; Ariane; L'VII; Le Pont de l'Epée. Honours: Prix du Goëland, 1943; Prix Mediterranée, 1954; Prix de Poésie, Académie Française, 1966. Address: 53 Avenue Gambetta, Courbevoie-92, France.

VAN SERTIMA, Ivan Gladstone, b. 26 Jan. 1935. Novelist; Critic; Broadcaster. Educ: London Univ. Schl. of Oriental & African Studies, 1969. m. Maria Nagy, 1964. Positions held: Press & Broadcasting Off., Govt. Info. Servs., British Guiana, 1957-59; Broadcaster, Central Off. of Info., London, U.K., 1960-. Published works: River and the Wall, 1958. Contbr. to: (anthologies) Schwarzer Orpheus, 1964; New Sum of Poetry from the Negro World, 1968. Address: 9 Arkwright Mansions, Finchley Rd., London N.W.3, U.K.

VAN TOORN, Peter, pen name **VAN TOORN, P.; P.V.T.,** b. 13 Jul. 1944. Teacher. Education: McGill Univ., Montreal, B.A. Positions held: many, including: Theme Reader, McGill Univ., 1968-71; Instr., Sir George Williams Univ., Montreal, 1971-73; Instr., John Abbott Coll., Montreal, 1972-74. Membership: League of Canadian Poets, 1972-74. Published works: Leeway Grass, 1970; In Guildenstern County, 1973. Contbr. to: The Antigonish Review; The Canadian Forum; Copperfield; The Fiddlehead; Prism; Vanderbilt Poetry Review; Four Montreal Poets (anthol., 1973); Almanac: 17 Poets (anthol., 1970); Radio & TV. broadcasts: Enviro (CTV, Montreal). Recip. Canada Council Awards, 1968-69, 1971-72. Address: John Abbott Coll., St. Anne De Bellevue, Quebec, Canada.

VAN VLIET, Eddy, b. 11 Sept. 1942. Lawyer. Education: Classical studies, Royal Atheneum of Antwerp, 1954-60; law degree, The Free Univ. of Brussels, 1965. Married, 2 children. Positions held: Mbr. of the Anti-Censorship Comm., 1968-; Pres., International Cultural Ctr., 1973-. Memberships: PEN (Direction); Editl. staff, Dutch periodical 'Kentering'. Published works: Het lied van ik, 1964; Duel, 1967; Columbus tevergeefs, 1969; Van bittere tranen, kollebloemen e.a. blozende droefheden, 1971; Verzamelde gedichten, 1962-72. Contbr. to: Avenue; Elseviers Weekblad; Poetry Int.; Dietsche Warande & Belfort; Impuls; Nieuw Vlaams Tijdschrift; Delta; De Geus; Soma; Kentering; Ruimten; Snoecks Almanak; Kruispunt/Sumier; Pan; Artisjok; De Nieuwe Stem; De Gids; Septentrion; Vandaag 12; Tydskrif vir Letterkunde; Literair Akkoord. Transl. into English, French, German & Russian. Honours, awards: Reina Prinsen Geerligs Prize, Amsterdam, 1967; Prize of the Flemish Poetry Days, Meise, 1968; Ark Prize of the Free Word, Brussels, 1971. Address: Mechelsesteenweg 205, Antwerp, Belgium.

VARMA, Monika, b. 5 Aug. 1916. Housewife; Agriculturist; Author. Education: Privately through tutors and teachers at home, non-academic. Personal details: daughter of Lalit Mohan Banerji, lawyer & judge of Allahabad High Court, U.P., India, and granddaughter of Sir Pramada Charan Banerji, authority on law & judge of Allahabad High Court for 32 yrs. Married to Brigadier K.K. Varma; 2 s. Membership: World Poetry Soc. Intercontinental. Published works: Dragonflies Draw Flame, 1962; Gita Govinda and Other Poems, 1966; A Bunch of Tagore Poems, 1966; Jayadeva's Gita Govinda - The Monika Varma Translation, 1968; Green Leaves and Gold, 1970; Quartered Questions and Queries, 1971; Past Imperative, 1972. Contbr. to anthols.: Modern Indian Poetry in English; Modern Indo-Anglian Poetry; Young Poets From India; Temple Carvers; One Hundred And One. Contbr. to magazines, newspapers: The Illustrated Weekly of India; Miscellany; Poet; Thought; Caravan; East & West; Man in India, Dialogue; Transition. Recip. Poetry Prize, Caravan Mag. Poetry Competition, 1956 and 1958; World Poetry Soc. Intercontinental Distinguished Service Citation, 1971 and 1973. Address: Sokra Nala Farm, P.O. Krishak Nagar, Raipur, M.P., India.

VARMA, Shrikant, b. 18 Sept. 1931. Journalist. Education: M.A. (Hindi Lit.), Univ. of Nagpur, India, 1956. Married; 1 s. Positions held: Editor, Nayee Disha, 1955-56; Editor, Kriti, 1958-63; Chief Sub-Editor, Dinaman, 1964-65; Special Correspondent, Dinaman, since 1966; Lectures delivered on mod. Indian Poetry (with reading of own poems) at the Univs. of Iowa, 1970; Berkeley, 1970; Hamburg, 1973; Heidelberg, 1973. Published works: (in Hindi) Bhatka Megh, 1957; Dinarambh, 1967; Maya Darpan, 1967; Jalsaghar, 1973; Faisle Ka Din, 1971; (in English) Otherwise and Other Poems. Contbr. to: Times of India; Hindustani Times; all leading journals and periodicals in India. Writings translated and published in USA, USSR, UK, West Germany, Cuba, Bulgaria, Japan. Awards: Fellowship for Internat. Writing, Internat. Writing Prog. of the Univ. of Iowa, USA, 1970-71; Honoured for contrib. to poetry by the State Govt. of M. Pradesh (India), April, 1973. Address: c/o Dinaman, Times of India, New Delhi, India.

VARNAI, Zseni, b. 25 May 1890. Poet. Published works: Katonafiamnak (To My Soldier Son); Vörös tavasz (Red Spring); Anyasziv (Mother Heart): A fájdalom könyve (Book of Grief); Gracchusok anyja (Mother of the Gracchi): Orömök kertje (Garden of Joys); A meséló erdö (The Forest of Tales); Im itt az irás (Lo, Here Is The Writing); Korus szopranban (Soprano Choir); Fekete bárány (Black Lamb); Mint viharban a talevel (Like A Leaf In The Tempest); Aldott asszonyok (Blessed Women); Száz vers a szabadságért (100 Poems for Liberty); Varnai Zseni válogatott versei; Féltámaddás; Peace!; Légy boldog te Világ! (O World, Be Happy); Elök, vigyázzatok! (People, be on your guard); Nem volt hiába (It was not in vain); & others. Honours: Silver Degree of Order of Liberty for work in the movement of nat. resistance during German occupation; Golden Degree of Order of Works, 1965.

VASCONCELLOS, Alma (Delia Ríos de Pagola Repetto), b. 25 Apr. 1927. Writer; Journalist. Education: studied langs., lit., philos. & dramatic art. Married Miguel Angel Pagola Repetto, 1 daughter. Positions held: 'Agregat Culturel', Embassy of Haiti; Public Rels. & 'Agregat Culturel', Instuto Panamericano de Cultura. Memberships incl: Hon. Pres., Asamblea Magna de Periodistas Ecuador, 1961; Hon. Mbr., Delegada Permanente, Asociación Internacional de Prensa, 1961; Collab. Mbr., Academia de Artes y Letras de Petrópolis, Brazil, 1965; Academia Interamericana de Letras, Argentina, 1965. Published works: Cardos y orquideas, 1954; Cumbres y abismos, 1956; Marmol y arcilla, 1959, 3rd ed., 1961; Puente hacia el alba, 1962; Bronce y cristal, 1964; Lumbre y tiniebla, 1966; Alma de América, 1967; Fuego sagrado, 1971; Long Play Poems, 1972. Contbr. to var. jrnls. & newspapers inclng: El Día, El

País, El Plata, El Debate; El diario Español, Norte, Acción, Antología Perfiles, Uruguay; Revista de la Casa de la Cultura, Ecuador; A tarde, Brazil; Patria & La tribuna, Paraguay; La Nación & La información, Chile, etc. Honours, awards incl: Gold medal, Caa artística de America, CADA, 1967 for her book 'Bronce y cristal'; First Gold Medal, Salón Juana de América, 1969; 2nd Prize Am., Poem 'Yuyeri-Tai'; Guest of Hon., 2nd World Cong. of Poets, 1973; Guest, Repub. of China govt., 1974. Address: Vicente Basagoiti 4333 ap. 3, Montevideo, Uruguay, S. Am.

VAS DIAS, Robert, b. 19 Jan. 1931. Poet. Education: B.A., Grinnell Coll., Iowa, 1953; grad. study, Columbia Univ., N.Y.C., 1958-59. Married Susan McClintock, 1 son. Positions held: Instr., Dept. of Engl., L.I. Univ., Brooklyn, N.Y., 1964-66; Dir., Aspen Writers' Workshop, Aspen, Colo., 1964-67; Instr., Dept. of Engl. & Am. Lang. Inst., Wash. Sq. Campus, N.Y. Univ., 1966-71; Poet-in-Res. & Tutor, Thomas Jefferson Coll. of The Grand Valley State Colls., Allendale, Mich., 1971-74; Dir., first & second Nat. Poetry Fest., Thomas Jefferson Coll., Allendale, 1971 & 73. Published works: The Counted, 1967; Ed., Inside Outer Space: New Poems of the Space Age, 1970; Speech Acts & Happenings (poems), 1972; The Life of Parts (long poem), 1972. Contbr. to: Chelsea; Choice; Colo. Qtly.; Cultural Affairs; Maps; Mulch; The Nation; The New Yorker; Partisan Review; Poetry; Stony Brook; Sumac; WIN Mag. Address: 1040 Park Ave., N.Y., NY 10028, U.S.A.

VASVARI, István, b. 19 Dec. 1916. Poet; Librarian. Education: Univ., Budapest. Positions held: Clerk, 1939-42; Tchr., 1942-44; in Nazi concentration camp, 1944; Jrnlst., 1945-50; Writer, 1950-57; Jrnlst., Ed., 1957-60; Chief Libn., Municipal Lib., Budapest, 1960–. Memberships: PEN; United Poets Laureate Int.; Assoc. of Hungarian Writers. Published works: Ifjukori lángok (Flames of Youth), 1935; A szépség zsoldjában (For Beauty), 1937; Tizenkét lépés (Twelve Steps), 1939; Férfizsoltár (Man's Psalm), 1942; Fegyvertelenül (Without Arms), 1945; Torlódó nyár (Gathering Summer), 1947; Tizediziglen (To the Tenth Generation), 1957; Izzó öszben (In A Glowing Autumn), 1963; Tíz kicsi ló (Ten Little Horses), 1964; Végső áron (To The Last Price), 1964; A lélek naplójaából (From A Soul's Diary), 1966. Contbr. to: Laurel Leaves; Vszvszvit, Kiev; Sovjetski vojn; Zivol; Forum, Hamburg; Eco del Sur, Mexico City; Göteborgs Tidningen; The American Hungarian Review; Kortárs; Látóhatár; Elet és irodalom; Jelenkor. United Poets Laureate Int., 1966; Dr., Quezon City Univ., 1967; Medal for work, Hungary. Address: Szabo Ervin Ter. 1, Budapest, VIII Hungary.

VATSEND, Helge Anton, b. 25 Nov. 1928. Writer. Member, Den norske Forfatterforening. Published works: Du, 1958; Stenbruddet, 1963; Blindpassasjerer, 1967; Nakent ansikt, 1970; En dags lys, 1971. Contbr. to: Verdens Gang., 1948; Dagbladet, 1961–; Profil, No. 1, 1962; Nye navn i norsk kunst (anthol.), 1962. Address: Ravnkollbakken 9, Oslo 9, Norway.

VAUGHN, Cleo (Christeen), b. 7 June 1913. Homemaker. Married (1928); widowed (1968). Membership: Acad. of American Poets; Poetry Club; (past member: Poetry Soc. of Michigan; Sounding Board; U.A.P.). Published work: Rambling, Rhyming Thoughtful Poetry, 1970. Contbr. to: (anthols.): The Best in Poetry, 1968; Personal Poetry, vols. 1 & 2; Poetry Dial, 1968; Poetry Parade, 1968; Poetry Pageant, 1969, etc. (newspapers, mags.): Progressive Farmer; Piggott Banner; Altoona Mirror; Skylines; Koshkonog Herald; Words With Wings; Sunrise-Sunset; Tejas; Author-Poet; Bardic Echoes; Poetry Club Advanced Monticellonian; Nutmegger; Staten Island Verse; Palmetto Casino; Santa Fe New; Daily Record Gazette; Normal News; Delight; Lit. Newsette; Bay Shore Breeze; The Sainte; Spearman Publications; Over The Ozarks; Angel Hour; Jean's Journal; Gems of Memory; The Show Case; Hoosier Challenger; Poetry Preview; Joy in Faith; The Muse;

American Evangelist; Poetry Parade; Tumblin Weeds; The Fairy Stone; The Lamp-lighter; Blue Nosed Rambler; Peninsula Poets; Country Janes Weekly Round Up; Ray's Triangle; Robbins Song; Modus Operandi; Mary's Scrap Book; Flint Journal; Gospel Light; Poetry Parlor; Poets On Parade; Poetry Dial; Sounding Board; Gainesville Bulletin (Arkansas); Flint Bulletin (Michigan); Paragould Bulletin (Arkansas). Awards: Internat. Who's Who in Poetry, 1970-71; Spearman (2) in 1968; NY State Poetry Contest, 1968; 1st Qtr. Amateur Press, etc. Address: 419 E. Garland Ave., Paragould, AR 72450, USA.

VAUGHT, Lucile Kathryn, pen name **VALOIS, Lucile,** b. 28 Aug. 1918. Poet. Education: Geo. Pepperdine Coll., L.A.; Wash. Schl. of Art. Memberships: United Poetry Soc. of Am.; Am. Mosaic Mbr. Published works: Cricket Wing Songs, 1970; Willow Leaf Poems, 1971. Contbr. to: Tweed; Gems; Sprigs; Paul's Poetry Corner; Phoenix Fires; Hyacinths & Biscuits; Canzoni; Modern Haiku; Friendship Ferry; Am. Bard; Jean's Jrnl.; Haiku Highlights; Echoes; Encore; Orphic Lute; Scimitar & Song; The Angels; Fireflower; Fullerton News Tribune; Haiku & Tanka Anthol.; Am. Poets' Best Anthol.; Melody of the Muse; Fragments of Faith Anthol., etc. Recip. of num. hons. & awards inclng: Dream Contest, Judson Dicks book award for In Dreams I Search, The Angels, 1966; Youth Today Contest, book award, The Sacred Flame, Jean's Jrnl., 1968; Angel Hour, book award, The Ship Came In, 1968; United Amateur Press Assn. Laureate Award, Sunrise at Luxor, Driftwood, 1969. Address: 8431 Santa Fe Dr., Buena Pk., CA 90620, U.S.A.

VAZAKAS, Byron, b. 24 Sept. 1905. Poet. Official Poetry Readings incl: Poetry Ctr., YM-YWHA, N.Y.C. (w. Tennessee Williams); Harvard Univ. (Morris Gray Fund), Cambridge, Mass.; Brown Univ., Providence, R.I.; Albright Coll., Reading, Pa; Kutztown State Coll. Pa.; Berks Co. Arts Fest., 1971; Poetry-in-the-Schools Prog., 1972 & 73; var. readings for private & profl. orgs. Published works: (books) Transfigured Night, 1946; The Equal Tribunals, 1961; The Marble Manifesto, 1966; Nostalgias For A House of Cards, 1970. Rep. in following anthols: Am. Writing; Accent Anthol.; An Am. Sampler; Contemporary Poetry; Cross Section; Focus 4; 100 Modern Poems; Modern Am. Poetry; Modern Poetry. Contbr. to over 50 mags. inclng: Ariz. Qtly.; Beloit Poetry Jrnl.; Commonweal; Harpers Bazaar; Hudson Review; Kenyon Review; The Nation; New World Writing 3; N.Y. Times; Partisan Review; Poetry (Chicago); Saturday Review; Sewanee Review; Va. Qtly. Recip., Amy Lowell Traveling Fellowship in Poetry, 1962 & other awards. Address: c/o Alexander K. Vazakas, 1623 Mineral Spring Rd., Reading, PA 19602, U.S.A.

VEGA, Celestino M., pen name **DE VILLA, Cordelia M.,** b. 6th Apr. 1910. Journalist; Poet. Positions held: Reporter, var. Philippine newspapers; Staff Mbr., Taliba; P.R. Officer, Home Financing Commn. Memberships: Panitikan (Tagalog Lit. Soc.); Acting Pres., Makata, Inkorporada (Tagalog Poets Assn.); Nat. Press Club of the Philippines; Dir., ibid, 1958-59; V.P., Bus. & Econ. Reporters Assn. of the Philippines. Published works: Poems in Tagalog, 1968. Contbr. to: Women's Outlook; Weekly Women's Mag.; Weekly Nation; Philippine Mag.; Philippine Review, etc. Honours, awards: Poet of the Year in Tagalog, 1967-68. Address: 37 Seattle, Cubao, Quezon City, Philippines.

VEILLEUX-FORTIN, Thérèse, b. 12 Oct. 1932. Educator; Poet. Educ: Dip. for Teaching of Domestic Scis.; Brevet Complémentaire, Ecole Normale, 1949; Brevet A, 1971. m. Laval Fortin, 1953, 1 s., 4 d. Positions held incl: Tchr., 1949-53, 1959–. Memberships: Soc. of French-Canadian Poets; Dir., ibid, 1972–; Soc. of Canadian Writers; Centro Studi e Scambi Int., Rome. Published works incl: Pleins Feux Sur Ma Nuit, 1973. Contbr. to: Poésie (Revue of Soc. of French-Canadian Poets). Honours, awards: Schlrship. for Studies, 1970-71; Named Mme. Châtelaine, La Revue Châtelaine, 1971. Address: 1 Pl.

Louis-Fréchette, Saint-Anselme, P.Q., Canada.

VELMANS, Michel (Henri), b. 17 Dec. 1926. Notary; Writer; Poet. Memberships: Pres. de l'Association des Ecrivains de l'Ouest, 1972; Fndr., Pres., Rencontres Poètiques du Mont Saint-Michel. Published works: De gueules sur Azur, 1952; Moi le chêne, 1961; Rencontres, 1968; La geste du poète et due Mont Saint Michel, 1972. Contbr. to: Journal des Poètes, Brussels; Le Thyrse, Brussels; Le Goëland; Sources; Alternances; Présence de L'Ouest; Fénix; Le Puits de l'Ermite. Awards: Prix du Poèsie du Goëland, 1955. Address: 7 Rue La Campion, Granville, Manche 50400, France.

VENABLES, Greg(ory) James, b. 6 Dec. 1949. Teacher. Education: Kingston Polytechnic; Christ Church Coll. Married, 1 son. Positions held: Computer Processing Officer, pharmaceutical firm; Teacher. Memberships: Poets Vigilantes; C.H.S. Lit. & Debating Soc. Published works: Look to the Scars, 1973. Contbr. to: Radix; Malenka; Reflections. Address: 2 Westcliff Terrace Mansions, Pegwell Rd., Ramsgate CT11 OJD, U.K.

VENABLES, Roger Evelyn Cavendish, b. 4 Mar. 1911. Lecturer. Education: Beaumont Coll., 1925-29; M.A., Christ Church, Oxford Univ., U.K., 1939. Positions held: W.E.A. Lect., 1936-40; War Serv., 1940-46; Lectr., Army Coll., Welbeck, 1946-52; Lectr., Coll. of Further Educ., Lytham St. Annes, 1955. Mbr., Lancashire Authors. Published works: Combe Valley, 1942, reprint, 1950; Images of Power, 1960; The Night Comes, 1961; Leaves & Seasons, 1961; Forebodings, 1963; D: Portrait of a Don, 1967; Combe Revisited, 1973. Address: Atlanta, Pendeen, Penzance, Cornwall, U.K.

VENKATESWARARAO, Kammisetty, pen name, **MAHASWAPNA,** b. 28 Sept. 1940. Poet. Memberships: Leading Poet, Digambara Movement. Published works: Agnisikhalu-Manghujadulu; Digambara Kavalu, 3 issues. Contbr. to: Bharati (Telugu monthly); Andhraprable (Telugu weekly); Andhrapatrika (weekly); Srijana (quarterly); Dharmayng (Hindi Weekly); Antorcitica (Hindi annual), etc. Address: Lingasamudram PO, Kandukar, Gngole (Dt) AP, India.

VENTADOUR, Fanny, Writer. Education: B.A., Tulane Univ.; Pa. Acad. of Fine Arts; grad. work, French. Tulane Univ.; Univ. of Mex. Married & widowed twice, 2 children. Positions held: worked on Cultural programmes, French Radio; Freelance newspaper work; Aide in Occupational Therapy; Saleswoman in Paris Haute Couture, 6 yrs. Published works: (book of poems) Blue is Recessive as in Irises, 1966. Rep. in following anthols: Anthol. of foreign poets writing in French, 1956; Borestone Poetry Annual, 1967; Avalon Anthol., 1958; Anthol. of Southern Poetry Today, 1962; Contbr. to: Discourse; Forum, 1968; The Laurel Review, 1969; DeKalb Lit. Jrnl., 1969; Cape Rock Jrnl., 1968; The Greenfield Review, 1970; Epos, 1957–; Voices; Wis. Review, 1971; Human Voice Qtly., 1967, '71, '72; Mich. Qtly.; The Wormwood Review, 1967; The Hartford Times, 1956-65; The Waukegan News Sun; News & Courier; South & West Review; The Fiddlehead, etc. Address: 236 Sylvan Blvd., Winter Pk., FL 32789, U.S.A.

VERCAMMEN, Jan, b. 7 Nov. 1906. Educational Inspector. Education: Univ. of nt. Positions held: Tchr.; Insp. of Elem. Schls.; Chief Insp. of Elem. Schls. Memberships: Hon. Pres., Assn. of Flemish Authors; Pres. of two provincial assns. of authors; Maatschappij van Nederlandse Letterkunde, Leiden; Zuid-Nederlandse Maatschappij voor Taal-en Letterkunde en Geschiedenis; Felibrige, France; Int. PEN; Die Kogge, Germany. Published works: Eksode, 1929; Reven, 1931; Credo, 1936; Het tweede Land, 1936; Het dode Kindje Eric, 1936; De rozen rijpen, 1938; Chibiabos zong, 1938; Volubile, 1939; Suite voor Cello, 1939; Drie suites, 1941, 42, 44; Repetitie, 1943; De Parelvisser, 1946; Verbroken Zegel, 1952; Ophelia,

1954; Tussen twee Woestijnen, 1958, 59; Zonder Berouw, 1966; Magnetisch Veld, 1967; Het Huis ten Einde, 1971. Contbr. to: Nieuw Vlaams Tijdschrift; Vlaamse Gids; Cyanuur; Dietse Warande en Belfort; Europa; Forum; De Gemeenschap; Helicon; Iris; Klaverendrie; Kontrast; Nieuw Gewas; De Periscoop; De Tijdstroom; Heibel, etc. Honours: Officer, Order of the Crown; Kt., Order of Leopold; Civil Cross 1st class. Address: Domeindreef 10, B 8200 Brugge-St.-Michiels, Belgium.

VERCRUYSSEN, Marie-Josée, b. 25 July 1915. Teacher; Poet. Memberships: Int. PEN Club; Union of Flemish Authors; (SA BAM) Belgian Soc. of Authors, Composers & Editors. Published works: (poetry) Lente, 1964; Intuïtie, 1965; Schoonheid, 1965; Beschaving – Evolutie, 1965; Poëzie – Lichtbron – Mens, 1970; (poetry story books for children) De Kleine Zanger, 1971; De Witte Vogelen met de Wondervisjes, 1972. Contbr. to: Le Bonheur; Spiegel van de nederlandse poëzie 4. Address: Lange Leemstraat 204, 200 Antwerp, Belgium.

VERGARA, Lautaro G., b. 23 Apr. 1913. Physician. Education: Grad., Schl. of Med., Santiago, Chile; extensive work in Epidemiology under Dr. Rudolph Kraus of Vienna; Marine Hosp.; Rockefeller Inst.; Presbyterian Med. Ctr., N.Y.C. Married Maria Casillas, 3 children. Positions held: Mbr., team of doctors from U.S. Public Hlth. Serv. studying conditions in New Mex.; currently in private practice. Memberships: State Poetry Soc. & Histl. Soc. of N.M. Published works: Luz y Sombra (in Spanish, 1st & 2nd edns.) 1960 & 65; Thirteen English Translations, 1967; Ecos Serranos, 1970. Contbr. to: Encore; Poet, & var. mags. & newspapers in New Mex., Mex., Peru & Chile (poetry & articles on health & med.). Address: 1034 La Font S.W., Albuquerque, NM 87105, U.S.A.

VERHEGGHE, Willy Omer Celesta, pen name **VERHEGGHE, Willie,** b. 22 June 1947. Journalist. Education: Jrnlsm., 'Press-house', Brussels, Belgium. Mbr., Soc. of Flemish Writers. Published works: Met Ikaros op schoot, 1969; De vlaamse guerillero's, 1971; De adem van Amor, 1973; Vlaanderen 1914-18, Vietnam, 1946-73, 1973. Contbr. to: Morgen; Avenue; Vooruit; Yang. Address: de brabanterstraat 76, 9470 Denderleeuw, Belgium.

VERKENNES, Geneva Alice, pen name **PIXIE** or **GINGER VERKENNES,** b. 30 Sept. 1914. Writer & Artist. Education: Flint Art Inst.; Honolulu Conserv. of Music. Positions held: Histn., Flint Cosmetologists; Ed., Aeolian-Harp Booklets; Compiler of a poetry anthol.; Ed., booklets on Hawaii. Memberships: Flint Poetry Forum; worked on Programs, Express Mag. Published works: (poetry booklet) Treasures of Truth; Aloha to Hawaii (w. E. Rosanova); Aeolian-Harp Anthol. (collected poems), 1968; Flowers of Hawaii, 1972-73. Contbr. to: Anthol. of Am. Poetry, Book IV, 1962, Book V, 1963, Book VI, 1964, Book VII, 1965, Book VIII, 1966; Harbor Lights Mag.; Jean's Jrnl.; Peninsula Poets of Mich.; Joy-Bearer; Handicaps. Poems read over radio, & has appeared on TV w. Mich. Water-Wonderland Poets-Writers. Address: 1395 James St., Flint, MI 48507, U.S.A.

VERMA, Ravi, pen name, **JWALA,** b. 30 Oct. 1933, Chhindwara, India. Poet & Journalist. Education: B.A., Saugar Univ., Madhya Pradesh State, 1957. Positions held: Special Corres., Dainik Madhyadesh, Bhopal; Poetry Rdr., Mandla Govt. Degree Coll., 1969, Badkuhi Schl., 1969. Eklehra Higher Secondary Schl., 1970, Bal Badi Betul, 1971; Authorised Correspondent to Nagpur Times. Memberships: Advsr., San Kalp, lit. soc. of Chhindwara; Sugam Manas Mandal, lit. soc., ibid. Author of Mati Ka Moh, pending publication. Contbr. to the following newspapers, mags. & books: Dainik Madhya Desh; Dainik Jagran; Jagwani; Maikalwani; Inkalab; Saras Sandesh; Maneesha; Gandhi Darshan; Sanchaya; Kawyanjali. Honours: various, including poems broadcast. Address: Nagpur Rd., Chhindwara, M.P., India.

VERNON, John Edward, b. 3 June 1943. University Professor. Education: B.A., Boston Coll., 1965; M.A., Univ. of Calif., 1967; Ph.D., ibid, Davis Campus, 1969. Positions held: Asst. Prof., Univ. of Utah, 1969-71; Asst. Prof., State Univ. of N.Y. at Binghamton, 197. Contbr. to: Chicago Review; Am. Review; Paris Review; Iowa Review; Dragonfly; Western Humanities Review; Poetry Northwest; Hanging Loose; Quartet; Epoch; Iowa Review; Cafe Solo; Brown's Window; The Mysterious Barricade; The Ohio Review; Poetry of Departures, anthol., etc. Recip., 1st Prize, Utah State Coun. of the Arts Poetry Contest, 1970. Address: Engl. Dept., State Univ. of N.Y., Binghamton, NY 13901, U.S.A.

VERTOMMEN, Karel, b. 25 Jan. 1907. Teacher. Education: Lic. Germ. Filol., Univ. Louvain. Married Louisa Bruynseels, 6 children. Positions held: Tchr., Athénée Royal, Chimay & Koninklijk Atheneum, Berchem-Antwerp; Ed., De Vlaamse Linie; Tchr., Sint Jan Berchmanscollege, Antwerp & Sint Vincentiuslyceum, Mortsel. Memberships: Pres., Katholieke Vlaamse Hogeschooluitbreiding, Antwerp; V.P., Kunstenaars voor de Jeugd; Kempische Schrijvers; Christelijk Vlaams Kunstenaarsverbond; PEN. Published works: Neuriën, 1934; Peillood, 1937; Brood, 1939; Uut herten vri, 1944; Het Veer, 1948; Vluchtig Schoon, 1954; Balladen en Gedichten, 1957; Diapositieven, 1967; Soms wuift een hand, 1969. Texts for musical compositions: Gedachtenis, comp. Renaat Veremans, 1954; Kleine Jaarkrans, comp., Gaston Feremans, 1960; Sneeuwtriptiek, comp., Gaston Feremans, 1960; Het Liefdegebod, comp., Lodewijk De Vocht, 1964; Emmanuel, comp., Renaat Veremans, 1966; Tijl Uilenspiegel, comp., Otto Rosenberger, 1968. Contbr. to var. anthols. & mags. Honours, awards: Prijs voor Poëzie van de Provincie Antwerpen, 1956; Ridder in de Leopoldsorde, 1964. Address: Strijdhoflaan 93, B 2600 Berchem, Belgium.

VERZOSA, Mauro, b. 3 May 1889. Lawyer. Education: LL.D., 1909; Bar Exam., 1910. Personal details: married (1) Encarnacion Foz, 1914; 12 children; married (2) Priscilla Casilama. Positions held: Mbr. of Congress House of Representatives in 1916-19; Member of Congress 1st Nat. Assembly in 1935-38, and of 2nd Nat. Assembly, 1939-41; Presided some sessions of Congress as Speaker Pro-tempore, and Commission & committees – Special Delegate Filipino Guerrilla in 1945; Presidential Delegate in 1945; Pres. Techn. Asst. in 1960. Memberships: UPLI; Director of the United Ilocamos, Inc.; Vice-pres., Timpuyog ti Amiamam; Regional Knight Commander of Knights of Rizal; Correspondent of the Acad. Filipina de Lengua Espanol. Published work: Granos de Aficion, 1970. Contbr. to various newspapers, journals, etc. Awards: Recip. of sev. awards, including Doctor of Lit. Leadership (h.c.), 1971. Address: Ilagam, Isabela Province, Philippines.

VESPER, Guntram, b. 28 May 1941. Author. Memberships: Verband deutscher Schriftsteller in der IG Druck und Papier (Delegierter für den AFM – Ausschuss); PEN Int.; Gruppe 47. Published works: Politische Flugschrift, poems, 1964; Fahrplan, poems, 1965; Gedichte, 1965; Kriegerdenkmal ganz hinten, prose, 1970; 14 Hörspiele (alle Sender der ARD); 7 rundfunk – features. Contbr. to: Frohburger Wochenblatt; Frankfurter Allgemeine Zeitung; Frankfurter Rundschau; Spiegel; Akzente; Neue Deutsche Literatur, etc. Honours, awards incl: Förderpreis für Literatur des Landes Niedersachsen, 1968; Hörfunkpreis der Arbeitsgemeinschaft der Rundfunkanstalten Deutschlands, 1970; Preis Junge Lyrik Niedersachsen, 1972. Address: Schonebergerstr. 15, 34 Gottingen, German Fed. Repub.

VIERECK, Peter, b. 5 Aug. 1916. Poet; University Professor. Education: B.S., Harvard Univ., 1937; M.A., 1939; Ph.D., 1942; Henry Fellow, Christ Ch., Oxford Univ., U.K., 1937-38. Married 1) Anya de Markov, div., 1 son, 1 daughter, 2) Betty Martin Falkenberg. Positions held: Vis. Lectr., Russian Hist., Smith Coll.,

1948-49; Assoc. Prof., Modern European, Russian Hist., Mount Holyoke Coll., 1948-55; Prof., ibid, 1955–; Vis. Lectr., Am. Culture, Oxford Univ., U.K., 1953; Whittal Lectr. in Poetry, Lib. of Congress, 1954, '63; Fulbright Prof., Am. Poetry & Civilization, Univ. Florence, Italy, 1955; Elliston Chair in Poetry, Univ. of Cinn., 1956, etc. Memberships: Am. Hist. Assn.; Oxford Soc.; Poetry Soc. Am.; PEN; Phi Beta Kappa. Published works incl: Terror & Decorum (poems), 1948, reprinted 1973; Strike Through the Mask! 1950, reprinted 1973; The First Morning, 1952, reprinted 1973; The Persimmon Tree, 1956; The Tree Witch (verse drama), 1961, reprinted 1973; Metapolitics: The Roots of the Nazi Mind, 1961 (up-dated expansion of his 1941 book of same title); Conservatism Revisited & The New Conservatives: What Went Wrong, rev. paperback edns., 1962, '65; New & Selected Poems, 1932-67, 1967. Honours, awards: Tietjans Prize for Poetry, 1948; Pulitzer Prize for Poetry (Terror & Decorum), 1949; Most Disting. Alumnus Award, Horace Mann Schl. for Boys, 1958. Address: 12 Silver St., South Hadley, MA 01075, U.S.A.

VIGEE, Claude, b. 3 Jan. 1921. University Professor (French Literature). Education: Coll. Classique Bischwiller; Univ. of Strasbourg, Caen, Toulouse, Ohio State Univ. Degrees: Bacc. phil., 1938, M.A., 1945; Ph.D., in Romance Studies, 1947. Married to Evelyn Meyer; children, Claudine, Daniel. Positions held: Asst. Prof. of French Lit. at Ohio State Univ., 1947-49; Visiting Lecturer, Wellesley Coll., 1949-50; J.S. Guggenheim Fellow, 1951; Assoc. Prof. (1952) and Prof. of French Lit., Brandeis Univ., Chairman, Dept. of European Lit., 1956-59, Chairman School of Humanities, 1958-59. Since 1960, Prof. of Mod. French Lit., Hebrew Univ., Jerusalem, Israel, and Chairman, Dept. of Comparative Lit., 1970-71. Memberships: Soc. des gens de lettres de France; Hebrew Writers' Union; Academie d'Alsace, etc. Published works: L'Eté Indien, 1957; Les Artistes de la Faim, 1960; Révolte et Louanges, 1962; Moisson de Canaan, 1967; La Lune d'Hiver, 1970; Le Soleil sous la Mer (collected poems), 1972; (In German translation) Netz des Windes, 1969; vols. of translations from German, English, Hebrew, Russian poetry. Contbr. to: Mercure de France; Nouvelle Revue Francaise; Cahiers du Sud; Preuves; Table Ronde; Médiations; Esprit; Le Monde; Etudes; Partisan Review; Southern Review; Modern European Poetry, and various anthols. Awards: Capri Internat. Poetry Award, Sirena d'Oro, 1959; French Acad. M. de Régnier Poetry Award, 1972. Address: 27 Ben Maimon Ave., Jerusalem, Israel.

VIIRLAID, Arved, b. 11 Apr. 1922. Poet; Novelist. Education: State Coll. of Fine Arts, Tallinn, Estonia. Positions held: Co-Ed., State Publishing House, Tallinn; Farm-hand; Labourer; Seaman; Compositor. Memberships: Estonian PEN Ctr., Exec. Comm.; Int. PEN Canadian Ctr.; PEN in-exile, Toronto; Estonian Authors' Assn.; United Poets Laureate Int.; Inst. för Estniska Spraket och Litteraturen, Stockholm; Estonian Ctrl. Coun. in Canada. Published works: (poetry) Hulkuri evangeelium (A Vagabond's Gospel), 1948; Uks Suveõhtune naeratus (A Summer Night's Smile), 1949; Jäätanud peegel (The Frosted Mirror), 1962; Müürilaulud (Songs of Longing), 1967; (novels) Tormiaasta I & II (Yr. of Storms), 1949; Ristideta hauah I & II (Graves without Crosses), 1952; Seitse kohtupäeva (Seven Days of Judgement), 1957; Vaim ja ahelad (Spirit & Shackles), 1961; Kustuvad tuled (The Fading Flames), 1965; Sadujökke (Rain for the River), 1965; Bambuskardina ees (A serial, At the Bamboo Curtain), 1970. Works have appeared in Estonian, Latvian, French, Swedish, Spanish, English, Finnish, Lithuanian, & Ukrainian. Contbr. to: Looming; Tulimuld; Mana; Canadian Lit.; CBC; Laurel Leaves; The PEN in exile, etc. Honours, awards: Estonian Lit. Prize of Hõllalaulud, 1968; 5 lit. prizes for prose, 1950-69; Kt.Cmdr., World Order of Human Merit, 1962; Karta & Pres. Medal as Disting. Creative Writer, United Poets Laureate Int. 1967. Address: 63 Glen Davis Cres., Toronto, Ont. M4E 1X7. Canada.

VILLA, Jose Garcia, b. 5 Aug. 1914. Instructor. Education: B.A., Univ. of New Mex.; Postgrad. work, Columbia Univ. Positions held: Assoc. Ed., New Directions Books, 1949-51; Instr., Poetry Workshop, N.Y.C. Coll., 1952-60; Instr., Poetry Workshop, The New School, 1964-. Published works: Footnote to Youth, 1933; Have Come, Am Here (poetry), 1942; Volume Two (poetry), 1949; Selected Poems & New, 1958; Many Voices, 1939; Poems by Doveglion, 1941; Poems Fifty-Five, 1962; Poems in Praise of Love, 1962; Selected Stories, 1962; The Portable Villa, 1963; The Essential Villa, 1965. Edited: E.E. Cummings Number, The Harvard Wake, 1946; Marianne Moore Issue, Qtly. Review of Lit., 1947; A Celebration for Edith Sitwell, New Directions, 1948. Rep. in num. anthols. Honours, awards: Guggenheim Fellowship, 1942; Am. Acad. Arts & Letters Award, 1942; Bollingen Fndn. Fellowship, 1951-53; Shelley Meml. Award, 1959; Hon.D.Litt., Far Eastern Univ., 1959; Philippines Pro Patria Award, 1961; Philippines Cultural Heritage Award, 1962; Rockefeller Fndn. Fellowship, 1963; Pres. Adviser on Cultural Affairs, Philippine Govt., 1968-; elected National Artist in Literature, 1973; L.H.D., Univ. of the Philippines, 1973. Address: 780 Greenwich St., N.Y., NY 10014, U.S.A.

VILLANEUVA, Tino, b. 11 Dec. 1941. Lecturer. Education: B.A., Southwest Tex. State Univ., 1969; M.A., Univ. of Buffalo, 1971; doctoral cand. currently at Boston Univ. Positions held: Instrs. Asst., SWTSU, 1968-69; Tchng. Asst., Univ. of Buffalo, 1969-71; Tchng. Fellow, Boston Univ., 1971-73; Lectr., ibid, 1973-74. Published works: Hay Otra Voz Poems, 1972. Contbr. to: The San Antonio Express; The San Antonio News; The North Am. Mentor; Caribbean Review; Magazin; El Grito; El Espejo/The Mirror; The Hays County Citizen; Hispamérica; Revista Chicano-Riquena; Entre nosotros. Address: P.O. Box 450, San Marcos, TX 78666, U.S.A.

VILLASENOR, Laura Wells de, b. 10 Oct. 1919. Housewife; Librarian; Poet. Education: A.B., Vassar Coll., 1940; Radcliffe Coll. Grad. Student, 1941-42; B.S., Columbia Univ., Schl. of Lib. Serv., 1947. Memberships: Poetry Soc. of Am.; World Poetry Soc. Intercontinental. Translator of Muerte Sin Fin (Death Without End), by José Gorostiza, published 1969 by Univ. of Tex. & 1971 by the Ark Press, G.B. Translator of Piedra de Sol (Sun Stone), by Octavio Paz, printed in The Tex. Qtly, 1970. Contbr. to: Columbia Univ. Forum; The Tex. Qtly.; Mex. Qtly. Review; Vassar Review; Mundus Artium. Address: Reyna 39, San Angel, Mexico 20, D.F., Mexico.

VILLEGAS, Antonio J., b. 9 Jan. 1928. Lawyer. Education: Assoc. of Arts, (Summa Cum Laude) Far Eastern Univ., Manila, Philippines; LL.B., (Magna Cum Laude) Manuel L. Quezon Univ., 1953. Positions held: Exec. Sec., Anti-Communist League, Philippines; Legal Officer, Vice Chmn., Presidential Complaints & Action Comm., 1954-57; Vice-Mayor, City of Manila, 1960-62; Mayor, ibid, 1962-. Published works: Libre'Ng Pilipino, 1969. Bakit Ako Tumula, 1967; Contbr. to: Laurel Leaves; Mabuhay; School Organs. Honours, awards: Distinguished patron of Int. Poetry, United Poets Laureate Int., 1968; Hon. Poet Laureate Mayor, ibid, 1968; LL.D., (Honoris Causa) McGregor Schl. of Law, Sacramento, Calif. Address: Office of the Mayor, Maharnilad, Manila, Philippines.

VIMAL, Ganga Prasad, born 3rd June 1939. Teacher. Education: M.A. (Hindi); Ph.D. (Symbols & Images in Poetry). Positions held: Awarded Fellowship to work on Modern Poetry; Tchr. to Foreign Students; Freelance Writer; Tchr., Hindi Lit., Coll. of Delhi Varsity. Memberships: Pres., Hindi Literary Soc., Punjab Univ., 1960-61; Sec., Literary Soc., ibid. Publications: Viggap; 2 vols. of criticism, 3 novels, 2 collections of short stories, & ed., several books & magazines. Contbr. to major Hindi jrnls.; Century; Indian Lit.; Indian Writing Today. Address: 26/53 Ramjas Rd., Karol Bagh, New Delhi 110005, India.

VINZ, Mark, b. 27 Sept. 1942. Teacher. Education:

B.A. & M.A., Univ. of Kansas; Ph.D., Univ. of New Mex. Positions held: Tchr., Moorhead State Coll., Minn.; Ed. of Dacotah Territory, a mag. of poetry & comment. Memberships: Minn. State Arts Coun., Literature Panel, & the Minn. Poets-in-the-Schools prog. Contbr. to: S.D. Review; The Lamp in the Spine; The Nation; West Coast Poetry Review; Wis. Review; The Smith; The Little Mag.; The Cottonwood Review; Steelhead; Crazy Horse; Kansas Qtly.; Cafe Solo; From the Belly of the Shark (anthol.), etc. Address: Box 775, Moorhead, MN 56560, U.S.A.

VIOLI, Paul Randolph, b. 20 July 1944. Poet. Education: B.A., Engl. Lit., Boston Univ., Coll. of Liberal Arts. Published works: (poetry) In Baltic Circles; Waterworks; Automatic Transmissions; She'll Be Riding Six White Horses; Sunoco. Contbr. to: Sun; The World; N.Y. Times; East Village Other; One; Toothpaste; Search for Tomorrow; Mulberry; Blue Suede Shoes; Connections; Milk Qtly.; The Harris Review; Intrepid; Penumbra; Gum; Matchbook; Extensions; The Herald; Miami Chapbook. Address: 68 Sleepyhollow Rd., Briarcliff Manor, N.Y., U.S.A.

VIOSCA, Renée Anne, b. 25 Nov. 1934. Librarian. Education: B.A., Loyola Univ., New Orleans. Personal details: daughter of Civil District Judge. Positions held: Hospital Receptionist; Teacher, 6th, 7th, and 8th grades; Librarian, St. Leo the Great School, New Orleans; Freelance Writer for newspapers and poetry publications. Memberships: New Orleans Chapter of the Louisiana State Poetry Soc.; Internat. Clover Poetry Assoc. Published works: Tribute in Verse, 1970. Contbr. to: St. Leo the Great Church Bulletin; We Sing (anthol.); State Yearbook, Louisiana State Poetry Soc.; Dominican Coll. Lit. Mag.; Nat. Poetry Assoc. Anthol.; etc. Awards: Hon. Mention, Louisiana State Poetry Soc. Festival, 1973; Cert. of Merit, 1973, from Dr. George Wm. Cooper, Poet Laureate of Louisiana. Address: 2825 St. Bernard Ave., New Orleans, LA 70119, USA.

VIRAY, Manuel, pen names **MARINO, Robert S., PATINO, Carlos, BORJA, N.A.,** b. 13 Apr. 1917. Diplomat. Educ: Ph.B., Univ. of the Philippines, Manila. m. Rosario S. Viray, 3d. Positions held: Mbr., Philippines Dept. of For. Affairs, 1952-68; Min., Philippine Embassy, Bad Godesberg, W. Germany, 1969-. Published works: After This Exile, 1965; Shawl from Kashmir (short stories), 1968; Ed., Heart of the Island, 1947; Ed., Philippine Poetry Annual, 1949. Contbr. to: Beloit Poetry Journal; Literary Review; Antioch Review; Talisman; Pacific Spectator; (anthologies) Philippine Writing 1953; Philippine Writing in English, 1955; New Writing from the Philippines, 1966. Recip., Carlos Palanca Lit. Award, 1966.

VIRET, Margaret Mary-Buchanan, pen name **VIRET, Margaret,** b. 18 Apr. 1913. Artist; Poet. Education: Business Coll., NYC.; Miami Art School; Terry Art School, Miami; Univ. of Miami Extension courses; Laramore Rader Poetry School; also private teachers of art. Married to Frank Ivo Viret. Positions held: Vice-Pres., Florida Fed. of Art, 1955; State Art Chairman, Florida Fed. of Women's Clubs, 1958, also Lit. Chairman, 1960; Poetry Director, Miami Woman's Club, 1967, also Art Director many times up to 1973-74; Laramore Rader Poetry Group, Pres., 1970-72, and now Director; Founder Member, Poetry Soc. of Florida; Member, Florida Fed. of Womens Clubs Poets, etc. Published work: Singing in the Sun, 1965; Poetry Soc. of Florida Poetry Book, 1969; many small pamphlets, etc. Contbr. to: Miami Herald; Miami News; Miami Beach Reporter-Sun; NY Times. Recip. Chamber of Commerce – Miami Poetry Award, 1964; Laramore Rader Poetry Award, 1969-70; Miami Palette Club Poetry Award, 1973; Miami Woman's Club Poetry Award, 1968, etc. Address: 294 N.E. 55th Terr., Miami, FL 33137, USA.

VIRGIL, Anita, b. 23 Nov. 1931. Housewife. Education: studied Art, night classes, N.Y. Univ. Married Andy Virgil. Positions held: Asst. to Art Dir., Town &

Planning Mag., N.Y.C., 1949-51; Costume Researcher, Rahl Studios, N.Y.C., 1951-57. Pres., Haiku Soc. of Am., N.Y.C. Contbr. to: Cats Mag.; Haiku West; Laurel Review; Haiku Spotlight (Japan); Haiku Highlights; Haiku (Toronto); Modern Haiku; Haiku Mag.; SCTH; Haiku Byways; The Haiku Anthol., 1974. Address: Cutlass Rd., Kinnelon, NJ 07405, U.S.A.

VIRGILIO, Nicholas Anthony, b. 28 June 1928. Poet & Lecturer. Education: Coll. of South Jersey, Camden, 1950; B.A., Temple Univ., Phila., Pa., 1952. Positions held: Profl. Radio Artist, 15 yrs.; Substitute Tchr., Camden City Schls., 2 yrs.; Book Salesman; Clerk; U.S. Navy, 1946-48; Creative writing (poetry), 1957-; Co-Dir., First Int. Haiku Fest., Univ. of Pa., Phila., 1971. Mbr., Haiku Soc. of Am. Has lectured at num. colls., univs., schls. & libs. Contbr. to: Leatherneck Mag.; Bitterroot; The Green World; Am. Haiku; Haiku West; Modern Haiku; Fiddlehead, Canada; Caravan; Creative Review; Ariz. Qtly.; Japan Times (Tokyo), etc. Poetry has been read on sev. radio stns. & featured on TV. Has exhibited at var. libs. & univs. Address: 1092 Niagara Rd., Camden, NJ 08104, U.S.A.

VIRTUE, Vivian (Lancaster), b. 13 Nov. 1911. Retired Civil Servant. Education: Kingston Coll., Jamaica. Positions held: served the Govt. of Jamaica, 1929-61, in var. clerical, exec. & admin. posts until retirement as Sr. Labour Officer in the Min. of Labour. Memberships: former Hon. Asst. Sec. & Libn., V.P., 1951-61, Poetry League of Jamaica; Fndr. Mbr., Exec. Comm. Mbr., V.P., –1961, Jamaica Ctr. Int. PEN; Advisory Bd., The Pioneer Press, Kingston; Co-Fndr., The New Dawn Press; Royal Soc. of Lit.; Fellow, Royal Soc. of Arts. Published works: Wings of the Morning, 1938. Rep. in following anthols: Treasury of Jamaican Poetry, 1949; Poetry of the Negro, 1949; Poetry for Children, 1950; Independence Anthol. of Jamaican Lit., 1962; Verse & Voice, 1965; New Poems, 1966; Caribbean Voices, vol.I, 1966, vol.II, 1970; New Voices of the Commonwealth, 1968; West Indian Poetry, 1971; Jamaica, Portrait of an Island, 1955; var. other works of ref. Contbr. to var. newspapers & jrnls. Participated in the Commonwealth Arts Fest., London, 1965. Frequent broadcaster in the former Caribbean Voices prog. of the BBC O'seas Serv. Recip., Musgrave Silver Medal for Poetry, Inst. of Jamaica, 1960 & The Constance Hollar Meml. Prize for Poetry, Poetry League of Jamaica, 1950. Address: 28 Horbury Cres., London W.11, U.K.

VISSER, Audrae Eugenie, b. 3 June 1919. Teacher. Education: B.S., S.D. State Univ., 1948; M.A., Univ. of Denver, 1954. Positions held: Tchr., Federal Indian Schl., Pierre, S.D., 1950-51; Am. Village Schl., Nagoya, Japan, 1954-55; Acquisitions Libn., S.D. State Univ., 1955-56; Tchr., High Schls., Flandreau, Pierre, Elkton, DeSmet, S.D. & Windom, Minn., 1958-71. Memberships: Regl. V.P., S.D. State Poetry Soc., 1960's; Co-Pres., ibid, 1967; Bd.Mbr., 1972-75; Recording Sec., 1974–. Published works: Rustic Roads, 1961; Poems For Brother Donald, 1974. Rep. in following anthols: Prairie Poets, I, 1949, II 1958, III 1966; Am. Sonnets & Lyrics, 1941; Am. Sonnets & Lyrics, 1945. Contbr. to: Sioux Falls Daily Argus Ldr., S.D.; Rapid City Jrnl., S.D.; Elton Record, S.D.; Medford Mail Tribune, Ore., etc. Honours, awards incl: Hon. doctorates from Univ. of Free Asia, Pakistan, 1968, Coll. of Heraldry, Barcelona, 1971; Great China Arts Coll. of World Univ., Hong Kong, 1972; Five Hon. Mentions in Nat. Poetry Contests, 1973; Grand Prize for Poetry, S.D. State Fair, 1972; Hope Massie Award for Creative Writing, 1972. Work read on radio. Address: Elkton, SD 57026, U.S.A.

VISWAM, Aripirala, b. 11 Oct. 1936. Lecturer. Education: M.A. & Ph.D., Visarad Hindi. Memberships: Fndr., Jt.-Sec., Affiliated Coll. Tchrs. Assn., A.P.; Convenor of Darsana Study Circle; Freeverse Writers Workshop; Sec., Sahitya Kalakendra; Pres., Taraka Organisers; Exec. Mbr., World Poetry Soc. Intercontinental, Indian Br.; Guest Ed., Poet, Great World Poets of Andhra Number; Nauyasahiti Samiti;

Andhraviswa Sahiti; Ed., Who's Who of Telugu Poets in English; Adjudicator, Ctrl. & State Sahity Acad. Awards. Published works: (in Telugu) Nidura Kannelu, 1962; Kaalam Geestunnagitalu; Aswaghoshudu; Darsana; Repati Swargam; Manas; Halebidu; Kalacherigi Poneeku Nestam; Man & Nature in Modern Telugu Poetry; Jaladevatalu; (in English) River my Guru, 1972. Contbr. to var. jrnls. Recip. var. awards for short story writing & The World Poetry Award, World Poetry Soc., 1973. Address: Dept. of Langs., New Sci. Coll., P.G. Ctr., Narayanagud, Hyderabad 500029, Andhrapradesh State, India.

VITORITTO, Elvira Lanza, b. 5 Aug. 1900. Retired Educator & Social Worker. Education: Tchng. Degree, Carroll Robbins Training Schl.; Tchng. Degree in Bus., Finance & Accty., Rider Coll., Trenton, NJ. Married Anthony Vitoritto. Positions held: Tchr., Elem. & Jr. High Schls.; Soc. Work, Settlement House & Internat. Inst., Trenton. Memberships: World Poetry Soc. Intercontinental; Centro Studi E Scambi; Poet Laureate Comm. of 100, Md. Bd. of Trustees; Hon., Iowa State Poetry Soc.; Eastern Ctr., Poetry Soc. of London; World Poets Resource Ctr., NY; Am. Poetry League. Published some 12 brochures & 3 books on poetry, including: Amaranth & Tumbleweed, 1967; Above The Roar of Silence, 1969; Gentle on the Wind, 1969-70; Dropping Pebbles in the Pond, 1969; Mediterranean Mood, 1970. Contbr. to: (anthols.) Heart of Angels; Pacific Breeze; Choice of the Angels; Ardentia Verba; The Best in Poetry; The Explorer; New Poetry; Badge of Promise; Selected Poems for 1967 & 1968 (Fla. State Poetry Soc., Inc.); Dr. Etta Josephean Murfey Mem. Book, 1967-69; Internat. Hall of Fame I, II, III & IV; Quorum of Cats; Am. Poetry Fellowship Annual Anthols. 1967-68; Poets 69; Laurel Leaves Anthol.; NJ Poetry Soc. Anthol.; Sweet Seventies Anthol.; Star Borne, NJPS Inc.; Best Broadcast Poetry II; Prairie Poetry Anthol. 1970; Am. Poet Anthol.; Inky Traile Anthol.; 1970 Potpourri of Poetry; Selected Poems, 1969-70; 70 Poets; Moon Age Poets; Echoes of Love Anthol. (jrnls.) Exploere; Caravan; Golden Circle; Writer's Notes & Quotes; The Angels; Angel Hour; Phylis; Hoosier Challenger; Ideals; Mod. Maturity; NRTA Jrnl.; Bay Shore Breeze; Showcase UAPA/A; Prairie Poet; Am. Poet; United Poets; Major Poets; Laurel Leaves; Southside Jrnl.; The Saint; Am. Bard; Penman; Cardinal; Bell's Letters; Echoes; Karyn; Pixie Angel; Author-Poet; UAPA-Forum; Flamingo; Inky Trails; Trenton Evening Times; Trentonian; Russell Times; NY Herald-Trib.; LI Kernel; Educ. Method; Progressive Educ.; Friendship Ferry; Fireflower; Ulmas; Tempo; Scimitar & Song; Am. Voice; Am. Poetry League; Albo D'Doro; Quaderni Di Poesia; Linda; Times Bull., Mt. Lakes News, Booton, NJ. Honours: Poems on death of J.F. Kennedy accepted for John F. Kennedy Mem. Lib.; Gold Laurel Wreath, Pres. Marcos of Philippines; Decretum, United Poets Laureate Internat; Certs. of Recognition, FSPS, 1969-70; Merit Award, Personal Poetry, 1970; Cinquain Legacy Citation, LS Cheney, 1970; Edna St. Vincent Millay Award, Comm. of 100, Md., 1970. Address: PO Box 116, W Trenton, NJ 08628, USA.

VOELCKER, Hunce, b. 28 June 1940. Poet. Education: A.B., Villanova Univ.; grad. classes, City Univ. of N.Y. Positions held: Tchr.; Typist; Book store clerk. Published works: The Hart Crane Voyages, 1967; Joy Rock Statue Ship, 1968; Logan, a novel, 1969; Songs for the Revolution, 1970; Parade of Gumdrop Prose Pictures, 1971; Brian, 1973; Sillycomb, 1973; A Mantra for the Campaign, Election & Term of George McGovern as the President of the United States, 1972. Contbr. to: The Lynx; Contact; Cow; The World; Sebastian Quill; Manroot; Kaliflower; Empty Elevator Shaft; Gay Sunshine; The Philadelphia Scene. Honours, awards: 1st prize, Philadelphia Regl. Writers' Conf., 1960; a Sprite Subsidy/Life Time Grant, 1973–. Address: Box 11, Duncans Mills, CA 95430, U.S.A.

VOGELSANG, Arthur, b. 31 Jan. 1942. Poet; Editor. Education: B.A., Univ. of Md., 1965; M.A., Johns Hopkins Univ., 1966; M.F.A., Univ. of Iowa, 1970.

Positions held: Editing Supvsr., McGraw-Hill Book Co., N.Y.; Grad. Asst., Univ. of Iowa; Instr., Wichita State Univ.; Ed., The Ark River Review, Wichita, Kans.; Dir., Kans. Poetry & Fiction Workshops, Wichita; Editl. Asst., The Am. Poetry Review, Phila. Published works: Stanzas Done for Alberta Coke, 1969. Contbr. to: Abraxas; Ark River Review; Calvert Review; The Croupier; Greenfield Review; Gum; Iowa Review; Kans. Qtly.; The Little Mag.; The Midwest Qtly.; N.Y. Qtly.; Northwest Review; Out of Sight; Panache; Ploughshares; Poetry Newsletter; Salted Feathers. Address: 519 Montgomery Ave., Haverford, PA 19041, U.S.A.

VOGT, Anton. Lecturer; Radio Reviewer. Positions held: Former Lectr., Engl., Wellington Tchrs. Coll., N.Z.; Reviewer, Wellington radio. Published works: Anti All That, 1940; Poems for a War, 1943; Love Poems, 1952; Poems Unpleasant (w. James K. Baxter & Louis Johnson), 1952; The Night Shift: Poems on Aspects of Love (w. others), 1957. Contbr. to (anthologies) A Book of New Zealand Verse 1923-50; New Zealand Poetry Yearbook, 1956-60; An Anthology of New Zealand Verse, 1956.

VOLTZ, Henry Thomas, b. 29 Jan. 1921. Teacher. Education: B.S., Central Mich. Univ., 1948; B.A., Univ. of Akron, 1951; M.Ed., Loyola Univ., New Orleans, 1956; also 30 grad. hours. Positions held: Night Libn., Loyola Univ., New Orleans; Classroom Tchr., H.S. & Elem. Divs. Memberships: V.P., La. State Poetry Soc., New Orleans Chapt.; IBA. Published works: Grains of Sand (poetry book), 1973. Contbr. to: We Sing Anthol., books I & II, 1973; U.S. Congressional Record, 1971; a sonnet 'On The Death of Franklin D. Roosevelt' placed in the Hyde Park, N.Y. Collection by Eleanor Roosevelt, 1950. Nom. for Hon. Doctorate from the Int. Boswell Inst., to be given at Loyola Univ. Address: 570 Walnut St., New Orleans, LA 70118, U.S.A.

VOM SCHEIDT, Martha, pen name **SAALFELD, Martha,** b. 15 Jan. 1898. Writer. Education: studied Hist. of Art & Philos. Married. Memberships: PEN, 1949–; Deutschen Akademie fur Sprache und Dichtung, Darmstadt, 1959–. Published works: Gedichte, 1931; Der unendliche Weg, sonnets, 1932; Staub aus der Sahara, Schauspiel, 1932; Beweis fur Kleber, Ttagikom, 1932; Deutsche Landschaft, poems, 1946; Idyll in Babensham, 1947; Der Wald, 1949; Pan ging vorüber, novel, 1954; Anna Morgana, novel, 1956; Herbstmond, poems, 1958; Mann im Mond, novel, 1961; Judengasse, novel, 1965; Isi oder die Gerechtigkeit, novel, 1970; Gedichteu/Erzählungen, 1973. Contbr. to: Die Neue Rundschau; Literarische Welt; Neue Zeitung; Die Ziet; Der Mittag, etc. Honours, awards: Literaturproic der Bayer. Akademie der Schönen Künste, 1955; Staatspreis des Landes Rheinland-Pfalz, 1963. Address: Zeppelinstr. 13, 6748 Bad Bergzabern, German Fed. Repub.

VONCK, Theo, pen name, **CUWART, Flore,** b. 28 June 1900. Author; Poet; Art Critic. Education: College St. Stanislas, Antwerp. Married, 5 Children. Positions held: Clerk; Tchr., Langs. & Piano; Jrnlst., 1944-65; Art Critic. Memberships: Soc. of Flemish Authors. Published works include: (in 5 langs.) Gitanella; European Cocktail, 1960; Flemish Cocktail, 1963; Preludes, 1966; 8 booklets of polyglot poetry; Many songs, in sev. langs. inclng. Anthem of Europe; (short stories) Reporters on Chase; The Rendez-Vous. Contbr. to the following jrnls. & mags: Gazet van Antwerpen; Vlaanderen, etc. Honours, awards: 1st Int. Prize, Festival, Capri, Italy, 1956; 2nd Prize, Art Coun. of Europe, Brussels, 1964. Address: 19 Marcel Aubertin Av., 2600 Berchem, Antwerp, Belgium.

VON NUMERS, Lorenz T.G.G., pen name (for columns & light verse only) **TVESKGG,** b. 25 Jan. 1913. Diplomat. Education: Helsinki Univ., Finland. Married, 2 daughters. Positions held: Jrnlst. & Writer: Editor of 'Sesam' (Lit. review, Stockholm), 1947; Mng. Ed. of 'Obs', Stockholm, 1948-52; Ed., literary page, Svenska Dagbladet, Stockholm, 1955-59; Cultural Attaché of the Finnish Embassy in Paris, 1967–. Memberships: Finland's Svenska Författarförening, 1934–; Sveriges Författarförbund. Published works: Svart harnesk, 1934; Porträtt med blomma, 1936; Havslyktan, 1942; Lyrical chapters in Drottningens handelsmän, 1964; some poems in Manen är en säl, 1953; var. essays & novels. Address: Ambassade de Finlande, 2 rue Fabert, 75007 Paris, France.

VON POKORNY, Rosamund Mary, pen name **GREENWOOD, Rosamund,** b. 12 June 1907. Actress. Education: Central Schl. of Speech & Drama; London Univ. Dip. of Dramatic Art. Widow of Leo von Pokorny, 1 son, 1 daughter. Acted in many plays at the old Vic., in Repertory, Provinces & West End of London; also broadcasts, films & TV. Memberships: Exec. Comm. & Readings Comm., Poetry Soc. of London, 1954-64; Manifold, 1964-70; Camden Poetry Grp., 1970–. Published works: Broadcast of Song, London, 1943; Broadcast of Poem, N.Z., 1964, and monologue BBC, 1974; Slide Into Poetry, 1973. Contbr. to: Without Adam (anthol.), 1968; Poetry Review, 1951; Manifold, 1967; South China Morning Post, 1971; Country Life, 1974. Honours, awards: Premium Prize, Poetry Review, 1951; Shelley Prize & Wordsworth Prize, Oxford Verse Speaking Contest (John Masefield), 1928. Address: c/o Fraser & Dunlop, 91 Regent St., London W.1., U.K.

VON SCHOULTZ-BERGMAN, Solveig Margereta, pen name **VON SCHOULTZ, Solveig,** b. 5 Aug. 1907. Author. Education: studies in psychology & pedagogy. Married the composer Erik Bergman. Memberships: Bd. Mbr., Finland's Svenska Författareförening, 1947-69; PEN Club; Finnish Dramatists Soc. Published works: (books)˙ Min Timme, 1940; Den bortvända glädjen, 1943; Eko av ett rop, 1945; Nattlig äng, 1949; Allt sker nu, 1952; Nätet, 1956; Terrassen, 1959; Sänk ditt ljus, 1963; Klippbok, 1968. Honours, awards: The States Lit. Prize, 1946, 48, 52, 57; The States Scholarships, 1963-65, 71-73; The Swedish Academy's big Lit. Prize, 1972; sev. prizes from Svenska Litteratursällskapet. Address: Bergg. 22, C, 52, Helsinki 10, Finland.

Von SPAKOVSKY, Anatol. b. 27 Feb. 1895. Professor; Emeritus; Writer; Poet. Education: Univ. of Moscow, Russia, 1914-15; Ph.D., Lyublyana Univ., Yugoslavia, 1921-25; Prof. of Philos. Degree, ibid, 1927; Univ. of Nancy, France, 1926. Married, Edeltraud Glaueser, 3 s., 2 d. Positions held: Prof. of Philos. & French, diff. Colls., Yugoslavia, 1927-41; Prof. of Philos., Volkshochschule, Munich, Germany, 1948-50; Prof. of Philos., World Univ. Serv., 1950-51; Prof. of Sociol., Russian & German, Jacksonville State Univ., Ala., USA, 1957-65; Prof. of German Humanities & Sociol., Athens Coll., 1965-68, '69-70; Prof., Sociol., Philos. & French, Miles Coll., Birmingham, 1968-69; Lecturer in Russian, Univ. of Alabama in Huntsville, 1971-72. Memberships: PEN Club, Europe; Ala. Writers Assn.; The International Poetry Society, England. Writer of numerous works on philos. & sociol. in various langs. Author of booklet of poems: On the Roads of Life & Thought, 1962. Contbr. to: The Aryan Path (Bombay). Internat. Who's Who in Poetry Anthology. Address: 10020 Hampshire Dr., SE, Huntsville, Ala. 35803, USA.

VOSKUIL, Duane Martin, b. 26 Mar. 1938. Professor of Philosophy. Education: B.A., Hope Coll.; M.A., Emory Univ.; Ph.D., Univ. of Mo., Columbia. Divorced, 3 children. Positions held: Tchr., secondary schl., 3 yrs.; Instr., Univ. of Mo.; Asst. Prof., Univ. of N.D. Contbr. to: Flame, Dianoia; Opus. Address: Philosophy Dept., Univ. of N.D., Grand Forks, ND 58201, U.S.A.

VOSS, John Allen, b. 11 Jan. 1945. Teacher; Researcher; Administrator. Education: B.S. in Sociol., State Coll. of Ark., Conway, 1967; M.A. in Sociol., Univ. of Ark., Fayetteville, 1970. Positions held: H.S. Tchr., Mayflower H.S., Ark., 1967-68; Instr. of Sociol., Lamar Univ., 1969-71; Researcher, Univ. of Ark., 1971-72; City Planner, City of Houston, Tex., 1973; Ctr. Coordinator (Asst. Dir.), Multicultural Ctr..

Houston, Tex., 1973–. Contbr. to Poet. Address: Rt. 2, Conway, AR, U.S.A.

VOZNESENSKY, Andrei, b. 12 May 1933. Poet. Education: Architectural Inst., Moscow. Memberships: USSR Writers' Union; Bd. Mbr., ibid; German Acad. of Fine Arts; Am. Acad. of Arts & Letters. Published works: Mosaics, 1960; Parabola, 1960; The Triangled Pear, 1962; The Antiworlds, 1964; Achillean Heart, 1966; Selected Poems, 1967; Shadow of Sound, 1970; A Look, 1972 (all colls. of poems); Save Your Faces, 1970 (play). Address: 52 Vorovsky St., Moscow, USSR.

VRBOVSKA, Anča. Author; Poet; Editor. Education: Bryn Mawr Coll., Phila., Pa.; N.Y. Univ.; CCNY; Hunter Coll., N.Y.C. Positions held: Ed., History of Czechoslovak Press in U.S.A.; Fndng. Ed., Pegasus Poetry Qtly., Greenwich Village, N.Y.C.; Ed., New Orlando Poetry Anthol.; Ed., Am. Dialog (now suspended); Translator of German, Czech., Hungarian, Polish, etc. Memberships: Poetry Soc. of Am.; Fndn. Pres., The Greenwich Village Poetry Soc.; Caliope Poetry Soc.; Hon. Mbr., Academia de Ciencas Humanisticas y Relaciones, Mex.; Dip. de Membre d'Honneur, Les Violetti et Normands, Paris, France, 1959; Membre d'Honneur, Club des Intellectuels Francais, Paris, 1959. Published works: Cyclme, poetry & prose, 1934; The Other Selves, 1951; The Gate Beyond the Sun, 1970. Contbr. to: New Orlando Poetry anthols.; Raven Poetry Anthol.; Dasein; Pegasus Poetry Qtly.; Writers' Forum; The Writing on the Wall; Poet; New Yorsky Dennik; Svu; Zápisnik, etc. Address: 39 Bedford St., N.Y., NY 10014, U.S.A.

VRKLJAN, Irena Vesna Ingeborg, b. 21 Aug. 1930. Writer. Education: Archaeol. & German, Univ. of Zagreb, 1949-51; Acad. for Film & TV, West Berlin, 1966-69. Married 1) Zvonimir Golob, div., 2) Benno Meyer-Wahlack. Positions held: Designer, Trick-Film Studio, Zagreb-Film; Own Film Prog., Radio-TV Zagreb, 10 yrs.; Writes & produces 'Films About Art & Poetry'; Writes TV & Radio plays together with husband. Memberships: Croatian & Yugoslav Lit. Socs.; Croatian & Yugoslav Fed. of Jrnlsts.; Croatian Soc. of Translators. Published works: (books of poetry) Krik je samo tisina, 1954; Paralele, 1957; Stvari vec daleke, 1963; Doba prijateljstva, 1963; Soba, taj strasan vrt, 1966; (w. B. Meyer-Wehlack) Modderkrebse, a play, 1971. Contbr. to: Telegram; 15 dana; Forum; Knjizevnost; Mogucnosti; Literatura; Danas; Letopis Matice Srpske; Krugovi; The Bridge, etc. Honours, awards: Prize for Screenplay 'Painting in the 19th Century', 1963; Prize of the TV Fest. for the screenplay, 'The Painter, Gabriel Stupica', 1965. Address: Mommsenstr. 56, 1 Berlin 12, Germany.

VROMAN, Leo, b. 10 Apr. 1915. Physiologist. Education: B.S., Univ. of Utrecht, Netherlands, 1937; M.S., Med. Coll., Djakarta, Indonesia, 1941; Ph.D., Univ. of Utrecht, 1958. Positions held: Asst. Zool., Med. Coll., Djakarta, Indonesia, 1941; Rsch. Assoc., New Brunswick, NJ, USA, 1947-55; Hematology Dept., Mt. Sinai Hosp., NYC, 1955-58; Sr. Physiologist, Dept. of Animal Behavior, Am. Museum of Nat. History, 1958-61; Physiologist, Veterans Admin. Hosp., Brooklyn, 1961–. Mbr., PEN. Published works include: Fedichten, 1946; Vroegere en Latere, 1949; Poems in English, 1953; Inleiding Toteen Leegte, 1955; Wit Slaapwandelen, 1957; De Ontvachting en andere gedichten, 1960; Twee gedichten, 1961; Fabels, 1962; Manke Vliegen, 1963; 126 gedichten, 1964; Almanak, 1965; Twee gedichten, 1966; God en Godin, 1967; 114 Gedichten, 1969. Contbr. to the following publs: Algameen Handelsblad; Gids; Tirade; Merlyn; Eibertinage; Maatstaf; Poetry (Chicago); Approach; Prairie Schooner, etc. Honours, awards include: Artists Resistance Award, 1965; PC Hooft Prize for Poetry (Nat. Poetry Prize), 1965. Address: 2365 E. 13th St., Brooklyn, NY 11229, USA.

VUAGNAT, Luc, b. 11 Dec. 1927. Writer; Artist; Poet. Positions held: Swiss Del., Office français d'information culturelle; ibid, de Main de la Main; etc.

Memberships: Mbr. of the Jury, Prix de l'Expression Francaise; ibid, Société des artistes et poètes de France; etc. Published works: Flammes Dans La Nuit, 1952; La Maison Du Soleil, 1954; Les Pas de Rêve, 1956; Choix de Poèmes, 1957; Trouées Dans L'Irréel, 1958; L'Ecoute Emerveillée, 1962; Les Comètes du Songe, 1964. Gramophone Record of his poems, L'Académie de Disque de Poésie, Paris. Contbr. to following anthols. & jrnls: Poètes Suisses, 1950; La Suisse; Le Courrier, Geneva; Le Monde; Le Figaro Littéraire; La Nouvelle République de Centre Ouest; Bulletin d'Information et da Pressa, Brussels; Butinons; Le Progrès; Le Bulletin du Livre, Paris; Bibliographie de France, Paris; La Montagne; Journal d'Esch; Bulletin de l'Académie Berrichonne; Les Roses D'Anjou; La Liberté; Tribune de Lausanne; Feuille d'Avis du Valais; Fauille d'Avis de Neuchâtel; La Dépêche du Midi; Poésie Francaise, Paris; Il Giornale dei Poeti, Rome; 10, France; Pour l'Art, Lausanne; Main dans la Main; Le Courrier de l'Académie, France; Lettres, Niort; Le Livre Suisse, Berne; Le Meridional, Marseille. Awards & Honours: Officier de la Renaissance des Lettres et des Arts; Officier du Génie Francais; Officier du Mérite Poétique; Grand Prix, La Haute Académie Internationale de Lutèce; Grand Prix de Feraudy, Paris, 1967. Address: Val d'Aire, 1213, Onex, Geneva, Switzerland.

VUCICEVIC, Stojan, b. 7 July 1941. Writer. Education: Fac. of Philos., Zadar, Yugoslavia; B.A. in Yugoslav Lit. & French Lang. Married. Positions held: Ed., Republika Lit. Review, Zagreb, 1968-73; Freelance Writer. Member, Association of Croatian Writers, 1964–. Published works: Pjesme (Poems), 1964; Greben (Cliff), 1965; Siga (Stalactite), 1966; Cavli (Nails), 1969; Sibanica (The Sibanica), 1971. Contbr. to: Forum; Kolo; Republika; Telegram; Savremenik; Polja; Odjek; Kultura; Secolul 20, etc. Honours, awards: The Skoj Prize for Poetry, 1970; The A.B. Simić Fndn. First Prize, 1970; The Zora Publishing Comp. First Prize, 1972. Address: Društvo Književnika Hrvatske, Trg Republike 7/I, 41000 Zagreb, Yugoslavia.

VUJOVIC, Slobodan, b. 18 Jan. 1939. Teacher of Literature. Education: Lic. in French Letters. Personal details: born in Yugoslavia; Father was principal of High School. Membership: Soc. des Poètes Canadiens-Francais. Published work: Minute Apres Minuit, 1973. Contbr. to La Poésie (Quebec), etc. Address: 9535 Av. Royale, Ste-Anne-de-Beaupre, Quebec, Canada.

VUKELICH, George, b. 5 July 1927. Radio Announcer; Book Editor. Education: Univ. of Wis. Married Helen Gutensohn Frisbie, 5 children. Member, Madison Lit. Club. Contbr. to: Poetry out of Wisconsin, 1961; New Poetry out of Wisconsin, 1969; Idiom; Beloit Poetry Jrnl.; Botteghe Oscure, Rome; Poet Lore; Hawk & Whippoorwill Recalled; Poet of India; Am. Poetry; Wis. Trails; The Capital Times; Wis. Hist. in Poetry. Honours, awards: Best Narrative Poem, 1971; First Prize (for Old Sailor), Poet Lore of Boston. Address: 3934 Plymouth Circle, Madison, WI 53705, U.S.A.

W

WADDELL, David Bruce, b. 20 Apr. 1953. Student. Education: currently studying anthropol. & maths., Univ. of Ark., Little Rock. Contbr. to: New Equinox (Univ. of Ark. Yrly. Publ.); Iced Ink (Univ. of Ark. Yrly. Publ.) Address: 5201 Nelbrook Dr., N. Little Rock, AR 72118, U.S.A.

WADDINGTON, Miriam (Dworkin), pen name **MERRITT, E.B.,** b. 23 Dec. 1917. University Teacher. Education: B.A., Univ. of Toronto, 1939; M.S.W., Univ. of Pa., 1945; M.A., Univ. of Toronto, 1968. Divorced, 2 sons. Positions held: Social Worker until 1964; Tchr., McGill Schl. of Soc. Work, Montreal, 1946-49; Taught Engl. & Canadian Lit., York Univ., 1964–; currently

Prof. Member, Int. PEN Club, Canadian Ctr. Published works: Green World, 1945; The Second Silence, 1955; The Season's Lovers, 1958; The Glass Trumpet, 1966; Call Them Canadians, 1968; Say Yes, 1969; The Dream Telescope, 1972; Driving Home: Poems New & Selected, 1972. Contbr. to num. jrnls., mags., anthols. inclng: The Nation (N.Y.); Poetry Review (London); New Statesman (London); Harper's (N.Y.); Canadian Forum; Prism Int. (Vancouver); Contemporary Poetry (Balt.); Queen's Qtly. (Kingston); Sat. Night (Toronto); Tamarack Review (Toronto); PEN Anthol. Honours, awards: Sr. Fellowship in Poetry, Can. Coun., 1962-63 & 1970-71; Borestone Mt. Awards, 1958, '63; Y.Y. Segal Prize for Best Canadian Book (poetry & prose) with Jewish content, 1972. Address: 32 Yewfield Cres., Don Mills, Ont., Canada M3B 2Y6.

WADDINGTON-FEATHER, John, b. 10 July 1933. Schoolmaster. Education: B.A., Leeds Univ., U.K., 1954; St. Mary's Hosp. Med. Schl., London, 1956-57; Keele Univ., 1972-74. Positions held: Commissioned into Intelligence Corps, qualified as Paratrooper in Airborne Div., 1954-56; Housemaster, HMS 'Worcester', 1957-59; Churchwarden & Prison Visitor. Memberships: Fndr./Co-Ed., Poetry & Audience, Leeds Univ., 1953; Fndr. Mbr., Pennine Platform Poetry Grp., 1967; Fndr. Mbr., Yorkshire Poets Assn., 1970; Fndr. Fellow, Int. Poetry Soc., 1971; Life Mbr., Yorks. Dialect Soc.; Life Mbr., Bronte Soc. Assoc. Ed., Orbis; Ed., Summer Bulletin, Yorks. Dialect Soc. Published works: A Collection of Verse, 1963; Northern Aspect (Ed.), 1965; Of Mills, Moors & Men, 1967; Garlic Lane (verse play), 1971; Easy Street (verse play), 1973. Co-Ed., First Int. Poetry Soc. Anthol., 1973. Contbr. to: Yorkshire Post; Rapport (Canada); Texas Opera News (U.S.A.); Dalhousie Review (Canada); The Listener; Orbis; Pennine Platform; Anglo-Welsh Review; Poetry & Audience; Here Now; Contemporary Review. Address: Fair View, Old Coppice, Lyth Bank, Shrewsbury, Salop, U.K.

WADE, David Lawson, pen names **BROTHER DIMITRIOS, HO CHU TAI, EMIL ROSTOV,** b. 24 Apr. 1934. Lecturer in Creative Writing. Education: B.A., Fla. State Univ., 1956; M.A., Ind. Univ., 1961. Positions held: Lectr., Univ. of Tampa, Fla., 1962; St. Leo Coll., Fla., etc.; Lit. Advisor/Co-Ed., Folio (Ind. Univ.), The Encounter, (St. Leo Coll.), The Stoney Lonesome (Bloomington, Ind.). Has had over 200 poems, short stories, aphorisms, interviews & articles published in univ. & little mags. Produced, in 1966 with two younger writers, the longplay recording 'Four New Poets'. Published works: Death of A Chinese Paratrooper (vol. of 16 poems). Contbr. of articles, reviews, short stories & poetry to num. mags. inclng: St. Petersburg Times; The Spectator, Ind Univ.; American, Wash. D.C.; The Encounter, Fla.; Folio; South & West; Etchings; Trace; Edge (Canada); Poetry Review; Kauri; South Fla. Review; Congress; The Ballantonian, etc. Recip., Fla. Poet of the Year Award, 1962. Address: 515 W. Kirkwood, Apt. 6, Bloomington, IN 47401, U.S.A.

WADE, (Mrs.) Gwendolen, pen name **WADE, Gwen,** b. 24 Aug. 1904. Artist. Education: Queen Margaret's School, Scarborough, 1915-23. Memberships: Internat. Poetry Soc. (Fellow); formerly member, Pennine Poets. Published works: The Golden Galloway, 1966; Anthol. of West Riding Dialect Verse (Editor), 1966. Contbr. to: Country Life; The Lady; Yorkshire Post; The Dalesman; Halifax Courier; Spring Anthol.; Orbis; Platform; Yorkshire Dialect Soc. Transactions; My North Country (Wilfred Pickles); Northern Broadsheet (Dorothy Una Ratcliffe); 'Twixt Thee and Me: an anthol. of Yorkshire and Lancashire Verse and Prose (Joan Pomfret); Anth. West Riding Dialect Verse; Verse from the Ridings. Award: Yorkshire Dialect Soc. prize poem, 1950. Address: The Mount, Littlethorpe Lane, Ripon, Yorks. HG4 1UD, UK.

WADE, John Stevens, b. 8 Dec. 1927. Poet; Painter; Translator. Education: B.S., Conn. State Coll. Published works: First Poems, 1954; Climbs, 1961;

Two From Where It Snows (w. John Judson), 1964; Drowning In the Dark, 1965; Small World, 1966; Poems from The Lowlands, 1967; Gallery, 1969; The Cats In the Colosseum, 1973. Contbr. to approx. 350 publs. inclng: The Nation; Colo. Qtly.; West Coast Review; Prisms Int.; Lit. Review; Voices; New Mex. Qtly.; Kans. Qtly.; El Corno Emplumado; Carleton Miscellany; Confrontation; Prairie Schooner; The Little Review; Wormwood Review; Fiddlehead; Trace; N.Y. Times; South & West, etc. Address: P.O. Box 14, Mt. Vernon, ME 04352, U.S.A.

WADE, Rosalind Herschel, b. 11 Sept. 1909. Novelist; Journalist; Lecturer. Married William Kean Seymour, 2 sons. Positions held: Ed., Contemporary Review, 1970–; Dir. (w. husband), Writers Craft courses, Moor Park Coll., Farnham, Surrey, 1962–. Memberships: Comm., Engl. PEN, 1934-38; Coun., Poetry Soc., 1962-66; Chmn., Soc. Women Writers & Jrnlsts., 1961-64; V.P., ibid, 1965–; Chmn., Alresford Histl. Soc., 1968-70; Lit. Panel, Southern Arts Assn., 1973–; Comm., West Country Writers Assn., 1953-64; Fndr. Fellow, Int. Poetry Soc. Has published over 30 novels. Rep. in following anthols: Happy Christmas, 1968; People Within, 1973; I.W.W.P. Anthol., 1973. Contbr. to: Surrey Advertiser; Outposts; Hampshire Poets; Yorkshire Poets; Weyfarers; Overspill; Books and Bookmen; Hampshire; Contemporary Review; Poetry Review; Surrey Today; Coming Events in Britain; Envoi. Honours, awards: 1st Prize, Hampshire Fed. Community Ctrs.; I.W.W.P. Contest, 1972. Address: White Cottage, Old Alresford, Hants., U.K.

WAGNER, Charles Abraham, b. 10 Mar. 1901. Journalist; Poet. Education: B.A., M.A., Columbia Univ.; Nieman Fellow, Harvard Univ. Positions held: Book Reviewer, Feature Writer, former NY World Book Reviewer, art Critic; Sunday Mag. Ed-in-Chief, NY Mirror, 1933-65; Exec. Sec., Poetry Soc. of Am., 1965–; Mbr., Edit. & Advisory Bd., Int. Who's Who in Poetry, 1969–. Published works: Poems of the Soil & Sea,1923; Nearer the Bone; New Poems, 1930; Harvard: Four Centuries & Freedoms, 1950. Ed., Prize Poems, 1932. Contbr. to the following anthols., jrnls., newspapers, etc: The Nation; Poetry; Sat. Review of Lit.; Bookman; Measure; Voices; Contemp. Verse; NY Times; NY Herald Trib.; Chicago Trib.; Coronet; NY Post; NY Mirror; Poetry Review, etc. Honours, awards: 1st Prize, Poetry Mag., Chicago, 1929; 1st Prize, Stratford Mag., 1930; 1st Prize, Edwin Markham Award, 1932; 1st Prize, Poetry Soc. of Am. Award, 1971. Address: The Poetry Soc. of Am., 15 Gramercy Park, New York, NY 10003, USA.

WAGNER, Georg-Michael, b. 8 Mar. 1924. Actor & Author. Mbr., Poesie Vivante, Geneva. Published works: Nikolaus von Kues–Den Landen zu Frijden, 1961; Christopher Perret-Memorial vol., 1967. Contbr. to: Das Magazin; Neue Zeit; Ekran; Mitteldeutsche Nachrichteu; Der Morgen; LDZY Filmspiegel; Der Neue Weg; Begegnung; Die Union; Sibylle; Jahr des Herrn 1967; Poesie Vivante; St. Hedwigsblatt (Berlin); Tag des Herrn (Leipzig). Honours: Arany-Janos-Medaille (bronze), Budapest, Hungary, 1959, '70. Address: Buschallee 3, 112-Berlin-Weissensee, German Democratic Republic.

WAGNER, Linda Welshimer, b. 18 Aug. 1936. Professor of English. Education: Ph.D., Bowling Green Univ., Ohio; Univ. of BC, Canada. Positions held: Instr., Engl., Bowling Green Univ.; Asst. Prof., Engl., Wayne State Univ., Mich.; Assoc. Prof. of Engl., then Prof., Mich. State Univ. Memberships: Detroit Women Writers. Published works include: Intaglios: Poems, 1967, & many books & essays of criticism. Contbr. to the following publications: Sumac; Cyclo-Flame; Am. Weave; Mainline; Borderline; Essence; Quartet; PS; Fiddlehead; Penny Poems; Caraval; South & West; Zeitgeist; Poet Lore; Goliards; Poetry Review; Human Voice Quarterly; Intermission; Mich. Poets anthol., 1969; Poems From Bowling Green, 1966; Poetry Northwest, etc. Address: Engl. Dept. Mich. State Univ., E Lansing, Mich., 48823, USA.

WAGNER, Marjorie Jeane, pen names **WAGNER, Marje & LLOYD, Marjeane,** b. 15 Apr. 1921. Housewife. Married, 4 children. Positions held: Sunday Schl. Tchr.; Church Clerk; Pastor's Sec.; Tchr. of Tchr. Trng. Classes. Memberships: First V.P., Ala. State Poetry Soc., 1968-70; DeKalb Poets; United Amateur Press; Fndr.-Dir., Christian Amateur Press, 1973. Ed. & Publsr: The Poet Witness, 1968; Keep Christ in Christmas, 1970; Alabama Poet Bulletin, 1968; The Fundamental Watchword, 1968-73; My Cup of Coffee, 1969; The Christian Pen, 1971; Alabama State Poetry Soc. Newsletter, 1968-70; Church Bulletins; Bible Baptist Banner, 1968-73; Pen of a Ready Writer, 1972; Three Thieves & the King, 1972; Unto Us a Child is Born, 1972; What's Going On? (book compiled for local radio stn.), 1968; Mustard Seed Anthol., 1974; Mustard Seed Newsletter, 1973; Crown Jewels, 1973. Contbr. to jrnls., mags., newspapers. Honours, awards incl: 1st pl., Joybells Contest, 1970; Named Poet Laureate of the Scriptures by the Ladies Prayer Band Bible Bapt. Ch., Fort Payne, Ala., 1973; 3rd Prize, Clover Int. Collection of Verse, & Author/Poet; Hon. Mention, for 'Fundamental Watchword', UAP, 1974. Address: 812 Lincoln Ave., N.E., Route 1, Fort Payne, AL 35967, U.S.A.

WAGONER, David Russell, b. 5 June 1926. Professor of English. Education: B.A., Penn State, 1947; M.A., Ind. Univ., 1949. Positions held: Engl. Tchr., DePauw Univ., Penn State & the Univ. of Wash. Published works: Dry Sun, Dry Wind, 1953; A Place to Stand, 1958; The Nesting Ground, 1962; Staying Alive, 1966; New & Selected Poems, 1969; Riverbed, 1972; Sleeping in the Woods, 1974. Contbr. to: The New Yorker; Harper's; Saturday Review; Southern Review; Kenyon Review; Poetry; Yale Review; Chicago Review; Shenandoah; Ohio Review; Salmagundi; Kayak, etc. Honours, awards: Guggenheim Fellowship, 1956; Ford Fellowship, 1964; Poetry Mag.'s Zabel Prize, 1967; Nat. Inst. of Arts & Letters Award, 1967; Nat. Endowment of the Arts Award, 1969. Address: 1075 Summit Ave. E., Seattle, WA 98102, U.S.A.

WAH, Frederick James, b. 23 Jan. 1939. English Teacher. Educ: B.A., Univ. of B.C., Vancouver, Canada, 1962; M.A., S.U.N.Y., Buffalo, U.S.A. Positions held: Tchr., Engl., Selkirk Coll., Castlegar, B.C., Canada, 1967-. Published works: Lardeau, 1965; Mountain, 1967. Contbr. to: Magazine of Further Studies; New Wave Canada (anthology), 1966. Recip., Macmillan Prize for Poetry, 1963. Address: South Slocan, British Columbia, Canada.

WAIN, John (Barrington), b. 14 Mar. 1925. University Professor. Education: B.A., St. John's Coll., Oxford, 1946; M.A., 1950. Positions held: Lectr., Engl. Lit., Univ. of Reading, 1947-55; Churchill Vis. Prof., Univ. of Bristol, 1967; Vis. Prof., Centre Universitaire Expérimental, Vincennes, France, 1969. Fellow, Royal Soc. of Lit., 1960. Published works: Mixed Feelings, 1951; A Word Carved on a Sill, 1956; Weep Before God, 1961; Wildtrack, 1965; Letters to Five Artists, 1969; (fiction) Hurry On Down, 1953; Living in the Present, 1955; The Contenders, 1958; A Travelling Woman, 1959; Nuncle & Other Stories, 1960; Strike the Father Dead, 1962; The Young Visitors, 1965; Death of the Hind Legs & Other Stories, 1966; The Smaller Sky, 1967; A Winter in the Hills, 1970; Ed. & Contbr. various publs. Address: c/o Macmillan & Co. Ltd., Little Essex St., London, WC2, UK.

WAKE, Brian, b. 6 Nov. 1945. Founder & Editor of Driftwood Publications. Positions held: Ed., poetry mags. Matrix, 1966, Asylum, 1967, Driftwood Quarterly, 1968; currently running Driftwood Publs. Published works: Love Poems (for the insane), w. Tony Dash, 1967; Old & Pneumatic Poems, w. Tony Dash, 1967; Ghost of Myselves, 1969; Stars, 1972. Contbr. to: Ambit; Peace News; Iconolatre; Second Aeon; Oasis; Expression; North; Capella; Imprint; The English Intelligencer; Scrip; Mofussil; Contrasts; Grass Eye; Somethings; Arts Alive Merseyside; BBC Radio 3, 4 & Merseyside. Address: 58 Exeter Rd.,

Bootle 20, Lancs., U.K.

WAKOSKI, Diane, b. 3 Aug. 1937. Poet & Lecturer. Education: B.A., Univ. of Calif. at Berkeley, 1960. Positions held: Freelance poetry readings on coll. campuses (approx. 400 colls.), 1967-; Writer in Res., Calif. Inst. of Technol., Spring, 1972, Univ. of Va., Fall, 1972, '73, Wilamette Univ., Spring 1974. Memberships: PEN; Coun. Mbr., Authors' Guild, 1973. Published works: (collections) Coins & Coffins, 1962; Discrepancies & Apparitions, 1966; The George Washington Poems, 1967; Inside the Blood Factory, 1968; The Magellanic Clouds, 1970; The Motorcycle Betrayal Poems, 1971; Smudging, 1972; Dancing on the Grave of a Son of a Bitch, 1973; Trilogy (reprint of first three titles), 1974; Virtuoso Literature for Two & Four Hands, 1975; (slim volumes) Greed: Parts I & II; Greed: Parts III & IV; Greed: Parts 5-7; Greed: Parts 8, 9 & 11; Thanking my Mother For Piano Lessons; & others. Contbr. to var. mags., jrnls., etc. Honours, awards incl: Nat. Endowment Anthol. Prize, 1970; N.Y. State Cultural Coun. Grant, 1971; Nat. Endowment for the Arts Grant, 1973. Address: P.O. Box 4786, Grand Central Stn., N.Y., NY 10017, U.S.A.

WALCOTT, Derek, b. 23 Jan. 1930. St. Lucia, Windward Islands, W Indies. Writer. Positions held: Art Critic, Sunday Guardian, Trinidad; Book Reviewer; Playwright. Published works: (Plays) Sea at Dauphin; Ione; Drums & Colours; Dream of Monkey Mountain, 1969; (poems) In A Green Night; Selected Poems, 1964; The Gulf, 1969, UK & 1970, USA. Contbr. to: The New Statesman; The London Magazine; Encounter; Evergreen Review; The Caribbean Quarterly; Tamarack Review, etc. Honours & Awards: Guinness Award for Poetry, UK; Royal Soc. of Lit. Award; Cholmondeley Prize for Poetry, 1969; Participant, Poetry Int. Festival, London, 1969; Fellowship, Eugene O'Neill Fndn.-Wesleyan Univ. Fellowship for Playwrights. Address: 165 Duke of Edinburgh Ave., Petit Valley, Port of Spain, Trinidad, W. Indies.

WALDMAN, Anne (Lesley), b. 2 Apr. 1945. Poet. Education: Friends Seminary, N.Y.C.; B.A. Literature, Bennington College, Vermont. Co-Editor (with Lewis Warsh) of Angel Hair Magazine and Books, 1965-, Asst. Director, 1966-1968; Director, The Poetry Project at St. Mark's Church In-the-Bowery, N.Y.C., 1968-; Editor, The World Magazine, 1966-. Pubs. On the Wing, 1967; O My Life!, 1969; Baby Breakdown, 1970; Giant Night (selected .poems), 1970; No Hassles, 1971; Memorial Day (in collab. with Ted Berrigan), 1971; The West Indies Poems, 1972; Spin-Off, 1972; Self-Portrait (in collab. with Joe Brainard), 1972; Life Notes (poems), 1973; Editor of 2 anthologies: The World Anthology, 1969; Another World, 1971. Contrib. to: The Paris Review; Yale Lit. Magazine; Changes; Mademoiselle; Newsweek; Rolling Stone; Audit; The Floating Bear; The University Review; Blue Suede Shoes; Adventures in Poetry; Telephone; Poetry Chicago; Contact; Best & Company; Unnatural Acts; The World; Alternative Press; The Iowa Review; Juillard; 49 SoughSouth; Oink!; The Young Am. Poets; Rising Tides; Dial-A-Poem Poets Record, ed. by John Giorno. Recipient, Dylan Thomas Memorial Award, 1967; Poets Foundation Award, 1969. Nat. Literary Anthology Award, 1970. Address: 47 Macdougal Street, New York, N.Y., 10012, USA.

WALDRAFF, Catharine Albright, b. 2 Sept. 1894. Artist & Writer. Education: var. writing courses; Cumnock Schl. of Expression; Univ. of N.M.; studied sculpture under Prof. Gage, Chouinard Schl. of Art & at Univ. of So. Calif. Married Paul H. Waldraff. Positions held: Actress, appearing in Irish plays & Shakespeare; character parts at the Belasco Theatre. Sculptures shown at art galls & sold in many stores. Memberships: Acad. of Am. Poets; Sec., La Mesa Writers Club (now Showcase Writers), 1966; Foothills Art Assn.; San Diego Poetry Soc. Published works: Prose & Poetry, 1968; Inner Light, 1971. Rep. in following anthols: Mitre Press, 3 anthols., 1971-73; Bouquet of Poems, 1972-73; Living Lyrics Anthol.,

1967; Poets on Parade, 1970; Poets Guild Anthol., 1972, etc. Contbr. to: Am. Bard; Bardic Echoes; Encore; Fireflowers, 1973; Hyacinths & Biscuits; Kans. Kernels, etc. Honours, awards incl: Dip., Centro Studi Int., 1972; Book Award, Quintessence, 1972; Cit., Poet of the Month, Poet Laureate, 1972; Gold Medal, 1972. Address: 8557 Roach Dr., La Mesa, CA 92041, U.S.A.

WALKER, Edward Joseph, pen name **WALKER, Ted,** b. 28 Nov. 1934. Writer. Education: St. John's Coll., Cambridge (B.A. Hons., 1956). Married, Lorna Ruth Benfell; 2 s., 2 d. Positions held: Asst. Master, North Paddington Sec. School; Head of French Dept., Southall Tech. School; Head of Languages Dept., Bognor Regis School; Asst. Master, Chichester HS for Boys; Poet-in-Residence, New England Coll., Arundel, from 1971. Memberships: Soc. of Authors; Poetry Soc. (UK). Published works: Those Other Growths, 1964; Fox on a Barn Door, 1965; The Solitaries, 1967; The Night Bathers, 1970; Gloves to the Hangman, 1973. Contbr. to: The New Yorker; The Observer; NY Times; Encounter; The Sunday Times; The London Mag.; The Poetry Review; The Transatlantic Review; The BBC Third Programme; The Critical Qtly.; The Spectator; The Listener; Tribune; Outposts; Times Lit. Supp.; Priapus; Stand; Sunday Telegraph, etc. Recip. The Eric Gregory Award, 1964; The Cholmondeley Award, 1966; The Alice Hunt Bartlett Award, 1968; Major Arts Council of G.B. Bursary, 1972. Address: Argyll House, The Square, Eastergate, Chichester, Sussex.

WALKER, Lois Virginia, b. 23 Oct. 1929. Teacher. Education: B.A., Univ. of Kansas, 1951; B.S., ibid, 1954; grad. study, Victorian Lit., Columbia Univ., 1957-59; New Schl. for Soc. Rsch. Married & divorced. Positions held: Tchr., Lee Ave. Schl., Hicksville, N.Y., 1954–. Memberships: Poetry Soc. of Am.; Acad. of Am. Poets. Contbr. to: Nat. Coll. Anthol. of Poetry; Writers Notes & Quotes; The Am. Poet; The Prairie Poet; The Hartford Courant; The English Record; College English; The Small Pond Mag. of Lit.; Yearbook of Modern Poetry. Address: 485 Front St., Apt. 312, Hempstead, NY 11550, U.S.A.

WALKER, Margaret Abigail. Teacher; Poet. Educ: B.A., Northwestern Univ., Evanston, Ill., 1935; M.A., Univ. of Iowa, 1940. Positions held: Tchr., Livingston Coll., Salisbury, N.C.; Tchr., W. Va. State Coll., Inst. Published works: For My People, 1942; Ballad of the Free, 1966. Contbr. to: (anthologies) Negro Caravan, 1941; Poetry of Freedom, 1945; Poetry of the Negro, 1949; Story Poems, 1957; American Negro Poetry, 1963; Modern Religious Poems, 1964; Black Voices, 1968. Recip. Yale Series of Younger Poets Award, 1942.

WALKER, Nigel John, b. 19 Jan. 1950. Writer. Married. Held var. positions from Office Worker to Broadcaster. Memberships: Merseyside Poetry Festivals Comm.; Treas., Southport Poetry Comm.; Poets Conf.; Poetry Soc.; London Poetry Secretariat; Nat. Poetry Secretariat; Chmn., Poetry Educ. Comm. for Merseyside. Published works: Seaside Revisited (poster), 1972; Collage One, 1972; An Oriental Affair, 1973; Aspects, 1974. Ed., 'Clips', An Anthol. of Poetry of the Cinema. Contbr. to: Pink Peace; Meridian; Caret; Lines; Merseyside Arts Alive; Medium; (anthols.) Roll The Union On, 1973; Granby Is Cool, 1973; Poems from the 3rd World War, etc. Co-presenter (w. Spencer Leigh) of 'No Holds Bard' & later Producer of Poetry Broadcast 'Close Up', both for BBC Radio Merseyside. New poetry broadcast for commercial radio due in April 1974. Address: 14 Lyra Rd., Waterloo, Liverpool, L22 0NT, U.K.

WALKER, Pauline S., b. 23 Apr. 1913. Piano Teacher; Homemaker; Poet. Education: Grad. of Plummer HS; Musical Education at MacPail Center for the Performing Arts, affiliated with Univ. of Minnesota. Personal details: Married, Martin Eldon Walker; 1 s. (Martin Paul). Author, The Things I Love, (poems), 1973. Contbr. to: Pen; Ideals; On the Line; The War Cry; American Bard; The Muse; Writers Notes &

Quotes; The Farmer; Grit; The Kindergartner; Knights of Columbus Minn. Bulletin; Modern Haiku; Haiku West; Haiku Highlights, and The Waif's Messenger. Recip. 2nd Prize, Nat. Camellia Poetry Contest, Capitol Poets Chapter, Calif. Fed. Chaparral Poets, 1968; Winning Poem, Haiku Highlights, 1969; Special Mention, Haiku West, 1970; Hon. Mention, Modern Haiku, 1970, and 1973. Address: P.O. Box 165, Oklee, MN 56742, USA.

WALLACE-CRABBE, Chris(topher) (Keith), b. 6 May 1934. Senior Lecturer in English. Education: Scotch Coll., Hawthorn, Victoria, and Univ. of Melbourne. Married, 1 s., 1 d. Currently, Senior Lecturer in Engl., Univ. of Melbourne; Visiting Fellow, Exeter Univ., 1973. Publications: No Glass Houses, 1956; The Music of Division, 1959; Eight Metropolitan Poems, 1963; In Light and Darkness, 1964; The Rebel General, 1967; Where the Wind Came, 1971; Selected Poems, 1973; Chris Wallace-Crabbe Reads from His Own Work (booklet & record), 1973. Contrib. to many journals, etc. Awarded Farmer's Poetry Prize, Sydney, 1971. Address: 52 Glenard Dr., Heidelberg, Victoria, Australia.

WALLENSTEIN, Barry Jay, b. 13 Feb. 1940. Assistant Professor. Education: B.A., N.Y. Univ., U.S.A., 1962; M.A., ibid, 1963; Ph.D., 1972. Positions held: Instr., Stern Coll., 1964-65; Lectr., The Cooper Union, 1965–; Instr., City Coll. of N.Y., 1965-72; Asst. Prof., 1972–. Member, The Modern Language Assn. Contbr. to: Aurora; The Transatlantic Review; The Washington Square Review; Ararat; Open Places; The Mass. Review; Anon; Gnosis; Dimensions; The N.Y. Times; The Humanist; The Nation; Pot-Hooks & Hangers; (anthols.) The American Experience: A Radical Reader, 1970; Doctor Generosity's Almanac: 17 Poets, 1970. Address: 588 West End Ave., N.Y., NY 10024, U.S.A.

WALPOLE, Terence, b. 24 June 1949. Chef. Education: Highbury Technical Coll., Portsmouth, Hants. Memberships: Ver Poets; The Writers, Friends Meeting House, Edgware. Published works: Alphabet Acrobat, 1972; Perhaps But Not Necessarily, 1972; Infinite Illusions, 1973. Contbr. to: Moonshine; Ver Poets Voices; Grass Eye. Address: c/o Ver Poets, 8A Brickets Rd., St. Albans, Herts, U.K.

WALSH, Chad, b. 10 May 1914. English Professor. Educ: A.B., Univ. of Va., Charlottesville, 1938; Ph.D., Univ. of Mich., 1943. m. Eva May Tuttle, 1938, 4d. Positions held: Rsch. Analyst, U.S. Army Signal Corps, 1943-45; Fac. Mbr., Engl. Dept., Beloit Coll., Wis., 1945–; Wis. Prof., Wellesley Coll., Mass., 1958-59. Published works: The Factual Dark, 1949; Eden Two-Way, 1954; The Psalm of Christ, 1964; The Unknowing Dance, 1964; The End of Nature, 1969. Ed., Doors into Poetry, 1962; Today's Poets: American & British Poetry since the 1930's, 1964; Garlands for Christmas, 1965; The Honey and the Gall: Poems of Married Life, 1967. Contbr. to: Saturday Review; New York Times; Spirit; Sewanee Review; Georgia Review; (anthologies) Heartland, 1967; Poems from Hospital, 1968. Honours, awards: Major Hopwood Award, 1939; Spirit Award, 1964; Coun. for Wis. Writers Award, 1965; Golden Anniversary Poetry Award, 1965. Address: 745 Church St., Beloit, WI 53511, U.S.A.

WALTER, Nina Willis, b. 11 June 1900. Free-lance Writer & Lecturer; Emeritus Professor of English. Education: A.B., Univ. of Calif. at Los Angeles; M.A., Univ. of Southern Calif. Positions held: Tchr., LA Elem. Schls.; Tchr., LA City High Schls.; Prof. of Engl., LA City Coll., currently Emeritus. Memberships: Poetry Soc. of S Calif.; Writers Club of Whittier; Am. Poetry League; Calif. Fed. of Chaparral Poets; Pasadena Writers Club; Fndr. & 1st Pres., Creative Writing Tchrs. Assn. of LA, & others. Published works include: Brush Strokes, 1948; People-Watching, 1966; Let Them Write Poetry, 1962; Flame in the Clod, 1973. Contbr. to the following jrnls. & mags: Personalist; Poet Lore; Fine Arts Discovery; Ave Maria; Bapt. Leader; Westminster; Poetry Forum; Catholic World; Chicago

Jewish Forum; Chicago Trib.; Christian Advocate; Christian Home; Christian Living; Cardinal; Driftwood; Discourse; Encore; Husk; Human Voice; Imprints; Interaction; Kans. Quarterly; Laurel Review; McCall's; Time of Singing, & many others. Recip. of sev. poetry awards, including Plaque, City of Pico Rivera, for outstanding achievement in the field of poetry, 1968. Address: 9331 Cosgrove St., Pico Rivera, Calif. 90660, USA.

WALTERS, Bryan, pen name **CYNFYN.** Poet; Writer; Literature Officer, West Midlands Arts Association. Identifies himself with the medieval Welsh poets and, in particular, Dafydd ap Gwilym. Has translated a number of medieval Welsh poems into English. Memberships: (listed) London Poetry Secretariat; The Nat. Poetry Secretariat. Published works: Between Dawns, 1972; Tir-na-Nog, 1973; ...To Remember, 1973; Images of Stone, 1973; Cloud Flowers, 1973; Seen but not Scenery, 1974; From the Welsh (translations of Medieval Welsh poems), 1974; George Borrow, A Biography, 1973; Long Play Recording, Bryan Walters & Bryn Griffiths read their own poetry (Decca/Argo PLP 1189), 1973. Poetry Editor for 2 yrs. of Midland United Newspapers. Contbr. to numerous newspapers, mags. etc. Also reads his poetry regularly on BBC-TV and Radio. Address: 18/19 Cartway, Bridgnorth, Shropshire, UK.

WALTERS, Dorothy May. Teacher; Housewife; Poet. Education: Coll. of Educ., Leeds, UK; Courses, Nottingham Univ. & Bristol Univ. Married, Gerald Walters, Univ. prof., 1948. Positions held: Music Chmn., Bath Fed. Townswomans Guilds; Sec. Bath. Conservative Womens Coun.; Chmn., Soc. Studies Grp., Bath. Memberships: City of Bath Lib. & Mus. Comm.; Conservative Pol. Ctr.; Exec. Comm., Friends of Holburne Mus.; Nat. Nats. Rep., Nat. Coun. of Women; Union of European Women; Commonwealth Coun.; Norwood Soc.; Bath. Univ. Ladies Assn. Published Works: And Will the Robin Sing Again, 1965; This Little Paradise, 1969; Because A Rainbow Danced, 1970; In the East A Star (verse play), 1970; A Journey to Bethlehem (verse readings, performed Bath Abbey), 1969; The Virgin's Lullabye (sung, Bath Abbey), 1967. Contbr. to: The Technol.; Technol. & Society; Ilkeston Pioneer; Nottingham Guardian Jrnl.; Derbyshire Advertiser; Spring Anthol., 1970, '71. Recip., Human Rights Award, Bath, 1968. Address: Queen Anne House, The High St., Batheaston, Bath BA1 1RA, Somerset, UK.

WALTERS, Florine (Saia) Petkoff, b. 10 Dec. 1911. Clerk, Secretary, Typist, Poet. Education: Course in Creative Writing, Phillips Community Coll., Helena, Ark. Married (1st), George Petkoff, 1936; 2 s., 1 d.; Widowed, 1965; Married (2nd), Andrew J. Walters, Sr., 1970. Positions held: Receptionist-Secretary; Clerk Typist; Asst. Officer Worker; Clerk-Sec., American Bakeries (for 18 yrs.). Memberships: Sec., East Central Branch, Ark. Poet's Roundtable (also past Pres., past Vice-Pres.); Poet's Roundtable of Ark., since 1967. Contbr. to: Memphis Commercial Appeal; Helena West; Helena World; Twin City Tribune; Courier-Index; Saline County News; Saline County Pacesetter; North Little Rock Times; Reliable Round Robin; Poems by Poet's Roundtable of Ark. Anthol., 1970, 1971, 1972, 1973. Awards: 1st Place, Poet Laureate Award, Ark. Poetry Day, 1971; Top Honor, monthly contest, Poet's Roundtable of Ark., Nov. 1969; Book Award, for best monthly poem published by Poet's Forum, Apr., 1971; Sev. hon. mentions for best monthly poems contests, East Central Branch of Ark. Poets (at intervals), 1968-1973. Address: 504 College St., Helena, AR 72342, USA.

WALTERS, Ollie Pauline, b. 24 Jan. 1912. Poet. Married L.H. Walters. Positions held: Mgr., Children's Foster Home, 1942-52; Dental Nurse, 1952-55; Bookkeeper, 1956; Private Duty Nurse, 1957-67; Publisher & Writer, 1967-71; V.P., Desert Writers Workshop of Imperial Valley, 1972; Chmn. of the Bd. of Directory in the United Amateur Press, 1972; Owner, Yuha Desert Press, 1973-; Publisher, Poets

on Parade. Memberships: Pres., Desert Writers' Workshop of Imperial Valley; Pres., United Amateur Press Assn. of Am.; Poetry Soc. of Tex.; Nat. Press Assn.; The Am. Amateur Press Assn.; Int. Platform Assn.; V.P., Waller Family Assn. Published works: My Heart Remembers, 1963; I Remember, 1969; Thoughts From My Pen, 1969; From My Album of Memories, 1970; My Happiness, 1971. Contbr. to: Hyacinths & Biscuits; Writers Bulletin; Golden Harvest Anthol.; The Last U.S. Frontier Anthol., etc. Recip. sev. awards inclng: Readers Companion Award, 1969; Ozark Cardinal Award, 1971. Address: 644 S. 7th St., El Centro, CA 92243, U.S.A.

WALTON, Peter, b. 28 June 1936. Town & Country Planner. Education: B.A., Fitzwilliam Coll., Cambridge Univ., U.K.; Dip. in Town & Country Planning, Univ. of Manchester. Married Elisabeth, 2 sons (David & Robert). Positions held: Planning Asst., Cheshire Co. Council; Town Planner in pvte. prac.; Sr. Planning Officer, Dept. of the Environment. Published works: Poetry from Cambridge, 1958 & Poetry Workshop, 1973, included in anthologies; A Crown for David, 1970. Contbr. to: Delta (Cambridge); The Anglo-Welsh Review. Address: 33 Finney Dr., Wilmslow, Ches. SK9 2ES, U.K.

WANG, Jyh-jiann, pen name, **SHANG, Guan-Yui,** b. 24 Oct. 1928. Education: B.A., Nat. Taiwan Univ. Married; 2 s., 1 d. Positions held: Member, Editing & Screening Committee, Chinese TV Service; Sec.-Gen. of Chinese Poets' Assoc., 1958-67; Deputy-Chief of School of New Poetry, Chinese Artist & Poets' Assoc., since 1968; Assoc. Prof. of Poetry, World Journalism Coll., since 1968. Membership: Chinese Writers' & Artists' Assoc. (Deputy Chief); Chinese Youth Assoc. (Chief, Seminar for Creation of New Poetry). Published works: Sea, 1944; The Fatherland is Calling, 1951; Song of Liberty, 1955, 2nd ed., 1957; Banner Keeper, 1965; Flower of Thousand Leaves, 1968; Poem Collections of Ten Years' Work, 1958; Treasure of Chinese Poems of these 60 Years, 1973; In Praise of May (in progress); On Literature, 1967; Chinese Poems in the Past Fifty Years, 1963. Contbr. to: Central Daily News; United Daily News; Taiwan Hsin Sheng Pao; China Daily News; Literature Monthly; Literature Mag. Recip. of several awards from Chinese Lit. Scholarship Committee, Chinese Writers' & Artists' Assoc., Chinese Lit. Scholarship Assoc., etc. Address: Apt. 3, 17 Lane 390, Tun Hwa South Rd., Taipei, Taiwan, Repub. of China.

WANG, Si-Chiu, pen name **SHU, Tik,** b. 3 Jan. 1905. Publisher. Memberships: Chinese Pen Ctr., Hong Kong. Published works: Examination of Traditional Chinese Calligraphy; Autobiog. of an Anonymity; Coll. of Homeward Poems; Concept–Nat. Defence; The New Thesis of Chinese Intellectuals; The New Thesis of Chinese Poets; The Life of Chuo Yuen; Retrospects on Chinese Culture; 25 Chuo Yuen's Poems in Pak Hua Translation; Philippine Travel Diaries in the South. Contbr. to: Hong Kong Times; Kung Sheung Daily News; Wah Kiu Yat Po; The Observatory Review; Eastern & Western Culture; The Nation; The Observation Post; Current Democracy; Current Lit.; The Liberty. Honours: Philippine Assoc. of Drs. in Law; Internat. Acad. of Leadership; United Poets Laureate Internat. Address: Alpha House, Flat E, 5th Floor, 27-33 Nathan Rd., Kowloon, Hong Kong.

WANG, Ta-jen, b. 19 Oct. 1912. Member of the Legislative Yuan, Repub. of China. Education: B.A., Nat. Northeast Univ.; Hon. Doctorate, Hongkong Tahan Univ. Married to Kuei-yung Tung; 2 s. Positions held: Member of the Legislative Yuan; Prof., Nat. Chengchi Univ. Memberships: Dr. Sun Yat-sen's Teaching Research Inst.; Chung Hsing Poetry & Songs Research Soc.; Personnel Admin. Inst. Published works: General Statement of Dr. Sun Yat-sen's Teachings, 1960; Contemporary Education, 1963; Manchurian Literature Review, 1971; Ta-jen Poem Collection, 1965. Contbr. to: Oriental Mag.; New Power Mag.; Parliamentary Mag. Award: 1st Prize, New Year Poem Contest, 1971. Address: No. 84 Chiu-

Kang St., Mucha, Taipei, Taiwan, Repub. of China.

WANG JUNG-CHIH (Mrs. Han Jen Tsun), pen name, **YUNGTZE,** b. 4 May 1928. Member of Sr. Staff of Chinese Government Radio Administration. Education: Experimental Course, Ginling Women's Coll.; Chien Chun Agricultural Coll. Personal details: Married to poet and critic, Lomen. Positions held: Teacher; Sr. Staff of C.G.R.A.; Editor of poetry mag.; Instructor; Speaker as Prof. on poetry and childrens lit. in colls. and univs.; Lecturer to overseas Chinese young writers in Manila, Philippines; Chief of the poetry section, Summer Seminar of Lit.; Judge to the poetic prize of young poets of Repub. of China. Memberships: Standing Supervisory Bd., Chinese Young Writers' Assoc.; Vice-Dir., Creative Poetical Writing Comm., Chinese Writers & Artists Assoc.; Bd. of Directors, Chinese Women Assoc.; Commissioner of Chinese Cultural Renaissance, Taipei Branch; Member, Chinese Ctr. of Internat. PEN; UPLI. Published works: The Blue Bird, 1953; South, in July, 1961; Yungtze Poem, 1965; City of the Innocent, 1967; Verna Liza Suites, 1969; Flute & Harp at Noontide, 1974. Contbr. to numerous anthols., journals, newspapers. Recip. of numerous honours (UPLI, and Gold Medal, President Marcos, Philippines, 1966; World Congress of Poets, Manila, 1969; H.L.M. (Hon.), Int. Acad., Hull, U.K., 1970; Hon. Ph.D., World Acad. of Philosophy, Brazil, 1972), etc. Address: C.G.R.A., Corner of Sinyi & Hangchow South Rd., Taipei, Taiwan, Repub. of China.

WANG TZAY-JIUN, b. 8 Aug. 1920. Poet. Education: Military Acad. (21st Infantry Br.). Married Alice Lee, 3 children. Positions held: Capt., Company Commdr., Newsman & Editor; Publsr., The Vine Yard, the Poetry Qtly.; Publsr.-Ed. in Chief, Entrepreneur Mag. Publ. Inc.; Dir., New Poetry Assn.; Advisor, Tzun Yuan Oil Mfg. Co. Ltd.; General Manager, Entrepreneur Communication Ltd. Memberships: Chmn., Vine Yard Poetry Qtly.; Dir., Chinese New Poetry Assn.; Rep. to World Congress of Poets. Published works: Rain & Tears, 1969; Heart Lake, due for publ. Contbr. to newspapers, mags. Recip., Decretum of Award, issued by Second World Congress of Poets. Address: Entrepreneur Mag. Publ. Inc., No. 6, Lane 14, Nanking East Rd., Section 3, Taipei, Taiwan, Rep. of China.

WANG-YAO, Wu, b. 1 May 1932. Chemical Industrialist. Education: Chemical Engineer. Married; 4 children. Positions held: 1965–, Shareholders & Gen. Manager, Viso Co., Vietnam; 1969–, Pres., Tico Co., Vietnam. Membership: Blue Stars Club, Taiwan. Published work: Song of the Soul, 1955; The Horizon, 1958; City of the Roses, 1958. Contbr. to: (Taiwan) United Daily News; Blue Stars; Cosmorama; Literature Mag.; Central Daily News; Modernist Poetry Qtly.; (Vietnam) Everybody Daily News; Success Daily News. Address: 121-A An-Binh St., Saigon, South Vietnam.

WANTLING, Wm. (Dewein), b. 7 Nov. 1933. Poet. Education: B.S. Ed., 1971, M.S., 1973, Ill. State Univ. Academic Appointee, Instr. in English and Creative Writing, Ill. State Univ., 1973. Member: COSMEP. Publications: The Search, 1964; Five Poem Songs, 1964; Machine and Destiny, 1965; Head First, 1965; Heroin Haikus, 1966; Down, Off and Out, 1966; The Source, 1967; The Awakening, 1967; 1968; Sick Fly, 1970; Obscene & Other Poems, 1972; 10,000 RPM, 1973. Contrib. to: Penguin Modern Poets 12, 1969, and to more than 300 magazines, newspapers, and anthols. Recip. Hart Crane Mem. Fund Poetry Award, 1969; Pentabarf Poet of the Year Award, 1971. Address: R.1, Towanda, Ill. 61776, USA.

WARBURG, Joan Emma Violet, b. 13 Nov. 1902. Child Psychotherapist. Education: King's Coll., London Univ. Positions held: Child Psychotherapist, London Hosp. & other hosps. Memberships: PEN; Poetry Soc., London; English Assn. Published works: (books of poetry) Gossamer & Honey, 1918; Poems, 1935; The English Year, 1943; The Secret Spring, 1958; The

Golden Boy, 1966; The Listening Ground, 1971. Contbr. to: The Christian Sci. Monitor; Country Life; The Countryman; The Field; The Observer; The Dublin Review. Poems collected for Harvard Univ. under special award scheme, U.S.A. Address: 22 Marlborough Ct., Pembroke Rd., London W.8, U.K.

WARBURTON, Thomas Henry, b. 4 Mar. 1918. Publisher's Editor; Translator. Married. Positions held: Literary Ed., Holger Schildts, publishers, 1944–. Memberships: Finland's Svenska Författareförening; Corres. Mbr., Svenska Litteratursällskapet i Finland. Published works: (colls. of poetry) Du, människa, 1942; Bröd av lera, 1945; Slagruta, 1953; Kort parlör, 1966; Leve revisionismerna!, 1970; (translations) Mitt i ett krig (Engl. & Am. poetry), 1945; Det langbenta betet (Engl. & Am. poetry), 1952; Helkasanger by Eino Leino (from Finnish), 1963; Spoon River Anthol. by Edgar Lee Masters, 1967. Contbr. to: BLM, Stockholm; Nya Argus, Helsinki; Parnasso, Helsinki; etc. Recip., Awards from Svenska Litteratursällskapet, 1946, 54, 67, 71. Address: Ostra Allen 16B, 00140 Helsinki 14, Finland.

WARD, Gabrielle Stephanie, pen name **JACK-O-LANTERN,** b. 11 Jan. 1908. Councillor. Widow. Positions held: County Alderman; Member of Gloucestershire County Council, 1952–. V.P., Cheltenham Poetry Soc. Contbr. to: Cheltenham Poets, 1971; People Within, 1973. Honours, awards: Winner of Appleby Cup, Cheltenham Competitive Fest., 1971; Winner, local comp., 1973; 2nd at Watford Fest. Poetry Comp., 1972. Address: Fieldgate House, Bishop's Cleeve, Glos., U.K.

WARD, John Powell, b. 28 Nov. 1937. University Lecturer. Education: Univ. of Toronto, Canada; Univ. of Cambridge, UK. Positions held: Ran Youth Club, Southampton, 1961-63; Lectr. in Educ., Univ. Coll. of Swansea, Wales, 1963–. Mbr., Poetry Soc. of GB. Published work: The Other Man, 1969. Contbr. to: Listener; Times Lit. Supplement; Tribune; Transatlantic Review; 20th Century; Delta; London Mag.; Poetry Wales: Anglo-Welsh Review; etc. Address: Bridge Cottage, Cheriton, Gower, S. Wales, UK.

WARD, Lois (Merritt), pen name **WARD, Lois Merritt,** b. 17 Jul. 1920. Administrative Clerk, U.S. Government. Pubs. World's Fair Anthology of Verse, 1937; Journey in the Sun, 1973. Address: Route 4, 300 Williamson Valley Road, Prescott, Arizona 86301, USA.

WARD, Martin Lindsay, b 28 Aug 1945 Librarian. Education: Jesus Coll., Cambridge Univ.; Coll. of Librarianship, Wales. Contbr. to: Hampshire Poets. Address: 14 Oakmount Ave., Southampton, SO2 1DR, Hants., U.K.

WARD, Mary B., pen names, **LATHAM, Linn; ATCHISON, Amy; ORDWAY, Jack.** Poet; Editor; Lecturer. Education: Univ. of Ala. Personal details: widow of Herbert J. Ward. Positions held: Ed., The Gammadion, a Lit. Mag., 1925-27; Contbng. Ed., Yankee Humor, 1926-27; Assoc. Ed., Poetry Forum, 1930-31; Feature Writer, Birmingham News, Ala., 1932-33; Edit. Staff, The Ala. Fed. of Women's Club Mag., 1935-36; Poet Laureate of Ala., 1954-59; Ala. Ch. Nat. Poetry Day, 1949-55, etc. Memberships: Charter Member, Birmingham Quill Club, Pres., 1925; Pres., Birmingham Poetry Club, 1930-31; Also Charter Member, Pres., First Ala. Poetry Soc., 1940; Charter Member and 2nd V.P., Ala. State Poetry Soc., 1968 when organized; Pres., Birmingham Branch of NLAPW, 1938-39; Pres., Ala. Writers' Conclave, 1938-39; Moderator numerous Panels Poetry & Juvenile fiction; Dean of Poetry, Ala. Conclave, Samford Univ.; Life Member, Ala. Fed. Women's Clubhouse; Charter Member, Birmingham Chap. Nat. Soc. Arts & Letters; Charter Member, Ala. Council Nat. Soc. Patriotic Women of Am. Inc., Press, 1960-62; Life Member, Ala. Libns. Assoc.; Co-Ch., 7th Municipal Garden Club Show; Member, Avon Internat. Poetry Soc.;

Birmingham Hist. Assoc.; Ala. Historical Assoc.; Arlington Hist. Assoc.; Nat. Fed. of State Poetry Socs.; Birmingham Museum of Arts Assoc.; Ed. Bd. of Ala. Poetry, 1945; Co-author, Historic Homes & Gardens of Ala., 1935. Published in every issue to-date of The Sampler, Ala. State Poetry Soc. vol. Published works: Heavenly Bundles, 1956; Thicket Clearers, 1960; Selected Poems, 1967, and 1968; Thoughts at Christmas, 1969. Contbr. to: Hall of Fame Poets, 1969; Am. Poetry; NLAPW; Pictorial Review; Sat. Eve. Post; Good Housekeeping; Psychology; Progressive Farmer; Liberty; Extension; Sat. Rev. of Lit.; Sewanee Review; Ave Maria; Catholic Home; Golden Book; Town Topics; Christian Observer; Christian Advocate; Ind. Business Women; Birmingham Bus. Woman; Pen Woman; Ala. Hist. Qtly.; The Furrow, NY Times; Washington Star; CS Monitor; Portland Oregonian; Charlotte Observer; Charleston Eve. Post; KC Star; Birmingham News; Birmingham Post Herald; Montgomery Advertiser, etc., also many poetry mags. Awards: Elberta Clark Walker Award, 1939; Gold Poet Laureate of Ala. Medal, 1954; Citation SW Writers' Conf., 1955; Avon Int. Award, 1958; U.N. Day Award of Honor, 1968; DIB Cert. of Merit, 1968; Award of Honor, Ala. State Poetry Soc., 1969, and numerous other state, national, and Internat. Poetry Awards and Honors. Address: 512 So. 55th St., Birmingham, AL 35212, USA.

WARD, Philip, b. 10 Feb. 1938. Librarian. Education: Profl. qualifications in Librarianship. Married, 2 daughters. Positions held: Has worked abroad in dev. of Lib. Services, most recently as UNESCO Co-Mgr. of the Nat. Lib. Serv. Proj. for Indonesia, based in Jakarta. Memberships: Fndng. Sec. of Private Libs. Assn., 1956 & for 7 yrs. Ed. of 'The Private Library'. Published works incl: Collected Poems, 1960; Loakrime, poem, 1967; Seldom Rains, poems, 1967; Poems for Participants, 1968; At the Best of Times, poems, 1968; A Musical Breakfast, play, 1968; Apuleius on Trial at Sabratha, essay, 1968; Touring Libya: the Eastern Provinces, 1969; A Lizard & Other Distractions, stories, 1969; Tripoli: Portrait of a City, 1969; The Fiction List of Murdoch, Lenz, 1969; Maps of the Ceiling, poems, 1970; Spanish Literary Appreciation, 1970; Sabratha, 1970; Touring Lebanon, 1971; Touring Cyprus, 1971; Touring Iran, 1971; Come With Me To Ireland, 1972; A House on Fire, poems, 1973. Contbr. to many lit. mags. & jrnls. Recip., Guinness Poetry Prize for poem 'Neither in that far Corn-Summer', 1961. Address: c/o United Nations Dev. Prog., P.O. Box 2338, Jakarta, Indonesia.

WARD, Wm. Fletcher, b. 7 Nov. 1900. Merchant; Farmer; Rancher; English & Music Teacher. Education: B.F.A., Univ. of Okla., 1928; Masters degree, ibid, 1948; 3 months study at Nottingham Univ., U.K., 1948; course of Hist. of Art & Music, Cambridge Univ., U.K. Positions held: Tchr. of Music & Engl., H.S. of Okla.; Rancher, 1936-47; Merchant, Norman, Okla., 1948-73. Member, Okla. Poetry Soc. Published works: Bobbed Tailed Versis & One Long Tale, poetry, 1967; Uncommon Clay Poems, 1971. Contbr. to: Okla. Today mag.; Restricted Domain; Persimmon Hill; Cottonwood Trees; South Canadian River; Spring Anthol., 1972. Address: 1016 West Lindsay Rd., Norman, OK 73069, U.S.A.

WARDEN, Bette Ruth Coker, pen names **COKER, Bette & SPECK, Bette,** b. 4 Mar. 1925. Writer of Poetry & Fiction. Education: Basic Psychol., Univ. of Monticello, Ark., 1966. Married, 2 sons, 1 daughter (dec.). Positions held: Bookkeeping Machine Op., Federal Govt.; wrote radio commercials for KOTN Radio, Pine Bluff; Asst. Soc. Ed.-Feature Writer, Pine Bluff Commercial, 1958-59; Asst. Mgr., Variety store, Stockton, Calif., 1959, etc. Memberships: South & West Inc.; World Poetry Soc. Intercontinental; Southeast Arts & Sci. Ctr. Contbr. to: Grit newspaper; Mark Twin Jrnl.; The Muse; Monticellian Advance; Radio KCLA, Pine Bluff; Contemporary Poets of Ark., 1971; Prog. 'Pine Bluff in Review'; Radio KHBM AM FM 'Afterglow'; Pine Bluff News; Cummins Jrnl.; Poet

(India); Christian Herald, etc. Honours, awards: Hon. Mention, Young Romances, 1971; Won Blue Ribbons, St. Luke United Ch. Fest., 1973; Blue Ribbon, Pine Bluff Dist. Fair, 1973 & Little Rock (State) United Meth. Conf. Fair & Fest., 1973. Address: 66 Western Dr., Pine Bluff, AR 71601, U.S.A.

WARDLAW, Catherine, b. 6 Dec. 1902. Retired School Teacher. Education: B.A., Univ. of Tex. Memberships: Poetry Soc. of Tex.; Histn., Odessa Chapt., ibid; The Odessa Creative Writers; American Poetry League; Ill. State Poetry Soc.; United Amateur Press; Am. Poetry Fellowship Soc. Contbr. to: Encore; Cyclo-Flame; Sweet 70s Anthol.; Shore Line Anthol.; American Poets; United Poets; Major Poets; Prairie Poets. Awards: Five 1sts & two 2nds, Odessa Poetry Soc., 1971. Address: 1710 Royalty, Odessa, Tex. 79760, USA.

WAREHAM, John, b. 31 Oct. 1941. College Lecturer. Education: B.Sc. (Hons.). Member, The Poetry Soc. Contbr. to: Equator; The Listener; Hampshire Poets; Sousaphone; Platform; BBC Radio Three 'Poetry Now'. Address: 235 North Ave., Southend-on-Sea, Essex. SS2 4EJ, U.K.

WARNER, Francis, b. 21 Oct. 1937. Lecturer & Fellow. Education: Christ's Hosp., St. Catharine's Coll., Cambridge. Married, 2 daughters. Positions held: Fellow & Tutor in Engl. Lit., St. Peter's Coll., Oxford, 1965-; Univ. Lectr. in Engl. Published works: (poetry) Perennia, 1962; Early Poems, 1964; Experimental Sonnets, 1965; Madrigals, 1967; The Poetry of Francis Warner, 1970; (plays) Maquettes, a trilogy of one-act plays, 1972; Lying Figures (Part One of Requiem, a trilogy), 1972; Meeting Ends, (Part Three of Requiem, a trilogy), 1974. Contrb. to var. mags., jrnls., etc. Recip., Messing Int. Award for disting. contbns. to the world of literature, 1972. Address: St. Peter's Coll., Oxford, U.K.

WARNER, Rex, b. 9 Mar. 1905. Novelist; Teacher; Poet. Educ: Wadham Coll., Oxford, U.K. m. Frances Chamier Grove, 2s., 2d. Positions held: Dir., British Inst., Athens, Greece, 1945-47; Tallman Prof., Bowdoin Coll., Brunswick, Me., U.S.A., 1962-63; Tchr., Univ. of Conn., Storrs, 1968-. Published works: Poems, 1937; (novels) The Wild Goose Chase, 1938; The Professor, 1939; The Aerodrome, 1947; Escapade: A Tale of Average, 1953; Imperial Caesar, 1960; Pericles the Athenian, 1963; The Converts, 1967. Contbr. to: (anthologies) Poems of Today, 1938; A New Anthology of Modern Verse, 1920-1940, 1951; Poetry of the Present, 1949; Penguin Book of Contemporary Verse, 1950. Honours, awards: Cmdr., Royal Order of the Phoenix, Greece, 1963; D.Litt., Rider Coll., Trenton, N.J., U.S.A., 1968. Address: Univ. of Conn., Storrs, CT, U.S.A.

WARNER, Val, b. 15 Jan. 1946. Freelance Copy Editor. Education: Somerville Coll., Oxford Univ., 1965-68. Published works: These Yellow Photos, (pamphlet), 1971; Under the Penthouse, (book), 1973; The Centenary Corbière (translation), 1974. Contbr. to: Poetry Review; Ambit; Carcanet; The Dublin Mag.; Ostrich; Tribune; Workshop; Critical Quarterly; Anglo-Welsh Review (translation); Southern Arts Review; Caret; Antaeus; Poetry Nation. Recip., Dip., Engl. Section of Gradara Poetry Comp., Italy, 1971. Address: c/o 15 Bouverie Grdns., Kenton, Harrow, Middx., HA3 0RQ, U.K.

WARREN, Eileen. Poet. Positions held: Served on Editl. Co-operative of Workshop New Poetry, 1971-72; Inaugurated a scheme for the sale of poetry books by living poets in a Supermarket & instigated a Display of Workshop Press Poetry, at the Ideal Homes Exhib., 1973. Memberships: The Poetry Soc.; Poets' Workshop; Poets' Conf.; Nat. Poetry Secretariat. Published works: A Match in the Dark, 1970. Contbr. to: Country Life; This England; Manifold; Scrip; Outposts; Workshop New Poetry; Expression I; Envoi; Samphire; Pink Peace; Ore; Towards Survival; Caret; Reading Mercury; Berkshire Mercury; Cork Weekly

Examiner; Poetry Soc. Newsletter; Ver Poets Poetry Post, etc. Rep. in following anthols: Landemus Te, Manifold, 1967; Versewise, 1968. Poetry Readings at: Hammersmith Town Hall; Friends Int. Ctr.; Nottingham Poetry Soc.; Running Horse Pub; Poetry Soc., etc. Honours, awards: Manifold Award, 1968; Poetry Soc. Premium Comp. Winner, 1972; Poetry Soc. Silver Medal in Poetry Reading & in Verse Speaking. Address: 23 Hereford House, 370 Fulham Rd., London S.W.10, U.K.

WARREN, Francis Eugene, pen name **GINO,** b. Oct. 1941. Teacher. Education: B.A., Kans. State Tchrs. Coll., Emporia, 1966; M.A., ibid, 1967. Married, 4 children. Positions held: Instr. in Engl., Univ. of Mo., Rolla., 1967-73; Asst. Prof. of Engl., ibid, 1973-. Memberships: N.Y. C.S. Lewis Soc.; Fine Arts Fellowship; Conf. on Christianity & Literature; Order of the Golden Elbow (First Master Klastidator). Published works: Christographia, 1973; The Fifth Season, 1974. Contbr. to: Folio; Green River Review; CHRISTIANITY Today; Eternity; Human Voice; Kansas Qtly.; The Mennonite; Poetry Bag; Quill; The Good Seed; (anthols.) Adam Among the Television Trees; Poets of the Resurrection, etc. Address: 107 South Rolla, Rolla, MO 65401, U.S.A.

WARREN, Hamilton, b. 16 Feb. 1898. Retired Businessman. Education: Litt.B., Princeton Univ. Married Janet Ward, 1 son, 1 daughter. Positions held: V.P., Nat. Carbon Co. (Div. of Union Carbide). Memberships: The Poetry Soc. of Am. Contbr. to: The Golden Year, 1960; The Diamond Anthol., 1971; Award Winning Poems, 1966 & 67; N.Y. Times; Sat. Evening Post; Unitarian-Universalist Register Ltr., Boston, Mass.; The Villager, N.Y.C.; Household Mag.; The Richard Wagner Qtly. Honours, awards: 1st Prize, Annual Award, Poetry Soc. of Am., 1965, 2nd Prize, 1965, 1st prize, 1970; 3rd prize, Rochester Fest. of Religious Arts, 1967, etc. Address: Shearer Rd., Washington, CT 06793, U.S.A.

WARREN, James Edward, Jr., born 11th December, 1908. Teacher. Education: B.A. & M.A.T., Emory Univ., Ga.; Ga. State Coll.; Yale Univ.; Cambridge Univ. Positions held. Tchr., Atlanta Public Schl. System, 1933-59; Part-time Instr., Ga. Inst. of Technol., 1958-60; Hd., Engl. Dept., The Lovett Schl., 1959-; Assoc. Ed., Verse Craft, 1933-46; Reviewer of Poetry Books, Atlanta Jrnl., Atlanta Times, Verse Craft, etc.; Sponser of Signature lit. mag., The Lovett Schl.; Former Ed., Ga. Engl. Counselor; currently Ed., Creative Writing Issues. Memberships: Trustee, Ga. Writers Assoc.; Poetry Soc. of Am.; Fellow, Internat. Inst. of Arts & Letters; Poetry Soc. of Va.; Poetry Soc. of Ga.; Atlanta Writers Club. Publications: This Side of Babylon, 1938; Against the Furious Men, 1946; Altars & Destinations, 1964; Trembling Still For Troy, 1965; Greener Year, Whiter Bough, 1966; Selected Poems, 1967; The Winding of Clocks, 1968; Listen, My Land, 1971; Mostly of Emily Dickinson, 1972. Contbr. to: Atlantic Monthly; Saturday Review; Western Humanities Review; Good Housekeeping; The Lyric; Ga. Review; Southern Poetry Review; Prairie Schooner; Emory Univ. Quarterly; Envoi; Manifold; Delphi Quarterly; La Voix des Poetes; Step Ladder; South & West; Cresset; Engl. Jrnl.; Educ. Forum; Classical Outlook; Classical Bull.; N. Am. Review; Sewanee Review; N.Y. Times; Deutsche Tagespost; Fiddlehead; Canadian Poetry Mag; Wis. Poetry Mag; Ga. Mag; Essence; Zebra Am. Weave; DeKalb Lit. Arts Jrnl; Archon; Poetry Digest; Verse Craft; Thistle; Sparrow; Poetry Review; Voices; East Anglian Mag; N.Y. Herald-Trib.; Kaleidograph; Yank; Poet Lore; Husk; & many other jrnls. & anthols. Contbr. to transls. of Horace, Catullus, Propertius, Tibullus, Martial & Sulpicia to various classical jrnls., etc. Honours: Annual Award, Poetry Soc. of Am., 1937; Barrow Prize, 1945, 1947; Leitch Mem. Prize, 1967; Ga. Writers Assoc. Lit. Achievement Award in Poetry, 1967; Aurelia Austin Writer of the Year Award, 1968; Nathan Haskell Dole Prize, 1971; Maywood Prize, 1972. Address: 544 Deering Rd., N.W., Atlanta, Ga. 30309, U.S.A.

WARREN, Robert Penn, b. 24 Apr. 1905. Writer. Education: B.A., Vanderbilt Univ., 1925; M.A., Univ. of Calif., Berkeley, 1927; Yale Grad. Schl., 1927-28; B.Litt., Oxford Univ., 1930. Positions held: Asst. Prof., Southwestern Coll., Memphis, Tenn., 1930-31; Asst. Prof., Vanderbilt Univ., 1931-34; Asst. Prof., La. State Univ., 1934-36; Assoc. Prof., ibid, 1936-42; Prof., Univ. of Minn., 1942-44; Chair of Poetry, Lib. of Congress, 1944-45; Prof., Univ. of Minn., 1945-50; Prof. of Playwriting, Yale, 1951-56; Prof., Engl., Yale, 1961-73. Memberships: Bd. Mbr., Am. Acad. of Arts & Letters; Chancellor, Am. Acad. of Poets. Published works incl: XXXVI Poems, 1936; Eleven Poems on the Same Theme, 1942; Selected Poems, 1944; Brother to Dragons, 1953; Promises, 1957; You, Emperors & Others, 1960; Selected Poems, New & Old, 1966; Incarnations: Poems, 1966-68, 1968; Audubon: A Vision, 1969. Contbr. to: Fugitive; Nation; Yale Review; New Republic; Encounter; Poetry Mag.; Southern Review; N.Y. Review of Books, etc. Recip. many poetry honours & awards inclng: Millay Award, Am. Poetry Soc., 1958; Nat. Book Award for Poetry, 1958; Pulitzer Prize for Poetry, 1958; Bollingen Prize for Poetry; Nat. Medal for Lit., 1970. Address: 2495 Redding Rd., Fairfield, CT 06430, U.S.A.

WARSAW, Irene, b. 26 Nov. 1908. Administrator. Positions held: Sec., State Office, Fed. Life Ins. Co.; Private Sec. to Pres. of ind. trust co., later, Peoples Nat. Bank & Trust Co. of Bay City, Mich.; VP & Trust Officer, ibid. Memberships: Nat. League of Am. Pen Women (Mbr. at large); Detroit Women Writers: Poetry Soc. of Mich. (Edit. Cons.); Pa. Poetry Soc.; Poets' Study Club of Terre Haute, Ind.; Nat. Fed. of State Poetry Socs.; Am. Acad. of Poets; Int. Platform Assn. Published works include: A Word in Edgewise, 1964, 1966, 1969, 1973. Contbr. to the following anthols.; jrnls., mags. etc.: Golden Quill anthols.; The Sat. Evening Post; Wall St. Jrnl.; The Christian Home; Good Housekeeping; McCall's; The Atlantic; Maclean's; Chatelaine; Writer's Digest; Christian Sci. Monitor; Cosmopolitan; Nation's Business; 1000 Jokes; Author & Journalist; Denver Post Empire; The Rotarian; Kan. City Poetry Mag.; Reflections; Greater Works, Pen Mag.; Am. Weave; NY Times Mag.; Purpose; Reader's Digest; The Pen Woman, etc. Recip. of num. prizes & awards. Address: 1309 6th St., Bay City, Mich. 48706, USA.

WARSH, Lewis, b. 9 Nov. 1944. Poet. Education: B.A., City Coll. of N.Y., U.S.A., 1966. Positions held: Co-Editor, Angel Hair Books & The Boston Eagle. Published works: The Suicide Rates, 1967; High Jacking, 1968; Moving Through Air, 1968; Chicago (w. Tom Clark), 1969; Dreaming As One, 1971; Long Distance, 1972: Part of my History, 1972. Contbr. to: Big Sky; Adventures in Poetry; The Ant's Forefoot; The World; This; The Paris Review; The End; Poetry; Telephone; The Harris Review, etc. Honours, awards: Poets Fndn. Award, 1968 & 72. Address: 216 E. 10th St., N.Y., NY, U.S.A.

WARSHAUER, Rose Virginia, b. 30 Jul. 1917. Secretary. Education: Grad. of P.S. 44, Queens; Grad. of Far Rockaway HS; NY Univ. 1 yr.; Ann Reno Teachers Training, 2 yrs.; Editorial Courses, NY Univ. with Beatrice Cole; Poetry Courses, New School for Social Research with Jose Garcia Villa. Positions held: Sec.-Treas., Weaver Organization Inc.; Sec.-Treas., Rayette Fabrege; Sec., Mal Klein Associates. Memberships: Eastern Center of Poetry Soc. (London), World Poets Resource Center; American Guild of Authors & Composers (Public Relations and Recruiting); American Soc. of Authors, Composers and Publishers. Published works: World Poets Resource Center Serail Paper Back Qtly., 1971; World Poets 3, 1971; lyrics for "Gee It's Love", 1968. Awards: Special Award, 1st Annual Internat. Poets Workshop, 1971. Address: 123 Washington Pl., New York, NY 10014, USA.

WARTER, LOUIS, b. 3 Feb. 1900. Retired. Lectr. or Guest Speaker at classes teaching the Humanities at: N.Y. Univ.; L.I. Univ.; The Henry George Schl., etc.;

Fndr.-Dir., Aquarian Publishers, N.Y. Memberships: Past Pres., Speakers' Club, N.Y., the Vegetarian Soc. of N.Y., the Tri-State Br. (N.Y., N.J., Conn.) of the Nat. Hlth. Fed.; currently Sec., N.Y. Poetry Forum, Inc. Published works: 'I Am a Giant' (a 2000 word poem glorifying the redwood trees of Calif., published in booklet form), 1968. Contbr. to: Sat Sandesh; Ahimsa. Address: 180 East 163rd St., Bronx, NY 10451, U.S.A.

WASSERMAN, Leib, b. 27 Aug. 1913. Economist and Book-keeper. Pubs. Silent Light (poems); My Nights and Days (poems). Contrib. to: The Word; Free Labor Voice; The Future; Jewish Combatant; On the Threshold; Our Time; Almanac. Awarded Carl Rotman Fund Prize (World Congress for Jewish Culture). Address: 1185 Lebanon Street, Apt. 1-K, Bronx, New York 10460, USA.

WATERMAN, Paul, b. 3 July 1903. Farmer (semi-retired). Education: Grad., HS, Worcester, NY; Cazenovia Seminary, NY (now a Jr. Coll.); Cornell Univ., B.A., 1926. Memberships: American Haiku Soc., NYC.; Western World Haiku Soc., Portland, Oregon; Ulmas. Published works: Boy for a Blond, 1932; Cabin for two, 1934; Love to the Town, 1955; Whimseys, 1968; Brief Candles, 1968; Wee Wings, 1967; Five Lines to Limerick, 1965; Those Brats From Limerick, 1966; Mad Land of Limerick, 1965. Contbr. to: Haiku Highlights; Jean's Journal; Echoes; The Saint; Poetry Preview; Harbor Lights; Mizpah Messenger; Nutmegger; The Written Word; Pacific Breeze; Cats Mag.; Hunting & Fishing; United Poets; Am. Poets; Prairie Poet; Friendship Poetry; Tempo; Bay Shore Breeze; Tejas; The Cazenovian; Worcester Times; Cornell Sun; Modern Haiku; Dragonfly, etc. Honours, Awards: Cert. of Recognition for Merit in Poetry, NY State Poetry Contest, 1968; 1st & 2nd for Haiku, Nutmegger; 5th in limerick & 1st, internal rhyme. Haiku Highlights; 4th in Haiku & 1st in limerick, Tajas; 1st, winter issue, Mod. Haiku, 1970; Hon. Mention, Modern Haiku, 1973. Address: Magnolia Hotel, Starke, FL 32091, USA.

WATKINS, Gordon R., b. 24 Dec. 1930. Writer; Director; Producer; Composer; Conductor. Education: B.S., M.S. in Voice, Juilliard Schl. of Mus., 1953-60; Jarahal Schl. of Music-Voice, Rep., Acting; Katherine Dunham Schl. of Dance; M.A., Directing, Hunter Coll., Grad. Schl. of Theatre, 1974; New Schl. for Soc. Rsch.-Film Directing. Married, 1 daughter. Positions held: Profl. Performer, TV, Theatre, Concerts & Nightclubs, 1963-67; Exec. Dir., Mount Calvary Theatre, N.Y.C., 1967; Asst. to Dir./Instr., Champlain Shakespeare Fest., 1968; Prod./Dir., Community Theatre Prof., Queen of Angels Ch., Newark, N.J., 1968-69; Assoc. Dir., Hudson Guild, N.Y.C., 1968-69; Instr., Rutgers Univ., N.J., 1968-70; Exec. Dir., Rutgers Community Theatre Workshop, 1969-70; Producer, WCBS TV, 1970-71; Prod./Dir./Writer, 'What Happened to Brownsville' WNBC's N.Y. Illustrated series, 1972; Pres., The Toussaint Grp., Inc., 1971-. Performed and/or published works incl: Expostulations of a Watkins (coll. of poems & essays); Tinkerman to the Promised Land (mus. drama); A Lion Roams the Streets (a poetic protest ritual drama w. full musical score); Sojourner Truth (a poetic play). Honours, awards incl: Nat. Assn. of TV Prog. Executives Award for Excellence in the Performing Arts, 1971; Ohio State Award for Excellence in TV Prod. Address: The Toussaint Grp., Inc., 420 East 51st St., Suite LD, N.Y., NY 10022, U.S.A.

WATSON, Robert, b. 26 Dec. 1925. Poet. Education: Williams College, B.A., The Johns Hopkins Univ., Ph.D. Instructor of English, Williams and Johns Hopkins; Prof. of English, The Univ. of N.C. at Greensboro; Visiting Prof. and Poet in Residence, Univ. of California at Northridge, 1968-69. Pubs. A Paper Horse, 1962; Advantages of Dark, 1966; Christmas in Los Vegas, 1971; Selected Poems, 1974; Contrib. to: Poetry; American Scholar; New Yorker; Kenyon Review; Sewanee Review; Transatlantic Review; Southern Poetry Review; The New York Times; Antaeus; The Above Ground Review;

Shenandoah Review; Impetus; Red Clay Reader; New American Review. Honours: American Scholar, 1959. Address: 527 Highland Avenue, Greensboro, N.C. 27403, USA.

WATSON, Roderick, b. 12 May 1943. University Lecturer (in English). Education: Aberdeen Univ., U.K., 1961-65; Ph.D., Peterhouse, Cambridge Univ., 1966-69. Married, 1 son. Positions held: Lectr. in Engl., Univ. of Victoria, B.C., Canada, 1965-66; Rsch. Student & Writer, 1966-71; Lectr. in Engl., Dept. of Engl. Studies, Univ. of Stirling, 1971-. Member, Assn. for Scottish Lit. Studies. Published works: 28 Poems (w. James Rankin), 1964; Roderick Watson, Parklands Poets No. 7, 1970; Trio (w. Paul Mills & Val Simmons), 1971. Rep. in sev. Scottish Poetry anthols. & in a forthcoming Carcanet anthol. of Contemporary Scottish Poetry. Contbr. to: Aberdeen Univ. Review; Akros; Lines; Scottish Int.; Delta; Spirit (N.J.); Cairn. Short stories & poems broadcast on Radio 3 & Radio 4. Has done many readings at Art Council programmes, Edinburgh Festival, Writers in School. Schemes, Poetry Socs., etc. Recip., Scottish Arts Coun. Bursary, 1970-71. Address: 19 Millar Pl., Stirling FK8 1XD, U.K.

WATSON, Wilfred. Professor. Educ: Univ. of B.C., Vancouver, Canada; Ph.D., Univ. of Toronto. Positions held: Served, Canadian Navy; Prof., Am. Lit., Univ. of Alta., Edmonton, current. Published works: Friday's Child, 1956. Contbr. to: Canadian Literature; Fiddlehead; (anthologies) Penguin Book of Canadian Verse, 1958; Oxford Book of Canadian Verse, 1960; Poetry 62, 1961. Honours, awards: British Coun. Fellowship for Creative Writing, 1955-56; Canadian Gov.-Gen. Award for Poetry, 1956. Address: Dept. of Engl., Univ. of Alta., Edmonton, Alberta, Canada.

WATTER, Lola Sheila, b. 13 Jan. 1925. Teacher; Art Critic. Educ: Univ. of Witwatersrand, Johannesburg, S. Africa; B.A., Univ. of S. Africa, Pretoria; Nat. Art Tchrs. Dip., Witwatersrand Tech. Coll. Art Schl. Positions held: Hd., Art Dept., Athlone Girls' H.S., Johannesburg, 1959-; Art Critic, Arts Review, S. African Broadcasting Corp., 1966-. Contbr. to: Contrast; New Coin; Purple Renoster; Wurm; New Nation; De Arte; Lantern. Address: 95 13th St., Orange Grove, Johannesburg, S. Africa.

WATTERS, Eugene Rutherford, pen name **TUAIRISC, O. Eugman,** b. 3 Apr. 1919. Author; Poet; Novelist; Playwright. Education: M.A., Univ. Coll., Dublin, Eire. Positions held: Commn., Army of the Rep. of Ireland; Primary Tchr.; Ed., Feasta; Author. Memberships: Soc. of Gaelic Writers. Published works include: The Week-End of Dermat & Grace, 1965; Lux Aeterna, 1965. Contbr. to the following anthols., jrnls.; mags., etc.: PEN Anthol.; Feasta; Combat; Irish Times; Irish Press. Honours, awards: Douglas Hyde Mem. Award, 1965; Arts Coun. Prize for Verse Drama, 1960; Oireachtas Prize, 1962. Address: The Cross, Knockananna, Arklow, Co. Wicklow, Ireland.

WAUTELET, Josephine LeGrave, pen name **WAUTELET, Josie,** b. 20 Feb. 1915. Housewife; Former Teacher. Education: Grad., Door Kewaunee Co. Tchrs. Coll.; Wis. State Univ., Madison. Married Edward Wautelet, 2 sons, 3 daughters. Memberships: Pres. & Treas., Christian Mothers; Pres. & Sec., Homemaker Club; Sec., Door Co. Deanery; Chmn., County Cultural Arts; County Cancer Comm.; Pres., Parish Coun.; Parish Rep. to Vicariate; Family Affairs Chmn. for Vicariate (4 counties); Wis. Fellowship of Poets; Wis. Regl. Writers Assn.; Door Co. Writers. Published works: Homespun, pamphlet of poetry, 1971; story in 'I Remember' paperback book, 1973. Contbr. to: Ideals; The Spirit; Writers Showcase; Door Co. Advocate; Landhandler; Farm Wife News. Recip., 2nd Prize, Wis. Regl. Writers Jade Ring Contest, 1972. Address: R.1, Brussels, WI 54204, U.S.A.

WAUTERS, Marcel, b. 9 Oct. 1921. Poet. Member, Flemish PEN Ctr. Published works: Er is Geen Begin en Geen Einde, 1950; Apoteek, 1958; Anker en Zon,

1960; Hipoteek, 1962; Nota's Voor een Portret, 1967; Als de Nachtegaal Toeslaat, 1969; Voor een Waterdruppel (Tekeningen). Contbr. to Flemish & Dutch lit. publs. Recip., Dirk Martens Prize, 1963. Address: 175 Dikke Beuklaan, 1020 Brussels, Belgium.

WAUTIER, André, pen names **THIERRY, André, LAURE, Thierry & d'HYVER, Jean,** b. 11 Mar. 1918. Civil Servant. Education: LL.D. Memberships: Fondation Charles Plisnier (Legal Advisor); PEN; Centro Studi e Scambi Int. (Mbr., Int. Comm.) Published works: Lyre, 1939; Cendre et Guirlande, 1941; Prismes, 1944; Du Souvenir au Rêve, 1947; Orphée aux Enfers, 1948; Frissons, 1949; Artémis désarmée, 1950; Eros et Psyché, 1951; Mystères, 1954; Errances, 1960. Has translated poems from Dutch, English, Italian & from French to English. Contbr. to: La revue irréaliste (Brussels); Le Miroir des Muses wallonnes (Brussels); Fair-Play (Liège); Amérique Française (Montreal); Marches de France (Alost); OEuvres nouvelles (Lodève); Le Bayou (Houston); Momentum (Balerna), etc. Address: 18 rue Fred. Pelletier, 1040 Brussels, Belgium.

WAZYK, Adam, pen name **WAZYK,** b. 17 Nov. 1905. Writer. Married, 2 daughters. Member PEN Club. Published works: Semafory (The Semaphores), poems, 1924; Oezy i usta (Eyes & Mouth), poems, 1925; Mity rodzinne (The Family Myths), novel, 1938; Serce granatu (Heart of Grenade), war poems, 1945; Poemat dla dorostych (Poem for Adults), 1956; Epizod (Episode), novel, 1960; Labirynt (The Labirynthe), poems, 1961; Wagon, poems, 1963; Kwestia gustu (Matter of Taste), essay, 1966. Contbr. to: Zwrotnica, 1925-26; Kuźnica, 1946-49; Tworczosc, 1951-55. Honours, awards: Prize of PEN Club for translation, 1951; State Prize, 1953. Address: Aleja Roz 8, 00556 Warsaw, Poland.

WEARNE, Alan Richard, b. 23 July 1948. Writer. Positions held: Commonwealth Public Servant, 1969 & 72. Published works: Public Relations, 1972. Contbr. to: The Age; Makar; Poetry Australia; New Poetry. Address: c/o State Savings Bank of Victoria, Bush House, The Strand, London, U.K.

WEAVER, Clarence Lahr, b. 5 Nov. 1904. Cataloger/Librarian (retired); Poet; Editor. Education: A.B., Ohio Wesleyan Univ., Delaware, 1926; B.S. in L.S., Western Reserve Univ. School of Library Science, Cleveland, Ohio, 1934; M.S. in L.S., Univ. of Michigan Library School/Horace H. Rackham School of Grad. Studies, 1959. Married Gertrude Viola Pratt, 1926 (dec. 1970); Children: Eleanor Janet; Kenneth Harmon; Charles Albert; Carol Lynne. Positions held: Clerk, Order of Bookfellows (publishers of The Step Ladder, a lit. journal), Chicago, 1926; Apprentice proofreader & cut-room Asst., The Lakeside Press, Chicago, 1926-30; Landscape gardener, Cleveland, Ohio, area, 1931; Dairy farmer, South Euclid, Ohio, 1932-33; Head cataloger & asst. editor (Library/Publications), Ohio Hist. Soc., Columbus, 1934-46; Chief Catalog & Order Dept., Public Library, Grand Rapids, Michigan, 1946-69; Library Consultant, Grand Rapids Teachers Credit Union, 1971-. Memberships: Engl. Writers Club, Ohio Wesleyan Univ.; Verse Writers Guild of Ohio; Ohio Poetry Day Assoc. (Treas., 1939-41); The Bards, Grand Rapids (Chaplain, 1957-66); Poetry Soc. of Michigan (Vice-Pres., 1972 onwards); American Lib. Assoc.; Michigan Lib. Assoc.; Michigan Reg. Group of Catalogers (Pres., 1953); Theosophical Soc. of America (Pres., Grand Rapids Lodge, since 1970); Kent Philatelic Soc., Grand Rapids (Vice-Pres., 1972-73); etc. Published works: Editor & Publisher: The Quickening Seed (poetry qtly.), 1933-46; Bardic Echoes (poetry qtly., The Bards) since 1960; Bardic Echoes Brochures (Echoes series, v. 1-6), 1967-73; With All My Love, 1936; A Bard's Prayers, 1967. Contbr. to numerous newspapers, journals, anthols., etc. Recip. of sev. awards. Address: 1036 Emerald Av., N.E., Grand Rapids, MI 49503, USA.

WEAVER, James E(dwin), pen name **JAMES, Dwin,** b. 14 Oct. 1942. Librarian; Poet; Artist. Education: A.B., Philos. & Religion, McPherson Coll., 1964; M. Div., Ministry, Bethany Theological Seminary, 1968; M.L.S., Librarianship, Indiana Univ., 1972. Positions held: Asst. Libr., Armour & Co. Food Res. Div., Oak Brook, Ill., 1965-67; Liby. Asst., McPherson College, McPherson, Ks., 1968-70; Pastor, Germantown Brick Church of the Brethren, Rocky Mount, VA., 1970-72; Librarian, Marion Correctional Inst., Marion, OH., 1972-. Member, Pennsylvania Poetry Soc; Assn. for the Arts in the Church of the Brethren. Contrib. to: Brethren Life and Thought; Messenger; American Coll. Poetry Soc. Anthology (1962); America Sings (1963); Here Not in Vain Are We (1961); Collage; A Collection of Thoughts...of the McPherson College Community (1970); Internat. Who's Who in Poetry Anthology, (1972-73), etc. Address: 1001 Bermuda Drive, Marion, OH 43302, USA.

WEAVER, Marvin Eugene, b. 12 Sept. 1944. Teacher; Horse Trainer. Education: B.A., Univ. of Ala., 1966; M.F.A., ibid, 1968. Positions held: Instr., Univ. of Ala. Middle Tenn. State Univ., Univ. of N.C. at Greensboro; Vis. Poet, N.C. 'Poetry in the Schools' prog.; Lectr., Soul City Learning Lab. Contbr. to: The Hollins Critic; Kansas Qtly.; The Greensboro Review; The Arlington Qtly.; The Miss. Review; The North Carolina Anvil; Brown Bag; Comment. Recip., Prize for Lyric Poetry, Norfolk, Va. Lit. Fest., 1972. Address: Rte. 2, Box 481-C, Hillsborough, NC 27278, U.S.A.

WEBB, Bernice Larson. University Professor. Education: B.A., Univ. of Kan., U.S.A., 1956; M.A., ibid, 1957; Ph.D., 1961. Positions held: Instr., Engl., Univ. of Kan., 1958-59 & 1960-61; Asst. Prof., Engl., Univ. of Southwestern La., 1961-67; Assoc. Prof., Engl., ibid, 1967-. Memberships: Nat. Fed. of State Poetry Socs., Inc.; Ed., La. Poetry Soc., 1970-; Corres. Sec., ibid, 1970-; Publicity Chmn., Southwest Br., La. State Poetry Soc., 1970-. Contbr. to approximately 80 publs. (jrnls., mags., newspapers, anthols.) inclng: AAUP Bulletin; The Kan. City Times; The Denver Post; The Horn Book Mag.; Essence; The Lyric; The Fiddlehead; Ball State Univ. Forum; Quoin; Epos; Voices; Voices Int.; Cyclo-Flame; The Laurel Review; The New Laurel Review; Encore; Personal Poetry: Best Broadcast Poetry (anthol.); The Best in Poetry (anthol.); Dance of the Muse (anthol.) Recip. of approx. 85 poetry prizes from 1946-73. Address: Box 861, Univ. of Southwestern La., Lafayette, LA 70501, U.S.A.

WEBB, Ethel, pen name (occasionally) **ROCH, Dalby,** b. 3 July 1925. Housewife; Writer. Education: B.A., Univ. of Western Australia. Married Colin Webb, 4 children. Positions held: Tchr. of Engl., Maths & Econs., St. Hilda's C. of E. Girls' Schl., Perth; Mss Appraisals for Australian Writers Profl. Service. Memberships: Australian Soc. of Authors; Australian Writers Professional Service; Fellowship of Australian Writers; Australian Soc. of Women Writers. Contbr. to: Twentieth Century (Australia); Westerly; Poetry Mag.; Poetry Australia; Poet, India. Honours, awards: Commended, Patterson Poetry Prize, N.S.W., 1963 & '65; 3rd Prize, Bunbury Poetry Prize, W.A., 1973; 1st Prize, Goondiwindi Poetry Prize, Qld., 1973. Address: 29 Napier St., Cottesloe, W.A. 6011, Australia.

WEBB, Francis Charles, b. 8 Feb. 1925. Poet. Educ: Sydney Univ., Australia. Positions held: Served w. Royal Australian Air Force, WWII; Worked for Canadian publishers. Published works: A Drum for Ben Boyd, 1948; Leichhardt in Theatre, 1952; Birthday, 1953; Socrates and Other Poems, 1964; The Ghost of the Cock, 1964; Collected Poems, 1969. Contbr. to: Meanjin; (anthologies) New Voices, 1959; Literature of Australia, 1964. Recip., Commonwealth Lit. Fund Fellowship, 1960. Address: c/o K. Snell, "Brewarrina", Thomas Rd., Galston, N.S.W., Australia.

WEBB, Harri, b. 7 Sept. 1920. Librarian Education: Nat. Schl. & Glanmore Schl., Swansea; Magdalen

Coll., Oxford. Positions held: Published; Bookselling; Chief Libn., Mountain Ash, 1964–. Memberships: Yr. Academi Cymreig; Lit. Panel, Welsh Art Coun. Published works include: The Green Desert, 1969. Contbr. to the following anthols., jrnls., mags., etc.: Wales; Life & Letters; Welsh Republican; Poetry Wales; Cilmeri. Honours, awards: Welsh Art Coun. Prize, 1970. Address: The Central Lib., Dyffryn Rd., Mountain Ash, Glamorgan, Wales, UK.

WEBB, Phyllis, b. 1927. Poet. Educ: Univ. of B.C., Vancouver, Canada; McGill Univ., Montreal, P.Q. Published works: Trio (w. others), 1954; Even Your Right Eye, 1956; The Sea Is Also a Garden, 1962. Contbr. to: Saturday Night; Tamarack Review; Canadian Literature; (anthologies) Penguin Book of Canadian Verse, 1958; Oxford Book of Canadian Verse, 1960. Recip., Canadian Government Overseas Fellowship, 1957-58.

WEBER, Hulda, pen name of **KATZ, Hilda,** b. 2 June 1909. Artist; Poet. Memberships: Authors League of Am.; Poetry Soc. Am.; Int. Poets Shrine; Life Fellow, Metropolitan Mus. Art. Represented in permanent collections: Metropolitan Mus. Art; Nat. Gall. Art; N.Y. Pub. Lib.; Nat. Collection Fine Arts; US Nat. Mus.; Univ. of Me. Art Mus.; Lib. of Congress; Nat. Air & Space Mus. Publs: (Children's Short Stories) Juan & the Prize; One Small Cruise; Why is this Night Different; The Synagogue of Yourself; The Sabbath is a Delight; The Good Deed; Jose & Sea Mamma. Contbr. to: (anthols.) Blue River Anthol., 1959; Treasures of Parnassus – Best Poems, 1962; The Cavalcade of Poetry – Best Poems, 1963; Melody of the Muse – Best Contemp. Poetry, 1964; Personal Poetry – Best Broadcast Poetry, 1969, '70; Avalon Anthol., 1960; Golden Harvest Anthol. – Best Contemp. Poetry, 1967; 1st Int. Poetry Soc. Anthol.; (jrnls.) Poetry Digest; Flatbush Mag.; The Christian; Blue River Poetry; Hartford Times; Vespers; Orphic Lute; Lutheran Companion; Scimitar & Song; Wis. Poetry Mag.; Villager; The Explorer; Am. Bard – Impression Portraits; Hartford Courant; Dasein Mag.; Poetry Personalities Page; My Baby Mag.; We Do It Together Mag.; The Christian Home; Am. Bard – The Experimentalist; Ch. Schl. Mag.; Bitterroot Mag.; etc. Broadcast on Personal Poetry, WHPL-AM, NBC. Honours: Rep. in Internat. Poetry Shrine; 2nd Award, Am. Bard, Am. Indian Contest, 1961; Hon. Mention, Writers Mag., 1958; 2nd Award, Wis. Poetry Mag., 1962; Ed's. Award, Orphic Lute, 1963; 1st Award, Relig. Poetry, The Explorer, 1961; Award Plaque, Exec. & Profl. Hall of Fame, 1966; Award Plaque, Community Ldrs. of Am., 1969, '70; Daughter of Mark Twain, 1970; Fndr. Mbr., Int. Poetry Soc.; Bettie Payne Wells Award, Am. Bard, 1972, & many other poetry & art awards. Address: 915 West End Ave. Apt. 5D, New York, NY 10025, USA.

WEBER, Marc Lee, b. 26 Nov. 1950. Poet. Education: B.A., Univ. of Colo., 1972; currently working on M.A., ibid. Married Linda Ruth Bohe. Positions held: Operator of Granite Harp Bookstore, Colo. Springs, 1972-73; Ed.-in-Chief, Riverrun; Poetry Ed. of New Day, 1972; Poetry Ed. of Weasel, 1972-73. Published works: 48 Small Poems, 1973. Recip., Int. Poetry Forum's U.S. Award for 1972. Address: 2 N. 24th St., Colo. Springs, CO 80904, U.S.A.

WEBER, Richard, b. 2 Sept. 1932. Poet; Lecturer; Book-Reviewer. Education: Nat. Coll. of Art, Dublin, 3 yrs; B.A., Univ. of Mass., U.S.A. Positions held: Asst. Ed., publishing mag. in London; Sec. to Percy Lubbock, C.B.E. (author of The Craft of Fiction), Italy; Vis. Lectr. in Engl., Mount Holyoke Coll., South Hadley, Mass., U.S.A., 1967-70. Published works: O'Reilly Poems, 1957; The Time Being, a long poem, 1957; Lady & Gentleman, poems, 1963; Stephen's Green Revisited, poems, 1968; A Few Small Ones, poems, 1971. Contbr. to: The Times Lit. Supplement; The Irish Times; Transatlantic Review; The Observer; The N.Y. Times; The Irish Press; The Mass. Review; Studies; Time & Tide; The Dubliner; The Nation; The Dublin Mag.; Poetry Ireland; Irish Writing; Truth;

Dolmen Miscellany; Broadsheet; Icarus; Delta; Univ. Review; The Irish Independent; Hibernia; Continuum; Chanticleer; Satis; The Malahat Review; The Kilkenny Mag.; The Fortnightly; Threshold; Review of English Lit.; Gemini. Address: Ballyknockan, Valleymount, Co. Wicklow, Ireland.

WEBER, Sarah Appleton, pen names **APPLETON, Sarah** (for poetry) & **WEBER, Sarah Appleton,** (for criticism), b. 4 Apr. 1930. Writer; Teacher. Education: B.A., Vassar Coll., 1952; M.A., Ohio State Univ., 1957; Ph.D., ibid, 1961. Married Joseph G. Weber, 1 son, 1 daughter. Positions held: Tchng. Asst., Ohio State Univ., 1955-61; Instr., Smith Coll., 1962-65; Poetry Ed. for Literature East & West, 1967-68; Radcliffe Inst. Scholar, 1970-72. Published works: Theology & Poetry in the Middle English Lyric: A Study of Sacred History & Aesthetic Form, 1969; The Plenitude We Cry For, long poem, 1972. Contbr. to: Commonweal; Am.; Midwest Engl. Review; Forum; Anthol. of Mag. Verse for 1958. Readings at Ohio State, Smith Coll., Everson Mus. at Syracuse, etc. Address: 124 Dorset Rd., Syracuse, NY 13210, U.S.A.

WEBLEY, Julia Mary, b. 16 June 1956. Student. Education: Purbrook Park Co. Grammar Schl.; Balls Park Tchrs. Trng. Coll., Hertford. Member, Poetry Soc. of Am. Contbr. to: Hampshire Co. Mag.; The Purbrookian. Honours, awards: Jt. Winner, Int. Who's Who In Poetry Contest, 1972-73; Winner, Poets & Painters (Oxfam) Comp.; Winner, Own Poem Sect., Portsmouth Arts Fes., 1972. Address: 176 Hazleton Way, Horndean, Hants. PO8 9DZ, U.K.

WEBSTER, Mary Morison, b. 26 Jan. 1894. Edinburgh, Uk Book Critic; Author. Education: Edinburgh Colls. Personal details: Sister of Elizabeth Charlotte Webster, novelist. Published works: To-Morrow, 1922; The Silver Flute, 1930; Alien Guest, 1933; Garland in the Wind, 1938; Flowers from Four Gardens, 1957; Mercury Book of English Verse. Contbr. to num. anthols. Recip. of Pringle Award for Lit. Criticism, 1965. Address: 22a Pietersen St., Johannesburg, S Africa.

WEDER, Heinz, b. 20 Aug. 1934. Medical Publisher. Ed. of: Gegenwart und Erinnerung, a collection of German-Swiss prose, 1961; Eduard Korrodi: Aufsätze Zur Schweizer Literatur, 1962; Fritz Ernst: Aufsätze zur Literatur, 1963; Ludwig Hohl: Wirklichkeiten, Prose, 1963; Briefe von Albin Zollinger an Ludwig Hohl, 1965; Gottfried Keller über Jeremias Gotthelf, 1969; Jean Cassou: Oeuvre lyrique/Das lyrische Werk, 1971; Hommage an Carl Spitteler, 1971; Ulrich-Bräker-Lesebuch, 1973. Published works: Klaus Tonau, Prose, 1958; Kerbel und Traum, Poems, 1962; Kuhlmann, Prose, 1962; Figur und Asche, Poems, 1965; Niemals wuchs hier Seidelbast, Poems, 1967; Walter Kurt Wiemken: Manifeste des Untergangs, 1968; Johann Gaudenz von Salis-Seewis, 1968; Der Makler, Prose, 1969; Gegensätze, Poems, 1970; Die Schwierigkeiten mitdem Mülleimer, 1970; Uber Rodolphe Töpffer, 1970; Am liebsten wäre ich Totengräber geworden, an arrangement for 7 voices, 1971; Ansichten, Poems, 1972; Der graue Kater, Prose, 1972; Die letzten Augenblicke des Herrn Xaver Rytz, a play in 6 scenes, 1973; Poems in Junge Lyrik, 1958 & Junge Schweizer Lyrik, 1958; Prose & Poems in Gut zum Druck, 1972. Honours, awards: Lions Prize (St. Galler Rheintal), 1964; Literature Prize of the City of Bern, 1965; Förderungspreis Stiftung Pro Helvetia, 1970. Address: P.O.D. 73, CH 3000 Bern 9, Switzerland.

WEEKS, Robert Lewis, b. 9 July 1924. Professor of English. Education: A.B., W. Va. Univ., 1948; M.A., ibid, 1949; Ph.D., Ind. Univ., 1956. Married, 2 children. Positions held: Instr., W. Va. Univ., 1949-51; Tchng. Assoc., Ind. Univ., 1951-54; Instr. to Full Prof., Wis. State Univ., Eau Claire, 1954-63; Prof., Stephen F. Austin State Univ., Tex., 1963-66; Prof., Colo. Women's Coll., Denver, Colo., 1966–. Published works: To the Maker of Globes, & Other Poems, 1964; For Those Who Waked Me, & Other Poems, 1968; The

Master of Clouds (chapbook), 1972. Contbr. to: The New Yorker; Mass. Review; Prairie Schooner; Beloit Poetry Jrnl.; Southwest Review; Poetry Northwest; Shenandoah; Carleton Miscellany; Denver Qtly.; Choice, etc. Address: Engl. Dept., Colo. Women's Coll., Denver, CO 80220, U.S.A.

WEHRLI, Peter K., pen names **SAUVAGE, Germain,** b. 30 July 1939. Journalist; Writer; TV Director. Education: Hist. of Art, Univ., Zurich, Switz. Positions held: Stage Dir., 'Jugendbühne Leimbach'; Co-Ed., 'Dieses Buch ist gratis' Publishing; Fndr., 'Clown Trio Treu'. Memberships: Swiss Writers Union 'Gruppe Olten'; Swiss Press Assn. VSP. Published works: Ankünfte (Arrivals), 1969; Catalogue of the 134 most important observations during a long railway journey, 1973; Catalogue of Everything, 1973. Contbr. to: Los Angeles Free Press, U.S.A.; Il polz, Malta; Das Pult, Austria; Gut Zum Druck, Switz.; Neue Literatur, Rumania; Rolls Royce Jrnl., Switz., etc. Honours, awards: World Poetry Translator Laureate, World Acad. of Langs. & Lit., 1971; Disting. Serv. Cit., World Poetry Soc., 1972; Award of Acknowledgement, Govt. of the Canton of Zurich, 1972. Address: Ankenweid 24, 8041 Zurich, Switzerland.

WEIDEMANN, Anton Frederick, pen name **WEIDEMANN, Anton F.,** b. 26 March 1917. Vegetable Farmer. Education: Grammar School, North Dakota; HS., Huntington Beach, Calif. Personal details: Mother was born in UK (came to USA in 1908); Father, of Norwegian ancestry, born in Belview, Minnesota, USA. Positions held: Slaughterhouse Foreman; Packing House Superintendent; Ranch Foreman; Ranch Owner and Operator. Membership: United Amateur Press Assoc. Published work: My Golden Years of Youth, 1973. Contbr. to: Special Song; Orphic Lute; Texas Treveler; El Paisano; Times Advocate; Commerce Journal; Southern Calif. Rancher; My Brothers Keeper; Womens Household; Friendly Neighbors; Good Old Days; Radio Dial; Lamplighter; Poetry Classical and Contemporary (anthol.); KFMB-Radio; The Sentinel; San Marcos Observer; The Express; Pacific Potpourri; Age Outlook; Sunrise Lions Bulletin; Pacific Greenery; The Friendly Way; Rancho Calif. News; Blue Bonnets and Silver Spurs. Recip. 2nd Prize, San Diego Poets Assoc., 1966; 1st Prize, Southern Calif. Exposition, 1967; 1st Prize, Womens Household, 1968; Winner (poem) Apollo XI Contest KFMB Radio 1969; 1st Floral Award, Add Enchantment Associates, 1973; Book Award, Special Song (poem & article), 1973. Address: Star Route, Box 407, Pala, CA 92059, USA.

WEINBAUM, Eleanor Perlstein (Mrs.). Estate Management Executive; Author. Education: Ward Belmont Coll. Positions held: Trustee, Manie Gordon Perlstein Trust; Ptnr., 23rd St. Shopping Ctr.; Owner of Real Estate. Fndr., Eleanor Poetry Room, Lamar Univ., Beaumont. Assisted in establishing lit. mag. PULSE, Lamar Coll., 1968. Donor, new Poetry Room, Southern Meth. Univ., 1967. Critic Judge, Tex. Poetry Soc., 1967. Memberships: Am. Poets Fellowship Soc.; Poetry Soc. of Tex.; Composers, Authors & Artists of Am.; Am. Poetry League; Chmbr. of Comm., Beaumont, Tex.; League of Women Voters; Heritage Soc. of Beaumont; United Poets Laureate Internat.; World Poetry Soc. Publications: From Croup to Nuts, 1941; The World Laughs With You, 1950; Jest For You, 1954; Shalom America, 1970; Biog. of Hyman Asher Perlstein (forthcoming). Author of numerous poems, short stories & articles in various periodicals & anthols. Honours: 1st Prize, Seydell Quarterly, 1964; 1st Prize, Quatrain Contest, CAAA, 1965; MHD, Int. Acad., Sovereign Order of Alfred the Great; Disting Serv. Citation, World Poetry Soc.; Fellow Intercontinental Biog. Assn.; L.H.D., Free Univ. of Asia, Africa & Am., 1973, & many others. Address: 203-A Gilbert Bldg., Beaumont, Tex. 77701, USA.

WEINER, Beatrice L., b. 8 Feb. 1915. Secretary. Education: M.A., Univ. of Pa. Positions held: Sec.; Medical Sec.; School Social Worker; Engl. Tchr. Memberships: Recording Sec., Penn Laurel Poets,

Phila. Contbr. to Pennsylvania Prize Poems. Recip., Prize, Pa. Poetry Soc., 1971. Address: 4856 N.8 St., Philadelphia, PA 19120, U.S.A.

WEINIG, Jean Maria, (Sister Mary Anthony Weinig), b. 19 May 1920. College Professor. Education: B.A., Rosemount Coll., 1942; M.A., Fordham Univ., 1951; Ph.D., ibid, 1957. Entered the Soc. of the Holy Child Jesus, 1940. Positions held: Tchr., H.S., 1942-56; Tchr., Rosemont Coll., 1956–. Member, MLA. Published works: Fire in the Well, 1966; Rain in the Chimney, 1972. Contbr. to: America; Commonweal; Christian Century; Sign; Ave Maria; Torch; Delta Epsilon Sigma Bulletin; Approach; Four Quarters; Sparrow; Hawk & Whippoorwill; Southern Humanities Review; Rapport; Today; Western Humanities Review; South & West, etc. Address: Rosemont Coll., Rosemont, PA 19010, U.S.A.

WEIR, John Edward, b. 25 Apr. 1935. University Lecturer & Catholic Priest. Education: M.A., Univ. of Canterbury, 1969. Positions held: Tchr., St. Bede's Coll., Christchurch, 1962-68; Lectr. in Engl., Univ. of Canterbury, Christchurch, 1970-73. Published works: The Sudden Sun, 1963; The Iron Bush, 1970. Contbr. to: Arena; Arts Yearbook; New Voices of the Commonwealth; N.Z. Poetry Yearbook; The Bulletin (Australia); N.Z. Listener; N.Z. Tablet; Poet (India); Poetry East/West (USA); Queens Qtly. (Canada); Twentieth Century (Australia); Canta; Comment; The Listener (UK), etc. Recip., The MacMillan Brown Prize, 1962, '63, '64. Address: Dept. of Engl., Univ. of Canterbury, Christchurch 1, New Zealand.

WEISS, Theodore Russell, b. 16 Dec. 1916. Poet; Professor; Editor & Publisher, Qtly. Review of Lit. Education: A.B., Muhlenberg Coll.; M.A., Columbia Univ. Married to Renee Karol. Positions held: Instr., Univ. of Md., Univ. of NC & Yale Univ.; Prof., Band Coll.; Vis. Prof., MIT; Prof., Princeton Univ. Memberships: PEN Club. Published works include: The Catch, 1951; Outlanders, 1960; Gunsight, 1962; The Medium, 1965; The Last Day and the First, 1968; The World Before Us, Poems 1950-70, 1970. Contbr. to num anthols., jrnls., mags. etc. Recip. of many hons. & awards, inclng: 1st Prize, Wallace Stevens Awards, 1956. Address: 26 Haslet Ave., Princeton, NJ 08540, USA.

WEISSBORT, Daniel, b. 30 Apr. 1935. Translator. Education: Queens Coll., Cambridge Univ., U.K.; L.S.E., London. Married Jill Anderson, 3 children. Positions held: Ed., Modern Poetry in Translation, 1965; Advsry. Dir., Poetry Int., 1971; Hon. Fellow in Lit., Univ. of Iowa, 1973. Memberships: Nat. Book League; Mbr., Gen. Coun., Poetry Soc., 1972–. Published works: The Leaseholder, 1971, In an Emergency, 1972; Scrolls, Selected Poems of Nikolai Zabolotsky (transl.), 1970; Post-War Russian Poetry, 1974; Natalya Gorbanevskaya, Selected Poems (transl.), 1972. Contbr. to: Ambit; Twentieth Century; Encounter; Times Lit. Supplement; Oasis; Stand; The Nation (US); Micromegas (US); Carcanet; New Measure; Cambridge Review; The Guardian; The Scotsman; European Judaism; The Jewish Chronicle; The Iowa Review; Solstice; Critical Qtly.; Poetry Nation; Poetry. Address: 10 Compayne Gdns., London NW6 3DH, U.K.

WEISSTUB, David Norman, b. 26 Oct. 1944. Professor of Law. Education: B.Sc., Columbia Univ., 1963; M.A., Univ. of Toronto, 1965; J.D., Yale Law Schl., 1970. Positions held: Lectr., Berkeley & Davenport Colls., Yale Univ., 1969-70; Chmn. of Yale Law Forum, 1969-70; Vis. Hoyt Fellow, Yale Univ., 1971; Vis. Lectr., Univ. of Toronto, Fac. of Arts, 1971-72, '72-73; Fac. Lectr., Centro Intercultural de Documentacion (CIDOC), Cuernavaca, Mexico, 1972; Fac. Guest Lectr., Univ. of Iowa Law Schl., April 1972; Guest Lectr., The Law Soc. of Upper Canada, April 1973; Vis. Mbr. of Sr. Common Room, St. Edmund Hall, Oxford Univ., May-June 1973; Mbr. of the Exec. Comm., Fed. Govt. Task Force on Privacy (Depts. of Justice & Communications), 1971-72; var. consultantships.

Guest lectures & readings at CBC, Public Libs., & var. colls. Published works incl: Heaven Take My Hand, vol. of poetry, 1968; var. legal publs. Contbr. to: The Canadian Forum; Canadian Dimension; Canadian Jrl. of Theol.; The Queen's Univ. Qtly.; Anthol. of Literature. Recip., Hon. Mention, Norma Epstein Nat. Writing Comp., 1968. Address: Osgoode Hall, Yor Univ., 4700 Keele St., Downsview, Ont., Canada M3J 2R5.

WELBURN, Ron (Ronald Garfield), b. 30 Apr. 1944. Writer; College Instructor. Education: B.A., Lincoln Univ., 1968; M.A., Univ. of Ariz., 1970. Married Eileen D. Millett. Positions held: IBM-machine Clerk, N.Y.C., 1962 & Philadelphia, 1963-64; Grad. Tchng. Asst., Univ. of Ariz., 1969-70; Instr. in Humanities, Lincoln Univ., 1968; Instr./Asst. Prof. of Lit. (Afro-Am. Studies), Syracuse Univ., 1970-74. Published works: Peripheries: Selected Poems 1966-68, 1972; Along the Estabon Way, poems, 1974; Moods, Bright & Indigo, Selected Poems, 1974; Brownup, & Other Poems, pending publ. Contbr. to: Axiom; The Angry I; Negro Digest (& Black World); Jrnl. of Black Poetry; The Ash Tree; (anthols.) Black Fire; The New Black Poetry; Am. Sings; Pegasus; The Poetry of Black America, etc. Recip., Edward S. Silvera Award, Lincoln Univ., 1967, '68. Address: Box 51, University Stn., Syracuse, NY 13210, U.S.A.

WELCH, Lew, b. 16 Aug. 1926. Poet. Educ: Coll. of the Pacific, Stockton, Calif.; B.A., Reed Coll., Portland, Ore.; Univ. of Chgo. Positions held: Served, USAC, WWII. Published works: Wobbly Rock, 1960; Hermit Poems, 1965; On Out, 1965. Contbr. to: (anthologies) Beat Scene, 1960; New American Poetry, 1960; A Poetry Folio, 1963; 12 Poets and 1 Painter, 1964; New Writing in the U.S.A., 1967.

WELCH, Mary Ross, b. 30 May 1918. Clerk; Poet. Memberships: 1st Pres., Writers Guild of Mid-Hudson Valley; Bd. Dirs., St. Davids Christian Writers Assoc.; Treas., Writers Guild; Nat. Writers Club; Am. Poets Fellowship Soc. Publications: (poetry) Bury Me Deep, 1948; Trying For Purple, 1953; Prouder Than Wine, 1965; (novel) Color of Loneliness, 1958; The Cross Will Splinter, 1970. Contbr. to: Spirit; Baptist Ldr.; Prairie Poet; Tidings; Waterwheel; Hoosier Challenger; Am. Bard; Major Poets; Orphic Lute; Bag Press Annual; Adventure Time; Queen; Clover Collection of Verse; United Poets; Cyclotron; Estater, etc. Recip. of Sev. poetry awards. Address: PO Box 898, Poughkeepsie, NY 12602, USA.

WELCH, Michael Irene, b. 13 May 1940. Teacher. Education: Barat Coll., Lake Forest, Ill., B.A. Readings and workshops in the city through the Ill. Arts Council. Published works: Gnosis, 1971; For Now, 1971. Contbr. to: Chicago Sun-Times mag. on poems of inner-city children. Address: 1743 N. Sedgwick, Chicago, IL 60614, USA.

WELKER, Robert Louis, b. 26 June 1924. University Professor. Education: Austin Peay State Univ.; Univ. of Conn.; B.A., Geo. Peabody Coll.; 1948; M.A., Vanderbilt Univ., 1952; Ph.D., ibid, 1958. Positions held: Tchng. Fellow, Vanderbilt Univ., 1954-55; Instr., ibid, 1955-56, '57-61; Asst. Prof., 1961-64; Assoc. Prof., Univ. of Ala., Huntsville, 1964-66; Prof. of Engl., ibid, 1966-; Chmn., Engl. Dept., 1964-70, 1973-; Ed., Poem, 1971-, Assoc. Ed., 1967-71. Pres. of Huntsville Lit. Assn., 1971-72. Address: English Dept., Univ. of Alabama in Huntsville, PO Box 1247, Huntsville, Ala. 35807, USA.

WELLES, Bettie Payne. Teacher; Writer of Poetry, Juvenile Stories & Travel articles. Education: B.S., Sam Houston State Univ., Huntsville, Tex. Widow of Thomas Welles, 1 daughter. Positions held: Tchr. of Hist., Engl. & Am. Lit., & Beginners Spanish, North Zulch H.S.s, 1930-33; Tchr., Centerville H.S., 1933-34; Tchr., Adult Creative Writing, Ebell of Los Angeles, 1958-66; Tchr., Adult Educ. Class, Glendale YWCA, 1958-66; Poetry Ed. for Ben Hunter's mag., The Limb, for radio KFI, Hollywood, Calif., 12 yrs. Memberships

incl: Nat. League of Am. Pen Women; Past Pres., Glendale Br., ibid, 1970-72; Am. Inst. of Fine Arts; Calif. Fed. of Chaparral Poets; State V.P., ibid, 1968-70. Published works: Harbor Hunger, 1948; Nantucket House, 1958; This is my Legacy, 1969. Contbr. to var. publs. inclng. anthols. Recip. var. awards inclng: Gold Medal, Int. Poets Shrine, for This is my Legacy, 1969. Address: 1356 Thompson Ave., Glendale, CA 91201, U.S.A.

WELLS, Brain Hadley, pen name **NEMA,** b. 28 July 1930. Clerical Officer. Married, 2 children. Positions held: var. positions inclng. Clerical Officer III, Hd. of Staff Section, National Carriers Ltd., Portsmouth. Treas., Portsmouth Poetry Soc. Published works: And The Wind Spoke, 1971; (pamphlets) Preferences, 1973; Vectis Quintet, 1973; Recent Poems, 1974. Contbr. to: The News, Portsmouth (newspaper); Hampshire Poets mag. Honours, awards: Cert. of Merit, London Musical Competitions Fest. (Lit. Sect.), 1972 & 1st Prize, Silver Medal, 1973; 2nd Prize, Dorothy Mauger Lit. Comp., Portsmouth Fest., 1973. Address: 256 Powerscourt Rd., Portsmouth PO2 7JR, U.K.

WELLS, Nigel Bernard Caleb, b. 10 Mar. 1944. Farm Worker & Cottage Restorer. Married, 2 children. Positions held: served w. R.A.F.; worked for Pest Control Dept. of M.A.F.F. Published works: Venturing Out From Trees, 1970. Contbr. to: Expression; Magnus (Mexico); Road Apple Review (USA); Prism International (Canada); Southern Arts; Anglo Welsh Review; Poetry Wales; Mole. Address: Caecarrog, Aberhosan, Machynlleth, Montgomeryshire, U.K.

WELSH, Anne, b. 19 Sept. 1922. Lecturer. Educ: Univ. of Witwatersrand, Johannesburg, S. Africa; Somerville Coll., Oxford, U.K. Married, four children. Positions held: Lectr., Economics, Univ. of Witwatersrand, S. Africa. Published works: Set in Brightness, 1968; Ed., Africa South of the Sahara, 1951. Contbr. to: New Coin; Contrast; (anthologies) A Book of South African Verse, 1959; African Writing Today, 1967; Penguin Book of South African Verse, 1968. Address: 10 Cecil Ave., Melrose, Johannesburg, S. Africa.

WENGER, Clara H., b. 18 May 1909. Teacher. Education: B.S., Longwood Coll., Farmville, Va., U.S.A.; grad. work, Univ. of Richmond & Va. Commonwealth Univ. Positions held: Principal, Elem. Schl.; Tchr., Eng. & French; Personnel Clerk, IBM, Wash., D.C.; Tchr. of Engl. & Latin. Memberships: Pa. Poetry Soc.; Poetry Soc. of Va.; Mbr. of Contest Comm. N.Y. Poetry Forum, 1974; Nat. Fed. of State Poetry Socs.; Acad. of Am. Poets (affil.) Published works: (coll. of poems) Hyacinths & Heather, 1973. Contbr. to: Torchbearer, The Torch of Beta Sigma Phi; The Rotunda; The Virginian; Prize Poems of Pa. Poetry Soc.; IWWP Anthol., 1973. Honours, awards: Rosa Dillard Award, Woman's Club of Lynchburg, 1971; Timbrook Award, Woman's Club of Lynchburg, 1972; 1st Prize, Pa. Poetry Soc. Annual Contest, 1973 & other awards; 2nd Prize (tied) N.Y. Poetry Forum, 1971. Address: 8710 Arran Rd., Richmond, VA 23235, U.S.A.

WERTHEIM, William Jay, pen name **BILL,** b. 7 Dec. 1944. Writer; Teacher. Education: B.A., Engl., Columbia Coll.; Columbia Univ., 1965; M.A., Engl., State Univ. of N.Y. at Stony Brook, 1972. Positions held: Public Schl. Tchr., N.Y.C., 1966-70; Lectr., Engl., State Univ. of N.Y. at Stony Brook, 1970-72; Instr., Poets-in-the-Schools Prog., N.Y. State, 1972-. Memberships: Directory of Am. Poets; Coordinating Coun. of Lit. Mags.; Coun. of Small Mag. Editors and Publishers. Published works: Beginning, a book of early poems, 1965. Editor: Talkin' About Us, an anthol. of teenage writers, 1970. Editor & Publisher: First Issue, a lit. mag., 1968-. Contbr. to: Hawaii Review; Columbia Review; Schist; Loon; West End; Sun; First Issue. Address: 503 West 122nd St., Apt. 11, N.Y., NY 10027, U.S.A.

WERTHMULLER, Hans, b. 23 June 1912. Bookseller.

Education: German Philology. Positions held: Jrnlst.; Publsr.; Bookseller (own shop in Basel). Member, Schweizerischer Schriftsteller – Verband BR. Published works: Erleuchtete Fensterzeile (poems), 1962; Jahr des Augenblicks (poems), 1965; Basler Texte Nr. 3, Basel, 1970; Der Rolladen (poems), 1972. Contbr. to: Basler Nachrichten; National-Zeitung Antaios, Neue Zürcher Zeitung; Stuttgart; Die Ernte, Basel; Blätter des Basler Literaturkredits; Jahresring, Stuttgart; Akzente, Munich; Spektrum des Geistes, Ebenhausen. Honours, awards: Berner Literaturpreis, 1963; Schweizerische Schillerstiftung, 1972. Address: Lützelstr. 3, CH-4055, Basel, Switzerland.

WESCOTT, Roger Williams, b. 28 April 1925. College Professor. Education: B.A., Engl. & Hist., Princeton Univ., 1942; B.A., Gen. Humanities, ibid., 1945; M.A., Oriental Studies, 1947; Ph.D., Linguistic Sci., 1948; B. Litt., Social Anthropol., Oxford Univ., 1952. Positions held: Asst. Prof., Hist. & Human Rels., Mass. Inst. of Tech. & Boston Univ., 1953-57; Assoc. Prof., Engl. & Soc. Sci., Mich. State Univ., 1957-62; Prof. of Anthropol. & Hist., S Conn. State Coll., 1962; Linguist, Bur. of Applied Soc. Rsch., Columbia Univ., 1963-64; Lectr. in Sociol. & Anthropol., Wilson Coll., 1964-66; Prof. of Anthropol. & Linguistics, Drew Univ., 1966–; Chmn., Anthropol. Dept., ibid., 1966–. Ed., Gallup Poll, 1952. Cons. Ed., Jrnl. of African Langs., 1962–; Poetry Ed., The Interpreter, 1962–. Mbr., Edit. Bd., The Jrnl. of Poetry Therapy, 1970–. Memberships: Pres., Princeton Univ. Literary Society, 1943-45. Pres., Mich. State Univ. Linguistic Soc., 1958-62; Pres., Mich. State Univ. Fed. of Tchrs., 1958-62; Am. Assn. Adv. of Sci.; Vis. Lectr., Am. Anthropol. Assoc., Wash., DC, 1966–; Mbr.; Speakers' Bur., NJ Acad. of Sci., Newark, NJ, 1969–, etc. Publications: A Comparative Grammar of the Albanian Language, 1955; Introductory Ibo, 1961; Bini Phonology, 1961; Bini Morphology, 1962; Bini Lexemics, 1963; An Outline of Anthropology, 1965; The Divine Animal, 1969. Co-author: The Spring Anthol. of Verse, 1965; Reconstructing African Hist., 1967; Culture: Man's Adaptive Dimension, 1968; Folk Song Cycle & Culture, 1968; Problems in African Hist., 1968. Contbr. of poetry, translations, essays, etc. to: Isis (Oxford Univ.); Siege; Fiddlehead; Classical Outlook; Anthropol. Linguistics; Green Revolution; Poets' Meat; The Gadfly; The Commentator; Phylon Review; Coll. Quarterly; Spartan; Graphica; Nat. Poetry Anthol., 1963; Voices; The Interpreter; The Free Humanist; The Independent; Torch Internat.; Bucknell Review; Poetry & the Therapeutic Experience. Also contbr. of a no. of scholarly articles to prof. jrnls. Honours: Sophomore Engl. & Hist. Prizes, Princeton Univ., 1943; Pres., Princeton Lit. & Debating Socs., 1944; Rhodes Scholar, Oxford Univ., UK, 1948-50; Ford Fellow, Ethnohist., Univ. of Ibadan, Nigeria, 1955-56, & many others. Address: 11 Green Hill Rd., Madison, N.J. 07940, USA.

WEST, Harold C., Jr., b. 3 Oct. 1930. Songwriter. Education: Univ. of Vermont, U.S.A.; Roberts Wesleyan. Positions held: Advertising Clerk; ARA Employee. Contbr. to: Orphic Lute; The Newark Gazette; Poetry Parade; Hoosier Challenger; Cyclotron; Cyclo-Flame; Post Standard; Oswego Valley News; The Fulton Patriot. Recip., Prize, Major Poets Contest, 1973. Address: 308 Leitch St., Fulton, NY 13069, U.S.A.

WEST, Thomas A., Jr., b. 20 Oct. 1928. Teacher. Education: B.A., Oberlin Coll.; M.A. of Ed., Tufts Univ. Memberships: Poetry Soc. of Am. Published works: Fifteen Minutes (chapbook), 1972. Contbr. to: Transatlantic Review; Literary Review; Quaderni di Poesia (Rome); Trace; New Orleans Review; Works; Wis. Review; Zahir; Poet Lore; Pyramid; Premiere; N.H. Poetry Soc.; The Writer; Human Voice; Voices Int.; New England Review; Sunburst; Am. Poet; Young Publications anthol.; New Renaissance; Epos; Ann Arbor Review; Am. Jrnl. of Nursing; Cats Mag.; Modern Images; Fine Arts Discovery. Address: 133-2 Chestnut Hill Rd., RR 3, Killingworth, CT 06417, U.S.A.

WESTBURG, John Edward, b. 24 Mar. 1918. Political Scientist. Education: B.A., Univ. of S.C., 1949; M.A., ibid, 1951; M. of Foreign Serv., Schl. of Int. Rels., Univ. of So. Calif., 1954; M.A., Comp. Lit., 1956 & Ph.D., Pol. Sci., 1958. Positions held: Tchng. Asst., Pol. Sci., Univ. of So. Calif., 1951-53; Sr. Rsch. Assoc., Nev. Legis. Coun. Bur., Carson City, Nev., 1953-56; Instr., Engl., Univ. of Ala., B'ham Ctr., Ala., 1956; Assoc. Prof., E. Ctrl. Okla. State Coll., Ada, Okla., 1957; Assoc. Prof., Hist. & Govt., Pan Am. Coll., Edinburg, Tex., 1958-60; Ed., San Diego Classroom Tchr., Exec. Sec., San Diego Fed. of Tchrs., 1960-61; Prof. & Dir., Div. of Public Admin., Bir Zeit Coll., Jordan, 1962-63; Assoc. Prof., Engl., St. Ambrose Coll., Davenport, Iowa, 1964-69; Assoc. Prof., Pol. Sci., Univ. of Wis., Platteville, 1969-72; Dir., Legis. Ref. Bureau, City of Milwaukee, 1973; Dir., Nutrition Proj. for the Elderly, Grant Co., Wis., 1974. Ed. & Publsr.; N. Am. Mentor Mag., 1964–; Ivan McShane, The First Selected Poems of Ivan McShane, 1965; N. Am. Mentor Anthol. of Poems, 1965; Maxim Konecky, Poet in Pomfret, 1968; An Anthol. of Poetry for the Sixties, 1966. Ed: Forum on Public Affairs, Univ. of Wis., Platteville, 1965-72; General Politics Qtly., 1966. Contbr. to var. jrnls. & reviews. Address: Fennimore, WI 53809, U.S.A.

WESTRING, Dorothy, b. 23 May 1904. Freelance Writer; Housewife. Education: B.A., Univ. of Wis. Married, 2 sons. Positions held: Lib. Asst.; Reporter & Feature writer; Medical sec.; Rschr. in med. studies. Memberships: Wis. Fellowship of Poets; Wis. Regl. Writers Assn. Contbr. to: Driftwind; Talaria; The Lantern; The Sat. Evenng Post; Jr. Cath. Messenger; The Little Folks; local & church publs. Honours, awards: First, Third & Fifth prizes, Gem Stone Award, Marathon Co., Wis., Histl. Soc. Contest; 1st Prize, Poetry, Rhinelander Schl. of Arts, 1971; 3rd Pl., Poetry, ibid, 1972. Address: 5360 N. Berkeley Blvd., Whitefish Bay, Milwaukee, WI 53217, U.S.A.

WEVILL, David Anthony, b. 15 Mar. 1935. Writer; Poet; Translator. Education: B.A., Cambridge Univ., 1957, UK. Positions held: Lectr., Mandalay Univ., Burma, 1958-60; Sci. Writer, Glaxo Labs.; Advtg. Copywriter; Publr.'s Reader; Ed., Delos, Univ. of Tex.; Nat. Translation Ctr., Austin, Tex. Published works: Penguin Modern Poets 4, 1963; Birth Of A Shark, 1964; A Christ of the Ice-Floes, 1966; Selected Poems of Ferenc Juhasz, 1969; Firebreak, 1971. Contbr. to: Penguin Book of Canadian Verse, 1967; Poetry, Chicago; Delta; Delos; Observer; Times Lit. Supplement; Spectator; Malahat Review; New Yorker; Ambit; Listener; Yorkshire Post; Prism; Pluck; Sewanee Review. Sev. Art Council awards. Address: c/o The National Translation Center, 2621 Speedway, Austin, Tex. 78705, U.S.A.

WEYRAUCH, Wolfgang Karl Joseph, b. 15 Oct. 1907. Writer. Education: Johann Wolfgang Goethe-Universität, Frankfurt am Main; Humboldt Universität, Berlin. Married, 4 children. Positions held: Lektor, Berliner Tageblatt, 1934-38; Ed., Ulenspiegel, Berlin 1946-48; Lektor, Rowohlt Verlag, Hamburg, 1950-58; Freelance Writer, 1958–. Memberships: PEN, W. German Ctr.; German Acad. for Language & Poetry, Darmstadt. Published works incl: Von des Glücks Barmherzigkeit, poems, 1947; An die Wand geschrieben, poems, 1950; Gesang, um nicht zu sterben, poems, 1956; Die Spur, poems, 1963; Etwas geschieht, story, 1966; Das erste Haus hiess Frieden (SOS-Children-villages), 1966; Ich bin einer, ich bin keiner, radio play, 1967; Geschichten zum Weiterschreiben, stories, 1969; Ein Clown sagt, story for children, 1971; Mit dem Kopf durch die Wand, stories, poems, essays & a radio play, 1972; Dostojevskij, radio play, 1974. Contbr. to var. anthols., jrnls., etc. Honours, awards incl: Johann-Heinrich-Merck-Ehrung der Stadt Darmstadt, 1972; Andreas-Gryphius-Preis, 1973; Juror des Leonce-und-Lena-Preises für neue Lyrik. Address: Alexandraweg 23, D-61 Darmstadt, German Fed. Repub.

WHALEN, Philip Glenn. b. 20 Oct. 1923. Lecturer.

Educ: B.A., Reed Coll., Portland, Ore., 1951. Positions held: Served, U.S.A.F., 1943-46; Part-time Tchr., Contemporary lit., 1955–. Published works: Three Satires, 1951; Like I Say, 1960; Memoirs of an Interglacial Age, 1960; Every Day, 1964; Monday in the Evening, 1964; Highgrade, 1965; The Education Continues Along, 1967; On Bear's Head: Selected Poems, 1969; You Didn't Even Try (novel), 1967. Contbr. to: Paris Review; Angel Hair; Noose; Coyote's Journal; Wild Dog; (anthologies) A New Folder: Americans, 1959; Helgon and Hetsporrar, 1960; New American Poetry, 1960; Junge Amerikanische Lyrik, 1961; Beat Poets, 1961; Acquainted with the Night, 1967. Honours, awards: Poets Fndn. Award, 1962; Am. Acad. of Arts and Letters Grant-in-Aid, 1965.

WHEATCROFT, John, b. 24 July 1925. Professor of English. Education: B.A., Bucknell Univ., U.S.A., 1949; M.A., Rutgers Univ., 1950; Ph.D., ibid, 1960. Married Joan Osborne, 2 sons, 1 daughter (Allen, David, Rachel). Positions held: Instr. in Engl., 1950-58; Asst. Prof. of Engl., 1958-62; Assoc. Prof. of Engl., 1962-66; Prof. of Engl., Bucknell Univ., Lewisburg, Pa., 1966–. Mbr., MLA. Published works: Death of a Clown, 1964; Prodigal Son, 1967; Ofoti, 1970. Contbr. to: Harper's Bazaar; Mademoiselle; Ladies' Home Jrnl.; Yankee; N.Y. Times; N.Y. Herald Tribune; Chicago Tribune; Carleton Miscellany; Univ. Review; Beloit Poetry Jrnl.; Epoch; Lit. Review; Northwest Review; AAUP Bulletin; Minn. Review; Carolina Quarterly; Ga. Review; New Orleans Review; Salmagundi; Colo. Quarterly; Denver Quarterly; The Far Point; Descant; Epos; Best Articles & Stories; The Humanist; Forum; Cimarron Review; Four Quarters; Shenandoah, etc. Address: Dept. of Engl., Bucknell Univ., Lewisburg, PA 17837, U.S.A.

WHEELOCK, John Hall. Critic; Translator. Educ: A.B., Harvard Univ., 1908; Univ. of Gottingen; & Sr. Ed., Charles Scribner's Sons, N.Y.C., 1911-57; V.P., Poetry Soc. of Am., 1944-46; Chancellor, Acad. of Am. Poets, 1947-71; VP, Nat. Inst. of Arts and Letters. Published works: Verses by Two Undergraduates (w. Van Wyck Brooks), 1905; The Human Fantasy, 1911; Beloved Adventure, 1912; Dust and Light, 1919; The Black Panther, 1922; The Bright Doom, 1927; Poems Old and New, 1956; The Gardener, 1961; Dear Men and Women: New Poems, 1966; (literary criticism) Alan Seeger: Poet of the Foreign Legion, 1918; What Is Poetry?, Roosevelt, 1920; The Face of a Nation, 1939; Editor to Author: The Letters of Maxwell E. Perkins, 1950; Poets of Today, 1954-61. Contbr. to: (anthologies) Contemporary Poetry, 1923; Book of American Poetry, 1934; Modern American Poetry, 1950; Faber Book of Modern American Verse, 1956; Poet's Choice, 1962; Modern Religious Poems, 1964; Earth Is the Lord's, 1965. Honours, awards: New England Poetry Soc. Golden Rose, 1937; Torrence Mem. Award, 1956; Bollingen Prize, 1962; L.H.D., Otterbein Coll., Westerville, Ohio, 1954. Address: 350 E. 57th St., N.Y., NY 10022, U.S.A.

WHIGHAM, Peter George, b. 6 Mar. 1925. Teacher. m. Priscilla Minn, 3 children. Positions held: Tchr., Verse Composition, Univ. of Calif., Santa Barbara, 1966; Fac. Mbr., Comparative Lit. Dept., Univ. of Calif., Berkeley, 1969–. Published works: Clear Lake Comes From Enjoyment, 1959; The Marriage Rite, 1960; The Ingathering of Love, 1967; The Blue Winged Bee, 1969; The Fletcher Song Book, 1969; Astapovo; or, What We Are to Do, 1970; (translations) The Detail and the Design by Umberto Mastroianni, 1963; Black Eros by Boris de Rachewiltz, 1964; Introduction to African Art by Boris de Rachewiltz, 1965; The Poems of Catullus, 1969. Contbr. to: Agenda; New Measure; Arion; Spectrum. Address: 1799 Spruce St., Berkeley, CA 94709, U.S.A.

WHISTLER, Laurence, b. 21 Jan. 1912. Glass Engraver; Writer. Education: B.A., 2nd class hons., Engl. Lit. & Lang., Balliol Coll., Oxford Univ., U.K. Memberships: Fellow, Royal Soc. of Lit.; Authors' Soc. Published works incl: The World's Room, 1949; The View From This Window, 1956; Audible Silence, 1961; The Initials in the Heart, 1966; To Celebrate Her Living,

1967; Fingal's Cave, 1963; For Example, 1969; works on arch. and his brother, Ree Whistler. Honours, awards: Royal Gold Medal for Poetry, (1st Award), 1935; 1st Prize, Cheltenham Fest., 1959; 3rd Prize, ibid, 1957; O.B.E., 1955; C.B.E., 1973. Address: Little Place, Lyme Regis, Dorset, U.K.

WHITACRE, Agnes Lucile Finch, pen name
WHITACRE, Agnes Finch, b. 5 Apr. 1911. Homemaker. Education: Ind. Univ., Kokomo Campus, 1950-51; studied oil painting, Hazel McMinn Studio, 1969–. Positions held: Pres., Parent-Tchrs., Ervin Grade Schl., 1948-50; Northwestern H.S., 1961-62; Exec. Dir., Youth Temperance Coun., Ind., 1953-57; Ed., Indiana Memo, 1953-57; Encampment Dir., Youth Camp, 1953-57; P.R. Dir., Woman's Christian Temperance Union of Ind., 1960-63; Promotion Sec., 1963-68; Pres., Ind. WCTU, 1968-74; Kokomo Dist. Pres. Member, Kokomo Poetry Circle (Sec., 1969-73). Published works: Ideals, Easter Greetings, 1962; Mother's Day Greetings, 1959; Easter Greetings, 1971; Arizona Highways, 1960-67; Country Guide (Canada), 1964; He Touched Me (poems), 1972; num. poems to The Methodist Publishing House, The Christian; Ch. of the Brethern; Conventual Francisian Fathers & Brothers; Poet Int. Monthly, etc. Regular contbr. to The Farmnews & The Message. Address: Rte. 1, Box 317, Kokomo, IN 46901, U.S.A.

WHITBREAD, Thomas Bacon, b. 22 Aug. 1931. Professor; Critic; Editor. Educ: B.A., Amherst Coll., Mass., 1952; M.A., Harvard Univ., 1953; Ph.D., ibid, 1959. Positions held: Instr., Engl., Univ. of Tex., Austin, 1959-62, Asst. Prof., 1962-65; Assoc. Prof., 1965–. Published works: Four Infinitives, 1964; Ed., Seven Contemporary Authors: Essays on Cozzens, Miller, West, Golding, Heller, Albee and Powers, 1967. Contbr. to: Harper's; New Yorker; Shenandoah; Virginia Quarterly Review; Massachusetts Review; Carleton Miscellany; Texas Observer; Perspective; (anthologies) Of Poetry and Power, 1964; Sprints and Distances, 1965; Harvard Advocate Centennial Anthology, 1966; Southwest Writers Anthology, 1967; American Literary Anthology 1, 1968; East of America, 1969; New Yorker Book of Poems, 1969. Honours, awards: O. Henry Award, 1962; Tex. Inst. of Letters Poetry Award, 1965; Nat. Endowment for the Arts Award; Aga Khan Prize for Fiction. Address: Dept. of Engl., Univ. of Tex., Austin, TX 78712, U.S.A.

WHITE, Charles Edwin, b. 28 Dec. 1908. Retired. Education: Attleboro HS, 1926; Marine Corps Inst., 1928-31. Positions held: US Marine Corps, 1927-31; various jobs, 1931-37; Metals & Controls Corp. later merged with Texas Instruments, Inc. various positions through production, Personnel (Asst. to Director of Pers.), Sales Product Specialist, Production Control Supervisor, and Stores Administrator, 1937-70. Memberships: Midwest Poetry League (past mbr., and poetry analyst, 1948); New England Antiquities Research Assoc., 1970-71; Poetry Soc. of America, 1971-72; Massachusetts Archaeological Soc.; Viking Soc. for Northern Research, UK (Assoc. mbr.). Works published privately: A Sheaf of Straw; A Few Poppies; Iceland Lyrics; Ballad of Grettir Asmundsson; A Saga Man's Library (bibliography). Contbr. to: Kaleidograph; The Garret; The Bard; Driftwind; Versecraft; Country Bard; Akeley Herald; Boston Herald; Westminster Mag.; Cycle; Pirate's Gold; Prairie Wings; American Poetry Mag.; Reflections; The Leatherneck; Jack & Jill; Iceland Review; Sixty Five Degrees (Iceland); Yearbook of Mod. Poetry (1971). Awards: Henry Gershwin Award, 1943; 1st Prize, Midwest Poetry League Contest, 1944; 1st Prize, Reflections, 1944; Hartsock Mem. Prize, Westminster Mag., 1943; Henry Harrison Prize, Prairie Wings, 1943. Address: 130 E. Washington St., Lot No. 38, North Attleboro, MA 02760, USA.

WHITE, (Mrs.) Claude Porter, b. 30 Apr. 1907. Musician (Composer, Performer, Teacher); Poet; Writer; Editor-Publisher. Education: B.A., Southwestern Univ., Texas; Northwestern Univ. School of Music, Ill.; Special study in studio, clinical sessions, conventions & conferences in NYC, Washington DC; Rocky Ridge Music Center, Colo.; Aspen School & Festival, Colo.; Southern Methodist Univ. Fine Arts, Dallas; Univ. of Texas Fine Arts, Austin. Positions held: Concert soloist; Supervisor public school music; Choir director; Voice teacher; Composer (piano, organ, Irish harp, ensembles, grass roots opera); Official & active yrs. in Church, Civic, Club, Political local & State affairs; present Opera Chr. (Texas Fed. Music Clubs); Originator, Editor & Publisher, Texas Opera News; Dallas Civic Opera Women's Bd.; Metropolitan Hosp. Comm., etc. Memberships: Poetry Soc. of Texas; Nat. Fed. Poetry Socs., Inc. Published works: Fruits Of My Spirit, 1955; Beauty For Ashes; Three Moods And Observations; Kinship; libretti in verse for own operas. Contbr. to: Texas Anthol. of Poetry; Poets Corner (Baylor Univ., Waco, Texas); Poets Classical and Contemporary; Texas Opera News. Various awards, including Cert. of Merit, 1970-71; Med. of Honor Diploma, CSSI, 1972. Address: 1945 Bowie Dr., Corsicana, TX 75110, USA.

WHITE, Eric Walter, b. 10 Sept. 1905. Writer. Education: Clifton Coll., Bristol., 1916-24; Balliol Coll. Oxford Univ., 1924-27. Positions held: Asst. Sec. of CEMA, 1942-45; Asst. Sec., Arts Coun. of G.B., 1945-71; Lit. Dir., Arts Coun., 1966-71. Sec., The Poetry Book Soc., 1954-71. Published works: The Room & Other Poems, 1927; A Tarot Deal & Other Poems, 1962; On a Drowned Girl, 1973. Address: 21 Alwyne Rd., London N1 2HN, U.K.

WHITE, Ivan, b. 23 May 1929. Teacher. Education: B.A., Univ. of York, 1969; Working on M.A., Univ. of Manchester. Married, 2 children. Positions held: Admnstr., Unilever Ltd., London, 1945-54 & The Sutton Dwellings Trust, 1954-66. Memberships: Gen. Coun. & Readings Comm., Poetry Soc. Inc. (Exec., 1957-58). Published works include: Cry Wolf, pamphlet, 1962; Crow's Fall, 1969. Contbr. to the following anthols., jrnls., mags., etc: Tribune; The Spectator; The Aylesford Review; Socialist Commentary; Outposts; Envoi; Skeletons; Yorick; New Voices of the Commonwealth; Extra Verse; Ambit; Poet Int. Monthly; The Poetry Review; BBC Third Programme; The Poet's Voice; Poetry Now; BBC Scottish Home Serv., Life & Letters. Honours, awards: 2nd Prize, Guinness Poetry Competition, Cheltenham Festival, 1964. Address: 28 Pikes Lane, Glossop, Derbyshire, U.K.

WHITE, Jon Manchip, b. 22 June 1924. English Professor. Educ: St. Catharine's Coll., Cambridge, U.K. m. Valerie Leighton, 1946, 2d. Positions held: Served, Royal Navy & Welsh Guards, WWII; Mbr., U.K. For. Serv., 1952-56; Assoc. Prof., Engl. Lit., Univ. of Tex., El Paso, U.S.A., 1967–. Published works: Dragon, 1942; Salamander, 1944; The Rout of San Romano, 1952; (novels) Mask of Dust, 1953; Build Us a Dam, 1954; The Girl from Indiana, 1956; No Home But Heaven, 1957; The Mercenaries, 1958; Hour of the Rat, 1961; The Rose in the Brandy Glass, 1965; Nightclimber, 1968; (other) Ancient Egypt, 1970; Anthropology, 1954; Marshal of France, 1962; Everyday Life in Ancient Egypt, 1964; The Land God Made in Anger, 1969. Address: c/o Lloyds Bank, 39 Piccadilly, London W.1, U.K.

WHITE, Kenneth, b. 28 Apr. 1936. Lecturer; Poet; Translator. Education: Univ. of Glasgow, U.K.; Univ. of Munich, Germany; Univ. of Paris, France. Positions held: Lectr., Engl., Sorbonne, Paris, France, 1962-63; Lectr., French lang. & lit., Univ. of Glasgow, U.K., 1963-67; Lectr., Engl., Univ. of Bordeaux at Pau, France, 1967-68; currently Maître de Conférences, Univ. of Paris VII. Published works: En toute Candeur, 1964; The Cold Wind of Dawn, 1966; The Most Difficult Area, 1968; Letters from Gourgounel, 1966; Selected Poems of André Breton, 1969; Ode to Charles Fourier by André Breton, 1969. Contbr. to: Lettres Nouvelles, Paris; NRF, Paris; Le Nouveau Commerce, Paris; Traverse, Paris; Raster, Amsterdam; Ishmael, Madrid; Alif, Tunis; Decal, Wales. Address: Résidence d'Aspin III, 64000 Pau, France.

WHITE, Louise Welk, b. 14 Jan. 1895. Teacher; Poet. Education: A.B., Univ. of Denver; Univ. of Chicago; Univ. of So. Calif. Married, 1 daughter. Positions held: Tchr., 1915-19, '37-41; Writer, Ed., Engrng. Dept., Convair, 1943-45; Writer, Ed., Underwater Sound, Navy Electronics Lab., 1945-48; Convair, 1953-58. Memberships: Nat. League of Am. Pen Women, San Diego Br.; V.P., San Diego Poets' Assn., 1971; Pres., ibid, 1972, '73, '74; Calif. Fed. of Chaparral Poets; Pres., San Diego Browning Soc., 1959-60, '63-64; Fellow, Int. Poetry Soc.; Fndn. Mbr., The Delta Kappa Gamma Soc., Epsilon Chapt. Contbr. to: IWWP Anthol., 1972; The Fantasia Anthol. Series, Vol.1, Grains of Sand, 1971; Calif. Anthol., & others; Durango Herald; San Diego Union; Daily Meditation; Author/Poet; Modern Haiku, etc. Address: 4598 Edgeware Rd., San Diego, CA 92116, U.S.A.

WHITE, Marion Gingrich, b. 17 Sept. 1905. Co-Owner, General Insurance Agency. Education: Daniel Baker Coll., Univ. of Tex., 3 yrs. Positions held: Sec.; Schl. Tchr.; Owner & Mgr., General Insurance Agency; Ed.; small weekly newspaper, 1 yr. Memberships: Reporter, Creative Writers' Club; Pres., Fed. Study Club, 2 terms; Prog. Chmn., Creative Writers' Club; Contest Chmn., ibid; Pres., Odessa Chapt., Poetry Soc. of Tex., 2 terms; Pres., Creative Writers' Club, 2 terms; Poetry Soc. of Tex. Contbr. to: Major Poets; Encore; Tumbleweed Poets; Yearbook, Poetry Soc. of Tex.; Columnist, Patterns in Poetry, Grandfalls Gazette. Honours, awards: 1st prize, Western Dist., TFWC, Poet Laureate Contest, 1969, '70, '71, '72, '73; Jan. Monthly Award, Poetry Soc. of Tex., 1973, etc. Address: 800 W. 19th, Odessa, TX 79763, U.S.A.

WHITEHEAD, Elena Goforth, b. 20 Jan. 1917. Editor; Writer. Education: B.S. in Bus., Univ. of Denver, Colo., 1937. Married Carleton Whitehead. Positions held: Sec. positions in Denver, Colo., 1937-50, San Francisco, Calif., 1950-56, Carmel, Calif., 1960-62; Ed., Creative Thought, religious devotional mag., 1965–. Memberships: Recording Sec., Poets & Patrons (Chicago); Chicago Br., Nat. League of Am. Pen Women; Friends of Am. Writers, Chicago; Nat. Writers Club, Denver, Colo.; Ill. State Poetry Soc. Published works: Lyrics of Living, 1972; Attitudes (sonnets), 1973. Contbr. to Science of Mind mag.; Weekly Unity. Honours, awards: 1st Prize, Poetry, Nat. Writers Club, Denver, 1968 & '74; 2nd Prize, Poetry, Nat. League of Am. Pen Women, Phoenix, 1972; 1st Prize, Lyric, Poets & Patrons, Chicago, 1973 & 1st Prize, Heroic Blank, 1973; Special Recognition, Poetry, Ala. State Poetry Soc., 1974; 2nd Prize, Shakespearean Sonnet, Poets Club of Chgo., 1969; 1st Prize, Donor's Competition & 2nd Prize, Non-mbrs. Competition, Okla. State Poetry Soc., 1974; 2nd Prize, Light Verse, Utah State Poetry Soc., 1974, etc. Address: 70 East Cedar St., Chicago, IL 60611, U.S.A.

WHITEHEAD, James Tillotson, b. 15 Mar. 1936. Writer; Teacher. Education: B.A., Philos., Vanderbilt Univ.; M.A., Engl., ibid; M.F.A., Writing, Univ. of Iowa. Married, 7 children. Positions held: Co-Dir., Prog. in Creative Writing, Univ. of Ark. Published works: Domains, 1966; Joiner, 1971. Contbr. to: Denver Qtly.; Shenandoah; Concerning Poetry; Southern Poetry Review; Contemporary Poetry in Am., anthol., etc. Recip., Robert Frost Fellowship, 1967. Address: Dept. of Engl., Univ. of Ark., Fayetteville, AR 72701, U.S.A.

WHITING, Clay, b. 15 Jan. 1885. Farmer; Oil & Gas Lessor & Producer; Timber Merchant; Writer; Lecturer. Memberships: Poetry Soc. of Am.; World Poetry Day; Poetry Soc. of Pa.; W.Va. Poetry Soc.; Am. Poetry League, etc. Contbr. to: Quaderni di Poesie, 1970; Centennial Verse of West Virginia, 1963; Fate Mag.; Am. News; Echoes of the West Virginia Poetry Soc.; From Sea to Sea in Song; Keystone Folklore Qtly.; W.Va. Schl. Jrnl.; The Morning Press, Bloomfield, Pa.; The Glenville Democrat. Recip., number of prizes from the Pa. Poetry Soc. Contests, 1950-57. Address: P.O. Box 54, Glenville, WV 26351, U.S.A.

WHITING, Nathan, b. 24 Feb. 1946. Research Assistant. Education: Okla. State Univ., 1964-65; State Univ. of Iowa, 1966-67. Positions held: Rsch. Asst., Curriculum Rsch. & Dev. Ctr. in Mental Retardation, Yeshiva Univ., N.Y.C., 1972-73. Published works: While Courting The Sergeant's Daughter, 1969; Buffalo Poem, 1970; Transitions, 1972. Address: Stand; Choice (Chicago); Extensions; Minn. Review; Cloud Marauder; Sumac; Metamorphoses; Antioch Review. Address: 537 E. 5th St., N.Y., NY 10009, U.S.A.

WHITIS, Margaret Elizabeth, pen names **WHITIS, Margaret Thurston & THURSTON, Margaret,** b. 26 Nov. 1912. Clerk-Typist; Receptionist. Married, 2 daughters. Memberships: Exec. Bd., Tacoma Writers' Club; Am. Poetry League; Northwest Writers' Conf. Published works: since 1960 approx. 250 poems in var. newspapers & poetry mags.; Overlappings (poetry booklet), 1971; Burlap & Velvet (poetry booklet), 1972. Contbr. to: Am. Poetry League Anthol. & Bulletins; Cat Mag.; Creative Review; Cyclo-Flame; Durango-Cortez Herald; Fed. Way News Advertiser; Poetry Guild; Haiku Highlights; Imprints Quarterly; The Messenger; Midwest Chaparral; Modern Haiku; The Muse; Nutmegger; Pep Talk; Personal Poetry; Poems of America; Poetic License; The Swordsman; Tacoma News Tribune (Wash. Verse); Oregonian Verse; Wash. Farmer; The Written Word Anthol.; Young Publications Anthol. Has had poetry read over var. radio stns. Honours, awards: 3rd Prize, Poetry Contest, Tacoma Writers' Club, 1966; 3rd Prize, Poetry Contest, Midwest Chaparral, 1971 & .1st Pl., ibid, 1973. Address: 3903 E. 112 St., Tacoma, WA 98446, U.S.A.

WHITMAN, Ruth, b. 28 May 1922. Poetry Scholar. Educ: B.A., Radcliffe Coll., Cambridge, Mass., 1944. m. Morton Sacks, 3 children. Positions held: Dir., Poetry Readings & Poetry Workshop, Cambridge Ctr. for Adult Educ., Cambridge, Mass., 1966-68; Scholar in Poetry, Radcliffe Inst., 1968–. Published works: Blood and Milk Poems, 1963; The Married Wig and Other Poems, 1968; (translations) Selected Poems of Alain Bosquet (w. others), 1962; Short Friday by Isaac Bashevis, 1966; The Seance by Isaac Bashevis, 1968. Contbr. to: New York Times; New Yorker; Nation; Midstream; Atlantic; (anthologies) New Orlando Poetry Anthology, 1963; An Anthology of Modern Yiddish Poetry in Translation, 1966. Honours, awards: MacDowell Colony Fellowship, 1962 & '64; Reynolds Lyric Award, 1962; Jennie Tane Award, 1964; Alice Fay di Castagnola Award, 1968; Kovner Award, 1969. Address: 15 Bellevue Ave., Cambridge, MA 02140, U.S.A.

WHITNEY, J.D., b. 23 Sept. 1940. Writer; Educator. Education: B.A. & M.A., Univ. of Mich., U.S.A. Positions held: currently Asst. Prof. of Engl., Univ. of Wis., Marathon Ctr., Wausau, Wis. Published works: Hello, 1965; Hello, 2nd ed., 1967; Tracks, 1969; The Nabisco Warehouse, 1971; sd, 1973. Contbr. to: El Corno Emplumado; Caterpillar; Epoch; Beloit Poetry Jrnl.; Tuatara; Work; Dust; Apple; Lillabulero; The Far Point; Cafe Solo; Odda Tala; Is; Hearse; Elizabeth; Crazy Horse; Shuttle; For Now; Asphodel; Occurence. Address: 614 Adams St., Wausau, WI 54401, U.S.A.

WHITNEY, Lena M., b. 19 Apr. 1895. Teacher. Education: Grad., Ind. Univ., Bloomington; Postgrad. work, Univ. of Colo., Ariz. State Univ. & Univ. of So. Calif. Positions held: Special Searcher for Bureau of War Risk Insurance, U.S. Treasury Dept., Wash. D.C.; Tchr. for 36 Yrs. in elem. & high schls. of Indiana, Colorado & Arizona. Has written articles for mags. in U.S.A. & U.K. Memberships: Ariz. State Poetry Soc.; Nat. Fed. of State Poetry Socs.; Phoenix Poetry Soc.; Nat. League of Am. Pen Women; World Poetry Soc. Intercontinental; Past Pres. of Phoenix Writers Club; Past Chmn., Creative Writing Grp. of AAUW, Phoenix Br. Contbr. to: Sing Naked Spirit (anthol. of Ariz. State Poetry Soc.), 1972; Ariz. Republic; Cats Mag.; Cyclo-flame; Poet; Premier Poets Pancontinental; Phoenix Fires, etc. Poetry recordings for radio progs. & tapes

for coll. Engl. classes in India. Recip. var. poetry awards inclng: 1st Award for Gen. Poetry & 1st Hon. Mention in Free Verse, Ariz. State Poetry Nat. Contest, 1971; 2nd Award, ibid, 1972; 4th Award, 1973; 2nd Hon. Mention, Nat. Fed. State Poetry Socs., 1973. Address: 1314 N. First St., No. 406, Phoenix, AZ 85004, U.S.A.

WHITTAKER, George Simon, pen name **WHITTAKER, George S.,** b. 13 Oct. 1897. Editor of Poetry Magazine (Driftwood, a literary mag., currently published in Woodburn, Oregon). Education: Grammar School; HS.; 1 yr. State Univ.; Course completed in Photoplay Writing (Palmer School of Authorship). Positions held: School Teacher; Railroad Ticket Clerk & Telegrapher; Freelance Writer (prose and poetry), US Mail Clerk; Apiculturist. Memberships: Oregon State Poetry Assoc. (hon.). Published works: Blazing Altars, 1925; Of Various ods, 1931. Contbr. to: Overland Monthly; Muse & Mirror; Lariat; The Buccaneer; Orphic Lute; Quoin; The Guild; Poets' Scroll; Tom-Tom; Driftwood; Legend; Encore; The Circle; Northern Light; Pleiades; Mustang Review; The Oregonian; Oregon Journal; Los Angeles Times; Boston Transcript; East Oregonian; Albany Democrat; Portland Telegram. Recip. 200-dollar prize limerick (contest) Blue Ribbon Malt, Chicago. Address: 1008 Hardcastle Ave., Woodburn, OR 97071, USA.

WHITTEMORE, (Edward) Reed, b. 11 Sep. 1919. Professor of English. Education: Yale Univ., B.A., 1941. Married to Helen Lundeen; Four children. U.S. Air Force (Captain), 1941-45; Professor, Carleton Coll., 1947-66; Professor, Univ. of Maryland, 1968–; Lit. Editor, New Republic Magazine, 1968-73. Pubs. Heroes & Heroines, 1946; An American Takes A Walk, 1956; The Self-Made Man, 1959; The Boy from Iowa, 1961; The Fascination of the Abomination, 1963; Poems New and Selected, 1967; From Zero to the Absolute, 1968; 50 Poems 50, 1970. Contrib. to: New Republic; New Yorker; Poetry; Carleton Miscellany; Virginia Quarterly Review; Saturday Review; Commentary. Recipient Emily Balch Prize of the Virginia Quarterly Review, 1962; Award of Merit, American Academy of Arts and Letters, 1970. Address: 3509 Macomb St. N.W., Washington, D.C. 20016, USA.

WHYATT, Frances, b. 3 Aug. 1945. Poet. Education: Univ. of Minn., 1968. Positions held: Publisher & Editor, Equal Time. Fellow, MacDowell Colony. Contbr. to: Equal Time Anthol., 1972; Loves Etc. Anthol., 1972; The New Republic; The Nation, 1972; The N.Y. Times; The Southern Poetry Review; The World; Penumbra; Mulberry; Choice; West End; First Issue; Sojourner; Telephone, etc. Address: Westbeth, 463 West St., Apt. 116G, N.Y., NY 10014, U.S.A.

WIBKING, Gladys, b. 14 Mar. 1898. English Teacher. Education: B.S., Ill. State Univ.; M.S., ibid. Married, 1 son. Positions held: Grade Schl. Tchr., 1918-21, '41-44; H.S. Tchr., 1921-25, '44-45, '46 50, '51-65. Published works: Sonnet Sequences, No. 244, 1948; Sonnet Sequences, No. 264, 1950; Scenes of the Road, 1966; Time, 1968; Living, 1971. Contbr. to: Poet Lore; Chicago Tribune Sunday Mag.; South & West; The Human Voice; Voices Int.; Encore; Imprints Qtly.; Timeless Treasures; Poetry Parade; Poet (India). Honours, awards: Deep South Award, 1967; Stephen Vincent Benet Award, 1971 & '72; Deep South Award, 1972; Festival Contest, Memphis, 1973. Address: 801 West Main, Genoa, IL 60135, U.S.A.

WICHMAN, Eva Aline, pen names **WICHMAN, Eva and EWn. E.Wn.,** b. 28 Mar. 1908. Writer; Author. Educ: New Swedish Co-educl. Schl.; Dept. of Graphic Art, Commercial Art Schl. Memberships: Soc. of Swedish Authors in Finland. Published works: (poetry) Ormöga, 1946; Den Andra Tonen, 1948; Dikt I Dag, 1951; De Levande, 1954; Färgernas Strand, 1956; Dikter 1960, 1960; Diktarväg, 1961; Orientering, 1967; (prose) Mania, 1937; Här Ar Alit Som Förut, 1938; Molnet Sag Mig, 1942; Ohörbart Vattenfall, 1944; Där Vi Gar, 1949; Smakryp I Blasten, 1954; Andarnas

Flykt, 1957; Se Dig Omkring!, 1962. Contbr. to: Arbetarbladet; Nya Argus; Ord Och Bild, etc. Honours, awards incl: Gold Medal, Triennale di Milano, Italy, 1933, & Expo, Paris, 1937. Address: Finlands Svenska Författareförening, Runebergsg. 32C, Helsingfors, Finland.

WICKRAMASINGHE, Nalin Chandra, b. 20 Jan. 1939. Fellow, Jesus College, Cambridge. Educ: B.Sc., Univ. of Ceylon; Royal Coll., Colombo, Ceylon; M.A. & Ph.D., Trinity Coll., Cambridge, U.K. m. Nelum Priyadarshini. Positions held: Fellow, Jesus Coll., Cambridge, U.K., 1963; Staff Mbr., Univ. of Cambridge Inst. of Theoretical Astronomy. Published works: Poems, 1958; Interstellar Grains (astronomy), 1967. Contbr. to: Young Commonwealth Poets '65 (anthology), 1965. Recip., Powell Prize for Poetry, 1962. Address: 10 King's Grove, Barton, Cambridge, U.K.

WIENERS, John Joseph, b. 6 Jan. 1934. Author. Education: B.A., Boston Coll., 1954; Black Mtn. Coll., 1955-56; M.A., SUNY, Buffalo, 1973. Positions held: Tchng. Fellow, The Dept. of Eng., SUNY, N.Y. Memberships: Acad. of Am. Poets. Published works: Youth, 1970; Idyll; L'Abysse; King Solomon's Magnetic Quiz; Broadside; Larders, 1970; Asylum Poems, (mimeograph), 1970; Chinoiserie San Francisco, (100 copies), 1966; God is the Organ of Novelty; Unhired, (booklet). Contbr. to: The Boston Phoenix; The Boston Eagle; Emerson College's Beacon St. Review; The Milk Qtly., Chicago, Ill.; The Poetry Review, etc. Honours, awards: The Nat. Endowment for the Arts & Humanities Awards, 1966 & '67; Recip. awards, The Comm. on Poetry, Inc. Trust & Grants, 1970, '71, '72, '73; The Poets' Fndn. Award, 1961; The New Hope Fndn. Award, 1963. Address: 44 Joy St., Boston, MA 02114, U.S.A.

WIENIAWA-KLIMASZEWSKI, (Count) Witold, b. 16 Mar. 1947. Writer. Education: De La Salle Coll.; Cardiff HS for Boys; London University; Cardiff Coll. of Music and Drama (8 yrs.). Founder of a folk club, Cardiff. Memberships: Cardiff Youth Theatre (founder member); Orbit Theatre. Currently writing TV documentary scripts, and compiling first book in poetry form, etc. Contbr. of verse translations into English (Lermontov), etc. Address: Talon House, Llandaff, Cardiff, Wales, UK.

WIESNER, Heinrich, b. 1 July 1925. Teacher. Education: Tchng. Seminars, 1941-45. Currently Tchng. special classes, Reinach, Basel. Memberships: Schweizerischen Schriftstellerverbad, resigned 1968; Gruppe Olten. Published works: Der innere Wanderer, poems, 1951; Leichte Boote, poems, 1958; Lakonische Zeilen, 1965; Lapidare Geschichten, prose, 1967; Schauplätze. Eine Chronik, 1969; Der Jass, 1970; Rico. Ein Fall, 1971; Neue Lakonische Zeilen, 1972; Notennot, 1973. Contbr. to: Neue Deutsche Hefte; Hortulus; Drehpunkt: Neue Zürcher Zeitung; Die Zeit. Honours, awards: Arbeitsbeitrag der Basellandschaftlichen Literaturkommission, 1969; Förderpreis der Stiftung pro Helvetia, 1970; Erzählpreis der Stadt fonds des Schweizerischen, Bankvereins, 1973. Address: Im Pfeiffengarten 38, 4153 Reinach BL, Switzerland.

WIGHT, Doris Teresa, b. 26 Jan. 1929. Writer. Education: B.S. in Engl., Univ. of Wis., 1950; studied Ballet & Modern Dance, N.Y., Wis. & Calif. Married Douglas A. Wight, 3 sons. Positions held: Tchr. of Dance to Adults, Univ. of Wis. Extension (short courses), 1971, '72, '73; Tchr. of a course in Ballet for students, Baraboo H.S., 5 weeks in Spring 1974; Tchr. of Creative Writing course, Univ. of Wis., Baraboo-Sauk County Campus, Spring semester 1974. Memberships: Phi Kappa Phi; Ky. State Poetry Soc., 1972, '73, '74; Midwest Fed. of Chaparral Poets, 1973, '74; Fortnightly Lit. Club, Baraboo, Wis.; South & West Inc., 1972. Contbr. to num. jrnls., mags. reviews inclng: Bitterroot; Bardic Echoes; Cardinal Poetry Qtly.; Christian Sci. Monitor; DeKalb Lit. Arts Jrnl.; Hyacinths & Biscuits; Midwest Chaparral; Midwest Poetry 1972; Orphic Lute; Pennons of Pegasus;

Poetry Club; Poetry Parade; Quintessence; Sunburst Anthol., 1973; Voices Int., etc. Honours, awards: Hon. Mention, Ky. State Poetry Soc. Contest, 1972; Poet-of-the-Month, South & West, Inc., 1972; Two 1st Prizes, One Hon. Mention, Ky. State Poetry Soc. Contest, 1973; 1st Prize, Spring Contest, Midwest Fed. of Chaparral Poets, 1973, etc. Address: 122 8th Ave., Baraboo, WI 53913, U.S.A.

WIGHTMAN, George Brian Hamilton, b. 5 June 1933. Poet. Education: M.A., Trinity Coll., Cambridge Univ., U.K. Memberships: Chmn., Dev. Comm., Poetry Soc.; Fndr., Nat. Poetry Secretariat; Fndr., Exec., London Poetry Secretariat; Fndr., Convenor, Poetry Consortium; Fndr. & Chmn., 1965-67, Poets' Workshop; Fndr., Hon. Sec., Poets in Public. Published works: Birds Through a Ceiling of Alabaster, 1969; The Fox & the Pig, 1973. Contbr. to: New Statesman; Tribune; Micromegas; Acquarius; Dial-a-Poem; Poetry Now; also BBC 3 radio. Honours, awards: Guinness Poetry Judge, Cheltenham Fest. of Lit., 1968 & 69. Address: 11 Bramham Gdns., London S.W.5, U.K.

WIKKRAMASINHA, Lakdasa, b. 3 Mar. 1941. English Teacher. Educ: St. Thomas' Coll., Mt. Lavinia, Ceylon. Positions held: Tchr., English, Central Province, Ceylon. Published works: Lustre Poems, 1965; Janakiharane ha venat kavi, 1967; 15 Poems, 1970. Address: Kandy, Repub. of Srilanka.

WILBUR, Richard, b. 1 Mar. 1921. English Professor. Educ: B.A., Amherst Coll., Mass., 1942; M.A., Harvard Univ., 1947. Positions held: Asst. Prof., Engl., Harvard Univ., 1950-54; Assoc. Prof., Engl., Wellesley Coll., Mass., 1955-57; Prof., Engl., Wesleyan Univ., Middletown, Conn., 1957-. Memberships: Soc. of Fellows, Harvard, 1947-50; Nat. Inst. of Arts and Letters; Am. Acad. of Arts and Scis. Published works: The Beautiful Changes, 1947; Ceremony, 1950; Things of This World, 1956; Advice to a Prophet, 1962; Poems of Richard Wilbur, 1963; Walking to Sleep: New Poems and Translations, 1969. Ed., A Bestiary (w. A. Calder), 1955; Complete Poems of Poe, 1959; Poems of Shakespeare (w. A. Harbage), 1966. Contbr. to: New Yorker; New York Review of Books; Nation; Hudson Review; Atlantic; Poetry; (anthologies) Faber Book of Modern American Verse, 1956; Modern Verse in English, 1956; New Poets of England And America, 1957; Chief Modern Poets of England and America, 1962; Contemporary American Poetry, 1962. Honours, awards: Prix de Rome, 1954; Pulitzer Prize, 1956; Nat. Book Award, 1956; Bollingen Translation Prize, 1964. Address: Box KK, Wesleyan Station, Middletown, CT 06457, U.S.A.

WILD, Peter, b. 25 Apr. 1940. Professor. Education: B.A., Univ. of Ariz., 1962; M.A., ibid, 1967; M.F.A., Univ. of Calif., Irvine, 1969. Positions held: Asst. Prof. of Engl., Sul Ross State Univ., 1969-71; Asst. Prof. of Engl., Univ. of Ariz., 1971-. Published works: The Afterncon In Dismay, 1968; New & Selected Poems, 1973; Cochise, 1973. Contbr. to: Kayak; Lillabulero; Minn. Review; Poetry; Tri-Qtly.; Univ. of Windsor Review. Honours, awards: Grant from the Hart Crane & Alice Crane Williams Meml. Fund, 1969; Nominee for Pulitzer Prize, 1973. Address: Engl. Dept., Univ. of Ariz., Tucson, AZ 85721, U.S.A.

WILDMAN, John Hazard, b. 22 Jan. 1911. Professor of English. Education: Ph.B., Brown Univ., 1933; M.A., ibid, 1934; Ph.D., 1937. Positions held: Instr. in Engl., Brown Univ., 1937-40; Instr. in Engl., La. State Univ., Baton Rouge, 1940-46; Asst. Prof. of Engl., ibid, 1946-51; Assoc. Prof. of Engl., 1951-58; Prof. of Engl., 1958-. Memberships: Catholic Poetry Soc. of Am.; MLA; South Ctrl. MLA; La. Folklore Soc. Published works: (books) Sun on the Night, 1962; Forgotten Land: Another Look, 1966. Contbr. to: America; The Catholic World; Spirit; The Commonweal; Today; N.Y. Times; The Sewanee Review; Poet; Shoreline; Reck; Penny Poems from Midwestern University; Two Centuries of Brown Verse 1764-1964, 1966; N.Y. Times Book of Verse, 1970. Address: 1809 Spring Hill

Ave., Mobile, AL 36607, U.S.A.

WILEY, Vivian, b. 12 Dec. 1896. Positions held: School Teacher, 1917-1921; Housewife, 1921-32; Book-keeper & Secretary, 1932-39; Executive Secretary, 1939-62; retired in 1962. Memberships: Kentucky State Poetry Soc.; The Acad. of American Poets; Nat. Fed. of State Poetry Socs., Inc. Published work: A Spring-Tide Bouquet, 1971. Contbr. to: Kentucky State Poetry Soc. Anthol.; The Paintsville Herald; Internat. Who's Who in Poetry Anthol. Address: P.O. Box 529, Paintsville, KY 41240, USA.

WILFORD, Sarah Kathleen, pen name **KAY, Sarah,** b. 20 Sept. 1921. Freelance Writer; Housewife. Married, 4 children. Memberships: Sec., Coventry Br., John o'London's Lit. Circle, 1963-65; Coventry Writers' Grp., 1962-. Contbr. to: Poets Mag., 1973; Pantomimes in Verse for local drama soc., 1970-71. Selected by John Hewitt for Readings in Herbert Art Gall., Dec. 1972. Was highly commended at Nuneaton Fest. of Art, 1973. Address:e40 Torbay Rd., Coventry CV5 9JW, Warwickshire, U.K.

WILKINS, William R., b. 3 Nov. 1933. Accountant; Tax Consultant. Education: Univ. of Okla., 1951; A.A., Columbia Basin Coll., 1959. Married Patricia A. Wilkins, 5 children. Positions held: U.S.A.F. Aministrative, 1951-55; Payroll Analyst, General Electric Co., 1955-58; self employed Accountant & Tax Consultant, 1959-. Memberships: Authors' Guild; Authors' League of Am.; World Poets; United Poets; Int. Platform Soc.; Intercontinental Biographical Assn. Published works: A Whisper in the Wind, 1962; Something Personal, 1974. Contbr. to: Nola Express; Brass Ring; Avant Garde Anthol.; Jean's Jrnl.; The Hartford Courant; Cardinal Qtly.; J. & C's Anthol.; Scimitar & Song; Overflow; Zahir; Poet's Roundtable; World Poet's Qtly.; Best in Poetry; Bardic Echoes; The Denver Post; Sunburst; Angel Hour; Young Publs.; Am. Poets; Lincoln Log; United Poets, etc. Address: 331 W. Bonneville, Pasco, WA 99301, U.S.A.

WILKINSON, Rosemary Challoner, b. 21 Feb. 1924. Poet. Married, with 4 children. Positions held: Hosp. Administration, 10 yrs. (4 yrs. as Supvsr.); Co-ordinator of Hospital Audiences, Inc., Burlingame, Calif. Chapt. Memberships: Pres., Toyon Chapt., Calif. Fed. of Chaparral Poets, Palo Alto, 1972-74; Ill. State Poetry Soc.; Am. Poets Fellowship Soc.; Eastern Ctr. of Poetry Soc. of London; World Poets Resource Ctr., Inc., N.Y.; United Poets Laureate Int.; Int. Clover Poetry Assn., Wash. D.C.; Ina Coolbrith Circle, San Francisco; Peninsula Poets, L.A. Published works: A Girl's Will, 1973. Honours, awards incl: Cert. w. title of 'Danae', Int. Clover Poetry Assn., 1973; Cert. of Merit, Am. Poets Fellowship Soc., 1973; Medal & Chain from Dr. Amado Yuzon at Second World Congress of Poets, Taipei, Taiwan, 1973, also Plaque & Marble Award from Dr. Tin-wen Chung. Address: 1239 Bernal Ave., Burlingame, CA 94010, U.S.A.

WILKINSON, Sylvia, b. 3 Apr. 1940. Writer. Education: B.A., Univ. of N.C., Greensboro, 1962; M.A., Hollins Coll., Va., 1963; Special Fellow, Stanford Univ., 1965-66. Positions held: Instr., Engl., Art, Drama, Univ. of N.C., Asheville, 1963-65; Instr., Engl. & Creative Writing, William & Mary Coll., 1966-67; Lectr. & Vis. Writer, Univ. of N.C., Chapel Hill, 1967-70, etc. Member, Authors Guild & League of Am. Published works: (novels) Moss on the North Side, 1966; A Killing Frost, 1967; Cale, 1970; The Stainless Steel Carrot, 1973; var. articles & short stories. Ed., Change, 1971. Contbr. to var. mags. & jrnls. Has had 8 one-woman art exhibs. Honours, awards incl: Mademoiselle Merit Award, Literature, 1966; Sir Walter Raleigh Award for Fiction, A Killing Frost, 1968; Nat. Endowment for the Arts Grant for 4th novel, 1973-74. Address: 109 Williams St., University Heights, Chapel Hill, NC 27514, U.S.A.

WILL, Frederic, b. 4 Dec. 1928. Professor. Educ: Ph.D., Yale Univ., 1954. m. Elizabeth Lyding. Positions held: Prof., Comparative Lt., Univ. of Iowa, current;

Ed., Micromegas poetry mag., current. Published works: Mosaic, 1959; A Wedge of Words, 1962; Planets, 1966; (other) Literature Inside Out, 1966; From a Year in Greece, 1966; Archilochos, 1969. Contbr. to: Poetry; Kayak; Tri-Quarterly; Paris Review; New Mexico Quarterly; Prairie Schooner; Southwest Review; Accent; (anthologies) Best Poems of 1963: The Borestone Mountain Poetry Awards, 1964; Of Poems, 1966. Honours, awards: Voertmann Prize, Tex. Inst. of Letters, 1962 & '64; Fulbright Awards. Address: 1425 Buresh Aven., Iowa City, IA, U.S.A.

WILLCOX, Jean, b. 5 July 1945. Musician; Poetry & Music Recitalist. Education: Guildhall, London, U.K.; Royal Conservatoire de Musique, Brussels, Belgium. Memberships: Poetry Soc., U.K.; Int. Poetry Soc. Published works: Symbolisms, 1967. Contbr. to: Poets Platform; Viewpoints; Poesie Vivante Exhibition, Geneva, Switzerland; The Informer; Manuscript; Country Quest; New Melody; Ore; Tamarisk; London Poetry Secretariat Newsletter; Ocarina; Tribune; Int. Poetry Soc. Anthol. Address: Highfields House, Hoe Lane, Ware, Hertfordshire, U.K.

WILLETTE, Florence Hynes, b. 22 Feb. 1901. Housewife. Education: Coll., 2 yrs.; Art Schl. Married to Donald Willette; 1 d., 5 s., 32 grandchildren. Memberships: Spirit; Minnesota Presswomen; Nat. Fed. of Press Women. Published works: A Handful of Straw, 1958; Shadows & Light, 1969. Contbr. to: Spirit Mag.; Tidings; Household; Poetry & Feature Page, Columbia Mag.; Manuscript; Oregonian; New York Times; Rural Life, etc. Awards: Nat. Fed. of Press Women; Minnesota Presswomen, 11 awards; Nat. Archives, Lib. of Congress, Wash. DC. Address: Delavan, MN 56023, USA.

WILLIAMS, Alan Moray, pen name **ROBERT THE RHYMER,** b. 17 June 1915. Foreign Correspondent of British Newspapers in Scandinavia & the USSR. Education: M.A., King's Coll., Cambridge Univ., 1941; Cand. mag., Copenhagen Univ., Denmark, 1969. Married 1) Annelise Ellekilde, 2) Erkel Christiansen, 2 sons, 1 daughter. Positions held: Accredited as a Scandinavian corres. of many papers inclng: Sunday Times & Kemsleys, 1949-52; News Chronicle; Daily Sketch; Daily Herald; currently accredited in Denmark to the Sunday Times & the Guardian. Memberships: Soc. of Authors; Dansk Forfatterforening; Int. PEN. Published works: The Road to the West: Poems from the Russian (w. V. de Sola Pinto), 1947; Children of the Century, 1948; Autumn in Copenhagen, 1964, etc. Contbr. to: New Strand Mag.; John o'London's; Spectator; Listener; Tribune; World Digest; Modern Reading; News Chronicle; Daily Worker; New Leader; Oxford Mag., etc. Address: Postbox 4, 3450 Allerod, pr. Copenhagen, Denmark.

WILLIAMS, Alberta N., pen name **DAVIS, Sonia,** b. 22 Apr. 1908. Housewife & Writer. Education: Business Coll., Fayetteville, Ark.; two corres. courses in writing. Married Billy Williams. Positions held: worked for Anna Rand, Court Reporter in Denver; worked for Haskins & Sells, Court Reporter in Denver; worked for Ralph Mayo & Co., Court Reporter in Denver; Ranch Sec. & Bookkeeper, Apache Creek Ranch. Memberships: E.S.O. Chmn. (S.E. Dist.), 1969-70. Contbr. to: World's Fair Anthol., 1970; Golden Harvest; Second Biennial Anthol. of C.F.W.C.; Ark. Valley Jrnl., La Junta, Colo.; Colo. City Sun; Colo. Poetry Soc.; Greenhorn Valley News; Centennial Edn., Rye United Meth. Ch. Booklet, 1972. Honours, awards incl: 1st pl., Wapiti, 1960; 1st hon. mention, My Son, 1962; hon. mention, Sparkling Jewels, 1965; hon. mention, Possession, 1969. Address: Lascar Rt., Box 75, Rye, CO 81069, U.S.A.

WILLIAMS, Barrie, b. 16 Jan. 1933. Lecturer. Education: B.A., Emmanuel Coll., Cambridge Univ., 1954; M.A., ibid, 1958; Ripon Hall, Oxford, 1962-63; M.Litt., Bristol., 1971. Positions held: School Master, 1955-65; Lectr. at Coll. of Sarum St. Michael, 1965-. Memberships: Chmn., Salisbury Poetry Circle; V.-Chmn., Salisbury Writers Circle. Published works: Flowers of All Hue, 1960; Three Voices (w. others),

1973. Contbr. to: The Church Times; The Cork Weekly Examiner; The Catholic Standard; The Window; Salisbury Circle Poets. Address: 23 Cornwall Rd., Salisbury, Wilts. SP1 3NH, U.K.

WILLIAMS, C(harles) K(enneth), b. 4 Nov. 1936. Poet. Education: B.A., Univ. of Pennsylvania, 1959. 1 d. Contributing Editor, The American Poetry Review, 1972–. Published works: A Day for Anne Frank, 1968; Lies, 1969; I Am The Bitter Name, 1972. Contbr. to: The American Poetry Review; The New Yorker; The New American Review; Poetry; Transpacific Review; December; Colo. State Review; Iowa Review; Ironwood; Carleton Miscellany; Lillabulero, etc. Address: 506 Delancey St., Philadelphia, PA 19106, USA.

WILLIAMS, David Arthur, b. 23 Nov. 1947. Teacher. Education: Caerleon Coll. of Educ., 1966-69. Memberships: The Poetry Soc., London. Contbr. to: Poetry Australia; The Curiously Strong. Address: 52 Penrhiw Rd., Clase, Swansea, Glam , U.K.

WILLIAMS, David Gwyn, pen name **WILLIAMS, Gwyn,** b. 24 Aug. 1904. Professor of English Literature. Education: Port Talbot Co. Schl.; B.A., Univ. Coll. of Wales, Aberystwyth; M.A., Jesus Coll., Oxford. Married, 5 children. Positions held: Lectr. in Engl., Cairo Univ., Egypt; Asst. Prof. of Engl., Alexandria Univ. & Univ. of Libya, Benghazi; Prof. of Engl. Lit., Istanbul Univ., Turkey. Memberships: Yr Academi Gymreig; The Soc. of Authors. Published works include: The Burning Tree, 1956; Inns of Love, 1970; (transls. from Welsh) The Rent That's Due to Love, 1950; Against Women, 1952; In Defence of Woman, 1961. Contbr. to the following anthols., jrnls., mags., etc: Welsh Review; Wales; Poetry London: London Mag.; Penguin New Writing; Life & Letters; Poetry Wales; Mabon; Barn; Valeurs; Listener; Hudson Review; Burning Tree. Address: Treweithan, Trefenter, Aberystwyth, Wales, UK.

WILLIAMS, Diana Gruffydd, b. 21 Oct. 1944. Beauty Therapist; Poet. Education: Chelmsford Co. HS, UK; Trinity Coll., Carmarthen; Christine Shaw Schl., London. Positions held: Tchr., St. James Schl., Collyhurst, Manchester, 1966-67; Tchr., Arts Educ. Trust Schl., Tring, Herts., 1967-68; Rep., Cosmetic House, 1969; Free-lance writer, 1970–. Memberships: Comm., London Br., Plaid Cymru; Poetry Soc., London; Cardiff Theatre Soc.; BBC Welsh Lit. Soc.; Assn. of Beauty Therapists, London; Sec., Visual Arts Soc., Trinity Coll., Carmarthen, 1965-66. Author of I Did Not Have the Excuse of Insanity, 1971. Contbr. to the following anthols. & jrnls: Dock Leaves Anthol.; Gardens of Within; New Poems & Poems in Honour (Dock Leaves); Poems & Stories, 1968; Gwerinwr, 1969-70; London Welshman, 1970; Planet, 1970; Mental Health, 1971. Broadcast poem on World This Weekend, BBC, 1969. Awards: 1st Prize, Ford Trust Award, 1962; Highly Commended, Dock Leaves Anthol., 1968; 2nd Prize, ibid, 1967. Address: 1, Kyveilog St., Cardiff, Wales, UK.

WILLIAMS, Geoffrey Nathaniel, pen name **WILLIAMS, Jeff,** b. 3 Nov. 1941. Poet. Education: North Tex. State Univ., 1960. Has written poetry & essays since 1961. Address: 2732 University, Houston, TX 77005, U.S.A.

WILLIAMS, Grace Franklin, b. 18 May 1915. Homemaker; Songwriter; Vocalist; Poet. Education: corres. schls., N.Y. Schl. of Writing, Newspaper Inst. of Am.; Creative Writing at Mnpls. Pub. Lib.; Univ. of Minn. Ext. classes w. Vermelle Messer. Widow, 4 children. Memberships: Mnpls. Writers' Workshop; Midwest Fed. of Chaparral Poets. Contbr. to: Counterpoint, 1966; Kitchen-Klatter, 1973; Mnpls. Sun, 1973. 2nd Prize for best unrhymed poetry, Mnpls. Writers' Workshop Contest, 1973. Address: 1635 Vincent Ave. N., Minneapolis, MN 55411, U.S.A.

WILLIAMS, Herbert Lloyd, b. 8 Sept. 1932. Writer. m. Dorothy Edwards, 1954, 4s., 1d. Positions held: Feature Writer, South Wales Echo, Cardiff, Wales.

Published works: Too Wet for the Devil, 1963; The Dinosaurs, 1966; The Trophy, 1967; A Lethal Kind of Love (verse play), 1968. Contbr. to: Poetry Wales; Anglo-Welsh Review; Tribune; (anthologies) Welsh Voices, 1967; The Lilting House, 1969. Address: 27 Fern Place, Fairwater, Cardiff, Wales, U.K.

WILLIAMS, Hugo, b. 20 Feb. 1942. Poet; Editor. Positions held: Asst. Ed., The London Mag., 1961–. Published works: Symptoms of Loss, 1965; Sugar Daddy, 1970; All the Time in the World (travel), 1966; Ed., London Magazine Poems, 1961-1966, 1966. Contbr. to: (anthologies) New Lines 2, 1963; London Magazine Poems, 1966. Recip., Eric Gregory Award for Poetry, 1966. Address: 3 Raleigh St., London N.1, U.K.

WILLIAMS, John Edwin Stuart, pen name **WILLIAMS, John Stuart,** b. 13 Aug. 1920. Lecturer. Education: B.A., Univ. Coll., Cardiff, U.K.; M.A. & Cert. Educ. (Wales), ibid. Married Sheelagh Williams, 2 sons (Michael & Gavin). Positions held: Sr. Engl. Master, Whitchurch Grammar Schl.; Hd. of Dept. of Engl. & Drama, City of Cardiff Coll. of Educ. Mbr., The Welsh Acad., Engl. Sect. Published works: Last Fall, 1962; Green Rain, 1967; Dic Penderyn & Other Poems, 1970. Ed. of: Dragons & Daffodils (w. Richard Milner), 1960; Poems '69, 1969; The Lilting House (w. M. Stephens), 1969. Contbr. to: Prospect; English; Wales; Dock Leaves; The Anglo-Welsh Review; Poetry Wales; Poet; Decal Int.; Utter; Transatlantic Review; Planet; Scythe; Magpie; Western Mail; Country Quest; London Welshman; BBC; var. anthols.; W.A.C. Dial-a-Poem, etc. Recip., Welsh Arts Coun. Lit. Prize, 1971. Address: 52 Dan-y-Coed Rd., Cyncoed, Cardiff, U.K.

WILLIAMS, Jonathan Chamberlain, b. 8 Mar. 1929. Poet. Executive Dir., The Jargon Soc., Inc. Published works: Garbage Litters The Iron Face of the Sun's Child, 1951; Red/Gray, 1951; Four Stoppages, 1953; The Empire Finals at Verona, 1959; Amen/Huzza/Selah, 1960; Elegies & Celebrations, 1962; In England's Green &, 1962; Emblems For The Little Dells, & lNooks & Corners of Paradise, 1962; LTGD (Lullabies Twisters Gibbers Drags), 1963; Petite Country Concrete Suite (pamphlet); Lines About Hills Above Lakes, 1964; Twelve Jargonelles From the Herbalist's Notebook, 1965; Ten Jargonelles From the Herbalist's Notebook, 1966; Four Jargonelles From the Herbalist's Notebook, 1966; Paean to Dvorak, Deemer & McClure, 1966; Eight Jargonelles From the Herbalist's Notebook, 1967; Affilati Attrezzi per i Giardini di Catullo, 1967; Mahler Becomes Politics, Beisbol, 1967; 50! EPIphytes, -taphs, -tomes, -grams, -thets! 50!, 1967; Les Six Pak; A French 75! (Salut Milhaudious), 1967; Polycotyledonous Poems, 1967; Sharp Tools For Catullan Gardens; The Lucidities, 1968; Descant on Rawthey's Madrigal, 1968; Ripostes, 1969; An Ear in Bartram's Tree, Selected Poems 1957-67, 1969; On Arriving at the Same Age as Jack Benny, 1969; Mahler, 1969; Slow Owls (as Theodore Chamberlain with R. Johnson), 1969; Six Rusticated, Wall-Eyed Poems; The Apocryphal, Oracular Yeah-Sayings of Mae West; The New Architectural Monuments of Baltimore City; Strung Out With Elgar on a Hill; The Plastic Hydrangea People Poems; Blues & Roots/Rue & Bluets: A Garland for the Appalachians, 1970. Awarded Hon. Degree of Dr. of Humane Letters, Md. Inst. Coll. of Art, 1969. Address: Highlands, NC 28741, USA.

WILLIAMS, Kemble, b. 24 Feb. 1908. Ophthalmic Optician. Education: Bristol Grammar School. Married; 5 children. Co-editor, Samphire (new poetry). Published works: The Kind Woman, 1967; Uses of Culture, 1972. Contbr. to: Tribune; Poetry Review; Iconolatre; Poetry Workshop; Daylight; Lysismos; Larvae; The Journal; BBC (Midland Poets); Samphire; Prism; Caret. Address: Heronshaw, Fish Pond Lane, Holbrook, Ipswich, Suffolk, UK.

WILLIAMS, Lowell Allen, b. 3 Jan. 1907. Teacher. Education: Mo. Valley Coll., Marshall, Mo.; Univ. of Louisville; Univ. of Ky. (Ext.); Murray State Univ. Am.

Landscape Schl.; Ph.D., Bernadean Univ., Las Vegas, 1971. Married Gladys Lovelace, 1 son, 1 daughter. Positions held: Civil Technologist; Landscape Architect; Quality Control Inspector, Atomic Energy Program; Mathematician; Jrnlst.; Tchr. Published works: Poems for Remembering, 1955; Home is My Kentucky, 1956; This Life We Live, 1948; Across the Wide, Green Valley, 1960 '61, rev. '65 & Series II, 1966; New Voices, Am. Poetry, 1971. Contbr. to: Grounds Maintenance; Organic Gardener; Carlisle Co. News; Ballard Yeoman; Oak Ridge Jrnl.; La Plata Press. Honours, awards: a Kentucky Poet Laureate, 1956; West Kentucky Voc-Tech Poet Laureate, 1968–. Address: Box 502, Cunningham, KY 42035, U.S.A.

WILLIAMS, Margaret Frances Howell, pen name, **WILLIAMS, Frances Howelle,** b. 25 Jan. 1912. Second Grade Teacher; Poet. Education: Andrew Coll. Acad., Cuthbert, Ga.; Abraham Baldwin Coll., Tifton, Ga.; Valdosta State Coll., Ga., A.B.; Grad. work, Birmingham Southern and Univ. of Ala. Married, Howard Eldridge Williams; 1. s. (Michael Barrett), 1 d. (Frances Marilyn Guyer). Positions held: 2nd Grade, Alapaha, Ga., 1st & 3rd Grade, Talladega County; 27 yrs. in City of Birmingham, Glen Iris School; Taught in Jefferson County (previously). Memberships: Ala. State Poetry Soc.; Nat. Fed. of State Poetry Socs.; Affiliate, Acad. of American Poets; Ala. Writers' Conclave; Huntsville Lit. Assoc. Contbr. to: New Voices In The Wind, 1969; Yearbook of Modern Poetry, 1971; Lyrics of Love, 1972; Internat. Who's Who in Poetry Anthol., 1973; Major Poets; The Sampler (Ala. State Poetry publication), 1970, 1971, 1972, 1973; Shades Valley Sun; Talladega Daily Home; Birmingham News. Awards: Best Lyric Poem, Ala. Writers' Conclave, 1966, and Best Religious Lyric, 1968; Hon. Mention for Shakespearean Sonnet, Ala. St. Poetry Soc., 1970, etc. Address: 215 West Linwood Dr., Birmingham, AL 35209, USA.

WILLIAMS, Miller, b. 8 Apr. 1930. Professor of English. Education: B.S. (Biology), Ark. State Coll., 1950; M.S. (Zool.), Univ. of Ark., 1952. Positions held: Instr., La. State Univ., 1962-63; Vis. Prof., Univ. of Chile, 1963-64; Asst. Prof., La. State Univ., 1964-66; Assoc. Prof., Loyola Univ., New Orleans, 1966-69; Fulbright Prof., Nat. Univ. of Mex., 1970; Assoc. Prof., Univ. of Ark., 1971-73; Prof., ibid, 1973–. Fndr. & Ed., New Orleans Review, 1968-70. Published works: A Circle of Stone (poems), 1964; Recital (poems), 1964; 19 Poetas de Hoy en los Estados Unidos, 1966; Southern Writing in The Sixties: Fiction (w. John Wm. Corrington), 1966; Southern Writing in The Sixties: Poetry (w. John Wm. Corrington), 1967; Poems & Antipoems (transl. from Nicanor Parra), 1967; So Long at the Fair (poems), 1968; Chile: An Anthology of New Writing, 1968; The Achievement of John Ciardi, 1968; THE Only World There Is (poems), 1971; The Poetry of John Crowe Ransom, 1971; Emergency Poems (transl. from Nicanor Parra), 1972; Contemporary Poetry in America, 1972; Halfway from Hoxie: New & Selected Poems, 1973, etc. Contbr. to var. jrnls., anthols., etc. Recip. var. hons. & awards. Address: Dept. of Engl., Univ. of Ark., Fayetteville, AR 72701, U.S.A.

WILLIAMS, Opal Euphemia (Coffman), pen name **MOORE, Amelia,** b. 16 May 1917. IBM Keypunch Operator. Education: Okla. Bapt. Univ., Shawnee, 1 yr.; Southeastern State Tchrs. Coll., Durant, Okla., 1 yr.; Computer Programming, Tarrant Co. Jr. Coll., Ft. Worth, Tex. Positions held: Beautician, Dallas, Tec.; Keypunch Operator, Ft. Worth. Memberships: Asst. Recording Sec., Composers, Authors, Artists of Am., Ft. Worth Chapt.; Poetry Soc. of Am. (Tex. Soc.), Ft. Worth Chapt. Published works: The Handiwork of God (in Poetry Sect., Ft. Worth Pub. Lib.); poem 'Please Lord, Not All of Me', accepted for Mr. Connally's book, 'Prayers in Poetry'. Recip., 2nd Prize for 'The Handiwork of God', Tarrant Co. Contest, 1971. Address: 2251 Lipscomb, Ft. Worth, TX 76110, U.S.A.

WILLIAMS, Pieter Daniel de Wet, pen name **WILLIAMS, Pieter,** b. 29 July 1929, Natalspruit,

Germiston, Transvaal, South Africa. School Vice-Principal. Education: Univ. of the Witwatersrand, Johannesburg, Transvaal; Univ. of Edinburgh, Scotland, UK; Univ. of Stellenbosch, Cape Province; Univ. of South Africa, Pretoria, Transvaal; Tchr. Trng., Johannesburg Coll. of Educ.; B.A., B.Ed., T.T.C. Positions held: currently, Vice-Prin., Queen's Park High Schl., Cape Town. Memberships: South African Coun. for Engl. Educ.; South African Poetry Soc. Contbr. to the following anthols., mags., newspapers, etc: Canadian Forum; Cardinal Poetry Quarterly; Contrast; De Arte; The Field, London; Jewish Affairs; New Coin; New Nation; Personality; The Sailor; S-B Gazette; Volume 63; Weed; Williamsburg News; also: short stories, translations & lit. articles in lit. mags. in South Africa & USA. Honours, awards: 2nd Prize, Poetry Competition, Dept. of Cultural Affairs, 1967; Gold Diploma, Poetry, Cape Town Eisteddfodd, 1966; Prize, Goethe Inst., trans. of German Poetry, 1953. Address: 8 Basil Rd., Plumstead, Cape Province, South Africa.

WILLIAMS, Richard, b. 20 Oct. 1944. Education: B.A., Spanish, Univ. of S.C., U.S.A.; M.A., Spanish, Univ. of N.C. Published works: Suburban Blues, 1972. Contbr. to: Lillabulero; The Carolina Qtly.; Miscellany; The St. Andrews Review; Ironwood. Recip., Acad. of Am. Poets Award, 1967. Address: P.O. Box 563, Chapel Hill, NC 27514, U.S.A.

WILLIAMS, Sandra Beth Anne, pen name **WILLIAMS, Sandre,** b. 23 Oct. 1948. Writer/Model. Education: Temple Univ., Phila., Pa.; Yale Univ., New Haven, Ct. Positions held: Actress, 1968-70; Poet (readings), 1968-71; Radio Work, 1969-70; Playwright, 1969-73; Dance Tchr., 1970; Dancer, 1970-71; Singer, 1972; Lectr. (writing – theatre, film), 1972-73; Creative Writing Tchr., N.Y.C., 1972-73. Member of Poets, Writers, N.Y., 1972–. Published works: Sylus, 1969; Night Comes Softly, edited, 1969. Recip., Playwrighting Grant, Creative Artists Public Serv. Prog., N.Y., 1972-73. Address: 836 Boston Post Rd., Madison, CT 06443, U.S.A.

WILLIAMS, Ursula Moray, b. 19 Apr. 1911. Writer of Children's Books. Education: Schl. in France, 1 yr.; Winchester Coll. of Art. Married C.S. John. Positions held: Justice of the Peace, County of Worcester; Chmn. of Juvenile Panel (Evesham Br.); Governor of Vale of Evesham Schl. Memberships: West of England Writers Assn.; Nat. Book League. Published works: Grandfather, 1934; Jean-Pierre, 1932. Contbr. to: Noel Streatfield's Spring Holiday Book, 1974; Barbara Willard's Hullabaloo, 1972 & Happy Families, 1974; Cricket, U.S.A. Address: Court Farm, Beckford, Nr. Tewkesbury, Glos., U.K.

WILLIAMS, Wendy Elizabeth Ann, b. 22 Sept. 1933. Medical Research. Education: Northwood coll., Middlesex, UK. Married, Donald Graham Corrie. Positions held: Student Nurse, The Westminster Hosp., London; with Statistical Rsch. Unit, Med. Rsch. Council; staff trng. with firm of Mgmt. Cons.; Med. Rsch., Clin. Rsch. Ctr., Harrow. Memberships: The Poetry Soc., London; The Arts Theatre Club, London; Hon. Mbr., Hampstead Theatre Club, London. Published works: In The Circle of My Feet, 1965; Letters To The Nagging World, 1969. Contbr. to: Breakthru; Manifold; Loophole; News & Views. Address: 28 Romney Ct., Haverstock Hill, Hampstead, London NW3, UK.

WILLIAMSON, Craig Burke, b. 26 Aug. 1943. Professor. Education: B.A., Stanford Univ., 1965; M.A., Harvard Univ., 1966; Ph.D., Univ. of Pa., 1973. Married, 1 daughter. Positions held: Tchng. Asst., Univ. of Pa., 1970-71; Instr., Swarthmore Coll., 1972-73; Asst. Prof. of Engl., ibid, 1973–; participant in Poets-in-the-Schools project funded by Nat. Endowment for the Arts, 1971–. Memberships: MLA; Mediaeval Acad. of Am. Published works: African Wings, 1969. Contbr. to: Era; College English. Address: Engl. Dept., Swarthmore Coll., Swarthmore, PA 19081, U.S.A.

WILLIAMSON, Moncrieff, b. 23 Nov. 1915. Lecturer; Museum Director. Educ: Edinburgh Coll. of Art, Scotland. m. Pamela Upton Fanshawe, 1s. Positions held: Dir., Art Exhibitions Bureau, London, U.K., 1953-57; Staff Mbr., Extension Servs., Art Gall. of Gtr. Victoria, B.C., Canada, 1957-60; Dir., Art Dept., Glenbow Fndn., Calgary, Alta., 1960-63; Curator, Art. Gall., Victoria, 1963-64; Lectr., Fine Art, Univ. of Vic., 1963-64; Art Critic, Victoria Times, 1957-60, 1963-64; Dir., Confederation Art Gall. & Mus., Charlottetown, P.E.I., 1964–; Asst. Prof., Fine Art, Univ. of P.E.I., 1966–. Published works: Four Poems, 1944; The Fluid Idol, 1952. Contbr. to: (anthologies) Old Line, 1943; Notes on a Native Land, 1969. Recip., Canadian Centennial Medal, 1967. Address: P.O. Box 848, Charlottetown, P.E.I., Canada.

WILLIAMSON, Robin, b. 24 Nov. 1943. Composer; Songwriter. Education: George Watson's, Edinburgh. Married Janet Shankman. Published works: Poetry of Rock, edited Richard Goldstein, 1969; Incredible String Band Song Book, 1968; Home Thoughts from Abroad, 1972; Other Voices of Albion, edited Mike Horovitz, 1974. Records (mostly w. lyric sheets) Incredible String Band; 5000 Spirits or the Layers of the Onion; The Hangman's Beautiful Daughter; Wee Tam & the Big Huge; Changing Horses; I Looked Up; Liquid Acrobat as Regards the Air; Earth; Span; No Ruinous Feud; Myrrh (solo record). Address: c/o Island Records, 10 Basing St., London W.11, U.K.

WILLIAMSON, Ruth Carol Tharin Smith, pen name **WILLIAMSON, Tharin,** b. 6 June 1944. Poet; Housewife. Education: Assoc. of Gen. Studies, Stratford Coll., Danville, Va., 1964. Married John Robert Williamson, 3 sons. Memberships: Sec., Clemson Chapt. Jaycee-ettes, 1968-70; Mother's March of Dimes Chmn., ibid, 1968; Prog. Chmn., 1968-69; Mag. Co-Ed., 1968-69; Area Chmn., Cancer Fund, 1969; Ways & Means Comm., Morrison Elem. Schl. PTA, Clemson, 1973; World Poetry Soc. Intercontinental; Acad. of Am. Poets; Am. Poetry League; Nat. Fed. of State Poetry Socs.; Poetry Soc. of S.C.; Ky. State Poetry Soc.; W.Va. Poetry Soc.; Poets' Study Club of Terre Haute, Ind.; Ind. State Fed. of Poetry Clubs; Stratford Coll. Alumnae Assn., 1964–; French Huguenot Life Mbrship; Book Review for the State Newspaper, Columbia, S.C., 1968-69. Contbr. to: Orphic Lute; Bethel Meth. Ch. Bulletin; Stratford Coll. Alumnae Mag.; Poetry Soc. of S.C. Yrbook; Echoes of Faith; A Treasury of Religious Poetry (anthol.); Poet, etc. Recip. var. hons. & awards inclng: 1st pl. in Onomastic Award category, Poetry Soc. of S.C., & 1st pl. in Regional Prize, 1973. Address: Rte. 1, Beechwood Parkway, Englewood, Anderson, SC 29621, U.S.A.

WILLIOT-PARMENTIER, André, b. 19 Nov. 1931. Professor of French and Secular Ethics. Educ: Prof. agrégé; Dip., Inst. of Hebrew Knowledge, Paris. Positions held: French Prof., Tech. schls.; French Prof., Lycée; Prof., Secular Ethics, Lycée; Mbr., Ethics Commn., Coun. for Improvement of Teaching. Memberships: Assn. of Belgian Writers; Royal Assn. of Walloon Writers. Published works incl: Meandres, 1948; La Rose des Vents & Météore, 1952; La Chanson Limpide & Corolles, 1957; Panoplie du Coeur et de la Raison, 1960; Le Chantier d'Entre les Ronces, 1967. Contbr. to: Jeunes Lettres hennuyères; La Toile d'Araignée. Honours, awards: Gold Laurel, 1st Prize of Acad. of Poetry Recording, 1972. Address: Rue de la Bruyère 2, 7588 Saint-Sauveur, Belgium.

WILLY, Margaret Elizabeth, b. 25 Oct. 1919. Writer & Lecturer. Education: Goldsmiths Coll., Univ. of London, 1936-40. Positions held: Lectr., British Council, 1950–; at the City Lit. Inst., London, 1956–; at Goldsmiths Coll., Univ. of London, 1959–; at St. Marylebone Lit. Inst., 1966-72; at Morley Coll., London, 1973–. Has lectured in Germany & Poland. Memberships: The English Assn. (Ed. of its jrnl. 'English', 1954–); Fellow, Royal Soc. of Lit. Published works: The Invisible Sun, 1946; Every Star a Tongue, 1951 & other books. Rep. in following anthols: The

Distaff Muse, 1949; The Voice of Poetry, 1950; Images of Tomorrow, 1953; An Anthology of Contemporary Verse, 1953; Poetry, Prose & Play Series, 1953; An Anthology of Spoken Verse & Prose, 1957; PEN New Poems, 1954; PEN New Poems, 1958; The Albemarle Book of Modern Verse, 1961; The School Book of Modern Verse, 1962; Poems of Today: Fifth Series, 1963; Commonwealth Poetry of Today, 1967; Without Adam, 1968; Poems from Hospital, 1968. Contbr. to: The Observer; Times Lit. Supplement; Time & Tide; The Adelphi; John o'London's Weekly; Country Life; Poetry Quarterly; Outposts; Punch & many other jrnls. & mags. Recip., Atlantic Award in Lit., Rockefeller Inst., 1946. Address: 1 Brockmere, 43 Wray Pk. Rd., Reigate, Surrey, U.K.

WILSHIRE, George Henry, pen name **WILSHIRE, Lewis,** b. 22 June 1922. Public Relations Officer. Positions held: Jrnlst., 1948-54; Registrar, 1954-56; Ed. (Industrial), 1957-65; Public Relations Officer; w. Property Dept. of Brewery Co. Memberships: West Country Writers Assn.; Fellow, Royal Soc. of Lit.; Inst. of Public Relations. Published novels (1949-52) & topographical books of West Country interest. Contbr. to: English; West Country Mag.; Facet; Argosy; John o'London's. Address: Walden, 162 Whittucks Rd., Hanham, Bristol, U.K.

WILSON, Emily Herring, b. 11 June 1939. Teacher. Education: B.A., Univ. of N.C. at Greensboro; M.A., Wake Forest Univ. Married Edwin G. Wilson, 1 son, 2 daughters. Positions held: Engl. Instr., Wake Forest Univ., 1962-64 & Salem Coll., 1964-65; Editl. Writer, Winston-Salem, N.C. Jrnl. & Sentinel, 1968-71; Tchr., N.C. Poetry in the Schls., 1971-72, '72-73, '73-74. Member, N.C. Arts Coun. Poetry Readings. Published works: Down Zion's Alley, 1972. Contbr. to: Southern Poetry Review; Greensboro Review; Southern Pines Pilot, N.C.; N.C. Poetry, 1970; Raleigh, N.C., News & Observer. Address: 3381 Timberlake In., Winston-Salem, NC 27106, U.S.A.

WILSON, (Gladys) Mary, b. 12 Jan. 1917. Poet. Educ: Congregational Boarding Schl. Married James H. Wilson, M.P., ex Oxford don, Prime Minister, U.K., 1964-70 & 1974–; two sons. Positions held: Typist, Lever Brothers Ltd., Port Sunlight, Cheshire. Memberships: The Labour Party; League of Labour Women; Hampstead Garden Suburb Free Church, London. Published works: Selected Poems, 1971. Recip. of several awards for poetry. Address: 10 Downing St., London SW1, U.K.

WILSON, Keith, b. 26 Dec. 1927. Professor of English; Writer. Education: B.S., US Naval Acad.; M.A., abd, Univ. of New Mexico. Positions held: Regular Naval officer, 1950-54; Instr. of Engl., Univ. of Nevada; Instr. of Engl., Univ. of Arizona; presently, Resident Poet and Assoc. Prof. of Engl., New Mexico State Univ., Las Cruces, NM. Published works: Sketches for a New Mexico Hill Town, 1966 & 1967; 11 Sequences, 1967; The Old Car, 1967; Graves Registry & Other Poems, 1969; Homestead, 1969; Rocks, 1971; The Shadow of Our Bones, 1971; The Old Man & Others, 1971; Midwatch, 1972. Contbr. to: College English; Evergreen Review; Poetry; N. American Review; Tri-Qtly. Review; Prairie Schooner; Grossteste Review; Kayak; Southwest Review; NM Qtly.; Sumac; Wild Dog; Sur; Athanor; Expatriates Review, and many others; (anthols.) Poems Southwest, 1968; 31 New American Poets, 1969; Inside Outer Space, 1970; The NOW Voices, 1971; Accent: USA, 1972; America: A Prophecy, 1973; The Belly of the Shark, 1973, and many others. Awards: D.H. Lawrence Creative Writing Fellowship, 1972; P.E.N.-American Center Writing Grant, 1971; Westhafer Award for Creative Activity, 1972. Address: 1500 Locust, Las Cruces, NM 88001, USA.

WILSON, Keith Stewart, b. 28 May 1951. Writer. Education: B.A. in Hist., Univ. of Birmingham, U.K., 1973. Positions held: Jt. Ed., Black Columbus, Birmingham Univ. Poetry Mag., 1970-72; Chmn., Birmingham Univ. Guild Arts Soc., 1971-73. Has appeared on local radio, Univ. TV, & Lanchester Arts Fest. Memberships: Second City Poets, Birmingham, 1971-72; Whitehaven Writers' Club, 1970-72. Published works: The Tragic Roundabout, 1972. Contbr. to: Muse; Black Columbus; The Little Word Machine; Midland Read (Midlands Anthol. 1973); West Cumberland '71 Anthol. Address: 56 Wodow Rd., Thornhill, Egremont, Cumberland, U.K.

WILSON, Margaret Ann, b. 12 June 1927. Poet. Married Col. M.F.A. Wilson, O.B.E. Positions held: Ed., History of the Swanage Sailing Club. Published works: Star in the Cupboard, 1971. Broadcast to the British Forces Broadcasting Service, Cologne, Germany, 1972. Contbr. to: Swanage Times; Schl. of Infantry Newsletter; Dialogue, Montreal, Canada; Spring Anthol., 1971, '72, '73. Honours, awards: Runner Up, World Poetry Day, 1970. Address: 8 Church Hill, Swanage, Dorset, U.K.

WILSON, Oliver Whitwell, b. 19 Apr. 1901. Retired Architect; Engineer; U.S. Government Research Analyst. Education: Schl. of Archt., Columbia Univ., N.Y.C., 1919-24. Married Marjorie Jenkins. Positions held: Chief Designer; Architect; U.S. Army Corps of Engrs., Rsch. & Dev.; Rsch. Analyst, Engr. Intelligence, ibid; Defense Intelligence Agency (ret'd 1971). Memberships: Pres., V.P., Sec. & Treas., Federal Poets of Wash. D.C., 1973-74; Assoc. Mbr., N.Y. Poetry Forum; Centro Studi e Scambi Int., Rome. Published works: In Memoriam (to Pres. Kennedy), 1963; Centennial Memories (First Presbyn. Ch.), 1972. Contbr. to: Federal Poet, Wash. D.C.; Arlington News; ALA, Buenos Aires, Argentina; Scribe; (anthols.) The Unsung, Vol. I, 1964; In Commemoration (of Pres. Kennedy), 1964; Bouquets of Poems, 1971 & '72. Honours, awards: First Prize, serious poem & Hon. Mention, light verse, Federal Poets Contest, 1972. Address: 868 N. Kentucky St., Arlington, VA 22205, U.S.A.

WILSON, Patrick Seymour, b. 2 Dec. 1926. Lecturer in Philosophy of Education. Education: M.A., Ph.D., Univ. of New Zealand; G.T.L.C.; Trinity Coll. of Music, London, UK. Positions held: Primary Schl. Tchr.; Bethnal Green, London; Lectr., St. Mark's & St. John's Coll., Chelsea & Goldsmiths' Coll., New Cross. Published works include: The Bright Sea, 1951; Staying at Ballisodare, 1960. Contbr. to Landfall. Honours, awards: Jessie Mackay Award, 1954. Address: 2 Granville Rd., Ilford, Essex, UK.

WILSON, Raymond, b. 20 Dec. 1925. Professor. Educ: London Univ., U.K. Positions held: Former Hd., Engl. Dept., Dulwich Coll., London; Prof., Educ., Univ. of Reading, Berkshire, 1968–. Published works: Ed., A Coleridge Selection, 1962. Contbr. to: Listener; Times Literary Supplement; London Magazine; Transatlantic Review; Critical Quarterly; (anthologies) New Poems, 1963; New Voices of the Commonwealth, 1968. Address: Roselawn, Station Rd., Shiplake, Henley-on-Thames, Oxfordshire, U.K.

WILSON, Royce, pen name **T.O.,** b. 14 Apr. 1950. School Teacher. Education: B.S.E., State Coll. of Ark., Conway, 1972; M.S.E., Henderson State Coll., Arkadelphia, 1973. Married. Member, Am. Amateur Press Assn. Contbr. to: Biennial Coll. Poetry Review, L.A., 1969; Pegasus, 1970; The Creative Review, Mo., 1971, '72, '73; The Archer, 1971; Contemporary Poets of Ark., 1969; Poetry Prevue, 1972; The Best In Poetry, 1972; Poetry of the Year, 1973; Cycloflame, 1973; Images; Fla. Notes; Inky Trails; Pacific Greenery; Author/Poet; Poetry Hall of Fame; Twigs; Merlin's Magic, etc. Honours, awards: Poetry Hall of Fame, North Babylon, N.Y., 1973. Address: 911 East Richmond St., Ashdown, AR 71822, U.S.A.

WILTBANK, Milo Charles, b. 9 Oct. 1902. Farmer; Rancher. Married Mae Hale, 5 children. Has held var. church positions (Latter Day Saints). Published works: Gramma Grass Wisdom, 1st & 2nd edns.; Spittin' & Whittelin'; Wind Through Barren Branches; Wiff of the West. Contbr. to local newspapers. Address: 61 South Miller, Mesa, AZ 85204, U.S.A.

WIMMER, Paul, b. 18 Apr. 1929. Writer; Radio Producer; Translator; Poet. Education: D.Phil., Univ. of Vienna. Positions held: Producer, Lit. Progs. & Dramas, Radio Stn., Austrian Broadcasting serv. Memberships: Sec.-Gen., Austrian Writers' Assn.; Mbr. of Bd., Goethe Club, Vienna; Bd., Writers' Soc.; Bd., working Grp. for Arts & Scis.; Sci. Advr., Int. Lenau-Gesellschaft; PEN; Soc. for Theatre Rsch., Vienna, etc. Published works: Unterwegs, 1963; Das Wort freiheit Klingt so schön, by Herwig Hensen (transl. from Flemish), 1965; Der Dichter in der technischen Welt, 1968; Goethe in der Sicht des 20. Jahrhundert, 1968; Flämische Lyrik, 1971; Der Zeitgenössische Roman in Belgien, 1971. Contbr. to: Reallexicon der deutchen Literatur; Lexicon der Weltliteratur un 20. Jahrhundert; Wort in der Zeit; Neues Osterreich; Wiener Zeitung; Le Giornale dei Poeti; Dialogi; Ortam; Das Zeitlose Wort, 1964; Die Barke, 1960; Lebendige Stadt, 1962; Osterreichische Akademische Blatter; Die Presse Het Laatste Nieuws; Nieuw Vlaams Tijdschrift; De Vlaamse Gids. Awards: Theodor Korner Prize, 1958; Art Fund Prize, City of Vienna, 1963; Promotion Prize for Lit., Vienna, 1970. Address: A 1050 Wien V, Krongasse 3, Austria.

WINANS, Allan Davis, pen name **WINANS, A.D.,** b. 12 Jan. 1936. Writer. Education: A.B. in Sociology, San Francisco State Univ., 1962. Positions held: Social Worker; Juvenile Probation Officer; Special Agent, Office of Naval Intelligence. Memberships: C.C.L.M.; C.O.S.M.E.P. Published works: Carmel Clowns, 1970; Crazy John Poems, 1972; Venus in Pisces, 1973. Editor-Publisher, Second Coming Mag. Contbr. to: Amphora; Argot; Arx; Atom Mind; Cardinal Poetry Qtly.; Cave; Desperado; Erratica; Grande Ronde Review; The Miscellany; New Dawn; Poetry Venture; Overflow; Project; Greenfield Review; Harrison Street Review; Heirs; Hey Lady; The Lace Review; Pacifica; Willow Leaves; Mendocino Robin; Hyperion; Invisible City; The Mag; Mandala; Meatball; Overflow; Living Underground; Poesie; Second Coming; Tulsa Poetry Qtly.; Unfold; Vagabond; IS; Starweb; Suspicious Humanist; Poetry Parade; Titmouse; Nausea One; Jeans Journal; The Shore Review; Wagtail; Outcast; Gato; Neo; Gallimaufry; Poetry Australia, etc. Address: P.O. Box 31246, San Francisco, CA 94131, USA.

WINANT, Francine, b. 28 Oct. 1943. Mbr., Poetry Soc. Am. Author, Looking At Women, 1971. Contbr. to: Art & Archaeol. Newsletter; Cape Rock Jrnl.; Folio; Gallary Series Three; Hanging Loose; Kan. Quarterly; Spero. Recip., Bernice Kavinoky Isaacson Award, New Schl. for Soc. Rsch., 1967-68. Address: PO Box 398, New York, NY 10009, USA.

WINCH, Harriet Gragg, pen names **WINCH, Sally G. & GRAY, Carla,** b. 14 Aug. 1908. Retired. Education: A.B., Ind. Univ., Bloomington, Ind., 1930. Widow of Leland S. Winch. Positions held: w. Ind. Dept. Conservation (now Dept. Natural Resources), 1932-40 & again 1951-53, as Rsch. Asst. to Chas. C. Deam, botanist, Rsch. Forester, Author, in prep. of Botanical Texts & Reference Books. Memberships: Regent, Gen. de Lafayette Chapt., Daughters of the Am. Revolution, 1970-72; Ind. St. Ch. Insignia, ibid, 1972-73; Ind. Cent. Dist. Dir., 1973–; World Poetry Soc. Intercontinental. Contbr. to: Northwest Ind. Conf. News (Methodist); Eleusis of Chi Omega (Qtly.); Horseshoe Herald (Theta Beta Chapt. of Chi Omega, Ind. Univ.); 50th Anniversary Hist. of Theta Beta of Chi Omega; Indiana State Day News; Poet, India. Address: 128 Seneca Lane, West Lafayette, IN 47906, U.S.A.

WINCHELL, Wallace, b. 8 Mar. 1914. College Faculty Member. Education: B.A., Montclair State Tchrs. Coll., N.J., 1936; M. Div., Union Seminary, N.Y.C., 1944; M.A., Wayne Univ., Detroit, Mich., 1954. Married, 3 children. Positions held: Field Officer, The Salvation Army, 1936-43; Pastor, United Church of Christ, 1943-69; Adjunct Fac. Mbr., Univ. of Hartford, 1962-65; Fac. Mbr., Manchester Community Coll., 1970–.

Memberships: Poetry Soc. of Am. 1965–; Maine Soc. of Poets. Published works: The Poetry of the Shakers, 1970; The House of Bethlehem, 1972; Century-Spanning Significance, 1974. Contbr. to: Chicago Sunday Tribune mag.; The Lyric; The Lit. Review; Scimitar & Song; Ukrainian Review; The War Cry; Christian Advocate, etc. Honours, awards: Geo. Wash. Honor Medal, Freedoms Fndn., 1959; Suffield Writers Award, 1965; co-winner, The Di Castagnola Award of the Poetry Soc. of Am., 1970; Lyric Mag. Award, Winter 1971. Address: Manchester Community Coll., Manchester, CT 06040, U.S.A.

WINCHESTER, Olive May, b. 5 Oct. 1919. Writer. Married, 1 son, 1 daughter. Memberships: New Zealand Women Writers' Soc. Inc.; World Poetry Soc.; Playwrights' Assn. of N.Z. Contbr. to: Animal World; Pause; Te Ao Hou; Farmer; Hunting & Fishing; Zealandia; Cycling; Northland; Listener; Gardener; Thursday; Penpoint; Poet Int. (India); Ala (Buenos Aires). Address: 82 Panorama Rd., Mt. Wellington, Panmure, Auckland 6, New Zealand.

WINDHAGER, Juliane, b. 12 Oct. 1912. Writer; Poet. Married. Memberships: PEN Club, Austria; Austrian Author's Soc.; Die Kogge; Authors' assn. of western countries. Published works: Der Friedtäter (novel), 1948; Der linke Engel (poetry), 1959; Die Distelreppe (poetry), 1960; Staubflocken (2 plays), 1965; Talstation (poetry), 1967. Contbr. to num. mags., jrnls., etc. Honours, awards: Georg Trakl-Prize, Salzburg, 1956; Osterreichischer Staatspreis für Horspiel, Vienna (Nat. Prize for Lit.), 1964; Concordia-Lyrikpreis (Prize Boga Tinti), Vienna, 1969; Silberner Heine-Taler, Hamburg, Germany, 1966; Erster Hörspielpreis der Stadt Klagenfurt, 1969 (1st prize for radio plays of the town of Klagenfurt). Address: 5020 Salzburg, Robert Munzstrasse 9, Austria.

WINGFIELD, Sheila, b. 23 May 1906. Poet. m. Viscount Powerscourt, 1932, 2s., 1d. Published works: Poems, 1938; Beat Drum, Beat Drum, 1946; A Cloud Across the Sun, 1949; A Kite's Dinner: Poems 1938-1954, 1954; The Leaves Darken, 1964; Real People (autobiography), 1952. Contbr. to: Dublin Magazine; London Mercury; Times Literary Supplement; New Statesman; London Magazine; Listener; Time and Tide; (Anthologies) Behold This Dreamer, 1939; Oxford Book of Irish Verse, 1958. Address: c/o Barclays Bank Ltd., 8 W. Halkin St., London S.W.1, U.K.

WINKLER, Manfred, b. 27 Oct. 1922. Archivist & Editor. Education: B.A., Univ. of Jerusalem, 1963. Married, 1 daughter. Positions held: Official, 1946-55; Writer & Jrnlst., 1955-58; Archivist & Ed., 1964-74. Memberships: Hebrew Writers Assn. in Israel; PEN Center in Israel. Published works: Tief Pflügt Das Leben, 1956; Kunterbunte Verse, 1957; Fritzchens Abenteuer, 1958; Shirim, 1965; Bein Etzbhot Hair, 1970. Contbr. to: Moznaim; Keshet; Eked; Gazit; Haouma; Davar; Haaretz; Al Hamishmar; Maariv; Lamerhaw; Ariel; Die Horen; Neue Literatur; Schongeist – Belle Esprit, etc. Address: Bolivar St. 7, Kiriat Jowel, Jerusalem, Israel.

WINSETT, Marvin Davis, b. 13 Feb. 1902. Author; Editor; Lecturer; Poet. Education: Austin Coll. Prep. Dept., 1919; Southern Meth. Univ. 1922-24; L.H.D., honoris causa, l'Univ. Libre (Asie). Memberships: VP, Nat. Fed. State Poetry Socs., 1963, '67-68; Pres., 1964-66; Hon. Life Mbr., Poetry Soc. of Tex.; Treas., 1956-61; Pres., 1962-65; Mbr., Advsry. Bd., Vachel Lindsay Assn.; Chmn., Tex. Coun. for Promotion of Poetry; Founder, Acad. of American Poets; Lambda Chi Alpha; Life Mbr., Sigma Delta Chi; Hon. Mbr., United Poets Laureate Int.; Associes Etranger, Academie Francaise de la Poesie; Southern Rep., South & West; Life Fellow, Int. Inst. of Arts & Letters, Switzerland; Fellow, Royal Soc. of Arts, UK; Editor, State Poetry Societies Section, Int. Who's Who in Poetry; Edit. & Advsry. Bd., Dictionary of Int. Biog.; Edit. & Advsry. Bd., Int. Who's Who in Poetry, 1970–; Edit. Bd., Royal Blue Book, 1968. Originator,

nationally-known Cyclus verse form. Published works: Winding Stairway, 1953; April Always, 1956; Remembered Earth, 1962; Basic Ad Writing (prose) 1954; Some Uses of Words, 1969. Contbr. to the following anthols., jrnls., newspapers, etc: Kaleidograph; Quicksilver; Poet Lore; Am. Bard; Seydell Quarterly; South & West; Green World; Creativity; Creative Review; Hoosier Challenger; Christian Herald; Surf; Stars; Stone Anthol. of Tex. Poets, 1961; Southwestern Anthol., 1937; The Guild Anthol., 1966; Sci. of Mind; Western Outdoors; Ft. Worth Press; Memorabilia Anthol., 1965; The Minds Create Anthol., 1961; Sing Loud for Lovliness Anthol., 1962; Yearbooks, Poetry Soc. of Tex., var. years; Dallas News; Dallas Times Herald; Progressive Farmer; Cyclo-Flame; Poet; Biblical Recorder; Carovana, Italy; Flame; Peninsula Poets; Ideals; Presby. Survey; Tex. Freemason; Internat. Who's Who in Poetry Anthol.; Golden Book Anthol.; The Paper; Anthol. of American Poetry Book III; Union Christian News (Korea); Mich. State News; Sea to Sea in Song anthols., 1957, 58, 59, 60, 61, 62, 63; Laurel Leaves; Southwester Mag.; Southwester Anthol.; Hawk & Whippoorwill Recalled; Avalon Anthol. of Texas Poets; Spring Anthols. (UK) 1961, 62, 63, 64, 65, 66, 67, 68; Muse Anthols., 1962, 1963; Lone Star Gardener; Forney Messenger; Port Arthur News; Lufkin News; Pikeville (Ky.) News; Sunday Mag.; Dallas Times Herald; Eureka Springs Times-Echo; Hockaday Fourcast; The Numismatist; Numismatic Scrapbook; Nacogdoches Daily Sentinel; Home Life Mag.; The Guild Anthol.; Idaho Poets' & Writers' Guild Mag. Manifold, & many others in UK, India, Belgium, Italy, Korea, Philippines, US, etc. Honours, awards, etc: App. Poet Laureate of Tex., 1962, by State Legislature; Recip. Pres; Macapagal Gold Medal & named UPLI Hon. Poet Laureate Ldr. w. Citation & Laurel Wreath, 1965; Pres., Marcos UPLI Gold Medal, 1968; Citation, Poetry Soc. of Tex. for Disting. Serv., 1966; Citation, South & West, Inc., for Disting. Contbns. to Poetry, 1968; Deanne Settoon Mernagh Sonnet Award, Kaleidograph, 1957; Winner, 30 awards, Poetry Soc. of Tex. Contests & awards in other contests, jrnls. & anthols. Chosen as Speaker, Vachel Lindsay Assn. Annual Meeting, Springfield, Ill., 1966. Included in The 2000 Men of Achievement, 1969. Address: 3936 Colgate Av., Dallas, TX 75225, USA.

WIRPSZA, Witold, b. 4 Dec. 1918. Poet & Translator. Education: studies in law & music. Married Maria Kurecka, 2 children. Positions held: Hd. of Cultural Section of the bi-weekly PO PROSTU, 1956-57; Mbr., Editl. Bd., Nowa Kultura, Warsaw, 1957-58; Guest Lectr., Technische Universität, Berlin & at the Freie Universität, Berlin, 1971-72. Memberships: Polish Writers' Assn.; Int. PEN Club. Published works: (books of poetry) Sonata, 1949; Stocznia, 1949; Polemiki i piesni, 1950; Pisane w kraju, 1951; Dziennik Kozedo, 1951; List do zony, 1953; Z mojego zycia, 1956; Poematy i wiersze wybrane, 1956; Maly gatunek, 1960; Don Juan, 1960; Komentarze do fotografii, 1962; Drugi opor, 1965; Przesady, 1966; Traktat sklamany, 1968; Bruchsünden und todstücke, 1967. Contbr. to var. jrnls. in Poland, France & Germany. Honours, awards: The Literary Award of Szczecin, 1955; Award for Translation by ZAIKS, Warsaw, 1961; Translation Award of the 'Deutsche Akademie für Sprache und Dichtung', 1967. Address: Elkesteig 4, D-1 Berlin West 28, German Fed. Repub.

WIRTZ, Adele Watson. Writer. Education: B.A., Univ. of Tex., U.S.A. Widow of Lewis Milton Wirtz, 1 daughter. Positions held: Tchr. of H.S. Engl., 1 yr.; Pvte. Sec. to bus. exec.; Writer of Prose & Poetry. Memberships: Acad. of Am. Poets; Poetry Soc. of New Hampshire; Poetry Soc. of Tex.; Pres., Houston Chapt., ibid; Treas., Austin Chapt. Rep. in the following anthols: Three Voices, 1960; Golden Quill Anthols., 1962, 66, 67, 68, 69; This Friendly Shore, 1955; Today the Stars, 1960; Surf, Stars & Stones, 1961; This Singing Earth, 1959; Avalon Golden Book, 1961; Avalon Anthol. of Tex. Poets, 1963; From Sea to Sea in Song, 1962 & 64; Flame, 1965; Not From The

Victor, 1965; Variations of Mulberry (haiku), 1971; IWWP, 1971. Contbr. to num. jrnls., newspapers, mags., inclng: Christian Sci. Monitor; Denver Post; Portland Oregonian; S.C. News & Courier; Detroit News; The Writer's Voice; The Archer; Homelife; Cyclo Flame; Lyric; Am. Weave; The Muse; Hoosier Challenger; Am. Haiku; Univ. of Tex. Qtly. Recip. num. poetry awards. Address: 1801 Lavaca St., Apt. 12M, Austin, TX 78701, U.S.A.

WISE, Alice Caroline Holt, b. 26 Oct. 1922. Elementary School Librarian & Homemaker. Education: B.S. in Home Econ., Iowa State Univ., 1945; B.S. in Elem. Educ., Univ. of Minn., 1965; Lib. Certification, ibid, 1970. Married Ernice Wise, 6 children. Positions held: Asst. Dir., Nursery Schl., Univ. of Chicago Settlement House, 1945-46; Therapeutic Dietician, St. Olaf's Hosp., Austin, Minn., 1959-61; Elem. Schl. Tchr., Anoka, Minn., 1961-70; Elem. Schl. Libn., Anoka, Minn., 1970-. Memberships: Midwest Fed. of Chaparral Poets; Minn. League of Poets; former mbr., Chi Delta Phi, & Writers' Round Table, Iowa State Univ. Contbr. to: Mnpls. Midweek Sun; Coon Rapids Herald; Mnpls. Tribune. Honours, awards: Babcock Award for patriotic poem, Midwest Fed. of Chaparral Poets, 1972. Address: 1216 Banfill Circle, Minneapolis, MN 55444, U.S.A.

WISEMAN, Christopher S., b. 31 May 1936. Univ. Teacher. Education: M.A. (Cantab.); M.A.; Ph.D., Strathclyde Univ. Positions held: Lectr., Univ. of Strathclyde; Assoc. Prof., Univ. of Calgary, Alberta, Canada. Published works include: Waiting for the Barbarians. Contbr. to the following anthols., jrnls., mags., etc: Ambit; Stand; Transatlantic Review; English; Twentieth Century; Phoenix; Vigilante; The Scotsman; The Glasgow Review; December; White Pelican; Malahat Review; Queen's Qtly.; The Canadian Forum; The Seneca Review; Black Swamp Review; Oxford Opinion; The Sunday Times; Scottish Poetry I; Midland: An Anthol. Address: Dept. of Engl., Univ. of Calgary, Calgary, Alberta T2N 1N4, Canada.

WITHEFORD, Hubert, b. 18 Mar. 1921. Information Officer. Educ: Wellesley Coll., N.Z.; M.A., Victoria Univ., Wellington. m. Noel Brooke, 1s. Positions held: Joined N.Z. Civil Serv., 1939; Employed w. N.Z. Prime Minister's Off., 1939-45; N.Z. War Hist. Br., 1945-53; Civil Servant, Central Off. of Info., London, U.K., 1954-; Hd., Overseas Sect., Ref. Div., London, 1968-. Published works: Shadow of the Flame, 1949; The Falcon Mask, 1951; The Lightning Makes a Difference, 1962; A Native, Perhaps Beautiful, 1967. Contbr. to: Landfall; (anthologies) New Zealand Poetry Yearbook, 1951-54; An Anthology of New Zealand Verse, 1956; Penguin Book of New Zealand Verse, 1966; Young Commonwealth Poets '65, 1965. Recip., Jessie Mackay Prize for Poetry, 1963. Address: 88 Roxborough Rd., Harrow, Middlesex, U.K.

WITHERUP, William Allen, b. 24 Mar. 1935. Teacher. Education: Univ. of Wash., 2 yrs. Positions held: Tchr. in Performing Arts, Inst. of Am. Indian Arts, Santa Fe, N.M., 1963-64; Tchr. in Creative Writing, Evening Div., Monterey Peninsula Coll., Calif., 1971-; Tchr. in Creative Writing, Soledad Prison, Calif., 1971-72. Published works: This Endless Malice, co-translations of the Chilean poet, Enrique Lihn, 1969; Sangre de Cristo Mountain Poems, 1970; Horsetails (w. Stephan Taugher), 1970; Love Poems, 1970; Public & Private Poems, 1972; I Go Dreaming Roads, co-translations of Antonio Machado, 1973. Contbr. to: Poetry Northwest; Northwest Review; Lillabulero; Prairie Schooner; The Nation; Kayak; Stooge; Changes; New Am. & Canadian Poetry; Granite, etc. Honours, awards: Nat. Endowment of the Arts Award, 1967; Hart Crane & Alice Crane Williams Award, 1970. Address: Bixby Canyon, Coast Rte., Monterey, CA 93940, U.S.A.

WITT, Harold Vernon, b. 6 Feb. 1923. Writer. Education: B.A., Univ. of Calif., Berkeley, 1943; B.L.S., ibid, 1953; M.A., Univ. of Mich., 1947. Married, 3 children. Positions held: Ref. Libn., Washoe Co. Lib., Reno, Nev., 1953-55 & San Jose State Coll. Lib., 1956-

59; Free-lance Writer, 1959-. Memberships: Poetry Soc. of Am; International Poetry Soc. Published works include: Family in the Forest, 1956; Superman Unbound, 1956; The Death of Venus, 1958; Beasts in Clothes, 1961; Winesburg by the Sea: a Preview, 1970; Pop. by 1940: 40,000, 1971. Contbr. to the following anthols., jrnls., mags., etc: Hearse; Sat. Review; The New Yorker; Poetry; The Atlantic; The New Republic; Commonweal; The Nation; The Reporter; The Carleton Miscellany; Poetry NW; Mich. Qtly.; The Hudson Review; The Kenyon Review; NY Times; The Paris Review; Beloit Poetry Jrnl.; Poet Lore; The Antioch Review; Pebble; The Dragonfly; Qtly. Review of Lit., etc. Honours, awards: Hopwood Award for poetry, 1947; James D. Phelan Award for Narrative Poetry, 1960; Co-winner, San Francisco Poetry Ctr. Competition for Poetic Drama, 1963; 3rd Prize, Poet Lore's Stephen Vincent Benet Competition for narrative verse, 1969. Address: 39 Claremont Ave., Orinda, Calif. 94563, USA.

WITTLER, Janet Marie, b. 30 Jan. 1947. Teacher; Editor. Education: B.S., Univ. of Wis., Madison, 1970; M.A., ibid, 1974. Positions held: Editl. & Prodn. Asst., AMA, Dearborn St., Chgo., 1970; Lang. Arts Tchr., Sr. H.S., Green Bay, Wis., 1970-71; Engl. Tchr., Title III Reading, Jr. H.S., Green Bay, 1971-; Housefellow, Univ. of Wis., Madison, 1972-73; Editl. Asst., Law Alumni Assn., Madison, 1973. Memberships: Nat. Fed. of State Poetry Socs.; Wis. Fellowship of Poets. Published works: Creation, anthol., 1971; Heart's Chord, coll. poems, 1974. Contbr. to: Shore Poetry Anthol. mag.; Flight; The Twisted Dial; The Badger Herald Octopus; Apostrophe mag.; The Concord Saunterer. Honours, awards: Annual Award, AAUW, Green Bay Br., 1972; Cert. of Merit, Apostrophe, S.C., 1973; Breadloaf Writers Auditorship in Poetry, 1971-72 & Contbr. in Poetry, 1973. Address: 67 Berwick St., Belmont, MA 02178, U.S.A.

WITTLIN, Joseph (Jozef), b. 17 Aug. 1896. Writer. Education: studied Philos., Univ. of Vienna, 1915-16; Studied at Univ. of Lwow, Poland, 1918-19. Married Halina Handelsman, 1 daughter. Positions held: Tchr., Polish Lang. & Lit., Gymnasium, Lwow, 1919-1921; affil. w. the Grp. of Polish Expressionists in Poznan, Zdroj, 1919-20; Lit. Dir., Municipal Theatre & Lectr. Schl. of Drama, Lodz (Co-Fndr.), 1921-24; Writer, transl., adapter from Italian & German, Warsaw, 1927; Co-Ed., N.Y. Polish weekly, Tygodnik Polski, 1941-43; Co-Ed., The Democratic Heritage of Poland, 1953; worked for Radio Free Europe, 1952. Memberships: Int. PEN; Pen in Exile (Chmn., 1960-63); Polish Writers Assn. in Exile; Corres. Mbr., German Acad. of Poetry & Language, 1971. Published works incl: Hymns, coll. of poems, 1920; Gilgamesh, new version, 1922; transl. of Homer's Odyssey from Greek into Polish, 1924; War, Peace & a Poet's Soul, book of essays & addresses, 1925; The Odyssey, 2nd version, 1931; Etaphy (stages), travel sketches, 1933; The Salt of the Earth, first part of the Saga of the Patient Footsoldier, 1935, 2nd edn. 1941, new Polish edn., 1954, German edn., 1969 (transl. into 6 langs); Your Freedom & Ours, an anthol. of Polish Democratic Thought, 1943, '44; Moj Lwow, 1946; Polish transl. of John Hersey's Horoshima, 1948; Orpheus in the Inferno of the Twentieth Century, book of essays & other prose, 1963. Recip. awards for The Salt of the Earth from var. orgs. Address: 5400 Fieldston Rd., N.Y., NY 10471, U.S.A.

WOESSNER, Warren, b. 31 May 1944; Research Chemist. Education: B.A., Cornell Univ., 1966; Ph.D., Univ. of Wis., Madison, Wis., 1971. Positions held: Postdoctoral Rsch. Assoc., Schl. of Pharmacy, Univ. of Wis., Madison, Wis.; Ed., Abraxas Mag. Published works include: The Forest and the Trees, 1968; The Rivers Return, 1969; Inroads, 1970; Cross-Country, 1972; Landing, 1973. Contbr. to the following anthols., jrnls., mags., etc: Poetry Chicago; Poetry NW; Epoch; December; Sumac; Quixote; Bones; Hearse; Wis. Review; The N Stone Review; The Greenfield Review; Abraxas; Modine Gunch; The Trojan Horse; The Nation; Kaleidoscope; Connections; Cronopious;

View. Honours, awards: Wis. Mem. Union Creative Writing Competition Awards, 1967-70. Address: 1831 S Park St.(9), Madison, Wis. 53713, USA.

WOFFORD, Grace Kirk, pen name **HOPE, Evelyn,** b. 9 Dec. 1914. Manager. Education: B.A., Blue Mountain Coll., 1934; post grad. studies, Univs. of hicago & Miss. Married George C. Wofford, 4 daughters. Positions held: H.S. Tchr.; Pres., Women's Soc. of Christian Serv.; V.P., Blue Mountain Coll. Nat. Alumnae Assn.; Mgr., Ctrl. Whse. Miss. State D.P.W. Memberships: State Pres., Delta Br. Pres., Nat. Letters Bd., Nat. League of Am. Pen Women; Miss. Poetry Soc.; Pres., Drew Culture Club. Published works: Lyric Poems, 1964. Rep. in following anthols: Singing Mississippi, 1938; Toward the Stars, 1948; The Muse, 1944; Am. Anthol. of Poetry, 1963. Contbr. to var. jrnls. & newspapers. Honours, awards: 1st Prize, Miss. Poetry Soc., 1941 & '45; 1st prize, Southeast Region, Nat. League Am. Pen Women, 1962; Gemstone Award, Mid-South Poetry Fest., 1969; Wrote official poem for founding Southern Lit. Fest., 1937. Address: 123 N. 3rd St., Drew, MS 38737, U.S.A.

WOLCOTT, Katharyn, b. 24 Aug. 1899. Poet; Writer; Critic; Lecturer. Education: Aff., Columbia Univ.; grad., Famous Writers Schl.; R.N. Married John H. Grouls, Jr. Positions held: Vol. Chmn., Am. Red. Cross; Mbr., N.H.C. Exec.Bd., Am. Red. Cross during WWII; Reader, Borestone Mt. Poetry Awards, 1960-70; Poet Laureate, H. Wolcott Soc., 1973. Memberships: Poetry Soc. of Am.; Pen & Brush Club, N.Y.; Treas., N.Y. Women Poets, 1953-60. Published works: (book) Wind Across The Threshold, 1948. Rep. in following anthols: Columbia Poetry; New Voices; Am. Poets; N.J. History; Int. Who's Who in Poetry Anthol., 1973. Contbr. to: N.Y. Times; Christian Sci. Monitor; Wash. Post; Educational Forum; Fiddlehead, etc. Honours, awards: Pat Davis Meml. Prize for Poetry, Pen & Brush, 1968; 3 annual poetry prizes of N.Y. Women Poets, 1955, '65, 68; Candice Stevenson Meml. Prize for Poetry, 1970; Pen & Brush 1st Prize for Short Story, 1970-72. Address: 72 Riverside Ave., Apt. 39, Red Bank, NJ 07701, U.S.A.

WOLGAMOT, John Barton, pen names **WALDROP, Keith, WALDROP, Rosmarie, CAMP, James,** b. 24 Aug. 1925. Poet. Education: B.A., Harvard Univ., 1947; M.A., Organic Chemistry, Princeton Univ., 1948; Ph.D., Astronomy, ibid, 1954. Positions held: Instr. in Astronomy, Kantian Coll. of Metaphysics, 1954-60; Astronomer in Residence, Bemidji Coll., 1960-64; Mgr., The Little Carnegie, 1965-70; Poet-in-Res., Regent Coll., 1970-. Published works: In Sarah, Mencken, Christ & Beethoven there are Men & Women, 1944; A Windmill near Calvary, 1900; An Ediot from the Emperor, 1969; Camp Printing, 1970; Body Image, 1971; To the Sincere Reader, 1971; The Aggressive Ways of the Casual Stranger, 1972. Contbr. to: New Yorker; Antioch Review; Harper's Bazaar; Prism Int., etc. Honours, awards: Hopwood Award, 1960; Borestone Poetry Award, 1961; Aardvark Prize, 1967; Am. Poetry Soc. Award, 1967. Address: 71 Elmgrove Ave., Providence, RI 02906, U.S.A.

WONG, Alan Yun Sang, pen name **WONG, Alan L.,** b. 28 June 1938. Poet; Painter. Education: St. John's Coll., Southsea, Hants., U.K.; Bachelor hons. degree in French Lit., Columbia Univ., N.Y., U.S.A. Positions held: Taught at Dalton Schl., N.Y. & Univ. of Hong Kong Extra-Mural Dept., Hong Kong. Published works: (books in English published in London) Drift, 1963; Shailo & Other Poems, 1967; From The Silence, 1968; Chinese Sonnets, 1968; Deeper Spring, 1969; The Pillar of Wisdom, 1971; Angel in the Dark, 1972; A Gathering of Dusty Grains, 1973; The Orphan of China, 1973; (plays & essays in Chinese published in Taiwan) The Last Champagne, 1963; And to Think I Had It, 1964; La Morale d'Henry de Montherlant, 1971. Recip., Pres. Marcos Gold Medal, 1969. Address: 24 Park Gate, Ealing, London, W.5, U.K.

WONG MAY, b. 16 Nov. 1944. Poet. Educ: B.A., Univ. of Singapore; M.A. Univ. of Iowa, U.S.A. Published works: A Bad Girl's Book of Animals, 1969. Contbr. to: American Scholar; Poetry; Epoch; (anthologies) Intro 2, 1969; Midland II, 1970. Honours, awards: Univ. of Iowa Writers Prog. Fellowship, 1966-67; Aspen Writers Workshop Poetry Scholarship, Aspen, Colo., 1967. Address: c/o Harcourt Brace & World, 757 Third Ave., N.Y., NY, U.S.A.

WONG PHUI NAM, b. 20 Sept. 1935. Economist. Educ: B.A., Univ. of Singapore. Positions held: Economist, Malaysian Indl. Dev. Finance Berhad, Kuala Lumpur, Malaysia. Published works: How the Hills are Distant, 1968. Contbr. to: Tenggara; Poetry Singapore; (anthologies) Bunga Emas, 1964; Young Commonwealth Poets '65, 1965; Seven Poets, 1969. Address: Malaysian Industrial Development Finance Berhad, 117 Jalan Ampang, Kuala Lumpur, Selangor, Malaysia.

WONODI, Okogbule, b. 27 Aug. 1936. Educator. Education: B.A. (Hons.) in Engl., Univ. of Nigeria, Nsukka, 1965; M.A., Univ. of Iowa, Iowa City, U.S.A., 1966. Married Eunice Wonodi, 3 sons, 1 daughter. Positions held: Lectr. in Engl., Univ. of Nigeria, Nsukka, 1966-70; Personnel Mgr., Nigerian Tobacco Co. Ltd., Port Harcourt, Nigeria, 1970-72; Vis. Prof. of African Lit. & Participant, Int. Writing Prog., Univ. of Iowa, U.S.A., 1972-74; Gen. Mgr., Rivers State Newspaper Corp., Port Harcourt, Nigeria. Fellow, Iowa Writing Prog. Published works: Icheke & Other Poems, 1964; Two Poems for Leaders of Thought, 1967; Dusts of Exile, 1971. Contbr. to: Young C'wealth Poets '65; West African Verse, 1968; New Voices of the C'wealth, 1968; Poetry from Africa, 1968; The Poetry of Dance, 1971; New African Writing, 1969; Nigeria Mag.; Transition; Black Orpheus; Lit. Review, N.J., U.S.A. Address: P.O. Box 834, Port Harcourt, Nigeria.

WOOD, Eleanor Chaffee, pen names: **CHAFFEE, Eleanor Alletta; RODMAN, Frances.** Editor & Writer. Membership: Poetry Soc. of America. Contbr. to: Saturday Eve. Post; Saturday Review; Ladies' Home Journal; NY Times; McCall's Mag., etc. Address: 145 Walnut St., Ridgewood, NJ 07450, USA.

WOOD, Leland Foster, b. 9 May 1885. Minister. Education: B.A., Univ. of Rochester, 1908; M.A., ibid, 1914; Dip., Rochester Theol. Sem., 1911; B.D., ibid, 1914; Ph.D., Univ. of Chicago, 1923. Positions held: Missionary, Am. Bapt. Foreign Mission Soc., Congo Mission, 1911-20; Prof. of Relig. Educ., Bucknell Univ., 1923-25; Prof. of Christian Sociol., Social Ethics Rochester Theol. Sem., 1925-28, continuing in the same merged w. Colgate Theol. Sem. to become Colgate Rochester Divinity Schl., 1928-32, Sec. tof the Commn. on Marriage & the Home, Federal Coun. of the Churches of Christ in the U.S.A., 1932-50. Member, Rochester, N.Y. Poetry Soc. Published works: Beatitudes for the Family, 1935. sev. edns., rev. as Beatitudes For the Family & Other Verses, 1952; Fourteenth printing, ibid, 1974; Verses for Fun, 1958; Help-Tell Bible Verses, 1960. Contbr. to: The Am. Family; The Christian Home; The Christian Century; Rochester, N.Y. Democrat & Chronicle; The Gleam, Annual of Rochester Poetry Soc. Address: 12 Brighton St., Rochester, NY 14607, U.S.A.

WOOD, Marguerite. Chartered Physiotherapist. Education: Devonshire Royal Hosp., Buxton, Derbys. Married, 2 children. Positions held: Gov., Brentwood Co. H.S.; Justice of the Peace for County of Essex; Mbr., Probation & Aftercare Comm.; Deputy Chmn., Juvenile Bench (B'wood); Assoc. Ed., Envoi. Memberships: Poetry Soc.; Suffolk Poetry Soc.; Fellow, Int. Poetry Soc.; Essex Naturalists Trust; Essex Archaeological Soc. Published works: Stone of Vision, 1964; Windows Are Not Enough, 1971; Where Lurks My Soul, in prep. Contbr. to: (anthols.) Without Adam, 1968; Look Through a Diamond (Canada), 1971; Poems of the Sixties, 1970; Suffolk Poetry, 1970; Lamda VIII, 1973; Int. Poetry Anthol., 1974; (mags.) Outposts; Scrip; East Anglian. Address: 69 Mount Cres., Brentwood, Essex, U.K.

WOODALL, Stella, b. 15 Jan. 1899. Professional Writer; Poet. Education: HS Grad.; Coll. & extra writing courses, 6 years; Engl. & Creative Writing, Tex. Univ.; Famous Writers' Schl., etc. Personal details: daughter of Railroad Executive; traveled extensively throughout USA & Mexico; married. Positions held: Free-lance Profl. Writer. Memberships: Pres., Poetry Soc. of San Antonio, Tex.; Chmn., The Stella Woodall Circle, Meth. Ch., San Antonio, 8 years; Chmn., Strategy Round Table & Reporter, Round Table of Letters, San Antonio Women's Club.; PR Chmn. & Poet Laureate Chmn., Alamo Dist., Tex. Fed. of Women's Clubs; Int. Platform Assn.; Nat. Advsry. Bd. & Nat. Contest Chmn., Am. Poetry League; Past Pres., Armed Forces Writers' League; Past Pres., Sr. Citizens Club. Published works include: 12 Air Force Histories (one of which selected as Model History for Flying Airforce Bases throughout the world); Most Asked For Poems 1971; Inspirational Poems, 1972; Golden Treasures, 1973. Contbr. to the following anthols., jrnls., mags., newspapers, etc: Ideals; Poet; Progressive Life; Best in Poetry; American Voice; American Poetry League; Armed Forces Writer; Air Force Times; Tex. Methodist; Poetry Ed., Free Press; Travis Park News; Ralls Banner; San Marcos Record; San Antonio Express-News; SW Tex. Historical Yearbook. Honours, awards: Poet Laureate of Texas Alternate, 1973-74. Award for poem submitted to Alamo Dist., Tex. Fed. of Women's Clubs, 1971; KBAT-TV Tex. Star Award, 1971; Churchmanship Award, Travis Park United Meth. Ch., 1971; Patron of Poetry, 1971; Hon. Mbrship. & Dir., Beautify San Antonio, 1972. Address: 3915 SW Military Dr., San Antonio, Tex. 78211, USA.

WOODCOCK, George, b. 8 May 1912. Editor and Writer. Education: Sir Wm. Borlase's School, Marlow. Married. World traveller. Lecturer and subsequently Asst. Prof. of English, Univ. of Washington, 1954-56; Asst. and later Assoc. Prof. of English and Lecturer in Asian Studies, Univ. of B.C., 1956-63; Editor of Now, 1940-47; Editor of Canadian Literature, 1959–. Member, League of Canadian Poets; Royal Soc. of Canada; Royal Geographical Soc. Pubs. The White Island, 1940; The Centre Cannot Hold, 1943; Imagine the South, 1947; Selected Poems, 1967; plus some 30 vols. of prose. Verse plays produced by the Canadian Broadcasting Corporation: Maskerman; The Island of Demons; The Floor of the Night; The Benefactor; The Empire of Shadows; The Brideship. Contrib. to: Partisan Review; Tomorrow; Saturday Review; Tribune; New Verse; Twentieth Century Verse; Poetry London; Poetry Folios; Poetry Quarterly; Poetry Review; Contemporary Verse (Canada); Poetry Northwest, etc. Honours, Awards: LL.D., Univ. of Victoria, 1967; D.Litt., Sir George Williams Univ., 1970; Molson Prize of the Canada Council, 1973. Address: 6429 McCleery Street, Vancouver 13, B.C., Canada.

WOODS, Alice Edna, b. 21 Dec. 1891. Teacher. Education: B.A., Iowa State Tchrs. Coll., 1920; Univ. of SC, 1924. Tchr., Iowa High Schls., 1916-21, '22-23; Tchr., SD High Schls., 1921-22; Tchr., Engl. & Soc. Studies, Elem. & High Schls., Los Angeles, Calif., 1924-57. Memberships: Chmn., Mbr.-at-Large, Calif. Fed. Chaparral Poets, 1963-65; Fla. State Poetry Soc. Inc.; Iowa Poetry Day Assn.; Southern Calif. Womens Press Club; Eastern Star; Retired Tchrs. Assn., etc. Publications: Voices of My Century, 1972. Contbr. to: Velvet Paws in Print Vol. 2, 1967; The Wagging Tale, 1969; Pageant of Poetry, 1947; Talent-Songwriters & Poets, 1947; Am. Bard; Flamingo; Selected Poems, Fla., 1967, '68, '69, '70; Limericks, 1967; Mem. Poems, 1967, '68, '69, '70; Brochure of Poems, Iowa, 1967, '69, '70. Recip. of sev. poetry hons. & awards. Address: 849 W 69th St., Los Angeles, Calif. 90044, USA.

WOODS, Barbara Gullo, b. 27 Nov. 1934. Writer; Teacher. Education: B.A., San Jose State Coll., 1956; M.A., Univ. of Iowa, 1967. Positions held: Engl. Tchr., Salt Lake City, Utah; Dept. Chmn., Engl. Dept., Highland HS, Salt Lake City. Contbr. to the following anthols., jrnls., mags., etc: Haiku Highlights, 1968, '71; Bachaet, 1969; Am. Bard, 1969; Shore Poetry Anthol.;

Yearbook of Mod. Poetry, 1971; Poetry of Our Time, 1972; Lyrics of Love, 1972; Cimarron Review, 1972. Address: 633 Stowell Dr., Rochester, N.Y. 14616, USA.

WOODS, John (Warren), b. 12 Jul. 1926. Professor of English. Education: B.A. (1949), M.A. (1955), Indiana Univ.; Advanced study, Univ. of Iowa. Married to Emily Newbury; Two sons, David and Richard. Grad. Asst., Indiana Univ., 1950-51; Instructor, Morgan Park Military Academy, Chicago, 1951-55; Prof., Western Michigan Univ., 1955–; Prof., Univ. of California at Irvine, 1967. Pubs. The Deaths at Paragon, Indiana, 1955; On the Morning of Color, 1961; The Cutting Edge, 1966; Keeping Out of Trouble, 1968; Turning to Look Back; Poems, 1955-1970, (1972); The Knees of Widows, 1970; Alcohol, 1973; Bone Flicker, 1973. Contrib. to: Folio; Kenyon Review; Poetry New York; Chicago Review; Epoch; The Western Review; Poetry; Paris Review; Kayak; Fresco; Calliope; The Saturday Review; Prairie Schooner; Poetry Northwest; Massachusetts Review; The Critic; Chelsea; Tennessee Poetry Review; Choice; New York Quarterly; CCC Journal; Western Humanities Review; Shenandoah; Niobe; American Weave; Southern Poetry Review; North American Review; Northwest Review; Mad River Review; Westigan Review; Hudson Review; Sumac; Windless Orchard; December; Jeopardy; Hearse; Concerning Poetry; Field. Recipient Theodore Roethke Prize, Poetry Northwest, 1968; Award, National Endowment of the Arts, 1969. Address: English Dept., Western Michigan Univ., Kalamazoo, Mich., 49001, USA.

WOODWARD, (Chevalier) John William, b. 19 Sept. 1920. Author; Publisher; Editor; Poet; Playwright. Positions held: Libn., Rolls-Royce; Admin., Personnel, Employment & Welfare Off., ibid; Chmn., Four Names Publng. Co.; Mbr., Editl. Bds., Royal Blue Book.; Bibliog. of Monaco; Cecil Day-Lewis, The Poet Laureate, A Bibliog.; IWWP, etc.; Advsry. Bd., Dict. of Pub. Affairs. Memberships: Life Fellow, Int. Inst. of Arts & Letters; Life Pres., Int. Writers' Guild & Soc. of New Authors; V.P., Int. Poetry Soc.; Life Pres., Derby Writers' Guild; Life Pres., Derby & Derbyshire Dumas Assn.; Fellow, Intercontinental Biog. Assn.; Life Pres., Derby Int. Writers' Guild; Kt. M.T.; Int. Mbrship Advsr., & Fndr.-Fellow, Int. Poetry Soc.; Life Mbr., Lancs. Authors Assn.; New Arts Theatre Club. Published works: (poems) Beyond the Dawn, 1949; Prelude, 1952; Four Names Anthol., 1954-56; Purrings of Pussycat, Ph.D., 1957-58; Mss. Anthol., 1958; Jeptha Young, His Life & Works, 1954; Fugue, 1962; Pebbles in the Pool, 1965; Though Roses Die, 1967; The Haunted Ballroom, 1965; Hold Back The Dawn, 1969; Lucifer Reflects, 1970; Not Bread Alone, 1971; The Agony & The Ecstacy, 1971; The Tapestry, 1972; num. plays. Contbr. to num. jrnls., anthols., etc. in many countries & to Int. Writers' Guild, Soc. of New Authors publs. & IBA Mag. Honours, awards: from Int. Writers' Guild & Soc. of New Authors, 1950-52; Derby Poetry Circle, 1953-54; Derby Writers' Guild, 1955-57; Derby Int. Writers' Guild, 1958-64; Dip., Int. Inst. of Arts & Letters, 1963; Cert. of Merit, DIB, 1967, '70, Nottingham Poetry Soc., 1968, IBA, 2000 Men of Achievement, IWWP, Nat. Register of Prominent Ams. & Int. Notables, all 1970; Elected 'Prominent Am', 1970; Kt. of Grace, Sovereign Order of St. John of Jerusalem (Chevalier, OSJ), 1971; Hon. Mbr., Eastern Ctr., N.Y. of The Poetry Soc. of London, 1970; Int. Award of Hon. Medallion & Dip. of Distinction, Int. Acad. of Leadership & World Inst. of Drs., 1969; Hon. Life Mbr., Int. Coun. of Ldrs. & Scholars, 1969, etc. Address: Abbots Lodge, 2 Madeley St., Derby DE3 8EX, U.K.

WOODWARD, Margaret R., b. 4 Feb. 1945. Chief Adoption Caseworker. Education: B.A. in Engl., Calif. Bapt. Coll.; currently enrolled for M.F.A., Univ. of Alaska, Anchorage. Positions held: Clerk Typist, Procurement Office, Elmendorf AFB, summer 1964; Asst. Sec., Pub. Rels. Office, Calif. Bapt. Coll., 1964-65; Accounts Payable Personnel, Bus. Office, ibid, 1965-67; Clerk Typist, Info. Office, Elmendorf AFB,

1967-68; Sec. to Command Histn., ibid, 1968-69; Adoption Case Wkr., Catholic Charities, Anchorage, Alaska, 1969–. Memberships: World Poetry Soc. Intercontinental; Poetry Soc. of Alaska. Contbr. to: Anchorage Times; Anchorage Daily News; Raven; Poet (WPSI); Haiku Drops from the Great Dipper (anthol. published by Poetry Soc. of Alaska). Recip., cash prize (3rd pl. winner), Anchorage Daily News Winter Contest, 1967. Address: 2752 West 42nd Pl., No. 3, Anchorage, AK 99503, U.S.A.

WOOLF, Henry, b. 1930. Hackney, UK. Professional Actor. Education: Hackney Downs Grammar Schl.; Exeter & Bristol Univs.; Wm. & Mary Coll., Va., USA. Married to Susan Williamson, actress, 3 children. Author of one volume of poems. Contbr. to: Ambit; Tribune; PEN Anthology; Recorder; Dial-a-Poem. Address: Folkestone, UK.

WORKS, Elberta Benschoton, b. 27 Feb. 1896. Housewife. Education: Univ. of Bowling Green, Ohio, 2 yrs.; special course in writing poetry under Lilith Lorraine. Married, 1 daughter. Memberships: Poetry Soc. of Va.; Avalon. Contbr. to: The Mitre Press Anthol., 1967; IWWP Anthol., 1971; Golden Anniversary Anthol. of the Poetry Soc. of Va.; Flame; Cycloflame; Cardinal; Different, etc. Recip. var. awards from mags. Address: Rt. 1, Box 242, Five Forks Teacherage, Williamsburg, VA 23185, U.S.A.

WOROSZYLSKI, Wiktor, b. 8 June 1927. Writer. Education: Med. studies, Univ. of Lodz; studies of Polish lang., Univ. of Warsaw; studied of Russian lang., Maksym Gorki's Inst. of Lit., Moscow, 1956; Dr. of Russian Philol. Married Janina Witczak, 1 son, 1 daughter. Positions held: Ed.-in-Chief, 'Nowa Kultura', weekly, 1956-58. Memberships: Polish Sect., PEN Club; Polish Writers Assn. Published works: Smierci nie ma, 1951; Z rozmów, 1955, '56; Wanderjahre, 1960; Twój powszedni morderca, 1962; Niezgoda na uklön, 1964; Przygoda w Babilonie, 1969; Zagläda gatunków, 1970; Po zagladzie, 1974; Wybór wierszy, 1974; biog. books on Saltykov-Scedrin, Mayakovsky, Jesenin & Pushkin. Contbr. to lit. jrnls. Recip., Nat. Award, 1951. Address: ul. Mickiewicza 30 m. 46, 01-616 Warsaw, Poland.

WRAY (The Chevalier) William Henry, pen name, **WRAY, Bill,** b. 20 Nov. 1932. Area Organiser. Education: Correspondence courses in many subjects; Dip. Graphology; Doctorates in Theol., Div., Litt., Musicology, etc. Married Marlene Ellis; 3 children. Memberships: numerous, including Internat. Poetry Soc. (Fellow); Royal Philharmonic Soc. (Fellow); Richard III Soc.; Royal Soc. of St. George; Max Steiner Music Soc.; Assoc., Songwriters Guild of GB, and of the Light Music Soc., GB.; Brit. Music Hall Soc.; Cinema Theatre Assoc.; Chinese Poets Assn. (Taiwan); World Writers Org., Sao Paulo (Patron); Free World Int. Acad. (Academician); UPLI; Geneva Arts Club; Imperial Byzantine Soc. (life); Bards of Grand Rapids; The Heraldry Soc.; Philosophical Soc. of England; World Univ. Roundtable, Arizona, etc. Published works: The Common Sense of Christianity, 1964; The Self is One, 1970; Ode to the Samarinesi, 1971. Contbr. to many newspapers, journals, including: Daily Mail (Hull); Hull Times; Jrnl. of World Congress of Poets, 1973; Fate; Laurel Leaves; Amman Review; IWWP (anthol.). As composer & lyricist has produced many short pieces and songs. Recip. of many honours and awards, including World Poetry Medal, UPLI, 1970; Acad. of Merit, Free World Internat. Acad.; Pres. Marcos Award for Relig. Literature (Philippines); Awards from Gt. China Arts Coll. (Hong Kong), St. Thomas Acad. (Montreal); K.O.S.J. (Malta); Col.-A.D.C., La., USA; Hon. Citizen, New Orleans, and numerous decorations from many countries. Address: 411 Bowness House, Walker Street, Hull, Yorkshire HU3 2NJ, UK.

WRIGHT, Celeste Turner, b. 17 March 1906. University Professor. Education: A.B., Univ. of Calif., Los Angeles, 1925; M.A. (1926), Ph.D. (1928), Univ. of Calif., Berkeley. Married, Vedder Allen Wright; 1 s.

(Vedder, Jr.). Positions held: (Since 1928) Member, Dept. of Engl., Univ. of Calif., Davis; Prof. since 1948; Chairman, Engl. Dept., 1928-55; Faculty Research Lecturer for the Academic Senate, U.C. Davis, 1963. Membership: Poetry Soc. of America. Published works: Etruscan Princess and Other Poems, 1964; A Sense of Place, 1973. Contbr. to: Alentour; The American Bard; The American Poet; American Weave; The Archer; The Arizona Qtly.; The Beloit Poetry Journal; Cimarron Review; Different; Down East; Essence; The Florida Mag. of Verse; Imprints Qtly.; Harper's Kaleidograph; The Laurel Review; The Lyric; Maelstrom; Midwestern Univ. Qtly.; Poet Lore; Poetry (Chicago); The Poetry Chapbook; Poetry Poetry Venture; Prairie Schooner; Queen's Qtly.; Quoin; South & West; The Southern Poetry Review; The Univ. Review; Versecraft; Voices; The West Coast Review; Westward; Wings; The Yale Review; The New Mexico Qtly. Review; NY Herald-Tribune; The Winged Word; The Northwest Review; Cycle; The Pacific Spectator; The Western Humanities Review. Awards: Reynolds Lyric Prize, 1963; Grand prize, Ina Coolbrith Circle contest, 1961, 1965, 1970; Fellow, Univ. of Calif. Inst. for Creative Arts, 1966-67 (writing poetry full time for the year); Commencement Speaker, Univ. of Calif., Davis (Coll. of Letters and Science), 1973. Address: Dept. of Engl., Univ. of Calif., Davis, CA 95616, USA.

WRIGHT, Charles, b. 25 Aug. 1935. Teacher. Education: B.A., Davidson Coll.; M.F.A., Univ. of Iowa. Positions held: Asst. Prof., Univ. of Calif. at Irvine, 1966–; Lectr., N. Am. Lit., Univ. of Padua, Italy, 1968-69. Published works: The Dream Animal, 1968; The Grave of the Right Hand, 1970; Venice Notebook, 1971; Back Water, 1973; Hard Freight, 1973. Contbr. to: The New Yorker; The Nation; Poetry; The New Orleans Review; The N. Am. Review; The NW Review. Recip., Eunice Tietjeus Award, Poetry Mag., 1969. Address: Dept. of Engl., Univ. of Calif., Irvine, Calif. 92664, USA.

WRIGHT, David John Murray, b. 23 Feb. 1920. Editor; Translator; Poet. Educ: B.A. Oriel Coll., Oxford, U.K. m. Phillipa Reid, 1951. Published works: Poems, 1949; Moral Stories, 1954; Monologue of a Deaf Man, 1958; Adam at Evening, 1965; Nerve Ends, 1969; (verse translations) Beowulf, 1957; The Canterbury Tales, 1965; (other) Roy Campbell, 1960; Algarve (w. P. Swift), 1965; Minho and North Portugal (w. P. Swift), 1968; Deafness: A Personal Account, 1969. Ed., The Faber Book of Twentieth Century Verse (w. John Heath-Stubbs), 1965; Longer Contemporary Poems, 1966; The Mid-Century English Poetry, 1940-1960, 1965. Contbr. to: London Magazine; Agenda; Chirimo; New Coin; Poetry; (anthologies) Chatto Book of Modern Poetry, 1915-1955, 1956; A Book of South African Verse, 1959; 100 Postwar Poems, 1968. Honours, awards: Atlantic Award in Lit., 1950; Guinness Poetry Award, 1958, '60; Gregory Fellowship in Poetry, 1965-67. Address: c/o A.D. Peters Ltd., 10 Buckingham St., Adelphi, London W.C.2, U.K.

WRIGHT, Elizabeth Prince (Weil), b. 5 Feb. 1905. Retired Teacher. Education: B.A., Radcliffe, 1927; Cert., Special Educ., Western Mich., 1968. Married, 2 sons. Positions held: Sec. to Dean, St. Lawrence Univ., 1930-37; H.S. Engl. Tchr., 1940-41; Substitute Tchr., 1944-62; Tchr., Kambly Schl. for Retarded, 1962–. Member, Mich. Poetry Soc. Contbr. to: Peninsula Poets; World Poetry; Ludington News; AAUW Newsletter. Recip. num. poetry prizes. Address: 1003 North Ave., Battle Creek, MI 49017, U.S.A.

WRIGHT, Frank William Nielsen, pen name **WRIGHT, Neil,** b. 30 Sept. 1935. University Teacher. Education: M.A., Victoria Univ. of Wellington, New Zealand. Married, 1 child. Published works include: The Park, 1963; The Mythologist, 1963; A Baffled Paradise, 1963; The Imaginings of the Heart, 1965; A Mid-Winter Garland, 1966; Beyond Nonsense, 1967; The Divine Parody, 1967; Man and No Man, 1968; The Elegant Barbarian, 1968; The Brazen Tower, 1969; The

Crocodile Dances, 1969; Only a Bullet Will Stop Me Now, 1970. Address: Engl. Dept., Victoria Univ., POB 196, Wellington, New Zealand.

WRIGHT, George T., b. 17 Dec. 1925. Professor of English. Education: B.A. Columbia College, 1946; M.A. Columbia University, 1947; Univ. of California (Berkeley), Ph.D., 1957. Married to Jerry Honeywell. Instr. and Asst. Prof. (of English), Univ. of Kentucky, 1957-60; Asst. Prof., San Francisco State College, 1960-61; Assoc. Prof., Univ. of Tennessee, 1961-68; (Fulbright Lecturer in American Lit., Univ. d'Aix-Marseille, 1964-66); Prof. Univ. of Minnesota, 1968-. Contrib. to: New Yorker; Nation; American Review; Sewanee Review; Arizona Quarterly; Tennessee Poetry Journal; North Stone Review; Counter/Measures; Druid; Berkeley Review; East and West; Circle. Address: 1205 Upton Avenue N., Minneapolis, Minnesota 55411, USA.

WRIGHT, James Arlington, b. 13 Dec. 1927. English Instructor. Educ: B.A., Kenyon Coll., Gambier, Ohio; M.S. & Ph.D., Univ. of Wash., Seattle. m. Edith Anne Runk, 2s. Positions held: Former Instr., Univ. of Minnesota, Mpls.; Former Instr., Macalester Coll., St. Paul, Minnesota; Instr., Engl. Dept., Hunter Coll., N.Y., current. Published works: The Green Wall, 1957; Saint Judas, 1959; The Branch Will Not Break, 1963; Shall We Gather at the River, 1968; (verse translations) The Rider on the White Horse, by Theodor Storm, 1964; Twenty Poems by Georg Trakl, 1963; Twenty Poems of Cesar Vallejo, 1964; Twenty Poems of Pablo Neruda (w. Robert Bly), 1968. Contbr. to: New Yorker; Hudson Review; Chicago Review; Poetry; (anthologies) Poetry for Pleasure, 1960; Contemporary American Poetry, 1962; Erotic Poetry, 1963; American Poems, 1964; Poems on Poetry, 1965; An Introduction to Poetry, 1967; Heartland, 1967; Poems of Our Moment, 1968. Honours, awards: Fulbright Schlrship., 1952-53; Nat. Inst. of Arts & Letters Grant; Guggenheim Grant; Oscar Blumenthal Award, 1968.

WRIGHT, Judith Arundell (Mrs. McKinney), pen name **WRIGHT, Judith,** b. 31 May 1915. Writer. Education: Sydney Unlv., Australia. Positions held: Sec. work until 1948; Univ. Statistician, Univ. of Queensland, 1948-49; Writer, 1949-. Has lectured in lit. at Univ. of Queensland & as Guest Lectr. at most other Australian Univs. Memberships: Councillor, Australian Soc. of Authors. Published works: The Moving Image, 1946; Woman to Man, 1949; The Gateway, 1953; The Two Fires, 1955; Australian bird poems (pamphlet), 1961; Birds, 1962; Five Senses, 1963; City Sunrise (pamphlet), 1964; The Other Half, 1966; Collected Poems, 1970; Alive, 1973. Contbr. to: Southerly; Meanjin; Australian Poetry; Sydney Bulletin; Poetry Mag.; Austrovert; Vision;.Ern Malley's Jrnl.; Overland; London Mag.; Quadrant; Salient; Australian Letters; Tex. Quarterly; Australian Book Review; Lit. Review; The Lit. Criterion; Times Lit. Supplement; Sydney Morning Herald; Hemisphere; The Australian, & many others. Honours, awards: F.A.H.A., 1970; D.Litt., Unlv. of Queensland, 1964 & Univ. of New England, 1965; Ency. Britannica. Award, 1964; Grace Leven Prize, 1950 & (aeq.) 1972. Address: Calanthe, Long Rd., North Tamborine 4272, Australia.

WYNAND, Derk, b. 12 June, 1944. Assistant Professor. Education: B.A., Univ. of B.C., 1966; M.A., ibid, 1969. Married. Positions held: Instr. of Engl., Berlitz Schl. of Langs., Montreal, P.Q., 1967; Vis. Lectr., Dept. of Engl., Univ. of Victoria; 1969; Lectr., Dept. of Engl., Univ. of Victoria, 1971; Asst. Prof., Dept. of Creative Writing, ibid, 1973; Editl. Asst., Contemporary Literature in Translation, Vancouver, B.C., 1968-69; Asst. Ed., The Malahat Review, Victoria, B.C., 1972-. Published works: Locus, 1971. Contbr. to: Poet & Critic; The Fiddlehead; Univ. of Tampa Review; The Far Point; Expression; le puits de l'ermite (Paris); Quarry; Edge; Wascana Review; Copperfield; Occident; The New Orleans Review; Tuatara; Trace; Encore; The Malahat Review; Prism Int.; Extensions; Mundus Artium; Poetry; The Canadian Forum; Cronopios; Wendigo; Mainline;

Karaki; The Lit. Review; Cloud Nine: Vancouver Island Poems, etc. Address: Dept. of Creative Writing, The Univ. of Victoria, Victoria, B.C., Canada.

WYNANT, Vivienne Leslie, b. 14 Apr. 1948. Art Teacher. Positions held: Tchr. of Art. & Engl., Islington Secondary Schl., 1969-71; Asst. Libn., 1972-73; Asst. Children's Libn., 1973-; Freelance poster/illustration work. Memberships: Unity Poets (Unity Theatre); Cockpit Poets (Cockpit Theatre). Helped organise var. 'mini' poetry festivals. Asst. Ed. of var. small poetry mags. inclng. graphic/illustration/design. Published works: Within These Walls of White, 1969; Will You Step a Little Closer? (pamphlet), 1972; Recent Poems: 1972-73 (pamphlet). Contbr. to: Sigma; Obelisk; Pod; Next Wave Poets; Outburst; var. anthols. Address: 57 Primrose Gdns., Hampstead, London NW3 4UJ, U.K.

WYNESS, Jean Mildred, b. 3 Jan. 1917. Schoolteacher. Education: qualified as a Tchr. in Primary Schls., New Zealand. Married Rev. Stuart Wyness, 3 children. Positions held: Permanent & Substitute tchng. positions in N.Z. Schls.; Reporter for a N.Z. provincial newspaper; Market Rsch. Agent for var. cos.; Subs. Tchng. in U.S.A. Memberships: Pa. Poetry Soc.; Past Mbr., N.Z. Penwomen's Club; var. offices in ch. orgs. Contbr. to: (N.Z.) Mirror; Exporter; Northland; Outlook; Christchurch Star; Farmer; (U.S.A.) The Christian; Vital Christianity; Grit; Broadcast Poetry; sev. anthols., etc. Honours, awards: Citation List for two poems in Pa. Poetry Soc. Contest, 1972; Mentioned for Merit, Experimental Poetry Class, Pa. State Poetry Contest, 1974. Address: 174 Main St., Sayreville, NJ 08872, U.S.A.

WYN GRIFFITH, Llewelyn, b. 30 Aug. 1890. Civil Servant. Positions held: Former Asst. Sec., Inland Revenue; Former Vice Chmn., Arts Coun. of Gt. Britain. Published works: Branwen, 1934; The Barren Tree, 1945; (other) Up to Mametz, 1931; Spring of Youth, 1935; The Wooden Spoon, 1937; The Way Lies West, 1945; The Welsh, 1948; Wales in Colour, 1958; Pryderi, 1962. Contbr. to: (anthologies) Modern Welsh Poetry, 1944: Up the Line of Death, 1964; Lilting House, 1969. Honours, awards: D. Litt., Univ. of Wales; O.B.E.; C.B.E.; Croix de Guerre avec Palmes. Address: 4 Park View Rd., Berkhamsted, Hertfordshire, U.K.

Y

YAGUCHI, Yorifumi, b. 1 Nov. 1932. Associate Professor. Education: B.A., Tohoku Gakuen Coll.; M.A., Int. Christian Univ.; B.D., Goshen Coll. Biblical Sem. Positions held: Assoc. Prof., Am. Lit., Hokusei Gakuen Coll., Sapporo. Memberships: Poetry Nippon (Ed.); Hokkaido Poetry Soc. Published works include: A Shadow, 1966; A Myth in Winter, 1967; A Fisherman, 1969; Resurrection, 1970. Contbr. to the following anthols., jrnls., mags., etc: Poetry Nippon; Hokkaido Newspaper; Hokkaido Anthol. of Poetry; Poetry (Tokyo); Poetry Australia; Poets' Village; Embers; Mennonite; nat. Poetry Anthol., USA; Anthol. of Kushire Lit. Address: Kita 35, Heiwadori 9 Chome, Shiroishi, Sapporo, Japan 062.

YALAN-STEKELIS, Miriam, b. 26 Aug. 1900. Librarian. Education: Univ. of Kharkov; Hochschule für Wissenschaft des Judentunes, Berlin; Ecole des Bibliothecaires, Paris. Positions held: Hd., Slavonic Dept., Hebrew Univ. Lib., Jerusalem, Israel. Member, Authors' Assn., Israel. Published works: Shir ha-gedi Yesh li sod, & Bahalomi, 1963; Maase be-pharohet, 1952; Vetvi (in Russian), 1967; In the Woods (in English), 1972; As-safra ila jazirat Yumkin, 1972, etc. & a no. of prose works & translations. Many poems put to music. Contbr. to: Davar; Davar le-yeladim; Mfaariv; Masa; Ha-ooma; Vestnik Israilia; Shalom; Nasha Strana; Et asher bakharti be-shira, etc. Honours, awards: Israel Prize, 1957; Title of Hon., City of Jerusalem, 1968; Cert. of Merit, IWWP, 1971. Address: 31 Abarbanel Str., Jerusalem 92477, Israel.

YALDIZCIYAN, Zareh, pen name **ZAHRAD,** b. 10 May 1924. Trader. Education: studied at Fac. of Med., Univ. of Istanbul, Turkey. Married. Positions held: Chief Ed. & Co-Ed., 'San' Lit. Review, Istanbul, 1948-73; Editl. Staff, 'Shoghagat'. Published works: Medz Kaghaki (The Big City), 1960; Koonavor Sahmanner (Bounderies in Colour), 1968; Gigo Poems (Engl. Transl.), 1969; Pari Yergink (Happy Skies), 1971; collect. of poems in series featuring contemporary Armenian Poetry in the Diaspora, Paris, 1971. Contbr. to: (in Armenian) Jamanak; Marmara; Badger; Djarakait; Tar; San; Ahegan; Shirag; Karoon; Shoghagat, etc. Anthols. in Istanbul, in Beirut, (French transl.) in Paris. Broadcast over: Radio Erevan, USSR, 1968, 71; Radio France – Culture, Paris, 1973. Var. other translations. Honours, awards: United Poets Laureate Award for translation of Jose Risal's Poster Adios Poem, 1972; Dip. of Merit, Philippines Rep., 1973. Address: Uzun Carsi 138, Istanbul, Turkey.

YANKAH, Kojo, pen name **YANKAH, Mike,** b. 16 Aug. 1946. Teacher. Education: B.A., Engl., Univ. of Ghana, Legon, 1972. Positions held: Ed., Adisadel Coll. Mag. 'The Santa Claus', 1965-66; Mbr., Commonwealth Hall, Univ. of Ghana, Jrnl. Editl. Bd., 1969-70; Pres., Commonwealth Hall Jr. Common Room, 1970-71; Ed.; Commonwealth Hall Jrnl., 'The Echo', Editl. Adviser, Univ. Student Rep. Coun. Jrnl. 'The Forum', Sub-Ed. of Dept. of Engl. Jrnl. 'The Legacy' & Sec. of Socialist Soc. of Legon, 1971-72. Memberships: Gen. Sec., Ghana Assn. of Writers, 1973; Exec. Mbr., Univ. of Ghana's Writers Forum, 1971-72; Nat. Assn. of Writers, 1973–; Creative Writers Soc., 1972–. Published works: Take Care (vol. of poems), 1974; co-author, Appreciation of West African Verse, 1974. Contbr. to: Daily Graphic (Ghana); The Forum (Univ. of Ghana); The Echo (Univ. of Ghana). Honours, awards: Langston Hughes Prize, 1971 & Davidson Nichol Prize, 1972, Univ. of Ghana. Address: Adisadel Coll., P.O. Box 83, Cape Coast, Ghana, West Africa.

YAOS-KEST, Itamar, b. 3 Aug. 1934. Poet; Editor. Education: B.A. Married, 2 children. Positions held: Ed., Eked. Member, Org. of Hebrew Writers. Published works: Angel Without Wings (poems), 1959; Eyes Heritage (poems), 1965; Nof-Beashan (poems), 1960; Collected Poems, 1967; Summer of Viola (poems), 1973; At the Slope of Her House (poems), 1969; In the Window of the Traveling House (novel), 1970; The Shadow of the Bird (novel), 1971; The Incandescent Line (novel), 1972; Night Carriage (short stories), 1973; Gidrai Laila (play), 1965; Light That Failes (play), 1965. Recip., Talpir prize, 1967; Hersel prize, 1972. Address: Nahmani St., 5i Tel Aviv, Israel.

YAP CHIOR HIONG, Arthur, 11 Jan. 1943. Teacher; Editor; Painter. Educ: B.A., Univ. of Singapore, 1965; Cert. of Educ., Singapore, 1967. Positions held: Exec. Off., Min. of Educ., Singapore, 1965; Tchr., 1965–; Co-Ed., Saya, current. Contbr. to: Poetry Singapore; Tumasek Prospect; Focus; Pelita; New Voices of the Commonwealth (anthology), 1968. Address: 236 Kim Seng Rd., Singapore 9.

YARBROUGH, Anna Nash, born 19th January, 1897. Writer. Positions held: Ed., Poet's Forum, Saline Co. News, Benton, Ark.; Poetry Market Ed., The Penwoman. Memberships: Pres. & Dir., Ark. Writers Conf.; Pres., Ark. Poets Roundtable; Past State Pres. & Br. Pres., Nat. League Am. Pen Women; Past Pres., Authors, Composers & Artists Soc. of Ark. Publications: Flower of the Field, 1962; Building With Blocks, 1965; Poetry Patterns, 1968; Laurel Branches (co-author), 1969. Contbr. to Am. Legion & other nat. mags., & to Denver Post & other newspapers. Honours: 1st Place, Shakespearean Sonnet, N.L.A.P.W., 1966; Cinquain, Ark. Writers' Conf., 1967; Poet of the Present Award, by Rosa Marinoni, Poet Laureate of Ark., 1967; Allard Cup, 1956; Life Mbr., South & West, Inc.; Many awards from local poetry contests. Address: 510 E. St., Benton, Ark. 72015, U.S.A.

YATES, J. Michael, b. 10 April, 1938, in Fulton, Missouri, USA (now Canadian citizen). Writer and Publisher. Education: Schools in Germany, Mexico, and USA; Univ. of Kansas City, B.A., M.A.; Univ. of Michigan, Ann Arbor; studied with Austin Warren at Michigan. Positions held: Instr. in Engl. and Creative Writing, Ohio Univ., 1964-65; Special Lecturer in Lit. and Creative Writing, Univ. of Alaska, Fairbanks, 1965-66; Assoc. Prof. of Creative Writing, Univ. of Brit. Columbia, Vancouver, 1966-71; Visiting Full Prof. of Engl. and Creative Writing, Univ. of Arkansas, Fayetteville, fall semester, 1972. Since 1971, Pres., the Sono Nis Press, Mission, B.C. Poetry Editor, Prism International, 1966-71; Co-editor, Contemporary Lit. in Translation; Member, editorial bd., Mundus Artium. Memberships: Internat. PEN (London); League of Canadian Poets (Member of Executive). Published works: Spiral of Mirrors, 1967; Hunt In An Unmapped Interior, 1967; Canticle for Electronic Music, 1967; Man in the Glass Octopus, 1968 (and in paperback, 1970); The Great Bear Lake Meditations, 1970; Parallax, 1971; Contemp. Poetry of Brit. Columbia, Vols. 1 & 2 (Ed.), 1970, 1972; Volvox: Poetry from the Unofficial Languages of Canada in Engl. Translation (Ed.), 1971; Contemp. Fiction of Brit. Columbia (Ed.), 1971; The Abstract Beast, 1971; Canadian Ecological Poetry (Ed., with Andreas Schroeder), 1972; Exploding, 1972; Selected Poems, 1972, etc. Contbr. to many journals, newspapers, anthols., and to radio and television progs. Awards: Univ. of Kansas City Poetry Prize, 1960; Internat. Broadcasting Award; 1961 & 1962; Major Hopwood Award for Poetry, 1964; Major Hopwood Award for Drama, 1964; Contributors Prize, The Fair Point Mag., 1970; Canada Council Grant, 1968, 1969, 1971, and sev. Canada Council Travel Grants between 1966 and 1971. Address: 4565 Church St., Delta, British Columbia, Canada.

YATES, Katherine Louisa, b. 8 Feb. 1907. Secretary; Sub-postmistress. Positions held: Sec.; Tchr.; Sub-Postmistress. Memberships: Soc. of Women Writers & Jrnlsts.; London Writers Circle; W.E.A. Tutorial Grp.; Sub-Ed., Envoi Poetry Mag.; Fndr. Fellow, Int. Poetry Soc.; Writers' Summer Schl. Published works: A Murmur on the Monsoon, 1974. Contbr. to: The Writer; Woman & Home; Sense Waves, USA; Breakthru; Southern Cross, S. Africa; Manifold; Quintessence, USA; Envoi; Glasgow Herald; Expression One; This England; Int. Poetry Soc. Anthol. No. 1; IWWP Anthol., etc. Honours, awards: 3rd prize, The Writer, 1965; Book Award, Spearman Publs., USA, 1966; Cert. of Merit, The Writer, 1966 & 3rd prize; 3rd prize, Envoi, 1968; 2nd prize, Townswomens Guild Vista, 1969 comp. Address: 54 Lakeside Rd., Palmers Green, London N.13 4PR, U.K.

YEE, Ta-Teh, pen name, **PEI, Tai,** b. 21 Sept. 1908. National Assemblyman and College Professor. Education: B.A., Shanghai Law Coll.; Grad., Chinese Military Acad.; Grad., Nat. War Coll. Married; 3 s., 5 d. Positions held: Lieut.-General; Chief of Political Sections of Division, Army, Army Corps, and Hs. of C-in-C Chinese Army; Deputy Director of Military Council; Chairman of Political Warfare Planning Commission, Ministry of Nat. Defense; Lecturer, Vice Dean of Nat. War Coll.; Nat. Assemblyman; Prof., Chinese Coll. of Culture. Memberships: Deputy Chief, Poetry Research Inst., Chinese Academic Council; Pres., Chinese Poetry Monthly; Vice-Pres., Union of Chinese Poetry Assocs.; Vice-Chairman, Arrangement Committee, Second World Congress of Poets, also member of Presidium, and Deputy Chief, Chinese Delegation. Publications in progress: Chinese Traditional Thought; Chinese Poems. Contbr. to: Ta Hua Eve. News; Independence Eve. News; Min Tzu Eve. News; Chinese Poetry Monthly; Sprint & Autumn Mag.; Asian Poetry Forum, etc. Address: c/o Nat. Assembly, City Hall, Taipei, Taiwan, Republic of China.

YELLEN, Samuel, b. 7 July 1906. Professor of English Lit. Education: B.A., Western Reserve Univ., 1926; M.A., Oberlin Coll., 1932. Married Edna Bard, 2 children. Positions held: Instr. in Engl., Ind. Univ.,

1929-40; Asst. Prof., ibid, 1941-46; Assoc. Prof., 1947-52; Prof., 1953-62; Univ. Prof., 1963-73; Univ. Prof. Emeritus, 1973. Published works: In the House & Out, & Other Poems, 1952; New & Selected Poems, 1964; The Convex Mirror: Collected Poems, 1971. Contbr. to: Am. Mercury; Am. Scholar; Antioch Review; Atlantic Monthly; Christian Sci. Monitor; Commentary; Commonweal; Good Housekeeping; Nation; New Republic, etc. Address: Dept. of Engl., Ind. Univ., Bloomington, IN 47401, U.S.A.

YELLOTT, Barbara Leslie, pen name **JORDAN, Barbara Leslie,** b. 30 Sept. 1915. Poet. Education: Poetry Workshop, Columbia Univ., N.Y., U.S.A. under Joseph Auslander & Leonora Speyer, 1933-34; New Schl. for Soc. Rsch. Married John I. Yellott, 2 sons by previous marriages. Positions held: City Ed., N.Y. Jr. League Mag., 1934-35; currently Treas. & V.P., John Yellott Engrng. Assocs., Inc.; Lectr., schls., colls. & univs. Memberships: Poetry Soc. of Am.; N.Y. Women Poets; Nat. Soc. of Arts & Letters (Valley of the Sun Br.). Published works: Web of Days, 1949; Comfort The Dreamer, 1955. Contbr. to: N.Y. Times; N.Y. Herald Tribune; Christian Sci. Monitor; Poetry Chap-Book; Fla. Mag. of Verse; Talaria; Ariz. Repub.; Denver Post; Wings; Kaleidograph; Am. Weave; The East Hampton Star; Wings; Driftwind; Variegation; The Wash. Star; Quicksilver; Folio; Hippocrene; Voices; Westminster Mag.; The Lyric; The Toledo Blade; Albatross; The Bonacker; The Lantern. Address: 901 West El Caminito, Phoenix, AZ 85021, U.S.A.

YELTON, Marjorie (Ledbetter), b. 12 Jan. 1916. Executive Sec., Braniff Internat. Airlines (27 yrs.). Education: Honor Grad., Carrollton HS; Secretarial training, Metropolitan Business Coll.; attended Dallas Coll. of Southern Methodist Univ., with special emphasis on Engl., literature, creative writing. Married: Harold Monroe Yelton; 1 d. Memberships: Southwest Writers (Pres., 1966, 1967, 1969, 1970, 1971); Poetry Soc. of Texas (Director & Membership Chairman, member of Editorial Committee, 1969-74); Elm Fork Echoes, historical journal (Vice-Pres. & Chairman of Editorial Committee, 1973, re-elected for 1974); Headed Texas delegation to World Congress of Poets, Taipei, Taiwan, 1973, and served as Advisor to World Congress, and elected Chancellor. Published works: In Loving Memory (edited, this tribute to her father, the late E.E. Ledbetter, a Baptist minister and freelance writer); Ledbetters from Virginia (edited), 1964. Honours & Awards: various from Poetry Soc. of Texas; Southwest Writers; Hon. Dr. of Humane Letters, Univ. of Free Asia, 1973; Patroness of the Congress of Poets award given by Imelda Romualdez Marcos, 1st Lady of the Philippines at World Congress of Poets, Taipei, 1973, etc. Address: 5703 West Greenbrier Dr., Dallas, TX 75209, USA.

YEVTUSHENKO, Yevgeny Alexandrovich, b. 1933. Poet. Education: Moscow Lit. Inst. Positions held: Geol. Expeditions w. his father, 1948-50; visited France, Africa, USA, Cuba, UK, Germany, 1960-63; Mbr., Moscow Section, Union of Soviet Writers. Published works: Scouts to the Future (collected poems), 1952; The Third Snow, 1955; The Highway of Enthusiasts, 1956; Zima Junction, 1956; The Promise (collected poems), 1959; Conversation With A Count; Moscow Goods Station; At the Skorokhod Plant; The Nihilist; The Apple; A Sweep of The Arm, 1962; Tenderness, 1962; A Precocious Autobiography, 1963; On The Banks of the Dniepr River; A Woman and A Girl; Do The Russians Want War?; Bratskaya Hydro-Electric Power Station, 1965; Poems Chosen By The Author (transl: Peter Levi & Robin Milner-Gulland), 1966; The Bratsk Station and 9ther Poems (intro. by Peter Levi), 1967; Poems (Ed: H. Marshall), 1967; Poetry 1953-65 (English & Russian), 1967. Address: c/o Union of Soviet Writers, ul. Vorovskogo 52, Moscow, USSR.

YINCHOW, Sy, b. 16 Mar. 1919. Editor-in-Chief. Positions held: Ed.-in-Chief, Manila New Day (English Daily), 1945, Chiang Kai Shek Press (Chinese), 1946-48, Great China Press (Chinese), 1948-72, United Daily News (Chinese & Engl.), 1973-. Mbr., United Poets Laureate Int. Translations: The World's Best Poems, 1965; Selected Modern Poems, 1969; The World's Great Poems, 1972 (these three completed the translator's life time work of thirty yrs. - Anthol. of World Poetry); Shakespeare: Sonnets (Chinese transl. in Shakespearian sonnet form). Contbr. to: leading newspapers & mags. in Taipei, Hong Kong & Manila inclng: United Daily News; China Times; The Crown Mag.; Lit. Monthly; Young Lion Lit. Monthly; etc. Honours, awards: Outstanding Chinese Poet Award, UPLI, 1965; Golden Lion Prize, 1966; Outstanding Translator of Poetry Award, UPLI, 1967; Chiang Kei Shek Prize, 1968 & 70. Address: P.O. Box 1747, Manila, Philippines.

YONATHAN, Nathan, b. 20 Sept. 1923. Lecturer. Education: Hebrew Univ. of Jerusalem. Positions held: Tchr., Dir. of HS; Hd., Educ. Dept., Jewish Youth Org., USA; Tchr., Kibbutz Ctrl. Tchrs. Coll., Israel. Mbr., Hebrew Writers Assn. of Israel. Published works: Paths of Soil, 1951; To the Grey Furrows, 1954; That We Loved, 1957; Songs Along the Shore, 1962; Songs of Soil & Wind, 1965; Poems, 1969. Contbr. to: Al-Hamishmar; Davar; Maariv; Moznaim. Honours: Landau Prize, 1960; Minhan Haazmant, 1962. Address: Kibbutz Sarid, Israel.

YOON SOOK, Hong, pen name **YEO SA,** b. 19 Aug. 1925. College Lecturer. Education: Coll. of Educ., Seoul Nat. Univ. Married, 1 son, 3 daughters. Positions held: Newspaper Reporter, 1947-49; H.S. Tchr., 1949-50; Coll. Lectr., 1970-. Memberships: Exec. Comm., Korean Ctr., Int. PEN; Exec. Comm., Korean Writers' Assn.; Exec. Comm., Korean Poets' Assn.; Exec. Comm., Korean Women Writers' Assn. Published works: (poetry) Yeo Sa Poetry, vol. I, 1962; A Wind Mill, vol. II, 1964; An Ornamentation, vol. III, 1965; Sound of Clock in Dailyness, vol. IV, 1971; (poetic drama) This City After Eden, 1967; (essay) Liberty & Of Momentary World, 1972. Contbr. to: Hankuk; Chosun; Dong-A; Modern Lit.; Monthly Lit.; Modern Poetry; Poetic Lit.; Korean Lit.; Sam-Ted; Doksoshinmun; Catholic Shibo. Address: 50-13, 1st Chang Chung Dong, Chung-gu, Seoul, Korea.

YOUNG, Albert James, pen name **YOUNG, Al,** b. 31 May 1939. Poet-Novelist. Education: Univ. of Mich., 1957-61; Stanford Univ., 1966-67; Univ. of Calif. at Berkeley, 1968-69; B.A. in Spanish. Married, 1 son. Positions held: Instr., Writing Workshop, Berkeley Neighborhood Youth Corps, 1968-69; Writing Instr., Teenage Workshop, San Francisco Mus. of Art, 1968-69; Edward H. Jones Lectr. in Creative Writing, Stanford Univ., 1969-73; Ed., Yardbird Reader (bi-annual jrnl. of new writing), 1972-. Memberships: Authors Guild; Authors League; Writers Guild of Am., West, Inc. Published works: Dancing, 1969; The Song Turning Back Into Itself, 1971; Some Recent Fiction, 1974; (novels) Snakes, 1970; Who Is Angelina?, 1974. Contbr. to: Yardbird Rdr.; Evergreen; Mass. Review; Chicago Review; Essence, Alas; Decal; Jrnl. for the Protection of All Being; New Directions; Jrnl. of Black Poetry, etc. Honours, awards: Joseph Henry Jackson Award, San Francisco Fndn., 1969; Nat. Arts Coun. Awards, 1968 & '69. Address: c/o Creative Writing Ctr., Stanford Univ., Stanford, CA 94305, U.S.A.

YOUNG, Andrew John, b. 29 Apr. 1885. Clergyman (Rtr.); Author. Education: Royal High Schl., Edinburgh; M.A., Univ., Edinburgh; New Coll., Edinburgh. Positions held: Min., Hove Presby. Church, 1919-38; Vicar, Stonegate, Sussex; Canon, Chichester Cathedral. Memberships: FRSL. Published works include: Collected Poems, 1960; Out of the World & Back, 1961 & 13 Other books of poems. Contbr. to num. anthols., jrnls., mags., etc. Honours, awards: Queen's Gold Medal for Poetry, 1953; Cooper Mem. Prize. Address: Park Lodge, Church Lane, Yapton, Arundel, Sussex, UK.

YOUNG, Celia, b. 3 Oct. 1948. Graduate Student. Education: B.A., Univ. of Wis., Milwaukee; M.A., Johns Hopkins Univ., Balt., Md. Positions held: Tchng.

Fellow, Johns Hopkins Univ. Member, Am. Acad. of Poets. Published works: Brewing: 20 Milwaukee Poets, 1972; Poems for Madeline Swansen, 1972. Contbr. to In mag.; Collection of Words, lit. mag. Recip., Am. Acad. of Poets Award, 1971. Address: 11219 Wornall Rd., Kansas City, MO 64114, U.S.A.

YOUNG, Charlotte, pen names **GENEVA, THORNEDYKE, & GENEVA-OF-THE-HILLS,** b. 11 June 1878. Educator. Education: Carson-Newman Coll., Tenn.; Grad., Western Carolina Coll., 1942 (now w. N.C. Univ.). Positions held: Prin., Denver H.S., N.C.; Tchr. of German & Art. Cullowhee Jr. Coll. Memberships: Pres., N.C. Poetry Soc., 1950-53; Pres., Poetry Coun. of N.C., 1960's. Published works: The Heart Has Reasons, 1953, 2nd printing 1956; Speak to us of Love, 1959. Contbr. to: Kaleidograph; Talaria; Classical Jrnl.; Primary Tchr. (N.Y.); The State (Raleigh, N.C.); H.S. Jrnl. & var. anthols. inclng. A Time For Poetry. Honoured by the North Carolina Poetry Soc., 1966 & 72. Address: 104 Arnold Rd., Asheville, NC 28805, U.S.A.

YOUNG, David Pollock, b. 14 Dec. 1936. Associate Professor; Editor. Educ: B.A., Carleton Coll., Northfield, Minnesota, 1958; Ph.D., Yale Univ., 1965. Positions held: Fac. Mbr., Oberlin Coll., Ohio, 1961-; Assoc. Prof., Engl., ibid, 1969-; Ed., Field: Contemporary Poetry & Poetics, Oberlin, 1969-. Published works: Sweating Out the Winter, 1969; Six Poems from Wang Wei, 1969; Thoughts of Chairman Mao, 1970; Ed., Twentieth Century Interpretations of "2 Henry IV", 1968. Contbr. to: Kayak; New American Review; Tri-Quarterly. Honours, awards: Tane Prize, 1965; U.S. Award, 1968. Address: 220 Shipherd Circle, Oberlin, OH 44074, U.S.A.

YOUNG, Douglas Cuthbert Colquhoun, b. 5 June 1913. Professor of Greek. Education: Univ. of St. Andrews, 1930-34; New College, Oxford, 1934-38. Married Helena Gossaree Auchterlonie, 2 daughters. Positions held: Lectr. in Greek, Univ. of Aberdeen, 1938-41; in Latin, Univ. Coll., Dundee, 1947-55; in Greek, Univ. of St. Andrews, 1955-68; Prof., Univ. of Minn., 1963-64; McMaster Univ., 1968-70; Paddison Prof. of Greek, Univ. of N.C., 1970-. Memberships: Int. PEN; Scottish Ctr. Pres., ibid, 1960-63. Published works: Auntran Blads, 1943; A Braird o Thristles, 1947; The Puddocks of Aristophanes, 1958; The Burdies of Aristophanes, 1959; The Oresteia of Aeschylus, 1973. Contbr. to: Observer; Glasgow Herald; Scotsman, etc. Address: Dept. of Classics, Murphey Hall, Univ. of N.C., Chapel Hill, NC 27514, U.S.A.

YOUNG, Eleanor May, b. 10 Apr. 1888. Teacher. Education: B.A., Wellesley Coll., 1910; M.A., Columbia Univ., 1915; Tchrs. Coll., Columbia Univ., Cornell Univ., Univ. of So. Calif. Positions held: Prof. of Engl. Comp., Tift Coll., Forsyth, Ga.; Hd. of Engl. Dept., The Wolcott Schl., Denver, Colo.; Tchr. of Engl. in West N.Y., N.J. & Mt. Vernon, N.Y., 1926-50. Memberships: Colo. Authors' League; Past Pres., Denver Br., Nat. League of Am. Pen Women; Wellesley Club; Book Review Clubs, etc. Published works: Forgotten Patriot: Robert Morris, 1950; Biographical Sketch of Robert Morris (by request) for American Oxford Ency., 1967. Contbr. to: Aspire (Divine Sci. Mag.); Improvement Era; The Poetry Forum of The Denver Post; Modern Maturity; Laugh Book, etc. Recip., 1st, 2nd, third prizes & hon. mention in contests of The Denver Br. of Nat. League of Am. Pen Women. Address: 4829 E. Kentucky Circle, Denver, CO 80222, U.S.A.

YOUNG, Elizabeth, b. 14 Apr. 1923. Writer. Education: Int. Schl., Geneva, Switz.; Downe House, Newbury, U.K.; Somerville Coll., Oxford Univ. Married, 6 children. Published works: (poetry) Time is as Time Does, 1958. Contbr. to: Botteghe Oscure; Springtime; Sunday Times; 'Best articles & Stories', etc. Address: 100 Bayswater Rd., London W.2, U.K.

YOUNG, Helen Lorene Rooney, pen name **YOUNG,**

Helen Rooney, & others, b. 16 Mar. 1904. Housewife; Secretary; Poet. Education: Bus. Coll. Grad.; Tchrs. Cert., Sherwood Schl. of Mus. Ext. Course. Married Issac Jonathan Young II, 5 children. Positions held: Sec. before marriage; Writer & Poet for over 30 yrs. Memberships: Hon. Rep., Centro Studi e Scambi Int. (Stati Uniti 1972-73); Pres., Springfield Writers' Club, 1944-56, '73-74; Sec., Ohio Poetry Day Assn.; Verse Writers Guild of Ohio; Am. Poetry League; Fellow, Int. Poetry Soc., 1973; Poetry Soc. of San Antonio, Tex. Published works: Poesy Book, 1952; Sonnets to An Outstanding Woman, 1956; Flowers of Diplomacy, 1965; Contbr. to the following anthols., jrnls., mags: Urbana Daily Citizen; Upper Sandusky Chief Union; Columbus Citizen; Sidney Daily; Nelsonville Tribune; Springfield Daily News; Springfield News & Sun; The New Hampshire Sunday News; The Normal News; Now; Ohio State Jrnl.; Ore. Beacon; Review; The Am. Gold Star Mothers, Inc.; Horizon; Ohio Anthol., Bd. of Educ.; From Sea to Sea in Song; Ohio Singing; Our Best to You; The Muse of 1944; Am. Sonnets & Lyrics; Contemporary Ohio Poetry; Prairie Poet; The Singing Quill; Golden Quill Anthol.; Bouquets of Poems; IWWP Anthol., 1973, etc. Honours, awards incl: 1st, Poesy Book, Mansfield, Ohio, 1944; Hon. mention, 1st Chapbook Contest, Verse Writers' Guild of Ohio, 1962; 1st Prize, ibid, 1971; Certs. of Merit, Centro Studi e Scambi Int., 1962, '65, '68; Silver, Gold & Bronze Medals, ibid, 1962-68; Hon. Mention, Am. Poetry League Nat. Contest, 1973. Address: 225 South Douglas Ave., Springfield, OH 45505, U.S.A.

YOUNG, Ian George, b. 5 Jan. 1945. Writer. Education: Malvern Collegiate Inst., Toronto, Canada; Victoria Coll., Univ. of Toronto. Positions held: Press Sec., Univ. of Toronto Homophile Assn., 1969-72; Chmn., Univ. of Toronto Homophile Assn., 1972-73; Treasurer, Gay Alliance Toward Equality (Toronto), 1973-. Published works: (books) White Garland: 9 poems for Richard (co-authored w. Richard Phelan), 1969; Year of the Quiet Sun, 1969; Double Exposure, 1970; Cool Fire (co-authored w. Richard Phelan), 1970; Curieux d'Amour (Translator), 1970; Lions in the Stream (co-authored by Richard Phelan), 1971; Some Green Moths, 1972; The Male Muse: A Gay Anthol. (Ed.), 1973;eCommon-or-Garden Gods, forthcoming. Rep. in following anthols: T.O. Now: The Young Toronto Poets, 1968; Poets of Canada 1969; Notes for a Native Land, 1969; Fifteen Winds, 1969; Printed Matter: An Anthol. of Black Moss, 1970; Storm Warning, 1971; The Book Cellar Anthol., 1971; New Am. & Canadian Poetry, 1971; Contemporaries: Twenty-Eight New Am. Poets, 1972; Voice & Vision, 1972. Contbr. to var. periodicals, reviews, etc. Honours, awards: Canada Coun. Grant, 1969 & Bursary, 1972-73; Ont. Coun. for the Arts Grant, 1970. Address: 315 Blantyre Ave., Scarborough, Ont., Canada.

YOUNG, Mary Clemewell, pen name **YOUNG, Clemewell,** b. 21 Dec. 1925. English Teacher. Education: M.A., Univ. of Conn., 1972; B.A., Syracuse Univ., 1948; Wellesley Coll., 1944-46. Married, 3 daughters. Positions held: p/t Reporter for local newspaper, 1963-70; p/t Lectr. in Engl., Manchester Community Coll., 1970-73; Instr., ibid, 1973-. Asst. Ed., Poet Lore, 1969-. Member, Poetry Soc. of Am. Contbr. to: Poet Lore; Cardinal Poetry Qtly.; Bitterroot; Lyric; Educational Forum; Hartford Courant; Meriden Record; Commonweal; Christian Sci. Monitor; Cat Fancy; Gourmet Mag.; South & West; Poems by Poets, anthol., 1974; United Ch. Herald, etc. Recip., 3rd Prize, Descriptive Poem, Poet Lore, 1968. Address: 123 Notch Rd., Bolton, CT 06040, U.S.A.

YOUNG, Ruth Eloise Rogers, b. 18 Dec. 1920. Housewife & Poet. Education: Univ. of Toledo, Ohio. Married Roy O. Young. Memberships: Okla. Writers Fed. (w. Nat. affiliation); Pres., Enid Writers Club, 1973-74; Okla. Poetry Soc.; Nat. Poetry Soc.; Sec. & Past Pres., Truitteers. Contbr. to Carboneer (a quarterly publ. of Great Lakes Carbon Corp.) Honours, awards: 1st pl. Award, 1968,e69, 72, 2nd pl. Award, 1971, Enid Writers Club Annual Contest; 2nd pl.

Award, Truitteers Poetry Contest, 1971; 1st pl. Award, ibid, 1973; One of Top Ten, Okla. Writers Fed. Summer Contest, 1970, etc. Address: 1013 Seneca, Enid, OK 73701, U.S.A.

YUZON, Amado M., b. 30 Aug. 1906. Lawyer. Education: A.B., B.S.E., B.S.D.F.S., LL.B., M.A., M.S.B.A. & LL.M., Philippines. Married, 6 children. Positions held: Mbr., 1st Philippine Congress, 1946-49; Tech. Asst. under 4 Presidents of the Rep., 1952-65; First Acting Nat. Commnr. of Culture, 1965-66; Del. to the Philippine Constitutional Conven., 1970-73; Chmn. of Comm. on Arts & Culture; Mbr., Interim Nat. Assembly, 1973-. Memberships: Fndr.-Pres., 1st World Congress of Poets, Philippines, 1969; Co-Sponsor, Advsr., Pres.-Emeritus, 2nd World Congress of Poets, Repub. of China, 1973; Pres. for Life, United Poets Laureate Int.; Hon. Pres., Accademia Int. de la Valliere, Rome; Patron, Am. Jr. Poetry Soc., N.Y.; Hon. For. Dir., French Acad. of Poetry, Paris; Patron, World Poetry Soc. Int., etc. Published works: (in Filipino) Salitang Paka Bersu; Kasakmal a Bulaklak & 20 unpublished Mss; (in Engl.) Simple Verses; Rizal's Ultimo Pensamiento & Translations; The Citizen's Poems; The Life Story of Lam-ang (a transl. & 12 unpublished Mss). Ed., Laurel Leaves (official organ of UPLI). Advisory & Editl. Bd. Mbr., Dict. Int. Biog., London. Recip. num. poetry prizes & hons. inclng: Poet Laureate of Pampanga, 1930; Poet Laureate of Far Eastern Univ., 1934-36; Nat. Poet Laureate of Philippines, 1959; Hon. Int. Poet Laureate, 1965, 16 times, (Vienna, Rome, Liberia, Ill., N.Y., etc.); IPA Poet Laureate, Wash. D.C., 1972; Nobel Prize Nominee for Peace (3 times) & for Lit. (twice), 1966-73, & 37 hon. doctorates. Address: UPLI-Yuzon 'The Poets Corner', Makyapo, Guagua, Pampanga, Philippines.

Z

ZAGOREN, Ruby, b. 9 Dec. 1922. Author; Poet. Education: A.B., Connecticut Coll., New London, U.S.A., 1943. Married, 2 children. Positions held: Country Corres., Hartford (Conn.) Times, 1935-39; Reporter & Asst. State Ed., Hartford Courant, 1943-46; Feature Writer, Hartford Times; Instr., Univ. of Conn., Torrington Br., 1966-. Mbr., Authors' Guild of Am. Published works: New England Sampler (book), 1965; Israel My Israel, (book), 1968; Meandering Meditation (book), 1939. Contbr. to: Calcutta, India, Review; N.Y. Times; Scimitar & Song; Univ. Review; N.Y. Herald Tribune; The Christian; Prairie Schooner; Christian Sci. Monitor; Young Judaean; Horn Book; Kans. City Star; The Lantern; Lyric; Portland Oregonian; Canadian Nature Mag.; Denver Post; Hartford Times; Country Guide; Christian Home; Washington D.C. Star, etc. Address: Felicity Lane, Torrington, CT 06790, U.S.A.

ZAGORSKI, Jerzy, pen names incl. **J. ZAG., MAGISTER JURAS, ZAG.,** b. 13 Dec. 1907. Writer; Poet; Essayist; Playwrite; Art Critic; Translatoreof Poetry. Education: M.A., Law Fac., Stefan Batory Univ., Vilna, 1936. Positions held: Co-Ed., Zagary, Vanguard Monthly Lit. Review, Vilna, 1931-34; Radio work, Vilna, Lodz & Warsaw, 1936-39; Co-Ed., Apel Lit. Supplement to Kurier Poranny, 1938; Co-Ed., anthol. of resistence Slowo Prawdziwe & Co-Ed., Kulura Jutra (underground Press), 1943-44; Cultural Attaché in the Polish Embassy in Paris, 1947-48. Memberships: Union of Polish Writers; V.P., ibid, 1947; Chmn., Poetry Sect., Cracow, 1950-56; Chmn., Poetry Club, Warsaw, 1972-; V.P., Polish PEN Club, 1970-; S.E.C.; I.T.I. Published works: Ostrze mostu, 1933; Przyjście wroga (Enemy Has Come), 1934; Wyprawy, 1937; Wieczór w Wieliszewie (Evening in Welishew), 1947; Wiersze wybrane, 1951; Meskazpieśń, 1954; Czas Lota (Time of Loth), 1956; Krawedź, 1959; Bajka pienińska, 1961; Oto nurt, 1963; Bialy bez, 1963; Pancerni, 1964; Królestwo ryb, 1967; Rykoszetem (Stray Bullet), 1969; Wiersze, 1972. Translations: Aragon, poetry, 1954; Lermontoff, poetry, 1955; Lermontoff, plays, 1963; Rusthaweli,

poems, 1966. Contbr. to var. mags., jrnls., newspapers. Honours, awards incl: 1st Prize, Comp. of Letters, Gazeta Polska, 1931; 1st Prize in comp. conspiracy for underground poetry about Warsaw, 1943; Hon. Award, Min. of Defence for poem 'Pancerni' (People in Armour), 1964; Prize, Polish PEN, for poetical transl., 1964. Address: Ul. Mickiewicza 18 m. 32, 01-517 Warsaw, Poland

ZAMAKHSHARY, Tahir, b. 1913. Retired Government Official. Education: Intermediate. Has held sev. Government positions. Published works: Seven volumes of Arabic poetry. Address: c/o The Higher Committee for Arts & Sciences, Ministry of Education, Riyadh, Saudi Arabia.

ZAPATA-ACOSTA, Ramón, b. 4 Nov. 1917. University Professor. Education: B.A., Educ., Univ. of Puerto Rico, 1940; M.A., ibid, 1945; Ph.D., Columbia Univ., N.Y., 1970. Married to Mabel Oliveras de Zapata, 2 sons, 1 daughter. Positions held: Prof. of Spanish, Puerto Rico High Schls., 1941-45; Prof. of Spanish, Polytech. Inst. of P.R., 1945-55; Prof. of Spanish, Cath. Univ. of P.R., 1955-; Dept. Chmn., ibid, 1961-71. Memberships: Soc. of Puerto Rican Authors; Pres., Atheneum of Ponce, 1957-. Published works: Canciones de ruta & sueño, 1954; Espejos y figuras, 1963, '68. Contbr. to: El Mundo; El Día; Alma Latina; La Nao; Horizontes; Polygraph; Revista Hispánica Moderna; Caracola. Address: Catholic Univ., Ponce, Puerto Rico 00731.

ZAPFFE, Peter Wessel, b. 18 Dec. 1899. Author. Education: Examen Artium, 1918; Cand. jur., 1924; Dr. philos., 1941. Positions held: Constituted City Judge; Asst. Tchr. in Logics, Univ. of Oslo. Memberships: Den norske Forfatterening; Kunstnerforeningen. Published works: Den fortapte sonn (play in XI Acts about Jesus), Oslo, 1951; Dikt og Drama, Oslo, 1970. Contbr. to: Tromsoe Stiftstidende; Ordet; Farmand; Morgenbladet. Address: Nedre Baastad vei 6, 1370 Asker, Norway.

ZARAGOZA, Francisco, pen name **HAMLET,** b. 29th Jan. 1914. Librarian; Archivist; Poet. Positions held: Dir., Via Comercial Weekly; oprietor & Dir., La Mujer, Mag.; Dir., Rélampages, lit. & critical Mag.; 1930; Hd. of Nat. Archives, 8 years; currently Curator & Libn., Fndn. Claro M. Recto; Cultural Councellor to the Speaker, Philippine Congress; Libn., Philippine Acad. Memberships: Philippine Acad.; Corres., Royal Spanish Acad.; Hon., United Poets Laureate Int.; Nat. Philippine Assn. of Writers; Dir. Bd., Claro M. Recto Fndn. Published Works: El Insagani de Rizal (w. Claro M. Recto), 1954; Marella y la Inquietud Romántica de la Revolución, 1954; Castalia Intima; 6 vols. of prose. Contbr. to num. newspapers & jrnls. Honours: Nobel Poetry Prize, for Castalia Intima, 1964; 1st Prize, Poetry Contest, United Poets Laureate Int., 1968. Address: Manila, Philippines.

ZASLOW, Edmund M., pen name **PENNANT, Edmund,** b. 28 Apr. 1917. Educator. Education: B.A., Coll. of the City of N.Y.; M.A., Grad. Fac., New Schl. for Soc. Rsch. Married Doris Kahn, 3 daughters. Positions held: Tchr., N.Y. City H.S's.; Prin., Glen Oaks Schl., N.Y. Currently V.P., Poetry Soc. of Am. Published works: I, Too, Jehovah (poems), 1952. Rep. in following anthols: The Golden Year, 1960; The New Orlando, II, 1963; The Voice of Cyprus, 1965; New Orlando III, 1968; Illustrated Treasury of Poetry for Children, 1970; The Diamond Anthol., 1971. Contbr. to: Sat. Review; N.Y. Times; Poet Lore; Am. Scholar; The Lit. Review; Antioch Review; N.Y. Qtly.; Commonweal; Denver Post; Poet; Bitterroot; Am. Weave, etc. Honours, awards: Nat. Prize, Poetry Soc. of Am., 1962; Hart Crane Award, Am. Weave Assn., 1963; Poet Lore Annual Prize, 1967. Address: 29-02 210 St., Bayside, NY 11360, U.S.A.

ZATURENSKA, Marya, b. 12 Sept. 1902. Poet: Editor. Educ: Valparaiso Univ., Ind.; Univ. of Wis. m. Horace Gregory, 1s., 1d. Published works: Threshold and Hearth, 1934; Cold Morning Sky, 1937; The Listening

Landscape, 1941; Golden Mirroe, 1943; Selected Poems, 1954; Terraces of Light, 1960; Collected Poems, 1965. Ed., The Mentor Book of Religious Verse (w. Horace Gregory), 1957; The Crystal Cabinet: An Invitation to Poetry (w. Horace Gregory), 1962: Collected Poems of Sara Teasdale, 1966. Contbr. to: Poetry; New Republic; Tiger's Eye; Contemporary Verse; New Poetry; (anthologies) New Voices, 1928; Pulitzer Prize Poems, 1941; Treasury of Great Poetry, 1942; Twentieth Century American Poetry, 1944; Modern American Poetry, 1950; Faber Book of Modern American Verse, 1956. Honours, awards: John Reed Mem. Award, 1922; Shelley Mem. Award, 1935; Guarantor's Award, 1937; Pulitzer Prize, 1938. Address: Closter Rd., Palisades, Rockland County, NY 10964, U.S.A.

ZAVADA, Vilém, b. 22 May 1905. Librarian. Education: Ph.D., Univ. of Prague. Published works: Panychida, 1927; Pašijový týden, 1931; Siréna, 1932; Cesta pěšky, 1937; Hradní věž, 1940; Povstání z mrtvých, 1946; Město světla, 1950; Polní kvítí, 1955; Jeden život, 1962; Na prahu, 1970; Selected Poems; Básně, 1954; Vzduch a světlo, 1960; Beze jména, 1970. Honours, awards: State Prize Winner, 1956, '71; Nat. Poet Laureate. Address: Na pěkné vyhlídce 1, 16200 Prague 6, Střešovice, Czechoslovakia.

ZAWACKI, Franklin George, b. 14 Sept. 1939. Teacher. Education: A.B. in Engl., Univ. of Calif., Davis, 1966; M.A. in Engl., ibid, 1968; M.A. in Creative Writing, Brown Univ., 1972. Positions held: H.S. Tchr., 1968-70; Writing Instr., Brown Univ., 1970-72; Freelance Poet, 1972-73; Writer in Res., State of Rhode Island, 1973–. Published works: Motley, 1963-66; Hellcoal Annual, 1970, '71. Recip., 1st Prize, Univ. of Calif., Davis, Poetry Contest, 1965. Address: 689 Hope St., Providence, RI 02906, U.S.A.

ZECHENTER, Witold, b. 29 Dec. 1904. Writer. Education: Univ. Jagiellonski, Cracow, Poland & Sorbonne, Paris, France. Married Beata Choloniewska, 1 daughter. Memberships: Soc. of Polish Writers; PEN Club, Warsaw. Published works: (books of poetry) Ręka na sterze, 1929; Niebieskie i zlote, 1932; Linia prosta, 1932; Inne chwile, 1939; Strzępy ekupacji, 1945; Wiersze wybrane, 1967; (books of pamphlets & parodies) Guzy dla Muzy, 1939; W mojej razurze, 1954; Parodie, 1956; Parodie, ed. II, 1960; Fraszki, 1962; Z Pegazem pod gazem, 1965; Trzecie parodie, 1969; Drobiazdzki z przejazdzki, 1970; Grymasy z komentarzem, 1973; Gabinet uśmieché, 1974. Contbr. to: Zycie literackie; Poezja; Kamena; Literatura; Magazyn kulturalny; Gazeta krakowska; Dziennik Polski. Address: ul Dluga 84 m. 6, 31-146 Krakow, Poland.

ZEKOWSKI, Arlene, b. 13 May 1922. Author; Educator. Education: B.A., Brooklyn Coll., 1944; M.A., Duke Univ., 1945; Licentiate-es-lettres, Univ. of Paris, 1949; post grad. work, La. State Univ., 1958-63. Married Stanley Berne. Positions held: Asst. Prof. in Engl., Eastern N.M. Univ., Portales, 1963-67; Assoc. Prof., ibid, 1968–. Memberships: PEN; Comm. of Small Mags., Eds., and Publrs.; Coord. Coun. of Literary Mags.; New England Small Press Assn.; Chmn. of the Bd., Am.-Canadian Publsr. Ltd., Portales, N.M. Published works: Thursday's Season, 1950; A First Book of the Neo-Narrative, 1954; Cardinals & Saints, 1958; Concretions, 1962; Abraxas, 1964; Seasons of the Mind, 1969; The Age of Iron & Other Interludes, 1973. Contbr. to: Breakthrough Fictioneers, 1973; Tigers Eye; New World Writing No. 11; S.D. Review; Kayak; Boundary II, etc. Address: Dept. of Engl., Eastern N.M. Univ., Portales, NM 88130, U.S.A.

ZELDIS, Chayym, b. 7 Oct. 1927. Publicity Director, Women's American ORT. Education: Univ. of Michigan, 2 yrs.; New School for Social Research, B.A. Membership: Poetry Soc. of America. Published works: Seek Haven, 1968. Contbr. to: (anthol.) A Treasury of Jewish Poetry, 1957; (newspapers, journals) Commentary; Accent; Midstream; Jewish Frontier; The Reconstructionist; Egret. Recip. Avery

Hopwood Award, Univ. of Michigan, 1946. Address: 140 Ocean Parkway, Brooklyn, NY 11218, USA.

ZELIFF, Viola Tompkins Rhoades, b. 26 Feb. 1896. Professor of English. Education: B.S., Columbia Univ., 1916; M.A., ibid, 1934; Ph.D., N.Y. Univ., 1946. Married. Positions held: Instr., Newark State Tchrs. Coll., 1917-21; Asst. Prof., ibid, 1920-21; Assoc. Prof. & Dept. Hd., Jersey City State Coll.; Ed., Contemporary Life Mag. Memberships: Nat. League Am. Pen Women; Pres., Ft. Lauderdale Br., ibid; Fla. State Treas., 1968-69; Fla. State Auditor, 1970-71; W. Va. Poetry Assn.; Am. Nat. Poetry Assn. Contbr. to following anthols., newspapers, mags.: Contemporary Life: Poems, 1944-54; Poetry Anthol. of Children's Verse, 1930; Anthol. of Prize Poems, 1955 & 56; Newark Evening News; Contemporary Mag.; Cat Mag.; Understanding Mag. Recip. prizes awarded by Fla. Poetry Assn., Spring Contest, 1955, Winter, 1955, March '54 & by Cat Mag., 1957. Address: 2025 S.E. 17th St., Pompano Beach, FL 33062, U.S.A.

ZERZAN, Joan C., b. 12 Oct. 1953. Pre Medical Student. Education: currently in 3rd year at Portland State Univ. Member, World Poetry Soc. Intercontinental. Published works: The Reunion, 1974. Contbr. to World Poetry Mag. Has written var. short stories as well as poems. Public readings of own poems for Speech Classes. Address: 6364 S.E. McNary Rd., Milwaukie, OR 97222, U.S.A.

ZIDICH, Igor, b. 10 Feb. 1939. Editor. Education: Law, Fac. of Law, Zagreb Univ., 1957-58; Grad., Comparative Lit. & Art Hist., Fac. of Arts & Scis., ibid, 1964. Positions held: Ed. of review Razlog (The Reason), 1961-64; Ed. of Fine Art mag., Zivot umjetnosti (The Art's Being), 1966-70; Ed.-in-Chief, lit. monthly review, Kolo (The Circle), 1968-71; Ed., series Kolo (Contemp. Croatian writers), 1969-71; the prime-mover & first-time Ed.-in-Chief of cultural weekly paper Hrvatski tjednik, 1971. Memberships: Sec., Matica hrvatska (Cultural & Sci. Soc. of Croatie), 1966-68; Croatian Writers Soc., 1961–. Published works: Uhodeći more (Spying of the Sea), 1960; Kruh s grane (Bread from the Bough), 1963; Blagdansko lice (Holiday Face), 1969; Lointain (16 poems in French transl. by J. Matillon), 1969, etc. Contbr. to var. lit. publs. Address: Nakladni zavod Matice hrvatske, Maticina 2, 41000 Zagreb, Yugoslavia.

ZIMMER, Paul Jerome, b. 18 Sept. 1934. Publisher. Education: B.A., Kent State Univ. Married, 2 children. Positions held: Mgr., San Francisco News Co.; Mgr., U.C.L.A. Bookstore; Asst. Dir., Univ. of Pittsburgh Press. Published works: Seed on the Wind, 1960; The Ribs of Death, 1967; The Republic of Many Voices, 1969. Contbr. to: Field; Poetry Northwest; Northwest Review; Prairie Schooner; Yankee; Mass. Review; Ohio Review; Southern Poetry Review; Va. Qtly. Review, etc. Honours, awards: Borestone Mountain Poetry Awards, Best Poems of 1970. Address: 5515 Hobart St., Pittsburgh, PA 15217, U.S.A.

ZIMUNYA, Bonus, b. 14 Nov. 1952. Student. Education: Univ. of Rhodesia. Memberships: Chmn., a Young Writers Club & Ed. mag. 'Young Voice'; Poetry Soc. of Rhodesia. Contbr. to: Chirimo, 1969; Two Tone, 1970, '71 & '72; Rhodesian Poetry '70, 1970; New Coin, 1970; Umtali Post, 1971; Rhodesia Poetry Soc., 1972; SGM Speaks, 1973; Young Voice, 1970. Honours, awards: 1820 Settlers' Prize for Poetry, 1970; Univ. of Rhodesia Principal's Prize for Verse Composition in Engl. Address: c/o J. Zimunya, U.G.H.S., Box 95, Umtali, Rhodesia.

ZINNES, Harriet Fich. Poet; Professor of English. Education: B.A., Hunter Coll.; M.A., Brooklyn Coll.; Ph.D., NY Univ. Married to Prof. Irving I. Zinnes; 1 s., 1 d. Positions held: Assoc. editor, Harper's Bazaar; Tutor, Hunter Coll.; Lecturer, Rutgers Univ. (Univ. Coll.), New Brunswick, NJ.; Assoc. Prof. of Engl., Queens Coll., Flushing, NY.; Visiting Prof. of American Lit., Univ. of Geneva, Switzerland. Memberships: American Center of P.E.N.; Acad. of American Poets;

Poetry Soc. of America; Published works: Waiting and Other Poems, 1964; An Eye For An I, 1966; Entropisms, New Directions 27, 1973. Contbr. to: Poetry; NY Times; Chelsea; Choice; Centennial Review; Prairie Schooner; Voyages; Mademoiselle; Carleton Miscellany; NY Qtly.; For Now; Ante; The Nation; Folder; Canadian Forum; Aylesford Review, etc. Awards: Resident Fellowship, MacDowell Colony, Peterborough, New Hampshire, 1972, 1973. Address: Dept. of Engl., Queens Coll., Flushing, NY 11367, USA.

ZIVKOVIC, Peter D., b. 10 July 1929. College Professor. Education: B.S., Univ. of Ill., 1957; M.A., ibid, 1959; Writers Workshop, Univ. of Iowa, 1959-60. Married, 3 children. Positions held: Asst. Prof., Auburn Univ., Auburn, Ala., 1960-66; Asst. Prof., Ga. Tech., 1967-69; Assoc. Prof., Fairmont St. Coll., W. Va., 1969-. Memberships: Nat. Fed. of State Poetry Socs.; W. Va. Poetry Soc.; Ga. Writers Assn.; Avalon World Arts Acad. Published works: Bezich, 1969; Little Book, Little Book, Where Have You Been? 1973. Contbr. to: Lit. Review; Southwest Review; Poem; Epos; Yes; Story; So. Humanities Review; Folio; Ariz. Quarterly; Descant; South & West; S.C. Review; Poet Lore; The Personalist; Chicago Review; Ga. Review; Human Voice Quarterly; Approaches; N.Y. Times Book Review; The Prairie Poet; Bitterroot; Mass. Review; Univ. of Kans. City Review; Cyclo Flame; Carleton Miscellany; Athanor; Infinity Review; Sunday Clothes, etc. Honours, awards: 1st Prize Award, Rocket Writer Contests, 1965; Lilith Lorraine Meml. Awards, 1970; 1st Prize Awards, Ga. Writers Assn., 1971 & W. Va. Poetry Soc., 1970; 1st Hon. Mention, Nat. Fed. of State Poetry Socs., 1973; 1st Prize Awards, W. Va. Poetry Soc., 1973. Address: Rte. 4, Box 577, Fairmont, WV 26554, U.S.A.

ZMORA, Israel, b. 7 May 1899. Writer; Publisher; Owner of Publishing House 'Mahbarot Leisfrut'. Married Ada Kremiansky, 2 children (Zvi & Ohad). Positions held: Mbr., Coun. for Art & Culture, Min. of Educ. & Culture & Chmn. of its Lit. Div.; Ed., 'Mahbarot le-Sifrut' (monthly); Mbr., Editl. Bd., 'Turim'; Ed., 'Moznayim'; Ed., Lit. Sect., 'Koi Israel'. Published works: Ameshet (poetry); Lamed Sonetolh (poetry); author of works on Rilke & Gnessin; 'Last Prophets'; transl. over 20 books from Russian, English, French, German, etc. Address: 5 Gnessin St., Tel-Aviv, Israel.

ZOLA, Marion Joy, b. 19 June 1945. Writer. Education: B.A. & M.A. in Literature. Positions held: formerly Engl. Tchr., Bronx H.S. of Science; currently Writing full time. Member, Poetry Soc. of Am. Contbr. to: N.Y. Herald Tribune; P.S.A. Diamond Anthol., 1972; Best in Poetry, Winter 1972. Address: 205 West End Ave., N.Y., NY 10023, U.S.A.

ZUCKER, Jack S., b. 23. Jan. 1935. Teacher of English. Education: B.A., City Coll. of NY.; M.A., NY Univ. Married, 2 children. Positions held: Teacher, Garden School, NY., NY.; Asst. Instr., Ohio State Univ., Columbus, Ohio; Asst. Prof., Newark State Coll., Union, NJ.; Asst. Prof., Babson Coll., Wellesley, Mass.; Instr., Phillips Acad., Andover, Mass. (currently). Memberships: Poetry Soc. of America; New England Poetry Club (Member, Governing Bd.). Contbr. to: PSA Diamond Anthol., 1970; Best Poems of '72 (Borestone Mountain Awards, 1973); Epos; The Island; Calif. Review; Laurel Review; South; South & West; Pembroke Mag.; Trace; Hellcoal Annual; Gissing Newsletter; Boston Spectator; Caravel; Prospero's Cell; Ab Intra; New Laurel Review; Literary Review; Folio; Southern Poetry Review; The Lyric; Premiere, etc. Address: Stearns House, Chapel Ave., Andover, MA 01810, USA.

ZUKOFSKY, Louis, b. 23 Jan. 1904. Retired Associate Professor of English; Writer; Poet. Educ: M.A., Columbia Univ., 1924. m. Celia Thaew, 1s. Positions held: Tchr., Univ. of Wis., 1930-31, Colgate Univ., Hamilton, 1947; Assoc. Prof., Engl., Polytechnic Inst., Brooklyn, 1947-66. Published works: Some Time, 1956; All: The Collected Short Poems, 1923-1958, 1965; All: The Collected Short Poems, 1956-1964, 1967; Catullus (w. Celia Zukofsky) (verse translation), 1969; Ferdinand/It Was, 1968; Ed., An "Objectivists" Anthology, 1932; Ed., A Test of Poetry, 1964. Contbr. to: Poetry; (anthologies) A Controversy of Poets, 1965; New Writing in the U.S.A., 1967; American Literary Anthology 1, 1968. Honours, awards: Longview Fndn. Award, 1961; Union League Civic and Arts Fndn. Prize, 1964; Nat. Endowment for the Arts Award, 1968.

ZULAWSKI, Juliusz, b. 7 Oct. 1910. Poet; Prose Writer; Essayist; Translator of Poetry. Memberships: V.P., Polish PEN; Polish Writers' Assn. Published poetical works: Pole Widzenia, 1948; Wiersze Z Notatnika, 1957; Kartki Z Drogi (in press). Translations of: El Molino, 1954, El Anzuelo De Fenisa, 1955, Lope de Vega; The Curse of Minerva, Byron, 1954; Selected Poetry, Robert Browning, 1969; approx. 50 Engl. & Am. poets, 1954-72, in separate vols. & in anthol. 'Poeci Jezyka Angielskiego, 3 vols., 1969-74. Contbr. to: Droga, 1933; Wiadomosci Literackie, 1934; Wiadomosci Polskie, 1942; Nowa Polska, 1946; Kuznica; Nowa Kultura; Tworczosc; Poezja; Swiat; Tygodnik Powszechny. Honours, awards: Polish PEN Award, 1969; Kister Meml. Award, Am. PEN, 1970; The Alfred Jurzykowski Fndn. Award, 1972. Address: Iwicka 8-A, m 8, 00-735 Warsaw, Poland.

FOR PSEUDONYMS AND PEN NAMES OF INCLUDED POETS PLEASE SEE PAGE 870

THE INTERNATIONAL
WHO'S WHO IN POETRY
$3,000 AWARDS

Nearly six thousand entries (5,898 to be exact) were submitted for the *International Who's Who in Poetry* $2,500 Awards – later increased to $3,000 by the addition of the Charles Baudelaire $500 Prize for a young poet under 21 years of age. The entries came from 1,473 poets in twenty-eight countries. Many poets sent in multiple entries (the largest was 128 poems!) and the average was four poems per person. Every poem submitted was read and marked by each of the adjudicators. Ernest Kay, Hon. General Editor of the *International Who's Who in Poetry*, was chairman of the panel of judges.

This section concerns only the original $2,500 Awards: the Charles Baudelaire Prize will be dealt with in the section which follows.

The *International Who's Who in Poetry Awards*, now judged for the third time, are among the most substantial in the world.

For the current Awards the standard of poems was extremely high: many of the poets who submitted entries are known internationally. But the adjudicators had no knowledge of the names of the poets as each entry was numbered and the name of the poet obliterated.

It was the unanimous decision of the judges that the first prize of $1,000 should be awarded to Madeline Mason, of New York City, for her "Portrait". Madeline Mason, who is the wife of the artist, Malcolm Forbes McKesson, is a Vice President of the Poetry Society of America and conducts regular poetry workshops at the P.S.A. headquarters in Gramercy Park, New York City. She is, of course, the inventor of the Mason Sonnet. Her $1,000 prize-winning poem is:

PORTRAIT

And is this really she?
This old sick woman in her late hour.....

Memory guards her from time:
Years do not touch a loved image,
The classic grace of young face,
The firm, slim nose, calm brow,
Thought-subtle eyes
Where blues glimmer like the changing hues
Of sky-stain over the soft greys
Of gently moving waters,
Her thrush-brown hair smoothly curving
To the proud shape of her head.

She talks and laughs at a dinner table,
Gala occasions her daily fare.
She does not know I watch her there
Among us all, and think
I have not seen so perfect
A beauty ever before.

I visit her to-day; hair
Grisled and abused,
The body she rejects neglected,
Weak and uncaring,
She waits for tardy death.

"Kiss me", she says. I kiss her.
What is there left to say?
"You must get well – I need you."
The words are selfish.
She has no need of the world,
And she would go.

The ambulance is come; the stretcher takes her.
A grieving husband follows helplessly.
Time-stung, I look in the mirror,
And will not see what I see.

MADELINE MASON

The second prize of $500 goes to Charles A. Wagner, also of New York City, for his "New World Triptych" – the only poem he submitted for the Awards. Charles Wagner is the Executive Secretary of the Poetry Society of America.

NEW WORLD TRIPTYCH

1.

They're back in the Yard* if you've eyes but to see
and at midnight they dance round Rebellion Tree;
cavorting in shadow, the stout with the lank,
are Johnny, John Quincy and Teddy and Frank.
The Roosevelts show Adamses everything new,
the Adamses mark how their house portraits grew,
but never a word do you hear about rank
from Johnny, John Quincy or Teddy or Frank.
They're home again, home again trying their chairs
and racing each other up Littauer stairs
rejoined there forever, the stout with the lank --
young Johnny, John Quincy and Teddy and Frank.

*Five U.S. Presidents (John Adams, John Quincy Adams, Theodore Roosevelt and Franklin D. Roosevelt are referred to here: the fifth was John F. Kennedy) were graduates of Harvard College, where the Yard is located. This fantasy celebrates the fact that by far the greatest number of Presidents graduated from Harvard.

2.

The printed book has found its peer
in ocean stanzas written here
song-enchanted scroll on scroll
as merging mist-millennia roll
their taped recordings shell by shell
in calcium lines that store their spell
distant as Circe's cunning cry
or Cheops boat-chant on the sky.
Listen! The breakers roar their rage
in reticence to turn the page!

3.

Beneath the beat of heart and wheel
time annotates its special steel
with careless stride so that its flood
bears no relationship with blood

its computation keyed to sense
set in the soul's circumference
yet drawing on some secret power,
some overt mystery of hour

like heard occurrence unoccurred
or meaning never reaching word
direction taking any turn
or ash implicit in the burn

time passing long before it came
and bearing namelessness for name

CHARLES A. WAGNER

The third prize of $250 was awarded to David Holbrook, of Cambridge, England, for "Listening to Mahler While Packing". He is Assistant Director of English Studies at Downing College, University of Cambridge, and the author of four books of poetry.

LISTENING TO MAHLER WHILE PACKING

You are dead, and your joy with you,
And Alma, and Bruckner, and Schoenberg, too
Are dead: and the mocking laughter
Wahs out from the trombones, and the percussion
Beats hell out of us all. A mother's voice
Sobs to us from the strings --- but that is art.

Progressive tonality! The glockenspiel
Escaping into Eternity ! Continuity !
Or so we say. When our Mutterlein
Comes in at the door, I seem to see your face.
I seem to see you, Mahler, in the wood
Loving and fearing Pan in the green woodpecker,
Or in the cranky rabbit running across my lawn.

Dust, and paper: sonic scratches,
Columns of electronic air: all art is death.

So, I unhusk myself to your music
Packing, dismantling all my paper world.

So, it is all in boxes, in a shed,
And all I am, an aching, sweating man,
Homeless and unsupported by my scaffolding.
Your long serpenting horn-call in my head

Fills the night's spaces with its grandness,
So does the death-march on an infant tune.
I retreat from the world, become unreal, sordid,
Into your structures: out of place and time:
The stuff it teaches is but schattenhaft.

Yet, among coils of wire, the dust fur,
Our naked love is real, passionate play,
My hard flesh like col legno *on her thighs,*
Stirred like dark violas, in rising throes.

Wie ein schwerer Kondukt, *this house-move,*
Leaving this place of sorrow and despair
Into a new key, towards resolution.
Wanderers, all our lives, reflections, paper.
Shall we end up, in some more sunken key?
God save us from your horn-calls of non-meaning,
Even if brutal thuds shall bury us,
And let us have our winks of your bright triad gold!

DAVID HOLBROOK

The winner of the fourth prize of $125 is Bernard Grebanier, of New York City, for his Mason Sonnet, "Spring Afternoon". He was for 33 years Professor of English at Brooklyn College, New York, and is now Professor Emeritus.

SPRING AFTERNOON
(A Mason sonnet)

Mad!--with desk-tasks waiting for me still--
to stretch upon the grass in Maytime's light
without in cranium one thought profound!--
rather, busy tracing every frill
the filmy clouds are making in their flight
I snatch a dandelion deep from the ground;
the cat-bird's call (unconvincing sound)
could tempt what dog? The cardinal's crest too bright
for sun, I edge between my teeth blade-grass;
a squirrel flees a hound in pretended fright;
two frantic sparrows decide to mock with will
a baptism in the dust. With sudden pass
a thrush soars up a gaping oak's crevasse,
demanding world's attention to his trill.

BERNARD GREBANIER

While United States poets won three of the major awards to the United Kingdom's one, the position was reversed in the case of the twenty-five prizes of $25 each. These consisted of twelve poets from the United Kingdom, eight from the United States and one each from India, Dominica, Sweden, Australia and New Zealand.

The $25 prize-winning poems are:

THE SLEEPERS

Tolerance for the sleepers.
Eutychus, who slumped into somnolence
While Paul, moved by the Spirit, expounded divine truths,
To look up and see Eutychus toppling through the window
To hit the ground three storeys below. And the helmsman Palinurus
Lulled by the sun's music on the waves,
Slid overboard without so much as a word of goodbye
For Aeneas or his crew. I too come
From a family of sleepers. My brother was noted
For sleeping on his feet when propelled through cathedrals.
Plucked from my bunk to be held aloft
To see erupting Stromboli I remembered nothing.
And one of my son's eyes set like the dying sun
On the words of my wisdom.

Tolerance for the sleepers.

MICHAEL IVENS
London N W 8, England

Michael Ivens, a former Editor of "Twentieth Century", is now Director of Aims of Industry, a private enterprize organization in London, England. He is author of several books.

AN INDIAN MANGO VENDOR

She squats
on the dust-broomed pavement
behind a pyramid of mangoes
washed with her youth's milk
tinctured with the musk-rose in her hair.
 Through the slits
 of her patched blouse
 one bare shoulder
 two white moons
 pull all horses
 off the track.

This old man's leery eyes –
idle birds
pecking at the mango-nipples.
 Buy something, man
 or move on
 to the crypt
 where Death's ferrous fingers
 will pull the remaining stray hair
 from your green skull.

      SHIV K. KUMAR
      Hyderabad, India

Professor Kumar is Chairman of the Department of English at Osmania University, Hyderabad. He has written two books of poetry and contributed to many newspapers and periodicals throughout the world.

THE RICHES AROUND HIM.

The peasant's dog at dawn disturbs
the music of the rain, and stirs
the man from his bed; the scene
begins again as he opens the screens
which kept spirits from his dreams.
His wife from the kitchen sets down coffee;
he sips, his eyes roving the valley
as a chorus of rain swells over the crest
of the hills, and soars to the west.
He reviews his bananas growing in ranks
to the top, where giant ferns in groves
wave below the gomier trees. By the river banks,
his cows take water, his mangoes
ripen and the garden he cleaned
prospers with potatoes, yams and dasheen.
Behind his home, smoke wafts from charcoal pits
where breadfruit grows and foraging pigs
eat avocado pears. His child sucks
a sugar cane, as passing trucks
head for the capital. He must pick grapes
box and despatch, saw wood, set traps,
repair the roof, fix a shoe, clean his gun,
then sit on his steps, day done, while the sun
sinks into the sea and he seeks his release
in the riches around him, this poor man at peace.

ROYSTON ELLIS,
Dominica, West Indies.

Royston Ellis, an Administrator in Dominica since 1966, has the distinction
of being an Honorary Duke of the tiny Caribbean island of Redonda. He is
the author of numerous books of poetry and prose.

CYPRESSES

Primal Gothic towers, as vibrant flame-augur shells
we spiral into deep green elongation. Vertical
we stream beyond our apex into descending light;
elegant in our capes of sun; or in a wind, wild.

At twilight, we allow swift black swallows to flit
about us, but they do not alight:
We do not invite the intimacy of swallows.

Or black and angular against silver of moonlit
cemeteries where the Dead congregate, we conceal
within our velvet robes, or reveal
to those who can see in the dark, that we are barque
and Ark, temple, crucifix, and door: – And we endure.

DAISY ALDAN
New York, N.Y. 10022, U.S.A.

Dr. Aldan, a member of the Executive Board of the Poetry Society of America, has edited various poetry anthologies and written many books of poems. She is a teacher at the High School of Art and Design, New York City.

YOUNG DANTE ALIGHIERI
(Inspired by a marble statue in the Town Hall of Palermo)

The carved nostrils of his marble profile
Seem to vibrate. The earnest lips of a
Slender youth are sealed by
Silence
And the bowing head so sadly – demurely
Reconciled to Fate –

As if he poignantly felt in the
Very depths of his boyish self
The bitter reluctance of
Renouncement,
The shaping of inmost pain
Into sheer poetry:

His brilliant inheritance through
Centuries to come – to all the
Trivial bearers of minor roles
Of the pitiful,
The "Earthly Comedy", hélàs,
Not the Divine ...

Did the sculptor ever grasp it when
Coughing from dust of a chiselled stone
Which was to yield
The image
Of a noble offspring with the sad and
The silent hands –

Did the artist imagine that in his own
Odd way he made live for times
Eternal –
Past atom-weapons and data –
The ardent venerator, the all-penetrating
Wanderer

As a thoughtful youth,
Almost breathing,
In yellow-veined
Stone?

KARIN SAARSEN,
Bandhagen, Sweden

Mrs. Karlstedt, who writes under the name of Karin Saarsen, was born in Estonia and is an official of the Association of Free Estonian Writers, Stockholm, Sweden. She is a teacher of modern languages and the author of books of poetry in Estonian.

WHITE-CHAPEL CHURCH YARD
Skid Row

Who are you? Lying down there, dirty and grimy, tattered clothes, and legs all
bare?
Sodden with meth, and without a care?
What is your story? for one there must be,
Lying there drunk for the whole world to see.
I see, laying on chest,
Military medals, four abreast.
Back in time were you once a War hero? Honoured with a citation
In the Military Gazette? What started your skid?
Was it unemployment? Was it stealing that got you the sack?
Or perhaps a wife's infidelity, in another shack?
Or was it your experience in war, that left you mentally maimed?
Who are we, to scorn you and judge,
But from our comfort, to help you we won't budge.
Can we guarantee to be secure?
What fate is knocking on our door?
As the great poet, John Donne, once said.
'Don't ask for whom the bell tolls, it tolls for thee.
And so to you, fellow human, I accord you dignity.'
Farewell, brother, farewell.

JACK DASH
London E.1, England.

Jack Dash, who was orphaned at an early age and left school at 14, became
famous in England as the leader of the dockers (longshoremen). He holds
the highest award of the British Trades Union Congress. His poetry has now
been officially recognized in Britain and the Poetry Society (London)
recently asked him to raise £275,000 ($680,000) for a new centre.

O, ENGLAND
A Mason Sonnet

O, England, land eternal, noble Isle,
When first my foot felt firm your vibrant earth,
The rivers of my Anglo-Saxon strain
Ran high. I saw you through traumatic smile
and broad peripheral dream. On boundless girth
Of sea, your honed horizons swam with rain
and mist and fog, and on to sun again.
Enormities of time divide: The birth
of my ancestral seed lies buried deep
within your sacred womb. Its valiant worth
lives on in me for my life's transient while.
O, England, my adoring heart shall keep
Your vigils, mark your triumphs and shall weep
for your defeats . . . down storied, gloried mile.

GLADYS MUNGEN BROWN,
New York, N.Y. 10010, U.S.A.

Gladys M. Brown has the double distinction of being a descendant of both Lady Jane Seymour and of George Washington. She is a member of the Board of Directors of the New York Poetry Forum.

OCCIDENTALLY

Japanese girl
in leaf-green tunic and pants,
you grew in our eyes to an island
where jewel-birds wavered and sang,
and we curved in towards you
like Hokusai's wave tipping over
to a long prostration
upon your shores.

Your torrent of jet-black hair
poured in vivid strands
past your lifted cheeks
and over your shoulders
which moved like a cat's
when you turned to answer our questions,
and each English word
crept out between your lips
with all the stealth
of an alien syntax.

But when with laquered nails
you plucked your new guitar
and tossed your hair aside
to free your face
for cameras we could not see
to feed upon,
our hearts were one sonometer
for your eastern song –

but you sang occidentally
as our girls sing,
and if we wished to understand you less
and find the stranger where the mask had torn
we'd have to spend much more
than this one hour with you.

DAVID GILL
High Wycombe, England.

David Gill, a College Lecturer, is the official translator to Ondra Lysohorsky, the great Czechoslovakian poet. He has already published two important books of his own poetry in England.

ROSE OF THE WORLD

Whatever the future may hold,
Let's make this moment shine bright
As a diamond studded with light –
Alive with the sun's throbbing gold.

Whatever Fate may intend,
Escape with me now to the place
Where happiness shows in each face
And of beautiful things there's no end.

Whatever fear may impose,
Let's be gay, eager and brave;
With high hearts let's be ready to save
Love's forever crimson Rose.

P. BRIAN COX
Melbourne, Victoria, Australia.

Dr. Cox, who has been described as "the greatest living love poet", is the author of three books of poetry and a contributor to anthologies and periodicals in many parts of the world. He is the founder of the Cosmosynthesis League.

BROWN GIRL

Around your thigh
you smoothe the cocoa stocking-top
with firm and self-caressing hands.
The ripple of your skin snakes lazily
as waves on far-off sands.

The dark mysterious Continent of your flesh
ridged and ranged by mountain bone
glints velvet as it surfaces
these shy and narcissistic lands.

Here early-breeding flowers will spring
and pine-cones opening their tangs
reveal the silken chestnut, sweetbriar wood
and deep mahogany's red tinge.

Now, like a photo still the moment stands:
your gesture smoothes the past
and all the future out
with calm, untroubled hands.

NORMAN HIDDEN
London N.4, England

Norman Hidden was Chairman of the Poetry Society of Great Britain from
1968 to 1971. He is the author of several books of poetry and an Editor and
Publisher of poetry.

CHILDHOOD

Deep into those
distant waters dive
retrieving treasures tossed
on the tides of Time,
coloured by changing seas
that rage and chime
as childhood's joys and fears
break on the flowering years
yet still survive.

Was it so long ago
a child by another sea
building castles of sand,
I saw the world's mystery,
beautiful, slow,
unfolding in waves; and shells
clutched in my hand
sang all the magic spells
of a far land?

Beauty and love were there;
and they have sung
through all the years between
keeping that Springtime young;
and here in this mellow sun
where the waves thunder
I feel in the Autumn air
as if life had just begun,
that sense of wonder.

DOUGLAS GIBSON
Leigh-on-Sea, England.

Douglas Gibson, a former Editor of "Quest" literary magazine, has published two important books of poetry and contributed to many journals. He is a Lecturer for the Eastern Arts Association of Great Britain.

THE EMPTY HOUSE

I went into an empty house;
The walls and floors were bare;
A single tear fell on my blouse;
No sign of life was there.
  It was my house.

I looked into an empty room;
Thick dust lay on the floor;
No sunshine could dispel the gloom
And sadness that it were.
  It was your room.

I saw, in mind, a poster bed
It held so long ago.
The image there, with touselled head
Was one I used to know.
  It was your bed.

I pictured, too, an empty chair ---
The one you loved so much;
And saw again, a loved one there
With pens and books and such.
  It was your chair.

The clothes; the shoes; the banners; rings;
The skis; the racquets; skates ---
Came rushing back, as if on wings,
And crashed at Reason's gates.
  They were your things.

I looked into an empty heart,
Squeezed dry of joy and pain ---
A stone would be its counterpart . . .
It will not weep again.
  It was my heart.

MILDRED BREEDLOVE
San Bernadino, California 92405, U.S.A.

Mildred Breedlove, a former Poet Laureate of the State of Nevada, is the President of the Nevada Poetry Society. She has written many books of poetry, including the well-known narrative, "Nevada".

A NEW SONG

Let me sing a new song
As the way I travel,
Let it every winding road
Cheer and unravel.

Let it seek a metre
Wide and high and free,
Let it strike a sweeter
Melody ›

Chords to run like thunder
Through my days
To beat in heartfelt wonder,
Fervent praise,

For the joy of knowing
Fellowship of gold
Like a river flowing
Till my days are told:

And as the stream winds onward
Through the land
Let me sing this new song
Loud and grand.

ROBERT ARMSTRONG
London, N2, England.

Robert Armstrong was Chairman of the Poetry Society of Great Britain 1948-50 and 1961. He is the author of books of poems published in the U.K. and U.S.A. and contributor to many journals.

IN PRAISE OF ALL POETS

The druids, ovates and the bards in grace
in ancient Britain had no means to write,
but taught their knowledge in a leaf-green space
open to all from tribal dawn to night;
their memories the records of the race,
the spoken words formed in the eye of light.

Like planets orbiting a central light
– a sun as old as time in outer space
which moves maternally through day and night,
true poets and their works absorb the grace
from she between whose magnet arms they write
of all the love and landscape of the race.

For the Muse instils the vigours of the race
by magnetizing all these sons of light
who use her mother-power, relaying grace;
and each true word advanced she helps them write
– a presence like a star which fills the space
between the tree arms of an empty night.

Their books like field corn wait from day to night,
potentially a nourishment to grace
the eyes of those soon born to read and write,
yielding their grains of wisdom to the race
on the table of the mind at proper light
while scientists launch the bodies into space.

And when from interplanetary space
in passage through the black galactic night
the poets of the future send the race
those thoughts of truth illumining like light
all base intention, then they act in grace
with those before who were impelled to write.

Let records honour poets who read and write;
they are the Muse's regents of the race,
the leaders to the avenues of light,
the shepherds through immensities of space.
And men and women born to day and night
find in their truthful words the terms for grace.

Assemble all those records which they write
like bands of secret silver lining space
to reflect eternally the Muse's light!

ERIC RATCLIFFE
Stevenage, England.

Eric Ratcliffe, who is an Information Scientist by profession, is the author of nine books of poetry. He has contributed to anthologies and journals in many parts of the world.

THE THIRD PRESENCE

Near the cliff's brow, high above
The restless, dark, white-stippled sea,
A man and woman walk as one;
Their languid steps rhyme perfectly.

The sun is loverlike; is fierce
And yet caressing; jealous, too:
It won't permit a single pale
Intruder to disturb the blue.

Gorse sweetens the warm soft breeze;
The man and woman pause to kiss
And then move on. Suddenly
He feels disquiet he can't dismiss,

A chilling breath, a faceless fear,
And in this English sun can't guess
Why, amidst green abundance, he
Should glimpse a white blind wilderness,

Great plains of snow and ice, except
That somewhere he has read or heard
Of two furred lost explorers who
Sensed – as he can now – a third.

VERNON SCANNELL
Sherborne, England.

Vernon Scannell, a Fellow of the Royal Society of Literature (U.K.), is the author of nine books and a contributor to literary journals in the U.K. and U.S.A. He won the famed Heinemann Award for Literature in 1960.

STRANGE REMINDER

Why should her face
For a flash replace
The one I approach to kiss?
Why should her eyes
Like a dream, surprise
My heart that its beat should miss?

Whose is the hair
That seems to bear
The scent I can still recall?
Are these the lips
And the tongue's small tip
That once meant all in all?

The fancy flies;
I regain my eyes.
She loves me whom I embrace,
Happy to find
Once more her kind,
Her dear, forgiving face.

That sharp, sweet glance
From a brief romance,
How did it slip my guard?
Did a thought by her
Unwittingly stir
Some ember yet uncharred?

Or could it be
She was sending me
The gift I was loth to take –
Her parting kiss?
I shall call it this
When my heart has ceased to ache.

DOUGLAS FRASER
Edinburgh, Scotland.

Douglas Fraser, a retired insurance official by profession, is the Hon. Secretary of the Edinburgh Poetry Club. He has published two books of poetry and contributed to many magazines.

SONG OF NORWAY

Where have we ever met,
Save by grey harbours,
Cabins or ships or some dockside hotel?
Time for a cigarette,
Question and answer
Ere the last siren and one more farewell.

Not for us sun and sand,
Sound of fiesta,
Church-bells and roses and streets full of stars;
Where did we ever stand
Save on wet gangways,
Hemmed in by fish-boxes, Custom Sheds, cars?

These made the pattern of
Meeting and parting ---
And when the last time comes let there be snow,
Friendship, a little love,
Sad seagulls crying,
As when it all began, long, long ago.

                    JOAN POMFRET
                Great Harwood, England

Joan Pomfret (Mrs. Douglas C. Townsend), a Fellow of the Royal Society of
Arts (U.K.), has been writing poetry since she was a schoolgirl. She has
published eight books of poetry and edited several poetry anthologies.

DEAF AND DUMB

Cannot hear birds, wind in trees,
small field noises,
thunder of brooks at flood time,
sighs, echoes,
or any music;
I groan in my throat like a beast,
eager to praise with my mute tongue.
Yet know, by touch, heart of stone,
hair like wire on moth's back,
knife-edge of grass
death in an autumn leaf.
And see what you do not see,
details you miss at casual glance,
strange flower in ruined garden,
pad of fox, first corn shoot,
the wordless look.
Can only come to you
where you talk in closed companies
when eyes speak, a finger beckons.
And then, reading your lips,
I walk unchained on soundless feet,
wait in the shadows for tears to fall,
huge as waterfalls,
on your dumb hands,
my deaf ears.

LEONARD CLARK,
London N.6. England.

Leonard Clark, joint winner of the last I.W.W.P. Awards first prize, is a Fellow of the Royal Society of Literature (U.K.) and a Freeman of the City of London. He is the author of many books of poetry and prose and a contributor to learned publications in the U.K. and U.S.A.

NOT BREAD ALONE

Give me a dream – I do not ask
For freedom from the irksome task,
Or happiness that holds no pain,
Only, though torments fall again
To endless seem –
That I may dream....

Give me a dream – for I am bound
By mortal chains to tread this ground,
When music from a million strings
Could bear me hence on tireless wings
To Truth supreme –
And bid me dream....

Give me a dream that I may seek
The deathless glory of the meek,
And shining through the former dark,
O mystic, and immortal spark
Of Love divine,
In dreams be mine....

Give me a dream when I am old,
Ill-comforted by earthly gold –
When labours of the past seem vain –
When ghosts of dreams which died for gain
To Justice scream –
Then let me dream.

Give me a dream – that I may see
The prisoner who still is free,
The sinned-against who yet forgive,
The crucified, who, dying, live,
The heathen pray –
As dream I may.

Give me a dream – I do not ask
For freedom from the irksome task,
Or happiness that holds no pain,
Only, though torments fall again
To endless seem –
That I may dream.

JOHN W. WOODWARD,
Derby, England

John Woodward, Life President of the International Writers' Guild and Society of New Authors (U.K.), has published many books of poems and contributed to numerous literary journals in many parts of the world.

ON THE CREST

There was a high road
And at that plateau
The point on the crest
Where cedars uprose

I read the raucous shouts of stranger birds.

Travellers of roads
Across oceans plains
From territories
Subconscious long guessed

I encountered moving into sun light.

Squawking the chorus
Suddenly silenced
Peered through the cedars
Their eyes waterdrops

I sensed staring down glints of sharp needles.

Now the archetypals
Drew close in circle
Grey coated people
A red frocked woman

I saw in glimmering landscape talk.

HELEN SHAW,
Auckland 5, New Zealand

Helen Shaw (Mrs. Hofmann) is one of the best known poets in New Zealand. She has published two important volumes of poems and contributed world-wide.

DOWN AT THE OLD WATERGATE

(The London Times was 100% correct in criticizing
the attitude of the Washington Post on Watergate)

In the recent election the President won by a landslide vote,
Now leftist liars in vengeance would make him the goat,
     Piling venomous hearsay and lies at a fanatical rate ---
        Down at the old Watergate !

This whole thing would be over in two minutes flat
If the people themselves could take up the bat ---
     It would soon be all over if someone would just tell it straight ---
        Down at the old Watergate !

When a state faces revolution, subversion and treason,
We must act and act quickly without rhyme or reason ---
     When the nation's safety is threatened and the danger is great
        Down at the old Watergate !

We all know that politics is a most dirty game
And often the things that go wrong are just nobody's blame ---
     So now men are fishing with falsehoods and fables as bait
        Down at the old Watergate !

We are witnessing an orgy of recrimination,
A parade of black lies and wildest exaggeration
     That is spreading antagonism, falsehood and hate
        Down at the old Watergate !

In this Watergate mess there is something that smells very queer ---
The truth is it's just a gigantic political smear
     That threatens our nation with a most tragic fate
        Down at the old Watergate !

> VINCENT GODFREY BURNS
> Annapolis, Maryland 21401, U.S.A.

Vincent Godfrey Burns, Poet-Laureate of Maryland, U.S.A., wrote the best selling book of the 1930s – "I Am a Fugitive From a Chain Gang" which became a famous film, starring Paul Muni. Much of his poetry has also concerned his years in a Georgian chain gang.

HOLINESS

There is no
Holiness in
Resignation or
Silence,
Or in repeating
What is known
To be absurd.

There is no
Holiness in
Believing the
Incredible
Or assenting
To the cruel
And tawdry.

There is no
Holiness in
Being sensible
When the heart
Says no.

There is
Holiness only
In the slow
Kiss of love
And the trusting
Look of a child.

CHARLES ANGOFF
New York, N.Y. 10024 U.S.A.

Professor Angoff, a former President of the Poetry Society of America, has been Professor of English at Fairleigh Dickinson University, New Jersey, U.S.A., since 1954 and Editor of The Literary Review since 1957. He has written more than forty books of poetry and prose.

ICE-CREAM PARLOR

In gelatin light of summer late afternoon,
A quarter to no time, two lovers floated
Into the ice-cream parlor. They saw on shelves
The bottles, glassy carafes, the crystal containers,
Transparent boxes (with lozenged licorice),
Admiring themselves in mirrors all around.

The sighs of the lovers interviewed the menu:
Hot butterscotch boasting of walnuts softly embedded;
Velvety hot fudge; strawberry parfait;
Succulent hot caramel and rich marshmallow,
Redolent of myrrh or exotic incense.
Nectared syrup lucent with mellow honey;
Banana ice-cream, bragging of pineapple juices;
Sundaes, luxuriating with cinnamon spices,
Like perfumes of Arabia; sweetened fruits;
Sherberts, soft and rose-petaled; chocolate ice-cream,
Arrogant with whipped cream and heaps of sprinkles;
Ice-cream, haughty with candied reserves and confections,
Unburdening themselves of honeysuckle fragrance,
Like poppy and mandragora to dizzy one.

(John Keats would have loved to be with these lovers here
To drug his spirit with sensuous delights,
And, with these lovers, let his senses fall,
Like drunken pirates, on these voluptuous riches
To loot them all of essences they cached.)

As wonders jostled each other, the lovers arose
To see the objects about them – the display cases,
The tables and chairs – now became porous with
The luminous glow of their love. The lovers left
To feel the ice-cream store's enchantments fade
Before the feasts their hearts made of each other.

                              LOUIS GINSBERG,
                    Paterson, N.J. 07504, U.S.A.

Louis Ginsberg, a teacher at Rutgers University, New Jersey, U.S.A., is one
of America's outstanding living poets. He has published numerous works.
One of his sons, Allen Ginsberg, is America's leading "beat" poet.

THE FORGOTTEN ORCHARD

Un-
withering
the old trees stand
in a garden lost
in the world's new wilderness
burdened with the fruit of choice
now as in the beginning.

Unwithering
the tree of life
stands by the tree of death
the tree of bread by the tree of stone
the tree of delight by the tree of thorns.

Unwithering
the tree of evil
stands by the tree of good
the tree of grief by the tree of joy
the tree of lost hope by the tree of promise
the tree of old surprises by the tree of new song.

Unwithering
the trees stand
in a lost garden
where no fruit
is forbidden
where each may
pick what he will --
now, as in the beginning.

CORNEL LENGYEL
Georgetown, California 95634, U.S.A.

Cornel Lengyel, winner of an *I.W.W.P.* Award in 1972, also received the Alice Fay di Castagnola $3,500 Award for a work-in-progress from the Poetry Society of America. He is a distinguished poet and his work has been published all over the world.

THE SLEEPING BEAUTY

She seems to sleep, the woman there.

The peaceful picture of her sleeping
builds itself against the air
as if the blue were part of her.
A drift of dandelion hair
ripples in sunlight toward the slope
of her full breast, the planted field
which holds the farmer's hidden hope,
the milk of life in earth concealed.

She seems to sleep. Yet deep inside
apparent languor engines move
where spring's explosive kiss of love
sparks into action a machine
whose motion is harmonious as
the laziest landscape ever seen.

Below the earth the matted roots
reach out in writhing energy
to catch the seeping damp. It shoots
up through the bole of bush and tree
to spurt out in a jet of leaves
from which the twanging wires of birds
flow back and forth from nest to ground
where excavating worms abound
and tractor caterpillars creep.

The tiny insect spindles fly;
the season's mighty pistons beat;
the small rain weaves;
the great storms ply;
the master sun strides down the sky
cracking his gentle lash of heat.

The waking woman sways like wheat.

DOROTHY LEE RICHARDSON
Cambridge, Mass. 02140 U.S.A.

Dorothy Lee Richardson won the first prize in the 1970 I.W.W.P. Awards.
She is a member of the Executive Committee of the Poetry Society of
America and a distinguished poet in her own right.

The "Highly Commended" poems exceeded a hundred and the judges had the greatest difficulty imaginable in reducing them to a publishable number. Many poems of considerable merit had, therefore, to be excluded. It is the hope of the Hon. General Editor and of the adjudicators that unsuccessful poets will try again for the I.W.W.P. Awards to be organized in connection with the Fifth Edition of the *International Who's Who in Poetry*.

The following are the "Highly Commended" poems:

PICTURES

Paintbox colours summon visions
of bright pictures;
landscapes,
seascapes
and the sky's great arc
in every mood;
Portraits of friends,
family pets.
My mind frets
to retain fleeting memories,
elusive inspirations,
fix them for ever on canvas
framed on a wall..!

My unresponsive brush
useless as a pickaxe
kills each artistic hope.
Ships aground on a sea of mud,
floating flour bags above;
grandpa, baby,
so unlike,
yet so alike reproaching mutely.
The gulf between
the eager dream
and its fulfilment
appals me.

Confidently
I write a verbal picture,
draw a mental image,
from the colours of my mind.
They do not stare reproachfully
from walls,
but hide their imperfections
between closed covers;
but my mind's fret
has been eased.

MARY BALDWIN
Melton Mowbray, Leicestershire, U.K.

I HAVE BEEN MADE AWARE

I have been made aware of many things
Which do not wring the heart without reply,
And I have seen that multitudes go by
More unsubstantial than the smoky rings
Which scent the cottage gardens' winnowings
Of golden sunflakes through green fruit-boughs high;
Where cool and silent thoughts suspended lie,
Where roses shatter and the last bird sings.
All this I know; and yet those folk unreal
My heart must wring more than the shining staves
Which sing so clear of heavenliness to me;
These multitudes could live, the mind's all-heal
Sweeter than pungent plant, or dim enclaves
Of heady smokedrift poised in ecstasy.

MARJORIE BALDWIN
Horsham, Sussex, U.K.

TIMOTHY HUGH

Timothy Hugh went to Timbuctoo
With a Chimpanzee he met at the Zoo,
But he lost his purse and he lost a shoe
And he started to cry with a Boo-hoo-hoo,
When along came a terribly friendly Gnu,
And a little black boy, his hat all askew,
Who said that his name was Itchypaloo
And asked was there anything they could do?
"I want to go back to my home in Kew"
Said Timothy Hugh, "And the Chimp does, too."
"In that case I'll build you a Catamaroo"
Said Itchypaloo. "That's a sort of Canoe
And a Catamaran all mixed in two."

So all day long with hammer and screw
They worked and made such a hullabaloo,
The folk from the village came out to view
The four of them building the Catamaroo,
Bringing them bowls of a savoury stew
And Cacao beans, like chocolate, to chew.
And that way the Catamaroo soon grew.
And when it was finished, Itchypaloo
Said "The Gnu and I will act as your crew."

So they climbed aboard with a "Toodle-oo"
And sailed away on the ocean blue
Till they reached the Thames and sailed on to Kew,
And there on the bank was somebody who
Timothy Hugh most certainly knew.
It was Daddy, looking around for a clue
As to what might have happened to Timothy Hugh.
Then they climbed ashore in an orderly queue,
And right at the end came Itchypaloo,
Saying politely, "How do you do?
I've brought your little boy home for you."
And Daddy could hardly believe it was true.
But that was the story Timothy Hugh told his Mummy.

ELSIE E. SELMAN
Knowle, Bristol, U.K.

THIS LAND IS OURS
A Poem Devoted to African Freedom Fighters

I talk to the mountains
And the mountains talk to me,
The mountains,
My ancestors worshipped;
Talking loud,
Crying high,
Evoking the powers,
The powers of my ancestors,
Who fought and spilled
their blood,
For this land.
This land of ours;
This is our land,
This is our property,
This is our country,
Our beloved country,
We shall continue to fight
for our land,
The land of our ancestors.
We are deprived,
We are forsaken,
We are ruined of our liberties,
We are enslaved of our freedom,
We are enslaved of our liberty,
Yes, the battle still continues,
And we shall continue to fight the foe,
We shall continue to fight the enemy,
We shall continue to battle with the enemy,
'Cause we want our freedom,
This is our land
This is our property,

This is our country.

G. KWESI ANNOH
Accra, Ghana

THE FEMALE HUNT

She--triple mirrored
  In scarlet coat--
White cravat glinting
  At slender throat--

Settles her black cap,
  Flicks at a boot,
Eyes bright with malice,
  Voice like a lute.

"There must be hunters
  And a quarry," says she,
"Not just for pleasure--
  For ecology."

This is her life style,
  Like a second skin
Or electric aura
  Of the one she's in.

Some shocked vixen
  Must bear the brunt,
Tagged as the target
  Of the Female Hunt--

Whose jaunty Mistress,
  Fearsomely gay,
Is in no mood for
  A grounding today.

Hard to escape her
  If she rode alone,
Which will not happen--
  Horse is her throne,

And a brave coterie
  Hunts at her back.
They like her dashing style,
  They like the crack

Of a long whip
  In frosty air,
And they prize--the immunity--
  Behind her there.

Ah! She is raising
  The horn. Tally ho!
Run, little fugitive,
  Give them a show.

CATHARINE N. FIELEKE
Momence, Illinois, U.S.A.

TO ONE IN MEDITATION

Wanderer through time and twilight,
Sorrow and pain and stress,
Bounded by walls and clocks,
Reach down for Boundlessness.

Like buds of water lilies
Along a woodland pond,
Widening at sunrise, open
To sight and sense and sound.

Stretch out! Breathe one with all worlds,
Earth and the salt dark sea.
Know spaces more than this whole
Starry immensity.

For in you –– aura-rainbowed ––
Whose wise self wakes and sings,
Cosmos interblends, aware,
As flute-notes tune with strings.

Sweetness past wine or fragrance,
Beauty within all hue,
Good health in the mind's mansion
Hold and encircle you!

WALLACE WINCHELL,
Manchester, Connecticutt, U.S.A.

COELACANTH

Once I lay in rivers, ribbon waters,
Basking as trout do,
Dreaming as trout do,
On the current's edge; sedge and the streaming weed
My dream was.
Sun, sun and the restless waters
My day was: moon and the oblique stars
My night was.

Waters that ribboned without resting,
To the world's end questing.....
Thither went I
To where the broad sea was,
Shell-sung the surf was,
The moon's road my journey.
To the world's end went I
By sea-road and moon-road,
Bitter salt tasting.

Down, down, down, down,
Falling a thousand ages,
Falling as shells do,
Writing Time's pages
On drift and dune, runes that the rock holds,
Cave, cranny, sea-cleft and left
By wave-wash and sea-song.
Down where the deeps are sea-night,
Green-dark, and the strange sad creatures
Slip and twist, kiss in the green-night
And sometimes lie dreaming
In the abyss,
Dreaming as I do.

Note: The species Coelacanth is believed to have been a river fish early in its development.
Lately believed extinct, several coelacanths have been caught by fishermen in deep sea waters in
this present half-century.

EILEEN M. HAGGITT
Birmingham, U.K.

NIGHT TRAIN

They have all left with the declining sun
Indifferent, some content, they have all passed
Into the weightless landscape.

Processions of the night, window on window,
Transparent in their blackness
Pass me by.

I seem not to be moving
And the empty train
Is still in the night's darkness
Upon the tangent of some greater motion

Some motion that I cannot touch
Or measure, one that goes
To no point of the compass
I hear the black surf of the night
That pounds upon some distant surface
Pointless, without content
And yet encompasses me on the periphery
Of its indifference.

Sometimes in a corridor of light
I pass my shadow on the glass
Touch it but with no contact.

I watch the book under the lamp
My finger's shadow moves between the lines
Trying to feel the words
The words that lie
Beside each other, each
Private, opaque.

I go into the corridor and touch
My shadow as it moves
Upon the surface of another motion.

But we exist
In different dimensions like the sea
Pounding
On a transparent plastic shore.

TILOTTAMA RAJAN,
London, Ontario, Canada

SMALL HOURS

Small hours have I known, indeed small hours,
Conceived in wretchedness: erection short
Of minute hand the hour overpowers.

Small hours have I known, poor sounds, lone chord
In foggy blue-smoked bars and cheap cafés
That sell you blurring spirits by the quart;

Some murky juice for coffee – as a brace.
Small hours have I known of sleeplessness;
And of fighting sleep – on sentry-go at the base.

Small hours of a heavy loneliness –
My men spread out in shifty sleep, in dreams
About their loves, while I just see their deaths.

I'm staring at the minute hand; it seems
My greatest wish is to achieve that zero,
The moment when the rocket flares and beams.

Although I know a dead man is no hero,
That war is sordid and its hours so small,
Yet do I sit here like a petty Nero.

But all small hours are not bitter gall:
I've known such hours when I heard the grass
Of poems grow and saw the rhymes rise tall.

I kissed the rhyming blades as lips of lass
And breathed with them and swayed with them in tune.
Alas, such splendid hours quickly pass.

Still others have I known that flit so soon
As later to be thought of just as dreams;
But in my mind they live, are not je-june.

These hours when a golden fire gleams
And burgeons into flaming tenderness,
As silent tide of strength flows from my limbs

Into the pool of magic realness –
The alembic, the "eternal feminine",
Of all inspired matter genesis.

Indeed, such great small hours have I seen.

WALTER M. BARZELAY,
Tel-Aviv, Israel.

SUN-MOON LAKE

As I close my eyelids, you emerge to my gaze –
The lake of infinite expanse and unplumbed depths,
First awakening after a rain-shower,
A light mist seems to be wrapped around you.

A dim illusion   wells up from the bottom of the lake
With the shimmering glow of a flowing spring,
                    with an indistinct phosphorescence.
Spirit waves roll in from the distance   and call softly to me;
A rainbow bridge extends from Dream Island   and invites me to cross.

How Joyous!   How overwhelming!
As I gaze up at the blue sky,
                    the blue sky is reflected within the water;
As I distantly view the white clouds,
                    the white clouds are floating upon the water,
Like bud after bud of blossoming, sleeping lotus.

Unfathomable, deeply reflecting water margin:
Immeasurable, Limpidly reflecting shore-line:
I'd like to plant a thousand willows upon your drooping eyelash
And become a piece of bright crystal
Thrown into that lake of pure clarity.

CHEN MIN-HWA
Taipei, Taiwan, Republic of China

A PLACE TO GO

My shoes are shined.
I have some dough.
I only need
A place to go.

My hair is combed.
My teeth all glow.
I only need
A place to go.

It's really sad to be a lad
Who has to stay at home
Especially when like other men
You get the urge to roam.

My black tie forms
A perfect bow.
I only need
A place to go.

I'd like to leave
Before I grow.
Won't someone show me
Where to go?

KEITH HALL, JR.
Santa Ana, California, U.S.A.

BALLAD OF EXPANDING DIMENSIONS

When God decreed "Let There Be Light"
  Space shone out everywhere
He next formed man with thinking brain
  A brain beyond compare.

Great Dante thought of distant space
  Including red-hued Mars
His Divine Comedy took him
  To realms among the stars.

And Ariosto visualized
  A place upon the moon
To send love-sick Orlando's brain
  Some centuries too soon.

Now man has sailed around the earth
  And probed beneath the sea
Brave men have faced the Arctic ice
  To solve its mystery.

Men fly the skies and shorten time
  Communications bloom
The Planets draw creative minds
  That fear no wrathful doom.

Columbus found a Continent
  Astronauts orbit earth
Computers calculate the task
  Of scientific worth.

At Houston men control the craft
  So Astronauts dare seek
New continents in outer space
  With dreams of realms unique.

For surely God impelled man's mind
  To each discovery
Inspired him to search and strive
  Through all Eternity.

LIBORIA ROMANO
Brooklyn, N.Y., U.S.A.

ARGUMENTS

We have no eyes but can see the harmattan dust
descending on cracked flesh;
we have no ears but do hear the she-owl
hooting on our thatched roof;
we have no heart but do feel the shock of blood
bartering our life away.

Miracles are rare
Miracles have fled the world:
Surgery is unconsecrated murder
X-ray is unhallowed light
Moon-landing is unblessed feat
Water-made-wine is but for the poor.

We can rightly ignore the dread
of an invisible distant Father;
and rightly be insensate to pangs
of the bleeding tree;
and deaf to the call
of the dove's flippant wings;
True fear is of faith gone right.

Our river drains into the crack
on desiccated carcass,
our fish tunnels into decayed mud
in pursuit of hooded worm,
parts of our fervid feat
to harvest life out of death
like God did at Easter!

How wise not to believe
God has wedded a human;
How wise not to believe
jewish murder is life insurance
How wise not to believe
autopsy at Mass is not filthy
how wise not to believe
heaven is no place nowhere;
how wise not to believe
we kill a lion with a wish;
how equally wise not to believe
poison can taste sweet.

ROMANUS N. EGUDU
Lagos, Nigeria

LIFE IN JEOPARDY

What hazards lie ahead of casual trips,
what destination for the daily going?
A man commutes each morning without knowing
whether he will return at night. Chance rips
apart the pattern of a life; storm whips
up vicious tides, obscures the shore-line, blowing
small vessels off their mortal course. A growing
uncertainty mounts trains, boards planes and ships.

No one immune from universal danger,
no man too undramatic to be drawn
into some network of bizarre design:
the passer-by at gunpoint of a stranger,
the harmless passenger a helpless pawn
of alien forces lurking down the line.

ANNE MARX
Hartsdale, N.Y., U.S.A.

COAST ROAD – TRINIDAD.

The sun silvers the sea below the coastal road,
Tipping the wave shapes,
Tearing them apart in shining jewels
Like diamond facets, in the morning light.
Dark faces peer through curtains, checked or flower'd,
Greeting the morning,
Taking for granted all that sunlight and that spread of sea
Washing the softly rounded coast
And guarding the quiet bays, the little questing boats.
Once smugglers hid in caves along these shores,
Hiding their guilty loot in the dark, dank sea-washed caves
And went upon fresh plunder of the unsuspecting ships
Sailing these self-same seas,
Where now the sunlight shatters all the shadows and no pirate lurks.
Green vines entwine the trees
Along the coastal road,
And gay-hued birds have kingdom in the leaves.
The singing boys, gay clothed, with garlanded guitars,
Sit lounging in the shade and know no flight of hours,
Nor heed the flies and floating flecks of dust.
The windless air draws heat and spreads it like a shawl,
Across the fruitful earth, with all its wealth of green,
To lose itself in cool brown shade of nutmeg groves,
Where restless butterflies pursue their mating;
And the day goes singing, lazy, dreaming,
On the coastal road above the timeless sea.

MAVIS A. DOWLING
Vaucluse, N.S.W., Australia

DEATH STALKS LIFE

Whether living is important or not
We are aware no form of life can escape death !
Death is following me
Darkness engulfs the once vivid air. Death !
I can't see you.
But I know you are behind me.
After searching for the meaning of you.
This is what I found:
Death you have meaning only as life has had significance.
I am as ready as will ever be.
Yet, I am proud to be alive and here.
But as strange as it may seem death opens the door.
The door to senseful being,
Personal relatedness to life,
And much, much more.
Yet, the natural response to death is fear.
Non-considered that no form of life can escape death.
I know what has flowed through me,
Also flows through my children,
Through work accomplished and service rendered,
And on and on, to more and more.
Suddenly one senses life's essence,
Growth and Creativity.
People helped, work accomplished and service rendered
Makes death unimportant.

JOSEPH MASON ANDREW COX
New York, N.Y., U.S.A.

STOP YOUR TEARS

Spring has come, stop your tears –
Forget once more, your hopes and fears,
Ah, with the rose the spring will fly
And all its lovely emblems die !

Bring forth the cup of joy and mirth,
Watch how the flowers peep out from earth,
Let's sing a note of love from heart,
Since like the spring we soon depart.

If once we part, we meet no more,
Fate casts us off to unknown shore
Love weeps in loneliness at night,
Youth fades away like candle light.

Let's live in peace while we are near
Smile and all clouds will disappear,
Comrades, be happy, blithe and gay,
Like blossoms short lived is our stay !

BANO TAHIRA SAYEED
Hyderabad 28, India

FAR

Far is there where we stand
Wearing our distrusting solitude --

It is there -- but then far is sometimes also here
And so much here so very near that we touch thigh to thigh --
That we cling tightly to one another
A refuge for each other against common fears --
-- Or we melt passionately together with millenary yearnings --
The salt and the wet of our flesh mingles

But then suddenly we realize that far is precisely there
Where we stand separate I in my you in your we in our worlds
Even though near -- thigh to thigh --
Even though melted -- flesh to flesh --
But suddenly
Realizing that we are simply strangers to each other

Far is there where we go
To don our distrusting solitude

Translated from Turkish by Ralph Setian

ZAREH YALDIZCIYAN (ZAHRAD)
Instanbul, Turkey

THE MAGNET

Far stars we are, of wild, domestic light,
born of ourselves, each a miracle.
A world, cold and hard as anthracite
is each one to another, a pinnacle

of doubt, a gravitative pull to home
--the scald excitement of it, how it changes
overnight to quite a different Rome,
blocked its roads behind to other ranges.

But how softly, firstly brinks the touch of two,
how clingly met to fusion farther on,
how crossed, how tangled all the I and you
locked in the angles of the polygon.

From our far stations each provoking glove
is choiceless flung. We are made of love.

LAURA W. de VILLASENOR
Mexico 20., D.F., Mexico

LOAN

How can the immaculate atom come out of its trance
from beyond Time
and divest itself altogether
of its impersonal glory to become incarnate
in the blood and bone and brain that are my embroilment!
Does it not soar in its own awareness,
in valences,
in relevances of behavior, known and unknown,
trailing its platoons of protons, neutrons, neutrinos,
its exquisitely patterned concentric spherical shells,
glowing with dazzling electrons,
invisible, inviolate?

And this is the stuff I am made of, packed into molecules
in trillions of googols,
but how does this profit the atom?
When the entity of atoms that is I is dissolved in death,
each atom will be free as before it was ever a part of me,
its principal intact,
but with no accrual of interest.
How then! No profit for the agony of incarnation
in the bar-brittle bone,
the frangible flesh that is I,
in order that the gift of consciousness might be mine!

For this high favor, how great is my debt to the atom,
this immortal intangible that offers no reckoning,
asks none:
the ineffable component of galaxies and quasors,
now my consenting servant in uncounted millions,
if I so much as bend my finger or speak a word.

I should be proud as a peacock,
humble as a mole,
for the loan of these star-shine fragments of the universe!

LILY PETER
Marvell, Arkansas, U.S.A.

CANINE ELEGY

Your body
was many years ago
covered with cinders;
and later on, a brownish powder,
was slowly spread
on a rose.

You barked at noon
Nostalgia in the neighbours
Your sharp throat
watchful ears
insomnia;
your legs,
forty thousand times fast
and that desperation
in your attachment to me.

Your body,
a brownish powder
on a rose.
And my tears
on the terrace floor,
Diana.

Translated from Spanish by Leopoldo Chizzini Melo

MARELI ECHENIQUE POSSE
Cordoba, Argentina

YOU CAN

After a drought
the fields yield plentiful grain,
after the night
follows the day
and after death
comes resurrection.

Why should not I dare to hope,
when hope is my bread?!
Why should not I dare to believe,
when faith is my land?!
Why should not I dare to sing
when the morning is yet to come.

Truly,
mountains move
and seas evaporate,
my smile vanishes
and tears are exhausted,
but my faith remains!

Heads up, my people,
hope and endure,
walk with songs through the night!

Heads up, my people!
Eat the dark bread of
    God's Mills
– you can bear it,
because you are
to whom bows
        a new day!

Translated from Estonian by Taimi Ene Moks.

ARVED VIIRLAID
Toronto, Ontario, Canada.

I greet you my new world
who wrap around me
with a whir
like a big wind
in the days of my youth
you roar and dance on my seas
in the sunrises
in you
in me
in all of us
each drop is born anew
each sun into other myriads
into light
into stardust
into delight and in that into pain
that I live and we live
in order to know
about the birth of our knowledge
about love and death
in order to dance our dance
again and anew
without ever giving up
in an other way
but riding on the torch of the sun ever breeding
sleeping and waking
in the wings of your winds
falling in love more and more
to grasp new glittering
in the thread of each moment
in each fold of life
where new foetuses are born
into different days and nights
into tomorrows and the days after tomorrow that are coming
give me
what is mine
give always
so that I won't turn away from you
like others
I am not like others
I am me

KALEVI RAHIKAINEN
Leppavaara, Finland

TRAPPED

I am trapped
Yes I am
In the mine
Of my benefactors
In the rich ore
Of the soil
Of my uninvited guests.

My head
My Heart
My Limbs
They are revolting
They are revolting
The echoes
Of the brutality
Of the wallsides which fall on me.

I am down
Down in the pit
Of my employers –
Here I spit
Spit
At the faces of my free ancestors
And grin
Grin
At the whiteness of my spit
Which smells
Of nothing other than
The bitterness of the soil
Under which
I am trapped.

KOJO YANKAH
Cape Coast, Ghana

THE CHARLES BAUDELAIRE $500 PRIZE

This prize, presented by Dr. and Mrs. B.H. Makar, of Jersey City, New Jersey, U.S.A., in memory of the French poet, is awarded for the first time in conjunction with the publication of this Fourth Edition of the *International Who's Who in Poetry*. It is open to poets under 21 years of age who need the money for the pursuance of their poetry.

Entries in the main I.W.W.P. Awards from qualifying young poets were considered by the adjudicators. In this case, *all* poems submitted were taken into account.

The judges decided unanimously to award the prize to Julia Mary Webley of Horndean, Hampshire, England. At the time of judging, Julia was 17 years old. She is a Grammar School student and she intends to be a teacher. She was the joint winner, at the age of 15, of the first prize in the I.W.W.P. $1,000 Awards organised with the publication of the Third Edition and her prize was presented to her by the Lord Mayor of Portsmouth at a civic ceremony in 1972.

The following are the poems which won her the Charles Baudelaire $500 Prize:

COMMUNION

I came full circular with goodness
And sweet holy thoughts.
I came with a friend, for comfort and
Money.
I stood, with the nail handful, who piously
Adjusted pink petals and grey felts.
Bending their heads in civilised thought.
We read, not too loudly, from a rusty
Clipped paper, trembling, grimacing in gesture
Over the mistakes my tongue made.

Then in all the godly silence, we knelt.
Friend and I, before the stiff prayer coated
Rail.
And I watched.
So many cupped hands, fluttering eyelids
Straining to close, to be quiet.
Can you be quiet with flesh in your palm,
And blood dripping from your fingers?
Can you watch the minister give to the
Cripple? Jesus bent double in grief of age?

We stood again, and lived again,
A thousand Christs dead in our
Throats.

THE EXORCIST

I watched you very quietly cross the street
And mount the stairs, riding thumpily
Up the stairs; the followers that
Silently, modestly crept like monkeys
Behind you.
"Here" you yelled like the echoing sun,
"Here". Hear me, hear me.
We are not all whitened, chalk chiseled
With bloated tongues and wide-spread
Fingers.

Having sat you out, brown-faded and
Curly edged; the children of my image
Photograph are dirty, and wedged in the loft.
I have cared over you as a child for
Rag dolls.
Merely the air, merely the kiss chuffed
Birds.
The flowers you laid to death in the
Pollen polished room, here,
Decorate me, hang in my hair like a
Countrychild.

Books and bells both ring with psalms.
I cannot go. I was never here,
Hear me.

STORM

Yet I am running, screaming to clutch
The rain.
The brown-skin hood rings my hair,
My legs long to fill the folds of the
Wind swirling cotton.

Why are we running when it would be so
Easy, if we tried?
The one-lifed song; poppies and flax
For the poor man's hair-life and
Time for those that die.
Noah builds the ark dark clouds and
Anvils of sorrow.
Splinters of steel strike the earth,
And fold into comforting
Softness.

I would go, in this slim blue-jeaned way
To Africa and teach.
I would design silver in Siam
And work the theatres with a
Knowledge I cannot write.

Please, silent lady — stir the rattling
Winds — let them
Beat the Earth drums
Until the skin pierces people.

The runner-up (who does not receive a prize under the terms of the Award) was Rohini Gupta, a 20-year-old student, of Bombay, India. Rohini received the Nehru Award (gold medal) for a collection of twenty-six poems in 1968, and has contributed to various periodicals in India and elsewhere.

The following two poems were submitted for the I.W.W.P. Awards:

THAT MAN IS

Against the half lit, sun drenched sky
And breaker upon breaker
Walks
The bubble that man is.

Sheath on sheath, half understood
With the seedlings of emotion
Grey as the sky
A tiny wave
Vibrating with sensation, waking
To an outside world
Slowly, moving with care
Gentle finger tips spread
In a zone not seen before
Feeling without haste.

Meeting vibrations from
A force of thought, an energy of
A mind.
One of many
The wave laps at its sides
Seeking
Self concealed. A hidden groping
For things that are not
While the mind moves in worlds not felt before.

A FLAME

The moment explodes
A flame fleck reaches flame
And there licking pauses
The iced wind outside, leaf edged, blown
With flowers, hesitates
Behind the unseen shield of mind
It waits as worlds do
When time clashes on time
That glimpse of an eternity
When candle meets sun and flame fleck merges in flame.

An eternal mind
Its vibrations met, lances out
Reaching, stooping that
The flame might light again
From the incense end of light.

A flash
And the thought forms of the world respond
Vibrate.
Blazing, speared through them all
The flame fleck merges in flame.

PHOTOGRAPHIC APPENDIX

Within the following thirty-one pages are the photographs of ninety-seven poets from many countries whose biographies appear in this Edition of the *International Who's Who in Poetry*. Some of them are Poets-Laureate; some are *I.W.W.P.* Award winners; some are authors and poets of distinction. Most of them are living poets.

This is believed to be the largest number of photographs of individual poets ever to appear in one international poetry reference work of this kind.

Easy reference can be made to the life and work of most of these poets by consulting the biographical section of this book.

Madeline Mason (New York), winner of the $1,000 First Prize in the I.W.W.P. Awards

Charles A. Wagner (New York), winner of the Second Prize of $500.

Bernard Grebanier (New York), I.W.W.P. Award winner.

Julia Webley (Horndean, England), winner of the I.W.W.P. $500
Charles Baudelaire Prize.

Rohini Gupta (Bombay, India), runner-up for the Charles Baudelaire Prize.

Vivian Trollope-Cagle

Vesta Kimble

Dr. George William Noel Cooper

Rt. Rev. Gregory Fontain, S.S.B.

P. Brian Cox

Faqir Mohammed

Basil Payne

Royston Ellis

Mildred Breedlove

Robby K. Mitchell

Lorena Simon

Jean Sterling

Ronald Criswell

William Henry Wray

Dr. Frances Clark Handler

Ethel Green Russell

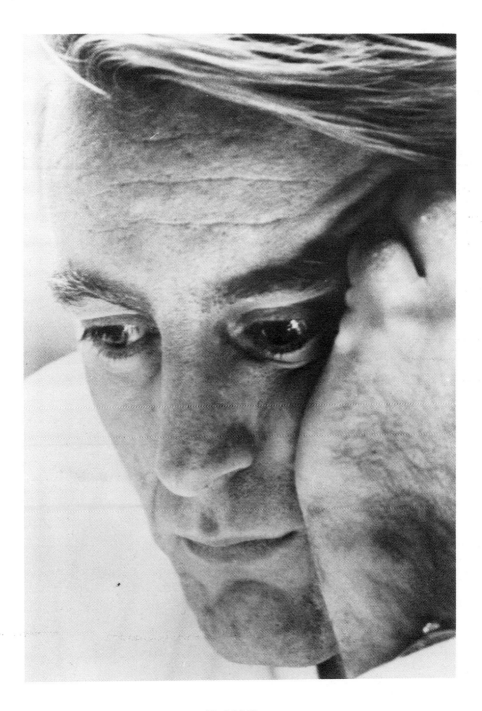

Rod McKuen

Dr Tin-Wen Chung, World Congress of Poets

Joan E. Morgan

Delphia Frazier Smith

John Haines

M. P. John

Patricia A. Sullivan

Anne Bonner Marley

Geraldine F. Kruesi

Sudie Stuart Hager

Oliver Page Everette

Leslie A. McRill

Orville Crowder Miller

Edwin Carlisle Litsey

Virginia Bagliore

Agnes Cochran Bramblett

Eugene McCarthy

Gwendolyn Glassberg

Vincent Godfrey Burns

Leonard Clark

Ruby Fogel

Lily Peter

Princess Chandanena

Percival R. Roberts, III

Robert Armstrong

Milford E. Shields

Richard Eberhart

Dr. Marvin Davis Winsett

Stella Woodall

Esther York Burkholder

Samuel William Scantlan

Wilbur Knox

Deborah Jean Castellano

Virginia Conkey

Freda E. Blanard

Natalie Robins

Marie Tschumperlin

Ethel McDonald deLiesseline

Stephen Morris

Michael H. McBride

Margaret Wilson

Ann Thompson Jester

Judson Campbell Crews

Celestino M. Vega

Lou LuTour

Alfonso Mann

El Gilbert

Professor Yar Slavutych

Jim Strickland

Roy Lee Harmon

Elvira Lanza Vitoritto

Joyce Frances Carpenter

Geoffrey Handley-Taylor

Ruth Lisa Schechter

Genevieve Sargent

Godfried Kwesi Annoh

Sister M. Albertina

William R. Wells

Auriel Bessemer

Kerstin Korning-Strid

Dr Jonas Negalha

Min Hwa Chen

Joseph Albion Joyce

James Humphrey

Carol B. Hayman

Nissim Ezekiel

Joan George

Mary Louise Busching

Wauneta Hackleman

Mildred D. Cathcart

Beryl Baigent

Peter Edward Clarke

Ossie E. Tranbarger

Dr Harold S. Gulliver

David Ray

Maralee Davis

APPENDIX A

QUEEN'S GOLD MEDAL FOR POETRY

The King's/Queen's Gold Medal for Poetry was instituted by King George V in 1933 at the suggestion of the then Poet Laureate, John Masefield. Since then a small committee, under the chairmanship of the Poet Laureate, has been created to choose the annual recipient of the medal. The choice is approved by the Queen and the honour conferred at Buckingham Palace.

The following is a list of the recipients of the King's/Queen's Gold Medal from the date of the medal's inception.

1934 Laurence Whistler
1936 W.H. Auden
1940 Michael Thwaites
1952 Andrew Young
1953 Arthur Waley
1955 Ruth Pitter — 1st woman recipient. Medal personally presented by
H.M.
1956 Edmund Blunden
1957 Siegfried Sassoon
1959 Frances Cornford
1960 John Betjeman
1962 Christopher Fry
1963 William C. Plomer
1964 Rev. Ronald S. Thomas
1965 Philip Larkin
1967 Charles Causley
1968 Robert Graves
1969 Miss Stevie Smith — presented personally by H.M.
1970 Professor Roy Fuller
1971 Stephen Spender
1973 John Heath-Stubbs

POETS LAUREATE OF THE UNITED KINGDOM

The title of Poet Laureate in England was conferred back as far as the 17th century in the form of a pension which specifically recognized the poet's services to the Crown. The laureateship has become the reward for eminence in poetry and is recognized as a Royal office to be filled automatically when vacant.

The following is a list of the Poets Laureate of the United Kingdom from the date of inception of that honour.

Samuel Daniel — 1599
Ben Jonson — 1619
Sir William D'Avenant — 1637
John Dryden — 1670
Thomas Shadwell — 1688
Nahum Tate — 1692
Nicholas Rowe — 1715
Rev. Laurence Eusden — 1718
Colley Cibber — 1730
William Whitehead — 1757
Rev. Thomas Warton — 1785
Henry James Pye — 1790
Robert Southey — 1813
William Wordsworth — 1843
Lord Tennyson — 1850
Alfred Austin — 1896
Robert Bridges — 1913
John Masefield — 1930
Cecil Day-Lewis — 1967
Sir John Betjeman — 1972

OXFORD PROFESSORSHIP OF POETRY

The Professorship of Poetry was established in 1708 from funds left by Henry Birkhead who was a scholar of Trinity College, Oxford, from 1635, and a Fellow of All Souls College from 1638-57.

The Professor's appointment procedure is totally unlike that for other professorships. Appointments are made by panels of nine people including specialists in the subject of the professorship. Convocation, consisting of all the holders of the degree of M.A. from Oxford University, then elects the Professor. In order to vote for the Professorship it is necessary to attend in person at Oxford and give one's vote to the Vice-Chancellor or his representative.

By way of duties, the Professor, by Statute, has to deliver a public lecture each term. The position carries a small salary for the five year term of office.

The following is a list of holders of the Professorship of Poetry from the date of the chair's inception. Only in recent times has the Professor been primarily a poet so the list contains many purely professorial names.

Joseph Trapp	1708-18
Thomas Warton	1718-28
Joseph Spence	1728-38
John Whitfield	1738-41
Robert Lowth	1741-51
William Hawkins	1751-56
Thomas Warton	1756-66
Benjamin Wheeler	1766-76
John Randolph	1776-83
Robert Holmes	1783-93
James Hurdis	1793-1802
Edward Copleston	1802-12
John Josias Conybeare	1812-21
Henry Hart Milman	1821-31
John Keble	1831-42
James Garbett	1842-52
Thomas Legh Claugnton	1852-57
Matthew Arnold	1857-67
Sir Francis Hastings Charles Doyle	1867-77
John Campbell Shairp	1877-85
Francis Turner Palgrave	1885-95
William John Courthope	1895-1900
Andrew Cecil Bradley	1901-06
John William Mackail	1906-11
Sir Thomas Herbert Warren	1911-16
William Paton Ker	1920-23
Heathcote William Garrod	1923-28

Ernest de Selincourt	1928-33
George Gordon	1933-38
Adam Fox	1938-43
Sir Cecil Maurice Bowra	1946-51
Cecil Day-Lewis	1951-55
Wystan Hugh Auden	1956-61
Robert Ranke Graves	1961-66
Edmund Charles Blunden	1966-68
Roy Broadbent Fuller	1968-73
John Barrington Wain	1973—

Vacancies occurred from 1917-19 and from 1944-45.

OFFICIAL STATE POETS LAUREATE OF THE USA

by Marvin Davis Winsett

The following list of official State poets laureate of the USA has been revised and updated since its original appearance in the Second Edition of the *International Who's Who in Poetry*. However, it is still possible that our information is not complete. Therefore, the editors would welcome any corrections or additions which may be included in a future edition of the *International Who's Who In Poetry*.

Only official State poets laureate, appointed either by the State Governors or by leglislative action, appear on the list. It does not include the various poets laureate appointed by some literary groups.

The editors wish to express their thanks for the co-operation they received from State governmental sources in compiling this list. Those States omitted from the list do not observe the poets laureate tradition.

ALABAMA

Dr. Samuel Minturn Peck, served 1929-38 (deceased)
Mrs. Mary P. Ward, Birmingham, served 1954-59
Mr. Bert C. Henderson, Montgomery, serving 1960—.

ALASKA

Margaret Mielkie, served 1963-65
Dr. Oliver Everette, served 1965-67 (deceased)
Carol Beery Davis, Juneau, served 1967-69
John Haines, serving 1969—

ARKANSAS

C.T. Davis, first poet laureate (deceased)
Mrs. Rosa Zagnoni Marinoni, served 1953-70 (deceא. ⅃)
Ercil Brown, served 1970
Lily Peter, serving currently

CALIFORNIA

Ina Coolbrith, served 1919-28 (deceased)
Henry Meade Bland, served 1929-31 (deceased)
John Steven McGroarty, served 1933-44 (deceased)
Gordon W. Norris, served 1953-61 (deceased)
Charles B. Garrigus, serving 1966—.

COLORADO

Alice Polk Hill, served 1919-21
Nellie Burget Miller, served 1921-52
Margaret Clyde Robertson, served 1952-54
Milford E. Shields, Durango, serving 1954—.

DELAWARE

Edna Deemer Leach, Wilmington, served 1947-50
Jeanette Slocomb Edwards, Wilmington, served 1950-54
Frances Shannon McNeal, Wilmington, served 1954-55
Katharine King Johnson, Dover, served 1955-56
David Hudson, Wilmington, served 1956-60
Alice Kimball Bradford, Wilmington, served 1960-61
Marguerite Eleanor Weaver, Wilmington, served 1961-63
Mother Aloysius Peach, O.S.U., Wilmington, served 1963-65
Dr. Percival R. Roberts, III, Newark, served 1965-67
Joyce M. Carlson, Wilmington, served 1967-69
Antonia Bissell Laird, Wilmington, served 1969-71
Dr. Harry O. Eisenberg, serving 1971—.

FLORIDA

Mrs. Vivian Laramore Rader, Miami, serving, 1929—.

GEORGIA

Frank Lebby Stanton, Atlanta, served 1925-27 (deceased)
Ernest Neal, Calhoun, served 1927-43 (deceased)
Wichtman Fletcher Melton, Atlanta, served 1943-44 (deceased)
Oliver (Ollie) Franklin Reeves, Atlanta, served 1944-63 (deceased)
Agnes Ezell (Cochran) Bramblett, Forsyth, serving 1963—.

IDAHO

Mrs. Irene Welch Grissom, Idaho Falls, served 1923-48
Mrs. Sudie Stuart Hager, Kimberly, serving 1949—.

ILLINOIS

Howard B. Austin, Springfield, served 1936-62
Carl Sandburg, Galesburg and Chicago, served 1962-68 (deceased)
Gwendolyn Brooks, Chicago, serving 1968–.

INDIANA

Emory A. Richardson, Evansville, serving 1929–.

IOWA

Gladys Gibson Pagel, Allison, served 1957-68 (deceased)

KENTUCKY

James T. Cotton Noe, Lexington, served as first poet laureate (deceased)
Jesse Hilton Stuart Greenup serving Eastern Kentucky 1969–.
Edwin Carlisle Litsey, Beechland, serving Central Kentucky 1969–.

LOUISIANA

Mrs. Robert Emery (deceased)
Ethel Green Russell, served 1970
Dr. George William Noel-Cooper serving currently

MARYLAND

Maria B. Crocker, Baltimore, served 1959-62 (deceased)
Vincent Godfrey Burns, Annapolis, serving 1962–.

MICHIGAN

Edgar A. Guest, Detroit, (deceased)

MISSISSIPPI

Mrs. M.L. Prenshaw

NEBRASKA

John G. Neihardt, Bancroft, serving 1921–.

NEVADA

Mildred Breedlove, Las Vegas, appointed in 1957 and again in 1959
Norman Kaye, Las Vegas, present poet laureate

NEW HAMPSHIRE

Paul Scott Mowrer, Chocorua, served 1967-71 (deceased)

NORTH CAROLINA

Arthur Talmadge Abernethy, Burke County, served 1935-53 (deceased)
James Larkin Pearson, Wilkes County, serving 1953—.

NORTH DAKOTA

Cal Waldron, Minot, serving 1968—.

OKLAHOMA

Violet McDougal
Paul Maurice Kroeger (David Nash)
Jenny Harris Oliver
Della I. Young
Ann R. Semple
Bess Truitt
Leslie A. McRill

OREGON

Edwin Charles Markham, served 1921-51 (deceased)
Ben Hur Lampman, served 1951-57 (deceased)
Ethel Fuller (Romig), served 1957-65 (deceased)
William Stafford serving 1974—.

SOUTH CAROLINA

Dr. Archibald Rutledge, Hampton, near McClellanville, serving 1934—.

SOUTH DAKOTA

Miss Adeline Jenny, Valley Springs, present poet laureate.

TEXAS

Judd Mortimer Lewis, Houston, served 1932-34 (deceased)
Aline T. Michaelis, Austin, served 1934-36 (deceased)
Grace Noll Crowell, Dallas, served 1936-39 (deceased)
Lexie Dean Robertson, Rising Star, served 1939-41 (deceased)
Nancy Richey Ranson, Dallas, served 1941-43 (deceased)
Dollielee Davis Smith, Cleburne, served 1943-45
David Russell, Dallas, served 1945-47 (deceased)
Aline B. Carter, San Antonio, served 1947-49 (deceased)
Carlos Ashley, Llano, served 1949-51
Arthur M. Sampley, Denton, served 1951-53
Mildred Lindsey Raiborn, San Angelo, served 1953-55
Dee Walker, Texas City, served alternate 1953-55 (deceased)
Pierre Bernard Hill, Hunt, served 1955-57 (deceased)
Margaret Royalty Edwards, Waco, served 1957-59 (deceased)
Van Chandler, Kingsville, served 1959-61 (deceased)
Edna Coe Majors, Colorado City, served alternate 1959-61 (deceased)
Lorena Simon, Port Arthur, served 1961
Marvin Davis Winsett, Dallas, served 1962
Gwendolyn Bennett Pappas, Houston, served 1963
Vassar Miller, Houston, served alternate 1963
Jenny Lind Porter, Austin, served 1964-65
Edith Rayzor Canant, Texas City, served alternate 1964
Bessie Maas Rowe, Port Arthur, served 1966, alternate 1967 (deceased)
Grace Marie Scott, Abilene, served alternate 1965-66
William E. Bard, Dallas, served 1967
Kathleen Henry Harris, Waco, served 1968
Sybil Leonard Armes, El Paso, served alternate 1968
Anne B. Marley, Austin, served 1969 (deceased)
Rose Davidson Speer, Brady, served alternate 1969 (deceased)
Mrs. Robby Koons Mitchell, McKinney, served 1970
Faye Carr Adams, Dallas, served alternate 1970-71
Terry Fontenat, Port Arthur, served 1971
Mrs. Clark Gresham, Burkburnett, served 1972
Marion J. McDaniel, Enoch, served alternate 1972
Violette Newton, Beaumont, served 1973
Stella Woodall, San Antonio, served alternate 1973
Lila Todd O'Neill, Port Arthur, serving 1974
C.W. Miller, San Antonio, alternate serving 1974

VIRGINIA

Ruby Altizer Roberts, Christiansburg, appointed 1950
Guy Carleton Drewery, present poet laureate

WEST VIRGINIA

Vera Andrew Harvey, Huntington, first poet laureate
Roy Lee Harmon, Beckley, present poet laureate

APPENDIX B

INTERNATIONAL POETRY SOCIETIES

CENTRO STUDI E SCAMBI INTERNAZIONALI

Via Corrado Segre 7, Rome, Italy

President General:
Professor Harry Elstrom, Professor at the University of Louvain and at the Institut Superieur d'Architecture et des Arts Decoratifs, Belgium.

Vice-Presidents:
S.E. Maurice de Hanot d'Hartoy, Dr. es Sciences politiques, Dr. es Lettres. Former Minister Plenipotentiary to the S.d.N.; former Permanent Delegate, ONU; Laureate, French Institute, Paris.
S.E. Giuseppe Guido Loschiavo, Magistrate and Writer. President, Tribunale Superiore delle Acque; former Pres. di Sez. della Suprema Corte di Cassazione, Italy.
Professor Leo Magnino, Dr. of Political Science. University Lecturer and Writer (Italy).
Rev. Monseigneur Prof. Maurice Orban, Professor, Catholic University of Mons, Belgium.

General Secretary, President, International Executive:
Dr. Armando Troni, International Director and Writer.

Members of the Board:
Mme. Suzanne Collon-Gevaert, Professor of History & Art, University of Liege, Belgium.
Professor Charles Gilbert, Director, Royal Academy of Fine Arts and Institut Superieur d'Architecture, Belgium.
Professor Gustave E. Von Grunebaum, Professor of History and Director, Near Eastern Center, University of California, USA.
Professor A.N.J. Den Hollander, Director, Sociologisch Seminarium Universiteit van Amsterdam, The Netherlands.
Professor Charles J. Jacobs, University of Bridgeport, USA.
S.E. Dott. Giuseppe Marchegiano, President di Sezione On. della Súprema Corte di Cassazione: Legal Adviser, Minister of Foreign Affairs, Italy.
Professor Dr. Avv. Jean Moruzi, Professor, University of Bucharest; Director, Revue Internationale de doctrine et de legislation comparée, Rumania.

Professor Pierre Sometchin Nginn, Professor, University Sisavanvong; former Director, Information and Press Services, Laos.

Mrs. Collice Portnoff, A.B., A.M., Ph.D., Department of English, Arizona State University, USA.

S.E. Professor Emile Tyan, Professor, Faculty of Law, University of Beirut; former First President, Cour de Cassation, Liban.

Vice-Secretary General:

M. Ettore Rubcich, Secretary, International Executive.

The 'Centro Studi e Scambi Internazionali' was the first association founded in Italy immediately after World War II, for the purpose of promoting the resumption and development of international cultural exchanges. The Centre has the purpose of serving the cause of sciences, letters and art, but, above all, of furthering international relations among scholars, artists and writers, thus facilitating the exchange of cultural and scientific information. (The term 'scientific' is to be understood in the widest sense of the word and consequently it includes all the humanistic and social branches of learning as well.)

International Committee for Scientific Information:

In order to contribute to the diffusion of scientific and cultural information, the Centro Studi e Scambi has organised an International Committee for Scientific Information, with the task of grouping scholars in various branches of learning and promoting enquiries to be conducted by the Centre at universities, cultural institutions and associations throughout the world.

Members in the Fifteen International Commissions are grouped under the following subject headings:

(1) Architecture; (2) Fine Arts; (3) Law; (4) Geography & Ethnology; (5) History & Archaeology; (6) Mathematics & Astronomy; (7) Medicine & Veterinary; (8) Music & Theatre; (9) Cinema, Radio & Television; (10) Numismatics, Bibliophily & Philately; (11) Philology, Linguistics & Letters; (12) Philosophy, Pedagogy, Theology & Religion; (13) Applied Sciences & Technology; (14) Economic, Political and Social Sciences; (15) Natural Sciences in general.

Programme:

In addition to a yearly meeting (General Conference), the Centre will organize a display of Painting, Sculpture and Architecture (projects) which will give members an opportunity of exhibiting their work publicly. Authors of literary or scientific publications will also be able to show and sign their works.

The Members of the International Committee will, on request, be appointed 'Honorary Representatives' with the task of representing the Centre in their towns of residence.

Membership cards for the current year will be forwarded to all members free of charge.

In accordance with article 4 of the social rules, an artistic Nomination Diploma will be given free to the Members of the International Committee after the ratification of the appointment.

With a view to furthering international relations among writers, critics and journalists and in order to make the contemporary poets of various countries better known to each other, the Centro Studi e Scambi will provide for the publication and diffusion of a series of 'Bouquets of Poems'. The authors who would like to have a specimen of this series, are asked to remit $1 (one dollar) on receipt of which, 3 books by Italian, American and Australian writers, previously published by this organization will be sent on by registered mail.

Literary and scientific competitions are organized through the medium of the International Information Bulletin *Mondo*. The latter is the organ of the Center and an indispensable means of contact with its members. It is published monthly, in Italian, English and French. The Contents include: (a) Full information on every type of activity of the Centre; (b) Short bio-bibliographic hints introducing new members; (c) Full information on the activities of members (publications and appointments); (d) Full information on international cultural matters (e.g., Constitutions of new associations, new publications, prizes, artistic and literary competitions, etc.); (e) The UNESCO Features; (f) An address list of cultural institutions, translators, editors, magazines, collectors, members, etc., all over the world; (g) A list of forthcoming international meetings.

The International Exchange Section brings collectors and correspondents in all parts of the world into close touch with one another by publishing their names and addresses together with their enquiries in the bulletin. A special form is addressed free on request to all members.

The Centre of Studies and International Cultural Exchange is a non-profit making, non-political association. The Centre is an affiliate of the Union of International Associations and appears in the UNESCO Handbook of international exchanges of publications.

DELEGUES — HONORARY REPRESENTATIVES — DELEGATI

AFRIQUE DU SUD — M. Steinberg Coert — Sculpeur — Pretoria

ALLEMAGNE — (Rep. Federale) — Fritz Petsch — Peintre — Bonn Bad Godesberg

ALLEMAGNE — Dr. Friedrich Rasenberger — Koch — Berlino

ARGENTINE — Prof. Carlos Enrique Larrosa — Buenos Aires

AUSTRALIE — Mrs Jessie Goode — Writer & Poet — Melbourne

AUTRICHE — Prof. Ernest J. Gorlich — Wien

BELGIQUE — M. Pierre Vandendries — Jounaliste — Bruxelles

BRASIL — Prof. Jonas Negalha — Sao Paulo

BULGARIE — Nicolai Dontchev — Homme de Lettres — Sofia

CANADA — Stanley Lewis — Writer & Poet — Montreal

CEYLAN— Sri Ramanathan Thiagarajah — Proctor Supreme Court — Colombo

CHINE — Prof. Ivano Foti D'Inardo — Pechino

CHYPRE — M. Andreas K. Righas — Fonctionnaire de Police — Nicosia

COTE D'IVOIRE — M.me Denise Massida — Femme de Lettres — Abdjan

DAHOMEY — M. Raymond Akpan — Yikpon-Ecrivain — Cotonou

DENMARK — Mr. Mogens Amdrup — A. Peintre — Roskilde

EQUATEUR — Prof. Carlos Carrera Barreto — Quito

ESPAGNE — M. Francisco J. Bracero — Organisateur — Madrid

ETATS UNIS D'AMERIQUE — Mrs. Jasmine Texoon — Peintre — New York

FINLANDE — M. Erkki Talari — A. Peintre Helsinki

FRANCE — M.me la Baronne Ines de Freville — Paris

FRANCE — (Vice) M.me Germaine Michelet — A. Peintre — Paris

GHANA — Dr. Joseph Y. Ewusie — Accra

GRANDE BRETAGNE — Dr. Ernest Kay — Homme de Lettres — Londres

GRECE — Hon. Jean Coutsocheras — Avocat — Athenes

GUINEE — M.me Sarah Laverna Sharp — Ecrivain — Conakry

HAITI — Prof. Benique Vernio — Port-au-Prince

HAUTE VOLTA — Prof. Ki-Zerbo — Ouagadougo

HONGRIE — M. Adam Wurtz — A. Peintre — Budapest

INDE — Dr. Krishna Srinivas — Editor — Madras

IRAN — Dr. Moosa Hekmat — Teheran

IRLANDE — M. Christopher Campbell — Ecrivain — Dublin

ISLANDE — M. Johann Kristjansson — Ecrivain — Reykkjavik

JAPON — M.me Chiyoko Nakatani — A. Peintre — Tokyo

LAOS — Prof. Pierre Somtchine Nginn — Vientiane

LIBAN — M. Moussa Prince Avocat — Beyrouth

LUXEMBOURG — M. Camille Frieden — Architecte — Luxembourg

MALAISIE — Dr. Sambanthanathan Underwood — Kuaka Kangsar

MALGACHE rép. — M. Randriamarozaka — Journaliste — Tananarive

MALI — M. Guy Boucher Conseiller Ped. — Diré

MALTE — Rev. Prof. Amante Buontempo — La Valletta

MAROC — M. Henri Levivalle — Ecrivain — Casablanca

MEXIQUE — M. Vincenzo Totoro Nieto — Avocat — Mexico

MONACO P.TE — M.me Emma de Sigaldi — Sculpteur — Monaco

NIGERIE — Dr. Isu Okogeri —Journaliste — Afikpo
NORVEGE — M.me Laura Hovland — A. Peintre — Oslo
NOUVELLE ZELANDE — M. Frederich Parmee — Ecrivain — Auckland
PAKISTAN — M. Ghulam Alî Allana Poète — Karachi
PAYS BAS — M. Felix Leon Homme de Lettres — Amsterdam
PHILIPPINES — Rev. Prof. Isidoro Dino — Sorgoson
POLOGNE — M. Andrzej Janota — A. Peintre — Varsavie
PORTUGAL — M. Sebastiâo J. de Sousa Diniz — Lisbonne
RHODESIE — M.me Philippa Berlyn — Ecrivain — Salisbury
ROUMANIE — Mihu Vulcanescu — A. Peintre — Bucarest
SENEGAL — M. Iba N'Diaye — A. Peintre — Dakar
SINGAPORE — M. C.G.J. Médecin — Singapore
SUEDE — M. Olle Baertling — A. Peintre — Stockholm
SUISSE — M.me Rose Marie Eggmann — A. Peintre — Genève
SYRIE — Prof. Mahmoud Dadouch — A. Peintre — Damas
TCHECOSLOVAQUIE — M. Miloslav Troup — A. Peintre — Prague
TURQUIE — M. Ilgi Adalan — A. Peintre — Istanbul
URUGUAI — Prof. Eugenio Relgis — Montevideo
VENEZUELA — Dr. Maria Sonni — Femme de Lettres — Caracas
VIET NAM DU SUD — M. Le Linh — Journaliste — Saigon
YOUGOSLAVIE — M. Stojan Troumitch — A. Peintre — Pantchevo
ZAIRE — Rep. Prof. Emmanuel Mahieu — Lumbubashi
ZAMBIE — M. Romus Chee Wong — Architecte — Lusaka

THE UNITED POETS LAUREATE INTERNATIONAL

OBJECTIVE: "WORLD BROTHERHOOD AND PEACE THROUGH POETRY"

By Amado M. Yuzon

Promoting the First World Congress of Poets in Manila, Philippines, in 1969, and again suggesting, co-promoting and advising the Second World Congress in Taipei, Republic of China, in November of 1973, the United Poets Laureate International (UPLI) now finds itself leading a movement unique in the history of poetry, which is the mobilization of the poetry forces of all nations, large and small, towards "world brotherhood and peace through poetry".

UPLI is trying its best to give poetry a purpose more than "art for art's sake". This idea was reiterated by me in my keynote speech before an audience of thousands of leaders of thought and high government dignitaries including the 300 delegates at the inaugural session of the Taipei World Congress of Poets on November 12, 1973.

I said: "Poetry, worthy of its name, must have a purpose more than art for art's sake, a purpose that is humane, humanistic, and humanitarian, that is, the maximation or perfection of man's love for his fellow men, a nation's love for other nations, a kind of love that can only promote a lasting peace for the world."

Certainly, the UPLI World Congress of Poets movement has caught fire. Various countries, states and organizations vie for the privilege of holding a World Congress of Poets. One of such is a consortium of invitations addressed to me by Governor Marvin Mandel of Maryland, Mayor William Donald Schafaer of Baltimore, Walter Orlinsky, President of the City Promotion Council, Thomas J. Foster, Esq., the Executive Director of the City Council. Referred to the Second World Congress of Poets, the Maryland invitation was unanimously accepted by the three hundred delegates.

The third World Congress of Poets will, thus, be held in Baltimore, Maryland, U.S.A., sometime in 1976 during the bi-centennial celebration of American Independence.

In retrospect, the UPLI was inaugurated at the Hotel Filipinas on 30 September 1963. The constitution provides for: (a) the promotion of friendly relations among nations of the world through the exchange of poetry by the best living poets, and (b) the cultivation of poetry as an art, irrespective of race, religion and ideology, by giving the most gifted and inspired poets the incentive to write. In other words, the aim of UPLI is to promote world brotherhood and peace through poetry.

Implementing this objective, UPLI has undertaken by cultural tours, the Laurel Leaves publication, correspondence and world congresses, the recognition of meritorious poets and poetry organizations in the form of laureateships, medals, decretum of award and commendations. It has involved itself practically with every major Poetry Society and leading poet of the world.

Summing up the UPLI objective, Dr. Mildred Breedlove, Honorary Narrative Poet Laureate of North America, made the following observation in a speech delivered in the First World Congress of Poets in Manila in 1969.

"Through UPLI all the great works of member nations may be made available to each other and to the world at large as gems of thought and speech from all countries, as incorporated into the language of each. Poetry truly creates the universal language. And we, who write the poetry, must realize that, as we write, so the history of the world is molded. If we strive for brotherhood, we achieve brotherhood. But, if we advance the qualities of hatred, injustice and unbeautiful, we achieve destruction."

Let us dedicate ourselves to the composition of the beautiful; the just; the philosophy of universal harmony. If we can make these qualities the theme of our poetry, we will not need to bear arms for justice and brotherhood. Surely, no person may underestimate the power of the weapon we hold.

THE WORLD POETRY SOCIETY INTERCONTINENTAL

by Orville Crowder Miller

The Parnassian family now known as World Poetry Society Intercontinental was founded in 1960 by Dr. Krishna Srinivas of India when he launched his journal 'POET'. Originally conceived by him as a non-profit making, often gratuitous service to his growing group of receptive poets and readers in centres throughout the entire literary world, it has since become not only that but much more.

At first a quarterly, 'POET' as the voice of an organization for a new world movement dedicated to peace through poetry, became, in three years, a monthly which, early in 1964, announced that fifty centres of World Poetry Society had already been launched in five of the world's six continents.

Twenty-six of these centres were in America—twenty-four in eighteen states of the USA in such cities as New York, San Francisco, Salt Lake City, Iowa City, Chicago, Las Vegas, Tucson, Corpus Christi, Batesville, Dillsburg, and DeLand, with others, Toronto and Halifax, in two Canadian Provinces,

In Europe, London, Oxford, Dublin, Paris, Budapest, Milan and Rome had centres, as did Baghdad in the Middle East. Africa had five, spread from Salisbury, South Rhodesia and Mombasa, Kenya to Algiers, Algeria. Australia had centres at both Sydney and Ashburton, while those in Asia were at Tokyo, Kyoto, Hong Kong, Lae, Quezon City, New Delhi, Calcutta and other places in India.

The following are a few representatives of American WPS centres and/or contributors to 'POET' which our research of that earlier period reveals: Will Inman, Lilith Lorraine, Robert Sward, Ruth Sherry, William Taylor, Vera La Claustra, Guy Owen, Alice Swaim, Hale Hatfield, Christine Oppenheimer, Frank Ankenbrand Jr., Emma Crobaugh, Robert Avret, Magny Jensen, Sam Bradley, Maude Rubin, Menke Katz, Rosemary Trott, George Montgomery, Frances Brinkley, Leonard Opalov, Gigi Lord, Frances Price, Robert Chute, Violette Newton, James Northe, Roberta Goldstein, Marvin Winsett, Leona Hamilton, Tracy Thompson, Stella Tremble, Kenneth Beaudoin, Barbara Holland, Charles Shaw, Rachel Graham, Albert Tallman, A.J. Christenson and William Beyer.

Likewise, Canadian, George Bowering, Mabel Baird, Raymond Souster; Australian, Cyril E. Goode, Patricia Daniel, A.R. Chisholm, Fairlie Apperly; European, Vera Rich, Norman Hidden, Jessie B. Heard, Jon Stallworthy, Jaques Cordonnet, Joseph Bognar, *Salvatore Quasimodo, *Tarjei Vesaas, *Arnulf Overland; African, Douglas Livingston, Neoline Buttress, L. Minyan, Mary Fourie, Domini Keeble, Kathleen Searle; and Asian, *G. Allana, P. Lal, R. Ganesh and B.S.R. Swamy.

WPS soon gave the world new evidence that its American centres and poets were particularly cooperative participants when it published the January 1967 American Women Poets and March 1968 American University Poets issues of 'POET'. The former of these was guest edited by Fort Smith, Arkansas editor Sue Abbott Boyd of South and West, while the latter was compiled by Urbana, Illinois Professor Orville Crowder Miller, editor of the Abraham Lincoln Trilogy. Each was an anthology of one hundred poets representing all active states of the USA. The latter included *Robert Lowell, *Peter Viereck, *Howard Nemerov, *Kenneth Rexroth, *Richmond Lattimore, *Delmore Schwartz, *John Ciardi, *Allen Ginsberg, *Marvin Malone, *Leonie Adams and many other noted editors, university professors and affiliates. Soon thereafter other eminent poets published in 'POET' included *Denise Levertov, *Anne Sexton, *Stanley Kunitz, *W.H. Auden, *Cecil Day Lewis, *Steven Spender and *Jon Stallworthy. Thousands of copies of these issues reached readers worldwide and brought much favourable comment.

Through all of this, Dr. Srinivas was very appreciative of all national issues of 'POET' which his guest editors had afforded him by now from all six continents. But he developed an especially keen admiration for America, born of deep gratitude for her ardent support of WPS from its very beginning. Moreover, his admirer, Dr. Amado M. Yuzon*, encouraged him in his desire to give more tangible thanks to all who had made possible these and other meritorious services to world poetry.

But others of Dr. Srinivas' associates were also mindful of the pressing need to share more widely the problems of financially undergirding an enduring future for WPS, which problems the founder had thus far borne too much alone. With the membership growing slowly not only in numbers but in the sense of personal indebtedness without self-adulation, it was felt imperative that WPS members be further encouraged to seek the noble awards which they might best earn themselves, rather than through Dr. Srinivas' financial undergirding of WPS.

Hence, in mid-summer of 1968, Dr. Srinivas asked that the author of this article accept the presidency of WPS, to reorganize and enlarge still further its membership, activities and aims—the going beyond self, to the goal of self-giving by all its members. The recipient of this generous offer of the presidency declined. However, he did counter with a similar plan for WPS which retained Dr. Srinivas as both perpetually acknowledged Founder and honoured President-for-life. This plan thus not only incorporated the above mentioned ideals but also introduced the concept of a society 'where Knights of East and West mass orphic aims of peace in poetry . . . whose voice for peace is "POET" '. Thus it was that the writer of this paper became involved in pan-continental administration of WPS reorganized as World Poetry Society Intercontinental.

Following an advisory meeting with Dr. Percival R. Roberts III, ninth poet laureate of the State of Delaware, and Constance Adele Henning, editor of the forthcoming American Mosaic of Poets (and later exchange of letter with these and many others), the newly installed executive Chancellor caused to be drawn up, and approved by the Founder, the constitution under which WPSI now functions, with each new member ratifying it when joining. He also set up a General Secretariat and began naming national directors and representatives-at-large.

Soon authorized letters of citation with attractively printed proclamations were forwarded honouring many (and granting honorary and liaison memberships to a select few) who had performed past sacrificial services for and through World Poetry Society. Projects were also promoted to afford suitable Archives for World Poets as repositories of books, holographs and audio recordings of members' poems for posterity. Parnassian heraldic, poet laureate and poet-in-residence titles were instituted, as were also distinguished service citations and world poet awards.

Late in the fall of 1970, in addition to the twelve 48— to 64—page issues of their monthly journal 'POET', each member received a free copy of the Society's first biennial anthology, *Pancontinental Premier Poets*, edited in America by the author of this article and printed in India. And when he became Vice President and the headquarters office of WPSI was moved from Urbana, Illinois to Phoenix, Arizona, USA in January of 1971, the second official WPSI biennial anthology was published in 1972 as scheduled and under the now permanently established same title. This volume, edited by Mabelle A. Lyon, Wallace H. Fuller, Alfarata Hansel and Margaret-Mary Eitzen, contained a poem from each of 200 poets, twice the number in the first biennial volume.

Having been re-elected recently to another 3-year term, Drs. Lyon, Fuller and Hansel are now compiling a third biennial anthology to be published by WPSI in the fall of 1974. Such uninterrupted regularity of publication of poetry from all continents has afforded a grateful membership "not merely a promise but an accomplished fact" and for Dr. Lyon an appreciative nomination which afforded her an honorary Litt.D. She and Dr. Srinivas represented the officialdom of WPSI at the 1973 Second World Congress of Poets in Taipei, Taiwan, Republic of China where WPSI was one of five co-sponsors.

All six continents and more than forty states of the United States are now represented in the considerable membership of World Poetry Society. Furthermore, the following international and national poetry groups have been noted on application forms as being represented by WPSI members: United Poets Laureate, Studi e Scambi Internazionali and Accademia Leonardo da Vinci, Cosmosynthesis League, Poesie Vivante, World Avalon, International Poets Shrine, Poets Corner, World Poetry Day Association, PEN, Poetry Society (of Great Britain, of Australia, of America), and numerous groups in America including its academy of Poets, Pen Women, Poets Fellowship, Poetry League, Catholic Poetry, South and West, Chaparral Poets, National Federation of State Poetry Societies, National Poetry Day Committee, Canadian Authors, and many state poetry societies.

The WPSI constitution provides that members be chosen, and honours granted, not alone by reputation but chiefly by quality of published poems submitted as specimens to be carefully examined in the light of the WPSI ideals. The preamble shows that these ideals rest upon the premise that there is already enough filth in the world, and that there are now too many (and too much encouragement given) free-riding poets devoted to 'self-adulation and material aggrandizement' without the levelling sense of 'self-giving in gracious sharing as well as in achievement of . . . quality'. It decries that there is too little 'charitable brotherhood of understanding'. It opposes 'prejudices as to race, religion, ideology, or poetic pattern, style or habitat'. It offers means to seek to overcome ignorant lack of universal appreciation for 'lawful literary liberty' and affords ways to do away with vague perceptions of 'the aspirations and practices of divergent cultures, freedoms and reverences'.

The honorary title citation here indicated was conferred in 1968 upon *His Excellency President Ferdinand E. Marcos: Poet-in-Residence for Mate and Home; *The Honourable Dr. Amado M. Yuzon*; Sir Galahad of Parnassus; His Supreme Highness Prince M.C. Chand: Poet Laureate of the Orient; Chief Minister of Tamil Nadu, M. Karunanidhi: Poet Laureate of Tamil Culture; and Honorary Poet Laureate Della Crowder Miller, Litt.D.: World Premier Epic Biography Sonneteer.

Also in 1968, a Distinguished Service Citation was presented to each of the following guest editors of the special issue of 'POET' indicated: African, Phillippa Berlyn; African, David Botes; American, Will Inman; American Women Poets, Sue Abbott Boyd; American University Poets, Orville Crowder Miller; Australian, Grace Perry; Australian, P. Brian Cox; British, Howard Sergeant; Canadian, John Robert Colombo; Canadian, Padraig O'Brion; Greek, Hugh MacKinley; Hungarian, Thomas Kabdebo; Indian, Bejan J. Daruwalla; Italian, Armando Troni; Japanese, Yuzuru Katagiri; Jewish, Ish Yair; Malayan, Edwin Thruboo; Maltese, Victor French; New Zealand, Helen Shaw; Norwegian, Magny Landstad Jensen; Philippine, Amado M. Yuzon; Portuguese, Jonas Negalha; Rumanian, Roy MacGregor-Hastie; Russian, Eugeny Dolmatovsky; and Scottish, Maurice Lindsay. In 1969-70: Welsh, Peter Finch; Modern Telugu, Nikhileswar; French, Guy Foreau; German, Andreas P. Schroeder; World Poetry Day 1970, Milford E. Shields; as well as to *Ondra Lysohorsky of Czechoslovakia for his two Lachian issues which he contributed as Guest Poet and nominee for the Nobel Prize in Literature for 1970.

During 1971-74, Distinguished Service Citations have been awarded to Chen Min-Hwa, Taiwan Radio-TV personality and poetry magazine editor; Dr. Johann Gunert of Austria, world poetry day chairman for Europe and outstanding leader of European letters; Dr. Chung Tin-Wen, National Poet Laureate of China (Nationalist), for leadership in Asian poetry; Dr. Greta De La Valliere, President of the Accademia Internazionale de la Valliere of Rome, Italy; Dr. William Kean Seymour, VP of the Poetry Society of England and UPLI Vice President for the British Isles; Dr. Martin-Saint-René, President of the French Academy of Poetry and Poet Laureate of the French Regions (Traditional Poetry); Dr. Ivete Tanus of Brazil, for outstanding modern verse; Dr. Cyril Goode of Australia, for New Sonnet Forms; Dr. Peshoton S. Dubash, President of l'Universite Libre (Asie) of Pakistan, for his Golden Jubilee Leadership in Arts, Sciences and Letters; Dr. Emilie Glen of New York, for poetry and dramatic arts; and Dr. Wallace H. Fuller, Alfarata Hansel, Margaret-Mary Eitzen, Frances Brown Price, Dr. Mary Eleanor Cox, Kenneth L. Beaudoin, Dr. Percival R. Roberts III, Hyacinthe Hill, Ruth Kilcher Mariott, Dr. Sue Abbott Boyd and Jeanne Bonnette of the USA, for guest editing one or more issues of 'POET'.

Other distinguished service citations and world poet awards were conferred upon highly qualified members of WPSI for their most outstanding poem or self-giving service contributed during each biennium,

1969-74. These recipients were chosen, as were also the hundred poets featured in the first biennial *Pancontinental Premier Poets* anthology, from among those who had volunteered unselfish service or a previously unpublished poem, as part of a regular WPSI-sponsored project, without knowing that such contribution was to be judged for possible special recognition.

The following are Honorary, General and Continental officers of World Poetry Society Intercontinental—that original small family of receptive readers and poets now become a rewarding pan-continental Society serving peace by gracious non-profit unprejudiced poetry of high ideals and technique:

Honorary: Patron—*Amado M. Yuzon, United Poets Laureate International; Liaison Patron—Ernest Kay, International Who's Who in Poetry; Liaison—Norman Hidden, Writers' Workshop (London); P. Lal, Writers' Workshop (Calcutta).

General: Founder-President—Dr. Krishna Srinivas (East); Vice-President—Dr. Orville Crowder Miller, 1971—; Executive Chancellor—Dr. Miller, 1968-71; Dr. Mabelle Lyon, 1971—; Executive Vice-Chancellor—Dr. Stella Craft Tremble, 1969-71, Dr. Wallace H. Fuller, 1971— (West).

Continental: Regent and Parnassian Jurist, respectively — Africa——Phillippa Berlyn, Michael Dei-Anang; Anglo America——Sue Abbott Boyd, *Howard Nemerov; Asia——Rabindranath Menon, Prince Chand; Europe——Hugh McKinley, Guy Foreau; Latin America——Jonas Negalha, *Miguel Asturias; and Oceania——P. Brian Cox, William E. Morris.

General Secretariat Headquarters: 8801 N. 17th St., Phoenix, Arizona 85021, USA.

*Honorary members' names are starred when listed above. Two are recipients of the Nobel Prize, four the Pulitzer Prize, one the Nordic Prize and two Poet Laureate of his nation.

INTERNATIONAL P.E.N.

P.E.N. is a world association of writers, editors and translators in all branches and classes of literature – belles-lettres, poetry and drama, fiction, history and biography, science and philosophy. Founded in 1921, its aim is to promote and maintain friendship and intellectual co-operation between men of letters in all countries in the interests of literature, freedom of expression and international goodwill.

Membership is open to all professional writers, editors and translators without regard to nationality, race, colour or religion who accept the P.E.N. Charter.

There are eighty Centres of P.E.N. An International Executive Committee and International Rules govern the practices of the Association as a world organisation, but each Centre is autonomous, makes its own rules, and fixes its own subscription. Membership of any one Centre implies membership of the world association. The headquarters are at Glebe House, Glebe Place, Chelsea, London S.W.3, England. The present International President is the German novelist, Heinrich Böll.

International Centres:

ARGENTINA
    Miguel Alfredo Olivera (President)
    Basavilbaso 1396
    Buenos Aires
    Argentina

AUSTRALIA (Melbourne)
    Miss Innes Cameron (Secretary)
    5 Denham Street
    Hawthorn
    Victoria 3122
    Australia

AUSTRALIA (Sydney)
    Frank Trist (Secretary)
    45 Noonbinna Crescent
    Northbridge
    N.S.W. 2063
    Australia

AUSTRIA
    Prof. Hilde Spiel (Secretary)
    Concordia Haus
    Bankgasse 8
    Vienna 1
    Austria

BELGIUM (Flemish)
Willem M. Roggeman (Secretary)
Diksmuidelaan 40
Brussels 1000
Belgium

BELGIUM (French)
Baron Carlos de Radzitzky d'Ostrowick (Secretary)
110 Avenue Fond'Roy
Brussels 18
Belgium

BOLIVIA
Senora Yoland Bedregal de Conitzer (Secretary)
Casilla 149
Calle Goitia 17
La Paz
Bolivia

BRAZIL (Sao Paulo)
Ernesto de Merais Leme (Secretary)
Rua Tupi 425
Sao Paulo
Brazil

BRAZIL (Rio de Janeiro)
Miss Maria Cecilia Ribas Carmeiro (Secretary)
Avenida Nilo Pecanica
26-13-ZC-D
Rio de Janeiro
Brazil

BULGARIA
Nikolai Antonov (Secretary)
Rue Anghel Kantchev 5
Sofia
Bulgaria

CATALONIA
Dr. J.M. Battista i Roca (Secretary)
5 Lyndewode Road
CAMBRIDGE
U.K.

CANADA
Miss Eileen Goodman (Secretary)
5025 Macdonald Avenue 104
Montreal 248
Quebec
Canada

CANADA (French)
Jacques Lamarche (Secretariat)
2140 Cote Vertue
Montreal 9
Quebec
Canada

CEYLON
Eamon Karyakarawana (Secretary)
P.O. Box 1428
Colombo 15
Ceylon

CHILE
Senorita Chela Royes (Secretary)
Casilla 2061
Instituto Nacional
Santiago
Chile

CHINA (Hongkong)
William Hsu (Secretary)
Victoria Park Mansion
15th Floor, Flat A
Paterson Street
Hongkong
China

CHINA (Taipei)
Dr. Lin Yutang (President)
P.O. Box 4025
277 Roosevelt Avenue, Sec. 3
Taipei
Taiwan
China

CUBA
Alejo Carpentier (President)
Salvador Bueno
Cuban National Commission to UNESCO
Avenida Kohly 151
Nuevo Vedado
Havana
Cuba

CZECHOSLOVAKIA
Miss Marta Kadlecikova (Secretary)
U. Rajske Zahrady 1839/1B
Prague 3
Czechoslovakia

DENMARK
Miss Kirsten Bredsgaard (Secretary)
Forlaget Spectator A/S
Klareboderne 6
Copenhagen
Denmark

EGYPT
Col. Youssef El-Sibai (Secretary)
104 Kast El-Eini Street
Cairo
Egypt

Mursi Saad el-Din (Secretary)
c/o United Arab Republic (Cultural Councillor)
4 Chesterfield Gardens
London W.1
U.K.

ENGLAND
David Carver, O.B.E. (Secretary)
Glebe House
62-63 Glebe Place
London S.W.3
U.K.

ESTONIA
Asta Willmann-Linnolt (Secretary)
3 Pinnacle Ridge Road
Farmington
CT 06032
U.S.A.

FINLAND
Kaleri Haikara (Secretary)
Kustannusosakeyhtio Otava
Uudenmaankatu 8–12
Helsinki 12
Finland

FRANCE
Jean de Beer (Secretary)
Maison Internationale des P.E.N. Clubs
6 rue François Miron
Paris
France

GERMANY (German Federal Republic)
  Thilo Koch (Secretary)
  c/o P.E.N.
  61 Darmstadt
  Sandstr. 10
  West Germany

GERMANY (German Democratic Republic)
  Werner Ilberg (Secretary)
  108 Berlin
  Friedrichstra. 194—199
  East Germany

GERMAN SPEAKING AUTHORS ABROAD
  Dr. Gabriele Tergit (Secretary)
  315 Upper Richmond Road
  London S.W.15
  U.K.

GREECE
  John Coutsoheras (President)
  60A Skoufa Street
  Athens 144
  Greece

GUYANA
  Sheik M. Sadeek (Secretary)
  100 D'Andrade Street
  Newton, Kitty
  Georgetown
  Guyana

HUNGARY
  Iván Boldizsár (President)
  Vörös Marty ter 1
  Budapest 5
  Hungary

ICELAND
  Kristjan Karlsson (Secretary)
  Solheimar 23
  Reykjavik
  Iceland

ALL INDIA CENTRE
  Prof. Nissim Ezekiel (Secretary)
  Theosophy Hall
  40 New Marine Lines
  BOMBAY 20 BR
  India

IRAN
  Dr. Z. Rahnema (Secretary)
  Boulevard Elizabeth N. 344
  Teheran
  Iran

IRELAND (Belfast)
  Prof. Arthur Terry (President)
  42 Annadale Avenue
  Belfast 6
  Ireland

IRELAND (Dublin)
  Desmond Clarke (Secretary)
  St. Maur
  22 Palmerston Park
  Dublin 6
  Ireland

ISRAEL
  Dr. David Lazer (Secretary)
  6 Kaplan Street
  Tel Aviv
  Israel

ITALY
  Prof. Rosario Assunto (Secretary)
  c/o Annamaria Gobbi Belcredi
  Via Muzio Clementi 64
  I—00193 ROME
  Italy

IVORY COAST
  Christophe Assamoi (Secretary)
  P.B. 1718
  Abidjan
  Ivory Coast

JAMAICA
  Mrs. Annette Dundas (Secretary)
  c/o Institute of Jamaica
  14-16 East Street
  Kingston
  Jamaica W.1
  West Indies

JAPAN
  Hiroyuki Agawa (Secretary)
  The Japan P.E.N. Club
  Room 265 Syuwa Akasaka RH
  9-1-7 Akasaka
  Minato-ku
  Tokyo 107
  Japan

JORDAN
M.S. Juneidi (Secretary)
Ministry of Education
Amman
Jordan

KOREA
Dr. Chull Paik (President)
163 Ankuk-dong
Jongno-ku
Seoul
Korea

LANGUE D'OC
Jean Tournot (Secretary General)
4 Rue Desarcieux
30 Nîmes
Gard
France

LATVIA
Martin Ziverts (President)
Box 797
10131 Stockholm 1
Sweden

LEBANON
Camille Aboussouan (President)
12 Avenue Madame Curie
Beirut
Lebanon

MEXICO
Rosario Castellanos (Secretary)
Constituyentes 171
Mexico 18 DF

MONACO
A.G. Bernard (Secretary)
7 Avenue des Citronniers
Monte Carlo
Monaco

THE NETHERLANDS
Hans van de Waarsenburg (Secretary)
Pergamijndonk 92
Maastricht
The Netherlands

NORWAY
Mrs. Karna Dannevig (Secretary)
Haslekbroken 7 b
Oslo 5
Norway

NEW ZEALAND
Mrs. Dora Somerville (Secretary)
142 Upland Road
Kelburn
Wellington 5
New Zealand

THE PHILIPPINES
F. Sionil Jose (Secretary)
Solidaridad Publishing House
531 Padre Faura
Ermita
Manila
The Philippines

POLAND
Wladyslaw Bartoszewski (General Secretary) .
Palac Kultury i Nauki
Warsaw
Poland

PUERTO RICO
Ernesto Juan Fonfrias (Secretary)
Apartado 4692
San Juan
Puerto Rico 0093

RHODESIA
Mrs. D.E. Finn (Secretary)
22 Bradfield Road
Hillside
Salisbury E.61
Rhodesia

ROMANIA
All Correspondence to:
Horia Lovinescu
"Casa Scriitorilor Mihail Sadoveanu"
Bukarest
Romania

SCOTLAND
Miss Mary Baxter (Hon. Secretary)
20 Canniesburn Road
Bearsden
Glasgow
Scotland

SENEGAL
Ousmane Soce Diop (President)
Deputé a l'Assemblée Nationale
Dakar
Senegal

SOUTH AFRICA
Miss Mary Renault (Chairman)
Delos
Glen Beach
Campsbay
Cape Province, South Africa

SOUTH AFRICA (Cape Town)
Mrs. Adele Naude (Secretary)
217 Montebello
Montrose Street
Newlands
Cape Town
South Africa

SOUTH AFRICA (Johannesburg)
Mrs. Amelia Brown (Secretary)
P.O. Box 17191
Hillbrow
Johannesburg
South Africa

SWEDEN
Dr. Thomas von Vegesack (Secretary)
Norstedt Publishers
Box 2052
S–10312
Stockholm
Sweden

SWITZERLAND (Centre de Suisse Romande)
Suzanne Deriex (Secretary)
Les Armillaires
Praz-Berthoud 25
1010 Lausanne
Switzerland

SWITZERLAND (Basel)
  Dr. Dieter Fringeli (Secretary)
  Laufenstrasse 42
  4000 Basel
  Switzerland

SWITZERLAND (Italienisch-Romanisch)
  Eros Bellinelli (Secretary)
  Via del Sindacatori 11
  6900 Lugano
  Massagno
  Switzerland

SWITZERLAND (Zurich)
  Dr. Hans Schumacher (Secretary)
  Lehanstrabbe 74
  Zurich 10/37
  Switzerland

THAILAND
  K. Direk (Secretary)
  2 Pichai Road, Dusit,
  Bangkok 3
  Thailand

TURKEY
  Fikret Adil (Secretary)
  Cagaloglu Yokusu 40
  Istanbul
  Turkey

UNITED STATES OF AMERICA
  Mrs. Kirsten Michalski (Executive Secretary)
  156 Fifth Avenue
  NEW YORK
  NY 10010
  U.S.A.

UNITED STATES OF AMERICA (Hawaii)
  Professor John Young (Chairman)
  Dept. of Pacific and Asian Languages
  University of Hawaii
  Honolulu
  Hawaii
  U.S.A.

UNITED STATES OF AMERICA (Los Angeles)
Gloria D. Miklowitz (Secretary)
5255 Vista Miguel Drive
La Canada
CA 91011
U.S.A.

URUGUAY
Dra. Sarah Bollo (President)
Constituyente 1711
Montevideo
Uruguay

VIETNAM
Prof. Thanglang (President)
36/59 Cô-Bac
Saigon
Vietnam

WRITERS IN EXILE (Germany)
K.G. Werner (President)
61 Darmstadt
Graupnerweg 9
Germany

WRITERS IN EXILE (London)
Mrs. Velta Snikere (Secretary)
46 Crouch Hall Road
London N.8
U.K.

WRITERS IN EXILE (New York)
Mr. Dragomir Nenoff (Hon. Secretary)
28 Stirling Place
Edgewater
NJ
U.S.A.

Tibor Florian (Asst. Hon. Secretary)
3 Mt. View Drive
New Milford
CT 06776
U.S.A.

WRITERS IN EXILE (Paris)
Pavel Tigrid (Secretary)
"La Berchellerie"
Etiolles (Essonne)
France

YIDDISH
Samson Apter (Secretary)
66-66 Thornton Place
Rego Park
NY 11374
U.S.A.

YUGOSLAVIA (Belgrade)
Mrs. Jara Ribnikar (President)
Francuska br. 7
Belgrade
Yugoslavia

YUGOSLAVIA (Ljubljana)
Mrs. Mira Mihelic (President)
Tomsiceva 12
Ljubljana (Slowenien)
Yugoslavia

YUGOSLAVIA (Skopje)
Tomé Momirovski (President)
Maksima Gorkog 18
91000 Skopje
Yugoslavia

YUGOSLAVIA (Zagreb)
Marijan Matkovic (President)
Croatian Writers Association
Trg Republike 7/1
Zagreb (Kroatien)
Yugoslavia

THE INTERNATIONAL POETRY SOCIETY

by Robin Gregory
Youlgrave, Bakewell, Derbyshire, England.

President:	Christopher Fry
Vice-Presidents:	John Woodward (England);
	Ronald Bottrall (Italy);
	John Cremona (Malta).
Honorary Fellows:	Sir John Betjeman
	Edmund Blunden
	Kingsley Amis
	John Heath-Stubbs
	Ondra Lysohorsky
	Edmund Rubbra
	Derek Stanford
Director-General:	Robin Gregory
Council:	Cal Clothier
	Robin Gregory
	Norman S. Jackson
	Mike Shields
	Frederic Vanson
	John Waddington-Feather.
Public Relations:	Malcolm Payne.

*   *   *   *   *   *   *

The International Poetry Society is an organisation of poets and poetry lovers. It has no political bias beyond a wish for international understanding.

In many respects the growth of the International Poetry Society has been remarkable. Whereas most literary societies find, *after* their formation, that there is a need for some members' magazine or newsletter, the I.P.S. really grew as a natural development out of an *existing* Magazine, ORBIS. Orbis had started in 1969 as a regional arts magazine covering the north and midlands of England; but its Editor, Robin Gregory found (perhaps because of his own literary tastes) that his magazine was attracting contributions from poets from the four corners of the Earth. It thus seemed natural to form an international society, and the International Poetry Society was the result. Gradually Orbis became the official journal of the I.P.S., and from 1972 onwards it was almost exclusively literary, with the emphasis on poetry.

Although the organisation has remained deliberately loose, a clear policy has emerged. This policy is related to some fundamental, but unstated, beliefs about human life: and is best understood by a consideration of the sort of person who becomes a member. All members have a very deep belief in the importance of poetry, and an (often intuitive) feeling that a free and friendly exchange of ideas between members makes for vigour and health. If one looks at the list of Honorary Fellows one will appreciate that they all have in common some indefinable quality which lifts their work somehow above any mere "commercial" valuation: this quality (like electricity) is hard to define but immediately recognised. The President, Christopher Fry, is the author of many outstanding verse-dramas (including that great cycle of seasonal plays: "The Lady's Not for Burning", "A Yard of Sun", "Venus Observed" and "The Dark is Light Enough"). Sir John Betjeman (the Poet

Laureate), Edmund Blunden and John Heath-Stubbs are poets of quite remarkable sensitivity and insight. Ondra Lysohorsky is a Czechoslovak poet who has had to overcome much political persecution, yet remains a warm human being and fine writer. Derek Stanford, as Poetry Critic of "Books and Bookmen" and author of numerous critical works, works unceasingly to further the cause of poetry and poets. Edmund Rubbra, the distinguished musician, is one of the finest "setters to music" of poetry, possessed of an unusual ear and appreciation of art in others. John Woodward has worked unceasingly for the dissemination of understanding through poetry and is himself a sensitive writer and editor. Kingsley Amis's achievements embrace a wide spectrum of literature.

The I.P.S. magazine, Orbis, goes out quarterly to poets in many lands: not only in Britain and the United States, but in Japan, New Zealand, Italy, France, Holland, Germany, Canada, Australia, Iceland, and many more. It is a handsome letterpress publication which prints not only poetry by members, but also articles by such formidable contributors as Harold Hobson (Drama Critic of the Sunday Times), Cal Clothier (winner of the Guinness International Poetry Prize), Hugh McKinley (Literary Editor of the Athens Daily Post) and Derek Stanford. Yet it remains a *membership* magazine, never preferring a "big-name" article simply because it *is* a big-name article. The sizeable editorial board (which includes many editors of little press publications) ensures that all aspects are covered and all work properly considered.

Members, besides Orbis, receive a quarterly Newsletter and information about numerous poetry publications. Through the publishers of Orbis (Hub Publications Ltd) many members find their work published in book or pamphlet form, and a regular hardback Anthology is planned. (The first I.P.S. Anthology should be ready by the time this article appears in print.) Editorial Consultants in America, Germany, Holland, Greece and elsewhere feed information and comment into the Derbyshire headquarters; and a real feeling of "participation" is thus ensured. Many exciting new developments are just beginning, including the issue of tapes of poets reading their own work: already tapes are available ranging from some translations of the Russian poems of Boris Pasternak, through Cal Clothier's love poetry, to the remarkable dialect verse of Yorkshireman Fred Brown. A poetry competition is being organised, and should become a regular feature.

Full details of membership (and of Fellowship) may be obtained from the Director General, Robin Gregory, at Youlgrave, Bakewell, Derbys., England.

THE INTERNATIONAL WRITERS' GUILD AND SOCIETY OF NEW AUTHORS.
(established 1939)

by Robin Gregory

For many years the International Writers' Guild and Society of New Authors enjoyed a high reputation and a vigorous membership. It counted among its members poets, novelists, biographers and others, and provided a forum which was particularly valuable for the writer of talent who was only just beginning his literary career.

Of late, though, the Guild suffered a number of grievous blows in the death of some of its most active supporters; and it all but disappeared from the literary map. A few valiant and dedicated members, though, kept, the flag flying, notably Dr John Woodward; and it is through his concern for every author's welfare and reputation that active steps are at this very moment being taken to re-establish and revitalise the organisation. The following officers have already been named (all of them operating on an entirely voluntary basis):

Life President: Chev. John W. Woodward, Kt.M.T., O.S.J., D.Litt.,
                              F.I.A.L., F.I.B.A., F.F.I.P.S.
Director-General: Robin Gregory, B.A., F.F.I.P.S.
Associate Director: J. Waddington-Feather, B.A., F.F.I.P.S.
Metropolitan Secretary: Rita Spurr, B.A., F.F.I.P.S.
Special Representatives: Lou Lu Tour, D.Phil., F.F.I.P.S.
                              Albert Dobson.
                              Ron Muschamp, A.T.D.

It is intended that the I.W.G.A.S.O.N.A. will maintain close ties with other literary groups. It is entirely non-political; and has plans to publish for members books, pamphlets, magazines, newsletters and portfolios.

Writers of whatever field of literary endeavour are invited to contact the Director-General, Robin Gregory, at his home address, which is "Rose House", Youlgrave, Bakewell, Derbyshire.

THE COSMOSYNTHESIS LEAGUE

By P. Brian Cox.

It is well known that I have been a biographee of *International Who's Who in Poetry* since 1958, when Dr. Geoffrey Handley-Taylor published his original edition and in which year I founded the Cosmosynthesis League, of which Dr. Ernest Kay, now Hon. General Editor of IWWP, is Chancellor for the United Kingdom. Founder and Director is my style in this worldwide organization with headquarters in Melbourne, Australia, and I am Grand Magus of its Hermetic Order to which membership is available only by invitation and in which numbers are restricted to one hundred.

The origin of the League lay in a poem entitled AVE ATQUE VALE! and subtitled *A Sequence for Resurgence*. This was published in HOODED FALCON in 1957 as one of a selection of poems written in Japanese P.O.W. camps under conditions of stress. The message was tantamount to restoration of wholeness through practice or study of the arts in association with mysticism of a positive rather than negative type — optimism about love, especially the *yang* and *vin*, sun and shadow, which is man and woman warring towards union; optimism, yet in full awareness of the nuclear Damoclean sword of perpetual menace. *Afflatu illuminatio* (illumination through inspiration) is the League's motto.

Meetings in Melbourne have been mainly attended by my associate Cyril E. Goode and by other magi and sibyllae James Kerr, Shirley Thomas, Fairlie Szacinski (née Apperly), Alvie Egan and Rudel O'Dowd (deceased). Overseas Chancellors are Dr. Orville C. Miller (the Americas), Mme Ligaya Yuzon (Europe), Dr. Amado M. Yuzon (Eastern Asia). Regents: Gaston-Henry Aufrère (Belgium), Allison Johnn-St. Johnn, Ph.D. (New England, U.S.A., and Canada), Rêva Rémy (France), Dr. Krishna Srinivas (India), Estelle Trust (Louisiana, U.S.A.), Prince Chand (Thailand). Many other distinguished persons throughout the world are members of the League, for whose official address please turn to my biography.

APPENDIX C

AMERICAN POETRY SOCIETIES AND RELATED ORGANIZATIONS

NATIONAL FEDERATION OF STATE POETRY SOCIETIES, INC.

by Marvin Davis Winsett

Organized in Baton Rouge, Louisiana, October 17th, 1959
Constitution adopted in Philadelphia Pennsylvania, June 18th, 1960
Incorporated in Madison, Wisconsin, July 15th, 1966

The Idea of a National Federation of State Poetry Societies was conceived by Mary B. Wall while she was president of the Louisiana State Poetry Society in 1955-56.

In March 1956, she called a meeting of the Louisiana State Poetry Society Board to take place in New Orleans for the purpose of laying before it her plan for the project. Since the idea was to be a union of State Poetry Societies, her own society would be the first and sponsoring group. At that time board members of the Louisiana State Poetry Society were: Mary B. Wall, President; Ruth Voss, First Vice-President; Thelma Adams, Second Vice-President; Felix Howland, Third Vice-President; Charline Hayes Brown, Recording Secretary; Alice Claudel, Corresponding Secretary; and Ethel Eikel Harvey, Treasurer. Gertrude B. Saucier was also present, unofficially.

Upon returning home, Mary B. Wall wrote to the two members who could not be present at the meeting, Thelma Adams of Shreveport, and Charline Brown of Monroe, receiving immediate approval from them. In October the plan was presented at the State meeting and enthusiastically endorsed.

Finally, after two and a half years of correspondence with various State societies, the effort seemed promising and Mary B. Wall decided that the time had come to call a convention and finalize plans.

In 1959, during the tenure of Gertrude B. Saucier as president of Louisiana State Poetry Society, Ethel Eikel Harvey was asked to be convention chairman for a meeting to take place on October 17th. Joining at this meeting or coming in later during the year as charter members were: First State Writers of Delaware; Louisiana State Poetry Society; Pennsylvania Poetry Society; Utah State Poetry Society; West Virginia Poetry Society; Wisconsin Fellowship of Poets. Members, in addition to the above, at present are: Alabama State Poetry Society; Arizona State Poetry Society; Poet's Roundtable of Arkansas; California State Poetry Society; Poetry Society of Colorado; District of Columbia State Poetry Society;

Illinois State Poetry Society; Indiana State Federation of Poetry Clubs; Kentucky State Poetry Society; Maryland State Poetry Society, Inc.; Massachusetts State Poetry Society; Poetry Society of Michigan; Poetry Society of New Hampshire; New Jersey Poetry Society; New Mexico Poetry Society; North Carolina Poetry Society; Ohio Poetry Society; Poetry Society of Oklahoma; South Dakota State Poetry Society; Poetry Society of Tennessee; Poetry Society of Texas.

The first elected officers of the National Federation of State Poetry Societies were: Cecilia Parsons Miller, President; Dr. Clinton F. Larson, First Vice-President; Mary Alice Hart, Second Vice-President; Robert D. West, Third Vice-President; William Gresham, Fourth Vice-President; Dr. Louis E. Dollarhide, Recording Secretary; and Mary B. Wall, Treasurer.

Past Presidents of the National Federation are: Cecilia Parsons Miller, 1959; Dr. Clinton F. Larson, 1960; Robert D. West, 1961; Edma Meudt, 1962–63; Dr. Marvin Davis Winsett, 1964–65; Dr. Max C. Golightly, 1966–67; Dr. Hans Juergensen, 1968–69; Russell Ferral, 1970–71.

The National Federation of State Poetry Societies is a non-profit making organization dedicated solely to the furtherance of poetry and the sustaining of poets on the national level. It exists to promote State societies and to help organize them in States where none has been formed. There are no individual memberships. An individual can join only through his State society, or by applying through a State which is a member.

The purpose of the National Federation of State Poetry Societies, as set forth in Article XII of its Constitution reads as follows:

> *'. . . To enrich the cultural background of the nation; to preserve our national heritage of poetry; to give poetry its rightful recognition among the arts; to stimulate an awareness of its solacing and joy-giving qualities; to join poetry and poetry lovers throughout the land in harmony and co-operation. Moreover, national and international problems arising from the inability of persons and groups adequately to communicate with each other and of its self-imposed duty to lead the way to understanding through the artistic use of language. It recognizes that metaphorical language, as against abstract language, has the greater power to persuade and educate human beings; it recognizes that lack of satisfactory contexts for words incites fear; it recognizes that poets, wherever they may be, work for human understanding by offering linguistic contexts that appeal to the mind and spirit of man. It contends that if national and international authorities understand the ability of poets to appeal successfully to the whole man, they will avail themselves of the services of poets and the National Federation of State Poetry Societies, which is the official organization for the nation's poets. It further contends that world peace will be attained chiefly through language accurately and significantly used; it therefore offers its services in whatever way it can to achieve this goal.'*

The National Federation meets annually in a different State and conducts a large annual prize programme, offering a wide variety of prizes ranging from $10.00 to $200.00. The Federation has established a library of books and holograph poems by members, housed at Provo, Utah, and a repository for archives and memorabilia at Baton Rouge, Louisiana.

It is the custom of the National Federation each year to name some distinguished poet as Honorary Chancellor. This award is given in recognition of outstanding literary excellence. Poets who have been thus honored are: *Joseph Auslander, 1961; John Crowe Ransom, 1962; *Glen Ward Dresbach, 1963; Jesse Stuart, 1964; *Grace Noll Crowell, 1965; *Jean Starr Untermeyer, 1966; *Loring Williams, 1968; Harry Meacham, 1969; John Williams Andrews, 1970; *August Derleth, 1971. Present officers are: Mrs. Jean Jenkins, President; Catherine Case Lubbe, First Vice President; Dr. Glenn Swetman, Second Vice President; Dr. Frederick L. Morey, Third Vice President; Will Pollard, Fourth Vice President; Mary Manningham, Chancellor; Athaleen LaHaise, First Vice Chancellor; Carl P. Morton, Second Vice Chancellor; Jeanne Bonnette, Secretary; Wauneta Hackleman, Treasurer; Dr. Max Golightly, Librarian; Gertye B. Saucier, Historian; Mr. Lee Mays, Contest Chairman; Mrs. Osa Mays, Contest Clerk; Alice Briley, Editor, Strophes; Catherine Case Lubbe, Chairman, Sponsorship Committee and Brochures; Russell Ferrall, Chairman, NFSPS Inc. Anthology Fund; Frederick L. Morey, Chairman, Constitution and By-Laws; Glenn Swetman, Membership Chairman; Richard G. Beyer, National Publicity Chairman; Dr. N. Scott Momaday, Honorary Chancellor.

The members of the National Federation of State Poetry Societies, Inc., are:

ALABAMA STATE POETRY SOCIETY
Carl P. Morton, President, 1732 Shades View Lane, Birmingham, AL 35216.

ARIZONA STATE POETRY SOCIETY
Alfarata Hansel, President, 35 E. Indianola, Phoenix, AZ 85012.

POET'S ROUNDTABLE OF ARKANSAS
Roberta E. Allen, Secretary, 6604 Kenwood Road, Little Rock, AR 72207.

CALIFORNIA STATE POETRY SOCIETY
Mrs. Romayne Dowd, President, 8501 S. Sepulveda Blvd. Los Angeles, CA 90045.

THE POETRY SOCIETY OF COLORADO
Mrs. Lenabell Sloan Martin, President, 1195 South Vine Street, Denver, CO 80210.

FIRST STATE WRITERS OF DELAWARE
Mrs. Sandra S. Michel, President, 608 Whilby Drive, Sharplay, Wilmington, DE 19803; Ms. Jeanette Edwards, Vice President, 5 Hillcrest Avenue, Wilmington, DE 19809.

DISTRICT OF COLUMBIA STATE POETRY SOCIETY

ILLINOIS STATE POETRY SOCIETY
Stella Craft Tremble, President, 902 10th Street, Charleston, IL 61920.

INDIANA STATE FEDERATION OF POETRY CLUBS
Mrs. Esther Alman, President, 826 South Center Street, Terre Haute, IN 47807.

KENTUCKY STATE POETRY SOCIETY
Linda Reeder, President, Route 10, Ridgemont Road, Paducah, KY 42001.

LOUISIANA STATE POETRY SOCIETY (see article I)
Glenn R. Swetman, President, 638 Fairway Drive, Thibodaux, LA 70301; Bernice Larson Webb, Corresponding Secretary, 159 Whittington Drive, Lafayette, LA 70501.

MARYLAND STATE POETRY SOCIETY, INC.
Mr. Leonard Paul, President, 3315 Shelburne Road, Baltimore, MD 21208.

MASSACHUSETTS STATE POETRY SOCIETY
Mrs. Mary Manningham, President, 4 Russet Lane, Winchester, MA 01890.

POETRY SOCIETY OF MICHIGAN
S. Geneva Page, President, 256 Burr Street, Battle Creek, MI 49015; Clarence L. Weaver, Vice President, 1036 Emerald N.E., Grand Rapids, MI 49503; Gloria Anderson, Secretary-Treasurer, 3555 Burton S.E., Apt. 10, Grand Rapids, MI 49506; Elizabeth K. Wathen, Corresponding Secretary, 1474 Beach Street, Muskegon, MI 49441.

POETRY SOCIETY OF NEW HAMPSHIRE (see article III)
Miss Priscilla T. Daneau, 19 Montgomery Street, Concord, NH 03301.

NEW JERSEY POETRY SOCIETY (see article VI)
Vivian M. Meyer, President, 6 Park Avenue, Mine Hill, Dover, NJ 07801; Mildred Wohlgemuth, Corresponding Secretary, 10 Prospect Street, Mendham, NJ 07945.

NEW MEXICO POETRY SOCIETY
Dr. Peter Dechert, President, P.O. Box 636, Santa Fe, NM 87501.

NORTH CAROLINA POETRY SOCIETY, INC.
Samuel L. McKay, President, Box 268, Broadway, NC 27505; Mrs. Betty M. Daly, Corresponding Secretary, Box 108, Broadway, NC 27505.

OHIO POETRY SOCIETY
Mrs. Howard R. Evans, 679 Ardleigh Drive, Akron, OH 44303.

POETRY SOCIETY OF OKLAHOMA
Barbara Rasmussen, President, 5517 N. Shawnee, Oklahoma City, OK 73112.

PENNSYLVANIA POETRY SOCIETY, INC.
Will Pollard, President, Box 380, Harrisburg, PA 17108; Jessie Ruhl Miller, Treasurer, 670 W. Louther Street, Carlisle, PA 17013.

SOUTH DAKOTA STATE POETRY SOCIETY
Dr. Harold M. Jordan, President, 917 Ridgecrest Drive, Vermillion, SD 57069.

POETRY SOCIETY OF TENNESSEE
Dr. Rosemary Stephens, President, 64 N. Yates Road, Memphis, TN 38117; Ruth Peal Harrell, Vice President; Isabel J. Glaser, Recording Secretary; Rubye T. Simpson, Corresponding Secretary; James Clifford Middleton, Treasurer.

POETRY SOCIETY OF TEXAS (see article VII)
Jack E. Murphy, President, 10436 Creekmere Drive, Dallas, TX 75218; Faye Carr Adams, Corresponding Secretary, 4244 Skillman Avenue, Dallas, TX 75206.

UTAH STATE POETRY SOCIETY, INC.
Kathryn Kay, President, 982 Jasper Circle, Salt Lake City, UT 84106.

WEST VIRGINIA POETRY SOCIETY
Thursa A. Pratt, President, 1625 Oak Street, Parkersburg, WV 26101; Ann Wiestling, Recording Secretary; Kimberly Dunham, Corresponding Secretary; Ethel W. Rittenhouse, Treasurer, 449 White Avenue, Morgantown, WV 26505.

WISCONSIN FELLOWSHIP OF POETS (see article IX)
Frances May, President, 309 Joliet Avenue, Sturgeon Bay, WI 54235.

ARTICLE I

THE LOUISIANA STATE POETRY SOCIETY

by Dr. George W. Noel-Cooper

The Louisiana State Poetry Society was organized in Baton Rouge in October, 1953, by Ethel Eikel Harvey and Mary B. Wall. The past presidents of the society are Clement Cook, J. Ashton Greene, Mary B. Wall, Ethel Eikel Harvey, Alice Moser Claudel, Gertrude B. Saucier, Clara T. Wilkinson, Grace T. Granger, Mattie Belle Singletary, Faye Phillips Niles, Calvin Claudel, Edna Campbell, Jerry White, George W. Noel-Cooper, and Katherine V. Letteer.

An annual high school poetry contest is sponsored by the society with participation invited by all the high schools of the state, thus encouraging the love and writing of poetry in the young people of the state.

Four anthologies of poetry by the members have been published, entitled, Lyric Louisiana, Volumes I, II, III and IV. Poetry Day, October 15th, is annually celebrated with a State meeting, at which time officers are elected, poems read, and a recognized speaker heard. At the Spring Poetry Festival in April, fellowship of poets is stressed, and contests are featured, also with a speaker and a workshop.

The current officers are Dr. Glen R. Swetman, Betty Cassidy, Ruth Voss, Thelma Adams, May Lacassagne, Bernice Larson Webb, Dr. James A. Mitchell, and Dr. George W. Noel-Cooper.

The three years of work by Mary B. Wall in organizing the National Federation of State Poetry Societies was sponsored by the Louisiana State Poetry Society, culminating in October 1959, with this organization becoming a reality, now the largest organization of poets in the world. LSPS gave Mary B. Wall its heartiest cooperation in this project, and many names could be cited, except for space considerations; two in particular being Ethel Eikel Harvey and Gertrude B. Saucier.

Mary B. Wall is Chairman of the Board of Regents of LSPS, while Katherine V. Letteer and Dr. George William Noel-Cooper, COPA, having each served two terms as president, were voted titles of President Emeritus. Dr. James A. Mitchell and Mary B. Wall are trustees of finance and property.

ARTICLE II

THE BROOKLYN POETRY CIRCLE

by Estelle J. Ellisson

The Brooklyn Poetry Circle was founded on November 2, 1935, by Marie-Louise d'Esternaux, Maude Clark Hough, and Laura Spofford Wiltsie Lake. The Founders were subsequently successive Presidents of the Circle, Marie-Louise d'Esternaux holding that office for several years.

From the beginning, the Circle was organized as a study group under the guidance of Anna Hempstead Branch as Critic, and later under Gertrude Ryder Bennett. Dr. Edwin Markham was very interested in its progress, presenting the Circle with his famous quatrain "Outwitted". This is used as the motto of the Circle and is repeated in unison at each meeting. The Circle has joined in many group activities throughout the years, including World's Fair Poetry Day.

Annual medals were instituted by Marie-Louise d'Esternaux for lyric and dramatic poetry, and authentic ballads on the American scene, and a gold medal is awarded annually by Countess d'Esternaux in honor of her daughter since 1946.

Many of the members have published volumes of poetry, have also appeared in various magazines, and have won numerous contests and prizes, besides participating in other branches of creative art.

There are a number of traditional events throughout the year; an Annual Dinner late in May; Founders' Day in November; a Christmas Party; and the celebration of Mother's Day. The Annual Dinner is generally held at the National Arts Club in New York City, and is largely attended by the membership, and by many distinguished guests and speakers.

Among the honorary members are the names of Dr. Markham, Anna Hempstead Branch, Dr. Robert MacGowan, Faith Van Valkenburgh Vilas, and Dr. Percy MacKaye, distinguished poets, professors of English, artists and dramatists.

ARTICLE III

THE POETRY SOCIETY OF NEW HAMPSHIRE

by Winona B. Richardson

The Poetry Society of New Hampshire, founded in 1963 with a substantial number of charter members, is a very definite factor in the State cultural scene; in fact it is the only State-wide organized poetry group.

The Society on a continual basis averages about 200 members. Over 80 of these are resident New Hampshire writers; the others are out-of-state members, representing states from Maine to Florida and New Jersey to California.

We hold five meetings a year: January, March, June (Founders' Day), August and October. New Hampshire has 6 distinctive regions: White Mountains, Dartmouth-Lake Sunapee, Lakes (Winnipesaukee area), Merrimack Valley (central NH), Monadnock (southwestern area), and Seacoast. We have members in all these areas and thus hold meetings in various locations.

The Poetry Society of New Hampshire is a most versatile organization, promoting poetry projects and involving itself in the cultural life of the community. Six of its related activities are:

POETRY CONTESTS

Contests in writing specific types of poems are held at each meeting. Assignments are made in advance, and awards for the best poems submitted are presented at such times. These five contests are open to *all members of the Society.*

SHIRLEY BARKER AWARD—a national award open to all poets everywhere, awarded in June each year.
PAUL SCOTT MOWRER AWARD—a national award open to all poets everywhere, awarded annually in January.
WINONA B. RICHARDSON ANNUAL SHAKESPEAREAN SONNET AWARD—open only to resident New Hampshire poets who are members of the Society and awarded in January.

ROUND ROBIN POETRY LETTERS

Approximately 8 to 10 poets are assigned to one Robin. Each submits an original poem, giving constructive suggestions to the other poets on their submitted poems and, in turn, receiving their suggestions as to his own poem.

PROGRAM

The agenda varies. Outstanding speakers have addressed the group at various intervals. At other times excellent, constructive workshops are held.

NEWSLETTER

Under the capable supervision of Editor-in-Chief, Leighton W. Bryne, this Society publishes a well-organized and informative NEWSLETTER, containing many items of interest; namely, articles on various phases of poetry, book reviews, news items about literary activities of PSNH members, poetry contest announcements, prize-winning poems, writers' conferences, etc.

NEWSPAPER POETRY COLUMNS

Poetry Review in NH Sunday News features on a weekly basis poems by all members in the group. *Voice of New Hampshire Poets* is a bi-weekly column in the *Concord Shoppers News* emphasizing on the first

Wednesday of the month a *NH POET OF THE MONTH* and on the third Wednesday poets (3) of a specific region—Lakes, Merrimack Valley, etc. This latter column publishes only the poems of New Hampshire residents who are Society members.

POETRY PUBLICATIONS
Under the progressive leadership of the current President of PSNH, Lawrence A. Wiggin, the Society will undertake the annual publication of anthologies of the poems of group members. The first, to be released in 1971, is an anthology of haiku entitled 'Variations in Mulberry'.

The Poetry Society of New Hampshire is a member of the National Federation of State Poetry Societies (NFSPS), an organization comprising many poetry groups and totalling several thousand members.

In an effort to contribute to community service one member has recently organized a Poetry Club for patients at the New Hampshire Hospital. Although not designed as a specific poetry therapy program, nevertheless, the fellowship enjoyed in the reading and discussion of poetry and in the creative writing of their own poems is producing very creditable results in the members involved. Original poems are displayed in the Hospital Library, and a quarterly publication of their original poems is planned for the near future.

Our Society participates annually in the observance of National Poetry Day (October 15th) and New Hampshire Poetry Week (October 15th—22nd). The Governor of our state issues an Annual Poetry Proclamation; the late Paul Scott Mowrer, our former Poet Laureate, used to write a poem for the occasion; articles are released to newspapers; attractive exhibits are arranged in public and school libraries on a state-wide basis; radio interviews are held; poetry programs are conducted, etc.

ARTICLE IV

FLORIDA STATE POETRY SOCIETY, INC.

by Dr. Frances Clark Handler

On May 28th, 1965, the Florida Bankers' Association in cooperation with the Florida Development Commission conducted a conference at Homestead Air Force Base, Homestead, Florida. Frances Clark Handler as a past president of the Hotel Accountant's Association attended this conference. From the notes taken that day it appeared that the one factor above all the others that kept Florida from growing industrially and educationally was its cultural lack.

This bothered Mrs. Handler for this was her adopted state. She was a member of over 20 poetry societies of the United States and 2 International Societies. She was Membership Chairman of United Poets Laureates International, the International Platform Association, National League of American Penwomen, Member-at-Large, and past treasurer of the Coral Gables Branch. At that time she was Co-Chairman of the National Poetry Day Committee, since becoming National Director and incorporating this organization. She was also a member of many work-shop groups over the state. Naturally with this background Mrs. Handler decided to do something about the cultural lack in Florida.

Thousands of letters were written and every state in the United States was studied as to their associations and their culture. Seventeen countries were asked what they had for societies and when all data was compiled plans were formed for the Florida State Poetry Society, Inc., the first and the only one the state of Florida ever had.

On September 1, 1965 the Charter was signed at Tallahassee, Florida making this a non-profit literary cultural organization to be known as the Florida State Poetry Society, Inc. Commander Frank Stevenson Handler, USN, RTD became President and Frances Clark Handler, Litt. D., Secretary-Treasurer and National Director.

This is an endowed society. The estate of the Handlers is willed to this society, and that will is in trust at the First National Bank of Miami, who are the Executors and Honorary Officers. Other State Officials are Honorary Life Members and Directors. Florida State Poetry Society, Inc., in the eight years since it was founded has maintained its membership list at 3,000 plus members. It has been lauded as the most outstanding State Society in the United States today and is one of the few states with an accredited State Poetry Society Charter. Letters are on file from all over the world acclaiming the achievements of this poetry group.

Dr. Etta Josephean Murfey was the first Poet Laureate of Florida — State Poetry Society, Inc. Other claims have been made but this office of Poet Laureate is a registered one and cannot be misrepresented. Dr. Murfey died April 1, 1966. After one year of memoriam, Dr. Frances Clark Handler was voted by the Executive Committee to be Life Poet Laureate of the Florida State Poetry Society, Inc. in honor of her work founding this organization in 1965.

The Florida State Poetry Society, Inc. is a member of All National State Poetry Societies, Sponsor National Audubon Society, Arts-Literature-Poetry Society, United Poets Laureate International Membership Chairman, National Arts Council — Advisory Board, Florida Arts Council (and Several Affiliates), National Business Committee on the Arts, National Platform Association, USA — Government Board on Youth Affairs, Danae — Clover Association (Life), Charter — Smithsonian Institute, Charter — National Historical Society, All National Environmental groups, Third Century and Florida Bicentennial Celebration Committee, National League of American Penwomen (Member-at-Large), Life Poets Committee of One Hundred — Maryland. It is affiliated with National Poetry Day Committee, Inc. and World Poetry Day Committee, Inc.

ARTICLE V

IDAHO POETS' AND WRITERS' GUILD

by Dr. Marvin Davis Winsett

The Idaho Poets' and Writers' Guild was organized on 10 November 1959. The founders and first officers of the organization were: Helen Gee Woods, President; Williard Adams and William Walter DeBolt, Vice-Presidents; Edith B. Johannesen, Treasurer; Marna Holm Adams, Recording Secretary.

An editorial note from an early issue of THE GUILD, the official publication, states the following about the founding of the group: 'If poets are yet the unrewarded leglislators of mankind, they are bound by all enlightening attributes that develop the fine art of poetry. As many have experienced, it has accomplished what no other human utterance has accomplished. It is a cry of urgency and longing. It serves as a means to bridge the soul across chaos and disintegration to unity. It has not only social, and universal, but also cosmic implications. These are what the true poet seeks out to present. So it is that the birth of a writers organization in Idaho has come into its own. It is the IDAHO POETS' AND WRITERS' GUILD.'

The Guild meets monthly and functions on the state and national levels. It has published two anthologies and two books on Idaho history, besides publishing THE GUILD QUARTERLY, which is edited by Helen Gee Woods.

ARTICLE VI

THE NEW JERSEY POETRY SOCIETY

by Vivian M. Meyer

The purpose of the New Jersey Poetry Society is to work toward the advancement of the poetic arts.

Among the benefits offered by the New Jersey Poetry Society, Inc. to its members are the following: a monthly newsletter containing lessons, contests, book reviews, poetry, etc.; an annual anthology of poetry by the members; workshops held at Princeton University twice a year.

Our chapters hold monthly workshop meetings.

The New Jersey Poetry Society, Inc. has three types of membership: Full (for chapter members); Associate (for out-of-State members and all others who cannot attend chapter meetings); Affiliate (for those who enjoy poetry but do not write it). In addition to this we accept Probationers as prospective members. These are persons who have not yet mastered the art but desire to learn it.

N.J.P.S. officers are: President, Vivian M. Meyer, 6 Park Ave. Mine Hill, Dover, N.J. 07801; Executive Vice President, Caryl Appeld, Box 378C, RD 2, Hackettstown, N.J. 07840; Vice President, Anthologies, Richard K. Wright, Box 300, Dept. of English, County College of Morris, Randolph Twp., Dover, N.J. 07801; Vice President, Publicity, Howard R. Reeves, Box 33, RD 2, Boonton, N.J. 07005. Recording Secretary, Jane Leary, 205 Porter St., Easton, Pa. 19042; Corresponding Secretary, Mildred Wohlgemuth, 10 Prospect St., Mendham, N.J. 07945; Executive Treasurer, Louise G. Friedman, 145 Wootton St., Boonton, N.J. 07005.

ARTICLE VII

THE POETRY SOCIETY OF TEXAS

by Dr. Marvin Davis Winsett
Founded 5 November 1921
Charter issued by the State of Texas, 26 January 1922

The purpose of the Poetry Society of Texas as set forth in Article II of the Constitution is as follows: 'The purpose of the Society shall be to secure fuller public recognition of the art of poetry, to encourage the writing of poetry by Texans, and to kindle finer and more intelligent appreciation of poetry, especially the work of living poets who interpret the spirit and heritage of Texas.'

Charter members were: *Hilton Ross Greer, President; *Karle Wilson Baker, Vice-President; *Clyde W. Hill, Second Vice-President; *Therese Lindsey, Corresponding Secretary; Jewel Wurtzbaugh, Recording Secretary; *Whitney Montgomery, Director; *Louella Styles Vincent, Director.

The Society operates under a Constitution and By-Laws adopted at the time of organization and amended in 1950, 1956, and 1969, printed in the 1951, 1967, and 1968 Yearbooks.

Past Presidents of the Society are: *Hilton Ross Greer; *David Russell; Arthur M. Sampley; William D. Barney; Martin Shockley; and Marvin Davis Winsett.

Present officers are: Jack E. Murphy, President; Guy Malone, Vice-President; Martin Benno, Treasurer; Faye Carr Adams, Corresponding Secretary; Roberta Pipes Bowman, Recording Secretary; Catherine Case Lubbe, Director; Marjorie Ledbetter Yelton, Director; Pat Stodghill, Director. Honorary Officers are: *Walter R. Adams, Honorary Vice-President; *Aline B. Carter, Honorary Vice-President; John A. Lubbe, Treasurer Emeritus.

The Society began with less than a score of members and has grown consistently through the years. The 1922 Yearbook lists 182 members and the current Yearbook lists in excess of 800. From the beginning its standards have been high. Its membership and officers have included many of the nation's most distinguished poets.

For several years the Society has maintained a permanent collection of books and pamphlets by members, now numbering over 1,000 items, housed in the Texas Room of the Dallas Public Library. Catherine Case Lubbe is Librarian of the collection.

The regular monthly meetings are held on the second Saturday of each month at 8 pm in the Umphrey Lee Student Center, Southern Methodist University, Dallas, Texas. No meetings are held during July, August and September. The reading of poems submitted in monthly contests and the awarding of prizes are features of the meetings. Writers of distinction and members with recently published books appear on the programme. The June meeting is traditionally a June Festival and the November meeting is the Annual Awards Dinner.

One of the reasons the Society has maintained its high standard through the years is the large cash prize programme. Annual prizes totalling more than $3,000.00 in various categories are offered, open only to active members except where otherwise specifically stated. Another contributing factor in keeping the standards high is the selection of distinguished judges for the contests.

To keep in touch with members throughout the State and elsewhere, a monthly bulletin is published. Once each year, usually in March, the Society publishes a volume known as A Book of the Year, which in reality is an anthology of monthly and annual first place prose poems. It also contains a list of members, new books by members, a condensed record of the monthly meetings, a list of poets laureate of Texas, and other interesting information.

Membership as defined by the Constitution: Active Members: native Texans, citizens of Texas, or former citizens of Texas who were members while residing in Texas. Associate members: All others who desire to affiliate. Libraries, schools and universities are classified Associate members. Dues are $7.50 per year for Active and Associate members.

Other types of memberships are provided for individuals, business firms, corporations, associations, or societies desiring to have a part in the work of the Poetry Society and in the furtherance of the writing and appreciation of poetry.

For information write to: Marjorie Ledbetter Yelton, Membership Committee Chairman, 5703 West Greenbrier Drive, Dallas, Texas 75209. All other matters related to the Society should be directed to Faye Carr Adams, Corresponding Secretary, 4244 Skillman, Dallas, Texas 75206.

*Deceased

ARTICLE VIII

THE INA COOLBRITH CIRCLE

Ina Donna Coolbrith, born in 1841 in Nauvoo, Illinois, was the first white child to enter California through the Beckwourth Pass. Her family settled in Los Angeles, where the Los Angeles Times published her first verses in 1854.

At the 1915 Panama Pacific International Exposition she was titled "loved, laurel-crowned poet of California", later officially appointed by the State Legislature. Her place in California literary life has never been equalled, spanning seventy years until her death in 1928. Articles, lectures, radio and TV programs based on her life and activities continue to the present day.

For over half a century her home was a center of artistic interest where poets, musicians and artists gathered. Spontaneously this group of friends grew into a formal organization in 1919, with its expressed objects the promotion of the art of poetry, the study of the history and literature of the Golden State, the discussion of its writers' works and the assembling and preservation of their personal and literary reminiscences. Honorary members have included Gertrude Atherton, James D. Phelan, Dr. Francis Meehan (Brother Leo), Charles Keeler, to name a few. The Circle meets monthly, September through May, on the last Sunday, in Room 401, Marines' Memorial Building, San Francisco, at 2:30 p.m. and presents programs on literary and topical subjects, and poetry readings.

To carry out the principal objective of encouragement of poetry, the Circle conducts an annual Poetry Contest climaxing in a Banquet in October, featuring a prominent speaker and awards to the winning poets; a biennial contest for newspaper verse; and the publication of a biennial Anthology of Poems by Circle members.

Some of the special Circle projects through the years have been the dedication of bronze plaques in the State Library Building in Sacramento honoring the four official Poets Laureate of California — Ina Coolbrith, Henry Meade Bland, John Steven McGroarty and Gordon Norris; the successful campaign to preserve "Ina Coolbrith Park"; and the sponsoring of youth poetry contests to awaken the talents of the nation's future poets.

The Circle welcomes writers and artists in all fields, and especially those interested in the art of poetry, the study of California history and the furthering of cultural activities in the Golden State.

ARTICLE IX

WISCONSIN FELLOWSHIP OF POETS

The Wisconsin Fellowship of Poets, organized in 1949, is a state-wide organization of 150 poets who became members upon the recommendation of a credentials committee. The group has two state-wide meetings a year and publishes a quarterly magazine entitled 'Muse Letter' which is available to its members. The group also sponsors two contests in the National Federation of State Poetry Societies' annual contest. The current President is Mr. Russell Ferrall.

To date the Fellowship has published three hard-cover anthologies of Wisconsin poetry; the last anthology, 'Poems Out of Wisconsin', vol. III, was published with the help of a Federal grant on the recommendation of the Wisconsin Arts Foundation & Council. In December 1969 the group's fourth anthology was published entitled 'New Poetry Out of Wisconsin'. This publication was edited by August Derleth, a prominent Wisconsin publisher and author who is a member of the Wisconsin Fellowship of Poets. This latest book contains the work of Wisconsin's most widely published poets, both members and non-members of the Fellowship.

ARTICLE X

THE IOWA POETRY ASSOCIATION

by Aletha Humphreys

The Iowa Poetry Association was formally organized on October 21, 1945. The original name was Iowa Poetry Day Association, but the "Day" was dropped from the name in 1949, since the aim of the association is the promotion of poetry itself and not a specific day. Brochures of poems have been published annually since 1946, and in 1948 'Lyrical Iowa' was the name adopted for the anthology. Poems for the anthology are selected from submissions to the annual contest. Cash prizes are given in five adult categories and for college and high school poems. IPA is entirely self-supporting from dues and the sale of 'Lyrical Iowa'. Poetry workshops with two outstanding poet-critics, usually Iowa College professors, are held twice yearly in Des Moines. The Association is experiencing steady growth in membership, attendance at workshops and, very markedly, in the number of submissions to the annual contest.

ARTICLE XI

THE KOKOMO POETRY CIRCLE

The Kokomo Poetry Circle was founded in January 1931, by Maud McKinsey Butler with seven charter members. The membership represented three schools of poetry: Standard or Conventional; Modern and Semi-modern. The object of the organization is the mutual development in the creative writing of poetry; also to become proficient in the application of poetry technique as it pertains to the various forms of rhythm in contemporaneous poetry. In addition, the aim is to cultivate the imagination, which is necessary in being able to clothe ideas with the imagery required for true poetic expression.

Most of the sixteen mmbers of the Circle have had their work accepted for publication in a wide range of periodicals and several have had books published. The number of members is kept small to facilitate entertainment and criticism of each member's poems. The Circle conducts a poetry contest each year.

ARTICLE XII

THE MAINE POETRY DAY ASSOCIATION

by James Edwin Trott

The Maine Poetry Day Association was founded in October, 1950 by Dr. Rosemary Clifford Trott, Honorary Poet Laureate of Nature, U.P.L.I. She served several times as its president, and also on its Board of Judges for the annual poetry competition, which the Association sponsors to promote "Maine Poetry Day, and Week", and to encourage student poets, and others aspiring to write poetry.

The purpose of The Maine Poetry Day Association was, and is to foster the writing and reading of good poetry, and to, from time to time, publish anthologies of Maine poetry, but, more specifically, to promote the observance of "Maine Poetry Day with the week following to be known as 'Maine Poetry Week.'"

Maine joins the nation, and the world in observing October 15th as "Poetry Day", but has a week of its own, known as "Maine Poetry Week", of which Dr. Trott is the founder.

Every year since 1950, a poetry competition has been held under the sponsorship of the Association. Silver Cups engraved with name of the winner have been awarded many years, in addition to book prizes, which were donated by Dr. Trott, and which she received as review copies, for her work as a poetry reviewer. During the past few years United States Saving Bonds have been awarded as first prize.

Many well-known poets, and educators have served on the Board of Judges for this competition, including Dr. Kenneth C. M. Sills, late president of Bowdoin College, Dr. Marguerite Cook, former English professor, University of Maine, Professor Louis Coxe of Bowdoin, Mrs. Kenneth C. M. Sills, wife of Dr. Sills, and Dr. Trott.

An award tea has been given each year, with many poets being invited to read their works, and to give brief biographical talks about themselves.

In 1957, Dr. Trott requested legislation for "Maine Poetry Day," and "Maine Poetry Week". Representative Benjamin Crockett, Freeport, presented the bill, which was passed without a dissenting vote.

Qualified poets throughout the world may become associate members of the Maine Poetry Day Association. Those desiring to so affiliate may contact the Executive Secretary, James Edwin Trott, D.V.S., P.O. Box 143, Yarmouth, ME 04096, U.S.A.

ARTICLE XIII

HISTORY OF POETRY DAY
AND
NATIONAL POETRY DAY COMMITTEE, INC.

by Dr. Frances Clark Handler

It all started in 1936. It had been a dream all of Tessa Sweazy Webb's life to find a way to "honor poets" and she talked with everyone who would listen to her plans. Finally she was introduced to Ohio Senator Williams and through this contact she was able to get a joint resolution S.J.R. No. 39, called the Grubbs-Myers-Marshall Resolution introduced and passed in January 1938, by Ohio's 92nd General Assembly naming the third Friday of October of each year as Ohio Poetry Day. The Day was to be set aside to honor Poets of Ohio; to give special programs and observances in the schools and in the public places.

Other states followed Ohio slowly but no concerted effort was made to make this a National Day or a National Poetry Day in all states until Lucia Trent of Texas, spearheaded the movement and called this the National Poetry Day Committee. It was not incorporated until Dr. Frances Clark Handler took over the National Directorship and incorporated the name for its protection in 1966. Lucia Trent enlisted the aid of Will Strong of California who was Vice-President of Poets of the Pacific (since disbanded). This organization covered ten states in the west and far west but had no Charter and no National organization.

Instead of the third Friday in October which was being used by Ohio and and still is as well as October 15th, for the National Poetry Day, Lucia Trent selected October 15th for her National Poetry Day to honor Ralph Cheney, a noted poet and her husband, who died on that day in 1941. This now was the year, 1947. There are some groups who for convenience sake name other days and even weeks and months as Poetry Days, weeks and months, but the official day for National Poetry Day remains annually October 15.

This Day is celebrated in 50 United States and 40 foreign countries. October 15 is listed in all almanacs as Poetry Day. The National Poetry Day Committee, Inc. is listed in Encyclopedia of Associations, and is known all over the world.

Since the first Texas Proclamation in 1947 issued by the Governor of Texas, Beauford Jester, 49 other states have come into the fold. Thirty-eight states have legislation naming October 15 Poetry Day and the one state that does not celebrate October 15th does celebrate another day as Poetry Day on its own.

In 1949, Dr. Etta Josephean Murfey was named National Director of the National Poetry Day Committee, Inc. and this position she held until her death April 1, 1966. All 50 states of the United States have a state chairman and most of them are the same ones appointed by the first National Director, Dr. Etta Josephean Murfey. A small few have resigned due to age or ill health, but the Chairmanship is readily filled from a long waiting list. Dr. Etta Josephean Murfey had appointed as her Co-Chairman for Florida, Dr. Frances Clark Handler. Then knowing her health was a factor Dr. Murfey appointed Dr. Handler Co-Chairman for the United States.

Dr. Frances Clark Handler took over the National Director's Chair on April 1, 1966. National Poetry Day Committee, Inc. was then incorporated as a non-profit organization for the name's protection.

Legislation has been introduced in the 89—90—91—92 and this first session of the 93rd Congress of the United States by Congressman Claude Pepper and Congressman Dante Fascell. Legislation calls for a Mandatory issuance of a Poetry Day Proclamation annually by the President of the United States. There is indication that this will pass if only by our insistence over the years. Maybe this year will see a successful bill passed. When National Poetry Day Committee, Inc. achieves this goal for poets, they will have reached a summit never before attained by any cultural group.

ARTICLE XIV

THE NEW YORK POETRY FORUM

by Miss Dorothea Neale

The New York Poetry Forum was founded by Dorothea Neale in 1958 for the purpose of bringing poets before an appreciative audience and to advance the cause of poetry. For nine years it was conducted as a monthly program, held primarily at the Ligoa Duncan Arts Centre, and presenting Poets of the Month and sometimes an entire group as Poetry Club of the Month. Poets were selected on the basis of the quality of their work and upon their dedication to poetry, and groups both through achievement by members and through some particular contribution in the field of poetry. During these years the programs were open to the public without charge and there were no memberships, though the latter was frequently suggested.

The closing of the Arts Centre and other problems forced a lapse in the programs following the 1967 National and World Poetry Program.

With the 1968 National and World Poetry Day Celebration held on October 12th at the Hotel Berkshire, The New York Poetry Forum became a membership organization, with greatly increased and widened opportunities for accomplishment. Membership in The New York Poetry Forum is open to all lovers of poetry everywhere, both poets and non-poets. Besides the public programs, membership meetings are held, awards have been established, workshops and study groups are in operation, and a Poetry Forum Theatre in the planning stage.

Current Officers are: Dorothea Neale, Director & President; Jeffrey Escoffier, Vice-President; Bessie Wherry Nóe, Treasurer; Louis Warter, Secretary; Sylvia Argow, Historian.

For further information contact Miss Dorothea Neale, Director, The New York Poetry Forum, Inc., P.O. Box 855, Madison Square Station, 149 East 23rd Street, New York, NY 10010.

ARTICLE XV

THE PASADENA WRITERS' CLUB

by Dr. Vivian Bonine

Two young men, one about twenty, the other four years younger, were walking down a small community street. The elder waved his arm in a wide sweep and said, "One day my name will be emblazoned upon these buildings." That young man became immortal as James Whitcomb Riley. His friend was Albert William Macy. They remained friends for several years before their trails parted, and Mr. Macy was greatly influenced by Mr. Riley (who sometimes wrote under the pen name of "Doc Marigold.") Both men became established writers.

On the first Saturday afternoon of June, 1922, after a picnic luncheon under the carob trees in the park, THE WRITERS' CLUB OF PASADENA, CALIFORNIA was organized, and Mr. Albert William Macy was the first president. A Mr. Aspinwall was elected secretary. Other charter members were Mrs. Jeanette Benadum, Miss Elizabeth Pingree, Miss Anna Maria Wirth, Miss Mary Catherine Judd, Mrs. Ruth Rea Irwin Lambert, and Mrs. (Louise) C. F. Huddleston.

The club grew and newspaper, magazine and photo-play writing were studied. There were also programs on writing short stories, novels, poetry and songs. In September, 1923, the organization was officially renamed THE PASADENA WRITERS' CLUB.

It met in members' homes or libraries. It became the custom to hold a picnic or patio luncheon annually, which it still does.

One of its early "fun things to do" was holding a regularly scheduled writing contest. Manuscripts were placed in a jar, with no identifications, and later judged for first, second and third honors. The contributions became such spicy, whimsical, cleverly written short notes that the contest became known as The Ginger Jar, and on those meeting days, candied ginger was served to all present.

On October 22, 1928, Mrs. Caroline Converse founded THE ROUNDTABLE, a group of poets, some of whom belonged to The Pasadena Writers' Club. This provided more time for discussion of both prose and poetry, since the two groups met on different days. It was sometimes called a "by-product of the writers' club." However, it has always functioned as the verse section of the original unit. Many joint meetings were held after that, but on January 26, 1974 the two groups merged again under the old name of THE PASADENA WRITERS' CLUB.

Besides Mrs. Converse, charter members of The Roundtable were Dr. Odell I. Fellows, Mrs. Mary Augsbury, Mrs. Kate K. Church, Miss Nellie Mortensen, Mr. Edwin K. Hurlburt and Mr. Macy. Joining before the year was out: Miss Louise A. Frye, Mrs. Nora L. Brown, Mrs. Sarah Stansbury, and Mrs. Ruby Robinson Wise. Although the parent organization required nominal dues, the entire constitution and by-laws, purpose and dues policy was formulated for The Roundtable in the following hokku written by Miss Caroline West:

> *"Oh, we love the Muse,*
> *Flirting with all forms of verse,*
> *No blue laws, no dues."*

Mrs. Caroline Converse and Mrs. Ruby Robinson Wise are still members of The Pasadena Writers' Club today. It is Mrs. Converse's fiftieth year of membership and Mrs. Wise's forty-fifth year. At a club meeting in 1939, Occidental College of Los Angeles, California, honored Mrs. Wise (who was a graduate of that institution) by awarding her the Phi Beta Kappa Key. Both Mrs. Converse and Mrs. Wise are still writing prize-winning poetry.

One other member, though not a poet, deserves to be mentioned here. Mrs. Leila Hiser is in her forty-ninth year of membership. Although she no longer writes, she still enjoys the fellowship of club members who visit her in the convalescent home where she now lives. She was the club historian for fourteen years.

On March 30, 1929, Chief Standing Bear and three other "First Americans" entertained with Indian customs, folk lore and legends.

During the 1932 Olympic Celebrations, Pasadena Writers' Club members were chosen to welcome foreign visitors, serve refreshments and show visitors the city. They secured flags of all the nations represented in the Olympic games, outlined the walks in the park with big umbrellas and wicker chairs, where the ladies in pretty, colorful gowns flitted through the crowds attending visitor needs.

On January 9, 1932 the Pasadena Post published the first VERSE SECTION of poems from Pasadena Writers' Club members. The Pasadena Post became the Pasadena Star-News, and through the efforts of Barbara Miller Smales, the Star-News continued to publish the poems until 1946. The newspaper also agreed to pay for the poems. This money was saved in a special fund for financing publication of an anthology. Eventually three anthologies resulted: POEMS FROM PASADENA, Vol. I (1937); Vol. II (1943); and Vol. III (1948). A fourth anthology was published by the club under the direction of Mrs. Ruby Robinson Wise in 1971. This Vol. IV was titled "POETRY AND PROSE FROM THE WRITERS' CLUB of Pasadena," and contained short stories and articles as well as poetry.

In 1942 a music department was organized with Mrs. Leota McKnight appointed Chairman. This gave the club three sections: Prose, Poetry and Music. Other charter members of this group were Sadie Ashford Garnett, Ferne Downing Sanders, and Mae Metzler. Membership increased, but regretfully after ten years it disbanded.

Through years of peace, prosperity, depression and wars, The Pasadena Writers' Club carried on. In the club year 1946-47 alone, members sold to 130 different publications, including Saturday Evening Post, Ladies Home Journal, Children's Activities, Good Housekeeping, The Christian Science Monitor, Progressive Farmer, Denver Post, Writer's Digest, Child Life, Woman (a London magazine) as well as literary, religious, and other organs of both major and minor importance. In 1949, Barbara Miller Smales had 41 radio episodes broadcast (children's fiction). Total membership has always ranged between fifty and seventy-five creative people. The public is always invited to attend either regular or special progams.

On October 31, 1949, Radio Station KAGH (later changed to KALI) broadcast the first of a two year program called POETRY TRAILS, in which from six to fifteen poems were used on each presentation. Mrs. Edna Wherritt, Chairman, and Mrs. Leota McKnight, Co-Chairman, guided the project which was broadcast the first Sunday afternoon of each month. Mr. Hugh Wherritt, narrator; Violet Severy, pianist; and Rosemary McNamee, violinist presented nineteen broadcasts, ending in May, 1951. Some of the programs were recorded.

The club has had many outstanding guest speakers in the field of poetry ... including James Neil Northe, Joseph Joel Keith, Nina Willis Walter, Will Strong (who was instrumental in getting most states of the U.S. to co-ordinate in making October 15th of each year to be called POETRY DAY, with a proclamation from each state governor stating so). . . Ethel Jacobson and Helen Hinckley Jones (both now life members), and three California State Poet Laureates . . . John Steven McGroarty (who was a life member of The Pasadena Writers' Club), Mr. Gordon W. Norris, who followed Mr. McGroarty, and the current Poet Laureate, Mr. Charles B. Garrigus.

In 1955, Pasadena City College and Pasadena Writers' Club co-sponsored a WRITER'S WEEK. Helen Hinckley Jones chaired a committee from the college while Ferne Downing Sanders, President of Pasadena Writers' Club, worked with her committee. The two groups planned and beautifully executed a marvelous four-day program with speakers scheduled for both morning and evening sessions. Poetry was certainly included on the programs. 1974 will be the nineteenth year in which this event is to be held. One major change has taken place: the college is predominantly responsible for its sponsorship, but many cultural organizations throughout the San Gabrial Valley now participate in its planning. Mr. Williard C. Hyatt is the 1974 Writers' Club representative. Both Mrs. Jones and Mrs. Sanders are honorary life members for their outstanding contributions of service to the organization.

Ferne Downing Sanders is also quite adept in the field of photography. She has prepared both movies and still photography with musical backgrounds for poetry reading entertainment, which she and her husband, Mr. Edwin C. Sanders, have presented at county fairs, educational, civic, and cultural events over the entire Southern California area.

Under the presidency of Vivian Bonine, eight issues of a workshop magazine, SCRIPTORIUM ARBORETUM - "The Writing Room In A Garden Of Trees," - were published (1963–65) and two paper back books by the same title (1966 and 1968). Some of these contained original music as well as prose and poetry. It won a UPLI award, and Mrs. Bonine (as owner, editor and publisher) received notices from as far away as Africa and Canada.

About 1964, Mrs. Ruby Robinson Wise began using watercolor illustrations to decorate poetry submitted by Writers' Club members to be displayed in picture frames at the Pasadena City Outdoor Art Fair each Autumn. Her lovely artwork has attracted many people who would not otherwise have enjoyed our literary contributions. She is still continuing this work.

Following is the entire list of presidents, given in the order in which they served their term or terms of presidencies:

1. Mr. Albert William Macy
2. Mrs. Jeanette Benedum
3. Mrs. Louise Huddleston
4. Mrs. Anna Lucky
5. Mrs. A. McConnell
6. Dr. J. Franklin Kelly
7. Mr. George Cary
8. Dr. Odell T. Fellows
9. Mrs. Caroline Converse
10. Miss Anna Maria Wirth
11. Mrs. Mabel Clapp
12. Mr. Luther Fentress
13. Mrs. Genevieve Weight
14. Mrs. Gertrude McCarthy
15. Mrs. Irene Waage
16. Mrs. Christine Roome
17. Mrs. Jessie Pierce
18. Mrs. Elizabeth Sawyer
19. Mrs. Barbara Smales
20. Mrs. Ruth Coleman
21. Mrs. Leota McKnight
22. Mrs. Ruth Lambert
23. Mrs. Ivy Stone
24. Mrs. Bertha L. Plant
25. Mrs. Caroline Converse
26. Mrs. Joy McCartney
27. Mrs. Dorothy M. Keesling
28. Miss Ferne Downing
29. Mrs. Mary Vivian Small
30. Mrs. Ferne Downing Sanders
31. Dr. Vivian Way Small Bonine
32. Mrs. Ruby Robinson Wise
33. Mrs. Lillian M. Keahey

ARTICLE XVI

THE POETRY FELLOWSHIP OF MAINE

by Miss Barbara Coonley Hollis

Historical Sketch, 14 November 1969

On 1 March 1931, the first poetry group in the State of Maine, USA, was formed. Organized as The Poets' Club of Waterville, the group included women interested in the study of versification and the writing of poetry. Mrs. Elsia Holway Burleigh was the founder, residing in Waterville. Mrs. Burleigh was elected first president and continued in the office for ten years.

Shortly after the Poets' Club of Waterville was founded, another group was formed, known as the Dover-Foxcroft Poetry Circle. With several other poetry and literary clubs appearing, Mrs. Burleigh felt that a state poetry fellowship would be of advantage.

On 31 October 1936, the Waterville Poets' Club entertained the Poetry Circle of Dover-Foxcroft at a luncheon meeting at Hinckley, Maine, and the Poetry Fellowship of Maine was formally organized. Five years of planning had preceded this meeting. Members of the Scribblers' Club of Rockland and the Omar Club of Rockport were invited to join in the new Poetry Fellowship of Maine.

Invitations to become Honorary Members were extended to Edna St. Vincent Millay, Laura E. Richards, Robert Peter Tristram Coffin, Harold Trowbridge Pulsifer, Wilbert Snow, and Harold Vinal, all distinguished Maine poets. The Poetry Fellowship of Maine invited Louise Bogan (Mrs. Raymond Holden), to become Honorary President.

The first poetry Fellowship of Maine officers were Miss Ida M. Folsom, Dover-Foxcroft, President; Mrs. Elsia Holway Burleigh, Waterville, and Miss Bessie C.H. Cooper, Dover-Foxcroft, Vice-President; Miss Beatrice Hussey, Waterville, Recording Secretary; Mrs. Argie Lord Buzzell, Waterville, Treasurer; Miss Anna Shaw Buck, Dover-Foxcroft, Corresponding Secretary; Miss Alice Frost Lord, Scribe; Mrs. Blanche Wass Brown and Rev. Mary A. Hurd, both of Dover-Foxcroft, Project Committee; Miss Helen Dyer Paine, Dover-Foxcroft, and Mrs. Burleigh, Program Committee. Hospitality Committee: Mrs. Ellen Webber, Dover-Foxcroft; Mrs. Nellie Hinckley and Mrs. Charlotte T. Hill, both of Waterville. Membership Committee: Mrs. Helen Burpee Larsen, Waterville, and Mrs. Charlotte J. Buffam, Dover-Foxcroft.

Eligibility for membership depended upon having had published one or more volumes of poetry, or submitting for approval to a board of review three poems. The latter membership requirement continues to be observed, although limited memberships are now open for non-poets. A poetry contest for Maine High School students was an early project, discontinued in 1969 after enjoying many years of success. Publications of the Fellowship have been: As Maine Writers, An Anthology; REED, Poetry of Members, published in 1950, 1952, 1953, 1955; A Poetry Fellowship of Maine Anthology: Juniper and White Pine, published in 1961; A Poetry Fellowship of Maine Anthology, Rock Ledge and Apple Blossoms, published in December 1971.

The Poetry Fellowship of Maine has stressed the need for study of verse forms, and has afforded opportunity in assigned projects for members to practice and acquire skills in recognized forms. Judges for assigned projects may be members of the Fellowship, or faculty members for Maine institutions of higher learning.

The Poetry Fellowship of Maine was for a few years affiliated with the National Federation of State Poetry Societies. Individual members of the Fellowship are associated with the National group through various other organizations, and at present the Fellowship is not nationally affiliated as a group.

The current President is Barbara Bond, 89 Ferry Road, Saco, ME 04072.

ARTICLE XVII

THE POETRY SOCIETY OF AMERICA

by Charles Wagner

The officers for 1973–1974 are: Richard Eberhart, Honorary President; Richard V. Lindabury, President; Vice-Presidents Corliss Lamont, Madeline Mason, Edmund Pennant; Governing Board: Gertrude Ryder Bennett, Patricia Coffin, Lisa Grenelle, Dorsha Hayes, Mary Kennedy, Joseph Francis Murphy, Dorothy Lee Richardson, Judith Johnson Sherwin, Jack Stadler, Brian Swann and Charles A. Wagner, Executive Secretary, 15 Gramercy Park South, New York, N.Y. 10003. Telephones 254–9628, 9683 (Area code 212).

Among officers and members of the society, past and present are included: Conrad Aiken, W.H. Auden, Joseph Auslander, Stephen Benet, William Rose Benet, Richard Burton, Witter Bynner, Willa Cather, Bliss Carman, Stanton Coblentz, Robert P.T. Coffin, Padraic Colum, George Dillon, Theodore Dreiser, Richard Eberhart, John Erskine, Arthur Davison Ficke, John Gould Fletcher, Robert Frost, Oliver St. John Gogarty, Arthur Guiterman, Du Bose Heyward, Robert Hillyer, Robinson Jeffers, Thomas S. Jones Jr., Joyce Kilmer, Alfred Kreymborg, Christopher La Farge, Henry Goddard Leach, Ludwig Lewisohn, Vachel Lindsay, Amy Lowell, Edwin Markham, John Masefield, Edgar Lee Masters, Phyllis McGinley, Joaquin Miller, Marianne Moore, David Morton, Robert Nathan, Alfred Noyes, Lizette Woodworth Reese, Edwin Arlington Robinson, Carl Sandburg, Alan Seeger, Anne Sexton, Leonora Speyer, Wallace Stevens, Sara Teasdale, Ridgely Torrence, Louis Untermeyer, Mark Van Doren, John Hall Wheelock, George Edward Woodberry, Elinor Wylie, Marya Zaturenska.

The Poetry Society of America was founded in 1910 and has been in continuous existence ever since. It is the parent organization of many regional groups throughout the country.

It was responsible for the Pulitzer prizes in poetry. It initiated open forums for the discussion of poetry. It established a poetry collection at the New York Public Library. It sponsors many notable awards such as the Shelley, di Castagnola, Cane, Ficke, Dylan, Masefield, Davidson, Emily Dickinson, Reedy, Morley, Hemley, Joyce, Ford, and Coffin poetry contests, aggregating more than $10,000 annually. On occasion, the society awards its Gold Medal for distinguished achievement in poetry.

Some of the country's outstanding writers, editors, critics, scholars, and poets have appeared before the society as speakers or readers. Many of them are members and have served as officers.

In 1946 the society published *The Poetry Society of America Anthology*, featuring the work of 223 members, past and present. In 1950 it published *In Fealty to Apollo*, a pictorial history of the society, paralleling the golden age of poetry in this country, from the early 1900's to the first half of the present century. In 1960, in observance of the society's 50th anniversary, it published its second anthology, *The Golden Year*. In 1966, a series of

Centenary Memorial volumes was begun, with the publication of *Richard Le Gallienne*, a memoir-anthology. Other titles now include: *Edgar Lee Masters, George Sterling, Edwin Arlington Robinson* and in October 1972, *The Diamond Year*, a third PSA Anthology is due to appear.

The society's monthly Bulletin, issued eight times a year, keeps members and friends informed of activities during the society's sessions. Unless otherwise announced, meetings are held the last Thursday of the month, October to May, at 122 East 58th St., New York. Admission to these meetings is free to the public. In April, in lieu of a regular meeting, there is an annual dinner.

PSA AWARDS for 1973 include: John Ashbery, co-winner of the Shelley Award ($1,800.) for published work; Helen Bryant, winner of the PSA Gassner Award; Virginia Moran Evans, winner of the James Joyce Award; Norma Farber, winner of the Christopher Morley Award; George Keithley, co-winner of the Alice Fay di Castagnola Award; Jerome Mc Gann, winner of the Melville Cane Award, for his book *Swinburne: An Experiment In Criticism*; Sandra McPherson, winner of the Emily Dickinson Award; Sallie W. Nixon, winner of the Gustav Davidson Award; Mary Oliver, co-winner of the Alice Fay di Castagnola Award; Elisavietta Ritchie, winner of the William Marion Reedy Award; Margaret Rockwell, winner of the PSA Award, 2nd Prize; Larry J. Rubin, winner of the PSA Award 1st Prize; Heidi Schmidt, winner of the Elias Lieberman High School Award; Sarah Singer, winner of the Consuelo Ford Award; Helen Sorrells, winner of the Cecil Hemley Award, and Richard Wilbur, co-winner of the Shelley Award.

ARTICLE XVIII

POETS AND PATRONS, INC.

Poets And Patrons, Inc. was organized in the early 1940's for the purpose of studying how to write poetry. It has grown to a large membership, about 160, and these members are drawn from many writing groups in the Chicago area. Isabelle G. Young was the founder, and she was president until her death in 1967.

Miss Young was very active in the Poets' Club of Chicago and for this reason the two groups have been closely allied. However, usually six to eight poetry writing groups are affiliated.

Lillian B. Foster followed Miss Young as president, and in 1972 Evelyn Schmidt of Brookfield became president.

The group has an annual awards dinner on October 15, honoring National Poetry Day. Twenty contests are offered with $10 first and $5 second prizes as well as first and second Honorable Mentions. A grand prize of $50 is awarded, due to a gift of stock from W. Clement Stone. This prize was supplied by Mr. Stone to honor a club member, Ella Kracke, who was his high school teacher. It goes to the poem considered best of all the first prize winners. Cliff and Anne Nolan present an award called "On Second Thought". This award of $25 goes to the best of the second place winners. It is given in honor of the late Hazel Frazee.

Workshops are held four times annually where members may have their poetry criticized anonymously. Panelists for the criticism sessions are chosen from the English Departments of Chicago area colleges and from other competent sources.

The officers for 1974 are: Evelyn Schmidt, President, 4205 Madison Avenue, Brookfield, IL 60513; Anne Nolan, First Vice President, 9524 S. Colfax Avenue, Chicago, IL 60617; John Pineda, Second Vice President, 5219 S. Blackstone Avenue, Chicago, IL 60615; Elena Whitehead, Recording Secretary, 70 E. Cedar Street, Chicago, IL 60611; Gladys Cook, Treasurer, 1628 W. Touhy Avenue, Chicago, IL 60626; Lillian Foster, Auditor, 5738 W. 63rd Street, Chicago, IL 60638; Wilma Burton, Workshop Chairman, 519 N. President Street, Wheaton, IL 60187; Hazel Broadus, Publicity Chairman, 4914 Prospect Avenue, Downers Grove, IL 60515.

ARTICLE XIX

POETS' CLUB OF CHICAGO

Poets' Club of Chicago had its beginning in the mid-30's, the time of depression. It came about when a group of Chicago teachers from Hirsch Highschool met in the evenings to find enjoyment in reading poetry. These sessions developed into a poetry writing group and moved out of the highschool into a more centrally located meeting place where other Chicago area poets might join them.

Members bring several copies of an original unsigned poem and it is then criticized by the entire group. For practical purposes the club has been kept small in number but it has prospered. Members feel they benefit greatly by the excellent suggestions they receive from their colleagues.

Poets' Club of Chicago sponsors an annual Shakespearean sonnet contest which attracts entries from all over United States and sometimes from foreign countries. Awards are $20 first, $10 second and $5 third prizes. There are also first, second and third Honorable Mentions.

The officers of Poets' Club of Chicago for 1974 are: Gladys M. Cook, President, 1628 W. Touhy Avenue, Chicago, IL 60626; Lillian B. Foster, Vice President, 5738 W. 63rd Street, Chicago, IL 60638; Mary Torode, Secretary and Contest Chairman, 1541 N. Avers Avenue, Chicago, IL 60651; Anne Nolan, Treasurer, 9524 S. Colfax Avenue, Chicago, IL 60617.

ARTICLE XX

POETS' TAPE EXCHANGE

The Poets' Tape Exchange is a tape recording exchange for poets and lovers of poetry. It was founded by Frances Brandon Neighbours, the current president, with the purpose of establishing by the medium of the tape recorder, a method of verbal communication between poets, in order to promote a better appreciation of poetry by sound. Reels of poetry and discussion by the members, as well as listening reels on which the work of other poets is recorded, are sent from member to member and are later collected in the PTE Library. Only reel to reel tape recorders are used in the Exchange.

The PTE library consists of tapes of original poetry sent in by the members, completed Reel Rounds (a tape for the purpose of reading and discussing poetry, including the biographical study of poets), Listening Reels, and other material contributed or selected as educational matter. Members may borrow any listed tape for the period of two weeks by sending a written request, enclosing postage to cover the cost of mailing. There is a Reference Shelf for the Blind. From this source blind poets may borrow taped material that is helpful in the writing of all forms of poetry, including haiku.

Poetry contests are conducted, with prizes of money, books and tapes. Each member is eligible to enter all contests offered by Poets' Tape Exchange.

Membership in the Exchange is extended to both poets and lovers of poetry. Anyone wishing to become a member may, by request, receive an application for membership. Subscription is $4 per year.

Address all communication to Poets' Tape Exchange, Frances Brandon Neighbours, 109 Twin Oak Drive, Lynchburg, VA 24502.

ARTICLE XXI

ST. LOUIS POETRY CENTER

by Kathrene Casebolt

The St. Louis Poetry Center was founded in March 1946 by Mrs. Fred Armstrong, with the support of a few poets and interested persons for the purpose of encouraging poets by reading and criticizing their writing by whatever form of recognition was available. In addition the Center would provide a meeting place where the poets could come free of charge — an Open Door. Throughout its 23 years the Center has maintained this policy.

The Center was incorporated in 1963 and organized with two boards, a ruling and administrative body of nine Directors, and a literary body composed of outstanding members of the community who sponsor and support the Center's effort toward quality or excellence in writing. This is not direct financial support, but rather moral and prestige support.

The Center has no actual membership in the sense of dues-paying. It is supported entirely by donations. The monthly paper, Poetry Center Speaking, is mailed to 300 poets and interested persons throughout the season of nine months, October through May. Subscriptions cost $3.00.

Workshop meetings take place monthly (Oct.–May) on the 3rd Sunday in the afternoon. Formerly the Center met at the St. Louis Public Library where it still gives instruction and holds classes in poetry one evening a week for ten week sessions. The classes have continued for 10 years at the Public Library and are free. Beginning in October 1969 the Center moved to the Bishop Tuttle Memorial Building of Christ Church Cathedral at 1210 Locust St., St. Louis.

Each year culminates in a Poetry Concert when two prizes are offered: one first prize of $75 for the best poem in the concert and the Edmée B. Nash Prize for $50. Both are local.

Critics, teachers, poets, writers, act as the critic for the monthly workshops. No fee is charged or paid to those who give their time, professional experience, and guidance through interest. A radio programme called 'Poets and People', which was conducted for four years by Kathrene Casebolt, teacher at the Poetry Center, was broadcast on KFUO, when poets and teachers of the area were interviewed.

The new president of the St. Louis Poetry Center is Jon Johnson, 223 Tiffcn Street, St. Louis, MO 63135.

ARTICLE XXII

TEXAS COUNCIL FOR THE PROMOTION OF POETRY

by Dr. Marvin Davis Winsett

In 1947, Beauford H. Jester, Governor of Texas, issued a proclamation designating October 15th as Poetry Day in Texas. On that date a group of interested poets met at the home of Aline B. Carter, Poet Laureate of Texas, to celebrate the first Texas Poets Day. This meeting resulted in the formation of the Texas Council for the Promotion of Poetry. The first Poets Day honoured the memory of the late Ralph Cheyney, poet, critic and lecturer, and the husband of Lucia Trent. Lucia Trent founded the Council with Aline B. Carter as co-founder who was named Honorary Chairman and Lucia Trent Executive Chairman.

Members of the first Council were: Dr. A.J. App; Artemisia Bowden; Dr. Van Chandler; Doris H. Connerly; Grace Noll Crowell; Angel Cano Del Castillo; Oscar J. Fox; Agnes James; Pauline Griffin; Bishop Everett H. Jones; Fania B. Kruger; Lillian Holloway; May Laufenburg; Max Reiter; Lexie Dean Robertson; David Russell; Dr. Arthur M. Sampley; Effa Stark Sanders; Dollilee Davis Smith.

An early issue of *The Texas Poet*, the official publication, states the purposes of the Texas Council for the Promotion of Poetry as follows: 'The Council will try to foster an appreciation of poetry in all ages and cultures, but especially the work of contemporary writers. It will endeavour to make Texans more poetry-minded and appreciative of the poets in their midst and through the arts to help build a more spiritual age, and age of peace and security for all. The Council will encourage poetry recitals, verse choirs, poetry columns in the press and poetry readings on the air.

'It will endeavour to acquaint the public with the role of the poet and his functions in society. It will act as a bureau of information on poetry groups and advise on mechanical training for poets. It will co-operate with poetry groups in other states. It will promote poetry in our schools, colleges and universities. It will promote Texas Poets Day throughout the state through poetry meetings, radio programs, book displays, and other methods of bringing poetry to the attention of the people of Texas'.

Local chairmen for the observance of the first Poets Day in Texas were: Faye Carr Adams, Wichita Falls; Mary Miller Beard, Amarillo; Dr. Van Chandler, Kingsville; Lillian Durham Dickson, Fort Worth; Pauline Griffin, Houston; Rose Jasper Nickell, Lubbock; Mildred Lindsey Raiborn, San Angelo; Effa Stark Sanders, Corpus Christi; Dr. Arthur M. Sampley, Denton; Rita Barr, San Antonio; and Mrs Eugene W. Staph, San Antonio.

Those who have served as state officers are: Hobart W. Enoch, Margie B. Boswell, and Stella James Boren as secretaries. Eleanor Perlstein Weinbaum, Lillian Durham Dickson, and Dr. Van Chandler as co-chairmen.

Honorary Chairmen are: William D. Barney, Aline B. Carter, Dr. Athur

M. Sampley, Lucia Trent, and Dee Walker.

The State Chairman of the Texas Council for the Promotion of Poetry is Marvin Davis Winsett. The State Secretary-Treasurer is Charles B. Hanna.

ARTICLE XXIII

THE VACHEL LINDSAY ASSOCIATION

by Dr. Marvin Davis Winsett

A dozen people called together by Frank R. Bohnhorst and Robert O. Schulze, met in 1946 to discuss forming an association. An invitation through the press was extended to a meeting convened in the Lincoln Library. Fifty-five persons were present at this meeting and organized The Vachel Lindsay Association. Mrs. Harry C. Blankmeyer was elected the first president.

Through the kindness of Oliver J. Keller, the group secured the St. Louis Symphony Orchestra for an 11 February concert. The Association assumed responsibility for the sale of tickets. The net proceeds were used to get started.

On 21 May 1947, the Association was granted incorporation papers as a tax-free, non-exclusive, and non-profit-making organization.

The purpose of The Vachel Lindsay Association is: 'to stimulate interest in the significance of the life, writings, and ideals of the poet, Vachel Lindsay'. The Association maintains the Lindsay Home at 603 S. Fifth Street, Springfield, Illinois, as a permanent literary shrine housing Lindsayana treasures and memorabilia including twenty framed designs of Lindsay's drawings, paintings, and letterings; fifty books of Lindsay autographed by him; unprinted poems, recordings by the poet of his own poems, old 78 records not available elsewhere, out-of-print booklets, original manuscripts and other unpublished documents.

Officers for 1971 are: Robert D. Furry, President; Miss Lillian Scalzo, Vice-President; Miss Elizabeth E. Graham, Corresponding Secretary; Mrs. J.A. Eastham, Recording Secretary; Mrs. A.A. Hoffman, Treasurer. Other officers are Savoy Wollan, Alton Hall, and Clarissa Jorgensen.

Past Presidents of The Vachel Lindsay Association are: 1946-48, Mrs. Helen Van Cleve Blankmeyer; 1948-52, Miss Elizabeth E. Graham; 1952-54, Mr. Ewing Baskette; 1954-55, Ruth Black; 1955-58, E. Carl Lundgren; 1958-64, Mrs. Clarissa Jorgensen; 1964-69, Mr. Robert D. Furry.

It is the custom of the Association to present some outstanding speaker on the anniversary of the poet's birth, 10 November. On 10 November 1947, the series of annual birthday celebrations began with Reverend Alan Jenkins of Galesburg, Illinois, as the speaker. In 1948, Isadora Bennett, who acted with Vachel Lindsay at the University of Chicago when he read his own poetry, recited some of his poems. In April 1948, Albert Edmund Trombly gave an anniversary lecture on Vachel Lindsay which was later published. In April 1950, Hiram College Centennial Choir gave a program of the poet's poems set to music. In November 1950, Gertrude Johnson read a series of Lindsay poems. In 1951, Arno L. Bader discussed the poet's legends and epic poems. In 1952, George S. Bonn gave a lecture entitled, 'We Need More Lindsay-Hearted Men', which was published. In 1953, Dr. Paul Graebel read poems. In 1954, Mrs. Charles Boynton gave 'A Literary Pilgrimage'. In 1955, Eleanor Dougherty (nee Madam Francois Trives) and her daughter, Helene, gave a eurhythmy program in costume. Olive Wakefield read some of Lindsay's poems. In 1956, David Virgil Felts, editorial writer for Lindsay-Schaub Newspapers, gave a lecture entitled, 'Thanking Rhymes for Bread', which was published. In 1957, the poet's cousin, Eudora Lindsay South, gave a lecture on her recollections of Lindsay. In 1958, a three-part program by local talent was given on 'The Prose and Poetry of Nicholas Vachel Lindsay'. In 1959, the first open house was held at Lindsay Home, whose rehabilitation had been in process since August 1958. A program of music and talks discussed the aims and purposes of The Lindsay Home. In November 1960, Ralph Schroeder lectured on 'Such Stuff as Dreams Are Made Of'. In 1961, three dance programs were given: one directed by Betty Jo Mack on the Fantasies. George Ecklund composed 29 musical settings for 29 children's fantasies for this dance program. A second dance program was directed by Lorrayne Touch, and the third dance program was by Mildred Caskey, 'These are the Young'. In 1962, the Lanphier A Capella Choir of 130 verse-speaking Lanphier students was directed by Esther Duncan. In 1963, Vachel Lindsay Week, 77 people appeared on broadcasts and telecasts as the schools gave programs prepared by students and teachers. In 1964, Ralph Sprecklemeyer had his SHS. A Capella Choir perform George Ecklund's setting of 'The Congo', printed by The Vachel Lindsay Association. In November of 1964, Frances Ridgely read a chapter of her forthcoming book on Springfield as the background used by the poet Lindsay. In March 1965, a guided tour of the Lindsay Home was taken by members of the Association. In August 1965, programs of 'Three Poets of Illinois' were given at the Illinois State Fair. This was repeated at the Illinois Education Building by young people of the state. In November 1965, Radford B. Kuykendall of Western Michigan University spoke on the topic, 'The Legacy of Vachel Lindsay'. In November 1966, Marvin Davis Winsett gave a lecture on 'Some Uses of Words', which was published. In November 1967, Alex Gehlman recounted experiences with the poet and read poems, and Frances Ridgely showed drawings for her book and read her chapter on Altgeld. In August 1968, a Decatur group, The Loft Players, put on the Lindsay program which the college students had prepared for The Vachel Lindsay Association.

In 1969, a group of young people met at the Museum, read and recited their own poems. Also, ten people reminisced about Vachel Lindsay at their literary school, or city clubs, or in their homes. The 1970 speaker was Ann Massa who is the author of 'Vachel Lindsay Field Worker for the American Dream'.

Types of membership in The Vachel Lindsay Association are: Junior at 50c per year; Regular at $2.00 per year; Contributing at $5.00 per year; Sustaining at $10.00 per year; Life at $150.00. Membership fees should be directed to the Treasurer, Mrs. A.A. Hoffman, 2428 Whittier Avenue, Springfield, Illinois, 62404.

ARTICLE XXIV

WORLD POETS RESOURCE CENTER, INC.

The World Poets Resource Center, Inc. is a non-profit organization which promotes clean, choice poetry which in no way refers to race, creed, color or national origin in a derogatory way.

The aim of the organization is four fold: 1. to collect Poetry Anthologies in all languages from all over the world; pictures of poets; manuscripts and books, pictures etc. of those in the field of the allied arts; 2. to create and maintain a Resource Center for Poetry and other forms of art to meet the needs of poets and other artists interested in clean, choice material by or about poets and other artists the world over; 3. to promote the art and skill of writing and reading poetry; and to promote beginning poets, writers and painters as well as to promote the appreciation and understanding of poetry and the allied arts; 4. to promote clean, choice poetry and give financial assistance through scholarships and fellowships to deserving youth who show an interest in/or are talented in writing or reading poetry which in some way fits in with the motto of the Resource Center, 'Love, Peace, and World Brotherhood Through Poetry'; to inspire and help individuals and groups through "Poetry in Action" Workshops (the depressed, the bereaved, shutins, those in Nursing Homes, senior citizens, etc.) developing the realization of inner strength and the creative ability of participants.

The Center's activities include poetry workshops for children, poetry readings, verse speaking competitions, annual international verse speaking festival (May), annual awards' luncheon (June).

The founder and president of the World Poets Resource Center, Inc. is Lou LuTour, 1270 Fifth Avenue, Apt. 2F, New York, NY 10029; Honorary President: Dr. Ernest Kay (England); Honorary Consultant: Dr. Amado M. Yuzon (Philippines); Honorary Chairman: Huntington Hartford (U.S.A.); Honorary Patron: Dr. John Woodward (England).

POETRY SOCIETIES (OTHER THAN STATE) AND RELATED ORGANIZATIONS IN THE U.S.A.

AKRON POETRY SOCIETY
President: Donna J. Dougherty, 4623 Provens Drive, Akron, OH 44319.

AMERICAN JUNIOR POETRY SOCIETY
Director: Miss Emilia DeLisa, Renee Gate, Rt. 6, Main Street, Laurie Road, Peekskill, NY 10566.

AMERICAN POETRY LEAGUE
President: Truth Mary Fowler, 10419 Audrey Drive, Sun City, AZ 85351; Vice President & Editor: Alfarata Hansel, 35 E. Indianola Ave., Phoenix, AZ 85012; Secretary & Treasurer: Genevieve Sargent, P.O. Box 15092, Phoenix, AZ 85060.

The League was founded in 1922 for people who write poetry. It provides the opportunity for members to have their poetry published in the American Poetry League Bulletin; sponsors numerous minicontests with modest prizes to motivate members to write in a pattern never tried before; sponsors an annual maxicontest; provides information on other contests open to all poets, market tips, writing skills.

AMERICAN POETS FELLOWSHIP SOCIETY
President: Stella Craft Tremble, 902 10th Street, Charleston, IL 61920.

ARKANSAS WRITERS' CONFERENCE
Director: Anne Nash Yarbrough, 510 East Street, Benton, AR 72015.

The Thirtieth Annual Arkansas Writers' Conference was held at the Sam Peck Hotel, Little Rock, Arkansas on June 7th and 8th, 1974.

AUSTIN POETRY SOCIETY
See Poetry Society of Texas — Austin Chapter.

BERGEN POETS
President: Ruth C. Falk, 197 Delmar Avenue, Glen Rock, AR 07452.

BRAILLE POETS GUILD
148 Washington Street, Tanton, MA.

BREAD LOAF WRITERS' CONFERENCE
Middlebury College, Middlebury, VT 05753.

BROOKLYN POETRY CIRCLE (see Article II)
Secretary: Gabrielle Lederer, 61 Pierrepont Street, Brooklyn, NY 11201; President: David F. Gosnell, 12 Gales Road, Edison, NJ 08817.

CALIFORNIA FEDERATION OF CHAPARRAL POETS

President: Dr. Charles Welch, 6604 La Jolla Blvd., La Jolla, CA 92037; Corr. Secretary: Mary E. Cox; Editor CFCP Newsletter: Maud O'Neil, 11214 Bellaire Street, Loma Linda, CA 92354.

CALIFORNIA FEDERATION OF CHAPARRAL POETS — APOLLO CHAPTER

Secretary: Dr. Mary F. Lindsley, 13361 El Dorado, 201H Seal Beach, CA.

CALIFORNIA FEDERATION OF CHAPARRAL POETS — ROBERT FROST CHAPTER

Vice President: Edwin A. Falkowski, 208 W. Latimer Ave., Campbell, CA 95008.

CALIFORNIA FEDERATION OF CHAPARRAL POETS — TOYON CHAPTER

President: Mrs. Rosemary Wilkinson, 1239 Bernal Avenue, Burlingame, CA 94010.

CALIFORNIA OLYMPIAD OF THE ARTS

Secretary: Miss Gwendolen B. Penniman, 22100 Mount Eden Road, Saratoga, CA.

A California Olympiad of the Arts is held in the beautiful Garden Theatre at Villa Montalvo, Saratoga, every four years at the time of the Olympic Games. Awards are given for original poetry, musical composition, literature and poetic drama; a winner is laurel crowned and prize-winning works are presented.

Senator James D. Phelan, Montalvo's genial host, and a poet in his own right, was the first sponsor of a 'Poesy Olympiad' on June 2, 1928. He, and California's Poet Laureate, Dr. Henry Meade Bland, envisioned such Olympiads as carrying on the spirit of the ancient Olympic Games which included contests in the arts as well as in sports. The idea was revived by The Edwin Markham Poetry society with an Olympiad in 1956, under the Chairmanship of Gwendolen Brooks Penniman. It has since been held every four years (next one in 1976), at the time of the Olympic Games, with the help of cultural groups and of distinguished judges. It is sponsored by the Quadrennial Contests in the Arts.

CALIFORNIA POETRY READINGS CIRCUIT

Director: Charles Wright, Department of English, University of California at Irvine, Irvine, CA 92664.

THE CANTON POETRY SOCIETY

1205 Broad Avenue, Canton, OH 44708.

THE CLEVELAND STATE UNIVERSITY POETRY CENTER

Director: Dr. Alberta Turner, 482 Caskey Court, Oberlin, OH 44074.

This Center, founded in 1963, conducts monthly public workshops, gives readings by nationally and locally known poets, and publishes a series of poetry booklets, containing the work of Cleveland-Area Poets.

CLOVER INTERNATIONAL POETRY ASSOCIATION
Mrs. Evelyn Petry, P.O. Box 4989, Washington, DC 20008.

COMMITTEE FOR THE REVITALIZATION OF THE POETRY SOCIETY OF AMERICA
Chairperson: Hyacinthe Hill, 166 Hawthorne Avenue, Yonkers, NY 10705; Honorary President: W. H. Auden.

The Committee was established in lieu of the need, expresed by various members, to revitalize the Poetry Society of America. The revitalization program proposes that the business meetings open to all members be held once a year, with budgets, proposals and proxies sent to all members in advance; that the Board make efforts to attract members from various social groups and that recruitment be made without regard to age, sex, religion, or race; that the PSA burst out with greater poetic activity, such as a monthly magazine of poetry, a book club, an annual anthology, more poetry readings on radio and T.V.

CONNECTICUT POETRY CIRCUIT
Director: Mrs. Jean Maynard, The Honors College, Wesleyan University, Middletown, CT 06457.

THE DAYTON POETRY FORUM
1220 Patterson Road, Dayton, OH 45420.

THE DAYTON POETS ROUNDTABLE
4430 Grange Hall Road, Dayton, OH 45430.

DIAL-A-POEM POETS
Originator: John Giorno, c/o Giorno Poetry Systems, 222 Bowery, New York, NY 10012.

The Dial-A-Poem Poets are an open-ended poetry group.

THE EDGAR ALLAN POE SOCIETY OF BALTIMORE
President & Acting Secretary: Alexander G. Rose, 402 E. Gittings Avenue, Baltimore, MD 21212.

EMILY DICKINSON SOCIETY
c/o Higginson Press, 4508 38th Street, Brentwood, MD 20722.

FAIRMONT POETRY SOCIETY
President: Dr. Ruth Ann Musick, Colonial Apts. No. 2, East Garden Lane, Fairmont, WV 26554.

FEDERAL POETS OF WASHINGTON, D.C.
President: Oliver Whitwell Wilson, 868 N. Kentucky Street, Arlington, VA 22205.

FLORIDA STATE POETRY SOCIETY, INC. (see Article IV)
National Director: Dr. Frances Clark Handler, 1110 North Venetian Drive, Miami Beach, FL 33139.

FOREST HILLS LITERARY CLUB
President: Mr. R. James Bryant, 666 Highland Avenue, Newark, NJ.

FORT LAUDERDALE POETRY WORKSHOP
Secretary: Mrs. Henry Wilke, 5307 NE 32nd Avenue, Fort Lauderdale, FL 33308.

GANSVOORT PIER POETS
Gansvoort Street & West St. Pier, New York, NY 10014.

GEM STATE WRITERS GUILD
President: Mrs. Eleanor Bensòn, 1702 N. 23rd, Boise, ID 83702.

GEORGIA WRITERS ASSOCIATION, INC.
President & Director: Mrs. Raymond Massey, 18 Collier Road NW, Atlanta, GA 30309.

THE GREATER CINCINNATI WRITERS LEAGUE
2413 Ohio Avenue, Cincinnati, OH 45219.

HAIKU SOCIETY OF AMERICA
Japan House, 333 East 47th Street, New York, NY 10017
    The Haiku Society of America is open to the general public. There are no requirements for membership, except an interest in haiku and other forms of Japanese poetry. At the moment members include haiku writers, editors of haiku magazines in U.S., England, Australia as well as individuals with only an interest in Haiku and related topics. An annual awards program has been initiated for outstanding work in the field. Virginia Brady Young is the President for 1974–75, 12 Chetelat Drive, Mansfield Center, CT 06250.

IDAHO POETS' AND WRITERS' GUILD (see Article V)
President: Mrs. Helen Gee Woods, 317 6th Street, Idaho Falls, ID 83401.

IDAHO STATE POETRY SOCIETY
Miss Hazel Alrich, Homedale, ID 83628.

THE INA COOLBRITH CIRCLE (see Article VIII)
Room 401, Marines' Memorial Building, San Francisco, CA.

INKY TRAILS POETS
Pearl Kirk, Editor, Inky Trails Publication, Route No. 2, Box 2028, Nampa, ID 83651.

INTERNATIONAL CULTURAL, POETRY & EFFICIENCY SOCIETY
Director of Public Relations: Mrs. Loretta Jean Skibbe, 13604 Summer Hill Drive, Phoenix, MD 21131.

INTERNATIONAL POETRY FORUM
Director: Dr. Samuel Hazo, 4400 Forbes Avenue, Pittsburgh, PA 51213.

INTERNATIONAL POETS' SHRINE
Founder-Director: Dr. Henry Picola, 1060 N. St. Andrews Place, Hollywood, CA 90038; Japanese Representative: Keiko Manago; Far East Representative: Amado M. Yuzon; Representative for France: R. Dion Levesque; Art Director: Dr. Marjorie Sharp Carter; Corresponding Secretary: James Glackin.

INTERNATIONAL WRITING PROGRAM
Director: Paul Engle, The University of Iowa, Iowa City, Iowa 52240.

Thirty-five years ago Paul Engle began the still existent Iowa University Writer's Workshop. During that time he raised more than one million dollars to enable writers to go to Iowa to write and study. The fame of the program has spread across the world and writers from such places as Nigeria, Romania, Israel, Chile, Korea, Ghana, Taiwan and India have attended sessions. Some of the noted authors who have attended the program are Anthony Hecht, Robert Bly, Jane Cooper, W.D. Snodgrass and Flannery O'Connor.

IOWA POETRY ASSOCIATION (see Article X)
President: Mrs. Eleanora Miller, 208 South Church Street, Leon, IA 50144; First Vice President: Max S. Barker, 509 N. 16th Street, Marshalltown, IA 50158; Second Vice President: Gloria A. Martin, 829 26th Avenue, Council Bluffs, IA 51501; Secretary: Jauvanta M. Walker, 3620 Story Street, Ames, IA 50010; Treasurer: Lucille E. Morgan, 2325 61st Street, Des Moines, IA 50311.

IOWA POETRY DAY ASSOCIATION
Director: Mrs. Margaret J. Heinrich, 2614 East Avenue N.E., Cedar Rapids, IA.

Iowa Poetry Day Association observes 15 October as National Poetry Day. An annual meeting is held on or near this day, on which the State Governor of Iowa extends the Governor's Proclamation in observance of National Poetry Day.

KANSAS AUTHORS CLUB
State President: Sister Emmanuela O'Malley, Asst. Professor of English, Marymount College, Salina, KS 67401.

KOKOMO POETRY CIRCLE (see article VI)
President: Mrs. Barry Peterson; Secretary: Mrs. Emily Spindler, 1418 West Jefferson Street, Kokomo, IN 46901.

LAKELAND POETRY WORKSHOP
Director: Dr. Ethel Walker Jacobsen, 810 East Bella Vista, Apt. 203, Lakeland, FL 33801; Chairman: Dr. Leona Will Caldwell.

The Workshop, organized in 1966, is made up of a group of dedicated poets who meet once a month to read their poems. Members offer constructive criticism before a poem is sent out for publication. Meetings are open to the public.

LARAMORE RADER POETRY GROUP
President: Maylen Newby Pierce, 300 Mendoza Avenue, Apt. 4, Coral Gables, FL 33134; Secretary: Amelia Lummis, 3800 LeJeune Road, Coral Gables, FL 33134.

The first meeting of this Group met at the home of Vivian Yeiser Laramore to study poetry in 1931. Since then it has met every third Tuesday of the month without fail. Members include graduate students and 110 top writers of the South U.S.A. Large poetry festivals have been sponsored for the last seven years and since 1970 a World Poetry Week (10th–17th October) has also taken place. Poetry readings take place in most of the bigger libraries in Dade County and guest poets of renown are invited to participate. The Group is affiliated to the Academy of American Poets.

LEAGUE OF MINNESOTA POETS
President: Norman R. Boe, 131 Nineteenth Avenue North, South St. Paul, MN 55075.

LONG ISLAND WRITERS
President: Mrs. Muriel Von Weiss, 30 Skidmore Place, Valley Streem, NY 11581.

THE MACDOWELL COLONY, INC.
General Director: Conrad S. Spohnholz, Peterborough, NH 03358.

MAINE POETRY DAY ASSOCIATION (see article VII)
Executive Secretary: James Edwin Trott, D.V.S., P.O. Box 143, Yarmouth, ME 04096.

MANUSCRIPT CLUB OF LOS ANGELES
Program Chairman: Frances I. Nauman, 1100 South Ninth Street, Alhambra, CA 91801.

MIDWEST FEDERATION OF CHAPARRAL POETS
National Director: Lucille E. Klemmack, 3447 S. Garfield Avenue, Minneapolis, MN 55408.

This federation includes over 30 states of the Midwest U.S.A. Each state observes a semi-annual meeting of members, a spring meeting and an autumn meeting. A journal of poems, Midwest Chaparral, is published semi-annually.

MIDWEST FEDERATION OF CHAPARRAL POETS – MINNESOTA CHAPTER
Lucille E. Klemmack, 3447 S. Garfield Avenue, Minneapolis, MN 55408.

MISSISSIPPI POETRY SOCIETY
President: Mrs. Winifred Hamrick Farrar, 2322 36th Street, Meridian, MS 39301; Recording Secretary & Treasurer: Miss Goldie Jane Feldman, 765 Avalon Road, Jackson, MS 39206.

MISSOURI STATE COUNCIL OF THE ARTS
Executive Director: Mrs. Frances Poteet, Suite 213, 7933 Clayton Road, St. Louis, MO 63117.

MODERN POETRY ASSOCIATION
Secretary & Editor: Henry Rago, 1018 North State Street, Chicago 10, IL.

This association was founded in 1946 as a non-profit making corporation to sponsor the continuation of Poetry Magazine, a monthly publication founded in 1912. It holds annual meetings in Chicago.

MORGANTOWN POETRY SOCIETY
President: Mrs. Melba Dungey, 101 Jones Avenue, Morgantown, WV; Secretary: Mrs. Ethel Rittenhouse, 449 White Avenue, Morgantown, WV 26505; Vice President: Mrs. Georgia Heaster, Rt. 7, Morgantown, WV; Treasurer: Miss Kimberley Dunham, 673 Bellaire Drive, Morgantown, WV.

NATIONAL LEAGUE OF AMERICAN PEN WOMEN, INC.
1300 17th Street, NW, Washington, DC 20036.

National Executive Board 1972–74 – President: Helen Lakin Trueheart; Recording Secretary: Charlotte R. Budd; Corresponding Secretary: Louise A. Baldwin; Treasurer: Orpha B. Russell; Librarian: Seletha A. Brown; Editor 'The Pen Woman': Lee M. Waldrop.

NATIONAL LEAGUE OF AMERICAN PEN WOMEN – ARIZONA STATE
President: Frances Nelon Cole, 1701 E. Cinnabar, Phoenix, AZ 85020.

NATIONAL LEAGUE OF AMERICAN PEN WOMEN – POETRY WORKSHOP OF CORAL GABLES BRANCH
Chairman: Dorothy Bechhold, 1100 Sorolla Avenue, Coral Gables, FL 33134.

NATIONAL LEAGUE OF AMERICAN PEN WOMEN – MANTTOON BRANCH
President: Stella Craft Tremble, 902 10th Street, Charleston, IL 61920.

NATIONAL LEAGUE OF AMERICAN PEN WOMEN – NEW MEXICO CHAPTER
President: Mrs. Henry Mullin, 1140 Alameda Road, NW, Albuquerque, NM 87107.

NATIONAL POETRY DAY COMMITTEE (see Article XIII)
National Director: Dr. Frances Clark Handler, 1110 North Venetian Drive, Miami Beach, FL 33139.

This is an organization of poets who are seeking to secure the annual observance on October 15th of a National Poetry Day. It sponsors an annual poetry contest and maintains a library of 1,000 volumes. It publishes a monthly Newsletter and a Yearly book of Selected Poems. It is affiliated with the Florida State Poetry Society, Inc. and holds a convention or meeting every year.

THE NEW ENGLAND POETRY CIRCUIT
See Connecticut Poetry Circuit and Northern New England Poetry Circuit.

THE NEW ENGLAND POETRY CLUB
President: Victor Howes; Vice President: Martin Robbins; Treasurer: Joseph Cohen; Secretary: Jean Harper, 43A Joy Street, Boston, MA 02114; Membership Chairman: Mrs. Kinereth Gensler, 45 Gale Road, Belmont, MA 02178.

NEW JERSEY POETRY SOCIETY, INC. – DELAWARE VALLEY POETS CHAPTER
President: Ms. Kitty Druck, 13 Penlaw Road, Lawrenceville, NJ 08648.

NEW JERSEY POETRY SOCIETY, INC. – LEAVES OF GRASS CHAPTER
President: Geraldine C. Little, 519 Jacksonville Road, Mt. Holly, NJ 08060.

NEW JERSEY POETRY SOCIETY, INC. – MUSCONETCONG CHAPTER
Secretary: Miss Florence Firth, 685 Belvidere Road, Phillipsburg, NJ 08865.

THE NEW ORLEANS POETRY FORUM
Directors: Vaughn L. Duhamel, 3404 Louisiana Avenue Pkwy., New Orleans, LA 70125 and Lee Grue, 828 Lesseps Street, New Orleans, LA 70117.

THE NEW YORK POETRY CIRCUIT
Coordinator: Robert Koch, Dean of University College, Harkness Hall, University of Rochester, River Campus Station, Rochester, NY 14627.

THE NEW YORK POETRY FORUM (see Article XIV)
Director and President: Miss Dorothea Neale, The New York Poetry Forum, Inc., P.O. Box 855, Madison Square Station, 149 East 23rd Street, New York, NY 10010; Secretary: Louis Warter; Vice President: Jeffrey Escoffier.

NEW YORK POETS COOPERATIVE
Barbara Holland, 14 Morton Street, New York, NY 10014.

NEW WRITERS GROUP
c/o A.G. Sobin, English Department, University, Wichita, KS 67208.

NORTH CAROLINA POETRY CIRCUIT
Ronald Bayes, Laurinburg, NC 28372.

NORTH CAROLINA POETRY SOCIETY – STATESVILLE BRANCH
President: Eleanor T. McLaughlin, 304 Gregory Road, Statesville, NC 28677.

NORTHERN NEW ENGLAND POETRY CIRCUIT — Does not exist at present but may be revised in 1975.

NORTHWEST CONNECTICUT VISITING POETS PROGRAM
Director: William DeVoti, Falls Village, CT 06031.

THE NORTHWEST POETRY CIRCUIT
Director, Division of Continuing Education, University of Oregon, 1736 Moss Street, Eugene, OR 97403.

OHIO POETS ASSOCIATION
Richard Snyder, RD 4, Box 131, Ashland, OH 44805.

OVERSEAS CHINESE POETS CLUB
President: Mr. Loo Koon Lai, 54 Catherne St., 15J, New York, NY.

OZARK WRITERS & ARTISTS GUILD
President: Mrs. Florence Rupert Wray, 1110 Valley View Drive, Fayetteville, AR 72701.

PACIFIC NORTHWEST POETS
Director: Mrs. Beth Bentley, 8762 25th Place NE, Seattle, WA 98115.

PAN
P.O.B. 24C45, Los Angeles, CA 90024.
   Pan is a group of poets working in Los Angeles. There are twenty members to date.

PASADENA WRITERS' CLUB (see Article XV)
President: Lillian M. Keahey, 5403 Bartlett Avenue, San Gabriel, CA 91776; Secretary: Florence Duncan Long, 85 N. Madison Avenue, No. 27, Pasadena, CA 91101; Treasurer: Coral Nilsson; 1st Vice President (Program): Willard Hyatt; 2nd Vice President (Publicity): Dorothy Keesling.

PEN AND BRUSH CLUB
President: Mrs. Louise Hausen, 713 South 34th Street, Terre Haute, IN 47803.

PENN LAUREL POETS OF PHILADELPHIA
President: Emma Wood, 27 W. Mt. Pleasant Avenue, Philadelphia, PA 19119.

PENNSYLVANIA POETRY SOCIETY — BEAVER COUNTY BRANCH
Corr. Secretary: Miss Catherine Jasper, 1526 5th Avenue, Beaver Falls, PA 15010.

THE PENROCK WRITERS
President: Mrs. Dolores Clines, 424 McKinley Street, Waupun, WI 53963.

PHILADELPHIA Y POETRY CENTER
Staff Director: Stephen Parker, 401 South Broad Street, Philadelphia, PA 19417.

PHILLIS WHEATLEY LITERARY CLUB
President: Mrs. V. Blackmon, 21 Enfield Avenue, Montclair, NJ.

POETRY AND PHILOSOPHY GROUP
President: Mrs. Jeanne Robert Foster, 1762 Albany Street, Schenectady, NY 12304.

THE POETRY CENTER, SAN FRANCISCO STATE UNIVERSITY
Director: Kathleen Fraser, 1600 Holloway Avenue, San Francisco, CA 94132; Secretary: Barbara Wright.

THE POETRY CENTER, 92nd STREET YM–YWHA
Director: June Fortess, 92nd Street YM–YWHA, Lexington Avenue at 92nd Street, New York, NY 10028.

POETRY CIRCUIT OF OHIO
Director: Robert W. Daniel, Box 247, Gambier, OH 43022.

POETRY CLUB
P.O. Box 279, Clinton, AR 72031.

POETRY FELLOWSHIP OF MAINE (see Article XVI)
President: Barbara Bond, 89 Ferry Road, Saco, ME 04072.

POETRY FORUM
Mark Soifer, 633 Wood Street, Vineland, NJ 08360.

POETRY FORUM OF VIRGINIA COMMONWEALTH UNIVERSITY
Vice Chairman: Mrs. Harry A. Wolfe, 118 Seneca Road, Richmond, VA 23226.

POETRY SOCIETY OF ALASKA, INC.
President: David Dillman, Box 433, Juneau, AK 99801.

THE POETRY SOCIETY OF AMERICA (see Article XVII)
Executive Secretary: Charles A. Wagner, 15 Gramercy Park South, New York, NY 10003.

POETRY SOCIETY OF BEDFORD
Mrs. John W. Sale, Route 5, Bedford, VA 24523.

POETRY SOCIETY OF GEORGIA
President: Rev. M. Tom Dunlap, 65 Cronwell Road, Savannah, GA 31404.

POETRY SOCIETY OF SAN ANTONIO, TEXAS
President: Mrs. Stella Woodall, 3915 S.W. Military Drive, San Antonio, TX 78211.

POETRY SOCIETY OF SOUTH CAROLINA
President: Col. John Robert Doyle, Jr., The Citadel, Charleston, SC 29409.

THE POETRY SOCIETY OF SOUTHERN CALIFORNIA
Mrs. Irene Gaertner, 338 N. Kenmore Avenue, Los Angeles, CA 90004.

POETRY SOCIETY OF TEXAS – AUSTIN CHAPTER
Secretary: Mrs. Christine Stedman, Ambassador Apartments, No. 316, 407 W. 18th Street, Austin, TX 78701.

POETRY SOCIETY OF VIRGINIA
President: Mr. Louis C. Carlton, 3213 Seminary Avenue, Richmond, VA 23227.

POETRY WORKSHOP OF THE LYNCHBURG WOMAN'S CLUB
Chairman: Dr. Roberta D. Cornelius, Parkmont Apartments, Rivermont Avenue, Lynchburg, VA 24503.

POETRY WORKSHOP OF THE STATE UNIVERSITY OF IOWA
Director: John Leggett, University of Iowa, Iowa City, IA 52240.

POETS AND PATRONS, INC. (see Article XVIII)
President: Evelyn Schmidt, 4205 Madison Avenue, Brookfield, IL 60513.

POETS AND WRITERS, INC.
Director: Galen Williams, 201 West 54 Street, New York, NY 10019.

Poets & Writers, Inc. is a non-profit, tax exempt corporation organized for educational and literary purposes. Poets & Writers compiled and published 'A Directory of American Poets', a unique reference work. The Directory provides a comprehensive listing of poets living and working in the United States. The primary purpose of the Directory is to assist in locating the writers for readings, workshops, and other assignments. It is, however, a useful reference work for libraries, book and magazine publishers, and poets themselves. "Coda", a supplement to the Directory, presents up-dated and additional information.

POETS' CLUB OF CHICAGO (see Article XIX)
President: Gladys M. Cook, 1628 W. Touhy Avenue, Chicago, IL 60626; Secretary and Contest Chairman: Mary Torode, 1541 N. Avers Avenue, Chicago, IL 60651.

POETS STUDY CLUB
President: Mrs. Louise Nelson, 302 N. 3rd Street, Marshall, IL 62441.

POETS TAPE EXCHANGE (see Article XX)
Founder and Director: Frances Brandon Neighbours, 109 Twin Oak Drive, Lynchburg, VA 24502.

PURCHASE POETS CLUB
President: Tom Perkins, c/o Mid-Continent Bible College, 502 N. 15th Street, Mayfield, KY 42066.

RIDGE POETRY ASSOCIATION
President: Mr. Michael Miller, Fedhaven, Lake Wales, FL 33853.

RIMERS OF TUCSON, ARIZONA
Mrs. Irene Taylor, 2246 East Mabel Street, Tucson, AZ 85719.

ROANOKE POETRY SOCIETY
President: Mr. R. Irving Broughton, 1117 2nd Street, Roanoke, VA 24061.

THE ROCHESTER POETRY SOCIETY
President: Mrs. Dale Davis, 155 S. Main Street, Fairport, NY 14450;
Corresponding Secretary: Mrs. Carol Oliver, 24 Pine Cone Road, Pittsford,
NY 14534.

ROCHESTER WORLD POETRY DAY COMMITTEE
Assistant Directors: Larry and Duverne Farsace and Vera Bishop Konrick,
P.O. Box 1101, Rochester, NY 14603.

ROUND TABLE POETS OF FORT SMITH
President: Kathleen Knox, 6510 Meadowcliff, Fort Smith, AR 72901.

RUTH STEPHEN POETRY CENTER
Director: Lois Shelton, 1086 North Highland, Tucson, AZ 85719.

ST. LOUIS POETRY CENTER (see Article XXI)
President: Jon Jonson, 223 Tiffen Street, St. Louis, MO 63135.

ST. PETERSBURG POETRY ASSOCIATION
President: Miss Nan Hunt, 775 123rd Avenue, Treasure Island, FL 33706.

SHELLEY SOCIETY OF NEW YORK
President: Annette B. Feldman; Vice President: Dorothea Neale, 221 East
28th Street, New York, NY 10016.
   This society was founded in November of 1973.

THE SOCIETY OF MIDLAND AUTHORS
L. Ellsworth Laflin, Jr., 205 N. Mayflower, Lake Forest, IL 60045.

SOUTH AND WEST, INC.
President: Sue Abbott Boyd, 2601 South Phoenix, Fort Smith, AR 72901.

SOUTHWEST MICHIGAN WRITERS SOCIETY
Co-Chairman: Gwendolyn A. Niles, 706 Pipestone, Benton Harbor, MI.

SPOKESMAN POETS
Director: The Rev. Dr. Daniel J. Rogers, Department of English, Loras
College, Dubuque, IA 52001.

STATE POETRY SOCIETY OF IOWA
President: Dorothy B. North, Box 218, Plainfield, IA 50660.

STATEN ISLAND POETRY SOCIETY
President: Ted Lovington Jr., 25 Washington Place, Staten Island, NY 10302; Secretary: Louise Wright, 786 Brighton Avenue, Staten Island, NY 10301.

TENNESSEE POETRY CIRCUIT
Director: Prof. Paul Ramsey, Dept. of English, The University of Chattanooga, Chattanooga, TN 37401.

TEXAS COUNCIL FOR THE PROMOTION OF POETRY (see article XXII)
State Chairman: Dr. Marvin Davis Winsett, 3936 Colgate Street, Dallas, TX 75225.

UNIVERSITY OF ARIZONA POETRY CENTER
Director: Lois Shelton, 1086 North Highland Avenue, Tucson, AZ 85719; Secretary: Miss Phyllis Gibbs.

VACHEL LINDSAY ASSOCIATION (see Article XXIII)
Treasurer: Mrs. A.A. Hoffman, 2428 Whittier Avenue, Springfield, IL 62404; President: Robert D. Furry.

VERDIGRIS VALLEY WRITERS
President: Mrs. Ossie Tranbarger; Vice-President: Mrs. Valorie Smith; Secretary and Treasurer: Miss Ethel Bretches, 213 W. Locust, Independence, KS 67301.

WASHINGTON POETRY CENTER
Director: Roderick Jellema, c/o Department of English, University of Maryland, College Park, MD 20742.

WASHINGTON STATE POETRY FOUNDATION, INC.
5727 35th NE, Seattle, WA 98105.

WAUSAU POETRY SOCIETY
Founder: Mrs. Anne Marie Stubbe, 905 South 6th Avenue, Wausau, WI 54401.

WILMINGTON POETRY SOCIETY AND DELAWARE WRITERS, INC.
President: Mr. David Hudson, P.O. Box 1005, Wilmington, DE 19899.

WISCONSIN ARTS COUNCIL
Secretary: Jane Tainter, P.O. Box 3356, Madison, WI 53704.

WISCONSIN ARTS FOUNDATION AND COUNCIL
President: Mr. William Cary, P.O. Box 90191, Milwaukee, WI 53202.

WISCONSIN REGIONAL WRITERS ASSOCIATION
President: Dorothy House Guilday, Box 146, Rhinelander, WI 54501;
Secretary: Helen Fehrbach, 193 W. 4th Street, Menasha, WI 54952;
Treasurer: Hilbert Mueller, 2630 N. 8th Street, Sheboygan, WI 53081.

WORLD POETRY DAY
World Director: Emma S. Wood, 27 W. Mt. Pleasant Avenue, Philadelphia,
PA 19119.

WORLD POETS RESOURCE CENTER, INC. (see Article XXIV)
Founder & President: Lou Lutour, 1270 5th Avenue, New York, NY 10029;
Executive Secretary: Carol Hill.

WRITER'S ASSOCIATION OF THE ITHACA AREA
President: Mrs. Paulene Rebeles, 106 E. State Street, Ithaca, NY 14850.

APPENDIX D

POETRY SOCIETIES AND RELATED ORGANISATIONS IN THE U.K. AND REPUBLIC OF IRELAND

ABERDEEN LITERARY SOCIETY
Hon. Secretary: Mr. C. Milton, 54 Tillydrone Ave., Aberdeen, AB2 2TN Scotland.

ALEXANDRIA BURNS CLUB
Secretary: Mr. J. Barton, 126 Middleton Street, Alexandria, Dumbarton, Scotland.

ANON
Secretary: Mrs. E. Labrom, 131 Ridge Road, Sutton, Surrey.

This is a group which organizes regular public poetry readings, where poets are invited to read their work. In addition to these readings, informal private meetings are held to discuss various aspects of poetry, as well as planning future programmes. The emphasis at both types of meeting is on contemporary poetry, but of course it is impossible to discuss the work of modern writers without relating it to the past.

The public readings are usually held in a room over a pub, the private meetings in the houses of members. Financial support is received from the local Arts Council and grants for some of the readings from the London Poetry Secretariat. Without this assistance, the society could not function. Collections are made after public readings instead of charging for admission. Membership cards are sold at 20p. each.

Audiences at the public readings vary between 18 and 50 in number, and usually average 25-30. At the private meetings, the 'hard core' membership comprises about eight people. The group was actually formed two and a half years ago.

APOLLO SOCIETY
16 Eccleston Square, London SW1.

The Apollo Society membership is confined to one hundred poets, musicians and readers. An average of 25 recitals a year are given in such places as the Recital Room of the Royal Festival Hall, London, and the festivals at Edinburgh, Stratford, King's Lynn, Bath, York, Devon, The Hague; also schools, universities, music clubs, etc.

The aim of the Apollo Society is to present poetry and music side by side so that the one art illuminates or contrasts with the other, to their mutual advantage.

ARTS COUNCIL OF GREAT BRITAIN
105 Piccadilly, London W1V OAU. Chairman: Patrick Gibson; Secretary-General: Sir Hugh Willatt.

ARTS COUNCIL OF NORTHERN IRELAND
Bedford House, Bedford Street, Belfast BT2 7FX, Ireland. President: Captain Peter Montgomery; Director: Kenneth Jamison; Assistant Director/Literature & Education: Michael Longley.

ARVON FOUNDATION LTD.
Administrator: Mr. Peter F. Mason, Totleigh Barton Manor, Sheepwash, Beaworthy, Devon.

Arvon is an educational venture devised, directed and conducted entirely by artists of one sort or another. Its aim is to afford opportunity to those who so wish to meet and, in a completely informal situation, to consult and work with artists. The method Arvon employs is simply to arrange for small groups of students to live for a number of days at the Foundations's Centre in the company of two artists (musicians, poets, painters, playwrights, etc.). From this encounter with practising artists, the student gains some knowledge of the excitements and rigours of working full time with the imagination.

ATTINGHAM WRITERS
Secretary: Mary Barnett, 9 Meadow View Road, Whitchurch, Shropshire.

BASILDON POETRY GROUP
Secretary: Gillian Fisher, 54 Beaufort Road, Billericay, CM12 9JL, Essex.

THE BIRMINGHAM CENTRAL LITERARY ASSOCIATION
Hon. Secretary: J.H. Edge, "Crossmeads", Vicarage Hill, Tamworth-in-Arden, Warwickshire.

The Birmingham Central Literary Association was founded in 1856. It is now an affiliated Society of the Birmingham and Midland Institute. Meetings are held at the Institute on alternate Thursday evenings from October to March, a Shakespeare Celebration Dinner is held annually, and other activities take place.

The Central Literary Magazine has been issued regularly since 1873. It is printed by the Oxford University Press. At present it is published annually, and is devoted entirely to contributions from *members only* and it contains *Poetry*, short stories and articles; also a record of the activities of the Association.

Each year one of our meetings is an Evening with the Poets, and the writing and appreciation of poetry is an important part of the activities.

BIRMINGHAM POETRY CENTRE
Secretary: Valerie Leon, 158 Long Nuke Road, Northfield, Birmingham B31.

BLACKHEATH POETRY SOCIETY
Secretary: Mrs. Fiona Gardner, Applewell, 7 Manorbrook, Blackheath, London, SE3 9AW.

BLACKPOOL WRITERS' CIRCLE
Secretary: Mr. Frank Byrne, 55 Preston Old Road, Blackpool, Lancs.

BOLTON WRITERS' CIRCLE
Oak Room, Deansgate YMCA, Bolton.

The Bolton Writers' Circle has been in existence exactly six years. Quite a number of the members write poetry. The circle is small but enthusiastic and meets every other Thursday evening in the Oak Room, Deansgate YMCA of Bolton. Lectures and talks are given by well known people such as Phoebe Hesketh and anyone is welcome to attend.

BOURNEMOUTH WRITERS' CIRCLE
Secretary: Mrs. E. Denton, 51 Salisbury Road, Fordingbridge, Hants.

BRADFORD WRITERS' CIRCLE
Secretary: Mrs. W. St. Q. Willcock, 38 Grove House Road, Bolton Road, Bradford 2, Yorks.

BRENTWOOD WRITERS' CIRCLE
Hon. Secretary: Mrs. I. P. Moore, 5 Chestnut Grove, Brentwood, Essex.

THE BROWNING SOCIETY OF LONDON
Hon. Secretary: Mr. Roy Bolton, The Browning Society of London, London N14.

The New York Browning Society, aided by the London Society and many other groups launched an appeal for $77,000 to restore the historic Browning apartment in Casa Guidi. Visitors to Florence will be pleased to hear that 90 per cent of the amount has been raised and that the home of Robert and Elizabeth Barrett Browning from 1848 to 1861 is once again open to the public. The eight room apartment is on the second floor of the 15th century palazzo in the piazza S. Felice near the Pitti Palace.

CALDER VALLEY POETS
President, Hon. Secretary & Treasurer: Mrs. Maud Fearnley, 3 Callis Wood Bottom, Charlestown, Hebden Bridge, HX7 6PY, Yorks.

THE CAMDEN POETRY GROUP
President: A. Stanley King; Chairman: Rita Spurr, 7 Netherhall Gardens, Hampstead, NW3 5RN.

The Camden Poetry Group originated from a selection of poets in the Borough of Camden who were invited to present readings of their own poetry at two successive Camden Festivals. A number of these poets then wished to remain together and have been meeting regularly over the past three years. This is a small group of dedicated and creative poetry lovers, the majority of professional status. A collection of the Group's work is now published in an anthology of 'Visual Poems', entitled "Slide into Poetry", edited by Rita Spurr. 40pp. price 40p. plus 5p. postage, obtainable from the above address.

CARDIFF ARTS CENTRE
Market Road, Canton, Cardiff.

CARDIFF WRITERS' CIRCLE
President: Mr. W. Beynon; Hon. Secretary: Mrs. Margery Humble, 20 West Rise, Llanishen, Cardiff, Wales.

CENTRE 17 (The Walthamstow Poetry Group)
Chingford Community Centre, Friday Hill, Chingford, London E4.
  The Walthamstow Poetry Group is known as Centre 17 which is also the title of the magazine it publishes. At present the group meets on the first Wednesday of each month at 7:30 p.m. in the Chingford Community Centre at the above address.

CHICHESTER POETS CO-OPERATIVE
Secretary: John Bennett, 44 Little Breach, Chichester.

CINQUE PORT POETS SOCIETY
Chairman: Robert Denis Smith, Palm Beach 17, Seaview Road, Greatstone, Kent.

THE COOL WEB
Organizers: Hugh Dickson, 4a Colinette Road, London SW15 and David Brierley, 1 Zenobia Mansions, London W14.
  The Cool Web is a platform for good verse from all sources to be presented in a relaxed atmosphere. A small group of experienced readers, all professional actors, select a programme and are joined by a well-known poet. The guest poet is invited to use one part of the evening in any way he likes: to read his own poems or other people's, to make critical, political or polemical points, to involve the actors, or to integrate with the rest of the programme.
  50 successful programmes have already taken place. Some time is also set aside for readings from the audience.

COSMIC MEDIA (formerly PM Poetry Events)
D. Cunliffe, 1 Spring Bank, Salesbury, Blackburn, BB1 9EU, Lancs.
  Cosmic Media does gigs, street shows and open events in the North West. Poets associated with open readings at Amamus Bookshop are Ian Ross, Chris Broadhead, Frank Riding, Tina Morris, Nigel Gray, Euleen Sharples, Neil Sowerby, Keith Sowerby, Nigel Thompson, Renee Duckworth.

COUNTESTHORPE COMMUNITY COLLEGE POETRY WORKSHOP
Organizing Tutor: Mrs. Emma Tindall, 15 Orange Street, South Wigston, Leicester.

COVENTRY WRITERS' GROUP
Hon. Secretary: P.L. Moore, 38 Biggin Hall Crescent, Coventry; Chairman: Mr. H. Jones, 267 Allesley Old Road, Coventry.

DERBY POETRY SOCIETY
Hon. Secretary: Mrs. I.C. Danson, 63 Ferrers Way, Darley Abbey, DE3 2BB, Derby.
  The Circle was formed in 1928. The President is Miss Teresa Hooley.

Meetings are held on the second Friday of every month, except August, usually in the Prince Charlie Room, Derby Art Gallery, at 7.30 pm. The subscription is £1 per annum; Visitors, 10p each meeting.

Meetings comprise: Talks, Poetry Competitions, Poetry Workshop (for criticism and mutual help in the writing of poetry), Members' Evening, and an Afternoon School held in conjunction with the WEA in St. Helen's House, Derby. Poetry Recitals are given occasionally, and various social events arranged. The season begins in September. Visitors are welcome to all meetings.

DUMBARTON BURNS CLUB
President: Mr. George S. Begg; Hon. Secretary: Mr. T. Wilson, 111 Brucehill Road, Dumbarton.

THE DUNEDIN SOCIETY
Hon. Secretary: William MacLellan, 104 Hill Street, Glasgow, Scotland.

The Society provides a focal point through which the creative artist in Scotland can find an interested audience. Founded in 1911 to encourage creative arts in Scotland.

EALING WRITERS CIRCLE
Secretary: Mrs. Kathleen Allison, 17 Barn Close, Northolt, Middlesex.

EAST ANGLIAN WRITERS
President: Correlli Barnett, F.R.S.L.; Secretary: Hilda Nickson, Artilda, The Street, Dilham, North Walsham, Norfolk.

Membership is open to writers who have had at least one book published or one play professionally acted and produced. Membership is automatically open to poets whose work has been published in book form.

EASTERN ARTS ASSOCIATION
30 Station Road, Cambridge, CB1 2JH.

EAST MIDLANDS ARTS ASSOCIATION
1 Frederick Street, Loughborough, Leicestershire, LE11 3BH.

EDINBURGH POETRY CLUB
Hon. Secretary: Douglas J. Fraser, 2 Keith Terrace, Edinburgh, EH4 3NJ

THE ENGLISH ASSOCIATION
29 Exhibition Road, London S.W.7.

The object of the English Association is to promote the knowledge and appreciation of the English language and of English Literature, and to uphold the standards of English Writing and speech.

The Association holds conferences, lectures, and poetry recitals, and publishes a journal 'English' three times a year; the Presidential Address, The Year's Work in English Studies, and Essays & Studies annually; and also other books, papers and leaflets to further its objects.

ESSEX POETRY AND PROSE SOCIETY
Secretary: S. Cutress, The Lodge, Great Ruffins, Wickham Bishops, Witham, Essex.

FYLDE POETS
Chairman: Miss Olive Dewhurst, 41 Ormont Avenue, Cleveleys, Nr. Blackpool, Lancs.; Secretary: Mrs. Potter, 38 Manor Drive, Cleveleys.

GOSPORT WRITERS GROUP
Secretary: Mrs. S. Jones, 8 Bury Hall Lane, Gosport.

GREATER LONDON ARTS ASSOCIATION
Garrick House, 27 Southampton Street, London, WC2E 7JL.

GREENWICH POETRY SOCIETY
Secretary: Mrs. Jane Hooppell, 52 Dallin Road, London, SE18 3NX.

The Greenwich Poetry Society was founded in November 1970. It is affiliated to the Greenwich Community Council, and the Woolwich Arts Council. Weekly Meetings take place on Tuesdays, 8-10 pm, Shrewsbury House Community Centre, Bushmoor Crescent, London SE18. No subscription is required. There is only a small membership so far; activities are mainly reading of members' own poems, encouragement of writing, occasionally on a set theme, and discussion.

One duplicated magazine of members' work, called *Dumbdumb*, has been published and there is another in preparation. Members' work only can be accepted. About 300 copies of the first were sold or distributed (mostly sold, locally). Copies available 5p each: stamp appreciated. New members are sought.

GUILDFORD AND WEST SURREY CENTRE OF THE POETRY SOCIETY
President: William Kean Seymour, F.R.S.L.; Hon. Secretary: Mr. Peter Owtram, 14 Busbridge Lane, Godalming, Surrey.

THE GWENT POETRY SOCIETY
Secretary: Mr. John E. Williams, 107 St. Julian's Road, Newport, Mon.

Headquarters of The Gwent Poetry Society are at Dolman Theatre, Kingsway, Newport, Mon. The Society has published their Eighteenth Anthology to which 26 members contributed. Co-founders of the society are F. Platts and John E. Williams.

HAROLD HIKINS FAMOUS MERSEYSIDE ARTS ASSOCIATION POETRY CIRCUS
Mr. Harold Hikins, 14 Harringay Ave., Liverpool, L18 1JE.

'Harold Hikins' Famous Merseyside Arts Association Poetry Circus' was formed in April 1970 as a promotion of the MAA. Booking is made through the MAA. The Circus is available to local societies and institutions, to present an evening of poetry and music. No charge is made to the organization making the booking, and the performers' expenses are met from the funds of the MAA. The performers are drawn from a panel of some

20 Merseyside poets and about 10 musicians, all experienced in this kind of presentation. The normal team is four poets and one musician.

The Circus has made about 30 appearances to date, at venues varying from public halls and theatres to village shows and public houses. In this way, poetry has been introduced to many audiences who might otherwise disregard it, and the scope for the poets to present their work has been much widened.

HAVANT AND DISTRICT POETS SOCIETY
Secretary: Mr. P.I. Edwardes, Kenilworth, Portsdown Hill Road, Cosham, Portsmouth.

HAVANT ARTS COUNCIL
C.H. Lawrence, Esq., Brambledene, New Cut, Havant Road, Hayling Island.

HULL ARTS CENTRE
Spring Street, Hull, HU2 8BR.

The Hull Arts Centre no longer has regular poetry writers workshops but do have a programme of readings by local and national poets. Poetry activities are supervised by Roy McGregor Hastie who is a lecturer in English at Hull College of Education.

HUMBERSIDE POETRY SOCIETY
Secretary: Peter Fenton, 1 Beech Grove, Marshall Street, Kingston-upon-Hull.

INNER CIRCLE POETRY/MEDIA GROUP
Secretary: S.H. Sneyd, 4 Nowell Place, Almondbury, Huddersfield, HD5 8PB.

The Inner Circle, started December 1969, aims to promote the live presentation of poetry and other media (ie, experimental music, folk music, improvisational theatre, blues, etc.) in Huddersfield, both by encouraging local poets and other creative people to do live presentations of their work, and by inviting guests from outside. It meets the first Tuesday of every month, currently at the Plough Hotel, Westgate, Huddersfield, as well as arranging occasional events elsewhere and exchange visits by the members to other such groups.

The Group receives a small grant from the Yorkshire Arts Association towards the cost of bringing guest poets to Huddersfield, and took part in the Huddersfield Arts Festival earlier this year. Members of the group were also responsible for launching a primarily local-based poetry magazine, *Ludds' Mill*.

INSTITUTE OF CONTEMPORARY ARTS LTD.
Nash House, 12 Carlton House Terrace, London SW1. President: Sir Roland Penrose, C.B.E.; General Manager: Joe Aveline.

Since the foundation of the Institute in 1947 it has consistently given poetry readings by distinguished living poets and by young lesser known poets. In addition, there has been an uninterrupted flow of lectures and discussions on poets and on literary criticism.

The ICA's main contribution to poetry in 1973 was *Poetry International* held at the I.C.A. June 25th to 28th and at the Queen Elizabeth Hall from June 29th to June 30th. Poetry International comprised of numerous lectures and poetry readings by poets such as Richard Eberhart, Allen Ginsberg, Hugh MacDiarmid, W.H. Auden and Basil Bunting.

INTERNATIONAL SOCIETY OF LITERATURE
109 Main Street, Burley-In-Wharfedale, West Yorkshire.

The International Society of Literature is a fellowship of Writers and Poets. It is a member of the Poetry Society and the Society of Authors. Editor: C.L. Riley; Ass. Secretary: Christine Parrington; Hon. Overseas Secretary: Mrs. P. Fussell, Waerenga-A-Hika, New Zealand; Finance Secretary: Miss E. Gunson, 40 Norman Ave., Eccleshill, Bradford 2.

IRISH ARTS COUNCIL
70 Merrion Square, Dublin 2, Ireland.

JARROW AND HEBBURN POETRY GROUP
Tony Henderson, Esq., 31 Burn Heads Road, Hebburn, Co. Durham.

KEATS-SHELLEY MEMORIAL ASSOCIATION
Hon. Secretary: Mrs. C.M. Gee, Keats House, Keats Grove, Hampstead, London, NW3 2RR.

Preserves the house, 26 Piazza di Spagna, Rome, where Keats died, and cares for the graves of Keats, Shelley, Severn and Trelawny in the Protestant Cemetery. This Memorial, beautiful in itself and situated by the famous Spanish Steps, exhibits, in the rooms inhabited by Keats, manuscripts, first editions and relics of Keats, Shelley, Byron and Leigh Hunt, all poets who at one time or another lived in Italy. There is also a fine library of over 10,000 volumes available free to students and to Friends.

The Association publishes annually their Bulletin, a literary illustrated magazine containing articles or research or critism on the Romantic poets and their circle. This is distributed free to Friends and can be otherwise obtained from the Memorial House in Rome, from Keats House, Hampstead, London NW3 2RR; or Longfield Cottage, Longfield Dr., London SW14, or by order from any bookseller.

KENT AND SUSSEX POETRY SOCIETY
Hon. Secretary: Mrs. Iris Munns, 40 St. James' Road, Tunbridge Wells.

KILMARNOCK BURNS CLUB
Secretary & Treasurer: Miss M. Caldwell, Mid Gartocharn Farm, Gartocharn, By Alexandria, Dunbartonshire. President: Dr. John Galloway.

LANCASHIRE AUTHORS' ASSOCIATION
Hon. General Secretary: Mr. J.R. Sutcliffe, "Sea Winds", 22 Lune View, Knott End on Sea, Fylde Coast, Lancs. FY6 OAG.

The Association was founded in 1909 to promote the welfare of

Lancashire Literature, History and Fellowship. Meetings are held quarterly in the various Lancashire towns, where members have an opportunity of visiting places of local literary and historic interest, listen to lectures and talks, and take part in reading their own and fellow members' work.

The Association's official publication *The Record* is published four times per year, (free to members) and forms a valuable link between members resident in the County and those in other parts of England and overseas. In addition to this a Manuscript Magazine of original poetry and prose is circulated, and members also have access to their own extensive collection of Lancashire books which is housed in the Manchester Central Library.

A number of competitions are held annually for both Standard English Poetry and Prose and Lancashire Dialect Poetry and Prose. Cups and other prizes are awarded, including the "Writer of the Year" Trophy.

Annual Subscription from 1st January 1974— £2 per individual member; £3.50 husband and wife (jointly); 50 pence Juniors (12 to 16 years); £25 Individual life membership.

THE LANCASHIRE POETRY ASSOCIATION
Chairman: Jim Blackburn, 2 Kintore Drive, Great Sankey, Warrington, Lancs.

The Group has a large membership in both Lancashire and Cheshire and continues to hold monthly readings or 'Platforms' where poets and poetesses are invited to read their work to public audiences. The group will travel to give readings to colleges, schools, clubs and associations for expenses and small fee. The travelling group (usually five) is very fluid and is not necessarily the same five each time.

LEEDS POETRY GROUP
Secretary: Mr. Trevor Dickinson, 11 Rutford Ave., Yeadon, Nr. Leeds.

LEICESTER POETRY SOCIETY
President: G.S. Fraser; Chairman: Alan Bates; Secretary: Mrs. E. Tindall, 15 Orange Street, South Wigston, Leicester; Treasurer: Mrs. E. Fowler.

LEICESTER WRITERS CLUB
Secretary: H.L. Watkins, 143 Shanklin Drive, Leicester, LE2 3QG; President: Mrs. B. Taylor.

LINCOLNSHIRE ASSOCIATION
County Centre, Burton Road, Lincoln.

LITERARY SOCIETY OF THE CITY LIT
Stukeley Street, Drury Lane, London WC2. B5 LJ

The first meeting of the Society at the City Lit Centre for Adult Studies was in October 1947 and there have been six meetings a year ever since. Membership is open to all students at The City Lit, the largest centre of adult education in the country. Meetings, on the third Saturday of the month from October to May at 6. pm, consist of lecture followed by discussion.

The opening lecture was delivered by Patric Dickinson, and several other well-known speakers have since appeared on the platform including, Elizabeth Bowen, Richard Church, Christopher Hassall, John Lehmann, Margaret Drabble, Martin Esslin, Stephen Spender, Robert Speaight, Kathleen Raine and Terence Tiller. The aim of the Society as stated on the membership card is to 'bring together in the spirit of fellowship all students interested in literature'.

LONDON WRITER CIRCLE
Hon. General Secretary: Miss M.E. Harris, 308 Lewisham Road, London, SE13 7PA; President: Paul Scott; Chairman: Trevor Allen; Hon. Enrolment Secretary: Mrs. Arda Lacey, 48 Lower Camden, Chislehurst, BR7 5JA, Kent.

The circle offers mutual help among writers of all grades. Lectures at Caxton Hall and study groups, MS Clubs, discussions and competitions are all features of the club. Subscriptions: £2 (town), £1 (country).

LUTON ARTS COUNCIL
Executive Officer of Literature, 200 Barton Road, Luton, Beds.

LUTON WRITERS' GUILD
Secretary: Mick Doherty, 96 Kinross Crescent, Luton, Beds.

MALVERN POETRY CIRCLE
Secretary: Miss H.B. Webber, 7 Davenham Close, Worcester.

MANCHESTER POETRY CENTRE
Director: Professor C.B. Cox, The University, Manchester, M13 9PL

MERSEYSIDE ARTS ASSOCIATION
6 Bluecoat Chambers, School Lane, Liverpool, LI 3BX.

NEW RICHMOND POETRY GROUP
Secretary: Mrs. Margo Laird, 15 Park Court, Hampton Wick, Kingston, Surrey.

1970's POETS GROUP
Secretary: Miss Marcia Andrews, Rose Vale, 40 Robin Hood Lane, Walderslade, Chatham, Kent.

NORTHERN ARTS
31 Bridge Street, Newcastle-Upon-Tyne, NE1 8JY.

NORTH WALES ASSOCIATION FOR THE ARTS
9—11 Wellfield House, Bangor, Caernarvonshire.

NORTH WEST ARTS ASSOCIATION
David Pease, 52 King Street, Manchester, M2 4LY.

NOTTINGHAM POETRY SOCIETY

Secretary: N.E. Findlay, 82 Kentwood Road, Sneiton Dale, Nottingham; Treasurer: Connie M. Ford, M.B.E., 49 Rivermead, West Bridgford, Nottingham.

Meetings are held at the Y.W.C.A. (corner of Shakespeare/Sherwood St.) at 2.45 p.m. on the third Saturday of each month except August. The £1.25 subscription entitles members to receive a copy of *Poetry Nottingham*, the magazine of members' work. Two poetry competitions are held each year, one for members only, with a prize of £2.10 and an Open Competition for Adults and Juniors with prizes of £10 and £5 respectively.

Meetings include talks by well-known poets or authoritative lectures, and talks about their own work by member poets. Other meetings are devoted to Poetry Workshop, where criticism and help can be obtained. It is affiliated to the London Poetry Society.

NOTTINGHAM WRITERS CLUB

President: Mr. Eric Malpass, 216 Breedon Street, Long Eaton, Nottinghamshire; Secretary: Miss Mary Suggitt, 24 Vernon Road, Wilford, Nottingham.

OSWESTRY WRITERS

Secretary: Mrs. B. Leatham Thomas, Rock House, Kinnerley, Oswestry, Shropshire.

OXFORD POETRY GROUP

Hon. Secretary: Miss Kathleen Fison, 327 Woodstock Road, Oxford.

OXFORD WRITERS' CIRCLE

Hon. Secretary: Miss M. Von Kahler, 1 Bainton Road, Oxford.

THE PENMAN CLUB

262 London Road, Westcliff-on-Sea, Essex, SS0 7JG. President: Trevor J. Douglas; General Secretary: Leonard G. Stubbs, F.R.S.A.; Assistant Secretary: John Upton.

The Penman Club is open to poets of all nationalities throughout the world. There are many poets amongst the members and in many cases the club was pleased to have been able to help them to get their works published for the first time. They try and pay special attention to the new and coming poets whenever they feel that their works show promise.

PENNINE POETS

Secretary: Mrs. Joan Lee, Sun Vale, Brunley Road, Luddenden Foot, Yorks, HX2 6AH.

The Pennine Poets' Group was founded in the mill-town of Elland in the West Riding of Yorkshire. The local library provided encouragement and help for the founding of the group, which grew to include writers living within a thirty mile radius of Elland. The group has been established eight years and include making recordings of poetry for regional broadcasts among their activities. They are also available for public readings. Their quarterly magazine *Pennine Platform* is supported by the Yorkshire Arts Association.

PENTAMETERS POETRY CIRCLE
Secretary: Miss Léonie Scott-Matthews, 57 Belsize Avenue, Hampstead, London N.W.3.

Pentameters was founded by Léonie Scott-Matthews in the summer of 1968. It was started to bring poets and small audiences together for informal poetry readings, and it has been a success from the beginning. A compelling feature is the informality, and there are now well over 1,000 members.

Among the first poets who appeared were Dannie Abse, George Barker, Pete Brown, John Heath-Stubbs, Adrian Henri, Christopher Logue, Roger McGough, Brian Patten and Stevie Smith. Others who have taken part include Sinclair Beiles, Gerard Benson, Bob Cobbing, Ivor Cutler, John Horder, Michael Horovitz, George MacBeth, Adrian Mitchell and Edward Lucie Smith.

Although the main idea is to get poets to read their own latest or published poems, there have also been many readings of poems that are traditional, or by poets other than the reader. Pentameters has also provided a stage for hundreds of new or unknown poets. It meets currently in the Three Horse Shoes, 28 Heath Street, Hampstead, NW3, on Wednesday evenings.

PETERSFIELD LITERARY SOCIETY
Chairman: Mr. Ray Sparkes, 23 Inmans Lane, Sheet, Petersfield, Hants.

POETRY AND PLAYS IN PUBS
Sponsors of the Scheme: John Masefield, O.M., former Poet Laureate; Sir Ernest Barker, Litt.D., D.Lit., LL.D., etc., Emeritus Professor of Political Science in the University of Cambridge; The Rt. Rev. C.S. Woodward, M.C., D.D.; The Very Rev. The Dean of St. Paul's K.C.V.O., D.D., D.Lit.; Dame Sybil Thorndyke, LL.D.; H.L. Bradfer-Lawrence, F.S.A.; Sir Cecil Wakeley, Bt., K.B.E., C.B., P.R.C.S.; Sir Charles Tennyson, C.M.G.; Dr. J.J. Mallon, C.H.; Sir Robert Ewbank, C.S.I., C.I.E.; Sir Sydney Nevile; E.H.F. Fuller; Nowell Smith; Louis MacNeice. Henry McCarthy, Organizer: St. Stephen's House, Westminster, London SW1.

THE BARROW POETS
The Society of Barrow Poets was founded in 1951 by a number of students at the University of London and the Slade School with the idea of selling their poems and paintings from a barrow during the Festival of Britain. This attempt failed for lack of a site, but an appeal made to 'A Committee for Verse and Prose Recitation' enabled them to present programmes of poetry and music in public houses. Thus they became part of this organization, formed in 1937 with financial assistance of a group of brewers.

Programmes last approximately forty minutes and are given fortnightly in a round of pubs all over London.

Pub audiences on the whole prefer the best. They like poems whose language and rhythms seem to be those of men's speech of the time they were written. For this reason ballads, Chaucer, Donne, Suckling, Wordsworth, Hardy, and Pound are all listened to with attention.

THE POETRY BOOK SOCIETY LTD.
105 Piccadilly, London, W1V OAU.

The Poetry Book Society, founded in 1954, is non-profit-making, and is helped financially by the Arts Council of Great Britain. Membership costs £5 per year and brings post free the following:

1. A book of new poetry every quarter.
2. With the book, the Society's Bulletin with contributions from the authors of the books chosen and recommended.
3. A special Poetry Supplement at Christmas.
4. A yearly check list of books of new verse.

The quarterly book of poetry is chosen for members by Selectors appointed every year by the Society's Board of Management. It is always a book of new poems. During the Society's existence some of the most interesting poetry of the day has come to members on publication.

The Selectors also recommend, every quarter, any other books of special merit. The recommendations are announced in the Society's Bulletin which also prints specimen poems from them or unpublished poems by their authors. In addition to books of new poems, volumes of collected poems and anthologies of contemporary poetry are eligible for recommendation (but not for choice).

Since a subscription costs no more than the published price of the books members receive, an obvious benefit is derived from membership. In addition a member knows that the book he receives has been carefully selected by experts, usually practising poets or critics.

It need hardly be said that the Society serves the needs of organizations such as schools (many of which are in membership) as well as those of individuals, since one result of continued membership is the building up of a representative library of the best modern verse.

There are hidden advantages too: the Society's existence certainly encourages publishers to publish books of new poetry and to keep their price to the minimum. To become a member of the Society is a practical way of helping the art and dissemination of poetry.

The Society promotes an annual festival of international poetry each summer in London. Advance details are supplied to all members, from The Secretary, The Poetry Book Society, 105 Piccadilly, London W1V OAU.

POETRY FESTIVALS COMMITTEE
Harold Hikins, Esq., 14 Harringay Ave., Liverpool, L18 1JE.

This was formed in 1968, and is now a registered Charity. It is a self-elective group whose primary function is to promote the composition and presentation of poetry, a function which it conducts on Merseyside, basically through the annual Merseyside Festivals of Poetry.

(These Festivals began in 1968; they have hitherto consisted of seven recitals spread over a single week, at a variety of different venues. All people composing poetry in the Merseyside area are invited to take part — without payment — and numbers involved have varied from 70 to 110. This includes all the well-known 'Liverpool Poets'. Admission is charged, and donations made to selected charities from the proceeds.)

The Committee also provides teams of local poets to visit schools for recitals and discussions; has begun work in compiling an anthology of

Merseyside poetry; presents periodically a series of one-night events at which important poets from outside Merseyside are presented.

The Committee has about 25 members (there is no fixed figure) most of whom are either leading active poets, or are closely involved in poetry affairs of Merseyside. There is no subscription. The members reflect most aspects of Merseyside poetry.

The Committee has no funds other than the income it manages to derive from its activities (which in some important cases are supported by guarantees from the Merseyside arts Association, to whom the Committee is affiliated as a member society).

POETRY IN MOTION
Secretary: Mrs. Jan Falkiner, 37 Salisbury Road, Barnet, Herts.

THE POETRY LOVERS' FELLOWSHIP
President: Dr. Oliver C De C Ellis, "Otterbrook", Chinley, Derbyshire; Hon. Director: Dilys M. Gibbons-Turner; Hon. Secretary General: Marjorie Dawson, Unicorn Meadow, Clee Saint Margaret, via Craven Arms, S. Shropshire, SY7 9DT; Secretary of North Region Poetry Lovers' Fellowship: Mr. Wm. Gutteridge, Chinley, via Stockport, SK12 6AH.

This is a body founded in 1928 by a research-scientist editor of the *Poetry Review* in response to Thomas Hardy's 'forlorn hope' of 'an alliance between Religion and Complete Rationality, which must come,' he said, 'unless the world is to perish, by means of the interfusing effect of poetry.' He foresaw, what has since come terribly to pass, 'owing to unabashed selfishness in all classes' and the growing trends to 'outrageous stimulation' on which Wordsworth had already sounded the alarm, 'a New Dark Age'. Since the first president, Charles H. Herford (d. 1931), presidential guidance has been afforded by Lascelles Abercrombie (d. 1938) Walter de la Mare (d. 1956) and Gilbert Murray (1957).

Hardy's suggested alliance is considered in detail in *Rational Religious Belief* and *Rational Religious Practice*. Our internationalism does not seek to reduce the colours and structures of the world to one hideous and indistinguishable mess: it seeks to continue, as far as in us lies, the clean and enormous characteristic English contribution to the world's enrichment. The current decay to a Pidgin English or 'Basic English' as a 'World Language' must be resisted at all costs. In *For English Undefiled*, a stand is made against the mis-used and mutilated English devised by the press both for home consumption and export. In *Speech Exercises (6th Revn)* Spoken English is sought to be preserved against the innovations and suppressions of the broadcast, a travesty of English which is all the English that the majority of our conscripted children now ever hear or–the youngest–have ever heard.

Besides devoting itself to the maintenance of high standards in conduct and in language, the Fellowship promotes every aspect of individual dignity and independence. The citizen proudly pays his rates and taxes when these are fairly levied and honestly used for the provision of social necessities and amenities. He resists compulsory questionnaires and official intrusions on his home. He is responsible for the education and the moral and spiritual welfare of his children, and this responsibility cannot be delegated. He upholds and assists the police in their thankless struggle against crime, but he resents employees who turn themselves into 'authorities' and run municipalities as if they were limited companies or tourist concerns. At the present time, rates and taxes are imposed under penalty of imprisonment, and the Fellowship neither invites nor receives 'grants' from monies so levied and so squandered. Nor will any Fellow accept any benefit, direct or indirect, from 'compulsory purchase', which is theft.

Adherents of the Fellowship make a serious and sustained effort to advance the welfare of the Fellowship and to promote its aims and activities at every opportunity that their particular circumstances afford. Applicants for membership should write stating agreement with our aims and the intention to help positively in their attainment. The annual subscription of £2.10 is payable by bankers' order on admission. Every member is expected unceasingly to conduct himself as a living protest and enemy to the various squalid bedlams that masquerade as 'modern' art. The *Prospectus* gives full information on courses, examinations, diplomas and medals. Members so bitten will be kept informed of the prizes offered from time to time for successful competitive verse-writing. A money prize is offered each year for an essay of about 5,000 words on some aspect of our crusade 'The Struggle Against The Cad'. There is a critical service for writers covering both verse and prose. A book prize can be won at any time by a well-written and knowledgeable criticism of any broadcast weather-report, news-reading, book at bed-time, etc.

POETRY ONE
Alex Smith, 4 MacDonald Way, Hornchurch Essex.

The group, over ten years old now, meets every other Monday at Fair Kytes Art Centre, Hornchurch, Essex. It is an informal gathering of people of all ages who write poetry. Efforts are being made to recruit new faces into the group. Publication of their anthologies continue and after this year the name Poetry One will be changed to Assega.

THE POETRY SOCIETY
21 Earls Court Square, London SW5. President: Basil Bunting; Chairman: John Cotton; Hon. Treasurer: Stuart Montgomery; General Secretary: Michael Mackenzie; Education Secretary: Christopher Wright.

"The Society was founded in 1909. Since its inauguration it has honoured the great names of poetry, and encouraged new talent.

Over recent years it has secured the support and recognition of the Arts Council of Great Britain, who have committed themselves to endorsing the Society's efforts for the good of poetry. At the same time, the Society has worked in co-operation with other major organisations, such as the National Book League, the I.C.A. and the regional arts associations. Such liaison has resulted in major poetry events on the South Bank in London, and the Edinburgh, Aldeburgh and other festivals.

The programme of events at the National Poetry Centre has become increasingly varied, with readings by over 60 poets a year, including leading poets, such as MacDiarmid, Auden, Spender, Plomer, Bunting and Kathleen Raine, and by numerous younger poets, covering every conceivable style from the most traditional to the most avant garde. At the same time, there have been lecture series, poetry and music events, and a series of anthology programmes chosen by celebrities such as Trevor Huddleston, Spike Milligan, Jack Dash, Edna O'Brien and Lord Soper.

Of its multifarious other interests, the following should be mentioned: Poetry Review, widely regarded as a leading poetry magazine, the extensive system of verse-speaking examinations which are held for children and adults throughout the country, a commercially sponsored 'Poets in Schools' scheme, open poetry competitions, an information service which is used by people all over the world, the club bar and other facilities offered to members at N.P.C., and workshops and discussion groups both for poets just beginning to write, and for published poets. Weekend courses are held in London and at provincial universities."

The National Poetry Secretariat was set up in 1973. Run by the Poetry Society, it acts as an agency for poets giving readings all over the British Isles, provides assistance to arts organisers setting up poetry events, supplies up to date information about poets, standardises contracts with poets, sets minimum fees, subsidises readings and arranges poets' tours.

A Poetry Resources Centre is being established which will supply material connected with poetry (tapes, films, books, magazines, etc.). This will be available in all regions to organizations such as schools and colleges, as well as to individuals.

Individual membership is open to anyone, whether or not they write poetry. Subscription rates: Adult members (London) £3 and (Country) £2.25; Associate Members (ie. full time students, or under 18) £1.50; Life Members £30; Corporate Membership (ie. schools, colleges) £4; Affiliated Membership (ie. other societies, literary groups) £3.

The following are Poetry Society Centres outside London.

UNITED KINGDOM

Guildford and West Surrey Centre
Hon. Secretary: Mr. Peter Outram, 14 Busbridge Lane, Godalming, Surrey.

Nottinghamshire Centre
Hon. Secretary: N. E. Findlay, 82 Kentwood Road, Sneiton Dale, Nottingham.

Suffolk Centre
Hon. Secretary: Mrs. H. Dell, 'Doggers', Copdock, Ipswich, Suffolk, 1P8 3JF.

U.S.A.

Eastern Centre
Chairman: Miss Lou LuTour, 1270 Fifth Ave. 2F, New York, NY 10029, U.S.A.

Chicago Centre
Secretary: Miss Anna T. Mulligan, 569 North Laramie Ave., Chicago, IL, U.S.A.

CANADA
  Nova Scotia Centre
  Hon. Secretary: Mrs. S. MacLeod, 9 Mayo Street, Armdale, Nova
  Scotia, Canada.

INDIA
  Hyderabad Centre
  Hon. Secretary: Mrs. Bilkiz Alladin, 'Shangrila', 8-2-584 Jubilee Hills,
  Road No. 9, Hyberabad-34, AP India.

Affiliated Organizations: Brighton Poetry Society; Browning Society of
  London; Bruton Poetry Society; Cheltenham Poetry Society; Francis
  Thompson Society; Institute of Directors; The 'Open House' Society;
  Plymouth Writers Circle; Shortlands Poetry Circle; Swansea & District
  Writers' Circle; Tennyson Research Centre; Torbay Poetry Centre;
  U.S. Embassy; Ver Poets (St. Albans); York Poetry Society.

THE POETRY SOCIETY OF CHELTENHAM
Hon. Secretary & Treasurer: Miss W. K. Allardyce, 'Kilworth', 8
Cleevelands Drive, Cheltenham, Glos., GL50 4QF.

POETRY SOCIETY, TRINITY AND ALL SAINTS COLLEGES
Brownberrie Lane, Horsforth, Leeds, LS18 5HD

POETRY TRIANGLE
Organizer: Brian Dunn, 33 Grangecliffe Gardens, London, SE25 6SY.

POETRY WORKSHOP
Con Moore, 6 Balmoral Road, Bristol, BS7 9AZ.

POETS CONFERENCE
Chairman: Mr. Bob Cobbing, 262 Randolph Avenue, London W9.

POET'S VIGILANTES
Chairman & General Secretary: Malcolm Payne, 4 Wealden Close,
Crowborough, Sussex.
  Poet's Vigilantes is an organization formed to help aspiring/emerging
poets to have a fuller understanding of the various methods of poetry
publication available in the U.K. and U.S.A.
  Members are able to use the PV Poets Panel to get opinion/criticism on
their work; send work for consideration of publication in the PV Poets
Series, or for the PV Publications — Radix & Nucleus; to receive the three
annual issues of PV Newsletter, which gives information on poetry markets,
poetry publishing publications, other organisations & societies, reviews,
articles etc.
  Founder, Chairman & General Secretary: Malc Payne, F.I.P.S.; Co-
Founder, London Rep. & Public Relations: Margaret George, F.I.P.S.;
Midlands Rep.: Mike Park; Scottish Rep.: W. L Herd, M.A.; U.S.A. Rep.,
Mia Albright, F.I.P.S.

POETS' WORKSHOP

Secretary: Laurie Smith, 26 Albion Court, Albion Road, Sutton, Surrey.

"Poet's Workshop is the leading poetry discussion group in London. It is the successor of 'The Group', some of whose members helped to found it in 1965. Members include poets, both published and unpublished, critics, in fact anyone with a genuine interest in poetry.

Three times a year, all members receive a booklet containing new unpublished poems by fellow members. At each meeting, a member reads his poems one at a time from the booklet and each is discussed in detail by those present.

All types of poetry are welcome. Discussion tends to be good-humoured but frank, a wide variety of views being expressed. The aim is always to help the poet to judge the effectiveness of his work from the response of an informed and sympathetic audience and to encourage him with honest and constructive criticism. Above all, the Workshop aims to overcome the sense of isolation from which many new poets suffer, by providing a friendly atmosphere in which they can share the experience of discussing new work with other poets.

Members of the Workshop have included Dannie Abse, Fleur Adcock, Leo Aylen, Alan Brownjohn, John Daniel, Christopher Hampton, Philip Hobsbaum, Edward Lucie-Smith, George Macbeth, Jean Overton-Fuller, Peter Porter, David Tribe and Donald Ward. Some of these, including Alan Brownjohn and George Macbeth, are still regular contributors at the Workshop".

Meetings are held at the National Poetry Centre, 21 Earls Court Square, at 8 p.m. on alternate Fridays from October to July. Subscriptions: Full Member, £3; Associate Member, £1.50; Student Member, £1.50.

PORTSMOUTH POETRY SOCIETY

Secretary: Howard F. Wood, 78 Hartley Road, North End, Portsmouth, PO2 9HX.

The Portsmouth Poetry Society aims to promote the study and writing of poetry and when possible have a well-known poet read and discuss his work. A Chairman is appointed for each meeting and meetings are held fortnightly on alternate Tuesdays and Wednesdays; venues vary according to the availability of premises at the Society's disposal. Subscription is by payment per meeting.

Treasurer: Brian H. Wells, 256 Powerscourt Road, Portsmouth, Hants., PO2 7JR.

PRESTON POETS' SOCIETY

Hon. Secretary: Mrs. Celia Harvey, 8 Whitefield Road E., Penwortham, Preston, Lancs.

RICHMOND HILL LITERARY SOCIETY

Miss Ogilvie, 5 Kinross Road, Talbot Woods, Bournemouth, Hants.

RICHMOND POETRY GROUP

c/o Expression One, 117 Forest Rise, Waltham Forest, London E17 3PW.

RICHMOND WRITERS' CIRCLE

Hon. Secretary: Miss M. Farrell, Richmond Community Centre, Room 4, Richmond, Surrey; Chairman: Mr. Lee Brown; Vice-Chairman: Mr. Chetwynd-Hayes; Hon. Treasurer: Mrs. D. Whyte; Librarian: Miss Mabel Bethell.

"Writers, whether it be short stories, novels, factual articles or poetry, all have something to say and the ability to express it, the Circle provides the ideal outlet". The Circle is now in its 25th year of existence. They meet every Wednesday at Richmond Community Centre at 8 p.m.

ROYAL SOCIETY OF LITERATURE

1 Hyde Park Gardens, London, W2 2LT. President: The Rt. Hon. Lord Butler, C.H.; Chairman of the Council: The Rt. Hon. The Earl of Birkenhead; Secretary: Mrs. J. M. Patterson.

SALISBURY POETRY CIRCLE

Secretary: Miss K. Munday, 57 Bouverie Avenue, Salisbury; President: Dr. Elsie Smith, Ph.D.; Chairman: The Rev. B. Williams, M.Lit.; Hon. Treasurer: Miss P. B. Amey, 5 Belle Vue Road, Salisbury.

THE SALTIRE SOCIETY

Administrative Secretary: Mrs. Sylvia Fennell, Gladstone's Land, 483 Lawnmarket, Edinburgh, EH1 2NT.

SCAFFOLD

John Gorman Esq., Hillcote, Hoylake Road, Bidston, Birkenhead, Cheshire.

SCOTTISH ARTS

Secretary: Thomas R. Moffatt, C.A., 24 Rutland Square, Edinburgh, EH1 2BW.

THE SCOTTISH ARTS COUNCIL

Assistant Director: Trevor Royle, 19 Charlotte Square, Edinburgh, EH2 4DF.

SCOTTISH ASSOCIATION FOR THE SPEAKING OF VERSE

President: Dr. C. M. Grieve (Hugh McDiarmid); Chairman, Edinburgh Branch: Prof. John MacQueen; General Secretary: Miss K. Morrison, 36A Esslemont Road, Edinburgh, EH16 5PY; Treasurer: Mr. Douglas Fraser, 2 Keith Terrace, Edinburgh, EH4 3NJ.

This association was started in 1924 as a result of a suggestion by John Masefield who became its first president. Branches were formed in Aberdeen, Edinburgh, Inverness, Glasgow and Perth. But there are now only two branches, those of Edinburgh and Glasgow.

The Association's main object is to further the causes of Spoken Verse; it also endeavours to foster a general appreciation of Poetry by inviting to its platform Poets and Speakers of Poetry.

The Association celebrates its 50th anniversary this year. Activities for 1974 include Maurice Lindsay, Robert Nye and Kathleen Raine reading their own poems and the Jubilee Poetry Competition.

SCOTTISH LITERATURE AND SONG ASSOCIATION
President: Mr. Cyril G. Pope, 108 Rosemount Viaduct, Aberdeen, AB1 1NX; Secretary: Mrs. A. Anderson, 76 Union Street, Aberdeen, AB1 6SA.

SECOND CITY POETS
Birmingham and Midland Institute, Margaret St., Birmingham, B3 3BS.

This is the main group in the area and caters for all needs in the field of poetry. The Poetry Centre itself is comprised of about 40 members (rising steadily) and has various affiliations with the other small groups in the area. Activities include monthly national poetry readings, monthly local pub readings and regular discussion groups. Publications include a quarterly magazine *Muse*, a monthly newsletter of local and national news and reviews, called *Poetry News* and Anthologies of Local Poets. The society also acts as agent for members and local poets.

THE SHAKESPEARE BIRTHPLACE TRUST
The Shakespeare Centre, Stratford-Upon-Avon. Chairman: Mr. Dennis L. Flower; Director: Dr. Levi Fox, O.B.E., D.L.

The annual *Stratford-Upon-Avon Poetry Festival* is arranged by the Shakespeare Birthplace Trust. It usually consists of readings by poets and actors on nine consecutive Sunday evenings, beginning in late June or early July.

SHORTLANDS POETRY CIRCLE
President: Miss Margaret Paice, 103 Masons Hill, Bromley; Hon. Secretary: Mrs. E. Rutt, 5 Dairsie Court, 163 Widmore Road, Bromley, Kent, BR1 3AX; Writers' Group Secretary: Mr. Arthur Gerard; Hon. Treasurer: Mrs. Phyllis Cook.

Shortlands Poetry Circle was founded in 1911 by Miss Catherine Punch. Its aim was to hold meetings for the study and reading aloud of poetry; and from time to time to invite professional speakers and to organise Open Meetings. The Writers' and Drama Groups meet once a month. In 1947 the Circle became the North-West Branch of the English Association and is also affiliated to the Poetry Society.

SHREWSBURY POETRY CIRCLE
Secretary: Mrs. Isobel Scott Mills, 41 St. John's Hill, Shrewsbury, SY1 1JQ.

THE SOCIETY OF AUSTRALIAN WRITERS
Australia House, Strand, London, WC2B 4LA.

The Society of Australian Writers was formed in 1952 to further the cause of Australian writing and to act as an advice and information centre for Australian writers in the U.K.

THE SOCIETY OF AUTHORS
84 Drayton Gardens, London SW10. President: Dame Veronica Wedgwood, O.M., D.B.E., LL.D.

The Society of Authors is a non-profit making organisation with the purpose of promoting the interests of authors, and defending their rights whenever and wherever they are challenged. Founded in 1884 by Sir Walter

Besant, it has a long history of devoted service by leading writers of the day, including such men as Shaw, Hardy, Wells, Eliot, Masefield, and Forster.

Although admission to membership is at the discretion of the Committee of Management, an author (including poets) will normally be made a full member of the Society if he has a full-length work published in the U.K. by a member of the Publishers Association, or if he has an established reputation in another medium, e.g. stage or radio.

The Society is responsible for numerous awards including two poetry awards — The Eric Gregory Award and the Cholmondeley Award.

SOCIETY OF CIVIL SERVICE AUTHORS
Secretary: Sydney Dobson, 17 Abbotsford Road, Goodmayes, Ilford, Essex.

The aim of the Society is to encourage writing both by present and past members of the Civil Service. Literary competitions are held annually for members.

SOLIHULL WRITER'S WORKSHOP
Secretary, Solihull Writers' Workshop, The Manor House, Solihull, Warwicks.

THE SOUTHAMPTON POETRY CIRCLE
Chairman: Mrs. Olive Cox, 3 Peterscroft Avenue, Ashurst, Southampton, SO4 2AB.

The Southampton Poetry Circle began in 1970 and, at the moment, is a small group who meet informally once a month at the house of one of the members. In 1972 they produced their first small anthology 'Mayflower' which sold 500 copies. Their second effort has recently been published.

SOUTH EAST ARTS ASSOCIATION
c/o Marlowe Theatre, St. Margaret's Street, Canterbury, Kent.

SOUTH EAST WALES ARTS ASSOCIATION
c/o Welsh Arts Council, Holst House, 9 Museum Place, Cardiff, CF1 3NX.

SOUTHERN ARTS ASSOCIATION
Literature Officer: Christopher Kerr, South Side Offices, Law Courts, Winchester, Hampshire.

This is the Regional Arts Association for Berkshire, Hampshire, the Isle of Wight, West Sussex and Wiltshire. Activities include support for art, drama, literature, music and festivals including the promotion of poetry readings and other literary events.

SOUTHPORT POETRY COMMITTEE
Secretary: Spencer Leigh, 8 Mersey Road, Crosby, Liverpool, L23 3AG. L23 3AG.

SOUTH WESTERN ARTS ASSOCIATION
23 Southernhay East, Exeter, Devon.

SPECTRO GALLERY
M. Tilley Esq., 18 Station Road, Whitley Bay, Northumberland.

STRATFORD-UPON-AVON POETRY FESTIVAL
See The Shakespeare Birthplace Trust

SUFFOLK POETRY SOCIETY
Hon. Secretary: Mrs. H. Dell, 'Doggers', Copdock, Ipswich, 1P8 3JF

The activities of the society take the form of monthly meetings during the summer (April to September inclusive) at various places in the country, e.g. Melton Grange Hotel, Woodbridge; White Lion Hotel, Eye, etc. A well-known speaker lectures on some poet or group of poets or some aspect of poetry.

During the winter months, group readings are arranged by certain members in their homes. These are monthly or fortnightly as the group wishes.

The president of the society is R.N. Currey and the Chairman is R.I. Redfern.

The George Crabbe Memorial Competition is organised by the society. This is open to anyone who was born, educated or resides in Suffolk. A different theme is set each year for a poem of not more than 50 lines in length. Book tokens are awarded as prizes.

SUNDERLAND ARTS CENTRE
17 Grange Terrace, Stockton Road, Sunderland.

SWANSEA & DISTRICT WRITERS' CIRCLE
Hon. Secretary: Lorna Byran, 3 Bryn Terrace, Mumbles, Swansea.

THE FRANCIS THOMPSON SOCIETY
3 Kemplay Road, Hampstead, London NW3. President: Henry Williamson; Hon. Secretary: Dr. G. Krishnamurti.

Mainly The Francis Thompson Society examines the research done on the life and work of Francis Thompson but they do arrange lectures, poetry readings and exhibitions at intervals.

TORBAY POETRY CENTRE
Mrs. Armitage Hargreaves, Church Style, Bovey Tracey, Newton Abbot, Devon.

THE TRANSLATORS ASSOCIATION
84 Drayton Gardens, London, SW10 9SD.

The Translators Association is a specialist unit within the Society of Authors.

THE UMBRELLA CLUB
Tudor House, 14 Spon Street, Coventry, CV1 3BA.

The Umbrella Club is a multipurpose arts club; there is a poetry group within the club.

VER POETS
Chairman: Ray Badman; Hon. Secretary & Treasurer: May Badman, 61 & 63 Chiswell Green Lane, St. Albans, Herts.

Ver Poets exists to promote poetry and to help poets. The group meets in St. Albans, runs a Poetry Bookstall, operates the only Poetry Parlour in the world, has a Poetry Reading Group, publishes the work of members in pamphlets and broadsheets, runs internal and international competitions, gives help, advice and encouragement whenever they are sought. Membership costs £1.20 per annum (students 60p).

THE WALTHAMSTOW POETRY GROUP
See Centre 17

THE WELSH ARTS COUNCIL
Holst House, 9 Museum Place, Cardiff, CF1 3NX, Wales.

THE WEST COUNTRY WRITERS' ASSOCIATION
President: Christopher Fry, F.R.S.L.; Chairman: William Kean Seymour, Hon. D.Litt., F.R.S.L.; Hon. Secretary: Dr. R. A. Cooper, M.B., L.M.S.S.A., The Dene, The Street, Aldermaston, Berks.

The Association was founded 22 years ago with the aims of fostering a love of literature in the West Country and to give writers an opportunity for social and professional contact and the exchange of ideas through informal meetings, through the Newsletter, and through the Annual Conference which is held on a weekend in May at different West Country towns.

WEST MIDLANDS ARTS ASSOCIATION
Lloyds Bank Chambers, Market Street, Stafford.

WEST MIDLANDS WRITERS' CIRCLE
Secretary: Ms. Maureen Owen, 4 Pine Walk, The Highlands, Lickhill Lodge, Stowport-on-Severn, Worcs.

WEST WALES ASSOCIATION FOR THE ARTS
Dark Gate, Red Street, Carmarthen.

WIGAN POETS
Dennis Lysons, 18 Sycamore Avenue, Golborne, Nr. Warrington, Lancs.

WINCHESTER POETRY CIRCLE
Chairman: T. Roy Sparkes, 8 Taplings Road, Weeke, Winchester.

WINCHESTER WRITERS' CIRCLE
Secretary: Mrs. Pat Barton, 84 Old Kennels Lane, Olivers Battery, Winchester, Hants.

WORCESTER WRITER'S CIRCLE
Secretary: Mrs. Joan Reeves, 15 Lynn Close, Leigh Sinton, Nr. Malvern Worcs.

THE WRITERS

Founder & Organizer: Mrs. Marta Dannheisser, 35 Rundell Crescent, London, NW4 3BS.

The group aims at quality, rather than quantity, of writers, both of poetry and prose. The Writers is a writers' workshop: apart from reading work by members, they write during sessions. The discussions are on work done by the members as well as on questions of general interest to writers.

YORK POETRY SOCIETY

President: Robert Armstrong; Director: Kathleen Bell, 33 Chestnut Avenue, York; Secretary: Mrs. N. Wallis, 7 Castle Close, Sheriff Hutton, York.

YORKSHIRE ARTS ASSOCIATION

Glyde House, Glydegate, Bradford, Yorkshire, BD5 OBQ.

THE YORKSHIRE DIALECT SOCIETY

Hon. Secretary: Ian Dewhirst, 14 Raglan Avenue, Fell Lane, Keighley, Yorks, BD22 6BJ.

The aims of the Society are to encourage interest in all dialect speech, the writing of dialect verse and prose, and the publication of dialect literature. Annual subscription is 50p; life membership is £10.50.

YORKSHIRE POETS ASSOCIATION

Chairman: Margaret Perkins, 64 Broomgrove Road, Sheffield, S10 2NA; Secretary: Lyn Cooper, 24 Laverdene Drive, Totley, Sheffield.

The aims of the society are: (a) to encourage the writing, speaking and publication of poetry in Yorkshire; (b) to act as a forum for the discussion of matters pertaining to poets and poetry in Yorkshire; and (c) to be a means of communication between poets, publishers and the public in Yorkshire.

It is hoped that the association will hold a minimum of three meetings a year in various parts of Yorkshire; and also publish an annual journal and run a poetry competition for members.

YR ACADEMI GYMREIG

President: Dr. Kate Roberts; Chairman: Prof. J.E. Caerwyn Williams; Secretary: Dr. John Rowlands, Dôl Bebin, Pen-y-garn, Bow Street, Ceredigion, Cards., SY24 5BE, Wales.

Founded in 1959, the society promotes literature in the Welsh language and provides a platform for young writers. The society publishes a literary magazine, 'Taliesin', and awards an annual prize for a Welsh book of merit. It is a society of creative writers, whether in poetry or prose.

YR ACADEMI GYMREIG: ENGLISH LANGUAGE SECTION

President: A. G. Prys-Jones; Chairman: Glyn Jones; Joint Secretaries: Mrs. Alison Prosser Bielski, The Cottage, Itton Common, Chepstow, Monmouthshire, NP6 6BX and Mrs. Sally Roberts Jones, 3 Crown Street, Port Talbot, Wales.

Founded in 1968, this section provides a meeting point for writers of Welsh origin who write in English or who take Wales as their main theme. Membership is invited. At the moment 34 out of the 49 members are poets.

APPENDIX E

POETRY SOCIETIES AND RELATED ORGANIZATIONS IN COUNTRIES OTHER THAN U.S.A. AND U.K.

AFRICA

Cameroon
Association Nationale des Poètes et Ecrivains Camerounais, René Philombe, Secretary, B.P. 2180, Yaounde-Messa, Cameroon.

Ghana
Creative Writers Association, The National Organizer, c/o Institute of African Studies, University of Ghana, Legon-Accra, Ghana.

Ghana Association of Writers, Mr. Atukwei Okai, President, P.O. Box 4414, Accra, Ghana.

National Association of Writers, Mr. Kwabena Asiedu, Secretary, The Arts Council of Ghana, P.O. Box 2738, Accra, Ghana.

The National Association of Writers is the only Government sponsored association of writers and poets in Ghana. It has just been inaugurated as a branch of the Arts Council of Ghana.

Writers Forum, The Secretary, c/o S.R.C. Office, University of Ghana, Legon-Accra, Ghana.

The University of Ghana Writers Forum is a student literary group at the University. The group meets on Friday evenings to read and criticise their own poems.

Rhodesia
Poetry Society of Rhodesia, Colin Style, Chairman, P.O. Box A294, Avondale, Salisbury, Rhodesia.

Shona and Sindebile Writers' Association, Salisbury, Rhodesia.

South Africa
The South African Poetry Society, c/o The English Department, University of Rhodes, Grahamstown, South Africa.

Sudan
National Council for Culture, Ministry of Culture and Information, Khartoum, Sudan.

ASIA

Republic of China
Chinese Poets Association, Dr. Tin-wen Chung, President, P.O. Box 58508, Taipei.

Chinese Writers' and Artists' Association, Mr. Jyh-jiann Wang, Deputy Chief, Apt. 3, 17 Lane 390, Tun Hwa South Road, Taipei.

Chun Jen Poetry Association, Mr. Chang Hsi, Secretary, 27 Han Kou Street, Sec. 2, Taipei.

Ying Ming Poetry Association, Mr. Chu Ping-yi, Secretary, 24-2 Alley 32, Lane 417, Sungshan Road, Taipei.

Hong Kong
Sun Lui Poetry Association, Dr. Lam Yan-Chiu, President, 107 Sai Yeung Choi Street, 9/P Flat C, Kowloon, Hong Kong.

Indonesia
Dewan Kesenian Jakarta (The Arts Council of Jakarta), Jalan Cikini Raya 73, Jakarta, Indonesia.

Israel
Hebrew Writers Association, Mr. D. Chomsky, 6 Kaplan Street, Tel Aviv, Israel.

The Kibbutzs' Authors Association, Mrs. Judith Kafri, Secretary, Kibbutz Shoval 85320, Israel.

Korea
Korean Literary Men's Association, In-Hyeon, Cho, Director General, Room No. 706, Doctor's Building, No. 3, 1-Ka, Chongro-Ku, Seoul, Korea; Yoon-Seong, Kim, Standing Director.

Malaysia
The Sirius Poetry Society, Mr. Bernard Woon Swee Tin, Chairman, U—31 Theatre Street, Bidor, Perak, Malaysia.

Pakistan
National Book Centre of Pakistan, M.A. Chiragh, Research Assistant, 1 Montgomery Road, Lahore, Pakistan.

Pakistan Writers' Guild, 16/B Sindhi Muslim Housing Society, Karachi —3, Pakistan.

Sindhi Adabi Board, Amin Manzil, Garri Khata, Hyderabad (Sind), Pakistan.

Saudi Arabia
Higher Council for Sciences, Literature and Arts, Mr. Hassan Abdullah Al-Shaikh, Chairman, Office of the Minister, Ministry of Education, Riyadh, Saudi Arabia.

AUSTRALIA & NEW ZEALAND

Australian Literature Society, Mrs. A. Egan, Secretary, c/o 221 Clarendon Street, South Melbourne 3205.

Australian Society of Authors, Deirdre Hill, Secretary, 6th Floor, 252 George Street, Sydney 2000.

Australian Writers' Workshop, Mrs. Verna Mary Clarke, Director, 31 Salkeld Street, Tarragindi, Queensland 4121.

Fellowship of Australian Writers, Mrs. Maureen Freer, Federal President, "Coottha Coottha", 445 Simpsons Road, Bardon, Brisbane, Queensland 4065.

Canberra: L.F.H. Rees, Hon. Secretary, 50 Booroondara Street, Reed, A.C.T. 2601.

New South Wales: Jean Abbey, Secretary, 2/2 Holbrook Avenue, Kirribilli, N.S.W. 2061.

Queensland: A.A. Daniels, Hon. Secretary, 14 Kanumbra Street, Coorparoo, Queensland 4151 and Pat Price, Hon. Secretary, Wellington Road, Red Hill, Queensland 4059.

South Australia: Veda Swain, Secretary, 122 Osmond Terrace, Norwood, South Australia 5067.

Tasmania: Don Griffiths, Hon. Secretary, 11 Fowler Street, Montrose, Tasmania 7010.

Tasmania-Launceston Regional: Secretary, Private Mail Bag 77, Launceston, Tasmania 7250.

Tasmania-North Regional: Mrs. E. Brown, Secretary, Box 464 P.O., Burnie 7320.

Victoria: J.S. Hamilton, Hon. Secretary, 1/317 Barkers Road, Kew, Victoria 3101.

Victoria-Geelong Regional: John Prescott, President, 41 Shackleton Street, Belmont, Victoria 3216.

Victoria-North Central Regional: Tony Gallagher, Secretary, 15 Coomboona Street, Shepparton, Victoria 3630.

Victoria-Western Districts Regional: Mrs. R.E. Wilson, Secretary, Yarambe, North Hamilton, Victoria 3300.

Western Australia: Hon. Secretary, c/o Tom Collins House, 9 Servetus Street, Swanbourne, Western Australia 6010.

Western Australia-Albany Regional: Hon. Secretary, P.O. Box 310, Albany, Western Australia 6330.

Western Australia-Geraldton Regional: Mrs. E.V. Ford, Hon. Secretary, 151 Brede Street, Geraldton 6530.

Hervey Bay Writers' Workshop Albert Crawfoot, Secretary, 47 Truro Street, Torquay, Queensland 4657.

New Zealand Women Writers Society, Mrs. E.G. Stahl, Hon. Secretary, 75 Hall Crescent, Lower Hutt, New Zealand.

The Poetry Society of Australia, The Secretary, Box 110, George Street North, Sydney, N.S.W. 2001.

Toowoomba Ladies' Literary Society, Mrs. M. Schumann, 3 Kent Street, Queensland 4350.

CANADA

Canadian Authors' Association, 22 Yorkville, Toronto, Ontario, M4W 1HA; President: Cdr. C.H. Little; Secretary: A.L. Fosbrooke.

Full Tide (Vancouver Poetry Society), R. Charles Summers, President, 2964 West 8th Avenue, Vancouver 8, British Columbia.

League of Canadian Poets, 106 Avenue Road, Toronto, Ontario, M5R 2H2; Chairman: Douglas Barbour, 13 Merryvale Crescent, Sherwood Park, Alberta, T8A 0N4.

Nova Scotia Centre of the Poetry Society, Hon. Secretary, Mrs. S. MacLeod, 9 Mayo Street, Armdale, Nova Scotia.

Saskatchewan Poetry Society, Mrs. A.H. Campbell, President, 201 2500 Victoria Avenue, Regina, Saskatchewan.

Scotian Pen Guild, Hazel Firth Goddard, President, P.O. Box 173, Dartmouth, Nova Scotia, B2Y 3Y3.

The Wilson MacDonald Poetry Society of Canada, Langford Dixon, President, 66 Burnaby Blvd., Toronto 12, Ontario. (See Article I)

CENTRAL AND SOUTH AMERICA

Argentina
Sociedad Argentina de Escritores, Mexico 524, Buenos Aires, Argentina.

Ecuador
Casa de la Cultura Ecuatoriana, Departamento de Secretaria y Biblioteoas, Avenida 6 de Diciembre 332, Quito, Ecuador.

Club Femenino de Cultura, Manabi 309, Quito, Ecuador.

Mexico
Centro Mexicano de Escritores A.C., Valle Arizpe 18, Mexico D.F.

Peru
Instituto Nacional de Cultura, 390 Ancash, Lima, Peru.

EUROPE

Austria
Osterreichische Gesellschaft Für Literatur, Dr. Hans Haider, Palais Wilczek, 1010 Wien 1, Herrengasse 5, Austria.

Belgium

Association des Ecrivains Belges, Adrien Jans, President, Maison Camille Lemonnier, Maison Des Ecrivains, 150 Chaussee de Wavre, B 1050 Brussels, Belgium.

Association Royale Des Ecrivains Wallons, Max Siemons, General Secretary, Rue de la Carrière 41, 1080 Brussels, Belgium; Emile Poumon, President, Rue d'Aubremé 31, 1800 Vilvorde, Belgium.

Centre International D'Etudes Poétiques, Fernand Verhesen, Boulevard de l'Empereur 4, 1000 Brussels, Belgium.

Maison Internationale de la Poésie, Pierre Bourgeois and Arthur Haulot, Directors, 147 Chaussée de Haecht, B 1030 Brussels, Belgium.

Bulgaria

The Union of Bulgarian Writers, 'Angel Kantchev' Street, No. 5, Sofia, Bulgaria.

Denmark

Dansk Forfatterforening (Danish Authors Society), Nyhavn 21, 1051 Copenhagen K, Denmark.

Finland

Finlands Svenska Forfattareforening (Association of Swedo-Finnish Authors), Ms. Agneta Glad, Secretary, Runebergsgatan 32 C, 00100 Helsinki 10, Finland.

Lounais Suomen Kirjailijat r.y., Kai Kaukovalta, Kyosti, Puolalanpuistv 3-5, sf 20100 Turku 10, Finland.

Suomen Kirjailijaliitto (Association of Finnish Authors), Ms. Liisa Silander, Runeberginkatu 32 C 28, 00100 Helsinki 10, Finland.

Svenska Osterbottens Litteraturforening, Ms. Wava R. Sturmer, Chairman, Pedersespl. 12, 68 620 Jakobstad 2, Finland.

France

Club des Poètes, 30 rue de Bourgogne, 75 Paris 7e, France.

Société des Gens de Lettres, Philippe Dumaine, Secretary General, Hotel De Massa, 38 rue du Faubourg-Saint-Jacques, 75 Paris 14e, France.

Société des Poètes Français, 38 rue du Faubourg-Saint-Jacques, 75 Paris 14e, France.

Syndicat des Ecrivains, 38 rue du Faubourg-Saint-Jacques, 75 Paris 14e, France.

Union des Ecrivains, 6 Passage Charles Dallery, 75 Paris lle, France.

Germany

Der Tukan-Kreis Intn. literarische Gesellschaft, 8000 Munich 40, Moosacherstr. 47, Germany.

Deutsche Akademie für Sprache und Dichtung, Dr. Ernst Johann, General Secretary, 6100 Darmstadt, Alexandraweg 23, Germany.

Deutscher Autoren-Verband e. V., Dr. Werner Dittschlag, President, 3000 Hannover, Sophienstr. 2, Germany.

Gesellschaft für deutsche Sprache e. V., 6200 Wiesbaden, Taunusstr. 11, Germany.

Interessengemeinschaft deutschsprachiger Autoren e. V., Ms. Ursula Völkel, 415 Krefeld-Holterhöfe, Am Rotforn 7, W. Germany.

Literary Union, President: Wolfgang Durben, Petersbergstrasse 82, D-66 Saarbrucken 6, W. Germany. (See Article II)

Verband deutscher Schriftsteller (VS) e. V., Ursula Brauning, General Secretary, 8000 Munich 40, Clemensstr. 58, Germany.

Verband Deutscher Schriftsteller (VS) in Hamburg e. V., 2000 Hamburg 1, Glockengiesserwall 2, Germany.

Hungary
Magyar Irók Szövetsége (Union of Hungarian Writers), Gabor Garai, Secretary General Assistant, Budapest VI, Bajza Utca 18, Hungary.

Iceland
Félag islenzkra rithöfunda, c/o Thoroddur Gudmundsson, Olduslód 3, Hafnarfjördur, Iceland.

Rithöfundafélag Islands, c/o Mrs. Vilborg Dagbjartsdóttir, Vonarstraeti 12, Reykjavik, Iceland.

Italy
Sindacato Nazionale Scrittori (Writers' Union), Via Sansovino 6, 00196 Rome, Italy.

Grand Duchy of Luxembourg
Chambre syndicale des Arts et des Lettres, Madame Maggy Neiers-Stein, Secretary General, 2 rue Bessemer, Esch/Alzette, Grand Duchy of Luxembourg.

Institut grand-ducal, Section des Arts et Lettres, 19 Côte d'Eich, Luxembourg, Grand Duchy of Luxembourg.

Lochness-Verlag Luxemburger Autoren, 17 rue J.P. Koenig, Luxembourg, Grand Duchy of Luxembourg.

Société des Ecrivains Luxembourgeois de Langue Française, Mlle. Rosemarie Kieffer, 10 rue de l'Abbé Lemire, Luxembourg, Grand Duchy of Luxembourg.

The Netherlands
Circle of Authors of Sallard and East-Veluwe, A.J. de Weerd, Secretary, Wessel Zulselerstraat 6, Deventer, The Netherlands.

Maatschappij der Nederlandse Letterkunde, Sjoerd Leiker, Secretary, West 50 Hoorn (N.-H.), The Netherlands.

Norway
Den Norske Forfatterforening (The Norwegian Authors' Association), Mrs. Annicken Sogn Ness, Secretary, Fr. Nansens plass 6, Oslo 1, Norway.

Poland
Agencja Autorska (Authors' Agency Ltd.), Leopold Rybarski, Acting General Manager, 00-950 Warsaw, ul. Hipoteczna 2, Poland.

Zwiazek Literatow Polskich (Polish Writers' Association), Warsaw, Krakowskie Przedmiescie 87/89, Poland.

Portugal
Sociedade Portuguesa de Autores, Dr. Luiz Francisco Rebello, President, Av. Duque de Loule, 111-1°, Lisbon, Portugal.

Romania
The Writers Union of the Socialist Republic of Romania, Laurentiu Fulga, Vice President, Soseaua Kiseleff, 10, Sectorul 1, Bucarest, Romania.

Spain
Sociedad General de Autores de Espana, Fernando VI, 4, Madrid 4, Apartado 484, Spain.

Sweden
Sveriges Forfattarforbund, Box 5252, 102 45 Stockholm 5, Sweden.

Switzerland
Schweizer Autorengruppe 'Gruppe Olten', Mr Hans Muhlethaler, Secretary, Siedlung Halen 43, CH 3037 Stuckishaus, Switzerland.

Société Suisse des Ecrivains, Ernest-François Vollenweider, Secretary, Kirchgasse 25, 8001 Zurich, Switzerland.

U.S.S.R.
Union of Soviet Writers, ul. Vorovskogo 52, Moscow, U.S.S.R.

Yugoslavia
Szvez Knjizevnika Jugoslavije, 11000 Belgrade, Francuska 7, Yugoslavia.

ARTICLE I

THE WILSON MACDONALD POETRY SOCIETY OF CANADA

by Jacob Kisner
(Member of the Executive Committee)

The Wilson MacDonald Poetry Society of Canada, with headquarters in Toronto, Ontario, had its inception in the Spring of 1953. Its dual purpose, as stated succinctly in its constitution and charter, is 'to encourage the development and an understanding of Canadian poetry and, in particular, the poetry of the Canadian poet, Wilson MacDonald'. In 1963, it became the first incorporated poetry society in Canada.

The early organization group was headed by Dr. E. Crosley Hunter and the Rev. Murdock McKinnon. The late John M. Elson was Chairman of this first historic meeting, at which Mrs. C.W. King was elected President. Originally, there was a board of directors, later discontinued, of seven prominent members 'to manage, advise and guide the financial affairs of the society'.

The membership list of The Wilson MacDonald Poetry Society could serve as a virtual Who's Who in Canada, with internationally known names such as Langford Dixon (Canadian poet), Stanley G. Moyer (artist), Dean Miner (concert violinist), Ken Muma (photographer), Jacob Kisner (American poet), Bonnie Day (Canadian poet), Dr. A.J.W. Myers, Wallace Havelock Robb, the late Nathaniel Benson, the Rev. Harvey Howey, Ethel Brant Monture, Dennis Critoph, Clayton Moyer—to name just a few. Among the Society's recently honored guests can be included the late Wilson MacDonald (1880-1967), Mahir Lal Mitra from India, Pijush Kanti Paul from Malaysia, John Robert Colombo, Judge John Grudeff, Aba Biefsky, and Dr. Mary Needler.

Each meeting of The Wilson MacDonald Poetry Society, as a matter of course, features at least one selection from the Society's patron-poet, Wilson MacDonald. Of late, there has been a keen interest in Eskimo and Indian poetry, although one could hardly say that the French and English influences, which have made Canada largely what it is, are neglected. With the world growing smaller every day, the Society is now endeavoring to include an international potpourri of poets whenever feasible.

Special poetry recitals are held annually, and each year on the fifth of May the Society holds a meeting in honor of Wilson MacDonald, who was born on that date at Cheapside, Ontario. At Cheapside, The Wilson MacDonald Memorial School Museum was recently established as a lasting tribute to the author of Canada's all-time poetry best-sellers, *Out of the Wilderness and A Flagon of Beauty*. A visit to the Museum is a must for all tourists and poetry lovers. The Museum maintains a delightful selective collection of memorabilia with much priceless material on Canada's literary past. Prospective visitors to the Museum may contact the curator, the Rev. E.M. Sider, R.R.2, Nanticoke, Ontario, Canada.

The current President, Langford Dixon, is as well Co-Ordinator of Poets for the international School-to-School Project of the Ontario Department of Education. The Society publishes a magazine called View, with contributions from some of the world's great poets.

International visitors are always welcome at the Society's meetings. Further information regarding The Wilson MacDonald Poetry Society of Canada can be obtained by writing to Langford Dixon, President, Wilson MacDonald Poetry Society of Canada, 66 Burnaby Blvd., Toronto 12, Ontario, Canada. In the United States, information on membership in the Society can be obtained from Jacob Kisner, 750 Park Avenue, New York, N.Y. 10021.

ARTICLE II

THE LITERARY UNION

The Literary Union is an international organization of poets, writers, men of letters and of all literary-minded people who are deeply interested in a cultural exchange free from any political or religious bias. The union was founded (under the name of the 'Literary Circle') in Saarbrücken in 1956. Nowadays its members and supporters are to be found all over this tense, anxious and inhuman world of ours... which has so great a need of tolerance and humanism.

The Literary Union aims at the gathering together of all literary powers, the furtherance of both the interests of literature and the international exchange of culture (particularly in the field of literature), the promotion of all authors who are members of the Union and the establishment of contact between literary-minded people and societies. The special aims of the Union include the publication of an international literary magazine (UNIO appears quarterly and English language versions are integrated in the manuscript), the publication of anthologies of poetry and prose in several languages whereby the circle of authors will in no way be restricted in the expression of their philosophical or political convictions, the arrangement of lecture tours abroad for authors of the Literary Union, the organization of reading and discussion sessions.

The address of the Central Committee is D—66 Saarbrücken 6, Petersbergstr. 82, Germany. Address of President Wolfgang Durben is D—6639 Beckingen/Saar, Schulstr. 8, Germany.

Members of the Presidial Committee: Sivar Arnér (Sweden), Prof. Aron Borélius (University of Lund), Prof. Maurice Boucher (Sorbonne), Prof. Dr. Tin-wen Chung (Taiwan, Republic of China; President of the Chinese Poets Association), Dr. Brian Cox (Australia, Vice President of United Poets Laureate International), Friedr. Dürrenmatt (Switzerland), Johannes Edfelt (President of Swedish P.E.N.), Dr. Manfred Hausmann (Germany), Baroness Marie-Luise von Kaschnitz-Weinberg (Germany), Halldór

Laxness (Iceland), Marianne Linder (Sweden), Dr. Lou LuTour (U.S.A., President, World Poets' Resource Centre, Inc.), Prof. Gabriel Marcel and Baron Pierre Guillet de Monthoux (France), Mohamed Mzali (Tunis, Ministre de la Santé Publique, ancien Ministre de l'Education Nationale), Prof. Jonas Negalha (Brazil, Pan Continental Editor of 'Poet'), Eugene Roth (Germany), Prof. Albert Schneider (University of Nancy), Dr. Krishna Srinivas (India, President of the World Poetry Society Intercontinental), Jos Vandeloo (Belgium), Prof. Dr. Amado Yuzon (Philippines, President of the United Poets Laureate International).

APPENDIX F

MAGAZINES AND PUBLISHERS
INTERESTED IN POETRY

The entries in this appendix have been taken from reliable sources and it is believed that the list is as comprehensive as possible. Letters were written to every editor for confirmation but some did not reply. Those who did not reply are marked with an asterisk at the beginning of the entry.

Our special thanks are due to the International Directory of Little Magazines and Small Presses, Ninth Edition 1973-74; Dust Books, Len Fulton, Editor & Publisher, 5218 Scottwood Road, Paradise, CA 95969, U.S.A.; The Poetry Society of America Bulletin Supplement 1973; and Poets and Writers Inc., U.S.A. – 'Publishing Houses Interested in Poetry'.

Thanks are also offered to *International Who's Who in Poetry* biographees who also publish poetry journals which they sent to us for inclusion in this listing.

AB INTRA (Hellric Publs.), Dolores Stewart, Ed., 32 Waverley St., Belmont, MA 02178, USA. Gut Poetry. Qtly.; $2.50/yr.; 75 cents/ea.; 28-32 pgs.; 200 circ. Reports 3-6 wks. Pays 5 copies plus 1 yr. sub.

ABBEY (White Urp Press), David Greisman, Co-Ed., 5011-2 Green Mountain Cir., Columbia, MD 21044, USA. Poetry & gen. lit. Qtly.; Free; 8 pgs.; 200 circ. Pays copies only.

* ABBOTSBURY PUBLICATIONS, David Boadella, Ed., Abbotsbury Primary Schl., Abbotsbury, Dorset, UK.

* ABELARD-SCHUMAN, LTD., 158 Buckingham Palace Rd., London S.W.1, UK.

ABOVE GROUND REVIEW, George Roland Wood, Sr., Ed., P.O. Box 337, Arden, NC 28704, USA. Poetry & gen. lit. 2/yr.; $5.75/3 issue vol.; $2/ea.; 1500 circ. Reports 1 wk.-2 mos. $10 for best poem ea. issue.

ABRAXAS, Warren Woessner, Ed., 1831 S. Park St., Madison, WI 53713, USA. Poetry & reviews. 2/yr.; $2/yr.; $1/ea.; 40 pgs.; 300 circ. Reports 3 wks. Pays copies only.

ABYSS, Gerard Dombrowski, Ed., P.O. Box C, Somerville, MA 02143, USA. Poetry & gen. lit. Qtly.; $4/yr.; $1/yr.; 40 pgs.; 500 circ. Reports 6 wks. Pays copies only.

* ACADEMY, Mike Finley, Ed., 115 Johnson Hall, Univ. of Minn., Mpls. MN 55455, USA.

ACORN PRESS, Lesley Macdonald, Ed., 7 Harley Gdns., London S.W.10 9SW, UK. Poetry.

* ADLARD (Norman) & CO. (Smiths Suitall Ltd.), 33 Upper Orwell St., Ipswich, IP4 1HN, UK.

ADVENT BOOKS, Brian Coffey, Ed., 13 Elms Ave., London N10, UK. Poet. Single poems up to 1000 lines. Bilingual texts accepted. 6 books/yr.; 1020 pgs.; 250 circ. Reports at sight. Payment 10% royalty.

AESOP'S FEAST, Michael Walton, 540 S. Gaylord, Denver, CO 80209, USA. Poetry, solicited material only, chapbook & small poetry pamphlet. Irreg.; $1/ea.; 40 pg.; 500 circ. Pays 10 cents/line, $1 min. plus copies.

AGENDA, (Agenda Edits.), William Cookson, Ed., 5 Cranbourne Ct., Albert Bridge Rd., London SW11 4PE, UK. Poetry & gen. lit. Recognizable contemporary Engl. poetry. No 'concrete' or sound poetry. £2/yr.; 45 pence/ea.; 96 pgs.; 2 million circ. Reports 1 mo., only if accompanied by SAE. Pays £1/pg. poetry.

THE AGNI REVIEW (Eidolon Press), Ashold Melnyczuk, Ed., Box 764, Sparta,

NJ 07871, USA. Poetry & gen. lit. 3 or 4/yr.; $1/2 issues; 50 cents/ea.; 38 pgs.; 300 circ. Reports 3 wks. Pays only by special arrangement, 3 copies.

AISLING, Paul Shuttleworth, Ed., Devlin's, 2526 42nd Ave., San Fran., CA 94116, USA. Poems of Clarity & Vision; New qtly. of Irish & Am. poetry. $4/yr.; $1/ea.; 20-40 pgs.; 300 circ.

AKROS, See Akros Publs.

AKROS PUBLICATIONS, Duncan Glen, Ed., 14 Parklands Ave., Penwortham, Preston, Lancs. PR1 0QL, UK. Poetry, no restrictions on length or lang.; specializes in Scottish poetry. 3/yr.; £1/4 issues; 30 pence/ea.; 80 pgs.; 750 circ. Reports a few days. Pays £2 per pg.

AKWESASNE NOTES, Rarihokwats, Part-Ed., Mohawk Nation, via Rooseveltown, NY 13683, USA. Poetry & gen. lit. 9/yr.; donation; 48 pgs.; 44 million circ. Reports vary. Pays copies.

* ALASKA REVIEW, Robert Bowen, Ed., Alaska Meth. Univ., Anchorage, AK 99504, USA.

ALBION VILLAGE PRESS, Iain Sinclair, Ed., 28 Albion Dr., London E.8 4ET, UK. Poetry & gen. lit.; generally publish unpubld.; any length & style.

* ALDEN MOWBRAY PRESS LTD., Osney Mead, Oxford, UK.

ALICE JAMES BOOKS, 46 Brattle St., Cambridge, MA 02138, USA. Poetry, esp. by women. 4/yr.; $25/signed copies 1st 6 books.; $4.25/ea.

ALL IN WALLSTICKERS (Allin), Nina Steane, Ed., 31 Headlands, Kettering, Northants., UK. Poetry; short poems considered; poetry usually contracted for. 1-2/yr.; 15-20 pence/ea. Reports 1-2 wks. Pays copies only.

ALL THIS & LESS PUBLISHERS, see Star-Web Paper.

ALL-TIME FAVORITE POETRY (J. Mark Press), Dr. Barbara Fischer, Ed., 133 W. 6th St., Deer Park, NY 11729, USA. Poetry & reviews; 3-16 lines, all subjs. & styles; no humour. Qtly.; $4.95/soft, $7.95/hard; 30 pgs.; Reports 2 wks. Pays 2-10 cents a line.

ALL YOU CAN EAT, 391 George St., New Brunswich, NJ 08903, USA. Poetry, gen. lit. 12/yr.; $5/yr.; 24 pgs.; 25 million circ. Pays copies only.

ALLIN, see All in Wallstickers.

ALLISON & BUSBY LTD., 6A Noel St., London W1V 3RB, UK.

ALTERNATIVE PRESS QUARTERLY, Ken & Ann Mikolowski, Eds., 4339 Avery, Detroit, MI 48208, USA. Poetry. Qtly.; $10/yr.; $2.50/ea.; 500 circ. Reports erratic. Pays copies only.

AM HERE BOOKS, Richard Aaron, Ed., 1867 Ollon, Vaud, Switzerland. Poetry & gen. lit.; books only. Reports 1 mo. Pays copies only.

* AMANUENSIS, James Gash, Ed., Dept. of Engl., Univ. of Ky., Lexington, KY 40506, USA.

AMARANTHUS (Pilot Press Books), L. Eric Greinke, Poetry Ed., P.O. Box 2662, Grand Rapids, MI 49501, USA. Poetry & gen. lit.; solicits "Trans-Symbolist" work. 3/yr.; $3.75/yr.; $1.25/ea.; 120 pgs.; 1 million circ. Reports 2 wks. Pays 2 copies.

AMBER, Hazel Firth Goddard, Ed., P.O. Box 173, Dartmouth, N.S. B2Y 3Y3, Canada. Contemporary poetry; prefer haiku, lanterne, good free verse & blank verse, not over 14 lines; like sonnets. Qtly.; $2/yr.; 50 cents/ea.; 24 pgs.; 100 circ. Reports not over 3 mos. Pays free copies. Sev. poetry awards.

AMBIT, Dr. Martin Bax, Ed., 17 Priory Gdns., London N6, UK. Poetry & gen. lit. Qtly.; 75 pence/yr.; 25 pence/ea.; 48 pgs.

AMERICA, Donald R. Campion, S.J., Ed., 106 W. 56th St., N.Y. NY 10019, USA. Wkly. jrnl. of opinion, occasionally poetry. $12/yr.; 40 cents/ea.; 32 pgs.; 48,000 circ. Reports 4 wks. Pays $10-$20 for poetry. Annual poetry award.

AMERICAN-CANADIAN PUBLISHERS, LTD., Arthur Goodson, Dir., P.O. Box 2078, Portales, NM 88130, USA. Poetry & prose of seventies & beyond; gen. lit.; books only on invitation; Neo-Narrative Newsletter & Anthol. of Post-Modern in prep. 6/yr.; $3.95/ea. Reports 3 mos. Pays copies only.

THE AMERICAN CONFERENCE OF THERAPEUTIC SELFHELP SELFHEALTH SOCIAL CLUBS, see Constructive Action for Good Health Magazine.

* AMERICAN DIALOG, Joseph North, Ed., 853 Braodway, Room 2105, N.Y., NY 10003, USA.

* AMERICAN FORESTS, James B. Craig, Ed., 919 17th St., N.W., Wash., DC 20006, USA. Outdoor themes.

* AMERICAN HAIKU, James & Gayle Bull, Eds., Box 73, Platteville, WI 53818, USA.

* AMERICAN LEGION MAGAZINE, 345 6th Ave., N.Y., NY 10019, USA. Light Verse.

AMERICAN POET (Prairie Press), Stella Craft Tremble, Ed., 902 10th St., Charleston, IL 61920, USA. Poetry. Qtly.; $4/yr.; $1.50/ea.; 30 pgs.

AMERICAN POETRY LEAGUE BULLETIN, Truth Mary Fowler, Ed., 10419 Audrey Dr.,

Sun City, AZ 85351, USA. Qtly.

AMERICAN POETRY REVIEW (World Poetry, Inc.), Stephen Berg, Part-Ed., 401 S. Broad St., Phila., PA 19147, USA. Poetry & gen. lit. 6/yr.; $5/yr.; $1/ea.; 56 pgs.; 30 million circ. Reports 3-4 mos.

* AMERICAN-SCANDINAVIAN REVIEW, Eric J. Friss, Poetry Ed., 127 E. 73rd St., N.Y., NY 10021, USA. Poetry about Scandinavia.

AMERICAN SCENES (J. Mark Press), Dr. Barbara Fischer, 133 W. 6th St., Deer Park, NY 11729, USA. All subjs. & styles. Qtly.; $4.95/soft, $7.95/hard; 30 pgs.; 1 million circ. Reports immediate. Pays 2-10 cents per line.

* AMERICAN SCHOLAR, Hiram Haydn, Ed., 1811 Q St. N.W., Wash DC 20009, USA.

* AMERICAN WEAVE, Alfred Cahen, Ed., 23728 Glenhill Dr., Cleveland, OH 44121, USA.

AMPERS & MAGAZINE (X Cathedra), John R. Mackay, Ed., 816 S. Hancock St., Phila., PA 19147, USA. Poetry and gen. lit. 6/yr.; $3/yr.; 75 cents/ea.; 44 pgs.; 5 million circ. Reports 1 mo. Pays $15 per poem.

AMS PRESS, see Works: A Quarterly of Writing.

ANA EXCETERA (Anna Eccetera-Edizioni AE), Martino & Anna Oberto, Eds., Via Montallegro 32A/43 16145 Genoa, Italy. Poetry, art, & criticism; Mag. on abstract philos. & lang. L2000 plus postal charges for. mail/ea.; 60 pgs.

ANCHOR PRESS, Miss Elizabeth Deighton, Ed., 325 Barnsley Rd., Cudworth, Barnsley, Yorks., UK. Poetry suitable for children's & adult's recitationo. 1/yr.; 25 pence/ea.; 12-20 pags.; 3-400 circ. Reports about 2 wks.

AND (Writers Forum), John Rowan, Co-Ed., 262 Randolph Ave., London W9, UK. Concrete Poetry; submissions not required. Irreg.; 25 pence/ea.; 500 circ.

* ANGEL HOUR, 388 Sun Park Pl., San Jose, CA 95136, USA.

* THE ANGELS, Judson Dicks, Ed., 70 Snowberry Ln., Central Islip, NY 11722, USA.

* ANGLO-SOVIET JOURNAL, 118 Tottenham Court Rd., London W.1, UK.

ANGLO-WELSH REVIEW, Roland Mathias, Ed., Deffrobani, Maescelyn, Brecon LD3 7NL, UK. Poetry by Welsh writers who write in Engl.; limited space for non-Welsh contbns. 3/yr.; £1.50/yr.; 60 pence/ea.; 275 pgs.; 1500 circ. Reports 3 mos. Payment varies, no poem less than £1.50.

ANGUS & ROBERTSON (U.K.) LTD., 2 Fisher St., London WC1R 4QA, UK.

* ANN ARBOR REVIEW, Fred Wolven, Poetry Ed., 2118 Arlene St., Ann Arbor, MI 48106, USA.

ANTAEUS (The Ecco Press), Daniel Halpern, Ed., 1 W. 30th St., N.Y., NY 10001, USA. Poetry & gen. lit. Qtly.; $8/yr.; $2.50/ea.; 160 pgs.; 2500 circ. Reports 1 mo. Pays copies only.

ANTHONY HARRIS LITTLE PRESS (AHLP), Dr. Anthony Harris, Co-Ed., 16 Glebe St., London W4, UK. Poetry & gen. lit. 10 pence-£100/ea.; 10-400 pgs. Pays by arrangement.

THE ANTIGONISH REVIEW, R.J. MacSween, Ed., St. Francis Xavier Univ., Antigonish, N.S., Canada. Poetry & gen. lit. Qtly.; $5/yr.; $1.50/ea.; 110 pgs.; 500 circ. Reports 1 mo. Pays copies only.

THE ANTIOCH REVIEW, Lawrence Grauman, Jr., Ed., P.O. Box 148, Yellow Springs, OH 45387, USA. Poetry & gen. lit. Qtly.; $6/yr.; $1.75/ea.; 144 pgs.; 6 million circ. Reports 4-6 wks. Pays $8/pg., 3 copies.

ANVIL PRESS, see Raven Books.

ANVIL PRESS POETRY, Peter Jay, Ed., 69 King George St., London SE10 8PX, UK. Poetry. Reports vary. Payment royalty.

APALACHEE QUARTERLY (Dixie Dung Beetle Press, Inc.), David Mr. Morrill, Co-Ed., 502 W. Jefferson, Tallahassee, FL 32301, USA. Poetry & gen. lit. 3/yr.; $4/yr.; $1/ea.; 44 pgs.; 300 circ. Reports 1 mo. Pays copies only.

APHRA/the feminist literary magazine, Elizabeth Fisher, Co-Ed., Box 893, Ansonia Stn., N.Y., NY 10023, USA. Poetry; concerned w. feminist art. Qtly.; $4.50/yr.; $1.25/ea.; 72 pgs. Reports 3-6 mos. Pays copies only.

THE APOLLO (Northwoods Press), James Romnes, Ed., Bigfork Schl., Bigfork, MN 56623, USA. Poetry & gen. lit.; mag. exclusively for h.s. students. 3/yr.; $5/yr.; $18 hard/yr.; $2/ea., $5.95 hard/ea.; 100 pgs.; 500+ circ. Reports up to 60 days. Pays royalty only.

APOSTROPHE, Tom Parks, Co-Ed., P.O. Box 5985, Columbia, SC 29250, USA. Poetry, no restrictions. Qtly.; $2/yr.; 75 cents/ea.; 40 pgs.; 2 million circ. Reports 2 wks. Pays 1 yr. subscription, framable cert.

* APPROACH, Albert & Helen Fowler, Eds., 114 Petrie Ave., Rosemont, PA 19010, USA.

* APPROACHES, Joy Bale, Ed., 110 S. Maple, Elizabethtown, KY 42701, USA.

THE AQUILA PUBLISHING COMPANY LTD. (see also PROSPICE), J.C.R. Green, Co-Ed., 18 Atherstone Close, Shirley, Solihull, Warwickshire B90 1AU, UK. Poetry & gen. lit. 12-100 pgs. Pays by arrangement.

ARBITRARY CLOSET PRESS, see Screen Door.

ARC PUBLICATIONS, Anthony Ward, Ed., 11 Byron Rd., Gillingham, Kent, UK. Poetry, poems rarely exceed 24 pgs. Irreg.; from 15 pence/ea.; 20 pgs.; 250-500 circ.

* ARCADE RECORDING CIRCUIT, 23 Arcadian Gdns., London N22 5AG, UK.

* ARCADIA PRESS, 38 George St., London W.1, UK.

* ARCADIAN, 154 Montrose Dr., Port Jefferson Stn., NY 11776, USA.

* THE ARCHER, Elinor Brown, Ed., Box 9646, N. Hollywood, CA 91609, USA.

* ARENA, Anthony Trotman, Ed., 42 Lake Rd., Wimbledon, London SW19, UK.

ARENA: a Literary Magazine (The Handcraft Press), Noel Farr Hoggard, Ed., P.O. Box 6188, Te Aro, Wellington, New Zealand. Poetry up to 80 lines; New Zealand writers only. Irreg.; 28 pgs.; 600 circ. Reports 1 mo. Pays copies only.

ARETE INK, see Good News.

* ARIZONA HIGHWAYS, Raymond Carlson, Ed., 2039 W. Lewis Ave., Phoenix, AZ 85009, USA.

ARIZONA QUARTERLY, Albert Frank Gegenheimer, Ed., Univ. of Ariz., Tucson, AZ 85721, USA. Poetry & gen. lit. Qtly.; $2/yr.; 50 cents/ea.; 96 pgs. Reports 2-4 wks. Pays copies only.

ARIZONA STATE POETRY SOCIETY, see the Sandcutters.

THE ARK PRESS, Kim Taylor, Brushford, Dulverton, Somerset, UK. Poetry & gen. lit.; rarely books in translation; no length restriction.

THE ARK RIVER REVIEW, Jonathan Katz, Part-Ed., 348 N. Ohio, Wichita, KS 67214, USA. Poetry & gen. lit.; prefer minimum of 2 pgs. per poem or poet. Qtly.; $2/yr.; 75 cents/ea.; 52 pgs.; 700 circ. Reports 3-6 wks. Pays 20 cents per line poetry plus 2 copies. Annual awards prog.

* ARLINGTON QUARTERLY, Box 336, Univ. Stn., Arlington, TX 76110, USA.

* ARMADILLO, P.O. Box 392, Sarasota, FL 33578, SA.

* ARNOLD (E.J.) (SCOTLAND), LTD., Fac-

tory No. 18, 27-35 Napier Pl., W. Park N., Cumbernauld, Dumbarton, U.K.

ARTS ALIVE MERSEYSIDE (Merseyside Arts Assn.), 6 Bluecoat Chambers, Schl. Lane, Liverpool L1 3BX, UK. Poetry & arts. Monthly; Free.

ART & LITERARY DIGEST, Roy Cadwell, Ed., Tweed, Ont., Canada. Poetry & gen. lit. 4/yr.; $2/yr.; 50 cents/ea.; 4 pgs.; 2 million circ. Reports 1 mo. Pays 1 cent/word.

* ART LIVING, 9 Rochdale Pl., Kirkintilloch, Glasgow, UK.

ARTISANS ALMANACK, Pressing On-printing and graphics, Q.K. Simms, Ed., P.O. Box 628, San Anselmo, CA 94960, USA. Poetry & gen. lit.; natural earth poetry. 1/yr.; 90 pgs.; 7500 circ. Reports 45 days. Pays $100-$500.

* ARTS IN SOCIETY, Morgan Gibson, Ed., Univ. of Wis. Ext., Madison, WI 53706, USA.

ASIA PUBLISHING HOUSE LTD., P.S. Jayasinghe, Publr., 447 Strand, London WC2R OQU, UK. Engl. Lang. Poetry.

THE ASHLAND POETRY PRESS, Robert McGovern, Co-Ed., Ashland Coll., Ashland, OH 44805, USA. Poetry; anthols. & individual poets; rarely read unsolicited mss. Pays 10% on books, $5 anthols.

ASPECT, Edward J. Hogan, Co-Ed., 66 Rogers Ave., Somerville, MA 02144, USA. All styles & genres of poetry; fiction & non-fiction essays. 6/yr.; $5/yr.; 75 cents/ea.; 40-48 pgs.; 100-250 circ. Reports 30 days. Payment, 2 copies.

ASSEMBLING, Henry Korn, Co-Ed., Box 1967, Brooklyn, NY 11202, USA. Poetry & gen. lit. 1/yr.; $2.50/yr.; 200 pgs.; 1 million circ. Reports 1 mo. Pays copies only.

ATEN PRESS, see Pink Peace.

ATHANOR, Douglas Calhoun, Ed., P.O. Box 582, Clarkson, NY 14430, USA. Poetry & gen. lit.; poetry w. highly charged lines. 2/yr.; $5/yr.; $1.50/ea.; 72 pgs.; 600 circ. Reports 1 wk. plus. Pays copies only.

ATHENEUM, 122 E. 42nd St., N.Y., NY 10016, USA.

THE ATLANTIC ADVOCATE, John Braddock, Ed., Glesner Bldg., Phoenix Sq., Fredericton, N.B., Canada.

THE ATLANTIC MONTHLY, Robert Manning, Ed., 8 Arlington St., Boston, MA 2116, USA. Poetry of all types. Monthly; $11.50/yr.; $1/ea.; 104 pgs.; 325,000 circ. Reports 6-8 wks. Pays $2 per line & depends on author & quality of poem.

ATLANTIC PRESS, 122 Grand Bldgs., Trafalgar Sq., London WC2N 5EP, UK.

ATLANTIC PRESS, 520 Fifth Ave., N.Y., NY 10036, USA.

ATLANTIS EDITIONS, Richard O'Connell, Ed., 4910 N. 12th St., Phila., PA 19141, USA. Poetry.

* ATLAS, Malcolm Muir, Jr., Poetry Ed., 1180 Sixth Ave., N.Y., NY 10036, USA.

* AUDIT/POETRY, Geo. Butterick, Ed., 180 Winspeare Ave., Buffalo, NY 14214, USA.

AUGTWOFIVE, Craig Ellis, Ed., c/o Abyss, P.O. Box C, Somerville, MA 02143, USA. Poetry & gen. lit. Irreg.; $1.50/ea. Pays copies plus hopper bux.

AUTHOR, Soc. of Authors, 84 Drayton Gdns., London SW10 9SD, UK.

* AUTHOR POET, Box 1024, Birmingham, AL 35201, USA.

AXIS BAG (Goofy Publs.), Mike George, Ed., 123 Holland Rise, Rochdale, Lancs., UK. Poetry & fiction; primarily small-press modern poets. Irreg.; 15 pence/ea.; 30 pgs.; 300 circ. Reports at time of printing. Pays copies only.

AZYMOTE (Ramah), Rob Miller, Co-Ed., Box 516, Union, OR 97883. Poetry & letters; no mss. solicited yet.

B AND H BOOKS, see Fur Line Press.

* BABY CARE, 52 Vanderbilt Ave., N.Y., NY 10017, USA.

BABY JOHN, James Evans, Ed., 5406 Latona Ave. N.E., Seattle, WA 98105, USA. Poetry & gen. lit.; no restrictions length or style. Irreg.; $3/4 issues; 50 cents/ea.; 36 pgs.; 250 circ. Reports 3-6 wks. Pays copies only. $5 prize for best work ea. issue.

BACHY, William Mohr, Poetry Ed., Papa Bach Bookstore, 11317 Santa Monica Blvd., L.A., CA 90025, USA. Largely unpublished poets. 2/yr.; $3.50/yr.; $2/ea.; 150 pgs.; 1500 circ. Reports immediately to 6 wks. Pays $2 per pg. & 1 copy.

THE BALEEN PRESS, see Inscape.

BALTHUS: Fantasy Literature & Folk-Lore, Jon M. Harvey, Ed., 18 Cefn Rd., Mynachdy, Cardiff CF4 3HS, UK. Poetry & gen. lit. 2/yr.; 60 pence/3 issues; 20 pence/ea.; 350 circ. Reports max. time 1 mo. Pays copies only.

BALL STATE UNIVERSITY FORUM, Merrill Rippy, Co-Ed., Ball State Univ., Muncie, IN 47306, USA. Poetry & gen. lit. Qtly.; $3/yr.; $1/ea.; 80 pgs.; 1500 circ. Reports 3 mos. Payment 10 copies.

BANTAM BOOKS, LTD. (Transworld Publrs. Ltd.), Cavendish House, 57-59 Uxbridge Rd., Ealing, London W5 5SA, UK.

BARDIC ECHOES, Clarence L. Weaver, Ed., 1036 Emerald Ave., N.E., Grand Rapids, MI 49503, USA. Poetry not over 40 lines. Qtly.; $2/yr.; 50 cents/ea.; 24 pgs.; 500 circ. Reports 1-3 mos.

BARTLEBY'S REVIEW, Albert Stainton, Co-Ed., Box 332, Machias, ME 04654, USA. Poetry & reviews; poems under 100 lines. 2/yr.; $1.75/yr.; 48 pgs.; 500 circ. Reports 1 mo. Pays 3 copies.

* BASILDON DISTRICT ARTS ASSOCIATION, c/o Mr. B. Harris, 28 Paprills, Basildon, Essex, UK.

BASILISK PRESS, David Lunde, Co-Ed., P.O. Box 71, Fredonia, NY 14063, USA. Poetry. 3-4/yr.; $1.95/ea.; 64 pgs.; 600 circ. Reports 3-6 mos. Pays copies only.

BATSFORD (B.T.) LTD., 4 Fitzhardinge St., London W1H OAH, UK. Publish "Batsford Book of Children's Verse".

BAUHAN (William L.), PUBLISHER, W.L. Bauhan, Ed., Dublin, NH 03444, USA. Poetry & New England regional books.

BB BKS (see also GLOBAL TAPESTRY JOURNAL), David Cunliffe, Ed., 1 Spring Bank, Salesbury, Blackburn, Lancs. BB1 9EU, UK. Contemporary Poetry & creative prose.

* BBC PUBLICATIONS, 35 Marylebone High St., London W1M 4AA, UK.

BEACON PRESS, see The Prickly Pear.

BEAU GESTE PRESS, see Schmuck.

BEAVER COSMOS, see Imago.

BEDSITTER ANNUALS, Olive Rhodes Teugels, Ed., 6 Clapham Mansions, Nightingale Ln., London SW4 9AQ, UK. Poetry & gen. lit. 2/yr.; 50 pence/yr.; 30 pence/ea.; 100 + pgs.; 800 circ.

* BEE & BLACKTHORN PRESS, 6 Perth Rd., Beckenham BR3 2PP, UK.

BELLSTONE JOURNAL, E.G. White-Swift, Ed., P.O. Box 1643, Portland, OR 97207, USA. Poetry, criticism, reviews; experimental poetry & criticism. 6/yr.; $4.50/yr.; $1/ea.; 48-144 pgs.; 500 + circ. Reports 1-2 mos. Pays copies.

BELLSTONE PRESS (see also BELLSTONE JOURNAL), E.G. White-Swift, Ed., P.O. Box 1643, Portland, OR 97207, USA. Poetry at least 32 pgs.

BELOIT POETRY JOURNAL, Robert Glauber, Part-Ed., Box 2, Beloit, WI 53511, USA. Poetry & reviews. Qtly.; $3/yr.; 75 cents/ea.; 40 pgs.; 1200 circ. Reports immediately to 4 mos. Pays 3 copies.

BENN (Ernest) LTD., Keon Hughes, Chmn., Sovereign Way, Tonbridge, Kent TN9 1RW, UK. Publish only 2 books of poetry by Robert Service.

* BERG (Norman S.), PUBLISHERS, Sellanraa, Dunwoody, GA 30338, USA.

BEST IN POETRY (J. Mark Press), Dr. Barbara Fischer, Ed., 133 W. 6th St., Deer Park, NY 11729, USA. Poetry & reviews; send 1-4 poems, 3-16 lines to ed. & wait for reply. Qtly.; $4.95/soft; $7.95/hard; 30 pgs.; 1 million circ. Reports immediate. Pays 2-10 cents per line.

* BETTISCOMBE PRESS, Bettiscombe, Bridport, Dorset, UK.

* BEYOND BAROQUE, P.O Box 806, Venice, CA 90291, USA. Avant-Garde Poetry.

* BIBLO & TANNEN BOOKSELLERS & PUBLISHERS INC., 63 Fourth Ave., N.Y., NY 10003, USA.

ALISON BIELSKI, The Cottage Itton Common, Chepston Moor NP6 6BX, UK. Poetry & art; emphasis on layout of shaped poetry. 2/yr.

BIG BOULEVARD, William Robson, Ed., P.O. Box 5580, Long Beach, CA 90805, USA. Poetry & gen. lit. 12/yr.; $7/yr.; 75 cents/ea.; 13 pgs. Reports 1 mo. Pays copies only.

BIG D PRESS, see Softball.

BIG DEAL PRESS, see Chernozem.

BIG SKY, Bill Berkson, Ed., Box 272, Bolinas, CA 94924, USA. Poetry & gen. lit. Qtly.; $5/yr.; $1.50/ea.; 80 pgs.; 800 circ. Reports 1-2 mos. Pays copies only.

BIRMINGHAM POETRY CENTRE, see Muse.

BITTERROOT, Menke Katz, Ed., Blythebourne Stn., P.O. Box 51, Brooklyn, NY 11219, USA. Poetry only. Qtly.; $4/yr.; $1.50/ea.; 32-52 pgs.

BLACK BOOKS BULLETIN (Institute of Positive Education), Don L. Lee, Co-Ed., 7848 S. Ellis Ave., Chgo., IL 60619, USA. Poetry & gen. lit. Qtly.; $8/yr.; $2/ea.; 60 pgs.; 5 million circ. Reports 3-4 wks. Pays copies only.

BLACK BOX, Alan Austin, Part-Ed., 3725 Jocelyn St., N.W., Wash. DC 20015, USA. Poetry & gen. lit. that can be published on tape. 6/yr.; $20/yr.; $5/ea.; 3 hrs.; Reports 1 mo. Payment $2 per min. on publ.

THE BLACK COLLEGIAN, N.R. Davidson, Co-Ed., 3217 Melpomene Ave., New Orleans, LA 70125, USA. Poetry & gen. lit. 6/yr.; $2.50/yr.; 50 cents/ea.; 56 pgs.; 75 million circ. Reports 2 mos. Pays copies only.

BLACK PUBLICATIONS, Miss A. Gilbertson, Ed., Room 12, Top Flat, 32 Vinicombe St., Glasgow G12 8BE, UK. Poetry.

BLACK SPARROW PRESS, John Martin, Ed., P.O. Box 25603, L.A., CA 90025, USA. Poetry & fiction. 15-20 books/yr. Reports 30-60 days. Pays 10% Royalty.

* BLACK SWAMP REVIEW, Engl. Dept., Bowling Green Univ., Bowling Green, OH 43402, USA.

THE BLACKBIRD CIRCLE, Dean Deter, Co-Ed., Box 218, Cazenovia, NY 13035, USA. Poetry. Irreg.; $6/3 issues; 32 pgs.; 500 circ. Reports 6 wks. Pays copies only.

* BLACKIE & SON, LTD., Bishopbriggs, Glasgow, G64 2NZ, and 5 Fitzhardinge, London WIH ODL, UK.

BLACKWOOD'S MAGAZINE (William Blackwood & Sons Ltd.), Douglas Blackwood, Ed., 32 Thistle St., Edinburgh EH2 1HA, UK. Poetry & articles. 12/yr.; £3/yr.; 24 pence/ea.; 96 pgs.; 11,250 circ. Reports by return. Pays on publication.

BLEB, George Ryan, Ed., Box 322, Times Sq. Stn., N.Y., NY 10036, USA. Poetry, concrete art. 2/yr.; $1/yr.; 75 cents/ea.; 32 pgs.; 500 circ. Reports 3 wks. Pays copies only.

BLEEDING PHANTOM (see also BROKEN COBWEBS), A.J. Lindenberg & others, Eds., 686 Greenhills Dr., Ann Arbor, MI 48105, USA. No unsolicited mss.

* BLES (Geoffrey) LTD., 59 Brompton Rd., London S.W.3, UK.

* BENJAMIN BLOM INC., 2521 Broadway, N.Y., NY 10025, USA.

THE BLUE CLOUD QUARTERLY (Graphic Arts/Blue Cloud Abbey), Brother Benet Twedten, O.S.B., Blue Cloud Abbey, Marvin, SD 57251, USA. Poetry & gen. lit. Qtly.; $1/yr.; 25 cents/ea.; 12-16 pgs.; 2,718 circ. Reports immediately. Pays copies.

BLUE DRAGON, see Stardance.

BLUE WIND PRESS (see also SEARCH FOR TOMORROW), George Mattingly, Ed., Box 1189, Iowa City, IA 52240, USA. Open to submission of mss.

* BLUESTONE, Loker Raley, Ed., Box 355, Woodstock, NY 12598, USA.

THE BODLEY HEAD, Sir Hugh Greene, Chmn., 9 Bow St., Covent Gdn., London WC2E 7AL, UK. No new poetry; well estab. series of poetry selections on children's list.

BOGG (Fiasco Publs.), George Cairncross, Ed., 31 Belle Vue St., Filey, E. Yorks., UK. Poetry & gen. lit. Qtly.; 60 pence/yr.; 15

pence/ea.; 30 pgs.; 150 circ.

* BONEFOLD IMPRINT, see Zam Is Dat.

BONES (White Bones Press), Katherine Greef, Co-Ed., R.D.1, Box 265, Otego, NY 13825, USA. Poetry & gen. lit. 1-2/yr.; $2/2 issues; $1.25/ea.; 80 pgs.; 1 million circ. Pays 2 copies.

THE BOOKSTORE PRESS, David Silverstein, Co-Ed., 39 Housatonic St., Lenox, MA 01240, USA. Poetry & gen. lit.

* BOSTON UNIVERSITY JOURNAL, Box 357, Boston Univ. Stn., Boston, MA 02215, USA.

BOUNDARY 2: A Journal of Postmodern Literature (State Univ. of N.Y. at Binghamton), William V. Spanos, Co-Ed., Dept. of Engl., SUNY-Binghamton, Binghamton, NY 13901, USA. Poetry & gen. lit.; restricted to postmodern lit. 3/yr.; $5/yr.; $2/ea.; 260 pgs.; 500 circ. Reports 1 mo. Payment variable.

BOX 749 (Seven Square Press), David Ferguson, Part-Ed., P.O. Box 749, Old Chelsea Stn., N.Y., NY 10011, USA. Poetry & gen. lit. Qtly.: $7/yr.; $2/ea.; 64-80 pgs.; 1 million circ. Reports 2-4 mos. Pays 2 copies.

* BOYDELL PRESS, P.O. Box 24, Ipswich IP1 1JJ, UK.

GEORGE BRAZILLER INC., Richard Howard, Gen. Ed., 1 Park Ave., N.Y., NY 10016, USA. Braziller Series of Poetry.

BRECHT TIMES, Peter Langford, Ed., Alexandra Cottage, Kimpton Rd., Welwyn, Herts., UK. Poetry & art; Socialist poetry. 3/yr.; 25 pence/yr.; 10 pence/3a.; 25 pgs.; 400 circ. Reports 1 mo. No payment.

* BREWHOUSE PRIVATE PRESS, The Orchard, Wymondham, Melton Mowbray, UK.

BRIDGE, A POETRY QUARTERLY (Bridge Publs.), Nanlee Haston Pitts, Ed., 3726 Hibiscus St., Coconut Grove, FL 33133, USA. Poetry, experimental & traditional. Qtly.; $8/yr.; $2.50/ea.; 30 pgs.; 300 circ. Reports 6 wks. max. Pays copies & 1 yr. sub. Cash prizes.

BRIDGE PUBLICATIONS (see also BRIDGE, A POETRY QUARTERLY & TROLL), Nanlee Haston Pitts, Ed., 3726 Hibiscus St., Coconut Grove, FL 33133, USA.

* BRITISH PUBLISHING COMPANY LTD., 3 Brunswick Sq., Gloucester GL1 1UQ, UK.

BRO-CARDS, see Success.

BROADSIDE SERIES, Dudley Randall, Ed., 12651 Old Mill Pl., Detroit, MI 48238,

USA. Black poetry & criticism. 12/yr.; $6/yr.; 50 cents/ea.; 100 circ. Pays $10 a poem.

BROKEN COBWEBS (Bleeding Phantom), A.J. Lindenberg & others, Eds., 686 Greenhills Dr., Ann Arbor, MI 48105, USA. Poetry & fiction; no unsolicited mss. Irreg.; 75 cents/ea. Pays copies only.

* BRUCE (David) & WATSON, 44 Gt. Russell St., London W.C.1, UK.

BRUCE BABBITT, 24 Evelyn Gdns., London S.W.7, UK.

BUGLE-AMERICAN, 2909 N. Humboldt Blvd., Milwaukee, WI 53201, USA. Poetry & gen. lit.; newspaper. 52/yr.; $9/yr.; 48 pgs.; 20 million circ.

THE BUMMER, Brian C. Felder, Ed., 1915 N. Prospect Ave., Apt. 19, Milwaukee, WI 53202, USA. Poetry. Irreg.; 25 cents/ea.; 24 pgs.; 500 circ. Reports 90 days. Pays copies only.

BURNING DECK PRESS, see Diana's Bimonthly.

BURKE PUBLISHING CO., LTD., 14 John St., London WC1N 2EJ, UK.

BURROUGHS BULLETIN (House of Greystoke), Vern Coriell, Ed., 6657 Locust, Kan. City, MO 64131, USA. Poetry & gen. lit. Qtly.; $5/mbrship.; $2/ea.; 28-32 pgs.; 2200 circ. Reports 30 days. Pays copies only.

* BURROW (Ed. J.) & CO. LTD., Imperial House, Lypiatt Rd., Cheltenham, Glos. GL50 2QL, UK.

MICHAEL BUTTERWORTH PUBLICATIONS, see Corridor.

THE BYRON PRESS PUBLICATIONS, John Lucas, Part-Ed., Engl. Dept., Univ. Park, Nottingham, UK. Poetry vols. & pamphlets by contemporary poets of Engl.-speaking world.

BYWAYS, Gerry Loose, Ed., Hedda's Cottage, Arkesdew, Saffron Walden, Essex, UK. Poetry 48/yr.; 80 pence/yr.; 23 pence/ea.; 30 pgs.; 300 circ. Reports 1 mo. Payment negotiable.

* CAFE BOOKS, 1B Kensington Church Walk, London W8 4NB, UK.

CAFE SOLO (The Solo Press), Glenna Luschei, Ed., 1209 Drake Cir., San Luis Obispo, CA 93401, USA. Poetry & gen. lit.; plans special issues inclng. single poet issues. 3/yr.; $2.50/yr.; $1.50/ea.; 60 pgs.; 500 circ. Reports 2 wks.

CAITHNESS BOOKS, John Humphries, Ed., Janet St., Thurso, Caithness, UK. Poetry by Scottish writers only.

CALDER AND BOYARS LTD., John Calder, Part Dir., 18 Brewer St., London W1R 4AS, UK. Poetry inclng. 'New Russian Poets' & 'Contemporary Scottish Verse'.

THE CALIFORNIA QUARTERLY, Elliot Gilbert, Part Ed., 100 Sproul Hall, Univ. of Calif., Davis, CA 95616, USA. Poetry & gen. lit.; like Calif. material. Qtly.; $5/yr.; $1.50/ea.; 83 pgs.; 400 circ. Reports 4-6 wks. Pays 2 copies plus subscription.

* CALIFORNIA CROSSROADS, Robert Shaver, Ed., 1101 University Ave., Fresno, CA 93724, USA.

* CALIFORNIA REVIEW, Bill Richardson, Ed., 280 E. Mountain Dr., Santa Barbara, CA 93102, USA.

CALDER VALLEY POETS' SOCIETY, see The Parnassian.

CALVERT, Ruthellen Quillen, Poetry Ed., 46C Taliaferro, Univ. of Md., College Pk., MD 20742, USA. Poetry & gen. lit. 2/yr.; No subscription; Student supported; 40 pgs.; 33,000 circ. Reports 1 mo. No payments.

CAMBRIDGE REVIEW, 7 Green St., Cambridge, UK.

CAMELS COMING NEWSLETTER, Richard Morris, Ed., P.O. Box 703, San Francisco, CA 94101, USA. Poetry & gen. lit.; Poetry submissions not wanted. Irreg.; $7/12 issues; 4-8 pgs.; 1500 circ. Reports 1 wk. Pays copies only.

* CANADIAN FORUM, Milton Wilson, Ed., 56 Esplanade, Toronto 1, Ont., Canada.

THE CANADIAN MONARCHIST, now MONARCHY CANADA (The Monarchist League of Canada), John L. Aimers, Ed., 559 Roslyn Ave., Montreal 217, P.Q., Canada. Poetry, criticism & satire; Patriotic Poetry. 5/yr.; $3.50/yr.; 25 cents/ea.; 8 pgs.; 6 million circ. Reports 30 days. Pays copies only.

* CANADIAN POETRY, Arthur S. Bourniot, Ed., 290 Acacia Ave., Rockliffe, Ottawa, Ont., Canada.

CANADIAN/WHOLE EARTH/RESEARCH, see Northern Comfort.

CANTALOUPE (Woodhix Press), Raymond Zdonek, Co-Ed., 717 W. 4th, Bloomington, IN 47401, USA. Poetry & gen. lit. $2 & up/ea.; 20-100 pgs. Reports 4-5 wks.

* CAPE GOLIARD PRESS, see Cape (Jonathan) Ltd.

CAPE (JONATHAN) LTD., 30 Bedford Sq., London WC1B 3EL, UK.

* CAPE ROCK QUARTERLY, Peter Hilty, Ed., S.E. Missouri, Cape Girardeau, MO 63701, USA.

CAPELLA (Tara Telephone Publs.), Peter Falcon, Ed., 19 Oakdown Rd., Dublin 14, Ireland. Poetry & cartoons. Irreg.; 15 pence/ea.; 36 pgs.; 1200 circ. Pays copies only.

CAPRA PRESS (formerly Capricorn Press), Noel Young, Ed., 631 State St., Santa Barbara, CA 93101, USA. Poetry & gen. lit. Reports 1 mo.

* CARAVEL, Ben Hagglund, Ed., 1065 Runnymede St., E. Palo Alto, CA 94303, USA.

CARBON PRESS, see Harrison Monthly Review.

* CARCANET PRESS, 266 Councillor Lane, Cheadle House, Cheadle SK8 5PN, UK. Corres. to: c/o Dept. of Engl., Univ. of Manchester, Manchester M13 9PL, UK.

* THE CARDINAL, Tim Walton, Ed., Wesleyan Stn., Middletown, CT 06458, USA.

* CARDINAL POETRY QUARTERLY, Eda Casciani, Ed., 10418 W. Drummond Pl., Melrose Park, IL 60164, USA.

CARDINELL LTD., see International Times.

CARE– the magazine for people who care about race relations, Thomas Oliver Newham, Ed., 12 Phillip Ave., Auckland 7, New Zealand. Poetry, articles, reviews. 4/yr.; $1/yr.; 25 cents/ea.; 20 pgs.; 3 million circ. Reports 2 wks. Pays copies only.

CARET, Trevor McMahon, Co-Ed., 31 Marlborough Pk. Ctrl., Belfast BT9 6HN, Northern Ireland. Poetry & short stories. 3/yr.; 50 pence/yr.; 15 pence/ea.; 36 pgs.; 600 circ. Reports 10 days. Pays copies.

* CARLETON MISCELLANY, Erling Larsen, Ed., Carleton Coll., Northfield, MN 55057, USA.

CAROLINA QUARTERLY, Bruce M. Firestone, Ed., Box 1117, Chapel Hill, NC 27514, USA. Poetry & gen. lit. 3/yr.; $4/yr.; $1.50/ea.; 112 pgs.; 2 million circ. Reports 6-8 wks. Pays $5 per pg. plus 3 copies.

* CARR (J.L.), 27 Milldale Rd., Kettering, Northants., UK.

* CASS (FRANK) & CO. LTD., 67 Gt. Russell St., London WC1B 3BT, UK.

* CASSELL & CO. LTD., 35 Red Lion Sq., London W.C.1, UK.

THE CASTALIAN (The Crabcalf Press), Jeff Riggenbach, Co-Ed., P.O. Box 75182, Los Angeles, CA 90075, USA. Poetry & gen. lit. Qtly.; $5/yr.; $1.50/ea.; 24 pgs.; Reports 4-8 wks. Pays $10, poetry & reviews.

* CASTLELAW PRESS, W. Linton, Peebleshire, UK.

CATALYST, Ian Young, Ed., 315 Blantyre Ave., Scarborough, Ont., Canada M1N 2S6. Poetry & fiction; 2-3 chapbooks per yr. w. poetry by gay & non-gay authors. All books $2. Reports very fast.

* CAT FANCY, Leslie S. Smith, Ed. 11760 Sorrento Valley Rd., San Diego, CA 92101, USA. Poems about cats.

CATS MAGAZINE, Jean A. Laux, Ed., P.O. Box 4106, Pittsburgh, PA 15202, USA. 12/yr.; $6.50/yr.; $1/ea.; 48 pgs.; 46,000 circ. 1 page of poetry. Pays on publication, 20 cents per line.

CAT'S PAJAMAS PRESS, John Jacob, Ed., 602 S. Austin, Apt. 2-C, Oak Park, IL 60304, USA. Poetry & gen. lit. Irreg.; 8-28 pgs.; 250 circ. Reports 3-4 wks. Pays copies.

CAVE (Caveman Press), Trevor Reeves, Ed., P.O. Box 1458, Dunedin, New Zealand. Poetry & gen. lit.; No limit on length of mat.; like concrete poetry. 3/yr.; $NZ3/yr.; $NZ1/ea.; 72 pgs.; 700 circ. Reports 3 mos. Pays copies only.

CAXTON PRESS, see New Zealand Monthly Review.

CELTIC EDUCATIONAL SERVICES LTD., Celtic House, St. James' Gdns., Swansea SA1 6EA, UK. Poetry & gen. lit.

* CENTAUR PRESS, LTD., Fontwell, Arundel, Sussex, UK.

CENTER FOR CONTEMPORARY POETRY, John Judson, Ed., Murphy Lib., Univ. of Wis., La Crosse, WI 54601, USA. Poetry, articles, interviews; emphasis on midwestern poetry; 3 poets per volume. 1/yr.; $6/yr.; $6/ea.; 88 pgs.; 500 circ.

CENTER FOR WRITERS, see Mississippi Review.

CENTRE 17 (Walthamstow Poetry Grp.), Stanley J. Thomas, Co-Ed., 115 Old St., London EC1V 9JR, UK. Poetry & Prose. Qtly.; 50 pence/yr.

CENTRE SPAN, Martyn C. Offord, Ed., 2 Valetta Rd., Arnold Nottj, UK. Poetry & reviews; purpose to foster community spirit. 12/yr.; 3 pence/ea.; 6-8 pgs.; 1 million circ. Pays £40/mo.

* CHALLENGE, Leland Stewart, Ed., 2865 W. 9th St., Los Angeles, CA 90006, USA.

CHAPBOOKS, see David R. Godine Publisher.

CHAPMAN, Walter Perrie, Ed., 10 Spottiswoode Rd., Edinburgh EH9 1BQ, UK. Poetry & gen. lit.; Serious orientation, partly philosophical. Qtly.; £1.10/yr.; 30 pence/ea.; 32-48 pgs.; 750 circ. Reports 14 days. No payment.

CHARAS, Claire Levenhagen, Ed., 1224 N. Jay, Apt. 2, Tacoma, WA 98403, USA. Poetry. 3/yr.; $4.50/yr.; $1.75/ea.; 85 pgs. Reports 1 mo. Pays copies only.

* CHATELAINE, Doris Anderson, Ed., 481 Univ. Ave., Toronto, Ont., Canada.

CHATTO AND WINDUS LTD., I.M. Parsons, Part-Dir., 40-42 William IV St., London WC2N 4DF, UK. Poetry & gen. lit.; Some Engl. translations of for. poetry.

* CHELSEA, P.O. Box 242, Old Chelsea Stn., N.Y., NY 10011, USA.

CHERNOZEM (Big Deal Press), Steven L. Deal, Co-Ed., Box 404, Gothenburg, NB 69138, USA. Poetry of any length & style. Irreg.; $1/ea.; 20-30 pgs.; 200 circ. Reports within 30 days. Pays copies only.

CHICAGO REVIEW, Alexander Besher, Ed., Univ. of Chgo., Chgo., IL 60637, USA. Poetry & gen. lit.; No length on submissions. Qtly.; $5/yr.; $1.50/yr.; 200 pgs.; 2 million circ. Reports 1-2 mos. Pays prizes, 3 copies & 1 yr. subscription. Offers $100 poetry prize.

CHICAGO TRIBUNE MAGAZINE, Marcia Lee Masters, Poetry Ed., 435 N. Michigan Ave., Chgo., IL 60611, USA. Today's Poets, weekly column of poetry, published in Sunday Issues of Chgo. Tribune; Poems up to 35 lines. Prices vary. Payment.

* CHILMARK PRESS, INC., 201 E. 50th St., N.Y., NY 10022, USA.

* CHOICE, Engl. Dept., SUNY, Buffalo, NY 14214, USA.

* THE CHRISTIAN LIVING MAGAZINE, Daniel Hertzler, Ed., Mennonite Publng. House, Scottsdale, PA 15683, USA.

* THE CHRISTIAN MOTHER, Wilma Schaffer, Ed., 8121 Hamilton Ave., Cincinnati, OH 45231, USA. Inspiration for mothers.

THE CHRISTIAN SCIENCE MONITOR, Henrietta Buckmaster, Ed., 1 Norway St., Boston, MA 02115, USA. Poetry on Home Forum Page, 5 days per wk. Reports within days. Payment on acceptance varies $20-$40.

CHRISTOPHER'S BOOKS, (see also TREE), Melissa Albers, Ed., 1819 Sycamore Canyon, Santa Barbara, CA 93108, USA. Poetry & gen. lit. Reports 3 wks. Payments depends upon particular publ.

* CHURCH INFORMATION OFFICE, Church House, Dean's Yard, London SW1P 3NZ, UK.

CIMARRON REVIEW, Clinton C. Keeler, Ed.-in-Chief, Okla. State Univ., Stillwater, OK 74074, USA. Poetry & gen. lit.: emphasis on Man Triumphant in technological soc. Qtly.; $6/yr.; $2/ea.; 78 pgs.; 1500 circ. Payment in copies.

CINOLUTION, D. Forney, Ed., 710 21st St., Sacramento, CA 95814, USA. Poetry, criticism, reviews. Qtly.; $5/yr.; $1.25/ea.; 52 pgs.; 1 million circ. Reports 1 wk. to 1 mo. Payment negotiable.

* CIRCLE IN THE SQUARE PUBLICATIONS, see Poetry of the Circle in the Square.

CITY LIGHTS BOOKS, INC., 1562 Grant Ave., San Francisco, CA 94133, USA. Pocket Poets Series.

* CITY LIGHTS JOURNAL, Lawrence Ferlinghetti, Ed., 261 Columbus Ave., San Francisco, CA 94116, USA.

CIVIL SERVICE POETRY (Emma), Ernest Meadowcroft, Co-Ed., S. Corner, Burses Way, Hutton, Brentwood, Essex, UK. Poetry; incls. poetry from European Civil Serv., UK Civil Serv. & guest poets. 1/yr.; 20 pence/ea.; 36 pgs.

CLAM PRESS, Mike Leniman, Ed., 206 Montpelier Row, Blackheath Village, London SG23, UK. Poetry.

CLARE MARKET, (LSE Students Union), John Stathatos, Ed., Students Union, London Schl. of Econs., Houghton St., Aldwych, London WC2 UK. Poetry & gen. lit. 2/yr.; £2/4 issues; 50 pence/ea.; 80 pgs.; 500 circ. Reports 2-3 mos. Pays copies only.

* CLO-BEAG, 6 Lilybank Gdns., Glasgow W2, UK.

CLOUD NINE-SOFT PRESS (VICTORIA) REVIEW, see Soft Press.

CLOUD NINE: Vancouver Island Poems, (Soft Press), Robert Sward, Ed., 1050 St. David St., Victoria, B.C., Canada. Poetry & photos; No unsolicited mss. 1/yr.; $3/yr.; 1 million circ. Reports 3 mos. Pays copies only.

CLOVEN HOOF, Rosemary Polzin, Ed., Box 925, Saginaw, M 48606, USA. Poetry & gen. lit. Irreg.; $2/4 issues; 50 cents/ea.; 50 pgs.; 500 circ. Reports 1 mo. Pays copies only.

CLUB LEABHAR, F.G. Thompson, Dir., 31 Braeside Pk., Balloch, Inbhirnis IV1 2HJ, UK. Poetry mainly in Gaelic Lang.

COBRA PRESS, G.W. Sherman, Ed., 15381 Chelsea Dr., San Jose, CA 95124, USA.

COG PRESS, see Enigma.

COLLEGES POETRY, Poetry Soc., Trinity & All Saints Colls., Brownberrie Ln., Horsforth, Leeds LS18 5HD, UK. Poetry; annual anthol. of poetry from students of colls. of further educ. in England & Wales. 1/yr.; 20 pence plus postage/ea.

* COLLET'S HOLDINGS, LTD., Denington Estate, Wellingborough, Northants., UK.

COLLINGS (REX) LTD., G.R. Collings, Co-Dir., 6 Paddington St., London W1M 3LA, UK. Poetry.

* COLLINS (WALTER) LTD., London Rd., Bowbridge, Stroud, Glos., UK.

COLLINS (WILLIAM) SONS & CO. LTD., 14 St. James's Pl., London SW1, UK. Occasionally publish poetry.

* COLUMBIA, Elmer Feldt, Ed., P.O. Drawer 1670, New Haven, CT 09507, USA.

THE COLUMBIA FORUM, Erik Wensburg, Ed., 612 W. 114th St., N.Y., NY 10025, USA. Poetry & gen. non-fiction. 3-5 poems/issue; 48 pgs.; 10,000 circ. plus newsstand sales. Reports up to 6 mos. Pays $75 per poem.

* COLUMBIA UNIVERSITY PRESS LTD., 70 Gt. Russell St., London W.C.1, UK.

* COMBRIDGE (C.) LTD., Wrentham St., Birmingham B5 6QT, UK.

* COMMENTARY, 165 E. 56th St., N.Y., NY 10022, USA.

COMMONWEAL, James O'Gara, Ed., 232 Madison Ave., N.Y., NY 10016, USA. Weekly; $14/yr.; 50 cents/ea.; 24 pgs.; 27,000 circ. Reports 2-3 wks. Pays 40 cents/line poetry.

COMMUNICATIONS COMPANY, Dan Dorman, Ed., The Communication Co., P.O. Box 6723, Columbus, OH 43209, USA. Poetry & gen. lit. Irreg. Reports 4 wks. Payment varies.

COMMUNITIES, Lime Saddle, Rte. 1, Box 191, Oroville, CA 95965, USA. Poetry & gen. non-fiction. 6/yr.; $6/yr.; $1/ea.; 72 pgs.; 6 million circ. Reports 3 mos.

COMMUNITY OF FRIENDS, Moses Yanes, Ed., 13850 Big Basin Way, Boulder Creek, CA 95006, USA. Poetry & gen. lit. 3/yr.; $3/yr.; $1.25/ea.; 30 pgs.; 300 circ. Reports 2-6 wks. Pays copies only.

CONCERNING POETRY, L.L. Lee, Ed., Western Wash. State Coll., Bellingham, WA 98225, USA. Poetry & gen. non-fiction. $3/yr.; $1.50/ea.; 85 pgs.; 300 circ. Pays copies only.

CONFRONTATION, Martin Tucker, Ed., Engl. Dept., Long Island Univ., Brooklyn, NY 11201, USA. Poetry & gen. lit. 2/yr.; $2/yr.; $1/ea.; 90 pgs.; 2 million circ. Reports 4-6 wks. Pays $15-$100, 1 copy.

CONNECTIONS MAGAZINE, Toni Zimmerman, Co-Ed., 100 W. 94th St., N.Y., NY 10025, USA. Poetry & gen. lit. 2/yr.; $2/yr.; $1/ea.; 60 pgs.; 300 circ. Reports immediately. Pays copies only.

* CONSTABLE & CO. LTD., 10 Orange St., Leicester Sq., London WC2H 7EG, UK.

CONSTRUCTIVE ACTION FOR GOOD HEALTH MAGAZINE (The American Conf. of Therpeutic Selfhelp/Selfhealth/Social Clubs), Miss Shirley Burghard, Ed., 2nd Fl. Rear Apt., 710 Hickory St., Syracuse, NY 13203, USA. Poetry & gen. lit. 12/yr.; $5/yr.; 50 cents/ea.; 35-40 pgs.; 500 circ. Reports 1 mo. Pays copies only.

CONTAC, John Freeman, Ed., 6 Main View, Thorne Rd., Stainforth, Nr. Doncaster, Yorks. DN7 5BU, UK. Poetry, art, criticism, reviews, music. Qtly.; 80 pence/yr.; 17 pence/ea.; 28 pgs.; 200 circ.

* CONTACT, Ruth Kentfield, Ed., 3030 Bridgeway, Sausalito, CA 94965, USA.

CONTEMPORA, Paul G. Putney, Co-Ed., P.O. Box 673, Atlanta, GA 30301, USA. Poetry & gen. lit. Qtly.; $4.50/6 issues; $1/ea.; 48 pgs.; 2500 circ. Reports 2 wks.

CONTEMPORARY REVIEW (incorporating the Fortnightly), Rosalind Wade, Ed., 37 Union St., London S.W.1, UK. Poetry & gen. lit.; Ideal maximum length 2500-3000 words. 12/yr.; £4.02/yr.; 30 pence/ea.; 56 pgs. Reports 1 mo. Pays £2.50 per thousand.

CONTINUING EDUCATION PRESS, John Fisher, Ed., Div. of Continuing Educ., Draper Annex, Univ. of Mass., Amherst, MA 01002, USA. Poetry & gen. lit.

CONTINUUM, (Trelawney Press), Robert Schware, Co-Ed., Univ. of Lancaster-Bowland Coll., Lancaster, UK. Literary contbns. of outstanding univ. writers & young persons. 2/yr.; 10 pence/ea.; 25 pgs.; 1 million circ. Reports 1 mo. Pays copies only.

* CONTRASTS, Russell Pemberton, Ed., 76 Rosedale Ave., Gt. Crosby, Liverpool L23 0UQ, UK.

THE COOPERATOR (Int. Coop. Coun.), Louis K. Acheson, Jr., Ed., 17819 Roscoe Blvd., Northridge, CA 91324, USA. Poetry & gen. lit.; Poetry of less than 40 lines. 2/yr.; $3.50/2 yrs.; $1/ea.; 24-32 pgs.; 1500 circ. Reports 2 mos. Pays complimentary copies.

CORDUROY, Richard Immersi, Ed., 406 Highland Ave., Newark, NJ 07104, USA. Poetry & gen. lit. 2/yr.; $2.50/3 issues; $1/ea.; 50 pgs.; 300 circ. Reports 2 wks. Pays copies only.

CORGI BOOKS, LTD. (Transworld Publrs. Ltd.), Cavendish House, 57-59 Uxbridge Rd., Ealing, London W5 5SA, UK.

* CORINTH BOOKS, 29 Perry St., N.Y., NY 10003, USA.

CORNHILL MAGAZINE, Osyth Leeston, Ed., 50 Albemarle St., London W1X 4BD, UK. Poetry & gen. fiction. Qtly.; £1.40/yr.; 30 pence/ea.; 74 pgs. Payment by agreement.

* CORNELL UNIVERSITY PRESS, 124 Roberts Pl., Ithaca, NY 14850, USA.

CORRIDOR: New Writings Quarterly (Michael Butterworth Publs.), Michael Butterworth, Ed., 61 Seymour St., Radcliffe, Manchester, UK. Poetry & gen. lit. Qtly.; 60 pence/yr.; 15 pence/ea.; 24-28 pgs.; 1 million circ. Reports no more than 2 wks. No payment.

* COSMEP, Andrew Curry, Ed., Box 123, El Cerrito, CA 94530, USA.

COTTONWOOD REVIEW, Chris Suggs, Poetry Ed., Box J, Kan. Union, Univ. of Kan., Lawrence, KS 66044, USA. Poetry & gen. lit. 2/yr.; $3/yr.; $1.50/ea.; 85 pgs.; 1 million circ. Reports 2 mos. No payment, copies only.

COTYLEDON, Michael Mayer, Ed., Rte. 4, Box 276, Traverse City, MI 49684, USA. Poetry & gen. lit. 6/yr.; 75 cents/yr.; 16 pgs.; 5 million circ. Reports 1-2 wks. Pays copies only.

* COUNTER/MEASURES, X.J. Kennedy, Ed., Box 431, Bedford, MA 01730, USA.

* COUNTRY BEAUTIFUL, Dana Kellerman, Ed., 15330 Watertown Plank Rd., Elm Grove, WI 53122, USA.

* COUNTRY GUIDE, 1760 Ellice Ave., Winnipeg 21, Man., Canada.

* COUNTRY LIFE, 2-10 Tavistock St., Covent Garden, London W.C.2, UK.

* COUNTRYGOER BOOKS, LTD., The School House, 12 Market St., Buxton SK17 6LD, UK.

THE COUNTRYMAN, Crispin Gill, Ed., Sheep St., Burford, Oxfordshire, OX8 4LH, UK. Poetry & gen. non-fiction. Qtly.; $5.50/yr.; 35 pence/ea.; 208 pgs.; 60 million circ. Reports 1-2 wks. Pays £10 per thousand words.

COURRIER DU CENTRE INTERNATIONAL D'ETUDES POETIQUES, Musée de la Littérature, Bibliothèque Royale, Blvd. de l'Empereur 4, 1000 Brussels, Belgium.

* COVENT GARDEN PRESS LTD., 80 Long Ave., London WC2E 9NG, UK.

* COWLES BOOK COMPANY INC., 488 Madison Ave., N.Y., NY 10022, USA.

CPHJ NEWSLETTER, Comm. for Prisoner Humanity & Justice, 1029 Fourth St., No. 37, San Rafael, CA 94901, USA. Poetry & gen. non-fiction; much of mat. comes from prison inmates. Irreg.; Free; 8 pgs.; 2500 circ. Reports up to 3 mos. Pays copies only.

CRAB GRASS, John Gilbert, Ed., 7 Rugby Rd., Belfast 7, Northern Ireland. Poetry & gen. non-fiction. 15 pence/ea.; 40 pgs.; 1200 circ. No payment.

THE CRABCALF PRESS, see The Castalian.

THE CRANNER-SKIBB REPRODUCTION ENGINE, see Nunquam Mens.

* CRAZY HORSE, Philip Dacey, Ed., S.W. Minn. State Coll., Marshall, MN 56258, USA.

CREATIVE MOMENT (Poetry Eastwest), Syed Amanuddin, Ed., P.O. Box 391, Sumter, SC 29150, USA. Poetry; esp. world poetry written in Engl. 2/yr.; $3/yr.; $1.50/ea.; 40 Pgs.; 500 circ. Reports 6-8 mos. Pays 1 copy.

* CREATIVE REVIEW, 1718 S. Garrison, Carthage, MO 64836, USA.

CRITICAL QUARTERLY (Manchester Univ. Press), C.B. Cox, Co-Ed., Dept. of Engl., Univ. of Manchester, Manchester M13 9PL, UK. Poetry, criticism, longpoems. Qtly.; £1.50/yr.; 40 pence/ea.

* CRONOPIOS, James Stephens, Ed., 138 S. 13th St., La Crosse, WI 54601, USA.

CROSS-CULTURAL COMMUNICATIONS, Stanley H. Barkan, Publr., 239 Wynsum Ave., Merrick, NY 11566, USA.

THE CROSSING PRESS (see also NEW: AMERICAN & CANADIAN POETRY), John Gill, Ed., R.D.3, Trumansburg, NY 14886, USA. New Am. & Canadian poetry; individual vols.; minority anthols.; gay poetry anthol.; women's poetry anthol.; Am. Indian anthol.

* THOMAS Y. CROWELL CO., 201 Park Ave. S., N.Y., NY 10003, USA.

CURTAINS (Pressed Curtains), Paul Buck, Ed., 12 Foster Clough, Hebden Bridge, Yorks., HX7 5QZ, UK. Poetry & gen. lit.; translations of mod. French poetry since 2nd World War. Qtly.; $4/yr.; $1/ea.; 40 pgs.; 400 circ. Reports 1 wk. Pays copy only.

THE CURWOOD COLLECTOR, Ivan A. Conger, Ed., 1825 Osaukie Rd., Owosso, MI 48867, USA. Poetry & gen. lit.; anything pertaining to James Oliver Curwood. 3-4/yr.; $2/4 issues; 50 cents/ea.; 8-14 pgs.; 200 circ.

CYCLO*FLAME, Vernon Payne, Ed., 212 W. First St., San Angelo, TX 76901, USA. Poetry. 1/yr.; $4/yr.; $4/ea.; 120 pgs.; 500 circ. Reports 1 mo. Pays $1 on acceptance.

DACOTAH TERRITORY, Mark Vinz, Ed.,

P.O. Box 775, Moorhead, MN 56560, USA. Poetry & reviews; biased against merely acad. of linguistic. Irreg.; $2.50/3 issues; $1/ea.; 64 pgs.; 1 million circ. Reports 1 wk. to 2 mos. Pays copies only.

* DAILY MEDITATIONS, Ruth S. Paterson, Ed., P.O. Box 2710, San Antonio, TX 78206, USA.

DAILY WORD, Martha Smock, Ed., Unity Village, MO 64063, USA. Poetry & prayers & meditations. 12/yr.; $2/yr.; 25 cents/ea.; 48 pgs.; 825,000 circ. Reports 2-3 wks. Pays $1 per line of poetry.

DAMASCUS ROAD, Charles Shahoud Hanna, Ed., 6271 Hill Dr., Wescosville, PA 18106, USA. Poetry. Irreg.; $1.95/ea.; 70 pgs.; 500 circ. Pays copies only.

* DASEIN, Percy Johnston, Ed., G.P.O. Box 2121, N.Y., NY 10001, USA.

DATR, John Noyce, Ed., 67 Vere Rd., Brighton BN1 4NQ, Sussex, UK. Poetry; shorter mat. bias; no aversion to concrete & typewriter poetry. Irreg.; 20 pence/ea.; 24 pgs.; No Payment.

DAWN (Wichita Falls Alternative), Craig Canan, Ed., P.O. Box 1822, Wichita Falls, TX 76307, USA. Poetry & gen. non-fiction. 6/yr.; $6/yr.; 25 cents/ea.; 20 pgs.

* DAWSONS OF PALL MALL, Cannon House, Folkestone, Kent, UK.

DAY BY DAY (The Loverseed Press), Ronald Mallone, Mng. Ed., Woolacombe House, 141 Woolacombe Rd., Blackheath, London S.E.3, UK. Poetry & gen. lit.; short poems. 12/yr.; £1.40/yr.; 10 pence/ea.; 14 pgs.; 11 million circ. Reports 3-21 days. Pays by arrangement.

DECAL POETRY REVIEW, Meic Williams, Ed., 52 Can-Y-Coed Rd., Cyncoed, Cardiff, UK. Poetry & gen. lit. 2/yr.; £1/yr.; 50 pence/ea.; 80 pgs.; 600 circ. Pays copies only.

DECEMBER MAGAZINE, Curt Johnson, Co-Ed., Box 274, Western Springs, IL 60558, USA. Poetry & gen. lit. 1-2/yr.; $6/4 issues; $2/ea.; 196 pgs.; 2 million circ. Reports 6-8 wks. Pays 2 copies.

DECIDUOUS, Christopher Franke, Ed., 3212 Lorain Ave., No. 15, Cleveland, OH 44113, USA. Poetry & gen. lit. Irreg.; $1/yr.; 1 pg. Pays copies usually.

DEFACATION PRESS, see Suck.

DEFENDERS OF WILDLIFE NEWS, Mary Hazell Harris, Ed., 2000 N St. N.W., Suite 201, Wash. DC 20036, USA. Incls. poetry on wildlife or environment. 6/yr.; copies to mbrs. of Defenders of Wildlife; mbrship. $5/yr.; 130 pgs.; 40,000 circ.

* DEFINITION, Martha Baird, Ed., 39 Grove St., N.Y., NY 10014, USA.

DEKALB LITERARY ARTS JOURNAL, Mel McKee, Ed., DeKalb Coll., Clarkston, GA 30021, USA. Qtly.; $5/yr.; $1.25/ea.; 100 pgs.: 1500 circ. Reports 6 wks. Pays 1 copy. Yearly poetry contest.

DELTA, Michael Launchbury, Co-Ed., 524 Fulwood Rd., Sheffield 10, UK. Poetry & gen. lit. 3/yr.; 75 pence/3 issues; 50 pgs. No payment.

DELTA CAN, Glen Siebrasse, Ed., 351 Gerald St., Lasalle 690, Montreal, Canada. Poetry; only contemporary Canadian work. 38 titles. Reports 3 wks.

J.M. DENT & SONS LTD. PUBLISHERS, F.J. Martin Dent, Chmn., Aldine House, 26 Albemarle St., London W1X 4QY, UK. Occasional poetry; gen. lit.

* DENVER POST, Henry W. Hough, Ed., 615 15th St., Denver, CO 80202, USA.

DENVER QUARTERLY, (Univ. of Denver), Burton Feldman, Ed., Univ. of Denver, Denver, CO 80210, USA. Qtly.; $6/yr.; $1.50/ea.: 140 pgs. Reports 1 mo. min. Pays $10 per printed pg. of poetry.

DESCANT (Tex. Christian Univ. Press), Betsy Feagan Colquitt, Ed., Dept. of Engl., Tex. Christian Univ., Ft. Worth, TX 76129, USA. No restriction on poetry style; generally no longer than 40 lines; 10-15 pgs. poetry ea. issue. $3/4 issues; $1/ea.; 56 pgs.; 600 circ. Reports no longer than 6 wks. Pays copies only.

DEUTSCH (ANDRE), LTD., 105 Gt. Russell St., London WC1B 3LJ, UK.

* DIALOGUE CALCUTTA, 12/2/1 Palm Ave., Calcutta 19, India.

DIANA'S BIMONTHLY (Burning Deck Press), Tom Ahern, Ed., 71 Elmgrove Ave., Providence, RI 02906, USA. Poetry & fiction. Irreg.; $5/yr.; 50 cents/ea.; 50 pgs.; 250 circ. Reports 1 wk.-1 mo. Pays 3 copies.

EMILY DICKINSON BULLETIN (Higginson Press), Frederick L. Morey, Ed., 4508 38th St., Brentwood, MD 20722, USA. Info. on Emily Dickinson. 2/yr.; $5/yr. for individuals; $10/yr. for institutions, invoices: 50 pgs.

DILDO PRESS, see The Reginald A Fessenden Mem. Radio/Times/Are.

DIMENSION (Univ. of Tex. at Austin), A. Leslie Willson, Ed., P.O. Box 7939, Dept. of Germanic Langs., Austin, TX 78712, USA. Poetry & gen. lit.; contemporary lit. in German w. face-pg. translations. 3/yr.; $6/yr.; $2.50/ea.; 200 pgs.; 600 circ. Reports vary. Pays copies.

* DISINHERITED, Peter Hoida, Ed., 7 Evesham Rd., Cheltenham, Glos., UK.

DISPOSABLE PAPER PRESS, see Little Magazines/Small Presses, Moongoose.

DIXIE DUNG BEETLE PRESS, see Apalachee Quarterly.

DOBSON BOOKS LTD., Dennis Dobson, Co-Ed., 80 Kensington Church St., London W8 4BZ, UK. Poetry & gen. lit.

* DOCK LEAVES PRESS, Ty Newydd, Lodge Hill, Caerleon NP6 1DA, UK.

* DODD, MEAD & CO., 79 Madison Ave., N.Y., NY 10016, USA.

DODO, Steve Kuttner, Ed., 63 Victoria Rd., Whalley Range, Manchester 16, Lancs., UK. Poetry & art. 3/yr.; 45 pence/yr.; 15 pence/ea.; 50 pgs.; 600 circ.

DOGGERAL PRESS (see also FOUR DOGS MOUNTAIN SONGS), Alice Karle, Co-Ed., P.O. Box 448, Inglewood, CO 80110, USA. Poetry & chapbooks.

DOLPHIN BOOK CO. LTD., J.L. Gili, Part-Dir., 1A Southmoor Rd., Oxford OX2 6RY, UK. Some poetry books translated from Hispanic langs.

SEAN DORMAN MANUSCRIPT SOCIETY, see Writing.

* DORSET NATURAL HISTORY & AR-CHAEOLOGICAL SOCIETY, c/o The County Museum, Dorchester, Dorset, UK.

* DORSET PUBLISHING COMPANY, Milborne Port, Sherborne, Dorset, UK.

DOUBLEDAY & CO., 277 Park Ave., N.Y., NY 10003, USA.

* DRAGON BOOKS, Bala, Merioneth, UK.

DRAGON'S TEETH PRESS, El Dorado Nat. Forest, Georgetown, CA 95634, USA. Living Poets' Library series.

DRAGONFLY, Duane Ackerson, Ed., Box 147, Idaho State Univ., Pacatello, ID 83201, USA. Poetry, satire, criticism, reviews. Qtly.; $3.50/yr.; $1/ea.; 60 pgs.; 350 circ. Reports vary. Pays copies only.

DRAGONFLY: A Quarterly of Haiku, Lorraine Ellis, Ed., 4102 N.E. 130th Pl., Portland, OR 97230, USA. Engl. lang. classical/traditional haiku only. Qtly.; $5/yr.; $1.25/ea.; 500 circ. Reports ss than 30 days. No Payment. Num. cash awards & book prizes.

DRIFTWOOD EAST, Marjorie Drake, Ed., 95 Carter Ave., Pawtucket, RI 02864, USA. Qtly.; $5/yr.; $1.50/ea.; 70 pgs.; 950 circ. No payments.

DRIFTWOOD PUBLICATIONS, Brian Wake, Ed., 58 Exeter Rd., Bootle Lancs. L20 7SA, UK. Engl. poetry only; concentrate on pamphlets & books of 20-30 pgs. 6/yr.; £1.50/yr.; 20 pence/ea.; Reports vary. Pays copies only.

* THE DRUID, Eric Ratcliffe, Ed., 77 Carlton Ave., Dulwich, London SE21, UK.

* DUCKWORTH (GERALD) & CO., LTD., The Old Piano Factory, 43 Gloucester Cres., London NW1 7DY, UK.

* THE DUBLIN MAGAZINE, Rivers Carew, Ed., Haccombe Parva, Dublin, Co. Killiney, Ireland.

DUENDE PRESS, see Fervent Valley.

DUFOUR EDITIONS INC., Booksellers & Publrs., Jeanne H. Dufour, Pres., Chester Springs, PA 19425, USA. Poetry; no for. lang. mat.

* DUNDALGAN PRESS (W. TEMPEST), LTD., Francis St., Dundalk, Ireland.

DUSTBOOKS, (see also SMALL PRESS REVIEW), Len Fulton, Ed., 5218 Scottwood Rd., Paradise, CA 95969, USA. Poetry, non-fiction, fiction, photos, longpoems.

DUTTON (E.P.) & CO., 201 Park Ave. S., N.Y., NY 10003, USA.

DWARF NEWS (Dwarf Ministry of Info.), Tony Brantingham, Ed., 3 Pant Glas, Harmerhill, Shropshire, UK. Poetry, articles, cartoons. 12/yr.; £1/yr.; 10 pence/ea.; 20 pgs.; 500 circ.

EARTH'S DAUGHTERS, Judith Kerman, Co-Ed., 944 Kensington Ave., Buffalo, NY 14215, USA. Poetry & gen. lit. 2-4/yr.; $3/6 issues; 75 cents/ea.; 1 million circ. Pays copies only.

EARWIG MAGAZINE (Earwig Graphics), John Milne, Part-Ed., 10 Norfolk St., Auckland 2, New Zealand. Poetry & gen. lit. Qtly.; 40 cents/ea.; 48 pgs.; 5 million circ.

EAST CAROLINA UNIVERSITY POETRY FORUM PRESS, see Tar River Poets.

EAST TEXAS STATE UNIVERSITY, see Sadakichi Hartmann Newsletter.

THE ECCO PRESS, see Antaeus.

* ECHOES, Florence Unangst, Ed., 88 Church St., Brooklyn, NY 11218, USA.

ECOLIT, Gerald Haslam, Ed., Dept. of Engl., Sonoma State Coll., Rohnert Park, CA 94928, USA. Poetry & gen. lit.; aimed at introducing environmental awareness in Engl. classes. 2/yr.; $1/yr.; 50 cents/ea.; 50 pgs.; 300 circ. Reports 2 wks. Pays 2 copies.

EDGE, Don Long, Part-Ed., Whitcombe & Tombs Ltd., Mag. Dept., P.O. Box 1465, Christchurch, New Zealand. 3/yr.; $1.50 (NZ)/ea.

* EDGE, Henry Beisse, Ed., Box 4067, Edmonton, Alta., Canada.

EDIBLE MAGAZINE, Allen Fisher, Part-Ed., 54 Mayes Ct., New Park Rd., London SW2 4EX, UK. Poetry & graphics. 30 pgs. Reports vary. Payment varies, copies sometimes.

EDINBURGH UNIVERSITY PRESS, 22 George Sq., Edinburgh EH8 9LF, UK. Poetry & gen. lit.

EGG – A Literary Quarterly, Bill Linehan, Part-Ed., P.O. Box 289, Surfside, CA 90743, USA. Poetry & gen. lit. Qtly.; $3.50/yr.; $1/ea.; 52 pgs.; 500 circ. Reports 1-2 mos. Pays 4 copies.

* EGRET, J. Pierre Boenig, Ed., 84 Seventh Ave., Brooklyn, NY 11215, USA.

EIDOLON PRESS, see The Agni Review.

* EIKON, Bob Fay, Ed., 111 Woodbridge St., S. Hadley, MA 01075, USA.

EL GRITO, (Quinto Sol Publs., Inc.), 2150 Shattuck Ave., No. 606, Berkeley, CA 94704, USA. Chicano poetry & gen. lit. Qtly.; $5/yr.

ELAN poétique littéraire et pacifiste, Louis Lippens, Ed., 31 rue Foch, 59126 Linselles, France. Poetry & gen. lit. 3/yr.; 12F/yr.

ELBOW DRUMS, Marjo Price, Prog. Dir., Calgary Indian Friendship Soc., 140 2nd Ave. S.W., Calgary, Alta. T2P OB9, Canada. Poetry & gen. lit. 12/yr.; $3.50/yr.; 25 cents/ea.; 10 pgs.; 350 circ.

ELEK (PAUL) LTD., Paul Elek, Part-Ed., 54-58 Caledonian Rd., London N1 9RN, UK. Engl. poets & Engl. lang. only.

* ELEVENTH FINGER, Paul Matthews, Ed., 1 Charletta St., Brighton 7, Sussex, UK.

THE ELIZABETH PRESS, James L. Weil, Ed., 103 Van Etten Blvd., New Rochelle, NY 10804, USA. Poetry.

ELLIS (AIDAN) PUBLISHING LTD., Cobb House, Nuffield, Henley-on-Thames, Oxon RG9 5RU, UK. Gen. lit.; will consider poetry.

EMBER PRESS, see Flowers From The Printshop, New Headland, Littack.

EMMA, see Civil Service Poetry.

EMPTY BELLY (Orphan Press), Charles Tidler, Ed., Box 14, Ganges, B.C., Canada. Poetry & gen. lit. Irreg.; $1/ea.; 24-32 pgs.; 200 circ. Reports 2 wks. Pays 2 copies.

EMPTY BOAT, Ben Goldberg, Ed., P.O. Box 42, Brandywine Stn., Schenectady, NY 12304, USA. Poetry & gen. lit. Irreg.; $2/3 issues; $1/ea.; 45 pgs.; 500 circ. Reports 2 wks.-1 mo. Pays copies only.

EMPTY ELEVATOR SHAFT, Bruce Leary, Ed., P.O. Box 27004, San Francisco, CA 94127, USA. Poetry & gen. lit. Qtly.; $4/yr.;

$1.25/ea.; 60 pgs.; 500-1 million circ. Reports vary, 10 days average. Pays 2 copies.

* ENCORE MAGAZINE, 1121 Major Ave. N.W., Albuquerque, NM 87107, USA.

ENCOUNTER, Melvin J. Lasky, Co-Ed., 59 St. Martins Ln., London WC2N 4JS, UK. Poetry & gen. lit. 12/yr.; $14/yr.; $1.25/ea.; 96 pgs.

* ENCOUNTER, Herbert Prizeman, Poetry Ed., P.O. Box 96, St. Leo, FL 33574, USA.

THE ENGLISH RECORD, Daniel J. Casky, Ed., State Univ. Coll., Oneonta, NY 13820, USA. Poetry & gen. lit. Qtly.; $10/yr.; $2/ea.; 100 pgs.; 3 million circ. Reports 1 mo. Pays 2 copies.

ENIGMA, (Cog Press), Rigby Graham, Ed., 396 Aylestone Rd., Leicester, UK. Poetry & gen. lit.; hardbound mag. limited to 50-60 copies max. Irreg.; £3.50/ea.; 140 pgs.; 50 circ. Reports very slow. Pays copy.

ENITHARMON PRESS, Alan Clodd, Ed., 22 Huntingdon Rd., E. Finchley, London N2 9DU, UK. Poetry. Reports 2 mos. Pays royalty.

ENSIGN (Ch. of Jesus Christ of Latter-Day Saints), Doyle L. Green, Ed., 50 E. N. Temple St., Salt Lake City, UT 84150, USA. Religious, spiritual, uplifting, hopeful poetry. 12/yr.; $4/yr.; 80-144 pgs.; 370,000 circ. Reports 6 wks. Pays 3-5 cents per word, straight copy, up to 40 cents a line for poetry. Poetry contest open to mbrs. of Relief Soc. of Ch. of Jesus Christ of Latter-day Saints.

ENVOI, J.C. Meredith Scott, Ed., Lagan Nam Bann, Ballachulish, Argyll, Scotland, UK. Poetry. 3/yr.; £1/yr.; 20 pgs. Reports before next issue. Pays by arrangement.

* ENVOI, Baxter Hathaway, Ed., "Seven Levels", N. Place, 159 Goldwin Smith, Cornell Univ., Ithaca, NY 14850, USA.

EPOCH, Baxter Hathaway, Part-Ed., 245 Goldwin Smith Hall, Cornell Univ., Ithaca, NY 14850, USA. Poetry & fiction; contemporary, previously unpubld. 3/yr.; $4/yr.; $1.50/ea.; 700 circ. Reports 2-3 mos. Pays copies.

EPOS, (Rollins College Press), Evelyn Thorne, Co-Ed., Crescent City, FL 32012, USA. Poetry. Qtly.; $3/yr.; $1/ea.; 32 pgs.; 500 plus circ. Reports 1 wk. Pays 2 copies.

EQUAL TIME, Hugh Seidman, Ed., 463 West St., Apt D1016, N.Y., NY 10014, USA. Poetry; conceived as anthol. w. work of 65 poets from all around country. 100 pgs.; 1 million circ.

EQUALITY, Richard Fichter, Ed., 6 Frankfurt-Main, Postfach 2803, German Fed. Repub. & 28 E. Vine, Oxford, OH 45056, USA. Poetry & gen. lit. Irreg.;

Donation; 16 pgs.; 500 circ. No payment.

ERISIAN IMPRINTS INK, see Pentabarf.

ERRATICA, Don Dorrance, Ed., 626 Milwaukee, S. Milwaukee, WI 53172, USA. Poetry & gen. lit. Irreg.; $2/yr.; 50 cents/ea.; 40 pgs.; 200 circ. Reports 2-4 wks. Pays copies only.

ESPRESSO, Robert Mann, Co-Ed., Box 1466, Pacifica, CA 94044, USA. Qtly.; $1/ea.; 100 pgs.; 1 million circ.

ESSENCE, Sharyn J. Skeeter, Poetry Ed., 300 E. 42nd St., N.Y., NY 10017, USA. Mag. for today's Black woman; prefer poetry under 35 lines. 12/yr.; $6/yr.; 75 cents/ea.; 96 pgs.; 304,000 circ. Reports 1-6 wks. Pays $25-50 for poems; fees vary w. length.

ESTUARY PRESS, see Tangent Poetry Quarterly.

ETC: A Review of General Semantics (Int. Soc. for Gen. Semantics), Dr. Thomas Weiss, Ed., Aptdo 19, Comala, Colima, Mexico. Poetry & poetry reviews. Qtly.; $6/yr.; $1.50/ea.; 112 pgs.; 5 million circ. Reports 60 days. Pays copies only.

* ETHNOS PRESS, 46 Gallowhill Rd., Kirkintilloch, Glasgow, UK.

EUREKA, Alan Burgis, Ed., Tellusborgsvagen 45b, 3tr., 126 33 Hagersten, Stockholm, Sweden. Mag. of poetry, prose & art; seeking Am. contbrs.

EUROPEAN JUDAISM, Anthony Rudolf, Ed., Kent House, Rutland Gdns., London S.W.7, UK. Poetry & gen. lit. 2/yr.; $3.30/yr.; 65 pence/ea.; 56 pgs. Reports 1 mo.

* EUROSPAN, LTD., 3 Henrietta St., London W.C.2, UK.

EVANS BROTHERS LTD., Montague House, Russell Sq., London SC1B 5BX, UK. Poetry anthols.

EVENT, David Evanier, Ed., Douglas Coll., P.O. Box 2503, New Westminster, B.C., Canada. Poetry & gen. lit. $4/yr.; $1.50/ea.; 88 pgs.; 1 million circ. Reports 1 mo. Payment arranged.

* EVERGREEN REVIEW, Barney Rosset, Ed., 80 University Pl., N.Y., NY 10003, USA.

EVERYMAN MAGAZINE, (Cuyahoga Community Coll.), Christopher Franke, Ed., 2900 Community Coll. Ave., Cleveland, OH 44115, USA. Poetry & gen. lit. 1/yr.; $1/yr.; 40 plus pgs.; 500 circ. Payment 2 copies.

* EVIDENCE, Alan Bevan, Ed., Box 245, Stn. F, Toronto, Ont. Canada.

EXILE (Atkinson Coll., York Univ.), Barry

Callaghan, Ed., Box 546, Downsview, Ont., Canada. Poetry & gen. lit. Qtly.; $7/yr; $2/ea.; 140 pgs. Reports 3-4 wks. Payment varies.

EXIT, John Hall, Ed., 818 Osmaston Rd., Allentown, Derby, UK.

THE EXPATRIATE REVIEW, Roger W. Gaess, Co-Ed., P.O. Box D, N.Y. (Staten Island), NY 10301, USA. Poetry & gen. lit. 2/yr.; $2.50/yr.; $1.25/ea.; 48 pgs.; 750 circ. Reports 1 wk.-1 mo. Pays copies only.

EXPEDI PRINTING, see Tlaloc.

EXPERIMENT, Carol Ely Harper, Ed., 6565 N.E. Windermere Rd., Seattle, WA 98105, USA. Poetry, longpoems, poetic plays.

* EXPRESS, P.O. Box 834, Palatka, FL 32077, USA.

* EXPLORER, Raymond Elar, Ed., 1047 Elliot St., S. Bend, IN 46624, USA.

EXP/PRESS, (see also Specimen), G.J. de Rook, Ed., P.O. Box 14012, Utrecht, Netherlands.

EXPRESS, Andrew Kowal, Co-Ed., 113 Broadway, Hicksville, NY 11801, USA. Poetry & gen. lit. 52/yr.; $9/yr.: 25 cents/ea.; 24 pgs.; 25 million circ. Reports mo. or less. Pays copies only.

EXPRESSION ONE, Les Surridge, Ed., 117 Forest Rise, Waltham Forest, London E17 3PW, UK. Poetry & articles. Qtly.; $1.50/yr.; 15 pence/ea.; 24 pgs.

EXTENSIONS, Suzanne Zavrian, Co-Ed., P.O. Box 383, Cathedral Stn., N.Y., NY 10025, USA. No restrictions on type mat. used. Irreg.; $4/yr.; $1/ea.; 96 pgs.; 4 million circ. Reports 2 mos. Pays copies only.

* EXTRA VERSE, Barry Cole, Ed., 18 Gt. Percy St., Islington, London W.C.1, UK.

* EYRE METHUEN, LTD., 11 New Fetter Ln., London EC4P 4EE, UK.

FABER AND FABER LTD., P.F. du Sautoy, Chmn., 3 Queen Sq., London WC1N 3AU, UK. Poetry & gen. lit.

THE FALCON, W.A. Blais, Poetry Ed., Mansfield State Coll., Mansfield, PA 16933, USA. Poetry & short stories. 2/yr.; $2/yr.; $1/ea.: 100 pgs.; 1500 circ. Reports 1 mo. Pays copies only.

* FAMILY WEEKLY, Robert Fitzgibbon, Ed., 405 Park Ave., N.Y., NY 10022, USA.

* FANTASIA PUBLICATIONS, C.D. Stephens, Ed., Box 124, Petersburg, TX 79250, USA.

FAPTO, 441 Northdown Rd., Margate, Kent, UK. Poetry & gen. lit. 36/yr.; £3.50/yr.; 15 pence/ea.; 32 pgs.; 12 million circ. Payment by arrangement.

* FARM JOURNAL, Peal L. Patterson, Ed., Wash. Sq., Phila., PA 19105, USA.

* FARRAR, STRAUS & GIROUX, 19 Union Sq. W., N.Y., NY 10003, USA.

THE FAULT, Terrence Ames, Ed., 41186 Alice Ave., Fremont, CA 94538, USA. Poetry & gen. lit. 2/yr.; $1.50/yr.; 75 cents/ea.; 52 pgs.; 500 circ. Reports 1 wk. Pays copies & profits.

FELLOWSHIP IN PRAYER, Paul Griffith, Ed., 200 E. 36th St., N.Y., NY 10016, USA. Poems & short stories promoting prayer. 6/yr.; $3/yr.; 50 cents/ea.; 36 pgs.; 2000 circ. No payments.

FEMALE LIBERATION INC., see The Second Wave.

THE FEMINIST PRESS, Box 334, Old Westbury, NY 11568, USA. Poetry, fiction, plays.

FERRY PRESS, 177 Green Lane, London SE9, UK. Poetry; new writing in Engl. & Am.

FERVENT VALLEY (Duende Press), Larry Goodell, Ed., Box 571, Placitas, NM 87043, USA. Poetry & art. Irreg.; $4/yr.; $1.50/ea.; 40 pgs.; 500 circ.

* FESTIVAL PUBLICATIONS, 29 Malone Rd., Belfast, N. Ireland, UK.

FIASCO PUBLICATIONS, see Bogg.

THE FIDDLEHEAD, Dr. Kent Thompson, Ed., Observatory, Univ. of N.B., Fredericton, N.B., Canada. Poetry & gen. lit. Qtly.; $4.50/yr.; $1.25/ea.; 120 pgs.; 850 circ. Reports 4 wks. Pays $5/pg.

THE FIELD, Wilson Stephens, Ed., 8 Stratton St., London W1X 6AT, UK. Short poems. 52/yr.; £9.85/yr.; 15 pence/ea.; 50-70 pgs. Payment at discretion of Ed.

FIFTH ESTATE NEWSPAPER, 4403 Second, Detroit, MI 48201, USA. Poetry & gen. lit. 36/yr.; $5/yr.; 25 cents/ea.; 24 pgs.; 19,500 circ. Reports vary. Payments varies.

* FIFTH ESTATE PRESS, 64 Muswell Hill Rd., London N10 3JR, UK.

FIGHT BACK, see Rita Notes.

FIGTREE, Joe Ribar, Ed., Star Rte., Box 91, Claverack, NY 12513, USA. Poetry & gen. lit.

* FILMBANK PUBLICATIONS, 70 Middle Abbey St., Dublin 1, Ireland.

* FINE ARTS DISCOVERY MAGAZINE, P.O. Box 7193, Kan. City, MO 64113, USA.

* FIREFLOWER, Box 2170, Whitehorse, Yukon, Canada.

1ST CASUALTY PRESS, Basil T. Paquet, Part-Ed., P.O. Box 518, Coventry, CT 06238, USA. Poetry & gen. lit.; lit. coming from veterans of war in Indochina; 3 publd. anthols. of veterans. Reports 1 mo.

FIVE ARCHES PRESS, (H.G. Walters (Publrs.) Ltd.), G.A. Walters, Mng. Dir., Knowling Mead, Tenby, Pembrokeshire, UK.

* FLAME, (Different Press), 5009 Anthony St., Corpus Christi, TX 78415, USA.

FLEET PRESS CORP., 160 Fifth Ave., N.Y., NY 10010, USA.

FLEET PUBLISHING CORP., 230 Park Ave., N.Y., NY 10017, USA.

* FLORIDA EDUCATION, c/o Dr. Wm. Taylor, Stetson Univ., Deland, FL 32720, USA.

* FLORIDA NOTES, 1819 Nigel St., Pittsburgh, PA 15212, USA.

* FLORIDA QUARTERLY, 207 Anderson Hall, Univ. of Fla., Gainesville, FL 32601, USA.

FLOWERS FROM THE PRINTSHOP (Ember Press), A.L. Shearn, 11 Ember Gdns., Thames Ditton, Surrey KT7 OLL, UK. Some poetry. Irreg.; 4-40 pgs.; 200-250 circ. Reports within 7 days. Pays copies only.

FLY BY NIGHT MAGAZINE, Fredric Koepell, Ed., 3436 Carnes, Memphis, TN 38111, USA. Poetry & gen. lit.; prefer poetry showing strains of subjectivity. Irreg.; 40 cents/ea.; 35-45 pgs.; 450-500 circ. Reports 3-4 wks. Pays 2 copies.

FOCUS/MIDWEST, Charles L. Klotzer, Ed., P.O. Box 3086, St. Louis, MO 63130, USA. Poetry & gen. lit. 6/yr.; $5/yr.; 85 cents/ea.; 40 pgs.; 10,000 circ. Reports 1-2 mos. Payment depends upon publication.

* FOLLET PUBLISHING COMPANY, 1010 W. Washington Blvd., Chgo., IL 60607, USA.

FORUM, Archibald Henderson, Poetry Ed., Univ. of Houston, Houston, TX 77004, USA. 3/yr.; $3/yr.; $1/ea.; 40-48 pgs. Reports 1-2 mos. Payment in reprints & copies.

FORUS, Paul Holden, Ed., 8 Thormanby Rd., Howth, Co. Dublin, Ireland,. Poetry & gen. lit. 12/yr.; 10 pence/ea.; 16 pgs.; 1500 circ. Reports vary. Pays when possible.

FOUR DOGS MOUNTAIN SONGS (Doggeral Press), Alice Karle & Thor, Eds., P.O. Box 448, Engelwood, CO 80110, USA. Poetry & art. 1/yr.; $4/yr.; $6/ea.; 20-60 pgs.; 240 circ. Reports 2 wks. Pays 1 copy or more by request.

FOUR QUARTERS, John J. Keenan, Ed., La Salle Coll., Phila., PA 19141, USA. Poetry & gen. lit. Qtly.; $3/yr.; 75 cents/ea.; 48 pgs.; 700 circ. Reports 6 wks. Pays $5 per poem.

FOXFIRE, (The Foxfire Fund, Inc.), Eliot Wigginton, Ed., Rabun Gap, GA 30568, USA. Occasionally poetry; Southern Appalachians emphasis. Qtly.; $5/yr.; $1.25/ea.; 80 pgs.; 10 million circ. Reports 3 wks. Pays copies.

A FRAGMENT, F.G. Bissenden, Ed., 41 Fabian Rd., Fulham, London SW6 7TY, UK. Articles; poetry occasionally. Irreg.; Free; 8 pgs.; 200-300 circ. No payment.

FRAGMENTS, Neil Greenberg, Ed., 54 W. 88th St., N.Y., NY 10024, USA. Poetry & articles. Irreg.; $4/yr.; $1.25/ea.; 60 pgs.; 400 circ. Reports irreg. Pays copies only.

THE FREE LANCE, A Magazine of Poetry & Prose, Russell Atkins, Part Ed., 6005 Grand Ave., Cleveland, OH 44104, USA. 2/yr.; $2/yr.; $1/ea.; 80-115 pgs.; 1000 circ. Reports 4 mos. Pays copies.

FREE PEOPLE PRESS, 1232 Laura St., Jacksonville, FL 32206, USA. Producers of Both Sides Now & Penny Press. Irreg.; $2/12 issues; 25 cents/ea.; 20 pgs.; 4-5 million circ. Pays copies only.

FREWIN (LESLIE) PUBLISHERS, LTD., 5 Goodwin's Ct., St. Martins Lane, London WC2N 4LL, UK. Poetry must make up into full-length book.

* THE FRIENDLY WAY MAGAZINE, Isabelle Scarset, Ed., Box 95, Westbrook, MN 56183, USA.

FRIENDS OF THE WESTERN BUDDHIST ORDER MAGAZINE, Stephen Parr, Ed., Aryatara Community, Sarum House, 3 Plough Ln., Purley, Surrey CR2 3QB, UK. Poetry & gen. lit.; Mahayana Buddhism. £1/yr.; 25 pence/ea.; 30 pgs.; 700 plus circ. Reports 1 mo. in adv.

* FROM A WINDOW, Paul Malanga, Ed., P.O. Box 3446, College Stn., Tucson, AZ 85700, USA.

FROM HERE (From Here Press), William J. Higginson, Ed., Box 2702, Paterson, NJ 07509, USA. Poetry & gen. lit. Qtly.; $5/yr.; sub. only; 40 plus pgs.; 200 plus circ. Reports up to 4 wks. Pays copies only.

FROM HERE PRESS, see From Here.

FRONTIER PRESS, Harvey Brown, P.O. Box 448, W. Newbury, MA 01985, USA. Poetry & fiction.

FTA WITH PRIDE, see Rita Notes.

* FULCRUM PRESS, 20 Fitzroy Sq., London W.1, UK.

FUR LINES PRESS (B and H Books), E.

Chandler, Ed., 330 Paloma Ave., San Rafael, CA 94901, USA. Poetry.

* FURBALO, 3400 Main St., Buffalo, NY 14214, USA.

GABERBOCCHUS PRESS LTD., 42a Formosa St., London W.9, UK. Poetry & gen. lit.

GAIRM, Derick S. Thomson, Ed., 29 Waterloo St., Glasgow G2, Scotland, UK. Poetry & gen. lit.; all mat. printed in Gaelic. Qtly.; £1.20/yr.; 25 pence/ea.; 100 pgs.; 2 million circ. Payment nominal.

GALLERY BOOKS (Tara Telephone Publs.), Peter Falcon, Ed., 19 Oakdown Rd., Dublin 14, Ireland. Poetry & gen. lit. Qtly.; 20-40 pence/ea.; 36 pgs.; 2 million circ. Pays copies/royalties, negotiable.

GALLERY SERIES/POETS (Harper Sq. Press), Phyllis & Arthur Choyke, Eds., c/o Artcrest Products Co., Inc., 401 W. Ontario St., Chgo., IL 60610, USA. Poetry & art. Irreg.; 1 million circ. Reports few wks. to few mos. Pays copies only.

* GALLIARD, LTD., Queen Anne's Rd., Great Yarmouth, Norfolk, UK.

GALLIMAUFRY, (Warren Waller Press), Mary MacArthur, Co-Ed., 123 Leroy Alley, San Francisco, CA 94109, USA. Poetry & gen. lit. Qtly.; $2/yr.; 50 cents/ea.; 50 pgs.; 5 million circ. Reports max. 3 mos. Pays copies.

GAMBIT INC., 53 Beacon St., Boston, MA 02108, USA. Poetry & gen. lit.

* GAMUT, Frank Radford, Ed., 8-13 Compton Union Bldg., Wash. State Univ., Pullman, WA 99163, USA.

* GANGLIA, B.P. Nichol, Ed., 477 Brunswick Ave., Toronto 4, Ont., Canada.

THE GAR, Hal & Carolyn Wylie, Eds., Box 4793 Austin, TX 78765, USA. Local monthly of "community affairs and the arts". 12/yr.; $3/yr.; 25 cents/ea.; 24-30 pgs.; 2,500 circ. Reports 2-3 mos. Pays copies only.

GARFIELD LAKE REVIEW (Whale Publng. Co.), James Coleman, Ed., Box 397, Olivet, MI 49076, USA. Poetry, fiction, art, photos. Irreg.; $1/ea.; 90 pgs.; 1 million circ. Reports vary. Pays copies only. Nat. poetry contest, Abbie M. Copps Poetry Contest.

GARGANTUA (Rejection Press), Robert Ensor, Ed., 134 Hollybank Rd., Birmingham B13 ORL, Warwickshire, UK. Poetry & gen. lit. Irreg.; 10 pence plus/ea.; 48 pgs.; 500 circ. Reports 2 wks. max. Pays copies.

* GARNSTONE PRESS LTD., 59 Brompton Rd., London SW3 1DS, UK.

GARRETT ARTS, John Schofield, Ed., 12 Rankeillor St., Edinburgh EH8 9HY, UK. Poetry.

* GARRETT PRESS, INC., 250 W. 54th St., N.Y., NY 10019, USA.

* GATO, John Snyder, Ed., Box 654, Los Gatos, CA 95030, USA.

GAY NEWS, Denis Lemon, Part-Ed., 34D Redcliffe Sq., London SW10, UK. Poetry & gen. lit. 26/yr.; £2.30/yr.; 10 pence/ea.; 16 pgs.; 10 million circ. Reports vary. Payment negotiable.

GAY SUNSHINE (Gay Liberation Newspaper), Winston Leyland, Ed., P.O. Box 40397, San Francisco, CA 94140, USA. Poetry & gen. lit. 6/yr.; $5/yr.; 50 cents/ea.; 20 pgs.; 10 million circ. Reports 2 wks. Pays copies only.

GAYZETTE, Joseph Raphael, Ed., P.O. Box 5019, Crosse Pointe, MI 48236, USA. Poetry & gen. lit.; newspaper of gay liberation.

GEE & SON, see Gwasg Gee.

GEGENSCHIEN QUARTERLY, Phil Smith, Ed., 211 Ada Ave., Bowling Green, OH 43402, USA. Poetry & gen. lit.; 2-3 poems per poet. 4/yr.; $5/yr.; $1.50/ea.; 50 pgs.; 200-300 circ. Reports 2 wks. to 2 mos. Pays copies.

GEMINI PRESS, see Madrona.

* GENERATION, Anne Richmond, 420 Maynard, Ann Arbor, MI 48103, USA.

* GENESIS: GRASP, David Giannini, Co-Ed., 173 Elizabeth St., N.Y., NY 10012, USA.

THE GEORGIA REVIEW (Univ. of Ga. Press), Edward Krickel, Ed., Lustrat House, Univ. of Ga., Athens, GA 30601, USA. Qtly.; $3/yr.; $1/ea.; 128 pgs.; 1,800 circ. Reports 1-2 mos. Pays 50 cents per line.

GERALDTON GRAPHIC (Geraldton Br., Australian Fellowship of Writers), Mrs. E.V. Ford, Sec., 151 Brede St., Geraldton, W.A., Australia. Poetry & gen. lit.

GHOST DANCE, Hugh Fox, Ed., ATL/EBH/MSU, E. Lansing, MI 48823, USA. Poetry & art. Qtly.; $2.50/yr.; 75 cents/ea.; 36 pgs.; 500 circ. Reports 1 day.

GIDRA, The Monthly of The Asian American Experience, P.O. Box 18649, L.A., CA 90018, USA. Poetry & gen. lit.; mat. done by and about Asians in Am. 12/yr.; $2.50/yr.; 25 cents/ea.; 28 pgs.; 20 million circ. Reports within 1 mo.

THE GILIGIA PRESS, David Kherdian, Ed., Lyme Center, NH 03769, USA. Poetry.

* GILL & MACMILLAN, LTD., 2 Belvedere Pl., Dublin 1, Ireland.

* GLAZEBROOK/N.V.C.P. PUBLICATIONS, 294 Birchfield Rd., E., Northampton NN3 2SY, UK.

GLOBAL TAPESTRY JOURNAL, (BB Books), Dave Cunliffe, Ed., 1 Spring Bank, Salesbury, Blackburn, Lancs. BB1 9EU, UK. Poetry & gen. lit. Qtly.; £1/yr.; 25 pence/ea.; 32 pgs.; 1000 circ. Reports as soon as possible. Pays 1 copy.

* GNOSIS, Stanley Nelson Ed., 372 Pacific St., Brooklyn, NY 11217, USA.

GNOSTICA NEWS (Llewellyn Publs.), Ronald M. Wright, Ed., P.O. Box 3383, St. Paul, MN 55165, USA. Poetry & gen. lit. 8/yr.; $2.50/yr.; 25 cents/ea.; 24 pgs.; 40 million circ. Reports 1 mo. Pays 1 cent per word.

THE GODDARD JOURNAL (304 publs.), Box 595, Goddard Coll., Plainfield, VT 05667, USA. Poetry & gen. lit. 2/yr.; $1.50/yr.; $1/ea. Pays 4-6 copies.

GODINE (DAVID R.), PUBLISHER, 306 Dartmouth St., Boston, MA 02116, USA. Poetry & gen. lit.

GOLD DUST PRESS, see Kyoi.

GOLDEN ATOM PUBLICATIONS, Larry & Duverne Farsace, Eds., P.O. Box 1101, Rochester, NY 14603, USA. Poetry & gen. lit. 12-100 pgs.; 500 plus circ. Reports 2 wks. Pays 25 cents per line poetry.

* GOLDEN EAGLE PRESS, 55 Vaughan Way, Leicester LE1 4NT, UK.

GOLDEN ROSE POEMS (Headland Publs.), Editl. Corres.: Gerald England, 745 Abbeydale Rd., Sheffield S7 2BG, UK. Bus. Corres.: Vivienne Finch, 56 Blakes Ln., New Malden, Surrey KT3 6NX, UK. Poetry; limited editions. 4 pgs. Reports vary. Pays 10% royalty or 50 copies plus 10 signed.

GOLF DIGEST, Nick Seitz, Ed., 297 Westport Ave., Norwalk, CT 06856, USA. 1 poem per mo. 12/yr.; $7.50/yr.; 75 cents/ea.; 128 pgs.; 650,000 circ. Reports within 2 wks. Payment averages $25.

GOLGONOOZA PRESS, B.J. Keeble, Ed., 76 Suffolk Rd., Ipswich, Suffolk, UK. Poetry, articles, longpoems. 3/yr. Reports 1 mo. Payment varies.

* GOLIARDS, P.O. Box 1292, Bellingham, WA 98225, USA.

GOLLANCZ (VICTOR) LTD., Livia Gollancz, Mng. Dir., 14 Henrietta St., London WC2E 8QJ, UK. Poetry & gen. lit.

GONE SOFT, Ron Bogan, Co-Ed., Salem State Coll., Engl. Dept., Salem, MA 01970, USA. Poetry & gen. lit. 2/yr.; $2/yr.; $1/ea.; 50 pgs.; 4 million circ.

GONG, (Univ. of Nottingham Press), Nick Kent, Ed., 56 Ditton Ct. Rd., Westcliff-on-Sea, Essex, UK. Poetry & gen. lit. 1-2/yr.; 30 pence/yr.; 15 pence/ea.; 50-100 pgs.; 700 circ. Reports vary.

* GOOD BUSINESS, James A. Decker, Ed., Lee's Summit, MO 64063, USA.

GOOD ELF/VISST (Good Elf Publs.), Lawrence Upton, Ed., c/o Clairview Rd., Streatham, London SW16, UK. Poetry & gen. lit.; Visst is review sect., Good Elf. 2-3/yr.; 16 pence/ea.; 45 pgs.; 1 million circ. Reports 1-10 days. Pays 1 copy.

* GOOD HOUSEKEEPING, 959 8th Ave., N.Y., NY 10019, USA.

GOOD NEWS (Arete Ink), Steve Kraus, Ed., 239 E. 2nd St., N.Y., NY 10009, USA. Poetry & gen. lit. Irreg.; 25 cents/ea.; 20 pgs.; 10 million circ. Reports 1 wk. Pays copies only.

GOODBYE TO ALL THAT, Box 3092, San Diego, CA 92103, USA. Poetry & gen. lit.; feminist paper. 12/yr.; $4/yr.; 25 cents/ea.; 16 pgs.; 2 million circ.

THE GOODLY CO., G.R. Morgan, Ed., Jackson Ave. & Rte. 45, Mantua, NJ 08051, USA. Poetry & gen. lit.; prefer brevity. 3/yr.; $3/yr.; $1/ea.; 40 pgs. Pays 2 copies.

GOOFY PUBLICATIONS, see Axis Bag.

* GOOSEBERRY, John & Susan Cornillon, Eds., 3805 Grosvenor Rd., Cleveland, OH 44118, USA. or Point Pleasant, PA 18950, USA.

* GORDON (GILES), 9 St. Ann's Garden, London NW5 4ER, UK.

* GOURMET MAGAZINE, 777 Third Ave., N.Y., NY 10017, USA.

GRANDE RONDE REVIEW, Ben L. Hiatt, Ed., 907 River Way, Folsom, CA 95630, USA. Poetry & gen. lit. Qtly.; $6/yr.; $1/ea.; 60 pgs.; 500 circ. Pays 2 copies.

GRANITE, Anselm Parlatore, Poetry Ed., Box 774, Hanover, NH 03755, USA. Poetry & gen. lit. 2-3/yr.; $5/3 issues; $2/ea.; 150 pgs.; 1 million circ. Reports 2 wks. Pays copies only.

GRANNY SOOT PUBLICATIONS, Colin Browne, Ed., P.O. Box 171, Saanichton, B.C., Canada. Poetry & gen. lit.

GRANVILLE PRESS, Graham Carey, Ed., 6 Granville Terr., Bingley, Yorks., UK. Poetry 40 pence/ea.

GRAPE PRESS, see Tom Veitch Magazine.

GRAPHIC ARTS/BLUE CLOUD ABBEY, see The Blue Cloud Quarterly.

GREAT SOCIETY PRESS, Angelo De Luca, Ed., 101 Morris St., Phillipsburg, NJ 08865, USA. Poetry. 35 cents/ea.; 16 pgs.; 300 circ. No payment.

THE GREATER LLANO ESTACADO SOUTHWEST HERITAGE, J.L. Burke, Jr., Poetry Ed., P.O. Box 2446, Hobbs, NM 88240, USA. Qtly.; $4/yr.; $1/ea.; 44 pgs.; 1300 circ. Pays copy.

GREATER LONDON ARTS/LONDON POETRY SECRETARIAT NEWSLETTER, G.A. Rankmore, Co-Ed., 27 Southampton St., London WC2, UK. Poetry & gen. lit. London Poetry Secretariat 2/yr. 12/yr.; £2/yr. mbrship.; 5 pence/ea.; 4 pgs.; 5,500 circ.

GREEN GINGER, Hull University Literary Magazine, Peter Read, Ed., The Univ., Hull, Yorks., UK. Poetry & gen. lit. Seasonal; 5 pence/ea.; 32 pgs.; 650 circ. Reports 1 mo. No payment.

THE GREEN HORSE FOR POETRY, Richard Behm, Co-Ed., c/o Creative Writing Prog., Bowling Green Univ., Bowling Green, OH 43402, USA. 3/yr.; $3/yr.; $1/ea.

GREEN KNIGHT PRESS, Ritchie Darling, Ed., P.O. Box 512, Amherst, MA 01002, USA. Reports 6 wks. to 6 mos. Pays $10 per poem.

GREEN RIVER REVIEW, Raymond Tyner, Ed., 515 Stockton St., Owensboro, KY 42301, USA. Poetry, Short fiction, essays. 3/yr.; $5/yr.; $1.75/ea.; 56 pgs. Reports 2 mos. Pays copies.

* GREEN WORLD, Faye P. Niles, Ed., P.O. Drawer LW, Univ. Stn., Baton Rouge, LA 70803, USA.

GREENFIELD REVIEW, Joseph Bruchac, Ed., Greenfield Center, NY 12833, USA. Poetry & gen. lit.; 1 issue per yr. devoted to contemporary African poetry. Qtly.; $4/yr.; $1/ea.; 750 circ. Reports 1-4 wks. Pays $5 per pg. plus copies.

GREENFIELD REVIEW PRESS, Joseph Bruchac, Ed., Greenfield Center, NY 12833, USA. Mostly Third World authors; usually publish 500 copies. Split of profits – 50% on sales.

GREEN'S MAGAZINE, David Green, Ed., Box 313, Detroit, MI 48231, USA. Poetry & fiction; poems to 40 lines preferred. Qtly.; $3/yr.; $1/ea.; 48 pgs.; 1 million circ. Reports 6 wks. Pays $10-$25.

GR/EW BOOKS, see Grosseteste Review.

* GRIAN-AIG PRESS, 36 Margaret St., Greenock, Renfrewshire, UK.

* GRIMSAY PRESS, 2 Springfield Ln., Salford M3 7JN, UK.

* GRIST, John Fowler, Ed., 1237 Oread, Lawrence, KS 66044, USA.

* GRIST WEST, Box 132, Berkeley, CA 94704, USA.

GROSSETESTE REVIEW, Grosseteste Review Books (GR/EW Books), Tim Longville, Ed., 10 Consort Cres., Commonside, Pensnett, Staffs., UK. Poetry & gen. lit.; bias towards contemporary poetry. Qtly.; £1/yr.; 30 pence/ea.; 64 pgs.; 300 circ. Reports 2 wks. Pays copies only.

GROSVENOR BOOKS, 54 Lyford Rd., London SW18 3JJ, UK. Occasional books of poetry.

* GROVE PRESS, INC., 214 Mercier St., N.Y., NY 10012, USA.

* GROVE PUBLICATIONS, c/o Mrs. Margaret Perkins, 64 Broomgrove Rd., Sheffield S10 2NA, UK.

* THE GUILD, Helen G. Woods, Ed., 317 Sixth St., Idaho Falls, ID 83401, USA.

GUILDFORD POETS PRESS, see Overspill.

GULFSTREAM, Michael Scearce, Part Ed., Rte. 3, Box 501A, Baton Rouge, LA 70808, USA. Poetry & fiction. 3/yr.; $3/3 issues; $1.50/ea.; 44 pgs.; 400 circ. Reports 1 mo. Pays 3 copies plus subscription.

GUM (The Happy Press), Dave Morice, Ed., Box 585, Iowa City, IA 52240, USA. Short poetry & fiction. Irreg.; 75 cents/ea.; 80 pgs.; Reports irreg. Pays copies only.

GWASG GEE (Gee & Son), Charles Cledlyn, Chmn., Chapel St., Denbigh, UK. Poetry & gen. lit.; primarily Welsh lang.

GWASG GOMER, see Lewis (J.D.) & Sons Ltd.

* GWASG Y MORESG, Llanystumdwy, nr. Cricieth, Wales, UK.

GYPSY TABLE, (Mother's Hen), P.O. Box 99592, San Francisco, CA, USA. Poetry. Seasonal; $2.25/3-5 issues; $1/ea.; 40-60 pgs. Reports 1-3 wks.

RUSS HAAS PRESS, see Nausea One.

* HACHETTE C.P.D., BOOKS DIVISION, 4 Regent Pl., London W1R 6BH, UK.

HAIKU MAGAZINE, Eric W. Amann, Ed., 61 Macdonnell, Toronto, Ont. MGR 2A3, Canada. Poetry & articles. Qtly.; $4/yr.; $1.25/ea.; 40 plus pgs.; 300 circ. Reports mo. plus. No payment.

* HAIKU HIGHLIGHTS, Jean Calkins, Ed., Box 15, Kanona, NY 14856, USA. Verse to 8 lines.

HALE (ROBERT) & CO., 63 Old Brompton Rd., London SW7 3JU, UK.

THE HALLAMSHIRE & OSGOLDCROSS

POETRY EXPRESS (Headland Publs.), Editl. Corres: Gerald England, 745 Abbeydale Rd., Sheffield S7 2BG, UK. Bus Corres: Vivienne Finch, 56 Blakes Ln., New Malden, Surrey KT3 6NX, UK. Poetry, criticism, reviews. Irreg.; $2/life subscription; postage/ea.; 6 pgs.; 1 million circ. Reports very long. Pays copies.

* HAMILTON (HAMISH), LTD., 90 Gt. Russell St., London SC1B 3PT, UK.

* HAMLYN PUBLISHING GROUP LTD., Hamlyn House, 42 The Centre, Feltham, Middx., UK.

HAMPSHIRE POETS, Ms Katharine Sparks, Ed., 7 Leep Ln., Alverstoke, Hants. PO12 2BE, UK.

THE HANDCRAFT PRESS, see Arena.

HANDSEL, (Shenco Printers), G.W. Zeitz, Ed., P.O. Box 558, Lexington, KY 40501, USA. Poetry & gen. lit. 3-4/yr.; $4/4 issues; $1.25/ea.; 60 pgs.; 500 circ. Reports 1 mo. Pays 2 $10 prizes, copies.

HANGING LOOSE, Robert Hershon, Part Ed., 231 Wyckoff St., Brooklyn, NY 11217, USA. Poetry. Qtly.; $3.50/yr.; $1/ea.; 72 pgs.; 850 circ. Reports 2-3 mos. Pays $5/1 poem, $10 for more than 1, 3 copies.

HAPPINESS HOLDING TANK (Stone Press), Albert Drake, Ed., P.O. Box 227, Okemos, MI 48864, USA. Poetry & literary info. 3/yr.; $3.50/yr.; $1/ea.; 50 pgs.; 500 circ. Reports 1 wk. Pays copies.

THE HAPPY PRESS, see Gum.

HARBOUR LIGHTS, 1710 Oakwood Dr., Shoreview, MN 55112, USA.

HARBOUR PUBLISHING, see Raincoast Chronicles.

* HARCOURT, BRACE & JOVANOVICH INC., 757 Third Ave., N.Y., NY 10017, USA.

HARCOURT BRACE JOVANOVICH LTD., 24/28 Oval Rd., London NW1, UK.

HARPER & ROW, 10 E. 53rd St., N.Y., NY 10022, USA. 4-6 books of poetry per yr.; no restrictions.

HARPER & ROW, LTD., 28 Tavistock St., London WC2E 7PN, UK.

HARPER SQUARE PRESS, see Gallery Series/Poets.

* HARPER'S BAZAAR, Alice S. Morris, Poetry Ed., 572 Madison Ave., N.Y., NY 10022, USA.

* HARPER'S MAGAZINE, 2 Park Ave., N.Y., NY 10016, USA.

HARRAP (GEORGE G.) & COMPANY LTD., 182/184 High Holborn, London WC1V 7AX, UK. Poetry & gen. lit.; currently publng. anthols. only.

THE HARRIS REVIEW, Harris Schiff, Ed., Box 516, Cuba, NM 87013, USA. Poetry, poems generally 1 or 2 pgs. Irreg.; $5/yr.; $1/ea.; 25 cents/ea.; 45 pgs.; 250 circ. Reports variable. Pays 2 copies.

HARRISON MONTHLY REVIEW, (Carbon Press), Steven & Gordon Harrison, Eds., 213 Indian Ln., Media, PA 19063, USA. Poetry & gen. lit. Irreg.; $20/yr.; $1/ea. Reports immediately. Pays Varies, dep. on quality.

THE HARTFORD COURANT, Malcolm Johnson, Ed., 285 Broad St., Hartford, CT 06015, USA. Newspaper publng. short poems. 365/yr., poetry only on Sat.; $40.56/yr.; 15 cents/ea.; 62 pgs. No reports or payments.

* HARTFORD TIMES, Doris Smith, Poetry Ed., Prospect St., Hartford, CT 06101, USA.

* HARVARD REVIEW, 52 Dunster St., Cambridge, MA 02138, USA.

HARVILLE PRESS LTD., Sir William Collins, Chmn., 30a Pavilion Rd., London SW1X 0HJ, UK. Occasional book of poetry.

HEADLAND PUBLICATIONS (see also GOLDEN ROSE POEMS, THE HALLAMSHIRE & OSGOLDCROSS POETRY EXPRESS), Editl. Corres.: Gerald England, 745 Abbeydale Rd., Sheffield S7 2BG, UK. Bus. Corres.: Vivienna Finch, 56 Nlakes Lns., New Malden, Surrey KT3 6NX, UK. Poetry, longpoems; booklets of poetry. Reports 1-6 mos. Payment varies.

HEARSE, E.V. Griffith, Ed., 3118 K St., Eureka, CA 95501, USA. Poetry jrnl. Irreg.; $3.50/4 issues; $1/ea.; 80 pgs.; 1500 circ. Reports 1-30 days. Pays 2 contrib. copies.

* HEINEMANN (WILLIAM), LTD., 15-16 Queen St., Mayfair, London W1X 8BE, UK.

HEIRS MAGAZINE, Alfred Garcia, Part-Ed., 657 Mission St., San Fran., CA 94105, USA. Poetry & gen. lit. $4.50/yr.; $1.25/ea.; 64 pgs.; 1 million circ. Reports 6 wks. Pays copies.

HELIOS PRESS, see Starworlds.

HELLCOAT ANNUAL, Bruce McPherson, Ed., Box 4 S.A.O., Brown Univ., Providence, RI 02912, U.S.A., Poetry & gen. lit. 1/yr.; $2.50/yr.; 175 pgs.; 1 million circ. Reports 6 wks. or less. Pays copies only.

HELLRIC CHAPBOOK SERIES, Ottone M. Riccio, Ed., 32 Waverley St., Belmont, MA 02178, U.S.A. Longpoem series, Pyramid Pamphlets. Pays royalties arranged w. authors.

HELLRIC PUBLICATIONS, see Hellric Chapbook Series, Ab Intra, Espontaneo, Pyramid.

HERE NOW, Tom Kelly, Ed., 22 Torquay

Parade, Hebburn, Co. Durham NE31 2AD, UK. Poetry, short stories, articles. Qtly.; 75 pence/yr.; 15 pence/ea.; 48 pgs.; 500 circ. Pays £1 to ea. contributor publd.

HERITAGE, Paul Breman, Ed., 1 Rosslyn Hill, London NW3 5UL, UK. Poetry; 1 author to ea. issue; Black authors only. 4-6/yr.; $2/yr.; $2/ea.; 24 pgs.; 500 circ. Reports long.

HERO PRESS, see Witchcraft Digest, WICA Newsletter.

HEY LADY (Morgan Press), Edwin H. Burton II, 1819 N. Oakland Ave., Milwaukee, WI 53202, U.S.A. Poetry, art, photos. 6/yr.; free; 24-32 pgs.; 300-500 circ. Reports about 2 wks. Pays 10-200 copies.

HIEROPHANT PRESS, Thomas Kerrigan, Ed., 15141 Sutton St., Sherman Oaks, CA 91403, USA. Poetry. 1/yr.; $2/ea.; 2 million circ. Reports 3 wks. Pays 2 copies.

HIGGINSON JOURNAL OF POETRY (Higginson Press), Frederick L. Morey, Ed., 4508 38th St., Brentwood, MD 20722, U.S.A. Poetry, articles. 2/yr.; $5/yr.; $3/ea.; 50 pgs.; 200 circ. Reports 2-4 wks. Pays copies only.

HIGGINSON PRESS, see Emily Dickinson Bulletin, Higginson Journal of Poetry.

HIRAM POETRY REVIEW, Hale Chatfield & others, Eds., P.O. Box 162, Hiram, OH 44234, U.S.A. Poetry from unsolicited submissions. 2/yr.; $2/yr.; $1/ea.; 34 pgs.; 500 plus circ. Reports 1 mo. Pays 2 copies plus 1 yr. sub.

* HODDER & STOUGHTON, St. Paul's House, Warwick Ln., London EC4P 4AH, UK.

* THE HOGARTH PRESS, LTD., 40-42 William IV St., London WC2N 4DG, UK.

THE HOLLINS CRITIC, John Rees Moore, Ed., Box 9538, Hollins Coll., VA 24020, USA. Short poems in every issue. 5/yr.; $2/yr.; 45 cents/ea.; 15 pgs.; 1 million circ. Reports 2-3 mos. Pays $20 poems.

* HOLLOW ORANGE, Clifford Burke, Ed., 642 Schrader, San Fran., CA 94110, USA.

HOLMES MCDOUGALL LTD., Peter I. Murby, Ed., 30 Royal Terr., Edinburgh EH7 5AL, UK. Schl. Anthols.; original children's verse.

* HOLT-BLOND, LTD., 120 Golden Ln., London EC1Y 0TU, UK.

* HOLT, RINEHART & WINSTON, INC., 383 Madison Ave., N.Y., NY 10012, USA.

HOLY BEGGARS' GAZETTE (House of Love & Prayer Publs.), Steven Maimes, Co-Ed., 1456 Ninth Ave., San Fran., CA 94122, USA. Poetry, articles. S/yr.; $5/yr.; $1/ea.; 24 pgs.; 1500 circ. Reports 2 wks. Pays copies only.

HOLY DOORS ANTHOLOGY William J. Robson, Ed., P.O. Box 5580, Long Beach, CA 90805, U.S.A. Poetry & gen. lit. 1 time; $3/ea.; 140 pgs.; 500 circ.

HOME LIFE, George W. Knight, Ed., 127 Ninth Ave., N., Nashville, TN 37234, USA. 5 or 6 short poems ea. issue; prefer inspirational-devotional poetry of 8-12 lines. 12/yr.; $4.25/yr.; 66 pgs.; 800,000 circ. Reports 6 wks. Pays $5-$10 on acceptance.

* HOOFS & HORNS, Willard H. Porter, Ed., 4425 E. Ft. Lowell Rd., Tucson, AZ 85716, USA.

* HOOSIER CHALLENGER, 8365 Wicklow Ave., Cinn., OH 45236, U.S.A.

HORSEHEAD NEBULA PRESS, see Shithook.

HOT APPLES PRESS, see Michigan Hot Apples.

* HOUGHTON MIFFLIN, 53 W. 43rd St., N.Y., NY 10017, U.S.A.

HOUSE OF GREYSTOKE, see Burroughs Bulletin.

HOUSE OF LOVE AND PRAYER PUBLICATIONS, see Holy Beggars' Gazette, Tzaddikim.

HUB PUBLICATIONS LTD., see Orbis.

* THE HUDSON REVIEW, 65 E. 55th St., N.Y., NY 10022, USA.

* HUMAN VOICE QUARTERLY, J.H. Frederick, Ed., P.O.D. 1409, Homestead, FL 33030, USA.

HUMMINGBIRD PRESS, see Hyacinths & Biscuits.

HUMORAMA, INC., Ernest N. Devver, Ed., 100 N. Village Ave., Rockville Ctr., NY 11570, USA. Popular Jokes; Cartoon Parade; Joker; Popular Cartoons. Qtly.; 50 cents/ea. Reports 30 days. Pays 50 cents per line.

HUTCHINSON PUBLISHING GROUP LTD., R.A.A. Holt, Chmn., 3 Fitzroy Sq., London W1P 6JD, UK. Engl. lang. poetry only.

HYACINTHS & BISCUITS (Hummingbird Press), Jane R. Card, Ed., P.O. Box 392, Brea, CA 92621, USA. Poetry, cartoons, satire. 4-6/yr.; $5/6 issues; $1/ea.; 60 pgs.; 8 million circ. Reports 1 to 2 mos. Pays $1-$10, up to 25 copies w. poem.

HYPERION (Thorp Springs Press), Paul Foreman, Ed., 2311-C Woolsey St., Berkeley, CA 94705, USA. Poetry, prolitarian fiction. Qtly.; $4/yr.; $1/ea.; 56 pgs.; 1 million circ. Reports 6 mos. Pays copies at presrrt.

* I.B.E.G., LTD., 2-4 Brook St., London W1Y 1AA, UK.

ICARUS, Margaret Diorio, Ed., P.O. Box 8, Riderwood, MD 21139, USA. Poetry. Qtly.; $2/yr.; 75 cents/ea.; 600 circ. Reports 1-2 mos. Pays 4 copies.

ICONOCLAST, Doug Baker, Jr., Ed., P.O. Box 7013, Dallas, TX 75209, USA. Poetry & gen. lit. 52/yr.; $10/yr.; 25 cents/ea.; 24 pgs.; 10 million circ. Reports 2 mos. Pays 1 cent per word.

* IDELLA, Hazel Firth Goddard, Scotian Pen Guild, P.O. Box 173, Dartmouth, N.S., Canada.

* IDIOM, Univ. of Manchester Union, Oxford Rd., Manchester 13, UK.

* THE IDLER, Sam Smith, Ed., 125 Fifth St., N.E., Wash. DC 20002, USA.

THE IDLER, An Entertainment, James Parkhill-Rathbone, Ed., The Old Crown, Wheatley, Oxford, UK. Poetry & gen. lit. Qtly.; 8 pgs.; Reports 4 wks. Pays £2 per 1,000.

* IKON, Doug Sandle, Ed., Univ. Union, Leeds 2, UK.

ILLINGWORTH BROS., see Pennine Platform.

ILLUMINATIONS, Norman Moser, Ed., 1601 W. 6th St., Austin, TX 78703, USA. Poetry & gen. lit. 3-4/yr.; $4/yr.; 50 cents/ea.; 16 pgs.; 2,500 circ. Reports 3-4 mos. Pays copies only.

IMAGO (Beaver Cosmos), George Bowering, Ed., 2521 Balaclava St., Vancouver 8, B.C., Canada. Poetry & longpoems. 3/yr.; $2/yr.; 75 cents/ea.; 44 pgs.; 300 circ. Reports 1 mo. Pays copies only.

* IMPRINTS QUARTERLY, 900 Monroe Ave., Apt. 1, Rochester, NY 14620, USA.

THE IMPROVEMENT ERA, see The Ensign.

INDEX, Michael Scammell, Part Ed., 32 Bow St., London WE2R 7AU, UK. Poetry & gen. lit.; Original poetry & prose must be examples of censored material. Qtly.; £2/yr.; 50 pence/ea.; 130 pgs.; 2 million circ. Reports 1-2 mos. Pays £10 per 1000.

* INDIANA UNIVERSITY PRESS, 10th & Morton Sts., Bloomington, IN 47401, USA.

INFORMER, Keith Armstrong, Co-Ed., Circle Books, 16 Davenant Rd., Oxford OX2 8BX, UK. Poetry & gen. lit. Irreg.; £1/4

issues; 25 pence/ea.; 64 pgs.; 1 million circ. Reports irreg. Pays 1 copy.

* INGENUE, Susan Thaler, Ed., 750 Third Ave., N.Y., NY 10017, USA.

INKY TRAILS, Peral L. Kirk, Ed., Rte. No. 2, Box 2028, Nampa, ID 83651, USA. Poetry, articles; 16 lines or less. 3/yr.; $5/yr.; $2/ea.; 50-70 pgs.; 200 circ. Reports 2-4 wks. Num. poetry prizes.

INLAND WRITERS MAGAZINE, Ed Rimbaugh, Ed., 1051 Western Ave., Colton, CA 92324, USA. Poetry, illustrations; poetry not too long, 36 lines. Qtly.; $2/yr.; $1/ea.; 24 pgs.; 100 circ. Reports 2-3 wks. Pays copies only.

INLET, Bruce Guernsey, Ed., Va. Wesleyan Coll., Norfolk, VA 23502, USA, Poetry & fiction. Mss. read Sept.-Mar. only. 1/yr.; free; 36 pgs. Reports 1 mo. Pays 3 copies.

* INSCAPE, Joseph P. Griffin, Ed., Dept. of Engl., Univ. of Ottawa, Ottawa, Ont., Canada.

INSCAPE (The Baleen Press), Ramona Weeks, Co-Ed., Box 13448, Phoenix, AZ 85002, USA. Poetry, art. Qtly.; $5/yr.; $1.50/ea.; 32 pgs.; 300 circ. Pays copies only.

INSTITUTE OF POSITIVE EDUCATIONS, see Black Books Bulletin.

INTAK' (Yorkshire Poets' Assn.), Lyn Cooper, Sec., 24 Laverdene Dr., Totley Rise, Sheffield S17 4HH, UK. Poetry, articles, criticism. 1/yr.; £1/mbrship.; 20 pence/ea.; 20 pgs.; 200 circ.

INTERIM BOOKS, see Magazine (Six).

INTERMEDIA PRESS, see The Poem Company.

INTERNATIONAL COOPERATION COUNCIL, see The Cooperator.

INTERNATIONAL POETRY REVIEW, Dr. Henry Picola, Ed., 1060 N. St. Andrews Pl., Hollywood, CA 90038, USA.

INTERNATIONAL SOCIETY FOR GENERAL SEMANTICS, see Etc.

INTERNATIONAL TIMES (IT), (Cardinell Ltd.), 11B Wardour Mews, London W1, UK. Poetry & gen. lit. 26/yr.; £4.80/yr.; 15 pence/ea.; 24 pgs.; 25 million circ. Reports vary. Payment varies.

INTERNATIONAL WHO'S WHO IN POETRY, Ernest Kay, Gen. Ed., Int. Biographical Ctr., Cambridge CB2 3NJ, UK.

INTERSECTION NEWSLETTER, Paul Kleyman, Ed., 756 Union St., San Fran., CA 94133, USA. Poetry & gen. lit.; max. 30

lines for poetry. Irreg.; free; 8 million circ. Pays copies only.

* INTRANSIT, c/o Bill Thomas, 338 W. 22nd Ave., Eugene, OR 97401, USA.

* INTREPID, Allen DeLoach, Ed., 297 Oakmont Ave., Buffalo, NY 14215, USA.

INTRO, Walton Beacham, Ed., Va. Commonwealth Univ., Acad. Ctr., Richmond, VA 23220, USA. Submissions through creative writing prog.; No direct submissions.

INVISIBLE CITY (The Red Hill Press), John McBridge, Co-Ed., 6 San Gabriel Dr., Fairfax, CA 94930, USA. Poetry & reviews. 3-4/yr.; $2/3 issues; 75 cents/ea.; 16 pgs.; 1 million circ. Reports 2 wks. Pays copies only.

* IN WYOMING, Grace Curl Cochran, Poetry Ed., Box 2108, Casper, WY 82601, USA.

* IOWA REVIEW, Marvin Bell, Poetry Ed., Univ. of Iowa, Iowa City, IA 52240, USA.

* IRISH UNIVERSITY PRESS (INTERNATIONAL), LTD., 60 Russell Sq., London WC1B 4HP, UK.

IS (The Transient Press), Ken Saville, Ed., P.O. Box 297, Albuquerque, NM 87103, USA. Poetry & fiction. Once; free; 16 pgs.; 500-1 million circ. Reports 2 wks. Pays copies only.

ISTHMUS, J. Rutherford Willems, Ed., 1429 Leavenworth St., No. 303, San Fran., CA 94109, USA. Poetry & fiction. 2/yr.; $4/yr.; $2/ea.; 120 pgs.; 800 circ. Reports 6 wks. Pays copies only.

* IT, J.D. Whiting, Ed., 336 Luther St., Detroit, MI 48217, USA.

ITHACA HOUSE, Baxter Hathaway, Part-Ed., 108 N. Plain St., Ithaca, NY 14850, USA. Poetry & fiction. Reports 3 mos. Pays copies only.

J & C TRANSCRIPTS, see Dragonfly & Jean's Journal.

JABBERWOCKY, Anne Clark, Ed., The Lewis Carroll Soc., Rm. 17A, S. Block, The County Hall, London SE1 7PB, UK. Literary & Hist. articles rel. to Lewis Carroll. 4/yr.; £2/yr.; 24 pgs.; 400 circ. No payment.

JAM TO-DAY, Rita & Mike Conley & others, Eds., P.O. Box 249, Northfield, VT 05663, USA. Poetry, pref. short. 2/yr.; $2.50/yr.; $1.50/ea.; 32 pgs.; 500 circ. Reports 3-6 wks. Pays 2 copies to ea. poet printed.

* JANAY PUB. CO. LTD., 60 North St., Chichester, PO19 1NB, UK.

JANUS-SCTH, (Sangre de Cristo), Rhoda

del. Jewell, Ed. 1325 Cabrillo Ave., No. 12, Venice, CA 90291, USA. Poetry. Reviews. Qtly.; $2.50/yr.: 65c./ea.; 42 pgs.; 350 circ. Reports 2 wks.

JEAN'S JOURNAL (J & C Transcripts), Jean Calkins, Ed., Box 15, Kanona, NY 14856, USA. Poetry. Qtly.; $5/yr.; $1.25/ea.; 70 pgs.; 500 circ. Reports 2-3 wks. Cash & Book awards; Contest ea. issue.

* JENNINGS (JOHN) GLOUCESTER LTD., Brunswick Rd., Gloucester, UK.

JEOPARDY, Ed. changes annually, Viking Union 218, W.W.S., Bellingham, WA 98225, USA. Poetry, articles. 1/yr.; $1/yr.; 125 pgs.; 2000 circ. Pays 2 copies.

JET CADET, Dana Eynon, Ed., 8121 Hamilton Ave., Cincinnatti, OH 45231, USA. Poetry, short stories/articles etc. Wkly.; $2/yr.; 12 pgs. Reports 4-6 wks. Pays up to 1½ cents per word.

* JEWISH CHRONICLE PUBLS., 67 Gt. Russell St., London WC1B 3BT, UK.

* JOHNS (R.H.) LTD., 20 Daniel St., Newport, Mon. NPT 2TH, UK.

* JOHNSON PUBLS. LTD., 11-14 Stanhope Mews W., London S.W.7., UK.

* JONGLARS, Clark Collidge, Ed., 292 Morris Ave., Providence, RI, 02906, USA.

* JOURNAL OF BLACK POETRY, Joe Gonclaves, Ed., 1308 Masonic Ave., No. 4, San Francisco, CA 94117, USA.

JOURNAL OF CYBERNATION & PUBLIC AFFAIRS, see R.U.R.

JOURNAL OF POPULAR CULTURE (Popular Press), Ray B. Browne, Ed., 101 Univ. Hall, Bowling Green State Univ., Bowling Green OH 43403, USA. Poetry, fiction, reviews, plays. Qtly.; $15/yr.; $3/ea.; 196 pgs.; 1800 circ. Reports 6 wks.

THE JOURNAL OF THE SHAW SOCIETY, see The Shavian.

JOURNAL PUBLICATIONS, see The Weekly Journal & Poet's Nook.

JOURNALISM LABORATORY PRESS, see Shenadoah.

* JUNIOR LIFE, Standard Publications, 8121 Hamilton Ave., Cincinnatti, OH 45231, USA.

JUNIPER PRESS, see Juniper/Northeast Books.

* KALEIDOSCOPE, P. Brian Cox, Ed., P.O. Box 21085, Melbourne, Vic., Australia.

* THE KANSAS CITY STAR, Kansas City, MO 64108, USA.

KANSAS KERNELS, Carol Robbins, Ed., Box 26, Valley Centre, KS 67147, USA. Poetry & non-fiction. Qtly.; $4/yr.; $1.25 ea.; 48 pgs.; 400 circ. Reports 3-4 wks.

KANSAS QUARTERLY, Harold W. Schneider & Ben Nyberg, Eds., Denison Hall, Kansas State Univ., Manhattan, KS 66506, USA. Poetry, fiction & non-fiction. Qtly.; $7.50/yr.; $2/ea.; 128 pgs.; 1 million circ. Reports 2-3 months. Pays 2 copies.

KARAMU, Allen Neff, Ed., English Dept., E. Ill. Univ., Charleston, IL 61920, USA. Short poems & stories. 1/yr.; $3/4 issues; $1/ea.; 100 pgs.; 300 circ. Reports 3-4 months. Pays 2 copies.

* KAURI, c/o Will Inman, Box 429, Am. Univ., Mass. & Nebr. Aves., Wash D.C. 20016, USA.

KAYAK, George Hitchcock, Ed., Bonny Doon Rd., Santa Cruz, CA 95060, USA. Poetry & Criticism. Qtly.; $3/yr.; $1/ea.; 72 pgs.; 1400 circ. Reports 2 wks. Pays copies.

KEEPSAKE POEMS, Shirley Toulson, Roy Lewis, Eds., 26 Sydney Rd., Richmond, Surrey, UK. Illust. poems. 8/yr.; £1.75/yr.; 25p/ea.; 4 pgs.; 180 circ. Reports 2/3 wks. Pays by agreement.

KENFIG PRESS, (British amateur press assn.), Arthur Smith, Ed., 41 Heol Fach, Cornelly, Pyle, Glam., S. Wales CF33 4LN, UK. Poetry, fiction, articles. 4 pgs.; 150 circ. Pays copies.

KENTUCKY FOLKLORE RECORD, Charles S. Guthrie, Ed., Box 169, W. Ky. Univ., Bowling Green, KY, USA. Folk Poetry. Qtly.; $3/yr.; $1/ea.; 24 pgs.; 350 circ. Reports 4 wks. Pays 3 copies.

* KEVIN PRESS, 17 Cathcart Place, Edinburgh, EH11 2HF, UK.

KINESIS, Virginia Kidd, Ed., Box 278, Milford, PA 18337, USA. poetry, restricted amt. 50 cents ea.; 24 pgs.; 100 circ. Reports same day. Pays copies.

KING JAMES* VERSION, (Quicksilver Printing), Carole & Daniel McGinley, 225 S. Main St., Wilkes-Barre, PA 18701, USA. Poetry, reviews, fiction etc. Qtly.; $2/yr.; 50 cents/ea.; 24 pgs. Reports 4 wks. Pays copies.

* ALFRED A. KNOPF, 201 E. 50th St., N.Y., NY 10022, USA.

KNOW INC., see Know News.

KNOW NEWS (Know, Inc.), Anne Pride, Ed., P.O. Box 86031, Pittsburg, PA 15221, USA. Occ. poetry w. feminist bias. 10/yr.; $4/yr.; 1300 circ.

* KODANSHA INTERNATIONAL/USA,

599 College Ave., Palo Alto, CA 94306, USA.

KONGLOMERATI, Richard Mathews, Ed., 5719 29th Ave. S., Gulfport, FL 33707, USA. Poetry, fiction, reviews etc. 2/yr.; $2/50 yr.; $1.50/ea.: 60 pgs.; 300 circ. Reports 2 wks. Pays copies.

KONTEXTS, Michael Gibbs, Ed., 31 Pinhoe Rd., Exeter, Devon, UK. I experimental poetry. Irreg.; 15-20 pence/ea.; 2-300 circ.

KRAKEN PRESS, see You Kill Me.

KRAX, G.A. Rhodes, Flat 3, 60 York Place, Harrogate, Yorks., UK. Poetry, fiction, reviews. Qtly.; 60 pence/yr.; 15 pence/ea.; 20 pgs.; 300 circ. Reports 2 months.

KROKLOK, (Writers Forum), Dom Silvester Houedard, Bob Cobbing, Eds., 262 Randolph Ave., London W9, UK. Sound-poetry. Irreg.; 25 pence/ea.; 32 pgs.; 500 circ. Reports 1 mo. Pays copies.

KROPOTKIN'S LIGHTHOUSE PUBLICATIONS, Jas. Huggon, Ed., c/o Housmans Bookshop, 5 Caledonian Rd., London N1, UK. Occ. poetry pamphlets, w. political bias.

KULCHUR FOUNDATION, Lita Hornick, Ed., 888 Park Ave., N.Y., NY 10021, USA. Poetry, fiction.

KYOI: A Backcountry Writers Forum, (Gold-dust Press), Dale Pendell James Ekedal, Eds., Box 334, Redway, CA 95560, USA. Poetry, articles etc. w. rural emphasis. 2/yr.; $1/yr.; 50 cent/ea.; 32 pgs.: 500 circ. Reports 1 wk–1 mo. Pays 5-10 copies.

L.A. JOURNAL OF SOUND, Garry Lauher, 19641 Rosita St., Tarzana, CA 91356, USA. Poetry fiction, reviews etc. Qtly.; $3.50/yr.; $1/ea.; 40 pgs.; 500 circ. Reports 1-3 wks. Pays copies.

THE LADDER, Ms. Gene Damon, Ed., P.O. Box 5025, Wash. Stn., Reno, NV 89503, USA. Lesbian poetry etc. 6/yr.; $7.50/yr.; $1.25/ea.; 56 pgs.; Reports 15 days. Pays copies.

THE LADYSMITH PRESS, Sean Haldane, Marnie Pomeroy, Eds., The Ladysmith Press, Ladysmith, Quebec, J0X 2AO, Canada. Var. poetry books & pamphlets.

THE LAKE SUPERIOR REVIEW, Cynthia Willoughby, Ed., Box 724, Ironwood, MI 49938, USA. Poetry, fiction & non-fiction. 3/yr.; $2.75/yr.; $1/ea.; 42-48 pgs.; circ. 225. Reports 6-8 wks. Pays 2 copies.

LAME DUCK PRESS, see Sixpack.

* THE LAMP, Rev. Ralph Thomas, S.A., Ringgold St., Peekskill, NY, 10566, USA.

THE LAMP IN THE SPINE, James Moore, Patricia Hampl, Eds., P.O. Box 3372, St.

Paul, MN 55165, USA. Poetry, fiction etc. of a topical nature. 3/yr.; $3/yr.; $1/ea.; 108 pgs.; 900 circ. Reports 2 wks. Pays 5 copies. Some contests.

THE LANCASHIRE AUTHOR'S ASSOCIATION, see The Record & Red Rose.

LANE (Allen), (The Penguin Press), 21 John St., London W1N 2BT, UK. Poetry anthologies & books.

* LARVAE, Leland S. Meyerzove, Ed., 3273 Phillips Ave., Santa Rosa, CA 95401, USA.

THE LAST COOKIE, David Arnold, Ahmos Zu-Bolton II, Pinkie Gordon Lane, 765 Lakeview San Francisco, CA 94112, USA. Poetry. 2/yr.; $1/ea.; 60 pgs.; 1 million circ. Reports 2 wks.-3 mos. Pays copies.

* LATITUDES, Robert Bonazzi, Ed., 6102 Sherwood, Houston, TX 77021, USA.

THE LAUREL PRESS, see Openspaces.

* LAUREL REVIEW, Leonard Roberts, Ed., W. Va. Wesleyan Coll., English Dept., Buckhannon, WV 26201, USA.

LAVA, G.P. Vimal, Ed., 26/53 Ramjas Rd., Karol Bagh, New Delhi 110005, India. Poetry.

SEYMOUR LAWRENCE, INC., Seymour Lawrence, Ed., 90 Beacon St., Boston, MA 02108, USA. Poetry & poetry translations.

* LEATHERNECK, Ronald D. Lyons, Ed., P.O. Box 1918, Wash. DC 20013, USA. Poetry rel. to The Marines.

LEEDS LARYNX (Poetry & Audience), Peter Popham, Ed., Poetry & Audience, The Univ. of Leeds, UK. Poetry, reviews, etc. 15 pence/ea. 40 pgs.

LEGEND, Bonnie E. Parker, Ed., 39213 Gloucester, Westland, MI 48185, USA. Poetry. Qtly.; $4/yr.; $1/ea.; 64 pgs.; Reports 1-3 wks. Pays 1 copy. Occ. prizes.

LEMMING, Rex Burwell, Ed., 3551 42nd St., San Diego, CA 92105, USA. Poetry. Qtly.; $4/yr.; $1/ea.; 30 pgs.; 200 circ. Reports 1 wk. Pays copies.

* LEOPARDESS, Queen Mary Coll. Union Soc., Mile End Rd., London E.1, UK.

LES ETUDES POETIQUES, Martin-Saint-Rene, Ed., 3 Square La Fontaine, Paris XVI, France. Poetry, reviews. Qtly.; 15 francs/yr.; 3.95 francs/ea. 15-20 pgs.; Occ. prizes.

* HAROLD LEVENSON ASSOCIATES, Harold Levenson, Ed., 7080, Hollywood Boulevard, Suite 422, Hollywood, CA 90028, USA.

LEWIS (J.D.) & SONS LTD., John H. Lewis, Ed., Gomer Press, Llandysul, Cardiganshire, Wales, UK. Welsh Poetry w. Anglo-Welsh poets only.

LIBERA -a new womans journal, (Womans Press Collective), 516 Eshleman Hall, Univ. of Calif., Berkeley, CA 94720, USA. Poetry, fiction etc., contbns. by women only. 3/yr.; $3/yr.; $1/ea.; 56 pgs.; 10 million circ. Reports 4 mos. Pays copies.

LIBERATION, Gwenda Blair, Dave Dellinger, Bruce Brown, Eds., 339 Lafayette St., N.Y., NY 10012, USA. Poetry, articles, reviews w. Left-wing, feminist bias. 12/yr.; $7/yr.; $1/ea.; 44 pgs.; 6 million circ. Reports 1 mo.

LIBRARIANS FOR SOCIAL CHANGE, (Smoothie Publications), John Noyce, Ed., 67 Vere Rd., Brighton, Sussex, BN1 4NQ, UK. Poetry w. rel. to Libraries. 3/yr.; 50 pence/yr.; 20 pence/ea.; 30 pgs.; 400 circ.; Reports 1-4 wks. Pays copy.

LIFEFORCE, (Pacific Life Press), Gordon Harrison, Kaspar Schmidt, Anne Ladof, Eds., 213 Indian Lane, Media, PA 19063, USA. Poetry, reviews etc. 12/yr.; 25 cents/ea.; 25 pgs.; 1300 circ. Reports immediately. Pays copies.

LIGHT, A Poetry Review, Roberta C. Gould, Ed., 315 E. 18th St., N.Y., NY 10003, USA. 3/yr.; $3/yr.; $1.25/ea.; 64 pgs.; 1 million circ. Reports 2 mos. Pays copies.

* LILAC TREE PRESS, Wallasey, Cheshire, UK.

* LILLABULERO, William Matthews, Ed., Krums Corners Rd., RD No. 3, Ithaca, NY 14850, USA.

THE LINCOLNSHIRE ASSOCIATION, see Lincolnshire Writers.

LINCOLNSHIRE WRITERS, Mary Gibson, Ed., 2 Vetner Terrace, Lincoln, UK. Poetry etc. from Lincolnshire residents only. 2/yr.; 30 pence/yr.; 15 pence/ea.; 48 pgs.; Pays 50 pence/pg. & 1 copy.

* LINES REVIEW, Alan Riddell, Ed., 12 Richmon Lane, Edinburgh, Scotland, UK.

LINES REVIEW, (M. MacDonald), Robin Fulton, Ed., M. MacDonald, Edgefield Rd., Loanhead, Midlothian, Scotland, UK. Poetry etc., w. particular ref. to Scotland. Qtly.; $3/yr.; $1/ea.; 50-60 pgs.; 700 circ. Reports by return. Pays by arrangement.

LIONHEAD PUBLISHING, see Roar.

LIP, (Middle Earth Books), Samuel Amico, Ed., 1134 Pine St., Phila., PA 19107, USA. Occ. poetry on particular themes. 2/yr.; $4/yr.; $1.25-$1.75/ea.; 128-160 pgs.; 2500 circ. Pays $2.50/poem, $2/pg. prose & 2 copies.

THE LISTENER, B.B.C., 35 Marylebone High St., London, W1M 4AA, UK.

THE LITERARY REVIEW, Charles Angoff, Ed., Fairleigh Dickinson Univ., Rutherford, NJ 07070, USA. Poetry, sketches, etc. Qtly.; $7/yr.; $2/ea.

* LITERARY SERVICES & PRODUCTION LTD., 2 Denbigh Close, London W11 2QH, UK.

THE LITERARY SUPPLEMENT (Nothing Doing (formally in London)), Anthony Barnett, Ed., Johan Grundt Tanum, Karl Johans Gate 43, Oslo 1, Norway. Occ. poetry, unpublished only. Irreg.; 4 pgs.; 150 circ. Reports immediately.

THE LITERARY SUPPLEMENT, WRIT-INGS (Nothing Doing (formally in London)), Anthony Barnett, Ed., 25 Woodhall Drive, London SE21 7HJ, UK. Poetry Irreg. 20 pgs.; 200 circ.

* LITERARY TIMES, Jay Robert Nash, Ed., Box 4327, Chgo., IL 60680, USA.

LITERARY UNION, see Unio.

LITTACK (Ember Press), William Oxley, Ed., 27 Brook Rd., Epping. Essex, UK. Poetry, reviews. 3/yr.; £1/yr.; 40 pence/ea.; 80 pgs.; 300 circ. Reports 1 mo. Pays by arrangement.

* LITTLE, BROWN & CO LTD., 34 Beacon St., Boston, MA 02106, USA.

THE LITTLE DWARF (Village Underground Press), David Legg, Ed., 57 Silver St., Gt. Barford, Bedford MK44 3HX, UK. short poems & articles Qtly.; 40 pence/yr.; 8 pence/ea.; 15 pgs.; 500 circ. Reports for next issue. Pays copies.

THE LITTLE MAGAZINE, Thomas T. Beeler, Co-Ed., P.O. Box 207, Cathedral Stn., N.Y., NY 10025, USA. Poetry, reviews etc. Qtly.; $5/yr.; 64-80 pgs.

THE LITTLE REVIEW, John McKernan, W.G. Webster, Eds., P.O. Box 2321, Huntington, WV 25724, USA. Poetry, reviews etc. 2/yr.; $3/yr.; $1.50/ea.; 40 pgs.; 1000 circ. Reports 1-3 mos.

THE LITTLE WORD MACHINE, (L.W.M. Publications), Nick Toczek, Ed., 103 Moorhead Lane, Shipley, Yorks, UK. Poetry & short fiction. Qtly.; £1/yr.; 28 pence/ea.; 50-60 pgs. 1 million circ. Reports up to 2 mos. Pays 1-2 copies.

*LIVERPOOL UNIVERSITY PRESS, 123 Grove St., Liverpool, L7 7AF, UK.

LLEWELLYN PUBLICATIONS, see Gnostica News.

* LLYFRFA'R METHODISTIAID CAL-

FINAIDD, Caernarvon, Caerns., UK.

* THE LOCK HAVEN REVIEW, Vincent Stewart, Ed., Russell Hall 5, Lock Haven State Coll., Lock Haven, PA 17745, USA.

* LODENEK PRESS, 14-16 Market St., Padstow, Cornwall, UK.

LOL (Y Lolfa), Robat Gruffud, Ed., Talybont, Cardiganshire, SY24 5ER, Wales, UK. Occ. poetry w. pro Welsh bias.

THE LONDON COLLECTOR (Wolf House Books), Richard Weiderman, Ed., 1420 Pontiac Rd., S.E., Grand Rapids, MI 49506, USA. Poetry w. rel. to Jack London. Irreg.; $1/yr.; 50 cents/ea.; 20 pgs.; 130 circ. Reports immediately. Pays 12 copies.

LONDON LITERARY EDITIONS LTD., 29 Avenue Chambers, Vernon Place, London W.C.1., UK.

LONDON MAGAZINE EDITIONS, Alan Ross, Ed., 30 Thurloe Place, London SW7, UK. Poetry, reviews etc. 2/mth.; £5/yr.; 90 pence/ea.; 160 pgs. Pays about £5/pg.

LONG ISLAND REVIEW, Stephen Sossaman, Ed., Box 10, Cambria Hts., NY 11411, USA. Poetry & fiction. 3/yr.; $3/yr.; $1/ea.; 32 pgs.; 300 circ. Reports 3 wks. Pays copies.

THE LOON, D.L. Emblen, Ed., P.O. Box 11633, Santa Rosa, CA 95406, USA. Poetry. 2/yr.; $1/ea.; 50-60 pgs. Reports 2-3 wks. Pays copies.

* LORRIMER PUBLISHING, LTD., 47 Dean St., London W1V 5HL, UK.

LOUISIANA STATE UNIVERSITY PRESS, (see also THE SOUTHERN REVIEW), Leslie E. Phillabaum, Assoc. Dir. and Ed., Baton Rouge, LA 70803, USA. Book-length poetry in Engl. only.

* LOVE/WOMAN, Poetry Corporation VII, English Dept., Univ. of Wisconsin, Milwaukee, WI 53201, USA.

THE LOVERSEED PRESS, see Day By Day.

LSE STUDENTS UNION, see Clare Market.

LUCKIAMUTE, Gary L. Lark, Ed., Rt.1, Box 288A, Corvallis, OR 97330, USA. Oregon Poets only. 1/yr.; $2/yr.; 130 pgs.; circ. 1 million. Reports 1 mo. Pays copies.

LUDD'S MILL (Hilltop Press), Steve Sneyd, Ed., 4 Nowell Place, Almondbury, Huddersfield, Yorks., UK. Poetry, fiction etc. Qtly.; 40 pence/yr.; 12½ pence/ea. 22 pgs.; 500 circ.

LUNCH MAGAZINE, Ruan Bone, Ed., 16 Avon Court, Keswick Rd., Putney SW15 2JU, UK. Homosexual interests. 12/yr.; £2.80/yr.; 25 pence/ea.; 32 pgs.; 3 million circ.

* LUZAC & CO., LTD., P.O. Box 157, 46 Gt. Russell St., London WC1B 3PE, UK.

* LYREBIRD (LONDON), LTD., 14 Cornwall Gdns., London, SW7 4AN, UK.

THE LYRIC, Ruby Altizer Roberts, John Nixon Jr., Eds., Bremo Bluff, VA 23022, USA. Poetry. Qtly.; $2/yr.; 50 cents/ea.; 24 pgs.

THE LYRIC PLAYERS THEATRE, see Threshold.

LYRICAL IOWA, (Sutherland Printing Co., Inc.), Ruth Delong Peterson, Ed., New London, IA 52645, USA. Poetry by Iowa residents only. 1/yr.; $2/yr.; 128 pgs.; 700 circ. Reports April, Pays prizes.

* MACABRE, Joseph P. Brenner, Ed., 26 Fowler St., New Haven, CT 06516, USA.

* Mc'CALLS, Bette-Jane Raphael, Poetry Ed., 230 Park Ave., N.Y., NY 10017, USA.

* MacDONALD & CO. (PUBLISHERS), LTD., St. Giles House, London W1A 2LG, UK.

M. MACDONALD, see Lines Review.

* MCGILL-QUEENS UNIVERSITY PRESS, 70 Gt. Russell St., London W.C.1, UK.

* MCGRAW-HILL BOOK CO. (U.K.) LTD., McGraw-Hill House, Shoppenhagers Rd., Maidenhead, SL6 2QL, UK.

* MCGRAW-HILL COMPANY, 330 Sixth Ave., N.Y., NY 10022, USA.

MCKEE PUBLISHING COMPANY, see This Issue.

* MACLELLAN (WILLIAM) LTD., 104 Hill St., Glasgow C3, Scotland, UK.

MACMILLAN LONDON LIMITED, 4 Little Essex St., London WC2R 3LF, UK. Engl. lang. only.

* MACMILLAN & COMPANY, 866 Third Ave., N.Y., NY 10022, USA.

MADEMOISELLE, 350 Madison Ave., N.Y., NY 10017, USA. Poetry on any topic, prefer short poems; fiction; non-fiction. 12/yr.; $7/yr.; 75 cents/ea. Pays from $25 for poetry.

MADRONA (Gemina Press), J.K. Osborne, Co-Ed., 502 12th Ave. E., Seattle, WA 98102, USA. Poetry, fiction, criticism. 3/yr.; $5/yr.; $1.50/ea.; 80 pgs.; 500 circ. Reports 1 mo. Pays 1 yr. subscription.

MAG, John Kay, Co-Ed., 3802 La Jara, Long Beach, CA 90805, USA. Poetry, fiction, criticism; like poems that can be followed. 3/yr.; $1/ea.; 60 pgs.; 400 circ. Reports 1 mo.

MAGAZINE (SIX), (Interim Books), Kirby Congdon, Ed., Box 35, N.Y., NY 10014, USA. Poetry, articles, criticism. 2/yr.; $10/ea.; 500 circ. Reports 2 wks. Pays copies only.

* THE MAGDALENE SYNDROME, David Tammer, Ed., 446 Cole St., San Francisco, CA 94101, USA.

MAGIC CIRCLE PRESS, Valerie Harms Sheehan, Co-Ed., 31 Chapel Ln., Riverside, CT 06878, USA. Poetry, fiction, articles, etc. Reports 1 mo. Pays depends, 15% authors royalty.

* THE MAGNIFICAT, Sister Mary Walter, Ed., Box 15, 131 Laurel St., Manchester, NH 03105, USA. Poems from 4-16 lines.

* MAGPIE PRESS LONDON, 36 Sherard Rd., London S.E.9, UK.

* MAGUEY, P.O. Box 385, El Cerrito, CA 94530, USA.

MAINLINE, Eugene McNamara, Co-Ed., P.O. Box 61, Sandwich Stn., Windsor, Ont., Canada. Poetry. 3/yr.; $2/yr.; 75 cents/ea.; 30 pgs.; 500 circ. Reports swift. Pays 2 copies.

* MAINLY, Carregraff, Craig Las, Talybent-on-Usk, Brecon, Wales, UK.

THE MALAHAT REVIEW, Robin Skelton, Ed., Univ. of Vic., Victoria, B.C., Canada. Poetry & gen. lit. Qtly.; $5/yr.; $1.50/ea.; 148 pgs. Reports less than 3 mos. Pays on acceptance at rate of $10.00 per poem or pg. of poetry.

* MANALA, 1623 Superior Bldg., Cleveland, OH 44114, USA.

* MANDALA, Tim Hildebrand, Ed., 818 Terry Pl., Madison, WI 53711, USA.

MAN-ROOT, Paul Mariah, Co-Ed., P.O. Box 982, S. San Francisco, CA 94080, USA. Poetry, fiction, etc. 2-4/yr.; $5/yr.; $1.50/ea.; 96-120 pgs.; 1 million circ. Reports 5-60 days. Pays $2/pg. if grant, copies normally.

MANY SMOKES, Sun Bear, Wabun, Eds., P.O. Box 5895, Reno, VN 89503, USA. Poetry, articles, interviews dealing w. Native Ams. Qtly.; 2/yr.; 50 cents/ea.; 20 pgs.; 6 million circ. Reports vary. Pays copies only.

MAPS, John Taggart, Ed., 311 E. Garfield St., Shippensburg, PA 17257, USA. Poetry, art, criticism, etc. 1/yr.; $2.50/yr.; 115-130 pgs.; 500 circ. Reports 2 wks. Pays copies only.

J. MARK PRESS, see All-Time Favorite Poetry, American Scenes, Best in Poetry, Poetry of Our Time.

MARK TWAIN JOURNAL, Cyril Clemens, Ed., Kirkwood, MO 63122, USA. Some poetry, mostly articles on Engl. & Am. authors. $3/yr.; $1/ea.

MARTIN BRIAN & O'KEEFFE LTD., 37 Museum St., London WC1, UK. Few poetry titles.

MARVELL PRESS, 3/33 Compayne Gdns., London NW6 3DD, UK. Poetry collections.

THE MASSACHUSETTS REVIEW, John Hicks, Co-Ed., Memorial Hall, Univ. of Mass., Amherst, MA 01002, USA. Poetry, fiction, reviews, pub. affairs. Qtly.; $9/yr.; $2.50/ea.; 200 pgs.; 1500 circ. Reports vary. Pays 35 cents/line poetry, $8 min. Presents Jsees Tane Award of $100 for best poem in previous vol.

MATRIX: For She of the New Aeon, Idell, Ed., Box 4218, N. Hollywood, CA 91607, USA. Poetry, fiction, articles, etc. 50 pgs.; 600 circ. Pays copies only.

MAYFLOWER, (Southampton Poetry Circle), Olive Cox, Chmn., 3 Peters Croft Ave., Ashurst, Southampton SO4 2AB, UK. Anthol. of Southampton Poetry Circle. 1/yr.; 15 pence/ea.

MAYNARD PRESS, Cedric Cullingford, Ed., 8 Rangers Sq., Greenwich, London SE10, UK. Poetry.

MEANJIN QUARTERLY, C.B. Christesen, Ed., Univ. of Melbourne, Parkville, Vic., Australia. Poetry, fiction, articles, etc. Qtly.; $10/yr.; 144 pgs.; 3500 circ. per quarter. Reports 2 mos. Pays upon publication.

* MEASURE, Howard McCord, Ed., 317 Coll. Hall, Wash. State Univ., Pullman, WA 99163, USA.

* MEDITERRANEAN REVIEW, Orient, NY 11957, USA. Poetry, criticism, reviews.

* MEDUSA PRESS, 21 Lynford Gdns., Seven Kings, Ilford, Essex, UK.

MELE, Stefan Baciu, Ed., Dept. of European Lang., Univ. of Hawaii, Honolulu, HI 96822, USA. Poetry, any length, any lang., w. Engl. translation.

MEMBRANE PRESS (see also STATIONS), Karl Young, Ed., P.O. Box 5431, Shorewood, Milwaukee, WI 53211, USA.

THE MENARD PRESS, Anthony & Brenda Rudolf, Eds., 1 Primrose Gdns., London NW3 4UJ, UK. Poetry, translated.

THE MERCIER PRESS LTD., Capt. J.M. Feehan, Mng. Dir., 4 Bridge St., Cork, Ireland. Poetry & gen. lit.; no restrictions as to lang. or length.

MERIDIAN, Poetry Magazine, (Rondo Publications Ltd.), Trevor Kneale, Ed., 10 Pall Mall, Liverpool L3 6HJ, UK. Engl. lang. poetry only. Qtly.; 25 pence.

MERLIN'S MAGIC, Merlin F. Teed, Ed., 318-81 St., Brooklyn, NY 11209, USA. Poetry, fiction, articles, reviews. 6/yr.; 30 cents/ea.; 4 pgs.; 350 circ. Reports 2 wks. to a mo. No payment.

* MERMAID, Gay Search, Ed., Birmingham Univ. Union, Edgbaston Rd., Birmingham 15, UK.

MERSEYSIDE ARTS ASSOCIATION, see Arts Alive Merseyside.

* METAMORPHOSIS, Michael Roloff, Ed., 301 W. 19th St., N.Y., NY 10011, USA.

EYRE METHUEN LTD., (Associated Book Publishers Ltd.), John D. Cullen, Chmn., 11 New Fetter Ln., London EC4P 4EE, UK. Poetry in Engl., no length restrictions.

* MHC PUBLICATIONS, Morris Harvey Coll., Charleston, WV 25304, USA.

MHP – Montgomery – Hyde Park, Jeri Herrmann, Ed., 2505 St. Louis Ave., St. Louis, MO 63106, USA. Poetry, fiction, articles, etc. for low-income, inner-city resident audience. 12/yr.; $5/yr.; 50 cents/ea.; 8 pgs.; 3 million circ. Reports 10 days. Pays copies only.

MICHAEL deHARTINGTON PUBLISHERS, 60 Oxford St., London W1A 4WD, UK. Poetry, fiction; gay orientation.

MICHIGAN HOT APPLES (Hot Apples Press), P.O. Box 238, Bloomfield Hills, MI 48013, USA. Poetry, fiction.

MICHIGAN QUARTERLY REVIEW (Univ. of Mich.), Radcliffe Squires, Ed., 3032 Rackham Bldg., Ann Arbor, MI 48104, USA. Poetry, fiction, articles, etc. Qtly.; $6/yr.; $1.50/ea.; 100 pgs.; 3 million circ. Reports 2-3 wks. Pays 50 cents/line poetry plus 3 copies.

MIDDLE EARTH BOOKS, see Lip.

MIDNAG PUBLICATIONS, (Mid Northumberland Arts Group), Northumberland Co. Tech. Coll., Coll. Rd., Ashington, Northumberland, UK. Poetry, posters.

* MIDNIGHT PUBLICATIONS, 405 N. Woodside Rd., Glasgow W2, Scotland, UK.

* MIDWEST, R.R. Cuscaden, Ed., 289 E. 148th St., Harvey, IL 60426, USA.

* MIDWEST CHAPARRAL, 5508 Osage Ave., Kan. City, KS 66196, USA.

MIKROKOSMOS, Courtney Frobenius, Co-Ed., Dept. of Engl., Wichita State Univ., Wichita, KS 67208, USA. Poetry, prose, etc. $4/4 issues; $1/ea.; 125 pgs. Reports 2 wks. Pays copies. $25 award ea. issue for poetry, prose & art.

THE MILK QUARTERLY, (The Yellow

Press), Richard Friedman, Co.-Ed., 7724 Marshfield, Chgo., IL 60626, USA. Poetry, no unsolicited submissions from people who haven't seen mag. Qtly.; $4/yr.; $1/ea.; 80 pgs.; 400 circ. Reports 2 wks. Pays copies only.

* MILLER (J. GARNET), LTD., 1-5 Portpool Ln., London EC1N 7SL, UK.

* MIMEO, Sam Cornish, Ed., 10 R Centre St., Cambridge, MA 02138, USA.

* MINERVA PRESS, 27 Southampton St., Strand, London WC2E 7JA, UK.

MINNESOTA POETRY ANTHOLOGY, Chris Boros & students, Eds., Atwood Ctr., St. Cloud State Coll., St. Cloud, MN 56301, USA. Poetry, art, photos; best poetry by writers in Minn./Upper Mid-W. area. 1/yr.

THE MINNESOTA REVIEW, Roger Mitchell, Ed., Box 5416, Milwaukee, WI 53211, USA. Poetry, fiction, drama, criticism. 2/yr.; $3.50/yr.; $2/ea.; 120 pgs.; 1000 circ. Reports 1-2 mos. Pays copies.

MISSISSIPPI POETRY JOURNAL, Miss Goldie Jane Feldman, Ed., 765 Avalon Rd., Jackson, MS 39206, USA.

MISSISSIPPI REVIEW (Center for Writers), Gordon Weaver, Ed., Southern Stn., Box 37, Hattiesburg, MS 39401, USA. Poetry, fiction, reviews, etc. 3/yr.; $3/yr.; $1.75/ea.; 85 pgs.; 500 circ. Reports 1 wk.- 2 mos. Pays $5/poem.

MITCHELL BOOKS, John Yamrus, Ed., 94 Oliver St., Swoyerville, PA 18704, USA. Poetry, fiction; Mss. of no more than 50 pgs. 30 pgs. Reports 1 wk. Pays percentage.

THE MITRE PRESS (Imprint of Fudge & Co. Ltd.), 52 Lincoln's Inn Fields, London WC2, UK. Poetry collections.

* MODERN AGE, Eugene Davidson, Ed., 154 E. Superior St., Chgo., IL 60611, USA.

* MODERN BRIDE, Helen Gray, Ed., 1 Park Ave., N.Y., NY 10016, USA. Poems appealing to young married couples.

MODERN IMAGES, Roy Douglass Burrow, Ed., 1400 N. Jefferson, El Dorado, AR 71730, USA. Emphasis on free verse & mod. poetry. Qtly.; 100 circ. No payment, acquires all rights.

MODERN POETRY IN TRANSLATION, Daniel Weissbort, Ed., 10 Compayne Gdns., London NW6 3DH, UK. Poetry, fiction, articles, etc.; in translation only. Qtly.; £2/yr.; 50 pence/ea.; 32 pgs.; 1500 circ. Reports 3 mos. Payment varies.

MOJO NAVIGATOR(E) (Cat's Pajamas Press), John Jacob, Ed., 102 S. Austin, Apt. 2-C, Oak Park, IL 60304, USA. Poetry, fiction, articles, etc. Irreg.; $3.50/yr.;

$1/ea.; 32-40 pgs.; 250-500 circ. Reports 2-3 wks. Pays copies, small cash payment.

THE MONARCHIST LEAGUE OF CANADA, see The Canadian Monarchist.

MONDAY MORNING PRESS, Tom Montag, Ed., 2912 N. Hackett, Milwaukee, WI 53211, USA. Primary interest Wis. & Mid-W.

MONDAY MORNING WASH (Monday Morning Press), Tom Montag, Ed., 2912 N. Hackett, Milwaukee, WI 53211, USA. Poetry, fiction, etc.

THE MONTHLY or THE ASIAN AMERICAN EXPERIENCE, see Gidra.

MONUMENT in Cantos and Essays, Victor Myers, Ed., Rte. 10, Columbia, MO 65201, USA. Poetry, fiction, etc. 1/yr.; $1/yr.; $1/ea.; 50 pgs.; 300 circ. Reports 3 mos. Pays 1 $25 prize annually, 2 copies.

MOONBIRD PUBLICATIONS, Robert Richardson, Ed., 52 Holtspur Ave., Woodburn Green, High Wycombe, Bucks., UK. Poetry, fiction, etc. 30 pgs. Pays by arrangement.

MOONGOOSE (Disposable Paper Press/Moongoose Press), Ralph Alfonso, Ed., 5252 Borden, Montreal 265, P.Q., Canada. Poetry, art, cartoons, satire. Qtly.; $1.50/yr.; 50 cents/ea.; 30-50 pgs.; 200 circ. Reports 2 wks. Pays 2 copies only.

MOONSHINE, Tina Fulker, Ed., 6 Oxford Close, Edmonton, London N.9, UK. Poetry, art. Irreg.; 10 pence/ea.; 30 pgs.; 'grapevine' circ. No payment.

MORGAN PRESS, see Hey Lady.

MORNING STAR PRESS, see The Phoenix.

MORTEN (ERIC J.), 46 Warburton St., Didsbury, Manchester 20, UK. Poetry collects.

* MOTHER, Peter Schjeldahl, Ed., Box 94, Stuyvesant Stn., N.Y., NY 10009, USA.

MOTHER'S HEN, (see also GYPSY TABLE, MUCHOS SOMOS), P.O. Box 99592, San Francisco, CA, USA.

MOUNTAIN GAZETTE, Mike Moore, Ed., 1801 York St., Denver, CO 80206, USA. Poetry, fiction, articles, etc. relating to mtns., environment, sport. 1/yr.: $5/yr.: 50 cents/ea.; 32 pgs.; 6 million circ. Reports 2-4 wks. Pays 75 cents per col. inch.

* MOUTH, Les Weichselbaum, Ed., 17 Oxford, Buffalo, NY 14209, USA.

* MT. ADAMS REVIEW, George Thompson, Ed., 4 Riverview Pl., Cincinnatti, OH 45202, USA.

MUCHOS SOMOS (Mother's Hen), P.O.

Box 99592, San Francisco, CA, USA. Poetry pamphlets; 75 cents; 20 pages; any style & subject matter; English lang.

* MULLER (FREDERICK), LTD., Ludgate House, 110 Fleet St., London EC4A 2AP, UK.

MUNDUS ARTIUM: A Journal of International Literature and the Arts, Rainer Schulte, Ed., Ellis Hall 303, Ohio Univ., Athens, OH 45701, USA. Bilingual jrnl. publng. contemporary int. poetry, fiction, & photographic reproduction of art works. 2/yr.; $6/yr.; 150 pgs.; 1 million circ. Reports 1 mo. Payment varies.

MUSE (Birmingham Poetry Centre), Geoff Charlton, Ed., B.M.I., Margaret St., Birmingham B3 3BS, UK. Poetry mainly from Engl. midlands, poems small to medium length. 2/yr.; 50 pence/yr.; 20 pence/ea.; 60 pgs.; 500 circ. Reports 6 wks.

* THE MUSE, Mildred Moon Howell, Ed., Cathlamet, WA 98612, USA.

* THE MUSIC JOURNAL, Robert Cumming, Ed., 200 W. 57th St., N.Y., NY 10019, USA. Will consider poems about music.

MUSTANG REVIEW, Marjorie Appell, Co-Ed., 212 S. Broadway, Denver, CO 80209, USA. Poetry, prefer 12-24 lines. 2/yr.; $2/yr.; $1/ea.; 24 pgs.; 400 circ. Reports 2 wks. Pays copy.

THE MYSTERIOUS BARRICADES, Henry Weinfield, Ed., 425 Riverside Dr., No. 12E, N.Y., NY 10025, USA. Poetry, fiction, articles, etc. 2/yr.; $1.25/yr.; 50 cents/ea.; 50 pgs.; 500 circ. Reports 2 wks. Pays copies only.

NASA REC (OUR WORD), D. Tochitch, Ed., 53 Hawthorn Dr., Harrow, Middlesex HA2 7NU, UK. Yugoslav mag. publng. poetry, short stories, film & lit. reviews.

NASE DELO (OUR WORK), D. Tochitch, Ed., 53 Hawthorn Dr., Harrow, Middlesex HA2 7NU, UK. Lib. in Serbo-Croat lang., incls. poetry. Irreg.

NASH PUBLISHING CORP., Janet Shepard, Mng. Ed., 9255 Sunset Blvd., Los Angeles, CA 90069, USA. Some poetry.

THE NATION, Grace Schulman, Poetry Ed., 333 Sixth Ave., N.Y., NY 10014, USA. Poetry of high quality by new & estab. writers. 48/yr.; $15/yr.; 50 cents/ea. Annual poetry contest.

NAUSEA ONE (Russ Haas Press), Leo Mailman, Co-Ed., P.O. Box 4261, Long Beach, CA 90804, USA. Poetry, fiction, art, etc.; prefers works not over 10 pgs. in length. Qtly.; $2.75/yr.; 75 cents/ea.; 48 pgs.; 400 circ. Reports 1 mo. Pays 2 copies.

* NEBRASKALAND, Neb. Game & Parks

Commn., P.O. Box 30370, Lincoln, NB 68503, USA.

NEGRO AMERICAN LITERATURE FORUM (Ind. State Univ.), John F. Bayliss, Ed., Schl. of Educ., Ind. State Univ., Terre Haute, IN 47809, USA. Poetry, fiction, short novels, etc. Qtly.; $4/yr.; $1/ea.; 36 pgs.; 1 million circ. Reports 2 wks.

* NEO MAGAZINE, R.L. Peters, Ed., 1112 Park Ave., N.Y., NY 10028, USA.

NEON SUN, Clive Matson, Ed., P.O. Box 2191 Stn. A, Berkeley, CA 94702, USA. Poetry, longpoems.

NEVERSELL MONTHLY, Robert L. Griffiths III, Poetry Ed., 3006 Porter St. N.W., Wash. DC 20008, USA. Poetry, fiction, articles, etc. 12/yr.; $10/yr.; $1/ea.; 156 pgs.; 12 million circ. Reports no longer than 1 mo. Pays $30 per pg.

NEVILLE (GARY), Printer & Stationer, The Print Shop, High St., Stonehouse, Glos., UK. Engl. lang. only.

NEW: American & Canadian Poetry (The Crossing Press), John Gill, Poetry Ed., R.D. 3, Trumansburg, NY 14886, USA. Poetry, articles, criticism, etc. 3/yr.; $2.75/yr.; $1/ea.; 64 pgs.; 1 million circ. Reports 6 wks. Pays copies only.

* NEW AMERICAN REVIEW, Richard Howard, Poetry Ed., Bantam Books, 666 Fifth Ave., N.Y., NY 10019, USA.

NEW COLLAGE MAGAZINE, A.McA. Miller, Ed., P.O. Box 1898, Sarasota, FL 33578, USA. Poetry. 3/yr.; $3/yr.; $1/ea.; 32 pgs.; 3 million circ. Reports 3 wks. Pays only by prior arrangement & if solicited, copies usually.

NEW DEPARTURES, Michael Horovitz, Ed., Mullions, Piedmont, Bisley, Glos. GL6 7BU, UK. Poetry, art, photos, etc. Irreg.; £1/3 issues; 40 pence/ea.; 60 pgs.; 10 million circ. No submissions required now. Pays by arrangement.

NEW DIRECTIONS PUBLISHING CORP., 333 Sixth Ave., N.Y., NY 10014, USA. Poetry & prose, few bilingual titles.

NEW EARTH TRIBE NEWSPACK (R.V.K. Publng. Co.), S.P. Stavrakis, Ed., P.O. Box 264du, Menomonee Falls, WI 53051, USA. Poetry used on reg. basis along w. articles, art, etc. 10/yr.; $5.43/yr.; 8-32 pgs. Reports 1-3 mos. Pays $5-15 involvement.

THE NEW ENGLAND GALAXY, Catherine Fennelly, Ed., Old Sturbridge Village, Sturbridge, MA 01566, USA. Poetry w. New England theme. Qtly.; $4/yr.; $1/ea.; 60 pgs.; 11000-12000 circ. Reports 1-2 mos. Pays $50 per poem.

NEW ENGLAND POETRY CLUB, see Writ.

* NEW ENGLISH LIBRARY, LTD.,

Barnard's Inn, Holborn, London EC1N 2JR, UK.

* NEW FRONTIERS, Raymond Gaboriault, Ed., Box 908, Fairfield Univ., Fairfield, CT 06430, USA.

* NEW HAMPSHIRE PROFILES, Paul E. Estaver, Ed., 1 Pleasant St., Portsmouth, NH 03801, USA.

NEW HEADLAND (Ember Press), William Oxley, Ed., 27 Brook Rd., Epping, Essex, UK. Poetry, articles, criticism, reviews. Qtly.; £1/yr.; 25 pence/ea.; 35 pgs.; 200 circ. Reports 1 wk. Pays copies only.

THE NEW INFINITY REVIEW, James R. Pack, Ed., P.O. Box 412, S. Point, OH, USA. Poetry, fiction, non-fiction; No length limit on poems, submit 4-12 poems and autobiographical statement. $2.50/yr.; 75 cents/ea.; 48 pgs.; 500 circ. Reports 4 wks.

NEW LETTERS, David Ray, Ed., Univ. of Mo.-Kan. City, 5100 Rockhill Rd., Kan. City, MO 64110, USA. Poetry, critical articles, short stories, etc. Qtly.; $8/yr.; $5/ea.; 128 pgs. Small payment upon publication.

* NEW MEASURE, Peter Jay, Ed., 1A Littlegate St., Oxford, UK.

NEW MEXICO MAGAZINE, Stanley Noyes, Poetry Ed., 113 Washington Ave., Santa Fe, NM 87501, USA. Poetry pg. 'The Cloud Terrace', ea. issue; interested in short poems relating to S.W. US & its Indian, Hispano, & Anglo-Am. cultures. 6/yr.; $3.25/yr.; 75 cents/ea.; 48 pgs.; 72012 circ. Reports 2 mos. No payment.

NEW ORLEANS REVIEW, Francis Sullivan, Poetry Ed., Loyola Univ., New Orleans, LA 70118, USA. Poetry & gen. lit. Qtly.; $6/yr.; $1.50/ea.; 96 pgs.; 1000 circ. Reports 2 wks. to 2 mos. Pays 10 per poem per 1 pg. Winner of best poem of ea. vol. given 1 pg. in upcoming issue for any poem he wishes to publish.

NEW POETRY — journal of the Poetry Society of Australia, Robert Adamson, Ed., P.O. Box 110, Grosvenor St. Post Off., Sydney, Australia 2000. Contemporary poetry by new & estab. poets. 6/yr.; $9/yr.; $2/ea.; 64 pgs.; 1000 circ. Reports 1 mo. Pays min. $7.50 per poem. $100 New Poetry Award held annually.

* NEW REPUBLIC, 1244 19th St. N.W., Wash. DC 20013, USA.

THE NEW REVIEW, Ian Hamilton, Ed., 11 Greek St., London W1, UK. Poetry, fiction, interviews, etc. 12/yr.; £12/yr.

NEW RIVERS PRESS, C.W. Truesdale, Ed., P.O. Box 578, Cathedral Stn., N.Y., NY 10025, USA. Poetry collections. Reports 2-3 mos. Pays 15% royalties.

THE NEW SALT CREEK READER (Windflower Press), Ted Kooser, Ed., 1720½ C. St., Lincoln, NB 68502, USA. Poetry, art, interviews, etc. Qtly.; $3.50/yr.; $1/ea.; 40 pgs.; 400 circ. Reports 1 mo. Pays copies only.

* NEW STATESMAN, Gt. Turnstile, London W.C.1, UK.

* NEW STUDENT REVIEW, Steven Bigwood, Ed., The Circle, Box 40, Norton Union, SUNY, Buffalo, NY 14205, USA.

NEW UNITY, Box 891, Springfield, MA 01101, USA. Poetry, articles, art, etc.; pro-labor & wkr. 12/yr.; $2.50/yr. donation; 10 cents/ea. donation; 8 pgs.; 5 million circ. Reports vary. No payment.

NEW VOICES MAGAZINE, Alexander Pazandak, Ed., P.O. Box No. 251, Orange, NJ, U.S.A. Poetry, short stories, articles. Qtly.; $2/yr. There is no recent issue of New Voices Mag. due to lack of poetry worthy of publication.

NEW WORLD REVIEW (N.W.R. Publs., Inc.), Jessica Smith, Ed., Suite 308, 156 Fifth Ave., N.Y., NY 10011, USA. Poetry, articles, reviews, interviews concerned w. Socialist countries. Qtly.; $4/yr.; $1.25/ea.; 128 pgs.; 7 million circ. Reports vary. Payment varies.

NEW WRITING FROM ZAMBIA, David Simpson, Ed., P.O. Box 1889, Lusaka, Zambia, Africa. Poetry, fiction mainly from Zambia; no overseas submissions. Qtly.; 84 ngwee/yr.; 21 ngwee/ea.; 28 pgs.; 900 circ.

NEW YORK QUARTERLY, William Packard, Ed., Room 603, Columbia Univ. Club, 4 W. 43rd St., N.Y., NY 10036, USA.

* THE NEW YORK REVIEW OF BOOKS, 250 W. 57th St., N.Y., NY 10019, USA.

* THE NEW YORK TIMES, 229 W. 43rd St., N.Y., NY 10036, USA.

NEW ZEALAND MONTHLY REVIEW (Caxton Press), P.V. Neavy, Ed., Box 345, Christchurch, New Zealand. Poetry, fiction, articles, etc. 12/yr.; $NZ5/yr.; 30 cents/ea.; 24 pgs.; 2100 circ. Reports immediate.

NIMROD, Francine Ringold, Ed., Univ. of Tulsa, 600 S. College, Tulsa, OK 74104, USA. 2/yr.; $3/yr.; $1.50/ea.; 96 pgs.; 500 circ. Reports 1-5 mos. No payment.

THE NISHNAWBE NEWS, Michael J. Wright, Ed., 140 Univ. Ctr., N.M.U., Marquette, MI 49855, USA. Poetry, articles, art, etc.; paper serving Gt. Lakes area, Canada, & Am. Indians. 12/yr.; $5/yr.; 50 cents/ea.; 8 pgs.; 8 million circ. Reports 6 wks. No payment.

* NOBE, L. Steven Zwerling, Ed., 202 Columbia Heights, Brooklyn, NY 11201, USA.

* NOETICS, Robert Morrison, Ed., 113 Marshall St., Syracuse, NY 13201, USA.

* NOLA'S BIRTHDAY TWIN BULLETIN, 1303 Ave. A, No. 16, S. Houston, TX 77587, USA.

NORTH AMERICAN MENTOR MAGAZINE (Westburg Assocs.), John & Mildred Westburg, Eds., 1730 Lincoln Ave., Fennimore, WI 53809, USA. Poetry, fiction, articles, etc. Qtly.; $7/yr.; $2.50/ea.; 40 plus pgs.; 450 circ. Reports 3-6 mos. Pays copy. Annual poetry contest.

THE NORTH AMERICAN REVIEW, Peter Cooley, Poetry Ed., Univ. of Northern Iowa, Cedar Falls, IA 50613, USA. Poetry, fiction, articles, etc. Qtly.; $6/yr.; $1.50/ea.; 80 pgs.; 3 million circ. Reports 8 wks. Pays $10/pub. pg.

NORTH COUNTRY ANVIL, Jack Miller, Ed., Box 252, Millville, MN 55957, USA. Poetry, fiction, articles, etc. rel. to alternatives to Am. way of life. 6/yr.; $4/yr.; 75 cents/ea.; 80 pgs.; 3 million circ. Reports 1 mo. Pays copies only.

THE NORTH STONE REVIEW, James Naiden, Ed., Univ. Stn., Box 14098, Mpls., MN 55414, USA. Poetry, short stories, nonfiction, etc. 2-3/yr.; $3.50/3 issues; $1.50/ea.

NORTHEAST (Northeast/Juniper Books, Juniper Press), John Judson, Ed., 1310 Shorewood Dr., La Crosse, WI 54601, USA. Poetry, criticism, reviews, longpoems. 2/yr.; $6/yr.; $1/ea.; 44-48 pgs.; 500 circ. Reports 3-6 wks. Pays copies only.

NORTHERN COMFORT (Canadian/Whole Earth/Research), Box 6, 341 Bloor W., Toronto "F", Canada. Poetry, fiction, articles, etc.

* NORTHERN HOUSE PAMPHLET POETS, 58 Queen's Rd., Jesmond, Newcastle-On-Tyne, NE2 2PR, UK.

NORTHERN JOURNEY, Fraser Sutherland, Co-Ed., 112 Driveway, Ottawa K2P 1E6, UK. Poetry, fiction, articles, etc.; mat. only from Canadians, or on Canadian subjs. 1/yr.; $2/ea.; 100 pgs.; 2 million circ. Reports 4 wks. Nominal payment on publication plus 2 copies.

NORTHWEST PASSAGE, Roxanne Park, Co-Ed., 105 S. Bell Stn., Bellingham, WA 98225, USA. Poetry, fiction, articles, etc. rel. to 'alternative culture'. 26/yr.; $6/yr.; free/ea.; 32 pgs.; 8 million circ. Reports 4 wks. No payment.

NORTHWEST REVIEW, Patricia Brooks, Ed., Univ. of Ore., Eugene, OR 97454, USA. Poetry, fiction, art, photos, etc. 3/yr.; $4/yr.; $1.50/ea.; 128 pgs. Reports 3 mos. or less. Pays 3 comp. copies.

* NORTHWESTERN UNIVERSITY PRESS, 1735 Benson, Evanston, IL 60201, USA.

NORTHWOODS NEWSLETTER (Northwoods Press), Robert W. Olmsted, Ed., Box 24, Bigfork, MN 56628, USA. Reviews, etc. to promote circ. Irreg.; 20 cents/ea. Reports 2 wks. No payment.

NORTHWOODS PRESS, (see also THE APOLLO, NORTHWOODS NEWS-LETTER), Genevieve Sargent, Ed., P.O. Box 15092, Phoenix, AZ 85060, USA. 3 anthols. In the Wake of the Dragon, Side Effects of Living, & The Other Poetry Book.; wants imaginative poems. Pays 8 copies per reserved pg. plus 10% royalties on all sales attributed to your influence.

* NORTON BAILEY & CO., 103 Lonsdale Rd., London SW13, UK.

* NORTON (W.W.) PRESS, 55 Fifth Ave., N.Y., NY, USA.

NOSFERATU PRESS, see Stoney Lonesome.

* A NOSEGAY IN BLACK, Winifred & Thomas Blevins, Eds., 1414 S. 2nd St., Lafayette, IN 47904, USA.

NOTHING DOING (formally in London), (see also THE LITERARY SUPPLEMENT and THE LITERARY SUPPLEMENT, WRITINGS), Anthony Barnett, Mgr., 25 Woodhall Dr., London SE21 7HJ, UK.

NUCLEUS (Poet's Vigilantes Press & Publs.), Malcolm R. Payne, Fndr. & Gen. Sec., 4 Wealden Close, Crowborough, Sussex, UK. Annual anthol. of PV mbrs.' work. 1/yr.; 25 pence/ea. Pays copy.

NUNQUAM MENS (The Cranner-Skibb Reproduction Engine), Pat Crabb, Ed., 127 Radnor Ave., Welling, Kent, UK. Poetry, articles, art, etc. 12/yr.; 12 pence plus s.a.e./yr.; s.a.e./ea.; 4-50 pgs.; 100 circ.

OASIS (formerly EXPRESSION), Ian Robinson, Ed., 12 Stevenage Rd., London SW6 6ES, UK. Poetry, fiction, etc. 4/yr.; 80 pence/yr.; 20 pence/ea.; 70 pgs.; 500 circ. Reports 3 wks. Pays copies.

OBERON PRESS OTTAWA (CANADA), (publd. in UK by Dobson Books Ltd.), 80 Kensington Church St., London W8 4BZ, UK.

* OCCIDENT, Eshleman Hall, Univ. of Calif., Berkeley, CA 94720, USA.

OCCULT GAZETTE, Dick Speller, Ed., The Schl. of Universal Philos., 6 Phillimore Pl., Kensington, London W.8, UK. Some poetry. 6/yr.; £2/yr.; 25 pence/ea.

OCCUM RIDGE REVIEW, Richard Schaaf, Ed., P.O. Box 68, S. Willington, CT 06265, USA. Poetry, fiction, articles, longpoems.

2/yr.; $1.80/yr.; 90 cents/ea.; 40 pgs.; 500 circ. Reports 2-4 wks. No payment, copies only.

* OCTOBER HOUSE, 55 W. 13th St., N.Y., NY 10011, USA.

OFF OUR BACKS, 1346 Conn. Ave. N.W., Room 1013, Wash. DC 20036, USA. Work relevant to & by women. 12/yr.; $5/yr.; 35 cents/ea.; 28 pgs.; 8 million circ. Reports as soon as possible. No payment.

* OHIO MOTORIST, A.K. Murway, Ed., 6000 S. Marginal Rd., Cleveland, OH 44103, USA. Prefer short, humorous poems.

THE OHIO REVIEW: A Journal of the Humanities, S.W. Lindberg, Mng. Ed., 346 Ellis Hall, Ohio Univ., Athens, OH 45701, USA. Poetry, fiction, articles, etc. 3/yr.; $5/yr.; $2/ea.; 112 pgs.; 900 circ. Reports 8-10 wks. Pays copies usually, but varies.

OINK! MAGAZINE (Oink! Books), Paul Hoover, Co-Ed., c/o Jim Leonard, 438 W. Belden, Chgo., IL 60614, USA. Poetry of any length. Qtly.; $3/yr.; $1/ea.; 50 pgs.; 400 circ. Reports 1 wk. Pays copies only.

OLD ADOBE PRESS, Julio Hasley, Ed., P.O. Box 115, Penngrove, CA 94951, USA. Poetry, fiction, scholarly. Reports 3 wks. Pays standard.

THE OLD RED KIMONO, Ken Anderson, Ed., Floyd Jr. Coll., P.O. Box 789, Rome, GA 30161, USA. No long poems. Qtly.; 10 pgs.; 300 circ. Reports 1 mo. Pays 2 copies.

* OLDMAN (GEORGE), 4 Elmfield Ave., Aberdeen, Scotland, UK.

THE OLEANDER PRESS, 28 Parkfield Cres., Harrow HA2 6JZ, UK & 210 Fifth Ave., N.Y., NY 10010, USA. Oleander modern poets series; no restriction on lang. or length.

OLIVANT PRESS, see Weid.

OLIVER & BOYD, Croythorn House, 23 Ravelston Terr., Edinburgh EH4 3TJ, UK. Mainly anthols. for use in primary or secondary schls.

OMENS, G.S. Fraser, Ed., c/o John Martin, 9 Roundhay Rd., Leicester, UK. Poetry only. Qtly.; 80 pence/yr.; 25 pence/ea.; 36 pgs.; 500 circ. Reports 3 wks. Pays 3 copies.

100 FLOWERS, John McChesney, Co-Ed., c/o Lit. Dept., Antioch Coll., Yellow Springs, OH 45387, USA. Poetry, fiction, art, etc. Qtly.; $4/yr.; $1/ea.; 50 pgs.

* THE OPEN LETTER, Frank Davey, Ed., Canservcol Royal Rds., Victoria, B.C., Canada.

OPEN PLACES, Eleanor M. Bender, Ed., Box 2085, Stephens Coll., Columbia, MO 65201, USA. Poetry, fiction, reviews. 2/yr.; $3/yr.; $1.50/ea.; 64 pgs.; 600 circ. Reports 6 wks. Pays copies only.

* OPEN UNIVERSITY PRESS, Walton Hall, Walton, Bletchley, Bucks., UK.

OPENSPACES (The Laurel Press), Elizabeth Brown, Co-Ed., 1360 N. Laurel Ave., L.A., CA 90046, USA. Poetry. 2/yr.; $5/yr.; $2.75/ea.; 40 pgs.; 500 circ. Reports 2 wks. Pays 2 copies.

OPINION, James E. Jurtz, Co-Ed., P.O. Box 688, Evanston, IL 60204, USA. Poetry, articles, art, etc. 12/yr.; $5/yr.; 50 cents/ea.; 8 pgs.; 3 million circ. Reports immediately. Pays copies only.

ORBIS (Hub Publs. Ltd.), Robin Gregory, Co-Ed., Orbis, Youlgrave, Bakewell, Derbyshire, UK. Poetry, articles, criticism, etc.; mag. of int. poetry soc. Qtly.; £1.20/yr.; 30 pence/ea.; 48 pgs.

ORE MAGAZINE (Ore Publs.), Eric Ratcliffe, Ed., 11 High Plash, Cuttys Ln., Stevenage, Herts., UK. Poetry, articles & reviews on mystizue of early Britain, nature gods, Arthur, etc. Irreg.; 17 pence/ea.; 40 pgs.; 1300 circ. Reports 3 wks.

ORE PUBLICATIONS (see also ORE MAGAZINE), Eric Ratcliffe, Ed., 7 The Towers, Stevenage, Herts. SG1 1HE, UK. Poetry, inclng. Chariot Poets series.

OREGONIAN VERSE, Howard McKinley Corning, Ed., The Oregonian, Portland, OR 97201, USA. Poetry col. publd. weekly in Sunday Oregonian; limit 24 lines. Pays $5 per poem used. Poetry prizes offered are regional and by local writers only.

* ORIEL PRESS, 32 Ridley Pl., Newcastle-upon-Tyne NE1 8LH, UK.

ORIGINAL WORKS, Robert M. Flores, Ed., Dept. of Hispanic & Italian Studies, Univ. of Victoria, B.C., Canada.

* ORIGINS/DIVERSIONS, Michael J. Dyke, Ed., 8 Court Dr., Sutton, Surrey, UK.

ORPHAN PRESS, see Empty Belly.

ORPHIC LUTE, Viola Gardner, Ed., 3815 Mercier, Kan. City, MO 64111, USA. Poetry, little prose. Qtly.; $5/yr.; $1.35/ea.; 300 circ. Reports at once. Pays prizes, 1 copy.

OSGOLDCROSS REVIEW (Poets' Press of Osgoldcross), Gerald England, Ed., 50 Chiltern Dr., Ackworth, Pontefract WF7 7DW, UK. Poetry, longpoems. Irreg.; 40 pence/2 yrs.; 5 pence plus post/ea.; 8 pgs.; 150 circ. Reports 6 wks. Pays 5 copies.

OSIRIS, Robert & Andrea Moorhead, Eds.,

1065 Univ. Pl., Schenectady, NY 12308, USA. Poetry, fiction, articles, etc. 2/yr.; $3/yr.; $1.50/ea.; 44 pgs.; 500 circ. Reports 1 mo. Pays 2 copies.

OTHER SCENES & NOMAD, John Wilcock, Ed., BCM-NOMAD, London WC1V, UK. Poetry & gen. lit.; Nomad pieces must be short. Irreg.; £4/yr.; $1/ea.; 12 pgs.; 2 million circ. Reports 1 wk. Pays minimal.

* OTHER VOICES, Jane Johnson, Ed., 1226 Richmond St., London, Ont., Canada.

OUR FAMILY, A. James Materi, O.M.I., Ed., Box 249, Battleford, Sask. SOM OEO, Canada. All types of mat. 11/yr.; $3/yr.; 40 cents/ea.; 32 pgs.; 8784 circ. Reports 2-4 wks. Pays $3-10 per poem.

OUT OF THE ASHES FLASHFOOD SERVICE, Norman Solomon, Ed., Out of the Ashes Press, P.O. Box 42384, Portland, OR 97242, USA. Poetry, fiction, art, etc. 12/yr.; free; 16 pgs.; 200 circ. Reports 3 wks. Pays 'good vibrations' and free copy.

OUT THERE MAGAZINE (Pedestrian Press), Stephen M.H. Braitman, Ed., 11133 Rose Ave., No. 15, L.A., CA 90034, USA. Poetry, fiction, articles, etc.; previously sci. fiction oriented. Irreg.; 50 cents/ea.; 25 pgs.; 500 circ. Reports 1 mo. Pays 5 copies.

OUTPOSTS, Howard Sergeant, Ed., 72 Burwood Rd., Walton on Thames, Surrey, UK. Poetry; poems no more than 150 lines. Qtly.; $5/yr.; $1.25/ea.; 36 pgs.; 1500 circ. Reports 2 wks. Pay varies.

OUTPOSTS MODERN POETS SERIES (Outposts Publs.), Howard Sergeant, Ed., 72 Burwood Rd., Walton on Thames, Surrey, UK. Booklets by individual poets.

OUTPOSTS PUBLICATIONS (see also OUTPOSTS, OUTPOSTS MODERN POETS SERIES), Howard Sergeant, Ed., 72 Burwood Rd., Walton on Thames, Surrey, UK. Poetry in Engl., some translations.

* THE OUTSIDER, John E. & Gypsy Lou Webb, Eds., 1009 E. Elm, Tucson, AZ 85702, USA.

* OVERFLOW, P.O. Box 24, Salem, OR 98175, U.S.A.

OVERSPILL (Guildford Poets Press), Eric Harrison, Ed., April Cottage, 3 Grantley Close, Shalford, Surrey, UK. Poetry, up to 300 lines. 5/yr.; £1/yr.; 20 pence/ea. Pays copies.

OXFORD UNIVERSITY PRESS, Ely House, 37 Dover St., London S1X 4AH, UK. Poetry & gen. lit.

OXFORD UNIVERSITY PRESS, 200 Madison Ave., N.Y., NY 10016, USA.

Poetry & gen. lit.

OYEZ REVIEW, Civia Cohen, Ed., Roosevelt Univ., 430 S. Michigan Ave., Chgo., IL 60605, USA. Poetry & gen. lit. 3/yr.; $1.50/ea.; 3000 circ. Reports 8 wks. Pays copies only. Poetry contest twice a yr. offers prizes of $30 & $20.

P.V. PUBLICATIONS, see Radix.

PACIFIC LIFE PRESS, see Lifeforce.

* PAIDEUMA, Univ. of Me., Orono, ME 04473 U.S.A.

THE PAN AMERICAN REVIEW (Funch Press), Seth Wade, Ed., 1100 W. Samano, Edinburg, TX 78539, USA. Poetry, fiction, articles, etc.; need translations of Latin Am. work. 2/yr.; $3.50/yr.; $2/ea.; 80 pgs.; 500 circ. Reports 1 day-2 mos. Pays copies only.

* PAN BOOKS, LTD., 33 Tothill St., London S.W.1, UK.

PANJANDRUM – A Record Magazine of Poetry, Dennis Koran, Ed., 99 Sanchez St., San Francisco, CA 94114, USA. Record Mag. w. poets reading their works. 1-2/yr.; $15/3 issues; $5/ea.; 500 circ. Reports 1 mo. Pays copies only.

PANTAGRAPH PRESS, see The Sou'Wester.

* THE PAPER, P.O. Box 1793, Dallas, TX 75221, USA.

PAPER PUDDING, Steve Minkin, Ed., P.O. Box 712, Monte Rio, CA 95462, USA. Poetry, fiction, articles, art, etc. Qtly.; $2/yr.; 50 cents/ea.; 112 pgs.; 2 million circ. Reports 1-3 mos. Pays copies only.

PAPER TIGER (Running Dog), 16 Cloyster Wood, Edgware, Middx. HA8 6RS, UK. Poetry, articles, art, etc. 12/yr.; £1.20/yr.; 5 pence/ea.; 20 pgs.; 500 circ.

THE PARIS REVIEW, 45-39 171 Pl., Flushing, NY 11358, USA. Poetry, fiction, art, etc.

THE PARNASSIAN, (Calder Valley Poets' Soc.), Mrs. A.H. Earnshaw, Ed., 9 Watty Cottages, Bacup Rd., Todmorden, Lancs., UK. Poetry.

PARTISAN REVIEW, William Phillips, Ed., Rutgers Univ., 1 Richardson St., New Brunswick, NJ 08903, USA. Poetry, fiction, articles, etc. Qtly.; $5.50/yr.; $1.50/ea.; 140 pgs.; 10 million circ. Reports 3 mos. Pays 1½ cents per word/40 cents per line poetry.

PEACE & PIECES PRESS (see also PEACE & PIECES REVIEW), Box 99394, San Francisco, CA 94109, U.S.A. Pamphlet Poetry Series; humor/satire, poetry, short fiction, & non-fiction. No payment, copies to author.

PEACE & PIECES REVIEW (Peace & Pieces Press), Maurice Custodio, Ed., Box 99394, San Francisco, CA 94109, USA. Poetry. Qtly.; $3.50/yr.; $1/ea.; 25-40 pgs.; 1 million plus circ. Reports 3 wks. Pays copies only.

* PEBBLE, Greg Kuzma, Ed., 1031 Charleston St., Lincoln, NB 68508, USA.

PEDESTRIAN PRESS, see Out There Magazine.

PEGASUS (Vinyard Press), O.F. Gibb, Ed., Green Island, Ardleigh, Essex CO7 7SL, UK. 1/yr.; 65 pence/yr.

PELICAN PUBLISHING CO. INC., 630 Burmaster St., Gretna, LA 70053, USA. No 'ashcan' schl. of poetry.

PEN (PUBLIC EMPLOYEES NEWS) MAGAZINE, Jean Blair Ryan, Ed., 444 Sherman St., Denver, CO 80203, USA. Poetry limited to 16 lines, fiction, articles. 12/yr.; $3/yr.; 25 cents/ea.; 32 pgs. Pays 50 cents/line.

* PENDULUM, 79-66 77th Ave., Glendale, NY 11227, USA.

PENGUIN BOOKS LTD., 21 John St., London WC1N 2BT, UK. Poetry and gen. lit.; no unsolicited poems.

* PENMAN, Barbara Fischer, Ed., 133 W. Sixth St., Deer Park, NY 11729, USA.

THE PEN WOMAN, Mrs. Lee M. Waldrop, Ed., Nat. League of Am. Pen Women, Inc., 1300 17th St. N.W., Wash. DC 20036, USA. All poetry forms. 9/yr.; $4/yr.; 50 cents/ea.; 32 pgs.; 5700 circ. Reports 30-45 days. No payment.

PENINSULA POETS (Poetry Soc. of Mich.), Joseph Cherwinski, Ed., 1207 Walsh St., Lansing, MI 48912, USA.

PENNINE PLATFORM (Illinsworth Bros.), Mabel Ferrett, Ed., 2 Vernon Rd., Heckmondwike WF16 9LU, UK. Poetry, articles, criticism, etc. Qtly.; 80 pence/yr.; 20 pence/ea.; 26 pgs.; 200 circ. Reports 3 mos. No payment.

PENNY PRESS, see Free People Press.

PENNY DREADFUL, Dara Wier, Co-Ed., 201 Univ. Hall, Bowling Green State Univ., Bowling Green, OH 43403, USA. Poetry, fiction, short plays, etc. 5/yr.; $1.25/yr.; 25 cents/ea.; 16 pgs.; 1 million circ. Reports immediately-2 wks. Pays copies.

PENTABARF (Erisian Imprints Ink), Bill & Ruthie Wantling, Eds., R. No. 1, Towanda, IL 61776, USA. Poetry, fiction, cartoons, etc. Irreg.; postage/ea. Reports sev. mos. Pays copies only.

PENUMBRA, Charles Haseloff, Ed., GPO Box 1501, N.Y., NY 10001, USA. Poetry. 1-2/yr.; $5/2yr.; $1/ea.; 40 pgs.; 500 circ. Reports 4-8 wks. Pays copies only.

* PEOPLE, William H. Stephens, Ed., 127 Ninth Ave. N., Nashville, TN 37203, USA. Poetry w. a message.

PEOPLESMEDIA, see Rama Pipien.

THE PEOPLESMEDIA DIGEST, see Rama Pipien.

* PER SE, Robin White, Ed., Box 2377, Stanford, CA 94307, USA.

* PERGAMON PRESS, LTD., Headington Hill Hall, Oxford, OX3 OBW, UK.

* PERSONALIST, Robert Beck, Ed., Schl. of Philos., Univ. of Southern Calif., Los Angeles, CA 90007, USA.

PERSPECTIVE: A Magazine of Modern Literature, Jarvis Thurston, Co-Ed., Wash. Univ., Box 1122, St. Louis, MO 63130, USA. Poetry, fiction, articles, etc. Irreg.; $4/yr.; $1/ea.; 64 pgs.; 1 million circ. Reports 2 mos. Pays copies only. $150 prize for best poem or poems ea. vol.

* PHAEDRA, INC., 49 Park Ave., N.Y., NY 10016, USA.

PHANTHOM FINGER PRESS, see Portland Review.

PHOENIX, Harry Chambers, Ed., 8 Cavendish Rd., Heaton Mersey, Stockport SK4 3DN, UK.

THE PHOENIX (Morning Star Press), James Cooney, Ed., Morning Star Farm, W Whately, RFD Haydenville, MA 01039, USA. Poetry, fiction, articles, art, etc. Qtly.; $8/yr.; $3/ea.; 220 pgs.; 3100 circ. Reports 3 wks. Pays hon. sub. & copies.

* PICTON PUBLISHING, Citadel Works, Bath Rd., Chippenham, Wilts., UK.

PIKEVILLE COLLEGE PRESS, see Twigs.

* PILGRIM PUBLICATIONS, Church St., Wilbarston, Market Harborough, Leics., UK.

PILOT PRESS BOOKS (see also AMARANTHUS), L. Erick Greinke, Poetry Ed., P.O. Box 2662, Grand Rapids, MI 49501, USA. Full-length books & pamphlet series; Trans-Symbolist poetry anthol. Pays 10% royalties books, 50 copies pamphlets.

PINK PEACE (Aten Press), John Rice, Ed., 93 Biggins Wood Rd., Folkestone, Kent, UK. Poetry, articles, art, etc. 3/yr.; 65 pence/yr.; 20 pence/ea.; 40 pgs.; 500 circ. Pays copies only.

* PLAINSONG, Franklin Brainard, Ed., Box 2613, New Brighton, MN 55113, USA.

* PLAINTIFF, Darrel Hunter, Ed., Room 205 Centennial Student Union, Mankato State Coll., Mankato, MN 56001, USA.

PLATFORM, Andrew & Jim Cozens, Co-Eds., 'Avalon', London Rd., Stockbridge, Hants., UK. Poetry, articles, art, etc. 4-5/yr.; 50 pence/yr.; 15 pence/ea.; 50 pgs.; 350 circ. Reports 1 mo. No payment as yet.

* PLATFORM, Mrs. Joan Lee, Ed., 'Sun Vale', Burnley Rd., Luddenham Foot, Halifax, UK.

PLOUGHSHARES, DeWitt Henry, Co-Ed., Box 529, Cambridge, MA 02139, USA. Poetry, fiction, articles, art, etc.; biased towards new writers & discovery of neglected writers. 3/yr.; $8/4 issues; $2/ea.; 112-128 pgs.; 1500 circ. Reports max. 3 mos. Pays copies.

THE PLUMED HORN (El Corno Emplumado), Sergio Mondrajon, Poetry Ed., Apartado Postal No. 13-546, Mexico D.F. 13, Mexico.

PN3 VERBAL EXPERIMENTATION (Poetry Newsletter), Wally Depew, Co-Ed., 819-17 St., Sacramento, CA 95814, USA. Poetry, fiction, articles, art, etc.; all work anonymous & must be verbal experimentation. Irreg.; $1/ea.; 125 circ. Reports 1 mo. Pays copies only.

PN2 NONVERBAL POETRY (Poetry Newsletter), Wally Depew, Co-Ed., 819-17 St., Sacramento, CA 95814, USA. Poetry, fiction, articles, art, etc.; all work anonymous. Irreg.; $1/ea.; 125 circ. Reports 1 mo. Pays copies only.

POEM, Robert L. Welker, Ed., P.O. Box 1247, W. Stn., Huntsville, AL 35807, USA. Poetry only. 3/yr.; $3.50/yr.; $1.50/ea.; 70 pgs.; 500 circ. Reports 1 mo. Pays $5 per poem on publication.

THE POEM COMPANY (Intermedia Press), Mr. Poem, Co-Ed., Box 8915 Stn. H, Vancouver, Canada. Poetry, art, photos, etc. 52/yr.; free; 8 pgs. No reports or payment.

* POEMS FROM THE HILLS, Morris Harvey Coll., Charleston, WV 25304, USA.

POESIE SONORE INTERNATIONALE A GENEVE, Isaïe Goldman, Ed., 4 rue Bonivard, Geneva, Switzerland. Poetry & prose in almost all langs.; anti-racist, courteous, tolerant. Qtly.; free; 16-20 pgs.; 500 circ.

POESIE VIVANTE, Isaïe Goldman, Ed., 4 rue Bonivard, Geneva, Switzerland.

* POET, John T. Campbell, Ed., 2174 34th St., Sacramento, CA 95801, USA.

POET -International Monthly, Dr. Krishna Srinivas, Litt.D., Ed., 20 A Venkatesan St., Madras 600017, India. Poetry only. 12/yr.; $1.25/ea.; 100 pgs.; 2 million circ. Reports 3 mos. Pays 1 copy.

POET & CRITIC (Iowa State Univ. Press), Richard Gustafson, Ed., Engl., 210 Pearson Hall, Iowa State Univ., Ames, IA 50010, USA. Poetry, articles, art, etc. 3/yr.; $3/yr.; $1/ea.; 48 pgs.; 500-1 million circ. Reports immediately-8 wks. Pays copies only.

* POET LORE, John Williams Andrews, Ed., Box 688, Westport, CT 06880, USA.

* POET AND PAINTER, 36 Halstead Rd., London E.11, UK.

* POETPURRI, Portland Sunday Telegram, Portland, ME 04106, USA. Poetry by Maine writers only.

POETRY, Daryl Hine, Ed., 1228 N. Dearborn Pkwy., Chgo., IL 60610, USA. Poetry, reviews. 12/yr.; $12/yr.; $1/ea.; 64 pgs.; 10 million circ. Reports 6 wks. Pays $1/line poetry.

POETRY & AUDIENCE, Peter Popham, Co-Ed., Schl. of Engl., Univ. of Leeds, Leeds, Yorks., UK. Poetry, art. 26/yr.; 75 pence/yr.; 2 pence/ea.; 18 pgs.; 500 circ. Reports vary. No payment.

POETRY & AUDIENCE PUBLICATIONS, see Poetry & Audience, Leeds Larynx.

POETRY AUSTRALIA (South Head Press), Grace Perry, Ed., 350 Lyons Rd., Five Dock, Australia 2046. Qtly.; $7.50/yr.; $2/ea.; 80 pgs.; 1800 circ. Reports 2 mos. Pays $8-10 per pg.

POETRY EASTWEST, (see also CREATIVE MOMENT), Syed Amanuddin, Ed., P.O. Box 39 1, Sumter, SC 29150, USA. Poetry empathizing w. world poetry movement; only unpublished poems & translations under 30 lines. 1/yr.; $2/yr.; 44 pgs., 500 circ. Reports 6-8 mos. Pays copies only.

* POETRY GLASGOW, 15 Bank St., Glasgow W2, Scotland, UK.

POETRY INFORMATION, Peter Hodgkiss, Ed., 17 Carungford Rd., London NW3, UK. Poetry reviews & index. Qtly.; 50 pence/yr.; 15 pgs.; 500 circ.

POETRY NATION, C.B. Cox, Co-Ed., Dept. of Engl., Univ. of Manchester, Manchester M13 9PL, UK. Poetry in Engl., translations, essays on mod. Engl. lang. poetry. 2/yr.; £2.90/yr.; £1.60/ea.; 128 pgs.; 2-3000 circ.

POETRY NEWSLETTER, Richard O'Connell, Ed., Dept. of Engl., Temple Univ., Phila., PA 19122, USA. Poetry, interviews, etc. 12/yr.; free single; 24 cents ea. by mail; 12-14 pgs. Reports 1 mo. Pays copies only.

POETRY NEWSLETTER, see PN3 Verbal

Experimentation, PN2 Nonverbal Poetry, Poetry Newsletter Special Issue.

POETRY NEWSLETTER SPECIAL ISSUE, PN, Wally & Linda Depew, Eds., 819-17 St., Sacramento, CA 95814, USA. Poetry, fiction, articles, art, etc. Irreg.; 50 cents/ea.; 12-30 pgs.; 150 circ. Reports 1 mo. Pays copies only.

POETRY NORTHWEST, David Wagoner, Ed., Univ. of Wash., Parrington Hall, Seattle, WA 98195, USA.

POETRY OF OUR TIME (J. Mark Press), Dr. Barbara Fischer, Ed., 133 W. 6th St., Deer Park, NY 11729, USA. Poetry, reviews; send 1-4 poems, 3-16 lines then wait for reply. Qtly.; $4.95/soft; $7.95/cloth; 30 pgs.; 1 million circ. Reports immediately. Pays 2-10 cents line.

POETRY OF THE CIRCLE IN THE SQUARE (Circle in the Square Publs.), Bill Pickard, Ed., Bristol Arts Ctr., King Sq., Bristol 2, UK. Poetry. 5 pence/ea.; 20 pgs.

POETRY PAGE OF THE NEWSPAPER OF WICHITA, D. Clinton, Poetry Ed., 2148 N. Broadway, P.O. Box 4203, Wichita, KS 67204, USA. Poetry, area articles & interviews, etc. 52/yr.; $10/yr.; 25 cents/ea.; 1 pg. to poetry; 8500 circ. Reports 3 wks. max. Pays $10 per poem, 2 copies.

POETRY/PEOPLE (RVK Publng. Co.), S.P. Stavrakis, Ed., P.O. Box 264du, Monomonee Falls, WI 53051, USA. Poetry, photos, line-art; experimental poetry. 2/yr.; $10/yr.; $6.25/ea. Pays over $100 cash awards & prizes ea. issue.

POETRY REVIEW, Eric Mottram, Ed., The Poetry Soc., 21 Earls Ct. Sq., London SW5, UK.

* POETRY SINGAPORE, c/o Dept. of Engl., Univ. of Singapore, Bukit Timan Rd., Singapore 10.

POETRY SOCIETY OF MICHIGAN, see Peninsula Poets.

POETRY SOCIETY OF SAN ANTONIO TEXAS MAGAZINE, Mrs. Stella Woodall, Ed., Publr., Pres., 3915 S.W. Military Dr., San Antonio, TX 78211, USA. Poetry by mbrs. $2/ea.

POETRY VENTURE (Valkyrie Press, Inc.), Marjorie Shuck, Ed., 8245 26th Ave. N., St. Petersburg, FL 33710, USA. Poetry, articles, criticism, etc.; anthol. Poetry Ventured. 2/yr.; $3/yr.; $1.50/ea.; 64 pgs.; 1 million circ. Reports 8-16 wks. Pays copies plus 1 yr. sub.

POETRY WALES, Meic Stephens, Ed., 42 Church Rd., Witchurch, Cardiff, Wales, UK. Poetry, articles, interviews, etc.; publd. w. support of Welsh Arts Coun. Qtly.; £1.52/yr.; 38 pence/ea.; 120 pgs.; 850-1

million circ. Reports 2-3 wks. Pays by arrangement.

POETRY WORKSHOP, Stephen Morris, Ed., Fac. of Art & Design, The Polytechnic, Wolverhampton, UK. Poetry, letters, parts-of-novels, longpoems. 2/yr.; 25 pence/yr.; 10 pence/ea.; 16 pgs.; 500 circ. Reports 1 mo. Pays 2 copies.

* POETS' AND PAINTERS' PRESS, 146 Bridge Arch, Sutton Walk, London SE1, UK.

POET'S CROSSROADS, (W.Va. Poetry Soc.), Jean Smith O'Connor, Ed., Apt. 4-K, Plaza East, 4300 N. Ocean Blvd., Ft. Lauderdale, FL 33308, USA.

* POETIS GUILD, 317 6th St., Idaho Falls, ID 83401, USA.

POET'S NOOK (Journal Publs.), Silvia Sheafer, Ed., 6416 S. Western Ave., Whittier, CA 90606, USA.

POETS' PRESS OF OSGOLDCROSS, (see also OSGOLDCROSS REVIEW), 50 Chiltern Dr., Ackworth, Pontefract WF7 7DW, UK. Poetry, longpoems; plans anthol. dedicated to Lewis Carroll & anthol. of poetry in Yorks. dialect. 5 pence plus post/ea. Reports irreg. Pays by arrangement.

POET'S VIGILANTES PRESS & PUBLICATIONS (see also RADIX, NUCLEUS, PV POET'S SERIES, PV POET'S HANDBOOK, PV NEWSLETTER), Malcolm R. Payne, Fndr. & Gen. Sec., 4 Wealden Close, Crowborough, Sussex, UK.

* POLISH CULTURAL FOUNDATION, 9 Charleville Rd., London W.14, UK.

POMMEGRANATE, Marie Freeman, Co-Ed., 28 Richmond Pk. Rd., Bristol 8, UK. Poetry, fiction, articles, etc. 2/yr.; 12 pence/ea.; 20-30 pgs.; 800 circ. Reports 1 mo. Pays copies only.

* POND PRESS, 46 St. Augustine's Ave., Ealing, London W5 1ED, UK.

THE PONI PRESS, Tom Buchan, Co-Ed., 10 Pittville St., Edinburgh EH15 2BY, UK. Poetry, satire, parts-of-novels, longpoems, plays.

POPULAR PRESS, see Journal of Popular Culture.

* PORCUPINES, 19 Pilton St., Barnstaple, Devon, UK.

PORTLAND REVIEW: An Oregon Quarterly of Literature & Thought (Phanthom Finger Press), E.G. White-Swift, Ed., P.O. Box 751, Portland, OR 97207, USA. Poetry, fiction, articles, etc. Qtly.; $4.50/yr.; $1.50/ea.; 96 pgs.; 1 million circ. Reports 1-3 mos. Pays copies only.

* PORTLAND (MAINE) SUNDAY TELE-GRAM, (see also POETPURRI), Portland, ME 04101, USA.

POT-HOOKS & HANGERS, J. Richard Patton, Co-Ed., P.O. Box 718, Old Chelsea Stn., N.Y., NY 10011, USA. Poetry. 2/yr.; $2.50/yr.; $1.25/ea.; 48 pgs.; 550 circ. Reports 2-4 wks. Pays 2 copies.

* POYNTER (DAVIS), LTD., 10 Earlham St., London WC2H 9LP, UK.

THE PRAIRIE PRESS (see also AMERICAN POET, WORLD POETS), Iowa Writers Bookshop, Univ. of Iowa, Iowa City, IA, USA.

PRAIRIE SCHOONER (Univ. of Neb.), Bernice Slote, Ed., 201 Andrews Hall, Univ. of Neb., Lincoln, NB 68508, USA. Poetry, fiction, articles, etc. Qtly.; $4.50/yr.; $1.50/ea.; 100 pgs.; 1 million circ.

* PREMIERE, 39 Quahog Rd., Acton, MA 01720, USA.

PRESSED CURTAINS, see Curtains.

PRESSING ON, see Artisans Almanack.

THE PRICKLY PEAR (Beacon Press), Calif. State Coll., San Bernardino, 5500 State Coll. Pkwy., San Bernardino, CA 92407, USA. Poetry, fiction, art, etc. 1-2/yr.; free; 20-50 pgs.; 500 circ. Reports 1-3 mos. Pays some cash prizes.

* PRISM INTERNATIONAL, Jacob Zibler, Ed., Dept. of Creative Writing, Univ. of B.C., Vancouver 8 B.C., Canada.

* PROGRESS HOUSE (PUBLICATIONS), LTD., 270 N. Circular Rd., Dublin 7, Ireland.

* PROMENADE, Clarissa deVillers, Poetry Ed., 40 E. 49th St., N.Y., NY 10017, USA

* THE PROMETHEAN LAMP, John T. Campbell, Ed., 2174 34th St., Sacramento, CA 95801, USA.

* PROSPERO'S CELL, Box G, Queen Anne's Stn., Seattle, WA 98109, USA.

PROSPICE (The Aquila Publng. Co. Ltd.), J.C.R. Green, Co-Ed., 18 Atherstone Close, Shirley, Solihull, Warks, B9O 1AU, UK. Poetry, articles, art, etc.; mainly poetry in translation & Engl.-speaking poets' work. 3/yr.; £1/yr.; 25 pence/ea.; 60 pgs. Reports vary. Pays 10 offprints plus 2 copies.

PROTEUS, Frank & Cathy Gatling, Eds., 225 E. Mason Ave., Alexandria, VA 22301, USA. Poetry, fiction, art, etc. Qtly.; $3.50/yr.; $1/ea.; 50 pgs.; 600 circ. Reports 1-6 wks. Pays copies only.

THE PROVIDENCE REVIEW, Jessica Murray, Co-Ed., 64 Elmgrove Ave.,

Providence, RI 02906, USA. Poetry, fiction, articles, cartoons, etc.; mat. relating to or by inhabitants of R.I. 12/yr.; 50 cents/ea.; 48 pgs.; 200 circ.

* PS (POEMS AND STORIES), 2659 S. York St., Denver, CO 80210, USA.

PSYCHOLOGICAL   PERSPECTIVES, J'nan Sellery, Assoc. Ed. Poetry, 595 E. Colorado Blvd., Suite 503, Pasadena, CA 91101, USA. Poetry, short fiction, articles, essays, commentaries. 2/yr.; $6r.; $3a.; 100 pgs.; 2000 circ. Reports 2 mos. Pays copies.

THE PTA MAGAZINE (Nat. Congress of Parents & Tchrs.), Donal Mahoney, Ed., 700 N. Rush St., Chgo., IL 60611, USA. Poetry, fiction, articles, art, etc. 10/yr.; $3.50/yr.; 50 cents/ea.; 44 pgs.; 80 million circ. Reports vary. Pays copies in addition to money. $10 poems.

PULP PRESS, see 3 cent Pulp.

PULSE -Finger Press, Orion Roche, Ed., Box 16697, Phila., PA 19139, USA. Poetry, fiction, articles; book-length. Reports 3 mos. Standard payment.

* PUTNAM & CO. LTD., 9 Bow St., London WC2E 7AL, UK.

* G.P. PUTNAM & SONS, 200 Madison Ave., N.Y., NY 10016, USA.

PV POET'S HANDBOOK (Poet's Vigilantes Press & Publs.), Malcolm R. Payne, Fndr. & Gen. Sec., 4 Wealden Close, Crowborough, Sussex, UK. Info. for poets wishing to have poetry publd. 45 pence/ea.

PV NEWSLETTER (Poet's Vigilantes Press & Publs.), Malcolm R. Payne, Fndr. & Gen. Sec., 4 Wealden Close, Crowborough, Sussex, UK. Poetry news & contacts, reviews, letters, etc. 3/yr.; free to mbrs.; 10-11 pgs.

PV POET'S SERIES (Poet's Vigilantes Press & Publs.), Malcolm R. Payne, Fndr. & Gen. Sec., 4 Wealden Close, Crowborough, Sussex, UK. Poetry collections by mbrs. after at least 10 publs. in poetry mags. 20 pence/ea.

PYRAMID (Hellric Publs.), Ottone M. Riccio, Ed., 32 Waverley St., Belmont, MA 02178, USA. Poetry, fiction, articles, art, etc.; no limit on poetry. Qtly.; $5/yr.; $1.50/ea.; 78 pgs.; 500 circ. Reports 4-8 wks. Pays $3-20 pg. on publication plus 5 copies & 1 yr. sub.; arrangement by author starting 1973.

QUAKER FELLOWSHIP OF THE ARTS, see Reynard.

QUARRY, John Kucich, Co-Ed., College V, UCSC, Santa Cruz, CA 95060, USA. Poetry, fiction, parts-of-novels, etc. 2-3/yr.; $1/ea.; 90plus pgs.; 1500 circ. Reports 1-2 mos. Pays 3 copies.

* QUARRY, W.J. Barnes, Ed., Box 1061, Kingston, Ont., Canada.

QUARTERLY REVIEW OF LITERATURE, Theodore Weiss, Co-Ed., 26 Haslet Ave., Princeton, NJ 08540, USA. Poetry, stories, plays, translations. 2 double issues/yr.; $20/hardcover; $10/paper; 25,000 circ. Reports 6 wks. Pays per pg.

QUARTET, Richard Hauer Costa, Ed., 1119 Neal Pickett Dr., College Station, TX 77840, USA. Qtly.; $4/yr.; $1/ea.; 40 pgs.; 700 circ. Reports 6 wks.-3 mos. Pays copies only.

* QUARTET, 186 Ridge Rd., Utica, NY 13501, USA.

THE QUARTO PRESS, B.L. Pearce, Ed., 69 Swan Rd., Feltham, Middlesex, TW13 6PE, UK. Poetry; new pamphlet series. 3-4/yr.; 12 pgs. Reports 1 mo. Pays by negotiation.

QUEEN'S QUARTERLY, Kerry McSweeney, Ed., Queen's Univ., Kingston, Ont., Canada. Some poetry, mainly Canadian authors. Qtly.; $8.25/yr.; $2/ea.; 160 pgs.; 2100 circ. Reports up to 1 mo. Pays $10 per poem.

* THE QUEST, P.O. Box 207, Cathedral Stn., N.Y., NY 10025, USA.

QUICK COPY CENTER, TEXAS A&M UNIVERSITY, see Stanley (from beneath the earth).

QUICKSILVER PRINTING, see King James* Version.

QUIGGLEOUTS, see Quixote.

QUILDFORD POETS PRESS, see Weyfarers.

* QUILL, Michal Thomas, Ed., 2 The Drive, Mardleyhill, Welwyn, Herts., UK.

* QUINTESSENCE, 166 Albany Ave., Shreveport, LA 71105, USA.

QUINTO SOL PUBLICATIONS, INC. (see also EL GRITO), 2150 Shattuck Ave., No. 606, Berkeley, CA 94704, USA.

QUIXOTE (Quiggleouts), 933 Spaight, Madison, WI 53703, USA. Poetry, fiction, articles, art, etc. 12/yr.; $10/yr.; $1/ea.; 40-120 pgs.; 1 million circ. Reports 2 wks. Pays copies only.

R.U.R., Journal of Cybernation and Public Affairs, T.D.C. Kuch, Co-Ed., Box 5833, Bethesda, MD 20014, USA. Poetry, articles, cartoons, etc. rel. to impact of computers on soc. Qtly.; $3/yr.; $1/ea.; 20 pgs.; 500 circ. Reports 2 wks. Pays occasional small honorarium, usually copies.

* RADIX, Stephen Sherman, Ed., 163 College Ave., Somerville, MA 02143, USA.

RADIX (Poet's Vigilantes Press & Publs.), Malcolm R. Payne, Fndr. & Gen. Sec., 4 Wealden Close, Crowborough, Sussex, UK. Poetry, art, prose. 3/yr.; 75 pence/yr. Pays copy.

THE RAG, 2330 Guadalupe, Austin, TX 78705, USA. 1 pg. Poetry per issue. 52/yr.; $8/yr.; 10 cents/ea.; 16 pgs.; 3000 circ. No payment.

RAGNAROK PRESS, D.H. Stefanson, Co-Ed., 3416 Davis, Sioux City, IA 51106, USA. Poetry, fiction, art, photos, parts-of-novels. Pays 3 copies of book to author.

RAINCOAST CHRONICLES (Harbour Publng.), Howard White, Co-Ed., Box 119, Madeira Park, B.C., Canada. Poetry, articles, reviews, parts-of-novels. Qtly.; $4/yr.; $1.75/ea.; 56 pgs.; 10 million circ. Reports 2 mos. Pays $50-75 per article.

* RALEIGH (N.C.) NEWS-OBSERVER, Samuel Ragen, Poetry Ed., S. McDowell St., Raleigh, NC 27601, USA.

RAMA PIPIEN (The Peoplesmedia Digest, Peoplesmedia), Charles A. Raisch, Ed., 1380 Howard, San Francisco, CA 94103, USA. Poetry, fiction, articles, art, etc.; basically radical left perspective. 6/yr.; $7/yr.; $1/ea.; 64 pgs.; 10 million circ. Reports 1-2 mos. Pays few dollars & copies.

RAMAH, see Azymtote.

* RAMPARTS, Harry Stiehl, Ed., 1182 Chestnut St., Menlo Park, CA 94025, USA.

RAMSAY HEAD PRESS, 36 Castle St., Edinburgh EH2 3BN, UK. Poetry & gen. lit.; Engl. & Scots lang. only.

* RANDOM HOUSE, 201 E. 50th St., N.Y., NY 10022, USA.

* RAPP & WHITING, LTD., 105 Gt. Russell St., London WC1B 3LJ, UK.

RAPPORT (The Slow Loris Press), Tony Petrosky, Co-Ed., 95 Rand, Buffalo, NY 14216, USA. Poetry, interviews; pamphlet series invitation only. Irreg.; $4/yr.; $1/ea.; 60 pgs.; 1 million circ. Reports 1-2 mos. Pays 5 copies.

RAT & MOLE PRESS, Ritchie Darling, Ed., P.O. Box 111, Amherts, MA 01002, USA. Reports 6 mos. or 6 wks. Pays 10 per poem, adjusted for prose.

RATCLIFFE (ERIC), (Ore Publs.), 7 The Towers, Stevenage, Herts. SG1 1HE, UK.

RAVEN, Adelaide Blomfield, Co-Ed., 2407 E. Northern Lights Blvd., Anchorage, AK 99504, USA. Poetry, articles, interviews, etc. 3/yr.; $3.50/yr.; $1.50/ea.; 48 pgs.; 500 circ. Reports 1-3 mos. Pays copies only.

RAVEN BOOKS (Anvil Press), Susan P. Place, Co-Ed., c52 The Temple, 24 Dale St., Liverpool L2 5RL, UK. Memories of old Liverpool.

READING UNIVERSITY ARTS MAGAZINE, see Tamesis.

REBEL PRESS, Ronald Duncan, Ed., 2 Derby St., London W1, UK. Poetry, criticism, longpoems.

THE RECORD (Lancashire Authors' Assn.), R.Y. Digby, Ed., 222 Stanley St., Accrington, Lancs., UK. Poetry by members. Qtly.; £2/yr.; 24 pgs.; 200 circ. Offers var. prizes inclng. The Batty Cup for best poem in Standard Engl., Scholes Cup for Lancs. Dialect poem.

RED BRIDGE BLACK STONE, Bill Costley, Co-Ed., Box 2477 Eastside Stn., Providence, RI 02906, USA. Poetry, fiction, articles, etc. Qtly.; $3/yr.; $1/ea. Reports few days. Pays copies.

* RED CEDAR REVIEW, 325 Morrill Hall, Mich. State Univ., E. Lansing, MI 48823, USA.

RED DUST INC., Joanna Gunderson, Ed., 218 E. 81st St., N.Y., NY 10021, USA. Poetry, fiction. 2-4/yr.; 128 pgs. Reports 1 mo. Pays $300 plus reg. royalties.

RED FOX PUBLICATIONS, N.S. Thompson, Ed., The Studio 193, Todmorden Rd., Littleborough, Lancs., UK. Poetry.

THE RED HILL PRESS, John McBride, Co-Ed., 6 San Gabriel Dr., Fairfax, CA 94930, USA. Publishes 'Invisible City' & individual vols.

RED ROSE (Lancashire Authors' Assn.), John P. Berry, Ed., "Homelands", Bryning Ln., Wrea Green, Preston PR4 2NL, UK. Poetry, plays & prose submitted for Annual Competitions of Assn. 1/yr.; 80-100 pgs.: 300 circ. Offers var. prizes & awards.

* REFLECTIONS, Robert V.N. Brown, Ed., The Free South Reveiw, Box 109, Chapel Hill, NC 27514, USA.

* REGENCY PRESS (LONDON & NEW YORK), LTD., 43 New Oxford St., London W.C.1, UK.

THE REGINALD A FESSENDEN MEMORIAL RADIO/TIMES/ARE (Dildo Press), Douglas S. Cruickshank, Co-Ed., 5 Univ. Ave., Los Gatos, CA 95030, USA. Poetry, articles, criticism, etc. rel. to experimental community radio broadcasting & technol. 24/yr.; $3/yr.; 10 cents/ea.; 16 pgs.; 3 million circ. Pays copies only.

* HENRY REGNERY CO., 114 W. Illinois St., Chgo., IL 60610, USA.

* REID (ALEX P.) & SONS, 28 Market St., Aberdeen AB9 2EQ, UK.

* REINHARDT (MAX), LTD., 9 Bow St., London WC2E 7AL, UK.

REJECTION PRESS, see Gargantua.

THE REMINGTON REVIEW, Dean Maskevich, Poetry Ed., 505 Westfield Ave., Elizabeth, IIJ 07208, USA. Poems not over 100 lines. 2/yr.; $2/yr.: $1/ea.; 72 pgs. Reports 2-3 mos. Pays 2 copies.

* REPLOY, LTD., Barracks Rd., Newcastle-under-Lyme ST5 1LG, UK.

REYNARD (Quaker Fellowship of The Arts), Robert Ward, Ed., 2 Gaveston Dr., Berkhamsted, Herts. HP4 1JE, UK. Poetry, fiction, articles, art, etc. w. Quaker viewpoints. 1/yr.; 75 pence/mbrship.; 32 pgs.; 500 circ.

RHODESIAN POETRY (The Poetry Soc. of Rhodesia), Colin Style, Chmn., P.O. Box A 294, Avondale, Salisbury, Rhodesia. Poetry by Rhodesians only. Biennial; $1.25/ea.; 36 pgs.

RHODESIAN POETRY SOCIETY, see Rhodesian Poetry.

RIPPLES, Jim & Karen Schaefer, Eds., P.O. Box 52, Ann Arbor, MI 48107, USA. 1st 3 issues of yr. are newsletters of mat. being worked on, 4th is formal format. Qtly.; $3/yr.; 20 pgs.; 500 circ. Reports 1 day. Pays copies only.

RITA ACT, see Rita Notes.

RITA NOTES (Rita Act), Ritas & Fritas, Eds., D-69 Heidelberg, Marstallstr. 11A, German Fed. Repub. Poetry, fiction, articles, etc. Irreg.; $25/30 issues; $2/ea.; 1-25 pgs.; 1-10 million circ.

RIVER CITY ENTERPRISES, see River City Review.

RIVER CITY REVIEW (River City Enterprises), James M. Godown, Ed., P.O. Box 12725, Memphis, TN 38112, USA. Poetry, fiction, articles, art, etc. of 100 words or less. 12/yr.; $3.50/yr.; 30 cents/ea.; 28 pgs.; 20 million circ. Reports 1 wk. before printing. Pays copies only.

RIVERSIDE QUARTERLY, Leland Sapiro, Ed., Box 40, Univ. Stn., Regina, Canada. Poetry, fiction, articles, art, etc. Qtly.; $2/yr.; 60 cents/ea.; 80 pgs.; 1340 circ. Reports 10 days. Pays copies only.

ROAD APPLE REVIEW (Road Runner Press), Brian Salchert, Ed., 334 Linden St., Fond du Lac, WI 54935, USA. Poetry, art, interviews, reviews, longpoems. Qtly.; $3/yr.; $1/ea.; 64 pgs.; 300 plus circ. Reports 1 mo. Pays 2 copies.

ROAD RUNNER PRESS, see Road Apple Review.

* ROADRUNNER, Nina M. Booth, Ed., Am. Bapt. Bd. of Educ. & Publication, Valley Forge, PA 19481, USA.

* ROANOKE REVIEW, R.R. Walter, Ed., Engl. Dept., Roanoke Coll., Salem, VA 24153, USA.

ROAR (Lionhead Publng.), Martin J. Rosenblum, Ed., 5416 N. Christiana Ave., Chgo., IL 60625, USA. Poetry, interviews, criticism, reviews, longpoems. 1/yr.

* ROCKY MOUNTAIN REVIEW, 2320 W. Pikes Peak Ave., Colorado Springs, CO 80904, USA.

RONDO POETRY PAMPHLET SERIES, (Rondo Publications Limited), Trevor Kneale, Ed., 10 Pall Mall, Liverpool L3 6HJ, UK.

RONDO PUBLICATIONS LIMITED (see also MERIDIAN Poetry Magazine, RONDO POETRY PAMPHLET SERIES), Trevor Kneale Mng. Dir., 10 Pall Mall, Liverpool L3 6HJ, UK.

ROOTS, Anton Stewart, Co-Ed., 30 Basegreen Ave., Sheffield S12 3FA, UK. Poetry, fiction, articles, interviews, etc. rel. to definiton of character of man. 5/yr.; 50 pence/yr.; 12½ pence/ea.; 24 plus pgs.; 200 circ. Reports 1 mo. Pays copies only.

ROOTS, 6 Lonsdale Terr., Edinburgh 3, UK. Poetry, articles, photos, etc. 12/yr.; £1/yr.; 6 pence/ea.; 20 pgs.; 1 million circ. Reports vary. No payment, copies usually.

* THE ROTARIAN, Karl K. Kruger, Ed., 1600 Ridge Ave., Evanston, IL 60204, USA.

* THE ROUNDUP, Henry Hough, Poetry Ed., The Denver Post, Denver, CO 80202, USA.

* ROUNDWOOD PRESS (PUBLISHERS), LTD., Kineton, Warks., UK.

* ROUTLEDGE & KEGAN PAUL, LTD., 68-74 Carter Ln., London EC4V 5EL, UK.

THE RUFUS (Gyst Publs.), Patricia Ann Bunin, Ed., & Publr., P.O. Box 75982, Los Angeles, CA 90075, USA. Poetry any length, articles on poetry movement. 3/yr.; $5/yr.; $2/ea.; 70 pgs.; 300 circ. Reports 4-6 wks. Pays copies plus 3 cash awards ea. issue.

RUNNING DOG, see Paper Tiger.

RUSTY KARMA PRESS, see Two Charlies.

* RUTGERS UNIVERSITY PRESS, 30 College Ave., New Brunswick, NJ 08903, USA.

RVK PUBLISHING (see also NEW EARTH TRIBE NEWSPACK, POETRY/PEOPLE), Steve P. Stavrakis, Ed., P.O. Box 264du, Monomonee Falls, WI 53051, USA. Poetry books.

SADAKICHI HARTMANN NEWSLETTER (E. Tex. State Univ.), Richard Tuerk, Ed., Dept. of Lit. & Langs., E. Tex. State Univ., Commerce, TX 75428, USA. Poems, essays & stories about Sadakichi Hartmann. 3/yr.; $2.50/yr.; 8 pgs.; 280 circ. Reports 2 wks. Pays 2 copies.

ST. ANDREWS REVIEW, Malcolm Doubles, Mng. Ed., St. Andrews Coll., Laurinburg, NC 28352, USA. Poetry, fiction, articles, etc. 2/yr.; $3.50/yr.; $2/ea.; 75 pgs.; 650 circ.

* ST. GILES PRESS, 224 Causewayside, Edinburgh 9, Scotland, UK.

SALT LICK, James Haining, Co-Ed., P.O. Box 1064, Quincy, IL 62301, USA. Poetry, fiction, articles, etc. 2/yr.; $3/yr.; $1/ea.; 60 pgs.; 1200 circ. Reports 2 wks. Pays copies.

SALTED IN THE SHELL, Gary Lawless, Ed., 40 High St., Belfast, ME 04915, USA. Poetry, interviews, satire, reviews, longpoems influenced by natural world. 6-8/yr.; 25 cents/ea.; 15 pgs.; 350-400 circ. Reports 2-3 wks. Pays copies.

THE SALTIRE SOCIETY, Gladstone's Land, 483 Lawnmarket, Edinburgh EH1 2NT, UK. Scottish poetry.

SAMMY'S DOT PRESS, Charles S. Preston, Ed., 411 Lakeview Dr., York, PA 17403, USA. Poetry, satire, plays; left-wing.

SAMPHIRE, Kemble Williams, Co-Ed., S. Bank, Spring Rd., Ipswich, UK. Poetry, fiction, articles, reviews, letters. Qtly.; 60 pence/yr.; 18 pence/ea.; 32 pgs. Pays copies only.

* SAN FRANCISCO REVIEW, June Oppen Degnam, Ed., 2808 Laguna St., San Francisco, CA, USA.

THE SANDCUTTERS (Ariz. State Poetry Soc.), Genevieve Sargent, Ed., P.O. Box 15092, Phoenix, AZ 85060, USA. Poetry by mbrs. & guest authors. Qtly.; $3.50/yr. mbrship.; 75 cents/ea.; 20-52 pgs.; 250 circ. Monthly & annual contests.

SANGRE DE CRISTO, see Janus-SCTH.

THE SATURDAY CENTRE, Patricia Laird, Ed., Box 140, P.O. Cammeray, N.S.W., Australia 2062. Publishes The Saturday Centre Poets' Series & The Saturday Club Book of Poetry.

THE SATURDAY CENTRE POETS' SERIES, see The Saturday Centre.

THE SATURDAY CLUB BOOK OF POETRY, see The Saturday Centre.

* SATURDAY EVENING POST, Post Scripts Ed., 641 Lexington Ave., N.Y., NY 10022, USA.

SATURN, see This Is Not A Magazine.

* SCENE PUBLICATIONS, 52 Market St., Wigan, Lancs., UK.

* SCEPTER PUBLISHERS, LTD., 11 Ely Pl., Dublin 2, Ireland.

SCEPTRE PRESS, Martin Booth, Publr., 15 Keats Way, Rushden, Northants. NN10 9BJ, UK. Poetry in booklet & broadsheet form; Mss. must be accompanied by s.a.e. or Int. Reply Coupon.

SCHISM: A Journal of Divergent American Opinions, Donald L. Rice, Ed., 1109 W. Vine St., Mt. Vernon, OH 43050, USA. Poetry, articles, art, cartoons, etc.; no unsolicited mss. Qtly.; $7.50/yr.; $2/ea.; 64 pgs.; 1100 circ.

SCHIST, Sandy Dorbin, Ed., P.O. Box 836, Flagstaff, AZ 86001, USA. Poetry, art, photos. Irreg.; $5/4 issues; $1.50/ea.; Reports vary. Pays 2 copies.

* SCHOFIELD & SIMS, LTD., 35 St. John's Rd., Huddersfield, UK.

SCHMUCK (Beau Geste Press), David Mayor, Ed., Beau Geste Press, Langford Ct., S., Cullompton, Devon EX15 1SQ, UK. Poetry, fiction, articles, art, etc. Irreg. Reports vary.

* SCOTIA, Morven View, Reaster, Lyth, by Wick, Caithness, UK.

SCOTIAN PEN GUILD, see Amber.

* SCOTTISH ARTS COUNCIL, 11 Rothesay Terr., Edinburgh 3, Scotland, UK.

SCOTTISH INTERNATIONAL REVIEW, Robert Tait, Ed., 23 George Sq., Edinburgh EH8 9LD, UK. Poetry, fiction, articles, photos, etc. 10/yr.; £1.50/yr.; 15 pence/ea.; 40 pgs.

SCREEN DOOR & Review Broadsides (Arbitrary Closet Press), Richard Neva, Ed., Box 54, Onondaga, MI 49264, USA. Poetry, art, photos, etc. Reports immediately. Pays copies only.

* SCRIBNER'S, 597 Fifth Ave., N.Y., NY 10017, USA.

SCRIP, David Holliday, Ed., 67 Hady Cres., Chesterfield, Derbyshire S41 OEB, UK. Poetry, reviews; prefers short poetry. Qtly.; 60 pence/yr.; 15 pence/ea.; 28 pgs.; 350 circ. Reports as soon as possible. Pays 2 copies.

* SCROGIE, (P.) LTD., 17 Chapel St., Peterhead, Aberdeen, Scotland, UK.

SCROTUM, John C. Currier, Jr., Ed., 7 Harrison Ave., Gloucester, MA 01930, USA. Poetry, fiction, satire, parts-of-novels, etc. Irreg.; $2/yr.; $1/ea.; 50 pgs.; 200 circ. Reports 4-6 wks. Pays 2 copies.

SEARCH FOR TOMORROW (Blue Wind Press), George Mattingly, Ed., Box 1189, Iowa City, IA 52240, USA. Poetry, fiction, art, photos, etc. Irreg.; $3/4 issues; $1/ea.; 64 pgs.; 1500 circ. Reports 2 wks. Pays copies only.

* SECKER (MARTIN) & WARBURG, LTD., 14 Carlisle St., London W1V 6NN, UK.

SECOND AEON, Peter Finch, Ed., 3 Maplewood Ct., Maplewood Ave., Llandaff N., Cardiff CF4 2NB, UK. Poetry, fiction, articles, art, etc. 3/yr.; £1.50/yr.; 150 pgs.; 2 million circ. Reports 2 wks. Pays copies only.

SECOND AEON PUBLICATIONS (see also SECOND AEON), Peter Finch, Ed., 3 Maplewood Ct., Maplewood Ave., Llandaff N., Cardiff CF4 2NB, UK. Poetry, art, long-poems, collages, etc.; books & booklets. 12/yr.; £1.50/yr. Reports 2 wks. Pays by arrangement.

SECOND COMING, A.D. Winans, Ed., P.O. Box 31246, San Francisco, CA 94131, USA. Poetry, fiction, articles, art, etc. 3/yr.; $3.25/yr.; $1.25/ea.; 48-60 pgs.; 500-1 million circ. Reports 1-6 wks. Pays copies only.

THE SECOND WAVE, Box 344, Cambridge A, Cambridge, MA 02139, USA. Few short poems ea. feminist or women's liberation pt. of view. issue; Qtly.; $3/yr.; 48 pgs.; 5000 circ. Reports 3 mos.

SEIZURE MAGAZINE, Steven Granger, Co-Ed., P.O. Box 5462, Eugene, OR 97405, USA. Poetry, fiction, art, parts-of-novels, collages, plays. 2/yr.; $2/yr.; $1/ea.; 60 pgs.; 500 circ. Reports 1 wk.-5 mos. Pays copies only.

SELF KNOWLEDGE, 29 Chepstow Villas, London W11 3DR, UK. Some poetry books & some poems in jrnl. Qtly.

SENECA REVIEW, Ira Sadoff, Co-Ed., Hobart & William Smith Colls., Geneva, NY 14456, USA. Poetry, fiction, art, interviews, reviews. 2/yr.; $2/yr.; $1.25/ea.; 80 pgs.; 1 million circ. Reports 2-6 wks. Pays copies plus sub.

SEQUOIA, Michael Dana Gioia, Ed., Storke Publs. Bldg., Stanford, CA 94305, USA. Poetry & fiction of any length. Qtly.; $4/yr.; $1/ea.; 40 pgs.; 1 million circ. Reports 1-2 mos. Pays 3 copies.

* THE SERIF, Dean H. Keller, Ed., Kent State Univ. Lib., Kent, OH 44240, USA.

SESHETA, Richard Downing, Co-Ed., 32 Pinfold Ln., Skerton, Lancaster LA1 2BJ, UK. Poetry, prose, fiction, etc.; prefer collections from individual authors. 3/yr.; £1.50/yr.; 50 pence/ea.; 86 pgs.; 250 circ. Reports 3 wks. Pays 1 copy.

SEVEN, James Neill Northe, Ed., 21½ N. Harvey, Okla. City, OK 73102, USA. Poetry.

Irreg.; $4/4 issues; $1.25/ea.; Reports 30 days. Pays $3 per poem on acceptance.

* SEVEN DIALS PRESS, 6 Frethern Chambers, Welwyn Garden City, Herts., UK.

SEVEN SQUARE PRESS, see Box 749.

THE SEVENTIES (The Seventies Press), Robert Bly, Ed., Odin House, Madison, MN 56256, USA. Poetry. Irreg.; $4/yr.; $1/ea.; 82 pgs.; 3 million circ. Reports long. Pays $10/pg.

THE SEVENTIES PRESS, see The Seventies.

THE SEVENTY-FIVE PRESS (see also THE SPICY MEATBALL), Tchrs. Writers Collaborative, 236 Clinton St., Brooklyn, NY 11201, USA. Elem. Schl. writings.

THE SEWANEE REVIEW, George Core, Ed., Univ. of the South, Sewanee, TN 37375, USA. Poetry, fiction, articles, etc. Qtly.; $7/yr.; $2/ea.; 185 pgs.; 3800 circ. Pays 60 cents/line verse.

* SEYDELL QUARTERLY, Mildred Seydell, Ed., P.O. Box 7072, Stn. C, Atlanta, GA 30304, USA.

* SF KEEPER'S VOICE, Alexander Weiss, Ed., 1263 Sixth Ave., San Francisco, CA 94965, USA. Zoological subjs.

SHADES OF LIGHT, Gregory S. Reisig, Advsr., Crete-Monee H.S., W. Exchange St., Crete, IL 60417, USA. Poetry, fiction, non-fiction by student body of Crete-Monee H.S. only.

THE SHAKESPEARE NEWSLETTER, Louis Marder, Ed., Univ. of Ill. at Chgo., IL 60680, USA. Poetry, articles, criticism. Qtly.; $2/yr.; 50 cents/ea. Reports vary. Pays copies only.

SHAMELESS HUSSY REVIEW (formerly Remember Our Fire), Alta, Ed., Box 424, San Lorenzo, CA 94580, USA. Poetry. 1/yr.; 75 cents/ea.; 40 pgs.; 1 million circ. Pays 2 copies.

SHANTI SADAN, see Self Knowledge.

SHANTIH, John S. Friedman, Co-Ed., P.O. Box 125, Bay Ridge Stn., Brooklyn, NY 11220, USA. Poetry, fiction, interviews, criticism. Qtly.; $5/yr.; $1.25/ea.; 1000 circ. Reports immediately. No payment.

THE SHAVIAN– Journal of the Shaw Society, Eric Ford, Exec. Ed., High Orchard, 125 Markyate Rd., Dagenham. Essex RM8 2LB, UK. Mat. rel. to Shavian life work & times. 2/yr.; £2/yr.; £1.60/ea.; 24 pgs. Reports 3 mos. Payment negotiable.

THE SHAW SOCIETY, see The Shavian.

SHENADOAH (Journalism Laboratory Press), James Boatwright, Ed., P.O. Box 722, Lexington, VA 24450, USA. Qtly.; $4/yr.; $1.25/ea.; 100 pgs.; 1 million circ. Pays by arrangement.

SHENCO PRINTERS, see Handsel.

SHITHOOK (formerly Throb), (Horsehead Nebula Press), F.A. Nettelbeck, Co-Ed., 12655 Flat St., Boulder Creek, CA 95006, USA. Poetry, fiction, articles, art, etc. Qtly.; $3/yr.; $1/ea.; 60-80 pgs.; 550 circ. Reports 1 day-1 mo. Pays 2 copies.

THE SHORE, Olive Dewhurst, Ed., Allegro, 41 Ormont Ave., Cleveleys, Blackpool, UK.

SHORTLANDS POETS (Shortlands Poetry Circle), Mrs. E. Rutt, Hon. Sec., 5 Dairsie Ct., 163 Widmore Rd., Bromley BR1 3AX, UK. Poetry by circle mbrs.

* SIDGWICK & JACKSON, LTD., 1 Tavistock Chambers, Bloomsbury Way, London WC1A 2SG, UK.

* SILO, Bennington Coll., Bennington, VT 05201, USA.

* SIMON & SCHUSTER, 630 Fifth Ave., N.Y., NY, USA.

SINTER, D.E. Steward, Ed., Jurastrasse 18, 4053 Basel, Switzerland. Irreg.; free; 3 pgs. Reports immediately. No payment.

SIXPACK (Lame Duck Press), Pierre Joris, Ed., 34 Stanhope Gdns., London SW7, UK. Poetry, fiction, articles, art, interviews, etc.; prefer 5-10 pgs. by 1 author. 4 or 2 doubles/yr.; £1/yr.; 30 pence/ea.; 50 pgs.; 500 circ. Pays copies only.

THE SIXTIES, see The Seventies.

* THE SKIPPER, 305 E. 56th St., N.Y., NY 10022, USA. Boating subjs.

SKYWRITING, Martin Grossman, Co-Ed., 2917 Madison, Eugene, OR 97405, USA. Poetry, fiction, articles, interviews, criticism, reViews. 3/yr.; $3/yr.; $1.25/ea.; 40-50 pgs.; 500 circ. Reports 3 wks. Pays 2 copies.

THE SLOW LORIS PRESS, see Rapport.

SMALL POND MAG OF LITERATURE, Napoleon St. Cyr, Ed., 10 Overland Dr., Stratford, CT 06497, USA. Poetry, fiction, articles, art, etc. 3/yr.; $2.50/yr.; $1/ea.; 36-40 pgs.; 275 circ. Reports 1-15 days. Pays 2 copies only.

SMALL PRESS REVIEW (Dustbooks), Len Fulton, Ed., 5218 Scottwood Rd., Paradise, CA 95969, USA. Poetry, articles, etc. rel. to small presses & little mags. 6/yr.; $5/yr.; $1/ea.; 32-40 pgs.; 2 million circ. Reports 1-2 wks. Pays by arrangement.

* SMALL PUBLISHERS CO., 276 Park Ave., S., N.Y., NY 10010, USA.

THE SMITH, Harry Smith, Publr., 5 Beekman St., N.Y., NY 10038, USA. Poetry books.

* SMOKEY HILL REVIEW, Ft. Hays Kan. State Coll., Ft. Hays, KS 67601, USA.

SMOOTHIE PUBLICATIONS (see also LIBRARIANS FOR SOCIAL CHANGE, DATR), John Noyce, Ed., 67 Vere Rd., Brighton, Sussex, BN1 4NQ, UK.

* SMYTHE (COLIN), LTD., Gerrards Cross, SL9 8EL, UK.

SNAIL MAGAZINE, Peter Blake, Ed., 16 Silver St., Barnstable, N. Devon, UK. Poetry, articles, photos, etc.; esp. 18-25 age grp. 12/yr.; £1.50/yr.; 15 pence/ea.; 24 pgs.; 3 million circ. Reports 15th of mo. previous. Pays nominal/expenses.

* SNAP, Univ. of Manchester Union, Oxford Rd., Manchester 13, UK.

SNOWY EGRET, Humphrey A. Olsen, Co.-Ed., 2L5 S. Ninth St., Williamsburg, KY 40769, USA. Poetry, fiction, articles, criticism, etc. rel. to natural hist. 2/yr.; $1.50/yr.; 75 cents/ea.; 40 pgs.; 250 circ. Reports 1 mo. Pays $4/pg. poetry.

* SOCIETY FOR PROMOTING CHRISTIAN KNOWLEDGE, Holy Trinity Ch., Marylebone, London NW1 4DU, UK.

SOFT PRESS (see also CLOUD NINE, SOFT PRESS REVIEW), Robert Sward, Co-Ed., 1050 Saint David St., Victoria, B.C., Canada. Poetry, art, photos, etc. 1/yr.; $5.50/yr.; 100 pgs.; 750 circ. Reports 3 mos. Pays copies.

SOFT STONE, An International Journal of the Arts, Karl Wang, Ed., 102-40 62nd Ave., Apt. 6C, Forest Hills, NY 11375, USA. Poetry, fiction, articles, art, etc. 3/yr.; $3/yr.; $1/ea.; 100 plus pgs ; 1 million circ. Reports 2 wks. Pays 2 or 3 copies.

SOFTBALL (Big D Press), Ann Shaftel, Co-Ed., 69 Harvey St., Cambridge, MA 02140, USA. Poetry, fiction, art, photos, etc. Qtly.; $3/yr.; $1/ea.; 50 pgs.; Reports 2-4 wks. Pays 1 copy plus extras for 50 cents.

THE SOLO PRESS, see Cafe Solo.

* SOLSTICE, Phil Short, Ed., 6B Castle St., Cambridge, UK.

SOLSTICE, Kenneth Dana Lyon, Ed., Union Bldg., Univ. of Utah, Salt Lake City, UT 84112, USA. Poetry, fiction, art, photos, etc.; contbns. only from artists associated w. Univ. of Utah. 6/yr.; 50 cents/yr.; 64 pgs.; 3 million circ. Reports 2 mos. Pays copies only.

SOME FRIENDS, Terry J. Cooper, Ed., 2931 Tanglewood, Tyler, TX 75701, USA. Poetry, fiction, art, etc. Qtly.; $2.75/yr.; 75 cents/ea.

SOME OF US PRESS, Terry Winch, Co-Ed., 4110 Emery Pl. N.W., Wash. DC 20016, USA. Poetry; 1 chapbook of 1 poet's work every mo. 12/yr.; $1/ea.; 20-40 pgs.; 500 circ. Reports 1 mo. Pays copies only.

* SOME/THING, Jerome Rothenberg, Ed., 600 W. 163rd St., N.Y., NY 10032, USA.

SONO NIS PRESS, J. Michael Yates, Co-Ed., Box 94, Port Clements, Queen Charlotte Islands, B.C., Canada. Poetry, fiction, plays; 45 pg. typescript min. Reports 3-5 mos.

THE SONUS PRESS, Edwin Tarling, Ed., 3 Bewick Grove, Hull, Yorks. HU9 3QY, UK. Poetry only; also little mag. Wave.

* SOUTH AND WEST, Sue Abbott Boyd, Ed., 2601 S. Phoenix, Ft. Smith, AR 72901, USA.

SOUTH DAKOTA REVIEW, John R. Milton, Ed., Box 111, Univ. Exchange, Vermillion, SD 57069, USA. Poetry, fiction, articles, art, etc. Qtly.; $4/yr.; $1.25/ea.; 100 pgs.; 800 circ. Reports 1-4 wks. Pays copies only.

SOUTHAMPTON POETRY CIRCLE, see Mayflower.

SOUTHERN HUMANITIES REVIEW, Eugene Current-Garcia, Co-Ed., Auburn Univ., Auburn, AL 36830, USA. Poetry, essays, short fiction. Qtly.; $4/yr.; $1.25/ea.; 110 pgs.; 500 circ. Reports 1 mo. No payment.

SOUTHERN POETRY REVIEW, Guy Owen, Co-Ed., Dept. of Engl., N.C. State Univ., Raleigh, NC 27607, USA. No light verse or nature poems. 3/yr.; $3/yr.; $1.50/ea.; 60 pgs.; 700-1 million circ. Reports 1 wk.-1 mo. Pays $3 per poem plus contrib. copy.

THE SOUTHERN REVIEW, Donald E. Stanford, Co-Ed., Drawer D. Univ. Stn., Baton Rouge, LA 70803, USA. Poetry, fiction, literary criticism, novel excerpts, articles on hist. & culture of the S. Qtly.; $5/yr.; $1.50/ea.; 250 pgs.

* SOUTHSIDE (PUBLISHERS), LTD., 6 Sciennes Gdns., Edinburgh EH9 1NR, UK.

* SOUTHWEST BREEZE, P.O. Box 37215, Los Angeles, CA 90037, USA.

SOUTHWEST REVIEW, Margaret L. Hartley, Ed., Southern Meth. Univ., Dallas, TX 75222, USA. Some poetry. Qtly.; $5/yr.; $1.50/ea.; 120 pgs.; 1000 circ. Reports 3 mos. Pays $5/poem on pub. plus 2 contrib. copies.

* SOUVENIR PRESS, LTD., 95 Mortimer St., London W1N 8HP, UK.

THE SOU'WESTER (Pantagraph Press), David H. Rathbun, Ed., Engl. Dept., Humanities Div., Southern Ill. Univ., Edwards-ville, IL 62025, USA. Poetry, fiction, arti-clès, etc. 3/yr.; $3/yr.; $1/ea.; 60 plus pgs.; 500 circ. Reports 3 wks. Pays 2 copies.

THE SPARROW MAGAZINE (publrs. of Vagrom Chap Books), Felix & Selma Stefa-nile, Eds., 103 Waldron St., W. Lafayette, IN 47906, USA. Poetry. 2/yr.; $2/yr.; $1/ea.; 48 pgs.; 880 circ. Reports 4-8 wks. Pays $25 prize per issue & copies.

* SPECIAL SONG, Box 74, Woodmont Station, CT 06460, USA.

SPECIMEN, Marten Hendriks, Ed., Ommershofse-laan 8, Velp, Netherlands. Poetry & gen. lit. dealing w. visual arts. Irreg.; 50-60 pgs.

* THE SPECTATOR, 99 Gower St., London W.C.1, UK.

SPECTRUM, Terry Schwartz, Ed., P.O. Box 14800, UCSB, Santa Barbara, CA 93016, USA. Poetry, prose, fiction, critiques. 1/yr.; $2.50/yr.: $1.50/ea.; 100 pgs. Pays copies. Offers $100 prize for best work in poetry & $100 for best work in prose fiction.

* SPHERE BOOKS (ABACUS), LTD., 30-32 Gray's Inn Rd., London WC1X 8JL, UK.

THE SPICY MEATBALL (Seventy Five Press), Sue Willis, Co-Ed., Tchrs. Writers Collaborative, 236 Clinton St., Brooklyn, NY 11201, USA. Poetry, fiction, articles, art, etc.; mostly work by kids at P.S. 75 in Manhattan. 2/yr.; $3/yr.; $2/ea.; 64-100 pgs.; 1 million circ.

* SPIRIT: A MAGAZINE OF POETRY, David M. Rogers, Ed., Seton Hall Univ., S. Orange, NJ 07079, USA.

SPRING RAIN PRESS, Karen Sollid, Co-Ed., P.O. Box 15319, Seattle, WA 98115, USA. Poetry, longpoems; ea. books contains 3-4 poems by 8 authors. Qtly.; $3/yr.; $1/ea.; 45 pgs.; 400 circ. Reports 6 wks. Pays copies only.

SRIMITAR AND SONG, Jean Stirling, Ed., P.O. Box 151, Edgewater, MD 21037, USA.

* STACEY PUBLICATIONS, 1 Hawthorndene Rd., Hayes, Bromley BR2 7DZ, UK.

STAINER & BELL LTD., 82 High Rd., E. Finchley, London N2 9PW, UK. Var. poetry books.

STANBROOK ABBEY PRESS, Callow End, Worcester WR2 4TD, UK. Deluxe limited editions of poetry; mainly religious poetry.

STAND: A Quarterly of the Arts, Jon Silkin, Co-Ed., 58 Queens Rd., Newcastle-upon-Tyne NE2 2PR, UK. Poetry, fiction, articles,

criticism, etc. rel. to contemporary culture. Qtly.; $3.50/yr.; 95 cents/ea.; 80 pgs.; 2500 circ. Reports 6-8 wks. Pays £2/pg.

STANLEY (from beneath the earth), (Quick Copy Center, Tex. A & M Univ.), Bradley D. Ellis, Ed., Box 5475, College Station, TX 77840, USA. Poetry, fiction, articles, art, etc. rel. to sci. fiction. 8/yr.; free; 12 pgs.; 350 circ.

STARDANCE (Blue Dragon), Marek Urba-nowicz, Ed., 49 Sheen Park, Richmond, Surrey, UK. Poetry. Irreg.; 10 pence/ea.; 6 pgs.; street circ.

STAR-WEB PAPER (All This & Less Publrs.), Thomas Michael Fisher, Co-Ed., St. Andrews Coll., Laurinburg, NC 28352, USA. Poetry, art, photos, longpoems. $5/4 issues; $1/ea.; 30 pgs. Reports 2 wks. or less. Pays copies.

STARWORLDS (Helios Press), Verne O'Brian, Ed., c/o 1320 Arthur Ave., Las Vegas, NV 89101, USA. Poetry, fiction, articles, art, etc. rel. to sci. fiction. Irreg.; $1/4 issues; 30 cents/ea.; 30 pgs.; 300 circ. Pays copies or free sub.

STATIONS (Membrane Press), Karl Young, Ed., P.O. Box 5431, Shorewood, Milwaukee, WI 53211, USA. Emphasis on longpoems. 2/yr.; $4/3 issues; $1.50/ea.; 80 pgs. Pays in copies.

* STEIN & DAY PUBLISHERS, 7 E. 48th St., N.Y., NY 10017, USA.

STEPPENWOLF, Philip Boatright, Co-Ed., P.O. Box 55045, Omaha, NB 68155, USA. Poetry, articles, criticism, reviews; interest in longer poems, translations. 1/yr.; $2/yr.; 70 pgs.; 500 circ. Reports 1-2 wks. Pays copies only.

STEREO HEADPHONES, Nicholas Zurbrugg, Ed., Church Steps, Kersey, nr. Ipswich, Suffolk, UK. Poetry, criticism, reviews, concrete art. Irreg.; £1.25/yr.; 25 pence/ea.; 44 pgs.; 500 circ. Pays copy.

* STILLBORN, Stewart Brown, Ed., 39 Exeter Rd., Forest Fields, Nottingham, UK.

STINKTREE, Thomas Johnson, Ed., P.O. Box 14762, Memphis, TN 38114, USA. Prefer short poems relying on image. 2/yr.; $3/yr.; $1.50/ea.; 36-48 pgs.; 400 circ. Reports 1 mo. Pays copies only.

STONE DRUM, Joseph Colin Murphey, Poetry Ed., Box 2234, Huntsville, TX 77340, USA. Special issues mag. 2/yr.; $3/yr.; $1.50/ea.; 64 pgs.; 500 circ. Reports 6 wks. Pays copies only.

STONE PRESS (see also HAPPINESS HOLDING TANK), Albert Drake, Ed., Box 227, Okemos, MI 48864, USA. Poetry books, posters, etc.

* THE STONE REVIEW, 1925 S. 21st St., Milwaukee, WI 53204, USA.

STONE SOUP POETRY, Jack Powers, Co-Ed., 315 Cambridge St., Boston, MA 02114, USA. Poetry. 6/yr.; $5/yr.; $1/ea.; 32 pgs.; 250 circ. Reports 1 mo. Pays copies only.

STONEY LONESOME (Nosferatu Press), Richard Pflum, Co-Ed., 420 N. Washington, Bloomington, IN 47401, USA. Poetry, art, concrete art. 1/yr.; $1.75/yr.; 80-90 pgs.; 300 circ. Reports 2 mos. or less. Pays 1 copy per poet.

* STONY BROOK, Box 1102, Stony Brook, NY 11790, USA.

* STORNOWAY GAZETTE LTD., 10 Francis St., Stornoway, Isle of Man, UK.

* STORY, George Dickerson, Poetry Ed., Four Winds Press, 53 W. 43rd St., N.Y., NY 10036, USA.

* STUDENT, A. Flegon, Ed., 24 Chauncey Ln., London W.C.2, UK.

* STUDIO VISTA, PUBLISHERS, Blue Star House, Highgate Hill, London N19 5NY, UK.

SUBVERS, Hans Clavin, Ed., Dennekoplaan II, Ymuiden, Netherlands. Poetry, art, photos, collages, concrete art. Qtly.; FL20/yr.; 300 circ.

SUCCESS (Bro-Cards Plymouth England), Kate Dean, Ed., 17 Andrews Cres., Paston Ridings, Peterborough PE4 6XL, UK. Poetry, articles, interviews, criticism, etc. 6/yr.; £1.20/yr.; 20 pence/ea.; 32 pgs.; 200 circ. Reports immediately. Pays 1 copy plus reviews.

* SUCCESSFUL FARMING, 1716 Locust St., Des Moines, IA 50318, USA.

SUCK (Defacation Press), C. Marks, Ed., 12655 Boulder Creek, CA 95006, USA. Poetry, fiction, articles, art, etc. Irreq.; $2/yr.; 50 cents/ea.; 50 pgs.; 200 circ. Reports 2 wks. Pays 2 copies.

THE SUMAC PRESS, Dan Gerber, Co-Ed., P.O. Box 39, Fremont, MI 49412, USA. Poetry, fiction; no unsolicited mss.

SUMMER BULLETIN (Yorkshire Dialect Society), John Waddington-Feather, Ed., Fair View, Old Coppice, Lyth Bank, Shrewsbury SY3 0BW, UK. Poetry, articles, reviews rel. mainly to Yorks. dialect. 1/yr.; 50 pence/yr.; 30 pgs.; 800 plus circ. Reports by return usually.

* SUMMIT PUBLICATIONS LTD., Red House, Eaton Bishop, Hereford, UK.

* SUMUS, Kip Ward, Ed., P.O. Box 469, Chapel Hill, NC 27514, USA.

SUNBURST ANTHOLOGY, Clarence Poulin, Ed., 87 High St., Penacoock, NH 03301, USA. Poetry, reviews; poetry of traditional form, 3-30 lines plus short biog.

of author. 1/yr.; $1.50/ea.; 36 pgs.; 250 circ. Reports 2 wks. No payment.

THE SUNSTONE REVIEW, Jody Ellis, Ed., P.O. Box 2321, Santa Fe, NM 87501, USA. Poetry, fiction, photos, criticism. Qtly.; $5/yr.; $1.50/ea.; 300 circ. Reports 30 days. Pays copies only.

* SURFER MAGAZINE, Steve Pezman, Ed., Box 1028, Dana Point, CA 92629, USA. Poetry concerning surfing.

* SUSSEX, John Hedge, Ed., Sussex Grad. Assn., Univ. of Sussex Union, Falmes House, Brighton, Sussex, UK.

SUTHERLAND PRINTING CO., INC., see Lyrical Iowa.

THE SWALLOW PRESS, INC., 1139 S. Wabash Ave., Chgo., IL 60605, USA.

* SYCAMORE PRESS, 4 Benson Pl., Oxford, UK.

SYDON, INC., Dr. Sy M. Kahn, Ed., 451 S. Regent St., Stockton, CA 95204, USA. Poetry book. Irreg.; 60 pgs. Reports 3 mos. Pays 10% royalty.

TAGR PRESS, see Above Ground Review.

* TALBOT PRESS, LTD., 89 Talbot St., Dublin, Ireland.

* TALMY FRANKLIN, LTD., 124 Knightsbridge, London S.W.1, UK.

* THE TAMARACK REVIEW, Robert Weaver, Ed., Box 159, Stn. K, Toronto 12, Ont., Canada.

TARA TELEPHONE PUBLICATIONS, see Gallery Books, Capella.

T.A.S.C. in POETRY, Trinity & All Saints Colls., Brownberrie Ln., Horsforth, Leeds L318 SHD, UK. Poetry, 12/yr.; 60 pence/8 issues. Reports 7 wks. Pays copies only.

TALISMAN, Blythe Ayne, Ed., Box 80713, Lincoln, NB 68501, U.S.A., Poetry, fiction, art, photos. $2.50/6 issues. 39 cents/ea.

TAMESIS (Reading Univ. Arts Mag.), Edward P. deG. Chaney, Ed., Hampden Lodge, 22 Fairfield Rd., Oxbridge, Middx., UK. Poetry, fiction, articles, art, satire, criticism. 1/yr.

TANGENT POETRY QUARTERLY (Estuary Press), Robert D. West, Ed., 9075 River Styx Rd., Wadsworth, OH 44281, USA. Poetry. Qtly.; 32 pgs.; 120 circ. Reports 6-8 wks. Pays copies only.

TAR RIVER POETS (E. Carolina Univ. Poetry Forum Press), Vernon Ward, Ed., P.O. Box 2707, Greenville, NC 27834, USA. Poetry, art, photos, reviews; work usually by ECU Poetry Forum mbrs. Irreg.; $1.50/ea.; 64 pgs.; 1 million circ. Pays

$100 to guest poet, copies to forum poets.

TAURUS PRESS OF WILLOW DENE, Paul Peter Piech, Ed., 2 Willow Dene, Bushey Heath, Herts. WD2 1PS, UK. Poetry, articles, art, letters. Pays 150-200 copies.

* TEJAS, Box 866, Barry, TX 75102, USA.

TELEPHONE, Maureen Owen, Ed., 412 W. 110th St., Apt. 42, N.Y., NY 10025, USA. Poetry, fiction, cartoons, parts-of-novels, longpoems, etc. 3/yr.; $3/yr.; $1/ea.; 54 pgs.; 400 circ. Reports fairly quickly. Pays copies only.

* TEMPO, Bonnie McConnell, Poetry Ed., 982 Parkview Ave., Windsor 16, Ont., Canada.

* TENNESSEE POETRY PRESS, Box 196, Martin, TN 38237, USA.

TENTACLE (Umbilical Cord Press), Prudence Juris, Ed., 811 Henderson, Big Rapids, MI 49307, USA. Poetry, fiction, articles, art, etc. in unfamiliar forms. Irreg.; $4/yr.; $1/ea.; 40 pgs. Pays copies only.

TEXAS CHRISTIAN UNIVERSITY PRESS, see Descant.

* TEXAS QUARTERLY, Harry H. Ranson, Ed., Box 7517, Austin, TX 78712, USA.

* THAMES & HUDSON, LTD., 30 Bloomsbury St., London W.C.1., UK.

THIS IS NOT A MAGAZINE (Saturn), P.A.H. Bower, Ed., 14 Watling Knoll, Radlett, Herts., UK. Poetry, fiction, art, photos, etc. Irreg.; free single; 16 pgs.; 200 circ. No payment.

THIS ISSUE (McKee Publng. Co.), Mel McKee, Ed., Box 15558, Emory Univ. Stn., Atlanta, GA 30333, USA. Poetry, fiction, articles, art, etc. Qtly.; $4.50/yr.; $1.25/ea.; 40 pgs.; 25 million circ. Reports 6 wks. Pays $5 min. poem.

THORP SPRINGS PRESS (see also HYPERION), Paul Foreman, Ed., 2311-C Woolsey St., Berkeley, CA 94705, USA. Poetry, proletarian fiction.

THREE/FOUR, Betty M. Buerki, Ed., 201 Eighth Ave. S., Nashville, TN 37203, USA.

3 cents PULP (Pulp Press), Stephen Osborne, Ed., Box 8806, Stn. H, Vancouver 5, B.C., Canada. Poetry, fiction, articles, art, etc. 26/yr.; $10/yr.; 3 cents/ea.; 4 pgs.; 1 million circ. Reports 2 wks. Pays copies only.

304 PUBLICATIONS, see The Goddard Journal.

THREE RIVERS POETRY JOURNAL, Gerald Costanzo, Ed., P.O. Box 21, Carnegie-Mellon Univ., Pittsburgh, PA 15213, USA. 2/yr.; $4/4 issues; $1.25/ea.; 38 pgs.; 500 circ. Reports 1 wk.-1 mo. Pays

copies only.

THRESHOLD (The Lyric Theatre), Joan P. Burks, Exec. Mgr., Ridgeway St., Stranmillis Rd., Belfast 9, UK. Poetry, articles, short stores. 2/yr.

TIMES CHANGE PRESS, Su Negrin, Co-Ed., Penwell Rd., Washington, NJ 07882, USA. Poetry, articles, art, photos, cartoons, criticism.

* TIMES LITERARY SUPPLEMENT, Printing House Sq., London EC4 P4DE, UK.

TITMOUSE REVIEW, Avron Hoffman, Co-Ed., 3152 W. 7th Ave., Vancouver 8, B.C., Canada. Poetry, fiction, cartoons, satire, music, letters. Irreg.; $3.50/yr.; $1/ea.; 53½ pgs.; 500 circ. Reports 1 mo. Pays copies only.

TLALOC (Expedi Printing), Francisco Arturo Alvarado, Ed., Spanish Dept., SUNY at Stony Brook, Stony Brook, NY 11790, USA. Poetry, fiction, articles, art, etc. 2/yr.; free; 84 pgs.

* TODAY'S GIRL, Margaret Adams, Ed., 1518 Walnut St., Philadelphia, PA 19102, USA.

TOLAR CREEK SYNDICATE, Bill Thompson, Ed., Box 192, Dell City, TX 79837, USA. Poetry. Irreg.; $1/yr.; 50 cents/ea.; 10 pgs.; 250 circ. Reports 1 mo. Pays copies only.

TOM VEITCH MAGAZINE (Grape Press), Tom Veitch, Ed., 461 Wilde St., San Francisco, CA 94134, USA. Poetry, fiction, articles, art, etc.; doesn't accept submissions.

THE TOOTHPASTE PRESS, Allan Kornblum, Ed., Box 546, W. Branch, IA 52358, USA. Poetry; mostly Iowa City Poets. Reports erratic. Pays 10% copies run.

TORC, Patrick Benham, Ed., Avalon House, 7 The Batch, Ashcott, Bridgwater, UK. Poetry, fiction, articles, art, etc. biased toward the Mystical/Occult. 4-5/yr.; 50 pence/yr.; 10 pence/ea.; 24 pgs.; 300-400 circ.

TOTS TO TEENS (Inky Trails Publs.), Pearl L. Kirk, Ed., Rte. No. 2, Box 2028, Nampa, ID 83651, USA. Poetry, articles, art, cartoons, etc.; mat. written for young people & by young people. 3/yr.; $4/yr.; $1.50/ea.; 30 pgs.; Reports 2-3 wks.

TOTTEL'S, Ron Silliman, Ed., 3565 Sacramento, San Francisco, CA 94118, USA. Poetry, longpoems, concrete art; lang.-centered. Irreg.; 20 pgs.; 125 circ. Reports days. Pays copies.

THE TOUCAN PRESS, Mt. Durand, St. Peter Port, Guernsey, Channel Islands, UK. Engl. lang. only.

TOULOUSE PRESS, Sylvia Hikins, Dir., 14

Harringay Ave., Liverpool L18 1JE, UK. Books & booklets inclng. poetry.

* TOWN & COUNTRY PRESS, LTD., 42 Rectory Ln., Bracknell, Berks., UK.

TRACTOR, Barbara Szerlip, Ed., 1900 Eddy, No. 18, San Francisco, CA 94115, USA. Poetry, fiction, art, satire, etc. 2/yr.; $2/yr.; $1.50/ea.; 55 pgs.; 500 circ. Reports 2-4 wks. Pays 5 copies per contbr.

TRANSATLANTIC REVIEW, J.F. McCrindle, Ed., Ennismore Gdns., London SW7 1AE, UK; and Box 3368 Grand Ctrl. Stn., N.Y., NY 10017, USA. Poetry, fiction, art, interviews. Qtly.; $3/yr.; $1/ea.; 176 pgs.; 3 million circ. Reports 2 mos. Pays according to length.

THE TRANSIENT PRESS (see also IS), Ken Saville, Ed., P.O. Box 297, Albuquerque, NM 87103, USA. Local mss.

TRANSPACIFIC, Robert Mezey, Poetry Ed., c/o Nicholas Crome, Antioch Coll., Yellow Springs, OH 45387, USA. Poetry, fiction, art, etc. Irreg.; $4/4 issues; $1/ea.; 60 pgs.; 1 million circ. Reports 2-5 wks. Nominal payment.

TRANSWORLD PUBLISHERS LTD., Cavendish House, 57-59 Uxbridge Rd., London W5 5SA, UK. Poetry & gen. lit.

TRAUMWALD PRESS, Helen Bugbee, Ed., 3550 Lake Shore Dr., Suite 10, Chgo., IL 60657, USA. Poetry, fiction.

TREE (Christopher's Books), David Meltzer, Ed., P.O. Box 365, Bolinas, CA 94924, USA. Poetry, articles, rel. to Jewish mystical tradition. 2/yr.; $6/yr.; $3/ea.; 172 pgs.; 1200 circ. Report 2 wks. Pays copies only.

TRELAWNEY PRESS, see Continuum.

TRELLIS, Margaret Anderson, Co-Ed., Box 656, Morgantown, WV 26505, USA. Poetry, articles, criticism. Qtly.; $5/yr.; $2/ea.; 100 pgs. Reports 2 wks. Pays copies only.

* TRIDENT PRESS, 630 Fifth Ave., N.Y., NY, USA.

TRIGRAM PRESS LTD., Asa Benveniste, Co-Ed., Blue Tile House, Stibbard, Fakenham, Norfolk, UK. Poetry books.

TROLL (Bridge Publs.), Nanlee Haston Pitts, Ed., Bridge Publs., 3726 Hibiscus St., Coconut Grove, FL 33133, USA. Annual collection of experimental & traditional poems, short play & pen/ink drawings.

TRUCK, David Wilk, Ed., Box 10, Enosburg Galls, VT 05450, USA. Poetry, fiction, articles, art, etc.; bias towards ecology, natural hist., localism. 3/yr.; $3/yr.; $1.50/ea.; 96 pgs.; 500 circ. Reports 2-3 mos. Pays 3-5 copies.

* TUCKER (ALAN & JOAN), The Bookshop, Station Rd., Stroud, Glos., UK.

* TURRET BOOKS (PUBLISHERS), 1B Kensington Church Walk, London W8 4NB, UK.

TUVOTI BOOKS, see The Unspeakable Visions of the Individual.

TWIGS, (Pikeville Coll. Press), Lillie D. Chaffin, Poetry Ed., Coll. Box 2, Pikeville Coll., Pikeville, KY 41501, USA. Poetry, fiction, articles, etc.; poetry limited to 25 lines. 2/yr.; $5/yr.; $3/ea.; 140 pgs.; 250 circ. Reports 3-6 wks. Pays copies, awards.

TWO BAGS PRESS, John Jacob, Ed., 488 Fairview, Glen Ellyn, IL 60137, USA. Poetry, art, photos, criticism, letters. Irreg.; 1-32 pgs. Reports vary.

TWO CHARLIES (Rusty Karma Press), Charlie Walsh, Co-Ed., P.O. Box 361, Scappoose, OR 97056, USA. Poetry, art, reviews, letters, concrete art. 2/yr.; $2.50/yr.; $1.25/ea.; 50 pgs.; 400 circ. Reports 1 mo. Pays copies only.

TWOWINDOWS PRESS, Don Gray, Ed., 2644 Fulton St., Berkeley, CA 94704, USA. Poetry, longpoems. 32 pgs.; 500-1 million circ.

TZADDIKIM (House of Love & Prayer Publs.), Steven Maimes, Ed., 224 Judah St., No. 1, San Francisco, CA 94122, USA. Poetry, reviews, criticism; newsletter of Chassidic, Kabbalistic & selected Judaic books. 2/yr.; $1/yr.; 16 pgs.; 1500 circ.

* UKRAINIAN PUBLISHERS, LTD., 200 Liverpool Rd., London N1 1LF, UK.

* ULSTERMAN PUBLICATIONS, 56 Univ. St., Belfast BT7 1HB, UK.

UMBILICAL CORD PRESS (see also TENTACLE), Prudence Juris, Ed., 811 Henderson, Big Rapids, MI 49307, USA.

* UNDERSTANDING, Daniel W. Fry, Ed., P.O. Box 206, Merlin, OR 96522, USA.

UNFOLD (Zetetic Press), Donald E. Jenkins, Ed., P.O. Box 6, Folsom, CA 95630, USA. Poetry, short stories, articles, illustrations. $10/yr.; $1.50/ea.; 40 pgs.; 1000 circ. Reports 1 mo.

UNICORN: A Miscellaneous Journal, Karen S. Rockow, Ed., 1153 E. 26 St., Brooklyn, NY 11210, USA. Poetry, fiction, articles, art, etc. 3/yr.; $2.50/yr.; $1/ea.; 32 pgs.; 500 circ. Reports 2-4 wks. Pays copies & offprints.

UNICORN JOURNAL, Teo Savory, Ed., P.O. Box 3307, Greensboro, NC 27402, USA. Poetry, fiction, articles, art, etc. 1/yr.; $2/yr.; 128 pgs.; 3 million circ. Reports 3 mos. Pays $5/pg. plus 2 copies.

* UNICORN PRESS, Studio 126 El Paseo, Santa Barbara, CA 93101, USA.

UNIO, (Literary Union), Wolfgang Durben, Fndr.-Pres., 6639 Beckingen-Saar, den, Schulstrasse 8, German Fed. Repub. Poetry, short stories, translations, essays, etc.; mainly in German. Qtly.; $4/yr.

* UNITED POETS, Stella C. Tremble, Ed., 915 Jackson St., Charleston, IL 61920, USA.

* UNITED WRITERS PUBLICATIONS, Travail Mill, Zennor, St. Ives, Cornwall, UK.

UNITY PRESS, Stephen Levine, Co-Ed., P.O. Box 1037, Santa Cruz, CA 95061, USA. Poetry, fiction, articles, art, photos.

* UNIVERSITY OF CALIFORNIA PRESS, 25 W. 45th St., N.Y., NY 10036, USA.

* UNIVERSITY OF CHICAGO PRESS, 5750 Ellis Ave., Chicago, IL 60637, USA.

* UNIVERSITY OF CHICAGO PRESS, LTD., 126 Buckingham Palace Rd., London SW1W 9SD, UK.

* UNIVERSITY OF DENVER QUARTERLY, Burton Feldman, Ed., Univ. of Denver, Denver, CO 80210, USA.

* UNIVERSITY OF LONDON PRESS, LTD., St. Paul's House, Warwick Ln., London, EC4P 4AH, UK.

UNIVERSITY OF MASSACHUSETTS PRESS, Amherst, MA 01002, USA. 2 poetry books ea. yr.

* UNIVERSITY OF NORTH CAROLINA PRESS, Chapel Hill, NC 26514, USA.

UNIVERSITY OF PITTSBURGH PRESS, 127 N. Bellefield Ave., Pitts., PA 15260, USA. Only considers 1st mss. of poetry annually through US Award competition.

UNIVERSITY OF UTAH, see Western Humanities Review.

* UNIVERSITY OF WALES PRESS, Merthyr House, James St., Cardiff CF1 6EU, UK.

UNIVERSITY OF WINDSOR REVIEW, Dr. Eugene McNamara, Ed., Sunset Ave., Windsor 11, Ont., Canada. Poetry, fiction, articles, criticism, art, etc. 2/yr.; $2.50/yr.; $1.25/ea.; 100 pgs.; 200 circ. Reports 3-4 mos. No payment.

* UNIVERSITY REVIEW, Alexander P. Cappon, Ed., Univ. of Mo., Kansas City, MO 64110, USA.

UNMUZZLED OX, Michael Andre, Ed., Box 374, Planetarium Stn., NY 10024, USA. Poetry. Qtly.; $4/yr.; $1/ea.; 80 pgs.; 1600 circ.

THE UNSPEAKABLE VISIONS OF THE INDIVIDUAL, Arthur & Glee Knight, Eds., Box 439, California, PA 15419, USA. Poetry, fiction, articles, art, etc. 3/yr.; $5/yr.; $2/ea.; 50 pgs.; 600-1 million circ. Reports 2 wks.

UP FROM UNDER, 339 Lafayette St., N.Y., NY 10012, USA. Poetry, fiction, articles, art, etc. $3/5 issues; 60 cents/ea.; 64 pgs.; 12 million circ. Pays copies only.

UT REVIEW, Duane Locke, Ed., Univ. of Tampa, Tampa, FL 33606, USA. Poetry anthol. $2.50/4 issues.

VAGABOND, John Bennett, Ed., P.O. Box 2114, Redwood City, CA 94061, USA. Poetry, fiction, articles, art, interviews. Irreg.; $3/yr.; $1/ea.; 72 pgs.; 500 circ. Reports quickly. Pays 3 copies.

VALKYRIE PRESS, see Poetry Venture.

* VALLENTINE, MITCHELL & CO., LTD., 67 Gt. Russell St., London WC1B 3BT, UK.

VALLEY VIEWS, Nelson P. Bard, Ed., P.O. Box 39096, Solon, OH 44139, USA. Poetry, stories, cartoons, art, photos. Qtly.; $2/yr.; $1/ea.; 44 pgs.; 5400 circ. Reports 3 wks. Pays copies.

* VENDURE, P.O. Box 395, Oyster Bay, NY 11771, USA.

VER POETS VOICES/BROADSHEET-/POETRY POST (Ver Poets), May E. Badman, Ed., 10 Oldfield Rd., London Colney, Herts. AL2 1JA, UK. Poetry by mbrs. only. 6/yr.; £1.20/mbrship.; 15 pence/ea.; 24 pgs.; 200 circ. Internal competitions.

VERITAS, Grace Russell Jaco, Ed. & Publr., 622 Jefferson Ave., Cape Girardeau, MO 63701, USA. Poetry.

* VERTIGO PUBLICATIONS, 4 Colville St., Nottingham, UK.

* THE VIKING PRESS, INC., 625 Madison Ave., N.Y., NY 10022, USA.

* THE VILLAGE REVIEW, Quenton Lane, Ed., Lapboard, Newport, Essex, UK.

VILLAGE UNDERGROUND PRESS, see The Little Dwarf.

THE VILLAGER, (Bronxville Women's Club), Mrs. Ted W. Proudfoot, Poetry Ed., 135 Midland Ave., Bronxville, NY 10708, USA. 9/yr.; $2.75/yr.; 35 cents/ea. No payment.

THE VINEYARD POETRY QUARTERLY, Min-Hwa Chen, Ed.-in-Chief, 71-16 Section, Chung Hsiau Ed. Rd., Taipei, Taiwan, Repub. of China.

VIOLET PRESS, Fran Winant, Ed., P.O. Box 398, N.Y., NY 10009, USA. Poetry, articles, art. 16-64 pgs.; 3 million circ. Reports 1 mo.-1 yr. Pays copies only.

VINEYARD PRESS, see Pegasus.

* VIRGINIA QUARTERLY REVIEW, Charlotte Kohler, Ed., 1 W. Range, Charlottesville, VA 22901, USA.

* VISION PRESS, LTD., 157 Knightsbridge, London SW1X 7PA, UK.

* VOICES INTERNATIONAL, Frances T. Brinkley, Ed., Box 325, Piggott, AR 72454, USA.

WALDEN PRESS, F.W. Hamilton, Ed., 423 S. Franklin Ave., Flint, MI 48503, USA. Poetry, fiction.

WARREN WALLER PRESS, see Gallimaufry.

* WARREN HOUSE PRESS, Southrepps Lower St., Norwich NOR 35Y, UK.

WASCANA REVIEW, H.C. Dillow, Ed., Engl. Dept., Univ. of Sask., Regina Campus, Regina, Sask. S4S 0AZ, Canada. Poetry, fiction, articles, satire, criticism, reviews; poems 4-100 lines. 2/yr.; $2.50/yr.; $1.50/ea.; 95 pgs.; 350 circ. Reports 4-6 wks. Pays $10/pg. poetry, 2 copies.

* WATTS (FRANKLIN), LTD., Third floor, 1 Vere St., London W1N 9HQ, UK.

WAVE, Edwin Tarling, Ed., The Sonus Press, 3 Bewick Grove, Hull, Yorks, HU9 3QY, UK.

WAVES, Bernice Lever, Co-Ed., Room 141, Petrie Sci. Bldg., York Univ., Downsview 463, Ont., Canada. Poetry, fiction, articles, photos, etc. 3/yr.; $3/yr.; $1.50/ea.; 80 pgs.; 1 million circ. Reports 1 mo. plus. Pays copies only.

WAYSIDE EDITIONS, see The Wayside Review.

THE WAYSIDE REVIEW (Wayside Editions), R. Clarence Allard, Ed., 6 Alta Ave., Salem, NH 03079, USA. Poetry, art, longpoems. 6/yr.; $4.50/yr.; $1.25/ea.; 32 pgs.; 500 plus circ. Reports as soon as possible. Pays 2-3 copies.

THE WEEKLY JOURNAL (formerly Montebello Journal), (Journal Publs.), Silvia Sheafer, Ed., 6416 S. Western Ave., Whittier, CA 90606, USA.

* WEEKLY UNITY, Unity Village 1, MO 64063, USA.

WEID: The Sensibility Revue (Olivant Press), Charles Guenther, Poetry Ed., P.O. Drawer 1409, Homestead, FL 33030, USA. Poetry, fiction, articles, art, etc. 3/yr.; $5/yr.; 150 pgs.; 500-1 million circ. Reports 2 mos. Pays copies only.

* WEIDENFELD (GEORGE) & NICHOLSON, LTD., 11 St. John's Hill, London SW11 1XA, UK.

WESLEYAN UNIVERSITY PRESS, 356

Washington St., Middletown, CT 06457, USA. Poetry books & gen. lit.

WEST COAST POETRY REVIEW, Wm. Fox, Co-Ed., 1127 Codel Way, Reno, NV 89503, USA. Poetry, articles, art, photos, etc. Qtly.; $5/yr.; $1.50/ea.; 64 pgs.; 2 million circ. Reports 2-3 wks. Pays copies only.

WEST COAST REVIEW, Frederick H. Candelaria, Ed., Simon Fraser Univ., Burnaby 2, B.C., Canada. Poetry, music, fiction, bibliographies, etc. Qtly.; $6/yr.; $1.50/ea.; 64 pgs.; 500 circ. Reports vary. Pays $5-25.

WEST END, John F. Crawford, Ed., Dept. of Engl., Herbert Lehman Coll., Bronx, NY 10468, USA. Poetry, fiction, interviews, longpoems. Qtly.; $5/yr.; $1/ea.; 48 pgs.; 400 circ. Reports immediately-3 mos. Pays copies only.

WEST HIGHLAND FREE PRESS, Brian Wilson, Ed., Kyleakin, Isle of Skye, Scotland, UK. 52/yr.; £4.50/yr.; 8 pgs.; 6500 circ. Reports immediately. Payment negotiable.

WEST VIRGINIA POETRY SOCIETY, see Poet's Crossroads.

WESTBURG ASSOCIATES, see North American Mentor Magazine.

WESTERN HUMANITIES REVIEW (Univ. of Utah), Dr. Jack Garlington, Ed., Dept. of Engl., Univ. of Utah, Salt Lake City, UT 84112, USA. Poetry, fiction, articles, interviews, satire, etc. Qtly.; $5/yr.; $1.50/ea.; 100 pgs.; 1 million circ. Reports 4-6 wks. Pay varies.

* WESTERN REVIEW, Dr. Lewis A. Richards, Ed., Western N.M. Univ., Silver City, NM 88061, USA.

WESTIGAN REVIEW OF POETRY, John Knapp II, Co-Ed., Swetman Hall, State Univ. Coll., Oswego, NY 13126, USA. Poetry, reviews. Irreg.; $2/4 issues; 50 cents/ea.; 36 pgs.; 300 circ. Reports 1 mo. Pays 2 copies.

* WESTMINSTER PUBLICATIONS, LTD., Westminster Theatre, Palace St., Buckingham Palace Rd., London SW1E 5JB, UK.

* WESTWAYS, David Dutton, Ed., 14120 Magnolia Blvd., Van Nuys, CA 91403, USA.

WETLANDS, Thomas S. Zawyrucha, Ed., Box 252, W. Islip, NY 11795, USA. Poetry, fiction, articles, art, etc; environment oriented. Qtly.; $2/yr.; 50 cents/ea.; 32 pgs.; 1 million circ. Reports 1 wk. Pays copies only.

WEYFARERS (Guildford Poets Press), Eric Harrison, Ed., April Cottage, 3 Grantley Close, Shalford, Guildford, Surrey, UK.

WHALE PUBLISHING CO., see Garfield

Lake Review.

* WHENEVER WHATEVER, Grace Adkins, Ed., Am. Bapt. Bd. of Educ., Valley Forge, PA 19482, USA.

WHITE BONES PRESS, see Bones.

THE WHITE ELEPHANT, Stephen Morse, Co-Ed., 4455 Howe St., Oakland, CA 94611, USA. Poetry, fiction, articles, art, etc. Qtly.; $3.50/yr.; $1/ea.; 40 pgs.; 1500 circ. Reports 2 wks.-1 mo. Pays 2 copies.

* WHITE LION PUBLISHERS, LTD., 138 Park Ln., London W1Y 3DD, UK.

WHITE URP PRESS, see Abbey.

WICA NEWSLETTER (Hero Press), Dr. Leo Louis Martello, Ed., Suite 1B, 153 W. 80th St., N.Y., NY 10024, USA. Poetry should be similar to Dr. Martello's book on witchcraft. 10/yr.; $4/yr.; 50 cents/ea.; 3 million circ.

THE WIDENING CIRCLE, Richard Centing, Ed., 111 W. Hudson, Apt. 2-C, Columbus, OH 43202, USA. Poetry & prose. Qtly.; $3/yr.; 24 pgs. Pays $5-15 per poem.

WILD HAWTHORN PRESS, Stonypath, Dunsyre, Lanark, Scotland, UK. Poetry, no restrictions on lang. or length; no gen. submissions.

* WILDING & SON, LTD., 33 Castle St., Shrewsbury SY1 2BL, UK.

WIN, Maris Cakars, Ed., P.O. Box 547, Rifton, NY 12471, USA. Poetry, artiles, art, photos, etc. rel. to nonviolent revolution. 52/yr.; $7/yr.; 20 cents/ea.; 16 pgs.; 5 million circ. Reports vary. No payment, 3 copies.

WIND, Quentin R. Howard, Ed., RF Rte. 1, Box 810, Pikeville, KY 41501, USA. Poetry, short stories, 1-act plays, etc. Qtly.; $4/yr.; $1.25/ea.; 56 pgs.; 250 circ. Reports less than 1 mo. Pays copies.

WINDFLOWER PRESS, see The New Salt Creek Reader.

THE WINDLESS ORCHARD, Robert Novak, Ed., Sect. of Engl., Purdue Univ., Ft. Wayne, IN 46805, USA. Poetry, articles, art, photos, criticism, reviews; poetry w. contemporary or avant-garde techniques only. Qtly.; $3.75/yr.; $1/ea.; 50 pgs.; 300 circ. Reports 1-6 wks. Pays 2 copies.

THE WINE PRESS, James Ramholz, Ed., 4504 McVicker, Chgo., IL 60630, USA. Poetry, fiction, interviews, criticism, parts-of-novels, longpoems, plays.

* WINTER HOUSE LTD., 1123 Broadway, N.Y., NY 10010, USA.

* WISCONSIN POETRY, A.M. Sterk, Ed., 2821 E. Belleview Pl., Milwaukee, WI 53202, USA.

* WM. H. WISE & CO. INC., 336 Mountain Rd., Union City, NJ 07087, USA.

WITCHCRAFT DIGEST (Hero Press), Dr. Leo Louis Martello, Ed., Suite 1B, 153 W. 80th St., N.Y., NY 10024, USA. Poetry similar to that of Dr. Martello's book on witchcraft. 1/yr.; $1.20/ea.; 24-32 pgs.; 3 million circ. Pays copies only.

* WOBURN PRESS, LTD., 67 Gt. Russell St., London WC1B 3BT, UK.

WOLF HOUSE BOOKS, see The London Collector.

* WOLFE PUBLISHING LTD., 10 Earlham St., London WC2H 9PL, UK.

WOMEN'S LIBERATION REVIEW (Women's Literature Collective), 14 Argyll Mansions, London W14, UK. Poetry, articles, short stories rel. to women's liberation.

WOMANS PRESS COLLECTIVE, see Libera.

WOMEN: A Journal of Liberation, WJL Collective, 3028 Greenmount Ave., Balt., MD 212-18, USA. Poetry, fiction, articles, art, etc. rel. to women's liberation. Qtly.; $4/4 issues; $1/ea.; 72 pgs. Reports 3-4 mos. Pays copies only.

WOODHIX PRESS, see Cantaloupe.

* WOOLF (CECIL & AMELIA), 10 Kingly Ct., 10 Kingly St., London W.1, UK.

THE WORD, see Rita Notes.

* WORDENS OF CORNWALL, LTD., 11 Parade St., Penzance, Cornwall, UK.

WORDS ETCETERA (Words Press), Julian Nangle, Co-Ed., Crane Bookshop, High St., Haslemere, Surrey, UK. Poetry, fiction, articles, art, etc. 2/yr.; £4/yr.; £2/ea.; 50-60 pgs.; 250 circ. Reports immediately. Pays 1 copy.

WORDS PRESS, see Words Etcetera.

WORKS: A Quarterly of Writing (AMS Press, Inc.), Lee Hatfield, Co-Ed., 56 E. 13 St., N.Y., NY 10003, USA. Qtly.; $5/yr.; $1.50/ea.; 100 pgs.; 3 million circ. Reports 4-8 wks. Payment varies.

WORKSHOP NEW POETRY (Workshop Press), Norman Hidden, Ed., 2 Culham Ct., Granville Rd., London N4 4JB, UK. Poetry, occasional articles & reviews. 4/yr.; £1.50/yr.; 40 pence/ea.; 40 pgs.; 2000 circ. Pays by arrangement if solicited; copies for unsolicited.

WORKSHOP PRESS, see Workshop New Poetry.

WORLD POETRY, INC., see The American Poetry Review.

WORLD POETS (Prairie Press Books), Box 35, Charleston, IL 61920, USA. Qtly.; $4/yr.; $1.50/ea.; 30 pgs.

* WORLD PUBLISHING CO., 110 E. 59th St., N.Y., NY 10009, USA.

THE WORMWOOD REVIEW, Marvin Malone, Ed., P.O. Box 8840, Stockton, CA 95204, USA. Poetry, art, interviews, satire, etc. Qtly.; $3.50/yr.; $1.50/ea.; 44 pgs.; 800 circ. Reports 2-7 wks. Pays 3-7 copies or cash equivalent.

WRIT (New England Poetry Club), Dorothy Burnham Eaton, Ed., Prospect Hill Rd., Harvard, MA 01451, USA.

WRITER'S VIEWPOINT, Dorothy Dalton, Ed., 1125 Valley Rd., Menasha, WI 54952, USA. Poetry View poetry col. in Sunday Mag. Sect. of View Appleton Post-Crescent. Pays $3/poem.

WRITERS FORUM (see also KROKLOK, AND), Bob Cobbing, Co-Ed., 262 Randolph Ave., London W9, UK. Poetry, fiction, art, music, etc. Irreg.; 250-500 circ. Reports 1 mo. Pays copies only.

* WRITER'S NOTES & QUOTES, Bill & Lanelle Greer, Eds., 142 W. Brookdale Pl., Fullerton, CA 92631, USA.

WRITING (Sean Dorman Manuscript Soc.), Sean Dorman, Ed., 4 Union Pl., Fowey, Cornwall PL23 1BY, UK. Poetry, articles; poetry 8-20 lines. 6/yr.; $2/yr.; $1/ea.; 65 pgs.; 1 million circ. Reports immediately. Pays $2.50 article or poem.

X-UNDERGROUND JOURNAL OF OCCULT, Rod Frye, Ed., P.O. Box 7374, Hampton, VA 23666, USA. Poetry, articles, art, photos, etc. on occult. Irreg.; $5/6 issues; $1/ea. Reports 3-4 wks. No payment, copies only.

X. CATHEDRA, see Ampers & Magazinc.

Y LOLFA, see Lol.

* THE YALE REVIEW, J.E. Palmer, Ed., 28 Hillhouse Ave., New Haven, CT 06510, USA.

YALE UNIVERSITY PRESS, 149 York St., New Haven, CT 06520, USA.

* YALE UNIVERSITY PRESS, LTD., 20 Bloomsbury Sq., London WC1A 2NP, UK.

YANKEE, Jean Burden, Poetry Ed., Dublin, NH 03444, USA. Poetry, fiction, articles, humor, etc. rel. to New England. 12/yr.; $5/yr.; 60 cents/ea.; 650000 circ. Reports 4-6 wks. Pays $25 per poem, all rights.

YELLOW BUTTERFLY, Laurence & Guadalupe Fallis, Eds., Box 50, WNMU, Silver City, NM 88061, USA. Poetry, longpoems; ea. issue devoted to special theme. Irreg.; $3/yr.; $1/ea.; 40 pgs. Reports 2-4 wks. Pays 1 copy.

YELLOW PRESS, (see also MILK QUARTERLY), Bob Rosenthal, Co-Ed., 7724 N. Marshfield, Chgo., IL 60626, USA. Limited edition poetry books.

YES (A Magazine of Poetry), Virginia Elson, Co-Ed., Smith Pond Rd., Avoca R.D. No. 1, NY 14809, USA. Poetry, photos, interviews, longpoems. 3/yr.; $3/yr.; $.50/ea.; 48 pgs.; 400 circ. Reports 2 wks. Pays 2 copies.

YORK POETRY SERIES (York Poetry), Colin Simms, Ed., 37 Ouse Lea, Shipton Rd., Clifton, York, UK. Poetry, longpoems; esp. regional work. Qtly.; £1/yr.; 20 pence/ea.; 12-40 pgs.; 250-500 circ. Reports vary. Pays copies only.

YORKSHIRE DIALECT SOCIETY, see Summer Bulletin.

YORKSHIRE POETS' ASSOCIATION, see Intak'.

YOU KILL ME (Kraken Press), Mike Finley, Ed., 1212 E. 21st St., Minneapolis, MN 55404, USA. Poetry, fiction, rare essays. $5/life sub. & everything publd. by Kraken Press; $1/ea.; 300-500 circ.

YOUNG PUBLICATIONS, Lincoln B. Young, Ed., 69 W. Main St., Appalachia, VA 24216, USA. Poetry, longpoems; collections in book form only. Reports up to 6 mos. No payment.

* YOUNG WORLD, 1100 Waterway Blvd., Indpls., IN 46202, USA.

ZAHIR, Diane Kruchkow, Ed., c/o Engl. Dept., Hamilton-Smith Hall, Durham, NH 03824, USA. Poetry, fiction, art, photos, etc. 2/yr.; $2/yr.; $1/ea.; 60 pgs.; 700 circ. Reports 2-4 wks. Pays 2 copies.

ZAM IS DAT (Bonefold Imprint), Bernard Joseph Kelly, Ed., 68 Parkhill Rd., London NW3, UK. Poetry, interviews, satire, criticism, music, letters. Qtly.; 60 pence/yr.; 40 pgs. No payment.

ZEITGEIST, Gary Groat, Ed., Box 595, Saugatuck, MI 49453, USA. Poetry, fiction, articles, art, photos, satire. $3.50/yr.; $1/ea.; 100 pgs.; 500 circ. Reports 1 wk. Pays copies only.

ZERO ONE, Arthur Moyse, Co-Ed., 39 Minford Gdns., W. Kensington, London W14 OAP, UK. Poetry, fiction, articles, art, etc. w. anarchist orientation. 3/yr.; £3/yr.; £1/ea.; 300 pgs.; 350 circ.

ZETETIC PRESS, see Unfold.

APPENDIX G

POETRY AWARDS, PRIZES AND CONTESTS

The following list of awards, prizes, contests, fellowships, grants, etc., connected with poetry, has been compiled from a multitude of sources in many parts of the world by the Research Department of the *International Who's Who in Poetry*. Grateful thanks are expressed to so many organizations and individuals for their valued co-operation.

In some instances, especially in the case of poetry contests, the rules, number of awards and amounts of prizes vary from year to year. Much of the information in this Appendix applies to the year 1974 (and in some cases 1973) and readers are urged to contact the sponsors personally for the latest information.

The hundreds of items are listed under the name of the sponsor but, where this is not known, under the name of the award or prize.

Additional information, for publication in the Fifth Edition of the *International Who's Who in Poetry*, will be warmly welcomed by the Hon. General Editor.

ABOVE GROUND REVIEW George Roland Wood, Sr. Editor P.O. Box 337 Arden NC 28704 U.S.A.

Pays $10 for the best poem in each issue.

ALABAMA STATE POETRY SOCIETY Information from: Lee Mays 310 Cedarcrest Drive Ripley WV 25271 U.S.A.

Alabama State Poetry Society Award $25 1st prize is offered for a love poem of 40 lines or less of any form.

AMBER Hazel Firth Goddard Editor Scotian Pen Guild P.O. Box 173 Dartmouth Nova Scotia Canada

Hazel's Hangup Souvenir offered by the editor for the best poem published in Amber during the year.

Jerry's Gem Souvenir offered by the cover artist, Jerry O'Brien, for the best poem published in Amber during the year.

Best poem each issue will receive a book from comments editor.

AMERICA Donald R. Campion, S.J. Editor 106 West 56th Street New York NY 10019 U.S.A.

Annual Poetry Award $250 to author of the best poem or collection of poems published in America magazine in the previous calendar year.

AMERICAN ACADEMY OF ARTS AND LETTERS The National Institute of Arts and Letters 633 West 155 Street New York NY 10032 U.S.A.

Arts and Letters Awards For encouragement to artists, composers and writers who are not members of the Institute. Nomination only. Ten Awards of $3,000 are awarded annually for literature.

Russell Loines Award for Poetry To an American or British poet. One award of $1,000 given periodically. Nomination only.

Award of Merit A medal and a monetary prize is given to an outstanding American poet, novelist or dramatist who is not a member of the Institute. The award of $1,000 may not be applied for and is given periodically.

Marjorie Peabody Waite Award Given in rotation to an older artist, writer or composer for continuing achievement in his art. $1,500 given annually. Open to U.S.A. residents. Nomination only.

Morton Dauwen Zabel Prize Given in rotation to an American poet, writer of fiction or critic. One prize of $2,500 awarded annually. May not be applied for.

AMERICAN ACADEMY OF ARTS AND SCIENCES 280 Newton Street Brookline Station Boston MA 02146 U.S.A.

Emerson-Thoreau Medal For recognition of distinguished achievement in the broad field of literature. Nomination only.

AMERICAN POETRY LEAGUE Truth Mary Fowler President 10419 Audrey Drive Sun City AZ 85351 U.S.A.

Contest open to members only.

AMERICAN POETS FELLOWSHIP SOCIETY Stella Craft Tremble President 902 10th Street Charleston IL 61920 U.S.A.

The Society sponsors various contest and awards. Information available from above address.

THE ANGELS Judson Dicks Editor 70 Snowberry Lane Central Islip NY 11722 U.S.A.

Prizes offered for poems which appear in The Angels magazine.

THE ANGLO-WELSH REVIEW Roland Mathias Editor Deffrobani Maescelyn Brecon Wales LD3 7NL

Poetry prizes given occasionally.

Anisfield-Wolf Award. See Saturday Review.

APPROACH Albert & Helen Fowler Editors 114 Petrie Avenue Rosemont PA 19010 U.S.A.

Prizes are offered for poems which appear in the magazine.

ARIZONA QUARTERLY Albert Frank Gegenheimer Editor University of Arizona Tucson AZ 95721 U.S.A.

Poetry prizes are offered to poems which appear in Arizona Quarterly magazine.

ARIZONA STATE POETRY SOCIETY Alfarata Hansel President 35 E. Indianola Phoenix AZ 85012 U.S.A.

Arizona State Poetry Society Award Annual national contest. $25 1st prize offered for a poem of any subject, any form, 50 lines or less.

Monthly contests open to members only.

THE ARTS COUNCIL OF AUSTRALIA (N.S.W. DIVISION) 162 Crown Street Darlinghurst N.S.W. 2010 Australia

Farmer's Poetry Prize, 1975 Section A open to all ages; $250 for a poem 60 lines or more, or a group or sequence of shorter poems. Section B open to all poets under 25 years; $100 for a poem of any length on any theme. Section C open to Australian school students under 18 years: $50 for a poem of any length on any theme. Closing date for entries is June 1, 1975. All entries to Farmer's Poetry Prize, South Head Press, 350 Lyons Road, Five Dock, N.S.W. 2046, Australia. Prize offered every two years.

THE ARTS COUNCIL OF GREAT BRITAIN 105 Piccadilly London U.K. WIV OAU

Grants to Writers On the recommendation of publishers, literary editors, and other responsible members of the literary profession, grants may be awarded by the Arts Council to a writer of fiction, poetry, criticism and biography who is a British subject or Commonwealth subject resident in Great Britain.

Grants to Translators Arts Council grants are available, on publishers' recommendations, for the translators into English of approved works of foreign fiction, biography and autobiography, travel, poetry or other kinds of creative writing, which have been proposed for publication

THE ATHENAEUM OF PHILADELPHIA Literary Awards Committee 219 E. Washington Square Philadelphia 6 PA 19106 U.S.A.

The Athenaeum of Philadelphia Literary Award For any volume of general literature (fiction, history, biography, drama, belles lettres) written by a Philadelphian. Nominations for this annual prize to be made before December 31 of each year to the Literary Award Committee at the above address by the author or publisher. Award is a bronze medal bearing the name of the award, the title of the book, the name of the author and the year conferred.

BAVARIAN ACADEMY OF FINE ARTS 8 Munich 22 Max-Joseph-Platz 3 Germany

The Literature Prize of the Bavarian

Academy of Fine Arts This prize is usually awarded annually; it is awarded by the decision of the literary section of the Academy and, therefore, is not applied for.

BEREA COLLEGE College Box 2336 Berea KY 40403 U.S.A.

W.D. Weatherford Award The value of the basic Award is $500, but a Special Award of $200 may be given. Entries must be published works about the Southern Appalachian region and its people. The writing in these works may be of any kind, tone and point of view; the work may consist of one individual piece or a series of pieces. They may be published in newspapers, magazines or anthologies, or they may be complete books in themselves. Closing date is 31 of each year. Submit entries to Thomas Parrish, Chairman of the Award Committee, Appalachian Center, CPO 2336, Berea, KY 40403, U.S.A.

BITTERROOT MAGAZINE Blythebourne Station P.O. Box 51 Brooklyn NY 11219 U.S.A.

Bitterroot Lyric Poetry Contest Open to any form or subject within the framework of a lyric; length not to exceed 30 lines. Poems must be original and unpublished. Contestants need not be subscribers. $100 first prize; life-time subscription to Bitterroot, second prize; five year subscription, third prize.

BLACK ACADEMY OF ARTS AND LETTERS 475 Riverside Drive New York NY U.S.A.

Annual Awards given to black authors for outstanding work in poetry, fiction, history, drama and biography.

THE VERA BLADEN MEMORIAL AWARD c/o Peter Bladen P.O. Box 19 Quorn South Australia 5433 Australia

The Vera Bladen Memorial Award Award for the longer unpublished poems by a writer born or domiciled in Australia. A minimum annual award of $500 is expected. Closing date for the first award is December 31, 1974.

B'NAI B'RITH COMMISSION ON ADULT JEWISH EDUCATION 1640 Rhode Island Avenue, NW Washington DC 20036 U.S.A.

B'nai B'rith Book Award A single annual award of $500 is given to a single book of quality dealing with some aspect of Jewish life. Book to be published in the preceding year. Open to U.S.A. residents. Nomination only.

Jewish Heritage Award For Excellence in Literature One award of $1,000 is given annually to a U.S.A. resident for his contribution to contemporary Jewish literature. Nomination only.

BOOKS ABROAD, AN INTERNATIONAL LITERARY QUARTERLY 401 W. Brooks, Room 45-A University of Oklahoma Norman OK 73069 U.S.A.

Books Abroad/Neustadt International Prize for Literature An award for distinguished and continuing artistic achievement in the fields of poetry, drama or fiction. The award consists of a medallion, an award certificate and $10,000. Books Abroad dedicates one issue to laureate. The University of Oklahoma Press will seriously consider the publication of a book by or on the recipient. Given every other year. Nomination by one member of the jury only.

BORESTONE MOUNTAIN POETRY AWARDS Box 653 Solana Beach CA 92075 U.S.A.

Borestone Mountain Poetry Awards Cash awards are available but may not be applied for. Poetry direct from poets is *not* accepted.

BRANDEIS UNIVERSITY Waltham MA 02154 U.S.A.

Brandeis University Creative Arts Awards "Medals and citations are presented annually in four major fields: Sculpture, Painting or Architecture; Poetry, Non-Fiction or Fiction; Music or Dance; and Theater Arts or Film by professional juries selected by the Creative Arts Awards Commission. Medals are awarded to established artists in recognition of a life-time of distinguished achievement, and citations are conferred on particularly talented artists actively engaged and/or in mid-career. Since 1964, the Creative Arts Awards Commission has presented a special award for Notable achievement in Creative Arts. A one-thousand dollar honorarium accompanies each award".

BREAD LOAF WRITERS' CONFERENCE Middlebury College Middlebury VT 05753 U.S.A.

Robert Frost Fellowship in Poetry Candidates must be nominated by an editor, agent, published writer, or a teacher of writing before April 15th of each year. Fellowships pay all fees for the two weeks of the Conference (board, room, and tuition; fees that amount to $340 in 1974), but do not pay traveling expenses.

Scholarships Nomination procedure is the same as above. Scholarships pay whole or partial tuition (up to $215) but not room and board.

BRIDGE PUBLICATIONS Nanlee Pitts Editor 3726 Hibiscus Street Coconut Grove FL 33133 U.S.A.

Several cash prizes are awarded each issue of Bridge, A Poetry Quarterly, for poems which appear in the magazine. Several annual prizes are also available.

BRITISH ACADEMY Burlington House Piccadilly London U.K. W1V ONS

Rose Mary Crawshay Prize To a woman for a critical work on a subject connected with English Literature. Preference is given to a work on one of the poets Byron, Keats or Shelley. £100 awarded annually.

THE BROOKLYN POETRY CIRCLE Miss Gabrielle Lederer Secretary 61 Pierrpont Street Brooklyn NY 11201 U.S.A.

Marie-Louise d'Esternaux Poetry Scholarship presented annually to young students of 1 — 21 years of age. $50 will be awarded for an original, unpublished poem of not more than 24 lines. The English Dept. of each school will select the poem to be submitted. "The object of the scholarship is to encourage young people to study poetry, to seek to express poetry, and thus to enrich themselves". Deadline date is April 7 of each year.

AGNES C. BROTHERS MEMORIAL FUND Information from: Lee Mays 310 Cedarcrest Drive Ripley WV 25271 U.S.A.

Agnes C. Brothers Significant Poetry Contest $75 1st prize is offered for a literary poem of merit on a personal theme. 50 lines or less. Second and Third prizes are $50 and $25.

CALDER VALLEY POETS' SOCIETY Mrs. Maud Fearnley Secretary 3 Callis Wood Bottom Charlestown Hebden Bridge Yorks. HX7 6PY U.K.

The George Camp Poetry Competition Open to members of the Calder Valley Poets' Society. An annual competition with three classes. Length of poems between 14 and 42 lines. Entry fee of 30p. per competitor.

CALIFORNIA FEDERATION OF CHAPARRAL POETS Zelma Dennis Contest Chairman 13020 Gabbett Drive La Mirada CA 90638 U.S.A.

California Poetry Competition Annual contest with classes open to all poets in the U.S.A., California poets only, and Chaparral members and associates only. Deadline is February 1 and prizes range from $50 first prize to $10 third prize. A one dollar entry fee is required of all non-members for each contest entered.

The Golden Pegasus Trophy will be awarded in a surprise presentation at the closing Festival banquet to the poet whose poem has been judged best of all the prize-winning poems.

Annual Poetry Contest for Junior and Senior High School Students Open to California residents for original unpublished poems. Categories open to Jr. & Sr. students with cash prizes of $20, $15 and $10; The Laban & Ethel Johnston Memorial Award is open to Jr. High School students only; one category open to Sr. High School students only with the same cash prizes. Entries to School Contest Chairman, Terese Aikens, 4748 Oliva Street, Lakewood, CA 90712, U.S.A. Deadline is March 1st.

Pony Pegasus Sweepstakes Award will go to the student whose poem is judged best of all prize winning poems in all the high school contest classifications.

CALIFORNIA FEDERATION OF CHAPARRAL POETS, ROBERT FROST CHAPTER P.O. Box 464 San Jose CA 95103 U.S.A.

Robert Frost Chapter Annual Contest offers prizes of $7, $5 and $3 in three categories for CFCP members. Deadline is September 21.

Jewel Award $25 will be given to the poem that "best crystallizes a facet of beauty".

CALIFORNIA OLYMPIAD OF THE ARTS Sponsored by the Quadrennial Contests in the Arts 22100 Mount Eden Road Saratoga CA 95070 U.S.A.

The Henry Meade Bland Award for a poem in the English language.

The Florence Brooks Sonnet Award For a sonnet in English and a sonnet in French.

CALIFORNIA STATE POETRY SOCIETY Romayne Dowd President 8501 S. Sepulveda Blvd. Los Angeles CA 90045 U.S.A.

Annual Competitions Please write for details.

THE CALIFORNIA WRITERS' CLUB Mrs. Ila Berry 761 Sequola Woods Place Concord CA 94520 U.S.A.

Annual Poetry Contest Please write for details.

CANADA COUNCIL 140 Wellington Street Ottawa 4 Ontario Canaoa

Literary Awards For the professional artist (including literature) who wants time to studyt orr to work freely from eight to twelve months. Over 60 awards offered annually. Awards up to $7,000. Open to Canadian citizens or landed immigrants. Deadline is October 1 of each year.

Bursaries For artists starting their professional careers to study or work freely from eight to twelve months. Over 150 bursaries up to $4,000 awarded annually. Open to Canadian citizens or landed immigrants. Deadline is November 15 of each year.

Short Term Grants Available to artists up to three months; $250 to $450 per month. Open to Canadian citizens or landed immigrants. Apply to Arts Division at above address.

Travel Grants For travel important to the professional career of the artist. Up to $350 offered to Canadian citizens or landed immigrants. Apply to Arts Division at above address.

THE CARDINAL Tim Walton Editor Wesleyan Station Middletown CT 06458 U.S.A.

Prizes Offered for poems which appear in the magazine.

THE CARLISLE POETS' WORKSHOP Contest Chairman Kay M. Freiberg R.D. No. 4 Carlisle PA 17013 U.S.A.

Carlisle Poets Award Open to all poets for unpublished serious poetry of 32 lines or less. Entry fee $1.00 per poem. Prizes: $10, $5, $3 plus Hon. Mentions.

Florence Mort Kent Memorial Award Open to all poets for unpublished humorous or light verse, any form, 32 lines or less. Entry fee $1.00 per poem. Prizes: $5, $3, $2 plus Hon. Mentions.

Gidda Finsterwald Strauss Memorial Award Student category open to young people under 18 years of age for unpublished poetry of any form, 32 lines or less. No entry fee. Prize is $5 plus Hon. Mentions.

In all instances please write for the subject of the competition.

CINTAS FELLOWSHIP PROGRAM Institute of International Education 809 United Nations Plaza New York NY 10017 U.S.A.

Cintas Fellowships The fellowships "are intended to foster and encourage the professional development and recognition of talented creative artists in the fields of architecture, painting, sculpture, the graphic arts, music composition and literature". They are not awarded for the furtherance of academic or professional study. Limited to young professionals in these arts who are of Cuban citizenship or lineage. Six fellowships are awarded annually in the amount of $4,000 each. Applications are received by the Institute of International Education from January 1 to April 1 of each year.

COMMONWEALTH CLUB OF CALIFORNIA Durward S. Riggs Secretary Literature Medal Awards Monadnock Arcade 681 Market Street San Francisco CA 94105 U.S.A.

California Literature Medal Awards Authors and publishers are invited to submit entries for this competition before January 31 of each year. Author must be a California resident. A number of medals are awarded for various classifications including one silver medal for the best book of poetry and three silver medals for the next best entries regardless of classification.

COMMONWEALTH INSTITUTE AND NATIONAL BOOK LEAGUE Kensington High Street London U.K. W8 6NQ

Commonwealth Poetry Prize The £250 prize is awarded annually for a first book of poetry in English published by an author from a Commonwealth country other than Great Britain. Manuscripts and typescripts will not be accepted. Seven copies of the book should be sent to The Librarian, Commonwealth Institute at the above address to arrive not later than June 30 of each year.

THE INA COOLBRITH CIRCLE Room 401 Marines' Memorial Building San Francisco CA U.S.A.

Annual Poetry Contest "To carry out the principal objective of encouragement of poetry". Awards.

Biennial Newspaper Verse Contest Please write for details.

Youth Poetry Contests "To awaken the talents of the nation's future poets". Write for details.

THE DUFF COOPER MEMORIAL PRIZE The Warden New College Oxford U.K. OX1 3BN

The Duff Cooper Memorial Prize The Prize is awarded annually for a work of literature in the fields of history, biography, politics or poetry. There are five judges. The sum involved varies from year to year and the award made toward the end of the calendar year.

COUNCIL OF INTERRACIAL BOOKS FOR CHILDREN 1841 Broadway New York NY 10023 U.S.A.

Annual Contest African American, Asian American, American Indian, Chicano and Puerto Rican writers who are unpublished in the children's book field are invited to submit manuscripts for children's books that are free of racist and sexist stereotypes. Any literary form (picture or story books, poetry, fiction or non-fiction) is acceptable. For rules send stamped, self-addressed envelope to the contest chairman of above address. Five $500 prizes are awarded.

COUNCIL FOR WISCONSIN WRITERS P.O. Box 212 Milwaukee WI 53216 U.S.A.

Wisconsin Writers' Awards Four awards of $250 each are awarded to residents of Wisconsin for a scholarly book, best poetry collection, less than book length fiction or non-fiction. Awarded annually to encourage creative work in Wisconsin.

CREATIVE ARTISTS PUBLIC SERVICE PROGRAM 250 West 57th Street Room 430 New York NY 10019 U.S.A.

The Creative Artists Public Service Program This independent program was designed to purchase the professional services of New York state artists in various art fields. The program funds approximately ten poets each year with $1,500 to $5,000 to either create a new work or complete a work in progress. A panel of professional artists in each of the art fields recommend the artists. The poets must be New York State resident and can not be either an undergraduate or graduate student.

CUMBRIAN LITERARY GROUP Stonecroft Beresford Road Windermere U.K.

Roderick Webb Prize Open to members of the Cumbrian Literary Group only.

DAILY TELEGRAPH 135 Fleet Street London EC4 U.K.

Young Writer of the Year Annual competition open to poets under 24 years of age. Pergamon Press presents cash prizes to twelve best entries.

DEKALB LITERARY ARTS JOURNAL Mel McKee Editor DeKalb College Clarkson GA 30021 U.S.A.

Annual Poetry Contests

EMILY DICKINSON BULLETIN Frederick L. Morey Editor 4508 38th Street Brentwood MD 20722 U.S.A.

The Maryland Award $25 1st prize is offered for a lyric line length poem of any form, 25 lines or less on a personal salvation theme.

DRAGONFLY: A QUARTERLY OF HAIKU Lorraine Ellis Harr Editor 4102 N.E. 130th Place Portland OR 97230 U.S.A.

Numerous cash awards and book prizes are offered for poems which appear in Dragonfly.

THE ENSIGN Doyle L. Green Editor 50 East North Temple Street Salt Lake City UT 84150 U.S.A.

Poetry Contests Open to members of the Relief Society of The Church of Jesus Christ of Latter-day Saints. Write for details.

THE EXPLICATOR Virginia Commonwealth University 901 West Franklin Street Richmond VA 23284 U.S.A.

The Explicator Award An annual award for the best book of explication de texte published in the preceding year in the field of English or American literature. Book must be written in English and must be submitted, one copy to each judge on the Board of Judges, by April 1 of each year. Monetary prize of $200 and an engraved bronze plaque.

FABER & FABER LTD. 3 Queen Square London U.K. WCIN 3AU

The Geoffrey Faber Memorial Prize £250 is awarded annually for a volume of verse and for a volume of prose fiction in alternate years. The volume must be first originally published in U.K. during the two years preceding the year in which the award is given. Writer must not be more than 40 years old and be a citizen of the U.K. or Commonwealth. Editors are invited to submit nominations; no submissions for the prize are made.

FEDERATION INTERNATIONALE DES TRADUCTEURS Secretariat Permanent 5 Square Thiers 75 Paris XVI France

The FIT International Translation Prize A grant of 10,000 Swedish Kroner is awarded to an outstanding translator or translation in the literary and nonliterary fields. The grant is divided for one literary and one scientific translation and is awarded every 3 yrs. as grants are available. Translators should be sponsored by a member society of FIT.

FLORIDA STATE POETRY SOCIETY, INC. Dr. Francis Clark Handler National Director 1110 North Venetian Drive Miami Beach FL 33139 U.S.A.

Numerous contests and awards are sponsored by the Society. Please write for details.

FRIENDS OF LITERATURE AWARD Mrs. Hazel R. Ferguson President 1500 Chicago Avenue Evanston IL 60210 U.S.A.

Friends of Literature Award $100 annual award for poetry or essay by a present or former resident of Metropolitan Chicago. Available only to U.S.A. citizens.

FRIENDS OF THE RICHARDS LIBRARY Newport NH 03773 U.S.A.

The Sarah Josepha Hale Award Given annually in August by the Friends of the Richards Library in the field of literature and letters. The recipient, in some way associated with New England, is chosen by a national board of judges. No applications are accepted. The award is a bronze medal.

JOHN SIMON GUGGENHEIM MEMORIAL FOUNDATION 90 Park Avenue New York NY 10016 U.S.A.

Fellowships to Assist Research and Artistic Creation The fellowships were established "to improve the quality of education and the practise of the arts and professions, to foster research, and to provide for the cause of better international understanding". They are awarded through two annual competitions (one open to citizens and permanent residents of the U.S. and Canada, and the other open to citizens and permanent residents of the other American states, the Caribbean, the Philippines, and the French, Dutch and British possessions in the Western Hemisphere) to men and women "of high intellectual and personal qualifications who have already demonstrated unusual capacity for productive scholarship or unusual creative ability in the fine arts". Applications to be made in writing by the candidates themselves on or before October 1 of each year for the United States and Canada competition and December 1 for the Western Hemisphere and Philippines competition.

HAIKU SOCIETY OF AMERICA 333 East 47 Street New York NY 10017 U.S.A.

Awards will be given "for meritorious work, not necessarily haiku poems but anything related to the subject published in haiku magazines (poems, book reviews, sequences, haibun, anything which advances the improvement of haiku)" Awards will not be given if work of merit is not published. Whenever such work is published HSA will be on the lookout for it and will try to see that it receives the recognition it deserves.

HOSPITALIZED VETERANS WRITING PROJECT, INC. 333 E. Huron Street Chicago IL 60611 U.S.A.

Hospitalized Veterans Writing Contests Open to U.S.A. Armed Forces hospitalized veterans for unpublished work in the following categories: poems, articles, stories, light verse, patriotic essays. $5 awarded per poem.

ILLINOIS STATE POETRY SOCIETY Stella Craft Tremble President 902 10th Street Charleston IL 61920 U.S.A.

Illinois State Poetry Society Contest $25 1st prize offered for a poem on any subject, any form, 50 lines or less.

INDIANA STATE FEDERATION OF POETRY CLUBS Mrs. Esther Alman President 826 S. Center Street Terre Haute IN 47807 U.S.A.

Indiana Contest $25 1st prize offered for a poem on any subject, any form, 50 lines or less.

INTERNATIONAL P.E.N. AMERICAN CENTER 156 Fifth Avenue New York NY 10010 U.S.A.

The P.E.N. Fund for Writers Several grants up to $500 are given annually to U.S.A. established writers to help them through financial difficulties.

INTERNATIONAL P.E.N. AMERICAN CENTER AND COLUMBIA UNIVERSITY SCHOOL OF THE ARTS Mathematics Building 307A Columbia University School of the Arts New York NY 10027 U.S.A.

Translation Fellowships The fellowships are awarded by the Translation Center which is a joint project of Columbia School of the Arts and P.E.N. American Center. The awards are for $10,000 each and are for American writers of proven excellence to perfect themselves in the study of one of the more difficult and neglected languages, such as Chinese, Thai, Bengali and the African languages, with the intention of going on to translate from that language. Application forms and information sheets are available from Mrs. Constance Hirsch, Translation Coordinator, 307A Mathematics Building.

INTERNATIONAL P.E.N. ENGLISH CENTRE 62-63 Glebe Place Chelsea London U.K. SW3 5JB

The P.E.N. Awards (formerly The Silver Pen Awards) Publishers and P.E.N. members are requested to submit recommendations for two categories The Novel and Biography/Autobiography (poetry is included). Published in the preceding year to which the award is made, the books must be written in English (translations not accepted) and must have been published initially in the U.K. An award of an illuminated scroll and book tokens to the value of £50 will be presented to the winner in each category.

INTERNATIONAL P.E.N. NEW ZEALAND CENTRE Mrs. Dora Somerville Secretary 142 Upland Road Kelburn Wellington 5 New Zealand

Jesse Mackay Poetry Award $100 will be awarded for poetry of a New Zealand poet written within the year for which it is applied.

INTERNATIONAL P.E.N. RHODESIA CENTRE P.O. Box 1900 Salisbury Rhodesia

Book Centre of Rhodesia Literary Prize The prize, valued at $400 will be awarded annually to advance the cause of outstanding literature in Rhodesia. It is hoped that by creating this prize, authors, journalists, poets, playwrights and persons directly involved in promoting literature in Rhodesia will be spurred to enhance the standards of writing in the country. Open to Rhodesians by birth, domicile, or long association for a published work in the immediately preceding year. Deadline date is March 31st of each year.

INTERNATIONAL POETRY FORUM University of Pittsburg Press Pittsburg PA 15260 U.S.A.

United States Award $2,000 is awarded to a U.S.A. citizen who has not published a volume of poetry. The manuscript must be original poetry in English and at least 48 pages (typewritten). Application forms are not necessary. Entries must be submitted between February 1 and April 1 of the year for which the application is made. Manuscripts should be mailed to The International Poetry Forum's United States Award at the above address.

INTERNATIONAL POETS' SHRINE Mr. James Glackin Corr. Secretary 1060 N. St. Andrews Place Hollywood CA 90038 U.S.A.

The Golden Trophy Award Given every year for the best poetry book published.

Edna St. Vincent Millay Award $100 prize for the best sonnet (English or Italian) in the manner of Edna St. Vincent Millay.

Golden Medal Awards Five medals will be given in 1974.

Annual Poetry Contest Any subject, length, and form. $1.00 entry fee.

IOWA POETRY ASSOCIATION Eleanora Miller President 208 South Church Street Leon IA 50144 U.S.A.

The following contests are open to residents of Iowa.

Dwight G. McCarty Awards Open to adults for nature poetry. Poems must be original and unpublished. $10 and $5 are given as prizes.

Harlan Miller Memorial Awards $10, $5 and $3 for 4 to 6 line light verses. Open to adults. Poems must be original and unpublished.

Carl Stiefel Awards For poems on current events (16 line limit). $15 and $10 offered as prizes. Poems must be original and unpublished. Adults contest.

College Contest $10, $5 and $3 prizes are offered for original unpublished poems by college students.

High School Contest $10, $5 and $3 prizes are offered for original unpublished poems by high school students.

Grade School Contest: Grades K through 4 $3, $2 and $1 prizes for poetry by grade school students.

Grade School Contest: Grades 5 through 8 $3, $2 and $1 prizes.

THE IRISH ARTS COUNCIL 70 Merrion Square Dublin 2 Ireland

The Denis Devlin Memorial Award for Poetry "£350 awarded once every three years in respect of the best book of poetry in English by a poet who is an Irish citizen, and which was published during the previous triennial period. The next award will be made in 1976 in respect of a book of poetry published during the period 1973-1974-1975".

An Chomhairle Ealaíon Prize "£300 for the best book of poetry in the Irish language published in the preceding three years. The next award will be made in 1974 in respect of the best book published in the triennial period 1971-1972-1973".

JEAN'S JOURNAL Jean Calkins Editor Box 15 Kanona NY 14856 U.S.A.

Poetry Contests for each issue of the journal with cash and book awards given.

JEOPARDY Viking Union 218 West Washington State College Bellingham WA 98225 U.S.A.

Prizes Poetry prizes are only offered to students at the present time, but efforts are being made to establish prizes for poetry and fiction for non-student contributors sometime in the next few years.

JEWISH BOOK COUNCIL OF THE NATIONAL JEWISH WELFARE BOARD 15 East 26th Street New York NY 10010 U.S.A.

Harry and Florence Kovner Memorial Awards for Books of Poetry $500 and a citation will be given to a United States or Canadian citizen for a published book of poetry of Jewish interest. The book may be written originally in English or translated from another language into English. From 1970, the award has been given for a book published in Yiddish, the next year for a book published in English and the third year for a book published in Hebrew. The award is given to the author of a book published during the three preceding calendar years.

ALFRED JURZYKOWSKI FOUNDATION, INC. 200 Park Avenue New York NY 10017 U.S.A.

The Jurzykowski Foundation Awards Awards are granted to writers of Polish ethnic background for distinguished services to the arts and sciences. Translation grants are also available to the translators of Polish; translators do not have to be of polish ethnic background. Nomination only.

KANSAS CITY POETRY CONTESTS P.O. Box 5313 Kansas City MO 64131 U.S.A.

Devins Award Given to a book length poetry manuscript. This annual award of $500 advance against royalties is for an original unpublished manuscript.

Hallmark Honor Prize Six prizes of $100 each are given for single poems by full-time undergraduates of colleges and universities.

Kansas City Star Awards Four prizes of $100 each are open to U.S.A. residents for single poems.

Sharp Memorial Awards Four prizes of $25 each are given to High School students of Missouri or bordering states for a single poem.

KENTUCKY STATE POETRY SOCIETY Linda Reeder President Route 10 Ridgemont Road Paducah KY 42001 U.S.A.

The 1974 Kentucky State Poetry Contest offered 30 different awards and prizes including:

Grand Prix Open to all. $5 entry fee. Limit to 32 lines. Award $50.

This Heaven, This Hell, This Kentucky Open to Kentucky residents only. $2 entry fee. Award $25.

Jesse Stuart Award Sponsored by James B. Goode for a poem with a Kentucky theme. Awards were books by Stuart.

Blaine Hall Award KSPS members only. $10, $6, $4 for lyric poetry to 24 lines. Sponsored by Blaine Hall.

Lucia Clark Markham Memorial Award Open to all poets. $15, $10, $5, 2 books sponsored by Priscilla White for sonnets.

World Peace Award Open to all. Sponsored by Mary G. Faulconer for a poem with a peace theme. Awards: $10, $5, Book.

MARTIN LUTHER KING MEMORIAL PRIZE c/o Midland Bank Ltd. 122 Finchley Road London NW3 U.K.

Martin Luther King Memorial Prize Awarded annually for a literary work (poem, novel, story etc.) published in the preceding calendar year. Work to reflect the ideals of Dr. Martin Luther King.

KOKOMO POETRY CIRCLE Mrs. Emily Spindler Secretary 1418 West Jefferson Street Kokomo IN 46901 U.S.A.

Annual Cup Contest Open to members only. Cups or similar gold mementoes are given to the first, second and third place winners.

THE LANCASHIRE AUTHORS' ASSOCIATION Mr. J.R. Sutcliffe General Secretary "Sea Winds" 22 Lune View Knott End on Sea Fylde Coast Lancs. U.K. FY6 OAG

The Batty Cup Open to members only for the best poem in Standard English. Holder will receive award from the Simon Trust Fund.

The Scholes Cup Open to members only for the best poem in Lancashire Dialect. Holder will receive an award from the Harry Craven Mem. Trust Fund.

Writer of the Year For the most outstanding entry chosen from the six cup winners including the two mentioned above. The holder of this title will receive an award from the Handley-Taylor Trust Fund.

LARAMORE RADER POETRY GROUP Maylen Newby Pierce President 300 Mendoza Avenue Apt. 4 Coral Gables FL 33134 U.S.A.

Monthly Popular and Judge's Prizes Open to members only. Each prize is $3.

'Vivian's Choice' Special Award Offered by Sadie Frenkil Eisenberg as a tribute to Vivian. $25 for poem of poet's choice not to exceed 24 lines.

Helen Knaus Memorial Award Open to members only. Offered by Helga Eason for a poem of poet's choice not to exceed 24 lines. $15 award.

Vivian Laramore Rader's Special Award $5 given for best poem submitted by out-of-town members for the June monthly contests.

Vivian Laramore Rader's Special Popular Votes Award $10 given annually to the member whose poems had the most popular votes throughout the year.

LEGEND Bonnie E. Parker Editor 39213 Gloucester Westland MI 48185 U.S.A.

Poetry Prizes Each issue of Legend is judged separately. Books and/or subscriptions are given to the best poems in each issue.

LITERARY TIMES Jay Robert Nash Editor Box 4327 Chicago IL 60680 U.S.A.

Prizes Given to poems published in Literary Times.

LONDON LITERARY EDITIONS 29 Avenue Chambers Vernon Place London WC1 U.K.

Keats Poetry Prize Competition £2,000. Please write for details.

LOUISIANA STATE POETRY SOCIETY Dr. Glenn R. Swetman President Dept. of English Nicholls State University Thibodaux LA 70301 U.S.A.

Louisiana State Poetry Society Award $25 given for a poem on any subject, any form, 40 lines or less. Open to all Poets.

Emma Wilson Emery High School Poetry Contest Open to Louisiana High School students only.

Annual Spring Poetry Festival Contest Several cash prizes of $5 each. Open to Louisiana State Poetry Society members only.

LOUISIANA STATE POETRY SOCIETY, BATON ROUGE BRANCH Information from: Lee Mays 310 Cedarcrest Drive Ripley WV 25271 U.S.A.

Cora R. Phillips Memorial Contest $25 given for a poem on any theme or subject in any sonnet form.

THE LYRIC Bremo Bluff VA 23022 U.S.A.

The Lyric Memorial Prize $100

The Nathan Haskell Dole Prize $100

The Roberts Memorial Prize $100

The Leitch Memorial Prize $50

The Virginia Prize $50

The New England Prize $50

The Phyllida Prize $25

The Georgia Prize $25

$100 Yearly in Quarterly Awards of $25 each

Awards as listed above are for poets whose poems appeared in The Lyric.

The Lyric Foundation For Traditional Poetry Award An award of $100 "will be made for the best original and unpublished poem of 32 lines or less, written in the traditional manner by an undergraduate student enrolled in any American or Canadian college or university. There will also be a second prize of $50 and a number of honorable mentions, each in the amount of $25. An honorarium of $100 will be made to the library of the college in which the winner of the first prize is enrolled, provided the library is on the list of subscribers to The Lyric. Deadline date is June 1, 1974.

MADEMOISELLE MAGAZINE 350 Madison Avenue New York NY 10017 U.S.A.

Mademoiselle College Poetry Competition Two prizes of $100 each are offered for poems by undergraduates. For rules write to College Poetry Competition at the above address.

MARYLAND STATE POETRY SOCIETY, INC. AND MARYLAND ARTS COUNCIL Entries to: Mr. Walter H. Kerr 6602 Wells Parkway Hyattsville MD 20782 U.S.A.

Serious Verse Contest 30 lines or less, any subject. Cash prizes.

Light Verse Contest 25 lines or less, any subject. Cash prizes.

Maryland Contest 50 lines or less, about Maryland. Cash prizes.

Short Form Contest 10 lines or less, any subject. Cash prizes.

The Lucy Robertson Stavely Awards Offered by Margaret Stavely Payne in memory of her grandmother. Poems to be judged by Margaret Stavely Payne. Poems to be 50 lines or less, any theme or form.

These contests are open to all poets for an entry fee of $1 per poem entered. M.S.P.S. members do not pay this handling fee.

Youth Contest Offered to students of Maryland colleges, universities, senior and junior high schools whether they are members of MSPS or not. 28 lines or less, any subject or form. There is no handling fee for this contest.

THE MASSACHUSETTS REVIEW Memorial Hall University of Massachusetts Amherst MA 01002 U.S.A.

Jesse Tane Award $100 is offered for the best poem published in the previous volume of The Massachusetts Review.

MASSACHUSETTS STATE POETRY SOCIETY Mrs. Mary Manningham President 4 Russet Lane Winchester MA 01890 U.S.A.

Massachusetts State Poetry Society Award $25 1st prize is offered for a poem any subject, any form. 20 lines or less.

NATIONAL BOOK COMMITTEE, INC. 1564 Broadway New York NY 10036 U.S.A.

The National Book Awards "Now America's most prestigious literary laurels, these $1,000 awards are presented annually in ten categories". Poetry is one of these categories and the award is conferred for a book published in the preceding calendar year by an American citizen.

National Medal For Literature Beginning in 1973 this medal includes a cash award of $10,000 for the total body of work by a living American writer. Previously, the cash award was $5,000. The current recipient is Vladimir Nabokov.

NATIONAL BOOK LEAGUE See Commonwealth Institute and National Book League.

NATIONAL FEDERATION OF STATE POETRY SOCIETIES, INC. Lee Mays Contest Chairman 310 Cedarcrest Drive Ripley WV 25271 U.S.A.

NFSPS Grand Prize $500 1st prize is offered for a poem of 100 lines or less, any subject, any form. Entry fee is $3 per poem.

In addition to the NFSPS Grand Prize, information on the following awards, prizes and contests can be obtained from the above address.

Fidelia Van Antwerp Ballac Award

Lubbe Cinquain Award

Humorous Poetry Award

Lyric Poem Award

Gertrude Saucier Lyric Award

C. Faye Bennett Memorial Award

Sarah Curtis Memorial Award

The August Derleth Memorial Award

Clement Hoyt Memorial Haiku Award

Walter R. Lovel Memorial Award

Anne and Cicero Maxwell Memorial Award

Lloyd Frank Merrell Memorial Lanterne Award

Walter E. Pratt Memorial Award

Kate Spalding Memorial

Evans Spencer Wall Memorial Award

Grafikon Award

The Tennant Award

Beaudoin Gemstone Award

Youth Award

Little Twigs Award

The above contests are open to all poets but those who are not a member of the NFSPS are required to pay an entry fee of $1 for each contest entered.

The following contests are open to NFSPS members only:

NFSPS Award

NFSPS Award-Traditional

Kate Heanue Memorial Award

The Spoon River Award

Colorado Award

Poet Laureate of Louisiana Contest

The Bible Award

Susan A. Callahan Award

Eternity Award

Kaleidograph Award

The Lisa Lyric Prize

The Manningham Award

Alma Partello Carlson Memorial Award

THE NATIONAL INSTITUTE OF ARTS AND LETTERS see The American Academy of Arts and Letters The National Institute of Arts and Letters

NATIONAL LEAGUE OF AMERICAN PEN WOMEN Louise A. Baldwin Corres. Secretary 1300 17th Street NW Washington DC 20036 U.S.A.

The NLAPW Poetry Contest Annual contest.

NEW DEPARTURES Michael Horovitz

Editor Mullions Piedmont Bisley Glos. U.K. GL6 7BU

Prizes are given for poems which appear in the magazine.

NEW ENGLAND POETRY CLUB Jean Harper Secretary 43A Joy Street Boston MA 02114 U.S.A.

The Golden Rose To a New England poet for distinguished achievement in poetry. The hand-made gold rose is awarded annually.

Joyce Glueck Poetry Prizes Open to young women poets at New England colleges. Cash award presented annually.

THE NEW JERSEY POETRY SOCIETY Vivian Meyer President 6 Park Avenue Mine Hill Dover NJ 07801 U.S.A.

Annual competitions Write for details.

NEW MEXICO POETRY SOCIETY Information from: Lee Mays 310 Cedarcrest Drive Ripley WV 25271 U.S.A.

Franc Johnson Newcomb Memorial Award $25 1st prize is offered for a poem not exceeding 20 lines, any form, on the subject of the American Indian heritage.

NEW ORLEANS REVIEW Francis Sullivan Editor Loyola University 6363 St. Charles Avenue New Orleans LA 70118 U.S.A.

 oetry Prizes Author of the best poem published in each volume of the Review is given one page in an upcoming issue for any poem he wishes to publish.

NEW POETRY: JOURNAL OF THE POETRY SOCIETY OF AUSTRALIA Robert Adamson Editor P.O. Box 110 Grosvenor Street Post Office Sydney N.S.W. 2000 Australia

New Poetry Award $100 awarded annually for previously unpublished work. Contest usually closes around August of each year.

NEW STATESMAN 10 Great Turnstile London U.K. WC1V 7HJ

The New Statesman is about to set up an annual poetry prize, starting in 1974. It is restricted to poems which appear in the paper over the year.

THE NEW YORK POETRY FORUM Miss Dorothea Neale Director Box 855 Madison

Square Station 149 East 23rd Street New York NY 10010 U.S.A.

The New York Poetry Forum has conducted its Fifth Annual Awards Contest offering prizes in twenty-two categories, with a total of over four hundred dollars in cash, plus book and membership prizes, and readings at Forum programs. The annual awards contest closes November 15th of each year and are open to all poets who write in English. A number of the categories are repeated annually but a few are dropped and new ones added.

Mary F. Lindsley Award

Henry Rago Memorial Award

Bessie Wherry Noe Award

Maurice Farnelle Award

Gustav Davidson Memorial Award

Katherine Lee Bates Award

Sam Negrin Award

Eleanor Otto Award

Robert Martin Award

Louise Louis Award

A. Gordon King Award

Louise Bogan Memorial Prize in Poetry

East Side Herald Award

Will Anthony Madden Memorial Award

Lillian Steinhauer Award

Richard Alan Miller Award

Mayves Zantell Lyric Award

Beatrice Feldmann Award

Gladys Brown Award

Mason Sonnet Award

Sylvia Argow Awards – Love Sonnet Award

Sylvia Argow Awards – Argonelle Award

NORTH AMERICAN MENTOR MAGAZINE 1730 Lincoln Avenue Fennimore WI 53809 U.S.A.

Poetry Contest $100 cash awards for poems not exceeding 50 lines. $9 entry fee which includes a one-year subscription to the magazine. Fee is not required for paid subscribers for the year of the contest entered. Send poems no later than September 1 to Contest Editor, Mentor, Drawer 69, Fennimore, WI 53809.

NORTH CAROLINA FEDERATION OF WOMEN'S CLUB

Separk Sonnet Cup

John Henry Bonner Poetry Lover's Cup

NORTH CAROLINA POETRY SOCIETY, INC. Mrs. Betty Daly Corres. Secretary Box 108 Broadway N.C. 27505 U.S.A.

Thomas H. McDill Award Open to North Carolina residents only. Entrance fee to all non-members of NCPS Inc. General category, any subject, any form up to 24 lines.

Sidney Lanier Award Open to North Carolina residents only. Entrance fee for non-members. Any traditional sonnet form.

Caldwell W. Nixon Award Open to North Carolina residents only. Entrance fee for non-members. Any subject, any form, to 32 lines, to be written for children ages 2–12 years of age.

Brotherhood Award Open to all poets writing in English. Entrance fee for non-members. Any form, to 24 lines, on the subject of brotherhood.

Carl Sandburg Award Open to all poets writing in English. Entrance fee for non-members. Any subject, experimental forms, to 24 lines.

Ogden Nash Award Open to all poets writing in English. Light verse, any form, to 24 lines.

Student Contest Open to North Carolina residents only. Any subject, any form, to 24 lines, by High School students.

Travis Jordan Contest Open to children in grades 3 to 8 who are residents of North Carolina. Any subject, any form, to 24 lines.

All annual contests close on March 1 of each year. Contest chairman varies from year to year; please write for updated information.

THE FRANK O'HARA FOUNDATION 145 West 45th Street New York NY 10036 U.S.A.

The Frank O'Hara Award for Poetry To a poet who has not yet had a book of poetry published or accepted for publication. $1,000 given annually.

OHIO UNIVERSITY PRESS Administration Annex Ohio University Athens OH 45701 U.S.A.

Cecil Hemley Poetry Prize $1,500 awarded every two years for an outstanding volume of poetry or verse translation from another language published by the Ohio University Press.

OTHER VOICES Jane Johnson Editor 1226 Richmond Street London Ontario Canada

Prizes are offered for poems which appear in 'Other Voices'.

THE OUTSIDER John E. & Gypsy Lou Webb Editors 1009 E. Elm Tucson AZ 85702 U.S.A.

Prizes are offered for poems which appear in 'The Outsider'.

OYEZ REVIEW Ms. Civia Cohen Editor 430 S. Michigan Avenue Chicago IL 60605 U.S.A.

Poetry Contest Held twice a year offering prizes of $30 and $20 plus publication.

PENN LAUREL POETS Information from: Lee Mays 310 Cedarcrest Drive Ripley WV 25271 U.S.A.

Eleanor Aman Crump Memorial Award $25 first prize is offered for a poem of any form, 30 lines or less, on the subject of "Mysticism of the Soul-Reincarnation, etc.".

PENNSYLVANIA POETRY SOCIETY Ms. Jessie Ruhl Miller Treasurer 670 W. Louther Street Carlisle PA 17013 U.S.A.

The Eunice Pond Laselle Memorial Award Open to all juniors and seniors of English and Creative Writing Classes in the High Schools of the Commonwealth of Pennsylvania. $10 first prize and $5 second prize offered for the best poems on any subject, any form, 16 line limit.

The Bruce De Marco Memorial Award Restrictions as in the above award. $6 1st prize and $4 2nd prize offered to the best poems on the future, any form, 16 line limit.

Light Verse Award Restrictions as above. One prize of $5 for a poem of 9 lines or less.

Deadline for these awards in the Pennsylvania Pegasus Contest is February 1. Mail to: Contest Chairman, Pennsylvania Pegasus awards, 10 Cherry Lane, Wynnewood, Pa. 19096, U.S.A.

In the Annual Contest the following categories are open to all poets.

Grand Prize Any subject, any form, 50 lines or less. Entry fee to all contestants $2 per poem, limit 3 poems. One prize of $50.

Colonel Henry W. Shoemaker Memorial Award Three prizes of $10, $6 and $4 are sponsored by the Harrisburg Workshop & Proceeds from Endowment Fund for poems on Pennsylvania History or Folklore, any form, 24 lines or less. Entry fee for non-members.

Katherine Lyons Clark Award Three prizes of $10, $6 and $4 are sponsored by Katherine Lyons Clark for free verse, 20 lines or less. Entry fee for non-members.

Edna Shoemaker Award Three prizes sponsored by Edna Shoemaker for poems of any form, 24 lines or less. Entry fee for non-members.

Edna Groff Diehl Memorial Award Two prizes sponsored by Amelia Reynolds Long & Carlisle Poets Workshop for narrative poems, any form, 28 lines or less. Entry fee for non-members.

Experimental Poetry Award Will S. Pollard sponsors one prize of $25 for a poem with originality of subject, construction and approach. 28 lines or less. Entry fee for non-members.

Kate Heanue Award Georgia Pierce sponsors one prize of $15 for a rhymed poem of 12 lines or less. Entry fee for non-members.

Sylvia Plath Award One prize of $25 is sponsored by Ingrid Gleeson for a poem on woman's identity, any form, 28 lines or less. Entry fee for non-members.

The following categories in the Annual Contest are open to Pennsylvania Poetry Society members only.

Blanche Whiting Keysner Memorial Award Three monetary prizes are offered for Petrarchan or Shakespearean sonnets.

C. Sterling Clifton Award Three monetary prizes from $4 are offered for portraits, any form, 24 lines or less.

Sans Souci Award Sponsored by Louise Clayton Young. $10 offered for light verse, 8 lines or less.

THE PERPETUAL TRUST CO. LTD. 33-39 Hunter Street Sydney NSW 2000 Australia

Grace Leven Prize for Poetry $200 offered. Contestants submitting a volume of poetry published during the preceding 12 months must be Australian born or resident for at least 10 years.

PHOENIX POETRY SOCIETY Information

from: Lee Mays 310 Cedarcrest Drive Ripley WV 25271 U.S.A.

Phoenix Poetry Society Award $25, $15 and $5 are offered for poems of any form, 50 lines or less, on the Phoenix Bird.

POESIE SYMBOLISTE RENAISSANTE Information from: M. Herve Anglard 32 rue de la Conque 87 Limoges France

Prix de Poesie Symboliste Renaissante

POET AND CRITIC Richard Gustafson Editor 210 Pearson Hall Iowa State University Ames IA 50010 U.S.A.

Prizes are offered to poets whose poems are published in the Poet and Critic.

POET LORE John William Andrews Editor-in-Chief 52 Cranbury Road Westport CT 06880 U.S.A.

Stephen Vincent Benet Narrative Poem Award Contestants need not be subscribers to Poet Lore. First prize $500, second prize $100, three third prizes $25 each, one Honorable Mention, ten Special Mentions. Only unpublished manuscripts will be accepted. Submit only narrative poems, not lyrics or collections of lyrics. Competition closes December 31.

The following are annual poetry awards offered by Poet Lore. Poems accepted for publication by Poet Lore are automatically eligible, when published, to compete for these awards.

Narrative Poem — $35, $30, $25

Subjective Poem $35, $30, $25

Descriptive Poem $35, $30, $25

Translation $35, $30, $25

Love Poem $35, $30, $25

POETRY LOVERS' FELLOWSHIP AND INTERNATIONAL FELLOWSHIP OF LITERATURE Miss Marjorie Dawson Hon. Secretary General Unicorn Meadow Clee Saint Margaret S. Shropshire U.K. SY7 9DT

Poetry Lovers' Fellowship Essay Prize Essay prize of £5 awarded annually for essay in English of 5,000 words.

POETRY MAGAZINE 1228 North Dearborn Parkway Chicago IL 60610 U.S.A.

Blumenthal-Leviton-Blonder Prize $200

George Dillon Memorial Prize $100

Bess Hokin Prize $100

Levinson Prize $500

Frank O'Hara Prize $500

Eunice Tietjens Prize $100

Union League Civic & Arts Foundation Prize $100

The Harriet Monroe Memorial Prize $100

POETRY SOCIETY 21 Earls Court Square London SW5 U.K.

The Alice Hunt Bartlett Prize "This prize will be awarded annually to the poet the Society most wishes to honour and encourage. The Prize of £200 will be awarded to him for his poems in a book published in English and presented in duplicate to the Society's Library in the year of publication. The closing date in each year is December 31st. Special consideration to newly emerged poets will be shown as far as merit warrants and to first published collections of their work. In such collections there should be not less than 20 poems or 400 lines. In the event of the poems being translated into English, the original poet must be alive and the prize will be divided equally between that poet and the translator".

The Greenwood Competition "The sum of £20 is offered as the Shirley Carter Greenwood Prize for the best single poem in open competition". Only one poem (unpublished) may be submitted by any one competitor, the length not to exceed 250 lines. Closing date in each year is July 31.

The Premium Competition Open to Society members only. Held three times a year with the total entrance fees as prize money. Only one poem may be entered by each competitor.

The Arnold Vincent Bowen Competition £10 is offered for the best single lyric poem in open competition. Only one poem up to 30 lines per contestant may be entered. Closing date is February 28 of each year.

The Gold Medal for Verse Speaking This is held twice a year in May and November. Entries should be received two months in advance.

POETRY SOCIETY OF AMERICA 15 Gramercy Park New York NY 10003 U.S.A.

The following contests are open to PSA members only.

The Gustav Davidson Memorial Award The award of $500 annually is for an unpublished sonnet, or sonnet sequence not to exceed three sonnets; any sonnet form.

Alice Fay di Castagnola Award This award of $3,500 annually is offered for a work-in-progress (prose or verse).

The Emily Dickinson Award $100 is awarded annually for a poem inspired by Emily Dickinson, although not necessarily in imitation of her style, not exceeding 30 lines, unpublished.

The Consuelo Ford Memorial Award The award of $250 annually is for an unpublished lyric poem not to exceed 50 lines.

The Cecil Hemley Memorial Award $300 is awarded annually for an unpublished lyric poem on a philosophical theme, up to 100 lines.

James Joyce Award $300 is awarded annually for an original, unpublished poem in French form.

The Alfred Kreymborg Memorial Award $100 for an original and unpublished poem of merit in any form or freedom, not to exceed 100 lines.

The Lucille Medwick Memorial Award For an original, unpublished poem on an humanitarian theme, any form, up to 100 lines. $500 annually.

The Christopher Morley Memorial Award $500 annually for an unpublished poem of light verse, not to exceed 100 lines.

The Poetry Society of America Awards Three awards of $300, $200, and $200 are awarded annually for the three poems chosen as best among those which won awards in the PSA monthly contests. The awards are given to the poets whose poems (printed anonymously) received the highest votes.

The Devil's Advocate Award $200 is given to the poet whose poem is judged best among the poems which appeared on the monthly contest sheets but which failed to win prizes.

William Marion Reedy Memorial Award $300 for an original, unpublished poem in free form on any theme, up to 100 lines.

The following awards are open to all poets:

The Elias Lieberman Student Poetry Award $100 is awarded annually for the best unpublished poem by a high school or preparatory school student in the U.S.A.

Melville Cane Award $500 is given annually by Harcourt, Brace Jovanovich, Inc. for a book of poems or a prose work on a poet or on poetry. Books must be submitted by the publisher.

Shelley Memorial Award This award of $1,800 annually is non-competitive and is given for a poet's entire work. Selection is made by a jury and, therefore, applications are not accepted.

The John Masefield Memorial Award $500 given annually for an unpublished narrative poem, up to 200 lines, written in English.

POETRY SOCIETY OF GEORGIA Rev. M. Tom Dunlap President 65 Cronwell Road Savannah GA 31404 U.S.A.

The Poetry Society of Georgia Contest $200 in prizes.

POETRY SOCIETY OF MICHIGAN Elizabeth K. Wathen Corres. Secretary 1474 Beach Street Muskegon MI 49441 U.S.A.

Annual Competitions Please write for details.

POETRY SOCIETY OF NEW HAMPSHIRE, INC. 19 Montgomery Street Concord NH 03301 U.S.A.

Annual Competitions Please write for details.

POETRY SOCIETY OF OKLAHOMA 5517 N. Shawnee Oklahoma City OK 73112 U.S.A.

Annual Competitions including the Mize Award.

POETRY SOCIETY OF TENNESSEE Dr. Rosemary Stephens President 64 N Yates Road Memphis TN 38117 U.S.A.

Poetry Society of Tennessee Award $25 is offered for a poem of 30 lines or less, any subject, any form.

POETRY SOCIETY OF TEXAS Faye Carr Adams, Corres. Secretary, 4244 Skillman Avenue Dallas TX 75206 U.S.A.

Aline B. Carter Peace Prize $50 awarded annually for best poem on world harmony. 40 lines or less. U.S.A. resident.

Cyclotron Prize $25 awarded annually. To all poets writing in English.

Lan & Willie Davis Award $100 awarded annually. 100 lines or less on conflict between the old and young generations.

Harry Kovner Memorial Award $25 awarded annually. U.S.A. resident.

The Nyogen Senzaki Memorial Haiku

Award $25 to any poet for best traditional Haiku.

Abbie Frank Smith Memorial Award To a resident of U.S.A. for a poem of 100 lines or less on the rights of Americans to own protective weapons. $100 given annually.

POETRY SOCIETY OF TEXAS, ODESSA CHAPTER Information from: Lee Mays 310 Cedarcrest Drive Ripley WV 25271 U.S.A.

Poetry Society of Texas Odessa Chapter Award $25 awarded for poem of 50 lines or less, any form, southwestern theme.

POETRY SOCIETY OF VIRGINIA Louis Carlton President 3213 Seminary Avenue Richmond VA 23227 U.S.A.

The Helen Rushfeldt Duff Memorial Prize $75 for an in memoriam sonnet on any one of these subjects: Edgar Allan Poe, Virginia Clemm Poe, Sidney Lanier. Form to be either Petrarchan, Spenserian or Shakespearean. Restricted to Poetry Society of Virginia members.

The Leitch Memorial Prize $50 for a poem in any form, not to exceed 28 lines, on the sea. Open to PSV members only.

The Keats Memorial Sonnet Prize $50 for a sonnet. Open to residents of Virginia.

The Keats Memorial Lyric Prize $50 for a lyric not exceeding 42 lines. Open to residents of Virginia only.

The Stanley Corprew Paul Memorial Prize $25 for a poem on peace.

The Mason Sonnet Prize $50 for the best Mason sonnet.

The Mildred Hutzler Memorial Prize $25 for light verse not to exceed 28 lines.

POETRY WORKSHOP OF THE LYNCHBURG WOMAN'S CLUB Dr. Roberta D. Cornelius Chairman Parkmont Apartments Rivermont Avenue Lynchburg VA 24503 U.S.A.

Annual Competitions Please write for details.

POETS AND PATRONS, INC. Evelyn Schmidt President 4205 Madison Avenue Brookfield IL 60513 U.S.A.

Annual Awards Twenty contests are offered with first and second prizes of $10 and $5 respectively. Grand prize of $50 is awarded to the poem considered best of all first prize winners.

'On Second Thought' Award $25 to the best of the second place winners. Offered by Cliff and Anne Nolan to honor late Hazel Frazee.

POETS' ROUNDTABLE OF ARKANSAS Geneva I. Crook Treasurer 2304 E. 2nd Street North Little Rock AR 72114 U.S.A.

Annual Competitions The Poets' Roundtable of Arkansas observes annual National Poetry Day on October 15. Announcement of the contests for 1974 will not be made until August 1974 when the contest chairman will be elected. Until then we do not know what categories there will be for members and non-members. The 1973 contests had 33 categories with a total prize money of $1,115. Please write for details.

POETS' CLUB OF CHICAGO Mary Torode Contest Chairman 1541 N. Avers Avenue Chicago IL 60651 U.S.A.

Annual Shakespearean Sonnet Contest Three awards for first, second and third ($20, $10, $5)

POETS' STUDY CLUB OF TERRE HAUTE, INDIANA Mrs. Vera Koppler Contest Chairman Route 2, Box 243 Marshall IL 62441 U.S.A.

Serious Poems $20, $15 and $5 will be awarded for best serious poems written in English. Open to all poets. February 1, 1975 is deadline for the 1974-75 contest.

Light Verse $10 and $5 will be given to best light verse written in English. Deadline is Feb. 1, 1975. Open to all poets but only one poem per contestant may be entered.

Haiku Prize is $5. Poem must be in English, only one per contestant, open to all poets. Deadline is Feb. 1, 1975.

POETS TAPE EXCHANGE Frances Brandon Neighbours Director 109 Twin Oak Drive Lynchburg VA 24502 U.S.A.

Contests Contests will be conducted with prizes of money, books and tapes. Each member is eligible to enter all contests offered by the Exchange.

PRESTON POETS' SOCIETY Mrs. Celia Harvey Hon. Secretary 8 Whitefield Road East Penwortham Preston Lancs. U.K.

MacKenzie Cup

Pomfret Cup

PRISM INTERNATIONAL Jacob Zibler

Editor Dept. of Creative Writing University of British Columbia Vancouver 8 British Columbia Canada

Prizes Please write for details.

PRIX ANTONIN ARTAUD Rules from: Mme. Christiane Burucoa 68 Avenue Jean-Jaures 12 Millau France

Prix Antonin Artaud This prize will be given for the 23rd time on April 20, 1974. It will be for a collection of French poems edited since 1972. Winner receives 1000 Francs sponsored by The General Council of Aveyron, Municipal Council of Rodez and Rodez Savings Bank.

PRIX CLAUDE SERNET Rules from: Mme. Christiane Burucoa 68 Avenue Jean-Jaures 12 Millau France

Prix Claude Sernet 500 Francs will be given for the 6th time in 1974. Contest may not be entered as a Jury selects winner from collections of poems which appeared during the past 2 years. This prize is given through a private endowment.

PRIX ILARIE VORONCA Rules from: Mme. Christiane Burucoa 68 Avenue Jean-Jaures 12 Millau France

Prix Ilarie Voronca This prize is given for manuscripts of French poems which will then be published by Jean Subervie. Sponsored by General Council of Aveyron, Municipal Council of Rodez, Rodez Savings Bank.

PRIX INTERNATIONAUX DE POESIE CLASSIQUE JULES SOTTIAUX (Jules Sottiaux International Prizes for Classical Poetry) Information from: M. Paul Philippe 189 rue de Marchienne 6110 Montigny-Le-Tilleul Belgium

Prix Internationaux De Poesie Classique Jules Sottiaux For unpublished poems, no limit as to subject or length, classical style. Art objects worth 10,000 Belgian Francs will be distributed to winners of this prize and the Roger Desaise International Prizes for Free Verse or Classical Poetry. Entry fee of 50 Belgian Francs for each poem. Deadline date is May 30 of each year.

PRIX INTERNATIONAUX DE POESIE LIBRE OU CLASSIQUE ROGER DESAISE (Roger Desaise International Prizes for Free Verse or Classical Poetry) Information from: Mr. Paul Philippe 189 rue de Marchienne 6110 Montigny-Le-Tilleul Belgium

Prix Internationaux De Poesie Libre Ou Classique Roger Desaise This prize will be presented for the fourth time in 1974. For Free Verse or Classical Poetry, no limit as to subject or length. Art objects worth 10,000 Belgian Francs will be distributed between the winners of this prize and the Jules Sottiaux International Prizes for Classical Poetry. Entry fee of 50 Belgian francs per poem. Deadline date is May 30 of each year.

THE PROMETHEAN LAMP John T. Campbell Editor 2174 34th Street Sacramento CA 95801 U.S.A.

Prizes Please write for details.

PULITZER PRIZE Trustee of Columbia University New York NY 10027 U.S.A.

The Pulitzer Prizes Several prizes of $1,000 each are awarded annually to American authors for the most distinguished book of poetry, non-fiction, biography, history, novel or play. Nomination only.

Queen's Gold Medal For Poetry Awarded for a book of verse from a British subject. May not be applied for.

QUINTO SOL PUBLICATIONS, INC. P.O. Box 9275 Berkley CA 94709 U.S.A.

Premio Quinto Sol For Literature Annual literary prize of $1,000. For the best literary work of the year (novel, collection of short stories, book-length essay, poetry, experimental writing). Restricted to writers of Mexican descent who are residents of the U.S.A. Deadline date is January 31.

Chicano Perspective Award $2,000 plus royalties from publication of winning entry. Deadline date is September 30.

REAL ACADEMIA ESPANOLA Felipe IV No. 4 Madrid Spain

Premio Fastenrath First given five years ago; next award will be made in October, 1976. Last winner was Dr. Aquilino Duque Gimeno for his poetry.

RICHMOND WRITERS' CIRCLE Room 4 Richmond Community Centre Richmond Surrey U.K.

Nesbitt-Kemp Cup Competition

ROANOKE-CHOWAN GROUP Through the N.C. Literary & Historical Association Box 1881 Raleigh NC 27602 U.S.A.

Roanoke-Chowan Cup For Poetry Open to North Carolina residents for a book of poetry published in the twelve months preceding June 30 of the year for which the award is applied for.

THE DOROTHY ROSENBERG POETRY AWARD Barbara Greenberg 47 Dilphin Road Newton MA 02159 U.S.A.

The Dorothy Rosenberg Poetry Award $50 for the best poem on the spirit of man.

ROYAL NATIONAL EISTEDDFOD OF WALES Swyddfa'r Eisteddfod Rhyd-y-Môr Criccieth Caernarvonshire Wales

The Awdl A poem of 250 to 300 lines on a set subject — 1975 subject is Afon (River) — written in strict metrical verse, according to the Welsh code known as "cynghanedd". The Eisteddfod Chair and a money prize of £100 is awarded. Entries must be submitted in the Welsh language by the 1st of April preceding the Eisteddfod.

The Pryddest A poem of 250 to 300 lines in the measure of the poet's own choice. Subject for 1975 is Pridd (Soil or Earth). The Eisteddfod Crown and a money prize of £100 is awarded. Entries must be submitted in the Welsh Language by the 1st of April preceding the Eisteddfod.

There are 10 to 12 other poetry competitions sponsored by the Royal National Eisteddfod of Wales which is held annually during the first week of August. Please write for details.

THE ROYAL SOCIETY OF LITERATURE 1 Hyde Park Gardens London W2 2LT U.K.

The Royal Society of Literature Award Under the W.H. Heinemann Bequest Publishers are invited to submit books for this award. Books submitted must have been published during the current year and must be written in the English language (no translations). The closing date is December 31. Open for poetry, biography, criticism, philosophy, history, novels etc. Up to three prizes may be given.

ST. LOUIS POETRY CENTER Jon Johnson President 223 Tiffen Street St. Louis MO 63135 U.S.A.

Annual Competitions Please write for details.

SAN FRANCISCO FOUNDATION 425 California Street Suite 1602 San Francisco CA 94104 U.S.A.

James S. Phelan Award For unpublished partly completed book-length works of fiction, non-fiction, drama and poetry. Applicants must have been born in California and be between the ages of 20 and 35. $2,000.

Joseph Henry Jackson Awards For unpublished partly completed book length works of fiction, non-fiction and poetry. Applicants must have been residents of Northern California or Nevada for the three years preceding the year for for which the award is given and be between the ages of 20 and 35. $2,000. Write to The San Francisco Foundation Awards Office for further information.

SATURDAY REVIEW 25 West 45th Street New York NY 10036 U.S.A.

The Anisfield-Wolf Award in Race Relations The first award is for a scholarly book published in the field of race relations and the second is given to the best book concerned with racial problems in the field of creative literature. Works of fiction, drama, poetry, biography or autobiography are eligible. The awards consist of $1,500 for each of the two books chosen.

SCHOCKEN FOUNDATION c/o F. Harry Brown 280 Park Avenue New York NY 10017 U.S.A.

Grants A few grants are available annually to U.S. citizens as a means of assistance to needy artists and writers.

THE SCOTTISH ARTS COUNCIL Dept. of Literature 19 Charlotte Square Edinburgh EH2 4DF Scotland

Book Awards and New Writing Awards "A limited number of awards, value of £300 each, are made each year by The Scottish Arts Council to published books of literary merit written by Scots or writers resident in Scotland. The Awards fall into two categories: Scottish Arts Council New Writing Awards for first books and Scottish Arts Council Book Awards for established authors. All types of books are eligible for consideration and the closing date is the 31st October of each year. Books are sponsored by the authors' publisher who is asked to submit two copies of each title to the Council's Literature Dept."

Writers Bursaries "Each year the Council makes a number of awards to Scottish writers or writers resident in Scotland to enable them to devote themselves more fully to their art. Writers are asked to submit examples of their published and unpublished work and in some cases the Council will ask for candidates to be sponsored by other writers. Editors, literary agents, and academics are invited to bring suitable names to the Council's attention."

Travel Grants A limited number of travel grants are available each year.

University Fellowships The Council helps to maintain Writers in Residence posts at the Universities of Strathclyde and Glasgow. Each post is tenable for a single academic year and neither is confined to Scottish Writers. For further information contact the Professor of English at each University.

Writers in the Community A new type of Writers in Residence post was founded by the Council in Aberdeen in 1973. The writer will be based in Aberdeen Art Gallery but the entire community will have open access to him. A similar post will be founded in 1974 for a Gaelic writer on the Isle of Skye. The Council hopes to start other fellowships of this kind in other parts of Scotland.

SEVEN 21½ North Harvey (Terminal Arcade) Oklahoma City OK 73102 U.S.A.

Jesse Stuart Contest International, annual contest for the best unpublished poems in the Jesse Stuart tradition; any form or free verse; no restrictions on length. Monetary prizes of $25, $15, $10, and $5. Closing date is February 1 of each year.

SHENANDOAH COLLEGE AND CONSERVATORY OF MUSIC Bruce Souders Chairman Arts and Sciences Faculty Shenandoah College and Conservatory of Music Winchester VA 22601 U.S.A.

The Poetry Contest of the Shenandoah Festival of the Arts The contest is open only to college students at the undergraduate or graduate school level under the age of 30. Individual poems should not exceed 30 lines and be of lyric form. Limit of 2 poems per contestant. Entry fee. $50 first prize, $25 second prize, and $10 third prize. Deadline date is usually around January 15 of each year.

W.H. SMITH & SON LTD. Strand House Portugal Street London WC2 U.K.

The W.H. Smith & Son Annual Literary Award The £1,000 award is presented annually for the book which, in the opinion of the panel of independent judges, represents "the most outstanding contribution to English literature for the year in question". The winning book in 1972 was a collection of poems by Kathleen Raine. Entries are not sought or accepted from authors, publishers or others.

THE SOCIETY OF AUTHORS 84 Drayton Gardens London S.W.10 U.K.

The Eric Gregory Trust Fund Award These annual awards are made for the encouragement of young poets under the age of 30. Candidates must be British subjects by birth but not nationals of Eire or any of the British Dominions or Colonies and ordinarily resident in the United Kingdom or Northern Ireland. The sum varies from year to year but in a recent year there were four awards amounting to £1,000.

The Somerset Maugham Awards Poetry, fiction, criticism, biography, history, philosophy, belles-lettres, travel books are all eligible for the awards of about £500 each. Authors entering for the awards must be British subjects by birth but not Nationals of Eire or any of the British Dominions; ordinarily resident in the United Kingdom or Northern Ireland; be under the age of 35. The winners are required to use the money for a period of foreign travel of not less than three months.

Cholmondeley Award for Poets Non-competitive.

SOCIETY OF MIDLAND AUTHORS 2020 N. Howe Street Chicago IL 60614 U.S.A.

Midland Poetry Award For a collection of poetry by an author who is resident in the mid-west of America. Monetary prize of $250 is awarded annually.

SONS OF THE REPUBLIC OF TEXAS 2426 Watts Road Houston TX 77025 U.S.A.

Summerfield G. Roberts Prize Poetry books are eligible for this annual prize of $1,000. Open to U.S.A. citizens for a book which describes or represents the Republic of Texas.

SOUTH DAKOTA STATE POETRY SOCIETY AND SOUTH DAKOTA BICENTENNIAL COMMISSION Dr. Harold M. Jordan President S. Dakota State Poetry Society 917 Ridgecrest Drive Vermillion S.D. 57069 U.S.A.

National Bicentennial Poetry Contest Monetary prizes of $100, $50 and $25 are offered for poems of 50 lines or less, any form, on the subject of Festival U.S.A.

SOUTH AND WEST INC. Ms. Sue Abbott Boyd President 2601 S. Phoenix Ft. Smith AR 72901 U.S.A.

Poetry Book Publication Award Open to members of National Federation of State Poetry Societies. Books of poems are eligible. Author will receive 50 copies of book gratis. Closing date was April 1, 1974.

SPECTRUM P.O. Box 14800 University of California Santa Barbara CA 93107 U.S.A.

The magazine offers a poetry prize of $100 for the best work in poetry.

STORY MAGAZINE George Dickerson Poetry Editor 53 W. 43rd Street New York NY 10036 U.S.A.

Prizes offered for poems which were published in the magazine.

TEXAS INSTITUTE OF LETTERS Martin Shockley Secretary-Treasurer N. T. Box 5712 Denton TX 76203 U.S.A.

The Voertman's Poetry Award $200 is given to the best book of poetry. Books by Texas authors (one who was born in Texas, who presently resides in Texas, or who spent formative years in Texas) or books about Texas are eligible.

The Texas Collectors' Institute Award (Best Book Design) Books entered for the above award may also be entered for this award.

THE TRANSLATORS' ASSOCIATION 84 Drayton Gardens London S.W.10 U.K.

The John Florio Prize $200 awarded annually for the best translation into English of a 20th century Italian work. Work to have been published in the preceding year by British publisher.

The Schlegel-Tieck Prize Awarded annually for best translation of a 20th century German work published by a British publisher in the preceding year.

Classical Prize Bi-annual award for new translation of works written before 1900.

The Scott-Moncrieff Prize £400 awarded annually for best translation of 20th century French work published by a British publisher in the preceding year.

UNIVERSITY OF CHICAGO Division of the Humanities 1010 East 59th Street Chicago IL 60637, U.S.A.

Harriet Montroe Poetry Award One award of $500 is given periodically to a poet of achievement or promise who is a citizen of the U.S.A. Open only by nomination.

UNIVERSITY OF LIVERPOOL The Registrar P.O. 147 Liverpool L69 3BX U.K.

Felicia Hemans Prize for Lyrical Poetry Open to past and present members and students of University College or of the University of Liverpool. Prize will consist of a bronze medal and monetary prize. Deadline date is May 1 of each year.

UNIVERSITY OF MINNESOTA PRESS 2037 University Avenue S.E. Minneapolis MN 55455 U.S.A.

McKnight Awards One award of $1,000 and two awards of $750 each are awarded annually to the authors of the most distinguished books published by the University of Minnesota Press in the year under review.

UNIVERSITY OF SHEFFIELD The Registrar & Secretary Sheffield S10 2TN U.K.

The Arthur Markham Memorial Prize A group of six poems or a single poem are eligible for this prize. Candidates must fall into one of the following classes: men or youths who are engaged as manual workers in or about a coal mine in England or Scotland or Wales, earning weekly or daily wages; men or youths who have at some time been engaged in such occupation and have been injured in their employment. A sum of about £75 will be available for the prize.

UTAH STATE POETRY SOCIETY Kathryn Kay President 982 Jasper Circle Salt Lake City Utah 84106 U.S.A.

Utah State Award $25 first prize is offered for a poem of 42 lines or less, any subject, any form.

VER POETS The Secretary 61-63 Chiswell Green Lane St. Albans Herts U.K.

Michael Johnson Memorial Poetry Competition £20 first prize is offered for an original, unpublished poem, 40 lines or less, any subject.

VERSE WRITERS GUILD OF OHIO

Information from: Lee Mays 310 Cedarcrest Drive Ripley WV 25271 U.S.A.

Verse Writers Guild of Ohio Contest $25 first prize is offered for a poem of 24 lines or less, any form, about birds or a bird.

THE VILLAGER Mrs. Ted W. Proudfoot Poetry Editor 135 Midland Avenue Bronxville NY 10708 U.S.A.

Prizes Offered for poems which appear in the Villager.

VIRGINIA COMMONWEALTH UNIVERSITY English Department 910 West Franklin Street Richmond VA 23220 U.S.A.

$25 is offered for a poem in Marlowe's mighty line blank verse which is iambic pentameter unrhymed. Open to college students only.

VIRGINIA QUARTERLY REVIEW 1 West Range Charlottesville VA 22903 U.S.A.

Emily Clark Balch Prizes Three prizes from $250 to $1,000 are given annually for short stories and poetry alternately. Poetry award is 1974 and short story award is 1975. Open to U.S.A. citizens.

WELSH ARTS COUNCIL Museum Place Cardiff, Wales CF1 3NX

The Welsh Arts Council Awards to Writers A number of awards are open to Welsh and Anglo-Welsh authors who have contributed to the literature of Wales.

WEST VIRGINIA POETRY SOCIETY Thursa A. Pratt President 1625 Oak Street Parkersburg WV 26101 U.S.A.

Annual competitions The contests are primarily open to members of WVPS only. There is a deadline date of August 1st each year and the contest chairman, the sponsors and rules are all subject to change each year. There are, however, four permanent categories open to all poets: Traditional, $25; Modern, $15; Limerick, $10; Haiku, $5. There are 17 categories sponsored by WVPS Chapters and individuals open to members only.

WICHITA FALLS POETRY SOCIETY Information from: Lee Mays 310 Cedarcrest Drive Ripley WV 25271 U.S.A.

Wichita Falls Poetry Society Award $25 first prize is offered for a poem of 40 lines or less, any form, on the subject of finding joy in living.

THE WISCONSIN FELLOWSHIP OF POETS Frances May President 309 Joliet Avenue Sturgeon Bay WI 54235 U.S.A.

Wisconsin Poetry Contest $35 first prize is offered for a poem of 50 lines or less, any subject, any form.

WISCONSIN POETRY A.M. Sterk Editor 2821 E. Belleview Place Milwaukee WI 53202 U.S.A.

Prizes Offered for poems which are published in Wisconsin Poetry.

WORLD FESTIVAL OF NEGRO ARTS LITERARY PRIZES National Book League 7 Albemarle Street London W.1 U.K.

World Festival of Negro Arts Literary Prizes A collection of poetry in English or French is eligible for these prizes. Open only to Negro authors. Awarded every four years (awarded in 1974). One "Grand Literary" prize and various others in cash.

WRITER'S DIGEST 9933 Alliance Road Cincinnati OH 45242 U.S.A.

Writer's Digest Creative Writing Contest For articles, short stories and poetry (not to exceed 16 lines). Prizes of typewriters, cassette recorders etc.

YALE UNIVERSITY LIBRARY New Haven CT 06520 U.S.A.

Bolligen Prize in Poetry of the Yale University Library "The Prize is awarded biennially to the American poet whose work, in the opinion of the Committee of Award, represents the highest achievement in the field of American poetry during the two-year period under review. The award, in the amount of $5,000 is based upon published work and, if possible, upon work published during the two-year period, although prior achievement may be taken into consideration. Individuals who are citizens of the United States, either by birth or naturalization, are eligible for the prize". The prize will next be awarded in January 1975; the two years under review at that time will be 1973 and 1974. Authors and publishers are *not* encouraged to submit work for consideration.

YALE UNIVERSITY PRESS 92A Yale Station New Haven CT 06520 U.S.A.

The Yale Series of Younger Poets Open to any writer under forty years of age who has not previously published a volume of poetry. The winning manuscript (48 to 64 pages, with no more than one poem on a page) is published by the Yale University Press and the author receives the usual royalties.

YANKEE, INC. Dublin NH 03444 U.S.A.

Yankee Poetry Contest The best three poems published in the magazine during the previous year are awarded prizes by the judges. The prizes are $100 first prize; $50 second prize; $25 third prize.

YR ACADEMI GYMREIG Dr. John Rowlands Secretary Dôl Bebin Pen-y-garn Bow Street Ceredigion Cards. Wales SY24 5BE

Gwobr Goffa Griffith John Williams (The Griffith John Williams Memorial Prize) Awarded annually for a volume of creative literature by an author who is not a member of Yr Academi Gymreig. The volume can be in any form, and volumes of poetry have in the past been awarded the prize.

APPENDIX H

POETRY ON RECORD AND TAPE

Angel Records

Hollywood and Vine Streets, Hollywood 28, CA, U.S.A.
This company records classical music primarily. However, the following poetry recordings are available.

B–3505 T.S. ELIOT. Murder in the Cathedral. Two record set.

60042 Shakespeare: 20 Sonnets. Read by Dame Edith Evans, T.S. Eliot, and Noel Rawsthorne. Practical Cats: read by Robert Donat with the Philharmonia Orchestra, Rawsthorne conducting.

Argo Records

115 Fulham Road, London S.W.3, U.K.

AUTHORS AND THEIR WORKS

PLP 1049 ARNOLD, CLOUGH, FITZGERALD
Arnold: Palladium, Dover Beach, To Marguerite (II), Growing Old, The Scholar Gipsy, others. Clough: It Fortifies my soul to know, Say Not the Struggle, The Latest Decalogue, others. Fitzgerald: Numerous stanzas from The Rubaiyat of Omar Khayyam. Read by Marius Goring, Ian Holm, Derek Jacobi.

PLP 1062 AUDEN, Wystan Hugh
Homage to Clio, The Shield of Achilles, Metalogue to the Magic Flute, The Hard Question, others. Read by the author.

ZPL 1058 The Battle of Maldon and other Old English Poems In translations by Kevin Crossley-Holland.
The Battle of Maldon, Eleven Riddles and a Charm, The Ruin, The Wife's Lament, Caedmon's Hymn, The Wanderer, The Dream of the Rood. Read by Frank Duncan, David King, George Rylands, Prunella Scales, Peter Orr, Gary Watson.

PLP 1118 BELLOC, Hilaire
Four Sussex poems: The South country, Duncton Hill, My own country, Ha'nacker Mill; Heroic poem in praise of wine, others. Read by Robert Speaight.

SW 506 BELLOC, Hilaire
Cautionary Tales read by Peter Ustinov.

ZPL 1057 BEOWULF
Includes Beowulf comes to Denmark and to Heorot, Beowulf kills Grendel, Beowulf fights the dragon, others. Read by Frank Duncan, Kevin Crossley-Holland, Peter Orr, George Rylands, Prunella Scales, David King, Gary Watson.

PLP 1067 BETJEMAN, John
Includes Harrow-on-the-Hill, Upper Lambourne, Wantage bells, The heart of Thomas Hardy, The arrest of Oscar Wilde, In a Bath teashop, Matlock Bath, others. Read by the author.

PLP 1069 BETJEMAN, John
Summoned by Bells – selections from the autobiography. Read by the author.

PLP 1035 BLAKE, William
Selections from Songs of Innocence, Songs of Experience, Poetical Sketches, Gnomic Verses, others. Read by Alan Bates, Yvonne Bonnamy, William Devlin, Richard Johnson, Richard Marquand, Peter Orr.

PLP 1110/1 BRATHWAITE, Edward
Rights of Passage. Includes Prelude, New World A-comin', Tom, The Emigrants, South, others. Read by the author.

PLP 1047 BROWNING, Robert
Record One: Includes Love in a Life, Life in a love, Meeting at night, Parting at Morning, The lost mistress, Confessions, others. Read by Max Adrian, Alan Bates, Frank Duncan, Denis McCarthy.

PLP 1048 BROWNING, Robert
Record Two: Includes From The Ring and The Book, A Face, One Way of Love, Porphyria's Lover, Love Amoung the Ruins, others. Read by Max Adrian, David King, Gary Watson.

SW 506 BROWNING, Robert
The Pied Piper of Hamelin. Read by Peter Ustinov.

PLP 1040 BYRON, George Gordon (Lord)
Selections include She Walks in beauty, Childe Harold (Canto IV), Don Juan (Canto III), The Isles of Greece, So we'll go no more a-roving. Read by Frank Duncan, Richard Johnson, Peter Orr.

PLP 1041 BYRON, George Gordon (Lord)
Don Juan. Selections from Canto I and Canto II. Read by Peggy Ashcroft, Richard Johnson, Janette Richer.

PLP 1013 CAMPION, JONSON, HERRICK
Campion: Give beauty all her right, Now winter nights enlarge, Never love unless you can, My sweetest Lesbia, others. Jonson: On my first daughter, Epitaph on Elizabeth L.H., Tonight grave sir, Have you seen but a bright lily grow, Drink to me only, others. Wither: Shall I, wasting in despair. Drummond: This life, which seems so fair. Herrick: To Electra, Delight

in disorder, An Ode to Ben Jonson, Grace for a child, others. Shirley: The glories of our blood and state. Read by Peggy Ashcroft, Ian Holm, Richard Johnson, Peter Orr, John Stride.

ZTA 501/2 CARROL, Lewis
Alice In Wonderland.

ZTA 503/4 CARROL, Lewis
Through the Looking Glass.

SW 506 CARROL, Lewis
You Are Old Father William and The Walrus and the Carpenter. Read by Peter Ustinov.

PLP 1001 CHAUCER, Geoffrey
Prologue To The Canterbury Tales. Read in Middle English by Nevill Coghill, Norman Davis, John Burrow.

PLP 1002 CHAUCER, Geoffrey
The Nun's Priest's Tale. Read in Middle English by Nevill Coghill, Lena Davis, Norman Davis, John Burrow.

ZPL 1003/4 CHAUCER, Geoffrey
Troilus and Criseyde. Read in Middle English by Gary Watson, Prunella Scales, Richard Marquand, Derek Brewer, Peter Orr.

PLP 1039 COLERIDGE, Samuel Taylor
The Rime of the Ancient Mariner, Dejection: an ode, The Pains of Sleep, Lines from Christabel, others. Read by Yvonne Bonnamy, Richard Burton, William Devlin, John Neville, Robert Hardy.

PLP 1012 DONNE, John
Selections include: Goe, and catche a Falling Starre; The Indifferent; The Sunne Rising; The Canonization; A Valediction: Of Weeping; A Valediction: Forbidding Mourning; others. Read by Richard Johnson, Peter Orr and William Squire.

ZPL 1027 DRYDEN, John
Includes: Lines from Absalom and Achitophel, Part 1 and Part 2; To the memory of Mr. Oldham; Nell Gwynne's Epilogue to tyrannic love; Prologue to An Evening's Love; others. Read by Freda Dowie, David King and Richard Pasco.

PLP 1044 Early Victorian Poetry
Clare, Emily Bronte, Charlotte Bronte, Anne Bronte, E.B. Browning, Meredith. Read by Gary Watson, Jill Balcon, Freda Dowie and Ian Holm.

PLP 1108 ELIOT, Thomas Stearns
The Waste Land; Love Song of J. Alfred Prufrock; The Hollow Men; Ash Wednesday. Read by Robert Speaight.

PLP 1109 ELIOT, Thomas Stearns
Four Quartets. Burnt Norton; East Coker; The Dry Salvages; Little Gidding. Read by Robert Speaight.

SW 504 ELIOT, Thomas Stearns
Old Possum's Book of Practical Cats. The naming of cats; The old Gumbie cat; The Rum Tum Tugger; The song of the Jellicles; Mr. Mistoffelees; others. Read by the author.

PLP 1009 Elizabethan And Jacobean Lyric
Wyatt: What should I say; And Wilt Thou Leave Me Thus; others. Queen Elizabeth: When I was fair and young. Sidney: My true love hath my heart. Oxford: Were I a king. Lodge: Love in my bosom. Marlowe: Come, live with me. Munday: I serve a mistress. Dyer: The lowest trees. Nashe: Adieu, farewell earth's bliss. Others. Read by Peggy Ashcroft, Ian Holm, Richard Johnson, John Stride.

PLP 1010 Elizabethan Sonneteers And Spenser.
Surrey, Sidney, Greville, Daniel, Drayton, Constable, Barnes, Barnfield, Stirling, Davies of Hereford, Drummond, Spenser. Read by Ian Holm, Richard Johnson, George Rylands, John Stride.

PLP 1152 FORSTER, Edward Morgan
What I believe, The road from Colonus. Read by the author.

PLP 1063 GRAVES, Robert Ranke
The Bards, Full moon, It was all very tidy, To walk on hills, Prometheus, others. Read by the author.

PLP 1053 HARDY, Thomas
Record One: Great Things, My Spirit will not haunt the Mound, Lausanne – In Gibbon's Old Garden, Tess's Lament, The Phantom Horsewoman, others. Read by Ian Holm, Richard Pasco, Barbara Jefford.

PLP 1054 HARDY, Thomas
Record Two: He revisits his First School, The Youth who carried a Light, The Christening, The Tresses, The Haunter, others. Read by Ian Holm, Richard Pasco, Barbara Jefford, David King.

PLP 1051 HOPKINS, Gerard Manley
Pied Beauty, God's Grandeur, The Caged Skylark, The Wreck of the Deutschland, Peace, The May Magnificat, others. Read by Michael Redgrave, Barbara Jefford, George Rylands and Richard Pasco.

PLP 1093 JONES, David
The Anathemata (Excerpts), In Parenthesis (Excerpts), The Hunt. Read by David Jones.

PLP 1043 KEATS, John
On first looking into Chapman's Homer, A thing of beauty, La Belle Dame Sans Merci, Ode to Autumn, Ode on Melancholy, others. Read by Tony Church, Derek Godfrey, Richard Johnson, Margaretta Scott, Gary Watson.

PLP 1055 KIPLING, Rudyard
The River's Tale, Romulus and Remus, The Pirates in England, The Holy War, others. Read by Michael Bates, Richard Johnson, Patrick Wymark.

ZPL 1005/6 LANGLAND, William
Visions From Piers Plowman. Read by

Yvonne Bonnamy, Freda Dowie, Frank Duncan, David King, Ann Morrish, Peter Orr, Richard Pasco, George Rylands.

PLP 1052 Late Victorian Poetry
Poets include Wilde, J. Thomson, Dowson, Johnson, Stevenson, Mary Coleridge, Bridges, F. Thompson, Housman. Read by Frank Duncan, David King and Ian Holm.

PLP 1153 LEWIS, Cecil Day
Translation of the Georgics of Virgil, selections. Read by Cecil Day Lewis.

PLP 1065 MACNEICE, Louis
Conversation, Invocation, Dublin, The gone tomorrow, The cyclist, Rites of war, Death of an old lady, others. Read by the author.

PLP 1014 The Metaphysical Poets
Record 1 – Religious: John Donne's Holy Sonnets, Good Friday, Hymne to God My God in My Sickness, A Hymne to God the Father. Francis Quarles' A Good-night, On Zacheus. Thomas Traherne's A Salutation. George Herbert's Affliction, The Agonie, Vertue, Easter, Conscience, The Collar, others. Henry Vaughan's Ascension, The World, The Retreate, others. Read by Tony Church, Richard Marquand, Peter Orr, William Squire.

PLP 1015 The Metaphysical Poets
Record 2 – Secular: Thomas Carew's Ask me no more, I was foretold, others. Sir John Suckling's Why so pale and wan, Oh for some honest lover's ghost, others. Richard Lovelace's If to be absent were to be, The Scrutinie, others. Thomas Stanley's La Belle Confidente, The Repulse. Poems also by Henry King, Abraham Cowley, Montrose, Edmund Waller, Katherine Philips, Andrew Marvell. Read by Yvonne Bonnamy, Robin Holmes, Peter Orr, John Stride, Gary Watson.

PLP 1017 MILTON, John
Paradise Lost, Book I. Read by Tony Church, Denis McCarthy, Michael Redgrave.

PLP 1018 MILTON, John
Paradise Lost, Book II. Read by Sheila Burrell, Tony Church, William Devlin, Denis McCarthy, Peter Orr, Michael Redgrave, George Rylands, Patrick Wymark.

PLP 1019 MILTON, John
Paradise Lost, Books III & IV. Selections. Read by Tony Church, Richard Johnson, Michael Redgrave, John Stride.

PLP 1020 MILTON, John
Paradise Lost, Books V & VI. Selections. Read by Tony Church, Michael Hordern, Richard Johnson, Michael Redgrave, Prunella Scales, Gary Watson.

PLP 1021 MILTON, John
Paradise Lost, Books VII & IX. Selections. Read by Tony Church, Michael Redgrave, Richard Johnson, Prunella Scales.

PLP 1022 MILTON, John
Paradise Lost, Books IX, X, XII. Selections. Read by Tony Church, Michael Redgrave, Michael Hordern, Richard Marquand, Richard Johnson, Prunella Scales, William Squire.

PLP 1023 MILTON, John
Paradise Regained. Selections. Read by Ian Holm, Denis McCarthy, John Neville.

PLP 1016 MILTON, John
The Shorter Poems. Including: How soon hath Time, On Time, On the Morning of Christ's Nativity, At a Solemn Musick, L'Allegro, When I consider how my Light is spent. Read by William Devlin, William Squire, Gary Watson.

PLP 1075 OWEN, Wilfred
Wilfred Owen read by Richard Johnson, Harold Owen read by Tony Church, Siegfried Sassoon read by Frank Duncan. Includes: Arms and the Boy, The Send-off, Letter to Mrs. Owen 4 January 1917, The Sentry, Letter to Mrs. Owen 16 May 1917, Anthem for doomed Youth, Futility, others.

PLP 1029 POPE, Alexander
Selections from Windsor Forest, Essay on Man, Essay on Criticism, Epilogue to the Satires, others. Read by Max Adrian, Frank Duncan, Keith Michell, George Rylands.

PLP 1030 POPE, Alexander
The Rape of the Lock. Read by Peggy Ashcroft, Margaret Field Hyde, Joan Hart, Denis McCarthy, John Nettleton, Janette Richer, George Rylands, Prunella Scales.

PLP 1050 The Pre-Raphaelites
Includes selections by D.G. Rossetti, A.C. Swinburne, C. Rossetti, Morris. Read by Gary Watson, Peter Orr, Flora Robson.

PLP 1143 READ, Herbert
Echoes Of My Life. Includes: The Pond, Pasturelands, Childhood, Curfew, Night, Fear, The Autumn of the World, September Fires, The Seven Sleepers, others. Read by Herbert Read, Yvonne Bonnamy, Peter Orr.

PLP 1124 SANSOM, Clive
The Witnesses. Includes: Mary of Nazareth I, The Innkeeper's Wife, A Villager, John the Baptist, The Woman of Samaria, others. Read by Ruth and Clive Sansom.

ZPL 1006 Scots Chaucerians
Robert Henryson: The Testament of Cresseid; William Dunbar: Sweit Rosi of Vertew, To the City of London, On his Heidake, Of Lyfe, Lament for the Makaris, From the Golden Targe. Read by Duncan McIntyre and Freda Dowie.

ZPR 254–6 SHAKESPEARE
The Sonnets. Read by George Rylands, John Barton, Tony Church, Tony White, Anthony Jacobs, Gary Watson, Richard Marquand, David Gibson. Set of 3 records.

PLP 1042 SHELLEY, Percy Bysshe
From the defence of poetry, England in 1819, selections from The Mask of Anarchy, Prometheus Unbound, Epipsychidion, others. Read by Patrick Garland, Richard Marquand, Gary Watson.

ZPL 1008 Skelton and Early Lyric
Includes: Adam lay I bounded, The wells of Jesus wounds, I sing of a maiden, Christ calls man hime, A song in his Lady's absence, others. Read by David King, John Stride, Yvonne Bonnamy, Duncan McIntyre.

PLP 1061 SPENDER, Stephen
Word, The hawk, Not to you I sighed, Beethoven's death mask, Elegy for Margaret, Song, others. Read by the author.

PLP 1011 SPENSER, Edmund
The Faerie Queene. Selections from Books I, II, IV, VI, and Mutability Cantos. Read by Tony Church, Prunella Scales, Margaretta Scott, William Squire, Gary Watson.

PLP 1045 TENNYSON, Alfred (Lord)
Record One. Includes: A spirit haunts, The Lotus-Eaters, The splendour falls, Ulysses, Crossing the bar, others. Read by Tony Church, Frank Duncan, Denis McCarthy, Margaretta Scott, Gary Watson.

PLP 1046 TENNYSON, Alfred (Lord)
Record Two. Includes: The Lady of Shalott, Idylls of the King, From Guinevere, A Farewell, From The Vision of Sin, others. Read by Michael Hordern, Frank Duncan, David King.

SW 503 THOMAS, Dylan
Poems. Includes: In my craft and sullen art, Before I knocked, The hunchback in the park, Fern Hill, Lament, Poem in October, And death shall have no dominion, others. Read by Richard Burton.

PLP 1060 Homage To Dylan Thomas
The memorial performance recorded at the Globe Theatre, London, on 24 January 1954. Louis MacNeice: Requiem Canto. Dylan Thomas: Return journey, The hunchback in the park, Poem in October, A visit to Grandpa's, Fern Hill. Read by Louis MacNeice, Hugh Griffith, Richard Burton, Emlyn Williams.

TA 509/10 Emlyn Williams as Dylan Thomas in A Boy Growing Up. Record One: Introduction, Memories of Childhood, Who Do You Wish Was With Us, The Fight, The Outing, The Reminiscence of a Schoolmaster, Just Like Little Dogs.
Record Two: Self Portrait, Adventures in the Skin Trade, A Child's Christmas, A Visit to America, A Visit to Grandpa's.

PLP 1036 WORDSWORTH, William
Record One. Selections from The Sword in the Stone. Read by Alan Bates, Tony Church, Derek Godfrey, Michael Hordern, Peter Orr.

PLP 1037 WORDSWORTH, William
Record Two. Includes: The solitary reaper, Seven sonnets, She was a phantom of delight, Personal talk, Ode to duty, others. Read by Alan Bates, Tony Church, Derek Godfrey, Michael Hordern, Peter Orr.

PLP 1038 WORDSWORTH, William
The Prelude. Selections from Books I, II, II, VI, VII, X, XI, XII. Read by Peter Orr, William Squire.

PLP 1056 YEATS, William Butler
Includes: The Lamentation of the Old Pensioner, The Lover pleads with his friend, The Fiddler of Dooney, A Dialogue of Self and Soul, The Delphic Oracle upon Plotinus, A Last Confession, others. Read by Arthur O'Sullivan, Jim Norton, Chris Curran and Sheila Manahan.

ZPL 1091 YEATS, William Butler
Noh Plays. Record One. At the Hawk's Well, The Dreaming of the Bones. Read by Chris Curran, Cait Lanigan, Jane Carty, Eamonn Keane, Arthur O'Sullivan, Jim Norton, Gerard Victory, Daphne Carroll. Music by Gerard Victory.

ZPL 1092 YEATS, William Butler
Noh Plays. Record Two. The Cat and the Moon, Resurrection. Read by Chris Curran, Cait Lanigan, Jane Carty, Eamonn Keane, Arthur O'Sullivan, Jim Norton, Ronnie Walsh. Music by Gerard Victory.

THE POET SPEAKS
An anthology of contemporary poets reading their own works. Recorded in association with The British Council and the Poetry Room in the Lamont Library of Harvard University. Edited by Peter Orr.

PLP 1081 Volume One
James Reeves: Old and Young, This is your Elegy, Honeysuckle Smell, Music in the Wood, The Stone Gentleman. David Jones: The Fatigue. William Plomer: The Last Train, At the Supermarket, LimeFlower-Tea. C. Day Lewis: The Christmas Tress, Flight to Italy, The Fox.

PLP 1082 Volume Two
Norman Nicholson: Millom Old Quarry, Cleator Moor, The Pot Geranium, Bond Street, others. Stevie Smith: Tenuous and Precarious, Thoughts about the Person from Porlock, The Wedding Photograph, others. W.R. Rodgers: Four Poems for Easter, Express A Last Word for Louis Macneice. Vernon Watkins: Ballad of Culver's Hole, Moonrise, Buried Light, others. Edward Lowbury: Time for Sale, The Huntsman, Surgery of a Burn, Nothing.

PLP 1083 Volume Three
John Heath-Stubbs: In Every Sense of the Word; To Edmund Blunden on his Sixtieth Birthday, Song of the Death-Watch Beetle. Thomas Blackburn: Trewarmett, The Judas Tree, Mark. Laurence Whistler: The Guest, A Form of Epitaph, Flowers for her

Grave, Now there is only Following. John Press: Farewell, The Seagull, Winter Landscape, others. Julian Ennis: Wire-Dancer, Cold Storage, Elegy on Two Pets, others.

PLP 1084 Volume Four
Tony Conner: A Rather Public Statement, Elegy for Alfred Hubbard, Mrs. Root, others. Thomas Kinsella: Cover her Face, An Old Atheist Pauses by the Sea, Mirror in February, others. Elizabeth Jennings: My Grandmother, Harvest and Consecration, Two Deaths, others. Peter Redgrove: In Case of Atomic Attack, The Archaeologist, For No Good Reason.

PLP 1085 Volume Five
Ted Hughes: Her Husband, Bowled Over, Still Life, others. Peter Porter: Beast and the Beauty, Made in Heaven, Who Gets the Pope's Nose, others. Thom Gunn: Epitaph for Anton Schmidt, Elegy on the Dust, The Allegory of the Wolf Boy, others. Sylvia Plath: Lady Lazarus, Daddy, Fever 103°.

PLP 1086 Volume Six
John Arden: Here I Come. Michael Baldwin: Death on a Live Wire. Taner Baybars: Going Home to meet Myself. Patricia Beer: Ballad of the Red-Headed Man. George MacKay Brown: The Seven Houses: In Memory of John F. Kennedy. John Fuller: An Exchange between the Fingers and the Toes. Michael Harnett: They Drag Me Raw. Poems also by Hamish Henderson, David Holbrook, James Liddy, George MacBeth, Christopher Middleton, Adrian Mitchell, Ruth Pitter, Herbert Read, Edward Thomas, Anthony Thwaite, Rosemary Tonks, David Wevill.

PLP 1087 Volume Seven
John Betjeman: A Shropshire Lad, Before the Anaesthetic, others. Robert Graves: The Devil's advice to Storytellers, Welsh Incident, Two Grotesques. Stephen Spender: Earth Treading Stars, Seascape, To My Daughter. Kathleen Raine: Statues, The Eternal Child. W.H. Auden: The Hard Question, Song, The More Loving One, others. Basil Bunting: Mesh Cast for Mackerel, Let Them Remember Samangan. William Empson: Legal Fiction, To An Old Lady. Patric Dickinson: Song, This Cold Universe, Lincoln Cathedral. R.S. Thomas: Pisces, The Last of the Peasantry, others. Hilary Corke: The Early Drowned.

PLP 1088 Volume Eight
Philip Larkin: Wants, Coming, Nothing to be Said, others. Roy Fuller: Florestan to Leonora. Laurie Lee: Milkmaid, April Rise, Day of these Days. Charles Causley: I am the Great Sun, At The British War Cemetery, others. Geoffrey Hill: Canticle for Good Friday, In Piam Memoriam, The Assisi Fragments. Ken Smith: Fossil, Grass. Dom Moraes: Craxton, Jason. Charles Tomlinson: At Wells: Polyphony, The Hand at Callow Hill, others. Jon Stallworthy: A Letter from Berlin. Jon Silkin: To My Friends, Bowl, Asleep?, others.

PLP 1089 Volume Nine
Hugh MacDiarmid: First Love, In The Children's Hospital, Skald's Death, Under the Greenwood Tree, others. Sydney Goodsir Smith: The Winter O' The Hert, Simmer Nichtsang, Largo, The Reid Reid Rose, others. Norman MacCaig: You Went Away, Assisi, Smuggler. Iain Crichton Smith: Old Woman, Girl with Orange Sunshade. Louis MacNeice: Carrickfergus, Meeting Point, Prayer before Birth. Seamus Heaney: Follower, Poor Women in a City Church, Poem for Marie, others. Austin Clarke: Summer Lightning, Wandering Men, Marriage, others.

PLP 1090 Volume Ten
Edmund Blunden: Forefathers, The Author's Last Words to his Students. Andrew Young: Last Snow, The Stars, Secret Wood. Edwin Muir: The Two Brothers, The Desolations. Geoffrey Grigson: Hollowed Stone, About Owls. John Wain: Reason for not writing orthodox Nature poetry, Anecdote of 2 am, others. George Barker: I Stare Into, The Seraph Ascends, There is no sky, When the Babe, others. W.S. Graham: The Constructed Space, The Beast in the Space. Christopher Logue: I was born on a board. Edward Lucie-Smith: For Max Ernst, Gallipoli, Fifty years after. Edward Brathwaite: The Making of the Drum. B.S. Johnson: Great Men, Restoration.

ANTHOLOGIES
PLP 1072 The Barrow Poets
The Barrow Poets entertain. They believe that poetry is written not only to be appreciated in the silence and privacy of the home, but also to be enjoyed in the company of others. Their lively performances of poetry and music are heard in pubs, in festivals, recital rooms, colleges, and schools throughout the country. Selections include poems by Wallace Stevens, A.E. Housman, Sir Frances Bernard, Rameau, Robert Graves, James Stephens, W.B. Yeats, J. Hughes, Laurie Lee, Shakespeare, Henry Reed, others.

PLP 1071 Beyond the Blues.
American Negro Poetry. Poets include: Leslie M. Collins, Margaret Danner, Paul Vesey, Robert E. Hayden, Julia Fields, Gwendolyn Brooks, Owen Dodson, Sterling Brown, Ted Jones, Langston Hughes, and others.

PLP 1064 Robert Donat
Favourite Poems At Home. Includes poems by William Wordsworth, John Keats, Rudyard Kipling, Robert Bridges, T.S. Eliot, Wilfred Owen, Whan Chei, Robert Browning, William Shakespeare. Poems At Christmas Time: Includes poems by Thomas Hardy, T.S. Eliot, J. Alexander Chapman, Walter de la Mare, John Betjeman, Hilaire Belloc, and others.

PLP 1059 Robert Donat Reads Selected Poetry.
Poems by John Keats, William Wordsworth, Percy Bysshe Shelley, A.E. Housman, Rupert Brooke, Wilfred Owen, Siegfried Sassoon, Arthur Quiller-Couch, John Betjeman, Coventry Patmore, Ben Jonson, Walter Raleigh, and others.

PLP 1155 Poets of Wales
Abse: Letter to Alex Comfort, Albert, Elegy for Dylan Thomas, The Game, Return to Cardiff, others. Norris: Skulls, A girl's song, Ransom, Early frost, Pheasants, Burning the bracken, others. Read by the authors.

PLP 1156 Poets of Wales
Garlick: August Country, Ancestors, Agincourt, Waterloo, Shalom, Judgement Day, others. Ormond: My Grandfather and his Apple-tree, Johnny Randall, After a death, Design for a tomb, others. Read by the authors.

SW 506 Peter Ustinov Reads Cautionary Verse
Browning: The Pied Piper of Hamelin. Carroll: The Walrus and the Carpenter, You are Old Father William. Belloc: Cautionary Tales.

ZPL 1077-80 Rhyme & Rhythm
An anthology of poetry and music for Children. Spoken by Tony Church, Michael Hordern, Spike Milligan, Janette Richer, Prunella Scales, Margaretta Scott, Gary Watson, Patrick Wymark. Sung by Pat Shuldham-Shaw, Esme Lewis. These records have been made from four books of the same title published by MacMilliam & Co. Ltd. In the case of Record One (Red Book) and Record Two (Blue Book) the records follow the printed anthology closely and include almost all the printed material. Records Three (Green Book) and Four (Yellow Book) contain a selection of the material used in these books. The age groups for which the records and books are intended are approximately 7-8 (Red), 8-9 (Blue), 9-10 (Green), 10-11 (Yellow). All records and books are available separately.

ZPL 1094-1107 Poetry And Song
A companion anthology to Rhyme and Rhythm, designed for older children. Artists appearing in the Poetry and Song series are: Tony Church, The Critics Group, Choir of St. John's College, Cambridge, Michael Hordern, Barbara Jefford, Richard Johnson, Eamon Keane, Laurie Lee, Ewan MacColl, Peter Orr, Prunella Scales, Peggy Seeger, William Squire, Gary Watson, Patrick Wymark. Book One (Age 12-13) Records ZPL 1094-6; Book Two (Age 13-14) Records ZPL 1097-99; Book Three (Age 14-15) Records ZPL 1100-3; Book Four (Age 15-16) Records ZPL 1104-07.

ENTERTAINMENTS

MPR 262/3 Poetry International '69.
Poems by Auden, Holub, Clarke, Pilinszky, Ritsos, Nash, Bly, Brathwaite, Walcott, Popa. Poems read by the authors.

ZTA 513/4 Poetry and Jazz in Concert.
Record One: Adrian Mitchell reads Nostalgia – Now Threepence off Time and Motion Study, Veteran With a Head Wound, Pals. Dannie Abse reads Sunday Evening, extract from the Abandoned Odd, Epithalamion, Victim of Aulis. The Michael Garrick Trio with Joe Harriott and Shake Keane play Salvation March and Wedding Hymn. Record Two: Jeremy Robson reads Approaching Mount Carmet (With jazz), Winter fears, While Troops Moved In, others. Laurie Lee reads First Love, Juniper, Spring, April Rise, Stork in Jerez, others. The Michael Garrick Trio with Joe Harriott and Shake Keane play Vishnu and She's Like a Swallow.

RADIO BALLADS

DA 139 The Ballad of John Axon.
A Radio Ballad by Ewan MacColl and Charles Parker. Set into song by Ewan MacColl.

DA 140 The Big Hewer.
A Radio Ballad by Ewan MacColl and Charles Parker.

DA 141 The Fight Game.
A Radio Ballad by Ewan MacColl and Charles Parker. Musical direction and orchestration by Peggy Seeger.

DA 142 Singing The Fishing.
A Radio Ballad by Ewan MacColl and Charles Parker. Lyrics and music by Ewan MacColl.

PLP 1074 What Passing Bell.
A commemoration in poetry and prose of the 50th anniversary of the outbreak of the First World War. Contributors: Lt. Rupert Brooke (died on active service 23 April 1915), Lt-Col. Rowland Feilding, Field-Marshall the Viscount French of Ypres, Capt. the Hon. Julian Grenfell (died of wounds 26 May 1915), Field-Marshall the Earl Haig of Bemersyde, Thomas Hardy, Lt. Melville Hastings (died of wounds 3 October 1918), Pte. David Jones, Mrs. Jack May, 'A Little Mother', Lt. Wilfred Owen (killed in action 4 November 1918), Pte. Frank Richards, Pte. Isaac Rosenberg (killed in action 1 April 1918), Capt. Siegfried Sassoon, Capt. Charles Hamilton Sorley (killed in action 13 October 1915), Capt. Arthur Graeme West (killed in action 3 April 1917). Read by Jill Balcon, Hugh Burden, C. Day Lewis, Michael Hordern, John Stride, Gary Watson, Patrick Wymark.

ZPR 261 Will It Be So Again?
Poetry and prose of the Second World War read by Beatrix Lehmann, Robert Hardy, Ian Holm, Gary Watson. Poems by C. Day

Lewis, H. Read, A. Lewis, R. Hillary, D. Thomas, Henry Reed, Edith Sitwell, A. Rook, R. Campbell, C. Causley, S. Spender, others.

DOCUMENTARY RECORDINGS

History Reflected – Volumes I–VI.
12 long-play records covering six periods of English history from Agincourt to the Second World War. Presented by the Apollo Society, and directed by Peter Orr, the artists include Sir Michael Redgrave, Dorothy Tutin, Virginia McKenna, Donald Sinden, Richard Pasco, and Ian Holm, reading drama, poetry and prose of the times, with music from Yonty Solomon, Geoffrey Shaw, and the Purcell Consort of Voices.

ZPR 101/2 Volume I Agincourt 1415 – The Decline of Chivalry.

ZPR 103/4 Volume II Elizabeth I – The Armada 1588.

ZPR 105/6 Volume III Charles I – Court and Commons.

ZPR 107/8 Volume IV Liberty: Equality: Fraternity.

ZPR 109/10 Volume V The Great Exhibition 1851.

ZPR 111/2 Volume VI World Wars – 1914:1939.

RECENT ARGO SPOKEN WORD RECORDINGS
PLP 1031 The English Poets – Gray And Collins.
Read by Richard Bebb, John Neville, George Rylands, and William Squire.

PLP 1032 The English Poets – Johnson, Goldsmith and Cowper.
Read by John Neville, George Rylands and William Squire.

PLP 1033 The English Poets – Crabbe.
Read by Ian Holm, Clifford Rose, and Gabriel Woolf.

PLP 1034 The English Poets – Burns.
Read by Isla Blair, Julian Glover, Duncan McIntyre.

PLP 1180 Poets of Wales – David Jones.
Including the Wall, The Tribune's Visitation, and excerpts from The Sleeping Lord.

ZPL 1181 Poets of Wales – Idris Davies.
Read by Richard Bebb, Yvonne Bonnamy and William Squire.

PLP 1182 Cricket – Sovran King of Sports.
An anthology of the poetry and prose of cricket, read by John Arlott, Valentine Dyall, Robin Holmes, Russell Napier, and Michael Parkinson.

PLP 1183 Masks By Edward Brathwaite.
Read by the author.

PLP 1184/5 Islands By Edward Brathwaite.
Read by the author.

ZPL 1186 An Evening With Sybil Thorndike.
Browning, Hopkins, Shaw, etc. Read by Sybil Thorndike with John Casson and Jane Casson.

ZSW 508 Outpatients – The Barrow Poets.

ZSW 511 Magic Egg – The Barrow Poets.
A record for children.

SPA 200 The World of Children.
Excerpts from Alice in Wonderland, The Wind in the Willows, etc. Read by Jane Asher, Michael Hordern, Spike Milligan, Peter Ustinov, Patrick Wymark, etc.

PA 166 The World of Dylan Thomas.
Excerpts from Under Milk Wood, short stories and poems, read by Richard Burton, Richard Bebb, Emlyn Williams, etc.

Broadside Records

Pioneer Record Sales Corporation, 701 7th Ave., New York, NY 10036 U.S.A.
BR 461 New Jazz Poets.
Compiled and Edited by Walter Lowenfels. The poets on this record are adding a new dimension to American prosody. Their reading goes beyon the oral poetry now being heard by thousands throughout the country. A few of the poems featured on the record are Jutterbugging in the Streets The Second Coming, etc. 1–12" 33–⅓ rpm, notes $5.79.

BR 465 Poems for Peace.
Recorded and Edited by Ann Charters. The twelve poets on this record represent a cross-section of the talent drawn to this affair in the cause of peace. The occasion: A benefit reading for the New York Workshop in Non-Violence at St. Mark's Church in the Bouwerie. A few of the poems featured on the record are Auto Poesy to Nebraska, Elegy, Poems from Oklahoma. 1–12" 33-⅓ rpm, notes $5.79.

BR 470 To Live and Die in Dixie. John Beecher, Rebel and poet. John Beecher cuts at racial injustice with knifesharp precision. Bigotry and the indifference of man to the suffering of others is dramatized in a selection of his poetry and read by Beecher:
A few of the poems featured on the record are In Egypt Land, Chaney, The Convict, etc. Complete text and intro. 1–12" LP. notes $5.79.

BR 651 A reading of Primitive and Archaic Poetry.
How did the World begin? Who am I? What is death? In a world where conceptions of the proper role of man are undergoing a severe examination, primitive poetry offers a rare and moving experience. Mind and

imagination of primitive man are revealed in this collection compiled and read by poets J. Rothenberg, D. Antin and others. A few of the poems featured are A Maori Poem on the Creation of Light, Death Song-Papago, etc. Complete text inc. 1–12" LP, notes $5.79.

BR 652 From a Shaman's Notebook.
Primitive and Archaic Poetry. Through the centuries . . . The Medicine Man speaks . . . unchartered depths of human experience are explored . . . language barriers are shattered . . . ancient secrets revealed. Compiled, translated and read by poets J. Rothenberg, D. Antin and others. A few of the poems featured are, Song of the Ghost Dance Religion, Circumcision Rite, etc. Complete Text provided. 1–12" LP, notes $5.79.

ASCH MANKIND SERIES
(Ethnic series)
AHM 4126 The Four Vedas.
Introduction and Notes by Prof. J.F. Staal. Recordings by John Levy and J.F. Staal. Consists of a body of hymns, sacrificial formulas, chants, etc. which together constitute the four Vedas. The whole of the broad anthology has been handed down by word of mouth. Rgveda, Black Yajurveda etc. English and complete transliteration, illustrated notes. 2–12" LP's, $15.90.

Caedmon Records Inc.

505 Eighth Avenue, New York, NY 10018, U.S.A.

ENGLISH POETRY

TC 1023 ARNOLD, Matthew
Sohrab and Rustum. Alfred Drake reads the dramatic poem. On the reverse side, Omar Khayyam's Rubaiyat. 1–12" LP.

TC 1161 ARNOLD, Matthew
Beowulf and Other Poetry in Old English. J.B. Bessinger, Jr. reads Beowulf (selections), Caedmon's Hymn, The Dream of the Rood, A Wife's Lament, others. All in Old English, accompanied by the Sutton Hoo harp. Original text and modern translation included. 1–12" LP.

TC 4001 ARNOLD, Matthew
Beowulf, in Old English (Complete). Kemp Malone reads. Original text and modern translation included. 4–12" LPs.

TC 1101 BLAKE, William
The Poetry of William Blake. Ralph Richardson reads from Songs of Innocence and Songs of Experience. 1–12" LP.

TC 1071 BROWNING, Elizabeth Barrett
Sonnets From the Portuguese. Katharine Cornell reads I Thought Once How Theocritus Had Sung, How Do I Love Thee? Let Me Count The Ways, others. 1–12" LP.

TC 1075 BROWNING, Robert
The Pied Piper. Boris Karloff, aided by some slithery pied-piper music, reads. 1–12" LP.

TC 1048 BROWNING, Robert
The Poetry of Robert Browning, Volume I. James Mason reads The Bishop Orders His Tomb, Andrea del Sarto, Fra Lippo Lippi. Text included. 1–12" LP.

TC 1201 BROWNING, Robert
My Last Duchess and Other Poems, Volume 2. James Mason reads My Last Duchess, How They Brought the Good News from Ghent to Aix, Home Thoughts from Abroad, and others. 1–12" LP.

TC 1103 BURNS, Robert
The Poetry of Robert Burns and Border Ballads. Frederick Worlock reads these best-loved poems of Burns: To a Mouse, The Banks o'Doon, Auld Lang Syne, and others. C.R.M. Brookes reads these Scottish Border Ballads: Sir Patrick Spens, The Twa Corbies, The Lament of the Border Widow, and others. 1–12" LP.

TC 1042 BYRON, George Gordon
The Poetry of George Gordon Byron. Tyrone Power reads Don Juan (Canto 1), She Walks in Beauty, On This Day I Complete My 36th Year, and others. 1–12" LP.

TC 1078 CARROLL, Lewis/LEAR, Edward
Nonsense Verse. Beatrice Lillie, Cyril Ritchard and Stanley Holloway do Jabberwocky, The Walrus and the Carpenter, Will You Walk a Little Faster, The Owl and the Pussycat, and other nonsense. 1–12" LP.

TC 1226 CHAUCER, Geoffrey
The Parliament of Fowls and Six Other Poems in Middle English. J.B. Bessinger, Jr. reads in Middle English The Parliament of Fowls, Merciless Beauty, and others. Includes text in Middle English. 1–12" LP.

TC 1092 COLERIDGE, Samuel Taylor
The Poetry of Samuel Taylor Coleridge. Ralph Richardson reads in its entirety The Rime of the Ancient Mariner, together with Dejection, an Ode, Kubla Khan, This Lime Tree Bower My Prison, Frost At Midnight. 1–12" LP.

TC 1094 COWARD, Noel
Noel Coward Reading His Poems. Noel Coward and Margaret Leighton read Coward's sophisticated verses, and perform the hilarious Shaw interlude between King Magnus and his mistress. 1–12" LP.

TC 1046 DE LA MARE, Walter
Walter de la Mare Speaking and Reading. A Conversation: 1) Isn't It a Lovely Day, 2) A Little About Witches, and twelve poems which include Peace, The Veil, The Railway Junction. 1–12" LP.

TC 1141 DONNE, John
The Love Poems of John Donne. Richard Burton reads The Good Morrow, Song: Go and Catch a Falling Star; and others.112" LP.

TC 1125 DRYDEN, John
The Poetry of John Dryden. Paul Scofield reads Song: The Zambra Dance, Prologue from an Evening's Love, An Ode in Honor of St. Cecilia's Day, Absalom and Achitophel (abridged), and others. 1–12" LP.

TC 1066 GRAVES, Robert
Robert Graves Reads From His Poetry and The White Goddess. From The White Goddess, The Haunted House, Outlaws, Allie and others. 1–12" LP.

TC 1140 HARDY, Thomas
The Poetry of Thomas Hardy. Richard Burton reads In Tenebris 1, The Souls of the Slain, Shut Out That Moon, At Casterbridge Fair: I,II,III,IV, and VII and others. 1–12" LP.

TC 1111 HOPKINS, Gerard Manley
The Poetry of Gerard Manley Hopkins. Cyril Cusack reads Windhover, God's Grandeur, The Starlight Night, Pied Beauty, and others. 1–12" LP.

TC 1203 HOUSMAN, A.E.
A Shropshire Lad and Other Poetry. James Mason reads from A Shropshire Lad: 1877, Loveliest of Trees, the Cherry Now, The Recruit, and others. From More Poems: Stone, Steel, Dominions Pass; Parta Quies; and others. 1–12" LP.

TC 1087 KEATS, John
The Poetry of John Keats. Ralph Richardson reads Ode to a Nightingale, Ode on a Grecian Urn, To Autumn, Ode on Melancholy, When I have Fears That I May Cease to be; and others. 1–12" LP.

TC 1147 MASEFIELD, John
John Masefield Reading Sea Fever and Other Poems. Sea Fever, The West Wind, Cargoes, and others. 1–12" LP.

TC 1356 MILNE, A.A.
When We Were Very Young. Judith Anderson reads poems from When We Were Very Young and Now We are Six which include Buckingham Palace, Puppy and I, The King's Breakfast, If I Were King, and many others. 1–12" LP.

TC 1259 MILTON, John
The Poetry of John Milton. Anthony Quayle reads L'Allegro, Il Penseroso, Lycidas, On Shakespear, On the Morning of Christ's Nativity, and others. 1–12" LP.

TC 2008 MILTON, John
Paradise Lost, Books One and Four. Anthony Quayle reads Book One, complete and Book Four, selections. 2–12" LPs.

TC 2034 MILTON, John
Paradise Lost, Books Two and Three. Anthony Quayle reads. 2–12" LPs.

TC 2028 MILTON, John
Samson Agonistes. With Michael Redgrave, Max Adrian, Faith Brook, and Neil McCarthy. 2–12" LPs.

TC 1171 POPE, Alexander
The Poetry of Alexander Pope, Volume I. Michael Redgrave reads selections from The Rape of the Lock, Cantos I and II; Epistle to Dr. Arbuthnot; Selections from An Essay on Man; and others. 1–12" LP.

TC 1311 POPE, Alexander
The Poetry of Alexander Pope, Volume 2. Claire Bloom reads Eloisa to Abelard; Ode on Solitude. Max Adrian reads an Essay on Criticism, Part II. 1–12" LP.

SRS 239 SHAKESPEARE, William
The Rape of Lucrece and Other Poems. Richard Burton reads The Rape of Lucrece; Edith Evans and Donald Wolfit read the Passionate Pilgrim; and others. Complete text included. 2–12" LPs.

SRS 241 SHAKESPEARE, William
Sonnets. John Gielgud reads one hundred and twenty Shakespearean sonnets. Complete Text included. 2–12" LPs.

SRS 240 SHAKESPEARE, William
Venus and Adonis and A Lover's Complaint. Max Adrian reads Venus and Adonis; Claire Bloom reads a Lover's Complaint; complete text included. 2–12" LPs.

TC 1094 SHAW, Bernard
The Apple Cart, Interlude. Noel Coward and Margaret Leighton read Coward's sophisticated verses, and perform the hilarious Shaw Interlude between King Magnus and his mistress. 1–12" LP.

TC 1059 SHELLEY, Percy Bysshe
The Poetry of Percy Bysshe Shelley. Vincent Price reads Music, When Soft Voices Die; Ozymandias; Ode to the West Wind; and others. 1–12" LP.

TC 1016 SITWELL, Edith
Edith Sitwell Reading Her Poems. Three poems from Façade: The Wind's Bastinado, Trio for Two Cats and a Trombone, Said King Pompey; Spinning Song; and others. 1–12" LP.

TC 1013 SITWELL, Osbert
Osbert Sitwell Reading From His Poetry. From Wrack at Tidesend: Preface, Lousy Peter, The Three Miss Coltrums, Mrs. Busk; and others; from England Reclaimed and Selected Poems: Fool's Song, Journalist's Song, and others. 1–12" LP.

TC 1126 SPENSER, Edmund
The Faerie Queene and Epithalamion. Michael MacLiammoir reads Book III, and Cantos XI and XII from the Faerie Queene, and the Epithalamion, slightly abridged. 1–12" LP.

TC 1077 STEVENSON, Robert Louis
A Child's Garden of Verses. Judith Anderson reads The Swing, Happy Thought, Escape at Bedtime, A Good Play; and others. 1–12" LP.

TC 2022 TENNYSON, Alfred
Idylls of the King: Lancelot and Elaine and The Passing of Arthur. Basil Rathbone reads these two poetic sections describing Elaine's forlorn love for the great knight Lancelot, and the final days of the Round Table. 2–12" LPs.

TC 1285 TENNYSON, Alfred
Idylls of the King: Geraint and Enid. Anthony Quayle reads the poem which recounts Geraint's tests of Enid's love. 1–12" LP.

TC 1080 TENNYSON, Alfred
The Poetry of Alfred Tennyson. Sybil Thorndike and Lewis Casson read the Lady of Shalott; Ulysses; Tears, Idle Tears; Now Sleeps the Crimson Petal; and others. 1–12" LP.

TC 1343 THOMAS, Dylan/SITWELL, Edith
Dylan Thomas and Edith Sitwell Read and Discuss Her Poetry. Dylan Thomas reads Harvest; The Two Loves; The Shadow of Cain; and others while Edith Sitwell discusses how she came to write these specific poems. 1–12" LP.

TC 1294 THOMAS, Dylan
A Personal Anthology. Dylan Thomas broadcast for the BBC a series of readings called A Personal Anthology, consisting of poetry he loved. This recording contains selections from these programs including the poetry of Vernon Watkins, W.H. Davies, Alun Lewis, Edward Thomas, Wilfred Owen, W.B. Yeats, Gerard Manley Hopkins, D.H. Lawrence and John Milton. 1–12" LP.

TC 1002 THOMAS, Dylan
Dylan Thomas Reading, Volume 1. A Child's Christmas in Wales (short story); Fern Hill; Do Not Go Gentle; and others. 1–12" LP.

TC 1018 THOMAS, Dylan
Dylan Thomas Reading, Volume 2. Lament; Poem on His Birthday; Should Lanterns Shine; There Was a Saviour; and others. 1–12" LP.

TC 1043 THOMAS, Dylan
Dylan Thomas Reading, Volume 3. A Few Words of a Kind; On the Marriage of a Virgin; Over Sir John's Hill; and others. 1–12" LP.

TC 1061 THOMAS, Dylan
Dylan Thomas Reading, Volume 4. His irreverent preamble, A Visit to America, together with his readings of poetry by contemporary poets: De la Mare, W.H. Auden, Henry Reid, Edward Thomas and Thomas Hardy. 1–12" LP.

TC 1132 THOMAS, Dylan
Dylan Thomas Reading, Volume 5. Quite Early one Morning; Reminiscences of Childhood; A Visit to Grandpa's; Holiday Memory. 1–12" LP.

TC 2014 THOMAS, Dylan
Dylan Thomas Reading His Complete Recorded Poetry. Author's Prologue; If I Were Tickled by the Rub of Love; Light Breaks Where No Sun Shines; and others. 2–12" LPs.

TC 1157 THOMAS, Dylan
An Evening With Dylan Thomas Reading His Own and Other Poems. An Irreverent Introduction; The Traveler's Curse; After Misdirection, translated from the Welsh; and others of his poems, and poems by James Stephens, W.H. Davies, Thomas Hardy, Alun Lewis, John Betjeman, W.H. Auden, Andrew Young and W.B. Yeats. 1–12" LP.

TC 1281 THOMAS, Dylan
Dylan Thomas: In Country Heaven – The Evolution of a Poem. A unique and dramatic experience in hearing the development of a major poem, line by line, from the first rough draft to the published work, with Dylan Thomas, Hugh Griffith, Basil Jones, Douglas Cleverdon and Humphrey Searle. Included are: Over Sir John's Hill; In Country Sleep; In the White Giant's Thigh. 1–12" LP.

TC 1342 THOMAS, Dylan
Dylan Thomas Reading From His Work and the Works of Sean O'Casey and Djuna Barnes. Dylan Thomas reads his hilarious recounting of his fat uncle's pub-crawling in Wales entitled A Story; an essay called Laugharne and another poem Especially When the October Wind; He also reads from Sean O'Casey: a section from Chapter 2 of I Knock at the Door and Djuna Barnes: Nightwood – "Watchman, What of the Night?". 1–12" LP.

TC 1354 THOMAS, Dylan
Return Journey to Swansea. The original BBC broadcast with Dylan Thomas and full cast reading Return Journey to Swansea and Thomas reading the poetry of Robert Graves: Welsh Incident; Counting the Beats; John Betjeman: On a Portrait of a Deaf Man; Senex; and others. 1–12" LP.

TC 1353 THOMAS, Dylan
Dylan Thomas Reads the Poetry of W.B. Yeats and Others. Dylan Thomas reads the Speech of Oedipus at Colonus; Three Things; The Circus Animals; Leda and the Swan; and other poems by W.B. Yeats, and poems by Louis MacNeice, George Barker, Walter de la Mare, W.H. Davies, D.H. Lawrence, W.H. Auden and Christopher Marlowe. 1–12" LP.

TC 1231 TOLKIEN, J.R.R.
Poems and Songs of Middle Earth. J.R.R. Tolkien reads The Adventures of Tom Bombadil, The Mewlips, The Hoard, Perry-the-Winkle, The Man in the Moon Came

Down Too Soon, and others. William Elvin sings Donald Swann's The Road Goes Ever On, a song cycle based on Tolkien's poetry. The composer plays the piano accompaniment. 1–12" LP.

TC 1026 WORDSWORTH, William
The Poetry of William Wordsworth. Cedric Hardwicke reads Composed Upon Westminster Bridge, Sept. 3, 1802; Strange Fits of Passion Have I Known; Tintern Abbey; and others. 1–12" LP.

TC 1081 YEATS, William Butler
The Poetry of William Butler Yeats. Siobhan McKenna and Cyril Cusack read The Song of Wandering Aengus; The Wild Swans at Coole; Leda and the Swan; and others. 1–12" LP.

ENGLISH POETRY ANTHOLOGIES

TC 1049 17th Century Poetry
Cedric Hardwicke and Robert Newton read metaphysical and love lyrics by Herbert, Browne, Suckling, Lovelace, Cartwright, Strode, Traherne, Vaughan, Crashaw, Cowley, Marvell. Text included. 1–12" LP.

TC 4002 18th Century Poetry and Drama.
Max Adrian, Claire Bloom and Anthony Quayle read the works of Finch, Prior, Swift, Congreve, Addison, Watts, Gay, Berkeley, Carey, Pope, Warton, The Elder, Blair, Johnson, Gray, Collins, Warton, Goldsmith, Cowper, Bickerstaffe, Sheridan, Burns. 4–12" LPs.

TC 3005 English Romantic Poetry.
Claire Bloom, Anthony Quayle, Frederick Worlock and Ralph Richardson read the poetry of Coleridge, Landor, Moore, Hunt, Peacock, Byron, Shelley, Blake, Burns, Wordsworth, Scott, Clare, Keats, Hood, Beddoes. 3–12" LPs.

TC 2011 Golden Treasury of English Poetry.
Claire Bloom, Eric Portman and John Neville read a generous selection from the Palgrave Anthology of English lyric poetry including Marlowe, Shakespeare, Barnfield, Wyatt, Dryden, Gray, Rogers, Burns, Byron, Arnold, others. 2–12" LPs.

TC 1021 Hearing Poetry, Volume 1.
A spoken anthology of English poetry, introduced by Mark Van Doren with readings by Hurd Hatfield, Jo Van Fleet and Frank Silvera. Includes: Chaucer, Spenser, Marlowe, Dekker, Shakespeare, Jonson, Donne, Milton, Herbert. Text included. 1–12" LP.

TC 1022 Hearing Poetry, Volume 2.
A spoken anthology of English poetry introduced by Mark Van Doren, with readings by Hurd Hatfield, Jo Van Fleet and Frank Silvera. Includes: Dryden, Congreve, Pope, Blake, Coleridge, Wordsworth, Keats, Shelley, Byron, Browning. Text included. 1–12" LP.

TC 3004 Victorian Poetry.
Max Adrian, Claire Bloom and Alan Howard read the poetry of Henry, E.B. Browning, Fitzgerald, Tennyson, Thackeray, Browning, Lear, C. Bronte, E. Bronte, Clough, Kingsley, Eliot, Arnold, Meredith, D. Rossetti, Carroll, Hardy, others. 3–12" LPs.

AMERICAN POETRY
TC 1039 AIKEN, Conrad
Conrad Aiken Reading. A Letter from Li Po; The Blues of Ruby Matrix; Two poems from Time in the Rock. 1–12" LP.

TC 1260 ANTONINUS, Brother
The Savagery of Love: Brother Antoninus Reads His Poetry. The Way of Life and the Way of Death; Immortal Strangeness; The Rose of Solitude; and others. 1–12" LP.

TC 1019 AUDEN, W.H.
W.H. Auden Reading. In Memory of W.B. Yeats; In Praise of Limestone; The Capital; School Children; and others. 1–12" LP.

TC 1337 BENET, Stephen Vincent
The Poetry of Stephen Vincent Benét read by the Author and Joseph Wiseman. Includes: The Death of Stonewall Jackson; The Ballad of William Sycamore; others. 1–12" LP.

TC 1244 BROOKS, Gwendolyn
Gwendolyn Brooks Reading Her Poetry. She reads poems from A Street in Bronzeville, Annie Allen, The Bean Eaters, Black Expression, others. 1–12" LP.

TC 1387 CONKLING, Hilda
Hilda Conkling Reading Her Poetry. For You Mother; Silver Horn; Velvets; There Is a Star; Little Mouse in Grey Velvet; and others.

TC 1206 CRANE, Hart
The Poetry of Hart Crane. Tennessee Williams reads poems from The Bridge, White Buildings, Key West, and Uncollected Poems. 1–12" LP.

TC 1400 CULLEN, Countee
The Poetry of Countee Cullen. Ruby Dee and Ossie Davis read The Black Christ; and other poems. 1–12" LP.

TC 1017 CUMMINGS, E.E.
E.E. Cummings Reading His Poetry. HIM, the acrobat passage; EIMI, Lenin's tomb; when serpents bargain for the right to squirm; and others. 1–12" LP.

E.E. Cummings, Lecturing and Reading Six Nonlectures.
These are the Charles Eliot Norton Lectures delivered by E.E. Cummings at Sanders Theatre in Cambridge, Mass., in 1952-53. Autobiographical in nature, they cover the development of the poet with emphasis on influences that affected him in his childhood surroundings and thereafter, and the evolution of his creed as a poet and a man. In the course of the Nonlectures, the poet reads his own

poems and those of other poets. Each record may be purchased individually.

TC 1186 Nonlecture One: i & my parents. 1–12" LP.

TC 1187 Nonlecture Two: i & their son. 1–12" LP.

TC 1188 Nonlecture Three: i & selfdiscovery. 1–12" LP.

TC 1189 Nonlecture Four: i & you & is. 1–12" LP.

TC 1190 Nonlecture Five: i & now & him. 1–12" LP.

TC 1191 Nonlecture Six: i & am & santa claus. 1–12" LP.

TC 1333 DICKEY, James
James Dicky Reads His Poetry. In the Tree House at Night; The Scarred Girl; The Celebration; and other poems, and a section from his novel Deliverance.

TC 1119 DICKINSON, Emily
Poems and Letters of Emily Dickinson. Julie Harris reads This is my letter to the world; The soul selects her own society; Hope is the thing with feathers; and others. 1–12" LP.

TC 2026 DICKINSON, Emily
A Self-Portrait. Julie Harris creates a remarkably well-rounded portrait of the gifted poet by reading selections from her letters and poems which include To make a prairie it takes a clover and one bee; and others. 2–12" LPs.

TC 1243 EBERHART, Richard
Richard Eberhart Reading His Poetry. From Collected Poems: The Fury of Aerial Bombardment; and others. From Selected Poems: Sea-Hawk; and others. From the Southern Review, Winter 1967: The Mastery; Marrakech; and others. 1–12" LP.

TC 1045 ELIOT, T.S.
T.S. Eliot Reading Poems and Choruses. The Love Song of J. Alfred Prufrock; Portrait of a Lady; Preludes; Ash Wednesday; others. 1–12" LP.

TC 1326 ELIOT, T.S.
T.S. Eliot Reading The Waste Land and Other Poems. 1–12" LP.

TC 1359 EMERSON, Ralph Waldo
The Poetry of Ralph Waldo Emerson. Archibald McLeish reads Each and All; Hamatreya; The Snow-Storm; Give All to Love; and others. 1–12" LP.

TC 1035 FAULKNER, William
William Faulkner Reading. The Nobel Prize Acceptance Speech; selections from As I Lay Dying: Tull, Darl, Vardaman (two); A Fable, section; The Old Man, section. 1–12" LP.

TC 1298 FIELD, Eugene
Wynken, Blynken, and Nod and Other Poems by Eugene Field. Julie Harris reads the title poems; Gold and Love for Dearie; The Sugar-Plum Tree; others. 1–12" LP.

TC 1060 FROST, Robert
Robert Frost Reading. The Road Not Taken; The Pasture; Mowing; Birches; and others. 1–12" LP.

TC 1185 HEMINGWAY, Ernest
Ernest Hemingway Reading. This is the only recording of Hemingway's voice, and includes the Nobel Prize acceptance speech; Second Poem to Mary in London; In Harry's Bar in Venice; and others. 1–12" LP.

TC 1302 HOLMES, Oliver Wendell
Old Ironsides and Other Poems by Oliver Wendell Holmes. Ed Begley reads Old Ironsides; The Last Leaf; The Living Temple; and others. 1–12" LP.

TC 1272 HUGHES, Langston
The Poetry of Langston Hughes. Ruby Dee and Ossie Davis read poems from Selected Poems of Langston Hughes, The Panther and the Lash, One-Way Ticket and Ask Your Mama. 1–12" LP.

TC 1315 HUGHES, Langston
Poems From Black Africa Edited by Langston Hughes. James Earl Jones reads oral traditional and contemporary poetry from Sierra Leone, Nyasaland, Ghana, Nigeria, South Africa, The Congo, Liberia, Madagascar, Gabon, Rhodesia and Ethiopia. 1–12" LP.

TC 1424 JARRELL, Randall
Randall Jarrell Reads and Discusses His Poems Against War. A Lullaby; Mail Call; The Lines; Death of the Ball-Turret Gunner; Eighth Air Force; others. 1–12" LP.

TC 1364 JARRELL, Randall
The Bat Poet. Randall Jarrell reads this story for children. 1–12" LP.

TC 1297 JEFFERS, Robinson
The Poetry of Robinson Jeffers. Judith Anderson reads Divinely Superfluous Beauty; To the Sone-Cutters; Night; Boats in a Fog; and others. 1–12" LP.

TC 1216 LINDSAY, Vachel
The Poetry of Vachel Lindsay. Nicholas Cave Lindsay, the poet's son reads the most representative poems, including The Sorceress; The Kallyope Yell; What the Hyena Said; and others. 1–12" LP.

TC 1041 LINDSAY, Vachel
Vachel Lindsay Reading. The Congo; The Flower-Fed Buffaloes; The Moon's The North Wind's Cooky; and others. 1–12" LP.

TC 1107 LONGFELLOW, Henry Wadsworth
Best Loved Poems of Longfellow. Hal Holbrook reads Paul Revere's Ride; The

Village Blacksmith; The Wreck of the Hesperus; and others. 1–12" LP.

TC 1179 LONGFELLOW, Henry Wadsworth
Evangeline. Hal Holbrook reads this great American idyllic poem retaining all the best-known passages and the complete story in this abridged version. Text included. 1–12" LP.

TC 1009 MacLEISH, Archibald
Archibald MacLeish Reads His Poetry. The Old Man to the Lizard; They Come No More, Those Words, Those Finches; What Any Lover Learns; and others.

TC 1152 MASTERS, Edgar Lee
Spoon River Anthology. Julie Harris and forty-six townspeople of Milwaukee read fifty-six poems from this American epic, the epitaph of the small town. 1–12" LP.

TC 1295 MERWIN, W.S.
W.S. Merwin Reading His Poetry. From Green With Beasts, The Drunk in the Furnace, The Moving Target and The Lice. 1–12" LP.

TC 1024 MILLAY, Edna St. Vincent
The Poetry of Edna St. Vincent Millay. Judith Anderson reads Renascence; Not in This Chamber Only at My Birth; Love Is Not All; It Is Not Meat Nor Drink; and others. 1–12" LP.

TC 1123 MILLAY, Edna St. Vincent
Edna St. Vincent Millay Reading Her Poetry. Renascence; Recuerdo; I Shall Forget You Presently, My Dear; and others. 1–12" LP.

TC 1025 MOORE, Marianne
Marianne Moore Reading Her Poems. The Fish; The Steam Roller; Spenser's Ireland; Nevertheless; and others. 1–12" LP.

TC 1015 NASH, Ogden
Ogden Nash Reads Ogden Nash. Kind of an Ode to Duty; Portrait of the Artist as a Prematurely Old Man; and others. 1–12" LP.

TC 1323 NASH, Ogden
Ogden Nash reads The Christmas That Almost Wasn't; An Untold Adventure of Santa Claus; and others. 1–12" LP.

TC 1282 NASH, Ogden
Ogden Nash's Parents Keep Out Read by Ogden Nash. The Dog; The Kitten; Pediatric Reflection; Reflection on Babies; and others. 1–12" LP.

TC 1307 NASH, Ogden
Ogden Nash's Reflections On A Wicked World, Read by Ogden Nash. Reflection on a Wicked World; Reflections on Ice-Breaking; The Parent; Cat Naps Are Too Good For Cats; and others. 1–12" LP.

TC 1300 PATTEN, Brian
Brian Patten Reading His Poetry. A Small Dragon; A Creature to Tell the Time By; A Theme for Various Murders; and others. Graham Layden, accompanying himself on the guitar, sings and Patten reads Unisong; Somewhere Between Heaven and Woolworth's. 1–12" LP.

TC 1122 POUND, Ezra
Ezra Pound Reading His Poetry, Volume 1. Hugh Selwyn Mauberley; Cantos I, IV, XXXVI, and LXXXVI; Moeurs Contemporaines; Cantico del Sole. 1–12" LP.

TC 1155 POUND, Ezra
Ezra Pound Reading His Poetry, Volume 2. Cantos XLV, LI, LXXVI, second hald; The Gypsy; The Exile's Letter; Canto 99. 1–12" LP.

TC 1351 ROETHKE, Theodore
Theodore Roethke Reads His Poetry. Where Knock Is Open Wide; Give Way, Ye Gates; My Papa's Waltz; Pickle Belt; The Cycle; Dinky; and others. 1–12" LP.

TC 1150 SANDBURG, Carl
Carl Sandburg Reading His Poetry. Prairie Waters by Night; Southern Pacific; Prayers of Steel; In Tall Grass; White Ash; and others. 1–12" LP.

TC 1124 SANDBURG, Carl
Carl Sandburg discusses for children What Is Poetry? and reads his poems: Buffalo Dusk; Phizzog; Chicago Poet; The Abracadabra Boys; Young Sea; Jazz Fantasia; and others. 1–12" LP.

TC 2023 SANDBURG, Carl
The People, Yes. Carl Sandburg reads his favorite poems from The People, Yes, his poetic portrait of America; and from the new section of Complete Poems: Mr. Longfellow and His Boy; The Long Shadow of Lincoln; and others. 2–12" LPs.

TC 1253 SANDBURG, Carl
Carl Sandburg Reading Fog and Other Poems. Fog; Child; Broken-face Gargoyles; and others. 1–12" LP.

SERVICE, Robert William
The Poetry of Robert William Service. Ed Begley reads the shooting of Dan McGrew; The Cremation of Sam McGee; The Ballad of Pious Pete; and others. 1–12" LP.

TC 1084 SPENDER, Stephen
Stephen Spender Reading His Poetry. My Parents Kept Me; What I Expected; Who Live Under the Shadow; and others. 1–12" LP.

TC 1050 STEIN, Gertrude
Gertrude Stein Reads From Her Works. If I Told Him; Matisse; The Making of Americans, Parts 1 and 2; Madame Recamier; others. 1–12" LP.

TC 1068 STEVENS, Wallace
Wallace Stevens Reading His Poems. The Theory of Poetry; The Idea of Order at Key West; Credences of Summer; The Poem That Took the Place of A Mountain; and others. 1–12" LP.

TC 1233 WHITMAN, Walt
Crossing Brooklyn Ferry and Other Poems.
Ed Begley reads Crossing Brooklyn Ferry;
Song of Myself, section 26; I Sing the Body
Electric; and others. 1–12" LP.

TC 1037 WHITMAN, Walt
Leaves of Grass, Volume 1. Ed Begley
reads I Hear America Singing; A child said
What is the grass?; When I Heard the
Learn'd Astronomer; and others. 1–12"
LP.

TC 1154 WHITMAN, Walt
Leaves of Grass, Volume 2. Ed Begley
reads Song of the Open Road; From Song
of Myself: Twenty-eight young men (11);
When Lilacs Last in the Dooryard Bloom'd;
O Captain, My Captain. 1–12" LP.

TC 1308 WHITTIER, John Greenleaf
The Barefoot Boy and Other Poems by
John Greenleaf Whittier. Includes Snow-
Bound complete. 1–12" LP.

TC 1248 WILBUR, Richard
Richard Wilbur Reading His Poetry.
Walking to Sleep; Running; A Wood;
Under Cygnus; Seed Leaves; Complaint;
The Lilacs; The Proof; and others. 1–12"
LP.

TC 1005 WILLIAMS, Tennessee
Tennessee Williams Reading From His
Works. From The Glass Menagerie:
Opening Monologue and all the final
scenes from the breaking of Laura's glass
horse to the bitter end; Cried the Fox; The
Eyes; and other poems. 1–12" LP.

TC 1047 WILLIAMS, William Carlos
William Carlos Williams Reads His Poetry.
The Descent; To Daphne and Virginia; The
Orchestra; For Eleanor and Bill Monahan;
and others. 1–12" LP.

AMERICAN POETRY ANTHOLOGIES

TC 1204 American Patriotism in Poems
and Prose.
Ed Begley, Julie Harris and Frederick
O'Neal read The Star-Spangled Banner;
America; America the Beautiful; Yankee
Doodle; The Battle Hymn of the Republic;
and others. 1–12" LP.

TC 2041 Classics of American Poetry for
the Elementary Curriculum.
Eddie Albert, Ed Begley, Helen Gahagan
Douglas, Robert Prost, Julie Harris, Hal
Holbrook, Eartha Kitt, Frederick O'Neal,
Brock Peters, Vincent Price, Basil
Rathbone, and Carl Sandburg read a
selection of poems chosen especially for
classroom listening at upper elementary
levels: Included are poems by Dickinson,
Emerson, Frost, Holmes, Hughes,
Longfellow, Poe, Sandburg, Whitman,
Whittier, and others. 2–12" LPs.

TC 1207 Favorite American Poems
Ed Begley reads Thayer: Casey at the Bat;
Woodworth: The Old Oaken Bucket;
McCrae: In Flanders Fields; Lowell: The
First Snowfall; and others. 1–12" LP.

TC 2009 Great American Poetry.
Vincent Price, Eddie Albert, Julie Harris,
Ed Begley and Helen Gahagan Douglas
read 17th, 18th, and 19th Century classics
by Taylor, Bradstreet, Freneau, Bryant,
Longfellow, Emerson, Whittier, Holmes,
Whitman, Melville, Dickinson, and others.
2–12" LP.

OTHER WORKS

TC 1379 An Anthology of West Indian
Poets Reading Their Own Poetry. Edited
by John J. Figueroa.
The Anthology includes the works of
Edward Brathwaite, John J. Figueroa,
Anthony McNeill, Mervyn Morris, Frank
Collymore, Eric M. Roach, H.A. Vaughn,
Dennis Scott, Derek Walcott. 1–12" LP.

TC 2006 The Caedmon Treasury of
Modern Poets Reading Their Own Poetry.
Includes the poetry of Aiken, Auden,
Cummings, Eberhart, Eliot, Empson, Frost,
Graves, MacLeish, MacNeice, Moore,
Pound, Sitwell, Spender, Stein, Stevens,
Thomas, Wilbur, Williams, Yeats. 2–12"
LPs.

TC 1023 KHAYYAM, Omar
The Rubaiyat. Alfred Drake reads the well
loved translation by Edward Fitzgerald.
1–12" LP.

TC 1316 MORGENSTERN, Christian
The Poetry of Christian Morgenstern – The
Gallows Songs. Ogden Nash reads
selections from Christian Morgenstern's
Gallows Songs using the much-acclaimed
Max Knight translation of these satirical
and whimsical poems. 1–12" LP.

TC 1315 Poems From Africa
James Earl Jones reads oral traditional
and contemporary poetry from Sierra
Leone, Nyasaland, Ghana, Nigeria, South
Africa, the Congo, Liberia, Madagascar,
Gabon, Rhodesia and Ethiopia. 1–12" LP.

POETRY TEACHING TOOLS

TCp 1156 Discovering Rhythm and Rhyme
in Poetry.
Julie Harris and David Wayne read. The
skillful selection by Louis Untermeyer
makes this album an ideal way to introduce
children to the rhythms and rhymes basic
to poetical expression, including the Owl
and the Pussycat, The Three Billy-Goats-
Gruff, sections of the Pied Piper of
Hamelin and many Mother Goose rhymes.
Portfolio contains complete text in large
print for easy reading by children. 1–12"
LP.

TCp 1279 LEAR, Edward
Edward Lear's Nonsense Stories and
Poems. Claire Bloom reads the History of
the Seven Families of the Lake Pipple-
Popple, and other stories which illustrate
the right words used wrongly and short
words used longly, with such hilarity that
children stretch their vocabularies to laugh
harder and better. 1–12" LP.

TC 1339 MERRIAM, Eve
Catch a Little Rhyme: Poems for Activity
Time. This is a new and exciting kind of
activity record, in which Eve Merriam
reads those of her poems which invite
children to respond both verbally and with
their whole bodies. The poems include
Catch a Little Rhyme; Ollie's Polly; Toaster
Time; among others. 1–12" LP.

FOREIGN LANGUAGE AND LITERATURE

TC 1072 German Lyric Poetry
Lotte Lehmann reads, in German, Poetry
of Goethe, Morike, Heine, Rilke, von
Hofmannsthal, and Muller. German/
English text included. 1–12" LP.

TC 1128 RILKE, Rainer Maria
The Poetry of Rainer Maria Rilke. Lotte
Lehmann reads in German Die Weise von
Liebe und Tod; Das Marienleben. German
text included. 1–12" LP.

**TC 1034 Classics of Greek Poetry and
Prose.**
Pearl C. Wilson reads, in Greek, selections
from the Iliad, the Odyssey, Plato's
Republic, the poetry of Sappho and
Mimnermus, and an Anacreontic.
Greek/English text included.

TC1277 SEFERIS, George
The Poetry of George Seferis Read in
Greek by the Author and in English by the
translator, Edmund Keeley.
Erotikos Logos (Parts 4 & 5); In the
Goddess' Name I Summon You; Spring
A.D.; others. 1–12" LP.

**TCp 1296 Classics of Latin Poetry and
Prose.**
Voces Romanae, originating at the
University of Texas at Austin read in Latin:
Caesar's Gallic Wars, selections; Cicero's
Orations, selections; The Poetry of
Catullus; others. 1–12" LP.

TCp 2036 Classical Russian Poetry
Yevgeny Yevtushenko reads on one side
of the album in Russian poems by Fyodor
Tyutchev, Aleksandr Blok, Vladimir
Mayakovsky, Sergey Yessenin, Anna
Akhmatova, and others. Morris Carnovsky
reads the same poems in English on the
other side. 2–12" LPs.

TCp 1232 PASTERNAK, Boris
Poetry. Yevgeny Yevtushenko on one side
of the album reads in Russian and Morris
Carnovsky on the other side reads in
English these Pasternak poems: A
Testament; Autumn; Fragment from a
Sublime Malady; On Early Trains; To a
Friend; and others. 1–12" LP.

TC 1153 YEVTUSHENKO, Yevgeny
Yevtushenko Reads Babii Yar and Other
Poems. Yevgeny Yevtushenko reads in
Russian and Alan Bates reads in English
famous Yevtushenko poems: Babii Yar;
Envy; A Career; Prologue; and others.
1–12" LP.

TC 1215 NERUDA, Pablo
Pablo Neruda Reading His Poetry. Las
Alturas de Macchu Picchu (complete);
Arte Poetica; Solo la Muerte; Oda a los
Calcetines; others. 1–12" LP.

FOR CHILDREN

**TC 1227 Miracles: Poems Written by
Children.**
Collected by Richard Lewis. Read by Julie
Harris and Roddy McDowall. Richard
Lewis, under the auspices of UNESCO,
traveled the English-speaking world to
collect these poems written by children.
They are arranged by such themes as
Morning, Spring, The Wind, Playing, etc.
1–12" LP.

TC 1091 Mother Goose
Cyril Ritchard, Celeste Holm and Boris
Karloff in a production of the best loved
verses and songs, including Lady Bird,
Lady Bird; Who killed Cock Robin; Old
King Cole; and many others. 1–12" LP.

See other listings for further children's
recordings.

CBS Records

A Division of Columbia Broadcasting
System Inc., 51 West 52nd Street, New
York, NY 10019, U.S.A.
OL6400 Love Respelt.
Old and New Poems by Robert Graves.
Read by the author.

OS6590 Antiworlds.
The Poetry of Andrei Voznesensky. Poems
read in Russian by the author and in
English by W.H. Auden, William Jay Smith,
Stanley Kunitz and Richard Wilbur.

CMS Records Inc.

14 Warren Street, New York, NY 10007,
U.S.A.
CMS 510 Selections From Spanish Poetry.
An anthology tracing the development of
Spanish poetry from its early beginnings.
Complete English-Spanish text included.
Recommended as an aid in language
study. Read in English and Spanish by
Seymour Resnick. Suggested price $5.95.

CMS 511 Selections From Russian Poetry
and Prose.
Read in English and Russian by Marshall
Shatz. Includes works by Pushkin,
Lermentov, Gogol, etc. Complete Russian-
English text included. Recommended for
language study.

CMS 522 Alistair Reid.
Oddments Inklings Omens Moments and
other poems read by the author. Mr. Reid's
poetry provides a sensitivity, touched with
humor, in his approach to life.

CMS 523 John Updike Reads John
Updike.

Mr. Updike reads excerpts from his novel "The Centaur," his complete short story "Lifeguard", and several of his poems.

CMS 541 Wm. Shakespeare – The Great Sonnets and Soliloquies.
Sixteen sonnets read by David Allen with music for harp in the Elizabethan manner, and 12 famed soliloquies.

CMS 542 John Donne – No Man Is An Island & Other Great Poems.
Read by David Allen. Elegy Written in a Country Churchyard, Thomas Gray; No Single Thing Abides, Lucretius; No Man Is An Island, John Donne; When I Have Fears That I May Cease To Be, Keats; Written On The Eve Of His Execution, Chidiock Tichborne; Ozymandias, Shelley.

CMS 543 Walt Whitman – Leaves of Grass.
Read by David Allen. Featuring the great Lincoln Elegy: When Lilacs Last in the Dooryard Bloom'd: Song of Myself (excerpts), Out of the Cradle Endlessly Rocking, Vigil Strange I Kept on the Field One Night, others.

CMS 544 Great Poems Of The English Language, Vol. I.
"Shakespeare to Dylan Thomas" – includes over 25 selections by Donne, Milton, Blake, Wordsworth, Emerson, Browning, Whitman, Millay, Cullen, Sandburg, etc. Read by David Allen.

CMS 545 Great Poems Of The English Language, Vol. II.
1550–1850 "Marlowe to Poe" – 30 selections by Marlowe, Raleigh, Pope, Goldsmith, Shelley, Longfellow, Poe, etc. Read by David Allen.

CMS 546 Great Poems Of The English Language, Vol. III.
The 19th Century A Challenge to Tradition. Over 25 selections including Lowell, Melville, Arnold, Rossetti, Dickinson, Hardy, Keats. Read by David Allen.

CMS 571 Leonard Wibberley Reads His Poetry For Children.
The best selling author performs the story-poems The Ballad of the Pilgrim Cat and The Ballad of Dopey Mick.

CMS 576 The Brownings – Elizabeth Barrett and Robert.
An autobiography in poetry read by Esther Benson & Martin Donegan.

CMS 577 Spoken Greek Verse.
With complete English text. Homer, Sappho, Pseudo Anacreon, Aeschylus, Sophocles, Euripedes, Aristophanes, Callemachus.

CMS 592/2 Short Stories of Edgar Allan Poe, Vol. V – "The Gold Bug & Selected Poems".
Read by Martin Donegan. Complete short story & poems: Romance, Evening Star, The Lake, Spirits of the Dead, Conqueror Worm, Dreams, Dreamland, Eldorado, A Dream Within A Dream. 2 record set–$11.90. Also available on cassette CMS–X4592/2.

CMS 614 Robert Burns – In Poetry, Song and Prose.
A Program of Burns' material presented in the manner of "Burns reading Burns". A truly superb collection performed by Arnold Johnston with complete text.

CMS 615 "Word-Music" – Tobie Lurie– Reads His Poetry– A Poetic Happening.
Word images developed thru dynamics of sound and rhythm formation. Lurie is one of the most inventive of the "Avant-Garde" poets.

CMS 617 The World's Great Poets, Vol. I–"America-Today"
Celebrated poets reading from their own works – Allen Ginsberg, Lawrence Ferlinghetti & Gregory Corso.

CMS 618 The World's Great Poets, Vol. II – "England".
British poets reading – Stephen Spender; Charles Tomlinson; P.J. Kavanagh.

CMS 619 The World's Great Poets, Vol. III – Ezra Pound Reading His Cantos III, XVI, XLIX, LXXXI, XCII, CVI, CXV.

CMS 620 The World's Great Poets, Vol. IV – "The Spanish Poets".
Two of the most renowned of the Spanish Language poets read their works – Rafael Alberti and Homero Aridjis – reading in Spanish with complete English texts.

CMS 621 The World's Great Poets, Vol. V – "Poets of Latin America".
Three celebrated Latin-American poets read their works – Jose Emilio Pacheco (Mexico); Octavio Paz (Mexico); and Tamara Godoy (Chile) – read in Spanish with complete English text.

CMS 622 The World's Great Poets, Vol. VI – "The Italian Poets, Album 1".
Poets include Giuseppe Ungaretti, Nello Risi and Mario Luzi.

CMS 623 The World's Great Poets, Vol. VII – "The Italian Poets, Album 2".
Poets include Vittorio Sereni and Alfonso Gatto – read in Italian with complete English text.

CMS 627 Robert Penn Warren Reads His Poetry.
Included are selection from Selected Poems – New and Old 1923-1966; from Incarnations: 1966-1988 and others.

CMS 638 Victorian Poetry 1830-1890.
Read by John Gielgud, Jill Balcon, Carleton Hobbs and Edward Campion. Poets include Tennyson, Arnold, Swinburne, Fitzgerald, E. Bronte, C. Rossetti, The Brownings, etc.

CMS 639 Alfred Lord Tennyson – Portrait Of A Poet.

John Betjeman introduces various poems by Tennyson and reminiscences by the poet's grandson. Includes a recording made in 1890 of Tennyson, himself, reading from "Maud". Other poems read by Robert Donat, Peggy Ashcroft, Sybil Thorndike, Cecil Day Lewis, Jill Balcon, etc.

CMS 647 Do Not Go Gentle.
12 poems by Shakespeare, Yeats, Byron, Housman, Sappho, Langston Hughes, Robert Burns and Dylan Thomas. Sung by Tom Glazer with guitar, flute and recorders.

CMS 109 Ho Chi Minh: The Prison Diary.
A collection of poetry read by Martin Donegan.

CMS 114 My Flute – The Poetry & Teachings & Philosophy Of Sri Chinmoy.
The famed Indian Guru reads poems from his critically acclaimed book.

CHILDREN'S RECORDS AND CASSETTES
CMS 506 Poetry Programs For Children, Vol. I.
A dramatic presentation created and performed by Elinor Basescu. This series is designed to acquaint children of all ages with poetry and to help them understand its various forms and meanings. This is accomplished through the use of various poems, graduated in complexity, and with thoughtful concise introductions. A complete text of all poems is included. This volume contains poems by Lear, Farjeon, Stevenson, Conkling, Longfellow, Tennyson, etc. Also available on cassette (CMS–X4506).

CMS 526 Poetry Programs For Children, Vol. II.
"For the Very Young". Same format as Vol. I – with text-selections by Carroll, Rossetti, Riley, Field, Stevenson, etc. Also available on cassette (CMS–X4526).

CMS 530 Poetry Programs For Children, Vol. III.
"For Upper Elementary Grades 4 Thru 7". The format is identical to Vols. I & II. The selections used on this volume are more sophisticated – Lear, Dickinson, Browning, Wylie, Longfellow, etc. – with text. Also available on cassette (CMS–X4530)

CMS 510 Selections From Spanish Poetry.
Read by Seymour Resnick in English and Spanish. A bi-lingual anthology of poetry, perfect as an aid to high school students. With complete English/Spanish text.

CMS 511 Selections From Russian Poetry and Prose.
Read in English and Russian by Marshall Shatz. A bi-lingual edition with text. Recommended for high school and college levels.

CMS 571 Leonard Wibberley Reads His Poetry For Children.

The best selling author performs the story-poems The Ballad of the Pilgrim Cat and The Ballad of Dopey Mick a soon-to-be-published story-poem which is a parallel of the classic Moby Dick.

CMS 628 William Jay Smith Reading His Poems For Children, Vol. I.
Mr. Smith and Other Nonsense, Puptents and Pebbles, A Nonsense ABC, If I Had A Boat.

CMS 631 William Jay Smith Reading His Poems For Children, Vol. II.
Boy Blue's Book of Beasts, What Did I See, Ho For A Hat.

The Decca Record Company Limited

Decca House, 9 Albert Embankment, London, S.E.1, U.K.
KCPAA 166 The World of Dylan Thomas.
In my craft or sullen art(a); Memories of childhood(b); Under Milk Wood – Excerpt*(a,c & d); Poem in October(c); Adventures in the Skin Trade – Excerpt(b); Do not go gentle into that good night(a); A visit to America(b); The hunchback in the park(c); Fern Hill(c); And death shall have no dominion(c). Speakers: (a) Richard Bebb, (b) Emlyn Williams, (c) Richard Burton, (d) Cast; *produced by Douglas Cleverdon and issued with the co-operation of the B.B.C. Tape (musicassette).

Discourses Limited

High Street, Royal Tunbridge Wells, Kent, U.K.
JUR OOB7 Ten Contemporary Poets (A Jupiter recording).
Originally published as part of a junior anthology, this record has new poems by Michael Baldwin, Charles Causley, Leonard Clark, Patric Dickinson, Roy Fuller, C. Day Lewis, Micahel Raper, James Reeves, Vernon Scannell and Hal Summers.

jep OC16 Laurie Lee and Christopher Logue (A Jupiter recording).
Two contemporary poets read a selection of their own poems.

jep OC17 Marius Goring (A Jupiter recording).
Five poems by George Herbert, and three by John Milton.

Educational Audio Visual Inc.

Pleasantville, NY 10570, U.S.A.
99RR 964 American Poetry to 1900 – Vol. 1.
Poems by Bradstreet, Freneau, F. Hopkinson, Adams, J. Hopkinson, Pierpont, Drake, Woodworth, Halleck, Bryant, Pinkney, Emerson, Longfellow, Whittier, Poe, Holmes, Thoreau.

Dickinson, Whitman. Read by David Allen, Nancy Marchand, David Hooks. Set of 2 LPs–$13.00.

99RR 965 American Poetry to 1900 – Vol. 2.
Poems by Taylor, Freneau, Dwight, Trumbull, Dana, Bryant, Morris, Longfellow, Whittier, Holmes, Poe, Lowell, Whitman, Read, Dickinson, Sill, Lanier. Read by Robert Burr, Diana Barth, Theodore Weiss. Set of 2 LPs–$13.00.

99RR 936 American Story Poems.
Poems by Thayer, Anon, Holmes, Harte, Longfellow, Poe, Hay, Thompson; read by John Randolph, Paul Sparer. Set of 2 LPs–$13.00.

99R 927 Poems of Edgar Allan Poe.
An anthology of Poe's great lyric poems: The Raven, To Helen, Lenore, The Bells, City in the Sea, Haunted Palace, The Sleeper, To One in Paradise, Israfel, To Science, El Dorado, Dreamland. Read by David Hooks. LP–$6.50.

95R 440 God's Trombones – James Weldon Johnson.
Side 1: A reissue of the original recording of 1937 in which James Weldon Johnson reads four of his poems. The Creation; Go Down, Death; The Prodigal Son; Listen Lord. Side 2: Alice Childress and P. Jay Sidney read selected 20th century Negro poetry by Paul Laurence Dunbar, Countee Cullen, Waring Cuney, Langston Hughes, Robert Hayden, and Margaret Walker. LP–$6.50.

99T 395 Beowulf – Chaucer.
Excerpts read by Helge Kokeritz and John C. Pope. Beowulf: The Prologue, Beowulf's Voyage to Denmark; Fight with Grendel; The Conclusion; others. Chaucer: The General Prologue to the Canterbury Tales; Prologue to: Prioress, the Clerk of Oxford, The Wife of Bath, The Prioress's Tale. Tape (5″ dual track)–$8.00.

99R 962 Early English Ballads.
Read from original texts. Fortune, My Foe; Fair Margaret and Sweet William; The Three Ravens; Greensleeves; The Bailiff's Daughter of Islington; others. Read by Richard Hampton, Ann Penfold, Peter Howell. Sung by David Chatterton. Lutenist, Richard Pumphrey. LP–$6.50.

96RF 205 The Time, Life and Works of Chaucer.
Pictures contemporary to Chaucer's time are used to evoke the social and intellectual climate in which he lived and wrote. The filmstrip is correlated with one side of an LP. The other side offers a reading in Middle English of "The Tale of the Wyf of Bathe" with an introduction in modern English. The set includes teacher's notes, full text of the narration, and a special twelve-page Study Guide containing the full text of "The Tale of the Wyf of Bathe" as well as a glossary of

Middle English Words and phrases. Study Guides for students' use are available in packages of 35. Set of LP/filmstrip–$14.50; 99BB 997 35 study guides–$10.50.

99RF 233 Chaucer's Canterbury Pilgrims.
This filmstrip presents the characters described in the Prologue to The Canterbury Tales in medieval materials. The portraits of the individual pilgrims are reproduced from the illuminated Ellesmere Manuscripts; a portrait of Chaucer is included. The journey of the pilgrims, from the Tabard Inn to the town of Canterbury, is traced. A newly-added feature is a correlated LP record (available separately for those who already own the filmstrip) describing the pilgrims in excerpts from the Prologue, read on one side in modern English, and on the other side in Middle English. Teacher's notes and full text of the narration. Set of LP and filmstrip–$13.75; LP only (code 99R 124)–$6.50.

95RB 148 Seven Old English Poems.
An LP prepared and read by Professor John C. Pope is accompanied by an Old English text with fully annotated translations. Titles include: Caedmon's Hymn; The Battle of Brunanburh: The Dream of the Rood; The Seafarer. Set of LP/book–$11.00.

96RF 735 The Time, Life and Works of Shakespeare.
The life and achievements of Shakespeare are viewed against the social and intellectual developments of the period. This sound film strip set traces the major events of Shakespeare's life, from his birth in 1564, through his career as an "actor sharer" as well as a playwright, to his death in 1616. The illustrations are paintings, prints, and woodcuts of the period; the narration includes pertinent passages from Shakespeare's plays. One side of the record (or tape track) is correlated with the filmstrip; the other side, which has lock grooves, presents twenty-two of Shakespeare's sonnets. Teacher's notes and full text of the narration. Set of LP/film strip–$14.50; Set of tape/filmstrip (code 99TF 915)–$14.50.

96RF 164 Silas Marner.
The story of the weaver of Raveloe, told in a series of color illustrations. One side of the record, correlated with the filmstrip, tells the story; the other side presents a selection of George Eliot's poetry. Set of LP/film strip–$14.50.

98RF 780 The Time, Life and Works of Wordsworth.
This sound filmstrip set uses contemporary prints, paintings, and photographs to show the world the author knew, the people and places important to his development, and the historical events of his era that influenced his work. Side one of the LP is correlated with the film-strip. Side two,

which has lock grooves, contains a selection of Wordsworth's poems. Set of LP/filmstrip–$14.50.

99R 963 Poems by Robert Burns and Scottish Border Ballads.
Selections are: Afton Water; Mary Morison; To a Louse; John Anderson; Ye Banks an' Braes; Bonnie George Campbell; The Twa Corbies; Young Beichan; others. Read by Gordon Jackson and Ann Penfold. Sung by David Chatterton. Adrienne Simpson, piano; Richard Pumphrey, lute. LP–$6.50.

99R 926 Keats and Shelley.
Keats: Ode to a Nightingale, Three Sonnets, La Belle Dame Sans Merci, Ode on a Grecian Urn, Ode on Melancholy, Song About Myself. Shelley: Ode to the West Wind, Ozymandias, To a Skylark, Love's Philosophy, Hymn to Intellectual Beauty, Summer and Winter, To Night. Read by Theodore Marcuse. LP–$6.50.

92RF 380 The Rime of the Ancient Mariner.
As a vivid and dramatic presentation of Coleridge's classic poem – one of the most widely read in the English language – this sound filmstrip set will engage students' interest and aid understanding of the poem. Beautifully drawn illustrations enhance this telling of the tale of the mariner who killed a bird of omen. In addition to the correlated narration, there are readings of other Coleridge poems. Teacher's notes and full text of the poems. Set of LP/film-strip–$14.50.

99RF 510 The Ballad Tradition.
This new sound filmstrip set is a unique opportunity to hear ballads as they were intended to be heard. It presents three of the finest traditional examples – The Daemon Lover, The Wife of Kelso, and Tam Linn – as sung by Ewan MacColl, accompanied by Peggy Seeger. They also present material about the British ballad tradition and about each ballad. The ballads are illustrated in typical broadsheet style by Irish artist Dave Scott. One record is correlated with the filmstrip; the second consists of MacColl's and Seeger's performances of a number of British and American variants of the three ballads, and explanation of the process by which ballads are adapted and changed. Teacher's notes and full text of the ballads and narration. Set of 2 LPs/ filmstrip–$20.00.

99RR 938 Forms of Poetry.
A comprehensive collection of poems illustrating the classic forms in which poetry has been written. The notes illustrate metric feet and give a brief explanation of each poetic form, followed by the text of the poems used. The forms include: Ballad, Ballade, Blank Verse, Couplet, Limerick, Octave, Quatrain, Sestet, Sonnet, Triolet, Villanelle. Set of 2 LPs–$13.00.

Anthology of English and American Poetry.

99R 931 Vol. 1. Ballads; poetry of: Shakespeare, Marlowe, Jonson, Donne, Dryden, Milton, Suckling, Lovelace, Drayton, and Pope. Read by Nancy Marchand, James Ray, Paul Sparer. LP–$6.50.

99R 932 Vol. 2. Poetry of: Douglas, Carey, Gray, Cowper, Goldsmith, Freneau, Blake, Burns, Lindsay, Southey, Lamb, Wordsworth, and Coleridge. Read by Nancy Marchand, James Ray, Paul Sparer. LP–$6.50.

99R 933 Vol. 3. Poetry of: Moore, Campbell, Hunt, Scott, Southey, Cunningham, Byron, Keats, Shelley, and Landor. Read by David Hooks, Heidy Mayer, Dean Almquist. LP–$6.50.

99R 934 Vol. 4. Poetry of: Bryant, Emerson, Whittier, Longfellow, Hood, and Tennyson. Read by David Hooks, Heidy Mayer, Edward Asner. LP–$6.50.

99R 935 Vol. 5. Poetry of: Poe, R. Browning, E. Browning, Arnold, Howe, Whitman, Markham, Read, and Lowell. Read by Nancy Marchand and Paul Sparer. LP–$6.50.

99RR 930 Set of the 5 LPs–$31.50.

91RF 119 How To Read and Understand Poetry.
This sound filmstrip set has been designed to develop a sense of what poetry is and an appreciation for it. Paintings, photographs, and other visual materials are used both to explain technique and to suggest and portray ideas. Poetry readings and comments from poets about their art are used extensively throughout the narration. The technical aspects of poetry are also presented with a new clarity. The set is divided into four parts. Part 1: Poetry: Its Content; Part 2: Poetry: Its Form; Part 3: Interpretation: Reading and Meaning; Part 4: The Interpretation of a Poem. Parts 1 and 2 consist of an LP record correlated with filmstrips. Parts 3 and 4 are audio only. Set of 2 LPs/2 filmstrips–$30.00.

E.M.I. (Australia) Limited

301 Castlereagh Street, Sydney, N.S.W. 2000, Australia.

SOELP 10006 Verse By Young Australians.
Spoken by the pupils of Cammeray Primary School. Themes include: Bush, Things, Animals, Sea, People, Thoughts and Things, War.

The Everest Record Group

10920 Wilshire Boulevard, Suite 410, Los Angeles, CA 90024, U.S.A.

Tradition 501 Countess Cathleen by W.B. Yeats.

Everest 3361 Laura Huxley Narrates Recipes for Living and Loving

Folkways Records

701 Seventh Avenue, New York, NY 10036, U.S.A.
THE SPOKEN WORD (2–12″ –$13.96)
9578 Medieval Romance Poetry.

9580 Poems of Federico Garcia Lorca.

9595 Poemontages: 100 Years of French Poetry.

THE SPOKEN WORD – ENGLISH (12″ –$6.98)
9703 Serenade: Poets of N.Y.
Read by Aaron Kramer.

9704 The Poems of Norman Rosten.

9710 "Boss Soul" Sarah W. Fabio, Poet.
Rhythms, Soul Background. Stereo.

9711 Soul Ain't: Soul Is.
Poems by Sarah Webster Fabio.

9717 Selected Poems of Kenneth Patchen.

9718 Kenneth Patchen Reads With Jazz.

9719 Kenneth Patchen Reads His Love Poems.

9721 Of Poetry And Power.
2–12″ –$13.96.

9733 Derry Down Derry.

9736 Words For The Wind.

9737 Padraic Colum Reading From His Irish Tales and Irish Poems.

9751 New Jazz Poets.

9752 Read-in For Peace In Vietnam.

9765 Poems For Peace.

9776 Early English Plays.
Whitman – Frost Poetry.

9782 Mark Van Doren Reads From His Collected And New Poems.

9788 God's Trombones.

9789 The Best of Simple: Langston Hughes.

9790 Sterling Brown And Laneston Hughes.

9791 Anthology Of Negro Poets.

9792 Anthology Of Negro Poets In The U.S.A.

9793 Sonia Sanchez Reads Her Poetry.

9794 16 Poems By Sterling Brown, Read By The Poet.
America's foremost authority on black literature reads from his own works.

9801 Reading Of Primitive And Archaic Poetry.

9802 From A Shaman's Notebook Primitive And Archaic Poetry.

9805 Six Montreal Poets.

9806 Six Toronto Poets.

9818 The Poems Of Rupert Brooke.

9865 Poems Of St. John Of The Cross.

9867 The Poems Of Heinrich Heine.

9869 The Poetry of Yevtushenko.

9877 Poems And Letters Of Robert Burns.

9879 Anthology Of 20th Century English Poetry (Part 3)

9882 English Lyric Poems And Ballads.

9883 English Romantic Poetry.

9886 Anthology Of 20th Century English Poetry (Part 1).

9887 Anthology Of 20th Century English Poetry (Part 2).

9890 The Jupiter Book of Ballads.

9891 Anthology of English Verse, Vol. 1.

9892 Anthology of English Verse, Vol. 2.

9893 Christian Poetry And Prose.

9894 Poems By W.B. Yeats, Others.
Includes Thomas Hardy, Robert Graves.

FOREIGN LANGUAGE (12″ –$6.98)
9905 Voix De 8 Poetes Du Canada.

9914 Modern Brazilian Poe Poetry.

9915 Modern Portuguese Poetry.

9916 Poetry of Eriedrich Von Schiller.

9918 The German Ballad: The Classical Age.

9921 Chinese Poems Of The Tang And Sung Dynasties.

9924 Poesie De La Negritude.

9925 Catalina Levinton: Recital Poetico.

9932 San Juan De La Cruz: Poesias.

9936 19th Century French Poetry.

9943 20th Century French Poetry.

9944 L'Honneur Des Poetes.

9947 The Poetry Of Abraham Sutzkever.

9960 Russian Poetry.

9961 Russian Poetry And Prose.

9962 Modern Soviet Poetry And Humor.

9967 Roman Love Poetry.

9984 Ancient Greek Poetry.
Read in Greek by J.F.C. Richards.

9985 Homer (Greek Poetry).

CHILDREN'S RECORDINGS

7114 An Anthology Of Negro Poetry For Young People.
Compiled and read by Arna Bontemps; poets included are Paul Lawrence Dunbar, Beatrice L. Murphy, Waring Cuney, Langston Hughes, Countee Cullen, Arna Bontemps, Claude McKay, Wesley Curtright, Frank Horne, Josephine Copeland,
Helene Johnson, Fenton Johnson, Sterling A. Brown, Georgia Douglas Johnson. $5.00.

Giorno Poetry Systems

222 Bowery, New York, NY 10012, U.S.A.
The Dial-A-Poem Poets LP Stereo Album.
Features 27 poets reading their work.

Hub Publications Limited

Youlgrave, Bakewell, Derbyshire, England.
Have One: "Pasternak Brother and Sister".
Recorded by Lydia Pasternak Slater in her Oxford home. She reads ten of her own poems (nine in English, one in Russian), and five poems by Boris Pasternak in the original Russian and in translations by Lydia herself. Supplied with a wealth of printed material, including a hardback book. Tape –£4.00 or $12.00.

Have Two: "Love Time".
Nineteen sensitive love poems written and read by Cal Clothier. Supplied with booklet giving full texts. Tape –£3.33 or $10.00.

The Marvell Press

3/33 Compayne Gardens, London, NW6 3DD, U.K.
The Marvell Press presents Listen Records 'The Poets Voice Series' edited by George Hartley.

LPV1 Philip Larkin reads The Less Deceived.

LPV2 Robert Graves reads selected poems.

LPV3 William Empson reads selected poems.

LPV4 Thom Gunn reads On the Move.

LPV5 Kingsley Amis reads A Case of Samples.

LPV6 Philip Larkin reads The Whitsun Weddings.

LPV7 Stevie Smith reads selected poems.

National Council of Teachers of English

1111 Kenyon Road, Urbana, IL 61801, U.S.A.
These recordings are produced on many of the major labels.

AMERICAN POETRY

78971R Beyond The Blues.
American Negro Poetry. Poems by Gwendolyn Brooks, Countee Cullen, Langston Hughes, and others read by Brock Peters, Vinette Carroll, Gordon Heath, and Cleo Laine. From the anthology edited by Rosey E. Pool.

79104R Classic Poems Of Suspense And Horror.
Marvin Miller reading The Ballad of Reading Gaol, The Highwayman, The Bells, and The Raven.

79300R Spoon River Anthology.
Fifty-six of Masters's poems read by townspeople of Milwaukee. Introduction by Julie Harris.

81306R Twelve Contemporary Poets.
1966 Houston Poetry Festival poets reading selections of their own works: Robert Bly, Robert Creeley, Richard Eberhart, Donald Hall, Galway Kinnell, Carolyn Kizer, W.S. Merwin, Josephine Miles, Gary Snyder, William Stafford, May Swenson, Reed Whittemore. Edited by William J. Scannell.

MODERN POETRY

82001R An Album of Modern Poetry, Vol. I.
An anthology read by the poets: T.S. Eliot, Robert Frost, Archibald MacLeish, William Carlos Williams, Marianne Moore, Conrad Aiken, and others. With text.

82010R An Album of Modern Poetry, Vol. II.
An anthology read by the poets: W.H. Auden, Ogden Nash, Oscar Williams, Allen Tate, Richard Eberhart, and others. With text.

82029R An Album of Modern Poetry, Vol. III.
An anthology read by the poets: E.E. Cummings, Edgar Lee Masters, Robert Lowell, Richard Wilbur, Theodore Roethke, and others. With text.

79809R Robert Frost.
Frost reading Mending Wall, Birches,

Mowing, and other poems.

79907R Great American Poetry.
Poems by Bradstreet, Longfellow, Emerson, Thoreau, Bryant, Whittier, Holmes, Crane, Whitman, and others. Read by such interpreters as Vincent Price, Eddie Albert, Julie Harris, Helen Gahagan Douglas, and Ed Begley. Two records.

80003R Golden Treasury of American Verse.
Nancy Wickwire and Alexander Scourby read poems by Whittier, Lowell, Whitman, Holmes, Bryant, Dickinson, Poe, and Longfellow. Musical accompaniment.

80101R Langston Hughes Reads and Talks About His Poems.
A wide range of poems and personal anecdotes. Among the poems: The Negro Speaks of Rivers, Midnight Raffle, Ku Klux, Refugee in America.

80263R Vachel Lindsay.
Lindsay reading The Congo and other poems.

80307R The Best Loved Poems of Longfellow.
Paul Revere's Ride, The Village Blacksmith, The Courtship of Miles Standish, The Wreck of the Hesperus, and others read by Hal Holbrook.

80600R Ogden Nash Reads Ogden Nash.
Nash reads Kind of an Ode to Duty, Portrait of the Artist as a Prematurely Old Man, and others.

80851R Promises . . . To Be Kept.
Eighth graders read 74 poems of their own. Selected and edited by their teacher, Susan Sherman.

86800R The Great Tales And Poems Of Edgar Allan Poe.
Eight stories plus selected poems read by Marvin Miller. Four 16rpm records.

ENGLISH POETRY

82500R The Canterbury Tales.
Includes the General Prologue, Prologue to the Parson's Tale, and Chaucer's Retraction. Read in Middle English.

82920R Early English Poetry.
Caedmon's Hymn and excerpts from Seafarer, Beowulf, Sir Gawain and the Green Knight, and others. Read in Old and Middle English by Charles Dunn. Text, translation, introduction, and notes included.

82966R Eighteenth Century Poetry And Drama.
Includes works by Prior, Swift, Congreve, Addison, Isaac Watts, Gay, Pope, Dr. Johnson, Gray, Collins, Goldsmith, Cowper, Sheridan, and Burns. Read by Max Adrian, Claire Bloom, Anthony Quayle, and others. Four records.

83000R T.S. Eliot Reading Poems And Choruses.
Eliot reads The Love Song of J. Alfred Prufrock and others of his best-known poems.

83180R English Romantic Poetry.
Poems by Beddoes, Blake, Burns, Byron, Clare, Coleridge, Hood, Hunt, Keats, Landor, Moore, Peacock, Scott, Shelley, and Wordsworth. Read by Claire Bloom, Anthony Quayle, Ralph Richardson, and Frederick Worlock. Three records.

83206R The English Romantic Poets.
Poems by Blake, Burns, Wordsworth, Coleridge, Byron, Shelley, and Keats, read by Bramwell Fletcher. In the Enjoying Poetry series. With text.

83457R Idylls Of The King.
Basil Rathbone reads Lancelot and Elaine and The Passing of Arthur. Two records.

83705R A Kipling Collection.
Gunga Din, Danny Deever, Mandalay, Recessional, The Mark of the Beast, The Man Who Would Be King, and others. Two 16 rpm records.

84054R Nonsense Verse Of Lewis Carroll And Edward Lear.
Beatrice Lillie, Cyril Ritchard, and Stanley Holloway read Jabberwocky, The Owl and the Pussycat, and other selections.

84241R Poetry Of The Early Seventeenth Century.
Selections from Herrick, Jonson, Lovelace, Donne, Marvell, King, Waller, Suckling, Fletcher, Vaughan, others. Read by Peter Jeffrey, David King, Ann Morrish, Peter Orr.

84633R Dylan Thomas Reading His Complete Recorded Poetry.
More than 20 poems read by the author. Two records.

84642R An Evening With Dylan Thomas Reading His Own And Other Poems.
Thomas reads The Traveller's Curse and others, plus poems by Hardy, Auden and Yeats.

84704R A Treasury Of Great Poetry.
Short introduction to each poet and his work. Milton, Suckling, Pope, Dryden, Gray, Goldsmith, Blake, Burns, Wordsworth, Coleridge, Byron, Bryant and others. Three 16 rpm records.

WORLD LITERATURE

92802R The Glory Of Negro History.
Music, poetry, and song trace the last four centuries of Negro history. Script and narration by Langston Hughes.

93017R Poems From Black America.
James Earl Jones reads oral traditional and contemporary poetry from Sierra Leone, Nyasaland, Ghana, Liberia, Nigeria, South Africa, and other countries.

Edited by Langston Hughes. Sixth grade and up.

PRIMARY GRADES

95275R Classics of English Poetry For The Elementary Curriculum.
The Lay of the Last Minstrel, Incident of the French Camp, The Owl and the Pussycat, How Do I Love Thee?, The Charge of the Light Brigade, My Last Duchess, Gunga Din, The Law of the Jungle, The Highwayman, and others.

95248R Classics Of American Poetry For the Elementary Curriculum.
Twenty-six familiar poems including Old Ironsides, The Village Blacksmith, I Hear America Singing, Barbara Frietchie, The Concord Hymn. Two records.

96201R You Read To Me, I'll Read To You.
John Ciardi and his children read more than 30 poems.

Peerless Record Company Limited

Bercourt House, York Road, Brentford, Middlesex, TW8 OQP, U.K.

PRCS 112 Selections From Russian Poetry And Prose.
Read in English and Russian by Marshall Shatz. Includes works by Pushkin, Lermentov, Gogol, etc. Complete Russian-English text included. Recommended for language study.

PRCS 114 Robert Burns – In Poetry, Song and Prose.
A programme of Burns' material presented in the manner of "Burns reading Burns". A truly superb collection performed by Arnold Johnston with complete text.

PRCS 115 The World's Great Poets, Vol. I – "America – Today".
Celebrated poets reading from their own works – Allen Ginsberg, Lawrence Ferlinghetti & Gregory Corso. Recorded at Spoleto Festival of Two Worlds.

PRCS 116 The World's Great Poets, Vol. II – Ezra Pound Reading His Cantos III, XVI, XLIX, LXXXI, XCII, CVI, CXV. Recorded at Spoleto.

Plantagenet Productions

Westridge, Highclere, Newbury, Berks., U.K.

In Sure And Certain Hope.
A sequence of thought from Christian poetry and prose. Includes, from St. Paul, 1 Cor. 15; Wordsworth's Ode On Intimations of Immortality, Bacon's essay 'Of Death', with shorter poems and prose by Addison, Donne, Milton, Pope, Shakespeare. LP–£2; Tape £1.50; will be reproduced on cassette as wanted.

The Rubaiyat Of Omar Khayyam.
Full length arrangement from several translations by Edward Fitzgerald. Read by Dorothy Rose Gribble. LP–£2; Tape–£1.50; will be reproduced on cassette as wanted.

This Powerful Rhyme.
1) A changing mood from Shakespeare, including 'The Phoenix and the Turtle' and reflective passages from his poetry and plays. 2) An Elizabethan sequence, with sonnets by Sidney, Spenser, Drayton, lines from 'The Faery Queen', Raleigh's 'The Lie', and representing Queen Elizabeth 1, Ben jonson, Marlowe, Gascoigne, Tichbourn. Read by Dorothy Rose Gribble and Mhicheil Kennedy. LP–£2; Tape–£1.50; will be reproduced on cassette as wanted.

Sea Change.
Poetry and narrative. Brave Alum Bey (Gilbert), The Jumblies (Lear), from Colin Clout's come home again (Spenser), Nature and the Poet (Wordsworth), The Revenge (Tennyson) etc. Read by Dorothy Rose Gribble. LP–£2; Tape–£1.75; will be reproduced on cassette as wanted.

Enchantments.
An Anthology for All Hallowe'en. The Witch of En-dor (The Bible), La Belle Dame sans merci (Keats), a passage from Undine, The Hand of Glory (Barham) etc. Read by Gipsy Ellis and Dorothy Rose Gribble. Tape–£1.75; LP by special order.

Alexander Pope.
Studies in contrast; 1. The Wife of Bath, her Prologue from Chaucer. 2. Eloise to Abelard, from her letters. Read by Dorita Curtis-Hayward. Tape–£2.25; LP by special order.

John Clare, Countryman.
Selected poetry and prose read by David Allister. LP–£2.25; Tape–£1.75.

Christabel.
By Samuel Taylor Coleridge; read by Dorothy Rose Gribble. Tape–£1.75; LP by special order.

These Chaucer Wrote.
Sir Thopas, Thisbe of Babylon Balades: Trouthe, Lak of Steadfastnesse Fortune; Compleynt to his empty Purs; Proverbs. Chaucer's English, modified pronunciation. Read by Dorothy Rose Gribble. LP–£2; Tape–£1.75; will be reproduced on cassette as wanted.

The Nonne Preestes Tale.
Chaucer's English, modified pronunciation. Read by Dorothy Rose Gribble. LP–£2; Tape–£1.75; will be reproduced on cassette as wanted.

Poetry of Charles Graves.
Chosen by the author. Includes The Spark, Deaf Mute at the Dance, Myrrha and Damon, The Pool of Narcissus, Echo and Narcissus, Summer Night. Read by Dorothy Rose Gribble and Mhicheil

Kennedy. LP–£2.25; Tape–£1.75; will be reproduced on cassette as wanted.

Alice V. Stuart.
Selected poems. Read by Katharine Page and Dorothy Rose Gribble. LP–£2; Tape–£1.75; will be reproduced on cassette as wanted.

From My Fireside.
Poems of Leonard Clark spoken by the author. LP–£2; Tape–£1.75; will be reproduced on cassette as wanted.

Poetry And Stories For Children.
By Rita Spurr; music by Claire Yool. Read by Dorita Curtis-Hayward and Dorothy Rose Gribble. LP–£2; Tape–£1.75; will be reproduced on cassette as wanted.

Malcolm H. Tattersall.
Thirty sonnets recorded for the author. Read by Dorothy Rose Gribble and Noel Lloyd. LP–£2; Tape–£1.50; will be reproduced on cassette as wanted.

'And I Am a Doggerel Bard'.
Written and recorded by Dorothy Rose Gribble. LP 75p. Issued on tape with Tall Trees of Jerusalem written and recorded by David Hadda – £1.75.

Lyrics of Ronsard.
Translated by Charles Graves and read by Noel Lloyd. On tape with Poet's Choice written and read by Edgell Rickword. Tape–£1.75; LPs later.

RCA Records

1133 Avenue of the Americas, New York, NY 10036, U.S.A.

VDM–114 Everybody Knows The Trouble I've Seen.
(Ogden Nash) A Word to Husbands; The Hunter; Unfortunately it's the only Game in Town; A Limerick; Ft. Worth; The Strange Case of the Entomologist's Heart; Another Limerick: Rodent; The Stilly Night; The Perfect Husband; Anybody for Money; Tune for an ill-Tempered Clavichord; How to Be Married Without a Spouse; Another Limerick: Soprano; Crossing the Border; A Man Can Complain Can't He?; Another Limerick: Umpire; John Peel–Shake Hands with 37 Mamas; Exit, Pursued by a Bear; Everybody Tells Me Everything; All's Brillig in Tin Pan Alley; A Caution to Everybody; Brief Lives Are Not So Brief–Part I; Brief Lives Are Not So Brief–Part II; What, No Sheep?; Samson Agonistes; The Purist; The Terrible People; I Never Even Suggested It; The Axolotl; Don't Look Now, but There's Something Behind the Curtain; Another Limerick: A Princess; You'll Drink Your Orange Juice and Like It; Another Limerick: Lady of Natchez; The Buses Headed for Scranton; Come, Come Kerovac, My Generation Is Better Than Yours; Tweedle Dee and Tweedledoom; I Know Exactly Who Dropped the Overalls in Mrs. Murphy's Chowder; How Can Echo Answer What Echo Cannot Hear?; As I Was Saying to St. Paul Just the Other Day; Medusa and the Mot Juste; The Carcajou and the Kircajou; O Tempora, O, Oh; The Nymph and the Shepherd, or She Went That-A-Way; Another Limerick: Avant guard; So Penseroso; Try it Sundays and Holidays; I'll Met by Flourescence; I Will Arise and Go Now; For a Good Dog; So I Resigned from the Chuchin Chowder and Marching Club; Thoughts Thought While Waiting for a Pronouncement from a Doctor, an Editor, a Big Executive, the Department of Internal Revenue, or Any Other Momentous Pronouncer.

VDM–102 Personal Choice.
A (Dynagrove) Alec Guiness (E.E. Cummings): Sweet Spring Is Yours, When Faces Called Flowers Float Out the Ground, O the Sun Comes, The Moon Looked into My Window; (Edith Sitwell): I Do Like to Be Beside the Seaside, Polka; Tarantella (Hilaire Belloc); Romance (Walter James Turner); Through Nightmare (Robert Graves); Strange Meeting (Wilfred Owen); Hearing of Harvest Rotting in the Valley (W.H. Auden); (Anon.); Clerk Saunders, King John and the Abbot of Canterbury; Henry VI, Part 3; Act II, Scene 5; Soliloquy (William Shakespeare); A Toccata of Galuppi's (Robert Browning); Serviette in a Lovely Home (Ogden Nash); Spectator ab Extra (Arthur Hugh Clough); Night (William Blake); The Leaden Echo and the Golden Echo (Gerard Manley Hopkins).

LM–1812 Poet's Gold.
'The Day Is Done' (Longfellow); The Children's Hour (Longfellow); A Child's Laughter (Swinburne); The Lamb (Blake); The Tiger (Blake); Happy Thought (Stevenson); Whole Duty of Children (Stevenson); Good and Bad Children (Stevenson); My Shadow (Stevenson); The Land of Counterpane (Stevenson); Paul Revere's Ride (Longfellow); The Concord Hymn (Emerson); O Captain! My Captain (Whitman); Barbara Frietchie (Whittier); The Deacon's Masterpiece (Holmes); There Was a Child Went Forth (Whitman); Little Boy Blue (Field); The Owl and the Pussy-Cat (Lear); Jabberwocky (Carroll); The Law of the Jungle (Kipling); Rime of the Ancient Mariner (Coleridge).

LM–1813 Poet's Gold.
'The Rubaiyat of Omar Khayyam' and Other Poetry. Helen Hayes; Raymond Massey; Thomas Mitchell. Rubaiyat of Omar Khayyam (Fitz-Gerald); Ode on a Grecian Urn (Keats); The Ballad of the Harp-Weaver (Millay); The Raven (Poe); The Fiddler of Dooney (Yeats); The Lake Isle of Innisfree (Yeats); 'When You Are Old' (Yeats); On First Looking into Chapman's Homer (Keats); On Seeing the Elgin Marbles (Keats); My Last Duchess (Browning); Elegy Written in a Country Church-Yard (Gray); The Battle of Blenheim (Southey); Tomlinson (Kipling); Battle-Hymn of the Republic (Howe);

Recessional (Kipling).

VDS-106 Program of Poems By Edith Sitwell.
A John Gielgud; Irene Worth (John Gielgud): Colonel Fantock, The Sleeping Beauty: No. 8 Still Falls the Rain, Heart and Mind, Song: The Queen Bee Sighed; (Irene Worth): On the Vanity of Human Aspirations, Eurydice, Dirge for the New Sunrise; (John Gielgud and Irene Worth): Poems from 'Facade'; I Do Like to Be Beside the Seaside, En Famille, Trio for Two Cats and a Trombone, Hornpipe, By the Lake, Scotch Rhapsody, Lullaby for Jumbo, Waltz.

The Record Collectors Guild Inc.

507 Fifth Avenue, New York, NY 10017, U.S.A.

GR 901 The Poems Of John W. Clark.
Read by the poet.

GR 902/903/904 Spoken Word Poetry, Drama, Humour. An Album of Modern Poetry, British and American.
An anthology read by 44 poets. 3 record sets $14.37. Available singly $4.79.

GR 905 The Poems of Allan Dowling.
Read by the poet.

GR 907 Breathing Of First Things Speak To Me, Child.
New poems by Hy Sobiloff. Read by the poet.

GR 900 Great Shakespearean Actors.

Satori

1600 N. Willis Drive, Bloomington, IN 47401, U.S.A.

Four New Poets
Special long-playing recording features Ray Newton, Brother Dimitrios, David Wade, Richard Jaworski. $3.79.

Scholastic Audio-Visual Center

904 Sylvan Avenue, Englewood Cliffs, NJ 07632, U.S.A.

POETRY FOR CHILDREN

LC R-70-750961 Selections From The Arrow Book of Funny Poems. Twenty-seven fun-filled poems and limericks from the book. Includes Lewis Carroll's Father William, John Ciardi's The Reason for the Pelican, other verse with special appeal for children. 0736 7" LP and book – $1.95; 0636 Record only – $1.25.

LC R-68-3724 Selections From The Arrow Book of Poetry. Fourteen poems by Carl Sandburg, John Masefield, Langston Hughes, others. 0711 7" LP and book – $1.95; 0618 Record Only – $1.25.

LC 77-752362 Selections From Faces and Places: Poems For You. Excerpts from the book. A rich collection of poems both light and serious by Carl Sandburg, the Benets, Edna St. Vincent Millay, John Ciardi, and many others. For all ages. 1703 7" LP and book – $1.95; 1603 Record only – $1.25.

LC R-58-379 An Anthology of Negro Poetry For Young People. Poet Arna Bontemps reads lyric poetry especially appropriate for young listeners – simple, compelling poems that speak of heaven and earth, North and South, love and hate, the rich and the poor. Works of Langston Hughes, Countee Cullen, Paul Laurence Dunbar, anonymous traditional poets, many others. Complete text included. $4.50.

ENGLISH POETRY AND PROSE

9891 Anthology of English Verse, Vol. 1.
Masefield, de la Mare, James Stephens, Kipling, Housman, others. Text. LC R-64-609 12" LP–$6.50.

9892 Anthology of English Verse, Vol. 2.
Tennyson, Wordsworth, Lewis Carroll, Robert Graves, others. Text. LC R-64-609 12" LP–$6.50.

9886 Anthology of 20th Century English Poetry (Part 1)
Richard Church, Laurie Lee, C. Day Lewis, John Betjeman and 4 others read their own poetry. Also works of 13 other poets. LC R-61-1854 12" LP–$6.50.

9851 Early English Poetry.
Heroic, courtly, and comic masterpieces of early English poetry, read in Old and Middle English by Charles W. Dunn. Includes Caedmon's Hymn, Chaucer's The Wife of Bath's Tale, excerpts from Beowulf, Sir Gawain and the Green Knight, more. Complete text, modern English translations and background notes. LC R-59-65 12" LP–$6.50.

9882 English Lyric Poems and Ballads.
Selected works of Tennyson, Keats, de la Mare, Browning, others, read by Kathleen Danson Read. Text. LC R-59-63 12" LP–$6.50.

9883 English Romantic Poetry.
Wordsworth, Coleridge, Shelley, Keats, read by John S. Martin. Includes Kubla Khan, Ode to a Nightingale, Ozymandias, more. Text. LC R-62-1395 12" LP–$6.50.

AMERICAN PROSE

9745 Stephen Crane.
Jared Reed reads selected poems, excerpts from the Red Badge of Courage and The Veteran. LC R-64-619 12" LP–$6.50.

AMERICAN POETRY

9735 Anthology of Contemporary American Poetry.
Outstanding collection of modern verse edited and read by poet George Abbe. 28

selections by such poets as John Ciardi, Theodore Roethke, Kenneth Patchen, Richard Wilbur, Karl Shapiro, David Morton, others. LC R-62-135 12" LP–$6.50.

9791 Anthology of Negro Poets
A unique listening experience, as 6 distinguished Negro poets read from their own works. Voices of Langston Hughes, Sterling Brown, Claude McKay, Margaret Walker, Countee Cullen, and Gwendolyn Brooks give added power to the musical and intellectual appeal of their poetry. Booklet has biographical notes by the editor Arna Bontemps. LC R-55-646 12" LP–$6.50.

9792 Anthology of Negro Poets In The U.S.A.
The inspired expression of American Negro poets from 1746 to 1949. Poet Arna Bontemps reads from his own works and those of Langston Hughes, Claude McKay, Countee Cullen, Sterling Brown, Paul Laurence Dunbar, James Weldon Johnson, Phillis Wheatley, others. LC R-55-643 12" LP–$6.50.

0671 The Death of Lincoln.
A dramatization and poems on Lincoln's death. Includes excerpts from Walt Whitman's O Captain, Edwin Markham's Lincoln the Man of the People, Carl Sandburg's Tje People, Yes. 7" LP–$1.25.

9733 Derry Down Derry.
Twenty-eight Robert Frost poems read by his daughter, Lesley. Suitable for elementary grades. Text. LC R-63-271 12" LP–$6.50.

7774 The Dream Keeper.
Negro poet Langston Hughes reads 29 of his poems appropriate for elementary grades. Simple, powerful lines evoke his boyhood dreams, memories of far-away places and people. Poems on the Negro's heritage tell of a soul-weary blues player, a "darker brother" who loses his dreams, others who keep their dreams alive. Hughes' connective narration adds depth and warmth to the presentation. Complete text. LC R-55-644 12" LP–$6.50.

9753 Emily Dickinson's Letters.
A reminiscence by Thomas Wentworth Higginson written for the Atlantic Monthly in 1891. Includes Emily's letters to Mr. Higginson, written from 1862 until her death in 1886. Read with a critical introduction by Samuel Charters. Notes. LC R-62-1496 12" LP–$6.50.

9502 Evangeline.
Complete poem, read by broadcaster Harry Fleetwood. Appropriate for elementary graders. Complete text in accompanying paper back book. LC R-60-497. 2–12" LPs and book–$13.00.

9788 God's Trombones.
Excerpts from James Weldon Johnson's book of verse based on the Bible. Read by

actor Bryce Bond, with an original musical score. Notes with text. LC R-65-1755 12" LP–$6.50.

0604 The Light and Serious Side of Theodore Roethke.
The poet reads from his serious works; professional narrators, from his fun and nonsense verse. Appropriate for elementary grades. Poems used by permission of Doubleday and Co. 7" LP–$1.25.

11008 Poems and Ballads From 100 Plus American Poems.
Favorite selections from the book. Readings include Donald Hall's The Sleeping Giant, Langston Hughes' Mother to Son, Carl Sandburg's Localities, and others. Ballads sung by Pete Seeger, Peter LaFarge, and Guy Carawan. LC 74–751726 12" LP–$6.50.

9750 Readings From Walt Whitman.
Excerpts from Leaves of Grass, read by the University Players with Wallace House. Complete Text. LC R-59-137 12" LP–$6.50.

11007 Reflections On a Gift of Watermelon Pickle. Light modern verse especially suitable for high school English classes. Ellen Holly and Paul Hecht read poems by John Ciardi, Theodore Roethke, Carl Sandburg, others. LC R-67-3710 12" LP–$7.00.

1603 Selections From Faces and Places: Poems For You.
A rich collection of poems both light and serious, by Carl Sandburg, the Benets, Edna St. Vincent Millay, John Ciardi, and many others. 7" LP–$1.25.

9730 The Song of Hiawatha.
Dramatic excerpts from Longfellow's classic Indian tale, suitable for elementary grades. Harry Fleetwood reads Hiawatha's Childhood, The Hunting of Pau-Puk–Keewis, Hiawatha's Departure, more. Booklet has text. LC R-59-52 12" LP–$6.50.

9790 Sterling Brown and Langston Hughes.
Brown reads his early poems; Hughes, from his Simple Speaks His Mind. Illustrated text. LC R-59-652 12" LP–$6.50.

11001 Today's Poets: Their Poems-Their Voices, Vol. 1.
Contemporary poets Donald Hall, Louis Simpson, Joseph Langland and Robert Francis read their own works. Complete text, biographies of poets, bibliographies. LC R-66-3642 12" LP–$6.50.

11002 Today's Poets: Their Poems–Their Voices, Vol. 2.
Features May Swenson, David Wagoner, Josephine Miles, William Stafford. Text, biographies, bibliographies. LC R-66-342 12" LP–$6.50.

11003 Today's Poets: Their Poems-Their Voices, Vol. 3.
Features Denise Levertov, Robert Creeley, James Wright, David Ignatow. Text, biographies, bibliographies. LC R-68-3002 12" LP–$6.50.

11004 Today's Poets: Their Poems-Their Voices, Vol. 4.
Features Philip Booth, Robert Hayden, Adrienne Rich, Gary Snyder. Text, biographies, bibliographies. LC R-68-3275 12" LP–$6.50.

11005 Today's Poets: Their Poems-Their Voices, Vol. 5.
Features Michael Benedikt, Robert Bly, Galway Kinnel, John Logan. Text, biographies, bibliographies. LC R-68-3668 12" LP–$6.50.

9736 Words For The Wind.
Theodore Roethke reads his own works, including Elegy for Jane, I Knew a Woman, The Renewal, more. Text. Poems used by permission of Doubleday and Co. LC R-62-851 12" LP–$6.50.

WORLD LITERATURE

9871 Dante: The Inferno.
Poet John Ciardi reads 8 complete cantos from his English translation. Text. LC R-59-760 12" LP–$6.50.

11006 The Sound of World Poetry.
Melodic qualities of 15 languages explored through poetry. Introduction in English to each language followed by readings of poems in French, German, Russian, Chinese, Hindu, Swahili, English, more. Notes include complete text, transliteration of poems, bibliography, explanatory section on Techniques of Poetic Sound. LC R-67-3338 12" LP–$6.50.

BLACK LITERATURE

12012 The Black Hero.
Dramatizations of Winds of Change by Loyle Hairston; An Indignation Dinner by James David Carrothers; and Distrust (excerpt from Native Son) by Richard Wright. Readings of Strong Men by Sterling Brown; The Negro Mother by Langston Hughes; and Still Here by Langston Hughes. 12" LP–$7.00.

12021 Black Perspectives.
Dramatizations of God Bless America by John O. Killens and a scene from Five on the Black Hand Side by Charlie L. Russell. Readings of We Have Been Believers by Margaret Walker; Mother to Son by Langston Hughes; America by Claude McKay; A Poem to Complement Other Poems by Don L. Lee; Black Bourgeoise by LeRoi Jones; Boker T. and W.E.B. by Dudley Randall; The New Integrationists by Don L. Lee; and If We Must Die by Claude McKay. 12" LP–$7.00.

12011 The Journey.
Dramatization of The Drinking Gourd by Lorraine Hansberry. Readings of I Couldn't Hear Nobody Pray, I, Too, Sing America, and My People by Langston Hughes; Incident by Countee Cullen; What Color Is Black? by Barbara D. McHone; Black Power by Raymond Patterson; Outcast by Claude McKay; and The Emancipation of George Hector (A Colored Turtle) by Mari E. Evans. 12" LP–$7.00.

12020 Major Black Writers.
Dramatizations of The Scapegoat by Paul Laurence Dunbar and The Man Who Saw the Flood by Richard Wright. Readings of Go Down Death by James Weldon Johnson; Brown River Smile by Jean Toomer; Theme for English B by Langston Hughes; Notes for a Hypothetical Novel by James Baldwin; The Death of Nick Charles by LeRoi Jones; and beware; do not read this poem by Ishmael Reed. 12" LP–$7.00.

12018 The Scene.
Dramatizations of How the Snake Got His Rattles by Julius Lester and The Angel of the Candy Counter by Maya Angelou. Readings of Lift Every Voice and Sing by James Weldon Johnson; Good Morning Blues by Kristin Hunter; When Malindy Sings by Paul Laurence Dunbar; and But He Was Cool: or he even stopped for green lights by Don. L. Lee. 12" LP–$7.00.

12019 The Search.
Dramatizations of Sweat by Zora Neale Hurston and The Wife of His Youth by Charles Waddell Chesnutt. Readings of Customs and Culture by Ted Jones; For a Lady I know by Countee Cullen; and Let America Be America Again by Langston Hughes. 12" LP–$7.00.

UNDERSTANDING LITERATURE

9120 Understanding and Appreciation of Poetry.
Illuminating discussion using well-known works to illustrate special literary qualities of poetry-rhythms, sensory and emotional appeal, expressive figures of speech, metrical patterns, more. Includes poems by Sandburg, Poe, Masefield, Shelley, Coleridge, others. Complete text. LC R-61-1832 12" LP–$6.50.

SPANISH STORIES AND POEMS

9926 Oral Anthology: Spanish-American Poetry of The 20th Century.
Poetry of Mistral, Reyes, Vocos-Lescand, others, read in Latin American Spanish by Octavio Corvalan. Bilingual Text. LC R-63-446 12" LP–$6.50.

7824 Paso A Paso (Step by Step).
Richly varied selection of nursery rhymes, aphorisms, poems, and short stories read in Latin American Spanish by Octavio Corvalan especially for elementary graders. Progresses from simple poems and phrases for beginning students to short stories and poems for the second or third year. Bilingual text. LC R-67-1849 12" LP–$5.95.

9580 Poems of Federico Garcia Lorca. Twenty-eight poems read in classic Spanish by Jorge Juan Rodriguez. Text. LC R-61-1962 2–12" LPs–$13.00.

AFRO-AMERICAN HISTORY AND CULTURE RECORD UNITS

Unit 1318 Cultural Flowering: Music and Literature.
The black experience in America, evoked in the poems of Langston Hughes and Sterling Brown, the music of Leadbelly, the sounds of big city jazz bands, and more. 7 albums–$56.30.

Unit 1319 Negro Songs, Stories and Poetry For Young People.
Two collections of African folk tales, a documentary recording of New York City children at play, a brief history of jazz in America, folk songs, the poetry of Langston Hughes and others, inspire and instruct elementary grade students. 8 albums–$41.80.

Unit 1337 Negro History Sound Capsule.
A survey of Negro history and culture, containing five albums carefully selected from other Afro-American study units. 5 albums–$28.95.

RECORD LIBRARY UNIT

Unit 1212 Songs, Stories, and Poetry, Primary.
A richly varied collection of songs and stories – old and new – includes lullabies from around the world, Afro-American blues, stories-in-song about everyday experiences, West African parables, old English animal songs, and more. Performed by Pete Seeger, Leadbelly, Charity Bailey, Harold Courlander and others. 7 albums–$35.85.

Unit 1265 Today's Poets: Their Poems-Their Voices.
Distinguished American poets read from their own works, adding an exciting dimension to the study of modern poetry in secondary school and college. Each record is accompanied by a booklet which includes complete text, biographies of the poets, and a bibliography. 5 albums–$32.50.

Unit 1312 Civil War.
Songs, documents and speeches, an autobiographical account, poetry, and excerpts from a classic Civil War novel recreate an important period of American history. 5 albums–$36.25.

Schwann Long Playing Records

This is a monthly guide to long playing records. For further information write to: W. Schwann, Inc., 137 Newbury St., Boston, Mass. 02116, USA. (The pages quoted here are taken from the March 1969 catalogue).

POETRY, PROSE, SPEECH:

Abbe, George–Poetry (12-61) Folk. 9164.

American & British Poetry (4-64)–3-Gry, 902/4.

American Famous Story Poems (7-60) 2-Lex 7610/15.

American Poetry–To 1900–2-Lex 7550/5 Vol. 2. Burr. Barth, Weiss 2-Lex. 7698/9. Contemporary Anthology (1-62) Folk. 9735. Favorite Poems–Begley Caed. 1207. Historical Anthology (6-65) 2-Argo 245/6. 19th Cent. Anthology (6-67) Sp. Arts 963. Poems of Patriotism–Begley. Harris Caed. 1204.

Anthology of Modern Verse–Schol. 11007 Antoninus, Brother–Savagery of Love (12-68) Caed. S-1260.

Arnold. Clough, Fitzgerald–Poems–Holm, Goring, Jacobi Argo RG-521.

Arnold, Matthew–Sohrab & Rustum-Speaight Sp. Arts 975 Treasury-Speaight Sp. Arts 974.

As If (John Ciardi) Folk. 9780.

Auden, W.H. Caed. 1019. Poems–Auden Sp. Arts 999. Poems–Auden (High School Vers.) Sp. Arts 999-HS. Reading (11-60) Sp. Arts 780.

Ballad of Robin Hood–Quayle (11-63) Caed. 1177.

Baudelaire–Fleurs du Mal (F) Caed. 1029. Flowers of Evil–Mimieux, U.A.A. Khan. Misra (2-68) Conn. S-2007.

Baxter, Frank C.–Nature of Poetry Sp. Arts 703.

Beckett, Samuel–Cusack (11-63) Caed. 1169.

Belloc. H. & W.S. Gilbert–Bab Ballads & Cautionary Tales–Grenfell & Holloway Caed. 1104.

Beowulf † Chaucer 10" Lex. 5505. Davis. Coghill (10-66) Sp. Arts 918. Malone (complete) 4-Caed. 4001.

Beowulf & Other Poetry In Old English Caed. 1161.

Betjeman, John–Golden Treasury Sp. Arts 710. Vols. 1/2 (5-64) 2-Argo 225, 273.

Bhagavad-Gita (Song of God)-Selections-Mohyeddin (12-68) Caed. S-1249.

Blake, William–Richardson Caed. 1101. Bates, Bonnany, Johnson, Orr (6-65) Argo 428. Speaight (12-61) † Hopkins Sp. Arts. 814.

Brooke, Rupert–Poems–Waring (11-65) Folk. 9818.

Browning, Eliz. B.–Sonnets From Portuguese (Cornell) Caed. 1071. Sonnets From the Portuguese–Lee Sp. Arts 973.

Browning, Robert–Mason Caed. 1048. Anthology † Tennyson (2-67) Sp. Arts 934. My Last Duchess etc. Caed. 1201. Rylands, Adrian, etc. (565) Argo 346. Speaight (11-63) Sp. Arts 861.

Burns, Robert–Love Songs (6-59) Sp. Arts 754. Poems & Letters (2-61) Folk. 9877. Poetry–Worlock (3-59) Caed. 1103.

Byron–Tyrone Power Caed. 1042. Don Juan (Cantos 1, 2) Argo 374. Rylands, Duncan, etc. (5-64) Argo 344. Treasury–Orr (10-66) Sp. Arts 908.

Canadian Poets–Voices of 8 (9-59) Folk. 9905. Six Montreal Poets (12-57) Folk. 9805. Six Toronto Poets (3-59) Folk. 9806.

Catholic Verse–Brady, Callan Sp. Arts 712.

Chanson de Roland (F) 2-Folk. 9587.

Chaucer–Canterbury Tales–Ross Caed. 1008. Canterbury Tales–Prologue Argo 401. Miller's Tale & Reeve's Tale (4-67) Caed. 1223. Nun's Priest's Tale (1-67) Argo 466.
Coghill, Davis (10-66) Sp. Arts 919.
General Prologue In Middle English Caed. 1151. Kaplan Folk. 9859.
MacLiammoir, Holloway (excerpts) Caed. 1130.
Poetry † Beowulf 10″ Lex. 5505.
Poetry in Middle English (8-67) Caed. 1226.
Wife of Bath–Ashcroft Caed. 1102.

Chinese Poems, Tang & Sung Dynasty Folk. 9921.

Christian Poetry & Prose–Guinness (7-61) Folk. 9893.

Clark, John W.–Poems (7-64) Gry. 901.

Cocteau, Jean–Reads His Poetry & Prose [F] (2-63) Caed. 1083.

Coleridge–Poetry (Richardson) (8-58) Caed. 1092. Rime Of Ancient Mariner (10-66) Sp. Arts 910.

Conversation Pieces–Poems (4-67) Folk. 9880.

Coward, Noel–Duologues Caed. 1069. Poems (& Shaw: 'Apple Cart') Caed. 1094.

Dante–Inferno [1] Folk. 9977. Inferno–Ciardi Folk. 9871.

de la Mare, Walter–Reading Caed. 1046.

Derwood, Gene–Poetry of Sp. Arts 736.

Dickinson, Emily–Poems (4-60) Sp. Arts 761. Poems–Harris Caed. 1119.

Dicky, James–Poems–Dicky Sp. Arts 984.

Donat, Robert–Favorite Poems (2-63) Sp. Arts 848. Selected Poetry–Donat (1-66) Argo 437.

Donne, John–Love Poems–Burton Caed. 1141. No Man Is An Island, etc.–Allen (11-68) CMS 542. Treasury–Speaight (11-63) Sp. Arts 859. 26 Poems–Johnson. Orr (6-65) Argo 403.

Dowling, Allan–Poems (7-64) Gry. 905.

Dryden, John–Scolfield Caed. 1125. Treasury (11-63) Sp. Arts 866.

Durrell, Lawrence–Love Poems Sp. Arts 818. Grecian Echoes 2-Sp. Arts LVA-1003/4. Irish Faust Sp. Arts LVA-201.

Eberhart, Richard (2-66) Dec. 9145. Reading His Poetry (5-68) Caed. S-1243.

Eliot, T.S.–Reading Caed. 1045. Four Quartets (Eliot reading) Ang. 45012. Four Quartets (Speaight) Argo 11. Four Quartets Sp. Arts 765. Old Possum's Practical Cats–Eliot Argo 116. Old Possum's Practical Cats–Eliot Sp. Arts 758. Wasteland & Others–Speaight Argo 10. Wasteland & Others Sp. Arts 734. Oliver Twist–Mason Dec. 9107.

Elizabethan Love Poems (2-65) Sp. Arts 896.

Emerson, Ralph Waldo–Lynn (10-62) Sp. Arts 842. Essays, Poetry & Journals (3-63) Folk. 9758.

English & Amer. Poetry 5-Lex. 7510,-15,-20,-25,-30.

English Ballads Folk. 9881.

English Lyric Poems & Ballads Folk. 9882.

English Poetry–17th Century Caed. 1049. Campion, Jonson, Herrick (11-66) Argo 486.

Early English Poetry–Dunn Folk. 9851. Early 17th Cent.–Jeffery, King Sp. Arts 994. 18th & 19th Cent. (2-64) Brit. 1006. Elizabethan & Jacobean Lyric (1-67) Argo 484. Elizabethan Sonneteers (11-66) Argo 485. Goldsmith/Gray/Collins (10-66) Sp. Arts 927. Here Today–Parts 1/2 (10-66) 2-Sp. Arts 944/5. Lyrics From Old English Folk. 9858. Romantic Poetry Folk. 9883. 16th Cent.–Jeffrey, King, Morrish Sp. Arts 993. 16th & 17th Cent. (2-64) Brit. 1005. Thomas, Stephens, Lewis, etc. (5-64) Brit. 1001. 20th Cent. Anthology (1-62–) 2-Folk. 9886/7.

English Verse–Anthology (12-61) 2-Folk. 9891/2.

Famous American Documents & Poems (5-68) CMS 532.

Famous Poems that Tell Great Stories Dec. 9040.

Ferlinghetti, Lawrence–Poems Fan. 7004.

Forms Of Poetry (9-60) 2-Lex. 7620/5.

French Poetry–15th, 16th, 17th Cent. [F] Per. 1522. Anthology–Guilloton (2-64) Caed. 1184. 18th, 19th Cent. [F] Per. 1523. 19th Cent–Mankin [F] (12-61) Folk. 9936. 20th Cent.–Mankin (3-66) Folk. 9943. 100 Years Of [F] 2-Folk. 9595.

French Verse [F]–Jean Vilar Sp. Arts 711. 6th Cent. (13th-18th) (5-62) [F] Folk. 9934. Verlaine, Rimbaud, Mallarme [F] Per. 1524.

Frost, Robert–Reads Dec. 9033. Derry Down Derry–L. Frost (12-61) Folk. 9733. Reading His Poetry Caed. 1060. Reads Own Works (1-66) Dec. 9127.

Gather Ye Rosebuds GC 31010.

German Ballad (Classical Age) (8-65) Folk. 9918.

German Poetry–Lotte Lehmann [G] Caed. 1072. Anthology–Rothschild [G] (12-68) Sp. Arts 998. Invitation Dover 9892.

German Verse–Schnitzler [G] Sp. Arts 701.

Ginsberg, Allen–Howl & Others Fan. 7006.

Golden Treasury–Amer. Verse (9-60) Sp. Arts 772. English–Bloom, Portman, Neville 2-Caed. 2011.
Of Apollinaire, Cocteau, etc. (6-62) Sp. Arts 801.
Of French Literature (6-62) Sp. Arts 822.

Golden Treasury–Amer. Verse (9-60) Sp. Arts 772. English–Bloom, Portman, Neville 2-Caed. 2011. Of Apollinaire, Cocteau, etc. (6-62) Sp. Arts 801. Of French Literature (6-62) Sp. Arts 822. Of Italian Verse (9-60) Sp. Arts 771. Of Milton, Keats, Shelley (9-60) Sp. Arts 768. Of Nerval, Baudelaire, etc. (9-60) Sp. Arts 764. Of Spanish American Poetry (10-62) Sp. Arts 839. Of Spanish Poetry–Florit (10-62) Sp. Arts 829.

Graves, Robert–Graves (5-65) Argo 191. His Poetry (3-59) Caed. 1066. Love Respelt–Graves (1-66) Col. OL-6400 Rubaiyat of Omar Khayyam/Poems–Graves (9-68) Sp. Arts 1010.

Great American Poetry (6-62) 2-Caed. 2009.

Great Poems of the English Lang.– Vol. 1/3 (11-68) 3-CMS 5446.

Greek Modern Heroic Poetry (2-60) (Gr) Folk. 4468.

Greek Poetry, Ancient (Gr) (7-61) Folk. 9984.

Hardy, Thomas–Poetry (Richardson) (8-58) Caed. 1140.

Hearing Poetry 2-Caed. 1021/2.

Heart Speaks–Lyrics of Love Dec. 9043.

Heine, Heinrich–Poems–Luce Folk. 9867.

Heroic Soul–Poems of Patriotism Dec. 9044.

Homer–Iliad & Odyssey (Gr) (7-61) Folk. 9985. Bk XVI–Redgrave. Dobie, etc. Sp. Arts 926. Books 15, 16, 18 (excerpts)–Quayle Caed. 1196. Ch. 16, Death of Patroclus (E) Folk. 9863. Rees (E) Sp. Arts 833. Odyssey–Books 9/12–Quayle 3-Caed. 3001.

Honneur des poetes (8-65) Folk. 9944.

Hopkins, Gerard Manley–Poetry (6-59) Caed. 1111. Speaight (12-61) † Blake Sp. Arts 814.

Horace, Odes Of (2-60) Folk. 9968. Pei (L) (5-62) † Virgil Folk. 9964.

Housman, A.E.–Shropshire Lad. etc. Caed. 1203.

How To Read & Understand Poetry 2-Lex. 7700/1.

Irish Verse–Colum Sp. Arts 706. Siobhan McKenna Sp. Arts 707.

Keats–Poetry (Richardson) (8-58), Caed. 1087.

Keats & Shelley–Marcuse Lex 7505.

Khayyam, Omar–Rubaiyat–Dhiogh CMS 527 Rubaiyat (tr. Fitzgerald/tr. Graves & Ali-Shah) (9-68) Sp. Arts 965.

Latin Amer. Poets–Corvalan (Sp) Folk. 9926.

Lawrence, D.H.–Lady Chatterley Caed. 1116. Poetry & Prose–Moore Folk. 9837.

Lewis, C. Day–Reads Own Works (2-66) Dec. 9139.

Lincoln, Abraham–Sandburg, Whitman, etc. Dec. 8515.

Lincoln Treasury–Welles, Sandburg, Huston (2-59) † Musicals: Lonesome Train Dec. 9065.

Lindsay, Vachel Caed. 1041. Poetry (6-67) Caed. 1216.

Longfellow, Henry W.–Evangeline 2-Folk. 9502. Best Loved Poems–Holbrook (7-66) Caed. 1107.

Evangeline–Holbrook (abridged) Caed. 1179. Song of Hiawatha Folk. 9730. Treasury–Hall (2-67) Sp. Arts 898.

Lorca, Federico Garcia–Poesia y Drama Caed. 1067. Lament on Death of Bullfighter (Sp.) Van. 9055. Rodriguez (4-61) (Sp.) 2-Folk. 9580.

Lowell, Robert Reads Own Works (1-66) Dec. 9129.

MacLeish, Archibald Caed. 1009.

MacNiece, Louis–MacNiece (5-64) Argo 196. Reads Own Works (1-66) Dec. 9141.

Marshall, Lenore G.–Poetry (5-58) Sp. Arts 746.

Masefield, John–Story of Ossian (6-59) Sp. Arts 75. Fortune Of The Sea (5-64) Argo 230. Fox's Day (5-64) Argo 224. Reading Sea Fever (3-64) Caed. 1147. Story of Ossian–Masefield Argo 178.

Masters, Edgar Lee–Spoon River Caed. (S) 1152. Spoon River Anthology Col. OS-2410.

Maupassant Guy de–Treasury, Vols. 1/3 (1-66) 3-Sp. Arts 921/2,930.

Maurois, Andre–Treasury (1-66) 2-Sp. Arts 911/2.

Medieval Romance Poetry–Pei (E.F.I.Sp., Port) (5-62) 2-Folk. 9578.

Metaphysical Poets–Religious (6-65) Argo 404. Secular (6-65) Argo 427.

Millay, Edna St. Vincent (Anderson) Caed. 1024. Reading From Her Poetry Caed. 1123.

Milton, John–Paradise Lost, Books 1 & 4 Caed. 2008. Books 1 & 2–Redgrave, etc. (1-66) 2-Argo 431/2. Books 3 & 4–Redgrave, etc. Argo 463. Books 5 & 6 (1-67) Argo 464. Books 7, 9, 10, 12, (7-67) 2-Argo 508/9.
Paradise Regained (excerpts)–McCarthy, Neville, Holm Argo RG-510.
Samson, Agonistes 2-Caed. (9)2028.
Shorter Poems–Devlin, etc. (1-66) Argo 433. Treasury–Speaight & Eddison (11-63) Sp. Arts 067.

Modern Brazilian Poetry–Nuns (3-66) Folk. 9914.

Modern Soviet Poetry & Humour Folk. 9962.

Moore, Marianne Caed. 1025. Reads Own Works (1-66) Dec. 9135.

Nash, Ogden Caed. 1015. Everybody Knows (6-67) Vic. VDM-114.

Negro Poets–Anthology Folk. 9791. Beyond The Blues (5-64) Argo 338. Negro Poets in USA Folk. 9792.

New Jazz Poets (11-67) Broad 461.

Nonsense Verse of Carroll & Lear (3-58) Caed. 1078.

Ovid–Richards (L) Folk. 9970.

Parker, Dorothy–Poems, Story Sp. Arts

726. Short Stories–Booth Caed. 1136.

Pasternak, Boris–Poems (R) (6-59) Sp. Arts 756.

Patchen, Kenneth–Jazz in Canada (2-60) Folk. 9718. Reads His Love Poems (2-61) Folk. 9719. Selected Poems (11-59) Folk. 9717.

Poe, Edgar A.–Poems–Hooks (7-60) Lex. 7600. Poems & Stories–Olmsted (1-60) Van. 9046. Raven, The Bells, etc. (1-69) Sp. Arts 1023.

Poems for Peace (10-67) Broad. 465.

Poet Speaks, Vols. 1/6 (6-66) 6-Argo 451/6. Vols. 7/9 3-Argo RG-517/9.

Poetry & Jazz (6-65) 2-Argo (Z) DA-26/7. In the Cellar–Ferlinghetti & Rexroth Fan. 7002.

Poet's Gold 2-Vic, LM-1812, 1813.

Pope, Alexander–Poetry (11-63) Caed. 1171. Rape Of the Lock Argo 373. Rape Of the Lock Sp. Arts 961. Rylands, Adrian, etc. (5-64) Argo 343. Treasury–Speaight, Audley (6-67) Sp. Arts 962.

Portuguese Poetry, Modern (Port) (1-62) Folk. 9915.

Pound, Ezra (5-60) (11-62) 2-Caed. 1122, 1155.

Prevert, Jacques–Poems Sp. Arts LVA-34.

Primitive & Archaic Poetry–Rothenberg, Antin, MacLow, Owens (1-69) Broad. 651.

Ransom, John Crowe (2-66) Dec. 9147.

Reid, Alastair–Poetry–Reid CMS 522.

Rilke, R.M.–Poetry–Lotte Lehmann (G) Caed. 1128.

Roethke, Theodore–Words For the Wind–Roethke Folk. 9736.

Roman Love Poetry–Richards (L) (7-61)' Folk. 9967.

Rosten, Norman–Poems (5-63) Folk. 9704.

Rubaiyat: Sohrab & Rustum Caed. 1023.

Russian Poetry–Gatova (3-59) (R) Folk. 9950. Poetry & Prose–Markov (R) (12-61) Folk. 9961.

SanJuan de-la Cruz–Poesias (Sp.) (8-65) Folk. 9932. Vol. 2–Dhiegh (E) (8-65) Folk. 9865.

Sandburg, Carl–Fog, etc.–Sandburg (11-68) Caed. S-1253. Reading His Poetry (10-62) Caed. 1150. Reads Sandburg. Dec. 9039.

Shreiber, Morris-Understanding & Appreciation Of Poetry (2-61) Folk. 9120.

Service, Robert W.–Poetry (8-67) Caed. 1218.

Seton, Ernest Thompson (5-67) Caed. 1217. 7 Old English Poems–Pope Lex. 7645.

Shakespeare–Great Actors (4-64) Gry. 900. Barrymore, John (7-63) 2-Audio Rarities 2280/1 Cleopatra–Luce (7-64) Folk. 9845. Elizabethan Life Lex 7693. Great Sonnets & Soliloquies–Allen (11-68) CMS 541. Hamlet (Readings)–Vaughn (9-67) MGM S-4488. Homage–E. Evans, Gielgud, Leighton Col. OL-7020; OS-2520. Homage to Shakespeare (7-64) Argo (Z) NF-4 Immortal Scenes & Sonnets Dec. 9041. Life Lex. 7696. Love in Shakespeare (11-64) Sp. Arts 901. Men & Women–Gielgud, Worth (9-67) Vic VDS-115. Midsummer Night's Dream Folk. 9872 Phoenix & Turtle (see Plays, Tempest) 3-Argo 216/8. Quayle Sp. Arts 729. Rape Of Lucrece–Poems 2-Caed. SRS-(S)239. Speaight, Audley Sp. Arts 943. Scenes–Paul Rogers Sp. Arts 723. Scenes–McMaster (9-60) 2-Sp. Arts 766/7 Scenes from the Comedies (1-64) Argo DA-2. Scenes from the Histories (1-64) Argo DA-3. Scenes from the Tragedies (1-60) 2-Argo DA-1, 4. Selections–Evans (12-63) Dec. 9110 Shakespeare At Stratford (1906-61) (6-67) Argo (5) 289. Shakespeare's London Lex. 7694. Shakespeare's Stage Production Lex. 7697. Shakespeare's Theatre Lex. 7695. Soliloquies & Scenes–MacLiammoir & Edwards (10-62) 2-Sp. Arts 836/7. Sonnets (complete) 3-Argo 142/4. Sonnets (complete)–Gielgud 2-Caed. SRS-241. Sonnets–Speaight: Nos. 1/53-Sp. Arts 947/9. Sonnets–E. Evans (20) (6-67) Sera. 60042. Sound & Sweet Airs–Casson (1-66) Sp. Arts 900. Speaking of Shakespeare's Verse (1-69) Sp. Arts 1022.

Shelley–Price Caed. 1059. Garland, Marquand, Watson (2-65) Argo 380. Scott (5-64) Argo 23. Treasury–Speaight & Eddison (11-63) Sp. Arts 869.

Sitwell, Edith–Poems Caed. 1016. Gielgud, Worth (2-66) Vic. VDS-106.

Sitwell, Osbert–Poems Caed. 1013.

Sound of World Poetry (11-67) Schol. 11006.

Spanish Poetry–Garcia Lorca (12-60) (Sp) Miami 1231. Hernandez, Jose–Fierro (3-63) Folk. 9927. Invitation Dover 9894. Levinton, Catalina Folk. 9925. Minstral, Jorge–Poems (9-65) 2-Mus. 602, 724. Modern Verse–Florit (10-66) Sp. Arts 913. Neruda, Pablo–Poetry (9-67) Caed. 1215. Poema del Renunciamento (11-62) Miami 1276. Poesias Gauchos (3-62) Fluentes 0023. Poetas Colombianos (4-61) (Sp) Miami 1252. Poetas Latino-americanos (8-62) (Sp) Miami 1256. Selections–Resnick (5-66) CMS 510. Sirgo, Otto–Poemas de amor (12-65) Puch. 577.

Speaight, Robert–Gray, Goldsmith, Collins (2-63) Sp. Arts 849.

Spender, Stephen–His Poetry (4-58) Caed. 1084. Poems–Spender (5-65) Argo 88. Poems–Spender (6-61) Sp. Arts 804. Selected Poems–Spender (2-67) Sp. Arts 953.

Spenser, Edmund–Faerie Queene, etc. Caed. 1126. Faerie Queene (excerpts) Argo 488.

Stephens, James–Poems (2-59) Sp. Arts 744. Sutzkeyer, Abraham–Poetry Of (Yi) Folk. 9947.

Szowacki, Juliusz–Poetry (Pol) Folk 9401.

Tennyson, Alfred Lord–Poetry Caed. 1080. Anthology † Browning (2-67) Sp. Arts 934. Idylls Of the King–Rathbone 2-Caed. 2022. Rylands, Church, etc. (5-65) Argo 342. Selections–Massey Dec. 9108. Treasury–Speaight (11-63) Sp. Arts 858.

Thomas, Dylan 5-Caed. 1002, 1018, 1043, 1061, 1132. Complete Recorded Poetry (2-64) 2-Caed. 2014. Evening–Thomas (11-63) Caed. 11-57. Homage (5-64) Argo 29. Poems–Burton (5-65) Argo 43. Poems–Burton (2-61) Sp. Arts 789.

Today's Poets (11-67) Schol. 11001.

Tolkien, J.R.R.–Poems & Songs Caed. (9) 1231.

Treasury of Modern Poets Reading 2-Caed. 2006.

Virgil–Georgics–C. Day Lewis Sp. Arts 733. Aeneid–Hadas (L) Folk. 9973. Aeneid, Books 1, 3, 4, 6–Richards (L) Folk. 9969. Pei (L) † Horace Folk. 9964.

Watkins, Vernon (2-66) Dec. 9142.

Whitman, Walt–Leaves Of Grass Folk, 9750. Allen (11-68) CMS 543. Begley–Vols. 1/2 2-Caed. 1037, 1154. Scourby, Vols. 1/2 (10-66) 2-Sp. Arts 907, 946.

Wilbur, Richard–Poems (2-59). Sp. Arts 747.

Poetry–Wilbur (9-68). Caed. S-1248.

Williams, William Carlos (3-58). Caed. 1047.

Wordsworth, William–Hardwicke Caed. 1020. Prelude (selections)–Orr, Squire Argo 429. Treasury–Speaight (11-63) Sp. Arts 860. Vols. 1/2 (5-64) 2-Argo 345, 347.

Yeats, Wm. Butler–McKenna, Cusack Caed. 1081. Poems (2-59) Sp. Arts 753. Poems & Memories (2-59) Sp. Arts 751.

Yevtushenko–Selected Poems (3-66) Folk. 9869.

Yevtushenko, Yevgeny (7-66) Caed. 1153.

Yevtushenko & Voznesensky (8-64) Mon. 113.

Topic Records Limited

27 Nassington Road, London, NW3 2TX, U.K.

12T188 Deep Lancashire.
Songs and ballads of the industrial North-West.

12T204 'Owdham' Edge.
Popular Song and Verse from Lancashire.

12TS206 Oldham's Burning Sands.
Ballads, Songs, and Daft Ditties of The Oldham Tinkers.

12TS219 Canny Newcassel, Ballads and songs from Newcastle and thereabouts.

W & G Record Processing Co. Pty. Ltd.

185 a'Beckett Street, Melbourne, 3000 Australia.

RECORDS   FOR   SCHOOLS   AND KINDERGARTENS

WG 25/5003 The Best of Banjo (Paterson). John Clements.

WG 25/5196 The Best of Banjo Vol. 2. John Clements.

WG 25/5006 The Legend That Is Lawson. John Clements.

APPENDIX I

LITERARY RECORDINGS IN THE LIBRARY OF CONGRESS, WASHINGTON, D.C., U.S.A.

The Library of Congress has a rich literary reservoir of recordings made at the Library. It consists of poetry readings held in the Library's Coolidge Auditorium or in the Whittall Pavilion and visiting poets' readings of their poems in the Recording Laboratory, recordings of poets reading elsewhere for the archive, and recordings received through occasional gifts, exchanges or purchases.

At present, because of the Library's limited facilities for playing records, their use is somewhat restricted.

The following list of poetry readings was taken from 'Literary Recordings – A Checklist of the Archive of Recorded Poetry and Literature in the Library of Congress'.

ABBE, George. LWO 2896, reel 10. Reading his poetry on the program "The Reading Rail," Station KUSC, Los Angeles, Calif., in the 1958-59 series.

ABBE, George. LWO 3218, reels 1-4. Reading his poems with commentary at York Sight-Sound Productions, Inc., Troy, N.Y., on Nov. 22, 1960.

ADAMS, Léonie. LWO 2689. Reading her poetry in the Coolidge Auditorium, Sept. 15, 1949.

ADAMS, Léonie. LWO 2689, reel 1. Reading her poems in the Recording Laboratory, Oct. 7, 1949.

ADAMS, Léonie. LWO 1963, reel 5. Reading her poems in New York City, in 1951. Includes discussion.

ADAMS, Léonie. LWO 3993, reel 7. Guest on Florence Becker Lennon's program "Enjoyment of Poetry," broadcast over Radio Station WEVD, New York City, May 20, 1962. They discuss "Survival of the Lyric."

AIKEN, Conrad Potter. LWO 1963, reels 1 & 2. Reading his poems Apr. 6 and Oct. 7, 1951, at Potosi, Glen Rock, Pa.

AIKEN, Conrad Potter. LWO 1274. Reading his poetry at Harvard University, May 12, 1948.

AIKEN, Conrad Potter. LWO 2057. Reading his poems at Potosi, Glen Rock, Pa., June 12, 1952.

AIKEN, Conrad Potter. LWO 2986. Reading his poems in New York City, Aug. 27, 1959.

AIKEN, Conrad Potter. LWO 2058. Recorded at Glen Rock, Pa., July 2, 1952.

AIN, Josephine. LWO 2896, reel 12. Reading her poetry on the program "Poetry and Talk," Station KUSC, Los Angeles, Calif., in the 1957 – 1958 series.

ALDAN, Daisy. LWO 3083, reel 1. Reading her poems in 1960.

ALDAN, Daisy. LWO 4267. Reading her poems with commentary in the Recording Laboratory, Apr. 27, 1964.

ALDINGTON, Richard. LWO 2048, reel 1. Poems recorded at the City College of New York, Apr. 4, 1940.

ALTROCCHI, Julia. LWO 3848. Reading her poems entitled "Astronaut to Vega," at Radio Station KPFA, Berkeley, Calif., May 18, 1962.

AMIS, Kingsley. LWO 2713. Reading his poems with commentary in the Recording Laboratory, Oct. 13, 1958.

AMIS, Kingsley. LWO 2708. Reading his poems and novels in the Coolidge Auditorium, Oct. 13, 1958.

AMMONS, A.R. LWO 4119. Reading his poems with commentary, Oct. 22, 1963, in the Recording Laboratory. Some of the poems are from Ommateum and others are selections from a manuscript to be published. Howard Nemerov introduces Mr. Ammons and talks with him during the reading.

ANDERSON, Lee. LWO 2493, reels 1 & 2. Reading his poems at Potosi, Glen Rock, Pa., Oct. 26, 1956.

ANTONINUS, Brother William Everson. LWO 3336. Reading his poems with commentary in the studio of the Sound Recorders, Inc., San Francisco, Calif., on Mar. 20, 1961.

ARMOUR, Richard. LWO 3472. Reading his poetry with commentary at the recording studio of Pomona College, Pomona, Calif., Nov. 8, 1961.

ARMSTRONG, Phyllis Eleanor. LWO 3034. Commentator on a program presented on Radio Station WGMS, Washington, D.C., Oct. 1951, featuring recordings of four Pullitzer Prize winning poets reading their poems.

ARMSTRONG, Phyllis Eleanor. LWO 3144. Reading her poems with commentary in the Recording Laboratory, July, 11. 1960.

AU-YOUNG, Sum Nung. LWO 2048, reel 7. Reading his poems at the City College of New York, Apr. 12, 1938.

AUDEN, Wystan Hugh. LWO 2048, reel 1. Poems recorded at the City College of New York, June 4, 1940.

AUDEN, Wystan Hugh. LWO 2689. reel 1. Reading his poems in the Recording Laboratory, Jan. 24, 1948.

AUDEN, Wystan Hugh. LWO 2946. Reading his poems on Mar. 18, 1959 in New York City.

BAKER, Howard. LWO 2689, reels 1 & 2. Reading his poetry in the Recording Laboratory, July 9, 1948.

BARKER, George. LWO 2848. Reading his poems and those of other poets.

BARKER, George. LWO 2749. Reading from his poetry in the Coolidge Auditorium, Dec. 15, 1958.

BARKER, George. LWO 2748. Reading his poems with commentary in the Recording Laboratory, Dec. 15, 1958. Includes interview by Katherine Garrison Chapin.

BARKER, George. LWO 2976. Reading his poems in New York City, June 8, 1959.

BARO, Gene. LWO 3124. Reading his poems in the Recording Laboratory May 20, 1960.

BARTLETT, Elizabeth. LWO 3524. Reading her poems at Los Gatos, Calif., May 20, 1961.

BASLER, Roy Prentice. LWO 2414. Reading his poetry at Glen Rock, Pa., Oct. 1955.

BASLER, Roy Prentice. LWO 2935. Reading his poetry at Potosi, Glen Rock, Pa., May 3, 1959.

BAXTER, Frank C. LWO 2342. "The Unfaltering Lamp: Homage to Thirteen Centuries of English Poetry," presented in the Coolidge Auditorium, Mar. 28, 1955.

BEACH, Joseph Warren. LWO 2588, reels 1 & 2. Reading his poems at his home in Minneapolis, Minn., Mar. 25, 1957.

BEECHER, John. LWO 3980. Reading his poetry with comment in the Recording Laboratory, Apr. 10, 1963. Louis Untermeyer introduces Mr. Beecher.

BELITT, Ben. LWO 2947. Reading his poetry with commentary, Apr. 18, 1958, at Bennington, Vt.

BELL, Charles G. LWO 4622. Reading his poems with commentary in the Recording Laboratory, June 9, 1965. Introduced by Reed Whittemore.

BENET, Laura. LWO 2727. Reading her poems with commentary in the Recording Laboratory, Nov. 12, 1958.

BENET, Laura. LWO 3993, reel 1, side A. Guest on Florence Becker Lennon's program "Enjoyment of Poetry" broadcast over Radio Station WEVD, New York City, Apr. 17, 1960. They discuss "A Family of Poets."

BENET, Stephen Vincent. LWO 2529, reel 1. Reading his poems with commentary in the Coolidge Auditorium, May 29, 1941.

BENET, William Rose. LWO 2048, reels 1 & 2. Poems recorded at the City College of New York, May 8, 1938.

BENNETT, Joseph. LWO 2987. Reading his poems in New York City, Aug. 27, 1959.

BENTLEY, Beth. LWO 3415. Reading her poems with commentary at Station KCTS-TV, University of Washington at Seattle, Apr. 13, 1960.

BERRIGAN, Daniel. LWO 3486. Reading his poems in the Recording Studio of Le Moyne College, Syracuse, N.Y. in Nov. 1961.

BERRY, Francis. LWO 3900. Reading his poems with commentary on Dec. 7, 1962, at the Sheffield City Central Library, Sheffield, Eng.

BERRYMAN, John. LWO 2689, reel 2. Reading his poetry in the Recording Laboratory, Feb. 13. 1948.

BERRYMAN, John. LWO 1963. reel 3. Reading his poetry at his home in Princeton, N.J. in 1951.

BERRYMAN, John. LWO 2609. Reading his poems with commentary in the Coolidge Auditorium, Feb. 24, 1958.

BEUM, Robert. LWO 3219. Reading his poems in the studio of the University of Nebraska, Dec. 13. 1960.

BISHOP, Elizabeth. LWO 2689. reel 2. Reading her poetry at the ABC Studio, New York City, Oct. 18 1947.

BISHOP, Elizabeth. LWO 1519. Reading her poetry in the Recording Laboratory, Sept. 15, 1949.

BISHOP, John Peale. LWO 2048, reel 1. Poems recorded at the City College of New York, Mar. 28, 1941.

BLACKMUR, Richard P. LWO 2689, reel 2. Reading his poetry in the Recording Laboratory, Apr. 16, 1948.

BLACKMUR, Richard P. LWO 1830, reel 1. Reading his poems at his College Office, Princeton, N.J., in 1951, at the home of Donald Stauffer, and in his own home in 1953.

BLOOD, Albert M. LWO 3143. Mr. Blood, 90 years old — reads poems of James Whitcomb Riley with commentary in June 1960.

BLY, Robert, LWO 3106. Reading his poems with commentary in the Recording Laboratory, May 2, 1960.

BOCK, Frederick. LWO 3077. Reading his poetry in the Recording Laboratory, Apr. 4, 1960.

BODE, Carl. LWO 3102. Reading his poems with commentary in the Recording Laboratory, Apr. 27, 1960.

BODENHEIM, Maxwell. LWO 2529, reel 1. Reading his poetry in the Recording Laboratory, June 1. 1945.

BOGAN, Louise. LWO 2689, reel 3. Reading her poetry in the Recording Laboratory, Nov. 17 and 18, 1944.

BOGAN, Louise. LWO 2689. reel 2. Reading poetry to the Writers' Club of the Library of Congress, June 4, 1946.

BOGAN, Louise. LWO 1648. Reading poetry at ABC, New York City in Oct. 1, 1948.

BOGAN, Louise. LWO 1963. reel 2. Poems recorded in New York City in 1951.

BOGAN, Louise. LWO 2986. Reading her poems in New York City, Aug. 27, 1959.

BOGAN, Louise. LWO 2987. Reading her poems in New York City, Aug. 27, 1959.

BOGARDUS, Edgar. LWO 2588, reel 2. Reading his poems in the home of John Crowe Ransom, Gambier, Ohio, March 2, 1957.

BONTEMPS, Arna. LWO 4016. Reading his poems with commentary at Radio Station WPLN, Nashville Public Library, May 22, 1963.

BOOTH, Philip E. LWO 2883. Reading his poetry with commentary at Cambridge, Mass, Apr. 13, 1958.

BOSQUET, Alain. LWO 3014. Reading from his poems and translations of his poems by other poets in the Recording Laboratory, Jan 13, 1960. Includes discussion with Richard Eberhart.

BOYLE, Kay. LWO 3979. Reading her poems and a short story with commentary on Apr. 8, 1963, in the Coolidge Auditorium. Louis Untermeyer introduces Miss Boyle.

BOYLE, Kay. LWO 3999. Reading her poems and a short story with commentary on a program presented at Wesleyan University, Apr. 11, 1963.

BRINNIN, John Malcolm. LWO 1003. Reading his poetry. From Harvard Vocarium recordings.

BRINNIN, John Malcolm. LWO 2689, reel 3. Reading his poetry in the Recording Laboratory, July 15, 1945.

BRINNIN, John Malcolm. LWO 1830, reel 2. Reading his poetry at his home in Cambridge, Mass., May 1951.

BRINNIN, John Malcolm. LWO 2493, reel 2. Reading his poetry at Cambridge, Mass., Aug. 6, 1956.

BROOKS, Gwendolyn. LWO 3237. Reading her poems with comment in the Recording Laboratory, Jan 19, 1961.

BROOKS, Gwendolyn, and Peter Robert Edwin VIERECK. LWO 2863, reel 2. Recording of a joint reading by the two poets at the YMHA Poetry Center, New York City.

BROUGHTON, James. LWO 3370. Reading his poems with commentary at the studio of H Jacobs, Sausalito, Calif., June 13, 1961.

BROWN, Spencer. LWO 2925. Reading his poetry with commentary in New York City, Mar. 23, 1958. Includes discussion.

BROWNING, Robert. LWO 3037. Browning recites the first four lines of his poem "How they Brought the Good News from Ghent to Aix." on a tape given to the Library of Congress by the British Broadcasting Corporation in 1958. The original recording, a wax cylinder was made by Thomas Edison's agent in England, Colonel George Gouraud. Colonel Gouraud addresses Edison, stating that he is sending him the voice of "One of England's and America's most distinguished poets, the voice of Robert Browning." Browning comments on the "astonishing sensation" produced upon him by this "wonderful invention."

BURDEN, Jean. LWO 4148. Reading her poems with comment in the Recording Laboratory, Nov. 14, 1963. Howard Nemerov introduces Miss Burden.

BURFORD, William. LWO 1830, reel 4. Reading his poems in Dallas, Texas. Mar. 24, 1951.

BURNSHAW, Stanley. LWO 3888. Reading his poems with commentary in the Recording Laboratory, Nov. 28, 1962. Louis Untermeyer introduces Mr. Burnshaw.

BURR, Gray. LWO 1830. reel 3. Reading his poetry at Wheaton College, Norton, Mass. May 15, 1951.

BYNNER, Witter. LWO 2689, reel 3. Reading his poetry in the Recording Laboratory, Dec. 13, 1947.

BYNNER, Witter. LWO 2896, reel 7. Reading his poetry with commentary at Station KUSC, Sante Fe, N.M. for broadcast over KUSC–FM, Los Angeles, Calif., on the program "Poetry and Talk," in the 1957 – 58 series.

CANE, Melville. LWO 2048, reel 1. Poems recorded at the City College of New York, Feb. 28, 1941.

CANE, Melville. LWO 3069. Reading his poems with commentary in the Recording Laboratory, Mar 25, 1960.

CARDONA-HINE, Alvaro. LWO 2896, reel 8. Reading his poetry on the program "Poetry and Talk" Station KUSC, Los Angeles, Calif., in the 1957 – 58 series.

CAREY, Denis. LWO 2048, reel 2. Reading from poems and plays at the City College of New York in 1938.

CARR, Peter. LWO 2896, reel 1. Reading his poetry with commentary on the program "Poetry and Talk" Station KUSC, Los Angeles, Calif, in the 1957 – 58 series.

CARRIER, Constance. LWO 2493, reel 3. Reading her poems, July 28, 1956, in Hartford, Conn.

CARRUTH, Hayden. LWO 3039. Reading his poems with commentary in his home at Pleasantville, N.Y., Jan. 1959.

CASTO, Robert Clayton. LWO 3226. Reading his poems with commentary in the Recording Laboratory, Jan 10, 1961. Richard Eberhart introduces Mr. Casto.

CASTO, Robert Clayton. LWO 3993. reel 1, side A. Guest on Florence Becker Lennon's program "Enjoyment of Poetry" broadcast over radio Station WEVD, New York City, Jan 1, 1960 and Sept. 11, 1960. They discuss "The Growth Principle in Poetry."

CHAPIN, Katherine Garrison. LWO 2792, reel 1. Reading her poetry in the Recording Laboratory, Mar. 20, 1943.

CHAPIN, Katherine Garrison. LWO 2689, reel 3. Reading her poetry in the Recording Laboratory, Mar. 31, 1947.

CHAPIN, Katherine Garrison. LWO 2185. A reading of Emily Dickinson and other women poets in the Coolidge Auditorium, Dec 14, 1953.

CHAPIN, Katherine Garrison. LWO 3205. Reading her poems with commentary in the Recording Laboratory, Nov. 30, 1960. Richard Eberhart introduces Miss Chapin.

CHURCH, Richard. LWO 3507. A recording made by Recorded Sound, London, Eng., on Nov. 30, 1961, of Mr. Church reading his poems with commentary.

CIARDI, John. LWO 2372, reel 1. Reading his poetry in New York City, Apr. 20, 1955.

CITY COLLEGE POETRY COLLECTION. LWO 2048, reel 7. Poets reading the same Shakespeare sonnet at the City College of New York during the period 1938 to 1941.

CLAPP, Frederick Mortimer. LWO 2048, reels 2 & 3. Poems recorded at the City College of New York, Mar. 21, 1941.

CLARK, John W. LWO 3523. Reading his poems with commentary at the Columbia Records Studio, New York City, July 14, 1961. Includes interview by Oscar Williams.

CLARK, Saville Trice. LWO 2529. Reading his poetry in the Recording Laboratory, Dec. 11, 1943.

COFFIN, Robert Peter Tristram. LWO 2529, reels 1 & 2. Reading his poetry in the Recording Laboratory, May 25, 1945.

COLEMAN, Elliott. LWO 2529, reel 2. Reading his poetry in the Recording Laboratory, June 4 and 7, 1947.

COLEMAN, Elliott. LWO 2940. Reading his poetry with commentary in Baltimore, MD, Oct, 29. 1958. Includes interview.

COLUM, Padraic. LWO 2048, reel 1. Reading from his poems and from James Joyce at the City College of New York, June 4, 1941.

COLUM, Padraic. LWO 2824. Lecture and reading given in the Coolidge Auditorium, Apr. 13, 1959.

COLUM, Padraic. LWO 2827. Reading his poems with commentary in the Recording Laboratory, Apr. 14, 1959.

COMBS, Tram. LWO 2896, reel 9. Reading his poems with musical accompaniment. Recorded in the West Indies and broadcast on the program "The Reading Rail," Station KUSC, Los Angeles, Calif., in the 1958 — 59 series.

CONQUEST, Robert. LWO 3096. Reading his poems in the Recording Laboratory, Apr. 21, 1960.

COOK, Albert. LWO 3091. Reading his poems in the Recording Laboratory, Apr. 22, 1960.

COOK, Robert Lee. LWO 3993, reel 1, side B. Guest on Florence Becker Lennon's program "Enjoyment of Poetry," broadcast over Radio Station WEVD, New York City, Nov. 20, 1960. They discuss "Fourth Dimension in Poetry."

CORMAN, Sidney. ("Cid"). LWO 3175. Reading his poems with comment in the Recording Laboratory, Oct. 14, 1960. Richard Eberhart introduces Mr. Corman. Mr. Corman prefaces his reading with a selection from a series of "statements" by Louis Zukofsky from "A — 1 to 12."

CORSO, Gregory. LWO 2799. Reading his poems with commentary in the Recording Laboratory, Feb. 27, 1959.

COWLEY, Malcolm. LWO 2279. Reading his poems in the Recording Laboratory, Nov. 18, 1954.

COXE, Louis O. LWO 3182. Reading his poems with commentary at the Stapleton Studios, Dublin, Ireland, Aug. 1960.

CRAWFORD, Cheryl, and Greg Morton. LWO 1975. Reading poems and letters of John Keats, May 1952.

CREELEY, Robert. LWO 3348. Reading his poems with commentary in the Recording Laboratory, June 1, 1961.

CROWDER, Richard. LWO 2916. Lecturing and reading from the poetry of Edward Arlington Robinson, Oct. 26, 1959, in the Coolidge Auditorium.

CUMMINGS, Edward Estlin. LWO 2689. reel 3. Reading his poetry at NBC in New York City. June 26, 1946.

CUMMINGS, Edward Estlin. LWO 2863, reel 3. Reading from his poems at the YMHA Poetry Centre, New York City, Oct. 20, 1959.

CUNNINGHAM, James Vincent. LWO 2886. Reading his poetry with commentary, Apr. 15, 1958 at Cambridge, Mass.

CURNOW, Allen. LWO 2529, reels 2 & 3. Reading his poems in the Recording Laboratory, Apr. 3, 1950.

CURNOW, Allen. LWO 3343. Reading his poems with comment in the Recording Laboratory, June 2, 1961. Richard Eberhart introduces Mr. Curnow.

DANIELS, Guy. LWO 2896, reel 9. Reading his translations on the program "The Reading Rail" Station KUSC, Los Angeles, Calif., in the 1958 -59 series. Includes opening remarks on Mikhai Lermontov.

DANNENBAUM, Raymond. LWO 2529, reel 3. Reading his poetry in the Recording Laboratory, Aug. 29, 1944.

DAVIDSON, Donald. LWO 1731. Reading his poetry in the Recording Laboratory, Nov. 24, 1950.

DAVIDSON, Donald. LWO 3475. Reading his poems with commentary in the studio of the RCA Victor Record Division, Nashville, Tenn., Nov. 30, 1961.

DAVIDSON, Gustav. LWO 3759. Reading his poems with commentary in the Recording Laboratory, June 5, 1962.

DAVISON, Edward Lewis. LWO 2529, reel 3. Reading his poetry in the Recording Laboratory. Sept. 11, 1944.

DAVISON, Edward Lewis. LWO 2113. Presenting "An Evening's Anthology of Poetry" in the Coolidge Auditorium, Mar 23, 1953.

DAY-LEWIS, Cecil. LWO 3508. Reading his poems with comment at the studios of Recorded Sound, Ltd., London, Eng., Nov. 23, 1961.

DE HIRSCH, Storm. LWO 3083, reel 6. Reading her poems in 1960.

DENBY, Edwin. LWO 2984. Reading his poetry at the CBS Studio, New York City, May 26, 1959.

DENNEY, Reuel. LWO 2493, reel 2. Reading his poems with commentary at his home in Chicago, Feb. 21, 1956.

DE PALCHI, Alfredo. LWO 4562. Mr. De Palchi and his wife, Sonia Raiziss, reading selections from the work of contemporary Italian poets, including Vincenzo Cardarelli, Giuseppe Ungaretti, Eugenio Montale, and Leonardo Sinisgalli at Radio Station WBAI, New York City, Dec. 7, 1964. Introduction by Sonia Raizisa.

DERWENT, Clarence. LWO 2324. Reading poems by various authors in the Coolidge Auditorium, Feb. 14, 1955.

DERWOOD, Gene. LWO 2529. Reading her poetry in the Recording Laboratory, May 28, 1945.

DEUTSCH, Babette. LWO 2529, reel 3. Reading her poems in the Recording Laboratory, Mar. 25, 1947.

DEUTSCH, Babette. LWO 1830, reel 5. Reading her poetry in New York City, May 22, 1951.

DEUTSCH, Babette. LWO 3396. Reading her poems with comment at Station WRVR, Riverside Radio Studio, New York City, on Apr. 27–28, 1961.

DEUTSCH, Babette. LWO 3417. Reading her poems in the Coolidge Auditorium on Oct. 9, 1961.

DEVLIN, Denis. LWO 2529. reels 3 & 4. Reading poetry with commentary for the Writers' Club of the Library of Congress in the Coolidge Auditorium, Jan 3, 1956.

DICKEY, James. LWO 3092. Reading his poems in the Recording Laboratory, Apr. 22, 1960.

DODSON, Owen. LWO 3212. Reading his poems with comment in the Recording Laboratory, Dec. 13, 1960. Richard Eberhart introduces Mr. Dodson.

DORO, Edward, LWO 4315. Presentation of Edward Doro's dramatic narrative poem Shiloh by the faculty of the Department of Interpretation in Lutkin Hall, Northwestern University, on Jan. 9, 1962. Ellis Schuman composed the original music for the performance.

DORO, Edward. LWO 3750. Reading his poems with commentary in the Recording Laboratory, May 25, 1962. Louis Untermeyer introduces Mr. Doro.

DOWLING, Allan. LWO 3613. Reading his poems at the Columbia Records Studio, New York City, Mar. 26, 1962. Includes interview by Oscar Williams.

DOYLE, Charles. LWO 2896, reel 5. Reading his poetry on "The Reading Rail" Station KUSC, Los Angeles, Calif., in the 1958 – 59 series.

DUFAULT, Peter Kane. LWO 3993, reel 1, side B. Guest on Florence Becker Lennon's program "Enjoyment of Poetry," broadcast over Radio Station WEVD, New York City, Oct. 18, 1959. They discuss "The Trouble with Poetry."

DUGAN, Alan. LWO 3834. Reading his poems with commentary at Stereo Sound Studios, New York City, July 6, 1962.

DUNCAN, Robert Edward. LWO 2058, reel 2. Reading his poems in Berkeley, Calif., Mar. 22, 1952.

DUNSANY, Edward John Moreton Drax Plunkett. Baron. LWO 2331. "Poets I have known," a lecture and poetry reading in the Coolidge Auditorium, Feb. 28, 1955.

EASTMAN, Max. LWO 2728. Reading his poetry with commentary in the Recording Laboratory, Nov. 17, 1958.

EASTMAN, Max. LWO 3993, reel 2 side A. Guest on Florence Becker Lennon's program "Enjoyment of Poetry," broadcast over Radio Station WEVD, New York City, Apr. 27, 1958. They discuss "What Poetry is and How to Enjoy It."

EATON, Charles Edward. LWO 2948. Reading his poems with commentary at the Yal Audio-Visual Center, Nov. 20, 1958. Includes interview.

EBERHART, Richard. LWO 2689, reel 3. Reading his poetry in the Recording Laboratory, Dec. 2, 1944.

EBERHART, Richard. LWO 1830, reel 1. Reading his poems at his home in Cambridge, Mass., May 13, 1951.

EBERHART, Richard. LWO 2195. Reading his poems at a recording studio in Storrs, Conn., in 1953.

EBERHART, Richard. LWO 2426. Reading his poems in the Coolidge Auditorium. Mar. 12, 1956.

EBERHART, Richard. LWO 2908. Reading his poems with commentary in the Coolidge Auditorium, Sept. 26, 1959.

EBERHART, Richard. LWO 3185. Reading his poems with commentary in the Coolidge Auditorium, Oct. 24, 1960.

EBERHART, Richard. LWO 3339. Reading his poems with commentary in the Coolidge Auditorium, May 15, 1961.

ELIOT, Thomas Stearns. LWO 3016. Recorded at the Sanders Theatre, Harvard University, in the Spring of 1945.

ELIOT, Thomas Stearns. LWO 977. Reading his poems in the NBC Studio, New York City, July 26, 1946.

ELIOT, Thomas Stearns. LWO 2529, reels 9 & 10. Reading his poems with commentary at the National Gallery of Art, Washington, D.C., May 23, 1947. Includes short introduction.

EMPSON, William. LWO 2689, reel 4. Reading his poetry at Kenyon College, Gambier, Ohio., on Nov. 7, 1948.

EMRICH, Duncan. LWO 2529 & 2689. Reading his poetry in the Recording Laboratory, Mar. 13, 1947.

ENGLE, Paul. LWO 1003. Taken from Harvard Vocarium recordings.

ENGLE, Paul. LWO 2550. Reading his poems with commentary in the Coolidge Auditorium, Mar. 11, 1957.

ENGLE, Paul. LWO 3890. Reading his poems with commentary in the Recording Laboratory, Nov. 29, 1962. Louis Untermeyer introduces Mr. Engle.

ENSLIN, Theodore. LWO 1830, reel 4. Reading his poems in Boston, May 17, 1951.

EVANS, Abbie Houston. LWO 4203. Reading her poems in the Recording Laboratory, Jan. 22, 1964.

FACTOR, Donald. LWO 2896, reel 15. Reading his poetry on the program "The Reading Rail," Station KUSC, Los Angeles, Calif., in the 1958 − 59 series.

FANDEL, John. LWO 3027. Reading his poems in the Recording Laboratory, Feb. 4, 1960. Includes short discussion with Richard Eberhart.

FERRIL, Thomas Hornsby. LWO 1734. Reading his poems in the Recording Laboratory, Dec. 1, 1950.

FERRY, David. LWO 2931. Reading his poetry with commentary at Cambridge, Mass., Mar. 12, 1959. Includes discussion.

FICKE, Arthur Davison. LWO 2048, reel 2. Poems recorded at the City College of New York, Mar. 13 and May 10, 1940, May 9, 1941. Includes interview by Kimball Flaccus.

FINKEL, Donald. LWO 3132. Reading his poems with commentary. Recorded at Vassar College Studios, Poughkeepsie, N.Y., on Feb. 27, May 14, and May 21, 1960.

FITTS, Dudley. LWO 2926. Reading his poems and translations at Andover, Mass., Apr. 16, 1958. Includes discussion.

FITZGERALD, Robert. LWO 2689, reel 4. Reading his poems in the Recording Laboratory, June 7, 1948.

FITZGERALD, Robert. LWO 2588, reel 1. Reading his poems at Notre Dame, Ind., Apr. 12, 1957.

FLACCUS, Kimball. LWO 2048, reel 2. Poems recorded at the City College of New York, Jan. 12, 1942.

FLETCHER, Bramwell. LWO 3879. Reading selections from English and American poets in the Coolidge Auditorium, Nov. 5, 1962.

FLETCHER, John Gould. LWO 1003. Reading a poem taken from a Harvard Vocarium recording.

FOLDER, I. LWO 3083, reel 4. Poets reading their poems at the home of Daisy Aldan, in Nov. 1953. The poems are published in Folder 1, a portfolio of poems and drawings, edited by Daisy Aldan and Richard Miller.

FORD, Edsel. LWO 4612. Reading his poems with commentary in the Recording Laboratory, May 17, 1965.

FRANKENBERG, Lloyd. LWO 2048, reel 3. Poems recorded at the City College of New York, Dec. 13, 1940.

FRANKENBERG, Lloyd. LWO 1963, reel 6. Reading his poems in New York City, Nov. 4, 1951.

FROST, Elizabeth Hollister. LWO 2048, reels 2 & 3. Poems recorded at the City College of New York, Mar. 14, 1940.

FROST, Frances Mary. LWO 2372, reel 4. Reading her poems in New York City, Apr. 16, 1955.

FROST, Robert. LWO 2529, reel 4. Reading his poems with commentary in the Coolidge Auditorium, Mar. 29, 1941. The theme of Mr. Frost's introduction remarks was "The Poet in a Democracy."

FROST, Robert. LWO 2689, reels 4 & 5. Reading his poems with commentary in the Coolidge Auditorium, Mar. 17, 1948.

FROST, Robert. LWO 2689, reels 4 & 5. Reading his poems in the Recording Laboratory, Mar. 18, 1948 and Dec. 10, 1949.

FROST, Robert. LWO 2382. Reading his poems with commentary in the Coolidge Auditorium, Oct. 24, 1955.

FROST, Robert. LWO 2744. Reading his poems in the Coolidge Auditorium, Dec. 8, 1958.

FROST, Robert. LWO 2815. Reading his poems with commentary in the Coolidge Auditorium, Mar. 30, 1959. The theme of his introductory remarks was "Government by Disagreement."

FROST, Robert. LWO 2819. Reading his poems in a joint meeting of the Chesapeake Chapter of the American Studies· Association and the Folger Seminar in the Folger Shakespeare Library, Washington, D.C., Mar, 31, 1959.

FROST, Robert. LWO 2846. Reading his poems with commentaries and introductory remarks in the Coolidge Auditorium, May 18, 1959.

FROST, Robert. LWO 2849. Robert Frost is interviewed by Randall Jarrell in the Recording Laboratory, May. 19, 1959.

FROST, Robert. LWO 2850. Reading his poems in the Recording Laboratory, May 21, 1959, for the "Talking Books for the Blind."

FROST, Robert. LWO 3104. Reading his poems with commentary in the Coolidge Auditorium, May 2, 1960.

FROST, Robert. LWO 3105. Informal talk and poetry reading before members of Congress and their families in the Coolidge Auditorium, May 4, 1960.

FROST, Robert. LWO 3334. Reading his poems with commentary in the Coolidge Auditorium, May 3, 1961.

FROST, Robert. LWO 3656. Reading his poems with commentary in the Coolidge Auditorium, May 7, 1962. L. Quincy Mumford introduces Mr. Frost.

FROST, Robert. LWO 3972. Reading his poems with commentary at the University of Detroit, Nov. 14, 1962. Before Mr. Frost begins his reading, the University of Detroit Chorus sings "The Gift Outright" which is set to music by Mr. Don Large, Director of the chorus.

FROST, Robert. LWO 4121. Presenting a talk and poetry reading at Dartmouth College, Hanover, N.H., Nov. 27, 1962.

FROST, Robert. LWO 4173. Mark Van Doren reading poems of Robert Frost at a memorial service for Mr. Frost held in Johnson Chapel, Amherst College, Amherst, Mass, Feb. 17, 1963. Taped by Radio Station WAMF.

FRUMKIN, Gene. LWO 2896, reel 14. Reading his poetry on the program "The Reading Rail," Station KUSC, Los Angeles, Calif., in the 1958 – 59 series.

FULLER, Roy Broadbent. LWO 2900. Reading his poetry in London, Eng., 1959.

GALLER, David. LWO 3033. Reading his poetry at the Rockhill Recording Studio in New York City, Jan. 24, 1960.

GARDNER, Isabella. LWO 2195. Reading her poems in Chicago, Ill., 1953.

GARDNER, Isabella. LWO 2896, reel 7. Reading her poetry with commentary. Recorded at Station KUSF, Santa Fe, N. Mex. for broadcast over Station KUSC–FM, Los Angeles, Calif., on the program "Poetry and Talk," (1957 – 58 series).

GARDNER, Isabella. LWO 2588, reel 1. Reading her poetry in Chicago, Ill., Apr. 10, 1957.

GARRETT, George. LWO 3993, reel 2, side A. Guest on Florence Becker Lennon's program "Enjoyment of Poetry," broadcast over Radio Station WEVD, New York City, Nov. 8, 1959. They discuss "Clarity in Poetry."

GARRIGUE, Jean. LWO 1830, reel 5. Reading her poems in New York City, May 1, 1951.

GARRIGUE, Jean. LWO 2977. Reading her poetry in New York City, Oct. 1959.

GARRIGUE, Jean. LWO 3993, reel 2, side B. Guest on Florence Becker Lennon's program "Enjoyment of Poetry," broadcast over Radio Station WEVD, New York City, Feb. 21, 1960. They discuss "Poetry of Dreams and Changes."

GARRIGUE, Jean. LWO 4553. Reading her poems with commentary in the Coolidge Auditorium, Mar. 8, 1965.

GASCOYNE, David. LWO 1887. Reading his poems in the Recording Laboratory, Nov. 27, 1951.

GEIGER, Don. LWO 2922. Reading his poetry with commentary at the University of California, Sept. 23, 1958. Includes discussion.

GHISELIN, Brewster. LWO 3302, reels 3 & 4. Reading his poems with commentary at the University of Utah in Salt Lake City, June 1960, and Apr. 28, 1961. Richard Eberhart introduces Mr. Ghiselin.

GHISELIN, Brewster. LWO 3302, reels 1 & 2. Reading his poems with commentary at Salt Lake City, Utah, Feb. 25 and Mar. 7, 1961.

GIBSON, Walker. LWO 4003. Reading his poems with commentary in the Office of Radio-Television at New York University, May 8 – 9, 1963.

GILBERT, Jack. LWO 4144. Reading his poems with commentary in the Recording Laboratory, Nov. 7, 1963. Howard Nemerov introduces Mr. Gilbert.

GINSBERG, Allen. LWO 2799. Reading his poetry with commentary in the Recording Laboratory, Feb. 27, 1959.

GOGARTY, Oliver St. John. LWO 2056. Reading poems by A.E. Housman, Robert Bridges, Ralph Hodgson, and William Watson with Commentary in the Coolidge Auditorium, Dec. 15, 1952.

GOLL, Claire. LWO 2048, reel 7. Reading one of her poems in French. Recorded at City College of New York, May 28, 1940.

GOLL, Iwan. LWO 2048, reel 7. Reading one of his poems in French. Recorded at City College of New York, May 28, 1940.

GOODMAN, Paul. LWO 3128. Reading his poems with commentary in the Recording Laboratory, June 6, 1960.

GORDON, Donald Alexander. LWO 2896, reel 11. Reading his poetry on the program "The Reading Rail," Station KUSC, Los Angeles, Calif., in the 1958 – 59 series.

GORDON, Ralph. LWO 2048, reel 3. Poems recorded at the City College of New York, May 2, 1941.

GRAHAM, William Sydney. LWO 1887. Reading his poetry in the Recording Laboratory, Nov. 27, 1951.

GRAVES, Robert. LWO 2540. Reading his poetry with commentary in the Coolidge Auditorium, Feb. 11, 1957.

GREGORY, Horace. LWO 1272. Reading his poetry at the ABC Studios, New York City, Oct. 21, 1948.

GREGORY, Horace. LWO 2689, reel 5. Reading his poetry in the ABC Studios, New York City, May 9, 1949.

GREGORY, Horace. LWO 1963, reel 5. Reading his poetry in New York City, Nov. 9, 1951.

GUEST, Barbara. LWO 3129. Reading her poems in the Recording Laboratory, June 6, 1960.

GUITERMAN, Arthur. LWO 2048, reel 3. Poems recorded at the City College of New York, Dec. 6, 1940.

GUTHRIE, Ramon. LWO 3002. Reading his poems with commentary in the Recording Laboratory, Dec. 15, 1959.

GUTHRIE, Ramon. LWO 3993, reel 2, side B. Guest on Florence Becker Lennon's program "Enjoyment of Poetry," broadcast over Radio Station WEVD, New York City, Dec. 13, 1959. They discuss "The Paradox of Poetry."

HAFEN, Ann Woodbury. LWO 3235. Reading her poems with commentary in the Recording Laboratory, Jan. 17, 1961, Richard Eberhart introduces Miss Hafen.

HALL, Carol. LWO 2372, reels 1 & 2. Reading her poetry in Seattle, Wash., Apr. 18, 1955.

HALL, James. LWO 2372, reel 2. Reading his poems at Seattle, Wash., Apr. 18, 1955.

HAMBURGER, Michael. LWO 3119. Reading his poems with commentary. Recorded by the British Council, 59 Oxford Street, London, Eng., Apr. 1960.

HAMEIRI, Avigdor. LWO 1987. Reading his poems and a short story (in Hebrew) in the Recording Laboratory, July 18, 1952.

HAMMER, Peter. LWO 3993, reel 7, side B. Guest on Florence Becker Lennon's program "Enjoyment of Poetry," broadcast over Radio Station WEVD, New York City (1959?).

HANSON, Kenneth O. LWO 3268. Reading his poems with commentary in Portland, Ore., on Apr. 21, 1960.

HAY, Sara Henderson. LWO 2048, reel 3. Poems recorded at the City College of New York, June 7, 1938 and May 16, 1940.

HECHT, Anthony. LWO 2889. Reading his poems with commentary at Northampton, Mass., 1958.

HELTON, Roy Addison. LWO 2048, reel 3. Poems recorded at the City College of New York, Mar. 29, 1938.

HERSCHBERGER, Ruth. LWO 2985. Reading her poetry at the CBS Studio, New York City, May 26, 1959.

HERZING, Albert. LWO 3355. Reading his poems with commentary at Fairleigh Dickinson University, Teaneck, N.J., on May 31, 1961.

HILL, Lewis. LWO 2937. Reading his poetry at Berkeley, Calif., Mar. 24, 1952.

HILLYER, Robert Silliman. LWO 2393. Reading his poetry in the Recording Laboratory, Nov. 21, 1955.

HILLYER, Robert Silliman. LWO 2392. Poetry reading in Coolidge Auditorium, Nov. 21, 1955.

HOCHMAN, Sandra. LWO 4278. Reading her poems at the Rockhill Studios, New York City, on Apr. 15, and 20, 1964.

HOFFMAN, Daniel G. LWO 2372, reel 3. Reading his poems at Wheaton College, Norton, Mass., Apr. 24, 1955.

HOFFMAN, Daniel G. LWO 3375. Reading his poems with commentary in the Recording Laboratory, July 27, 1961.

HOLDEN, Raymond Peckham. LWO 2048, reel 3. Poems recorded at the City College of New York, May 31, and May 16, 1940.

HOLDEN, Raymond Peckham. LWO 3677. Reading his poetry with commentary in the Recording Laboratory, May 10, 1962. Louis Untermeyer introduces Mr. Holden.

HOLLANDER, John. LWO 2953, reels 1 & 5. Reading his poems with commentary at New London, Conn., Mar. 10, 1959. Includes interview.

HOLMES, John. LWO 1830, reel 2. Reading his poems at Medford, Mass., May 15, 1951.

HOLMES, John. LWO 2493, reel 3. Reading his poems with commentary at Cambridge, Mass., 1956.

HONIG, Edwin. LWO 2976. Reading his poems in New York City, June 8, 1959.

HONIG, Edwin. LWO 4558. Reading his poems with commentary in the Recording Laboratory, Mar. 15, 1965.

HOPE, A.D. LWO 3964. Reading his poems with commentary at the Australian Broadcasting Commission, Canberra, Australia, on Feb. 25, 1963.

HOWES, Barbara. LWO 1963, reel 8. Reading her poetry at Potosi, Pa., July 2, 1951. Includes discussion.

HOWES, Barbara LWO 2950. Reading her poetry at North Pownal, Vt., Apr. 22, 1958.

HOWES, Barbara. LWO 4301. Reading her poems with commentary at the Fassett Recording Studio, Boston, Mass., May 6, 1964.

HUGHES, Langston. LWO 2838. Reading his poems with commentary in the Recording Laboratory, May 1, 1959.

HUGHES, Langston. LWO 3993, reel 3 side A. Guest on Florence Becker Lennon's program "Enjoyment of Poetry," broadcast over Radio Station WEVD, New York City, Jan 18, 1959. They discuss "Poetry of the Blues."

HUGHES, Ted. LWO 2938. Reading his poetry with commentary at Springfield, Mass., Apr. 18, 1958. Includes interview.

HUGO, Richard. LWO 3363. Reading his poems with commentary at Station KCTS—TV, Seattle, Wash., May 19. 1961.

HUMPHRIES, Rolfe. LWO 2884. Reading his poems with commentary in his home at Belvedere, N.J., June 16, 1958.

IGNATOW, David. LWO 3833. Reading his poems with commentary at WBAI Studios, New York City, May 1962.

INGALLS, Jeremy. LWO 1830. reel 3. Reading her poetry at Medford, Mass., May 15, 1951.

JACOBSEN, Josephine. LWO 2945. Reading her poems with commentary at Potosi, Glen Rock, Pa., Dec. 6, 1958.

JARRELL, Randall. LWO 2689, reel 6. Reading his poetry in the Recording Laboratory, June 9, 1947.

JARRELL, Randall. LWO 2689, reels 5 & 6. Reading his poetry in the Recording Laboratory, Nov. 28, 1947.

JARRELL, Randall. LWO 2689, reel 6. Reading his poems in the Recording Laboratory, Mar. 29 and 30, 1948.

JARRELL, Randall. LWO 1963, reel 1. Reading his poems in the home of Donald Stauffer, Princeton, N.J., Sept. 28, 1951.

JEFFERS, Robinson. LWO 2529, reels 4 & 5. duplicated on LWO 2792, reel 8. Reading his poems with commentary in the Coolidge Auditorium, Feb. 27, 1941.

JEFFERS, Robinson. LWO 2048, reel 4. Poems recorded at the City College of New York, Mar. 7, 1941.

JEFFERS, Robinson. LWO 3835. Robinson Jeffers Memorial Program on Feb. 14, 1962, at the Theatre of the Golden Bough, Carmel, Calif. Introduction by Dr. Louis Balsam and reading of Robinson Jeffers' poems by Dr. Balsam, Kenneth H. Ford, Rochard K. Barker and Ray Simpson.

JEROME, Judson. LWO 3293. Reading his poetry with commentary in the basement of the American Embassy in London, Feb. 3, 1961.

JOHNS HOPKINS POETRY FESTIVAL. (The First). LWO 3905, reels 1 — 10. Poets delivering lectures and reading their poems with commentary, at the first Johns Hopkins Poetry Festival, held at Johns Hopkins University, Baltimore, Md., Nov. 5–11, 1958.

JOHNS HOPKINS POETRY FESTIVAL. (The Second). LWO 3558–3566. Poets reading their own poems and the works of others, with commentary, at the second Johns Hopkins Poetry Festival, Johns Hopkins University, Baltimore, Md., Oct. 24–26, 1961. Theodore Roethke was originally scheduled to appear but, because of his illness, Richard O'Connell replaced him.

JONES, Leroi. LWO 2831. Reading his poems with commentary in the Recording Laboratory, Apr. 17, 1959.

JUSTICE, Donald Rodney. LWO 2880. Reading his poems with commentary at Station WSUI, State University of Iowa, May 1, 1958.

KAUFMAN, Max. LWO 3484. Reading his poems with commentary in the studio of Radio Station WPAD, Paducah, Ky., in 1959.

KEES, Weldon. LWO 2058. Reading his poetry at Berkeley, Calif., Mar. 22, 1952.

KEITH, Joseph Joel. LWO 2896, reel 8. Reading his poetry on the program "The Reading Rail," Station KUSC, Los Angeles, Calif., in the 1958 — 59 series.

KEITH, Joseph Joel. LWO 3110. Reading his poems in the Recording Laboratory, May 9, 1960.

KEITH, Joseph Joel. LWO 3278. Reading his poetry with commentary at Los Angeles City College, Feb. 8, 1961.

KENNEDY, X. J. LWO 3830. Reading his poems with commentary in the Recording Laboratory, June 28, 1962.

KESSLER, Jascha. LWO 3019. Reading his poems with commentary in the Recording Laboratory, Jan. 19, 1960. Includes discussion with Richard Eberhart.

KINNELL, Galway. LWO 2942. Reading his poems with commentary in New York City, Mar. 20, 1959.

KIRKUP, James. LWO 2936. Reading his poems with commentary at the BBC Studios, Bristol, Eng., July 1958.

KIZER, Carolyn. LWO 2927. Reading her poetry with commentary in Seattle, Wash., Sept. 16, 1958.

KOCH, Kenneth. LWO 3111. Reading his poems with commentary in the Recording Laboratory, May 9, 1960.

KREYMBORG, Alfred. LWO 2048, reel 4. Poems recorded at the City College of New York, Mar. 17, 1938 and Feb. 14, 1941.

KREYMBORG, Alfred. LWO 2529, reels 5 & 6. Reading his poems in the Recording Laboratory, May 15, 1945. Includes a number of poems read with music on the mandolute.

KREYMBORG, Alfred. LWO 3993, reel 3, side B. Guest on Florence Becker Lennon's program "Enjoyment of Poetry," broadcast over Radio Station WEVD, New York City. Dec. 29, 1957. They discuss "Imagism in Poetry."

KROLL, Ernest. LWO 4007. Reading his poems with commentary in the Coolidge Auditorium. May 24, 1963. Louis Untermeyer introduces Mr. Kroll.

KUMIN, Maxine W. LWO 3145. Reading her poems with commentary at the Fassett Recording Studio, Boston, Mass., May 1960.

KUNITZ, Stanley Jasspon. LWO 3058. Reading his poems with commentary in the Coolidge Auditorium, Mar. 21, 1960.

KUNITZ, Stanley Jasspon. LWO 2979. Reading his poetry in New York City, Oct. 2, 1959.

KUNITZ, Stanley Jasspon. LWO 2887. Reading his poems with commentary in New York City, Mar. 16, 1959. Includes discussion.

KUNITZ, Stanley Jasspon. LWO 3993, reel 6, side B. Guest on Florence Becker Lennon's program "Enjoyment of Poetry," broadcast over Radio Station WEVD, New York City. Feb. 2. 1950. They discuss "Poetry of Vision."

LA FOLLETTE, Melvin Walker. LWO 3360. Reading his poems with comment in San Jose. Calif., May 1960.

LANGLAND, Joseph. LWO 3009. Reading his poems with commentary in the Recording Laboratory, Jan. 18, 1960.

LARSEN, Carl. LWO 2896, reel 13. Reading his poetry on the program "The Reading Rail." Station KUSC, Los Angeles, Calif., in the 1958 – 59 series.

LATOUCHE, John Treville. LWO 2529. Reading his poem "Ballad for Americans" in the Recording Laboratory, July 2, 1946.

LATTIMORE, Richmond Alexander. LWO 2896, reel 11. Reading his poetry with commentary on the program "The Reading Rail," Station KUSC, Los Angeles, Calif., in the 1958 – 59 series.

LATTIMORE, Richmond Alexander. LWO 2660. Reading his poems with commentary in the Recording Laboratory, Apr. 25, 1958.

LAUGHTON, Charles. LWO 2169. "An evening with Charles Laughton," a reading presented in the Coolidge Auditorium, Nov. 23, 1953.

LAYTON, Irving. LWO 3161. Reading his poems with commentary in the Recording Laboratory, Aug. 8, 1960.

LEE, Muna. LWO 3088. Reading her poems in the Recording Laboratory, Apr. 25, 1960.

LEHMANN, John. LWO 3521. Reading his poems with commentary at the studios of Recorded Sound Ltd., London, Eng., Jan. 9, 1962.

LENGYEL, Cornel. LWO 3433. Reading his poems with commentary in the Recording Laboratory, Oct. 20, 1961.

LESLIE, Kenneth. LWO 2048, reel 4. Recorded by the City College of New York, Apr. 19. 1937.

LEVERTOV, Denise. LWO 2882. Reading her poems with commentary in New York City. June 15, 1958. Includes discussion.

LEVINE, Philip. LWO 3353. Reading his poems with commentary in Fresno, Calif., during the Christmas vacation of 1960.

LEVINE, Philip. LWO 3818. Reading his poems with commentary on June 1, 1962, at Fresno. Calif.

LEVY, Newman. LWO 3522. Reading his poems with commentary in Stereo Sound Studios. New York City, Feb. 5, 1962.

LE WINTER, Oswald. LWO 3337. Reading his poems with commentary at the studio of Station KPFA, Berkeley, Calif., Oct. 24, 1960.

LEWIS, Janet. LWO 2689, reel 6. Reading her poetry in the Recording Laboratory, June 28, 1948.

LIEBERMAN, Elias. LWO 2048, reel 4. Poems recorded at the City College of New York, Dec. 6, 1940.

LINK, Gordden. LWO 3222. Reading his poems with commentary in the Recording Laboratory, Jan. 3, 1961. Richard Eberhart introduces Mr. Link.

LIVING THEATRE. LWO 3083, reel 3. Readings by the authors of a number of poems from A New Folder: Americans: Poems and Drawings: edited by Daisy Aldan. Recorded at the Living Theatre, New York City, June 12, 1959.

LLEWELLYN, Alun. LWO 3993, reel 7, side B. Guest on Florence Becker Lennon's program "Enjoyment of Poetry," broadcast over Radio Station WEVD, New York City (1959?)

LOGAN, John. LWO 2588, reel 3. Reading his poems at Notre Dame, Ind., Apr. 12, 1957.

LONG, William (Peter Yates, pseud.) LWO 2896, reel 5. Reading his poetry with commentary on the program "The Reading Rail," Station KUSC, Los Angeles, Calif., in the 1958 — 59 series.

LOWELL, Robert. LWO 2689, reels 6 & 7. Reading his poetry in the Recording Laboratory, Sept. 15, 1948.

LOWELL, Robert. LWO 2372, reel 2. Reading his poetry in his home at Boston, MASS., Apr. 27, 1955.

LOWELL, Robert. LWO 3188. Reading his poetry in the Coolidge Auditorium, Oct. 31, 1960.

LOWENFELS, Walter. LWO 3897. Reading his poems with commentary in the Recording Laboratory, Dec. 17, 1962.

MAAS, Willard. LWO 2529, reel 9. Reading his poetry in the Recording Laboratory, May 28, 1945.

McCORD, David. LWO 3442. Reading his poems with commentary in the Recording Laboratory, Nov. 2, 1961. Louis Untermeyer introduces Mr. McCord.

MacDIARMID, Hugh, pseud. of Christopher Murray Grieve. LWO 3756. Reading from his Collected Poems, with commentary in Scotland, Jan. 17, 1962.

McGINLEY, Phyllis. LWO 3148. Reading her poems with commentary at Aura Recording Studio, New York City, July 1960.

McGRATH, Thomas. LWO 2896, reel 6. Reading his poetry on the program "The Reading Rail," Station KUSC, Los Angeles, Calif., in the 1958 — 59 series.

McGRATH, Thomas. LWO 3147. Reading his poems at Radio Station KPFK, Los Angeles, Calif., Feb. 18, 1960.

McKNIGHT, Floyd. LWO 2048, reel 5. Poems recorded at the City College of New York, May 10, 1958.

MacLEISH, Archibald. LWO 2792, reel 10. Reading his poem "For This we Fight," in the Library of Congress, Aug. 21, 1943.

MacLEISH, Archibald. LWO 1649. Reading his poetry in Boston, Mass., Feb. 8, 1950. Recorded by Trans-Radio Production.

MacLEISH, Archibald. LWO 1649. Reading his poetry in the Recording Laboratory, Mar. 27, 1950.

MacLEISH, Archibald. LWO 2511. Reading his poems with commentary in the Coolidge Auditorium, Dec. 4, 1956.

MacLEISH, Archibald. LWO 3998. Reading his poetry with comments in the Coolidge Auditorium, May 13, 1963. Louis Untermeyer introduces Mr. MacLeish.

MacLEOD, Norman. LWO 2529, reel 6. Reading his poems in the Recording Laboratory, Apr. 21, 1945.

MANNES, Marya. LWO 3933, reel 3 side A. Guest on Florence Becker Lennon's program "Enjoyment of Poetry," broadcast over Radio Station WEVD, New York City, June 21, 1959. They discuss "Poetry and Politics."

MARKHAM, Edwin. LWO 2792, reel 10. Reading his poems. The poems were copied from a record owned by William LeRoy Stidger.

MARSHALL, Lenore Guinzburg. LWO 2885. Reading her poetry with commentary in New York City, Mar. 16, 1958.

MASON-MANHEIM, Madeline. LWO 2438. Reading her poetry with commentary in the Coolidge Auditorium, Apr. 9, 1956. Includes discussion of the Sonnet.

MASTERS, Edgar Lee. LWO 2048, reels 4 & 7. Poems recorded at the City College of New York, Mar. 13, Mar. 19, and Nov. 29, 1940. Includes discussion with Arthur Davison Ficke.

MATCHETT, William H. LWO 3050. Reading his poems at the Radio Station of the University of Washington, Seattle, Feb. 10, 1960.

MAY, James Boyer. LWO 2896, reel 2. Reading his poetry on the program "The Reading Rail," Station KUSC, Los Angeles, Calif., in the 1958 — 59 series.

MAY, James Boyer. LWO 2896, reel 4. Reading poems by Curtis Zahn on the program "The Reading Rail," Station KUSC, Los Angeles, Calif., in the 1958 — 59 series.

MAY, James Boyer. LWO 2896, reel 1. Giving (on July 1, 1959) a resume of the two year (1957–59) history of poetry readings broadcast over Station KUSC, Los Angeles (operated under the auspices of the University of Southern California). The Library of Congress has in its Poetry Archives copies of 29 KUSC readings from two series, "Poetry and Talk," and "The Reading Rail".

MAYHALL, Jane. LWO 1830, reels 4 & 5. Reading her poetry in New York City, May 21, 1951.

MEREDITH, Burgess. LWO 2792, reel 11. Reading the poetry of Stephen Vincent Benet in the Coolidge Auditorium, Mar. 18, 1943.

MEREDITH, Burgess. LWO 1809. Reading the poetry of Edwin Arlington Robinson in the Coolidge Auditorium, May 1, 1951, with commentary by Cleanth Brooks.

MEREDITH, Burgess. LWO 1906. Program entitled "The Paradox of Poe" presented in the Coolidge Auditorium, Jan. 7, 1952, with commentary by Dr. Frederick Wertham.

MEREDITH, William. LWO 2689, reel 7. Reading his poetry in the Recording Laboratory, Aug. 8, 1947.

MEREDITH, William. LWO 2915. Reading his poems in the Coolidge Auditorium, Oct. 19, 1959.

MEREDITH, William. LWO 3872. Reading his poems with commentary in the Recording Laboratory, Oct. 25, 1962. Louis Untermeyer introduces Mr. Meredith.

MERRIAM, Eve. LWO 3429. Reading her poems with commentary in the Recording Laboratory, Oct. 19, 1961. Introduced by Louis Untermeyer.

MERRILL, James Ingram. LWO 2652. Reading his poems with commentary in the Recording Laboratory, Apr. 15, 1958.

MERWIN, William S. LWO 2932. Reading his poems and translations with commentary. Recorded by Fassett Recording Studios, Boston, Mass., Mar. 18, 1958.

MERWIN, William S. LWO 3309. Reading his poems with comment in the Coolidge Auditorium, Apr. 10, 1961.

MEYERS, Bert. LWO 2896, reel 13. Reading his poetry in the program "The Reading Rail," station KUSC, Los Angeles, Calif., in the 1958 — 59 series.

MEYNELL, Francis. LWO 4286. Reading his poems, together with much commentary on other members of the illustrious Meynell family, at Recorded Productions Studio, London, Eng., Nov. 1963.

MEZEY, Robert. LWO 3369. Reading his poems at Fresno, Calif., May 1961.

MICHELINE, Jack. LWO 2896, reel 15. Reading his poetry with clarinet background on the program "The Reading Rail" Station KUSC Los Angeles, Calif., in the 1958 — 59 series.

MILES, Josephine. LWO 2930. Reading her poems with commentary at Berkeley, Calif., Sept. 20, 1958. Includes discussion.

MILLAY, Edna St. Vincent. LWO 2859. Obtained by special permission from the Radio Corporation of America for inclusion in An Album of Modern Poetry: An Anthology Read by the Poets, edited by Oscar Williams.

MILLAY, Norma. LWO 2999. Reading poems of her sister, Edna St. Vincent Millay in the Recording Laboratory, Dec. 8, 1959.

MILLER, Hugh. LWO 3468. In a recital of drama and poetry, "An Actor's Sketch Book," in the Coolidge Auditorium, Dec. 11, 1961.

MILLER, Mary Owings. LWO 2955, reels 1—4. Reading her poetry with commentary at Potosi, Glen Rock, Pa., May 9, 1959. Includes discussion.

MOORE, Marianne. LWO 1003. Reading poems taken from Harvard Vocarium recordings.

MOORE, Marianne. LWO 2048, reel 5. Poems recorded by the City College of New York, Feb. 14, 1941. Kimball Flaccus interviews Alfred Kreymbrog and Miss Moore.

MOORE. Marianne. LWO 1963, reel 7. Reading her poetry in New York City, Nov. 7, 1951.

MOORE, Marianne. LWO 3993, reel 3, side B. Guest on Florence Becker Lennon's program "Enjoyment of Poetry," broadcast over Radio Station WEVD, New York City, June 7, 1959. They discuss "A Poem Should Praise All It Can."

MOORE, Marianne. LWO 4118. Reading her poems with commentary in the Coolidge Auditorium, Oct. 21, 1963. Introduced by Howard Nemerov.

MOORE, Merrill. LWO 1907. Reading his poetry in the Recording Laboratory, Jan. 7, 1952.

MOORE, Merrill. LWO 2195. Reading his poetry in Boston, Mass., May 9, 1953.

MOORE, Merrill. LWO 2971, reels 1—12. Recordings presented to the Library of Congress by the Estate of Merrill Moore in 1958. The first eight reels are from a series of programs "Science of the Sonnet," broadcast in 1954.

MOORE, Richard. LWO 2058, reel 2. Reading his poetry at Berkeley, Calif., Mar. 23, 1952.

MORROW, Helen. LWO 2048, reel 5. Poems recorded at the City College of New York, Apr. 4, 1940.

MORSE, Samuel French. LWO 2493, reels 2 & 3. Reading his poems at Cambridge, Mass., July 31, 1956.

MORTON, David. LWO 2792, reel 10. Lecture and poetry reading in the Coolidge Auditorium, Apr. 2, 1946.

MOSS, Howard. LWO 2372, reel 1. Reading his poetry in New York City, Apr. 19, 1955.

MOSS, Howard. LWO 4565. Reading his poems with commentary in the Whittall Pavilion, Mar. 22, 1963. Introduced by Roy P. Basler.

MOWRER, Paul Scott. LWO 3476. Reading his poetry with commentary at the studio of Dartmouth College Films, Fairbank Hall, Hanover, N.H., on Nov. 20, 1961.

MOWRER, Paul Scott. LWO 3993, reel 7, side A. Guest on Florence Becker Lennon's program "Enjoyment of Poetry," broadcast over Radio Station WEVD, New York City, Dec. 25, 1960.

MUIR, Edward. LWO 2398. Reading his poems with commentary in the Recording Laboratory, Dec. 12, 1955.

MUNRO, Mrs. Harold. LWO 3367. Reading the poems of her husband with commentary in the Recording Laboratory, July 12, 1961.

NAPIER, John. LWO 3248. Reading his poetry with comment in the Recording Laboratory, Feb. 2, 1961.

NASH, Ogden. LWO 2982. Reading his poetry at Columbia Records, New York City, July 3, 1959. Includes interview by Oscar Williams.

NASH, Ogden. LWO 3968. Reading his poems with commentary in the Coolidge Auditorium, Mar. 25, 1963. Introduced by L. Quincy Mumford.

NATHAN, Robert. LWO 3733. Reading his poems with comment at his home in Los Angeles, Calif., in Apr. 1962.

NATIONAL POETRY FESTIVAL. LWO 3868, 3869, and 3870. Recording of the National Poetry Festival, held in the Coolidge Auditorium, Oct. 22 – 24 1962.

NEMEROV, Howard. LWO 2881. Reading his poems with commentary, Apr. 19 and 20, 1958, at Bennington, Vt. Includes discussion.

NEMEROV, Howard. LWO 3626. Reading selections from his poems in the Coolidge Auditorium. Apr. 16, 1962.

NEMEROV, Howard. LWO 4244. Reading his poems with commentary in the Recording Laboratory, Mar. 19, 1964, for the "Talking Books for the Blind."

NEMEROV, Howard. LWO 4282. Reading his poems in the Coolidge Auditorium, May 11, 1964. Introduced by L. Quincy Mumford.

NIMS, John Frederick. LWO 2529, reel 6. Reading his poetry in the Recording Laboratory, Dec. 30, 1946.

NIMS, John Frederick. LWO 2588, reel 2. Reading his poetry on the Notre Dame Campus, Apr. 11, 1957.

O'CONNOR, William Van. LWO 2588, reel 3. Reading his poems and a short story at Minneapolis, Minn., Mar. 24, 1957.

O'GORMAN, Ned. LWO 2997. Reading his poems in the Recording Laboratory, Dec. 1, 1959.

ORLOVITZ, Gil. LWO 2896, reel 4. Reading his poetry on the program "The Reading Rail," Station KUSC, Los Angeles, Calif., in the 1958 – 59 series.

ORLOVITZ, Gil. LWO 2954. Reading his poems in New York City, May 18, 1959.

ORLOVSKY, Peter. LWO 2799. Reading his poems with commentary in the Recording Laboratory, Feb. 27, 1959.

OSTROFF, Anthony, J. LWO 2897, reels 1-4. Reading his poetry with commentary in New York City, Mar. 15, 1959. Includes discussion.

PACK, Robert. LWO 3021. Reading his poems in the Recording Laboratory, Jan. 18, 1960.

PACKARD, William. LWO 4263. Reading his poems and excerpts from his plays, with commentary in the Recording Laboratory, Apr. 23, 1964.

PARKINSON, Thomas. LWO 4013. Reading his poems with commentary at the University of California, Oct., 1962.

PARKINSON, Thomas. LWO 4012. Reading his poems with commentary at Station KPFK in Berkeley, Calif., Jan. 25, 1963.

PATCHEN, Kenneth. LWO 2896, reel 3. Reading his poetry with commentary. Recorded at Station KUSF, Santa Fe, N.M., for broadcast over the program "Poetry and Talk," Station KUSC–FM, Los Angeles, Calif., in the 1957–58 series.

PAUKER, John. LWO 4510. Reading his poems with commentary in the Recording Laboratory, Feb. 2, 1965. Introduced by Reed Whittemore.

PENNEY, Edmund. LWO 2896, reel 13. Reading the poetry of Fred Cogswell on the program "The Reading Rail," Station KUSC, Los Angeles, Calif., in the 1958–59 series.

PHELPS, Lyon. LWO 3183. Reading his poems with commentary in Boston, Mass., June 2, 1960.

PHILBRICK, Charles H. LWO 3263. Reading from his poetry with comment before friends of the Library of Brown University, Dec. 5, 1960, in the John Hay Library, Providence, R.L.

PHILBRICK, Charles H. LWO 3263. Reading his poems with commentary at Brown University, Providence, R.L., Dec. 28, 1960.

PILLIN, William. LWO 2896, reel 10. Reading his poems on the program "Poetry and Talk," Station KUSC, Los Angeles, Calif., in the 1957 – 58 series.

PITTER, Ruth. LWO 3510. Reading her poems with commentary at Star Sound Studios, Ltd., Rodmarton St, London, W.L., Eng., on Dec. 20, 1961.

PLATH, Sylvia. LWO 2939. Reading her poems at Springfield, Mass., Apr. 18, 1958. Includes discussion.

PLOMER, William Charles Franklyn. LWO 3506. Reading his poems with commentary at the Recorded Sound Studios, London, Eng., Dec. 1, 1961.

PLUTZIK, Hyam. LWO 2966. Reading his poetry with commentary at the Eastman School of Music, Rochester, N.Y., June 18, 1959.

POETRY SOCIETY OF AMERICA. LWO 3059. The Fiftieth Anniversary Dinner held in the Waldorf-Astoria in New York City, Jan. 21, 1960. Recorded by Station WNYC, New York City.

POMEROY, Ralph. LWO 3929. Reading his poems with commentary in the Recording Laboratory, Feb. 11, 1963.

PRESS, John. LWO 3606. Reading his poems with commentary in the Recording Laboratory, Apr. 9, 1962. Introduced by Louis Untermeyer.

PRICE, Vincent. LWO 3955. Presenting a poetry reading entitled "America the Beautiful," in the Coolidge Auditorium, Mar. 11 and 12, 1963.

PRINCE, Frank Templeton. LWO 3708. Reading his poems with commentary at the British Council, Recorded Sound Department, Albion House, 59 New Oxford Street, London, W.C.1, Eng., on Jan. 10 1962.

PRITCHARD, Sheila. LWO 3889. Reading her own poems with commentary at Wayne State University, Radio Division, Detroit, Mich., on Oct. 16, 1962.

PRITCHARD, William Errol. LWO 3031. Reading his poems with commentary in the Studio of Radio Station KUOW, the University of Washington, Seattle, during 1959.

PUTNAM, Howard Phelps. LWO 1274. Reading his poem "Ballad of a Strange Thing," on a Harvard Vocarium recording.

QUASIMODO, Salvatore. LWO 3100. Reading his poems in Italian in the Recording Laboratory, Apr. 22, 1960.

RABOFF, Paul. LWO 2896, reel 12. Reading his poetry with commentary on the program "The Reading Rail," Station KUSC, Los Angeles, Calif., in the 1958 – 59 series. Includes discussion.

RAGO, Henry. LWO 2493, reel 3. Reading his poems at Cambridge, Mass., Aug. 1, 1956.

RAGO, Henry. LWO 3470. Reading his poems with comment in the Recording Laboratory, Dec, 4, 1961. Introduced by Louis Untermeyer.

RAINE, Kathleen J. LWO 1887. Reading her poems in the Recording Laboratory, Jan. 21, 1952.

RAINE, Kathleen J. LWO 3596. Reading her poems in the Recording Laboratory, Mar. 19, 1962.

RAIZISS, Sonia. LWO 3706. Reading her poems and translations from Italian by herself and Alfredo de Palchi in the Recording Laboratory, May 16, 1962.

RANSOM, John Crowe. LWO 2689, reels 7 & 8. Reading his poems with commentary to the Writer's Club of the Library of Congress and in the Recording Laboratory, Jan. 28, 1945.

RANSOM, John Crowe. LWO 2689, reels 8 & 9. Reading his poems in the Recording Laboratory, Apr. 12, 1948.

RANSOM, John Crowe. LWO 2588, reels 2 & 3. Reading his poems with commentary at his home in Gambier, Ohio, Mar. 1 and 2, 1957.

RANSOM, John Crowe. LWO 2609. Lecture "American Poetry at Mid Century" presented in Coolidge Auditorium, Jan. 13, 1958.

RANSOM, John Crowe. LWO 2628. Reading his poems and discussing them with Randall Jarrell in the Recordig Laboratory, Jan. 14, 1958.

RATHBONE, Basil. LWO 1961. Reading in the Coolidge Auditorium, Mar. 23, 1952.

RATHBONE, Basil. LWO 3891. Presenting, in conjunction with The Consort Players, a program of Elizabethan poetry and music in the Coolidge Auditorium, Nov. 29, and 30, 1962.

RAYFORD, Julian Lee. LWO 2048, reel 5. Chanting and singing folk songs and his poems at the City College of New York, Feb. 28, 1941. Interviewed by Kimball Flaccus.

READ, Sir Herbert Edward. LWO 2689, reel 9. Reading his poetry in the Recording Laboratory, Apr. 12, 1948.

READ, Sir Herbert Edward. LWO 3112. Reading his poems with commentary in the Recording Laboratory, May 9, 1960.

REDGROVE, Peter. LWO 3854. Reading his poems at Electronic Service, Ltd. Leeds, Eng., Aug. 14, 1962.

REDMOND, Liam. LWO 2048, reel 5. In a reading recorded at the City College of New York, Jan. 27, 1939.

REED, Henry. LWO 2859. Recorded by CBS in New York City for inclusion in An Album of Modern Poetry: An Anthology Read by the Poets, edited by Oscar Williams.

REID, Alastair. LWO 3249. Reading his poetry with comment at the Rockhill Recording Studios, New York City, on Jan. 9, 1961.

REXROTH, Kenneth. LWO 2529, reel 7. Reading his poetry in the Recording Laboratory, Oct. 31, 1948.

REXROTH, Kenneth. LWO 2896, reel 3. Reading poetry with commentary on the program "The Reading Rail," Station KUSC, Los Angeles, Calif., in the 1958 – 59 series.

RICH, Adrienne Cecile. LWO 1830, reels 1 & 2. Reading her poetry in the home of Richard Eberhart, Cambridge, Mass., May 1951.

RICH, Adrienne Cecile. LWO 2890. Reading her poetry in Boston, Mass., Jan. 30. 1959.

RICHARDS, Edward Ames. LWO 3312. Reading his poems with commentary in the Recording Laboratory, Apr. 13, 1961. Introduced by Richard Eberhart.

RICHARDS, Ivor Armstrong. LWO 3134. Reading his poems at Telavix Film and Recording Studios, 216 Tremont Street, Boston, Mass., May 5, 1960.

RICHARDS, Ivor Armstrong. LWO 3204. Reading his poems with commentary in the Coolidge Auditorium, Nov. 28, 1960.

RIDLAND, John M. LWO 3965. Reading his poems with commentary at the University of California, Santa Barbara, Calif., on May 28, 1962, and Mar. 1, 1963.

RIDLER, Anne Bradley. LWO 3736. Reading her poems with commentary at Isis Recording Studios, Oxford, Eng., in Mar. 1962.

RILEY, James Whitcomb. LWO 2964. Reading his poems. Purchased by the Library of Congress from the Historical Society, Indianapolis 20, Ind.

RODGERS, William Robert. LWO 2965. Reading his poems with commentary in London, Eng., in 1959. Includes discussion.

RODMAN, Selden. LWO 2048, reel 5. Reading his poetry at the City College of New York, June 4, 1940.

RODMAN, Selden. LWO 2529, reel 7. Reading his poetry in the Recording Laboratory, Sept. 1, 944.

ROETHKE, Theodore. LWO 2689, reel 9. Reading his poetry in the Recording Laboratory, Jan. 3, 1947.

ROETHKE, Theodore. LWO 2863, reel 1. Reading his poems and those of other poets at the YMHA Poetry Center, New York City.

ROETHKE, Theodore. LWO 2859. Recorded by CBS in New York City for inclusion in An Album of Modern Poetry: An Anthology Read by the Poets, edited by Oscar Williams.

ROSKOLENKO, Harry. LWO 3008. Reading his poems with commentary at Station KPFA, Calif., Feb. 19, 1957.

ROSKOLENKO, Harry. LWO 3008. Guest on Florence Becker Lennon's program "Enjoyment of Poetry," broadcast over Radio Station WEVD, New York City, May 31, 1959. They discuss " The Wandering Poet."

ROSS, David. LWO 2562. Presenting a program "Poet's Gold," in the Coolidge Auditorium, Apr. 8, 1957.

ROSTEN, Norman. LWO 3464. Reading his poems with comment in the Recording Laboratory, Nov. 28, 1961. Introduced by Louis Untermeyer.

RUKEYSER, Muriel. LWO 2689. Reading her poetry in the Recording Laboratory, Nov. 2, 1950.

RUKEYSER, Muriel. LWO 2933. Reading her poems with commentary in New York City, Mar. 21, 1959. Includes discussion.

RUKEYSER, Muriel. LWO 2976. Reading her poems and Emily Dickinson's in New York City, June 8, 1959 at CBS Studios.

RUKEYSER, Muriel. LWO 3627. Reading her poems with commentary in the Recording Laboratory, Apr. 17, 1962. Introduced by Louis Untermeyer. Includes discussion.

RUKEYSER, Muriel. LWO 4576. Reading her poems with commentary in the Whittall Pavilion, Apr. 5, 1965. Introduced by L. Quincy Mumford.

RUTLEDGE, Archibald Hamilton. LWO 2924. Reading his poetry with commentary at Spartanburg, S.C., in 1958.

SALOMON, Isidore Lawrence. LWO 3000. Reading his poems in the Recording Laboratory, Dec. 9, 1959. Includes interview by Richard Eberhart.

SALOMON, Isidore Lawrence. LWO 3338. Reading his poems with comment in the Stereo Sound Studios in New York City, Apr. 3, 1961.

SANDBERG, Carl. LWO 2529, reel 7. Lecturing on "The Poet in a Democracy," reading his poems, and singing folk songs in the Coolidge Auditorium, Apr. 24, 1941.

SANDBURG, Helga. LWO 4006. Reading her poems with commentary in the Coolidge Auditorium, May 23, 1963. Introduced by Louis Untermeyer.

SARTON, May. LWO 3022. Reading her poems with commentary in the Recording Laboratory, Jan. 20, 1960.

SCANNELL, Vernon. LWO 3923. Reading his poems with commentary at Recorded Sound, Ltd., 27-31 Bryanston Street, Marble Arch, London, W.1, Eng., on Jan 9, 1963.

SCHEVILL, James Erwin. LWO 2929. Reading his poetry at the Audio-Visual Center, University of California, Berkeley, Calif., Sept. 21, 1958. Includes discussion.

SCHEVILL, James Erwin. LWO 4362. Reading his poems with commentary in the Coolidge Auditorium, Oct. 19, 1964. Introduced by L. Quincy Mumford.

SCHWARTZ, Delmore. LWO 2689, reel 9. Reading his poems at the ABC Studio in New York City, Apr. 1948.

SCHWARTZ, Delmore. LWO 2609. Lecture "American Poetry at Mid-Century" presented in the Coolidge Auditorium, Jan. 20, 1959.

SCHWARTZ, Delmore. LWO 2859. Recorded by CBS in New York City for inclusion in An Album of Modern Poetry: An Anthology Read by the Poets, edited by Oscar Williams.

SCOTT, Winfield Townley. LWO 1830, reels 3 & 4. Reading his poems with commentary at Providence, R.L., May 16, 1951.

SCOTT, Winfield Townley. LWO 2195. Reading his poetry at his home in Hampton, Conn., Oct. 6, 1953.

SETHI, Narendra Kumar. LWO 3993, reel 4, side A. Guest on Florence Becker Lennon's program "Enjoyment of Poetry," broadcast over Radio Station WEVD, New York City, Mar. 12, 1961. They discuss "New dimensions in Hindi Poetry."

SEXTON, Anne. LWO 3146. Reading her poems with commentary. Recorded at the Fassett Recording Studio, Boston, Mass., in May 1960.

SEXTON, Anne. LWO 3993, reel 4, side A. Guest on Florence Becker Lennon's program "Enjoyment of Poetry," broadcast over Radio Station WEVD, New York City, Apr. 9, 1961. They discuss "Poetry as Therapy."

SHAPIRO, Harvey. LWO 3474. Reading his poems with commentary in the studio of Radio Station WBAI—FM, New York City, in the summer of 1961.

SHAPIRO, Karl Jay. LWO 2689, reel 9. Reading his poetry in the Recording Laboratory, June 6, 1945.

SHAPIRO, Karl Jay. LWO 2558. Reading his poems with commentary in the Coolidge Auditorium, Mar. 25, 1957.

SHAPIRO, Karl Jay. LWO 3993, reel 4, side B. Guest on Florence Becker Lennon's program "Enjoyment of Poetry," broadcast over Radio Station WEVD, New York City, Aug. 8, 1960. They discuss "Poems of a Jew."

SHAPIRO, Karl Jay. LWO 4206. Delivering a lecture entitled "American Poet?" in the Coolidge Auditorium, Jan. 27, 1964. Introduced by Roy P. Basler. The second of a 2—lecture series titled The Writer's Experience. The first lecture was by Ralph Ellison, item 230.

SHUSTER, George N. LWO 2048, reels 5 & 6. Recorded at the City College of New York, Apr. 25, 1941.

SIMPSON, Louis. LWO 2934. Reading his poems with commentary in New York City, Mar. 19, 1959.

SITWELL, Edith. LWO 2346. Reading her poetry in the Recording Laboratory, Mar. 31, 1955.

SITWELL, Sir Osbert. LWO 2347. Reading his poetry in the Recording Laboratory, Mar. 31, 1955.

SLAVITT, David R. LWO 3993, reel 4, side B. Guest on Florence Becker Lennon's program "Enjoyment of Poetry," broadcast over Radio Station WEVD, New York City, Nov. 13, 1960. They discuss "The Narrative Poem."

SLAVITT, David R. LWO 4654, reel 1. Reading his poems with commentary at the Fassett Recording Studio, Boston, Mass., Aug. 4, 1965.

SLOBODKIN, Salem. LWO 3032. Reading her poetry at the Fassett Recording Studio, Boston, Mass., Jan. 9, 1960.

SMITH, Thomas Vernor. LWO 2189. Reading his poems and those of other poets in the Coolidge Auditorium, Mar. 15, 1954.

SMITH, William Jay. LWO 1963. Reading his poetry at Potosi, Glen Rock, Pa., July 1, 1951.

SMITH, William Jay. LWO 2949. Reading his poems and translations, Apr. 21, 1958. Includes Interview.

SMITH, William Jay. LWO 4621. Reading his poems and the poems of Andrei Voznesensky in the Recording Laboratory, June 9, 1965. Introduced by Reed Whittemore.

SMYTHE, Daniel. LWO 2529, reel 8. Reading his poems with commentary in the Coolidge Auditorium, Apr. 17, 1946.

SNODGRASS, William De Witt. LWO 2892. Reading his poems with commentary at the University of Rochester School of Music, June 9, 1959.

SNODGRASS, William De Witt. LWO 3273. Reading his poems with comment in the Coolidge Auditorium, Feb. 27, 1961.

SOBILOFF, Hy. LWO 2427. Reading his poetry in the Recording Laboratory, June 12, 1956.

SOBILOFF, Hy. LWO 3103. Reading his poems in the Recording Laboratory, May 2, 1960. Interviewed by Oscar Williams and Richard Eberhart.

SOBILOFF, Hy. LWO 4518. Introducing the presentation of his poetry in three color feature films, shown in the Coolidge Auditorium, Feb. 8, 1965. The sound tracks of the films were not tape recorded. The films, presented by special permission of Three Arts Films, New York City, were "Montauk," narrated by Ed Begley, "Central Park," narrated by Jason Robards, Jr., and "Speak to Mr. Child," narrated by David Wayne. Mr. Sobiloff is introduced by L. Quincy Mumford.

SPENCER, Theodore. LWO 2689, reel 10. Reading poems taken from Harvard Vocarium recordings.

SPENDER, Stephen. LWO 2689, reel 10. Reading his poems in the Recording Laboratory, Jan. 16, 1948.

SPENDER, Stephen. LWO 2372, reel 3. Reading his poetry in the home of the President of Wheaton College, Norton, Mass., Apr. 23, 1955.

SPENDER, Stephen. LWO 2353. Reading his poems in the Recording Laboratory, May 19, 1955.

SPENDER, Stephen. LWO 2958. Reading his poetry in the Recording Laboratory, Nov. 2, 1959. Includes discussion between Mr. Spender and Richard Eberhart.

SPENDER, Stephen. LWO 2959. Reading his poetry in the Coolidge Auditorium, Nov. 2, 1959.

SPEYER, Lenora Von Stosch. LWO 2048, reel 6. Reading her poems at the City College of New York, May 20, 1940 and Feb. 7, 1941.

SPINGARN, Lawrence Perry. LWO 2896, reel 6. Reading his poetry on the program "The Reading Rail," Station KUSC, Los Angeles, Calif., in the 1958 – 59 series.

STAFFORD, William Edgar. LWO 2928. Reading his poems with commentary at Lewis and Clark College, Portland, Ore., Sept. 18, 1958. Includes discussion.

STALLMAN, Robert Wooster. LWO 2372, reel 3. Reading his poems with commentary in his home in Storrs, Conn., Apr. 28, 1955.

STANFORD, Ann. LWO 3430. Reading her poetry with commentary at Station KPFK, Los Angeles, Calif., July 5, 1961.

STARBUCK, George. LWO 2943. Reading his poems with commentary at Cambridge, Mass., in 1959.

STARBUCK, George. LWO 3993, reel 5, side A. Guest on Florence Becker Lennon's program "Enjoyment of Poetry," broadcast over Radio Station WEVD, New York City, June 28, 1959. They discuss "The Poet Takes a Stand."

STEAD, William Force. LWO 3440. Reading his poems with commentary in the Recording Laboratory, Oct. 31, 1961. Introduced by Louis Untermeyer.

STEVENS, Wallace. LWO 2863, reels 1 & 2. Reading his poems at the YMHA Poetry Center, New York City, Apr. 14, 1954.

STONE, Ruth. LWO 2879. Reading her poetry at Vassar College, Apr. 15, 1958. Includes interview by her husband, Walter Stone.

STONE, Ruth. LWO 3993, reel 5 Side A. Guest on Florence Becker Lennon's program "Enjoyment of Poetry," broadcast over Radio Station WEVD, New York City, Nov. 6, 1960. They discuss "The Image in Poetry."

STUART, Jesse. LWO 2529, reel 8. Reading his poems and one of his stories in the Recording Laboratory, Sept. 9, 1944.

SULLIVAN, Aloysius Michael. LWO 2048, reel 6. Reading his poetry at the City College of New York, Jan. 9, 1939 and Jan. 10, 1941.

SWALLOW, Alan. LWO 3517. Reading his poems with commentary in Denver, Colo., Jan. 19, 1962.

SWARD, Robert. LWO 3287. Reading his poems with commentary at the BBC Studios, Feb. 2, 1961.

SWARD, Robert. LWO 3315. Reading his poems with commentary before an audience in the U.S. Embassy, London, Eng., on Feb. 27, 1961.

SWENSON, May. LWO 2941. Reading her poems with commentary in New York City, Mar. 15, 1958.

TAGGARD, Genevieve. LWO 2048, reel 6. Reading her poems at the City College of New York, May 27, 1940.

TAGLIABUE, John. LWO 3136. Reading his poems in Tokyo, Japan. Recorded in Apr. 1960.

TANDY, Jessica and Hume Cronyn. LWO 2280. Joint reading entitled "Face to Face," presented in the Coolidge Auditorium, Nov. 22, 1954.

TATE, Allen. LWO 2048, reel 6. Reading his poetry at the City College of New York, Mar. 4, 1941.

TATE, Allen. LWO 2689, reel 10. Reading his poetry in the Recording Laboratory, Dec. 8, 1947.

TATE, Allen. LWO 2195. Reading his poetry in his home in Princeton, N.J., in 1953.

TATE, Allen. LWO 2863, reel 1. Reading his poems at the YMHA, Poetry Center, New York City.

TATE, Allen. LWO 2756. Reading his poems in the Coolidge Auditorium, Jan. 12, 1959.

THOMAS, Dylan. LWO 2529, reel 9. Reading his poems in the Recording Laboratory, Mar. 9, 1950.

THOMAS, Dylan. LWO 2848. Dylan Thomas reading poetry in the home of Mrs. Marcela DuPont, Washington, D.C., Mar. 3, 1952. Concludes with a short statement by Mrs. DuPont.

THOMPSON, George. LWO 3448. Reading his poetry with musical background at the Wise Temple, Reading Road, Cincinnati, Ohio, Mar. 16, 1961.

THOMPSON, George. LWO 3364. Reading his poems with short comment at 5541 Hanley Park Road, White Oak, Ohio, Mar. 26, 1961.

THOMPSON, John. LWO 2985. Reading his poetry at the CBS Studio, New York City, May 26, 1959.

TOMLINSON, Charles. LWO 3087. Reading his poems in the Recording Laboratory, Apr. 18, 1960.

TORRENCE, Frederic Ridgely. LWO 2048, reel 6. Reading his poetry at the City College of New York, May 2, 1940.

TORRENCE, Frederic Ridgely. LWO 1706. Reading his poetry in the Recording Laboratory, Oct. 10, 1955.

TRIEM, Eve. LWO 3307. Reading her poems with commentary in the studio of Station KUOW, University of Washington, Seattle, Wash., on Feb. 1 and Mar. 13, 1961.

TRIMMER, John. LWO 1963. Reading his poetry at Potosi, Glen Rock, Pa., Nov. 23, 1951.

TRIMPI, Wesley. LWO 3181. Reading his poems with comment. Recorded on home recorder at Stanford, Calif., Sept. 1960.

TURCO, Lewis. LWO 3013. Reading his poems with commentary in the Audio Laboratory, East Hall, State University of Iowa, Iowa City, Dec. 30, 1959.

TUSIANI, Joseph. LWO 3986. Reading his poems with comment in the Recording Laboratory, Apr. 18, 1963. Introduced by Louis Untermeyer.

UNTERMEYER, Jean Starr. LWO 2048, reels 6 & 7. Recording her poems at the City College of New York, Mar. 28, 1941.

UNTERMEYER, Jean Starr. LWO 3243. Reading her poems with comment at the Pathe Sound Studios, New York, Jan. 5, 1961.

UNTERMEYER, Louis. LWO 3125. Reading his poems with commentary in the Recording Laboratory, May 26, 1960. Includes interview by Robert H. Land, Assistant Chief, General Reference and Bibliography Division of the Library of Congress.

UNTERMEYER, Louis. LWO 3276. Lecturing on the subject "Play in Poetry" and reading his poems and parodies in the Coolidge Auditorium, Mar. 6, 1961.

UNTERMEYER, Louis. LWO 3413. Lecturing on "What Makes Modern Poetry Modern," and reading poetry in the Coolidge Auditorium, Oct. 2, 1961.

UNTERMEYER, Louis. LWO 3607. Reading his poems with commentary in the Coolidge Auditorium, Apr. 11, 1962.

VAN DOREN, Mark. LWO 2048, reel 2. Reading his poetry at the City College of New York, Mar. 14, 1941.

VAN DOREN, Mark. LWO 511. Reading his poetry at the NBC Studio in New York City, May 27, 1944.

VAN DOREN, Mark. LWO 1830, reel 4. Reading his poetry in New York City, May 20, 1951.

VAN DOREN, Mark. LWO 2304. Lecture "Whitman The Poet" presented in the Coolidge Auditorium, Jan. 17, 1955.

VAN DOREN, Mark. LWO 3993, reel 5, side B. Guest on Florence Becker Lennon's program "Enjoyment of Poetry," broadcast over Radio Station WEVD, New York City, June 1, 1958. They discuss "Love in Poetry."

VAN DOREN, Mark. LWO 3357. Reading his poems with commentary at the NBC Studio in New York City, Jan. 16, 1961.

VAN DUYN, Mona. LWO 2588, reel 1. Reading her poetry at her home in St. Louis, Mo., Mar. 16 and 17, 1957.

VIERECK, Peter Robert Edwin. LWO 3752. Reading his poems and the poems of William Ernest Henley, Thomas Lovell Beddoes, and Roy Campbell with commentary at Weslayan University during the winter of 1961–62. He also reads excerpts from The Tree Witch at an unspecified place and time.

VINAL, Harold. LWO 2048, reel 7. Reading his poetry at the City College of New York, Jan. 10, 1941.

WAGONER, David. LWO 2923. Reading his poems with commentary at Seattle, Wash., Sept. 17, 1958. Includes discussion.

WAIN, John. LWO 2738. Reading his poems with commentary in the Recording Laboratory, Dec. 1, 1958.

WAKOSKI, Diane. LWO 3993, reel 5, side B. Guest on Florence Becker Lennon's program "Enjoyment of Poetry," broadcast over Radio Station WEVD, New York City, Feb. 5, 1961. They discuss "Surrealism in Poetry."

WALCOTT, Derek. LWO 4363. Reading his poems with commentary in the Recording Laboratory, Oct. 20, 1964.

WARREN, Robert Penn. LWO 2689, reel 10. Reading his poetry in the Recording Laboratory, Dec. 6, 1944.

WARREN, Robert Penn. LWO 3149, reel 10. Reading his poems in the Recording Laboratory, June 7, 1945.

WARREN, Robert Penn. LWO 2396. Reading his poetry with commentary in the Coolidge Auditorium, Dec. 5, 1955.

WATKINS, Vernon Phillips. LWO 2981. Reading his poems. Recorded by the Auslitone Recording Company, Pontardawe, Wales, in 1959.

WEISBURD, Mel. LWO 2896, reel 14. Reading his poetry on the program "The Reading Rail," Station KUSC, Los Angeles, Calif., in the 1958 – 59 series.

WEISS, Theodore Russell. LWO 2951. Reading his poems with commentary at Potosi, Glen Rock, Pa., Feb. 9, 1959. Includes discussion.

WELCH, Livingston. LWO 2972. Reading his poems and stories in New York City, Sept. 29, 1959.

WHALEN, Philip. LWO 3918. Reading his poems with commentary in the studios of Musical Engineering Associates, Sausalito, Calif., on Jan. 18, 1963.

WHEELOCK, John Hall. LWO 2048, reel 7. Reading his poems with commentary at the City College of New York, Dec. 4, 1937, and Feb. 7, 1941.

WHEELOCK, John Hall. LWO 2414. Reading his poems with commentary in New York City, Oct. 18, 1955.

WHEELOCK, John Hall. LWO 2609. Lecture "American Poetry at Mid Century" presented in Coolidge Auditorium, Jan. 27, 1958.

WHEELOCK, John Hall. LWO 2721. Reading his poems in the Coolidge Auditorium, Oct. 27, 1958.

WHITTEMORE, Reed. LWO 3089. Reading his poems at KARL Studio, Northfield, Minn., Mar. 11, 1960.

WHITTEMORE, Reed. LWO 4239. Reading his poems with commentary in the Coolidge Auditorium, Mar. 9, 1964. Introduced by Howard Nemerov.

WHITTEMORE, Reed. LWO 4616. Reading his poems with commentary in the Coolidge Auditorium, May 24, 1965. Introduction and closing remarks made by L. Quincy Mumford.

WINTERS, Yvor. LWO 2944. Reading his poems with commentary at the Stafford Hotel, Baltimore, Md., Nov. 9, 1958.

WOODS, John. LWO 2962. Reading his poetry in Kalamazoo, Mich., Sept. 1959.

WRIGHT, James. LWO 2891. Reading his poems at the University of Minnesota, May 25, 1958.

YARON, Ahuva and Mariam Schneid. LWO 3993, reel 6, side B. Guests on Florence Becker Lennon's program "Enjoyment of Poetry," broadcast over radio Station WEVD, New York City, May 15, 1960. They discuss "Two Israel Poets."

YOUNG, Andrew. LWO 3579. Reading his poems with commentary at his home, Park Lodge, Church Lane, Yapton, Arundel, Sussex, Eng., on Jan. 28, 1962.

ZABRISKIE, George. LWO 4620, reel 1. Reading his poems with commentary in the Recording Laboratory, May 26, 1965. Introduced by Reed Whittemore.

ZATURENSKA, Marya. LWO 1273. Reading her poems at the ABC Studio in New York City, Oct. 21, 1948.

ZATURENSKA, Marya. LWO 2689, reel 5. Reading her poetry at the ABC Studio in New York City, May 9, 1949.

ZUKOFSKY, Louis. LWO 3247. Reading his poems with commentary at the Polytechnic Institute of Brooklyn, Brooklyn, N.Y., on Nov. 4, 1960.

APPENDIX J

WORLD CONGRESS OF POETS

The Second World Congress of Poets was held in Taipei, Taiwan, Republic of China, November 12-15, 1973, under the sponsorship of the Chinese Poets' Association with the co-sponsorship of United Poets-Laureate International (UPLI), World Poetry Society Intercontinental (WPSI), International Who's Who in Poetry (IWWP), World Poets' Resource Center, Inc. (WPRC) and its affiliate Eastern Centre of The Poetry Society of England (ECPSE). Attending the Congress were more than 300 poets from Argentina, Australia, Britain, Canada, Cyprus, Denmark, Dominica, Free Estonia, France, West Germany, Guam, Hong Kong, Free Hungary, India, Indonesia, Italy, Japan, Khmer, South Korea, Luxemburg, Free Latvia, Malta, Malaysia, Nicaragua, Pakistan, Panama, Philippines, Portugal, Saudi Arabia, Thailand, Turkey, Uruguay, U.S.A., Vietnam and the host country, Republic of China. The Congress was also supported by poets and/or Poetry Societies from Austria, Belgium, Bangladesh, Bolivia, Gambia, Greece, Guatemala, Honduras, Ireland, Ivory Coast, Jordan, Mexico, Netherlands, New Zealand, Paraguay, Peru, Rhodesia, Singapore, Spain, Sweden and Switzerland. Most of the sessions took place at the Grand Hotel, one of the ten best hotels in the world.

The Congress had a very impressive opening ceremony in the Taipei City Hall on the morning of November 12, 1973. Aside from Congress delegates, about 1,000 guests from various Chinese poetry societies, literary organizations, and civic bodies also attended this memorable event.

Dr. Tin-wen Chung, President of the Chinese Poets' Association and Chairman of the Arrangements Committee for the 2nd WCP announced the formal opening and expressed his heartfelt thanks to the distinguished poets from all parts of the world. He added that November 12 was also the birthday of Dr. Sun Yat-sen, founding father of Republic of China, and the Chinese Cultural Renaissance Day.

Dr. Yen-shih Tsiang, Minister of Education of the Republic of China, said in his inspiring speech that poetry is the basis of Chinese education and poetry is vital to the future of mankind. A congratulatory message from President Chiang Kai-shek was read in which he asked the international poets to voice common ideals, to praise the brightness of freedom, and to extol justice and righteousness according to the aims of the Congress, viz., World Brotherhood and Peace Through Poetry. Messages were also received from Madame Imelda Romualdez Marcos, First Lady of the Philippines; Mr. C.K. Yen, Vice President of the Republic of China; Dr. Ernest Kay, Hon. General Editor of IWWP; Mr. Meta Mayne Reid, Ex-President of International P.E.N., Irish Center; Ieronymos Archbishop of Athens and All Greece; Mr. Carol Wilson, President of the Canadian Authors' Association; Mr. Edirge Pesce Gorini of Italy, on behalf of Associazione Internazionale di

Poesia & Il Giornale dei Poeti; Dr. Jose Antonio Nino of Mexico and many others.

Dr. Amado M. Yuzon, President of UPLI and founder of WCP requested a one-minute silence to commemorate Dr. Sun Yat-sen and other deceased poets before his speech which was followed by Dr. Margarita Ausala. Poetess-in-Exile from Latvia and President of the P.E.N. Center of Writers-in-Exile, London.

A preparatory meeting, chaired by Dr. Yuzon, was convened in the afternoon. Dr. Tin-wen Chung was unanimously elected President of the 2nd WCP. Forty-six Chancellors, 41 Floor-Leaders, and 15 Judges were also elected. The Congress met again and was chaired by Dr. Krishna Srinivas of India, President of WPSI, and featured the international reading of poems by delegates from different countries. Poems received from poets who did not attend the Congress were printed and distributed. In the evening, the group went to the College of Chinese Culture to enjoy a show of Chinese folk dance and Chinese costumes of different dynasties.

On the second day, November 13, 1973, the first plenary session was held and chaired by Dr. Lou LuTour of the U.S.A., President of WPRC & ECPSE. Dr. Yuzon presented a trophy as a prize for World Leadership in Poetry to the Chinese Poets' Association on behalf of UPLI. The guest speaker, Prof. Kuang-tsu Hsing, a famous Chinese poet and scholar. lectured on "Poetry and Music". Before the end of the session. a congratulatory telegram was received from Pope Paul VI.

The second plenary session was held in the same afternoon at the National Palace Museum, with Dr. Jeno Platthy, Poet-in-Exile from Hungary and Professor at Harvard University, U.S.A., as chairman. Dr. George K.C. Ych, Minister Without Portfolio, an eminent diplomat. poet. and painter, lectured on "Poetry and Painting". After the speech and discussion, the delegates went to see the Chinese art treasures of the museum which houses a unique collection of nearly 24,000 pieces of Chinese cultural heirlooms.

After dinner the group heard a reading of Chinese poems at the Shih Chien College of Home Economics. The reading was synchronized by enchanting dances with rhythmical beauty.

On the third day, November 14, 1973, the third plenary session of the Congress was chaired by Mrs. Bertha A. Johnstone of Australia. President of International P.E.N., Melbourne Center. The guest speaker on "Poetry and Life" was Prof. Thome Fang, a well-known philosopher. After the lecture. several papers on the same subject were read.

A special session was convened in the afternoon by the President to accept six precious gifts (worth U.S.$35,000) from His Royal Highness Prince Abdullah Al Faisel Al Saud, of Saudi Arabia. The Hon. Sheikh Kannan Al Khatib, delegate of Saudi Arabia, read the message and poems from the Prince and then, as prizes for Leadership in Poetry, he awarded a gold sword to 2nd WCP, a silver sword to the Chinese Poets' Association, a gold dagger to IWWP, a silver dagger to WPSI, and two silver incense burners to UPLI & WPRC on His Royal Highness' behalf. To reciprocate, the Congress presented a plaque from Madame Imelda Romualdez Marcos to the Prince of Saudi Arabia. Meanwhile, Dr. Amado M. Yuzon on behalf of UPLI. crowned the Hon. Sheikh Kannan Al Khativ as a Laureate Poet

International. In the Evening, the party went to Taiwan Television Enterprise to see the Chinese opera.

On the fourth day, November 15, 1973, the fourth general session was chaired by Mme. Youn-Sook Moh of Korea, Vice President of Korea P.E.N. Center. Mrs. Loretta Jean Skibbe, delegate from Baltimore, Maryland, U.S.A., presented to the President a joint Invitation from Governor Marvin Mandel of Maryland; Mayor William Donald Schaefer of Baltimore; Mr. Walter S. Orlinsky, President of Baltimore City Council, and Mr. Thomas J. Foster, Executive Director of Baltimore Convention & Visitors Bureau, requesting the honor of holding the Third WCP in Baltimore in 1976.

A draft charter of WCP was read and discussed. At that juncture, a telegram was received from President Joaquin Balaguer of the Dominican Republic announcing that October 21, the birthday of Mrs. Salome Urena, a great poetess and educator of Dominica, should be set as Poets' Day in his country every year to commemorate the inauguration of WCP.

In the afternoon, two resolutions were passed. One was to accept the invitation from Governor Mandel, Mayor Schaefer, Mr. Orlinsky, and Mr. Foster to hold the 3rd WCP in Baltimore in 1976. The other was to express the Congress' opposition to the use of force anywhere and to the occupation of foreign territories by troops. Also, it was unanimously agreed that the WCP Charter should be revised and adopted by the sponsor & co-sponsors of the 2nd WCP.

An extra session was chaired by Mrs. Maria-Magdalena Durben of West Germany, member of the Central Committee of Literary Union, for the reading of new poems written by participants after their arrival. More than ten poets read their poems to express their impressions about Taiwan.

Mr. Wei-han Chang, Honorary President of the Chinese Poets' Association, chaired the closing ceremony. Dr. Domenico M. Morina of Luxemburg, on behalf of the judges, announced the list of winners of Congress Prizes for distinguished poets as follows:

Miss Maria Elisa-Echenique Posse, Argentina
Mrs. Bertha A. Johnstone, Australia
Dr. Cyril E. Goode, Australia
Dr. Patrick Brian Cox, Britain
Pro. Arved Viirlaid, Canada
Hon. Costas Montis, Cyprus
Mr. Jorgen Sonne, Denmark
Dr. Enriquillo Rojas Abreu, Dominica
Mr. Wolfgang Durben, West Germany
Mrs. Elizabeth H. Perry, Guam
Mr. Taufiq Ismail, Indonesia
Mr. Yutaka Akiya, Japan
Miss Kazue Shinkawa, Japan
Mr. Ok Nall, Khmer
Prof. Byung-Hwa Cho, Korea
Prof. Jaihiun Kim, Korea
Dr. Domenico M. Morina, Italy
Can. Dr. Amante Buontempo, Malta
Mr. Bernard Woon Swee Tin, Malaysia
Mr. Baharuddin Zainal, Malaysia

Mr. Pedro Rafael Gutierrez, Nicaragua
Dr. Arthur Lambert de Fonseca, Portugal
Mr. L. Sami Akalin, Turkey
Hon. Edison Bouchaton, Uruguay
Mrs. Carol Berry Davis, Alaska, U.S.A.
Dr. Mary Lindsley Jaffee, California, U.S.A.
Mme. Mary E. Cox, California, U.S.A.
Mrs. Grace C. Callahan, California, U.S.A.
Mrs. Naomi Young Armstrong, Illinois, U.S.A.
Mrs. Rosemary Clifford Trott, Maine, U.S.A.
Mrs. Loretta Jean Skibbe, Maryland, U.S.A.
Dr. Vivian Trollope-Cagle, Nevada, U.S.A.
Miss Eugenia E. Shelley, New York, U.S.A.
Mrs. Cleoral Lovell, New York, U.S.A.
Mrs. S. Wayne O'Keefe, Texas, U.S.A.
Mme. Marjorie L. Yelton, Texas, U.S.A.
Dr. Jeno Platthy, Washington, D.C., U.S.A.
Mrs. Mong Tuyet That Tieu Muoi, Vietnam

The session was highlighted by awarding plaques, trophies, prizes and laurels to the deserving participants.

The post-Congress tours of Central Taiwan and Kinmen were made on November 16 and 17.

THE KEYNOTE SPEECH DELIVERED AT THE INAUGURAL SESSION BY DR. AMADO M. YUZON

You are most cordially welcome to the Second World Congress of Poets. We have come here to rally in a united front for the cause of humanity, to reiterate as one man and one world our faith and dedication to the objectives of the First World Congress of Poets, held in Manila in 1969, that is "World Brotherhood And Peace Through Poetry."

This cause calls for concerted action, for militant implementation not in the battlefield of an armed conflict but in the lilting parnassus of poets where the pen, the lyre and the silver tongue can be the only consistent weapons in the entire campaign.

We are called upon from the various regions of the universe, to unite, indeed, as one man and one world irrespective of race, creed, or ideology, to help other forces and institutions in the pursuit of a common destiny, a common brotherhood of man and nation for the peace and happiness of all mankind.

Since time immemorial war, destructive war has become a permanent institution as if man is born not only with the right to live but also the duty to commit suicide and to destroy himself. Peace, the ideal obsession of all the prophets from Buddha to Mohammed, has always been a golden but certainly an elusive dream.

Religion in all these thousands of years has provoked religious wars among nations; politics has divided the world into two opposing arm camps, each raring to settle the ideological dispute on the battlefield. Economic imperialism has always proved to be the most irritating factor in the relations of nations; and among men. Science has given the world not only devices to lengthen human life, but also the deadliest and most powerful weapons for human death and disaster.

The Congress of Vienna, the Treaty of Versailles and the League of Nations, all failed miserably to establish a just and lasting peace. The United Nations Organization itself has its hands full with the South East Asia and the Middle East problems.

In the queer face of this persistent armed disturbances of nations, the poets of the world cannot afford to remain indifferent and fence-sitting witnesses to the whole ghastly and sanguinary tragedy, living isolated in their ivory towers, lilting only on beautiful and romantic subjects, and contented only with writing poetry for art's sake.

My friends, I contend that such indifference constitutes criminal omission. Poetry must have a purpose more than "Art for Art's Sake", a purpose that is humane, humanistic and humanitarian, that is, the maximation of perfection of man's love for his fellow men, a nation's love for other nations, a kind of love that can only promote a lasting peace in the world.

Poets can be dramatic poets, epic poets, lyric poets, satirical poets, humorists and sonneteers. Poets can be traditional or modernists, they may write on any subject of human interests, but in general they must contribute militant poetry for the education of mankind towards universal brotherhood and peace.

Pertinent to this suggestion you may ask: how powerful is the poet. Perhaps history can give us the answer.

In language pure and simple, most of the greatest poets of history were miserable dependents of rich men.

But what a paradox! You may not know any Greek name in history but certainly you remember Homer who wrote the immortal Iliad and the Odessey.

With all the glories of the Caesars, the great Roman Empire fell to pieces, but the names of poets such as Virgil, Horace, Dante, Tasso, and Petrarch have remained imperishable.

Kaisers and dictators fluctuated and perished with their imperial ambitions but the names of Schiller and Goethe have remained towering in German history. The British Empire is no more. But the empire of Shakespeare's and Milton's poetry still remains and dominates half of the globe.

Certainly, the names of Lao-tze, Li-Po and Tu-Fu, are common denominators in the hectic history of the Chinese people.

For, as Wadsworth said: "The poet binds together by passion and knowledge the vast empire of human society as it is spread over the whole earth and over all time." And according to William Cullen Bryan, "The poet will always commune with the distant ages." And the philosopher, Spinoza, confirms what Plato said: "The poet speaks the language of God."

Ladies and gentlemen of the Congress, listen to music, whether on the screen, on the platform or over the T.V. and radio, music can have a pleasing sound but hardly a mind and heart without poetry. Hence, such musical lyrics as "Love is a Many Splendored Thing", "Ave Maria", "Old Lang Syne", "Sunshine of your Smile".

Nations, great and small, must have National Anthems, and National Anthems must have their lyrics or poetry, if they are to stir love of country in the hearts of their citizens.

On the basis that the sacred Scriptures are written in verse, God the Almighty can only speak and will always articulate in the language of poetry.

King David of Israel was a poet, Jesus Christ was a poet, George Santayana was a poet. Philosophers and prophets moved the world and made history by their inspirations as poets *per se*.

The late John F. Kennedy summarized the overwhelming and far-reaching and consequential power of poetry in this wise: "When power leads man to arrogance, poetry reminds him of his limitations: when power narrows the areas of man's concern, poetry reminds him of the diversity and richness of his existence; when power corrupts, poetry cleanses, for art establishes the basic truths which must serve as the touchstones of human judgements."

Ladies and gentlemen of the Congress, such is the tremendous power of poetry. Such is the power in your hands, the power of the poets of the world. For, as Shelley said: "The poets are the unacknowledged legislators of the world." Was it not Aristotle who said that "The orator speaks like a learned man but the poet speaks like God"?

In seeking the solution to the problem of world peace today, this is the primordial reason why we have convened for the second time this World Congress of Poets.

The Sovereigns and Governors of mankind, individually and collectively, will try to vindicate their frustrations in all these thousands of years; ideologies, imperialism and the United Nations will, like the Knights of the Round Table, go on in seeking the Holy Grail of World Peace and we, too, the poets of the world, cannot remain silent and be blind to these problems of world insecurity without being guilty in our utter and cold indifference to the cause of humanity.

Hence, these World Congresses of Poets.

It was Galileo who said: "Give me a place where to stand and I will move the world."

Ladies and gentlemen, for us, the poets, this World Congress of Poets is the place where to stand to move heaven and earth for world brotherhood and peace through poetry.

In congratulating the Chinese Poets' Association for the booming success of this Congress may I, in the name of my country, the United Poets Laureate International and the other co-sponsoring organizations, present to the Chinese Poets' Association this loving trophy the UPLI prize for world leadership?

CHARTER OF THE WORLD CONGRESS OF POETS

PREAMBLE

WE, the poets of the various nations of the world have decided to mobilize and organize our kind into a World Congress of Poets to substitute peace for war in the minds of men, by educating mankind with love of peace and of fellowmen, that is, the promotion of world brotherhood and peace through poetry.

ARTICLE I.
The World Congress of Poets

Section 1. There shall be convened a World Congress of Poets at least once every three years, or more often when necessary and expedient, which may be prepared and called by a literary organization or organizations of good reputation, after an effective consultation with the Presidents of previous World Congresses of Poets.

Section 2. A World Congress of Poets shall be composed of Poets of good reputation, patrons of poetry, poetry magazine editors, professors of poetry and the like, irrespective of race-origin. Membership in the Congress shall be by invitation of the sponsoring organizations.

Section 3. A regional Congress of Poets may be called by a reputable literary organization after consultation with a World Congress President in the area.

ARTICLE II.
Officers

Section 1. The Congress shall elect by viva-voce a President, 8 Chancellors and 10 Floorleaders.

Section 2. The President shall preside over all sessions, guide the Congress in all deliberations and debates and create necessary committees and boards, unless he delegates some of these powers to any or a number of Chancellors. He shall also sign any and all documents and papers pertaining to the affairs of the Congress.

Section 3. The Chancellors will act as the Vice-Presidents of the Congress.

Section 4. The Floorleaders shall act as coordinators between the floor and the chair.

Section 5. A Secretary-General, Treasurer, Auditor and all other officers and employees of the Congress shall be appointed by the President.

Section 6. The President shall come from the host country or host organization.

Section 7. Presidents of previous congresses shall be Presidents Emeritus of succeeding Congresses.

ARTICLE III.
Rules of Procedures

Section 1. The Congress shall adopt the standard rules of parliamentary procedure in democratic countries. Debates and deliberations shall be done with the utmost freedom, honour and dignity.

ARTICLE IV.
An Academy of Arts and Culture

Section 1. An Academy of Arts and Culture of the World Congress of Poets may be established with a board of Trustees not more than 8 in number, including the Presidents of past Congresses and six other Congress delegates whom the past Presidents may appoint. The Academy may award to deserving poets and men of letters literary distinctions, honours and citations, including laureateships and cultural degrees.

ARTICLE V.
Amendments

Section 1. This Charter may be amended by an absolute majority vote of the delegates of future Congresses.

APPROVAL

By virtue of the power vested in us by the Second World Congress of Poets (Res. No. 2, Nov. 16, 1973), we have approved, as we hereby approve the foregoing Charter of the World Congress of Poets.

SIGNED at Taipei, Taiwan, Republic of China, this 17th day of November 1973.

DR. CHUNG TIN-WEN
President – Sec. World Congress of Poets & Chairman, WCP Arrangement Committee

DR. KRISHNA SRINIVAS
President, World Poetry Society Intercontinental

DR. AMADO M. YUZON
Founder-President, First World Congress of Poets and United Poets Laureate Intl.

DR. LOU LUTOUR
President, World Poets Resource Center and its affiliate The Eastern Centre of the Poetry Society of England

PSEUDONYMS AND PEN NAMES
OF INCLUDED POETS

Abbott, Anne – Bratt, Nina Elois
Abelardo – Delgado, Abelardo
Ace Space Co – Atchley, Dana Winslow
Adair, V.H. – Hamilton, M. Virginia
Adam, Cornel – Lengyel, Cornel Adam
Adams, Anna – Adams, Anna T.
Adams, B.B. – Adams, Barbara
Adams, Barbara Block – Adams, Barbara
Adams, Carmen Boitel – Boitel Adams, Carmen
Adams, Perseus – Adams, Peter Robert Charles
Adler, Marnie – Adler (Kinbor), Marnie Faustine
Aeon – Theis, Ed Edmund G.
Aesonius – Theis, Ed Edmund G.
Agape, Fedelis – Barranda, Natividad 'Natty' Gatbonton
Ahmad Nadeem Qasimi – Ahmed Shah, Nadeem
Ailor, Hazel Norwell – Ailor, Hazel Lea Nowell
Alanah, Patricia – Rosenfeld, Patricia Alanah
Albertina, M. – Mason, (Sister) M. Albertina
Albertina, Sister M. – Mason, (Sister) M. Albertina
Alder, B. – Fischer, Barbara
Alexander, A.J. – Ostroff, Anthony J.
Alice, G.A. – Dilke, Linda Helen
Allan, Jonathan – Rice, John
Allen, Billie – Allen, Alma
Allen, Mary – Stroh, Ruth Kathryn
Allison, Kathleen – Allison, Winifred Kathleen
Alomin – Tanny, Shlomo
Alurista – Urista Heredia, Alberto Baltazar
Ambi – Srinivasarajagopalan, Thirunarayanan
Amoako, Kwabena – Amoako, Alex Agyarko
Amor, Amos – Harrell, Irene Buck
Ample, Fanny – Lee, Betty Merritt
A.M.V. – Cruickshank, Helen Burness
A.N.A. – Cruickshank, Helen Burness
Anderson, Marlene – Spracklin, Myrtle Lilly
Anderson, Violet – Anderson, Violet Louise
Andrew, James – Kirkup, James
Andrzej, E – Falkowski, Edwin Andrzej
Anika – Irelan, Annislea
Ann, Avocado – Coffin, Ellen
Annand, Peter – Annand, Peter Geoffrey Grant
Anona – Egan, Alvie Mary
Anthony, P.F. – Fericano, Paul Francis
Apipo – Natachee, Allan
Appleton, Sarah – Weber, Sarah Appleton
April, Ruth – Stroh, Ruth Kathryn
Aquarius – Oppenheimer, Joel L(ester)
Araya – Tarlow, Idell Rose
Archer, Myrtle – Spacklen, Myrtle Lilly
Armstrong, Phil – Armstrong, Phyllis Eleanor
Arun – Nagarajan, R.

Ashford, Shirley Agin – Ashford, Shirley Ann
Ashour, Brierly – Ashour, Gladys Brierly
Askia Akhnaton – Eckels, Jon
Aspira – Petry, C(linton) B(rowning)
Asya – Abramoff, Asya
Atchison, Amy – Ward, Mary B.
Augustine, Luther – Coutermash, John H.
Austen, Vera – Scott, Vera Evelyn
Austin, A. Nash – Clendenning, Anna Martha Utterback
Avalon – Blasen, Robin
Avnira – Chamiel, Haim Itzchak
Aya – Tarlow, Idell Rose
Azcona-Cranwell, Elizabeth – Azcona-Cranwell, Elena-Ines Gurpegui
B2 – Havenne, Edgard Emile Laurent
Baldwin, Marjorie – Baldwin, Bertha Marjorie
Balkenbush, Michael – Balkenbush, Michael Lee
Bamdad – Shamlu, Ahmad
Ban, Eva – Ban, Eva Maria
Barfield, Steve – Barfield, Stephen Leonard
Barnhill, Myrtle Fait – Barnhill, Myrtle Annie
Barrett, Lucian – Coutermash, John H.
Barry, Noeline – Buttress, Noeline E. Barry
Bart, Gunther – Brattman, Steven Ronald
Barton, Geri – Barton, Geraldine Dolores
Batang Elias – Tolentino, Guillermo E.
Bat-Hedva – Amir-Pinkerfeld, Anda
Battaglia, Bette – Battaglia, Elizabeth Louise
Baucom, Margaret – Baucom, Margaret Dean
Bayliss, Timothy – Baybars, Taner
Beard, Amy Carol – Beard, Amy Carolina
Beech, Norah – Fisher, Gillian Christine
Belan – Batusic, Slavko
Bell, Viviane – Galloy, Alice
Belsen, Patricia – Thvoz, Jacqueline
Ben Ephraim – Chamiel, Haim Itzchak
Ben-Hanagar, Sidrophel – Regelson, Abraham
Bennett, Louise – Bennett-Coverley, Simone Louise
Bennett, Stefanie – Bennett, Sandra
Bennett, Valerie – Stout, Dorothy L.
Bereg, Eli – Bartura, Avraham Elieser
Beresford, Anne – Hamburger, Anne Ellen
Berg, Nina Stevenson – Berg, Helen Christina
Bergmann, A. – Bartura, Avraham Elieser
Berimont, Luc – Leclercq, Andre
Berkelaar, Willy – Rutten, Mathieu Jacques Henri
Berl-Lee, Maria – Lee, Maria Berl
Berlyn, Phillippa – Christie, Phillippa Mary
Berrigan, Ted – Berrigan, Edmund J., Jr.
Berrington, John – Brownjohn, Alan Charles
Bertini, K.A. – Bertini, Aharon

Beulah – Kershaw, Beulah Frances

Bill – Wertheim, William Jay

Bill O' Bows – Heyworth, Clifford

Bimgo – Margolis, William J.

Bishop, Mary – Bishop, Mary Cameron

Bissell, O. (Ole) – Bissell, Olin Cecil

Black, Wilma Fritz – Black, Wilma Elizabeth Fritz

Blank, Margaret – Barze, Marguerite Enlow

Blankenship, Frank – Blankenship, F. Anthony

Bligh, Aurora – Fabilli, Mary

Blight, John – Blight, Frederick John

Blumenkron, Carmen – Blumenkron, Carmen Virginia

Blumenthal-Weiss – Blumenthal, Ilse Rosa

Blunden, David – Stringer, David Allan

Boanerges – Egea, Norma Edith

Boet, Bugs – Sladek, John

Boisseau, Albertine – Boisseau, Marie-Antoinette-Albertine

Bokhari, Ustad – Sayed, Ahmed Shah Bokhari

Bolen, J. Carpenter – Lynes, Ruth C.

Bollard – Carter, Graeme

Bolton, Deric – Bolton, Frederic James

Bomkauf – Kaufman, Bob Garnell

Bonine, Vivian Small – Bonine, Vivian

Bonine, Vivian Way – Bonine, Vivian

Book, M.K. – Malone, Marvin H(erbert)

Borja, N.A. – Viray, Manuel

Boru – Joyce, Brian Charles

Bothwell, Shirley Oakes – Bothwell, Shirley Marie

Boyce, McKinley – Beaudoin, Kenneth Lawrence

Boyd, Melba J. – Boyd, Melba Joyce

Boyer, Gwen Roberts – Boyer, Gwen

Bradford, Jan – Badtke, Frances

Bradomin – O'Neill, Lisa

Bradshaw, Irene A. – Bradshaw, Irene Amelia

Brady, D. Kingsley – Brady, Derek Kingsley

Brahan, Leigh – Eitzen, Margaret-Mary

Bratt, Ronald – Brattman, Steven Ronald

Bredon, John – Eng, Stephen Richard

Breen, B.A. – Breen, Barry Andrew

Breighner, H. Daniel – Breighner, Harry Daniel, Sr.

Brel, Jennifer – Pearce, Carol Ann

Brewer, Jane – Heselton, Lette

Brian – Gabriel, Marie-Cruz

Bridge, John – Peters, Robert

Brobst, Sarah H. – Brobst, Sarah Elizabeth Heiney

Brock, Gavin – Lindsay, John Morris

Brooks, Sue Settie – Jackson, Sue Settie

Broome, Joanna – Doyle, Winefride

Broome, Winefride – Doyle, Winefride

Brophy, Jim – Brophy, James Joseph

Brother Antoninus – Everson, William Oliver

Brother Dimitrios – Wade, David Lawson

Brown, Gladys Lef erts – Brown, Gladys Mungen

Brown, Laurel (Mrs.) – Tuson, Sheila Irene Mary

Brown, Marel – Brown, Margaret Elizabeth Snow

Browning, Peter – Petry, C(linton) B(rowning)

Brownlow, Timothy – Brownlow, David Timothy

Budgie – Garden, David Kenday

Bulbul – Singh, Gurvir Inder

Bunin, Patricia Ann – Fletcher, Patricia Ann

Burns, Bobby – Burns, Vincent Godfrey

Burns, Picasso – Garden, David Kenday

Burton, Cleo M. – Burton, Cleo May

Burton, Wilma Wicklund – Burton, Wilma

Busching, Mary Wood – Busching, Mary Louise

Byrd, Lloyd – Lloyd, Cecil Robert

Byron, Christopher – Coutermash, John H.

Cagle, Billie Trollope – Trollope-Cagle, Vivian Jewel

Calbre, Zo – Shaw, Izola E.

Camp, James – Wolgamot, John Barton

Candido – Guerrero, Luis Beltran

Candidus – Harrison, Joseph

Cannady, Criss E. – Cannady, Criss Ellen

Canusi, Jose – Barker, Squire Omar

Cape, Judith – Irwin, Patricia Kathleen

Carm Mac & Keith X – Armstrong, Keith Francis Whitfield

Carpenter, Miles – Carpenter, Maurice

Carroll, Nina – Steane, Nina

Carter, Marjori S. – Sharp-Carter, Marjorie Elizabeth

Cassegrain, William – Briggs, John

Cassidy, Vin – Cassidy, Vincent Harold

Cathbad, Sean – McMahon, Bryan T(homas)

Cavalcante, Salome Diehl – Cavalcante, E. Salome

Cayer, Patrick – Duffy, Maureen Patricia

Ceso – Sebastian, Processo

Chaffee, Eleanor Alletta – Wood, Eleanor Chaffee

Chaffin, Randall – Chaffin, Lillie D.

Chaillie, Jean Humphrey – Chaillie, M. Jean Humphrey

Champa, Suhrid – Rege, Purushottama Shivarama

Chand – Rajani, Mom Chao (Prince) Chand

Chang Mo – Chang Teh-Chung

Chappell, Jeanette – Kalt, Jeanette

Charles, Timothy – Stanford, Derek

Chattelerault, Victor de – Beaudoin, Kenneth Lawrence

Chennai Sa Maniyarasan – Manickam, T. Sambasiva

Cherno, Julie – Hutner, Julie Sarah

Chiaro, Lee Bain – Chiaro, Lee

Chi Hsien – Lu Yu

Childs, C. Sand – Childs, (Sister) Maryanna

Chilton, Tracey – Chilton, Teresa Ann

Chizu Suzuki – Shindo Suzuki, Chizu

Cho-El – Kim Yang-Shik

Chung-Lei – Chai, Chun-Shih

Cifuentes, Jaime – Fontain, (Rt. Rev. Archimandrite) Gregory

Civasaqui, Jose – Shibasaki, Sosuke

Clandenning, Anne – Clendenning, Anna Martha Utterback

Clark, Frances Jamia – Handler, Frances Clark

Clark, Robert – Clark, Robert John

Clifford, John – Bayliss, John Clifford

Cloaca – Carter, Graeme

Clouser, Carolyn E. – Clouser, Carolyn Ruth

Cochrane, Micky – Morris, Linda Marlene (Cochrane)

Cogswell, Fred – Cogswell, Frederick William

Coker, Bette – Warden, Bette Ruth Coker

Cole, Cannon – Cook, Arlene E.

Cole, Casey – Cole, Katherine Cecelia Keller

Cole, Florence – Sitwell, Phronsie Irene

Coleman, Mary Ann Braunlin – Coleman, Mary Ann

Colette – Turmeau, Constance Evelyn

Colledge, Margaret – Crooke, Joan Theresa

College-Boy – Bhattacharya, Jagadish

Collins, Ellen E.H. – Redknap, Ellen Edith Hannah

Colvin Norma Thomas – Colvin, Norma Lucille Thomas

Combs, Tram – Combs, Elisha Trammell, Jr.

Constable, Patricia Anna – Constable, Patricia Ann

Connors, Bruton – Rohen, Edward

Constant De Horion – Constant, (Baron) Jean Theophile Joseph

Cook, G.L. – Cook, Gerald Lawrence

Cook, Gladys Moon – Cook, Gladys May

Cook, R. Graham – Cook, Ramona Graham

Corley, Vi. – Corley, Viola C.

Cornett, Fran – Cornett, Frances Boggs

Corti, Doris – Stump, Doris Joyce

Cortney, Michelle – Buonocore, Michaelina

Cramer, Hallie – Cramer, Hallie Agnes

Cranwell, Andi – Cranwell, Andrew, Jr.

Croat, Aurel – Tomicic, Zlatko

Crobaugh, Emma – Crobaugh, Emma Adelia

Crowbate, Ophelia Mae – Smith, C.U.

Crue, Norma Jones – Stremich, Norma Florence

Csepeli Szabo Bela – Szabo, Bela

Cunning, Alfred – Holliday, David

Currey, R.N. – Currey, Ralph Nixon

Cuwart, Flore – Vonck, Theo

Cynfyn – Walters, Bryan

Dahlhouse, The. – Gilbert, Robert L.

Danger, A. – McMahon, Bryan T(homas)

Dangerfield, Harlan – Gallup, Richard John

Dangerfield, Harlan – Padgett, Ron

Darlon, Christopher – Staley, Ronald Christopher

Das, S.N. – Das, Salilendra Nath

d'Auria, Gemma – d'Auria, Gemma Abkazoff

Davis, Georgianna – Drake, Marjorie Davis Look

Davis, Maralee – Gibson, Mary Elizabeth G.

Day, Donald – Harding, Donald E.

D'Cruz, Alvin Ajatashatru – Mukhopadhyay, Durgadas

Deane, Mark Anderson – McCall, Margaret Dole

Decaunes, Luc – Decaunes, Lucien Daniel

De Fonseca, Arthur Lambert – De Barboza Carneyro E Fonseca, Arthur Lambert

Degani, Assi – Degani, Asarel

Dell, Nevada – Lawrin, Lura Dell

de Radzitzky, Carlos – de Radzitzky d'Ostrowick, (Baron) Carlos

Deugd Verheut – Rutten, Mathieu Jacques Henri

De Vreede, Mischa – De Vreede, Henny

De Vreese, Dani – Denissen, Frans

De Wilde, Frans – Gilliams, Eugene

Dheorsa, Maclain – Hay, George Campbell

Diablo, Martian – Nolan, Pat 'Rocky'

Diana, O.G. – Nagarajan, R.

Dickey, R.P. – Dickey, R(obert) Preston

Dickie, M.M. – Eitzen, Margaret-Mary

Dickinson, Emily – Musgrave, Susan

Disch, Tom – Disch, Thomas Michael

Diwalaan – Mercado, Simon A(lvarez)

Dockeray, Malcolm – Dockeray, John Malcolm

Dofton – Jonsmoen, Ola

Dole, Margaret Aliona – McCall, Margaret Dole

Domini, Rey – Lorde, Audre Geraldin

Donovan, Maira – Kinsella, Mary D.

Dorbin, Sandy – Dorbin, Sanford

Douglas, John Cameron – Malek, John Francis, II

Doyle, Charles – Doyle, Charles Desmond

Doyle, Mike – Doyle, Charles Desmond

Dresse, Paul – Dresse De Lebioles, Paul Charles Marie

Drinan, Adam – MacLeod, Joseph Todd Gordon

Driver, C.J. – Driver, Charles Jonathan

Dromi, M. – Dor, Moshe

dsh – Houedard, Pierre Thomas Paul (dom Sylvester)

Duberstein, Helen – Lipton, Helen Laura Duberstein

Dubrau, Louis – Scheidt, Louise

Duce, Sacro – Dino, (Rev. Fr.) Isidoro D.

Du Givna, Henry – Henry, Fernand D.G.G.

Dunbar, Helen – Pelosi, Helen Priscilla

Dutz – Davis, Mary Octavia Roberta

Dycus, Webb – Dycus, Frances W

Eastlund, Madelyn – Hickey, Madelyn Eastlund

Echenique Posse, Mareli – Echenique Posse, Maria Elisa del Rosario

Eckhart, Katherine Nielsen – Eckhart, Katherine Lawrence

Eddy, Roberta – Roberts, Edna

Edgar, Judy – Edgar, June Elizabeth

Edwards, Dan – Harding, Donald E.

Edwards, Donald Earl – Harding, Donald E.

Eglite, Karina – Eglite-Berzins, Karina

Eigner, Larry – Eigner, Laurence Joel

Eitzen, Maggie – Eitzen, Margaret-Mary

Elaine, Marsha – Kash, Marsha Elaine (Katzman)

Elcy, Mabel – Stafford, Mabel E.

El Gilbert – Gilbert, Elizabeth

Elias – Mercado, Simon A(lvarez)

Elliot, Jean – Elliott, Jean Pirnie Robertson

Ellis, Carolyn – Ellis, Carolyn Hargus

Ellis, Lorraine – Harr, Lorrain Ellis

El Troubadour – Bradley, Maurice

Elvesmere Rose – Penn, Emily Josephine

Emars – Mazani, Eric Charles Fambai

Emerson, Ethelyn – Righton, Marian Castle

Emil Rostov – Wade, David Lawson

Emily, G.H. – Emily, Geneva Hargis

Empire-Statement – Booker, Clifford Harvey

Erne, Nino – Erne, Giovanni Bruno (Nino)

Erskine, Edith Deaderick – Erskine, Edith Lanier

Eskridge, Audeen Bunyard – Eskridge, Audeen

Esohg, Lama – Ghose, Amal

Esox – Klinkenberg, Jean-Marie

Espinosa, Rudy – Espinoza, Rudolph L.

Espy Bee – Sreenivos, Prathivadi Bhayankaram

Etain Whitethought – Brennan, Henry

Etter, Dave – Etter, David Pearson

EWn. E. Wn. – Wichman, Eva Aline

Faiz – Faiz, Ahmed Faiz

Fan-Ts'Ao – Chung, Tin-wen

Fareystone, Elizabeth – Lyman, Irene Vera Ponting

Farfalla, Angelica – Malanga, Gerard

Faulkner, Pete – Faulkner, Peter William

Fehr, Martha Morgan – Dawson, Martha Morgan

Femora – Brodey, James Miles

Ferry, David – Ferry, David Russell

Field, Delia – Howe, Fanny

Figar, Dilawar – Dilawar, Husain

Finlay, Michael – Roberts, Edna

Finley, Laura Dewey – Finley, Dewey Gibson

Finn, D.E. – Borrell, Dorothy Elizabeth

Fisher, Allen – Fisher, Thomas Allen

Fletcher, Marilyn Lowen – Lowen, Marilyn

Floro, Ruben – Sibug, Brigido B.

Forward, Luke – Patrick, J(ohnstone) G(illespie)

Frankhouser, Floyd R. – Frankhouser, Floyd Richard

Fraser, Margaret Kimball – Lampson, Margaret Fraser

Frazier, April – Cook, Audrey

Freeman, J. – Freeman, John

Friedman, Elias – Friedman, John

Friedman, Ken – Friedman, Kenneth Scott

Fries, Mardi – Fries, Marjorie Fifield

Frisby, Katie – Oughton, Edith

Frobisher, Mark – Bashford, Rosemary

Frost, Diana – Rudberg, Gertrude Jones

Gage, Paul – Anderson, Lila Pauline Gage

Garioch, Robert – Sutherland, Robert Garioch

Garland, Margaret Wolff – Garland, Margaret J.C. Wolff

Garrison, Peggy – Garrison, Margaret Ellen (Peggy)

Gause, Lynne – Gause, Emilyn

Gay, Ellen – Tracy, Pauline Aloise

Gaye, Jay – Thompson, Jessie Grace Cowan

Gee, Dee Jay – Grace, Dorman John

Gelder, Jack – Gelder, John Thomas

Geneva-Of-The-Hills – Young, Charlotte

Geneva – Young, Charlotte

George, Margaret – George, Peggy

George, Phil – George, Phillip William

Gerber, Dan – Gerber, Daniel Frank, Jr.

Gervais, C.H. – Gervais, Charles Henry Marty

Ghani – Khan, Ghani

Gibson, M. Munro – Hoole, Margaret Mary

Gilbert, Ruth – Mackay, Florence Ruth

Gilbert, Sister Mary – De Frees, Mary Madeline

Ginger, – Sargent, Genevieve

Ginger Verkennes – Verkennes, Geneva Alice

Gino – Warren, Francis Eugene

Gioseffi, Daniela – Gioseffi, Dorothy Daniela

Givens, V. – Givens, Violet (Banks-Robinson)

Glass, Helen B. – Glass, Helen Bernice (Lemansky)

Glem – Brooker, Irene

Glen, Emilie – Glen, Emilie Carolyn

Glenn, Rose – Holloway, Glenna

Glinka, Konstanty – Jastrzebski-Glinka, Kristof Konstanty

Goddard, Hazel Firth – Goddard, Hazel Idella

Golden, Anthony – Goulet, Antoine

Golden, Rima – Calkins, A. Jean

Goldthorpe, Judy – Goldthorpe, Judith Mary

Goltra, L. – Moore, Lucia

Goodwyn, Margaret – Goodwyn, Margaret Sturgis

Gordon, Guinevere – Koppler, Guinevere

Gosnell, Betty – Gosnell, Elizabeth Duke Tucker

Goswin, Rob – Goossens, Robert

Gourriet, Mel – Hudson, Sylvia Constance

Gracefield, Robert H. – Mohammed, Faqir

Graft, Guillaume Van Der – Barnard, Wilhelmus

Graham, Lola Beall – Graham, Lola Amanda

Graham, Ramona – Cook, Ramona Graham

Grant, Mary – Tilden, Lorraine Henrietta Frederick

Graves, R. Steven – Graves, Robert Steven

Gray, Carla – Winch, Harriet Gragg

Gray, Douglas – Barrows, Margaret Hamilton

Gray Green – Green, Graham Martin

Gray, Penelope – Hudson, Sylvia Constance

Gray, Rosemary – Badtke, Frances

Greeff, Adele – Greeff, Adele Montgomery Burcher

Green, J.C.R. – Green, James

Green, Thomas – Brattman, Steven Ronald

Greenfield, Bernadotte – Darby, Edith M.

Greenwood, Rosamund – Von Pokorny, Rosamund Mary

Greneforst, Leif – Olson, Robert Glen Kennith Leif

Grenelle, Lisa – Munroe, Elizabeth Grenelle

Griffiths, Bryn – Griffiths, Brywllyn David

Groupe, Darryl R. – Bunch, David Roosevelt

Groves, Dale – Groves, Dale Young

Guillevic – Guillevic, Eugene

Guinness, Bryan – Guinness, Bryan Walter (Lord Moyne)

Gunn, Thom – Gunn, Thomson William

Gyinaye, Kojo – Kyei, Kojo Gyinaye

Haddo, Oliver – Puechner, Ray

Hafeez (Jallandhari) – Hafeez, Abulasar Jallandhari Hilaale

Hagstrom, Joy Gresham – Hagstrom, Mary Joy

Hahn, Lola E. – Hahn, Lola Elizabeth Fessenden

Haines, John – Haines, John Meade, Jr.

Haines, Stacy Shannon – Canfield, Joan Giltner

Halin, Maciej – Jozef Maciej

Hall, Alice Clay – Hall, Alice Elizabeth

Hall, Hadessa – Shafer, Mabel Hadessa Hall

Hall, Ibby – Bellamy, Virginia

Halladay, Geneva – Halliday, Geneva Rose

Ham, Barbra A. – Ham, Barbra Allen

Hamlet – Zaragoza, Francisco

Hammell, Andre – Hudspeth, Betty Sue

Hanley, Elizabeth – Picker, Elizabeth E.

Hanley, Evelyn A. – Hanley, Evelyn Alice

Hannibal Ra – Brown, Clemson

Hansen, Norma Jones – Stremich, Norma Florence

Hanson, Elayne Clipper – Hanson, Elayne June

Hanson, Freddie Phelps – Peteron, Freddie Phelps

Hanson, H. – Guardino, Leonard J.

Harrington, Ann – Lyman, Irene Vera Ponting

Harris, Dorothy D. – Harris, Dorothy Dix

Harrison, Jim – Harrison, James Thomas

Hart, Paul – Hart, Paul Joseph

Harvey, Pippa – Harvey, Celia

Harvey-Booker, C. – Booker, Clifford Harvey

Haupt, Quita Ruth M. – Haupt, Quita Ruth Moore

Hawtre, Sharon Howard – Canfield, Joan Giltner

Hayden, Mrs. Charles L. – McGinley, Phyllis

Hayes, Thornton – Littlewood, Francis Desmond

Hemschemeyer, Judith – Rosenfeld, Judith

Henderson, Mildred Rowan – Henderson, Mildred Inez (Rowan)

Henrietta – Tilden, Lorraine Henrietta Frederick

Hereford, Eula Shaw – Hereford, Eula Frances

Herman, Betty – Herman, Anne Elizabeth

Herndon, Brodie – Herndon, Brodie Strachan, Jr.

Hertel, Francois – Dube, Rodolphe

Hess, Alice Shoup – Hess, Alice Leona

Hess, J.M., Mrs. – Hess, Alice Leona

Heywood, Pip – Heywood, James Philip

Hicks, Betty Brown – Hicks, Alice

Higgins, Dick – Higgins, Richard Carter

Hill, Hyacinthe (Dame) – Anderson, Virginia Rose (Cronin)

Hilton, Josephine – Roberts, Edna

Hitchings,Mary T. – Meehan, Mary Taft Hitchings

Ho Chu Tai – Wade, David Lawson

Holender, Mrs. H. William – Holender, Barbara D.

Holland, B. Adams – Holland, Barbara A.

Holmes, Charlotte – Dallas, Charlotte Holmes

Holmes, John – Souster, Raymond Holmes

Holmes, Liz – Holmes, Elizabeth Anne

Holmes, Raymond – Souster, Raymond Holmes

Holzappel, Rudolf Patrick – Holzappel, Rudi

Hompson, Davi Det. – Thompson, David E.

Hooper, Peter – Hooper, Hedley Colwill

Hoosier Hannah – Miner, Virginia Scott

Hope, Evelyn – Wofford, Grace Kirk

Horsley, E. Laurie – Bavin, Frances

Hoskins, Katherine – Hoskins, Katherine de Montalant Lackey

Hossier Hank – Miner, Virginia Scott

Houstan, Logan – Keller, Edith Light

Houston, Erin – Miller, Roger Dale

Hruska-Cortes, Elias – Hruska, Elias Nicolas

Hubbell, Patricia – Hornstein, Patricia

Hubert, Ann – Jonas, Ann

Hughes, Cyril – Hodges, Cyril

Hughes, Margery Edwards – Hughes, Marjorie Ethel

Hull, Edna – McCleery, Edna

Hunt, Inez Whitaker – Hunt, Sylvia Inez

Hunter, Lorraine – Hunter, Elsie Theresa

Hurkey, Rooan Hurkey – Holzappel, Rudi

Husain, Syed Akbar – Husain, Adrian

Hutner, Julie – Hutner, Julie Sarah

I.B.L. – Leath, Ida Belle

Idell – Tarlow, Idell Rose

Idell Tarlow – Tarlow, Idell Rose

Ijimere, Obotunde – Beier, Ulli

Ingram, Gloria – Roberts, Fay Ingram

Iny, Yvonne – Bachrach, Yvonne Iny

Irving, Henry – Upton, Lawrence John

Irving, Joan – Fischer, Barbara

Isapu – Natachee, Allan

Issac Awd – Grampound, Martin (Josiah Hepplethwaite)

Ivimy, May – Badman, May

Iyo, Dahil Sa – Mercado, Simon A(lvarez)

Jackie – Earley, Jacqueline

Jack-O-Lantern – Ward, Gabrielle Stephanie

Jackson, Wm. Dean – Jackson, William Hargadine

Jacob – Devanayagom, D. Jacob

Jacobsen, Ethel Walker – Jacobsen, Ethel Dorothy

Jacquemin, Jean – Sor, Daniel

Jaffe, Dan – Jaffe, Daniel Freeman

Jah – Hirschman, Jack Aaron

James, Cliff – James, Clifford Thomas

James, Dwin – Weaver, James Edwin

James, Susan – Lloyd, Susan Jacqueline

Jamil Malik – Malik, Abdul Jamil

Jamila Yaminah – Neal, Arnethia Murdock

Janet, Sister, CC. – Benish, (Sister) Janet Claughton

Jan Wos – Ozog, Jan Bolestaw

Jan Zdeb – Ozog, Jan Bolestaw

Jane – Knight, Helen Jane Craigen

Jasper, Bright – McWhorter, Bright Jasper

Javor, Pavel – Skvor, Jiri Jan

Jawa – Apronti, Eric Ofoe

Jay, Neva – Pappas, Neva J. (Flansburg)

Jayadeva – Pranchu, Joseph Kalarickal

Je-Chee – Chakravorty, Jagannath

Jeffries, Christie – Jeffries, Christie Frances

Jemmett, Doralee – Bean, Doralee Jemmett

Jenkins, Philip – Jenkins, Nigel Philip

Jespersen, Mary S. – Jespersen, Mary Sperry

Jodorowsky, Raquel – Prullansky, Raquel Jodorowsky

Johnson, Jenny – Johnson, Jennifer Hilary

Johnson, Robin – Johnson, Roberta Orban Lamon

Jones, H. Wendy – Jones, Helen Symons

Jonson, Hal – Johnson, Harold Leland

Jordan, Albert – Ivanisevic, Drago

Jordan, Barbara Leslie – Yellott, Barbara Leslie

Jordan, Khalid Walid Muhammad ibn – Jordan, Thornton Waddell

Jordan, Maude – Jordan, Anna Maude

Jordan, Troy – Jordan, Thornton Waddell

Joseph – Pigg, Arthur Carnes

Joyner, Anne – Saunders, Patricia Anne

Jubilate – Coppedge, George Herman, Jr.

Julie of Colorado Springs – Robbins, Julie

Justa Nabor – Brobst, Sarah Elizabeth Heiney

Jwala – Jwala, Ravi Verma

Kamalakanto – Kamalakanto, Mukherjee

Kane, Teddy – Eldridge, Jessie Cannon

Kastan, A – Falkowski, Edwin Andrzej

Kastel, Dee – Kastel, Daisylea Carl

Katthak, Roop – Rege, Purushottama Shivarama
Katz, Hilda – Weber, Hulda
Kaufman, Bob – Kaufman, Bob Garnell
Kay, Sarah – Wilford, Sarah Kathleen
Keane, Shake – Keane, Ellsworth McGranahan
Keating, Norma – Mattlin, Norma R.
Keeran, Laurence – Macentee, Sean
Keesing, Nancy – Keesing, Nancy Florence
Keighley, Gladys – Bradley, Gladys
Kelley, H.M. – Kelley, Helen Joyce
Kelly, Hannah – Hobsbaum, Hannah
Kelly, Maureen – Fischer, Barbara
Kendall, Lace – Stoutenburg, Adrien Pearl
Kennedy, X.J. – Kennedy, Joseph
Kent, Allison – Cobb, Winifred Mary Bradley
Kent, Julia Ann – Miller, Jessie Ruhl
Kenward, Jean – Chesterman, Jean
Kern, Canyon – Raborg, Frederick Ashton, Jr.
Kern, W. Bliem – Kern, William Bliem, Jr.
Kerry, Frances – Kerigan, Florence
Kesheth, Yeshurun – Kesheth, Jacob Joshua
Kesri – Srinivas, Krishna
Kesteman – Kesteman, Emile
K.G. – Jastrzebski-Glinka, Kristof Konstanty
K.G. – Menon, Kavungai Gangadhara
Kilbourne, Irene – Gaertner, Irene Kilbourne
Kim – Clancy, Barbara Anne
Kimrey, Grace Saunders – Kimrey, Grace Evelyn Saunders
King, R.T. – King, Ruby Thompson
Kiplinger, David – Miner, Virginia Scott
Kirill – Simonov, Konstantin Mikhailovich
Kisner, Jack – Kisner, Jacob
Kistner, Art – Kistner, Arthur Leroy
Kleiner, Pesca – Fischl, Ruth
Knight, Katherine – Knight, Anne Katherine
Knot, Bill – Knott, William Kilborn
Knye, Cassandra – Sladek, John
Kolker, Eleanor – Kolker, (Sister) Delphine
Kopland, Rutger – Hoofdakker, Rudi Rutger Hendrik van den
Koppler, Vera – Koppler, Guinevere
Kornedeplov, Mitya – Herman, Ira H.
Koz – Lyttle, Cosima Lucille Venet
Koz Venet – Lyttle, Cosima Lucille Venet
Kraus, Marci – Kraus, Marcella
Kreuz, Ilieronymo – Stiehl, Harry Charles Christopher
Kroman, G.G. – Glassberg, Gwendolyn Revilda Darling
Kroman, Gwen G. – Glassberg, Gwendolyn Revilda Darling
Kruger, Paul – Sebenthall, Roberta Elizabeth
Krzemien, Pawel – Drozdowski, Bohdan Otto
Kumalo – Clarke, Peter Edward
Kuprian, Hermann – Kuprian, Hermann Josef
Kutty, Madhavi – Kamala Das, Madhavi Kutty
Kuya – Culla, Daniel
Ladnek, Odlaw – Kendall, Carlton
Lador, Riva – Rubin, Riva Regina
Laird, Antonia B. – Laird, Antonia Bissell

Lam, Philip Y.C. – Lam, Yan-Chiu
Lambert, Cecily – Knechtel, Cecily Lambert
Lambertus – Rutten, Mathieu Jacques Henri
Land, Beatrice M. – Land, Beatrice Marie
Lane, M. Travis – Lane, Millicent Elizabeth (Travis)
Lantier, Nadine – Lantier, Nadine Marie Jez
Larter, Bob – Larter, Robert Oswald
Lates, Patricia – Kopetka, Patricia Christine
Latham, Linn – Ward, Mary B.
Laure, Thierry – Wautier, Andre
Lawrence, Audrey – Cole, Audrey
Layton, Jean – Shriver, Donna Newcomer
Leath, Mrs. John R. – Leath, Ida Belle
Lecerf, M. – Dudley, Austin Edison
Leckey, Hugo – Leckey, Hugo McClelland
Lee, Ai – Lee, Alfred Matthew
Lee, B. – Lee, Betty Merritt
Lee, Betty M. – Lee, Betty Merritt
Lee, Brad – Slattery, Bradley
Lee, Mariel – Lane, Mary Louisa
Lee, Oneida – Martin, Lillis Oneida
Lee, P.H. – Malone, Marvine H(erbert)
Lee Su-Ying – Lee Su
Lee Tseng-Chung – Lee Su
Leeds, Lynne – Gause, Emilyn
Le Fer Brun – Brennan, Henry
Leister, Lois Anderson – Leister, Lois
LeNoir, Ivy Anita – LeNoir, Ivy Anita (Darensbourg)
Leo – Nagarajan, R.
Leola – Archer, Lee Ola
Leprechaun – McHugh, Terence
Leumas, WM. S. – Scantlan, Samuel William
Leve, Mrs. Harvey – Hochman, Sandra
Levertov, Denise – Levertoff, Denise
Lewanae Palsapi – Khan, Ghani
Lewis, Pamela – Lewis, Pamela Rozalia
Li, Lin – Tiang, Seng-yong
Lib Ro – Romano, Liboria Elizabeth
Lilley, Merv, Mrs. – Hewett, Dorothy Coade
Lincoln, Anne – Jacobs, Florence Burrill
Linden, Ronald – Vaky, James Russell
Lingard, Christopher – Armstrong, Phyllis Eleanor
Lingham – Bantleman, Lawrence
Link, Gordden – Link, S. Gordden
Lisle, Lilia – Shepherd, Barbara Lilian
Litsey, Sarah – Nye, Sarah Litsey
Littlebird, Harold – Bird, Harold F.
Lloyd, J.B. – Blackburn, Beatrice Bray
Lloyd, Marjeane – Wagner, Marjorie Jeane
Lo Fu – Mo Lo-Fu
Locke, Lucie – Price, Lucie
Lodge, Edith – Lodge, Edith Bennett
Lomar, Martha – Lopez De Victoria, Maria
Lomen – Han Jen Tsun
Long, Bee Bacherig – Long, Beatrice Powell
Lorel, Phil – De Piftro, Albert
Love, Alice H. – Love, Alice Hellena Lowery Jezeski
Lovell, Mrs. Edward J. – Lovell, Cleoral A.
Lowly, Sable – Babalola, Adeboye Solomon Oladele

Lowrey, Joy – Durkee, Joycelyn Joan
Ludlow, George – Kay, Ernest
Lunn, Sally – Lunn, Hilda Beatrice Ellen
Luster, Helen – Sherry, Helen Luster
Lyberg – Hallstrom, Karin Lyberg
Lynds, Clara – Rudberg, Gertrude Jones
Lynn, Ross K. – Roskolenko, Harry
Lysohorsky, Ondra – Goy, Erwin
Lysons, Dennis – Lysons, William Dennis
Macartney, Frederick T. – Macartney, Frederick Thomas
McAfee, Thomas – McAfee, James Thomas
McCarty, Raymond – McCarty, Raymond M.
McCoin, Mac – McCoin, Joseph Young, Jr.
McConnell, Bonnie – Parker, Bonnie Elizabeth
McConnell, Evelyn – Staley, Ronald Christopher
McCormick, A.E. – Lewis-Smith, Anne Elizabeth
McCormick, Mary – McCormick, Mary Thelma
McCoy, Billie – McCoy, Mary Maurine
McDaniel, Esther Koerner – McDaniel, Esther C.
McDiarmid, Hugh – Grieve, Christopher Murray
McDonald, Nan – McDonald, Nancy May
MacGavin, Elizabeth Cushing – MacGavin, Elizabeth Louise Cushing
McGregor, A.E. – Lewis-Smith, Anne Elizabeth
Mackall, Virginia Woods – Bellamy, Virginia
McKeown, Tom – McKeown, Thomas S.
McLaren, Davis – Coutermash, John H.
McLaughlin, Emma S. – McLaughlin, Emma Jeanette Seiders
McLaughlin, William – McLaughlin, William DeWitt
Macnair, Mrs. D.C. – Livesay, Dorothy
McNear, Elizabeth – Rossini, Sarah Lois
Macpherson, Jay – Macpherson, Jean Jay
McWhorter, Bright – McWhorter, Bright Jasper
Madhu Vandu, S. – Sreenivos, Prathivadi Bhayankaram
Mag – Gordon, Marek Henryk
Magellan, Ellen – Coffin, Ellen
Magister Juras – Zagorski, Jerzy
Mahaswapna – Venkateswararao, Kammisetty
Mahr, David – Mahr, Allan David
Maize, Zea – Struthers, Dorothy M.
Makahiya – Mercado, Simon A(lvarez)
Malaka – Natachee, Allan
Mallory-Beck – See, Margielea Stonestreet
Malouf, David – Malouf, George Joseph David
Mammana, Camille Louise – Mammana, Louise Carmela
Maner, Loren – Ehrman, George Loren
Mani – Manickam, T. Sambasiva
Manjula – Bhaskaran, M.P.
Mann, Jan – Kuprian, Hermann Josef
Mansfield, Margery Swett – Mansfield, Margery
Marge – Friday, Marjorie H.
Marijnen, Joannes – Matthyssen, Joannes Michael
Marine, J.J. – Oppitz, Rene Charles
Marino, Robert S. – Viray, Manuel
Mark, Benita Marek – Marek, Benita Louise
Markham, Beulah Raines – Mark`iam, Beulah Belle
Marks, J. – Marks-Highwater, Jamake

Marshall, Inez – Marshall, Inez Mildred
Marshall, Tom – Marshall, Thomas Archibald
Marr, Lem – Carson, Robert
Marriott, Anne – McLellan, Joyce Anne
Martin, Michael – Mayer, Pam
Martland, Patricia – Brierley, Patricia Anne
Marx, Patricia – Lantay, Patricia Joan Marx
Maryam – Lowen, Marilyn
Mason, Tyler – Mason, Madeline
Mason, Val – Mason, Wauneta Hackleman
Mathews, A. – Mathews, Antoinette Mary
Mathews, Lorraine – Tilden, Lorraine Henrietta Frederick
Mathews, Toni – Mathews, Antoinette Mary
M. Bar-Ya'Akov – Dor, Moshe
Meehan, Mary H. – Meehan, Mary Taft Hitchings
Meher Baba – Horder, John Pearson (Peter)
Meletusa – Argow, Sylvia
Melmoth – Tullett, Denis John
Menon, R.R. – Menon, R. Rabindranath
Menusy, Didi – Menusy, Yedidia
Merritt, E.B. – Waddington, Miriam
Merritt, Si – Hoyer, Mildred N.
Meyland, Frank – Ascoop, Hubert
Michaelson, Michael – Michaelson, Louis W.
Michaud, E.G. – Mitchell, (Sister) Elaine
Middleton, Laura – Middleton, Laura Mary
Mihangel – Higgins, Michael
Miller, Agnes Allen – Miller, Martha Agnes Allan
Miller, Lion – Miller, Henry Lionel
Miner, Scott – Miner, Virginia Scott
Minerva – Cannon, M.
Mintz, Mattie – Mintz, Martha Annie
Miodownik, Eva – Oppenheim, Eva
Mistral – O'Neill, Lisa
Mitchell, K.L. – Lamb, Elizabeth Searle
Mizer, Ray – Mizer, Raymond Everett
M.M. Lover – Sreenivos, Prathivadi Bhayankaram
Mock Yang Min – Kim, Kyung Sooh
Mo Jen – Chang Wan-Hsi
Mong Tuyet That Tieu muoi – Suu, Thai Thi
Montal, Robert – Frickx, Robert
Moore, Amelia – Williams, Opal Euphemia
Moore, Lane – Moore, Lucia
Moore, Leona Goodwin – Moore, Leona Pearl
Moore, Rosalie – Brown, Rosalie Moore
Morden, Veatrice Victoria – Morden, Veatrice (Buck)
Moreau, Lucette – Schoene, Mary Patricia
Moreau, Lucie – Schoene, Mary Patricia
Moreland, Catherine S. – Quinn, Catherine Schroeder
Morgan, Patrick – Amidon, Bill
Morina, Mimmo – Morina d'Agira, Domenico Maria
Morisot, Simone – Mammatt, Doreen Rosalie
Morgan, Mary Martha – Dawson, Martha Morgan
Mork, Helen Ruth – Freeman, Helen Ruth
Morris, Bernie – Morris, Bernard Newth
Morris, B.J. – Fischer, Barbara
Morris, Michael – Morris, Michael Spence Lowdell
Morrison, Edward – Humphrey, Paul

Mullins, Helene – Mullins-Johnson, Helene

Mundi, Dolores – Harr, Lorrain Ellis

Munginni, Gladys – Brown, Gladys Mungen

Murphy, Marybeth Magnenat – Murphy, Mary Elizabeth

Mutocort, J. ten – De Groot, Jan Hendrik

Myhhb, Cesi – Buffington, Tiny Louise

Nachant, Frances Grant – Nachant, Mary Frances Grant

Nakagawa, Onsey – Nakagawa, Atsuo

Nam Poh – Lee Peng Jin

Nathan, Jo – Fruits, Wanda Fae Hardin

Nathan, Leonard – Nathan, Edward Leonard

Nedrow, Ella Castle – Nedrow, Ella L.

Nelson, Starr – Nelson, Doris Starr

Nema – Wells, Brain Hadley

Net, Thomas – Fisher, Thomas Allen

Nicol, Abioseh – Nicol, Davidson Sylvester Hector Willoughby

Nicole – Nicholson, Nicole N.

Nikhileswar – Kubam, Yadov Reddy

Niraj – Srinivasarajagopalan, Thirunarayanan

Nirapo, Nirago – Agaronian, Leon Roman

Noble, Virginia – Skawron, Virginia

Noel-Cooper, George – Cooper, George William Noel

Nokan, Zegoua (Charles) – Konan, Kakou

Noll, Bink – Noll, Lou Barker

Nonnie Nu Nu – Cox, Hardin Charles

Noone, Willard – Sladek, John

Norden, Charles – Durrell, Lawrence (George)

Nowell, Hazel Lea – Ailor, Hazel Lea Norwell

Noyes, Stanley – Noyes, Stanley Tinning

Oates, Titus – Bell, Martin

Ochester, Ed – Ochester, Edwin Frank

O'Connor, Bryn – Johnson, Kathryn

O'Fry, Evelyn Mills – Fry, L Evelyn

O'Handley, Robert – O'Handley, Robert Gerard

Ojo – Jonsmoen, Ola

Olbrechts, Maura – Page, Maura June Ann

Old Coyote, Sally – Old Coyote, Elnora A. (Stenersen)

Ole Dofton – Jonsmoen, Ola

Oliver, Emogene – Sletten, Madra Rix Oliver

Oliver, Madra Imogene – Sletten, Madra Rix Oliver

Oliver, M.R. – Sletten, Madra Rix Oliver

Oliver, Rix Madra – Sletten, Madra Rix Oliver

Ol Jonsa – Jonsmoen, Ola

O'Neall, James Benjamin – Johnson, Kathryn

O'Neil, Terrence – O'Neil, Terrence (William)

One-Minus-One – Trollope-Cagle, Vivian Jewel

Opalov, Leonard – Podoksik, David

O'Penyon, Anne – Stief, Willie Gay Morgan

Oppenheimer, Christine Backus – Oppenheimer, C.B.

Ordway, Jack – Ward, Mary B.

Orley, Van L. – Spellmon, Fronzell Lincoln

Oscien, Zygmunt – Piechal, Marian

Overy, Claire May – Bass, Clara May

Owen, Richard – Roberts, EdnEdna

Pacheco, Henry L. – Pacheco, Henricus Luis

Padraic Fiacc, O'Connor, Patrick Joseph

Page, Geneva – Page, Sarah Geneva

Page, P.K. – Irwin, Patricia Kathleen

Page, S. Geneva – Page, Sarah Geneva

Palma, Peggy – Palma, Margaret Tanghe

Palmer, Lynn – Palmer, Pamela Lynn

Parrish, Buchanan – Parrish, Jemima Buchanan

Parrish, Eugene – Harding, Donald E.

Parsons, Geoffrey C. – Parsons, Geoffrey Charles

Parsons, Kitty – Recchia, Kitty Parsons

Pasdeloup, Jean-Marie – Durben, Wolfgang

Pasek, Mya Kern – Pasek, Catherine (Mya) Louise Kern

Pasley, Beth – Pasley, Mary Beth

Pater, Elias – Friedman, John

Paterson, A.I.H. – Paterson, Allister Ian Hughes

Paterson, Alistair – Paterson, Allister Ian Hughes

Patino, Carlos – Viray, Manuel

Patrick, Connie – Constable, Patricia Ann

Patrick, Robert – O'Connor, Robert Patrick

Pearce, Bess Browning – Pearce, Bessie Belle

Pederek, Simon – Thomas, Peter Derek

Pedrito – Santaliz, Pedro

Peeper, Peter – Nolan, Pat 'Rocky'

Pei, Tai – Yee, Ta-Teh

Pelinegro – Sebastian, Processo

Pendleton, Conrad – Kidd, Walter Evans

Pennant, Edmund – Zaslow, Edmund M.

Penniman, Gwen – Penniman, Gwendolen Brooks

Perry, Kay – Perry, Etta May Kenyon

Peter Pan – Isaac. Charles Abraham

Peters, Patricia – Settle, Patricia Claire Peters

Petro – Trower, Peter Gerard

Phil, Phil – Nolan, Pat 'Rocky'

Philomela – Parker, Mabel

Philothea – Pelley, Ruth

Phoenice, Jay – Fox Hutchinson, Juliet Mary

Pibbss – Sreenivos, Prathivadi Bhayankaram

Pickard, Bill – Pickard, William Priestley

Pickard, Tom – Pickard, Thomas Mariner

Picker, Eliza – Picker, Elizabeth E.

Pield, Jean – Diamond, Florence Jean

Pinongo, Avaisa – Natachee, Allan

Piper, Ivonne – Bishop, Mary Elizabeth

Pitu – Santaliz, Pedro

Pixie – Verkennes, Geneva Alice

Platt, Eugene – Platt, Eugene Robert

Ploughman, Nina – Sutcliffe, Pavella Dolores

Poe, Marian M. – Poe, Marian Gloyd McNabb

Pogonowska – Pogonowska-Oplustil, Anna

Pointer, Jacqueline – Ives, Jacqueline Rose

Pomfret, Joan – Townsend, Joan

Pordellorar, Adrian – Cawein, Madison

Porter, Bern – Porter, Bernard Harden

Porter, Grace Kelly – Porter, Grace Ann

Post, Marie J. – Post, Marie J. (Tuinstra)

Poulin, A., Jr. – Poulin, Alfred Maurice

Pounds, Kara McFadden – Pounds, Kara Esther

Powell, Patsy – Long, Beatrice Powell

Pramuanmark, P. na – Rajani, Mom Chao (Prince)

Chand
Priya Bhaashi – Sreenivos, Prathivadi Bhayankaram
Publius II, Jr. – Theis, Ed Edmund G.
Purnell, Idelia – Stone, Idella Purnell

P.V.T. – Van Toorn, Peter
Qla – Culla, Daniel
Quixote De Extramuros – Espino, Frederico Licsi, Jr.
Raamah, Ingra – Babcock, Alberta
Rabindranath, R. – Menon, R. Rabindranath
Rahulan – Srinivasarajagopalan, Thirunarayanan
Raingoud, Ronald E. – Guardino, Leonard J.
Ralston, S. Scott – Ralston, Sonia Murray Scott
Random, Alan – Kay, Ernest
Ravi – Pandit, Raghunath Vishnu
Rawley, Callman – Rakosi, Carl
Reber, Clara Smith – Reber, Clara Belle Smith
Reed, Kelly – Stout, Dorothy L.
Reed, Lucy – Hazelton, Lucy Clare Elizabeth Schaeffer Reed
Reilly, Michael – Riley, Cyril Leslie
Rein, Carolus – Rein, Karl Carolus Hilding Gabriel
Renaldo, Kathryn – Musgrove, Virginia Margaret
Rene, Danilo – Fontain, (Rt. Rev. Archimandrite) Gregory
Rennob, Enna – Marley, Anne Augusta Bonner
Resin – McClintock, Michael Windsor
Reverb, Max – Nolan, Pat 'Rocky'
Reyes Y Basoalto, Ricardo Eliezer Neftail – Neruda, Pabio
Rhada – Bhaskaran, M.P.
Rhys, Elwy – Price, Ken
Rick Du Calme – Gilfillan, Merrill
Ricketts, Elizabeth – Ricketts, Elizabeth Page Mayer
Ricq, Anne – Richeboeuf, Suzanne
Riggs, Dionis Coffin – Riggs, Dionis
Rik – Orr, Richard Wayne
Ritchie, Elisavietta – Ritchie, Elisavietta Artamonoff

Roberson, Ed. – Roberson, Charles Edwin
Robert The Rhymer – Williams, Alan Moray
Roberts, Dorothy – Leisner, Dorothy Roberts
Roberts, Lotus Knowlton – Roberts, Lotus Lorraine
Roberts, Percy – Roberts, Percival R., Jr.
Robertson, Olive – Robertson, Olive Hope
Robertson, Pete – Robertson, Peter
Roch, Dalby – Webb, Ethel
Rodman, Frances – Wood, Eleanor Chaffee
Rogers, Mary Bee – Rogers, Mary Bernadette
Rohini – Gupta, Rohini
Rose, Ila Elizabeth – Swick Ila Elizabeth Rose
Rosen, Ayn – Finley, Dewey Gibson
Rosher, Rosamund – Bayley, Uria Marjorie
Ross, Colin – Roskolenko, Harry
Rosseeuw & Guilmain, Ray, Jill – Guilmain, Ray
Rovin, Alex – Russo, Albert
Rowe, Tony – Rowe, Tony Clara
Rowland, Gertrude – Rowland Du Puy, Gertrude
Russell, Dick – Russell, Richard Michael Friend
Russell, Euna – Mignault, Euna Maxine Hoyden
Russell-Mignault, Euna – Mignault, Euna Maxine Hoyden

Ryan, Teresa – McGilley, (Sister) Mary Janet
Saalfeld, Martha – Vom Scheidt, Martha
Saarsen, Karin – Karlstedt, Karin Marie
Saha, P.K. – Saha, Prosanta Kumar
St. Claire, Dorothy – Sharp-Carter, Marjorie Elizabeth
Saint Geraud – Knott, William Kilborn
Saint Gil, Phillippe – Gillet, Phillippe Claude Marie Jean
Saint-Lo, Michele – Bedeau, Rosemary
St. M. – Michael, Hjalmar Fridolf Martin
Saint-Remy – de Muynck, Remy
Salena – Burghard, Shirley Mae
Sally – Scott, Vera Evelyn
Samuel, Gutkin – Lowenstein, Tom
Sanders, Sandi – Sanders, Mary Alberta
Sandoval, Sandy Roberto – Sandoval, Roberto L.
Sands, Eleanor – Sands-Smith, Eleanor
Saner, Reg – Saner, Reginald
Santayana, Adrian – Coutermash, John H.
Santos, E.T. – Santos, Emmanuel Tiu
Santos, Noli – Santos, Emmanuel Tiu
Saqib – Ali Khan, (Mir) Naqi
Sarwech Sujawali – Tararo, Muhammed Siddique
Satish – Satish, Uma Shankar
Saunders, Patricia M. – Godsiff, Patricia Mary
Sauvage, Germain – Wehrli, Peter K.
Sayeh, H.A. – Ebtehaj, Hushang
Schaefer, Oda – Lange, Oda
Schmidt, Tom – Schmidt, Thomas Victor
Schneider, Dolli – Schneider, Dorothy Fay
Schroeder, Cathernie M. – Quinn, Catherine Schroeder
Scoggins, Faye – Bigelow, Faye Scoggins
Scott, Elena – Pelosi, Helen Priscilla
Scott, Marilyn Eynon – Eynon, Marilyn Martha Theresa Scott
Scott, Tom – Scott, Thomas McLaughlin
Scribner, Lucille – Rook, Pearl Lucille
Seese, Ethel Gray – Seese, Ethel Thelma Gray
Seferis, George – Seferiades, George
Settle, Claire – Settle, Patricia Claire Peters
Shain, Rick – Shain, Richard Arthur
Shalder – Jamieson, Peter
Shang, Guan-Yui – Wang, Jyh-jiann
Shantih, Philia – Barranda, Natividad 'Natty' Gatbonton
Sharp, Margery – Sharp-Carter, Marjorie Elizabeth
Shaver, Helen Ruth – Shaver, Helen Ruth Manning
Shaw, Helen – Hofmann, Helen Lilian
Sh. Baron – Shrira, Shoshana
Sheaff, Ardeana Hamlin – Sheaff, Ardeana
Shepard, Ellen – Hazelton, Lucy Clare Elizabeth Schaeffer Reed
Shepherd, Erle – Srinivas, Talwar Sampath
Sherrard, Dave – Canfield, Joan Giltner
Shiffert, Edith Marcombe – Shiffert, Edith Marion
Shishkov, Vasiliy – Nabokov, Vladimir
Shoshana Sh – Shrira, Shoshana
Shoup, Si – Hess, Alice Leona
Sh. Shani – Shrira, Shoshana

Sh-Sh-Sh – Shrira, Shoshana

Shu, Tik – Wang, Si-Chiu

Shuford, Gene – Shuford, Cecil Eugene

Shun-Ou – Chang, Wei-Han

Sid – Boughtwood, Alice Marian

Sikkema, Haje – De Groot, Jan Hendrik

Silliman, Ron – Silliman, Ronald Glenn

Simaoka, Sin – Shimaoka, Akira

Singer, Elsie – Singer, Elsie S.

Sirin, V. – Nabokov, Vladimir

Sisson, C.H. – Sisson, Charles Hubert

Sister Mary Jeannette – Fantuzzo, Carmen

Skelton, Roger – Horn, Peter (Rudolph Gisella)

Slater, Lydia Pasternak – Slater, Lydia Elizabeth

Slavko – Mader, Miroslav

Slesinski, Judy – Slesinski, Judith

Smalacombe, John – MacKay, Louis Alexander

Smaldon, Judith Elizabeth – Lovin, Judith Elizabeth Olive

Small, Mary Vivian – Bonine, Vivian

Smallwood, Jason – Kisner, Jacob

Smith, C. Busby – Smith, John

Smith, Latta C. – Smith, Latta Conway

Smith, Maggie Aldridge – Smith, Maggie

Snow, A.H. – Snow, Alfred Herbert

Snow, Jade – Greenfield, Lois Jean

Sol – Ozog, Jan Bolestaw

Solvin, Lois C. – Solvin, Lois Lorene Chinn

Sopher, Phil O. – Ditto, Roy Waymon

Sotirakopoulou, Agnes – Skina, Agnes

Spaceco – Atchley, Dana Winslow

Sparks, Joseph – Mtshali, Oswald Mbuyiseni

Sparks, Katherine – Sparks, Hypatia Katherine

Speaker, William – Holliday, David

Spear, Bino – Connor, Tony

Spears, Heather – Goldenberg, Marion Heather

Speck, Bette – Warden, Bette Ruth Coker

Spicer, Marcy – Spicer, Marcella

Squires, Phil – Barker, Squire Omar

Sri Sri – Srinivasarao, Srirangam

Stahl, Virginia – Stahl, Virginia McDaniel

Stalowy, Andrzej – Piechal, Marian

Stanford, Don – Stanford, Donald Elwin

Stanley, Alison – Bartholomew, Edna

Stanley, F.R. – Rajiva, Stanley Frederick

Starling, Lirrel – Gardella, Elsie May

Starr, Bill – Starr, Billie Joe

Starr, B.J. – Starr, Billie Joe

Starr Fish – Lurie, Hannah Ross

Starr, Saguaro – Starr, Billie Joe

Stephen, Sid – Stephen, Sidney James

Sterling, – Martin, Adele Lee

Stevens, Jean-Edouard – Stevens, Jean

Stevens, Leslie – Barrows, Margaret Hamilton

Stevens, William Christopher – Allen, Steve

Stevenson, Mabel B. – Stevenson, Mabel Brollier

Stevenson, Mary B. – Stevenson, Mary Blanche

Stopple, Libby – Carrie, Elizabeth

Street, Louise – Archer, Louise (Nellie Louise Barnes)

Stremich, Norma Jones – Stremich, Norma Florence

Stuart, Kenneth – Cox, Patrick Brian

Sturhahn, Joan – McNutt, Joan Sturhahn

Suburbanite – Bayley, Uria Marjorie

Summers, Diana – Farsace, Duverne Konrick

Summers, Hal – Summers, Henry Forbes

Sundar, R. – Sundaresan, Ramamurthy

Sundaresan, R. – Sundaresan, Ramamurthy

Sunshine – McNichol, Vera Luella

Sutton, Henry – Slavitt, David Rytman

Sutton, John – Tullett, Denis John

Swank, Ann Hefner – Swank, Ann Dashner

Sweet William – Seals, William Harold

Swett, Margery – Mansfield, Margery

Sykes, Ruth Welch – Sykes, Ruth

Sypher, A. – Malone, Marvin H(erbert)

Tadlock, Lila Swindell – Tadlock, Lila Clementa

Tait, Elizabeth Leeds – Tait, Elizabeth

Tan/Emcee/Sri – Rajani, Mom Chao (Prince) Chand

Tang-Sze – Lee Peng Jin

Tarsicio, Fray – Fontain, (Rt. Rev. Archimandrite) Gregory

Tawney – Ames, Barbara Dorothy

Taylor, Ann – Brodey, James Miles

Taylor, Jessie – Amidon, Bill

Taylor, May Ola – Taylor, Mary Ola

Taylor, Selman – Selman, Elsie E.

Teague, Christopher – Ghigna, Charles Vincent

Telois, Maurice – Browne, William

Teofil – Gordon, Marek Henryk

Terahata, Jun – Kirkup, James

Terry, D.E. – Hazelton, Lucy Clare Elizabeth Schaeffer Reed

Thangappa, M.L. – Thangappa, Mathanapandian Lenin

Thatcher, Amelia – Miner, Virginia Scott

The Bastard from the Bush – Robinson, Roland Edward

The Cajun Poet – Martin, Albert Anthony

The Gloster Ode Construction Company – Houedard Pierre Thomas Paul (dom Sylvester)

The Lass – Harkey, Vada George

The Pearl – Despain, Wilma Morley

The Very Young Man – Farsaci, Litterio B. (Larry Farsace)

Therfu – Criswell, Ronald

Thibeau, Jack – Thibeau, John G.

Thierry, Andre – Wautier, Andre

Thomas, Jessie Brown – Thomas, Jessie Leah

Thomas, Stelleta Angel – Thomas, Stelleta Marie Angel

Thompson, Amanda Meade Brewer – Thompson Amanda Meade

Thompson, Fannie Lee McCondiehie – Thompson Fannie Lee

Thorndyke – Young, Charlotte

Throde, Gith – Miles, Joel Eugene

Thurston, Margaret – Whitis, Margaret Elizabeth

Tiger, Jack – Puechner, Ray

Tikkanen, Juhani – Tikkanen, Jarmo Juhani

Tillion, Diana Rystbaek – Tillion, Diana

Tira, J. – Tan Pai, Joshua

T.O. – Wilson, Royce

Toczek, Nick – Toczek, Nicholas

Todany, Alex de – Beaudoin, Kenneth Lawrence

Tomlin, Gene – Tomlin, Eugene Edward

Tomos Radyr – Stevenson, James Patrick

Tournier, Ann Catherine – Sitwell, Phronsie Irene

Townsend, Timothy – Robey, Timothy Lester Townsend

Tracy, Aloise – Tracy, Pauline Aloise

Trelawney – Jones, Phyllis Marjory

Tremblay, Bill – Tremblay, William Andrew

Trezel – Lories, Robert

Trijntje Fop – Stip, Kees

Trott, R.C. – Trott, Rosemary Clifford

Troubadour, Ernest – McLaughlin, Laurence Leclair

Trumpet Brewster – Neal, Arnethia Murdock

Tsuyuki, Shigeru – Kirkup, James

Tuairisc, O. Eugman – Watters, Eugene Rutherford

Tunstall, Shana Barrett – Tunstall, Velma Barrett

Tveskgg – Von Numers, Lorenz T.G.G.

Twa – Abram, Theresa

Twichell, Chase – Twichell, Penelope Chase

Tyler, Lillian – Fountain, Helen Van Alstyne

Tynni, Aale – Tynni-Haavio, Aale Maria

Uhuru – Baradi, Mauro

Ulla K – Culla, Daniel

Uncle Pek – Gunn, Richard M. 'Pek'

Upton, Lawrence – Upton, Lawrence John

Urragi – Dave, Mukund R.

Vallis, Val. – Vallis, Valentine Thomas

Valois, Lucile – Vaught, Lucile Kathryn

Van Brunt, H.L. – Van Brunt, Howell Lloyd

Van Duyn, Mona – Thurston, Mona Jane

Van Toorn, P. – Van Toorn, Peter

Vasalis, M. – Leenmans, Margaretha

Vasconcellos, Alma – Repetto, Delia Rios De Pagola

Van Creme, Rachel – Archer, Eva L.

Veitch, Tom – Padgett, Ron

Verhegghe, Willie – Verhegghe, Willy Omer Celesta

Very, Alice – Brown, Alice Needham Very

Vesey, Paul – Allen, Samuel Washington

Victor, Charles B. – Puechner, Ray

Villaneuva, Jesus – Jesus, Ramon de

Vinayak – Gokak, Vinayak Krishna

Violette – Jahnke, Violette Louise

Viret, Margaret – Viret, Margaret Mary-Buchanan

Von Schoultz, Solveig – Von Schoultz – Bergman, Solveig Margereta

Wacken, Francoise – Biebuyck, Francine

Wadd, Roberta – Selby, Bernard Allen, Jr.

Wade, Gwen – Wade, Gwendolen

Wagner, Marje – Wagner, Marjorie Jeane

Waldrop, Keith – Wolgamot, John Barton

Waldrop, Rosemarie – Wolgamot, John Barton

Walenty, Ryk – Skiba, Henry Patrick

Wales, George Henry – Guardina, Leonard J.

Walker, Ted – Walker, Edward Joseph

Wally – Horder, John Pearson (Peter)

Wa-Na-Ka – Falkowski, Edwin Andrzej

Ward, Charles – Taylor, John Alfred

Ward, Lois Merritt — Ward, Lois

Ward, R. Patrick — Holzappel, Rudi

Wardd, Robert — Selby, Bernard Allen, Jr.

Water-Lily — Sibug, Brigido B.

Wautelet, Josie — Wautelet, Josephine LeGrave

Waylan, Mildred — Harrell, Irene Buck

Wazyk — Wazyk, Adam

Wegman, Helen Ruth — Freeman, Helen Ruth

Wendolin — Durben, Wolfgang

Wentworth, Nina — Rudberg, Gertrude Jones

Wheeler, Norma Jones — Stremich, Norma Florence

Wichman, Eva — Wichman, Eva Aline

Whitewing — Vandall, Donna Mae Whitewing

Whitney, Leona — Hutner, Julie Sarah

Wilcox, Hannah Sims — Miner, Virginia Scott

Will Friar — Margolis, William J.

Williams, Frances Howelle — Williams, Margaret Frances Howell

Williams, Gwyn — Williams, David Gwyn

Williams, Jeff — Williams, Geoffrey Nathaniel

Williams, John Stuart — Williams, John Edwin Stuart

Williams, Kyle H. — Hardin, Mary Frances

Williams, Pieter — Williams, Pieter Daniel de Wet

Willibald, Graf — Durben, Wolfgang

Wills, C.M. — Barnett, Mary

Wilshire, Lewis — Wilshire, George Henry

Winans, A.D. — Winans, Allan Davis

Winch, Sally G. — Winch, Harriet Gragg

Windsor, Betty — Tilden, Lorraine Henrietta Frederick

Windsor, Elizabeth — Musgrave, Susan

Winter, Mary — Krauss, Mary

Witherby, Diana — Cooke — Diana

Witsend, Dipso — Lyall, Charles Leslie

Wolf, Frances — Nauman, Frances I.

Wolfe — Cannon, M.

Wonders, Anne — Passel, Anne

Wong, Alan L. — Wong, Alan Yun Sang

Wongly Guerilla Pooh — Horder, John Pearson (Peter)

Worley, Stella — Johnson, Stella Gertrude

Worried of Barnsley — Grampound, Martin (Josiah Hepplethwaite)

Wright, Neil — Wright, Frank William Nielsen

Yair, Ish — Shtern, Israel Hirsh

Yankah, Mike — Yankah, Kojo

Yeo Sa — Hong, Yoon Sook

Yolanda — Lux, Yolanda Attianese

York, Esther Baldwin — Burkholder, Esther York

Young Woon — Mho, Youn Sook

Yungtze — Wang Jung-Chih

Zag — Zagorski, Jerzy

Zag, J. — Zagorski, Jerzy

Zagoni, Erzsebet — Szentkereszty, Elizabeth

Zaheer Kashmiri — Pirzada, Dastgir Zaheer

Zahrad — Yaldizciyan, Zareh

Zarellio, Florian — Painton, Ivan Emory

Zeri, F. Mar — Ramirez, Francisco M.

Zia Jallundhri — Ahmed, Zia Nisar

Zurndorfer, Lotte — Troupp, Lotte